Jobfile

2011-12

the essential careers handbook

Jobfile 2011-12
ISBN: 978-1-905854-94-3

First published in 2001 by Babcock Lifeskills

Babcock Lifeskills, First Floor, 24 West Street, Fareham, Hants. PO16 0LF Tel: 01329 229138 Fax: 01329 229159
Internet: http://www.babcocklifeskills.co.uk E-mail: info@babcocklifeskills.co.uk

Typesetting and production by Wordcraft. Tel: 01483 560735 E-mail: wordcraft_ts@btconnect.com

Jobfile 2011-12

Contents

Welcome to Jobfile 2011-12

This edition contains information on 929 jobs and careers at all occupational levels. As well as covering the most popular jobs, we have also included many specialised careers, and some unconventional ones too.

Each year a great deal of careful research goes into the gathering of the information, but changes do occur between updates. Please remember that factors such as entry qualifications, salary information, addresses and website details may change at any time, so you must check carefully.

We are always keen to learn about ways in which we can improve our software products and publications. If you would like to make any comments or complaints, or would like to suggest ideas for new job titles, then please contact us; details are on the back cover.

Using the Information

The jobs in this book appear in alphabetical order by title for quick and easy reference and are arranged as follows:

Accountant: Industry & Commerce

Gives the main or most popular title of the job.

also known as:

Lists alternative job titles (also listed in the job title index).

CRCI: Financial Services

Refers to the Connexions Resource Centre Index (page 1161) and indicates the name of the occupational area. CRCI is a system of classification used in careers libraries, particularly in England, Wales and Northern Ireland.

CLCI: NAB

Refers to the Careers Library Classification Index and indicates the code for the occupational area. The CLCI system of classification may be used in careers libraries, and particularly in Scotland.

Job Band: 4 to 5

Indicates the main entry route(s) for the job.

Job Description

Gives a general introduction to the job or career and highlights the main activities and responsibilities.

Work Details

Tells you more about the job and what is involved. May also include hours worked, any travel involved, whether the job is office based, and other useful details, such as the work environment.

Qualifications

Babcock Lifeskills software and resources are used throughout the UK, so two sets of qualifications are provided for each job. The first gives information for England, Wales and Northern Ireland. The second set is for students in Scotland.

Entry qualifications are based on the minimum requirements. You should not assume that you will be accepted automatically for a job or course, even if you meet these minimum requirements. Qualifications, entry routes and training requirements can vary significantly throughout the UK. A great deal depends on the amount of competition for the job or course, so it is essential to check local requirements carefully before seriously pursuing any specific occupation.

It is also possible to enter a job or course with different qualifications. For details of equivalent/similar qualifications, see page vii.

Degree Information

States whether a specific degree is required for entry to the job. May also suggest degree subjects that can be useful, where a degree is required for entry, but no subject is specified.

Adult Qualifications

Provides details on entry standards or any specific requirements for older applicants such as special entry routes. Information on courses or training is covered in separate notes for adults in the 'Entry and Training' section.

Work Experience

Provides useful information on the type of work experience that is helpful prior to entering the job or course.

Entry and Training

Gives information on the type and length of training that is available and the entry qualifications usually required for the job. May also include details of useful courses and examinations, such as S/NVQs, professional qualifications, and specific training routes or pro grammes. This section also includes additional information for mature applicants.

Opportunities and Pay

Provides details of where jobs are generally available, whether UK based, and if there are opportunities for working abroad. Also indicates promotion prospects and whether there is a formal career structure. May state the current demand for a particular job. The information provides a guide to what you may expect to be paid depending on your qualifications and experience. Provides details of approximate annual salaries, or for some jobs, hourly, daily or weekly wages.

Health

This section is only included if there are any special requirements to take into consideration, such as specific medical conditions, the standard of physical fitness required, and whether a medical test is required for the job.

Skills and Qualities

Look here for a summary of the qualities required for the job or career. You are not expected to have all of them, but those listed provide you with an idea of the ones that are important.

Relevant Subjects

Lists subjects that are most relevant to the job, career or course.

Further Information

Lists book titles, careers leaflets, websites, magazines or other resources that also provide useful information.

Addresses

Gives address details, including websites of organisations and/or professional associations that provide additional information.

Similar Jobs

Lists other jobs in Jobfile 2011-12 that may interest you.

Using the Indexes

The Job Titles Index (page 1183) is a quick and easy alphabetical list of over 2,200 job titles that also includes many alternative ones. Use this index if you know the name of a job or career in which you are interested. The index shows the job title and page number.

The Occupational Areas Index begins on page 1161. Use this index if you don't have a particular job in mind, but know the general type of work in which you are interested. This index lists jobs in occupational areas using the Connexions Resource Centre Index (CRCI) headings used in many careers libraries (particularly in England, Wales and Northern Ireland) for filing books, leaflets and other related information. The CRCI icons and their headings are shown as follows:

Administration, Business and Office Work
- Business and Management Services
- Civil Service
- Local Government Administration
- Office and Secretarial Work

Building and Construction
- Architecture
- Construction
- Surveying, Housing, Property and Planning

Catering and Hospitality

Computers and IT

Design, Arts and Crafts

Education and Training

Engineering
- Aerospace Engineering
- Agricultural Engineering
- Biomedical Engineering
- Chemical and Materials Engineering
- Electrical, Electronics, Telecommunications and Power Engineering
- Machinery Maintenance and Metal Work
- Marine Engineering and Shipbuilding
- Mechanical Engineering
- Mining, Quarrying and Extraction
- Motor Vehicle Engineering

Environment, Animals and Plants
- Agriculture and Fisheries
- Landscape and Plants
- Veterinary Services and Animal Care

Financial Services
- Accounting
- Banking/Building Society Work
- Finance Services
- Insurance/Actuarial Work

Healthcare
- Alternative Therapies
- Complementary Medicine
- Dental Services
- Environmental Health
- Health Administration
- Medical Technology and Laboratory Services
- Medical Therapies
- Medicine and Surgery
- Nursing and Paramedical Services
- Ophthalmic Services
- Pharmacy and Pharmacology

Languages, Information and Culture

Legal and Political Services

Leisure, Sport and Tourism
- Leisure/Recreation
- Sport and Outdoor Pursuits
- Travel and Tourism

Manufacturing and Production
- Chemical Products
- Clothing
- Food and Drink
- Glass and Ceramics
- Iron, Steel and Other Metals
- Leather and Footwear
- Paper and Paper Products
- Plastics, Polymers and Rubber
- Production/Manufacturing Work
- Textiles and Industrial Fabrics
- Woodworking and Furniture

Marketing and Advertising

Media, Print and Publishing

- Broadcasting and Film
- Journalism and Writing
- Photography
- Printing and Publishing

Performing Arts

Personal and Other Services

- Burial and Cremation
- Cleaning and Caretaking
- Hairdressing and Beauty Care

Retail Sales and Customer Services

- Customer Service/Call Centres
- Retail Sales
- Trading Standards/Consumer Protection
- Wholesaling

Science, Mathematics and Statistics

- Food Science and Technology
- Geography, Geology and other Earth Sciences
- Mathematics and Statistics
- Scientific Research and Laboratory Science

Security and Armed Forces

- Armed Forces
- Fire and Rescue Services
- National Border Security
- Police Service and Related Work
- Prison Service
- Security

Social Work and Counselling Services

Transport and Logistics

- Air Transport
- Logistics, Distribution and Freight Forwarding
- Purchasing
- Rail Transport
- Removals and Storage
- Road Transport
- Sea and Water Transport

Qualification Bands

The route by which you enter a job depends on the exam passes and the study and/or training needed for the job, as well as any previous related experience. In Jobfile 2011-12, the information provided for each job indicates both the qualifications required and the entry routes, divided into Jobfile job bands. You can also get a quick idea about a job's entry route by looking at the figures under the CRCI heading for each job. For example, a job at job bands **4** to **5** indicates that there are **two** main qualification entry routes.

If you are thinking of jobs that are at:

- **Bands 1-2**

  Usually no formal academic qualifications required though some GCSEs/S grades at any level, a Foundation Diploma, or equivalent vocational qualifications may help. S/NVQs at levels 1-2 are also useful. Often these types of jobs require particular qualities and skills rather than formal qualifications.

- **Bands 3-4**

  Usually need some GCSEs (A*-C)/S grades (1-3), a Higher Diploma or other equivalent vocational qualifications, including BTEC/SQA national awards, S/NVQs at levels 3-4, or similar.

- **Bands 4-5**

  Requires advanced qualifications such as higher national awards, foundation degrees, degrees or postgraduate diplomas. Entry to these jobs/courses usually requires 1-3 A levels/H grades and some GCSEs/S grades, or equivalent qualifications, such as an Advanced Diploma, Scottish Group Award (SGA), International Baccalaureate, Welsh Baccalaureate (advanced diploma), Scottish Baccalaureate, S/NVQs at levels 4-5, or BTEC/SQA awards.

Qualification Bands (continued)

The table below explains these different bands in more detail:

Job Entry Band	Job Examples	Training and Study for Young People	Training and Study for Adults
1 Usually no formal qualifications required	Hospital Cleaner RSPCA Animal Collection Officer Caretaker, Cloakroom Attendant Courier, Kitchen Porter Port Operative, Park Warden Waterway Operative	On-the-job training is usually less than one year.	On-the-job training lasting up to three months. Relevant work experience can be an advantage.
2 Some qualifications (academic or vocational) are helpful	Switchboard Operator, Locksmith Car Rental Agent Firefighter, Kinesiologist Optical Technician Builders' Merchant Film, TV & Theatre Craftsperson	Training is usually at least 1-2 years. Sometimes a short course or a part-time course is also required.	Mainly on-the-job training lasting several months. Possible short courses run by an employer or college. Relevant work experience can be an advantage.
3 Usually require some GCSEs (A*-C)/S grades (1-3) or equivalent vocational qualifications	Air Conditioning Technician Rail Transport Fitter/Electrician Farrier, Taxidermist Accounting Technician Spa Therapist, Volunteer Manager Prosthetic/Orthotic Technician	Training usually around 1-3 years, often including a part-time or short course at a college.	Possibility of short, full-time courses, followed by on-the-job training. Relevant work experience can be an advantage.
4 Usually require qualifications such as A levels/H grades or their equivalent	Municipal Engineer Computer Games Animator Public Relations Officer Magazine Features Editor Trading Standards Officer Quality Manager, Forensic Scientist	Training takes at least 3-4 years. Study is either full or part time in higher education.	Training and study usually 2-4 years. Some short, full-time courses may be available. Relevant work experience may reduce study time.
5 Advanced qualifications	RAF Officer, Building Society Manager Industrial Pharmacist, Website Developer Bilingual Secretary, Zoologist Probation Officer, Clinical Psychologist Solicitor, Surgeon Teacher, Transport Planner	Study/training is at least 3-5 years. A degree or equivalent qualification is required, and often with postgraduate qualification and continuing professional development (CPD).	Degree necessary; sometimes with a postgraduate qualification. Alternatively, extensive experience followed by further formal qualification may be acceptable.

Adults please note: Qualifications required for mature entry can vary greatly and often you may get credit for your current experience and/or qualifications when applying for a similar or related job/course.

Qualifications

England, Wales and Northern Ireland

The National Qualification Framework (NQF) provides a single structure for qualifications in England, Wales and Northern Ireland and sets out nine levels at which existing qualifications can be recognised (entry level to level eight). The inside front cover of this book displays full details of the NQF.

- Diplomas are available in fourteen subjects in most areas of England. They are 14-19 qualifications that combine essential skills and knowledge, hands-on experience, and employer-based learning. They are available at three levels. Foundation Diplomas are equivalent to 5 GCSEs at grade D-G, Higher Diplomas are equivalent to 7 GCSEs at A*-C and Advanced Diplomas are equivalent to 3.5 A levels.
- Qualifications such as the Welsh Baccalaureate (Advanced Diploma), International Baccalaureate (IB), or a BTEC (Edexcel) national diploma, are alternative qualifications (to A levels) for entry to a degree course. Those with an IB require a minimum of 24 points or more for competitive courses.
- A foundation degree (FdA in the arts/FdSc in the sciences) offers academic study combined with work-related skills and is offered in a wide variety of subjects. There are no set standard entry requirements and progression to further study of an honours degree is possible.
- Young Apprenticeships are a route at Key Stage 4 that enables young people aged 14-16 to pursue industry-specific vocational qualifications with employers and training providers. Pupils are based in school and follow the core national curriculum subjects. For two days a week (or equivalent), they also work towards nationally recognised vocational qualifications.

Changes to the NQF aim to offer a more flexible and greater choice of qualifications so that you can combine both academic and vocational qualifications of a similar value. Applicants should therefore check with universities and colleges at an early stage when making enquiries about individual course entry requirements. For further information, please visit the relevant websites:

- **Qualifications and Curriculum Development Agency (QCDA)** at http://www.qcda.gov.uk or telephone 0300 303 3011.
- **Department for Education** at http://www.education.gov.uk or telephone 0370 000 2288
- **Department for Business, Innovation and Skills** http://www.bis.gov.uk or telephone 020 7215 5000
- **Diplomas** at http://www.direct.gov.uk/diplomas/
- **Foundation Degrees** at http://www.findfoundationdegree.com
- **Apprenticeships** at http://www.apprenticeships.org.uk
- **Young Apprenticeships** at http://www.skillsactive.com/training/
- **Welsh Department for Children, Education, Lifelong Learning & Skills (DCELLS)** http://new.wales.gov.uk/topics/educationandskills/?lang=en or telephone 0845 010 3300.
- **NI Council for the Curriculum, Examination and Assessment (CCEA)** at http://www.rewardinglearning.org.uk or telephone 02890 261200.

Changes in Careers Guidance

From September 2011 there will be new arrangements for careers guidance in England. Building on the best practice of Next Step and Connexions, it will provide the first countrywide all-age careers service. It will be fully operational by April 2012.

Addresses

Food & Drink Qualifications
PO Box 141, Winterhill House, Snowdon Drive, Milton Keynes MK6 1YY
Phone: +44 (0)1908 231 062
Web: www.fdq.org.uk

Food Standards Agency (FSA)
Aviation House, 125 Kingsway, London WC2B 6NH
Phone: +44 (0)20 7276 8000
Web: www.food.gov.uk/

Scottish Meat Training
8-10 Needless Road, Perth PH2 0JW
Phone: +44 (0)1738 637785
Web: www.meattraining.net

Similar Jobs

Butcher: Retail, Butcher: Wholesale, Fish Farm Worker

Accountant: Industry & Commerce

also known as: Cost Accountant, Finance Manager: Private Sector, Management Accountant
CRCI:Financial Services
CLCI:NAB
Job Band: 4 to 5

Job Description

Accountants working in industry and commerce collect, analyse, and interpret financial information and focus on financial management. Management accountants specialise in preparing accounts, auditing accounts, monitoring cash flow, giving financial advice, budgeting, pricing or taxation. Examine different aspects of a business operation (internal auditing) to ensure efficient and effective work procedures, and investigate any irregularities. Aim to improve profitability and increase market share for their employer's business.

Accountants prepare financial statements and reports for company shareholders, HM Revenue & Customs, bank managers and external auditors. Use computers widely in much of the work. They may also manage bookkeepers and accounts clerks within the financial team.

Work Details

Usually work in an office from 9am to 5pm, five days a week, though may often have to work long hours at evenings or weekends, or spend time away from home. The work involves consulting with clients, colleagues and other professionals. Giving sound, accurate advice is essential. A lot of the storage and analysis of financial information is done by computer.

Qualification

- **England, Wales and Northern Ireland**

Band 4: For direct entry to accountancy training or BTEC higher national course in a relevant subject, such as business and finance: a minimum of two A levels and some GCSEs (A*-C) including maths and English, or equivalent.

Band 5: For entry to a degree course: 2-3 A levels and some GCSEs (A*-C) including maths and English, or equivalent. Exact requirements depend on the degree you take.

- **Scotland**

Band 4: For direct entry to accountancy training, or for an SQA higher national course in a relevant subject, eg accounting, you need at least three H grades and some S grades (1-3) including maths and English, or similar.

Band 5: For a degree: 3-5 H grades and some S grades (1-3) including maths and English, or similar qualifications. Exact requirements depend on the degree you take.

Degree Information

A degree in any subject is acceptable for entry to accountancy training. Degrees in accountancy, economics, law, mathematics, business studies/administration, computing, statistics, and financial management/banking are useful, and some lead to exemption from parts of the professional exams. Check with the appropriate professional body. Relevant postgraduate courses are also available.

Adult Qualifications

Formal entry requirements may be relaxed for those over 21 with relevant financial or accountancy experience. The accountancy professional bodies each have their own arrangements, which include special schemes for mature applicants. There are also special entry arrangements for adults applying for degree and higher national courses, including Access courses; check with the universities and colleges for details.

Work Experience

Relevant work or voluntary experience is always useful and improves your chances in application for entry to this career. Consider work experience in an accountant's practice or in the accountancy department of a central government department or local authority. Experience of other jobs involving finance is also valued by employers. Becoming involved in a work-related enterprise scheme, such as 'Young Enterprise', can enhance your chances when applying for a training contract.

Entry and Training

Most entrants are graduates with a relevant degree, such as accountancy, economics or business and finance. Accountants working in industry and commerce usually take the qualifications offered by the Association of Chartered Certified Accountants (ACCA), the Chartered Institute of Management Accountants (CIMA), the Institute of Chartered Accountants in England & Wales (ICAEW), the Institute of Chartered Accountants of Scotland (ICAS), or the Chartered Institute of Public Finance Accountants (CIPFA). Continuing professional development is also offered by the professional organisations and is an important part of ongoing training.

Broadly, students must complete a training contract with an authorised training firm to qualify. The contract lasts between three and five years depending on entry level and the individual firm. Some companies allow a greater number of attempts at exams than others. Training includes on-the-job experience combined with part-time courses and study in your own time. Some degree and higher national courses include work experience, which may count towards your training period.

There are also relevant full and part-time foundation degrees available, including some distance learning courses. A Diploma/ Welsh Baccalaureate in business, administration and finance may be available in your area. It is possible to begin training without a degree though training places are limited and entry is very competitive. You can also enter as a Certified Accountancy Technician (CAT) and work towards qualification as an accountant in two years. See the job profile for accounting technician and/or visit the Association of Accounting Technicians (AAT) website. An ability in foreign languages is very useful.

There are a number of training and development opportunities on offer across Scotland that can help you secure your first job in financial services or support your career development if you are already working in the sector.

Mature applicants should contact the professional bodies such as CIMA, CIPFA and ACCA, which have a mature entry route and also offer distance learning. Entry qualifications may be waived, though a good basis in maths, English and computing skills are usually necessary for the professional exams. A business or finance-related background is an advantage. All entrants train in exactly the same way as those starting from full-time education.

Opportunities and Pay

The demand for accountants has increased in recent years due to changes in taxation, and the fact that many people have become self-employed and require the services of an accountant. Despite the economic downturn, there is still demand for accountants and particularly in the specialist areas of tax, treasury and audit. Employers throughout the UK include retail and service industries, manufacturing, transportation and distribution. Jobs are also available in a large number of commercial and service organisations such as banks, building societies and insurance companies. Experienced accountants may set up their own firms and become consultants. It is possible to gain promotion within an organisation or by moving to another firm.

Many accountants in industry and commerce become financial directors/controllers or managing directors. You can specialise in a particular aspect of accountancy, such as forensic accounting, taxation or insolvency, or in a particular type of industry. It is possible to work abroad with some of the larger international companies.

Salaries can vary considerably and generally depend on the size and location of the firm. Graduate trainees can expect to earn around £19k-£26k a year. Once fully qualified, the average salary is around £38k a year. A top graduate employed by a large London firm can earn a starting salary of around £30k. Successful accountants can earn in the region of £50k-£100k a year.

Skills and Qualities

able to cope under pressure, able to manage a budget and keep records, analytical skills, good communication skills, good concentration level, good interpersonal skills, IT skills, logical, numeracy skills, tactful & discreet

Relevant Subjects

Business and accounting, Economics, English, ICT/Computer studies, Law, Mathematics

Further Information

Accountancy (Wolters Kluwer (UK) Limited) - www.accountancymagazine.com

Accountancy Uncovered (Trotman 2010) - www.trotman.co.uk

Accounting Web - www.accountingweb.co.uk

AGCAS: Accountancy and Business Services (Job Sector Briefing) (AGCAS) - www.prospects.ac.uk/

Diploma in Business, Administration and Finance - www.baf-diploma.org.uk/

Finance and Accounting (Pearson Publishing) - www.pearsoned.co.uk

Financial Services Skills Council - sector skills council for financial services, accountancy & finance - www.fssc.org.uk/

Inside Careers Guide: Management Accountancy - www.insidecareers.co.uk

TARGETjobs: City and Finance (GTI Specialist Publishers Ltd) - www.groupgti.com

Welsh Baccalaureate - www.wbq.org.uk

▶Working in maths (2009) (Babcock Lifeskills) - www.babcock-lifeskills.com/

Young Enterprise - www.young-enterprise.org.uk/pub/

Addresses

Association of Accounting Technicians (AAT)
140 Aldersgate Street, London EC1A 4HY
Phone: +44 (0)20 7397 3000
Web: www.aat.org.uk

Association of Chartered Certified Accountants (ACCA) UK
29 Lincoln's Inn Fields, London WC2A 3EE
Phone: +44 (0)20 7059 5000
Web: www.accaglobal.com

Association of International Accountants (AIA)
Staithes 3, The Watermark, Metro Riverside, Newcastle upon Tyne NE11 9SN
Phone: +44 (0)191 493 0277
Web: www.aiaworldwide.com

Chartered Institute of Management Accountants (CIMA)
26 Chapter Street, London SW1P 4NP
Phone: +44 (0)20 8849 2251
Web: www.cimaglobal.com

Chartered Institute of Public Finance and Accountancy (CIPFA)
3 Robert Street, London WC2N 6RL
Phone: +44 (0)20 7543 5600
Web: www.cipfa.org.uk

Institute of Chartered Accountants in England & Wales (ICAEW)
Chartered Accountants' Hall (Moorgate Place), PO Box 433, London EC2R 6EA
Phone: +44 (0)20 7920 8100
Web: www.icaew.com

Institute of Chartered Accountants in Ireland (ICAI) (Belfast)
The Linenhall 32-38 Linenhall Street, Belfast BT2 8BG
Phone: +44 (0)28 9043 5840
Web: www.icai.ie

Institute of Chartered Accountants of Scotland (ICAS)
CA House, 21 Haymarket Yards, Edinburgh EH12 5BH
Phone: +44 (0)131 347 0100
Web: www.icas.org.uk

Institute of Financial Accountants (ifa)
Burford House, 44 London Road, Sevenoaks, Kent TN13 1AS
Phone: +44 (0)1732 458080
Web: www.ifa.org.uk

Similar Jobs

Accountant: Private Practice, Accountant: Public Sector, Accounting Technician, Bank Manager, Company Secretary, Economist

Accountant: Private Practice

also known as: Chartered Accountant, Public Practice Accountant

CRCI:Financial Services
CLCI:NAB Job Band: 4 to 5

Job Description

Accountants in private practice work for an accountancy firm that provides a range of financial services and advice to fee-paying clients, including businesses and individual clients. May do consultancy work, helping individual clients or a company to manage money more efficiently, advising on taxation and giving financial advice. They deal with the financial affairs of companies or people who are declared bankrupt. May act as a trustee or an executor of a will. Some specialise in auditing, examining company accounts and certifying them as true and fair. The range of work varies from firm to firm and can depend on its size and location. Computers are widely used in much of the work.

Work Details

Mostly work around 35-40 hrs a week, Monday to Friday. You may have to work long hours, including evenings and weekends, and spend time away from home. The work is divided between time spent in the office and time out meeting clients, e.g. auditing is done on the client's premises. This is a demanding and challenging job and you may have to work long hours, including evenings and weekends, and spend time away from home. You have to be able to keep up to date with changes in financial regulations and work out the implications of changes for clients, using numerical and computer skills. Formal dress code is usual.

Accountants who qualify with one of the other professional bodies, such as the Association of Chartered Certified Accountants (ACCA), the Association of International Accountants (AIA), or the Chartered Institute of Management Accounts (CIMA), can choose to specialise in public finance, and can qualify for the CIPFA through a nine month fast track scheme. Continuing professional development is also offered by the professional organisations.

Those who have completed the full Association of Accounting Technicians (AAT) qualification can do the AAT Fast Track module to become fully qualified with CIPFA in two years.

Entrants who are over 21 can start training with the Chartered Institute of Public Finance Accountancy (CIPFA) with three years' relevant experience and the support of their employer. Those over 25, with five years' relevant experience, may be able to gain exemptions for some modules. There is also a fast track route available through the Warwick Postgraduate Diploma in Public Finance and Leadership. See the CIPFA website for full details.

Opportunities and Pay

You can work in various civil service agencies and departments, local authorities, the NHS, the National Audit Office, Audit Commission, or the Accounts Commission. Public finance accountants can also work in public sector industries, such as gas, electricity and water, or for charitable organisations, educational institutions, police authorities and housing associations. In the national audit organisations, there is a set career structure. Otherwise, pay and promotion depends on the employer, but it is possible to move between employers to gain experience and promotion, and to move into industry and commerce.

Salaries vary across sector, region and through each organisation. A trainee typically earns around £19k-£26k a year, depending on qualifications, location or employer, and around £30k-£40k when qualified. Experienced accountants earn around £40k-£120k a year, depending on location and level of responsibility.

Skills and Qualities

able to work to a budget, able to work to deadlines, accurate, analytical skills, attention to detail, good communication skills, good interpersonal skills, IT skills, patient, problem-solving skills

Relevant Subjects

Business and accounting, Economics, English, ICT/Computer studies, Law, Mathematics

Further Information

Accountancy Uncovered (Trotman 2010) - www.trotman.co.uk

Accounting Web - www.accountingweb.co.uk

AGCAS: Accountancy and Business Services (Job Sector Briefing) (AGCAS) - www.prospects.ac.uk/

AGCAS: Government & Public Administration (Job Sector Briefing) (AGCAS) - www.prospects.ac.uk

Diploma in Business, Administration and Finance - www.baf-diploma.org.uk/

Finance and Accounting (Pearson Publishing) - www.pearsoned.co.uk

Financial Services Skills Council - sector skills council for financial services, accountancy & finance - www.fssc.org.uk/

Inside Careers Guide: Chartered Accountancy - www.insidecareers.co.uk

Welsh Baccalaureate - www.wbq.org.uk

▶Working in maths (2009) (Babcock Lifeskills) - www.babcock-lifeskills.com/

Young Enterprise - www.young-enterprise.org.uk/pub/

Addresses

Association of Accounting Technicians (AAT)
140 Aldersgate Street, London EC1A 4HY
Phone: +44 (0)20 7397 3000
Web: www.aat.org.uk

Association of International Accountants (AIA)
Staithes 3, The Watermark, Metro Riverside, Newcastle upon Tyne NE11 9SN
Phone: +44 (0)191 493 0277
Web: www.aiaworldwide.com

Chartered Institute of Management Accountants (CIMA)
26 Chapter Street, London SW1P 4NP
Phone: +44 (0)20 8849 2251
Web: www.cimaglobal.com

Chartered Institute of Public Finance and Accountancy (CIPFA)
3 Robert Street, London WC2N 6RL
Phone: +44 (0)20 7543 5600
Web: www.cipfa.org.uk

Similar Jobs

Accountant: Industry & Commerce, Accountant: Private Practice, Accounting Technician, Bank Manager, Credit Manager, Economist, Police Financial Investigator

Accounting Technician

also known as: Accounting Assistant, Finance Technician

CRCI:Financial Services
CLCI:NAB Job Band: 3

Job Description

Accounting technicians collect, check and analyse financial information that enables accountants or business managers to make sound decisions. Work in all branches of accountancy as a qualified accounting professional. May work as an audit or credit control assistant, bookkeeper, payroll assistant, income supervisor or accounts manager. May do financial accounting and calculate sales, profit analysis, stock value, wages and salaries.

Some technician work includes checking financial records, examining expenses and looking at tax returns. In financial accounting, may collate and analyse financial and statistical information for business managers. Some technicians assist accountants with audits.

Work Details

Usually work a basic 35-39 hr week, from around 9am to 5pm, Monday to Friday. Extra hours may be required at crucial times in the financial calendar, to meet deadlines or at the end of month/year accounts. Accounting technicians are office based, though there may be some local travel to clients' premises. Some employers offer flexitime, part-time and home-based work.

You need to work quickly and accurately and to keep up to date with changes in financial practices. Team work is usual, but you also have to be able to work on your own. A lot of your work is done on computer, using spreadsheets and databases, and you may deal with clients, often by telephone.

Qualification

• England, Wales and Northern Ireland

Band 3: There are no set qualifications required for training as an accounting technician. However, most employers require 4 GCSEs (A*-C) including English and maths, or another numerate subject. Many entrants have A levels or equivalent qualifications.

• Scotland

Band 3: There are no set qualifications required for training as an accounting technician. However, most employers require four S grades (1-3) including English and maths, or another numerate subject. Many entrants have H grades or similar qualifications.

Adult Qualifications

A reasonable standard of literacy and numeracy is needed. Experience in accounting, clerical or computing work is an advantage and can help towards vocational qualifications at levels 3-4.

Work Experience

Relevant work or voluntary experience is always useful and can improve your chances in application for entry to this job. Experience that gives you the opportunity to improve your administration and numeracy skills is particularly useful. In some areas there is a young apprenticeship (14-16) scheme that provides an extended work placement and eventual achievement of a relevant level 2 qualification whilst at school.

Entry and Training

Most accounting technicians undertake on-the-job training with their employer combined with study for a professional qualification. An accounting technician may gain qualifications through the Association of Accounting Technicians (AAT), or the Association of Chartered Certified Accountants (ACCA).

The AAT offers a number of courses and vocational qualifications that include a three-stage programme at foundation, intermediate and technician levels, leading to S/NVQs at levels 2-4 or a diploma in accounting, depending on how you study. Each stage usually takes around a year. You can gain exemption from some of the exams if you have certain A levels/H grades or equivalent, or a BTEC/SQA national award in a relevant subject, such as business and finance or accounting. A degree in accounting leads to substantial exemptions from the examinations and you may be able to complete the programme in a year. Courses for the AAT scheme can be either full or part time, through day release, evening classes or distance learning. Some employers have company training schemes which lead to the AAT exams.

The Financial Services Skills Council (FSSC) offers apprenticeships for both new and existing employees. The apprenticeship is made up of a technical certificate which represents a professional qualification, an NVQ/SVQ and the opportunity to obtain, key, core and essential skills. Contact the FSSC for further details.

To qualify as a certified accounting technician (CAT) through the ACCA scheme, a similar course of study combined with practical experience is offered, and exemptions are given for those with relevant qualifications. Exams are split into three levels and you can train from the age of 16.

The Institute of Chartered Accountants in England and Wales (ICAEW) and the AAT have a Fast Track direct route for qualifying as a chartered accountant, enabling those with full accounting technician qualifications to progress to chartered accountant status in as little as two years. Training programmes, including apprenticeship schemes and the Diploma/Welsh Baccalaureate in business, administration and finance, may be available in your area. Advanced apprenticeships leading to qualification at level 3 can also be a route into higher education.

Adult entry is common in this profession and there are opportunities to study for the professional examinations through part-time and distance-learning courses.

Opportunities and Pay

Despite the economic downturn, there is still demand for qualified accounting technicians. Opportunities are available throughout the UK, particularly in large towns and in cities. You can work in a range of organisations, including manufacturing companies, central and local government, financial organisations such as insurance companies and banks, and private accountancy practices. Technicians often move from one organisation to another to gain experience and promotion, and qualified and experienced technicians can undertake further study and move into a senior position, such as supervisor, financial director or company accountant.

Those who are trained to technician level can gain exemption from some of the exams of the professional accountancy bodies, and can carry on to train as professional accountants. Self-employment is also possible, providing a range of accounting services to businesses.

Salaries depend on the size and location of the firm, but are highest in London. Trainees can expect a starting wage of around £11k-£18k a year, rising to around £29k with experience and a technician qualification. Managers and self-employed technicians may earn up to £40k-£45k a year.

Skills and Qualities

able to work both on your own and in a team, accurate, analytical skills, attention to detail, discreet, good spoken communication, IT skills, logical, methodical, numeracy skills

Relevant Subjects

Business and accounting, Economics, English, ICT/Computer studies, Mathematics

Further Information

Accountancy (Wolters Kluwer (UK) Limited) - www.accountancymagazine.com

Accountancy Uncovered (Trotman 2010) - www.trotman.co.uk

Accounting Technician online (AAT) - www.aat.org.uk

Accounting Web - www.accountingweb.co.uk

Apprenticeship Schemes (National Apprenticeship Service) - www.apprenticeships.org.uk

Diploma in Business, Administration and Finance - www.baf-diploma.org.uk/

Financial Services Skills Council - sector skills council for financial services, accountancy & finance - www.fssc.org.uk/

Student Guide to the AAT Accounting Qualification (Association of Accounting Technicians) - www.aat.org.uk/

Training Schemes - www.direct.gov.uk/en/educationandlearning

Welsh Baccalaureate - www.wbq.org.uk

▶Working in maths (2009) (Babcock Lifeskills) - www.babcock-lifeskills.com/

Addresses

Association of Accounting Technicians (AAT)
140 Aldersgate Street, London EC1A 4HY
Phone: +44 (0)20 7397 3000
Web: www.aat.org.uk

Association of Chartered Certified Accountants (ACCA) UK
29 Lincoln's Inn Fields, London WC2A 3EE
Phone: +44 (0)20 7059 5000
Web: www.accaglobal.com

Institute of Chartered Accountants in England & Wales (ICAEW)
Chartered Accountants' Hall (Moorgate Place), PO Box 433, London EC2R 6EA
Phone: +44 (0)20 7920 8100
Web: www.icaew.com

Institute of Chartered Accountants in Ireland (ICAI) (Belfast)
The Linenhall 32-38 Linenhall Street, Belfast BT2 8BG
Phone: +44 (0)28 9043 5840
Web: www.icai.ie

Institute of Chartered Accountants of Scotland (ICAS)
CA House, 21 Haymarket Yards, Edinburgh EH12 5BH
Phone: +44 (0)131 347 0100
Web: www.icas.org.uk

Similar Jobs

Accountant: Private Practice, Accountant: Public Sector, Clerk: Accounts, Law Costs Draftsman, Payroll Officer, Pensions Administrator

Acoustics Physicist

also known as: Acoustician

CRCI:Science, Mathematics and Statistics
CLCI:QOF Job Band: 5

Job Description

Acoustics physicists research and study the physics of sound and vibration. They may research methods of controlling noise levels in the workplace, to improve sound quality in the entertainment or communication industries, or to develop medical ultrasound testing. Generally work with those in industry or medicine to investigate acoustic problems, and recommend solutions. They interpret data and report scientific results using sophisticated equipment. May also work in the entertainment industry to develop and improve the sound quality in places that include recording studios, theatres and stadia.

Work Details

Usually work around 35-40 hrs a week, Monday to Friday, with early starts/late finishes. Some weekend/evening work is required at times. Works in a laboratory, office or on industrial premises that usually involves sitting at a desk. Standing and bending, as well as lifting and installing equipment and instruments, is also a feature of this job. You are responsible for devising experiments, analysing data, presenting reports and supervising staff. The work requires a high degree of accuracy and you usually work as part of a team with other professional scientists. Protective clothing is often worn.

Qualification

• England, Wales and Northern Ireland

Band 5: For degree courses: 2-3 A levels, including physics and preferably maths or chemistry, and some GCSEs (A*-C) usually including English, science and maths, or equivalent. Exact requirements depend on the degree you take.

• Scotland

Band 5: For degree courses: 3-5 H grades, including physics and preferably maths or chemistry, and some S grades (1-3), usually including English, science and maths, or similar qualifications. Exact requirements depend on the degree you take.

Degree Information

A degree in physics or acoustical engineering is required. There are specialist degrees that include physics with acoustics, and there are physics and applied physics degrees that also include the study of acoustics. Postgraduate MSc and diploma courses are available, such as acoustics and noise control.

Adult Qualifications

Entry requirements may be relaxed for adults applying for higher education courses. Access or foundation courses give adults without qualifications a route onto degree courses.

Work Experience

Universities and employers may prefer candidates who have relevant work or voluntary experience. Ideally you can shadow or work with somebody who is currently involved in the work, but alternatively something involving general physics is also relevant.

Entry and Training

Almost all acoustics physicists are graduates. Degree courses last three to four years and can be full time or sandwich. Southampton University is home to the Institute of Sound and Vibration Research. It is possible to study for a BSc and a post graduate MEng. Salford offers specialist degree courses such as physics with acoustics, acoustical engineering and electro acoustics with an option to continue on to a MPhys.

Training is mainly on the job and usually combined with in-house training such as a structured graduate training programme. Postgraduate study is an advantage. Acoustic physicists can take the one or two-year part-time postgraduate diploma in acoustics and noise control offered by the Institute of Acoustics. This may be studied at a college/university or through distance learning. Membership of the Institute of Acoustics (IOA) can lead to registration with the Engineering Council as a professional engineer (chartered status).

The Institute of Physics (IOP) offer qualifications such as a postgraduate diploma in acoustics noise control as well as certificates of competence in subjects that include workplace noise risk assessment. Membership of the IOP can be attained by graduates with 4-5 years' relevant experience.

Mature applicants with previous experience in acoustics technical work or in sound engineering may have an advantage. A formal qualification such as a degree and up-to-date scientific knowledge is usually essential. Financial support for postgraduate study may be available from organisations that include the Engineering and Physical Sciences Research Council (EPSRC) and the Science and Technology Facilities Council (STFC).

Opportunities and Pay

Opportunities arise throughout the country, mostly in large towns or cities. Employers include communications, broadcasting, manufacturing, construction, civil engineering, medical, aerospace, transportation and offshore industries, government departments or research councils. Many acoustics physicists are employed in the aircraft industry, working on engine design and manufacture, or airport controls. Others investigate the effects of noise and vibration in marine engineering. Progression is to more senior grades with increasing responsibility. Promotion can be easier with higher qualifications. Some experienced acoustic physicists work as independent consultants.

The Institute of Acoustics (IOA) has around 3,000 members, 900 of which are employed in industry, commerce and consultancies, 400 in education and research, and nearly 500 in public authorities.

Pay and career progression depends on the type of employer, but graduate entrants earn around £18k-£24k a year, rising to £35k a year with experience. Those in more senior posts may earn more than £50k a year.

Health

This job requires normal hearing and colour vision.

Skills and Qualities

able to report accurately, analytical skills, aptitude for teamwork, flexible approach, initiative, IT skills, numeracy skills, precise, technical aptitude

Relevant Subjects

Biology, Chemistry, Design and technology, English, ICT/Computer studies, Mathematics, Physics, Science

Further Information

Acoustics Bulletin (Institute of Acoustics) - www.ioa.org.uk/bulletin.asp

Tomorrow's Engineers - www.tomorrowsengineers.org.uk/careers.cfm

▶Working in science (2007) (Babcock Lifeskills) - www.babcock-lifeskills.com/

Addresses

Engineering and Physical Sciences Research Council (EPSRC)
Polaris House North Star Avenue, Swindon, Wiltshire SN2 1ET
Phone: +44(0)1793 444 100
Web: www.epsrc.ac.uk

Institute of Acoustics (IOA)
77a St Peter's Street, St Albans, Hertfordshire AL1 3BN
Phone: +44 (0)1727 848 195
Web: www.ioa.org.uk

Institute of Physics (IOP)
76 Portland Place, London W1B 1NT
Phone: +44 (0)20 7470 4800
Web: www.iop.org

Science and Technology Facilities Council (STFC)
Polaris House, North Star Avenue, Swindon, Wiltshire SN2 1SZ
Phone: +44 (0)1793 442 000
Web: www.scitech.ac.uk

SEMTA - Engineering Careers Information Service
14 Upton Road, Watford WD18 0JT
Phone: 0845 643 9001 (UK only)
Web: www.semta.org.uk

University of Salford
Salford, Greater Manchester M5 4WT
Phone: +44 (0)161 295 5000
Web: www.salford.ac.uk

University of Southampton
School of Psychology Shackleton Building Highfield, Southampton, Hampshire SO17 1BJ
Phone: +44(0)23 8059 3995
Web: www.psychology.soton.ac.uk

Similar Jobs
Audiological Scientist, Engineer: Broadcast, Geophysicist, Physicist, Teacher: Physical Sciences

Actor
CRCI:Performing Arts
CLCI:GAB Job Band: 1 to 5

Job Description
Actors assume a character created by an author or playwright and communicate this to an audience in live theatre productions, or for television, film or radio, using speech, movement and body language. They study the part to understand the character, memorise lines (vocal text) and rehearse the performance, following a director's instructions. Work includes both live performances and recordings. Some actors specialise by working with a classical theatre company, or in musicals, comedy, mime or puppetry.

Actors may work in TV and radio, including 'soaps', drama or documentaries. Some use their talent in community theatre, education and training, and also in a therapeutic role to help people to improved health or recovery from accidents and trauma. Some actors may also direct plays or teach.

Work Details
You work in a theatre, studio, or out on location, sometimes abroad, maybe travelling a good deal, and staying away from home for long periods. Work involves long hours, in the evenings and at weekends. A lot of time is spent learning parts and rehearsing. Rehearsal rooms are not always very comfortable and may be cold and draughty. If you are employed by a repertory company you may have to rehearse next week's play during the day, while performing the current play in the evenings. In film and television work, there may be a lot of hanging around while the scene is set and cameras are put in place.

Qualification
There is no one route to becoming an actor. Talent and determination are essential. Luck also plays a part - being in the right place at the right time. A degree in drama or HND in performing arts improves your chances because it provides experience. Many actors begin through fringe or amateur theatre.

Degree Information
It is possible to enter this job with a degree in any subject, but acting, drama, musical theatre and performing arts are most relevant. Drama can be studied within a teacher training course that leads to a BEd, though the National Council for Drama Training advises further vocational training and experience, before working as a professional actor. It may be useful to take a postgraduate course in directing, stage management, scriptwriting or dramatherapy.

Adult Qualifications
It is extremely difficult to enter this profession without talent and relevant experience, and most entrants have also attended drama school. Most colleges do not ask for formal qualifications from adults. Entry to a course is by audition and interview. There are a few one-year drama courses for graduates and mature entrants.

Work Experience
It is essential to get involved in drama through school, college/university, amateur dramatics or youth theatre and develop your skills and talent. Further experience, including front of house duties, directing, lighting, or editorial production of programmes, etc, is very useful. Working as an extra in productions is also useful experience.

Entry and Training
Most people enter the profession after taking a specialist course, degree or attending drama or stage school, but a few gain entry directly. Entry to both training courses and the profession is highly competitive. Often those entering courses have experience in school drama or youth theatre work. Selection for non-graduate courses is by audition and usually an interview. Check that the course you have chosen is accredited by the National Council for Drama Training (NCDT) and the Conference of Drama Schools. Courses last for 2-3 years and lead to a recognised professional diploma or BA in acting, as well as membership of Equity, the performers' trade union.

Graduates from courses that are not NCDT accredited may have more difficulty getting work. It may be worth training in singing and dance to widen your employment prospects. You can also train to direct, write scripts, teach, or work in dramatherapy. An annual dance and drama award is available from the government for the most talented dance/drama students from accredited providers in the UK.

A Diploma/Welsh Baccalaureate in creative and media may be available in your area. Check university entry requirements carefully in case there is an additional specialist learning requirement with the diploma. See the diplomas website for further information.

You need to be very proactive to find work and normally have to attend auditions to get a job. Once in work, you may have specific training for a part, such as a dance routine or special accent.

Adult applicants may find that some drama schools set upper age limits. Check requirements with individual schools. Government training opportunities, such as apprenticeships, may be available in your area. You can also gain recognition of previous experience through Accreditation of Prior Learning (APL) or by working towards relevant S/NVQs. Contact your local careers office, Jobcentre Plus, Next Step service or Learning and Skills Council (LSC) Local Enterprise Company (LEC) for details of training schemes, including apprenticeships for adults.

Opportunities and Pay
There is limited job security in acting. Jobs are often short term unless you are employed for a season with a repertory theatre, or in a regular television production. Many actors spend a lot of time 'resting' between jobs. Prospects vary according to the time of the year, such as at Christmas/New Year, when more jobs are available in pantomime. Most jobs are in large cities with commercial theatre companies, films, television, radio, TV

commercials, stunt work, children's and community theatres, promotional and training videos. There are also opportunities to work overseas or on cruise ships.

Many actors use an agent to find work. Costs can be high and probably include an agent's fee and professional subscriptions, although it is no longer essential to belong to Equity. You can also join a casting service such as The Spotlight to find work.

Pay is usually low and can be irregular, so you may need to have another job or source of income. According to Equity, pay is calculated on four factors; the category of the theatre, the performance schedule, the job of the actor and the actor's schedule. Many actors must take jobs paid by the day when starting and receive between £70 and £120 for walk-on parts or around £90 as supporting actors. Equity has negotiated minimum rates with all the main users of actors. Check the website for details. An actor in the chorus for a West End (London) show might earn around £500 a week, but £350 elsewhere. Successful actors earn very much more than this, although it is impossible to generalise earnings as they vary so much.

Health
You need to be physically fit and in good health to be an actor.

Skills and Qualities
able to withstand criticism, aptitude for teamwork, clear speaking voice, creative flair, good communication skills, good memory, reliable, self confident, stamina, versatile

Relevant Subjects
English, Media and communication studies, Performing arts

Further Information
Actors Centre - www.actorscentre.co.uk/

Apprenticeship Schemes (National Apprenticeship Service) - www.apprenticeships.org.uk

Conference of Drama Schools (CDS) - www.drama.ac.uk

Creative Choices - www.creative-choices.co.uk

Dance and Drama Awards - www.direct.gov.uk/en/EducationAndLearning

Diplomas (Foundation, Higher and Advanced) - http://yp.direct.gov.uk/diplomas

National Association of Youth Theatres - www.nayt.org.uk

National Youth Theatre of Great Britain - www.nyt.org.uk

Royal Academy of Dramatic Art (RADA) - http://rada.org/

The Spotlight - www.spotlightcd.com

The Stage Online - www.thestage.co.uk

Universal Extras - www.universalextras.co.uk

Welsh Baccalaureate - www.wbq.org.uk

▶Working in creative & media (2007) (Babcock Lifeskills) - www.babcock-lifeskills.com/

Addresses
Equity
Guild House, Upper St Martin's Lane, London WC2H 9EG
Phone: +44 (0)20 7379 6000
Web: www.equity.org.uk

National Council for Drama Training (NCDT)
249 Tooley Street, London SE1 2JX
Phone: +44 (0) 20 7407 3686
Web: www.ncdt.co.uk

Royal National Theatre
South Bank, London SE1 9PX
Phone: +44 (0)20 7452 3400
Web: www.nationaltheatre.org.uk

Similar Jobs
Dancer, Dramatherapist, Entertainer, Film/TV Stunt Performer, Presenter: Radio & TV, Teacher: Drama, Theatre Producer

Actuary
also known as: Insurance Actuary

CRCI:Financial Services
CLCI:NAJ Job Band: 4 to 5

Job Description
Actuaries apply mathematical theories and statistics to help the financial world and governments assess the long-term financial implications of their decisions, and to minimise losses associated with uncertain events. Traditionally work in pensions and insurance to design policies and calculate premiums so that the company does not make a loss. They also play a valuable role in other areas such as healthcare, banking, risk assessment and business management, and help the government to formulate public policies.

Actuaries collect and analyse data, such as medical and social factors affecting the life expectancy of different groups of people, and make predictions (work out the odds), according to the theory of probability. Design pension and insurance schemes, calculate risks, policy premiums and dividends. They use a computer to help in the analysis.

Work Details
Usually work a 35-39 hr week, Monday to Friday. This is mainly an office-based job, but if you work as a consultant, you spend a lot of time travelling and visiting clients. You are part of a team or consult with insurance underwriters and investment managers. This can be a very demanding job, involving forecasting trends, planning ahead and negotiating with other professionals such as accountants and lawyers.

Qualification
• England, Wales and Northern Ireland
Band 4: To register as a student member of the Institute of Actuaries, you need at least two A levels, including maths at grade B or higher.

Band 5: For degree courses: 2-3 A levels and some GCSEs (A*-C) usually including English and maths, or equivalent. For actuarial training, you need A level maths at grade B. Exact requirements depend on the degree you take.

• Scotland
Band 4: To register as a student member of the Faculty of Actuaries, you need at 3 H grades, including maths at grade A.

Band 5: For degree courses: 3-5 H grades and some S grades (1-3), usually including English and maths, or similar qualifications. For actuarial training, H grades must include maths at grade A or above. Exact requirements depend on the degree you take.

Degree Information
There are several degree and postgraduate courses available in actuarial science and combined studies, such as actuarial mathematics and statistics, but degrees in any discipline are accepted. However, employers often prefer a good honours degree in a mathematical or statistical subject. Other degrees, such as economics, computer science, engineering and physics, are also useful.

Adult Qualifications
There are usually special entry standards for adults applying for degree courses. Check with the universities for information. The Institute of Actuaries prefers entrants to start training within four years of achieving their entry qualifications.

Work Experience
Relevant work or voluntary experience is always useful and improves your chances in application for entry to this job. Any work in the finance sector is relevant and shows enthusiasm and commitment to the work. Time spent in a government office, an

accountancy firm or insurance company gives you a good basis and insight into the profession. The Actuarial Profession website has details of companies who offer work experience placements.

Entry and Training

Most entrants are graduates, usually with a degree in mathematics, statistics, or financial and actuarial science, or a related subject, and many employers look for a 2.1. Training is by practical experience, as well as study for the professional exams of the Institute of Actuaries, or the Faculty of Actuaries in Scotland, known jointly as the Actuarial Profession. Exams are held twice a year and it takes an average of 3-6 years to complete them and qualify as an actuary. The study programme covers topics such as statistical modelling, financial and actuarial maths, economics, and traditional areas of actuarial work, including life/general assurance, asset management, investment, pensions and employee benefits.

A degree/postgraduate degree in actuarial science offers the possibility of exemption from some of the professional syllabus. Most trainees take distance-learning courses and, although employers usually allow some time for study, you still have to do a great deal in your own time. Actuaries are expected to undertake continuing professional development to keep up to date.

Mature entrants with a numerate or science-based degree may take a postgraduate course in actuarial science. Most entrants are younger, and mature entrants should consider studying for one or two actuarial exams independently before applying. Exceptions may be considered for those with proven aptitude and experience, particularly in the insurance or pensions industry. Some financial support for relevant higher education study may be available from the Worshipful Company of Actuaries Charitable Trust Fund. It is useful to speak with someone within the actuarial profession before committing to a course.

Opportunities and Pay

Employers are usually concentrated around London and the South East and Edinburgh, though opportunities are increasing, regionally and worldwide. The majority of actuaries work for insurance or life assurance companies. Others work as consultants, or in the Government Actuary's Department, or the Stock Exchange. A few work in industry, commerce or education. Although this is a small profession there are good opportunities for actuaries in the UK, with many progressing to senior management jobs.

Actuaries are employed all over the world, and especially in the USA, Australia, Canada, New Zealand, the West Indies, South Africa and the Far East.

Salaries can vary considerably and generally depend on the size and location of the firm. The starting salary for graduate trainees is around £31k a year. Qualified actuaries can earn in the range of £43k-£53k and managers earn from £74k - £100k a year. Those who work their way up to partner in a firm can earn up to £180k a year.

Skills and Qualities

analytical skills, attention to detail, good at calculating risks, good concentration level, good written English, information handling skills, IT skills, numeracy skills, problem-solving skills, sound judgement

Relevant Subjects

Business and accounting, Economics, English, ICT/Computer studies, Law, Mathematics

Further Information

AGCAS: Accountancy and Business Services (Job Sector Briefing) (AGCAS) - www.prospects.ac.uk/

Association of Consulting Actuaries (ACA) - www.aca.org.uk

Inside Careers Guide: Actuaries - www.insidecareers.co.uk

Insurance Careers (CII) (CII) - www.cii.co.uk/

The Actuarial Profession - www.actuaries.org.uk

The Actuary (Incisive Media Ltd.) - www.the-actuary.org.uk

The Association of British Insurers (ABI) - www.abi.org.uk

▶Working in maths (2009) (Babcock Lifeskills) - www.babcock-lifeskills.com/

Worshipful Company of Actuaries - www.actuariescompany.co.uk/

Addresses

Faculty of Actuaries
Maclaurin House, 18 Dublin Street, Edinburgh EH1 3PP
Phone: +44 (0)20 7632 2100
Web: www.actuaries.org.uk

Government Actuary's Department (GAD)
Finlaison House, 15-17 Furnival Street, London EC4A 1AB
Phone: +44 (0)20 7211 2601
Web: www.gad.gov.uk

Institute of Actuaries
Napier House, 4 Worcester Street, Oxford OX1 2AW
Phone: +44 (0)1865 268 211
Web: www.actuaries.org.uk

Similar Jobs

Economist, Insurance Underwriter, Investment Analyst, Pension Fund Manager, Pensions Adviser, Statistician

Acupuncturist

CRCI:Healthcare
CLCI:JOD — Job Band: 4 to 5

Job Description

Acupuncturists aim to improve a client's health through holistic treatment (treating the whole body rather than isolated symptoms), and insert extremely fine needles into parts of the skin at particular points on the body to improve health. The principle aim is to recover the body's physical, spiritual and emotional balance by releasing endorphins which block pain. They examine the patient's health and lifestyle in detail and advise on diet and exercise. Then prescribe a course of treatment using acupuncture, a 3,000 year old system of traditional Chinese medicine which motivates the body's energy, known as Qi, and the healing power of the body.

Acupuncturists treat a range of conditions including respiratory problems such as asthma, digestive disorders and high blood pressure, arthritis and back pain, migraines and anxiety, reproductive problems and addictions (such as alcohol and drugs) and mental illness. They can also use acupuncture as an anaesthetic without the need for additional orthodox drugs, and for pain relief. May also heat the needles and treat them with herbs before insertion.

The use of electrical energy (electro-acupuncture) has been developed and introduced alongside traditional methods of treatment. Acupuncture is a medical technique recognised by the World Health Organisation.

Work Details

You work in consulting rooms and may be able to choose your own working hours. Some acupuncturists work from home, provided they have suitable facilities. You examine patients, advise and treat them. There is contact with people of all ages, who may be in pain or ill and possibly upset. You are responsible for careful work and giving sound advice. Work may be stressful at times and you have to cope with some standing and bending.

Qualification

Some institutions may consider applicants without formal academic qualifications if you can demonstrate an ability to study at the required level, have enthusiasm for the subject and the appropriate personality.

Acupuncturist

• England, Wales and Northern Ireland

Band 4: For HND, Diploma of Higher Education or foundation degree: 1-2 A levels ncluding science subjects, and some GCSEs (A*-C) usually including English and maths, or equivalent.

Band 5: For degree courses or equivalent qualifications in a medical or related field: 2-3 A levels including science subjects, and some GCSEs (A*-C) usually including English and maths, or equivalent. Exact requirements depend on the degree you take.

• Scotland

Band 4: For entry to training courses, SQA higher national and professional development awards, usually 2-3 H grades, preferably including chemistry and biology, and some S grades (1-3), including English and maths, or similar qualifications.

Band 5: For degree courses or equivalent qualifications in a medical or related field: 3-5 H grades including science subjects and some S grades (1-3), usually including English and maths, or similar qualifications. Exact requirements depend on the degree you take.

Degree Information

Degrees are available in acupuncture and specific subjects such as complementary medicine or Chinese medicine (acupuncture). Degrees in orthodox medicine and related subjects, such as a medical science, radiography, osteopathy, biology or nursing may be preferred for entry to some professional courses. There are also relevant postgraduate courses available.

Adult Qualifications

Entry requirements may be relaxed for adults applying for higher education courses. Access or foundation courses give adults without qualifications a route onto degree courses. It is an advantage to have experience in nursing, biology, medicine or a related field.

Work Experience

Relevant work or voluntary experience is always useful and can improve your chances in application for entry to this job. Consider work which involves helping people or working with the public. Work in a medical field such as volunteering at a hospital is very relevant.

Entry and Training

A degree or HND in life/medical sciences is useful, but not essential. There are several specific degrees in acupuncture. The British Acupuncture Council (BAcC) is the UK's main regulatory body for the practice of acupuncture. The British Acupuncture Accreditation Board offers training through a three-year full-time or part-time equivalent course. The Board is part of the BAcC which approves standards of training and can supply a list of recognised college courses. Applicants are carefully selected and personal suitability is very important. Some courses require a qualification in orthodox medicine or a medically-related area.

The British Medical Acupuncture Society runs courses for UK-registered healthcare professionals who wish to use acupuncture as an additional skill to traditional medicine. This includes registered doctors and dentists, vets, osteopaths, physiotherapists, podiatrists, midwives and nurses. Acupuncture is currently a self-regulated profession but this is likely to change in the near future.

Training generally lasts for two years part time, or three years for nurses or similarly qualified students. Training costs can be substantial. Students do not automatically receive loans or bursaries for some training courses and many are self-financing. Continuing professional development (CPD) is important and the BAcC runs a CPD programme for members.

A Diploma/Welsh Baccalaureate in society, health and development may be available in your area and be relevant to this job.

Mature entrants in their late 20s or early 30s are common. Entry requirements to some courses may be relaxed for those without the required academic qualifications, if you have relevant work experience and enthusiasm. It is an advantage to have experience in nursing, biology, medicine or a related field. Specific training courses are available through the British Medical Acupuncture Society for qualified dentists, doctors and vets. You may be able to receive funding (loans/bursaries) from the relevant professional bodies.

Opportunities and Pay

This is a small, but fast-growing profession, particularly in large towns and cities. Around 3,000 acupuncturists are registered with the British Acupuncture Council but many more than this practise in the UK. There is a shortage of qualified practitioners in some areas. Currently, the majority of acupuncturists are self-employed and work in private practice, but there are also opportunities to work in complementary therapy clinics, private healthcare schemes and hospitals, drug rehabilitation projects, pain clinics and local healthcare initiatives. A small number of acupuncturists now work for the NHS too. Prospects may depend on your willingness to move to another area.

As most acupuncturists are self-employed it is difficult to summarise earnings. Most charge around £40 a session (up to £90 in London), depending on location and experience. Over the year earnings can range from around £20k to more than £40k a year, depending on the number of clients/sessions.

Health

This job requires good colour vision for certain areas of work.

Skills and Qualities

analytical skills, business awareness, good listening skills, methodical, patient, precise, reassuring, scientific approach, steady hand, tactful

Relevant Subjects

Biology, Chemistry, English, Health and social care, Mathematics, Physics, Psychology

Further Information

Acupuncture in Medicine Journal (quarterly) (British Medical Acupuncture Society) - www.aim.bmj.com

Acupuncture Today (MPA Media) - http:/www.acupuncturetoday.com

Diplomas (Foundation, Higher and Advanced) - http://yp.direct.gov.uk/diplomas

Skills for Health - sector skills council - www.skillsforhealth.org.uk
Welsh Baccalaureate - www.wbq.org.uk

Addresses

Acupuncture Association of Chartered Physiotherapists (AACP)
AACP Limited, Southgate House, Southgate Park, Bakewell Road, Orton Southgate, Peterborough PE2 6YS
Phone: +44 (0)1733 390007
Web: www.aacp.uk.com

Acupuncture Society
27 Cavendish Drive, Edgware HA8 7NR
Phone: 0773 4668 402
Web: www.acupuncturesociety.org.uk

British Acupuncture Council (BAcC)
63 Jeddo Road, London W12 9HQ
Phone: +44 (0)20 8735 0400
Web: www.acupuncture.org.uk

British Acupuncure Accreditation Board (BAAB)
63 Jeddo Road, London W12 9HQ
Phone: +44 (0)20 8735 0466
Web: www.baab.co.uk

British Medical Acupuncture Society (BMAS)
BMAS House, 3 Winnington Court, Northwich, Cheshire CW8 1AQ
Phone: +44 (0)1606 786 782
Web: www.medical-acupuncture.org.uk/

Complementary Medicine Centre and Scottish College of Complementary Medicine
11 Park Circus, Glasgow G3 6AX
Phone: +44 (0)141 332 4924
Web: www.complementarymedicinecentre.co.uk

Similar Jobs

Aromatherapist, Kinesiologist, Medical Herbalist, Naturopath, Osteopath, Reflexologist

Administrator/Administrative Assistant

also known as: Office Junior, Typist, Word Processing Operator

CRCI:Administration, Business and Office Work
CLCI:CAT Job Band: 2

Job Description

Administrators produce letters, memos, minutes, reports and other documents using a computer. They check the layout, grammar and spelling on a screen and make any changes before printing. Usually work from a draft or from an audio message. Then proofread the document before printing the number of copies needed and saving the document on the computer so it can be changed and reprinted, if required. In some companies, they may use a document management system.

May do other office duties, such as filing, faxing or copying documents. May also sort the post, order stationery and answer the phone. Administrators are sometimes required to do other basic tasks, such as making tea or coffee, passing on messages and running errands.

Work Details

Usually work 35-39 hrs a week, Monday to Friday. Part-time work, flexitime, temporary work and job-sharing are possible. Your work must be accurate even when you are very busy and you need to be able to work under pressure. You may have to spend a long time each day sitting at a desk using a computer.

Normally you need to treat what you produce as confidential. In this type of work you have to be able to learn how to use new word-processing packages, and possibly new machines. For audio-typing you may have to wear headphones.

Qualification

- **England, Wales and Northern Ireland**

Band 2: For BTEC/OCR qualifications or an equivalent course: usually some GCSEs (A*-C) including English and maths, or equivalent vocational qualifications. Some employers may expect the same.

- **Scotland**

Band 2: For SQA/OCR qualifications or a similar course: usually some S grades (1-3) including English and maths, or similar qualifications. Some employers may expect the same.

Adult Qualifications

Employers and colleges do not always specify minimum qualifications, though many expect a good general level of education. Typing speed and relevant experience may be more important.

Work Experience

Relevant work or voluntary experience is always useful and can equip you with skills that you can use in the future and that you can add to your CV. Temporary holiday work in offices via employment agencies is useful, particularly if you can develop good keyboard skills and a knowledge of the most popular software packages. In some areas there is a young apprenticeship (14-16) scheme that provides an extended work placement and eventual achievement of a relevant level 2 qualification whilst at school.

Entry and Training

You may need to take a typing test to get into this job. Typing speeds of around 40-50 words per minute may be required. Training is often on the job, perhaps by work-shadowing a more experienced member of staff. You may attend a company induction to introduce you to company policy, practice and procedure.

There are a wide range of formal office skills courses available. Some people take a one-year full-time course first. Others begin as an office junior and study for exams part time through day release or evening course, if required. Courses can lead to qualifications from BTEC/SQA, OCR and London Chamber of Commerce and Industry (LCCI).

Distance-learning courses are available, including those offered by Cheltenham Tutorial College. Relevant S/NVQs at levels 1-2 are also available, such as in administration. Training programmes, including apprenticeship schemes in business administration, may be available in your area. Advanced apprenticeships leading to qualification at level 3 can also be a route into higher education.

A Diploma/Welsh Baccalaureate may be available in your area in business, administration and finance. The advanced level is equivalent to 3.5 A levels but for some university courses, the additional and specialist learning (ASL) component of the diploma needs to include specific A levels. Check entry requirements carefully with the individual institutions. See the diplomas website for further information.

Mature applicants can take refresher courses that are sometimes available for those returning to work and there may be special government training schemes in some areas. You can also gain recognition of previous experience through Accreditation of Prior Learning (APL) or by working towards relevant S/NVQs. Previous experience in office practice is an advantage though there are courses for complete beginners and courses to upgrade existing skills.

Opportunities and Pay

You may be employed by many types of organisation, such as the civil service, industry and commerce, and the armed forces. You can also get contract work through agencies or do this work from home. Your promotion prospects are better in larger companies. With further training you can move into other work with computers or secretarial work.

Pay varies depending on area and employer. Starting salaries are likely to be around £12k-£14k, rising to around £14k-£18k a year with further experience. Higher earners can achieve around £18k-£21k a year.

Health

Audio typists need to be able to hear tape recordings, usually through headphones. The positioning of work screens and the position and height of office chairs are subject to health and safety regulations. Any person who uses a VDU in their employment is also entitled to a free sight test paid for by their employer.

Skills and Qualities

able to follow instructions, able to work quickly, able to work well with others, accurate, attention to detail, good communication skills, good concentration level, good written English, IT skills, manual dexterity, methodical, reliable

Relevant Subjects

Business and accounting, English, ICT/Computer studies

Further Information

Apprenticeship Schemes (National Apprenticeship Service) - www.apprenticeships.org.uk

Apprenticeships in Scotland (Careers Info Scotland) - www.apprenticeshipsinscotland.com/about/

Council for Administration (CfA) - www.cfa.uk.com

Diplomas (Foundation, Higher and Advanced) - http://yp.direct.gov.uk/diplomas

Institute of Chartered Secretaries and Administrators (ICSA) - www.icsa.org.uk

Institute of Professional Administrators (Institute of Professional Administrators) - www.inprad.org

Local Government Careers (Improvement and Development Agency) - www.lgcareers.com/publications/

Real Life Guide to Business & Administration (Trotman 2009) - www.trotman.co.uk

Training Schemes - www.direct.gov.uk/en/educationandlearning

►Working in business, administration & finance (2010) (Babcock Lifeskills) - www.babcock-lifeskills.com/

►Working in English (2007) (Babcock Lifeskills) - www.babcock-lifeskills.com/

Addresses

Cheltenham Tutorial College
292 High Street, Cheltenham GL50 3HQ
Phone: +44 (0)1242 241279
Web: www.cheltenhamlearning.com

Similar Jobs

Clerk: Accounts, IT Data Input Operator, Local Government Administrative Assistant, Receptionist, Secretary

Adult Guidance Worker

CRCI:Social Work and Counselling Services
CLCI:KED Job Band: 4 to 5

Job Description

Adult guidance workers provide adults with advice and guidance on their education, training and employment options by linking their skills and interests to realistic career choices. Guidance is provided at adult centres or by telephone and email. Adult guidance workers arrange individual appointments or may work on a drop-in basis. For guidance to be successful, workers must first gain the clients' trust. By asking the right questions and listening carefully to the client's answers, they can identify and understand any barriers to the client's goals. Also help clients to decide on the best and most realistic way forward to achieve those goals.

Guidance workers help clients use up-to-date information resources such as computer guidance software, assessment tools and psychometric testing to help make informed choices and decisions. They use the Internet and printed publications as sources of information. May access educational course databases and liaise with training organisations and other agencies that provide opportunities. Some guidance workers give presentations to groups, or run courses and workshops. Others specialise in working with vulnerable groups such as homeless people, or those with learning difficulties.

Work Details

Usually work a basic 39 hr week, Monday to Friday, in a public office in or near a town/city centre, or near a university/college. Part-time work, flexi-time and job share may be available at some centres. You interview/advise people, deal with enquiries and provide information. Sometimes the work may be pressurised.

Qualification

- **England, Wales and Northern Ireland**

Band 4: For entry to some courses: 1-2 A levels and some GCSEs (A*-C), or equivalent. There are no set academic entry requirements for the NVQ level 4 in advice and guidance or the Qualification in Career Guidance (QCG).

Band 5: For degree courses: 2-3 A levels and some GCSEs (A*-C) usually including English, or equivalent. Exact requirements depend on the degree you take.

- **Scotland**

Band 4: For entry to some courses: 2-3 H grades and some S grades (1-3) or similar. There are no set academic entry requirements for the SVQ level 4 in advice and guidance or for the Qualification in Careers Guidance (QCG).

Band 5: For degree courses: 3-5 H grades and some S grades (1-3), usually including English. Exact requirements depend on the degree you take.

Degree Information

A degree in any subject is acceptable. Subjects such as psychology, education, and the social sciences give useful background knowledge. There are relevant postgraduate courses in careers guidance and education, and in careers management and counselling.

Adult Qualifications

Applicants without a degree or a similar qualification must convince selectors of their ability to cope with the academic and intensive nature of the Qualification in Career Guidance (QCG), similar to that of a postgraduate course.

Work Experience

Those who have relevant paid or voluntary experience have an advantage. This includes anything dealing with adults and the public in a helping capacity, such as at community centres or with adult groups and organisations. Any observation or direct experience in the caring professions is an advantage. Teaching, social work, youth work, probation or personnel work are all relevant to a career in adult guidance.

Entry and Training

Many guidance workers are graduates and have the Qualification in Career Guidance (QCG) or in Scotland the Qualification in Career Guidance and Development (QCGD), awarded by the Institute of Career Guidance (ICG). This can be obtained through one-year of full-time study or two years' part-time study at 11 universities across the UK and two in Scotland. Entry to this course does not necessarily require a first degree but you must prove that you can study at the level required for a postgraduate qualification. A relevant qualification and/or experience in social science or social studies, municipal or public administration, management studies or political science can therefore be useful.

There is also a postgraduate certificate/diploma/masters in career education, information and guidance in HE offered by the Association of Graduate Careers Advisory Services (AGCAS) and Reading University. This is an in-service course for those working in higher education. A recognised teaching qualification, PGCE, diploma in higher education, vocational guidance or relevant HND are also suitable. Most important are the right personal qualities such as good communication and motivational skills, and an ability to listen carefully and respond to the client's individual needs.

S/NVQs are available at levels 3-4 in advice and guidance for those already working in guidance-related areas. New work-based vocational qualifications for those who currently work in or wish to work in the adult guidance sector will replace these S/NVQs in 2011. Contact Lifelong Learning UK for details of the new qualifications and ICG for details of all routes to qualifying.

The National Open College Network offers awards and certificates in information, advice or guidance at NQF levels 1-3. The minimum age for entry to courses is 18. Contact your local Open College Network for further information.

Mature applicants with experience or skills in guidance or a related context have an advantage. Experience in social work, probation work, counselling, teaching or youth work, commerce and industry is useful, though adult entry from other fields is also common. Mature candidates without a degree can enter the Qualification in Career Guidance course if they can demonstrate commitment and relevant experience.

Opportunities and Pay

Information, advice and guidance services are provided by Next Step in England. Other typical employers are careers service companies, Employment Service/Jobcentre Plus offices, adult education and community centres, and some colleges/libraries. There are also private careers consultancies that provide a fee-paying service to adults. Those with experience and qualifications can become self-employed consultants.

Guidance workers earn around £15.5k-£18k a year, rising to around £22k-£29k with experience. Those with more responsibility earn around £29k-£35k a year, and senior managers can earn over £40k.

Skills and Qualities

able to prioritise work, able to work both on your own and in a team, efficient record keeping, excellent communication skills, good at writing reports, good interpersonal skills, good listening skills, information handling skills, IT skills, self confident, tactful & discreet

Relevant Subjects

English, Psychology, Sociology

Further Information

Careers Guidance Today (quarterly) (Institute of Careers Guidance (ICG) - www.icg-uk.org/career_guidance_today.html

ENTO (Employment National Training Organisation) (ENTO (Employment National Training Organisation)) - www.ento.co.uk

LLUK (Lifelong Learning UK) - sector skills council for the professional development of staff working in the lifelong learning sector - www.lluk.org

National Open College Network - www.nocn.org.uk

▶ Working in advice & counselling (2007) (Babcock Lifeskills) - www.babcock-lifeskills.com/

▶ Working in Careers Guidance (Institute of Careers Guidance (ICG) - www.icg-uk.org/workinginguidance.html

Addresses

Association of Graduate Careers Advisory Services (AGCAS)
Millenium House, 30 Junction Road, Sheffield S11 8XB
Phone: +44 (0)114 251 5750
Web: www.agcas.org.uk

Institute of Career Guidance (ICG)
Ground Floor Copthall House 1 New Road, Stourbridge, West Midlands DY8 1PH
Phone: +44 (0)1384 376 464
Web: www.icg-uk.org

National Association for Educational Guidance for Adults (NAEGA)
c/o SAS Event Management The Old George Brewery
Rollestone Street, Salisbury, Wiltshire SP1 1DX
Phone: +44 (0) 1722 415 154
Web: www.naega.org.uk

National Institute for Careers Education and Counselling (NICEC)
Sheraton House, Castle Park, Cambridge CB3 0AX
Phone: +44 (0)1223 460277
Web: www.crac.org.uk/nicec

Similar Jobs

Advice Worker, Careers Adviser, Counsellor, Personal Adviser (Connexions) (England), Psychologist: Occupational, Recruitment Consultant

Advertising Account Executive

also known as: Advertising Account Handler

CRCI:Marketing and Advertising
CLCI:OD — Job Band: 4 to 5

Job Description

Advertising account executives work in an advertising agency and are responsible for the day-to-day running of an advertising campaign. They act as a link between the agency and the client, interpreting the client's wishes. Executives may suggest background research and coordinate the work of different departments, such as copywriting or art, to create the advertisement. They oversee the budget and ensure the work is completed on time and in budget, keeping in close contact with both the client and agency, and discusses campaign progress. They usually have several 'accounts', each dealing with a different product.

Advertising agencies can be traditionally creative helping to develop a communications strategy for a brand, or they can be media agencies or increasingly, digital agencies. Often, these different types of agency work together on campaigns.

Work Details

Usually works Monday to Friday, though the hours are sometimes long and irregular, and may include early mornings, evenings and weekends, when tight deadlines approach. This job is mainly office based, although you may travel throughout the country to meet clients and promote the business. You may also travel abroad on business. The work involves advising and negotiating with clients. You work as a member of a team within an agency, manage a budget, and liaise closely with clients and colleagues. Legal regulations about advertising standards must be followed. Your work may be pressurised at times.

Qualification

• England, Wales and Northern Ireland

Band 4: For HND, Diploma of Higher Education or foundation degree: 1-2 A levels and some GCSEs (A*-C) usually including English and maths, or equivalent. There are a few courses related to advertising, as well as courses in business, administration or business studies, which include an advertising/marketing option.

Band 5: For degree courses: 2-3 A levels and some GCSEs (A*-C) usually including English and maths, or equivalent. Exact requirements depend on the degree you take.

• Scotland

Band 4: For entry to SQA higher national and professional development awards, usually 2-3 H grades and some S grades (1-3), including English and maths, or similar qualifications. There are a few courses related to advertising, as well as courses in business or administration, which include an advertising/marketing option.

Band 5: For degree courses: 3-5 H grades and some S grades (1-3), including English and maths, or similar qualifications. Exact requirements depend on the degree you take.

Degree Information

A degree in any subject is acceptable although degrees in advertising, communications, marketing, English, business or management may be an advantage.

Adult Qualifications
Those with a period of relevant work experience and with a minimum standard of entry qualifications may be accepted by the smaller, more specialist agencies and able to study for a Communication Advertising and Marketing (CAM) Education Foundation diploma course. Entry requirements for higher education may be relaxed for adults with previous experience in marketing or communications. Check with universities or colleges.

Work Experience
Entry to this job is competitive and it is important that you try to do some relevant work or voluntary experience before applying. Direct experience in advertising is ideal, but gaining experience in marketing, sales and public relations is also useful. The Institute of Practitioners in Advertising (IPA) website lists member agencies offering work experience and runs a summer school each year offering students the opportunity to win placements at advertising agencies.

Entry and Training
Entry to this work is very competitive. Most entrants are graduates, or move into account handling from another advertising job such as a copywriter or visualiser. Many of the larger agencies have a training programme for new entrants, learning from experienced members of staff. This can involve gaining experience in different departments within the agency, or working under the supervision of a mentor who oversees your work and gives advice.

D&AD runs advertising, design and digital workshops. You can also take professional courses organised by the Institute of Practitioners in Advertising (IPA), including the IPA Excellence Diploma once you have three years work experience. The Communication Advertising and Marketing (CAM) Education Foundation offers diploma courses in marketing, communications, digital marketing and managing digital media that can be studied at a range of study centres or through distance learning. Other short courses to support continuing professional development are offered by the IPA and the Account Planning Group.

A Diploma/Welsh Baccalaureate in creative and media may be offered in your area and can be a good route into this career. Foundation degrees in marketing and advertising are also available. Postgraduate professional qualifications are not essential though the professional diploma in marketing, offered by the Chartered Institute of Marketing, is very useful.

Entry requirements may be relaxed for adults applying for higher education courses. Access or similar courses give adults without qualifications a route onto degree courses. Mature applicants with relevant experience, such as advertising or sales, have an advantage.

Opportunities and Pay
Around 4,000 people work as advertising account executives in the UK, but advertising is a small industry and most agencies employ fewer than 50 staff. Few vacancies occur each year, and many of those that do are with larger agencies based in London and other major cities. Some agencies deal with all aspects of advertising but others specialise, for example, in consumer industries. You can move between agencies to broaden your experience or to gain promotion to account manager or director. With qualifications and experience, you may be able to set up your own agency. Despite the economic downturn, advertising opportunities are still available and certain sectors, such as digital/internet advertising, are growing in strength.

Salaries vary depending on size and location of the agency. A graduate trainee can expect around £18k-£20k rising to £30k-£45k a year with experience. Senior account directors can earn more than £50k a year.

Skills and Qualities
able to cope under pressure, aptitude for teamwork, business awareness, good communication skills, good interpersonal skills, good organisational skills, IT skills, motivated, persuasive, resourceful

Relevant Subjects
Business and accounting, Economics, English, Mathematics, Media and communication studies, Psychology, Retail and distribution

Further Information
Creative & Cultural Skills - sector skills council for advertising, crafts, cultural heritage, design, literature, music, performing & visual arts - www.ccskills.org.uk

Diplomas (Foundation, Higher and Advanced) - http://yp.direct.gov.uk/diplomas

Marketing Uncovered (Trotman 2010) - www.trotman.co.uk

Marketing Week (Centaur Media Plc) - www.marketingweek.co.uk/

Welsh Baccalaureate - www.wbq.org.uk

▶Working in business, administration & finance (2010) (Babcock Lifeskills) - www.babcock-lifeskills.com/

▶Working in marketing, advertising & PR (2008) (Babcock Lifeskills) - www.babcock-lifeskills.com/

Working with languages (2010) (Babcock Lifeskills) - www.babcock-lifeskills.com/

Addresses
Account Planning Group (APG)
16 Creighton Avenue, London N10 1NU
Phone: +44 (0)20 8444 3692
Web: www.apg.org.uk

Chartered Institute of Marketing (CIM)
Moor Hall, Cookham, Maidenhead, Berkshire SL6 9QH
Phone: +44 (0) 1628 427120
Web: www.cim.co.uk

Communication Advertising and Marketing (CAM) Foundation Ltd
Moor Hall, Cookham, Maidenhead, Berkshire SL6 9QH
Phone: +44 (0)1628 427 120
Web: www.camfoundation.com

D&AD
9 Graphite Square, Vauxhall Walk, London SE11 5EE
Phone: +44 (0)207 840 1111
Web: www.dandad.org

Institute of Practitioners in Advertising (IPA)
44 Belgrave Square, London SW1X 8QS
Phone: +44 (0)20 7235 7020
Web: www.ipa.co.uk

Similar Jobs
Advertising Copywriter, Advertising Media Buyer, Advertising Media Planner, Brand Manager, Marketing Manager, Public Relations Officer

Advertising Art Director
CRCI:Marketing and Advertising
CLCI:OD
Job Band: 4 to 5

Job Description
Advertising art directors work in the creative department of an advertising agency, to produce a suitable and persuasive image which helps to sell a product. They aim to encourage people to view the product or message positively so that they want to buy or act on it. Directors may work on TV, newspaper and magazine,

poster, direct mail and internet adverts. They work closely with a copywriter who supplies the words for the advert. and ensures the project keeps to budget and deadlines.

They discuss the client's brief with the account executive, find out about the product or message, who the advertising is aimed at and what the client's competitors are doing. Works with the copywriter on a selection of attention-grabbing ideas for the advert and ensures everything complies with advertising regulations. Puts the ideas to the creative director for approval an produces sketches or storyboards to show ideas to the client. Makes any changes required by the client and finds people with the right skills to work on the project.

Advertising art directors have a clear idea of how to combine written words and images on paper or screen to create the greatest impact. They brief photographers, film crews, artists and graphic designers on what is required and may choose locations, models or actors. Goes to photo and film shoots and oversees the editing of each advert to produce the finished product.

Advertising agencies can be traditionally creative, helping to develop a communications strategy for a brand, or they can be media agencies or increasingly, digital agencies. Often, these different types of agency work together on campaigns.

Work Details

Usually works a 40hr week, Monday to Friday. May have to work evenings or weekends to meet deadlines or to get the right conditions for photo shoots. The work is mainly office or studio based and may involve sitting for long periods at a drawing board or computer, using art and design packages.

Works very closely with a copywriter and with the account team managing each client's projects. Also spends time with clients, photographers, film crews, artists and graphic designers. Travels to meetings, photo and film studios and locations. Often works on several projects at once. Working to tight deadlines and receiving negative feedback from clients can be stressful. In many agencies, the dress code is informal.

Qualification

• England, Wales and Northern Ireland

Band 4: For art and design foundation studies courses: usually 1-2 A levels and some GCSEs (A*-C). For HND, Diploma of Higher Education or foundation degree: successful completion of a foundation studies, a BTEC national award, or an equivalent qualification. Applicants may be accepted with an art A level and 4 GCSEs (A*-C). Equivalent qualifications may be accepted.

Band 5: For degree courses: 2-3 A levels and some GCSEs (A*-C) usually including English and maths, or equivalent. Exact requirements depend on the degree you take. Most students take an art and design foundation studies course first.

• Scotland

Band 4: For entry to SQA higher national and professional development awards, usually 2-3 H grades and some S grades (1-3), including English and maths, or similar qualifications.

Band 5: For degree courses: 3-5 H grades and some S grades (1-3), including English and maths, or similar qualifications. Exact requirements depend on the degree you take.

Degree Information

Relevant degrees include graphic design, advertising design, creative advertising, fine art and illustration. Some courses may have options related to advertising. A good portfolio of work is expected. There are also postgraduate courses in art direction, advertising, graphic design, illustration, film and TV, digital media and visual communications.

Adult Qualifications

Entry requirements may be relaxed for adults applying for higher education courses in art and design, but a good portfolio of work is usually required. Access to art and design or foundation courses provide those without the required qualifications a route onto degree courses.

Work Experience

Relevant work or voluntary experience is always useful and can improve your employment prospects when applying for courses or jobs. Some courses include work placements or the opportunity to take part in real commissions. The Institute of Practitioners in Advertising website lists member agencies offering work experience and runs a summer school each year offering students the opportunity to win placements at advertising agencies.

Working with someone who wants to be a copywriter on developing ideas to include in your portfolio is worthwhile. D&AD runs advertising workshops for people looking for their first job in this field. They can provide help in building your portfolio and making contacts. This organisation also offers a graduate placement scheme for design and advertising graduates who have taken part in its programmes.

Entry and Training

Competition for entry is fierce and many entrants are graduates, with a background in graphic design or visual communication. Many entrants have previous experience in digital media or graphic design and knowledge of photography, typography and printing techniques. New entrants usually learn on the job from experienced staff by observing how others are working and showing initiative in your own work until you have gained the experience needed. You need to show a good portfolio of work when applying for art and design courses and design jobs in advertising agencies.

Most people going into this area of work as a junior advertising art director have an art and design degree or HNC/HND. Foundation degrees are also available in art and design subjects and marketing and advertising. You need to show a good portfolio of work when applying for art and design courses and design jobs in advertising agencies. Employers often appoint people who already have experience of working in an advertising agency. Some may be more interested in taking on an art director and copywriter team that works well together, rather than individuals.

Entry level jobs may not be advertised, so making contact with prospective employers, getting placements and working with a good copywriter on building a portfolio is important. Training is mostly on the job learning from experienced staff, observing how others are working and showing initiative in your work until you have gained the experience needed. You may get the opportunity to attend external courses to improve your knowledge and skills in certain areas. Some large agencies run training schemes for new graduates.

You need to keep up to date with the latest trends and developments in the advertising industry. The Institute of Practitioners in Advertising (IPA) offers relevant courses and continuing professional development (CPD) programmes. These include online examination courses, short courses and workshops. D&AD runs advertising, design and digital workshops at different levels to support CPD.

A Diploma/Welsh Baccalaureate in creative and media may be offered in your area and can be a good route into this career.

Mature applicants with a background in art and design are welcome. Many advertising art directors start out as graphic or other designers in companies involved in advertising before moving into this role. You usually need a portfolio of your work. Access to art and design courses or similar give adults without qualifications a route onto degree courses.

Opportunities and Pay

This is a fast moving and highly competitive career area, but with strong growth in digital/internet advertising, the industry is finding it hard to fill creative and IT roles. Almost 70% of people employed in the industry work in London, with others based mainly in the UK's larger cities. Most advertising art directors work for advertising agencies. There are also jobs in the marketing departments of large companies and overseas.

You can progress into senior art director roles and perhaps go on to become a creative director. To progress, usually you need to move to other or larger advertising agencies. Staff turnover is high and the industry views this as a good way of keeping ideas fresh and new. Some advertising art directors go on to set up their own agencies. You can also move into management or other fields such as TV or film making. Experienced advertising art directors with a network of contacts may be able to get freelance work.

Junior advertising art directors earn in the region of £20k-£25k a year and more experienced staff earn £30k-£50k a year. Senior advertising art directors earn up to £70k and some can earn over £100k a year.

Health

You need normal colour vision to do this job.

Skills and Qualities

able to cope under pressure, able to withstand criticism, attention to detail, business awareness, creative flair, design ability, good interpersonal skills, good organisational skills, research skills, specialist IT skills

Relevant Subjects

Art and Design, English, ICT/Computer studies, Media and communication studies, Performing arts, Psychology, Sociology

Further Information

Advertising Association (AA) (Advertising Association) - www.adassoc.org.uk/aa/

Creative & Cultural Skills - sector skills council for advertising, crafts, cultural heritage, design, literature, music, performing & visual arts - www.ccskills.org.uk

Creative Choices - www.creative-choices.co.uk

Creative Review (Centaur) - www.creativereview.co.uk

Diagonal Thinking - www.diagonalthinking.co.uk

Diplomas (Foundation, Higher and Advanced) http://yp.direct.gov.uk/diplomas

Welsh Baccalaureate - www.wbq.org.uk

▶Working in marketing, advertising & PR (2008) (Babcock Lifeskills) - www.babcock-lifeskills.com/

Young Creatives Network (YCN) - www.ycnonline.com

Your Creative Future (Design Council) (Design Council) - www.yourcreativefuture.org

Addresses

Advertising Association (AA)
7th Floor North, Artillery House, 11-19 Artillery Row, London SW1P 1RT
Phone: +44 (0)20 7340 1100
Web: www.adassoc.org.uk

D&AD
9 Graphite Square, Vauxhall Walk, London SE11 5EE
Phone: +44 (0)207 840 1111
Web: www.dandad.org

Institute of Practitioners in Advertising (IPA)
44 Belgrave Square, London SW1X 8QS
Phone: +44 (0)20 7235 7020
Web: www.ipa.co.uk

Similar Jobs

Advertising Account Executive, Advertising Copywriter, Film/TV Director, Graphic Designer, Illustrator, Website Designer

Advertising Copywriter

CRCI:Marketing and Advertising
CLCI:OD Job Band: 4 to 5

Job Description

Advertising copywriters work in the creative department of an advertising agency alongside the art director, to produce an original, suitable and persuasive message to sell a product. They write the words, slogans and phrases that are seen and heard in scripts and advertisements on TV, radio or the Internet, or text for posters, magazines, the press, text messaging, and brochures. Copywriters work closely with the advertising art director to ensure that the words complement the visual images, choosing text carefully, so that it has the required impact, within time and space requirements, and legal restrictions. What is said in an advertisement has to conform to the advertising code of practice.

They may also work with account executives to understand the client's requirements and helps present the idea to a client, making any modifications if needed. Spends time in meetings with other colleagues. May liaise with production companies, photographers, printers and designers. In smaller agencies, may be expected to combine art direction with copywriting.

Work Details

Usually works Monday to Friday, but hours are sometimes long and irregular and may include evenings and weekends, when tight deadlines approach. You need to work as part of a team and the work involves sitting and discussing for lengthy periods. You must be able to write well and to be able to define technical subjects in language that is easy to understand. May also spend time visiting film or recording sessions at various locations or visiting clients, TV and radio studios.

Qualification

• England, Wales and Northern Ireland

Band 4: For HND, Diploma of Higher Education or foundation degree: 1-2 A levels and some GCSEs (A*-C) usually including English and maths, or equivalent. There are a few courses related to advertising, as well as courses in business, administration or business studies, which include an advertising/marketing option.

Band 5: For degree courses: 2-3 A levels and some GCSEs (A*-C) usually including English and maths, or equivalent. Exact requirements depend on the degree you take.

• Scotland

Band 4: For entry to SQA higher national and professional development awards, usually 2-3 H grades and some S grades (1-3), including English and maths, or similar qualifications. There are a few courses related to advertising, as well as courses in business or administration, which include an advertising/marketing option.

Band 5: For degree courses: 3-5 H grades and some S grades (1-3), including English and maths, or similar qualifications. Exact requirements depend on the degree you take.

Degree Information

A degree in any subject is acceptable although degrees in design or advertising, communications or marketing, business, media journalism or management may be an advantage. There is a choice of specialist postgraduate and diploma courses available in copywriting or creative advertising.

Adult Qualifications
Entry requirements for higher education may be relaxed for adults with previous experience in marketing or communications. Those without the required qualifications may complete a foundation or Access course leading to relevant HNDs or accredited degrees. Check with universities or colleges.

Work Experience
Entry to this job is competitive and it is important to gain experience in creative writing for a school/university magazine or a local newspaper if possible. Work or voluntary experience in an advertising environment, or in marketing and public relations is useful background. Some agencies may offer summer internships and work placements for degree students. The Institute of Practitioners in Advertising website lists member agencies offering work experience and runs a summer school each year offering students the opportunity to win placements at advertising agencies.

Entry and Training
There are no set minimum qualifications to become a copywriter but most entrants are graduates and some may be able to enter training with an HNC/HND. You usually have to approach employers directly as vacancies are not often advertised, and a portfolio of your creative work is required. Work is very competitive and you may have to take several unpaid placements to gain relevant experience. D&AD runs creative talent shows each year which give new graduates a chance to display their work. Some agencies give copy tests at interview.

Employers usually organise an on-the-job training programme for new entrants, but there are few formal graduate training schemes. D&AD runs advertising, design and digital workshops. Professional courses are also offered by the Institute of Practitioners in Advertising (IPA) for those working in IPA member agencies and many of these are online.

Trainees may also be expected to study for a professional qualification, such as the Communication, Advertising and Marketing Foundation diploma, through day release or evening classes. A Diploma/Welsh Baccalaureate in creative and media may be offered in your area and can be a good route into this career. A foundation degree in marketing and advertising is also available in some areas.

Mature applicants usually require specialist experience in broadcasting, graphic design, work as a newspaper/magazine journalist, or in marketing, as advertising is largely a young person's industry. Employers may prefer applicants to have a postgraduate qualification in advertising. There are relevant distance-learning courses available, such as those offered by the Publishing Training Centre. The Institute of Practitioners in Advertising (IPA) also offers professional courses online.

Opportunities and Pay
The advertising industry is a small employer in the UK and most agencies employ fewer than 50 staff. Few vacancies occur each year, and many of those that do are with larger agencies based in London and other major cities. Some agencies deal with all aspects of advertising but others specialise. Copywriters work for advertising agencies or are freelance. There is fierce competition for jobs.

Promotion is possible within larger agencies, to positions such as creative director or senior copywriter. Despite the economic downturn, advertising opportunities are still available and certain sectors, such as digital/internet advertising, are growing in strength. International work is possible in Europe or other areas abroad, particularly in the areas of IT, telecoms and finance.

Salaries vary depending on size and location of the employing agency. Starting salaries in London for junior copywriters are around £20k-£25k a year, rising to £30k-£50k with three to five years' experience. Very successful copywriters, particularly in specialist sectors such as medical advertising, can earn £50k-£70k, and a senior copywriter/creative director may earn over £100k a year.

Skills and Qualities
able to withstand criticism, aptitude for teamwork, business awareness, clear-thinking, creative flair, good written English, IT skills, resilient, self-motivated

Relevant Subjects
Art and Design, English, Media and communication studies, Psychology, Sociology

Further Information
Creative & Cultural Skills - sector skills council for advertising, crafts, cultural heritage, design, literature, music, performing & visual arts - www.ccskills.org.uk

Creative Review (Centaur) - www.creativereview.co.uk

Marketing Week (Centaur Media Plc) - www.marketingweek.co.uk/

Welsh Baccalaureate - www.wbq.org.uk

▶Working in English (2007) (Babcock Lifeskills) - www.babcock-lifeskills.com/

▶Working in marketing, advertising & PR (2008) (Babcock Lifeskills) - www.babcock-lifeskills.com/

Young Creatives Network (YCN) - www.ycnonline.com

Addresses
Communication Advertising and Marketing (CAM) Foundation Ltd
Moor Hall, Cookham, Maidenhead, Berkshire SL6 9QH
Phone: +44 (0)1628 427 120
Web: www.camfoundation.com

D&AD
9 Graphite Square, Vauxhall Walk, London SE11 5EE
Phone: +44 (0)207 840 1111
Web: www.dandad.org

Institute of Practitioners in Advertising (IPA)
44 Belgrave Square, London SW1X 8QS
Phone: +44 (0)20 7235 7020
Web: www.ipa.co.uk

Publishing Training Centre at Book House
45 East Hill, Wandsworth, London SW18 2QZ
Phone: +44 (0)20 8874 2718
Web: www.train4publishing.co.uk

Similar Jobs
Advertising Account Executive, Advertising Media Planner, Copy Editor, Journalist, Screenwriter, Writer: Technical

Advertising Installer
also known as: Bill Fixer, Bill Poster

CRCI:Marketing and Advertising

CLCI:OD Job Band: 1 to 2

Job Description
Advertising installers place advertisements and posters on the sides of buildings and hoardings in built-up areas of towns and cities, or into separate glass and plastic or digital display units in shopping centres, airports and rail stations. Increasingly, installers works with electronic signage. They take off the old adverts and posters and put and paste new ones in place, often working from a ladder or suspension cradle. Makes up large posters by matching smaller pieces together and may also help to put up hoardings and to repair them.

In places such as by escalators, in bus shelters and on trains, unscrews the cover of display units and takes out the old poster or reprogrammes the digital display unit. Slots in a new advert and puts back the cover securely. Some posters are now made of vinyl and these can be clipped in and out of poster frames and can also be reused. Handheld scanning systems may also be used to check structures and feedback on any repairs that are needed. Installers also clean and maintain advertising display units.

Work Details

Usually works a basic 39 hr week, Monday to Friday, including some weekends, and may be required to start early or finish later in the day. Some evening work may be required when traffic is quieter and there are fewer people about. The work can be outdoors, so you may be out in all weathers and may get cold, wet and dirty at times. Some work is inside, usually in light and airy places, such as airports and shopping malls. You travel to different sites either alone or with a team of workers, particularly if you are working at heights.

The work requires you to stand for most of the day, use ropes and harnesses or climb ladders. You usually wear overalls and possibly a safety helmet. You need to pay great attention to safety procedures.

Qualification

• England, Wales and Northern Ireland

Band 1: For entry to jobs, no minimum qualifications are needed, but you are expected to have a good level of general education and relevant experience. Some formal/vocational qualifications at any level are useful.

Band 2: For entry to jobs and electrician training courses, no minimum qualifications are needed, but it is an advantage to have some GCSEs (A*-C) or equivalent in subjects that include English, maths and science. Craft or technology subjects are useful, but not essential.

• Scotland

Band 1: For entry to jobs, no minimum qualifications are needed, but you are expected to have a good level of general education and relevant experience. Some formal/vocational qualifications at any level are useful.

Band 2: Although academic qualifications are not specified for this job, it is an advantage to have some S grades (1-3) in subjects that include English and maths, or similar. For most electrician training courses it is an advantage to have several S grades (1-3) including English, maths and science, or similar. Craft or technology subjects are useful, but not essential.

Adult Qualifications

Some formal qualifications are helpful for mature entry to training courses. Those with relevant work experience may be accepted for some college courses without needing any formal entry requirements.

Work Experience

Any work experience can equip you with skills that you can use in the future and add to your CV. Practical skills in building work, such as carpentry, joinery or electrical work, are very useful.

Entry and Training

Training is mainly on the job working with a skilled installer. Some employers provide a short induction programme for entrants, to ensure they learn the basic practical skills. The Outdoor Advertising Association (OAA) introduced a health and safety passport scheme in 2005 and all employees need to pass this scheme within three months of being appointed. During this time, you can work under the supervision of an employee with a passport.

If working at heights with ropes and harnesses, you must hold an Industrial Rope Access Trade Association (IRATA) qualification at level 1. Courses are available at training centres throughout the country. Level 2 and 3 courses are also available for those wanting to learn more skills, including supervisory training. HSS Training Solutions also runs one and two day courses in harness and height safety training.

Increasingly, installers need to be trained in electrical installation to work with digital advertising screens. An electrical installation apprenticeship may be a good route into this job. A full driving licence is usually necessary for you to travel from job to job and you must be physically fit.

Mature people are often preferred for this job, particularly when work at nights and weekends is needed. You must be physically fit.

Opportunities and Pay

Despite the economic downturn and its effect on advertising, outdoor advertising is stable and the use of more electronic and computerised signs is growing. These have replaced many older advertising hoardings and displays. Employers include advertising agencies, outdoor advertising companies and specialist bill posting companies. Installers tend to work for contractors for outdoor advertising site owners. Some companies have contract work all over the UK, but most are based in larger towns and cities, or near transport networks.

With experience, some advertising installers go on to set up their own business or work freelance for advertising companies. You can expect a starting pay of around £10.5k a year, rising to £16k with experience. A few may earn as much as £25k a year.

Health

You have to be fit and able to climb ladders and work at heights. It is useful to have normal colour vision.

Skills and Qualities

able to work both on your own and in a team, able to work quickly, attention to detail, careful, good balance, head for heights, manual dexterity, stamina

Further Information

Apprenticeship Schemes (National Apprenticeship Service) - www.apprenticeships.org.uk

Creative & Cultural Skills - sector skills council for advertising, crafts, cultural heritage, design, literature, music, performing & visual arts - www.ccskills.org.uk

Addresses

HSS Training Solutions
Circle House, Lostock Road, Manchester M41 0HS
Phone: 0845 766 7799 (UK only)
Web: www.safeonsite.com

Industrial Rope Access Trade Association (IRATA)
Kingsley House Ganders Business Park Kingsley, Bordon, Hampshire GU35 9LU
Phone: +44 (0)1420 471619
Web: www.irata.org

Outdoor Advertising Association of Great Britain (OAA)
Summit House, 27 Sale Place, London W2 1YR
Phone: +44 (0)20 7973 0315
Web: www.oaa.org.uk

Similar Jobs

Cleaner: Windows, Electrician, Painter & Decorator, Plasterer, Roofer, Scaffolder

Advertising Media Buyer

also known as: Media Buyer, Media Executive, Media Space Buyer

CRCI:Marketing and Advertising
CLCI:OD Job Band: 4 to 5

Job Description

Advertising media buyers use a 'brief' from the media planner to negotiate with media companies to buy advertising space in different kinds of media, including television, radio, posters, the internet, and in cinemas, newspapers, magazines and other printed material. Working within an agreed budget, they try to get the best deal for the client, often competing with other buyers. They build good working relationships with media owners and develop and implement different buying strategies to get the best result.

Media buyers are responsible for booking the space or airtime once the campaign plan has been agreed with the client, managing the client's budget throughout the advertising campaign, meeting media targets and may also monitor the effectiveness of the campaign. They work on several accounts at the same time, and in smaller agencies may combine this role with that of the advertising media planner.

Work Details

Usually works Monday to Friday, but you must be willing to work long hours at times, including evenings and weekends, to meet deadlines. The work is office based, but may involve going out to meetings with companies that sell advertising space. You have to be good at negotiating with people and must be able to work to an agreed budget.

A lot of the work involving the analysis of the effectiveness of different types of media is done on a computer. Buying also involves spending a lot of time on the phone or using email. You need to keep up with social and economic trends in advertising.

Qualification

- **England, Wales and Northern Ireland**

Band 4: For HND, Diploma of Higher Education or foundation degree: 1-2 A levels and some GCSEs (A*-C) usually including English and maths, or equivalent. There are a few courses related to advertising, as well as courses in business, administration or business studies, which include an advertising/marketing option.

Band 5: For degree courses: 2-3 A levels and some GCSEs (A*-C) usually including English and maths, or equivalent. Exact requirements depend on the degree you take.

- **Scotland**

Band 4: For entry to SQA higher national and professional development awards, usually 2-3 H grades and some S grades (1-3), including English and maths, or similar qualifications. There are a few courses related to advertising, as well as courses in business or administration, which include an advertising/marketing option.

Band 5: For degree courses: 3-5 H grades and some S grades (1-3), including English and maths, or similar qualifications. Exact requirements depend on the degree you take.

Degree Information

A degree in any subject is acceptable, but useful subjects include advertising, media or communication studies, statistics, management or business studies, and operational research.

Adult Qualifications

Entry requirements may be relaxed for adults applying for higher education courses. Adults with previous experience in marketing or communications may have an advantage. Access or foundation courses provide those without the required qualifications a route onto degree courses.

Work Experience

Entry to this job is competitive and it is important to gain relevant work or voluntary experience before applying to demonstrate your keen interest. Experience in an advertising environment is useful background, but sales skills are also very important, so gaining experience of marketing, sales and public relations is helpful. Some agencies may offer summer internships and work placements for degree students. The Institute of Practitioners in Advertising website lists member agencies offering work experience and runs a summer school each year offering students the opportunity to win placements at advertising agencies.

Entry and Training

There are no set entry requirements, but most entrants are graduates, or move into media buying from other advertising jobs. Many agencies have a training programme for new entrants that includes on-the-job training with an experienced colleague. Agencies encourage their entrants to gain an understanding of audience research figures and the best use of online resources.

You can take courses organised by the Institute of Practitioners in Advertising (IPA). It runs a range of courses from those for junior staff to the IPA Excellence Diploma once you have three years work experience. The Media Research Group also offers a range of courses for new entrants to media research. Other relevant courses include the Communication Advertising and Marketing Foundation diploma course, that can be studied at centres or through distance learning.

A Diploma/Welsh Baccalaureate in creative and media may be offered in your area and can be a good route into this career. Foundation degrees in marketing and advertising are also available. Postgraduate professional qualifications are not essential although the professional diploma in marketing, offered by the Chartered Institute of Marketing, is very useful.

Mature applicants with specialist experience in advertising sales for a media firm have an advantage, as advertising is largely a young person's industry. Employers may prefer applicants to have a postgraduate qualification in advertising. Online and distance learning courses are available from the Communication, Advertising and Marketing Foundation and from the Institute of Practitioners in Advertising.

Opportunities and Pay

The advertising industry is a small employer in the UK and most agencies employ fewer than 50 staff. Few vacancies occur each year, and many of those that do are with larger agencies based in London and other major cities. Some agencies deal with all aspects of advertising but others specialise. Media buying employs around 3,000 people. You can work for an advertising agency or a company specialising in media buying.

This type of work is highly competitive and promotion prospects depend on proven success in the business. There may be opportunities to work abroad if you work for a multinational agency, and freelance work is possible.

Salaries vary widely depending on qualifications, experience and the number of advertisements you sell, but graduate starting salaries tend to be around £19k-£24k a year rising to £28k-£45k with three to five years' experience. Successful and senior media buyers may earn up to £80k a year.

Skills and Qualities

able to cope under pressure, able to work to a budget, good communication skills, good interpersonal skills, good organisational skills, IT skills, negotiating skills, numeracy skills, quick thinking, resourceful

Relevant Subjects

Business and accounting, Economics, English, ICT/Computer studies, Mathematics, Media and communication studies, Psychology

Further Information

AGCAS: Media (Job Sector Briefing) (AGCAS) - www.prospects.ac.uk

Creative & Cultural Skills - sector skills council for advertising, crafts, cultural heritage, design, literature, music, performing & visual arts - www.ccskills.org.uk

Diplomas (Foundation, Higher and Advanced) - http://yp.direct.gov.uk/diplomas

Internet Advertising Bureau (IAB) - www.iabuk.net

Media Circle - www.mediacircle.org

Media Research Group - www.mrg.org.uk

Welsh Baccalaureate - www.wbq.org.uk

Winning Edge (6 x year) (Institute of Sales & Marketing Management) - www.ismm.co.uk/magazine.php

▶ Working in marketing, advertising & PR (2008) (Babcock Lifeskills) - www.babcock-lifeskills.com/

Addresses

Chartered Institute of Marketing (CIM)
Moor Hall, Cookham, Maidenhead, Berkshire SL6 9QH
Phone: +44 (0) 1628 427120
Web: www.cim.co.uk

Communication Advertising and Marketing (CAM) Foundation Ltd
Moor Hall, Cookham, Maidenhead, Berkshire SL6 9QH
Phone: +44 (0)1628 427 120
Web: www.camfoundation.com

Institute of Practitioners in Advertising (IPA)
44 Belgrave Square, London SW1X 8QS
Phone: +44 (0)20 7235 7020
Web: www.ipa.co.uk

Similar Jobs

Advertising Account Executive, Advertising Copywriter, Advertising Media Planner, Market Research Executive, Retail Buyer

Advertising Media Planner

also known as: Media Planner

CRCI:Marketing and Advertising

CLCI:OD Job Band: 4 to 5

Job Description

Advertising media planners work closely with others in the advertising team to decide on the most effective way of advertising a product. They consider the market and select the media, such as TV, radio, the internet and text messaging, newspapers, outdoor posters or hoardings, or the cinema. They aim to reach the maximum number of people for the minimum cost so base the choice of media on research data and available budget. Develops evaluation techniques to prove the value of the media contribution and feeds this information back to the client, either directly or indirectly.

Media planners provide a 'brief' to the media buyer of the information researched, including the selected media, number of people they expect in their catchments and the available budget. They set objectives for the media buying team and keep them informed of any changes in the marketplace. They often manage client relationships and aim to gain their respect and trust for future campaigns. May work on several accounts at the same time, and in smaller agencies may combine this role with that of the advertising media buyer.

Work Details

Usually works Monday to Friday, but has to be willing to work long hours at times, including evenings and weekends, to meet deadlines. The work is office based, but also involves going to strategy meetings with clients and giving presentations. This may involve short stays away from home. A lot of the work involving the analysis of the effectiveness of different types of media is done on a computer. You need to keep up to date with social and economic trends in advertising.

Qualification

• England, Wales and Northern Ireland

Band 4: For HND, Diploma of Higher Education or foundation degree: 1-2 A levels and some GCSEs (A*-C) usually including English and maths, or equivalent. There are a few courses related to advertising, as well as courses in business, administration or business studies, which include an advertising/marketing option.

Band 5: For degree courses: 2-3 A levels and some GCSEs (A*-C) usually including English and maths, or equivalent. Exact requirements depend on the degree you take.

• Scotland

Band 4: For entry to SQA higher national and professional development awards, usually 2-3 H grades and some S grades (1-3), including English and maths, or similar qualifications. There are a few courses related to advertising, as well as courses in business or administration, which include an advertising/ marketing option.

Band 5: For degree courses: 3-5 H grades and some S grades (1-3), usually including English and maths, or similar qualifications. Exact requirements depend on the degree you take.

Degree Information

A degree in any subject is acceptable, but useful subjects include advertising, media or communication studies, statistics, management or business studies, and operational research.

Adult Qualifications

Entry requirements may be relaxed for adults applying for higher education courses. Adults with previous experience in marketing or communications may have an advantage. Access or foundation courses provide those without the required qualifications a route onto degree courses.

Work Experience

Entry to this job is competitive and it is important to gain relevant work or voluntary experience before applying to demonstrate your keen interest. Experience in an advertising environment is useful background, but sales skills are also very important, so gaining experience of marketing, sales and public relations is also relevant. Some agencies may offer summer internships and work placements for degree students. The Institute of Practitioners in Advertising website lists member agencies offering work experience and runs a summer school each year offering students the opportunity to win placements at advertising agencies.

Entry and Training

There are no set entry requirements, but most entrants are graduates, or move into media planning from other advertising jobs. Many agencies have a training programme for new entrants that includes on-the-job training with an experienced colleague. Agencies encourage their entrants to gain an understanding of audience research figures and the best use of online resources.

You can take courses organised by the Institute of Practitioners in Advertising (IPA). It runs a range of courses from those for junior staff to the IPA Excellence Diploma once you have three years work experience. The Media Research Group also offers a range of courses for new entrants to media research. Other relevant courses include the Communication Advertising and Marketing Foundation diploma course, that can be studied at a range of study centres or through distance learning.

A Diploma/Welsh Baccalaureate in creative and media may be offered in your area and can be a good route into this career. Foundation degrees in marketing and advertising are also available. Postgraduate professional qualifications are not essential though the professional diploma in marketing, offered by the Chartered Institute of Marketing, is very useful.

Mature applicants with specialist experience in advertising sales for a media firm have an advantage, as advertising is largely a young person's industry. Employers may prefer applicants to have a postgraduate qualification in advertising. Online and distance learning courses are available from the Communication, Advertising and Marketing Foundation and from the Institute of Practitioners in Advertising.

Opportunities and Pay

The advertising industry is a small employer in the UK and most agencies employ fewer than 50 staff. Few vacancies occur each year, and many of those that do are with larger agencies based in London and other major cities. Some agencies deal with all aspects of advertising but others specialise.

You may work for an advertising agency or a company specialising in media planning and buying. This type of work is highly competitive and promotion prospects depend on proven success in the business. The job of a media planner may be available, or the post of media executive may combine both media planning and buying or supervise the two areas. There may be opportunities to work abroad if you work for a multinational agency, and freelance work is possible.

Salaries vary widely depending on qualifications, experience and the number of advertisements you sell, but graduate starting salaries tend to be around £19k-£24k a year rising to £28k-£45k with three to five years' experience. Successful and senior media planners may earn up to £80k a year.

Skills and Qualities

able to cope under pressure, able to work to a budget, business awareness, good communication skills, good organisational skills, IT skills, negotiating skills, numeracy skills, quick thinking, resourceful

Relevant Subjects

Business and accounting, Economics, English, ICT/Computer studies, Mathematics, Media and communication studies, Psychology

Further Information

AGCAS: Media (Job Sector Briefing) (AGCAS) - www.prospects.ac.uk

Creative & Cultural Skills - sector skills council for advertising, crafts, cultural heritage, design, literature, music, performing & visual arts - www.ccskills.org.uk

Diplomas (Foundation, Higher and Advanced) - http://yp.direct.gov.uk/diplomas

Internet Advertising Bureau (IAB) - www.iabuk.net

Marketing Uncovered (Trotman 2010) - www.trotman.co.uk

Marketing Week (Centaur Media Plc) - www.marketingweek.co.uk/

Media Circle - www.mediacircle.org

Media Research Group - www.mrg.org.uk

Welsh Baccalaureate - www.wbq.org.uk

Winning Edge (6 x year) (Institute of Sales & Marketing Management) - www.ismm.co.uk/magazine.php

▶Working in marketing, advertising & PR (2008) (Babcock Lifeskills) - www.babcock-lifeskills.com/

Addresses

Account Planning Group (APG)
16 Creighton Avenue, London N10 1NU
Phone: +44 (0)20 8444 3692
Web: www.apg.org.uk

Chartered Institute of Marketing (CIM)
Moor Hall, Cookham, Maidenhead, Berkshire SL6 9QH
Phone: +44 (0) 1628 427120
Web: www.cim.co.uk

Communication Advertising and Marketing (CAM) Foundation Ltd
Moor Hall, Cookham, Maidenhead, Berkshire SL6 9QH
Phone: +44 (0)1628 427 120
Web: www.camfoundation.com

Institute of Practitioners in Advertising (IPA)
44 Belgrave Square, London SW1X 8QS
Phone: +44 (0)20 7235 7020
Web: www.ipa.co.uk

Similar Jobs

Advertising Account Executive, Advertising Copywriter, Advertising Media Buyer, Public Relations Officer

Advice Worker

also known as: Advice Centre Worker

CRCI:Social Work and Counselling Services
CLCI:KEG Job Band: 3 to 5

Job Description

Advice workers provide free, impartial and confidential advice to members of the public to help them cope with a problem. They have a broad understanding of the many factors that affect people's lives. They talk with and question people to gain a clear picture of their concerns. Then they discuss possible solutions. Advice workers explain what people's rights are with regard to housing and consumer laws, employment issues, boundary and neighbourhood disputes, welfare benefits, etc. Give advice and explore the options or possible actions that the client might take. May assist with the completion of forms, writing letters, or making phone calls on the client's behalf. Some specialise in the areas of drug dependency or immigration.

If necessary, advice workers refer people to other agencies and professionals such as a solicitor, benefits staff or social worker. Assist with the preparation of cases and sometimes represent clients at meetings or tribunals. Keep up-to-date records of each appointment and outcomes of each visit.

Work Details

Usually work a basic 36-40 hr week, Monday to Friday. Volunteer advice workers work for an agreed number of hours each week. Sometimes you may have to work extra hours. Work involves listening and asking questions, informing and advising, providing encouragement and support, and dealing with confidential information. The job can be emotionally demanding and stressful at times. You work with a wide range of people who are members of the local community, some of whom may be upset or demanding. Occasionally, you may be confronted with threatening behaviour.

Work is on a one-to-one basis with clients, but you also liaise with other workers. Advice centre workers need to understand legal technicalities and keep up to date with changes in legal regulations and local facilities.

Qualification

Employers look for basic English language and numeracy skills. Qualifications for this job vary depending on the applicant, though good communication skills and the ability to listen are essential. Degrees and/or professional qualifications are an advantage, but are not specified. Knowledge of an ethnic minority language may be useful for some posts.

Adult Qualifications

Personal qualities, maturity and experience of life are often more important to employers than formal qualifications.

Work Experience

Entry to this job is competitive and it is important to do some relevant work or voluntary experience before applying. Useful experience includes dealing with people in a helping capacity, the legal professions, social work, using listening skills and any observation or direct experience in the advice professions. This is sometimes difficult to obtain because of client confidentiality. Another option is to take a short introductory course in counselling to gain a good awareness of and grounding in counselling and listening skills.

Entry and Training

School leavers are not able to enter this job as it requires a broader life experience. Specific courses are not always required, but many organisations run their own training schemes. These often include short specialised courses on a modular basis, followed by supervised practical experience on the job. The Citizens Advice organisation offers nationally approved training courses, both for its workers and for advisers working outside of the organisation. In England and Wales this can lead to a Citizens Advice Bureau certificate in generalist advice work, equivalent to NVQ level 3.

The job requires regular training to keep up to date. Relevant S/NVQs include advice and guidance at levels 2-4.

Mature entrants are welcomed and those with experience of working in law, healthcare, social work or jobs working with people, may have an advantage. Government training opportunities, such as apprenticeships, may be available in your area. You can also gain recognition of previous experience through Accreditation of Prior Learning or by working towards relevant S/NVQs. Contact your local careers office, Jobcentre Plus, Next Step service or Learning and Skills Council (LSC)/Local Enterprise Company (LEC) for details of all training opportunities and schemes, including apprenticeships for adults.

Opportunities and Pay

You can work with a number of different organisations, but major employers are local authorities and the NHS. Citizens Advice is the UK's largest advice centre organisation, though many of its workers are volunteers. Other opportunities for advice workers are with universities and colleges of further education, professional organisations, and with some trade unions. Promotion prospects are limited, but with training and experience you can progress to coordinator or manager roles. Part-time, temporary and flexible working arrangements are possible.

Pay varies widely depending on location, employer and experience but is likely to be around £13k-£20k a year, rising to £21k-£27k with more experience. Higher earners can earn around £30k a year. Professional and specialist workers may earn more.

Skills and Qualities

able to explain clearly, able to get on with all kinds of people, able to understand other people's problems, efficient record keeping, good at writing reports, information handling skills, IT skills, non-judgemental, supportive, tactful & discreet

Relevant Subjects

Business and accounting, Economics, English, Government and politics, Law, Mathematics, Psychology, Sociology

Further Information

Adviser Magazine (bi-monthly) (Citizens Advice Bureau) - www.citizensadvice.org.uk/index/adviser_resources/adviser_magazine.htm

AGCAS: Charity & Development Work (Job Sector Briefing) (AGCAS) - www.prospects.ac.uk

ENTO (Employment National Training Organisation) (ENTO (Employment National Training Organisation)) - www.ento.co.uk

Addresses

Citizens Advice
Myddleton House, 115-123 Pentonville Rd, London N1 9LZ
Phone: +44 (0)20 7833 2181
Web: www.citizensadvice.org.uk

National Association for Voluntary Community Action (NAVCA)
The Tower, 2 Furnival Square, Sheffield S1 4QL
Phone: +44 (0)114 278 6636
Web: www.navca.org.uk

Similar Jobs

Adult Guidance Worker, Careers Adviser, Community Development Worker, Community Learning & Development Officer (Scotland), Counsellor, Debt Counsellor, Personal Adviser (Connexions) (England)

Advocate (Scotland)

also known as: Counsel: Advocate, Lawyer: Advocate (Scotland)

CRCI:Legal and Political Services
CLCI:LAB — Job Band: 5

Job Description

Advocates give independent, specialist legal advice and present cases in court on behalf of clients and some professional bodies. Represent their client in court, at arbitrations, tribunals, planning enquiries, disciplinary bodies etc. Discuss each case with the instructing solicitor, through whom contact with the client is made. They study relevant statutes and previous cases and give legal opinions. Argue the case in the House of Lords or supreme courts of Scotland and sometimes the sheriff and district courts. Usually practise in both civil and criminal cases.

In civil cases the advocate prepares written pleadings which form the foundation of a client's case. They offer advice on a wide range of legal problems, both general and specialist (often termed counsel's opinion), and can work on a wide range of cases. Advocates are sole practitioners who work independently of each other.

Work Details

Advocates work in court and in an office, or from home. Travel is necessary, with nights away from home. Very long hours are involved, including evenings and weekends. It is often necessary to take work home. The work involves consultation with people, such as solicitors and other professionals. Court cases are sometimes passed to the advocate at very short notice, so details have to be analysed and facts assimilated very quickly. Advocates spend a considerable time preparing case for presentation in court.

The work can be pressurised and stressful at times and can involve making difficult decisions. Most advocates tend to specialise in one or two areas, but are still capable of handling a wide variety of cases. Advocates wear formal dress and have to observe the traditions and formality associated with the job.

Qualification

- **Scotland**

Band 5: For a law degree: five H grades, usually including English, maths or a science and perhaps a modern language, and some S grades (1-3) or similar qualifications. Good H grades are required, preferably passed at one sitting.

Degree Information

A good honours degree (or ordinary degree with distinction) in Scottish law from a Scottish university is required for training. Alternatively, a good honours degree in another subject from a UK university followed by an ordinary degree (second class or above) in Scottish law from a Scottish university is acceptable. This must be followed by a diploma in legal practice.

Adult Qualifications
The study and training routes are common for all entrants though certain exemptions may apply. Solicitors who wish to become advocates should contact the Faculty of Advocates.

Work Experience
Entry to this job is competitive and it is important that you try to do some relevant work or voluntary experience before applying. Useful practical experience includes court attendance or work at a firm of solicitors.

Entry and Training
In order to practise at the Scottish Bar you must be a member of the Faculty of Advocates. The process of becoming an advocate is currently under review, but at present candidates, known as 'Intrants', must satisfy the educational and professional training requirements of the faculty. As well as a suitable degree in Scottish law from a Scottish university, an 'Intrant' must pass or gain exemption from the faculty's examination in law and obtain or gain exemption from the diploma in legal practice at a Scottish university. To become an 'Intrant' you must go through the process of matriculation which involves submitting references and the presentation of a petition to the Court.

'Intrants' must undergo 21 months' salaried training in a solicitor's office and then serve a period of about nine months as a pupil to a member of the Bar (known as devilling) and pass the faculty examination in Evidence, Practice & Procedure. Each year the faculty awards one or more scholarships to 'Intrants' commencing pupillage. Contact the Faculty of Advocates for further details on this and admission requirements.

Following admission, the faculty runs a continuing professional development (CPD) scheme which requires all practising members to complete a total of 10 hours' accredited professional development training each year.

Mature entrants with previous experience of working in a legal environment have an advantage for training. Certain exemptions may apply for mature applicants wishing to train. For those not already qualified in law, the lengthy training time should be considered carefully. Scottish solicitors who wish to become advocates are exempt from the diploma in legal practice if they already have three years of professional practice. Contact the Faculty of Advocates for details of training routes, qualifications and funding.

Opportunities and Pay
There are around 460 advocates who practise at the bar in Scotland at present. Most work for the Scottish Bar from the Advocates Library in Parliament House, Edinburgh. After about 12 years of practice, successful advocates with outstanding ability have the opportunity to become a sheriff or Queen's Counsel ("taking silk") and to take up judicial office.

Training provides a useful basis for a range of other occupations and there are openings for advocates in other fields such as the procurators-fiscal service, the legal section of a government department, or within industry, commerce or higher education. There are opportunities to specialise in European or international law, and to work or travel overseas. It is possible to be an advocate and a solicitor at the same time, and also to transfer between the two professions.

Advocates are self-employed and income is by fee rather than a regular salary and depends on the ability of the individual and their reputation. Income varies considerably and can be quite low during the first few years, but can rise rapidly through merit. Experienced advocates earn between £35-£100k a year, while some top advocates can earn up to and over £400k a year.

Skills and Qualities
able to inspire confidence, analytical skills, articulate, discreet, honest, information handling skills, integrity, objective, public speaking ability, sound judgement

Relevant Subjects
Business and accounting, Economics, English, Government and politics, History, Law, Performing arts, Psychology, Sociology

Further Information
A Career at the Scottish Bar (Faculty of Advocates 2008)
Scottish Court Service - www.scotscourts.gov.uk
Skills for Justice - sector skills council for the UK justice system - www.skillsforjustice.com
TARGETjobs: Law Scotland (GTI Specialist Publishing Ltd.) - www.groupgti.com
▶Working in politics & law (2010) (Babcock Lifeskills) - www.babcock-lifeskills.com/

Addresses
Faculty of Advocates
Parliament House, Edinburgh EH1 1RF
Phone: +44 (0)131 226 5071
Web: www.advocates.org.uk

Similar Jobs
Civil Service EU Administrator, European Law Solicitor, Procurator Fiscal (Scotland), Sheriff (Scotland), Solicitor

Agricultural Consultant/Adviser
also known as: Farming Adviser
CRCI:Environment, Animals and Plants
CLCI:WAB — Job Band: 4 to 5

Job Description
Agricultural consultants give specialist business and technical advice and support those in the land-based industry (farmers, landowners, conservation organisations, growers, etc) on all aspects of agricultural business and production. They work to develop farms and farming enterprises as well as forestry and horticulture. Also give specialist advice on issues such as EU and government agricultural programmes, and environmental management.

Consultants play an important part in farm planning and development. They usually act as either a technical consultant dealing with crops, livestock and nutrition, or a business consultant, looking at the financial management of an agricultural business. Must keep up to date on governmental and EU laws and regulations that apply to the land-based industry. Also assist with applications for government/EU funding or grants that may be available.

May specialise in any aspect of agriculture such as dairy farming, general animal nutrition, agricultural science or crop production. Consultants visit farms, undertake telephone consultations, attend agricultural shows, run training programmes, may run discussion groups and give presentations on aspects of work.

Work Details
Usually work 39 hrs a week, Monday to Friday, but early starts and late finishes are common. Some weekend work may be required. Though office based, you spend much time away from the office, sometimes outdoors and in all weather conditions. Crop consultants can expect to spend more time out of the office. Daily travel and time spent overnight away from home varies according to the nature of the job.

Qualification
• England, Wales and Northern Ireland
Band 4: For BTEC higher national award: 1-2 A levels and some GCSEs (A*-C) usually including English and maths, or equivalent.

Band 5: For a degree: 2-3 A levels, including at least one science subject and some GCSEs (A*-C), including maths, or equivalent qualifications. Chemistry and biology are often required at A level depending on the degree course. Exact requirements depend on the degree you take.

- **Scotland**

Band 4: For SQA higher national certificate courses: usually 2-3 H grades, including chemistry or biology, and some S grades (1-3) including maths and English, or similar qualifications. Entry requirements depend on the degree you take.

Band 5: For a degree: 3-5 H grades, including at least one science subject and some S grades (1-3), including maths. Chemistry and biology are often required at H grade depending on the degree course. Many universities also accept similar qualifications.

Degree Information

Employers expect you to have a degree in agriculture, or a related subject such as agricultural science, soil science, environmental science, agricultural engineering or land and property management. Relevant full/part-time and distance-learning postgraduate courses are available, though not essential.

Adult Qualifications

Course entry qualifications vary for mature applicants and there may be special entry requirements. Check with the university or college concerned. Foundation and Access courses may be available, as well as a number of distance-learning courses for those who have not followed a traditional academic route. Funding help with courses may be available from the Biotechnology and Biological Sciences Research Council.

Work Experience

Entry to this job is competitive and it is important that you try to do some relevant work or voluntary experience before applying for a course/job. This is ideally with an agricultural consultant, farm manager/estate manager, or some form of conservation work, but any work in business, management or any sort of consultancy can be helpful. Experience of work on the land on a farm offers useful background experience.

Entry and Training

Entrants usually have a good honours degree (NFQ Level 8) in agriculture or a related subject. Sometimes it is possible to enter with an appropriate HNC/HND, but you also need plenty of experience. There are also several full or part-time foundation degrees in agriculture and related subjects. Those specialising in agricultural business consultancy may have a business degree together with agricultural experience. The larger firms of agricultural consultants may run graduate training schemes, involving induction, mentoring schemes to provide support and short training courses.

You spend a number of years gaining experience on the job and many improve their prospects through a directly relevant MSc/PhD; especially those in technical consultancy. Continuing professional development (CPD) through membership of a professional body is also expected in order to keep up to date with developments and enhance knowledge in a specialist area of work. Relevant professional bodies include the British Institute of Agricultural Consultants (BIAC) and the Association of Independent Crop Consultants (AICC).

Further training is mainly through short courses and attendance at specialist conferences though this may be at your own expense. The Open University, Open Business School, colleges of agriculture, and Lantra also offer relevant professional development courses.

Mature applicants require considerable relevant and up-to-date experience and qualifications in agriculture or a related subject. A background in business, finance and commerce is also useful. You can study for a relevant course either part time or through distance learning, including postgraduate courses.

Opportunities and Pay

Most new entrants are graduates and competition for jobs is intense. Employers include the Agricultural Development and Advisory Service (ADAS), which is the leading consultancy and research organisation to the land-based industries, agricultural/horticultural companies, non-governmental organisations (NGOs), farming cooperatives, environmental and conservation bodies, and independent agricultural consultancies. You should be prepared to move to a different part of the country to improve your prospects.

Self-employment is possible, though you need to gain considerable experience if you wish to set up your own consultancy. There are opportunities for flexible and part-time work. Temporary contracts are often available with a foreign government.

Salaries vary, but generally, agricultural consultants earn around £20k-£26k. High earners can make more than £45k a year.

Health

This job requires good stamina and physical fitness. Some jobs may require you to have good colour vision.

Skills and Qualities

analytical skills, business awareness, good interpersonal skills, good listening skills, good spoken communication, good written English, initiative, IT skills, problem-solving skills, scientific approach, sound judgement

Relevant Subjects

Biology, Business and accounting, Chemistry, Economics, English, Geography, Land and Environment, Mathematics, Science

Further Information

ADAS - Agricultural Development and Advisory Service - www.adas.co.uk

AGCAS: Environment & Agriculture (Job Sector Briefing) (AGCAS) - www.prospects.ac.uk

Farmer's Weekly Interactive (Reed International) - www.fwi.co.uk

Lantra - The Sector Skills Council for environmental & land-based sector (Lantra) - http:/www.lantra.co.uk

Lantra Careers (A Future In...) (Lantra) - www.afuturein.com

Scottish Farmer (weekly) (Newsquest Media) - www.thescottishfarmer.co.uk/

Addresses

Association of Independent Crop Consultants (AICC)
Agriculture Place, Drayton Farm, East Meon, Petersfield, Hampshire GU32 1PN
Phone: +44 (0)1730 823881
Web: www.aicc.org.uk

Biotechnology and Biological Sciences Research Council (BBSRC)
Polaris House North Star Avenue, Swindon, Wiltshire SN2 1UH
Phone: +44 (0)1793 413 200
Web: www.bbsrc.ac.uk

British Institute of Agricultural Consultancies (BIAC)
The Estate Office, Torry Hill, Milstead, Sittingbourne, Kent ME9 0SP
Phone: +44 (0)1795 830100
Web: www.biac.co.uk

Department for Environment, Food & Rural Affairs (DEFRA)
Customer Contact Unit , Eastbury House, 30 - 34 Albert Embankment, London SE1 7TL
Phone: 0845 933 5577 (UK only)
Web: www.defra.gov.uk

Department of Agriculture and Rural Development
Training & Development Dundonald House Upper Newtownards Road, Belfast BT4 3SB
Phone: +44 (0)28 9052 4999
Web: www.dardni.gov.uk

Similar Jobs
Agricultural Research Scientist, Engineer: Land-based, Farm Manager, Horticultural Scientist, Soil Scientist

Agricultural Research Scientist
CRCI:Environment, Animals and Plants
CLCI:WAB Job Band: 4 to 5

Job Description
Agricultural research scientists conduct research to develop new and more efficient methods of feeding, breeding and managing of livestock, and also large-scale planting and production of field crops. They investigate ways to increase crop yields, control diseases and protect the natural habitat and wildlife. Also research environmental issues such as soil erosion, pollution and public health concerns, including genetically modified (GM) crops or diseases, such as foot and mouth disease in cattle. May be involved in more complex interdisciplinary studies such as genetic engineering and the molecular biology of crops and livestock.

Scientists provide current information on pest control, the use of chemicals, fungicides etc and may make on-site visits to farmers and growers. May also provide advice on the best use of soils and methods to improve crop production. Some scientists are involved in marketing or teaching, as well as in advisory or research work. Most scientists choose to specialise in a particular area.

Work Details
Usually work 35-39 hr, Monday to Friday, though in some jobs is expected to work shifts or at weekends. You are based in an office or laboratory, but the work can involve visiting farms, perhaps travelling over quite a wide area. You may also have to advise farmers and growers, and collect, collate and analyse information, carry out tests on soil, and prepare and present reports. The work involves meeting clients, such as seed companies or pesticide producers, and you may be involved in teaching or training.

Qualification
- **England, Wales and Northern Ireland**

Band 4: For HND, Diploma of Higher Education or foundation degree: 1-2 A levels and some GCSEs (A*-C) usually including English and maths, or equivalent.

Band 5: For a degree: usually 2-3 A levels, including at least one science subject some GCSEs (A*-C) that also include your A level subjects, plus English and maths, or equivalent. Chemistry and biology are often required at A level depending on the degree course.

- **Scotland**

Band 4: For entry to SQA higher national and professional development awards, usually 2-3 H grades chemistry or biology, and some S grades (1-3), including English and maths, or similar qualifications.

Band 5: For a degree: usually 3-5 H grades, including at least one science subject, and around five S grades (1-3) that also include your H grade subjects, plus English and maths. Chemistry and biology are often required at H grade depending on the degree course. Many universities also accept similar qualifications.

Degree Information
Degrees in relevant subjects include agricultural science, biological sciences, crop science, plant or animal science, and chemistry. Higher degrees or postgraduate diplomas are available, and specialisms include crop protection and tropical ecosystems.

Adult Qualifications
A degree, or perhaps an HND in a relevant subject is usually required. Entry qualifications vary for mature applicants to these courses and there may be special entry standards for adults. Check with the university or college concerned. Foundation and Access courses may also be available. The Studley College Trust offers funding for land-based courses. See their website for details.

Work Experience
Employers and universities may prefer candidates who have relevant work or voluntary experience. Experience in an industrial or commercial laboratory is ideal, but if it proves difficult to gain, then experience in other scientific and agricultural areas is relevant. Experience of work on the land, such as a farm, also offers useful background experience.

Entry and Training
Entrants usually have a relevant degree and for some jobs you may need to have postgraduate qualifications, eg MSc/PhD for entry. Previous practical experience in agriculture may be needed for entry to courses. After a degree, training is usually on the job for 1-2 years, with a programme of short courses, mentoring and site visits. If you work in a laboratory you are expected to take short courses on good laboratory practice. Relevant short courses on other agricultural research topics are available from a number of organisations including the Scottish Agricultural Science Agency.

Those with a good honours degree can apply for a postgraduate studentship with a research organisation that allows you to work towards a higher degree whilst being employed. In some areas of the country there are foundation degrees in agriculture and in science subjects that lead onto the third year of a degree course. Those with a relevant HND or foundation degree are likely to enter at technician level.

Mature applicants require relevant and up-to-date experience and qualifications in agriculture or a closely related subject. Some research posts may enable progression towards a postgraduate qualification whilst working.

Opportunities and Pay
You can find work with a variety of different types of employer, such as a manufacturing company, research organisation, local and central government offices, Agricultural Development and Advisory Service (ADAS), Biotechnology and Biological Sciences Research Council (BBSRC), a university or college. More opportunities are being created with the expansion of genetic engineering, whilst the more 'traditional' research and development work is diminishing. Work is also available abroad.

Pay varies depending on location and type of employer. Salaries for graduates are generally around £22k-£27k a year, rising to £30k-£50k.

Health
You may find this job difficult if you are allergic to animals or if you have hay fever. This job requires good health. Some posts may require good colour vision.

Skills and Qualities
accurate, aptitude for teamwork, good communication skills, good organisational skills, information handling skills, IT skills, methodical, patient, problem-solving skills, scientific approach

Relevant Subjects
Biology, Chemistry, Economics, English, Geography, ICT/Computer studies, Land and Environment, Mathematics, Science

Further Information
ADAS - Agricultural Development and Advisory Service - www.adas.co.uk

AGCAS: Environment & Agriculture (Job Sector Briefing) (AGCAS) - www.prospects.ac.uk

Lantra Careers (A Future In...) (Lantra) - www.afuturein.com

Studley College Trust - www.studleytrust.co.uk

Addresses

Biotechnology and Biological Sciences Research Council (BBSRC)
Polaris House North Star Avenue, Swindon, Wiltshire SN2 1UH
Phone: +44 (0)1793 413 200
Web: www.bbsrc.ac.uk

Department for Environment, Food & Rural Affairs (DEFRA)
Customer Contact Unit , Eastbury House, 30 - 34 Albert Embankment, London SE1 7TL
Phone: 0845 933 5577 (UK only)
Web: www.defra.gov.uk

Department of Agriculture and Rural Development
Training & Development Dundonald House
Upper Newtownards Road, Belfast BT4 3SB
Phone: +44 (0)28 9052 4999
Web: www.dardni.gov.uk

Scottish Agricultural Science Agency (SASA)
Roddinglaw Road, Edinburgh EH12 9FJ
Phone: +44 (0)131 244 8890
Web: www.sasa.gov.uk

Similar Jobs

Agricultural Consultant/Adviser, Biologist, Biotechnologist, Botanist, Horticultural Scientist, Microbiologist, Soil Scientist

Aid Worker

also known as: International Aid/Development Worker, NGO Aid Worker

CRCI:Social Work and Counselling Services
CLCI:KEZ Job Band: 4 to 5

Job Description

Aid workers work for a charity or non-governmental organisation (NGO) such as the Red Cross in the UK, or overseas in developing countries or regions. Aim to help improve the lives of people who live in very difficult and/or impoverished conditions. Do a variety of work depending on the location and employer. May work in areas that include teaching or education development programmes, conduct detailed research into a health problem, assist in agricultural projects, or help build facilities such as wells, schools and houses.

May also be involved in fundraising and publicity work in the UK. Some workers also organise and supervise teams of voluntary workers.

Work Details

Work conditions vary according to the job. Workers that live abroad in developing countries may encounter uncomfortable conditions, including extreme heat and poor sanitation. This can be emotionally demanding work that requires full commitment. If office-based in the UK, you usually work a standard 39 hr week, Monday to Friday.

Qualification

- **England, Wales and Northern Ireland**

Band 4: For BTEC higher national award: 1-2 A levels and some GCSEs (A*-C) usually including English and maths, or equivalent.

Band 5: For degree courses: 2-3 A levels and some GCSEs (A*-C) usually including English and maths, or equivalent. Exact requirements depend on the degree you take.

- **Scotland**

Band 4: For SQA higher national award: 2-3 H grades and some S grades (1-3) usually including English and maths, or similar qualifications.

Band 5: For degree courses: 3-5 H grades and some S grades (1-3), usually including English and maths, or similar qualifications.

Degree Information

Degrees can be in any subject but there are courses in third world development, international development and in development studies. Relevant postgraduate courses are available.

Adult Qualifications

Course entry requirements are usually relaxed for suitable mature applicants. Those without the required qualifications may complete a foundation or Access course leading to relevant HNDs and degrees.

Work Experience

Voluntary or charity work experience is essential for this job. Previous voluntary experience is usually expected by many employers to show a working knowledge of how these institutions operate and a commitment to the type of work. Professional experience in research and management are also particularly valued. Check the websites of some of the larger aid agencies for a better feel of their individual cultures and approaches.

Internships are more common in larger charities like Oxfam and Christian Aid. Smaller organisations are a useful source of volunteering opportunities at home or abroad. Voluntary Service Overseas is a good source of information. An internship provides you with the field experience that may also lead to permanent employment.

Entry and Training

Entry is very competitive for positions of responsibility within non-governmental organisations (NGOs) and charities. Most entrants are graduates and many have a degree or postgraduate qualification in a relevant subject such as international development, third world studies or a social science. Employers usually have an in-house induction and training programme but you are expected to continue your professional development throughout your employment. It may be possible to enter with a relevant qualification at higher national certificate/diploma level.

NGOs need all types of professionals so many aid workers are qualified in other fields and transfer their skills and experience later in their careers. The Development Studies Association (DSA) of the UK and Ireland provides a course guide for those seeking to study development-related courses. Contact the DSA for details. Knowledge of a foreign language may be useful and French, Spanish and Portuguese are often requested.

Mature applicants are welcome and there is no official upper age limit for this profession. It may be difficult to find a salaried position in an international agency without previous field experience or a relevant graduate degree. Aid agencies require many types of skills, so many of their workers transfer from other professions, eg teachers, IT professionals and engineers.

Opportunities and Pay

You can be employed by a non-governmental organisation (NGO) such as a charity, pressure group, research institute, professional association or a community care group. Many NGOs have headquarters in London but there are exceptions, eg World Vision UK in Milton Keynes and Skillshare International in Leicester. The Department for International Development employs aid workers in Scotland as well as London. There are a few opportunities to work as a freelance consultant for several institutions once well established and respected. There is often no clear promotion structure, but prospects are better with the larger funds and charities.

Pay varies considerably and depends on the type of employer, the issue you deal with, and in which capacity you work. As a rough guide, a researcher or administrator based in the UK may earn around £19k-£25k a year, rising to £26k-£40k for a senior post, of which there are few. Overseas field-based posts attract a salary of £18k-£35k a year. Principal posts may attract a salary of £30k-£45k a year.

Health
For some jobs, particularly when working overseas, you need to be physically fit.

Skills and Qualities
able to cope under pressure, committed, emotionally strong, enthusiastic, flexible approach, IT skills, resilient, resourceful, sense of humour, tolerant, willing to live and travel in basic conditions

Relevant Subjects
Biology, Chemistry, Economics, English, Geography, Government and politics, Health and social care, Land and Environment, Mathematics, Psychology, Science, Sociology

Further Information
Aid Workers Network - www.aidworkers.net

IDS Bulletin (annual) (Institute of Development Studies (IDS)) - www.ids.ac.uk/go/bookshop/ids-bulletin

ReliefWeb (UN Office for the Coordination of Humanitarian Affairs) - www.reliefweb.int/

UN Volunteers - www.unv.org

Volunteering Made Easy - www.do-it.org.uk

▶Working with languages (2010) (Babcock Lifeskills) - www.babcock-lifeskills.com/

Addresses
Department for International Development (DFID)
1 Palace Street, London SW1E 5HE
Phone: 0845 300 4100 (UK only)
Web: www.dfid.gov.uk

Development Studies Association (DSA)
PO Box 108, Bideford, Devon EX39 6ZQ
Phone: +44 (0)845 519 3372
Web: www.devstud.org.uk

Northern Ireland Volunteer Development Agency
129 Ormeau Road, Belfast BT7 1SH
Phone: +44 (0)28 9023 6100
Web: www.volunteering-ni.org

Scottish Council for Voluntary Organisations (SCVO)
Mansfield Traquair Centre, 15 Mansfield Place, Edinburgh EH3 6BB
Phone: +44 (0)131 556 3882
Web: www.scvo.org.uk

Voluntary Service Overseas (VSO)
Carlton House, 27a Carlton Drive, London SW15 2BS
Phone: +44 (0)20 8780 7200
Web: www.vso.org.uk

Volunteering England
Regents Wharf, 8 All Saints Street, London N1 9RL
Phone: 0845 305 6979 (UK only)
Web: www.volunteering.org.uk

Wales Council for Voluntary Action
Baltic House, Mount Stuart Square, Cardiff Bay CF10 5FH
Phone: 0800 2888 329 (UK only)
Web: www.wcva.org.uk

Similar Jobs
Charity Fundraiser, Community Development Worker, Social Worker, Volunteer Manager

Air Cabin Crew
also known as: Cabin Crew, Flight Attendant, Steward/ Stewardess: Airline

CRCI:Transport and Logistics
CLCI:YAB
Job Band: 2 to 3

Job Description
Air cabin crew are responsible for the comfort, safety and welfare of passengers travelling in aircraft. They attend a pre-flight briefing, and carry out a number of routine tasks before passengers board. These include checking the aircraft has been properly cleaned and tidied, and in-flight meals and refreshments are stored safely. They check that any passenger requests for a particular meal have been added. Also check stocks of duty-free goods to be sold during the flight.

Cabin crew welcome people aboard, supervise seating of passengers and stowing away of hand luggage. They explain emergency procedures, demonstrate the safety equipment, and make other flight announcements. They check passengers are seated prior to take-off and ensure that seat belts are fastened securely. They also serve drinks and meals during the flight, and usually sell goods such as alcohol, perfume, tobacco and jewellery.

Cabin crew assist passengers travelling with babies and children, and those requiring particular assistance such as those with limited mobility. They help any passenger who may be anxious about flying or who becomes unwell; giving first aid if necessary, and dealing with emergencies. Also ensure that the passengers disembark safely at the end of the flight. Writing a report after each flight, which includes completing customs and health forms and checking and recording duty-free stock transactions, is also part of this job.

Work Details
You need to live within easy reach of the airport at which you are based and are expected to work on a rota basis. Sometimes the hours are long and you spend time away from home. You work in a team, looking after people. Among your passengers are people who do not speak your language and those who are nervous or upset. Some passengers can also be awkward or demanding.

You spend a lot of time on your feet and may have to cope with jet lag when crossing time zones. The cabin of a plane is enclosed, noisy and can be cramped. There is a risk of air traffic accidents and you have to remain calm under pressure and during any emergencies. There are opportunities for part-time work though the hours are still irregular and unsocial. Airline companies require you to wear a corporate uniform and most do not allow visible body piercing (except one earring per ear) or tattoos. You can expect to spend 75-85 hours a month in the air.

Qualification
For employers, your previous work experience and personality is more likely to be of interest than formal qualifications, though all applicants are expected to have a good secondary education, with some academic qualifications or equivalent. Some applicants have higher educational qualifications including a higher national award, foundation degree or degree.

• England, Wales and Northern Ireland
Band 2: Although academic qualifications are not specified for this job, it is an advantage to have some GCSEs (A*-C) in subjects that include English and maths, or equivalent. The ability to speak a foreign language is preferred.

Band 3: For entry: usually at least 4 GCSEs (A*-C) including English and maths, or equivalent, as well as conversational ability in a foreign language. Check with individual airlines for entry requirements.

- **Scotland**

Band 2: Although academic qualifications are not specified for this job, it is an advantage to have some S grades (1-3) in subjects that include English and maths, or similar qualifications. The ability to speak a foreign language is also preferred.

Band 3: Although there are no set qualifications, usually at least four S grades (1-3) are needed, including English and maths or similar, as well as conversational ability in a foreign language. Check with individual airlines for entry requirements.

Adult Qualifications

Most applicants are between 19 and 35. Airlines do not recruit anyone under 18 so there may be opportunities for mature candidates with relevant experience.

Work Experience

Relevant work or voluntary experience can equip you with skills that you can use in the future and add to your CV. There are often opportunities available for voluntary work that give you experience of working with people.

Entry and Training

You need a valid passport to work for some airlines and all applicants must undergo a Criminal Records Bureau (CRB)/ Disclosure Scotland check due to increased security measures at airports. New entrants are usually aged 19-35 and some airlines retire employees at age 50-55, though this should not deter older applicants. Candidates are usually employed through a selection process involving a series of tests, group work and the opportunity to present yourself to others. Most airlines specify a minimum height and weight needs to be in proportion to height. Most airlines expect you to be able to swim approximately 25 metres.

All airlines have their own training programmes that usually last 4-6 weeks and include practical and written tests. As part of Safety & Emergency Procedures (SEP) training topics such as passenger service, galley management, safety and security issues, currency exchange, customs procedures and first aid are covered. This is followed by 3-6 months' probation, which includes on-the-job training with experienced crew. During this period your performance is monitored and assessed by a company trainer or senior cabin crew members.

Once you have passed this initial training you become part of the cabin crew team. Ongoing assessment and appropriate training for each new post is usual. Some colleges offer courses that prepare people who are interested in becoming air cabin crew. These courses can last up to a year and lead to air cabin crew qualifications, which ensure a national standard of assessment and training.

Courses include a level 2 qualification in aviation operations in the air - cabin crew, preparation for air cabin crew service, an intermediate certificate in air cabin crewing, and a level 3 qualification in aviation operations in the air - cabin crew. There are also qualifications in first aid, food hygiene, a foreign language, British Airways' certificate in ticketing and sign language for deaf people. Edexcel runs a BTEC level 2 certificate in preparation for air cabin crew service and a certificate or diploma in aviation operations. A Diploma/Welsh Baccalaureate in travel and tourism may be available in your area, providing a useful route into this career.

Mature applicants should be aware that some airlines prefer at least one-year of experience working with the public. Previous work as a nurse, paramedic, care work, catering, customer service, sales/retail work, or working for a travel agent, as well as other airport work, is an advantage. Fluency in a second language is an asset.

Opportunities and Pay

You are employed by a national or international airline company. The airline market has changed in recent years with a growth in the number of smaller airlines offering low-price flights and increased routes. Although there are opportunities, the economic downturn has had an effect on the number of flights and there is fierce competition for jobs. You may only be able to find seasonal or short term contract work at first, and then with experience move into a permanent job. Promotion prospects vary between airlines. You can be promoted to purser or cabin services manager/director, a crew controller, or move into the recruitment and training of cabin staff.

Pay varies according to the individual employer but there are usually allowances for working unsociable hours. You have subsidised travel and may be paid a living costs allowance when working away from home. Other benefits may also be part of your package. As a guide, salaries start at around £14k a year for new recruits, rising to £16k-£23k with experience. Senior crew earn up to £25k a year. A flight allowance is included in these figures.

Health

You have to take a medical test and must have a high standard of physical fitness. Good hearing and eyesight is also essential. The wearing of contact lenses is usually acceptable but some airlines do not allow glasses.

Skills and Qualities

ability in one or more languages, able to cope under pressure, able to get on with all kinds of people, aptitude for teamwork, business awareness, cash handling, including foreign currencies, diplomatic, energetic, friendly, smart appearance

Relevant Subjects

English, Hospitality and catering, Leisure, travel and tourism, Modern Foreign Languages

Further Information

AGCAS: Transport and Logistics (Job Sector Briefing) (AGCAS) - www.prospects.ac.uk

Cabin Crew - www.cabincrew.com

Diplomas (Foundation, Higher and Advanced) - http://yp.direct.gov.uk/diplomas

Flight International Magazine (Flight Global) - www.flightglobal.com/mediapack/

GoSkills - sector skills council for passenger transport - www.goskills.org

Welsh Baccalaureate - www.wbq.org.uk

▶Working in airports (2010) (Babcock Lifeskills) - www.babcock-lifeskills.com/

▶Working in travel & tourism (2010) (Babcock Lifeskills) - www.babcock-lifeskills.com/

Similar Jobs

Airline Customer Service Agent, Airport Information Assistant, Customer Services Adviser, Tour Operator, Travel Consultant, Waiter/Waitress

Air Traffic Controller

also known as: ATCO

CRCI:Transport and Logistics

CLCI:YAB — Job Band: 4 to 5

Job Description

Air traffic controllers (ATCOs) issue instructions, advice and information to pilots by radio to keep air traffic flying safely, efficiently and quickly. They regulate and control the movement of aircraft, either in flight, on approach to landing, or at airports. The efficient flow of air traffic and ensuring that all planes are a safe distance apart are also their responsibility. They work with complex radar and computer systems, making calculations and checking flight plans. They also give advice and relay instructions to pilots. It is important that ATCOs take account of factors such as weather conditions, aircraft requiring emergency help and other unexpected events.

ATCOs may be area/terminal controllers, controlling the progress of the flight and tracking the exact position of the aircraft. Some work as approach controllers who take over contact with pilots as they approach airports and sequence the landing order, or aerodrome controllers who guide an aircraft through landing to its parking stand. They also make sure that an aircraft gets from its parking stand to the runway and takes off safely.

Work Details

Air traffic control is a 24-hour business that requires shift work including weekends and public holidays. You may need to move location at your employer's request. The work requires a high degree of accuracy and is very demanding so shifts tend to be short with regular breaks. You must have sound judgement. The work can be highly demanding and stressful at times. The lighting in your workplace may be subdued, to enable radar screens to be seen clearly. You must have good normal colour vision and have to wear headphones.

Qualification

- **England, Wales and Northern Ireland**

Band 4: For National Air Traffic Services (NATS) student training: at least five GCSEs, or equivalent, at Grade C or above, including English and maths. However, you need to be at least 18 to start training so many undertake further study at A level or take a relevant BTEC national award.

Band 5: For degree courses: 2-3 A levels and some GCSEs (A*-C) usually including English and maths, or equivalent. Exact requirements depend on the degree you take.

- **Scotland**

Band 4: For National Air Traffic Services (NATS) student training: at least four S grades (1-3) including English and maths, or similar. However, you need to be at least 18 to start training so many undertake further study at H level or take a relevant BTEC national award.

Band 5: For degree courses: 3-5 H grades and some S grades (1-3), usually including English and maths, or similar qualifications. Exact requirements depend on the degree you take.

Degree Information

A degree in any discipline is acceptable. Mathematics and computer science give useful background.

Adult Qualifications

Educational qualifications or work experience showing ability in maths and English language are necessary, or equivalent qualifications such as national/higher national awards. Entry requirements may be relaxed for adults applying for higher education courses. Access or foundation courses give adults without qualifications a route on to degree courses.

Work Experience

Entry to this career is highly competitive and it is essential you have some relevant work or voluntary experience before applying for courses or posts. You can visit the College of Air Traffic Control in Bournemouth to find out more of the practicalities of the work. Work experience may be possible at a national control centre. Enthusiasm for aviation and an interest in technological developments is useful for entrants.

Entry and Training

You must be at least 18 at the date of your training application. Entry is highly competitive and many entrants are now graduates. There are nationality, residency and strict security regulations. Training is through the National Air Traffic Services (NATS) Student Air Traffic Controller Scheme, BAE Systems or Aviation Services Training and Consultancy (ASTAC) courses. It includes assessment of English language proficiency. You may be able to get sponsorship from an air traffic control provider or self-fund your training. It is recommended that you have a Civil Aviation Class 1 medical examination before applying for training posts.

The NATS course includes a salary, and lasts for six to twelve months, including eight weeks' holiday. You study courses at the Civil Aviation Authority (CAA) College of Air Traffic Control in Bournemouth, have practical training on high-tech computer simulators, and also training at airports and air traffic control centres. BAE training is based in Cwmbran and ASTAC courses at Shoreham or Gloucester. You have to pass a series of assessments and exams to obtain the CAA licences, which are needed before you can work as an air traffic control officer (ATCO). This licence enables you to work in the EU. After qualification and experience as an operational ATCO you can apply for a five-year secondment to train new ATCOs. There is ongoing in-service training.

Air traffic controllers are also trained and employed by the armed forces, for example, the Fleet Air Arm branch of the Royal Navy. You can apply from the age of 17 and must satisfy entry qualifications. There is also graduate entry, some opportunities for sixth-form scholarships, sponsorship programmes or bursaries for degree courses at designated universities. ATCOs attend flying aptitude and assessment tests at RAF Cranwell in Lincolnshire and if successful, professional training begins at the Britannia Royal Naval College in Dartmouth in Devon, for up to 12 months, as well as training on simulators at RAF Shawbury in Shropshire. A further 12 months at one of the Royal Naval Air Stations follows under the supervision of fully experienced ATCOs. After this you are awarded the ATCO certificate of competency.

Mature entrants with experience in aviation have an advantage but the upper age limit for National Air Traffic Services (NATS) training is 36. Military air traffic controllers can have their prior experience assessed and may gain exemption from some of the training course or may be able to attend a specially designed course. Contact the Civil Aviation Authority (CAA) or NATS for further information.

Opportunities and Pay

Air traffic control is a nationwide activity with several main centres. If you train with NATS who employ 80% of ATCOs, you are likely to work at one of the larger UK airports or one of the area control centres located at Swanwick, Prestwick, West Drayton and Manchester. ATCOs also work in airport control towers at UK regional, national/international airports. If you train with BAE or ASTAC, you are likely to be employed at a medium or smaller airfield that employs staff directly. Your employer may also be a private or local authority airport, or the armed forces.

The airline market has changed in recent years with a growth in the number of smaller airlines offering low-price flights and increased routes. Although there are still good opportunities and a shortage of qualified controllers, the economic downturn has had an effect on the number of flights. There are over 2,500 ATCOs in the UK but opportunities are dependent on the volume of air traffic. Promotion is by a grade system, beyond which there are opportunities to move into management, training and planning. Some work is possible at British Commonwealth and English-speaking airports in other countries, though these have their own licensing regulations.

On completion of the NATS training scheme you earn between £15k-£18k a year, with benefits. Once fully qualified, salaries can be between £40k-£46k a year, plus shift allowances. Experienced controllers at the busiest centres can earn over £75k a year.

Health

You have to pass a medical test before entry and also have to pass a thorough medical examination every two years up to the age of 40, then every year after that. This job requires a high standard of physical fitness, and you must have normal colour vision, full hearing, good eyesight and clear speech. Wearing glasses or contact lenses is acceptable within certain limits.

Skills and Qualities
able to cope under pressure, attention to detail, clear speaking voice, decisive, good communication skills, good concentration level, problem-solving skills, responsible attitude, spatial awareness, technical aptitude

Relevant Subjects
English, Geography, ICT/Computer studies, Mathematics, Physics, Science

Further Information
AGCAS: Transport and Logistics (Job Sector Briefing) (AGCAS) - www.prospects.ac.uk

Air Traffic Management - www.airtrafficmanagement.net

GoSkills - sector skills council for passenger transport - www.goskills.org

▶Working in airports (2010) (Babcock Lifeskills) - www.babcock-lifeskills.com/

Addresses
Aviation Services Training and Consultancy (ASTAC)
Gloucestershire Airport, Cheltenham GL51 6SP
Phone: +44 (0)1452 715630
Web: www.astac.co.uk

BAE Systems Training College
Cwmbran Training College, Beacon House, William Brown Close, Llantarnam Park, Gwent NP44 3AB
Phone: +44 (0) 1633 835123
Web: www.cwmbrancollege.com

Civil Aviation Authority (CAA)
HR Department London Team Room 703 CAA House
45-59 Kingsway WC2B 6TE
Phone: +44 (0)20 7453 6040
Web: www.caa.co.uk/

National Air Traffic Services (NATS)
Corporate and Technical Centre 4000 Parkway Whiteley, Fareham, Hampshire PO15 7FL
Phone: +44 (0) 1489 616001
Web: http://natscareers.co.uk

Royal Aeronautical Society (RAES)
4 Hamilton Place, London W1J 7BQ
Phone: +44 (0) 20 7670 4300
Web: www.aerosociety.com

Similar Jobs
Airline Pilot: Civil, Airport Load Planning Officer, Helicopter Pilot: Commercial, Meteorologist, RAF Airman/Airwoman, RAF Officer, Royal Navy Officer

Aircraft Engineering Technician
also known as: Engineer: Aircraft Maintenance, Flight Engineer

CRCI:Engineering
CLCI:RAC

Job Band: 1 to 3

Job Description
Aircraft maintenance engineers help to check, service and repair aircraft between flights and during a planned maintenance schedule. Those trained in mechanical engineering usually specialise in looking after the engines and the structure of aircraft. Those with knowledge of avionics maintain the electrical and electronic equipment such as instruments for navigation, automatic pilot and radar/radio communication. Both carry out routine runway and safety checks and maintenance on aircraft between flights, as well as overhauling aircraft in workshops and hangars during regular inspections. Some work as flight engineers and oversee the performance of engines during flights.

Work Details
Most engineers work a 39-40 hr week, Monday to Friday, with the possibility of shifts or irregular hours. Your place of work is either in a hangar or outside, working on planes parked on the tarmac. Meticulous procedures need to be followed to ensure safety. You need to be able to solve problems quickly and the work can be demanding. Constant retraining to cope with new equipment is necessary.

The job involves considerable physical exertion, climbing in and out of aeroplanes and sometimes into enclosed and cramped places. Your surroundings may be noisy and dirty and there can be a risk of accidents from equipment. You need to wear overalls, and at times, ear protectors and safety glasses.

Qualification
• England, Wales and Northern Ireland
Band 3: For entry to jobs, training programmes or an HNC or a relevant Diploma course, usually at least 4 GCSEs (A*-C) including English, maths and a science subject, preferably physics, or equivalent. A technical or engineering subject is useful.

• Scotland
Band 3: For entry to jobs, training programmes or for some college courses: usually at least four S grades (1-3) including English, maths, and a science subject, preferably physics, or similar. A technical or engineering subject is useful.

Adult Qualifications
Some colleges have entry tests for those with no relevant qualifications. Experience in a relevant engineering field is an advantage. There are special part-time and short courses for those with a mechanical or electrical/electronic engineering background.

Work Experience
Entry to training positions and qualified posts is competitive and selection procedures are thorough, so it is important to gain some related work experience prior to your application. However, it may not always be possible for young people to gain such experience as it is an area that involves security, safety and insurance regulations. Relevant experience may be in something similar such as mechanical or motor vehicle engineering.

Entry and Training
An aircraft maintenance engineer's licence, awarded by the Civil Aviation Authority (CAA), is necessary for this job. Entry can be highly competitive and a special selection procedure of practical and written tests is often used. Training to obtain a licence is usually through a recognised industry apprenticeship scheme leading to S/NVQ level 3. There are also CAA approved college courses that last from one to four years. Contact the CAA for advice on routes to obtaining a licence. You can also contact your local armed forces office for information on how to qualify through the armed forces.

Once qualified, aircraft maintenance engineers can apply to the Engineering Council for registration as an Engineering Technician (EngTech). Application is normally made through the Royal Aeronautical Society and the process involves gaining experience and going through a professional review and interview.

The Engineering Development Trust runs a range of nationwide schemes for 11-21 year olds who are interested in engineering as a career. See the website for details. A Diploma/Welsh Baccalaureate may be available in your area in engineering. Relevant training programmes, including apprenticeship schemes, may also be available. Advanced apprenticeships leading to qualification at Level 3 can be a route into higher education. Tomorrow's Engineers has lots of useful careers information including a route map and guide to engineering activities from primary school through to higher education. Visit the website for details.

Mature applicants may find it difficult to obtain apprenticeships but college courses, short and part time, are available for all ages. Employment opportunities may be available for candidates with a basic electrical/electronic or mechanical engineering background. Equivalent armed forces training enables you to transfer to this job. For example, RAF engineers usually achieve the CAA Aircraft Maintenance Engineer's Licence before leaving the service.

Contact your local careers office, Jobcentre Plus, Next Step service or Learning and Skills Council (LSC)/Local Enterprise Company (LEC) for details of training schemes.

Opportunities and Pay

The UK has one of the largest aerospace industries in the world and employs over 250,000 people. Most engineers are employed by commercial airlines and the armed forces. Some have jobs with air-taxi operators, manufacturing companies or with flying schools. Jobs are available only in certain areas and there have been recent cutbacks in the manufacturinf sector due to the economic downturn. There are a few opportunities overseas with British airlines where you supervise local service engineers. Promotion to supervisor depends on becoming a licensed engineering technician and obtaining a CAA Category B2 licence.

Pay varies depending on location and type of employer, but generally, earnings start at around £20k, rising to £25k-£30k a year with experience. Higher earners can make up to £40k a year.

Health

This job requires normal colour vision and there may be a medical test on entry.

Skills and Qualities

able to work in confined spaces, able to work quickly, agile, alert, attention to detail, good concentration level, methodical, responsible attitude, safety conscious, technical aptitude

Relevant Subjects

Design and technology, Engineering, ICT/Computer studies, Mathematics, Physics, Science

Further Information

Air Service Training - www.airservicetraining.co.uk

Apprenticeship Schemes (National Apprenticeship Service) - www.apprenticeships.org.uk

Apprenticeships in Scotland (Careers Info Scotland) - www.apprenticeshipsinscotland.com/about/

Army Careers Website - www. army.mod.uk

Diplomas (Foundation, Higher and Advanced) - http://yp.direct.gov.uk/diplomas

Engineering Scotland (SEMTA) - www.engineeringscotland.org

SEMTA - sector skills council for science, engineering and manufacturing technologies - www.semta.org.uk

Tomorrow's Engineers - www.tomorrowsengineers.org.uk/careers.cfm

Training Schemes - www.direct.gov.uk/en/educationandlearning

Addresses

Association of Licensed Aircraft Engineers (ALAE)
Bourn House, 8 Park Street, Bagshot, Surrey GU19 5AQ
Phone: +44 (0)1276 474888
Web: www.alae.org

Civil Aviation Authority (CAA)
HR Department London Team Room 703 CAA House
45-59 Kingsway WC2B 6TE
Phone: +44 (0)20 7453 6040
Web: www.caa.co.uk/

Engineering Council
246 High Holborn, London WC1V 7EX
Phone: +44 (0)20 3206 0500
Web: www.engc.org.uk

Engineering Development Trust (EDT)
Ridgeway, Welwyn Garden City, Hertfordshire AL7 2AA
Phone: +44 (0)1707 871520
Web: www.etrust.org.uk

Royal Aeronautical Society (RAES)
4 Hamilton Place, London W1J 7BQ
Phone: +44 (0) 20 7670 4300
Web: www.aerosociety.com

Similar Jobs

Electrical Engineering Technician, Engineer: Aeronautical, Fitter: Maintenance, Marine Engineering Technician, RAF Airman/Airwoman

Airline Customer Service Agent

also known as: Passenger Services Agent: Airline

CRCI:Transport and Logistics

CLCI:YAB Job Band: 2 to 3

Job Description

Customer service agents work for an airline at an airport terminal, checking in and helping passengers. They usually work at a check-in desk or at the boarding/flight gate, making sure that passengers' travel documents are in order. They weigh and check in baggage, give out boarding passes and luggage labels, and allocate seat numbers. Also work out any excess baggage charge and receive payment by cash or credit card. They see that luggage and other supplies are loaded on to the correct plane and prepare the papers that are needed for customs clearance.

Customer service agents sometimes escort passengers to and from an aircraft; especially taking care of any elderly and less able passengers. They also assist unaccompanied children. Some airlines employ customer service agents to communicate with customers who contact the airline by telephone, in writing or via web-based enquiries or complaints.

Work Details

Usually work a basic 40 hr week, probably on a shift basis that includes evenings, weekends and public holidays. It is necessary to live within easy reach of the airport where you work. You meet a wide variety of people from many different countries and cultures. You are expected to work quickly, solve problems and deal with any complaints. The work can be demanding at times and you may have to spend a lot of time on your feet. A uniform is provided by the employer and you are expected to have a smart appearance.

Qualification

- **England, Wales and Northern Ireland**

Band 2: Although academic qualifications are not specified for this job, it is an advantage to have some GCSEs (A*-C) in subjects that include English and maths, or equivalent. The ability to speak a foreign language is also preferred.

Band 3: For entry to many airlines: at least 4 GCSEs (A*-C) including English and maths, or equivalent. The ability to speak a foreign language is also preferred.

- **Scotland**

Band 2: Although academic qualifications are not specified for this job, it is an advantage to have some S grades (1-3) in subjects that include English and maths, or similar. The ability to speak a foreign language is also preferred.

Band 3: For entry to many airlines: usually at least four S grades (1-3) including English and maths, or similar.

Adult Qualifications

Formal entry qualifications vary from airline to airline and you should therefore contact the airline of your choice for specific details. Applicants fluent in another language have an advantage.

Work Experience
Relevant work or voluntary experience can equip you with skills that you can use in the future and add to your CV. There are often opportunities available for voluntary work which give you experience of working with people. A background in travel and tourism or customer service skills is useful.

Entry and Training
For entry there is usually a series of written tests and you need to pass an interview. Training is on the job, together with short courses that cover the airport emergency and evacuation procedures, health and safety, customer care, and airport layout and services. You may also take part in group exercises and role play activities and shadow existing staff.

S/NVQs such as providing or coordinating aviation operations on the ground are available at levels 2-3. Edexcel offers a level 3 award, certificate and diploma in aviation operations. You can also take specialist courses in fares and ticketing.

Other relevant qualifications which may provide a useful route into this career include a GCSE in Leisure and Tourism, BTEC/SQA awards in travel and tourism and customer service and S/NVQs in travel services and customer service. A Diploma/Welsh Baccalaureate in travel and tourism may be available in your area. Training programmes, including apprenticeship schemes may also be available. Advanced apprenticeships leading to qualification at level 3 can also be a route into higher education.

Adults may be preferred for their experience and maturity and may be able to enter this work through a government-funded training programme. Government training opportunities, such as apprenticeships, including those for adults, may be available in your area.

You can also gain recognition of previous experience through Accreditation of Prior Learning or by working towards relevant S/NVQs. Contact your local careers office, Jobcentre Plus, Next Step service or Learning and Skills Council (LSC)/Local Enterprise Company (LEC) for details of training schemes. It is an advantage to have experience of working in the travel and tourism industry and to speak a second language.

Opportunities and Pay
Jobs are available at airports throughout the UK, but concentrated at Gatwick, Heathrow, Stansted and Manchester. Competition for jobs is fierce and the economic downturn has reduced the number available. Employers can be airlines, but most are airport servicing or handling agents. Increasingly, the check-in procedure can be on-line or via machines at airports, so the nature of the job is changing. With experience, promotion to supervisory and management jobs is possible. Some customer service agents go on to apply for cabin crew jobs. Part-time, seasonal and overseas work is often possible.

Pay varies and depends on the employing airline or company, but usually starts at around £12k-£14k a year, rising to around £15k-£20k with experience. There are usually additional payments for unsocial hours. Perks of the job can include a number of free or heavily subsidised flights a year.

Health
There may be a medical test. Some airlines have height and weight restrictions. A good level of general fitness is required. You should have clear speech.

Skills and Qualities
ability in one or more languages, able to cope under pressure, aptitude for teamwork, diplomatic, friendly, good communication skills, good interpersonal skills, good written English, polite, smart appearance

Relevant Subjects
English, Hospitality and catering, ICT/Computer studies, Law, Leisure, travel and tourism, Media and communication studies, Modern Foreign Languages

Further Information
AGCAS: Transport and Logistics (Job Sector Briefing) (AGCAS) - www.prospects.ac.uk

Apprenticeship Schemes (National Apprenticeship Service) - www.apprenticeships.org.uk

Diplomas (Foundation, Higher and Advanced) - http://yp.direct.gov.uk/diplomas

GoSkills - sector skills council for passenger transport - www.goskills.org

Training Schemes - www.direct.gov.uk/en/educationandlearning

Welsh Baccalaureate - www.wbq.org.uk

▶ Working in airports (2010) (Babcock Lifeskills) - www.babcock-lifeskills.com/

Addresses
British Airports Authority (BAA)
BAA Airports Limited, The Compass Centre, Nelson Road, London Heathrow Airport, Hounslow TW6 2GW
Phone: +44 (0)20 8745 9800
Web: www.baa.com

International Academy of Travel (IAOT)
Waterford Regional Airport, Terminal Building, Killowen, Co Waterford
Phone: +353 (0)51 843365
Web: http://iaot.net

Similar Jobs
Air Cabin Crew, Freight Forwarder, Holiday Representative, Hotel Receptionist, Tourist Information Centre Assistant, Travel Consultant

Airline Pilot: Civil
also known as: Pilot: Civil Airline

CRCI:Transport and Logistics
CLCI:YAB — Job Band: 3 to 5

Job Description
Pilots are responsible for the safe and efficient operation of an aircraft on long and short-haul flights worldwide, for business, commercial and leisure purposes. They have overall responsibility for the aircraft, crew and passengers. They direct the crew, monitor information from computer systems and operate the controls to fly an aeroplane. It is important that they study the flight plan, check the weather conditions and brief the crew. Before take-off, pilots also supervise loading and refuelling and check the flight deck instruments.

Pilots maintain radio contact with air traffic control to receive information and instructions. They make in-flight announcements to give passengers information. Also write a flight log at the end of each trip and record any problems experienced.

Work Details
You may travel worldwide, need to spend nights away from home and you may need to live within a specified travelling distance of the airport. You usually work on a rota basis. The work requires sound judgement and can be stressful at times. You have to cope with sitting for hours in an enclosed space, which is noisy, and you may have to cope with jet lag. There is a risk of accidents. You need to wear a uniform and earphones.

Qualification

- **England, Wales and Northern Ireland**

Band 3: Minimum entry to a Civil Aviation Authority (CAA) approved training school: 5 GCSEs (A*-C) including English, maths and a physical science, preferably physics. Alternative qualifications may also be considered.

Band 4: For entry to training sponsored by airlines: normally two A levels preferably in maths and physics, plus a minimum of 5 GCSEs (A*-C) including maths, English and a science subject, or equivalent.

Band 5: For degree courses: 2-3 A levels preferably in maths and physics and some GCSEs (A*-C) usually including English and maths, or equivalent. Exact requirements depend on the course you take.

- **Scotland**

Band 3: Minimum entry to a Civil Aviation Authority (CAA) approved training school: five S grades (1-3) in English, maths and a physical science, preferably physics, or similar.

Band 4: For entry to training sponsored by airlines: normally three H grades preferably including maths and physics, plus a minimum of five S grades (1-3) including maths, English and a science subject, or similar qualifications.

Band 5: For degree courses: 3-5 H grades preferably including maths and physics and some S grades (1-3), usually including English and maths, or similar qualifications.

Degree Information

A degree in any subject is acceptable. Physics, aeronautical engineering, mathematics or computing science subjects, meteorology or systems and control engineering give useful background. Some degrees include pilot training.

Adult Qualifications

Flying experience with the armed forces or a private pilot's licence is almost essential. There are conversion or short courses for armed forces pilots up to the age of 35. Entry requirements may be relaxed for adults applying for higher education courses. Access or foundation courses give adults without qualifications a route on to degree courses.

Work Experience

Entry to this career is highly competitive, and the nature of the job makes work experience very hard to obtain. It does improve your chances at interview if you have some work experience that can develop your skills in relevant areas, such as aeronautical engineering or airport work, particularly linked to meteorology or air traffic control.

Entry and Training

Applicants are typically aged 18-24, or under 26 for graduates. There may be height and weight restrictions. Check with individual airlines. There are three ways to train as a civil airline pilot. These are: as a trainee commercial pilot via sponsorship or self-funding, or obtaining a private pilot's licence and taking commercial training modules, or in the armed services and then converting to civil aviation. Entry is highly competitive, training is expensive and many applicants are graduates. Alternatively, some universities offer degree courses that include pilot training.

Most pilots pay for their own training and private training courses can cost £50k-£65k. It may be possible to gain sponsorship or be awarded a scholarship, but this is increasingly difficult. It may be possible to pay an airline a bond of £15k-£30k towards your training which is repaid to you if you continue to work for the airline for a specific time period. It is advisable to take a pilot aptitude test, run by the Guild of Air Pilots and Air Navigators (GAPAN) at RAF Cranwell, and have a medical with the Civil Aviation Authority (CAA) before you start paying for private training.

The minimum qualification is a 'frozen' Airline Transport Pilot Licence (ATPL) which consists of written exams and 200 hours flying. You are then awarded the full ATPL based on additional flying hours and experience. You must be at least 21 to hold an APTL. City University and London Metropolitan University offer specific degrees that include pilot training to 'frozen' ATPL level. You must also have a Commercial Pilot's Licence (CPL) with instrument rating (IR) awarded by the CAA.

Cabair College of Air Training publishes a list of companies who may provide sponsorship and you may also apply to the Air League Educational Trust. The cheaper training route is to gain a Private Pilot's Licence (PPL) logging 45 hours flying time and taking short courses and written and practical exams. You are expected to undertake continuing professional development throughout your career.

Mature applicants should be aware that most airlines only train those up to the age of 24 unless you are an experienced armed forces pilot. Some scholarships or sponsorship may be available from the Air League Educational Trust.

Opportunities and Pay

Employers are scheduled, charter and freight airlines of all sizes. Over 10,000 pilots work in the UK but most vacancies are for those with experience, and due to the economic downturn opportunities may be limited. You usually begin as a co-pilot or second officer. Promotion to senior posts, such as first officer, captain and chief pilot, is possible after 5-7 years' experience. There are further opportunities in management and training. Some pilots may use their experience to become crop sprayers or move into aerial surveying, or courier, cargo and air taxi operations. Pilots trained in the UK are often employed by foreign airlines.

Pay depends on the individual airline, responsibility and experience, but is usually high. Perks include subsidised travel and you are given a subsistence allowance when working away from home. Starting salaries are from £30k a year, rising steeply for training captains, type rating instructors and examiners. Salaries tend to be lower for turboprop aircraft captains at £33k-£40k a year. Jet aircraft captains can expect to earn £45k-£85k, or more.

Health

This job requires a high standard of physical fitness, perfect colour vision, good hearing and good eyesight. Entrants have to have a medical test each year and medical checkups. There may be restrictions on height.

Skills and Qualities

able to communicate effectively, able to cope under pressure, able to cope with emergencies, good co-ordination, information handling skills, problem-solving skills, quick reactions, self confident, sound judgement, spatial awareness

Relevant Subjects

Engineering, English, Geography, ICT/Computer studies, Mathematics, Physics, Science

Further Information

A Career in Aviation (British Women Pilots' Association (BWPA)) - www.bwpa.co.uk/page7.html

AGCAS: Transport and Logistics (Job Sector Briefing) (AGCAS) - www.prospects.ac.uk

Air Cadets - www.raf.mod.uk/aircadets/

British Air Line Pilot's Association (BALPA) - www.balpa.org

Civil Aviation Authority: Publications List (Civil Aviation Authority) - www.caa.co.uk/default.aspx?categoryid=33

GoSkills - sector skills council for passenger transport - www.goskills.org

Guide to Becoming a Professional Pilot (ATPL 2009) - www.afeonline.com/shop/index.php

How to become a Commercial Pilot (BALPA) - www.balpa.org/intranet/How-to-bec/How-to-become-a-pilot.pdf

So you want to be a pilot? (GAPAN & RAeS) - www.gapan.org/career-matters/careers-information/sywtbap/

What's it like to be a Pilot? (A&C Black 2009)

▶ Working in airports (2010) (Babcock Lifeskills) - www.babcock-lifeskills.com/

Addresses

Air League Educational Trust
Broadway House, Tothill Street, London SW1H 9NS
Phone: +44 (0)20 7222 8463
Web: www.airleague.co.uk

British Air Line Pilot's Association (BALPA)
BALPA House, 5 Heathrow Boulevard, 278 Bath Road, West Drayton UB7 0DQ
Phone: +44 (0) 20 8476 4000
Web: www.balpa.org.uk

British Women Pilots' Association
c/o Brooklands Museum, Brooklands Rd, Weybridge, Surrey KT13 0QN
Web: www.bwpa.co.uk/

Cabair Group of Aviation Companies
Elstree Aerodrome, Borehamwood, Hertfordshire WD6 3AQ
Phone: +44 (0)20 8236 2400
Web: www.cabair.com/

Civil Aviation Authority (CAA)
HR Department London Team Room 703 CAA House
45-59 Kingsway WC2B 6TE
Phone: +44 (0)20 7453 6040
Web: www.caa.co.uk/

Guild of Air Pilots and Air Navigators (GAPAN)
Cobham House, 9 Warwick Court, Gray's Inn, London WC1R 5DJ
Phone: +44 (0) 20 7404 4032
Web: www.gapan.org

Royal Aeronautical Society (RAES)
4 Hamilton Place, London W1J 7BQ
Phone: +44 (0) 20 7670 4300
Web: www.aerosociety.com

Similar Jobs

Air Traffic Controller, Engineer: Aeronautical, Helicopter Pilot: Commercial, Pilot: Armed Forces, RAF Officer

Airport Baggage Handler

CRCI:Transport and Logistics
CLCI:YAB — Job Band: 1

Job Description

Baggage handlers load and unload passenger luggage, freight and mail cargo into and out of the holds of aircraft. They use a range of specialist equipment such as baggage trucks, conveyors and lifting equipment, as well as barcode recognition scanners. May use a computer-controlled system for loading and unloading the baggage or freight. For outgoing passenger baggage, they check and sort each piece of luggage, making sure that each item goes on to the correct aircraft in time for the flight. They also remove incoming baggage from the aircraft and load it on to the correct carousel for passengers to collect.

In smaller airports, baggage handlers help to clean aircraft inside and out. They deliver prepared meals to planes and may assist disabled passengers to and from an aircraft. Use a two-way radio to maintain contact with other ground staff, including security. They report any suspicious items to security or the airport police. May also help airport security to keep runways free from debris, snow, ice or birds. Experienced handlers are called lead ramp hands and also direct aircraft to their stands in preparation for the next flight.

Work Details

Usually work a basic 39 hr week that involves shifts, including evenings, weekends and public holidays. You work in the airport building and warehouses, as well as outdoors and also spend time in parts of aircraft, where it is enclosed and cramped.

Work near planes can be noisy and you have to be careful with the baggage/freight, even when you are very busy and under pressure. There is a lot of bending, lifting and carrying in this job, which can cause back problems or other injuries. You are provided with a uniform and safety clothing, such as ear protectors. You follow strict rules about security at all times.

Qualification

• England, Wales and Northern Ireland

Band 1: No minimum qualifications are required, but you are expected to have a good level of general education. However, some formal/vocational qualifications at any level are useful.

• Scotland

Band 1: No minimum qualifications are required, but you are expected to have a good level of general education. However, some formal/vocational qualifications at any level are useful.

Adult Qualifications

You have to pass tests in reading, writing and numeracy but employers do not usually request formal qualifications. You can improve your skills and qualifications by working through the Foundation Learning programme. This involves taking credit-based units and qualifications to help you progress.

Work Experience

Any work experience can equip you with skills that you can use in the future and add to your CV and can either be unpaid or voluntary or holiday/part-time work that you have organised yourself. Consider experience such as warehouse and building yard work or goods delivery.

Entry and Training

Applicants must be at least 18. You train on the job and take short courses from time to time to keep up to date. Your background is checked for security reasons and you may need to have a medical. A current full driving licence, possibly an LGV or forklift truck licence is desirable. Some employers test your driving skills. Employers may also provide short courses, including manual lifting and handling, how to deal with lost items, health and safety, use of barcode recognition equipment and methods for dealing with suspicious packages.

Relevant S/NVQs are available at level 2 in providing aviation operations on the ground, and at level 3 in co-ordinating aviation operations on the ground. Edexcel (BTEC) offers a National Certificate and Diploma in Aviation Operations at level 3. Training programmes, including apprenticeship schemes, may be available in your area. Advanced apprenticeships leading to qualification at level 3 can also be a route into higher education.

Mature applicants with experience in warehouse work, cleaning or portering may have an advantage. Government training opportunities, such as apprenticeships, may be available in your area. You can also gain recognition of previous experience through Accreditation of Prior Learning or by working towards relevant S/NVQs. Contact your local careers office, Jobcentre Plus, Next Step service or Learning and Skills Council (LSC)/Local Enterprise Company (LEC) for details of training schemes.

Opportunities and Pay

There are about 5,000 baggage handlers in the UK and opportunities for employment are obviously dependent on air traffic. The economic downturn may mean that there are fewer vacancies. Employment is with airport authorities, airlines, handling agents or transport service companies, and is based at airports around the country. With experience you can move into other jobs, such as marshalling aircraft onto stands, arranging transport for crews, or take on a supervisory or training role. It is usually possible to get seasonal temporary jobs.

Pay varies depending on location and employer but most baggage handlers earn from £14k-£17.5k a year. Supervisors can make around £22.5k a year, and allowances for shiftwork and overtime may increase earnings.

Health
You may have to pass a medical test. You must be fit and in good health and have normal colour vision.

Skills and Qualities
able to work quickly, aptitude for teamwork, honest, reliable, security conscious, strong, technical aptitude

Further Information
AGCAS: Transport and Logistics (Job Sector Briefing) (AGCAS) - www.prospects.ac.uk

Apprenticeship Schemes (National Apprenticeship Service) - www.apprenticeships.org.uk

Foundation Learning (QCDA) - www.qcda.gov.uk

GoSkills - sector skills council for passenger transport - www.goskills.org

▶Working in airports (2010) (Babcock Lifeskills) - www.babcock-lifeskills.com/

Similar Jobs
Builders' Yard Assistant, Hospital Porter, Warehouse Worker

Airport Information Assistant

CRCI:Transport and Logistics
CLCI:YAB Job Band: 2 to 3

Job Description
Information assistants work in an airport terminal, dealing with passenger enquiries, such as flight details, and providing information on airport and airline services. They work mainly at a customer information desk providing information such as directions to the correct terminal, airline check-in desks, airport shopping areas, toilet facilities, currency exchange bureau and so on. Also deal with lost property and handling any complaints. Assistants inform a supervisor or manager if the complaint requires further assistance.

An assistant is responsible for monitoring and updating the airport's computerised flight information display system to ensure that the latest information on all the aircraft is made available to passengers. They make announcements on a public address system when necessary. In smaller airports they may also book hire cars and hotels for passengers, or work in the currency exchange bureau.

Work Details
Usually work a basic 39 hour week including some weekend work. The airport information desks must be open 24 hours a day to pass on details to passengers, therefore working shifts is highly probable. Work is mainly indoors and employers usually provide a smart uniform. The ability to work in a fast-paced customer environment is vital. Due to the busy summer and Christmas seasons, temporary work around these times is often available.

Qualification

• England, Wales and Northern Ireland
Band 2: Although academic qualifications are not specified for this job, it is an advantage to have some GCSEs (A*-C) in subjects that include English and maths, or equivalent. The ability to speak a foreign language is an advantage.

Band 3: For entry: usually at least 4 GCSEs (A*-C) including English and maths, or equivalent.

• Scotland
Band 2: Although academic qualifications are not specified for this job, it is an advantage to have some S grades (1-3) in subjects that include English and maths, or similar. The ability to speak a foreign language is an advantage.

Band 3: For entry: usually at least four S grades (1-3) including English and maths, or similar.

Adult Qualifications
Generally, you are expected to have the minimum entry qualifications, which can vary. Applicants fluent in another language are often preferred.

Work Experience
Relevant work or voluntary experience is always useful and can improve your employment prospects when applying for entry to jobs. It is an advantage to gain experience through seasonal or temporary work at an airport and to have knowledge of an airport's procedures, layout and services. Any experience of working with the public, including reception desk work, is very useful. Work experience abroad in a non-English speaking country is also an advantage.

Entry and Training
Requirements vary between employers, but usually you must be aged at least 18 though some airports only recruit people from 20 years old. Some airport information assistants are recruited from other jobs at an airport, including airline customer service agents. Training is usually on the job, plus short courses, presentations and DVDs on subjects that include the airport emergency and evacuation procedures, customer care, airport layout and services, health and safety, and how to use the public address and computerised flight information system.

Role-play sessions may include how to deal with confused, drunk or aggressive passengers. Qualifications such as the BTEC national certificate/diploma or award in airline and airport operations may be studied either full or part time. Relevant S/NVQs at levels 2-3 are available. There is also a level 4 in controlling airport operations for those at supervisory/management level. A Diploma/Welsh Baccalaureate in travel and tourism may be available in your area, providing a useful route into this career. Training programmes, including apprenticeship schemes, may also be available. An advanced apprenticeship leading to qualification at level 3 is also a route into higher education.

Mature entry is possible, especially for those with experience of customer service and travel and tourism. Government training opportunities, such as apprenticeships, may be available in your area. You can also gain recognition of previous experience through Accreditation of Prior Learning or by working towards relevant S/NVQs. Contact your local careers office, Jobcentre Plus, Next Step service or Learning and Skills Council (LSC)/Local Enterprise Company (LEC) for details of training schemes.

Opportunities and Pay
Airport jobs are highly competitive and although available throughout the UK, the economic downturn has reduced the number available. Employers are either individual airports or airline and airport servicing companies such as Servisair/Globeground. Promotion to supervisory and management jobs is possible and some airport information assistants apply for cabin crew jobs with an airline company. Overseas work is also possible.

Salary depends on where you work and the size of the employing organisation, but usually starts at around £11k-£14k a year. This rises to £17k-£24k a year with experience and extra responsibility.

Health
There may be a medical test and you should have good stamina and be physically fit.

Skills and Qualities
able to cope under pressure, able to put people at ease, aptitude for teamwork, diplomatic, friendly, good communication skills, good interpersonal skills, IT skills, outgoing personality

Relevant Subjects
English, ICT/Computer studies, Leisure, travel and tourism, Modern Foreign Languages

Further Information
AGCAS: Transport and Logistics (Job Sector Briefing) (AGCAS) - www.prospects.ac.uk

Apprenticeship Schemes (National Apprenticeship Service) - www.apprenticeships.org.uk

Diplomas (Foundation, Higher and Advanced) - http://yp.direct.gov.uk/diplomas

GoSkills - sector skills council for passenger transport - www.goskills.org

Training Schemes - www.direct.gov.uk/en/educationandlearning

▶Working in airports (2010) (Babcock Lifeskills) - www.babcock-lifeskills.com/

Working with languages (2010) (Babcock Lifeskills) - www.babcock-lifeskills.com/

Addresses
British Airports Authority (BAA)
BAA Airports Limited, The Compass Centre, Nelson Road, London Heathrow Airport, Hounslow TW6 2GW
Phone: +44 (0)20 8745 9800
Web: www.baa.com

Similar Jobs
Air Cabin Crew, Airline Customer Service Agent, Car Rental Agent, Tourist Information Centre Assistant, Travel Consultant

Airport Load Planning Officer
also known as: Flight Dispatcher, Load Controller
CRCI:Transport and Logistics
CLCI:YAB Job Band: 3 to 4

Job Description
Load planning officers are responsible for the safe and economic loading of aircraft so that they can get airborne, fly, land and turn around efficiently. This involves seating passengers and locating cargo in the most appropriate way. They use a computer with specially designed software to work out the best seating arrangements for passengers and to load balance the cargo. Also produce information for pilots about the load of the aircraft, the weight and size of freight and luggage, and the number of passengers on board.

Load planners work with several aircraft at once. They spend time on a computer advance planning and preparing for flights. Work closely with check-in staff and cargo agents who accept cargo for transportation, often using a two-way radio.

Work Details
You usually work a shift system as airlines operate on a 24-hour basis each day of the year. This includes early mornings, evenings, weekends and bank holidays and nights. You may also be expected to work overtime on occasions when there are delays at the airport. Part-time work may be possible.

You are based in an office environment but also spend time outside on the airport apron liaising between baggage handlers and flight deck staff. Working on the airfield can be cold, wet and noisy. You may be issued with ear defenders, a high visibility jacket and steel toe-capped boots for working outside.

Qualification
- **England, Wales and Northern Ireland**

Band 3: For entry to the job: usually at least 4 GCSEs (A*-C) including English and maths, or equivalent.

Band 4: For BTEC higher national award: 1-2 A levels and some GCSEs (A*-C) usually including English and maths, or equivalent.

- **Scotland**

Band 3: For entry: usually at least four S grades (1-3) including English and maths, or similar.

Band 4: For SQA higher national award: usually 2-3 H grades and some S grades (1-3), often including English and maths, or similar qualifications.

Adult Qualifications
Entry requirements may be relaxed for adults applying for higher education courses. Access or foundation courses provide those without the required qualifications a route onto degree courses.

Work Experience
Relevant work or voluntary experience can equip you with skills that you can use in the future and add to your CV. There are often opportunities available for voluntary work which give you experience of working with people. A background in travel and tourism is useful.

Entry and Training
Entrants to this job need GCSE/S grades including English and maths. IT skills are also desirable and you need a Criminal Records Bureau (CRB)/Disclosure Scotland check to work as a load planning officer. Some enter air transport work as apprentices and later progress to load planning work and many have experience in an area such as passenger services which helps in the supervision of gate staff.

Initial training is usually carried out within the working environment and also includes experience of the work of a check-in agent and using computer databases. Specific training in load planning involves instruction in the manual weight and balance concepts of aircraft, and in computerised load planning. There is usually a short period of continual assessment before you are awarded a licence to work as a load planning officer. Training may also involve gaining recognised qualifications within the industry. This may be an NVQ level 3 in coordinating aviation operations on the ground or planning aircraft payloads. Edexcel offers a level 3 award, certificate and diploma in aviation operations.

Other relevant qualifications which may provide a useful route into this career include a GCSE in Leisure and Tourism, BTEC/SQA awards in travel and tourism and customer service and S/NVQs in travel services and customer service. A Diploma/Welsh Baccalaureate in travel and tourism may also be available in your area.

Mature applicants with experience in passenger services or working with aircraft may have an advantage. Employers look for common sense, the ability to think quickly and to work well as part of a team.

Government training opportunities, such as apprenticeships, may be available in your area. You can also gain recognition of previous experience through Accreditation of Prior Learning or by working towards relevant S/NVQs. Contact your local careers office, Jobcentre Plus, Next Step service or Learning and Skills Council (LSC)/Local Enterprise Company (LEC) for details of training schemes.

Opportunities and Pay
Some large airlines such as British Airways employ their own load planning officers. However, most officers are employed by ground handling companies working on behalf of airlines. These can be large international organisations or small regional companies. The number of load planning officers is increasing.

With experience, you can move on to become a duty manager or trainer. Some airports may offer opportunities for promotion to positions such as load planning manager, flight operation officer or airport duty manager.

Salaries for load planning officers start at around £15k a year. With more experience, it is possible to earn around £16k-£19k. Pay can be increased by working overtime.

Health

There may be a medical test. Some airlines have height and weight restrictions.

Skills and Qualities

able to cope under pressure, able to work both on your own and in a team, confident, decisive, excellent communication skills, good interpersonal skills, IT skills, numeracy skills, quick thinking

Relevant Subjects

English, ICT/Computer studies, Leisure, travel and tourism, Mathematics

Further Information

AGCAS: Tourism (Job Sector Briefing) (AGCAS) - www.prospects.ac.uk

Apprenticeship Schemes (National Apprenticeship Service) - www.apprenticeships.org.uk

Diplomas (Foundation, Higher and Advanced) - http://yp.direct.gov.uk/diplomas

GoSkills - sector skills council for passenger transport - www.goskills.org

Inside Careers Guide: Logistics & Transport Management - www.insidecareers.co.uk

Welsh Baccalaureate - www.wbq.org.uk

▶Working in airports (2010) (Babcock Lifeskills) - www.babcock-lifeskills.com/

Addresses

British Airports Authority (BAA)
BAA Airports Limited, The Compass Centre, Nelson Road,
London Heathrow Airport, Hounslow TW6 2GW
Phone: +44 (0)20 8745 9800
Web: www.baa.com

Similar Jobs

Air Cabin Crew, Airport Baggage Handler, Flight Operations Officer, Logistics Manager, RAF Airman/Airwoman, RAF Officer

Alexander Technique Teacher

CRCI:Healthcare
CLCI:JOD Job Band: 1 to 3

Job Description

Alexander Technique Teachers teach the principles of the Alexander Technique and show individuals how to apply it to their daily life and benefit from the technique. These may be athletes and artists, or those with disability, pain, illness or injury. They teach people to become self-aware, to think about the way they move and breathe, and identify and change any bad postural habits they have that may cause stress or pain. They also help people to re-establish the relationship between the head, neck and back, improving their confidence, strength and stamina, and reducing stress, aches and pains.

Teachers assess each student by talking about any health concerns. They watch behaviour such as attitude, ease of movement, coordination and breathing efficiency, then adjust the lesson according to the pupil's needs. They use gentle hands-on guidance and verbal explanations to help people with simple movements and everyday activities.

Work Details

Alexander Technique teachers work variable hours which may include some evenings and weekends. Your place of work is usually at your home, or may involve travelling to your pupils' homes. You may also work at a music or drama school, college, or at a therapy centre. Your students can be of all ages and have a range of different needs.

You mainly give individual tuition on a one-to-one basis, although you may also organise small introductory group sessions from time to time. You need to be physically fit to teach this technique. Work can involve kneeling, bending and standing for long periods.

Qualification

• England, Wales and Northern Ireland

Band 1: For entry to jobs, no minimum qualifications are needed, but you are expected to have a good level of general education and relevant experience. Some formal/vocational qualifications at any level are useful.

Band 2: For entry to jobs, no minimum qualifications are needed, but it is an advantage to have some GCSEs (A*-C) or equivalent in subjects that include English, maths and biology.

Band 3: For entry to jobs, HNC or a relevant Diploma, usually at least 4 GCSEs (A*-C) including English, maths and biology, or equivalent.

• Scotland

Band 1: For entry to jobs, no minimum qualifications are needed, but you are expected to have a good level of general education and relevant experience. Some formal/vocational qualifications at any level are useful.

Band 2: Although academic qualifications are not specified for this job, it is an advantage to have some S grades (1-3) in subjects that include English, maths and biology, or similar.

Band 3: For entry to some jobs: usually at least four S grades (1-3) including English, maths and biology, or similar.

Adult Qualifications

No pre-entry qualifications are usually required though some academic/vocational qualifications at any level are an advantage. English, maths and biology are useful subjects.

Work Experience

Relevant work or voluntary experience can equip you with skills that you can use in the future and that you can add to your CV. Experience of learning the technique through taking individual lessons is most important for training. Any experience of teaching, training or work in healthcare also provides useful experience.

Entry and Training

There is no fixed route to becoming an Alexander Technique teacher and teachers are not yet regulated. Two professional bodies run or approve training courses in the UK. Previous experience of learning the technique for your own personal development is more important than academic qualifications for entry to courses. To register with the Society of Teachers of the Alexander Technique (STAT) you must take an approved three-year full-time course, leading to a STAT teaching certificate. You can then join STAT as a teaching member. There are currently 18 approved courses throughout the UK. Contact STAT for a list of courses. STAT run a number of residential courses and workshops in the UK and overseas to help with continuing professional development.

The Professional Association of Alexander Teachers (PAAT) runs a four-year training course, with qualification through written examination and practical demonstration. Applicants for the course must have at least one year of individual lessons, or attended a course run by a PAAT member at college or university.

Applicants must also attend the association's recreational course and be at least 18 years of age. Tuition takes place during the evenings and at weekends.

You can also take a part time four-year course at Trinity College, Bristol, via the Interactive Teaching Method Association.

Maturity is an asset for teaching the Alexander Technique, and life experience is more important than qualifications, so this is a popular second career. Experience working as a teacher, trainer or counsellor is useful.

Opportunities and Pay

Around 2,000 teachers of the Alexander Technique are registered in the UK. Most are self-employed, although some work at music and drama schools. There are lots of opportunities for part-time work. Members of STAT can also teach abroad in countries where there are affiliated societies. Currently there are good opportunities for this work as interest in the technique continues to grow, although this depends on where you live and the level of competition from other teachers. Some teachers specialise in teaching particular groups such as sports professionals or children.

Salaries are difficult to gauge as most teachers are self-employed. Starting salaries can be around £15k or more, but this depends on the fees you charge and the number of pupils you have. Your charges per hour are likely to be £30-£60. Experienced teachers may earn £25k-£30k a year. If you have a good reputation and customer base you may earn around £40k a year.

Health

This job requires a good general level of fitness.

Skills and Qualities

able to explain clearly, able to inspire confidence, able to motivate others, able to understand other people's problems, enquiring mind, good listening skills, manual dexterity, observational skills, self-motivated, supportive

Relevant Subjects

Biology, English, Health and social care, Psychology, Science

Further Information

Alexander Technique Bibliography - www.mouritz.co.uk

Alexander Technique International (ATI) - www.ati-net.com

Alexander Trust - www.alexandertrust.org.uk

Interactive Teaching Method Association (ITM) - www.alexandertechnique-itm.org

STATnews (newsletter of STAT, 3 times a year) (STAT) - www.stat.org.uk

The Alexander Journal (Soc. of Teachers of the Alexander Technique (STAT)) - www.stat.org.uk

Addresses

Professional Association of Alexander Teachers (PAAT)
Room 706, 'The Big Peg' 120 Vyse Street, Birmingham, West Midlands B18 6NF
Phone: +44 (0)1743 236195
Web: www.paat.org.uk

Society of Teachers of the Alexander Technique (STAT)
1st Floor, Linton House, 39-51 Highgate Road, London NW5 1RS
Phone: +44 (0)20 7482 5135
Web: www.stat.org.uk

Similar Jobs

Chiropractor, Counsellor, Osteopath, Physiotherapist, Reflexologist, Sports Therapist

Ambulance Care Assistant

also known as: Patient Transport Service (PTS) Driver, PTS Driver: Ambulance

CRCI:Healthcare
CLCI:JOC — Job Band: 1 to 2

Job Description

Ambulance care assistants usually deal with non-emergency cases, transporting frail or elderly people to and from outpatient clinics and day centres, or dealing with non-urgent transfers. They are responsible for patients on the journey and while being transferred to and from the vehicle. Also have specialist driving skills and are trained in patient care, including basic life-support and general first-aid treatment.

All ambulance personnel have common duties that include keeping the ambulance clean and tidy, and stocked with first aid equipment and other necessary supplies. They also check the petrol, tyres, water and oil and complete log sheets.

Work Details

You need to travel around an area and usually work 39 hours a week; Monday to Friday. The job involves driving a health service vehicle that picks up patients and takes them to hospital or to clinics for appointments and treatment. Sometimes this may be an ambulance that allows access by wheelchairs or stretchers. Ambulance care assistants usually work in pairs, one driving the ambulance and the other looking after the patients, but you may work alone. You work with people, often the elderly, who are ill, possibly in pain and upset.

Work requires coping with the sight of blood. At times, work may be upsetting and you need to cope with unpleasant sights. The work involves bending and heavy lifting. You may need to work outside in all weathers. You need to wear a uniform and sometimes protective clothing.

Qualification

Qualifications for entry vary according to the individual ambulance service. Check with your local service HQ for details.

- **England, Wales and Northern Ireland**

Band 1: For entry to jobs, no minimum qualifications are needed, but you are expected to have a good level of general education and relevant experience. Some ambulance services do ask for qualifications so some formal/vocational qualifications at any level are useful.

Band 2: Some ambulance services ask for some GCSEs (A*-C) in subjects that include English and maths, or equivalent.

- **Scotland**

Band 1: For entry to jobs, no minimum qualifications are needed, but you are expected to have a good level of general education and relevant experience. Some ambulance services do ask for qualifications so some formal/vocational qualifications at any level are useful.

Band 2: Some ambulance services may ask for some S grades (1-3) in subjects that include English and maths, or similar.

Adult Qualifications

Usually a good standard of education is required that may include some formal qualifications or equivalent.

Work Experience

Work experience gives you an insight into what you enjoy and don't enjoy about a job or working environment, as well as the opportunity to acquire new skills. It also provides valuable information to add to your CV and improves your course application and future employment prospects.

Try to visit an ambulance station to discuss the work or consider some voluntary work with the ambulance service. Any work, either paid or voluntary, that gives experience of working in a caring capacity with people is very useful. Gaining first-aid certificates and knowledge of life-saving techniques also demonstrates commitment.

Entry and Training

Entry requirements depend on the employer, but you need a full, clean UK driving licence and to undergo a driving assessment test and a police check. You must be over 18 and for some ambulance services, over 21. You usually take an in-house course over two to three weeks which is followed by an assessment and a written examination. Training continues on the job, under supervision for a probationary period which varies according to your employer. You receive training to upgrade your driving skills, in basic patient skills, first-aid techniques and instruction on the safe moving and handling of patients. In some ambulance services, oxygen therapy administration training is given. You may also be able to get a licence to drive larger vehicles.

You may be able to train to work as part of a high dependency team which transports patients with particular medical conditions. If you have the aptitude and motivation, you can go on to train as a paramedic.

Mature entrants with relevant experience or qualifications in healthcare may have an advantage. Ambulance services welcome mature entrants and for some this can be a second career. All entrants must have the right level of physical fitness.

Opportunities and Pay

Most ambulance care assistants are employed by NHS trusts at one of the ambulance services across the UK. In Wales ambulance care assistants are also known as Patient Care Services (PCS) personnel. There are also opportunities to train and work for the armed forces. Progression to work as a paramedic, or to posts in other health service departments, such as operations management, administration, health and safety, training or personnel is possible. Part-time work is available. When trained and experienced you can also work for a private ambulance service.

Pay is on a nationally agreed scale and is more if overtime is worked. Salaries vary depending on the individual ambulance service but are around £14k-£17k a year, and £18k-£26k for higher level ambulance assistants.

Health

You need to be physically fit to handle the lifting and transport parts of the job. A medical assessment is required to establish your level of physical fitness and that you have good eyesight.

Skills and Qualities

able to get on with all kinds of people, aptitude for teamwork, calm, caring, good communication skills, good interpersonal skills, patient, reassuring, responsible attitude

Relevant Subjects

Biology, English, Health and social care, Science

Further Information

AGCAS: Armed Forces & Emergency Services (Job Sector Briefing) (AGCAS) - www.prospects.ac.uk

NHS Careers (NHS Careers) - www.nhscareers.nhs.uk

NHS Careers Scotland - www.infoscotland.com/nhs

NHS Careers Wales - www.wales.nhs.uk

Skills for Health - sector skills council - www.skillsforhealth.org.uk

Addresses

Ambulance Service Network
The NHS Confederation, 3rd Floor, 29 Bressendon Place, London SW1E 5DD
Phone: +44 (0)20 7074 3200
Web: www.nhsconfed.org/networks/ambulanceservice/

London Ambulance Service
NHS Trust Recruitment Centre St Andrew's House St Andrews Way Bow, London E3 3PA
Phone: +44 (0)20 3069 0260
Web: www.londonambulance.nhs.uk

Northern Ireland Ambulance Service (NIAS) Health and Social Care Trust
Ambulance Headquarters, Site 30 Knockbracken Healthcare Park, Saintfield Road, Belfast BT8 8SG
Phone: +44 (0)28 9040 0999
Web: www.niamb.co.uk

Scottish Ambulance Service
National HQ, Tipperlinn Road, Edinburgh EH10 5UU
Phone: +44 (0)131 446 7000
Web: www.scottishambulance.com

Welsh Ambulance Service NHS Trust
HM Stanley Hospital, St Asaph, Denbighshire LL17 0RS
Phone: +44 (0)1745 532 900
Web: www.ambulance.wales.nhs.uk

Similar Jobs

Ambulance Paramedic, Emergency Care Assistant/Ambulance Technician, Hospital Porter, Nurse: Adult, Social Care Worker

Ambulance Paramedic

also known as: Emergency Care Practitioner: Ambulance, Paramedic

CRCI:Healthcare

CLCI:JOC — Job Band: 4 to 5

Job Description

Ambulance paramedics are senior members of an accident and emergency ambulance crew working in ambulances, air ambulances or on motorcycles/bicycles. They respond to 999 calls and give emergency treatment to accident victims, or people who have been taken seriously ill, and transport them to hospital. Paramedics are trained to use the more advanced forms of equipment such as life-support equipment and can administer a range of drugs for the immediate treatment of medical and trauma conditions. They may need to carry out further emergency treatment such as resuscitation, deal with broken bones or set up an intravenous drip and are also qualified in coronary care. Paramedics travel with the patient to hospital, monitoring breathing, blood pressure, etc, during the journey. They complete a report for hospital medical staff. Often work alongside the police and fire brigade.

Community paramedics work together with GPs and practice nurses, providing care in the surgery and visiting patients at home. All ambulance personnel have common duties, which include keeping the ambulance clean and tidy with stocks of first aid equipment and other necessary supplies. They also regularly check that their equipment works properly.

Work Details

Usually work around 40 hrs a week of rotating shifts, including nights, weekends and public holidays. You work with people who are ill, possibly in pain and upset. You are expected to cope with the sight of blood and at times, some unpleasant sights. Your work requires sound judgement in observing and assessing the condition of the patients you are called out to help. You are usually one of a two-person ambulance crew but if you are seconded to work in rapid response or motorcycle units, you may need to work on your own.

Ambulances are clinical environments and you work with a range of emergency care equipment. You usually spend your time in a vehicle and on the move, in all weather conditions, and at all times of the day and night. The work involves bending and some heavy lifting. You are expected to wear a uniform.

Ambulance Paramedic

Qualification

You need to secure a student paramedic position with an ambulance service trust, or attend an approved full-time course in paramedic science at a university to qualify. Check with your local service HQ for details.

• England, Wales and Northern Ireland

Band 4: For entry to a training post and Health Professions Council (HPC) approved foundation degree or Diploma of Higher Education (DipHE): usually 1-3 A levels including a life science or natural science, and 5 GCSEs (A*-C), including English, maths and science, or equivalent.

Band 5: For degree in paramedic science: 2-3 A levels, preferably including a science subject and psychology or sociology, plus GCSEs (A*-C) in English, maths and science, or equivalent.

• Scotland

Band 4: For direct entry to ambulance technician training prior to training as a paramedic: two H grades plus 3-5 S grades (1-3), including English, maths and science-based subject.

Degree Information

A degree in paramedic science is needed. The NHS website has details of approved courses.

Adult Qualifications

Qualifications for entry may differ between some ambulance services, so check with your preferred employer. It is helpful to have qualifications in first aid and life-saving techniques. If you want to do a degree course first, you may be able to gain entry with an Access or foundation course in science.

Work Experience

Work experience gives you an insight into what you enjoy and don't enjoy about a job or working environment, as well as the opportunity to acquire new skills. It also provides valuable information to add to your CV and improves your course application and future employment prospects. Try to visit an ambulance station to discuss the work or consider some voluntary work with the ambulance service. Any work, either paid or voluntary, that provides experience of working in a caring capacity with people, is very useful. Gaining first-aid certificates and knowledge of life-saving techniques also demonstrates commitment.

Entry and Training

You can qualify as a paramedic in England and Wales by securing a student paramedic position with an ambulance service trust and studying part time, or attending a full-time course in paramedic science at a university. The Health Professions Council (HPC) approves a number of courses leading to a diploma, foundation degree and/or BSc honours degree in paramedic science. Courses last between two and five years, depending on whether you study full or part time. Clinical training lasts around ten to twelve weeks and includes several weeks in various hospital departments under the supervision of senior doctors. Check course entry requirements with the university and the ambulance service trust you want to work for.

After you have completed the course you are monitored for six months and once qualified, you must register with the HPC to work for the NHS and keep your skills and knowledge up to date throughout your career. The British Paramedic Association offers an online continuing professional development scheme for its members. Paramedics can undertake extended training to become Emergency Care Practitioners (ECPs).

You cannot enter the Scottish Ambulance Service as a paramedic, and generally work your way up from an ambulance care assistant to an ambulance technician and then train as a paramedic. There is no higher education entry route.

For all services, you are accepted with a provisional C1 driving licence, but need a full licence before you start training. Some ambulance services support training for employees who need an upgraded licence, but you may need to organise this yourself.

Mature entrants with relevant experience or qualifications in healthcare may have an advantage. Ambulance services welcome mature entrants and for some this can be a second career. This job also requires a considerable level of physical fitness. You may be at an advantage if you have a background in the ambulance service as an ambulance care assistant, technician or emergency care assistant. Contact your local ambulance service for further details.

Opportunities and Pay

There are around 15,000 paramedics working in the UK and most are employed by the NHS, mainly in cities or in large towns. The demand for qualified paramedics is good. Other opportunities exist in the armed forces, private ambulance services, or large industrial organisations with small on-site ambulance services. Paramedics may also work in a GP's surgery. There are some opportunities for overseas work, such as voluntary service overseas (VSO). Promotion to supervisory and management posts is possible. With further experience and qualifications, you may progress to become an Emergency Care Practitioner (ECP).

Pay is on a nationally agreed scale for those working in the NHS. Salary scales for paramedics vary depending on which trust you work for, but when fully qualified you can expect to earn around £21k-£28k a year. ECPs can earn around £25k-£34k a year.

Health

This job requires a medical test on entry and you are expected to be physically fit. This job requires good hearing and eyesight with normal colour vision. The work may involve a risk of infection.

Skills and Qualities

able to cope under pressure, able to cope with emergencies, able to inspire confidence, able to make important decisions, able to work both on your own and in a team, calm, decisive, good communication skills, not squeamish, quick reactions

Relevant Subjects

Biology, Chemistry, English, Health and social care, Psychology, Science

Further Information

AGCAS: Armed Forces & Emergency Services (Job Sector Briefing) (AGCAS) - www.prospects.ac.uk

British Paramedic Resource Centre - www.paramedic-resource-centre.com

NHS Careers (NHS Careers) - www.nhscareers.nhs.uk

NHS Careers Scotland - www.infoscotland.com/nhs

NHS Careers Wales - www.wales.nhs.uk

What's it like to be an Emergency Nurse? (A&C Black 2009)

Addresses

Ambulance Service Network
The NHS Confederation, 3rd Floor, 29 Bressendon Place, London SW1E 5DD
Phone: +44 (0)20 7074 3200
Web: www.nhsconfed.org/networks/ambulanceservice/

College of Paramedics
The Exchange Express Park Bristol Road, Bridgwater, Somerset TA6 4RR
Phone: +44 (0) 1278 420014
Web: https://www.collegeofparamedics.co.uk/home/

Health Professions Council (HPC)
Park House, 184 Kennington Park Road, London SE11 4BU
Phone: +44 (0)20 7582 0866
Web: www.hpc-uk.org

London Ambulance Service
NHS Trust Recruitment Centre St Andrew's House
St Andrews Way Bow, London E3 3PA
Phone: +44 (0)20 3069 0260
Web: www.londonambulance.nhs.uk

Northern Ireland Ambulance Service (NIAS) Health and Social Care Trust
Ambulance Headquarters, Site 30 Knockbracken Healthcare Park, Saintfield Road, Belfast BT8 8SG
Phone: +44 (0)28 9040 0999
Web: www.niamb.co.uk

Scottish Ambulance Service
National HQ, Tipperlinn Road, Edinburgh EH10 5UU
Phone: +44 (0)131 446 7000
Web: www.scottishambulance.com

Welsh Ambulance Service NHS Trust
HM Stanley Hospital, St Asaph, Denbighshire LL17 0RS
Phone: +44 (0)1745 532 900
Web: www.ambulance.wales.nhs.uk

Similar Jobs

Emergency Care Assistant/Ambulance Technician, Firefighter, Health Visitor, Nurse: Adult, Nurse: Children, Police Officer

Anaesthetist

CRCI:Healthcare
CLCI:JAB Job Band: 5

Job Description

Anaesthetists are doctors who prevent patients from feeling pain whilst they undergo surgical operations and other medical procedures. They work in pain management with people recovering from surgery, giving birth, or suffering from conditions that cause long-term pain, such as cancer. They talk to patients and assess their condition prior to surgery or other procedures. Administer either a general or local anaesthesia as appropriate. They monitor patients who are under anaesthetic and supervise them during the recovery period. Also supervise patients who are in intensive care. Some anaesthetists are involved in teaching other healthcare professionals.

It is possible to specialise in a particular branch of anaesthesia such as cardiac, paediatric, intensive care or chronic pain management.

Work Details

You are expected to work irregular and relatively long hours, especially as a junior doctor. You usually work shifts to provide 24-hour care, seven days a week. You have contact with people who are ill, in pain, upset or depressed. You have to make decisions about the most appropriate anaesthesia for their condition and keep accurate records. Work may be emotionally demanding, and requires coping with the sight of blood. You work in operating theatres, intensive care units, recovery units, hospital wards and accident and emergency departments. You need to work closely as a team with surgeons and nurses. This job is very satisfying for those wishing to work in a caring profession.

Qualification

- **England, Wales and Northern Ireland**

Band 5: For honours degree course in medicine: usually 3 A levels with good grades in chemistry and two from physics, biological sciences and maths, plus 5 GCSEs (A*-C), including English and maths, or equivalent. Some medical schools offer a one-year pre-medical course for students with A levels in Arts or mixed subjects. Check with individual schools for details.

- **Scotland**

Band 5: For honours degree course in medicine: usually five H grades, with good grades in chemistry and two from physics, biology and maths, plus five S grades (1-3) including English and maths, or similar. Normally science subjects not held at H grade should be offered at S grade. Some medical schools offer a one-year pre-medical course for students whose H grades do not include the required science subjects. Check with individual schools for full details.

Degree Information

A first degree in medicine awarded by a university medical school and recognised by the General Medical Council is essential, followed by specialist anaesthetist training.

Adult Qualifications

Entry requirement standards are not normally relaxed for mature applicants, though those who consider applying should contact the individual university for advice. Graduates with a good honours degree in a related subject may obtain exemptions from certain options within the medical degree course.

Work Experience

Work experience gives you an insight into what you enjoy and don't enjoy about a job or working environment, as well as the opportunity to acquire new skills. It also provides valuable information to add to your CV and improves your course application and future employment prospects. Entry to this career is highly competitive. It is essential that you have some relevant work or voluntary experience before applying to train as a doctor. All applicants need to demonstrate a long-term commitment to medicine. Evidence of this can come in the form of relevant paid or voluntary work in a healthcare setting such as in a hospital, residential care home or similar.

Entry and Training

To qualify as an anaesthetist takes seven years, depending on the rate at which necessary competences are achieved. Anaesthetists must first qualify as medical doctors by completing a medicine degree, pass the postgraduate two-year Foundation Programme and register as a doctor with the General Medical Council (GMC). For full details of medical training see the job article Doctor: Hospital.

Once you have completed the Foundation Programme, there is competitive entry for two-year postgraduate anaesthetist training which covers all aspects of anaesthetic, intensive care medicine and pain management. You then have to apply for posts for a minimum of three years' further training in the specialism. Progress is based on achieving competences, and leads to the Certificate of Completion of Training (CCT). Once you have achieved the CCT, you can join the specialist register (SpR) of the GMC and apply for a post as a consultant. You are expected to update your professional knowledge continually throughout your career. Contact the Royal College of Anaesthetists for details of courses, bursaries and training routes.

Mature entrants are welcomed by medical schools and especially suitably qualified mature students. Some medical schools may have reserved places for mature/graduate entrants. There are Access courses to medicine and pre-medical foundation courses. Some Open University credits at distinction level may be accepted at some medical schools. Check with individual medical schools for details of all opportunities.

Opportunities and Pay

There are around 6,000 consultant anaesthetists in the UK and this is the largest of the medical specialisms. Anaesthetists are usually employed by the NHS, private hospitals or the armed forces. Prospects may depend on willingness to move to another area to gain experience and obtain promotion. There may be opportunities to work part time or job share. There are opportunities to work abroad, especially in the USA and Middle East, and also with voluntary organisations, but pay is usually low.

Within the NHS, junior doctors earn a basic salary and are usually paid a supplement for extra hours worked. Basic salaries are around £33k a year (including a 50% supplement for extra hours), rising to £43k-£68k (including 50% supplement) for a doctor in specialist training. A consultant can earn £73k-£174k a year. These salaries do not include on-call payments, private income or London weighting allowances.

Health

There is a risk of infection. You should have no allergies and a good level of general fitness.

Skills and Qualities

able to cope under pressure, able to put people at ease, analytical skills, aptitude for teamwork, attention to detail, decisive, good communication skills, good interpersonal skills, not squeamish, observant

Relevant Subjects

Biology, Chemistry, English, Health and social care, Mathematics, Physics, Psychology, Science, Sociology

Further Information

British Journal of Anaesthesia (Royal College of Anaesthetists) http://bja.oxfordjournals.org/

Modernising Medical Careers - www.mmc.nhs.uk

NHS Careers (NHS Careers) - www.nhscareers.nhs.uk

NHS Careers Scotland - www.infoscotland.com/nhs

NHS Careers Wales - www.wales.nhs.uk

Addresses

British Medical Association (BMA)
BMA House, Tavistock Square, London WC1H 9JP
Phone: +44 (0)20 7387 4499
Web: www.bma.org.uk

General Medical Council (GMC)
Regents Place, 350 Euston Road, London NW1 3JN
Phone: +44 (0)161 923 6602
Web: www.gmc-uk.org

Royal College of Anaesthetists (RCoA)
Churchill House, 35 Red Lion Square, London WC1R 4SG
Phone: +44 (0)20 7092 1500
Web: www.rcoa.ac.uk

Similar Jobs

Cardiologist, Doctor: General Practitioner, Doctor: Hospital, Obstetrician/Gynaecologist, Ophthalmologist, Surgeon

Anatomical Pathology Technician

also known as: Mortuary Technician

CRCI:Healthcare
CLCI:JOZ Job Band: 2 to 3

Job Description

Anatomical pathology technicians (APTs) carry out a range of tasks related to mortuary service work. One of the primary tasks is to assist pathologists at post-mortems, which are carried out to establish the cause of an unexpected or suspicious death. They are responsible for the day-to-day administration and maintenance of the mortuary and post-mortem room. Ensure all instruments are clean, sterile and secure. Prepare and lay out instruments, make notes during examination and weigh human organs as they are removed.

Technicians take and record samples for toxicology or histopathological analysis. Keep accurate records of the identity of a body and its possessions. Replace organs, stitch and clean the body ready for storage or release to an undertaker. Prepare the bodies to be viewed or identified by relatives, through embalming, washing and dressing the body so that the deceased looks presentable and at peace. Liaise with the police, doctors, coroner's office and funeral directors.

Also help with the training of other healthcare professionals such as junior doctors, medical students, paramedics, nurses and porterage staff, who need to know of the mortuary practices and procedures. Use a computer to store records, information and write reports. Ensure all legal documentation is dealt with correctly and efficiently. May specialise in assisting forensic pathologists with examinations of murder victims.

Work Details

You are based in a hospital or a mortuary, usually working 37-40 hours a week with additional overtime and on-call work. Work can be emotionally demanding and requires coping with the sight of blood and some unpleasant sights and smells. This job also requires some lifting, carrying, bending and continuous standing at times. Some technicians have contact with people who are upset and therefore need to deal with them sympathetically and tactfully. APTs wear full safety clothing during post-mortem examinations, including theatre scrub suit, visor, gloves, apron and boots. A respirator is also worn during high-risk examinations.

Qualification

• England, Wales and Northern Ireland

Band 2: No set entry requirements, but employers prefer applicants to have GCSEs (A*-C), including English, maths and science (particularly biology), or equivalent qualifications.

Band 3: For entry as a trainee: usually at least 4 GCSEs (A*-C), including English, maths and science (particularly biology), or equivalent. The Association of Anatomical Pathology Technology recommends that entrants have at least 5 passes (A*-C) at GCSE. Preference may be given to those with a GCSE in human biology.

• Scotland

Band 2: No set entry requirements, but employers prefer applicants to have S grades (1-3), including English, maths and science (particularly biology), or equivalent qualifications.

Band 3: For entry as a trainee: usually at least four S grades (1-3), including English, maths and science (particularly biology), or equivalent. The Association of Anatomical Pathology Technology recommends that entrants have at least five S grades (1-3). Preference may be given to those with S grade in biology.

Adult Qualifications

No minimum entry qualifications are required for this job but most employers expect education to a good general standard. The Association of Anatomical Pathology Technology recommends that entrants have at least 5 passes (A*-C) at GCSE, or equivalent qualifications. Ability in science is an advantage.

Work Experience

Work experience gives you an insight into what you enjoy and don't enjoy about a job or working environment, as well as the opportunity to acquire new skills. It provides valuable information to add to your CV and improves your employment prospects.

Work or voluntary experience in a medical or healthcare setting such as a hospital or residential care home can be useful, or any work that demonstrates responsibility and practical manual skills. Some experience of record keeping and dealing with legal issues is an advantage. In some areas there is a young apprenticeship (14-16) scheme that provides an extended work placement and eventual achievement of a relevant level 2 qualification whilst at school.

Entry and Training
Many trainee technicians start straight from school though some employers may prefer to appoint those over the age of 20. Increasingly, those with higher level qualifications are applying. As a trainee technician, you begin with a short period of watching, listening and asking questions and move on to on-the-job training that involves working under supervision with an experienced technician or a pathologist. Technicians are expected to have some knowledge and respect for the different religious and cultural attitudes about death. All trainees are expected to develop a good understanding of health and safety issues regarding mortuary work, including the control of substances hazardous to health, manual handling, and infection control.

There are two qualifications available for APTs and awarded by the Royal Society for Public Health (RSPH). The first course takes around 40 hours, either by day or block release. Topics include anatomy and physiology, post-mortem room techniques, hygiene, hazards and precautions, legislation and codes of practice, administration and documentation. Training usually takes around two years to complete, and you then become eligible to take the RSPH's qualifying certificate in anatomical pathology technology. This certificate combines written and oral work.

After further work experience, you can take the RSPH diploma, which involves practical assessment 12 months after you obtain the RSPH certificate and enables you to apply for full membership of the RSPH. It also equips you with the ability to perform more intricate work, such as forensic and high-risk examinations. The Association of Anatomical Pathology Technology (AAPT) encourages qualified APTs to voluntarily register with the Voluntary Registration Council (VRC) in preparation for formal registration with the Health Professions Council (HPC) in the future. Check the VRC website for more details. If you have the RSPH certificate plus two-years experience, the RSPH diploma or six years training and experience, you can also join the AAPT who represent the profession and support continuing professional development.

Mature entrants are welcomed as experience of life is an advantage. Previous experience of responsible or health-related work is also useful.

Opportunities and Pay
This is a small profession of around 1,000 people but there are opportunities mainly working for a hospital trust or health authority. Some APTs are also employed by local authority mortuaries or those operated by the police/procurator fiscal in Scotland. There are prospects for promotion to senior technician posts through an established career structure. APTs are likely to be affected by changes to the regulation of mortuary pratice in the future.

After training, some technicians specialise in areas such as embalming or post-mortem work. Some may move into a related occupation, such as working as a funeral director. There may be opportunities to work abroad, in areas such as the Middle East.

Starting salaries for trainees are around £16k-£19k a year. With experience and on completion of professional qualifications this can rise. Higher level APTs can earn up to £27k and those with managerial responsibility can earn up to £45k a year. Rates are higher in London.

Health
There is a risk of infection especially when dealing with deaths from infectious diseases such as HIV/AIDS and hepatitis. This job requires good general fitness and normal colour vision.

Skills and Qualities
able to follow instructions, aptitude for teamwork, attention to detail, good communication skills, IT skills, not squeamish, safety conscious, tactful, technical aptitude

Relevant Subjects
Biology, Health and social care, Science

Further Information
Apprenticeship Schemes (National Apprenticeship Service) - www.apprenticeships.org.uk

Association of Anatomical Pathology Technology (AAPT) - www.aaptuk.org/

Health Professions Council (HPC) - www.hpc-uk.org

NHS Careers (NHS Careers) - www.nhscareers.nhs.uk

NHS Careers Scotland - www.infoscotland.com/nhs

NHS Careers Wales - www.wales.nhs.uk

Voluntary Registration Council (VRC) - www.vrcouncil.org

What is an anatomical pathology technologist? (AAPT) - www.aaptuk.org/go/careers

Addresses
Association of Anatomical Pathology Technicians UK (AAPTUK)
12 Coldbath Square, London EC1R 5HL
Phone: +44 (0)20 7278 2151
Web: www.aaptuk.org

Royal Society for Public Health (RSPH)
3rd Floor Market Towers, 1 Nine Elms Lane, London SW8 5NQ
Phone: +44 (0)20 3177 1600
Web: www.rsph.org.uk

Similar Jobs
Crematorium Technician, Embalmer, Funeral Director, Operating Department Practitioner, Pathologist, Police Scenes of Crime Officer

Animal Care Assistant
also known as: Animal Welfare Assistant, Cattery Worker, Kennel Worker

CRCI:Environment, Animals and Plants
CLCI:WAM — Job Band: 1 to 3

Job Description
Animal care assistants look after and care for cats and dogs that spend time in a cattery or in kennels due to their owners being away from home. Others may work in animal rescue centres where animals have been abandoned and ill-treated or at an animal sanctuary. They clean out the animals' accommodation by sweeping, hosing down and disinfecting the animals' living area, and also change their bedding. They also feed animals and may have to prepare and provide a special diet for them. Groom the animals and check for signs of any disease, skin conditions or infestation, such as fleas or ticks.

Assistants check vaccination records, liaise with veterinary staff and may have to look after any sick animals. They exercise the dogs in a yard or field, or take them out for walks. An animal care worker may also have clerical duties, such as taking bookings, handling payments and answering enquiries from visitors or owners.

Work Details
Hours vary between 37.5 hrs to 40 hrs a week, usually starting at around 7.30am. You may need to live-in, work early mornings, weekends and possibly at night. You usually work a rota to cover seven days a week. A lot of the work is outdoors in all sorts of weather. It can be cold, wet and dirty, and kennels are often noisy and smelly. If you work in hunt or racing kennels, you may need to travel to events. You need to have no fear of cats and dogs. There can be a risk of attack or injury from animals.

Animal Care Assistant

Qualification

- **England, Wales and Northern Ireland**

Band 1: For entry to jobs, no minimum qualifications are needed, but you are expected to have a good level of general education and relevant experience. Some formal/vocational qualifications at any level are useful.

Band 2: For entry to jobs, no minimum qualifications are needed, but it is an advantage to have some GCSEs (A*-C) or equivalent in subjects that include English and maths. Biology is also useful.

Band 3: For entry: usually at least 4 GCSEs (A*-C) including English and maths, or equivalent. A science subject is also useful.

- **Scotland**

Band 1: For entry to jobs, no minimum qualifications are needed, but you are expected to have a good level of general education and relevant experience. Some formal/vocational qualifications at any level are useful.

Band 2: Although academic qualifications are not specified for this job, it is an advantage to have some S grades (1-3) in subjects that include English and maths, or similar. A science subject is also useful.

Band 3: For entry: usually at least four S grades (1-3) including English and maths, or similar. A science subject is also useful.

Adult Qualifications

Formal qualifications are not usually needed, but experience with animals is an advantage.

Work Experience

Relevant work or voluntary experience is always useful and can improve your employment prospects when applying for entry to jobs. Any work that involves cats and dogs, such as a Saturday job or holiday work, provides valuable experience. Contact the various organisations/societies and canine welfare charities (listed in addresses) for opportunities to gain some work and voluntary experience.

Entry and Training

There are no set qualifications to enter this work, but some entrants do a college course prior to starting work. You can take a BTEC/SQA course in animal care, either full or part time. A level 3 certificate in animal care is also available from ABC or the National Proficiency Test Council (NPTC). Once in work, training is usually on the job.

A level 2 national certificate in small animal care is available through distance learning from the Animal Care College. They offer a series of courses at levels 1-3 and advanced short courses, such as a certificate in canine/feline first aid, or advanced care and management.

Animal care workers who are also required to groom dogs may need to obtain an intermediate/advanced certificate in grooming, which is offered by NPTC. There are also some courses at private colleges. S/NVQs in animal care at levels 1-3 are available. Relevant training programmes, including apprenticeship schemes, may be available in your area. Advanced apprenticeships leading to qualification at level 3 can also be a route into higher education.

Mature applicants may be able to benefit through local training opportunities. You can also gain recognition of previous experience through Accreditation of Prior Learning (APL) or by working towards relevant S/NVQs. Contact your local Connexions or careers office, Jobcentre Plus, Next Step service or Learning and Skills Council (LSC)/Local Enterprise Company (LEC) for details of all training opportunities and schemes. There are relevant distance learning courses available from the Animal Care College.

Opportunities and Pay

There are over 3000 people in the UK working in kennels and catteries, and there is strong competition for jobs. You can also work for organisations such as animal welfare centres or animal sanctuaries. Employers include organisations such as the Guide Dogs for the Blind Association (GDBA) or Hearing Dogs for Deaf People, or may be maintained by animal welfare and rescue organisations, such as the Blue Cross, RSPCA/SSPCA/USPCA. A private cattery or kennels may specialise in breeding, boarding or quarantine. Changes in the law have reduced the demand for workers in quarantine kennels.

There are posts in the armed forces or with a police authority. Civilian animal care workers, working with the armed forces and who have no formal qualifications, complete a basic care (dogs) course at their animal centre in Leicestershire.

Some establishments may provide accommodation. There may be opportunities for part-time or voluntary work. You can be self-employed, but you need quite a lot of money to set up a business.

Pay varies depending on location and employer, although a trainee without experience may earn around £9k-£10k rising to around £13k-£16k a year, with experience. Animal care staff working for the GDBA usually start at around £14k a year.

Health

You would find this job difficult if you are allergic to animals. You have to be physically fit to do this job.

Skills and Qualities

able to follow instructions, aptitude for teamwork, calm, energetic, firm manner, good at handling animals, not squeamish, patient, reliable

Relevant Subjects

Biology, Science

Further Information

Apprenticeship Schemes (National Apprenticeship Service) - www.apprenticeships.org.uk

Careers with animals (British and Irish Association of Zoos and Aquariums) - www.biaza.org.uk/

Lantra - The Sector Skills Council for environmental & land-based sector (Lantra) http:/www.lantra.co.uk

Lantra Careers (A Future In...) (Lantra) - www.afuturein.com

So you want to work with Animals (Wayland) - www.waylandbooks.co.uk

Training Schemes - www.direct.gov.uk/en/educationandlearning

►Working with animals (2009) (Babcock Lifeskills) - www.babcock-lifeskills.com/

Addresses

Animal Care College
Index House High Street, Ascot, Berkshire SL5 7ET
Phone: +44 (0)1344 636436
Web: www.animalcarecollege.co.uk/

Guide Dogs for the Blind Association (GDBA)
Burghfield Common, Reading, Berkshire RG7 3YG
Phone: +44 (0)118 983 5555
Web: www.guidedogs.org.uk

Hearing Dogs for Deaf People
The Grange, Wycombe Road, Saunderton, Princes Risborough, Buckinghamshire HP27 9NS
Phone: +44 (0)1844 348 100
Web: www.hearingdogs.org.uk/

RSPCA
Wilberforce Way, Southwater, Horsham, West Sussex RH13 9RS
Phone: 0300 1234 555 (UK only)
Web: www.rspca.org.uk

Scottish SPCA
Kingseat Road, Halbeath, Dunfermline KY11 8RY
Phone: +44 (0)3000 999 999
Web: www.scottishspca.org

Support Dogs
21 Jessops Riverside, Brightside Lane, Sheffield S9 2RX
Phone: +44 (0)114 261 7800
Web: www.support-dogs.org.uk

Similar Jobs
Dog Groomer, Guide Dog Trainer, Veterinary Animal Nursing Assistant, Veterinary Nurse

Animal Nutritionist
also known as: Nutritionist - Animal

CRCI:Environment, Animals and Plants
CLCI:WAL Job Band: 5

Job Description
Animal nutritionists specialise in managing and adapting food plans to meet the dietary needs of all animals, including agricultural animals, zoo animals and pets. They ensure that an animal is receiving a diet with the necessary nutrition to keep them healthy and avoid disease. They do this through evaluating the nutritional content of the feed. Nutritionists decide what needs to be added to an animals diet to maximise growth and, particularly in the case of breeding animals, to supply any additional vitamin or mineral supplements.

May work in an academic environment, carrying out research into different types of feed by performing trials in the laboratory. If a new foodstuff is developed, the nutritionist records changes in composition and monitors the affect on the animals. As part of this research, may split animals into separate groups and feed them different food. The nutritionist then logs data on the effectiveness of different feeds. May teach courses on animal nutrition.

Give advice to farmers, vets, the government and other pet owners on what is best for the animal concerned. Advise on changes in nutritional trends and any regulatory changes. Liaise with animal feed manufacturers on the development and marketing of new food products to deal with nutritional disorders. Must also take cost and shelf life of the product into consideration.

Work Details
Animal nutritionists tend to be self-employed, so hours are generally flexible. You can expect to work a 30-40 hr week. You travel to farms, laboratories and food production facilities as part of the job. If working in academia, you may be class room based and work on trials in laboratories.

Qualification

- **England, Wales and Northern Ireland**

Band 5: For degree courses: 2-3 A levels and some GCSEs (A*-C) usually including English and maths, and sciences or equivalent. Exact requirements depend on the degree you take.

- **Scotland**

Band 5: For degree courses: 3-5 H grades and some S grades (1-3), including English and maths, and sciences or similar qualifications. Exact requirements depend on the degree you take.

Degree Information
Specific degrees and foundation degrees in animal management and animal science are available. Other relevant degrees include dietetics, biology, biochemistry and biomedical sciences.

Adult Qualifications
Mature entry is common and academic entry requirements for courses may be relaxed for adults, particularly if you have relevant experience. Some enter with existing professional experience and/or qualifications in areas that include agricultural science, animal science, animal management or bioscience. There are Access and foundation courses that enable you to enter a higher education degree course.

Work Experience
Relevant work or voluntary experience is always useful and can improve your chances in application for entry to relevant courses. The types of work experience to consider are those that involve working in an animal care facility, a food production area or in an agricultural environment.

Entry and Training
Most entrants to this profession have a good science degree in biology, agriculture or zoology although it is possible to enter with an appropriate HNC/HND and plenty of experience. Some have a background in veterinary science. Degrees in animal management with agriculture are available and most nutritionists have some post graduate qualifications in areas such as animal nutrition. It is usual for students to try and secure some part-time internship work to gain experience while studying.

A Diploma/Welsh Baccalaureate may be available in your area in society, health and development. The advanced level is equivalent to 3.5 A levels but for some university courses, the additional and specialist learning component of the diploma needs to include specific A levels. Check entry requirements carefully with the individual institutions. See the websites for further information. There are also a range of foundation degrees in animal care, welfare and management.

Continuing professional development (CPD) through membership of a professional body is also expected to keep up to date with developments and enhance knowledge in a specialist area of work. Relevant professional bodies include the Nutrition Society and the Health Professions Council. Both have details of approved courses on their websites. The Scottish Agricultural College also has useful information on consulting and diversification on their website.

The Department for the Environment and Rural Affairs has details of its animal health and welfare strategy on its website. This covers areas such as animal husbandry and nutrition. The Shire Consulting website has lots of useful information on animal nutrition and also has a jobs section for those seeking employment.

Mature entry is common and some enter with existing professional experience and/or qualifications in a related area, such as agricultural or animal science.

Government training opportunities, such as apprenticeships, may be available in your area. You can also gain recognition of previous experience through Accreditation of Prior Learning (APL) or by working towards relevant S/NVQs. Contact your local careers office, Jobcentre Plus, Next Step service or Learning and Skills Council (LSC) Local Enterprise Company (LEC) for details of training schemes.

Opportunities and Pay
With experience, it is possible to work as a self-employed consultant, specialising in work with particular animals e.g. dairy cattle. You can move on to work for a large feed manufacturer, supplying expert advice on nutritional requirements. There may be opportunity to work overseas in a developing economy.

Pay varies depending on location and employer. New graduates can expect to earn in the region of £20k a year. With postgraduate qualifications, such as a PhD, earnings can rise up to £30k a year. If employed in academia and/or consulting roles, pay can range from £30k-£50k a year.

Health
Allergies to certain grain or pollen may cause discomfort.

Skills and Qualities
analytical skills, business awareness, encouraging, good communication skills, good interpersonal skills, methodical, perceptive, scientific approach, tactful

Relevant Subjects
Biology, Chemistry, Design and technology, English, Land and Environment, Science

Further Information
AGCAS: Environment & Agriculture (Job Sector Briefing) (AGCAS) - www.prospects.ac.uk

British Society of Animal Science - www.bsas.org.uk/

Career with Animals - www.careerwithanimals.co.uk/

Diplomas (Foundation, Higher and Advanced) - http://yp.direct.gov.uk/diplomas

How Do You Become An Animal Nutritionist - www.ehow.com/

Lantra - The Sector Skills Council for environmental & land-based sector (Lantra) http:/www.lantra.co.uk

Scottish Wider Access Programme (SWAP) - www.scottishwideraccess.org/

Shire Consulting - www.shireconsulting.co.uk/

Welsh Baccalaureate - www.wbq.org.uk

Addresses
Department for Environment, Food & Rural Affairs (DEFRA)
Customer Contact Unit , Eastbury House, 30 - 34 Albert Embankment, London SE1 7TL
Phone: 0845 933 5577 (UK only)
Web: www.defra.gov.uk

Scottish Agricultural College
West Mains Road, Edinburgh EH9 3JG
Phone: +44 (0) 131 535 4000
Web: www.sac.ac.uk/

Similar Jobs
Agricultural Consultant/Adviser, Animal Care Assistant, Dietitian, Naturopath

Animal Physiotherapist
also known as: Veterinary Therapist

CRCI:Environment, Animals and Plants

CLCI:WAL

Job Band: 5

Job Description
Animal physiotherapists use physical techniques for the treatment of injuries and movement dysfunction in animals, such as horses, cats and dogs, and in particular elite animals like racehorses and greyhounds. They work out a treatment and exercise programme that aims to reduce pain, improve the animal's mobility and prevent the recurrence of injury. Physiotherapists apply skilled hand massage and also use modern therapeutic technologies such as soft tissue mobilisation, ultrasound, H wave, joint mobilisation, neuromuscular stimulators, pulsed magnetic field therapy and hydrotherapy. They work closely with veterinary surgeons and need to obtain authorisation from the vet before beginning any treatment.

Work Details
Hours of work vary according to clinic times or hours of mutual convenience between you and the animal owner. Work is likely to be part of a vet's practice where clients can bring smaller animals to a clinic. However, for larger animals, such as horses, you usually need to travel around, holding sessions at different centres, or visiting a client at home. A driving licence is useful. This work can be very demanding and can require coping with the sight of blood. This job requires considerable physical exertion and sometimes heavy lifting.

Qualification
- **England, Wales and Northern Ireland**

Band 5: For degree courses: usually three A levels, preferably including biology, and at least 5 GCSEs (A*-C), taken at one sitting including English, maths and two science subjects, or equivalent. Exact requirements depend on the degree you take.

- **Scotland**

Band 5: For degree course: usually five H grades (AAABB), including English and a minimum of two science subjects, achieved at one sitting, and some S grades (1-3) with English, maths and physics sometimes specified, or similar qualifications. Exact requirements depend on the degree you take.

Degree Information
To qualify as an animal physiotherapist you need to have an approved degree in human physiotherapy and then complete a relevant postgraduate course. Entry to courses is very competitive.

Adult Qualifications
Applications are welcomed from mature people (over 21) who can show evidence of recent successful study at an appropriate level, such as an Open University Level I course in science or an appropriate foundation or Access course.

Work Experience
Entry to this career is competitive. It is important that you try to gain some relevant work or voluntary experience before applying to degree courses. Work experience in any aspect of healthcare is useful to you. Admissions tutors want to ensure that you have the ability to communicate well with all ages and sections of the community, and can cope with illness and disability.

It is also important to gain experience of working with animals before applying to a relevant postgraduate course in animal physiotherapy or physiology.

Entry and Training
Most entrants qualify first as a human physiotherapist and then complete a relevant postgraduate course. See the article Physiotherapist for full details. Once you are a chartered physiotherapist and a member of the Association of Chartered Physiotherapists in Animal Therapy, you can then take a part-time postgraduate diploma/MSc with either the Royal Veterinary College in Hertfordshire or Hartpury College in Gloucestershire. Successful completion enables the holder to use the title of 'veterinary physiotherapist'.

You are expected to maintain clinical knowledge and competence throughout your career through relevant continuing professional development (CPD).

If you are not qualified as a human physiotherapist, you can train in animal physiotherapy through either the National Association of Veterinary Physiotherapists (NAVP) or the College of Animal Physiotherapy. The NAVP is in the process of setting up an MSc course in collaboration with Harper Adams College for those with a relevant degree, such as in veterinary nursing. The College of Animal Physiotherapy runs a distance learning course with practical placements.

Mature applicants wishing to train as physiotherapists and animal physiotherapists are welcomed and numbers are increasing. Contact the Chartered Society of Physiotherapists for a list of approved courses and further career details.

Opportunities and Pay
Once qualified there are numerous opportunities to work with vets who are in private practice, as well as the opportunity to specialise in treating a particular group of animals such as horses, cats or dogs. Some animal physiotherapists move into teaching, consultancy or research work. Many treat people, as well as animals and are usually self-employed.

Pay varies depending on location and experience. The likely hourly rate is around £30-£70 if not more, for up to two hours, depending on the type of treatment involved. Mileage rates may also be added. Salaries for experienced animal physiotherapists can range from around £25k to over £65k a year depending upon experience, client base and number of hours worked.

Health

This job requires good general fitness and requires a medical test on entry.

Skills and Qualities

able to explain clearly, able to inspire confidence, aptitude for teamwork, firm manner, good at handling animals, IT skills, manual dexterity, patient, perseverance

Relevant Subjects

Biology, Chemistry, English, Health and social care, Mathematics, Physical education and sport, Physics, Psychology, Science, Sociology

Further Information

Animal Physiotherapy Career Information (ACPAT) - www.acpat.org.uk/

Association of Chartered Physiotherapists in Animal Therapy - www.acpat.org

NHS Careers (NHS Careers) - www.nhscareers.nhs.uk

Real Life Guide to Working with Animals & Wildlife (Trotman) - www.trotman.co.uk

▶ Working with animals (2009) (Babcock Lifeskills) - www.babcock-lifeskills.com/

Addresses

Chartered Society of Physiotherapy (CSP)
14 Bedford Row, London WC1R 4ED
Phone: +44 (0)20 7306 6666
Web: www.csp.org.uk

College of Animal Physiotherapy
Tyringham Hall, Cuddington, Aylesbury, Buckinghamshire
HP18 0AP
Phone: +44 (0)1844 290512
Web: www.animaltherapy.org

Hartpury College
Hartpury House, Gloucester GL19 8BE
Phone: +44 (0)1452 702345
Web: www.hartpury.ac.uk

National Association of Veterinary Physiotherapists
(Website only),
Web: www.navp.org.uk

Royal Veterinary College (Hertfordshire)
Hawkshead Lane North Mymms, Hatfield, Hertfordshire AL9 7TA
Phone: +44 (0)1707 666333
Web: www.rvc.ac.uk

Similar Jobs

Chiropractor, Osteopath, Physiotherapist, Sports Therapist, Veterinary Pathologist, Veterinary Surgeon

Animal Technician/Technologist

also known as: Animal Laboratory Technician

CRCI:Science, Mathematics and Statistics

CLCI:QOX — Job Band: 3 to 4

Job Description

Animal technicians/technologists are responsible for the care and welfare of animals used in scientific research. They are in daily contact with animals, 85% of which are rodents, which are kept in a range of suitable environments. Technicians look after their general welfare, keep them clean and control the light and temperature conditions. They make sure that the animals are comfortable and that they do not suffer unnecessary pain or distress. Also keep meticulous records detailing all procedures and developments.

Technicians may have to destroy animals humanely and prepare them for dissection. May also be involved with breeding programmes. Some are also involved in experimental work or designing studies. Increasingly, some routine procedures that were previously conducted by researchers are now being done by experienced technicians/technologists.

Work Details

Usually work a 35-40 hr week, Monday to Friday and may be expected to work shifts, weekends and evenings. You usually work in a laboratory within a university, teaching hospital or other establishment. Some experiments are conducted in a wide variety of working environments, including outdoors such as with farm animals.

This is a controversial area of work so confidentiality and awareness of ethical issues is important. This work can also be emotionally demanding and can involve the sight of blood. You are responsible for animal welfare, hygiene and keeping to legal regulations. There is a risk of minor injuries and you often need to wear full protective clothing, including a lab coat, apron, masks, overshoes and gloves.

Qualification

Qualifications specialising in animal technology are open only to those already working in the industry.

• England, Wales and Northern Ireland

Band 3: For entry to jobs, HNC or a relevant Diploma, usually at least 4 GCSEs (A*-C) including English, science and maths, or equivalent.

Band 4: For HND, Diploma of Higher Education or foundation degree: 1-2 A levels, preferably biology and another science subject, and some GCSEs (A*-C) usually including English, science and maths, or equivalent.

• Scotland

Band 3: For entry as a trainee: usually at least four S grades (1-3) including English, science and maths, or similar.

Band 4: For entry to SQA higher national and professional development awards, usually 2-3 H grades, including biology and preferably another science subject, and some S grades (1-3), including English, science and maths, or similar qualifications.

Adult Qualifications

Qualifications are not essential but are an advantage. Preference is given to those with experience of working with animals.

Work Experience

Experience of working with animals is very useful and this can be either paid or voluntary work. This can include working with domestic animals or in a science laboratory, as preference is given to those with experience. Working in a kennels or cattery, volunteering at an animal rescue centre or assisting at a veterinary centre are all appropriate.

Entry and Training

Many begin their career as a trainee animal technician and work towards a first certificate in animal husbandry. In-house training also covers subjects such as health checks, handling animals, and animal behaviour and welfare. Entry requirements vary depending on the individual employer and the applicant's previous experience. Training is mainly on the job, and usually combined with workplace training, day release and distance learning for the Institute of Animal Technology's (IAT) certificates, membership or fellowship, or for a relevant BTEC/SQA national/higher national certificate.

Registration and a licence to practise is gained from the Home Office after sufficient experience. Graduates with relevant degrees may claim exemptions from some subjects though traditionally this is not a graduate career. However, the IAT is currently developing a graduate programme, leading to degree level qualifications and fellowship (FIAT) of the IAT. The graduate programme is based around a foundation degree that leads to a BSc (Hons) degree in animal technology. It is also possible to pursue qualifications to MSc and PhD level through the IAT's structured career path.

S/NVQs in animal technology are available at levels 2-3. Training programmes, including apprenticeship schemes, may be available in your area. Advanced apprenticeships leading to qualification at level 3 can also be a route into higher education.

Mature applicants should note that preference is given to those with experience of working with animals, and any experience of laboratory work is an advantage. There may be accelerated training for those already qualified as an animal nurse, or similar.

Opportunities and Pay

Animal technicians/technologists are a small, but growing, specialist group of people who work for a university, pharmaceutical company, teaching hospital, a medical or veterinary college, specialist research institute, government departments such as ADAS and the Department for Environment, Food & Rural Affairs (DEFRA), or animal breeding companies. In some jobs there may be a chance of promotion to more senior posts after gaining experience. You can also specialise in areas such as breeding, immunology or training and management. A move to a different area may be necessary to secure promotion. Some may move into management posts.

Around 5,000 animal techicians/technologists work in the UK and although employment is predicted to decline in both research and pharmaceutical sectors, it is expected to increase in the education and medical sectors, and there is currently a demand for technicians/technologists. It may be possible to job share or work part time and there may be opportunities abroad.

Salaries vary depending on location and employer. Trainees earn in the region of £13k to £15k a year, rising to around £20k a year when qualified. Those in senior posts with managerial responsibility can earn more than £35k a year. Overtime pay is usual and in addition to salary. Some areas of the country attract additional salary weighting.

Health

A good standard of physical fitness is required. You may need normal colour vision for some posts. The work involves a risk of infection. You should not be allergic to animals.

Skills and Qualities

able to follow instructions, aptitude for teamwork, aware of legal and ethical considerations, emotionally strong, good communication skills, IT skills, not squeamish, observant, responsible attitude, scientific approach

Relevant Subjects

Biology, Chemistry, Mathematics, Science

Further Information

A Career as an Animal Technologist (Institute of Animal Technology (IAT 2008)) - www.medicalmouse.org.uk/documents/careersleaflet.pdf

Animal Technology & Welfare (Institute of Animal Technology) - www.iat.org.uk/

Animal Welfare (quarterly) (Universities Federation for Animal Welfare) - www.ufaw.org.uk

Lantra - The Sector Skills Council for environmental & land-based sector (Lantra) http:/www.lantra.co.uk

▶Working in science (2007) (Babcock Lifeskills) - www.babcock-lifeskills.com/

Addresses

ADAS
Woodthorne, Wergs Road, Wolverhampton WV6 8TQ
Phone: 0845 766 0085 (UK only)
Web: www.adas.co.uk

Department for Environment, Food & Rural Affairs (DEFRA)
Customer Contact Unit , Eastbury House, 30 - 34 Albert Embankment, London SE1 7TL
Phone: 0845 933 5577 (UK only)
Web: www.defra.gov.uk

Institute of Animal Technology (IAT)
5 South Parade, Summertown, Oxford OX2 7JL
Web: www.iat.org.uk

Similar Jobs

Farm Manager, Laboratory Technician: Science, Veterinary Animal Nursing Assistant, Veterinary Nurse, Veterinary Pathologist, Zoo Keeper

Animator

CRCI:Media, Print and Publishing
CLCI:ED Job Band: 4 to 5

Job Description

Animators work to create a concept or design style that visually interprets and conveys the required idea, information or story, using new and traditional animation techniques. They produce a drawing on paper or a cel (transparent sheet of celluloid), or use models and puppets which, when photographed in sequence, give an impression of movement. Traditionally, both backgrounds and characters are created by drawing, painting and the use of hand tools. However, computer-generated imagery (CGI) is increasingly used, enabling images to be made faster, more economically and with digital special effects.

Also liaise with clients and initially produce a storyboard using sketches and illustrations that cover both the story and narrative. May use a range of materials and technical software, such as Flash or 3D Studio Max. Animation is used in commercials, videos, short and long feature films, computer games and interactive videos, or special effects in film and television. May also be used in commercial products, including magazine covers, books and newspapers, stationery and on clothing, such as T-shirts.

Work Details

The hours are typically 9-5; Monday to Friday, but you may have to work extra hours, including weekends, to meet deadlines. Work is mainly in an open plan office or in a studio. You have to cope with the pressure of work, tight deadlines, and may need to travel to meet clients. You may spend a lot of time putting ideas to clients and selling your services to customers, particularly if you are freelance.

Qualification

- **England, Wales and Northern Ireland**

Band 4: For HND, Diploma of Higher Education or foundation degree: 1-2 A levels and some GCSEs (A*-C) usually including English and maths, or equivalent.

Band 5: For degree courses: 2-3 A levels and some GCSEs (A*-C) usually including English and maths, or equivalent qualifications. Exact requirements depend on the degree you take. Most students take a foundation course first.

- **Scotland**

Band 4: For entry to SQA higher national and professional development awards, usually 2-3 H grades and some S grades (1-3), including English and maths, or similar qualifications.

Band 5: For degree courses: 3-5 H grades and some S grades (1-3), usually including English, or similar. Exact requirements depend on the degree you take.

Degree Information
This area of work is open to all graduates, but there are some degrees that specialise in film and animation, and it is also available as an option on many digital media or visual effects courses. Other useful subjects include multimedia design, art and design, computer-aided design (CAD), 3-D design and spatial design. There are postgraduate courses in animation.

Adult Qualifications
Those with outstanding portfolios, or relevant experience, may not need the standard entry requirements for higher education. Entry requirements may be relaxed for adults applying for higher education courses and Access or foundation courses give adults without qualifications a route on to degree courses.

Work Experience
Entry to this job/career is highly competitive and it is essential to have some relevant work or voluntary experience before applying. The British Film Institute (BFI) requests the help of volunteers during the BFI annual film festival in London; this type of experience is useful. Direct experience with a graphic design or animation company, or with a department within a television or film group is the most relevant, but art-based computing work may also help with applications and add to your CV.

Entry and Training
This is a highly competitive field and most animators have a degree or HND in animation or related subject. Skillset, the sector skills council for the audio-visual industries, has a list of accredited degree courses on its website. Job vacancies are rarely advertised, and applicants need to be proactive and approach companies directly. A showreel of animated work is essential for potential employers and for entry to postgraduate courses. It is useful to have working knowledge of computer programming and of some of the current software packages. Training is mainly on the job, often with an experienced animator, and is usually supported by short courses.

You may be able to enter this job by first becoming a runner or production assistant (see job articles) in the film and TV industry and progressing to a job at assistant level. Most people who enter this way have a relevant degree. The National Centre for Computer Animation offers a range of appropriate courses, including a BA (Hons) in computer visualisation and animation, and MA/MSc courses in computer animation. There are also a number of relevant foundation degrees available. Skillset has worked with employers in the animation sector and produced a framework to ensure consistency in the delivery of foundation degrees and to check that the content meets the current and future skills needs.

You may have the opportunity to gain an MA in animation if working for a large company. Some specialist courses, including storyboarding for animators, can be via evening, weekend or summer schools. A list of animation courses is available from the British Film Institute. Throughout your career, you need to keep up to date with new techniques and specialist computer software.

Training may be available for people starting out in the TV and film industry. Contact organisations such as Skillset and Cyfle for information. A Diploma/Welsh Baccalaureate may be available in your area in creative and media. This can be a useful introduction to this type of career as you gain practical experience while studying. See the diplomas website or Skillset for further information.

Mature applicants should be aware that this is a relatively young industry and it may be difficult to enter this career in later years, unless with considerable talent and some industry experience. Those with a relevant first degree may be able to take a postgraduate qualification in animation, which can be full time or through distance learning.

Opportunities and Pay
Over 2000 people work in animation in the UK, with about two fifths either self-employed or on short term contracts. There are around 300 companies offering a range of animation services. Recent developments in digital computer animation and stop-frame videos have seen an increase in animation, with Britain playing a large part in the industry. Consequently there are increasing opportunities for those who demonstrate talent. There are a number of large animation studios in the UK, but the majority of animators work for small, independent production companies on a freelance basis. Some may work for magazines, design agencies or publishing companies.

Most opportunities are in London, Bristol, Dundee, Manchester and Cardiff. Some animators work abroad, mainly in Europe and the USA. Many animators work as independent film producers, trying to win commissions from broadcasting companies, advertising agencies or video producers. It is possible for experienced animators to become animation directors.

Typical starting salaries range from £12k-£18k a year, rising quickly with experience. Salaries are low to start with as entrants need to gain experience and develop a network of contacts. Highly successful animators can earn up to £60k and some may earn six figure salaries.

Health
This job requires normal colour vision.

Skills and Qualities
able to work both on your own and in a team, able to work to deadlines, artistic ability, attention to detail, creative flair, drawing ability, eye for visual effect, good interpersonal skills, IT skills, numeracy skills

Relevant Subjects
Art and Design, Design and technology, ICT/Computer studies, Media and communication studies

Further Information
Animation Magazine (Animation Magazine Inc) - www.animationmagazine.net

British Film Institute (BFI) - www.bfi.org.uk

Creative Review (Centaur) - www.creativereview.co.uk

Diplomas (Foundation, Higher and Advanced) - http://yp.direct.gov.uk/diplomas

Imagine (Imagineanimation) - www.imagineanimation.net/

Skillset - sector skills council for the creative media, fashion and textiles industries - www.skillset.org

►Working in art & design (2009) (Babcock Lifeskills) - www.babcock-lifeskills.com/

Addresses
Cyfle (Wales)
Galeri 13, Victoria Dock, Caernarfon LL55 1SQ.
Phone: +44 (0) 1286 685 242
Web: www.cyfle.co.uk

National Centre for Computer Animation
The Media School Bournemouth University Talbot Campus, Fern Barrow, Poole, Dorset BH12 5BB
Phone: 08456 501501 (UK only)
Web: http://ncca.bournemouth.ac.uk/

National Film and Television School
Beaconsfield Studios, Station Road HP9 1LG
Phone: +44 (0)1494 731 425
Web: www.nftsfilm-tv.ac.uk

Similar Jobs
Artist, Computer Games Animator, Film/TV & Theatre SFX Technician, Graphic Designer, Illustrator, Model Maker

Antiques Dealer

CRCI:Retail Sales and Customer Services
CLCI:OFM Job Band: 3 to 5

Job Description

Antique dealers buy antiques (old objects), collectables and objects of artistic value and sell them to the public or to other dealers for profit. Attend auctions, trade fairs and house clearances, and visit private houses to examine and buy goods. May restore an item before selling it in a shop, a market, or at an auction. Offer a valuation service for customers, providing the age and history (provenance) and maker of the item, if established. Some deal in a range of antiques, but many specialise in one type of object, such as furniture, clocks, ceramics, glassware, silver, books, or paintings, drawings and prints. Some may also buy and sell 'collectables', which are popular items that are not yet classified as antiques.

Work Details

Usually work a 40 hr week, which may involve very long hours, including weekends and some evenings. You work in a shop or a salesroom, or possibly in an antiques market. Some travel may be required to national and local sales exhibitions, or to visit clients at home. The work involves acquiring expert knowledge about the products you are selling. You also negotiate and consult with people, or give advice to customers. Sometimes you may have to cope with heavy lifting.

Qualification

Specialised knowledge and expertise may be more important than academic qualifications.

• England, Wales and Northern Ireland

Band 3: For some employers: a minimum of 4 GCSEs (A*-C) including English, or equivalent.

Band 4: For some companies: at least 1-2 A levels and some GCSEs (A*-C) usually including English and maths, or equivalent.

Band 5: For degree courses: usually 2-3 A levels and some GCSEs (A*-C) including English and maths, or equivalent. Exact requirements depend on the degree you take.

• Scotland

Band 3: For some employers: a minimum of four S grades (1-3) including English, or similar.

Band 4: For some companies: at least 2-3 H grades and some S grades (1-3) usually including maths and English, or similar qualifications.

Band 5: For degree courses: usually 3-5 H grades and some S grades (1-3) including English and maths, or similar qualifications. Exact requirements depend on the degree you take.

Degree Information

Although any degree is acceptable for entry to this job, subjects that give entrants an advantage include history of art, fine art, history, fashion design, interior design, and possibly business studies or business administration. Specific degree subjects include antiques and design, arts market and visual arts practice. Postgraduate courses are also available.

Adult Qualifications

Entry requirements may be relaxed for adults applying for higher education courses. Access or foundation courses give adults without qualifications a route onto degree courses. However, an interest in antiques or broad artistic background, some knowledge of how to run a business and sound financial back-up, can be more important than academic qualifications.

Work Experience

Entry to this job is competitive and it is important that you try to do some relevant work or voluntary experience before applying. The most relevant experience includes working alongside an expert antiques dealer, attending local/national auctions as an observer, or approaching local auctioneers for a part-time job and helping at an auction. Experience of retail and knowledge of history, particularly in specialist areas, also helps. Visits to places such as museums, sale rooms and dealers' shops also provide useful background knowledge.

Entry and Training

There are a number of different routes into this work. A Diploma/ Welsh Baccalaureate in retail business may be available in your area. It is possible to learn on the job as an assistant working with an experienced dealer. Training can also be gained by working as a porter or assistant in an auction house or salesroom. Entrants may be graduates, either with a related degree such as fine arts valuation, or with a qualification in business.

Entry to all types of training is highly competitive. There are some private specialist training courses which take a shorter amount of time than degrees, but these can be very expensive. Colleges, museums and major auction houses often run courses on specialist topics. The auction house Christie's offers a specialist training programme for graduates. It consists of 4-6 work placements over a two-year period. Entry is competitive and is via a selection process. Contact Christie's Education for further details.

There are foundation degrees that provide a route to relevant specialist degree subjects. Evening classes and museum/gallery lectures can provide useful knowledge, as can self-learning through reading and studying under your own initiative. The Open University offers courses in the history of art, which can lead to a humanities with history of art degree. There are no formal entry requirements and you study through distance learning.

Mature entrants are often those seeking a good second career, but it is a very competitive field, and relevant experience is important. There are specialised distance-learning courses, including foundation certificates, certificates and degrees, in subjects that include fine arts, fine arts valuation, art law and antiques.

Opportunities and Pay

Employment is possible with an auction house or salesroom, or with a small private company or shop. Many dealers are self-employed, but this requires capital investment. The majority of jobs are in towns and cities. Opportunities for promotion may depend on your flair for the business. There is scope for specialisation and there may be opportunities to work part time.

Many antiques dealers earn around £15k-£20k, rising to around £24k-£35k a year with experience. High earners make up to £40k, though highly successful and specialist dealers can earn more than £50k a year.

Health

For certain types of work, good colour vision is required.

Skills and Qualities

business awareness, cash handling skills, decisive, eye for shape/ colour, friendly, good memory, IT skills, negotiating skills, networking skills, persuasive

Relevant Subjects

Art and Design, Business and accounting, English, History, Retail and distribution

Further Information

British Antique Dealers' Association (BADA) (BADA) - www.bada.org/

Christie's Education - www.christieseducation.com

Diplomas (Foundation, Higher and Advanced) - http://yp.direct.gov.uk/diplomas
Open University - www.open.ac.uk
Sotheby's Institute of Art - www.sothebysinstitute.com/
Welsh Baccalaureate - www.wbq.org.uk

Addresses

British Antique Dealers' Association (BADA)
20 Rutland Gate, London SW7 1BD
Phone: +44 (0)20 7589 4128
Web: www.bada.org

London and Provincial Antique Dealers' Association (LAPADA)
535 King's Road, Chelsea, London SW10 0SZ
Phone: +44 (0)20 7823 3511
Web: www.lapada.co.uk

Similar Jobs

Archivist, Auctioneer, Market Stall Trader, Museum/Art Gallery Curator

Anti-Social Behaviour Officer

also known as: Anti-Social Behaviour Coordinator

CRCI:Social Work and Counselling Services
CLCI:KEB Job Band: 3 to 5

Job Description

Anti-social behaviour (ASB) officers investigate cases of anti-social behaviour in a given area and make sure that issues are effectively resolved. Cases may include harassment, vandalism, abusive or noisy neighbours and littering. Work closely with and support other professionals and departments, including the police, social workers, probation officers, local councils, landlords and teachers. Aim to link communities, local government and the police.

ASB officers provide mediation to parties involved in neighbourly disputes and conduct interviews if required. They work to prevent issues from arising, but may need to use enforcement at times. May act as a witness, prepare relevant legal paperwork and attend court. ASB officers also provide support to witnesses and victims of crime and disorder.

Work Details

You can work for the police, local council, housing association or a multi-agency department. You usually work a basic 37 hr week, though you may be expected to work unsociable hours including evenings and weekends. You are based in an office, but depending on your role and who you work for, may spend much of your time in the community visiting individuals, working with groups and attending meetings. You may need to travel around an area and, if rural, this may be over quite a wide area.

You meet people of all ages and have to deal with people who are upset, aggressive or are suspected of breaking the law. You may be confronted with threatening behaviour. You need to be able to approach and tackle sensitive issues with confidence. The job can be emotionally demanding and stressful at times.

Qualification

• England, Wales and Northern Ireland

Band 3: For entry to jobs, HNC or a relevant Diploma: usually at least 4 GCSEs (A*-C) including English and maths, or equivalent.

Band 4: For HND, Diploma of Higher Education or foundation degree: 1-2 A levels and some GCSEs (A*-C) usually including English and maths, or equivalent.

Band 5: For degree courses: 2-3 A levels and some GCSEs (A*-C) usually including English and maths, or equivalent. Exact requirements depend on the degree you take.

• Scotland

Band 3: For entry to jobs: usually at least four S grades (1-3) including English and maths, or similar.

Band 4: For entry to SQA higher national and professional development awards, usually 2-3 H grades and some S grades (1-3), including English and maths, or similar qualifications.

Band 5: For degree courses: 3-5 H grades and some S grades (1-3), including English and maths, or similar qualifications. Exact requirements depend on the degree you take.

Degree Information

A degree in any subject is acceptable for entry to this job, though there are a wide variety of courses that are relevant, such as law, youth community studies, police studies, criminology and criminal justice. Social science fields are useful. Postgraduate courses are available.

Adult Qualifications

Mature applicants who have experience in an appropriate field, may be accepted for courses without the standard formal qualifications. Access courses leading to relevant degree courses may be available in some areas.

Work Experience

Work or voluntary experience is always useful and can improve your chance of success when applying for jobs. Some employers look for paid or voluntary experience of community service. Anything that shows that you are interested in your community, that you can deal with and resolve conflict and that you are a team player is helpful.

Entry and Training

Entry requirements vary depending on the organisation and department you work for. Some are seconded to this role from the police force and some move into it from other council teams/departments. You need a good standard of general education and many employers ask for a minimum of HNC/HND level, with a background in conflict resolution. Previous experience of dealing with anti-social behaviour cases, working with members of the public and providing quality advice and training is essential. You need to have excellent communication and reasoning skills. Some training is given on the job, such as crime prevention and diversion, legislation and case conferencing with partnership agencies.

If working for a housing association or housing department, you may need membership or be working towards membership of the Chartered Institute of Housing (CIH). There are various levels of membership and routes to qualification. Contact the CIH for details. The YMCA George Williams College runs a Dip HE/BA in Informal Education (youth work and community learning and development) that can be studied full time for two years or part time/distance learning for three years. There are also S/NVQs in community development work at levels 2-4 and at levels 2-3 in youth work. Contact the professional organisations (listed in addresses) for details of all relevant qualification and training opportunities.

Employers usually require enhanced Criminal Records Bureau/Disclosure Scotland checks and a full UK driving licence to do this role. Training programmes, including apprenticeship schemes, may be available in your area for entry to this job. Advanced apprenticeships leading to qualification at level 3 can also be a route into higher education.

Mature entry is welcomed and any previous related experience is an advantage. You need to be able to engage and communicate with all members and age groups of a local community. Some employers may look for those applicants with experience of social work or community service. If you work for the police you need to pass their admission criteria, such as a health and fitness test.

Opportunities and Pay
Vacancies in this area are increasing as local authorities and the police focus more on tackling anti-social behaviour and work with the community. You may be employed by the police, a local authority, local community organisation or housing association. Promotion to more senior posts is possible after gaining experience, but opportunities are limited. There are often opportunities to work part time.

Pay depends on your employer, area and level of experience. Anti-social behaviour coordinators employed by local authorities earn from £15k, rising to around £26k a year with experience. You can earn up to £37k a year with the police and other agencies, depending on your experience and qualifications. There are additional allowances for overtime and working shifts.

Health
You should have good stamina and be physically fit.

Skills and Qualities
able to inspire confidence, able to make important decisions, able to motivate others, able to relate well to children and young people, able to work both on your own and in a team, diplomatic, tactful & discreet, good at writing reports, good communication skills, good interpersonal skills, resilient

Relevant Subjects
English, Health and social care, Law, Psychology, Sociology

Further Information
Community Development Exchange - www.cdx.org.uk

Could you? Police (Home Office) - www.policecouldyou.co.uk/

Local Government Careers (Improvement and Development Agency) - www.lgcareers.com/publications/

NYA Guide to Youth Work & Youth Services (NYA) (NYA) - www.nya.org.uk/catalogue/workforce-1

▶Working in advice & counselling (2007) (Babcock Lifeskills) - www.babcock-lifeskills.com/

▶Working in police, fire & security (2009) (Babcock Lifeskills) - www.babcock-lifeskills.com/

Addresses
Chartered Institute of Housing (CIH)
Octavia House Westwood Way, Coventry CV4 8JP
Phone: +44 (0)24 7685 1700
Web: www.cih.org

Chartered Institute of Housing (Scotland)
6 Palmerston Place, Edinburgh EH12 5AA
Phone: +44 (0)131 225 4544
Web: www.cih.org

YMCA George Williams College
199 Freemasons Road, Canning Town, London E16 3PY
Phone: +44 (0)20 7540 4900
Web: www.ymca.ac.uk

Similar Jobs
Advice Worker, Community Development Worker, Community Warden (Scotland), Police Community Support Officer (England & Wales), Police Family Liaison Officer

Arboriculturist
also known as: Local Government: Tree Officer, Woodland Consultant

CRCI:Environment, Animals and Plants
CLCI:WAF Job Band: 2 to 5

Job Description
Arboriculturists manage and supervise the cultivation and care of trees and woodlands in areas that are open to the public, or manage woodlands solely for commercial or private use. They work in towns and cities as well as the countryside and responsibilities include overseeing the planting, propagation, maintenance, tree surgery, and the prevention and eradication of disease. Arboriculturists undertake tree inspections and surveys to British Standard (BS) levels. As a local government tree officer, they administer tree protection law, particularly over privately owned trees, and also manage a council's own trees, advising on tree health and safety.

They use a range of specialised equipment, including computers, for detailed investigation and analysis. May develop new amenity woodlands or be more concerned with conservation of existing areas. Arboriculturists aim to improve the environment to its full advantage. They liaise and work with other professionals, such as town planners, civil and structural engineers, architects and landscape architects, and also those in environmental and land management.

May advise on land development, including proposals on the reclamation of abandoned industrial sites, and the use of tree planting for other development sites. Can also be involved in financial planning and management of resources. They are responsible for staff training and their development and the supervision of subcontracted work.

Work Details
Hours vary depending on the work and location, though you may be required to be on call for any emergencies. The work is mainly outdoors, usually in an urban area, although in some posts, you may work in the countryside. Travelling a large distance is not uncommon, whether you are self-employed or not, so your day may start and finish later. Emergency work, such as supervising the clearing of dangerous, fallen trees and branches during stormy weather or those causing road blockages, may involve out-of-hours work, at night and weekends.

Most of your time is spent in parks, gardens, woods or forests. Safety regulations must be observed at all times. A hard hat, gloves and protective clothing are usually provided.

Qualification

• England, Wales and Northern Ireland
Band 3: For course entry: usually at least 4 GCSEs (A*-C) including English and maths, or equivalent.

Band 4: For HND, Diploma of Higher Education or foundation degree: 1-2 A levels and some GCSEs (A*-C) usually including English and maths, or equivalent.

Band 5: For degree courses: 2-3 A levels, preferably including maths and science subjects, and some GCSEs (A*-C) including English, or similar qualifications. Exact requirements depend on the degree you take.

• Scotland
Band 3: For entry to jobs, usually at least four S grades (1-3) including English and maths, or similar.

Band 4: For entry to SQA higher national and professional development awards, usually 2-3 H grades and some S grades (1-3), including English and maths, or similar qualifications.

Band 5: For degree: 3-5 H grades, preferably including maths and science subjects, and some S grades (1-3) including English, or similar qualifications. Exact requirements depend on the degree you take.

Degree Information
A degree in arboriculture, arboriculture and urban forestry, horticulture (arboriculture), urban forestry management, or a related subject, such as forest sciences, is usually required. Other useful subjects include various forestry and woodland management subjects. Postgraduate degrees are also available.

Adult Qualifications
People entering this job usually have qualifications, such as a national/higher national award or a degree. The standard entry requirements for courses may be relaxed for adults. Check with the university or college for details. Experience in forestry or horticulture is usually needed.

Work Experience
Employers or colleges/universities prefer candidates who have relevant work or voluntary experience. This can include horticulture, outdoor pursuits/climbing experience, using practical skills, and using machinery and equipment. It is sometimes difficult to gain practical experience with an arboriculturalist because of the nature of some tasks and the implications for health and safety, but work shadowing opportunities are still an advantage. Organisations working in forestry and conservation may offer work placements.

Entry and Training
You can either enter this job at craft level as an arboricultural worker and gain relevant qualifications that enable you to progress further to more senior positions, or take relevant courses before you start work. Myerscough is one of the colleges that specialises in arboriculture courses.

Appropriate full and part-time BTEC/SQA courses in arboriculture and related subjects are available at a number of colleges, and relevant degree/postgraduate courses are also available at some universities. There are only a few specialist arboriculture degree courses, but some horticulture and forestry courses have options in arboriculture. There are also foundation degrees in arboriculture, which can be studied in 2-3 years, full or part time, or through distance learning. The Institute of Chartered Foresters (ICF) has a list of ICF validated courses on their website.

You need to gain certificates of competence through short courses in areas such as chainsaw use and maintenance, climbing trees and aerial rescue techniques, or in utility arboriculture. These certificates are offered through the National Proficiency Tests Council (NPTC) or the Scottish Skills Testing Service (SSTS). If you enter this job at craft level, you require a level 2 certificate in arboriculture (or equivalent) in order to gain the technician's certificate of the Arboricultural Association (AA).

Further professional qualifications (certificates/diplomas) in arboriculture are offered at various levels from organisations, including the AA, the Institute of Chartered Foresters (ICF) and the Royal (and Royal Scottish) Forestry Society (RFS/RSFS). For work as a consultant, the AA offers the Arboricultural Association Registered Consultant (AARC) scheme and the ICF also offers accreditation to become a chartered arboriculturist. Continuing professional development (CPD) is expected and is offered by the trade and professional organisations.

A Diploma/Welsh Baccalaureate may be available in your area in environment and land-based studies. S/NVQs in arboriculture are available at levels 2-3. Training programmes, including apprenticeship schemes, may be available in your area. Advanced apprenticeships leading to qualification at level 3 can also be a route into higher education.

Mature entrants as an arboricultural consultant usually have relevant experience, such as that gained through working as an arboricultural assistant, a contractor, or through general forestry work. Government training opportunities may be available in your area. Contact your local Connexions or careers office, Jobcentre Plus, Next Step service or Learning and Skills Council (LSC)/Local Enterprise Company (LEC) for details of training schemes.

Opportunities and Pay
Due to a current skills shortage, opportunities are good for those with skills and qualifications, particularly in amenity and conservation work areas. However, competition is keen for those jobs that are offered in the more well-established companies and organisations. Most arboriculturists work for local authorities, utility companies, universities, conservation organisations, botanical gardens, or commercial contractors. There are also some opportunities with large landscape and garden centres, national parks, private estates and woodland contractors.

Employment prospects abroad are good for experienced and trained arboriculturists, especially in the USA, New Zealand, Australia and Germany. However, this is a relatively new field and career patterns are still developing. Self-employment is possible.

Salaries for craft level work start at around £15k-£20k a year. Those with management/supervisory responsibilities earn around £22k-£38k.

Health
A good level of physical fitness and strength is required for this job.

Skills and Qualities
adaptable, agile, eye for visual effect, good co-ordination, head for heights, methodical, quick reactions, responsible attitude, safety conscious, technical aptitude

Relevant Subjects
Biology, Chemistry, Geography, Land and Environment, Mathematics, Science

Further Information
AGCAS: Environment & Agriculture (Job Sector Briefing) (AGCAS) - www.prospects.ac.uk

Apprenticeship Schemes (National Apprenticeship Service) - www.apprenticeships.org.uk

Arboricultural Journal (Aboricultural Association) - www.trees.org.uk

Diplomas (Foundation, Higher and Advanced) - http://yp.direct.gov.uk/diplomas

International Journal of Forestry Research (Hindawi Publishing Corporation) - www.hindawi.com/journals/ijfr/

Jobs and the Natural Heritage (leaflet) (Scottish Natural Heritage) - www.snh.org.uk/

Lantra - The Sector Skills Council for environmental & land-based sector (Lantra) http:/www.lantra.co.uk

Training Schemes - www.direct.gov.uk/en/educationandlearning

Treeline (International Society of Arboriculture) - www.isa-arboriculture.org

Addresses
Arboricultural Association
Ullenwood Court, Ullenwood, Cheltenham GL53 9QS
Phone: +44 (0)1242 522152
Web: www.trees.org.uk

Institute of Chartered Foresters (ICF)
59 George Street, Edinburgh EH2 2JG
Phone: +44 (0)131 240 1425
Web: www.charteredforesters.org

International Society of Arboriculture (ISA)
UK & Ireland Chapter, 148 Hydes Road, Wednesbury,
West Midlands WS10 0DR
Phone: +44 (0)121 556 8302
Web: www.isa-arboriculture.org

Myerscough College
Bilsborrow, Preston, Lancashire PR3 0RY
Phone: +44 (0)1995 642222
Web: www.myerscough.ac.uk

National Proficiency Test Council (NPTC)
City & Guilds Land Based Services Building 500 Abbey Park,
Stareton, Warwickshire CV8 2LY
Phone: +44 (0) 24 7685 7300
Web: www.nptc.org.uk

Royal Forestry Society (RFS)
102 High Street, Tring, Hertfordshire HP23 4AF
Phone: +44 (0)1442 822 028
Web: www.rfs.org.uk

Royal Scottish Forestry Society (RSFS)
Website contact only,
Web: www.rsfs.org

Scottish Skills Testing Service
Young Farmers Centre, Ingliston, Edinburgh EH28 8NE
Phone: +44 (0)131 333 2040
Web: www.sayfc.org/ssts/

Similar Jobs

Agricultural Consultant/Adviser, Countryside/Conservation Officer/Manager, Forest Officer, Horticultural Manager, Landscape Architect, Tree Surgeon

Archaeologist

CRCI:Languages, Information and Culture
CLCI:FAH Job Band: 4 to 5

Job Description

Archaeologists investigate the past through the study of ancient objects and other material remains, ranging from microscopic organisms to buried tombs, towns or cities. Most archaeologists specialise in an historical period, or a style/type of artefact, such as pottery, tools, coins or jewellery, or specific geographical areas. Some undertake field or marine excavations ('digs') as part of a team and survey, excavate or preserve objects and sites. Post-excavation interpretation of findings is an important aspect of an archaeologist's role.

Others work in museums, identifying and classifying material to define its age and purpose. Some teach in universities or colleges. Different skills may be needed for archaeologists working in an academic environment and those in contract work.

Can also be involved with planning applications that may involve an archaeological site, or in the protection and maintenance of sites or buildings. Uses photography, computer-aided design programs (CAD), geographical information systems (GIS), measured drawings and detailed notes to identify and record their work in precise detail. In most jobs, archaeologists have to write reports for a varied audience, often using a computer.

Work Details

Usually works 37-39 hrs a week, with overtime, late evenings and some weekends necessary if working on site. Depending on the area of expertise, your place of work may be an office, a museum, a laboratory or out on fieldwork. Travel may be necessary over quite a wide area and, on fieldwork, you may need to work for long periods in isolated places, living in a tent, hut or caravan. On site visits you have to cope with walking over rough ground, bending down, kneeling and sometimes working in extremes of heat and cold. Your work environment varies according to the type of site.

Qualification

- **England, Wales and Northern Ireland**

Band 4: For foundation degree in archaeology or history, heritage and archaeology: one A level preferably in archaeology, history, geography, classical civilisation or physical science, and some GCSEs, including maths and English, or a science (not biology alone) at grade C or above.

Band 5: For degree courses in archaeology: 2-3 A levels (good grades) and some GCSEs (A*-C) usually including English and maths, or equivalent. Exact requirements depend on the degree you take. History, geography, geology, sciences and foreign languages may be specified.

- **Scotland**

Band 4: For a certificate or diploma in Scottish archaeology from Aberdeen university centre for lifelong learning: two H grades preferably in archaeology, history, geography, classical civilisation or physical sciences, and some S grades, including maths and English, or a science (not biology alone), or similar.

Band 5: For degree in archaeology: usually 3-5 H grades (good grades) and at least some S grades (1-3), usually including English and maths, or similar qualifications. Exact requirements depend on the degree you take. History, geography, geology, sciences and foreign languages may be specified.

Degree Information

Entry can be with a first degree such as archaeology, archaeological sciences, history or heritage management, or with a postgraduate course. A good first degree in subjects such as classics, history, anthropology or geography is required for entry to postgraduate courses. In some specialisms a science degree, for example in geology, conservation, zoology or botany, may be more useful.

Adult Qualifications

Mature applicants for undergraduate courses are considered with a variety of entry qualifications such as Open University credits, Access courses and their formal academic equivalents. Some universities may offer relevant certificate/diploma courses particularly for mature students. Check with individual institutions because entry requirements vary.

Work Experience

Work experience gives you an insight into what you enjoy and do not enjoy about a job or working environment, as well as the opportunity to acquire new skills. It also provides valuable information to add to your CV and improves any course application and your future employment prospects. Paid work or voluntary experience on archaeological digs is very useful, as well as attending practical workshops, taster courses or summer schools. Showing this sort of commitment and interest in the work can help with applications for jobs and help build a portfolio of experience.

Entry and Training

Most archaeologists have a degree, HND or foundation degree. Universities usually expect at least four weeks experience in archaeological excavation as part of their entrance requirements. Entry to undergraduate and postgraduate courses is highly competitive. Postgraduate courses usually cover just one specialist area of archaeology, such as Egyptian archaeology. Training requires excavation and placement experience, as well as academic study. Most archaeologists are members of one of the professional bodies, such as the Institute for Field Archaeologists (IFA), the Council for British Archaeology (CBA) or the Council for Scottish Archaeology (CSA). Membership usually requires an appropriate honours degree and relevant experience.

The CBA coordinates the Young Archaeologists Club for those under 17 who are interested in archaeology as a career. The IFA offers an NVQ in archaeological practice at level 3 and level 4. Level 5 is in development. There is a cost associated with this work-based training but the IFA is exploring funding opportunities. Consult the IFA website for further details.

Entry to degree courses at some universities may also be through a foundation degree in archaeology or perhaps computing, due to the increasing use of computers, geographical information systems (GIS) and computer aided design (CAD) in archaeological projects. Contact the CBA or CSA for further details of routes to training and qualification. For a list of courses, check the website of the British Archaeological Jobs Resource (BAJR), or the Training Online Resource Centre for Archaeology (TORC).

Mature entry to archaeology is common, particularly from applicants with a keen interest in archaeology and a background in science or computing. Practical fieldwork experience is essential. It is also helpful to be a member of an archaeological society. There are distance-learning postgraduate courses available, as well as full and part-time postgraduate courses. Contact the Council for British Archaeology or Council for Scottish Archaeology for details. Short specialist courses are also available from organisations like English Heritage or Historic Scotland.

Opportunities and Pay

Jobs are available in many different locations, both in the UK and abroad, so you may need to move home frequently. This is a small profession and there are few vacancies. Employers include university departments, museums, heritage bodies or local authority planning departments. Some archaeologists work for organisations like the National Trust that covers England, Wales and Northern Ireland, the National Trust for Scotland, Forestry Commission, or for electricity, gas and water companies. Archaeologists are also employed by organisations such as the Council for British Archaeology, Council for Scottish Archaeology and Cadw.

Many people work freelance on short-term contracts. There may also be opportunities to teach or do research. The competition for full-time jobs is tough and promotion prospects are limited. Part-time work is possible on site.

Starting salaries for site assistants and evacuators are usually around £15k-£17k a year. Graduates with some qualifications and some experience earn around £20k, rising to around £30k a year. Pay varies hugely between the public and private sectors, and is often below average for equivalent level roles in other fields.

Health

This job requires good general fitness.

Skills and Qualities

able to communicate effectively, able to work both on your own and in a team, analytical skills, aptitude for fieldwork, interest in cultural heritage, IT skills, project management skills, research skills, scientific approach, willing to travel

Relevant Subjects

Chemistry, Classical studies, English, Geography, History, ICT/ Computer studies, Land and Environment, Mathematics, Science

Further Information

British Archaeological Jobs Resource (BAJR) - www.bajr.org

British Archaeology (bi-monthly) (Council for British Archaeology (CBA)) - www.britarch.ac.uk

Current Archaeology magazine (Current Publishing) (Current Publishing) - www.archaeology.co.uk

Open University - www.open.ac.uk

The Archaeologist (quarterly) (Institute for Archaeologists) - www.archaeologists.net

Training Online Resource Centre for Archaeology - www.torc.org.uk

▶Working in cultural heritage (2007) (Babcock Lifeskills) - www.babcock-lifeskills.com/

Young Archaeologist Magazine (Council for British Archaeology)

Addresses

Archaeology Scotland
Suite 1a, Stuart House, Eskmills, Station Road, Musselburgh EH21 7PB
Phone: 0845 872 3333
Web: www.scottisharchaeology.org.uk

Cadw
Welsh Assembly Government, Plas Carew, Unit 5/7 Cefn Coed, Parc Nantgarw, Cardiff CF15 7QQ
Phone: +44 (0)1443 33 6000
Web: www.cadw.wales.gov.uk

Council for British Archaeology (CBA)
St Mary's House, 66 Bootham, York YO30 7BZ
Phone: +44 (0)1904 671 417
Web: www.britarch.ac.uk

Institute for Archaeologists (IFA)
SHES Whiteknights University of Reading PO Box 227, Berkshire RG6 6AB
Phone: +44 (0)118 378 6446
Web: www.archaeologists.net

Institute of Archaeology
University College London, 31-34 Gordon Square WC1H OPY
Phone: +44 (0)20 7679 7495
Web: www.ucl.ac.uk/archaeology

Similar Jobs

Archivist, Cartographer, Conservator-Restorer, Geophysicist, Illustrator: Archaeological, Museum/Art Gallery Curator

Architect

CRCI:Building and Construction
CLCI:UB — Job Band: 5

Job Description

An architect plans and designs buildings of all types and manages construction projects through to their completion. As building work progresses, they regularly conduct site visits and inspections. Also, plans alterations and extensions for existing buildings. Ideas and designs are discussed with clients and architectural drawings are then prepared, often using computer-aided design (CAD) and 3D visualisation technology. After further consultation with the client, the architect advises on costs and negotiates with contractors and other professionals. Contracts are drawn up and any necessary planning consents are obtained. A specific programme of work is planned for the project . Architects also use their expertise to help conserve old buildings and redevelop parts of towns and cities.

An architect always aims for buildings of good appearance, best value, comfort, and environmental and consumer efficiency. They work closely with surveyors, engineers, landscape architects and contractors, ensuring time and costs are within agreed limits.

Work Details

Architects usually work around 39 hrs a week, though sometimes weekend and evening work may be required. You may need to spend nights away from home. This career is mainly office based, but you can be out on sites, so travel over quite a wide area may be necessary. You work with a wide range of people, including clients, local authority planners, building control officers, site managers, civil engineers and surveyors. You need to deal with legal documents and procedures.

Qualification

• England, Wales and Northern Ireland

Band 5: For degree courses: usually 2-3 A levels, preferably a mixture of arts, maths and science, and at least 5 GCSEs (A*-C), usually including English language, maths and science, or equivalent qualifications. A portfolio of work as proof of design and technical drawing ability is usually required. Check exact requirements with individual universities.

• Scotland

Band 5: For degree courses: usually 4-5 H grades, preferably with a mixture of arts, maths and science, and at least three S grades (1-3) usually including English, maths and science, or similar qualifications. A portfolio of work as proof of design and technical drawing ability is usually required. Check exact requirement details with individual universities.

Architect

Degree Information
Degrees must be those approved by the Royal Institute of British Architects (RIBA) and Architects Registration Board (ARB) for full professional status. Courses in general architecture lead to an honours degree and those students aiming for full professional status take a further two-year course, such as the diploma in architecture (Dip Arch), and then complete a year's practical training prior to RIBA's part 3 examination. There are postgraduate courses available, such as a master of architecture (MArch), including a distance-learning diploma.

Graduates may also choose to follow a non-professional route to achieve their masters degree (MA in architectural studies) through research.

Adult Qualifications
Mature applicants should contact academic institutions for details of any special schemes or degree entry standards for adults. There is special provision for those with related degrees, such as building, planning or engineering. Access, foundation courses and advanced apprenticeships provide a route to higher education.

Work Experience
Entry to this career is highly competitive and it is essential that you have some relevant work or voluntary experience before applying. Ideally, time spent in an architect's office or department is useful but related occupations, such as civil engineering, also give an idea of what is involved in the work.

Entry and Training
It takes a minimum of seven years (full time) to qualify as an architect. To enter the register of architects, you must complete and pass all three stages of the Royal Institute of British Architects (RIBA) designated training route. Stage one is a recognised degree programme, which is usually divided into two parts: a 3-4 year degree (RIBA part one), followed by a further two years of advanced undergraduate study (RIBA part two). Entry to training courses at a school of architecture is highly competitive and a portfolio of work as proof of relevant skills in art and design is usually required. Many schools of architecture accept BTEC qualifications, or equivalent. Most schools also ask candidates to attend an interview. Courses must be approved by RIBA and the Architects Registration Board (ARB).

The second stage consists of a minimum of two years' professional experience in an architect's office, or equivalent. One year is usually taken after RIBA part one, and the other after RIBA part two. This is followed by gaining the RIBA part three examination in professional practice and management, which enables you to register as an architect with the ARB and become a chartered member of RIBA.

Part-time training, such as day release or distance learning, is also available in some schools of architecture for students working in architects' offices and having already completed several years' experience. An S/NVQ is available in architectural practice at level 5. There are also relevant foundation degrees available. Ongoing training can include knowledge and use of the latest versions of computer drawing packages.

Short courses are available from both RIBA and the Royal Incorporation of Architects in Scotland (RIAS) in specialised subjects, such as urban design or planning law. You may also receive training through an employer, or through a local branch of RIBA, including talks from specialists/manufacturers on a variety of subjects/topics, or arranged visits to sites/buildings of architectural interest.

The 'Inspire Scholarships' scheme, offered through CITB-ConstructionSkills, the Sector Skills Council for the construction industry, offers scholarships of up to £9k to help fund a construction-related degree, such as civil engineering, architecture, surveying and construction management.
More information about the scheme is available at www.bconstructive.co.uk

Mature entrants with experience of working in an architect's office for a minimum of three years and having gained suitable qualifications, can apply for the RIBA Examination in Architecture for Office-Based Candidates. This route enables you to become a qualified architect without studying at a school of architecture. Contact RIBA for further details. Schools of architecture offer part-time study, including day-release or modular based programmes, for those who have some work experience as an architectural technologist.

Opportunities and Pay
Considerable talent is required for success. Most architects work in private practice for many types of organisations, including local authorities and central government, the NHS, industry and commerce. Many are self-employed and work as a consultant on a freelance basis. Jobs are located throughout the UK and there are also opportunities abroad. Availability of work depends on the state of the building trade and the national economy. Currently there is a downturn in the housing market which means there may be a shortage of vacancies. There is, however, a growth in demand for architects skilled in the design of timber-framed buildings.

Salaries for trainees start at £17k a year. Average earnings for a junior architect are between £25k-£35k a year, depending on size of firm and location. Experienced architects earn in the region of £32k-£42k, whilst an associate earns £39k-£45k. Partners can earn over £50k a year.

Health
Good colour vision is necessary for certain areas of work.

Skills and Qualities
able to follow drawings and plans, able to take responsibility, creative flair, drawing ability, eye for visual effect, imaginative, problem-solving skills, spatial awareness, specialist IT skills, technical aptitude

Relevant Subjects
Art and Design, Business and accounting, Classical studies, Construction and built environment, Design and technology, Economics, English, History, ICT/Computer studies, Mathematics, Physics, Science

Further Information
Architects' Journal (EMap Ltd) - www.architectsjournal.co.uk/index.html

Architecture Careers UK (RIBA) - www.architecture.co.uk

RIBA Appointments - www.ribaappointments.com

TARGETjobs: Construction & Building Services (GTI Specialist Publishers Ltd) - www.groupgti.com

Touchstone - Architecture in Wales (2 x year) (Royal Society of Architects in Wales (RSAW)) - www.wirad.ac.uk/journals/touchstone/

▶ Working in construction & the built environment (2007) (Babcock Lifeskills) - www.babcock-lifeskills.com/

Addresses
Architects Registration Board (ARB)
8 Weymouth Street, London W1W 5BU
Phone: +44 (0) 20 7580 5861
Web: www.arb.org.uk

Royal Incorporation of Architects in Scotland (RIAS)
15 Rutland Square, Edinburgh EH1 2BE
Phone: +44 (0)131 229 7545
Web: www.rias.org.uk

Royal Institute of British Architects (RIBA)
66 Portland Place, London W1B 1AD
Phone: +44 (0)20 7580 5533
Web: www.architecture.com/

Royal Society of Architects in Wales
4 Cathedral Road, Cardiff CF11 9LJ
Phone: +44 (0)29 2022 8987
Web: www.riba.org

Royal Society of Ulster Architects
2 Mount Charles, Belfast BT7 1NZ
Phone: +44 (0)28 9032 3760
Web: www.rsua.org.uk

Similar Jobs
Architectural Technician, Architectural Technologist, Furniture Designer, Landscape Architect, Surveyor: Quantity, Town Planner

Architectural Technician

CRCI:Building and Construction
CLCI:UB Job Band: 3 to 4

Job Description
Architectural technicians are specialists in applying the technical plans and drawings for architecture, building design and construction projects. They support the work of architects, architectural technologists, surveyors and engineers. May support the design and construction of new buildings, bridges, extensions, conversion work on existing buildings, and historical and conservation projects. Technicians also help to collect, organise and analyse the technical information.

Architectural technicians prepare the initial design proposals, often using computer-aided design (CAD) packages, such as AutoCAD. May also use traditional drawing techniques. They assist with design stage risk assessments. May also advise on the refurbishment, repair, re-use and deconstruction of buildings. Technicians also liaise and negotiate with design and construction teams and attend contract/project meetings and make site visits.

Work Details
Usually works around 39 hrs a week, though may be required to work weekends or evenings at times. The work is mainly office based, but could also be out on site, so some travel is necessary, perhaps over quite a wide area. Site visits are in all weather conditions and can involve climbing ladders and scaffolding, so protective clothing, boots and a safety helmet need to be worn.

Qualification
- **England, Wales and Northern Ireland**

Band 3: For relevant courses, such as BTEC national awards: usually at least 4 GCSEs (A*-C) including English, maths and a science, or equivalent qualifications. Art and technology subjects are also useful.

Band 4: For BTEC higher national award: 1-2 A levels and some GCSEs (A*-C) usually including English and maths, or equivalent.

- **Scotland**

Band 3: For relevant courses such as SQA national award: usually at least four S grades including English, maths and a science, or similar qualifications. Art and technology subjects are also useful.

Band 4: For SQA higher national award: usually 2-3 H grades and some S grades (1-3), often including English and maths, or similar qualifications.

Adult Qualifications
Course entry requirements are often relaxed for suitable mature applicants, particularly those with relevant skills and experience. Those without the required qualifications may complete an Access course, or similar, that leads to higher education qualifications.

Work Experience
Entry to this job is competitive and it is important that you try to do some relevant work or voluntary experience before applying for a course or job. Work in an architectural firm or a related job within the construction industry is an advantage. Any work that provides an opportunity to get involved with design projects, technical drawing and using office skills is very helpful.

Entry and Training
In order to train as an architectural technician, most entrants usually need to have taken A levels/H grades or their equivalent. You must also complete a Chartered Institute of Architectural Technologists (CIAT) accredited course that leads to professional qualification as an architectural technician (TCIAT) and technician membership of CIAT. Relevant accredited courses include a higher national certificate/diploma or a foundation degree in architectural technology.

Courses may be full or part time at a college and usually include work experience with an employer. When you have successfully passed an accredited course you can then apply for a job and complete the professional training. This takes around one to two years and involves a workplace assessment process known as the CIAT Professional and Occupational Performance Record (POP record). Those with existing relevant qualifications may have exemption from certain parts of the POP Record.

Architectural technicians are respected as professionals in their own right. However, some may choose to progress and to qualify as a chartered architectural technologist. Training programmes, including apprenticeship schemes, may be available in your area. Advanced apprenticeships leading to qualification at level 3 can also be a route into higher education.

Mature applicants may be accepted without the usual minimum requirements if they have relevant or useful experience in the building industry. Exemptions on some courses may apply if you have previous experience and/or qualifications.

Opportunities and Pay
Architectural technicians cannot practise on their own account, but are an integral part of the design process. Work is available throughout the UK but availability depends to some extent on the state of the building trade and the national economy. Currently there is a downturn in the housing market which means there may be a shortage of vacancies. Most work for private architectural firms, but some are employed by the building and construction industry, commercial companies, housing associations, the civil service or local government. Some work is contractual. You may be self-employed or in a partnership. There may be opportunities for some part-time work.

Salaries vary depending on location and size of firm. Junior architectural technicians earn around £17k-£26k a year, rising to £30k plus with experience. Senior associate or partner technicians can earn over £40k a year.

Health
Good colour vision is needed for certain areas of work.

Skills and Qualities
aptitude for teamwork, attention to detail, drawing ability, good communication skills, good organisational skills, negotiating skills, numeracy skills, spatial awareness, specialist IT skills, technical aptitude

Relevant Subjects
Art and Design, Construction and built environment, Design and technology, ICT/Computer studies, Mathematics, Physics

Further Information
ConstructionSkills - sector skills council for the construction industry - www.cskills.org

TARGETjobs: Construction & Building Services (GTI Specialist Publishers Ltd) - www.groupgti.com

▶ Working in art & design (2009) (Babcock Lifeskills) - www.babcock-lifeskills.com/

▶ Working in construction & the built environment (2007) (Babcock Lifeskills) - www.babcock-lifeskills.com/

Addresses

Chartered Institute of Architectural Technologists (CIAT)
397 City Road, London EC1V 1NH
Phone: +44 (0)20 7278 2206
Web: www.ciat.org.uk

Similar Jobs

Architect, Architectural Technologist, CAD Technician, Civil Engineering Technician, Construction Site Supervisor/Manager, Surveying Technician, Town Planning Support Staff

Architectural Technologist

CRCI:Building and Construction
CLCI:UB Job Band: 4 to 5

Job Description

Architectural technologists work on the technological aspects of design and construction, including new buildings, bridges, extensions, conversion work and historical conservation projects. They work closely with architects, surveyors and other professionals who are involved in building projects. They specialise in the science of architecture, building design and construction.

Technologists form the link between concept and construction. They collect and analyse the technical information required and carry out design stage risk assessments. Computer-aided design (CAD) and 3D visualisation technology, as well as traditional techniques are used in the design process. Technologists also produce and evaluate feasibility studies.

Architectural technologists are qualified to negotiate and manage all aspects of architectural and construction contracts. They obtain and evaluate tenders and agree contracts whilst also ensuring compliance with design, legal, statutory and professional requirements. Technologists organise construction work, liaise with contractors and clients, check schedules and ensure satisfactory completion of work. They administer contracts and project certification and coordinate associated professionals. May also advise on the refurbishment, repair, re-use and deconstruction of buildings.

Work Details

Architectural technologists usually work around 39 hrs a week, though you may be required to work weekends or evenings at times. The work is mainly office based. However, site visits are also usual, where some hazards may be encountered, and protective clothing is needed. Some travel is therefore necessary, perhaps over quite a wide area. You are responsible for organising work schedules, monitoring work progress and checking that the completed work meets the exact requirements and legal obligations. There may be opportunities for some part-time work.

Qualification

• England, Wales and Northern Ireland

Band 4: For BTEC higher national award: 1-2 A levels and some GCSEs (A*-C), usually including English, maths and a science, or equivalent. Physics, chemistry or technology are usually preferred.

Band 5: For degree courses: 2-3 A levels and some GCSEs (A*-C) usually including English, maths and a science, or equivalent. Exact requirements depend on the degree you take. Candidates with a relevant higher national award may transfer to a top-up degree course.

• Scotland

Band 4: For relevant SQA higher national award: usually 2-3 H grades and some S grades (1-3) in other subjects, or similar qualifications. English, maths, physics or chemistry are usually preferred.

Band 5: For degree courses: 3-5 H grades plus five S grades (1-3) usually including English, maths and a science, or similar qualifications. Candidates with a relevant higher national award may transfer to a top-up degree course. Entry requirements depend on the degree you take.

Degree Information

The Chartered Institute of Architectural Technologists (CIAT) approved degrees include those in architectural technology, architectural technology and innovation, architectural design technology and production, architectural technology and design/management/and the environment. Completion of one of one of these means you are qualified for membership of CIAT, which is expected by most employers.

Subjects covering the built environment with a technology base, including architecture, are normally also acceptable. Relevant subjects also include computer-aided engineering, civil/structural engineering, architectural engineering and surveying.

Adult Qualifications

Mature applicants can apply for places on full-time courses. Requirements vary and may be relaxed for adults with existing skills and experience. Those without the required qualifications may complete a foundation or Access course leading to relevant HNDs or accredited degrees.

Work Experience

Entry to this job is competitive and it is important that you try to do some relevant work or voluntary experience before applying. Work experience with an architectural firm or a related job within the construction industry is relevant and also any work that gives you the opportunity to get involved with design projects, technical drawing and using office skills.

Entry and Training

Most enter by first completing a degree in architectural technology (or related subject). To become a qualified architectural technology professional and gain full membership (MCIAT) of the Chartered Institute of Architectural Technologists (CIAT), you then need to complete a workplace assessment. This process is known as the CIAT Professional and Occupational Performance Record (POP Record). Those with existing relevant qualifications may have exemption from certain parts of the POP Record. The process is likely to take three years and is followed by a Professional Practice Interview.

Alternatively, relevant HNCs/HNDs are available in subjects such as architectural technology, building studies, construction, architectural design, or similar. Completion of an approved course enables you to apply for associate membership (ACIAT) of CIAT. From there you can either join a degree course, or progress to qualification as an architectural technologist by first becoming a qualified architectural technician. There are relevant foundation degrees available. Post qualification study also includes continuing professional development (CPD).

The 'Inspire Scholarships' scheme, offered through ConstructionSkills, the Sector Skills Council for the construction industry, offers scholarships of up to £9k to help fund a construction-related degree. This includes courses such as engineering, architecture, surveying and construction management. More information about the scheme is available at www.bconstructive.co.uk

You may be able to work for an appropriate S/NVQ at level 4 in architectural technology. Advanced apprenticeships leading to qualification at level 3 can also be a route into higher education.

Mature applicants with relevant experience and qualifications in the construction industry, including experience in computer-aided design (CAD) or 3D visualisation, may have an advantage for entry to courses. Formal qualifications can be relaxed for mature students. Open and distance-learning courses in architectural technology and in computer-aided design are also available.

Opportunities and Pay
There are over 8,000 professionals working in this field throughout the UK. Most work for private architectural firms, but some are employed by the building industry, commercial companies such as banks and building societies, or the public sector and housing corporations. You can be self-employed or in a partnership. Work may be located anywhere in the UK and also abroad. Availability of work depends to some extent on the state of the building trade and the national economy. Currently there is a downturn in the housing market which means there may be a shortage of vacancies.

Salaries vary depending on location and size of firm. Starting salaries are around £18k to £25k a year, rising to £25k to £35k a year with experience. A senior technologist earns up to £42k a year.

Health
Good colour vision is needed for certain areas of work.

Skills and Qualities
aptitude for teamwork, attention to detail, good communication skills, leadership qualities, negotiating skills, planning skills, problem-solving skills, spatial awareness, specialist IT skills, technical aptitude

Relevant Subjects
Art and Design, Construction and built environment, Design and technology, ICT/Computer studies, Mathematics, Physics

Further Information
Chartered Institute Of Architectural Technologists (CIAT)
http:www.ciat.org.uk

ConstructionSkills - sector skills council for the construction industry - www.cskills.org

▶Working in art & design (2009) (Babcock Lifeskills) - www.babcock-lifeskills.com/

▶Working in computers & IT (2010) (Babcock Lifeskills) - www.babcock-lifeskills.com/

▶Working in construction & the built environment (2007) (Babcock Lifeskills) - www.babcock-lifeskills.com/

Addresses
Chartered Institute of Architectural Technologists (CIAT)
397 City Road, London EC1V 1NH
Phone: +44 (0)20 7278 2206
Web: www.ciat.org.uk

Royal Incorporation of Architects in Scotland (RIAS)
15 Rutland Square, Edinburgh EH1 2BE
Phone: +44 (0)131 229 7545
Web: www.rias.org.uk

Royal Institute of British Architects (RIBA)
66 Portland Place, London W1B 1AD
Phone: +44 (0)20 7580 5533
Web: www.architecture.com/

Similar Jobs
Architect, Architectural Technician, CAD Technician, Model Maker, Surveyor: Quantity, Town Planning Support Staff

Archivist
also known as: Records Manager

CRCI:Languages, Information and Culture
CLCI:FAG Job Band: 5

Job Description
Archivists work with documents and other records of historical value, selecting and recording those which should be kept for present and future generations. They acquire, manage and maintain books, manuscripts, maps, photos, computer records, microfilm etc, which are no longer in current use. Often using a computer., they read, identify, date and classify material and enter details into catalogues and indexes Material is maintained in a good condition by storing it well, although increasingly, archives are being made available via the Internet. May specialise in archive conservation and arrange for the repair of damaged material.

Archivists also respond to enquiries to help the public find, read and interpret information they require for research purposes or personal interest. Provides them with access to historical documents in alternative formats, such as photocopies, microfiche, through publications and computer-assisted tools. May also promote access to archives through presentations, tours and local and national exhibitions and talks.

Work Details
Usually works 36-40 hrs a week, Monday to Friday, either in an office, library or reading room. Travel may be necessary to visit or work on different sites. You work mainly on your own, but deal with enquiries from all sorts of different people. You are responsible for accurate work and for providing detailed information. This work is intellectually demanding. You may also have to cope with lifting piles of books and occasionally climbing ladders. Sometimes your work environment may be dusty and dirty.

Qualification
- **England, Wales and Northern Ireland**

Band 5: For degree courses: 2-3 A levels and some GCSEs (A*-C) usually including English and maths, or equivalent. Exact requirements depend on the degree you take.

- **Scotland**

Band 5: For degree courses: 3-5 H grades and some S grades (1-3), including English and maths, or similar qualifications. Exact requirements depend on the degree you take.

Degree Information
Any degree is acceptable, but first degrees in archive and museum studies, media studies and computing science, history, classics, literary studies, modern languages (European or non-European), English, information science/management, or archaeology are preferred.

A postgraduate qualification in archive studies, administration or records management is usually required. The Forum for Archives and Records Management Education provides guidelines on the experience you need to be accepted onto a postgraduate course.

Adult Qualifications
For mature entrants, a degree is necessary followed by a postgraduate qualification. Access or foundation courses provide those without the required qualifications a route onto degree courses.

Relevant work experience is necessary for entry to postgraduate studies. Distance learning courses are also available. The Forum for Archives and Records Management Education and Research provides guidance on the experience you need to be accepted onto a postgraduate course.

Work Experience
Work experience gives you an insight into what you enjoy and do not enjoy about a job or working environment, as well as the opportunity to acquire new skills. It also provides valuable information to add to your CV and improves any course application and your future employment prospects. You need significant work experience to be accepted onto a postgraduate course. Ideally you need to gain experience in archiving, such as in a county or national records office or a library, in paid employment or voluntary work. Conservation or museum work is also very useful. The ARCHON directory lists all archive repositories in the UK and may be a useful source of information for arranging work experience.

Entry and Training
Most in-service training depends on the employer and its size and type. You need a degree and postgraduate qualification approved by the Society of Archivists (SoA) to enter this work and many also have library work experience. Specialist postgraduate courses in archives administration and records management in the UK generally include practical experience which may be supported by an employer. These are available at the universities of Liverpool, Aberystwyth, Northumbria, Dundee, Glasgow, Dublin and University College London (UCL). Courses can be studied full time for one year or part time for two, three or four years. It is an advantage to have experience in languages and in computing, and to have a reading knowledge of Latin.

Normal requirements for admission are a first or second class honours degree and a year's experience in paid or voluntary employment with an established archives or records service. However, it may be possible to start as a searchroom assistant and qualify while working.

Some institutions and the SoA offer correspondence courses for those who are in related employment and also programmes of continuing professional development (CPD), that include short courses, workshops and seminars in various areas of specialism. Some institutions offer one-year, paid graduate traineeships. Many employers require membership of the SoA. Further information on training, traineeships and qualifications is available from the SoA.

There is a modern apprenticeship in cultural heritage available in Scotland and this may be a good route into this career. Lifelong Learning UK offers a Level 2 certificate and a level 3 diploma in libraries, archives and information services which may also provide a good basis to progress to higher education to qualify and train as an archivist.

Mature entry may not be easy because of the small number of vacancies. Qualifications and experience in related areas of work, such as a library, information work, or archaeology, are useful for entry. Many archivists are those who have changed their career following qualification in a related area.

The SoA offers a certificate in archive conservation which is an entry-level work-based course for members who already work in archive conservation. Lifelong Learning UK offers two qualifications for assistants, working in libraries and archives and information settings.

Opportunities and Pay
This is a small, all graduate profession of around 1500 in the UK so entry is highly competitive, but there is a shortage of archivists, particularly in London. Jobs are mainly in cities. Most archivists are employed by local authorities, in museums, libraries or in national record offices. There are also jobs in universities, with professional bodies and a few with commercial companies. Numbers of archivists are increasing with the main growth in commercial and industrial work. There may also be opportunities to do research. Employment and promotion prospects may depend on your willingness to move to another part of the country or overseas.

Pay varies depending on location and employer, but graduate entrants usually earn £21k-£26k, rising to around £30k-£50k a year for experienced senior archivists. Head archivists are likely to earn more, maybe up to £60k a year. Business repositories, central government and universities may offer higher salaries.

Health
This job requires good eyesight and general fitness.

Skills and Qualities
able to get on with all kinds of people, accurate, analytical skills, good concentration level, information handling skills, interest in cultural heritage, IT skills, logical, methodical, research skills

Relevant Subjects
Classical studies, English, History, ICT/Computer studies, Modern Foreign Languages

Further Information
A Career in Archives (SoA) (Society of Archivists (SoA)) - www.archives.org.uk

ARCHON - www.nationalarchives.gov.uk/archon

Forum for Archive & Records Management Education & Research (FARMER) - www.digicult.info/farmer

Journal of the Society of Archivists (2 x year) (Society of Archivists (SoA)) - www.archives.org.uk/publications/journalofthesocietyofarchivists.html

LLUK (Lifelong Learning UK) - sector skills council for the professional development of staff working in the lifelong learning sector - www.lluk.org

Local Government Careers (Improvement and Development Agency) - www.lgcareers.com/publications/

► Working in cultural heritage (2007) (Babcock Lifeskills) - www.babcock-lifeskills.com/

Addresses
Museums, Libraries and Archives Council (MLA)
Grosvenor House, 14 Bennetts Hill, Birmingham B2 5RS
Phone: +44 (0)121 345 7300
Web: www.mla.gov.uk

National Archives
Kew, Richmond, Surrey TW9 4DU
Phone: +44 (0)20 88763444
Web: www.nationalarchives.gov.uk

National Archives of Scotland
HM General Register House, 2 Princes Street, Edinburgh EH1 3YY
Phone: +(0)131 535 1314
Web: www.nas.gov.uk

Records Management Society
14 Blandford Square, Newcastle upon Tyne NE1 4HZ
Phone: +44 (0)191 244 2839
Web: www.rms-gb.org.uk

Society of Archivists (SoA)
Prioryfield House, 20 Canon Street, Taunton, Somerset TA1 1SW
Phone: +44 (0)1823 327030
Web: www.archives.org.uk

Similar Jobs
Conservator-Restorer, Genealogist, Information Scientist, Library & Information Manager, Museum/Art Gallery Curator

Army Officer
CRCI:Security and Armed Forces
CLCI:BAF — Job Band: 4 to 5

Job Description
Army officers command, train and lead a fighting unit in a combat regiment/corps or administer one of the many specialist areas that provide essential support. This may include transport and logistics, finance and human resources, or IT and communications. May work in the engineering corps, or the military police, or in catering, law, medicine or music, and also in administration. Have responsibility for the general welfare, discipline and career development of those in their team. Are also responsible for overseeing security, and organising equipment and weapons.

Work Details
The hours can often be long and irregular, especially when on exercises and operations. Officers can be posted to serve anywhere in the UK and abroad where the environment can sometimes vary from extreme heat to cold. This can be a very

demanding job, which involves enforcing discipline and making unpopular decisions. The job requires a great deal of personal commitment. In the course of your duties you have to deal with people who are in need of support, nervous or perhaps in pain.

Sometimes you are expected to serve in dangerous situations where you are at risk of being injured or killed and you must be able to cope with the sight of blood. This is also a physically demanding job and it is necessary to maintain a high standard of fitness and stamina. You are required to wear a uniform and sometimes protective clothing.

Qualification

Some regiments or corps require entrants to have passes in specific exam subjects and may ask for higher than average qualifications. Check with your local armed forces careers office for information on exact requirements or contact the army careers information line.

• England, Wales and Northern Ireland

Band 4: For direct entry to a commission: minimum two A levels (180 UCAS points) and seven GCSEs (A*-C) normally including English, maths and either a science subject or a foreign language (total 35 ALIS points). Applicants with alternative qualifications, such as BTEC national awards are considered on their own merits.

Band 5: For degree course leading to graduate entry to a commission: at least two A levels and some GCSEs (A*-C) normally including English and maths, are required. The exact requirements depend on the degree you take.

• Scotland

Band 4: For direct entry to a commission: minimum three H grades (180 UCAS points) and seven S grades (1-3) normally including English, maths and either a science subject or a foreign language (total 35 ALIS points). Applicants with alternative qualifications such as SQA national awards are considered on their own merits.

Band 5: For degree course leading to graduate entry to short or regular commission: at least 3-5 H grades and some other S grades (1-3), normally including English and maths. Alternative qualifications such as an SQA awards may also be acceptable for entry to some courses. Exact subjects needed depend on the degree course you take.

Degree Information

Any degree discipline is acceptable for entry to this job. However, some regiments/corps require or prefer specific subjects or a professional qualification. These include the medical, dental, veterinary or engineering corps, legal services and chaplain's department.

Adult Qualifications

Standard entry requirements apply to applicants of any age. Entry requirements may be relaxed for adults applying for higher education courses and Access or foundation courses give adults without qualifications a route on to degree courses.

Work Experience

Relevant work or voluntary experience is always useful and can improve your chances in application for entry to this career. Choose activities that give you the opportunity to practise leadership or supervisory skills such as in a local army cadet organisation or in jobs such as a youth leader or scout/guide leader. Often you can gain valuable experience from a school's Combined Cadet Force (CCF). If you are looking at specialising in a certain area or trade, then work experience in this specialist area is an advantage.

Many universities run a university officer training corp (UOTC). This gives you experience of the army while you are studying, and there is no commitment to join the army once you have graduated.

Entry and Training

There are strict nationality and residence requirements for entry to the army. Entry is competitive and selection is based on aptitude, character and personality. Applicants attend the Army Officer Selection Board, that combines written examinations and physical tests designed to measure leadership potential. You must also pass a medical test. For entry to a commission, applicants must be at least 17 yrs and 9 mths, and are usually aged under 29. If you join under 18, you can leave on your 22nd birthday. If you join over 18, then your commission lasts 4 yrs 3 months, but in both cases you can choose to stay in the army for a maximum of 22 years.

The army awards cadetships for those studying to be doctors, nurses and vets. Cadets are paid an army salary while studying and must serve in the army for a minimum of five years after graduation. The army also awards bursaries for university study. Students who receive an army bursary must serve in the army for three years after completing the degree course. It is also possible to receive an army scholarship while studying for A levels/H grades at school. Successful candidates must serve in the army for at least three years after leaving school.

The armed forces also have their own sixth form residential college. Science and technology based A level courses at Welbeck College last for two years and successful students may go on to a degree course at either a civilian university, the Royal Military College of Science at Shrivenham, or straight to the officer training programme at the Royal Military Academy, Sandhurst.

After attending and completing a commissioning course at Sandhurst (11 months), during which you are trained to acquire/enhance skills such as decision making, negotiating, self-confidence, mental agility, leadership and communication, all officer entrants are given specialist training in the corps in which they are to serve. For those with the right professional qualifications there is the Professionally Qualified Officer's (PQO) course that offers a faster route to becoming an officer (four weeks). Those who are eligible are doctors, dentists, barristers, solicitors, chaplains and vets, and also qualified nurses with at least two years' post registration experience. Lawyers and chaplains must also show that they have professional experience prior to applying.

Officers are expected to continue training throughout their career and also have the opportunity to earn recognised academic qualifications, including an MA/MSc and military MBA. Currently, women are not eligible for a commission in the Infantry, Royal Armoured Corps or the Household Cavalry.

Mature entry is usually up to the age of 29 years but different upper age limits operate for certain corps and regiments. Check current regulations carefully. The Professionally Qualified Officers' (PQO) course is a fast route to becoming an officer. It has two intakes a year and takes ten weeks to complete. There are six types of eligible professions; doctors, dentists, nurses (with at least two years' post registration experience), barristers and solicitors, vets and chaplains. Lawyers and chaplains also require prior professional experience before applying.

Opportunities and Pay

There are around 14,000 officers in the regular army at present. There are good opportunities for promotion and prospects are improved by taking further training. The terms and length of service depends on the type of commission you hold (short, intermediate regular or regular). You are given accommodation in an officers' mess and must complete a minimum length of service. This can sometimes be a short career but the training and qualifications gained in this job provide an excellent basis for a range of occupations in civilian life.

Pay increases with promotion. Officer cadets earn £15K, whilst graduate officer cadets and second lieutenants earn £24k a year. Lieutenants earn around £30k-£32k and captains earn £37k-£44k.

Health
Applicants must pass a medical test before being accepted for officer training. Normal colour vision is necessary for certain areas of work.

Skills and Qualities
able to discipline, able to inspire confidence, able to manage a budget and keep records, able to take responsibility, aptitude for teamwork, decisive, good communication skills, leadership qualities, prepared to go into combat, quick thinking

Relevant Subjects
Design and technology, Engineering, English, Geography, Government and politics, Mathematics, Physical education and sport, Physics, Psychology, Science

Further Information
AGCAS: Armed Forces & Emergency Services (Job Sector Briefing) (AGCAS) - www.prospects.ac.uk

Army Careers Website - www. army.mod.uk

Careers Information - Job Explorer, Army - www.armyjobs.mod.uk/

Real Life Guide to Armed Forces (Trotman 2009) - www.trotman.co.uk

Skills for Work (Scottish Qualifications Authority) - www.sqa.org.uk/sqa/31390.html

TARGETjobs: Public Service (GTI Specialist Publishing Ltd.) - www.groupgti.com

▶Working in business, administration & finance (2010) (Babcock Lifeskills) - www.babcock-lifeskills.com/

▶Working in police, fire & security (2009) (Babcock Lifeskills) - www.babcock-lifeskills.com/

Addresses
Welbeck - Defence Sixth Form College
Forest Road, Woodhouse, Loughborough, Leicestershire
LE12 8WD
Web: www.dsfc.ac.uk/

Similar Jobs
Police Officer, Prison Governor, RAF Officer, Royal Marines Officer, Royal Navy Officer

Army Soldier
also known as: Soldier: Army Serviceman/Servicewoman

CRCI:Security and Armed Forces
CLCI:BAF Job Band: 1 to 2

Job Description
Army soldiers serve as a member of a fighting (combat) unit or work in one of the many specialist areas that provide essential support, such as transport and logistics, finance, IT and communications, engineering, military police, catering, human resources, law, medical and veterinary services, music, administration and clerical. Are trained primarily for combat together with other specialised training, though women do not take part in the work of front line troops.

Carry out a wide range of military duties and exercises. Are qualified and experienced in a trade or skill that is essential for maintaining an efficient and high performance army. Take part in UN/NATO exercises and operations throughout the world, including humanitarian and peacekeeping duties.

Keep physically fit and maintain a high level of combat skills. Are able to use a sophisticated range of equipment and advanced weaponry. Work as part of a team.

Work Details
Soldiers usually work an eight-hour shift but are on call at all times. The hours may be long and irregular during exercises, and you can be posted to serve in many different parts of the UK and overseas. Work is likely to be physically and mentally demanding. The environment varies depending on what branch of the army you are serving in, but conditions can be tough, particularly if you are on active duty when you can be at risk of being injured or killed. You are required to accept strict discipline. A uniform is provided and other protective clothing as needed.

Qualification
The Scottish Qualifications Authority (SQA) launched a new Skills for Work course in 2008. This course introduces candidates to the uniformed and emergency services and is particularly suited to those considering a career in the Army, Royal Navy, Royal Air Force or Royal Marines. Check the website for details.

• England, Wales and Northern Ireland
Band 1: No formal qualifications are required, though some GCSEs, or equivalent, are useful.

Band 2: For entry to Army training: some GCSEs (A*-C) are preferred usually in maths, English, science or technology subjects. For particular jobs in the Royal Signals/Intelligence Corps, entrants need GCSEs (A*-C) in English, maths and a modern language. Applicants with alternative qualifications such as BTECs are also considered.

• Scotland
Band 1: No formal qualifications are required though some S grades or similar are useful.

Band 2: For entry to some Army training: some S grades (1-3) are preferred usually in maths, English, science or technology subjects. For some jobs in the Royal Signals and the Intelligence Corps entrants need S grades (1-3) in English, maths and a modern language. Applicants with alternative qualifications such as SQAs are also considered.

Adult Qualifications
Certain jobs in the Army may require some formal/vocational qualifications, but generally there are no specific formal entry requirements.

Work Experience
Relevant work or voluntary experience is always useful and can improve your chances when applying for entry to the armed forces. It can help you to decide which trade or branch of the armed services is most appropriate for you. As a young person, getting involved in groups such as a local army cadet organisation, or the Scouts/Guides, helps show enthusiasm and commitment. Often you can gain valuable experience from a school's Combined Cadet Force (CCF). Physical fitness is a requirement for the armed forces, so evidence of an interest in keeping fit is also useful.

Entry and Training
All applicants must take the Army Entrance Test, known as the BARB (British Army Recruit Battery) and do well at the interview, regardless of the academic qualifications they have or expect to gain. This test is a common sense and multiple-choice test on a touch screen that takes around 30 minutes to complete, and which helps you decide which area of the Army best suits you and your talents. It also tests which area of training is most suitable for you. Entrants must also meet nationality requirements. Following the test you spend two days at the Army Development and Selection Centre, where you can find out more about Army life and have a medical and a physical assessment.

Those between the age of 16 and 17 have a choice of routes into the army. You can attend the Army Foundation College in Harrogate. They offer a 50 week course, relevant to both technical and non-technical recruits, which includes 25 weeks' military training, 5 weeks' leadership and 12 weeks' vocational training, leading to S/NVQs at levels 2-3. Courses take place twice yearly, beginning in September and January. The other option is to join the Army Training Regiment at Bassingbourn, where you do 14 weeks' military training, plenty of sport to build up physical fitness and can study for industry-recognised qualifications. This is followed by phase two training in specific regiments.

Entrants over 17 join one of three Army Training Regiments (Lichfield, Pirbright or Winchester). Basic training takes 14 weeks and includes use of weapons, health and safety, drill and fieldcraft. This is followed by phase two training with a specific regiment. There are many career options available in the Army, but you are a soldier first and foremost, and trained to fight and survive in any situation. Training can be both on the job and by short courses, or you may be able to take a full or part-time further education course to gain a City & Guilds or BTEC/SQA award. Training leads to the award of relevant S/NVQs at levels 1-3.

The army can also offer a residential sixth-form, science-based A level college course (Welbeck College) that prepares students for potential officer careers in the technical services branches.

At whatever age, those who are unsuccessful at their first attempt at selection are told whether they can apply again later. There are various age restrictions for entry to different branches of the service. Women are currently not eligible for the Infantry, Royal Armoured Corps, or for the Household Cavalry.

It is important to check with your local armed forces careers office for detailed information on all current opportunities and requirements, or contact the army careers information line.

Mature applicants need to be aware that there are strict upper age limits that vary depending on the area of work for which you are applying. Recruits aged up to 33 yrs are preferred, however exceptions are made to the upper age limit for those with appropriate specialist skills, certain professional qualifications or previous military experience. Check current regulations carefully. Relevant work experience is an advantage. Adult infantry entrants have their basic 24 week combat training at Catterick Camp (Infantry Training Centre). This combines both phase one and phase two training.

Opportunities and Pay

The army offers a wide range of possible jobs depending on skill and personal choice. A soldier can add to their skills by choosing from over 130 trades and professions currently available. There is a constant demand for new recruits offering good opportunities for promotion and skilled experience, and nationally recognised qualifications, particularly if you have taken further training.

There is an agreed length of service (engagement) though all soldiers may leave after four years, from age 18 or date of entry, whichever is later and by giving one year's notice. Recruits also have a right to leave after 28 days of service depending on the age of entry. On leaving the army, there are excellent opportunities to use your training and the qualifications gained in civilian work.

Upon entry, the standard training salary is £13k a year, rising to £17k once initial training is completed. Lance corporals earn from £20k; corporals from £26k and sergeants from £30k a year. Warrant officers, the highest rank for a non-commissioned officer, earn from £36k a year. Pay increases with promotion and extra pay is usually awarded to those doing particular jobs, serving overseas or living away from their families. There are also good allowances for accommodation and other benefits such as sporting facilities, medical and dental services.

Health

You must pass a medical test on entry. It is important to have a good level of general fitness. It is essential to have perfect colour vision for certain areas of work. You undergo regular medical check ups.

Skills and Qualities

able to cope under pressure, able to follow orders, aptitude for teamwork, good stamina and physically fit, practical skills, prepared to go into combat, quick reactions, responsible attitude, self-disciplined, technical aptitude

Relevant Subjects

Engineering, Physical education and sport

Further Information

AGCAS: Armed Forces & Emergency Services (Job Sector Briefing) (AGCAS) - www.prospects.ac.uk

Army Careers Website - www. army.mod.uk

Careers Information - Job Explorer, Army - www.armyjobs.mod.uk/

Real Life Guide to Armed Forces (Trotman 2009) - www.trotman.co.uk

Skills for Work (Scottish Qualifications Authority) - www.sqa.org.uk/sqa/31390.html

▶Working in police, fire & security (2009) (Babcock Lifeskills) - www.babcock-lifeskills.com/

Addresses

Welbeck - Defence Sixth Form College
Forest Road, Woodhouse, Loughborough, Leicestershire
LE12 8WD
Web: www.dsfc.ac.uk/

Similar Jobs

Army Officer, Merchant Navy Deck Rating, Merchant Navy Engine-room Rating, RAF Airman/Airwoman, Royal Marines Commando, Royal Navy Rating

Aromatherapist

CRCI:Healthcare
CLCI:JOD
Job Band: 2 to 3

Job Description

Aromatherapists treat clients with essential plant oils to improve physical, psychological and emotional conditions. Oils are absorbed through the skin into the bloodstream to stimulate healing and promote relaxation. They take a detailed medical history from the client, including information on their current health, any allergies, lifestyle and diet. Then they select appropriate oils, which are extracted or distilled from flowers, herbs, fruit or spices to treat the client. They blend oils and administer them by therapeutic massage or through inhalation, and may also provide the client with recommended oils to use at home.

If appropriate, an aromatherapist refers the client to other therapists and medical practitioners. As well as aromatherapists working in complementary medicine, some beauty therapists also use aromatherapy techniques.

Work Details

Many aromatherapists are self-employed and choose to work hours that suit themselves and their clients. You may have to work flexible hours and be available during evenings and weekends. Most consulting rooms are quiet, pleasant and have soothing music to help the client relax. You work mainly with adults, some of whom have injuries or are ill, in pain or under emotional stress.

Although aromatherapy massage is gentle, you are constantly active and on your feet for most of the time. The work is physically and emotionally demanding. The treatment room and equipment must be hygienic at all times and the environment kept warm, relaxing and tidy for each client. You may wear a white coat or tunic and trousers.

Aromatherapist

Qualification

For entry to many courses, formal qualifications are not usually required. However, subjects such as English, maths, biology, anatomy, pathology and physiology may be necessary for courses at a higher level.

- **England, Wales and Northern Ireland**

Band 2: For entry to jobs, no minimum qualifications are needed, but it is an advantage to have some GCSEs (A*-C) or equivalent in subjects that include English, maths and biology, or equivalent. For some courses, a good knowledge of anatomy is required.

Band 3: For entry to jobs, HNC or a relevant Diploma, usually at least 4 GCSEs (A*-C) including English, maths and two science-related subjects, or equivalent.

- **Scotland**

Band 2: Although academic qualifications are not specified for this job, it is an advantage to have some S grades (1-3) in subjects that include English, maths and biology, or similar. For some courses a good knowledge of anatomy and biology is required.

Band 3: For entry to jobs, usually at least four S grades (1-3) including English, maths and two science-related subjects, or similar.

Adult Qualifications

Maturity is an advantage. Applicants may be exempt from entry requirements for some courses or entry requirements may be relaxed for adults applying for higher education courses. Access or foundation courses give adults without qualifications a route onto degree courses and credit may be given for relevant experience. Check with individual colleges and universities for specific entry requirements.

Work Experience

Relevant work or voluntary experience can equip you with skills that you can use in the future and that you can add to your CV. There are often opportunities available for voluntary work in the care/health sector that give you experience of working with people.

Entry and Training

Some courses in aromatherapy are only available at private colleges and these can range from courses taking a few days to full training that is approved by the Aromatherapy Council (AC). The AC accredits courses that can be studied part time, in the evenings and weekends over two years, or full time over nine months. Courses cover anatomy, physiology, massage and aromatherapy. Students are required to complete 94 hours in the classroom, a period of supervised practice, 60 treatments outside the classroom and several case studies. Some private courses can be expensive. The AC has a college recognition scheme for aromatherapy training "centres of excellence". See the website for details.

There is a Level 3 qualification in complementary therapy offered by the Vocational Training Charitable Trust (VTCT) and a Level 2 certificate in anatomy and physiology for complementary therapies which may be a good place to start. There are also many short, basic, introductory courses available. The International Federation of Aromatherapists (IFA), the VTCT and the International Therapy Examinations Council have developed a diploma in aromatherapy course which can be studied part time over 6-18 months.

Make sure that your chosen course is accredited to be eligible for professional insurance. The IFA and the AC websites provide a list of professional organisations that offer training courses which meet the requirements of the National Occupational Standards and the AC's Core Curriculum. Meeting these requirements means that you can register with the General Regulatory Council for Complementary Therapists.

Route-specific courses in aromatherapy are available at degree level in complementary therapy or health sciences, but you must check that the course has substantial work-placement training content. A purely academic course does not provide the necessary skills and experience to practice as an aromatherapist. Relevant foundation degrees are also available. Check the UCAS website for details. There are also a number of other vocationally-related qualifications in aromatherapy at Level 3.

Mature entry is common and working as an aromatherapist is often a second career choice. Adults with a caring attitude are welcome, particularly if you have previous experience or qualifications in medically-related areas. Many entrants have previous relevant work experience such as in nursing. Distance-learning courses are available at several centres but these may not be recognised by the Aromatherapy Council.

Opportunities and Pay

The popularity of aromatherapy has increased rapidly, with many opportunities throughout the UK, particularly for self-employment, when experienced. Some aromatherapists work in clinics, a holistic medicine centre or a multi-discipline complementary health centre. If self-employed you may use private consulting rooms, work from home or in clients' own homes. There are opportunities for working in day or residential care homes, health spas and fitness centres, prisons, NHS and private hospitals, and hospices.

There is no structured promotion system and your prospects are governed by the extent of your client base. You may have the opportunity to run your own business, or become a partner in a business with other complementary practitioners offering additional therapies. Some train in other complementary therapies to offer a wider choice of treatments to customers.

As most aromatherapists are self-employed it is difficult to summarise earnings. Broadly speaking, they earn around £30-£60 an hour, depending on location and experience. Annually, earnings could range from around £16k to more than £30k, depending on success. A successful and experienced aromatherapist in their own practice can earn up to £50k a year.

Health

This job involves physical effort and some bending and stretching so requires good general fitness. You also need a good sense of smell.

Skills and Qualities

able to put people at ease, caring, friendly, good adviser, good listening skills, good sense of touch, good stamina and physically fit, strong hands, supportive, tactful

Relevant Subjects

Biology, Chemistry, Health and social care, Science

Further Information

Aromatherapy Council (AC) - www.aromatherapycouncil.co.uk

Aromatherapy Times (quarterly) (International Federation of Aromatherapists) - www.ifaroma.org

Complementary and Natural Healthcare Council (CNHC) - www.cnhc.org.uk

General Regulatory Council for Complementary Therapists (GRCCT) - www.grcct.org

Institute for Complementary and Natural Medicine - www.i-c-m.org.uk

Skills for Health - sector skills council - www.skillsforhealth.org.uk

Addresses

Aromatherapy & Allied Practitioners' Association
PO Box 36248, London SE19 3YD
Phone: +44 (0)20 8653 9152
Web: www.aapa.org.uk/

Aromatherapy Trade Council (ATC)
PO Box 387, Ipswich IP2 9AN
Phone: +44 (0)1473 603 630
Web: www.a-t-c.org.uk

European College of Natural Therapies
16 North Parade, Belfast BT7 2GG
Phone: +44 (0)28 9064 1454

International Federation of Aromatherapists (IFA)
7B Walpole Court, Ealing Green, London W5 5ED
Phone: +44 (0)20 8567 2243
Web: www.ifaroma.org

International Federation of Professional Aromatherapists (IFPA)
82 Ashby Road, Hinckley, Leicestershire LE10 1SN
Phone: +44 (0)1455 637987
Web: www.ifparoma.org

UCAS
Customer Services Unit, PO Box 28, Cheltenham GL52 3LZ
Phone: +44 (0)871 468 0468
Web: www.ucas.com

Vocational Training Charitable Trust (VTCT)
Eastleigh House, 3rd Floor , Upper Market Street, Hampshire
SO50 9FD
Phone: +44 (0)2380 684 500
Web: www.vtct.org.uk

Similar Jobs
Beauty Therapist, Massage Therapist, Medical Herbalist, Naturopath, Reflexologist, Spa Therapist

Art Exhibitions Organiser
also known as: Art Exhibition Adminstrator, Exhibitions Officer
CRCI:Languages, Information and Culture
CLCI:FAE Job Band: 5

Job Description
Art exhibition organisers plan, arrange and supervise the setting up of exhibitions, usually in an art gallery, museum or studio. Displays can be of paintings, ceramics, prints, textiles, jewellery and of books by artists. They design publicity material, promote events and handle funding. Organisers carry out research, advise customers and liaise with artists/exhibitors and other galleries. They may also negotiate with other collections for loans of artefacts. Plans and organises opening events to advertise the exhibition and organises the transport of items, insurance and security. Receives deliveries, deals with framing, hanging, packing and any claims for damage.

They also keep detailed information on each exhibit and also of any sales, if appropriate. Checks all details and liaises with curators, artists and exhibition staff to ensure that the exhibition runs efficiently. Supervises the health and safety requirements to ensure visitors and staff can leave the area quickly and safely if necessary.

Work Details
Usually works a basic 35-37.5 hr week, though some evening and weekend work may be necessary. Works in an office and at the exhibition site, often away from the office. May work with colleagues such as curators and marketing specialists.

Work may be demanding at times and you often have to work long hours, especially in the run up to an exhibition. You are responsible for the mounting and display of exhibits and for overall management, including budget management, marketing and administration. There may be some lifting and bending and working with ladders.

Qualification
- **England, Wales and Northern Ireland**

Band 5: For degree courses: 2-3 A levels and some GCSEs (A*-C) usually including English and maths, or equivalent. Exact requirements depend on the degree you take.

- **Scotland**

Band 5: For degree courses: 3-5 H grades and some S grades (1-3), including English and maths, or similar qualifications. Exact requirements depend on the degree you take.

Degree Information
Any degree discipline is acceptable for entry to this job. Subjects that give useful background knowledge include applied arts, fine art and history of art. Some knowledge of business studies, marketing or administration is an advantage.

Adult Qualifications
Entry requirements may be relaxed for adults applying for higher education courses. Access or foundation courses provide those without the required qualifications a route onto degree courses.

Work Experience
Entry to this job is competitive and it is important you try to do some relevant work experience before applying for jobs. This includes arts administration and working in a museum or art gallery in a different role or on a voluntary basis. Events management also gives you the opportunity to gain relevant organisational and networking skills.

Entry and Training
Entrants are usually graduates and many also have postgraduate qualifications. A foundation course in art and design, arts and events management or art and design enterprise followed by a specialised degree is common, and courses such as art galleries administration are available. Most job entrants have some previous training and practical experience in a related area of work, such as sales and marketing. Often specialist knowledge, related to the interests of the gallery, is required and short courses or relevant foundation degrees are available.

There is also an NVQ at Level 4 in cultural heritage and at Level 5 in cultural heritage management. Other useful courses include those in business studies, conference and exhibition management or promotions and events management, which are offered at some specialised colleges. The Diploma in creative and media may be a helpful start and in Scotland, there may be a modern apprenticship in culural heritage available.

Training is often on the job, working with an experienced person. Some exhibition administrators choose to become members of the Association of Event Organisers Limited (AEO), which offers short courses and training events on aspects of organising an exhibition, including sales, sponsorship, promotion and marketing opportunities, and health and safety. The Museums Association also runs regular relevant events. Organisers often become members of the Visual Arts & Galleries Association.

Mature entrants are welcomed and often personality and experience are more important than academic qualifications. Many galleries welcome adults with business and marketing experience. Relevant experience is important, so adults with an appropriate background in art and design or museum work may have an advantage.

Opportunities and Pay
Jobs are available mainly in towns and cities. Employers are usually a private gallery or a local/national gallery, but some galleries are run by local authorities. You may be employed on short contracts for specific projects and there may be opportunities to work part time. This is a small profession and there are few vacancies, so obtaining a first position may be difficult. Many experienced people work freelance on particular contracts.

Pay varies depending on location and employer, but salaries start at around £16k-£20k rising to £28k a year with experience. Those in senior gallery positions can earn £35k-£60k a year.

Health

This job will require good general fitness and normal colour vision to help with installing exhibitions.

Skills and Qualities

able to manage people, able to work to a budget, able to work to deadlines, aptitude for teamwork, creative flair, good communication skills, imaginative, methodical, networking skills, problem-solving skills, project management skills

Relevant Subjects

Art and Design, Business and accounting, Classical studies, English, History, Media and communication studies

Further Information

Arts Council - www.artscouncil.org.uk

Creative & Cultural Skills - sector skills council for advertising, crafts, cultural heritage, design, literature, music, performing & visual arts - www.ccskills.org.uk

Diplomas (Foundation, Higher and Advanced) - http://yp.direct.gov.uk/diplomas

Museums Association - www.museumsassociation.org

▶Working in art & design (2009) (Babcock Lifeskills) - www.babcock-lifeskills.com/

▶Working in business, administration & finance (2010) (Babcock Lifeskills) - www.babcock-lifeskills.com/

▶Working in cultural heritage (2007) (Babcock Lifeskills) - www.babcock-lifeskills.com/

Addresses

Arts Council of England
National Service Centre, The Hive, 49 Lever Street, Manchester M1 1FN
Phone: 0845 300 6200 (UK only)
Web: www.artscouncil.org.uk

Arts Council of Northern Ireland
77 Malone Road, Belfast BT9 6AQ
Phone: +44 (0)28 9038 5200
Web: www.artscouncil-ni.org

Arts Council of Wales
Bute Place, Cardiff CF10 5AL
Phone: 0845 8734 900 (UK only)
Web: www.artswales.org

Arts Marketing Association (AMA)
7a Clifton Court, Clifton Road, Cambridge CB1 7BN
Phone: +44 (0)1223 578078
Web: www.a-m-a.org.uk

Association of Event Organisers Ltd (AEO)
119 High Street, Berkhamsted, Hertfordshire HP4 2DJ
Phone: +44 (0)1442 285810
Web: www.aeo.org.uk

Scottish Arts Council
12 Manor Place, Edinburgh EH3 7DD
Phone: +44 (0)131 226 6051
Web: www.scottisharts.org.uk

Visual Arts & Galleries Association (VAGA)
The Old Village School Witcham, Ely, Cambridgeshire CB6 2LQ
Phone: +44 (0)1353 776356
Web: www.vaga.co.uk

Similar Jobs

Arts Administrator, Conservator-Restorer, Event & Exhibition Organiser, Exhibition Designer, Museum/Art Gallery Curator, Project Manager

Art Therapist

also known as: Art Psychotherapist

CRCI:Healthcare
CLCI:JOD

Job Band: 5

Job Description

Art therapy is a form of psychotherapy which uses artistic activities to help people who have emotional, physical or psychological problems. People referred to art therapists often cannot communicate easily with others or may have lost touch with their feelings. Therapists encourage their clients to express themselves, clarify their feelings and relieve tension through a variety of basic art materials, such as paint and paper, clay and collage. Art therapy is particularly helpful for younger children who may not be able to communicate well through speech. Therapists work on a one-to-one basis with individuals or groups of clients, helping them to create and understand images and develop personally and emotionally.

May also use art techniques to help medical staff make a diagnosis, or to assess mental or emotional disorders and pinpoint special problems. Can work in a variety of settings, such as palliative care and hospices, hospitals, special education units, forensic medicine and the prison service, child guidance clinics, family or marital therapy clinics, and drug or alcohol dependency units.

Work Details

Usually work 37 hrs a week; Monday to Friday, but may include some evening and weekend work. Art therapists work with all kinds of people, including those with learning difficulties, children, the elderly, people with physical impairment, those with eating disorders or who have progressive conditions such as HIV/Aids, Alzheimer's or Parkinson's disease, psychiatric patients or people in prison. You counsel people in need of support, who may be depressed, aggressive, anxious or upset. Therapists help people to express their thoughts and feelings through art work. Work can be emotionally demanding.

Qualification

- **England, Wales and Northern Ireland**

Band 5: For degree followed by a postgraduate qualification: 2-3 A levels and some GCSEs (A*-C), usually including English and maths, or equivalent. Exact requirements depend on the degree you take.

- **Scotland**

Band 5: For degree followed by postgraduate qualification: 3-5 H grades and some S grades (1-3), usually including English and maths, or similar qualifications. Exact requirements depend on the degree you take.

Degree Information

A degree in an art and design subject, fine art/visual art, or creative and expressive therapies is usually required for entry to the postgraduate course. However, applicants with degrees or professional qualifications in occupational therapy, psychology, education, nursing, medicine or social work may also be considered for the postgraduate course. A list of institutions offering validated qualifications can be obtained from the British Association of Art Therapists.

Adult Qualifications

Entry requirements for courses leading to a first degree or equivalent qualification in art or a related field may be relaxed for mature applicants. Contact individual universities and colleges for details of special entry standards for adults. Entry to postgraduate courses in art therapy is very competitive but many applicants are mature students.

Work Experience
Entry to this career is highly competitive and it is essential that you have some relevant work or voluntary experience before applying. Experience in the caring professions or working with people in a helping capacity is useful. BAAT states that many universities require an applicant to have completed a set number of hours working with those who have mental health difficulties, disabilities or related problems.

Entry and Training
You need to complete a postgraduate diploma or a masters course approved by the British Association of Art Therapists (BAAT). Applicants to the postgraduate course are usually art and design graduates or qualified art teachers, although other graduates or those with relevant professional qualifications, such as social workers, teachers and psychologists are also considered. Several institutions offer two-year full-time courses or part-time courses over three years. A few preliminary foundation courses, and full or part-time specialist MA courses are also available. Candidates are expected to present a portfolio of recent art work.

Most students are in their late 20s or early 30s. Before postgraduate training, some experience in a relevant field is required; this can include caring work, education, community work or experiential workshops. Students usually finance their own training courses, although a few are seconded by employers. Art therapists are required to possess the postgraduate diploma in art therapy or art psychology to become state registered with the Health Professions Council and BAAT, and must undertake continuing professional development (CPD) to maintain competence as a therapist.

BAAT offers specialised short courses and workshops to support CPD. There is also a one-day 'Introduction to the Profession of Art Therapy' course, designed for potential entrants to the profession, and a one-week Art Therapy Foundation Course, for potential entrants and healthcare workers who want to gain a better understanding of art within a care context. Contact BAAT for details on routes to qualification and a list of the seven accredited courses in the UK.

A Diploma/Welsh Baccalaureate may be available in your area in society, health and development. The advanced level is equivalent to 3.5 A levels but for some university courses, the additional and specialist learning (ASL) component of the diploma needs to include specific A levels. Check entry requirements carefully with the individual institutions.

Mature entrants are often those who have worked in a related area, such as social care, art and design or occupational therapy. Most students are in their late 20s or early 30s. Maturity is seen as an asset and it may be possible to get sponsorship for postgraduate courses from some employers, or to receive financial help from relevant medical trusts and charity organisations. It is possible to gain an art therapy or psychotherapy degree through a part-time course.

Opportunities and Pay
This is a small, but developing profession of around 2,500 people in the UK. Jobs are available mainly in cities or large towns and most art therapists work in the NHS. You can also work in a social services or education department, the prison service or perhaps a voluntary organisation. Work is available in trauma clinics, maybe with those who have head or stroke injuries, in drug and alcohol services, palliative care and hospices and in forensic medicine and psychiatry. Some specialise in working with children, teenagers or adults, particularly the elderly.

Experienced therapists may move into a training, supervisory or management role. Others go on to take further training in psychotherapy. This job is particularly suitable for part-time work, self-employment or employment on a sessional basis, and there are opportunities to work overseas.

Pay depends largely on the type of employer, but may be on a nationally agreed scale. You may be paid by fees and not by a regular salary. A newly qualified art therapist working for the NHS earns from £25k a year, rising to £34k-£38k with experience. Art therapist principals can earn up to £46k a year. Jobs in London and the South East attract an additional allowance and cost of living supplement.

Health
This job requires normal colour vision.

Skills and Qualities
able to put people at ease, artistic ability, emotionally strong, encouraging, flexible approach, good communication skills, good interpersonal skills, patient, resourceful, tactful

Relevant Subjects
Art and Design, Biology, English, Health and social care, Psychology, Sociology

Further Information
Art therapy career information pack (BAAT) (The British Association of Art Therapists) - www.baat.org/career.html

Diplomas (Foundation, Higher and Advanced) - http://yp.direct.gov.uk/diplomas

Health Professions Council (HPC) - www.hpc-uk.org

International Journal of Art Therapy (Routledge) - www.informaworld.com

NHS Careers (NHS Careers) - www.nhscareers.nhs.uk

NHS Careers Scotland - www.infoscotland.com/nhs

NHS Careers Wales - www.wales.nhs.uk

Welsh Baccalaureate - www.wbq.org.uk

Addresses
British Association of Art Therapists (BAAT)
24-27 White Lion Street, London N1 9PD
Phone: +44 (0)20 7686 4216
Web: www.baat.org

Northern Ireland Group for Art as Therapy (NIGAT)
c/o Centre for Psychotherapy, Shimna House, Knockbracken Healthcare Park, Saintfield Road, Belfast BT8 8BH
Web: www.nigat.org

Similar Jobs
Dramatherapist, Music Therapist, Occupational Therapist, Psychologist, Psychotherapist, Teacher: Art

Artist
also known as: Fine Artist, Painter
CRCI:Design, Arts and Crafts
CLCI:ED Job Band: 3 to 5

Job Description
Artists create fine art consisting of original pictures and designs using a variety of techniques and materials. They may specialise in a particular medium, for example oil, watercolour or ink, and in a subject matter, such as portraits, landscapes or still life, or use a combination of materials. Some take commissions from clients such as commercial companies, large organisations, publishing companies, or private individuals, for which they need to do research, make sketches and work to a brief. The finished art work may be for an entrance foyer or board room of a company building, an illustrated book cover, a retirement or wedding gift or other celebratory present.

Some artists provide educational art demonstration workshops for people of all ages, or secure a position in a school as an 'artist in residence'. Most artists sell their work through exhibitions, competitions, contact with shops, art galleries and museums, book publishers, or on the Internet through art websites and online art galleries.

Work Details

Self-employed artists usually choose the hours they work, which can be long or irregular, since the work is often combined with other full or part-time employment. May work indoors in a studio/workshop or outside, on location. Many artists work from home and may choose to work in the evenings and at weekends. Some schools and institutions employ artists-in-residence, who work a basic 35-40 hrs a week, Monday to Friday, though may be expected to work longer hours to complete a project, or to help set up an exhibition. Artists may have to promote their work and negotiate with dealers, shop/gallery owners and organisers of exhibitions.

Qualification

• England, Wales and Northern Ireland

Band 3: For entry to jobs, HNC in art and design or a relevant Diploma, usually at least 4 GCSEs (A*-C) including English and maths, or equivalent. For some diploma in foundation studies courses: usually at least 5 GCSEs (A*-C) or equivalent.

Band 4: For diploma in foundation studies (art & design): usually at least one A level and 4 GCSEs (A*-C). For BTEC higher national award: a BTEC national award, successful completion of a foundation studies course, or equivalent qualification.

Band 5: For degree courses: 2-3 A levels and some GCSEs (A*-C) usually including English and maths, or equivalent. Most students take a foundation studies course first. Exact requirements depend on the degree you take.

• Scotland

Band 3: For entry: usually at least four S grades (1-3), including English and maths, or similar.

Band 4: For entry to SQA higher national and professional development awards, usually 2-3 H grades and some S grades (1-3), including English and maths, or similar qualifications.

Band 5: For degree courses: 3-5 H grades and some S grades (1-3) usually including English and maths, or similar qualifications. Exact requirements depend on the degree you take.

Degree Information

Relevant degrees include fine art, applied art, fine art painting, and fine art contemporary media. Course titles and content vary, so check prospectuses carefully. There are also postgraduate courses available in fine art.

Adult Qualifications

Mature applicants with outstanding portfolios of work may be accepted for courses without the standard entry requirements. There are Access and foundation courses or similar in some areas, which give adults without qualifications a route into degree courses. Check with individual institutions.

Work Experience

Entry to this job/career is highly competitive and it is essential you have some relevant work or voluntary experience before applying. As most artists are self-employed and often self taught, it is difficult to gain direct relevant work experience. However experience in a publishing company, design studio or art gallery is relevant and helps to build up a good portfolio of work. Many aspiring artists join local art clubs and societies to widen their knowledge.

Entry and Training

Many artists are self-taught and whilst talent is very important, most artists also have formal training. Exceptional ability is needed for entry to most art courses and you have to provide a portfolio of work. Most artists are educated to HNC/HND or degree level and entry to reputable art courses is highly competitive. Talented applicants without qualifications can occasionally obtain college places with an exceptional portfolio of work. Check course requirements carefully.

Students usually take a foundation course in art and design before taking a three-year degree course. A foundation degree is also available in fine art and there are distance-learning courses available. In Scotland, degree courses last for four years, the first year is general before specialising in a particular area of art and design.

Mentoring from an established artist is very helpful. Membership of the Association of Illustrators (AOI) may be useful and the Artists Information Company website is also a good source of information. The Crafts Council fund a scheme to provide graduates with space to work, funds for materials and advice from established artists. Grants may also be available from the Arts Council.

Mature applicants need a good portfolio of work for entry to art and design courses at a college or university. There are part-time courses available for mature students over 21. Work experience in the art and design field is an advantage. Distance learning in art and design is also available at various levels of qualification, including those offered by the Open College of the Arts or the London Art College. Some private courses may be costly and you should choose carefully.

There is a wide range of courses available at adult education centres and colleges that offer day/evening art and design courses.

Opportunities and Pay

There is no recognised career path for artists. Success depends on what you are able to sell and on your reputation. There is strong competition for work and opportunities are limited. Some start work as an artist's or studio assistant. Many artists are self-employed, though few can support themselves solely by selling their work. It can take many years, often with little income, to build up a reputation. Most have supplementary jobs such as teaching, advertising, community art work, art therapy or art administration. Many are in gallery and sale room work, exhibition organising, or conservation and restoration.

Income varies according to ability and reputation and well-established artists can earn considerable salaries. Some artists enter into business arrangements with dealers and galleries, as well as with agents, who charge commission fees.

Health

Good eyesight is needed and an appreciation of colour is important, so normal colour vision is preferable.

Skills and Qualities

able to cope under pressure, able to withstand criticism, artistic ability, creative flair, dedicated, eye for shape/colour, good communication skills, hand-to-eye co-ordination, imaginative, self-disciplined

Relevant Subjects

Art and Design

Further Information

Artists & Illustrators (The Chelsea Magazine Co. Ltd.) - www.artistsandillustrators.co.uk/

Artists Information Company - www.a-n.co.uk

Artist's Magazine (F&W Media Inc.) - www.artistsnetwork.com/artistsmagazine/

Creative & Cultural Skills - sector skills council for advertising, crafts, cultural heritage, design, literature, music, performing & visual arts - www.ccskills.org.uk

Creative People - www.creativepeople.org.uk

NSEAD: Careers in Art, Craft & Design (National Society for Education in Art and Design) - www.nsead.org/resources/careers.aspx

Real Life Guide to Creative Industries (Trotman 2009) - www.trotman.co.uk

The Artists Fees Toolkit (Richard Murphy) (Artists Information Company) - www.a-n.co.uk/knowledge_bank/article/203835

▶ Working in art & design (2009) (Babcock Lifeskills) - www.babcock-lifeskills.com/

Writers' & Artists' Yearbook (A&C Black) (A&C Black) - www.writersandartists.co.uk

Addresses

Arts Council of England
National Service Centre, The Hive, 49 Lever Street, Manchester M1 1FN
Phone: 0845 300 6200 (UK only)
Web: www.artscouncil.org.uk

Arts Council of Northern Ireland
77 Malone Road, Belfast BT9 6AQ
Phone: +44 (0)28 9038 5200
Web: www.artscouncil-ni.org

Arts Council of Wales
Bute Place, Cardiff CF10 5AL
Phone: 0845 8734 900 (UK only)
Web: www.artswales.org

Association of Illustrators (AOI)
2nd Floor, Back Building, 150 Curtain Road, London EC2A 3AT
Phone: +44 (0)20 7613 4328
Web: www.theaoi.com

Crafts Council (CC)
44a Pentonville Road, Islington, London N1 9BY
Phone: +44 (0)20 7806 2500
Web: www.craftscouncil.org.uk

London Art College
PO Box 22, Milnthorpe LA7 7WY
Phone: 0800 3280 465 (UK only)
Web: www.londonartcollege.co.uk

National Society for Education in Art and Design (NSEAD)
3 Masons Wharf Potley Lane, Corsham, Wiltshire SN13 9FY
Phone: +44 (0)1225 810134
Web: www.nsead.org

Open College of the Arts
Michael Young Arts Centre, Redbrook Business Park, Wilthorpe Road, Barnsley S75 1JN
Phone: 0800 731 2116 (UK only)
Web: www.oca-uk.com

Scottish Arts Council
12 Manor Place, Edinburgh EH3 7DD
Phone: +44 (0)131 226 6051
Web: www.scottisharts.org.uk

Similar Jobs

Art Therapist, Graphic Designer, Illustrator, Photographer, Sculptor, Teacher: Art, Website Designer

Arts Administrator

also known as: Arts Manager, Festival Organiser

CRCI:Languages, Information and Culture
CLCI:GAV Job Band: 4 to 5

Job Description

Arts administrators are responsible for organising and promoting artistic, musical or cultural events and activities, on behalf of theatres, orchestras, art galleries, concert halls, museums and arts centres and other cultural organisations. They liaise closely with performers, artistic directors/promoters and venue managers and can specialise in different areas, such as marketing, publicity, fundraising or finance. Administrators may arrange a schedule of programmes for concerts, festivals or tours. They also plan exhibitions, buy equipment, make grant applications and book artists/musicians.

Some administrators also find venues, handle publicity and ticket sales, and perhaps arrange sponsorship. They manage and supervise staff, with some responsibility for recruitment and training. Work closely with local/national newspapers, TV and radio and may write contributions for event related publicity.

Work Details

Hours vary but you may work long, irregular hours and some evenings or weekends. This job is office based but you may have to travel widely and perhaps work on sites away from home. Duties vary according to the type of job, but you need good general administrative, organising, financial and budgeting skills. Many organisations in this field need to secure funding from the Arts Councils or from sponsors, so good negotiating skills are important. Also requires specialist knowledge of the arts, cultural and creative industries.

Qualification

- **England, Wales and Northern Ireland**

Band 4: For HND, Diploma of Higher Education or relevant foundation degree: 1-2 A levels and some GCSEs (A*-C) usually including English and maths, or equivalent.

Band 5: For degree courses: 2-3 A levels and some GCSEs (A*-C) usually including English and maths, or equivalent. Exact requirements depend on the degree you take.

- **Scotland**

Band 4: For entry to SQA higher national and professional development awards, usually 2-3 H grades and some S grades (1-3), including English and maths, or similar qualifications.

Band 5: For degree courses: 3-5 H grades and some S grades (1-3), including English and maths, or similar qualifications. Exact requirements depend on the degree you take.

Degree Information

Usually specialist knowledge in one field of the arts is expected for this job, so appropriate degree subjects include applied arts, fine art, history of art, drama and music. Some universities offer an arts and/or events management degree. Any business management or administration degree, provided you can show an in-depth knowledge of the arts, is acceptable. There are also relevant foundations degrees and some postgraduate diplomas and MA/MSc courses in arts administration. Some of these may require relevant work experience.

Adult Qualifications

For a career in arts administration, previous experience in at least one arts sector is very important. Academic requirements may be waived for experienced applicants, especially those with a performing or production background. Some colleges run HNC/HND courses in arts/events management or arts administration, and mature students with relevant experience may be accepted. Foundation degrees in community arts and arts mangement may be helpful.

Work Experience

Work experience gives you an insight into what you enjoy and do not enjoy about a job or working environment, as well as the opportunity to acquire new skills. It also provides valuable information to add to your CV and improves any course application and/or your future employment prospects. Entry to this job is competitive. Relevant experience may include work in an art gallery or theatre, taking temporary work with arts festivals or involvement with an amateur production. Office administration and computer skills are also useful.

Entry and Training

Many entrants to arts administration have an arts degree supplemented by specific short courses, though there is no particular career structure or training for this job. Entrants come from a wide variety of backgrounds and you usually train on the job. It is usual for administrators to have specialised knowledge of their area of work, perhaps from working as an artist or performer, plus business or teaching experience and training. Experience can be built up from work with student theatre or orchestras and from holiday jobs.

There are also postgraduate courses available in subjects such as visual arts enterprise and enterprise in art and design for the creative arts, and specialist HND courses, for example in music industry management. Useful training courses include those offered by the Arts Marketing Association and the Independent Theatre Council, and include fundraising, project budgeting, arts marketing, venue management, negotiating and contracts.

Creative & Cultural Skills is the Sector Skills Council for advertising, crafts, cultural heritage, design, music, performing, literary and visual arts, and coordinates and promotes training and skills development. The Cultural Leadership Programme is a government-funded initiative promoting excellence in leadership in creative and cultural industries.

You are expected to continue your professional development throughout your career to keep up to date in areas that include law, accountancy, human resources, and marketing. There are also options to work for S/NVQs level 3 in business administration and in cultural heritage management.

Relevant training programmes, including creative apprenticeship schemes in community arts management, may be available in your area and provide an alternative route into this career. Advanced apprenticeships leading to qualification at level 3 can be a route into higher education. The Museums, Libraries and Archives Council has pledged funding for up to 50 apprenticeships in museums over the next two years. There are also relevant foundation degrees and a Diploma in creative and media. In Scotland, there is a modern apprenticeship in cultural heritage which may be helpful.

Mature entrants may find it useful to have previous professional experience in a relevant field, such as business administration, accounting, the arts or management. Skills in bookkeeping and word processing are also useful.

Opportunities and Pay

Despite the economic downturn, the arts industry is growing but competition for jobs is still strong. Employers include regional arts councils, theatres, concert halls, dance companies, local festival committees, orchestras, community programmes or organisations such as regional arts projects and national Arts Councils. Jobs are mainly in cities and large towns. Promotion is usually gained by moving to another, larger organisation where there are opportunities to specialise in programming, sponsorship or public relations. The British Council employs administrative staff, some of whom may have overseas responsibility for displaying British art. Part-time work is common and freelance work as a consultant is possible, particularly for lottery-funded projects and increasingly with European arts companies.

Salaries vary widely, but new entrants generally earn £15k-£17k a year, increasing to £20k-£30k a year when experienced. More senior or strategic posts can pay up to £50k a year. Freelance work may be more highly paid depending on the contract. Some administrators move on to work in general management or to work for international arts projects.

Skills and Qualities

able to work to a budget, commercial awareness, creative flair, flexible approach, good communication skills, good organisational skills, good telephone manner, information handling skills, IT skills, networking skills, project management skills

Relevant Subjects

Art and Design, Business and accounting, Economics, English, History, Leisure, travel and tourism, Mathematics, Media and communication studies, Music, Performing arts

Further Information

Apprenticeship Schemes (National Apprenticeship Service) - www.apprenticeships.org.uk

British Arts Festivals Association (BAFA) (British Arts Festival Association (BAFA)) - www.artsfestivals.co.uk

British Council - www.britishcouncil.org

Creative & Cultural Skills - sector skills council for advertising, crafts, cultural heritage, design, literature, music, performing & visual arts - www.ccskills.org.uk

Diplomas (Foundation, Higher and Advanced) - http://yp.direct.gov.uk/diplomas

Knowledge Services for Arts Management - www.ksam.org.uk

National Association of Local Government Arts Officers (NALGAO) - www.nalgao.org.uk

The Artists' Information Company - www.a-n.co.uk

▶ Working in creative & media (2007) (Babcock Lifeskills) - www.babcock-lifeskills.com/

Addresses

Arts Council of England
National Service Centre, The Hive, 49 Lever Street, Manchester M1 1FN
Phone: 0845 300 6200 (UK only)
Web: www.artscouncil.org.uk

Arts Council of Northern Ireland
77 Malone Road, Belfast BT9 6AQ
Phone: +44 (0)28 9038 5200
Web: www.artscouncil-ni.org

Arts Council of Wales
Bute Place, Cardiff CF10 5AL
Phone: 0845 8734 900 (UK only)
Web: www.artswales.org

Arts Marketing Association (AMA)
7a Clifton Court, Clifton Road, Cambridge CB1 7BN
Phone: +44 (0)1223 578078
Web: www.a-m-a.org.uk

Independent Theatre Council (ITC)
12 The Leathermarket Weston Street, London SE1 3ER
Phone: +44 (0)20 7403 1727
Web: www.itc-arts.org

Museums, Libraries and Archives Council (MLA)
Grosvenor House, 14 Bennetts Hill, Birmingham B2 5RS
Phone: +44 (0)121 345 7300
Web: www.mla.gov.uk

Scottish Arts Council
12 Manor Place, Edinburgh EH3 7DD
Phone: +44 (0)131 226 6051
Web: www.scottisharts.org.uk

Similar Jobs

Art Exhibitions Organiser, Charity Fundraiser, Event & Exhibition Organiser, Museum/Art Gallery Curator, Public Relations Officer, Volunteer Manager

Assembler: Light Industry

also known as: Production Fitter

CRCI:Manufacturing and Production
CLCI:SAB Job Band: 1 to 2

Job Description

Assemblers work in light industrial premises, often on an assembly line, putting together parts to make completed products. They help with the production of everyday goods such as cars, electrical goods, telephones, furniture, lawn mowers, and computer equipment. May sit at a workbench or conveyor belt system fitting together parts of each product or, if working on large products such as cars and aeroplanes, stands and walks round the part. Some work can be simple and routine; other work requires following detailed diagrams and instructions. Assemblers use powered screwdrivers and also hand tools such as pliers and spanners to be able to work more quickly. They also use soldering irons, drills and microscopes for some of their work.

Assemblers can have other duties such as monitoring the production line and making simple quality checks. Reporting any faults or problems in the assembly process to a line manager is important.

Work Details

Assemblers usually work around 37-40 hrs a week from Monday to Friday. May be required to work shifts that include early starts, late finishes and weekend work. Part-time work is possible. Usually works in factories, which can sometimes be noisy. The work may require you to sit in one place for a long time or stand all day. In certain jobs you may have to do some lifting. Sometimes there are accidents with machines and you may have to wear special boots, safety glasses or gloves to protect you.

Qualification

• England, Wales and Northern Ireland

Band 1: You do not require formal qualifications to do this work though an employer may ask you to take a practical test to assess your manual dexterity. However, some formal/vocational qualifications at any level are useful.

Band 2: Although academic qualifications are not specified for this job, it is an advantage to have some GCSEs (A*-C) in subjects that include English, technology and maths, or equivalent.

• Scotland

Band 1: You do not require formal qualifications to do this work though an employer may ask you to take a practical test to assess your manual dexterity. However, some formal/vocational qualifications at any level are useful.

Band 2: Although academic qualifications are not specified for this job, it is an advantage to have some S grades (1-3) in subjects that include English, maths and a technical subject or similar.

Adult Qualifications

No pre-entry qualifications are usually required though some academic/vocational qualifications at any level may be an advantage. English and maths are useful subjects.

Work Experience

Work or voluntary experience is always useful. It can add to your CV and improve your chances when applying for jobs or apprenticeships in the manufacturing industry. Your personal or adult guidance adviser should be able to advise you about how to get some work experience.

Entry and Training

It is possible to enter this job at 16 though you have to be over 18 for shift work. You may have to take a test to show that you can work well with your hands. Training usually starts with a short course about the company and on health and safety. Then you train either on the job, working beside someone with experience, or at a training centre. Your training can last from a day to a few weeks. Some employers give day release for a relevant course. Training programmes, including apprenticeship schemes, may be available in your area. Advanced apprenticeships leading to qualification at level 3 can also be a route into higher education.

Various relevant S/NVQs may be available depending on the type of light industry work. For instance there are S/NVQs at levels 1-2 in performing manufacturing operations and at levels 2-3 in electrical assembly or installation. A Diploma/Welsh Baccalaureate in either engineering or manufacturing and product design may be available in your area.

Government training opportunities, such as apprenticeships, may be available in your area. You can also gain recognition of previous experience through Accreditation of Prior Learning (APL) or by working towards relevant S/NVQs. Contact your local careers office, Jobcentre Plus, Next Step service or Learning and Skills Council (LSC) Local Enterprise Company (LEC) for details of training schemes.

Opportunities and Pay

There are around 400,000 people employed in assembly work in the UK at the moment. You usually work for a manufacturing company or a firm that supplies assembled parts to them. Once you have experience, you can become a charge hand or a supervisor. You may be able to go on to train as an engineering craft worker. However, opportunities at assembler level in some industries continue to decline. This is due to the increasing use of automatic assembly processes and importation of ready-assembled units.

Pay depends on the employer. Starting wages are likely to be around £10k-£12k a year, rising to £14k-£15k a year when experienced. Supervisors can earn up to £20k a year. Overtime and shift work can increase your earnings.

Health

You need good eyesight in jobs where you work with very small parts. Sometimes good colour vision is also needed.

Skills and Qualities

able to follow drawings and plans, able to follow instructions, able to work quickly, accurate, aptitude for teamwork, good concentration level, manual dexterity, methodical, practical skills, prepared to do repetitive tasks

Relevant Subjects

Manufacturing

Further Information

Apprenticeship Schemes (National Apprenticeship Service) - www.apprenticeships.org.uk

Diplomas (Foundation, Higher and Advanced) - http://yp.direct.gov.uk/diplomas

SEMTA - sector skills council for science, engineering and manufacturing technologies - www.semta.org.uk

Tomorrow's Engineers - www.tomorrowsengineers.org.uk/careers.cfm

Training Schemes - www.direct.gov.uk/en/educationandlearning

Welsh Baccalaureate - www.wbq.org.uk

Addresses

Engineering Training Council (NI)
Interpoint, 20-24 York Street, Belfast BT15 1AQ
Phone: +44 (0)28 9032 9878
Web: www.etcni.org.uk

Scottish Engineering
Training Officer, 105 West George Street, Glasgow G2 1QL
Phone: +44 (0)141 221 3181
Web: www.scottishengineering.org.uk

Similar Jobs

Electronics Assembler, Engineering Machine Operative, Packer: General, Warehouse Order Picker/Assembler, Welder

Astronaut

CRCI:Science, Mathematics and Statistics
CLCI:RAC Job Band: 5

Job Description

Astronauts train to travel and work in space, although most of the time is spent on the ground. They are usually highly trained scientists or pilots of jet fighters with many flight hours logged. They fly and dock space vehicles and carry out scientific research and technical operations during the mission. Also repair, maintain and install space stations in orbit around the Earth. A few are pilots who fly the space shuttles.

Mission specialists carry out a range of experiments and research in the space station. The laboratory work focuses on research into fluid physics, materials and life sciences, for example the effects of radiation and weightlessness. They also observe the Earth and collect data to help our understanding of the ozone layer and other features that affect the planet.

A British astronaut was selected in 2009 to join a highly select group of international astronauts from member states of Europe. They are trained at the European Astronaut Centre (EAC) in Cologne, Germany, to man the International Space Station (ISS). Many who train for space travel do not actually go into space but carry out research and development work as part of a large ground team.

Work Details

At the EAC you work around 37 hours a week, Monday to Friday. You may go on only one or two space missions during your entire career. The preparation and missions themselves are physically and mentally demanding. You need to be able to work in very unusual conditions, including zero gravity and outside the space station, which may cause physical exhaustion. In space, you live and work with a small group of similarly trained people for up to 6 months at a time. There is the risk of a strain on normal family life. You need to wear protective and specialised clothing, especially on missions and during certain training exercises.

Qualification

• England, Wales and Northern Ireland

Band 5: For degree courses: 2-3 A levels and some GCSEs (A*-C) usually including English and maths, or equivalent. Exact requirements depend on the degree you take.

• Scotland

Band 5: For degree courses: 3-5 H grades and some S grades (1-3), usually including English and maths, or similar qualifications. Exact requirements depend on the degree you take.

Degree Information

A degree in a physical or natural science subject or medicine, engineering, information technology or maths is most useful. Postgraduate qualifications are usually expected.

Adult Qualifications

Entry requirements may be relaxed for adults applying for higher education courses. Access or foundation courses provide those without the required qualifications a route onto degree courses.

Work Experience

It is impossible to have work experience for this job, but experience as a diver or a pilot is valuable. The selection process identifies candidates who have experience of working in tightly knit teams and who show resilience in survival situations. Many astronauts in the American space programme have a background in scouting.

Entry and Training

The selection process for astronaut training is hugely rigorous and the opportunities extremely limited. Medical and psychological tests are a constant feature of your training and ongoing throughout your career.

All candidates should have a first degree, and many mission specialists also have a PhD. Sciences, especially physics, life sciences, engineering, maths and related subjects are very important. At least three years at a very high level of scientific, technological or military work is usually required prior to application for astronaut training.

Budding astronauts should look at the European Space Agency (ESA) website for details of its astronaut programme, which selects and trains European astronauts. The UK is a member of ESA so UK nationals can apply to take part. Priority is usually given to candidates from countries that fund the manned space missions. Current UK space policy supports unmanned, robotic missions, so the UK does not fund the ESA human space flight programme. However, in 2009 a British helicopter pilot with 18 years military flight experience was accepted onto the latest International Space Station (ISS) programme. The four previous British astronauts, one of whom was a woman, have either had to secure private funding or change nationality to be part of Russian or American programmes.

The training programme is in three parts over about 3.5 years. You first complete a year of basic training, during which you learn about space technology and science, basic medical skills, and how the ISS works. You may also learn to scuba dive as preparation for space walking. On successful completion of this year, you spend the second year learning more about the ISS, the experiments and the transport vehicles, and the involvement of ground control. Then you may be assigned to a mission, during which you work with the other crew members and learn about special tasks. You also become familiar with weightlessness doing parabolic flights.

You spend most of your time during training and once qualified in ground based work, as space flight is extremely costly and missions are rare. Over several years, you get to know your colleagues very well. You visit training centres in the USA, Russia, Japan, Canada and Europe. Fluent Russian is an advantage and the EAC offers lessons. English is the official language of the EAC.

Astronauts do not qualify straight from either undergraduate or postgraduate university courses, but from a career in another field, for example as a pilot in the armed forces or experience in a specialist scientific field. A pilot's licence or scuba diving expertise are useful, as is a commitment to rigorous physical fitness.

Opportunities and Pay

You spend most of your time during training and once qualified in ground based work, as space flight is extremely costly and missions are rare. The ESA plans to have a European astronaut flying an ISS mission every two years up to 2015 and beyond. This is in preparation for projected human exploration of the Moon and Mars.

While opportunities to be an astronaut are rare, there are other careers in the space industry. The UK is a world leader in space technology and science. Consult the Space Careers website for more information. Many astronauts move into management or research and development roles in space or similar organisations when they are no longer able to fly. There may also be teaching and media opportunities.

Salaries vary but range from around £44k to £75k a year. Allowances may also be available.

Health

Applicants must pass very strict medical tests before being accepted and there are regular medical check-ups throughout your career. You must have excellent levels of mental and physical fitness and stamina for this job.

Skills and Qualities

able to communicate effectively, able to cope under pressure, able to follow procedures, able to live and work closely with other people, able to use complex equipment, able to work in confined spaces, adventurous, aptitude for maths and science, problem-solving skills, resilient, willing to work in remote locations

Relevant Subjects
Biology, Chemistry, Design and technology, Engineering, English, ICT/Computer studies, Mathematics, Physical education and sport, Physics, Science

Further Information
European Space Agency (European Space Agency) - www.esa.int
NASA (National Aeronautics and Space Administration) - www.nasa.gov
National Space Centre Online - www.spacecentre.co.uk/
SEMTA - sector skills council for science, engineering and manufacturing technologies - www.semta.org.uk
Space Careers - www.space-careers.com
Women into Science, Engineering & Construction - www.wisecampaign.org.uk
▶Working in space (2010) (Babcock Lifeskills) - www.babcock-lifeskills.com/

Addresses
British National Space Centre (BNSC)
Polaris House North Star Avenue, Swindon, Wiltshire SN2 1SZ
Phone: +44 (0)20 7215 5000
Web: http://bnsc.gov.uk

International Space School Educational Trust (ISSET)
5 Herbert Terrace, Penarth CF64 2AH
Phone: +44 (0) 2920 710295
Web: www.isset.org/

Similar Jobs
Airline Pilot: Civil, Biomedical Scientist, Engineer: Aeronautical, Helicopter Pilot: Commercial, Nanoscientist/Nanotechnologist, Pilot: Armed Forces

Astronomer

also known as: Astrophysicist, Research Scientist: Astronomer
CRCI:Science, Mathematics and Statistics
CLCI:QOF
Job Band: 5

Job Description
Astronomers are research scientists in physical sciences who use satellites and powerful optical/radio telescopes to study the physics of the universe. They usually work as an observational or theoretical astronomer, often as part of a group working nationally and internationally. Astronomers examine the position, movement, structure and other characteristics of the sun, stars, planets and galaxies, and objects in space. They measure the different radiations emitted and interpret the findings involving calibrating instruments, logging data and analysing results by computer. Also write reports and publish professional papers about their findings.

Work Details
Usually work a basic 35-40 hr week that includes unusual hours when doing observational work. However, only some of the time is spent on observation and the emphasis is on the study of data. You may be required to work on space projects, telescopes or in observatories that are sited in other countries, including Hawaii, Australia and the Canary Islands. You usually work as part of a team with responsibility for collecting, analysing and interpreting data. This work is challenging and requires a high degree of accuracy.

Qualification

- **England, Wales and Northern Ireland**

Band 5: For degree courses: 2-3 A levels, including maths and physics, and some GCSEs (A*-C) usually including English, science and maths, or equivalent. Exact requirements depend on the degree you take.

- **Scotland**

Band 5: For degree courses: 3-5 H grades, including maths and physics, and some S grades (1-3), usually including English, maths and science, or similar. Exact requirements depend on the degree you take.

Degree Information
A degree in astronomy, astrophysics, physics, maths, geophysics or geology is preferred, but degrees offered in combination with astronomy or astrophysics are also acceptable. Computer science, software engineering and electronic engineering give useful background. The Royal Astronomical Society website lists courses.

Adult Qualifications
A degree or equivalent qualification and up-to-date scientific knowledge are necessary. A relevant PhD is required to undertake research.

Work Experience
Entry to this career is highly competitive. However, whilst work experience may be difficult to obtain, it improves your chances at interview for university degree courses. Any work experience that develops your skills in physics, IT or with using scientific equipment is very helpful.

Entry and Training
Training starts after obtaining a relevant first degree or after postgraduate qualification. An honours degree and usually a higher degree are required for research and development posts. It is useful to have previous experience of working with computers. The Royal Astronomical Society (RAS) and/or the Institute of Physics (IOP) offer membership to those who have relevant qualifications and experience. Membership leads to chartered scientist status (CSci) following at least four years of relevant post-graduation level experience. Astronomers must keep up to date with new developments and research techniques through national short courses/seminars, or via courses offered by an employer.

It is possible for those with backgrounds in mathematics, computer science or some branches of chemistry or engineering to move into this work, but mature entry as an astronomer is almost impossible without a postgraduate qualification. Graduates with a relevant first degree may be able to receive financial support from the Science and Technology Facilities Council (STFC).

Opportunities and Pay
There are around 1,250 professional astronomers in the UK working in research or academic posts, plus 750 postgraduate students. Astronomy is growing but there are still more applicants than vacancies. Most opportunities for newly qualified astronomers are in short-term research in universities, or in civil service observatories such as those in Cambridge, Edinburgh or the National Space Centre. Some jobs are in aerospace, meteorology and other government agencies/departments and opportunities exist in university teaching, maintaining and administering observatories and in instrument development. Promotion is limited by the small number of higher grade posts.

Students develop transferable skills during a PhD in Astronomy which are useful when seeking employment outside astronomy, for example, in aerospace industries, electronics and software engineering, teaching, scientific journalism, computing and accountancy.

As a new entrant, you may earn between £18k and £23k a year. An astronomer employed by a university earns up to £30k, but senior researchers and lecturers can earn up to £57k a year.

Skills and Qualities

able to work in abstract terms, analytical skills, aptitude for maths and science, attention to detail, good presentation skills, information handling skills, observant, perseverance, research skills, specialist IT skills

Relevant Subjects

Chemistry, Design and technology, Engineering, English, Geography, ICT/Computer studies, Mathematics, Physics, Science

Further Information

Astronomer Job Guide (Input Youth) - www.inputyouth.co.uk/jobguides/job-astronomer.html

Astronomy & Geophysics (Royal Astronomical Society) - www.blackwellpublishing.com

Astronomy Magazine - www.astronomy.com

Careers in Astronomy (Royal Astronomical Society (RAS)) - www.ras.org.uk

European Space Agency (European Space Agency) - www.esa.int

Journal of the British Astronomical Association (6 x year) (BAA) - www.britastro.org/baa

National Space Centre Online - www.spacecentre.co.uk/

▶Working in maths (2009) (Babcock Lifeskills) - www.babcock-lifeskills.com/

▶Working in science (2007) (Babcock Lifeskills) - www.babcock-lifeskills.com/

▶Working in space (2010) (Babcock Lifeskills) - www.babcock-lifeskills.com/

Addresses

British Astronomical Association (BAA)
Burlington House, Piccadilly, London W1J 0DU
Phone: +44 (0)20 7734 4145
Web: www.britastro.org

Institute of Physics (IOP)
76 Portland Place, London W1B 1NT
Phone: +44 (0)20 7470 4800
Web: www.iop.org

Royal Astronomical Society (RAS)
Burlington House, Piccadilly, London W1J 0BQ
Phone: +44 (0)20 7734 4582
Web: www.ras.org.uk

Science and Technology Facilities Council (STFC)
Polaris House, North Star Avenue, Swindon, Wiltshire SN2 1SZ
Phone: +44 (0)1793 442 000
Web: www.scitech.ac.uk

Women into Science, Engineering & Construction (WISE)
2nd Floor Weston House, 246 High Holborn, London WC1V 7EX
Phone: +44 (0)20 3206 0408
Web: www.wisecampaign.org.uk

Similar Jobs

Geophysicist, Meteorologist, Oceanographer, Operational Researcher, Physicist

Au Pair

also known as: Family Helper

CRCI:Social Work and Counselling Services
CLCI:KEZ Job Band: 1 to 2

Job Description

Au pairs help parents, single parents or guardians in a private home and work under their supervision. Help to look after babies and small children, usually by bathing, dressing, feeding and playing with them. Can also take them for walks and outings, read stories and generally keep them occupied, entertained and content. May have to do other tasks, including light shopping, babysit at night, light housework, launder and iron children's clothes, and collect older children from school.

Work Details

Usually work a 30-40 hr week. Exact hours are agreed with the employer and can often be long and irregular, including evenings, weekends and public holidays. You work in other people's homes, usually need to live-in and have to be active for most of the time. This job involves some kneeling, bending down and lifting. Work with young children can be noisy and messy at times.

Qualification

• England, Wales and Northern Ireland

Band 1: No qualifications are needed though some employers may ask for some GCSEs or equivalent.

Band 2: Although academic qualifications are not specified for this job, it is an advantage to have some GCSEs (A*-C) in subjects that include English and Maths, or equivalent.

• Scotland

Band 1: No qualifications are needed though some employers may ask for some S grades or similar.

Band 2: Although academic qualifications are not specified for this job, it is an advantage to have some S grades (1-3) in subjects that include English and Maths, or equivalent.

Adult Qualifications

No academic qualifications are needed though it is useful to have some qualifications, usually in English and maths.

Work Experience

Relevant paid or voluntary work experience can give you skills that you can use in the future and add to your CV. There are often opportunities for voluntary work that give you experience of working with people. Applicants with experience of working with and caring for young children, such as paid/unpaid work in a nursery school, helping at a playgroup, or assisting with childminding, may have an advantage.

Entry and Training

It is useful to have some experience of working with children. It is also helpful to have a driving licence, so that you can use your employer's car if required. Some families may prefer that you are a non-smoker. You may be asked to undergo a Criminal Records Bureau (CRB)/Disclosure Scotland check.

Training is on the job, though some employers look for vocational qualifications, such as those awarded by the Council for Awards in Children's Care & Education (CACHE). CACHE offer certificate courses at various levels in subjects such as Caring for a Child. Courses are available at many local colleges, often on a full or part-time basis. If employed by a private agency there is an initial in-house training period through short courses on various aspects of the job.

Mature entrants are welcomed, especially those who already have experience of working with babies and children. However, many au pairs are young adults aged 17-30.

There are a wide range of nationally-recognised qualifications available through distance learning. Government training opportunities, such as apprenticeships, may be available in your area. You can also gain recognition of previous experience through Accreditation of Prior Learning or by working towards relevant S/NVQs. Contact your local careers office, Jobcentre Plus, Next Step service or Learning and Skills Council (LSC)/Local Enterprise Company (LEC) for details of all training opportunities and schemes, including apprenticeships for adults.

Opportunities and Pay
You work in a private home and may use an agency to help you to find a job. Most jobs are temporary, for a few months, or for a year or more and it may be possible to work part time. Some au pairs progress to become a professional nanny. There are good opportunities to work abroad, often while learning a foreign language.

Pay varies widely, depending on your duties, location, the family you work for and your qualifications. An au pair should earn a minimum allowance of around £55-£75 a week, depending on the hours worked. Higher earners can make more than this. Food and accommodation are often provided.

Health
You need to be fit and able to cope with demanding children.

Skills and Qualities
able to cope with emergencies, cheerful, co-operative, energetic, even tempered, patient, practical skills, reliable, responsible attitude

Relevant Subjects
Biology, Health and social care, Hospitality and catering, Modern Foreign Languages

Further Information
Au Pairs JobMatch - www.aupairs.co.uk
IAPA, The International Au Pairs Association - www.iapa.org

Addresses
British Au Pair Agencies Association
Trafalgar House, Grenville Place, London NW7 3SA
Phone: +44 (0)7946 149 916
Web: www.bapaa.org.uk

CACHE: Council for Awards in Children's Care & Education
Apex House, 81 Camp Road, St Albans AL1 5GB
Phone: 0845 347 2123 (UK only)
Web: www.cache.org.uk

Similar Jobs
Childminder, Nanny, Nursery Worker, Teaching Assistant

Auctioneer
CRCI:Retail Sales and Customer Services
CLCI:UM Job Band: 3 to 5

Job Description
Auctioneers prepare, plan and carry out the sale of buildings and goods at auctions. They assess the value of what is to be sold and give the seller advice about expected prices. Research information regarding items for sale and write a detailed description for a catalogue or for an auction house website. Some auctioneers deal with all kinds of property including houses, country estates, farms and livestock. May auction a wide range of saleable items such as farm machinery, china, paintings, jewellery, toys, antiques and collectables, furniture, carpets, cars, electrical goods or office equipment. Others may specialise in one particular area of work.

Work Details
Usually work 35-40 hrs a week, Monday to Friday, though you may be expected to work some evenings/weekends and perhaps start early in the morning. You work in an office and salesroom, with time spent out and about in other locations, travelling over quite a wide area throughout the UK and perhaps abroad. This work requires some legal knowledge and involves preparation of sales catalogues, organising transportation and security of goods, insurance, storage, sales and some public speaking. You also require research skills in order to identify and value items for auction.

Qualification
There are various routes to becoming an auctioneer and no formal academic qualifications are specified.

- **England, Wales and Northern Ireland**

Band 3: For BTEC national award: 5 GCSEs (A*-C) including English and maths, or equivalent. Science subjects, history and geography are also useful.

Band 4: For BTEC higher national award: 1-2 A levels and some GCSEs (A*-C), or equivalent. English, maths, science subjects, geography or economics are preferred subjects.

Band 5: For degree courses: 2-3 A levels and some GCSEs (A*-C) including English, maths and preferably a science subject, or equivalent. Exact requirements depend on the degree you take.

- **Scotland**

Band 3: For SQA national award: five S grades (1-3) including English and maths, or similar. Science subjects, history and geography are also useful.

Band 4: For SQA higher national award: usually 2-3 H grades and some S grades (1-3), or similar qualifications. English, maths, science subjects, geography or economics are preferred subjects.

Band 5: For degree courses: 3-5 H grades and some S grades (1-3) including English, maths and preferably a science subject, or similar qualifications. Exact requirements depend on the degree you take.

Degree Information
Any degree is acceptable for entry to this job, though the following subjects are relevant: art history, antiques and design, fine art, building surveying, history, modern languages, business studies, or land and property management and surveying. Some postgraduate courses are available that are appropriate for obtaining professional qualifications.

Adult Qualifications
Entry requirements may be relaxed for adults applying for higher education courses and Access and foundation courses give adults without qualifications a route onto degree courses. Those with relevant work experience may be accepted for some college courses without meeting any formal entry requirements.

Work Experience
Entry to this job is competitive and employers or colleges/universities may prefer candidates who have relevant work or voluntary experience. This can include direct experience, usually through observation and attendance at auctions. Other related areas include work in valuation or surveyors' offices, property management or estate agency, and fine art and antiques dealerships.

Entry and Training
Entry routes to this profession vary, but many applicants have a relevant degree. Some of the large auction houses recruit a few graduates each year through an internship or graduate training programme. Others may enter the profession by first applying to an auction house as a valuer, cataloguer, porter or clerk, and gain relevant work experience. Some may join a small to medium-sized auction company as a general assistant. Few people become

auctioneers immediately and many gain experience in related fields such as property management. Several different professional qualifications are acceptable for this job, depending on the area in which you wish to specialise. For instance, to work as a property auctioneer it can be useful to train and qualify first as a valuer or surveyor.

Professional qualification is necessary for those wishing to become auctioneers in fine arts and artefacts, plant and machinery. The relevant professional body can supply lists of accredited courses. Entry requirements vary, depending on the institution and courses available. There are some exemptions from the professional exams for those with relevant degrees/diplomas. The Open University offers courses in the history of art, which can lead to a humanities with history of art degree. There are no formal entry requirements and you study through distance learning.

Some auction houses send their auctioneers on specialist courses, sometimes abroad. It is useful to have some knowledge of foreign languages. Auction houses such as Christie's and Sotheby's sometimes offer short courses in subjects that include decorative and fine arts. They also have an education department that offers undergraduate and postgraduate courses in relevant subjects. Fees can be expensive. Christie's offers a specialist training programme for graduates. It consists of 4-6 work placements over a two-year period. Entry is competitive and is via a selection process. Contact Christie's Education for further details.

Mature entrants may find it difficult to get started without relevant experience and/or qualifications. There are specialised distance-learning courses, including foundation certificates and degrees, in subjects that include fine arts, fine arts valuation, art law, and antiques.

Opportunities and Pay

Auctioneers are employed by auction houses and by estate agents. In an auction house you can specialise in a particular area, such as furniture, works of art, cars, books or machinery. Property auctioneering is part of an estate agency business and larger firms usually employ an auctioneer. You can specialise in commercial, industrial, residential or agricultural property. There is no formal promotion structure in this field, but there may be opportunities to become a partner.

Pay varies enormously and can be dependent on commission, and also location and type of company. Newly qualified auctioneers may earn around £20k-£23k, rising to around £24k-£36k a year with experience. Some senior or specialist auctioneers can earn around £40k-£50k a year.

Health

You need good hearing, good eyesight and clear speech. Normal colour vision is required for certain areas of work.

Skills and Qualities

able to estimate, alert, business awareness, IT skills, observant, public speaking ability, quick thinking, self confident, sound judgement

Relevant Subjects

Business and accounting, Construction and built environment, Economics, English, Geography

Further Information

Asset Skills - sector skills council for the places where we live and work - www.assetskills.org

Christie's Education - www.christieseducation.com

Open University - www.open.ac.uk

Sotheby's Institute of Art - www.sothebysinstitute.com/

Addresses

Institute of Revenues Rating and Valuation (IRRV)
41 Doughty Street, London WC1N 2LF
Phone: +44 (0)20 7831 3505
Web: www.irrv.org.uk

National Association of Estate Agents (NAEA)
Arbon House, 6 Tournament Court, Edgehill Drive, Warwick CV34 6LG
Phone: +44 (0)1926 496 800
Web: www.naea.co.uk

National Association of Valuers and Auctioneers
Arbon House, 6 Tournament Court, Edgehill Drive, Warwick CV34 6LG
Web: www.nava.org.uk

Royal Institution of Chartered Surveyors (RICS)
RICS Contact Centre Surveyor Court Westwood Way, Coventry CV4 8JE
Phone: +44 (0)870 333 1600
Web: www.ricscourses.org/pages/careers.aspx

Similar Jobs

Antiques Dealer, Estate Agent, Surveyor: General Practice, Surveyor: Rural Practice, Vehicle Sales Executive

Audiological Scientist

also known as: Clinical Scientist: Audiology

CRCI:Healthcare
CLCI:JOB — Job Band: 5

Job Description

Audiological scientists investigate and develop ways to measure and deal with hearing loss. They are part of a multi-disciplinary team, usually hospital-based; working directly with people, often children and the elderly, investigating problems with patients' hearing and balance. Audiology is a growing field of clinical science and technology which also uses techniques and equipment for diagnosing neurological diseases. They study problem cases found during routine tests and carry out further investigations. Work with medical and scientific staff to develop and assess new hearing-aids and equipment for people with a hearing impairment.

Audiological scientists adjust and calibrate equipment used for testing. May be responsible for managing a team of biomedical scientists and other support staff such as medical technologists, laboratory assistants and clerical assistants to develop audiological services.

Work Details

Your place of work is usually in a hospital, clinic, a laboratory or perhaps out in the community, working from 9am to 5pm, Monday to Friday, possibly with extra hours at times. You advise and help people or are involved in research for a university and perhaps teaching. There is contact with people of all ages, but particularly children and elderly people, some of whom can be distressed or are less able. Work can be demanding at times.

Qualification

- **England, Wales and Northern Ireland**

Band 5: For degree courses: 2-3 A levels usually including maths or psychology, or any science subject and some GCSEs (A*-C), usually including English, science and maths, or equivalent. Exact requirements depend on the degree you take.

- **Scotland**

Band 5: For degree courses: 3-5 H grades usually including maths or psychology, or any science subject, and some S grades (1-3), usually including English and maths, or similar qualifications. Exact requirements depend on the degree you take.

Degree Information

A good honours degree in audiology or an appropriate science subject, such as life and medical science, engineering, or physical, mathematical or applied science, is required. Other useful subjects include physics, biology, medical electronics, psychology or physiology, medicine, chemistry, speech science/therapy, biochemistry and biomedical science. This is followed by a postgraduate MSc or PhD in audiology/audiological science.

Adult Qualifications
Access or foundation courses may be available, which lead to first degree courses suitable for entry to the postgraduate audiology course. Competition for places on the limited number of courses is fierce. There may be occasional opportunities for scientists in audiological research, which may not require the postgraduate qualification.

Work Experience
Universities and employers may prefer candidates who have relevant work or voluntary experience. Ideally working with an audiological scientist is the most useful and you can contact them through human resources departments of hospitals. Similarly, any experience in the caring professions helps towards successful applications for employment and courses. It is useful to discuss this job with an employed audiological scientist prior to embarking on any course of study.

Entry and Training
There are two main ways to train as an audiological scientist: you can take a four-year BSc in audiology which includes a one-year clinical placement and the opportunity to register as an audiologist. Alternatively, you can train as a clinical scientist after achieving a good honours degree in an appropriate science subject and taking an MSc in audiology. This enables you to register as a clinical scientist (audiology). Both routes require a further period of supervised hospital-based, in-service training before you can join the Association of Clinical Scientists and register with the Health Professions Council (HPC). You must be registered with the HPC to practise. If you have a relevant science BSc, there is also a fast-track diploma available at Southampton, Manchester, University College London and Bristol universities. A good entry route for students taking the MSc route is to apply for an NHS-funded trainee scheme that offers a two-year, fixed-term contract to cover the basic training.

You are expected to follow a programme of continuing professional development (CPD) such as that offered by the British Academy of Audiology.

Mature applicants are welcome but must fulfil the entry requirements of an approved BSc in audiology followed by an MSc that is approved by the British Academy of Audiology, or take a one-year approved MSc following a science degree. A period of in-service training must be completed before applying to become state registered with the HPC. NHS funding may be available to assist students undertaking full-time university-based training. This may not cover the third year clinical placement of the BSc in audiology, though you are usually paid a salary during the period of placement.

Opportunities and Pay
This is a small profession but is expanding due to the advances in digital hearing aid technology, so prospects are good. Jobs are available only in certain cities or large towns and you work for the NHS, universities, private hospitals or the Medical Research Council. Some jobs exist in industry, particularly for companies that develop and manufacture hearing technology. There are also overseas opportunities, particularly in the USA and Australia, or in developing countries.

Pay for audiological scientists working for the NHS follows the salary bands for clinical scientists. Starting salaries for a trainee is around £24k-£32k, rising to £29k-£38k with experience and/or qualifications. Those in principal or consultant positions can earn up to £88k a year.

Health
This job requires normal hearing.

Skills and Qualities
able to explain clearly, able to get on with all kinds of people, aptitude for teamwork, careful, enquiring mind, imaginative, IT skills, patient, scientific approach, tactful

Relevant Subjects
Biology, Chemistry, English, Health and social care, Mathematics, Physics, Psychology

Further Information
Audiology Resources (Audiology in Ireland) - www.aud.org.uk/contents/regions/audiology_ireland.htm

Health Professions Council (HPC) - www.hpc-uk.org

NHS Careers (NHS Careers) - www.nhscareers.nhs.uk

NHS Careers Scotland - www.infoscotland.com/nhs

NHS Careers Wales - www.wales.nhs.uk

Addresses
Association of Clinical Scientists (ACS)
c/o Association of Clinical Biochemists, 130-132 Tooley St, London SE1 2TU
Web: www.assclinsci.org

British Academy of Audiology (BAA)
Resources for Associations, Association House, South Park Road, Macclesfield, Cheshire SK11 6SH
Phone: +44 (0)1625 504066
Web: www.baaudiology.org

British Society of Audiology (BSA)
80 Brighton Road, Reading, Berkshire RG6 1PS
Phone: +44 (0)1189 660 622
Web: www.thebsa.org.uk

Medical Research Council (MRC)
20 Park Crescent, London W1B 1AL
Phone: +44 (0)20 7636 5422
Web: www.mrc.ac.uk

Similar Jobs
Audiologist, Clinical Scientist: Medical Physicist, Engineer: Biomedical, Hearing Therapist, Microbiologist, Speech & Language Therapist

Audiologist
also known as: Audiological Technician, Clinical Physiologist: Audiology, Medical Technologist: Audiology, Physiological Measurement Technician: Audiology, Technical Audiologist

CRCI:Healthcare
CLCI:JOB Job Band: 5

Job Description
Audiologists works with other ear, nose and throat professionals, measuring the hearing capacity and balance of patients of all ages to establish the extent and nature of their hearing loss. They also measure a patient's middle ear function. Set up and use electronic measuring instruments for routine hearing tests. Select, fit and adjust appropriate hearing aids. They take impressions of the ear to make individually moulded ear inserts. Also teach patients how to use hearing aids to gain maximum benefit. Adjust and may repair aids for clinic patients.

Work Details
Usually work a basic 37 hr week, but may be required to work shifts if based in a hospital, on a rota to cover 24 hrs a day. You work in a hospital, a clinic, child assessment centre or a school.

You have contact with people of all ages, but mainly children and elderly people. You are responsible for a high standard of skilled work. A uniform or white coat is provided by your employer.

Qualification

• England, Wales and Northern Ireland

Band 5: For a degree in audiology: 3 A levels usually including maths or psychology (or any science subject) and some GCSEs (A*-C) usually including English, maths and science, or equivalent. Exact requirements depend on the degree you take.

• Scotland

Band 5: For a degree in audiology: 3-5 H grades usually including maths or psychology (or any science subject) and some S grades (1-3), usually including English, maths and science, or similar qualifications. Exact requirements depend on the degree you take.

Degree Information

A BSc degree in audiology is required, though a good science first degree is also acceptable, which can be followed by an accredited one-year postgraduate course, offered through the Clinical Scientist Training Scheme. Contact the British Academy of Audiology for a list of accredited courses.

Adult Qualifications

Entrants to this job are graduates with a degree in audiology. Those with a science degree may take an accredited one-year postgraduate course. Contact the British Academy of Audiology for details on accredited courses. Entry requirements may be relaxed for adults applying for higher education courses and Access or foundation courses give adults without qualifications a route on to degree courses.

Work Experience

Work experience gives you an insight into what you enjoy and don't enjoy about a job or working environment, as well as the opportunity to acquire new skills. It also provides valuable information to add to your CV and improves your employment prospects. Consider work experience with the public in a caring capacity and in different hospital departments. There is sometimes a waiting list for work experience in hospitals so it is best to enquire early.

Entry and Training

New entrants to this job are usually graduates with a BSc in audiology. This takes four years to complete with the first two years spent at university, followed by clinical placement in an audiological department or clinic. The BSc degree in audiology must be accredited by the British Academy of Audiology (BAA), and lead to state registration with the Health Professions Council (HPC) which regulates the profession. You can also take an accredited one-year postgraduate diploma course or an MSc in audiology, followed by a period of in-house training. You usually need a good relevant science degree to enter an accredited MSc course. Both routes require a period of in-service training to gain a certificate of audiological competence (CAC) from the BAA.

Those who study for higher degrees may also become clinical scientists (audiology) upon completion of the CAC. Contact the BAA for a full list of accredited degrees and MSc courses, or NHS Careers for details.

Note that from 2011 the degree programmes may be replaced by a new programme, currently under development as part of Modernising Scientific Careers. This is to include an audiology pathway with exiting students eligible to work in the NHS as audiologists. It is to be 3 years long and include clinical placement. Contact the BAA for further information.

Mature applicants are welcome but must fulfil the entry requirements of an approved BSc in audiology followed by an MSc that is approved by the British Academy of Audiology, or take a one-year approved MSc following a science degree. A period of in-service training must be completed before applying to become state registered with the HPC. NHS funding may be available to assist students undertaking full-time university-based training. This may not cover the third year clinical placement of the BSc in audiology, though you are usually paid a salary during the period of placement.

Opportunities and Pay

This is currently a small but growing profession and the need for audiology services is increasing. Jobs are available mainly in cities and large towns throughout the UK. You can be employed by the NHS in a hospital or community clinic, by a local authority or the armed forces. There are a few opportunities with private companies. Promotion is often through a formal career structure leading to departmental senior officers and manager posts. Most specialise in an area such as paediatrics or balance. Those who acquire a higher degree may also become clinical scientists.

Pay is usually on a nationally agreed scale and increases with promotion. Those working in the NHS follow a salary scale divided into levels of experience. Starting salary for a newly-qualified audiologist is around £21k-£28k a year, senior audiologists can earn around £23k-£31k and specialists can earn from £35k-£44k.

Health

This job requires normal hearing and a clear speaking voice.

Skills and Qualities

able to explain clearly, able to put people at ease, attention to detail, enquiring mind, IT skills, manual dexterity, methodical, observant, patient

Relevant Subjects

Biology, Design and technology, English, Health and social care, Mathematics, Physics, Science

Further Information

Audiology Resources - www.aud.org.uk
Health Professions Council (HPC) - www.hpc-uk.org
NHS Careers (NHS Careers) - www.nhscareers.nhs.uk
NHS Careers Scotland - www.infoscotland.com/nhs
NHS Careers Wales - www.wales.nhs.uk

Addresses

British Academy of Audiology (BAA)
Resources for Associations, Association House, South Park Road, Macclesfield, Cheshire SK11 6SH
Phone: +44 (0)1625 504066
Web: www.baaudiology.org

British Society of Audiology (BSA)
80 Brighton Road, Reading, Berkshire RG6 1PS
Phone: +44 (0)1189 660 622
Web: www.thebsa.org.uk

Similar Jobs

Audiological Scientist, Cardiac Physiologist, Hearing Therapist, Neurophysiologist, Respiratory Physiologist, Speech & Language Therapist

Auditor

also known as: Accountant - Audit

CRCI:Financial Services
CLCI:NAB Job Band: 4 to 5

Job Description

An auditor is responsible for checking company accounts and making sure all accounting activities comply with current regulations and legislation. External auditors can work for accountancy firms, the National Audit Office or the Audit Commission and are contracted in to examine the accounts and business transactions of firms. Checks to ensure that the business practises are in line with current legislation. Looks to see that the accounts present a true and reasonable reflection of the firms business activities and, when involved in the audit of public service organisations, checks that public funds are being used in the most cost effective way. On completion of an audit, a report is drawn up for presentation to management and shareholders.

Internal auditors are permanent employees of the firm in which they are working and work consistently to ensure that the firm is operating in compliance with current regulations and standards. Can work on a contract basis but represent the interests of the firm and not an external body. Seeks ways to improve the overall efficiency of the accounting practices and minimise risk within the business.

Work Details

Mostly works around 35-40 hrs a week, Monday to Friday. This is a demanding and challenging job and you may have to work long hours, including evenings and weekends, and spend time away from home. The work is divided between time spent in the office and time out meeting clients, e.g. auditing is done on the client's premises. You have to be able to keep up to date with changes in financial regulations and work out the implications of changes for clients. Formal dress code is usual.

Qualification

• England, Wales and Northern Ireland

Band 4: For direct entry to accountancy training or BTEC higher national course in a relevant subject, eg business and finance: a minimum of two A levels and some GCSEs (A*-C) including maths and English, or equivalent qualifications.

Band 5: For entry to a degree course: 2-3 A levels and some GCSEs (A*-C) including maths and English, or equivalent. Exact requirements depend on the degree you take.

• Scotland

Band 4: For direct entry to accountancy training or for an SQA higher national course in a relevant subject, eg accounting, you need at least three H grades and some S grades (1-3) including maths and English, or similar qualifications.

Band 5: For entry to a degree course: 3-5 H grades and some S grades (1-3) including maths and English, or similar qualifications. Exact requirements depend on the degree you take.

Degree Information

A degree in any subject is acceptable for entry to accountancy training. Degrees in accountancy, economics, law, mathematics, business studies/administration, computing, statistics, and financial management/banking are useful, and some lead to exemption from parts of the professional exams. Check with the appropriate professional body. Relevant postgraduate courses are also available.

Adult Qualifications

Formal entry requirements may be relaxed for those over 21 with relevant financial or accountancy experience. The accountancy professional bodies each have their own arrangements, which include special schemes for mature applicants. There are also special entry arrangements for adults applying for degree and higher national courses, including Access courses. Check with the universities and colleges for details.

Work Experience

Entry to this career can be competitive and it is important that you try to gain some relevant work or voluntary experience before applying. Time spent with an accountant's practice or in the accountancy department of a central or local authority, shows enthusiasm and commitment. Experience of other jobs involving finance is also valued by employers. Becoming involved in a work-related enterprise scheme, such as 'Young Enterprise', can enhance your chances when applying for a training contract.

Entry and Training

There are a number of routes into an auditing career. Employers look for evidence of training with one of the major accounting bodies and accountancy work experience. Students can study full time, part time or by day/block release. Although a degree is not always necessary, some auditors decide to take a law degree before entering this field.

Some enter the profession by working as a trainee accountant and sitting their exams simultaneously. Others train as an accounting technician through the Association of Accounting Technicians (AAT) or the Association of Chartered Certified Accountants (ACCA). They are then exempt from some papers in the professional accountancy exams. Once fully qualified as an accountant and registered with one of the chartered accountancy bodies in the UK, you can then sit exams to become an auditor.

The National Audit Office (NAO) runs AAT fast track scheme. For the 2010 intake, you must have a minimum of five GCSEs/S (or equivalent), grades A to C, including English and maths, and either have or expect to obtain A levels/H grades or equivalent worth at least 300 UCAS points.

The scheme runs for two years and includes paid time off for study leave and exams. On completion of the scheme, you continue your professional training by studying for the Institute of Chartered Accountants in England and Wales (ICAEW) exams. The NAO also runs a graduate recruitment scheme where graduates commit to studying for the ICAEW exams.

External auditors must have worked as a qualified accountant for a minimum of two years and have completed audit training with one of the professional accountancy bodies. The ICAEW stipulates that all ACA exams are completed and a specified period of work experience must be served with a firm of registered auditors. Check websites for current qualification requirements.

Internal auditors can complete the Institute of Internal Auditors (IIA) Certificate in Internal Audit and Business Risk or the IIA Diploma in Internal Audit Practice, then the Advanced Diploma in Internal Auditing and Management or the IT Audit Certificate. Whether internal or external, all auditors must commit to continuing professional development (CPD) throughout their career.

Full and part-time foundation degrees are available in subjects such as accounting and finance and business accounting. A Diploma/Welsh Baccalaureate may be available in your area in business, administration and finance. The advanced level is equivalent to 3.5 A levels but for some university courses, the additional and specialist learning component of the diploma needs to include specific A levels. Check entry requirements carefully with the individual institutions.

Mature applicants are judged on individual merit. The professional associations usually offer an adult entry route, including distance learning, and the number of mature entrants is increasing. Entry qualifications may be waived, though a good basis in maths, English and computing skills are usually necessary for the professional exams. A business or finance-related background is an advantage.

Opportunities and Pay

Opportunities for qualified auditors are increasing both in private practice and public service. Roles are available in external and internal audit and it is possible to progress to senior management positions. As regulations in the financial sector become more complex, it is likely there will be increased demand for more auditors with specialised training. This can include forensic, taxation and insolvency auditing. Companies are also becoming increasingly reliant on their internal audit departments to ensure that all aspects of the business are operating in accordance with financial regulatory rules.

Employers can range from small practices to firms with several partners or large international practices, in the UK and abroad. Despite the economic downturn, there is still demand for auditors, particularly in specialist areas. Auditors move from company to company to get experience in a particular type of work or to gain promotion. There are opportunities for self employment.

Trainee auditors studying for accountancy exams at the National Audit Office earn up to £26k a year in London. This rises to £35k while training and reaches £47k once qualified. Salaries in private practice can be higher with senior audit managers in large organisations earning up to £90k and audit directors or heads earning up to £150k a year.

Skills and Qualities

able to cope under pressure, able to prioritise work, analytical skills, attention to detail, good at writing reports, good concentration level, integrity, IT skills, numeracy skills, tactful & discreet

Relevant Subjects

Business and accounting, Economics, English, ICT/Computer studies, Law, Mathematics

Further Information

Accountancy (Wolters Kluwer (UK) Limited) - www.accountancymagazine.com

Accountancy Uncovered (Trotman 2010) - www.trotman.co.uk

Accounting Web - www.accountingweb.co.uk

AGCAS: Accountancy and Business Services (Job Sector Briefing) (AGCAS) - www.prospects.ac.uk/

Diplomas (Foundation, Higher and Advanced) - http://yp.direct.gov.uk/diplomas

Finance and Accounting (Pearson Publishing) - www.pearsoned.co.uk

Financial Services Skills Council - sector skills council for financial services, accountancy & finance www.fssc.org.uk/

Institute of Internal Auditors - www.iia.org.uk

Welsh Baccalaureate - www.wbq.org.uk

► Working in business, administration & finance (2010) (Babcock Lifeskills) - www.babcock-lifeskills.com/

Young Enterprise - www.young-enterprise.org.uk/pub/

Addresses

Association of Accounting Technicians (AAT)
140 Aldersgate Street, London EC1A 4HY
Phone: +44 (0)20 7397 3000
Web: www.aat.org.uk

Association of Chartered Certified Accountants (ACCA) UK
29 Lincoln's Inn Fields, London WC2A 3EE
Phone: +44 (0)20 7059 5000
Web: www.accaglobal.com

Association of International Accountants (AIA)
Staithes 3, The Watermark, Metro Riverside, Newcastle upon Tyne NE11 9SN
Phone: +44 (0)191 493 0277
Web: www.aiaworldwide.com

Chartered Institute of Management Accountants (CIMA)
26 Chapter Street, London SW1P 4NP
Phone: +44 (0)20 8849 2251
Web: www.cimaglobal.com

Institute of Chartered Accountants in England & Wales (ICAEW)
Chartered Accountants' Hall (Moorgate Place), PO Box 433, London EC2R 6EA
Phone: +44 (0)20 7920 8100
Web: www.icaew.com

Institute of Chartered Accountants in Ireland (ICAI) (Belfast)
The Linenhall 32-38 Linenhall Street, Belfast BT2 8BG
Phone: +44 (0)28 9043 5840
Web: www.icai.ie

Institute of Chartered Accountants of Scotland (ICAS)
CA House, 21 Haymarket Yards, Edinburgh EH12 5BH
Phone: +44 (0)131 347 0100
Web: www.icas.org.uk

National Audit Office (NAO)
157-197 Buckingham Palace Road, London SW1W 9SP
Phone: +44 (0)20 7798 7000

Similar Jobs

Accountant: Industry & Commerce, Accountant: Private Practice, Accountant: Public Sector, Accounting Technician, Actuary, Civil Service Tax Inspector, Company Secretary

Aviation Security Officer

also known as: Airport Security Officer

CRCI:Transport and Logistics
CLCI:MAG
Job Band: 1 to 2

Job Description

Aviation security officers screen everybody entering and exiting, and items being taken into, restricted zones in an airport. They help to ensure the safety and security of passengers and of the airport as a whole. This involves searching passengers for prohibited items, using an x-ray machine to screen passengers hand luggage and making sure that unauthorised people cannot enter the restricted zones. They also answer passengers enquiries. May carry out patrols of the terminals where required.

Work Details

You work an average of 40 hours a week on a shift system, including nights. As the service operates every day of the year, you have to work on bank holidays, with time off in lieu. You work as part of a team on the same shift pattern, alongside other teams of guards, airline staff, private security companies, the police and UK Border Agency officers. You work in different areas of the airport, which may lead to doing different tasks, such as screening and searching passengers or segregating incoming and outgoing passengers.

You use specialist equipment to check for security threats. This includes an x-ray screening machine, hand-held and archway metal detectors, trace detection swabs to detect explosives and a biometrics photo-capturing machine to check peoples identities. You are provided with a uniform. It is an advantage to live close to the airport at which you work, so a driving licence is desirable.

Qualification

• England, Wales and Northern Ireland

Band 1: For entry to jobs, no minimum qualifications are needed, but you are expected to have a good level of general education and relevant experience. Some formal/vocational qualifications at any level are useful.

Band 2: For entry to jobs, no minimum qualifications are needed, but it is an advantage to have some GCSEs (A*-C) or equivalent in subjects that include English and maths.

• Scotland

Band 1: For entry to jobs, no minimum qualifications are needed, but you are expected to have a good level of general education and relevant experience. Some formal/vocational qualifications at any level are useful.

Band 2: Although academic qualifications are not specified for this job, it is an advantage to have some S grades (1-3) in subjects that include English and maths, or similar.

Adult Qualifications
Although no formal qualifications are required, you are expected to have a good general standard of education.

Work Experience
Any relevant work experience can equip you with skills that you can use in the future and add to your CV. This can either be unpaid/ voluntary, or holiday/part-time work that you have organised yourself. Experience of working in the aviation sector, or a security or customer service role is valuable.

Entry and Training
Applicants should be over 18 and must undergo identity and Criminal Records Bureau (CRB)/Disclosure Scotland checks. You are trained on the job in a range of relevant skills, such as identifying potential threats to security and using X-Ray equipment. You are re-tested regularly to ensure that high standards are maintained. You must complete the Department for Transport x-ray competency test.

Customer service qualifications, such as NVQs at levels 2 and 3 are available. For some positions, security officers must hold specific security qualifications to qualify for a licence.

Any previous experience of dealing with members of the public is useful in this sort of work. Experience of working in the aviation sector, or a security or customer service role is especially valuable. Language skills can be an advantage. Government training opportunities, such as apprenticeships, may be available in your area. You can also gain recognition of previous experience through Accreditation of Prior Learning or by working towards relevant S/ NVQs. Contact your local careers office, Jobcentre Plus, Next Step service or Learning and Skills Council (LSC)/Local Enterprise Company (LEC) for details of training schemes.

Opportunities and Pay
There are opportunities in all UK airports. Contact individual airports for details of vacancies. It is possible to progress to a supervisory or management role.

Pay varies depending on the airport; however security officers can earn £12.5k-£20k a year. Salaries for security managers start from around £25k a year. Senior security managers may earn £50k or more. Company benefits may also be offered.

Health
You have to take a medical, which tests sight, hearing and smell. Full-colour vision is required for this job. You must be physically fit.

Skills and Qualities
able to follow procedures, able to report accurately, attention to detail, customer service skills, friendly but firm manner, good communication skills, observant, willing to work shifts

Addresses
British Airports Authority (BAA)
BAA Airports Limited, The Compass Centre, Nelson Road, London Heathrow Airport, Hounslow TW6 2GW
Phone: +44 (0)20 8745 9800
Web: www.baa.com

Similar Jobs
Door Supervisor, Emergency Services Control Room Operator, Police Officer, Prison Officer, Security Officer, Store Detective

Bailiff
also known as: Civil Enforcement Agent, Debt Collector, Enforcement Officer: Bailiff

CRCI:Legal and Political Services
CLCI:LAZ Job Band: 1 to 2

Job Description
Bailiffs enforce court orders to recover money owed to private clients or government. Court bailiffs deliver legal documents such as summonses or county court orders, mainly for debt recovery, possession of property or other aspects of civil law. Private or certificated bailiffs work for independent companies. They recover debts on behalf of their clients, such as banks, solicitors or local councils. Use several methods to try to obtain payment, including writing letters, visiting them at home or at their business premises.

Bailiffs try to negotiate an agreement to pay a small amount at a time. As a last resort, they are legally able to repossess a property or remove some goods. Write letters and complete paperwork. Must follow strict laws and guidelines.

Work Details
Most bailiffs work 37 hrs a week, Monday to Friday. You need to be flexible as you may be working early in the morning, evenings and weekends. You are based in an office but spend most of the time travelling and visiting debtors. You may need to spend time away from home, overnight or for several nights. Some heavy lifting may be required, especially if removing furniture or equipment from debtors' premises. You have to deal with people who can be angry, upset or destructive. Many bailiffs combine this work with another job. Part-time work and self-employment is possible.

Qualification
- **England, Wales and Northern Ireland**

Band 1: There are no set qualifications for entry to this type of work. A good level of general education is an advantage and the ability to read and write is essential. Good communication skills and life experience are more important than qualifications.

Band 2: No set minimum educational entry requirements, though some GCSE passes including English and maths, or equivalent, are an advantage.

Adult Qualifications
No entry qualifications are specified, though some employers prefer certificated bailiffs.

Work Experience
Work experience equips you with skills that you can use in the future and add to your CV. This can either be unpaid or voluntary or can be holiday or part-time work that you have organised yourself.

Entry and Training
Most entrants are aged 21-45. Bailiffs employed by private companies are usually trained on the job. However, it is an advantage to become a certificated bailiff, which enables you to undertake certain types of work, such as collecting parking fines and rent arrears for local authorities.

To become a certificated bailiff, you need a bailiff's general certificate. For this you have to appear before a county court judge and answer questions on bailiff law and procedures. You also have to pay a bond or other security of £10,000. If a debtor accuses you of acting unlawfully, and a judge agrees, then compensation can be paid out of this bond. The certificate is granted by a county court judge who declares that you are a 'fit and proper person'. No formal qualifications are required, but you do need knowledge of the law.

One way to acquire the necessary legal knowledge is to attend relevant seminars and training courses, such as those offered by the Institute of Credit Management and the Association of British Investigators. To become a bailiff your background may be checked for security reasons and you need to prove that you have no debt or criminal record. Some bailiffs choose to become members of the Enforcement Services Association.

Court bailiffs are civil servants employed by Her Majesty's Courts Service (HMCS). Entrants must satisfy strict nationality and residency requirements. In Northern Ireland, similar work is performed by an enforcement officer who is responsible to the Enforcement of Judgements Office (EJO). The officer must have a thorough knowledge of EJO legislation and office practices.

Mature entrants have an advantage for this type of work and particularly those with previous working experience of the law, in the armed forces or police force.

Opportunities and Pay

There is work in most towns throughout the UK. Bailiffs are employed by private companies or directly by county courts that employ around 1,000 bailiffs. There are around 1,300 certificated bailiffs. Some may work for firms that do not ask for the bailiff's general certificate. Promotion in firms is possible to senior bailiff and manager. County court bailiffs are civil servants and can be promoted to bailiff manager.

Pay varies with the type of work and whether you are employed or self-employed. Starting pay is around £12k-£14k a year and with experience £16k-£20k a year. This can rise to around £30k a year. Many firms pay a basic salary plus some form of commission or incentive payments.

Health

You may need to pass a medical and fitness assessment, as stamina and physical fitness are needed for this job. Normal colour vision is usually required.

Skills and Qualities

able to get on with all kinds of people, able to prioritise work, able to work both on your own and in a team, assertive, good communication skills, negotiating skills, self confident, sound judgement, understanding of legal technicalities

Further Information

Her Majesty's Courts Service - www.hmcourts-service.gov.uk

National Enforcement Services - www.enforcementofficers.co.uk

Skills for Justice - sector skills council for the UK justice system - www.skillsforjustice.com

▶Working in business, administration & finance (2010) (Babcock Lifeskills) - www.babcock-lifeskills.com/

Addresses

Association of British Investigators (ABI)
295/297 Church Street, Blackpool FY1 3PJ
Phone: +44 (0) 1253 297502
Web: www.theabi.org.uk

Enforcement of Judgements Office (EJO)
6th Floor, Bedford House Bedford St, Belfast BT2 7FD
Phone: +44 (0 2890 245 081
Web: www.courtsni.gov.uk

Enforcement Services Association (ESA)
Park House 10 Park Street, Bristol BS1 5HX
Phone: +44 (0)117 907 4771
Web: www.ensas.org.uk

Institute of Credit Management (ICM)
The Water Mill, Station Road, South Luffenham, Leicestershire LE15 8NB
Phone: +44 (0)1780 722900
Web: www.icm.org.uk

Similar Jobs

Civil Service Administrative Officer, Court Administrative Officer/Assistant, Credit Manager, Debt Counsellor, Private Investigator

Baker

CRCI:Manufacturing and Production
CLCI:SAC
Job Band: 1 to 3

Job Description

Bakers prepare, make and bake bread, cakes, biscuits, pies, pastries and savouries. Specialist breads can include wholegrain, organic and wholemeal bread, ciabatta, pitta bread, French loaves and croissants. They weigh and measure the ingredients, such as flour, water/milk or butter, following the recipe carefully. These ingredients are mixed together, divided and shaped, then put into tins and baked in an oven. Specialist (craft) bakers may do this by hand whilst plant bakery is mass-produced automated work using high-technology machinery. The different processes include moulding the dough, rising (proving), baking and cooling. The product is then ready for slicing and wrapping.

May make cakes for special occasions such as for Christmas, birthdays, christenings, anniversaries and weddings. Some products may require filling with cream or jam, covering with icing, or dipping in chocolate.

In-store/supermarket bakers, as well as craft bakers who work in specialist shops, are also trained to display their goods attractively, serve customers and handle sales. All bakers need to follow strict laws and guidelines regarding hygiene, health and safety when handling food and dealing with equipment.

Work Details

Bakers usually work a basic 39 hr week in a shop, supermarket/in-store bakery, or a plant bakery. In a plant bakery, you may have to work shifts that can include nights and weekends. If you work in an instore or craft bakery your working hours are likely to include Saturdays and Sundays. Early starts are common.

You have to cope with standing for many hours and possibly with some heavy lifting, and the place of work can often be hot. There may be a risk of burns and possibly accidents from equipment. You need to wear protective clothing as well as something to cover your hair. Long hair must be tied back and you must also wear suitable shoes.

Qualification

- **England, Wales and Northern Ireland**

Band 1: For some employers: qualifications are not essential though evidence of an interest in cooking is desirable.

Band 2: For some employers: qualifications are not essential, but some GCSEs (A*-C), preferably including maths, English, science and food technology, or equivalent qualifications, may be useful.

Band 3: For BTEC national certificate: 4 GCSEs (A*-C) preferably including English, maths and science, or equivalent.

- **Scotland**

Band 1: For some employers: qualifications are not essential though evidence of an interest in cooking is desirable.

Band 2: For some employers: qualifications are not essential, but some S grades (1-3), preferably including maths, English, science and food technology or similar, may be useful.

Band 3: For SQA national certificate/diploma: four S grades (1-3) preferably including English, maths and science, or similar.

Adult Qualifications

Some employers and colleges accept people with no qualifications but with relevant interest and experience. Others may ask for relevant basic qualifications.

Work Experience

Relevant work or voluntary experience is always useful and can improve your chances when applying for entry to jobs or apprenticeships in the manufacturing sector. Your personal or adult guidance adviser may be able to help you organise work experience with an employer.

There may be a young apprenticeship (for 14-16 year olds) available in your area in food manufacturing.

Entry and Training

Training can be done in a number of different ways, such as on-the-job training with an experienced employee, through an online course, or by a full or part-time course before entering a job. Apprenticeships in process bakery skills and craft bakery are available. See the Improve Ltd website for details. For those wanting to become managers or supervisors, BTEC runs a two year full-time National Diploma in Science (Baking Technology). SQA also run a national diploma in baking technology. There is a foundation degree in baking technology management available from the National Baking School at London South Bank University. This can be topped up to a BSc with a further year's study.

Employers may require you to study for certificates in health and safety, and in aspects of food hygiene. S/NVQs are available at level 2 in food manufacture: craft baking skills and food manufacture: process baking skills, and at level 3 in food manufacture: specialist craft baking skills. Short courses in bakery are run by the Federation of Bakers. Details of bakery schools can be found on the website of the National Association of Master Bakers.

A Diploma/Welsh Baccalaureate in manufacturing and product design may be available in your area. The food and drink section is particularly relevant for entry to this work.

Government training opportunities, such as an apprenticeship in food manufacture, may be available in your area. You can also gain recognition of previous experience through Accreditation of Prior Learning (APL) or by working towards relevant S/NVQs. Contact your local careers office, Jobcentre Plus, Next Step service or Learning and Skills Council (LSC) Local Enterprise Company (LEC) for details of training schemes.

Opportunities and Pay

The food and drink industry in the UK employs approximately 430,000 people nationwide. The bakery sector alone employs over 140,000 people made up of full and part-time workers. There is consistent demand for skilled bakers due to increased availability of jobs and replacement of those retiring.

Work is available throughout the UK with plant and craft bakeries, although in-store bakeries in supermarkets are increasing their market share. There are shortages of suitable applicants, and skilled craft bakers are in great demand. Promotion to supervisory level, product management, product development or sales and marketing, is possible. There are also opportunities for self-employment.

Pay varies depending on area and employer but starting salaries for over 18 year olds is around £11.5k-£14k, rising to £20k with experience. Very experienced bakers can earn over £25k a year. Overtime pay may increase your earnings.

Health

There are restrictions on certain skin complaints such as eczema or breathing difficulties such as asthma. There may be an allergy risk from flour. This job requires good colour vision for certain areas of work.

Skills and Qualities

able to operate equipment, able to work quickly, able to work well with others, adaptable, attention to detail, careful, good organisational skills, health & safety awareness, manual dexterity, numeracy skills

Relevant Subjects

Hospitality and catering, Manufacturing

Further Information

Apprenticeship Schemes (National Apprenticeship Service) - www.apprenticeships.org.uk

British Baker magazine - www.bakeryinfo.co.uk

Careers in Food & Drink - www.careersinfoodanddrink.co.uk

Course Information (Federation of Bakers) (Federation of Bakers) - www.bakersfederation.org.uk/home.aspx

Diplomas (Foundation, Higher and Advanced) - http://yp.direct.gov.uk/diplomas

Improve Ltd - sector skills council for food and drink manufacturing and processing - www.improveltd.co.uk

Training Schemes - www.direct.gov.uk/en/educationandlearning

Welsh Baccalaureate - www.wbq.org.uk

▶ Working in food & drink (2007) (Babcock Lifeskills) - www.babcock-lifeskills.com/

Addresses

Federation of Bakers
6 Catherine Street, London WC2B 5JW
Phone: +44 (0)20 7420 7190
Web: www.bakersfederation.org.uk

London Southbank University
90 London Road SE1 6LN
Phone: +44 (0)20 7815 6100

National Association of Master Bakers
21 Baldock Street, Ware, Hertfordshire SG12 9DH
Phone: +44 (0)1920 468 061
Web: www.masterbakers.co.uk

Scottish Association of Master Bakers
Atholl House, 4 Torphichen Street, Edinburgh EH3 8JQ
Phone: +44 (0)131 229 1401
Web: www.samb.co.uk

Worshipful Company of Bakers
Bakers Hall, Harp Lane, London EC3R 6DP
Phone: +44 (0)20 7623 2223
Web: www.bakers.co.uk

Similar Jobs

Cake Decorator, Chef/Cook, Food Service Assistant, Food Technician, Kitchen Assistant/Porter

Bank Manager

CRCI:Financial Services
CLCI:NAD — Job Band: 5

Job Description

Bank managers have overall responsibility for the efficient operation of a major bank branch, or for a number of smaller bank outlets within a local area. Oversee the day-to-day running of the bank including promoting the branch's services to acquire more business and to increase profit. Are also responsible for motivating and leading the staff, monitoring work practices and general personnel matters.

Spend a lot of time working with customers, identifying their needs and aiming to meet or exceed them. May work at management level in a specialist section, such as international banking, investment, personnel and training, IT or marketing. In specialist sections at regional or head office, managers are responsible for administering the work of staff in their section.

Work Details

Usually work a 37 hr week, Monday to Friday, with some Saturday mornings, but increasingly hours are becoming more flexible. You may spend a lot of time out of the office, meeting business clients on their own premises or travelling to head office and other branch locations, or to meetings and conferences. The working environment is usually modern, light and air-conditioned. This is a demanding job that can involve working long hours. There can also be short periods away from home. Formal business clothing is expected.

Bank Manager

Qualification

- **England, Wales and Northern Ireland**

Band 5: For degree courses: 2-3 A levels and some GCSEs (A*-C) usually including English and maths, or equivalent. Exact requirements depend on the degree you take. Check individual prospectuses.

- **Scotland**

Band 5: For degree courses: 3-5 H grades and some S grades (1-3), usually including English and maths, or similar qualifications. Exact requirements depend on the degree you take. Check individual prospectuses.

Degree Information

A degree in any subject is acceptable, but it may be an advantage to have a numerate subject, such as financial services, financial management, banking, accountancy, mathematics, statistics, law, business studies or economics. Marketing and business administration are also useful. There are postgraduate diplomas and MBAs in banking including distance-learning options, such as those offered by the University of London's external programme.

Adult Qualifications

Mature entrants usually have relevant previous experience in business, law, accountancy or finance. Entry requirements for courses may be relaxed for mature applicants. There are also foundation and Access courses which can help you to move onto higher education.

Work Experience

Relevant work or voluntary experience is always useful and improves your chances in application for entry to this job. Experience in a bank is obviously the most useful but any work experience in the finance sector is relevant and shows enthusiasm and commitment to the work. Time spent in an accountancy firm, an insurance company or even shadowing a financial adviser, gives you a good basis and insight into the profession. In some areas there is a young apprenticeship (14-16) scheme that provides an extended work placement and eventual achievement of a relevant level 2 qualification whilst at school.

Some larger finance companies offer summer internships, usually lasting ten weeks, for those in the penultimate year of their degree course.

Entry and Training

Entry is competitive and is usually via a graduate training scheme or through promotion. New entrants with a good honours degree (2:1 or better) usually follow a two year management training scheme, which is an accelerated programme leading to professional qualifications. Employees with A levels/H grades, an equivalent vocational qualification, such as the ifs School of Finance professional diploma in financial services management, or a relevant HNC/HND who show management potential, receive in-service training that may also lead to an accelerated training programme.

The Diploma/Welsh Baccalaureate in business, administration and finance may be available in your area and considered as an alternative to A levels. Check the additional and specialist learning (ASL) requirements for your course as you may need specific A levels for certain university courses.

Full and part-time foundation degrees are available in business, finance and management. The ifs School of Finance offers the foundation degree in financial markets and management and a range of professional qualifications. The Chartered Institute of Bankers in Scotland and the Chartered Insurance Institute also offer a wide range of professional certificates/diplomas. These qualifications can be gained through a variety of flexible options including day release, evening classes or distance learning, and are studied in your own time. In Scotland entrants can take the chartered banker programme to become members of the Chartered Institute of Banking in Scotland. This is studied by distance learning and takes 2-4 years.

Trainees with relevant degrees or higher national awards may be exempt from some examinations. Some banks offer sponsorship for degree courses. Continuing professional development is expected throughout your career.

Mature applicants should have relevant financial experience that includes supervisory management and customer service. A distance-learning option is to take a degree in banking that is offered by the University of London's external programme. Sponsorship or scholarships for study at degree level may be offered by some major high street banks. Graduates in disciplines such as financial services, banking, economics, accounting and computing have an advantage. Increasingly, foreign language skills are also very useful.

Opportunities and Pay

Most banks' head offices are located in the City of London with branch offices throughout the UK. With the increase of online and telephone banking, many high street branches are closing but some opportunities have transferred to bank call centres. Mergers with other banks, building societies and insurance companies are leading to a change in the more traditional areas of banking, with opportunities arising in non-traditional areas such as pensions and insurance. However, there are still about 12,000 high street banks serving consumers and businesses.

Promotion is based on performance as well as your qualifications, but you must be prepared to move around the country. Some managers move into specialist divisions such as human resources, card services or training as part of their promotion route. Opportunities exist with investment banks or with regulatory bodies such as the Financial Services Authority (FSA).

Pay varies depending on location and employer, but graduate trainees can expect around £19k-£25k a year. Generally, managers in their first post earn up to £40k a year, rising to £60k-£80k or more for senior managers with extensive responsibilities. Bank employees often have special subsidised mortgage rates and loans, pensions and insurance cover, and health insurance. Managers may also be provided with a car.

Skills and Qualities

able to take responsibility, analytical skills, clear-thinking, good communication skills, good interpersonal skills, IT skills, leadership qualities, negotiating skills, networking skills, sound judgement

Relevant Subjects

Business and accounting, Economics, English, ICT/Computer studies, Law, Mathematics

Further Information

AGCAS: Accountancy and Business Services (Job Sector Briefing) (AGCAS) - www.prospects.ac.uk/

British Bankers Association (BBA) - www.bba.org.uk

Diploma in Business, Administration and Finance - www.baf-diploma.org.uk/

Finance and Accounting (Pearson Publishing) - www.pearsoned.co.uk

Financial Services Skills Council - sector skills council for financial services, accountancy & finance - www.fssc.org.uk/

Inside Careers Guide: Banking, Securities & Investments - www.insidecareers.co.uk

Welsh Baccalaureate - www.wbq.org.uk

► Working in maths (2009) (Babcock Lifeskills) - www.babcock-lifeskills.com/

Addresses

Chartered Institute of Bankers in Scotland (CIOBS)
Drumsheugh House, 38b Drumsheugh Gardens, Edinburgh EH3 7SW
Phone: +44 (0)131 473 7777
Web: www.charteredbanker.com

Chartered Insurance Institute (CII)
42-48 High Road, South Woodford, London E18 2JP
Phone: +44 (0)20 8989 8464
Web: www.cii.co.uk

Financial Services Authority (FSA)
Membership Department, 25 The North Colonnade, Canary Wharf, London E14 5HS
Phone: +44 (0)20 7066 1000
Web: www.fsa.gov.uk

Financial Services Skills Council
51 Gresham Street, London EC2V 7HQ
Phone: 0845 257 3772 (UK only)
Web: www.fssc.org.uk

ifs School of Finance
IFS House, 4-9 Burgate Lane, Canterbury, Kent CT1 2XJ
Phone: +44 (0)1227 818609
Web: www.ifslearning.ac.uk

University of London
Information Centre Stewart House 32 Russell Square, London WC1B 5DN
Phone: +44 (0)20 7862 8360
Web: www.londonexternal.ac.uk

Similar Jobs

Accountant: Public Sector, Building Society Manager, Credit Manager, Financial Adviser/Planner, Investment Banker, Stockbroker

Bank Officer

also known as: Bank Customer Services Adviser, Cashier: Bank

CRCI:Financial Services
CLCI:NAD
Job Band: 2 to 3

Job Description

Bank officers work in a branch of a bank, doing administrative work or dealing with customers at the counter. Handle the paying in and withdrawal of cash and cheques, the payment of bills and other transactions at the bank counter. They process applications for mortgages and other loans. Deal with direct debits and standing orders, and may carry out other financial transactions for customers, such as buying and selling stocks and shares. Also arrange insurance or order foreign currency and travellers' cheques.

Carry out the routine and administrative day-to-day tasks such as dealing with post and ensuring that the tills balance at the close of business. Senior officers supervise other staff and oversee security and safety.

Other bank officers work in regional processing centres or telephone centres and do not have face-to-face contact with customers. Their duties are similar to those working in a branch, except that they do not deal with customers face-to-face or handle cash. They deal with customer accounts with instruction from customers over the phone. In all transactions they have to be very careful with client security.

Work Details

Usually work between 35-40 hrs a week, from 9am to 5pm, Monday to Friday, but hours vary from bank to bank. Many banks are open on Saturdays. Part time work and job sharing is widely available. Shift work is common in telephone and online retail banking centres. These are usually open six to seven days a week between the hours of 7am and 11pm. Flexible hours and overtime at busy times is very common.

Retail bank officers may split their time between processing administrative requests and handling cash transactions. In a contact centre, they work in a large open plan office at a computer desk, talking to customers over a telephone headset. Most of the work is done on a computer. Your work has to be accurate, and if the money and computer records do not balance you may have to stay late to find the mistake.

There are strict safety and security procedures of which each employee is aware. Bank employees who work in a branch are usually provided with a corporate uniform.

Qualification

• England, Wales and Northern Ireland

Band 2: Although academic qualifications are not specified for this job, banks expect applicants to have a good standard of literacy and numeracy. It is an advantage to have some GCSEs (A*-C) in subjects that include English and maths, or equivalent.

Band 3: For entry: most employers usually require at least 4 GCSEs (A*-C) including English and maths, or equivalent.

• Scotland

Band 2: Some banks do not require formal qualifications for this work though expect applicants to have a good standard of literacy and numeracy. Those with some S grades (1-3) including English and maths, or similar, may have an advantage.

Band 3: For entry: most employers usually require at least four S grades (1-3) including English and maths. Many entrants have H grades, or similar.

Adult Qualifications

There are no minimum formal entry qualifications though employers expect applicants to have a good standard of literacy and numeracy. Those with formal qualifications at any level may have an advantage.

Work Experience

Relevant work or voluntary experience is always useful and can improve your chances in application for entry to this job. Work with the public, retail and other work which involves handling cash and customer service is useful. In some areas there is a young apprenticeship (14-16) scheme that provides an extended work placement and eventual achievement of a relevant level 2 qualification whilst at school.

Entry and Training

Although there are no specific minimum entry qualifications, most employers expect you to be educated to at least GCSE (A*-C)/S grade (1-3) level and entrants may also have A levels/H grades or equivalent. Some employers may also require you to have a Criminal Records Bureau (CRB)/Disclosure Scotland and credit check carried out. You may also have to sit an aptitude test. Trainees learn on the job, working alongside an experienced bank officer. Most banks have their own company training programme, including short residential courses.

Many staff also study for the professional qualifications of the ifs School of Finance or those offered by the Chartered Institute of Bankers in Scotland (CIOBS). The ifs delivers tailored training courses for banks including certificates and diplomas in business and corporate banking. CIOBS offers similar courses including a certificate in call centre operations. Courses leading to these qualifications can be taken by day release, evening classes or distance-learning. A relevant BTEC/SQA national award can give you exemption from some parts of the professional exams; check with the professional institutions for details. Those with A levels/H grades or equivalent may receive accelerated training.

It is also possible to take a part-time foundation degree in business finance and law. Appropriate S/NVQs in customer service, retail financial services, contact centre professionals and providing financial services are available at levels 1-3. Training programmes, including Providing Financial Services apprenticeship schemes and the Diploma/Welsh Baccalaureate in business, administration and finance may also be available in your area. Advanced apprenticeships leading to qualification at level 3 can also be a route into higher education.

The ifs has also developed a foundation/intermediate certificate in personal finance aimed at 14-16 year-olds and college students, which is delivered at schools and colleges across the UK.

Mature entrants have increased in recent years as banks are recruiting people who have relevant experience, particularly in customer care, retail and any financial work. Any experience of cash handling within a retail or financial customer service setting is an advantage. IT, sales and marketing and office work skills are also helpful. Contact your local careers office, Jobcentre Plus, Nest Step service or Learning and Skills Council (LSC)/Local Enterprise Company (LEC) for details of all training opportunities and schemes, including apprenticeships.

Opportunities and Pay

The majority of banks have their head offices in the City of London but branch offices are located throughout the UK. Mergers with other financial services, such as building societies, has led to a reduction in staff in recent years. New technology, telephone and internet banking, has also resulted in fewer junior and middle level staff, and continued job cuts are likely due to the reduction in high street branches. However, opportunities do exist in the growing areas of bank call centres and specialised banking such as in supermarket outlets. Many call centres are based in south Wales, the North East and central Scotland.

The banks have structured promotion schemes, which usually depend on studying for professional qualifications as well as experience and merit. You can specialise or progress to become a supervisor or personal assistant to the manager. Promotions within banks are performance related and you may need to move between banks to progress. Part-time and temporary contracts are increasing.

Pay varies depending on location and employer but as a guide, officers are likely to earn in the region of £15k-£22k, rising to £25k a year with experience. High earners can earn over £30k a year. Employees can benefit from low-rate loans and mortgages, pension and health cover, and profit-sharing.

Skills and Qualities

accurate, aptitude for teamwork, good concentration level, good spoken communication, good written English, initiative, IT skills, logical, numeracy skills, trustworthy

Relevant Subjects

Business and accounting, Economics, English, ICT/Computer studies, Mathematics

Further Information

Apprenticeship Schemes (National Apprenticeship Service) - www.apprenticeships.org.uk

British Bankers Association (BBA) - www.bba.org.uk

Diploma in Business, Administration and Finance - www.baf-diploma.org.uk/

Financial Services Skills Council - sector skills council for financial services, accountancy & finance - www.fssc.org.uk/

Inside Careers Guide: Banking, Securities & Investments - www.insidecareers.co.uk

Training Schemes - www.direct.gov.uk/en/educationandlearning

Welsh Baccalaureate - www.wbq.org.uk

▶ Working in maths (2009) (Babcock Lifeskills) - www.babcock-lifeskills.com/

Addresses

Chartered Institute of Bankers in Scotland (CIOBS)
Drumsheugh House, 38b Drumsheugh Gardens, Edinburgh EH3 7SW
Phone: +44 (0)131 473 7777
Web: www.charteredbanker.com

Financial Services Skills Council
51 Gresham Street, London EC2V 7HQ
Phone: 0845 257 3772 (UK only)
Web: www.fssc.org.uk

ifs School of Finance
IFS House, 4-9 Burgate Lane, Canterbury, Kent CT1 2XJ
Phone: +44 (0)1227 818609
Web: www.ifslearning.ac.uk

Similar Jobs

Bank Manager, Building Society Officer, Clerk: Accounts, Insurance Broker, Insurance Technician, Retail Assistant

Barrister

also known as: Counsel: Barrister, Lawyer: Barrister

CRCI:Legal and Political Services

CLCI:LAB — Job Band: 5

Job Description

Barristers work within the legal system of England and Wales or in Northern Ireland in two main areas of the law, providing independent, specialist legal advice on complex issues, or representing and presenting cases in court on behalf of an individual client or clients. They represent their client in court at arbitrations, tribunals, planning enquiries etc. Prepare each case through research, read reports and statements, and discuss each case with the instructing solicitor, through whom contact with the client is made. Study relevant statutes and previous cases and give legal opinions.

Barristers argue the case before a judge and perhaps a jury. They may practise general common law, but usually specialise in a particular area such as company mergers, civil, criminal, litigation or chancery law (wills and trusts), patents or environmental legislation.

Work Details

Barristers work in court and in an office, or from home. Travel is necessary, with nights away from home. Very long hours are involved, including evenings and weekends. It is often necessary to take work home. The work involves consultation with solicitors and other professionals, including addressing audiences in the High Court, the Supreme Court and the Circuit Court. Court cases are sometimes passed to the barrister at very short notice, so details have to be analysed and facts assimilated very quickly.

The work can be pressured and stressful at times and can involve making difficult decisions. Barristers wear formal dress and have to observe the traditions and formality associated with the job.

Qualification

- **England, Wales and Northern Ireland**

Band 5: For degree: three A levels and some GCSEs (A*-C) including English and maths, or equivalent qualifications. Exact requirements depend on the degree you take.

Degree Information

In England and Wales, graduates should have either a good honours 'qualifying' degree in law or a non-law degree plus the common professional examination (CPE)/graduate diploma in law (GDL). This is known as the academic phase of the training.

In Northern Ireland, intending barristers must have a 'qualifying' honours degree in law before applying for the one-year full-time degree of Barrister-at-Law at Queen's University in Belfast. There is also a non-law degree route available.

Adult Qualifications

The study and training routes are common to all entrants though certain exemptions may apply. Solicitors who wish to become barristers should apply to the Joint Regulations Committee. For those not already qualified in law, the lengthy training time should be considered carefully.

Work Experience

Entry to this job is very competitive. It is almost essential that you try to do some relevant work or voluntary experience before applying. The Bar Council suggests that applicants to law degree courses should gain some practical experience by way of court attendance, in a barristers' chambers or at a firm of solicitors. University students can apply for a mini-pupillage, which lasts for one or two weeks and can be applied for through Pupillage Portal (formerly OLPAS). You should apply 18 months in advance.

Entry and Training

There are three stages in training to be a barrister - the academic stage, the vocational stage and the pupillage stage.

Before starting the vocational stage of training it is necessary to join one of the four Inns of Court (Gray's Inn, Lincoln's Inn, Middle Temple and Inner Temple) which provide social support as well as educational guidance for barristers and student barristers. You must then complete the one-year full-time or two-years part-time Bar Professional Training (BPTC). In Northern Ireland this is called the degree of Barrister-at-Law. Once completed, you are then 'called to the Bar' by your Inn.

A period of pupillage follows, consisting of two six-month periods (non-practising and practising) spent in either a barristers' chambers or other approved legal environment, under the guidance of an experienced barrister. A few annual scholarships are available to assist with training costs.

In the first three years of practice, new practitioners must complete 45 hours of continuing professional development (CPD), including nine hours of advocacy training and three hours of ethics. After three years, barristers must undertake 12 hours of CPD each year. Contact the Bar Standards Board for more information. Further career development is required and is aimed at becoming a Queen's Council (QC), which involves taking the extremely serious cases or as an assistant recorder, prior to selection as a judge.

Mature applicants over the age of 25 (29 in NI) may apply to be accepted as a student of law without the usual minimum qualifications. A standard level of education for entry applies and relevant work experience is an advantage, or may be required. An Access to law course is available, instead of A levels or similar, or you could take a foundation degree in law. Those with previous experience of working in a legal environment have an advantage for initial law training.

Contact the the Bar Council in England & Wales, or Bar Council of NI for specific entry requirements and details of any exemptions for other qualifications.

Opportunities and Pay

There are around 12,000 barristers in England and Wales. Barristers have chambers at the Inns of Court in London, with some based in provincial chambers. Most practising barristers are based in London with a further concentration in other cities throughout the UK. Outside London, a Northern Chancery Bar has been formed which reflects the increasing amount of work. Some are made a Queen's Counsel (QC) as a mark of outstanding ability and then usually become a senior judge. The Crown Prosecution Service also employs barristers to bring prosecutions on behalf of the police.

Training provides a useful basis for a range of other occupations, for example in consultancy or work in local authorities, industry or the civil service. This is a small profession and is highly competitive. Considerable talent is required for success. There are opportunities to specialise in European or international law, and to work or travel overseas.

Income is high for top achievers and is by fees rather than regular salary and depends on the level of cases the barrister's clerk is prepared to entrust to you. Most barristers are self-employed and so earnings can vary hugely. During the final years of training or pupillage, salaries are likely to be around £10k a year. Most qualified barristers earn between £25k-£150k a year, some top barristers earn over £500k-£1m a year.

Skills and Qualities

able to inspire confidence, analytical skills, discreet, excellent communication skills, good memory, honest, information handling skills, objective, public speaking ability, resilient

Relevant Subjects

Business and accounting, Economics, English, Government and politics, History, Law, Performing arts, Psychology, Sociology

Further Information

Bar Standards Board - www.barprofessionaltraining.org.uk

Her Majesty's Courts Service - www.hmcourts-service.gov.uk

Pupillage Portal (ex-OLPAS) (The General Council of the Bar) - www.pupillages.com/

Skills for Justice - sector skills council for the UK justice system - www.skillsforjustice.com

TARGETjobs: Law (GTI Specialist Publishing Ltd.) - www.groupgti.com

The Barrister (MMC Ltd) - www.barristermagazine.com

▶Working in English (2007) (Babcock Lifeskills) - www.babcock-lifeskills.com/

▶Working in politics & law (2010) (Babcock Lifeskills) - www.babcock-lifeskills.com/

Addresses

Bar Council
289-293 High Holborn, London WC1V 7HZ
Phone: +44 (0)20 7242 0082
Web: www.barcouncil.org.uk

Bar Council of Northern Ireland
The Bar Library, 91 Chichester St, Belfast BT1 3JQ
Web: www.barlibrary.com

Bar Standards Board
289-293 High Holborn, London WC1V 7HZ
Phone: +44 (0)20 7611 1444
Web: www.barstandardsboard.org.uk

The Crown Prosecution Service (CPS)
50 Ludgate Hill, London EC4M 7EX
Phone: +44 (0)20 7796 8000
Web: www.cps.gov.uk

Similar Jobs

Civil Service Fast Streamer, Coroner, European Law Solicitor, Judge, Magistrates' Court Legal Adviser, Solicitor

Barristers' Clerk

CRCI:Legal and Political Services
CLCI:LAZ Job Band: 3 to 4

Job Description

Barristers' clerks organise and coordinate work for barristers and are responsible for the overall administration of chambers (Inns of Court rooms). Plan the workload of each barrister. They decide which cases to accept, find a counsel for each case and negotiate fees. Junior clerks may act as a messenger, delivering documents by hand, or go to the court taking books, robes, papers and so on. Clerks are responsible for running the practice as a business and as a team. Arrange consultations, keep diaries, recruit and train junior clerks/messengers, and carry out administrative duties, such as accounts.

Clerks act as a link between the solicitor (who contacts the clerk if a counsel is required for a client) and the barrister. The historical title of 'clerk' is easily misinterpreted for a basic clerical position, when in fact it involves a managerial role of varying seniority. Experienced and senior clerks are often called clerk of chambers, practice managers, chief executives, chambers' managers or chambers' directors.

Work Details

Usually works a basic 39 hr week, Monday to Friday, but the hours can be long and you may have to work in the evenings and at weekends, and sometimes take work home. Deadlines have to be met, so the work can be pressured. You handle complex information, make good decisions quickly and also have to be very accurate and pay close attention to detail. Loyalty and discretion are important, since the work is confidential.

Clerks have to deal with solicitors and clients and a lot of the work is done by telephone and email. The formality and traditions of the legal world must be respected and you are expected to wear formal business clothes such as a dark suit.

Qualification

• England, Wales and Northern Ireland

Band 3: For entry: a minimum of 6 GCSEs (A*-C) in academic subjects. Equivalent qualifications may be considered, but the nature of this work demands a good standard of English and numeracy.

Band 4: Many applicants have one or more A levels, and some GCSEs (A*-C) in academic subjects, including English and maths, or equivalent qualifications.

Adult Qualifications

Mature entry is unusual. However, adults with legal experience, for example legal secretaries, are occasionally accepted. Experience in management and administration is also welcome.

Work Experience

Entry to this job is competitive and it is important that you try to do some relevant work or voluntary experience before applying. Chambers' practices may prefer those with good key skills and some previous experience. Gaining experience in an office environment improves your chances of getting into this job and demonstrate your organisational and administrative skills.

The majority of chambers have their own policies in placing students and some have affiliations to schools and colleges. You are advised to speak to your schools career adviser/teacher about making contact with individual chambers rather than the Institute of Barristers' Clerks, which is unable to help with work experience placements.

Entry and Training

Training is on the job working with experienced senior clerks (chambers' directors or practice managers). Most new entrants start as junior clerks after completing GCSEs or A Levels. A Diploma/Welsh Baccalaureate in business, administration and finance may be available in your area. However, an increasing number of new entrants have a degree, as the role of a clerk now focuses on business management and in particular, financial management and marketing of the chambers.

Juniors or deputies usually start with routine tasks, such as delivering messages and carrying books to court, and build up experience over the years. Entry is very competitive and it is very difficult to find a first job. The ability to type and to work with figures is an advantage.

It is possible to take a distance-learning course leading to the BTEC Advanced Award in Chambers Administration run by the Institute of Barristers' Clerks (IBC). The BTEC course is designed for junior clerks in the first five years of their career and it leads to IBC membership.

Becoming a barrister's clerk is not a route to professional qualification within the legal system, though the experience gained is clearly useful.

Mature entrants with relevant experience in law such as working as a solicitor's clerk or legal secretary, or court administration, have an advantage. However, many adult entrants are those with a degree.

Opportunities and Pay

There are around 1,500 barristers' clerks working in England, Wales and Northern Ireland. They are employed in chambers with 70-75% working in London. Chambers are also found in other cities throughout the UK. Once employed as a junior, promotion prospects to senior are quite good. A similar system operates in Northern Ireland. Some experienced clerks offer an online service to barristers working from home.

Clerks are now paid a salary, with commission less common. Barristers' clerks salaries start at around £12k rising to £30k. Senior clerks may earn £100k a year, or more. Clerks may also receive bonuses directly related to the income of the barristers.

Skills and Qualities

able to cope under pressure, administrative skills, aptitude for teamwork, awareness of confidentiality issues, good interpersonal skills, good organisational skills, initiative, negotiating skills, sound judgement, trustworthy

Relevant Subjects

Business and accounting, Economics, English, Law

Further Information

Diplomas (Foundation, Higher and Advanced) - http://yp.direct.gov.uk/diplomas

Skills for Justice - sector skills council for the UK justice system - www.skillsforjustice.com

TARGETjobs: Law (GTI Specialist Publishing Ltd.) - www.groupgti.com

Welsh Baccalaureate - www.wbq.org.uk

▶Working in politics & law (2010) (Babcock Lifeskills) - www.babcock-lifeskills.com/

Addresses

Institute of Barristers' Clerks (IBC)
289-293 High Holborn, London WC1 7HZ
Phone: +44 (0)20 7831 7144
Web: www.ibc.org.uk

Royal Courts of Justice
Chichester Street, Belfast BT1 3JF
Phone: +44 (0)28 9023 5111
Web: www.courtsni.gov.uk

Similar Jobs

Civil Service Administrative Officer, Company Secretary, Court Administrative Officer/Assistant, Law Costs Draftsman, Legal Executive, Office Manager

Bartender

also known as: Barperson

CRCI:Catering and Hospitality

CLCI:IC Job Band: 1 to 2

Job Description

Bartenders serve drinks from licensed bars in places such as pubs and restaurants, wine bars, hotels, leisure and holiday centres, clubs, airports, sports and social clubs. They also work at events such as agricultural/flower shows, major cricket, rugby, golf matches, etc. Bartenders make customers welcome, take their order and serve drinks with a pleasant and professional attitude. May serve beers, wines, spirits or soft drinks, and may mix cocktails and serve hot or cold meals and bar snacks.

They help to stock the bar and arrange bottles and glasses, and also prepare the bar area by putting out fresh beer mats, and bar snacks such as bowls of peanuts and crisps. Fills ice buckets and makes sure there is a supply of sliced lemons and cocktail cherries. May develop specialist knowledge of wines.

Bartenders are responsible for calculating customers' bills, collecting money and using a till. They may also deal with payments involving cheques or credit/debit cards. Regularly washes glasses or stacks an industrial dishwasher, and keeps the bar and tables clean and tidy at all times.

Bartenders may also help with bar entertainment events, including karaoke, theme and quiz nights. They stay alert for any trouble that may arise, and keep up to date with the licensing laws. After closing time, they collect the bottles and glasses and tidy and clean the bar area and tables.

Work Details

Usually works 37-40 hrs a week, including shift work, split shifts, early starts and late finishes, weekends and public holidays. There are times when you are very busy. In this job you meet many different people, some who may be awkward or aggressive at times. You spend most of the time on your feet and may have to move heavy crates of bottles and barrels around.

Work in licensed premises is often noisy and hot. High standards of hygiene and personal presentation are important for this job, and you must know the licensing laws and follow safe working practices.

Qualification

• England, Wales and Northern Ireland

Band 1: For entry to jobs, no minimum qualifications are needed, but you are expected to have a good level of general education and relevant experience. Some formal/vocational qualifications at any level are useful. Bar staff must usually be over 18.

Band 2: For entry to jobs, no minimum qualifications are needed, but it is an advantage to have some GCSEs (A*-C) or equivalent in subjects that include English and maths. Bar staff must be over 18.

• Scotland

Band 1: For entry to jobs, no minimum qualifications are needed, but you are expected to have a good level of general education and relevant experience. Some formal/vocational qualifications at any level are useful. Bar staff must usually be over 18.

Band 2: Although academic qualifications are not specified for this job, it is an advantage to have some S grades (1-3) in subjects that include English and maths, or similar. Bar staff must be over 18.

Adult Qualifications

No formal qualifications are required although a recognised certificate in food hygiene is useful.

Work Experience

Any work experience can equip you with skills that you can use in the future and add to your CV. There is often plenty of paid part-time catering work available, although you cannot work behind a licensed bar until you are 18. Holiday and seasonal work is usually widely available and training can be given on the job.

Entry and Training

Bar staff must usually be 18 but many are older. Those aged 16-17 can work as part of a training scheme, such as an apprenticeship. There is demand for qualified staff and professional training has increased. Most employers look for an outgoing personality and friendly manner, together with an ability in basic maths and English. Some employers may give a numeracy test. You may be trained on the job by a manager or by other bar staff. Staff in pubs owned by some breweries attend company training schemes.

The Wine & Spirit Education Trust offers a range of courses for the hospitality industry. A foundation certificate in wines is available for those in their first job. It provides basic product knowledge and skills in the service of wines. An intermediate certificate in wines and spirits, and a professional certificate in spirits are available at level two. A level 3 advanced certificate and a level 4 diploma in wines and spirits are also available for those who wish to progress to supervisory or management roles.

The BII offers a Professional Barperson's Qualification for bar staff working in licensed premises. This is made up of two units. One is an introduction to the skills required for customer and drinks service. The other provides an understanding of the licensing law, and the social responsibility of selling alcohol. Both units are covered in one day and assessed by a multiple-choice test. They also offer other relevant awards and national certificate qualifications, including several specific to Scotland. Contact the BII for further details.

Alcohol Focus Scotland, through training providers ServeWise and City & Guilds, offers a half day certificate course for staff working in Scottish licensed premises. This provides information on the sale and service of alcohol and is suitable for new or inexperienced bar staff. There are other ServeWise courses for licensees and managers.

S/NVQs in hospitality, food and drink service, customer service and hospitality supervision are available at levels 1-4. A Diploma/ Welsh Baccalaureate may be available in your area in hospitality or customer service. You may also choose to work towards a relevant national certificate or diploma in hospitality and catering. Training programmes, including apprenticeships leading to level 2 and advanced apprenticeships in hospitality leading to level 3, may also be available.

Mature applicants with experience of working with the public may have an advantage. Government training opportunities, such as apprenticeships in hospitality, may be available in your area. You can also gain recognition of previous experience through Accreditation of Prior Learning (APL) or by working towards relevant S/NVQs. Contact your local careers office, Jobcentre Plus, Next Step service or Learning and Skills Council (LSC) Local Enterprise Company (LEC) for details of training schemes

Opportunities and Pay

There are many jobs for bar staff in hotels, pubs and wine bars, on cruise ships and ferries, clubs, leisure centres and other licensed premises. Employers recruit young people who show an enthusiasm for the job and have the potential to progress. There is also temporary work at sporting events, music festivals etc. Many bar jobs are part time, and casual jobs are always available during busy times, such as at Christmas and during the holiday season. With experience you may progress to be a supervisor or manager. It is often possible to find work abroad.

Pay depends on the type and location of employer, but is likely to be around £10k-£14k a year, rising to around £16k with experience. Bar managers may earn up to £25k a year, or more. The basic pay for this job may not be high but staff may receive tips or free meals.

Health

To do this job you need to have good general fitness.

Skills and Qualities

able to get on with all kinds of people, aptitude for teamwork, energetic, friendly, good stamina and physically fit, numeracy skills, outgoing personality, sense of humour, smart appearance, trustworthy

Relevant Subjects

Hospitality and catering, Retail and distribution

Further Information

Apprenticeship Schemes (National Apprenticeship Service) - www.apprenticeships.org.uk

BII - Professional body for the Licensed Retail Sector (British Institute of Innkeepers) - www.bii.org/home

British Beer and Pub Association (BBPA) - www.beerandpub.com

CareerScope: Hospitality and Leisure (Springboard UK) - http://careerscope.springboarduk.net/

Diploma in Hospitality (People 1st) - www.hospitalitydiploma.co.uk

Diplomas (Foundation, Higher and Advanced) - http://yp.direct.gov.uk/diplomas

People 1st - sector skills council for hospitality, leisure, travel and tourism - www.people1st.co.uk

Publican's Industry Handbook (The Publican) (The Publican) - www.thepublican.com/

Real Life Guide to Hospitality & Event Management (Trotman 2010) - www.trotman.co.uk

Scottish Beer and Pub Association (SBPA) - www.scottishpubs.co.uk

Springboard UK (Springboard UK) - www.springboarduk.net

Springboard Wales (Springboard Wales) - http://wales.springboarduk.net/

UKSP - Guide to Success in Hospitality, Leisure, Travel & Tourism - www.uksp.co.uk

▶Working in food & drink (2007) (Babcock Lifeskills) - www.babcock-lifeskills.com/

▶Working in hospitality & catering (2009) (Babcock Lifeskills) - www.babcock-lifeskills.com/

Addresses

ServeWise, Alcohol Focus Scotland
166 Buchanan Street, Glasgow G1 2LW
Phone: +44 (0)141 572 6700
Web: www.alcohol-focus-scotland.org.uk

Wine & Spirit Education Trust (WSET)
International Wine & Spirit Centre, 39-45 Bermondsey Street, London SE1 3XF
Phone: +44 (0)20 7089 3800
Web: www.wset.co.uk

Similar Jobs

Food Service Assistant, Publican, Sommelier, Waiter/Waitress

Beauty Consultant

CRCI:Personal and Other Services
CLCI:IK Job Band: 1 to 2

Job Description

Beauty consultants sell and demonstrate the use of cosmetics and beauty products, such as perfume, skin creams, makeup and hair care products. They help customers to choose the right product and show them how to use it. Also hold demonstration sessions in the department store or chemist shop to advertise the products more widely.

Consultants may give facials or make-up sessions to a customer to help them choose or to show the benefits of a new product. They also give information about special offers or new products and send out mail shots to inform regular customers. Must keep accurate records of sales, order new stock, and arrange counter displays to attract customers.

Most consultants work in one department store and are usually employed by an individual cosmetics company. Others are employed by a large retail chain to sell more than one brand of cosmetics. Some beauty consultants travel around a number of stores. Some cosmetic counters are franchises run by self-employed consultants. It is possible to do this job as an independent beauty consultant, in which case you travel between clients and need a driving licence.

Work Details

Usually work a 37-40 hr week, over five days, often including one late evening. You may also have to work on a Saturday and possibly Sunday, but have time off during the week instead. You work on your own or in a small team and have constant contact with the public. Beauty consultants are required to be well groomed at all times and are expected to learn a great deal about their products.

Consultants usually wear the uniform of the company they represent, and are expected to use the company's products. You have to stand for many hours during both busy and quiet times. You may have to fetch products from a stockroom and carry these to your counter, which means some lifting, carrying and bending.

Qualification

Employers often look for a good general education, smart appearance and a keen interest or knowledge of cosmetics, rather than formal educational qualifications.

• England, Wales and Northern Ireland

Band 1: For entry to jobs, no minimum qualifications are needed, but you are expected to have a good level of general education and relevant experience. Some formal/vocational qualifications at any level are useful.

Band 2: For some employers/courses: 2-3 GCSEs (A*-C) including English, maths or a science, or equivalent.

• Scotland

Band 1: For entry to jobs, no minimum qualifications are needed, but you are expected to have a good level of general education and relevant experience. Some formal/vocational qualifications at any level are useful.

Band 2: For some employers/courses: 2-3 S grades (1-3) including English, maths or a science, or similar.

Adult Qualifications

Qualifications are not always needed. It is an advantage to have experience in selling or in related work, such as beauty therapy.

Work Experience

Relevant work or voluntary experience is always useful and can improve your chances when applying for entry to jobs in sales. It can equip you with skills that you can use in the future and add to your CV. Part-time and holiday employment in any type of shop is useful and is usually fairly easy to obtain. Work in a shop that sells cosmetics is most useful.

Entry and Training

When you start in this work, training is usually on the job, often following a short course at a company training centre to learn basic skills. Ongoing training is also required to learn about new products. There are several qualifications that are useful, but not essential for entry. These may be taken by either full or part-time courses. Both BTEC and City & Guilds offer a level 2 diploma in beauty consulting. The Vocational Training Charitable Trust offers courses in in cosmetic makeup and facial massage/skin care, both at level 2. The International Therapy Examination Council also offers a range of relevant courses. Private training courses are also available, but these may be expensive, so check details carefully.

Appropriate S/NVQs are available up to level 4 in subjects such as customer service and beauty therapy. Training programmes, including apprenticeship schemes, may be available in your area. Advanced apprenticeships leading to qualification at level 3 can also be a route into higher education. A Diploma/Welsh Baccalaureate in hair and beauty studies may be available in your area.

Mature applicants may be preferred if they are thought suitable, as beauty consultants are required to be well groomed and to maintain a high standard of personal appearance. Previous experience of retail work and customer care, is very useful. Adults may be able to enter this work through a government-funded training programme. Contact your local Connexions or careers office, Jobcentre Plus, Next Step service or Learning and Skills Council (LSC)/Local Enterprise Company (LEC) for details of all training opportunities and schemes, including apprenticeships for adults.

Opportunities and Pay

Beauty consultants usually work for individual cosmetics companies, though some stores employ staff to sell a number of different brands. There is a lot of competition for vacancies. Promotion to supervisor is possible, but chances are limited because of the small number of jobs. You may be able to work at airports, on cruise ships or ferries, in hotels, and at some residential health hydros.

Pay varies depending on where you work, but starting pay is usually around £12.5k-£16k a year, rising to £18.5k with experience. High earners can make around £19k a year. You are likely to be paid commission on the products you sell. Allowances for make-up and discounts on company products are usually available.

Health

There may be an allergy risk from skin irritants. Normal colour vision is required for this job.

Skills and Qualities

able to explain clearly, cash handling skills, customer service skills, friendly, good interpersonal skills, good personal grooming, outgoing personality, self confident, smart appearance, tactful

Relevant Subjects

Biology, Performing arts, Retail and distribution, Science

Further Information

Apprenticeship Schemes (National Apprenticeship Service) - www.apprenticeships.org.uk

Diplomas (Foundation, Higher and Advanced) - http://yp.direct.gov.uk/diplomas

Hair and Beauty Jobs - www.hairandbeautyjobs.com

Real Life Guide to the Beauty Industry (Trotman 2009) - www.trotman.co.uk

Skillsmart Retail - sector skills council for the retail industry - www.skillsmartretail.com

Training Schemes - www.direct.gov.uk/en/educationandlearning

Welsh Baccalaureate - www.wbq.org.uk

▶Working in retail & customer services (2008) (Babcock Lifeskills) - www.babcock-lifeskills.com/

Addresses

Hairdressing and Beauty Industry Authority (HABIA)
Oxford House, Sixth Avenue, Sky Business Park, Robin Hood Airport, Doncaster DN9 3EG
Phone: 0845 230 6080 (UK only)
Web: www.habia.org/

International Therapy Examination Council (ITEC)
2nd Floor , Chiswick Gate, 598-608 Chiswick High Road, London W4 5RT
Phone: +44 (0)20 8994 4141
Web: www.itecworld.co.uk

Vocational Training Charitable Trust (VTCT)
Eastleigh House, 3rd Floor , Upper Market Street, Hampshire SO50 9FD
Phone: +44 (0)2380 684 500
Web: www.vtct.org.uk

Similar Jobs

Beauty Therapist, Film/TV & Theatre Make-Up Artist, Hairdresser, Image Consultant, Retail Store Demonstrator, Spa Therapist

Beauty Therapist

also known as: Aesthetician

CRCI:Personal and Other Services

CLCI:IK — Job Band: 2 to 4

Job Description

Beauty therapists carry out a wide range of treatments to the face and body to improve a client's appearance and increase their feeling of well-being. The work includes applying make-up and doing facials, cleansing skin, using steam treatments, face packs and massage using special oils and creams. They also apply wax or sugar solutions to remove unwanted hair on the face or body and give eyebrow and eyelash treatment. May specialise in nail treatments and be known as a manicurist or nail technician (see separate job article).

In addition to the work of a beauty specialist, a beauty therapist, after extra training, may offer more advanced techniques, such as using electrotherapy to eliminate wrinkles, infra-red/ultra violet light treatments and tanning or slimming treatments.

Work Details

Usually work a 37-40 hr week, that may include a Saturday and/or evenings. There are usually opportunities for part-time or flexible working. Your work surroundings are usually hygienic, warm and pleasant with good lighting. Therapists usually work with one client at a time, in a private cubicle or room, though pedicurists and manicurists may also work alongside a hairdresser. Some jobs, like massage, are physically demanding.

Sometimes you may have to cope with clients who are not happy with their treatment or who are nervous and embarrassed. You should be able to provide a calm environment and put people at ease. You usually wear a uniform to protect your clothes and to give a clean, smart appearance.

Qualification

• England, Wales and Northern Ireland

Band 3: For BTEC national award or diploma in beauty therapy sciences and for most professional courses: usually 3-4 GCSEs (A*-C), preferably including biology or dual science, English and maths, or equivalent.

Band 4: For BTEC higher national certificate/diploma in beauty therapy sciences: usually one A level and some GCSEs (A*-C) including English and a science; preferably biology, or equivalent qualifications. Check individual prospectuses.

- **Scotland**

Band 3: For SQA national certificate modules and for most professional courses: usually 3-4 S grades (1-3) preferably including biology or a science subject and sometimes English, or similar.

Band 4: For SQA higher national certificate/diploma in beauty therapy sciences: usually 1-2 H grades and some S grades (1-3) including English and a science, preferably biology, or similar. Entry requirements vary so check prospectuses carefully.

Adult Qualifications

Some formal academic qualifications (or equivalent) are usually required for entry to training courses, but many colleges welcome mature entrants over 20 and may waive entry requirements. Colleges may have relevant Access and foundation courses that require no entry qualifications.

Work Experience

Entry to this job is competitive and it is important that you try to do some relevant work or voluntary experience before applying, such as Saturday or holiday work in a beauty or hairdressing salon. In addition, sales or reception experience can be useful, as well as other kinds of work with the public. Some therapists do voluntary work with the Red Cross, who train volunteers to work with patients in hospital, or with elderly people.

The Vocational Training Charitable Trust (VTCT) runs diploma courses in schools at three levels in beauty therapy and hairdressing. These are aimed at 14-19 year olds.

Entry and Training

Employers look for applicants who are well groomed and have a friendly and caring personality, artistic flair and good communication skills. Many salons require applicants to hold or work towards an S/NVQ in beauty therapy at level 3, although you may begin your training by assisting qualified staff, whilst initially working towards S/NVQ at level 2. City & Guilds courses, BTEC/SQA national/higher national awards can be studied full or part time at many further education colleges.

The Vocational Training Charitable Trust also offers national qualifications, including S/NVQs, certificates and diplomas/advanced diplomas in beauty therapy. The Confederation of International Beauty Therapy and Cosmetology (CIBTAC) offers a level 2 diploma in beauty therapy. The International Therapy Examination Council (ITEC) also offers courses; some of these lead to S/NVQs or a diploma. Comiti International d'Esthitique et de Cosmitologie (CIDESCO) offers an internationally recognised beauty therapy diploma that can be gained either by full or part-time training.

One and two-year full-time foundation degrees are available in subjects that include beauty therapy, beauty therapy and health studies, and beauty and spa services. Independent training schools also offer courses, some of which can be very expensive. The quality of these courses can vary and it is important to make sure that these qualifications are acceptable for professional insurance cover. Contact CIBTAC for advice on choosing a course and career development. Once trained you are expected to keep your skills and knowledge up to date.

Training programmes, including apprenticeship schemes, may be available in your area. Advanced apprenticeships leading to qualification at level 3 can also be a route into higher education. A Diploma/Welsh Baccalaureate in hair and beauty studies may be available in your area.

Mature applicants are welcomed by employers. You may be able to enter this work through a government-funded training programme. Contact your local Connexions or careers office, Jobcentre Plus, Next Step service or Learning and Skills Council (LSC)/Local Enterprise Company (LEC) for details of all training opportunities and schemes, including apprenticeships for adults.

Opportunities and Pay

The beauty industry changes rapidly and is increasingly competitive, so it is vital that you achieve nationally recognised training and qualifications. This is a growing profession and there are usually vacancies for qualified and experienced applicants. Beauty therapists usually start their careers working for a high street salon or hairdressers, a health farm, beauty clinic or a health spa. With experience and relevant qualifications, some work in a hospital specialising in remedial camouflage or using a range of skills to help patients who are recovering from mental and physical conditions. Others work in hotels, fitness and health centres, and on cruise ships.

Many become self-employed and either work from their own salons or make home visits to clients. For those working in salons, promotion prospects are usually good. Beauty therapists may also specialise in aromatherapy, Indian head massage, reflexology, hydrotherapy, stress management, nutrition and dietary advice, sport therapy, massage or fitness therapy and exercise.

Pay varies, depending on the salon, the area in which you work and the number of treatments you are qualified to offer. Beauty therapists earn around £11k-£20k a year. Tips from clients and commission for sales of services and products can supplement your salary.

Health

There may be an allergy risk from skin irritants. This job requires good general fitness as you are on feet for long hours. Some areas of work require good colour vision.

Skills and Qualities

able to inspire confidence, able to put people at ease, calm, eye for visual effect, friendly, good interpersonal skills, good listening skills, good personal grooming, manual dexterity, tactful

Relevant Subjects

Art and Design, Biology, Chemistry, English, Health and social care, Science

Further Information

Apprenticeship Schemes (National Apprenticeship Service) - www.apprenticeships.org.uk

Careers in Beauty Therapy (HABIA) (HABIA) - www.habia.org/

Diplomas (Foundation, Higher and Advanced) - http://yp.direct.gov.uk/diplomas

Hair and Beauty Jobs - www.hairandbeautyjobs.com

Real Life Guide to the Beauty Industry (Trotman 2009) - www.trotman.co.uk

Training Schemes - www.direct.gov.uk/en/educationandlearning

Welsh Baccalaureate - www.wbq.org.uk

▶ Working in hairdressing & beauty (2009) (Babcock Lifeskills) - www.babcock-lifeskills.com/

Addresses

Comité International d'Esthétique et de Cosmétologie
Waidstrasse 4a, 8037 Zurich
Phone: +41 44 448 22 00
Web: www.cidesco.com

Confederation of International Beauty Therapy and Cosmetology (CIBTAC)
Meteor Court, Barnett Way, Gloucester GL4 3GG
Phone: +44 (0)1452 623 114
Web: www.cibtac.com

Hairdressing and Beauty Industry Authority (HABIA)
Oxford House, Sixth Avenue, Sky Business Park, Robin Hood Airport, Doncaster DN9 3EG
Phone: 0845 230 6080 (UK only)
Web: www.habia.org/

International Therapy Examination Council (ITEC)
2nd Floor , Chiswick Gate, 598-608 Chiswick High Road, London W4 5RT
Phone: +44 (0)20 8994 4141
Web: www.itecworld.co.uk

Vocational Training Charitable Trust (VTCT)
Eastleigh House, 3rd Floor, Upper Market Street, Hampshire SO50 9FD
Phone: +44 (0)2380 684 500
Web: www.vtct.org.uk

Similar Jobs

Aromatherapist, Beauty Consultant, Hairdresser, Massage Therapist, Nail Technician, Spa Therapist

Bee Farmer

also known as: Apiarist, Beekeeper: Commercial

CRCI:Environment, Animals and Plants

CLCI:WAB Job Band: 1

Job Description

Bee farmers work on a commercial honey farm on either rented or privately owned land looking after many hives of bees, where the honey is collected and sold for a profit. There are routine tasks involved throughout the year. They make sure the bees are close to plants and trees with flowers/blossom that provide the nectar that the bees need to make honey. Also ensure the bees avoid disease and bee parasites, and keep to the rules and regulations of hygiene, health and safety. They provide new hives when the bees swarm to create a new colony and take care to prevent the bees from swarming away from the farm.

In autumn and winter bee farmers clean and repairs hives and feed the bees with a sugar solution. In summer, they regularly inspect the hives and remove the honeycomb after first quietening the bees with smoke. Then extract honey from the honeycomb using a machine called a honey extractor. May assist in putting the honey into labelled jars for sale, either direct to the public at the farm shop or visitor centre, or to other shops, a wholesaler, local cafis or garden centres.

Some may also help to produce bee-related products such as honey confectionery, soaps, lip balms, skin and hand creams, beeswax, candles and Royal Jelly. Some bee farmers may give informative talks about bee culture to farm visitors.

Work Details

Working hours can vary according to the number of bee hives and work is outside in all types of weather. Sometimes you have to work early in the morning or late at night to make sure that the bees don't swarm away from the land. It is busiest in the spring and summer when there are more flowers and blossoms for the bees. You need to wear boots, gloves and a protective bee suit that also covers your head.

Qualification

- **England, Wales and Northern Ireland**

Band 1: For entry to jobs, no minimum qualifications are needed, but you are expected to have a good level of general education and relevant experience. Some formal/vocational qualifications at any level are useful.

- **Scotland**

Band 1: For entry to jobs, no minimum qualifications are needed, but you are expected to have a good level of general education and relevant experience. Some formal/vocational qualifications at any level are useful.

Adult Qualifications

Formal qualifications are not specified for entry to this job, though it usually requires considerable skill and knowledge of the industry. You can improve your skills and qualifications by working through the Foundation Learning programme. This involves taking credit-based units and qualifications to help you progress.

Work Experience

Relevant experience is always useful and can improve your chances when applying for entry to jobs. You can join a local beekeeping association to gain knowledge of keeping bees. It is useful to gain work experience at a local honey farm, though any practical work on a farm is useful.

Entry and Training

You usually train on the job with an experienced bee farmer or you can take a course in beekeeping. Courses are available at some colleges of further education, including Newbury College, Eastleigh College and Northbrook College in Sussex. It is sometimes possible to do courses by distance learning, and some horticultural courses may have an option in beekeeping. Short, often one or two-day beekeeping courses are also run by local branches of the British (and Scottish) Beekeepers' Association, including introductory courses for potential bee farmers and apiary management courses. The courses are assessed to promote good standards for bee farmers.

There are legal requirements and regulations to be met when launching any enterprise which affects food production. You need to keep up to date with the legal implications (British and European) for keeping bees and selling the honey. It is useful to be good at woodwork, as you might need to make or repair the hives. You may need to have a driving licence if required to deliver the honey to commercial outlets, or to transport any swarm or hive to another site.

Mature entrants to this job are common. It is useful to have experience in business planning and marketing if you want to become self-employed and expand your business.

Opportunities and Pay

Jobs are mainly with commercial honey farms that are found in rural areas around the UK, though this is a small industry. There are only about 50 commercial farms, with the majority in southern England. Jobs are often seasonal or part time. However, there is a growing demand for high quality 'home' produce, so it is also possible to set up your own business. You need a garden that is big and sunny enough for the bees, and must have sufficient bee-farming experience (two years is recommended) and some business awareness. It can be hard to earn enough income in this way, so you may need another job. At the moment there is a shortage of honey bees following losses over the winter of 2007-8, and this may affect the ability to start a new business.

Pay depends on where you work, but usually starts at around £9k, rising to around £15k a year. Overtime pay is possible. Home-produced honey can sell from around £3-£8 a jar. Bee farmers also make some money by renting their hives to orchard and crop owners who 'hire' the bees for blossom pollination.

Health

You are not able to do this job if you are allergic to bee stings and may find this job difficult if you suffer from hay fever. You need good general health and fitness.

Skills and Qualities

able to work well on your own, business awareness, calm, careful, good organisational skills, patient, practical skills, strong

Relevant Subjects

Biology, Land and Environment, Science

Further Information

BBKA News (6 x year) (British Beekeepers' Assocation) - www.britishbee.org.uk/bbka_newsletters.php

Bee Farmers' Association UK - www.beefarmers.co.uk

Bee Improvement & Bee Breeders' Association (BIBBA) - www.bibba.co.uk

Bee Improvement and Conservation Magazine (3-4 times a year) (Bee Improvement and Bee Breeder's Association (BIBBA)) - www.bibba.com/guidelines.php

Beekeepers' Quarterly (Northern Bee Books) - www.beedata.com/bbq.htm

First Steps in Beekeeping (British Beekeepers' Assocation) - www.britishbee.org.uk/

Foundation Learning (QCDA) - www.qcda.gov.uk

Scottish Beekeeper's Association - www.scottishbeekeepers.org.uk

The Scottish Beekeeper (monthly) (Scottish Beekeeepers' Association (SBA)) - www.scottishbeekeepers.org.uk/index.html

▶ Working outdoors (2010) (Babcock Lifeskills) - www.babcock-lifeskills.com/

Addresses

British Beekeepers' Association (BBKA)
National Agricultural Centre, Stoneleigh Park, Coventry CV8 2LG
Phone: +44 (0)24 7669 6679
Web: www.bbka.org.uk

Similar Jobs

Farm Manager, Farm Worker: Livestock, Fish Farm Manager, Fish Farm Worker, Forest Worker, Gamekeeper

Betting Shop Manager

also known as: Bookmaker, Turf Accountant

CRCI:Leisure, Sport and Tourism
CLCI:GAK
Job Band: 1 to 3

Job Description

Licensed betting shop managers or bookmakers work in a betting shop and manage and coordinate all the betting shop activities. They aim to provide a friendly and efficient service. Managers use the in-shop equipment, including computerised tills and ensure that the counter and customer areas are kept clean and tidy. They offers odds and accept bets for sporting or other events. The job involves displaying information about the day's events on a notice board, accepting bets before the event starts and paying the winning bets later. They keep detailed records of bets placed and paid and use a computer for keeping records and issuing information.

Managers have overall responsibility for the business. This includes achieving profit targets, controlling costs, staff recruitment, including training and supervision, marketing, security and determining the betting odds. Also ensures that the shop operates within the law, and obeys the rules and regulations that govern gambling. Some are multi-site retail managers who are responsible for a number of betting shops.

Work Details

Usually works a basic 39 hr week in a high street shop. Your hours of work can be unsocial and normally include Saturdays/Sundays and sometimes evenings. There are opportunities for part-time work. Some bookmakers work outdoors at race meetings and need to travel to them, and occasionally stay away overnight. You meet all sorts of people, some of whom can be awkward or aggressive, especially if they have lost a bet. Work can be pressurised at times. Smart clothes or a company uniform are worn.

Qualification

• England, Wales and Northern Ireland

Band 1: For entry to jobs, no minimum qualifications are needed, but you are expected to have a good level of general education and relevant experience. Some formal/vocational qualifications at any level are useful for those wishing to become trainee managers, particularly GCSEs in maths and English. The ability to do simple figures is a requirement of this job.

Band 2: For entry to jobs, no minimum qualifications are needed, but it is an advantage to have some GCSEs (A*-C) or equivalent in subjects that include English and maths.

Band 3: For entry to jobs, HNC or a relevant Diploma, usually at least 4 GCSEs (A*-C) including English and maths, or equivalent.

• Scotland

Band 1: For entry to jobs, no minimum qualifications are needed, but you are expected to have a good level of general education and relevant experience. Some formal/vocational qualifications at any level are useful for those wishing to become trainee managers, particularly S grades in maths and English. The ability to do simple figures is a requirement of this job.

Band 2: Although academic qualifications are not specified for this job, it is an advantage to have some S grades (1-3) in subjects that include English and maths, or similar.

Band 3: For entry to jobs, usually at least four S grades (1-3) including English or maths, or similar.

Adult Qualifications

No formal qualifications are needed but the ability to do calculations quickly is important.

Work Experience

Work experience gives you an insight into what you enjoy and don't enjoy about a job or working environment. It gives you the opportunity to acquire new skills and provides valuable information to add to your CV. Work experience can be unpaid or voluntary. It may be holiday or part-time work that you have organised yourself. Any experience of working with customers and cashier work is useful.

Entry and Training

You must be at least 18 to work in a betting shop. Existing cashiers/customer service assistants who demonstrate ability for the job are often recruited as managers. Others may enter management with a range of higher qualifications, including A levels/H grades, BTEC/SQA awards, a degree, or equivalent. A Diploma/Welsh Baccalaureate may be available in your area in Business, Administration and Finance or Retail Business. Apprenticeships in leisure management, retail and/or customer service may also be useful. Although formal qualifications are not usually required, sometimes graduates are preferred for management posts. Most trainee vacancies are advertised in the shop window, in the local paper or The Racing Post.

You may be asked to do a maths test before you are accepted for this job, although further numerical training may be given on the job. It is useful to know about racing 'form' and have experience of working with cash and customers. Sometimes short courses are run by the company covering aspects such as company policy and administrative systems, bet calculation and legal requirements. Other training is given on the job. Trainee managers also receive an in-house management training programme. This can last for up to three months. Those with a bookmaker's permit may operate from a betting shop if they also hold a premises licence. Licensing authorities within local authorities are responsible for issuing licences and permits.

Mature entrants are often those who have previously worked as a junior cashier or a customer service assistant in a betting shop. You can work up to the job of deputy manager/manager with good customer service experience. However, any experience of cashier work is helpful.

Opportunities and Pay

There are a few very large employers who own most of the national chains and run betting shops. There are also independently owned shops of varying sizes. Jobs are available in most towns and cities. Many cashiers progress to become managers. They may then move to area or regional management. Some managers may become independent and set up their own licensed betting business. This sector is experiencing some slowdown in retail outlets due to the growth in online betting and the recent economic downturn. As a result, job opportunities on the high street may be limited.

Betting shop managers earn in the region of £11.5k-£18k a year, rising to around £23k with experience. A district manager earns around £30k and an area manager £35k-£50k. Regional directors can earn much more, up to £100k a year.

Skills and Qualities

able to communicate effectively, able to manage people, able to take responsibility, attention to detail, calm, firm manner, honest, IT skills, numeracy skills, quick thinking

Relevant Subjects

Business and accounting, ICT/Computer studies, Mathematics

Further Information

Apprenticeship Schemes (National Apprenticeship Service) - www.apprenticeships.org.uk

Careers in Racing (British Horseracing Authority) - www.careersinracing.com

Diplomas (Foundation, Higher and Advanced) - http://yp.direct.gov.uk/diplomas

Getting Started as a Bookmaker (ABB) - www.abb.uk.com/careers

People 1st - sector skills council for hospitality, leisure, travel and tourism - www.people1st.co.uk

Racing Post - www.racingpost.com

Springboard UK (Springboard UK) - www.springboarduk.net

Springboard Wales (Springboard Wales) - http://wales.springboarduk.net/

▶ Working in maths (2009) (Babcock Lifeskills) - www.babcock-lifeskills.com/

Addresses

Association of British Bookmakers (ABB)
Ground Floor, Warwick House, 25 Buckingham Palace Road, London SW1W 0PP
Phone: +44 (0)20 7434 2111
Web: www.abb.uk.com

Racecourse Association
Winkfield Road, Ascot, Berkshire SL5 7HX
Phone: +44 (0)1344 625912
Web: www.britishracecourses.org

Similar Jobs

Bank Manager, Cinema Manager, Croupier, Customer Services Manager, Leisure Manager, Retail Manager

Biochemist

CRCI:Science, Mathematics and Statistics
CLCI:QOD Job Band: 5

Job Description

Biochemists are responsible for research into the chemistry of animal or plant cells or tissues, and the way living organisms work. They study processes such as nutrition, fermentation, pollution or the action of substances such as vitamins, hormones, or drugs and their abuse. Some work on the analysis of body fluids and tissues, then interpret the results to assist in the diagnosis and treatment of patients. May advise doctors on the use and purchase of relevant equipment and commercial products. Others may work on production systems, development of new chemicals or causes of animal or plant disease.

May be responsible for managing a team of biomedical scientists and other support staff such as medical technologists, laboratory assistants and clerical assistants. Clinical biochemists usually have a teaching role when working in hospitals.

Work Details

Usually work a 37 hr week, Monday to Friday, that may include some evenings, weekends and being on call. Work is in a laboratory, hospital, university, college, industrial premises or office. Much time is spent standing or sitting at a bench. The work demands a high degree of accuracy. Depending on the kind of post, you may have responsibility for analysing results, presenting reports, teaching, training or supervising staff.

In a hospital, you provide information and advice for diagnosis and monitoring treatment as well as teaching students. Your work environment may be smelly and you may need to wear an overall, protective gloves, a mask and safety glasses.

Qualification

- **England, Wales and Northern Ireland**

Band 5: For degree courses: 2-3 A levels, including chemistry and preferably biology, physics or maths, and some GCSEs (A*-C) usually including English, science and maths, or equivalent. Exact requirements depend on the degree you take.

- **Scotland**

Band 5: For degree courses: 3-5 H grades, including chemistry and preferably biology, physics or maths, and some S grades (1-3), usually including English, science and maths, or similar qualifications. Exact requirements depend on the degree you take.

Degree Information

A degree in biochemistry or biochemical engineering is usually preferred, but degrees in molecular biology, biophysics, chemistry or biology may also be acceptable. Other biological science subjects provide useful background knowledge and can be followed by postgraduate study in biochemistry.

Adult Qualifications

Entry requirements may be relaxed for adults applying for higher education courses. Access or foundation courses give adults without qualifications a route on to degree courses. Check with universities for information.

Work Experience

Relevant work or voluntary experience can improve your chances for entry to this career. Experience in a hospital laboratory, university science department or in an industrial or commercial laboratory, such as in a pharmaceutical, brewing or agro-chemical company is ideal. Undergraduates on a relevant degree course may be able to apply for a 'Summer Vacation Studentship', which provides insight into working in a laboratory environment. Details are available through the Biochemical Society.

Entry and Training

Your training is through practical experience after obtaining a degree or postgraduate qualification. Some employers prefer to recruit entrants with postgraduate qualifications but may give graduates the opportunity to study for a relevant qualification whilst they are working. Many postgraduate courses are in specialist fields of biochemistry, such as agricultural biochemistry and biochemical pharmacology. Those with a relevant foundation degree/HND may be able to enter at technician level, and foundation degrees also lead to BSc degree courses.

Biologist

Biochemistry graduates seeking a professional career can join the Biochemical Society or the Society of Biology. Professional bodies require an honours degree and relevant work experience for membership. Biochemists working in the NHS have to be state registered via the Health Professions Council (HPC), and you also need to continue your professional development (CPD).

Mature applicants require a relevant degree or equivalent qualification, and up-to-date scientific knowledge. Those with laboratory technician experience may have an advantage for course entry, and employers welcome those with experience from industrial work placements. For those without a relevant degree, you can study through distance learning. Postgraduate study may be funded through the Biotechnology and Biological Sciences Research Council (BBSRC), Medical Research Council (MRC), or the National Environmental Research Council (NERC).

Opportunities and Pay

There are 550 bioscience companies in the UK employing more than 40,000 people, many of whom are biochemists. You can work for many different organisations including hospitals, the industrial sector, agriculture, laboratories and universities. Many are employed as clinical biochemists by the NHS or research establishments including the Medical Research Council (MRC), National Institute for Medical Research, and the Food Research Council. There are also jobs with pharmaceutical, brewing and food manufacturing companies. Promotion is based on ability and length of service and prospects are improved by studying to obtain professional qualifications.

Pay depends largely on the type of employer and may be higher in the private sector. Starting salaries in the NHS are £21k-£26k a year, rising to £27k-£35k for registered practitioners. Advanced practitioners can earn between £34k and £49k a year, and consultants £48k-£86k or more a year.

Health

This job can involve a risk of infection and there is an allergy risk from skin irritants. You need good colour vision for some areas of work.

Skills and Qualities

accurate, analytical skills, aptitude for teamwork, attention to detail, good communication skills, good concentration level, IT skills, observant, project management skills, research skills, scientific approach

Relevant Subjects

Biology, Chemistry, English, ICT/Computer studies, Mathematics, Physics, Science

Further Information

Biochemical Journal (Biochem. Society, monthly) (Portland Press) - www.biochemj.org

Careers in Clinical Biochemistry (The Association of Clinical Biochemists (ACB)) - www.acb.org.uk/site/faq.asp

Careers in the Pharmaceutical Industry (ABPI) (Association of British Pharmaceutical Industry (ABPI)) - www.abpi.org.uk/education/careers.asp

NHS Careers (NHS Careers) - www.nhscareers.nhs.uk

What Careers are there for Biochemists? (Biochemical Society) - www.biochemistry.org/education/careers.htm

▶Working in science (2007) (Babcock Lifeskills) - www.babcock-lifeskills.com/

Addresses

Biochemical Society
Charles Darwin House 12 Roger Street, London WC1N 2JU
Phone: +44 (0)20 7685 2400
Web: www.biochemistry.org

Biotechnology and Biological Sciences Research Council (BBSRC)
Polaris House North Star Avenue, Swindon, Wiltshire SN2 1UH
Phone: +44 (0)1793 413 200
Web: www.bbsrc.ac.uk

Health Professions Council (HPC)
Park House, 184 Kennington Park Road, London SE11 4BU
Phone: +44 (0)20 7582 0866
Web: www.hpc-uk.org

Institute of Biomedical Science (IBMS)
12 Coldbath Square, London EC1R 5HL
Phone: +44 (0) 20 7713 0214
Web: www.ibms.org

Medical Research Council (MRC)
20 Park Crescent, London W1B 1AL
Phone: +44 (0)20 7636 5422
Web: www.mrc.ac.uk

Natural Environment Research Council (NERC)
Polaris House North Star Avenue, Swindon, Wiltshire SN2 1EU
Phone: +44 (0)1793 411 500
Web: www.nerc.ac.uk

Royal Society of Chemistry (RSC)
Education Department, Burlington House, Piccadilly, London W1J 0BA
Phone: +44 (0)20 7437 8656
Web: www.rsc.org

School of Biological Sciences
The Queen's University of Belfast, Medical Biology Centre, 97 Lisburn Road BT9 7BL
Phone: +44 (0)28 9097 5787
Web: www.qub.ac.uk/bb

Society of Biology
9 Red Lion Court, London EC4A 3EF
Phone: +44 (0)20 7936 5900
Web: http://societyofbiology.org/home

Similar Jobs

Biomedical Scientist, Biotechnologist, Chemist: Analytical, Forensic Scientist, Immunologist, Microbiologist, Toxicologist

Biologist

CRCI:Science, Mathematics and Statistics
CLCI:QOD
Job Band: 5

Job Description

Biologists are scientists who are concerned with the study of human, animal and plant life. They work both in the laboratory and at outdoor sites, investigating the origin, structure and function of organisms/micro-organisms and their relationship with the environment. Usually specialise in one of the many branches of the discipline. Can be involved in the study of plants (botany) or animals (zoology). May collect and analyse field data, identify pests and diseases, assess effects of chemicals, develop routine tests or devise more efficient production processes. Some biologists lead and supervise teams of technicians, whose main responsibility is to perform the everyday laboratory tasks.

Work Details

Usually works a basic 35-40 hr week, Monday to Friday, in a laboratory at a university, college, industrial premises, hospital, school or in an office. In some posts you spend time on fieldwork. Depending on your job, you can be responsible for devising experiments, analysing data, presenting reports and also supervising staff. This work requires a high degree of accuracy. You may be monitoring quality standards or checking production schedules. Conditions are sometimes smelly and some jobs may involve having to cope with the sight of blood. A white coat or an overall and protective gloves are often needed.

Qualification

- **England, Wales and Northern Ireland**

Band 5: For degree courses: 2-3 A levels, including biology and preferably chemistry, maths or physics, and some GCSEs (A*-C) usually including English, science and maths, or equivalent. Exact requirements depend on the degree you take.

- **Scotland**

Band 5: For degree courses: 3-5 H grades and some S grades (1-3) usually including English, science and maths, or similar qualifications. Exact requirements depend on the degree you take.

Degree Information

An appropriate degree in a biological science is generally preferred, but some subjects with a biological basis may also be acceptable. Other related disciplines, such as a biomedical science or some of the agricultural sciences, can provide useful background knowledge.

Adult Qualifications

A formal qualification such as a degree and up-to-date scientific knowledge are essential. Entry requirements may be relaxed for adults applying for higher education courses, and Access or foundation courses give adults without qualifications a route onto degree courses.

Work Experience

Entry to this career is competitive. A degree in biology may not be sufficient to provide entry and further study may be appropriate. The Society of Biology advises that skills obtained outside an academic environment are highly valued by employers. These can be acquired through paid or voluntary work, sometimes building on a lifetime interest, for example, a love of animals or plants. Sustained efforts in this direction can help with entry to ecological, biological or museum work.

Entry and Training

A wide range of courses is available and you should choose your course carefully, depending on the area of work in which you wish to specialise. Most entrants are graduates; degree courses last for three or four years and can be full time or sandwich. Postgraduate study is an advantage and usually essential for a research post. Your training continues through practical experience in the workplace. Those with a relevant foundation degree/HND may be able to enter at technician level. Foundation degrees also lead to BSc degree courses.

Membership of the Society of Biology can be attained by graduates with appropriate qualifications and three years' relevant experience. This may lead to registration as a chartered biologist.

Mature applicants with laboratory technician experience may have an advantage for course entry, and employers welcome those with relevant scientific fieldwork, and experience gained on industrial work placements. Those without a relevant degree can study through distance learning. Postgraduate study may be funded through the Biotechnology and Biological Sciences Research Council (BBSRC).

Opportunities and Pay

You may be employed by a company that manufactures pharmaceuticals, agrochemicals or foodstuffs, working in research and development or in production. Biologists are also employed with a local authority and in central government, such as the Department for the Environment, Food and Rural Affairs (DEFRA), or government agencies. Other opportunities are in NHS laboratories or with water companies, research institutes and universities, or teaching in schools. You can specialise, for example in cell biology, virology or immunology.

Pay varies depending on location and employer. Starting salaries for research biologists are around £20k a year, and with experience £25k-£37k. University lecturers can earn between £34k-£43k a year, and professors around £60k.

Health

The work involves a risk of infection. There is an allergy risk from pollens or animals. You need good colour vision for some areas of work.

Skills and Qualities

analytical skills, enquiring mind, environmental awareness, good presentation skills, initiative, IT skills, logical, observant, problem-solving skills, research skills, scientific approach

Relevant Subjects

Biology, Chemistry, English, ICT/Computer studies, Land and Environment, Mathematics, Physics, Science

Further Information

Biologist (quarterly) (Society of Biology) - http://societyofbiology.org/

Biology for all - www.biology4all.com

Careers in the Pharmaceutical Industry (ABPI) (Association of British Pharmaceutical Industry (ABPI)) - www.abpi.org.uk/education/careers.asp

Civil Service - www.civilservice.gov.uk/jobs

Microbiology - Bioscience @ Work (Society for General Microbiology (SGM)) - www.biocareers.org.uk

NHS Careers (NHS Careers) - www.nhscareers.nhs.uk

Watsonia (bi-annual) (Botanical Society of the British Isles (BSBI)) - www.bsbi.org.uk/publications.html

► Working in science (2007) (Babcock Lifeskills) - www.babcock-lifeskills.com/

Addresses

BioIndustry Association (BIA)
14-15 Belgrave Square, London SW1X 8PS
Phone: +44 (0)20 7565 7190
Web: www.bioindustry.org

Biotechnology and Biological Sciences Research Council (BBSRC)
Polaris House North Star Avenue, Swindon, Wiltshire SN2 1UH
Phone: +44 (0)1793 413 200
Web: www.bbsrc.ac.uk

Department for Environment, Food & Rural Affairs (DEFRA)
Customer Contact Unit , Eastbury House, 30 - 34 Albert Embankment, London SE1 7TL
Phone: 0845 933 5577 (UK only)
Web: www.defra.gov.uk

Institute of Science & Technology (IST)
Kingfisher House, 90 Rockingham Street, Sheffield S1 4EB
Phone: +44 (0)114 276 3197
Web: www.istonline.org.uk

School of Biological Sciences
The Queen's University of Belfast, Medical Biology Centre, 97 Lisburn Road BT9 7BL
Phone: +44 (0)28 9097 5787
Web: www.qub.ac.uk/bb

Society of Biology
9 Red Lion Court, London EC4A 3EF
Phone: +44 (0)20 7936 5900
Web: http://societyofbiology.org/home

The Genetics Society (GS)
Roslin Biocentre, Wallace Building, Midlothian EH25 9PS
Phone: +44 (0)131 200 6392
Web: www.genetics.org.uk

Similar Jobs
Biomedical Scientist, Ecologist, Food Scientist/Technologist, Microbiologist, Teacher: Biological Sciences, Toxicologist, Zoological Scientist

Biomedical Scientist
also known as: Medical Laboratory Scientific Officer

CRCI:Science, Mathematics and Statistics
CLCI:JAX
Job Band: 5

Job Description
Biomedical scientists carry out a wide range of laboratory tests on samples of blood, tissue and body fluids to assist doctors in the diagnosis, monitoring and treatment of patients. They support patient care throughout the many hospital departments including accident and emergency, intensive care and operating theatres. Also test for diseases such as anaemia, leukaemia or diabetes, cancer and HIV/AIDS. May prepare tissue samples from autopsies and surgical operations to establish the cause of death or disease.

They use highly sophisticated and computer-controlled equipment, together with other high-tech equipment such as microscopes and electron microscopes. Scientists keep careful laboratory records of investigations and research, using a computer and help to write and maintain up-to-date policy and procedural documentation.

Work Details
Usually work a basic 37-40 hr week that can include shift work. Hospitals operating a 24 hr service may also require you to be on call for evening and weekend work. You work in a laboratory, often as one of a team of professional colleagues. The work demands accuracy. In a hospital, certain tests require you to spend some time with patients. Mostly you spend your time sitting or standing at a laboratory bench using specialised equipment.

You also have to deal with some unpleasant substances. While work involves some routine tasks, you are under pressure during busy times. Protective clothing is necessary including safety glasses, gloves and a face mask.

Qualification
- **England, Wales and Northern Ireland**

Band 5: For degree courses: 2-3 A levels and some GCSEs (A*-C) usually including English, maths and two sciences, or equivalent. Exact requirements depend on the degree you take.

- **Scotland**

Band 5: For degree courses: 3-5 H grades and some S grades (1-3), usually including English, maths and two sciences, or similar qualifications. Exact requirements depend on the degree you take.

Degree Information
A degree in biomedical science is usually preferred. A number of courses with principal focus on appropriate subjects such as animal physiology, biochemistry, biology, chemistry, human biology, microbiology, physics, or zoology, may also be acceptable. Degrees must be approved by the Institute of Biomedical Science (IBMS). A list of approved degree courses and top-up postgraduate courses can be obtained from the IBMS.

Adult Qualifications
Adults without the normal academic qualifications but who have relevant laboratory experience may be considered for some courses. Check with individual colleges or universities. Access and foundation courses may be available in some areas.

Work Experience
Universities and employers may prefer candidates who have relevant work or voluntary experience, including work in a hospital, a relevant university department, or an industrial or commercial laboratory. If it proves difficult to gain experience in this exact area, then similar or other scientific experience is still attractive to employers and admissions tutors.

Entry and Training
This is an all graduate profession and some degree courses incorporate the necessary in-service experience. Degrees must be approved by the Institute of Biomedical Science (IBMS). Most courses are full time, some with a sandwich year, but part-time courses are also available for trainees in suitable employment. There are also relevant foundation degrees that may lead on to an accredited honours degree course. To become a registered biomedical scientist, you need an IBMS accredited honours degree and at least one year's training in an approved laboratory (this may be included in a sandwich degree). You also require a Certificate of Competence Registration Portfolio and an IBMS Certificate of Competence, followed by registration with the Health Professions Council (HPC).

Once registered, you continue your professional development, such as part-time study for an MSc, which leads to fellowship of the IBMS. After qualification most biomedical scientists specialise. There are several branches you can choose from, including clinical chemistry, haematology, transfusion science, histopathology, cytology, medical microbiology, virology or immunology.

Applicants over 21 years of age may be accepted onto degree courses without the usual entry qualifications, particularly if they have relevant experience or qualifications. They may prepare for application to a degree course by taking an Access or foundation course. Mature entrants who gained an HND in medical laboratory science before 1995 may be accepted for training. Those with degrees that do not completely fulfil the requirements of the Institute of Biomedical Science (IBMS) may be eligible to take an IBMS accredited postgraduate top-up course.

Opportunities and Pay
Around 20,000 biomedical scientists practice in the UK, a number that has been stable for some time. Most posts are with the NHS but there is also work with government departments, private hospitals, the Public Health Laboratory Service, the National Blood Service, the food industry and laboratories, pharmaceutical firms, universities and research institute laboratories. Further opportunities exist in the armed services, VSO (Voluntary Service Overseas) and with the World Health Organisation (WHO).

Promotion prospects include laboratory or pathology service management, though these require a more advanced qualification. There are limited opportunities for work abroad, usually in Australia, Canada and Saudi Arabia. Agency work is also possible and occasionally, biomedical scientists may run a private laboratory. Self-employment opportunities are rare.

Trainees in the NHS earn around £15k a year. Newly qualified biomedical scientists working for the NHS earn around £20k-£26k a year and advanced level biomedical scientists can earn £32k a year. Additional payments may be made for overtime and on-call duties. Staff working in London receive an additional allowance. Benefits in the private sector are generally better.

Health
The work involves a risk of infection and there may also be an allergy risk from skin irritants. This job requires good colour vision for certain areas of work.

Skills and Qualities
Able to follow procedures, able to use complex equipment, able to work well on your own, accurate, analytical skills, aware of legal and ethical considerations, IT skills, not squeamish, observational skills, patient, scientific approach

Relevant Subjects
Biology, Chemistry, English, Health and social care, ICT/Computer studies, Mathematics, Physics, Science

Further Information

AGCAS: Health (Job Sector Briefing) (AGCAS) - www.prospects.ac.uk

British Journal of Biomedical Science (annual) (IBMS, Step Publishing) - www.bjbs-online.org

Careers in the Pharmaceutical Industry (ABPI) (Association of British Pharmaceutical Industry (ABPI)) - www.abpi.org.uk/education/careers.asp

NHS Careers (NHS Careers) - www.nhscareers.nhs.uk

▶ Working in science (2007) (Babcock Lifeskills) - www.babcock-lifeskills.com/

Addresses

Health Professions Council (HPC)
Park House, 184 Kennington Park Road, London SE11 4BU
Phone: +44 (0)20 7582 0866
Web: www.hpc-uk.org

Institute of Biomedical Science (IBMS)
12 Coldbath Square, London EC1R 5HL
Phone: +44 (0) 20 7713 0214
Web: www.ibms.org

Voluntary Service Overseas (VSO)
Carlton House, 27a Carlton Drive, London SW15 2BS
Phone: +44 (0)20 8780 7200
Web: www.vso.org.uk

World Health Organisation (WHO)
Avenue Appia 20, CH - 1211 Geneva 27
Phone: +41 22 791 2111
Web: www.who.int

Similar Jobs

Biochemist, Clinical Scientist: Medical Physicist, Forensic Scientist, Microbiologist, Pharmacist: Hospital, Pharmacologist

Biotechnologist

CRCI:Science, Mathematics and Statistics
CLCI:QOD Job Band: 5

Job Description

Biotechnologists specialise in using combined applications of biology and technology to provide new or improved processes or products in areas that include pharmaceuticals (such as vaccines), agriculture (crop management), healthcare (genetics) and the environment (such as recycling/waste management). They can be concerned with micro-organisms, genetic engineering, cell culture or the study and control of inherited diseases.

Some biotechnologists work on the development of new organisms. Others design and develop systems for industrial manufacture of materials such as fuels, animal foodstuffs or antibiotics. There are also opportunities in the development and production of medical devices.

Work Details

Usually work a 37 hr week in a laboratory, Monday to Friday. Additional hours may be necessary at times. You usually work with a multi-disciplinary team, advising, informing and consulting with them. Depending on your post, you can be responsible for analysing results, presenting reports, monitoring production schedules or safety standards. There can be a risk of accidents from equipment. You may need to wear a white coat or an overall and protective gloves.

Qualification

- **England, Wales and Northern Ireland**

Band 5: For degree courses: 2-3 A levels and some GCSEs (A*-C) usually including English, science and maths, or equivalent. Exact requirements depend on the degree you take.

- **Scotland**

Band 5: For degree courses: 3-5 H grades and some S grades (1-3), usually including English, science and maths, or similar qualifications. Exact requirements depend on the degree you take.

Degree Information

A degree in biotechnology or one with some biotechnology content is preferred. Other acceptable degrees include biochemical engineering, chemistry, chemical engineering, brewing, food science/technology and most of the biological sciences. Some other science and technology subjects provide a useful background. There are also relevant postgraduate courses.

Adult Qualifications

A relevant degree or equivalent and up-to-date scientific knowledge are essential. Some universities may offer a science foundation year prior to the degree for those who do not meet the traditional entry requirements. Access to science courses and Open University (OU) courses are also available.

Work Experience

Universities and employers may prefer candidates who have relevant work or voluntary experience. Work experience in a hospital, a relevant university department, or an industrial or commercial laboratory is ideal but, if it proves difficult to gain this exact experience, any work with a scientific background is attractive to employers and admissions tutors.

Entry and Training

Your training is by practical experience after obtaining a degree or postgraduate qualification in a biological science or related field. Degree courses can be full time or sandwich and last for three or four years. Several specialist first degree courses are available and some courses include biotechnology as part of a biological sciences course. Postgraduate qualifications are essential for research posts. There are relevant foundation degrees available that can lead to an honours degree course. Some employers provide structured training programmes and the opportunity to work part time towards a postgraduate qualification whilst in employment.

For those with relevant qualifications and experience, the Society of Biology offers membership that can lead to registration as a chartered biologist. Those with a relevant foundation degree/HND usually start at technician level, but may have the opportunity to study part time towards a degree, and move to technologist level.

Adults may be accepted onto a degree course without the usual entry qualifications, particularly if they have relevant experience. Mature applicants may be considered by some employers, especially those who have worked within the biotechnology industry as a laboratory technician. Postgraduate study may be funded through the Biotechnology and Biological Sciences Research Council (BBSRC).

Opportunities and Pay

The biotechnology industry is expanding and employs over 40,000 people. Biotechnologists are employed throughout the UK, with clusters of companies in London, the south east and the east of England, as well as in Scotland. Many biotechnologists work for companies that manufacture agrochemicals, pharmaceuticals, medical devices, chemicals, food and drink. Some are employed in waste management or by research institutes, the civil service or universities. There is a high demand for biotechnologists and new technology is fast creating more career opportunities.

It may be necessary to move between employers to gain promotion and some biotechnologists move between biotechnology sectors. It is also possible to move into sales, production, marketing, university lecturing or writing. There are excellent opportunities to work abroad, particularly in Europe and the USA.

Pay varies depending on location and type of employer and you may earn more in the private sector. Starting salaries for graduates are £21k-£26k a year, rising to £32k-£42k a year with experience. Experienced biotechnologists can earn more than £55k a year.

Health
The work involves a risk of infection and there is an allergy risk from skin irritants.

Skills and Qualities
analytical skills, clear-thinking, flexible approach, information handling skills, initiative, IT skills, methodical, precise, scientific approach, technical aptitude

Relevant Subjects
Biology, Chemistry, Design and technology, English, ICT/Computer studies, Mathematics, Physics, Science

Further Information
Careers in the Pharmaceutical Industry (ABPI) (Association of British Pharmaceutical Industry (ABPI) - www.abpi.org.uk/education/careers.asp

Open University - www.open.ac.uk

▶Working in science (2007) (Babcock Lifeskills) - www.babcock-lifeskills.com/

Addresses
BioIndustry Association (BIA)
14-15 Belgrave Square, London SW1X 8PS
Phone: +44 (0)20 7565 7190
Web: www.bioindustry.org

Biotechnology and Biological Sciences Research Council (BBSRC)
Polaris House North Star Avenue, Swindon, Wiltshire SN2 1UH
Phone: +44 (0)1793 413 200
Web: www.bbsrc.ac.uk

National Centre for Biotechnology Education (NCBE)
University of Reading 2 Earley Gate Whiteknights, Berkshire RG6 6AU
Phone: +44 (0)118 987 3743
Web: www.ncbe.reading.ac.uk

School of Biological Sciences
The Queen's University of Belfast, Medical Biology Centre, 97 Lisburn Road BT9 7BL
Phone: +44 (0)28 9097 5787
Web: www.qub.ac.uk/bb

Society of Biology
9 Red Lion Court, London EC4A 3EF
Phone: +44 (0)20 7936 5900
Web: http://societyofbiology.org/home

Similar Jobs
Agricultural Research Scientist, Biochemist, Biomedical Scientist, Food Scientist/Technologist, Laboratory Technician: Science, Microbiologist, Toxicologist

Blacksmith
also known as: Wrought Ironsmith

CRCI:Engineering
CLCI:SAW — Job Band: 1 to 3

Job Description
Blacksmiths use specialist skills and techniques to join and work metal, such as steel, iron, copper or bronze. They work on practical items and in creative and ornamental work. Blacksmiths usually work with mild steel or wrought iron using either traditional or modern forge-work techniques. They cut the metal to size, heat it in a furnace to make it soft and then shape it on an anvil using a hammer. They also uses other tools for twisting or bending the metal. In industry, blacksmiths often uses power tools such as air chisels, power hammers, drills and lathes to make the work easier. They rivet, weld and solder pieces of metal together to form anything from gates to candlesticks.

A blacksmith may also work as a farrier, using blacksmithing skills to make horseshoes. Only qualified farriers are permitted by law to shoe horses. See the Farrier job article for details.

Work Details
Usually work a basic 35-40 hr week that may include some early starts, late finishes and weekends. Forges and workshops vary in size but can be hot, noisy, uncomfortable and dirty. Work is often completed outdoors, so there may be extremes of temperature between a hot forge and possibly cold conditions outside. Travel around an area may be necessary to visit customers and collect supplies.

You are standing up most of the time and have to bend and lift heavy objects. There may be a risk of burns and accidents from equipment. You need to wear protective clothing and possibly gloves, boots, safety glasses and ear protectors.

Qualification
No formal qualifications are required to enter this job, although courses or qualifications in related areas are helpful. These can include appropriate NVQs/BTEC awards or equivalent. Areas such as engineering (welding/sheet metal work) or art and design qualifications in three-dimensional (3D) design (metalwork) are particularly relevant. Genuine interest and aptitude are essential.

• England, Wales and Northern Ireland
Band 1: For entry to jobs and many specialist blacksmithing courses , no minimum qualifications are needed, but you are expected to have a good level of general education and relevant experience. Some formal/vocational qualifications at any level are useful.

Band 2: For entry to jobs, no minimum qualifications are needed, but it is an advantage to have some GCSEs (A*-C) or equivalent in subjects that include English maths and a technical subject, or equivalent.

Band 3: For entry to some courses: usually at least 5 GCSEs (A*-C) including English, maths and a technical subject, or equivalent.

• Scotland
Band 1: For entry to jobs and many specialist blacksmithing courses, no minimum qualifications are needed, but you are expected to have a good level of general education and relevant experience. Some formal/vocational qualifications at any level are useful.

Band 2: Although academic qualifications are not specified for this job, it is an advantage to have some S grades (1-3) in subjects that include English and maths, or similar.

Band 3: For entry to some courses: usually at least five S grades (1-3) including English, maths and a technical subject, or similar.

Adult Qualifications
Mature entry is easier for those who have some experience of metal work, particularly forge skills. Specific entry requirements for courses may be relaxed for mature applicants.

Work Experience
Employers or colleges/universities may prefer candidates who have relevant work or voluntary experience. This can include any sort of practical metalwork. Your personal or adult guidance adviser may be able to advise you about how to organise work experience. The British Artists Blacksmiths Association has a list of companies who may be able to offer work experience.

Entry and Training

For those wishing to become an industrial blacksmith, training can be completed in a number of different ways, such as on the job, by an apprenticeship with an individual blacksmith or in metal processing, or via a training scheme or further/higher education course. Rural blacksmiths tend to work alone and it may be difficult to find an apprenticeship in this type of work. The Worshipful Company of Blacksmiths has a directory of blacksmithing firms on its website.

Training is usually by a full time or block-release course to study for a certificate or diploma in blacksmithing and metalwork. There are BTEC/SQA awards in blacksmithing and metalwork at national award/national certificate/diploma level, and also relevant courses in welding and fabrication. Part-time courses are available as well as special interest courses, run by private course providers. The British Artists Blacksmiths Association has details of courses on its website, some of which are outside the UK.

For those who are interested in the creative and craft design areas of blacksmithing, there are relevant HNDs and degrees available, such as the degree in artist blacksmithing from Hereford College of Arts. Check the Worshipful Company of Blacksmiths website for details of courses throughout the country and speak to the individual institutions for further details.

Mature entrants often take up blacksmithing as a second career. Relevant experience such as engineering, heritage work, or in the art and design field, is an advantage. Government training opportunities, such as apprenticeships, may be available in your area. You can also gain recognition of previous experience through Accreditation of Prior Learning or by working towards relevant S/NVQs. Contact your local careers office, Jobcentre Plus, Next Step service or Learning and Skills Council (LSC)/Local Enterprise Company (LEC) for details of training schemes, including apprenticeships for adults.

Opportunities and Pay

You can be employed by a number of different organisations, including industry, farming or engineering firms, but opportunities in this field are decreasing. This job can be combined with other types of business, such as work as a farrier. Promotion to supervisory level is possible. Many blacksmiths are self-employed in small businesses. In the early days of a new business, it may be necessary to have a second job to supplement your income. Increasingly, blacksmithing is becoming an artistic profession, building decorative pieces or specialised street furniture.

Pay varies between geographical areas and type of employment. There are no agreed rates of pay for apprentices and you may start on the minimum wage. Once qualified, blacksmiths can earn around £16k-£20k a year. Earnings for those who are self-employed are difficult to establish but may reach £25k a year or more for the most skilled.

Health

This job requires good general fitness, good eyesight and sometimes good colour vision for certain areas of work.

Skills and Qualities

able to work well on your own, creative flair, good concentration level, manual dexterity, patient, practical skills, safety conscious, strong, technical aptitude

Relevant Subjects

Art and Design, Design and technology, Engineering

Further Information

Apprenticeship Schemes (National Apprenticeship Service) - www.apprenticeships.org.uk

British Artists Blacksmiths Association (BABA) - www.baba.org.uk

Lantra - The Sector Skills Council for environmental & land-based sector (Lantra) http:/www.lantra.co.uk

Training Schemes - www.direct.gov.uk/en/educationandlearning

Addresses

Farriery Training Service
Sefton House, Adam Court, Newark Road, Peterborough PE1 5PP
Phone: +44 (0)1733 319 770
Web: www.farrierytraining.co.uk

Herefordshire College of Arts
Folly Lane, Hereford HR1 1LS
Phone: +44 (0)1432 273359
Web: www.hca.ac.uk

National Association of Farriers, Blacksmiths and Agricultural Engineers (NAFBAE)
The Bullock Building University Way, Cranfield , Bedford MK43 0GH
Phone: +44 (0)1234 750876
Web: www.nafbae.org

Worshipful Company of Blacksmiths
48 Upwood Road, Lee, London SE12 8AN
Phone: +44(0)20 8318 9684
Web: www.blacksmithscompany.org.uk

Similar Jobs

Engineering Craft Machinist, Farrier, Foundry Process Operative, Sheet Metal Worker, Welder

Boatbuilder

also known as: Yacht Builder
CRCI:Engineering
CLCI:ROF Job Band: 1 to 4

Job Description

Boatbuilders construct, repair and restore hulls and fittings of pleasure and small commercial crafts up to around 50 metres in length. They work on boats such as yachts, dinghies and canal/river barges (narrow boats). The job involves studying drawings of design and building the craft in a variety of materials, including wood, iron, steel, copper, aluminium and glass reinforced plastics (GRP). Also produce glass fibre mouldings and fit/secure parts to the exterior/interior of a GRP boat. Finally, they fix the rudder and may add the mast and rigging and install an engine.

Boatbuilders work with cloth material for internal furnishings and use a selection of paints. They select and match appropriate woods, and use woodworking skills to make a variety of straight and angled joints. Also make straight and curved items of boat joinery and interior furniture such as galleys, chart tables and bunk fronts. They use both hand and machine tools, and also moulds and clamps to finish off the interior and exterior of the boat.

They may also do skilled electrical and plumbing work, and welding. Depending on the size of the company, boatbuilders either specialise in parts of this work or, as in small businesses, may complete the whole project themselves. Some boatbuilders also work in the design field.

Work Details

Usually work a basic 37-39 hr week, Monday to Friday, though some employment may require you to work shifts or nights and weekends to complete a job. Work is in a small boatbuilding yard, a marina or workshop, and in all weather conditions for outside jobs. You assist other people and are responsible for working from precise instructions. The job is physically demanding and involves some lifting, climbing of ladders and kneeling or bending down. The environment can be cramped, dusty and noisy, with some time spent working at heights. There is a risk of minor injuries and you may need to wear protective clothing.

Boatbuilder

Qualification

• England, Wales and Northern Ireland

Band 2: For entry to jobs and some training programmes or college courses: no minimum qualifications are needed, but it is an advantage to have some GCSEs (A*-C) or equivalent in subjects that include English and maths.

Band 3: For entry to jobs, HNC or a relevant Diploma, usually at least 4 GCSEs (A*-C) including maths, English and a science, engineering or technology subject, or equivalent.

Band 4: For HND in marine engineering, Diploma of Higher Education or foundation degree: 1-2 A levels and some GCSEs (A*-C) usually including English, maths and science, or equivalent.

• Scotland

Band 2: Although academic qualifications are not specified for this job, it is an advantage to have some S grades (1-3) in subjects that include maths, science, English and technical or practical subjects, or similar.

Band 3: For entry to jobs and for many employers: usually at least four S grades (1-3) including including maths, English and a science, engineering or technology subject, or similar.

Band 4: For entry to SQA higher national award in marine engineering and professional development awards: 2-3 H grades, usually maths and physics, and some S grades (1-3), including English, maths and science, or similar qualifications.

Adult Qualifications

Course entry requirements are usually relaxed for suitable mature applicants.

Work Experience

Relevant work or voluntary experience is always useful and it can add to your CV and improve your chances when applying for entry to jobs or apprenticeships in boatbuilding. Practical and craft experience, and an interest in boats are important. You may be able to help out and gain valuable experience at a marina or boatyard.

Entry and Training

Training is usually on the job, sometimes by a marine industry apprenticeship, together with part-time study through a day-release or sandwich course at a college for relevant qualifications. However training varies, depending on the employer. Some courses can be full time and may be taken prior to finding a job. You can also study for a City & Guilds vocational related qualification (VRQ) in boatbuilding, maintenance and support at level 2-3, a BTEC/SQA national or higher national award, or other appropriate qualification, prior to starting a job.

It is also possible to progress to degree level in areas of marine engineering, including yacht and small boat design. Contact the Institute of Marine Engineering, Science and Technology or the British Marine Federation for details of all courses, qualifications and training. You may be expected to attend training courses away from home.

There are also short courses in boatbuilding, from basic skills to specialised craft skills at some colleges, including independent colleges. The International Boatbuilding Training College, the Boat Building Academy and some maritime museums offer relevant courses.

A Diploma/Welsh Baccalaureate may be available in your area in engineering. See the diplomas website for further information.

Craft skills such as plumbing and carpentry are an advantage when looking for work in a boatyard. Boatbuilding is often a second career and a mature attitude, motivation and enthusiasm is welcomed in the industry.

Mature applicants can benefit through training opportunities such as Work Based Learning/Training for Work that may be available in your area. You can also gain recognition of previous experience through Accreditation of Prior Learning or by working towards relevant S/NVQs. Contact your local careers office, Jobcentre Plus, Next Step service or Learning and Skills Council (LSC)/Local Enterprise Company (LEC) for details of training schemes, including apprenticeships for adults.

Opportunities and Pay

Jobs are usually available around the UK coast (and especially in southern England, Wales, East Anglia and west Scotland) with a marina or boatyard. Most firms are small. With more experience you can become self-employed. There is scope for specialisation, but prospects vary depending on where you live. You may be able to work overseas.

Pay varies depending on individual employer, but a trainee can earn up to £15k, rising to around £21k a year with some experience. Skilled and experienced boatbuilders earn around £25k-£30k. Overtime may increase your earnings. Self-employed boatbuilders may earn over £30k a year, depending on their success.

Health

This job requires good health, stamina and physical fitness.

Skills and Qualities

aptitude for teamwork, attention to detail, energetic, eye for visual effect, manual dexterity, numeracy skills, patient, problem-solving skills, technical aptitude

Relevant Subjects

Design and technology, Mathematics, Physics, Science

Further Information

Apprenticeship Schemes (National Apprenticeship Service) - www.apprenticeships.org.uk

Careers in the Marine Environment (IMarEST) - www.imarest.org/careers/

Diplomas (Foundation, Higher and Advanced) - http://yp.direct.gov.uk/diplomas

Engineering Scotland (SEMTA) - www.engineeringscotland.org

Sea Your Future: A Guide to Marine Careers (IMAREST) - www.imarest.org/membership/careers

SEMTA - sector skills council for science, engineering and manufacturing technologies - www.semta.org.uk

Training Schemes - www.direct.gov.uk/en/educationandlearning

▶ Working in manufacturing (2010) (Babcock Lifeskills) - www.babcock-lifeskills.com/

Your future in the boating industry (British Marine Federation) - www.britishmarine.co.uk/upload_pub/27441_bmf_your_future41.pdf

Addresses

Boat Building Academy (BBA)
Monmouth Beach, Lyme Regis, Dorset DT7 3JN
Phone: +44(0)1297 445545
Web: www.boatbuildingacademy.com

British Marine Federation (BMF)
Marine House, Thorpe Lea Road, Egham, Surrey TW20 8BF
Phone: +44 (0)1784 473 377
Web: www.britishmarine.co.uk

Institute of Marine Engineering, Science and Technology (IMarEST)
80 Coleman Street, London EC2R 5BJ
Phone: +44 (0)20 7382 2600
Web: www.imarest.org

International Boatbuilding Training College (IBTC)
Sea Lake Road, Oulton Broad, Lowestoft, Suffolk NR32 3LQ
Phone: +44 (0)1502 569663
Web: www.ibtc.co.uk

Maritime Skills Alliance
1 Hillside, Beckingham, Lincoln LN5 0RQ
Web: www.maritimeskills.org

Similar Jobs
Carpenter/Joiner, Fitter: Maintenance, Laminator, Marine Craft Worker: Ships, Mechanical Engineering Technician

Bookbinder: Handcraft

CRCI:Media, Print and Publishing
CLCI:SAR
Job Band: 2 to 5

Job Description
Handcraft bookbinders design and make special bindings by hand for books, journals and papers of value. Some work in traditional materials, while others use 21st century materials. Work is usually with collections of journals and papers or limited or special editions of books. They use specialist hand tools for making the outer cases for books. Covers are mostly made in leather but can be in other materials. They sew pages, glue them to the case and often decorates the cover in gilding or gold lettering. Some bookbinders also restore, clean and repair old or damaged books. May often work to a detailed client specification.

Work Details
Usually work a basic 39 hrs a week; Monday to Friday, but additional hours may be required when deadlines approach. If self-employed, your hours are at your own discretion. You work in a craft workshop/studio, or possibly at home. A high degree of accuracy is necessary. Customers may ask you for your advice concerning the condition and storage of the item.

You have to sit or stand in the same place for most of the day, but the workplace is quiet, light and airy. Some glues require you to wear a face mask and protective clothing.

Qualification

• England, Wales and Northern Ireland
Band 2: For entry to jobs, no minimum qualifications are needed, but it is an advantage to have some GCSEs (A*-C) or equivalent in subjects that include English and maths, plus a science, technology or art subject.

Band 3: For entry to jobs, HNC or a relevant Diploma, usually at least 4 GCSEs (A*-C) including English and maths, or equivalent.

Band 4: For HND, Diploma of Higher Education or foundation degree: 1-2 A levels and some GCSEs (A*-C) usually including English and maths, or equivalent.

Band 5: For degree courses: 2-3 A levels and a portfolio of creative work, and some GCSEs (A*-C) usually including English, or equivalent qualifications. Exact requirements depend on the degree you take.

• Scotland
Band 2: Although academic qualifications are not specified for this job, it is an advantage to have some S grades (1-3) in subjects that include English and maths, plus a science, technology or art subject.

Band 3: For SQA national award: no set qualifications, but some colleges ask for four S grades (1-3) or similar.

Band 4: For entry to SQA higher national and professional development awards, usually 2-3 H grades and some S grades (1-3), including English and maths, or similar qualifications.

Band 5: For degree courses: 3-5 H grades and a portfolio of creative work, and some S grades (1-3), usually including English, or similar. Exact requirements depend on the degree you take.

Degree Information
Degrees in fine art with options in printmaking and degrees in book arts are available. Subjects such as print media, graphic design or illustration, are also useful. Check course content carefully for bookbinding modules.

Adult Qualifications
Mature applicants with outstanding portfolios of work may be accepted for courses without the standard entry requirements. There are Access and foundation courses in some areas, which give adults without qualifications a route on to degree courses. Check with individual institutions.

Work Experience
Relevant work or voluntary experience is always useful and improves your chances in application for entry to this job. It may be difficult to find work experience with a bookbinder, but any experience that develops your technical craft skills or abilities in art and design is helpful. Work in a library provides experience of handling different types of old books and may include some book repair.

Entry and Training
Training can be by practical experience after an initial relevant college/university course, or on the job and combined with study in day or evening classes and specialist workshops. There are full time degree and graduate certificate/diploma courses in book arts, bookbinding and book restoration available at the University of the Arts in London. West Dean College in Sussex also offers full time courses in the conservation of books and library materials.

You can also take a short or weekend course, or day and evening classes in a range of bookbinding crafts. The Society of Bookbinders and Designer Bookbinders also run specialised weekend workshops. Both organisations list course providers on their websites. Designer Bookbinders also runs an annual competition for all UK trained bookbinders and an international competition is run in association with the Bodleian Library, Oxford. Check websites for details.

Vocational qualifications in bookbinding conservation and craft bookbinding are available at level 3. Training programmes may be available in your area.

The Institute of Bookbinding and Allied Trades have information on their website regarding bookbinding companies and suppliers of materials and equipment. Similarly, the Art Workers Guild aim to provide a forum, through their website, providing information on issues of craft education and apprenticeship training.

A Diploma/Welsh Baccalaureate may be available in your area in creative and media. This can be a useful introduction to this type of career as you gain practical experience while studying. See the diplomas website or Skillset for further information.

Experience in the art and design field is an advantage. Adults may be able to enter this work through a government-funded training programme. Contact your local Connexions or careers office, Jobcentre Plus, Next Step service or Learning and Skills Council (LSC)/Local Enterprise Company (LEC) for details of all training opportunities and schemes, including apprenticeships for adults.

Opportunities and Pay
You can be employed by a small printing firm, libraries and museums, or restoration workshops who may specialise in bookbinding or restoration. This is a specialist craft and opportunities for training and work are limited. Many specialist hand bookbinders are self-employed and work from home. You may have to buy your own tool kit. There may be opportunities for work on private collections.

A skilled bookbinder earns in the region of £16k-£20k a year; trainee salaries are much lower.

Health
There is an allergy risk from glue and other adhesives. This job requires good colour vision and good eyesight for certain areas of work.

Skills and Qualities
able to work well on your own, accurate, attention to detail, creative flair, manual dexterity, methodical, neat, patient, precise

Relevant Subjects
Art and Design, Design and technology

Further Information
Designer Bookbinders - www.designerbookbinders.org.uk

Diplomas (Foundation, Higher and Advanced) - http://yp.direct.gov.uk/diplomas

Institute of Bookbinding and Allied Trades - www.ibat.org.uk

Proskills UK - sector skills council for process and manufacturing industries - www.proskills.co.uk

Skillset - sector skills council for the creative media, fashion and textiles industries - www.skillset.org

Society of Bookbinders - www.societyofbookbinders.com

Training Schemes - www.direct.gov.uk/en/educationandlearning

Addresses
Art Workers Guild
6 Queen Square, Bloomsbury, London WC1N 3AR
Phone: +44 (0)20 7278 3009
Web: www.artworkersguild.org

University of the Arts - London College of Communication
Elephant & Castle, London SE1 6SB
Phone: +44 (0)20 7514 6569
Web: www.lcc.arts.ac.uk

West Dean College
West Dean, Chichester, West Sussex PO18 0QZ
Phone: +44 (0)1243 811301
Web: www.westdean.org.uk

Similar Jobs
Conservator-Restorer, Paintings Conservator-Restorer, Print Finisher, Reprographics Assistant

Bookshop Assistant
also known as: Retail Assistant: Books

CRCI:Retail Sales and Customer Services
CLCI:OFM Job Band: 2 to 5

Job Description
Bookshop assistants carry out a variety of tasks in a bookshop, including advising customers on the choice of books, maintaining stock in a well organised and attractive way, and handling sales. Receive new stock, fill, tidy and dust shelves and display tables. They also help people to find or trace book titles, sometimes from catalogues, computer databases, or microfiche. Give advice to all customers, although some larger shops have specialists in particular subjects. Read reviews and are aware of popular titles. Senior staff select and order new stock, which must be recorded, using a computer.

Work Details
Usually work a basic 39-40 hr week, including a Saturday (or a Sunday) and possibly one evening a week, but have other time off during the week instead. The work requires learning a great deal about the products you are selling. Occasionally you have to deal with customers' complaints and may have to cope with people who are being awkward. You are responsible for handling money and perhaps for keeping accounts. The work may require you to cope with standing for many hours and you may need to use a stepladder.

Qualification
There are no minimum academic qualifications specified for entry, though employers usually expect good general knowledge and a liking for literature. A wide range of people enter this job, from those with few formal academic qualifications to those with higher education qualifications. Some specialist bookshops, including academic bookshops, may prefer you to have degree level qualifications.

Adult Qualifications
No minimum qualifications are specified for entry to this job, though this varies depending on the employer. A good general education is usually essential.

Work Experience
Relevant work or voluntary experience is always useful and can improve your chances in application for entry to this job. The types of work experience to consider include retail, customer service, library work and any job involving administration experience. Jobs and tasks that widen your experience of working with the public are ideal, as is anything that increases your knowledge of book sales.

Entry and Training
The type of entry qualifications required depend on the individual employer. Some university bookshops and specialist bookshops may prefer those with higher qualifications, including degrees. Some employers prefer applicants with the right skills, such as customer service skills and sales ability, rather than formal qualifications. Training is usually given on the job, working with an experienced assistant or manager. Study for relevant vocational qualifications can be helpful, such as a BTEC/SQA award or a level 3 certificate/diploma in retail.

A Diploma/Welsh Baccalaureate in retail business may be available in your area. Training programmes, including apprenticeship schemes, may also be available. Advanced apprenticeships leading to qualification at level 3 can also be a route into higher education.

Mature entry may be highly competitive for some jobs in specialist areas of bookselling, so entry may depend on your previous work experience and level of qualification. Experience in a related field, such as library work or sales work, is useful, as well as retail work. Some experience in the use of computers can also be helpful.

Opportunities and Pay
You can be employed by a nationwide chain of bookshops or by an independent retailer. The growth in online book sales has caused a decline in the number of bookshops throughout the UK. There is scope for specialisation, such as antiquarian, academic or scientific bookselling. Promotion opportunities are generally better in larger organisations. Some larger bookshops also have a marketing department or mail order section. There may be opportunities for those with appropriate experience, skills and financial resources to become self-employed.

Sales assistants in bookshops are likely to earn around £10k-£12k, rising to £13k-£19k a year, depending on responsibility. Senior managers can earn more than £30k a year.

Health
There may be some lifting and bending, so a reasonable level of fitness is required.

Skills and Qualities
able to get on with all kinds of people, cash handling skills, customer service skills, efficient, good adviser, good memory, helpful, IT skills, patient

Relevant Subjects
English, Media and communication studies, Retail and distribution

Further Information
Apprenticeship Schemes (National Apprenticeship Service) - www.apprenticeships.org.uk

Book Careers - www.bookcareers.com

Bookselling Essentials (BA, newsletter) (Booksellers' Association) - www.booksellers.org.uk/organisation/ba_newsletter.asp

Diplomas (Foundation, Higher and Advanced) - http://yp.direct.gov.uk/diplomas

Real Life Guide to Retail (Trotman) - www.trotman.co.uk

Skillsmart Retail - sector skills council for the retail industry - www.skillsmartretail.com

Welsh Baccalaureate - www.wbq.org.uk

▶Working in English (2007) (Babcock Lifeskills) - www.babcock-lifeskills.com/

▶Working in retail & customer services (2008) (Babcock Lifeskills) - www.babcock-lifeskills.com/

Addresses

Booksellers Association of the United Kingdon and Ireland (BA)
Minster House 272 Vauxhall Bridge Road, London SW1V 1BA
Phone: +44 (0)20 7802 0802
Web: www.booksellers.org.uk

Similar Jobs

Editor: Publishing, Library Assistant, Retail Assistant, Retail Manager

Botanist

also known as: Plant Scientist

CRCI:Science, Mathematics and Statistics

CLCI:QOD Job Band: 5

Job Description

Botanists study plant life, both in the laboratory and in the natural environment. They collect and analyse field and statistical data to investigate the origin, structure and function of plants and carry out research into their relationship with the environment. Plant life such as algae, mosses and lichens, grasses, crops, flowering plants and trees are studied. They may be involved in finding and identifying plants and assessing their habitats (field botany) and the effect of pests and diseases on them. Can also be involved in research and development or conservation for environmental, agricultural/horticultural and forestry organisations. Some botanists take up teaching or lecturing posts. In research and education there may be a requirement to attend conferences and seminars and write papers for publication in scientific journals.

Can also assess the effect of chemicals and pollution on plants and crops. Increasingly, botanists assist in genetic modification (GM), particularly in the development of commercially grown crops, to increase their resistance to disease and crop-destroying insects. They develop routine tests and devise more efficient production processes. Use sophisticated technology, including electron microscopes, radio isotopes, digital imaging, geographical satellite information systems, as well as computer databases.

Work Details

In research and education usually work around 37-39 hrs, Monday to Friday. Fieldwork usually involves some late finishes and weekend work. You usually work in a laboratory, an office, or outdoors on fieldwork. This job demands a high degree of accuracy. Some jobs involve travel around an area, and sometimes abroad. You may be out in all weather conditions and in rough terrain. A white coat or an overall and protective clothing including a mask and eye protection are often worn for laboratory work.

Qualification

- **England, Wales and Northern Ireland**

Band 5: For degree courses: usually 2-3 A levels including biology and preferably chemistry, maths or physics and some GCSEs (A*-C) usually including English, maths and a science. Exact requirements depend on the degree you take.

- **Scotland**

Band 5: For degree courses: 3-5 H grades including biology and preferably chemistry, maths or physics and some S grades (1-3), usually including English, maths and a science. Exact requirements depend on the degree you take.

Degree Information

An appropriate degree in botany, applied plant science or plant science is generally preferred, but some subjects with a biological basis may also be acceptable. Combined subject courses, such as botany with geography, ecology, microbiology and molecular biology are available. Other related disciplines, including agricultural sciences, can provide useful background knowledge. This is usually followed with a relevant postgraduate qualification.

Adult Qualifications

Entry requirements may be relaxed for mature entrants to first degree courses provided they submit evidence of previous study, such as an Access/Open University (OU) course. Foundation courses are available at some universities for applicants who may not have the necessary science entry qualifications.

Work Experience

Knowledge and experience can be gained by attending field meetings of the Botanical Society of the British Isles (BSBI). For jobs that do not need a postgraduate qualification, it is an advantage if you have relevant experience. You can gain this by volunteering with an organisation like the National Trust or Scottish Natural Heritage, or working in botanic gardens. As a volunteer you may be trained in relevant areas such as conservation techniques and plant identification. Contact the British Trust for Conservation Volunteers (BTCV) for opportunities throughout the UK.

Entry and Training

Most botanists are graduates. Postgraduate study is essential for research posts and is an advantage if your first degree is in general biology. A wide range of full or part-time courses are available, including foundation degrees in botany or plant sciences, and you should choose any course carefully, depending on the area in which you wish to work. Some employers provide on-the-job training. The Botanical Society of the British Isles (BSBI) and the Field Studies Council (FSC) offer courses in biological recording that teach plant identification and other field skills. They also offer courses that allow participants to earn hours or points towards continuing professional development (CPD) schemes. Membership of the Society of Biology can be attained by graduates with appropriate qualifications and experience and can lead to chartered status.

Mature entry may be difficult unless with relevant qualifications or experience, such as scientific fieldwork.

Opportunities and Pay

There are about 5,000 botanists in the UK and competition for jobs can be fierce. Employers include universities, private research organisations, conservation organisations, local authorities, government agencies, nature reserves and country parks, botanical gardens and museums, and food and pharmaceutical companies. Field botanists may find employment in public gardens, parks and with countryside organisations such as the National Trust, Wildlife Trusts and Scottish Natural Heritage.

There is no established career structure for conservation and field research workers. Progression usually involves taking on more responsibility for projects and advising or managing others. In universities, botanists may be promoted from researcher to lecturer, then to higher grades. Botanists working in conservation, fieldwork or for multinational companies may have the opportunity to work overseas. Some experienced botanists/plant scientists may move into teaching or advisory/consultancy work and become self-employed.

Pay varies depending on the employer and location but starting salaries for graduates are likely to be around £18k-£20k a year, rising to £25k-£35k with experience. Higher earners can make up to £45k or more. Salaries for those working in private industry vary considerably. Salaries for lecturers in higher education are around £29k a year, with senior lecturers earning up to £55k.

Health
This job requires good general fitness and good colour vision and there is an allergy risk from pollens.

Skills and Qualities
able to report accurately, analytical skills, aptitude for fieldwork, aptitude for maths and science, initiative, IT skills, methodical, observant, problem-solving skills

Relevant Subjects
Biology, Chemistry, English, ICT/Computer studies, Land and Environment, Mathematics, Physics, Science

Further Information
Biology for all - www.biology4all.com

BSBI News (3 x year) (Botanical Society of the British Isles) - www.watsonia.org.uk/html/bsbi_news_1.html

Open University - www.open.ac.uk

Watsonia (bi-annual) (Botanical Society of the British Isles (BSBI) - www.bsbi.org.uk/publications.html

Addresses
Biotechnology and Biological Sciences Research Council (BBSRC)
Polaris House North Star Avenue, Swindon, Wiltshire SN2 1UH
Phone: +44 (0)1793 413 200
Web: www.bbsrc.ac.uk

Botanical Society of the British Isles (BSBI)
Botany Department, The Natural History Museum, Cromwell Road, London SW7 5BD
Web: www.bsbi.org.uk

British Trust for Conservation Volunteers (BTCV)
Sedum House, Mallard Way, Doncaster DN4 8DB
Phone: +44 (0)1302 388 883
Web: http://www2.btcv.org.uk

Field Studies Council (FSC)
Preston Montford Montford Bridge, Shrewsbury, Shropshire SY4 1HW
Phone: 0845 345 4071 (UK only)
Web: www.field-studies-council.org

National Institute of Agricultural Botany (NIAB)
Huntingdon Road, Cambridge CB3 0LE
Phone: +44 (0)1223 342200
Web: www.niab.com

Society of Biology
9 Red Lion Court, London EC4A 3EF
Phone: +44 (0)20 7936 5900
Web: http://societyofbiology.org/home

Similar Jobs
Biologist, Biotechnologist, Ecologist, Environmental Scientist, Lecturer: Higher Education, Marine Biologist, Microbiologist

Bottling Operative
CRCI:Manufacturing and Production
CLCI:SAC Job Band: 1 to 2

Job Description
Bottling operatives manage automatic machines that wash, fill and label bottles/jars with food or liquid on a production line. Products can include milk, baby food, sauces, medicines, perfume, soft or carbonated drinks, wine or beer. They ensure that there is an adequate supply of bottles/jars and checks there is a sufficient quantity of raw materials in the machine. May stand beside a conveyor belt on the production line. Any serious problems, such as a complex technical fault are reported to full-time maintenance staff, though operatives usually carry out routine machine maintenance and cleaning.

Operatives help to load and unload the lorries that transport the goods. In food and drink production, they ensure that the containers are fully sterilised before use. Awareness of the rules that govern health and safety is important.

Work Details
Bottling operatives usually work a basic 40 hr week, but may be expected to work shifts, including weekends. Work is supervised and you can be working in a team, often doing the same task over and over again. The environment is noisy and there is a risk of minor injuries. You may have to cope with standing for many hours and also do some lifting and bending. Overalls and protective clothing are provided, including a hat and perhaps something to cover your hair.

Qualification
- **England, Wales and Northern Ireland**

Band 1: No qualifications are needed.

Band 2: For some employers: 3-4 GCSEs (A*-C), including maths and English, or equivalent, are useful.

- **Scotland**

Band 1: No qualifications are needed.

Band 2: For some employers: 1-3 S grades (1-3), including maths and English, or similar, are useful.

Adult Qualifications
General secondary education is expected.

Work Experience
Relevant work or voluntary experience is always useful and can improve your chances when applying for entry to jobs or apprenticeships in the manufacturing sector. Your personal or adult guidance adviser is able to advise you how to organise work experience with an employer.

Entry and Training
Training is on the job with an experienced worker. Some employers are keen to employ people who can also do other tasks as well as bottling. This can include machine maintenance. This may mean that you have to gain some qualifications and additional training. The British Soft Drinks Association has details of training courses on their website, including courses in the manufacture of soft drinks, food safety in soft drinks and basic microbiology. The Institute of Brewers and Distilling (IBD) offers a course in the fundamentals of brewing and packaging for non-technical employees. Check the IBD website for details. Employees are expected to attend health and safety courses.

Appropriate S/NVQs at levels 1-3 may be available. Training programmes, including apprenticeship schemes, may also be available in your area.

Government training opportunities, such as apprenticeships, may be available in your area. You can also gain recognition of previous experience through Accreditation of Prior Learning (APL) or by working towards relevant S/NVQs. Contact your local careers office, Jobcentre Plus, Next Step service or Learning and Skills Council (LSC) Local Enterprise Company (LEC) for details of training schemes.

Opportunities and Pay
Jobs are available throughout the UK with a manufacturing company. However, the current economic downturn may mean there are less vacancies at the moment. With experience you can progress to become a supervisor or foreman/woman. There may be opportunities to work part time, and at times on a casual, temporary or seasonal basis.

Operatives are likely to earn around £11.5k a year, rising to £14k-£16.5k with experience. Overtime pay can make up a significant proportion of your earnings.

Health
This job requires good health and physical fitness. There are restrictions on certain skin troubles.

Skills and Qualities
able to operate equipment, able to work quickly, able to work well with others, alert, common sense, good co-ordination, health & safety awareness, manual dexterity

Relevant Subjects
Manufacturing

Further Information
Apprenticeship Schemes (National Apprenticeship Service) - www.apprenticeships.org.uk

Careers in Food & Drink - www.careersinfoodanddrink.co.uk

Improve Ltd - sector skills council for food and drink manufacturing and processing - www.improveltd.co.uk

Training Schemes - www.direct.gov.uk/en/educationandlearning

▶Working in food & drink (2007) (Babcock Lifeskills) - www.babcock-lifeskills.com/

Addresses
British Soft Drinks Association
20-22 Stukeley Street, London WC2B 5LR
Phone: +44 (0)20 7430 0356
Web: www.britishsoftdrinks.com

Food and Drink Federation (FDF)
6 Catherine Street, London WC2B 5JJ
Phone: +44 (0)20 7836 2460
Web: www.fdf.org.uk

Institute of Brewing & Distilling (IBD)
33 Clarges Street, London W1J 7EE
Phone: +44 (0)20 7499 8144
Web: www.ibd.org.uk

Scottish Food and Drink Federation (SFDF)
4a Torphichen Street, Edinburgh EH3 8JQ
Phone: +44 (0)131 229 9415
Web: www.sfdf.org.uk

Similar Jobs
Brewery Worker, Food Packaging Operative

Brand Manager
also known as: Product Manager

CRCI:Marketing and Advertising

CLCI:OB Job Band: 4 to 5

Job Description
Brand managers plan and implement all the marketing activity for particular products, and makes sure that everything a company does sends out the right message about the products. They aim to get people to think of and buy the company's brand when they think of that type of product. Brand managers ensure that the image of the brand reflects company values and encourages people to trust it. Produces brand guidelines to help anyone working with the brand to present it in the right way.

Brand managers undertake market and consumer research to find out what consumers like, spot trends and identify gaps in the market. They think of distinctive names for products and how to make the packaging eye-catching and memorable. Also works out the best price for products so they sell well and make a profit and checks that advertising, marketing and other activities associated with the brand follow brand guidelines. Managers are involved in the production of all advertising campaigns and marketing materials.

They also set up consumer research to find out how people react to the product and advertising. Briefs staff on new products and campaigns and attends events to launch the product to suppliers.

Work Details
Usually works a 37 hr week, Monday to Friday. May have to work evenings or weekends to meet deadlines or attend meetings, photo and film shoots, product launches or trade shows. May have to spend periods away from home, including travel overseas. Is based in an office, but visits other premises for meetings or to observe creative activity.

Works with marketing staff, product developers, market researchers and the legal team. Supervises junior staff. Liaises with advertising agencies, attends meetings and goes to studios and locations for photo and film shoots.

Qualification
- **England, Wales and Northern Ireland**

Band 4: For HND, Diploma of Higher Education or foundation degree: 1-2 A levels and some GCSEs (A*-C) usually including English and maths, or equivalent.

Band 5: For degree courses: 2-3 A levels and some GCSEs (A*-C) usually including English and maths, or equivalent. Exact requirements depend on the degree you take.

- **Scotland**

Band 4: For entry to SQA higher national and professional development awards, usually 2-3 H grades and some S grades (1-3), including English and maths, or similar qualifications.

Band 5: For degree courses: 3-5 H grades and some S grades (1-3), including English and maths, or similar qualifications. Exact requirements depend on the degree you take.

Degree Information
Any degree is accepted, although a degree in marketing or business studies is particularly relevant and may mean you are exempt from some professional examinations. Some courses cover brand management and a few universities offer degree courses in advertising and brand management/communication. You may be able to do a sandwich course and spend a year on a work placement. There are also several postgraduate courses in marketing.

Adult Qualifications
Entry requirements may be relaxed for adults applying for higher education courses. Access or foundation courses provide those without the required qualifications a route onto degree courses.

Work Experience
Entry to this area of work is competitive and work experience can give you an advantage. Brand management touches on many different areas, so paid or voluntary work experience in any of these is valuable. Direct experience of marketing, market research or advertising is particularly relevant. Some courses include work placements or the opportunity to take part in real marketing

projects. The CIM career partner scheme provides a marketing work placement service aimed at final year students and recent graduates interested in a career in marketing.

Entry and Training

Many entrants to this area of work are graduates, but actual entry requirements depend on the employer. A few large multinational companies have graduate training schemes for people wanting to get into brand management. Some people move into this area after starting in a marketing role without a degree and working towards Chartered Institute of Marketing (CIM) professional qualifications such as the CIM Professional Postgraduate Diploma in Marketing (DipM), which is recognised internationally. The CIM also offers an introductory certificate in marketing which may help progress towards a junior brand role.

Training is mostly on the job with experienced staff. You may spend time working with different teams or departments to learn about the products and the markets and work towards professional qualifications through full-time, part-time, distance learning and online courses. These are offered at different levels by organisations such as CIM, the Communication, Advertising and Marketing Foundation, the Institute of Direct Marketing and the Institute of Sales and Marketing Management.

There is an ABC vocationally-related qualification at level 3 in corporate identity and branding which may be useful and the Diploma/Welsh Baccalaureate in creative and media for those aged 14-19 may be available in your area and provide an alternative route into this career.

There are opportunities for adults in this area of work. Employers look for people with good teamworking and business skills. Work experience and professional qualifications may work in your favour. People often move into this job role from a marketing or product development background.

Opportunities and Pay

Large manufacturing, service and retail companies may employ one or more brand managers in their marketing departments. If you work for a multinational company, there may also be job opportunities abroad. Organisations such as charities, learning providers and public sector bodies may also employ brand managers. Internet advertising and therefore branding continues to be a growth area. New entrants often start as brand executives or junior brand managers. Some brand managers combine the role of marketing manager and brand manager. There are also jobs with marketing, direct marketing and advertising agencies where you can work with brands owned by several companies.

You can progress from junior to more senior roles in the company. Promotion can be to take charge of a group of brands or campaigns, have responsibility for the entire corporate brand or become the company's director of marketing or advertising. Experienced brand managers with a network of contacts may be able to get freelance work or set up their own agencies.

Assistant or junior brand managers earn up to £28k a year. Brand managers with experience in this area of work earn up to £45k a year. Senior brand managers can earn £45k-£65k or more.

Skills and Qualities

able to cope under pressure, able to empathise with customers, able to manage a budget and keep records, able to motivate others, analytical skills, business awareness, creative flair, excellent communication skills, good interpersonal skills, good organisational skills, good written English

Relevant Subjects

Art and Design, Business and accounting, Economics, English, ICT/Computer studies, Mathematics, Media and communication studies, Psychology, Retail and distribution

Further Information

ABC Awards - www.abcawards.co.uk

Campaign Magazine (Haymarket Business, weekly) (Haymarket Business) - www.campaignlive.co.uk

Creative & Cultural Skills - sector skills council for advertising, crafts, cultural heritage, design, literature, music, performing & visual arts - www.ccskills.org.uk

Creative Review (Centaur) - www.creativereview.co.uk

Diplomas (Foundation, Higher and Advanced) - http://yp.direct.gov.uk/diplomas

Get into Marketing - www.getintomarketing.com

Inside Careers Guide: Marketing & Sales - www.insidecareers.co.uk

Marketing Uncovered (Trotman 2010) - www.trotman.co.uk

Marketing Week (Centaur Media Plc) - www.marketingweek.co.uk/

Welsh Baccalaureate - www.wbq.org.uk

Winning Edge (6 x year) (Institute of Sales & Marketing Management) - www.ismm.co.uk/magazine.php

▶ Working in marketing, advertising & PR (2008) (Babcock Lifeskills) - www.babcock-lifeskills.com/

Addresses

Chartered Institute of Marketing (CIM)
Moor Hall, Cookham, Maidenhead, Berkshire SL6 9QH
Phone: +44 (0) 1628 427120
Web: www.cim.co.uk

Communication Advertising and Marketing (CAM) Foundation Ltd
Moor Hall, Cookham, Maidenhead, Berkshire SL6 9QH
Phone: +44 (0)1628 427 120
Web: www.camfoundation.com

Institute of Direct Marketing (IDM)
1 Park Road, Teddington, Middlesex TW11 0AR
Phone: +44 (0)208 977 5705
Web: www.theidm.com

Institute of Sales and Marketing Management (ISMM)
Harrier Court, Lower Woodside, Bedfordshire LU1 4DQ
Phone: +44 (0)1582 840 001
Web: www.ismm.co.uk

Similar Jobs

Advertising Account Executive, Market Research Executive, Marketing Manager, Press Officer, Public Relations Officer, Sales Executive

Brewer: Technical

CRCI:Manufacturing and Production
CLCI:SAC Job Band: 3 to 5

Job Description

Technical brewers plan, control and organise the entire production cycle of beer, which is a highly automated process in large breweries. They have responsibility for the raw materials from which the beer is made, the condition and smooth running of the plant and equipment and for managing the operators and technicians.

One of the main tasks is to make sure the taste, strength and appearance of each batch of beer remains consistent. To do this, the production process is monitored at regular intervals, samples are tested and any necessary adjustments are made. In large breweries may specialise in a single stage of production. May use a computer system to control the brewing process and also a personal computer for work such as technical calculations. In smaller breweries may be responsible for several or all aspects of the work. Brewing is constantly changing as new scientific and technological advances are made. Despite increasing automation this is still a hands-on job.

Work Details

Technical brewers usually work a basic 39 hr week, that often includes shift work and possibly night or weekend work in a brewery, perhaps in the production area, in a laboratory, or an office. You supervise and organise people and have to cope with some physical activity, including climbing ladders. Some larger breweries may require you to visit other plant locations which require you to be away from home for short or extended periods. The work environment can be hot, wet, noisy and sometimes dusty. You need to wear overalls, boots and sometimes ear protectors or a face mask.

Qualification

• England, Wales and Northern Ireland

Band 3: No specific qualifications but 4 GCSEs (A*-C) including English, maths or science, or equivalent are usually expected.

Band 4: For entry: 1-2 A levels in chemistry, physics or biology (or equivalent subjects) and some GCSEs (A*-C) usually including English and maths or equivalent. For appropriate HND: usually at least one A level and some GCSEs (A*-C) including English and maths, or equivalent.

Band 5: For degree course: usually 2-3 A levels and some GCSEs (A*-C) including chemistry, biology and maths/physics. Exact requirements depend on the degree you take.

• Scotland

Band 3: No specific qualifications, but four S grades (1-3) including English, maths and science, or similar are usually expected.

Band 4: For entry: usually 2-3 H grades including chemistry, physics or biology (or equivalent subjects), and some S grades (1-3) including maths and English, or similar qualifications or an appropriate HND.

Band 5: For degree course: 3-5 H grades and some S grades (1-3) including English, chemistry, biology and maths/physics, or similar qualifications. Exact requirements depend on the degree you take.

Degree Information

A degree in brewing and distilling is preferred by employers because of its specialist content. It also gives exemption from the first professional exam of the Institute of Brewing and Distilling (IBD). Heriot-Watt University in Edinburgh offers a first degree and a postgraduate course in this subject. Food science, chemistry, biochemical engineering, chemical engineering, biotechnology, biochemistry, microbiology and biology may also be acceptable.

Adult Qualifications

Entry requirements may be relaxed for adults applying for higher education courses. Access or foundation courses give adults without qualifications a route on to degree courses.

Work Experience

Relevant work or voluntary experience is always useful and can improve your chances in application for entry to this job. This can be direct experience in the brewing industry, if possible, or in other areas of science and technology. Brewlab, based at the University of Sunderland, offers a range of start-up courses in brewing.

Entry and Training

Entrants are mainly graduates who, once employed in a brewery, do both on and off-the-job training. Large breweries have graduate recruitment schemes, for those who want to do technical management, but entrance is very competitive. Others go straight into technical or scientific posts.

Once employed in the industry, technical brewers are expected to continue their education and training and pass the professional examinations of the Institute of Brewers and Distillers (IBD). The IBD offers qualifications in a number of areas including the diploma in brewing and the diploma in distilling, both of which then lead on the master brewer qualification. Exemptions to professional qualifications are granted for graduates of Heriot-Watt University who have completed the brewing and distilling courses. Check the IBD website for full details.

To achieve master brewer status you must first gain four or more years' experience and have passed the diploma in brewing. Brewers are expected to undergo continuing professional development (CPD) to keep up to date with new developments.

A Diploma/Welsh Baccalaureate may be available in your area in manufacturing and product design. The advanced level is equivalent to 3.5 A levels but for some university courses, the additional and specialist learning (ASL) component of the diploma needs to include specific A levels eg maths or physics. Check entry requirements carefully with the individual institutions. See the diplomas website for further information.

Mature entrants with relevant brewing experience, including laboratory-based research and development, or in quality control, or work in the general food and drink industry as a biochemist, or technologist/scientist, may have an advantage. Those already working as a brewing supervisor may have the opportunity to study for technical brewing qualifications. The Institute of Brewing and Distilling (IBD) offers the diploma in brewing as a distance-learning course. Contact the IBD for details.

Opportunities and Pay

There are nearly 15,000 people employed in beer manufacture in the UK, but the numbers are declining because of the increase in automation. You can work for a national brewing company or a smaller, more traditional business. Jobs are mainly available in eastern England, Yorkshire and Humberside and London, but there are few vacancies. Promotion to production director or technical director is possible but there is competition for these jobs. Self-employment is possible with experience, such as setting up a small brewery, often attached to a pub. The increasing interest in specialist local beers provides some opportunities for self-employment or freelance work.

Pay varies depending on location and individual brewery but, as a guide, trainees start from £18k-£21k a year, rising to around £25k-£30k. Senior brewers, such as head brewers, earn around £40k a year.

Health

There is an allergy risk from skin irritants. This job requires good general fitness and good hearing. For some areas of work good colour vision is necessary.

Skills and Qualities

able to motivate others, attention to detail, business awareness, efficient, good communication skills, good organisational skills, IT skills, problem-solving skills, scientific approach, technical aptitude

Relevant Subjects

Biology, Chemistry, Design and technology, English, ICT/Computer studies, Manufacturing, Mathematics, Physics, Science

Further Information

Brewlab - www.brewlab.co.uk

British Beer and Pub Association (BBPA) - www.beerandpub.com

Careers in Food & Drink - www.careersinfoodanddrink.co.uk

Diplomas (Foundation, Higher and Advanced) - http://yp.direct.gov.uk/diplomas

Guide to Technical Careers in the Brewing Industry (The Institute of Brewing & Distilling) - www.ibd.org.uk/careers/career-guide/

Improve Ltd - sector skills council for food and drink manufacturing and processing - www.improveltd.co.uk

Journal of the Institute of Brewing (Institute of Brewing & Distilling) - www.scientificsocieties.org/jib/

Real Life Guide to Manufacturing & Product Design (Trotman 2009) - www.trotman.co.uk

Welsh Baccalaureate - www.wbq.org.uk

▶Working in manufacturing (2010) (Babcock Lifeskills) - www.babcock-lifeskills.com/

▶Working in science (2007) (Babcock Lifeskills) - www.babcock-lifeskills.com/

Addresses

Heriot-Watt University
Edinburgh Campus EH14 4AS
Phone: 0131 449 5111
Web: www.hw.ac.uk

Institute of Brewing & Distilling (IBD)
33 Clarges Street, London W1J 7EE
Phone: +44 (0)20 7499 8144
Web: www.ibd.org.uk

Similar Jobs

Biochemist, Biotechnologist, Food Scientist/Technologist, Laboratory Technician: Science

Brewery Worker

CRCI:Manufacturing and Production
CLCI:SAC Job Band: 1 to 2

Job Description

Brewery workers assist with all the different stages of beer making in a brewery. They carry out a variety of jobs under the supervision of a technical brewer. May make 'wort' from sugar and barley or hops. This is then fermented with yeast to make beer. Workers also check the temperature of the beer, take regular samples, keep things sterile and help to pack and distribute the beer. Large breweries have computerised machines to do many of these jobs. These are monitored and controlled by brewery workers. Brewery workers ensure that all work processes and practices conform to health and safety rules and regulations. Sterilising equipment and keeping production areas very clean is an important part of the work.

Work Details

Brewery workers usually work a 39-40 hr week. This may include shift work and you may have to work weekends. You work under the supervision of a technical brewer and are active most of the time. The brewery can often be hot, wet, noisy and sometimes dusty. There is a risk of accidents when using machinery. You need to wear overalls and boots and sometimes a face mask or ear protectors.

Qualification

- **England, Wales and Northern Ireland**

Band 1: No minimum qualifications are required, but you are expected to have a good level of general education. However, some formal/vocational qualifications at any level are useful.

Band 2: Although academic qualifications are not specified for this job, it is an advantage to have some GCSEs (A*-C) in subjects that include English and maths, or equivalent.

- **Scotland**

Band 1: No minimum qualifications are required, but you are expected to have a good level of general education. However, some formal/vocational qualifications at any level are useful.

Band 2: Although academic qualifications are not specified for this job, it is an advantage to have some S grades (1-3) in subjects that include English and maths, or similar.

Adult Qualifications

There are no minimum entry qualifications, but a good secondary level of education is expected, as is some relevant experience.

Work Experience

Work or voluntary experience is always useful. This can improve your chances when applying for entry to jobs or apprenticeships. Your personal or adult guidance adviser should be able to advise you on how to organise work experience.

Entry and Training

Training usually takes place on the job, possibly through a company training scheme. Topics include company policies, health and safety rules and regulations, operation of brewing equipment, and hygiene. Those who do shift work are usually over 18.

The Institute of Brewing & Distilling (IBD) offers a range of courses relevant to the brewing industry. These include a course on the fundamentals of brewing and packaging. Those with experience may be able to move on to some of the more technical courses, some of which are available by distance learning. Check the IBD website for details.

S/NVQs are available at levels 1-3 in food manufacture. Relevant training programmes, including apprenticeship schemes, may be available in your area. Advanced apprenticeships leading to qualification at level 3 can be a route into higher education. A Diploma/Welsh Baccalaureate may be available in your area in manufacturing and product design. This may give relevant background for entry to this type of work.

Government training opportunities, such as apprenticeships, may be available in your area. You can also gain recognition of previous experience through Accreditation of Prior Learning (APL) or by working towards relevant S/NVQs. Contact your local careers office, Jobcentre Plus, Next Step service or Learning and Skills Council (LSC) Local Enterprise Company (LEC) for details of training schemes.

Opportunities and Pay

Approximately 15,000 people are employed in the brewing industry in the UK. There has been a steady increase in the number of breweries nationwide, but many of these are owned by multi-national industrial brewers and rely on increased mechanisation in production. Jobs are available with smaller independent breweries but they require less staff.

Jobs are only available in certain areas of the UK. With experience, there may be opportunities for promotion. You need further training to move into technical brewing.

Pay varies depending on location and employer. Trainees generally earn around £15k a year. With experience and extra responsibility, senior workers earn up to £30k a year. It is possible to earn extra pay for overtime work.

Health

This job requires good general fitness and normal colour vision.

Skills and Qualities

able to follow instructions, able to operate equipment, aptitude for teamwork, careful, health & safety awareness, numeracy skills, observant, practical skills, willing to learn

Relevant Subjects

Chemistry, Manufacturing, Science

Further Information

Apprenticeship Schemes (National Apprenticeship Service) - www.apprenticeships.org.uk

British Beer and Pub Association (BBPA) - www.beerandpub.com

Careers in Food & Drink - www.careersinfoodanddrink.co.uk

Diplomas (Foundation, Higher and Advanced) - http://yp.direct.gov.uk/diplomas

Improve Ltd - sector skills council for food and drink manufacturing and processing - www.improveltd.co.uk

Journal of the Institute of Brewing (Institute of Brewing & Distilling) - www.scientificsocieties.org/jib/

Training Schemes - www.direct.gov.uk/en/educationandlearning

Welsh Baccalaureate - www.wbq.org.uk

▶Working in food & drink (2007) (Babcock Lifeskills) - www.babcock-lifeskills.com/

Addresses

Institute of Brewing & Distilling (IBD)
33 Clarges Street, London W1J 7EE
Phone: +44 (0)20 7499 8144
Web: www.ibd.org.uk

Similar Jobs

Bottling Operative, Food Packaging Operative

Bricklayer

also known as: Builder, Stonelayer

CRCI:Building and Construction

CLCI:UF Job Band: 1 to 2

Job Description

Bricklayers build and repair interior and exterior walls, chimneys, arches and other constructions. They use different types of bricks, breeze blocks, patterned bricks, firebricks, concrete and mortar. Also use a variety of tools, including power tools, chisels, hammers and trowels. They work with different grades of standard and specialised bricks, including those that are hand made. May cut bricks and blocks to size. Bricklayers spread mortar and lay bricks, making sure they are straight and in line by using a plumb line and spirit level. They finish mortar with a special pointing trowel.

Some bricklayers create decorative features, such as ornamental walls and archways, by using the bricks as a feature. This may include a herringbone pattern, or setting the bricks in a spiral archway support. Some specialise in the maintenance or restoration of old and historic buildings. Others work on the linings of tunnels, or build extensions to existing properties. Some mainly work on new buildings, either on a small or large building site.

Work Details

Bricklayers usually work a 39 hr week, Monday to Friday. You may be expected to work some evenings and weekends to meet deadlines. The work is on site and you transfer to a new property or building project when each job is finished. Travel is required and sometimes you may need to stay away from home. Bricklaying involves heavy lifting, kneeling, bending, climbing ladders and working at heights on scaffolding. You work in a team with other construction workers, including joiners, plasterers and labourers. The work environment may be dirty, dusty and often cold, damp or muddy.

There may be a risk of injury, for example through falling from heights. A safety helmet and protective footwear is needed and sometimes protective eyewear. You also need to be able to read plans and drawings to work out how a structure needs to be built.

Qualification

- **England, Wales and Northern Ireland**

Band 1: No minimum qualifications are required, though a training programme approved by ConstructionSkills requires you to have had a good general education. Some formal/vocational qualifications at any level are useful.

Band 2: Although academic qualifications are not specified for this job, employers may expect some GCSEs (A*-C) in subjects such as English, maths, science, design and technology, or equivalent.

- **Scotland**

Band 1: No minimum qualifications are required, though a training programme approved by ConstructionSkills requires you to have had a good general education. Some formal/vocational qualifications at any level are useful.

Band 2: Although academic qualifications are not specified for this job, employers may expect some S grades (1-3) in subjects such as English, maths, science, design and technology, or similar.

Adult Qualifications

Entry requirements for courses may be relaxed for mature applicants with relevant work experience.

Work Experience

Relevant work or voluntary experience is always useful and can improve your chances when applying for entry to construction jobs and apprenticeships. It may be possible to gain work experience with a construction company whilst at school. The foundation certificate in building and craft occupations is available in some schools/ colleges in England and Wales. Health and safety issues may mean that there are certain jobs you can't do until you are over 16. Contact your local ConstructionSkills office for advice.

Entry and Training

Most young people enter aged 16-17 through specific schemes, with training usually extended by a nationally approved traineeship or apprenticeship. Some will have taken a Diploma or Welsh Baccalaureate in construction and the built environment prior to entry. In many areas of England and Wales there is a three-year Construction Apprenticeship Scheme. In Scotland the Scottish Building Apprenticeship and Training Council (SBATC) runs a four-year Scottish Building Apprenticeship Scheme (SVQ Level 3). Candidates for all schemes may be required to take an initial assessment. Training is on the job and by day release or a block-release course working towards nationally recognised qualifications. You also work towards gaining a level of competence card through the construction skills certification scheme (CSCS) to indicate your individual skill level.

There are a range of construction qualifications available throughout the country. There is a Scottish progression award/ skills for work award in building crafts and BTEC offer relevant courses at different levels, such as the introductory certificate and diploma in construction at level 1. NVQs in trowel occupations at levels 1-3 are available and an SVQ level 3 in construction: bricklaying.

The CSkills awards level 1 diploma in bricklaying replaces the foundation level Construction Award, which remain at intermediate and advanced level (England, Wales and Northern Ireland), and are available for those who are unable to gain workplace experience for NVQs. Foundation level is still available in trowel occupations. Intermediate Construction Award (ICA) qualified students may be eligible to join a Programme Led Apprenticeship; this enables you to receive on-the-job training with an employer who is committed to offering you a wide variety of work. Check the bconstructive website for details.

Specialist training is also available for those who wish to concentrate on achieving skills in restoration and heritage work. Contact the National Heritage Training Group has further information.

There are other routes to this job, including one and two-year full-time college courses in some areas of the country. You can also be trained and work for the Royal Engineers (Army) as a military engineer (bricklayer and concreter) and gain nationally recognised qualifications.

Mature applicants with relevant work experience in the building and construction trades have a reasonable chance of training opportunities. Contact your local careers office, Jobcentre Plus,

Next Step service or Learning and Skills Council/Local Enterprise Company for details of training opportunities, including apprenticeship schemes for adults.

Opportunities and Pay

Most work for building firms, civil engineering or construction companies. You can also work for the marine or gas industry, local authorities, or private homeowners. Availability of work depends on the state of the building trade and the national economy. Currently there is a downturn in the housing market which means there may be a shortage of vacancies for bricklayers. You can progress to technician level and move into construction/site management. There may be opportunities for contract work abroad. Many bricklayers are self-employed and work on their own on short or long-term contracts.

Bricklayers are mostly paid according to national industry rates, but pay can vary, depending on location and employer. A general building operative without specific qualifications earns £7.73 an hour. The basic standard hourly rate for qualified bricklayers is around £8.95-£10.41. The rate depends on your level of qualification. This can work out at around £18k-£21k a year. Those with a level 3 qualification earn from £21k and, with experience, up to £26k a year. Bonuses and overtime pay may be available. Employers may give allowances for travel and cost of lodgings. Self-employed annual incomes can be around £25k-£30k a year, or more.

Health

There may be an allergy risk from dust. You need good general fitness and stamina.

Skills and Qualities

able to follow drawings and plans, able to work both on your own and in a team, accurate measuring and calculating skills, enjoy working outdoors, head for heights, manual dexterity, methodical, safety conscious

Relevant Subjects

Construction and built environment, Design and technology

Further Information

Apprenticeship Schemes (National Apprenticeship Service) - www.apprenticeships.org.uk

Army Careers Website - www. army.mod.uk

bconstructive - www.bconstructive.co.uk/

Careers in Construction - www.bconstructive.co.uk

Construction Skills Certification Scheme (CSCS) - www.cscs.uk.com

ConstructionSkills - sector skills council for the construction industry - www.cskills.org

Diplomas (Foundation, Higher and Advanced) - http://yp.direct.gov.uk/diplomas

Welsh Baccalaureate - www.wbq.org.uk

What's it like to be a Builder (A&C Black 2008)

▶Working in construction & the built environment (2007) (Babcock Lifeskills) - www.babcock-lifeskills.com/

Addresses

National Heritage Training Group (NHTG)
Carthusian Court, 12 Carthusian Street, London EC1M 6EZ
Phone: 0300 456 5517 (UK only)
Web: www.nhtg.org.uk

Scottish Building Apprenticeship & Training Council (SBATC)
Crichton House, 4 Crichtons Close, Holyrood, Edinburgh EH8 8DT
Phone: +44 (0)131 556 8866
Web: www.sbatc.co.uk

Similar Jobs

Carpenter/Joiner, Construction Operative, Plasterer, Roofer, Steeplejack, Stonemason: Fixer

Broadcast Journalist

also known as: Journalist: TV/Radio, News Reporter: TV/Radio

CRCI:Media, Print and Publishing
CLCI:GAL

Job Band: 4 to 5

Job Description

Broadcast journalists research, investigate, write and present news items for television and radio across a range of news and current affairs topics, usually at short notice. They generate stories, attend press conferences, write reports, interview people, and may also comment on world events. Journalists set up and conduct interviews as part of the coverage and decide on the best way to present the item. They prepare carefully timed scripts and present directly to camera, radio or in a studio. They are often on location, indoors or outdoors.

Journalists work to tight deadlines and are often required to report 'live' to a viewing or listening audience, which can also be worldwide. They are also involved in meetings and briefings with other members of the news team.

Work Details

You may be working in an open plan, and usually hectic, newsroom, studio, or on location. Working hours depend on the programme, but are often unsocial and include early mornings, evenings and weekends. You may have to stay away from home overnight, and for some companies, travel abroad. Outdoor reporting is in all weathers and conditions. The work can be demanding and stressful, often requiring instant decision-making and working hard and fast, though maintaining accuracy. You have to meet with a wide range of people and need to be sensitive to their emotions.

Some people may be aggressive and hostile, so you need to keep calm. You need to have wide general knowledge, speak standard English clearly and naturally, and have a keen interest in current affairs. Knowledge of media law and ethics is essential.

Qualification

• England, Wales and Northern Ireland

Band 4: For pre-entry training course, such as a BTEC/HND in journalism, or direct entry to a traineeship: 1-2 A levels and some GCSEs (A*-C) usually including English, or equivalent.

Band 5: For degree courses, followed by a traineeship or postgraduate course: 2-3 A levels and some GCSEs (A*-C) usually including English or equivalent qualifications. Some degrees in journalism require A level English. Exact requirements depend on the degree you take.

• Scotland

Band 4: For SQA /HND course in journalism, journalism studies or direct entry to traineeship: 2-3 H grades and some S grades (1-3) usually including English, or similar.

Band 5: For a degree, followed by a traineeship or postgraduate course: 3-5 H grades and some S grades (1-3), usually including English, or similar. Some degrees in journalism require H grade English. Exact requirements depend on the degree you take.

Degree Information

There are degrees in journalism and broadcast journalism, but you can choose your preferred first degree specialist subject and follow this by formal journalism training. A first degree in business, finance, economics or government/politics can be useful. Employers look for a postgraduate diploma or MA in broadcasting, radio multimedia, TV or online journalism.

Adult Qualifications

Many entrants are adults, but they normally have several years' experience in print journalism. Mature entrants may not need the standard entry requirements for higher education courses. Previous relevant experience and an ability to study at the appropriate level is required.

Work Experience

Entry to this job/career is highly competitive and it is absolutely essential to have some relevant work or voluntary experience before applying for jobs or full-time training in journalism. Experience of student and community broadcasting, hospital radio, local radio and newspapers and amateur drama is extremely useful as you need to demonstrate your enthusiasm and commitment. Companies such as the BBC and Independent Television (ITV) offer short-term work experience opportunities.

Entry and Training

Most broadcast journalists are graduates with a proven interest in journalism. There are some news-training schemes run by broadcasting companies, such as the BBC, and independent broadcast companies, including Channel 4 and ITV. However, competition for places is fierce. Direct entry without a degree is theoretically possible, but unlikely, due to intense competition. Increasingly, applicants have completed a pre-entry course accredited by the Broadcast Journalism Training Council (BJTC). A list of accredited degrees and postgraduate courses is available on their website. This website also gives details of bursaries and sponsorship for postgraduate courses.

Many broadcast journalists do not start in this work until they are in their early twenties and have experience of key journalistic skills. Some people move into broadcasting from print journalism.

The majority of training is on the job, supplemented by short, in-service courses. Many broadcast journalists have training in the skills of being able to record and edit their own footage. Training in computer and web design applications is useful for getting into online journalism. Skillset/the British Film Institute produce the Media Courses Directory which has details of a very wide range of training opportunities in the industry. The National Union of Journalists also runs short training courses. Several foundation degrees in journalism, including a broadcast journalism course, are also available.

A Diploma/Welsh Baccalaureate may be available in your area in creative and media. This can be a useful introduction to this type of career as you gain practical experience while studying. See the diplomas website or Skillset for further information. Cyfle (Wales) also offers a range of training courses for new entrants to the industry and professional development for those already employed.

Mature entrants with relevant experience are often welcomed by employers, and those who are experts in a particular field may also be able to gain some freelance work. Distance-learning courses in journalism are available, such as those offered by the National Council for the Training of Journalists, and the London School of Journalism. Graduates can take a part-time (fast track) pre-entry postgraduate course in journalism.

Opportunities and Pay

Employers include local and national terrestrial television and radio broadcasters, cable and satellite broadcasting companies, and specialist news agencies. There are also jobs with independent production companies or with newspapers for online roles. Many companies are based in London, though local radio and TV stations are based in major towns and cities throughout the UK. Digitalisation has considerably increased the number of channels with some running 24 hr news channels, though competition for jobs is still intense.

You can progress to become a senior broadcast journalist, a studio-based presenter, news anchor or a correspondent.

Pay varies depending on the employing media company, but trainees generally earn £14k-£20k a year, and with several year's experience this can rise to up to £40k a year. Many work freelance and fees are based on experience. Salaries tend to be higher in TV than radio. Highly successful senior broadcast correspondents can earn up to £100k a year.

Skills and Qualities

able to cope under pressure, analytical skills, clear speaking voice, flexible approach, good communication skills, good interviewing skills, good written English, interest in current affairs, IT skills, quick thinking, self confident

Relevant Subjects

Economics, English, Geography, Government and politics, Media and communication studies

Further Information

Behind the Scenes: Television (Trotman 2009) - www.trotman.co.uk

Broadcast Magazine (weekly) (Emap) - www.broadcastnow.co.uk

Broadcast Now (Emap Ltd) - www.broadcastnow.co.uk

Careers Wales - www.careerswales.com/

Channel 4 - www.channel4.com

Community Media Association - www.commedia.org.uk

Cyfle (Wales) - www.cyfle.co.uk

Diplomas (Foundation, Higher and Advanced) - http://yp.direct.gov.uk/diplomas

Hospital Broadcasting Association - www.hbauk.com

ITV Jobs (ITV) - www.itvjobs.com

Journalism Uncovered (Trotman 2009) - www.trotman.co.uk

Media Week (weekly) (Haymarket Publishing Ltd) - www.haymarket.com/mediaweek/default.aspx

Media/Multimedia Courses Directory (BFI/Skillset) - www.bfi.org.uk/education/talkscourses/mediacourses/

National Council for the Training of Journalists (NCTJ) - www.nctj.com

Skillset - sector skills council for the creative media, fashion and textiles industries - www.skillset.org

The Broadcast Journalism Handbook (Longmans 2007)

Welsh Baccalaureate - www.wbq.org.uk

▶ Working in creative & media (2007) (Babcock Lifeskills) - www.babcock-lifeskills.com/

Addresses

BBC Recruitment Services
Recruitment BBC HR Direct, PO Box 1133, Belfast BT1 9GP
Web: www.bbc.co.uk/jobs

Belfast Metropolitan College
Gerald Moag Campus Millfield, Belfast BT1 1HS
Phone: +44 (0) 28 9026 5265
Web: www.belfastmet.ac.uk

Broadcast Journalism Training Council (BJTC)
18 Miller's Close, Rippingale, Nr. Bourne, Lincolnshire PE10 0TH
Phone: +44 (0)1778 440 025
Web: www.bjtc.org.uk

Chartered Institute of Journalists (CIoJ)
2 Dock Offices, Surrey Quays Road, London SE16 2XU
Phone: +44 (0)20 7252 1187
Web: www.cioj.co.uk

London School of Journalism
126 Shirland Road Maida Vale, London W9 2BT
Phone: +44 (0) 20 7432 8140
Web: www.home-study.com

National Union of Journalists (NUJ)
Headland House, 308-312 Grays Inn Road, London WC1X 8DP
Phone: +44 (0)20 7278 7916
Web: www.nuj.org.uk

Similar Jobs

Broadcast Researcher, Film/TV Producer, Journalist, Journalist: Magazine, Political/Parliamentary Researcher, Presenter: Radio & TV, Writer

Broadcast Researcher

also known as: Film Researcher, Programme Researcher, Radio Researcher, TV Researcher

CRCI:Media, Print and Publishing
CLCI:GAL

Job Band: 4 to 5

Job Description

Broadcast researchers check information, facts and figures for the production team in TV, film or radio programmes. They liaise with a producer and director to establish the production requirements, then originate and develop project ideas and present findings to programme producers. May research the location of relevant stills, film and tape archives or music, from sources such as museums, art galleries and government departments, specialist collections, and the Internet.

Researchers undertake preparatory reading, conduct preliminary fact-finding interviews by telephone and face to face, and prepare detailed background material for a scriptwriter. They may have to find and organise suitable programme guests, discussions, studio debates and phone-ins. Also write brief notes and sometimes scripts; checking the results for accuracy, style, legal and ethical considerations.

Some researchers specialise in areas such as documentaries or picture and archive research, in finding studio audiences for entertainment shows, including producing questions and contestants. Senior researchers manage other researchers and may also act as an assistant producer.

Work Details

Many jobs have regular office hours but can also include working unsocial hours. You may be called upon to go out with a voice recorder, radio car and television crew to record on-the-spot interviews. You may ask questions, interview people and extract information from all kinds of written and recorded material. The job requires you to contact many people, often by telephone, to encourage them to help you.

You take notes, analyse details and present the facts to the producer/director and need a sound knowledge of the best sources for your particular area of research. Often you work on your own. You need the ability to work under pressure.

Qualification

• England, Wales and Northern Ireland

Band 4: For HND, Diploma of Higher Education or foundation degree: 1-2 A levels and some GCSEs (A*-C) usually including English and maths, or equivalent.

Band 5: For degree courses: 2-3 A levels and some GCSEs (A*-C) usually including English, or equivalent qualifications. Exact requirements depend on the degree you take.

• Scotland

Band 4: For entry to SQA higher national and professional development awards, usually 2-3 H grades and some S grades (1-3), including English and maths, or similar qualifications.

Band 5: For degree courses: 3-5 H grades and some S grades (1-3), usually including English or similar. Exact requirements depend on the degree you take.

Degree Information

Any degree discipline is acceptable for entry to this job, but subjects such as history, English, broadcasting/media studies, politics, public relations and journalism, are useful.

Adult Qualifications

Entry requirements may be relaxed for adults applying for higher education courses. Access or foundation courses give adults without qualifications a route on to degree courses.

Work Experience

Entry to this job/career is highly competitive and it is essential to have some relevant work or voluntary experience in broadcasting, journalism or general research before applying. As this role is often freelance, it gives you an opportunity to build a portfolio of the work you have undertaken. Work experience is usually offered by broadcasting companies, including the BBC, though competition for places is fierce. The British Film Institute (BFI) requests the help of volunteers during the BFI annual film festival in London; this type of experience is useful.

Entry and Training

Some experience and/or training in broadcasting or journalism is vital. Entrants tend to be graduates, but those with relevant skills and work experience are also considered. Some entrants start as runners or production assistants, but it may be possible to start directly as a researcher with the right knowledge about a programme's content. It can be helpful to speak at least one foreign language. Foundation degrees are also available in some areas in subjects that include television production. IT skills and a current driving licence are also essential for this job.

There are some employer training schemes, but many entrants learn on the job working with an experienced team. Training providers for the film and TV industry include: Skillset, Scottish Screen, Cyfle (Wales), Indie Training Fund and the Top TV Academy. New entrants' schemes and some traineeships are available, but there is fierce competition for places.

While learning and gaining experience, it is vital to build up a portfolio of the programmes you have worked on. It may also be useful to become a member of an organisation such as the British Film Institute.

A Diploma/Welsh Baccalaureate may be available in your area in creative and media. This can be a useful introduction to this type of career as you gain practical experience while studying. See the diplomas website or Skillset for further information.

Mature entrants to this job need experience of working in journalism, lecturing, or perhaps as a broadcast production assistant. This job tends to attract young entrants.

Opportunities and Pay

This job is highly competitive and some people initially work unpaid to gain experience. There are some permanent posts for independent television or film production companies, but researchers are often offered short, fixed-term contracts. Many researchers are self-employed and work freelance. There is scope for specialisation, such as in music, science or current affairs. Most jobs are in factual programming. If successful, your career can progress into other jobs in broadcasting, such as a presenter or producer. You may move into other fields, such as films, books or publishing. Very occasionally, a researcher may be employed by a large permanent theatre organisation.

Pay varies depending on location and employer, but as a guide, starting salaries are likely to be around £18k-£22k, rising to £24k-£33k a year, with experience. Freelance researchers can earn around £150-£400 a day.

Skills and Qualities

able to cope under pressure, able to work both on your own and in a team, adaptable, attention to detail, aware of legal and ethical considerations, enquiring mind, good communication skills, good interpersonal skills, good written English, IT skills, perseverance, resourceful, self-motivated

Relevant Subjects

English, Government and politics, Media and communication studies

Further Information

BBC Recruitment Services (BBC) - www.bbc.co.uk/jobs

Behind the Scenes: Television (Trotman 2009) - www.trotman.co.uk
British Film Institute (BFI) - www.bfi.org.uk
Broadcast Now (Emap Ltd) - www.broadcastnow.co.uk
Diplomas (Foundation, Higher and Advanced) - http://yp.direct.gov.uk/diplomas
How to get a job in Television: Build your career from Runner to Series Producer (Methuen 2009)
Indie Training Fund - www.indietrainingfund.com
Irish Film Board - www.irishfilmboard.ie
Kemps - Film, Television, Commercials (KFTV) - www.kftv.com
Skillset - sector skills council for the creative media, fashion and textiles industries - www.skillset.org
Start in TV - www.startintv.com
Top TV Academy - www.toptvacademy.co.uk
▶ Working in creative & media (2007) (Babcock Lifeskills) - www.babcock-lifeskills.com/

Addresses

Cyfle (Wales)
Galeri 13, Victoria Dock,, Caernarfon LL55 1SQ.
Phone: +44 (0) 1286 685 242
Web: www.cyfle.co.uk

Scottish Screen
249 West George Street, Glasgow G2 4QE
Phone: 0845 300 7300 (UK only)
Web: www.scottishscreen.com

Similar Jobs

Broadcast Journalist, Film/TV Producer's Assistant, Film/TV Runner, Journalist, Picture Researcher, Screenwriter

Builders' Merchant

CRCI:Retail Sales and Customer Services
CLCI:OK Job Band: 2

Job Description

Builders' merchants sell building equipment, materials and products in bulk to the construction industry and retail goods to the general public. Often specialise in particular types of supplies, such as plumbing, electrical goods or timber. May also sell bricks, paving stones, sand and cement, kitchen and bathroom products, or DIY goods. Give information on products and advise on the suitability of materials for a particular use. Deal with customers and suppliers, both on the telephone and in person.

Merchants estimate quantities and costs of materials. Handle building materials and take payment from customers, sometimes for very large amounts. May have specialist responsibilities such as stock control. Order stock and deals with stock records, usually with the aid of a computer. Some companies also hire tools and equipment.

Work Details

Usually work a basic 39 hr week. Builders' yards usually open around 8am, Monday to Saturday. The work environment may be a store, warehouse or yard. You are on your feet most of the time. You must follow health and safety regulations to ensure there are no accidents, and you are likely to wear a uniform and sometimes protective clothing. You may have to move and lift heavy goods and materials.

Qualification

• England, Wales and Northern Ireland

Band 2: There are no set entry qualifications, but a good standard of general education is usually required. Most employers prefer good GCSEs (A*-C) including English and maths, or equivalent.

• Scotland

Band 2: There are no set entry qualifications but a good standard of general education is usually required. Most employers prefer good S grades (1-3) including English and maths, or similar.

Adult Qualifications

Although there are no set minimum qualifications, most companies prefer you to have a good standard of education. English and maths are useful subjects.

Work Experience

Relevant work or voluntary experience is always useful and can improve your chances when applying for entry to jobs in sales. It can equip you with skills that you can use in the future and add to your CV. Experience of working in the building/construction trade, particularly in a builder's yard, is the most useful.

Entry and Training

Training is provided on the job and also by attending short college courses, in such subjects as product knowledge, IT, health and safety, and management. The Builders' Merchant Federation (BMF) offers open learning modules in various aspects of product knowledge and essential skills. You are awarded a City & Guilds construction materials distribution certificate upon successful completion of five modules. The BMF also offers a diploma in merchanting, a self-study course suitable for existing and potential managers of builders merchants. The course is also suitable for those in the industry with specialist responsibilities such as stock control. Small businesses are more likely to offer informal on-the-job training. A driving licence is useful.

A Diploma/Welsh Baccalaureate in construction and the built environment may be available in your area. S/NVQs are available at levels 2-3 in distribution and warehousing, customer service, retail or business administration. Training programmes, including apprenticeship schemes such as those offered through the BMF, may be available in your area. Advanced apprenticeships leading to qualification at level 3 can also be a route into higher education.

Adults may be able to enter this work through a government-funded training programme. Contact your local careers office, Jobcentre Plus, Next Step service or Learning and Skills Council (LSC)/Local Enterprise Company (LEC) for details of all training opportunities and schemes, including apprenticeships. Those who have previous work experience of the building/construction trade, and particularly of working in a builders' yard or warehouse, may have an advantage. An interest in DIY is also useful.

Opportunities and Pay

There are a number of large firms of builders' merchants and many smaller companies throughout the UK. Some firms specialise in a particular type of product, such as timber or plumbing products. It is possible to progress to more senior management jobs. Some experienced builders' merchants start their own business. The current economic downturn may reduce opportunities.

Starting wages for a builders' merchant are likely to be around £11k, rising with experience to £20k a year. Those taking on more managerial responsibilities can earn around £25k a year, or more.

Health

You have to be fit to do this job. For some employers you may need to have normal colour vision.

Skills and Qualities

able to follow drawings and plans, business awareness, cash handling skills, friendly, good communication skills, health & safety awareness, honest, IT skills, numeracy skills

Relevant Subjects

Construction and built environment, Retail and distribution

Further Information

Apprenticeship Schemes (National Apprenticeship Service) - www.apprenticeships.org.uk

Diplomas (Foundation, Higher and Advanced) - http://yp.direct.gov.uk/diplomas

Training Schemes - www.direct.gov.uk/en/educationandlearning

Welsh Baccalaureate - www.wbq.org.uk

▶Working in construction & the built environment (2007) (Babcock Lifeskills) - www.babcock-lifeskills.com/

▶Working in retail & customer services (2008) (Babcock Lifeskills) - www.babcock-lifeskills.com/

Addresses

Builders' Merchants Federation (BMF)
15 Soho Square, London W1D 3HL
Phone: +44 (0)20 7439 1753
Web: www.bmf.org.uk

Similar Jobs

Builders' Yard Assistant, Stock Control/Replenishment Assistant, Vehicle Parts Operative, Warehouse Worker

Builders' Yard Assistant

CRCI:Retail Sales and Customer Services
CLCI:OK Job Band: 1

Job Description

Builders' yard assistants work in builders' merchant yards handling building equipment and materials such as bricks, cement, timber, paint or bathroom fittings. Also check in goods that have been delivered, display them, load goods onto vans or lorries for delivery and keep the yard tidy. May also assist with selling building products to those working in the construction industry or to the general public. Measure and cut certain goods to required size and move materials around the yard using trolleys, ladders and fork-lift trucks.

Work Details

Usually work a basic 39 hr week that generally includes Saturday morning and early starts. The work environment may be a store, warehouse or yard. You must follow health and safety regulations to ensure there are no accidents and are likely to wear an overall and sometimes protective clothing. You have to move and lift some heavy materials around the yard.

Qualification

- **England, Wales and Northern Ireland**

Band 1: Qualifications are not normally needed for this job but some GCSEs, or equivalent, are useful.

- **Scotland**

Band 1: Qualifications are not normally needed for this job but some S grades or similar, are useful.

Adult Qualifications

Formal qualifications are not normally needed for this job, but knowledge of basic maths and English may be required by employers. You can improve your skills and qualifications by working through the Foundation Learning programme. This involves taking credit-based units and qualifications to help you progress.

Work Experience

Relevant work or voluntary experience is always useful and can improve your chances when applying for entry to jobs in sales. It can equip you with skills that you can use in the future and add to your CV. Part-time and holiday employment with a builders' merchant or in any area where you meet the public is usually easy to obtain.

Entry and Training

Training is provided on the job and also by attending short college courses, in subjects such as product knowledge, IT, health and safety, and management. The Builders' Merchant Federation (BMF) offers open learning modules in various aspects of product knowledge and essential skills. You are awarded the City & Guilds construction materials distribution qualification upon successful completion of five modules. The BMF also offers a short training programme in fork-lift and other mechanical handling vehicles, and at the end of each course you take a test of practical ability. If successful you receive a certificate of competence. Contact the BMF for details of training and training providers.

Small businesses are more likely to offer informal on-the-job training. A driving licence is useful. A Diploma/Welsh Baccalaureate in construction and the built environment may be available in your area. S/NVQs are available at levels 2-3 in distribution and warehousing. Training programmes, including apprenticeship schemes such as those offered through the BMF, may also be available in your area. Advanced apprenticeships leading to qualification at level 3 can also be a route into higher education.

Mature applicants are usually welcomed by employers, especially those who have previous experience of the building/construction trade, or work in a warehouse. An interest in DIY is also useful.

Opportunities and Pay

There are a number of builders' merchants companies throughout the UK. Some firms specialise in a particular type of product, such as timber or plumbing products. It is possible to progress to become a builders' merchant.

Pay varies depending on the size of the company, but builders' yard assistants generally earn around £180-£210, rising to around £260-£320, a week. Income can be increased by overtime.

Health

You have to be strong and physically fit to do this job. For some employers you may need to have normal colour vision.

Skills and Qualities

friendly, health & safety awareness, honest, methodical, numeracy skills, punctual, reliable

Relevant Subjects

Construction and built environment, Retail and distribution

Further Information

Apprenticeship Schemes (National Apprenticeship Service) - www.apprenticeships.org.uk

Diplomas (Foundation, Higher and Advanced) - http://yp.direct.gov.uk/diplomas

Foundation Learning (QCDA) - www.qcda.gov.uk

Welsh Baccalaureate - www.wbq.org.uk

▶Working in construction & the built environment (2007) (Babcock Lifeskills) - www.babcock-lifeskills.com/

Addresses

Builders' Merchants Federation (BMF)
15 Soho Square, London W1D 3HL
Phone: +44 (0)20 7439 1753
Web: www.bmf.org.uk

Similar Jobs

Builders' Merchant, Construction Operative, Lift Truck Operative, Warehouse Order Picker/Assembler, Warehouse Worker

See where YOUR interests could take YOU!
Pathfinder live
www.pathfinderlive.com

Building Society Manager

CRCI:Financial Services
CLCI:NAF Job Band: 4 to 5

Job Description

Building society managers direct and coordinate the work of a building society branch and are responsible for its profitability. Manage and motivate staff so that the branch team achieve or exceed their set targets. Communicate with a wide range of people and deal with any complaints. Give advice to borrowers about mortgages and consider applications for loans. Discuss various methods of saving with investors. Try to increase business by attracting new investors and by keeping in touch with local professionals such as accountants, estate agents and solicitors. Market a range of products such as investment schemes and insurance.

Managers are responsible for security of the building and for the health and safety of employees and customers. Prepare reports and present management information for staff and for head office. Motivate the branch team to achieve top performance.

Work Details

Usually work a 35-40 hr week, Monday to Friday from 9am to 5pm, though building societies are often open six days a week and you may have to work on a Saturday. You also go out to meet clients and promote the society's business. Managers often have to work longer hours and may have to attend meetings, such as local business forums, early in the mornings or in the evenings. Formal business wear is expected. A driving licence is usually essential.

Qualification

• England, Wales and Northern Ireland

Band 5: For degree courses: 2-3 A levels and some GCSEs (A*-C) usually including English and maths, or equivalent. Exact requirements depend on the degree you take.

• Scotland

Band 5: For a degree: 3-5 H grades and some S grades (1-3), or similar qualifications. Exact subjects needed depend on the degree you take.

Degree Information

A degree or diploma in any subject is acceptable, but business studies/administration, accountancy, financial management, banking, mathematics and statistics are useful. Marketing or law also provide relevant background knowledge.

Adult Qualifications

Mature entrants usually have relevant previous experience in business, law, accountancy or finance. Entry requirements for courses may be relaxed for mature applicants. There are also foundation and Access courses which can help you to move onto higher education.

Work Experience

Relevant work or voluntary experience is always useful and improves your chances in application for entry to this job. Any work experience in the finance sector is relevant and shows enthusiasm and commitment to the work. Time spent in an accountancy firm, an insurance company or even shadowing a financial adviser gives you a good insight into the profession. In some areas there is a young apprenticeship (14-16) scheme that provides an extended work placement and eventual achievement of a relevant level 2 qualification whilst at school.

Some larger finance companies offer summer internships, usually lasting ten weeks, for those in the penultimate year of their degree course.

Entry and Training

Most direct management training programme recruits are graduates who receive on-the-job training, together with in-service courses that include practical experience of the work of an officer/cashier and short courses on specific aspects of the work. However, some management trainees are clerks or cashiers who have been selected for promotion from within the company. Most senior managers now join as graduate entrants and may receive accelerated training.

Employees who show management potential may receive in-service training that can lead to an accelerated training programme. It is necessary to have A levels/H grades or an equivalent vocational qualification such as the ifs School of Finance professional diploma in financial services management, or a relevant HNC/HND . The Diploma/Welsh Baccalaureate in business, administration and finance may be available in your area and considered as an alternative to A levels. The advanced level is equivalent to 3.5 A levels but for some university courses, the additional and specialist learning (ASL) component of the diploma needs to include specific A levels. Check entry requirements carefully with the individual institutions.

Building society management staff are expected to study for professional examinations offered by the ifs School of Finance or the Chartered Institute of Bankers in Scotland (CIOBS). Full and part-time foundation degrees are available in business, finance and management. The ifs School of Finance offers the foundation degree in financial markets and management and a range of professional qualifications. CIOBS and the Chartered Insurance Institute also offer a wide range of professional certificates/diplomas. These qualifications can be gained through a variety of flexible options including day release, evening classes or distance learning, and are studied in your own time.

Continuing professional development is expected throughout your career.

Mature applicants should have relevant financial experience that includes supervisory management and customer service. Graduates in disciplines such as financial services, accounting and computing have an advantage. A distance-learning option is to take a degree in banking that is offered by the University of London's external programme. Increasingly, foreign language skills are also very useful.

Opportunities and Pay

There are around 49 building societies in the UK but as a result of the current economic situation, the number may fall as societies merge. Head offices are usually in the North of England and the Midlands, and branch offices are situated throughout the UK. Several societies have already merged and closed a number of branch offices which, together with the rise in electronic and telephone banking facilities, has affected some management opportunities. Senior level posts are available in building society call centres.

Promotion prospects are performance related and increase if you are willing to work in other parts of the country to gain experience. It is possible to move into regional management and there are specialist management posts in head offices, e.g. in insurance or mortgage administration. Self-employment as an independent financial consultant is also possible.

Salaries vary depending on location and employer, but graduate trainees generally earn around £19k-£25k a year. Generally, experienced managers earn up to £40k, rising to £60k-£80k or more for senior managers with extensive responsibilities. Building society staff often have special subsidised mortgage rates and loans, pensions and insurance cover, and health insurance. Managers may also receive a company car as part of their package.

Skills and Qualities

able to get on with all kinds of people, analytical skills, business awareness, discreet, efficient, excellent communication skills, good organisational skills, IT skills, numeracy skills, trustworthy

Relevant Subjects
Business and accounting, Economics, English, ICT/Computer studies, Law, Mathematics

Further Information
Building Society Industry Factsheets (Building Societies Association) - www.bsa.org.uk/consumer/factsheets/careers

AGCAS: Accountancy and Business Services (Job Sector Briefing) (AGCAS) - www.prospects.ac.uk/

Building Societies Association - www.bsa.org.uk

Diploma in Business, Administration and Finance - www.baf-diploma.org.uk/

Finance and Accounting (Pearson Publishing) - www.pearsoned.co.uk

Financial Services Skills Council - sector skills council for financial services, accountancy & finance - www.fssc.org.uk/

Inside Careers Guide: Banking, Securities & Investments - www.insidecareers.co.uk

Welsh Baccalaureate - www.wbq.org.uk

▶Working in maths (2009) (Babcock Lifeskills) - www.babcock-lifeskills.com/

Addresses
Building Societies Association
6th Floor, York House, Kingsway, London WC2B 6UJ
Phone: +44 (0)20 7520 5900
Web: www.bsa.org.uk

Chartered Institute of Bankers in Scotland (CIOBS)
Drumsheugh House, 38b Drumsheugh Gardens, Edinburgh EH3 7SW
Phone: +44 (0)131 473 7777
Web: www.charteredbanker.com

Chartered Insurance Institute (CII)
42-48 High Road, South Woodford, London E18 2JP
Phone: +44 (0)20 8989 8464
Web: www.cii.co.uk

ifs School of Finance
IFS House, 4-9 Burgate Lane, Canterbury, Kent CT1 2XJ
Phone: +44 (0)1227 818609
Web: www.ifslearning.ac.uk

University of London
Information Centre Stewart House 32 Russell Square, London WC1B 5DN
Phone: +44 (0)20 7862 8360
Web: www.londonexternal.ac.uk

Similar Jobs
Accountant: Industry & Commerce, Accountant: Public Sector, Bank Manager, Credit Manager, Financial Adviser/Planner, Insurance Broker

Building Society Officer
also known as: Building Society Customer Adviser, Cashier: Building Society

CRCI:Financial Services
CLCI:NAF

Job Band: 2 to 3

Job Description
Building society officers work in a branch office, carrying out routine clerical tasks and dealing with clients. Receive and pay out cash to customers at the counter, recording details on a computer and ensuring that the day's transactions balance. They answer enquiries from clients and give out information or application forms. Help customers to open new accounts and advise investors on different options for saving money. Also advise clients of other products and services available, such as mortgages and insurance.

Officers in a building society deal with correspondence, answer telephone calls and process mortgage applications. Liaise with solicitors and surveyors. May manage a small team of clerical assistants. Some officers are now located in call centres where duties are similar to those working at a branch except that they do not deal with customers face-to-face or handle cash transactions. They deal with customer accounts with instruction from customers over the phone. In all transactions they have to be very careful with client security.

Work Details
Usually work a 35-40 hr week, Monday to Friday, 9am-5pm, though it may be necessary to work on Saturdays, usually on a rota basis, with time off during the week instead. Part time work and job sharing is widely available. Sometimes you may have to work late, especially if there are errors to be traced. If you are working in a call centre you may have to work shifts. The work is mainly office based and involves a lot of time on a computer. You are responsible for keeping accounts and handling cash. Employees are usually provided with a corporate uniform.

Qualification

• England, Wales and Northern Ireland
Band 2: Although academic qualifications are not specified for this job, building societies expect applicants to have a good standard of literacy and numeracy. It is an advantage to have some GCSEs (A*-C) in subjects that include English and maths, or equivalent.

Band 3: For entry: most building societies ask for 4 GCSEs (A*-C) including English and maths, or equivalent.

• Scotland
Band 2: Many building societies do not require formal qualifications for this work though expect applicants to have a good standard of literacy and numeracy. Those having some S grades (1-3) including English and maths, or similar, may have an advantage.

Band 3: For entry: most employers usually require at least four S grades (1-3) including English and maths. Many entrants have H grades, or similar.

Adult Qualifications
There are no minimum formal entry qualifications though employers expect applicants to have a good standard of literacy and numeracy. Those with formal qualifications at any level may have an advantage.

Work Experience
Relevant work or voluntary experience is always useful and can improve your chances in application for entry to this job. Work with the public, retail and other work which involves handling cash, and customer service jobs is useful. In some areas there is a young apprenticeship (14-16) scheme that provides an extended work placement and eventual achievement of a relevant level 2 qualification whilst at school.

Entry and Training
Although there are no specific minimum entry qualifications, most employers expect you to be educated to at least GCSE (A*-C)/S grade (1-3) level and entrants may also have A levels/H grades or equivalent. Some building societies set their own aptitude tests for new entrants. They may also require you to have a Criminal Records Bureau (CRB)/Disclosure Scotland and credit check carried out. On-the-job training with an experienced colleague is usual, together with short courses on the society's products and procedures.

Officers can study for professional qualifications from the ifs School of Finance, or Chartered Institute of Bankers in Scotland professional exams. BTEC/SQA awards are also available, which are flexible and can be studied part time, by day release, evening classes, or through distance learning. Those with A levels/H grades or equivalent may receive accelerated training. It is also possible to take a part-time foundation degree in business finance and law.

Appropriate S/NVQs in customer service, retail financial services, contact centre professionals and providing financial services are available at levels 1-3. Training programmes, including Providing Financial Services apprenticeship schemes and the Diploma/ Welsh Baccalaureate in business, administration and finance may also be available in your area. Advanced apprenticeships leading to qualification at level 3 can also be a route into higher education.

The ifs have also developed a foundation/intermediate certificate in personal finance aimed at 14-16 year-olds and college students, which is delivered at schools and colleges across the UK.

Mature entrants have increased in recent years and building societies are recruiting people who have relevant experience. Those with experience in banking, marketing and sales, office work, customer care, retail, and any financial work have an advantage. Contact your local careers office, Jobcentre Plus, Next Step service or Learning and Skills Council (LSC)/Local Enterprise Company (LEC) for details of all training opportunities and schemes, including apprenticeships.

Opportunities and Pay

There are branches throughout the UK with the head offices of larger societies often in the north of England and the Midlands. New technology, such as computer systems and automatic cash machines, has led to a decline in recruitment and some building societies have merged, leading to closure of branches. However there are still good opportunities in call centres run by the larger societies.

With experience, you can become a senior officer or manager's assistant, and you can specialise, e.g. in finance, personnel or computing. You can be promoted to management level from clerical jobs, depending on your qualifications, experience and performance. Part-time and temporary contracts are increasing.

Pay varies depending on location and employer. Officers are likely to earn around £12k-£16k, rising to £25k a year with experience and additional responsibilities. High earners can expect over £30k a year. Building society staff often have special subsidised mortgage rates and loans, pensions and insurance cover, and health insurance.

Skills and Qualities

Able to explain clearly, able to get on with all kinds of people, accurate, aptitude for teamwork, efficient, good spoken communication, good written English, IT skills, numeracy skills, tactful

Relevant Subjects

Business and accounting, Economics, English, ICT/Computer studies, Mathematics

Further Information

Building Society Industry Factsheets (Building Societies Association) - www.bsa.org.uk/consumer/factsheets/careers

Apprenticeship Schemes (National Apprenticeship Service) - www.apprenticeships.org.uk

British Bankers Association (BBA) - www.bba.org.uk

Building Societies Association - www.bsa.org.uk

Diploma in Business, Administration and Finance - www.baf-diploma.org.uk/

Financial Services Skills Council - sector skills council for financial services, accountancy & finance - www.fssc.org.uk/

Inside Careers Guide: Banking, Securities & Investments - www.insidecareers.co.uk

Welsh Baccalaureate - www.wbq.org.uk

▶Working in business, administration & finance (2010) (Babcock Lifeskills) - www.babcock-lifeskills.com/

▶Working in maths (2009) (Babcock Lifeskills) - www.babcock-lifeskills.com/

Addresses

Building Societies Association
6th Floor, York House, Kingsway, London WC2B 6UJ
Phone: +44 (0)20 7520 5900
Web: www.bsa.org.uk

Chartered Institute of Bankers in Scotland (CIOBS)
Drumsheugh House, 38b Drumsheugh Gardens, Edinburgh EH3 7SW
Phone: +44 (0)131 473 7777
Web: www.charteredbanker.com

ifs School of Finance
IFS House, 4-9 Burgate Lane, Canterbury, Kent CT1 2XJ
Phone: +44 (0)1227 818609
Web: www.ifslearning.ac.uk

Similar Jobs

Accounting Technician, Bank Officer, Building Society Manager, Clerk: Accounts, Post Office Counter Clerk

Buildings Conservation Officer

also known as: Conservation Officer: Buildings, Historic Buildings Adviser

CRCI:Languages, Information and Culture
CLCI:UX Job Band: 4 to 5

Job Description

Buildings conservation officers help to protect and enhance buildings to ensure that they remain part of our heritage in the future. They recommend buildings for conservation and may also find suppliers and craftspeople who can work with traditional building materials to maintain them.

They inspect and survey the building and write a report on its condition and any maintenance work that is required. Also estimate the cost of the conservation work and work out the best way to complete any work without damaging the building. They may also apply for funding to pay for the work and use a wide range of tools and historical, cultural, archaeological and community information to manage change in historically sensitive places. Buildings conservation officers usually work for a planning authority and historic building advisers work on behalf of bodies or clients in the private or voluntary sectors.

Work Details

Usually work in an office but also spends a lot of time visiting buildings. Working hours are often 9am-5pm, Monday to Friday. You may spend time working outdoors in all weather conditions, and in old buildings that are dusty and dirty.

You may also need to work in small spaces or at heights and spend time bending, lifting and climbing ladders. You wear protective clothing on site, including a hard hat and safety boots.

Qualification

• England, Wales and Northern Ireland

Band 4: For HND, Diploma of Higher Education or foundation degree: 1-2 A levels and some GCSEs (A*-C) usually including English and maths, or equivalent.

Band 5: For degree courses: 2-3 A levels and some GCSEs (A*-C) usually including English and maths, or equivalent. Exact requirements depend on the degree you take.

• Scotland

Band 4: For entry to SQA higher national and professional development awards, usually 2-3 H grades and some S grades (1-3), including English and maths, or similar qualifications.

Band 5: For degree courses: 3-5 H grades and some S grades (1-3), including English and maths, or similar qualifications. Exact requirements depend on the degree you take.

Buildings Conservation Officer

Degree Information

Degrees in architectural heritage and conservation, as well as building conservation and management are available. Other relevant degrees include planning, building/construction, civil/structural engineering, surveying and architecture. Postgraduate courses are also available in architectural and historical building conservation.

Adult Qualifications

Entry requirements may be relaxed for adults applying for higher education courses. Access to HE or foundation courses provide those without the required qualifications a route onto degree courses.

Work Experience

Entry to this career is highly competitive and it is essential that you have some relevant work or voluntary experience before applying. If you expect good A levels/H grades and intend to go to university, schemes such as 'A Year in Industry', enable you to spend a salaried year with a company to gain valuable work experience.

Voluntary work may be available with a number of organisations including the National Trust or your local authority. The IHBC website provides links to organisations that may need volunteers.

Entry and Training

The majority of entrants are graduates and many also hold a postgraduate qualification so entry without a degree or HND is unlikely. It may be possible to train as a planning technician and then move into building conservation with experience and on-the-job training courses.

Your degree must be accredited by the Institute of Historic Building Conservation (IHBC) and membership is usually a requirement for professional building conservation officers. You can also join the IHBC as a student member. If you have a degree that is not accredited by the IHBC, you can upgrade your qualifications by taking a conservation conversion course. See the IHBC website for details of all recognised postgraduate, undergraduate and certificate courses.

Creative Choices, part of Creative & Cultural Skills, is a useful source of information and provides information on heritage jobs, heritage courses, career advice and funding, leadership.

Training usually takes place in the workplace. Continuing professional development is important and the IHBC requires its members to complete 50 hours of professional development training every two years to keep up to date. The IHBC organises and supports a range of professional training courses and seminars and lists approved conservation and conservation-related courses on its website.

The Society for the Protection of Ancient Buildings (SPAB) and other heritage organisations offer scholarships. SPAB also runs several short courses, including a six-day course in the repair of old buildings, held in the Spring and Autumn each year. English Heritage offers a small number of work placements each year on the Historic Environment Traineeship scheme.

Mature entrants should note that this is a small and competitive field. Experience of working in a field related to buildings conservation is very useful.

Opportunities and Pay

Buildings conservation is a specialised area of work and although jobs are limited, opportunities have grown in recent years. Employers include local authority planning departments who employ conservation officers and historic buildings officers, and heritage organisations such as English Heritage and the National Trust. You can also work for private sector consultants, lottery-funded schemes and other government agencies.

There may be an opportunity to be promoted from building conservation officer to senior conservation officer or into a managerial role. With experience, you can move on to be self-employed.

Starting salaries are likely to be £18k-£26k a year, rising with experience to £36k or more at a senior level.

Health

A reasonable level of fitness and mobility is required as the work can be physically demanding.

Skills and Qualities

able to manage a budget and keep records, able to network and negotiate, aware of legal and ethical considerations, drawing ability, excellent communication skills, eye for visual effect, good presentation skills, initiative, project management skills

Relevant Subjects

Art and Design, Business and accounting, Classical studies, Construction and built environment, Design and technology, Engineering, English, History, ICT/Computer studies, Land and Environment, Law, Mathematics, Physics, Science

Further Information

Building Conservation - www.buildingconservation.com

Building Conservation Courses (Cathedral Communications Limited) - www.buildingconservation.com

Careers in Building Conservation and Restoration (NHTG) (National Heritage Training Group (NHTG)) - www.nhtg.org.uk/careers

Creative & Cultural Skills - sector skills council for advertising, crafts, cultural heritage, design, literature, music, performing & visual arts - www.ccskills.org.uk

Creative Choices - www.creative-choices.co.uk

The Civic Trust - www.civictrust.org.uk

▶Working in construction & the built environment (2007) (Babcock Lifeskills) - www.babcock-lifeskills.com/

Year in Industry (Engineering Development Trust) - www.yini.org.uk

Addresses

Ancient Monuments Society
St Ann's Vestry Hall, 2 Church Entry, London EC4V 5HB
Web: www.ancientmonumentsociety.org.uk

Cadw
Welsh Assembly Government, Plas Carew, Unit 5/7 Cefn Coed, Parc Nantgarw, Cardiff CF15 7QQ
Phone: +44 (0)1443 33 6000
Web: www.cadw.wales.gov.uk

Department of the Environment Northern Ireland
Clarence Court, 10-18 Adelaide Street, Belfast BT2 8GB
Phone: +44 (0)28 9054 0540
Web: www.doeni.gov.uk

English Heritage
1 Waterhouse Square, 138 - 142 Holborn, London EC1N 2ST
Phone: +44 (0)20 7973 3000
Web: www.english-heritage.org.uk/

Georgian Group
6 Fitzroy Square, London W1T 5DX
Phone: +44 (0)87 1750 2936
Web: www.georgiangroup.org.uk

Historic Scotland
Longmore House, Salisbury Place, Edinburgh EH9 1SH
Phone: +44 (0)131 668 8600
Web: www.historic-scotland.gov.uk

Institute of Historic Building Conservation (IHBC)
Jubilee House, Hight Street, Tisbury, Wiltshire SP3 6HA
Phone: +44(0)1747 873133
Web: www.ihbc.org.uk

National Trust
Heelis, Kemble Drive, Swindon, Wiltshire SN2 2NA
Phone: +44 (0)1793 817400
Web: www.ntjobs.org.uk

Society for the Protection of Ancient Buildings (SPAB)
37 Spital Square, London E1 6DY
Phone: +44 (0)20 7377 1644
Web: www.spab.org.uk

Society of Architectural Historians of Great Britain
16 Barnard Terrrace, Edinburgh EH1 1JZ
Web: www.sahgb.org.uk

The National Trust for Scotland
Wemyss House, 28 Charlotte Square, Edinburgh EH2 4ET
Phone: +44(0)844 493 2100
Web: www.nts.org.uk/Home/

The Victorian Society
1 Priory Gardens, Bedford Park, London W4 1TT
Phone: +44 (0)20 8994 1019
Web: www.victorian-society.org.uk

Similar Jobs

Architect, Conservator-Restorer, Energy Conservation Officer/Manager, Museum/Art Gallery Curator, Recycling Officer, Surveyor: Building

Business Analyst

also known as: Business Systems Analyst, IT Business Analyst

CRCI:Computers and IT
CLCI:CAV Job Band: 4 to 5

Job Description

Business analysts are IT professionals with business expertise who work with customers to understand and document their computer requirements in business terms. They focus on the mapping of business processes and activities and identify ways of improving productivity. May work on a new process or system, or modify an existing one. Analysts translate the requirements into technical terms so that a computer solution can be designed, developed and built by other specialist IT professionals. They present the proposals to clients and ensure that budget requirements are met.

May be involved in the testing of the system and overseeing the implementation of the project. Often provide workshops and training courses that are tailored to suit individual business and operational needs. Need to keep up to date with industry sector developments as well as technical innovations.

Work Details

Usually work 35-37 hrs a week, Monday to Friday, though may be expected to work extra hours as deadlines approach. The work is largely office-based, but you spend time working in different offices consulting with people, such as managers, business system users and other IT professionals. You may spend some time working away from home with occasional overnight stays.

Qualification

• England, Wales and Northern Ireland

Band 4: For a relevant higher national award: 1-2 A levels and some GCSEs (A*-C) including English and maths, or equivalent. For some courses you may need GCSEs in science, computer studies or information technology.

Band 5: For degree courses: 2-3 A levels including maths and science (computer studies or information technology for some courses) and some GCSEs (A*-C), usually including English, or equivalent. Exact requirements depend on the degree you take.

• Scotland

Band 4: For a relevant higher national award: 2-3 H grades and some S grades (1-3) including English and maths, or similar qualifications. For some courses you may need S grades in science, computer studies or information technology. Exact requirements depend on the degree you take.

Band 5: For degree courses: 3-5 H grades including maths and science (computer studies or information technology for some courses), and some S grades (1-3), usually including English, or similar qualifications. Exact requirements depend on the degree you take.

Degree Information

Employers mostly recruit graduates (usually with a 2:1) in computing or business subjects, or maths or science-based subjects, although these degrees are not essential. The Information Technology Management for Business degree is designed in partnership with some of the biggest employers in the IT industry. There are postgraduate courses in computing, and conversion courses are available for those without an IT-related degree.

Adult Qualifications

Mature applicants may not need to meet the standard entry requirements for higher education courses, particularly if your previous experience is relevant or you are able to show an ability to study at the appropriate level. There are many relevant full or part-time courses available at further/higher education colleges. Access to IT/computing and foundation courses are available for those who have no formal qualifications but wish to pursue a relevant degree.

Work Experience

Entry to this job is competitive and it is important that you try to do some relevant work or voluntary experience before applying. Paid work experience is usually preferred, either in general business, computing or in business analysis. However, internships and work placements as a student are a valuable introduction to the IT industry and enable you to make an informed choice. The British Computer Society offers a work placement service through its young professional group.

Other schemes, such as 'The Year in Industry', enable those who expect good A levels/H grades and intend to go to university, the opportunity to spend a salaried year with a company to gain valuable work experience.

Entry and Training

Business analysts are usually educated to degree level. Training is ongoing, on the job and by short in-house courses. These are likely to cover the development of your business and technical skills, analysis principles, project management, and other areas, such as presentation skills. Business analysts require knowledge of at least one major business area to have a good choice of opportunities. Specific training is given for work on particular projects when needed and continuing professional development (CPD) is essential.

Professional qualifications may be gained from organisations such as the British Computer Society (BCS), the Institution of Analysts and Programmers and the Institute for the Management of Information Systems.

The Open University offers courses in computing and maths that can lead to an appropriate computing degree through distance learning. A full or part-time foundation degree in IT is also available and a Diploma/Welsh Baccalaureate may be available in your area in IT. Several universities now offer the information technology management for business degree, developed by e-skills and employers to meet specific industry needs.

E-skills also runs a professional development programme which enables new IT professionals to fast-track their career. The programme is delivered through universities and participating employers. E-skills also offers an internship. Students are placed for a period of employment within an organisation, enabling them to develop valuable business and IT skills. Contact e-skills for details of all programmes and schemes.

Some business analysts work towards gaining Chartered IT Professional status through the BCS. Contact the BCS for further details.

Mature applicants need relevant experience in business and computing. It is sometimes possible to gain employment without a related degree if you have excellent analytical and business skills. A one-year IT postgraduate conversion course is an advantage. There are many full or part-time courses available at further/higher education colleges which give useful background knowledge.

Opportunities and Pay

There are jobs with all types of organisations throughout the UK, concentrated in London and the south east of England. These include software houses, manufacturing companies, local and national government, insurance companies, banks, and specialist firms such as IT consultancy services. Progress to more senior analyst posts, project management or strategic business planning is possible. Opportunities exist for experienced business analysts to work as self-employed consultants. There are many overseas opportunities with UK and foreign companies and international organisations.

Pay varies depending on location, size and type of employer. Starting salaries for graduates are likely to be around £24k-£35k, rising to £35k-£45k with experience. The most successful senior business analysts can earn up to £70k a year. Your salary may also include a profit-sharing scheme, performance-related pay or a company bonus.

Skills and Qualities

able to cope under pressure, analytical skills, attention to detail, business awareness, good communication skills, good presentation skills, information handling skills, IT skills, methodical, problem-solving skills

Relevant Subjects

Business and accounting, English, ICT/Computer studies, Mathematics, Science

Further Information

AGCAS: Information Technology (Job Sector Briefing) (AGCAS) - www.prospects.ac.uk

Computer Weekly (Reed Business Information) - www.computerweekly.com

Diplomas (Foundation, Higher and Advanced) - http://yp.direct.gov.uk/diplomas

e-skills UK - sector skills council for business and information technology - www.e-skills.com

Inside Careers Guide: Information Technology - www.insidecareers.co.uk

Open University - www.open.ac.uk

Real Life Guide to Information & Communications Technology (Trotman) - www.trotman.co.uk

Skills Framework for the Information Age (SFIA) (SFIA Foundation) - www.sfia.org.uk

TARGETjobs: IT (GTI Specialist Publishing Ltd.) - www.groupgti.com

Welsh Baccalaureate - www.wbq.org.uk

Year in Industry (Engineering Development Trust) - www.yini.org.uk

Addresses

British Computer Society (BCS)
First Floor, Block D North Star House North Star Avenue, Swindon, Wiltshire SN2 1FA
Phone: +44 (0)845 300 4417
Web: www.bcs.org

Institute for the Management of Information Systems (IMIS)
5 Kingfisher House, New Mill Road, Orpington, Kent BR5 3QG
Phone: +44 (0)700 002 3456
Web: www.imis.org.uk

Institution of Analysts and Programmers (IAP)
Charles House, 36 Culmington Road, London W13 9NH
Phone: +44 (0)20 8567 2118
Web: www.iap.org.uk

Similar Jobs

Geographical Information Systems Manager, IT Applications Developer, IT Systems Analyst/Designer, Management Consultant, Operational Researcher, Project Manager

Butcher: Retail

also known as: Craftbutcher

CRCI:Retail Sales and Customer Services
CLCI:OFM Job Band: 1 to 2

Job Description

Retail butchers store, display and cut up meat for sale in a shop, food market or supermarket. Use knives, power or hand saws to remove bones and to cut the meat into smaller pieces. Serve customers, weigh and wrap meat, and in smaller shops may also handle money transactions. Keep cutting tools sharp, clean equipment and check the workings of the cold store and deep freeze. May prepare processed meat products including pies and sausages, burgers and kebabs. Also prepare and display meat that is especially used for curries, barbecues or stir-fries.

Butchers are responsible by law for the safe and hygienic conditions of the shop/store. They must be aware of the rules and regulations that govern the sale of meat products.

Work Details

Usually work a basic 39-40 hr week, including Saturdays and possibly Sundays, but have a day or half days off during the week. The work may require you to start early in the mornings. This job requires you to serve customers and possibly give them advice about cooking the meat they have bought. It is important to be aware of hygiene and health regulations in this type of work. Your workplace can be messy and it is essential that you can cope with the sight of blood. Most of the time you are on your feet, and you also have to be able to lift heavy meat carcasses.

There is a risk of injuries and accidents from equipment, such as knives and power saws, and you need to wear protective clothing.

Qualification

- **England, Wales and Northern Ireland**

Band 1: For entry to the Meat Training Council's training programme: no minimum formal qualifications are required, though some GCSEs at any level are useful.

Band 2: For some jobs it may be an advantage to have some GCSEs (A*-D) in subjects that include English and maths, or equivalent.

- **Scotland**

Band 1: For entry to the Scottish Meat Training programme: no minimum formal qualifications are required, though some S grades at any level are useful.

Band 2: For some jobs it may be an advantage to have some S grades (1-4) in subjects that include English and maths, or similar.

Adult Qualifications

No formal qualifications are usually required and relevant experience may be more important. Adults with no academic qualifications can still be accredited with vocational qualifications by the Meat Training Council.

Work Experience
Relevant work or voluntary experience is always useful and can improve your chances when applying for entry to retail jobs. It can equip you with skills that you can use in the future and add to your CV. To get into this work it is useful to have had some experience in a butcher's shop or supermarket, through a Saturday or holiday job.

Entry and Training
Training involves a mixture of learning both on and off the job, through a training programme organised by the Meat Training Council (MTC). In Scotland and Northern Ireland, training is organised through the training arm of the Scottish Federation of Meat Traders, Scottish Meat Training. Most entrants complete a modern apprenticeship programme and successful completion of this training leads to the award of S/NVQ level 1-3 in meat and poultry processing. There are opportunities to extend your qualifications to advanced levels, such as the advanced certificate in meat and poultry or meat and poultry hygiene through MTC. Those who gain S/NVQ level 2 are eligible to become affiliates of the Worshipful Company of Butchers Guild.

There are other related S/NVQs and vocational certificates available at levels 1-4. Scottish Meat Training offers a level 2 food safety qualification which is taken through distance-learning in your own workplace. The MTC offers a food training international butchers' hygiene course. There are private training providers offering relevant courses.

A Diploma/Welsh Baccalaureate in retail business may be available in your area. Training programmes, including apprenticeship schemes, may also be available. Advanced apprenticeships leading to qualification at level 3 can also be a route into higher education.

Adults may be able to enter this work through a government-funded training programme. Contact your local careers office, Jobcentre Plus, Next Step service or Learning and Skills Council (LSC)/Local Enterprise Company (LEC) for details of all training opportunities and schemes, including apprenticeships for adults.

Opportunities and Pay
Jobs are available throughout the country. You can be employed by an independent butcher, a chain of butchers, a local food market, or a supermarket. You can specialise in the needs of some local communities who require a kosher or halal butcher. With experience, you may become self-employed, but this requires capital investment. With further training it is possible to become a meat inspector. There may be opportunities to work in the continental meat trade. However, due to the current economic downturn, there may be fewer openings.

Pay varies and depends on area and employer. As a trainee you are likely to earn around £180-£210 a week, rising to around £260-£350 a week. High earners with management responsibilities can earn £380-£540 a week.

Health
There are restrictions on certain skin conditions and allergies. This job requires good general fitness and stamina.

Skills and Qualities
careful, common sense, friendly, good communication skills, health & safety awareness, not squeamish, numeracy skills, steady hand, strong

Relevant Subjects
Biology, Hospitality and catering, Retail and distribution

Further Information
Apprenticeship Schemes (National Apprenticeship Service) - www.apprenticeships.org.uk

Be a Butcher (National Federation of Meat & Food Traders) - www.beabutcher.com/

Diplomas (Foundation, Higher and Advanced) - http://yp.direct.gov.uk/diplomas

Foundation Learning (QCDA) - www.qcda.gov.uk

Improve Ltd - sector skills council for food and drink manufacturing and processing - www.improveltd.co.uk

Meat Industry Careers (MTC) (Meat Training Council) - http://unix3.nildram.co.uk/~mtcunix/careers.htm

Meat Training Council (MTC) http://unix3.nildram.co.uk/~mtcunix/

National Federation of Meat and Food Retailers (NFMFT) - www.nfmft.co.uk/

Scottish Meat Training - www.meattraining.net

Training Schemes - www.direct.gov.uk/en/educationandlearning

Welsh Baccalaureate - www.wbq.org.uk

▶Working in retail & customer services (2008) (Babcock Lifeskills) - www.babcock-lifeskills.com/

Addresses
Food & Drink Qualifications
PO Box 141, Winterhill House, Snowdon Drive, Milton Keynes MK6 1YY
Phone: +44 (0)1908 231 062
Web: www.fdq.org.uk

Scottish Federation of Meat Traders
(Scottish Meat Training - SMT)
8-10 Needless Road, Perth PH2 0JW
Phone: +44 (0)1738 637472
Web: www.sfmta.co.uk

Worshipful Company of Butchers Guild
Butchers' Hall, 87 Bartholomew Close, London EC1A 7EB
Phone: +44 (0)20 7600 4106
Web: www.butchershall.com

Similar Jobs
Abattoir Operative, Butcher: Wholesale, Retail Assistant: Fish

Butcher: Wholesale
CRCI:Retail Sales and Customer Services
CLCI:OK Job Band: 1 to 2

Job Description
Wholesale butchers cut, bone, trim and pack meat for sale to local and overseas retail butchers, supermarkets, restaurants and hotels. They deal with animal carcasses from the abattoir. Store meat in chillers or freezers after packaging. They are responsible for cleaning tools and work area after use. Wear protective clothing, such as overalls, hats and wellington boots at all times. Making sure the work area is always hygienic and accident free, according to health and safety regulations, is a very important part of this job. They also make sure that tools and equipment, such as knives and band saws, are handled carefully to avoid accidents.

Work Details
Usually work a basic 39 hr week, with early starts, and weekend, evening and night work. You usually work in a covered market, factory or depot that is quite cold. You are on your feet for most of the time and need to lift heavy carcasses. You must be able to cope with the sight of blood. There are strict health and hygiene regulations that must be obeyed at all times. There is a risk of injury from equipment and you need to wear protective clothing, and possibly something to cover your hair.

Qualification

- **England, Wales and Northern Ireland**

Band 1: For entry to the Meat Training Council's training programme: no minimum formal qualifications are required, though some GCSEs at any level are useful.

Band 2: For some jobs it may be an advantage to have some GCSEs (A*-C) in subjects that include English, maths and a science, or equivalent.

- **Scotland**

Band 1: For entry to the Scottish Meat Training programme: no minimum formal qualifications are required, though some S grades at any level are useful.

Band 2: For some jobs it may be an advantage to have some S grades (1-3) in subjects that include English and maths, or similar.

Adult Qualifications
No formal qualifications are usually required and relevant experience may be more important. Adults with no academic qualifications can still be accredited with vocational qualifications by the Meat Training Council.

Work Experience
Relevant work or voluntary experience is always useful and improves your chances when applying for entry to jobs. It can equip you with skills that you can use in the future and add to your CV. Work at a food wholesalers or a butcher's shop is most relevant.

Entry and Training
Training involves a mixture of learning on and off the job, through a training programme usually run by the Meat Training Council (MTC). In Scotland, the Scottish Federation of Meat Traders (Scottish Meat Training - SMT) runs its own training programme. Some companies may provide their own in-house training. Successful completion of most training leads to the award of S/NVQ at level 1-2 in meat and poultry processing.

Further S/NVQs and vocational certificates are available at levels 1-4, such as meat and poultry processing at level 3 and meat processing management at level 4. Contact MTC or SMT for further details. Training programmes, including apprenticeship schemes, may be available in your area. Advanced apprenticeships leading to qualification at level 3 can be a route into higher education.

Adults may be able to enter this work through a government-funded training programme. Contact your local careers office, Jobcentre Plus, Next Step service or Learning and Skills Council (LSC)/Local Enterprise Company (LEC) for details of all training opportunities and schemes, including apprenticeships for adults.

Opportunities and Pay
Wholesale butchers normally work for private wholesale meat companies throughout the UK. In some areas, you can specialise in the needs of a local community which requires kosher or halal meat. There are opportunities to use butchery skills within other meat operations, such as retail butchers, manufacturing butchers and meat cutting factories. Promotion to a supervisory post is possible.

Pay rates vary but are in the region of £215-£240, rising to £280-£350 a week. Highly skilled workers earn around £420 a week.

Health
There are restrictions on certain skin conditions and allergies. This job requires good general fitness.

Skills and Qualities
careful, common sense, health & safety awareness, not squeamish, numeracy skills, practical skills, steady hand, strong

Relevant Subjects
Biology

Further Information
Apprenticeship Schemes (National Apprenticeship Service) - www.apprenticeships.org.uk

Foundation Learning (QCDA) - www.qcda.gov.uk

Meat Industry Careers (MTC) (Meat Training Council) - http://unix3.nildram.co.uk/~mtcunix/careers.htm

Training Schemes - www.direct.gov.uk/en/educationandlearning

Addresses
Food & Drink Qualifications
PO Box 141, Winterhill House, Snowdon Drive, Milton Keynes MK6 1YY
Phone: +44 (0)1908 231 062
Web: www.fdq.org.uk

Scottish Federation of Meat Traders
(Scottish Meat Training - SMT)
8-10 Needless Road, Perth PH2 0JW
Phone: +44 (0)1738 637472
Web: www.sfmta.co.uk

Worshipful Company of Butchers Guild
Butchers' Hall, 87 Bartholomew Close, London EC1A 7EB
Phone: +44 (0)20 7600 4106
Web: www.butchershall.com

Similar Jobs
Abattoir Operative, Butcher: Retail, Retail Assistant: Fish, Warehouse Worker

Cabinet Maker
also known as: Furniture Maker
CRCI:Manufacturing and Production
CLCI:SAJ Job Band: 1 to 4

Job Description
Cabinet makers produce all types of furniture, including tables and chairs, cupboards, shelves or drawers, usually out of wood or chipboard, but also using a variety of other materials such as metals and plastics. May produce drawings from customer specification or working drawings for production. The amount of timber is calculated and the appropriate wood is selected. It is then cut and planed to take full advantage of the grain. Some learn to apply wooden veneer to furniture and others work on finishing, spraying and polishing, or repair work. All use hand tools, sophisticated machinery and power tools.

In large firms, whilst hand tools may be used at times, the work is mainly through the high-tech machinery and power tools that are precisely set by the cabinet makers. Production processes can also be fully computerised in some manufacturers where the cabinet makers program the machines. Some may specialise as a craft cabinet maker, working to their own designs, or may specialise in restoration of period pieces of furniture.

Work Details
Usually works around 39 hrs a week, Monday to Friday, and may sometimes be required to work overtime. If self-employed, you may be able to have more flexible hours. You work for a furniture manufacturer in industrial premises or a workshop/studio. The work environment may be noisy and dusty although modern premises usually have extractor fans and are light and airy. A high degree of accuracy is required and, if design is involved, creativity and imagination. You may have to lift heavy pieces of wood and there is a risk of injury from toxic materials, so you may need to wear protective clothing, and possibly a face mask or goggles.

Qualification
- **England, Wales and Northern Ireland**

Band 2: Although academic qualifications are not specified for this job, it is an advantage to have some GCSEs (A*-C) for entry to particular training programmes and courses. Subjects that include English, technical subjects, science and maths, or equivalent are most useful.

Band 3: Some employers may look for 4 GCSEs (A*-C) possibly including maths, English and a science subject, or equivalent.

Band 4: For entry to a relevant foundation degree: usually 1-2 A levels and some GCSEs (A*-C), including English, maths and a science/technical subject.

- **Scotland**

Band 2: Although academic qualifications are not specified for this job, it is helpful for some training programmes and courses to have some S grades (1-3) in subjects that include English, technical subjects, science and maths, or similar.

Band 3: Some employers may look for four S grades (1-3), possibly including maths, English and a science subject.

Band 4: For entry to a relevant SQA higher national award: usually 2-3 H grades and some S grades (1-3), including English, maths and a science/technical subject.

Adult Qualifications

Qualifications may not be needed for entry if the applicant has proven woodworking ability.

Work Experience

Relevant work or voluntary experience is always useful and can improve your chances when applying for entry to jobs or courses. Your personal or adult guidance adviser should be able to advise you about how to organise work experience with a relevant employer. You should consider any work that develops your skills in woodworking, three-dimensional design or furniture restoration work.

Entry and Training

Entry to this job is usually through a work-based training scheme that involves a day or block-release course leading to S/NVQs. Some entrants choose to do a full-time college course prior to starting work in this field. City & Guilds runs a course in furniture making at levels 1-3. There are also several foundation degrees available in furniture making.

S/NVQs are available in making and installing furniture at levels 2-3 or in making and repairing handcrafted furniture and fittings at level 3. Training programmes, including apprenticeship schemes, may be available in your area. Advanced apprenticeships leading to qualification at level 3 can also be a route into higher education. A Diploma/Welsh Baccalaureate in manufacturing and product design may be available in your area.

Government training opportunities, such as an apprenticeship in cabinet making, may be available in your area. You can also gain recognition of previous experience through Accreditation of Prior Learning (APL) or by working towards relevant S/NVQs. Contact your local careers office, Jobcentre Plus, Next Step service or Learning and Skills Council (LSC) Local Enterprise Company (LEC) for details of training schemes. The Worshipful Company of Furniture Makers website has details of training opportunities for students.

Opportunities and Pay

Cabinet making is available all over the UK, with the main centres in the South East, London and the North West. Most firms are small or medium sized, but there are some larger manufacturers, and these firms employ over 40% of the workforce of this industry. There are opportunities for promotion to supervisory/managerial level and the training can lead to other similar jobs, including carpentry/joinery or furniture design. Once experienced you can become self-employed.

Pay varies, depending on location and employer. Salaries for trainees are likely to be around £14k a year, once trained this is likely to rise to £20k-£25k. Highly skilled cabinet makers can earn over £30k a year. Overtime pay may increase your salary.

Health

This job requires good health, as well as good eyesight and colour vision. There may be a risk of dermatitis or chest complaints. There may be a risk of allergy from dust.

Skills and Qualities

able to follow drawings and plans, accurate, attention to detail, creative flair, eye for shape/colour, IT skills, manual dexterity, numeracy skills, patient, practical skills

Relevant Subjects

Art and Design, Design and technology, Mathematics

Further Information

Apprenticeship Schemes (National Apprenticeship Service) - www.apprenticeships.org.uk

Cabinet Maker - www.cabinet-maker.co.uk

Careers in Furniture (Proskills) - www.prospect4u.co.uk

Diplomas (Foundation, Higher and Advanced) - http://yp.direct.gov.uk/diplomas

Proskills UK - sector skills council for process and manufacturing industries - www.proskills.co.uk

Real Life Guide to Carpentry and Cabinet Making (Trotman) - www.trotman.co.uk

Training Schemes - www.direct.gov.uk/en/educationandlearning

Welsh Baccalaureate - www.wbq.org.uk

Addresses

Guild of Master Craftsmen
166 High Street, Lewes, East Sussex BN7 1XU
Phone: +44 (0)1273 478449
Web: www.guildmc.com

Timber Trade Federation
The Building Centre 26 Store Street, London WC1E 7BT
Phone: +44 (0)20 3205 0067
Web: www.ttf.co.uk

Worshipful Company of Furniture Makers
Furniture Makers' Hall, 12 Austin Friars, London EC2N 2HE
Phone: +44 (0)20 7256 5558
Web: www.furnituremkrs.co.uk

Similar Jobs

Carpenter/Joiner, Furniture Designer, Furniture Polisher/Finisher, Musical Instrument Technician, Picture Framer, Upholsterer

CAD Technician

also known as: CAD Draughtsperson, Engineering Draughtsperson, Mechanical Engineering Draughtsperson

CRCI:Engineering
CLCI:RAB Job Band: 2 to 4

Job Description

Computer-aided design (CAD) draughtspeople prepare overall designs or detailed technical drawings using CAD systems. They work to a brief with a team or project leader and then produce clear and precise drawings of a design concept that gives instructions for making products and equipment. May design projects for a wide range of industries, including oil and gas, food processing and beverages, aerospace and defence projects, and electronic products. Some may use traditional technical drawing techniques for updating older or archived drawings.

Work Details

Usually work a 37-39 hr week, Monday to Friday, but may be expected to work late at times, especially when there are deadlines to meet. The work is office based and involves sitting for many hours at a PC or specifically designed workstation in a design or drawing office. The work needs a lot of concentration, so the working environment is likely to be quiet. Some CAD systems can be linked to others in the team working on different aspects of a project. You co-operate with designers and craft machinists and need to communicate in person and in writing. You may have to supervise other employees.

Qualification

• England, Wales and Northern Ireland

Band 3: For entry to jobs, HNC or a relevant Diploma or company training scheme, usually at least 4 GCSEs (A*-C) including English, maths and a science or engineering subject, or equivalent.

Band 4: For some companies, HND, Diploma of Higher Education or foundation degree: 1-2 A levels, usually including maths and physics or another acceptable science subject, and some GCSEs (A*-C) usually including English, maths and a science, or equivalent.

• Scotland

Band 3: For entry to some company training schemes: usually at least four S grades (1-3) including English, maths and a science subject, preferably physics, or similar. Technological studies is also useful.

Band 4: For entry to SQA higher national and professional development awards, usually 2-3 H grades, usually including maths and physics or another acceptable science subject, and some S grades (1-3), including maths, English and science subjects, or similar qualifications.

Adult Qualifications

Relevant experience is usually acceptable for entry to national/ higher national courses.

Work Experience

Employers or colleges may prefer candidates who have relevant work or voluntary experience. This can include experience in the engineering, design or computer industries. Many entry positions are for trainees or apprentices but relevant work experience will improve your application success. Colleges and training centres may also like to see examples of your work.

Entry and Training

Training is mainly on the job combined with day or block release to study at a local college for a relevant qualification. A Diploma/ Welsh Baccalaureate may be available in your area in engineering and can be a good introduction to this kind of work. You can take an apprenticeship and train for around three years. The first year is often at a training centre or a college. This is followed by on-the-job training with a company, combined with day or block release to college for BTEC/SQA awards in engineering. Alternatively, you can take a full-time college course leading to a national/higher national award. Relevant S/NVQs at level 3 are also available. City & Guilds and the British Computer Society also offer a range of relevant courses at several levels. Entry requirements are similar to those needed for a national award.

The Engineering Development Trust runs a range of nationwide schemes for 11-21 year olds who may be interested in engineering as a career. See the website for details.

With a combination of qualifications and experience you can progress to become an Engineering Technician (EngTech) or Incorporated Engineer (IEng). Relevant industrial training, initial professional development and further responsible experience are required before becoming fully qualified. You must also commit to continuing professional development throughout your career.

Mature applicants with engineering experience have an advantage and it is useful to have experience of working with computers. Contact your local careers office, Jobcentre Plus, Next Step service or Learning and Skills Council (LSC)/Local Enterprise Company (LEC) for details of training schemes.

The Open University (OU) runs a range of engineering courses and the Institution of Engineering Designers has accredited two OU engineering qualifications for professional registration. See the OU website for details.

Opportunities and Pay

You can work in all types of engineering, such as construction and civil engineering, the domestic appliance industry, office equipment manufacture, the car industry, aerospace, broadcasting and telecommunications. Jobs are also available in the armed forces, with design consultancies, and it is possible to find work abroad.

Pay varies depending on location and employer. A starting salary is likely to be around £18k a year, rising to £30k-£40k with experience.

Health

Normal colour vision may be required for some aspects of this work.

Skills and Qualities

able to manage people, accurate, analytical skills, attention to detail, good concentration level, imaginative, IT skills, numeracy skills, problem-solving skills, technical aptitude

Relevant Subjects

Art and Design, Design and technology, Engineering, ICT/ Computer studies, Mathematics, Physics, Science

Further Information

Apprenticeship Schemes (National Apprenticeship Service) - www.apprenticeships.org.uk

Apprenticeships in Scotland (Careers Info Scotland) - www.apprenticeshipsinscotland.com/about/

Diplomas (Foundation, Higher and Advanced) - http://yp.direct.gov.uk/diplomas

Engineering Connections - Apprenticeships - www.apprentices.co.uk

Open University - www.open.ac.uk

SEMTA - sector skills council for science, engineering and manufacturing technologies - www.semta.org.uk

Tomorrow's Engineers - www.tomorrowsengineers.org.uk/careers.cfm

Women into Science, Engineering & Construction - www.wisecampaign.org.uk

▶Working in art & design (2009) (Babcock Lifeskills) - www.babcock-lifeskills.com/

▶Working in manufacturing (2010) (Babcock Lifeskills) - www.babcock-lifeskills.com/

Addresses

Engineering Council
246 High Holborn, London WC1V 7EX
Phone: +44 (0)20 3206 0500
Web: www.engc.org.uk

Engineering Development Trust (EDT)
Ridgeway, Welwyn Garden City, Hertfordshire AL7 2AA
Phone: +44 (0)1707 871520
Web: www.etrust.org.uk

Institution of Engineering Designers (IED)
Courtleigh, Westbury Leigh, Wiltshire BA13 3TA
Phone: +44 (0)1373 822 801
Web: www.ied.org.uk

Similar Jobs

Architectural Technologist, Civil Engineering Technician, Engineer: Design, Mechanical Engineering Technician, Product Designer

Cake Decorator

CRCI:Manufacturing and Production
CLCI:SAC

Job Band: 1 to 2

Job Description

Cake decorators think up designs and decorate cakes to make them look interesting and attractive. They use icing, marzipan, chocolate, sweets and flowers to change the look of a cake. May add colourings to marzipan and different types of icing, which are then used to coat cakes or to make models to put on them. May pipe some types of icing to create swirls, letters and designs. Follows food hygiene and health and safety rules.

Some decorate cakes for bakeries and manufacturers to sell as part of their general product range. Often uses machine-made decorations for this to create the right design. Others decorate cakes to order. Decorators talk to customers to find out the type of cake and the sort of decoration they want. They make suggestions and put forward design ideas. May make the cake or arrange for someone else to do it. The cake is decorated as requested, made ready for delivery and sometimes, delivered in person.

Self-employed cake decorators buy ingredients, collect payments and complete any necessary paperwork. They market their services through advertising, flyers and often a website. May photograph cakes to show off their work to new customers.

Work Details

Employed cake decorators usually work a 37-40 hr week, Monday to Friday or Saturday. Self-employed cake decorators adapt their hours to suit the work they have and the deadlines they must meet. The amount of work varies with the time of year. Summer is a peak time for weddings; Christmas and Easter are busy too.

Usually works in a clean, cool room to keep icing and chocolate firm and easy to use. May sit or stand. In large bakeries or factories, works alongside other cake decorators. Decorators producing hand-crafted cakes may work with members of the public and staff in specialist retail outlets. May wear a uniform or overalls, or an apron and a head covering.

Qualification

- **England, Wales and Northern Ireland**

Band 1: No minimum qualifications are required, but you are expected to have a good level of general education. However, some formal/vocational qualifications at any level are useful.

Band 2: Although academic qualifications are not specified for this job, it is an advantage to have some GCSEs (A*-C) in subjects that include English, maths and science or food technology, or equivalent.

- **Scotland**

Band 1: No minimum qualifications are required, but you are expected to have a good level of general education. However, some formal/vocational qualifications at any level are useful.

Band 2: Although academic qualifications are not specified for this job, it is an advantage to have some S grades (1-3) in subjects that include English, maths and science or home economics, or similar.

Adult Qualifications

No formal qualifications are required, but you need basic maths skills for measuring, weighing and working out the right amounts of ingredients.

Work Experience

Work experience helps you find out what you enjoy and do not enjoy about a job. Paid or voluntary work that involves preparing food may be useful. Making and decorating cakes as a hobby lets you test and improve your skills. Talking to a cake decorator about their job gives you a valuable insight into the work.

In some areas you can do a young apprenticeship (14-16) in food manufacturing. You complete an extended work placement and a level 2 qualification whilst at school. For health and safety reasons there may be some jobs you cannot do until you are over 16.

Entry and Training

You can enter this area of work straight from school or do a relevant full-time course at a college. Employers and course providers look for people who are enthusiastic and able to cope with the demands of the job or course. At work you get on-the-job training with experienced staff. You may get day or block release to attend courses. Employers may want you to study for health and safety and food hygiene certificates. There are also relevant courses at levels 1 to 3 in food manufacture, cake decoration and a whole range of sugar decoration techniques. See the website of the National Skills Academy for Food and Drink Manufacturing for lists of relevant courses.

Apprenticeships in process bakery skills and craft bakery may be available in your area. There are no formal entry requirements.

Even if you are working from home, you must obey food hygiene and preparation regulations and register your business premises with the local authority. You need to keep up with trends and fashions, new techniques and materials.

Adult entry is common. Some decide to go into this area of work after taking adult education and leisure classes in cake decorating. Any previous practical experience of working in the food industry is useful.

Government training opportunities, such as apprenticeships, may be available in your area. You can also gain recognition of previous experience through Accreditation of Prior Learning (APL) or by working towards relevant S/NVQs. Contact your local careers office, Jobcentre Plus, Next Step service or Learning and Skills Council (LSC) Local Enterprise Company (LEC) for details of training schemes.

Opportunities and Pay

There are jobs for cake decorators with craft bakeries and cake manufacturers. Self-employed cake decorators usually work directly for customers. They may supply some retailers as well. You may build up your business and take on staff. If you are employed, you may be able to move into a role where you supervise, train or manage others. You may need a teaching qualification if you want to teach sugarcraft or cake decorating.

New entrants may earn £13k-£14k a year. Qualified or experienced cake decorators earn around £15k-£20k a year. Some may earn more. Earnings for self-employed cake decorators depend on the amount and type of work they do, costs and the prices they charge. For example, some cake decorators create highly bespoke creations for weddings or other celebrations and prices vary depending on the level of detail.

Health

You may not be able to do this type of work with certain skin conditions. There is a risk of allergy to flour and nuts. You need to have good colour vision.

Skills and Qualities

able to work to deadlines, attention to detail, creative flair, good listening skills, good organisational skills, health & safety awareness, manual dexterity, methodical, numeracy skills, patient

Relevant Subjects

Art and Design, Hospitality and catering

Further Information

Apprenticeship Schemes (National Apprenticeship Service) - www.apprenticeships.org.uk

Baking Excellence - www.bakingexcellence.co.uk

British Baker magazine - www.bakeryinfo.co.uk

Improve Ltd - sector skills council for food and drink manufacturing and processing - www.improveltd.co.uk

National Skills Academy for Food and Drink Manufacturing - http://foodanddrink.nsacademy.co.uk

Training Schemes - www.direct.gov.uk/en/educationandlearning

▶Working in food & drink (2007) (Babcock Lifeskills) - www.babcock-lifeskills.com/

Addresses

National Association of Master Bakers
21 Baldock Street, Ware, Hertfordshire SG12 9DH
Phone: +44 (0)1920 468 061
Web: www.masterbakers.co.uk

Scottish Association of Master Bakers
Atholl House, 4 Torphichen Street, Edinburgh EH3 8JQ
Phone: +44 (0)131 229 1401
Web: www.samb.co.uk

Similar Jobs

Baker, Caterer: Contract/Private, Ceramic Decorator, Chef/Cook

Car Rental Agent

CRCI:Retail Sales and Customer Services
CLCI:OFM
Job Band: 2

Job Description

Car rental agents work for a car rental firm, hiring out cars or vans. They answer enquiries about hire costs and vehicle availability and take bookings, mainly over the phone. Input booking details into the firm's car rental database. If working at a customer enquiry desk when clients come to collect their cars, they check driving licences, arrange insurance cover and complete hire agreement details. Some may arrange for the delivery of vehicles to hotels or airports.

Agents also deal with any problems that are reported by clients. They arrange servicing and repair work and, in smaller firms, may help to clean cars between hires. They also make up bills and keep records, often using a computer system.

Work Details

Mostly work 8am-6pm Monday to Saturday, though some firms open on a Sunday. Some jobs involve shift work, particularly those based at ports or airports. This work is mostly office based, but may also involve travel around the local area to deliver or collect vehicles. You deal with enquiries and give advice to customers. This can include visitors from overseas who may speak limited English.

You need to provide an efficient service for clients. This includes keeping careful records of transactions and doing some accounts and filing. The work can be demanding at times and you may have to spend a lot of time on the phone. A uniform may be provided.

Qualification

• England, Wales and Northern Ireland

Band 2: Some GCSEs (A*-C) including maths and English, or equivalent, may be expected.

• Scotland

Band 2: Some S grades (1-3) including maths and English or similar, may be expected.

Adult Qualifications

A good general secondary education is expected and some employers may ask for some formal qualifications in English or maths, or relevant experience.

Work Experience

Relevant work or voluntary experience is always useful and can improve your chances when applying for entry to jobs in sales. It can equip you with skills that you can use in the future and add to your CV. Part-time and holiday retail employment is useful and usually fairly easy to obtain. You may be able to find part-time or voluntary work experience in a car rental firm or garage.

Entry and Training

Training is on the job, through the employer's training scheme and possibly by a short course leading towards vocational qualifications. It is usually necessary to have a full, current driving licence and to be over 18. Keyboard skills are also very useful, and in particular, the use of a database and spreadsheets. You may be able to work towards relevant S/NVQs, such as customer service or travel and tourism services at levels 2-3. An S/NVQ at level 3 in vehicle sales is also useful for this job.

There are relevant vocationally-related qualifications (VRQs) such as the level 2 certificate in customer service for hospitality, leisure, travel and tourism. The Institute of the Motor Industry also offers a range of motor industry qualifications at levels 1-4, some of which are relevant to those already working in car rentals. The British Vehicle Rental and Leasing Association offers a range of qualifications for those working in the vehicle leasing and rental sectors. These include the City and Guilds rental operator exam and certificate in fleet consultancy programme. It also offers short training courses focusing on key industry knowledge and skills. Check the website for details.

A Diploma/Welsh Baccalaureate in retail business may be available in your area. Training programmes, including apprenticeship schemes, may also be available. Advanced apprenticeships leading to qualification at level 3 can also be a route into higher education.

Mature applicants with experience of working with the public, in particular customer services or car sales, have an advantage. IT skills are also useful, in particular the use of a database and spreadsheets. You may be able to enter this work through a government-funded training programme. Contact your local careers office, Jobcentre Plus, Next Step service or Learning and Skills Council (LSC)/Local Enterprise Company (LEC) for details of all training opportunities and schemes, including apprenticeships for adults.

Opportunities and Pay

Most jobs are with nationwide vehicle rental agencies and fleet management firms. There are also some smaller locally-based companies. Most jobs are in towns and cities, or near ports and airports. With larger firms, there may be opportunities for promotion to supervisory or management level. Perks may include special hire rates for employees.

Pay varies, depending on location and employer. Starting salaries are likely to be in the range of £12k-£16k a year. Salaries rise with experience to £18k-£20k a year. Pay often includes some form of commission, so very successful rental assistants can earn more.

Skills and Qualities

administrative skills, cash handling skills, customer service skills, efficient, good interpersonal skills, good organisational skills, IT skills, numeracy skills, smart appearance, time management skills

Relevant Subjects

Business and accounting, English

Further Information

Apprenticeship Schemes (National Apprenticeship Service) - www.apprenticeships.org.uk

British Vehicle Rental and Leasing Association (BVRLA) - www.bvrla.co.uk/Training_and_Careers/Homepage.aspx

Diplomas (Foundation, Higher and Advanced) - http://yp.direct.gov.uk/diplomas

Training Schemes - www.direct.gov.uk/en/educationandlearning

Welsh Baccalaureate - www.wbq.org.uk

▶Working in retail & customer services (2008) (Babcock Lifeskills) - www.babcock-lifeskills.com/

▶Working in travel & tourism (2010) (Babcock Lifeskills) - www.babcock-lifeskills.com/

Addresses

Institute of Customer Service (ICS)
2 Castle Court, St Peter's Street, Colchester, Essex CO1 1EW
Phone: +44 (0)1206 571716
Web: www.instituteofcustomerservice.com

Institute of the Motor Industry (IMI)
Fanshaws Brickenden, Hertford, Hertfordshire SG13 8PQ
Phone: +44 (0)1992 511 521
Web: www.motor.org.uk

Similar Jobs

Contact Centre Operator, Customer Services Adviser, Vehicle Sales Executive

Car Valet

CRCI:Personal and Other Services
CLCI:IJ Job Band: 1

Job Description

Valets provide a high quality cleaning and finishing service on the inside and outside of cars, vans and caravans. They use steam cleaners to clean the engine, wheel arches and underneath the car and wash down the outside using a powered water jet and a sponge or brush. Also polish windows, mirrors and paintwork, as well as metal, leather and plastic trims. May cover up small scratches in the paint, rub wax into the paintwork, put gels and other finishes on the bumpers and trims, and paint a rubber dressing on the sides of the tyres.

They use an electric buffer to do some polishing, but do a lot by hand. Also vacuum and shampoo the carpets and seats, and use chemicals to remove any stains. May collect the vehicle from customers or offer a service from a mobile cleaning unit.

Work Details

Usually work a basic 40 hr week, possibly including weekends, with early starts and late finishes. Some firms may have a shift system. The work is both indoors and outdoors, either in a garage or workshop, at the side of a road or in a customer's drive, so you can be out in all sorts of weather. Hand waxing and polishing is active and physical work and you are on your feet a lot of the time, often bending and stretching at difficult angles. The machines can be heavy and awkward to move around. The work may involve chemicals, so you need to wear gloves and safety glasses, at least some of the time.

Some firms may provide a uniform. Those working with a mobile unit can expect to drive around a fair amount as they go from customer to customer.

Qualification

- **England, Wales and Northern Ireland**

Band 1: You do not need qualifications, though GCSEs or equivalent in practical or technical subjects can be useful.

- **Scotland**

Band 1: You do not need qualifications, though S grades or similar in practical or technical subjects can be useful.

Adult Qualifications

You do not need formal qualifications. You can improve your skills and qualifications by working through the Foundation Learning programme. This involves taking credit-based units and qualifications to help you progress.

Work Experience

Any work experience can equip you with skills that you can use in the future and add to your CV. It can either be voluntary or part-time work that you have organised yourself. Any experience of cleaning, dry cleaning or work in the motor trade is useful.

Entry and Training

You need to be over the age of 17 as you usually need a full, clean driving licence to be able to move cars safely. Training is on the job, working with an experienced valet and learning how to use the equipment and materials safely. This may involve going on a short course (usually only for a day) with the company that makes the cleaning tools or chemicals. With a mobile valeting company, training can be for three to six months before you can work on your own and includes aspects such as health and safety and car polishing techniques.

The British Institute of Cleaning Science offers an in-house, car valeting certificate scheme. An S/NVQ in vehicle maintenance at level 1-2, including specific modules on valeting, may be available in your area. Training programmes, including apprenticeship schemes, may be available in your area. Certificates in principles of cleaning may be available as part of the scheme. Contact the Institute of the Motor Industry for more information.

Mature entrants with previous experience in the motor trade, or in carpet, upholstery, office or industrial cleaning, have an advantage. Some employers prefer mature entrants (over 25) who have held a driving licence for some time.

Opportunities and Pay

Many valets work for specialist car valeting firms, who have private customers, as well as contracts with car rental companies and car dealers. Some valeting companies specialise in dealing only with very expensive cars. Some rental firms and dealers employ their own valets. The work can be seasonal, especially when new cars come on to the market and more used cars are available. Some firms are large enough to have supervisors or area managers, so promotion is possible. Once you have experience and enough money, you can set up your own business or buy a franchise.

Income ranges from £10k-£12.5k a year, rising to around £16k a year with experience. High earners can make around £18k. Overtime/shift payments can increase basic earnings.

Health

The strong chemicals used can cause problems with skin allergies. You have to be reasonably fit for this job as there is bending and stretching. You must be able to see well, with or without glasses.

Skills and Qualities

able to follow instructions, able to work well on your own, attention to detail, business awareness, careful, methodical, reliable, safety conscious, self-motivated

Further Information

Apprenticeship Schemes (National Apprenticeship Service) - www.apprenticeships.org.uk

Asset Skills - sector skills council for the places where we live and work - www.assetskills.org

Cleaning Industry Handbook (BICSc) (BICSc) - www.bics.org.uk/

Foundation Learning (QCDA) - www.qcda.gov.uk

Institute of the Motor Industry (IMI) - sector skills council for the motor industry - www.motor.org.uk

Addresses

British Institute of Cleaning Science (BICSc)
9 Premier Court, Boarden Close, Moulton Park,
Northampton NN3 6LF
Phone: +44 (0)1604 678 710
Web: www.bics.org.uk

Similar Jobs

Caretaker, Chauffeur/Chauffeuse, Cleaner: Carpet & Upholstery, Cleaner: Industrial, Cleaner: Windows

Cardiac Physiologist

also known as: Cardiac Clinical Scientific Officer, Physiological Measurement Technician: Cardiology

CRCI:Healthcare

CLCI:JOB Job Band: 5

Job Description

Cardiac physiologists carry out tests using high-tech equipment to help doctors diagnose, monitor and treat heart disease. They use complex electrical and electronic equipment (electrocardiograms) to measure and record the electrical activity of a heart and how it is functioning. Monitor heart function of a patient during surgery and in intensive care. Attach electrodes to the patient. May measure the circulation of the blood in a particular part of the body or record the sounds or rhythm of a patient's heart. Carry out ultrasonic scanning known as echocardiography, analyse blood gases and record blood pressure. Results of tests enable medical staff to decide on the best method of treatment.

Cardiac physiologists work closely with patients who have pacemakers to ensure they continue to work effectively. They look after the equipment and prepare apparatus for heart tests and examinations. Also help to monitor the condition of patients after surgery.

Work Details

You work in a cardiology department in a hospital, in a clinical outpatient department, or on a ward. You usually work a basic 37 hour week which includes being on call and some evenings and weekends. Overtime may be necessary at busy times or in emergencies. There is frequent contact with people who may be anxious, need reassurance and an explanation of the procedures being carried out. Work can be demanding at times.

Qualification

- **England, Wales and Northern Ireland**

Band 5: For degree courses: 2-3 A levels including at least one science subject, and some GCSEs (A*-C) usually including English and dual science, or equivalent. Exact requirements depend on the degree you take.

- **Scotland**

Band 5: For degree courses: 3-5 H grades including two science subjects, and some S grades (1-3), usually including English and dual science, or similar qualifications. Exact requirements depend on the degree you take.

Degree Information

Trainee clinical physiologists are accepted from many degree disciplines, including cardiology, neurophysiology and respiratory physiology. However, you need to complete a specialism in cardiac physiology, approved by the Health Professions Council.

Adult Qualifications

Entry requirements may be relaxed for adults applying for higher education courses and Access and foundation courses give adults without qualifications a route on to degree courses.

Work Experience

Work experience gives you an insight into what you enjoy about a job or working environment, as well as the opportunity to acquire new skills. It provides valuable information to add to your CV and improves your employment prospects. Consider working with the public in a caring capacity and in different hospital departments. There is usually a waiting list for work experience in hospitals so enquire early. Arrange to visit other related departments if you can.

Entry and Training

New entrants to the profession are graduates with an accredited degree, who then follow a period of in-service clinical training specialising in cardiology before applying for state registration with the Health Professions Council which regulates the profession. Employers may offer a training post to applicants who demonstrate the ability to follow a part-time BSc course in clinical physiology (cardiology) while working. Swansea University offers a full-time BSc in clinical physiology with cardiology that includes in-service clinical training.

There are also foundation degrees available in medical sciences and applied medical technology. You can join the Society for Cardiological Science and Technology as a student and become an associate member on completion of your degree. You then follow a programme of continuing professional development (CPD) to keep up to date with the latest techniques.

Mature applicants are welcome but must fulfil the entry requirements of an approved BSc in clinical physiology. Existing hospital employees with clinical work experience may be offered the opportunity to train as cardiac physiologists if they demonstrate the ability to complete the academic study and practical training. If you have a degree in a relevant subject you may be offered a training post and then complete the BSc in clinical physiology. NHS funding may be available to assist students undertaking full-time university-based training.

Opportunities and Pay

Most cardiac physiologists are employed by the NHS. There are some opportunities in private hospitals, clinics, specialised investigation or research laboratories, and in the armed forces but there is a shortage of qualified staff in the UK. Promotion is often through a formal career structure and usually requires a more advanced qualification. Some may progress to senior officer and management posts; others with higher degrees may become clinical scientists. There are also opportunities to work overseas in countries such as New Zealand.

Pay is on a nationally agreed scale and increases with promotion. Those working in the NHS follow a salary scale divided into levels of experience. Starting salaries are around £21k-£28k a year. Specialists earn £35k or more a year. Those in managerial roles can earn up to £79k a year.

Skills and Qualities

able to cope under pressure, able to explain clearly, able to put people at ease, analytical skills, aptitude for maths and science, aptitude for teamwork, calm, good communication skills, IT skills, responsible attitude

Relevant Subjects

Biology, Chemistry, Health and social care, ICT/Computer studies, Mathematics, Physics, Science

Further Information

Cardiographer or Cardiac Physiologist Careers (SCST) (The Society for Cardiological Science and Technology) - www.scst.org.uk/careers/careers08.htm

Federation for Healthcare Science - www.fedhcs.net

Health Professions Council (HPC) - www.hpc-uk.org

NHS Careers (NHS Careers) - www.nhscareers.nhs.uk

NHS Careers Scotland - www.infoscotland.com/nhs

NHS Careers Wales - www.wales.nhs.uk

Addresses

Society for Cardiological Science and Technology (SCST)
Executive Business Support (EBS), City Wharf, Davidson Road,,
Lichfield WS14 9DZ
Phone: +44 (0)845 838 6037
Web: www.scst.org.uk

Swansea University
Singleton Park, Swansea SA2 8PP
Phone: +44 (0) 1792 205678
Web: www.swan.ac.uk/

Similar Jobs
Audiologist, Cardiologist, Clinical Technologist, Neurophysiologist, Perfusionist, Respiratory Physiologist

Cardiologist

CRCI:Healthcare
CLCI:JAB Job Band: 5

Job Description
Cardiologists deal with disorders of the heart and blood vessels and may specialise in an area such as congenital heart defects, coronary artery disease, heart failure and valvular heart disease. They decide on the most appropriate form of treatment. This can range from non invasive cardiology e.g. a pacemaker, to diagnosing abnormal heart rhythms through electrophysiology or interventional cardiology where clots are extracted or stents/ balloons are inserted through cannulation and pin hole surgery.

Consultant cardiologists also participate in the training of younger members of staff and have to comply with the Royal College requirements for training and assessment of junior doctors.

Work Details
Cardiology specialists can work fairly regular hours but are expected to be available for some on-call duties which may include nights and weekends. You work in consulting rooms, wards and outpatient clinics. Consultants divide their time between inpatient and outpatient duties. You make decisions about treatment and keep meticulous records.

Qualification

- **England, Wales and Northern Ireland**

Band 5: For degree in medicine: usually three A levels, with good grades in chemistry and two from physics, biological sciences and maths, plus 5 GCSEs (A*-C) including English, or equivalent. Some medical schools offer a one-year pre-medical course for students with A levels in arts or mixed subjects. Check with individual schools for full details.

- **Scotland**

Band 5: For degree in medicine: usually five H grades, with good grades in chemistry and two from physics, biology and maths, plus five S grades (1-3) including English and maths, or similar. Normally science subjects not held at H grade should be offered at S grade. Some medical schools offer a one-year pre-medical course for students whose H grades do not include the required science subjects. Check with individual schools for full details.

Degree Information
A degree in medicine awarded by a university medical school and recognised by the General Medical Council is essential, followed by specialist training.

Adult Qualifications
Entry requirement standards are not normally relaxed for mature applicants, though those who consider applying should contact the individual university for advice. Graduates with a good honours degree in a related subject may obtain exemptions from certain options within the medical degree course.

Work Experience
Entry to this career is highly competitive and it is essential that you have some relevant work or voluntary experience before applying to train as a doctor so that you are able to demonstrate a long-term commitment to medicine. Evidence of this can come in the form of relevant paid or voluntary work in a healthcare setting such as work in a hospital, residential care home, or similar. You can apply for voluntary work overseas that has a health education or medically-related programme.

Entry and Training
Entry to places at medical school is highly competitive, and most medical schools now require entrants to take the UK Clinical Aptitude Test (UKCAT) to aid the application process. There is a Royal College or a Faculty of a Royal College for each medical discipline which lays down the entry and training requirements for that discipline and sets examinations for membership/fellowship. Most medical degrees take five years. Candidates without science A/H levels may take a pre-medical course in science first.

All medical graduates must now enter a two-year Foundation Programme immediately after graduation. This forms a link between medical school and specialist hospital training and includes a series of placements in a variety of specialities and healthcare settings. Successful meeting of the standards for year one, leads to registration as a doctor with the General Medical Council (GMC).

During Foundation year two, you need to apply for a placement to train as a specialty registrar. Doctors wishing to undertake training in Cardiology must first complete 2 years of Specialty Training in a Core Medical Training programme or Acute Care Common Stem programme. On completion of your two years specialty training, all further training is specific to Cardiology. See the GMC link for full details on curriculum and assessment.

Suitably qualified mature applicants are welcomed by medical schools and some may have reserved places for mature/graduate entrants. There are access courses to medicine and pre-medical foundation courses. Open University credits at distinction level may be accepted at some medical schools. Check with individual medical schools for details of all opportunities.

Opportunities and Pay
Coronary heart disease is the biggest killer in the UK with one in every four men and one in every six women dying from the condition every year. In addition, over 300,000 people suffer a heart attack each year and in excess of a million people have angina. This means there is a steady demand for cardiology services.

The last decade has seen advances in technology that improve the prospects for those with cardiac disease. Much of the research in this area is trialled in clinical practice successfully, resulting in detection and treatment at an earlier stage for the patient. It is one of the fastest moving and most exciting areas of medicine to work in and cardiologists now treat many conditions previously treated by cardiac surgeons. There is a wide variety of opportunities for research in cardiology and the broader field of cardiovascular medicine.

Within the NHS, junior doctors earn a basic salary and are usually paid a supplement for extra hours worked. Basic salaries are around £33k a year (including a 50% supplement for extra hours), rising to £43k-£68k (including 50% supplement) for a doctor in specialist training. A consultant can earn £73k-£174k a year. These salaries do not include on-call payments, private income or London weighting allowances.

Health
There is a risk of infection. You should have no allergies and a good level of general fitness.

Skills and Qualities
able to cope under pressure, able to make important decisions, able to work both on your own and in a team, good communication skills, leadership qualities, planning skills, problem-solving skills

Relevant Subjects
Biology, Chemistry, English, Health and social care, Mathematics, Physics, Psychology, Science

Further Information
AGCAS: Health (Job Sector Briefing) (AGCAS) - www.prospects.ac.uk

British Cardiovascular Intervention Society - www.bcis.org.uk/pages/default.asp
British Cardiovascular Society - www.bcs.com/pages/default.asp
British Heart Foundation - www.bhf.org.uk/
British Medical Journal (weekly) (BMJ Publishing Group Ltd) - www.bmj.com/
Medical Speciality Training - www.mmc.nhs.uk/
Modernising Medical Careers - www.mmc.nhs.uk
NHS Careers (NHS Careers) - www.nhscareers.nhs.uk
NHS Careers Scotland - www.infoscotland.com/nhs
NHS Careers Wales - www.wales.nhs.uk
NHS Foundation Programme - www.foundationprogramme.nhs.uk/pages/home
The Lancet (weekly) (Elsevier Ltd) - www.thelancet.com/
UK Clinical Aptitude Test - www.ukcat.ac.uk

Addresses
British Medical Association (BMA)
BMA House, Tavistock Square, London WC1H 9JP
Phone: +44 (0)20 7387 4499
Web: www.bma.org.uk

General Medical Council (GMC)
Regents Place, 350 Euston Road, London NW1 3JN
Phone: +44 (0)161 923 6602
Web: www.gmc-uk.org

Open University (OU)
PO Box 197, Milton Keynes MK7 6BJ
Phone: +44 (0)845 300 6090
Web: http://www3.open.ac.uk

Royal College of Physicians (RCP)
11 St Andrew's Place, Regent's Park, London NW1 4LE
Phone: +44 (0)207 935 1174
Web: www.rcplondon.ac.uk

Similar Jobs
Anaesthetist, Cardiac Physiologist, Doctor: Hospital, Paediatrician, Plastic Surgeon, Surgeon

Care Home Manager
also known as: Social Worker: Residential
CRCI:Social Work and Counselling Services
CLCI:KEB
Job Band: 4 to 5

Job Description
Care home managers are responsible for the day-to-day running of care homes. Oversee all aspects of the home's administration, including managing the budget, recruitment and training of staff and ensuring quality standards are met. Clients may be older people, people with mental health problems, people with learning disabilities, young adults, the terminally ill or people with physical disabilities. Provide information, advice and support to residents, their families and carers. Arrange stimulating activities and encourage residents to get involved. Create the opportunity for residents to contribute to the local community and gain access to local services.

Care home managers work closely with other professionals including psychologists, probation officers, nurses, doctors, health and social care assistants.

Work Details
Hours can be irregular and you may be expected to work evenings, weekends and at night, perhaps on a rota basis or on shifts. Care home managers work in a variety of settings within the public, private, voluntary and charitable sectors. You have to assess an individual's care and support needs, be able to negotiate and manage a budget and to maintain accurate records. You also need knowledge of relevant legislation, local services and resources, and a good understanding of the medical conditions affecting service users. You are able to build effective working relationships with residents, their families, staff and other professionals.

You may not have to be resident, but you may need to live-in occasionally. Work is emotionally demanding and may involve making difficult decisions. Many of your clients are in need of support, so can be depressed, upset, anxious or negative.

Qualification

• England, Wales and Northern Ireland
Band 4: For BTEC higher national award: 1-2 A levels and some GCSEs (A*-C) usually including English and maths. Equivalent qualifications may also be acceptable. Check individual prospectuses.

Band 5: For degree courses: 2-3 A levels and some GCSEs (A*-C) usually including English, or equivalent qualifications. Exact requirements depend on the degree you take.

• Scotland
Band 4: For SQA higher national award: 2-3 H grades and some S grades (1-3) usually including English and maths. Similar qualifications are also accepted. Entry requirements vary so check prospectuses carefully.

Band 5: For degree courses: 3-5 H grades and some S grades (1-3), usually including English and maths, or similar. Exact requirements depend on the degree you take.

Degree Information
Degrees in psychology, sociology, social policy and administration, law, and in business-related subjects provide relevant background knowledge for this job. Some degrees give applicants exemptions from the NVQ Level 4 in Health & Social Care. You can also qualify in social work if you take a relevant postgraduate qualification such as a diploma or masters degree.

Adult Qualifications
For adults without the entry requirements for a degree, there are Access courses to social work that lead to further study at degree level. Some colleges also offer Accreditation of Prior Learning (APL). Those with a degree can qualify by taking a relevant postgraduate course.

Work Experience
Relevant work or voluntary experience is always useful and improves your chances in application for entry to this job. Consider work dealing with young people, the public in a helping capacity such as youth and community centre work, or in the caring professions. Although work experience is not an essential requirement, it demonstrates enthusiasm and commitment. The Community Service Volunteers website is a useful source of information.

Entry and Training
You are usually expected to have qualifications relating to the type of care home you are managing, eg a nursing background to manage a nursing home. It is not always necessary to have a degree as professional qualifications and relevant experience are also important. However, a degree in social work, psychology, social administration or a business-related subject may be useful.

Most employers require managers to have or be working towards a relevant S/NVQ Level 4 in Health and Social Care or in Leadership and Management for Care Services. Courses cover aspects of management, budgeting, marketing and human resources, as well as issues in the social care sector. Tuition fees may be paid for eligible students, including a bursary for social work courses through the NHS Business Services Authority. See their website for details. Postgraduate research degrees are also available in social work and social care.

Most training courses require applicants to have a period of relevant practical experience in a social work or a social care setting. Previous experience as an assistant or deputy manager is also useful.

Most people who become care home managers have already worked as an assistant or deputy, so they have started some training towards or hold the S/NVQ Level 4 in health and social care. Mature entrants are welcomed and considered on their relevant work/life experiences and academic qualifications.

Opportunities and Pay

You can work in a variety of settings within the public, private, voluntary and charitable sectors. There are a growing number of opportunities for qualified managers with private care companies providing services (especially for the elderly), as well as local authorities. There is currently a shortage of care home managers.

In a local authority, pay is on a nationally agreed scale and usually increased by allowances for unsociable hours. In the private sector it depends largely on the type of employer. Pay can also be increased by additional payments for working in deprived areas. Newly qualified care home managers generally earn around £20k-£28k, rising to around £30k-£40k a year and beyond with further experience and responsibilities. Pay can be higher in some private sector homes.

Skills and Qualities

able to manage a budget and keep records, able to understand other people's problems, good communication skills, good interpersonal skills, good listening skills, patient, problem-solving skills, sympathetic, tactful, tolerant

Relevant Subjects

English, Health and social care, Law, Psychology, Sociology

Further Information

Community Care - www.communitycare.co.uk

Community Service Volunteers - www.csv.org.uk

Compass: Complete Guide to Social Work and Social Care - www.compassjobsfair.com

NHS Business Services Authority - Social Work Bursary - www.nhsbsa.nhs.uk/

Skills for Health - sector skills council - www.skillsforhealth.org.uk

Social Care and Social Work Careers - www.socialworkandcare.co.uk

▶Working in social care (2010) (Babcock Lifeskills) - www.babcock-lifeskills.com/

Addresses

Care Council for Wales
South Gate House, Wood Street, Cardiff CF10 1EW
Phone: +44 (0)29 2022 6257
Web: www.ccwales.org.uk

General Social Care Council (GSCC)
Goldings House, 2 Hay's Lane, London SE1 2HB
Phone: +44 (0)20 7397 5100
Web: www.gscc.org.uk

Northern Ireland Social Care Council
7th Floor, Millennium House, 19-25 Great Victoria Street, Belfast BT2 7AQ
Phone: +44 (0)28 9041 7600
Web: www.niscc.info

Scottish Social Services Council (SSSC)
Compass House 11 Riverside Drive, Dundee DD1 4NY
Phone: +44 (0)845 60 30 891
Web: www.sssc.uk.com

Similar Jobs

Community Development Worker, Nurse: Mental Health, Prison Officer, Probation Officer, Psychologist: Counselling, Social Worker, Social Worker: Medical

Careers Adviser

CRCI:Social Work and Counselling Services
CLCI:KED
Job Band: 4 to 5

Job Description

Careers advisers help people to make informed and realistic decisions about their future education, training and employment. They listen carefully and ask questions to assess a client's interests, skills and abilities. May use psychometric tests to assist a client in their choices and decisions. Careers advisers provide guidance and advice on the various routes towards employment. They help clients to use up-to-date information resources such as computer guidance software, the Internet, and printed publications as sources of information.

Careers advisers contact local employers and training providers, colleges and universities to keep up to date with job vacancies and trends in employment, employment legislation, new courses, admission procedures, etc. They use a computer to produce reports and for general administrative tasks.

May currently work as a personal adviser for Connexions (England) with 13-19 year olds. Careers advisers support those who have issues that may affect their ability to take part in learning and work, and help them to raise their individual ambitions.

Work Details

Usually work a basic 37-39 hr week, Monday to Friday, in a public office in a major town or city, or in a college/university. Some occasional evening or weekend work may be required. Usually it is necessary to travel around a local area and sometimes further afield. You may be working with secondary school students, FE/HE students, young adults, parents, carers, disadvantaged young people and perhaps young people with special needs.

Duties include interviewing and advising people, dealing with enquiries, providing information and liaising with teachers, youth and community services, social workers and other professionals. Advisers also liaise with the employment service, benefits agency and other agencies, such as those who deal with drugs counselling and homeless people. Work may be pressurised at times.

Qualification

- **England, Wales and Northern Ireland**

Band 4: For BTEC higher national award: 1-2 A levels and some GCSEs (A*-C) usually including English and maths, or equivalent.

Band 5: For degree courses: 2-3 A levels and some GCSEs (A*-C) usually including English or equivalent. Exact requirements depend on the degree you take.

- **Scotland**

Band 4: For SQA higher national award: 2-3 H grades and some S grades (1-3) often including English and maths, or similar qualifications.

Band 5: For degree courses: 3-5 H grades and some S grades (1-3), usually including English and maths, or similar qualifications. Exact requirements depend on the degree you take.

Degree Information

A degree in any subject is acceptable, but psychology and the social sciences can be useful. There are relevant postgraduate courses, including careers guidance and education, and careers management and counselling. Contact the Institute of Careers Guidance (ICG) for details of courses.

Adult Qualifications

It is not necessary, though is helpful, to have a first degree. Applicants without a degree or an equivalent qualification must be able to convince selectors of their ability to cope with the academic and intensive nature of courses, similar to that of a postgraduate course. There are no set academic entry requirements for the NVQ at level 4 in advice and guidance, or for the Qualification in Career Guidance (QCG).

Work Experience
Employers or colleges/universities may prefer candidates who have relevant work or voluntary experience. This includes anything dealing with young people and the public in a helping capacity, such as at youth and community centres or with young peoples' groups and organisations. Any observation or direct experience in careers centres or in the caring professions is also an advantage.

Entry and Training
There are two main routes to become a fully qualified careers advisor. The Qualification in Career Guidance (QCG), or in Scotland the Qualification in Career Guidance and Development (QCGD), is the higher education route. Courses are offered by 11 universities in the UK and two in Scotland, either as a one-year full-time course or part time over two years. There are no set academic entry requirements, though most entrants are graduates and you must be able to cope at the level required for postgraduate study. You also need to pass a Criminal Records Bureau (CRB)/Disclosure Scotland check.

Alternatively a new work-based training route is available, which will replace NVQ levels 3-4 in advice and guidance in 2011. These include the level 4 Diploma in Career Information and Advice and the level 6 Diploma in Career Guidance and Development. Contact Lifelong Learning UK for details of the new qualifications and ICG for details of all routes to qualifying.

Those working in higher education can take an in-service specialist certificate/diploma/masters in career education, information and guidance in higher education, offered by the Association of Graduate Careers Advisory Services (AGCAS) and Reading University. Contact AGCAS for details.

The National Open College Network offers awards and certificates in information, advice or guidance at NQF levels 1-3. The minimum age for entry to courses is 18. Contact your local Open College Network for further information.

Mature applicants with relevant experience or skills in guidance or a related context may have an advantage. It is also an advantage to have experience in commerce, industry, social work, teaching or youth work. The Qualification in Career Guidance (QCG) is available through part-time study.

Opportunities and Pay
Employment is in towns and cities throughout the UK, with careers service companies, Connexions services, independent guidance agencies, further and higher education, and some sixth-form colleges. Training and education/industry initiatives are increasingly offering opportunities for qualified and experienced careers advisers. There are also private careers consultancies that provide a service to adults on a fee-paying basis.

It is possible to specialise in working with a particular group of clients, such as those with special needs, employer liaison or disadvantaged young people. There are opportunities for part-time work, job sharing and term-time work, and you can progress to become a self-employed consultant, researcher or writer.

Pay varies depending on the employer, but most newly-qualified careers advisers can expect to earn around £18k-£24k a year, rising to around £29k with experience. Those in senior posts can earn up to £35k a year, with senior managers and chief executives earning up to £55k.

Skills and Qualities
able to put people at ease, able to work both on your own and in a team, good communication skills, good interpersonal skills, good listening skills, good organisational skills, information handling skills, IT skills, self confident

Relevant Subjects
English, Psychology, Sociology

Further Information
Careers Guidance Today (quarterly) (Institute of Careers Guidance (ICG) - www.icg-uk.org/career_guidance_today.html

Connexions - www.connexions-direct.com

LLUK (Lifelong Learning UK) - sector skills council for the professional development of staff working in the lifelong learning sector - www.lluk.org

National Open College Network - www.nocn.org.uk

▶Working in advice & counselling (2007) (Babcock Lifeskills) - www.babcock-lifeskills.com/

Working in Careers Guidance (Institute of Careers Guidance (ICG) - www.icg-uk.org/workinginguidance.html

▶Working in schools & colleges (2007) (Babcock Lifeskills) - www.babcock-lifeskills.com/

▶Working in social care (2010) (Babcock Lifeskills) - www.babcock-lifeskills.com/

Addresses
Association of Graduate Careers Advisory Services (AGCAS)
Millenium House, 30 Junction Road, Sheffield S11 8XB
Phone: +44 (0)114 251 5750
Web: www.agcas.org.uk

Department for Employment and Learning
Careers Development Unit, Adelaide House, 39-49 Adelaide Street, Belfast BT2 8FD
Phone: +44 (0)28 9025 7777
Web: www.delni.gov.uk

Institute of Career Guidance (ICG)
Ground Floor Copthall House 1 New Road, Stourbridge, West Midlands DY8 1PH
Phone: +44 (0)1384 376 464
Web: www.icg-uk.org

National Association for Educational Guidance for Adults (NAEGA)
c/o SAS Event Management The Old George Brewery
Rollestone Street, Salisbury, Wiltshire SP1 1DX
Phone: +44 (0) 1722 415 154
Web: www.naega.org.uk

Similar Jobs
Advice Worker, Community Development Worker, Personal Adviser (Connexions) (England), Probation Officer, Psychologist: Counselling, Recruitment Consultant, Training & Development Officer/Manager

Caretaker
also known as: Premises Manager, School Caretaker/Janitor
CRCI:Personal and Other Services
CLCI:IJ
Job Band: 1 to 2

Job Description
Caretakers are responsible for the care and upkeep of large buildings and their grounds, such as schools and colleges, offices, hotels, community centres, leisure centres, or blocks of flats. They lock and unlock doors and check the security of the building. Also test fire alarms on a regular basis and may clean the building or organise other people to do this. They look after the central heating system and make sure equipment is working well. May maintain an on-site swimming pool or use a CCTV security system.

Sometimes caretakers work a switchboard, take messages, check deliveries and store supplies safely. They undertake small repairs and report larger jobs that need specialist attention. In some jobs, caretakers may supervise other staff such as cleaners and gardeners. Must understand health and safety and fire regulations. May act as a mobile caretaker and look after more than one building.

Work Details

Usually work a basic 37-39 hr week, which may include some weekend work, with early starts or late finishes, and you probably need to be on call for emergencies. Sometimes you may be required to live-in. You need to cope with all sorts of demands from different people in the building. The job requires you to be quite active, climbing ladders to fix lights or hang curtains, moving furniture and heavy objects. In some jobs, you may wear a uniform provided by your employer. If you are a mobile caretaker, you usually work from a specially equipped van.

Qualification

• England, Wales and Northern Ireland

Band 1: You do not need qualifications, though practical subjects such as metalwork, woodwork and technology are useful.

Band 2: Some GCSEs at any level in English and maths or equivalent are useful.

• Scotland

Band 1: You do not need qualifications, though practical subjects such as metalwork, woodwork and technology are useful.

Band 2: Some S grades at any level in English and maths or similar are useful.

Adult Qualifications

No academic qualifications are specified but qualifications/ experience in DIY, electrical or engineering work are useful.

Work Experience

Any work experience can give you skills to use in the future and add to your CV. This can either be unpaid or holiday/part-time work that you have sorted out yourself. Experience that shows your practical skills, such as DIY and woodwork, are most useful.

Entry and Training

People with practical skills, such as DIY, joinery, electrical/ engineering or security work, may be preferred. A knowledge of basic maths and reading and writing ability is also usually required. Those working in schools have to have a Criminal Records Bureau (CRB)/Disclosure Scotland check. You are trained on the job by a more experienced caretaker. You may take part in an induction course that gives a general introduction to the company/institution and its organisation. Larger organisations, including schools, hospitals and local government, may provide opportunities to work towards vocational qualifications.

A Diploma/Welsh Baccalaureate in construction and the built environment may be available in your area and have relevant modules for this job. There is a one-year level 3 certificate in housing available from the Chartered Institute of Housing. This includes a module on caretaking and concierge services. It may be studied at some colleges, by distance learning, or by work based training. Short courses are also available in subjects that cover health and safety, hazardous substances (asbestos), fire regulations and basic DIY skills. Relevant S/NVQs are available at levels 1-3. City & Guilds offers a level 2 award in cleaning principles (maintenance and minor repairs of property). Training programmes, including apprenticeship schemes, may be available in your area.

Mature applicants with experience in the building trades, in security work or portering may have an advantage. If working in a school, you need to have a Criminal Records Bureau (CRB)/ Disclosure Scotland check. There may be apprenticeships available in your area.

Opportunities and Pay

Jobs for caretakers can be found in all parts of the UK. You can work for a local authority, central government, a university, college or school, property companies, hotel chains, sport and leisure companies, hospitals and religious authorities. With experience, and additional qualifications, there may be chances for promotion. This may include supervising other staff. You may need to move jobs to gain promotion.

Pay varies, but most caretakers earn around £11k-£12k to start with. Experienced caretakers can earn upto £25k a year. You may be given free accommodation in some jobs.

Health

You have to have good general fitness to do this job.

Skills and Qualities

able to work both on your own and in a team, alert, co-operative, good organisational skills, hard working, honest, practical skills, punctual, reliable

Relevant Subjects

Construction and built environment

Further Information

Apprenticeship Schemes (National Apprenticeship Service) - www.apprenticeships.org.uk

Asset Skills - sector skills council for the places where we live and work - www.assetskills.org

Diplomas (Foundation, Higher and Advanced) - http://yp.direct.gov.uk/diplomas

Local Government Careers (Improvement and Development Agency) - www.lgcareers.com/publications/

The Caretakers Website - www.thecaretakers.net

▶Working in schools & colleges (2007) (Babcock Lifeskills) - www.babcock-lifeskills.com/

Addresses

Chartered Institute of Housing (CIH)
Octavia House Westwood Way, Coventry CV4 8JP
Phone: +44 (0)24 7685 1700
Web: www.cih.org

Similar Jobs

Cleaner: Industrial, Facilities Manager, Removals Operative, Security Officer, Warden: Sheltered Housing

Carpenter/Joiner

also known as: Joiner

CRCI:Building and Construction

CLCI:UF — Job Band: 1 to 3

Job Description

Carpenters/joiners repair or make things from wood. Joinery is usually done in a workshop and site work is usually called carpentry. They use skills to work with a wide variety of wood, from inexpensive types, which are used for basic construction, to expensive hardwoods that can be used for decorative features. Drawings are used to make calculations, and wood is then chosen and cut to size. Carpenters/joiners use hand tools, power tools and cutting machines. They make and fix objects and fittings with nails, glue and special joints.

Bench work joiners make items such as doors, window frames, staircases and roof timbers. Building site joiners fit floorboards, doors, staircases and window frames. Formwork joiners cut and fit the moulds ('formwork') that hold and shape wet concrete for construction work, such as motorways, multi-storey car parks and bridges. Shopfitters produce and fit shopfronts and interiors. They may specialise in one type of carpentry or use skills across all areas of work.

Work Details

Usually work a 39 hr week that may include Saturdays and some evenings to meet deadlines. Work can be on different sites, in a workshop or in people's houses. Travel is necessary and sometimes you may need to stay away from home. The job involves physical activity such as lifting, bending, kneeling, climbing ladders and working at heights on scaffolding. Work may be indoors or outdoors in all weathers.

You may work in a team with other craft workers including bricklayers, painters and plasterers, but sometimes you work alone. The work environment can be dirty, noisy, dusty and possibly cold, damp or muddy. There is a risk of minor injuries and you need to wear a safety helmet and protective footwear.

Qualification

• England, Wales and Northern Ireland

Band 2: Although academic qualifications are not specified for this job, GCSEs including maths, technical subjects, science and English, or equivalent, are helpful for some training programmes and courses. A training programme approved by ConstructionSkills requires you to have had a good general education.

Band 3: For entry to some courses, a number of GCSEs (A*-D) in subjects such as English, maths, science, design and technology, or equivalent qualifications, are required.

• Scotland

Band 2: Although academic qualifications are not specified for this job, S grades including maths, technical subjects, science and English, or similar are useful for some training programmes and courses. A training programme approved by ConstructionSkills requires you to have had a good general education.

Band 3: For entry to some courses, a number of S grades (1-4) in subjects such as English, maths, science, design and technology, or similar qualifications, are required.

Adult Qualifications

Entry requirements for some courses and training may be relaxed for adults with relevant work experience.

Work Experience

Relevant work or voluntary experience is always useful and can improve your chances when applying for entry to construction jobs and apprenticeships. It is useful to shadow an experienced carpenter/joiner or craft worker involved in construction, building or restoration work. For work experience, health and safety issues may mean that there are certain jobs you can't do until you are over 16. Contact your local ConstructionSkills office for advice.

Entry and Training

Most young people begin training at 16-17 through specific schemes, such as those offered by ConstructionSkills. A Diploma/ Welsh Baccalaureate in construction and the built environment may be available in your area. To enter a training scheme you may have to pass an initial assessment. Training can be on the job, and by a day or block-release course. Introductory vocational courses include basic carpentry and joinery skills offered by City & Guilds. Various colleges may also offer one or two-year full-time courses. There are also various levels of qualifications in carpentry and joinery that are offered by the Institute of Carpenters (IOC), including the master certificate scheme (Master Carpenter/Master Joiner).

Those who do not yet qualify for the scheme may be eligible for the IOC's membership card scheme, which is an enhancement of the government-required construction skills certification scheme (CSCS). Contact the IOC for details of its qualifications and membership requirements. Most contractors require proof of competence before allowing workers onto sites, which is provided by a CSCS card. It lists your qualifications and is valid for either three or five years.

You can be trained and work for the Royal Engineers (Army) as a military engineer (carpenter/joiner) and gain nationally recognised qualifications. Specialist training is also available for those who wish to concentrate on achieving skills in restoration and heritage work. Contact the National Heritage Training Group for further information.

S/NVQs in wood occupations are available at levels 1-3. Training programmes, including apprenticeships in carpentry and joinery leading to level 2 and advanced apprenticeships/construction apprenticeships leading to level 3, may be available in your area. There are also Construction Awards (England, Wales and Northern Ireland) at foundation, intermediate and advanced level, available for those who are unable to gain workplace experience for NVQs.

Mature applicants with relevant work experience in the building and construction trades have a reasonable chance of training opportunities. Government training schemes, including apprenticeships, may be available in your area. Contact your local careers office, Next Step service, Jobcentre Plus or Learning and Skills Council (LSC)/Local Enterprise Company (LEC) for details of training opportunities. The Carpenters' Company offers funding for wood-related courses undertaken in the UK through their charitable trust. Applications should be submitted by the end of June for consideration in July prior to the start of a course.

Opportunities and Pay

You can work for building firms, civil engineering companies and construction companies throughout the UK. Availability of work depends on activity in the building trade and the national economy. Currently there is a downturn in the housing market which means there may be a shortage of vacancies. However, timber-framed buildings are on the increase, so there may be a demand for your skills in some areas. A good proportion of carpenters and joiners are self-employed and work independently on short or long-term contracts.

Pay varies according to the employer and level of skill. Generally, an inexperienced worker may initially earn around £12.5k a year and when skilled and qualified, this can rise to £18k-£26k a year. Employers may give allowances for travel and cost of lodgings. Overtime and bonus payments may boost your income. Self employed carpenters and joiners are often paid a daily rate, negotiated with the customer.

Health

You need good general fitness and stamina. There may be an allergy risk from dust.

Skills and Qualities

able to follow drawings and plans, able to work both on your own and in a team, accurate measuring and calculating skills, attention to detail, eye for shape/colour, hand-to-eye co-ordination, head for heights, manual dexterity, steady hand

Relevant Subjects

Construction and built environment, Design and technology

Further Information

Apprenticeship Schemes (National Apprenticeship Service) - www.apprenticeships.org.uk

Apprenticeships in Scotland (Careers Info Scotland) - www.apprenticeshipsinscotland.com/about/

Army Careers Website - www. army.mod.uk

Careers in Wood (Proskills) - www.prospect4u.co.uk

Construction Skills Certification Scheme (CSCS) (CSCS) - www.cscs.uk.com/

ConstructionSkills - sector skills council for the construction industry - www.cskills.org

Real Life Guide to Carpentry and Cabinet Making (Trotman) - www.trotman.co.uk

▶Working in construction & the built environment (2007) (Babcock Lifeskills) - www.babcock-lifeskills.com/

Worshipful Company of Joiners and Ceilers - www.joinersandceilers.co.uk

Addresses

Carpenters' Company
Carpenters' Hall, Throgmorton Avenue, London EC2N 2JJ
Phone: +44 (0)20 7588 7001
Web: www.carpentersco.com

Institute of Carpenters (IOC)
Third Floor D , Carpenters' Hall, 1 Throgmorton Avenue, London EC2N 2BY
Phone: +44 (0)20 7256 2700
Web: www.instituteofcarpenters.com

National Heritage Training Group (NHTG)
Carthusian Court, 12 Carthusian Street, London EC1M 6EZ
Phone: 0300 456 5517 (UK only)
Web: www.nhtg.org.uk

Similar Jobs

Cabinet Maker, Ceiling Fixer, Construction Operative, Shopfitter, Timber Frame Erector, Wood Machinist

Carpet & Flooring Fitter

also known as: Carpet Fitter, Laminate/Wood Flooring Fitter, Vinyl Flooring Fitter

CRCI:Building and Construction
CLCI:OFZ Job Band: 1 to 2

Job Description

Carpet and flooring fitters use skills to lay floor coverings for private customers or businesses, including hotels, hospitals and offices. They work with materials such as carpet, vinyl, natural floor coverings (jute, coir and sisal), and underlay, cork, rubber, laminates and wood, and carpet/vinyl tiles. They study the plan of a room and calculate the amount of material needed to do the job. Fitters make sure that there is as little waste as possible. They may use computer generated floor plans to calculate the area to be fitted. The sub-floor is checked and issues such as how under floor heating may affect the installation of floor covering are investigated. Fitters check that the floor is level and in good, clean condition. When fitting a carpet, the fitter measures and cuts the carpet to fit the size of the room and may have to remove and re-hang doors, or move furniture.

They may fit an underlay to the floor surface first, to protect the carpet and enhance the quality. Certain types of carpet are glued straight onto the floor surface. Patterns are matched, and joins are completed by stitching, taping, heat-sealing or gluing. The carpet edges are then stretched over a spiked edging strip (gripper) to fix it. If fitting natural floor coverings, vinyl, tiles, laminates or wood boards, may need to prepare the floor surface by scraping off old glue, or putting down a layer of levelling compound. Sheets of hardboard, including moisture resistant (marine) plywood, may also be used and cut to size. Fitters need to be aware of the British Standards (BS) that are applied to floor coverings and their fitting.

Work Details

Usually work 39 hrs a week, though sometimes Saturday working may be required. Commercial jobs may be carried out during evening and weekends to minimise disruption. This job involves travelling around to different work sites, so a driving licence may be useful. You have to be able to cope with kneeling and must be able to lift heavy rolls of carpet/vinyl or boxes of tiles, and may need to move furniture. There may be a risk of minor injuries from working with cutting tools. Fitting and cutting floor coverings can be very dusty work, and there may also be strong fumes given off by some glues. You may need to wear overalls and knee pads, and sometimes a face mask and eye protection.

Qualification

- **England, Wales and Northern Ireland**

Band 1: No minimum qualifications are required, but you are expected to have had a good level of general education. However, some formal/vocational qualifications at any level are useful.

Band 2: Although academic qualifications are not specified for this job, it is an advantage to have some GCSEs, or equivalent. English, maths and design technology are useful subjects.

- **Scotland**

Band 1: No minimum qualifications are required, but you are expected to have had a good level of general education. However, some formal/vocational qualifications at any level are useful.

Band 2: Although academic qualifications are not specified for this job, it is an advantage to have some S grades, or similar. English, maths and design technology are useful subjects.

Adult Qualifications

Usually employers will take you on without qualifications, but they expect you to have a good standard of basic maths.

Work Experience

Relevant work or voluntary experience is always useful and can improve your chances when applying for entry to this job. Health and safety issues may mean that there are certain jobs you can't do until you are over 16. Contact your local ConstructionSkills office for advice.

Entry and Training

Most carpet fitters and floorlayers are trained on the job, working with an experienced fitter, and may also be sent on short courses offered by the Flooring Industry Training Association (FITA). For new entrants, FITA offers short basic carpet fitting courses that cover aspects such as carpet types, tools of the trade, methods of fitting, and also health and safety aspects. FITA also offers intermediate and advanced courses in carpet fitting, and specialised courses covering various subjects, such as estimating and planning, luxury vinyl tile fitting, essential/ intermediate wood fitting, laminate and floating wood fitting, and solid wood sanding and finishing. Courses are usually between 1-5 days.

Many carpet/floor fitters also work towards gaining a level of competence card through the Construction Skills Certification Scheme (CSCS) to indicate your individual skill level. A two-day Experienced Worker Practical Assessment is available for experienced fitters through FITA and this can be used to gain NVQ level 2 in floor covering. This is the minimum qualification needed for a CSCS card.

The UK Flooring Academy and Floortrain also run short training courses. The National Institute of Carpet and Floorlayers accredits master fitters by on site assessment or assessment at a training centre. S/NVQs are available at levels 1-3 in floor covering. Training programmes, including apprenticeships leading to level 2 and advanced apprenticeships/construction apprenticeships leading to level 3, may be available in your area.

Mature applicants with relevant experience, such as tiling or woodworking skills, may have an advantage. Contact your local careers office, Next Step service, Jobcentre Plus or Learning and Skills Council (LSC)/Local Enterprise Company (LEC) for details of all training opportunities and schemes, including apprenticeships for adults.

Opportunities and Pay
Jobs are available in most towns and cities throughout the UK. You can work for a carpet retailer, including individual shops or large stores, a specialist contractor or a floor covering warehouse. It may be possible to become a supervisor in a large company or an estimator. Many fitters are self-employed, and initial costs include buying your own tool kit and transport.

Pay varies depending on the size and type of employer. Most starting salaries are around £12k-£14k a year, rising to around £22k with experience or with managerial responsibilities. Overtime work is often available.

Health
This job requires normal colour vision and a good level of fitness and stamina. You may find this job difficult if you are allergic to dust, glue and other adhesives. There is a risk of developing knee problems.

Skills and Qualities
able to work both on your own and in a team, able to work quickly, accurate, hand-to-eye co-ordination, health & safety awareness, manual dexterity, numeracy skills, polite

Relevant Subjects
Construction and built environment

Further Information
Apprenticeship Schemes (National Apprenticeship Service) - www.apprenticeships.org.uk

Careers in Construction - www.bconstructive.co.uk

Careers in Wood (Proskills) - www.prospect4u.co.uk

Carpet and Flooring Review (Gearing Media Group) - www.cfr-magazine.com

ConstructionSkills - sector skills council for the construction industry - www.cskills.org

Diplomas (Foundation, Higher and Advanced) - http://yp.direct.gov.uk/diplomas

Floortrain - www.floortrain.co.uk

Foundation Learning (QCDA) - www.qcda.gov.uk

UK Flooring Academy - www.uk-flooring-academy.co.uk

Welsh Baccalaureate - www.wbq.org.uk

Addresses
Flooring Industry Training Association (FITA)
4C St Mary's Place, The Lace Market, Nottingham NG1 1PH
Phone: +44 (0)115 950 6836
Web: www.fita.co.uk

National Institute of Carpet and Floorlayers
4d St Mary's Place, The Lace Market, Nottingham NG1 1PH
Phone: +44 (0)115 958 3077
Web: www.nicfltd.org.uk

Similar Jobs
Carpenter/Joiner, Ceiling Fixer, Removals Operative, Tiler: Wall & Floor, Upholsterer

Cartographer
also known as: Map Editor, Map Maker, Mapping & Charting Officer

CRCI:Building and Construction
CLCI:UT — Job Band: 5

involve surveying, 3D visualisation imagery, aerial photography (photogrammetry), remote sensing (using satellites and aircraft) or social and economic research. Cartographers plan the production of maps, for which Geographic Information Systems (GIS) and digital-mapping techniques are used to scan, analyse, process and display data on screen using computer systems. They also produce topographic data for use in geographical databases. May also use computer-aided design (CAD) programs.

Map editing work may include working on the layout and choosing symbols, typefaces and colour schemes for maps. The print of the completed map is examined for accuracy and location of features and checks are made to ensure that all relevant information is included. Work may include the making of globes, charts and also models of the earth.

Work Details
Cartographers usually work 9am-5pm in an office at a work station, though occasionally may go out on fieldwork. Flexible working hours including shift work are common. Detailed research and analysis of data is involved. You make considerable use of information technology using GIS/CAD systems such as Intergraph, ESRI, MicroStation or AutoCAD and other design programs such as Freehand. You need to keep up to date as systems, equipment and techniques are changing all the time. Work can be pressurised at times and is intellectually demanding. You work with and may supervise technical staff.

Qualification

- **England, Wales and Northern Ireland**

Band 5: For degree courses: 2-3 A levels, including geography and science subjects, and some GCSEs (A*-C) including maths, or equivalent qualifications. Exact requirements depend on the degree you take.

- **Scotland**

Band 5: For degree courses: 3-5 H grades, including geography and science subjects, and some S grades (1-3) including maths, or similar qualifications. Exact requirements depend on the degree you take.

Degree Information
A degree in surveying and mapping sciences, geographical information science (GIS), and some geography degrees have direct relevance. Other courses may have modules relating to cartography such as topographic science. Degrees in geology or geophysics, depending on the course content, may also be acceptable. Postgraduate courses in geoinformation technology and cartography, applied geospatial technology, geographic information management and GIS are available.

Adult Qualifications
Some academic institutions may have special entry requirements for adults. Check with individual universities and colleges for details of entry schemes for mature applicants. Experience in geology, environmental matters, the use of computers or computer graphics is helpful.

Work Experience
Entry to this career is competitive. Those with some relevant work or voluntary experience may have an advantage. Surveying, environmental work and work with computers can also provide relevant skills and experience when applying for degrees or jobs.

Entry and Training
For entry you are expected to have a relevant degree. Although there are no specific undergraduate cartography courses in the UK, several degree courses include modules of cartography. A postgraduate qualification is also be helpful. Professional organisations such as the British Cartographic Society (BCS) can provide details about all the relevant courses on offer. There may be some opportunities for those with relevant HNDs in areas

of mathematical/physical and applied science, and land/urban studies. In government departments you may enter as a mapping technician (see job profile) and gain experience in several different departments before progressing to a more senior level.

Training is on the job by practical experience after obtaining your academic qualification. Most employers provide structured initial in-house training for new entrants, including courses such as digital mapping, GIS systems, topography and photogrammetry, and map design. Initial training may last from six months to two years. Many employers also provide sponsorship for postgraduate qualifications. Membership of the BCS or the Society of Cartographers may be helpful.

Mature applicants with previous relevant experience and qualifications have a good chance of entry, particularly those with up-to-date knowledge in GIS, digital-mapping techniques and CAD systems.

Opportunities and Pay

You can work for a central government department or agency such as the Ordnance Survey, Hydrographic Office, environmental, planning or transport departments, the Met office or UK defence departments. Other employers include companies and organisations such as British Geological Survey, public utility companies (water, gas and electricity), Forest Enterprise, British Telecom, and local authority planning and architect departments.

Entry is very competitive and you may have to take a post carrying out basic activities in order to start work in this area. There are some posts with oil exploration companies, large civil engineering contractors, commercial map publishers and universities. Those with knowledge of a second language may have good opportunities for working abroad in international mapping.

Salaries vary between employers in the public and private sectors. Typical starting salaries are around £18k-£20k whilst training, rising to around £29k with 3-5 years' experience. At senior level salaries are up to £45k a year. If working freelance, you may earn between £20 to £25 an hour and sometimes more, depending on your expertise and the type of work you do.

Health

This job requires good eyesight and normal colour vision.

Skills and Qualities

analytical skills, aptitude for maths and science, design ability, environmental awareness, geographical knowledge, information handling skills, methodical, patient, spatial awareness, specialist IT skills

Relevant Subjects

Art and Design, Design and technology, Geography, ICT/Computer studies, Mathematics, Physics

Further Information

AGCAS: Environment & Agriculture (Job Sector Briefing) (AGCAS) - www.prospects.ac.uk

British Cartographic Society, BCS - www.cartography.org.uk

Cartographic Journal (BCS) (British Cartographic Society (BCS) - www.cartography.org.uk

Geospatial Course Information - www.gogeo.ac.uk

Hydrographic Journal (International Federation of Hydrographic Surveyors) - www.hydrographicsociety.org/Publications/welcome.html

Hydrographic, Meteorological & Oceanographic Training Group (HMTG) (The Royal Navy) - www.royalnavy.mod.uk/

Society of Cartographers - www.soc.org.uk

Addresses

Association for Geographic Information (AGI)
5, St Helen's Place, Bishopsgate, London EC3A 6AU
Phone: +44 (0)20 7036 0430
Web: www.agi.org.uk

International Federation of Hydrographic Surveyors
PO Box 103, Plymouth PL4 7YP
Phone: +44 (0)1752 223512
Web: www.hydrographicsociety.org

Met Office
FitzRoy Road, Exeter, Devon EX1 3PB
Phone: 0870 900 0100 (UK only)
Web: www.metoffice.gov.uk

Ordnance Survey
Romsey Road, Southampton, Hampshire SO16 4GU
Phone: 0845 605 0505 (UK only)
Web: www.ordnancesurvey.co.uk

Similar Jobs

Geographical Information Systems Manager, Geophysicist, Mapping & Charting Technician, Surveyor: Geomatics/ Geospatial, Surveyor: Hydrographic

Caterer: Contract/Private

also known as: Outside Caterer

CRCI:Catering and Hospitality
CLCI:IB Job Band: 1 to 4

Job Description

Private or contract caterers provide food and drink for organisations and businesses on their own premises or at an event. They take the details, give advice on menus and work out the cost. May hire additional chefs, waiters and bar staff. Also hires tables and table linen, plates, cutlery and glasses. May also supply flowers, plants and ice-sculptures, if required.

Some caterers work for a contract company, supplying food and services to companies for functions and special events. Others supply airlines, hospitals and schools etc. You can be self-employed and work on a small scale. This involves organising, budgeting, cooking and delivering food for private parties, weddings, funerals, office events or meetings. Caterers can also arrange for everything to be cleared away. They may also arrange for the premises to be cleaned and tidied after the event or function.

Work Details

You may have to work irregular hours, including weekends and evenings. Work is available in large industrial catering units, business premises or in people's homes. Self-employed caterers often prepare food in their own kitchens and travel around delivering to different sites. Sometimes caterers serve the food or supervise workers at events and functions such as wedding receptions, barbecues, sporting events, antiques fairs etc.

It is important to follow health and safety regulations and pay attention to hygiene. You must be able to budget and provide food/ drinks within various price ranges. The work can be physically demanding as you are active and on your feet for most of the day.

Qualification

- **England, Wales and Northern Ireland**

Band 2: For entry to jobs, no minimum qualifications are needed, but it is an advantage to have some GCSEs (A*-C) or equivalent in subjects that include English and maths.

Band 3: For entry to jobs, HNC or a relevant Diploma, usually at least 4 GCSEs (A*-C) including English and maths, or equivalent.

Band 4: For HND, Diploma of Higher Education or foundation degree: 1-2 A levels and some GCSEs (A*-C) usually including English and maths, or equivalent.

- **Scotland**

Band 2: Although academic qualifications are not specified for this job, it is an advantage to have some S grades (1-3) in subjects that include English and maths, or similar.

Band 3: For entry to jobs, usually at least four S grades (1-3) including English or maths, or similar.

Band 4: For entry to SQA higher national and professional development awards, usually 2-3 H grades and some S grades (1-3), including English and maths, or similar qualifications.

Adult Qualifications
Course entry requirements are usually relaxed for suitable mature applicants. It is possible to set up on your own without any formal qualifications, but experience in catering is essential. Experience of running a business is an advantage.

Work Experience
Any work experience equips you with skills that you can use in the future and add to your CV. There is often plenty of paid part-time catering work available, although you cannot work behind a licensed bar until you are 18.

Entry and Training
It is usually necessary to be trained and have experience in catering before you can do this job. There are many different training options. You can study full or part time at a college for national/higher national certificates/diplomas that usually include work-based placements. Qualifications include BTEC/SQA certificates/diplomas in hospitality and catering, S/NVQs in professional cookery and in hospitality and catering at levels 1-3. City & Guilds' certificates/diplomas and awards in professional cookery and hospitality and catering are available. A Diploma/ Welsh Baccalaureate in hospitality and catering, and hospitality apprenticeships may be available in your area.

There are also short courses for specialist cooking, as well as cake making and decorating. Training on the job as a chef is also an option with day release to a local college to gain qualifications. Some people may wish to study for a relevant foundation degree.

There are also private fee-paying courses, but these can be expensive and may not offer opportunities for gaining nationally recognised qualifications, including S/NVQs. It may be necessary to study for certificates and other qualifications in areas such as health and hygiene or first aid in the workplace. You almost certainly need a driving licence.

This job is particularly relevant for mature applicants, many of whom run their own businesses. Government training opportunities, such as apprenticeships in hospitality and catering, may be available in your area. You can also gain recognition of previous experience through Accreditation of Prior Learning (APL) or by working towards relevant S/NVQs. Contact your local careers office, Jobcentre Plus, Next Step service or Learning and Skills Council (LSC) Local Enterprise Company (LEC) for details of training schemes.

Opportunities and Pay
Contract catering firms are expanding by managing canteens and restaurants for businesses and manufacturing firms. There are also opportunities with other employers, including the national health service (NHS), local government, schools, universities and the civil service. Independent caterers are increasing due to the demand for fine cuisine at private parties and at other events.

If self-employed, your set-up costs include buying equipment and a car or van. There are good opportunities for promotion within large companies if you have management skills. It is possible to find work abroad. Income depends on the success of your business. Demand can be seasonal with more work at times such as Christmas and New Year. An employee of a catering firm can earn from £11k-£16k a year, depending on experience and responsibility. Managers and self-employed caterers may earn £18k-£27k. The more successful can earn around £35k a year, and some may earn more.

Health
You require good health, a good sense of smell and a good sense of taste. People with certain skin problems may not be able to do this job.

Skills and Qualities
able to cope under pressure, able to work to a budget, adaptable, business awareness, creative flair, good communication skills, good organisational skills, resilient

Relevant Subjects
Business and accounting, English, Hospitality and catering

Further Information
Academy of Culinary Arts - www.academyofculinaryarts.org.uk

Apprenticeship Schemes (National Apprenticeship Service) - www.apprenticeships.org.uk

CareerScope: Hospitality and Leisure (Springboard UK) - http://careerscope.springboarduk.net/

Caterer and Hotelkeeper (weekly) (Reed Business Information) - www.caterersearch.com/Home/

Diploma in Hospitality (People 1st) - www.hospitalitydiploma.co.uk

Diplomas (Foundation, Higher and Advanced) - http://yp.direct.gov.uk/diplomas

Hospitality Magazine (Institute of Hospitality) - www.instituteofhospitality.org

People 1st - sector skills council for hospitality, leisure, travel and tourism - www.people1st.co.uk

Real Life Guide to Hospitality & Event Management (Trotman 2010) - www.trotman.co.uk

So you want to work in the Food Industry (Wayland) - www.waylandbooks.co.uk

Springboard UK (Springboard UK) - www.springboarduk.net

Springboard Wales (Springboard Wales) - http://wales.springboarduk.net/

Training Schemes - www.direct.gov.uk/en/educationandlearning

►Working in food & drink (2007) (Babcock Lifeskills) - www.babcock-lifeskills.com/

►Working in hospitality & catering (2009) (Babcock Lifeskills) - www.babcock-lifeskills.com/

Addresses
Institute of Hospitality
Trinity Court, 34 West Street, Sutton, Surrey SM1 1SH
Phone: +44 (0)20 8661 4900
Web: www.instituteofhospitality.org

Similar Jobs
Baker, Catering Manager, Chef/Cook, Food Service Assistant, Publican, Waiter/Waitress

Catering Manager
CRCI:Catering and Hospitality
CLCI:IB
Job Band: 3 to 5

Job Description
Catering managers provide organisations and businesses with good value food and drink at a high standard of hygiene and customer satisfaction. This may be for food and drink outlets in hotels, cruise ships, schools, business and factory canteens, hospitals and prisons, or at events etc. They organise the service to suit the client's requirements, check the quality of food and service and may be involved in planning menus. They are responsible for

recruitment and dismissal of staff, their work rotas, keeping staff motivated and their development and training. Also deals with budgets, stock control and accounts, usually using a computer.

Catering managers must ensure that hygiene, health and safety regulations are met at all times. They also deals with any complaints. Catering managers in larger organisations are likely to have a more administrative role than those with smaller operations.

Work Details

A working week is usually around 38-40 hours, but you may need to work long or unsociable hours, including public holidays, evenings and weekends. Senior managers are more likely to work regular office hours; Monday to Friday. The work can be busy and pressurised at times, so you must be able to remain calm. Sometimes conditions may be cramped, hot and noisy. You may work in one place or be responsible for a number of sites. A willingness to travel is important for catering events.

Qualification

• England, Wales and Northern Ireland

Band 3: For entry to jobs, HNC or a relevant Diploma, usually at least 4 GCSEs (A*-C) including English and maths, or equivalent.

Band 4: For HND, Diploma of Higher Education or foundation degree: 1-2 A levels and some GCSEs (A*-C) usually including English and maths, or equivalent.

Band 5: For degree courses in hospitality management: 2-3 A levels and some GCSEs (A*-C) usually including English and maths, or equivalent. Exact requirements depend on the degree you take.

• Scotland

Band 3: For entry to jobs, usually at least four S grades (1-3) including English or maths, or similar.

Band 4: For entry to SQA higher national and professional development awards, usually 2-3 H grades and some S grades (1-3), including English and maths, or similar qualifications.

Band 5: For degree courses in hospitality management: 3-5 H grades and some S grades (1-3), including English and maths, or similar qualifications. Exact requirements depend on the degree you take.

Degree Information

There are a wide range of relevant degree subjects, including hospitality management, business administration with hospitality management, and culinary arts management. Alternative courses include consumer studies, food science, nutrition or dietetics. Relevant postgraduate qualifications are beneficial, particularly for those without an appropriate first degree.

Adult Qualifications

Some colleges may consider applications from mature students without the usual standard of academic qualifications, especially if they have relevant work experience. Relevant foundation/Access courses may also be available.

Work Experience

Relevant work or voluntary experience is useful and can improve your application chances for entry to this career. Consider work in hotels, retail, customer service or anything that gives you relevant management or supervisory experience. Initially, work as a waiter/ waitress, bar work, kitchen work and office administration, gives useful 'hands-on' experience. Accounting and budgeting knowledge is also an advantage.

In some areas there is a young apprenticeship (14-16) scheme that provides an extended work placement and eventual achievement of a relevant level 2 qualification whilst at school.

Entry and Training

There are many routes into catering management and a degree/ HND is not necessarily required. It is possible to work your way up to the job by starting as a trainee and previous experience in a customer service environment is often more important to some employers than formal qualifications.

However, formal recruitment schemes may ask for a degree or equivalent level of qualification for entry. Entrants to management training schemes are often graduates or those who have a relevant BTEC/SQA higher national award, or professional qualifications. Hospitality management and culinary arts management are particularly useful subjects to study.

Training routes and nationally recognised qualifications at all levels are offered by professional organisations. These include qualifications from the Institute of Hospitality, such as a certificate/diploma in management at levels 3-4. Foundation degrees in hospitality management and other relevant subjects are also available. Many courses can be studied full time or part time whilst in employment.

Continuing professional development is also available and is encouraged. S/NVQs are available in hospitality supervision at level 3. A Diploma/Welsh Baccalaureate may be available in your area in hospitality. The advanced level is equivalent to 3.5 A levels but for some university courses, the additional and specialist learning (ASL) component of the diploma needs to include specific A levels. Check entry requirements carefully with the individual institutions. Training programmes, including hospitality and catering apprenticeship schemes, may be available in your area for entry to this job. Advanced apprenticeships leading to qualification at level 3 can also be a route into higher education.

Mature applicants with relevant experience in catering and managerial work are welcomed. Government training opportunities, such as apprenticeships in hospitality and catering, may be available in your area. You can also gain recognition of previous experience through Accreditation of Prior Learning (APL) or by working towards relevant S/NVQs. Contact your local careers office, Jobcentre Plus, Next Step service or Learning and Skills Council (LSC) Local Enterprise Company (LEC) for details of training schemes.

You can apply to the Savoy Educational Trust for financial support to study for hospitality industry-related courses. The Trust aims to support individuals who wish to make a career in hospitality.

Opportunities and Pay

Around 145,000 people work as catering or restaurant managers in the UK and there is a shortage of skilled and trained managers. Catering managers are likely to be employed either directly or by contract caterers in businesses, universities, prisons, schools, hospitals, the armed forces etc. Promotion to regional or area management exists for managers working in contract catering companies. If you are seeking promotion you need to be prepared to move around the country. Some catering managers move into hotel or leisure management, or set up their own contract catering business.

Pay varies considerably depending on location, size of organisation and level of responsibility. Trainee managers may earn around £16k-£20k a year, rising to £30k-£35k with experience. Senior catering managers earn more than this. Salaries tend to be higher in London and south-east England.

Health

This job requires good health, stamina and physical fitness. People with certain skin problems may not be able to do this job.

Skills and Qualities

able to motivate others, able to work to a budget, aptitude for teamwork, business awareness, calm, good communication skills, good interpersonal skills, good organisational skills, negotiating skills, problem-solving skills, smart appearance

Relevant Subjects
Business and accounting, Economics, English, Hospitality and catering, ICT/Computer studies, Mathematics, Modern Foreign Languages

Further Information
Academy of Culinary Arts - www.academyofculinaryarts.org.uk

Apprenticeship Schemes (National Apprenticeship Service) - www.apprenticeships.org.uk

British Hospitality Association (BHA) (British Hospitality Association) - www.bha.org.uk

Caterer and Hotelkeeper (weekly) (Reed Business Information) - www.catersearch.com/Home/

Diploma in Hospitality (People 1st) - www.hospitalitydiploma.co.uk

Diplomas (Foundation, Higher and Advanced) - http://yp.direct.gov.uk/diplomas

Hospitality Magazine (Institute of Hospitality) - www.instituteofhospitality.org

People 1st - sector skills council for hospitality, leisure, travel and tourism - www.people1st.co.uk

Real Life Guide to Hospitality & Event Management (Trotman 2010) - www.trotman.co.uk

So you want to work in the Food Industry (Wayland) - www.waylandbooks.co.uk

Springboard UK (Springboard UK) - www.springboarduk.net

Springboard Wales (Springboard Wales) - http://wales.springboarduk.net/

Training Schemes - www.direct.gov.uk/en/educationandlearning

►Working in hospitality & catering (2009) (Babcock Lifeskills) - www.babcock-lifeskills.com/

Addresses
British Hospitality Association (BHA)
Queens House, 55-56 Lincoln's Inn Fields, London WC2A 3BH
Phone: +44 (0)207 404 7744
Web: www.bha.org.uk

Institute of Hospitality
Trinity Court, 34 West Street, Sutton, Surrey SM1 1SH
Phone: +44 (0)20 8661 4900
Web: www.instituteofhospitality.org

Savoy Educational Trust
Queen's House 55-56 Lincoln's Inn Fields, London WC2A 3BH
Phone: +44 (0) 207 269 9692
Web: www.savoyeducationaltrust.org.uk

Similar Jobs
Caterer: Contract/Private, Chef/Cook, Hotel Manager, Off-Licence Manager, Publican, Restaurant Manager

Cavity Wall Insulation Technician
also known as: Cavity Wall Insulator

CRCI:Building and Construction

CLCI:UF Job Band: 1 to 2

Job Description
Cavity wall insulation technicians inject insulating materials into the space between the layers of brickwork that make up the outside wall of a building. They work from the outside of the building, drilling holes into walls and follow a set pattern. They calculate the amount of material needed and make use of a variety of insulating materials, such as foam, expanded polythene beads/granules or blown mineral wool. These act as a barrier to heat loss from the building. Technicians operate a machine to pump the insulation into the cavity space. A ventilation pipe is fitted where needed to conform to safety requirements for flues and chimneys.

When completed, the insulation technician fills the holes with mortar so that the work done is not obviously visible on the outside of the building. They also work inside a building to insulate lofts, or fit soundproofing and draughtproofing systems.

Work Details
Usually work over 40 hrs a week, which may include some overtime work, including weekends. The hours may be longer in the summer. Travel is necessary to different sites. You may need to work away from home at times. It is an advantage to have a driving licence. Work is outdoors and in all sorts of weather. Technicians are often expected to complete three jobs a day, depending on size.

In this job, you have to bend down a lot and lift heavy objects. Building sites are often dusty, dirty, muddy and oily and the ground is rough. You may have to climb up on scaffolding and ladders. A safety helmet, ear defenders, overalls, and boots are usually worn.

Qualification
- **England, Wales and Northern Ireland**

Band 1: No minimum qualifications are required, but you are expected to have had a good level of general education. However, some formal/vocational qualifications at any level are useful.

Band 2: Although academic qualifications are not specified for this job, it is an advantage to have some GCSEs (A*-C) in subjects that include English and maths, or equivalent.

- **Scotland**

Band 1: No minimum qualifications are required, but you are expected to have had a good level of general education. However, some formal/vocational qualifications at any level are useful.

Band 2: Although academic qualifications are not specified for this job, it is an advantage to have some S grades (1-3) in subjects that include English and maths, or similar qualifications.

Adult Qualifications
Generally, no formal qualifications are specified and adult entry is common. However, it is an advantage to have some level of qualifications in order to make calculations and keep accurate written records of each job.

Work Experience
Any work experience can help you to identify the things you enjoy doing. It can equip you with skills that you can use in the future and add to your CV. However, health and safety issues may mean there are certain jobs in the building industry that you can not do until you are 16. Your local ConstructionSkills office is able to advise you on this.

Entry and Training
Training is usually on the job, initially working with experienced cavity wall insulators. There may be off-the-job training offered by some companies/manufacturers on specialist topics, including specific materials and health and safety. It usually takes around three to six months to become fully trained. You are expected to eventually gain a level of competence card through a Construction Skills Certification Scheme (CSCS) that indicates your individual skill level.

A Diploma/ Welsh Baccalaureate in construction and the built environment may be available in your area. You can also work towards S/NVQs in insulation, such as insulation and building treatments (cavity wall insulation) at level 2. Training programmes, including apprenticeships leading to level 2 and advanced apprenticeships/construction apprenticeships leading to level 3, may be available in your area. They should all follow BSI British Standards and British Board of Agriment (BBA) regulations.

Mature applicants with relevant experience of building work may have an advantage when applying for this job.

Opportunities and Pay
Jobs are available throughout the UK, mainly in urban areas. Most jobs are with specialist insulation companies. Larger firms offer a route to chargehand/supervisor posts. When fully experienced, many become self-employed and start their own business. Although there is a downturn in the property market and building trade at the moment, employment prospects for insulator technicians are stable due to the government's promotion of energy efficiency.

Pay varies depending on area and employer. Trainees earn around £15k a year and after training around £20k. Those with experience earn around £25k a year. You may get paid for overtime.

Health
You must be physically fit with good eyesight and hearing. You should not be allergic to dust.

Skills and Qualities
able to follow instructions, able to work both on your own and in a team, accurate measuring and calculating skills, head for heights, health & safety awareness, practical skills, steady hand

Relevant Subjects
Construction and built environment, Design and technology

Further Information
Construction Skills Certification Scheme (CSCS) - www.cscs.uk.com

ConstructionSkills - sector skills council for the construction industry - www.cskills.org

Diplomas (Foundation, Higher and Advanced) - http://yp.direct.gov.uk/diplomas

Welsh Baccalaureate - www.wbq.org.uk

▶Working in construction & the built environment (2007) (Babcock Lifeskills) - www.babcock-lifeskills.com/

Addresses
British Board of Agriment (BBA)
Bucknalls Lane, Garston, Hertfordshire WD25 9BA
Phone: +44 (0)1923 665300
Web: www.bbacerts.co.uk/

National Energy Action
St Andrew's House, 90-92 Pilgrim Street, Newcastle Upon Tyne NE1 6SG
Phone: +44 (0)191 261 5677
Web: www.nea.org.uk

National Insulation Association
2 Vimy Court, Vimy Road, Leighton Buzzard LU7 1FG
Phone: 08451 636363 (UK only)
Web: www.nationalinsulationassociation.org.uk

Similar Jobs
Ceiling Fixer, Construction Operative, Damp Proofer, Engineer: Thermal Insulation, Mastic Asphalter, Roofer

Ceiling Fixer

CRCI:Building and Construction
CLCI:UF — Job Band: 1 to 2

Job Description
Ceiling fixers install ceilings inside buildings, often to cover air conditioning systems, wiring and pipe work. Some ceilings are decorative. They work on new and existing buildings, such as shops and offices, hospitals, airports, banks, nightclubs and cinemas. Ceilings can be suspended or with metal stud partitions. Others are specialist, such as acoustic ones in theatres, and damp and chemical resistant ones for swimming pools. Fixers may work on building restoration projects.

Ceiling fixers study drawings, site measurements and instruction sheets to work out job requirements. They may fit insulation material into the ceiling space before installing panels. A ceiling grid system is installed, and the fixer then fits ceiling tiles of varying design and materials. They mark out the position for the framework and check levels. Work is done from scaffolding or from a wooden platform and a range of hand tools, such as hacksaws, spirit or water levels, hammers, knives and metal cutters, as well as power tools are used. Ceiling fixers work with electricians, heating and ventilation engineers, plumbers, painters, and carpenters/joiners.

Work Details
Usually work a 39 hr week, though some evening and weekend work may be necessary. You work indoors and on different sites, so some travelling is necessary. A driving licence may be useful. You usually work in a team, but may also work on your own. You have to cope with working at heights on scaffolding/ladders and may have to work in confined spaces. Wearing a safety helmet and sometimes protective goggles is often required.

Qualification

• England, Wales and Northern Ireland
Band 1: No minimum qualifications are required, but you are expected to have a good level of general education. However, some formal/vocational qualifications at any level are useful.

Band 2: No minimum entry qualifications, but some GCSEs including maths, science, technical subjects and English, or equivalent, are useful.

• Scotland
Band 1: No minimum qualifications are required, but you are expected to have a good level of general education. However, some formal/vocational qualifications at any level are useful.

Band 2: No minimum entry qualifications, but some S grades including maths, science, technical subjects and English, or similar, are useful.

Adult Qualifications
No formal entry requirements, but it is useful to have practical ability in woodwork and some work experience in the construction industry.

Work Experience
Relevant work or voluntary experience is always useful and can improve your chances when applying for entry to construction jobs and apprenticeships. Health and safety issues may mean that there are certain jobs you can't do until you are over 16. Contact your local ConstructionSkills office for advice.

Entry and Training
Training is usually through a combination of on-the-job training and an approved programme offered by ConstructionSkills and City & Guilds. You may have to take an entrance test before you can start training. Most young people enter schemes at age 16-17 and train by working on the job, with a day-release or block-release course. A Diploma/ Welsh Baccalaureate in construction and the built environment may be available in your area. Training centres are located in certain areas throughout the UK; contact ConstructionSkills for details. Relevant one and two-year full-time college courses are also available. Training may also be available from manufacturers of suspended ceilings and partitioning.

Many ceiling fixers also work towards gaining a level of competence card through the Construction Skills Certification Scheme (CSCS) to indicate individual skill level. S/NVQs are available in interior systems (ceiling fixing) at level 2. This is the level of qualification required to gain CSCS accreditation. Training programmes, including apprenticeships leading to level 2 and advanced apprenticeships/construction apprenticeships leading to level 3, may be available in your area. There are also Construction Awards (England and Wales) available for those who are unable to gain workplace experience for NVQs. Further information is available from ConstructionSkills.

Mature applicants with related experience, such as woodworking/building skills, have a reasonable chance of entering this job. There may be special government training schemes in some areas. Contact your local careers office, Next Step service, Jobcentre Plus or Learning and Skills Council (LSC)/Local Enterprise Company (LEC) for details of training schemes, including apprenticeships for adults.

Opportunities and Pay
You can be employed by a small firm of builders, a large building contractor, or a specialist interior fit-out company. Availability of work depends on activity in the building trade and the national economy. Currently there is a downturn in the housing market which means there may be a shortage of vacancies for ceiling fixers. Some experienced ceiling fixers are sub-contractors, who are self-employed.

Ceiling fixers are mostly paid according to national industry rates, but pay can vary, depending on location and employer. Without qualifications, a general operative earns about £8 an hour. The basic standard hourly rate for qualified ceiling fixers is around £9-£13. The rate depends on your level of qualification. This can work out at around £18k-£24k a year. Bonuses and overtime pay may be available to increase your pay. Employers may also pay allowances for travel and cost of lodgings. Self-employed annual incomes can be around £25k-£35k a year, or more.

Health
This job requires good general fitness.

Skills and Qualities
able to follow drawings and plans, able to work both on your own and in a team, able to work in confined spaces, accurate measuring and calculating skills, head for heights, manual dexterity, safety conscious

Relevant Subjects
Construction and built environment, Design and technology

Further Information
Apprenticeship Schemes (National Apprenticeship Service) - www.apprenticeships.org.uk
Careers in Construction - www.bconstructive.co.uk
ConstructionSkills - sector skills council for the construction industry - www.cskills.org
Diplomas (Foundation, Higher and Advanced) http://yp.direct.gov.uk/diplomas
Training Schemes - www.direct.gov.uk/en/educationandlearning
Welsh Baccalaureate - www.wbq.org.uk
▶ Working in construction & the built environment (2007) (Babcock Lifeskills) - www.babcock-lifeskills.com/

Addresses
Association of Interior Specialists (AIS)
Olton Bridge, 245 Warwick Road, Solihull B92 7AH
Phone: 020 (0)121 707 0077
Web: www.ais-interiors.org.uk

Similar Jobs
Carpenter/Joiner, Carpet & Flooring Fitter, Cavity Wall Insulation Technician, Damp Proofer, Dry Liner, Plasterer

Cemetery Worker
also known as: Grave Digger

CRCI:Personal and Other Services
CLCI:IP Job Band: 1

Job Description
Cemetery workers dig graves, look after cemetery grounds and clean and maintain machinery. They inspect statues and gravestones and make them safe if needed, and keep the graves tidy. Use gardening equipment to trim the grass and look after plants. Workers follow health and safety rules and make sure legal requirements are met.

They measure and mark out where to dig each grave. Then, dig the hole with a mechanical digger or hand tools. Use special equipment to remove any water and put in wooden supports to stop the sides collapsing. Must make sure mourners can get to the grave safely and may lay down a walkway so they can stand at the edge of the grave. Fill the grave after the funeral service and place floral tributes on top.

Work Details
Usually work a 37 hr week, Monday to Friday and some weekends. You may start work early in the morning. Works outdoors in all weathers. Comes into contact with a wide range of people including funeral, crematorium, council and grounds staff. It is dirty and physically demanding work that involves a lot of bending and climbing. You may have to use heavy machinery and chemicals. Protective clothing is supplied by the employer.

Qualification

• England, Wales and Northern Ireland
Band 1: No minimum qualifications are required, but you are expected to have a good level of general education and reading and writing skills. However, some formal/vocational qualifications at any level are useful.

• Scotland
Band 1: No minimum qualifications are required, but you are expected to have a good level of general education and reading and writing skills. However, some formal/vocational qualifications at any level are useful.

Adult Qualifications
Adults can enter this area of work without formal qualifications, but reading and writing skills are required. You can improve your skills and qualifications by working through the Foundation Learning programme. This involves taking credit-based units and qualifications to help you progress.

Work Experience
It is useful to arrange work experience to see if you are suited to this type of work. Paid or voluntary experience of labouring or working outdoors is relevant. You can develop gardening skills through volunteering, paid work or as a hobby.

The Land-Force website lets you check how many of the skills you need you already have. For a small charge you can store your skills passport online to show employers. This lists your skills, practical experiences, achievements and qualifications.

Entry and Training
Training is on the job with experienced members of staff. You may go on courses to learn how to use horticultural equipment or machinery for digging graves. The Institute of Cemetery and Crematorium Management (ICCM) runs a cemetery operatives training scheme (COTS). This involves a series of courses covering health and safety, excavator operation, ground support and mowing. Health & safety and the burial process, excavator and dumper courses are now delivered and assessed by City & Guilds

NPTC qualified officers at your cemetery or at the Berkshire College of Agriculture (BCA). You may be able to work towards S/NVQ level 2 in amenity horticulture (cemeteries and graveyards).

Mature entrants who are fit enough to cope with the physical demands of the job are welcome. Experience of gardening or operating construction or agricultural machinery is useful.

Opportunities and Pay
There are over 1,800 cemeteries run by local councils in the UK. Others are run by parish councils, religious groups or are privately owned. Nationally, fewer than 30% of deaths are followed by burial. The number may be even lower in some places. There has been an increase in recent years in pet burials. There are not many chances to progress. You may have to move to another site to become a supervisor. With further training, some workers move into administration and management.

Cemetery workers earn around £14k-£18k a year. Senior or supervisory staff may earn £20k-£25k or more. Cemetery managers earn £28k-£40k or more a year, depending on the job role. Overtime allowances are sometimes paid.

Health
You need to be physically fit. There is an allergy risk from pollen, chemicals and dust.

Skills and Qualities
able to follow procedures, able to operate equipment, able to work both on your own and in a team, enjoy working outdoors, good communication skills, manual dexterity, practical skills, respectful, safety conscious, tactful

Further Information
Foundation Learning (QCDA) - www.qcda.gov.uk

Institute of Cemetery and Crematorium Management - www.bereavement-services.org/

Land-force ( ) - www.land-force.com

Lantra - The Sector Skills Council for environmental & land-based sector (Lantra) - http:/www.lantra.co.uk

Local Government Careers (Improvement and Development Agency) - www.lgcareers.com/publications/

Skills Passport - www.land-force.org.uk

▶Working outdoors (2010) (Babcock Lifeskills) - www.babcock-lifeskills.com/

Addresses
Association of Burial Authorities (ABA)
Waterloo House, 155 Upper Street, London N1 1RA
Phone: +44 (0)20 7288 2522
Web: www.burials.org.uk

Berkshire College of Agriculture (BCA)
Burchetts Green, Maidenhead, Berkshire SL6 6QR
Phone: +44 (0)1628 824 444
Web: www.bca.ac.uk

Institute of Cemetery and Crematorium Management (ICCM)
City of London Cemetery, Aldersbrook Road, Manor Park E15 5DQ
Phone: +44 (0)20 8989 4661
Web: www.iccm-uk.com

Similar Jobs
Construction Operative, Construction Plant Operative, Crematorium Technician, Farm Worker: Crops, Gardener

Ceramic Decorator

CRCI:Manufacturing and Production
CLCI:SAD Job Band: 1 to 2

Job Description
Ceramic decorators are skilled in applying the finishing touches and decorations to ceramic and pottery items, such as tableware and tiles. They work either for a manufacturer or in a craft pottery or studio and use a number of different methods to apply a design. These include painting freehand, filling in outlines, or by copying from a similar pattern design. Decorators choose brushes and then mix paints to make the right colour for the design. Techniques also include banding or lining, which adds bands/lines of colour. May use gilding techniques. Decorative details are added using precious metals such as gold and silver. May use machines that apply ink or paint to the ceramic object, or may work with transfers.

Work Details
Ceramic decorators usually work a basic 39 hr week, Monday to Friday, though may be required to work a shift system. You work for a manufacturer of domestic/household goods and kitchenware, or commemorative china and ornamental pieces, a craft workshop/studio, or possibly from home. Working conditions may be hot, but are usually well lit. Great care must be taken when painting small designs. In some jobs, you may have to do the same task over and over again. Most decorating work is done sitting down. Protective clothing is worn.

Qualification

• England, Wales and Northern Ireland
Band 1: No minimum qualifications are required, but you are expected to have a good level of general education. However, some formal/vocational qualifications at any level are useful, as is an aptitude for art and design.

Band 2: Although academic qualifications are not specified for this job, it is an advantage to have some GCSEs (A-C*) in subjects that include English and maths, or equivalent.

• Scotland
Band 1: No minimum qualifications are required, but you are expected to have a good level of general education. However, some formal/vocational qualifications at any level are useful, as is an aptitude for art and design.

Band 2: Although academic qualifications are not specified for this job, it is an advantage to have some S grades (1-3) in subjects that include English and maths, or similar.

Adult Qualifications
No pre-entry qualifications are usually required though some academic/vocational qualifications at any level may be an advantage. English and maths are useful subjects.

Work Experience
Work or voluntary experience is always useful. It can improve your chances when applying for jobs or apprenticeships. Your personal or adult guidance adviser should be able to advise you about how to get some work experience.

Entry and Training
To enter this job you may have to take a test to demonstrate that you can work well with your hands. Training is usually on the job with an experienced worker, or possibly by a day or block-release course leading to job-related qualifications. City & Guilds offers level 2/3 awards in creative techniques in ceramics - surface decoration. Relevant training programmes, including apprenticeship schemes, may be available in your area. Advanced apprenticeships leading to qualification at level 3 can be a route into higher education.

For those who want to work in craft potteries and develop freehand skills, there are a range of higher education courses available in ceramics. A portfolio of art and design work is usually needed, as well as higher entry qualifications, for these courses.

Government training opportunities, such as apprenticeships, may be available in your area. You can also gain recognition of previous experience through Accreditation of Prior Learning (APL) or by working towards relevant S/NVQs. Contact your local careers office, Jobcentre Plus, Next Step service or Learning and Skills Council (LSC) Local Enterprise Company (LEC) for details of training schemes.

Opportunities and Pay

The ceramics industry in the UK employs approximately 20,000 people and is in decline at present. You are usually employed by a large commercial pottery manufacturer. These are most likely located in the Potteries (West Midlands area of the UK). There are small craft potteries and studios throughout the UK. These are often in tourist areas. Some decorators may be able to work from home. Promotion to supervisory/team leader level is possible but there is limited opportunity.

Pay varies depending on employer and location but generally ranges from around £10k-£15k, rising to around £20k a year for supervisors. There may be opportunities to earn more money for shift work, bonuses and overtime.

Health

There is allergy risk from skin irritants. This job requires good eyesight and normal colour vision.

Skills and Qualities

able to work quickly, able to work well on your own, artistic ability, attention to detail, careful, eye for shape/colour, good concentration level, good co-ordination, patient, steady hand

Relevant Subjects

Art and Design, Manufacturing

Further Information

Apprenticeship Schemes (National Apprenticeship Service) - www.apprenticeships.org.uk

Ceramic Review (bi-monthly) (Ceramic Review Publishing Ltd) - www.ceramicreview.com/

Creative & Cultural Skills - sector skills council for advertising, crafts, cultural heritage, design, literature, music, performing & visual arts - www.ccskills.org.uk

Training Schemes - www.direct.gov.uk/en/educationandlearning

▶Working in art & design (2009) (Babcock Lifeskills) - www.babcock-lifeskills.com/

Addresses

Ceramic Industry Learning Network (CILN)
Unit 1 Riverside, 2 Campbell Road, Stoke-On-Trent ST4 4RJ
Phone: +44 (0)1782 747 828
Web: www.cilnweb.co.uk

Similar Jobs

Ceramic Designer, Ceramic Pottery Maker/Operative, Signwriter/Signmaker

Ceramic Designer

also known as: Ceramicist, Potter

CRCI:Manufacturing and Production
CLCI:EG — Job Band: 3 to 5

Job Description

Ceramic designers create designs for pottery products such as kitchenware, table and ovenware, bathroom fittings or floor and wall tiles. May produce designs for decorative/ornamental pieces, and also gift and commemorative items. They design articles made with ceramic materials such as hard porcelain, bone china, stoneware and earthenware. They work either for a large company that mass-produces a large variety of items, or can be self-employed, designing and producing one-off pieces, including jewellery, and selling them for a profit.

Designers need to ensure that the finished design is commercially viable and appealing to purchasers. In industry they work from a design brief that sets out the type of item required and the desired production costs. May oversee the design to final production. If self-employed, creates their own designs or works with a client's idea. Some designers also make the object by throwing it on a potter's wheel, by using moulds, or by rolling and shaping by hand. The product is then decorated and glazed before firing in a kiln (oven).

Self-employed designers may run a shop from their studio and hold exhibitions and demonstrations of their work. Also sells their items through craft shops, gift shops and galleries, direct to purchasers through a mail order catalogue and the Internet, or at craft fairs. Ceramic designers may conduct further research on a design idea or brief and also consider technical aspects, including decorative techniques and kiln temperatures. Needs to keep up to date with trends in the industry, and usually attends trade fairs and exhibitions to enhance their knowledge.

Work Details

Ceramic designers usually work a basic 37-39 hr week, Monday to Friday, though at times may be required to work extra hours to meet deadlines. Those who are self-employed or work freelance are able to choose their own working hours. Mostly works in a well-lit, warm environment in a studio or workshop, or from home. The work involves travel to clients, craft fairs, markets and exhibitions, and you may have to promote your own work and develop business skills.

Qualification

- **England, Wales and Northern Ireland**

Band 3: For entry: usually at least 4 GCSEs (A*-C) including English and maths or equivalent. For some art and design foundation courses: usually at least 5 GCSEs (A*-C).

Band 4: For relevant BTEC higher national award/foundation degree: 1-2 A levels and some GCSEs (A*-C) usually including English and maths, or equivalent.

Band 5: For degree courses: 2-3 A levels and some GCSEs (A*-C) usually including English and maths, or equivalent. Exact requirements depend on the degree you take.

- **Scotland**

Band 3: For entry: usually at least four S grades (1-3) including English and maths, or similar.

Band 4: For relevant SQA higher national award: usually 2-3 H grades and some S grades (1-3), often including English and maths, or similar qualifications.

Band 5: For degree courses: 3-5 H grades and some S grades (1-3), usually including English and maths, or similar qualifications. Exact requirements depend on the degree you take.

Degree Information

Degree subjects are often in ceramics, ceramic design, 3D design (ceramics) or design and applied arts (ceramics). There are relevant postgraduate qualifications available in ceramics. Graduates in other art and design subjects, such as fine art, can take postgraduate courses in ceramics.

Adult Qualifications

Those with outstanding portfolios of work may be accepted for courses without the standard entry requirements. There are Access and foundation courses in some areas, which give adults without qualifications a route on to degree courses. Check with individual colleges. Experience in the art and design field is an advantage.

Work Experience

Competition for college and university places in this area is high and those with relevant work or voluntary experience may be preferred. Any practical or design experience of work in a craft studio or workshop is very useful. Another way to build experience is to gain a wide range of contacts through craft fairs and galleries.

Entry and Training

Considerable talent is needed and competition for jobs is fierce. You require an excellent portfolio both for employers and colleges. Almost all ceramic designers take full-time courses first and many of those who obtain employment have a relevant higher education qualification. Students normally take a foundation or BTEC national course first, followed by a three-year degree course in their specialist subject. Those who have relevant craft skills and experience may have the opportunity to move into ceramic designing, but you should be able to demonstrate a high level of talent. Relevant foundation degrees are available in some areas.

Continuing professional development (CPD) is an important and key element throughout your career in order to keep up to date with the latest developments. A structured programme of CPD is offered by organisations such as the Chartered Society of Designers (CSD).

Training programmes, including apprenticeship schemes for the ceramics industry, may be available in your area. Advanced apprenticeships leading to qualification at level 3 can also be a route into higher education. City & Guilds have a range of accredited courses in creative techniques in ceramics and ceramics manufacture. Contact them directly for full details.

Adults with work experience in design, such as in a studio workshop may have an advantage for entry to courses. You require an up-to-date portfolio of your creative work and an understanding of the ceramics industry is also very useful.

Opportunities and Pay

There is strong competition for this type of work. There are some full-time opportunities with design teams that are employed by established ceramic manufacturers. These are mainly located in Derbyshire and Staffordshire and contract work may be available. Some major retail outlets also offer contractual work to those with substantial experience and flair. Self-employment is possible but you may not be able to earn a living solely as a designer. You can supplement your income with work in art-related areas such as gallery management/administration, or teaching.

It can take many years with very little income to build up a reputation and contacts. Sometimes there are grants available for people to start up a business, for example, from the Crafts Council.

Pay varies enormously and can range from £15k to around £25k a year. Extremely successful ceramics designers can earn much more. Those who are self-employed earn according to their success and the amount of work they produce.

Health

Pottery work is dusty and can cause problems for people with allergies or asthma. Colour matching is difficult for those who do not have normal colour vision.

Skills and Qualities

able to work well on your own, artistic ability, business awareness, creative flair, eye for shape/colour, good communication skills, good sense of touch, hand-to-eye co-ordination, practical skills, self-disciplined

Relevant Subjects

Art and Design

Further Information

Apprenticeship Schemes (National Apprenticeship Service) - www.apprenticeships.org.uk

Ceramic Review (bi-monthly) (Ceramic Review Publishing Ltd) - www.ceramicreview.com/

Chartered Society of Designers (Chartered Society of Designers) - www.csd.org.uk

Craft Potters Association (Craft Potters Association) - www.cpaceramics.co.uk

Creative & Cultural Skills - sector skills council for advertising, crafts, cultural heritage, design, literature, music, performing & visual arts - www.ccskills.org.uk

Scottish Potters Association - www.scottishpotters.co.uk

Training Schemes - www.direct.gov.uk/en/educationandlearning

▶Working in art & design (2009) (Babcock Lifeskills) - www.babcock-lifeskills.com/

▶Working in creative & media (2007) (Babcock Lifeskills) - www.babcock-lifeskills.com/

Addresses

Arts Council of Northern Ireland
77 Malone Road, Belfast BT9 6AQ
Phone: +44 (0)28 9038 5200
Web: www.artscouncil-ni.org

British Ceramic Confederation
Federation House, Station Road, Stoke-on-Trent ST4 2SA
Phone: +44 (0)1782 744631
Web: www.ceramfed.co.uk

City & Guilds
1 Giltspur Street, London EC1A 9DD
Phone: +44 (0)20 7294 2800
Web: www.cityandguilds.com

Crafts Council (CC)
44a Pentonville Road, Islington, London N1 9BY
Phone: +44 (0)20 7806 2500
Web: www.craftscouncil.org.uk

Scottish Arts Council
12 Manor Place, Edinburgh EH3 7DD
Phone: +44 (0)131 226 6051
Web: www.scottisharts.org.uk

Wales Craft Council
Henfaes Lane, Welshpool, Powys SY21 7BE
Phone: +44 (0)1938 555 313
Web: www.walescraftcouncil.co.uk

Similar Jobs

Artist, Ceramic Decorator, Jewellery Designer, Sculptor, Teacher: Art

Ceramic Pottery Maker/Operative

CRCI:Manufacturing and Production
CLCI:SAD
Job Band: 1 to 2

Job Description

Ceramic pottery makers are skilled in both traditional and mechanised processes that are used to create a large variety of clay products. They usually work in large commercial pottery manufacturers and may make small items such as wall tiles or teacups, or larger goods such as baths. Pottery makers load the machines and watch to make sure that the items are correctly made. May operate casting machinery that pours the slip (liquid clay) or plaster into moulds to make items such as teapots, figures and souvenirs. May use a jiggering machine to make flatware such as saucers or a jolleying machine to make hollowware like soup bowls. Some operatives may work on lathes that turn, shape and trim the item.

May use hand tools for some of this work and employ traditional methods such as a potters wheel. Most specialise in one part of the production process such as jiggering, firing or glazing. Must ensure that health and safety regulations are observed and report any faults to a supervisor.

Work Details

Most ceramic pottery makers/operatives work a 39 hr week over five days. Some companies operate a shift system over 24 hrs, so some evening or night work may be necessary. You may work in manufacturing premises, often doing the same task over and over again. In more traditional firms, you are likely to work in a small studio. You need a lot of energy for this work and need to be quite strong. The building is hot and possibly dusty, and you need to wear protective clothing.

Qualification

• England, Wales and Northern Ireland

Band 1: No minimum qualifications are required, but you are expected to have a good level of general education. However, some formal/vocational qualifications at any level are useful.

Band 2: Although academic qualifications are not specified for this job, it is an advantage to have some GCSEs (A-C*) in subjects that include English and maths, or equivalent.

• Scotland

Band 1: No minimum qualifications are required, but you are expected to have a good level of general education. However, some formal/vocational qualifications at any level are useful.

Band 2: Although academic qualifications are not specified for this job, it is an advantage to have some S grades (1-3) in subjects that include English, and maths, or similar.

Adult Qualifications

No pre-entry qualifications are usually required though some academic/vocational qualifications at any level may be an advantage. English and maths are useful subjects.

Work Experience

Work or voluntary experience is always useful. It can improve your chances when applying for entry to jobs or apprenticeships. Your personal or adult guidance adviser should be able to advise you about how to get some work experience.

Entry and Training

Training is usually on the job with an experienced worker learning basic techniques and routines, such as casting, and eventually leading to more advanced procedures, including jiggering and finishing. You also train in aspects of health and safety at work. A training programme may be offered that can lead to vocational qualifications. City & Guilds accredit many courses in ceramic manufacture. Check with them for a full listing.

Training programmes, including apprenticeship schemes, may be available in your area. Advanced apprenticeships leading to qualification at level 3 can also be a route into higher education. A Diploma/Welsh Baccalaureate in manufacturing and product design may be available in your area.

Government training opportunities, such as an apprenticeship in ceramics manufacturing, may be available in your area. You can also gain recognition of previous experience through Accreditation of Prior Learning (APL) or by working towards relevant S/NVQs. Contact your local careers office, Jobcentre Plus, Next Step service or Learning and Skills Council (LSC) Local Enterprise Company (LEC) for details of training schemes.

Opportunities and Pay

You are usually employed by a large commercial pottery manufacturer. They are most likely located in the Potteries (West Midlands area of the UK), although there has been a decline in this area recently. With experience, you can progress to become a team leader or supervisor.

Pay varies but trainees earn around £10k a year, rising to around £15k with experience. Supervisors may make £20k a year. You may receive piecework, bonus or overtime payments.

Health

There may be an allergy risk from skin irritants. You need to be physically fit and have stamina to do this work.

Skills and Qualities

able to operate equipment, able to work both on your own and in a team, attention to detail, awareness of production process, eye for shape/colour, good concentration level, good co-ordination, patient, steady hand

Relevant Subjects

Manufacturing

Further Information

Apprenticeship Schemes (National Apprenticeship Service) - www.apprenticeships.org.uk
Creative & Cultural Skills - sector skills council for advertising, crafts, cultural heritage, design, literature, music, performing & visual arts - www.ccskills.org.uk
Diplomas (Foundation, Higher and Advanced) http://yp.direct.gov.uk/diplomas
Training Schemes - www.direct.gov.uk/en/educationandlearning
Welsh Baccalaureate - www.wbq.org.uk
▶Working in art & design (2009) (Babcock Lifeskills) - www.babcock-lifeskills.com/

Addresses

British Ceramic Confederation
Federation House, Station Road, Stoke-on-Trent ST4 2SA
Phone: +44 (0)1782 744631
Web: www.ceramfed.co.uk

City & Guilds
1 Giltspur Street, London EC1A 9DD
Phone: +44 (0)20 7294 2800
Web: www.cityandguilds.com

Similar Jobs

Ceramic Decorator, Ceramic Technologist, Foundry Process Operative, Glassmaker: Operative

Ceramic Technologist

also known as: Materials Technologist: Ceramics, Pottery Technologist

CRCI:Manufacturing and Production
CLCI:SAD Job Band: 5

Job Description

A ceramic technologist is concerned with the development of ceramic materials, through research, analysis, production and quality control testing. May be involved in any or all stages of production from the extraction of raw material to supply of the finished article. They look at the structure and physical and chemical properties of raw materials and ceramic products. Such materials are used in building and construction, as electronic components or to line furnaces. May work on products used in the home such as washbasins, baths, kitchen sinks or tableware.

Technologists use X-ray imaging techniques and also high technology microscopes. They must develop strong knowledge of the qualities of these different products; they usually specialise in an area such as design or testing.

Work Details
Ceramic technologists usually work a basic 39 hr week, Monday to Friday, although it may be necessary to work late at times. Works in an office or industrial premises, a laboratory or workshop. Shift work is common if you are part of the production process. You usually work in a team with other scientists, technologists and technicians.

Qualification
• England, Wales and Northern Ireland
Band 5: For degree: 2-3 A levels, including maths, physics and preferably chemistry, and some GCSEs (A*-C) including English and maths. Exact requirements depend on the degree you take.

• Scotland
Band 5: For degree courses: 3-5 H grades, including maths, physics and preferably chemistry, and some S grades (1-3) including English and maths. Exact requirements depend on the degree you take.

Degree Information
A degree in materials science may be preferred, but degrees in closely related subjects such as polymer chemistry or materials engineering are normally acceptable. Other sciences that provide a useful background include applied chemistry, physics and some technology or engineering subjects. Relevant postgraduate courses are also available, including materials science.

Adult Qualifications
A formal qualification, preferably a relevant degree, is usually required and scientific knowledge must be up to date. Course requirements are usually relaxed for suitable mature applicants. Those without the required qualifications may complete a foundation or Access course leading to relevant degrees.

Work Experience
Employers may prefer candidates who have relevant work or voluntary experience. Ideally you shadow or work with someone who is currently involved in the industry. Alternatively, obtaining general experience to develop team-working, communication and IT skills is also useful.

Entry and Training
Most enter this job after a degree in materials science or a closely related subject, and many technologists also have a relevant postgraduate qualification. However, you may be able to enter at a lower level of qualification and work your way up to this job. First degree courses can be full time, part time or sandwich and usually last for 3-4 years. A wide range of courses are available and you should take care to select one with an appropriate content relating to ceramic materials. Some large companies provide specialised in-house training.

Mature applicants are valued by employers if they have previous work experience in the ceramics industry. There are a range of distance-learning courses in ceramic technology available from Staffordshire University. No formal educational requirements are necessary for entry as previous experience is considered to be more important. Courses are designed for new entrants and for those already working in the ceramics industry. Contact Staffordshire University for details.

There may be opportunities of funding for postgraduate courses from the professional organisations such as the Engineering and Physical Sciences Research Council (EPSRC).

Opportunities and Pay
Ceramic technologists are employed in the field of electronics and the development of fibre optics. Current research is also exploring the viability of using ceramics in other types of engineering. Employment prospects may be good in research fields, although there may be fewer vacancies in general given the current economic downturn.

You may be employed by one of the many manufacturing companies involved in producing ceramics and glass. Employers also include research organisations, and other industries such as telecommunications and electronics. A few technologists become self-employed when established and trusted within the industry.

Pay varies depending on location, type and size of employer. The starting salary for a graduate entrant is likely to be from around £22k-£25.5k a year, rising to £40k.

Health
Good eyesight (with or without spectacles/contact lenses) is usually necessary for laboratory work.

Skills and Qualities
analytical skills, aptitude for teamwork, good communication skills, IT skills, logical, numeracy skills, precise, problem-solving skills, scientific approach

Relevant Subjects
Chemistry, Design and technology, Engineering, ICT/Computer studies, Manufacturing, Mathematics, Physics, Science

Further Information
AGCAS: Engineering (Job Sector Briefing) (AGCAS) - www.prospects.ac.uk

Ceramic Review (bi-monthly) (Ceramic Review Publishing Ltd) - www.ceramicreview.com/

Materials World (monthly) (IOM) - www.iom3.org

▶Working in science (2007) (Babcock Lifeskills) - www.babcock-lifeskills.com/

Addresses
British Ceramic Confederation
Federation House, Station Road, Stoke-on-Trent ST4 2SA
Phone: +44 (0)1782 744631
Web: www.ceramfed.co.uk

Engineering and Physical Sciences Research Council (EPSRC)
Polaris House North Star Avenue, Swindon, Wiltshire SN2 1ET
Phone: +44(0)1793 444 100
Web: www.epsrc.ac.uk

Institute of Materials, Minerals and Mining (IOM3)
1 Carlton House Terrace, London SW1Y 5DB
Phone: +44 (0)20 7451 7300
Web: www.iom3.org

Staffordshire University
College Road, Stoke-On-Trent, Staffordshire ST4 2DE
Phone: +44 (0)1782 294 000
Web: www.staffs.ac.uk

Similar Jobs
Materials Scientist/Engineer, NDT Technician/Engineer, Polymer/Plastics Technologist

Chaplain

also known as: Padre

CRCI:Social Work and Counselling Services
CLCI:FAM Job Band: 4 to 5

Job Description

Chaplains provide, spiritual, pastoral, moral and religious care to individuals, families or groups of people. Often work as part of a multi-faith chaplaincy team across a broad range of faiths, but have usually been previously ordained in a particular faith.

Chaplains usually work in non-traditional church settings such as hospitals, prisons, armed forces bases, airports or police departments. Duties depend on the work setting but may include visiting patients and families in a hospital or hospice; providing spiritual leadership and pastoral support to military personnel and their families; providing moral guidance for new recruits to the armed forces, through teaching core values; leading services of worship; assisting police officers, families and victims of crime with emotional and spiritual guidance; offering prayer and spiritual direction to people from a range of faiths during their time at the airport.

Work Details

There are no set hours of work and chaplains need to be prepared to work each day of the year. Hours are irregular and depend on where you work, although some duties must take place at set times of the day or week. Chaplains have contact with a large number of people, often including those who are upset, in pain, vulnerable and in need of support. Work can be very demanding at times. Some religions may require you to wear formal dress on certain occasions.

Although you have an office, you go out and about to attend meetings or work in the community. Travel around an area is necessary to visit people in their homes or in other places such as a hospital. Chaplains in the armed forces can be posted to serve anywhere in the UK and abroad, where the environment can sometimes vary from extreme heat to cold. If doing operational duties abroad, you may be working in dangerous situations where you are at risk of being injured or killed and you must be able to cope with the sight of blood.

Qualification

You must first become an ordained minister with several years in the clergy before becoming a chaplain. Entry requirements for ministers vary across the major world religions now practised in Britain. Many ministers experience a vocational calling before joining. A strong belief in your faith, commitment, and active participation and observance of its rules and regulations are paramount.

• England, Wales and Northern Ireland

Band 4: For entry to training: usually two A levels and some GCSEs (A*-C). Useful subjects include English, history, religious studies, or equivalent.

Band 5: For degree course in theology: 2-3 A levels and some GCSEs (A*-C) including English, maths or equivalent qualifications. Exact requirements depend on the degree you take.

• Scotland

Band 4: For entry to training: usually three H grades and some S grades (1-3). Useful subjects include English, history, religious studies, or similar.

Band 5: For degree course in theology: 3-5 H grades and some S Grades (1-3) including English, maths or similar qualifications. Exact requirements depend on the degree you take.

Degree Information

Any degree is acceptable, though for ministerial training in some denominations, a degree in theology and religious studies usually leads to shortened vocational training. Postgraduate degrees and certificates are available in subjects such as health care chaplaincy and chaplaincy studies.

Adult Qualifications

Maturity is an advantage due to knowledge and life experience. Formal entry qualifications required for ministerial training are often relaxed for those with the right experience and attributes.

Work Experience

Relevant work or voluntary experience is always useful and can improve your chances in application for entry to this job. Maturity and life experience is often an entry requirement, so consider experience that gives you the opportunity of dealing with people in a helping capacity such as at youth and community work, or in the caring professions. Contact Community Service Volunteers for ideas.

Entry and Training

To become a chaplain you must first be an ordained minister recognised by one of the Sending Churches (Anglican, Roman Catholic, Methodist, Baptist/URC/Congregational, Church of Scotland/Presbyterian, Elim or Assemblies of God) and normally have at least 3 years' experience in full-time ministry. Most chaplaincy departments also require you to be a citizen of the United Kingdom or of a Commonwealth country and to have resided continuously in the United Kingdom for the 5 years immediately before applying.

Formal training, a professional qualification and practical experience are usually required to become a minister, although requirements vary between different employers/faiths. Theology and divinity courses are available at non-graduate, undergraduate and postgraduate levels, and chaplaincy courses at postgraduate level. Applicants must be at least 18 before a course can be started, though most entrants are older. Usually professional status is gained after a probationary period and this may include a ceremony to be ordained. Priests attend a seminary (training college).

You need a satisfactory recommendation and authorisation by your faith community to gain entry to chaplaincy. Once you are employed as a chaplain you undergo on-the-job training and specialist courses, depending on the sector you work in. For example, healthcare chaplains require specialist training and knowledge before they are considered suitable for work in a hospital. Army chaplains undergo training at the Armed Forces Chaplaincy Centre (AFCC) at Amport House and attend the four-week Professionally Qualified Course at the Royal Military Academy, Sandhurst. You are then posted to your first unit. Contact your local Armed Forces Careers Office for further details.

Periods of reflection, meditation and study of your own particular faith and others are usual. For some, this may involve spending time at a monastery or retreat.

Adult entry is common as this job is particularly suitable for older, more experienced people. The training period to become a minister may be shorter for older entrants. Formal training can be full or part time, or by distance learning, weekend (or longer) residential courses, and summer schools. Some theological colleges and institutes offer a variety of training programmes, including postgraduate study. A degree in religious studies is also available from the Open University.

Opportunities and Pay

Opportunities exist within the NHS, the police force, nursing homes, schools, airports, the Prison Service and the armed forces (Army, RAF and Royal Navy). In the NHS, you can work for a range of services, including ambulance trusts, hospitals, care homes and hospices.

Opportunities for progression depend on the employer and your experience/qualifications. In the NHS, for instance, there are at least four levels of chaplain: entry level chaplain, chaplain, senior chaplain, and chaplain manager or advanced practitioner/specialist. Entry level is considered as a transition between work as a faith community minister and that of a healthcare chaplain. A qualified chaplain will have proven additional skills and experience. At senior levels there is opportunity to study at postgraduate level in areas such as health care chaplaincy.

Salaries vary depending on your employer. Starting salaries for Chaplains in the armed forces are £37k-£43k a year. In the NHS, salaries are around £30k-£40k a year. Senior chaplains can over £45k a year.

Health
You need to be physically and emotionally strong for this job.

Skills and Qualities
able to inspire confidence, able to set an example, able to understand other people's problems, approachable, belief & commitment, good interpersonal skills, patient, public speaking ability, supportive, time management skills

Relevant Subjects
English, History, Psychology, Religious studies, Sociology

Further Information
AGCAS: Armed Forces & Emergency Services (Job Sector Briefing) (AGCAS) - www.prospects.ac.uk

Community Service Volunteers - www.csv.org.uk

Ministry in the Church of England - www.cofe-ministry.org.uk

NHS Careers (NHS Careers) - www.nhscareers.nhs.uk

Open University - www.open.ac.uk

RAF Careers - Chaplaincy (RAF) - www.raf.mod.uk/careers/jobs/chaplain.cfm

UK Priest - www.ukpriest.org

► Working in advice & counselling (2007) (Babcock Lifeskills) - www.babcock-lifeskills.com/

Addresses
Inter Faith Network for the UK
8A Lower Grosvenor Place, London SW1W 0EN
Phone: +44 (0)20 7931 7766
Web: www.interfaith.org.uk

Similar Jobs
Community Development Worker, Community Learning & Development Officer (Scotland), Counsellor, Religious Leader, Social Worker

Charity Fundraiser
also known as: Charity Organiser, Fundraiser

CRCI:Social Work and Counselling Services

CLCI:KEM — Job Band: 4 to 5

Job Description
Charity fundraisers raise funds from a variety of sources, usually for a voluntary organisation or charity. They work to raise public awareness of the aims and needs of the charity. Arrange local and national publicity appeals, fundraising events and press interviews. Organise mailing lists and approach individuals and organisations such as industry, local and central government bodies or commerce, to ask for help, sponsorship or donations.

Use volunteers to arrange and take part in events, carry out telephone canvassing and arrange collections. Write reports, attend meetings and record information using databases and spreadsheets, etc.

Work Details
Usually work a basic 39 hr week, though some evening and weekend work may be required. You are usually based in an office, but you may also go out and about, perhaps giving talks, visiting companies, etc. Duties include public speaking and contacting potential donors in writing, in person, by e-mail or telephone. The work involves meeting clients, persuading people and organising volunteers and events. This type of work is challenging and can be pressurised at times.

Qualification
- **England, Wales and Northern Ireland**

Band 4: For BTEC higher national award: 1-2 A levels and some GCSEs (A*-C) usually including English and maths, or equivalent.

Band 5: For degree courses: 2-3 A levels and some GCSEs (A*-C) usually including English and maths, or equivalent qualifications. Exact requirements depend on the degree you take.

- **Scotland**

Band 4: For SQA higher national award: usually 2-3 H grades and some S grades (1-3) often including English and maths, or similar qualifications.

Band 5: For degree courses: 3-5 H grades and some S grades (1-3), usually including English and maths, or similar qualifications. Exact requirements depend on the degree you take.

Degree Information
Any degree discipline is acceptable for entry to this job. Useful subjects include financial management/banking and marketing.

Adult Qualifications
There are no standard requirements for entry to this job. Entry requirements for degrees or national/higher national courses may be relaxed for mature applicants. Details should be obtained from the academic institution.

Work Experience
Employers or colleges/universities may prefer candidates who have relevant work or voluntary experience. This includes experience of accountancy or bookkeeping, marketing, public relations or working for a charitable organisation such as Community Service Volunteers (CSV).

Entry and Training
Entry qualifications vary but employers expect relevant post-school qualifications and many entrants are graduates. Employers look for fundraising experience and dedication to working for a charity. It is an advantage to have experience in accountancy, industry, social work, marketing or public relations. A degree in life science or a biomedical field is useful for a medical charity. Training is usually on the job, accompanied by short courses. Some major charities offer graduate training programmes, though all new entrants have on-the-job training, usually with experienced colleagues, to gain experience of a variety of fundraising roles.

You may take short courses that are offered by the Institute of Fundraising and the Directory of Social Change (DSC). Courses offered by the Institute of Fundraising range from a one-day Introductory Certificate to Fundraising, to specialist courses for experienced fundraisers. Courses may include topics such as corporate fundraising, donations and legacy. The Institute also offers a professional qualification route for fundraisers, the Certificate, Diploma or Advanced Diploma in Fundraising. Many employers look for membership of the Institute as evidence of professional status and commitment.

The Open University offers a short course for fundraisers entitled 'winning resources and support'. This is the distance-learning route to the Institute of Fundraising's Certificate in Fundraising Management. Fundraising Training Ltd offers a fundraising trainee programme for those new to fundraising. If working for a small local group, there are relevant external courses run by private agencies.

Sometimes it is possible to enter this job as a volunteer and work your way up to a permanent post. Postgraduate courses in voluntary sector organisations are offered by some universities.

Mature entrants are common as this job is suitable for those with experience, particularly if you have relevant skills and experience in a business-related field or social work. Previous work experience in public relations, financial management or marketing, advertising or administration is also useful.

Opportunities and Pay

You may be employed by a voluntary organisation, a charity, community, benevolent and philanthropic organisation, or you can work as a consultant or on a freelance basis for a number of different organisations. This job requires a great deal of personal commitment. Promotion prospects vary as there is no clear promotion structure. Some fundraisers may set up their own consultancy.

There are no set salaries for fundraisers and pay can vary greatly. You may receive a regular salary or your income can be dependent on commission or fees. Entrants are likely to start in the region of £17k-£22k a year, rising to around £24k-£38k with experience. Senior fundraisers in large charities can earn up to £60k.

Skills and Qualities

business awareness, enterprising, good communication skills, good interpersonal skills, good organisational skills, initiative, IT skills, persuasive, planning skills, resourceful

Relevant Subjects

Business and accounting, Economics, English, Mathematics, Psychology, Sociology

Further Information

AGCAS: Charity & Development Work (Job Sector Briefing) (AGCAS) - www.prospects.ac.uk

Civil Society - www.civilsociety.co.uk

Community Service Volunteers - www.csv.org.uk

Open University - www.open.ac.uk

▶Working in marketing, advertising & PR (2008) (Babcock Lifeskills) - www.babcock-lifeskills.com/

▶Working in social care (2010) (Babcock Lifeskills) - www.babcock-lifeskills.com/

Addresses

Directory of Social Change (DSC)
24 Stephenson Way, London NW1 2DP
Phone: 08450 77 77 07 (UK only)
Web: www.dsc.org.uk

Fundraising Training Ltd
PO Box 240, Wallingford OX10 9XZ
Phone: +44 (0)1491 202070
Web: www.fundraisingtraining.co.uk

Institute of Fundraising (IoF)
Park Place 12 Lawn Lane, London SW8 1UD
Phone: +44 (0)20 7840 1000
Web: www.institute-of-fundraising.org.uk

Northern Ireland Volunteer Development Agency
129 Ormeau Road, Belfast BT7 1SH
Phone: +44 (0)28 9023 6100
Web: www.volunteering-ni.org

Scottish Council for Voluntary Organisations (SCVO)
Mansfield Traquair Centre, 15 Mansfield Place, Edinburgh EH3 6BB
Phone: +44 (0)131 556 3882
Web: www.scvo.org.uk

Volunteering England
Regents Wharf, 8 All Saints Street, London N1 9RL
Phone: 0845 305 6979 (UK only)
Web: www.volunteering.org.uk

Wales Council for Voluntary Action
Baltic House, Mount Stuart Square, Cardiff Bay CF10 5FH
Phone: 0800 2888 329 (UK only)
Web: www.wcva.org.uk

Working for a Charity
NCVO, Regent's Wharf, 8 All Saints Street, London N1 9RL
Web: www.wfac.org.uk

Similar Jobs

Community Development Worker, Community Learning & Development Officer (Scotland), Event & Exhibition Organiser, Marketing Manager, Public Relations Officer, Volunteer Manager

Chauffeur/Chauffeuse

CRCI:Transport and Logistics
CLCI:YAD Job Band: 1

Job Description

Chauffeurs/chauffeuses are skilled drivers who drive a car, or a range of vehicles, for one person or for a company, government department, or hire car agency. They may drive official cars for functions, such as weddings or funerals. Some deliver children to and from school, or take VIPs to and from various destinations throughout the country, including embassies, airports and diplomatic missions. They collect the passenger at an appointed time, load luggage into the boot and drive to the destination.

May provide knowledge and information about the area and places of interest. Cleaning and looking after the car is part of the job. Sometimes they carry out car maintenance.

Work Details

Usually work a basic 39 hr week, though often need to work unsocial hours, including evenings, weekends and public holidays. You may have to spend nights away from home. There are long periods of time when you have to sit alone in the car, waiting for your passenger. Lifting of packages and luggage may be necessary and in some jobs you may also do other tasks, including gardening. In some jobs you can meet a wide range of people, such as business executives, politicians and foreign visitors. You are usually required to wear a uniform.

Qualification

• England, Wales and Northern Ireland

Band 1: No minimum qualifications are required, but you are expected to have a good level of general education. However, some formal/vocational qualifications, especially in English and maths, at any level are useful.

• Scotland

Band 1: No minimum qualifications are required, but you are expected to have a good level of general education. However, some formal/vocational qualifications at any level, especially in English and maths are useful.

Adult Qualifications

Previous driving experience is important, for example, as a taxi driver or in the armed forces. Those without existing qualifications can work through the Foundation Learning programme by taking credit-based units and qualifications.

Work Experience

Relevant work or voluntary experience can equip you with skills that you can use in the future and add to your CV. Driving experience is essential, particularly if this is with a range of different vehicles.

Entry and Training

You usually have to be over 21 for insurance reasons, and need a full and current driving licence, together with several years' driving experience. Training is usually on the job. Some companies provide training schemes and short courses for their drivers in safe driving, security work, first aid and in self-defence. Many chauffeurs take the advanced driving certificate issued by the Institute of Advanced Motorists. The British Chauffeurs Guild offers those over the age of 21 a security chauffeur training course that also leads to becoming a member of the Guild.

You can progress to the mobile security course that is taken over three days and looks at aspects such as defensive/evasive driving techniques, and risk assessment. There is also an S/NVQ in road passenger transport at level 2. Some knowledge of vehicle maintenance is useful and it is helpful to be good at reading maps, although satellite navigation is widely used.

Mature applicants with experience in a related job such as the police, taxi and minicab driving, security work, or armed forces military transport, have an advantage. Most chauffeurs have considerable driving experience and a mature outlook.

Government training opportunities, such as apprenticeships, may be available in your area. You can also gain recognition of previous experience through Accreditation of Prior Learning or by working towards relevant S/NVQs. Contact your local careers office, Jobcentre Plus, Next Step service or Learning and Skills Council (LSC)/Local Enterprise Company (LEC) for details of training schemes.

Opportunities and Pay

Most drivers are employed by an individual or a company such as a limousine company, although it is possible to be self-employed. It is difficult to find work in this type of driving. In some jobs you may be given a room or a flat to live in and have other duties. It is not uncommon for couples to be employed in jobs that include chauffeuring, gardening, cooking, cleaning and do-it-yourself tasks. There are few prospects for promotion though experienced chauffeurs may set up their own business.

Pay varies depending on employer but is likely to be in the region of £18k a year, with experienced chauffeurs earning around £25k-£30k. Overtime is sometimes available.

Health

You have to be physically fit and have good eyesight.

Skills and Qualities

diplomatic, discreet, friendly, good concentration level, helpful, patient, polite, punctual, quick reactions, smart appearance

Further Information

AGCAS: Transport and Logistics (Job Sector Briefing) (AGCAS) - www.prospects.ac.uk

Foundation Learning (QCDA) - www.qcda.gov.uk

GoSkills - sector skills council for passenger transport - www.goskills.org

The Chauffeur Magazine - www.thechauffeur.com

Training Schemes - www.direct.gov.uk/en/educationandlearning

Addresses

British Chauffeurs Guild Ltd
13 Stonecot Hill, Sutton, Surrey SM3 9HB
Phone: +44 (0)20 641 1740
Web: www.britishchauffeursguild.co.uk

Driving Standards Agency (DSA)
The Axis Building, 112 Upper Parliament Street, Nottingham NG1 6LP
Phone: +44 (0)115 936 6666
Web: www.dsa.gov.uk

Institute of Advanced Motorists (IAM)
510 Chiswick High Road, London W4 5RG
Phone: +44 (0)20 8996 9600
Web: www.iam.org.uk

Licensed Private Hire Car Association (LPHCA)
56 Austins Mead Bovingdon, Hemel Hempstead, Hertfordshire HP3 0LH
Phone: +44 (0)7956 329288
Web: www.lphca.co.uk

Similar Jobs

Car Valet, Courier, Driver: Bus, Driver: Coach, Driver: Taxi/Minicab, Driving Instructor

Checkout Operator

also known as: Supermarket Checkout Operator

CRCI:Retail Sales and Customer Services
CLCI:OE
Job Band: 1 to 2

Job Description

Checkout operators work at a cash till or cash register in a supermarket, DIY store or other large retail shop, or a trade warehouse. Most work with a computerised till system. They accept payment from customers for goods they wish to purchase. They pass each item over an electric barcode scanner to record its price or may enter the price by keying in numbers on the till keypad. Then, they press a key that produces an itemised bill and the total payment required. Must be able to deal with cash and give change, or take payments by credit/debit or store card, or in some stores a cheque. Finally, they hand a receipt to the customer.

May also need to enter or swipe a customer's discount/loyalty card through the till, and in some stores, weigh vegetables or fruit. May assist the customer in the packing of purchased items. Sometimes they help with other jobs around the store, such as filling shelves and re-stocking the fridges.

Work Details

Usually work 39 hrs a week that may involve early starts, including some weekends. Some shops are open very late in the evenings or operate a 24-hour service and require you to work shifts. Your place of work is usually clean, warm and well lit. A uniform is provided by the employer.

Qualification

• England, Wales and Northern Ireland

Band 1: No minimum qualifications are required, but you are expected to have a good level of general education. However, some formal/vocational qualifications at any level are useful.

Band 2: Although academic qualifications are not usually specified for this job, it is an advantage to have some GCSEs (A*-C) in subjects that include English and maths, or equivalent.

• Scotland

Band 1: No minimum qualifications are required, but you are expected to have a good level of general education. However, some formal/vocational qualifications at any level are useful.

Band 2: Although academic qualifications are not usually specified for this job, it is an advantage to have some S grades (1-3) in subjects that include English and maths, or similar.

Adult Qualifications

You need to be able to cope with basic maths and it is an advantage if you have had a good general education.

Work Experience

Relevant work or voluntary experience is always useful and can improve your chances when applying for entry to jobs in sales. It can equip you with skills that you can use in the future and add to your CV. Part-time and holiday employment in a wide range of shops is usually fairly easy to obtain.

Entry and Training

Employers look for basic numeracy and good communication skills and you may have to take a maths and an English test. Training is often combined in an on and off-the-job programme provided by the employer, or through a work-based training scheme aimed at achieving vocational qualifications. Initially, you work with an experienced operator or store supervisor. Practical training often includes customer service, health and safety at work, and how to handle cheques, credit/debit cards, store loyalty cards etc.

Relevant S/NVQs include retail skills at levels 1-2, and sales and/or customer service at levels 2-3. Other vocational qualifications are also available, such as the level 2 certificate in retail operations. A Diploma/Welsh Baccalaureate in retail business may be available in your area. Training programmes, including retail apprenticeship schemes, may be available in your area. Advanced apprenticeships leading to qualification at level 3 can also be a route into higher education. Contact Skillsmart Retail for details of all training options.

Mature applicants are increasingly welcomed by employers, and in particular those with previous experience in a customer service/retail industry.

Opportunities and Pay

Jobs are mainly in or close to towns and cities. You can work in a supermarket, superstore or warehouse. You can also work in DIY stores, hypermarkets or other large shops. There is a variety of work available for full/part time, or temporary employment. However, due to the current economic downturn, there may be fewer opportunities for work in the retail sector. Many firms actively encourage their workers to take part in training schemes that lead to qualifications. With experience, you can become a supervisor or move into management.

Pay varies, depending on where you live and who you work for. Starting salaries are around £10k a year. Pay rises with experience to around £12k-£17k a year. Checkout supervisors can earn around £18k-£20k a year.

Health

Stamina may be needed as you can be on your feet for long periods. There may also be some bending and lifting.

Skills and Qualities

able to work quickly, accurate, cash handling skills, customer service skills, good interpersonal skills, honest, IT skills, numeracy skills, smart appearance, trustworthy

Relevant Subjects

Retail and distribution

Further Information

Apprenticeship Schemes (National Apprenticeship Service) - www.apprenticeships.org.uk

Diplomas (Foundation, Higher and Advanced) - http://yp.direct.gov.uk/diplomas

Foundation Learning (QCDA) - www.qcda.gov.uk

Real Life Guide to Retail (Trotman) - www.trotman.co.uk

Skillsmart Retail - sector skills council for the retail industry - www.skillsmartretail.com

Welsh Baccalaureate - www.wbq.org.uk

▶Working in retail & customer services (2008) (Babcock Lifeskills) - www.babcock-lifeskills.com/

Similar Jobs

Customer Services Adviser, Forecourt Assistant: Fuel Service Station, Retail Assistant, Stock Control/Replenishment Assistant

Chef/Cook

also known as: Culinary Artist

CRCI:Catering and Hospitality

CLCI:IC Job Band: 1 to 5

Job Description

Chefs/cooks supervise and prepare the cooking of food and meals for diners in a hotel, restaurant, hospital, business canteen, college or university, etc. Those working in a hotel or restaurant kitchen are called chefs and those in schools and colleges, business canteens or hospitals may be called cooks. Actual duties depend upon the size of kitchen and they may work alone or perhaps with one or two staff, or in a large kitchen with many others as part of a team. They may plan complete menus, often working to a budget, and arrange supplies. Also supervises and oversees the training and development of other kitchen staff.

Some chefs specialise in a type of cooking such as Thai or vegetarian. Others specialise in an area of cooking. This can be preparing and cooking vegetables (chef entremettier), main meal and sauces (chef saucier), fish (chef poisonnier) or pastry preparation (chef patissier). Chefs are ranked from a trainee (aide) to assistant/junior (commis); section chef (chef de partie); deputy/second chef (sous chef) and head chef (chef de cuisine), or for those owning a restaurant, chef patron.

Chefs/cooks must make sure that food is of a high quality and looks appetising to the customer. They must also have knowledge of the regulations and law surrounding food preparation and hygiene and observe health and safety procedures.

Work Details

Chefs/cooks usually work a 37-40 hr week, with irregular hours or shifts, including evenings, weekends and public holidays. This work is physically tiring as you are on your feet all day and do a lot of lifting and carrying. Trainee chefs/cooks learn how to prepare and cook meats, vegetables, sauces and gravies, pastries and cakes, desserts etc. They learn how to safely handle kitchen equipment including ovens, meat cleavers, knives and mixing machines, and how to wash up and clean the kitchen hygienically.

Work in kitchens can be hot and stressful at busy times. You must remain calm even when you are very busy, follow health and safety rules and pay attention to hygiene. Cooking smells can cling to your clothes and hair. A uniform or protective clothing called 'whites' is usually worn. This may include a head covering.

Qualification

Commitment, creativity, enthusiasm and a passion for food are a strong advantage for this job.

• England, Wales and Northern Ireland

Band 1: For entry to jobs, no minimum qualifications are needed, but you are expected to have a good level of general education and relevant experience. Some formal/vocational qualifications at any level are useful.

Band 2: For entry to jobs, no minimum qualifications are needed, but it is an advantage to have some GCSEs (A*-C) or equivalent in subjects that include English and maths.

Band 3: For entry to jobs, HNC or a relevant Diploma, usually at least 4 GCSEs (A*-C) including English and maths, or equivalent.

Band 4: For HND in hospitality management or culinary arts, Diploma of Higher Education or foundation degree: 1-2 A levels and some GCSEs (A*-C) usually including English and maths, or equivalent.

Band 5: For degree courses in culinary arts and hospitality management: 2-3 A levels and some GCSEs (A*-C) usually including English and maths, or equivalent. Exact requirements depend on the degree you take.

- **Scotland**

Band 1: For entry to jobs, no minimum qualifications are needed, but you are expected to have a good level of general education and relevant experience. Some formal/vocational qualifications at any level are useful.

Band 2: Although academic qualifications are not specified for this job, it is an advantage to have some S grades (1-3) in subjects that include English and maths, or similar.

Band 3: For entry to jobs, usually at least four S grades (1-3) including English or maths, or similar.

Band 4: For entry to SQA higher national and professional development awards in professional cookery: usually 2-3 H grades and some S grades (1-3), including English and maths, or similar qualifications.

Band 5: For degree courses in culinary arts and hospitality management: 3-5 H grades and some S grades (1-3), including English and maths, or similar qualifications. Exact requirements depend on the degree you take.

Degree Information

Foundation degrees are available in culinary arts and hospitality management, and honours degrees in hospitality, business and events management and culinary arts.

Adult Qualifications

There are no formal entry requirements for direct entry to on-the-job training. Course entry requirements are sometimes relaxed for suitable mature applicants. Those without the required qualifications may complete a foundation/Access course leading to higher qualifications.

Work Experience

Employers or colleges may prefer candidates who have relevant work or voluntary experience in food preparation, though other catering/hospitality experience is helpful. There is often plenty of paid part-time catering work available, although you cannot work behind a licensed bar until you are 18. In some areas there is a young apprenticeship (14-16) scheme that provides an extended work placement and eventual achievement of a level 2 qualification whilst at school.

Entry and Training

To become a chef/cook you can combine on-the-job training in a kitchen with day or block release at a local college. It is also possible to do full-time courses leading to S/NVQs, Applied A levels or national awards/higher national awards in professional cookery or hospitality before entering employment. City & Guilds' certificates/diplomas and awards in professional cookery and hospitality and catering are available. There are degree courses for those wishing to progress to a higher level and specialise in culinary arts management. A Basic Food Hygiene Certificate is very useful.

There are numerous qualifications to choose from, so make sure you spend time working out the best route for you to become a chef/cook. People 1st, the sector skills for hospitality are planning to simplify and reduce the number of courses and encourage more people to train. Contact them for a list of chef schools.

Large restaurants and hotels may offer their own training schemes, usually for 16-19 year olds, where you can start as a kitchen aide. Private fee paying courses are also available, though these may be expensive. The Academy of Culinary Arts (ACA) supports specialised chefs' training programmes for young apprentices. The three-year scheme (currently south-east England only), leads to national qualifications with an opportunity to achieve the ACA's diploma in professional cookery (DPC). The Vegetarian Society has details of the Cordon Vert Diploma for meat-free cookery. This is for professional chefs only.

S/NVQs at levels 1-4 are available in many aspects of cookery and food preparation. A Diploma/Welsh Baccalaureate in hospitality and catering may be available in your area. Training programmes, including apprenticeship schemes in hospitality, may be available in your area for entry to this job. Advanced apprenticeships leading to qualification at level 3 can also be a route into higher education.

Mature applicants may benefit from government training opportunities, such as apprenticeships in hospitality and catering. You can also gain recognition of previous experience through Accreditation of Prior Learning (APL) or by working towards relevant S/NVQs. Contact your local careers office, Jobcentre Plus, Next Step service or Learning and Skills Council (LSC) Local Enterprise Company (LEC) for details of training schemes. You can also apply to the Savoy Educational Trust for financial support to study for hospitality industry-related courses. The Trust supports individuals who wish to make a career in hospitality.

Opportunities and Pay

Around 250,000 people work as chefs/cooks. The hospitality industry, and in particular the restaurant business, is struggling in the current economic climate. This may affect the number of opportunities available for chefs, although skilled chefs may still be in demand. Jobs are available throughout the UK and there is a growing interest in speciality food restaurants, bistros and tapas bars as well as pubs, hotels, cafis and restaurants. Jobs are also available on cruise ships or with catering contractors for offices, schools, the armed forces and in the NHS.

It is fairly easy to find part-time work and promotion opportunities are good. This usually follows the route from trainee (commis chef) to chef de cuisine/chef patron. There are many different options once you are trained. It is possible to open your own restaurant or move into catering management, or teaching. A few pursue a career in writing or television appearances. It is possible to specialise, for example in French, Japanese, Thai or vegetarian cuisine, or to work overseas. With further study, some move into related areas such as consumer science and food technology.

Pay varies enormously depending on area and type of employer. A cook in a school or residential home earns around £11k-£15k, rising to around £20k depending on experience and/or qualifications. Chefs tend to earn more. A commis chef (junior chef) earns around £12k-£19k a year. Chefs de partie (section chefs) earn between £14k and £25k. A head chef (chef de cuisine) earns in the region of £20k-£50k. Highly successful executive and celebrity chefs can earn more than this.

Health

This job requires good general fitness. People with certain skin problems may not be able to do this job.

Skills and Qualities

able to cope under pressure, able to work quickly, alert, aptitude for teamwork, creative and imaginative flair, good organisational skills, hard working, stamina

Relevant Subjects

Art and Design, Hospitality and catering

Further Information

Academy of Culinary Arts - www.academyofculinaryarts.org.uk

Apprenticeship Schemes (National Apprenticeship Service) - www.apprenticeships.org.uk

Apprenticeships in Scotland (Careers Info Scotland) - www.apprenticeshipsinscotland.com/about/

CareerScope: Hospitality and Leisure (Springboard UK) - http://careerscope.springboarduk.net/

Caterer and Hotelkeeper (weekly) (Reed Business Information) - www.caterersearch.com/Home/

Diploma in Hospitality (People 1st) - www.hospitalitydiploma.co.uk

Diplomas (Foundation, Higher and Advanced) - http://yp.direct.gov.uk/diplomas

Hospitality Magazine (Institute of Hospitality) - www.instituteofhospitality.org

People 1st - sector skills council for hospitality, leisure, travel and tourism - www.people1st.co.uk

Restaurant Magazine (William Reed Business Media) - http://restaurantmagazine.com/

So you want to work in the Food Industry (Wayland) - www.waylandbooks.co.uk

Springboard UK (Springboard UK) - www.springboarduk.net

Springboard Wales (Springboard Wales) - http://wales.springboarduk.net/

Vegetarian Society - www.vegsoc.org

What's it like to be a Chef? (A&C Black 2008)

▶Working in airports (2010) (Babcock Lifeskills) - www.babcock-lifeskills.com/

▶Working in hospitality & catering (2009) (Babcock Lifeskills) - www.babcock-lifeskills.com/

Addresses

British Hospitality Association (BHA)
Queens House, 55-56 Lincoln's Inn Fields, London WC2A 3BH
Phone: +44 (0)207 404 7744
Web: www.bha.org.uk

Institute of Hospitality
Trinity Court, 34 West Street, Sutton, Surrey SM1 1SH
Phone: +44 (0)20 8661 4900
Web: www.instituteofhospitality.org

Savoy Educational Trust
Queen's House 55-56 Lincoln's Inn Fields, London WC2A 3BH
Phone: +44 (0) 207 269 9692
Web: www.savoyeducationaltrust.org.uk

Similar Jobs

Baker, Cake Decorator, Caterer: Contract/Private, Catering Manager, Food Service Assistant, Publican

Chemical Plant Process Operative

also known as: Chemical Plant Process Worker

CRCI:Manufacturing and Production
CLCI:SAV — Job Band: 3

Job Description

Chemical plant process operatives start up, control, monitor and shut down the systems and machinery involved in production at a chemical plant. They may have to maintain some of the equipment and organise spare parts for repairs or replacement. Larger plants may have computerised control rooms from which a lot of the machines are managed.

In the chemical industry, they work at a plant converting raw materials into a range of everyday items used in the home and industry. This can range from toothpaste to fertiliser. Quantities of raw material must be carefully measured at the beginning of the production cycle. Quality control is an important part of the job and samples from output batches are checked routinely. All findings are recorded in a log in case they need to be referred to in the future. If there is some inconsistency in the batch output, adjustments have to be made using valves, gauges and meters.

Health and safety is very important. The working environment can be hazardous so strict guidelines and laws must be adhered to. There may be regular safety checks and protective clothing is usually worn.

Work Details

Usually works a 37-39 hr week, Monday to Friday, and this may include shift work. Shifts can be up to twelve hours long. There may be some opportunities for part-time work. Your place of work is most likely to be a chemical plant or industrial premises. You work as part of a small team throughout your shift and may have to move around, checking and adjusting equipment or, sit at a computer monitoring output.

The work environment can be noisy and smelly, and there may be a risk of exposure to hazardous chemicals. You may need to wear overalls or other protective clothing.

Qualification

- **England, Wales and Northern Ireland**

Band 3: For entry to jobs, usually at least 4 GCSEs (A*-C) including English and maths. Science, technology, computers and engineering are also useful.

- **Scotland**

Band 3: For entry to jobs, usually at least four S grades (1-3) including English and maths. Science, technology, computers and engineering are also useful.

Adult Qualifications

Those with relevant work experience may be accepted for college courses without meeting any formal entry requirements.

Work Experience

Work experience helps you find out what you enjoy and do not enjoy about a job, as well as the opportunity to acquire new skills. It also provides valuable information to add to your CV and improves your future employment prospects. Paid or voluntary work where you use machinery or do building or engineering work may be useful.

Entry and Training

You can enter this work with no formal qualifications, although you need a good standard of general education. A Diploma/Welsh Baccalaureate may be available in your area in engineering. With a foundation diploma, you can apply for a level 2 apprenticeship programme. Those with an advanced diploma can enter an advanced apprenticeship or apply for a foundation degree.

You can apply for an apprenticeship scheme with training largely on the job. This is normally under the supervision of experienced workers with day or block release to attend courses at college. The City and Guilds level 2 apprenticeship in process technology covers process operations, engineering maintenance and laboratory work in the chemicals sector. The level 3 advanced apprenticeship leads to a technician level qualification. Those with level 3 qualifications can apply for a HNC in an engineering programme, many of which are run as distance learning courses.

You can work towards a certificate in process technology. This new qualification is aimed at learners on an apprenticeship scheme seeking a technical certificate. Having a certificate in process technology is beneficial to chemical plant process workers wanting to further their careers. The certificate covers process science, calculations, health and safety and environmental issues, and communications and IT. The chemical pathway in this qualification has well developed learning packages and keen students can move on to a supplementary studies pathway which can lead to a foundation degree. Alternatively, you can progress on to the level 3 certificate in process technology. This qualification enables workers in the industry to move from junior to more senior positions.

City and Guilds also offers S/NVQs at levels 1-4 in chemical, pharmaceutical and petro-chemical manufacture. See the website for full details on this training route.

Through continuing professional development (CPD) or further training, it is possible to progress to supervisory or managerial positions. Safety awareness is very important in this job and health and safety training is provided.

Employers may look for evidence of relevant skills or experience in areas such as engineering, electrical or plant maintenance work. Government training opportunities, such as apprenticeships, may be available in your area. You can also gain recognition of previous experience through Accreditation of Prior Learning (APL) or by working towards relevant S/NVQs. Contact your local careers office, Jobcentre Plus, Next Step service or Learning and Skills Council (LSC) Local Enterprise Company (LEC) for details of training schemes.

Opportunities and Pay
The UK chemical industry continues to grow, accounting for approximately 12% of UK manufacturing, with turnover exceeding £57bn and over 180,000 employees. This, coupled with the availability of apprenticeships and S/NVQs, indicates good prospects for employment and training.

Apprentices earn an initial salary of £14k a year. Qualified chemical plant process operatives can earn in the region of £28k a year. With experience, qualifications and managerial responsibility earnings can be higher.

Health
You need normal colour vision for some areas of work and there is a risk of allergy from skin irritants.

Skills and Qualities
able to work both on your own and in a team, attention to detail, calm, efficient record keeping, good communication skills, health & safety awareness, methodical, practical skills, problem-solving skills, responsible attitude

Relevant Subjects
Biology, Chemistry, English, ICT/Computer studies, Mathematics, Physics, Science

Further Information
Apprenticeship Schemes (National Apprenticeship Service) - www.apprenticeships.org.uk

Chemistry and Industry (SCI) - www.soci.org/Chemistry-and-Industry/Cnl-Data/2009/19

Cogent - sector skills souncil for chemicals, pharmaceuticals, nuclear, oil & gas, petroleum & polymers - www.cogent-ssc.com

Diplomas (Foundation, Higher and Advanced) - http://yp.direct.gov.uk/diplomas

Welsh Baccalaureate - www.wbq.org.uk

▶Working in science (2007) (Babcock Lifeskills) - www.babcock-lifeskills.com/

Addresses
Chemical Industries Association (CIA)
Kings Buildings, Smith Square, London SW1P 3JJ
Phone: +44 (0)20 7834 3399
Web: www.cia.org.uk

Royal Society of Chemistry (RSC)
Education Department, Burlington House, Piccadilly, London W1J 0BA
Phone: +44 (0)20 7437 8656
Web: www.rsc.org

Society of Chemical Industry (SCI)
14-15 Belgrave Square, London SW1X 8PS
Phone: +44 (0)20 7598 1500
Web: www.soci.org

Similar Jobs
Chemist, Chemist: Analytical, Heat Treatment Operative, Laboratory Technician: Science, Polymer/Plastics Technologist, Teacher: Physical Sciences

Chemist
CRCI:Science, Mathematics and Statistics
CLCI:QOB
Job Band: 5

Job Description
Chemists are scientists who specialise in the properties of materials and how they react to certain conditions. Many are involved in production of everyday materials, such as types of foods, medicines or cosmetics. Some create new compounds for different applications in industry, agriculture or medicine. Others analyse compounds to determine their exact chemical composition. May also design systems for processing or testing of chemicals.

Chemists use specialised equipment and computers to carry out tests and to analyse results. They write reports and may publish professional papers on their findings. May have a teaching or research role, usually in universities and colleges.

Work Details
Usually work around 37-39 hrs, Monday to Friday, though some late finishes and weekend work may be required at times. You work in a laboratory, an office, college, university or industrial premises. Tasks can include advising, or consulting with colleagues and supervising or organising staff. Depending on the kind of post, you can have responsibility for production schedules, safety procedures, analytical data, research reports or quality standards.

This work requires a high degree of accuracy. Sometimes you can deal with unpleasant substances and there is a risk of minor injuries. You may need to wear a white coat or protective clothing that can include a face mask and eye protection.

Qualification
• England, Wales and Northern Ireland
Band 5: For degree courses: 2-3 A levels including chemistry and preferably maths or physics, and some GCSEs (A*-C) usually including English, maths and a science. Exact requirements depend on the degree you take.

• Scotland
Band 5: For degree courses: 3-5 H grades including chemistry and maths or physics, and some S grades (1-3), usually including English, maths and a science. Exact requirements depend on the degree you take.

Degree Information
A degree in chemistry is preferred, but degrees with a significant chemistry content can also be acceptable depending on the employer. Many courses have a specialised focus such as analytical, applied, environmental, medicinal or industrial chemistry. Combinations of chemistry with business, languages or law are also offered. Some other science or technology subjects provide useful background knowledge. There are postgraduate courses available.

Adult Qualifications
A formal qualification, usually a degree, and up-to-date scientific knowledge are essential. Course requirements may be relaxed for mature applicants. A foundation course may be available prior to the start of a science degree for those who do not have the usual science qualifications for direct entry to the degree. Check with universities or colleges for information. Credit is given for relevant experience, for example in a laboratory.

Work Experience
Increasingly, you are likely to need relevant work experience before applying for your first job. The Royal Society of Chemistry (RSC) website contains advice on how to gain work experience. Universities may also prefer candidates who have relevant work or voluntary experience such as hospital work, or experience of

working in an industrial or commercial laboratory. If this proves difficult to obtain then work in another scientific field is also an advantage.

Entry and Training

A range of courses is available and you should choose your course carefully depending on the work in which you wish to specialise. Most entrants are graduates; degree courses last for three or four years and can be full time, part time and distance learning. There are relevant foundation degrees in chemistry that can lead to an honours degree course. Postgraduate study is an advantage. Training continues through practical experience in the workplace, and is often supplemented by seminars or short courses to update knowledge. You can gain an S/NVQ level 5 in analytical chemistry through workplace training. As an experienced chemist with in-depth knowledge of your specialism, you may be able to satisfy the requirements for Chartered Chemist (CChem) or Chartered Scientist (CSci) status with the Royal Society of Chemistry (RSC). It is also possible to gain European Chemist (EurChem) status.

Alternatively, an additional year of part-time study gains licentiate membership of the society. Some chemists work as public analysts, food analysts and agricultural analysts and these are required to achieve the Mastership in Chemical Analysis (MChemA), an RSC qualification.

Mature entrants with laboratory experience gained on industrial work placements are valued by prospective employers. Sponsorship for research or postgraduate study may be available from the Engineering and Physical Sciences Research Council (EPSRC). You may receive funding for higher education courses through a prospective employer.

Opportunities and Pay

There are large numbers of chemists working throughout the UK and job opportunities are good. Most work in manufacturing or processing industries as industrial, analytical, or research and development chemists. Opportunities in pharmaceutical research or environmental agencies are growing. Chemists can work in chemical, agrochemical, food, drink and consumer goods, oil, water, paper, electrical equipment, metals and nuclear industries in research and development. Employers also include contract research organisations, food research associations and biotechnology industries. There may be work in the public sector including universities and government research establishments, or specialised publishing and patents, health and safety and forensic science.

Salaries vary depending on area and type of employer. A trainee graduate chemist is likely to earn £16k-£24k a year, rising to £25k-£35k. An experienced chemist with postgraduate/professional qualifications can earn £45k or more a year.

Health

You need good colour vision for some areas of work and there is an allergy risk from skin irritants.

Skills and Qualities

analytical skills, aptitude for maths and science, efficient record keeping, flexible approach, health & safety awareness, initiative, problem-solving skills, scientific approach, specialist IT skills, technical aptitude

Relevant Subjects

Biology, Chemistry, English, ICT/Computer studies, Mathematics, Physics, Science

Further Information

Association of the British Pharmaceutical Industry (ABPI) - www.abpi.org.uk/education

Chemist & Druggist Education (UBM Medica) - www.chemistanddruggist.co.uk/education

Chemistry and Industry (SCI) - www.soci.org/Chemistry-and-Industry/Cnl-Data/2009/19

Chemistry World (monthly) (Royal Society of Chemistry) - www.rsc.org/chemistryworld

Highlights in Chemical Science (monthly) (Royal Society of Chemistry (RSC)) - www.rsc.org/Publishing/ChemScience/

Royal Society of Chemistry Careers Gateway (Royal Society of Chemistry) - www.rsc.org/gateway/subject/careers/

► Working in science (2007) (Babcock Lifeskills) - www.babcock-lifeskills.com/

Addresses

Engineering and Physical Sciences Research Council (EPSRC)
Polaris House North Star Avenue, Swindon, Wiltshire SN2 1ET
Phone: +44(0)1793 444 100
Web: www.epsrc.ac.uk

Royal Society of Chemistry (RSC)
Education Department, Burlington House, Piccadilly, London W1J 0BA
Phone: +44 (0)20 7437 8656
Web: www.rsc.org

Similar Jobs

Biochemist, Chemist: Analytical, Chemist: Medicinal, Pharmacist: Industrial, Pharmacologist, Public Analyst, Teacher: Physical Sciences, Toxicologist

Chemist: Analytical

CRCI:Science, Mathematics and Statistics
CLCI:QOB Job Band: 4 to 5

Job Description

Analytical chemists analyse substances to identify and understand their chemical composition and how they behave under certain conditions. They use high tech techniques and instruments for the analysis of samples in several sectors, including pharmaceuticals, manufacturing, healthcare, forensics, food and retail product development. Then interpret and record data and report results, sometimes in scientific journals and at conferences.

In the pharmaceutical industry, they help to determine the stability and quality of drugs or may be involved in processes such as forensic analysis, toxicology and drug development. In other fields, chemists may conduct a range of tests such as those to determine contamination in soil or harmful engine emissions, as well as quality control. There is also an administrative aspect to the job which supports collaborative working with teams nationally and internationally, customer liaison and maintaining current standards of health and safety legislation, which may involve staff training. May also have to apply for product licences and help to produce the specifications for finished products.

Work Details

Hours vary according to the employer, but usually work around 35-40 hrs a week, Monday to Friday. May be required to work early mornings, evenings and weekends. You work in a laboratory, office or on industrial premises. Work can be stressful due to tight deadlines and pressure to solve problems as quickly as possible. This work requires a high degree of accuracy. You usually work as part of a team with other professional scientists. Protective clothing is often worn.

Qualification

• England, Wales and Northern Ireland

Band 5: For degree courses: 2-3 A levels including chemistry and preferably maths or physics, and some GCSEs (A*-C) usually including English, maths and science. Exact requirements depend on the degree you take.

• Scotland

Band 5: For degree courses: 3-5 H grades including chemistry and preferably maths and physics, and some S grades (1-3), usually including English, maths and science. Exact requirements depend on the degree you take.

Degree Information

Degrees such as analytical/applied chemistry, environmental science (physical), biochemistry, geochemistry, chemistry, marine sciences and oceanography, materials sciences/ technology may be advantageous but there are also many other relevant degrees, including physical, mathematical or applied science, life and medical science. A relevant first degree can also be followed by a specialist higher degree.

Adult Qualifications

A formal qualification, such as a degree and up-to-date scientific knowledge, are essential. Course requirements may be relaxed for mature applicants provided they submit evidence of previous serious study, such as a relevant Access course. A foundation course may be available prior to the start of a science degree for those who do not have the usual science qualifications for direct entry to the degree. Check with universities or colleges for information.

Work Experience

Universities and employers may prefer candidates who have relevant work or voluntary experience. Academic standards can be high and work experience in a hospital or in an industrial or commercial laboratory can be an asset. Alternatively, work in another scientific field is an advantage and demonstrates interest.

Entry and Training

Entrants are usually graduates with an honours degree in analytical chemistry or a chemistry degree with a significant analytical chemistry content. There are relevant foundation degrees in chemistry that can lead to an honours degree course. Postgraduate study can be an advantage, as is relevant work experience and the ability to use computers. Those already working in analytical chemistry may have the opportunity to upgrade their HND to a degree, or to undertake a PhD through part-time study. Training continues through practical experience in the workplace and is often supplemented by short or residential courses. Major employers have graduate training schemes.

Membership and chartered status (CChem) of the Royal Society of Chemistry (RSC) can be attained by graduates with appropriate qualifications and relevant experience. Alternatively, an additional year of part-time study gains licentiate membership of the society. The Analytical Science Network (ASN) also offers assistance to aspiring analytical chemists or existing chemists who wish to further their career.

Both the RSC and ASN offer informal regional meetings and information that includes accredited degree courses, professional membership and continuing professional development (CPD). There is an S/NVQ at level 5 in analytical chemistry that is the principal route onto the Analytical Chemists Register, and holders of the MChemA who can demonstrate two years of CPD are also eligible. Holders of the S/NVQ at level 5 are entitled to use the designation 'Registered Analytical Chemist'.

Mature entrants with laboratory experience gained on industrial work placements are valued by prospective employers. Sponsorship for research or postgraduate study may be available from the Engineering and Physical Sciences Research Council (EPSRC) and you may also receive funding for higher education courses through employers, such as the food and drink industry, or utility companies.

Opportunities and Pay

Demand for this work is increasing throughout the UK and the pharmaceutical industry has difficulty recruiting suitable qualified applicants. Other employers include chemical manufacturers, hospital laboratories, food producers, research laboratories, independent consultancies and environmental agencies. Competition can be fierce for entry to some major companies, and there are often only short term contracts available. Progression is to more senior grades with increasing responsibility and promotion can be easier with higher qualifications such as a PhD. Self-employment is not common.

Salary and career progression depends on location and the type of employer. Graduate entrants start on around £20k-£22k rising to £25k-£40k a year. A senior, experienced chemist with higher qualifications can earn £50k or more a year.

Health

You need normal colour vision for some areas of work and there is a risk of allergy from skin irritants.

Skills and Qualities

able to report accurately, able to work both on your own and in a team, analytical skills, aptitude for maths and science, efficient record keeping, health & safety awareness, methodical, objective, problem-solving skills, scientific approach, specialist IT skills

Relevant Subjects

Biology, Chemistry, English, ICT/Computer studies, Mathematics, Physics, Science

Further Information

AGCAS: Health (Job Sector Briefing) (AGCAS) - www.prospects.ac.uk

Analytical Science Network (ASN) (Royal Society of Chemistry) - www.asnetwork.org/

Association of Public Analysts (Association of Public Analysts) - www.publicanalyst.com

Chemistry and Industry (SCI) - www.soci.org/Chemistry-and-Industry/Cnl-Data/2009/19

Chemistry World (monthly) (Royal Society of Chemistry) - www.rsc.org/chemistryworld

Life beyond exams: Chemistry (Royal Society of Chemistry) - www.rsc.org/education/teachers/learnet/Life_Beyond_Exams.htm

▶ Working in science (2007) (Babcock Lifeskills) - www.babcock-lifeskills.com/

Addresses

Chemical Industries Association (CIA)
Kings Buildings, Smith Square, London SW1P 3JJ
Phone: +44 (0)20 7834 3399
Web: www.cia.org.uk

Engineering and Physical Sciences Research Council (EPSRC)
Polaris House North Star Avenue, Swindon, Wiltshire SN2 1ET
Phone: +44(0)1793 444 100
Web: www.epsrc.ac.uk

Royal Pharmaceutical Society of Great Britain (RPSGB)
1 Lambeth High Street, London SE1 7JN
Phone: +44 (0)20 7735 9141
Web: www.rpharms.com

Royal Society of Chemistry (RSC)
Education Department, Burlington House, Piccadilly, London W1J 0BA
Phone: +44 (0)20 7437 8656
Web: www.rsc.org

Society of Chemical Industry (SCI)
14-15 Belgrave Square, London SW1X 8PS
Phone: +44 (0)20 7598 1500
Web: www.soci.org

Similar Jobs

Biochemist, Chemist, Chemist: Medicinal, Laboratory Technician: Science, Public Analyst, Toxicologist

Chemist: Medicinal

CRCI:Science, Mathematics and Statistics
CLCI:QOB Job Band: 5

Job Description

Medicinal chemists apply principles of chemistry and biology to the design and synthesis of new drugs for treating diseases. They use acquired knowledge of chemistry, biochemistry and physiology to generate solutions to health-related problems. May work on the research and development of medical advances such as anti-cancer drug design. Also undertake research into new chemical compounds (substances that contain atoms of two or more bonded chemical elements) that may have a pharmaceutical value.

Chemists work as part of a multi-disciplinary team of scientists. They interact with a wide range of specialists, including biologists, chemical engineers, patent attorneys, molecular modellers, safety consultants and biologists.

Work Details

Usually work around 37-39 hrs; Monday to Friday, though some late finishes and weekend work may be required at times. Your tasks can include advising or consulting with colleagues and supervising or organising staff. Depending on the kind of post, you may have responsibility for production schedules, safety procedures, analytical data, research reports or quality standards.

This work requires a high degree of accuracy. Sometimes you can deal with unpleasant substances and there is also a risk of minor injuries. You may need to wear a white coat or protective clothing that can include a face mask and eye protection.

Qualification

- **England, Wales and Northern Ireland**

Band 5: For degree courses: 2-3 A levels including chemistry and preferably maths or physics and some GCSEs (A*-C) usually including English, maths and science. Exact requirements depend on the degree you take.

- **Scotland**

Band 5: For degree courses: 3-5 H grades including chemistry and maths or physics and some S grades (1-3), usually including English, maths ans science. Exact requirements depend on the degree you take.

Degree Information

There are degrees in medicinal chemistry, biological and medicinal chemistry, and combined medicinal chemistry subject degrees, but subjects such as organic chemistry or other chemical science degrees are also relevant. Some courses include a year of industrial experience. A relevant first degree can also be followed by a specialist higher degree.

Adult Qualifications

Course requirements may be relaxed for mature applicants provided they submit evidence of previous serious study, such as a relevant Access course. Some universities may offer a foundation year prior to the degree course. Check with universities or colleges for information.

Work Experience

Employers or universities may prefer candidates who have relevant work or voluntary experience, such as hospital work or in an industrial or commercial laboratory. If this proves difficult to obtain then work in another scientific field is also an advantage.

Entry and Training

New entrants are usually graduates with a good honours degree. Courses last for three or four years and can be full time or sandwich. There are relevant foundation degrees in chemistry that can lead onto an honours degree course, or to entry at technician level. Postgraduate study is an advantage, as is relevant work experience. Training continues through practical experience in the workplace, and is often supplemented by seminars or short/residential courses to update knowledge.

Membership and chartered status (CChem) of the Royal Society of Chemistry (RSC) can be attained by graduates with appropriate qualifications and relevant experience. Alternatively, an additional year of part-time study gains licentiate membership of the society.

Mature entrants require a formal qualification such as a degree/postgraduate degree, and up-to-date scientific knowledge is essential. Sponsorship for research or postgraduate study may be available, and you should contact the professional organisations for details. You may receive funding for higher education courses through a prospective employer.

Opportunities and Pay

There are opportunities throughout the UK, mostly in large towns or cities. Employers include pharmaceutical manufacturers and research laboratories. Competition can be fierce for entry to some of the major companies. Academic standards can be high and work experience is an asset. Progression is to more senior grades with increasing responsibility. Promotion is easier with higher qualifications such as a PhD.

Salary and career progression depend on location and the type of employer. Starting salaries for graduate entrants are generally £20k-£25k a year. Experienced medicinal chemists earn £25k-£48k a year. Those in some senior posts earn around £45k-£65k a year.

Health

You need good colour vision for some areas of work and there is a risk of allergy from skin irritants.

Skills and Qualities

able to report accurately, able to work both on your own and in a team, analytical skills, aptitude for maths and science, methodical, objective, problem-solving skills, safety conscious, scientific approach, specialist IT skills

Relevant Subjects

Biology, Chemistry, English, ICT/Computer studies, Mathematics, Physics, Science

Further Information

Association of the British Pharmaceutical Industry (ABPI) - www.abpi.org.uk/education

Highlights in Chemical Science (monthly) (Royal Society of Chemistry (RSC)) - www.rsc.org/Publishing/ChemScience/

Royal Society of Chemistry Careers Gateway (Royal Society of Chemistry) - www.rsc.org/gateway/subject/careers/

▶Working in science (2007) (Babcock Lifeskills) - www.babcock-lifeskills.com/

Addresses

Chemical Industries Association (CIA)
Kings Buildings, Smith Square, London SW1P 3JJ
Phone: +44 (0)20 7834 3399
Web: www.cia.org.uk

Medicines & Healthcare Products Regulatory Agency (MHRA)
10-2 Market Towers, 1 Nine Elms Lane, London SW8 5ND
Phone: +44 (0)20 7084 2000
Web: www.mhra.gov.uk

Royal Society of Chemistry (RSC)
Education Department, Burlington House, Piccadilly, London W1J 0BA
Phone: +44 (0)20 7437 8656
Web: www.rsc.org

Society of Chemical Industry (SCI)
14-15 Belgrave Square, London SW1X 8PS
Phone: +44 (0)20 7598 1500
Web: www.soci.org

Similar Jobs
Biochemist, Chemist, Chemist: Analytical, Forensic Scientist, Public Analyst, Teacher: Physical Sciences

Childminder
CRCI:Social Work and Counselling Services
CLCI:KEB Job Band: 1 to 2

Job Description
Childminders work in their own home, taking care of other people's children whose parents/carers are at work or studying. Hours can be from early morning until evening. Registered childminders usually care for up to six children under eight years old (under sixteen in Scotland), and only three of which may be under five. Make sure the children are clean, warm, fed, stimulated, safe and happy. Childminders play games, read stories and take children for walks.

Negotiate a written contract of care for each child, which may include specific arrangements, such as the child's diet and acceptable standard of behaviour. Contracts also give details of hours of work and payment.

Work Details
You work at home and may have to work long hours, but it is up to you to negotiate your hours of employment. It is possible to look after children all day, part time or perhaps just outside school hours. You work with babies and children of all ages but by law you can only look after a certain number of children. Childminding requires you to keep records and comply with the requirements of parents, health visitors, etc.

This work can be physically demanding as childminders are active most of the time. Working with babies and children can be noisy and messy.

Qualification
- **England, Wales and Northern Ireland**

Band 1: No qualifications are needed, but some formal/vocational qualifications at any level are useful.

Band 2: Although academic qualifications are not specified for this job, it is an advantage to have some GCSEs (A*-C) in subjects that include English and maths, or equivalent.

- **Scotland**

Band 1: No qualifications are needed, but some GCSEs are useful.

Band 2: Although academic qualifications are not specified for this job, it is an advantage to have some S grades (1-3) in subjects that include English and maths, or similar.

Adult Qualifications
Although there are no specified qualifications, all new childminders must complete a pre-registration course prior to registration. Formal qualifications or their equivalent at any level are useful.

Work Experience
Relevant work or voluntary experience can equip you with useful skills that you can add to your CV. There are often opportunities available for voluntary work. Applicants with experience of working with and caring for young children, such as paid/unpaid work in a nursery school, helping at a playgroup, or assisting with childminding, may have an advantage.

Entry and Training
The minimum age for a childminder is 18, but this job is particularly suitable for older people with experience of working with children and is not generally suitable for school leavers. If you work as a childminder in England or Wales, or provide day care for children under eight years old for more than two hours each day, you must register with the Office for Standards in Education (Ofsted) and may be inspected regularly. This is coordinated through your local children's information service and you need to undergo a check on general health, family and safety standards in your home, and a Criminal Records Bureau (CRB) check. In Scotland, you must register with the Scottish Commission for the Regulation of Care and have a Disclosure Scotland check.

Training is required for registered childminders. You must take a pre-registration course and a first aid course. Introduction to Childcare Practice (ICP) (Home-based), developed by the National Childminding Association (NCMA), is a nationally recognised award for those seeking registration. The registration process can take up to six months. Because ICP is the first unit of the Diploma in Home-based Childcare, there is opportunity for further childminder training studied by distance learning or at a local college.

NCMA Children Come First childminding networks offer a range of training opportunities for childminders. Contact the NCMA for details. There are relevant open and distance-learning courses in childcare offered by organisations including the National Open College Network. A qualification in nursery nursing is useful but not required for the job. S/NVQs in children's care, learning and development, and in playwork are available at levels 2-4.

Mature entrants are common as most new childminders are those with experience of bringing up their own child/children or have experience of working with children. You may be eligible for a start-up grant from your local authority under the Early Years Development and Childcare Partnership (EYDCP), which is part of the National Childcare Strategy. There are a wide range of nationally-recognised qualifications that are available through distance learning. Contact the relevant organisations (listed in addresses) for details on registration as a childminder, training routes and qualifications.

Opportunities and Pay
There are more than 70,000 registered childminders and it is possible for you to work anywhere in the UK. You are self-employed and your income varies depending on the number of children in your care. Your local authority can refer parents to you or you can advertise in your local press. Fees are negotiated with your clients. You can progress to become a local network coordinator supporting other childminders or a trainer for childcare services. Some move into nursery nursing or teaching.

Income is variable and most childminders work part time so it is hard to summarise earnings. You can set your own rates, usually around £6 an hour, and you need to meet the costs of food and buying toys and equipment. You also need to make your own arrangements for paying tax and insurance. The average income for a childminder is likely to be around £11k-£15k a year, rising to around £17k. In some areas of the country you may earn more.

Health
In some parts of the country you may have to pass a medical test before becoming registered as a childminder. For this job you need to have good general fitness.

Skills and Qualities
calm, caring, common sense, energetic, good stamina and physically fit, health & safety awareness, patient, practical skills, reliable, sense of humour

Relevant Subjects
Biology, English, Health and social care, Hospitality and catering, Psychology

Further Information
Become Childminder (NCMA) (NCMA) - www.ncma.org.uk/childminders/become_a_childminder.aspx

Children's Information Service - www.childrensinfo.org

Foundation Learning (QCDA) - www.qcda.gov.uk

How to Become a Registered Childminder in Wales (NCMA) (NCMA) - www.ncma.org.uk/childminders.aspx

Real Life Guide to Childcare (Trotman 2009) - www.trotman.co.uk
So you want to work with Children (Wayland) - www.waylandbooks.co.uk

Addresses

CACHE: Council for Awards in Children's Care & Education
Apex House, 81 Camp Road, St Albans AL1 5GB
Phone: 0845 347 2123 (UK only)
Web: www.cache.org.uk

National Childminding Association of England and Wales (NCMA)
Royal Court 81 Tweedy Road, Bromley, Kent BR1 1TG
Phone: 0845 880 0044 (UK only)
Web: www.ncma.org.uk

National Open College Network
The Quadrant, Parkway Business Park, 99 Parkway Avenue, Sheffield S9 4WG
Phone: +44 (0)114 227 0500
Web: www.nocn.org.uk

Northern Ireland Childminding Association
16-18 Mill Street, Newtownards, Co Down BT23 4LU
Phone: +44 (0)871 200 2063
Web: www.nicma.org

Scottish Childminding Association (SCMA)
7 Melville Tterrace, Stirling FK8 2ND
Phone: +44 (0)1786 445 377
Web: www.childminding.org

Scottish Commission for Regulation of Care
Compass House, 11 Riverside Drive, Dundee DD1 4NY
Phone: +44 (0)1382 207100
Web: www.carecommission.com

SureStart
Department for Education Castle View House East Lane, Runcorn WA7 2GJ
Phone: 0870 000 2288
Web: www.education.gov.uk/

Similar Jobs

Au Pair, Nanny, Nursery Worker, Pre-school Supervisor/Worker, School Lunchtime Supervisor, Teaching Assistant

Chimney Sweep

also known as: Chimney Service Technician

CRCI:Personal and Other Services
CLCI:IJ Job Band: 1

Job Description

Chimney sweeps clear soot and dirt from chimneys of open fires and flues of other cooking and heating systems, so that they work efficiently and do not become blocked. They travel to a customer's house in a suitably equipped van. The area around the fireplace is covered with sheets taped in place to trap the dirt. They use brushes on rods to shift soot and tar sticking to the inside of the chimney. Then use vacuum tools to draw out the dirt. Sometimes a metal ball is lowered down the chimney from the roof to clear places in the flue which are blocked. May carry out surveys of the state of chimneys using a video camera.

This job is often combined with related work, eg installing chimney linings, fixing cowls and caps, replacing chimney pots and installing fireplaces. May advise customers on the safe operation and maintenance of flues and chimneys.

Work Details

Usually work from 8.30am to 5.30pm, five days a week, with some Saturday work possible. Hours may be longer at busier times of the year, usually during spring and autumn months. Chimney sweeps have to travel around an area to their customers' homes. To do this job, you may need to climb ladders and work on roofs. You are active all day and do some lifting, kneeling, standing, and bending.

This is a dirty, dusty job, so you need to wear overalls and sometimes a face mask and helmet. You need to work carefully and safely. Chimney sweeps often write invoices for people and handle money or cheques.

Qualification

- **England, Wales and Northern Ireland**

Band 1: For entry to jobs, no minimum qualifications are needed, but you are expected to have a good level of general education and relevant experience. Some formal/vocational qualifications at any level are useful.

- **Scotland**

Band 1: For entry to jobs, no minimum qualifications are needed, but you are expected to have a good level of general education and relevant experience. Some formal/vocational qualifications at any level are useful.

Adult Qualifications

No formal academic qualifications are needed. You can improve your skills and qualifications by working through the Foundation Learning programme. This involves taking credit-based units and qualifications to help you progress.

Work Experience

Any work experience can give you skills to use in the future and add to your CV. Work experience can either be unpaid or can be holiday or part-time work that you have sorted out yourself. It may be useful for you to ask to accompany a local chimney sweep to find out more about the job.

Entry and Training

You are usually trained on the job working with an experienced person. The National Association of Chimney Sweeps (NACS) runs training courses for those already working as sweeps and offers courses for new entrants to the industry. NACS, together with the Heating Equipment Testing and Approval Scheme (HETAS) also offers a two-day solid fuels course which enables you to become 'HETAS approved'.

The Institute of Chimney Sweeps offers a one day training course covering all aspects of chimney sweeping. The Guild of Master Sweeps also offers training courses for new sweeps. Membership of the Guild or of NACS is an advantage as it shows customers that you have attained a good standard of knowledge. A driving licence is necessary for this job.

Other specific training is available from related professional organisations such as the National Association of Chimney Engineers. You can also work towards a ConstructionSkills NVQ level 2 in chimney engineering/cleaning.

This is often a second career for older applicants who have relevant skills and experience gained in the building and roofing trade.

Opportunities and Pay

Jobs may be with small firms of chimney sweeps, but most sweeps are self-employed. There is not usually enough work to earn a living doing chimney sweeping alone, and demand changes with the season. Sweeps may combine the work with another job, such as repairing roofs, cleaning gutters, working on heating systems or installing fireplaces.

Generally, the rate for each job is around £30-£70. Initial set-up costs for those who become self-employed include the purchase of a van and cleaning equipment. As a relatively dangerous job, insurance can be high for sweeps. Some sweeps supplement their income as a traditional 'Lucky Sweep', who attends weddings and receives a payment for each appearance.

Health
This job requires good general fitness. People who are allergic to dust may find this job difficult.

Skills and Qualities
able to get on with all kinds of people, able to work well on your own, careful, efficient record keeping, hard working, head for heights, health & safety awareness, honest, practical skills

Relevant Subjects
Construction and built environment

Further Information
ConstructionSkills - sector skills council for the construction industry - www.cskills.org

Foundation Learning (QCDA) - www.qcda.gov.uk

The Guild of Master Sweeps - www.guild-of-master-sweeps.co.uk/

Addresses
Heating Equipment Testing and Approval Scheme (HETAS)
Orchard Business Centre, Stoke Orchard, Gloucestershire
GL52 7RZ
Phone: 0845 634 5626
Web: www.hetas.co.uk

Institute of Chimney Sweeps
Unit G4, The Power Hub, St. Peters Street, Maidstone, Kent
ME16 0ST
Phone: +44 (0) 1622 691676
Web: www.instituteofchimneysweeps.co.uk/

National Association of Chimney Engineers Ltd (NACE)
PO Box 849, Metherington, Lincoln LN4 3WU
Phone: +44 (0)1526 322555
Web: www.nace.org.uk

National Association of Chimney Sweeps NACS)
Unit 15, Emerald Way, Stone Business Park, Staffordshire
ST15 0SR
Phone: +44 (0)1785 811 732
Web: www.chimneyworks.co.uk

Northern Ireland Association of Chimney Sweeps
c/o County Down Stoves and Flues 8 Main Street, Dundrum
BT33 0LU
Phone: + 44 (0) 284 375 1555
Web: www.niacs.co.uk

Similar Jobs
Cleaner: Industrial, Gas Service Engineer, Heating & Ventilation Fitter/Welder, Roofer

Chiropractor
CRCI:Healthcare
CLCI:JOD Job Band: 5

Job Description
Chiropractors use diagnostic techniques and manipulation to treat patients with mechanical disorders of the joints, ligaments, muscles and tendons of the body. They play an important part in relieving disorders, pain and discomfort arising from stress, tension headaches, poor posture, lack of exercise, accidents or illness. Chiropractors treat pain and other symptoms in several parts of the body, often in the back, neck, legs or various nerves. They use spinal manipulation techniques that do not involve the use of drugs or surgery.

Chiropractors discuss the patient's medical history, carry out a physical examination and maybe tests, such as X-rays, blood or urine tests, to determine that the condition is suitable for chiropractic treatment. Then they give manipulative treatment to relieve pain and correct the problem without surgery or drugs. The specific joints where movement is restricted are treated with adjustments by hand, directly to the problem area.

May support treatment with advice about work, diet and exercise. Some may provide advice on orthotics to help posture and the spine. Can refer the client to a health specialist or GP if a condition is detected that is not suitable for manipulation, and requires medical treatment. Some chiropractors work with babies or specialise in working with people with sports injuries or with animals, especially horses.

Work Details
Usually work around 35-40 hrs a week though the working hours may be flexible according to the workplace. Some evening and weekend work may be required at times. Most self-employed chiropractors work hours to suit themselves. You see patients in consulting rooms, assess their problems and give treatment and advice for the best recovery. Patients may be distressed, or in pain and therefore require careful reassurance. Work can be physically demanding and involves standing and bending. Chiropractors often attend events, such as athletics meetings or football matches.

Qualification
If you do not have the necessary qualifications for entry to a science degree course, you may be able to take a one-year preliminary course at a General Chiropractic Council approved institution, or a Foundation Certificate Chiropractic. Check with universities and colleges for course entry requirements at an early stage in your enquiries.

- **England, Wales and Northern Ireland**

Band 5: For a chiropractic degree course: a minimum of two A levels, preferably in chemistry, biology, human biology or physics, and normally five GCSEs (A*-C), including English and maths, physics, biology or human biology (or dual science) if not held at A level. Contact the individual institution for specific entry requirements.

- **Scotland**

Band 5: For degree course: 3-5 H grades, usually including chemistry, physics or human biology, plus five S grades (1-3) in those sciences, if not offered at H grade, plus maths and English, or similar. Exact requirements depend on the degree you take.

Degree Information
BSc degrees in chiropractic and chiropractic sciences are available in Bournemouth, Glamorgan and the McTimoney College of Chiropractic in Oxfordshire. All are recognised by the General Chiropractic Council and meet international standards. There are also foundation courses for applicants without the relevant science qualifications for entry. It is also possible to carry out postgraduate clinical training in Denmark, Norway and Switzerland, as well as in the UK.

Adult Qualifications
Mature entrants may be accepted without the usual requirements if you have a relevant Access or foundation course certificate or equivalent science qualification.

Work Experience
Employers or colleges/universities may prefer candidates who have relevant work or voluntary experience. This may include experience in the caring professions, or time spent with a qualified chiropractor or similar professional, such as a physiotherapist or osteopath.

Entry and Training
There are three accredited courses in the UK recognised by the General Chiropractic Council (GCC). These are at the Anglo-European College of Chiropractic, the Welsh Institute of Chiropractic at the university of Glamorgan and the McTimoney

College of Chiropractic in Oxfordshire. All offer four-year, full-time courses but a five-year BSc degree in chiropractic modular course is also offered by the McTimoney College of Chiropractic. Courses combine classroom and laboratory work with clinical experience. Training includes anatomy, biochemistry and physiotherapy as well as chiropractic techniques. Following qualification at degree level, most students complete an employed but supervised, postgraduate year in a clinic to gain membership of the British Chiropractic Association (BCA).

The McTimoney College of Chiropractic also offers a validated postgraduate animal chiropractic course and the Anglo-European College of Chiropractic, a postgraduate course. The Welsh Institute of Chiropractic offers a foundation certificate if you do not have the qualifications to take a science degree.

To practise as a chiropractor you must register with the GCC. Check your course details to make sure it leads to GCC registration which meets international standards and means that you can work anywhere in the world. The BCA is the largest chiropractic association in the UK and represents more than 50% of chiropractors. Most students are self-financing and training costs can be expensive. Bursaries and loans may be available from the relevant professional associations.

Continuing professional development is necessary throughout your career to keep your skills up to date, and the GCC requires at least 30 hours a year. The College of Chiropractors (CoC) also provides courses, seminars and journals to keep qualified chiropractors up to date. See the CoC website for details.

A Diploma/Welsh Baccalaureate in society, health and development may be available in your area and may be relevant to this job.

Maturity and life experience are important for chiropractors and mature entrants are often those who wish to make a career change. It is possible to enter some courses without the required qualifications. An Access or foundation course can also provide a route to higher education for those without the usual entry qualifications. Funding for chiropractic courses may be available from the British Chiropractic Association student trust fund.

Opportunities and Pay

There are over 2,500 practising chiropractors in the UK and the numbers are steadily increasing. Good opportunities exist for work, particularly in the UK and Europe. You are usually self-employed and work in private practice, possibly in a partnership with other health professionals. However, some chiropractors provide a service through the NHS with Primary Healthcare Trusts. Costs include financial investment and expenses which can be high, especially when establishing a practice. Some chiropractors specialise in an area such as pregnancy or sports injuries, or work with animals, particularly horses. General Chiropractic Council registration allows you to work overseas.

Pay depends on the size of your practice, and may be by fees, not a regular salary. As most chiropractors are self-employed it is difficult to summarise earnings. Broadly speaking, you can earn £30-£60 a session, depending on location and experience. Over the year earnings may range from £20k-£30k. A chiropractor with an established practice may earn from £30k-£50k a year and those at the top of their field may earn up to £70k.

Health

You need to have a good level of fitness for this job.

Skills and Qualities

able to inspire confidence, business awareness, good communication skills, good sense of touch, patient, perceptive, reassuring, scientific approach, strong hands, sympathetic

Relevant Subjects

Biology, Chemistry, English, Health and social care, Physical education and sport, Physics, Psychology, Science

Further Information

ChiroIndex - www.chiroindex.org

Clinical Chiropractic (College of Chiropractors) (Elsevier) - http://colchiro.org.uk/default

Diplomas (Foundation, Higher and Advanced) - http://yp.direct.gov.uk/diplomas

McTimoney Chiropractic Association (MCA) - www.mctimoney-chiropractic.org

Welsh Baccalaureate - www.wbq.org.uk

Addresses

Anglo-European College of Chiropractic (AECC)
13-15 Parkwood Road, Bournemouth, Dorset BH5 2DF
Phone: +44 (0)1202 436 200
Web: www.aecc.ac.uk

British Chiropractic Association (BCA)
59 Castle Street, Reading, Berkshire RG1 7SN
Phone: +44 (0)118 950 5950
Web: www.chiropractic-uk.co.uk

College of Chiropractors (CoC)
Chiltern Chambers 37 St Peters Avenue, Reading, Berkshire RG4 7DH
Phone: +44 (0)1189 469727
Web: www.colchiro.org.uk

General Chiropractic Council (GCC)
44 Wicklow Street, London WC1X 9HL
Phone: +44 (0)20 7713 5155
Web: www.gcc-uk.org

McTimoney College of Chiropractic
Kimber House 1 Kimber Road, Abingdon, Oxfordshire OX14 1BZ
Phone: +44 (0)1235 523336
Web: www.mctimoney-college.ac.uk

Scottish Chiropractic Association
1 Chisholm Avenue, Bishopton PA7 5JH
Phone: +44 (0)141 404 0260
Web: www.sca-chiropractic.org

Welsh Institute of Chiropractic
University of Glamorgan, Pontypridd CF37 1DL
Phone: 0800 716 925 (UK only)
Web: www.glam.ac.uk

Similar Jobs

Acupuncturist, Kinesiologist, Naturopath, Osteopath, Physiotherapist, Sports Therapist

Choreographer

CRCI:Performing Arts
CLCI:GAF

Job Band: 1 to 5

Job Description

Choreographers create dance and movement routines for dancers to perform on television, in films and on the stage. This can be in any sort of dance, ranging from classical ballet to ice dance, ballroom and contemporary dancing. They may design their own dance routine or work under an artistic director and create the effect required. Movement routines can be anything from a fight sequence to working with artists so that they can, for example, mimic the movement of an animal. They may use either Benesh movement notation or labanotation (dance/motion systems) to record the movements.

Some choreographers are involved in selecting dancers for a production and may also help to choose the music that accompanies the performance. They plan the rehearsal schedule and work with either large groups of dancers or with individuals. As many choreographers are freelance, they also have to manage the administrative side of their business and promote themselves to theatres and directors.

Work Details

Working hours can be long and irregular. Creating dance routines and rehearsals take place during the day, but you may also attend performances in the evening. You may be working on more than one performance at once, so at times the work can be very demanding. Part time work is sometimes available, especially for those who are freelance.

You work in rehearsal rooms or on stage in a theatre, in a film or television studio or in a nightclub. You may have to travel at times, and this can mean time away from home. You need to be physically fit and have plenty of stamina.

Qualification

Choreographers are almost always trained dancers and to train as a dancer there are no specified minimum requirements. However, some formal qualifications are useful for transfer to choreography or to dance teaching. Useful subjects include English, drama, music, biology, performing arts and dance. See the dancer job article for more details.

Degree Information

There is a wide range of degrees in dance, some of which specialise in choreography. Postgraduate courses are also available.

Adult Qualifications

Adult entrants must have training as a dancer and are likely to need to take a specialist course in choreography.

Work Experience

It is essential to begin your dance training at an early age and perform in amateur productions, and at school/dance school performances. Some voluntary/holiday or temporary work with a local theatre or dance company is useful, particularly if it involves organising and creating dance routines.

Entry and Training

Most choreographers are trained dancers. Training in dancing starts at an early age, and usually involves attending dance schools, some specialising in classical and some contemporary dance. The Council for Dance Education and Training accredits professional training programmes and has details of dance training available. If you are interested in choreography, you must make sure your formal dance training is in the style of dance that you want to work in.

Some move into this work while still dancing, while others use it as a second career when their dancing life is coming to an end. Dancers Career Development offers advice for professional dancers at the end of their career. While still dancing you may become a dance captain, ensuring the continuity of the dance, and then become an assistant choreographer. It is fairly common for trainee choreographers to work for no pay while they are training to find an opening into this work. Once trained you are expected to maintain your fitness and keep up to date with research into new dance styles.

A Diploma/Welsh Baccalaureate in creative and media may be available in your area. Check university entry requirements carefully in case there is an additional specialist learning requirement with the diploma. See the diplomas website for further information.

Degree and postgraduate courses in choreography are available at a range of universities and private dance schools. Dance UK offers support for choreographers and runs the UK Choreographers' Directory on their website.

This is a second career for many established dancers, but you need to be physically fit and active so that you can demonstrate routines. Many dancers start choreography in a small way while they are still following their dance careers.

Opportunities and Pay

There are around 200 dance companies in the UK. There may be work available in theatres, opera and ballet companies, with specialist dance theatres, with variety shows, in outdoor performances, on cruise ships and with fashion shows. However, entry to this work is very competitive and vacancies are rarely advertised, with most jobs being filled through a network of contacts. Real talent and enthusiasm are essential. Many choreographers are self-employed, and combine this work with dance teaching. The may also be opportunities to work overseas.

Some choreographers start work in a training role and earn little or no pay. Experienced dancers moving into this work may earn around £20k a year. Established choreographers can earn £40k or more a year.

Health

You must be physically fit and agile to do this work.

Skills and Qualities

able to motivate others, able to stimulate learners, creative and imaginative flair, dance skills, determined, even tempered, good communication skills, good interpersonal skills, leadership qualities, stamina

Relevant Subjects

Media and communication studies, Music, Performing arts, Physical education and sport

Further Information

Creative & Cultural Skills - sector skills council for advertising, crafts, cultural heritage, design, literature, music, performing & visual arts - www.ccskills.org.uk

Creative Choices - www.creative-choices.co.uk

Dance UK News (Dance UK) (Dance UK) - www.danceuk.org

Dancing Times (Dancing Times Ltd) - www.dancing-times.co.uk

Diplomas (Foundation, Higher and Advanced) - http://yp.direct.gov.uk/diplomas

The Stage Online - www.thestage.co.uk

Welsh Baccalaureate - www.wbq.org.uk

Addresses

Council for Dance Education and Training (CDET)
Old Brewer's Yard, 17 - 19 Neal Street, Covent Garden, London WC2H 9UY
Phone: +44 (0)207 240 5703
Web: www.cdet.org.uk

Dance UK
2nd Floor, Finsbury Town Hall , Rosebery Avenue, London EC1R 4QT
Phone: +44 (0)20 7713 0730
Web: www.danceuk.org

Dancers' Career Development
19-20 Hatton Place, London EC1N 8RU
Phone: +44 (0)20 7831 1449
Web: www.thedcd.org.uk

Laban Centre of Movement
Creekside, London SE8 3DZ
Phone: +44 (0)20 8691 8600
Web: www.laban.org

London Contemporary Dance School
The Place, 17 Duke's Road, London WC1H 9PH
Phone: +44 (0)20 7121 1000
Web: www.theplace.org.uk

Similar Jobs

Actor, Dancer, Entertainer, Fitness Instructor, Teacher: Dance

Cinema Manager

also known as: Entertainments Manager

CRCI:Leisure, Sport and Tourism

CLCI:GAN

Job Band: 3 to 5

Job Description

Cinema managers are responsible for the everyday running of a multiplex cinema, or a smaller art house cinema and its activities. They aim to provide entertainment for the public, and to produce a profit. This involves planning events, organising advertisements for films, managing a budget, keeping accounts, and arranging catering facilities. Also oversees booking systems and prepares regular reports on the state of business. Managers liaise with the media (press, radio and TV) during the promotion of film premieres, and are often involved in local events and arts festivals. Also recruits and manages the staff, and arranges in-house training. Advises on any career opportunities within the organisation.

Other parts of the job include dealing with any public complaints or concerns, looking after the condition of the premises, and ensuring that safety and legal regulations are kept.

Work Details

Usually works a basic 39 hr week, often working unsocial hours, including evenings and weekends, perhaps on a rota basis. This job is office based but you spend a great deal of time on site. You have contact with a large number of people of all ages and are responsible for their health and safety while on the premises.

Qualification

- **England, Wales and Northern Ireland**

Band 3: For entry to jobs, HNC or a relevant Diploma, usually at least 4 GCSEs (A*-C) including English and maths, or equivalent.

Band 4: For HND, Diploma of Higher Education or foundation degree in leisure management or related subject: 1-2 A levels and some GCSEs (A*-C) usually including English and maths, or equivalent.

Band 5: For degree courses in leisure management: 2-3 A levels and some GCSEs (A*-C) usually including English and maths, or equivalent. Exact requirements depend on the degree you take.

- **Scotland**

Band 3: For entry to jobs, usually at least four S grades (1-3) including English or maths, or similar.

Band 4: For entry to SQA higher national and professional development awards in leisure studies or related subject, usually 2-3 H grades and some S grades (1-3), including English and maths, or similar qualifications.

Band 5: For degree courses in leisure management: 3-5 H grades and some S grades (1-3), including English and maths, or similar qualifications. Exact requirements depend on the degree you take.

Degree Information

Courses in leisure studies/management, arts administration, events and entertainment management, are particularly relevant, but any degree is acceptable for entry to this job. The following subjects also provide useful background knowledge: hospitality management, administration, business studies, industrial relations, and marketing.

Adult Qualifications

Qualification requirements may be waived for adults with related experience. Access or foundation courses give adults without qualifications a route onto degree courses.

Work Experience

Relevant work or voluntary experience is always useful and can improve your chances in application for entry to this career. This can be in retail, business administration and work that helps you to gain skills in accounts, budgeting, marketing and human resources management. Other leisure management work, including working in restaurants or public houses, is also relevant. It is very useful to talk to a cinema manager about the job and to gain some casual work experience at a cinema complex.

Entry and Training

You need to be over 18 to work for most cinema chains due to film certification laws. Entry to this job is possible with a range of different qualifications and previous experience is often as important as qualifications. Many cinemas require applicants to have previous managerial experience from a similar industry such as leisure, retail or hospitality. It is also an advantage to be able to show experience of business or entertainment. Larger companies may have structured management training programmes but, more usually, training is on the job while working as an assistant manager.

Trainee managers may study for relevant qualifications while working. The professional body for the leisure industry is the Institute for Sport, Parks and Leisure (ISPAL). ISPAL offers professional qualifications and continuing professional development including tailored in-house training courses in categories such as leisure operations, leadership and management, and event management. For full membership, you have to achieve NVQ Level 4. Contact ISPAL for further details of courses, routes to membership and qualifications.

There are relevant vocational qualifications such as BTEC HNCs/HNDs in sport and leisure management at level 5 and S/NVQs in leisure management at level 3. A Diploma/Welsh Baccalaureate may be available in your area in business, administration and finance or retail business, and apprenticeships in leisure management, customer service and/or marketing and communications may also be helpful. Relevant foundation degrees and honours degrees are also available in leisure management and may be studied full or part time.

Mature entrants with relevant experience may be preferred by some employers. There is no fixed career pattern for this job, so it is often possible for those with relevant experience to move into management. The ability to deal with a wide cross section of people is an advantage.

Opportunities and Pay

Entry to jobs is highly competitive, especially from assistant manager to manager level. You are usually employed by a cinema chain within a large leisure company or group which has centres throughout the UK. Promotion prospects are usually good. However, it may be necessary to move location at times to progress your career.

Pay varies depending on location, type and size of business, and level of responsibility. A starting salary is likely to be around £15k-£20k a year. A manager of a small business earns in the region of £16k-£22k, whereas a manager in a larger organisation earns around £22k-£32k a year. A senior manager with significant experience and responsibilities may earn up to £50k a year. Often earnings are partly performance related so you may receive a bonus on top of your salary. Perks may include the use of facilities for your own leisure and recreation.

Skills and Qualities

able to get on with all kinds of people, able to withstand criticism, business awareness, enthusiastic, friendly, good organisational skills, imaginative, IT skills, outgoing personality

Relevant Subjects

Business and accounting, English, Hospitality and catering, Leisure, travel and tourism, Mathematics, Media and communication studies

Further Information

Apprenticeship Schemes (National Apprenticeship Service) - www.apprenticeships.org.uk

Diplomas (Foundation, Higher and Advanced) - http://yp.direct.gov.uk/diplomas

Leisure Management Magazine (The Leisure Media Company) - www.leisuremanagement.co.uk

Northern Ireland Screen (Northern Ireland Screen) - www.northernirelandscreen.co.uk

People 1st - sector skills council for hospitality, leisure, travel and tourism - www.people1st.co.uk

Real Life Guide to Sports & Active Leisure (Trotman 2009) - www.trotman.co.uk

Scottish Screen (Scottish Screen) - www.scottishscreen.com

Skillset - sector skills council for the creative media, fashion and textiles industries - www.skillset.org

Springboard UK (Springboard UK) - www.springboarduk.net

Springboard Wales (Springboard Wales) - http://wales.springboarduk.net/

UKSP - Guide to Success in Hospitality, Leisure, Travel & Tourism - www.uksp.co.uk/

▶Working in sport & leisure (2010) (Babcock Lifeskills) - www.babcock-lifeskills.com/

▶Working in travel & tourism (2010) (Babcock Lifeskills) - www.babcock-lifeskills.com/

Addresses

Cinemas Exhibitors' Association
22 Golden Square, London W1F 9JW
Phone: +44 (0)20 7734 9551
Web: www.cinemauk.org.uk/

Institute for Sport, Parks & Leisure (ISPAL)
Abbey Business Centre, 1650 Arlington Business Park, Theale, Reading RG7 4SA
Phone: 0844 418 0077 (UK only)
Web: www.ispal.org.uk

Similar Jobs

Arts Administrator, Betting Shop Manager, Event & Exhibition Organiser, Leisure Manager, Retail Manager

Cinema/Theatre Attendant

also known as: Front-of-House Assistant, Usher

CRCI:Leisure, Sport and Tourism
CLCI:GAN Job Band: 1 to 2

Job Description

Cinema and theatre attendants carry out a range of tasks in a cinema, concert hall or a theatre, such as assisting people and guiding them to their seats. They check tickets, answer any questions from the public and keep gangways and exits clear. May sell programmes before the show starts, or drinks and snacks. Also deals with any problems that happen during the show.

At the end of a show, they help the audience to leave the auditorium and make sure they have left the building. May check the cinema/theatre, tidy the seats and collect any items that people have left behind. Ensures public safety in the auditorium and, if an emergency occurs, is responsible for evacuating the premises. Attendants need to keep up to date with fire regulations and emergency procedures.

May also do other front-of-house duties, such as working in the box office selling and exchanging tickets. If so, usually operates a computerised till and a booking database. Takes payments from people using credit/debit cards, and also cash if at the cinema/theatre itself.

Work Details

Work is mainly during the afternoons and evenings, but some venues are open in the morning. Many theatres/cinema complexes are open seven days a week, so you have to work weekends, usually on a rota basis. You can be responsible for handling cash and the administration of debit/credit card payments. You are on your feet for much of the time and have periods of quiet and busy times. You meet all kinds of people and a few may be awkward or aggressive. A uniform may be provided.

Qualification

• England, Wales and Northern Ireland

Band 1: For entry to jobs, no minimum qualifications are needed, but you are expected to have a good level of general education and relevant experience. Some formal/vocational qualifications at any level are useful.

Band 2: For entry to jobs, no minimum qualifications are needed, but it is an advantage to have some GCSEs (A*-C) or equivalent in subjects that include English and maths.

• Scotland

Band 1: For entry to jobs, no minimum qualifications are needed, but you are expected to have a good level of general education and relevant experience. Some formal/vocational qualifications at any level are useful.

Band 2: Although academic qualifications are not specified for this job, it is an advantage to have some S grades (1-3) in subjects that include English and maths, or similar.

Adult Qualifications

No pre-entry qualifications are usually required, although some academic/vocational qualifications at any level may be an advantage. English and maths are useful subjects.

Work Experience

Any work experience can equip you with skills that you can use in the future and add to your CV. This can either be unpaid or voluntary, holiday or part-time work that you have organised yourself. It is useful to talk to a cinema manager about the job and to gain some casual work experience at a theatre or cinema complex. Any work that gives you experience of dealing with people is useful.

Entry and Training

Entrants to this job are usually over 18. This is a requirement if you are serving alcohol and to comply with film certification laws. Employers look for applicants with pleasant personalities who are good at dealing with the general public. An interest in cinema/theatre or the arts is useful. Training is on the job. Initially you work with experienced staff. You learn about company policies, issues of health and safety, and emergency procedures. You may receive formal in-house training if you work for a large cinema chain or leisure company.

Training programmes, including apprenticeship schemes in customer service, may be available in your area. Relevant S/NVQs may be available at level 1 and 2 such as in customer service. City & Guilds offer a level 2 award in principles of customer service in hospitality, leisure, travel and tourism. A Diploma/Welsh Baccalaureate may also be available in your area in hospitality and/or creative and media.

Mature entrants with experience in customer service work and handling money may have an advantage. You may be able to benefit from government training opportunities, such as an apprenticeship in hospitality or customer service, which may be available in your area. You can also gain recognition of previous experience through Accreditation of Prior Learning (APL) or by working towards relevant S/NVQs. Contact your local careers office, Jobcentre Plus, Next Step service or Learning and Skills Council (LSC) Local Enterprise Company (LEC) for details of training schemes, including apprenticeships for adults.

Opportunities and Pay

You can be employed by a cinema, theatre or concert hall, ranging from small independents to large multi-screen cinema complexes. Jobs are available mainly in towns and cities and there are many opportunities to work part time. With experience you can progress to a box office or management role. Despite the recent economic downturn, opportunities to work in the UK entertainment business are good.

Pay varies depending on area and employer but is likely to be £6-£8 an hour. Those who work full time tend to earn from £11k-£13k a year. You may be given free or reduced price cinema or theatre tickets.

Skills and Qualities

aptitude for teamwork, efficient, friendly, helpful, IT skills, numeracy skills, polite, self confident, smart appearance, trustworthy

Relevant Subjects

Media and communication studies

Further Information

Apprenticeship Schemes (National Apprenticeship Service) - www.apprenticeships.org.uk

Diplomas (Foundation, Higher and Advanced) - http://yp.direct.gov.uk/diplomas

Northern Ireland Screen (Northern Ireland Screen) - www.northernirelandscreen.co.uk

People 1st - sector skills council for hospitality, leisure, travel and tourism - www.people1st.co.uk

Scottish Screen (Scottish Screen) - www.scottishscreen.com

Skillset - sector skills council for the creative media, fashion and textiles industries - www.skillset.org

Springboard UK (Springboard UK) - www.springboarduk.net

Springboard Wales (Springboard Wales) - http://wales.springboarduk.net/

Training Schemes - www.direct.gov.uk/en/educationandlearning

▶Working in retail & customer services (2008) (Babcock Lifeskills) - www.babcock-lifeskills.com/

Addresses

Cinemas Exhibitors' Association
22 Golden Square, London W1F 9JW
Phone: +44 (0)20 7734 9551
Web: www.cinemauk.org.uk/

Similar Jobs

Bartender, Door Attendant, Hotel Porter, Retail Assistant, Theatre Stagehand

Civil Engineering Technician

also known as: Construction Engineering Technician, Structural Engineering Technician

CRCI:Building and Construction
CLCI:UN — Job Band: 3 to 4

Job Description

Civil engineering technicians provide technical support for construction projects, such as bridges, roads, tunnels, modern stadia, power stations, railways, airports, dams and harbours. They carry out a variety of tasks in a team headed by a qualified engineer. May assist in the planning of projects and decide on the labour and equipment needed for all stages of the project. They produce detailed drawings of the project, using a drawing board or computer-aided design (CAD) program. Technicians also become involved in estimating the type and quantities of the materials required and the costs involved and arrange for purchase and delivery of the materials at the appropriate time. They supervise and inspect the building work, checking what has been done on site by operatives and craft workers.

Civil engineering technicians monitor schedules and the ongoing costs of the scheme. May also deal with the legal paperwork required for a project. They are often responsible for health and safety aspects on site.

Work Details

Civil engineering technicians usually work around 35-40 hrs a week, Monday to Friday, including early starts and late finishes on some projects. May also be required to work some weekends to meet approaching deadlines. The work combines office duties and spending some time on site, depending on the employer and type of project. Schedules can be demanding at times. On-site conditions may be cold or damp and you need to be able to climb ladders and scaffolding. There is a risk of accidents from equipment, so you need to wear a safety helmet and protective footwear.

Qualification

• England, Wales and Northern Ireland

Band 3: For entry: usually at least 4 GCSEs (A*-C) including English, maths and a science subject (physics preferred), or equivalent.

Band 4: For BTEC higher national award: 1-2 A levels, preferably maths and physics, and some GCSEs (A*-C), including English, maths and a science, or equivalent qualifications. There are foundation courses available for those without appropriate A levels.

• Scotland

Band 3: For entry to a relevant course in civil engineering or building: four S grades (1-3) including English, maths and a science subject (preferably physics), or similar.

Band 4: For an SQA higher national award: 2-3 H grades, usually including maths and physics, and some S grades (1-3), including English, maths and a science, or similar qualifications. There are foundation courses available for those without appropriate H grades.

Adult Qualifications

Those with relevant work experience may be accepted for some college courses without formal entry requirements.

Work Experience

Entry to this job is competitive and it is important that you try to do some relevant practical work or voluntary experience before applying. Trainee positions for young people are few and for adults it can be difficult to gain entry without prior relevant experience or professional qualifications. Work in a related career in the construction industry, such as in an architect's firm or in computer-aided design, is relevant. The Institution of Civil Engineers (ICE) states that work experience, although not a requirement, shows enthusiasm and commitment, and that is what employers like.

Entry and Training

There are several routes to becoming a registered engineering technician with the Engineering Council UK (EngTech), depending on your qualifications. You can take a relevant national certificate/ diploma, or similar qualification, such as City & Guilds higher professional diploma, either full time before employment, or part time with on-the-job training. Or you can follow work-based training for an S/NVQ at level 3 in a variety of subjects that meet the academic entry requirements for registration. Subjects include technical design (built environment), construction site supervision, and construction contracting operations.

After an approved period (provided you are over 21) you can register as a technician with the Engineering Council and become a technician member of the Institution of Civil Engineers, Institution of Structural Engineers or Institute of Highway Incorporated Engineers. Further study, either part or full time, for a higher national certificate/diploma is common and you can also go on to study for a degree. There are part or full-time foundation degrees available in relevant subjects. Contact the professional organisations listed in addresses for further information.

A Diploma/ Welsh Baccalaureate in construction and the built environment may be available in your area. S/NVQs in relevant subjects are available at levels 1-3. Training programmes, including apprenticeship schemes, may be available in your area for entry to this job. Advanced apprenticeships leading to qualification at level 3 can also be a route into higher education.

Mature entrants are usually qualified and/or experienced in a related field of construction/engineering. Those who have craft level experience, and/or relevant qualifications, have an advantage. Contact your local careers office, Next Step service, Jobcentre or Learning and Skills Council (LSC)/Local Enterprise Company (LEC) for details of training schemes, including apprenticeships for adults.

Opportunities and Pay

Work is located throughout the UK and employers include building and civil contractors, public utility companies, engineering consultants, property developers and local authorities. Some also work for central government and the armed forces. Availability of work depends on the state of the building trade and the national economy. Currently there is a downturn in the housing market which means there may be a shortage of vacancies for technicians.

There may be opportunities for further training, which is sometimes offered in-house. You may be able to work towards becoming an incorporated engineer (IEng) and then progress to gaining the qualifications and experience for chartered engineer status (CEng). There are opportunities for work overseas.

Salaries vary depending on the employer and location. New entrants start on around £16k-£18k, rising to around £22k-£30k with experience. Some technicians can earn up to £38k a year.

Health

This job requires you to have stamina and be physically fit.

Skills and Qualities

able to work both on your own and in a team, accurate measuring and calculating skills, good communication skills, good organisational skills, health & safety awareness, logical, planning skills, project management skills, specialist IT skills

Relevant Subjects

Chemistry, Construction and built environment, Design and technology, ICT/Computer studies, Mathematics, Physics, Science

Further Information

Apprenticeship Schemes (National Apprenticeship Service) - www.apprenticeships.org.uk

Apprenticeships in Scotland (Careers Info Scotland) - www.apprenticeshipsinscotland.com/about/

ConstructionSkills - sector skills council for the construction industry - www.cskills.org

Diplomas (Foundation, Higher and Advanced) - http://yp.direct.gov.uk/diplomas

ICE Virtual Library (institute of Civil Engineers) (ICE) - www.icevirtuallibrary.com

The Institute of Structural Engineers (IStructE) - www.istructe.org.uk/

Welsh Baccalaureate - www.wbq.org.uk

▶Working in construction & the built environment (2007) (Babcock Lifeskills) - www.babcock-lifeskills.com/

Addresses

Engineering Council
246 High Holborn, London WC1V 7EX
Phone: +44 (0)20 3206 0500
Web: www.engc.org.uk

Institute of Highway Incorporated Engineers (IHIE)
De Morgan House, 58 Russell Square, London WC1B 4HS
Phone: +44 (0)20 7436 7487
Web: www.ihie.org.uk

Institution of Civil Engineers (ICE)
1 Great George Street, Westminster, London SW1P 3AA
Phone: +44 (0)20 7222 7722
Web: www.ice.org.uk

Institution of Structural Engineers (IStructE)
11 Upper Belgrave Street, London SW1X 8BH
Phone: +44 (0)20 7235 4535
Web: www.istructe.org.uk

Similar Jobs

Architectural Technologist, Construction Site Supervisor/ Manager, Engineer: Civil/Structural, Surveying Technician, Surveyor: Quantity

Civil Service Administrative Assistant

CRCI:Administration, Business and Office Work
CLCI:CAB Job Band: 2 to 3

Job Description

Administrative assistants in the civil service carry out day-to-day clerical tasks required in all central government departments and agencies, either in public or non-public offices. They work as part of a team that provides support to other staff. They operate computer systems; often keying in data or retrieving information. Check and update official records, file papers, open and distribute the mail, addresses envelopes. They may also order supplies, including stationery, and in some offices, prepare figures for accounts or compile statistical information. Some assistants deal with press reports, newsletters and employees' records such as absences, annual leave and expenses claims.

Administrative assistants use photocopiers, fax machines and other office equipment, such as a franking machine. May deal with incoming telephone enquiries or spend time at a reception desk answering visitor enquiries.

Work Details

Most administrative assistants are based in an office and usually work 36-37 hrs a week, Monday to Friday. Some agencies and departments work outside normal office hours. Staff also receive all public holidays and privilege days in addition to their annual leave. There may be flexitime, part time and job-share opportunities. Some travel may be required for attendance at meetings or conferences, or for training courses.

Your specific job may require you to be away from the office, or to make visits to various premises during the course of your everyday work. You often deal with confidential information. All government offices are open to public scrutiny and this may make the work stressful at times.

Civil Service Administrative Assistant

Qualification

• England, Wales and Northern Ireland

Band 2: For entry to jobs, no minimum qualifications are needed, but it is an advantage to have some GCSEs (A*-C) or equivalent in subjects that include English and maths.

Band 3: For some departments you may be required to have 4 GCSEs (A*-C) including English and maths, or equivalent.

• Scotland

Band 2: Although academic qualifications are not specified for this job, it is an advantage to have some S grades (1-3) in subjects that include English and maths, or similar.

Band 3: For some departments you may be required to have at least four S grades (1-3) including English, or similar.

Adult Qualifications

Generally mature entrants are expected to have the minimum entry qualifications, which can vary. However for some jobs suitable relevant experience is accepted instead of formal qualifications. Those without the minimum qualifications may be tested on their written, numerical and decision-making abilities, as well as communication, analytical and interpersonal skills.

Work Experience

It is important that you try to do some relevant work or voluntary experience before applying for a job. Applicants are expected to be competent in key administration skills.

Entry and Training

Entry requirements may vary depending on the department you are applying to. Those without formal qualifications may be accepted with suitable relevant experience. All administrative assistants have some form of on-the-job training. This is usually under the supervision of an experienced work colleague. It may be combined with specific part-time and short courses, including e-learning. Regular appraisals and job feedback take place throughout your career. You can take exams for civil service promotion and you may also have the opportunity to study for nationally recognised vocational qualifications in specific areas of work.

S/NVQs in administration are available at levels 1-2. Training programmes, including business administration apprenticeships, may be available in your area. Advanced apprenticeships leading to qualification at level 3 can also be a route into higher education. From September 2010, a diploma/welsh baccalaureate in public services is being introduced to the school curriculum in some areas. This includes the study of public services, local communities and health and wellbeing in communities. Diplomas are available at foundation, higher, progression or advanced levels. Check the website for further details.

The Welsh Assembly Government is responsible for delivering and implementing policies and programmes for all issues that have been devolved to Wales. Civil service jobs are available with the Welsh Assembly Government across Wales but applicants are usually expected to be able to speak Welsh.

Mature entrants with experience in clerical work/office administration or basic qualifications in administration, may have an advantage. Adults may be able to enter this work through a government-funded training programme, such as an apprenticeship. Contact your local Connexions or careers office, Jobcentre Plus, Next Step service or Learning and Skills Council (LSC)/Local Enterprise Company (LEC) for details of all training opportunities and schemes.

Opportunities and Pay

Jobs are available throughout the UK and are mainly in towns and cities. Nationality and residency requirements apply, but all jobs are open to British nationals, with 75% also open to EU nationals and Commonwealth citizens. There are many different government offices and agencies, such as the Department for Culture, Media and Sport, HM Revenue & Customs, Department for Work and Pensions, Crown Prosecution Service, Department of Health, and the Department for Children, Schools and Families. Jobs are usually advertised locally and also through the department/civil service recruitment website, and availability varies. Promotion, firstly to administrative officer, is on merit, and training can help your chances.

The civil service encourages further development and training through regular work appraisals and performance feedback. You can progress quickly to administrative officer level and opportunities exist for further progression to the first level of junior management. You may be able to get financial help for courses that are usually taken in your own time. You can also apply to the EU for B* grade administrative posts. B* administration posts are part of the assistants' grade (AST) in the EU. Entrants can start at junior filing clerk level and progress through the promotional levels leading to personal assistant. Check the EU website for details.

Salaries vary depending on department/location and tend to be higher in London. Typical starting salaries are around £12k-£15k, and with greater experience and responsibility this may rise to around £17k-£18.5k a year.

Health

You may have to take a medical test.

Skills and Qualities

able to get on with all kinds of people, able to work to deadlines, adaptable, aptitude for teamwork, attention to detail, good organisational skills, good spoken communication, good written English, IT skills, methodical, numeracy skills

Relevant Subjects

English, Government and politics, ICT/Computer studies

Further Information

AGCAS: Government & Public Administration (Job Sector Briefing) (AGCAS) - www.prospects.ac.uk

Careers in British Intelligence - www.careersinbritishintelligence.co.uk/

Careers in the Foreign & Commonwealth Office (Foreign and Commonwealth Office) - www.fco.gov.uk/en/

Careers Wales - www.careerswales.com/

Civil Service - www.civilservice.gov.uk/jobs

Civil Service Commissioners' Information Leaflet (Office of the Civil Service Commissioners) - www.civilservicecommissioners.org/

Diplomas (Foundation, Higher and Advanced) - http://yp.direct.gov.uk/diplomas

European Personnel Selection Office (EU Careers) (Office for Official Publications of the EC) - http://europa.eu/epso

Government Skills - sector skills council for central government - www.government-skills.gov.uk

National School of Government - www.nationalschool.gov.uk

TARGETjobs: Public Service (GTI Specialist Publishing Ltd.) - www.groupgti.com

Welsh Baccalaureate - www.wbq.org.uk

▶Working in business, administration & finance (2010) (Babcock Lifeskills) - www.babcock-lifeskills.com/

Addresses

Civil Service Commission (Northern Ireland)
HRConnect, PO Box 1089, 2nd Floor, The Metro Building,
6-9 Donegall Square South, Belfast BT1 9EW
Phone: 0800 1300 330
Web: www.irecruit.nicsrecruitment.gov.uk/

Northern Ireland Assembly
Communications Office Northern Ireland Assembly Parliament Buildings Ballymiscaw Stormont, Belfast BT4 3XX
Phone: +44 (0)28 9052 1333
Web: www.niassembly.gov.uk

Scottish Executive
St Andrew's House, Regent Road, Edinburgh EH1 3DG
Phone: +44 (0)131 556 8400
Web: www.scotland.gov.uk

Welsh Assembly Government
Cathays Park, Cardiff CF10 3NQ
Phone: 0845 010 3300 (UK only)
Web: www.wales.gov.uk

Similar Jobs

Administrator/Administrative Assistant, Civil Service Administrative Officer, Court Administrative Officer/Assistant, Local Government Administrative Assistant, Receptionist

Civil Service Administrative Officer

CRCI:Administration, Business and Office Work
CLCI:CAB Job Band: 3

Job Description

Administrative officers in the civil service support and supervise a team of administrative assistants that carry out the day-to-day clerical tasks required in all government departments and agencies. They also work closely with central government officials that formulate and implement national policies, depending on the department. Deal with incoming mail and reply to correspondence and telephone/email enquiries. Use a computer to update and maintain records. Interpret complex information, and compile statistics and reports.

May also manage work diaries and meetings for one or more people within the section. Duties may include supervising other administrative staff, planning the workload, delegating tasks, and organising staff training and development needs. Some officers purchase and maintain office supplies and equipment.

Work Details

Administrative officers mostly work normal office hours from Monday to Friday, though there may be flexitime, part-time and job-share opportunities. Staff receive all public holidays and privilege days in addition to their annual leave. You assist managers and other senior colleagues. If you are involved in dealing with the public, your clients may sometimes be upset or angry, which makes the work stressful at times. Smart/professional or smart-casual office dress code is usually expected and depends on the demands of the job.

Qualification

- **England, Wales and Northern Ireland**

Band 3: Usually at least 5 GCSEs (A*-C) including English, or equivalent qualifications or suitable relevant experience.

- **Scotland**

Band 3: Usually at least 5 S grades (1-3) including English, or similar qualifications, or suitable relevant experience.

Adult Qualifications

Those without the minimum educational qualifications may be able to take a written test and interview, or be accepted with relevant administrative experience.

Work Experience

It is important that you try to do some relevant work or voluntary experience before applying for a job. Applicants are expected to be competent in key administration skills. Experience of working abroad is also an advantage as is any experience of working with the public, particularly in roles that demonstrate strong communication skills.

Entry and Training

This job is open to those with qualifications up to diploma/degree level in relevant subjects, such as business, business administration and economics, but entry without an HND/degree is commonly possible. Although not essential, many applicants have A levels/H grades or equivalent. Relevant administrative experience can take the place of formal qualifications. There are strict nationality and residency requirements but all jobs are open to UK nationals, with 75% also open to EU nationals and Commonwealth citizens. Those working for the Welsh Assembly government are usually expected to be able to speak Welsh.

You are usually trained on the job through a comprehensive training programme, and often with a senior colleague or mentor who can provide helpful advice and guidance. Short courses, including e-learning, are available, which vary depending on the department or agency for which you work. You can take exams for civil service promotion and also have the opportunity to study for nationally recognised qualifications in specific areas of work.

The civil service expects you to commit to a programme of continuing professional development (CPD) and lifelong learning throughout your career. The National School of Government offers a range of courses, from foundation to advanced level, which are specifically aimed to provide or develop the necessary skills and knowledge required for working in the civil service.

Appropriate S/NVQs at levels 1-3 may be available. Training programmes, including business administration apprenticeships, may also be available in your area. Advanced apprenticeships leading to qualification at level 3 can also be a route into higher education.

From September 2010, a diploma in public services is being introduced to the school curriculum in some areas. This includes the study of public services, local communities and health and wellbeing in communities. Diplomas are available at foundation, higher, progression or advanced levels. Check the website for further details.

Mature entrants with experience in clerical work/office administration, or basic qualifications in administration, may have an advantage. Adults may be able to enter this work through a government-funded training programme, such as an apprenticeship. Contact your local Connexions or careers office, Jobcentre Plus, Next Step service or Learning and Skills Council (LSC)/Local Enterprise Company (LEC) for details of all training opportunities and schemes.

Opportunities and Pay

Jobs are available throughout the UK and are mainly in towns and cities. Jobs vary from department to department and may be advertised locally or nationally. There are many different government offices and agencies, such as HM Revenue & Customs, Department of Health, or Department for Children, Schools and Families. Once you have experience and have perhaps taken further training, promotion to first management level is possible. You can also apply to the EU for B* grade administrative posts. B* administration posts are part of the assistants' grade (AST) in the EU. Entrants can start at junior filing clerk level and progress through the promotional levels leading to personal assistant. Check the EU website for details.

The civil service encourages further development and training through regular work appraisals and performance feedback. There may be financial help available for courses studied in your own time.

Salaries vary depending on department/location and tend to higher in London. Typical starting salaries are in the region of £13.5k-£15k, and rise to around £21k a year (in London), with greater experience and responsibility.

Health
You may be asked to take a medical test.

Skills and Qualities
able to explain clearly, accurate, aptitude for teamwork, attention to detail, efficient, good communication skills, good interpersonal skills, good written English, IT skills, methodical, responsible attitude

Relevant Subjects
Business and accounting, English, Government and politics, ICT/ Computer studies

Further Information
AGCAS: Government & Public Administration (Job Sector Briefing) (AGCAS) - www.prospects.ac.uk

Careers in British Intelligence - www.careersinbritishintelligence.co.uk/

Careers in the Foreign & Commonwealth Office (Foreign and Commonwealth Office) - www.fco.gov.uk/en/

Civil Service - www.civilservice.gov.uk/jobs

Civil Service Commissioners' Information Leaflet (Office of the Civil Service Commissioners) - www.civilservicecommissioners.org/

Civil Service Fast Stream (Civil Service) - www.civilservice.gov.uk/jobs/faststream

Diplomas (Foundation, Higher and Advanced) - http://yp.direct.gov.uk/diplomas

European Personnel Selection Office (EU Careers) (Office for Official Publications of the EC) http://europa.eu/epso

Government Skills - sector skills council for central government - www.government-skills.gov.uk

National School of Government - www.nationalschool.gov.uk

Addresses
Civil Service Commission (Northern Ireland)
HRConnect, PO Box 1089, 2nd Floor, The Metro Building,
6-9 Donegall Square South, Belfast BT1 9EW
Phone: 0800 1300 330
Web: www.irecruit.nicsrecruitment.gov.uk/

Northern Ireland Assembly
Communications Office Northern Ireland Assembly Parliament Buildings Ballymiscaw Stormont, Belfast BT4 3XX
Phone: +44 (0)28 9052 1333
Web: www.niassembly.gov.uk

Scottish Executive
St Andrew's House, Regent Road, Edinburgh EH1 3DG
Phone: +44 (0)131 556 8400
Web: www.scotland.gov.uk

Welsh Assembly Government
Cathays Park, Cardiff CF10 3NQ
Phone: 0845 010 3300 (UK only)
Web: www.wales.gov.uk

Similar Jobs
Civil Service Administrative Assistant, Civil Service Diplomatic Executive Assistant, Civil Service EU Administrator, Civil Service Executive Officer, Court Administrative Officer/Assistant, Local Government Administrator

Civil Service Customs Officer

CRCI:Security and Armed Forces
CLCI:CAB — Job Band: 3 to 5

Job Description
Civil service customs officers work for HM Revenue & Customs (Border Protection) at UK ports and airports ensuring that people keep to the laws governing what can be taken out or brought into the country. They check passengers and their vehicles, freight vehicles and cargo ships, looking for illegal drugs and other prohibited items, such as obscene material, explosives, firearms, certain meat products and endangered species. Use sophisticated technical equipment to view inside suitcases, bags, lorries and cargo. May work with a highly trained sniffer dog to examine luggage and freight.

Customs officers check passengers' luggage and also their pet animals, including the scrutiny of pet passports. Stop and search any vehicle or person that arouses suspicion and confiscate the goods if necessary. They enforce laws on imported and exported goods and are involved in the documenting and removal of suspect goods from vehicles for forensic examination. Calculate and collect duty on imports when necessary.

Customs officers also work to prevent people from importing more tobacco or alcohol than is allowed for their own personal consumption. May need to attend court to give evidence when people are prosecuted.

Work Details
A working week of around 36 hours is usual though the work can involve shift work, including evenings, weekends and public holidays. You may have to strip-search people you suspect of smuggling drugs, and also give evidence in court. Searching planes, ships and warehouses can be dirty and physically demanding. Flexitime, part-time work and job-sharing may be available. A uniform and protective clothing are provided.

Qualification

• England, Wales and Northern Ireland
Band 3: For assistant officer entry: usually 5 GCSEs (A*-C) including English language and maths, or equivalent qualifications.

Band 4: For entry at officer level: two A levels and 5 GCSE passes, including English language, or equivalent.

Band 5: For degree course: 2-3 A levels and some GCSEs (A*-C). Exact requirements depend on the degree you take.

• Scotland
Band 3: For assistant officer entry: usually five S grades (1-3) including English language and maths, or similar qualifications.

Band 4: For entry: 3-4 H grades and some S grade passes, including English language, or similar qualifications.

Band 5: For degree course: 3-5 H grades and some S grades (1-3) or similar. Exact requirements depend on the degree you take.

Degree Information
Any degree discipline is acceptable for entry to this job, but degrees in modern languages, business studies or law are useful. For Fast Stream, a second class honours degree is required but most candidates have first or upper second class honours.

Adult Qualifications
Adults without the required qualifications are considered if they have relevant experience, or if they pass a written test and an interview. Entry requirements may be relaxed for adults applying for higher education courses. Access or foundation courses give adults without qualifications a route onto degree courses.

Work Experience
Work experience gives you an insight into what you enjoy and don't enjoy about a job or working environment, as well as the opportunity to acquire new skills. It is also provides valuable information to add to your CV and improves your course application and future employment prospects. The most relevant experience is in jobs involving administration, working in a team, or with the public. You can apply for paid or unpaid work experience in a government department or agency. Fast Stream also arranges summer placement schemes. Check the websites for details.

Entry and Training

Customs officers are part of the civil service, which has strict nationality and residency requirements for entry. It is unusual for new entrants to join as trainee customs officers. Most entrants to this work either join at assistant officer level and work their way up, or join at officer level in other departments of the civil service and transfer across after some experience. Candidates are also recruited centrally through the Civil Service Fast Stream open competition.

Once in post, you have familiarisation training, often involving a residential training course, followed by around nine months training on the job, under the supervision of experienced officers. There is a graduate 'fast track' scheme in the civil service that provides the opportunity to achieve senior management positions usually within four years. Graduates must have at least a 2:2 degree in any subject.

Keyboard skills and computer literacy are required for some jobs. S/NVQs at level 3 in supervisory management and levels 4-5 in management may be available. The Diploma/Welsh Baccalaureate (for 14-19 year olds) in public services may be a useful background for this career but check entry requirements with individual organisations carefully.

Mature entrants are welcomed and the civil service encourages applications from people of every background. Experience and/or qualifications in areas such as finance, administration or management are useful for this job.

Opportunities and Pay

HM Revenue and Customs has around 23,000 staff based in the UK. There is a clear promotion route in the civil service, linked to the appraisal system. There can be opportunities to develop specialisms in areas such as computing or auditing. Officers may have to relocate.

The Single European Market and changes to the work pattern has meant that there are fewer jobs available in this particular area at the moment. Competition for entry is fierce. Once trained, there may be opportunities to change your role (within HM Revenue & Customs) to other areas of work such as in excise and international trade, law enforcement, logistics, and business services and taxes.

Pay and conditions are currently set by HM Revenue & Customs. Uniformed officers usually enter at bands 5-6 and assistants at band 4. Salaries for uniformed officers are £19k-£25k a year; higher and senior officers earn £24k-£38k a year, rising to around £40k a year with experience. Salaries shown do not include London weighting allowance.

Health

You may be asked to take a medical test.

Skills and Qualities

able to cope under pressure, able to report accurately, fair minded, firm manner, good communication skills, honest, IT skills, numeracy skills, observant, tactful

Relevant Subjects

Business and accounting, English, Government and politics, Law, Mathematics, Psychology

Further Information

AGCAS: Government & Public Administration (Job Sector Briefing) (AGCAS) - www.prospects.ac.uk

Civil Service - www.civilservice.gov.uk/jobs

Civil Service Fast Stream (Civil Service) - www.civilservice.gov.uk/jobs/faststream

Diplomas (Foundation, Higher and Advanced) - http://yp.direct.gov.uk/diplomas

HM Revenue & Customs (HMRC) (HM Revenue & Customs) - www.hmrc.gov.uk

Skills for Justice - sector skills council for the UK justice system - www.skillsforjustice.com

TARGETjobs: Public Service (GTI Specialist Publishing Ltd.) - www.groupgti.com

Welsh Baccalaureate - www.wbq.org.uk

▶Working in police, fire & security (2009) (Babcock Lifeskills) - www.babcock-lifeskills.com/

Similar Jobs

Civil Service Excise/VAT Assurance Officer, Civil Service Executive Officer, Civil Service Immigration Officer, Civil Service Revenue Executive, Local Government Administrator, Trading Standards Officer

Civil Service Diplomatic Executive Assistant

also known as: Executive Assistant: Diplomatic Service

CRCI:Administration, Business and Office Work

CLCI:CAB Job Band: 3

Job Description

Diplomatic executive assistants work for the Foreign and Commonwealth Office (FCO), supporting the work of the Diplomatic Service, both in London and overseas. They may work in any of the following sections; registry (central filing system), communications, clerical/secretarial, administration, accounts or in immigration. The routine, though essential work, involves drafting letters, filing papers, retrieving files, handling and managing accounts, or sorting through visa applications. May also help to arrange the schedule for a major conference or for a Ministerial/Royal visit.

Work Details

The work is mainly office based and working 36-37 hrs a week, Monday to Friday, though you may be expected to work additional hours at times. Staff also receive all public holidays and privilege days in addition to their annual leave. There may be flexitime, part time and job-share opportunities. You need to be able to cope with pressure as well as completing many routine tasks on a daily basis. You often deal with confidential information.

Qualification

You must have had at least six months' experience using information technology and other office equipment in an office environment. A minimum of 30 wpm typing speed is essential and is tested.

- **England, Wales and Northern Ireland**

Band 3: Applicants should have a minimum of five GCSEs (A*-C) including English language and maths, or equivalent.

- **Scotland**

Band 3: Applicants should have a minimum of five S grades (1-3) including English language and maths, or similar.

Adult Qualifications

All applications are treated on merit, though mature entrants are expected to have the required minimum entry qualifications and experience.

Work Experience

Relevant work or voluntary experience is always useful and can equip you with skills that you can use in the future and that you can add to your CV. Temporary holiday work in offices via employment agencies is also useful, particularly if you can develop good keyboard skills and a knowledge of the most popular software packages. The civil service does offer a limited work experience placement schemes. Contact the Foreign & Commonwealth Office (FCO) for details.

Entry and Training

Those with PA and secretarial skills and experience have the best chance of entry. There are nationality and residency requirements, but all jobs are open to British nationals, with a good percentage also open to EU nationals and Commonwealth citizens. Your background is checked for security reasons and you have to take a medical test. New entrants take a three-week induction course, followed by training to prepare for their day-to-day work. You usually spend the first two years in London, followed by an overseas posting.

There is continuous on-the-job and in-service training, though this is a single-grade branch with no direct route to other grades in the Diplomatic Service. However, you can take an internal exam called the A to B Competition, which gives candidates the opportunity to transfer. Competition is tough and you are expected to be able to meet similar high standards as successful external applicants.

Training programmes, including business administration apprenticeships, may be available in your area. Advanced apprenticeships leading to qualification at level 3 can also be a route into higher education.

Mature entrants with experience in office skills of at least six months are preferred and you must have a minimum typing speed of 30wpm. Any other qualifications held are considered and relevant work experience is taken into account, in particular good IT and customer service skills. Those with previous experience as a personal assistant (PA) may have an advantage. An ability in another language is also an advantage.

Opportunities and Pay

You are usually based at the Foreign & Commonwealth Office (FCO) in London, and then for regular periods of time in Embassies, High Commissions and Consulates overseas in over 190 countries worldwide. Work may also be with the European Commission or United Nations. With experience and merit you can progress to a B*4 operational officer post. B* administration posts are part of the assistants' grade (AST) in the EU. Entrants can start at junior filing clerk level and progress through the promotional levels leading to personal assistant. Check the EU website for details.

In London, an executive assistant (A2) has a starting salary of £21,653 a year (inclusive of a £3k London allowance). This increases with experience. Additional allowances are paid for living overseas including rent-free accommodation, educational allowances for dependent children, and one or more fare-paid journeys to and from the UK.

Health

You have to pass a medical, to show that you are fit and healthy and able to cope with climates of different countries.

Skills and Qualities

able to cope under pressure, able to prioritise work, able to work both on your own and in a team, attention to detail, committed, flexible and adaptable, good communication skills, good written English, IT skills, patient, willing to train and work away from home

Relevant Subjects

Business and accounting, English, Geography, Government and politics, ICT/Computer studies, Modern Foreign Languages

Further Information

AGCAS: Government & Public Administration (Job Sector Briefing) (AGCAS) - www.prospects.ac.uk

British International Studies Association (British International Studies Association) - www.bisa.ac.uk

Careers in British Intelligence - www.careersinbritishintelligence.co.uk/

Careers in the Foreign & Commonwealth Office (Foreign and Commonwealth Office) - www.fco.gov.uk/en/

Civil Service - www.civilservice.gov.uk/jobs

Civil Service Commissioners' Information Leaflet (Office of the Civil Service Commissioners) - www.civilservicecommissioners.org/

Government Skills - sector skills council for central government - www.government-skills.gov.uk

National School of Government - www.nationalschool.gov.uk

Addresses

Civil Service Commission (Northern Ireland)
HRConnect, PO Box 1089, 2nd Floor, The Metro Building,
6-9 Donegall Square South, Belfast BT1 9EW
Phone: 0800 1300 330
Web: www.irecruit.nicsrecruitment.gov.uk/

Northern Ireland Assembly
Communications Office Northern Ireland Assembly Parliament Buildings Ballymiscaw Stormont, Belfast BT4 3XX
Phone: +44 (0)28 9052 1333
Web: www.niassembly.gov.uk

Scottish Executive
St Andrew's House, Regent Road, Edinburgh EH1 3DG
Phone: +44 (0)131 556 8400
Web: www.scotland.gov.uk

Welsh Assembly Government
Cathays Park, Cardiff CF10 3NQ
Phone: 0845 010 3300 (UK only)
Web: www.wales.gov.uk

Similar Jobs

Civil Service Administrative Officer, Local Government Administrative Assistant, Personal Assistant, Secretary, Secretary: Bilingual

Civil Service Diplomatic Officer

also known as: Diplomatic Service Officer (DSO)

CRCI:Administration, Business and Office Work
CLCI:CAB — Job Band: 5

Job Description

Diplomatic officers work for the Foreign and Commonwealth Office (FCO) to promote and protect British interests worldwide. They support the work of ministers of the government and advise on the formulation of Britain's foreign policy. May organise visits for ministers abroad. May report to London on political and economic developments in the host country. Also study the local trading environment and advise British businesses. May brief the local media and deal with general enquiries about the UK to promote British policy. Also work in consulates, high commissions, missions or embassies, giving help and advice to UK nationals abroad.

Managing staff is an important part of the work. This includes clerical staff in the UK and locally-engaged staff on overseas postings. First overseas postings usually involve work in the visa or consular section.

Work Details

Usually work 9am to 5pm, Monday to Friday, but additional hours may be required, including evening or weekends at times, and depending on the demands of the job. Often you may be on call 24 hours a day. You have to be prepared to work in any country in the world at any time. About two thirds of your working life is likely to be spent abroad. When working overseas there are no set working hours. You need to be flexible as you are likely to be posted to a new job every two to three years.

Diplomatic Service Officers (DSOs) come into contact with a wide range of people, such as senior officials of the host country and UK nationals at home and abroad. The work can be very demanding and you may have to make difficult decisions at times.

Qualification

- **England, Wales and Northern Ireland**

Band 5: For degree courses: 2-3 A levels and some GCSEs (A*-C) usually including English and maths, or equivalent. Exact requirements depend on the degree you take.

- **Scotland**

Band 5: For degree courses: 3-5 H grades and some S grades (1-3), usually including English and maths, or similar qualifications. Exact requirements depend on the degree you take.

Degree Information

A degree in any discipline is acceptable. Foreign languages, politics, history, international relations, law, geography (human), American studies and European studies all give useful background.

Adult Qualifications

All applications are treated on merit, though mature entrants are expected to have at least the required minimum entry qualifications and experience. An ability in one or more foreign languages is useful. Entry requirements may be relaxed for adults applying for degree courses or there may be special entry routes, such as Access courses. Check with universities for details.

Work Experience

Entry to this job is highly competitive and it is important that you try to do some relevant work or voluntary experience before applying. The most relevant areas of experience include any work that involves administration, team working or working with the public. You can also apply for paid or unpaid work experience in a particular government department or agency by contacting their human resources department directly, or through the civil service website.

The Foreign and Commonwealth Office (FCO) offers two annual placement schemes. These are open to university students in their second year of undergraduate study. Contact the FCO for details.

Entry and Training

There are strict nationality regulations and your background is checked for security reasons. The selection process is very competitive and applications are on an annual basis. There are two routes into this job; Operational Officer entry point, which deals with the more practical aspects of diplomatic work and the Policy entry point that helps to form political, economic and commercial policy. Those entering at Policy entry level require at least a second class degree, whilst those entering at Operational entry level usually require a degree, or a combination of academic qualifications, and set periods of work experience.

A Policy entry Fast Stream application programme is available to graduates who have a first or second class honours degree, or equivalent. This programme prepares entrants for a high level career within the civil service. Entry is highly competitive and involves on-line assessments and tests to gauge a candidate's verbal and numerical reasoning skills. This is followed by a job-related 'e-tray' exercise that takes place under test conditions at regional centres around the country. Successful candidates undergo a one-day assessment centre, followed by a Final Selection Board interview. Check www.faststream.gov.uk for details of the Fast Stream selection process and www.fco.gov.uk for details of all other routes in to the diplomatic service.

Knowledge of foreign languages and life/work abroad are taken into account. Postgraduate study is an advantage though not a requirement. All new entrants have an induction course on the work, structure and aims of the Service and on policy drafting. The first two years are based in London, following an agreed training plan involving on-the-job training and work-related courses, as well as courses to develop necessary skills, such as effective speaking and management skills. Before the first posting abroad, you receive training in relevant areas, including languages.

Mature entrants are welcomed, and in particular, applications from those with public administration, management and commercial experience, and/or an ability in one or more foreign languages.

Opportunities and Pay

You are employed by the Foreign and Commonwealth Office (FCO) and diplomatic missions overseas; known as High Commissions (Commonwealth countries) and Embassies (all other countries). Jobs are available in London and abroad. Competition is fierce for the very few vacancies. There is a formal graded promotion structure and promotion is strictly on merit and experience.

A diplomatic officer working for the Foreign Office has a starting salary of around £22.5k a year (inclusive of a £3k London allowance). A senior executive officer (SEO) can earn around £35k a year and a top civil servant can earn more than £60k a year. 'Fast stream' entrants start at around £24k, rising to around £39k after promotion. Additional allowances for living overseas include rent-free accommodation, educational allowances for dependent children, and one or more fare-paid journeys to and from the UK.

Health

You have to pass a medical assessment to show that you are physically fit, healthy and able to cope with the demands of working overseas.

Skills and Qualities

ability in one or more languages, able to report accurately, analytical skills, good communication skills, good interpersonal skills, good organisational skills, good written English, information handling skills, IT skills, motivated, objective, persuasive

Relevant Subjects

Business and accounting, Economics, English, Geography, Government and politics, History, Law, Mathematics, Modern Foreign Languages

Further Information

AGCAS: Government & Public Administration (Job Sector Briefing) (AGCAS) - www.prospects.ac.uk

British International Studies Association (British International Studies Association) - www.bisa.ac.uk

Careers in British Intelligence - www.careersinbritishintelligence.co.uk/

Careers in the Foreign & Commonwealth Office (Foreign and Commonwealth Office) - www.fco.gov.uk/en/

Civil Service - www.civilservice.gov.uk/jobs

Civil Service Commissioners' Information Leaflet (Office of the Civil Service Commissioners) - www.civilservicecommissioners.org/

Civil Service Fast Stream (Civil Service) - www.civilservice.gov.uk/jobs/faststream

Government Skills - sector skills council for central government - www.government-skills.gov.uk

How to Pass the Civil Service Qualifying Tests (2010) (Kogan Page) - www.koganpage.com

National School of Government - www.nationalschool.gov.uk

TARGETjobs: Public Service (GTI Specialist Publishing Ltd.) - www.groupgti.com

Addresses

Civil Service Commission (Northern Ireland)
HRConnect, PO Box 1089, 2nd Floor, The Metro Building,
6-9 Donegall Square South, Belfast BT1 9EW
Phone: 0800 1300 330
Web: www.irecruit.nicsrecruitment.gov.uk/

Northern Ireland Assembly
Communications Office Northern Ireland Assembly Parliament Buildings Ballymiscaw Stormont, Belfast BT4 3XX
Phone: +44 (0)28 9052 1333
Web: www.niassembly.gov.uk

Scottish Executive
St Andrew's House, Regent Road, Edinburgh EH1 3DG
Phone: +44 (0)131 556 8400
Web: www.scotland.gov.uk

Welsh Assembly Government
Cathays Park, Cardiff CF10 3NQ
Phone: 0845 010 3300 (UK only)
Web: www.wales.gov.uk

Similar Jobs

Civil Service Diplomatic Executive Assistant, Civil Service EU Administrator, Civil Service Fast Streamer, Civil Service Immigration Officer, Economist, Interpreter: European Union, Local Government Administrator

Civil Service EU Administrator

also known as: European Commission Administrator

CRCI:Administration, Business and Office Work
CLCI:CAG Job Band: 4 to 5

Job Description

EU administrators are involved in the development and implementation of European Union (EU) policies in areas such as agriculture, social affairs, law, transport, economy, or the environment. They work in the institutions of the European Commission (EC), the European Parliament, Council of Ministers and the Court of Justice. Work can include the management of a large economic aid programme to the third world, monitoring existing policies in areas such as health and agriculture, or working with external relations services overseas. Administrators draft reports, legislation and regulations, and proposals on EU issues. Also have responsibility for the management of people, finances and other resources.

Administrators have contact with individuals and organisations throughout Europe, as well as liaising with other EU institutions and officials. Also manage EU relations with non-member countries.

Work Details

The normal working week is 37 hours, Monday to Friday, although you are expected to be available for work at other times to meet important deadlines, or during negotiating sessions. The work is mainly office based with administrators spending a lot of time at their desks, in meetings and attending conferences.

Qualification

Graduates can apply for Administrator (AD) positions and non-graduates for Assistant (AST) grade positions. All entrants require a thorough knowledge of one official EU language and a satisfactory knowledge of another.

• England, Wales and Northern Ireland

Band 4: For entry to AST grade posts: two A levels and some GCSEs (A*-C) or equivalent. Applicants must also have two/three years' relevant work experience.

Band 5: For degree course: 2-3 A levels and some GCSEs (A*-C), usually including English and maths, or equivalent. Exact requirements depend on the degree you take.

• Scotland

Band 4: For entry to AST grade posts: three H grades and some S grades (1-3), or similar. Applicants must also have two/three years' relevant work experience.

Band 5: For degree course: 3-5 H grades and some S grades (1-3), usually including English and maths, or similar qualifications. Exact requirements depend on the degree you take.

Degree Information

A degree in any discipline is acceptable, though some posts may require a degree in law, economics, accounting or statistics. Modern European languages are also useful.

Adult Qualifications

For adult entry, a degree level qualification in any discipline is required for AD posts. Entry at AST grade is possible with relevant experience and/or professional training. Entry requirements may be relaxed for adults applying for degree courses or there may be special entry routes, such as Access or foundation courses. Check with universities for details. The Open University also offers a degree in European studies.

Work Experience

Entry to this job is highly competitive and it is important that you try to do some relevant work or voluntary experience before applying. Any experience of work abroad is an advantage as is any experience of working with the public, particularly in roles that demonstrate strong communication skills. Many of the EU institutions offer traineeships for graduates. These last between three and five months. Candidates must have a university degree. A modest living allowance is usually available. This is extremely advantageous for entry but gives no guarantee of a permanent job. Check the scheme website on www.eu-careers-gateway.gov.uk for details.

Entry and Training

There are strict nationality and residency requirements but all jobs are open to British and other EU nationals. Candidates must be fluent in one EU language and have a satisfactory knowledge of another. There is an open competition process of recruitment that is usually in three stages. Those who pass a series of tests and an interview over a period of several months have their names published on a reserve list and can then contact departments that interest them though there is no guarantee of a job offer. Notice of the open competitions is published in the Official Journal of the European Communities, on the main EU recruitment website and also in the national press. Recruitment can often take more than a year due to the complexity of advertising simultaneously in all member states.

There is one basic administrator grade of entry for graduates without significant professional experience. This is known as AD5. Higher levels of entry are also available, such as AD6, for graduates with a minimum of three years' relevant experience. Knowledge of a second official EU language to roughly A level/H grade standard is necessary, although no formal language qualification is required. Non-graduates with two to three years' professional experience can enter as 'Assistants' (AST) and can progress to AD grade.

After appointment, administrators receive a series of induction courses and professional training. Intensive language courses are also available and encouraged. Before promotion, officials need to demonstrate the ability to work in a third language. A Fast Stream Development Programme is available to graduates who have a first or second class honours degree or equivalent. This programme prepares entrants for a high level career within the civil service. Check the Fast Stream website www.faststream.gov.uk for details.

Mature applicants may require two or three years' relevant experience for some grades. For entrants between 18-25 years, there may be some financial support for a relevant short course, research visit or internship for European/international studies at higher education level. Contact the Gilbert Murray Trust or the British International Studies Association (BISA) for details.

Opportunities and Pay

Competition for entry is fierce, but currently there is a shortage of well-qualified British candidates. Most likely you will be based in Brussels or Luxembourg, although a small number of staff work in Commission offices in member states or in EU delegations throughout the world. Assistant grade (AST) staff may be promoted to more senior posts, or move to category Administrator (AD) by internal or open competition. There are also excellent prospects for category AD staff.

Those employed in the civil service as a European Fast Streamer work on EU policy issues and receive selective training to get through the EU entry competitions. If successful, you resign from the UK civil service and become an EU institution employee. If unsuccessful, you remain an employee of the UK civil service.

Salary rates are based on the highest member state and are usually attractive to UK applicants. They are also weighted according to the cost of living in the country concerned. Basic monthly commission salaries range from 2.3k a month for a newly recruited AST 1 to around 16k a month for a top level AD official with wide experience. For those working abroad, salaries are also enhanced by an expatriation allowance, equal to 16% of basic salary.

Further allowances are added according to personal circumstances such as a household allowance (for officials who are the principal earner in a household, equal to 5% of basic salary), educational allowances for dependent children, one or more fare-paid journeys to and from the UK, and a relocation package.

Skills and Qualities

ability in one or more languages, able to manage people, efficient, good communication skills, good written English, information handling skills, initiative, IT skills, motivated, objective, persuasive, sound judgement

Relevant Subjects

Business and accounting, Economics, English, Geography, Government and politics, History, Law, Modern Foreign Languages

Further Information

AGCAS: Government & Public Administration (Job Sector Briefing) (AGCAS) - www.prospects.ac.uk

British International Studies Association (British International Studies Association) - www.bisa.ac.uk

British International Studies Association (British International Studies Association) - www.bisa.ac.uk

Civil Service - www.civilservice.gov.uk/jobs

Civil Service Commissioners' Information Leaflet (Office of the Civil Service Commissioners) - www.civilservicecommissioners.org/

Civil Service Fast Stream (Civil Service) - www.civilservice.gov.uk/jobs/faststream

European Personnel Selection Office (EU Careers) (Office for Official Publications of the EC) http://europa.eu/epso

Government Skills - sector skills council for central government - www.government-skills.gov.uk

How to Pass the Civil Service Qualifying Tests (2010) (Kogan Page) - www.koganpage.com

National School of Government - www.nationalschool.gov.uk

Open University - www.open.ac.uk

TARGETjobs: Public Service (GTI Specialist Publishing Ltd.) - www.groupgti.com

The EU in the UK (EC) - www.ec.europa.eu/unitedkingdom

▶Working with languages (2010) (Babcock Lifeskills) - www.babcock-lifeskills.com/

Similar Jobs

Civil Service Administrative Officer, Civil Service Diplomatic Officer, Civil Service Executive Officer, Civil Service Fast Streamer, Interpreter: European Union, Local Government Administrator

Civil Service Excise/VAT Assurance Officer

also known as: Excise Officer, VAT Assurance Officer

CRCI:Administration, Business and Office Work

CLCI:CAB — Job Band: 3 to 5

Job Description

Excise officers ensure that businesses pay the correct amount of excise duty and/or value added tax (VAT) each year. This tax is charged on most business transactions made in the UK or the Isle of Man. It also includes goods and some services known as 'taxable supplies' such as renting and hiring out goods, selling new and used goods, or providing a service such as hairdressing or painting and decorating.

Officers visit business premises to check and audit their accounts and also to give advice on ways of accurately presenting and recording the required financial information. They prepare reports and ensure that each business pays within the agreed time. May be required to seek legal action to enforce the law and make businesses pay their calculated duty and/or taxes. Also work closely with other agencies, such as the Home Office and police authorities. On occasions, may need to attend a court of law as a prosecution witness.

Work Details

Work is based in an office, though you travel around a specified area to visit local businesses. Hours of work are usually 36 hrs a week over five days. Flexitime, part-time work and job-sharing may be available. Sometimes you may need to work on reports outside of office hours to complete the necessary paperwork.

Qualification

• England, Wales and Northern Ireland

Band 3: For assistant officer entry: usually 5 GCSEs (A*-C) including English language and maths, or equivalent qualifications.

Band 4: For entry at officer level: two A levels and some GCSEs (A*-C), usually including English and maths or equivalent.

Band 5: For degree courses: 2-3 A levels and some GCSEs (A*-C), usually including English and maths, or equivalent. Exact requirements depend on the degree you take.

• Scotland

Band 3: For assistant officer entry: usually five S grades (1-3) including English language and maths, or similar qualifications.

Band 4: For entry at officer level: 2-3 H grades and some S grades (1-3), often including English and maths or similar qualifications.

Band 5: For degree courses: 3-5 H grades and some S grades (1-3), usually including English and maths, or similar. Exact requirements depend on the degree you take.

Degree Information

Any degree discipline is acceptable for entry to this job, but degrees in modern languages, business studies or law are useful.

Adult Qualifications

Adults without the required qualifications are considered if they have relevant experience, or if they pass a written test and an interview. Entry requirements may be relaxed for adults applying for higher education courses. Access or foundation courses give adults without qualifications a route onto degree courses.

Work Experience

Work experience gives you an insight into what you enjoy and don't enjoy about a job or working environment, as well as the opportunity to acquire new skills. It also provides valuable information to add to your CV, and improves your course application and future employment prospects. HM Revenue &

Customs (HMRC) offers an eight-week summer internship scheme which is a graduate-level work placement open to all students in their penultimate year of study. Contact HMRC for details.

Entry and Training

Excise officers are part of the civil service (HM Revenue & Customs, HMRC), which has strict nationality and residency requirements for entry. Posts within the civil service are open to British nationals, as well as many that are open to European/ Commonwealth citizens.

Depending on your qualifications and/or experience, you can enter at administrative assistant level (job bands 1 and 2), administration officer level (job bands 3 and 4) or executive officer level (job bands 5 and 6). It is possible to progress through the job bands or come straight in at executive level if you have the requisite qualifications. Those without the required formal qualifications can take a suitability test before going through the rest of the selection process.

Administration officers and assistants attend an introductory course, have training on the job, under the supervision of an experienced member of staff and can also take part in local training programmes. Executive officers have a structured induction programme including a residential week and a foundation course. This is followed by technical on-the-job training for a further nine months. Keyboard skills are required for some jobs and it is also beneficial to be computer literate. You may be expected to study for relevant professional qualifications, such as becoming a chartered tax adviser, or for basic qualifications in indirect taxation. All civil service employees take part in a regular appraisal and staff development programme, which helps to identify your training needs throughout your career within the service.

Entry on to the graduate development programme leads to the Tax Professional Development Programme. This provides the opportunity to become a senior tax professional, usually within four years. Graduates must have at least a 2:2 degree in any subject. HMRC also run a Management Fast Track programme. This incorporates a six week core module, some of which is at your local office, and a two week residential course. After this, you begin studying for your Chartered Management Institute (CMI) exams. Trainee managers are appointed a mentor and development manager to support them and further on-the-job training (including a variety of six month placements) offers valuable work experience.

Mature entrants are welcome and those with relevant professional qualifications equivalent to degree level may apply for direct entry to specific recruitment programmes. The civil service encourages applications from people of every background. Experience and/or qualifications in areas such as finance, administration or management are useful for this job.

Opportunities and Pay

There are opportunities throughout the UK and you may be required to move to another part of the country. You can progress to a more senior officer grade, including higher officer and senior officer. The civil service has a structured promotion system and you may have the opportunity to move into other areas of work, such as logistics, auditing or IT.

Pay and conditions are currently set by HM Revenue & Customs (HMRC) and assistant officers start on a salary of £15k rising to £19k a year. Officers earn from £20k-£26k and graduate starting salaries range from £25k-£39k. With increased responsibility and experience, higher level salaries range from £43k-£66k. Salaries shown do not include London weighting allowance.

Health

You may be asked to take a medical test.

Skills and Qualities

Able to report accurately, able to work both on your own and in a team, analytical skills, enquiring mind, firm manner, good communication skills, good interpersonal skills, IT skills, logical, methodical, numeracy skills, observant, tactful

Relevant Subjects

Business and accounting, Economics, English, Government and politics, ICT/Computer studies, Law, Mathematics, Psychology

Further Information

AGCAS: Government & Public Administration (Job Sector Briefing) (AGCAS) - www.prospects.ac.uk

Civil Service - www.civilservice.gov.uk/jobs

Civil Service Commissioners' Information Leaflet (Office of the Civil Service Commissioners) - www.civilservicecommissioners.org/

Civil Service Fast Stream (Civil Service) - www.civilservice.gov.uk/jobs/faststream

Civil Service, Real Careers, Real Opportunities (Civil Service and Local Appointments Commissioners) - www.publicjobs.ie/downloads/careerinfo.pdf

Government Skills - sector skills council for central government - www.government-skills.gov.uk

HM Revenue & Customs (HMRC) (HM Revenue & Customs) - www.hmrc.gov.uk

How to Pass the Civil Service Qualifying Tests (2010) (Kogan Page) - www.koganpage.com

National School of Government - www.nationalschool.gov.uk

TARGETjobs: Public Service (GTI Specialist Publishing Ltd.) - www.groupgti.com

Addresses

Chartered Management Institute (CMI)
Management House, Cottingham Road, Corby NN17 1TT
Phone: +44 (0)1536 204 222
Web: www.managers.org.uk

Similar Jobs

Civil Service Customs Officer, Civil Service Executive Officer, Civil Service Fast Streamer, Local Government Administrator, Trading Standards Officer

Civil Service Executive Officer

also known as: Civil Service Junior Manager

CRCI:Administration, Business and Office Work

CLCI:CAB Job Band: 4 to 5

Job Description

Executive officers are the first line of management in the civil service and undertake general office work in a particular government department or agency. The work varies greatly from department to department. May manage a section overseeing the work, training and development of other administrative staff. Also allocate the staff's work/responsibilities and manage their performance and deal with personnel and welfare issues where appropriate. Support senior staff, arrange and attend meetings, prepare papers and statistics, write minutes and reports.

May carry out research, and produce and present written information in a variety of formats (mostly in Word, Excel, PowerPoint) and the civil service document management system. Also assist senior civil servants working on government policy and provide advice/information to the public. Can choose to specialise in areas such as tax and fraud investigation, immigration, accountancy, or customs and excise control.

Liaise with a wide range of people and organisations. Most of the civil service's computer programming and systems work is the responsibility of executive officers.

Work Details

Most executive officers are based in offices and work around 37 hours a week; Monday to Friday. Part-time work, flexitime and job-sharing are possible. The work of some executive officers involves visiting business premises or people's homes. A lot of time is spent on paperwork, statistics, numerical work and using computer systems. Many government offices, such as Jobcentre Plus offices and Benefit Agencies, are open to the public. You may deal with difficult telephone calls and complex queries. Some of your decisions may be unpopular and work can be stressful at times.

Qualification

• England, Wales and Northern Ireland

Band 4: For direct entry: usually two A levels and some GCSEs (A*-C) including English, or equivalent. Applicants with relevant experience and core competencies may be accepted without these qualifications.

Band 5: For degree, prior to executive officer entry: 2-3 A levels and some GCSEs (A*-C) usually including English and maths, or equivalent. Exact requirements depend on the degree you take.

• Scotland

Band 4: For direct entry: usually 3-4 H grades and some S grades (1-3) including English, or similar. Applicants with relevant experience and core competencies may be accepted without these qualifications.

Band 5: For degree, prior to executive officer entry: 3-5 H grades and some S grades (1-3), usually including English and maths, or similar qualifications. Exact requirements depend on the degree you take.

Degree Information

A degree in any discipline is acceptable for entry to this job. Management and business studies, or similar, give useful background knowledge.

Adult Qualifications

Adults may need the minimum entry qualifications. However some departments recruit on the basis of relevant experience and competences in certain areas, such as interpersonal or financial skills, rather than on academic qualifications. Entry requirements may be relaxed for adults applying for higher education courses.

Work Experience

Entry to this job is competitive and it is important that you try to do some relevant work or voluntary experience before applying for a job. The most relevant areas of experience include any work that involves administration, team working, or working with the public. You can also apply for paid or unpaid work experience in a particular government department or agency by contacting their human resources department directly, or through the civil service website. One or two-day visits may also be offered by some departments.

Entry and Training

There are strict nationality and residency requirements but all jobs are open to UK nationals, with 75% also open to EU nationals and Commonwealth citizens. Entry requirements vary depending on the department that you apply to, but competition is fierce and around half of entrants are graduates. Selection involves qualifying tests and selection boards. You can also become an executive officer by working up through the administrative grades. Those working for the Welsh Assembly government are usually expected to be able to speak Welsh. Check the Civil Service Recruitment Gateway (www.careers.civil-service.gov.uk) for a central source of information on vacancies and careers.

Training is on the job, usually following an induction course. There is ongoing in-service training for job-related skills and for the development of management skills. It is possible to study for higher qualifications. The National School of Government offers a range of courses, which are specifically aimed at providing the necessary skills and knowledge required by the civil service.

A Fast Stream Development Programme is available to graduates who have a first or second class honours degree or equivalent. This programme prepares entrants for a high level career within the civil service and many start at executive officer level. An option to prepare for working in the EU is also available. You may be able to obtain S/NVQ levels 3-5 in supervisory management or in management.

Mature applicants with relevant experience and/or qualifications are welcome to apply. Those who have gained experience as a civil service administrative officer may be promoted to an executive officer.

Opportunities and Pay

Jobs are available throughout the UK and are mainly in towns and cities. There are many different government offices and agencies such as HM Revenue & Customs, the Home Office, Department for Culture, Media and Sport, and the Cabinet Office. You can specialise, for example in defence issues or immigration control, educational policy, employment issues, social security, estate management or the environment. Promotion to higher management levels is on experience and merit.

Prospects are improved by training. The civil service encourages further development and training through regular work appraisals and performance feedback. You may get financial help for courses which you take in your own time. Work abroad is possible.

Pay varies depending on department and location, but generally starting salaries for an executive officer (EO) are around £19k-£23k and with more experience, salaries can rise to around £24k-£28k. Following promotion, you can earn £38k or more. Top civil servants can earn over £60k a year.

Health

You may be asked to have a medical examination.

Skills and Qualities

able to manage people, able to take responsibility, able to work to deadlines, analytical skills, good communication skills, good organisational skills, good written English, initiative, IT skills, leadership qualities, sound judgement

Relevant Subjects

Business and accounting, Economics, English, Government and politics, ICT/Computer studies

Further Information

AGCAS: Government & Public Administration (Job Sector Briefing) (AGCAS) - www.prospects.ac.uk

Careers in British Intelligence - www.careersinbritishintelligence.co.uk/

Civil Service - www.civilservice.gov.uk/jobs

Civil Service Commissioners' Information Leaflet (Office of the Civil Service Commissioners) - www.civilservicecommissioners.org/

Civil Service Fast Stream (Civil Service) - www.civilservice.gov.uk/jobs/faststream

Government Skills - sector skills council for central government - www.government-skills.gov.uk

How to Pass the Civil Service Qualifying Tests (2010) (Kogan Page) - www.koganpage.com

National School of Government - www.nationalschool.gov.uk

TARGETjobs: Public Service (GTI Specialist Publishing Ltd.) - www.groupgti.com

Addresses

Civil Service Commission (Northern Ireland)
HRConnect, PO Box 1089, 2nd Floor, The Metro Building,
6-9 Donegall Square South, Belfast BT1 9EW
Phone: 0800 1300 330
Web: www.irecruit.nicsrecruitment.gov.uk/

Northern Ireland Assembly
Communications Office Northern Ireland Assembly Parliament Buildings Ballymiscaw Stormont, Belfast BT4 3XX
Phone: +44 (0)28 9052 1333
Web: www.niassembly.gov.uk

Scottish Executive
St Andrew's House, Regent Road, Edinburgh EH1 3DG
Phone: +44 (0)131 556 8400
Web: www.scotland.gov.uk

Welsh Assembly Government
Cathays Park, Cardiff CF10 3NQ
Phone: 0845 010 3300 (UK only)
Web: www.wales.gov.uk

Similar Jobs

Civil Service Administrative Officer, Civil Service Diplomatic Officer, Civil Service EU Administrator, Civil Service Operational Research Analyst, Human Resources Officer/Manager, Local Government Administrator, Office Manager

Civil Service Fast Streamer

CRCI:Administration, Business and Office Work
CLCI:CAB Job Band: 5

Job Description

Fast stream civil servants are selected through a fast stream development programme for high levels of management early in their careers. They complete a series of job placements, moving frequently between different projects and sections within a particular department. They are required to have, or develop, in-depth knowledge of a subject area and act as a consultant/expert in their field. Their role is to support ministers in the government department to which they are assigned. This may be in departments that include defence, transport, environment, diplomatic and security, science and engineering, health, education and the arts, or in international development.

May also be posted to other departments and agencies for a period of time. This may include postings to Europe or to international partners such as the USA. Some choose to become a Clerk to the House of Commons or Lords, a statistician, or represent those in the European Parliament. Fast streamers may work on research and analysis of a particular area, and are often involved in forming government policy and assist in putting it into action.

Work Details

Officially work a basic 39 hr week, Monday to Friday, although very long hours, late nights and early mornings are common. Fast stream candidates have some choice in which department they work. The fast stream development programme is very demanding; work is often under pressure, with long hours and to tight deadlines. However, there are opportunities for working part time, flexible working, and for job sharing.

Qualification

- **England, Wales and Northern Ireland**

Band 5: For degree courses: 2-3 A levels and some GCSEs (A*-C) usually including English and maths, or equivalent. Exact requirements depend on the degree you take.

- **Scotland**

Band 5: For degree courses: 3-5 H grades and some S grades (1-3) often including English and maths, or similar qualifications. Exact requirements depend on the degree you take.

Degree Information

All subjects are acceptable though you need at least a 2:2 honours degree (2:1 for economists or technology in business) or equivalent. Some departments, such as the Ministry of Defence, require specialist degrees in their subject area. Relevant postgraduate courses are also available.

Adult Qualifications

Entry requirements may be relaxed for adults applying for degree courses or there may be special entry routes, such as foundation or Access courses. Check with universities for details.

Work Experience

Work experience is always useful as entry to this career is competitive; apply to individual government departments directly to arrange this. Vacation visits and sandwich course placements are also available in many departments. Voluntary work for charities, non-government organisations (NGOs) and other political institutions may also be useful, although impartiality is a quality looked for in applicants.

Entry and Training

To apply for the fast stream you must have at least a first or second class honours degree. Alternatively, those already employed in the civil service can be nominated by their department. Entry requirements can vary between departments. For example, if applying for the economist or science and engineering options you must have a relevant degree, and for the European fast stream you must be fluent in at least one other language. Applicants choose the fast stream option that is most of interest, such as the diplomatic service or central departments. Check the Civil Service Fast Stream website for further details.

There are strict nationality and residency requirements but all jobs are open to UK nationals, a few are also open to those from EU countries and the Commonwealth. All applicants must pass stages of competitive written and psychometric tests and interviews, and applications must be made online. Shortlisted candidates are invited to London for a one-day assessment. This whole process takes around eight months in total, and only around 2.5% of applicants are offered jobs.

Once accepted, fast streamers follow an individually tailored training programme, which can last up to five years. On-the-job training is supplemented by formal training courses and periods of self study. You do a series of work placements (each lasting between twelve and eighteen months). All training is geared towards developing competencies in flexible thinking, results orientation, decisiveness, relationship building and making an impact. There are a range of foundation courses at the National School of Government which help you develop the skills and knowledge needed. There are opportunities to study for professional qualifications, including an MBA. You are expected to continue your professional development (CPD) throughout your career.

There is no upper age limit for Fast Track application. Mature applicants, particularly with relevant work experience and qualifications, are welcomed.

Opportunities and Pay

Competition for posts is fierce. You are employed by the civil service in one of a wide range of departments or agencies, some of which may include: Environment, Food and Rural Affairs, Fisheries Research Services, Foreign and Commonwealth Office, Forestry Commission, Children, Schools and Families, Government Communications HQ, Defence Procurement, Culture, Media and Sport, Transport, and the Home Office.

Pay varies according to the department you work for but the average starting salary for fast streamers in London is £24.5k. On promotion salaries rise to around £39k year. With increased responsibility top civil servants are paid more than £60k a year. There is also a very good non-contributory pension scheme and other benefits that can include assistance with childcare, career breaks and crhche facilities.

Skills and Qualities

able to cope under pressure, able to prioritise work, able to work to deadlines, aptitude for teamwork, decisive, good communication skills, good interpersonal skills, good written English, information handling skills, public speaking ability, self-motivated

Relevant Subjects

Business and accounting, Economics, English, Government and politics, ICT/Computer studies, Mathematics, Modern Foreign Languages

Further Information

AGCAS: Government & Public Administration (Job Sector Briefing) (AGCAS) - www.prospects.ac.uk

Careers in British Intelligence www.careersinbritishintelligence.co.uk/

Careers in the Foreign & Commonwealth Office (Foreign and Commonwealth Office) - www.fco.gov.uk/en/

Civil Service - www.civilservice.gov.uk/jobs

Civil Service Commissioners' Information Leaflet (Office of the Civil Service Commissioners) - www.civilservicecommissioners.org/

Civil Service Fast Stream (Civil Service) - www.civilservice.gov.uk/jobs/faststream

European Personnel Selection Office (EU Careers) (Office for Official Publications of the EC) - http://europa.eu/epso

Government Skills - sector skills council for central government - www.government-skills.gov.uk

How to Pass the Civil Service Qualifying Tests (2010) (Kogan Page) - www.koganpage.com

National School of Government - www.nationalschool.gov.uk

TARGETjobs: Public Service (GTI Specialist Publishing Ltd.) - www.groupgti.com

The EU in the UK (EC) - www.ec.europa.eu/unitedkingdom

Similar Jobs

Civil Service Diplomatic Officer, Civil Service Executive Officer, Economist, Local Government Administrator, Political/ Parliamentary Researcher, Statistician

Civil Service Immigration Officer

also known as: Immigration Officer

CRCI:Security and Armed Forces

CLCI:CAB Job Band: 3 to 5

Job Description

Immigration officers (IOs) are based at airports and seaports around the UK, both large and small, and at the Channel Tunnel and are responsible for maintaining an effective immigration control. Check that those entering the UK have the correct documentation including passports, landing cards and other identification documents. Also have to detect forged passports and other illegal documents. Interview people who come from a wide range of nationalities, cultures and backgrounds. Ask them about the length and purpose of their visit to this country and sometimes decide to interview people in more depth.

Need to ask searching personal questions and perhaps prevent some people from immediately entering the country. Supervise and manage a team of assistants, organise surveillance and carry out intelligence-based activities. Undertake, with police assistance, immigration visits to identify people who have no authority to remain in the UK.

Assistant immigration officers (AIOs) provide administrative support and help set up interviews, take fingerprints, arrange passenger removals, carry out some surveillance work and deal with enquiries from other Agency offices.

Work Details

Work for the Border & Immigration Agency, which is part of the Home Office. All staff work around 36 hrs a week. Overtime is sometimes necessary. Immigration officers/assistants work shifts involving unsociable hours, weekends and public holidays. Usually you work indoors at a desk dealing with people arriving in the UK from all over the world, who may be unable to speak English. Some are upset, angry and perhaps aggressive and you have to remain helpful and sensitive towards them. Difficult decisions have to be made and some of your decisions are unpopular.

Qualification

Formal qualifications are not always required for some jobs but you need to demonstrate strong written and verbal communication skills. The ability to communicate in a foreign language is an advantage.

• England, Wales and Northern Ireland

Band 3: For entry as an assistant immigration officer: a minimum of 5 GCSEs (A*-C) including English, or other equivalent qualification.

Band 4: For direct entry as an immigration officer: 2 A levels and 5 GCSEs (A*-C) including English, or equivalent.

Band 5: For degree course, prior to entry: 2-3 A levels and some GCSEs (A*-C). Exact requirements depend on the degree you take.

• Scotland

Band 3: For entry as an assistant immigration officer: a minimum of five S grades (1-3) including English, or similar qualifications. Many applicants have H grades or similar.

Band 4: For direct entry as an immigration officer: 3-4 H grades and some S grades (1-3) including English and maths or similar.

Band 5: For degree course, prior to entry: 3-5 H grades and some S grades (1-3), including English or maths or similar. Exact requirements depend on the degree you take.

Degree Information

Any degree discipline is acceptable for entry to this job, but it is an advantage to have a degree in modern languages, law or business studies. For Fast Stream, a second class honours degree is required but most candidates have first or upper second class honours.

Adult Qualifications

Formal qualifications or their equivalent are not always required for some jobs but you need to demonstrate strong written and verbal communication skills. For other jobs you need to have some academic secondary education qualifications (or equivalent) or a higher education qualification, such as a degree.

Work Experience

Entry to this job is competitive and it is important that you try to do some relevant work or voluntary experience before applying. Experience of working with people, particularly in an area that enables you to develop your communication skills, is always very useful. You can also apply for paid or unpaid work experience in a particular government department or agency by contacting their human resources department directly or through the civil service website. One or two-day visits may also be offered by some departments.

Entry and Training

Immigration officer (IO) and assistant immigration officer (AIO) posts are open to those over 18 who are UK nationals and have been resident in the UK for more than five years. Entry is very competitive and selection is through an assessment centre, where you are tested on judgement, conflict management, communication skills and awareness of diversity and equal opportunities. You also have to obtain security clearance.

Initial training covers immigration law, customer care, report writing, regulations and procedures and interview techniques. This takes place near Heathrow airport, at Gatwick airport, in Dover or Manchester, and lasts for at least nine weeks (five weeks classroom based and four operational). Continuous in-service training is encouraged. Newly qualified immigration officers have a mentor assigned to them and receive a lot of support from qualified staff in their first appointment.

A fast stream graduate entry programme is available to graduates who have a first or second class degree or equivalent. This programme prepares entrants for a high level career within the civil service. It is also possible for staff in administrative grades to work up to officer level and beyond.

The Diploma/Welsh Baccalaureate (for 14-19 year olds) in public services may be a useful background for this career but check entry requirements with individual organisations carefully.

Mature entry is welcomed from those with a wide range of work experience. Formal qualifications are not always required for some jobs but you go through a formal selection process. The ability to communicate in a foreign language is an advantage.

Opportunities and Pay

Due to expansion of the Border & Immigration Agency, there are increasing opportunities in this area of work, but entry is still very competitive. Almost half of the Immigration Service is based in south-east England, around Heathrow, Gatwick and Dover/ Folkestone, though officers are employed at all of the air and sea ports (over 50 in total) around the UK. Promotion to chief immigration officer and beyond is on merit and experience, and prospects are improved by training. Experienced officers have the opportunity to serve in other branches of the civil service, and in embassies and high commissions overseas.

Salaries for assistant immigration officers start at around £21k-£22k a year, rising to around £31k a year for a senior officer. A shift disturbance allowance and overtime pay is additional to basic salary. London and Heathrow pay levels are higher.

Health

You may have to take a medical test.

Skills and Qualities

ability in one or more languages, able to cope under pressure, fair minded, firm manner, good communication skills, IT skills, perceptive, quick thinking, sound judgement, tactful

Relevant Subjects

English, Geography, Government and politics, Law, Modern Foreign Languages

Further Information

AGCAS: Government & Public Administration (Job Sector Briefing) (AGCAS) - www.prospects.ac.uk

Civil Service - www.civilservice.gov.uk/jobs

Civil Service Fast Stream (Civil Service) - www.civilservice.gov.uk/jobs/faststream

Diplomas (Foundation, Higher and Advanced) - http://yp.direct.gov.uk/diplomas

Skills for Justice - sector skills council for the UK justice system - www.skillsforjustice.com

Welsh Baccalaureate - www.wbq.org.uk

▶Working in airports (2010) (Babcock Lifeskills) - www.babcock-lifeskills.com/

▶Working in police, fire & security (2009) (Babcock Lifeskills) - www.babcock-lifeskills.com/

Addresses

Border & Immigration Agency (Home Office)
Lunar House, 40 Wellesley Road, Croydon CR9 2BY
Phone: 0870 606 7766 (UK only)
Web: www.bia.homeoffice.gov.uk

Similar Jobs

Civil Service Administrative Officer, Civil Service Customs Officer, Civil Service Diplomatic Executive Assistant, Civil Service Executive Officer, Police Officer, Trading Standards Officer

Civil Service Operational Research Analyst

CRCI:Administration, Business and Office Work
CLCI:CAB Job Band: 5

Job Description

Research analysts apply scientific methods to management problems, and aim to provide a rational basis for decision-making. They research and analyse detailed information that the government requires to make policy decisions on issues such as transport, child poverty, drug smuggling, illiteracy, disease, international trade, and failing schools. Use a variety of techniques including case studies, interviews, qualitative surveys and analysis of records. Also study the impact of present government policy and the potential impact of future policy. Then give advice on the most appropriate options for future action.

May conduct in-house research or manage research contracts, where projects are carried out by an external organisation. Prepare reports for multi-disciplinary teams.

Work Details

As a research analyst you are usually office based, working normal office hours from Monday to Friday, but you may be required to work additional hours at times. You liaise with other organisations, such as environmental groups, to gather information. You have to interpret data and present information clearly, occasionally under pressurised conditions. Flexitime, part-time and job-sharing is possible. You spend a lot of time using computers with the latest software packages.

Qualification

- **England, Wales and Northern Ireland**

Band 5: For degree courses: 2-3 A levels and some GCSEs (A*-C) usually including English and maths, or equivalent. Exact requirements depend on the degree you take.

- **Scotland**

Band 5: For degree courses: 3-5 H grades and some S grades (1-3), usually including English and maths, or similar qualifications. Exact requirements depend on the degree you take.

Degree Information

A first/upper second class honours degree in a numerate subject is preferred. Subjects for a first degree include operational research, maths, statistics, physics, chemistry, engineering, economics, life science, environmental science and psychology. Postgraduate training in research methods and quantitative techniques can be an advantage.

Adult Qualifications
A good honours degree or relevant postgraduate degree is required. There may be special entry routes for adults such as Access courses to certain degree courses. Contact the universities for details. Postgraduate experience in an appropriate area is valuable.

Work Experience
The civil service may prefer candidates who have relevant work experience. It looks for team players with well-developed communication and interpersonal skills. It is an advantage for new graduates to gain work experience in areas where they can develop team, communication and analytical skills. Various departments offer industrial placements to students, as part of their degree. Placement vacancies for GORS and other government departments are advertised on the Civil Service Recruitment Gateway website. One or two-day visits may also be offered by some departments.

Entry and Training
There are strict nationality and residency requirements but all jobs are open to UK nationals, with a good percentage also open to EU nationals and Commonwealth citizens. This is a graduate job and some relevant experience and/or knowledge of the analytical methods used in operational research and statistics may be preferred. However, you can be accepted by the Government Operational Research Service (GORS) at level 1 with little or no experience if you can demonstrate that you have the qualifications, ability and personal qualities required.

Applicants must apply to GORS, giving preferences for the department(s) that they wish to work for. If suitable, you are invited to a GORS recruitment day where you are given a problem structuring test and an interview. Those successful at this stage are invited to visit departments that are a good match for applicants' skill set and interests. One of these departments may then make a firm job offer.

Training is on the job, with in-service courses on research techniques, project management, communication skills and staff management. You may be able to study for further qualifications and day release and sponsorship may be given to study for a relevant postgraduate qualification. You are encouraged to develop your professional skills by presenting at conferences and preparing papers for publication. The Operational Research Society (ORS) also offers training and development courses, including one and two-day courses, events and conferences.

Mature applicants are welcomed. Applicants should be talented, numerate graduates with a first or upper second class degree. Relevant postgraduate experience or training may be an advantage when applying for vacancies.

Opportunities and Pay
Analysts work in operational research groups, mainly in departments that include the Home Office, HM Revenue and Customs, Departments for Work and Pensions, Health, Transport, and the Food Standards Agency. Promotion is on individual competencies and potential, and prospects can be improved with further training. The civil service encourages further development and training through regular work appraisals and performance feedback. You may be able to get financial help for courses studied in your own time.

Pay and conditions depend on the department in which you work. Typical starting salaries for junior analysts (GORS grade 1) are around £20k-£25k a year. Grade 2 analysts earn £23k-£28k a year and grade 3 earn £30k-£37k a year. This does not include any London allowances. Top civil servants can earn more than £60k a year. You have an option to join a final salary pension scheme.

Health
You may be asked to take a medical examination.

Skills and Qualities
able to report accurately, analytical skills, aptitude for teamwork, clear-thinking, good communication skills, good interpersonal skills, good reasoning power, information handling skills, IT skills, objective, public speaking ability

Relevant Subjects
Economics, English, Government and politics, ICT/Computer studies, Mathematics, Psychology, Sociology

Further Information
AGCAS: Government & Public Administration (Job Sector Briefing) (AGCAS) - www.prospects.ac.uk

Civil Service - www.civilservice.gov.uk/jobs

Civil Service Fast Stream (Civil Service) - www.civilservice.gov.uk/jobs/faststream

GORS (GORS) - www.operational-research.gov.uk

Government Skills - sector skills council for central government - www.government-skills.gov.uk

How to Pass the Civil Service Qualifying Tests (2010) (Kogan Page) - www.koganpage.com

Journal of the Operational Research Society (JORS) - www.palgrave-journals.com/jors/index.html

National School of Government - www.nationalschool.gov.uk

TARGETjobs: Public Service (GTI Specialist Publishing Ltd.) - www.groupgti.com

Addresses
Civil Service Commission (Northern Ireland)
HRConnect, PO Box 1089, 2nd Floor, The Metro Building,
6-9 Donegall Square South, Belfast BT1 9EW
Phone: 0800 1300 330
Web: www.irecruit.nicsrecruitment.gov.uk/

OR (Operational Research) Society
Seymour House, 12 Edward Street, Birmingham B1 2RX
Phone: +44 (0)121 233 9300
Web: www.orsoc.org.uk

Scottish Executive
St Andrew's House, Regent Road, Edinburgh EH1 3DG
Phone: +44 (0)131 556 8400
Web: www.scotland.gov.uk

Welsh Assembly Government
Cathays Park, Cardiff CF10 3NQ
Phone: 0845 010 3300 (UK only)
Web: www.wales.gov.uk

Similar Jobs
Civil Service Fast Streamer, IT Systems Analyst/Designer, Management Consultant, Operational Researcher, Statistician

Civil Service Revenue Executive
CRCI:Administration, Business and Office Work
CLCI:CAB Job Band: 4 to 5

Job Description
Revenue executives assist in the calculation, collection and investigation of tax and national insurance contributions that are owed to HM Revenue & Customs (HMRC). Money owed may cover income tax, inheritance tax, stamp duties, land and petroleum taxes, corporation tax, and capital gains tax. They also deal with the allocation and payment of tax credits to those people who are eligible. Answer queries and advise taxpayers on their level of contributions and method of payment. Use computer systems to work out the amounts that people need to pay. Casework may also include dealing with the taxation of a company.

Some assist in compliance work, such as investigating the cases of tax evasion, fraudulent claims, or non-payment of tax. May need to attend court to represent HMRC if there is a prosecution. They are often responsible for a team of clerical staff, and supervise and monitor the work of the team. Also take responsibility for their development and training needs.

Work Details

Most revenue executives are based in offices and usually work flexible office hours from Monday to Friday, though sometimes may be required to work extra hours in the evenings or at weekends. Part-time work and job sharing are also possible, as well as temporary or short-term contracts. The work can involve visiting business premises or people's homes. A lot of your time is spent on paperwork, statistics, numerical work and using computers.

If you are responsible for a team of people, you have to give them advice and deal with tax cases that are problematic. Some of your decisions can be unpopular and your work can be stressful at times.

Qualification

• England, Wales and Northern Ireland

Band 4: For entry at officer level: two A levels and some GCSEs (A*-C), usually including English and maths or equivalent.

Band 5: For degree courses: 2-3 A levels and some GCSEs (A*-C), usually including English and maths, or equivalent. Exact requirements depend on the degree you take.

• Scotland

Band 4: For entry at officer level: 2-3 H grades and some S grades (1-3), often including English and maths or similar qualifications.

Band 5: For degree courses: 3-5 H grades and some S grades (1-3), usually including English and maths, or similar qualifications. Exact requirements depend on the degree you take.

Degree Information

A first or second class honours degree in any discipline, or an acceptable equivalent qualification, is an advantage. Accountancy, law and statistics give useful background.

Adult Qualifications

The department may recruit on the basis of competencies in specific areas, such as interpersonal skills and financial ability, rather than academic qualifications. However, formal qualifications are an advantage. Entry requirements may be relaxed for adults applying for degree courses. Contact universities for details of special entry standards.

Work Experience

It is useful to try to do some relevant work or voluntary experience before applying for a job. The most relevant areas of experience are any work that involves finance, administration, teamworking, or working with the public. You can also apply for paid or unpaid work experience in a particular government department or agency by contacting their human resources department directly, or through the civil service website. One or two-day visits may also be offered by some departments.

An HM Revenue & Customs (HMRC) internship programme is available to undergraduates in their penultimate year of university, which offers an eight-week paid work placement during July/August. Contact HMRC for details.

Entry and Training

There are strict nationality and residency requirements but all jobs dealing with taxpayers are open to UK nationals. For entry at officer level it is an advantage to have the minimum qualifications specified, but you may be accepted without them if you pass an initial suitability test. Many people who apply are graduates. All applicants are tested on their skills and competencies and those who pass, may be invited for interview. Although not essential, knowledge of social policy and the tax system is an advantage.

Training is on the job with a more experienced or senior member of staff, and also at the HM Revenue & Customs (HMRC) training centre. There is ongoing, in-service training for job-related skills and for the development of management skills. You can also become a revenue executive by working up through the administrative grades of the civil service.

Further progression to become a tax inspector or manager is possible, after gaining experience as a revenue executive. Those with potential can apply through the Graduate Development Programme which is open to all staff, with or without a degree. The programme is available in three areas; tax professional development, management fast track and accountancy. Once accepted onto the programme, you are placed on a particular route e.g. the Tax Professional Development Programme. It then takes four years to complete your training and involves working as part of an experienced team. Contact HMRC for further information on all entry routes.

Mature entrants are welcomed and HM Revenue & Customs encourages applications from people of every background, with or without formal qualifications. Experience in areas such as finance, administration, supervisory or management is useful for this job.

Opportunities and Pay

Jobs are available throughout the UK, mainly in major towns and cities, and are advertised locally/nationally, and on the HM Revenue & Customs website. Promotion to higher management levels is on experience and merit. Your prospects are improved by training. The civil service encourages further development and training through regular work appraisals and performance feedback. You may get financial help for courses, which you take in your own time.

Salaries vary depending on your entry level and location, but officers start on around £19k a year, rising to £25k. Higher officers earn £24k-£31k a year and senior officers £31k-£38k a year. A London allowance may be paid on top of this, if applicable.

Health

You may be asked to have a medical examination.

Skills and Qualities

able to get on with all kinds of people, able to manage a budget and keep records, able to take responsibility, attention to detail, efficient, good communication skills, good written English, IT skills, numeracy skills, problem-solving skills, sound judgement

Relevant Subjects

Business and accounting, Economics, English, Government and politics, ICT/Computer studies, Mathematics

Further Information

AGCAS: Government & Public Administration (Job Sector Briefing) (AGCAS) - www.prospects.ac.uk

Civil Service - www.civilservice.gov.uk/jobs

Civil Service Commissioners' Information Leaflet (Office of the Civil Service Commissioners) - www.civilservicecommissioners.org/

Civil Service Fast Stream (Civil Service) - www.civilservice.gov.uk/jobs/faststream

Government Skills - sector skills council for central government - www.government-skills.gov.uk

HM Revenue & Customs (HMRC) (HM Revenue & Customs) - www.hmrc.gov.uk

How to Pass the Civil Service Qualifying Tests (2010) (Kogan Page) - www.koganpage.com

National School of Government - www.nationalschool.gov.uk

TARGETjobs: Public Service (GTI Specialist Publishing Ltd.) - www.groupgti.com

▶Working in maths (2009) (Babcock Lifeskills) - www.babcock-lifeskills.com/

Similar Jobs
Accountant: Public Sector, Civil Service Administrative Officer, Civil Service Excise/VAT Assurance Officer, Civil Service Executive Officer, Civil Service Tax Inspector, Local Government Administrator, Office Manager

Civil Service Scientific Officer

CRCI:Science, Mathematics and Statistics
CLCI:CAB Job Band: 4 to 5

Job Description
Scientific officers carry out research and development work for central government or its agencies in one of many scientific areas. They seek to develop aspects such as the protection and enhancement of the environment, or work in agricultural and veterinary science, the regulation and control of UK pesticides, food science and nutrition, and meteorological services. Scientific officers are also involved in defence projects, building methods, conservation or transport. They investigate new techniques and equipment, log data, interpret results and develop research methods. May also be involved in technical administration or advisory work, and some are involved in management and in advising on Government policy.

Work Details
Usually work in a laboratory or sometimes an office working normal office hours from Monday to Friday, but may be required to work additional hours at times. As an officer you have responsibility for accurate analysis of the data collected. A high standard of interpretation of your findings and clear presentation of your results is required. You usually work in a team, informing, consulting and liaising with colleagues.

Qualification
- **England, Wales and Northern Ireland**

Band 4: For HND, Diploma of Higher Education or foundation degree: 1-2 A levels and some GCSEs (A*-C) usually including English, science and maths, or equivalent.

Band 5: For degree courses: 2-3 A levels including science or maths, and some GCSEs (A*-C) usually including English, or equivalent. Exact requirements depend on the degree you take.

- **Scotland**

Band 4: For entry to SQA higher national and professional development awards, usually 2-3 H grades and some S grades (1-3), including English, science and maths, or similar qualifications.

Band 5: For degree courses: 3-5 H grades including science or maths and some S grades (1-3) including English, or similar qualifications. Exact requirements depend on the degree you take.

Degree Information
A range of first degree subjects are available that are specific to individual departments or agencies including mathematics, geophysics, meteorology, computer science, information technology, environmental sciences, veterinary science, engineering, communications, psychology, medical and related sciences.

Adult Qualifications
A formal qualification, such as a relevant degree (officer level) or higher national award, or equivalent is required. Scientific knowledge must be up to date.

Work Experience
Entry to this job is competitive. It is important that you try to do some relevant work or voluntary experience before applying. You can also apply for paid or unpaid work experience in a particular government department or agency by contacting their human resources department directly or through the civil service website. One or two-day visits may also be offered by some departments. Different civil service departments require varying experience according to their specialisms, but any experience of a job in science is of value.

Entry and Training
There are strict nationality and residency requirements but all jobs are open to British nationals, with a good percentage also open to EU nationals and Commonwealth citizens. All applicants must pass competitive written tests and interviews. Most entrants at officer level are graduates who have first completed a science degree, but some may enter as assistant officers, usually with a range of qualifications, including higher national awards or equivalent. Training is through practical experience, usually following an in-service programme. Specialised courses, which may be residential, are often available. The Science and Engineering Fast Stream Development Programme is available to graduates who have a first or second class honours degree or equivalent. This programme prepares entrants for a high level career within the civil service. Check the website for details.

Graduate scientists may also enter as administration trainees or take part in a Graduate Trainee Scheme, which is offered by departments and agencies to a number of students who are currently completing their science or science-related degree.

Mature entrants may have difficulty in finding employment unless they have previous relevant experience. A relevant degree is essential for entry.

Opportunities and Pay
You are employed by the civil service in a wide range of departments or agencies. The Ministry of Defence (MoD) and the Department for Business, Innovation and Skills (BIS) employ a network of scientists and technologists across the civil service. Other departments and agencies, such as the Centre for the Environment, Fisheries and Aquaculture, Forensic Science Service, Meteorological Office, Home Office, Environment, Food and Rural Affairs, Central Science Laboratory, Veterinary Medicines Directorate, Pesticides Safety Directorate, Forestry Commission, Patent Office and Government Communications HQ all have responsibilities associated with scientific research and development. Check the Civil Service Recruitment Gateway website for details.

Promotion prospects are good and those aiming for higher qualifications are encouraged. The civil service encourages further development and training through work appraisals and performance feedback. Financial help and time off for study are usually possible for courses relevant to your post. Flexitime, part-time work and job-sharing are possible.

Starting salaries for assistant scientific officers are from £23k a year and for higher scientific officers £27k-£31k a year. Senior scientists earn from £34k-£40k, depending on experience and level of responsibility and top civil servants can earn more than £60k a year. Salaries are generally higher in London.

Health
You should have good colour vision for certain areas of work. There may be an allergy risk from skin irritants in some jobs.

Skills and Qualities
able to report accurately, able to work both on your own and in a team, analytical skills, clear-thinking, good concentration level, IT skills, observant, perseverance, resourceful, scientific approach

Relevant Subjects
Biology, Chemistry, Design and technology, English, ICT/Computer studies, Land and Environment, Mathematics, Physics, Psychology, Science

Further Information

AGCAS: Government & Public Administration (Job Sector Briefing) (AGCAS) - www.prospects.ac.uk

Civil Service - www.civilservice.gov.uk/jobs

Civil Service Fast Stream (Civil Service) - www.civilservice.gov.uk/jobs/faststream

▶Working in science (2007) (Babcock Lifeskills) - www.babcock-lifeskills.com/

Addresses

Civil Service Commission (Northern Ireland)
HRConnect, PO Box 1089, 2nd Floor, The Metro Building, 6-9 Donegall Square South, Belfast BT1 9EW
Phone: 0800 1300 330
Web: www.irecruit.nicsrecruitment.gov.uk/

Northern Ireland Assembly
Communications Office Northern Ireland Assembly Parliament Buildings Ballymiscaw Stormont, Belfast BT4 3XX
Phone: +44 (0)28 9052 1333
Web: www.niassembly.gov.uk

Scottish Executive
St Andrew's House, Regent Road, Edinburgh EH1 3DG
Phone: +44 (0)131 556 8400
Web: www.scotland.gov.uk

Welsh Assembly Government
Cathays Park, Cardiff CF10 3NQ
Phone: 0845 010 3300 (UK only)
Web: www.wales.gov.uk

Similar Jobs

Agricultural Research Scientist, Biologist, Ecologist, Food Scientist/Technologist, Forensic Scientist, Meteorologist

Civil Service SIS Operational Officer

also known as: SIS Officer

CRCI:Administration, Business and Office Work
CLCI:CAB Job Band: 5

Job Description

Operational officers work for the Secret Intelligence Service (SIS), countering any threat to UK interests worldwide. They are part of a team that obtain secret foreign intelligence, and conduct covert operations in support of the UK's foreign policies and objectives. The role is primarily to mount and run intelligence operations to promote and protect British interests and security overseas, and to defend national security and the economic well-being of the United Kingdom. Endeavour to disrupt any threats to UK citizens and the country's assets.

Work can be in any of the three branches of the SIS: Intelligence, Executive, and Scientific and Technical, of which the latter has staff designing information and communications technology. Work varies depending on whether you are a case officer, targeting officer, analyst, or report officer. For example, operational analysts assimilate, process and interpret large amounts of information, whereas case officers plan and execute overseas operations. Work is often with partners such as the armed forces, the Ministry of Defence and the Home Office.

Work Details

Work for the SIS can be extremely pressured, for long hours and in uncomfortable surroundings, or it may be mainly administrative and office-based, in which case you normally work a basic week of around 39 hours. However, you must be flexible and work longer hours, evenings and weekends if the nature of the work demands it. You may also spend time away from home and overseas. You must have the ability to deal with potentially hazardous situations in a calm manner.

Qualification

- **England, Wales and Northern Ireland**

Band 5: For degree courses: 2-3 A levels and some GCSEs (A*-C) usually including maths and English, or equivalent. Exact requirements depend on the degree you take.

- **Scotland**

Band 5: For degree courses: 3-5 H grades and some S grades (1-3), usually including maths and English, or similar. Exact requirements depend on the degree you take.

Degree Information

All subjects are acceptable, though you need at least an upper second class honours degree or equivalent. Relevant postgraduate courses are also available.

Adult Qualifications

Entry requirements may be relaxed for adults applying for degree courses or there may be special entry routes, such as foundation or Access courses. Check with universities for details.

Work Experience

Entry to this job is highly competitive and it is important that you try to do some relevant work or voluntary experience before applying. The most relevant areas of experience is any work that involves working abroad, in the public service, or under severe pressure. You can also apply for paid or unpaid work experience in a particular government department or agency by contacting their human resources department directly, or through the civil service website. Although there is no possibility of work experience in the SIS, the Foreign and Commonwealth Office (FCO), for example, offers two annual placement schemes.

Entry and Training

The SIS is not formally part of the Home Civil Service and recruitment is therefore handled directly by the SIS. They look for 'high calibre graduates' with exceptional interpersonal skills for operational officer posts. Candidates are expected to have at least a first class or upper second honours degree. You must be able to show full commitment to working in security, and have a keen interest in foreign peoples and cultures. It is possible to enter the SIS with an academic background of GCSEs/S grades (A*-C/1-3) in an administrative role, which includes some basic work at operational level.

Because of the nature of the work, candidates must be British, with at least one parent a British national, and have lived for at least six of the last ten years in the UK. You need to pass an extensive security clearance process prior to joining. Potential candidates should not let others know of their application to the SIS, and failure to observe confidentiality may affect your eligibility for employment. A second language is desirable, though not essential, as you are given any necessary language tuition.

Training is on the job, starting with an induction programme, and further training is tailored to your specific area of work. Additional training to enhance or broaden professional skills may be provided during your career. This may include being sent on external training courses.

Mature applicants are welcomed, particularly those with public and private sector experience. Career change is common for those with a strong academic record, coupled with evidence of interest in foreign people and cultures and a commitment to public service. This is a job well suited to those with previous high calibre professional experience, although most recruits are less than 35 years of age.

Opportunities and Pay

The SIS offers long-term careers with the possibility of promotion to higher levels of responsibility for those who show promise. There are also a small number of posts for linguists with a high level of analytical ability.

Pay information for roles in the SIS are undisclosed. There are additional benefits such as pensions and healthcare schemes.

Health
A good level of physical fitness is required when working in the Intelligence branch. The recruitment process involves a detailed medical.

Skills and Qualities
able to cope under pressure, able to take responsibility, accurate, analytical skills, discreet, excellent communication skills, information handling skills, IT skills, resilient, self-motivated

Relevant Subjects
English, Geography, Government and politics, History, ICT/ Computer studies, Law, Mathematics, Modern Foreign Languages

Further Information
AGCAS: Government & Public Administration (Job Sector Briefing) (AGCAS) - www.prospects.ac.uk

British International Studies Association (British International Studies Association) - www.bisa.ac.uk

Careers in British Intelligence - www.careersinbritishintelligence.co.uk/

Careers in the Foreign & Commonwealth Office (Foreign and Commonwealth Office) - www.fco.gov.uk/en/

Civil Service Fast Stream (Civil Service) - www.civilservice.gov.uk/jobs/faststream

Government Skills - sector skills council for central government - www.government-skills.gov.uk

How to Pass the Civil Service Qualifying Tests (2010) (Kogan Page) - www.koganpage.com

National School of Government - www.nationalschool.gov.uk

TARGETjobs: Public Service (GTI Specialist Publishing Ltd.) - www.groupgti.com

Addresses
Secret Intelligence Service (SIS)
PO Box 1300, London SE1 1BD
Web: www.sis.gov.uk

Similar Jobs
Civil Service Diplomatic Officer, Civil Service Fast Streamer, Public Affairs Executive/Consultant

Civil Service Tax Inspector

CRCI:Administration, Business and Office Work
CLCI:CAB Job Band: 5

Job Description
Tax inspectors are experts on tax law who work for HM Revenue & Customs (HMRC). They make sure that employed individuals and companies pay an accurate amount of tax on their income and capital. Can specialise in areas that include the investigation of serious fraud, tax avoidance, oil taxation and international taxation. Have knowledge about the nature of a business, including e-commerce implications. May interview clients and also their accountants, examine business records and a company's economic state, looking at the accounts in fine detail, and particularly for any irregularities. Then negotiate payment of any unpaid taxes.

May look into the financial affairs of wealthy individuals or help small businesses to understand the law on taxation. Sometimes may be required to represent HMRC at an independent tribunal in cases of dispute.

Work Details
Tax inspectors are based in offices and have to be prepared to work anywhere in the UK, and to move at the request of the employer. Usually work standard office hours, though must be prepared to work additional hours, including evenings and weekends, at times. Often work within a team of inspectors, especially when involved in large and complex cases. Deal with a wide range of people, such as accountants, small business owners, company directors and private individuals. The work of a tax inspector is intellectually demanding and can be highly pressurised. You have to make unpopular decisions at times.

Qualification
- **England, Wales and Northern Ireland**

Band 5: For degree courses: usually 2-3 A levels and some GCSEs (A*-C), usually including English and maths, or equivalent qualifications. Exact requirements depend on the degree you take.

- **Scotland**

Band 5: For degree courses: usually 3-5 H grades and some S grades (1-3), usually including English and maths, or similar qualifications. Exact requirements depend on the degree you take.

Degree Information
A first or second class honours degree in any discipline or an acceptable equivalent qualification, is needed. Accountancy, law and statistics give useful background.

Adult Qualifications
Entry requirements may be relaxed for adults applying for degree courses. Contact universities for details of special entry standards.

Work Experience
Entry to this job is competitive and it is important that you try to do some relevant work or voluntary experience before applying. This can include accountancy or other work of a financial nature. You can apply for paid or unpaid work experience in a particular government department or agency by contacting their human resources department directly, or through the civil service website. One or two-day visits may also be offered by some departments.

An HM Revenue & Customs (HMRC) internship programme is available to undergraduates in their penultimate year of university, which offers a six to nine week paid work placement during July/ August. Successful applicants can return to university with a secure offer of a place on the Graduate Development Programme, following achievement of at least a 2:1 honours degree. Contact HMRC for details.

Entry and Training
HM Revenue & Customs (HMRC) rules mean that only UK nationals and British protected persons are eligible to work in jobs that deal with taxpayers. Most people enter this profession through the Civil Service Fast Stream or Customs Talent Recruitment Programme which are open to those with at least a 2:1 honours degree. Those already working for HMRC in a related role (such as revenue executive) may apply without a degree. Training takes around four years to complete and involves working as part of an experienced team. These programmes prepare entrants for a high-level career within the civil service. There is also an option to prepare for working in the EU. Contact HMRC for further information on all entry routes.

Mature entrants with professional qualifications equivalent to degree level may apply for direct entry to the Talent Recruitment Programme. Qualifications include those of the Association of Chartered Certified Accountants (ACCA), Institute of Chartered Accountants (ICAEW) and the Chartered Institute of Management Accountants (CIMA). Relevant professional experience including membership of, for example, the Chartered Institute of Public Finance and Accounting (CIPFA), is also acceptable for application. Equivalent postgraduate or overseas qualifications are also acceptable.

Opportunities and Pay

Jobs are available throughout the UK, mainly in towns and cities, and are advertised locally/nationally and on the HM Revenue & Customs (HMRC) website. There is fierce competition for positions. Promotion depends on experience and merit, and prospects are improved with further training. District inspectors are those who are in charge of an office, managing a team of inspectors, revenue executives and administrative staff.

Pay and conditions are set by HMRC and starting pay varies depending on qualifications, experience and location. Starting salaries for those on the graduate development programme are generally around £26k in London and £24k elsewhere. When qualified, salaries range from around £47.7k in London and £42.5k elsewhere. Senior tax inspectors can earn up to £60k a year.

Health

You may be asked to take a medical examination.

Skills and Qualities

able to manage people, able to take responsibility, able to work to a budget, analytical skills, efficient record keeping, good communication skills, good written English, impartial, information handling skills, integrity, numeracy skills, problem-solving skills

Relevant Subjects

Business and accounting, Economics, English, ICT/Computer studies, Law, Mathematics

Further Information

AGCAS: Government & Public Administration (Job Sector Briefing) (AGCAS) - www.prospects.ac.uk

Civil Service - www.civilservice.gov.uk/jobs

Civil Service Fast Stream (Civil Service) - www.civilservice.gov.uk/jobs/faststream

Government Skills - sector skills council for central government - www.government-skills.gov.uk

HM Revenue & Customs (HMRC) (HM Revenue & Customs) - www.hmrc.gov.uk

How to Pass the Civil Service Qualifying Tests (2010) (Kogan Page) - www.koganpage.com

National School of Government - www.nationalschool.gov.uk

TARGETjobs: Public Service (GTI Specialist Publishing Ltd.) - www.groupgti.com

Addresses

Institute of Indirect Taxation
Suite G1, The Stables, Station Road West, Oxted, Surrey RH8 9EE
Phone: +44 (0)1883 730658
Web: www.theiit.org.uk

Similar Jobs

Accountant: Industry & Commerce, Accountant: Private Practice, Accountant: Public Sector, Civil Service Fast Streamer, Civil Service Revenue Executive, Economist, Tax Adviser

Cleaner: Carpet & Upholstery

CRCI:Personal and Other Services
CLCI:IJ Job Band: 1

Job Description

Carpet and upholstery cleaners clean carpets, chairs, sofas and other upholstered items in shops, offices and people's homes using industrial cleaning machines. They fill the extractor with water at the right temperature, add chemicals and attach different tubes, depending on the type of material to be cleaned. They spray the material and then suck up the water and dirt. Use a dry cleaning chemical process for some upholstery and carpets. May also collect money or cheques when the job is completed. If self-employed, they need to keep records of work done and send out estimates and invoices.

Work Details

Usually work a basic 39 hr week, which may include some weekend work, with early starts or late finishes. You may have to drive a van or car with your equipment to customers within an area, and work in places such as offices, shops or people's houses. For much of the time you are either working on your own or with a colleague. You must be very careful not to damage the carpets or furniture. This is an active job and some of the machines that you use are quite heavy to lift. The places where you work may be dirty and dusty, and you may need to wear overalls and a mask to protect your mouth and nose.

Qualification

- **England, Wales and Northern Ireland**

Band 1: For entry to jobs, no minimum qualifications are needed, but you are expected to have a good level of general education and relevant experience. Some formal/vocational qualifications at any level are useful.

- **Scotland**

Band 1: For entry to jobs, no minimum qualifications are needed, but you are expected to have a good level of general education and relevant experience. Some formal/vocational qualifications at any level are useful.

Adult Qualifications

No qualifications are needed. You can improve your skills and qualifications by working through the Foundation Learning programme. This involves taking credit-based units and qualifications to help you progress.

Work Experience

Any work experience can equip you with skills to use in the future and add to your CV. Work experience can either be unpaid, holiday or part-time work that you have sorted out yourself. Any work related to cleaning is useful.

Entry and Training

Some employers recruit people at 16, but they often employ older people because this job may require a driving licence. You are usually trained on the job with an experienced worker, and you may also attend short training courses run by companies who sell the machines, shampoos and chemicals. Employers may also offer the opportunity for in-house vocational training. Two-day carpet and upholstery cleaning courses are offered by the National Carpet Cleaners Association, as well as courses on spot and stain removal, and flood and fire restoration. The British Institute of Cleaning Science (BICSc) also offers a cleaning operators proficiency certificate scheme.

Asset Skills (Sector Skills Council) maintains national occupational standards within the cleaning industry. This job can lead to an S/NVQ level 1/2 in cleaning & support services. Training programmes, including apprenticeship schemes, may be available in your area.

Adults may be able to enter this work through a government-funded training programme. Contact your local Connexions or careers office, Jobcentre Plus, Next Step service or Learning and Skills Council (LSC)/Local Enterprise Company (LEC) for details of all training opportunities and schemes, including apprenticeships for adults.

Opportunities and Pay

Jobs are available in most UK towns and cities. You can be employed by a private cleaning company or be self-employed. Some companies have a franchise system where they help you to set up your business and you are allowed to use their products and name. You need to pay an initial sum of money to do this and perhaps a percentage of your earnings.

Pay varies widely but you are likely to earn around £11k-£14.5k a year, rising to around £25k a year, depending on whether you are employed or self-employed. Earnings may be increased through overtime.

Health
This job requires good general fitness. People with certain skin problems or who are allergic to dust may find this job difficult.

Skills and Qualities
able to get on with all kinds of people, able to operate equipment, able to work well on your own, adaptable, careful, co-operative, customer service skills, honest, practical skills, reliable

Further Information
Apprenticeship Schemes (National Apprenticeship Service) - www.apprenticeships.org.uk

Asset Skills - sector skills council for the places where we live and work - www.assetskills.org

Cleaning and Support Services Association (CSSA) - www.cleaningindustry.org

Cleaning Industry Handbook (BICSc) (BICSc) - www.bics.org.uk/

Foundation Learning (QCDA) - www.qcda.gov.uk

Laundry & Cleaning Today (LCT) - www.laundryandcleaningtoday.com

Training Schemes - www.direct.gov.uk/en/educationandlearning

Addresses
British Cleaning Council (BCC)
478-480 Salisbury House London Wall EC2M 5QQ
Phone: +44 (0)20 7920 9640
Web: www.britishcleaningcouncil.org

British Institute of Cleaning Science (BICSc)
9 Premier Court, Boarden Close, Moulton Park, Northampton NN3 6LF
Phone: +44 (0)1604 678 710
Web: www.bics.org.uk

National Carpet Cleaners Association
62c London Road, Oadby, Leicester LE2 5DH
Phone: +44 (0)116 271 9550
Web: www.ncca.co.uk

Similar Jobs
Car Valet, Cleaner: Domestic, Cleaner: Industrial, Dry Cleaning Assistant/Manager, Laundry Assistant/Manager

Cleaner: Domestic
also known as: Domestic Cleaner

CRCI:Personal and Other Services

CLCI:IJ — Job Band: 1

Job Description
Domestic cleaners provide a household cleaning service in private homes. They dust, clean and polish all surfaces, including floors, furniture and mirrors. Also vacuum the house, clean windows and empty rubbish bins. May load/unload the dishwasher/washing machine or may wash and dry any dishes and pans. Clean bathroom surfaces such as the floor, washbasin, bath, shower and toilet. May be asked to iron clothing and bedding. Some cleaners may be asked to do a special 'blitz clean' or 'spring clean' when required, for an occasion such as after a party or when the owner is moving house. This work usually includes cleaning out kitchen cupboards and the inside of an oven, as well as cleaning paintwork, such as a room's skirting boards.

Work Details
Usually work Monday to Friday, though sometimes may be required to work at weekends. Self-employed cleaners choose their working hours to suit themselves and the homeowners, but agency cleaners may have a set number of working hours each week. Some cleaners work in pairs, or perhaps three or four people, depending on the job required. Cleaners travel around an area, usually in a car or van, so a clean driving licence may be useful.

Qualification
- **England, Wales and Northern Ireland**

Band 1: For entry to jobs, no minimum qualifications are needed, but you are expected to have a good level of general education and relevant experience. Some formal/vocational qualifications at any level are useful.

- **Scotland**

Band 1: For entry to jobs, no minimum qualifications are needed, but you are expected to have a good level of general education and relevant experience. Some formal/vocational qualifications at any level are useful.

Adult Qualifications
No qualifications are needed. You can improve your skills and qualifications by working through the Foundation Learning programme. This involves taking credit-based units and qualifications to help you progress.

Work Experience
Work experience gives you an insight into what you enjoy and don't enjoy about a job, as well as the chance to learn new skills. It also gives you useful information to add to your CV and improves your future job prospects.

Entry and Training
Employers look for applicants who have a pleasant and responsible attitude and who can understand and follow instructions. Training is usually on the job, working with an experienced domestic cleaner to learn the work routine and methods of cleaning. If working for an agency in-house training usually includes a session on their company policy. Health and safety aspects at work are important.

You may be able to gain a certificate in cleaning operators' proficiency that is organised through the British Institute of Cleaning Science (BICSc), or work towards a City & Guilds level 2 certificate in cleaning science. S/NVQs may also be available at level 1-2 in cleaning and support services. Asset Skills sets National Occupational Standards for the cleaning industry. See the website for details. It is useful if you have a current driving licence.

Mature applicants with previous experience of general domestic or industrial cleaning have an advantage.

Opportunities and Pay
There are many jobs throughout the country and there are often shortages in some areas. Domestic cleaners often work part time and are usually either self-employed or work for a cleaning agency. Most work for regular clients in a local area.

Pay varies depending on the employer and amount of hours worked each week, but can be around £170-£200 a week. This can rise to around £235-£270 a week, though some can earn around £335 a week. Hourly rates are from £6.50 to around £11.

Health
You should not be allergic to dust and must be physically fit.

Skills and Qualities
able to work well on your own, common sense, energetic, good organisational skills, hard working, honest, neat, practical skills, trustworthy

Further Information
Asset Skills - sector skills council for the places where we live and work - www.assetskills.org

Cleaning and Support Services Association (CSSA) - www.cleaningindustry.org

Cleaning Industry Handbook (BICSc) (BICSc) - www.bics.org.uk/

Foundation Learning (QCDA) - www.qcda.gov.uk

Laundry & Cleaning Today (LCT) - www.laundryandcleaningtoday.com

Addresses
British Cleaning Council (BCC)
478-480 Salisbury House London Wall EC2M 5QQ
Phone: +44 (0)20 7920 9640
Web: www.britishcleaningcouncil.org

British Institute of Cleaning Science (BICSc)
9 Premier Court, Boarden Close, Moulton Park, Northampton
NN3 6LF
Phone: +44 (0)1604 678 710
Web: www.bics.org.uk

Similar Jobs
Car Valet, Caretaker, Cleaner: Hospital, Cleaner: Industrial, Hotel Room Attendant

Cleaner: Hospital
also known as: Hospital Domestic Assistant, Ward Services Officer: Hospital

CRCI:Personal and Other Services
CLCI:IJ
Job Band: 1

Job Description
Hospital cleaners clean wards and other areas of the hospital, such as operating theatres, clinics, waiting rooms and offices. They use cloths and mops to clean worktops, sinks, tables and bathrooms, and use machines to clean and polish floors. Also take away dirty sheets, wraps and towels to the laundry and empty bins, ensuring that waste is disposed of correctly. Cleaners are responsible for safe procedures at all times and especially when working on floor surfaces. They must ensure that all areas and surfaces are cleaned in accordance with the rules of hygiene in the workplace to stop the spread of infections.

If working as a ward services officer, they also has to serve food to patients on the ward, as well as keeping the workplace clean and hygienic.

Work Details
Usually work a basic 39 hr week that can involve a shift system, including early mornings or late afternoons. You may be required to work some weekends but you have days off during the week. In this job you are on your feet most of the time. You also have to do a lot of bending, sometimes lifting heavy equipment, such as polishing machines. Patients in hospitals are often in pain, or upset, nervous or demanding, and you have to cope with this. Sometimes your work is messy and smelly. You have to cope with the sight of blood and need to wear a uniform or protective clothing.

Qualification
- **England, Wales and Northern Ireland**

Band 1: For entry to jobs, no minimum qualifications are needed, but you are expected to have a good level of general education and relevant experience. Some formal/vocational qualifications at any level are useful.

- **Scotland**

Band 1: For entry to jobs, no minimum qualifications are needed, but you are expected to have a good level of general education and relevant experience. Some formal/vocational qualifications at any level are useful.

Adult Qualifications
Formal qualifications are not needed. You can improve your skills and qualifications by working through the Foundation Learning programme. This involves taking credit-based units and qualifications to help you progress.

Work Experience
Any work experience can equip you with skills to use in the future and add to your CV. This can either be unpaid or voluntary, or holiday/part-time work that you have organised yourself. Any work related to cleaning is useful.

Entry and Training
Training is on the job working with a more experienced person. Some employers offer specialist short courses, such as health and safety at work, and also vocational training. Hospitals train all cleaners in hygiene procedures for controlling infections. You may be able to gain a healthcare professionals cleaning certificate that is organised through the British Institute of Cleaning Science (BICSc) or study for a City & Guilds qualification in cleaning and cleaning science on a part-time basis.

Asset Skills (Sector Skills Council) is responsible for setting National Occupational Standards for the cleaning industry. See the website for details. There are S/NVQs in cleaning and support services at level 1-2. Training programmes, including apprenticeship schemes, may be available in your area.

Mature applicants with previous experience of providing cleaning services may be preferred by some employers. Apprenticeship schemes for adults may be available in your area.

Opportunities and Pay
This work is usually done by cleaning agencies that provide services to hospitals, though some hospitals have housekeeping departments that may also employ cleaners directly. With experience, you may be able to become a supervisor.

Pay varies, but is around £5.50-£6.30 an hour. Supervisors can earn more than this.

Health
The work involves a risk of infection. To do this job you have to have good general fitness.

Skills and Qualities
able to follow instructions, aptitude for teamwork, common sense, conscientious, friendly, good communication skills, helpful, not squeamish, reliable

Relevant Subjects
Hospitality and catering

Further Information
Apprenticeship Schemes (National Apprenticeship Service) - www.apprenticeships.org.uk

Asset Skills - sector skills council for the places where we live and work - www.assetskills.org

Cleaning and Support Services Association (CSSA) - www.cleaningindustry.org

Cleaning Industry Handbook (BICSc) (BICSc) - www.bics.org.uk/

Foundation Learning (QCDA) - www.qcda.gov.uk

NHS Careers (NHS Careers) - www.nhscareers.nhs.uk

Addresses

British Cleaning Council (BCC)
478-480 Salisbury House London Wall EC2M 5QQ
Phone: +44 (0)20 7920 9640
Web: www.britishcleaningcouncil.org

British Institute of Cleaning Science (BICSc)
9 Premier Court, Boarden Close, Moulton Park, Northampton NN3 6LF
Phone: +44 (0)1604 678 710
Web: www.bics.org.uk

Similar Jobs

Cleaner: Domestic, Cleaner: Industrial, Hospital Porter, Hotel Room Attendant, Sterile Services Technician

Cleaner: Industrial

CRCI:Personal and Other Services
CLCI:IJ Job Band: 1

Job Description

Industrial cleaners clean many types of buildings, such as offices, shops, hotels, and theatres, and also buses, aircraft, ships and trains. They clean all surfaces, including floors, walls, furniture and stairs. Use vacuum cleaners, brushes, cloths, mops and sometimes an electrical floor scrubber and polisher. Also clean washrooms and lavatories, replacing items such as soap and toilet rolls. May clean equipment such as telephones, desks, computers and other office machines. Cleaners look after the cleaning equipment and see that it is kept in good and safe working order.

Work Details

Usually work a 35-39 hr week, Monday to Friday, but sometimes may be required to work shifts that include weekends. Often cleaners have to work early in the morning or late in the evenings, when buildings may be empty. In this job you are active for most of the time and some tasks require you to bend, kneel, lift and climb stairs. Since this sort of work can be dirty and dusty, you usually wear protective clothing.

Qualification

- **England, Wales and Northern Ireland**

Band 1: For entry to jobs, no minimum qualifications are needed, but you are expected to have a good level of general education and relevant experience. Some formal/vocational qualifications at any level are useful.

- **Scotland**

Band 1: For entry to jobs, no minimum qualifications are needed, but you are expected to have a good level of general education and relevant experience. Some formal/vocational qualifications at any level are useful.

Adult Qualifications

No qualifications are needed. You can improve your skills and qualifications by working through the Foundation Learning programme. This involves taking credit-based units and qualifications to help you progress.

Work Experience

Any work experience can equip you with skills to use in the future and add to your CV. This can either be unpaid or voluntary, or holiday/part-time work that you have organised yourself. Any work related to cleaning is useful.

Entry and Training

Employers look for applicants who have a responsible attitude and who can understand and follow instructions. Training is on the job working with a more experienced person. Some employers offer specialist short courses, such as health and safety at work, and also vocational training. You may be able to gain a cleaning operators proficiency certificate that is organised through the British Institute of Cleaning Science (BICSc) or study for a City & Guilds qualification in cleaning and cleaning science on a part-time basis.

Asset Skills (Sector Skills Council) set National Occupational Standards for the cleaning industry. See the website for details. There are S/NVQs in cleaning and support services at level 1-2. Training programmes, including apprenticeship schemes, may be available in your area. The BICSc also runs an assessment scheme for supervisors.

Mature applicants with experience of general domestic cleaning have an advantage. There may be apprenticeships for adults in your area.

Opportunities and Pay

Jobs are found throughout the UK, working with a cleaning contractor on jobs in different places, or with hotel or shop owners. Chances for promotion are rare unless you work for a large firm where you may be able to move to a supervisory role. Cleaners often work part time, though the number of full-time jobs is growing. Many cleaners are self-employed.

Pay can vary a lot, but is likely to be around £5.35-£7 an hour, depending on whether you are employed or self-employed. Most cleaners earn around £10.5k-£14k a year, rising to £15.5k, with experience. Some specialist cleaners earn up to £17k a year. Overtime pay is usually possible.

Health

This job requires good general fitness. You may find this job difficult if you are allergic to dust.

Skills and Qualities

able to work quickly, able to work well on your own, common sense, good organisational skills, hard working, honest, practical skills, trustworthy

Further Information

Apprenticeship Schemes (National Apprenticeship Service) - www.apprenticeships.org.uk

Asset Skills - sector skills council for the places where we live and work - www.assetskills.org

Cleaning and Support Services Association (CSSA) - www.cleaningindustry.org

Cleaning Industry Handbook (BICSc) (BICSc) - www.bics.org.uk/

Foundation Learning (QCDA) - www.qcda.gov.uk

Laundry & Cleaning Today (LCT) - www.laundryandcleaningtoday.com

Addresses

British Cleaning Council (BCC)
478-480 Salisbury House London Wall EC2M 5QQ
Phone: +44 (0)20 7920 9640
Web: www.britishcleaningcouncil.org

British Institute of Cleaning Science (BICSc)
9 Premier Court, Boarden Close, Moulton Park, Northampton NN3 6LF
Phone: +44 (0)1604 678 710
Web: www.bics.org.uk

Similar Jobs

Car Valet, Caretaker, Cleaner: Domestic, Cleaner: Hospital, Cleaner: Street, Cleaner: Windows

Cleaner: Street

also known as: Highways Cleaner

CRCI:Personal and Other Services

CLCI:IJ Job Band: 1

Job Description

Street cleaners work in towns, cities, villages and in the countryside, keeping streets/roads and public places free of litter and rubbish. They keep pavements, roads and gutters clean using a powered brush. May collect leaves/litter, by shovelling or vacuuming them into a hand pushed or battery operated trolley, or into a motorised ride-on vehicle. Also empty litter bins and may help to clear snow and spread grit. Some cleaners work in a team using a larger cleaning lorry. Others use a scrubber-dryer system for smooth tiled surfaces in shopping malls and centres. May use a special machine to remove chewing gum from pavements.

Work Details

Most street cleaners work a 37-40 hr week, Monday to Friday, and may have to start work as early as 6am to clean some public areas. May also need to work at weekends and overtime is also possible. Can work outdoors in all sorts of weather and sometimes you are cold and wet. This job requires you to be active most of the time, bending down, lifting, and walking around. This type of work is dirty, dusty, noisy and often smelly in hot weather. There may be a risk of injury from things like broken glass and 'sharps' (needles). You need to wear protective gloves, boots and overalls, which are provided by the employer. You may work on your own, but usually as part of a team.

Qualification

- **England, Wales and Northern Ireland**

Band 1: For entry to jobs, no minimum qualifications are needed, but you are expected to have a good level of general education and relevant experience. Some formal/vocational qualifications at any level are useful.

- **Scotland**

Band 1: For entry to jobs, no minimum qualifications are needed, but you are expected to have a good level of general education and relevant experience. Some formal/vocational qualifications at any level are useful.

Adult Qualifications

No qualifications are needed. You can improve your skills and qualifications by working through the Foundation Learning programme. This involves taking credit-based units and qualifications to help you progress.

Work Experience

Any work experience can equip you with skills that you can use in the future and add to your CV. Work experience can either be unpaid or voluntary or can be holiday or part-time work that you have organised yourself. Any experience of manual work or cleaning is useful.

Entry and Training

Entrants are usually over 18, and for some jobs you need a driving licence/LGV (large goods vehicle) licence. Training is on the job working alongside a more experienced street cleaner. You may be able to work towards a qualification, such as the cleaning operator's proficiency certificate of the British Institute of Cleaning Science (BICSc) or the City & Guilds certificate in cleaning science.

You may have the opportunity to work towards relevant work-based qualifications offered by the Waste Management Industry Training and Advisory Board, such as the certificates of competence at levels 1-3. Specific S/NVQs are available at levels 1-2 cleaning and support services.

Mature applicants with experience in labouring or other cleaning work may have an advantage.

Opportunities and Pay

There are around 20,000 street cleaners in the UK. Jobs are available mainly in towns and cities. You either work for a local authority or a private contractor which provides cleaning services to the council. There are also jobs at shopping centres, airports, stations, tourist and leisure parks. After experience, you may be able to move up to a supervisory job.

Average pay starts at around £11k-£14k a year, rising to around £16k a year. There may also be overtime pay and bonuses.

Health

You need to have good general fitness. You may find this job difficult if you are allergic to dust.

Skills and Qualities

able to work both on your own and in a team, enjoy working outdoors, hard working, prepared to do repetitive tasks, reliable, safety conscious, strong

Further Information

Asset Skills - sector skills council for the places where we live and work - www.assetskills.org

Foundation Learning (QCDA) - www.qcda.gov.uk

Local Government Careers (Improvement and Development Agency) - www.lgcareers.com/publications/

Addresses

British Institute of Cleaning Science (BICSc)
9 Premier Court, Boarden Close, Moulton Park, Northampton NN3 6LF
Phone: +44 (0)1604 678 710
Web: www.bics.org.uk

Waste Management Industry Training and Advisory Board (WAMITAB)
Peterbridge House, 3 The Lakes, Northampton NN4 7HE
Phone: +44 (0)1604 231 950
Web: www.wamitab.org.uk

Similar Jobs

Cleaner: Industrial, Cleaner: Windows, Groundsman/ Groundswoman, Refuse Collector, Road Worker, Street Lighting Operative

Cleaner: Windows

CRCI:Personal and Other Services

CLCI:IJ Job Band: 1

Job Description

Window cleaners remove dirt and polish windows to keep them clean and shiny. They also clean other parts of buildings that are made of glass, such as skylights and conservatory roofs. May use ladders to reach the windows or extended water-fed poles that enable the work to be done from the ground to a height of around 60 ft. May work on very high buildings and have to work from safety cradles. Some window cleaners do additional jobs, such as cleaning and painting or clearing gutters. Cleaners often have to ask the customer to sign for the work that has been done, or collect cash or cheques, which need to be taken to the employer.

Work Details

Usually work a basic 38-39 hr week, Monday to Friday, though some weekend work may be required. Hours in summer are likely to be longer. You work outside most of the time in all weathers. You may be asked to clean the inside of windows too. You need to travel around from customer to customer and perhaps cope with climbing ladders and working at heights. This job can be quite dangerous as there is the risk of falling. In some jobs, you work in a cradle on high buildings and usually wear a safety harness. It is important to know and obey safety rules for work at heights and you need to wear protective overalls.

Qualification

• England, Wales and Northern Ireland

Band 1: For entry to jobs, no minimum qualifications are needed, but you are expected to have a good level of general education and relevant experience. Some formal/vocational qualifications at any level are useful.

• Scotland

Band 1: For entry to jobs, no minimum qualifications are needed, but you are expected to have a good level of general education and relevant experience. Some formal/vocational qualifications at any level are useful.

Adult Qualifications

No qualifications are needed. You can improve your skills and qualifications by working through the Foundation Learning programme. This involves taking credit-based units and qualifications to help you progress.

Work Experience

Any manual work experience can equip you with skills to use in the future and add to your CV. This can either be unpaid or voluntary, or can be holiday/part-time work that you have organised yourself.

Entry and Training

Training is usually on the job, working with an experienced window cleaner. Some large contract companies run an induction programme that lasts 2-3 days, which introduces you to the health and safety aspects of the job, customer care, and handling the equipment, such as cradles, ladders and water-fed poles. Some employers may offer vocational training. S/NVQs in cleaning and support services (window cleaning) are available at level 2. Relevant training programmes, including apprenticeship schemes, may be available in your area. A driving licence may be useful.

The Federation of Window Cleaners (FWC) offers relevant training in subjects, such as health and safety and employment law. Contact FWC for details. The British Window Cleaning Academy runs courses throughout the year at training centres in Swindon and Newcastle, from basic techniques to roof access skills and glass restoration. See its website for details.

Mature applicants with previous work experience within the building and construction industry may have an advantage. It may be possible to gain some financial support to help towards setting up your own business. Contact your local Connexions or careers office, Jobcentre Plus, Next Step service or Learning and Skills Council (LSC)/Local Enterprise Company (LEC) for details of all training opportunities and schemes, including apprenticeships for adults.

Opportunities and Pay

There is work throughout the UK, with more opportunities available in towns and cities. You work for a local small firm of window cleaners dealing with shops and private houses, or for larger contract cleaners, working in gangs on extensive office blocks and high-rise buildings. Many people become self-employed once they have been trained. You have to be insured and this can be expensive.

Pay varies, but as a guide, employed window cleaners earn in the region of £13k a year, rising with experience to £16k a year. Work on multi-storey buildings usually attracts much higher salaries. If self-employed, your pay depends on the number of customers you have and your charge rate for each job.

Health

You need to be fit and strong to do this work.

Skills and Qualities

able to work both on your own and in a team, able to work quickly, careful, cash handling skills, enjoy working outdoors, head for heights, safety conscious, trustworthy

Further Information

Apprenticeship Schemes (National Apprenticeship Service) - www.apprenticeships.org.uk

Asset Skills - sector skills council for the places where we live and work - www.assetskills.org

Foundation Learning (QCDA) - www.qcda.gov.uk

Addresses

British Institute of Cleaning Science (BICSc)
9 Premier Court, Boarden Close, Moulton Park, Northampton NN3 6LF
Phone: +44 (0)1604 678 710
Web: www.bics.org.uk

British Window Cleaning Academy (BWCA)
Alpha House Star West Westmead Industrial Estate, Swindon, Wiltshire SN5 7SW
Phone: +44 (0)1793 497786
Web: www.bwca.co.uk

Federation for Window Cleaners (FWC)
Summerfield House Harrogate Road Reddish, Stockport SK5 6HQ
Phone: +44 (0)161 432 8754
Web: www.f-w-c.co.uk/

Similar Jobs

Car Valet, Cleaner: Industrial, Painter & Decorator, Scaffolder, Steeplejack

Clerk of Works/Site Inspector

CRCI:Building and Construction
CLCI:UD Job Band: 2 to 5

Job Description

Clerk of works/site inspectors are employed by a client as impartial inspectors to regularly check the quality of materials and workmanship of construction companies carrying out building contracts. They ensure that the client gets the best value for money and check the contractor's drawings and written instructions. They take measurements and samples on a site to ensure that work meets the standards and specification expected by the client and make sure that the work is on schedule. An inspector is up to date on the rules and regulations that surround construction, such as building regulations, planning law, health and safety requirements etc.

Site inspectors liaise regularly with the building site supervisor/ manager, architects, engineers and sub-contractors. May advise the client on minor changes that can be made, though does not have the authority to enforce these suggestions. They keep detailed records, and present a weekly report to the client, and/or planner/architect.

Work Details

Usually work around 35-40 hrs a week, Monday to Friday, though may be required to do some evenings and weekends. You usually spend time travelling to various sites and nights spent away from home are common. The job can be quite isolated as you work independently of contracted workers. You are normally based in a temporary office when visiting a site, but work requires inspections to be outside and in all weathers. You may have to work on scaffolding or in confined spaces on some sites. This requires protective clothing, boots and a hard hat.

Clerk of Works/Site Inspector

Qualification

- **England, Wales and Northern Ireland**

Band 2: Although academic qualifications are not specified for this job, it is an advantage to have some GCSEs (A*-C) in subjects that include English and maths, or equivalent.

Band 3: For entry: usually at least 4 GCSEs (A*-C) including English and maths, or equivalent.

Band 4: For BTEC higher national award: 1-2 A levels, preferably including maths or a science subject, and some GCSEs (A*-C), or equivalent.

Band 5: For relevant degree: usually 2-3 A levels, preferably including maths or a science subject, and some GCSEs (A*-C), usually including English and maths, or equivalent. Exact requirements depend on the degree you take.

- **Scotland**

Band 2: Although academic qualifications are not specified for this job, it is an advantage to have some S grades (1-3) in subjects that include English and maths, or similar.

Band 3: For entry: usually four S grades (1-3) preferably including English and maths, or similar.

Band 4: For SQA higher national award: usually 2-3 H grades, preferably including maths or a science subject, and some S grades (1-3), or similar.

Band 5: For relevant degree: usually 3-5 H grades, preferably including maths or a science subject, and some S grades (1-3) usually including English and maths, or similar. Exact requirements depend on the degree you take.

Degree Information

A degree in any subject related to construction work, such as construction management, building construction and management, building studies, or civil engineering, is most useful. Postgraduate courses are available in this area of work.

Adult Qualifications

Entry requirements may be waived for mature applicants, particularly those with experience in construction. There are relevant Access courses to higher education including construction or the built environment.

Work Experience

Relevant work or voluntary experience is always useful and can improve your chances when applying for entry to construction jobs and apprenticeships. In some areas there is a young apprenticeship (14-16) scheme that provides an extended work placement and eventual achievement of a level 2 qualification whilst at school. Health and safety issues may mean that there are certain jobs you can't do until you are over 16. Contact your local ConstructionSkills office for advice.

Entry and Training

Experience in construction is as important as academic qualifications for entry to this job. It is therefore common for a clerk of works/site inspector to have started their careers in construction at craft level and progressed to site inspection after a number of years' experience and qualification. Some employers may provide sponsorship for degree study. Some clerk of works/ site inspectors may already have a degree in a subject such as construction management, building construction management or civil engineering, and have followed an in-house training programme with an employer.

A relevant full or part-time foundation degree is also possible. You are required to apply for the Construction Skills Certification Scheme card that provides evidence of your professional achievement. Membership of the Institute of Clerks of Works (ICW) is via a professional practice interview; ICW usually requires qualifications of a minimum equivalent to S/NVQ level 3 and relevant experience. You can apply for student membership if you are studying for qualifications at this level. Increasingly, employers require you to be members of the ICW, which also offers a programme of continuing professional development.

After obtaining a degree and having had a period of appropriate work experience, you can apply for membership of the Chartered Institute of Building (CIOB) through a professional interview. You can join the CIOB without a degree if you have three years of construction management experience. It is also possible to achieve chartered engineer status and become a member of the Institution of Civil Engineers.

A Diploma or Welsh Baccalaureate in construction and the built environment may be available in your area. Relevant S/NVQs are available in site inspection at levels 3-4 and in construction management/project management at level 5. Training programmes, including apprenticeship schemes, may be available in your area for entry to this job. Advanced apprenticeships leading to qualification at level 3 can also be a route into higher education.

Mature entry is common because of the need for previous experience in the construction industry. Entry is possible with a wide range of qualifications such as S/NVQ level 3 or BTEC/SQA national/higher national awards. Applicants without the appropriate qualifications are expected to have had considerable relevant experience.

Opportunities and Pay

Work is located throughout the UK and major employers include local and central government, and large private firms, including general building contractors, a building/civil engineering contractor, or a large national/international organisation. Availability of work depends on activity in the building trade and the national economy.

An experienced site inspector may become a contracts manager or a director of a construction company. Others may move into research or teaching. Many site inspectors are self-employed and are contracted to one or several independent projects. There are opportunities to work abroad, particularly in developing countries.

Pay varies depending on area and employer. Salaries tend to start at around £20k a year, rising to over £25k with experience. Senior clerks of works may earn over £35k.

Health

This job requires you to have stamina and be physically fit.

Skills and Qualities

able to follow drawings and plans, able to manage a budget and keep records, able to report accurately, attention to detail, good communication skills, good organisational skills, head for heights, health & safety awareness, information handling skills, technical aptitude

Relevant Subjects

Business and accounting, Construction and built environment, Design and technology, English, ICT/Computer studies, Mathematics, Physics, Science

Further Information

Apprenticeship Schemes (National Apprenticeship Service) - www.apprenticeships.org.uk

Construction Skills Certification Scheme (CSCS) - www.cscs.uk.com

ConstructionSkills - sector skills council for the construction industry - www.cskills.org

Diplomas (Foundation, Higher and Advanced) http:// yp.direct.gov.uk/diplomas

Site Recorder (monthly) (Institute of Clerks of Works etc.) - www.icwgb.org/

Welsh Baccalaureate - www.wbq.org.uk

▶Working in construction & the built environment (2007) (Babcock Lifeskills) - www.babcock-lifeskills.com/

Addresses

Chartered Institute of Building (CIOB)
Englemere King's Ride, Ascot, Berkshire SL5 7TB
Phone: +44 (0)1344 630 700
Web: www.ciob.org.uk

Institute of Clerks of Works
28 Commerce Road Lynch Wood, Peterborough PE2 6LR
Phone: +44 (0)1733 405 160
Web: www.icwgb.org

Institution of Civil Engineers (ICE)
1 Great George Street, Westminster, London SW1P 3AA
Phone: +44 (0)20 7222 7722
Web: www.ice.org.uk

Similar Jobs

Civil Engineering Technician, Construction Site Supervisor/Manager, Engineer: Building Services, Surveyor: Building Control, Surveyor: Quantity

Clerk: Accounts

also known as: Accounts Clerk, Bookkeeper, Cashier: Office, Finance Clerk

CRCI:Financial Services
CLCI:CAT Job Band: 2 to 3

Job Description

Accounts clerks keep accurate records of the accounts and financial work of an organisation, educational establishment, or company. Prepare invoices and make payments for goods or services that the company has bought. May keep records of services or goods sold to customers, make up invoices and make sure that the correct payment is received on time. They help to prepare final accounts, such as profit and loss accounts and balance sheets. Use computerised accounting systems.

If working in a college or university, accounts clerks calculate, invoice and collect all fees such as tuition and accommodation fees.

Work Details

Usually work a basic 35-39 hrs a week, from 9am to 5pm, Monday to Friday. This job is mainly office based. You may have to spend a lot of time using computers and speaking to people on the phone. The work has to be done neatly and accurately. Flexitime and part-time working opportunities are possible. You are likely to spend a lot of the time each day working on a computer.

Qualification

- **England, Wales and Northern Ireland**

Band 2: Although academic qualifications are not specified for this job, it is an advantage to have some GCSEs (A*-C) in subjects that include English and maths, or equivalent, and have keyboard/computer skills. Subjects such as business studies and accounting are also useful.

Band 3: For entry: usually at least 4 GCSEs (A*-C) including English and maths, or equivalent.

- **Scotland**

Band 2: Although academic qualifications are not specified for this job, it is an advantage to have some S grades (1-3) in subjects that include English and maths, or similar, and have keyboard/computer skills. Subjects such as business studies and accounting are also useful.

Band 3: For entry: four S grades (1-3) including English and maths, or similar.

Adult Qualifications

There are no set entry qualifications, but some relevant office experience, working with figures or handling money is an advantage. Some employers may prefer mature applicants.

Work Experience

Relevant work or voluntary experience is always useful and can equip you with skills that you can use in the future and that you can add to your CV. Temporary holiday work in offices via employment agencies is useful, particularly if you can develop good keyboard skills and a knowledge of the most popular accounting software packages. In some areas there is a young apprenticeship (14-16) scheme that provides an extended work placement and eventual achievement of a relevant level 2 qualification whilst at school.

Entry and Training

Training is usually a mixture of on-the-job training and attendance on relevant courses. Some companies run their own training programmes or you may take a part-time college course, such as BTEC/SQA awards in subjects such as accounting, business studies or business and finance. The Association of Accounting Technicians (AAT) runs a bookkeeping certificate at level 2 and the International Association of Bookkeepers (IAB) offers a range of professional certificates/diplomas in bookkeeping, computerised accounting, accounting and financial management. These compliment the business, administration and finance Diploma/Welsh Baccalaureate which may also be available in your area.

The Institute of Certified Bookkeepers also offers a range of courses, including the certificate in basic bookkeeping and a qualification in small business financial control. These courses are available both face to face and by distance learning. Some accounts clerks go on to take the AAT accounting technician exams. Progression through further study can lead to accountancy qualifications.

You may also be able to gain S/NVQs at levels 1-3. Training programmes, including apprenticeship schemes, may be available in your area. Advanced apprenticeships leading to qualification at level 3 can also be a route into higher education. The Financial Services Skills Council (FSSC) offers apprenticeships for both new and existing employees. The apprenticeship is made up of a technical certificate which represents a professional qualification, an NVQ/SVQ and the opportunity to obtain, key, core and essential skills. Contact the FSSC for further details.

It is useful to have knowledge of programs such as Microsoft Access, Excel and accounting software, including Sage, TAS and QuickBooks.

Government training opportunities, such as apprenticeships, may be available in your area. You can also gain recognition of previous experience through Accreditation of Prior Learning (APL) or by working towards relevant S/NVQs. Contact your local Connexions or careers office, Jobcentre Plus, Next Step service or Learning and Skills Council (LSC)/Local Enterprise Company (LEC) for details of training schemes. Distance learning courses at all levels are available from the Institute of Certified Bookkeepers.

Opportunities and Pay

Accounts/finance clerks work in the accounts departments or offices of many different organisations, in private companies, educational institutions and in local and central government. Promotion prospects are usually better for staff who take courses in bookkeeping, accounting or business. Freelance work may be possible.

Pay varies depending on location and employer. Starting salaries are likely to be around £14k-£17k rising to around £19k a year with experience. Senior accounts clerks earn from £22k-£25k a year, depending on qualifications and experience.

Skills and Qualities
able to work both on your own and in a team, able to work to deadlines, accurate, good concentration level, good organisational skills, good spoken communication, good written English, methodical, numeracy skills, specialist IT skills

Relevant Subjects
Business and accounting, ICT/Computer studies, Mathematics

Further Information
Accountancy Uncovered (Trotman 2010) - www.trotman.co.uk

Apprenticeship Schemes (National Apprenticeship Service) - www.apprenticeships.org.uk

Diploma in Business, Administration and Finance - www.baf-diploma.org.uk/

Financial Services Skills Council - sector skills council for financial services, accountancy & finance www.fssc.org.uk/

Student Guide to the AAT Accounting Qualification (Association of Accounting Technicians) - www.aat.org.uk/

Training Schemes - www.direct.gov.uk/en/educationandlearning

Welsh Baccalaureate - www.wbq.org.uk

Addresses
Association of Accounting Technicians (AAT)
140 Aldersgate Street, London EC1A 4HY
Phone: +44 (0)20 7397 3000
Web: www.aat.org.uk

Institute of Certified Bookkeepers
1 Northumberland Avenue, Trafalgar Square, London WC2N 5BW
Phone: 0845 060 2345 (UK only)
Web: www.book-keepers.org

International Association of Bookkeepers (IAB)
Suite 30 , 40 Churchill Square Kings Hil, West Malling, Kent ME19 4YU
Phone: 0844 330 3527 (UK only)
Web: www.iab.org.uk

Similar Jobs
Accounting Technician, Bank Officer, Civil Service Administrative Assistant, Law Costs Draftsman, Legal Cashier, Payroll Officer, Pensions Administrator

Clinical Molecular Geneticist
also known as: Molecular Geneticist

CRCI:Science, Mathematics and Statistics
CLCI:QOD Job Band: 5

Job Description
Molecular geneticists examine DNA to identify single gene abnormalities or other genetic disorders. They use a range of state-of-the-art chemical techniques and methodologies in their analysis and work quickly and with meticulous accuracy. Geneticists Interpret results and provide advice on appropriate investigations to other healthcare professionals looking after patients and their families. They may confirm a diagnosis of a genetic disorder. In prenatal diagnosis, cells are examined for possible abnormalities in the foetus (unborn child) usually where single gene disorders have previously been identified in a family.

Can also detect from blood samples to identify whether a patient is a carrier of a particular genetic disorder or disease such as cystic fibrosis. Geneticists rarely have patient contact but are aware of the impact their research and tests may have on patients and their families.

Work Details
Usually work 36-38 hrs a week, Monday to Friday, in a laboratory, university, college or hospital. Depending on your employment, you may have responsibility for setting up experiments, analysing results and presenting reports. In hospital work, you provide information and advice for diagnosis and treatment of a patient and occasionally have direct contact with them. This work requires a high degree of accuracy at all times. Sometimes the work may be pressurised and intense.

At a senior level, you may be required to supervise trainees and junior members of staff. You may need to wear a white coat or overall and protective clothing, such as gloves.

Qualification

- **England, Wales and Northern Ireland**

Band 5: For degree courses: 2-3 A levels in appropriate science subjects and some GCSEs (A*-C) usually including English, maths and double science, or equivalent. Exact requirements depend on the degree you take.

- **Scotland**

Band 5: For degree courses: 3-5 H grades in appropriate science subjects and some S grades (1-3), usually including English, maths and double science, or similar. Exact requirements depend on the degree you take.

Degree Information
Degrees in genetics, molecular biology, biomedical science, biotechnology, biochemistry or medicine are preferred by employers. Some courses offer molecular or human genetics, or combine genetics with other biological sciences. Some other biological science degrees give a useful background.

Adult Qualifications
A degree and up-to-date scientific knowledge are essential. Course requirements may be relaxed for mature applicants provided they submit evidence of previous serious study, such as a relevant Access course. Credit is given for relevant experience, especially of laboratory work. It is also possible for those without the specified science qualifications to take a foundation year leading into the relevant degree. Check with individual colleges and universities for specific entry requirements.

Work Experience
Universities and employers often prefer candidates who have relevant work or voluntary experience in a hospital, a relevant university department or an industrial or commercial laboratory. If it proves difficult to gain this exact experience, then similar or other scientific backgrounds are still attractive to employers and admissions tutors.

Entry and Training
Training can be by practical experience after obtaining a degree or postgraduate qualification in genetics or a relevant biological science. Degree courses can be full time or sandwich and last for 3-4 years. A number of suitable first degree courses are available and there are also some relevant postgraduate courses. Some employers prefer to recruit entrants with postgraduate qualifications. Clinical molecular geneticists work towards the Clinical Molecular Genetics Society (CMGS)'s certificate of competence. There is a structured clinical scientist training programme provided by a number of UK molecular genetics laboratories. Your work is guided and monitored by the laboratory training officer.

The first two years covers modules in techniques, diseases, management, scientific and other elementary knowledge. Once assessed you can be awarded the postgraduate certificate of competence in clinical molecular genetics, which serves as the foundation for mandatory registration with the Health Professions Council (HPC) as a clinical scientist. The following two years broaden your clinical experience whilst under the supervision of a registered clinical scientist.

Successful completion leads to HPC full registration after which you must agree to undertake a programme of continuing professional development (CPD). Further training in this career can lead to membership of the Royal College of Pathologists (RCPath).

Mature applicants with research experience in clinical or pharmaceutical areas may have an advantage.

Opportunities and Pay

This is one of the fastest growing scientific fields and genetics is a rapidly developing discipline. Most molecular geneticists work in the regional genetics centres for the NHS, but there is also work with government agencies and departments, private laboratories, cancer research laboratories, pharmaceutical firms, the food industry, environmental organisations, agrochemical industry and universities. There are opportunities for work abroad, sometimes in developing countries.

Pay and promotion prospects depend largely on the type of employer, and are dependent on further training, additional responsibility and experience. The starting salary for a graduate clinical scientist trainee is £22k a year, rising to £27k-£35k for a registered clinical scientist. Principal clinical scientists can earn up to £42k and consultants up to £73k a year.

Health

There may be a risk of allergy from skin irritants or of infection. This job requires good colour vision for certain areas of work.

Skills and Qualities

accurate, analytical skills, aptitude for teamwork, good communication skills, IT skills, methodical, observant, problem-solving skills, research skills

Relevant Subjects

Biology, Chemistry, English, Health and social care, ICT/Computer studies, Mathematics, Physics, Science

Further Information

British Society for Human Genetics Newsletter (3 x year) (BSHG) - www.bshg.org.uk/

Clinical Molecular Genetics Society (CMGS) - www.cmgs.org

NHS Careers (NHS Careers) - www.nhscareers.nhs.uk

▶Working in science (2007) (Babcock Lifeskills) - www.babcock-lifeskills.com/

Addresses

British Society for Human Genetics (BSHG)
Clinical Genetics Unit, Birmingham Women's Hospital B15 2TG
Phone: +44 (0)121 627 2634
Web: www.bshg.org.uk

Health Professions Council (HPC)
Park House, 184 Kennington Park Road, London SE11 4BU
Phone: +44 (0)20 7582 0866
Web: www.hpc-uk.org

Royal College of Pathologists (RCPath)
2 Carlton House Terrace, London SW1Y 5AF
Phone: +44 (0)20 7451 6700
Web: www.rcpath.org

The Genetics Society (GS)
Roslin Biocentre, Wallace Building, Midlothian EH25 9PS
Phone: +44 (0)131 200 6392
Web: www.genetics.org.uk

Similar Jobs

Biochemist, Biologist, Biotechnologist, Cytogeneticist, Embryologist, Geneticist

Clinical Research Associate

also known as: Clinical Trials Scientist, Pharmaceutical Trials Scientist

CRCI:Science, Mathematics and Statistics
CLCI:QOB Job Band: 5

Job Description

Clinical research associates (CRAs) organise and supervise clinical trials on the effects, risks, side effects and benefits of a medicinal product. They design each trial, recruit the participants and investigators, and supervise the running of the trial. Trials use willing and healthy volunteers to confirm the results of laboratory tests. CRAs coordinate research, and liaise with other research staff and medical practitioners including GPs, hospital pharmacists and hospital doctors.

They analyse and interpret results, then write accurate and technical reports. Final analysis and report summaries are sent to the various regulatory bodies that approve the medicine/drug for safe and effective use. Work varies between companies. In some the CRAs are involved in the whole research process, in others they may be involved in the collection of data and then confirming results once the trial is complete.

Work Details

Usually work standard office hours, Monday to Friday in a laboratory, university, research institute or office. Sometimes may need to work early mornings, evenings or weekends. May have responsibility for analysing results, presenting reports, monitoring safety standards and ensuring guidelines covering the use of humans and animals in clinical trials are observed. You inform and consult with people and supervise staff.

It is often necessary to travel to different sites nationally and internationally. A driving licence is useful. Protective clothing may be necessary for some of the work.

Qualification

• England, Wales and Northern Ireland

Band 5: For degree courses: 2-3 A levels including biology, chemistry and other science subject or maths, and some GCSEs (A*-C) usually including English, science and maths. Exact requirements depend on the degree you take.

• Scotland

Band 5: For degree courses: 3-5 H grades including biology, chemistry and other science subject or maths, and some S grades (1-3), usually including English, science and maths. Exact requirements depend on the degree you take.

Degree Information

A life sciences or nursing degree is required. Subjects such as pharmacology, pharmacy, biology, biochemistry, immunology, medicine, physiology or toxicology, are particularly relevant. There are relevant postgraduate courses available.

Adult Qualifications

A formal qualification such as a degree and up-to-date scientific knowledge is essential. Course requirements may be relaxed for mature applicants provided they submit evidence of previous serious study, such as a relevant Access or foundation course. Check with universities or colleges for information. Credit is given for relevant experience.

Work Experience

Universities and employers may prefer candidates who have relevant work or voluntary experience, such as hospital work, work in a relevant university department or an industrial/commercial laboratory. If it proves difficult to gain this exact experience, then any work with a scientific background is attractive to employers and admissions tutors.

Entry and Training

Entry requirements usually include a life sciences degree. Degree courses last for three to four years and can be full time or sandwich. Postgraduate study may be an advantage, as is relevant work experience. You may be able to work towards a relevant postgraduate degree whilst in employment. The ability to use computers is also an advantage. Entry is usually at research associate level unless you are a medical doctor. With experience in handling one set of trials you may then progress to executive level that can involve up to three trial studies.

Training continues through practical experience in the workplace. Some institutions run trainee schemes, often supplemented by short or residential courses which include clinical and data management skills, standard operating procedures and ethical quality issues. Membership of the British Pharmacological Society (BPS) can be attained by graduates with appropriate qualifications and/or relevant experience.

Mature applicants to courses with previous experience in nursing, medical sales, clinical laboratory work or pharmaceutical research, have an advantage. It is also an advantage to have a relevant postgraduate degree, though some employers may sponsor a graduate on an MSc postgraduate course.

Opportunities and Pay

Once qualified and experienced, prospects are good. Opportunities arise in most large towns or cities but most pharmaceutical companies are based in the south of England. Other employers include health research organisations and universities. Progression is to more senior grades with increasing responsibility. Promotion can be easier with higher qualifications such as a PhD. Self-employment is not common though some contract research organisations may offer freelance or part-time work. Currently, there is a shortage of qualified clinical research associates (CRAs).

Salary varies depending on location, the type of employer, role and responsibility. Starting salaries average £20k-£23k a year, rising to around £25k-£35k a year with experience. The most experienced clinical research associates are equivalent in status to a consultant and can earn £50k a year. A car is often provided and bonuses may be paid.

Health

You need normal colour vision for some areas of work. There is a risk of allergy from skin irritants.

Skills and Qualities

able to communicate effectively, able to motivate others, able to report accurately, able to work to deadlines, administrative skills, analytical skills, aptitude for teamwork, IT skills, numeracy skills, responsible attitude, scientific approach

Relevant Subjects

Biology, Chemistry, English, ICT/Computer studies, Mathematics, Physics, Science

Further Information

Association of the British Pharmaceutical Industry (ABPI) - www.abpi.org.uk/education

Clinical Research Focus (10 x a year) (Institute of Clinical Research) - www.icr-global.org/crfocus/

NHS Careers (NHS Careers) - www.nhscareers.nhs.uk

▶Working in science (2007) (Babcock Lifeskills) - www.babcock-lifeskills.com/

Addresses

British Pharmacological Society (BPS)
16 Angel Gate City Road, London EC1V 2PT
Phone: +44 (0) 131 718 4457
Web: www.bps.ac.uk

Institute of Clinical Research (ICR)
Institute House, Boston Drive, Bourne End, Buckinghamshire SL8 5YS
Phone: +44 (0) 1628 536960
Web: www.icr-global.org

Royal Pharmaceutical Society of Great Britain (RPSGB)
1 Lambeth High Street, London SE1 7JN
Phone: +44 (0)20 7735 9141
Web: www.rpharms.com

Society of Biology
9 Red Lion Court, London EC4A 3EF
Phone: +44 (0)20 7936 5900
Web: http://societyofbiology.org/home

Similar Jobs

Biomedical Scientist, Microbiologist, Pathologist, Pharmacist: Industrial, Pharmacologist, Sales Executive: Medical, Writer: Technical

Clinical Scientist: Medical Physicist

also known as: Medical Physicist

CRCI:Healthcare

CLCI:JOB — Job Band: 5

Job Description

Medical physicists apply physical sciences to medicine to help prevent, diagnose and treat disease. They work with medical staff, planning the nature and extent of treatment for a patient. Calculate treatments such as radiotherapy, and give advice on radiation protection. Develop systems for capturing images and processes images to aid diagnosis. They keep up to date with the latest developments in X-rays, nuclear medicine, ultrasound imaging, laser Doppler blood flow measurement and magnetic resonance imaging (MRI). Make physiological measurements, using mathematical models of temperature, pressure, perfusion and flow of body fluids, which assists surgery and intensive therapy.

Medical physicists play a crucial role in the development of radiology, nuclear medicine and radiation oncology. Some also work in cardiology and neurology. May manage a team of biomedical scientists and other support staff such as medical technologists, laboratory assistants and clerical assistants. Many also teach and do research.

Work Details

Usually work around 37 hrs a week, Monday to Friday, though may be expected to work irregular hours. You advise and consult with medical staff and patients, and have contact with people who are ill or in pain. The job carries a responsibility for radiation safety and protection of staff and patients. This work requires knowledge of new technical developments and a high degree of accuracy. You need to be aware of regulations governing health and safety at work. There is a risk of exposure to radiation.

Qualification

- **England, Wales and Northern Ireland**

Band 5: For degree courses: 2-3 A levels including maths and physics, and some GCSEs (A*-C) usually including English and maths, or equivalent. Exact requirements depend on the degree you take.

- **Scotland**

Band 5: For degree courses: 3-5 H grades usually including maths and physics, and some S grades (1-3), usually including English and maths, or similar qualifications. Exact requirements depend on the degree you take.

Degree Information
Usually a good honours degree in physical science or a computing or engineering subject that is accredited by the Institute of Physics & Engineering in Medicine and followed by a postgraduate qualification, usually an MSc or PhD in the medical physics field.

Adult Qualifications
Some universities have special entry schemes for mature applicants. Check with individual universities for details. In some areas Access and foundation courses leading to appropriate degrees are available.

Work Experience
Universities and employers may prefer candidates who have relevant work or voluntary experience. Work experience in a hospital, a relevant university department or an industrial or commercial laboratory is ideal, but other scientific backgrounds are also attractive to employers and admissions tutors.

Entry and Training
You need a relevant degree accredited by the Institute of Physics and many entrants also have an appropriate postgraduate qualification, but it is possible to study for this while in employment. Training is through a two year in-service programme leading to an MSc and the diploma of the Institute of Physics & Engineering in Medicine (IPEM). As part of the programme of advanced training, there is then a further two years of supervised practice to achieve registration with the Health Professions Council who regulate this profession, or registration as a chartered scientist (CSci) or chartered engineer (CEng). Contact the IPEM for details of qualifications, training routes and state registration.

Vacancies are advertised by the NHS Clinical Scientists recruitment service. See the website for further details.

Mature entrants to this job in the NHS require an honours degree in a physics or engineering subject and follow the same training route towards an MSc and the diploma of the Institute of Physics & Engineering in Medicine. Those with an appropriate postgraduate qualification or relevant experience in the healthcare industry may have an advantage.

Opportunities and Pay
Over 1500 medical physicists are employed in the UK and opportunities are growing, but this is a small profession and a highly competitive area. Most medical physicists are employed by the NHS or healthcare industry, but there are also some posts in universities and research organisations and in manufacturing medical equipment. Jobs are available mainly in towns and cities and there are opportunities to work overseas. There is a well structured NHS progression route and promotion depends on obtaining professional qualification.

Pay for a medical physicist working for the NHS follows the salary scale for clinical scientists and is divided into levels of experience. Starting salary is around £25k-£34k a year, rising with experience to £38k. Top salaries can be £50k-£80k a year.

Skills and Qualities
able to cope under pressure, able to explain clearly, efficient record keeping, good communication skills, good interpersonal skills, problem-solving skills, reassuring, responsible attitude, scientific approach, technical aptitude

Relevant Subjects
Biology, Chemistry, Design and technology, Engineering, English, Health and social care, ICT/Computer studies, Mathematics, Physics, Science

Further Information
AGCAS: Health (Job Sector Briefing) (AGCAS) - www.prospects.ac.uk

European Federation of Organisations for Medical Physics - www.efomp.org

Health Professions Council (HPC) - www.hpc-uk.org

NHS Careers (NHS Careers) - www.nhscareers.nhs.uk

NHS Careers Scotland - www.infoscotland.com/nhs

NHS Clinical Scientists Recruitment Services - www.nhsclinicalscientists.info

▶Working in maths (2009) (Babcock Lifeskills) - www.babcock-lifeskills.com/

Addresses
Association of Clinical Scientists (ACS)
c/o Association of Clinical Biochemists, 130-132 Tooley St, London SE1 2TU
Web: www.assclinsci.org

Institute of Physics (IOP)
76 Portland Place, London W1B 1NT
Phone: +44 (0)20 7470 4800
Web: www.iop.org

Institute of Physics and Engineering in Medicine (IPEM)
Fairmount House, 230 Tadcaster Road, York YO24 1ES
Phone: +44 (0)1904 610 821
Web: www.ipem.ac.uk

Similar Jobs
Audiological Scientist, Biomedical Scientist, Clinical Technologist, Physicist, Radiographer: Diagnostic, Radiographer: Therapeutic

Clinical Technologist
also known as: Medical Physics Technician, Medical Technologist, Medical Technologist: Clinical Engineering, Medical Technologist: Medical Physics

CRCI:Healthcare
CLCI:JOB — Job Band: 4 to 5

Job Description
Clinical technologists monitor, maintain and operate a range of advanced and complex machinery and equipment used in medical diagnosis and treatment. They work closely with clinical scientists, physiological measurement technicians or doctors, as increasingly sophisticated equipment, instruments and techniques are developed and come into use. Work in one of a range of specialist areas, including radiotherapy, medical engineering or nuclear medicine where the clinical technologist is responsible for purifying radioactive materials, calculating the required dose, and ensuring the safe disposal of waste material.

Those specialising in radiotherapy, ultrasound or renal dialysis have a high degree of patient contact. Others working in areas such as lasers, radiation protection or engineering have little or no contact with patients. Can also be directly involved in the research and development of new equipment and techniques.

Work Details
You usually work a 37 hr week in a hospital assisting senior colleagues, but may be required to work shifts on a rota to cover 24 hrs a day, including some weekends. Overtime work is also possible. May need to visit patients' homes, to check and repair kidney dialysis equipment. You are responsible for radiation safety and protection of staff and need to be aware of the regulations governing health and safety at work. Work requires a high degree of accuracy. There is a risk of exposure to radiation. You need to wear a white coat or overall and perhaps protective clothing.

Qualification

- **England, Wales and Northern Ireland**

Band 4: For some employers: 1-2 A levels and some GCSEs (A*-C) usually including English, science and maths, or equivalent so that you are able to take a degree while training.

Band 5: For degree courses: 2-3 A levels, preferably two science subjects, and some GCSEs (A*-C) usually including English, maths and two science subjects or dual science. Exact requirements depend on the degree you take.

- **Scotland**

Band 4: For some employers: usually 2-3 H grades and some S grades (1-3), often including English, science and maths, or equivalent so that you are able to take a degree while training.

Band 5: For degree courses: 3-5 H grades, preferably two science subjects and some S grades (1-3), usually including English, maths and two science subjects, or dual science, or similar qualifications. Exact requirements depend on the degree you take.

Degree Information

A degree in clinical technology is available though subjects that include physical science, electronics, physics, medical physics, electrical, medical or mechanical engineering are also acceptable. Foundation degrees in clinical technology are also available.

Adult Qualifications

Entry requirements may be relaxed for adults applying for higher education courses and Access and foundation courses give adults without qualifications a route on to degree courses.

Work Experience

Work experience gives you an insight into what you enjoy about a job or working environment, as well as the opportunity to acquire new skills. It provides valuable information to add to your CV and improves your employment prospects. Consider working in electronics or engineering, or gaining experience in a variety of hospital departments. There is usually a waiting list for work experience in hospitals so enquire early.

Entry and Training

You usually become a clinical technologist by obtaining a relevant degree in physics or engineering, or by enrolling on a university vocational degree course in clinical technology. This can be in radiation-based subjects or in engineering-based subjects and studied over two years full time or three years part time. Make sure a course is accredited by the Institute of Physics & Engineering in Medicine (IPEM) and allows you to register on the IPEM training scheme for clinical technologists.

Some hospitals advertise for trainee clinical technologists and allow you to take the degree course on a part-time basis while working in a medical physics or clinical engineering department. If you already have post-A level qualifications these are valid and may shorten the training period for completion of the degree and enable state registration at an earlier date. Contact IPEM for details on all training opportunities and qualifications.

It is advisable to join the Voluntary Register of Clinical Technologists once you are qualified. Contact IPEM for details.

Mature applicants are particularly welcome though you usually require an accredited degree/postgraduate degree for direct entry. Competition for training posts is strong.

Opportunities and Pay

This is currently a small but growing profession. Jobs are available mainly in cities and large towns throughout the UK. You can be employed by the NHS in a hospital, by a local authority or the armed forces, or in a private medical institution or laboratory but there are few opportunities with private companies. Promotion is often through a formal career structure leading to departmental senior officers and managers and usually requires a more advanced qualification. Those who acquire a higher degree may become clinical scientists. It is also possible to offer independent services and work for yourself.

Pay in the NHS is on a nationally agreed scale and increases with promotion. Starting salaries for clinical technologists are between £21k-£27k a year. Specialist clinical technologists earn between £25k-£34k a year and those in senior posts may earn more.

Skills and Qualities

able to put people at ease, able to work both on your own and in a team, accurate, attention to detail, caring, excellent communication skills, IT skills, manual dexterity, responsible attitude, technical aptitude

Relevant Subjects

Biology, Chemistry, Design and technology, Engineering, Health and social care, ICT/Computer studies, Mathematics, Physics, Science

Further Information

NHS Careers (NHS Careers) - www.nhscareers.nhs.uk

NHS Careers Scotland - www.infoscotland.com/nhs

NHS Careers Wales - www.wales.nhs.uk

Voluntary Register of Clinical Technologists (VRCT) - www.vrct.org.uk

Addresses

Institute of Physics and Engineering in Medicine (IPEM)
Fairmount House, 230 Tadcaster Road, York YO24 1ES
Phone: +44 (0)1904 610 821
Web: www.ipem.ac.uk

Similar Jobs

Cardiac Physiologist, Clinical Scientist: Medical Physicist, Neurophysiologist, Perfusionist, Radiographer: Diagnostic, Respiratory Physiologist

Cloakroom Attendant

also known as: Luggage Attendant

CRCI:Catering and Hospitality
CLCI:IJ
Job Band: 1

Job Description

Attendants are responsible for the safe storage and return of a customer's clothing, umbrellas, bags, luggage and parcels. This can be in hotels, theatres, clubs, restaurants, conferences and exhibitions, museums, art galleries, civic and central government buildings, and other places of interest. Attendants take the item and put a numbered ticket, plastic identification disc or label on it, so that it can be found when the customer needs it. They may scan the item with an X-ray machine in places that operate with high security.

They usually give the person a receipt, and may take payment and give change. Also stores things tidily in a safe place until the owner returns. Attendants may offer to brush down a guest's jacket or coat. Some attendants supervise the washrooms, making sure that there are supplies of fresh towels, toilet rolls and soap etc. In some cloakrooms there may be items such as perfumes for the ladies and fragrances/colognes for the men.

Work Details

Usually works 39-40 hrs a week, on a shift basis that may include evenings, weekends and public holidays. You often work on your own but meet all kinds of people. Some people may be awkward. For example, at the end of a performance or event, large numbers of people require their coat or belongings at the same time. You need to be calm, polite and helpful while you find their belongings quickly. Attendants must also be careful and make sure that items in their care are not lost or damaged. You may have to lift cases and heavy bags.

Attendants who are responsible for looking after the washrooms must have excellent hygiene skills and be aware of the rules that govern health and safety. Attendants usually wear a uniform or protective clothing when necessary.

Qualification

• England, Wales and Northern Ireland

Band 1: For entry to jobs, no minimum qualifications are needed, but you are expected to have a good level of general education and relevant experience. Some formal/vocational qualifications at any level are useful. Employers look for people with good communication skills and a personable nature.

• Scotland

Band 1: For entry to jobs, no minimum qualifications are needed, but you are expected to have a good level of general education and relevant experience. Some formal/vocational qualifications at any level are useful. Employers look for people with good communication skills and a personable nature.

Adult Qualifications

No formal qualifications are required but employers expect good numeracy skills. You can improve your skills and qualifications by working through the Foundation Learning programme. This involves taking credit-based units and qualifications to help you progress.

Work Experience

Any work experience equips you with skills that you can use in the future and add to your CV. Experience of working with the public, perhaps in customer care or sales, is helpful. Saturday jobs and seasonal work are also useful.

Entry and Training

Training is usually on the job working with an experienced colleague. Larger employers may offer induction training to cover health and safety, security, evacuation procedures and customer care. You may be offered a training programme that includes qualifications such as S/NVQs in customer care, hospitality, housekeeping or in aspects of security. Some employers may provide the opportunity to gain relevant qualifications off the job at a local college, usually on a day-release basis.

The Hospitality Awarding Body (HAB) offers certificates and awards in customer service and conflict handling. Training programmes including apprenticeships at level 2 may be available in your area. Hospitality and Customer Service apprenticeships may include some cloakroom duties. A Diploma/Welsh Baccalaureate may be available in your area in hospitality.

Mature entrants are often preferred by employers and those with a background in security and/or experience in dealing with the public in a customer service role have an advantage.

Government training opportunities, such as apprenticeships, may be available in your area. You can also gain recognition of previous experience through Accreditation of Prior Learning (APL) or by working towards relevant S/NVQs. Contact your local careers office, Jobcentre Plus, Next Step service or Learning and Skills Council (LSC) Local Enterprise Company (LEC) for details of training schemes.

Opportunities and Pay

Around 6,000 people work as cloakroom attendants in the UK. There are full or part-time jobs in many different places. Employers include rail, airport and bus companies, large museums, owners of hotels and restaurants, large office buildings, clubs and theatres, and local and central government. There are opportunities with specialist luggage firms that offer a left-luggage storage facility at airports and rail stations, although these are fewer now due to security risks. Some companies that manage sport and entertainment events or business conferences employ cloakroom attendants. There may be opportunities for promotion to supervisory level.

Pay varies depending on area and employer. Many are paid an hourly rate based on the minimum wage (£4.83-£4.92 an hour if you are 18-20 and up to £5.93 an hour if you are over 21). Pay can be increased by tips or overtime work. A cloakroom attendant with supervisory responsibilities may earn up to £20k.

Skills and Qualities

able to work well on your own, alert, friendly, helpful, numeracy skills, polite, reliable, responsible attitude, trustworthy

Relevant Subjects

Hospitality and catering

Further Information

Apprenticeship Schemes (National Apprenticeship Service) - www.apprenticeships.org.uk
CareerScope: Hospitality and Leisure (Springboard UK) - http://careerscope.springboarduk.net/
Caterer and Hotelkeeper (weekly) (Reed Business Information) - www.catersearch.com/Home/
City & Guilds Hospitality Awarding Body - www.hab.org.uk
Diploma in Hospitality (People 1st) - www.hospitalitydiploma.co.uk
Foundation Learning (QCDA) - www.qcda.gov.uk
People 1st - sector skills council for hospitality, leisure, travel and tourism - www.people1st.co.uk
Real Life Guide to Hospitality & Event Management (Trotman 2010) - www.trotman.co.uk
Springboard Wales (Springboard Wales) - http://wales.springboarduk.net/

Addresses

Springboard UK
3 Denmark Street, London WC2H 8LP
Phone: +44 (0)20 7497 8654
Web: www.springboarduk.org.uk

Similar Jobs

Airport Baggage Handler, Cleaner: Industrial, Hotel Porter, Parking Attendant

Close Protection Officer/Bodyguard

also known as: Personal Protection Officer

CRCI:Security and Armed Forces
CLCI:MAG   Job Band: 1 to 3

Job Description

Close protection officers (CPOs) provide safety and security from unwanted attention for individuals or groups of people, including sports and media celebrities, politicians and diplomats, barristers and judges, high profile business executives, heads of state and royalty. Protection often extends to family members. They look at any situation that is potentially harmful for the client, such as a risk of kidnapping and the threat of physical violence. Whilst much of the work is discreet, you may need to provide a physical presence to protect the client (or clients) during business or social visits, or at crowded events to protect them from the enthusiasm of admiring fans or the inquisitive.

Accompany clients when attending and leaving venues, and also on trips abroad whether business or social. Check out the proposed indoor/outdoor premises, such as offices, conference suites, political rallies, corporate venues, sporting events, film premiers, restaurants, theatres, aeroplanes and hotels.

Close Protection Officer/Bodyguard

CPOs keep constantly alert and liaise regularly with other security personnel, often working in teams. Use highly specialised communication devices and equipment. Are also competent in a range of combative skills, both armed and unarmed. Some CPOs specialise in defensive and evasive driving, surveillance work, or in providing protection at a client's residence.

Work Details

Often work long shifts, which usually cover 24-hour protection. Evening and weekend work is common. Travel is often necessary and may include spending long periods away from home. A driving licence is essential. Much of the work entails planning tasks such as arranging hotels, acquiring transport, security/police liaising, assessing evacuation services, and public relations. May work indoors or at outdoor venues such as at political meetings. May need to stand in fixed positions for long periods.

Qualification

• England, Wales and Northern Ireland

Band 1: Formal qualifications are not specified though some GCSEs or equivalent at any level, are useful.

Band 2: Although academic qualifications are not specified for this job, it is an advantage to have some GCSEs (A*-C) in subjects that include English and maths, or equivalent.

Band 3: For BTEC national award: usually at least 4 GCSEs (A*-C) including English, or equivalent qualifications.

• Scotland

Band 1: Formal qualifications are not specified though some S grades or similar at any level, are useful.

Band 2: Although academic qualifications are not specified for this job, it is an advantage to have some S grades (1-3) in subjects that include English and maths, or similar.

Band 3: For SQA national award: usually at least four S grades (1-3), including English or similar qualifications.

Adult Qualifications

Whilst no formal qualifications are specified, people enter this job with a wide range of formal and vocational qualifications, or none. However, you are expected to have a good level of general education as this is vital when writing reports and plans.

Work Experience

Work experience gives you an insight into what you enjoy and don't enjoy about a job or working environment, as well as the opportunity to acquire new skills. It also provides valuable information to add to your CV and improves any course application and/or your future employment prospects. You can gain valuable experience as a volunteer for the army or naval service reserve or by developing specialist driving skills.

Entry and Training

It is now a legal requirement in England and Wales for CPOs to have a Security Industry Authority (SIA) licence. This licence can be a front-line or non front-line licence depending on the type of protection work you are involved in. Applicants must be aged over 18 and need to undergo criminal records and identity checks. Those with a criminal record are not necessarily excluded from obtaining a licence as the SIA looks at the seriousness and history of the offence.

To demonstrate the necessary skills, you must obtain an SIA approved level 3 qualification in close protection and a first aid certificate. Currently, there are three awarding bodies that offer the approved close protection qualification; City and Guilds (level 3 certificate in close protection), Edexcel (BTEC level 3 certificate in close protection operations), and Bucks New University (certificate in close protection security).

Successful completion of any of these courses means you have completed the requisite one hundred and fifty hours knowledge and practical skills training. The SIA approved first aid awards include the four day first aid at work course (HSE approved) and the first person on scene intermediate award from Edexcel (BTEC)/ HCD Health and Care Ltd). Further information on training providers and qualifications can be found on the SIA website. Private security firms such as TASK International also run close protection training and first aid courses.

Many who enter this profession were previously employed in the armed forces, the police/military police or prison services. Some have a background in martial arts. Part or full exemption from some of the SIA-approved training can be authorised for those who have some formal close protection training, but all entrants need to pass a minimum knowledge test and practical assessment. The growth of the security industry and a professional qualification route now allows entrants from all backgrounds. An ability and knowledge of a foreign language such as French or Spanish is desirable, though not essential.

Training is on the job together with specialist courses, some of which may need to be arranged privately or through the employer. For those who have obtained their SIA licence and work in the close protection industry, Bucks New University offers a foundation degree in protective security management

Employers value maturity for this job and a security background is an advantage. Previous work in the armed forces, police or in martial arts is also very useful when applying for training and jobs. Some may work in supervisory/management roles, rather than operational/front line work. A full driving licence is also necessary and you are expected to be physically fit as well as being presentable.

Opportunities and Pay

In the UK today, approximately 4,700 individuals hold valid licences issued by the Security Industry Authority. Employers vary from private individuals to those employed by the state and private organisations. Close Protection Officers (CPOs) are also employed by commercial firms and agencies. There is competition for jobs, although female CPOs are in demand to accompany and protect celebrities. Most CPOs are self-employed and can have long or short-term contracts that can range from a few days to a few years. Fully experienced CPOs may move into risk assessment consultancy, or set up their own company to offer training courses for clients, or to provide a security protection service.

Pay varies widely due to the length of contract, any risks involved, and the profile and wealth of a client. Daily rates can be around £150-£200 with a rate of around £500 for high-risk work. Newly qualified CPOs earn around £18k a year, rising to around £25k-£30k a year. Those working internationally and in high-risk jobs can earn up to £100k a year and some may earn more.

Health

Entrants must have stamina and be physically fit. Applicants should be more than 168cm (5ft 6) in height.

Skills and Qualities

able to cope under pressure, aptitude for teamwork, common sense, confident, discreet, good at calculating risks, good communication skills, observant, quick reactions

Relevant Subjects

Design and technology, English, Geography, Government and politics, Law, Modern Foreign Languages, Physical education and sport, Psychology

Further Information

Apprenticeship Schemes (National Apprenticeship Service) - www.apprenticeships.org.uk

Foundation Learning (QCDA) - www.qcda.gov.uk

International Professional Security Association (IPSA) (IPSA) - www.ipsa.org.uk/

Professional Security Magazine - www.professionalsecurity.co.uk

Skills for Security - sector skills council for security industry - www.skillsforsecurity.org.uk/

Why Security? - A Guide to Careers in the Security Industry (Security Industry Authority) - www.the-sia.org.uk

▶Working in police, fire & security (2009) (Babcock Lifeskills) - www.babcock-lifeskills.com/

Addresses

British Security Industry Association (BSIA)
Kirkham House, John Comyn Drive, Worcester WR3 7NS
Phone: +44 (0)845 389 3889
Web: www.bsia.co.uk

Bucks New University
Queen Alexandra Road, High Wycombe, Buckinghamshire HP11 2JZ
Phone: +44 (0)1494 522141
Web: www.bucks.ac.uk

Security Industry Authority (SIA)
PO Box 1293, Liverpool L69 1AX
Phone: 0844 892 1025 (UK only)
Web: http://sia.homeoffice.gov.uk/Pages/home.aspx

Skills for Security
Security House, Barbourne Road, Worcester WR1 1RS
Phone: +44 (0)8450 750111
Web: www.skillsforsecurity.org.uk

TASK International Limited
Inkerman House, 3-4 Elwick Road, Ashford, Kent TN23 1PF
Phone: +44 (0)1223 614796
Web: www.task-int.com

Similar Jobs

Army Officer, Door Supervisor, Police Officer, Private Investigator, Security Officer, Store Detective

Cloth/Garment Examiner

also known as: Garment Examiner: Clothing
CRCI:Manufacturing and Production
CLCI:SAH
Job Band: 1 to 2

Job Description

Cloth/garment examiners check material or items of clothing that have been manufactured. They look to see if there are any faults such as holes, bad sewing, loose threads, misplaced labels or no labels. They check for any stains or patterns that are incorrect and feel the material for knots and mark any mistakes with chalk or a piece of thread. Examiners keep careful note of all faults and checks the batch number so that the item can be sent back for correction. May use a machine roller to pull the cloth over the area where it is checked. Occasionally, examiners carry out small repairs.

Work Details

Cloth/garment examiners usually work a 37-39 hr week with perhaps an early finish on Fridays. You work in an industrial building or a workshop, which may be light and airy, although some are cramped, noisy and dusty. You may be expected to work shifts or overtime and be asked to do the same task over and over again. There may be opportunities to work part time.

Qualification

- **England, Wales and Northern Ireland**

Band 1: No academic qualifications are usually needed to enter this work.

Band 2: For some courses or training: 3-4 GCSEs or equivalent are useful.

- **Scotland**

Band 1: No academic qualifications are usually needed to enter this work.

Band 2: For some courses or training: 3-4 S grades or similar are useful.

Adult Qualifications

General secondary education is expected.

Work Experience

Relevant work or voluntary experience is always useful. It can improve your chances when applying for entry to jobs or apprenticeships in the manufacturing sector. Your personal or adult guidance adviser is able to assist you on how to organise relevant work experience with an employer.

Entry and Training

Most people who enter this work are experienced sewing machinists. A short induction course is usually provided as an introduction to the company and the work required. Aspects such as health and safety at work, and employment conditions are usually included. Training is on the job according to the requirements of the employing company.

Appropriate S/NVQs may be available at levels 1-3. Training programmes, including apprenticeships leading to level 2 and advanced apprenticeships leading to level 3, may be available in your area.

Government training opportunities, such as apprenticeships, may be available in your area. You can also gain recognition of previous experience through Accreditation of Prior Learning (APL) or by working towards relevant S/NVQs. Contact your local careers office, Jobcentre Plus, Next Step service or Learning and Skills Council (LSC) Local Enterprise Company (LEC) for details of training schemes.

Opportunities and Pay

Due to large scale production moving overseas, the industry is in decline. Also, due to the current downturn in the economy, there has been 30% less vacancies in the clothing industry. You can work for a small to large manufacturing company. There are fewer vacancies for examiners than for sewing machinists, as one examiner may oversee the work of 30-40 machinists.

Pay varies depending on area and employer, but a starting wage is likely to be around £13k-£16k a year. You may be able to increase your wages by working overtime and you can be paid extra for working shifts.

Health

This job may require an eyesight test as good eyesight and good colour vision are necessary for certain areas of work. There is an allergy risk from dust.

Skills and Qualities

able to work quickly, attention to detail, careful, good communication skills, good concentration level, good interpersonal skills, good sense of touch, observant, patient

Relevant Subjects

Manufacturing

Further Information

Apprenticeship Schemes (National Apprenticeship Service) - www.apprenticeships.org.uk

Skillset - sector skills council for the creative media, fashion and textiles industries - www.skillset.org

▶Working in fashion & clothing (2008) (Babcock Lifeskills) - www.babcock-lifeskills.com/

Similar Jobs
Clothing Pattern Cutter/Grader, Quality Assurance Controller/Inspector, Sewing Machinist, Textile Operative

Clothing Alteration Hand

CRCI:Manufacturing and Production
CLCI:SAH Job Band: 1 to 2

Job Description
A clothing alteration hand Is responsible for the skilled alteration and repair of clothing. Makes changes to all types of garments for people so that they fit them better. Unpicks stitching and re-sews clothes, either by hand or using a sewing machine. Can work with all kinds of clothes such as coats, suits, dresses and bridal wear. Jobs can include making jacket, trouser, dress or skirt hems shorter or longer, and taking in or letting out seams. Replaces buttons and zips, and may work on more specialised garments, repairing detailed beadwork or intricate designs that may have come unstitched. Presses the finished garment.

Work Details
Clothing alteration hands usually work a 39-40 hr week from Monday to Friday. Saturday work is also common, particularly if you work in a shop or dry cleaners. You may have to work extra hours at busy times. You may work in a shop or a workshop attached to a dry cleaners or laundry. You may be able to work from home. The work area is usually warm and well lit, but may be cramped.

Work is supervised and can involve giving advice to customers. You do the same task quite often. You are very busy at times and your workplace can be noisy. Much of the work involves sitting at a sewing table. It may involve close needlework, needing good light.

Qualification

- **England, Wales and Northern Ireland**

Band 1: Formal qualifications are not usually required.

Band 2: No minimum entry qualifications but many employers prefer some GCSEs, for example, English and maths.

- **Scotland**

Band 1: Formal qualifications are not usually required.

Band 2: Although academic qualifications are not specified for this job, it is an advantage to have some S grades in subjects that include English and maths, or similar.

Adult Qualifications
Good secondary education is required.

Work Experience
Relevant work or voluntary experience is always useful. It can improve your chances when applying for jobs or apprenticeships. Your personal or adult guidance adviser should be able to advise you about how to get work experience.

Entry and Training
All entrants need a good knowledge of garment construction, and many start as an assistant to a tailor or dressmaker. Training is on the job, possibly through a training scheme. Full-time and day-release courses are available and you may be able to study for relevant courses, such as ABC level 3 certificate in apparel manufacturing technology, ABC diploma in handcraft tailoring or ABC level 1-3 in fashion and textiles. Relevant training programmes, including apprenticeship schemes in manufacturing sewn products, apparel manufacturing technology and bespoke cutting and tailoring, may be available in your area.

Government training opportunities, such as apprenticeships, may be available in your area. You can also gain recognition of previous experience through Accreditation of Prior Learning (APL) or by working towards relevant S/NVQs. Contact your local careers office, Jobcentre Plus, Next Step service or Learning and Skills Council (LSC) Local Enterprise Company (LEC) for details of training schemes.

Opportunities and Pay
Due to large scale production moving overseas, the industry is in decline in the UK, and during the current economic downturn vacancies in the clothing industry are down by 30%.

You can be employed by a private company, possibly a small firm. After you have gained more experience, you may choose to become self-employed. There are opportunities to work part time. You can also specialise, maybe in women's or men's garments, or bridalwear. You can be promoted to a workshop supervisor.

Pay varies depending on location and employer. Salaries are around £11k a year though supervisors can usually earn up to £22k. You can increase your salary by doing piecework (where you are paid per item) and with overtime pay.

Health
This job requires good eyesight and good colour vision for certain areas of work.

Skills and Qualities
able to work quickly, able to work well on your own, accurate, attention to detail, careful, excellent sewing skills, eye for visual effect, good knowledge of garment construction, manual dexterity, neat

Further Information
ABC Awards - www.abcawards.co.uk

Apprenticeship Schemes (National Apprenticeship Service) - www.apprenticeships.org.uk

Skillset - sector skills council for the creative media, fashion and textiles industries - www.skillset.org

►Working in fashion & clothing (2008) (Babcock Lifeskills) - www.babcock-lifeskills.com/

Similar Jobs
Clothing Pattern Cutter/Grader, Clothing Presser, Dressmaker, Film/TV & Theatre Wardrobe Assistant, Sewing Machinist, Tailor

Clothing Packer

CRCI:Manufacturing and Production
CLCI:SAH Job Band: 1 to 2

Job Description
A clothing packer usually works in a warehouse or on a production line for a clothing manufacturer. Work involves folding garments and packing them into polythene bags, cartons or boxes for distribution. May need to repack imported or returned items, checking items for flaws. May fold certain items such as shirts, around pieces of cardboard. Then uses pins or clips to keep them in place. Uses a variety of packaging materials, including tissue paper or bubble wrap. Puts labels on the packages or boxes and organises delivery notes.

In large firms different people may do the folding and packing. In small firms one person does both of these jobs. Mass-produced garments may be packed by a machine. The machine operator loads and unloads the machine with the correct packaging materials, labels etc, ready for dispatch. Computers are sometimes used to print off labels.

Work Details
Clothing packers usually work a 37-40 hr week, that requires shift-work and may involve some work at night. Part-time work is common. You work for a clothing manufacturer and are part of a team of workers, often doing the same task over and over again, and sometimes standing or sitting for long periods of time. You may be expected to work overtime. Your work environment is usually a light and airy warehouse or on a production line with a similar environment. Some stretching and lifting may be required, and use of a ladder to reach products.

Qualification
- **England, Wales and Northern Ireland**

Band 1: Formal qualifications are not usually required.

Band 2: No minimum entry qualifications but many employers prefer some GCSEs, for example, English and maths.

- **Scotland**

Band 1: Formal qualifications are not usually required.

Band 2: Although academic qualifications are not specified for this job, it is an advantage to have some S grades in subjects that include English and maths, or similar.

Adult Qualifications
A reasonable standard of general secondary education is expected.

Work Experience
Work or voluntary experience is always useful. It can improve your chances when applying for entry to jobs or apprenticeships. Your personal or adult guidance adviser is able to advise you how to get work experience.

Entry and Training
Training is given on the job by a supervisor or team leader. A short induction course is usually provided as an introduction to the company and the work required. Training aspects such as health and safety at work, employment working conditions and how to operate equipment are usually included. S/NVQs for packing operations at levels 1-2 may be available.

Government training opportunities, such as apprenticeships, may be available in your area. You can also gain recognition of previous experience through Accreditation of Prior Learning (APL) or by working towards relevant S/NVQs. Contact your local careers office, Jobcentre Plus, Next Step service or Learning and Skills Council (LSC) Local Enterprise Company (LEC) for details of training schemes.

Opportunities and Pay
Due to large scale production moving overseas, the industry is in decline, and in the current economic downturn vacancies in the clothing industry are down by 30%.

Jobs are available mainly in towns and cities. These can be with garment manufacturers or mail order companies. Jobs can be found with wholesalers, department stores and shipping agents. Promotion to supervisory or charge-hand level is possible. Some packers can move into areas such as machining. Some move on to quality control inspection.

Starting salaries are around £10.5k a year rising to around £13k for experienced workers. Your pay may depend on how many pieces of work you complete (piece work). You may be able to work overtime and do shift work to increase your wages.

Skills and Qualities
able to follow instructions, able to work quickly, aptitude for teamwork, careful, health & safety awareness, manual dexterity, methodical, neat, prepared to do repetitive tasks

Further Information
Apprenticeship Schemes (National Apprenticeship Service) - www.apprenticeships.org.uk

Skillset - sector skills council for the creative media, fashion and textiles industries - www.skillset.org

▶ Working in fashion & clothing (2008) (Babcock Lifeskills) - www.babcock-lifeskills.com/

Similar Jobs
Food Packaging Operative, Packer: General, Removals Operative, Warehouse Order Picker/Assembler, Warehouse Worker

Clothing Pattern Cutter/Grader
also known as: Fabric Cutter

CRCI:Manufacturing and Production

CLCI:SAH Job Band: 2 to 4

Job Description
Pattern cutters take designers' original ideas and create a pattern to produce items of clothing. May use information technology to create the pattern using computer aided design (CAD) methods, which works out the most economical way to create a layout of the pattern on the cloth. They then create the correct body shape (called a block). Sometimes may adapt a previous 'block' from a similar garment. Some traditional pattern cutters create a pattern by draping the material over a dummy or live model and cutting the pattern pieces with hand shears.

Pattern graders then take the pattern template and re-size it. This is so garment manufacturers can produce one design in many sizes. Grading may be done by hand, using charts to alter pattern proportions, but increasingly this is being done by computer. In small companies the cutting and grading process may sometimes be done by the same person.

Work Details
Most pattern cutters/graders work a 37-39 hr week; Monday to Friday. Overtime may be needed at times to meet deadlines. Shift-work and part-time work is possible. You may work in a studio with clothing designers or in an industrial workshop that can be noisy at times. The environment is usually clean, warm and light. You may be required to sit for long periods at a computer working out the pattern pieces for a design, or spend time standing, stretching and bending when working with pattern pieces at a large table.

Qualification
- **England, Wales and Northern Ireland**

Band 2: Although academic qualifications are not specified for this job, it is an advantage to have some GCSE grades (A*-C) in subjects that include English and maths, or similar.

Band 3: For entry: usually 4 GCSEs (A*-C) or equivalent.

Band 4: For a relevant BTEC higher national award: 1-2 A levels and some GCSEs (A*-C) usually including English and maths, or equivalent.

- **Scotland**

Band 2: Although academic qualifications are not specified for this job, it is an advantage to have some S grades (1-3) in subjects that include English and maths, or similar.

Band 3: For entry: usually at least four S grades (1-3) preferably including English and maths, or similar.

Band 4: For a relevant SQA higher national award: usually 2-3 H grades and some S grades, often including English and maths, or similar qualifications.

Adult Qualifications
General secondary education is expected and some employers may also require a higher level of relevant qualifications.

Work Experience
Relevant work or voluntary experience is always useful and can improve your chances when applying for entry to jobs or apprenticeships in the manufacturing sector. Your personal or adult guidance adviser is able to advise you how to organise work experience with an employer.

Entry and Training
Many entrants to pattern cutting take relevant courses before they start work. These can include ABC level 2-3 in pattern cutting, ABC level 3 in pattern cutting and construction techniques and City & Guilds level 2-3 in creative techniques in fashion - pattern cutting. Some HNDs, foundation degrees and degrees also have modules in pattern cutting.

Some train through an apprenticeship where training is usually on the job and can include a day-release course or evening classes. The London College of Fashion runs a range of short courses on pattern cutting techniques. Relevant vocational qualifications are available in manufacturing sewn products at level 2, and pattern technology at level 3.

Graders often start as assistant graders, after completing an appropriate degree course. Some may train through apprenticeships.

Mature applicants can apply for most courses without having the formal entry requirements. Those with relevant practical experience in the clothing manufacturing industry may have an advantage. It is useful to demonstrate an interest in design and fashion.

Opportunities and Pay
There is a strong demand for those with relevant technical qualifications and jobs are available mainly in towns and cities. Employers range from exclusive designer and couture houses to manufacturing companies. Most companies are small to medium in size, but there are a few major firms. The main promotion route is to become head pattern cutter. With experience, you can progress to become a pattern grader, and then move into design or buying. There are opportunities to move into supervisory or management roles and to work abroad. Self-employment is also possible.

Pay varies widely, depending on area and employer. Starting salaries are around £11k-£18k a year, and with experience, rise to around £20k. Some pattern cutters/graders are paid 'piecework' and given a set amount for each pattern they produce. Overtime pay and bonuses are possible.

Health
There is an allergy risk from dust. This job requires good eyesight and normal colour vision.

Skills and Qualities
accurate, accurate measuring and calculating skills, aptitude for teamwork, attention to detail, eye for shape/colour, good knowledge of garment construction, IT skills, methodical, numeracy skills, steady hand

Relevant Subjects
Art and Design, Design and technology, ICT/Computer studies

Further Information
ABC Awards - www.abcawards.co.uk

Apprenticeship Schemes (National Apprenticeship Service) - www.apprenticeships.org.uk

Can you Cut it? - www.canucutit.co.uk

▶Working in fashion & clothing (2008) (Babcock Lifeskills) - www.babcock-lifeskills.com/

See where YOUR interests could take YOU!
Pathfinder live
www.pathfinderlive.com

Addresses
London College of Fashion
20 John Princes Street, London W1G 0BJ
Phone: +44 (0)20 7514 7344
Web: www.fashion.arts.ac.uk

Similar Jobs
Cloth/Garment Examiner, Clothing Alteration Hand, Costume Designer, Dressmaker, Tailor, Textile Designer

Clothing Presser
CRCI:Manufacturing and Production
CLCI:SAH — Job Band: 1

Job Description
Clothing pressers use pressing machines, which produce heat and steam, to smooth clothes and to shape them. May also press items such as curtains and sheets. They set the press for the right amount of steam for the type of material. The presser then puts the material between two pads and uses levers and pedals to bring the pads together and to release the steam. May use different machines for different types of garment. Can sometimes press clothes using a hand iron. Folds the finished garments ready for packing. May need to press a garment in between the stages of manufacture.

Work Details
Clothing pressers usually work around 39 hrs a week, working under supervision in industrial premises, a laundry or a workshop, perhaps doing the same task over and over again. Shift-work and early starts may be required. Part time working is common. You have to cope with standing for long periods and you may also have to do some lifting. The work environment may be hot and damp, and there is a risk of burns.

Qualification
- **England, Wales and Northern Ireland**

Band 1: Formal qualifications are not usually required.

- **Scotland**

Band 1: Formal qualifications are not usually required.

Adult Qualifications
General secondary education is expected. You can improve your skills and qualifications by working through the Foundation Learning programme. This involves taking credit-based units and qualifications to help you progress.

Work Experience
Work or voluntary experience is useful. It can improve your chances when applying for jobs. Your personal or adult guidance adviser can advise you on how to get work experience.

Entry and Training
There are no specific qualifications for entry to this work. Employers may set a practical test at interview and look for people who are reliable and good timekeepers. Training is on the job, working with an experienced presser or supervisor, and usually on rejected garments at first until you have reached the required level of skill and speed.

S/NVQs may be available at levels 1-2 in manufacturing sewn products.

Government training opportunities, such as apprenticeships, may be available in your area. You can also gain recognition of previous experience through Accreditation of Prior Learning (APL) or by working towards relevant S/NVQs. Contact your local careers office, Jobcentre Plus, Next Step service or Learning and Skills Council (LSC) Local Enterprise Company (LEC) for details of training schemes.

Opportunities and Pay
Clothing pressers can be employed in clothing manufacturing companies or in dry cleaners and laundries. Due to large scale production moving overseas, the clothing industry in the UK is in decline, and the current economic downturn has led to a large reduction in vacancies. Most companies are in the East Midlands, north-west Yorkshire, and parts of Scotland and Northern Ireland. Dry cleaners and laundries can be found in most towns and cities throughout the country.

With experience you can become a supervisor or an instructor. There may be opportunities to move into other roles such as sewing machining or you can work in quality control.

Pay varies according to the employer. It also depends on the amount of work completed (piecework). Trainees may start at around £10k a year. This can rise to £12.5k-£14k with experience. It may be possible to work overtime to increase your wages.

Health
This job requires normal colour vision, good eyesight and good health.

Skills and Qualities
able to work quickly, attention to detail, careful, manual dexterity, methodical, neat, prepared to do repetitive tasks

Further Information
Apprenticeship Schemes (National Apprenticeship Service) - www.apprenticeships.org.uk

Foundation Learning (QCDA) - www.qcda.gov.uk

Skillset - sector skills council for the creative media, fashion and textiles industries - www.skillset.org

▶Working in fashion & clothing (2008) (Babcock Lifeskills) - www.babcock-lifeskills.com/

Similar Jobs
Clothing Alteration Hand, Clothing Packer, Dry Cleaning Assistant/ Manager, Laundry Assistant/Manager, Textile Operative

Coastguard Watch Officer

CRCI:Security and Armed Forces
CLCI:MAZ Job Band: 1 to 2

Job Description
Coastguard watch officers develop and enforce high standards of marine safety and keep a constant watch over a designated area of UK coast. Send information about tides and weather to ships, listen for distress calls on the radio, contact other emergency services, such as RNLI lifeboats and RAF/Navy helicopters, and generally maintain the Channel Navigation Information Service (CNIS) together with its French counterpart. Work on specified areas of coast (per district) and also operate 1,000 miles into the North Atlantic sea. Check the coast for pollution, coastal erosion, smuggling, illegal fishing and immigration.

Coastguard watch assistants work in administration and in the operations room, handling emergency calls, monitoring equipment, updating logs and providing information. Coastguard watch officers (CWOs) coordinate rescue activities, assist in the training of voluntary rescue teams and, in some posts, are involved in arduous cliff rescues, coastal searches and boat work. Are also involved with raising awareness of the coastguard service through talks on coastguard activities to groups in schools and colleges or clubs, and give professional advice to owners of small vessels.

Work Details
The working week is 42 hours over five days. It can include night shifts and weekends. The work is mostly indoors, but those working at sector offices can be out in all weathers and sometimes in a small boat. Overtime is available. You have to be prepared to work at any of the UK's 19 maritime rescue coordination centres, though you can apply for a transfer once you have been in a centre for more than three years.

Some maritime rescue centres are located in very remote areas with few facilities. Some CWOs undertake strenuous rescue work, involving climbing, pulling and lifting, and you may have to work at heights, for example on cliff tops. Uniforms and protective clothing are provided.

Qualification

• England, Wales and Northern Ireland
Band 1: No formal qualifications are needed for entry, but good skills in English and maths are looked for.

Band 2: A minimum of 3 GCSEs (A*-C) or equivalent, ideally maths, IT and English, may be preferred.

• Scotland
Band 1: No formal qualifications are needed for entry, but good skills in English and maths are looked for.

Band 2: A minimum of three S grades (1-3) or similar, ideally maths, IT and English, may be preferred.

Adult Qualifications
All candidates must be able to demonstrate an acceptable level of competence in literacy and numeracy, so some secondary educational qualifications, particularly in English, maths and IT, or equivalent are an advantage.

Work Experience
Any work experience can equip you with skills that you can use in the future and add to your CV and can either be unpaid or voluntary, holiday or part-time work that you have organised yourself. Any involvement gained in maritime or outdoor activities or knowledge is very useful. Auxiliary coastguard membership, either paid/ unpaid, or membership of a local lifeboat rescue team is an advantage.

Entry and Training
Coastguard watch officers (CWOs) are civil servants and must be a British national or a member of the Commonwealth. Many entrants to this work start as coastguard watch assistants (CWAs), gain experience of the work and then move on to CWO level. CWAs require no previous maritime experience, though work as an auxiliary (volunteer) coastguard may count towards qualification in the coastguard service. Training is given on the job, under supervision.

Direct entry as a CWO usually requires at least six years' seagoing experience, for example, in the Royal Navy/RAF, Merchant Navy or the fishing industry, or three years' marine search and rescue experience, as well as a knowledge of communications or navigation. Training takes 9-12 months, depending on experience on entry, and is a combination of on-the-job training and periods at the Maritime and Coastguard Agency (MCA) training centre in Dorset. Training covers search planning, communications and signals, chart and map work, and coastal rescue. There is a proficiency exam at the end of the training. Once qualified, new CWOs continue to work under supervision for some time. All staff are encouraged to continue their own personal development.

The Maritime Skills Alliance and the Marine Society and Sea Cadets both have useful careers information on their websites. There are details of available courses and, in the case of the Sea Cadets, an opportunity to develop some useful skills to give you an advantage when later applying for work.

Mature entry is usual due to the work experience required and many officers are recruited from the Royal Navy/RAF. Applicants require knowledge of communications or navigation and at least six years' maritime experience, or three years' search and rescue experience. Applicants must also hold a full current UK driving licence and be a British subject or member of the Commonwealth.

Opportunities and Pay

The Maritime and Coastguard Agency (MCA) is part of the civil service. There are over 1,000 people employed in the service supported by over 3,000 axillary staff. Staff are based in one of the 18 Maritime Rescue Co-ordination Centres or at MCA headquarters in Southampton. Coastguard Watch Assistants (CWAs) are normally recruited locally, but recruitment for Coastguard Watch Officers (CWOs) is national. See the MCA website for details. There is a clear promotion structure and you have to pass exams and interviews to gain promotion to watch manager, section manager or beyond. However, there are only a small number of higher grade posts. There are opportunities to work part time.

A CWA earns around £12k-£15k a year, rising to around £18k-£23k for a CWO. Senior officers earn more. A performance bonus system and shift allowances are additional to basic pay and additional allowances are paid to those working in the Scottish Islands.

Health

You have to pass a medical test and have good eyesight and hearing.

Skills and Qualities

able to cope with emergencies, able to work both on your own and in a team, decisive, good communication skills, good coordinator, IT skills, observant, reliable, resourceful, responsible attitude

Relevant Subjects

English, Geography, ICT/Computer studies, Mathematics, Physical education and sport

Further Information

Careers with the Maritime and Coastguard Agency (MCA) (Maritime & Coastguard Agency) - www.mcga.gov.uk/

Foundation Learning (QCDA) - www.qcda.gov.uk

▶Working in police, fire & security (2009) (Babcock Lifeskills) - www.babcock-lifeskills.com/

Addresses

Centre for Search Research (The)
Office 03 Wansbeck Enterprise Workspace Green Lane, Ashington, Northumberland NE63 0EE
Phone: +44 (0)1670 528141
Web: www.searchresearch.org.uk

Marine Society & Sea Cadets
202 Lambeth Road, London SE1 7JW
Phone: +44 (0)20 7654 7000
Web: www.ms-sc.org

Maritime and Coastguard Agency (MCA)
Spring Place, 105 Commercial Road, Southampton, Hampshire SO15 1EG
Phone: +44 (0)2380 329 308
Web: www.mcga.gov.uk

Maritime Skills Alliance
1 Hillside, Beckingham, Lincoln LN5 0RQ
Web: www.maritimeskills.org

Similar Jobs

Ambulance Paramedic, Firefighter, Merchant Navy Deck/Navigating Officer, Police Officer, Royal Navy Officer

Commodity Broker

also known as: Futures Broker

CRCI:Financial Services

CLCI:NAM Job Band: 4 to 5

Job Description

Commodities brokers buy and sell contracts for physical commodities on behalf of clients. Act as a direct link between the commodity producer (the seller) and the consumer (the buyer). Negotiate a successful transaction for their clients and aim to achieve the highest possible price. Commodities can be foods, such as cocoa, coffee, sugar, or energy, including oil and gas, or base metals, such as tin, copper and zinc. Also deal in precious metals, including gold, silver or platinum.

They use the telephone and computer links to communicate with the producer, broker and consumer to agree a price. Often the buyer and seller are in different countries and the commodity under discussion is not bound for the UK, even though the business is handled through a UK-based broker. Draw up a contract and arrange the shipment, insurance and finance for the sale.

May also deal in derivatives (futures and options), which are contracts for a future date at a price agreed in advance. These may be for physical commodities or for financial futures, such as bonds, gilts or currencies. Commodity brokers monitor the world markets, stay in close contact with clients, and may advise investors and visit the country from which their commodity originates to ensure product quality. Most brokers tend to specialise in one or two commodities. Desk-based brokers are traditionally known as 'dealers' and floor-based brokers as 'traders'.

Work Details

Usually from 7am-7pm, Monday to Friday, but there may be longer hours and additional work at weekends. The work can be very competitive and stressful. You spend a great deal of time on the telephone or at a computer. The work involves consulting and negotiating with people, on the telephone, or via computer links and sometimes face to face, so you need to have strong interpersonal skills. You also need a strong interest in financial and current affairs.

Qualification

There are no rigid entry requirements. However most firms look for graduates, though personal characteristics, such as an extrovert personality, excellent communication skills, intuition and confidence, together with a flair for numeracy and computers, are often considered to be more important than formal qualifications. Employers expect a high standard of English and maths.

• England, Wales and Northern Ireland

Band 4: Many firms ask for 1-2 A levels and some GCSEs (A*-C) usually including English and maths, or equivalent. Computing, science, and foreign languages are also useful. Equivalent qualifications may also be acceptable.

Band 5: For degree courses: 2-3 A levels and some GCSEs (A*-C) usually including English and maths, or equivalent. Exact requirements depend on the degree you take.

• Scotland

Band 4: Many firms ask for 2-3 H grades and some S grades (1-3), often including English and maths, or similar qualifications. Computing, science subjects, and foreign languages are also useful.

Band 5: For degree courses: 3-5 H grades and some S grades (1-3), usually including English and maths, or similar qualifications. Exact requirements depend on the degree you take.

Degree Information
A degree in any discipline is acceptable though financial management, banking, accountancy, business studies, statistics, law or modern languages are particularly useful.

Adult Qualifications
Mature entrants are usually already qualified in accountancy, actuarial work, banking, or a related field. Those without the required academic qualifications can enter via a foundation or Access course that leads to a relevant degree, such as business-related subjects, maths, modern languages and economics.

Work Experience
Entry to this job is competitive and it is important that you try to do some relevant work or voluntary experience before applying. This needs to include wide experience in a financial or commercial organisation or via a degree in a related subject such as accountancy, finance or economics. Many 'blue-chip' companies offer work experience and summer internships to students. Contact companies directly or visit the professional websites for further information.

Entry and Training
Training programmes vary depending on which commodity you are dealing in, but to become an authorised floor broker, on-the-job training is traditionally carried out together with specific exams, which may involve a day-release college course, an evening class or distance learning. You may start as a market clerk (or runner), who passes messages between the floor brokers and back-office staff, and then progress onto the floor of the market, when successful. Trainee desk brokers follow a similar training route of on-the-job experience, but may have a more formalised training programme, particularly if you are a graduate employed by a larger firm.

All companies must meet the standards required by the Financial Services Authority (FSA). Part-time study is required for the FSA professional qualification and you are also expected to do some studying in your own free time. It is useful to have some knowledge of foreign languages and also experience in using computers.

Brokers are expected to do continuing professional development (CPD) to keep up to date with new developments. Organisations such as the London Metal Exchange and the CFA Society of the UK run short courses on relevant subjects. The Securities Investment Institute offers a CPD scheme and a range of appropriate professional qualifications. Check the website for details.

Mature entry may be difficult as this is often seen as a career for younger people. However, applicants who have considerable professional experience in aspects of financial work, may have an advantage.

Opportunities and Pay
This is a small profession and there is a lot of competition for jobs. Availability of jobs is very affected by changes in the economic climate. Due to increased reliance on technology in exchanges, floor broker numbers are dwindling though there are opportunities to move into desk-based broking and support jobs. You can work for a commodity firm or for a bank or securities house. Experienced brokers can become self-employed.

Some large manufacturing companies have their own broking departments. The majority of jobs are centred on the international exchanges in the City of London with organisations like the London International Financial Futures and Options Exchange (LIFFE), the International Currency Exchange (ICE) and the London Metal Exchange (LME).

Graduate entrants earn between £25k-£35k rising to £45k-£80k a year with experience. The most successful brokers earn more than £100k a year. Performance-related bonuses can increase these earnings by 50% or more.

Skills and Qualities
able to cope under pressure, able to evaluate, able to manage a budget and keep records, decisive, excellent communication skills, IT skills, motivated, numeracy skills, quick thinking, self confident

Relevant Subjects
Business and accounting, Economics, English, Geography, Government and politics, ICT/Computer studies, Law, Mathematics, Modern Foreign Languages, Retail and distribution

Further Information
Financial Services Skills Council - sector skills council for financial services, accountancy & finance www.fssc.org.uk/

ICE Futures - www.theice.com

Inside Careers Guide: Banking, Securities & Investments - www.insidecareers.co.uk

London International Financial Futures and Options Exchange (LIFFE) - www.liffe-commodities.com

Professional Investor (10 x year) (UK Society of Investment Professionals (UKSIP)) - www.marchpublishing.co.uk/pi.html

TARGETjobs: City and Finance (GTI Specialist Publishers Ltd) - www.groupgti.com

Addresses
CFA Society of the UK
2nd Floor 135 Cannon Street, London EC4N 5BP
Phone: +44 (0)20 7280 9620
Web: https://secure.cfauk.org/

Euronext Liffe
Cannon Bridge House, 1 Cousin Lane, London EC4R 3XX
Phone: +44 (0)20 7623 0444
Web: www.euronext.com

Financial Services Authority (FSA)
Membership Department, 25 The North Colonnade, Canary Wharf, London E14 5HS
Phone: +44 (0)20 7066 1000
Web: www.fsa.gov.uk

London Metal Exchange (LME)
56 Leadenhall Street, London EC3A 2DX
Phone: +44 (0)20 7264 5555
Web: www.lme.co.uk

Securities & Investment Institute (SII)
8 Eastcheap, London EC3M 1AE
Phone: +44 (0)20 7645 0600
Web: www.sii.org.uk

Similar Jobs
Investment Analyst, Investment Banker, Pension Fund Manager, Retail Buyer, Stock Market Trader/Market Maker, Stockbroker

Community Development Worker
also known as: Community Worker, Youth & Community Worker

CRCI:Social Work and Counselling Services
CLCI:KEG Job Band: 2 to 5

Job Description
Community development workers help people to improve their quality of life and tackle social inequality in their local area. Engage individuals, families and groups in communities in analysing the issues affecting their lives, and set goals for improvement and taking action. The work is often project-based, which means that they usually have a specific location or social issue to tackle. Provide leadership and help people to develop the skills to eventually run their own community groups.

They work closely with other professionals, including the police, social workers, probation officers, teachers and other agencies. Aim to link communities, local government and statutory bodies.

Work Details

Usually works a basic 37 hr week, though may be expected to work unsociable hours including some evenings and weekends. You are based in an office, but spend much of your time in the community visiting individuals or working with groups, giving advice and support or attending meetings.

Your work may involve supervising part-time and voluntary workers. Most community workers need to travel around an area and if rural, this may be over quite a wide area.

Qualification

- **England, Wales and Northern Ireland**

Band 3: For certificate or diploma recognised by the National Youth Agency: a minimum of 3 GCSEs (A*-C), preferably including English and maths, or equivalent.

Band 4: For entry to relevant foundation degree: usually at least 1-2 A levels and 3 GCSEs (A*-C), or equivalent.

Band 5: For degree courses: 2-3 A levels and some GCSEs (A*-C) usually including English and maths, or equivalent qualifications. Exact requirements depend on the degree you take.

Degree Information

A degree in any subject is acceptable for entry to this job, though there are a wide variety of courses in youth community studies or community work/studies. Social science fields are useful. Postgraduate courses are available.

Adult Qualifications

Mature applicants who have experience in an appropriate field, may be accepted for courses without the standard formal qualifications. Access courses leading to relevant degree courses may be available in some areas. Relevant postgraduate courses are also available.

Work Experience

Employers or universities prefer candidates who have relevant work or voluntary experience. This includes work in education, in a community or youth centre, work with young people in an advice or helping capacity or a youth activities organisation. It is essential to have relevant work experience before beginning a course.

Entry and Training

This job is only available in England, Wales and Northern Ireland. A similar job (Community Education Worker) is available in Scotland, but entry requirements and training are different. There are no formal entry requirements, though many enter this job with a degree/postgraduate qualification or a relevant HNC/HND. Many courses have a minimum age of 21 and this job is particularly suitable for older, more experienced people. Job applicants need to undergo a check by the Criminal Records Bureau (CRB). A criminal record does not automatically prevent entry to the job.

The YMCA George Williams College runs a Dip HE/BA in Informal Education (youth work and community learning and development) that can be studied full time for two years or part time/distance learning for three years. Postgraduate courses are usually one-year full time, or two-years part time. There are also S/NVQs in community development work at levels 2-4 and at levels 2-3 in youth work. Contact the professional organisations (listed in addresses) for details of all relevant qualification and training opportunities.

Maturity is an advantage and experience in social work, teaching or a related field is particularly useful.

Opportunities and Pay

Vacancies in this area are increasing as local authorities focus more on social inclusion. You may be employed by a local authority, local community organisation, Connexions service or voluntary organisations such as Barnardo's and the YMCA. Promotion to more senior posts is possible after gaining experience, but opportunities are limited. It is possible to specialise in one area such as youth work, anti-social behaviour or housing. There are often opportunities to work part time and to do voluntary work.

Community workers employed by local authorities earn from £14k, rising to around £25k a year. You can earn up to £36k a year, depending on your experience and qualifications.

Skills and Qualities

able to inspire confidence, diplomatic, tactful & discreet, efficient record keeping, good at writing reports, good communication skills, good interpersonal skills, initiative, non-judgemental, resilient, self-motivated

Relevant Subjects

English, Health and social care, Law, Physical education and sport, Psychology, Sociology

Further Information

Community Development Exchange - www.cdx.org.uk

Jobs for Youth Work - www.jobs4youthwork.co.uk

Local Government Careers (Improvement and Development Agency) - www.lgcareers.com/publications/

National Youth Agency - www.nya.org.uk

NYA Guide to Youth Work & Youth Services (NYA) (NYA) - www.nya.org.uk/catalogue/workforce-1

Real Life Guide to Care, Welfare & Community Work (Trotman 2010) - www.trotman.co.uk

▶Working in advice & counselling (2007) (Babcock Lifeskills) - www.babcock-lifeskills.com/

▶Working in social care (2010) (Babcock Lifeskills) - www.babcock-lifeskills.com/

Addresses

Federation for Community Development Learning
3rd Floor The Circle, 33 Rockingham Lane, Sheffield S1 4FW
Phone: +44 (0)114 273 6770
Web: www.fcdl.org.uk

YMCA George Williams College
199 Freemasons Road, Canning Town, London E16 3PY
Phone: +44 (0)20 7540 4900
Web: www.ymca.ac.uk

Similar Jobs

Aid Worker, Anti-Social Behaviour Officer, Care Home Manager, Counsellor, Personal Adviser (Connexions) (England), Social Worker

Community Learning & Development Officer (Scotland)

also known as: Community Education Worker, Community Educator, Youth & Community Worker

CRCI:Social Work and Counselling Services
CLCI:KEG Job Band: 5

Job Description

Community learning & development officers specialise in either youth work, community work or adult education. They work to identify learning needs and plan and evaluate learning opportunities. Help people to assume responsibility for their own development by encouraging them to develop socially, educationally and in their personal life. They also help to set up and run groups relating to social and community issues, tenants' groups, playgroups, job clubs or adult education classes.

May work on local youth projects, such as work with the homeless or young offenders. Work closely with other professionals such as social workers, the police, probation officers and teachers.

Work Details

Usually works a 35-37 hr week, but hours can be flexible and you may be expected to work during some evenings and weekends. Works from a base such as a school, community centre, or industrial premises, or as an outreach worker, making contact with people who are not involved with any organisations. You work with all sorts of people in the local community, such as young adults, elderly people, people from ethnic minorities and people who may be in need of support.

The work involves consulting with people, planning learning programmes and providing encouragement and support. You have to travel around your local area and for some jobs you may need to have a driving licence. Most of the time you work without supervision, but you are part of a professional team.

Qualification

• Scotland

Band 5: For degree courses: 3-5 H grades and five S grades (1-3) usually including English and maths, or similar qualifications. Entrants need experience of community education work before starting a course.

Degree Information

A degree in community education is preferred for entry to this job but any degree is acceptable for the postgraduate qualification. A degree in youth and community studies is particularly relevant, and may be preferred by some institutions. Social work and education give general background knowledge to this job.

Adult Qualifications

Entry to a degree course can be via an Access course or by Accreditation of Prior Learning. Opportunities also exist for entrants with appropriate experience but no formal academic qualifications, eg through the scheme of individual recognition operated by the Community Validation and Endorsement Committee (CeVe - Scotland). Some universities also accept HNCs endorsed by the CeVe or Open University credits. Check with individual institutions.

Entrants over 23 may be able to take a three-year course in two years. Postgraduate courses are available and entry is open to those with professional qualifications in social work or teaching.

Work Experience

Employers or colleges/universities may prefer candidates with relevant work or voluntary experience. This includes anything dealing with young people or adults in a helping capacity, such as at youth and community centres or in community-based adult learning. Areas using listening skills, and any observation or direct experience in the caring professions are also useful.

Entry and Training

This job only exists in Scotland. A similar job (community development worker) is available in the rest of the UK, but the entry requirements and training are different. Applicants for courses must be at least 18 but mature entry is preferred. Some practical experience is required before starting a degree course and it can be an advantage to have experience, including voluntary, in teaching, social work or any job working with people. You also need to pass an enhanced Scotland Disclosure check.

There are currently four approved degree courses in Scotland and some postgraduate programmes in community education/ community learning and development, or similar. These are at Strathclyde, Edinburgh, Dundee and Glasgow universities. Work placements are usually included during the degree period of study, which can be 3-4 years. A relevant Higher National Certificate (HNC) in working with communities is available through several colleges in Scotland. Check the Community Learning and Development (CLD) Standards Council for Scotland website for details of all approved courses.

Maturity is an advantage and experience in social work, teaching or a related field is particularly useful.

Opportunities and Pay

Most posts are in local councils, or you can be employed by a voluntary organisation. It is usually possible to find part time, voluntary or short-term work. There is a clear career structure but you may need to move around the country to gain experience and improve your promotion prospects. The voluntary sector has a less defined career path.

The pay for this job varies depending on your employer, but you may be paid extra for working unsociable hours. Newly qualified workers earn around £18k-£26k, rising to around £32k a year. Senior managers can earn more than £40k a year.

Health

This job requires good health.

Skills and Qualities

able to inspire confidence, creative flair, good communication skills, good interpersonal skills, good organisational skills, initiative, networking skills, resilient, resourceful, self-motivated

Relevant Subjects

English, Psychology, Sociology

Further Information

CLD Standards Council for Scotland - www.cldstandardscouncil.org.uk/
▶Working in social care (2010) (Babcock Lifeskills) - www.babcock-lifeskills.com/

Addresses

Federation for Community Development Learning
3rd Floor The Circle, 33 Rockingham Lane, Sheffield S1 4FW
Phone: +44 (0)114 273 6770
Web: www.fcdl.org.uk

Similar Jobs

Careers Adviser, Counsellor, Police Officer, Social Worker

Community Warden (Scotland)

CRCI:Social Work and Counselling Services
CLCI:KEG Job Band: 1 to 2

Job Description

Community wardens are usually employed to be the 'eyes and ears' of a community and a key person in tackling antisocial behaviour. Tasks change from day to day depending on the needs of the area. They work with local authorities, the police, community groups, the fire service and housing associations to decide on local needs. Help to put schemes in place to reduce crime and the fear of it (especially youth crime). Try to reduce vandalism and other antisocial behaviour to improve people's quality of life and local environment.

Community wardens patrol an area in pairs or small teams, to prevent criminal activity and reassure the public. Work with young people and give them information on social and leisure activities. Report any concerns of individuals and communities so that action can be taken. Also have the power to enforce laws and issue fines on a range of issues, including litter, fly-tipping and dog fouling.

Work Details
Usually works around 39 hours a week, on a shift system often between 8am and midnight, including weekends and bank holidays. Some communities have a system where shifts cover the full 24 hours a day, every day. Most time is spent outside in all weather conditions and on foot, with the occasional talks inside to groups. You may be required to wear a uniform.

Qualification

• Scotland
Band 1: You do not need qualifications, though some S grades in English, maths and science, or similar, at any level are useful. You are expected to have a good level of general education.

Band 2: Although academic qualifications are not specified for this job, it is an advantage to have some S grades (1-3) in subjects that include English and maths, or similar qualifications.

Adult Qualifications
There are no formal educational requirements for recruitment, and applications from adults are especially welcomed. However, you are expected to have a good level of general education and to be able to write accurate reports.

Work Experience
Work or voluntary experience is always useful and can improve your chance of success when applying for jobs. Some employers look for paid or voluntary experience of community service. Anything that shows that you are interested in your community and a team player is helpful.

Entry and Training
Training depends on your duties. These are linked to the Antisocial Behaviour etc (Scotland) Act 2004, which is about dealing with antisocial behaviour, antisocial behaviour orders (ASBOs), noise nuisance, fixed penalties, the environment, and parenting orders. On-the-job training is usually given on topics that are relevant to the area you work in. You must have a Disclosure Scotland check.

In-house training usually includes health and safety, understanding the problems of antisocial behaviour, care of victims, team building, and working with the community. Your employer may also support other training and development such as that offered by the Chartered Institute of Housing in Scotland. Full training usually takes 4-8 weeks. You may also be able to take an SVQ at levels 3-4 in community justice. Check the Scottish Qualifications Authority (SQA) website for details of relevant courses in community justice.

Adult entry is welcomed and any previous related experience is an advantage. You need to be able to engage and communicate with all members and age groups of a local community. Some employers may look for those applicants with experience of community service, either paid or voluntary.

Opportunities and Pay
There are more than 550 community wardens employed by local councils in Scotland, and there are jobs in most areas, including island communities. With experience you may move on to supervisory or training roles, or perhaps apply to become a police officer. This is quite a new occupation and is still developing.

Pay varies according to your area, but full-time starting salaries are around £16.5k a year. This can rise to around £18.5k-£22k with experience. There are additional allowances for overtime and working shifts.

Health
You should have good stamina and be physically fit.

Skills and Qualities
able to cope under pressure, aptitude for teamwork, calm, good communication skills, good interpersonal skills, good listening skills, resilient, sympathetic

Relevant Subjects
Law, Psychology, Sociology

Further Information
Antisocial Behaviour Scotland - www.antisocialbehaviourscotland.com

Scottish Government - Education and Training - www.scotland.gov.uk/Topics/Education

Skills for Justice - sector skills council for the UK justice system - www.skillsforjustice.com

Addresses
Chartered Institute of Housing (Scotland)
6 Palmerston Place, Edinburgh EH12 5AA
Phone: +44 (0)131 225 4544
Web: www.cih.org

Scottish Qualifications Authority (SQA)
The Optima Building 58 Robertson Street, Glasgow G2 8DQ
Phone: 0845 279 1000
Web: www.sqa.org.uk/sqa/41328.html

Similar Jobs
Community Learning & Development Officer (Scotland), Park Warden, Parking Attendant, Police Officer

Company Secretary
also known as: Chartered Secretary/Administrator

CRCI:Administration, Business and Office Work
CLCI:CAP Job Band: 3 to 5

Job Description
Company secretaries play a major part in an organisation's governance, being responsible for the legal, financial and day-to-day administrative and management aspects of a company or organisation. They have a high level of responsibility, advising the company on legal matters and making sure the organisation complies with current company law. Their duties include organising board and committee meetings, circulating the agenda, drafting minutes and seeing that decisions are passed on to staff. They also prepare reports, including annual reports, sign legal documents and negotiate contracts for the company or organisation.

Company secretaries keep a shareholders' register and call meetings; providing a link between directors and shareholders. They pay dividends (sums of money) to shareholders and administer share option schemes. Some may also organise a company pension and payroll scheme. Training non-executives and trainee employees is part of the role.

Work Details
Usually work normal office hours of 39 hrs, Monday to Friday, but this varies due to the demands of the job; occasionally longer hours and weekend work may be required. You are based in an office but may need to travel to meetings. The work can be demanding at times with deadlines that must be met. You liaise with managers and directors, and negotiate with lawyers, bankers and auditors. The work involves dealing with complex financial matters.

Qualification

• England, Wales and Northern Ireland
Band 3: For entry to the Certificate in Business Practice programme of the Institute of Chartered Secretaries and Administrators (ICSA): candidates are accepted without formal qualifications or with some GCSEs and/or A levels, or equivalent. Useful subjects include English and maths.

Band 4: For BTEC higher national award: 1-2 A levels and some GCSEs (A*-C) usually including English and maths, or equivalent.

Band 5: For degree courses: 2-3 A levels and some GCSEs (A*-C) usually including English and maths, or equivalent. Exact requirements depend on the degree you take.

- **Scotland**

Band 3: For entry to the Certificate in Business Practice programme of the Institute of Chartered Secretaries and Administrators (ICSA): candidates are accepted without formal qualifications or with some S grades and/or H grades, or similar. Useful subjects include English and maths.

Band 4: For SQA higher national award: usually 2-3 H grades and some S grades (1-3), often including English and maths, or similar qualifications.

Band 5: For degree courses: 3-5 H grades and some S grades (1-3), usually including English and maths, or similar qualifications. Exact requirements depend on the degree you take.

Degree Information

Any degree discipline is acceptable. Law, economics, accountancy and business studies are relevant subjects that may lead to exemptions from the Institute of Chartered Secretaries and Administrators (ICSA) professional qualifications. Business administration, financial management and banking give useful background. There are also several foundation degrees in business-related subjects. It is not necessary to have a pre-entry postgraduate qualification.

Adult Qualifications

Entry requirements may be relaxed for adults applying for higher education courses. Access or foundation courses provide those without the required qualifications a route onto degree courses. Those with relevant qualifications, eg accountancy, law, business studies or administration, may gain exemption from parts of the professional exams. ICSA also offers a Certificate in Business Practice programme for those without formal qualifications.

Work Experience

Entry to this job is competitive and it is essential that you try to do some relevant work or voluntary experience in related areas, such as legal, financial, bookkeeping, events management and administration, and in local/central government. Experience or knowledge of basic accounting techniques is also a distinct advantage. Many companies offer trainee placements that last from around two to three months, and often in the summer months. Contact the Institute of Chartered Secretaries and Administrators (ICSA) for details.

Entry and Training

Most entrants are graduates with relevant previous experience in administration. However, some entrants may first qualify as an accountant or lawyer and move into the role of a company secretary. All entrants are required to study for a professional qualification, usually those of the Institute of Chartered Secretaries and Administrators (ICSA). Qualifications are available through full or part-time courses, evening or weekend courses, flexistudy (distance learning with tutorials), or by distance learning whilst in a job. The ICSA International Qualifying Scheme offers four relevant stages/programmes: Certificate in Business Practice (open access that requires no formal qualifications), Diploma in Business Practice, and parts I and II of the Professional Programme. It usually takes around 2-3 years to complete the scheme, but less for graduates with relevant first degrees.

Successful completion of the scheme is recognised as a postgraduate qualification and leads to chartered secretary status. Professional examination exemptions from the ICSA are available for those with specific qualifications, such as a relevant degree, professional or postgraduate qualifications, an S/NVQ level 4 in administration, or equivalent. Alternatively, you can study at university with an ICSA university partner and gain a masters degree or postgraduate diploma from the university as well as being awarded Grad.ICSA status. This route meets the requirements of the Professional Programme examination of the ICSA. You can study on a part-time basis and continue working building your professional and academic qualifications at the same time.

ICSA also offers Self-Standing Awards to attract people from specific industry sectors such as local government, charities and education. Candidates for these awards must be employed in a relevant occupational field.

You are expected to continue your professional development (CPD) throughout your career as a company/chartered secretary and support varies between employers. The ICSA offers a series of seminars, workshops, and conferences to help update your professional knowledge, and to provide an opportunity for networking and shared working experiences.

Mature entrants to this job often have previous experience, including financial management, law, senior administration, pensions and insurance, or human resources/personnel. Recognition of past experience can be accredited through Accreditation of Prior Learning (APL). The Worshipful Company of Chartered Secretaries and Administrators Charitable Trust offers scholarships for higher education study for appropriate degree courses and ICSA examinations. It also offers an apprenticeship scheme for those aged 18-29. Check the website for details as you have to meet specific criteria to apply.

Opportunities and Pay

Currently, every UK registered company is required by law to have a company secretary, but competition for vacancies is intense. You can work in many different types of organisation, such as voluntary organisations, local authorities, civil service, schools, colleges and universities, financial organisations, charities, the NHS, industry, commerce, investment trusts, and manufacturing companies. Some specialise in pensions, administration, finance or personnel management. With experience you can become a general manager, a company director or partner. There are some part-time opportunities and work abroad is possible, particularly with international companies.

Recent changes to company law mean that private companies can choose whether they employ a company secretary or not. This may mean that more company secretaries will work for professional services firms that offer company secretary services and consultancy to a wide range of clients. It is important to keep up with changes in legislation and, if you are working for a large international company, proficiency in another language may be advantageous.

Pay varies depending on location, size of company, responsibility and experience, and is high for top achievers. A graduate entering this career can expect to earn around £28k-£32k. Experienced and qualified chartered secretaries earn £45k-£85k a year. Those at a more senior level or working for a FTSE 100 firm can earn more than £190k a year or £129k a year if working for a FTSE 250. Salaries with not for profit or private companies can range from £65k-£105k. Bonus schemes and performance-related pay are offered by some companies.

Skills and Qualities

able to work to deadlines, aptitude for figures, attention to detail, discreet, good communication skills, good organisational skills, good written English, information handling skills, IT skills, sound judgement

Relevant Subjects

Business and accounting, Economics, English, Government and politics, ICT/Computer studies, Law, Mathematics

Further Information

Chartered Secretary Magazine (ICSA) - www.charteredsecretary.net

Institute of Professional Administrators (Institute of Professional Administrators) - www.inprad.org

Real Life Guide to Business & Administration (Trotman 2009) - www.trotman.co.uk

▶Working in business, administration & finance (2010) (Babcock Lifeskills) - www.babcock-lifeskills.com/

Addresses

Companies House
Companies House, Crown Way, Maindy, Cardiff CF14 3UZ
Phone: +44 (0)303 1234 500
Web: www.companieshouse.gov.uk

Institute of Chartered Secretaries and Administrators (ICSA)
16 Park Crescent, London W1B 1AH
Phone: +44 (0)20 75804741
Web: www.icsa.org.uk

Worshipful Company of Chartered Secretaries and Administrators
Saddlers' House, 3rd Floor, 40 Gutter Lane, London EC2V 6BR
Phone: +44 (0)20 7726 2955
Web: www.wccsa.org.uk

Similar Jobs

Accountant: Industry & Commerce, Accountant: Public Sector, Human Resources Officer/Manager, Local Government Administrator, Pension Fund Manager, Solicitor

Compliance Officer

CRCI:Financial Services
CLCI:NAG Job Band: 5

Job Description

Compliance officers work for financial services organisations, and may specialise in a particular product area such as life insurance, pensions and investment, or mortgages. They have up-to-date knowledge of the laws and regulations of the financial services industry and are responsible for ensuring that the company behaves ethically and consistently in accordance with Financial Services Authority (FSA) requirements.

All company paperwork is thoroughly checked to make sure everything complies with FSA rules and regulations. Compliance officers supervise and advise front-office staff on all questions relating to a company's products and services within areas of compliance. May investigate customer complaints and any suspected breaches of the rules of the FSA. They need to keep up to date with all FSA requirements.

Work to improve the productivity and performance of staff by introducing methods of best practice. May develop and/or provide in-house training programmes for the company's employees on aspects of legal and regulatory issues. Review new company products and projects, and test that they also comply with rules and regulations.

Work Details

Usually work a basic 39 hr week, Monday to Friday, but may be required to work evenings and weekends on occasions. Work is in an office environment and can sometimes be under pressure. Smart dress is essential. Much of the time is spent in meetings and liaising with other sections of the company. Overseas travel is possible if working for an international company.

Qualification

There are no set minimum qualifications for entry, but employers often look for a background in law, accounts or auditing work, with a degree level qualification.

- **England, Wales and Northern Ireland**

Band 5: For degree courses: 2-3 A levels and some GCSEs (A*-C) usually including English and maths, or equivalent. Exact requirements depend on the degree you take.

- **Scotland**

Band 5: For degree courses: 3-5 H grades and some S grades (1-3), usually including English and maths, or similar qualifications. Exact requirements depend on the degree you take.

Degree Information

Employers may prefer a first degree in subjects that include finance, a business subject, economics or law. There is a masters degree in financial regulation and compliance management at London Metropolitan University and a diploma in capital markets, regulation and compliance at Reading University.

Adult Qualifications

Entry requirements may be relaxed for adults applying for higher education courses. Foundation and Access courses give adults without qualifications a route on to degree courses.

Work Experience

Entry is often competitive and previous experience in an advisory or insurance sales role is advantageous. Any work experience in the finance sector is relevant and shows enthusiasm and commitment to the work. Time spent in an accountancy firm, an insurance company or even shadowing a financial adviser gives you a good basis and insight into the profession. Some courses offer an option for a period of professional placement during the third year of a degree. You can also apply for an internship, usually taken during the Easter or summer vacation period.

Entry and Training

There are no specified entry requirements, although most entrants are suitably qualified graduates, often with at least two years' experience in finance, insurance sales, accounts or administration. You may be able to enter this job at a more junior level and work your way up. A Diploma may be available in your area in business, administration and finance. The advanced level is equivalent to 3.5 A levels. Check entry requirements carefully with the individual institutions.

As compliance is an area that exists across the financial services industry, many have entry level qualifications from professional bodies in areas such as banking, insurance, or investment. Some have a background in law.

Employers may expect you to have the Chartered Insurance Institute's (CII) certificate in financial planning. This develops an understanding of the industry and reflects the priorities of the Financial Services Authority and the Financial Services Skills Council. There are no minimum qualifications needed to study for this certificate. There are further qualifications from the CII that may also be appropriate. The ifs School of Finance, the Institute of Chartered Secretaries & Administrators and the Securities and Investment Institute also offer relevant qualifications, such as the ifs certificate for financial advisers.

Training is usually on the job together with short specialist courses. The International Compliance Association, in conjunction with the University of Manchester Business School, offers distance-learning courses and qualifications, including certificates and diplomas in areas of compliance practice. The Compliance Institute also offers a qualification for compliance staff, in partnership with the business, technology, leadership and management unit at the University of Warwick Business School.

You are required to update your knowledge through a programme of continuing professional development throughout your career.

Mature entrants are welcomed, especially those with experience and qualifications in financial planning, insurance or a related profession, such as accountancy or law. A career in compliance can also be entered via an administrative role if you do not have relevant experience.

Distance-learning courses for professional qualifications are available from the Chartered Institute of Insurance and the International Compliance Association. Normal entry requirements may be relaxed for those over 25 years of age. Many companies require a certificate in financial planning as a minimum.

Opportunities and Pay

Despite the economic downturn and the challenges the financial services industry faces at the moment, this is an expanding sector. The Financial Services Authority's (FSA) approach to regulation is increasing the skills and responsibilities expected of compliance staff, so employment and promotion prospects are good.

There are job opportunities with financial services, investment and insurance companies, independent financial advisers, life and pensions companies, stockbrokers and banks. All financial services companies need a compliance function and there is a concentration of jobs in major cities. The FSA recruits 40-50 new graduates a year to its training programme. You may be able to gain promotion to partner in a firm, branch or area manager, or a director.

Earnings vary depending on location and employer, but a starting salary can be around £30k a year, rising to around £40k-£50k for senior compliance officers with five to six years experience and at least one professional qualification. Directors of compliance can earn £70k or more a year.

Skills and Qualities

able to cope under pressure, accurate, analytical skills, diplomatic, tactful & discreet, enquiring mind, good communication skills, good interpersonal skills, good organisational skills, IT skills, meticulous

Relevant Subjects

Business and accounting, Economics, English, ICT/Computer studies, Law, Mathematics

Further Information

Diploma in Business, Administration and Finance - www.baf-diploma.org.uk/

Financial Services Skills Council - sector skills council for financial services, accountancy & finance www.fssc.org.uk/

TARGETjobs: City and Finance (GTI Specialist Publishers Ltd) - www.groupgti.com

The Association of British Insurers (ABI) - www.abi.org.uk

▶Working in maths (2009) (Babcock Lifeskills) - www.babcock-lifeskills.com/

Addresses

Chartered Financial Analyst (CFA) Institute
10th Floor, One Canada Square, Canary Wharf, London E14 5AB
Phone: 0800 1247 8132 UK only
Web: www.cfainstitute.org

Chartered Insurance Institute (CII)
42-48 High Road, South Woodford, London E18 2JP
Phone: +44 (0)20 8989 8464
Web: www.cii.co.uk

Compliance Institute
107 Barkby Road, Leicester LE4 9LG
Phone: +44 (0)116 246 1316
Web: www.complianceinstitute.co.uk

Financial Services Authority (FSA)
Membership Department, 25 The North Colonnade, Canary Wharf, London E14 5HS
Phone: +44 (0)20 7066 1000
Web: www.fsa.gov.uk

ifs School of Finance
IFS House, 4-9 Burgate Lane, Canterbury, Kent CT1 2XJ
Phone: +44 (0)1227 818609
Web: www.ifslearning.ac.uk

Institute of Chartered Secretaries and Administrators (ICSA)
16 Park Crescent, London W1B 1AH
Phone: +44 (0)20 75804741
Web: www.icsa.org.uk

International Compliance Association (ICA)
Wrens Court, 52-54 Victoria Road, Sutton Coldfield, Birmingham B72 1SX
Phone: +44 (0)121 362 7534
Web: www.int-comp.org

Securities & Investment Institute (SII)
8 Eastcheap, London EC3M 1AE
Phone: +44 (0)20 7645 0600
Web: www.sii.org.uk

Similar Jobs

Accountant: Industry & Commerce, Company Secretary, Financial Adviser/Planner, Insurance Broker, Insurance Business Development Manager, Investment Analyst, Pensions Adviser

Computer Assembly Technician

CRCI:Engineering
CLCI:RAL Job Band: 2 to 3

Job Description

Computer assembly technicians build computers from their individual parts and then test the completed system. They assemble parts such as circuit boards, modems, CD-ROM drives, external cases, processors, cables and switches. Then they perform tests to check that all parts are working correctly and to locate and correct any faults.

Technicians may upgrade computers by fitting new hardware to existing systems. They use tools such as screwdrivers, soldering irons and electronic testing equipment. For large companies, the work may be more routine and for smaller, specialist companies, based on custom-built systems for an individual customer's requirements. Technicians may deal directly with customers, servicing and upgrading machines.

Work Details

Usually work a basic 39 hr week, Monday to Friday, though may be expected to work a shift system. Overtime work is possible. Some components are very delicate. Technicians sometimes need to wear special outer clothing to reduce the risk of contaminating the part by dust and dirt, or to prevent damage to circuit boards through static electricity. You are supervised and expected to follow safety regulations. There may be a risk of accidents from equipment.

Qualification

- **England, Wales and Northern Ireland**

Band 2: For entry to jobs, no minimum qualifications are needed, but it is an advantage to have some GCSEs (A*-C) or equivalent. Useful subjects include English, maths, science and technology.

Band 3: For entry to jobs, HNC or a relevant Diploma, usually at least 4 GCSEs (A*-C) including including English, maths and preferably physics or another science subject, or equivalent.

- **Scotland**

Band 2: Although academic qualifications are not always specified for this job, some courses/employers may require some S grades (1-3), or similar. Useful subjects include English, maths, science and technology.

Band 3. For entry to jobs, usually at least four S grades (1-3) including English, maths and preferably physics or another science subject, or similar.

Adult Qualifications
Entry requirements may be relaxed for mature applicants. Previous experience in electronic assembly is useful.

Work Experience
It is important that you try to do some relevant work or voluntary experience before applying for this job. You can gain experience in areas that involve electronics and electrical equipment and also work of a practical nature. Work experience is not always so crucial for young people as many entry positions are for trainees or apprentices. For adults, relevant work experience or previous employment is more necessary and is widely asked for.

Entry and Training
Applicants are usually aged 16-17. To enter this job you may have to take a practical aptitude test to check whether you have the necessary skills and dexterity. Training is likely to be a combination of on-the-job training with an experienced employee and a day or block-release course at a local college. There are relevant full or part time BTEC/SQA awards/City & Guilds courses.

A popular industry-recognised entry-level qualification is the CompTIA A+ offered by the Computing Technology Industry Association (CompTIA). The course has been updated to reflect changes in technology. It also offers alternative validation paths for specific job environments, including a bench technician. Contact CompTIA for details of the range of available qualifications.

Relevant S/NVQs are available at levels 1-2 such as performing engineering operations and at levels 2-3 in electrical assembly. Relevant training programmes, including apprenticeship schemes offering a technical support route, may be available in your area. Advanced apprenticeships leading to qualification at level 3 can also be a route into higher education. You may be able to do a Diploma/Welsh Baccalaureate in engineering if they are available in your area.

Mature applicants are considered by employers but this depends on your experience. College courses are available for all ages.

Government training opportunities, such as apprenticeships for adults, may be available in your area. You can also gain recognition of previous experience through Accreditation of Prior Learning (APL) or by working towards relevant S/NVQs. Contact your local careers office, Jobcentre Plus, Next Step service or Learning and Skills Council (LSC)/Local Enterprise Company (LEC) for details of training schemes.

Opportunities and Pay
Jobs are available throughout the UK and employment can be with a manufacturing company, large retailer or a computer distributor. Larger organisations are likely to have more opportunities for advancement to a supervisory or management position. With experience, it may be possible to set up your own business.

Pay varies according to the type of employer but generally you can expect to earn around £18k-£20k a year after training. With experience, this may increase to £25k. It may also be possible to earn bonus payments.

Health
This job requires normal colour vision and a good standard of physical fitness and stamina.

Skills and Qualities
able to communicate effectively, able to work quickly, attention to detail, IT skills, manual dexterity, methodical, patient, practical skills, technical aptitude

Relevant Subjects
Design and technology, Engineering, ICT/Computer studies, Manufacturing, Mathematics, Physics, Science

Further Information
Apprenticeship Schemes (National Apprenticeship Service) - www.apprenticeships.org.uk

Computing Technology Industry Association (CompTIA) - www.comptia.org

Diplomas (Foundation, Higher and Advanced) - http://yp.direct.gov.uk/diplomas

e-skills UK - sector skills council for business and information technology - www.e-skills.com

SEMTA - sector skills council for science, engineering and manufacturing technologies - www.semta.org.uk

Welsh Baccalaureate - www.wbq.org.uk

Women into Science, Engineering & Construction - www.wisecampaign.org.uk

▶Working in computers & IT (2010) (Babcock Lifeskills) - www.babcock-lifeskills.com/

▶Working in manufacturing (2010) (Babcock Lifeskills) - www.babcock-lifeskills.com/

Addresses
British Computer Society (BCS)
First Floor, Block D North Star House North Star Avenue, Swindon, Wiltshire SN2 1FA
Phone: +44 (0)845 300 4417
Web: www.bcs.org

Similar Jobs
Electrical Engineering Technician, Electronics Assembler, IT Service Technician, Office Equipment Service Engineer

Computer Games Animator
CRCI:Computers and IT
CLCI:CAV Job Band: 3 to 5

Job Description
Computer games animators work as part of the art department team in the interactive and computer games industry and are responsible for the portrayal of movement and behaviour of the characters. They also create the setting of computer games and use specialist software (computer graphics programs) to create lifelike effects to entertain games players. Increasingly, computer games are also informative and educational and some animators may specialise in this area of work. Usually follow a 'storyboard', which can be a series of rough sketches outlining the characters and story of the game.

Work closely with games programmers and artists and are knowledgeable in all aspects of their discipline. Use techniques such as character modelling, skinning, rigging, basic cinematography and kinematics.

Work Details
Usually work a basic 37 hr week, Monday to Friday, but may have to work extra hours to meet deadlines. Work is mainly in an open plan office or studio. You have to cope with the pressure of work, tight deadlines, and may need to travel to meet clients. Must fit into the art department environment, working closely with programmers and artists. Good communication skills are essential as is knowledge of the overall production process.

Qualification

- **England, Wales and Northern Ireland**

Band 4: For BTEC higher national award: 1-2 A levels and some GCSEs (A*-C) usually including English and maths, or equivalent.

Band 5: For degree courses: 2-3 A levels and some GCSEs (A*-C) usually including English and maths, or equivalent. Entrance to art and design courses can be through an arts foundation course. Exact requirements depend on the degree you take.

- **Scotland**

Band 4: For SQA higher national award: 2-3 H grades and some S grades (1-3), often including English and maths, or similar qualifications.

Band 5: For degree courses: 3-5 H grades and some S grades (1-3), usually including English and maths, or similar qualifications. Entrance to art and design courses can be through an arts foundation course. Exact requirements depend on the degree you take.

Degree Information

Computer graphics is a rapidly expanding creative area and there are various computer games animation degrees. These either concentrate specifically on animation or are general art courses with animation components. Subjects include computer animation, computer visualisation, special effects, CAD, music technology, and many more. The Information Technology Management for Business degree is designed in partnership with some of the biggest employers in the IT industry.

However, employers often recruit talented graduates from more traditional academic degree courses that include computer science, programming, art, psychology, design, maths and physics. There are some specialised and relevant postgraduate courses, including an MA/MSc in computer animation, or in digital effects.

Adult Qualifications

Entry requirements may be relaxed for adults applying for higher education courses and Access or foundation courses give adults without qualifications a route onto degree courses. Postgraduate courses in computer animation, including distance-learning courses, may be available for those without a relevant first degree.

Work Experience

Work experience is desirable and is best found by contacting animation houses and software companies directly. Graduates who have taken a gap year to gain computer games industry experience may have an advantage with employers. In some areas there is a young apprenticeship (14-16) scheme that provides an extended work placement and eventual achievement of a relevant level 2 qualification whilst at school.

Other schemes, such as 'The Year in Industry', enable those who expect good A levels/H grades and intend to go to university, the opportunity to spend a salaried year with a company to gain valuable work experience. Some higher education courses offer work experience placements as part of the course.

Entry and Training

The majority of entrants are graduates with an animation or related degree, although some entrants are extremely talented and experienced amateurs. Experience of a computer animation package is important and a background in practical art is often required. Employers may also look for a background in maths and physics, computer science or programming. Some animators move into the games industry from film and television careers.

Being bright, flexible and naturally talented can be considered more useful than a vocation specific degree. There is a range of courses accredited by the sector skills council for creative media, Skillset. Contact them for details. The computer games industry currently looks for well-educated and talented individuals who have the ability and willingness to keep learning. Knowledge of at least one animation package, such as Maya, Character Studio, Flash, Action Script or 3D Studio Max, is useful.

There are also a number of foundation degrees available in aspects of computer animation and a Diploma/Welsh Baccalaureate in IT may also be available in your area. Training is mainly on the job and is usually supported by specialised short courses in animation packages and/or animation techniques. Some institutions offer specialist computer animation training, such as the National Centre for Computer Animation in Bournemouth.

Applicants for jobs are usually required to demonstrate their work and creative potential through a portfolio or 2-3 minute show reel (film/video) of their work. For more advice on training, qualifications and how to make an effective submission, contact Skillset Careers.

Mature entrants with previous experience in CAD or visual arts may have an advantage. Applicants are usually required to demonstrate their work and creative potential through a portfolio or show reel (film/video). Contact Skillset Careers for entry routes available for mature applicants.

Opportunities and Pay

Computer games animators often work for animation or development studios, or for interactive media designers and independent games publishers. They may also work for specialist games outsourcing companies. The main areas for work are London and the south east, Bristol, Dundee, Manchester and Cardiff.

There are about 30,000 people employed in the UK games industry working for games developers, publishers and retailers. There are over 250 games development studios. The UK has the biggest development community in Europe but it has been affected by the economic downturn. There are also good opportunities to work in France, the USA or Japan, though entry may be competitive. This is a young industry and those with relevant skills, with or without qualifications, can progress rapidly. There are also opportunities to move into game production or a multimedia career in graphic design.

Some computer animators start as runners, earning around £12k-£16k a year. Most graduates start at £16k-£24k a year, rising to £25k-£35k with experience. Lead animators can earn £30k-£40k and some very successful and talented animators earn considerably more. Unlike other media jobs, where work is paid project-by-project, experienced games animators are usually permanently contracted. Freelance animators are paid per project, or according to the Broadcasting, Entertainment, Cinematograph and Theatre Union guidelines. Employers may provide bonuses for project completion.

Health

This job requires normal colour vision.

Skills and Qualities

able to cope under pressure, able to work both on your own and in a team, artistic ability, attention to detail, creative flair, eye for visual effect, full motion video (FMV) knowledge, good communication skills, good presentation skills, spatial awareness, specialist IT skills

Relevant Subjects

Art and Design, Design and technology, English, ICT/Computer studies, Mathematics, Physics, Psychology, Science

Further Information

Broadcasting Entertainment Cinematographic and Theatre Union (BECTU) - www.bectu.org.uk

Computer Arts (Future Publishing) - www.computerarts.co.uk

Diplomas (Foundation, Higher and Advanced) http://yp.direct.gov.uk/diplomas

e-skills UK - sector skills council for business and information technology - www.e-skills.com

Futurelab - www.futurelab.org.uk/

Games Industry Information - www.gamesindustry.biz

National Centre for Computer Animation - http://ncca.bournemouth.ac.uk

Real Life Guide to Information & Communications Technology (Trotman) - www.trotman.co.uk

Skillset - sector skills council for the creative media, fashion and textiles industries - www.skillset.org

Tiga - www.tiga.org

Welsh Baccalaureate - www.wbq.org.uk

▶Working in computers & IT (2010) (Babcock Lifeskills) - www.babcock-lifeskills.com/

▶Working in creative & media (2007) (Babcock Lifeskills) - www.babcock-lifeskills.com/

Working in the Games Industry - www.workingames.co.uk

Year in Industry (Engineering Development Trust) - www.yini.org.uk

Addresses

British Computer Society (BCS)
First Floor, Block D North Star House North Star Avenue, Swindon, Wiltshire SN2 1FA
Phone: +44 (0)845 300 4417
Web: www.bcs.org

Similar Jobs

Animator, Computer Games Designer, Computer Games Programmer, Graphic Designer, Interactive Media Designer, Website Designer

Computer Games Designer

CRCI:Computers and IT
CLCI:CAV Job Band: 3 to 5

Job Description

Computer games designers create original and abstract ideas (concepts) for a computer game which can then be developed by computer games programmers and other development team members. They design games for a PC, a console (dedicated games machine), or increasingly games that are played on the Internet. May first write down thoughts and produce sketches, then outline the concept of how the game will look and be played. Also liaise with senior programmers, animators, graphic artists, musicians and writers.

Designers present the concept document for consideration to a games production company. If acceptable, they work with programmers and artists to build a game prototype. They demonstrate how the game will function and write the design document. Using tools such as storyboards, flowcharts and index cards, they interpret many different functions and conclusions to a game. May need to amend designs due to technical difficulties. Some designers work on one aspect/dimension of the design, or may work across the complete game. In some cases, designers also manage and oversee the project through to completion.

Work Details

Usually work a basic 37 hrs a week, Monday to Friday, though in practice work longer hours including evenings and weekends when deadlines approach. You are normally based at a desk or workstation. You have to cope with the pressure of work, tight deadlines, and may need to travel to meet clients. Must fit into the art department environment, working closely with programmers, other artists and animators.

Qualification

- **England, Wales and Northern Ireland**

Band 4: For a relevant BTEC higher national award: 1-2 A levels and some GCSEs (A*-C) including English and maths, and for some courses, preferably science, computer studies or information technology, or equivalent.

Band 5: For degree courses: 2-3 A levels including maths, science, computer studies or information technology for some courses, and some GCSEs (A*-C) usually including English and maths, or equivalent. Exact requirements depend on the degree you take.

- **Scotland**

Band 4: For a relevant higher national award: 2-3 H grades and some S grades (1-3) including English and maths, and for some courses preferably science, computer studies or information technology, or similar qualifications.

Band 5: For degree courses: 3-5 H grades including maths, science and computer technology for some courses, and some S grades (1-3), often including English and maths, or similar qualifications. Exact requirements depend on the degree you take.

Degree Information

There are many relevant degree courses such as computer games design, computer games and visual effects, computer games software development/illustration/animation and computer science (games technology). The Information Technology Management for Business degree (see e-skills UK) is designed in partnership with some of the biggest employers in the IT industry. There are also relevant postgraduate computing qualifications.

Adult Qualifications

Although predominantly a young industry, a track record of designing games is the only essential qualification. Mature entrants may not need to meet the standard entry requirements for higher education courses, particularly if your previous experience is relevant and you show the ability to study at the appropriate level.

Work Experience

Entry to this job is competitive and it is important that you try to do some relevant work or voluntary experience before applying. This includes designing games and using art work in a commercial company or at home, and producing a portfolio of your work. Computer programming experience can also provide a good basis.

Schemes such as 'The Year in Industry' enable those who expect good A levels/H grades and intend to go to university the opportunity to spend a salaried year with a company to gain valuable work experience.

Entry and Training

This is a very popular industry, entry is highly competitive and there is no set route into a job. It is possible to begin as a games playtester and work your way into the job, providing you have the skills and talent. However, game development is a highly complex, intensive process and many entrants have been educated to degree level and acquired a high level of industry experience. There is a range of computer games degree courses accredited by the sector skills council for creative media, Skillset. Contact them for details.

Some programming experience is required for entry, as well as experience of designing games either at home or in the games industry. Experience of software packages such as 3D Studio Max, Maya, Lightwave, Photoshop is useful as these are widely used. Employers also expect to see a portfolio of your work to date. Training is ongoing, both on the job and by short courses run by manufacturers. You need to keep ahead with game development and its technology throughout your career, by continually updating your skills.

E-skills run a professional development programme which enables new IT professionals to fast-track their career. The programme is delivered through universities and participating employers. E-skills also offers an internship. Students are placed for a period of employment within an organisation, enabling them to develop valuable business and IT skills.

The Open University offers courses in computing and maths that can lead to a computing degree. There are no formal entry requirements and you study through distance learning. Foundation degrees in IT, computer game design and development, computer games development, or in animation and games, are also available.

A Diploma/Welsh Baccalaureate in IT may be available in your area. An ICT higher apprenticeship is available through e-skills. This combines an apprenticeship with a foundation degree and can lead to a full honours degree. There are partnerships with colleges and universities throughout the UK. Contact e-skills for details of all programmes and schemes.

Mature applicants can enter higher education through Access, foundation or similar courses, which are available for those who have no formal qualifications but wish to pursue a relevant degree. There are many full or part-time courses available at further/higher education colleges for careers that do not require degree level entry. Some LSCs/LECs, Jobcentres (NI) and ELWa (Wales) run high technology courses. You can also gain recognition of previous experience through Accreditation of Prior Learning (APL) or by working towards relevant S/NVQs.

Opportunities and Pay

Around 7,000 people now work in the industry in over 250 games development studios in the UK. Companies are based throughout the UK, but particularly in major cities. With the explosion of PCs and consoles as a form of home entertainment, the computer games industry has become a profitable global business. In total, there are about 30,000 people employed in the UK games industry working for games developers, publishers and retailers. The UK has the biggest development community in Europe but it has been affected by the economic downturn. There are companies based in many parts of the country, though there are games industry 'clusters' in areas that include Dundee, Manchester, Liverpool, Yorkshire, Warwickshire, and the south east of England. This is a young industry and those with relevant skills, with or without qualifications, can progress rapidly. Employers are usually independent specialised companies or those owned by games publishers.

The UK industry has a reputation for producing many innovative and quality games and there are also good opportunities to work overseas, particularly in the USA, Canada, Japan and France. Designers often work freelance on long fixed-term contracts as games take a considerable time to develop. Self-employment is also possible.

Depending on the company, a graduate may expect to earn around £20k-£24k a year, rising to around £25k-£40k with experience. Lead designers can earn up to £55k a year and highly successful designers may earn more. Profit-sharing, performance-related pay or a bonus payment may be additional to your basic salary.

Skills and Qualities

able to cope under pressure, able to withstand criticism, able to work both on your own and in a team, creative and imaginative flair, good communication skills, information handling skills, inventive, logical, specialist IT skills

Relevant Subjects

Art and Design, Design and technology, English, ICT/Computer studies, Mathematics, Media and communication studies, Music

Further Information

AGCAS: Information Technology (Job Sector Briefing) (AGCAS) - www.prospects.ac.uk

Computer Arts (Future Publishing) - www.computerarts.co.uk

Develop Magazine (Intent Media) - www.develop-online.net

Diplomas (Foundation, Higher and Advanced) - http://yp.direct.gov.uk/diplomas

e-skills UK - sector skills council for business and information technology - www.e-skills.com

Games Industry Information - www.gamesindustry.biz

Open University - www.open.ac.uk

Real Life Guide to Information & Communications Technology (Trotman) - www.trotman.co.uk

Skills Framework for the Information Age (SFIA) (SFIA Foundation) - www.sfia.org.uk

Skillset - sector skills council for the creative media, fashion and textiles industries - www.skillset.org

Tiga - www.tiga.org

Welsh Baccalaureate - www.wbq.org.uk

▶Working in computers & IT (2010) (Babcock Lifeskills) - www.babcock-lifeskills.com/

▶Working in creative & media (2007) (Babcock Lifeskills) - www.babcock-lifeskills.com/

▶Working in manufacturing (2010) (Babcock Lifeskills) - www.babcock-lifeskills.com/

Working in the Games Industry - www.workingames.co.uk

Year in Industry (Engineering Development Trust) - www.yini.org.uk

Addresses

British Computer Society (BCS)
First Floor, Block D North Star House North Star Avenue, Swindon, Wiltshire SN2 1FA
Phone: +44 (0)845 300 4417
Web: www.bcs.org

Entertainment and Leisure Software Publishers Association (ELSPA)
167 Wardour Street, London W1F 8WL
Phone: +44 (0)20 7534 0580
Web: www.elspa.com

Similar Jobs

Computer Games Animator, Computer Games Programmer, Computer Games Technical Support Person, Interactive Media Designer, IT Applications Developer, Website Designer

Computer Games Playtester

also known as: Games Tester, QA Tester: Computer Games

CRCI:Computers and IT
CLCI:CAV — Job Band: 2 to 4

Job Description

Games playtesters (or quality assurance testers) test, tune and debug a game to ensure the quality and playability of the game before it is released for sale. They create a test plan and play-test the game over and over again in a systematic way during its development phase. They need to work out all the ways in which the game is likely to be played and test it accordingly. Testers evaluate the product and locate any flaws in the software. Often need to work on an isolated part of the program to check that each detail works properly. They act as the game's first audience and identify and report on any aspects that need to be improved, although testers have limited influence over the actual design.

Playtesters usually work in a team, sometimes playing the game together on a multi-player game. They look for compatibility with hardware such as processors and graphics cards. Some playtesters write reviews for game providers. Once a game is launched, they may help the customer support team with quality assurance issues.

Work Details

Work a basic 37 hr week, Monday to Friday, although you may need to work extra hours to meet deadlines. You are normally based at a desk or workstation and need to concentrate for long periods of time. Games development is very much a team effort and you need to consult regularly with colleagues.

Computer Games Playtester

Qualification

• England, Wales and Northern Ireland

Band 3: For most employers, or for a relevant BTEC national award: usually at least 4 GCSEs (A*-C) including English, maths and preferably computer studies, information technology, or equivalent.

Band 4: For some employers and BTEC higher national award: 1-2 A levels and some GCSEs (A*-C) usually including English, maths and preferably science, computer studies or information technology, or equivalent.

• Scotland

Band 3: For most employers, or a relevant SQA national award: usually several S grades (1-3) including English, maths and preferably computer studies or information technology, or similar.

Band 4: For some employers and SQA higher national award: 2-3 H grades and some S grades (1-3) often including English, maths and preferably science, computer studies or information technology, or similar qualifications.

Adult Qualifications

Although predominantly a young industry, a track record of playing/testing games is the only essential qualification. Mature entrants may not need to meet the standard entry requirements for higher education courses, particularly if your previous experience is relevant and you show the ability to study at the appropriate level.

Work Experience

Entry to this job is highly competitive and it is important that you try to do some relevant work or voluntary experience in aspects of the computing industry before applying. College courses or employers look for enthusiasm and commitment. Relevant work experience with computers and experience/knowledge of games titles in particular can demonstrate this and helps to improve your chances on application. Working in the retail computer games industry also gives background knowledge. A successful work experience placement can be an effective way into the job.

Entry and Training

This is a popular entry level job and there are no specific entry qualifications, although most testers have a relevant number of good GCSE/S grades (A*-C/1-3) or equivalent, and are able to document findings and communicate them to colleagues. As this is a popular industry for young people, entry is highly competitive, from applicants with few or no qualifications to those with a degree, or similar. Playtesters do need to have a good knowledge of ICT and must be experienced and proficient high level game players. Some programming knowledge or experience is desirable. Training is usually ongoing and on the job, as technology changes rapidly. You need to keep up with game development and its technology throughout your career, by continually updating your skills.

You can take the Information Systems Exam Board's foundation certificate in software testing which may improve your skills and employability. Check the British Computer Society website for details. Skillset's Games Testing Apprenticeship is now available nationally. Skillset are now in the process of piloting an advanced apprenticeship. Contact Skillset Careers for details. A Diploma/ Welsh Baccalaureate may also be available in your area in IT.

The Open University offers courses in computing and maths that can lead to a computing degree. There are no formal entry requirements and you study through distance learning. Foundation degrees in IT, in game production or in animation and games, are also available.

Mature applicants with knowledge or experience in programming, together with a good knowledge of games titles on the market have a fair chance of entry. There are many full or part-time courses available at further/higher education colleges for careers that do not require degree level entry. Some LSCs/LECs, Jobcentres (NI) and ELWa (Wales) run high technology courses. You can also gain recognition of previous experience through Accreditation of Prior Learning (APL) or by working towards relevant S/NVQs.

Opportunities and Pay

There are about 30,000 people employed in the UK games industry working for games developers, publishers and retailers and around 7,000 work in games development in over 250 studios. Companies are based throughout the UK, but particularly in major cities. With the explosion of PCs and games consoles as a form of home entertainment, the industry has become a highly profitable global business. Employers are usually specialised companies producing games for PCs or games consoles, or outsourced companies that test for a range of customers in the UK and overseas. The UK has the biggest development community in Europe, but has been affected by the economic downturn. The UK industry has a reputation for producing many innovative and quality games and there are also good opportunities to work overseas, particularly in the USA, Canada, Japan and France.

Progression to QA team leader or QA manager is possible and there are opportunities to move into design, production management, project management or marketing. More specialist areas of the game industry require relevant skills and aptitude, such as programming or 3D modelling. Self-employment is possible.

Depending on the size and location of company, starting salaries may be around £6.50-£7.50 per hour. Once experienced you can expect to earn around £15k-£18k a year, rising to around £25k. Profit-sharing, performance-related pay or a bonus payment may be additional to your basic salary.

Skills and Qualities

able to cope under pressure, able to work both on your own and in a team, attention to detail, good communication skills, good written English, IT skills, logical, methodical, perseverance, technical aptitude

Relevant Subjects

Art and Design, Design and technology, ICT/Computer studies, Mathematics, Physics, Science

Further Information

Computer Arts (Future Publishing) - www.computerarts.co.uk

Diplomas (Foundation, Higher and Advanced) - http://yp.direct.gov.uk/diplomas

e-skills UK - sector skills council for business and information technology - www.e-skills.com

Games Industry Information - www.gamesindustry.biz

Information Systems Exam Board (ISEB) - www.bcs.org/iseb

Open University - www.open.ac.uk

Skills Framework for the Information Age (SFIA) (SFIA Foundation) - www.sfia.org.uk

Skillset - sector skills council for the creative media, fashion and textiles industries - www.skillset.org

Tiga - www.tiga.org

Welsh Baccalaureate - www.wbq.org.uk

►Working in computers & IT (2010) (Babcock Lifeskills) - www.babcock-lifeskills.com/

Working in the Games Industry - www.workingames.co.uk

Addresses

British Computer Society (BCS)
First Floor, Block D North Star House North Star Avenue, Swindon, Wiltshire SN2 1FA
Phone: +44 (0)845 300 4417
Web: www.bcs.org

British Interactive Media Association (BIMA)
The Lightwell, 12-16 Laystall Street, Clerkenwel, London EC1R 4PF
Phone: +44(0)207 843 6797
Web: www.bima.co.uk

Entertainment and Leisure Software Publishers Association (ELSPA)
167 Wardour Street, London W1F 8WL
Phone: +44 (0)20 7534 0580
Web: www.elspa.com

Similar Jobs
Computer Games Designer, Computer Games Programmer, Computer Games Technical Support Person, Computer Operator, Interactive Media Designer, IT Service Technician, Software Tester

Computer Games Programmer
also known as: AI Programmer: Computer Games, Middleware Programmer: Computer Games, Tools Programmer: Computer Games

CRCI:Computers and IT
CLCI:CAV Job Band: 3 to 5

Job Description
Games programmers work at the heart of the game development process, translating the computer game designer's specifications and ideas into the code of a programming language that runs and controls the game. Different platforms (PCs, Internet, games consoles, handhelds, mobiles etc) require particular programming expertise, so may specialise in artificial intelligence (AI), physics programming, interface and control systems, or in 3D engine development. Programmers work closely with game designers, playtesters, sound, and graphics specialists in the development of a games program. Although similar in function to general computer programming, this work can be more creative because there is often no standard solution to a problem.

Usually work in a team of programmers who are each given a specific number of tasks to translate. Programmers may test and 'de-bug' the completed application, though in larger companies this is often done by a specialist games tester, who liaises and reports to the programmer.

Work Details
Work a basic 37 hr week, Monday to Friday, although you may need to work extra hours including evenings and weekends to meet deadlines. You are normally based at a desk or workstation. Those working as consultants need to travel to visit clients and spend some nights away from home. Games development is very much a team effort and you frequently need to consult with colleagues.

Qualification
- **England, Wales and Northern Ireland**

Band 4: For a relevant BTEC higher national award: 1-2 A levels and some GCSEs (A*-C) usually including English and maths, and for some courses science, computer studies or information technology, or equivalent.

Band 5: For degree courses: 2-3 A levels including science, computer studies or information technology for some courses, and some GCSEs (A*-C), usually including English and maths, or equivalent. Exact requirements depend on the degree you take.

- **Scotland**

Band 4: For a relevant higher national award: usually 2-3 H grades and some S grades (1-3), often including English and maths, and for some courses, science, computer studies or information technology, or similar qualifications.

Band 5: For degree courses: 3-5 H grades including maths, science, computer studies or information technology for some courses, and some S grades (1-3), usually including English and maths, or similar qualifications. Exact requirements depend on the degree you take.

Degree Information
The most relevant degree subjects are computer games programming, computer games software engineering, computer games development and computer science. The Information Technology Management for Business degree (see e-skills UK) is designed in partnership with some of the biggest employers in the IT industry. Degrees in maths, physics, or any first degree with a substantial programming element are also usually acceptable. There are also relevant postgraduate computing qualifications.

Adult Qualifications
Employers expect all applicants to have a proven aptitude for games programming and mature applicants need to show outstanding ability. You may not need the standard entry requirements for higher education courses, particularly if your previous experience is relevant and you show the ability to study at the appropriate level.

Work Experience
Entry to this job is competitive and it is important that you try to do some relevant work or voluntary experience before applying. Direct experience with a company specialising in this area is the most useful, but also experience of using a programming language and maybe even writing your own new short programs is considered relevant. Work placements are often available with game development studios who have links with some university courses, and this can often be a way into the industry.

The British Computer Society offers a work placement service through its young professional group. Other schemes, such as 'The Year in Industry', give those who expect good A levels/H grades and intend to go to university, the opportunity to spend a salaried year with a company to gain valuable work experience.

Entry and Training
This is a popular industry with young people and entry is highly competitive. All applicants need to display a proven aptitude for games programming. Most have a computing degree, and many also have a relevant postgraduate qualification, although unqualified applicants with an outstanding aptitude may be considered. There is a range of computer games degree courses accredited by the sector skills council for creative media, Skillset. Contact them for details.

The Open University offers courses in computing and maths that can lead to a computing degree. There are no formal entry requirements and you study through distance learning. Several universities now offer the information technology management for business degree, developed by e-skills and employers to meet specific industry needs. A full or part-time foundation degree in IT is also available. A Diploma/Welsh Baccalaureate may be available in your area in IT as a route into this career.

Training is ongoing, both on the job and by short courses to keep pace with technology. It is very important to keep up to date with the latest developments in the games industry. The ability to write in C, C++ and other languages is desirable, together with specific platform experience, such as PS2 or DirectX. Some programmers work towards gaining Chartered IT Professional (CITP) status through the British Computer Society (BCS). Contact the BCS for further details.

E-skills run a professional development programme which enables new IT professionals to fast-track their career. The programme is delivered through universities and participating employers. E-skills also offers an internship. Students are placed for a period of employment within an organisation, enabling them to develop valuable business and IT skills. Contact e-skills for details.

Mature applicants need to gain experience in computing and programming. You can enter higher education through Access, foundation or similar courses, which are available for those who have no formal qualifications but wish to pursue a relevant degree. A one-year IT postgraduate conversion course may be an advantage. There are also some full or part-time courses available at further/higher education colleges. Some LSCs/LECs, Jobcentres (NI) and ELWa (Wales) run high technology courses. You can also gain recognition of previous experience through Accreditation of Prior Learning (APL) or by working towards relevant S/NVQs.

Opportunities and Pay

The UK industry has a reputation for producing many innovative and quality games. There are about 30,000 people employed in the UK games industry working for games developers, publishers and retailers. There are over 250 games development studios. The UK has the biggest development community in Europe, but has been affected by the recent economic downturn. There are companies based in many parts of the country, though there are games industry 'clusters' in areas that include Dundee, Manchester, Liverpool, Yorkshire, Warwickshire, and the south east of England.

Employers are usually development studios that are publisher owned and independent, or middleware producers that provide cross-platform graphics, artificial intelligence (AI), game physics and other specialist tools. Other jobs are with localisation companies that translate and re-version games for different countries.

With experience you can move into project management or senior programming roles. Some experienced programmers may work as self-employed consultants. The computer games industry has become a highly profitable global business and there may be opportunities to work overseas, particularly in the USA, Canada, Japan and France. Short-term contract work is also possible.

Depending on the company, a graduate may expect to earn £20k-£23k a year, rising to around £34k with experience. Successful programmers can earn £35k-£45k a year, and some considerably more. Profit-sharing, performance-related pay or a bonus payment may be additional to your basic salary.

Skills and Qualities

able to work both on your own and in a team, able to work in abstract terms, accurate, analytical skills, logical and methodical, methodical, perseverance, problem-solving skills, specialist IT skills

Relevant Subjects

Art and Design, Design and technology, ICT/Computer studies, Mathematics, Physics, Science

Further Information

Computer Arts (Future Publishing) - www.computerarts.co.uk

Diplomas (Foundation, Higher and Advanced) - http://yp.direct.gov.uk/diplomas

e-skills UK - sector skills council for business and information technology - www.e-skills.com

Games Industry Information - www.gamesindustry.biz

Inside Careers Guide: Information Technology - www.insidecareers.co.uk

Open University - www.open.ac.uk

Real Life Guide to Information & Communications Technology (Trotman) - www.trotman.co.uk

Skillset - sector skills council for the creative media, fashion and textiles industries - www.skillset.org

Tiga - www.tiga.org

Welsh Baccalaureate - www.wbq.org.uk

▶Working in computers & IT (2010) (Babcock Lifeskills) - www.babcock-lifeskills.com/

Working in the Games Industry - www.workingames.co.uk

Year in Industry (Engineering Development Trust) - www.yini.org.uk

Addresses

British Computer Society (BCS)
First Floor, Block D North Star House North Star Avenue, Swindon, Wiltshire SN2 1FA
Phone: +44 (0)845 300 4417
Web: www.bcs.org

British Interactive Media Association (BIMA)
The Lightwell, 12-16 Laystall Street, Clerkenwel, London EC1R 4PF
Phone: +44(0)207 843 6797
Web: www.bima.co.uk

Entertainment and Leisure Software Publishers Association (ELSPA)
167 Wardour Street, London W1F 8WL
Phone: +44 (0)20 7534 0580
Web: www.elspa.com

Institution of Analysts and Programmers (IAP)
Charles House, 36 Culmington Road, London W13 9NH
Phone: +44 (0)20 8567 2118
Web: www.iap.org.uk

Similar Jobs

Computer Games Designer, Computer Games Playtester, Interactive Media Designer, IT Applications Developer, IT Systems Developer, Website Designer

Computer Games Technical Support Person

CRCI:Computers and IT
CLCI:CAV Job Band: 3 to 4

Job Description

Computer games technical support people answer telephone calls or emails from PC or console users who are having problems with games software. They work on a computer that allows them to communicate directly with the game user. They need to obtain information about the problem from the caller, attempt to diagnose the cause of the problem, explain the solution to the user, or email a response. Increasingly they may also operate/respond through web-based procedures. Where the problem appears to be caused by faulty software, technical support may arrange to have it returned or replaced.

Although similar to the role of a computer help desk operator (see separate job profile), technical support staff need specific technical knowledge and games playing experience related to games software. They may also be involved in research and testing of development kits and resolving technical problems for games developers. Also keep records of calls received, document the problems and solutions, and record any actions taken.

Work Details

Usually work a 35-37 hr week, Monday to Friday, though may be expected to work outside normal office hours, including some weekend or shift work over seven days. You need to be prepared to work overtime to solve difficult problems or meet a deadline. You have to sit at a desk for many hours at a time.

Qualification

• England, Wales and Northern Ireland

Band 3: For some employers or for a relevant BTEC national award: usually 4-5 GCSEs (A*-C) including English and maths, and preferably computer studies, information technology, or equivalent.

Band 4: For relevant BTEC higher national award: 1-2 A levels and some GCSEs (A*-C) usually including English and maths, and preferably science, computer studies or information technology, or equivalent.

- **Scotland**

Band 3: For some employers or for a relevant SQA national award: usually 4-5 S grades (1-3) including English and maths, and preferably computer studies or information technology, or similar.

Band 4: For a relevant SQA higher national award: 2-3 H grades and some S grades (1-3) often including English and maths, and for some courses preferably science, computer studies or information technology, or similar qualifications.

Adult Qualifications

Entry requirements may be relaxed for adults applying for relevant higher education courses. This is particularly true if your previous experience is relevant and you show the ability to study at the appropriate level.

Work Experience

Entry to this job is competitive and it is important that you try to do some relevant work or voluntary experience before applying. College courses or employers look for enthusiasm and commitment. Relevant work experience with computers and experience/knowledge of games titles in particular can demonstrate this and help to improve your chances on application. Working in the retail computer games industry also offers good background knowledge.

Entry and Training

Entry is highly competitive as this is a popular industry with young people. It is possible to enter with a varied range of qualifications and some entrants have an HND or a degree. However, most employers look for extensive knowledge of PCs/games consoles and considerable games playing experience. You may need to pass a practical aptitude test. Training is ongoing and on the job, which may include studying for qualifications through private sector suppliers, or a relevant professional organisation. It is very important to keep up to date with the latest developments in the games industry.

There are a range of computer support qualifications and S/NVQs for IT practitioners at levels 1-4 which are relevant to general service desk support. Foundation degrees are available and may be studied full or part time. The diploma for IT users (ITQ 2009) has been developed as part of a project that involved a full review of the National Occupational Standards (NOS) for IT users. See the e-skills uk website for details. A Diploma/Welsh Baccalaureate may also be available in your area in IT.

The Service Desk Institute offers industry-recognised qualifications and an e-learning programme of online courses in technical support. They also offer a service desk analyst qualification. Training programmes, including apprenticeship schemes, may also be available in your area. An ICT higher apprenticeship is available through e-skills. This combines an apprenticeship with a foundation degree and can lead to a full honours degree. There are partnerships with colleges and universities throughout the UK. E-skills also offers an internship. Students are placed for a period of employment within an organisation, enabling them to develop valuable business and IT skills. Contact e-skills for details of all courses.

This is a predominantly young industry and employers expect all applicants to have considerable games playing experience as well as technical support skills and/or qualifications. Some Jobcentre Plus offices, LSCs/LECs, Jobcentres (NI) and ELWa (Wales) offer courses relevant to general helpdesk support for adults.

Opportunities and Pay

The UK industry has a reputation for producing many innovative and quality games. There are about 30,000 people employed in the UK games industry working for games developers, publishers and retailers. There are over 250 games development studios. The UK has the biggest development community in Europe although it has been affected by the economic downturn. There are companies based in many parts of the country, though there are games industry 'clusters' in areas that include Dundee, Manchester, Liverpool, Yorkshire, Warwickshire, and the south east of England.

Employers are usually specialised companies producing games for PCs, the internet, mobiles or games consoles. Progress may be possible to supervisor level, games playtester or, for those with the aptitude for further training, to programming.

Depending on the type of company, a technical support person earns around £16k-£20k a year, rising to £28k with experience. Some earn more than £30k a year.

Skills and Qualities

able to explain clearly, able to work both on your own and in a team, good communication skills, good interpersonal skills, good telephone manner, helpful, logical, methodical, specialist IT skills, technical aptitude

Relevant Subjects

Design and technology, English, ICT/Computer studies, Mathematics, Science

Further Information

Apprenticeship Schemes (National Apprenticeship Service) - www.apprenticeships.org.uk

Computer Arts (Future Publishing) - www.computerarts.co.uk

Diplomas (Foundation, Higher and Advanced) - http://yp.direct.gov.uk/diplomas

e-skills UK - sector skills council for business and information technology - www.e-skills.com

Games Industry Information - www.gamesindustry.biz

Inside Careers Guide: Information Technology - www.insidecareers.co.uk

Real Life Guide to Information & Communications Technology (Trotman) - www.trotman.co.uk

Service Desk Institute (SDI) - www.sdi-europe.com

Skillset - sector skills council for the creative media, fashion and textiles industries - www.skillset.org

Support World (bi-monthly) (Service Desk 360) - www.servicedesk360.com/supportworld/

Tiga - www.tiga.org

Welsh Baccalaureate - www.wbq.org.uk

▶Working in computers & IT (2010) (Babcock Lifeskills) - www.babcock-lifeskills.com/

Working in the Games Industry - www.workingames.co.uk

Addresses

British Computer Society (BCS)
First Floor, Block D North Star House North Star Avenue, Swindon, Wiltshire SN2 1FA
Phone: +44 (0)845 300 4417
Web: www.bcs.org

British Interactive Media Association (BIMA)
The Lightwell, 12-16 Laystall Street, Clerkenwel, London EC1R 4PF
Phone: +44(0)207 843 6797
Web: www.bima.co.uk

Entertainment and Leisure Software Publishers Association (ELSPA)
167 Wardour Street, London W1F 8WL
Phone: +44 (0)20 7534 0580
Web: www.elspa.com

Similar Jobs

Computer Games Playtester, Computer Games Programmer, Computer Operator, IT Helpdesk Analyst/Operator, IT Service Technician

Computer Hardware Engineer

also known as: IT Hardware Engineer

CRCI:Computers and IT
CLCI:CAV Job Band: 4 to 5

Job Description

Computer hardware engineers are responsible for the design and development of computers and computerised parts of other products. They usually work on a specific area of hardware rather than the whole system, such as circuit boards, keyboards, printers or processing units. Sometimes engineers work on peripheral devices and computerised elements of appliances and machines.

Hardware engineers help turn new ideas and techniques into profitable products. They use computer-aided design (CAD) to produce designs and drawings that enable products to be made, and develop new hardware. May test and install equipment once it is made and identify any problems that occur. May also supervise the manufacturing of new computer products. Hardware engineers are part of a multi-disciplinary team, including electronic engineers, analysts, programmers and software engineers.

Work Details

Usually work around 37 hrs a week, Monday to Friday, though you must be prepared to be on call if problems occur outside normal hours. Work is based in a workshop, laboratory or office. You sit for long periods of time in front of a screen, working on your own, even though you are part of a team. You have to be able to meet deadlines and work under pressure as deadlines approach, often doing extra hours to complete the work. You may need to travel to different sites.

Qualification

• England, Wales and Northern Ireland

Band 4: For a relevant higher national award: 1-2 A levels and some GCSEs (A*-C) including English, maths and science, or equivalent.

Band 5: For degree courses: 2-3 A levels usually including maths and physics, and some GCSEs (A*-C), usually including English and maths, or equivalent. Exact requirements depend on the degree you take.

• Scotland

Band 4: For a relevant higher national award: usually 2-3 H grades and some S grades (1-3), often including English, maths and science, or similar qualifications.

Band 5: For degree courses: 3-5 H grades usually including maths and physics, and some S grades (1-3), often including English and maths, or similar qualifications. Exact requirements depend on the degree you take.

Degree Information

Subjects such as systems and control engineering, electronic engineering and other specialised degrees in computer engineering are relevant, including postgraduate computing qualifications. The Information Technology Management for Business degree (see e-skills UK) is designed in partnership with some of the biggest employers in the IT industry.

Adult Qualifications

Mature entrants may not need the standard entry requirements for higher education courses, particularly if your previous experience is relevant and you show the ability to study at the appropriate level.

Work Experience

Employers and universities may prefer candidates who have relevant work or voluntary experience. This can include spending time with electronic engineering or software engineering companies. Applicants to degree courses are encouraged to apply to the Year in Industry Scheme for a placement in industry prior to starting their studies. Students also have an opportunity to gain work experience in industry for a year between the penultimate and final years of their degree programme. This experience enhances job prospects on graduation.

Headstart is a well-established UK education programme. It aims to give A-level/H grade students the opportunity to learn about degrees leading to jobs in technology-based industries.

Entry and Training

Entry is usually with a good degree in electronic engineering, computer engineering or related subject. Courses are mainly full time, but there are also sandwich courses and sponsorship for training is possible. You may be able to start in a junior IT role, such as technical support, and progress into this role. Relevant industrial training, professional development and further experience are required before becoming fully qualified. You must also commit to continuing professional development throughout your career.

Some computer hardware engineers join the Institution of Engineering and Technology, or another professional body, and work to become professional engineers at incorporated (IEng) or chartered engineer (CEng) level. To register as a CEng or an IEng, you must become a member of one of the Engineering Council UK's (ECUK) nominated engineering institutions, such as the British Computer Society. The competences for the UK Standard for Professional Engineering Competence (UKSPEC) then need to be met. Check with the ECUK for details.

Foundation degrees are available in general engineering and computing subjects. S/NVQs are available in a range of IT subjects at levels 2-4. The new S/NVQ for IT users (ITQ 2009) has been developed as part of a project involving a full review of the National Occupational Standards for IT users. Training programmes, including IT and engineering apprenticeship schemes, may be available in your area for entry to this job. Advanced apprenticeships leading to qualification at level 3 can also be a route into higher education. A Diploma/Welsh Baccalaureate may be available in your area in IT and can be good background for entry to this work.

Those with considerable experience but who lack formal qualifications may be considered for the Technical Report Route (TRR) to qualify as a chartered/incorporated engineer with the Engineering Council. Sponsorship may be available for postgraduate courses from the Engineering and Physical Sciences Research Council. Contact the Engineering Council UK or the Institution of Engineering and Technology for details of all training opportunities.

You can gain recognition of previous experience through Accreditation of Prior Learning (APL) or by working towards relevant S/NVQs. Contact your local careers office, Jobcentre Plus, Next Step service or Learning and Skills Council (LSC)/Local Enterprise Company (LEC) for details of training schemes, including apprenticeships for adults.

Opportunities and Pay

Opportunities exist throughout the UK with computer manufacturers, electronic companies, IT consultants, telecommunications and retail companies, and software/systems manufacturers. It is possible to progress to senior hardware engineer, team or project leader or departmental manager. There are also opportunities for experienced engineers to work as self-employed consultants and work abroad may be available.

Pay varies depending on location and type of company. A graduate entrant can expect to earn around £20k-£27k, rising to around £35k-£40k a year. Successful hardware engineers can earn more.

Health

This job requires good eyesight and normal colour vision.

Skills and Qualities

able to work both on your own and in a team, accurate, good communication skills, good interpersonal skills, logical, methodical, problem-solving skills, scientific approach, specialist IT skills, technical aptitude

Relevant Subjects

Design and technology, Engineering, English, ICT/Computer studies, Mathematics, Physics, Science

Further Information

AGCAS: Information Technology (Job Sector Briefing) (AGCAS) - www.prospects.ac.uk

Diplomas (Foundation, Higher and Advanced) - http://yp.direct.gov.uk/diplomas

e-skills UK - sector skills council for business and information technology - www.e-skills.com

Headstart Scheme - www.headstartcourses.org.uk

Inside Careers Guide: Information Technology - www.insidecareers.co.uk

Real Life Guide to Information & Communications Technology (Trotman) - www.trotman.co.uk

SEMTA - sector skills council for science, engineering and manufacturing technologies - www.semta.org.uk

TARGETjobs: IT (GTI Specialist Publishing Ltd.) - www.groupgti.com

Welsh Baccalaureate - www.wbq.org.uk

▶Working in computers & IT (2010) (Babcock Lifeskills) - www.babcock-lifeskills.com/

Year in Industry (Engineering Development Trust) - www.yini.org.uk

Addresses

British Computer Society (BCS)
First Floor, Block D North Star House North Star Avenue, Swindon, Wiltshire SN2 1FA
Phone: +44 (0)845 300 4417
Web: www.bcs.org

Engineering and Physical Sciences Research Council (EPSRC)
Polaris House North Star Avenue, Swindon, Wiltshire SN2 1ET
Phone: +44(0)1793 444 100
Web: www.epsrc.ac.uk

Engineering Council
246 High Holborn, London WC1V 7EX
Phone: +44 (0)20 3206 0500
Web: www.engc.org.uk

Institution of Engineering and Technology (IET)
Michael Faraday House, Stevenage, Hertfordshire SG1 2AY
Phone: +44 (0)1438 313311
Web: www.theiet.org

Similar Jobs

Electrical Engineering Technician, Engineer: Electronics, Engineer: Telecommunications, IT Service Technician, IT Systems Developer, IT Technical Sales Specialist, Network Manager

Computer Operator

also known as: IT Computer Operator

CRCI:Computers and IT
CLCI:CAV — Job Band: 2 to 4

Job Description

Computer operators maintain the day-to-day running of mainframe computer systems in businesses, including banks, insurance companies, hospitals, offices, shops, universities and colleges. They are familiar with the business operations of the employer and help to run computerised jobs that are prepared by operations managers and computer programmers. Operators control the processing of jobs through a large mainframe computer, and use a keyboard and screen to start and monitor the operation. They also keep a log of all completed work and ensure all data is backed-up and stored on disk or tape in case of a serious failure of the system.

A growing number of operators now work on personal computers (PCs) and minicomputers. The tasks they perform are similar to those performed on large computers. May also run anti-virus checks, and organise routine servicing and cleaning of the machines. Operators check for faults by watching for error messages on the screen. They report the problem and call a service engineer or manager. May supervise the use of computer time to keep the work flowing smoothly.

Work Details

Usually work a standard 37-40 hr week, but this job often involves shift and weekend work. Some operators work permanent night shifts. The work environment is clean and usually air conditioned. You must be able to organise your work well, follow instructions carefully and work accurately, even at times of pressure. Even when the work is routine you have to be able to concentrate. You may need to sit for long periods of time and the area can be noisy, due to the machines.

Qualification

It may be possible to enter this job without formal educational qualifications, though employers expect a very good level of literacy and numeracy.

• England, Wales and Northern Ireland

Band 2: Although academic qualifications are not specified for this job, it is an advantage to have some GCSEs (A*-C) in subjects that include English and maths, or equivalent.

Band 3: For some employers or a BTEC national course: usually at least 4 GCSEs (A*-C) including English, maths and preferably computer studies, or equivalent.

Band 4: For most employers and for a BTEC higher national award: 1-2 A levels and some GCSEs (A*-C) usually including English and maths, or equivalent.

• Scotland

Band 2: Although academic qualifications are not specified for this job, it is an advantage to have some S grades (1-3) in subjects that include English and maths, or similar.

Band 3: For some employers, or for an SQA national course: usually at least four S grades (1-3) including English and maths, or similar.

Band 4: For most employers and for a SQA higher national award: 2-3 H grades and some S grades (1-3) often including English, IT and maths, or similar qualifications.

Adult Qualifications

For some employers, experience of working with computers is often more important than formal qualifications. Those with relevant work experience may be accepted for some college courses without meeting formal entry requirements.

Work Experience

It is important that you try to do some relevant work or voluntary experience before applying. College courses and employers look for enthusiasm and commitment. Relevant work experience with computers can demonstrate this and helps to improve your knowledge and chances on application. For adults, relevant and related work experience or previous employment is more necessary and widely asked for.

Entry and Training

Entry into a training post can be direct from school/college, though you may also need to pass a practical aptitude test. Experience in computing is an advantage and keyboard skills are useful, though operators may begin as a clerical worker and acquire and develop

IT skills in their work. Applicants must be at least 18 for shift work but you can start training before this. Training is usually on the job, often with day release to a local college, though many entrants take a full-time course first. You require regular training to keep up to date with changes in technology, perhaps by taking short courses run by computer manufacturers.

There are a wide variety of online qualifications from foundation level upwards. Choose your course carefully to ensure that the qualification is nationally recognised by the IT industry. There are also distance-learning courses and full or part-time foundation degrees. Professional qualifications are available via the British Computer Society and the Service Desk Institute. The Open University also offers courses in computing and maths, which can lead to an appropriate computing degree. There are no formal entry requirements and you study through distance learning.

S/NVQs for IT users are available at levels 2-4. The new S/NVQ for IT users (ITQ 2009) has been developed as part of a project involving a full review of the National Occupational Standards for IT users. A Diploma/Welsh Baccalaureate may also be available in your area in IT.

Training programmes, including IT apprenticeship schemes, may be available for entry to this job. Advanced apprenticeships leading to qualification at level 3 can also be a route into higher education. An ICT higher apprenticeship is available through e-skills. This combines an apprenticeship with a foundation degree and can lead to a full honours degree. There are partnerships with colleges and universities throughout the UK.

Mature applicants need to gain experience in computing. There are many full or part-time courses available at further/higher education colleges. You can benefit through training opportunities such as Work Based Learning/Training for Work which may be available in your area. You can also gain recognition of previous experience through Accreditation of Prior Learning (APL) or by working towards relevant S/NVQs. Contact your local careers office, Jobcentre Plus, Next Step service or Learning and Skills Council (LSC)/Local Enterprise Company (LEC) for details of all training opportunities and schemes, including apprenticeships for adults.

Opportunities and Pay

Employment is with a wide range of organisations in most parts of the country, such as local and central government, banks and insurance companies, the police, industry and commerce, the health service, education, chain stores, or public utility companies. Promotion to senior operator, higher technical or managerial positions is possible after further training.

Developments in data processing mean that mainframe computers have been replaced by individual users in some cases, resulting in fewer opportunities for computer operators. Many tasks performed by computer operators are also automated by software. These include scheduling, loading, and downloading programs, mounting tapes, re-routing messages, and running reports. As technology continues to advance, computer operators are likely to move into computer network operations, user support, and database maintenance. However, this role is still available and and there are still good opportunities, but the role is often centralised as part of a managed service for a number of organisations.

Pay varies depending on location and type of company. A trainee operator can expect to earn £15k-£18k, rising to £20k-£30k a year with experience. High earning senior operators can earn up to £40k a year.

Skills and Qualities

able to cope under pressure, attention to detail, careful, co-operative, logical, methodical, patient, responsible attitude, specialist IT skills, technical aptitude

Relevant Subjects

ICT/Computer studies, Mathematics

Further Information

AGCAS: Information Technology (Job Sector Briefing) (AGCAS) - www.prospects.ac.uk

Computer Weekly (Reed Business Information) - www.computerweekly.com

Diplomas (Foundation, Higher and Advanced) - http://yp.direct.gov.uk/diplomas

e-skills UK - sector skills council for business and information technology - www.e-skills.com

Open University - www.open.ac.uk

Service Desk Institute (SDI) - www.sdi-europe.com

Training Schemes - www.direct.gov.uk/en/educationandlearning

Welsh Baccalaureate - www.wbq.org.uk

▶ Working in computers & IT (2010) (Babcock Lifeskills) - www.babcock-lifeskills.com/

Addresses

British Computer Society (BCS)
First Floor, Block D North Star House North Star Avenue, Swindon, Wiltshire SN2 1FA
Phone: +44 (0)845 300 4417
Web: www.bcs.org

Institute for the Management of Information Systems (IMIS)
5 Kingfisher House, New Mill Road, Orpington, Kent BR5 3QG
Phone: +44 (0)700 002 3456
Web: www.imis.org.uk

Similar Jobs

Computer Games Technical Support Person, Database Administrator, IT Data Input Operator, IT Service Technician

Conservator-Restorer

also known as: Museum Conservator

CRCI:Languages, Information and Culture
CLCI:FAE

Job Band: 5

Job Description

Conservators reserve or restore objects of historical interest, buildings and works of art, usually for museums, art galleries or private collectors. They may specialise in working in one area, such as furniture, stone, fossils, glass and stained glass, ceramics, tapestries, carpets, armour, monuments, paintings, metals and photographic materials.

Conservators assess the condition of the relevant object and may research its origins and history. They use a variety of conservation techniques to clean, repair and maintain artefacts, monitoring and controlling the environment in which collections are stored or displayed to prevent deterioration. This requires a combination of scientific skill, art appreciation and historical knowledge. May supervise other staff or volunteers or students and may also be involved with costing projects and writing proposals of treatments.

Work Details

Usually works a basic 35-39 hrs a week, usually 9am-5pm, though may be expected to work irregular and longer hours at times. Works in a studio, workshop, laboratory or on site. You have to sit or stand for long periods concentrating on objects which may be intricate. Depending on your area of work, you may have to lift heavy objects or climb ladders. You inspect the work to be conserved, analyse the problem and give advice as to the treatment required and the best way to store the item. You may have to arrange for the transportation of items between sites. You have to work with a range of specialist tools and some chemicals.

Qualification

- **England, Wales and Northern Ireland**

Band 5: For degree courses: 2-3 A levels and some GCSEs (A*-C) usually including English, maths and chemistry or equivalent. Exact requirements depend on the degree you take. Check individual prospectuses as some courses may require an art foundation course to be taken first.

- **Scotland**

Band 5: For degree courses: 3-5 H grades and some S grades (1-3), including English, maths and chemistry or similar qualifications. Exact requirements depend on the degree you take.

Degree Information

There are specialist degrees in conservation-restoration, such as heritage and conservation, archaeology and history, conservation and history, archaeological or furniture conservation. Entry is also possible with degrees in history of art, fine art or science, usually chemistry.

Entry to postgraduate courses is possible with degrees in several subjects. An applied arts subject is preferred because of its specialist knowledge content. Architecture, archive studios, materials science or graphic art may also be acceptable for some postgraduate courses.

Adult Qualifications

Degree entry requirements may be relaxed for adults, particularly for those with appropriate skills and experience. Some conservation courses are designed for mature entrants with relevant work experience.

Work Experience

Entry to this job is very competitive. It is important that you try to do some relevant work or voluntary experience before applying. Colleges and universities may prefer applicants who have direct observation or practical experience of the type of work involved and of the environment. Antique dealers, specialist antique restorers, conservation studios and workshops and museums are the first point of contact to gain some practical or observational work experience. Voluntary work is very useful to build up a portfolio.

Entry and Training

Entrants are mainly graduates and an arts and science background is preferred for many courses. Graduates usually do an internship for a year in a museum or gallery, gaining on the job, supervised practical experience on a part-time basis. This is then followed by taking a postgraduate certificate/diploma or masters degree that usually requires evidence of skills and experience in conservation. Details of suitable courses, work-based learning schemes, training programmes and internships are available from the Institute of Conservation (ICON) and Creative & Cultural Skills. Voluntary work is needed to build up a portfolio.

A few people obtain traineeships working with an experienced conservator, but these are often unpaid. Once in employment there are many specialist short courses for continuing professional development. If working in a museum, you can also gain associateship of the Museums Association. Your work can also lead to an S/NVQ at levels 3-5 in subjects like cultural heritage. There are vocational qualifications in specific subjects such as bookbinding conservation and the restoration and conservation of clocks and watches. To work as a conservator of wallpaper or stone masonry, it may be possible to train on the job as part of an apprenticeship scheme.

The recognised professional qualification for experienced conservators is the Professional Accreditation of Conservator-Restorers. Additional professional qualifications are available, including the British Association of Paintings Conservator-Restorers Fellowship Scheme, and membership of the British Antique Furniture Restorers' Association. You may also wish to join the Conservation Register which lists accredited professionals in this area.

Mature entrants should note that this is a small and competitive field. For entry to a traineeship or apprenticeship with a qualified restorer or conservator, no formal qualifications are needed, though spaces are extremely limited. Experience of working in a field related to the area of conservation in which you are interested is very useful.

The Institute of Conservation and some employers are currently running a pilot for a new conservation technician qualification. This recognises those who support conservators and restorers. If you already work in conservation, this may be a route to qualification.

Opportunities and Pay

The UK has a long history of producing highly skilled conservators. However, there are not many vacancies and a large number of well-qualified people chasing work in this area. The major employers are museum conservation departments, art galleries and heritage organisations. Most people work freelance, on their own or in a small partnership, working for museums, commercial art galleries, historic or heritage sites, organisations such as the National Trust, antiques dealers, auction houses and for private individuals. Contract terms vary widely and can last from as little as three months or up to five years.

Numbers of those working in the private sector are increasing, but opportunities in the public sector remain steady. Experienced and trained conservators often work abroad, usually in Australia, Canada and the USA.

Salaries vary depending on location, type of employer and field in which you work. A restorer of paintings tends to earn more than a restorer working in archaeology. Graduate salaries start around £18k-£22k, rising with experience to £25k a year. The most skilled and experienced restorers earn £40k a year or more.

Health

This job requires normal colour vision and good eyesight. For some jobs you may need to have a good level of fitness.

Skills and Qualities

attention to detail, enquiring mind, good concentration level, health & safety awareness, interest in cultural heritage, IT skills, manual dexterity, practical skills, problem-solving skills, technical aptitude

Relevant Subjects

Art and Design, Chemistry, Classical studies, Design and technology, History, Science

Further Information

Apprenticeship Schemes (National Apprenticeship Service) - www.apprenticeships.org.uk

Conservation Register - www.conservationregister.com

Creative & Cultural Skills - sector skills council for advertising, crafts, cultural heritage, design, literature, music, performing & visual arts - www.ccskills.org.uk

Journal of the Institute of Conservation (ICON) (Routledge) - www.icon.org.uk/

Local Government Careers (Improvement and Development Agency) - www.lgcareers.com/publications/

Professional Accreditation of Conservator-Restorers (PACR-ICON Accreditation) (PACR) - www.icon.org.uk

▶ Working in cultural heritage (2007) (Babcock Lifeskills) - www.babcock-lifeskills.com/

Addresses

British Antique Furniture Restorers' Association (BAFRA)
The Old Rectory, Warmwell, Dorchester DT2 8HQ
Phone: +44 (0)1305 854822
Web: www.bafra.org.uk

British Association of Paintings Conservator-Restorers (BAPCR)
PO Box 258, Blofield, Norwich NR13 4WY
Phone: +44 (0)1603 516237
Web: www.bapcr.org.uk

Cadw
Welsh Assembly Government, Plas Carew, Unit 5/7 Cefn Coed, Parc Nantgarw, Cardiff CF15 7QQ
Phone: +44 (0)1443 33 6000
Web: www.cadw.wales.gov.uk

Historic Scotland
Longmore House, Salisbury Place, Edinburgh EH9 1SH
Phone: +44 (0)131 668 8600
Web: www.historic-scotland.gov.uk

Institute of Conservation (ICON)
1st Floor, Downstream Building 1 London Bridge Road SE1 9BG
Phone: +44 (0)20 7785 3807
Web: www.icon.org.uk

International Institute for Conservation of Historic and Artistic Works
6 Buckingham Street, London WC2N 6BA
Phone: +44 (0)20 7839 5975
Web: www.iiconservation.org

Museums Association (MA)
24 Calvin Street, London E1 6NW
Web: www.museumsassociation.org

Similar Jobs

Archivist, Chemist: Analytical, Library & Information Manager, Museum Assistant/Technician, Museum/Art Gallery Curator, Paintings Conservator-Restorer

Construction Estimator

also known as: Cost Engineer

CRCI:Building and Construction
CLCI:UD

Job Band: 3 to 4

Job Description

Construction estimators prepare, calculate and submit tenders for contracts in the building and construction industry. They make sure the employer makes a good profit on all the resources needed to fulfil the contract. They receive detailed specifications, including bill of quantities and architect's drawings for a job/project. Then assess costs of materials, labour and other expenses. Estimators prepare an estimate of all projected costs, taking into account materials required, any sub-contracting work, bonus payments, availability of parts and profit margin.

Conducting risk assessments of the job, looking at timescales and building in allowances to cover any contingencies are all part of the job description. Construction estimators work closely with other professionals such as architects, construction managers, quantity surveyors and planning engineers.

Work Details

Usually work around 37-40 hrs a week, Monday to Friday, though may be required to work late or at weekends when deadlines approach. This is mainly an office-based job, though travel to a client's premises may sometimes be required. Estimates often have to be prepared quickly, so you sometimes have to work under pressure. Often work as part of a team of estimators. Software packages and databases may be used to help with calculations.

You need to be able to deal with disappointment if contracts are awarded to competitors. Protective clothing, including a hard hat and boots, are required when conducting site visits.

Qualification

- **England, Wales and Northern Ireland**

Band 3: For BTEC national award: usually at least 4 GCSEs (A*-C) often including English, maths and science (preferably physics) and a technical or practical subject, or equivalent.

Band 4: For BTEC higher national award: 1-2 A levels and some GCSEs (A*-C) including English, maths and science (preferably physics) and a technical or practical subject, or equivalent qualifications.

- **Scotland**

Band 3: For SQA national award: usually at least four S grades (1-3) including English, maths and science (preferably physics) and a technical or practical subject, or similar.

Band 4: For SQA higher national award: usually 2-3 H grades and some S grades (1-3), often including English, maths and science (preferably physics) and a technical or practical subject, or similar qualifications.

Adult Qualifications

Relevant qualifications and experience of the appropriate work area are usually required for entry to this job. However, entry requirements may be waived for mature applicants, particularly those with experience in construction or costing. There are relevant foundation/Access courses to higher education including construction or the built environment.

Work Experience

Relevant work or voluntary experience is always useful and can improve your chances in application for this job. Direct work experience with a building and construction company is most suitable, but you can also consider work in a surveyor or valuer's office. Local government offices usually have such departments and are a good starting point as a contact.

Entry and Training

Many estimators first train to technician level in the building and construction industry; others are trained in a costing department. Some may complete a relevant BTEC/SQA day release or sandwich course while working on the job with an experienced person. However, others complete a full-time course first. Membership of the Association of Cost Engineers (ACostE) is gained through a minimum of S/NVQ level 4 and at least five years' relevant experience. They also offer a scheme of continuing professional development. Membership can lead to incorporated and chartered engineer status. Contact the Association of Cost Engineers for further details.

A Diploma or Welsh Baccalaureate in construction and the built environment may be available in your area. A wide range of relevant S/NVQs are available at levels 3-4, including construction contracting operations and project control. Training programmes, including apprenticeship schemes, may be available in your area for entry to this job. Advanced apprenticeships leading to qualification at level 3 can also be a route into higher education.

Mature entrants with appropriate work experience and who are fully trained may be preferred by some employers. Contact the professional organisations listed in addresses for details of training/qualification routes.

Opportunities and Pay

Jobs are located throughout the country and are in many sectors, including the building and construction industry, public utilities, oil/gas and chemical processing, and in engineering. Many work for contractors and sub-contractors, and some estimators work for consultancies. Availability of work depends on the state of the building trade and the national economy. Currently there is a downturn in the housing market which means there may be a shortage of vacancies for estimators. There may be more opportunities in urban areas.

In large companies you can progress to senior estimator or project leader/manager posts, and with experience and further training/qualifications, you may become a cost engineer, or progress to another senior role. There may be opportunities for work at home and abroad on contractual work.

Income increases with experience and there is scope for specialisation. Pay varies depending on area and type of company. Graduate entrants are likely to earn around £18k-£22k, rising to £25k-£40k with experience. Senior estimators earn in the region of £40k-£60k a year. An employer may also provide a company car or a car allowance, and other job-related benefits.

Skills and Qualities
able to work both on your own and in a team, able to work to deadlines, analytical skills, attention to detail, business awareness, good communication skills, good presentation skills, information handling skills, IT skills, numeracy skills

Relevant Subjects
Business and accounting, Construction and built environment, Design and technology, Economics, Engineering, English, ICT/Computer studies, Mathematics, Physics, Science

Further Information
Apprenticeship Schemes (National Apprenticeship Service) - www.apprenticeships.org.uk

ConstructionSkills - sector skills council for the construction industry - www.cskills.org

Engineering Construction Industry Training Board - www.ecitb.org.uk

Project Control Professional (monthly) (ACostE) - www.acoste.org.uk

SEMTA - sector skills council for science, engineering and manufacturing technologies - www.semta.org.uk

▶Working in construction & the built environment (2007) (Babcock Lifeskills) - www.babcock-lifeskills.com/

Addresses
Association of Cost Engineers (ACostE)
Lea House, 5 Middlewich Road, Sandbach, Cheshire CW11 1XL
Phone: +44 (0)1270 764 798
Web: www.acoste.org.uk

Chartered Institute of Building (CIOB)
Englemere King's Ride, Ascot, Berkshire SL5 7TB
Phone: +44 (0)1344 630 700
Web: www.ciob.org.uk

Similar Jobs
Surveying Technician, Surveyor: Building, Surveyor: Building Control, Surveyor: General Practice, Surveyor: Quantity

Construction Operative
also known as: Building Operative, Labourer: Building

CRCI:Building and Construction
CLCI:UF
Job Band: 1 to 2

Job Description
Construction operatives carry out a range of practical tasks to assist skilled construction workers on a building site or civil engineering project. They help to build roads and bridges, houses, factories and offices, airports, shopping malls, and other buildings and structures. They unload lorries, move and store items such as tools, barrows, sand, cement and bricks. Operatives set out the site area to be excavated using profiles (metal or wooden stakes) and usually erect site huts, signs and barriers, any scaffolding and ladders. They prepare material such as plaster, mortar and concrete and use drills, pumps and cement mixers.

Construction operatives may drive a fork-lift truck or other site vehicles. They lay pipes and drains, kerbs or paving and dig trenches. Keeping the site tidy, cleaning the tools and making sure they are safely locked away at the end of the day is important. They may be involved in specialist operations such as underpinning, deep drainage etc.

Work Details
Usually work a 39 hr week, Monday to Friday. Overtime work is common. Travel to different sites is required and work may sometimes be away from home. Work is outdoors and on site in all weathers. You work with a skilled construction worker, such as a bricklayer or plasterer. Have to cope with rough ground, bending, lifting, and working at heights on scaffolding and ladders.

Building sites and civil engineering projects are often dusty, dirty, muddy and noisy. Protective clothing is usually needed. This may include a safety helmet and reinforced boots, eye protection and ear defenders, plus high visibility and weather resistant clothing.

Qualification

• England, Wales and Northern Ireland
Band 1: No minimum qualifications are required, though you are expected to have a good general level of education. However, some formal/vocational qualifications at any level are useful.

Band 2: Although academic qualifications are not always specified, GCSEs in English, maths and technology, or equivalent, are useful.

• Scotland
Band 1: No minimum qualifications are required, though you are expected to have had a good general level of education.

Band 2: Although academic qualifications are not always specified, S grades in English, maths and technology, or similar, are useful.

Adult Qualifications
You can enter this job without formal qualifications. However, secondary qualifications in English, maths and technology, or equivalent, are useful.

Work Experience
Relevant work or voluntary experience is always useful and can improve your chances when applying for entry to jobs or apprenticeships in the building/construction industry. Your personal or adult guidance adviser should be able to advise you about how to organise work experience with an employer. Health and safety issues may mean that there are certain jobs you can't do until you are over 16. Contact your local ConstructionSkills office for advice.

Entry and Training
Most people enter this job via a training scheme, such as a construction apprenticeship scheme, and receive on-the-job training with a skilled worker or supervisor. A Diploma/ Welsh Baccalaureate in construction and the built environment may be available in your area. You may attend a training centre or local college on a day-release basis to gain vocational qualifications in construction skills. There are also ConstructionSkills awards available for those who are unable to gain workplace experience for S/NVQs. You are expected to gain a Construction Site Operative card through the Construction Skills Certification Scheme. Contact ConstructionSkills for further details.

S/NVQs and VRQs in construction and civil engineering services and in specialised plant and machinery operations are available at levels 1-2. Training programmes, including apprenticeships leading to level 2 and advanced apprenticeships/construction apprenticeships leading to level 3, may be available in your area.

Mature entrants with related experience in the building/construction industry are often welcomed by employers and considered for training if physically fit for the job. The National Construction College (ConstructionSkills) offers general construction courses for adults. Government training opportunities may also be available in your area. Contact your local careers office, Jobcentre Plus, Next Step service or Learning and Skills Council (LSC)/Local Enterprise Company (LEC) for details of training schemes, including apprenticeships for adults.

Opportunities and Pay

Work is located throughout the UK. Employers include building firms, civil engineering firms, local councils and public utilities companies. Tools and equipment are supplied by your employer. Self-employment, working on a labour-only basis, is common for this job. Some jobs are seasonal or short term. You can also work on contracts abroad. Availability of work depends on activity in the building trade and the national economy. A downturn in the housing market usually means there is a shortage of vacancies.

Pay varies depending on location and employer. Generally you are likely to start on around £15k a year. This rises to £20k with experience and/or qualifications. Some top earners make around £24k a year. Pay can be increased a good deal with overtime. You may be given a lodging allowance when working away from home.

Health

Good general fitness is required. There may be an allergy risk from dust.

Skills and Qualities

able to follow instructions, aptitude for teamwork, common sense, enjoy working outdoors, hard working, head for heights, practical skills, safety conscious

Relevant Subjects

Construction and built environment, Design and technology

Further Information

Apprenticeship Schemes (National Apprenticeship Service) - www.apprenticeships.org.uk

Apprenticeships in Scotland (Careers Info Scotland) - www.apprenticeshipsinscotland.com/about/

Careers in Construction - www.bconstructive.co.uk

Construction Skills Certification Scheme (CSCS) - www.cscs.uk.com

ConstructionSkills - sector skills council for the construction industry - www.cskills.org

Diplomas (Foundation, Higher and Advanced) - http://yp.direct.gov.uk/diplomas

Training Schemes - www.direct.gov.uk/en/educationandlearning

Welsh Baccalaureate - www.wbq.org.uk

▶Working in construction & the built environment (2007) (Babcock Lifeskills) - www.babcock-lifeskills.com/

Similar Jobs

Builders' Yard Assistant, Construction Plant Operative, Demolition Operative, Fence Installer, Quarry Operative, Rail Track Maintenance Worker

Construction Plant Operative

also known as: Construction Plant Operator, Plant Operative

CRCI:Building and Construction

CLCI:UV

Job Band: 1 to 2

Job Description

Construction plant operatives operate and control construction plant machinery, such as bulldozers, earth-scrapers and motorised diggers, used on building sites and roads. They also use rough terrain forklifts, excavators, trucks and mobile or static tower cranes. They work the levers to place tools, such as shovels or lifting gear, into the right position. Plant operatives excavate and move earth, sometimes hundreds of tonnes of earth in a day. May work with a ground level worker who guides the operative by using hand signals or radio, especially when visibility is poor. Many specialise in using one type of machine.

Plant operatives also carry out simple maintenance, servicing and repairs to plant equipment. They report any major faults to maintenance workers. An awareness of the health and safety aspects of the work is important when using equipment, as is awareness of the rules and regulations that govern a building site or project.

Work Details

Usually work around 37-39 hrs a week, Monday to Friday, though sometimes may need to work overtime on a Saturday. You work on your own but are in communication with other workers. The work is outdoors, sometimes in unpleasant weather and muddy conditions. Sites can be dusty, noisy and dirty. You have to cover rough ground and climb in and out of machines. This can be dangerous and you have to follow rules for using them safely.

Some machines involve working at heights. You may have to travel to different sites during a working week. Plant operatives wear protective clothing, including a safety helmet, ear defenders, gloves and safety footwear.

Qualification

• England, Wales and Northern Ireland

Band 1: No minimum requirements are required, but you are expected to have had a good level of general education. However some formal/vocational qualifications at any level are useful.

Band 2: For entry: some employers require a few GCSEs, or equivalent. English, maths and technology subjects are useful.

• Scotland

Band 1: There are no minimum entry requirements, but you are expected to have a good level of general education. However some formal/vocational qualifications at any level are useful.

Band 2: For entry: some employers require a few S grades, or similar. English, maths and technology subjects are useful.

Adult Qualifications

Those with relevant work experience may be accepted for some college courses without meeting any formal entry requirements.

Work Experience

Relevant work or voluntary experience is always useful and can improve your chances when applying for entry to jobs or apprenticeships in the building/construction industry. Your personal or adult guidance adviser should be able to advise you about how to organise work experience with an employer. Health and safety issues may mean that there are certain jobs you can't do until you are over 16. Contact your local ConstructionSkills office for advice.

Entry and Training

You normally receive training on the job with day or block release to a local college or training provider, leading to S/NVQs. Training is also available at a ConstructionSkills centre. Other options include one or two-year full-time courses at a college. If you are under 18 you cannot drive the machines, but you can start training at 16 or 17. A full driving licence is often required. You can also work towards gaining a level of competence card through the Construction Plant Competence Scheme that indicates your individual skill level.

A Diploma/ Welsh Baccalaureate in construction and the built environment may be available in your area. Relevant S/NVQs and VRQs are available at levels 1-3, such as specialised plant and machinery operations, plant maintenance and plant operations. Training programmes, including apprenticeships leading to level 2, and advanced apprenticeships/construction apprenticeships leading to level 3, may be available in your area. There are also ConstructionSkills Awards (England and Wales) available for those who are unable to gain workplace experience for NVQs. Contact ConstructionSkills or check the bconstructive website for details of all routes to training.

Mature entrants with related experience in the building/ construction industry, and also with driving and/or mechanical skills, are often considered for training if physically fit for the job. The National Construction College (ConstructionSkills) offers plant operation courses for adults. Government training opportunities may also be available in your area. Contact your local careers office, Jobcentre Plus, Next Step service or Learning and Skills Council (LSC)/Local Enterprise Company (LEC) for details of training schemes, including apprenticeships for adults.

Opportunities and Pay

Work is located throughout the UK. You can work for a building firm, a construction/civil engineering company, or a public utilities firm. Many plant operatives are self-employed and use either their own or the contractor's machines. There is seasonal, temporary and casual work for those who are self-employed or who work as a sub-contractor. Availability of work depends on the state of the building trade and the national economy. Currently there is a downturn in the housing market which means there may be a shortage of vacancies. Those with experience can progress to supervisory jobs.

Pay can vary greatly depending on location and employer. Trainees can earn around £12k-£15k a year. With experience and/or qualifications most earn £20k-£24k a year. Overtime pay is common. On some projects you may be paid an incentive bonus based on your work output. This can lead to higher earnings. You may also be given a lodging allowance when working away from home.

Health

You must be physically fit with good eyesight and good hearing. You should not be allergic to dust.

Skills and Qualities

able to follow instructions, able to work both on your own and in a team, enjoy working outdoors, good concentration level, mechanical skills, practical skills, quick reactions, safety conscious, steady hand, technical aptitude

Relevant Subjects

Construction and built environment, Design and technology

Further Information

Apprenticeship Schemes (National Apprenticeship Service) - www.apprenticeships.org.uk

Apprenticeships in Scotland (Careers Info Scotland) - www.apprenticeshipsinscotland.com/about/

bconstructive - www.bconstructive.co.uk/

Careers in Construction - www.bconstructive.co.uk

Construction Skills Certification Scheme (CSCS) - www.cscs.uk.com

ConstructionSkills - sector skills council for the construction industry - www.cskills.org

Diplomas (Foundation, Higher and Advanced) http://yp.direct.gov.uk/diplomas

Welsh Baccalaureate - www.wbq.org.uk

▶Working in construction & the built environment (2007) (Babcock Lifeskills) - www.babcock-lifeskills.com/

Addresses

Construction Plant-hire Association
27-28 Newbury Street, Barbican, London EC1A 7HU
Phone: +44 (0)20 7796 3366
Web: www.cpa.uk.net

Similar Jobs

Construction Operative, Crane Operator, Driver: Lorry, Lift Truck Operative, Quarry Operative

Construction Site Supervisor/Manager

also known as: Building Manager, Building Site Supervisor/ Manager

CRCI:Building and Construction
CLCI:UD Job Band: 3 to 5

Job Description

Construction site supervisors are responsible for organising and supervising the day-to-day progress on a building site, civil engineering project, or an architectural/conservation project. They work daily on site to ensure an efficient use of the workforce and construction materials. Supervisors encourage good industrial relations between all on-site construction workers and are responsible for discipline on the site. They liaise regularly with the site inspector (clerk of works), architects, engineers and sub-contractors and see that work proceeds according to the timescale and that costs are kept within an agreed budget. Quality of building materials and standard of work are checked.

Construction site supervisors implement and maintain health and safety standards, and arrange site security. They keep detailed construction progress reports for the site inspector and may work on more than one project at a time.

Work Details

Construction site supervisors usually work a basic 38-40 hour week, on site and outdoors, as well as in a temporary site office. The hours can sometimes be very long, including weekends and on-call duties. You may need to travel to sites away from home and perhaps stay away for long periods. Supervising and organising the labour force efficiently is a priority, as well as liaising with people, including buyers, estimators, architects and clients. You are responsible for planning and monitoring work progress, and for health and safety standards.

When inspecting work, you need to be able to cope with rough ground, ladders and scaffolding. You are often out in all sorts of weather, and sometimes have to wear a safety helmet and boots.

Qualification

• England, Wales and Northern Ireland

Band 4: For BTEC higher national award in construction: one A level and 4 GCSEs (A*-C) including maths, a science subject and English, or equivalent.

Band 5: For relevant degree: 2-3 A levels and some GCSEs (A*-C), usually including maths, a science subject and English, or equivalent. Sometimes A level maths is required. Exact requirements depend on the degree you take.

• Scotland

Band 4: For SQA higher national award: two H grades and four S grades (1-3) including maths, a science subject and English, or similar.

Construction Site Supervisor/Manager

Band 5: For relevant degree: 3-5 H grades and some S grades (1-3), usually including maths, a science subject and English, or similar qualifications. Exact requirements depend on the degree you take.

Degree Information

Degrees in construction, construction management, building construction management, building studies, or civil/structural engineering are normally preferred by employers. Degrees in architecture, building surveying or related subjects may also be acceptable.

Adult Qualifications

There are relevant foundation/Access courses to higher education, including construction and the built environment, and also distance-learning courses, including construction management. Colleges may accept applicants without academic qualifications, provided they have relevant experience.

Work Experience

Employers or colleges/universities may prefer candidates who have relevant work or voluntary experience. This can include making site visits or shadowing a trade professional, such as a carpenter or plumber. Depending on your age, there are health and safety regulations, which may prevent physical site visits. If this is the case then there are other related areas that are useful, such as working in an architect's, civil engineering or construction-based office. It is becoming increasingly important for prospective site supervisors/managers to have good IT skills.

Entry and Training

Some building site managers already have a degree in a subject, such as construction management, building construction management or civil engineering, and have followed an in-house training programme with an employer. Some employers may provide sponsorship for degree study. A relevant full or part-time foundation degree is also possible, as is an HNC/D in construction. The Chartered Institute of Building (CIOB) offers a level 3 Certificate in Site Supervisory Studies and a level 4 Diploma in Site Management. Courses are delivered through colleges, universities and companies. Holders of the Diploma are eligible for CIOB Associated Membership.

After obtaining an accredited degree and having had a period of appropriate work experience, you can apply for membership (MCIOB) of the CIOB through a professional review, and also become a chartered builder. However, there are several routes to full membership, including a route for those without a relevant degree, but with three years of professional experience. Members may apply for the Construction Skills Certification Scheme card that provides evidence of professional achievement. It is also possible to gain higher qualifications and to reach qualified engineer status. Contact the CIOB for information on membership, training and qualifications.

Some site supervisors/managers work their way up to assistant level by first learning on the job, and gaining qualifications in general construction site working and training in a particular craft. Others enter as technicians, having first taken a relevant further education course.

The 'Inspire Scholarships' scheme, offered through ConstructionSkills, the Sector Skills Council for the construction industry, offers scholarships of up to £6k to help fund a construction-related degree, such as civil engineering, architecture, surveying and construction management. More information about the scheme is available on the bconstructive website.

Relevant S/NVQs are available at levels 1-4 in construction, in construction site supervision at level 3 and in construction site management at level 4. Training programmes, including apprenticeship schemes, may be available in your area for entry to this job. Advanced apprenticeships leading to qualification at level 3 can also be a route into higher education.

Mature entry is possible for those with relevant experience in craft or supervisory jobs in building, civil engineering or surveying. Applicants may have their previous training experience recognised through Accreditation of Prior Learning. Some large construction companies may offer sponsorship for higher education courses in construction management.

Opportunities and Pay

Work is located throughout the UK. You can work for a general building contractor, a building/civil engineering contractor, or a large national/international organisation that carries out its own construction work. Availability of work depends on the state of the building trade and the national economy. Currently there is a downturn in the housing market which means there may be a shortage of vacancies. Opportunities are generally better in medium and large firms. Experienced building site/construction site managers can become independent site inspectors (clerks of works), contracts managers, or progress further to become a director of a construction company. There are also opportunities to work abroad.

Pay can vary considerably depending on location and employer. An assistant site manager typically earns around £16k-£20k and as a building site supervisor/manager, £26k-£37k a year or more. You may be given a lodging allowance when working away from home.

Health

This job requires good general fitness.

Skills and Qualities

able to communicate effectively, able to cope under pressure, able to manage people, able to work to deadlines, analytical skills, good at writing reports, good interpersonal skills, IT skills, planning skills, problem-solving skills

Relevant Subjects

Business and accounting, Construction and built environment, Design and technology, English, ICT/Computer studies, Mathematics, Physics, Science

Further Information

Apprenticeship Schemes (National Apprenticeship Service) - www.apprenticeships.org.uk

bconstructive - www.bconstructive.co.uk/

Construction Manager magazine (CIOB, 10 x year) (Construction Manager) - www.construction-manager.co.uk

Construction Skills Certification Scheme (CSCS) - www.cscs.uk.com

ConstructionSkills - sector skills council for the construction industry - www.cskills.org

TARGETjobs: Construction & Building Services (GTI Specialist Publishers Ltd) - www.groupgti.com

▶Working in construction & the built environment (2007) (Babcock Lifeskills) - www.babcock-lifeskills.com/

Addresses

Chartered Institute of Building (CIOB)
Englemere King's Ride, Ascot, Berkshire SL5 7TB
Phone: +44 (0)1344 630 700
Web: www.ciob.org.uk

Institution of Civil Engineers (ICE)
1 Great George Street, Westminster, London SW1P 3AA
Phone: +44 (0)20 7222 7722
Web: www.ice.org.uk

Similar Jobs

Civil Engineering Technician, Clerk of Works/Site Inspector, Engineer: Civil/Structural, Surveyor: Building Control, Surveyor: Quantity

Consumer Scientist

also known as: Home Economist, Local Government: Food Officer

CRCI:Science, Mathematics and Statistics
CLCI:ID Job Band: 4 to 5

Job Description

Consumer scientists are the link between consumers and manufacturers, measuring and interpreting consumer needs, tastes and preferences in areas that include household goods, food manufacture and product development, clothing and home management. They may do analytical work in a company laboratory or work in marketing and production, using high technology, including sophisticated and complex computer systems, to carry out their work. May write information articles and press releases, or organise exhibitions and produce advertising material. Also help food manufacturers or supermarket chains to develop new products by testing prototypes or recipes and reporting users' opinions. May work in the catering industry where their specialised research and advice can help restaurants, hotels, or the healthcare sector such as hospitals, residential homes etc.

In further and higher education, they provide advice on healthy living. May also advise families on budgeting and homemaking skills. Some consumer scientists teach and research subjects such as consumer science or hospitality and catering. As a food officer in local government, helps local businesses to produce and market their products, both locally and nationally. May provide ideas and information on incorporating local produce into menus at consumer outlets such as pubs and restaurants, or the shelves of supermarkets.

Work Details

Usually work around 36-40 hrs a week, Monday to Friday, that may include some evenings or weekends. In many jobs you may have to travel around a local area to different sites. Attendance at events/exhibitions may require you to sometimes stay away from home. In most jobs you work indoors in offices or schools, shops, kitchens and laboratories, and spend time sitting at a desk or standing to deliver a talk or lesson. You are also likely to spend time reading, researching and producing reports.

Qualification

- **England, Wales and Northern Ireland**

Band 4: For relevant HND, Diploma of Higher Education or foundation degree: 1-2 A levels and some GCSEs (A*-C) usually including English, science and maths, or equivalent.

Band 5: For degree courses: 2-3 A levels and some GCSEs (A*-C) usually including English, maths and a science, or equivalent. Exact requirements depend on the degree you take.

- **Scotland**

Band 4: For relevant SQA higher national and professional development awards, usually 2-3 H grades and some S grades (1-3), including English, science and maths, or similar qualifications.

Band 5: For degree courses: 3-5 H grades and some S grades (1-3), usually including English, maths and a science, or similar qualifications. Exact requirements depend on the degree you take.

Degree Information

Those wishing to enter this job at graduate level should have a degree in food and consumer science/studies, food and consumer management, consumer marketing and product development/ design or a related subject. Postgraduate courses are available in consumer science and related subjects, such as health promotion and marketing.

Adult Qualifications

Entry requirements may be relaxed for adults applying for higher education courses. Access or foundation courses give adults without qualifications a route on to degree courses.

Work Experience

Employers or colleges/universities may prefer candidates who have relevant work or voluntary experience. This can include retail, catering and training in a variety of situations that involve working with the public or giving advice to people.

Entry and Training

Most entrants have a higher education qualification in a consumer science or related subject. The term 'home economics' has been changed over recent years to reflect the growing public awareness of wider consumer issues, although there is a degree course available at Liverpool John Moores University in home economics (food design and technology). Many of the college and university courses include related work experience. Food producers, household equipment and appliance manufacturers run short courses about their products.

For information on routes into training and relevant courses in consumer science and home economy, contact the Design and Technology Association, the Institute of Food Science and Technology or the Trading Standards Institute. This job often requires a driving licence and it is an advantage to have skills in speaking to groups of people.

Requirements for mature entrants vary from employer to employer. Those without a relevant degree can benefit from gaining experience in food manufacturing or catering.

Opportunities and Pay

Consumer scientists/home economists can find a variety of employment in many different areas such as retail chains, including supermarkets or kitchen designers, food and drink manufacturing, gas and electricity companies, hotels and restaurants. May also work in education, local and central government, health authorities, public relations agencies, consumer pressure groups, consumer advice organisations, journalism, and in publishing.

Around 5,000 people work as consumer scientists in the food industry, but there are more than 25,000 working in the wider area of consumer affairs. Promotion opportunities vary widely and include moving between organisations, progressing to management or employment abroad working for international companies. It is possible to work on a freelance basis and part-time work is often available.

Pay varies depending on the employer but is likely to be around £18k-£20k a year, for newly qualified graduates, rising to around £25k-£30k a year, with experience. Senior professionals can earn more than £50k a year. Freelance earnings vary considerably.

Health

For some jobs there are restrictions for those people with certain skin conditions.

Skills and Qualities

able to get on with all kinds of people, analytical skills, excellent communication skills, good presentation skills, IT skills, problem-solving skills, research skills, self confident

Relevant Subjects

Business and accounting, Chemistry, Economics, English, Health and social care, Hospitality and catering, Mathematics, Science

Further Information

Improve Ltd - sector skills council for food and drink manufacturing and processing - www.improveltd.co.uk

Tomorrow's Engineers -
www.tomorrowsengineers.org.uk/careers.cfm
Trading Standards Careers - www.tradingstandards.gov.uk/jobs

Addresses

British Nutrition Foundation (BNF)
High Holborn House, 52-54 High Holborn, London WC1V 6RQ
Phone: +44 (0)20 7404 6504
Web: www.nutrition.org.uk

Design & Technology Association (D&TA)
16 Wellesbourne House, Walton Road, Warwickshire CV35 9JB
Phone: +44 (0)1789 470 007
Web: www.data.org.uk

Institute of Food Science and Technology (IFST)
5 Cambridge Court, 210 Shepherd's Bush Road, London W6 7NJ
Phone: +44 (0)20 7603 6316
Web: www.ifst.org.uk

Trading Standards Institute (TSI)
1 Sylvan Court, Sylvan Way, Southfields Business Park, Basildon, Essex SS15 6TH
Phone: 0845 608 9400 (UK only)
Web: www.tradingstandards.gov.uk/

Similar Jobs

Dietitian, Food Scientist/Technologist, Health Promotion Specialist, Nutritional Therapist, Teacher: Food Technology, Trading Standards Officer

Contact Centre Operator

also known as: Call Centre Operator, Telesales Operator
CRCI:Retail Sales and Customer Services
CLCI:OM
Job Band: 2 to 3

Job Description

Contact centre operators usually work in the customer services department of a company with a high level of telephone, email or internet customer enquiries. Tasks vary depending on the company, but usually include selling goods and services. They contact people by telephone to persuade them to buy goods or services. May sell advertising space and goods such as insurance, office equipment, house improvements or timeshare property. Operators use a prepared script to describe the product and try to convince people to accept more information by post, or a visit from a sales representative. Usually have to make a certain number of calls within a fixed period.

Some operators carry out market research to find out what people like, what they spend their money on and to gain a better knowledge of consumer trends. May work at a centre taking customer orders and dealing with credit/debit card payments. Others give advice about company products and answer complaints, or offer advisory services in areas such as counselling, welfare and benefits, or help with careers. They maintain a computerised database, update records on each customer and make notes about any further contact needed.

Work Details

Work is usually between 37-40 hrs over a five-day week, often including weekends and evenings, and you may need to work shifts. Your work place is usually a brightly lit and air-conditioned office. You have to sit in one position for long periods at a computer workstation. You need to be very persistent and persuasive, so that people consider buying the product or service you are telling them about. A headset is usually worn.

Qualification

Personality is more important than qualifications and there are no formal entry qualifications. A good general education is usually expected.

- **England, Wales and Northern Ireland**

Band 2: For entry to jobs, no minimum qualifications are needed, but it is an advantage to have some GCSEs (A*-C) or equivalent in subjects that include English and maths.

Band 3: For some employers/courses: at least 5 GCSEs (A*-C) including English and maths, or equivalent.

- **Scotland**

Band 2: Some employers may ask for a few S grades (1-3) in subjects that include English and maths, or similar.

Band 3: For some employers/courses: at least four S grades (1-3) including English and maths, or similar.

Adult Qualifications

A good standard of secondary education is needed.

Work Experience

Relevant work or voluntary experience is always useful and can improve your chances when applying for entry to jobs in sales. It can equip you with skills that you can use in the future and add to your CV. Part-time and holiday employment in a wide range of shops is usually fairly easy to obtain. Any work involving sales or customer services is useful.

Entry and Training

Most employers provide in-house training, which may consist of a short course in product knowledge followed by more specialised training in the company's products and systems. Smaller companies provide on-the-job training under the supervision of experienced staff. Some organisations may include S/NVQ assessment as part of their internal training programmes.

The Customer Contact Association (CCA) runs a range of courses for those wishing to become accredited. The CCA Certificate course is for people who are new to the job but have completed their company induction programme. The Diploma is awarded to those who have completed a further period of training, the Advanced Diploma is for those working at team leader level and the Executive Diploma is aimed at contact centre middle management. Contact the CCA for further details on all courses.

Higher qualifications are available for those who wish to progress, including relevant HNCs/HNDs. There are also professional qualifications offered by organisations such as the Institute of Direct Marketing and the Chartered Institute of Marketing. Relevant S/NVQs are available, including contact centre operations (levels 1-2), and contact centre professionals (levels 3-4).

A Diploma/Welsh Baccalaureate in retail business may be available in your area. Training programmes, including apprenticeship schemes in call centre operations may also be available in your area. Advanced apprenticeships leading to qualification at level 3 can also be a route into higher education.

Adults may be able to enter this work through a government-funded training programme. Contact your local careers office, Jobcentre Plus, Next Step service or Learning and Skills Council (LSC)/Local Enterprise Company (LEC) for details of all training opportunities and schemes, including apprenticeships for adults. Sales experience is an advantage and sometimes specialist product knowledge is required.

Opportunities and Pay

Jobs are available throughout the UK, especially in London, the south east and Scotland. There may be promotion opportunities to supervisory and management levels. Some companies have relocated their contact centres abroad, so job opportunities may be reduced.

The amount you are paid varies depending on the company you are working for, and you may only be paid commission on sales. Apprentices earn around £9k a year but an average starting salary can be around £13k-£15k a year, although this varies with employer and location. With experience, this rises to around £16k-£20k. Some team leaders and call centre managers earn up to £35k a year.

Health
You need to have good hearing and clear speech for this type of work.

Skills and Qualities
able to communicate effectively, able to work to targets, attention to detail, calm, customer service skills, discreet, good organisational skills, good telephone manner, IT skills, self confident

Relevant Subjects
English, Psychology, Retail and distribution

Further Information
Apprenticeship Schemes (National Apprenticeship Service) - www.apprenticeships.org.uk

CCF Online (Call Centres Focus) - www.callcentre.co.uk

Diplomas (Foundation, Higher and Advanced) - http://yp.direct.gov.uk/diplomas

e-skills UK - sector skills council for business and information technology - www.e-skills.com

Training Schemes - www.direct.gov.uk/en/educationandlearning

Welsh Baccalaureate - www.wbq.org.uk

▶Working in marketing, advertising & PR (2008) (Babcock Lifeskills) - www.babcock-lifeskills.com/

▶Working in retail & customer services (2008) (Babcock Lifeskills) - www.babcock-lifeskills.com/

Addresses
Chartered Institute of Marketing (CIM)
Moor Hall, Cookham, Maidenhead, Berkshire SL6 9QH
Phone: +44 (0) 1628 427120
Web: www.cim.co.uk

Customer Contact Association (CCA)
20 Newtown Place, Glasgow G3 7PY
Phone: +44 (0)141 564 9010
Web: www.cca.org.uk

Institute of Customer Service (ICS)
2 Castle Court, St Peter's Street, Colchester, Essex CO1 1EW
Phone: +44 (0)1206 571716
Web: www.instituteofcustomerservice.com

Institute of Direct Marketing (IDM)
1 Park Road, Teddington, Middlesex TW11 0AR
Phone: +44 (0)208 977 5705
Web: www.theidm.com

Similar Jobs
Airline Customer Service Agent, Car Rental Agent, Customer Services Adviser, Market Research Interviewer, Sales Executive

Copy Editor
also known as: Sub-editor

CRCI:Media, Print and Publishing

CLCI:FAD Job Band: 5

Job Description
Copy editors ensure that a writer's text (copy) is clear and readable, and that spelling, grammar and facts are correct, ready for publication. They also correct errors in punctuation, style and usage, ensuring that the copy is suitable for the intended audience, either in a book or on a computer screen. The work must be of the right length, including illustrations and captions where relevant, title page, table of contents, footnotes, glossary, appendices and index. The content and structure has to be logical. Liaising with the author to resolve queries and to make sure that the house style of the publication is maintained is an important part of the job.

Copy editors alert the publisher to potential legal issues, such as breaches of copyright and libel issues. They need to have enough knowledge about the technical side of publishing to be able to liaise with designers, typesetters or printers.

Copy editors working on newspapers and magazines may be called sub-editors. Their tasks may include composing headlines, writing introductory paragraphs (standfirsts), editing and laying out stories to a set page design. They work with newsroom and production colleagues.

Work Details
Hours of work vary depending on the quantity of work received. Many copy editors are freelance and work from home. Whether employed full time or freelance, you may need to work some evenings and weekends, to meet publishers' deadlines. Sub-editors on daily newspapers may work shifts, including early starts and late nights.

Work can be demanding at times and requires a high degree of accuracy. You usually work on a computer, editing on screen, but may also work with a printed (hard) copy of a manuscript. It is increasingly common to use a content management system (CMS) for editing text to fit into templates. There may be occasional travel for meetings.

Qualification
• England, Wales and Northern Ireland
Band 5: For degree courses: 2-3 A levels and some GCSEs (A*-C) usually including English and maths, or equivalent. Exact requirements depend on the degree you take.

• Scotland
Band 5: For entry to a degree course: 3-5 H grades and some S grades (1-3) including maths and English, or similar qualifications. Exact requirements depend on the degree you take.

Degree Information
Although there are no set qualifications, copy editors usually have a degree, often in a related subject, such as English, publishing, media or journalism. A degree in science, economics, business studies or law may enable you to work in a specialist field. There are postgraduate publishing qualifications.

Adult Qualifications
Entry requirements for higher education may be relaxed for adults with experience in publishing or journalism. There are foundation degrees in journalism and publishing.

Work Experience
It is important to build up a good track record, delivering work of a high standard on time. Freelance copy editors need to develop and maintain contacts. Some of the larger publishing companies may offer work experience placements or internships, but there is intense competition for places.

Membership of a professional organisation, such as the SfEP or Women in Publishing, can provide useful networking opportunities, support and advice.

Entry and Training
For copy editors employed by a company, it is usual to have a degree and gain experience in a junior role, such as editorial assistant. Sub-editors in newspapers and magazines may start as general reporters. You learn on the job with support from experienced colleagues.

In-house training may be offered. There are distance-learning and short courses in journalism, working freelance, copy editing, text editing and on-screen editing skills available at different levels. Those accredited by the National Council of Training for Journalists (NCTJ) and the Periodicals Training Council (through the Periodical Publishers Association) are recognised by the publishing industry. Consult the websites of the SfEP, United Kingdom Association for Publishing Education (UKAPE) and Skillset for useful information about available courses.

A Diploma/Welsh Baccalaureate in creative and media may be available in your area.

A publishing qualification is not essential but it can lead to valuable work experience and networking opportunities. Mature applicants who can show evidence of a good body of work may be preferred for freelance opportunities. Experience in publishing or a related area of work is useful.

Opportunities and Pay

You can be employed by a publishing company to work on a range of paper or online publications, such as books, journals, newspapers, magazines and websites. Many publishing companies use freelance copy editors, so competition is fierce and building a reputation for good work and meeting deadlines is important. However, there are also opportunities in organisations that use copy editors to support their communications activities. Nearly half of those working in publishing are based in London and the South East, but there are jobs in national, regional and local news media.

With experience, you may specialise in a particular area, such as medical, scientific or business publishing. In-house copy editors may move on to more senior roles in publishing, such as commissioning editor or editor. Experienced sub-editors can take on more management responsibilities to become a chief sub-editor or production editor.

Rates of pay vary, depending on employer and location, but start from around £16k a year, rising to around £35k with experience. Freelance copy editors negotiate their own fees. The National Union of Journalists and the Society for Editors and Proofreaders (SfEP) offer advice on freelance rates. The SfEP suggests a minimum rate of £20.75 an hour for copy-editing on paper, and £22.50 for on-screen work. Chief sub-editors on a national publication can earn up to £60k a year.

Skills and Qualities

able to network and negotiate, able to work to deadlines, attention to detail, diplomatic, flexible approach, good concentration level, good spelling, grammar and punctuation, good written English, IT skills, tactful

Relevant Subjects

Design and technology, English, ICT/Computer studies, Media and communication studies

Further Information

Careers in Book Publishing (The Publishers Association) - www.publishers.org.uk/

Diplomas (Foundation, Higher and Advanced) - http://yp.direct.gov.uk/diplomas

National Council for the Training of Journalists (NCTJ) - www.nctj.com

Skillset - sector skills council for the creative media, fashion and textiles industries - www.skillset.org

Society of Young Publishers - www.thesyp.org.uk/

United Kingdom Association for Publishing Education (UKAPE) - http://ukape.org/

Welsh Baccalaureate - www.wbq.org.uk

Women In Publishing - www.wipub.org.uk

Writers' & Artists' Yearbook (A&C Black) (A&C Black) - www.writersandartists.co.uk

Addresses

National Union of Journalists (NUJ)
Headland House, 308-312 Grays Inn Road, London WC1X 8DP
Phone: +44 (0)20 7278 7916
Web: www.nuj.org.uk

Periodical Publishers' Association (PPA) (Periodicals Training Council)
Queens House, 28 Kingsway, London WC2B 6JR
Phone: +44 (0)207 404 4166
Web: www.ppa.co.uk/

Publishers' Association
29b Montague Street, London WC1B 5BW
Phone: +44 (0)20 7691 9191
Web: www.publishers.org.uk

Publishing Training Centre at Book House
45 East Hill, Wandsworth, London SW18 2QZ
Phone: +44 (0)20 8874 2718
Web: www.train4publishing.co.uk

Society for Editors and Proofreaders (SfEP)
Erico House, 93-99 Upper Richmond Road, Putney, London SW15 2TG
Phone: +44 (0)20 8785 5617
Web: www.sfep.org.uk

Similar Jobs

Advertising Copywriter, Indexer, Journalist, Proofreader, Writer, Writer: Technical

Coroner

CRCI:Legal and Political Services
CLCI:LAB — Job Band: 5

Job Description

Coroners are independent officials, appointed and paid for by local authorities, who are responsible for investigating violent, unnatural deaths or sudden deaths of unknown cause and deaths in custody. They are usually barristers, solicitors or medical practitioners with at least 5 years experience. They receive reports of deaths that are considered not to be through any 'natural' cause. Deaths through industrial diseases such as mesothelioma (cancer associated with exposure to asbestos) are also reported.

Coroners collect all relevant information concerning the death in order that a conclusion can then be made about its cause, often consulting with GPs and pathologists. They arrange for a post-mortem (pathological examination of the dead body) if there are any questions arising from the cause of death. Coroners hold an inquest if it is concluded that a death was not from natural causes. However, it is not the coroners responsibility to establish who is to blame for such a death. Sometimes they are required to make a decision concerning the cremation of a body or of organ donation.

Coroners are required by law to ensure that correct procedures are carried out and that records are kept properly and accurately. Coroners are no longer responsible for making decisions on any treasure from a particular find in their area. Such decisions are now made by a national coroner for treasure, instead of at a local level.

In Northern Ireland coroners are either a barrister or solicitor (see individual job profiles), and in Scotland, the role is carried out by the procurator fiscal (see job profile).

Work Details

Full-time hours are 35-40 hr week, Monday to Friday, and you also work an on-call rota through weekends and evenings. You must be available to the public at all times as some procedures must be completed within a limited time. For example, most post-mortems are carried out within 24-hours following the discovery of a dead body. Travel is required to attend a court, or when there is a need to visit a crime scene, or visit other places, such as a pathology department.

You are helped by a deputy and assistant deputy coroner. Some are full time but many work part time in less densely populated parts of the country. You then work the rest of the time in your own practice.

Qualification

- **England, Wales and Northern Ireland**

Band 5: For degree courses: 2-3 A levels and some GCSEs (A*-C) usually including English and maths, or equivalent qualifications. Exact requirements depend on the degree you take.

Degree Information

The first degree is usually in law. Currently, in England & Wales only, a degree in medicine is also applicable though this is soon to change. See job profiles for a barrister, solicitor and doctor.

Adult Qualifications

You must first qualify as a solicitor, barrister or, currently, a medical practitioner, and have at least five years of experience following qualification. Some coroners may have a medical qualification as well as a law degree.

Work Experience

Entry to this job is highly competitive and only open to qualified barristers, solicitors, and medical practitioners. Any practical experience in working with the police is an advantage. Attendance at a court to observe a variety of post-mortems is also helpful.

Entry and Training

The Ministry of Justice is responsible for policy, the law and training for coroners. Its website has full details of recent changes likely to go through Parliament between 2010-2012.

This job is open to barristers, solicitors and doctors with at least five years of post-qualifying experience. All future applicants to become a coroner must be legally qualified. Transitional provision will be offered to existing coroners who have medical qualifications only.

Coroners are appointed by individual local authorities. To gain work as a coroner, it is usually necessary to first find a coroner able and willing to appoint you as their deputy or assistant deputy. Most are therefore trained in court proceedings and the necessary associated administrative tasks on the job. Contact the Coroners' Society to find details of a coroner local to you.

As there are constant changes in medical procedures, law, and administrative practices, continuous training to keep up to date is also a requirement. The Coroners Officers Association has developed a range of relevant short training courses for coroners and their staff. There is also a relevant postgraduate course at Staffordshire University in death, bereavement and human tissue studies.

Mature entrants need to qualify using the standard routes to professional qualification. However, maturity and experience is an advantage in this job.

Opportunities and Pay

Entry is very competitive as there are a limited number of posts. At the moment there are 106 different coroner districts. There are 32 full-time coroners, the rest are all part time and are called in when needed.

Coroners are appointed by a local authority in England, Wales and Northern Ireland. It may be necessary to move jobs around the country in order to gain experience. Promotion to senior posts is by competition when vacancies arise. A coroner can also move into civil service posts. There are many opportunities to work part time as this job is often combined with that of a practising lawyer.

Most coroners are paid according to the population in the local area they serve and the case load. However, full-time salaries are generally up to about £82k a year. Part-time coroners are paid according to their specific caseload.

Skills and Qualities

analytical skills, attention to detail, decisive, efficient record keeping, excellent communication skills, good interpersonal skills, information handling skills, not squeamish, sound judgement, tactful

Relevant Subjects

Biology, Chemistry, English, Law

Further Information

Coroners Officers Association (COA) - www.coronersofficer.org.uk

Coroners' Society of England and Wales - http:// www.coronersociety.org.uk

Ministry of Justice - www.justice.gov.uk

Skills for Justice - sector skills council for the UK justice system - www.skillsforjustice.com

TARGETjobs: Law (GTI Specialist Publishing Ltd.) - www.groupgti.com

▶Working in politics & law (2010) (Babcock Lifeskills) - www.babcock-lifeskills.com/

Addresses

Coroners' Service for Northern Ireland
Mays Chambers, 72 May Street, Belfast BT1 3JL
Phone: +44 (0)28 9044 6800
Web: www.coronersni.gov.uk/index.htm

Similar Jobs

Barrister, Doctor: Hospital, Police Officer, Solicitor

Costume Designer

CRCI:Design, Arts and Crafts
CLCI:EJ — Job Band: 3 to 5

Job Description

Costume designers research, design and prepare costumes for theatrical, film and TV productions. They study the script and take location, background and historical/period aspects into account, before producing ideas and sketches. May be required to travel nationally or internationally for research and ideas. Also use the Internet for research. Designers work closely with the director of photography, artistic director, production team, make-up artists and actors.

Usually present their designs using illustrations, either by hand or increasingly through computer aided design (CAD) and applications such as Adobe Photoshop. Also provide fabric samples for each design. May decide to create a dedicated costume workshop for an individual production. Then organise the hire or purchase of costumes if necessary, as well as arranging for the making of costumes by the wardrobe department or a tailor/ dressmaker. They often need to produce designs for wigs and may also need to buy accessories such as hats, scarves, jewellery, shoes or gloves.

Designers work within an agreed budget and work schedule. They are responsible for the return of hired costumes and for the sale or disposal of in-house costumes and accessories that are no longer required.

Work Details

Work around 39 hrs a week in a studio, office or sometimes from home, though hours vary according to deadlines. Weekend and evening work is also possible. Employment is with theatre, ballet, opera, repertory, advertising companies, TV, video and film companies throughout the UK, with major employers in the West End (London) and other UK major cities. Travel may be needed when searching for materials and accessories. Sometimes, costume designers in TV and film-making may be required to go on tour with a production, or work on location away from home.

Work involves coordinating a team of staff, including commercial hire companies, specialist craftspeople and the wardrobe staff who make the clothes and check the fit of each costume. There are usually frequent rehearsals and meetings with the director, production team and actors. Costume designers may work on more than one production at a time.

Qualification

• England, Wales and Northern Ireland

Band 3: For entry to jobs, HNC or a relevant Diploma, usually at least 4 GCSEs (A*-C) including English and maths, or equivalent. For some diploma in foundation studies courses: usually at least 5 GCSEs (A*-C) or equivalent.

Band 4: For diploma in foundation studies (art and design): usually at least one A level and 4 GCSEs (A*-C) usually including English and maths, or equivalent. For BTEC higher national award: a BTEC national award, successful completion of a foundation studies course, or equivalent qualification.

Band 5: For degree courses: 2-3 A levels and some GCSEs (A*-C) usually including English and maths, or equivalent qualifications. Most students take a foundation studies course first. An advanced creative and media diploma may be considered as an alternative to A levels for entry to some higher education courses. Exact requirements depend on the degree to be taken.

• Scotland

Band 3: For entry: usually at least four S grades (1-3), including English and maths, or similar.

Band 4: For entry to SQA higher national and professional development awards, usually 2-3 H grades and some S grades (1-3), including English and maths, or similar qualifications.

Band 5: For degree courses: 3-5 H grades and some S grades (1-3), usually including English and maths, or similar qualifications. Exact requirements depend on the degree you take.

Degree Information

Degrees in costume design/interpretation, performance design, design and applied arts and theatre costume are relevant. Graduates in any art and design subject may be acceptable, but have to gain experience and build up a portfolio of work. Postgraduate courses in costume are also available.

Adult Qualifications

Mature applicants with outstanding portfolios of work may be accepted for courses without the standard entry requirements. There are Access and foundation studies courses in art and design in some areas, which give adults without qualifications a route into degree courses. Check with individual colleges.

Work Experience

Entry to this job/career is highly competitive and it is necessary that you have some relevant work or voluntary experience before applying. Experience in drama productions and dressmaking is an advantage. It is essential that you gain an understanding of how different kinds of lighting, camera lenses, film stock and movement affect costumes.

Work or voluntary experience with local amateur theatrical groups, film companies or with drama productions at school or college, is extremely valuable. It may be possible to gain work experience with a theatrical costumier or supplier, or a textile design/manufacturing company.

Entry and Training

The role of a costume designer is not an entry-level position and most have gained knowledge and experience, together with a relevant foundation degree or BA honours degree in fashion, costume design or interpretation. A portfolio of art and design work is needed, which must be kept up to date throughout your career. Some full-time courses may include a practical placement.

Full and part-time foundation degrees are available in subjects that include fashion, costume construction for stage and screen, costume design and interpretation and applied art and design. A Diploma/Welsh Baccalaureate may be available in your area in creative and media and this may provide a route onto higher education courses. There is also an apprenticeship in sewn products at level 2 and an advanced apprenticeship in apparel at level 3 which may be available in your area.

Many costume designers, having gained their qualifications, begin their career as a trainee or costume assistant in the wardrobe department of a theatre. You need good knowledge of period costume, a high standard of creative ability and skills in design-related software such as Photoshop. Others have previously worked for a maker or supplier of theatrical or fancy dress costumes (costumier). You may be able to enter the film and television industry through a new entrants' training scheme. The BBC runs a one-year Design Trainee scheme to give talented young designers an introduction to the television, film and interactive design industry.

Another entry route is to transfer from the fashion industry, or with a drama degree that includes a high content of wardrobe or costume. A careers information pack for opportunities within the broadcasting film/video industry is available from Skillset, the profession's training organisation.

Mature applicants with relevant experience from a design workshop or studio, or costume department in an amateur/professional theatre, together with a good portfolio of work, are welcomed. Courses can be full or part time and some are run in the evening.

Opportunities and Pay

This is a highly competitive area and you need to gain early experience and qualifications to succeed. Personal contacts, initiative, talent and flair are important and may help you to gain promotion. When in full-time employment with the larger film, theatre and TV production/broadcasting organisations, you may progress to senior positions, including head of costume design. Self-employment is usual, working on a freelance basis for film and television production companies, theatre production companies or producers of music videos and commercials. Some designers work as a partner in a consultancy. It is also possible to work as a lecturer in colleges and drama schools, though you usually require a teaching qualification.

Income varies according to the type of employment, ability and reputation. Starting salaries in the theatre are around £18k-£22k a year, rising to around £25k-£40k with experience. Earnings in film and television can be much higher than in theatre, but pay depends on experience, the type of production and the budget available. Freelance designers can earn £3k-£6k per production. Some successful designers earn more than £50k a year. Equity can provide information on rates for working in the theatre and the Broadcasting Entertainment Cinematograph and Theatre Union (BECTU) for working in film and televison.

Health

Colour co-ordination may be difficult for those who do not have normal colour vision.

Skills and Qualities

able to cope under pressure, attention to detail, creative flair, drawing ability, eye for shape/colour, eye for visual effect, good interpersonal skills, good organisational skills, resourceful, specialist IT skills

Relevant Subjects
Art and Design, English, History, Media and communication studies, Performing arts

Further Information
AGCAS: Fashion & Design (Job Sector Briefing) (AGCAS) - www.prospects.ac.uk

BBC Design Vision Careers - www.bbc.co.uk/design/careers

Chartered Society of Designers (Chartered Society of Designers) - www.csd.org.uk

Costume Society - www.costumesociety.org.uk

Creative & Cultural Skills - sector skills council for advertising, crafts, cultural heritage, design, literature, music, performing & visual arts - www.ccskills.org.uk

Design Uncovered (Trotman 2009) - www.trotman.co.uk

Diplomas (Foundation, Higher and Advanced) - http://yp.direct.gov.uk/diplomas

Future Textiles - www.futuretextiles.co.uk

Get into Theatre - www.getintotheatre.org

Skillset - sector skills council for the creative media, fashion and textiles industries - www.skillset.org

▶Working in art & design (2009) (Babcock Lifeskills) - www.babcock-lifeskills.com/

▶Working in creative & media (2007) (Babcock Lifeskills) - www.babcock-lifeskills.com/

▶Working in fashion & clothing (2008) (Babcock Lifeskills) - www.babcock-lifeskills.com/

Addresses
BECTU
(Broadcasting Entertainment Cinematographic and Theatre Union)
373-377 Clapham Road, London SW9 9BT
Phone: +44 (0)207 346 0900
Web: www.bectu.org.uk

Equity
Guild House, Upper St Martin's Lane, London WC2H 9EG
Phone: +44 (0)20 7379 6000
Web: www.equity.org.uk

Society of British Theatre Designers (SBTD)
Theatre Design Department, Rose Bruford College,
Burnt Oak Lane, Sidcup DA15 9DF
Phone: +44 (0)20 8308 2664
Web: www.theatredesign.org.uk

Similar Jobs
Fashion Designer, Film/TV & Theatre Wardrobe Assistant, Film/TV & Theatre Wardrobe Supervisor, Hat Designer, Textile Designer, Wig Maker

Counsellor

CRCI:Social Work and Counselling Services
CLCI:KEK Job Band: 4 to 5

Job Description
Counsellors help people to explore, understand and come to terms with their personal problems. They give clients the opportunity to work through their feelings, by offering them time, attention and support, in complete confidence. Enable clients to talk freely, improve their self esteem, develop better relationships and discover more satisfactory ways of living. Usually work on a one-to-one basis and have to gain the client's confidence. May work in a specialist area such as victim support, health (including terminal illness), marriage guidance, bereavement or education, such as student counselling.

Work Details
Usually works a 37 hr week that may include some evenings and weekends. Most work part time and contact time with clients is recommended by professional bodies to be a maximum of 20 hours. This job can be emotionally demanding and stressful at times, as you work with people who are upset, in need of assistance, or perhaps depressed. The work involves listening and providing encouragement and support. People tell you things that are confidential and you need to have a non-judgemental attitude.

Qualification
Currently, formal educational qualifications are not essential, though the British Association for Counselling and Psychotherapy (BACP) has stringent ethical guidelines and training for its members. Most employers ask for BACP accreditation.

• England, Wales and Northern Ireland
Band 4: For BTEC higher national award: 1-2 A levels and some GCSEs (A*-C) usually including English and maths, or equivalent.

Band 5: For degree courses: 2-3 A levels and some GCSEs (A*-C) usually including English, maths and sometimes a science subject. Exact requirements depend on the degree you take.

• Scotland
Band 4: For SQA higher national award: usually 2-3 H grades and some S grades (1-3) usually including English, maths and sometimes a science subject, or similar.

Band 5: For degree courses: 3-5 H grades and some S grades (1-3), usually including English, maths and sometimes a science subject. Exact requirements depend on the degree you take.

Degree Information
Any degree is acceptable for entry to this job. There are degrees in counselling, and combined degrees, such as counselling and psychotherapy. Psychology, psychotherapy, sociology, philosophy, anthropology, theology/religious studies, or social work and nursing, provide useful background knowledge. Postgraduate qualifications in counselling are available. Contact the British Psychological Society (BPS) and BACP for details of accredited courses.

Adult Qualifications
Personal qualities, maturity and experience are more important than formal educational qualifications. A degree is sometimes useful, but not always essential. Entry requirements may be relaxed for adults applying for higher education courses. Access or foundation courses give adults without qualifications a route on to degree courses.

Work Experience
Entry to this job is competitive and it is important to do some relevant work or voluntary experience before applying to courses. Relevant work includes anything dealing with people in a helping capacity. Listening skills and observation or direct experience in the caring professions are also useful. Direct observation is not possible because of client confidentiality issues, but it is always useful to discuss the nature of the work directly with a trained counsellor.

You can apply for voluntary work with one of the many organisations, such as Cruse or Relate. Another option is to take part in a short introductory course in counselling to get a good grounding of what work is involved. These are practical, part-time courses that usually last about eight weeks.

Entry and Training
Young people are not usually accepted for training as this work requires a broader experience of life. You can train for this job in a number of ways and most start work as a volunteer. Accreditation by the British Association for Counselling and Psychotherapy

(BACP) is based on training, experience, supervision, development of skills and adherence to the BACP Code of Ethics and Practice. Courses are usually one-year full time or 2-3 years part time.

Courses can lead to a number of professional qualifications such as a postgraduate diploma, a diploma or an MA in counselling. The Institute of Counselling offers a range of courses, including a certificate in counselling theory, certificate in trauma counselling, and diplomas in general counselling skills, and in cognitive behavioural therapy. Contact the BACP for a list of accredited courses. For accredited counselling courses in Scotland you can also contact Counselling & Psychotherapy in Scotland (COSCA).

BACP accreditation can qualify you for membership of other professional bodies, such as the United Kingdom Register of Counsellors (UKRC). Voluntary work in counselling is available with agencies such as Relate (relationship counselling), Cruse (bereavement), the Anxiety Disorders Association and others, who select and train volunteers for counselling work within its own organisation. Some employers may require a Criminal Records Bureau (CRB)/Disclosure Scotland check.

Mature entrants are common as life experience and professional experience in an area of work involving people, such as social work, teaching or nursing, is usually expected.

Opportunities and Pay

The BACP has over 32,000 members and vacancies occur in a broad range of settings. You may be able to find work as a volunteer or possibly in a private practice or on a freelance basis. You can be employed by a voluntary organisation, a school, college or university, the NHS, or you can be self-employed. Promotion prospects vary since there is no clear promotion structure and many counsellors work as volunteers.

Pay can be low, so it may be necessary to have another job or source of income. Salaries vary widely depending on the employer, but range from £15k-£28k a year. Senior counsellors can earn up to £45k a year.

Skills and Qualities

able to communicate effectively, able to inspire confidence, able to understand other people's problems, awareness of confidentiality issues, emotionally strong, good listening skills, non-judgemental, perceptive, reassuring, tactful & discreet

Relevant Subjects

English, Health and social care, Psychology, Sociology

Further Information

Accreditation for Counsellors/Psychotherapists (COSCA) - www.cosca.org.uk/

British Journal of Social Psychology (BPS, quarterly) (British Psychological Society) - www.bpsjournals.co.uk/journals/bjsp

Careers in Counselling (BACP) (BACP) - www.bacp.co.uk/information/education

The Modern World of Counselling (Institute of Counselling) (Institute of Counselling) - www.collegeofcounselling.com

Training in Counselling & Psychotherapy Directory (BACP) (British Association for Counselling & Psychotherapy) - www.bacp.co.uk/information/education

▶Working in advice & counselling (2007) (Babcock Lifeskills) - www.babcock-lifeskills.com/

▶Working in social care (2010) (Babcock Lifeskills) - www.babcock-lifeskills.com/

Addresses

British Association for Counselling and Psychotherapy (BACP)
BACP House, 15 St John's Business Park, Lutterworth, Leicestershire LE17 4HB
Phone: +44 (0)1455 883300
Web: www.bacp.co.uk

British Psychological Society (BPS)
St Andrews House, 48 Princess Road East, Leicester LE1 7DR
Phone: +44 (0)116 254 9568
Web: www.bps.org.uk

Counselling & Psychotherapy in Scotland (COSCA)
16 Melville Terrace, Stirling FK8 2NE
Phone: +44 (0)1786 475 140
Web: www.cosca.org.uk

Institute of Counselling (IC)
40 St Enoch Square, Glasgow G1 4DH
Phone: +44 (0)141 204 2230
Web: www.collegeofcounselling.com

UK Council for Psychotherapy (UKCP)
2nd Floor Edward House , 2 Wakley Street, London EC1V 7LT
Phone: +44 (0)20 7014 9955
Web: www.psychotherapy.org.uk

Similar Jobs

Debt Counsellor, Psychoanalyst, Psychologist, Psychologist: Counselling, Psychotherapist, Social Worker

Countryside Ranger

also known as: Nature Reserve Warden, Warden: Countryside

CRCI:Environment, Animals and Plants
CLCI:WAR
Job Band: 2 to 5

Job Description

Countryside rangers help to manage, protect, maintain and promote areas such as national, regional or country parks, nature reserves, sites of specific scientific interest (SSSIs), and areas of outstanding natural beauty (AONB). They provide environmental information and help people to understand, enjoy and respect forests, hills or parks, as well as other areas of environmental significance, including coastal areas, canals and moorland. Also take visitors on educational guided walks and set up nature trails. Usually look after any rare plants, carry out practical maintenance, plant hedges and trees, lay footpaths, clearsexcess vegetation from river beds/ponds, collect litter, and erect signposts.

May organise or maintain a specific geographic area or nature conservation, such as heathland, wetlands or woodland habitat. Also conserve trees, shrubs, plants, animals, insects and birds within the area and work to enhance their surrounding environment. Rangers make sure people do not damage or disturb the wildlife and habitat and may patrol an area looking for signs of damage and reports on any illegal activities, such as signs of egg stealing from protected birds, or poaching.

Some rangers train and supervise other workers/volunteers who also carry out practical maintenance. They may keep records and lists of the number of plants and animals/birds in the area, and also write reports. Rangers are trained in first aid and help in emergencies, such as fire, floods and mountain rescue.

Work Details

Rangers/wardens normally work around 37-39 hrs a week and may be expected to work weekends. Work is mainly outdoors in all weathers, and you need to travel around the district. You may need to work in an isolated place, sometimes on your own. Some time may be spent in an office or visitor centre and sometimes at night attending meetings, or out observing wildlife. You inform, advise and deal with enquiries, as well as being responsible for security and dealing with people who break rules. Accommodation may be provided with some posts. The work requires a knowledge of any new legal regulations. Work can be very strenuous.

Qualification

No set minimum entry requirements for this job though many rangers/wardens are graduates or hold a relevant HND.

- **England, Wales and Northern Ireland**

Band 2: For entry to jobs, no minimum qualifications are needed, but it is an advantage to have some GCSEs (A*-C) or equivalent in subjects that include English and maths.

Band 3: For entry to jobs, HNC or a relevant Diploma, usually at least 4 GCSEs (A*-C) including English and maths, or equivalent.

Band 4: For HND, Diploma of Higher Education or foundation degree: 1-2 A levels and some GCSEs (A*-C) usually including English and maths, or equivalent.

Band 5: For degree courses: 2-3 A levels and some GCSEs (A*-C) preferably including biology, geography, maths and English, or equivalent. Exact requirements depend on the degree you take so check individual prospectuses.

- **Scotland**

Band 2: Although academic qualifications are not specified for this job, it is an advantage to have some S grades (1-3) in subjects that include English and maths, or similar.

Band 3: For entry to jobs, usually at least four S grades (1-3) including English and maths, or similar.

Band 4: For entry to SQA higher national and professional development awards, usually 2-3 H grades and some S grades (1-3), including English and maths, or similar qualifications.

Band 5: For degree courses: 3-5 H grades and some S grades (1-3), preferably including biology, geography, maths and English. Good H grades are required. Exact requirements depend on the degree you take.

Degree Information

Degrees include countryside management, biological sciences, environmental land management, countryside conservation, geology, geography (physical), geoscience, land and property management, ecology or environmental science.

Adult Qualifications

Qualifications are often not specified, but graduates are increasingly recruited. Entry requirements may be relaxed for adults applying for higher education courses. Access and foundation courses give adults without qualifications a route onto degree courses.

Work Experience

Entry to this job is highly competitive. A strong interest in this type of work is very important and extensive experience of some kind of conservation work is essential. Evidence of commitment to the work is looked for, such as paid or voluntary work in organisations such as the National Trust, RSPB, Groundwork UK and other conservation groups. You can also contact your local council to find out about work experience or work shadowing opportunities.

Entry and Training

Many entrants to this job have HND/degree level qualifications, though others start at a more practical level and work their way up in the job. On-the-job training is usual, perhaps including short specialist courses. Before entry, it is useful to have experience in this field, perhaps through voluntary work. You may also need to have a driving licence, and woodwork skills are also helpful.

An increasing number of applicants for this job now hold qualifications such as an appropriate degree, or a BTEC/SQA diploma, or a City & Guilds award, for example, in environmental conservation or countryside management. Relevant foundation degrees are also available. Organisations such as the National Trust offer 'careerships' that provide a training programme leading to qualifications in environmental conservation.

A Diploma/Welsh Baccalaureate may be available in your area in environment and land-based studies. S/NVQs are available at levels 2-4 in environmental conservation/management. Training programmes, including apprenticeship schemes, may be available in your area. Advanced apprenticeships leading to qualification at level 3 can also be a route into higher education.

Dedication to this type of work is very important and extensive experience of some kind of conservation work is essential. Often, mature people are preferred by some employers. Mature applicants may benefit through training opportunities such as Work Based Learning/Training for Work that may be available in your area. You can gain recognition of previous experience through Accreditation of Prior Learning (APL) or by working towards relevant S/NVQs. Contact your local Connexions or careers office, Jobcentre Plus, Next Step service or Learning and Skills Council (LSC)/Local Enterprise Company (LEC) for details of all training opportunities, apprenticeships and schemes.

Opportunities and Pay

Recently there has been a growth of jobs in all areas to do with the environment, but there has also been an increase in people with qualifications, so entry is very competitive. Most employment is with local authorities. Employment can also be with organisations such as the Forestry Commission, Royal Society for the Protection of Birds (RSPB), National Trust, Nature Conservancy Council, Countryside Council for Wales or the National Trust for Scotland. This job can be seasonal. Promotion prospects depend on the organisation for which you work but you can progress to work as a countryside officer or countryside manager.

Starting salaries are around £15.5k-£18k, rising to £21k-£26k a year. The job may also attract an anti-social hours allowance. You may be given free accommodation and possible use of a vehicle.

Health

Good general fitness and stamina are essential and you will find this job difficult if you have hay fever, or if you are allergic to animals.

Skills and Qualities

able to explain clearly, able to work both on your own and in a team, enjoy working outdoors, friendly but firm manner, good at writing reports, good spoken communication, observant, planning skills, practical skills, responsible attitude, strong interest in the environment

Relevant Subjects

Biology, Geography, Land and Environment, Leisure, travel and tourism, Science

Further Information

Apprenticeship Schemes (National Apprenticeship Service) - www.apprenticeships.org.uk

Countryside Jobs Service - www.countryside-jobs.com

Diplomas (Foundation, Higher and Advanced) - http://yp.direct.gov.uk/diplomas

Environmental Careers (Chartered Institution of Water and Environmental Management) - www.ciwem.org.uk/publications/careers/

Jobs and the Natural Heritage (leaflet) (Scottish Natural Heritage) - www.snh.org.uk/

Lantra - The Sector Skills Council for environmental & land-based sector (Lantra) http:/www.lantra.co.uk

Lantra Careers (A Future In...) (Lantra) - www.afuturein.com

Local Government Careers (Improvement and Development Agency) - www.lgcareers.com/publications/

Scottish Countryside Rangers' Association (SCRA) - www.scra-online.co.uk

Training Schemes - www.direct.gov.uk/en/educationandlearning

Wildlife Trusts http://wildlifetrusts.org

▶Working in cultural heritage (2007) (Babcock Lifeskills) - www.babcock-lifeskills.com/

Addresses

Countryside Council for Wales
Maes-y-Ffynnon, Penrhosgarnedd, Bangor, Gwynedd LL57 2DW
Phone: 0845 130 6229 (UK only)
Web: www.ccw.gov.uk

Countryside Management Association (CMA)
Writtle College Lordship Road Writtle, Chelmsford, Essex CM1 3RR
Phone: +44 (0)1245 424116
Web: www.countrysidemanagement.org.uk

Groundwork UK
Lockside, 5 Scotland Street, Birmingham B1 2RR
Phone: +44 (0)121 236 8565
Web: www.groundwork.org.uk

National Trust
Heelis, Kemble Drive, Swindon, Wiltshire SN2 2NA
Phone: +44 (0)1793 817400
Web: www.ntjobs.org.uk

Northern Ireland Environment Agency
Contact via website/telephone,
Phone: 0845 302 0008
Web: www.ni-environment.gov.uk

Scottish Natural Heritage (SNH)
Great Glen House Leachkin Road, Inverness IV3 8NW
Phone: +44 (0)1463 725000
Web: www.snh.gov.uk/

Similar Jobs

Arboriculturist, Countryside/Conservation Officer/Manager, Forest Officer, Forest Worker, Gamekeeper, Horticultural Manager

Countryside/Conservation Officer/Manager

also known as: Environmental Conservation Officer/Manager, Nature Conservationist, Woodlands Officer: Local Government

CRCI:Environment, Animals and Plants
CLCI:WAR Job Band: 4 to 5

Job Description

Countryside conservation officers are environmental specialists who are involved in the management, conservation and protection of the natural habitat of animals, trees and plants. They aim to promote public awareness of their natural environment, including areas such as country parks, nature reserves, woodlands, fishing areas, sites of specific scientific interest (SSSIs), areas of natural beauty (AONB) and rights of way. They encourage visitors to the countryside and promote a responsible attitude to their surroundings. Also study the effects of modern developments on the environment, advise on planning applications and are concerned with all aspects of countryside preservation and protection.

Conservation officers investigate ways in which farming procedures (eg the use of pesticides) or construction projects (eg laying of pipelines or road construction) interact with plant and animal life. They also examine changes in the balance of nature. May research and prepare legal or scientific report, write press releases and other publications such as information leaflets.

They advise the public and liaise with other scientists, the government and its agencies, landowners, organisations, economists and planners on nature conservation and environmental protection practice. Also enforce countryside and environmental regulations. May manage other workers including rangers, wardens and volunteers.

Officers may also manage and develop a visitor centre, gift shop and/or cafi on certain sites. At manager level, they are likely to have overall responsibility of a budget and other financial aspects relating to the management of the countryside and employee.

Work Details

Officers usually work 37-40 hrs a week, but in practice may work long and irregular hours, attending evening meetings or observing wildlife at night. Work can be in an office, a laboratory and out on fieldwork. Travel around the district is necessary. You inform, advise and consult with people, write reports and also have to cope with some physical activity eg when out on fieldwork.

Qualification

No set minimum entry requirements for this job though many countryside/conservation officers/managers are graduates, often with postgraduate (MSc/PhD) qualifications.

• England, Wales and Northern Ireland

Band 4: For HND, Diploma of Higher Education or foundation degree: 1-2 A levels and some GCSEs (A*-C) usually including English and maths, or equivalent.

Band 5: For degree courses: 2-3 A levels, including science subjects, and some GCSEs (A*-C) usually including English and maths, or equivalent. Exact requirements depend on the degree you take.

• Scotland

Band 4: For entry to SQA higher national and professional development awards, usually 2-3 H grades and some S grades (1-3), including English and maths, or similar qualifications.

Band 5: For degree courses: 3-5 H grades, including science subjects, and some S grades (1-3), usually including English and maths, or similar qualifications. Exact requirements depend on the degree you take.

Degree Information

Degrees include environmental sciences, countryside/environmental management, sustainable development, biology, ecology, conservation, surveying or geography. A relevant postgraduate course or higher degree is an advantage. For those with a relevant first degree, a postgraduate qualification in management can be useful. Those without a relevant first degree should take a postgraduate qualification in conservation, land management, ecology or similar.

Adult Qualifications

A degree is required unless you have considerable experience in conservation or natural history. Entry standards may be relaxed for adults applying for degree courses. Foundation and Access courses in science may be available. Check with the university concerned.

Work Experience

Entry to this job is highly competitive and it is essential that you have some relevant work or voluntary experience before applying for jobs. Evidence of commitment to the work is looked for, such as paid or voluntary work with organisations such as the British Trust for Conservation Volunteers, National Trust, Groundwork UK and other conservation/heritage groups. Membership of organisations such as the Wildlife Trusts can also be an advantage. Many degree courses offer vacation opportunities or placements during the course.

Entry and Training

Many countryside/conservation officers/managers are graduates, often with postgraduate (MSc/PhD) qualifications. Foundation degrees are available in aspects of environmental conservation. Part-time study for an MSc/PhD may be offered through distance learning from a university or the Open University (OU).

It may be possible to start in a lower-level job, such as a ranger/warden and work your way up. Whatever level you start at, considerable experience is often needed in conservation eg voluntary work with organisations that include the British Trust for Conservation Volunteers (BTCV), Groundwork UK, the Royal Society for the Protection of Birds or the National Trust. Knowledge of geographical information systems (GIS) is useful. It can also be an advantage to be able to drive as you may need to drive a 4x4 vehicle.

In-service training is provided by your employer on such topics as report writing, public speaking, time management, legal aspects, in-depth study of a particular habitat or species, and information technology. Courses on specialist topics are provided by organisations like the BTCV or the Field Studies Council. The Countryside Management Association (CMA) offers professional accreditation as well as a programme of continuing professional development (CPD).

A Diploma/Welsh Baccalaureate may be available in your area in environment and land-based studies. S/NVQs are available at levels 2-4 in environmental conservation/management.

Mature entrants require extensive experience and knowledge of natural history and conservation. Previous experience/ qualifications in planning, landscape/leisure management or teaching is helpful. There are suitable open learning and correspondence courses available such as Open University courses. Funding for courses may be available from the Nuffield Farming Scholarships Trust.

Opportunities and Pay

Over 50,000 people are employed by conservation organisations in the UK, with another 200,000 working as volunteers. Jobs are available only in certain areas, but, although this is a growing profession, competition is fierce among well-qualified and experienced applicants. Employment can be with a research organisation, a professional/voluntary organisation, local government, or a central government agency, such as English Nature, Countryside Agency, Scottish Natural Heritage, the Northern Ireland Environment Agency, Countryside Council for Wales, and national parks. Other opportunities are with charitable organisations such as Wildlife Trusts, Woodland Trusts, Royal Society for the Protection of Birds, the National Trust, and at field study centres.

Often qualified and experienced officers take on more management duties. Some become scientific specialists/ researchers, or advisors for wildlife or conservation trusts and other professional organisations and businesses. Some move into journalism, lecturing and teaching, and overseas work is often available.

Pay varies widely depending on the employer and level of responsibility. Starting salaries are around £14k-£17k, rising with experience to £28k-£30k a year.

Health

There is an allergy risk from pollen, animals or birds. This job may require good colour vision for certain areas of work.

Skills and Qualities

able to manage a budget and keep records, aptitude for fieldwork, confident, enthusiastic, good organisational skills, good spoken communication, good written English, information handling skills, IT skills, scientific approach, strong interest in the environment

Relevant Subjects

Biology, Chemistry, English, Geography, Land and Environment, Science

Further Information

AGCAS: Environment & Agriculture (Job Sector Briefing) (AGCAS) - www.prospects.ac.uk

Countryside Jobs Service - www.countryside-jobs.com

Diplomas (Foundation, Higher and Advanced) - http://yp.direct.gov.uk/diplomas

Environmental Careers (Chartered Institution of Water and Environmental Management) - www.ciwem.org.uk/publications/careers/

Jobs and the Natural Heritage (leaflet) (Scottish Natural Heritage) - www.snh.org.uk/

Lantra - The Sector Skills Council for environmental & land-based sector (Lantra) http:/www.lantra.co.uk

Lantra Careers (A Future In...) (Lantra) - www.afuturein.com

Local Government Careers (Improvement and Development Agency) - www.lgcareers.com/publications/

Nuffield Farming Scholarships Trust (Nuffield Farming Scholarships Trust) - www.nuffieldscholar.org

▶Working outdoors (2010) (Babcock Lifeskills) - www.babcock-lifeskills.com/

▶Working with animals (2009) (Babcock Lifeskills) - www.babcock-lifeskills.com/

Addresses

British Trust for Conservation Volunteers (BTCV)
Sedum House, Mallard Way, Doncaster DN4 8DB
Phone: +44 (0)1302 388 883
Web: http://www2.btcv.org.uk

Countryside Council for Wales
Maes-y-Ffynnon, Penrhosgarnedd, Bangor, Gwynedd LL57 2DW
Phone: 0845 130 6229 (UK only)
Web: www.ccw.gov.uk

Countryside Management Association (CMA)
Writtle College Lordship Road Writtle, Chelmsford, Essex CM1 3RR
Phone: +44 (0)1245 424116
Web: www.countrysidemanagement.org.uk

Field Studies Council (FSC)
Preston Montford Montford Bridge, Shrewsbury, Shropshire SY4 1HW
Phone: 0845 345 4071 (UK only)
Web: www.field-studies-council.org

Groundwork UK
Lockside, 5 Scotland Street, Birmingham B1 2RR
Phone: +44 (0)121 236 8565
Web: www.groundwork.org.uk

Northern Ireland Environment Agency
Contact via website/telephone,
Phone: 0845 302 0008
Web: www.ni-environment.gov.uk

Scottish Natural Heritage (SNH)
Great Glen House Leachkin Road, Inverness IV3 8NW
Phone: +44 (0)1463 725000
Web: www.snh.gov.uk/

Similar Jobs

Agricultural Research Scientist, Arboriculturist, Biologist, Countryside Ranger, Farm Manager, Forest Officer

Courier

also known as: Dispatch Rider, Motorcycle Courier

CRCI:Transport and Logistics
CLCI:YAT — Job Band: 1

Job Description

Couriers collect letters, packages and parcels for a customer and deliver them on the same day, usually within the same area such as a large town or city. They contact a controller in an employer's office, often using a mobile phone or hand-held computer to ask for job details. Travel to the collection point to collect item and delivery instructions, then travel to drop-off point, hand over the item and collect a signature. Couriers complete work sheet on paper or computer and communicate with office for next job. Cyclists usually work in the central area of large towns and cities carrying items between offices, shops, factories and private homes.

Motorcyclists may travel from town to town or carry larger parcels within a town. Van couriers may travel greater distances. Some personal couriers take packages by air, either within the UK, or abroad.

Work Details
Most couriers work during the day from Monday to Friday, but many companies operate 24 hrs each day and you may need to be on call during unsocial hours. You are outside in all weathers. There is a risk of road traffic accidents, especially in busy city centres. Couriers usually wear their own clothes, suitable for riding, and a protective helmet. A company provides a jacket and satchel for carrying parcels.

You need to have a good knowledge of your area and be able to travel quickly from place to place, even through heavy traffic. Map reading skills are essential, although satellite navigation is widely used.

Qualification
- **England, Wales and Northern Ireland**

Band 1: No minimum qualifications are required, but you are expected to have a good level of general education. However, some formal/vocational qualifications, especially in English and maths, at any level are useful.

- **Scotland**

Band 1: No minimum qualifications are required, but you are expected to have a good level of general education. However, some formal/vocational qualifications, especially in English and maths, at any level are useful.

Adult Qualifications
This job is often done by people with a wide variety of work experience, so there are opportunities for adults. Those without existing qualifications can work through the Foundation Learning programme by taking credit-based units and qualifications.

Work Experience
Relevant work or voluntary experience can equip you with skills that you can use in the future and add to your CV. Driving experience is essential, particularly if this is with a range of different vehicles.

Entry and Training
Due to the high cost of insurance, motorcycle couriers usually need to be at least 18, and to have a full motorcycle licence or have the compulsory basic training (CBT) qualification. It is helpful to be able to read maps and to know the area well. Training is on the job with an experienced courier, though courier training schemes may be available in some areas. It is possible to find work as a bicycle courier under the age of 18. You need your own cycle or motorcycle for some jobs.

There are private fee-paying companies that offer short training courses for various aspects of the job, including law and insurance, communication facilities, and code of conduct. With an employer, you may be able to work towards S/NVQs, such as carry and deliver goods at level 2 and driving goods vehicles at levels 2 and 3.

Employers prefer more experienced couriers over 21 (or over 25 for van driving) due to the high cost of motor insurance. Government training opportunities, such as apprenticeships, may be available in your area. You can also gain recognition of previous experience through Accreditation of Prior Learning or by working towards relevant S/NVQs. Contact your local careers office, Jobcentre Plus, Next Step service or Learning and Skills Council (LSC)/Local Enterprise Company (LEC) for details of training schemes. Courier Training offers free training in bicycle and motorcycle work for registered job seekers over 18 in London.

Opportunities and Pay
There are about 98,000 couriers in the UK, employed by companies offering a fast delivery service. They work in most major cities, some are large companies with offices throughout the UK but many are small local firms. Work is irregular and depends on the amount of work the company can get. The economic downturn may have affected the volume of work available for couriers.

Cyclists and motorcyclists are often self-employed, provide their own transport and are responsible for the maintenance and insurance of their bikes. Van drivers are usually employed by a company and earn a regular wage. Although there are few promotions, opportunities for self-employment running your own business are good. It is possible to become a member of the National Courier Association in the UK. Consult the website for further details.

You have to be able to move quickly, and have a good knowledge of an area as you may only be paid for the number of deliveries you do. Earnings vary a great deal, especially if you are self employed. Employed and experienced couriers/riders earn from £14k-£20k a year and some can expect to earn up to £30k, especially in London.

Health
You have to be fit to be a courier, particularly if you are riding a bicycle all day.

Skills and Qualities
able to follow instructions, able to work to deadlines, able to work well on your own, good communication skills, honest, punctual, reliable, safety conscious, technical aptitude

Further Information
AGCAS: Transport and Logistics (Job Sector Briefing) (AGCAS) - www.prospects.ac.uk
Courier Training - www.couriertraining.co.uk
Foundation Learning (QCDA) - www.qcda.gov.uk
National Courier Association (NCA) - www.thenca.co.uk
Skills for Logistics - sector skills council for freight logistics industries - www.skillsforlogistics.org
Training Schemes - www.direct.gov.uk/en/educationandlearning

Addresses
Despatch Association
Lamb's End House 36 Church Road Magdelen, King's Lynn, Norfolk PE34 3DG
Phone: +44 (0)1553 813 479
Web: www.despatch.co.uk/index.html

Institute of Couriers (IOC)
Green Man Tower 332 Goswell Road Islington, London EC1V 7LQ
Phone: 0845 601 0245 (UK only)
Web: www.ioc.uk.com

Similar Jobs
Chauffeur/Chauffeuse, Driver: Taxi/Minicab, Driver: Van, Postal Worker

Court Administrative Officer/Assistant
CRCI:Legal and Political Services
CLCI:LAG
Job Band: 2 to 3

Job Description
Court administrative officers carry out the clerical and administrative work of the courts. The UK has two legal systems, one in England, Wales and N. Ireland, and a separate one in Scotland. The House of Lords is the highest court in the land and covers all UK countries.

The roles of the job vary depending on the type of court the administrator works in, but may include the following: setting dates and times of cases, sending out related paperwork, allocating cases to court rooms, and following up judgements to include issuing orders or collecting fines. They deal with enquiries, mail and filing of documents. They also collect statistics and input data on a computer. In England, Wales and N. Ireland, administrators also ensure that appropriate court costs are paid by the defendant and prosecutor.

Court administrative officers carry out the clerical and administrative work of the courts. The UK has two legal systems, one in England, Wales and N. Ireland, and a separate one in Scotland. The House of Lords is the highest court in the land and covers all UK countries.

Court administrative officers carry out the clerical and administrative work of the Scottish Court Service (SCS), which consists of the Sheriff Courts, the Supreme Courts (including the Court of Session, the Accountant of Court's Office, and the High Court of Justiciary) and the headquarters offices. They have a variety of clerical/administrative tasks according to the area of SCS work, including setting dates and times of cases, sending out all paperwork needed for a case, following up judgements, answering phone enquiries and allocating rooms.

Administrators may also deal face to face with members of the public, who may be angry or upset. May also calculate and collect legal fees, as well as handle warrants, summonses and items of evidence.

Work Details

You usually work 37hrs a week, Monday to Friday, though sometimes you are required to work evenings or weekends if there is a special hearing. Your base is an office, with perhaps time spent in court, and you are likely to work in a team of around 12 people. You help to process the court's paperwork, which has to be dealt with quickly, accurately and efficiently. The courts are often very busy and you need to work well under pressure. You deal with enquiries from the public, both in person and by phone, and with defendants and solicitors, as well as with the justices' clerk or justices' chief executive.

You usually work 37-40 hrs a week, Monday to Friday, and is based in an office, with time also spent in court. The day-to-day work of the courts involves paperwork, which has to be dealt with quickly, accurately and efficiently. The work includes handling enquiries from members of the public, both in person and by phone/email. You may be involved in financial and accounting work and you often work under pressure, since the courts are very busy. Part-time work and job-sharing are possible.

Qualification

• England, Wales and Northern Ireland

Band 2: For entry as an assistant: 2-3 GCSEs (A*-C) including English and preferably maths, or equivalent qualification.

Band 3: For an officer: usually 5 GCSEs (A*-C) including English and preferably maths, or equivalent.

• Scotland

Band 2: For entry as an assistant: two S grades (1-3) including English and maths, or similar qualifications.

Band 3: For an officer: usually five S grades (1-3) including English and maths, or similar.

Adult Qualifications

Mature applicants are welcomed, especially those with relevant experience.

Work Experience

Any work experience can equip you with skills that you can use in the future and add to your CV. This can either be unpaid or voluntary, or can be holiday or part-time work that you have organised yourself. It is useful to visit a court to observe the proceedings and to gain some experience in clerical work and office administration.

Entry and Training

Entry to this work is usually with GCSEs, but some entrants have A levels or equivalent. Training is usually on the job, with an experienced colleague together with locally organised short courses. You may be given the opportunity to study for a relevant qualification, such as an NVQ. However, many people doing this job are working towards other legal training.

Applicants to the civil service must satisfy strict nationality and residency requirements. Entry to court jobs is very competitive. An interest in law is useful and good typing and/or administrative skills are important. An interview and Disclosure Scotland check form part of the selection criteria. Training is mostly on the job, gaining experience of different functions within the office. The Scottish Court Services (SCS) offer customised vocational qualifications according to the area and nature of the job. It is possible to move into court work from other civil service jobs. Vacancies are listed on the SCS website.

There are SVQs in court administration and court operation at levels 2-3.

Mature entry is common and clerical/administrative experience is an advantage, and in particular work in law or other related offices. Mature entrants with relevant experience in similar civil service, or with proven administrative skills, have an advantage.

Opportunities and Pay

Opportunities exist throughout the UK, though the number of staff is stable in most areas. In England and Wales you work for Her Majesty's Courts Service and in Northern Ireland the Northern Ireland Court Service.

There are opportunities to gain promotion from assistant to officer level, and then to executive officer or supervisory posts, through training, experience and merit. Prospects are greater if you are able to move to another area. Part-time work, flexitime and job sharing are possible. Some court administrative officers move on to other legal work such as that of a legal executive.

Pay varies depending on location and employer. Assistants start at around £12k rising to £15k a year with experience. Officers are likely to start at around £14k-£15k rising to £19k-£20k a year with experience.

Scottish court staff are civil service employees who work for the Scottish Court Service, which is an executive department that is part of the Scottish Executive Justice Department. There are over 100 staff employed at present. There are promotion opportunities within the civil service structure, though these may involve moving to another area. Some court administrative officers choose to move into paralegal work (see job profile).

Pay varies depending on location and employer. Assistants start at around £12k rising to £15k a year with experience. Officers are likely to start at around £14k-£15k rising to £19k-£20k a year with experience.

Health

Entrants may be required to have a health and fitness assessment on appointment as part of the civil service recruitment procedure.

Skills and Qualities

able to explain clearly, able to get on with all kinds of people, able to work both on your own and in a team, customer service skills, discreet, good communication skills, good organisational skills, IT skills, tactful

Relevant Subjects

Business and accounting, English, Law

Further Information

Criminal Justice System (CJS) - www.cjsonline.gov.uk

Skills for Justice - sector skills council for the UK justice system - www.skillsforjustice.com

▶Working in politics & law (2010) (Babcock Lifeskills) - www.babcock-lifeskills.com/

Addresses

Her Majesty's Courts Service (HMCS)
Customer Service Unit, Post Post 1.40, 1st Floor, 102 Petty France, London SW1H 9AJ
Phone: 0845 4568770 (UK only)
Web: www.hmcourts-service.gov.uk

Northern Ireland Court Service
Information Centre Communications Group Laganside House
23-27 Oxford Street, Belfast BT1 3LA
Phone: +44 (0) 28 9032 8594
Web: www.courtsni.gov.uk

Scottish Courts Service (SCS)
Saughton House Broomhouse Drive, Edinburgh EH11 3XD
Phone: +44 (0)131 444 3300
Web: www.scotcourts.gov.uk

Similar Jobs

Barristers' Clerk, Civil Service Administrative Assistant, Court Usher, Local Government Administrative Assistant, Local Government Administrator

Court Reporter

also known as: Stenographer, Verbatim Reporter

CRCI:Legal and Political Services
CLCI:LAG Job Band: 3 to 4

Job Description

Court reporters attend court hearings and use a stenograph machine or palantype to take down a complete record of the court proceedings for immediate and future reference. They must be able to work at high speed, usually at around 200 words per minute. Some may use computerised shorthand machines or computer-linked stenography, though computer-aided transcription (CAT) is more usual. They may also check legal details in libraries. Some work for political conferences or public inquiries, industrial tribunals, or may record live parliamentary debates.

Many reporters are bilingual and their work may take them to countries outside the UK. Reporters who provide a 'live' facility for the deaf or hearing impaired are speech-to-text (STT) real-time reporters, who work in the courts, in parliament, or for TV and theatre live captioning.

Work Details

You work 35-37 hrs a week, Monday to Friday, though the hours are variable since the courts can continue sitting into the evening. Usually, court sessions are between 10am and 4.30pm but can start earlier. Travel is expected as you need to go to the place of a court hearing. After the day's proceedings, transcription work sometimes may have to be done in the evenings, either in the office or at home. You have to be able to sit, concentrating fully, for long periods of time. The work is very demanding. Smart dress is expected in court.

Qualification

- **England, Wales and Northern Ireland**

Band 3: Entry requirements can vary and sometimes no formal qualifications are required. However, most courses and employers ask for up to 5 GCSEs (A*-C) including English, or equivalent qualifications.

Band 4: Many successful applicants for courses and for jobs have one or more A levels, or equivalent, and some GCSEs (A*-C) including English, or equivalent.

- **Scotland**

Band 3: Entry requirements can vary and sometimes no formal qualifications are required. However, most courses and employers ask for at least 3-4 S grades (1-3) and preferably more, including English and maths, or similar qualifications.

Band 4: Many successful applicants for courses and for jobs have one or more H grades, or equivalent, and some S grades (1-3) including English and maths, or similar qualifications.

Adult Qualifications

Many firms prefer mature entrants. It is an advantage to have qualifications/experience in word-processing, shorthand, typing or legal/medical secretarial work.

Work Experience

Relevant work or voluntary experience is always useful and can improve your chances of entering this job. Consider work experience with professions or companies linked to law and current affairs. It is helpful to visit the courts and become familiar with the processes and procedures involved. Experience or college courses that use and improve on your word processing or typing skills, shorthand or secretarial skills are also an advantage. It is also important to demonstrate your listening skills and your ability to handle information.

Entry and Training

Shorthand and typing courses are a useful starting point, but experience in shorthand, though useful, is not essential, except in Scotland. You must have a high standard of English language (vocabulary, grammar, spelling and punctuation). In England and Wales, companies usually expect new entrants to have taken courses and have qualifications in machine shorthand/stenotyping and to have a minimum speed of 160 to 180 words per minute (wpm) and 200+ wpm for real-time reporting.

A list of colleges with full-time or distance-learning courses can be obtained from the British Institute of Verbatim Reporters (BIVR). Training takes around two years. Membership of the BIVR requires a minimum shorthand speed of 180 wpm and an examination pass that demonstrates your ability to produce a transcript. Some companies may take trainees. For all new entrants, there is usually an on-the-job training period of three months to one year.

There are currently no specific training courses in Scotland. A certificate in shorthand with a minimum speed of 120 wpm is usually required. Further training is usually done on the job with an experienced reporter, gaining practice, increasing speeds and becoming familiar with court procedures.

Those who are members of the BIVR can apply for training with Signature (formerly the Council for the Advancement of Communication with Deaf People) in speech to text (STT) reporting. Signature is currently developing a level 3 qualification.

Mature entrants are usually those who already have skills and experience in shorthand and general secretarial work. Those who have legal secretarial work have an advantage. A list of colleges with full-time or distance-learning courses can be obtained from the British Institute of Verbatim Reporters.

Opportunities and Pay

There are currently around 600 court reporters working in the UK. They are usually self-employed, and may work part-time. Freelance reporters work for firms that are contracted to provide a service to the courts. In England and Wales, many firms are based in London, though some firms are in towns with a Crown Court. It is possible to move into working for Hansard which produces reports of the daily proceedings in the House of Commons and House of Lords.

Reporters may also work at conferences, or in providing subtitles or captions for broadcasting and in the theatre. Police forces in some areas are now using verbatim reporters to record interviews instead of taping an interview.

There is a shortage of court reporters in England and Wales. However, there are only a few firms in Scotland and these cover the whole country. Opportunities in Scotland are decreasing because proceedings in court are taped.

Salaries vary considerably though usually start at £12k rising to £20k a year. Highly skilled freelance reporters can make £40-£300 per day. Most court reporters provide their own machine, which can be expensive new, but may also be available second hand.

Health
You must have good hearing to do this job.

Skills and Qualities
able to report accurately, able to work quickly, able to work to deadlines, good concentration level, good listening skills, good written English, information handling skills, IT skills, keyboard/typing skills, understanding of legal technicalities

Relevant Subjects
English, ICT/Computer studies, Law

Further Information
Sorene Court Reporting and Training Services - www.sorene.co.uk
▶Working in politics & law (2010) (Babcock Lifeskills) - www.babcock-lifeskills.com/

Addresses
British Institute of Verbatim Reporters (BIVR)
The Secretary , 73 Alicia Gardens, Kenton, Harrow HA3 8JD
Phone: +44 (0)20 8907 5820
Web: www.bivr.org.uk

Her Majesty's Courts Service (HMCS)
Customer Service Unit, Post Post 1.40, 1st Floor, 102 Petty France, London SW1H 9AJ
Phone: 0845 4568770 (UK only)
Web: www.hmcourts-service.gov.uk

Scottish Courts Service (SCS)
Saughton House Broomhouse Drive, Edinburgh EH11 3XD
Phone: +44 (0)131 444 3300
Web: www.scotcourts.gov.uk

Signature
Mersey House Mandale Business Park Belmont, Durham DH1 1TH
Phone: +44 (0) 191 383 1155
Web: www.signature.org.uk/

Similar Jobs
Court Administrative Officer/Assistant, Court Usher, Paralegal, Secretary, Secretary: Legal

Court Usher

also known as: Court Officer (Scotland), Macer (Scotland)
CRCI:Legal and Political Services
CLCI:LAG Job Band: 3

Job Description
Court ushers work under the direction of court clerks, as part of a team ensuring the efficient operation of County and Crown courts. They are usually people's first contact with the court. They liaise between the court and all those involved with a case. They also ensure that everything required for a hearing is available.

Ushers prepare the courtroom for the day's hearings, show people into court, call witnesses, check that defendants are present and instruct people in how to take the oath. They also help to swear in of the jury. They hand evidence to the judge, sheriff or jury and pass messages between the clerk and lawyers. Ushers remain in court throughout the 'sitting' and help to keep order in the public area. They may also provide administrative support in the court offices. Some may operate the video link equipment, which allows nervous witnesses to give their evidence in another room.

In Scotland, court ushers are known as court officers in the Sheriff Court, and as macers in the Court of Session/High Court of Justiciary. They carry out similar jobs to an usher and also undertake further administrative tasks.

Work Details
Hours are variable, usually 8.30am-5.00pm, Monday to Friday, but some evening work may be required. You are normally based in a court with some time spent in an office. Travel between courts may be necessary and occasional nights away from home required. The work involves dealing with members of the public. Discretion is important as the work is of a confidential nature. Court ushers usually wear a dark, business-style suit, often with a calf-length black gown in court.

Qualification

- **England, Wales and Northern Ireland**

Band 3: Most courts look for at least 4 GCSEs grades (A*-C), including English and maths, or equivalent, or relevant clerical experience.

- **Scotland**

Band 3: Most courts look for at least four S grades (1-3), including English and maths, or similar, or relevant clerical experience.

Adult Qualifications
There are no set qualifications for mature entrants, though a good standard of education is expected. Mature applicants are welcomed.

Work Experience
Any work experience can equip you with skills that you can use in the future and add to your CV. This can either be unpaid or voluntary, or can be holiday or part-time work that you have organised yourself. It is useful to visit a court to observe the proceedings. Experience in clerical work, customer service work and/or office administration is an advantage.

Entry and Training
Mature applicants are usually preferred for entry to this work, preferably with a background in police work or the armed forces. Training is usually on the job under the supervision of experienced ushers or senior staff, and takes about a year. Good keyboard skills are required as you need to type basic lists etc. Previous experience of working with customers is useful and is sometimes required. It is also useful to have a driving licence.

Some courts run in-house training courses that cover court behaviour and procedure, dealing with the public, and identifying the role of different legal representatives, such as court reporters, clerks and solicitors. N/SVQs are available at levels 2-3 in court operations.

Maturity is an advantage for this type of work and experience of work in the police, prison services, armed services and/or customer service work is extremely useful.

Opportunities and Pay
Ushers in England, Wales and Northern Ireland, and court officers in Scotland, are part of the civil service. They work for the Court Service in Crown or County Courts, Courts of Appeal and High Courts. Jobs are available in cities and major towns throughout the UK, though entry is competitive. Ushers also work for magistrates courts in England and Wales, and are employed by local authorities.

Ushers can be promoted to supervisory positions or to clerk of the court. There are good opportunities for part-time work. Promotion prospects are limited.

Pay varies depending on location and experience, but most earn £12k-£15k, though this can rise to more than £19k a year for senior ushers. In London salaries are usually higher. Overtime payments may be paid in some courts for early morning and weekday evening court sittings.

Health
This job requires good general fitness.

Skills and Qualities
able to put people at ease, awareness of confidentiality issues, clear speaking voice, diplomatic, discreet, good communication skills, good organisational skills, methodical, patient, self confident

Relevant Subjects
Law

Further Information
Civil Service - www.civilservice.gov.uk/jobs

Criminal Justice System (CJS) - www.cjsonline.gov.uk

Skills for Justice - sector skills council for the UK justice system - www.skillsforjustice.com

▶Working in politics & law (2010) (Babcock Lifeskills) - www.babcock-lifeskills.com/

Addresses
Her Majesty's Courts Service (HMCS)
Customer Service Unit, Post Post 1.40, 1st Floor, 102 Petty France, London SW1H 9AJ
Phone: 0845 4568770 (UK only)
Web: www.hmcourts-service.gov.uk

Northern Ireland Court Service
Information Centre Communications Group Laganside House
23-27 Oxford Street, Belfast BT1 3LA
Phone: +44 (0) 28 9032 8594
Web: www.courtsni.gov.uk

Scottish Courts Service (SCS)
Saughton House Broomhouse Drive, Edinburgh EH11 3XD
Phone: +44 (0)131 444 3300
Web: www.scotcourts.gov.uk

Similar Jobs
Barristers' Clerk, Court Administrative Officer/Assistant, Police Front Office Staff, Receptionist

Crane Operator

CRCI:Building and Construction
CLCI:UV   Job Band: 1 to 2

Job Description
Crane operators drive cranes of all types to lift and move large and heavy loads on building sites, in ports, docks and harbours, shipyards, power stations, quarries, or heavy engineering worksites. May work on mobile cranes, including rough terrain cranes that are moved from site to site. May also work on fixed tower cranes, such as those on construction sites. Some cranes run on rails or may be mounted on a lorry. Operators position the crane into the precise area of work and use the controls (levers, pedals and switches) so that the hook or grab is ready to load or unload.

Crane operators work with a ground level worker called a banksman/woman, who guides the operator by using hand signals or through a cab-to-ground communication system. They carry out simple routine maintenance on a daily basis and report any major faults to a supervisor. Must be aware of the health and safety aspects of operating a crane, and of the rules and regulations that govern their work.

Crane operators can also work in the media and music industries, operating cranes with heavy camera and sound equipment.

Work Details
Crane operators usually work a basic 37-39 hr week, Monday to Friday, though there is often overtime, including some evenings and weekends. Travel may be necessary to different sites and you may have to work away from home. You work on your own, but are in contact with other workers. Although you are inside a cab, you may have to deal with difficult weather conditions. Sites can be dusty, noisy, dirty and muddy. You sometimes have to cover rough ground, and climb in and out of cranes.

Cranes can be dangerous and you have to follow rules for using them safely. You work at heights on some cranes, and need to wear a safety helmet, ear defenders and outdoor wear.

Qualification

• England, Wales and Northern Ireland
Band 1: No minimum qualifications are required, but you are expected to have had a good general level of education. GCSEs in English, maths, science and technology subjects, or equivalent, are useful.

Band 2: For entry as a trainee: it is an advantage to have a few GCSEs (A*-C) in subjects that include English, maths, science and technology subjects, or equivalent.

• Scotland
Band 1: No minimum qualifications are required, but you are expected to have had a good general level of education. S grades in English, maths, science and technology subjects, or similar, are useful.

Band 2: For entry as a trainee: it is an advantage to have a few S grades (1-3) in subjects that include English, maths, science and technology subjects, or similar.

Adult Qualifications
No formal qualifications required. However, GCSEs in English, maths, science and technology subjects, or equivalent, are useful.

Work Experience
Relevant work or voluntary experience is always useful and can improve your chances when applying for entry to construction jobs and apprenticeships. Health and safety issues may mean that there are certain jobs you can't do until you are over 16. Contact your local ConstructionSkills office for advice.

Entry and Training
Some enter as an experienced construction plant operator. Most complete a construction apprentice scheme run by the National Construction College (ConstructionSkills) and your employer. ConstructionSkills sets an assessment test for those wishing to join a training scheme. In Scotland, you take an apprenticeship through the Scottish Building Apprenticeship Training Council Scheme. Most practical training is on the job through your employer. You then take a variety of relevant courses in construction at an approved training centre, such as the crane operative course through the National Construction College. You learn to operate different types of crane.

As an apprentice, you can work towards a number of qualifications, including S/NVQs, a first aid certificate, key skills level 1, and a technical certificate. If you are under 18 you cannot drive the machines, but can start your training at 16. You need a driving licence to be able to drive a crane. You can also work towards gaining a level of competence card through the Construction Plant Competence Scheme which indicates your individual skill level and experience.

A Diploma/Welsh Baccalaureate in construction and the built environment may be available in your area. Relevant S/NVQs include specialised plant and machinery operations at level 2.

Training programmes, including apprenticeships leading to level 2, and advanced apprenticeships/construction apprenticeships leading to level 3, may be available in your area. Contact ConstructionSkills for details of all training and card schemes.

Mature applicants may be preferred and often employers train people who are already working on site. Any work in the construction industry, or experience as a building site worker, is useful. The National Construction College (ConstructionSkills) runs crane operator courses for adults. Government training opportunities may also be available in your area. Contact your local careers office, Jobcentre Plus, Next Step service or Learning and Skills Council (LSC)/Local Enterprise Company (LEC) for details of training schemes, including apprenticeships for adults.

Opportunities and Pay

Work is located throughout the UK. Employers include firms of builders, a construction/civil engineering firm, a port authority or a crane hire firm located throughout the UK. Availability of work depends on activity in the building trade and the national economy. Currently there is a downturn in the housing market which means there may be a shortage of vacancies. Crane operators can be self-employed and may use either their own or the contractor's machines. Some jobs are seasonal or short term. With experience you can become a site instructor and train others to operate the machines. Some also specialise in certain types of cranes.

Pay can vary greatly depending on location and employer. A starting wage is likely to be around £15k a year, rising to around £26k with experience. The most skilled and experienced operators can earn more than £36k a year. Overtime is common for which there is additional pay. You may also be given a lodging allowance when working away from home.

Health

You need to be physically fit, with no allergies to dust, and must have good eyesight and good hearing.

Skills and Qualities

able to follow instructions, able to work both on your own and in a team, alert, good concentration level, good co-ordination, head for heights, safety conscious, spatial awareness, steady hand, technical aptitude

Relevant Subjects

Construction and built environment

Further Information

Apprenticeship Schemes (National Apprenticeship Service) - www.apprenticeships.org.uk

Careers in Construction - www.bconstructive.co.uk

Construction Skills (CPA) - www.cskills.org

ConstructionSkills - sector skills council for the construction industry - www.cskills.org

Diplomas (Foundation, Higher and Advanced) - http://yp.direct.gov.uk/diplomas

Training Schemes - www.direct.gov.uk/en/educationandlearning

Welsh Baccalaureate - www.wbq.org.uk

▶Working in construction & the built environment (2007) (Babcock Lifeskills) - www.babcock-lifeskills.com/

Addresses

Construction Plant-hire Association
27-28 Newbury Street, Barbican, London EC1A 7HU
Phone: +44 (0)20 7796 3366
Web: www.cpa.uk.net

Scottish Building Apprenticeship & Training Council (SBATC)
Crichton House, 4 Crichtons Close, Holyrood, Edinburgh EH8 8DT
Phone: +44 (0)131 556 8866
Web: www.sbatc.co.uk

Similar Jobs

Construction Operative, Construction Plant Operative, Demolition Operative, Driver: Lorry, Lift Truck Operative, Quarry Operative

Credit Manager

also known as: Credit Controller, Credit Risk Manager, Credit Scoring Analyst, Finance Manager: Credit

CRCI:Financial Services

CLCI:NAK — Job Band: 3 to 5

Job Description

Credit managers work in a wide range of businesses and organisations, usually in consumer or trade credit areas. Within these, there are three main areas of work: risk assessment, insolvency issues and debt collecting. Credit managers aim to ensure that their organisation has a regular cash flow.

Trade credit is between two companies where one is the seller and the other the buyer of goods or services. Managers assess the creditworthiness of a customer and ensure that credit is only granted to companies that can afford to pay within the terms of an agreement. Consumer credit terms are offered and arranged for individual customers who take on a debt to pay for items such as a new car, electrical goods, or for digital cameras, TV systems etc. The debt is then paid off in regular instalments and the repayments are monitored by a credit manager on behalf of the company that sold the goods.

They are also responsible for any breaches of a credit agreement and take legal action if necessary to recover the costs. Usually manage and organise a team of credit control staff if working for a large company, and arrange staff training and development.

Work Details

Usually work a basic 35-40 hr week, Monday to Friday, though in some jobs you may be required to work weekends and public holidays. Longer hours than other staff are usual, together with early starts and late finishes to a working day. Your base is an office, though you may have to travel to some meetings. You are responsible for policy-making and company strategy.

Qualification

• England, Wales and Northern Ireland

Band 3: For direct entry to credit control: usually at least 4 GCSEs (A*-C) including English and maths, or equivalent.

Band 4: For BTEC higher national award: 1-2 A levels and some GCSEs (A*-C) usually including English and maths, or equivalent.

Band 5: For degree courses: 2-3 A levels and some GCSEs (A*-C) usually including English and maths, or equivalent. Exact requirements depend on the degree you take.

• Scotland

Band 3: For direct entry to credit control: usually at least four S grades (1-3) including English and maths, or similar qualifications.

Band 4: For SQA higher national award: usually 2-3 H grades and some S grades (1-3), often including English and maths, or similar qualifications.

Band 5: For degree courses: 3-5 H grades and some S grades (1-3), usually including English and maths, or similar qualifications. Exact requirements depend on the degree you take.

Degree Information

A degree in business or other finance-related subjects, such as accountancy, is particularly appropriate.

Adult Qualifications
There are special entry arrangements for adults applying for degree and higher national courses, including foundation and Access courses. Check with the universities and colleges for details. Universities offer relevant degrees and foundation degrees through various options of study, including full-time, distance-learning, part-time, modular and evening classes.

Work Experience
Relevant work or voluntary experience is always useful and can improve your employment prospects when applying for entry to jobs. Any experience that involves working with figures is useful. In some areas there is a young apprenticeship (14-16) scheme that provides an extended work placement and eventual achievement of a relevant level 2 qualification whilst at school.

Entry and Training
Entry requirements vary, but all employers look for a good general education. Qualifications such as national and higher national certificates in business studies are useful for entry. Some entrants start as credit controllers and work their way up to credit management. A good understanding of business accounts, sales ledgers and cash flow is also important. Some entrants are graduates, but all entrants receive on-the-job training and are likely to be encouraged to study for the Institute of Credit Management's (ICM) professional qualifications.

The ICM offers several levels of qualification and these can be achieved through evening classes, online learning and by supported and unsupported home study. The certificate in credit management (level 3) is an entry level qualification that requires candidates to pass units in accounting, business law and business environment. Passing this allows associate membership to the ICM. The level 5 diploma in credit management leads to full membership if the ICM.

Computerised accounting systems are widely used, so IT skills and a working knowledge of one or more of the widely used software packages is advantageous.

Thames Valley University runs a foundation degree in credit management. This is recognised by the ICM as entry to full membership. Contact the ICM for further details on all progression routes, membership and qualifications. Continuing professional development is encouraged by the ICM.

Mature entry is common and adults with related experience in areas such as accountancy and banking, building societies and insurance have an advantage.

Other financial experience, including work as an accounting technician or in bookkeeping is also very useful. You can study for various professional examinations through the Institute of Credit Management (ICM) through online learning or home study.

Opportunities and Pay
There are opportunities for credit managers in all types of business throughout the UK, and demand is constant. In the current economic climate, the emphasis on cash and collection functions is greater than ever and maintaining good cashflow is vital in developing successful companies.

Apart from trade and consumer credit in industry and commerce, you can also work in other areas such as export credit, credit insurance and insolvency practice, or in credit reporting. With qualifications and experience it is possible to work freelance as an interim credit manager on a short-term contract. There are also opportunities for work abroad, particularly in Europe.

Salaries depend on the size, type and location of the employing company, but are around £21k-£26k a year, rising to around £45k-£50k. High earners can earn up to £85k or more a year.

Skills and Qualities
able to manage a budget and keep records, accurate, aptitude for figures, diplomatic, discreet, good organisational skills, good spoken communication, good written English, IT skills, sound judgement

Relevant Subjects
Business and accounting, Economics, English, ICT/Computer studies, Law, Mathematics

Further Information
AGCAS: Accountancy and Business Services (Job Sector Briefing) (AGCAS) - www.prospects.ac.uk/

Credit Today - www.credittoday.co.uk

Financial Services Skills Council - sector skills council for financial services, accountancy & finance www.fssc.org.uk/

Inside Careers Guide: Banking, Securities & Investments - www.insidecareers.co.uk

Journal of the Institute of Credit Management (ICM, monthly) (Institute of Credit Management (ICM)) - www.icm.org.uk/

TARGETjobs: City and Finance (GTI Specialist Publishers Ltd) - www.groupgti.com

▶Working in maths (2009) (Babcock Lifeskills) - www.babcock-lifeskills.com/

Addresses
ifs School of Finance
IFS House, 4-9 Burgate Lane, Canterbury, Kent CT1 2XJ
Phone: +44 (0)1227 818609
Web: www.ifslearning.ac.uk

Institute of Credit Management (ICM)
The Water Mill, Station Road, South Luffenham, Leicestershire LE15 8NB
Phone: +44 (0)1780 722900
Web: www.icm.org.uk

Similar Jobs
Accountant: Private Practice, Accountant: Public Sector, Accounting Technician, Bank Manager, Building Society Manager

Crematorium Technician
also known as: Chapel Attendant

CRCI:Personal and Other Services
CLCI:IP Job Band: 1 to 2

Job Description
Crematorium technicians ensure that funerals run smoothly, the body is cremated and remains are stored safely. They clean the chapel, set up the music system to play selected music and get everything ready for the funeral service. Also greet the funeral party, show people where to go and answer questions. May help to carry the coffin.

Technicians check that the furnace equipment is working properly. They ensure the deceased is correctly identified and labelled, move the coffin into the furnace and set the equipment to begin the cremation process. Afterwards, they remove the ashes, grind them down and put them in a labelled container.

May scatter or bury ashes if asked to do so and show visitors to sites where ashes of loved ones have been scattered or buried. They also look after the grounds, keep records, follow health and safety rules and make sure legal requirements are met.

Work Details
Usually work a 37 hr week, Monday to Friday. Depending on crematorium opening times, may work shifts to cover evenings and weekends. May do chapel duty on one day and operate the

cremator the next. Most of the work is carried out indoors, but some tasks may take place outside. The work involves standing for long periods.

Comes into contact with a wide range of people including mourners, religious officials and funeral, council and grounds staff. You need to dress smartly and respectfully when working in the public areas. When working with the furnace, you wear protective clothing supplied by the employer.

Qualification

• England, Wales and Northern Ireland

Band 1: No minimum qualifications are required, but you are expected to have a good level of general education and reading and writing skills. However, some formal/vocational qualifications at any level are useful.

Band 2: Although academic qualifications are not specified for this job, it is an advantage to have some GCSEs (A*-C) in subjects that include English and maths, or equivalent.

• Scotland

Band 1: No minimum qualifications are required, but you are expected to have a good level of general education and reading and writing skills. However, some formal/vocational qualifications at any level are useful.

Band 2: Although academic qualifications are not specified for this job, it is an advantage to have some S grades (1-3) in subjects that include English and maths, or similar.

Adult Qualifications

Adults can enter this area of work without formal qualifications, but reading and writing skills are required.

Work Experience

It is an advantage to have experience of working with people who are upset or stressed. Paid or voluntary experience of administration and using ICT skills is also useful. You can develop gardening skills as a hobby or through volunteering or paid work.

Sometimes crematoria have open days where you can look behind the scenes and ask staff about their work. Most crematoria have signed up to the ICCM charter for the bereaved. This means you have the right to arrange a visit and view the cremation process in action.

Entry and Training

You train on the job with experienced members of staff. Before you can operate the cremator on your own, you must complete either the crematorium technicians' training scheme (CTTS) run by the Institute of Cemetery and Crematorium Management (ICCM) or the training and examination scheme for crematorium technicians (TEST) run by the Federation of British Cremation Authorities (FBCA).

Both schemes are offered through distance learning, so you can work at your own pace supported by a mentor at the crematorium. They involve both theory and practical tests. The CTTS scheme leads to BTEC accredited intermediate and advanced certificates for ICCM crematorium technical operations.

Often adults can offer a mature outlook and emotional detachment that is an advantage in this area of work. Experience in administration or of dealing with members of the public is useful.

Opportunities and Pay

There are over 250 crematoria in the UK. Nationally, over 70% of deaths are followed by cremation. This figure may be much higher in some places. Most crematoria are run by local councils, but some are privately owned. You may progress to senior technician roles and, with further training, into crematorium management. Some technicians move into administration roles. They may go on to become registrars. Crematoria employ relatively few staff, so you may have to move to another site to gain promotion.

Crematorium technicians earn around £14k-£17k a year. Senior technicians may earn from £20k-£25k a year. Crematorium managers earn £27k-£40k or more a year, depending on the job role. There may be overtime pay and allowances for living in London.

Health

You must be able to stand for long periods. The work involves some lifting and bending, so stamina and physical fitness are important.

Skills and Qualities

able to follow procedures, able to operate equipment, attention to detail, emotionally strong, good communication skills, good organisational skills, health & safety awareness, respectful, tactful

Further Information

Institute of Cemetery and Crematorium Management - www.bereavement-services.org/

Local Government Careers (Improvement and Development Agency) - www.lgcareers.com/publications/

Addresses

Cremation Society of Great Britain
2nd Floor, Brecon House, 16/16a Albion Place, Maidstone, Kent ME14 5DZ
Phone: +44 (0)1622 688292
Web: www.cremation.org.uk

Federation of Burial and Cremation Authorities (FBCA)
41 Salisbury Road, Carshalton, Surrey SM5 3HA
Phone: +44 (0)20 8669 4521
Web: www.fbca.org.uk/

Institute of Cemetery and Crematorium Management (ICCM)
City of London Cemetery, Aldersbrook Road, Manor Park E15 5DQ
Phone: +44 (0)20 8989 4661
Web: www.iccm-uk.com

Similar Jobs

Anatomical Pathology Technician, Cemetery Worker, Embalmer, Funeral Director, Gardener

Critical Care Technologist

also known as: Critical Care Scientist

CRCI:Healthcare

CLCI:JOB Job Band: 3 to 5

Job Description

Critical care technologists (CCTs) are trained healthcare scientists and experts in the use of the technology which is used to care for critically ill patients. This role enables nursing and medical staff to concentrate primarily on patient care. CCTs are responsible for a range of tasks including physiological monitoring, support and use of diagnostic technology such as respiratory machines, electrocardiograms (ECGs) which monitor heart rhythm and brain monitors. They also undertake patient tests such as blood analysis and take responsibility for for the scientific and technical training of medical and nursing staff in the use of the relevant technology.

CCTs organise the transfer of patients between hospitals, assess the use of new equipment for critical care and manage and maintain the equipment used. They also communicate with third party suppliers of services to critical care which may include electricity and gas supplies and ventilation.

Critical Care Technologist

Work Details
Usually work a basic 37.5 hr week and are expected to work unsocial hours and shifts to cover 24 hours a day. You work in a hospital as part of a team of healthcare professionals, including nurses, doctors, anaesthetists and therapists. There is contact with people who are ill and possibly in pain, upset or depressed. Work can be emotionally, physically and intellectually taxing as you must be able to respond quickly to changes in the function of equipment and the health of patients. You have to deal with emergencies and be able to cope with the sight of blood. A uniform is provided by your employer and protective clothing where relevant.

Qualification

• England, Wales and Northern Ireland
Band 3: For entry to jobs as a trainee: usually at least 4 GCSEs (A*-C) including English, maths and science, or equivalent.

Band 4: For HND in electronics, Diploma of Higher Education or foundation degree: 1-2 A levels and some GCSEs (A*-C) usually including biology, physics, chemistry or maths, or equivalent.

Band 5: For degree courses: 2-3 A levels and some GCSEs (A*-C) usually including English, maths and science, or equivalent. Exact requirements depend on the degree you take.

• Scotland
Band 3: For entry to jobs as a trainee: usually at least four S grades (1-3) including English, maths and science, or similar.

Band 4: For entry to SQA higher national and professional development awards in electronics, usually 2-3 H grades and some S grades (1-3), including biology, physics, chemistry or maths or similar qualifications.

Band 5: For entry to a degree course: 3-5 H grades and some S grades (1-3) including maths, science and English, or similar qualifications. Exact requirements depend on the degree you take.

Degree Information
A degree in a relevant engineering or life science subject is useful. In the future, a degree in clinical physiology/medical science specialising in critical care technology may be required.

Adult Qualifications
There are no formal entry requirements, but most hospitals expect a good secondary education and a mature attitude to work. Formal qualifications are important if you want to qualify for more advanced work later on.

Work Experience
Work experience gives you an insight into what you enjoy and don't enjoy about a job or working environment, as well as the opportunity to acquire new skills. It provides valuable information to add to your CV and improves your course application and future employment prospects. Consider some voluntary work in a hospital. Any work, either paid or voluntary, that provides experience of working in a caring capacity with people in a healthcare environment is very useful. Gaining first-aid certificates and knowledge of life-saving techniques also demonstrates commitment.

Entry and Training
There are currently no formal entry requirements but this will probably change in the near future as critical care technologists are likely to become a registered profession with the Health Professions Council. Most hospitals expect GCSEs/S grades (A-C/1-3), particularly if you want to qualify for more advanced work in the future. Increasingly, most entrants have A levels/H grades, or a relevant engineering or science degree. Trainees without a degree follow a training programme and attend college to study for the qualifications relevant to their work. Specialisms include audiology, cardiology, neurophysiology and respiratory physiology.

In the future, a vocational degree in clinical physiology/medical science specialising in critical care technology may be required for entry to this job. This will involve taking the professional exams of the Society of Critical Care Technologists. Entry will also be possible with a relevant degree followed by the professional exams.

The Diploma/Welsh Baccalaureate in society, health and development may be available in your area and provide an alternative route into this career. Check the diplomas website for details.

Mature entrants with relevant experience or qualifications in healthcare may have an advantage. This job requires a considerable level of physical fitness.

Opportunities and Pay
This is a relatively new profession, with around 500 critical care technologists (CCTs) employed nationally by the NHS. Jobs are available in larger hospitals with critical care and intensive care units. There may also be opportunities to work in private hospitals. Jobs are available in towns and cities across the UK.

Salaries for trainee CCTs are around £18k a year, rising to £25k-£40k with experience. Critical care managers can earn significantly more. Salaries may be higher in London.

Health
You need to be physically fit as the work may involve carrying heavy equipment and standing or sitting for long periods of time. There is also a risk of skin irritation from hazardous chemicals.

Skills and Qualities
able to cope under pressure, able to follow procedures, able to inspire confidence, able to take responsibility, aptitude for teamwork, attention to detail, good concentration level, interest in new technology, quick reactions, sensitive

Relevant Subjects
Biology, Chemistry, Design and technology, Engineering, English, Health and social care, ICT/Computer studies, Mathematics, Physics, Science

Further Information
Diplomas (Foundation, Higher and Advanced) - http://yp.direct.gov.uk/diplomas

Health Professions Council (HPC) - www.hpc-uk.org

NHS Careers (NHS Careers) - www.nhscareers.nhs.uk

NHS Careers Scotland - www.infoscotland.com/nhs

NHS Careers Wales - www.wales.nhs.uk

NHS Clinical Scientists Recruitment Services - www.nhsclinicalscientists.info

Skills for Health - sector skills council - www.skillsforhealth.org.uk

The Technologist (Society of Critical Care Technologists)

Voluntary Register of Clinical Technologists (VRCT) - www.vrct.org.uk

Welsh Baccalaureate - www.wbq.org.uk

Addresses
Intensive Care Society (ICS)
Churchill House, 35 Red Lion Square, London WC1R 4SG
Phone: +44 (0)20 7280 4350
Web: www.ics.ac.uk/

Society Of Critical Care Technologists (SCCT)
6 South Bar, Banbury, Oxfordshire OX16 9AA
Phone: +44 (0)23 8079 6123
Web: www.criticalcaretech.org.uk/

Similar Jobs
Clinical Scientist: Medical Physicist, Clinical Technologist, Emergency Care Assistant/Ambulance Technician, Operating Department Practitioner, Perfusionist, Sterile Services Technician

Croupier

also known as: Casino Croupier, Dealer: Casino

CRCI:Leisure, Sport and Tourism
CLCI:GAK Job Band: 2 to 3

Job Description

Croupiers have responsibility for running a gaming table in a licensed casino or gaming club. They work under close supervision of an inspector and must work to specific gambling guidelines. They usually deal with up to four main games such as roulette, poker, baccarat, and blackjack. Croupiers follow a set betting cycle and manage the game as it is being played. They welcome customers to the table and explain rules if necessary, seeing that all bets are placed before play starts. Deals cards, throws dice or spins roulette wheel and mentally calculates the winners' payouts. Collects the 'chips' (counters exchanged for money) from the losing players, pays out the winners and clears the table before starting another game.

Work Details

Usually works 8 hr shifts with regular breaks. You are expected to work very long and unsocial hours. Most gambling is done during the night and is busiest between 10pm and 4am, and at weekends. Work is highly pressurised and requires intense concentration. You are responsible for making quick decisions and calculations, and for providing an accurate and speedy service. Your work involves meeting clients and giving them instructions. You have contact with all kinds of people and sometimes they can be awkward and argumentative.

The work is usually in a casino/gaming club or possibly on board a cruise ship. Casinos are usually dimly lit and can often be hot and crowded. You need to wear a uniform, usually evening dress, and look very smart and tidy at all times.

Qualification

- **England, Wales and Northern Ireland**

Band 2: For entry to jobs, no minimum qualifications are needed, but it is an advantage to have some GCSEs (A*-C) or equivalent in subjects that include English and maths.

Band 3: For entry to jobs, HNC or a relevant Diploma, usually at least 4 GCSEs (A*-C) including English and maths, or equivalent.

- **Scotland**

Band 2: Although academic qualifications are not specified for this job, it is an advantage to have some S grades (1-3) in subjects that include English and maths, or similar.

Band 3: For entry to jobs, usually at least four S grades (1-3) including English or maths, or similar.

Adult Qualifications

There are no minimum entry qualifications for this job. Successful appointment depends on personality, appearance and numeracy skills.

Work Experience

Any work experience can equip you with skills for use in the future and add to your CV. This can either be unpaid or voluntary, holiday or part-time work that you have organised yourself. Any work that involves working with customers and doing mental calculations is useful.

Entry and Training

Applicants must be at least 18 to enter this job. You may have to take a test in manual dexterity, pass a selection interview and often take a maths test. You have to be able to make fast mental calculations. Some entrants have A levels/H grades, or similar, though they are not usually required. Entrants are often appointed through personal contact or direct approach. This job requires a personal functional licence (PFL) from the Gambling Commission. Your background is thoroughly checked and you must have no criminal convictions.

Training is via courses run by the employer or by an independent trainer. Initial training covers the management of one game, usually blackjack, and after some experience you are trained in other casino games. Training also includes appropriate customer service, gaming rules and regulations, dress and grooming. Croupiers work under the supervision of an inspector, whose role it is to make sure that all gaming regulations are adhered to.

There are relevant short courses available, such as the City & Guilds NVQ level 2-3 in gambling operations and the level 4 diploma in hotel and casino management. The London Gaming College offers an intensive 8-week casino croupier course. See the website for more details.

Blackpool and the Fylde College runs the level 2 NVQ in Gambling Operations for Casinos (Croupiers) through its National Gaming Academy. Courses cover roulette, blackjack, three card poker, customer service, health and safety and social responsibility. Entry for this course is by an interview. The college also offers a foundation degree in casino operations management, for those who wish to progress further. Some of the larger casino chains offer management training schemes for those who demonstrate aptitude for the job. Relevant Diplomas/Welsh Baccalaureates may be available in your area in subjects such as hospitality and apprenticeships in customer service may also be helpful.

Maturity is seen as an advantage and experience of using mental calculations in a job is very useful. Government training opportunities, such as apprenticeships in customer service, may be available in your area. You can also gain recognition of previous experience through Accreditation of Prior Learning (APL) or by working towards relevant S/NVQs. Contact your local careers office, Jobcentre Plus, Next Step service or Learning and Skills Council (LSC) Local Enterprise Company (LEC) for details of training schemes, including apprenticeships for adults.

Opportunities and Pay

There are 143 casinos in the UK, 25 of which are in London and business is good so there is a steady demand for croupiers. Staff turnover is high so there is a good demand for trainees, but entry to a training programme is often very competitive. Some of the larger casino companies offer a six week paid training course. Check the British Casino Association website for details.

Jobs are available only in certain towns and cities. After experience, there are good opportunities for work abroad, as British croupiers are known to be well trained. There are also jobs on cruise liners, which are not so well paid, but tips, which are forbidden in the UK, are allowed. Promotion prospects are good for long stay staff. There is a clear career pattern from dealer to inspector, to supervisor to manager. Candidates for promotion must meet the strict licence requirements.

Pay varies enormously depending on location, type of club and how skilled you are. Generally, croupiers earn in the region of £13k-£18k a year, rising to around £25k. Croupiers in London with a high level of experience may earn more. Some employers may pay an unsocial hours allowance and may also offer a pension scheme, profit-share scheme, and an annual bonus. Subsidised food and drink is often available or is sometimes free.

Health

This job requires normal colour vision and you need good hearing and clear speech.

Skills and Qualities

able to cope under pressure, alert, aptitude for figures, diplomatic, firm manner, friendly, good concentration level, hand-to-eye co-ordination, honest, quick reactions

Relevant Subjects
Leisure, travel and tourism, Mathematics

Further Information
Apprenticeship Schemes (National Apprenticeship Service) - www.apprenticeships.org.uk

Diploma in Hospitality (People 1st) - www.hospitalitydiploma.co.uk

Diplomas (Foundation, Higher and Advanced) - http://yp.direct.gov.uk/diplomas

London Gaming College - www.business-unit.why-choose-us/sectors/gaming

People 1st - sector skills council for hospitality, leisure, travel and tourism - www.people1st.co.uk

Skillsmart Retail - sector skills council for the retail industry - www.skillsmartretail.com

Springboard UK (Springboard UK) - www.springboarduk.net

Springboard Wales (Springboard Wales) - http://wales.springboarduk.net/

Training Schemes - www.direct.gov.uk/en/educationandlearning

UKSP - Guide to Success in Hospitality, Leisure, Travel & Tourism - www.uksp.co.uk/

Addresses
Blackpool and The Fylde College
Ashfield Road, Bispham, Blackpool FY2 0HB
Phone: +44 (0)1253 352352
Web: www.blackpool.ac.uk

British Casino Association (BCA)
38 Grosvenor Gardens, London SW1W 0EB
Phone: +44 (0)20 7730 1055
Web: www.britishcasinoassociation.org.uk

City & Guilds
1 Giltspur Street, London EC1A 9DD
Phone: +44 (0)20 7294 2800
Web: www.cityandguilds.com

Gambling Commission
Victoria Square House, Victoria Square, Birmingham B2 4BP
Phone: +44 (0)121 230 6666
Web: www.gamblingcommission.gov.uk

Similar Jobs
Bank Officer, Betting Shop Manager, Building Society Officer, Clerk: Accounts, Customer Services Adviser

Crown Prosecution Service Caseworker
also known as: CPS Caseworker, Paralegal Officer

CRCI:Legal and Political Services
CLCI:LAZ　　Job Band: 3 to 5

Job Description
Crown Prosecution Service (CPS) caseworkers support the work of the CPS legal teams, the body advising the police on prosecutions in England and Wales. They work in local teams around the country, handling the paperwork and liaising with the police and other agencies in the preparation of cases for court.

Administrative duties include registering files as they arrive and researching the background of cases to support the work of senior colleagues. They also handle data, arrange and support meetings and carry out a range of other administrative tasks.

Caseworkers summarise and prepare cases for prosecutors, making recommendations about charges to be brought. They attend court to support the legal team of barristers and solicitors. They also liaise with witnesses in court as well as other organisations in the criminal justice system. Complete administrative duties following a case and ensure accurate records are kept. Deal with correspondence and enquiries related to a case. Caseworkers are also sometimes known as paralegal officers or assistants.

Work Details
You usually work normal office hours, Monday to Friday, but often have to meet specific deadlines. The CPS has a flexible working hours scheme. Part-time work is also possible. You work in an office, but have to travel to police stations and to court. As a senior caseworker, you may have to travel throughout England and Wales.

Qualification

• England, Wales and Northern Ireland
Band 3: For entry to jobs, HNC or a relevant Diploma, usually at least 4 GCSEs (A*-C) including English and maths, or equivalent.

Equivalent qualifications which may be acceptable include the Higher Diploma, functional skills level 2, vocational qualifications at level 2 and Welsh Baccalaureate (intermediate diploma level). Check with individual institutions/employers. You may be able to follow an advanced apprenticeship scheme.

Band 4: For HND, Diploma of Higher Education or foundation degree: 1-2 A levels and some GCSEs (A*-C) usually including English and maths, or equivalent.

Equivalent qualifications which may be acceptable include the Advanced Diploma, vocational qualifications at level 3 and the International Baccalaureate/Welsh Baccalaureate (advanced diploma level). Check with individual institutions.

Band 5: For degree courses: 2-3 A levels and some GCSEs (A*-C) usually including English and maths, or equivalent. Exact requirements depend on the degree you take.

Equivalent qualifications which may be acceptable include the Advanced Diploma (with additional and specialist learning), Progression Diploma, HNC, CertHE, vocational qualifications at level 4 and the International Baccalaureate/Welsh Baccalaureate (advanced diploma level). Check with individual institutions.

Adult Qualifications
Entry requirements may be relaxed for adults applying for higher education courses. Access to HE or foundation courses provide those without the required qualifications a route onto degree courses.

Work Experience
Work experience gives you an insight into what you enjoy and don't enjoy about a job or working environment, as well as the opportunity to acquire new skills. It also provides valuable information to add to your CV and improves any course application and/or your future employment prospects. For this job it may be helpful to have experience of working in an office or in a legal environment.

Entry and Training
There are no set entry requirements, but most applicants have at least four GCSEs, grades A*-C, including English and maths. Many entrants also have A levels and/or degrees. A Diploma/Welsh Baccalaureate in Public Services may be available in your area. All applicants to the CPS have to complete a character enquiry form, a health declaration form, and a National Identification Service vetting form.

Caseworkers can enter the service at level A, an administrative role, or level B, supporting crown prosecutors, following a competitive interview. All new caseworkers follow an induction programme and are then teamed up with a senior caseworker and trained on the job. There are distance learning courses validated by the Institute of Legal Executives (ILEX) available, such as the Introduction to Criminal Prosecution for Level A caseworkers, providing an introduction to the English legal system and the principles of criminal law, CPS policies and procedures, and the role and responsibilities of CPS employees. The course is roughly equivalent to GCSE level and lasts six months, with three assignments to complete.

The Certificate in Criminal Prosecution is a compulsory course for Level B caseworkers, but is also available for Level A caseworkers who want to progress. The course provides a working knowledge of criminal law and procedure. It is roughly equivalent to A level standard and lasts one year with seven assignments.

The CPS encourages continuing professional development (CPD). The nature of the job and changes to legislation mean that training is ongoing to make sure caseworkers' skills are kept up to date. Training is delivered in-house, supported on occasion by external courses. You may also be able to study towards legal qualifications whilst working, via the Law Scholarship Scheme, which offers a development and qualification route from administrator/ caseworker through to crown prosecutor by way of a bursary. Sponsorship is guaranteed for the duration of the course and employees can study part time at a college or through distance learning.

If you complete the Legal Practice Course or Bar Vocational Course you can apply to the CPS legal trainee scheme to train as a solicitor or pupil barrister. On successful completion of this training you can then apply for posts as crown prosecutors.The Crown Prosecution Service (CPS) employs more than 8,500 staff, dealing exclusively with criminal cases. Caseworkers work in one of 42 CPS areas in England and Wales, as well as headquarters in London, Birmingham and York.

Caseworker vacancies may be advertised on the CPS website and on the Civil Service Recruitment Gateway. See the relevant website for details.

Experienced caseworkers or applicants with a suitable legal qualification may apply to become an associate prosecutor. This requires passing a selection process and completing a specialised training course.

Salaries start at £13k a year, rising to £15k- £19k a year. Senior caseworkers can earn over £25k a year.

While there are no set entry requirements, most applicants have at least four GCSEs, grades A*-C, including English and maths. Many entrants also have A levels and/or degrees. All legal training is provided after appointment. Keyboard skills are essential.

Opportunities and Pay

The Crown Prosecution Service (CPS) employs more than 8,500 staff, dealing exclusively with criminal cases. Caseworkers work in one of 42 CPS areas in England and Wales, as well as headquarters in London, Birmingham and York.

Caseworker vacancies may be advertised on the CPS website and on the Civil Service Recruitment Gateway. See the relevant website for details.

Experienced caseworkers or applicants with a suitable legal qualification may apply to become an associate prosecutor. This requires passing a selection process and completing a specialised training course.

Salaries start at £13k a year, rising to £15k- £19k a year. Senior caseworkers can earn over £25k a year.

Skills and Qualities

able to get on with all kinds of people, able to prioritise work, analytical skills, aptitude for teamwork, awareness of confidentiality issues, excellent communication skills, good organisational skills, IT skills, self-motivated, sound judgement

Relevant Subjects

English, Government and politics, ICT/Computer studies, Law

Further Information

Civil Service - www.civilservice.gov.uk/jobs

Diplomas (Foundation, Higher and Advanced) - http://yp.direct.gov.uk/diplomas

Law Uncovered (Trotman 2009) - www.trotman.co.uk

Skills for Justice - sector skills council for the UK justice system - www.skillsforjustice.com

▶Working in politics & law (2010) (Babcock Lifeskills) - www.babcock-lifeskills.com/

Addresses

Institute of Legal Executives (ILEX)
Kempston Manor, Bedfordshire MK42 7AB
Phone: +44 (0)1234 841 000
Web: www.ilex.org.uk

The Crown Prosecution Service (CPS)
50 Ludgate Hill, London EC4M 7EX
Phone: +44 (0)20 7796 8000
Web: www.cps.gov.uk

Similar Jobs

Barristers' Clerk, Legal Executive, Paralegal, Solicitor

Customer Services Adviser

also known as: Customer Services Assistant, Helpdesk Adviser

CRCI:Retail Sales and Customer Services

CLCI:OM Job Band: 2 to 3

Job Description

Customer services advisers give information and advice about a company's goods and services to customers by telephone, face to face, or by email. They work in a customer service team handling enquiries and complaints about services, staff or goods. They help customers to get the goods and services they need and handle credit/debit card payments over the phone.

Some advisers may handle calls at a centre for several organisations. Others work for a single large organisation such as a bank, and only handle enquiries about that organisation's products and services. Some centres may take calls from all over Europe.

Work Details

Work between 35-40 hrs in a five-day week, often including weekends and evenings. You may need to work shifts. Your work place is usually a bright and air-conditioned office or bank. You need to sit in one position for long periods, using a computer workstation for recording enquiries. If handling calls, a headset is usually worn and there is a digital display to inform you of how many callers are in the queue. You may need to wear a uniform or corporate dress.

Qualification

- **England, Wales and Northern Ireland**

Band 2: For entry: there are no set qualifications, though some employers may ask for some GCSEs (A*-C) including English and maths, or equivalent.

Band 3: For some employers/courses: at least 4 GCSEs (A*-C) including English and maths, or equivalent.

- **Scotland**

Band 2: For entry: there are no set qualifications, though some employers may ask for some S grades (1-3) including English and maths, or equivalent.

Band 3: For some employers/courses: at least four S grades (1-3) including English and maths, or similar.

Adult Qualifications
No particular academic qualifications are specified by employers, though a good general education is expected.

Work Experience
Relevant work or voluntary experience can equip you with skills that you can use in the future and add to your CV. Any work where you are dealing with the public is particularly relevant. There are often opportunities available for voluntary work that give you experience of working with people.

Entry and Training
Personality is often more important than qualifications. You may be asked to take an entry test. Most employers offer in-house training, which may consist of a short course in product knowledge, then more specialised training in the company's products and systems. Smaller companies provide on-the-job training with experienced staff. S/NVQ assessment is part of some internal training programmes. Introductory courses in call handling techniques, such as the City & Guilds certificate in contact centre skills, are offered at various UK colleges.

The Institute of Customer Service (ICS) offers a wide range of qualifications, including ICS professional award schemes, a student membership scheme, and relevant training and networking events. They also have details of apprenticeships on their website.

Relevant S/NVQs at levels 1-4 in customer service standards and contact centre operations, are widely available. Training programmes, including apprenticeship schemes in customer service, may be available in your area. Advanced apprenticeships leading to qualification at level 3 can also be a route into higher education. A Diploma/Welsh Baccalaureate in retail business may also be available in your area.

Adults may be able to enter this work through a government-funded training programme. Contact your local careers office, Jobcentre Plus, Next Step service or Learning and Skills Council (LSC)/Local Enterprise Company (LEC) for details of all training opportunities and schemes, including apprenticeships for adults.

Opportunities and Pay
Jobs are available throughout the UK, mainly in major towns and cities. Employers include the insurance industry, private health, motoring industry, telephone companies, electricity, gas and water suppliers, airlines, banks and building societies, computer industry, catalogue and recruitment companies, and department stores. There may be promotion opportunities, especially in the larger centres/organisations, to supervisory and management levels.

An average starting salary can be between £14k-£17k a year, although this varies with employer and location. With experience, this rises to around £24k a year. Some team leaders can earn up to £35k a year.

Health
You need to have good hearing and clear speech for this type of work.

Skills and Qualities
able to work quickly, aptitude for teamwork, attention to detail, clear speaking voice, customer service skills, discreet, good memory, good telephone manner, honest, IT skills

Relevant Subjects
English, Retail and distribution

Further Information
Apprenticeship Schemes (National Apprenticeship Service) - www.apprenticeships.org.uk

CCF Online (Call Centres Focus) - www.callcentre.co.uk

Customer First Magazine (bi-monthly) (Institute of Customer Service) - www.instituteofcustomerservice.com/Customerfirst.aspx

Diplomas (Foundation, Higher and Advanced) - http://yp.direct.gov.uk/diplomas

ICS Jobs Board - www.instituteofcustomerservicejobs.com

Skillsmart Retail - www.skillsmartretail.com/SR/Careers/Home/default.aspx

Training Schemes - www.direct.gov.uk/en/educationandlearning

Welsh Baccalaureate - www.wbq.org.uk

▶Working in retail & customer services (2008) (Babcock Lifeskills) - www.babcock-lifeskills.com/

Addresses
Customer Contact Association (CCA)
20 Newtown Place, Glasgow G3 7PY
Phone: +44 (0)141 564 9010
Web: www.cca.org.uk

Institute of Customer Service (ICS)
2 Castle Court, St Peter's Street, Colchester, Essex CO1 1EW
Phone: +44 (0)1206 571716
Web: www.instituteofcustomerservice.com

Similar Jobs
Airline Customer Service Agent, Contact Centre Operator, Customer Services Manager, Hotel Receptionist, Switchboard Operator, Travel Consultant

Customer Services Manager
also known as: Call Centre Manager, Customer Care Manager

CRCI:Retail Sales and Customer Services
CLCI:OFZ Job Band: 2 to 5

Job Description
Customer services managers ensure that all staff work to a company's standard in satisfying customer requirements, enquiries or complaints, in a pleasant and efficient manner. They are responsible for a team that may work in an office, a call centre or a central desk in a department store, supermarket, railway station or airport. Managers oversee the operation of telephones, computers and checkouts, depending on the place of work.

Help staff to handle queries from customers, either in person or by telephone and deal with more complex and difficult customer enquiries or complaints, as well as with refunds. Managers need to have a good level of knowledge about the company's products and services. May also be involved in the recruitment and training of staff.

Work Details
Usually work 35-40 hrs in a five-day week, including some evenings, Saturdays and possibly Sundays on a rota basis. The work is challenging and pressured at times and can involve making difficult decisions when dealing with customers. You need to cope with being on your feet for some of the time. Sometimes you have to stand or sit in one place for long periods of time.

Qualification

• England, Wales and Northern Ireland
Band 2: Although academic qualifications are not specified for this job, it is an advantage to have some GCSEs (A*-C) in subjects that include English and maths, or equivalent.

Band 3: For entry: usually at least 4 GCSEs (A*-C) including English and maths, or equivalent.

Band 4: For entry to some management training schemes: a minimum of 1-2 A levels and some GCSEs (A*-C), including English and maths, or equivalent.

Band 5: For degree course: 2-3 A levels and some GCSEs (A*-C) preferably including English and maths, or equivalent. Exact requirements depend on the degree you take.

• **Scotland**

Band 2: Although academic qualifications are not specified for this job, it is an advantage to have some S grades (1-3) in subjects that include English and maths, or similar.

Band 3: For entry: usually at least four S grades (1-3) including English and maths, or similar.

Band 4: For entry to some management training schemes: 2-3 H grades and three S grades (1-3), including maths and English, or similar.

Band 5: For degree course: 3-5 H grades and some S grades (1-3), preferably including English and maths, or similar.

Degree Information

Any degree is acceptable. It may be an advantage to have studied retail management or marketing. Business studies and business administration also give useful background knowledge. Alternatively, it is possible to take a postgraduate qualification, such as a Master of Business Administration (MBA), or MSc/ Diploma in marketing, with options in retail management.

Adult Qualifications

Entry requirements may be relaxed for adults applying for higher education courses and Access or foundation courses give adults without qualifications a route on to degree courses.

Work Experience

Entry to this job is competitive. It is important that you try to do some relevant work or voluntary experience before applying. Consider sales work, particularly in larger shops or stores, or any work dealing with the public. Part-time and holiday employment in a wide range of shops is usually fairly easy to obtain.

Entry and Training

Entry to management training schemes is very competitive. You can enter at different levels, according to your qualifications. It is possible to begin as an assistant in customer services or a call centre operator and work up to this job if you show management potential. You can attend management training courses, either run in-house or at a college. There are also full or part-time college BTEC/SQA courses such as contact centre supervisory skills at level 3. Training schemes usually include spending time working in different departments.

The Institute of Customer Service (ICS) offers a range of qualifications, including ICS professional award schemes, student membership scheme, and relevant training and networking events. Once your training is completed, you can gain an S/NVQ in customer service or contact centre professionals up to level 4. Membership of the ICS is open to full or part-time managers who have achieved an S/NVQ at levels 2-4. Many trainees are graduates or have a higher national award. The Institute of Leadership and Management also offers management and leadership courses ranging from level 2 certificates in team leading to level 7 qualifications for middle and executive management. See the website for further details.

Training programmes, including apprenticeship schemes in customer service, may be available in your area. Advanced apprenticeships leading to qualification at level 3 can also be a route into higher education. A Diploma/Welsh Baccalaureate in retail business may also be available in your area.

Adults may be able to enter this work through a government-funded training programme. Contact your local careers office, Jobcentre Plus, Next Step service or Learning and Skills Council (LSC)/Local Enterprise Company (LEC) for details of all training opportunities and schemes, including apprenticeships for adults. Previous management, sales or supervisory experience is desirable, as employers often prefer older staff, particularly those with experience of working with the public.

Graduate training schemes are available for those with degrees in any subject. There are also distance-learning courses in customer and consumer affairs.

Opportunities and Pay

Most customer services managers are employed in the retail trade, utility companies, transport industry, health care, hotel industry, banks, insurance and building societies, public transport, mail order companies, or perhaps with information providers, such as tourist agencies and libraries. Opportunities for promotion and overall prospects can be better in larger companies or organisations. However, to gain promotion, it is often necessary to move to work in another part of the country. The work is suitable for part time or job share.

Pay can vary considerably, depending on location and type of company. Salaries start at around £20k-£26k, rising to £30k-£45k a year, with increased experience and responsibility. Senior managers earn more than £60k a year. Some employers pay commission and offer bonus schemes.

Health

A good level of general fitness is needed for this job.

Skills and Qualities

able to manage people, able to motivate others, business awareness, customer service skills, discreet, good communication skills, good interpersonal skills, initiative, IT skills, problem-solving skills

Relevant Subjects

Business and accounting, Economics, English, ICT/Computer studies, Mathematics, Retail and distribution

Further Information

Apprenticeship Schemes (National Apprenticeship Service) - www.apprenticeships.org.uk

CCF Online (Call Centres Focus) - www.callcentre.co.uk

Customer First Magazine (bi-monthly) (Institute of Customer Service) - www.instituteofcustomerservice.com/Customerfirst.aspx

Diplomas (Foundation, Higher and Advanced) - http://yp.direct.gov.uk/diplomas

ICS Jobs Board - www.instituteofcustomerservicejobs.com

Inside Careers Guide: Management - www.insidecareers.co.uk

Institute of Leadership and Management (ILM) (ILM) - www.i-l-m.com/

Real Life Guide to Retail (Trotman) - www.trotman.co.uk

Training Schemes - www.direct.gov.uk/en/educationandlearning

Welsh Baccalaureate - www.wbq.org.uk

▶Working in retail & customer services (2008) (Babcock Lifeskills) - www.babcock-lifeskills.com/

▶Working with languages (2010) (Babcock Lifeskills) - www.babcock-lifeskills.com/

Addresses

Customer Contact Association (CCA)
20 Newtown Place, Glasgow G3 7PY
Phone: +44 (0)141 564 9010
Web: www.cca.org.uk

Institute of Customer Service (ICS)
2 Castle Court, St Peter's Street, Colchester, Essex CO1 1EW
Phone: +44 (0)1206 571716
Web: www.instituteofcustomerservice.com

Similar Jobs

Building Society Manager, Hotel Manager, Marketing Manager, Retail Manager

Cycle Mechanic

also known as: Bike Mechanic, Bike Technician

CRCI:Retail Sales and Customer Services

CLCI:OFM Job Band: 1 to 2

Job Description

Cycle mechanics work in an independent cycle shop or a national chain store, selling and repairing bicycles and their components. They mend punctures, chains and brakes and fit and adjust gears and specialist equipment. May put together and test new bikes or rebuild old ones. They give advice and help to customers, including advice on their choice of cycle. Stock ordering, keeping accounts and using a computer are all part of the job. Some shops operate a cycle hire service. May also specialise in the 'high-spec' end of the industry, including racing bikes, or perhaps electronic bikes. May assist in the shop by selling stock and cycle accessories.

Work Details

Usually work a basic 39 hr week, including some Saturdays, and perhaps Sundays, but have time off during the week instead. The job requires you to deal with enquiries, give advice to customers and also deal with complaints. You need to learn all about the products you are selling and keep up to date with information about new cycles or equipment. Often, you are expected to handle sales and deal with cash and credit/debit cards. If self-employed, you may spend time at home doing accounts and other paperwork. You may be on your feet all day and also have to lift cycles and heavy items equipment.

Qualification

• England, Wales and Northern Ireland

Band 1: No minimum qualifications are required, but you are expected to have a good level of general education. However, some formal/vocational qualifications at any level are useful and may be required by some employers.

Band 2: Although academic qualifications are not specified for this job, employers may ask for some GCSEs (A*-C) in subjects that include English and maths, or equivalent. These qualifications may also be needed for entry to courses in retailing.

• Scotland

Band 1: No minimum qualifications are required, but you are expected to have a good level of general education. However, some formal/vocational qualifications at any level are useful and may be required by some employers.

Band 2: Although academic qualifications are not specified for this job, employers may ask for some S grades (1-3) in subjects that include English and maths, or similar. These qualifications may also be needed for entry to courses in retailing.

Adult Qualifications

Formal qualifications are not essential to enter this job, though a good general education and any relevant practical qualifications are an advantage.

Work Experience

Relevant work or voluntary experience is always useful and can improve your chances when applying for entry to jobs in sales. It can equip you with skills that you can use in the future and add to your CV. Part-time and holiday employment in a wide range of shops is usually fairly easy to obtain. People employed in this type of work often have an interest in cycling and repairing bikes as a hobby.

Entry and Training

Training is usually by practical experience on the job, working with an experienced person, and perhaps taking courses in mechanics. Courses can be full or part time, short specialised courses, or evening classes.

The Association of Cycle Traders offers Cytech qualifications that are the industry-recognised standard for cycle mechanics and technicians. Cytech training and accreditation options are available to those already employed within the bike industry. There is also a Cytech technical theory distance-learning course that also offers an introduction to bike maintenance and which can be studied at home. With further practical assessment, this course may be upgraded to the Cytech technical one foundation course. Some Cytech courses are available to those wishing to develop their maintenance skills, prior to applying for a job.

You can work towards S/NVQs in retail skills at levels 1-2. A Diploma/Welsh Baccalaureate in retail business may be available in your area. Training programmes, including retail apprenticeship schemes, may also be available. Advanced apprenticeships leading to qualification at level 3 can also be a route into higher education. See the Skillsmart Retail website for details.

Adults may be able to enter this work through a government-funded training programme. Contact your local careers office, Jobcentre Plus, Next Step service or Learning and Skills Council (LSC)/Local Enterprise Company (LEC) for details of all training opportunities and schemes, including apprenticeships for adults. Previous experience in selling is helpful, as are workshop skills.

Opportunities and Pay

You can be employed by an independent retailer, perhaps a small firm, or a national chain of cycle shops. If you have enough money for stock, you can start up your own cycle shop and be self-employed. Promotion opportunities are limited, but may be better in larger stores.

Pay varies according to your employer and area. Most start on around £12k, rising to around £14k-£15k a year. Those working for larger firms/stores can earn more than £19k a year. Self-employed mechanics may earn significantly more than this.

Skills and Qualities

business awareness, customer service skills, enterprising, good communication skills, IT skills, methodical, patient, practical skills, strong hands, technical aptitude

Relevant Subjects

Design and technology, Retail and distribution

Further Information

Apprenticeship Schemes (National Apprenticeship Service) - www.apprenticeships.org.uk

Diplomas (Foundation, Higher and Advanced) - http://yp.direct.gov.uk/diplomas

Foundation Learning (QCDA) - www.qcda.gov.uk

Skillsmart Retail - sector skills council for the retail industry - www.skillsmartretail.com

Training Schemes - www.direct.gov.uk/en/educationandlearning

Welsh Baccalaureate - www.wbq.org.uk

▶Working in retail & customer services (2008) (Babcock Lifeskills) - www.babcock-lifeskills.com/

Addresses

Association of Cycle Traders
PO Box 5110, Hove BN52 9EB
Phone: +44 (0)845 618 7256
Web: www.act-bicycles.com

Similar Jobs

Assembler: Light Industry, Mechanic: Motorcycle, Retail Assistant, Vehicle Mechanic/Motor Vehicle Technician

Cytogeneticist

also known as: Clinical Cytogeneticist

CRCI:Science, Mathematics and Statistics

CLCI:JAX Job Band: 5

Job Description

Cytogeneticists investigate, detect and diagnose hereditary diseases and disorders. They carry out analysis on human cells, obtained through samples of blood, bone marrow or body fluid, to study chromosomes. May also obtain samples of foetal tissue or amniotic fluid. This leads to the detection of hereditary diseases and abnormalities and assists the management and treatment of, for example, mental and physical disorders, pre-natal defects, infertility and developmental problems.

Cytogeneticist use screening methods, including computer-assisted laboratory techniques and other high-tech equipment, then record data and write reports. May be responsible for managing a team of biomedical scientists and other support staff such as medical technologists, laboratory assistants and clerical assistants. Work closely with other health professionals, including paediatricians, clinical geneticists and obstetricians.

Work Details

Regular hours are usually worked, Monday to Friday in a laboratory, university, college, hospital, or perhaps an office. However, additional hours may be required to cover emergencies, weekends and bank holidays. Depending on the post, you may have responsibility for setting up experiments, analysing results and presenting reports, often to strict deadlines. Hospital work requires you to provide information and advice for diagnosis and treatment, which requires a high degree of accuracy. Some work can involve having to cope with the sight of blood. In some jobs you monitor quality standards, check production schedules or supervise staff. A white coat or overall and protective gloves may be worn at times.

Qualification

- **England, Wales and Northern Ireland**

Band 5: For degree courses: 2-3 A levels in appropriate science subjects and some GCSEs (A*-C), preferably including English, maths and sciences, or equivalent qualifications. Exact requirements depend on the degree you take.

- **Scotland**

Band 5: For degree courses: 3-5 H grades in appropriate science subjects and some S grades (1-3), preferably including English, maths and sciences, or similar qualifications. Exact requirements depend on the degree you take.

Degree Information

A good honours degree is required of which genetics is an essential component. Appropriate subjects, including genetics, biochemistry, biomedical science, molecular biology, biology, physiology and zoology are an advantage. Postgraduate degrees are available and in particular, an MSc/PhD related to human genetics is an advantage.

Adult Qualifications

Adults without the normal academic qualifications, but who have relevant laboratory experience may be considered for some courses. Access courses may be available in some areas. It is also possible for those without the specified science qualifications to take a foundation year leading into the relevant degree. Check with universities.

Work Experience

Universities and employers may prefer candidates who have relevant work or voluntary experience, such as work in a hospital, a relevant university department, an industrial or commercial laboratory. If it proves difficult to gain this exact experience, then similar or other scientific backgrounds are still attractive to employers and admissions tutors.

Entry and Training

There are two entry routes to the profession. The preferred one, recommended by the Association for Clinical Cytogenetics (ACC) is through an accredited training scheme in national training laboratories organised via the NHS Clinical Scientists Recruitment Office. Following a two-year period of in-service, continually assessed, competence-based training, successful trainees are awarded a postgraduate certificate in clinical cytogenetics from the ACC. Continuing professional development (CPD) is a job requirement to maintain registration with the Health Professions Council (HPC).

Not all laboratories offer this form of training and the second, less common route is to enter at a training level as a Grade A associate on a two-year traineeship as part of the laboratory's staffing quota. In this case, you also carry out a proportion of the diagnostic work. Trainee posts are very competitive with only a few NHS vacancies offered each year. An MSc may entitle you to an award of credit towards clinical cytogenetics training. Laboratory experience, especially genetics related, gained within studies and/or a hospital, is helpful.

When qualified you can register with the HPC, which is essential for work as a practising clinical scientist. It is important to check that employment offered is approved by the HPC for training. Some degree courses incorporate the necessary in-service experience.

Mature entry may be difficult from your early 40s. However, adults with extensive and relevant laboratory experience as an assistant or associate healthcare scientist have an advantage, and applications are welcomed.

Opportunities and Pay

Most posts are with the NHS and competition is intense, but there is also work with government departments, private laboratories, cancer research laboratories, pharmaceutical firms, and universities. After qualification most cytogeneticists specialise. Two major areas of specialisms are fertility problems and abnormalities in babies. Promotion usually requires a more advanced qualification such as membership of the Royal College of Pathologists (RCPath).

Agency work is possible and occasionally cytogeneticists become self-employed, running a private laboratory. Opportunities for work abroad are usually found in Australia, Canada and Saudi Arabia.

Typical starting salaries range from £24k a year. Once registered, and with more experience you can earn £29k-£36k a year. Principal scientists earn up to £52k and consultants up to £93k a year. In the NHS there are salary scales for each grade that include annual increments. Trust hospitals set their own rates locally and there are likely to be additional allowances for working in London.

Health

There is a risk of allergy from skin irritants and the work can involve a risk of infection. This job requires good colour vision for certain areas of work.

Skills and Qualities

able to work to deadlines, accurate, analytical skills, aptitude for teamwork, good at writing reports, IT skills, methodical, not squeamish, problem-solving skills, research skills, scientific approach

Relevant Subjects

Biology, Chemistry, English, Health and social care, ICT/Computer studies, Mathematics, Physics, Science

Further Information

Careers in Cytogenetics (Association of Clinical Cytogeneticists (ACC) - www.cytogenetics.org.uk/

New Scientist (weekly) (Reed) - www.newscientist.com

NHS Careers (NHS Careers) - www.nhscareers.nhs.uk

▶Working in science (2007) (Babcock Lifeskills) - www.babcock-lifeskills.com/

Addresses

Association for Clinical Cytogenetics (ACC)
Oxford Medical Genetics Laboratories, The Churchill, Old Road, Headington OX3 7LJ
Phone: +44 (0)1865 226001
Web: www.cytogenetics.org.uk

British Society for Human Genetics (BSHG)
Clinical Genetics Unit, Birmingham Women's Hospital B15 2TG
Phone: +44 (0)121 627 2634
Web: www.bshg.org.uk

Clinical Scientists Recruitment Office (ACB)
c/o Association of Clinical Biochemists, 130-132 Tooley Street, London SE1 2TU
Phone: +44 (0)20 7403 8001
Web: www.acb.org.uk

Health Professions Council (HPC)
Park House, 184 Kennington Park Road, London SE11 4BU
Phone: +44 (0)20 7582 0866
Web: www.hpc-uk.org

Royal College of Pathologists (RCPath)
2 Carlton House Terrace, London SW1Y 5AF
Phone: +44 (0)20 7451 6700
Web: www.rcpath.org

School of Biological Sciences
The Queen's University of Belfast, Medical Biology Centre, 97 Lisburn Road BT9 7BL
Phone: +44 (0)28 9097 5787
Web: www.qub.ac.uk/bb

Similar Jobs

Biochemist, Clinical Molecular Geneticist, Clinical Technologist, Geneticist, Microbiologist, Toxicologist

Damp Proofer

CRCI:Building and Construction
CLCI:UF Job Band: 1 to 2

Job Description

Damp proofers treat buildings (brickwork, woodwork, floors, walls, and roofs) against damp, fungal and insect attack. They carry out the treatment recommended by a damp-surveyor and use chemicals such as insecticides and fungicides and sometimes flame retardants. They inspect the property to check the extent of the problem and drill holes into masonry walls. Chemicals are injected at high pressure into the blocks and the damp proof course in buildings, mostly using injection equipment. Damp proofers ensure there is enough drainage around the building. May use hand and power tools and machines.

Work Details

Damp proofers usually work a basic 39 hr week. You may be expected to work overtime, in the evenings or at weekends to complete jobs. Work is usually outdoors and on-site in all weathers. You may also work indoors if treating woodwork, sometimes in confined spaces, such as lofts. Travel to different sites is necessary and sometimes you may be working away from home.

You have to cope with rough ground, bending, lifting and working at heights on scaffolding and ladders. Special protective clothing is needed when using chemicals. You must keep up to date with EU and health and safety regulations. A driving licence may be required.

Qualification

• England, Wales and Northern Ireland

Band 1: No minimum qualifications are required, but some formal/vocational qualifications at any level are useful.

Band 2: Although academic qualifications are not specified for this job, it is an advantage to have some GCSEs (A*-E) in subjects that include English and maths, or equivalent.

• Scotland

Band 1: No minimum qualifications are required, but some formal/vocational qualifications at any level are useful.

Band 2: Although academic qualifications are not specified for this job, it is an advantage to have some S grades (1-5) in subjects that include English and maths, or similar.

Adult Qualifications

You do not need educational qualifications to enter this job though employers may expect you to have a good level of general education.

Work Experience

Relevant work or voluntary experience is always useful and can improve your chances when applying for entry to construction jobs and apprenticeships. Health and safety issues may mean that there are certain jobs you can't do until you are over 16. Contact your local ConstructionSkills office for advice.

Entry and Training

Training is usually on the job, initially working with experienced damp proofers, or possibly through an employer's training scheme such as an apprenticeship. There may be off-the-job training offered through companies that produce damp proofing treatments or equipment. You may be expected to eventually gain a level of competence card through a Construction Skills Certification Scheme that indicates your individual skill level.

The Property Care Association (PCA) is the main trade body for water and damp proofing in the UK. They offer several qualifications including the technician qualification which is relevant to damp proofers. They also offer 1-3 day courses on a range of topics including structural waterproofing and technicians' training.

A Diploma/Welsh Baccalaureate in construction and the built environment may be available in your area. Practical work-related qualifications include the BTEC First Certificate/Diploma in Construction at level 2. An S/NVQ in insulation and building treatments is also available at level 2. Training programmes, including apprenticeships leading to level 2 and advanced apprenticeships/construction apprenticeships leading to level 3, may be available in your area. Contact ConstructionSkills or the PCA for details of all certified courses.

Mature entrants with related experience in construction or building work are often preferred. Applicants can take refresher courses that are sometimes available for those returning to work and there may be special government training schemes in some areas. If you have experience without formal qualifications, you can use On-Site Assessment and Training or the Experienced Worker Practical Assessment scheme to achieve a qualification. More information is available from the ConstructionSkills website.

Opportunities and Pay

You can work for specialist damp-proofing contractors, or building contractors throughout the UK. There may be some opportunities with related companies, such as pest control firms. Availability of work may depend on activity in the building trade and the national economy. Currently there is a downturn in the housing market which means there may be a shortage of vacancies.

When experienced it is possible to become self-employed. Tools and equipment may be supplied by the employer. Some jobs are seasonal or short-term. There may be opportunities to work on contracts abroad. Promotion is possible to supervisor posts.

Pay varies depending on area and employer. A trainee damp proofer earns around £12k-£15k a year; when skilled this rises to around £18k-£25k. The most skilled and experienced workers, including the self-employed, can earn up to £35k a year. Employers may give allowances for travel and cost of lodgings. Overtime and bonus payments can add to income.

Health
This job requires good stamina and physical fitness. The use of chemicals may be an issue if you have chest problems or allergies.

Skills and Qualities
able to follow instructions, able to work both on your own and in a team, able to work in confined spaces, agile, attention to detail, health & safety awareness, manual dexterity, practical skills, willing to travel

Relevant Subjects
Construction and built environment, Design and technology

Further Information
Careers in Construction - www.bconstructive.co.uk

Construction Skills Certification Scheme (CSCS) - www.cscs.uk.com

ConstructionSkills - sector skills council for the construction industry - www.cskills.org

Diplomas (Foundation, Higher and Advanced) - http://yp.direct.gov.uk/diplomas

Welsh Baccalaureate - www.wbq.org.uk

▶Working in construction & the built environment (2007) (Babcock Lifeskills) - www.babcock-lifeskills.com/

Addresses
Property Care Association (PCA)
Lakeview Court Ermine Business Park, Huntingdon, Cambridgeshire PE29 6XR
Phone: +44 (0)844 375 4301
Web: www.property-care.org

Similar Jobs
Bricklayer, Cavity Wall Insulation Technician, Construction Operative, Plasterer, Roofer, Tiler: Wall & Floor

Dancer

CRCI:Performing Arts
CLCI:GAF Job Band: 1 to 5

Job Description
Dancers perform dance and creative movement to portray a role or character without using words, usually before a live audience or in film and television. They usually interpret the work of a choreographer. Many dancers specialise, such as in ballet or contemporary dance. Some dancers perform in musical theatres and specialise in tap-dancing or jazz interpretation. Many are all-round dancers with a variety of dancing skills in ballroom, flamenco, Bollywood, bodypopping or breakdancing. All professional dancers spend most of their time exercising, rehearsing and performing. Dancers may train to teach their skills or become choreographers or producers.

Work Details
Dancers spend a great deal of time practising, rehearsing and performing, often at evenings and weekends, working in a theatre, studio, a club, in schools or on location. Hours are usually irregular and include long evenings and early starts. As you are extremely active, physical fitness is essential. There is always a risk that injury may end your career suddenly. On tour, travel is necessary and you may have to spend long periods away from home, sometimes abroad.

Qualification
No minimum academic qualifications are required for most performance courses, and entry requirements vary between dance schools. You are judged on your potential performance ability, personality, and your physique, rather than academic exam passes. However, some formal qualifications are useful as this may be a short career, and exam passes at any level help in the transfer to a second career. Useful subjects include English, drama, music, biology, performing arts and dance.

Degree Information
Dance and performing arts degrees are not intended as a training route for dancers, but can develop potential. You should be advised by your dance teacher.

Adult Qualifications
Adults are unlikely to be successful in this occupation unless they have been taking dance lessons from an early age and also have some experience.

Work Experience
It is essential to begin your dance training at an early age and perform in amateur productions, and at school/dance school performances. Some voluntary/holiday or temporary work with a local theatre or dance company is useful.

Entry and Training
Those who wish to work in ballet must begin ballet training at a young age, while joints and bones are still flexible. Many dancers start classes at age 4-5. Ballet schools, such as the Royal Ballet School, take pupils aged between 11-18 and offer specialist training for entry to an adult ballet company, though only the most exceptional dancers are successful. Courses include academic study as well as ballet, and may be residential. There may be minimum height requirements for ballet schools.

For contemporary dance there are two main schools which run a number of specialised courses - the London Contemporary Dance School and the Laban Centre for Movement. Many employers look for multi-skilled dancers, so it is an advantage to have experience in drama and music. The Council for Dance Education and Training holds a list of accredited courses on its website. Similarly, the British Theatre Dance Association has details of training courses on its website and Dance UK has lots of relevant information for dancers.

To be accepted for a course or a job, you usually have to pass an audition and an interview. An annual dance and drama award is available from the government for the most talented dance/drama students. A Diploma/Welsh Baccalaureate in creative and media may be available in your area. Check university entry requirements carefully in case there is an additional specialist learning requirement with the diploma. See the diplomas website for further information.

For information on training as a dance teacher or choreographer, see the job articles Teacher: Dance, and Choreographer.

Some contemporary dance schools accept mature applicants aged up to early thirties if you have exceptional talent.

Opportunities and Pay
There are around 200 dance companies in the UK and the dance industry employs about 30,000 people. There is strong competition for all jobs and these are usually short-term contracts which give limited job security. Considerable talent is required for success and it is usually a short career. A professional dancing career may not extend beyond the age of 35, but there are exceptions. Dancers Career Development offers advice for professional dancers at the end of their career.

You can start your career as a member of a troupe or corps de ballet; there are few soloists or principals. Most performers work with private dance companies, theatres, film and TV companies, nightclubs, cruise ships and in cabaret. Prospects vary according to the season with more jobs at Christmas and during the pantomime season. After performing it is possible to move into other areas such as teaching or choreography. There is a growing number of jobs with local authority community dance programmes and also with non-western dance, which includes African and South Asian dance groups. Dance/movement therapy is another growing area.

Pay varies depending on the type of dancer you are. You are usually paid per week or per performance. A dancer at the start of their career is likely to earn around £330 a week, rising to £350-£550. Performers with recognised 'star quality', such as soloists and principal dancers, earn much more. Equity negotiates minimum rates of pay for their members. Contact Equity for details.

Health
You must be well proportioned and have a high level of physical fitness and lots of stamina. A medical examination is usual for course entry.

Skills and Qualities
aptitude for teamwork, committed, competitive, determined, enthusiastic, good ear for music, hard working, self confident, self-disciplined

Relevant Subjects
Art and Design, Media and communication studies, Music, Performing arts, Physical education and sport

Further Information
Ballet Ireland - www.ballet-ireland.com

British Ballet Organisation (BBO) - www.bbo.org.uk

Creative Choices - www.creative-choices.co.uk

Dance and Drama Awards - www.direct.gov.uk/en/EducationAndLearning

Dancing Times (Dancing Times Ltd) - www.dancing-times.co.uk

Diplomas (Foundation, Higher and Advanced) - http://yp.direct.gov.uk/diplomas

Foundation for Community Dance - www.communitydance.org.uk

So you want to work in Music & Dance (Wayland) - www.waylandbooks.co.uk

The Stage Online - www.thestage.co.uk

Welsh Baccalaureate - www.wbq.org.uk

▶Working in creative & media (2007) (Babcock Lifeskills) - www.babcock-lifeskills.com/

▶Working in music (2007) (Babcock Lifeskills) - www.babcock-lifeskills.com/

Addresses
British Theatre Dance Association
The International Arts Centre, Garden Street, Leicester LE1 3UA
Phone: 0845 166 2179 (UK only)
Web: www.btda.org.uk

Council for Dance Education and Training (CDET)
Old Brewer's Yard, 17 - 19 Neal Street, Covent Garden, London WC2H 9UY
Phone: +44 (0)207 240 5703
Web: www.cdet.org.uk

Dance UK
2nd Floor, Finsbury Town Hall , Rosebery Avenue, London EC1R 4QT
Phone: +44 (0)20 7713 0730
Web: www.danceuk.org

Dancers' Career Development
19-20 Hatton Place, London EC1N 8RU
Phone: +44 (0)20 7831 1449
Web: www.thedcd.org.uk

Equity
Guild House, Upper St Martin's Lane, London WC2H 9EG
Phone: +44 (0)20 7379 6000
Web: www.equity.org.uk

Laban Centre of Movement
Creekside, London SE8 3DZ
Phone: +44 (0)20 8691 8600
Web: www.laban.org

London Contemporary Dance School
The Place, 17 Duke's Road, London WC1H 9PH
Phone: +44 (0)20 7121 1000
Web: www.theplace.org.uk

Royal Academy of Dance (RAD)
36 Battersea Square, London SW11 3RA
Phone: +44 (0)20 7326 8000
Web: www.rad.org.uk

Royal Ballet School
46 Floral Street, Covent Garden, London WC2E 9DA
Phone: +44 (0)20 7836 8899
Web: www.royal-ballet-school.org.uk

Similar Jobs
Actor, Choreographer, Entertainer, Fitness Instructor, Singer, Teacher: Dance

Database Administrator
also known as: DBA, IT Database Administrator

CRCI:Computers and IT

CLCI:CAV

Job Band: 3 to 5

Job Description
A database administrator (DBA) plans, develops, tests and maintains an organisation's computerised information, and is responsible for the accuracy, consistency, security and accessibility of each database. Ensures that the requirements of the Data Protection Act are met. Works closely with database users to locate and solve problems in the system. May also be responsible for ensuring that only authorised people can access certain information and for ensuring an adequate storage and data back-up system is in place.

May write database user documents and train staff to use the database. Recommends/implements improvements to the system. May set up reports for database users to run. Works on ways to make databases faster and easier to use. Other responsibilities may include the supervision of staff. Also works closely with programmers, analysts and other IT managers.

Work Details
Usually works 37-40 hrs a week, Monday to Friday, though may need to be on call if problems occur outside normal office hours. Some of your work on the database may need to take place at times when it is not in general use, such as evenings and weekends. The job involves sitting for a long time at a computer. You may be based at one site or travel between sites. Those visiting clients may be away from home at times. You frequently consult with managers and other IT professionals and you may need to lead a team of employees. An understanding of the organisation is important.

Qualification

• England, Wales and Northern Ireland
Band 3: For direct entry: usually at least 4 GCSEs (A*-C) preferably including English, maths and computer studies/information technology, or equivalent.

Band 4: For BTEC higher national award: 1-2 A levels and some GCSEs (A*-C) usually including English and maths, or equivalent. For some courses you need science, computer studies or information technology.

Band 5: For relevant degree course: 2-3 A levels including subjects such as maths, science, computer studies or information technology, and some GCSEs (A*-C) usually including English and maths, or equivalent. Exact requirements depend on the degree you take.

- **Scotland**

Band 3: For direct entry: usually at least four S grades (1-3) preferably including English, maths and computer studies or information technology, or similar.

Band 4: For SQA higher national award: 2-3 H grades and some S grades (1-3) including English and maths, or similar qualifications. For some courses you need science, computer studies or information technology.

Band 5: For relevant degree course: 3-5 H grades in subjects such as maths, science, computer studies or information technology, and some S grades (1-3) usually including English and maths, or similar qualifications. Exact requirements depend on the degree you take.

Degree Information

Most database administrators are graduates in computing subjects, including computer/software engineering. Operational research, maths and electronics are also useful. The Information Technology Management for Business degree (see e-skills UK) is designed in partnership with some of the biggest employers in the IT industry. There are postgraduate qualifications in computing that may improve your job prospects, especially if your first degree is not in a computing-related subject.

Adult Qualifications

Employers expect mature applicants to have relevant experience, particularly in technical areas of computing. Mature entrants may not need the standard entry requirements for higher education courses, particularly if their previous experience is relevant and they show the ability to study at the appropriate level. Access courses give adults without qualifications a route onto degree courses. Some Jobcentre Plus offices and Jobcentres (NI) offer specialised IT courses for adults.

Work Experience

Entry to this job is competitive and it is important that you try to do some relevant work or voluntary experience before applying. Relevant areas and skills are anything office based, using administration skills, or working with the public or a team of people. Experience or knowledge of database software packages and other IT techniques is a distinct advantage and sometimes a requirement. Internships and work placements are a valuable introduction to the IT industry, and enable you to make an informed career choice. The British Computer Society offers a work placement service through its young professional group.

Other schemes such as 'The Year in Industry', enable those who expect good A levels/H grades and intend to go to university, the opportunity to spend a salaried year with a company to gain valuable work experience.

Entry and Training

There are no set entry requirements, though database administrators usually have a good technical background in systems programming or design. Some move into this work from other business areas within the organisation. You need to know how to use structured query language (SQL) and the components of the database management system (DBMS). SQL Server, Oracle and Sybase are the main database systems to gain experience of.

Entrants often have a degree but it is possible to become a database administrator without a degree or HND if you have good all-round IT skills. Training is ongoing, both on the job and by short courses run by database systems providers, including Microsoft, IBM and Oracle. It is important to keep your skills up to date. Web-based services are growing so expertise in integrating web technologies with databases is increasingly useful.

Some employers may assist with study for professional qualifications, including those of the British Computer Society, the Skills Framework for the Information Age and the Institute for the Management of Information Systems. Skills that are currently in demand include Microsoft, Java and Unix. A popular industry-recognised entry-level qualification is the CompTIA A+ offered by the Computing Technology Industry Association (CompTIA) which offers alternative validation paths for specific job environments. Contact CompTIA for details.

The Open University offers courses in computing and maths that can lead to an appropriate computing degree through distance learning. Several universities now offer the information technology management for business (ITMB) degree, developed by e-skills and employers to meet specific industry needs. A full or part-time foundation degree in IT is available and a Diploma/Welsh Baccalaureate in IT may be available in your area for those aged 14-19.

E-skills run a professional development programme which enables new IT professionals to fast-track their career. The programme is delivered through universities and participating employers. E-skills also offers an internship. Students are placed for a period of employment within an organisation, enabling them to develop valuable business and IT skills. Contact e-skills for details of all programmes and schemes. Relevant S/NVQs for IT users are available at levels 2-4. The diploma for IT users (ITQ 2009) has been developed as part of a project involving a full review of the National Occupational Standards (NOS) for IT users and is backed by employers.

Training programmes, including apprenticeship schemes, may be available in your area. Advanced apprenticeships leading to qualification at level 3 can also be a route into higher education. An ICT higher apprenticeship is available through e-skills. This combines an apprenticeship with a foundation degree and can lead to a full honours degree. There are partnerships with colleges and universities throughout the UK.

Mature applicants need to gain experience in computing, though it is sometimes possible for a graduate to gain employment without experience. IT programming or systems operations experience is useful and a one-year IT postgraduate conversion course is an advantage for those without a relevant degree. There are many full or part-time courses available at further/higher education colleges and government training opportunities may be available in your area.

You can also gain recognition of previous experience through Accreditation of Prior Learning (APL). Contact your local careers office, Jobcentre Plus, Next Step service or Learning and Skills Council (LSC)/Local Enterprise Company (LEC) for details of all training opportunities and schemes.

Opportunities and Pay

Database administrators (DBAs) are employed in the UK with all types of organisation in industry and commerce, the financial sector, local and central government departments, health and voluntary sectors, and the armed services. Some work for specialist firms that provide a complete database service to clients. The increased use of interactive, database-driven websites offers new opportunities for DBAs. It is possible to progress to general management or transfer to other areas of computing, such as systems analysis and network management. There are also opportunities for experienced DBAs to work as self-employed consultants. Work abroad may also be available.

Salary depends on the location and type of company. On entry you may expect to earn between £18k-£22k a year, rising to around £25k-£35k with experience. Senior DBAs may earn £35k-£45k or more a year.

Relevant Subjects
Design and technology, English, ICT/Computer studies, Mathematics, Physics, Science

Further Information
AGCAS: Information Technology (Job Sector Briefing) (AGCAS) - www.prospects.ac.uk

Apprenticeship Schemes (National Apprenticeship Service) - www.apprenticeships.org.uk

Computer Weekly (Reed Business Information) - www.computerweekly.com

Computing Technology Industry Association (CompTIA) - www.comptia.org

Diplomas (Foundation, Higher and Advanced) - http://yp.direct.gov.uk/diplomas

e-skills UK - sector skills council for business and information technology - www.e-skills.com

Inside Careers Guide: Information Technology - www.insidecareers.co.uk

Open University - www.open.ac.uk

Real Life Guide to Information & Communications Technology (Trotman) - www.trotman.co.uk

Skills Framework for the Information Age (SFIA) (SFIA Foundation) - www.sfia.org.uk

TARGETjobs: IT (GTI Specialist Publishing Ltd.) - www.groupgti.com

Training Schemes - www.direct.gov.uk/en/educationandlearning

Welsh Baccalaureate - www.wbq.org.uk

▶Working in computers & IT (2010) (Babcock Lifeskills) - www.babcock-lifeskills.com/

Year in Industry (Engineering Development Trust) - www.yini.org.uk

Addresses
British Computer Society (BCS)
First Floor, Block D North Star House North Star Avenue, Swindon, Wiltshire SN2 1FA
Phone: +44 (0)845 300 4417
Web: www.bcs.org

Institute for the Management of Information Systems (IMIS)
5 Kingfisher House, New Mill Road, Orpington, Kent BR5 3QG
Phone: +44 (0)700 002 3456
Web: www.imis.org.uk

Similar Jobs
Computer Operator, Information Scientist, IT Applications Developer, IT Systems Developer, Network Manager, Website Developer

Debt Collector/Bailiff
also known as: Sherrif Officer (Scotland)
CRCI:Financial Services
CLCI:NAK

Job Band: 1 to 3

Job Description
Debt collectors/bailiffs help to collect money from people or companies who owe debts. Most work is with consumers, although a proportion of the work is with companies, some of which may want to collect debts from international organisations.

Use several methods to try to obtain payment from people who owe money, including telephoning and writing to debtors, or visiting them at their home or at their business premises. Attempt to sort out how the debt is to be paid, often in small amounts. If no agreement is reached, may legally be able to repossess a property or remove a debtor's goods. Write letters and complete any necessary paperwork.

In Scotland, sheriff officers or messengers-at-arms enforce court orders to recover money for private clients or government departments. They deal with particular sorts of debt recovery such as court orders or taxes. They also deliver legal documents such as summonses or county court orders, mainly for debt or possession of property.

Work Details
Most debt collectors work 37-39 hrs a week, Monday to Friday. They often work in the early mornings and evenings, depending on when people are available; some weekend work may be necessary. Much of the work is based in offices or call centres, contacting people by phone or mail. You may also have to spend time travelling and visiting debtors. This may mean spending time away from home, overnight or for several nights. Some heavy lifting may be required, especially if removing furniture or equipment from debtors' premises.

You have to deal with people who can be angry, upset or destructive. Many debt collectors combine this work with another job. Part-time work and self-employment is possible.

Qualification
- **Scotland**

Band 1: No minimum qualifications are required, but you are expected to have a good level of general education. However, some formal/vocational qualifications at any level are useful.

Band 2: Although academic qualifications are not specified for this job, it is an advantage to have some S grades (1-3) in subjects that include English and maths, or similar.

Band 3: For entry: usually at least four S grades (1-3) including English and maths, or similar.

Adult Qualifications
No entry qualifications are specified, though most employers prefer mature entrants with some experience in accounting or credit control.

Work Experience
Any work experience can equip you with skills that you can use in the future and add to your CV. Work experience can either be unpaid or voluntary or can be holiday or part-time work that you have organised yourself. Any experience that involves working with figures or dealing with the public is useful.

Entry and Training
There are no minimum qualifications required for entry to this work but most enter with S grades. Training takes place mainly on the job with an experienced debt collector. Employers may send new entrants on relevant short courses. Some companies run bespoke in-house training on Scottish debt recovery as the process is different to the rest of the UK.

The Institute of Credit Management has branches in Scotland and offers a range of relevant qualifications including diplomas in credit management at levels 3-5. Check the website for details. The Credit Services Association is also a useful source of information for those working in this industry.

Mature entrants have an advantage in this type of work and particularly those with previous working experience of the law, financial advice, security or credit control. Employers expect applicants to be able to deal with the public.

Opportunities and Pay
There are opportunities for part-time or full-time work in most urban areas and the use of collection agencies has grown in recent years. Debt collectors are employed by firms of debt collectors, credit insurers, mail order companies, or other companies with large credit control departments. There are also opportunities for self-employment. Promotion in firms is possible to senior debt

collector, assistant manager and manager. Alternatively, you may go on to work for the courts in Scotland as a sheriff officer (see job profile).

Earnings vary according to the type of work and whether you are employed or self-employed. Starting salaries for debt collectors are around £15k a year, rising to £20k-£25k. Many firms pay a basic salary plus some form of commission or incentive payments. Some companies may only pay commission on the money recovered.

Health
You need to have good stamina and be physically fit for this job.

Skills and Qualities
able to get on with all kinds of people, able to manage a budget and keep records, assertive, calm, decisive, negotiating skills, patient, perseverance, tactful

Further Information
Credit Services Association (CSA) - www.csa-uk.com

Society of Messengers-at-Arms and Sherrif Officers (SAMSO) - www.smaso.org

Addresses
Institute of Credit Management (ICM)
The Water Mill, Station Road, South Luffenham, Leicestershire
LE15 8NB
Phone: +44 (0)1780 722900
Web: www.icm.org.uk

Similar Jobs
Clerk: Accounts, Credit Manager, Financial Adviser/Planner

Debt Counsellor
also known as: Finance Adviser, Money Adviser

CRCI:Social Work and Counselling Services
CLCI:KEK Job Band: 3 to 5

Job Description
Debt counsellors help people to take control of their money and deal with their debts. They talk to clients to build a rapport and develop trust. Offer support and reassurance that there are steps people can take to improve their situation. Provide impartial and confidential advice. Contact organisations the client owes money to on the client's behalf, or helps clients to act for themselves. Refer clients to other organisations that can help. May go to court to help clients make their case.

Debt counsellors find out how much money the client has coming in from earnings, benefits and other sources. They check whether clients can pay less tax or get extra benefits and whether the amounts they owe are right. Work out how much they need for living expenses like food, heating, housing and travel. They see how much is left to pay off debts. Help clients to decide which debts they need to pay off first. They work out a realistic budget that leaves the client enough to live on and allows them to start paying back the money they owe. Negotiate with organisations that are owed money to reduce the debts, lower interest rates and get realistic repayment terms. Give advice about bankruptcy and going to court.

Work Details
Usually works a 37 hr week, Monday to Friday. Depending on the employer, you may do some evening or weekend work. Part-time work is quite common. Works in an office and uses a computer. Sometimes goes to court. Deals with clients face to face in an interview room or over the phone. Some debt counsellors visit clients at home or in the community. If you work for an organisation that provides a telephone helpline, you may wear a headset.

Clients are likely to be under a lot of stress and may be frightened or upset. They may be facing court action or losing their homes and possessions. Liaises with other advice workers and professionals such as social workers and solicitors.

Qualification
Employers look for at least basic English language and numeracy skills. Qualifications held by people entering this area of work vary widely. Good communication skills, especially the ability to listen, are essential. A degree and/or professional qualifications are an advantage, but not essential.

Adult Qualifications
Employers look for people with the right personal qualities, level of maturity and life experience rather than those with specific qualifications.

Work Experience
Usually you need at least a year's paid or voluntary experience as an advice worker if you want to work as a debt counsellor. Organisations such as Citizens Advice accept volunteers from the age of 16 and some actively encourage student volunteers. Experience of work that involves using listening skills and helping people is useful. Many colleges and adult education services offer courses that provide an introduction to counselling for people interested in developing these skills.

Entry and Training
Usually people move into debt counselling from general advice work. Most paid advice workers start out as volunteers. In some areas, being able to speak a second language is an advantage. Due to the nature of the work, it is likely that your employer will ask for a Criminal Records Bureau (CRB) or Disclosure Scotland check.

Many advice organisations run their own training schemes that include initial training and short specialised courses on topics related to money advice. You gain practical knowledge and skills on the job, supervised or mentored by experienced staff. Relevant S/NVQs include advice and guidance at levels 2-4. Ongoing training and continuing professional development (CPD) is an important aspect of this work. You need to keep up to date with the latest legislation and changes to taxes and benefits.

All advisers doing voluntary or paid work for Citizens Advice undertake a set training programme. In England and Wales this leads to a CAB certificate in generalist advice work, equivalent to NVQ level 3. You may then progress to specialist training in areas such as money advice.

The Institute of Money Advisers (IMA) provides training courses at various levels on a range of issues, many of which are accredited by the Law Society. The Money Advice Trust (MAT) provides training on all aspects of money advice work. They also run the Wiseradviser online training programme with their partners. In Scotland, if you want to be an approved money adviser under the Debt Arrangement Scheme (DAS), you can apply for free training from MATRICS and must then be assessed before approval is given. Check the Money Scotland website for details.

Adult entry is common as people usually choose to specialise in debt counselling after working as paid or voluntary general advice workers. Often adults can offer a mature outlook and life experience that is an advantage in this area of work. A background in law, welfare rights, consumer advice or debt recovery may be particularly helpful.

Opportunities and Pay
The most common problem experienced by people who use the Citizens Advice service is debt. Citizens Advice Bureaux (CABs) in England and Wales receive over 1.9 million debt enquiries a year. Other organisations are also experiencing high levels of demand. Advice organisations are diversifying into preventative measures by helping people to manage their money better and avoid debt problems.

Due to the current economic climate, opportunities for debt counsellors are good at present. There are jobs with public and voluntary sector general advice organisations and specialist money advice centres. Local authorities, colleges, universities and trade unions may employ debt counsellors. Due to the way they are funded, many jobs are fixed-term contracts which may or may not be renewed. With experience you may take on more complex cases, supervise others or go into management.

Trainee debt counsellors earn £12k-£18k a year. Experienced caseworkers earn £22k-£28k and those with supervisory or management roles may earn around £25k-£32k a year.

Skills and Qualities

able to explain clearly, able to get on with all kinds of people, able to inspire confidence, able to put people at ease, awareness of confidentiality issues, good listening skills, negotiating skills, non-judgemental, numeracy skills

Relevant Subjects

Business and accounting, Economics, English, ICT/Computer studies, Law, Mathematics, Psychology, Sociology

Further Information

AGCAS: Charity & Development Work (Job Sector Briefing) (AGCAS) - www.prospects.ac.uk

Citizens Advice - www.citizensadvice.org.uk

Citizens Advice Northern Ireland - www.citizensadvice.co.uk

Citizens Advice Scotland - www.cas.org.uk

Money Advice Trust Information Hub - www.infohub.moneyadvicetrust.org

Money Scotland - www.moneyscotland.gov.uk

Wiseradviser - www.wiseradviser.org

▶Working in advice & counselling (2007) (Babcock Lifeskills) - www.babcock-lifeskills.com/

▶Working in maths (2009) (Babcock Lifeskills) - www.babcock-lifeskills.com/

Addresses

Institute of Money Advisers (IMA)
Stringer House, 34 Lupton Street, Leeds LS10 2QW
Phone: 0845 094 2384 (UK only)
Web: www.i-m-a.org.uk

Similar Jobs

Advice Worker, Counsellor, Financial Adviser/Planner, Social Worker

Demolition Operative

CRCI:Building and Construction
CLCI:UZ — Job Band: 1 to 2

Job Description

Demolition operatives use tools or machinery to safely take apart and demolish buildings and other structures that are no longer needed. They work in one or more of three areas of demolition: manual (by hand), heavy plant demolition using demolition attachments, and explosive demolition. The structure is assessed prior to demolition and a decision is made on how to go about the process safely. Fences and screens are erected around the site, along with any scaffolding that may be needed. Roofs, floors and fittings are stripped out in advance. Demolition operatives cut timber and girders with a saw, special blowtorch, or oxy-fuel cutting equipment and use chisels, crowbars, axes and machinery, such as chain saws and pneumatic drills. They secure cables and may operate a winch, crane or grappling machine.

After demolition, the site is cleaned and graded and items such as bricks, timbers and special stone work are sorted for re-use. Awareness of health and safety legislation and regulation is essential in this work.

Work Details

Demolition operatives usually work a basic 37-39 hr week, Monday to Friday, though there is often overtime, including weekends. Work is outdoors and involves travel to different sites. You may need to spend nights away from home. The site can be dirty, dusty, muddy and noisy. There are safety rules which need to be followed carefully as there is a risk of falling or other accidents. You have to manage rough ground, climbing, lifting and working at heights on scaffolding and ladders. The job requires you to use power and hand tools. You need to wear a safety helmet, ear defenders, boots, gloves, and sometimes a face mask and safety glasses. For some jobs breathing equipment is provided.

Qualification

• England, Wales and Northern Ireland

Band 1: Academic qualifications are not always required, though some formal/vocational qualifications at any level are helpful. Maths, science, English or technical subjects are the most useful.

Band 2: For entry to jobs, no minimum qualifications are needed, but it is an advantage to have some GCSEs (A*-C) or equivalent in subjects that include English, maths and technology.

• Scotland

Band 1: Academic qualifications are not always required, though some formal/vocational qualifications at any level are helpful. Maths, science, English or technical subjects are the most useful.

Band 2: For entry as a trainee: although academic qualifications are not specified for this job, it is an advantage to have some S grades (1-3) in subjects that include English, maths and technology or similar.

Adult Qualifications

No formal educational qualifications required. However, secondary qualifications in English, maths, science and technology subjects, or equivalent, are useful.

Work Experience

Any work experience can equip you with skills that you can use in the future and add to your CV. Work experience can either be unpaid or voluntary or can be holiday or part-time work that you have organised yourself. Health and safety issues may mean that there are certain jobs you can't do until you are over 16. Contact your local ConstructionSkills office for advice.

Entry and Training

You train on the job, usually through an employer's training scheme that combines work-based training with day or block release at an approved training centre. Relevant training/courses are offered by ConstructionSkills and the National Demolition Training Group, such as the certificate of competence for demolition operatives at levels 1-3 (labourer, mattockman, topman). This can lead to qualification as a demolition supervisor, via a 12 week distance-learning course. Completion of the certificate of competence (plus S/NVQs in demolition for levels 2-3) leads to the Construction Skills Certification Scheme (CSCS) card, which indicates your individual skill and level of experience. You also complete a required safety awareness demolition operative course and test. You must be over 18 to start the training.

A Diploma/Welsh Baccalaureate in construction and the built environment may be available in your area. S/NVQs in demolition are available at levels 2 and 3. Training programmes, including apprenticeships leading to level 2 and advanced apprenticeships/ construction apprenticeships leading to level 3, may be available in your area.

Mature applicants are sometimes preferred and often employers train people who are already working on site. Any experience of working in the construction industry is useful. Government training opportunities may also be available in your area. Contact your local careers office, Jobcentre Plus, Next Step service or Learning and Skills Council (LSC)/Local Enterprise Company (LEC) for details of training schemes, including apprenticeships for adults.

Opportunities and Pay
You can work for a specialist demolition contractor or with building, construction and civil engineering firms throughout the UK. Availability of work depends on activity in the building trade and the national economy. Currently there is a downturn in the housing market which means there may be a shortage of vacancies. With experience you can become a supervisor or become self-employed. You can do seasonal, casual or temporary work.

The basic standard hourly rate for qualified demolition operatives is around £9-£10 per hour. The rate depends on your qualifications. This can work out at around £18k-£21k a year. Those with a level 3 qualification earn from £21k and, with experience, up to £26k a year. Bonuses and overtime pay may be available. Employers may give allowances for travel and cost of lodgings.

Health
You need to be physically fit as the job is physically demanding, with no allergies to dust. You must also have good eyesight and good hearing.

Skills and Qualities
able to follow instructions, agile, aptitude for teamwork, head for heights, practical skills, reliable, safety conscious, strong

Relevant Subjects
Construction and built environment

Further Information
Apprenticeship Schemes (National Apprenticeship Service) - www.apprenticeships.org.uk

Careers in Construction - www.bconstructive.co.uk

ConstructionSkills - sector skills council for the construction industry - www.cskills.org

Demolition & Dismantling (quarterly) (National Federation of Demolition Contractors) - www.demolition-nfdc.com

Diplomas (Foundation, Higher and Advanced) - http://yp.direct.gov.uk/diplomas

European Demolition Association - www.eda-demolition.com

Welsh Baccalaureate - www.wbq.org.uk

▶Working in construction & the built environment (2007) (Babcock Lifeskills) - www.babcock-lifeskills.com/

Addresses
National Demolition Training Group (NDTG)
Paradise, Hemel Hempstead , Hertfordshire HP2 4TF
Phone: +44 (0) 1442 217144
Web: www.ndtg.org

National Federation of Demolition Contractors (NFDC)
Resurgam House, Paradise, Hemel Hempstead HP2 4TF
Phone: +44 (0) 1442 217144
Web: www.demolition-nfdc.com

Similar Jobs
Builders' Yard Assistant, Construction Operative, Construction Plant Operative, Crane Operator, Quarry Operative, Steeplejack

Dental Hygienist

CRCI:Healthcare
CLCI:JAF — Job Band: 3 to 5

Job Description
Dental hygienists work as part of a team in all sectors of dentistry to improve oral and dental health, and have both clinical and health promotional responsibilities. They carry out treatments prescribed by a dentist; clean, scale and polish teeth. Also apply preventative materials, such as topical fluorides or fissure sealants, to prevent tooth decay and periodontal (gum) disease such as dental caries, as well as prophylactic and antimicrobial materials. They take dental radiographs and in hospitals may also deal with mouth hygiene before and after oral surgery, working alongside an orthodontist.

Hygienists promote aspects of dental care and oral hygiene. They plan, implement and evaluate educational programmes to prevent oral disease. These may include ways to control plaque or dietary advice to individual patients, or to groups of children or adults.

Work Details
Usually work between 8.30am and 5.30pm, Monday to Friday, though work may be required on some evenings or on a Saturday. Work is in a dental surgery, general practice, a dental hospital or clinic supporting the work of a dentist. Travel may be necessary around an area to other places of work, such as schools or community centres. You are responsible for careful and thorough work involving a variety of people, or working with one group, e.g children, geriatric patients or patients with special needs. You may have to cope with standing for many hours and need to wear protective clothing, such as gloves, face mask and safety glasses.

Qualification
Applicants to courses in dental hygiene are usually required to have experience as a dental nurse as well as the qualifications listed.

• England, Wales and Northern Ireland
Band 3: For entry to a training course: usually 5 GCSEs (A*-C) including English, maths and a biological science, or equivalent, plus a recognised dental nurse qualification.

Band 4: For some courses: two A levels and some GCSEs (A*-C) preferably including English, maths and a biological science, or equivalent, such as a recognised dental nursing qualification.

Band 5: For degree courses in dental hygiene and therapy: 2-3 A levels and some GCSEs (A*-C) usually including English and maths, or equivalent. Exact requirements depend on the degree you take.

• Scotland
Band 3: For entry to a training course: usually at least five S grades (1-3) including English, maths and a biological science, or similar, plus a recognised dental nurse qualification.

Band 4: For some courses: 3 H grades as well as some S grades (1-3), including English, maths and a biological science, or similar, such as a recognised dental nursing qualification.

Band 5: For degree courses: 3-5 H grades and some S grades (1-3), usually including English and maths, or similar qualifications. Exact requirements depend on the degree you take.

Degree Information
A three-year BSc in Oral Health Sciences is available at the universities of Manchester, Dundee, Edinburgh and the UHI Millenium Institute, or in Dental Hygiene and Dental Therapy at a number of universities.

Adult Qualifications
Dental schools do not normally relax entry requirements for adult entrants, but may do so if applicants have relevant work experience.

Work Experience
Relevant work or voluntary experience is always useful and can improve your chances in application for entry to this career. It is an advantage to have worked in a dental environment but any experience that gives you the opportunity to work with the public,

or in a scientific area, puts you at an advantage when applying for jobs and training. Try to speak to a qualified dental hygienist about their work and the training that is required.

Entry and Training

To practise as a dental hygienist you need to undertake an appropriate course approved by the General Dental Council (GDC). You must be qualified and registered with the GDC and entered on the register for dental care professionals (DCPs) before you can practise in the UK. The GDC also requires that you keep your skills up to date through continuing professional development (CPD) to learn new and advanced dental care techniques. CPD is offered by organisations such as the British Society of Dental Hygiene and Therapy (BSDHT).

Entry to dental hygiene courses is highly competitive and you must be at least 18 before you start training. The full-time diploma course in dental hygiene and/or dental therapy is usually two years (or up to 27 months) long and is offered by dental schools and also the Defence Dental Services Training Establishment. Courses include anatomy and physiology, preventive dentistry, dental health education, dental pathology and the management and care of patients. Several dental schools offer courses combining dental hygiene and dental therapy.

Alternatively, you can take a three-year BSc course in Oral Health Sciences. There are also opportunities to train with the armed forces. Check the BSDHT for all course details.

Mature applicants who are offered a place on a dental hygiene course can apply for an NHS bursary which covers the full course fees and provides a means tested grant.

Opportunities and Pay

There are around 6,000 dental hygienists in the UK. Most work in general dental practices and some work for hospitals, the community dental service or in industry. There are also a number of periodontal and orthodontic practices which employ hygienists. There are increasing opportunities for work with children and adults who have special needs. The armed forces train dental hygienists and occasionally has opportunities for civilians. You may progress to become a practice manager though there is no structure for career progression. Once qualified, there are also opportunities to work as an orthodontic therapist.

Some hygienists take a higher qualification in business studies, health sciences and education. Some opportunities exist for work abroad, particularly in Europe.

Pay varies considerably depending on area and type of employment. Starting pay for those who are qualified and working for the NHS is around £21k-£28k, rising to £37k for specialists with experience. Many hygienists are self-employed or work with a private practice where you may earn more. An experienced private dental hygienist can earn up to £50k a year.

Health

This job requires good eyesight.

Skills and Qualities

able to inspire confidence, able to put people at ease, calm, good communication skills, good concentration level, manual dexterity, not squeamish, patient, smart appearance, sympathetic

Relevant Subjects

Biology, Chemistry, English, Health and social care, Psychology, Science

Further Information

AGCAS: Health (Job Sector Briefing) (AGCAS) - www.prospects.ac.uk

British School of Dental Hygiene & Therapy (BSDHT) - www.bsdht.org.uk/index

NHS Careers (NHS Careers) - www.nhscareers.nhs.uk

NHS Careers Scotland - www.infoscotland.com/nhs

NHS Careers Wales - www.wales.nhs.uk

Addresses

Belfast School of Dental Hygiene
Royal Victoria Hospital Grosvenor Road, Belfast BT12 6BA
Phone: +44 (0)28 9063 2733

British Dental Association (BDA)
64 Wimpole Street, London W1G 8YS
Phone: +44 (0)20 7935 0875
Web: www.bda.org/

General Dental Council (GDC)
37 Wimpole Street, London W1G 8DQ
Phone: +44 (0)20 7887 3800
Web: www.gdc-uk.org

Similar Jobs

Dental Nurse, Dental Technician/Technologist, Dental Therapist, Health Promotion Specialist

Dental Nurse

also known as: Dental Surgery Assistant

CRCI:Healthcare
CLCI:JAF

Job Band: 2 to 3

Job Description

Dental nurses work closely with a dentist and are part of a team that provides care and treatment to patients. They prepare the surgery for each patient ensuring that it is hygienic, clean and tidy. This includes laying out the instruments and passing them to the dentist, hygienist or therapist. Dental nurses also mix filling compounds, sterilise equipment and process X-ray films. They welcome each patient and take them into the surgery. During treatment, they keep the patient's mouth clear using suction equipment. Also tidy the surgery after each treatment. Dental nurses must maintain sterile conditions and follow health and safety regulations.

They often have clerical duties, such as keeping records and filing. May also act as a receptionist, making appointments, answering the telephone and taking payments.

Work Details

Working hours are generally 8.30am to 5.30pm, Monday to Friday, though start and finish times may vary. Some evening or Saturday work may be required. Your place of work is a surgery, clinic or a hospital. There is contact with people of all ages, and some people are in pain or upset. Sometimes the work may be tiring and stressful. You are responsible for maintaining hygienic conditions. Work requires coping with the sight of blood. You have to stand for many hours and need to wear a uniform and often protective clothing, including gloves, safety glasses and a face mask.

Qualification

- **England, Wales and Northern Ireland**

Band 2: For most courses and employers: some GCSEs (A*-C) including English, biology or another science are usually needed. Equivalent qualifications may be acceptable.

Band 3: For courses offered at dental schools: usually 5 GCSEs (A*-C) including English and biology or human biology, or equivalent qualifications.

- **Scotland**

Band 2: For most courses and employers: some S grades (1-3) including English, biology or another science are usually needed. Similar qualifications may be acceptable.

Band 3: For courses offered at dental schools: usually at least five S grades (1-3) including English and biology, or similar qualifications.

Adult Qualifications

Some dental schools expect mature entrants to have the required academic entry qualifications, but others offer a written entrance test and interview in place of exam passes. Some employers may accept mature applicants on the basis of personality and experience. Check with individual dental schools and with employers.

Work Experience

Work experience can equip you with skills that you can use in the future to add to your CV. Employers may prefer candidates who have relevant work or voluntary experience in a medical or healthcare setting such as a hospital or residential care home. Try to speak to a qualified dental nurse about their work and the training that is required.

Entry and Training

All dental nurses have to be registered with the General Dental Council (GDC) or undertaking training. Trainees usually work in a dental surgery and combine this with a part-time evening study or day-release course approved by the GDC. Full-time courses are also available at dental schools and hospitals. It is also possible to train as a dental nurse in the armed forces. Contact your local armed forces careers office for details.

You usually need to obtain an S/NVQ level 3 in dental nursing, a dental hospital certificate of proficiency in dental nursing, a certificate of higher education in dental nursing, or have passed the national certificate of the National Examining Board for Dental Nurses. When qualified, specialist courses are available including oral health education, dental anaesthetic nursing and dental sedation nursing.

There is an orthodontic therapy programme for dental nurses at the University of Central Lancashire leading to a Certificate in Higher Education. Successful candidates then have the opportunity to complete a final exam and earn a diploma in orthodontic therapy. This new qualification makes it possible for dental nurses to play a much more active role within the dental team, providing treatment under the supervision of the dentist. There is a also foundation degree course in dental nursing available at the University of Bedfordshire.

Qualified dental nurses need to register with the GDC on the list for dental care professionals (DCPs) before they can practise in the UK. The register is administered by the British Association of Dental Nurses which also supports continuing professional development (CPD) throughout your career. The GDC requires you to have 150 hours of CPD over a five-year period.

A Diploma/Welsh Baccalaureate may be available in your area in society, health and development. This can provide a useful introduction to this career.

Mature applicants without the traditional academic requirements may be accepted by some hospital dental schools for training, though you need to pass an entrance test. Some employers may train mature applicants on the job, but there is an upper age limit for training in the armed forces. Contact the British Association of Dental Nurses and the General Dental Council for all training options.

Opportunities and Pay

There are around 44,000 dental nurses registered in the UK but there is a shortage of experienced staff in some areas. You can be employed in general dental practice, by a private dental practice, universities, hospital dental service, in industry, the community dental service or the armed forces. A few large companies have their own dental practice. Promotion usually requires a more advanced qualification.

After two years' experience and qualification, progression is possible to become a dental hygienist, dental therapist or oral health practitioner, orthodontic therapist, or a practice manager. Some may progress to becoming a tutor after first gaining a teaching qualification, such as the further and adult education teachers' certificate. There are opportunities to work abroad, particularly in the Middle East.

Pay varies considerably depending on area and type of employer. A trainee dental nurse in the NHS earns around £15.5k-£18.5k a year, rising to around £22k for an experienced and qualified nurse. A dental nurse specialist can earn around £27k a year. A private dental nurse can expect to earn around £10-£12 an hour.

Health

This job requires good health, stamina and fitness.

Skills and Qualities

able to put people at ease, calm, careful, efficient, friendly, methodical, not squeamish, practical skills, quick reactions, reassuring

Relevant Subjects

Biology, Chemistry, Health and social care, Science

Further Information

British Dental Nurses' Journal (BADN, quarterly) (BADN) - www.badn.org.uk/

Diplomas (Foundation, Higher and Advanced) - http://yp.direct.gov.uk/diplomas

NHS Careers (NHS Careers) - www.nhscareers.nhs.uk

NHS Careers Scotland - www.infoscotland.com/nhs

NHS Careers Wales - www.wales.nhs.uk

Welsh Baccalaureate - www.wbq.org.uk

Addresses

British Association of Dental Nurses (BADN)
PO Box 4 Room 200 Hillhouse International Business Centre, Thornton-Cleveleys, Lancashire FY5 4QD
Phone: +44 (0) 1253 338360
Web: www.badn.org.uk

British Dental Association (BDA)
64 Wimpole Street, London W1G 8YS
Phone: +44 (0)20 7935 0875
Web: www.bda.org/

General Dental Council (GDC)
37 Wimpole Street, London W1G 8DQ
Phone: +44 (0)20 7887 3800
Web: www.gdc-uk.org

National Examining Board for Dental Nurses (NEBDN)
110 London Street, Fleetwood, Lancashire FY7 6EU
Phone: +44 (0)1253 778417
Web: www.nebdn.org

School of Medicine, Dentistry and Biomedical Sciences
Queen's University Belfast Health Sciences Building
97 Lisburn Road BT9 7BL
Phone: +44 (0)2890 971 444
Web: www.qub.ac.uk/cd

University Central Lancashire
Preston, Preston , Lancashire PR1 2HE
Phone: +44 (0)1772 201 201
Web: www.uclan.ac.uk

Similar Jobs

Dental Hygienist, Dental Technician/Technologist, Dental Therapist, Healthcare Assistant, Operating Department Practitioner

Dental Technician/Technologist

also known as: Orthodontic Technician

CRCI:Healthcare

CLCI:JAF Job Band: 3 to 5

Job Description

Dental technicians are essential members of a dental team who use specialist equipment, including computer technology, to make or repair a range of dental appliances. They work to a dentist's prescription for each individual patient making dentures, crowns and bridges, clips, braces, springs and also splints for facial injuries. The job uses a high level of artistic, scientific and technical skill so technicians have a good knowledge of the properties of various metals and plastics. They assess the job from the dentist's notes, make a mould, cast plates and set teeth. Then finish the work with hand tools. Technicians rarely have contact with patients.

Some technicians work with dental and oral surgeons to help patients who have a facial or jaw injury, producing crucial parts, known as prostheses. These are sometimes known as maxillofacial technicians. Some dental technicians may become involved in hospital research or teaching.

Work Details

Work in a commercial dental laboratory, hospital, community service or a general dental practice, alone or as part of a team. If working for the NHS, you usually work a 35 hour week, though sometimes may need to work irregular hours, including on-call duty for emergencies. Commercial work may require additional hours during the week. If working in a hospital, you have direct contact with dental and oral surgeons. You are responsible for accurate and intricate work, which is mostly done sitting down. An overall and occasionally safety glasses are usually worn.

Qualification

- **England, Wales and Northern Ireland**

Band 3: For entry to BTEC national diploma in dental technology: usually 4 GCSEs (A*-C) including English, maths and 1-2 science subjects, or equivalent. Some dental schools may ask for GCSE (A*-C) in physics and biology for entry.

Band 4: For foundation degree courses in dental tenchnology: 1-2 A levels and some GCSEs (A*-C) usually including English, maths and a biological science, or equivalent.

Band 5: For degree courses: 2-3 A levels and some GCSEs (A*-C) usually including English, maths and a biological science, or equivalent. Exact requirements depend on the degree you take.

- **Scotland**

Band 3: For entry to SQA national certificate in dental technology: five S grades (1-3) usually English, maths and 1-3 science subjects, or similar. Some dental schools may ask for S grades (1-3) in physics and biology for entry.

Band 4: To enrol for the SQA higher national certificate in dental technology, satisfactory completion of the national certificate in dental technology, or accredited prior learning, plus interview.

Band 5: For degree courses: 3-5 H grades, one of which must be in a science or technology, and some S grades (1-3), usually including English and maths, or similar qualifications. Exact requirements depend on the degree you take.

Degree Information

Degree courses in dental technology and in dental materials are available.

Adult Qualifications

Academic requirements for college/hospital training may be relaxed for mature entrants. Credit may be given for relevant experience and qualifications.

Work Experience

Employers or colleges/universities may prefer candidates who have relevant work or voluntary experience. This can include voluntary experience in a dental laboratory, possibly a dental clinic or surgery or a hospital.

Entry and Training

Entrants are encouraged either to take the full-time foundation degree in dental technology or to take it on a part-time basis if employed as a trainee dental technician. Degrees are also available in dental technology at a number of universities.

You may be able to enter this career without A/H levels by training on the job and studying for the accredited BTEC national diploma in dental technology or the SQA national certificate in dental technology. Part-time study on a day-release basis with employment in a laboratory takes 4-5 years. You can also follow a three-year, full-time course before entry to a job. There is also a four-year block-release training programme for hospital dental technicians.

Qualified dental technicians/technologists must register with the General Dental Council's (GDC) register of dental care professionals (DCPs) before they can practise in the UK. Contact the Dental Technologists Association or the Dental Laboratories Association for a list of approved qualifications and details of the state registration scheme for qualified dental technicians. The GDC requires you to keep your skills up to date by following a programme of continuing professional development.

Training and employment is also offered by the Defence Dental Agency for the armed forces. Contact your local armed forces careers office for details. Relevant training programmes, including apprenticeship schemes, may be available in your area for entry to this job.

Mature applicants should apply to their prospective employer, such as a commercial laboratory or local health trust for details of training and funding opportunities.

Opportunities and Pay

There are an estimated 8,000 registered dental technicians in the UK and jobs are available mainly in towns and cities. Currently, there is a shortage of qualified technicians. Employment can be with a commercial or private practice laboratory, a dental practice, the national health service (NHS), an armed forces dental laboratory, or you may be self-employed and set up your own laboratory. There is scope for specialisation, eg in crowns and bridges, orthodontics or maxillofacial technology (reconstructive techniques). There are opportunities for self employment and to work overseas.

Prospects in commercial laboratories are generally good and in the NHS there is a clear promotion structure to senior or chief technician, related to experience and qualifications. Some technicians progress to teaching after completing the further and adult education teachers' certificate.

Pay varies depending on area and type of employer. Newly qualified technicians working for the NHS earn around £21k on a scale rising to £28k a year. Senior technicians earn £35k or more and there are opportunities to earn up to £45k for exceptional technicians. Dental laboratory managers can earn more.

Health

This job requires good eyesight, though wearing of glasses is acceptable, and you require normal colour vision. The environment can often be dusty when grinding, welding and polishing work is carried out, so this can affect people who suffer with respiratory problems, such as asthma.

Skills and Qualities
Attention to detail, eye for shape/colour, eye for visual effect, good concentration level, hand-to-eye co-ordination, information handling skills, IT skills, manual dexterity, scientific approach, technical aptitude

Relevant Subjects
Biology, Chemistry, Design and technology, Engineering, Health and social care, Mathematics, Physics, Science

Further Information
DentalLab Journal (10 x a year) (Dental Laboratories Association) - www.dla.org.uk

Ministry of Defence (MoD) (MOD) - www.mod.uk

NHS Careers (NHS Careers) - www.nhscareers.nhs.uk

NHS Careers Scotland - www.infoscotland.com/nhs

NHS Careers Wales - www.wales.nhs.uk

The Dental Technician News - www.dental-practice.org

The Dental Technology Student's Prospectus (DLA) - www.dla.org.uk/files/Students%20Handbook.pdf

▶Working in manufacturing (2010) (Babcock Lifeskills) - www.babcock-lifeskills.com/

Addresses
British Dental Association (BDA)
64 Wimpole Street, London W1G 8YS
Phone: +44 (0)20 7935 0875
Web: www.bda.org/

Dental Laboratories Association (DLA)
44-46 Wollaton Road, Beeston, Nottingham NG9 2NR
Phone: +44 (0)115 925 4888
Web: www.dla.org.uk

Dental Technologists Association
Waterwells Drive, Waterwells Business Park, Gloucester GL2 2AT
Phone: 0870 243 0753 (UK only)
Web: www.dta-uk.org

General Dental Council (GDC)
37 Wimpole Street, London W1G 8DQ
Phone: +44 (0)20 7887 3800
Web: www.gdc-uk.org

School of Medicine, Dentistry and Biomedical Sciences
Queen's University Belfast Health Sciences Building 97 Lisburn Road BT9 7BL
Phone: +44 (0)2890 971 444
Web: www.qub.ac.uk/cd

Similar Jobs
Clinical Technologist, Dental Hygienist, Dental Nurse, Laboratory Technician: Science, Prosthetist/Orthotist

Dental Therapist
also known as: Oral Health Practitioner

CRCI:Healthcare
CLCI:JAF Job Band: 3 to 5

Job Description
Dental therapists work as part of a dental team that provide clinical and educational care for children and adults of all ages. They work under a dentist's direction or by following written procedures and may be assisted by a dental nurse. Dental therapists carry out clinical work such as extracting milk teeth, drilling and filling minor cavities. They clean, scale and polish teeth, apply solutions, fissure sealants and gels to gums and teeth to help prevent decay, and take radiographs (x-rays) of teeth and gums.

Dental therapists may give patients a local anaesthetic for some treatments. They advise on dental health matters and may give talks to individuals or groups in a community about good dental care, hygiene and diet.

Work Details
Most therapists work 37 hrs a week, Monday to Friday, though sometimes may need to work a Saturday. Usually work in a clinic, school or a mobile clinic that travels around a district, visiting various surgeries or community centres, residential homes or a patient's own home. Sterile conditions must be maintained at all times. In this job, you advise and care for people who may be nervous, including children, people with special needs and the elderly.

Work requires coping with the sight of blood and you may need to stand for many hours. Protective clothing is worn including a coat/tunic, face mask, surgical gloves and eye protection.

Qualification
- **England, Wales and Northern Ireland**

Band 3: For the diploma in dental therapy: at least 5 GCSEs (A*-C) including English and biology or a biology-based subject such as human biology, or equivalent qualifications. It is an advantage to have a nationally recognised dental nursing qualification (sometimes together with a minimum of two years' dental nursing experience).

Band 4: For some courses: two A levels and 5 GCSEs (A*-C), preferably including English, biology or human biology, or equivalent. A nationally-recognised dental nurse qualification is also acceptable for entry.

Band 5: For degree courses: 2-3 A levels and some GCSEs (A*-C) usually including English, maths and biology or a biology-based subject, or equivalent. Exact requirements depend on the degree you take.

- **Scotland**

Band 3: For the diploma in dental therapy: at least five S grades (1-3), including English and biology or a biology-based subject such as human biology, or similar qualifications. It is an advantage to have a nationally recognised dental nursing qualification (sometimes together with a minimum of one year's dental nursing experience).

Band 4: For some courses: 2-3 H grades as well as five S grades (1-3), preferably including English, biology or human biology, or similar. A nationally-recognised dental nurse qualification is also acceptable for entry.

Band 5: For degree courses: 3-5 H grades and some S grades (1-3), usually including English, maths and biology or a biology-based subject, or similar qualifications. Exact requirements depend on the degree you take.

Degree Information
Degrees in oral health science and dental hygiene and therapy are available at universities throughout the UK.

Adult Qualifications
Entry requirements for adult applicants are the same as those for young people.

Work Experience
Relevant work or voluntary experience is always useful and can improve your chances in application for entry to this career. Competition for course places is fierce as there are still relatively few available, and you often need to have spent two years as a dental nurse before applying. If you see this as a long-term goal then work experience in the area of dental care is very useful. Also, any experience which gives you the opportunity to work with the public, or in a scientific area puts you at an advantage when applying for jobs and training.

Entry and Training
You must be at least 18 to train as a dental therapist and there are several ways to qualify. Applicants usually need 5 GCSEs (A-C)/S grades (1-3) including English and a biological science with two A

levels (A-C)/2-3 H grades (1-3) including biology and preferably one other science subject, or a nationally-recognised certificate in dental nursing. You then attend a full-time course for around 27 months. Full-time courses include combined diplomas in dental hygiene/dental therapy at schools of dentistry, dental hospitals and training centres throughout the country.

Alternatively, you can take a degree in dental hygiene and therapy or in oral health science. These courses are offered at a range of universities in the UK. If you are already qualified as a dental hygienist, you may be able to take a conversion course to become a dental therapist. The NHS sponsors some course places leading to professional qualification. Your course fees are paid and you may be eligible for a means-tested bursary and non-means tested loan. Check with individual schools for entry requirements as some require two-years' work experience before you can attend a course.

Contact the British Association of Dental Therapists (BADT) for a current list of schools of dentistry offering all qualifications, and details of registration. All qualified dental therapists are required to register with the General Dental Council's register for dental care professionals (DCPs) before practising in the UK. The BADT promotes continuing professional development throughout your career and you can become a member of the association if you hold a dental therapy qualification or are a student dental therapist.

Mature applicants are welcomed although entry requirements are not relaxed for those taking the diploma in dental therapy.

Opportunities and Pay

Dental therapists are enrolled with the General Dental Council and work in hospitals or clinics in the community, including the new Personal Dental Service set up by the NHS, and in the armed services. Around 1300 are currently registered in the UK. Posts are often for a combined dental therapist/dental hygienist. Some therapists are also known as oral health practitioners and may take the certificate in oral health education to specialise in health promotion. Others may progress to become practice managers. Some specialise as orthodontic therapists.

A dental therapist working in the NHS earns around £20k-£27k a year, rising to £35k or more for specialists with experience. Advanced oral health practitioners can earn more. Those working privately may earn in the region of £35k-£45k a year.

Health

The work may involve a risk of infection. Dentist therapists need to have good eyesight.

Skills and Qualities

able to explain clearly, able to inspire confidence, able to work both on your own and in a team, conscientious, efficient, manual dexterity, not squeamish, patient, reassuring, technical aptitude

Relevant Subjects

Biology, Chemistry, English, Health and social care, Psychology, Science

Further Information

British Association of Dental Therapists (BADT) - www.badt.org.uk

British School of Dental Hygiene & Therapy (BSDHT) - www.bsdht.org.uk/index

NHS Careers (NHS Careers) - www.nhscareers.nhs.uk

NHS Careers Scotland - www.infoscotland.com/nhs

NHS Careers Wales - www.wales.nhs.uk

Skills for Health - sector skills council - www.skillsforhealth.org.uk

Addresses

British Dental Association (BDA)
64 Wimpole Street, London W1G 8YS
Phone: +44 (0)20 7935 0875
Web: www.bda.org/

General Dental Council (GDC)
37 Wimpole Street, London W1G 8DQ
Phone: +44 (0)20 7887 3800
Web: www.gdc-uk.org

School of Medicine, Dentistry and Biomedical Sciences
Queen's University Belfast Health Sciences Building 97 Lisburn Road BT9 7BL
Phone: +44 (0)2890 971 444
Web: www.qub.ac.uk/cd

Similar Jobs

Dental Hygienist, Dental Nurse, Dental Technician/Technologist, Dentist, Health Promotion Specialist, Healthcare Assistant

Dentist

CRCI:Healthcare
CLCI:JAF Job Band: 5

Job Description

Dentists lead a team of healthcare professionals who provide dental care for their patients. They diagnose and treat diseases and disorders of the mouth, gums and teeth. They aim to prevent decay, as well as to give dental treatment, and are concerned with the appearance and general health of the patient. Dentists examine the patient's teeth and mouth, take x-rays, give local anaesthetics, extract teeth, drill and fill cavities. Also fit dental appliances, such as crowns, dentures, braces, bridges, and prescribe drugs.

Dentists manage a team that must include a dental nurse and, depending on the size of practice, can also include dental hygienists, a dental therapist and dental technician, as well as reception staff. In a small practice, the dentist also does the work of a hygienist. After graduating, most dentists work as general dental practitioners (GDPs) who provide NHS/private dental care for the general public. Some dentists work in community settings where patients have difficulty getting treatment that is not usually available in general dental care.

Others may specialise in non-clinical dental public health working to improve the dental health of the population rather than the individual. Some experienced dentists may teach or carry out research in a university, or work in a hospital doing specialised work, including surgery.

Work Details

Work in a comfortable environment that is clean and well lit; usually a dental surgery, dental hospital or a clinic. Your hours of work depend on the type of employment. In general practice you choose how many hours to work depending on the size of practice. Opening hours are usually between 8.30am and 6.00pm; Monday to Friday and Saturday mornings, but may include an evening and emergency service at other times. Hospital dentists may work shifts and also need to be on-call for emergencies.

You may work as part of a team including dental nurses and hygienists. There is contact with people of all ages, including those who are in pain or upset. Work can be very demanding and requires coping with the sight of blood. Sterile conditions are maintained at all times to prevent cross-infection. A protective coat or tunic, surgical gloves and safety glasses are usually worn.

Qualification

- **England, Wales and Northern Ireland**

Band 5: For degree course in dentistry: usually very good grades in three A levels, including two sciences (chemistry and biology preferred), and 5 GCSEs (A*-C) including English and maths, or equivalent. Some dental schools offer a one-year pre-dental course for students with A levels in non-science subjects. Exact requirements depend on the degree you take.

- **Scotland**

Band 5: For degree course: usually very good passes in 5 H grades, including two sciences (chemistry and biology preferred), and five S grades (1-3) including maths and English. Biology and physics may be needed at S grade if not offered at H grade. Some dental schools offer a one-year pre-dental course for students with H grades in non-science subjects. Exact requirements depend on the degree you take.

Degree Information

An approved degree in dentistry (BDS or BChD) is required to register with the General Dental Council at one of 16 dental schools in the UK.

Adult Qualifications

Entrance requirements are rarely relaxed for mature entrants because of the high level of competition for places at dental schools.

Work Experience

Entry to this career is highly competitive and it is essential that you have some relevant work or voluntary experience before applying, as universities and employers may give preference to candidates with experience. Working in a dental practice is the most suitable, but other work with the public or in a helping capacity is also relevant. Prospective students are strongly advised to shadow a dentist to find out whether they are suited to dentistry.

Entry and Training

Competition is fierce for places at dental school and you need to complete a course from a recognised university. A degree in dentistry (BDS or BChD) takes five years, and six years if a pre-dental year is included. A four-year accelerated course is offered to graduates who hold a 2:1 (or better) degree in a biology/chemistry subject. Academic study is combined with theoretical and practical training in all branches of dentistry. There are 16 undergraduate dental schools in the UK located in major cities.

After qualification you must first register with the General Dental Council (GDC) to be able to practise. Most dental graduates choose to become self employed as a general dental practitioner (GDP) though some choose general professional training and spend a year in vocational training as a vocational dental practitioner (VDP). Dentists working for the NHS work in general dental service, personal dental service, community dental service, hospital dental service, or in dental public health. Due to a current shortage of public health dental consultants, there are many training opportunities in this specialised area of work.

The armed forces offer cadetships (sponsorship) to candidates who have completed part of their training at a dental school. This leads to a short commission of five years or a post as a regular officer. There are 180 armed forces locations throughout the UK, as well as overseas postings, that provide a dental service to the army, navy and air force service personnel and their families.

Qualified dentists must commit to a programme of continuing professional development (CPD) to maintain their GDC registration. The British Dental Association represents 20,000 dentists in the UK and supports CPD.

Mature entry requirements are the same as for younger entrants and mature entry is welcomed. Those without the required academic qualifications may take a university Access course such as Access to Science or a one-year, pre-dental course if you do not have the required science A levels/H grades. Applicants with a degree in a relevant subject (minimum 2:1) such as medical or life sciences may also gain entry to a dental school, though places are limited. Contact the individual dental schools/universities for entry requirements and also the General Dental Council Charitable Trust for details of any funding opportunities.

Some funding may be possible from the NHS. Cadetships are sometimes available for the latter years of a dental degree from the armed forces. Direct entry into the armed forces is possible up to the age of 32. Contact your local armed forces careers office for details of current training opportunities.

Opportunities and Pay

There are around 30,000 dentists in the UK. Most work in general practice, are employed contractually by the NHS and if they wish, also treat some patients privately, either in a partnership, or as a self-employed dentist. There are also posts in the hospital dental service, community dental service, the armed forces and in voluntary organisations. Some large companies run their own dental practice. You can specialise in one area of dentistry, eg orthodontics or oral surgery, and there are also opportunities for university teaching and research. Dental public health is a relatively new and expanding speciality and there is a national shortage of consultants in this area of work. Cosmetic dentistry opportunities are also increasingly available.

Promotion depends on experience and usually requires a more advanced qualification. You may need to be prepared to move to an area where there is a demand for your services. Opportunities abroad include working in the European Union, Australia, New Zealand, South Africa and developing countries.

Pay varies considerably depending on the amount of work and type of employment. A trainee working in public dental health is likely to earn around £29k a year. The vast majority of qualified dentists work in general practices and are likely to earn £60k-£100k a year as a partner/owner. Dentists who work for the community dental service or the NHS earn £26k in the first year of working, rising to between £29k-£44k with experience and £74k-£176k as a consultant.

Health

The work may involve a risk of infection. Dentists need to have good eyesight and stamina.

Skills and Qualities

able to explain clearly, able to get on with all kinds of people, able to inspire confidence, careful, conscientious, good concentration level, IT skills, manual dexterity, patient, scientific approach

Relevant Subjects

Biology, Chemistry, English, Health and social care, ICT/Computer studies, Mathematics, Physics, Science

Further Information

AGCAS: Health (Job Sector Briefing) (AGCAS) - www.prospects.ac.uk

Becoming a Dentist (BDA) (British Dental Association) - www.bda.org/

Dentistry website - www.dentistry.co.uk

Ministry of Defence (MoD) (MOD) - www.mod.uk

NHS Careers (NHS Careers) - www.nhscareers.nhs.uk

NHS Careers Scotland - www.infoscotland.com/nhs

NHS Careers Wales - www.wales.nhs.uk

Addresses

British Dental Association (BDA)
64 Wimpole Street, London W1G 8YS
Phone: +44 (0)20 7935 0875
Web: www.bda.org/

General Dental Council (GDC)
37 Wimpole Street, London W1G 8DQ
Phone: +44 (0)20 7887 3800
Web: www.gdc-uk.org

School of Medicine, Dentistry and Biomedical Sciences
Queen's University Belfast Health Sciences Building 97 Lisburn Road BT9 7BL
Phone: +44 (0)2890 971 444
Web: www.qub.ac.uk/cd

Similar Jobs

Dental Nurse, Dental Technician/Technologist, Dental Therapist, Doctor: General Practitioner, Orthodontist, Surgeon

Desktop Publishing (DTP) Operator

also known as: Desktop Publishing Editor, DTP Operator, Electronic Publisher, Mac Operator

CRCI:Design, Arts and Crafts
CLCI:ED Job Band: 2 to 5

Job Description

DTP operators use a computer, perhaps an Apple-Macintosh (MAC), desktop publishing, image manipulation and page layout software to create publication documents for large scale publishing or small scale output and distribution. They usually work to a design brief provided by the customer to create the design and layout of books, newspapers, magazines and increasingly formats ready for the Internet. May use other publishing tools, such as scanners to capture photographs, images, or art as digital data.

DTP operators assemble all the elements of a design produced by graphic designers, typographers, photographers, customers and other specialists. They may scan photographs directly into a document and then make changes to the size, colour or shape. Work can include charts and diagrams, press advertisements, client reports, conference materials, presentation or marketing/publicity materials for internal/external use.

They use electronic publishing technologies such as hypertext markup language (HTML) and computer packages, such as Quark Xpress, Adobe InDesign, Photoshop and Microsoft Publisher. Usually print out a proof copy that is checked, sometimes by a proofreader or perhaps the customer, and then make any necessary amendments. May work in a team with other DTP operators. Must keep up to date with the latest computer technology and software.

Work Details

Usually work around 39 hrs a week; Monday to Friday, but may have to work extra hours to meet deadlines. Some employers, such as those producing daily/weekly publications, may operate a shift system that includes nights and weekends. Work is mainly in a clean and well-lit open-plan office or studio. It is essential to be extremely accurate and to reproduce exactly what is required.

You may have to cope with sitting for many hours at a computer screen and must have the ability to prioritise your work. Part-time work and working at home is possible. The work may be pressurised at times.

Qualification

• England, Wales and Northern Ireland

Band 2: For entry to jobs, no minimum qualifications are needed, but it is an advantage to have some GCSEs (A*-C) or equivalent in subjects that include English, ICT and maths, or equivalent.

Band 3: For entry to jobs, HNC or a relevant Diploma, usually at least 4 GCSEs (A*-C) including English and maths, or equivalent.

Band 4: For diploma in foundation studies, HND, Diploma of Higher Education or foundation degree: usually 1-2 A levels and some GCSEs (A*-C) usually including English and maths, or equivalent.

Band 5: For degree courses: 2-3 A levels and some GCSEs (A*-C) usually including English and maths, or equivalent. Most students take a foundation course first. Exact requirements depend on the degree you take.

• Scotland

Band 2: Although academic qualifications are not specified for this job, it is an advantage to have some S grades (1-3) in subjects that include English, ICT and maths, or similar.

Band 3: For entry: usually at least four S grades (1-3) including English and maths, or similar.

Band 4: For entry to SQA higher national and professional development awards, usually 2-3 H grades and some S grades (1-3), including English and maths, or similar qualifications.

Band 5: For degree courses: 3-5 H grades and some S grades (1-3), usually including English and maths, or similar qualifications. Exact requirements depend on the degree you take.

Degree Information

A degree in computer science or a computer related subject is an advantage.

Adult Qualifications

Entry requirements may be relaxed for adults applying for higher education courses with outstanding portfolios. Access or foundation courses provide those without the required qualifications a route onto degree courses.

Work Experience

Employers or colleges/universities may prefer candidates who have relevant work or voluntary experience. This includes any role working with computers and design, such as desktop publishing, or graphic design. Work on a school/student magazine or with a local newspaper/free press publication is very useful experience.

Entry and Training

DTP operators come from a variety of backgrounds and some have worked as studio juniors in graphic design, or in administration. Applicants usually need to produce a portfolio of artwork. It is possible to enter directly from school/college, though most employers expect previous experience of a range of desktop publishing and photo-imaging software. Entrants are increasingly graduates with a relevant degree/HND, usually in computing or graphic design. On-the-job training is usual and supported by short or part-time courses at a local college. You need to frequently update your skills as publishing packages are continually being replaced by new versions.

Larger companies often give more time to formal training, but smaller companies usually want employees to come with the necessary skills and knowledge. A high level of qualifications is not essential, but many entrants are graduates who use this post to move into graphic design.

A Diploma/Welsh Baccalaureate in creative and media may be available in your area. There is an ABC level 3 award in desktop publishing skills and S/NVQs at levels 1-3 for IT practitioners may also be available. City & Guilds offer desktop publishing courses at levels 1-3. Training programmes, including IT users apprenticeship schemes, may be available for entry to this job. Advanced apprenticeships leading to qualification at level 3 can also be a route into higher education.

Mature entrants need to be skilled users of DTP and image manipulation software, and have good keyboard skills. You may need to produce a portfolio of work that demonstrates your artistic/technical skills and ability. Any related experience is an advantage.

Opportunities and Pay

Opportunities occur throughout the UK, with a concentration in London and other major cities. You may be employed by a local/national newspaper or periodical company, printing, reprographics, publishing, advertising or graphic design company, or for a large organisation that has its own publishing section. Promotion is to more senior positions within your department, including supervisory roles or shift leader. It is possible for DTP operators to train as graphic or website designers. Self-employment is also possible. There are opportunities overseas, particularly in India and the Middle East.

Salaries vary depending on the location and type of employer. An operator can earn £16k-£18k a year, rising to around £25k. Experienced operators earn over £30k a year. Salaries in London can be up to £35k a year. Shift allowances are additional to salary. Hourly rates for those working freelance can vary from around £13-£25 an hour.

Skills and Qualities
able to cope under pressure, able to work both on your own and in a team, artistic ability, attention to detail, creative flair, eye for shape/colour, good organisational skills, imaginative, patient, specialist IT skills, technical aptitude

Relevant Subjects
Art and Design, Design and technology, English, ICT/Computer studies, Mathematics, Media and communication studies

Further Information
Apprenticeship Schemes (National Apprenticeship Service) - www.apprenticeships.org.uk

British Interactive Media Association (BIMA) - www.bima.co.uk

Creative Review (Centaur) - www.creativereview.co.uk

Diplomas (Foundation, Higher and Advanced) - http://yp.direct.gov.uk/diplomas

e-skills UK - sector skills council for business and information technology - www.e-skills.com

▶Working in art & design (2009) (Babcock Lifeskills) - www.babcock-lifeskills.com/

Your Creative Future - www.yourcreativefuture.org.uk

Addresses
British Printing Industries Federation (BPIF)
Farringdon Point, 29-35 Farringdon Road, London EC1M 3JF
Phone: 0870 240 4085 (UK only)
Web: www.britishprint.com

Graphic Enterprise Scotland
112 George Street, Edinburgh EH2 4LH
Phone: +44 (0)131 220 4353
Web: http://graphicenterprisescotland.org/

Similar Jobs
Administrator/Administrative Assistant, Graphic Design: Studio Junior, Graphic Designer, Illustrator: Technical/Scientific, Interactive Media Designer, Website Designer, Website Developer

Dietetic Assistant

CRCI:Healthcare
CLCI:JAV — Job Band: 1 to 2

Job Description
Dietetic assistants work in the community or a hospital under the guidance of a state registered dietitian (SRD). Those working in a hospital have various responsibilities but as a priority, ensure that patients are well nourished and on the correct diet for their condition. They assist patients who are referred to the dietetic department and who require a special diet. Help them to choose from the hospital menu, obtain details of a patient's food intake, and monitor their weight. Also gather information on a patient's dietary history and consult regularly with the dietitian about the patient's progress.

Dietetic assistants who work in a community setting assist a dietitian in analysing and assessing the health and dietary needs of residents. They help people to prevent disease by eating more healthily. Work with people who are on strict food regimes, such as those with kidney disease, HIV/AIDS, diabetes, cancer, eating disorders or digestive problems. Also provide general nutritional advice, including grocery shopping and food preparation to people such as pregnant women, the elderly, individuals with special needs, or to parents of young children.

Work Details
Usually work 9am to 5pm, Monday to Friday, though you may be expected to work outside normal hours, and have time off in lieu. The community dietetic assistant may have to regularly travel between local GP surgeries, patients' homes, nursing homes and other locations. There is contact with people who are ill, in pain or depressed. A uniform is usually provided by the employer.

Qualification
A mature, caring attitude is more important than academic qualifications.

• England, Wales and Northern Ireland
Band 1: For entry to jobs, no minimum qualifications are needed, but you are expected to have a good level of general education and relevant experience. Some formal/vocational qualifications at any level are useful.

Band 2: For entry to jobs, no minimum qualifications are needed, but it is an advantage to have some GCSEs (A*-C) or equivalent in subjects that include English and maths.

• Scotland
Band 1: No minimum qualifications are required, but you are expected to have a good level of general education. However, some formal/vocational qualifications at any level are useful.

Band 2: Although academic qualifications are not specified for this job, it is an advantage to have some S grades (1-3) in subjects that include English and maths, or similar.

Adult Qualifications
There are no formal educational requirements for recruitment and applications from adults are especially welcomed.

Work Experience
Work experience gives you an insight into what you enjoy about a job or working environment, and the opportunity to acquire new skills. It provides valuable information to add to your CV and improves any course application and/or your future employment prospects. Relevant work or voluntary experience in a healthcare setting is useful and can improve your employment prospects when applying for jobs.

Entry and Training
Most employers of dietetic assistants provide on-the-job training, working under the supervision of a state registered dietitian (SRD) and other medical staff. Posts for dietetic assistants are often advertised locally. Some assistants move into this work from other hospital support jobs.

Training is provided by the British Dietetic Association and dietetic assistants can become associate members. You can work towards the Royal Society for Public Health's level 2 certificate in health promotion. There are also nutrition/healthier food and special diets courses at levels 2 and 3.

Having experience as a dietetic assistant is very helpful if you want to become a SRD, but you need to gain a higher level of education such as a degree/foundation degree or Access course to progress. Look at the job article for a dietitian for entry and training information.

A Diploma/Welsh Baccalaureate may be available in your area in society, health and development. This can provide a useful introduction to this career. See the diplomas website for further information.

Experience and maturity are valued in this role so mature entrants are particularly suited for this job. Employers usually prefer applicants who show aptitude and motivation, and with a keen interest in nutrition. Previous experience of working in a caring capacity is an advantage.

Opportunities and Pay

At the moment there is a good demand for this work. You can be employed by the NHS to work in a hospital, in GP surgeries and clinics, patients' homes, schools, nursing homes and other community locations. Promotion opportunities are limited without achieving higher educational qualifications. There may be opportunities to work part time.

Pay starts around £15.5k and can rise to around £18.5k a year. Salaries can be higher in London or if you have added responsibilities.

Skills and Qualities

able to explain clearly, able to get on with all kinds of people, able to inspire confidence, aptitude for teamwork, caring, good organisational skills, helpful, persuasive, reassuring

Relevant Subjects

Biology, Health and social care, Hospitality and catering, Psychology, Science

Further Information

Dietetics Today (monthly) (British Dietetic Association) - www.bda.uk.com

Diplomas (Foundation, Higher and Advanced) - http://yp.direct.gov.uk/diplomas

Food Standards Agency - www.food.gov.uk

NHS Careers (NHS Careers) - www.nhscareers.nhs.uk

NHS Careers Scotland - www.infoscotland.com/nhs

NHS Careers Wales - www.wales.nhs.uk

Perspectives in Public Health (bi-monthly) (Sage Publications) - www.rsph.org.uk/en/publications-and-bookshop/Perspectives-in-Public-Health/

Welsh Baccalaureate - www.wbq.org.uk

Addresses

British Dietetic Association (BDA)
5th Floor, Charles House, 148-149 Great Charles Street, Queensway, Birmingham B3 3HT
Phone: +44 (0)121 200 8080
Web: www.bda.uk.com

British Nutrition Foundation (BNF)
High Holborn House, 52-54 High Holborn, London WC1V 6RQ
Phone: +44 (0)20 7404 6504
Web: www.nutrition.org.uk

Royal Society for Public Health (RSPH)
3rd Floor Market Towers, 1 Nine Elms Lane, London SW8 5NQ
Phone: +44 (0)20 3177 1600
Web: www.rsph.org.uk

Similar Jobs

Dietitian, Health Promotion Specialist, Nutritional Therapist

Dietitian

also known as: Food Adviser

CRCI:Healthcare

CLCI:JAV Job Band: 5

Job Description

Dietitians translate the science of nutrition into everyday information about food and work to prevent and treat disease through balanced eating. They plan and give practical dietary advice to patients in hospital or in the community. Dietitians use their skills to assess the dietary needs of individual patients who need a controlled diet because of their medical condition, eg diabetes or renal disease. Give general nutritional advice to people such as pregnant women or parents of young children. Is able to evaluate new clinical research and advances in food technology, and explain their importance to patients, nurses, health professionals, doctors, students and community groups.

Also consult with other medical staff, inform the hospital catering department of menus needed, and advise and encourage patients. May play an important role in health promotion and give talks on diet and nutrition, or work in research.

Work Details

Usually work a 9am to 5pm, Monday to Friday week, though you may be expected to work outside normal hours, and have time off in lieu. You work in a hospital, a clinic or a laboratory, though community dietitians work in GP surgeries, patients' homes, schools, nursing homes and other locations. You advise, teach and consult with people. There is contact with people who are ill, in pain or depressed. You may also have to produce leaflets, write articles, and write reports and letters about your patients to other professionals.

Qualification

- **England, Wales and Northern Ireland**

Band 5: For degree courses: 2-3 A levels, usually including chemistry and another science subject and some GCSEs (A*-C) usually including English, maths and science, or equivalent. Exact requirements depend on the degree you take.

- **Scotland**

Band 5: For degree courses: 3-5 H grades, including chemistry and another science subject, and some S grades (1-3), usually including English and maths, or similar qualifications. Exact requirements depend on the degree you take.

Degree Information

There are two qualification routes: either through an approved degree in dietetics or by taking a degree in a related discipline, such as biochemistry, biology, nutrition, human life science, medicine, food science/technology and physiology, followed by a two-year postgraduate diploma in dietetics.

Adult Qualifications

Competition for places on courses is very keen. Some institutions may accept adults who have completed an Access course in science or health-related studies.

Work Experience

Universities and employers may prefer candidates who have relevant work or voluntary experience. Working with a dietitian/nutritionist is the most useful. Contact them through hospitals, private practice, and GP surgeries or health centres. Related experience in other scientific or food-related industries is also useful.

Entry and Training

All qualified dietitians are required to be registered with the Health Professions Council (HPC) to be able to practise in the NHS. Training takes at least four years, or longer if you follow the postgraduate route. It is necessary to have a recognised degree, MSc or postgraduate diploma in nutrition and dietetics to work as a dietitian.

You need an HPC approved degree in dietetics or a postgraduate qualification, during which you study subjects such as human nutrition, biochemistry, microbiology and medicine. You also acquire interviewing/communication skills and clinical practice.

In a hospital, you usually spend six to twelve months gaining experience in various areas of work, such as surgery, oncology, medical and orthopaedic wards, and in outpatient's clinics, including those who see people with heart conditions, have weight problems or who are diabetic. Registered dieticians can become members of the British Dietetic Association which offers regular courses on a range of topics for continuing professional development. They also offer a structured Professional Development Award which takes five years to complete.

A Diploma/Welsh Baccalaureate may be available in your area in society, health and development. The advanced level is equivalent to 3.5 A levels but for some university courses, the additional and specialist learning (ASL) component of the diploma needs to include specific A levels. Check entry requirements carefully with the individual institutions.

Mature entrants with experience in a scientific, community/social or health setting have an advantage for entry to courses. Those with a relevant first degree that have a good level of biochemistry and human physiology, may take an accelerated two-year postgraduate course. There are a number of NHS-funded places on relevant university courses and you may also be eligible for a bursary or student loan.

Opportunities and Pay

This is an expanding profession in the UK. Most dietitians are employed by the NHS as clinical dieticians, but also by central government and its agencies, or on a freelance basis in advisory or research work. There are marketing, advertising and public relations opportunities with community education and nutrition organisations, and also posts in the pharmaceutical, food and catering industries, with major supermarkets, and as nutrition advisers to websites and health-related charities. An increasing number of dietitians now work in GP practices.

Following qualification you can remain in a general post or choose to specialise in, for example, oncology, renal or gastroenterology, working with elderly people or people with mental health problems. There may be opportunities in research or to teach, or you can take on a management role, eventually being responsible for controlling a budget and planning and marketing a dietetic service. Opportunities are available abroad, particularly with relief agencies in developing countries.

Pay is on a nationally agreed scale in the NHS. A newly qualified dietitian working for the NHS earns from £21k-£28k a year, rising to £34k as a dietitian specialist. Dietetic team managers can earn up to £40k a year.

Skills and Qualities

able to explain clearly, able to get on with all kinds of people, able to inspire confidence, aptitude for teamwork, good adviser, non-judgemental, patient, planning skills, scientific approach, self confident

Relevant Subjects

Biology, Chemistry, English, Health and social care, Hospitality and catering, Mathematics, Psychology, Science, Sociology

Further Information

BDA Career Choices - www.bdacareerchoices.com

Dietetics Today (monthly) (British Dietetic Association) - www.bda.uk.com

Diplomas (Foundation, Higher and Advanced) - http://yp.direct.gov.uk/diplomas

Health Professions Council (HPC) - www.hpc-uk.org

NHS Careers (NHS Careers) - www.nhscareers.nhs.uk

NHS Careers Scotland - www.infoscotland.com/nhs

NHS Careers Wales - www.wales.nhs.uk

Royal Society for Public Health (RSPH) - www.rsph.org.uk

Want a Career as a Dietitian (BDA) (BDA) - www.bda.uk.com/ent.html

Welsh Baccalaureate - www.wbq.org.uk

▶Working in science (2007) (Babcock Lifeskills) - www.babcock-lifeskills.com/

Addresses

British Dietetic Association (BDA)
5th Floor, Charles House, 148-149 Great Charles Street,
Queensway, Birmingham B3 3HT
Phone: +44 (0)121 200 8080
Web: www.bda.uk.com

Similar Jobs

Consumer Scientist, Food Scientist/Technologist, Health Promotion Specialist, Nutritional Therapist, Sport & Exercise Scientist

Digital Imaging Specialist

CRCI:Media, Print and Publishing
CLCI:EV Job Band: 2 to 4

Job Description

Digital imaging specialists work on enhancing and manipulating existing photographic images. They are not involved in the initial photography but work with designers and photographers to establish what the image will be used for. Between them, they agree what needs to be done to the image for it to be acceptable for its particular purpose.

They work at a computer workstation using sophisticated laboratory equipment, mini-labs and imaging equipment to scan images into the system. Manipulate the image for best effect and correct any colour imbalances. Use software such as Photoshop to edit the image e.g. change the background, combine sections from different images to create one new image or resize the whole picture. Can be involved in the restoration of old photos and archiving and cataloguing prints.

May use programmes such as Quark, Illustrator and InDesign when creating some new designs that have been commissioned by clients. Can be involved with producing large format prints, such as posters, fine art canvases, banners and exhibition stands. May also provide a specialist developing and printing service for professional photographers. Also set, monitor and adjust machinery, and refill as needed with paper, ink and chemicals.

Work Details

The hours are usually around 38-40 a week, Monday to Friday, though overtime and weekend work is possible. Some large companies may have a shift system. You usually work in a fast-paced computerised laboratory, which is clean and brightly lit. You may spend long hours sitting at a computer. The work requires attention to detail and a high degree of accuracy. You wear protective clothing, including goggles and gloves, when dealing with chemicals.

Qualification

• England, Wales and Northern Ireland

Band 2: For entry to jobs, no minimum qualifications are needed, but it is an advantage to have some GCSEs (A*-C) or equivalent in subjects that include English and maths.

Band 3: For entry to jobs, HNC or a relevant Diploma, usually at least 4 GCSEs (A*-C) including English and maths, or equivalent. ICT and art are also useful subjects.

Band 4: For HND, Diploma of Higher Education or foundation degree: 1-2 A levels and some GCSEs (A*-C) usually including English and maths, or equivalent. Art and ICT are useful subjects.

• Scotland

Band 2: Although academic qualifications are not specified for this job, it is an advantage to have some S grades (1-3) in subjects that include English and maths, or similar.

Band 3: For entry: usually at least four S grades (1-3) including English and maths, or similar. ICT and art are useful subjects.

Band 4: For entry to SQA higher national and professional development awards, usually 2-3 H grades and some S grades (1-3), including English and maths, or similar qualifications. ICT and art are useful subjects.

Adult Qualifications

Those with relevant work experience may be accepted for some college courses without meeting the formal entry requirements. Access or foundation courses may be available in your area.

Work Experience

Employers or colleges may prefer candidates with relevant work or voluntary experience. This is ideally in a photographic laboratory. Work that develops your computer skills, especially working with digital images, and experience in amateur photography is very useful.

Entry and Training

There are no set entry qualifications, but some experience or knowledge of photography is useful. Entrants are also usually expected to have good computing skills and a working knowledge of image manipulation software, such as Photoshop, Quark XPress, Illustrator or InDesign. You usually train on the job, working with experienced staff and perhaps taking short courses run by product and equipment manufacturers.

It is possible to take a full-time course first at a college, though entry to these courses is highly competitive. City & Guilds have redeveloped their digital imaging courses and offer part time and full time courses at levels 1-3 in photo imaging and photo image printing, or you can work for a BTEC HNC/HND in photography. Training programmes, including apprenticeship schemes, may be available in your area. Advanced apprenticeships leading to qualification at level 3 can also be a route into higher education.

The British Association of Picture Libraries and Agencies (BAPLA) has news of technological developments in printing and details of short courses. They also research and report on market developments and have details of job vacancies and volunteering opportunities. Registered members can also participate in the discussion forums and receive the BAPLA newsletter. Similarly, the Association of Photographers (AOP) has a JobShop section on their website, detailing employment opportunities. See the websites for details.

The British Institute of Professional Photography (BIPP) offers training to those wishing to achieve licentiateship, associateship or fellowship levels of membership. This can provide a good foundation on which to build your digital imaging skills. Approved courses are run at a selection of nine universities throughout the UK. See the BIPP website for details. The AOP produces 'Beyond the Lens', a publication that details all aspects of the industry.

A Diploma/Welsh Baccalaureate may be available in your area in creative and media. This can be a useful introduction to this type of career as you gain practical experience while studying. See the diplomas website or Skillset for further information.

Government training opportunities, such as apprenticeships, may be available in your area. You can also gain recognition of previous experience through Accreditation of Prior Learning (APL) or by working towards relevant S/NVQs. Contact your local Connexions centre, careers office, Jobcentre Plus, Next Step service or Learning and Skills Council (LSC)/Local Enterprise Company (LEC) for details of training schemes, including apppprenticeships for adults.

Opportunities and Pay

Many digital imaging specialists have traditionally progressed into this role after working in photofinishing and professional processing labs. Some may be employed in hospitals, research establishments, broadcasting companies, universities, colleges, digital picture libraries and in the armed forces. There has been a rapid expansion of laboratories over the past 15-20 years and to meet the requirements of the industry, new S/NVQs, specifically in digital imaging, have been introduced. This makes it easier for students to find work without having experience in this area.

Approximately 15,000 people work in this sector. There is a steady demand for skilled operators, especially in London and south-east England, though the rapid growth in downloading digital photographs directly to a PC may impact on future employment opportunities. High levels of computer skills are increasingly required. Many photographic laboratories are diversifying and producing large scale products such as posters and exhibition materials. Part-time work and self-employment are possible.

Pay varies depending on location and employer, but a trainee is likely to earn around £12k-£15k, rising to £25k a year, with experience. Highly skilled and experienced digital technicians can earn up to £45k a year.

Health

Good colour vision is essential for this job. The chemicals used can cause allergic reaction.

Skills and Qualities

able to work to deadlines, attention to detail, design ability, eye for shape/colour, eye for visual effect, good concentration level, methodical, numeracy skills, patient, specialist IT skills

Relevant Subjects

Art and Design, Chemistry, ICT/Computer studies, Media and communication studies, Physics, Science

Further Information

Apprenticeship Schemes (National Apprenticeship Service) - www.apprenticeships.org.uk
Beyond The Lens (Association of Photographers (AOP)) - www.beyond-the-lens.com
British Journal of Photography (weekly) (Incisive Photographic Ltd) - www.bjp-online.com
Diplomas (Foundation, Higher and Advanced) - http://yp.direct.gov.uk/diplomas
Photo Imaging (Skillset) (Skillset) - www.skillset.org/photo/careers/
Picture Research Association (PRA) - www.picture-research.org.uk
Professional Photographic Laboratories Association - www.pmai.org/ppla/
Skillset - sector skills council for the creative media, fashion and textiles industries - www.skillset.org
Welsh Baccalaureate - www.wbq.org.uk
▶Working in creative & media (2007) (Babcock Lifeskills) - www.babcock-lifeskills.com/

Addresses

Association of Photographers (AOP)
81 Leonard Street, London EC2A 4QS
Phone: +44 (0)20 7739 6669
Web: www.the-aop.org

British Association of Picture Libraries and Agencies (BAPLA)
18 Vine Hill, London EC1R 5DZ
Phone: +44 (0)20 7713 1780
Web: www.bapla.org

British Institute of Professional Photography (BIPP)
1 Prebendal Court Oxford Road, Aylesbury, Buckinghamshire HP19 8EY
Phone: +44 (0)1296 718530
Web: www.bipp.com

Similar Jobs

Laboratory Technician: Science, Photographer, Photographic Laboratory Machine Print Operative, Photographic Stylist, Print Finisher, Textile Colour Technologist

Diver

CRCI:Security and Armed Forces
CLCI:YAZ Job Band: 2 to 5

Job Description

Divers use professional skills to carry out a wide range of underwater activities depending on the industry in which they work and the type of diving equipment used. May dive in inland waters such as lakes, rivers, reservoirs and canals, or in oceans and seas. Work at depths varying from just a few metres down to around 200 metres, or 300 metres in some parts of the world, such as Brazil. Some work in docks, harbours, or on offshore oil and gas rigs, looking for any sign of deterioration, and carrying out repairs. May also work offshore in the exploration of sites for future construction work.

Divers carry out salvage work when recovering lost cargo, sunken boats, ships or vehicles that have gone off roads into deep water. Some work with the rescue services, such as the police, where a diver may be required to search in rivers, lakes and deep ponds, or offshore to look for and retrieve a missing person, or for vital evidence at a crime scene. Use a wide range of equipment, including pneumatic and hydraulic power tools as well as hand tools. They also work in branches of the armed forces such as the Royal Navy and Royal Engineers. May also have specialist skills in explosives, welding skills, or in underwater filming and photography.

May be required to spend time underwater in a special chamber (saturation diving), that allows them to live and work underwater for a period of up to 28 days. With the relevant academic qualifications, such as marine science and nautical archaeology, some take part in underwater exploration. Others may specialise in sport and recreational diving, and may teach underwater diving skills at a diving centre. May also lead a group of recreational divers and ensure that the strict rules and regulations surrounding each dive are safely followed.

Work Details

Hours are irregular and the work is physically demanding. Offshore work is usually in 12 hour shifts. You can be based on a ship or an oil rig and may need to spend nights away from home and long periods at sea. Conditions can sometimes be hazardous which makes jobs, such as welding or cementing, difficult. You may have to cope with long periods of inactivity in compression chambers. Decompression after deep diving can be hazardous to health and is tedious, but vital.

You must be able to work both on your own and as part of a team. The work environment can be dangerous, cold, wet, dark and possibly cramped. There is a risk of accidents from equipment or contact with dangerous materials.

Qualification

There are no set minimum qualifications and entry requirements vary depending on the employer. However, it is useful to have some level of qualifications in English, maths, and a science.

Adult Qualifications

Experience in mechanical/civil engineering or construction is an advantage. Fitness is more important than formal qualifications. However, entrants to the armed forces have to meet specific entry requirements.

Work Experience

Employers or colleges/universities may prefer candidates who have relevant work or voluntary experience, although diving experience may be difficult to gain, especially if under 18. It is useful to have experience in skilled technical areas such as construction, welding or engineering. You should also develop your skills in swimming and perhaps in sports diving.

Entry and Training

You must be at least 18 and ideally complete your training before you are 25. To enter this job you may have to have evidence of specialist knowledge, and you must have excellent swimming skills and pass a thorough medical. For conventional diving it is useful to combine diving ability with other technical skills such as welding, fitting, engineering and inspection skills. An employer's requirements depend on the nature of the job, such as police work, marine science and marine archaeology.

Professional divers are required to take courses approved by the Health & Safety Executive (HSE), although the police and armed forces have their own training schemes. Specialist diving qualifications such as those offered by The Underwater Centre and the Professional Diving Academy include welding and burning, non-destructive testing (NDT) and diver medic. Most trainees usually have to fund their own training which is costly. The International Marine Contractors Association details courses and careers on their website. For some offshore careers, you may need to have BOSIET (Basic Offshore Safety Induction and Emergency Training).

Those working in underwater scientific exploration may have a degree in marine biology or oceanography and those in marine archaeology usually have a degree in archaeology. Some degree courses such as marine biology, underwater technology and marine archaeology include diving training, but you should check the university prospectus carefully.

Mature applicants should be aware that most trainee divers are under 33, though the average age of experienced North Sea saturation divers is around 41. You must be in excellent physical condition to pass an annual medical examination.

Opportunities and Pay

You can work for an offshore oil and gas company, a civil engineering company, a diving contractor, a water company, fish farms, the armed forces or the police. There is competition for jobs, but at the moment there is a worldwide shortage of experienced divers. Advances in underwater technology have meant that people who combine a diving qualification with a degree or diploma in some branch of engineering, are becoming increasingly valuable. There are also some opportunities in film, television, video, and in marine science and archaeology.

There are few full-time jobs for divers and most work on short-term contracts, though opportunities are increasing for recreational diving instructors both in the UK and worldwide. With experience you can also become a dive supervisor or superintendent. Work is also possible in the Far and Middle East, or in under-developed countries and you may work on a self-employed basis.

Pay depends on the employer, but can be very high. Earnings vary considerably as most work is via short contracts and divers usually get paid by the day. The exceptions are the police and Royal Navy divers, who are paid according to their respective forces. Inshore divers are paid up to £120 a day. Offshore divers start earning around £170 a day, rising to around £275-£350 a day for a diver with proven experience. Those with supervisory responsibility can earn up to £450 a day, and saturation divers (further than 50m depth) can expect up to £1000 a day.

Health

You must have a high standard of physical fitness and have to pass a strict medical.

Skills and Qualities

able to work both on your own and in a team, calm, health & safety awareness, quick thinking, resourceful, responsible attitude, self-reliant, technical aptitude, vigilant

Relevant Subjects

Engineering, Mathematics, Physical education and sport, Physics, Science

Further Information

British Sub Aqua Club (BSAC) - www.bsac.com

Dive Magazine (Jellyfish) http://info.divemagazine.co.uk/homepage

Diving and Undersea Vehicles (Society for Underwater Technology (SUT) - www.sut.org.uk/

Health and Safety Executive - www.hse.gov.uk

I want to be a Diver (International Marine Contractors' Association (IMCA)) - www.imca-int.com

Underwater Technology (bi-annual) (SUT) (Society for Underwater Technology) - www.sut.org.uk/journal/default.htm

▶ Working outdoors (2010) (Babcock Lifeskills) - www.babcock-lifeskills.com/

Addresses

International Marine Contractors Association (IMCA)
52 Grosvenor Gardens, London SW1W 0AU
Phone: +44 (0)20 7824 5520
Web: www.imca-int.com/careers

National Diving Centre
Tidenham, Chepstow, Gloucestershire NP16 7LH
Phone: +44 (0)1291 630046
Web: www.ndac.co.uk

National Diving School
Stoneycove Sapcote Road, Stoney Stanton, Leicestershire LE9 4DW
Phone: +44 (0)1455 273089
Web: www.stoneycove.co.uk

Nautical Archaeology Society (NAS)
Fort Cumberland, Fort Cumberland Road, Portsmouth PO4 9LD
Phone: +44 (0)23 9281 8419.
Web: www.nasportsmouth.org.uk/

Professional Association of Diving Instructors (PADI)
Unit 7 St Philips Central Albert Road St Philips, Bristol, Avon BS2 0PD
Phone: +44 (0)117 300 7234
Web: www.padi.com

Professional Diving Academy
Unit 19, Sandbank Business Park, Dunoon, Argyll PA23 8PB
Phone: +44 (0)1 369 701701
Web: www.professionaldivingacademy.com

Society for Underwater Technology (SUT)
80 Coleman Street, London EC2R 5BJ
Phone: +44 (0)20 7382 2601
Web: www.sut.org.uk

Underwater Centre
Marine Walk Carmichael Way, Fort William, Invernesshire PH33 6FF
Phone: +44 (0)1397 703786
Web: www.theunderwatercentre.co.uk

Similar Jobs

Engineer: Marine, Life Support Technician: Diving, Marine Biologist, Oceanographer, ROV Pilot, Royal Navy Diver

DJ

also known as: Disc Jockey

CRCI:Performing Arts
CLCI:GAL — Job Band: 1 to 4

Job Description

DJs introduce and play music for a live audience at a club or event, or work in radio as a presenter. Many DJs own their own mobile equipment, including vinyl, CDs, MP3s, mixing desk, sound and lighting systems. They provide entertainment and music for a range of age groups at functions such as weddings, birthday and anniversary celebrations and other special events. The job involves unloading, setting up and dismantling equipment at the end of the event and transporting it home.

DJs need to maintain and repair the equipment. May also need to organise publicity and keep financial records. In local/national radio, they present and play music in a 'running order' agreed with the producer. The presentation may include interviews with people on a variety of subjects, guest celebrities, 'phone-ins', news, weather and travel bulletins. May also host quiz shows and broadcast advertisements.

If working in a club or pub, DJs need to keep their audience entertained with a steady flow of music, although the DJ may use a microphone to talk to the audience between tracks or to invite music requests. Club DJs use laptop computers and need to be familiar with music software. May specialise in a particular range of music, jazz or dance style, or from a decade, such as the 60s or 80s.

Work Details

Hours for DJs can be long and irregular, and involve working late evenings and weekends. DJs working in radio may be required to work early mornings. May work in village halls, pubs and public buildings, or outdoors at music events. If working in radio, you are likely to be in an air-conditioned studio, and spend a lot of your time sitting at a music console. In a club the atmosphere can be hot and very noisy. DJs should have regular hearing tests.

You need to prepare music before each broadcast or performance and maintain up-to-date knowledge of music. If conducting interviews, you need to put people at their ease. Those working in radio also need to keep up to date with current affairs. Work can be pressured at times.

Qualification

Formal qualifications are not needed for this job but a love of music is vital. An outgoing personality with good communication and technical skills is more important. You can therefore enter this job with qualifications at all levels.

Adult Qualifications

Formal qualifications are not needed for this job but a love of music is vital.

Work Experience

Entry to this job is competitive and it is important to gain some relevant work or voluntary experience before applying. The Community Media Association and the Hospital Broadcasting Association may be useful contacts. Any practical experience in school/college, local and hospital radio, or amateur plays and performances is useful.

Entry and Training

Formal educational qualifications are seldom specified, but relevant experience, such as hospital radio, university campus or community radio, is important. Those working in clubs or operating mobile equipment usually begin working part time, while still doing another job. Training is usually practical and on the job, but there are increasing numbers of relevant or specialised courses on offer throughout the UK in DJ skills, radio and media production and music technology. These range from short courses to part and full-time courses, including City & Guilds, BTEC/SQA national/higher national courses, degrees and postgraduate qualifications.

The Radio Academy in London offers careers advice, training and mentoring for those wishing to work in radio broadcasting. See the website for details. A Diploma/Welsh Baccalaureate in creative and media may be available in your area. Check university entry requirements carefully in case there is an additional specialist learning requirement with the diploma. See the diplomas website for further information.

Many DJs working in radio are graduates, but their degrees can be in any subject. Occasionally, there are opportunities for new entrants to the industry to participate in industry-based training, leading to vocational certificates in radio production at levels 1-2. A demo tape/CD of your work demonstrating your style can be helpful in finding work, especially in radio and night clubs.

Mature applicants usually require background experience in the music and entertainment industry. For some venues or radio employment, young DJs may be preferred. The Department for Employment and Learning offers a New Deal for Musicians, a programme to help unemployed musicians into music careers.

Opportunities and Pay

DJs are employed in local/national radio by the BBC and commercial/independent radio stations. Many are self-employed and find work in clubs, pubs, ferries, cruise ships and holiday centres. Those working in hospital radio, campus or community radio are usually unpaid volunteers. Many self-employed DJs initially work part time in the evenings and at weekends while doing another job, or studying during the day. There is limited job security and it can take years to build a reputation and the right techniques. Some opportunities exist abroad in popular tourist areas but this work is usually seasonal. Only a talented few achieve success. Some of the more well known DJs may work through an agent.

At the start of their careers many DJs work for very little (or even nothing) to gain experience and start building a reputation. Pay varies enormously, depending on your employer or on your popularity. Most DJs work freelance and are paid for the day/session. Self-employed DJs usually earn between £60-£400 a session, rising to £500-£1000 a session for someone with a high reputation. The most popular DJs can earn more than £100k a year.

Health

You need a clear speaking voice and good general fitness.

Skills and Qualities

able to cope under pressure, able to get on with all kinds of people, good ear for music, hand-to-eye co-ordination, motivated, outgoing personality, self confident, self-disciplined, sense of humour, technical aptitude

Relevant Subjects

Media and communication studies, Music, Performing arts

Further Information

BBC Recruitment Services (BBC) - www.bbc.co.uk/jobs

Community Media Association - www.commedia.org.uk

Creative & Cultural Skills - sector skills council for advertising, crafts, cultural heritage, design, literature, music, performing & visual arts - www.ccskills.org.uk

Creative Media Academy - www.s-s-r.com/

Department for employment and learning - www.delni.gov.uk/index.htm

Diplomas (Foundation, Higher and Advanced) - http://yp.direct.gov.uk/diplomas

Hospital Broadcasting Association - www.hbauk.com

National Association of Disc Jockeys (NADJ) - www.nadj.org.uk

RadioCentre - www.radiocentre.org

Skillset - sector skills council for the creative media, fashion and textiles industries - www.skillset.org

The DJ Handbook (PC Publishing)

Welsh Baccalaureate - www.wbq.org.uk

▶ Working in music (2007) (Babcock Lifeskills) - www.babcock-lifeskills.com/

Addresses

Radio Academy
5 Market Place, London W1W 8AE
Phone: +44 (0)20 7927 9920
Web: www.radioacademy.org

Similar Jobs

Broadcast Journalist, Entertainer, Film/TV & Theatre Lighting Technician, Film/TV/Radio & Theatre Sound Recordist, Presenter: Radio & TV

Doctor: General Practitioner

also known as: Family Doctor, GP

CRCI:Healthcare

CLCI:JAB — Job Band: 5

Job Description

Doctors in general practice (GPs) are responsible for the diagnosis and treatment of a wide range of illnesses, infections and diseases. They work in the primary care sector, usually for a primary care trust (PCT), and attend to patients in a general practice surgery, clinic, or in their home. Examine and talk to patients, give advice on health issues, carry out or refer the patient for tests, such as X-rays or blood tests, and arrange suitable treatment by specialists. They also prescribe medicine, issue certificates, keep case notes and may refer patients to a hospital or specialist healthcare professional.

GPs talk to and educate patients about healthy lifestyles and are responsible for adopting preventative medical programmes in surgery, eg family planning clinics or flu vaccinations. Take into account physical, psychological and social factors when assessing patients.

Work Details

Most GPs work 8.30am-6.30pm, Monday to Friday. Some work Saturday mornings and provide out of hours cover. Part-time work is common. You advise and help people. You have contact with people who are ill, in pain, upset or depressed. You have to make decisions about treatment and keep meticulous records. Work can be emotionally demanding and requires coping with the sight of blood. This job is very satisfying for those wishing to work in a caring profession.

Qualification

- **England, Wales and Northern Ireland**

Band 5: For degree in medicine: usually three A levels, with good grades in chemistry and two from physics, biological sciences and maths, plus 5 GCSEs (A*-C) including English, or equivalent. Some medical schools offer a one-year pre-medical course for students with A levels in arts or mixed subjects. Check with individual schools for full details.

- **Scotland**

Band 5: For degree in medicine: usually five H grades, with good grades in chemistry and two from physics, biology and maths, plus five S grades (1-3) including English and maths, or similar. Normally science subjects not held at H grade should be offered at S grade. Some medical schools offer a one-year pre-medical course for students whose H grades do not include the required science subjects. Check with individual schools for full details.

Degree Information

A degree in medicine awarded by a university medical school and recognised by the General Medical Council is essential.

Adult Qualifications

Entry requirement standards are not normally relaxed for mature applicants, though those who consider applying should contact the individual university for advice. Graduates with a good honours degree in a related subject may obtain exemptions from certain options within the medical degree course.

Work Experience

Entry to this career is highly competitive and it is essential that you have some relevant work or voluntary experience before applying to train as a doctor so that you are able to demonstrate a long-term commitment to medicine. Evidence of this can come in the form of relevant paid or voluntary work in a healthcare setting such as work in a hospital, residential care home, or similar. You can apply for voluntary work overseas that usually has a health education or medically-related programme.

Entry and Training

Entry to places at medical school is highly competitive, and most medical schools now require entrants to take the UK Clinical Aptitude Test (UKCAT) to aid the application process. There is a Royal College or a Faculty of a Royal College for each medical discipline which lays down the entry and training requirements for that discipline and sets examinations for membership/fellowship. Most medical degrees take five years. Those candidates without science A/H levels may take a pre-medical course in science first.

All medical graduates must now enter a two-year Foundation Programme immediately after graduation. This forms a link between medical school and GP training and includes a series of placements in a variety of specialisms and healthcare settings. Successful meeting of the standards for year one leads to registration as a doctor with the General Medical Council (GMC).

During Foundation year two, you need to apply for a placement for GP registrar training. This is competitive and involves three stages of application: on-line application, shortlisting using a written applied knowledge test, and an assessment centre process. General practice specialist training consists of three years in approved posts in hospital and general practice, followed by an examination leading to Membership of the Royal College of General Practitioners (MRCGP) and entry on the GP register of the GMC. All doctors have to undertake continuing professional development (CPD) throughout their career.

The armed forces offer medical cadetships for medical students. Contact your nearest armed forces careers office for details.

Mature applicants that are suitably qualified are welcomed by medical schools and some may have reserved places for mature/graduate entrants. There are access courses to medicine and pre-medical foundation courses. Some Open University credits at distinction level may be accepted at some medical schools. Check with individual medical schools for details of all opportunities.

Opportunities and Pay

There is a shortage of doctors in the UK and training provision for new staff has been increased. Most GPs are independent contractors to the NHS and are usually employed by a GP partnership, and work towards becoming a partner. You can also work towards becoming a GP with a Special Interest (GPwSI), eg in family planning or drug misuse. There are opportunities to become involved in hospital work, training of other GPs, local issues within the community, or working abroad with voluntary organisations in developing countries. Prospects may depend on your willingness to move to another area to gain experience and obtain promotion.

In general practice, income within the NHS depends on the size of the practice, number of patients and number of treatments carried out each year. The average salary for a GP is £53k-£80k a year, while self-employed GPs can earn around £80k-£120k a year. This may increase with fees from private work.

Health

There is a risk of infection. You should have no allergies and a good level of general fitness.

Skills and Qualities

able to put people at ease, able to take responsibility, analytical skills, aptitude for teamwork, compassionate, discreet, emotionally strong, good listening skills, not squeamish, scientific approach

Relevant Subjects

Biology, Chemistry, English, Health and social care, Mathematics, Physics, Psychology, Science, Sociology

Further Information

Becoming a Doctor (BMA) (BMA) - www.bma.org.uk/careers/becoming_doctor/index.jsp

Becoming a Doctor: Is Medicine really the career for you? (Matt Green & Tom Nolan, 2008) (Apply2 Ltd)

British Medical Journal (weekly) (BMJ Publishing Group Ltd) - www.bmj.com/

Foundation Programme - www.foundationprogramme.nhs.uk

Health Professions Admission Test (HPAT) - www.hpat-ireland.acer.edu.au

Medicine Uncovered (Trotman 2009) - www.trotman.co.uk

Modernising Medical Careers - www.mmc.nhs.uk

National Recruitment Office for GP Training - www.gprecruitment.org.uk

NHS Careers (NHS Careers) - www.nhscareers.nhs.uk

NHS Careers Scotland - www.infoscotland.com/nhs

NHS Careers Wales - www.wales.nhs.uk

So You Want to be a GP? (RCGP) (RCGP) - www.rcgp.org.uk/pdf/SYWTBGP%20Booklet.pdf

The Lancet (weekly) (Elsevier Ltd) - www.thelancet.com/

UK Clinical Aptitude Test - www.ukcat.ac.uk

Addresses

British Medical Association (BMA)
BMA House, Tavistock Square, London WC1H 9JP
Phone: +44 (0)20 7387 4499
Web: www.bma.org.uk

General Medical Council (GMC)
Regents Place, 350 Euston Road, London NW1 3JN
Phone: +44 (0)161 923 6602
Web: www.gmc-uk.org

Royal College of General Practitioners (RCGP)
14 Princes Gate, Hyde Park, London SW7 1PU
Phone: 0845 456 4041(UK only)
Web: www.rcgp.org.uk

Similar Jobs

Anaesthetist, Coroner, Doctor: Hospital, Pathologist, Pharmacist: Hospital, Surgeon

Doctor: Hospital

also known as: Physician

CRCI:Healthcare
CLCI:JAB — Job Band: 5

Job Description

Doctors use medical knowledge and skill in the diagnoses, care and treatment of illnesses, infections, diseases and general wellbeing of people. They work in a hospital and examine the patient in a ward or an outpatient clinic. They practise in a range of roles, from accident and emergency to medical genetics. Often specialise in a branch of medicine, for example pathology, radiology, psychiatry, paediatrics, ophthalmology or cardiology. Doctors carry out or refer the patient for tests, such as X-rays or blood tests, and arrange suitable treatment.

Doctors issue medical certificates and prescriptions and keep case notes on each patient both for a record of hospital treatment, and for referral to a patient's GP. They liaise closely and are supported by a team, including other doctors, nurses and other health professionals. May carry out research and assist in the teaching of trainee medics.

Work Details

You are expected to work irregular hours, weekends and be on call, and may sometimes work very long hours. Junior hospital doctors have to live in the hospital when on call. You advise and help people. There is contact with people who are ill, in pain, upset or depressed. You have to make decisions about treatment and keep meticulous records. Work can be emotionally demanding and requires coping with the sight of blood. This job is very satisfying for those wishing to work in a caring profession.

Qualification

• England, Wales and Northern Ireland

Band 5: For degree in medicine: usually three A levels, with good grades in chemistry and two from physics, biological sciences and maths, plus 5 GCSEs (A*-C) including English, or equivalent. Some medical schools offer a one-year pre-medical course for students with A levels in arts or mixed subjects. Check with individual schools for full details.

• Scotland

Band 5: For degree in medicine: usually five H grades, with good grades in chemistry and two from physics, biology and maths, plus five S grades (1-3) including English and maths, or similar. Normally science subjects not held at H grade should be offered at S grade. Some medical schools offer a one-year pre-medical course for students whose H grades do not include the required science subjects. Check with individual schools for full details.

Degree Information

A degree in medicine awarded by a university medical school and recognised by the General Medical Council is essential.

Adult Qualifications

Entry requirement standards are not normally relaxed for mature applicants, though those who consider applying should contact the individual university for advice. Graduates with a good honours degree in a related subject may obtain exemptions from certain options within the medical degree course.

Work Experience

Entry to this career is highly competitive and it is essential that you have some relevant work or voluntary experience before applying to train as a doctor so that you are able to demonstrate a long-term commitment to medicine. Evidence of this can come in the form of relevant paid or voluntary work in a healthcare setting such as work in a hospital, residential care home, or similar. You can apply for voluntary work overseas that usually has a health education or medically-related programme.

Entry and Training

Entry to places at medical school is highly competitive, and most medical schools now require entrants to take the UK Clinical Aptitude Test (UKCAT) to aid the application process. There is a Royal College or a Faculty of a Royal College for each medical discipline which lays down the entry and training requirements for that discipline and sets examinations for membership/fellowship. Most medical degrees take five years. Candidates without science A/H levels may take a pre-medical course in science first.

All medical graduates must now enter a two-year Foundation Programme immediately after graduation. This forms a link between medical school and specialist hospital training and includes a series of placements in a variety of specialisms and healthcare settings. Successful meeting of the standards for year one, leads to registration as a doctor with the General Medical Council (GMC).

During Foundation year two, you need to apply for a placement to train as a specialty registrar. This can take up to 7 years, depending on the specialty. There are more than 60 different specialties but training is initially broad based. Once completed you are eligible to be on the specialist register of the GMC. During the second year of the Foundation programme, you may decide not to follow the specialist training route, but instead to do shorter training and work in a hospital as a career post doctor. All doctors have to undertake continuing professional development (CPD) throughout their career.

The armed forces offer medical cadetships for medical students. Contact your nearest armed forces careers office for details.

Mature applicants that are suitably qualified are welcomed by medical schools of which some may have reserved places for mature/graduate entrants. There are access courses to medicine and pre-medical foundation courses. Some Open University credits at distinction level may be accepted at some medical schools. Check with individual medical schools for details of all opportunities.

Opportunities and Pay

There is a shortage of doctors in the UK and training provision for new staff has been increased. Doctors are usually employed by the NHS, a private hospital, research organisation, the armed forces or a university medical school. You can specialise in one of a number of areas of hospital work, eg geriatrics, paediatrics, or pathology. There are opportunities abroad with voluntary organisations in developing countries, but pay is usually lower.

Prospects may depend on willingness to move to another area to gain experience and obtain promotion. Some may teach or do research. There may be opportunities to work part time or job share.

Within the NHS, junior doctors earn a basic salary and are usually paid a supplement for extra hours worked. Basic salaries are around £33k a year (including a 50% supplement for extra hours), rising to £43k-£68k (including 50% supplement) for a doctor in specialist training. A consultant can earn £73k-£174k a year. These salaries do not include on-call payments, private income or London weighting allowances.

Health

There is a risk of infection. You should have no allergies and a good level of general fitness.

Skills and Qualities

able to put people at ease, able to take responsibility, analytical skills, discreet, emotionally strong, good listening skills, not squeamish, scientific approach, self confident, sympathetic

Relevant Subjects

Biology, Chemistry, English, Health and social care, Mathematics, Physics, Psychology, Science, Sociology

Further Information

AGCAS: Health (Job Sector Briefing) (AGCAS) - www.prospects.ac.uk

Becoming a Doctor (BMA) (BMA) - www.bma.org.uk/careers/becoming_doctor/index.jsp

Becoming a Doctor: Is Medicine really the career for you? (Matt Green & Tom Nolan, 2008) (Apply2 Ltd)

British Medical Journal (weekly) (BMJ Publishing Group Ltd) - www.bmj.com/

Foundation Programme - www.foundationprogramme.nhs.uk

Medicine Uncovered (Trotman 2009) - www.trotman.co.uk

Modernising Medical Careers - www.mmc.nhs.uk

NHS Careers (NHS Careers) - www.nhscareers.nhs.uk

NHS Careers Scotland - www.infoscotland.com/nhs

NHS Careers Wales - www.wales.nhs.uk

The Lancet (weekly) (Elsevier Ltd) - www.thelancet.com/

UK Clinical Aptitude Test - www.ukcat.ac.uk

Addresses

British Medical Association (BMA)
BMA House, Tavistock Square, London WC1H 9JP
Phone: +44 (0)20 7387 4499
Web: www.bma.org.uk

General Medical Council (GMC)
Regents Place, 350 Euston Road, London NW1 3JN
Phone: +44 (0)161 923 6602
Web: www.gmc-uk.org

Royal College of Physicians (RCP)
11 St Andrew's Place, Regent's Park, London NW1 4LE
Phone: +44 (0)207 935 1174
Web: www.rcplondon.ac.uk

Similar Jobs

Anaesthetist, Coroner, Doctor: General Practitioner, Pharmacist: Hospital, Psychologist: Neuropsychologist, Surgeon

Dog Groomer

also known as: Canine Beautician, Pet Stylist

CRCI:Environment, Animals and Plants
CLCI:WAM Job Band: 1

Job Description

Dog groomers groom, trim, cuts wash, dry and brush the coats of different breeds of dog and also advise the owner on caring for their dog. They lift the dog onto a hygienic work surface and check it for any skin problems. May need to cut a rough coat first by using scissors. They brush the dog's hair, comb and may cut its coat into an appropriate style for the breed. Also clean the dog's ears and teeth, clip the dog's nails and treat it for fleas and other external parasites. They wash the dog using a specialised shampoo and may also use a conditioner.

Groomers rinse and dry the coat with a specialist hairdryer. They use scissors, electric clippers or other specialised cutting equipment. May get dogs ready for dog competitions and shows. Some groomers operate a mobile service and visit an owner's home with a specially equipped 'dog wash' van.

Work Details

Usually work a 35-40 hr week, Monday to Friday, though may need to work a Saturday and have a different day off instead. Works indoors either in a pet shop or salon, or boarding and breeding kennels. If offering a mobile service, needs to travel around a local area to visit clients. It is important not to be scared of dogs as sometimes you need to work with those that may be nervous or try to bite you. The work environment may be hot and humid and you stand for most of the time. Protective and waterproof clothing is normally worn.

Qualification

- **England, Wales and Northern Ireland**

Band 1: For entry to jobs, no minimum qualifications are needed, but you are expected to have a good level of general education and relevant experience. Some formal/vocational qualifications at any level are useful.

- **Scotland**

Band 1: For entry to jobs, no minimum qualifications are needed, but you are expected to have a good level of general education and relevant experience. Some formal/vocational qualifications at any level are useful.

Adult Qualifications

Employers may tend to favour younger applicants for trainee places, though entry to fee-paying courses is equally open to mature candidates, as well as school leavers. You can improve your skills and qualifications by working through the Foundation Learning programme. This involves taking credit-based units and qualifications to help you progress.

Work Experience

Relevant work experience is always useful and can improve your job prospects. Any work that involves dogs, such as a Saturday job or holiday work, is very useful.

Entry and Training

Some entrants go straight into the job and receive on-the-job training with an experienced and usually qualified groomer. This can take about 18 months. You can also take a fee-paying course at a private college.

There is a City & Guilds/NPTC intermediate certificate in dog grooming available that includes three units - the work environment, preparation for bathing, and bath, dry and finish. Assessment is by practical tests and online questions. With over 18 months' experience you can go on to take the advanced certificate. The British Dog Groomer's Association (BDGA) also runs a higher diploma; successful completion of this means you can join the Guild of Master Groomers. See the website of the Pet Care Association/BDGA for full details and for a list of approved training centres.

You can also study full or part time at a college for national certificates/diploma in animal care before looking for employment. S/NVQs are available in dog grooming at levels 2-3. Training programmes, including apprenticeships leading to level 2 and advanced apprenticeships leading to level 3, may be available in your area.

Mature applicants can benefit through government training opportunities that may be available in your area. Contact your local Connexions or careers office, Jobcentre Plus, Next Step service or Learning and Skills Council (LSC)/Local Enterprise Company (LEC) for details of all training opportunities and schemes. Distance-learning courses in dog grooming are offered by the Animal Care College.

Opportunities and Pay

There are over 3,000 dog grooming parlours in the UK. The demand for dog grooming has grown in recent years, but the chance of working full time is limited and varies according to area and local demand. Pet shops, boarding and breeding kennels are now also offering grooming as an additional service. Demand for dog grooming is usually less in the winter months as owners may let their dogs' coats grow long for warmth. Some groomers are self-employed and travel to an owner's home. Larger employers may be able to offer senior posts for those who are qualified and experienced.

Pay varies a lot as most dog groomers are self-employed and many work part time. Starting pay is around £9k rising to around £12k-£16k a year. Self-employed dog groomers may charge around £25-£75 a session.

Health

This job is difficult to do if you are allergic to animals and some of the chemicals and shampoos used can irritate the skin.

Skills and Qualities

able to work well on your own, attention to detail, business awareness, careful, good at handling animals, good communication skills, good co-ordination, good organisational skills, manual dexterity, patient

Relevant Subjects

Art and Design, Biology

Further Information

Apprenticeship Schemes (National Apprenticeship Service) - www.apprenticeships.org.uk

Foundation Learning (QCDA) - www.qcda.gov.uk

Lantra - The Sector Skills Council for environmental & land-based sector (Lantra) http:/www.lantra.co.uk

Lantra Careers (A Future In...) (Lantra) - www.afuturein.com

Real Life Guide to Working with Animals & Wildlife (Trotman) - www.trotman.co.uk

Training Schemes - www.direct.gov.uk/en/educationandlearning

▶Working with animals (2009) (Babcock Lifeskills) - www.babcock-lifeskills.com/

Addresses

Animal Care College
Index House High Street, Ascot, Berkshire SL5 7ET
Phone: +44 (0)1344 636436
Web: www.animalcarecollege.co.uk/

Pet Care Trust/Dog Groomers' Association
Bedford Business Centre, 170 Mile Road MK42 9TW
Phone: +44 (0)1234 273933
Web: www.petcare.org.uk

Similar Jobs

Animal Care Assistant, Horse Groom, Pet Shop Assistant, Veterinary Nurse

Domestic Appliance Service Technician

also known as: Electrical Appliance Repairer, Field Service Engineer: White Goods

CRCI:Engineering
CLCI:ROK
Job Band: 1 to 3

Job Description

Domestic appliance technicians install, service and repair white (household) electrical goods, such as washing machines and dryers, irons, cookers, microwave ovens, kettles or electronic equipment, including TVs and DVD players. They study technical manuals of drawings, wiring and diagrams and then examine the appliance to identify and trace faults. They may use plug-in computerised diagnostic equipment to establish a fault in sophisticated electronic and computer systems, and a range of hand and power tools. Technicians may dismantle the appliance before repairing or replacing worn or damaged parts. Then they reassemble it and test that the appliance is working.

Technicians may work in a company workshop or visit customers in their own homes. They provide an estimate of the repair cost after initial examination of the appliance and may need to transport it to a workshop for further tests, if it can not be repaired on site.

Work Details

Usually work a basic 39 hr week that may include some evenings and Saturdays. You are based either in a workshop or a shop and may visit customers' homes. Travel around a geographical area is necessary. Sometimes you have to deal with complaints. The job involves a fair amount of physical activity, including some heavy lifting, kneeling and bending down. There may be a risk of minor injuries and you may need to wear overalls to protect yourself from dirt and dust.

Qualification

• England, Wales and Northern Ireland

Band 2: For entry to jobs, no minimum qualifications are needed, but it is an advantage to have some GCSEs (A*-C) or equivalent in subjects that include English, maths, science and technology.

Band 3: For entry to jobs, HNC or a relevant Diploma, usually at least 4 GCSEs (A*-C) including maths, physics and English, or equivalent.

• Scotland

Band 2: Although academic qualifications are not specified for this job, it is an advantage to have some S grades (1-3) in subjects that include English, maths, science and technology subjects, or similar.

Band 3: For entry to jobs, usually at least four S grades (1-3) including maths, physics and English, or similar.

Adult Qualifications

A good standard of secondary education is expected. A driving licence may also be required. Course entry requirements are usually relaxed for suitable mature applicants.

Work Experience

Relevant work or voluntary experience is always useful. It can add to your CV and improve your chances when applying for entry to jobs or apprenticeships in the engineering industry. Your personal or adult guidance adviser may be able to assist you on how to organise work experience. In some areas there is a young apprenticeship (14-16) scheme that provides an extended work placement and eventual achievement of a relevant level 2 qualification while at school.

Entry and Training

Most entrants train with an employer and this may be partly off the job at a training centre and partly on the job in a workshop, working with an experienced domestic appliance service engineer. The training given can vary depending on the employer. There are also short courses and refresher courses run by manufacturers and this job requires regular training to keep up to date. Successful craft-level trainees may convert to technician-level training and study for a BTEC/SQA award. A driving licence is usually required. Those working with gas appliances need to train to be on the Gas Safe Register. See the Gas Service Engineer article.

Relevant S/NVQs at levels 2-3 are available in electrical and electronic servicing. City & Guilds also offer a progression award in electrical and electronics servicing at levels 2-3. Training programmes, including apprenticeship schemes, may be available in your area. Advanced apprenticeships leading to qualification at level 3 can also be a route into higher education.

The Engineering Development Trust runs a range of nationwide schemes for 11-21 year olds who are interested in engineering as a career. See the website for details. A Diploma/Welsh Baccalaureate may be available in your area in engineering. See the diplomas website for further information.

Mature applicants with relevant experience or qualifications may be able to enter directly. It is an advantage to have qualifications or experience in electrical work, electronics or engineering. Government training opportunities, such as apprenticeships for adults, may be available in your area. You can also gain recognition of previous experience through Accreditation of Prior Learning or by working towards relevant S/NVQs. Contact your local careers office, Jobcentre Plus, Next Step service or Learning and Skills Council (LSC)/Local Enterprise Company (LEC) for details of training schemes.

Opportunities and Pay

Jobs are available mainly in towns and cities with electricity utility companies or manufacturing companies, domestic appliances rental firms, or electrical shops. There is a steady demand for qualified staff and you can specialise in a particular type or make of appliance. Promotion to more senior posts is possible after gaining experience. There is plenty of scope for self-employment once you have experience.

Pay can vary depending on location and employer. A starting wage is likely to be around £12k-£15k a year, rising to £18k with experience. The most skilled and experienced engineers can earn £22k-£27k a year and this may be more with bonuses. You may have the use of a company van.

Health

Normal colour vision and good general fitness are required.

Skills and Qualities

able to work quickly, able to work well on your own, IT skills, logical, manual dexterity, methodical, polite, problem-solving skills, responsible attitude, safety conscious

Relevant Subjects

Design and technology, Engineering, ICT/Computer studies, Mathematics, Physics, Science

Further Information

Apprenticeship Schemes (National Apprenticeship Service) - www.apprenticeships.org.uk

Diplomas (Foundation, Higher and Advanced) - http://yp.direct.gov.uk/diplomas

Energy & Utility Skills - sector skills council for gas, power, waste management & water industries - www.euskills.co.uk

Gas Safe Register - www.gassaferegister.co.uk

SEMTA - sector skills council for science, engineering and manufacturing technologies - www.semta.org.uk

Training Schemes - www.direct.gov.uk/en/educationandlearning

Addresses

Domestic Appliance Service Association (DASA)
2nd Floor, 145-157 St John Street, London EC1V 4PY
Web: www.dasa.org.uk

Engineering Development Trust (EDT)
Ridgeway, Welwyn Garden City, Hertfordshire AL7 2AA
Phone: +44 (0)1707 871520
Web: www.etrust.org.uk

Institute of Domestic Heating and Environmental Engineers (IDHEE)
P O Box 329, Southampton, Hampshire SO40 0BT
Phone: +44 [0] 23 80 66 89 00
Web: www.idhee.org.uk

Similar Jobs

Electrician, Fitter: Maintenance, Gas Service Engineer, IT Service Technician, Office Equipment Service Engineer

Domestic Energy Assessor

CRCI:Building and Construction
CLCI:UM Job Band: 2 to 3

Job Description

Domestic energy assessors are instructed by homeowners or estate agents to record the energy efficiency of domestic properties and issue an Energy Performance Certificate (EPC). This is now a requirement for all domestic properties that are built, put on the market or rented. They visit the home and survey the property; collect data on the building's construction, heating, hot water and dimensions. This information is then entered into a software programme, which produces the EPC.

The energy rating of the property is measured on a scale and compared with the rating that the owner or tenant needs to aim for. Recommendations are made for improving the energy performance and the client receives practical information on such things as cutting fuel bills, reducing emissions and using renewable energy sources.

Work Details

Domestic energy assessors usually work a 35-39 hr week, Monday to Friday, though you may be required to work longer hours at times to fit in with clients, including evenings and weekends. Work is mostly on site, in new buildings or at people's homes, with some time spent working from an office or at home. You spend a lot of time travelling around to visit property.

On-site inspections can involve some physical activity, such as climbing ladders and scaffolding, so you need to wear a protective helmet. You may be working outside in all weathers. Conditions on site can be damp, dirty or cramped. You usually need a driving licence to do this job.

Qualification

• England, Wales and Northern Ireland

Band 2: Although academic qualifications are not specified for this job, it is an advantage to have some GCSEs (A*-C) in subjects that include English and maths, or equivalent.

Band 3: For entry: it may be preferable to have at least 4 GCSEs (A*-C) including English and maths, or equivalent.

Adult Qualifications

Entry is possible without specific academic qualifications, though it is an advantage if you can demonstrate an aptitude for basic maths and English. Any entry requirements are usually relaxed for suitable mature applicants. Contact your local careers office, Jobcentre Plus, Next Step service or Learning and Skills Council (LSC) Local Enterprise Company (LEC) for details of training schemes.

Work Experience

Relevant work or voluntary experience is always useful and can improve your chances in application to this job or to a college course. The types of work experience to consider include work with home information pack (HIP) providers, work with an estate agent or surveyor's office or a related area, such as jobs in the construction industry or local government. In some areas there is a young apprenticeship (14-16) scheme that provides an extended work placement and eventual achievement of a level 2 qualification whilst at school.

Entry and Training

The main route to accreditation for those without relevant experience is to obtain an approved level 3 award or diploma in domestic energy assessment. This is available through either the Awarding Body for the Built Environment, City & Guilds or the National Federation of Property Professionals. Training for this award/diploma is offered by a range of training providers, including private training companies and colleges. Larger companies may provide training in-house. There are a range of study options, from full or part-time courses to distance learning. Lengths of courses vary depending on the course you choose, any prior experience and method of study. Contact the awarding bodies for details of all training options. Also, visit the Asset Skills website for details on accreditation schemes.

No previous qualifications are needed to enter training, though you need a good basic standard of literacy and numeracy. A Diploma/ Welsh Baccalaureate in construction and the built environment may be available in your area, and is a useful foundation for this job.

To practise as a domestic energy assessor you need to become a member of an approved accreditation scheme. Contact Asset Skills for a list of schemes. You must abide by their rules for membership, such as participating in continuing professional development (CPD) and maintaining professional indemnity. Those with prior experience of energy assessment can apply directly to an accreditation scheme and may be able to enter without qualification.

In Scotland energy performance certificates are undertaken by existing professionals, such as surveyors, architects and engineers. The work can only be carried out by members of a number of organisations/institutions specified by the Scottish Government. There are no specific qualifications for energy assessors in Scotland.

Mature applicants with experience in estate agency, the construction industry or surveying may have an advantage. Those already experienced in energy assessment work can apply directly for accreditation via the Accreditation of Prior Experiential Learning (APEL) route. Contact Asset Skills for details.

Opportunities and Pay

Typical employers include home information pack (HIP) providers, estate agents, solicitors, surveyors, valuers and service suppliers, such as energy retail organisations. Work is available throughout the UK, though mainly in towns and cities. Many work on a self-employed basis. Availability of work may depend on the property climate and the number of assessors at the time of entry to this work. Currently there is a downturn in the property market which means there may be a shortage of vacancies or less work available for those that are self-employed.

With additional training you can produce energy performance certificates (EPCs) for non-domestic buildings. Or you can do a 'top up' qualification and become a home inspector.

Salaries vary depending on the size and location of your company and who you work for. Starting salaries are in the region of £12k-£18k a year, rising to £18k-£25k with experience. Bonuses and travel allowances can boost your income. If self-employed, your pay depends on the number of EPCs that you do.

Health
You need good general fitness to do this job.

Skills and Qualities
able to get on with all kinds of people, analytical skills, attention to detail, environmental awareness, good communication skills, IT skills, methodical, numeracy skills, observational skills

Relevant Subjects
Construction and built environment, Mathematics

Further Information
Asset Skills - Energy Assessors - www.energy-assessors.org.uk

Asset Skills - sector skills council for the places where we live and work - www.assetskills.org

Communities and Local Government - Energy - www.communities.gov.uk/epbd

Diplomas (Foundation, Higher and Advanced) - http://yp.direct.gov.uk/diplomas

Home Condition Report Register - www.hcrregister.com

Home Information Packs - www.homeinformationpacks.gov.uk

Welsh Baccalaureate - www.wbq.org.uk

▶Working in maths (2009) (Babcock Lifeskills) - www.babcock-lifeskills.com/

Addresses
Awarding Body for the Built Environment (ABBE)
Room A045, Birmingham City University, Franchise Street, Perry Barr B42 2SU
Phone: +44 (0)121 331 5174
Web: www.abbeqa.co.uk

City & Guilds
1 Giltspur Street, London EC1A 9DD
Phone: +44 (0)20 7294 2800
Web: www.cityandguilds.com

National Association of Estate Agents (NAEA)
Arbon House, 6 Tournament Court, Edgehill Drive, Warwick CV34 6LG
Phone: +44 (0)1926 496 800
Web: www.naea.co.uk

Similar Jobs
Estate Agent, Surveying Technician, Surveyor: Building, Surveyor: Building Control

Domestic Services Manager
also known as: Accommodation Manager, Domestic Bursar, Hospital Manager: Domestic Services, Hotel Services Manager, Housekeeper, Housekeeping Manager

CRCI:Catering and Hospitality
CLCI:IB Job Band: 3 to 5

Job Description
Domestic services managers are responsible for accommodation and cleaning services in places such as hotels, holiday centres and health spas, residential and nursing homes, hospitals and universities. They are known as 'housekeepers' in the hotel industry and 'domestic bursars' in places like universities.

Managers are responsible for recruiting new staff and organising their training, usually with an experienced colleague. They plan work rotas and supervise the work of room attendants, cleaners, laundry and linen staff. Also orders and issues cleaning materials and linen supplies, including bedding and towels. They check equipment, furnishings, decoration, etc, and arrange any repairs and maintenance that is required. They also ensure that rooms are kept clean, tidy and welcoming and deal with lost property.

Domestic services managers write reports and complete other paperwork including health and safety audits, maintenance, stock checks, budgets and room check-sheets. They ensure that the laws, rules and regulations surrounding health and safety, security and fire safety are in place and are observed by staff at all times. In small hotels, they may also be involved directly in some of the cleaning.

Work Details
Usually works a basic 40 hr week over five days, though may need to work shifts and some weekends. Early starts and late finishes are usual. You are responsible for making sure that there are high standards of hygiene and that rooms are clean and comfortable. You may have an office, but the job requires you to work in all areas of the premises. You are on your feet for long periods of time, often going up and down stairs. You may live in your place of work.

Qualification
- **England, Wales and Northern Ireland**

Band 3: For entry to jobs, HNC or a relevant Diploma, usually at least 4 GCSEs (A*-C) including English and maths, or equivalent.

Band 4: For HND, Diploma of Higher Education or foundation degree: 1-2 A levels and some GCSEs (A*-C) usually including English and maths, or equivalent.

Band 5: For relevant degree courses: 2-3 A levels and some GCSEs (A*-C) usually including English and maths, or equivalent. Exact requirements depend on the degree you take.

- **Scotland**

Band 3: For entry to jobs, usually at least four S grades (1-3) including English or maths, or similar.

Band 4: For entry to SQA higher national and professional development awards, usually 2-3 H grades and some S grades (1-3), including English and maths, or similar qualifications.

Band 5: For relevant degree courses: 3-5 H grades and some S grades (1-3), usually including English and maths, or similar qualifications. Exact requirements depend on the degree you take.

Degree Information
Degrees in hospitality management, hotel hospitality management or hospitality business management are relevant to this job. Related courses in home economics/consumer studies or in business/management studies with relevant options are also acceptable.

Adult Qualifications
Entry requirements may be relaxed for adults applying for higher education courses. Access or foundation courses provide those without the required qualifications a route onto degree courses.

Work Experience
Colleges/universities may prefer entrants who have experience of the hospitality industry before beginning their course. Relevant work experience is very important for most employers. This includes various jobs in the hotel industry, particularly in hotel accommodation, and jobs where experience of administration and organisational skills are included. It is also useful to have experience and knowledge of other hotel departments such as kitchen, restaurant and bar work, and reception duties.

In some areas there is a young apprenticeship (14-16) scheme that provides an extended work placement and achievement of a level 2 qualification whilst at school.

Entry and Training

A degree/HND qualification is usually required for management training schemes. However, there are varied routes into this job and it is possible to start as a room attendant or junior housekeeper and work up to management level, gaining relevant qualifications and proving you are a good organiser whilst working. You may be able to take part-time courses at a local college, leading to S/NVQs, BTEC/SQA awards, or the Institute of Hospitality certificate or diploma. Many courses are available through distance learning. Relevant foundation degrees in subjects that include hospitality are available and may be taken full or part time, or as a sandwich course.

Managers of some student residences are often postgraduate students or administrative staff at the university or college. The Association for Student Residential Accommodation (ASRA) holds training days and conferences on a national basis.

S/NVQs in cleaning and support services, hospitality, multi-skilled hospitality services and housekeeping are available at levels 1-2, and hospitality supervision at level 3. A Diploma/Welsh Baccalaureate may be available in your area in hospitality. Training programmes, including apprenticeship schemes in hospitality or customer service, may be available in your area for entry to this job. Advanced apprenticeships leading to qualification at level 3 can also be a route into higher education.

Mature applicants are often promoted within the industry and have the option to enter as a receptionist or room attendant/junior housekeeper and gain qualifications and experience to be eligible for management roles. Experience of working in a customer service role is useful.

Government training opportunities, such as apprenticeships, may be available in your area. You can also gain recognition of previous experience through Accreditation of Prior Learning (APL) or by working towards relevant S/NVQs. Contact your local careers office, Jobcentre Plus, Next Step service or Learning and Skills Council (LSC) Local Enterprise Company (LEC) for details of training schemes.

You can also apply to the Savoy Educational Trust for financial support to study for hospitality industry-related courses. The Trust supports individuals who wish to make a career in hospitality.

Opportunities and Pay

This work is available throughout the UK in hotels and luxury health resorts, hospitals, residential or nursing homes, holiday centres, cruise liners and golf clubs, in schools, particularly the independent sector, universities or other student residencies. There is a shortage of experienced managers, particularly in London and the South East. Promotion opportunities are generally better in larger organisations and are improved if you are prepared to move around the country. Managers often move into similar occupations such as hotel or business facilities management. It is possible to find jobs abroad, particularly with an international hotel chain.

Pay varies depending on location, employer and level of responsibility, but you are likely to earn in the region of £15k-£28k a year, depending on your qualifications and/or experience. Some managers with more responsibility may earn up to and over £35k a year.

Skills and Qualities

able to motivate others, able to take responsibility, attention to detail, efficient, good communication skills, good interpersonal skills, good organisational skills, numeracy skills, smart appearance, tactful

Relevant Subjects

Business and accounting, English, Hospitality and catering, Leisure, travel and tourism

Further Information

Accommodation Management (United Kingdom Housekeeper's Association (UKHA)) - www.amuk.info

Apprenticeship Schemes (National Apprenticeship Service) - www.apprenticeships.org.uk

Association for Student Residential Accommodation (ASRA) - www.asra.ac.uk

CareerScope: Hospitality and Leisure (Springboard UK) - http://careerscope.springboarduk.net/

Caterer and Hotelkeeper (weekly) (Reed Business Information) - www.caterersearch.com/Home/

Confederation of Tourism & Hospitality (CTH) - www.cthawards.com

Diploma in Hospitality (People 1st) - www.hospitalitydiploma.co.uk

People 1st - sector skills council for hospitality, leisure, travel and tourism - www.people1st.co.uk

Real Life Guide to Hospitality & Event Management (Trotman 2010) - www.trotman.co.uk

Springboard UK (Springboard UK) - www.springboarduk.net

Springboard Wales (Springboard Wales) - http://wales.springboarduk.net/

UK Housekeepers Association (UKHA) - www.ukha.co.uk

UKSP - Guide to Success in Hospitality, Leisure, Travel & Tourism - www.uksp.co.uk

▶Working in hospitality & catering (2009) (Babcock Lifeskills) - www.babcock-lifeskills.com/

Addresses

British Hospitality Association (BHA)
Queens House, 55-56 Lincoln's Inn Fields, London WC2A 3BH
Phone: +44 (0)207 404 7744
Web: www.bha.org.uk

Institute of Hospitality
Trinity Court, 34 West Street, Sutton, Surrey SM1 1SH
Phone: +44 (0)20 8661 4900
Web: www.instituteofhospitality.org

Savoy Educational Trust
Queen's House 55-56 Lincoln's Inn Fields, London WC2A 3BH
Phone: +44 (0) 207 269 9692
Web: www.savoyeducationaltrust.org.uk

Similar Jobs

Catering Manager, Hostel Manager, Hotel Manager, Hotel Room Attendant, Restaurant Manager

Door Attendant

also known as: Commissionaire

CRCI:Catering and Hospitality
CLCI:IJ
Job Band: 1 to 2

Job Description

Door attendants greet guests/visitors at the door of a large hotel, restaurant or theatre, office block, exclusive shop or large departmental store. They open the door to allow guests to enter or leave the building and may help people from a car/taxi by opening and closing the vehicle's doors. If it is raining, they protect people arriving and leaving from getting wet by holding an umbrella over them. Also calls taxis if required and helps the elderly or less able people. Attendants may get porters to carry luggage/parcels and arrange for a parking attendant to park an owner's car. They may also enforce a dress code for the venue.

Attendants often provide guests with local information and directions. They keep an eye on security and may lock up at the end of the evening. At theatres, they make sure that queues are orderly and keep doorways and the front of the building clear. They may also collect performance tickets.

Work Details
Usually works a 37 hour week which may include shifts, including evenings, weekends and sometimes bank holidays. Door attendants meet many different people including visitors from overseas. Sometimes you have to cope with people who are awkward, so you need to remain calm and patient.

Shelter is usually provided in the lobby area, but you work outdoors and may be exposed to all weather conditions. This job requires you to be on your feet for many hours and you need to wear a smart uniform. Part-time and seasonal work is possible.

Qualification
- **England, Wales and Northern Ireland**

Band 1: For entry to jobs, no minimum qualifications are needed, but you are expected to have a good level of general education and relevant experience. Some formal/vocational qualifications at any level are useful.

Band 2: For entry to jobs, no minimum qualifications are needed, but it is an advantage to have some GCSEs (A*-C) or equivalent in subjects that include English and maths.

- **Scotland**

Band 1: For entry to jobs, no minimum qualifications are needed, but you are expected to have a good level of general education and relevant experience. Some formal/vocational qualifications at any level are useful.

Band 2: Although academic qualifications are not specified for this job, it is an advantage to have some S grades (1-3) in subjects that include English and maths, or similar.

Adult Qualifications
No formal qualifications are needed but employers expect a reasonable level of education, good personal appearance, and the right approach to the job.

Work Experience
Any work experience can help equip you with skills that you can use in the future and add to your CV. Experience of working with people helps to develop your communication and interpersonal skills.

Entry and Training
Training is on the job, initially helping experienced staff and learning company policies, issues of health and safety, and emergency/evacuation procedures. You also learn about customer service and complaints procedures. Employers generally look for people with good personal presentation and the right personality for the job, and you usually have to be age 18 or over. In some jobs it is necessary to gain knowledge of the local area and places of interest. In hotel work you may need to gain experience as a luggage porter before becoming a door attendant/commissionaire.

A Diploma/Welsh Baccalaureate may be available in your area in hospitality. S/NVQs in hospitality, customer care and front office may be available at level 2. Training programmes, including apprenticeships in hospitality or customer service leading to a level 2 qualification, may also be available in your area. You can also work towards Hospitality Awarding Body (HAB) qualifications in hospitality, customer service and conflict handling and prevention.

Mature applicants may be preferred by some employers and it is useful to have some experience of working with the public. Employers look for applicants with a pleasant personality who are able to deal with the general public. Adults may be able to enter this work through a government-funded training programme, such as an apprenticeship. Contact your local Connexions or careers office, Jobcentre Plus, Next Step service or Learning and Skills Council (LSC)/Local Enterprise Company (LEC) for details of all training opportunities and schemes.

Opportunities and Pay
Most jobs are in towns and cities where there are more hotels, offices, theatres, etc. Progression may be limited with some employers but in large organisations it is possible to move into supervisory and managerial roles.

Pay varies depending on location and employer. Door attendants usually earn around £11.5k-£15k a year, and some may earn more. Normal pay is often increased by tips, overtime and shift work. If you work in an hotel, you may be able to live in.

Health
You need to have good general fitness.

Skills and Qualities
able to get on with all kinds of people, alert, approachable, calm, common sense, friendly, helpful, polite, reliable, tolerant

Relevant Subjects
Hospitality and catering

Further Information
Apprenticeship Schemes (National Apprenticeship Service) - www.apprenticeships.org.uk

CareerScope: Hospitality and Leisure (Springboard UK) - http://careerscope.springboarduk.net/

Caterer and Hotelkeeper (weekly) (Reed Business Information) - www.caterersearch.com/Home/

Diploma in Hospitality (People 1st) - www.hospitalitydiploma.co.uk

Real Life Guide to Hospitality & Event Management (Trotman 2010) - www.trotman.co.uk

Springboard UK (Springboard UK) - www.springboarduk.net

Springboard Wales (Springboard Wales) - http://wales.springboarduk.net/

Training Schemes - www.direct.gov.uk/en/educationandlearning

▶Working in hospitality & catering (2009) (Babcock Lifeskills) - www.babcock-lifeskills.com/

Addresses
British Hospitality Association (BHA)
Queens House, 55-56 Lincoln's Inn Fields, London WC2A 3BH
Phone: +44 (0)207 404 7744
Web: www.bha.org.uk

Institute of Hospitality
Trinity Court, 34 West Street, Sutton, Surrey SM1 1SH
Phone: +44 (0)20 8661 4900
Web: www.instituteofhospitality.org

Similar Jobs
Cinema/Theatre Attendant, Cloakroom Attendant, Door Supervisor, Hotel Porter, Parking Attendant, Tourist Information Centre Assistant

Door Supervisor
also known as: Bouncer

CRCI:Security and Armed Forces
CLCI:MAG Job Band: 1

Job Description
Door supervisors control who is allowed into pubs, hotels, clubs and a wide variety of other licensed entertainment venues. Usually work in a pair or in a small team. They are involved in meeting and greeting customers and dealing with potential troublemakers. Perform a public relations role with face-to-face contact with the public. Assess situations as they arise, making quick decisions for action as needed.

Door Supervisor

Door supervisers, or 'bouncers', refuse entry to people who may be a risk to other customers or endanger the premises' licence. Such people may not meet the premises' requirements for entry. They may be under the influence of drink or drugs, have a reputation for violence, or be carrying offensive weapons. This job can involve searching, evicting and sometimes arresting members of the public. Some physical contact with troublemakers may be required.

Work Details

Door security personnel generally work three or four 4-8 hr shifts in a week. These are likely to be at unsociable hours when pubs, clubs, etc, are at their busiest. Some shifts may go on into the early morning. The conditions are likely to be busy, noisy and you are also on your feet for most of the time. You may be at risk of injury from potentially threatening customers but this depends a great deal upon the type of workplace.

Qualification

• England, Wales and Northern Ireland

Band 1: No academic qualifications are required, though employers look for good verbal and written communication skills, as well as a confident manner.

• Scotland

Band 1: No academic qualifications are required, though employers look for good verbal and written communication skills, as well as a confident manner.

Adult Qualifications

No specific educational qualifications are required. You can improve your skills and qualifications by working through the Foundation Learning programme. This involves taking credit-based units and qualifications to help you progress.

Work Experience

Health and safety requirements may prevent you from getting direct work experience with door supervisors until you are 18. Experience of working in other areas of security, perhaps with the police or armed forces, is also relevant.

Entry and Training

All door supervisors must obtain a licence to practise from the Security Industry Authority (SIA). You need to be over 18 and have to go through an identity and criminal records check. Those with a criminal record are not necessarily excluded from obtaining a licence as the SIA looks at the seriousness and history of the offence.

Before applying for a licence you need to take a level 2 certificate in door supervision. Full details are on the SIA website. The qualification is in two parts: part one - the role and responsibilities of a door supervisor, and part two - communication skills and conflict management. The course takes 30 hours in total and is available over four days, at weekends and/or evening sessions. Two exams form part of the training. Some other current qualifications may be used as an exemption from all or part of these qualifications. Contact the SIA for details. Door supervisors are further trained in additional skills such as physical intervention and search procedures.

It is possible to work for a BTEC level 3 in security management (head door supervision). This is a two day training programme, delivered by Rutherford Training, which builds on the training that you have already received and develops managerial and operational skills that are required to effectively manage an operational door security team. All candidates must possess a valid security industry authority door supervisor's licence or have successfully passed a nationally recognised level 2 award in a door supervision training programme. Check the Skills for Security website for full details.

Mature applicants with experience in the armed forces, security or the police, have an advantage. You may be able to enter this work through a government-funded training programme. Contact your local careers office, Jobcentre Plus, Next Step service or Learning and Skills Council (LSC)/Local Enterprise Company (LEC) for details of all training opportunities and schemes, including apprenticeships for adults.

Opportunities and Pay

There are over 120,000 licensed door supervisors employed throughout the UK. Many register with a security agency or are employed in pubs, hotels, clubs and other licensed venues. More experienced door supervisors may be put in charge of small teams or may move into area supervisor jobs. Some progress to more senior jobs in the security sector.

Pay depends upon the employer and location, but most are paid around £6-£15 an hour, though it is often more in inner cities, and can double in major cities, such as London.

Health

You need to have good stamina and be physically fit to do this job.

Skills and Qualities

able to cope under pressure, able to get on with all kinds of people, alert, aptitude for teamwork, assertive, firm manner, good communication skills, polite, quick thinking

Relevant Subjects

Physical education and sport

Further Information

Apprenticeship Schemes (National Apprenticeship Service) - www.apprenticeships.org.uk

Foundation Learning (QCDA) - www.qcda.gov.uk

Professional Security Magazine - www.professionalsecurity.co.uk

Skills for Security - sector skills council for security industry - www.skillsforsecurity.org.uk/

Training Schemes - www.direct.gov.uk/en/educationandlearning

Why Security? - A Guide to Careers in the Security Industry (Security Industry Authority) - www.the-sia.org.uk

▶Working in police, fire & security (2009) (Babcock Lifeskills) - www.babcock-lifeskills.com/

Addresses

Door Supervisor Training Organisation
298 Charminster Road, Bournemouth, Dorset BH8 9RT
Phone: 0800 652 9965
Web: www.dsto.co.uk

National Association of Security Professionals
34 Woodlands Avenue, Rayleigh, Essex SS6 7RD
Web: www.nasp.org.uk

Rutherford Training
Rutherford House, Chapel Lane, Wadebridge, Cornwall PL27 7NJ
Phone: +44 (0)1208 816 709
Web: www.rutherford-group.co.uk/

Security Industry Authority (SIA)
PO Box 1293, Liverpool L69 1AX
Phone: 0844 892 1025 (UK only)
Web: http://sia.homeoffice.gov.uk/Pages/home.aspx

Similar Jobs

Bartender, Close Protection Officer/Bodyguard, Door Attendant, Police Officer, Security Officer

Dramatherapist

CRCI:Healthcare
CLCI:JOD Job Band: 5

Job Description

Dramatherapists use drama and theatre techniques to give people experiences that are helpful socially, physically or emotionally. Work with people who have psychological or mental health issues, special learning needs or disabilities, or have personal or social problems, to improve their skills, imagination, creativity, confidence and self-knowledge. May also work with people who have to face a long-term illness. Use dance, theatre, mime, puppetry, storytelling, role-play and improvisation in a variety of settings such as health, education, probation work, prison service and social work.

Can work with small groups and individual clients. Dramatherapy can be used in management training. Liaise with other professionals, including psychiatrists, psychologists, doctors, nurses and other arts therapists.

Work Details

Usually work a basic 37 hour week that may include some evenings and weekends and may work on a sessional basis. Where you work depends on who your clients are. This may be in a hospital or clinic, a pupil referral unit or day care centre, for behaviour support services in a rehabilitation centre, in a prison, or a residential home. You may need to travel between various locations. You can deal with a wide range of people or may specialise in working with one group, such as those who are mentally ill, people with learning difficulties, ex-offenders or people with drug or alcohol problems. Work is emotionally demanding at times.

Qualification

- **England, Wales and Northern Ireland**

Band 5: For entry to degree course followed by postgraduate qualification in dramatherapy: 2-3 A levels and some GCSEs (A*-C) usually including English and maths, or equivalent. Exact requirements depend on the degree you take.

- **Scotland**

Band 5: For entry to degree course followed by postgraduate qualification in dramatherapy: 3-5 H grades and some S grades (1-3), usually including English and maths, or similar qualifications. Exact requirements depend on the degree you take.

Degree Information

A degree with a drama, theatre or performing arts content, sociology, psychology or anthropology is usually required for entry to an approved postgraduate course. Applicants with a professional qualification and experience in teaching, nursing, social work, youth work or professions supplementary to medicine, may also be acceptable. The postgraduate course is offered at specific universities in England. Check with the British Association of Dramatherapists for information on validated courses and routes to qualification.

Adult Qualifications

A relevant first degree is usually needed for entry to the postgraduate course. Entry standards may be relaxed for adults applying for degree courses; check with the universities for details. Entry to postgraduate courses may be possible for non-graduates with diplomas and relevant work experience.

Work Experience

Work experience gives you an insight into what you enjoy about a job or working environment, and the opportunity to acquire new skills. It provides valuable information to add to your CV and improves your employment prospects. It also demonstrates commitment when applying for entry to the postgraduate course. Consider teaching or working with people in a helping capacity, particularly those with mental health problems or learning disabilities. Working as a nursing assistant, support worker or in theatre or drama work is helpful. It is useful to approach a qualified dramatherapist to discuss their work.

Entry and Training

You usually need to be at least 23 for entry to training courses. Postgraduate training in a qualification approved by the British Association of Dramatherapists (BADth) leads to professional registration, and is required to enter this job. The postgraduate course runs at BADth approved universities and takes two years part time. Part-time students must be employed in a post where dramatherapy can be used. On completion of the course, you also need to register with the Health Professions Council. There are short introductory courses that you are advised to take if you are applying for a place on a postgraduate course. It is necessary to complete a minimum of 40 supervised sessions to apply for full membership of BADth.

You also need a Criminal Records Bureau or Disclosure Scotland check to work as a dramatherapist. Students do not automatically receive grants for training courses but are often funded by their employers, especially those employed within the NHS and local authority social services. Some teachers are funded by their Local Education Authority. Funding for course fees may be available from the Arts and Humanities Research Council. Once you are state-registered, continuing professional development is expected and consists of short courses, conferences, workshops and summer schools. Contact BADth for details.

A Diploma/Welsh Baccalaureate may be available in your area in society, health and development. The advanced level is equivalent to 3.5 A levels but for some university courses, the additional and specialist learning (ASL) component of the diploma needs to include specific A levels. Check entry requirements carefully with the individual institutions.

Mature entrants usually have experience of working in a related career such as teaching, psychology, acting, social work, counselling or in a professional healthcare setting, and this is often a second career. Relevant postgraduate study that is BADth validated to become registered with the Health Professions Council is necessary. You may be able to get some financial support from relevant medical trusts and charitable organisations. Check with BADth for information on validated courses and routes to training.

Opportunities and Pay

This is a small, but expanding profession of around 1,500 people. Most dramatherapists are employed by the NHS or a local authority social service department. Jobs also exist in educational establishments, voluntary organisations, prisons and the probation service. Once experienced you can become self-employed and work in private practice. Some go on to teach dramatherapy, lead a team, work in research or further train to be a psychotherapist. There may be opportunities to work part time or on a sessional basis. Some contracts can be temporary.

Pay depends largely on type of employer, but may be on a nationally agreed scale. Alternatively, you may be paid on a fees basis, not a salary. A newly qualified dramatherapist working for the NHS earns around £25k a year, rising to around £34k with experience. Senior dramatherapists may earn up to £46k and a principal therapist or consultant can earn £60k or more a year.

Skills and Qualities

able to explain clearly, able to inspire confidence, emotionally strong, enthusiastic, imaginative, outgoing personality, patient, perceptive, reassuring, tactful

Relevant Subjects

Art and Design, English, Health and social care, Music, Performing arts, Psychology, Sociology

Further Information

About Dramatherapy - Career Training (BADth) (BADth) - www.badth.org.uk/training
Diplomas (Foundation, Higher and Advanced) - http://yp.direct.gov.uk/diplomas
Dramatherapy Scotland - www.dramatherapyscotland.org.uk/
Health Professions Council (HPC) - www.hpc-uk.org
NHS Careers (NHS Careers) - www.nhscareers.nhs.uk
NHS Careers Scotland - www.infoscotland.com/nhs
NHS Careers Wales - www.wales.nhs.uk
Skills for Health - sector skills council - www.skillsforhealth.org.uk
Welsh Baccalaureate - www.wbq.org.uk

Addresses

British Association of Dramatherapists (BADth)
Waverley , Battledown Approach, Cheltenham GL52 6RE
Phone: +44 (0)1242 235 515
Web: www.badth.org.uk

Similar Jobs

Art Therapist, Music Therapist, Occupational Therapist, Speech & Language Therapist, Teacher: Drama, Teacher: Special Educational Needs

Dressmaker

CRCI:Manufacturing and Production
CLCI:SAH Job Band: 2 to 3

Job Description

Dressmakers produce items of clothing for a customer using an individual design or pattern. May specialise in making wedding and bridesmaid dresses, haute couture (high fashion) or children's clothing. They meet with clients to discuss what they like; usually referring to magazines and brochures for ideas of styles and fabrics. The dressmaker then takes the customer's measurements, and looks at their posture and general body shape.

Creates an estimate of the amount of fabrics, outer and lining, and any trimmings that may be required to provide a detailed cost. For some bespoke (made-to-measure) products, produces a rough sample using cheaper fabric that can be checked on the client before cutting the more expensive fabric. Either uses an existing design, creates their own pattern or may approach a designer for a completely new design.

Lays out the pattern and cuts the fabric. Pins and tacks the garment together and fits it on the customer or a model. Sews the garment by machine; finishes and presses it by hand. Some garments may require detailed stitching, including beadwork, sequins or lace. Some dressmakers may also repair or alter clothes.

Work Details

Employed dressmakers usually work a basic 37-40 hrs a week, usually including a Saturday. Self-employed dressmakers can choose their own hours, but they depend on the amount of work and if they have deadlines to meet. You work in a shop, away from the main customer area, in a workshop, or possibly at home, meeting customers and giving them advice, which requires you to have an awareness of current fashion trends. You have to have creativity and imagination and be able to cope with sitting for many hours. Work can be pressurised at times.

Qualification

• England, Wales and Northern Ireland

Band 2: No minimum entry qualifications but many employers prefer some GCSEs, for example, English, maths, art and design or similar.

Band 3: For course entry: usually at least 4 GCSEs (A*-C) including English, maths, art and design or equivalent.

• Scotland

Band 2: Although academic qualifications are not specified for this job, it is an advantage to have some S grades in subjects that include English, maths, art and design or similar.

Band 3: For entry: usually at least four S grades (1-3) preferably including English, maths and art or design, or similar.

Adult Qualifications

A good standard of secondary education is expected. Some colleges consider adults without formal qualifications but with relevant experience.

Work Experience

Relevant work or voluntary experience is always useful and can improve your chances when applying for entry to jobs or apprenticeships in the manufacturing sector. Your personal or adult guidance adviser is able to advise you how to organise work experience with an employer.

Entry and Training

Initially, you begin by learning basic tasks and skills under the guidance of an experienced worker. Training can be on the job, combined with day/block release or evening study leading to vocational qualifications. City & Guilds and ABC offer several qualifications for dressmakers, from introductory to higher level in creative studies. For those with appropriate higher qualifications, there are also a variety of full-time courses that can be studied before starting work, such as higher national diplomas that can also lead to a degree.

The London College of Fashion offers a range of courses, including specialist work such as bridal wear, that require no academic entry requirements. S/NVQs in manufacturing sewn products are available at levels 1-2 and in apparel manufacturing technology at level 3. Relevant training programmes, including apprenticeship schemes, may be available in your area. Advanced apprenticeships leading to qualification at level 3 can be a route into higher education.

Government training opportunities, such as apprenticeships, may be available in your area. You can also gain recognition of previous experience through Accreditation of Prior Learning (APL) or by working towards relevant S/NVQs. Contact your local careers office, Jobcentre Plus, Next Step service or Learning and Skills Council (LSC) Local Enterprise Company (LEC) for details of training schemes.

Opportunities and Pay

Work is available throughout the UK but can be limited. You can be employed by a couture (specialist fashion), or wholesale fashion house, a clothing manufacturer, or making and altering costumes for theatre, film and TV. Large retail stores also employ dressmakers to carry out any alterations to clothing purchases. Many work for a small company such as a dress shop. Promotion in larger companies or manufacturers can be to supervisory level. Some experienced and suitably qualified dressmakers are employed in further and adult education. With experience you can become self-employed.

Pay varies depending on location and employer. Trainees usually earn around £10k-£13k a year, rising to £17k, and with experience to around £20k. In haute couture highly experienced and successful dressmakers can earn much more.

Health

This job requires normal colour vision and good eyesight.

Skills and Qualities
attention to detail, creative flair, excellent sewing skills, eye for shape/colour, eye for visual effect, good communication skills, imaginative, manual dexterity, numeracy skills, patient

Relevant Subjects
Art and Design

Further Information
ABC Awards - www.abcawards.co.uk

Apprenticeship Schemes (National Apprenticeship Service) - www.apprenticeships.org.uk

Can you Cut it? - www.canucutit.co.uk

Skillset - sector skills council for the creative media, fashion and textiles industries - www.skillset.org

Training Schemes - www.direct.gov.uk/en/educationandlearning

▶Working in fashion & clothing (2008) (Babcock Lifeskills) - www.babcock-lifeskills.com/

Addresses
London College of Fashion
20 John Princes Street, London W1G 0BJ
Phone: +44 (0)20 7514 7344
Web: www.fashion.arts.ac.uk

Similar Jobs
Clothing Alteration Hand, Fashion Designer, Film/TV & Theatre Wardrobe Assistant, Sewing Machinist, Tailor, Upholsterer

Driver: Bus

CRCI:Transport and Logistics
CLCI:YAD Job Band: 1

Job Description
Bus drivers drive a bus taking passengers on local routes in and around towns and cities. They check the lights, brakes and tyres of the bus before setting off. Some may operate a rural service to villages and main towns. Bus drivers travel along a certain route, stopping for people to get on and off, and keeping to the service timetable. Most buses have a driver/conductor, so deal with the passengers and also take fares. Need to write reports on any accidents or incidents.

Drivers keep in contact with the operator's communication centre which enables information about traffic problems, breakdowns, weather conditions and any information involving the safety and security of both driver and passengers, to be passed on.

Work Details
Usually work a 39-40 hr week on an eight-hour shift basis, including early mornings, evenings, weekends and public holidays. This work involves sitting for long periods of time in a small cab, which is quite cramped. Bus driving can sometimes be a stressful job and you have to be able to maintain concentration and not be distracted. There is a risk of being threatened or attacked. A uniform is provided.

Qualification

• England, Wales and Northern Ireland
Band 1: No minimum qualifications are required, but you are expected to have a good level of general education. However, some formal/vocational qualifications at any level are useful, especially in English and maths, or equivalent. Drivers are expected to be competent in basic numeracy, writing and verbal skills.

• Scotland
Band 1: No minimum qualifications are required, but you are expected to have a good level of general education. However, some formal/vocational qualifications at any level are useful, especially in English and maths, or equivalent. Drivers are expected to be competent in basic numeracy, writing and verbal skills.

Adult Qualifications
Drivers are expected to be competent in simple arithmetic, writing and verbal skills. Formal qualifications are not specified, though some at any level are useful, especially in English and maths. Those without existing qualifications can work through the Foundation Learning programme by taking credit-based units and qualifications.

Work Experience
Relevant work or voluntary experience can equip you with skills that you can use in the future and add to your CV. Driving experience is essential, particularly if this is with a range of different vehicles.

Entry and Training
You must have a PCV (Passenger Carrying Vehicle) licence and you need to be 21 to obtain an unrestricted licence. It is possible to get a PCV licence at 18 but this only allows you to drive smaller vehicles such as minibuses. Because of insurance costs employers may prefer drivers to be over 21, or even over 25. You may have to take a basic arithmetic test and you need a full EU driving licence with a few years' driving experience.

It is an EU requirement that drivers hold a driver's certificate of professional competence (CPC) as well as a PCV. The driver's CPC must be approved by the Driving Standards Agency (DSA) and consists of a theory test of 4 hours with case studies, and a practical two-hour test. You can take it alongside your PCV. It lasts for 5 years, during which time you must complete 35 hours of 'periodic training'. This five-year cycle continues throughout your career and aims to improve standards in road safety. See the DSA Driver website for full details.

Experience of working with the public is an advantage. Employers now have their own flexible training schemes or send trainees to a training centre to take the PCV course. You can take the course and sit the test even if you do not have a job, as some companies prefer people who already have the licence. Some time is spent in a classroom, but there is also driving practice off and on the road, with a trainer.

Appropriate vocational related qualifications in transporting passengers by bus and coach are available, including an S/NVQ level 2 in road passenger transport and a level 3 in driving instruction. Training programmes, including a passenger carrying apprenticeship, may be available in your area. Advanced apprenticeships leading to qualification at level 3 can also be a route into higher education.

Adults with previous experience of driving vehicles, such as vans or minibuses with a PCV licence have an advantage. There are training courses for the PCV licence.

Government training opportunities, such as apprenticeships, may be available in your area. You can also gain recognition of previous experience through Accreditation of Prior Learning or by working towards relevant S/NVQs. Contact your local careers office, Jobcentre Plus, Next Step service or Learning and Skills Council (LSC)/Local Enterprise Company (LEC) for details of training schemes.

Opportunities and Pay
There has been a shortage of bus drivers in recent years but the economic downturn may have had an impact on the number of available vacancies. With experience you can apply for promotion to supervisor, service controller or driving instructor. Some move into administrative posts and progress to operations manager or garage manager. Bus and coach companies now offer flexible progression routes. Some bus drivers transfer to driving for tour operators or for day-trip operators.

You can also sit an exam for the certificate of professional competence (CPC), which means that you can set up your own business.

Pay varies depending on the location and type of company you work for. Salaries range from around £11k while training for the PCV licence to £16k-£23k as an experienced driver. Overtime and shift pay is often available. You may be able to travel free on buses operated by the company.

Health

You have to pass a medical test and must have a good standard of physical fitness and good eyesight. There can be restrictions on the wearing of contact lenses.

Skills and Qualities

calm, common sense, good communication skills, good concentration level, health & safety awareness, polite, punctual, quick reactions, responsible attitude, stamina

Further Information

AGCAS: Transport and Logistics (Job Sector Briefing) (AGCAS) - www.prospects.ac.uk

Apprenticeship Schemes (National Apprenticeship Service) - www.apprenticeships.org.uk

Coach & Bus Week Magazine - www.cbwonline.com/menus/main.asp

Driving Standards Agency - www.dsa.gov.uk

Foundation Learning (QCDA) - www.qcda.gov.uk

GoSkills - sector skills council for passenger transport - www.goskills.org

Training Schemes - www.direct.gov.uk/en/educationandlearning

Transport and Logistics (Business Link) - www.businesslink.gov.uk/bdotg/action/layer?topicId=1082103262

Addresses

Driver and Vehicle Licensing (DVLNI - Northern Ireland)
County Hall, Castlerock Road, Coleraine BT51 3TB
Phone: 0845 402 4000 (UK only)
Web: www.dvlni.gov.uk

Similar Jobs

Chauffeur/Chauffeuse, Driver: Coach, Driver: Lorry, Driver: Taxi/Minicab, Driver: Tram, Driving Instructor

Driver: Coach

CRCI:Transport and Logistics
CLCI:YAD Job Band: 1

Job Description

Coach drivers drive a coach that takes passengers on outings, tours or long-distance routes. They check tickets and bookings, pack away the luggage, give advice on routes and connections and deal with passengers' questions and problems. On tours and excursions, coach drivers may give information on places of interest. Can work on an express service or do private hire work. On some long distances they work in pairs to keep to the strict laws that govern driving time. Many companies operate excursions or holiday tours, including continental travel.

Work Details

You can drive over a small local area, but may also cover longer distances throughout the UK and also in Europe. You need to spend nights away from home and sometimes stay away for longer periods working unsociable hours, including weekends and public holidays. This work can be stressful at times. You have to concentrate well. Because of the amount of driving, there is a risk of being involved in traffic accidents.

Qualification

- **England, Wales and Northern Ireland**

Band 1: No minimum qualifications are required, but you are expected to have a good level of general education. However, some formal/vocational qualifications at any level are useful. Drivers are expected to be competent in basic numeracy, writing and verbal skills.

- **Scotland**

Band 1: No minimum qualifications are required, but you are expected to have a good level of general education. However, some formal/vocational qualifications at any level are useful. Drivers are expected to be competent in basic numeracy, writing and verbal skills.

Adult Qualifications

Drivers are expected to be competent in simple arithmetic, writing and verbal skills. Formal qualifications are not specified, though some at any level are useful, especially in English and maths. Those without existing qualifications can work through the Foundation Learning programme by taking credit-based units and qualifications.

Work Experience

Relevant work or voluntary experience can equip you with skills that you can use in the future and add to your CV. Driving experience is essential, particularly if this is with a range of different vehicles.

Entry and Training

You must have a PCV (Passenger Carrying Vehicle) licence and you need to be 21 to obtain an unrestricted licence. It is possible to get a PCV licence at 18 but this only allows you to drive smaller vehicles such as minibuses. Because of insurance costs employers may prefer drivers to be over 21 or even over 25. You may have to take a basic arithmetic test and you need a full EU driving licence with a few years' driving experience.

It is an EU requirement that drivers hold a driver's certificate of professional competence (CPC) as well as a PCV. The driver's CPC must be approved by the Road Safety Authority and consists of a theory part of 4 hours with case studies, and a practical two-hour test. You can take it alongside your PCV. It lasts for 5 years, during which time you must complete 35 hours of 'periodic training'. This five-year cycle continues throughout your career and aims to improve standards in road safety. See the Driving Standards Agency Driver website for full details.

Experience of working with the public is an advantage. Employers now have their own flexible training schemes or send trainees to a training centre to take a PCV course. You can take the course and sit the test even if you do not have a job as some companies prefer people who already have the licence. Some time is spent in a classroom, but there is also driving practice off and on the road, with a trainer.

Appropriate vocational related qualifications in transporting passengers by bus and coach are available, including an S/NVQ level 2 in road passenger transport and level 3 in driving instruction. Training programmes, including apprenticeships, may be available in your area. Advanced apprenticeships leading to qualification at level 3 can also be a route into higher education.

Adults with previous experience of driving vehicles, such as vans or minibuses have an advantage. In some areas there are training courses for the PCV licence.

Government training opportunities, such as apprenticeships, may be available in your area. You can also gain recognition of previous experience through Accreditation of Prior Learning or by working towards relevant S/NVQs. Contact your local careers office, Jobcentre Plus, Next Step service or Learning and Skills Council (LSC)/Local Enterprise Company (LEC) for details of training schemes.

Opportunities and Pay

There has been a shortage of coach and bus drivers in recent years but the economic downturn may have had an impact on the number of available vacancies. You can work for a coach company, a charter firm, a holiday tour operator, or be self-employed. There is more work in the summer. You may be given an accommodation allowance and free meals when working away from home.

Once you have experience you can take the certificate of professional competence (CPC), which means that you can set up your own business. Some may move into administrative posts and progress to operations manager, garage manager or similar. Bus and coach companies now offer flexible progression routes. With experience you can apply for promotion to supervisor, service controller or driving instructor.

Pay varies depending on the location and type of company you work for, but is likely to be around £14k-£22k a year, rising to about £26k with experience. You may be able to travel free on vehicles operated by the company. Overtime pay and tips are possible.

Health

You may have to pass a medical test and you must be in good health and have good eyesight. There may be restrictions on the wearing of contact lenses.

Skills and Qualities

able to get on with all kinds of people, calm, good concentration level, health & safety awareness, polite, punctual, quick reactions, stamina, tactful

Relevant Subjects

Leisure, travel and tourism

Further Information

AGCAS: Transport and Logistics (Job Sector Briefing) (AGCAS) - www.prospects.ac.uk

Apprenticeship Schemes (National Apprenticeship Service) - www.apprenticeships.org.uk

Coach & Bus Week Magazine - www.cbwonline.com/menus/main.asp

Driving Standards Agency - www.dsa.gov.uk

Foundation Learning (QCDA) - www.qcda.gov.uk

GoSkills - sector skills council for passenger transport - www.goskills.org

Training Schemes - www.direct.gov.uk/en/educationandlearning

Transport and Logistics (Business Link) - www.businesslink.gov.uk/bdotg/action/layer?topicId=1082103262

▶ Working in travel & tourism (2010) (Babcock Lifeskills) - www.babcock-lifeskills.com/

Addresses

Driver and Vehicle Licensing (DVLNI - Northern Ireland)
County Hall, Castlerock Road, Coleraine BT51 3TB
Phone: 0845 402 4000 (UK only)
Web: www.dvlni.gov.uk

Similar Jobs

Chauffeur/Chauffeuse, Driver: Bus, Driver: Lorry, Driver: Taxi/Minicab, Driver: Tram, Driving Instructor

Driver: Lorry

also known as: HGV Driver, Large Goods Vehicle (LGV) Driver, Truck Driver

CRCI:Transport and Logistics
CLCI:YAD — Job Band: 1 to 2

Job Description

Lorry drivers are responsible for the collection and delivery of goods throughout the UK and Europe, using a large goods vehicle (LGV) and sometimes articulated trucks. They ensure the load is safely secured and that the lorry is fit for the journey. Sometimes have to load and unload goods, and provide invoices or delivery notes to customers. Lorry drivers have to plan the quickest and most economical route, and keep records of mileage and deliveries. They are required to keep the rules and regulations regarding driving hours, speed limits, and load limits and restrictions.

Some LGV drivers work on car transporters, animal trailers or tankers loaded with dangerous or hazardous chemicals. May do minor repairs or clean the lorry.

Work Details

Usually work a basic 40 hr week though often work early mornings, at night and weekends. There are strict rules regarding the number of hours drivers can work in a 24 hr period. Depending on your employer you drive throughout the UK and possibly to Europe. You usually work on your own, or sometimes with a mate, and meet different people when delivering goods. Accurate records are required of your journeys and deliveries.

Driving for long periods can be stressful. The cab of a lorry is noisy and many hours are spent sitting in a cab. You may need to spend nights away from home and many lorries have sleeping facilities for overnight stops. There is a risk of road traffic accidents.

Qualification

• England, Wales and Northern Ireland

Band 1: No minimum qualifications are required, but you are expected to have a good level of general education. However, some formal/vocational qualifications at any level are useful and employers expect drivers to have basic maths and English ability. You may be asked to take a basic aptitude test.

Band 2: Although academic qualifications are not specified for this job, it is an advantage to have some GCSEs (A*-C) in subjects that include English and maths, or equivalent.

• Scotland

Band 1: No minimum qualifications are required, but you are expected to have a good level of general education. However, some formal/vocational qualifications at any level are useful and employers expect drivers to have basic maths and English ability. You may be asked to take a basic aptitude test.

Band 2: Although academic qualifications are not specified for this job, it is an advantage to have some S grades (1-3) in subjects that include English and maths, or similar.

Adult Qualifications

No pre-entry qualifications are usually required though some academic/vocational qualifications at any level may be an advantage. English and maths are useful subjects.

Work Experience

Relevant work or voluntary experience can equip you with skills that you can use in the future and add to your CV. Driving experience is essential, particularly if this is with a range of different vehicles.

Entry and Training

Employees are usually at least 21 and those over 25 are preferred by some employers because insurance costs are cheaper. Apprenticeship training is available for applicants aged 16-24, but most entrants to this scheme are over 19. You need an LGV licence to be a lorry driver. A category C licence is required to drive a vehicle up to 7.5 tonnes and a further category E licence is needed to drive heavier vehicles. Some employers prefer to take people who already have a licence, and you can take the course privately at an approved training centre.

The driver certificate of professional competence (CPC) has also been introduced for LGV drivers who drive professionally throughout the UK. The EU requires that new LGV drivers hold the CPC as well as an LGV licence. The driver's CPC must be approved by the Driving Standards Agency (DSA) and consists of a theory test of 4 hours with case studies, and a practical two-hour test. You can take it alongside your PCV. It lasts for 5 years, during which time you must complete 35 hours of 'periodic training'. This five-year cycle continues throughout your career and aims to improve standards in road safety. See the DSA Driver website for full details.

Drivers of dangerous goods (ADR drivers) should take a training course which leads to the ADR certificate. This is valid for driving in the UK and overseas. Training courses are available at approved training centres and modular, depending of the type of goods to be carried. There are specific courses for carrying petrol, explosives and propane gas cylinders, for example. Drivers of petrol tankers at airports may have responsibility for refuelling aircraft.

Most employers expect trainees to achieve relevant S/NVQs at levels 1-2. There is a driving goods vehicle course at levels 2 and 3. Training programmes, including apprenticeship schemes in driving goods vehicles, may be available in your area. Advanced apprenticeships in driving goods vehicles leading to qualification at level 3 can also be a route into higher education.

Government training opportunities, such as apprenticeships, may be available in your area. You can also gain recognition of previous experience through Accreditation of Prior Learning or by working towards relevant S/NVQs. Contact your local careers office, Jobcentre Plus, Next Step service or Learning and Skills Council (LSC)/Local Enterprise Company (LEC) for details of training schemes.

Most LGV drivers are over 25 due to reduced insurance costs, and some insurance companies insist that drivers are aged over 30. Previous experience of work in the road transport industry including warehouse delivery and distribution is very useful.

Opportunities and Pay

You can work for a haulage contractor, a distribution company, major retailer or a manufacturing company, or be self-employed. Work is available throughout the country and whilst there are shortages of LGV drivers in many areas, competition for work is still keen and the number of vacancies has been affected by the economic downturn. Some drivers move into office jobs as supervisors or in logistics planning, and many transport managers start as drivers. There are opportunities for self-employment.

Pay varies depending on employer and size of vehicle. Starting salaries for newly qualified drivers are likely to be around £15k a year, rising to £30k with experience. Drivers of fuel and chemical tankers with specialist training can earn £35k a year. You are usually paid extra allowances when you work away from home and for overtime.

Health

You must be physically fit and in good health and have good eyesight.

Skills and Qualities

able to work well on your own, basic understanding of vehicle maintenance, common sense, good concentration level, health & safety awareness, patient, quick reactions, reliable

Further Information

AGCAS: Transport and Logistics (Job Sector Briefing) (AGCAS) - www.prospects.ac.uk

Apprenticeship Schemes (National Apprenticeship Service) - www.apprenticeships.org.uk

Driving Standards Agency - www.dsa.gov.uk

Skills for Logistics - sector skills council for freight logistics industries - www.skillsforlogistics.org

The Professional LGV Driver's Handbook (2008) (Kogan Page)

Training Schemes - www.direct.gov.uk/en/educationandlearning

Transport and Logistics (Business Link) - www.businesslink.gov.uk/

Addresses

Freight Transport Association (FTA)
Hermes House, St John's Road, Tunbridge Wells, Kent TN4 9UZ
Phone: 0871 711 2222 (UK only)
Web: www.fta.co.uk/

Road Haulage Association
Roadway House, 35 Monument Hill, Weybridge, Surrey KT13 8RN
Phone: +44 (0)1932 841 515
Web: www.rha.uk.net/home

Similar Jobs

Driver: Bus, Driver: Coach, Driver: Taxi/Minicab, Driver: Van, Driving Instructor, Lift Truck Operative

Driver: Taxi/Minicab

also known as: Cabbie, Taxi Driver
CRCI:Transport and Logistics
CLCI:YAD Job Band: 1

Job Description

Taxi/minicab drivers take clients to their destination by the most direct route for a fee. Taxi drivers pick up passengers by waiting in a taxi rank, getting radio calls, or by looking for people signalling in the street. At the end of the journey, take fares, which are shown on a meter in the taxi, and give change. Minicabs are private hire vehicles that carry out similar duties but are not licensed to pick up passengers from a street or taxi rank.

Usually obtain business through a taxi-hire agency that passes on customer enquiries by two-way radio or computer, and charges the driver for the service. Drivers may help with luggage and must know the local area well. Clean the cab and carry out minor repairs.

Work Details

You often have to work long hours, although you may be able to choose your own hours. You may have to work early mornings, evenings and weekends and sometimes have to cope with passengers who are aggressive or awkward. Driving is a stressful job and you have to be able to concentrate well and stay calm, even when under pressure. There are times when you have to sit in your cab/car waiting for passengers. There is a risk of traffic accidents.

Qualification

• England, Wales and Northern Ireland

Band 1: No minimum qualifications are required, but you are expected to have a good level of general education. However, some formal/vocational qualifications at any level are useful.

• Scotland

Band 1: For entry to jobs, no minimum qualifications are needed, but you are expected to have a good level of general education and relevant experience. Some formal/vocational qualifications at any level are useful.

Adult Qualifications

Drivers are expected to be competent in simple arithmetic, writing and verbal skills. Formal qualifications are not specified, though some at any level are useful, especially in English and maths, or equivalent. Those without existing qualifications can work through the Foundation Learning programme by taking credit-based units and qualifications.

Work Experience

Relevant work or voluntary experience can equip you with skills that you can use in the future and add to your CV. Driving experience is essential, particularly if this is with a range of different vehicles.

Entry and Training
The minimum age is 21 (18 in Northern Ireland), although most entrants are over 25 because of the high cost of insurance for the under 25s. You need to have had a clean driving licence for at least 12 months (3 years in London), as well as a special licence from the local authority, or the DVLNI in Northern Ireland and the Public Carriage Office, (part of Transport for London) in London. Experience in car maintenance and some knowledge of foreign languages is useful in certain locations. You may also need a CRB/ Disclosure Scotland check and a medical assessment.

You may need to take a test of knowledge of your local area, and London black cab drivers must take 'the Knowledge' test. There are private schools that run training for 'the Knowledge' test and it can take nearly three years to learn all the set routes. Those who wish to work at a London airport must also take the 'All London' test. The Transport for London website gives full details of all training routes for taxi drivers in the Greater London area.

Vocational Related Qualifications (VRQ) are available in transporting passengers by taxi and private hire. An S/NVQ in road passenger transport, specialising in taxi or private hire is available at level 2.

Several years' driving experience is required and most entrants are over 25. Must be able to read maps and to learn recommended routes. Government training opportunities, such as apprenticeships, may be available in your area. You can also gain recognition of previous experience through Accreditation of Prior Learning or by working towards relevant S/NVQs. Contact your local careers office, Jobcentre Plus, Next Step service or Learning and Skills Council (LSC)/Local Enterprise Company (LEC) for details of training schemes.

Opportunities and Pay
You can find work in most towns and cities though there is usually a waiting list before you can buy your own taxi licence. Most taxi/ minicab drivers are self-employed and own their own vehicle. Some work for a fleet operator and may rent a vehicle from them. Some drivers work towards owning a fleet of vehicles. Business start-up information is available from the National Private Hire Association.

You are likely to earn £13k-£20k a year in a major city, but can earn up to £30k if you work long hours. Your earnings depend on the number of fares you take, on tips from passengers, and on whether you own or rent your car/cab. You have to pay your own driver licensing, fuel, car insurance and maintenance costs.

Health
You have to pass a medical test before being granted a licence. You need a good standard of physical fitness and good eyesight.

Skills and Qualities
able to work well on your own, calm, cash handling skills, good concentration level, good driving skills, good memory, honest, polite, punctual

Further Information
AGCAS: Transport and Logistics (Job Sector Briefing) (AGCAS) - www.prospects.ac.uk

Driving Standards Agency - www.dsa.gov.uk

Foundation Learning (QCDA) - www.qcda.gov.uk

GoSkills - sector skills council for passenger transport - www.goskills.org

How to become a licensed taxi cab driver (London) - www.taxiknowledge.co.uk

National Taxi Association: Taxi Trade Reports/Documents in PDF - www.national-taxi-association.co.uk

Private Hire and Taxi Monthly (PHTM) - www.phtm.co.uk

Training Schemes - www.direct.gov.uk/en/educationandlearning

Addresses
Driver and Vehicle Licensing (DVLNI - Northern Ireland)
County Hall, Castlerock Road, Coleraine BT51 3TB
Phone: 0845 402 4000 (UK only)
Web: www.dvlni.gov.uk

Licensed Private Hire Car Association (LPHCA)
56 Austins Mead Bovingdon, Hemel Hempstead, Hertfordshire HP3 0LH
Phone: +44 (0)7956 329288
Web: www.lphca.co.uk

Licensed Taxi Drivers Association (LTDA)
Taxi House, Woodfield Road, London W9 2BA
Phone: +44 (0)20 7286 1046
Web: www.ltda.co.uk

Transport for London
Palestra 4th Floor (Green Zone) 197 Blackfriars Road, London SE1 8N
Phone: 0845 602 7000 (UK only)
Web: www.tfl.gov.uk/

Similar Jobs
Chauffeur/Chauffeuse, Courier, Driver: Bus, Driver: Coach

Driver: Tram
also known as: Driver: Light Rail, Tram Driver

CRCI:Transport and Logistics

CLCI:YAD — Job Band: 1

Job Description
Tram drivers drive a tram or light rail train along fixed metal tracks, usually in towns and cities, as a passenger transport service. At the start of a shift, tram drivers check that the tram is in good order, going through a safety checklist. They control the tram by a lever and make sure that it is driven within speed limits. Usually work to a set timetable. Pick up and set down passengers at tram stops. May have to collect fares or check passes.

Tram drivers keep in contact with the communication centre which enables information to be passed on, such as breakdowns, weather and any information involving the safety and security of driver and passengers. May have to make announcements to passengers, letting them know which stop they have reached. They cope with any emergencies, such as breakdowns, accidents and problems with the track. Also write reports of anything that has occurred during the shift.

Work Details
Work around a 40 hr week, usually on a shift system, as trams run early in the morning until late at night, and also operate on weekends and public holidays. Part-time work may be available. This work involves sitting for long periods of time in a small cab, which can be quite cramped, but is heated and air conditioned. A uniform is usually provided by your employer. You deal with passengers, some of whom may be difficult or rowdy.

Qualification

• England, Wales and Northern Ireland
Band 1: For entry to jobs, no minimum qualifications are needed, but you are expected to have a good level of general education and relevant experience. Some formal/vocational qualifications at any level are useful. Drivers are expected to be competent in basic numeracy, writing and verbal skills.

• Scotland
Band 1: Although no formal qualifications are specified, some S grades at any level are useful, especially in English and maths, or similar. Drivers are expected to be competent in basic numeracy, writing and verbal skills.

Adult Qualifications
Mature entrants are expected to be competent in simple arithmetic, writing and verbal skills. Formal qualifications are not specified, though some at any level are useful, especially in English and maths. Those without existing qualifications can work through the Foundation Learning programme by taking credit-based units and qualifications.

Work Experience
Relevant work experience can give you the skills that you can use in the future and add to your CV. Driving experience is vital, particularly if this is with a range of vehicles.

Entry and Training
Some tram drivers start as trainee drivers, while others start as conductors first and then move to driving later. There are no set entry requirements, but many employers may look for GCSEs/S grades in English and maths. You also need to have a full UK driving licence and a few years' driving experience. Entrants are at least over 18 years old and have to pass a medical examination.

Training is usually on the job and includes operating procedures, basic tram/light rail mechanics, first aid, customer service and cash handling. Some drivers may work towards S/NVQs at level 2 in road passenger transport or rail transport operations, or work to gain a PCV (passenger carrying vehicle) licence. Training programmes, including apprenticeship schemes, may be available in your area.

GoSkills, the sector skills council for passenger transport, has developed occupational standards for tram drivers and is working with awarding bodies to set up an S/NVQ specifically for trams and light rail.

Adults with previous experience of driving vehicles, such as vans, minibuses or buses have an advantage. Government training opportunities, such as apprenticeships, may be available in your area. You can also gain recognition of previous experience through Accreditation of Prior Learning or by working towards relevant S/NVQs. Contact your local careers office, Jobcentre Plus, Next Step service or Learning and Skills Council (LSC)/Local Enterprise Company (LEC) for details of training schemes.

Opportunities and Pay
There are around 1,400 people working in the tram/light rail industry at the moment. Systems run in Birmingham, London Docklands, Tyne & Wear, Croydon, Manchester, Nottingham and in Blackpool, which has a vintage tram service. The use of trams and light rail is growing as they are much more environmentally friendly than bus services. More cities are likely to start tram systems and those that already have them are extending them over a wider area.

Once experienced, you can move on to duty manager, controller or become a driver trainer. Some drivers move into bus or coach driving, if they have their PCV licence.

Pay starts at around £15k a year, rising with experience to £35k. Overtime and shift pay are likely to increase this.

Health
You have to pass a medical test and must have a good standard of physical fitness and good eyesight.

Skills and Qualities
alert, calm, clear speaking voice, good concentration level, numeracy skills, patient, polite, punctual, quick reactions, responsible attitude

Further Information
AGCAS: Transport and Logistics (Job Sector Briefing) (AGCAS) - www.prospects.ac.uk

Apprenticeship Schemes (National Apprenticeship Service) - www.apprenticeships.org.uk

Foundation Learning (QCDA) - www.qcda.gov.uk

GoSkills - sector skills council for passenger transport - www.goskills.org

The Trams - http://thetrams.co.uk

Tramways and Urban Transit (LRTA) - www.tramnews.net/

Addresses
Confederation of Passenger Transport UK
Drury House, 34-43 Russell Street, London WC2B 5HA
Phone: +44 (0)20 7240 3131
Web: www.cpt-uk.org

Light Rail Transit Association (LRTA)
c/o 138 Radnor Avenue, Welling DA16 2BY
Phone: + 44 (0) 1179 517785
Web: www.lrta.org

Similar Jobs
Driver: Bus, Driver: Coach, Driver: Lorry, Driving Instructor, Rail Transport Train Driver

Driver: Van
also known as: Delivery Van Driver, Goods Van Driver, Van Driver

CRCI:Transport and Logistics
CLCI:YAD — Job Band: 1 to 2

Job Description
Drive a van or light truck to deliver goods to customers' businesses or household premises. Van drivers deliver a wide variety of goods, including floral arrangements, office stationery and computer supplies, frozen foods or carpets and furniture. May work for a supermarket chain delivering internet shopping orders to customers. Work out a route delivery plan and check the necessary paperwork.

Van drivers load the van so that goods are arranged in order of each delivery and ensure that they are secure. They unload or collect items according to the order/plan, and ask the customer to sign for receipt of the delivery. They are required to keep accurate records of each delivery and also to complete work timesheets. May be required to keep the van clean and sometimes do routine maintenance and minor repairs.

Some drivers cover long distances, and others work mostly in a small local area. Usually work on their own but some may have an assistant for deliveries/collection of heavier goods. May also deliver valuable items in specially adapted security vans with time-lock safes.

Work Details
Usually work a basic 39-40 hr week with some early starts and late finishes. Most of the time you are out and about in the van though you spend some time in a warehouse or depot. You may have to do heavy lifting and driving can sometimes be stressful. You have to cope with all kinds of weather and traffic conditions and you must be able to concentrate and remain alert. There is a risk of traffic accidents.

Qualification

• England, Wales and Northern Ireland
Band 1: For entry to jobs, no minimum qualifications are needed, but you are expected to have a good level of general education and relevant experience. Some formal/vocational qualifications at any level are useful.

Band 2: Although academic qualifications are not specified for this job, it is an advantage to have some GCSEs (A*-C) in subjects that include English and maths, or equivalent.

- **Scotland**

Band 1: For entry to jobs, no minimum qualifications are needed, but you are expected to have a good level of general education and relevant experience. Some formal/vocational qualifications at any level are useful.

Band 2: Although academic qualifications are not specified for this job, it is an advantage to have some S grades (1-3) in subjects that include English and maths, or similar.

Adult Qualifications
You do not need formal qualifications for this job, though employers expect a good standard of education and an ability in English and numeracy.

Work Experience
Relevant work or voluntary experience can equip you with skills that you can use in the future and add to your CV. Driving experience is essential, particularly if this is with a range of different vehicles. Experience of work with people is useful for jobs where you deliver to customers.

Entry and Training
Larger companies may run short introductory courses for new entrants, but often there is little formal training. Drivers either learn their routes alone or are taught the job and the route by a more experienced driver or supervisor. Satellite navigation systems are increasingly used to assist with the route. You must have a clean driving licence and be at least 18 to sit a test for a Category C licence to drive a light goods vehicle (LGV).

The initial driver certificate of professional competence (CPC) must be passed before you can pass the driver certificate of professional competence (CPC). You must then complete a periodic driver CPC, which is five days in every five year period, to maintain your licence. The driver CPC has also been introduced for LGV drivers who drive professionally. The EU requires that new LGV drivers hold the CPC as well as an LGV licence. Because of the high cost of insurance, most employers prefer employees over 21, or even 25.

Holders of the C1 licence can work towards S/NVQs distributive operations at level 1, and a level 2 in carry and deliver goods. Training programmes, including apprenticeship schemes, may be available in your area. Advanced apprenticeships leading to qualification at level 3 can also be a route into higher education. A driver transporting valuables or cash, must hold a Security Industry Authority cash and valuables in transit licence.

Mature applicants over the age of 25 may be preferred because insurance premiums are lower. Any sort of driving experience, or experience in sales or in running a small business is useful. Government training opportunities, such as apprenticeships, may be available in your area. You can also gain recognition of previous experience through Accreditation of Prior Learning or by working towards relevant S/NVQs. Contact your local careers office, Jobcentre Plus, Next Step service or Learning and Skills Council (LSC)/Local Enterprise Company (LEC) for details of training schemes.

Opportunities and Pay
There are over 200,000 van drivers in the UK. Opportunities have increased in recent years as a result of the growth in internet shopping, but the economic downturn has affected the number of jobs available. You can work for manufacturing firms, transport or delivery companies, haulage firms or shops. Many jobs are in towns and cities. Some drivers go on to take the LGV or PCV test and move into lorry or bus driving. Careers in Logistics can advise on approved training providers. Others become self-employed and run their own vans. In some companies experienced drivers can apply for promotion to supervisory or management jobs.

Pay varies depending on location and type of employer. The average salary for a van driver is £16k-£18k a year. High earners in more senior roles can make around £23k-£26k a year.

Health
You may have to pass a medical test and must have good eyesight.

Skills and Qualities
able to work well on your own, common sense, friendly, good memory, honest, quick reactions, responsible attitude, safety conscious

Relevant Subjects
Retail and distribution

Further Information
AGCAS: Transport and Logistics (Job Sector Briefing) (AGCAS) - www.prospects.ac.uk

Apprenticeship Schemes (National Apprenticeship Service) - www.apprenticeships.org.uk

Careers in Logistics - www.careersinlogistics.co.uk

Foundation Learning (QCDA) - www.qcda.gov.uk

Skills for Logistics - sector skills council for freight logistics industries - www.skillsforlogistics.org

Training Schemes - www.direct.gov.uk/en/educationandlearning

Addresses
Road Transport Industry Training Board
Access House, Halesfield 17, Telford, Shropshire TF7 4PW
Phone: +44 (0)1952 520 200
Web: www.rtitb.co.uk

Security Industry Authority (SIA)
PO Box 1293, Liverpool L69 1AX
Phone: 0844 892 1025 (UK only)
Web: http://sia.homeoffice.gov.uk/Pages/home.aspx

Similar Jobs
Driver: Bus, Driver: Coach, Driver: Lorry, Driver: Taxi/Minicab, Removals Operative, Van Driver: Sales

Driving Examiner

CRCI:Transport and Logistics
CLCI:YAD — Job Band: 1 to 2

Job Description
Driving examiners assess whether people drive safely enough to be awarded a full driving licence. Most test car drivers, but some assess motorcycle, large goods vehicle or passenger carrying vehicle drivers.

They meet the candidate at the test centre and go to their car. Ask them to read out or write down what is on a car number plate a set distance away. If the person cannot do this, examiners follow procedures to check their eyesight further. They ask two questions about safety checks that drivers should carry out. Begin the test. Give the candidate directions to take them round a planned route. Ask the driver to perform two reversing manoeuvres and sometimes an emergency stop. They make notes of any driver errors and can stop the test if they feel the driver is too unsafe to continue.

After the test, the examiner adds up the number of faults and reviews their severity to see if the driver has passed. They tell the driver whether they have passed or failed and provide feedback. Return to the centre and write a short report before meeting the next candidate.

Work Details
Usually work a 35 hr week from 8.30am-4.30pm, Monday to Friday. If you have to work longer than this, you are paid overtime. Testing also takes place on Saturdays and in the evenings during the summer months. You can volunteer to work these hours. Part-time examiners work at least two days a week.

You are based at one test centre, but may also work at other local centres to meet demand. Spend most of the day sitting in cars. Each test takes up to 45 minutes and examiners may carry out up to seven tests a day. You work as part of a team with other examiners. Candidates come from all walks of life. Many are young people aged 17 or 18. People are often nervous about taking the test and may be angry or upset if they fail.

Qualification

No formal qualifications are required for this job, but you need the skills you get from a good level of general education. You must have held a full UK or EU driving licence for at least four years and have no more than three current penalty points on it.

- **England, Wales and Northern Ireland**

Band 1: For entry to jobs, no minimum qualifications are needed, but you are expected to have a good level of general education and relevant experience. Some formal/vocational qualifications at any level are useful.

Band 2: For entry to jobs, no minimum qualifications are needed, but it is an advantage to have some GCSEs (A*-C) or equivalent in subjects that include English and maths.

- **Scotland**

Band 1: For entry to jobs, no minimum qualifications are needed, but you are expected to have a good level of general education and relevant experience. Some formal/vocational qualifications at any level are useful.

Band 2: For entry to jobs, no minimum qualifications are needed, but it is an advantage to have some GCSEs (A*-C) or equivalent in subjects that include English and maths.

Adult Qualifications

No formal qualifications are required for this job.

Work Experience

Work or voluntary experience can give you skills you can use in the future. Paid or voluntary work where you meet members of the public or provide customer service may be useful. The Driving Standards Agency (DSA) finds that people who do a lot of driving tend to be safer drivers. Safe drivers are more likely to pass the selection process. Having one or two lessons with an Approved Driving Instructor may help you prepare for the driving test.

Entry and Training

There are no set entry requirements, but you have to be 21 or over to do this job. The Driving Standards Agency (DSA) selection process is quite drawn out. There is a multiple choice theory test and a hazard-spotting test that uses film clips. If you pass, you can take the special driving test. This is an extended version of the normal driving test and includes an eyesight test. Successful applicants are then interviewed to see if they have the skills and abilities needed to be an examiner. Finally, the DSA carries out a Criminal Records Bureau (CRB) or Disclosure Scotland check.

You do a four-week residential training course at a training centre in Bedfordshire. You learn the assessment and people skills you need to be an effective examiner. You are then assigned to a driving test centre and can begin work. Managers may sit in a car and watch you handle a driving test at any point in your career to check your performance.

You update your knowledge, skills and working practices through further training and courses. When you have worked as a car test examiner for a year, you can train to test drivers of other types of motor vehicle.

There is an upper age limit of 63 for new entrants. Often adults can offer a mature outlook and a wealth of driving experience that is an advantage in this area of work.

Opportunities and Pay

The Driving Standards Agency (DSA) employs over 1,900 driving examiners in England, Scotland and Wales in over 400 test centres. Numbers are expected to remain constant for the next few years. They carry out over 1.8 million car tests each year. They also handle over 90,000 motorcycle and a similar number of lorry and bus tests. The Driver & Vehicle Agency employs examiners in Northern Ireland. You can progress to senior and supervising examiner roles. Some examiners focus on training.

New entrants earn around £21k a year, with an extra £3.7k for working in the London area. Senior examiners can earn up to £26k. Supervising driving examiners earn £32k a year.

Health

You have to be able to read a car number plate at a distance of 27.5 metres in good daylight, with glasses or lenses if needed.

Skills and Qualities

able to get on with all kinds of people, able to put people at ease, assertive, calm, fair minded, good communication skills, good concentration level, good driving skills, information handling skills, observant

Relevant Subjects

English

Further Information

Despatch Magazine (DSA, quarterly) (Driving Standards Agency) - www.dsa.gov.uk/welcome.asp

Addresses

Driver & Vehicle Agency (DVA)
County Hall , Castlerock Road, Coleraine BT51 3HS
Phone: 0845 601 4094 (UK only)
Web: www.dvtani.gov.uk/home/index.asp

Driving Standards Agency (DSA)
The Axis Building, 112 Upper Parliament Street, Nottingham NG1 6LP
Phone: +44 (0)115 936 6666
Web: www.dsa.gov.uk

Similar Jobs

Chauffeur/Chauffeuse, Driver: Bus, Driver: Lorry, Driver: Taxi/Minicab, Driving Instructor, Road Safety Officer

Driving Instructor

CRCI:Transport and Logistics
CLCI:YAD — Job Band: 1 to 2

Job Description

Driving instructors teach driving skills, road sense and safety, to learner drivers or those wishing to become advanced drivers. They prepare people for their driving test on an hourly instruction basis. Plan the route and lesson according to the client's ability. Explain and give practice in driving techniques and give advice on individual difficulties. Instruct the pupil in the highway code and supervise driving lessons under all kinds of traffic and weather conditions.

Driving instructors prepare the pupil for the practical and theory tests for a driving licence. Many also offer advanced driving training for those who wish to achieve the advanced driver's qualification. Keep accurate and up-to-date records of the learner's progress and payment of fees.

Work Details

Hours are irregular and you have to work evenings and weekends. The hours can be longer in the summer. You sit in a car for most of the day. The work is stressful at times and there is a risk of traffic accidents. You have to be able to teach and reassure people who are nervous, give them confidence, and be able to stay calm under pressure.

Qualification
Driving skills, the ability to relate well to other people and teaching ability are more important than formal qualifications.

• England, Wales and Northern Ireland
Band 2: For entry to jobs, no minimum qualifications are needed, but it is an advantage to have some GCSEs (A*-C) or equivalent in subjects that include English and maths.

• Scotland
Band 2: Although academic qualifications are not specified for this job, it is an advantage to have some S grades (1-3) in subjects that include English and maths, or similar.

Adult Qualifications
The minimum age for driving instructors is 21. Good driving ability and communication skills are required.

Work Experience
Relevant work or voluntary experience can equip you with skills that you can use in the future and add to your CV. Driving experience is essential, particularly if this is with a range of different vehicles. Any work that involves instructing or training others is also very useful.

Entry and Training
You must register and train as an approved driving instructor (ADI) with the Driving Standards Agency. To do this you have to be 21, but most entrants are at least 23. You must have held a clean driving licence for at least four years out of the last six, and you need to pass a three-part 'Register' qualifying exam. A Criminal Records Bureau/Disclosure Scotland check is needed to establish that you have no criminal or motoring convictions of any kind. The exam consists of a written paper, a driving test and a practical test of ability to instruct pupils.

When you have passed parts 1-2 you can apply for a trainee licence. This lasts for six months and with some supervision, it gives you the opportunity to gain paid experience in instructing pupils to drive before you sit part 3. Once fully registered you can join the ADI list, but must renew your certificate every four years. Some knowledge of car maintenance is also useful. It is possible to gain an S/NVQ level 3 in driving instruction. The Driving Instructors Association offers continuing professional development schemes.

Mature entrants require good and proven experience in driving ability and communication skills. Many employers prefer those over the age of 25 due to high levels of car insurance premiums for young drivers. Driving skills, the ability to relate well to other people and teaching ability are often more important than formal qualifications. You must register and train as an approved driving instructor (ADI) with the Driving Standards Agency.

Opportunities and Pay
There are an estimated 39,000 ADIs in the UK and the work is available mainly in towns and cities. You can work for a driving school or be self-employed. Some companies operate a franchise system and you can pay a fee each week/month. You may have to buy or hire a car, which can be expensive. A few driving instructors are employed by the armed forces or by transport companies. With experience you can tutor trainee instructors or become an examiner.

Income varies enormously and depends on the hours worked, location and whether you are self-employed or not. Lessons cost between £17-£30 a session and instructors can work up to 48 hours a week. Driving instructors generally earn around £15k initially, rising to £25k a year. High earners can earn up to £35k a year.

Health
You have to be able to read a car number plate at a distance of 27.5 metres in good daylight, with glasses or lenses if needed. Any medical restrictions listed on your driving licence are taken into account when you apply. You have to be able to pass the practical tests in a car with a manual gearbox.

Skills and Qualities
able to cope under pressure, able to explain clearly, able to get on with all kinds of people, able to give clear instructions, alert, basic understanding of vehicle maintenance, good driving skills, patient, quick reactions, tactful

Relevant Subjects
English

Further Information
Driving Instructor's Handbook (2009) (Kogan Page) - www.koganpage.com

Driving Standards Agency - www.dsa.gov.uk

GoSkills - sector skills council for passenger transport - www.goskills.org

So you want to be a Driving Instructor (DIA) - www.driving.org/becomeadrivinginstructor.html

Transport and Logistics (Business Link) - www.businesslink.gov.uk/bdotg/action/layer?topicId=1082103262

Your road to becoming an Approved Driving Instructor (DSA) (Driving Standards Agency) - www.drminstructortrainingcollege.co.uk/become.html

Addresses
Driver & Vehicle Agency (DVA)
County Hall , Castlerock Road, Coleraine BT51 3HS
Phone: 0845 601 4094 (UK only)
Web: www.dvtani.gov.uk/home/index.asp

Driving Instructors' Association (DIA)
Safety House Beddington Farm Road, Croydon CR0 4XZ
Phone: +44 (0)20 8665 5151
Web: www.driving.org

Similar Jobs
Driver: Bus, Driver: Taxi/Minicab, Driving Examiner, Outdoor Activities Instructor, Road Safety Officer

Drug/Alcohol Advice Worker
also known as: Alcohol/Drug Counsellor, Outreach Worker, Substance Misuse Worker

CRCI:Social Work and Counselling Services
CLCI:KEB Job Band: 2 to 4

Job Description
Drug/alcohol advice workers support young people and adults who have misused drugs, alcohol and other harmful substances. Do not judge the client but help them to make constructive changes to their lifestyle and find ways to reduce or stop using these substances. Offer support through these changes and keep records of client's progress. May specialise in one particular area of work such as assessing client's needs, counselling, education or testing for substance use.

May work in places such as schools, youth clubs, community centres, drop-in centres, specialist clinics, rehabilitation centres, prisons, police stations, or accompany police officers patrolling the streets. They work with a range of other professionals such as police, nurses, doctors, social workers and youth workers.

Drug/Alcohol Advice Worker

Work Details
Usually works 35-40 hours a week, but is often expected to work unsocial or varied hours, including evenings and weekends. You may have to work with people who are aggressive and uncooperative. Jobs are community based and the work involves travelling to different districts, possibly visiting substance users in their own homes. Part time work and job sharing may be available.

Qualification

• England, Wales and Northern Ireland
Band 2: For entry to jobs, no minimum qualifications are needed, but it is an advantage to have some GCSEs (A*-C) or equivalent in subjects that include English and maths.

Band 3: For entry to a BTEC national award in health and social care: usually at least 4 GCSEs (A*-C) including English and maths, or equivalent.

Band 4: For BTEC higher national award in health and social care: 1-2 A levels and some GCSEs (A*-C) usually including English and maths, or equivalent.

• Scotland
Band 2: For direct entry: usually some S grades (1-3) in subjects that include English and maths, or similar.

Band 3: For entry to a relevant national course: usually at least four S grades (1-3) including English and maths, or similar.

Band 4: For SQA higher national award: usually 2-3 H grades and some S grades (1-3), often including English and maths, or similar qualifications.

Adult Qualifications
Entry requirements for relevant courses are usually relaxed for mature entrants, particularly if you have suitable work experience.

Work Experience
Relevant work or voluntary experience is always useful and can improve your chances in applications for entry to this job. Consider experience that gives you the opportunity of dealing with young people and adults in a helping capacity such as at youth and community centres, the Samaritans or Victim Support.

Entry and Training
There are no set entry qualifications, but most entrants have previous experience and possibly a qualification in health and social care or counselling. Some may be professionals, qualified in nursing, teaching, youth work, probation or the prison service. All posts are subject to a Criminal Records Bureau or Disclosure Scotland check. Under 21s are rarely employed in unsupervised support roles. For over 18s, an Advanced Apprenticeship in Criminal Justice (Drugs and Alcohol Pathway) may be available in England and Wales.

Training is usually on the job and often includes an induction course. All entrants are well supervised while training and are often mentored by an experienced worker. Training may also include attendance at college on a part-time basis for courses in recognising and working with substance abuse, run by City & Guilds and Edexcel at levels 2-4. The Federation of Drug & Alcohol Professionals also offers a range of online, distance learning and face-to-face courses, specialist workshops and short courses. See their website for details. Employers encourage continuing professional development (CPD) to keep knowledge and skills up to date.

A Diploma/Welsh Baccalaureate may be available in your area in society, health and development.

Adult entry is common to this work as previous experience of working with people is considered vital. There are a range of qualifications dealing with drug and alcohol misuse organised by the Federation of Drug & Alcohol Professionals by online or distance learning. Adults may be able to enter this work through a government-funded training programme. Contact your local Connexions or careers office, Jobcentre Plus, Next Step service or Learning and Skills Council (LSC)/Local Enterprise Company (LEC) for details of all training opportunities and schemes, including apprenticeships for adults.

Opportunities and Pay
Over 30,000 people are employed in this type of work in the UK. This is with a variety of employers such as prisons, drug and alcohol support organisations, charities, housing agencies, local authorities and Connexions Services in England. With experience, some people may choose to do more training and go into counselling or social work.

Starting pay may be around £12k a year. Experienced workers may earn £20k-£35k a year. Project leaders can earn £40k or more.

Skills and Qualities
able to inspire confidence, able to understand other people's problems, able to work both on your own and in a team, emotionally strong, good interpersonal skills, good listening skills, good organisational skills, non-judgemental, observant, patient

Relevant Subjects
English, Health and social care, Psychology, Sociology

Further Information
Alcohol Concern - Making Sense of Alcohol - www.alcoholconcern.org.uk

Apprenticeship Schemes (National Apprenticeship Service) - www.apprenticeships.org.uk

Community Care Journal - http:///www.communitycare.co.uk

Diplomas (Foundation, Higher and Advanced) - http://yp.direct.gov.uk/diplomas

Drink and Drugs News (DDN) - www.drinkanddrugsnews.com

Druglink magazine (bi-monthly) - www.drugscope.org.uk/publications/druglink

Local Government Careers (Improvement and Development Agency) - www.lgcareers.com/publications/

Social Care and Social Work Careers - www.socialworkandcare.co.uk

Welsh Baccalaureate - www.wbq.org.uk

▶Working in advice & counselling (2007) (Babcock Lifeskills) - www.babcock-lifeskills.com/

▶Working in social care (2010) (Babcock Lifeskills) - www.babcock-lifeskills.com/

Addresses
Care Council for Wales
South Gate House, Wood Street, Cardiff CF10 1EW
Phone: +44 (0)29 2022 6257
Web: www.ccwales.org.uk

Federation of Drug & Alcohol Professionals
Unit 84, 95 Wilton Road, London SW1V 1BZ
Phone: 0780 763 6139 (UK only)
Web: www.fdap.org.uk

National Treatment Agency for Substance Misuse
6th Floor, Skipton House 80 London Road SE1 6LH
Phone: +44 (0)20 7972 1999
Web: www.nta.nhs.uk

Northern Ireland Social Care Council
7th Floor, Millennium House, 19-25 Great Victoria Street, Belfast BT2 7AQ
Phone: +44 (0)28 9041 7600
Web: www.niscc.info

Scottish Social Services Council (SSSC)
Compass House 11 Riverside Drive, Dundee DD1 4NY
Phone: +44 (0)845 60 30 891
Web: www.sssc.uk.com

Similar Jobs
Community Development Worker, Community Learning & Development Officer (Scotland), Counsellor, Prison Officer, Social Worker

Dry Cleaning Assistant/Manager
also known as: Dry Cleaning Technician

CRCI:Personal and Other Services
CLCI:IG Job Band: 1 to 3

Job Description
Dry cleaning assistants or manager work in a high street shop, and uses steam or chemicals to clean items that may not be washed. They accept the garments from a customer, check for damage or stains and label the items. Then provide the customer with a receipt and inform them of the cost. Sort items for cleaning and may need to remove some stains with chemicals or steam before processing. Then set and load the machines. Monitor progress of the cleaning processes, making adjustments if necessary.

They inspect the cleaned items when processed. Also press the clean clothes with a steam press, taking special care with pleats and delicate fabrics. Then pack the clothes ready for the customer and hang them on a rail for collection. Take payment by cash, credit/debit card or cheque, and use a computerised till. Some retail outlets offer a clothing repair and alteration service.

Managers are also responsible for organising the running of the business, training new staff and dealing with complaints. In smaller businesses, managers are likely to help in the shop, dealing with customers and assisting with the dry cleaning process if needed.

Work Details
Working hours are usually between 35-40 hrs a week, and may include Saturdays. You work in a shop or a large dry cleaning plant where you may be required to work shifts. Sometimes your job is very busy and you need to stand for a lot of the time. This type of work can be quite energetic, lifting clothes in and out of machines. Some of the machines are quite noisy and many of the chemicals you use give off unpleasant smelling fumes. You are often expected to wear an overall or protective clothing.

Managers may work partly in an office, keeping records and using a computer. As a result their work may be less physically demanding.

Qualification
• England, Wales and Northern Ireland
Band 1: For entry to jobs, no minimum qualifications are needed, but you are expected to have a good level of general education and relevant experience. Some formal/vocational qualifications at any level are useful.

Band 2: For entry to jobs, no minimum qualifications are needed, but it is an advantage to have some GCSEs (A*-C) or equivalent in subjects that include English and maths.

Band 3: For direct entry to manager training: usually at least 4 GCSEs (A*-C) including English and maths or equivalent qualifications.

• Scotland
Band 1: For entry to jobs, no minimum qualifications are needed, but you are expected to have a good level of general education and relevant experience. Some formal/vocational qualifications at any level are useful.

Band 2: Although academic qualifications are not always specified for this job, it is an advantage to have some S grades (1-3) in subjects that include English and maths, or similar qualifications.

Band 3: For direct entry as a manager: usually at least four S grades (1-3) including English and maths, or similar qualifications.

Adult Qualifications
No formal qualifications are needed, but, for entry as a manager, experience and/or qualifications in business/management are an advantage.

Work Experience
Any work experience can equip you with skills that you can use in the future and add to your CV. This can either be unpaid or voluntary, or holiday/part-time work that you have organised yourself. Any retail, customer service, or cleaning work provides useful experience.

Entry and Training
Training for a dry cleaning assistant is usually on the job with a more experienced worker. Training concentrates particularly on the safety aspects of using the cleaning products. Many employees also have the opportunity to take the Guild of Cleaners & Launderers (GCL) Qualification (Q) Star Scheme, through a local training provider, or other short courses, such as those offered by SATRA Fabric Care Division. SATRA provides most of the training, including short courses and seminars on specific techniques. It provides the training for the GCL Q Star qualifications, in areas such as dry-cleaning practice, stain removal, setting up a dry cleaning shop and aspects of health and safety.

The Dry Cleaning and Laundry Technology Centre offers a range of courses. The website of the Textile Services Association may also offer useful information. Appropriate S/NVQs at levels 1-2 are available in cleaning and support services. Training programmes, including apprenticeship schemes, may be available in your area.

With experience and training, assistants may move on to become managers. Some of the larger chains of dry cleaners may recruit graduates to manager posts, but this is not the normal route. Many management jobs are filled by staff promoted from within the company.

Adults may be able to enter this work through a government-funded training programme. Contact your local Connexions or careers office, Jobcentre Plus, Next Step service or Learning and Skills Council (LSC)/Local Enterprise Company (LEC) for details of all training opportunities and schemes, including apprenticeships for adults.

Opportunities and Pay
It is usually possible to find work in most towns and cities throughout the UK. You may be employed by a large nationwide chain or a small private company. Work is also available with large-scale dry cleaning companies that clean garments, household textiles and soft furnishings, under contract from a network of shops. Jobs with nationwide chains or large units may offer the best opportunities for progression, which can include moving into other areas, such as human resource management or research and development. It may be possible to set up your own business under a franchise system, but this requires capital investment.

Pay varies depending on area and location and employer, but as a guide, earnings for assistants are around £12.5k-£15k a year. Managers may earn £15k-£28k a year depending on the size of the business.

Health
You need good colour vision for certain areas of work. This job may not be suitable for people with certain skin conditions or asthma, as there is an allergy risk from some of the chemicals used for cleaning. In some posts, a good level of fitness is required.

Skills and Qualities
able to operate equipment, able to work quickly, attention to detail, business awareness, cash handling skills, customer service skills, good organisational skills, methodical

Relevant Subjects
Retail and distribution

Further Information
Apprenticeship Schemes (National Apprenticeship Service) - www.apprenticeships.org.uk

Cleaning Industry Handbook (BICSc) (BICSc) - www.bics.org.uk/

Laundry & Cleaning Today (LCT) - www.laundryandcleaningtoday.com

Training Schemes - www.direct.gov.uk/en/educationandlearning

Addresses
Dry Cleaning & Laundry Technology Centre (DTC & LTC Ltd)
Unit 10A, Drill Hall Business Centre, East Parade, Ilkley LS29 8EZ
Phone: +44 (0)1943 816545
Web: www.dtcltc.com

Guild of Cleaners & Launderers (GCL)
5 Portland Place, London , Middlesex W1B 1PW
Phone: 0845 600 1838 (UK only)
Web: www.gcl.org.uk

SATRA Fabric Care Research Division
SATRA Technology Centre,, Wyndham Way, Telford Way, Kettering, Northamptonshire NN16 8SD
Phone: +44 (0)1536 410 000
Web: www.satra.co.uk

Textile Services Association (TSA)
5 Portland Place, London, Middlesex W1B 1PW
Phone: +44 (0)20 8863 7755
Web: www.tsa-uk.org

Similar Jobs
Car Valet, Cleaner: Carpet & Upholstery, Clothing Presser, Laundry Assistant/Manager, Retail Assistant, Retail Manager

Dry Liner
also known as: Dry Lining Operative, Metal Stud Fixer

CRCI:Building and Construction

CLCI:UF — Job Band: 1 to 2

Job Description
Dry liners use dry finishes (instead of wet plaster) to fix up and join together plasterboard and wall boards before decoration. There are two trades for dry liners: fixers and finishers. Dry lining fixing involves building and putting up wall and ceiling linings and partitions. Fixers build the frame by measuring, cutting and laying metal tracks. Then they fill the frame, usually with plasterboard, and fix it in place. Dry lining finishing involves providing a smooth surface, ready for decoration. Joints between boards are filled, covered and plaster is applied where needed.

Dry liners work in the construction industry on a wide range of projects. These include houses and state-of-the-art buildings, such as airport terminals and hotels. They have specialist knowledge of the materials they work with. May work as part of a larger team, alongside plasterers, electricians, painters, plumbers and engineers. In Scotland, this job is done by a carpenter and joiner.

Work Details
Dry liners usually work a basic 39 hr week, Monday to Friday. You may have to work some evenings and weekends at times. You work mainly indoors. You may need to travel around the local area and sometimes sites are further away. This job requires a good level of fitness, an ability to read charts and diagrams, and basic numeracy skills for working out quantities.

The job involves lifting, bending, kneeling and working at heights on scaffolding and ladders. There is a risk of falling from heights. You usually need to wear a safety helmet, overalls, and sometimes gloves and safety glasses.

Qualification
- **England, Wales and Northern Ireland**

Band 2: No minimum qualifications but some GCSEs (A*-C) or equivalent, including maths, English, science or technical subjects, are required by some employers.

- **Scotland**

Band 2: No minimum qualifications but some S grades (1-3) or similar, including maths, English, science or technical subjects, are required by some employers.

Adult Qualifications
Course entry requirements are usually relaxed for suitable mature applicants, particularly for those with some knowledge of carpentry or plastering.

Work Experience
Relevant work or voluntary experience is always useful and can improve your chances when applying for entry to construction jobs and apprenticeships. In some areas there is a young apprenticeship (14-16) scheme that provides an extended work placement and eventual achievement of a level 2 qualification whilst at school. Health and safety issues may mean that there are certain jobs you can't do until you are over 16. Contact your local ConstructionSkills office for advice.

Entry and Training
Most entrants begin training through an approved ConstructionSkills scheme, such as a three-year construction apprenticeship scheme (four years in Scotland), which you can apply for in year 11 (January). Other schemes include work-based training at a ConstructionSkills centre and full-time work training with an employer, usually supported by day or block release to a local college. You may have to take an assessment test before you can start training.

There are also full and part-time college courses in construction, such as the level 3 BTEC Diploma in Construction and the Built Environment and the level 1 ConstructionSkills Certificate in Building Craft Occupations. The Federation of Plastering and Drywall Contractors (FPDC) has been successful in obtaining funding from ConstructionSkills to help deliver a number of new training programmes. These programmes can be delivered 'on demand' throughout the UK. Contact FPDC for further details.

A Diploma/Welsh Baccalaureate in construction and the built environment may be available in your area. Training programmes, including apprenticeships leading to level 2 and advanced apprenticeships or construction apprenticeships leading to level 3, may be available in your area. There are also Construction Awards (England and Wales) available for those who are unable to gain workplace experience for NVQs. Relevant S/NVQs include interior systems (dry lining fixing and finishing) at level 2 and plastering at level 2.

Mature applicants can take refresher courses that are sometimes available for those returning to work and there may be special training schemes in some areas. Training opportunities such as Work Based Learning/Training for Work may be available. Contact your local careers office, Jobcentre Plus, Next Step service or Learning and Skills Council (LSC)/Local Enterprise Company (LEC) for details of training schemes, including apprenticeships for adults.

Opportunities and Pay
Work is mostly with a firm of plasterers or a building contractor. Availability of work depends on activity in the building trade and the national economy. Currently there is a downturn in the housing market which means there may be a shortage of vacancies for dry liners. You may be able to progress to supervisory and management roles. With enough experience you can start your own business. Seasonal and short-term employment is possible. There are opportunities to work abroad.

Dry liners are mostly paid according to national industry rates, but pay can vary, depending on location and employer. Without qualifications, a general building operative earns £7.73 per hour. The basic standard hourly rate for qualified dry liners is around £8-£10 per hour. The rate depends on your level of qualifications. This can work out at around £18k-£21k a year. Those with a level 3 qualification earn from £21k and, with experience, up to £26k a year. Bonuses and overtime pay may be available. Employers may give allowances for travel and cost of lodgings. Many dry liners are self-employed and income depends on the success of the business. Top earners can make up to £40k a year.

Health
You need to be physically fit and have good eyesight. You should not be allergic to dust.

Skills and Qualities
able to follow drawings and plans, able to work both on your own and in a team, accurate, attention to detail, hand-to-eye co-ordination, head for heights, health & safety awareness, numeracy skills, strong

Relevant Subjects
Construction and built environment, Design and technology

Further Information
Apprenticeship Schemes (National Apprenticeship Service) - www.apprenticeships.org.uk

Careers in Construction - www.bconstructive.co.uk

ConstructionSkills - sector skills council for the construction industry - www.cskills.org

Diplomas (Foundation, Higher and Advanced) - http://yp.direct.gov.uk/diplomas

Specialist Building Finishes (bi-monthly) (FPDC) - www.fpdc.org/Specialist-Building-Finishes-Magazine.aspx

Training Schemes - www.direct.gov.uk/en/educationandlearning

Welsh Baccalaureate - www.wbq.org.uk

▶Working in construction & the built environment (2007) (Babcock Lifeskills) - www.babcock-lifeskills.com/

Addresses
Federation of Plastering and Drywall Contractors (FPDC)
4th Floor 61 Cheapside, London EC2V 6AX
Phone: +44 (0)20 7634 9480
Web: www.fpdc.org

Similar Jobs
Carpenter/Joiner, Ceiling Fixer, Construction Operative, Painter & Decorator, Plasterer, Tiler: Wall & Floor

Ecologist
CRCI:Science, Mathematics and Statistics
CLCI:QOD Job Band: 5

Job Description
Ecologists research the complex relationship between animals and plants, in particular their habitats and the impact of people on their environment. They are involved in habitat mapping, data collection and interpretation, and identifying new areas of conservation value. May assess the ecological impact of development proposals such as road building schemes or intensive farming. Also carry out field studies to record data about animal and plant life and note any rare and endangered species.

Ecologists set up and maintain ecological databases and may be involved in generating project bids for funds and grants. They also work as advisers to local and central government, industries, landowners and water companies, aiming to ensure that environmental regulations are upheld and standards are met. May attend conferences and research, write and present findings in a report.

Work Details
Usually work a 35-39 hr week, Monday to Friday, though may be required to make an early start, work late and sometimes at weekends. You may work in an office or laboratory, but fieldwork is more usual and often involves spending time away from home and working outdoors in all weathers. A great deal of travel is necessary and often to remote areas. You work with other scientists and professionals and may also supervise staff. The work can be physically active.

Qualification
• England, Wales and Northern Ireland
Band 5: For degree courses: 2-3 A levels including biology and preferably chemistry, maths or physics, and some GCSEs (A*-C) usually including English, science and maths, or equivalent qualifications. Exact requirements depend on the degree you take.

• Scotland
Band 5: For a degree: 3-5 H grades including biology and preferably chemistry, maths or physics and some S grades (1-3), including English, science and maths, or similar qualifications. Exact requirements depend on the degree you take.

Degree Information
Most ecologists are qualified to degree level. There are specialist degree courses in ecology, though other subjects may also be relevant, such as biological or life sciences, environmental studies, earth sciences, geography, agricultural science or urban and land studies or countryside management. Many ecologists also have a postgraduate qualification.

Adult Qualifications
Entry requirements may be relaxed for mature entrants to first degree courses provided they submit evidence of previous study, such as an Access/Open University course. It is also possible for those without the specified science qualifications to take a foundation year leading into the relevant degree. Check with universities.

Work Experience
Entry to this career is highly competitive and the profession demands high levels of commitment. Applicants need to demonstrate a high level of interest and work experience, often obtained through voluntary work. You can work for organisations such as natural history societies, wildlife trusts and voluntary conservation organisations, who are always keen to recruit enthusiastic volunteers for conservation projects. These offer the opportunity to help identify plants and animals, contribute to structured surveys, gain management experience of nature reserves, as well as valuable practical experience.

Entry and Training
Most entrants are graduates and many have a postgraduate qualification in a biological or environmental subject. Relevant degree courses last for 3-4 years, can be full time or sandwich and may also offer specialisms including plant/animal ecology. Postgraduate study is an advantage and is usually essential for research projects. Full membership of the Institute of Ecology and Environmental Management (IEEM) requires a relevant first or second class degree, plus three years' professional experience to gain chartered status (CEnv). Membership of the Landscape Institute (LI) can be obtained by studying for an approved degree or postgraduate award, followed by a period of professional experience and completion of the Institute's practice examination.

There are foundation degrees that can be studied full or part time in subjects such as ecology and conservation management, land management, wildlife management, and ecology and conservation, as well as biological/environmental subjects. The Chartered Institution of Water and Environmental Management (CIWEM) offers training and professional development initiatives in the UK and overseas.

Experience of relevant fieldwork provides useful background for course entry for mature applicants. There are opportunities for postgraduate or research funding from professional associations, such as the British Ecological Society (BES).

Opportunities and Pay

This is a small, though growing profession and competition is fierce. Ecologists are directly employed by local/central government (botanical gardens, environmental agencies, local government departments etc), and with universities and colleges, environmental consultants, NGOs (non-government organisations) and voluntary sector organisations, such as the National Trust, English Nature or Scottish Natural Heritage. There are also opportunities with statutory bodies, in publishing and with environmental consultancies. Some employers may offer work overseas.

Pay varies depending on location and employer. New entrants are likely to earn £16k-£23k a year, progressing to £24k-£40k as a senior ecologist. Ecologists or project leaders in senior positions may earn up to £45k a year, or more.

Health

This job requires good general fitness. You may find this job difficult if you have hay fever.

Skills and Qualities

adaptable, analytical skills, aptitude for fieldwork, aptitude for teamwork, attention to detail, environmental awareness, excellent communication skills, information handling skills, IT skills, observant, scientific approach

Relevant Subjects

Biology, Chemistry, English, Geography, ICT/Computer studies, Land and Environment, Mathematics, Physics, Science

Further Information

In Practice (quarterly) (Institute of Ecology & Environmental Management) - www.ieem.org.uk

Jobs and the Natural Heritage (leaflet) (Scottish Natural Heritage) - www.snh.org.uk/

Open University - www.open.ac.uk

Rooting for a Career in Ecology or Environmental management (BES) (British Ecological Society) - www.britishecologicalsociety.org/

The Ecologist (10 x year) (Ecologist Magazine) - www.theecologist.co.uk

▶Working in science (2007) (Babcock Lifeskills) - www.babcock-lifeskills.com/

▶Working with animals (2009) (Babcock Lifeskills) - www.babcock-lifeskills.com/

Addresses

British Ecological Society (BES)
Charles Darwin House 12 Roger Street, London WC1N 2JU
Phone: +44 (0)207 685 2500
Web: www.britishecologicalsociety.org

Chartered Institution of Water and Environmental Management (CIWEM)
15 John Street, London WC1N 2EB
Phone: +44 (0)20 7831 3110
Web: www.ciwem.org.uk

Environment Council
contact via website, London WC1V 7BF
Phone: +44 (0) 208 144 8380
Web: www.the-environment-council.org.uk

Institute of Ecology and Environmental Management (IEEM)
45 Southgate Street, Winchester, Hampshire SO23 9EH
Phone: +44 (0)1962 868 626
Web: www.ieem.net/

Landscape Institute (LI)
33 Great Portland Street, London W1W 8QG
Phone: +44 (0)20 7299 4500
Web: www.landscapeinstitute.org

Natural Environment Research Council (NERC)
Polaris House North Star Avenue, Swindon, Wiltshire SN2 1EU
Phone: +44 (0)1793 411 500
Web: www.nerc.ac.uk

Society for the Environment (SocEnv)
The Old School House, 212 Long Street, Atherstone, Warwickshire CV9 1AH
Phone: +44 (0)845 337 2951
Web: www.socenv.org.uk

Society of Biology
9 Red Lion Court, London EC4A 3EF
Phone: +44 (0)20 7936 5900
Web: http://societyofbiology.org/home

Similar Jobs

Agricultural Research Scientist, Biologist, Botanist, Countryside/ Conservation Officer/Manager, Environmental Scientist, Soil Scientist

Economist

CRCI:Financial Services
CLCI:QOK — Job Band: 5

Job Description

Economists analyse and research data, and forecast economic trends and their impact on the economy. Advise government departments, and help businesses, banks and other organisations to develop economic policy. May study and give advice on productivity, pricing and marketing policy, incomes or employment/unemployment. Help a company, government-related body or individuals to make the best use of their resources. Solve complex problems by the application of a range of economic analysis tools. Prepare reports and present findings to employers.

Some economists identify weaknesses in the import/export market and alert business managers to any significant economic changes that may affect the company. They often study the current economic state of other countries that may have an impact on a company's overseas business affairs.

Work Details

Usually work a basic 35-39 hrs a week, Monday to Friday, either on your own or as part of a small team. You may have to work longer hours or take work home.

Depending on your post, you may have responsibility for providing financial advice, forecasting trends or assessing cost benefits on a wide range of economic issues. Much of your work is done on computers, using specialist software. The job may involve presentations and seminars with clients, or the public, via the media. Some overseas travel or work may be required depending on the employer. This can be a demanding and pressured job at times.

Qualification

• England, Wales and Northern Ireland

Band 5: For degree courses: 2-3 A levels, preferably including maths or economics, and some GCSEs (A*-C) usually including English and maths, or equivalent. History and geography are also helpful. Exact requirements depend on the degree you take.

- **Scotland**

Band 5: For degree courses: 3-5 H grades, preferably including maths or economics, and some S grades (1-3), usually including English and maths, or similar qualifications. History and geography at S grade are also helpful. Exact requirements depend on the degree you take.

Degree Information

A good honours degree (first or 2:1) in economics is preferred, but financial management, banking, business studies, statistics and maths can provide a basis for postgraduate study. Some economics degrees are combined with maths, politics, law and management. A specialist higher degree may be expected by some employers.

Adult Qualifications

Entry requirements for degree courses are specified by individual universities and colleges. Many have special arrangements, including Access courses, for mature students who do not have the required qualifications. Check with universities for details.

Work Experience

Universities and employers may prefer candidates who have relevant work or voluntary experience. Ideally you can shadow or work with somebody who is currently involved in the job, but alternatively work involving finance or working with numbers, such as accountancy, is relevant. Any experience that involves the use of research skills is also an advantage.

It is useful to join student industrial societies and the Society of Business Economists, which demonstrates enthusiasm and commitment and also enables you to make contacts. The Government Economic Service offers a student and vacation placement service.

Entry and Training

There is a wide range of degree courses and you should choose carefully. Many are combined with other subjects, such as politics, statistics or languages. Courses are mainly full time for three or four years, but there are also some sandwich courses available. Training is by practical work experience, after obtaining a degree or further qualification. Postgraduate study is advisable, particularly if you wish to specialise. Some companies fund postgraduate study and provide study leave. You are expected to commit to continuing professional development and to manage your own training and development needs, within your own and employer's career expectations. Short courses are available on specialist topics.

Economists are increasingly using a wide variety of computer software packages to help compile and analyse statistics. Familiarity with these packages is essential.

Entrants as assistant economists to the Government Economic Service need a good honours degree in economics. Those with a joint honours degree need to have spent at least 50% of their time on economics and studied both macro and microeconomics. Entrants follow a fast stream programme and should achieve economic adviser level after 3-4 years. There are also opportunities to join the European Fast-Stream and work within the EU. The Bank of England runs a graduate training programme (Analyst Career Training) and provides sponsorship for postgraduate study. It also recruits economics PhD students for research economics posts.

In the private sector, you usually join as an economic research officer before progressing with experience to become a senior economist.

Mature entrants may have difficulty in finding employment unless they have previous relevant experience, particularly in finance and accountancy.

Opportunities and Pay

Despite the economic downturn, there are still opportunities to work in these sectors. However, this is a small profession and competition for posts is very keen. The largest single employer is the Government Economic Service. Other public sector employers include central government agencies and departments, large local and metropolitan authorities and some regional development agencies. Major employers also include financial institutions, including the Bank of England and other major retail banks, insurance companies and building societies.

Economists are also employed by industrial or commercial firms, research organisations, marketing and management services or a stock exchange. Some economists are self-employed and work as part of management consultancy groups. There may be opportunities abroad with, for example, the World Bank or the International Monetary Fund (IMF).

Pay varies hugely depending on location, type and size of employer. Assistant economists earn around £25k-£30k (higher for those with a Masters degree), which can rise to £32k-£42k a year with experience. The most successful economists in the City (London) often command £60k-£80k, and some can earn six-figure salaries.

Skills and Qualities

analytical skills, attention to detail, business awareness, good at forecasting trends, good communication skills, good interpersonal skills, information handling skills, IT skills, numeracy skills, research skills

Relevant Subjects

Business and accounting, Economics, English, Government and politics, ICT/Computer studies, Law, Mathematics

Further Information

AGCAS: Government & Public Administration (Job Sector Briefing) (AGCAS) - www.prospects.ac.uk

Bank of England - www.bankofenglandjobs.co.uk/

Civil Service - www.civilservice.gov.uk/jobs

Financial Services Skills Council - sector skills council for financial services, accountancy & finance - www.fssc.org.uk/

The Business Economist (SBE) (Society of Business Economists) - www.sbe.co.uk/

The Economist (weekly) (Economist Newspaper Ltd) - www.economist.com/

▶Working in maths (2009) (Babcock Lifeskills) - www.babcock-lifeskills.com/

Addresses

Government Economic Service (GES)
HM Treasury, 1 Horse Guards Road, London SW1A 2HQ
Phone: +44 (0)20 7270 4571
Web: www.ges.gov.uk

Society of Business Economists
Dean House, Vernham Dean, Andover, Hampshire SP11 0JZ
Phone: +44 (0)1264 737552
Web: www.sbe.co.uk

Similar Jobs

Accountant: Industry & Commerce, Actuary, Investment Analyst, Investment Banker, Operational Researcher, Statistician

Editor: Publishing

also known as: Commissioning Editor, Newspaper/Periodicals Editor

CRCI:Media, Print and Publishing
CLCI:FAD Job Band: 4 to 5

Job Description

Publishing editors control the content of a newspaper, book or magazine publication, from the original manuscript through to the printed copy. They oversee junior/section editors who are in charge of one part of a publication, eg spor and work with production staff overseeing final proof copies before printing. They make sure publications are produced smoothly, efficiently and on time. Editors are responsible for keeping costs within an agreed budget. May also assist with marketing and promotion.

Editors may work initially as a commissioning or copy editor. A commissioning editor organises and negotiates a price for work from freelance writers and photographers. A copy or desk-editor ensures that the finished written material is of a high standard and is consistent with the style of the publication. On smaller publications, the editor may help write articles, copy edit material and deal with the design and layout.

Work Details

You are based in an office and may spend a large part of your time sitting at a desk using a word processor. The job can consist of working long hours, and you have to be able to remain calm under pressure and when publication deadlines approach. The ability to get on with others is important as you need to liaise with writers, literary agents and printers. This job involves making difficult decisions, and you must be able to rely on your own judgement.

Qualification

• England, Wales and Northern Ireland

Band 4: For HND, Diploma of Higher Education or foundation degree: 1-2 A levels and some GCSEs (A*-C) usually including English and maths, or equivalent.

Band 5: For degree courses: 2-3 A levels and some GCSEs (A*-C) usually including English or equivalent qualifications. Exact requirements depend on the degree you take.

• Scotland

Band 4: For entry to SQA higher national and professional development awards, usually 2-3 H grades and some S grades (1-3), including English and maths, or similar qualifications.

Band 5: For degree courses: 3-5 H grades and some S grades (1-3), usually including English, or similar. Exact requirements depend on the degree you take.

Degree Information

Some employers prefer a degree in publishing but any degree is acceptable for entry to this job. A course in English language/ literature, communication studies or media studies gives useful background knowledge. There are postgraduate courses in publishing.

Adult Qualifications

Entry requirements may be relaxed for adults applying for higher education courses. Access or foundation courses give adults without qualifications a route on to degree courses.

Work Experience

Entry to this career is highly competitive and it is essential to have some relevant work or voluntary experience before applying for positions. The Publisher's Association advises that new entrants have some idea of the industry as a whole before embarking on job searching and that experience of other industries such as teaching, librarianship, book-selling and printing can be advantageous.

Entry and Training

There are few vacancies and fierce competition for the jobs that become available. Entrants are usually graduates, particularly those with a degree in publishing. Relevant foundation degrees are also available and may be taken full or part time. The Publishing Training Centre at Book House can provide details of relevant degrees. Some editors have worked their way up after experience as a journalist or from a position as an editorial assistant. They usually work first as a copy or commissioning editor. Some editors are recruited with specialist skills, such as knowledge and experience of a particular subject area.

You must be able to use word-processing packages and you need to keep your publishing and editing skills up to date with short and distance-learning courses such as those offered by the Publishing Training Centre at Book House and the Society for Editors and Proofreaders. The London School of Publishing and the Oxford International Centre for Publishing Studies at Oxford Brookes University also offer relevant training courses. Some employers train inexperienced staff on the job via their own training schemes or send their staff on external short courses.

Publishing Scotland runs a variety of courses for those wishing to hone their skills in a particular field e.g digital publishing. Similarly, the National Council for the Training of Journalists (NCTJ) offers bespoke in-house training in writing skills and, occasionally advertise trainee vacancies.

A Diploma/Welsh Baccalaureate may be available in your area in creative and media. This can be a useful introduction to this type of career as you gain practical experience while studying. See the diplomas website or Skillset for further information.

Mature entry to editor posts is common as experience and/or qualifications in journalism and publishing, or knowledge of the book trade, is an advantage. A suitable specialist background is helpful for specific fields of literature, such as science, law or education. It is also possible to work your way up to this job from copy editor or editorial assistant positions. The Publishing Training Centre regularly introduces new online courses on book publishing. Contact them for details.

Opportunities and Pay

The UK publishing industry is the second largest in Europe, employing in excess of 160,000 people, and keeping approximately 8,000 publishing companies in business. Jobs are mainly in London, the south of England and Edinburgh, but regional and local newspapers are published throughout the UK. The main opportunities are in books and magazines and increasingly online publishing. With advances in technology, many publishers now offer multimedia products and electronic publishing looks to be a future growth area. Many start work at a local newspaper and then work their way up through regional to national publications, and from there may branch into magazine publishing.

Salaries vary considerably depending on location and type of work; starting salaries for copy-editors and sub-editors are likely to be around £17k-£19k a year. Local newspaper and book editors can earn £16k-£25k as a starting salary. Section editors on a larger paper may earn £40k or more. Editors of large national publications can earn over £100k a year.

Skills and Qualities

able to make important decisions, able to work to deadlines, analytical skills, attention to detail, enthusiastic, good organisational skills, good spelling, grammar and punctuation, good spoken communication, good written English, imaginative, IT skills

Relevant Subjects

Business and accounting, Economics, English, ICT/Computer studies, Media and communication studies

Further Information

Behind the Scenes: Publishing (Trotman 2009) - www.trotman.co.uk

Careers in Book Publishing (The Publishers Association) - www.publishers.org.uk/

Diplomas (Foundation, Higher and Advanced) - http://yp.direct.gov.uk/diplomas

Editing Matters (bi-monthly) (Society for Editors & Proofreaders (SFEP) - www.sfep.org.uk/pub/mag/magazine.asp

How to get a job in Publishing (A&C Black)

Oxford International Centre for Publishing Studies - http://ah.brookes.ac.uk/publishing/

Skillset - sector skills council for the creative media, fashion and textiles industries - www.skillset.org

Society of Young Publishers - www.thesyp.org.uk/

Women In Publishing - www.wipub.org.uk

▶Working in creative & media (2007) (Babcock Lifeskills) - www.babcock-lifeskills.com/

▶Working in English (2007) (Babcock Lifeskills) - www.babcock-lifeskills.com/

▶Working in politics & law (2010) (Babcock Lifeskills) - www.babcock-lifeskills.com/

Addresses

London School of Publishing
David Game House, 69 Notting Hill Gate, London W11 3JS
Phone: +44 (0)207 221 3399
Web: www.publishing-school.co.uk

National Council for the Training of Journalists (NCTJ)
The New Granary , Station Road, Newport, Saffron Walden, Essex CB11 3PL
Phone: +44 (0)1799 544014
Web: www.nctj.com

Publishers' Association
29b Montague Street, London WC1B 5BW
Phone: +44 (0)20 7691 9191
Web: www.publishers.org.uk

Publishing Scotland
Scottish Book Centre, 137 Dundee Street, Edinburgh EH11 1BG
Phone: +44 (0)131 228 6866
Web: www.publishingscotland.co.uk/

Publishing Training Centre at Book House
45 East Hill, Wandsworth, London SW18 2QZ
Phone: +44 (0)20 8874 2718
Web: www.train4publishing.co.uk

Society for Editors and Proofreaders (SfEP)
Erico House, 93-99 Upper Richmond Road, Putney, London SW15 2TG
Phone: +44 (0)20 8785 5617
Web: www.sfep.org.uk

Similar Jobs

Bookshop Assistant, Editorial Assistant: Publishing, Journalist, Literary Agent, Magazine Features Editor, Proofreader

Editorial Assistant: Publishing

CRCI:Media, Print and Publishing
CLCI:FAD Job Band: 4 to 5

Job Description

Editorial assistants help senior editorial staff in the administration of the commissioning and production of books, newspapers, magazines and journals. The work can involve many tasks, including the issuing of contracts, checking proofs, correction of manuscripts, summarising written material as well as being a PA (personal assistant) to an editor. They also help in the planning of new titles and with the organisation of new book launches. May be involved in writing articles, collating work and using specialist computer software, such as QuarkXPress.

Other tasks include everyday office secretarial and administrative tasks such as answering the telephone, ordering office supplies and word-processing. Assistants liaise with other editorial and creative staff, including the marketing and production team. After some experience, they may be more involved with assessing the work of others, assisting with the design of a publication and sourcing new writers.

Work Details

Usually work a basic 37-39 hr week; Monday to Friday, and sometimes extra hours to meet deadlines. The work is office based and usually in an informal and creative environment. Many publishers use flexible contracts so career breaks, freelance, and part-time work are possible.

Qualification

- **England, Wales and Northern Ireland**

Band 4: For HND, Diploma of Higher Education or foundation degree: 1-2 A levels and some GCSEs (A*-C) usually including English and maths, or equivalent.

Band 5: For degree courses: 2-3 A levels and some GCSEs (A*-C) usually including English or equivalent qualifications. Exact requirements depend on the degree you take.

- **Scotland**

Band 4: For entry to SQA higher national and professional development awards, usually 2-3 H grades and some S grades (1-3), including English and maths, or similar qualifications.

Band 5: For degree courses: 3-5 H grades and some S grades (1-3), usually including English, or similar. Exact requirements depend on the degree you take.

Degree Information

Some employers prefer a degree in publishing but any degree is acceptable for entry to this job. A course in English language/ literature, communication studies or media studies gives useful background knowledge. There are postgraduate courses in publishing.

Adult Qualifications

Entry requirements may be relaxed for adults applying for higher education courses and Access or foundation courses give adults without qualifications a route on to degree courses.

Work Experience

Relevant work or voluntary experience is always useful and improves your chances in application for entry to this job. Writing and editing experience is very desirable to employers. Magazine editing staff often have experience in journalism, or sometimes in media sales. Other relevant experience includes working in a bookshop or library. Knowledge of the publishing industry is useful and can be gathered from trade publications such as Publishing News and The Bookseller.

Entry and Training

This job is open to all graduates though often personal qualities are more important than the subject studied. Many people in publishing have an arts and humanities background or a technical or scientific specialism relevant to the area of publishing. A postgraduate course or short course in publishing may give entrants an advantage as there is a lot of competition for few openings.

Entry without a degree or HND is occasionally possible through secretarial, sales and marketing departments in larger publishers. Relevant foundation degrees are available and may be taken full or part time.

Training is mainly on the job, supported by short courses held by organisations such as the Publishing Training Centre, Publishing Scotland and the London School of Publishing. The courses are often offered through distance learning or evening classes. Large publishers have comprehensive training programmes for new entrants.

A Diploma/Welsh Baccalaureate may be available in your area in creative and media. This can be a useful introduction to this type of career as you gain practical experience while studying. See the diplomas website or Skillset for further information.

Mature entry into this profession is possible, although relevant professional experience in journalism/administrative work or other related fields is required. Distance-learning courses are available in relevant subjects and are offered by organisations that include the National Council for the Training of Journalists and the National Extension College.

Opportunities and Pay

The UK publishing industry is the second largest in Europe, employing in excess of 160,000 people, and keeping approximately 8,000 publishing companies in business. Many publishers are in or around London and the major regional cities. Most publishing falls into three areas: books, magazines and academic/professional. With technology advances, many publishers now offer multimedia products and electronic publishing looks to be a future growth area. Competition for jobs is fierce and this job is recognised as an entry path to becoming an editor. Promotion prospects are better in larger publishing houses.

Entering competitions can be a good way to develop skill in this area and gain work experience. The Women in Publishing website has details of competitions for female writers.

Salaries depend on the size and type of employer and level of responsibility, although a starting salary is in the range of £16k-£20k a year, rising to around £26k with some employers. Assistants can supplement their income by freelance work in copy editing and proofreading. The Society for Editors and Proofreaders (SfEP) has lots of useful information on freelance working. See their website for details.

Skills and Qualities

able to cope under pressure, analytical skills, attention to detail, enthusiastic, good communication skills, good interpersonal skills, good organisational skills, good spelling, grammar and punctuation, initiative, IT skills, time management skills

Relevant Subjects

Business and accounting, English, ICT/Computer studies, Media and communication studies

Further Information

Behind the Scenes: Publishing (Trotman 2009) - www.trotman.co.uk

Careers in Book Publishing (The Publishers Association) - www.publishers.org.uk/

Diplomas (Foundation, Higher and Advanced) - http://yp.direct.gov.uk/diplomas

Editing Matters (bi-monthly) (Society for Editors & Proofreaders (SFEP)) - www.sfep.org.uk/pub/mag/magazine.asp

How to get a job in Publishing (A&C Black)

Skillset - sector skills council for the creative media, fashion and textiles industries - www.skillset.org

Society of Young Publishers - www.thesyp.org.uk/

The Bookseller (The Bookseller) - www.thebookseller.com/

Women In Publishing - www.wipub.org.uk

▶Working in creative & media (2007) (Babcock Lifeskills) - www.babcock-lifeskills.com/

▶Working in English (2007) (Babcock Lifeskills) - www.babcock-lifeskills.com/

Addresses

London School of Publishing
David Game House, 69 Notting Hill Gate, London W11 3JS
Phone: +44 (0)207 221 3399
Web: www.publishing-school.co.uk

National Council for the Training of Journalists (NCTJ)
The New Granary , Station Road, Newport, Saffron Walden, Essex CB11 3PL
Phone: +44 (0)1799 544014
Web: www.nctj.com

National Extension College (NEC)
The Michael Young Centre, Purbeck Road, Cambridge CB2 8HN
Phone: +44 (0)1223 400 200
Web: www.nec.ac.uk

Publishers' Association
29b Montague Street, London WC1B 5BW
Phone: +44 (0)20 7691 9191
Web: www.publishers.org.uk

Publishing Scotland
Scottish Book Centre, 137 Dundee Street, Edinburgh EH11 1BG
Phone: +44 (0)131 228 6866
Web: www.publishingscotland.co.uk/

Publishing Training Centre at Book House
45 East Hill, Wandsworth, London SW18 2QZ
Phone: +44 (0)20 8874 2718
Web: www.train4publishing.co.uk

Society for Editors and Proofreaders (SfEP)
Erico House, 93-99 Upper Richmond Road, Putney, London SW15 2TG
Phone: +44 (0)20 8785 5617
Web: www.sfep.org.uk

Similar Jobs

Editor: Publishing, Magazine Features Editor, Personal Assistant, Proofreader, Secretary

Education Administrator

also known as: College Administrator, University Administrator

CRCI:Education and Training

CLCI:COZ Job Band: 4 to 5

Job Description

An education administrator works within a central administrative department of universities and colleges of further and higher education as well as in individual faculties, sections and departments of an educational institution. Responsibilities vary but generally include day-to-day operational administration, often specialising in financial/budget control, management of resources, student and staff recruitment, marketing, or human resources management and public relations. Other areas of work include central administration, examinations and assessment processes, admissions, curriculum development, quality assurance, international office and external relations, or other specialised areas.

Duties include the writing and presenting of reports to committees and academic boards, contributing to policy and practice, the supervision of staff, and purchasing of goods and equipment as required. Also provides administrative support to lecturers, tutors and other academics, and liaises with government departments, external agencies and partner institutions.

Work Details

The work is mainly office based with hours worked from around 9am-5pm, Monday to Friday. However, administrators may work occasional overtime at busy times in the academic year, such as enrolment, examination periods and at academic quality inspection visits. A lot of time is spent collecting, collating and analysing information. Sometimes the work is stressful during busy times of the academic year. There may be opportunities to travel in the UK and possibly abroad where the job involves liaison with overseas partners.

Qualification

- **England, Wales and Northern Ireland**

Band 4: For HND, Diploma of Higher Education or foundation degree: 1-2 A levels and some GCSEs (A*-C) usually including English and maths, or equivalent.

Band 5: For degree courses: 2-3 A levels and some GCSEs (A*-C) usually including English and maths, or equivalent. Exact requirements depend on the degree you take.

- **Scotland**

Band 4: For entry to SQA higher national and professional development awards, usually 2-3 H grades and some S grades (1-3), including English and maths, or similar qualifications.

Band 5: For degree courses: 3-5 H grades and some S grades (1-3), including English and maths, or similar qualifications. Exact requirements depend on the degree you take.

Degree Information

A good honours degree in any discipline is acceptable, but a degree in education studies, English, information science/ management, social or public administration, statistics or business studies is useful.

Adult Qualifications

Government training opportunities, such as apprenticeships, may be available in your area. You can also gain recognition of previous experience through Accreditation of Prior Learning (APL) or by working towards relevant S/NVQs. Contact your local careers office, Jobcentre Plus, Next Step service or Learning and Skills Council (LSC) Local Enterprise Company (LEC) for details of training schemes.

Work Experience

Entry is competitive and it is likely that applicants are expected to show competence in key skills and administration skills gained by work experience or work shadowing in an office. This can be gained through a wide variety of companies and organisations, and particularly in an educational establishment, or in local and central government offices.

Entry and Training

Increasingly, a degree is an advantage and usually essential for entry to further and higher education sectors, though a postgraduate qualification is not often required. However, higher degrees or professional qualifications may help your prospects for progression to senior posts. Those with an HND find entry is more possible for junior grades or in further and tertiary education. You are offered in-house training that includes an induction programme to introduce the work of the institution and its procedures.

Continuing professional development (CPD) is encouraged and may include studying for the postgraduate certificate in professional practice that is offered by the Association of University Administrators (AUA). You need to have a first degree and be a member of the AUA to apply for the postgraduate qualification. However, those who can demonstrate relevant substantial work experience or have a comparable qualification or professional/other qualification, are also able to take the postgraduate certificate.

It is possible to update the postgraduate certificate to a diploma or MSc in management (higher education administration) at Loughborough University or the MBA in higher education management at the Institute of Education, University of London. Further opportunities to update your skills and knowledge are offered by the AUA through a programme of conferences, seminars and lectures. Some institutions may offer the facility to work towards an MBA, a diploma in management studies or a postgraduate qualification in educational administration.

Additional relevant qualifications include those offered by the Institute of Chartered Secretaries and Administrators and by the Institute of Administrative Management. S/NVQs at levels 3-4 are available in administration and there are relevant full or part-time foundation degrees.

Mature applicants with previous experience in formal office work, especially in an administrative capacity have an advantage. Experience gained in local or central government administration departments is particularly valuable. Those with relevant professional qualifications may also increase their promotion opportunities.

Opportunities and Pay

Employers are usually universities and colleges of further and higher education. Opportunities are increasing in independent colleges, specialist training colleges, or at tertiary colleges. There is keen competition for senior posts and you may need to change to an employer in another area to gain promotion. However, within an institution there is a very wide range of jobs in administration, so there are often opportunities to move into other areas of the work if you wish.

Salaries vary widely depending on the size of institution, its location and type as well as by job title, which also varies, but may start at around £20k-£25k a year rising to £25k-£45k with experience. At senior levels, equivalent to professors, the salary range is from around £45k-£90k.

Skills and Qualities

able to deal effectively with change, able to prioritise work, aptitude for teamwork, clear-thinking, efficient, flexible approach, good communication skills, good organisational skills, innovative, IT skills

Relevant Subjects

Business and accounting, Economics, English, ICT/Computer studies, Mathematics

Further Information

Institute of Education (IOE), University of London - www.ioe.ac.uk/

Addresses

Association of School and College Leaders (ASCL)
130 Regent Road, Leicester LE1 7PG
Phone: +44 (0)116 299 1122
Web: www.ascl.org.uk

Association of University Administrators (AUA)
AUA National Office, University of Manchester , Oxford Rd
M13 9PL
Phone: +44 (0) 161 275 2063
Web: www.aua.ac.uk

Institute of Administration Management (iam)
6 Graphite Square, Vauxhall Walk, London SE11 5EE
Phone: +44 (0)20 7091 2600
Web: www.instam.org

Institute of Chartered Secretaries and Administrators (ICSA)
16 Park Crescent, London W1B 1AH
Phone: +44 (0)20 75804741
Web: www.icsa.org.uk

Similar Jobs

Civil Service Administrative Officer, Civil Service Executive Officer, Company Secretary, Local Government Administrator, Office Manager, School Business Manager/Bursar

Education Inspector

CRCI:Education and Training
CLCI:FAZ Job Band: 5

Job Description

Education inspectors carry out independent inspections in nurseries, schools, colleges and other education providers, including local education authorities (LEAs), ensuring that they meet government standards. They also carry out joint inspections of services for children, including early years provision, residential schools and care homes. Inspecting learning and skills for adult and community learning and training, including in prisons, is also part of their job.

Inspectors prepare for inspections by reading documentation from and about the institution. Once on site, they interview members of staff, students, governors and parents. They observe teaching sessions and record their findings. They draw up a detailed report of the facilities and educational provision in each institute. They then feed back to the institution and publish the full report.

Work Details

Usually work freelance and from home. You work in groups of between two and twelve, under a lead inspector, and inspect an institution over a period of 3 days to two weeks.

The job involves a lot of travel and you may be regularly away from home. A driving licence is required. You are also required to have an enhanced Criminal Records Bureau (CRB)/Disclosure Scotland clearance.

Qualification

- **England, Wales and Northern Ireland**

Band 5: For degree courses: 2-3 A levels and some GCSEs (A*-C) usually including English and maths, or equivalent. Exact requirements depend on the degree you take.

- **Scotland**

Band 5: For degree courses: 3-5 H grades and some S grades (1-3), including English and maths, or similar qualifications. Exact requirements depend on the degree you take.

Degree Information

A degree in a subject related to education is useful. Inspectors coming to the job from a teaching role, may have a degree in their chosen subject area.

Adult Qualifications

Entry requirements may be relaxed for adults applying for higher education courses. Access or foundation courses provide those without the required qualifications a route onto degree courses.

Work Experience

Candidates are expected to have substantial teaching and/or training experience in schools, colleges of further education, youth work, higher education institutions, or in industrial/commercial training. Many have experience at senior levels in education or training and some have held senior posts in industry and commerce.

Entry and Training

As inspectors need extensive experience in the sector they are inspecting, this job is not open as a first career. Most inspectors have at least five years' recent experience of working in education and at least three years of relevant management experience, for example as a headteacher, deputy head or head of department. Therefore, you have a degree in a subject related to education, and professional qualifications. You must also have up-to-date knowledge of the curriculum as well as of recent developments and statutory requirements in education. Early years inspectors require experience as a nursery manager or similar role.

You may have experience at senior levels of training or have held senior posts in industry and commerce, often in more than one organisation. Before being appointed, you have to attend a course of training provided or approved by the Office for Standards in Education, Children's Services and Skills (Ofsted). As a newly appointed inspector, you serve a two-year probationary period. During this time you follow an induction programme and staff development, which includes training days, taking part in training inspections and support from a mentor. Professional development continues throughout your term of office and includes attending conferences and keeping up to date with educational matters.

Each team of inspectors is led by a registered inspector, who has passed an assessment of ability to lead the inspection and who has a legal duty to ensure the inspection is carried out properly.

This is not open as a first career. Mature applicants with considerable experience in education, usually in a management role, or in training within industry, possibly in more than one sector, are preferred.

Opportunities and Pay

In England HMIs (Her Majesty's inspectors) are employed directly by Ofsted. There are also additional inspectors, working under contract to Ofsted for one of the regional inspection service providers. Estyn is the education and training inspectorate in Wales. In Scotland you work for HM Inspectorate of Education. The Education and Training Inspectorate is responsible for inspections in Northern Ireland.

Additional training is provided on employment. All inspectors must ensure they keep their professional knowledge of education and training up to date. Experienced inspectors may progress to lead inspection teams or for management roles.

Salaries range from £28k a year for an early years inspector to around £48k-£61k a year for an HMI. The inspection team leader is at the upper level of that range. Freelance inspectors earn £300-£500 per day. Additional inspectors are usually paid a daily fee.

Skills and Qualities

able to follow procedures, able to work to deadlines, analytical skills, excellent communication skills, good at writing reports, impartial, information handling skills, observant, self-motivated

Relevant Subjects

English, Government and politics

Further Information

Education and Training Inspectorate (NI) - www.etini.gov.uk/

Her Majesty's Inspectorate of Education (HMIE) - www.hmie.gov.uk

Addresses

Estyn
Anchor Court, Keen Road, Cardiff CF24 5JW
Phone: +44 (0) 29 2044 6446
Web: www.estyn.gov.uk

Office for Standards in Education, Children's Services and Skills (Ofsted)
Royal Exchange Buildings, St Anne's Square, Manchester M2 7LA
Phone: +44 (0)845 649 4045
Web: http//:www.ofsted.gov.uk

Similar Jobs

Education Administrator, Information Scientist, Lecturer: Further Education, Management Consultant, Teacher: Secondary School

Education Welfare Officer (England)

also known as: Education Social Worker, Inclusion Officer

CRCI:Education and Training
CLCI:FAZ Job Band: 3 to 5

Job Description

Education welfare officers (EWOs) work closely with schools and families to resolve attendance issues, arranging school and home visits as necessary. They support children and families when children aged between 5 and 16 yrs are experiencing difficulties in school or when welfare issues are disrupting a child's education. Work with schools, parents, carers and children. Also work with other professionals such as social workers, home school link workers and educational psychologists, often as part of a multidisciplinary area team.

In schools, EWOs carry out regular register checks to verify attendance. They meet with key members of staff to identify areas of concern, which may lead to a referral and subsequent meetings with the child and its parents or carers. Discuss a plan with all parties to identify issues and improve school attendance. May involve external agencies to support the family in housing, counselling, bereavement and so on. Support excluded pupils and those who have had long-term illness on their return to school. May also advise the school in staff training and assemblies about ways of improving overall attendance.

Usually each EWO has a caseload of several schools. They keep detailed records of all conversations, meetings and interventions and writes letters to parents and agencies. May use this to compile evidence to be presented in court, usually by a colleague specifically trained for this role. Also have responsibility for enforcing employment law regarding children of school age.

Work Details

You work a regular 37 hr week, Monday to Friday, but may need to attend evening meetings. You are usually based in an office or in a school, depending on your caseload. It is expected that you meet children and their families in their own homes, but you also attend meetings in family centres or at school. You need a driving licence. Everybody working with children and vulnerable adults is required to undergo a Criminal Records Bureau (CRB) check. Smart/ professional dress is usually expected.

Qualification

• England, Wales and Northern Ireland

Band 3: For entry to jobs, HNC or a relevant Diploma, usually at least 4 GCSEs (A*-C) including English and maths, or equivalent.

Band 4: For HND, Diploma of Higher Education or foundation degree: 1-2 A levels and some GCSEs (A*-C) usually including English and maths, or equivalent.

Band 5: For degree courses: 2-3 A levels and some GCSEs (A*-C) usually including English and maths, or equivalent. Exact requirements depend on the degree you take.

Degree Information

Degrees in psychology, sociology, social policy, education or administration may provide relevant background knowledge for this job.

Adult Qualifications

Government training opportunities, such as apprenticeships, may be available in your area. You can also gain recognition of previous experience through Accreditation of Prior Learning (APL) or by working towards relevant S/NVQs. Contact your local careers office, Jobcentre Plus, Next Step service or Learning and Skills Council (LSC) Local Enterprise Company (LEC) for details of training schemes.

Work Experience

You are usually employed by a local authority in the Education Welfare Service, but some schools employ attendance officers or manage their own EWO.

Entry and Training

Entry requirements vary across the country, but increasingly education welfare officers are required to have a degree or a diploma in social work. Some authorities prefer a degree in teaching, social work or a related subject. In some authorities entry is at 'assistant' level which requires NVQ level 3 or 3 A levels. The National Association of Social Workers in Education (NASWE) colleges offer NVQ levels 3 and 4 in education welfare training. Consult the website for further details.

The Open University offers a level 3 certificate in working with vulnerable young people (QCF), which can be a stepping stone into higher education for people with few or no qualifications, but who have considerable experience of working with young people. Learners who successfully complete this award can progress onto the level 4 award. This can lead to acceptance onto FE or HE courses.

New staff are trained in-house by experienced colleagues. Short courses in safeguarding children, personal safety, and key areas of legislation are usually offered. It is also possible to complete training on the job such as the learning, development and support services (LDSS) levels 3 and 4 qualifications. The Children's Workforce Development Council website offers excellent information on LDSS and on requirements for this job.

The Department for Education provides the National Programme for Specialist Leaders of Behaviour and Attendance (NPSLBA), which offers qualifications of increasing interest to employers. Ongoing continuing professional development (CPD) is a key feature of this job. Networking with a range of other agencies involved with young people is also very important.

This is often a second career for a mature person. Some have previously worked in education as teachers or support staff, or in social work. Life experience is greatly valued by employers. Experience, either voluntary or paid, in youth or community work is also useful.

Opportunities and Pay

It is possible to specialise in a certain area of education welfare work, such as with primary school age children or re-integration of children into mainstream school. Promotion to more senior roles usually results in less involvement with specific casework and a more supervisory role. There may also be an increase in administrative responsibilities or court duties. It is also possible to move to another role within the children's services departments of local authorities.

Salaries vary across the country, but are generally in the range of £21k-£30k a year. Managerial roles may pay up to £55k a year.

Skills and Qualities

able to relate well to children and young people, administrative skills, aptitude for teamwork, awareness of confidentiality issues, good interpersonal skills, good listening skills, good organisational skills, observational skills, sound judgement, tactful

Relevant Subjects

English, Health and social care, Law, Psychology, Sociology

Further Information

Children's Workforce Development Council (CWDC) (CWDC) - www.cwdcouncil.org.uk

Local Government Careers (Improvement and Development Agency) - www.lgcareers.com/publications/

National Association of Social Workers in Education (NASWE) http://www/naswe.org.uk

Open University - www.open.ac.uk

Addresses

Department for Education
Castle View House East Lane, Runcorn, Cheshire WA7 2GJ
Phone: 0870 000 2288 (UK only)
Web: www.education.gov.uk/

Similar Jobs

Advice Worker, Careers Adviser, Counsellor, Drug/Alcohol Advice Worker, Personal Adviser (Connexions) (England), Social Worker

Electrical Engineering Technician

also known as: Electronics Engineering Technician

CRCI:Engineering
CLCI:RAL Job Band: 3 to 4

Job Description

Electrical engineering technicians are responsible for the safe and efficient working of electrical and electronic equipment in a workplace. Jobs can be in 'heavy' current, dealing with power generation and supply, or in 'light' current in the electronics industry, dealing with the wide range of electronic products used in homes and offices. Work is mainly in designing, researching or production, but can include areas such as testing, inspection, installation, maintenance or after-sales service. Technicians follow engineering instructions, use wiring and circuit diagrams and a range of tools to calibrate, test and inspect equipment.

Work Details

Usually work a basic 39-40 hr week, Monday to Friday, though for some employers you may be expected to work shifts and overtime, and you may be on call for emergencies. You are based on industrial premises, in a workshop or travel to various sites, such as factories and power stations. Initially you are under supervision. You are responsible for following safety regulations. The environment depends on the type of industry in which you are employed. There may be a risk of accidents from equipment.

Qualification

- **England, Wales and Northern Ireland**

Band 3: For entry to jobs, an apprenticeship, HNC or a relevant Diploma, usually at least 4 GCSEs (A*-C) including English, maths and physics or another science subject, or equivalent.

Band 4: For HND, Diploma of Higher Education or foundation degree: 1-2 A levels and some GCSEs (A*-C) usually including English, maths and science/technical subjects, or equivalent.

- **Scotland**

Band 3: For entry to jobs or an apprenticeship: usually at least four S grades (1-3) including English, maths and physics or another science subject, or similar.

Band 4: For entry to SQA higher national and professional development awards, usually 2-3 H grades and some S grades (1-3), often including English, maths and science/technical subjects, or similar qualifications.

Adult Qualifications

Course entry requirements are usually relaxed for suitable mature applicants, though this is at the discretion of the college. Candidates with relevant work experience have an advantage.

Work Experience

Entry to this job is competitive and it is important that you try to do some relevant work or voluntary experience before applying. The areas that are relevant are those involving electronics and electrical equipment and also work of a practical nature. Work experience is not always vital for young people as many entry positions are for trainees or apprentices. For adults, relevant work experience or previous employment is usually necessary and is widely asked for.

Entry and Training

Training usually follows a pattern recommended by SEMTA (the sector skills council for science, engineering and manufacturing technologies). Most entrants do an apprenticeship at age 16-17. Training lasts 2-3 years combined with day-release and block-release courses at a local college. Instead of an apprenticeship you can choose to take a full-time college course before you start work. Most study for a BTEC/SQA award or for City & Guild certificates in engineering or engineering systems maintenance. You may be able to obtain relevant S/NVQs at levels 2-3 while you work. Some may enter this type of work with a relevant degree.

Progression to qualification as a registered engineering technician (EngTech) with the Engineering Council is possible, and with further experience and qualification, you can qualify as an incorporated/chartered engineer. On-going training is important because of the constant advances in technology. A relevant foundation degree may be available in some areas. Advanced apprenticeships leading to qualification at level 3 can also be a route into higher education. Contact SEMTA or the Engineering Council UK for further details of routes to training.

A Diploma/Welsh Baccalaureate may be available in your area in engineering. See the diplomas website for further information.

Mature applicants are considered for training but entry depends on company policy and your experience. College courses are available for all ages. Training opportunities such as Work Based Learning/ Training for Work and government training opportunities, such as apprenticeships for adults, may be available in your area. You can also gain recognition of previous experience through Accreditation of Prior Learning (APL) or by working towards relevant S/NVQs. Contact your local careers office, Jobcentre Plus, Next Step service or Learning and Skills Council (LSC)/Local Enterprise Company (LEC) for details of training schemes.

Opportunities and Pay

Opportunities within this area of work can be good but may be limited due to the current economic climate. Employment can be with a wide range of industries, such as a manufacturing company, power company, at an airport, a broadcasting company or with the armed forces. Once experienced, you can choose to move into more technical work or into other areas, such as sales and marketing.

Pay varies depending on location, type and size of employer. Starting salaries are likely to be around £15k-£18k, rising to around £25k with experience. Senior technicians can earn £30k-£40k a year.

Health

This job requires normal colour vision.

Skills and Qualities

accurate, analytical skills, aptitude for teamwork, attention to detail, IT skills, manual dexterity, methodical, numeracy skills, problem-solving skills, technical aptitude

Relevant Subjects

Design and technology, Engineering, ICT/Computer studies, Mathematics, Physics, Science

Further Information

Apprenticeship Schemes (National Apprenticeship Service) - www.apprenticeships.org.uk

Apprenticeships in Scotland (Careers Info Scotland) - www.apprenticeshipsinscotland.com/about/

Diplomas (Foundation, Higher and Advanced) - http://yp.direct.gov.uk/diplomas

Energy & Utility Skills - sector skills council for gas, power, waste management & water industries - www.euskills.co.uk

Engineering Scotland (SEMTA) - www.engineeringscotland.org

SEMTA - sector skills council for science, engineering and manufacturing technologies - www.semta.org.uk

Welsh Baccalaureate - www.wbq.org.uk

Addresses

Engineering Council
246 High Holborn, London WC1V 7EX
Phone: +44 (0)20 3206 0500
Web: www.engc.org.uk

Engineering Training Council (NI)
Interpoint, 20-24 York Street, Belfast BT15 1AQ
Phone: +44 (0)28 9032 9878
Web: www.etcni.org.uk

Scottish Engineering
Training Officer, 105 West George Street, Glasgow G2 1QL
Phone: +44 (0)141 221 3181
Web: www.scottishengineering.org.uk

Similar Jobs

Computer Assembly Technician, Electrician, Electronics Assembler, Engineer: Electrical, Engineer: Electronics, Rail Transport Fitter/Electrician, Telecommunications Technician

Electrician

CRCI:Building and Construction
CLCI:RAK Job Band: 1 to 3

Job Description

Electricians install, maintain and repair electrical services, including heating, lighting, and power supplies, to a variety of buildings, both inside and out. They also work on fire, safety and security systems, including CCTV, and telecommunications networks. Work is in private homes, hospitals, industrial premises, offices and power stations. Electricians locate and repair faults using a variety of tools. These include power tools, such as screwdrivers, pliers and drills, to measure, cut, joint and fit cabling, wiring and equipment. May also work on street lighting and traffic lights.

Electricians work from technical plans and drawings when installing and maintaining lighting, sockets and switches, fuse boxes, cabling and appliances. They often need to follow diagrams of wiring circuits from architects' drawings. They are responsible for periodic testing to ensure that electrical installations are safe to use in accordance with health and safety regulations. May work alongside other skilled tradespeople, including carpenters/joiners, plumbers and bricklayers, and liaise with architects, builders and site managers.

Work Details

Electricians usually work a basic 39 hr week, Monday to Friday, though some employment may include weekend work and overtime. Ensuring that safety standards are met and that regulations are observed are amongst your key responsibilities. In older houses and premises you have to strip out the old wiring and install new cables. Sometimes the place in which you work is dusty or dirty and cramped.

In new houses you install power points, run the wiring and connect up the fitments, such as lights and immersion heaters. This involves kneeling down to take up floorboards, bending metal pipes that hold the wiring (conduit) and climbing ladders to fix light fittings. You may need to wear overalls.

Qualification

- **England, Wales and Northern Ireland**

Band 2: For most training courses and employers: it is an advantage to have several GCSEs (A*-C) including English, maths and science, or equivalent. Craft or technology subjects are useful, but not essential.

Band 3: For entry to some courses: at least 4 GCSEs (A*-C) preferably including English, maths and science, or equivalent.

- **Scotland**

Band 2: For most training courses and employers: it is an advantage to have several S grades (1-3) including English, maths and science, or similar. Craft or technology subjects are useful, but not essential.

Band 3: For entry to some courses: at least four S grades (1-3) preferably including English, maths and science, or similar.

Adult Qualifications

Some formal qualifications are helpful for mature entry to training courses. Those with relevant work experience may be accepted for some college courses without meeting formal entry requirements.

Work Experience

Relevant work or voluntary experience is always useful. It can add to your CV and improve your chances when applying for entry to jobs or apprenticeships. Your careers adviser may be able to advise you about how to organise relevant work experience. Health and safety issues may mean that there are certain jobs you can't do until you are over 16. Contact your local ConstructionSkills office for advice.

Entry and Training

Entrants are usually aged 16-19 and most train towards qualification through a 3-4 year apprenticeship. All applicants take a selection test and have an interview. Training is by practical experience on the job and through college courses after an initial period off the job to learn basic skills. Apprenticeships for electricians are usually managed by JTL and the Scottish Electrical Charitable Training Trust. Contact them for further details. Most apprentices work towards an S/NVQ in electrotechnical services at level 3 and a City & Guilds Certificate in Electrotechnical Technology at levels 2 & 3. You can study by day or block-release whilst working for an employer.

This is one route to meeting the requirements of the Electrotechnical Certification Scheme (ECS). The ECS is administered by the Joint Industry Board (JIB)/Scottish Joint Industry Board for the Electrical Contracting Industry. An Apprentice ECS card is also available for apprentices registered with JIB. To qualify as an Approved Electrician with JIB you must be registered as an apprentice, or similar; have an NVQ level 3 in electrical installation work, or equivalent, and be qualified in testing and inspecting installations. Finally you need two years' post-training experience as an electrician.

JIB also provides financial assistance for further education courses through a designated fund. Applicants should ideally be JIB graded operatives or apprentices. Contact JIB for details. Highly experienced electricians may be eligible to apply for professional registration as an engineering technician (Eng Tech). Contact the Institution of Engineering and Technology for details.

Mature applicants with relevant work experience in electrical installation have an advantage. Adult electricians can be assessed through the Crediting Electrotechnical Competence (CEC) scheme that leads to S/NVQ at level 3 and meets the requirements for the Electrotechnical Certification Scheme (ECS).

Manchester Open Learning offers electrical installation courses through distance learning. Joint Industry Board (JIB) approved courses may be available through government sponsored training, such as work-based learning schemes. The Scottish Electrical Charitable Training Trust also runs a training scheme aimed at adults over 22. Many employers train adults due to a shortage of school leaver trainees.

Opportunities and Pay

Jobs are available throughout the UK, with more opportunities in towns and cities. Currently, there is a shortage of skilled electricians. Employers range from small family-run businesses to large national firms of electrical contractors, local government, power generating and supply companies. Promotion prospects are improved with further training. Some electricians go on to take a relevant degree, sometimes with financial support from their employer.

With experience and qualifications you can become self-employed or work on a contracting basis. Set-up costs may include buying your own tool kit and transport.

Pay varies depending on area and employer; salaries for apprentices start at around £10k a year. An average basic salary is around £22k-£25k, rising to around £32k with experience and qualifications. Successful self-employed electricians may earn more. There may be additional pay through overtime, shift work, as well as travel allowances.

Health
This job requires good stamina and physical fitness, including perfect colour vision. A medical test may be required for entry. There may be an allergy risk from dust.

Skills and Qualities
able to follow drawings and plans, able to work both on your own and in a team, good communication skills, good concentration level, good interpersonal skills, manual dexterity, methodical, numeracy skills, problem-solving skills, safety conscious

Relevant Subjects
Design and technology, Engineering, Mathematics, Physics, Science

Further Information
Apprenticeship Schemes (National Apprenticeship Service) - www.apprenticeships.org.uk

Careers in Engineering Booklets (SEMTA) - www.semta.org.uk

Energy & Utility Skills - sector skills council for gas, power, waste management & water industries - www.euskills.co.uk

JTL - www.jtltraining.com

Manchester Open Learning - www.mol-openlearning.co.uk

Real Life Guide to Electrician (Trotman) - www.trotman.co.uk

Summitskills - sector skills council for building services engineering - www.summitskills.org.uk

Wiring Matters (quarterly) (The Institute of Engineering and Technology) - www.theiet.org/publishing/wiring-regulations/mag/

▶Working in construction & the built environment (2007) (Babcock Lifeskills) - www.babcock-lifeskills.com/

Addresses
Electrical Training Trust (ETT)
Units 57-59 Ballymena Business Development Centre
62 Fenaghy Road BT42 1FL
Phone: +44 (0)28 2565 0750
Web: www.ett-ni.org/

Institution of Engineering and Technology (IET)
Michael Faraday House, Stevenage, Hertfordshire SG1 2AY
Phone: +44 (0)1438 313311
Web: www.theiet.org

Joint Industry Board (JIB) for the Electrical Contracting Industry
Kingswood House 47-51 Sidcup Hill, Kent DA14 6HP
Phone: +44 (0)20 8302 0031
Web: www.jib.org.uk

Scottish Electrical Charitable Training Trust (SECTT)
The Walled Garden, Bush Estate, , Midlothian EH26 0SE
Phone: +44 (0)131 445 5659
Web: www.sectt.org.uk

Scottish Joint Industry Board for the Electrical Contracting Industry
The Walled Garden, Bush Estate, Midlothian EH26 0SB
Phone: +44(0)131 445 9216
Web: www.sjib.org.uk

Similar Jobs
Domestic Appliance Service Technician, Electrical Engineering Technician, Electrician: Auto, Heating & Ventilation Fitter/Welder, Lightning Conductor Engineer, Security Systems Installer, Telecommunications Technician

Electrician: Auto
also known as: Auto Electrician, Car Electrician, Vehicle Electrician

CRCI:Engineering
CLCI:RAE Job Band: 1 to 3

Job Description
Auto electricians find faults in the wiring and other electrical and electronic parts of a vehicle. They repair and service electrical and electronic equipment and checs parts and circuits using special tools and testing equipment. On modern cars, they may plug a computer into the vehicle's electronic control unit (ECU) to find faults. Also fix or change parts such as the electronic ignition, alternators or fuel injection systems. Then tests that everything is working.

Auto electricians may fit alarms and audio systems, car phones and satellite navigation systems. In buses or taxicabs, the may fit ticket and money machines. Some work on one type of vehicle. This may be light vehicles such as cars, vans and motorcycles, or heavy vehicles such as lorries, buses and coaches. Some electricians work on one make of vehicle.

Work Details
Usually work around 39 hrs a week with the possibility of overtime, including weekends. There may be shift work and in some companies, for example breakdown companies, you may have to be on call. The work is usually indoors, although workshop doors are large and normally left open. Workshops can be cold and noisy. Sometimes auto-electricians deal with breakdowns at the roadside. You have to be able to work quickly to find and repair problems so that vehicles can go back on the road as quickly as possible.

You need to be fit enough to be able to bend, kneel and stretch in quite awkward positions. You also have to lift mechanical parts out of the way and some of these are heavy. Working with cars is dirty and oily and this can cause skin problems, so auto electricians use barrier creams for protection.

Qualification

• England, Wales and Northern Ireland
Band 2: For some training programmes and entry to jobs: no minimum qualifications are needed, but it is an advantage to have some GCSEs (A*-C), including maths, English and a science, preferably physics, or equivalent. Practical and technology subjects are also useful.

Band 3: For entry to jobs, HNC or a relevant Diploma: usually at least 4 GCSEs (A*-C) including English, maths, a science (preferably physics), or technology or an engineering subject, or equivalent.

• Scotland
Band 2: Although academic qualifications are not specified for this job, for some training programmes: a few S grades (1-3), including maths, English and a science, preferably physics, or similar. Craft, design and technological studies are also useful.

Band 3: For entry to jobs, usually at least four S grades (1-3) including English, maths, a science (preferably physics), or a technology or engineering subject, or similar.

Adult Qualifications
It is possible for those over 21 to enter some courses without the required academic qualifications.

Work Experience
Relevant work or voluntary experience is always useful and it can add to your CV and improve your chances when applying for entry to jobs or apprenticeships in the engineering industry. Any relevant experience in electrical work and the ability to follow circuit diagrams is an advantage.

Entry and Training

Many trainees start on a training programme or apprenticeship at age 16-19. You usually train on the job, working with an experienced person, together with a local college course through either day or block release. Most work towards S/NVQs in vehicle maintenance and repair at levels 2-3. Level 2-3 diplomas in auto electrical and mobile electrical competence are also available. You can also study full/part time for a City & Guilds, or a BTEC/SQA award, prior to starting work or while in employment. This job may require a driving licence and you may have to pass a practical aptitude entrance test. National training providers of apprenticeships and automotive training include the training arm of the Retail Motor Industry Federation, remit, and Thatcham. See their websites for details.

The Institute of the Motor Industry (IMI) also offers nationally recognised vocationally related qualifications (VRQs) at levels 1-3 for those wishing to progress to technician level and onto higher education. VRQs at level 1 are also available as a pre-apprenticeship programme for school pupils aged 14-16 and provide the opportunity to 'fast track' onto higher level motor industry qualifications. Visit the Institute of the Motor Industry website for further career information and qualification routes.

A Diploma/Welsh Baccalaureate may be available in your area in engineering with automative specialist learning. Students complete the core compulsory units of a standard engineering diploma but also cover the foundation skills and knowledge required for working in the vehicle repair and maintenance sector. See the diplomas website for further information.

Relevant experience in electrical work and the ability to follow circuit diagrams is an advantage. Evidence of practical skill such as servicing your own car is helpful. Government training opportunities, such as apprenticeships, may be available in your area. You can also gain recognition of previous experience through Accreditation of Prior Learning (APL) or by working towards relevant S/NVQs. Contact your local careers office, Jobcentre Plus, Next Step service or Learning and Skills Council (LSC) Local Enterprise Company (LEC) for details of training schemes.

Opportunities and Pay

Employers include garages, specialist firms, transport companies, road haulage companies, local authorities, gas, electricity and water companies, or any other large firm with a lot of vehicles. Most auto electricians specialise, perhaps in cars or in a particular make of car, or in working with lorries or buses and coaches. There is a steady demand for skilled auto electricians. There are promotion prospects in larger companies, for example to supervisor or head of the servicing department. With experience and qualifications you can become self-employed.

Pay varies depending on location and employer. As an apprentice or trainee auto electrician you can earn around £8k-£12k a year. Qualified auto electricians generally earn around £14k-£17k and once experienced, £18k-£25k.

Health

You must have normal colour vision. You need to be physically fit with good stamina.

Skills and Qualities

able to follow drawings and plans, able to follow instructions, able to take responsibility, aptitude for teamwork, attention to detail, good communication skills, logical, manual dexterity, methodical, self-reliant

Relevant Subjects

Design and technology, Engineering, Mathematics, Physics, Science

Further Information

Apprenticeship Schemes (National Apprenticeship Service) - www.apprenticeships.org.uk

Autocity (IMI) - http://autocity.org.uk

Diplomas (Foundation, Higher and Advanced) - http://yp.direct.gov.uk/diplomas

Institute of the Motor Industry (IMI) - sector skills council for the motor industry - www.motor.org.uk

Motor Industry Magazine (monthly) (Institute of the Motor Industry (IMI)) - www.motor.org.uk/magazine/index.html

remit - www.remit.co.uk

SEMTA - sector skills council for science, engineering and manufacturing technologies - www.semta.org.uk

Thatcham - www.thatcham.org

Training Schemes - www.direct.gov.uk/en/educationandlearning

Addresses

Retail Motor Industry Federation (RMIF)
210 Great Portland Street, London W1W 5AB
Phone: +44 (0)20 7580 9122
Web: www.rmif.co.uk

Scottish Motor Trade Association
Palmerston House, 10 The Loan, South Queensferry EH30 9NS
Phone: +44 (0)131 331 5510
Web: www.smta.co.uk

Transport Training Services (TTS)
15 Dundrod Road, Nutts Corner, Crumlin, Co Antrim BT29 4SS
Phone: +44 (0)28 9082 5653
Web: www.transport-training.co.uk

Similar Jobs

Electrician, Engineer: Automotive, Mechanic: Motorcycle, Vehicle Breakdown Engineer, Vehicle Mechanic/Motor Vehicle Technician

Electricity Distribution Worker

also known as: Cable Jointer, Electrical Fitter, Overhead Linesman

CRCI:Engineering
CLCI:RAN Job Band: 1 to 3

Job Description

Electricity distribution workers install and maintain the equipment and machinery that supplies electricity to industrial, commercial and domestic premises. Power is supplied through overhead lines and underground cables. This job is divided into three distinct areas; cable jointers, overhead lineworkers or electrical fitters.

Cable jointers work on the underground electricity supply cables that connect to the central generating system and overhead lines. Responsibilities include maintenance of the connections, fault detection and overall repairs. Overhead lineworkers build, install and repair overhead lines that are supported by wooden poles and steel pylons. Work is often from harnesses, and ladders are used when lines and circuits are tested. Electrical fitters install and repair generating equipment such as transformers and switchgears and also install electricity meters. Work can be indoors or outdoors.

In all branches of this work, you work with other engineers to solve problems and may refer to drawings to complete an installation or carry out repairs. You may also be responsible for the maintenance of other substation equipment such as compressors or batteries.

Work Details

Usually work a basic 37-40 hr week, Monday to Friday, but may have to do paid overtime to get a job finished. You take turns on a stand-by rota for call out to emergencies at night, weekends or during bank holidays. Some of the work is outdoors in all weathers. It is physically demanding and dirty work, and may involve working in tight spaces or at heights. You usually work in teams of two or three.

Health and safety is important as you are working with materials and equipment that can cause serious injuries. You wear protective clothing provided by the employer such as high-visibility jackets, fireproof trousers, thick gloves, kneepads and insulated boots with rubber soles.

Qualification

- **England, Wales and Northern Ireland**

Band 1: For entry to jobs, no minimum qualifications are needed, but you are expected to have a good level of general education and relevant experience. Some formal/vocational qualifications at any level are useful.

Band 2: For entry to jobs, no minimum qualifications are needed, but it is an advantage to have some GCSEs (A*-C) or equivalent in subjects that include English and maths.

Band 3: For entry to jobs, HNC or a relevant Diploma, usually at least 4 GCSEs (A*-C) including English and maths, or equivalent.

- **Scotland**

Band 1: For entry to jobs, no minimum qualifications are needed, but you are expected to have a good level of general education and relevant experience. Some formal/vocational qualifications at any level are useful.

Band 2: Although academic qualifications are not specified for this job, it is an advantage to have some S grades (1-3) in subjects that include English and maths, or similar.

Band 3: For entry to jobs, usually at least four S grades (1-3) including English and maths, or similar.

Adult Qualifications

Mature entrants with relevant work experience may be accepted for college courses without meeting any formal entry requirements. You can improve your skills and qualifications by working through the Foundation Learning programme. This involves taking credit-based units and qualifications to help you progress.

Work Experience

Work experience helps you find out what you enjoy and do not enjoy about a job, as well as the opportunity to acquire new skills. It also provides valuable information to add to your CV and improves your future employment prospects. Paid or voluntary work outdoors, where you use machinery or do building or engineering work, may be useful.

Entry and Training

You can enter this work with no formal qualifications, although you need a good standard of general education. Alternatively, you can enter through an electricity industry apprenticeship scheme. Training is largely on the job, under the supervision of experienced workers, with day or block release to attend courses at colleges, or with training providers.

You can work for a diploma in electrical power metering or current/voltage transformer metering. S/NVQs are available at levels 2 and 3 in overhead lines, substation plant or underground cables. Apprenticeships in plant maintenance leading to level 2 and advanced apprenticeships leading to level 3 qualifications may be available in your area. Those with level 3 qualifications can apply for a HNC in engineering programme, many of which are run as distance learning courses.

Many of the major energy suppliers run their own trainee engineering schemes. For example, Scottish and Southern Energy run apprenticeships in mechanical and electrical fitting, overhead lines construction, maintenance and refurbishment and cable jointing in the north of Scotland and south of England. Training lasts 3-4 years. Scottish Power, E.ON and EDF offer similar training opportunities. Visit the Energy and Utility Skills website for details of training providers in your area.

The National Grid runs apprenticeships in overhead lines and substations. Once you successfully complete the apprenticeship, you transfer to a permanent craftsperson role. There is opportunity to progress as the National Grid runs a foundation engineer programme. To be eligible for this training programme you must have a diploma or HNC/HND in electrical, electronic or mechanical engineering.

AFAQ-ETA supports the professional training needs of electricity utility companies through the provision of a series of open learning courses. Distribution workers can study the high voltage safety and power system protection courses in modular format. The website of the Energy Networks Association has details on careers, industry information and listings of member companies.

Through continuing professional development or further training, it is possible to progress to supervisory or managerial positions. Safety awareness is very important in this job and health and safety training is provided. See the Energy and Utilities Skills Register for details of the Basic Electrical Safety Competence Scheme, which is an essential requirement in most jobs.

A Diploma/Welsh Baccalaureate may be available in your area in engineering. With a foundation diploma, you can apply for a level 2 apprenticeship programme. Those with an advanced diploma can enter an advanced apprenticeship or can apply for a foundation degree, such as the one offered by the National Grid.

Employers may look for evidence of relevant skills or experience in areas such as engineering, building services engineering, electrical or construction work.

Government training opportunities, such as apprenticeships for adults, may be available in your area. You can also gain recognition of previous experience through Accreditation of Prior Learning (APL) or by working towards relevant S/NVQs. Contact your local careers office, Jobcentre Plus, Next Step service or Learning and Skills Council (LSC)/Local Enterprise Company (LEC) for details of training schemes.

The Scottish Electrical Charitable Trust (SECTT) runs an adult training scheme for electricians. Candidates must be over 22 and no previous experience is necessary. Contact SECTT for full details.

Opportunities and Pay

There are over 75,000 people employed in the UK power industry. There are over 2,000 power stations in operation and work is available with regional electricity companies or large electrical contractors. You can contact your local electricity supplier directly to find out about job opportunities. There are also a number of specialist employment agencies that deal specifically with recruitment in this sector. This is a growth area, particularly in the area of renewable energy generation and developments in technologies. There is currently a shortage of skilled workers.

Apprentices earn an initial salary of £11k-£19k a year. Qualified distribution workers can earn in the region of £30k a year. With significant experience and responsibility you can earn up to £45k a year.

Health

You must have normal colour vision to work with electrical wiring. You need to be fit as this work can be physically demanding.

Skills and Qualities

able to work both on your own and in a team, able to work in confined spaces, attention to detail, enjoy working outdoors, good communication skills, head for heights, manual dexterity, mechanical skills, problem-solving skills, safety conscious

Relevant Subjects

Construction and built environment, Design and technology, Engineering, Mathematics, Physics, Science

Further Information

AFAQ-ETA - www.afaq-eta.com

AGCAS: Energy & Utilities (Job Sector briefing) (AGCAS) - www.prospects.ac.uk

Apprenticeship Schemes (National Apprenticeship Service) - www.apprenticeships.org.uk

Apprenticeships in Scotland (Careers Info Scotland) - www.apprenticeshipsinscotland.com/about/

Diplomas (Foundation, Higher and Advanced) - http://yp.direct.gov.uk/diplomas

e.on - www.eon-uk.com

EDF - www.edfenergy.com

Energy & Utlility Skills - sector skills council for gas, power, waste management & water industries - www.euskills.co.uk

National Grid - www.nationalgrid.com

Scottish and Southern Energy (SSE) - www.scottish-southern.co.uk

Scottish Power - www.scottishpower.co.uk

Utility Week (Reed Business Info) - www.utilityweek.co.uk

Welsh Baccalaureate - www.wbq.org.uk

Addresses

Energy and Utilities Skills Register (EUSR)
Friars Gate, 1011 Stratford Road, Shirley, Solihull B90 4BN
Phone: +44 (0)845 077 9922
Web: http://eusr.co.uk

Energy Networks Association
6th Floor Dean Bradley House 52 Horseferry Road, London SW1P 2AF
Phone: +44 (0) 20 7706 5100
Web: http://2010.energynetworks.org/

Engineering Council
246 High Holborn, London WC1V 7EX
Phone: +44 (0)20 3206 0500
Web: www.engc.org.uk

Scottish Electrical Charitable Training Trust (SECTT)
The Walled Garden, Bush Estate, Midlothian EH26 0SE
Phone: +44 (0)131 445 5659
Web: www.sectt.org.uk

Similar Jobs

Electrical Engineering Technician, Electrician, Electricity Generation Worker, Engineering Machine Operative, Gas Distribution Worker, Telecommunications Technician

Electricity Generation Worker

CRCI:Engineering
CLCI:RAN
Job Band: 1 to 3

Job Description

Electricity generation workers look after the equipment used to generate electricity, including the installation of machinery, day-to-day operations and carrying out any maintenance when the machinery malfunctions. Machinery can include waste heat recovery boilers, steam turbines, compressors, pumps and transformers. Generating stations are fuelled by gas, coal or nuclear energy. Increasingly, generating stations are using renewable energy.

They work with automated systems that control the instrumentation used in the running of the plant. Routine testing is carried out to keep the machines in good working order. Contingency plans must be in place in case of an emergency as machines may need to be shut down quickly. Once the machine is shut down, any fault must be identified and repaired as quickly as possible to minimise interuption to service. Strict safety procedures must be followed at all times.

Work Details

Usually work a 37-40 hr week, Monday to Friday but you may have to do paid overtime to get a job finished. Some jobs may be planned for nights or weekends. Takes turns on a stand-by rota for call out to emergencies at night, weekends or during bank holidays. Most of the work is indoors, in powerstations. The work environment can be a clean, light control room where you operate machinery remotely or it can be a noisy plant room where you work on the shop floor. At times, you may have to work in cramped positions. You may work as part of a team that is responsible for the maintenance of all equipment in a plant.

Health and safety is important as you must follow strict safety procedures. You wear protective clothing provided by the employer such as high-visibility jackets, hard hats and insulated boots with rubber soles.

Qualification

- **England, Wales and Northern Ireland**

Band 1: For entry to jobs, no minimum qualifications are needed, but you are expected to have a good level of general education and relevant experience. Some formal/vocational qualifications at any level are useful.

Band 2: For entry to jobs, no minimum qualifications are needed, but it is an advantage to have some GCSEs (A*-C) or equivalent in subjects that include English and maths. Technology and science subjects are useful but not essential.

Band 3: For entry to jobs, HNC or a relevant Diploma, usually at least 4 GCSEs (A*-C) including English and maths, or equivalent.

- **Scotland**

Band 1: For entry to jobs, no minimum qualifications are needed, but you are expected to have a good level of general education and relevant experience. Some formal/vocational qualifications at any level are useful.

Band 2: Although academic qualifications are not specified for this job, it is an advantage to have some S grades (1-3) in subjects that include English and maths, or similar. Technology and science subjects are useful, but not essential.

Band 3: For entry to jobs, usually at least four S grades (1-3) including English and maths, or similar.

Adult Qualifications

If you have relevant work experience you may be accepted for college courses without meeting any formal entry requirements.

Work Experience

Work experience helps you find out what you enjoy and do not enjoy about a job, as well as the opportunity to acquire new skills. It also provides valuable information to add to your CV and improves your future employment prospects. Paid or voluntary work outdoors, where you use machinery or do building or engineering work, may be useful.

Entry and Training

You can enter this work with no formal qualifications, although you need a good standard of general education. You can apply for an apprenticeship scheme with training largely on the job, under the supervision of experienced workers and day or block release to attend courses at college.

You may work towards qualifications such as S/NVQ levels 1-3 in engineering technology operations, level 2-3 in engineering technology maintenance or a VRQ level 2 in converting biomass into fuel and wind into energy. Apprenticeships leading to level 2 and advanced apprenticeships leading to level 3 qualifications may be available in your area. Those with level 3 qualifications can apply for a HNC in engineering programme, many of which are run as distance learning courses.

Many of the major energy suppliers run their own trainee engineering schemes. For example, Scottish and Southern Energy run apprenticeships in generation which last for around four years. Candidates work towards their modern apprentice qualification completing a City & Guilds technical certificate, S/NVQ level 3 and key skills. Scottish Power, E.ON and EDF offer similar training opportunities. Visit the Energy and Utility Skills website for details of training providers in your area.

The National Grid runs an apprenticeship in substations where you learn about the maintenance of high-voltage plant and equipment in electrical substations. The work is centred around mechanical, electrical and instrumentation systems with a mechanical bias. Once you successfully complete the apprenticeship, you transfer to a permanent craftsperson role. There is opportunity to progress as the National Grid runs a foundation engineer programme. To be eligible for this training programme, you must have a diploma or HNC/HND in electrical, electronic or mechanical engineering.

Through continuing professional development or further training, it is possible to progress to supervisory or managerial positions. Safety awareness is very important in this job and health and safety training is provided. See the Energy & Utilities Skills Register for details of the Basic Electrical Safety Competence Scheme which is an essential requirement in most jobs.

AFAQ-ETA supports the professional training needs of electricity utility companies through a series of open learning courses. Generation workers can study the operating power plant systems and power induction courses in modular format. See the website for details. The website of the Energy Networks Association has details on careers, industry information and listings of member companies.

A Diploma/Welsh Baccalaureate may be available in your area in engineering. With a foundation diploma, you can apply for a level 2 apprenticeship programme. Those with an advanced diploma can enter an advanced apprenticeship or can apply for a foundation degree, such as the one offered by National Grid.

Employers may look for evidence of relevant skills or experience in areas such as engineering, building services engineering, electrical or construction work.

Government training opportunities, such as apprenticeships for adults, may be available in your area. You can also gain recognition of previous experience through Accreditation of Prior Learning (APL) or by working towards relevant S/NVQs. Contact your local careers office, Jobcentre Plus, Next Step service or Learning and Skills Council (LSC)/Local Enterprise Company (LEC) for details of training schemes.

The Scottish Electrical Charitable Trust (SECTT) runs an adult training scheme for electricians. Candidates must be over 22 and no previous experience is necessary. Contact SECTT for full details.

Opportunities and Pay

There are over 75,000 people employed in the UK power industry. There are over 2,000 power stations in operation and work is available with regional electricity companies or large electrical contractors. You can contact your local electricity supplier directly to find out about job opportunities. There are also a number of specialist employment agencies that deal specifically with recruitment in this sector. This is a growth area, particularly in the area of renewable energy generation and developments in technologies. There is currently a shortage of skilled workers.

Apprentices earn an initial salary of £11k-£15k a year, rising to £20k. Qualified generation workers can earn in the region of £25k a year. With significant experience and responsibility you can earn up to £40k a year.

Health

You need normal colour vision and should be in good health.

Skills and Qualities

able to follow drawings and plans, able to work both on your own and in a team, able to work in confined spaces, good communication skills, health & safety awareness, practical skills, problem-solving skills, responsible attitude, steady hand

Relevant Subjects

Construction and built environment, Design and technology, Engineering, Mathematics, Physics, Science

Further Information

AFAQ-ETA - www.afaq-eta.com

Apprenticeship Schemes (National Apprenticeship Service) - www.apprenticeships.org.uk

Apprenticeships in Scotland (Careers Info Scotland) - www.apprenticeshipsinscotland.com/about/

Diplomas (Foundation, Higher and Advanced) - http://yp.direct.gov.uk/diplomas

e.on - www.eon-uk.com

EDF - www.edfenergy.com

Energy & Utility Skills - sector skills council for gas, power, waste management & water industries - www.euskills.co.uk

National Grid - www.nationalgrid.com

Scottish and Southern Energy (SSE) - www.scottish-southern.co.uk

Scottish Power - www.scottishpower.co.uk

Utility Week (Reed Business Info) - www.utilityweek.co.uk

Welsh Baccalaureate - www.wbq.org.uk

Addresses

Energy and Utilities Skills Register (EUSR)
Friars Gate, 1011 Stratford Road, Shirley, Solihull B90 4BN
Phone: +44 (0)845 077 9922
Web: http://eusr.co.uk

Energy Networks Association
6th Floor Dean Bradley House 52 Horseferry Road, London SW1P 2AF
Phone: +44 (0) 20 7706 5100
Web: http://2010.energynetworks.org/

Engineering Council
246 High Holborn, London WC1V 7EX
Phone: +44 (0)20 3206 0500
Web: www.engc.org.uk

Scottish Electrical Charitable Training Trust (SECTT)
The Walled Garden, Bush Estate, Midlothian EH26 0SE
Phone: +44 (0)131 445 5659
Web: www.sectt.org.uk

Similar Jobs

Electrician, Electricity Distribution Worker, Engineer: Electrical, Gas Service Engineer, Satellite Systems Technician, Telecommunications Technician

Electronics Assembler

also known as: Electrical Assembler

CRCI:Engineering
CLCI:RAL Job Band: 1 to 2

Job Description

Electronics assemblers fit microchips and wires, or insert coloured parts to an electronic circuit board for mass-produced products. These are mainly household appliances and equipment used in industry. They may work on automotive, aeronautical, medical and scientific equipment. May also work on items such as TVs/DVDs, washing machines and computers.

Assemblers fix the part or wire by dipping it into a solder bath or by using an electric soldering iron. They follow special instructions that may include a detailed diagram or technical drawing, and a parts list. They may only add a few parts to an item as it passes down the production line to the next assembler. For some jobs, may use tweezers and microscopes or magnifiers. Assemblers are also responsible for watching the machines (which are sometimes computer controlled) and examining or testing finished pieces.

Work Details

Usually work a basic 37-40 hr week, Monday to Friday, though you may be required to work shifts or early mornings. Part-time work is available. This work involves sitting or standing for many hours, usually doing the same tasks repeatedly. If you are working with small parts, you may be given regular breaks to avoid eye strain. Your working environment is well lit and dust free as some parts need to be assembled in sterile conditions. You may need to wear safety glasses and gloves, an overall, antistatic wrist or ankle bands and perhaps something to cover your hair. Using a soldering iron can be hot work.

Qualification

- **England, Wales and Northern Ireland**

Band 1: For entry to jobs, no minimum qualifications are needed, but you are expected to have a good level of general education and relevant experience. Some formal/vocational qualifications at any level are useful.

Band 2: For entry to jobs, no minimum qualifications are needed, but it is an advantage to have some GCSEs (A*-C) or equivalent in subjects that include English, maths and a science/technology subject.

- **Scotland**

Band 1: For entry to jobs, no minimum qualifications are needed, but you are expected to have a good level of general education and relevant experience. Some formal/vocational qualifications at any level are useful.

Band 2: Although academic qualifications are not specified for this job, it is an advantage to have some S grades (1-3) in subjects that include English, maths and a science/technology subject.

Adult Qualifications

General secondary education is expected, however practical ability and personal qualities are usually more important than qualifications. You can improve your skills and qualifications by working through the Foundation Learning programme. This involves taking credit-based units and qualifications to help you progress.

Work Experience

Relevant work or voluntary experience is always useful. It can add to your CV and improve your chances when applying for entry to jobs or apprenticeships in the electronics/engineering industry.

Entry and Training

Although entry at 16 is possible, there may be restrictions on the hours you work (such as night shifts) until you are 18. To enter this job you may have to take a practical test to show that you can work well with your hands and follow written instructions and diagrams. Training is on the job through an employer's training scheme, such as an apprenticeship following a precision engineering route, and possibly also with short external courses. You may be able to obtain S/NVQs at levels 1-2 in performing manufacturing operations.

A Diploma/Welsh Baccalaureate may be available in your area in engineering. See the diplomas website for further information.

Mature entrants may be preferred by some employers, especially those with relevant experience. Government training opportunities, such as apprenticeships for adults, may be available in your area. You can also gain recognition of previous experience through Accreditation of Prior Learning (APL) or by working towards relevant S/NVQs. Contact your local careers office, Jobcentre Plus, Next Step service or Learning and Skills Council (LSC/Local Enterprise Company (LEC) for details of training schemes.

Opportunities and Pay

Employers are based throughout the UK. You can work for a firm that assembles parts for domestic appliances. Others work on scientific, medical, audio or office equipment. With experience you can progress to supervisory level or to other jobs such as quality control. There may be opportunities for part-time work.

Pay varies according to the individual employer. Starting wages for assembly workers are likely to be around £11k a year, rising to £17k-£20k with experience. Overtime pay can make up a large proportion of your earnings.

Health

This job requires good eyesight and perfect colour vision. The work may involve a risk of eyestrain. There may be an allergy risk from skin irritants and you should have no respiratory problems.

Skills and Qualities

able to follow drawings and plans, able to work quickly, aptitude for teamwork, attention to detail, careful, good concentration level, literacy and numeracy skills, manual dexterity, methodical, patient

Relevant Subjects

Manufacturing

Further Information

Apprenticeship Schemes (National Apprenticeship Service) - www.apprenticeships.org.uk
Diplomas (Foundation, Higher and Advanced) - http://yp.direct.gov.uk/diplomas
SEMTA - sector skills council for science, engineering and manufacturing technologies - www.semta.org.uk
Tomorrow's Engineers - www.tomorrowsengineers.org.uk/careers.cfm
Training Schemes - www.direct.gov.uk/en/educationandlearning
Welsh Baccalaureate - www.wbq.org.uk
Women into Science, Engineering & Construction - www.wisecampaign.org.uk

Addresses

Engineering Training Council (NI)
Interpoint, 20-24 York Street, Belfast BT15 1AQ
Phone: +44 (0)28 9032 9878
Web: www.etcni.org.uk

Scottish Engineering
Training Officer, 105 West George Street, Glasgow G2 1QL
Phone: +44 (0)141 221 3181
Web: www.scottishengineering.org.uk

Similar Jobs

Assembler: Light Industry, Computer Assembly Technician, Electrical Engineering Technician, Engineering Machine Operative, Polymer/Plastics Process Operative

Embalmer

CRCI:Personal and Other Services
CLCI:IP — Job Band: 1 to 2

Job Description

Embalmers prepare the body of a deceased person using special treatments to preserve it before burial or cremation. They use chemical and physical treatments to slow down or prevent deterioration of body tissues, and to repair any visible signs of injury. Also make sure there are no health risks for all who come into contact with the body, by using hygienic fluids and germicidal soap. They ensure the body appears as life-like and normal as possible, so that it can be viewed by the bereaved.

May restore any damage to the body caused by accidents, disease or illness with the use of wax or plaster of Paris. Also apply cosmetics to bring skin tones back to a normal shade, wash hair and may shave a man's face. Embalmers are sensitive to the feelings of the bereaved and maintain a dignified and respectful manner.

Work Details

Usually work a basic 37-39 hr week, but may need to work irregular hours and sometimes be on call. Weekend work is sometimes needed. Your work environment is cool and clean, usually an operating room at a funeral director's premises. It may be necessary to travel around the district to visit different premises.

The job involves bending and you need to lift a body, which sometimes can be heavy. You may find this work very demanding and at times, you need to cope with some unpleasant sights. Protective clothing is usually worn.

Qualification

- **England, Wales and Northern Ireland**

Band 1: Generally, no set qualifications are required for entry to this job, though applicants may find that subjects such as English, maths, biology, chemistry and art, or equivalent, are very useful.

Band 2: Employers may expect some GCSEs (A*-C) including English, maths and science, or equivalent.

- **Scotland**

Band 1: Generally, no set qualifications are required for entry to this job, though applicants may find that subjects such as English, maths, biology, chemistry and art, or similar, are very useful.

Band 2: Employers may expect some S grades (1-3) including English, maths and science, or similar.

Adult Qualifications

No set academic qualifications are required for entry to this job, though subjects such as English, maths, biology, chemistry and art, or equivalent, are very useful.

Work Experience

It is difficult to get work experience with an embalmer/funeral director because of health and safety rules, and consideration for the family of the dead person. It is useful to visit and talk to an embalmer/funeral director, to find out as much as you can about their work. You need to show a keen interest in the career of an embalmer.

Entry and Training

Entrants to this job can be straight from school, but most are older. Most entrants start as a general funeral operative and move into embalming later. There are no specific entry requirements, but entrants are interviewed and may have to take an entrance test in English and maths. Training is often in-house, being trained on the job by an experienced embalmer. Most embalmers work for qualifications awarded by the International Examinations Board of Embalmers. Study areas include anatomy, physiology, bacteriology and practical embalming. Membership of the British Institute of Embalmers (BIE) is possible on completion of exams and may be required by some employers.

Some employers offer training through accredited tutors (off site) or may be accredited trainers themselves. On average training takes from 18 months to two years part time. A driving licence is often essential for this job.

Mature entry is common and encouraged as experience of life is an advantage for this job. Experience in the funeral service, mortuary work, business or administration is useful, as well as having practical manual skills.

Opportunities and Pay

Work is available throughout the UK, with a firm or perhaps a smaller, often family-run, company. Around 1,300 qualified embalmers are BIE members but this work may be hard to get into, due to a low staff turnover. Most opportunities are in the larger towns and cities. Professional training and promotion is more likely if you work for a larger company. You may also work as a funeral director as sometimes the roles are combined. Some embalmers may specialise in working with disaster teams, dealing with the victims of train or air accidents.

Part-time work and self-employment is possible, with some embalmers working for more than one company. Overseas work is also possible.

Pay varies depending on where you work and your level of responsibility, but starting pay is likely to be around £11k, rising to £18k a year, with experience. Overtime pay is also available.

Health

You need to be fit to do this work, as there is some lifting. There is a risk of allergy to certain chemicals.

Skills and Qualities

able to work well on your own, artistic ability, attention to detail, conscientious, emotionally strong, eye for visual effect, not squeamish, sensitive, tactful, technical aptitude

Relevant Subjects

Biology, Religious studies, Science

Further Information

Funeral Service Journal (monthly) (FSJ Communications) - www.fsj.co.uk

Addresses

British Institute of Embalmers (BIE)
21c Station Road, Knowle, Solihull B93 0HL
Phone: +44 (0)1564 778 991
Web: www.bioe.org.uk

National Association of Funeral Directors (NAFD)
618 Warwick Road, Solihull, West Midlands B91 1AA
Phone: 0845 230 1343 (UK only)
Web: www.nafd.org.uk

Similar Jobs

Anatomical Pathology Technician, Beauty Therapist, Film/TV & Theatre Make-Up Artist, Funeral Director, Laboratory Assistant, Prosthetist/Orthotist

Embryologist

also known as: Clinical Embryologist

CRCI:Science, Mathematics and Statistics
CLCI:QOX Job Band: 5

Job Description

Embryologists research and investigate the scientific causes of infertility through the study of an embryo, development of a foetus (unborn child) and human birth. They identify factors that prevent reproduction to assist patients through programmes of assisted reproduction, including IVF, under medical supervision. Work closely with doctors and other clinical and biomedical scientists to treat each individual patient's condition.

They usually lead a team that includes medical technical officers and medical laboratory assistants, together with clerical and administration staff. Embryologists use a range of highly specialised and sophisticated technical equipment, including computers, and are responsible for setting and maintaining quality and performance standards of all the work done.

Work Details

Usually work a 36-38hr week, Monday to Friday, in a laboratory, university, college or hospital. Depending on your employment, you may have responsibility for setting up experiments, analysing results and presenting reports. In hospital work you provide information and advice for diagnosis and treatment of a patient. Your work requires a high degree of accuracy at all times. Sometimes the work may be pressurised and intense.

At a senior level, you may be required to supervise trainees and junior members of staff. Some embryologists wear a white coat or overall, and protective clothing, such as gloves.

Qualification

- **England, Wales and Northern Ireland**

Band 5: For degree courses: 2-3 A levels in appropriate science subjects and some GCSEs (A*-C) preferably including English, maths and sciences, or equivalent. Exact requirements depend on the degree you take.

- **Scotland**

Band 5: For a degree: 3-5 H grades in appropriate science subjects and some S grades, preferably including English, maths and sciences, or similar qualifications. Exact requirements depend on the degree you take.

Degree Information

A first or upper second class honours degree in a relevant subject is required. Most commonly acceptable are degrees in life sciences (biology, microbiology, genetics or biochemistry). Science degrees relating to medicine such as biomedical science may also be considered.

Adult Qualifications

Adults without the required qualifications but having relevant laboratory experience may be considered for some courses. Access courses may be available in some areas. It is also possible for those without the specified science qualifications to take a foundation year leading into the relevant degree. Check with universities.

Work Experience

Employers or universities may prefer candidates who have relevant work or voluntary experience such as hospital work, a relevant university department or an embryology laboratory. If it proves difficult to gain this exact experience any work with a scientific background is useful.

Entry and Training

There are two entry routes to this profession, usually following a relevant first degree. The preferred option is through a training scheme in a national training laboratory offered via the Recruitment Centre for Clinical Scientists, within the NHS. However, not all laboratories offer this form of training and a less common route is to enter training as a Grade A associate on a two-year traineeship that is part of the laboratory's staffing quota. In this case, you also carry out a proportion of the diagnostic work. Embryologists are expected to undergo a formal, nationally recognised training programme that enables them to become state registered. The Association of Clinical Embryologists (ACE) certificate programme is the only recognised route for completion of Grade A training and state registration.

Trainees need to commit to a significant amount of private study outside normal working hours. To enrol for the certificate, you must be an associate or full member of ACE and already working in an HFEA (Human Fertilisation and Embryology Authority) licensed embryology laboratory. The diploma in clinical embryology is an additional qualification for experienced embryologists and takes two years to complete. It follows the successful completion of the certificate in clinical embryology, though there are exemptions. Training and/or qualifications can lead to an MSc and provide part of the requirements for entry to the first stage of full membership of the professional body.

Continuing professional development (CPD) is expected for scientists in career grade posts. Contact the ACE for details on membership and routes to qualification, as well as the CPD programme information.

Mature applicants with experience gained in work placements are welcomed by many employers. A postgraduate MSc in embryology or diploma is available through part-time study or distance learning. The Biotechnology and Biological Sciences Research Council and Medical Research Council may offer funding for postgraduate study and research.

Opportunities and Pay

Most embryologists are employed by the NHS, but there is also work with government departments, private laboratories, cancer research establishments, pharmaceutical firms, and universities. Embryology is in a state of rapid growth and there is a corresponding increase in opportunities for trained embryologists. In contrast to other areas of clinical medical science there are a significant number of opportunities outside the NHS. There are ever increasing opportunities for work abroad.

Rates of pay vary depending on employer, but for an NHS embryologist there are bands of pay within the career structure. New entrants usually start with a salary of £23k-£32k a year. Senior clinical embryologists earn £28k-£37k a year. Salaries in the private sector are likely to be higher, particularly in some senior positions.

Health

There may be a risk of allergy from skin irritants and the work can involve the risk of infection. This job requires good colour vision for certain areas of work.

Skills and Qualities

able to report accurately, accurate, analytical skills, aptitude for teamwork, aware of legal and ethical considerations, IT skills, methodical, observant, patient, scientific approach

Relevant Subjects

Biology, Chemistry, English, Health and social care, ICT/Computer studies, Mathematics, Physics, Science

Further Information

NHS Careers (NHS Careers) - www.nhscareers.nhs.uk

The Journal of Clinical Embryology (Quarterly) (Medical Market Consultants Inc.) - www.embryologists.com/

▶Working in science (2007) (Babcock Lifeskills) - www.babcock-lifeskills.com/

Addresses

Association of Clinical Embryologists (ACE)
Kelmer Court House, 102 Sale Lane, Manchester M29 7PZ
Phone: +44 (0)161 790 2020
Web: www.embryologists.org.uk/

Biotechnology and Biological Sciences Research Council (BBSRC)
Polaris House North Star Avenue, Swindon, Wiltshire SN2 1UH
Phone: +44 (0)1793 413 200
Web: www.bbsrc.ac.uk

Human Fertilisation and Embryology Authority (HFEA)
21 Bloomsbury Street, London WC1B 3HF
Web: www.hfea.gov.uk

Medical Research Council (MRC)
20 Park Crescent, London W1B 1AL
Phone: +44 (0)20 7636 5422
Web: www.mrc.ac.uk

Queen's University
University Road, Belfast BT7 1NN
Phone: +44 (0) 28 90245133
Web: www.qub.ac.uk

Royal College of Pathologists (RCPath)
2 Carlton House Terrace, London SW1Y 5AF
Phone: +44 (0)20 7451 6700
Web: www.rcpath.org

Similar Jobs

Biochemist, Biotechnologist, Clinical Molecular Geneticist, Clinical Scientist: Medical Physicist, Cytogeneticist, Haematologist, Microbiologist, Toxicologist

Emergency Care Assistant/Ambulance Technician

also known as: Emergency Medical Technician
CRCI:Healthcare
CLCI:JOC Job Band: 2 to 3

Job Description

Emergency care assistants (ECAs) respond to 999 calls as part of an accident and emergency crew, or sometimes as a first responder to safely move and observe patients and report any changes to the paramedic. They drive a range of ambulances under emergency and non-emergency circumstances and help to transport patients safely ensuring they get to hospital in the quickest time. May also work in air ambulances or on motorcycles. ECAs liaise with and take information from carers or others at the scene.

Can use defibrillation (electric shock treatment) on a patient with heart failure, and give a range of drugs under the supervision of a paramedic. May give treatment to control bleeding, care for wounds, splint broken bones or use equipment to help patients breathe.

ECAs work as part of a larger healthcare team including doctors and control room staff as well as paramedics. All ambulance personnel have common duties which include keeping the ambulance clean and tidy with stocks of first aid equipment and other necessary supplies. Also check the petrol, tyres, water and oil, and complete log sheets.

Work Details

You are based at a local ambulance station but need to travel around an area. You work rotating shifts, including nights and weekends over a 40 hr week. Shifts cover 24 hrs a day, seven days a week, including bank and public holidays. Ambulance staff usually work in pairs, one driving the ambulance and one looking after the patient. You work with people, often the elderly, who are ill, possibly in pain and upset. Work requires coping with the sight of blood. At times, work may be upsetting and you need to be able to cope with unpleasant sights.

Your work involves bending and heavy lifting. You may need to work outside in all weathers. There is a risk of danger and possibly road accidents. You need to wear a uniform and sometimes protective clothing.

Qualification

Qualifications for entry differ according to the individual ambulance service. A good general education is usually needed to work as an emergency care assistant (ECA). Check with your local service HQ for details.

- **England, Wales and Northern Ireland**

Band 2: For entry to job: many ambulance trusts require 3 GCSEs, NVQ level 2 or equivalent qualifications and/or relevant work experience.

Band 3: For entry at emergency care assistant level: 3-5 GCSEs (A*-C) may be preferred, particularly English, maths and a science-related subject, or equivalent qualifications. Employers sometimes ask for more qualifications. Applicants for training who show an aptitude for progressing to paramedic level need at least two A levels or equivalent.

- **Scotland**

Band 2: For entry at ambulance care assistant level: it is usual to have a minimum of three S grades, which include English and a scientific or numerate subject, or similar.

Band 3: For direct entry to ambulance technician training: 3-5 S grades (1-3) including English, maths and science, but employers sometimes ask for more qualifications. Applicants for training who show an aptitude for progressing to paramedic level need at least two H levels or equivalent.

Adult Qualifications

Usually a good standard of education is required that may include some formal qualifications or equivalent. A good level of fitness is also needed.

Work Experience

Work experience gives you an insight into what you enjoy and don't enjoy about a job or working environment, as well as the opportunity to acquire new skills. It provides valuable information to add to your CV and improves your course application and future employment prospects. Visit an ambulance station to discuss the work or consider some voluntary work with the ambulance service. Any work, either paid or voluntary, that provides experience of working in a caring capacity with people is very useful. Gaining first-aid certificates and knowledge of life-saving techniques also demonstrates commitment.

Entry and Training

All entrants require a full, clean, driving licence for the classification of vehicle they are to drive and have to undergo a police check. Ambulance services in Scotland may require you to first train as an ambulance care assistant (see the job article for more information). To train directly as an emergency care assistant/ambulance technician involves an initial six to nine week course (nine weeks for ambulance technician training in Scotland), including pre-hospital emergency care in moving and handling patients, resuscitation techniques, anatomy, physiology and safe emergency driving. In Scotland many ambulance technician posts are filled through internal recruitment of ACAs but vacancies do occur for direct entry too.

Courses include assessment and written practical examinations. Successful trainees are then attached to an ambulance station where they work under the guidance of a trained supervisor for a probationary period before working unsupervised. Further experience and training can lead to qualifying as a paramedic (see job article).

Mature entrants with relevant experience or qualifications in healthcare may have an advantage. Ambulance services welcome mature entrants and for some this can be a second career. This job requires a considerable level of physical fitness.

Opportunities and Pay

Jobs are available in most towns and cities. Most posts are with the NHS, but you can also be employed by a voluntary organisation, the armed forces, or a private company. Experienced assistants/technicians may be selected for paramedic training or be promoted to supervisory and management roles. There are a few opportunities to work overseas with, for example, the voluntary service overseas (VSO).

Pay is on a nationally agreed scale and is more if overtime is worked. Salary scales vary depending on the individual ambulance trust but, generally, qualified assistants/technicians earn around £17k-£21k a year.

Health
You need to have good hearing, good eyesight and normal colour vision. This job requires a medical test on entry. The work may involve a risk of infection.

Skills and Qualities
able to cope under pressure, able to cope with emergencies, able to get on with all kinds of people, able to put people at ease, adaptable, alert, aptitude for teamwork, calm, not squeamish, quick reactions

Relevant Subjects
Biology, English, Health and social care, Science

Further Information
NHS Careers (NHS Careers) - www.nhscareers.nhs.uk

NHS Careers Scotland - www.infoscotland.com/nhs

NHS Careers Wales - www.wales.nhs.uk

What's it like to be an Emergency Nurse? (A&C Black 2009)

Addresses
Ambulance Service Network
The NHS Confederation, 3rd Floor, 29 Bressendon Place,
London SW1E 5DD
Phone: +44 (0)20 7074 3200
Web: www.nhsconfed.org/networks/ambulanceservice/

London Ambulance Service
NHS Trust Recruitment Centre, St Andrew's House,
St Andrews Way, Bow, London E3 3PA
Phone: +44 (0)20 3069 0260
Web: www.londonambulance.nhs.uk

Northern Ireland Ambulance Service (NIAS) Health and Social Care Trust
Ambulance Headquarters, Site 30 Knockbracken Healthcare Park,
Saintfield Road, Belfast BT8 8SG
Phone: +44 (0)28 9040 0999
Web: www.niamb.co.uk

Scottish Ambulance Service
National HQ, Tipperlinn Road, Edinburgh EH10 5UU
Phone: +44 (0)131 446 7000
Web: www.scottishambulance.com

Welsh Ambulance Service NHS Trust
HM Stanley Hospital, St Asaph, Denbighshire LL17 0RS
Phone: +44 (0)1745 532 900
Web: www.ambulance.wales.nhs.uk

Similar Jobs
Ambulance Care Assistant, Ambulance Paramedic, Firefighter, Nurse: Adult, Police Officer

Emergency Services Control Room Operator

also known as: Call-Handler: Emergency Services, Communications Operator, Dispatcher: Emergency Services

CRCI:Security and Armed Forces
CLCI:MAB
Job Band: 2 to 3

Job Description
Emergency services control room operators answer emergency calls from the public and decide what action the emergency service should take. Some services split this role into call-takers who note the call details and dispatchers who decide what action to take. May work for fire, ambulance, police or a search and rescue service. Help to ensure any response time standards are met. The role may also include the operation of monitoring systems including CCTV and emergency services radio. Maintaining confidentiality is essential.

Control room operators get information from the caller and record the details on a computer. They assess how serious the incident is and the best way for the service to respond. May advise the caller on what to do at the scene. Tell the caller who to contact if the call is not an emergency. They send out emergency services teams as appropriate, making best use of the resources available. May use phones, radios and computers to stay in touch with the teams as they respond to the incident.

Work Details
Usually work a 37-40 hr week, including weekends and bank holidays. Often work on a shift basis to provide 24-hr a day cover. You may work long hours on a shift, but have blocks of time off as well. Part-time work may be available. You are based in a brightly-lit control room with phones, computer and radio equipment. Sit at a desk for long periods, working at a computer and wearing a headset. You usually wear a uniform supplied by your employer.

Work alongside other operators under the guidance of a team leader or control officer. Liaise with staff from their own and other emergency services and organisations to deal with incidents. The work can be stressful. You have to make important decisions quickly and deal with people who are frightened and upset.

Qualification
Qualifications in ICT, typing skills, modern languages and public service may be useful. A first aid qualification may be an advantage.

- **England, Wales and Northern Ireland**

Band 2: Although academic qualifications are not specified for this job, it is an advantage to have some GCSEs (A*-C) in subjects that include English and maths, or a BTEC first award in public services, or equivalent.

Band 3: For entry or for a BTEC national award in public services or uniformed public services: usually at least 4 GCSEs (A*-C) including English and maths, or equivalent.

- **Scotland**

Band 2: Although academic qualifications are not specified for this job, it is an advantage to have some S grades (1-3) in subjects that include English and maths, or similar.

Band 3: For entry: employers may look for four S grades (1-3) including English, maths and science, or SVQ level 2 in public services, or similar.

Adult Qualifications
Employers look for people with the knowledge and skills that come from a good level of secondary education.

Work Experience
Experience of working with people who are upset or stressed is very useful. Paid or voluntary community or customer service or enquiry work experience is an advantage. Police forces may take on volunteer support staff. Contact your local police force to find out more.

The Duke of Edinburgh's Award helps young people develop useful skills. Police forces may run cadet schemes that provide work experience.

Entry and Training
Employers look for people with good ICT and keyboard skills. In some areas, being able to speak a second language is an advantage. Map reading skills are also useful. For the ambulance service, knowledge of medical terms is an asset. You have to pass a Criminal Records Bureau (CRB)/Disclosure Scotland check, plus a medical. For some jobs you may have to take verbal reasoning, listening or keyboard skills tests before being accepted.

Training is mostly on the job with experienced staff. You may do some in-house training courses as well. You learn how to use the equipment, prioritise calls and give advice. In the ambulance service you learn first aid as you may have to tell callers what to do before the ambulance arrives.

Mature applicants are welcome. Often adults can offer a mature outlook and emotional detachment that is an advantage in this area of work. A background in handling enquiries in a public or customer service setting is an advantage.

Opportunities and Pay

There are jobs all over the UK. Fire, ambulance, police and search and rescue services employ control room operators. You may go on to become a supervisor, team leader or manager. Some people move into different roles within the service. Others go into customer service roles elsewhere.

Control room operators and call handlers earn around £14k-£18k a year. Dispatchers, more experienced staff and supervisors may earn £17k-£26k a year or more.

Health

Good hearing and clear speech is required for this type of work. You need to pass a medical.

Skills and Qualities

able to cope under pressure, able to prioritise work, awareness of confidentiality issues, decisive, good communication skills, good concentration level, information handling skills, IT skills, sensitive

Relevant Subjects

English, ICT/Computer studies, Psychology

Further Information

Could you? Police (Home Office) - www.policecouldyou.co.uk/

Fire & Resilience - www.communities.gov.uk/fire

NHS Careers (NHS Careers) - www.nhscareers.nhs.uk

▶Working in police, fire & security (2009) (Babcock Lifeskills) - www.babcock-lifeskills.com/

Similar Jobs

Contact Centre Operator, Health Records Clerk, Police Front Office Staff, Switchboard Operator

Energy Conservation Officer/Manager

CRCI:Administration, Business and Office Work
CLCI:COZ
Job Band: 4 to 5

Job Description

Energy conservation officers make improvements to the energy efficiency of public, private and commercial premises by evaluating energy use and offering practical solutions to promote the use of renewable, sustainable energy sources. They co-ordinate the way energy is used within an organisation or community to ensure that it is efficient, reduces waste, and is in line with national and European directives on emissions. They are responsible for raising public awareness about energy conservation through publicity and education. They look at carbon management issues, emissions, energy performance, waste management and sustainable/renewable resources. Their work often leads to the implementation of new policies.

Energy conservation officers carry out a range of tasks depending on the type of organisation they work for. They may advise on strategies to help entire communities, companies or individuals. Their duties include providing energy efficiency advice and training; liaising with contractors, local organisations, council services, voluntary and community groups; carrying out energy surveys and site inspections; and obtaining statutory approvals. They draw up specifications, cost estimates, drawings, feasibility studies, tender documents and work schedules; they also analyse data and collate information. Maintaining accurate records and writing regular progress reports is an important part of this job.

It is important that energy conservation officers keep up to date with changes in legislation such as the EU energy performance directives. They often attend meetings, events and conferences.

Work Details

You work generally 9am-5pm, sometimes with flexi-time. Some evening and weekend work may be required to attend meetings and promotional events. You may have to work to deadlines or meet targets. You are based in an office but make visits to sites, landlords, local businesses, home owners or tenants, which involves some travel, so a driving licence is useful. You may be part of a team or have to work on your own.

Qualification

• England, Wales and Northern Ireland

Band 4: For HND, Diploma of Higher Education or foundation degree: 1-2 A levels and some GCSEs (A*-C) usually including English and maths, or equivalent.

Band 5: For degree courses: 2-3 A levels and some GCSEs (A*-C) usually including English and maths, or equivalent. Exact requirements depend on the degree you take.

• Scotland

Band 4: For entry to SQA higher national and professional development awards, usually 2-3 H grades and some S grades (1-3), including English and maths, or similar qualifications.

Band 5: For degree courses: 3-5 H grades and some S grades (1-3), including English and maths, or similar qualifications. Exact requirements depend on the degree you take.

Degree Information

A degree in energy engineering, environmental health, environmental sciences or management, business studies or administration, surveying, engineering, building or construction, is appropriate.

Adult Qualifications

A degree is usually required. Entry standards may be relaxed for adults applying for degree courses. Foundation courses with an environmental or energy conservation focus may be available. A relevant postgraduate qualification, and experience of managing projects and supervising others is viewed favourably.

Work Experience

Relevant experience gained through holiday or sandwich placements and voluntary work is highly advantageous. A useful way of building on your experience is to choose a dissertation or an assignment linked to an employer.

Entry and Training

This is a relatively new profession, and entry routes are developing. In the past, the role evolved within an organisation. Increasingly, with the growth of legislation, public awareness and rising energy costs, employers are creating dedicated posts. Entry to this job usually requires an appropriate degree or HND in a subject such as environmental health, environmental sciences or management, business studies or administration, surveying, engineering, building or construction. With the development of renewable and sustainable energy, specialist degrees with an energy and the environmental focus, such as energy engineering, sustainable energy and climate change, have also become available.

An understanding of the energy market and legislation surrounding energy efficiency and carbon reduction is beneficial. See the Energy Saving Trust website for useful background and further links to regional information for Scotland, Northern Ireland and Wales.

Keeping up to date with legislation, compliance and reporting requirements through training and continuous professional development is very important. It is usual to take postgraduate qualifications part time whilst in employment. A relevant postgraduate qualification, experience of initiating and managing projects and supervising others is viewed favourably, especially for management posts. There are courses in energy management, some offering work placement. Consult the Energy Institute (EI) website for lists of accredited courses, including the Level 4 qualification, training in energy management through open learning (TEMOL), the Diploma in energy management and utilisation and the recently developed European energy manager qualification. The EI has recently launched the title of Chartered Energy Manager for members or fellows of the EI, following a professional assessment.

There are also training courses dealing with the effectiveness of energy conservation strategies. The basis of many of the courses is the Building Research Establishment Environmental Assessment Method (BREEAM), developed by the BRE, which is used to assess and improve the environmental performance of buildings. Specialist software is often used in this job and training is available on the job for this.

Many officers and managers specialise in specific areas, such as environmental protection, energy consulting or sustainability.

A relevant postgraduate qualification is useful. Experience of initiating and managing projects and supervising others is also viewed favourably. Health and safety training can be helpful, but is often given once in post.

Opportunities and Pay

Although energy conservation is currently a small profession, there has been and will continue to be an expansion in the number of job opportunities as a result of government and international environmental policies. Therefore, there is competition for posts. Most energy conservation officers are employed by health trusts, housing associations, higher education institutions, utilities, charities, energy agencies, voluntary and community organisations, and in the housing or environmental health departments of local authorities. There are also opportunities in the commercial sector with retailers, supermarkets, facilities management service providers and in the construction industry.

You can work in an energy efficiency advice centre, funded partly by the Energy Saving Trust, which works closely with utilities companies and local authorities to help them deliver their energy conservation targets and raise the profile of energy efficiency. Organisations that are large users of energy are likely to have someone responsible for energy saving, sometimes as part of another job.

It is possible to find part-time opportunities, but you must keep up to date with changes in legislation. Promotion opportunities depend on the organisation and sector you are in.

Pay varies depending on the type of organisation you work for, but is in the range of £22k-£33k a year, rising with experience to £30k-£62k.

Skills and Qualities

able to explain clearly, able to work both on your own and in a team, analytical skills, confident, excellent communication skills, good organisational skills, initiative, networking skills, project management skills, specialist IT skills

Relevant Subjects

Construction and built environment, Economics, Engineering, English, Geography, ICT/Computer studies, Land and Environment, Mathematics, Science

Further Information

AGCAS: Energy & Utilities (Job Sector briefing) (AGCAS) - www.prospects.ac.uk

Association for the Conservation of Energy (ACE) - www.ukace.org/

Careers in Renewable Energy (CRE) - www.careersinrenewables.co.uk/

Energy Institute (Institute of Petroleum (IOP) - www.energyinst.org.uk

The Energy Saving Trust (EST) - www.energysavingtrust.org.uk/

Addresses

BRE
Bucknalls Lane, Watford WD25 9XX
Phone: +44 (0)1923 664000
Web: www.bre.co.uk/index.jsp

Similar Jobs

Buildings Conservation Officer, Countryside/Conservation Officer/Manager, Engineer: Energy, Facilities Manager, Recycling Officer

Engineer: Aeronautical

CRCI:Engineering
CLCI:RAC Job Band: 4 to 5

Job Description

Aeronautical engineers apply scientific and technological principles to the design, development, testing and production of machines that can fly. These can be civil and military aircraft, weapons systems, space vehicles, missiles, satellites and their components. They use a combination of aerodynamics, avionics and mechanical engineering. Most specialise in a particular area of expertise, such as structural design of airframes, navigation and control, or hydraulics. Engineers may work in research and development, production or maintenance, or be involved with aerodynamics of craft, navigation or communication equipment. Development engineers have to meet tight specifications for cost and safety as well as considering performance, strength, environmentally-friendly fuels, etc.

Aeronautical engineers can also be employed in space research (applied, practical or blue sky which is pure research), or research into other high speed transport such as hovercraft. See the Aerospace Engineer job profile for full details. They work with a range of specialised software packages and often use computer-aided design (CAD), robotics, lasers and advanced electronics. May lead teams of engineering technicians and are responsible for meeting work deadlines and keeping within a specified budget.

Work Details

Usually work around 35-40 hrs a week, Monday to Friday, but sometimes in production work may need to work shifts. Additional hours may be necessary to meet contract deadlines. In production and testing you may be on your feet for most of the time in a noisy industrial environment. There may be a risk of accidents from equipment. In design, you may spend a lot of your time in a laboratory or working at a computer.

You work in a team advising, informing and consulting with people. Travel may be required, sometimes overseas, to attend international conferences and courses on aeronautical engineering. Work can be very demanding and may involve difficult and complicated decisions.

Qualification

- **England, Wales and Northern Ireland**

Band 4: For HND, Diploma of Higher Education or foundation degree: 1-2 A levels, usually including maths, physics or a technical subject, and some GCSEs (A*-C) usually including English, maths and science, or equivalent.

Band 5: For degree courses: 2-3 A levels, usually including maths and physics, and some GCSEs (A*-C), including English and sometimes chemistry, or equivalent. Exact requirements depend on the degree you take.

- **Scotland**

Band 4: For entry to SQA higher national and professional development awards, usually 2-3 H grades, including maths and physics, and some S grades (1-3), including English, maths and science, or similar qualifications.

Band 5: For degree courses: 3-5 H grades, usually including maths and physics, and some S grades (1-3), including English .maths and sometimes chemistry, or similar qualifications. Exact requirements depend on the degree you take.

Degree Information

A degree in aeronautical/aerospace engineering or avionics is most relevant. Degrees in mechanical, electrical or electronic engineering, applied physics, mathematics, computer software or software engineering are also acceptable. A relevant postgraduate degree is desirable for pre-entry to this job. An MSc in aeronautical/aerospace engineering is most useful when a first degree is in a different subject. The Royal Aeronautical Society (RAeS) has a list of accredited degrees on its website.

Adult Qualifications

A relevant higher education qualification, usually a degree, is required, together with a postgraduate qualification. Entry requirements may be relaxed for adults applying for higher education courses and Access or foundation courses give adults without qualifications a route onto degree courses.

Work Experience

Employers and universities may prefer candidates who have relevant work or voluntary experience. Most relevant experience is with an aeronautical engineering firm or in aircraft maintenance but if this proves difficult then any area of engineering is suitable and demonstrates enthusiasm and commitment to the job. Applicants to degree courses are encouraged to apply to the 'Year in Industry' scheme for a placement in industry prior to starting their studies. Students also have an opportunity to gain work experience in industry for a year between the penultimate and final years of their degree programme. This experience enhances your job prospects on graduation.

The Engineering Education Scheme runs programmes in England, Scotland and Wales giving young people the chance to be involved in a real engineering project for six months. Students commit to two to three hours work a week and some time at university residents' workshops. This valuable experience can contribute to any future university application and counts towards the Duke of Edinburgh award skills section. Check the website for details.

Similarly, Headstart offers students a chance to experience a week at university, designing, building and testing projects. As engineering careers can be quite diverse, a week of hands on experience can be helpful when trying to decide which field of engineering you want to train in. Check the website for details.

Entry and Training

Training usually takes place following a degree which can be full time, a sandwich course, or through semester and modular courses. There are relevant postgraduate courses available. If you are employed as a technician, you can study for a HNC/HND through a part-time course or, if prior to employment, a full-time or sandwich course. Relevant industrial training, initial professional development and further responsible experience is required before becoming fully qualified. This usually leads to membership of a professional institution such as the Royal Aeronautical Society. You must also commit to continuing professional development throughout your career. The Tomorrow's Engineers website has lots of useful careers information including a route map and guide to engineering activities from primary school through to higher education. Visit the website for details.

Most aeronautical engineers aim to become professional engineers at either incorporated or chartered engineer level. Both levels involve gaining experience and you need to keep detailed records of your development. Experience is followed by a professional review and an interview. There is no requirement for a specific period of experience; demonstration of competence and commitment are the sole criteria.

Incorporated engineers (IEng) need to be qualified to HNC/HND or BEng level, followed by a further year of learning known as a Matching Section. Another route is through an apprenticeship programme leading to S/NVQ at level 4, then to HNC/HND. Foundation degrees are available in general engineering subjects and in manufacturing engineering, but need to be extended to a full degree. Chartered engineers (CEng) may qualify through an accredited course leading to an MEng degree, or a BEng (Hons) followed by an appropriate masters degree. CEng can also qualify as European engineers (Eurlng) but need to be fluent in a European language.

A Diploma/Welsh Baccalaureate in engineering may be available in your area. The advanced level is equivalent to 3.5 A levels but for some university courses, the additional and specialist learning (ASL) component of the diploma needs to include specific A levels eg maths or physics. Check entry requirements carefully.

Mature applicants may be considered by employers depending on the company requirements, as well as the qualifications and experience of the candidate. Contact the Engineering Council for details.

The Open University (OU) runs a range of engineering courses and the Institution of Engineering Designers has accredited two OU engineering qualifications for professional registration. See the website for details.

Opportunities and Pay

Jobs are only available in certain geographical areas because the aeronautical industry is not widespread. There are jobs with aircraft manufacturing companies, civil airlines and air freight operators, the armed forces, further and higher education, government research agencies, or with the Ministry of Defence. There may be opportunities abroad and many engineers choose to undertake sub-contact work. Promotion is generally better in larger organisations and may involve moving into different areas of the work.

Pay varies depending on location and the particular industry. Starting salaries for graduates are likely to be in the region of £20k-£25k, rising to £35k-£45k with experience. Some may earn up to £65k a year.

Health

This job requires normal colour vision.

Skills and Qualities

able to work both on your own and in a team, analytical skills, attention to detail, good communication skills, good organisational skills, IT skills, problem-solving skills, safety conscious, scientific approach, technical aptitude

Relevant Subjects

Chemistry, Design and technology, Engineering, English, ICT/Computer studies, Mathematics, Physics, Science

Further Information

AeroSociety Jobs - www.aerosocietyjobs.com

AGCAS: Engineering (Job Sector Briefing) (AGCAS) - www.prospects.ac.uk

Apprenticeship Schemes (National Apprenticeship Service) - www.apprenticeships.org.uk

Diplomas (Foundation, Higher and Advanced) - http://yp.direct.gov.uk/diplomas

Engineering Education Scheme - www.engineering-education.org.uk/

Engineering Education Scheme Wales - www.eesw.org.uk
Engineering Scotland (SEMTA) - www.engineeringscotland.org
Headstart Scheme - www.headstartcourses.org.uk
Open University - www.open.ac.uk
Scenta - Careers Guide, Engineering, Technology and Science (Engineering Technology Board) - www.scenta.co.uk/careers.cfm
Scottish Wider Access Programme (SWAP) - www.scottishwideraccess.org/
SEMTA - sector skills council for science, engineering and manufacturing technologies - www.semta.org.uk
So you want to work in Engineering (Wayland) - www.waylandbooks.co.uk
TARGETjobs: Engineering (GTI Specialist Publishing Ltd.) - www.groupgti.com
The Aeronautical Journal (monthly) (Royal Aeronautical Society) - www.raes.org.uk
Tomorrow's Engineers - www.tomorrowsengineers.org.uk/careers.cfm
Women into Science, Engineering & Construction - www.wisecampaign.org.uk
▶Working in space (2010) (Babcock Lifeskills) - www.babcock-lifeskills.com/
Year in Industry (Engineering Development Trust) - www.yini.org.uk
Young Engineers - www.youngeng.org/

Addresses

Engineering Council
246 High Holborn, London WC1V 7EX
Phone: +44 (0)20 3206 0500
Web: www.engc.org.uk

Engineering Training Council (NI)
Interpoint, 20-24 York Street, Belfast BT15 1AQ
Phone: +44 (0)28 9032 9878
Web: www.etcni.org.uk

Royal Aeronautical Society (RAES)
4 Hamilton Place, London W1J 7BQ
Phone: +44 (0) 20 7670 4300
Web: www.aerosociety.com

Scottish Engineering
Training Officer, 105 West George Street, Glasgow G2 1QL
Phone: +44 (0)141 221 3181
Web: www.scottishengineering.org.uk

Women into Science, Engineering & Construction (WISE)
2nd Floor Weston House, 246 High Holborn, London WC1V 7EX
Phone: +44 (0)20 3206 0408
Web: www.wisecampaign.org.uk

Similar Jobs

Aircraft Engineering Technician, Engineer: Aerospace, Engineer: Control & Instrumentation, Engineer: Mechanical, Naval Architect

Engineer: Aerospace

also known as: Astronautical Engineer

CRCI:Engineering
CLCI:RAC — Job Band: 4 to 5

Job Description

Aerospace engineers, also known as astronautical engineers, deal with the science and technology of flight in space and design, create and maintain equipment and machinery for use in space travel. This includes rockets and space launchers, broadcasting and communications satellites, manned space vehicles and planetary probes. They work in ground control centres operating and maintaining earth-orbiting satellites and remote operated vehicles in space.

Aerospace engineers are employed in a number of areas dealing with radio and digital communications and computer and software engineering. Also deal with the electrical and mechanical engineering in the construction of spacecraft, thermal engineering to maintain environmental conditions and propulsion engineering or, as it is more commonly known, rocket science! May specialise in areas such as product assurance or payload engineering.

Can work as part of a team involved in mission and system design. Carry out analysis of projects and decide what changes need to be made. May follow a project through from initial concept to launch and operations. At times, have to compile reports outlining the various stages of development and may have to deliver presentations. May have responsibility for managing performance/cost ratios and making sure a project is within budget. Need to be aware of developments in their particular field and the impact of any future developments on design and operations

Work Details

Usually works around 35-40 hours a week, Monday to Friday, but may be required to work shifts. Additional or irregular hours may be necessary to meet deadlines, especially if involved in a mission. You may spend a lot of your time in a laboratory, workshop or working in front of a computer.

You work as part of a team, advising, informing and consulting with people. Travel may be required to attend conferences and training courses. Work can be stressful during missions as rapid responses and decision making are required at these times.

Qualification

• England, Wales and Northern Ireland

Band 4: For HND, Diploma of Higher Education or foundation degree: 1-2 A levels and some GCSEs (A*-C) usually including English and maths, or equivalent.

Band 5: For degree courses: 2-3 A levels and some GCSEs (A*-C), usually including English and maths, or equivalent. Exact requirements depend on the degree you take.

• Scotland

Band 4: For entry to SQA higher national and professional development awards, usually 2-3 H grades and some S grades (1-3), including English and maths, or similar qualifications.

Band 5: For degree courses: 3-5 H grades and some S grades (1-3), including English and maths, or similar qualifications. Exact requirements depend on the degree you take.

Degree Information

A university degree or equivalent in a space-related engineering discipline, computer science, or related discipline is needed.

Adult Qualifications

A relevant higher education qualification, usually a degree, is required together with a postgraduate qualification. Entry requirements may be relaxed for adults applying for higher education courses and Access or foundation courses give adults without qualifications a route onto degree courses.

Work Experience

Employers or universities may prefer candidates who have relevant work or voluntary experience. Applicants to degree courses can apply to the Year in Industry scheme for a placement in industry prior to starting their studies. This scheme is run by the Engineering Development Trust (EDT) to encourage career choices in engineering and science. Visit their website for details on other schemes such as Headstart and the Engineering Education Scheme (England and Scotland). All schemes provide students with valuable experience which can contribute to a university application and/or enhance job prospects.

Engineer: Aerospace

Entry and Training

Training can take place following a degree in a space science related subject such as mathematics, astrophysics, physics, space or design technology and robotics. Degree courses can be full time or part time and some offer the opportunity to study abroad for a year. Relevant postgraduate courses are available. Those employed as technicians can study for a HNC/HND through a part-time course. Relevant industrial training, initial professional development and further responsible experience is required before becoming fully qualified. This usually leads to professional membership of the Royal Aeronautical Society.

Incorporated engineers (IEng) need to be qualified to HNC/HND or BEng level, followed by a further year of learning known as the Matching Section. Apprenticeship programmes can lead to S/NVQ at level 4, then to HNC/HND. Chartered engineers (CEng) may qualify through an accredited course leading to an MEng degree, or a BEng (Hons) followed by an appropriate masters degree. Chartered engineers can also qualify as European engineers (EurIng) but need to be fluent in a European language.

Specific graduate development programme (GDP) opportunities exist with companies such as Astrium. Their GDP programme runs for two years and is open to graduates with limited post graduate work experience. Similarly, the European Space Agency (ESA) offers a one year training contract to help young graduates gain valuable work experience. See the ESA website for details.

Astrium also runs an apprenticeship scheme for those seeking to enter the industry without a degree. Apprentices spend the first year of their training at full-time college and the next two years gaining hands-on work experience. You also attend college in three separate blocks over the two year period. Disciplines covered include design, manufacturing and assembly, quality assurance and cost engineering. At the end of the three years, students gain an HNC qualification which covers both mechanical and electrical elements, as well as a Modern Apprenticeship which includes NVQ 3 in engineering.

A Diploma/Welsh Baccalaureate may be available in your area in engineering. The advanced level is equivalent to 3.5 A levels but for some university courses, the additional and specialist learning component of the diploma needs to include specific A levels e.g. maths and physics. Check entry requirements carefully with the individual institutions.

The International Space School Educational Trust runs courses for teachers to help bring space science into the classroom. Check their website for details of forthcoming courses and developments in the space industry in the United States.

Depending on the company requirements as well as the qualifications and experience of the candidate, mature applicants may be considered by employers. Experience in spacecraft hardware, software or operations is advantageous. Candidates should have good computer skills

Those wishing to gain incorporated/chartered engineer status and who lack the required academic qualifications, may apply to achieve registration through the Technical Report Route. This gives applicants without post 18 academic qualifications the opportunity to demonstrate, through the writing of a technical report, that they have acquired the necessary engineering knowledge. Contact the Engineering Council for details.

Opportunities and Pay

With the launch of the UK Space Agency, there is currently a lot of excitement and optimism around the space industry. Space science and research contributes more than £6.5 billion a year to the economy and employs nearly 19,000 highly qualified people. Jobs are available in research through university-based groups or in spin out companies that deal with satellite technology and communications. There may be opportunities to work abroad and to work on a contract basis. Promotion prospects are improved in larger organisations and may involve moving into different areas of work and widening your skill set.

Pay varies depending on location and the particular industry/ employer. Starting salaries for graduates are likely to be in the region of £20k-£25k, rising to around £35k-£45k with experience. Some may earn over £50k a year

Health

This job requires normal colour vision.

Skills and Qualities

able to work both on your own and in a team, analytical skills, aptitude for maths and science, design ability, good communication skills, IT skills, planning skills, problem-solving skills, safety conscious, technical aptitude

Relevant Subjects

Chemistry, Design and technology, Engineering, English, ICT/ Computer studies, Mathematics, Physics, Science

Further Information

AGCAS: Engineering (Job Sector Briefing) (AGCAS) - www.prospects.ac.uk

Apprenticeship Schemes (National Apprenticeship Service) - www.apprenticeships.org.uk

Astrium - www.astrium.eads.net/

Diplomas (Foundation, Higher and Advanced) - http://yp.direct.gov.uk/diplomas

Engineering Development Trust - www.go4set.org.uk/EDT.html

NASA (National Aeronautics and Space Administration) - www.nasa.gov

National Space Centre Online - www.spacecentre.co.uk/

Scottish Wider Access Programme (SWAP) - www.scottishwideraccess.org/

SEMTA - sector skills council for science, engineering and manufacturing technologies - www.semta.org.uk

Space Careers - www.space-careers.com

Space School UK http://spaceschool.co.uk/

UK Space Agency - www.ukspaceagency.bis.gov.uk/default.aspx

Welsh Baccalaureate - www.wbq.org.uk

Women into Science, Engineering & Construction - www.wisecampaign.org.uk

►Working in space (2010) (Babcock Lifeskills) - www.babcock-lifeskills.com/

Addresses

British National Space Centre (BNSC)
Polaris House North Star Avenue, Swindon, Wiltshire SN2 1SZ
Phone: +44 (0)20 7215 5000
Web: http://bnsc.gov.uk

Engineering Council
246 High Holborn, London WC1V 7EX
Phone: +44 (0)20 3206 0500
Web: www.engc.org.uk

International Space School Educational Trust (ISSET)
5 Herbert Terrace, Penarth CF64 2AH
Phone: +44 (0) 2920 710295
Web: www.isset.org/

Royal Aeronautical Society (RAES)
4 Hamilton Place, London W1J 7BQ
Phone: +44 (0) 20 7670 4300
Web: www.aerosociety.com

Scottish Engineering
Training Officer, 105 West George Street, Glasgow G2 1QL
Phone: +44 (0)141 221 3181
Web: www.scottishengineering.org.uk

Women into Science, Engineering & Construction (WISE)
2nd Floor Weston House, 246 High Holborn, London WC1V 7EX
Phone: +44 (0)20 3206 0408
Web: www.wisecampaign.org.uk

Similar Jobs
Astronaut, Engineer: Aeronautical, IT Applications Developer, IT Systems Developer, Nanoscientist/Nanotechnologist

Engineer: Automotive

CRCI:Engineering
CLCI:RAX Job Band: 4 to 5

Job Description
Automotive engineers are involved in the design, testing and production of light and heavy vehicles and their components. They work in a multi-disciplinary team of experienced electrical, mechanical and manufacturing engineering craftspeople, technicians and professional engineers. If working in design, they use computer-aided design (CAD) software and draught and modelling systems for converting initial ideas into blueprints, which are used for development and testing.

Engineers may work in research and development, turning the blueprints into prototypes for testing, with the use of sophisticated and highly technological computer systems. Also analyse and interpret technical data for reports. They may have to meet tight specifications for cost and safety, as well as considering performance, strength, fuels and emissions. Some engineers may be involved with the aerodynamics of the vehicle, or computer systems involved in fuel management, etc.

If working in production, engineers plan and monitor all processes to final phase production, and oversee quality control to ensure each finished product meets the set quality standards. Automotive engineers supervise technical teams, manage projects and write reports.

Work Details
Usually work normal office hours, Monday to Friday, though engineers in production may need to work shifts. In production and testing you may be on your feet for most of the time in a noisy industrial environment, where there may be a risk of accidents from equipment. You may also work outside during testing periods. In design work, you may spend a lot of your time in a laboratory, or working in front of a computer. If involved in the motorsport industry, the work may involve travel to events overseas.

Work in a team advising, informing and consulting with people. Work can sometimes be very demanding and involve difficult and complicated decisions.

Qualification

- **England, Wales and Northern Ireland**

Band 4: For HND, Diploma of Higher Education or foundation degree: 1-2 A levels, usually maths and a science subject, and some GCSEs (A*-C) including English, maths and science, or equivalent.

Band 5: For relevant degree courses: 2-3 A levels, preferably maths and a science subject, and some GCSEs (A*-C) usually including English, maths and a science subject, or equivalent. Exact requirements depend on the degree you take.

- **Scotland**

Band 4: For entry to SQA higher national and professional development awards, usually 2-3 H grades, including maths and a science subject, and four S grades (1-3) usually including English, maths and science, or similar qualifications.

Band 5: For relevant degree courses: 3-5 H grades, preferably including maths and physics, and some S grades (1-3) usually including English and a science subject, or similar qualifications. Exact requirements depend on the degree you take.

Degree Information
Most employers require degrees in subjects that include automotive engineering, electrical/mechanical engineering, materials engineering, engineering design and general engineering. There are also degrees available in motorsport engineering. It is important to study for a professionally accredited degree to become a chartered engineer. Contact the Institution of Mechanical Engineers for a list of accredited subjects. There are also relevant accredited postgraduate degrees.

Adult Qualifications
A degree or higher national award is normally required. Course entry requirements for mature applicants with appropriate experience may be reduced. There are also Access and foundation courses leading to engineering degrees.

Work Experience
Relevant work or voluntary experience is always useful and can improve your chances in application for entry to this career/job. The types of work experience to consider include work within automotive production or manufacturing engineering itself, or in related occupations, such as mechanical engineering. Applicants to degree courses are encouraged to apply to the 'Year in Industry' Scheme for a placement in industry prior to starting their studies. Students also have an opportunity to gain work experience in industry for a year between the penultimate and final years of their degree programme. This experience enhances job prospects on graduation.

The Engineering Education Scheme, run by the Engineering Development Trust, offers programmes in England, Scotland and Wales giving young people the chance to be involved in a real engineering project for six months. Students commit to two to three hours work a week and some time at university residents' workshops. This valuable experience can contribute to any future university application and counts towards the Duke of Edinburgh award skills section. Check the website for details. Similarly, Headstart offers students a chance to experience a week at university, designing, building and testing projects. Check the website for details.

Entry and Training
Training with an employer follows a degree or BTEC/SQA higher national award. Sponsorship for degree courses is often possible. The Institution of Engineering and Technology offers undergraduate and postgraduate scholarships. Check their website for details.

Most graduates begin with a formal company training scheme that lasts 12-24 months, and which usually introduces the trainee to the different departments/sections within the company. Most join a professional body such as the Institution of Mechanical Engineers (IMechE). Relevant industrial training, initial professional development and further responsible experience are required before becoming fully qualified. You must also commit to continuing professional development throughout your career.

Most automotive engineers aim to become professional engineers at incorporated or chartered engineer level with the Engineering Council (ECUK). This involves gaining experience and keeping detailed records of your development. Experience is followed by a professional review and an interview. There is no requirement for a specific period of experience; demonstration of competence and commitment are the sole criteria. Contact ECUK for details.

Incorporated engineers (IEng) need to be qualified to HNC/HND or BEng level, followed by a further year of learning known as a Matching Section. Another route is through an apprenticeship programme leading to S/NVQ at level 4, then to HNC/HND. Foundation degrees are available in general engineering subjects, but need to be extended to a full degree. Chartered engineers (CEng) may qualify through an accredited course leading to an MEng degree, or a BEng (Hons) followed by an appropriate masters degree. Chartered engineers can also qualify as European engineers (EurIng) but need to be fluent in a European language.

The Tomorrow's Engineers website has lots of useful careers information, including a route map and guide to engineering activities from primary school through to higher education. Visit the website for details. Similarly, the Institution of Engineering Designers has information on career routes, including apprenticeships.

The Engineering Development Trust runs a range of nationwide schemes for 11-21 year olds who are interested in engineering as a career. See the website for details. A Diploma/Welsh Baccalaureate may be available in your area in engineering with automotive specialist learning. Students complete the core compulsory units of a standard engineering diploma but also cover the foundation skills and knowledge required for working in the vehicle repair and maintenance sector. Check entry requirements carefully with the individual institutions. See the diplomas website for further information.

Those with considerable experience but who lack formal qualifications may be considered for the Technical Report Route to qualify as a chartered/incorporated engineer with the Engineering Council UK (ECUK). This gives applicants without post 18 academic qualifications the opportunity to demonstrate, through the writing of a technical report that they have acquired the necessary engineering knowledge. Applicants need to be employed in a job at an equivalent grade to a chartered engineer (CEng) or incorporated engineer (IEng). Contact the professional organisation, such as the Institution of Mechanical Engineers or ECUK, for details of mature entry routes to training and registration.

Sponsorship may be available for higher education courses from the Engineering and Physical Sciences Research Council. See their website for details.

Opportunities and Pay

There are many opportunities throughout the UK, particularly with companies that offer specialist services to the automotive industry. Many companies are concentrated in the Midlands and in southern England. Employment can be with one of the large automotive engineering companies, tyre manufacturers, design houses and test laboratories, or with a smaller manufacturing components company. Other opportunities are with motor sport teams, and fuel and oil companies. Promotion opportunities are generally better in larger organisations and may involve moving into different areas of management. The Institute of the Motor Industry has details of career pathways, training, employer links and events on their website.

Pay varies depending on location, type and size of company. Typical starting salaries for graduate entrants are generally around £23k-£30k a year, rising to £35k-£40k with experience. Those with managerial responsibility can earn £45k-£60k a year.

Skills and Qualities

able to prioritise work, able to work both on your own and in a team, analytical skills, aptitude for maths and science, attention to detail, good communication skills, good interpersonal skills, good reasoning power, IT skills, logical, technical aptitude

Relevant Subjects

Chemistry, Design and technology, Engineering, English, ICT/Computer studies, Manufacturing, Mathematics, Physics, Science

Further Information

AGCAS: Engineering (Job Sector Briefing) (AGCAS) - www.prospects.ac.uk

Apprenticeship Schemes (National Apprenticeship Service) - www.apprenticeships.org.uk

Automotive Engineer (monthly) (Professional Engingineering Publishing) - www.ae-plus.com

Careers in Engineering Booklets (SEMTA) - www.semta.org.uk

Diplomas (Foundation, Higher and Advanced) - http://yp.direct.gov.uk/diplomas

Engineering Education Scheme - www.engineering-education.org.uk/

Engineering Education Scheme Wales - www.eesw.org.uk

Headstart Scheme - www.headstartcourses.org.uk

Institute of the Motor Industry (IMI) - sector skills council for the motor industry - www.motor.org.uk

Motorsport Industry Association - www.the-mia.com

SEMTA - sector skills council for science, engineering and manufacturing technologies - www.semta.org.uk

Tomorrow's Engineers - www.tomorrowsengineers.org.uk/careers.cfm

Women into Science, Engineering & Construction - www.wisecampaign.org.uk

Year in Industry (Engineering Development Trust) - www.yini.org.uk

Addresses

Engineering and Physical Sciences Research Council (EPSRC)
Polaris House North Star Avenue, Swindon, Wiltshire SN2 1ET
Phone: +44(0)1793 444 100
Web: www.epsrc.ac.uk

Engineering Council
246 High Holborn, London WC1V 7EX
Phone: +44 (0)20 3206 0500
Web: www.engc.org.uk

Engineering Development Trust (EDT)
Ridgeway, Welwyn Garden City, Hertfordshire AL7 2AA
Phone: +44 (0)1707 871520
Web: www.etrust.org.uk

Institution of Engineering and Technology (IET)
Michael Faraday House, Stevenage, Hertfordshire SG1 2AY
Phone: +44 (0)1438 313311
Web: www.theiet.org

Institution of Engineering Designers (IED)
Courtleigh, Westbury Leigh, Wiltshire BA13 3TA
Phone: +44 (0)1373 822 801
Web: www.ied.org.uk

Institution of Mechanical Engineers (IMechE)
1 Birdcage Walk, Westminster, London SW1H 9JJ
Phone: +44 (0)20 7222 7899
Web: www.imeche.org.uk

Similar Jobs

Engineer: Control & Instrumentation, Engineer: Design, Engineer: Manufacturing, Engineer: Mechanical, Fork-Lift Truck Engineer, Quality Manager

Engineer: Biomedical

also known as: Bioengineer, Clinical Engineer, Rehabilitation Engineer

CRCI:Engineering
CLCI:RAM
Job Band: 5

Job Description

Biomedical engineers apply engineering principles and techniques to medicine, healthcare and biological problems. They aim to improve lives through a combination of engineering and medicine and often work in a multi-disciplinary team on a variety of problems.

Engineers design electromedical equipment such as prosthetic devices and materials to replace, support or repair lost/damaged body parts. They may be concerned with heart surgery, joint replacements, kidney dialysis machines, robotic surgical instruments, materials for bone repair, or aids for people with disabilities. They can also work with instruments for analysis, monitoring, etc. Also test prototypes, write reports and may be involved in solving problems with manufacturing or quality. Many engineers work in research and development and some also train technical or clinical staff.

Work Details

Usually work around 35-40 hrs a week, Monday to Friday, though you may need to work longer hours at times. In research and development you work in a laboratory or a workshop and consult with medical staff and perhaps with patients. You may have to travel to different locations to conduct research. In a hospital you are more directly involved with patient care and sometimes have to cope with the sight of blood. If working in a sterile environment you may need to wear special clothing.

Qualification

- **England, Wales and Northern Ireland**

Band 5: For degree in biomedical engineering: 3 A levels, often including maths, physics and another science, and some GCSEs (A*-C) including English and possibly chemistry and biology, or equivalent. Exact requirements depend on the degree you take.

- **Scotland**

Band 5: For degree in biomedical engineering: 3-5 H grades, often including maths, physics and another science, and some S grades (1-3) including English and possibly chemistry and biology, or similar qualifications. Exact requirements depend on the degree you take.

Degree Information

There are degree courses in biomedical science/engineering, medical engineering and in biomaterial science and tissue engineering, but many entrants have degrees in electronic engineering, mechanical engineering, medical physics or physics followed by an appropriate postgraduate course. Some medical science and other engineering subjects give useful background knowledge and help entry to postgraduate courses.

Adult Qualifications

A relevant degree is usually required. For graduates in a related discipline, specialist postgraduate qualifications are available. Requirements for entry to first degree courses may be reduced for suitably experienced candidates and Access and foundation courses are also available.

Work Experience

Universities and employers may prefer candidates who have relevant work or voluntary experience. This can include working with adults or children who require specialised facilities, including speech communication aids/computer software devices or specially designed/adapted furniture or wheelchairs. Time spent in a clinical engineering department at a hospital or laboratory is also ideal. Experience shows enthusiasm and commitment and also helps you decide whether this specific career is suited to you.

Schemes such as 'A Year in Industry' enable those who expect good A levels/H grades and intend to go to university the opportunity to spend a salaried year with a company to gain valuable work experience. The Engineering Education Scheme runs programmes in England, Scotland and Wales giving young people the chance to be involved in a real engineering project for six months. Students commit to two to three hours work a week and some time at university workshops. This valuable experience can contribute to any future university application and counts towards the Duke of Edinburgh award skills section. Check the website for details.

Similarly, Headstart offers students a chance to experience a week at university, designing, building and testing projects. As engineering careers are diverse, a week of hands on experience can be helpful when students are trying to decide which field of engineering they want to train in. Check the website for details.

Entry and Training

Most entrants have a background in physics or a relevant engineering field. First degrees are mainly full time for 3-4 years but some are sandwich courses. There are specialist postgraduate courses available in biomedical or clinical engineering; the Institute of Physics and Engineering in Medicine publishes a list of accredited courses. You can also visit the Tomorrow's Engineers website for details of careers and routes in specific branches of engineering.

There is a structured training programme leading to qualification as a state registered clinical scientist with the Health Professions Council. The clinical scientist route takes four years after entry (following completion of an accredited degree or masters degree) and is usually through the Association of Clinical Scientists and the NHS. Training includes a combination of formal study and practical supervised training in different laboratories and rotation between different hospitals. Relevant industrial training, initial professional development and further experience is required before becoming fully qualified. You must also commit to continuing professional development throughout your career.

Most biomedical engineers also aim to become professional engineers at chartered engineer level. This involves gaining experience so you need to keep detailed records of your development. Experience is followed by a professional review and an interview to demonstrate you r competence and commitment. Chartered engineers (CEng) may qualify through an accredited course leading to an MEng degree, or a BEng (Hons), followed by an appropriate masters degree. CEngs can also qualify as European engineers (EurIng) but need to be fluent in a European language.

A Diploma/Welsh Baccalaureate in engineering may bc available in your area. The advanced level is equivalent to 3.5 A levels but for some university courses, the additional and specialist learning (ASL) component of the diploma needs to include specific A levels e.g maths or physics. Check entry requirements carefully.

Mature applicants are considered for training, particularly if you have relevant work experience in areas that include engineering, medicine or healthcare. Contact the Engineering Council UK for details of training routes.

The Open University (OU) runs a range of engineering courses and the Institution of Engineering Designers has accredited two OU engineering qualifications for professional registration. See the OU website for details. You may be able to receive funding for higher education from one of the larger manufacturing/engineering companies and for postgraduate study from the Engineering and Physical Sciences Research Council.

Opportunities and Pay

This is a small profession and entry is very competitive, but opportunities are expanding due to new technology. The growing ageing population is also creating greater demand for cheaper medical devices and systems. This, combined with advances in computer assisted surgery and orthopaedic engineering, mean employment prospects are good.

Employment is with hospital trusts, medical schools, university research departments, manufacturing medical equipment companies, research organisations or charities. Jobs are only available in certain cities. Promotion opportunities vary.

Pay varies according to the type of employer and location but in the NHS, a trainee earns around £23k-£26k a year, rising to around £28k-£40k a year with experience. Senior biomedical engineers in industry may earn up to £80k a year.

Health

This job may require good colour vision for certain areas of work.

Skills and Qualities
analytical skills, attention to detail, creative and imaginative flair, good communication skills, good interpersonal skills, IT skills, problem-solving skills, scientific approach, spatial awareness, technical aptitude.

Relevant Subjects
Biology, Chemistry, Design and technology, Engineering, English, Health and social care, ICT/Computer studies, Mathematics, Physics

Further Information
AGCAS: Engineering (Job Sector Briefing) (AGCAS) - www.prospects.ac.uk

Careers in Engineering Booklets (SEMTA) - www.semta.org.uk

Diplomas (Foundation, Higher and Advanced) - http://yp.direct.gov.uk/diplomas

Engineering Education Scheme - www.engineering-education.org.uk/

Engineering Education Scheme Wales - www.eesw.org.uk

Headstart Scheme - www.headstartcourses.org.uk

New Scientist (weekly) (Reed) - www.newscientist.com

NHS Careers (NHS Careers) - www.nhscareers.nhs.uk

Open University - www.open.ac.uk

Scenta - Careers Guide, Engineering, Technology and Science (Engineering Technology Board) - www.scenta.co.uk/careers.cfm

SEMTA - sector skills council for science, engineering and manufacturing technologies - www.semta.org.uk

TARGETjobs: Engineering (GTI Specialist Publishing Ltd.) - www.groupgti.com

Tomorrow's Engineers - www.tomorrowsengineers.org.uk/careers.cfm

Women into Science, Engineering & Construction - www.wisecampaign.org.uk

Year in Industry (Engineering Development Trust) - www.yini.org.uk

Addresses
Association of Clinical Scientists (ACS)
c/o Association of Clinical Biochemists, 130-132 Tooley St, London SE1 2TU
Web: www.assclinsci.org

Engineering Council
246 High Holborn, London WC1V 7EX
Phone: +44 (0)20 3206 0500
Web: www.engc.org.uk

Institute of Physics and Engineering in Medicine (IPEM)
Fairmount House, 230 Tadcaster Road, York YO24 1ES
Phone: +44 (0)1904 610 821
Web: www.ipem.ac.uk

University of Ulster
Cromore Road, Coleraine, Ulster BT52 1SA
Phone: 0870 040 0700 (UK only)
Web: www.ulster.ac.uk

Similar Jobs
Audiological Scientist, Biomedical Scientist, Clinical Scientist: Medical Physicist, Engineer: Electronics, Nanoscientist/Nanotechnologist, Prosthetist/Orthotist

Engineer: Broadcast
also known as: Broadcast Engineer, Radio Broadcast Engineer, TV Broadcast Engineer

CRCI:Media, Print and Publishing
CLCI:RAL Job Band: 4 to 5

Job Description
Broadcast engineers are responsible for the broadcast of sound and vision for TV and radio programmes and ensure that they are broadcast on time and to a high standard. They are also concerned with a wide range of advanced and sophisticated technology such as digital coding equipment, much of it computerised. They set up and maintain equipment, diagnose and repair faults in studios and on outside broadcasts. Also ensure networks, transmitters and radio links are established and effective. Engineers are involved in the research and continuing development of online internet services and of digital terrestrial TV. They may also advise on studio design, improvement of services or purchase of equipment.

Work Details
Usually work a basic 37-40 hr week, though may be required to work long and irregular hours, shifts, weekends and public holidays. Place of work is a studio or on location, where travel may be necessary over quite a wide area. You may need to regularly stay away from home.

Quick problem-solving skills and an ability to remain calm when under pressure are vital. New equipment is always being introduced, so you must be able to adapt to new techniques. On location, the work environment can sometimes be overcrowded, enclosed or uncomfortable. Work can also be pressurised at times.

Qualification
- **England, Wales and Northern Ireland**

Band 4: For HND, Diploma of Higher Education or foundation degree: 1-2 A levels, preferably maths and physics or a technical subject, and some GCSEs (A*-C) usually including English, maths and science, or equivalent.

Band 5: For degree courses: 2-3 A levels, preferably including maths and physics, and some GCSEs (A*-C) usually including English, maths and science, or equivalent. Exact requirements depend on the degree you take.

- **Scotland**

Band 4: For entry to SQA higher national and professional development awards,or direct entry to training scheme: 2-3 H grades, usually maths and physics or a technical subject, and some S grades (1-3), often including English, maths and science, or similar qualifications.

Band 5: For degree courses: 3-5 H grades, usually including maths and physics, and some S grades (1-3) often including English, maths and science, or similar qualifications. Exact requirements depend on the degree you take.

Degree Information
A degree in electronic, electrical or communication engineering is preferred but some other engineering subjects and physics may be acceptable for entry.

Adult Qualifications
A relevant qualification, such as a higher national award or a degree, or relevant work experience in engineering, is usually required. Formal entry requirements to college courses may be relaxed for mature applicants. Access or foundation courses provide those without the required qualifications a route onto degree courses.

Work Experience

Entry to this job is competitive and it is important that you try to do some relevant work or voluntary experience before applying for jobs or even degree courses. Spending time with a broadcasting company is ideal. The BBC offers work experience placements, but there can be a lengthy waiting list.

Experience in a related area of engineering is also relevant and demonstrates enthusiasm and commitment to the job. Applicants to degree courses are encouraged to apply to the 'Year in Industry' scheme for a placement in industry prior to starting their studies. Students also have an opportunity for work experience in industry for a year between the penultimate and final years of their degree programme. This experience enhances your job prospects on graduation.

The Engineering Education Scheme runs programmes in England, Scotland and Wales giving young people the chance to be involved in a real engineering project for six months. Students commit to two to three hours work a week and some time at university residents' workshops. This experience can contribute to any future university application and counts towards the Duke of Edinburgh award skills section. Check the website for details.

Similarly, Headstart offers students a chance to experience a week at university, designing, building and testing projects. A week like this can be really helpful when you are trying to decide which field of engineering you want to study and work in. Check the website for details.

Entry and Training

Most broadcasting companies provide a mixture of in-house training by practical experience and formal courses. The training pattern depends on your entry level. Training is usually after obtaining a degree or BTEC/SQA higher national award. Higher education courses can be full time, part time or sandwich courses, and include relevant foundation degrees. Relevant industrial training, initial professional development and further responsible experience are required before becoming fully qualified. You must also commit to continuing professional development throughout your career.

The British Kinematic, Sound and TV Society offers training for its members on a range of topics such as HD and broadcast technology. The BBC sometimes offers schemes for trainee engineers who have studied up to A level/H grade in maths and physics or BTEC/SQA HND in electronics, as well as a training programme for graduate engineers. The training centres are only in certain areas. Check the BBC website for placement details and registration.

Many broadcast engineers aim to become professional engineers with the Engineering Council at either incorporated or chartered engineer level. Both levels involve gaining experience and keeping detailed records of your development. Experience is followed by a professional review and an interview.

The Tomorrow's Engineers website has lots of useful careers information including a route map and guide to engineering activities from primary school through to higher education. The Engineering Development Trust also runs a range of nationwide schemes for 11-21 year olds who may be interested in engineering as a career. See the websites for details.

A Diploma/Welsh Baccalaureate may be available in your area in engineering. The advanced level is equivalent to 3.5 A levels but for some university courses, the additional and specialist learning component of the diploma needs to include specific A levels eg maths or physics so check entry requirements carefully. See the diplomas website for further information.

Mature entry is possible if you have related qualifications and experience in electronic engineering and communication equipment. It is also possible for graduates with non-relevant degrees to achieve employment and training, though you must be able to demonstrate a technological aptitude and display an active interest in the work.

The Open University (OU) runs a range of engineering courses. See their website for details.

Opportunities and Pay

Jobs are in broadcasting engineering, development or project management with a terrestrial, satellite or cable broadcasting company. Facilities houses and independent production companies are mainly located in London and the south east of England. The growth of digital broadcasting has led to increased opportunities, and there is currently a shortage of well qualified engineers. Promotion prospects depend on your willingness to travel or move to another area. With experience, there may be opportunities to become self-employed and to work on a freelance basis.

Starting salaries for trainees are likely to be in the region of £18k a year. Qualified broadcast engineers working for a large company are likely to earn between £22k-£28k, rising to £35k-£40k a year, depending on experience and level of responsibility. Senior engineers can earn around £50k a year.

Health

This job requires normal colour vision.

Skills and Qualities

able to cope under pressure, able to work quickly, attention to detail, good communication skills, good interpersonal skills, IT skills, methodical, problem-solving skills, scientific approach, technical aptitude

Relevant Subjects

Design and technology, Engineering, English, ICT/Computer studies, Mathematics, Physics, Science

Further Information

AGCAS: Engineering (Job Sector Briefing) (AGCAS) - www.prospects.ac.uk

Behind the Scenes: Television (Trotman 2009) - www.trotman.co.uk

British Kinematograph, Sound and Television Society - http://n12.orbital.net.bksts

Broadcast Engineering (Penton Media Inc.) - www.broadcastengineering.com

Broadcast Now (Emap Ltd) - www.broadcastnow.co.uk

Diplomas (Foundation, Higher and Advanced) - http://yp.direct.gov.uk/diplomas

Engineering Education Scheme - www.engineering-education.org.uk/

Engineering Scotland (SEMTA) - www.engineeringscotland.org

Headstart Scheme - www.headstartcourses.org.uk

How to get a job in Television: Build your career from Runner to Series Producer (Methuen 2009)

Image Technology (British Kinematograph, Sound and Television Society) - www.imagetechnology.info/main/

Open University - www.open.ac.uk

SEMTA - sector skills council for science, engineering and manufacturing technologies - www.semta.org.uk

Skillset - sector skills council for the creative media, fashion and textiles industries - www.skillset.org

TARGETjobs: Engineering (GTI Specialist Publishing Ltd.) - www.groupgti.com

Tomorrow's Engineers - www.tomorrowsengineers.org.uk/careers.cfm

Women into Science, Engineering & Construction - www.wisecampaign.org.uk

Year in Industry (Engineering Development Trust) - www.yini.org.uk

Addresses

BBC Recruitment Services
Recruitment BBC HR Direct, PO Box 1133, Belfast BT1 9GP
Web: www.bbc.co.uk/jobs

Engineering Council
246 High Holborn, London WC1V 7EX
Phone: +44 (0)20 3206 0500
Web: www.engc.org.uk

Engineering Development Trust (EDT)
Ridgeway, Welwyn Garden City, Hertfordshire AL7 2AA
Phone: +44 (0)1707 871520
Web: www.etrust.org.uk

Institution of Engineering and Technology (IET)
Michael Faraday House, Stevenage, Hertfordshire SG1 2AY
Phone: +44 (0)1438 313311
Web: www.theiet.org

Scottish Screen
249 West George Street, Glasgow G2 4QE
Phone: 0845 300 7300 (UK only)
Web: www.scottishscreen.com

Similar Jobs

Engineer: Control & Instrumentation, Engineer: Electronics, Engineer: Mechanical, Engineer: Telecommunications, Film/TV Camera Operator, Film/TV/Radio & Theatre Sound Recordist

Engineer: Building Services

also known as: Engineer: Environmental

CRCI:Building and Construction
CLCI:UJ Job Band: 4 to 5

Job Description

Building services engineers design services, such as power, ventilation, air conditioning, lifts and escalators, that control the working or living environment of buildings. May work with new or existing buildings. These can include offices, private homes, colleges/universities, hotels, hospitals and industrial premises. They liaise with architects, construction managers, civil engineers and surveyors to incorporate gas, electricity, water supply, air conditioning, safety systems and fire protection, telephone and computer cabling etc. into buildings.

Building services engineers prepare the design, often using computer-aided design (CAD) software. The design must be cost effective and environmentally sound. The use of environmentally friendly technologies is becoming increasingly important. Engineers ensure the design also meets the required health and safety rules. They estimate the costs, put work and supply of goods out to tender and negotiate contracts. Overseeing the installation and monitoring the operation of the system is an important part of the job.

Work Details

Building services engineers usually work a basic 40 hr week, Monday to Friday, but may do weekend or evening work if required. Travel to different sites is necessary, perhaps throughout the UK or sometimes abroad. Discussing requirements with your clients as well as professional colleagues is central to the job. You are responsible for checking the progress of work and ensuring that all services are correctly installed and working. You may also be involved in maintenance work. When visiting sites you need to wear a safety helmet and boots.

Qualification

• England, Wales and Northern Ireland

Band 4: For BTEC higher national award: two A levels, usually maths and physics, and some GCSEs (A*-C) often including English, maths and science, or equivalent.

Band 5: For relevant degree: 2-3 A levels, preferably maths and physics, and some GCSEs (A*-C) usually including English, or equivalent. Exact requirements depend on the degree you take.

• Scotland

Band 4: For SQA higher national award: at least two H grades, usually maths and physics, and some S grades (1-3) often including English, maths and science, or similar qualifications.

Band 5: For relevant degree: 3-5 H grades, preferably maths and physics, and some S grades (1-3) usually including English, or similar qualifications. Exact requirements depend on the degree you take.

Degree Information

Chartered Institution of Building Services Engineers (CIBSE) and the Engineering Council UK accredited degrees include building services engineering, building environment engineering, environmental engineering, architectural engineering and building design engineering. Electrical, mechanical, electronic or systems control engineering may also be acceptable; check with the CIBSE. Relevant accredited postgraduate courses are available, including sustainable environmental design, environmental engineering and facility and environmental management.

Adult Qualifications

Colleges and universities often have special entry standards for adults applying for degree and higher national courses; contact individual universities or colleges. Access and foundation courses to higher education include engineering. Relevant Open University degrees are also available.

Work Experience

Relevant work or voluntary experience is always useful and can improve your chances in application for entry to this job. The types of work experience to consider are with a construction company, an architect's practice or with a civil engineering company. Applicants to degree courses are encouraged to apply to the Year in Industry Scheme for a placement in industry prior to starting their studies. The Engineering Education Scheme in England and Scotland links year 12 students with local companies to work on real engineering problems. A similar scheme operates in Wales.

Students also have an opportunity to gain work experience in industry for a year between the penultimate and final years of their degree programme. This experience enhances your job prospects on graduation.

Entry and Training

An engineering or technology degree is required and you need an accredited master of engineering (MEng) degree to become a chartered engineer. A BEng (Hons) degree leads to incorporated engineer (IEng) status. There are alternatives to accredited degrees, such as an Open University degree, Engineering Council examinations, cognate degrees (such as maths, physics or chemistry) plus relevant experience. Appropriate foundation degrees are also available, which can be studied full or part time. S/NVQs at level 5 in construction project management and in built environment design and consultancy are also possible.

Membership of the Chartered Institution of Building Services Engineers (CIBSE) is obtained through a combination of academic qualifications and practical experience. It may be possible to be sponsored by an employer. Relevant industrial training, initial professional development and further responsible experience are also required before becoming fully qualified. Once accepted as a Member of CIBSE you can apply for registration as a Chartered Engineer (CEng) with the Engineering Council. Throughout your career you must commit to continuing professional development. CIBSE can assist with this.

Training programmes, including apprenticeship schemes, may be available in your area for entry to this job at building services engineering technician level. Advanced apprenticeships leading to qualification at level 3 can also be a route into higher education. There are also HNC/HND qualifications in building services engineering.

A Diploma/Welsh Baccalaureate may be available in your area in construction and the built environment. The advanced level is equivalent to 3.5 A levels but for some university courses, the additional and specialist learning (ASL) component of the diploma needs to include specific A levels eg maths or physics. Check entry requirements carefully with the individual institutions.

Mature entrants may have difficulty in finding employment unless they have previous relevant experience or relevant qualifications. There is a Technical Report Route (TRR) offered by the Chartered Institution of Building Services Engineers (CIBSE) for those who wish to gain chartered engineer status (CEng) but who do not have the required formal academic qualifications. Applicants without the appropriate qualifications are therefore expected to have considerable relevant experience of at least 15 years; those with an accredited HNC/HND at least 10 years. There are also options for CEng status for those who are existing associate members of the CIBSE, including the TRR.

The Open University also offers an MEng degree course and there are other options of flexible or distance-learning courses. Contact CIBSE for details of all options for qualification as a building services engineer.

Opportunities and Pay

Work is located throughout the UK. Most employment is through the construction industry, such as within building firms, architects' practices, design consultancies and civil engineering companies. Some work for equipment manufacturers, NHS Trusts, power stations and local authorities. Availability of work depends to some extent on activity in the building trade and the national economy. Currently there is a downturn in the housing market which means there may be a shortage of vacancies for building services engineers.

Some people are in private practice, working on short-term contracts or as consultants. It is possible to specialise, for example in design, energy management, public health engineering or acoustics. Building services engineers are increasingly more involved with environmental issues, such as pollution and conserving energy.

Depending on the size and location of the firm, a graduate entrant can expect a starting salary in the region of £20k-£26k a year. A chartered building services engineer earns around £36k-£50k, and some senior managers may earn more than £70k a year.

Skills and Qualities

able to communicate effectively, able to cope under pressure, aptitude for teamwork, attention to detail, good coordinator, planning skills, problem-solving skills, safety conscious, specialist IT skills, technical aptitude

Relevant Subjects

Chemistry, Construction and built environment, Design and technology, Engineering, English, ICT/Computer studies, Mathematics, Physics, Science

Further Information

AGCAS: Engineering (Job Sector Briefing) (AGCAS) - www.prospects.ac.uk

Apprenticeship Schemes (National Apprenticeship Service) - www.apprenticeships.org.uk

Building Services & Environmental Engineer (monthly) (BSEE) - www.bsee.co.uk/

ConstructionSkills - sector skills council for the construction industry - www.cskills.org

Diplomas (Foundation, Higher and Advanced) - http://yp.direct.gov.uk/diplomas

Engineering Education Scheme - www.engineering-education.org.uk/

Engineering Education Scheme Wales - www.eesw.org.uk

Open University - www.open.ac.uk

SEMTA - sector skills council for science, engineering and manufacturing technologies - www.semta.org.uk

Summitskills - sector skills council for building services engineering - www.summitskills.org.uk

TARGETjobs: Construction & Building Services (GTI Specialist Publishers Ltd) - www.groupgti.com

Welsh Baccalaureate - www.wbq.org.uk

▶Working in construction & the built environment (2007) (Babcock Lifeskills) - www.babcock-lifeskills.com/

Year in Industry (Engineering Development Trust) - www.yini.org.uk

Addresses

Association for Consultancy and Engineering (ACE)
Alliance House, 12 Caxton Street, London SW1H 0QL
Phone: +44 (0)20 7222 6557
Web: www.acenet.co.uk

Building Engineering Services Training
The Priory, Stomp Road, Burnham, Bucks SL1 7LW
Phone: +44 (0)1628 607800
Web: www.best-ltd.co.uk

Chartered Institution of Building Services Engineers (CIBSE)
222 Balham High Road, Balham, London SW12 9BS
Phone: +44 (0)20 8675 5211
Web: www.cibse.org

Engineering Council
246 High Holborn, London WC1V 7EX
Phone: +44 (0)20 3206 0500
Web: www.engc.org.uk

Society of Environmental Engineers
The Manor House, High Street, Buntingford,
Hertfordshire SG9 9AB
Phone: +44 (0)1763 271209
Web: www.environmental.org.uk

Women into Science, Engineering & Construction (WISE)
2nd Floor Weston House, 246 High Holborn, London WC1V 7EX
Phone: +44 (0)20 3206 0408
Web: www.wisecampaign.org.uk

Similar Jobs

Engineer: Civil/Structural, Engineer: Electrical, Engineer: Fire, Engineer: Mechanical, Engineer: Municipal, Surveyor: Building Control

Engineer: Chemical

also known as: Process Engineer: Chemical
CRCI:Engineering
CLCI:RAG — Job Band: 4 to 5

Job Description

Chemical engineers are involved in the design, construction and operation of large scale manufacturing processes for producing the chemicals we use in everyday life. They work in research, design, planning, commissioning, installation, operation and maintenance of industrial plants that produce a variety of materials. These include petrochemicals, fertilisers, cosmetics, fuels, plastics, dyes, pharmaceuticals and paper. May specialise in research in areas such as plant design, tissue engineering, pollution control, molecular recognition, water and waste treatment, or energy management, including nuclear energy management. Engineers ensure that all the processes used are safe and cost effective.

Engineer: Chemical

Work Details

Usually work a basic 37-40 hr week, Monday to Friday, in an office, a laboratory or on site at a processing plant. In process work you may be expected to work shifts or be on call. You are responsible for safety and efficient production. In research work you are mainly in a laboratory testing designs or in small-scale process plants. Work is possible abroad in exploration or processing sites, requiring long periods away from home.

The work environment can be noisy and dirty but depends on the kind of product. In some places you need to wear protective clothing, special footwear and a helmet. There can be a risk of exposure to harmful substances and accidents from equipment.

Qualification

• England, Wales and Northern Ireland

Band 4: For HND, Diploma of Higher Education or foundation degree: 1-2 A levels, preferably maths, chemistry or physics, and some GCSEs (A*-C) usually including English, maths and science, or equivalent.

Band 5: For degree courses: 2-3 A levels, usually maths, chemistry and physics, and some GCSEs (A*-C) including English, or equivalent. Exact requirements depend on the degree you take.

• Scotland

Band 4: For entry to SQA higher national and professional development awards: 2-3 H grades, usually maths, chemistry or physics, and some S grades (1-3), including English, maths and science, or similar qualifications.

Band 5: For degree courses: 3-5 H grades, usually maths, chemistry and physics, and some S grades (1-3) including English, or similar qualifications. Exact requirements depend on the degree you take.

Degree Information

Relevant degrees include either BEng or MEng in chemical engineering, biochemical engineering, environmental engineering, nuclear engineering, or a degree in subjects such as applied chemistry, chemistry, or polymer science/technology. Many graduates continue on to a relevant Masters degree.

Adult Qualifications

A higher education qualification, usually a degree or higher national award, is usually required. Mature entrants who do not have the required entry qualifications may be able to enter higher education via an Access or foundation course. Experience in a relevant field is an advantage.

Work Experience

Employers and universities may prefer candidates who have relevant work or voluntary experience, ideally with a chemical engineering company. If this proves difficult then any area of engineering is relevant and demonstrates enthusiasm and commitment to the job. Similarly, work involving experience in a laboratory or with computers is helpful. If you expect good A levels/ H grades and intend to go to university, schemes such as 'A Year in Industry' provide the opportunity to spend a salaried year with a company to gain valuable work experience.

The Engineering Education Scheme runs programmes in England, Scotland and Wales giving young people the chance to be involved in a real engineering project for six months. Students commit to two to three hours work a week and some time at university residents' workshops. This experience can contribute to any future university application and counts towards the Duke of Edinburgh award skills section. Check the website for details.

Similarly, Headstart offers students a chance to experience a week at university, designing, building and testing projects. As engineering careers can be quite diverse, a week of hands on experience such as this can be really helpful when students are trying to decide which field of engineering they want to train in. Check the website for details.

Entry and Training

Entrants are almost always graduates. Training takes place after obtaining a degree and often after a postgraduate qualification. A few entrants have BTEC/SQA higher national diplomas, but they usually enter at technician grade level. Higher education courses are mainly full time, but there are some sandwich courses available. There are good opportunities for sponsorship on these courses. The website of the Institution of Chemical Engineers (IChemE) has details of all accredited courses.

The Tomorrow's Engineers website has lots of useful careers information including a route map and guide to engineering activities from primary school through to higher education. The Engineering Development Trust also runs a range of nationwide schemes for 11-21 year olds who may be interested in engineering as a career. See the websites for details.

Entrants often train through graduate training schemes and are usually expected to join the IChemE. Relevant industrial training, initial professional development and further responsible experience is required before becoming fully qualified. The IChemE has details of companies that run accredited training schemes. You must also commit to continuing professional development throughout your career.

Most chemical engineers aim to become professional engineers at incorporated or chartered engineer level with the Engineering Council. This involves gaining experience and keeping detailed records of your development. Experience is followed by a professional review and an interview.

Incorporated engineers (IEng) need to be qualified to HNC/HND or BEng level, followed by a further year of learning known as a Matching Section. Another route is through an apprenticeship programme leading to S/NVQ at level 4, then to HNC/HND. Foundation degrees are available in general engineering subjects, but you need to then extend to a full degree. Chartered engineers (CEng) may qualify through an accredited course leading to an MEng degree, or a BEng (Hons) followed by an appropriate masters degree. Chartered engineers can also qualify as European engineers (EurIng) but need to be fluent in a European language.

A Diploma/Welsh Baccalaureate may be available in your area in engineering. The advanced level is equivalent to 3.5 A levels but for some university courses, the additional and specialist learning (ASL) component of the diploma needs to include specific A levels eg maths or physics so check entry requirements carefully. See the diplomas website for further information.

Mature applicants are welcomed by employers and college courses are available for all ages. Your success depends on company requirements, and your qualifications and experience.

The Open University (OU) runs a range of engineering courses. See the OU website for details. You may also be able to receive funding for higher education from one of the larger manufacturing/ engineering companies and for postgraduate study from the Engineering and Physical Sciences Research Council.

Opportunities and Pay

There is usually a steady demand for qualified staff in the UK and abroad, particularly with the increased emphasis on sustainability. Employment is with the extremely wide and varied chemical industry and allied products field. There are good opportunities in central government and its agencies, tissue engineering, the oil, gas and water industry and increasingly, with engineering contract companies that design and construct production plant. Promotion opportunities to senior posts in management are quite good.

Starting salaries for graduate entrants are around £26k a year, rising to around £33k with experience. Average salaries for chemical engineers are around £47k a year. Engineers with chartered status can earn up to £70k a year.

Health
There is an allergy risk from chemicals. Normal colour vision may be needed for certain areas of work.

Skills and Qualities
able to take responsibility, able to work both on your own and in a team, analytical skills, careful, good communication skills, good interpersonal skills, health & safety awareness, IT skills, problem-solving skills, scientific approach

Relevant Subjects
Chemistry, Design and technology, Engineering, English, ICT/Computer studies, Manufacturing, Mathematics, Physics, Science

Further Information
AGCAS: Engineering (Job Sector Briefing) (AGCAS) - www.prospects.ac.uk

Cogent - sector skills souncil for chemicals, pharmaceuticals, nuclear, oil & gas, petroleum & polymers - www.cogent-ssc.com

Diplomas (Foundation, Higher and Advanced) - http://yp.direct.gov.uk/diplomas

Engineering Education Scheme - www.engineering-education.org.uk/

Engineering Education Scheme Wales - www.eesw.org.uk

Engineering Scotland (SEMTA) - www.engineeringscotland.org

Engineering Services SKILLcard - www.skillcard.org.uk

Headstart Scheme - www.headstartcourses.org.uk

Open University - www.open.ac.uk

Scenta - Careers Guide, Engineering, Technology and Science (Engineering Technology Board) - www.scenta.co.uk/careers.cfm

SEMTA - sector skills council for science, engineering and manufacturing technologies - www.semta.org.uk

TARGETjobs: Engineering (GTI Specialist Publishing Ltd.) - www.groupgti.com

The Chemical Engineer (Institution of Chemical Engineers) - www.tcetoday.com

Tomorrow's Engineers - www.tomorrowsengineers.org.uk/careers.cfm

Welsh Baccalaureate - www.wbq.org.uk

Why Not Chemical Engineering? (Insitution of Chemical Engineers) - www.whynotchemeng.com

Women into Science, Engineering & Construction - www.wisecampaign.org.uk

▶Working in engineering (2010) (Babcock Lifeskills) - www.babcock-lifeskills.com/

Year in Industry (Engineering Development Trust) - www.yini.org.uk

Young Engineers - www.youngeng.org/

Addresses
Engineering and Physical Sciences Research Council (EPSRC)
Polaris House North Star Avenue, Swindon, Wiltshire SN2 1ET
Phone: +44(0)1793 444 100
Web: www.epsrc.ac.uk

Engineering Council
246 High Holborn, London WC1V 7EX
Phone: +44 (0)20 3206 0500
Web: www.engc.org.uk

Engineering Development Trust (EDT)
Ridgeway, Welwyn Garden City, Hertfordshire AL7 2AA
Phone: +44 (0)1707 871520
Web: www.etrust.org.uk

Engineering Training Council (NI)
Interpoint, 20-24 York Street, Belfast BT15 1AQ
Phone: +44 (0)28 9032 9878
Web: www.etcni.org.uk

Institution of Chemical Engineers (IChemE)
Davis Building Railway Terrace, Rugby, Warwickshire CV21 3HQ
Phone: +44 (0)1788 578 214
Web: www.icheme.org

Scottish Engineering
Training Officer, 105 West George Street, Glasgow G2 1QL
Phone: +44 (0)141 221 3181
Web: www.scottishengineering.org.uk

Similar Jobs
Biotechnologist, Engineer: Biomedical, Engineer: Fire, Engineer: Gas, Engineer: Mechanical, Food Scientist/Technologist

Engineer: Civil/Structural
CRCI:Building and Construction
CLCI:UN

Job Band: 4 to 5

Job Description
Civil/structural engineers work on the design and construction of major engineering projects. These may include modern sports stadia, bridges, buildings, roads, railways, airports, dams, reservoirs, harbours and other large-scale projects including nuclear and hydroelectric power installations. They ensure that such structures withstand the forces and pressures they will encounter, including people, traffic, wind and/or water pressure, or machinery. The project is discussed with clients, contractors and architects, and plans are prepared. Civil engineers use computers in their work, including the use of computer-aided design (CAD) simulation programs, to calculate the strains, pressures and stress factors of the design. They are responsible for seeing the project through from conception and design to construction and completion.

Duties may include making decisions about what materials and labour are needed. Engineers oversee the initial work of surveying the site and examining the subsoil. They check that agreements about the design, time, cost and safety are being met and often work in partnership with architects.

Work Details
Civil/structural engineers usually work around 35-40 hrs a week, Monday to Friday, though to meet deadlines it may be necessary to work some evenings and weekends. In some posts you may be on call. You are mostly based in an office, but travel to different sites, perhaps throughout the UK or even abroad. Duties involve supervising and organising staff and their work schedules, administration, planning and finance.

On site visits you have to cope with rough ground and climbing scaffolding and ladders; it may be cold and damp and you are out in all sorts of weather. On site you need to wear protective footwear and a safety helmet.

Qualification
• England, Wales and Northern Ireland
Band 4: For BTEC higher national award: 1-2 A levels, preferably maths and physics, and some GCSEs (A*-C), including English, maths and a science, or equivalent. There are foundation courses available for those without appropriate A levels.

Band 5: For degree courses: 2-3 A levels, preferably maths and physics/engineering science, and some GCSEs (A*-C) usually including maths, English and science, or equivalent. Exact requirements depend on the degree you take. There are foundation courses for those without appropriate A levels.

• Scotland
Band 4: For SQA higher national award: usually 2-3 H grades, preferably maths and physics, and some S grades (1-3), often including English, maths and a science, or similar qualifications. There are foundation courses available for those without appropriate H grades.

Band 5: For degree courses: 3-5 H grades, preferably including maths and physics/engineering science, and some S grades (1-3) including English and a science subject, or similar qualifications. Exact requirements depend on the degree you take.

Degree Information

A degree in civil/structural engineering, general engineering, and numerate subjects, including physics, maths and geology are particularly relevant. Qualifications are also available in timber engineering, reflecting the huge growth in demand for timber-framed buildings.

Adult Qualifications

Recent qualifications, such as an appropriate degree or higher national award, are usually required. Adults applying for courses should check with individual academic institutions for details of mature entry requirements. Those with relevant qualifications and/ or experience in a related area may be considered. Access or foundation courses may also be available.

Work Experience

Entry to this job can be competitive and it is important that you try to do some relevant work or voluntary experience before applying to degree courses or jobs. The types of work experience to consider are with a civil engineering company, a construction company, or an architect's practice. Applicants are encouraged to apply to the Year in Industry Scheme for a placement in industry prior to starting their studies. The Engineering Education Scheme in England links year 12 students with local companies to work on real engineering problems . A similar scheme operates in Wales.

Students also have an opportunity to gain work experience in industry for a year between the penultimate and final years of a degree programme. This experience enhances job prospects on graduation. The professional societies can offer placements to engineering students, which are usually part of a sandwich degree course or summer holiday placement.

Entry and Training

You can train after getting a relevant degree or BTEC/SQA higher national certificate/diploma; courses for these can be full time, part time or sandwich. Relevant foundation degrees are also available. All trainees must progress through a period of initial professional development that leads to a final examination and a professional review interview with qualified engineers. Membership of the Institution of Civil Engineers or Institution of Structural Engineers is therefore obtained through a combination of academic qualifications and practical experience. Many qualify with both institutions to gain more career flexibility.

You can also apply for Incorporated Engineer (IEng) status through the Engineering Council. You need to be qualified to HNC/HND or BEng level. Chartered engineers (CEng) must hold an MEng or accredited equivalent, plus satisfy all the requirements of the Chartered Professional Review. Chartered engineers can also qualify as European engineers (EurIng) which is recognised in Europe. The minimum age for registration as a chartered engineer is 25, although the study and training can be completed earlier.

The 'Inspire Scholarships' scheme, offered through ConstructionSkills, the Sector Skills Council for the construction industry, offers scholarships of up to £9k to help fund a construction-related degree, such as civil engineering, architecture, surveying and construction management. More information about the scheme is available on the bconstructive website. It might be possible to gain sponsorship from an employer.

A Diploma/Welsh Baccalaureate may be available in your area in construction and the built environment. The advanced level is equivalent to 3.5 A levels but for some university courses, the additional and specialist learning component of the diploma needs to include specific A levels eg maths or physics. Check entry requirements carefully with the individual institutions.

Continuing professional development (CPD) is an important and key element of your career to keep up to date with the latest developments. The professional institutions and societies offer programmes of CPD that include workshops, conferences and short courses on a range of subjects.

Mature entrants may have difficulty in finding employment unless they have previous relevant experience. There is a Technical Report Route (TRR) offered by the Institution of Civil Engineers (ICE) and Institution of Structural Engineers (IStructE) for those who wish to gain chartered engineer (CEng) or incorporated engineer (IEng) status, but who do not have the required formal academic qualifications. Applicants without the appropriate academic qualifications are expected to have had a substantial period of relevant experience, which can vary, according to the training route.

There are also options for CEng status for those who are existing associate members of the ICE/IStructE, including the TRR. Contact ICE/IStructE for details of all training routes and qualification information.

Opportunities and Pay

Work is available throughout the UK and employers include building and civil engineering contractors, public utility companies, engineering consultants, property developers, and local authorities. Some also work for central government and its agencies, research establishments, the armed forces, or as teachers and lecturers. Civil/structural engineers can also work in private practice or as a self-employed consultant. Availability of work depends to some extent on the state of the building trade and the national economy. Currently there is a downturn in the housing market which means there may be a shortage of vacancies.

Opportunities for promotion are generally better in larger organisations and it helps if you are willing to move around the country to gain experience. There are opportunities for international work, particularly in times of crisis, such as conflict and war zones, earthquakes and floods. Career breaks are also possible in this profession.

Salaries vary according to the size and type of organisation/ company, but starting salaries for graduate trainees are around £22k-£30k a year. Experienced civil engineers earn in the region of £25k-£40k. Chartered engineers can earn around £35k-£50k or more a year. Allowances may be given for travel costs and travelling time, a company car may be provided and perhaps also fringe benefits for work abroad.

Skills and Qualities

analytical skills, aptitude for maths and science, aptitude for teamwork, attention to detail, excellent spoken and written communication, planning skills, problem-solving skills, specialist IT skills

Relevant Subjects

Art and Design, Chemistry, Construction and built environment, Design and technology, English, Geography, ICT/Computer studies, Mathematics, Physics, Science

Further Information

AGCAS: Engineering (Job Sector Briefing) (AGCAS) - www.prospects.ac.uk

bconstructive - www.bconstructive.co.uk/

ConstructionSkills - sector skills council for the construction industry - www.cskills.org

Diplomas (Foundation, Higher and Advanced) - http://yp.direct.gov.uk/diplomas

Engineering Education Scheme - www.engineering-education.org.uk/

Engineering Education Scheme Wales - www.eesw.org.uk

ICE Virtual Library (institute of Civil Engineers) (ICE) - www.icevirtuallibrary.com

International Journal of Engineering Education (IJEE) - www.ijee.dit.ie

New Civil Engineer (Emap) - www.nce.co.uk

TARGETjobs: Civil & Structural Engineering (GTI Specialist Publishing Ltd.) - www.groupgti.com

The Institute of Structural Engineers (IStructE) - www.istructe.org.uk/

The Structural Engineer (fortnightly) (ISE) - www.istructe.org/

Welsh Baccalaureate - www.wbq.org.uk

▶Working in construction & the built environment (2007) (Babcock Lifeskills) - www.babcock-lifeskills.com/

Year in Industry (Engineering Development Trust) - www.yini.org.uk

Addresses

Engineering Council
246 High Holborn, London WC1V 7EX
Phone: +44 (0)20 3206 0500
Web: www.engc.org.uk

Engineering Training Council (NI)
Interpoint, 20-24 York Street, Belfast BT15 1AQ
Phone: +44 (0)28 9032 9878
Web: www.etcni.org.uk

Institution of Civil Engineers (ICE)
1 Great George Street, Westminster, London SW1P 3AA
Phone: +44 (0)20 7222 7722
Web: www.ice.org.uk

Institution of Structural Engineers (IStructE)
11 Upper Belgrave Street, London SW1X 8BH
Phone: +44 (0)20 7235 4535
Web: www.istructe.org.uk

SEMTA - Engineering Careers Information Service
14 Upton Road, Watford WD18 0JT
Phone: 0845 643 9001 (UK only)
Web: www.semta.org.uk

Women into Science, Engineering & Construction (WISE)
2nd Floor Weston House, 246 High Holborn, London WC1V 7EX
Phone: +44 (0)20 3206 0408
Web: www.wisecampaign.org.uk

Similar Jobs

Civil Engineering Technician, Engineer: Building Services, Engineer: Municipal, Surveyor: Building Control, Surveyor: Planning & Development, Surveyor: Quantity

Engineer: Control & Instrumentation

also known as: Measurement & Control Technician, Process Engineer

CRCI:Engineering
CLCI:RAL — Job Band: 4 to 5

Job Description

Control and instrumentation engineers research, design, develop and manage the equipment that controls industrial processes and automated systems. They are concerned with automatic monitoring of processes, such as those in chemical plants or power stations and may work on gas analysis and detection systems. They use complex test instrumentation for precise and technologically advanced analysis. May work with different systems such as programmable logic controllers that track mechanical handling devices, and with distributed control systems that use measuring devices, such as control valves and flow meters. Engineers use the information from different parts of the process to control output efficiently and ensure safety.

Engineers prepare and test the designs using mathematical models and computer simulations. They may write the software required for a system that analyses data from the instruments. Also train staff or lead teams to operate the system, including other engineers, technicians and craft workers. This is a very multidisciplinary role and involves working closely with colleagues in operations, purchasing and design.

Work Details

Usually work around 35-40 hrs a week, Monday to Friday, though sometimes you may be expected to work additional hours. Some employers may require you to be on call in case any faults develop out of normal working hours. If you are involved in a continuous process, you may need to work shifts. You work as part of a team and are responsible for efficient production and safety. The work environment depends on the type of industry and can vary from pharmaceutical industrial premises to outdoor chemical plants. In some places there may be a risk of accidents from equipment and you may need to wear protective clothing.

Qualification

• England, Wales and Northern Ireland

Band 4: For HND, Diploma of Higher Education or foundation degree: 1-2 A levels, preferably including maths and physics, and some GCSEs (A*-C) usually including English, maths and a science, or equivalent.

Band 5: For degree courses: 2-3 A levels, usually including maths and physics, and some GCSEs (A*-C) usually including English, maths and sometimes chemistry or another science, or equivalent. Exact requirements depend on the degree you take.

• Scotland

Band 4: For entry to SQA higher national and professional development awards: 2-3 H grades, usually maths and physics, and some S grades (1-3), including English, maths and a science, or similar qualifications.

Band 5: For degree courses: 3-5 H grades, usually including maths and physics, and some S grades (1-3), including English, maths and sometimes chemistry or another science, or similar qualifications. Exact requirements depend on the degree you take.

Degree Information

A degree in systems and control engineering, electrical/electronic engineering, mechanical engineering, physics/applied physics, computer or chemical engineering are most useful. Aeronautical engineering with a component of control engineering may be acceptable, depending on the employer and the number of applicants. Computer science and software engineering provide useful background knowledge, although degrees in these subjects may not be acceptable for entry. If your first degree does not give direct entry, there are several suitable postgraduate courses.

Adult Qualifications

A degree or higher national award is usually required. Access and foundation courses to undergraduate engineering courses may mean formal qualifications are not essential.

Work Experience

Employers and universities may prefer candidates who have relevant work or voluntary experience. Ideally this is with an electrical engineering company or in any other area of engineering which is relevant and demonstrates enthusiasm and commitment to the job. Similarly, careers involving experience with machinery or computers also helps. Many employers run summer placement schemes, though you should apply early.

Applicants to degree courses are encouraged to apply to the 'Year in Industry' scheme for a placement in industry prior to starting their studies. Students also have an opportunity to gain work experience in industry for a year between the penultimate and final years of their degree programme. This experience enhances job prospects on graduation.

Engineer: Control & Instrumentation

The Engineering Education Scheme runs programmes in England, Scotland and Wales giving young people the chance to be involved in a real engineering project for six months. Students commit to two to three hours work a week and some time at university residents' workshops. This experience can contribute to any future university application and counts towards the Duke of Edinburgh award skills section. Check the website for details.

Similarly, Headstart offers students a chance to experience a week at university, designing, building and testing projects. As engineering careers can be diverse, a week of hands on experience can be helpful when you are trying to decide which field of engineering you want to train in. Check the website for details.

Entry and Training

A degree or BTEC/SQA higher national certificate/diploma is required. Courses are usually full time and some are sandwich courses. Funding for postgraduate courses may be available from the Engineering and Physical Sciences Research Council. See the website for details. Relevant industrial training, initial professional development and further experience are required before becoming fully qualified. You must also commit to continuing professional development throughout your career. Many entrants join the Institute of Measurement and Control. Contact them for different membership grades.

Many control and instrumentation engineers also aim to become professional engineers at incorporated or chartered engineer level with the Engineering Council. This involves gaining experience, and keeping detailed records of your development. Experience is followed by a professional review and an interview.

Incorporated engineers (IEng) need to be qualified to HNC/HND or BEng level, followed by a further year of learning. Another route is through an apprenticeship programme leading to S/NVQ at level 4, then to HNC/HND. Foundation degrees are available in general engineering subjects, but need to be extended to a full degree. Chartered engineers (CEng) may qualify through an accredited course leading to an MEng degree, or a BEng (Hons) followed by an appropriate masters degree. Chartered engineers can also qualify as European engineers (EurIng) but need to be fluent in a European language.

The Tomorrow's Engineers website has lots of useful careers information including a route map and guide to engineering activities from primary school through to higher education. The Engineering Development Trust also runs a range of nationwide schemes for 11-21 year olds who may be interested in engineering as a career. See the websites for details.

A Diploma/Welsh Baccalaureate may be available in your area in engineering. The advanced level is equivalent to 3.5 A levels but for some university courses, the additional and specialist learning component of the diploma needs to include specific A levels e.g maths or physics so check entry requirements carefully. See the diplomas website for further information.

Mature applicants are usually considered but this depends on your qualifications and experience. Managerial and technological expertise is an advantage. Contact the Engineering Council for details.

The Open University (OU) runs a range of engineering courses and the Institution of Engineering Designers has accredited two OU engineering qualifications for professional registration. See the OU website for details.

You may be able to receive funding for higher education from one of the larger manufacturing/engineering companies and for postgraduate study from the Engineering and Physical Science Research Council. Contact the Institute of Measurement and Control or the Engineering Council UK for more information on mature entry.

Opportunities and Pay

Jobs are available throughout the country and exist in a wide range of industries including the chemical, oil and gas or water industries, the food and drink, aerospace or defence industries. You can work for a manufacturing or robotics company, a power generating company or a research organisation. Many move into consultancy work, design and project management, or into senior positions in planning, general management or operations. Job and promotion prospects are generally good due to the continuing increase in new technology.

Pay varies depending on location and type of company. A graduate entrant can expect to earn around £20k-£25k, rising to £38k a year. Successful senior control and instrumentation engineers earn more than £40k a year.

Health

This job requires normal colour vision.

Skills and Qualities

analytical skills, aptitude for teamwork, attention to detail, business awareness, clear-thinking, good communication skills, good interpersonal skills, IT skills, problem-solving skills, scientific approach

Relevant Subjects

Chemistry, Design and technology, Engineering, English, ICT/Computer studies, Manufacturing, Mathematics, Physics, Science

Further Information

AGCAS: Engineering (Job Sector Briefing) (AGCAS) - www.prospects.ac.uk

Apprenticeship Schemes (National Apprenticeship Service) - www.apprenticeships.org.uk

Diplomas (Foundation, Higher and Advanced) - http://yp.direct.gov.uk/diplomas

Engineering Education Scheme - www.engineering-education.org.uk/

Engineering Education Scheme Wales - www.eesw.org.uk

Engineering Scotland (SEMTA) - www.engineeringscotland.org

Headstart Scheme - www.headstartcourses.org.uk

Open University - www.open.ac.uk

SEMTA - sector skills council for science, engineering and manufacturing technologies - www.semta.org.uk

TARGETjobs: Engineering (GTI Specialist Publishing Ltd.) - www.groupgti.com

Tomorrow's Engineers - www.tomorrowsengineers.org.uk/careers.cfm

Welsh Baccalaureate - www.wbq.org.uk

Women into Science, Engineering & Construction - www.wisecampaign.org.uk

Year in Industry (Engineering Development Trust) - www.yini.org.uk

Addresses

Engineering and Physical Sciences Research Council (EPSRC)
Polaris House North Star Avenue, Swindon, Wiltshire SN2 1ET
Phone: +44(0)1793 444 100
Web: www.epsrc.ac.uk

Engineering Council
246 High Holborn, London WC1V 7EX
Phone: +44 (0)20 3206 0500
Web: www.engc.org.uk

Engineering Development Trust (EDT)
Ridgeway, Welwyn Garden City, Hertfordshire AL7 2AA
Phone: +44 (0)1707 871520
Web: www.etrust.org.uk

Engineering Training Council (NI)
Interpoint, 20-24 York Street, Belfast BT15 1AQ
Phone: +44 (0)28 9032 9878
Web: www.etcni.org.uk

Institute of Measurement and Control
87 Gower Street, London WC1E 6AF
Phone: +44 (0)20 7387 4949
Web: www.instmc.org.uk

Scottish Engineering
Training Officer, 105 West George Street, Glasgow G2 1QL
Phone: +44 (0)141 221 3181
Web: www.scottishengineering.org.uk

Similar Jobs

Engineer: Aeronautical, Engineer: Broadcast, Engineer: Electronics, Engineer: Manufacturing, Engineer: Mechanical, IT Systems Analyst/Designer

Engineer: Design

also known as: Industrial Designer

CRCI:Engineering
CLCI:ROZ Job Band: 4 to 5

Job Description

Design engineers use innovative engineering, technical skills and processes to create and shape products that we use in our day-to-day life. They work in a variety of industries such as aeronautical/ automotive industry, civil engineering, electrical/electronics industry, power generation, consumer goods and mechanical engineering. May work on a brand new product or the improvement and modification of an existing one. Designs range in scale from tiny medical implants and mobile phones, to motor vehicles and aircraft.

Engineers often specialise in one area of design and use specialist knowledge to create and develop products that are functional, appealing and competitive. They need to take into account safety and reliability and the production costs from the original concept and research to the completed product. With the design of new products, they must also consider any adverse impact on the environment. Engineers work with initial sketches, computer-aided design (CAD) systems, prototypes and models and test each product prototype to ensure it fulfils the concept/process and also works effectively. May have to solve problems that occur during production.

Design engineers work closely with other engineers, designers and technicians, and sometimes with ergonomists, as well as professionals in other areas, including sales and marketing. May lead a team of CAD staff or design draughtspeople.

Work Details

Work in a shared studio or drawing office, usually a basic 39 hr week, Monday to Friday. Overtime is possible, since tight deadlines have to be met. However, additional hours do not generally involve weekends or shift work. May spend a large portion of time at a computer screen, usually working with a computer-aided design (CAD) system. There may be some travel required for visits to a site or to a client so you may need to be away from home overnight at times.

Qualification

- **England, Wales and Northern Ireland**

Band 4: For relevant HND, Diploma of Higher Education or foundation degree: 1-2 A levels and some GCSEs (A*-C) usually including maths, English and a science subject, or equivalent. Subject entry requirements vary, so check with colleges.

Band 5: For degree courses: 2-3 A levels, including maths, and some GCSEs (A*-C) including maths, a science subject and English, or equivalent. Exact requirements depend on the degree you take.

- **Scotland**

Band 4: For entry to SQA higher national and professional development awards, usually 2-3 H grades and some S grades (1-3), including English, maths and a science subject, or similar qualifications. Subject entry requirements vary, so check with colleges.

Band 5: For degree courses: 3-5 H grades, including maths and a science, and some S grades (1-3) usually including maths and English, or similar qualifications. Exact requirements depend on the degree you take.

Degree Information

Relevant courses include mechanical, materials or electrical engineering, industrial/design engineering, industrial design, industrial design and technology, CAD engineering, aeronautical design technology, or design and technology. There are relevant postgraduate and masters qualifications available.

Care should be taken when choosing your course as those that lead to BA degrees are generally art and design focused and are aimed more at product designers than design engineers.

Adult Qualifications

Colleges may accept mature applicants without the standard entry qualifications. There are Access and foundation courses in some areas that give adults without qualifications a route onto degree courses. Mature entrants who have experience, such as through an engineering apprenticeship, may be able to continue training by taking a distance-learning degree or studying part time while working.

Work Experience

Entry to this job is competitive and it is important that you try to do some relevant work or voluntary experience before applying. Any work experience where you learn about the design processes involved in engineering is most beneficial, such as using CAD software or perhaps working in an engineering company. Most degree courses include a work placement and companies such as BAE systems run industrial placements in engineering, technology, business and finance. Candidates who impress may have their final year's university fees paid and in some cases, an offer of employment at the end of their degree.

If you expect good A levels/H grades and intend to go to university, schemes such as 'A Year in Industry' may give you the opportunity to spend a salaried year with a company and gain valuable work experience.

The Engineering Education Scheme runs programmes in England, Scotland and Wales giving young people the chance to be involved in a real engineering project for six months. Students commit to two to three hours work a week and some time at university residents' workshops. This valuable experience can contribute to any future university application and counts towards the Duke of Edinburgh award skills section. Check the website for details.

Similarly, Headstart offers students a chance to experience a week at university, designing, building and testing projects. As engineering careers can be diverse, a week of hands on experience can be helpful when students are trying to decide which field of engineering they want to train in. Check the website for details.

Entry and Training

It is very difficult to get into work without at least a relevant HNC/ HND, and most entrants are graduates. Course titles and content vary, so check prospectuses carefully to ensure that the course is relevant to the particular area of work you wish to specialise in. Foundation degrees are also available. Specialist courses, or courses with an industrial design option, are available at BTEC/SQA higher national level, and at degree level. It is useful to choose a course that offers an industrial placement.

Postgraduate qualifications may offer an advantage in some areas of work. Contact the Institution of Engineering Designers and the Institution of Engineering and Technology for routes to qualification and a list of accredited courses. Tomorrow's Engineers has lots of useful careers information including a route map and guide to engineering activities from primary school through to higher education. The Engineering Development Trust also runs a range of nationwide schemes for 11-21 year olds who may be interested in engineering as a career. See the websites for details.

Training is mainly on the job with in-house courses that may include product knowledge or enhancement of CAD (computer-aided design) training in the design packages used within the company. It is becoming increasingly important in some areas of work to become professionally qualified and gain Incorporated Engineer (IEng) or Chartered Engineer (CEng) status. This is awarded through the Engineering Council but assessed through one of the professional engineering institutions following membership. You need to keep your knowledge up to date throughout your career by undergoing a programme of continuing professional development (CPD). The IET runs a range of short courses that are suitable for CPD.

A Diploma/Welsh Baccalaureate may be available in your area in engineering. The advanced level is equivalent to 3.5 A levels but for some university courses, the additional and specialist learning (ASL) component of the diploma needs to include specific A levels eg maths or physics. Check entry requirements carefully with the individual institutions.

Mature applicants with related experience in engineering may be welcome. There are a range of part-time courses including degrees/foundation degrees and diplomas. Some courses may be taken through distance learning but course titles and content vary and you should ensure that you choose a course that is particularly relevant to the engineering design area you wish to work in.

The Open University (OU) runs a range of engineering courses and The Institution of Engineering Designers has accredited two OU engineering qualifications for professional registration. See the OU website for details.

You may be able to receive funding for higher education from one of the larger manufacturing/engineering companies and for postgraduate study from the Engineering and Physical Science Research Council.

Opportunities and Pay

There is generally a high demand for experienced design engineers, particularly if you have experience of designing products that are better for the environment. Employers include manufacturing companies, design consultancies, and consulting design engineering companies. There are good prospects for promotion to senior design engineer or project manager. Professional status as an incorporated or chartered engineer is increasingly desirable. Work abroad is possible, especially if you are employed by a multinational company. There are also opportunities for self-employment.

Pay varies depending on location and the particular industry. Starting salaries for graduates are likely to be up to £28k a year, rising to £35-£45k with experience. Some may earn over £50k a year.

Health

Normal colour vision is required.

Skills and Qualities

able to explain clearly, aptitude for maths and science, aptitude for teamwork, creative and imaginative flair, eye for shape/colour, logical, manual dexterity, perseverance, problem-solving skills

Relevant Subjects

Art and Design, Design and technology, Engineering, ICT/Computer studies, Manufacturing, Mathematics, Physics, Science

Further Information

AGCAS: Engineering (Job Sector Briefing) (AGCAS) - www.prospects.ac.uk

Become an Engineer (IET) (Institution of Engineering and Technology (IET) - www.theiet.org/education/becomingengineer/makeyourchoice/

Diplomas (Foundation, Higher and Advanced) - http://yp.direct.gov.uk/diplomas

Engineering Connections - Apprenticeships - www.apprentices.co.uk

Engineering Designer (bi-monthly) (Institute of Engineering Designers) - www.engineeringdesigner.co.uk

Engineering Education Scheme - www.engineering-education.org.uk/

Engineering Education Scheme Wales - www.eesw.org.uk

Engineering Scotland (SEMTA) - www.engineeringscotland.org

Headstart Scheme - www.headstartcourses.org.uk

Open University - www.open.ac.uk

Scenta - Careers Guide, Engineering, Technology and Science (Engineering Technology Board) - www.scenta.co.uk/careers.cfm

SEMTA - sector skills council for science, engineering and manufacturing technologies - www.semta.org.uk

So you want to work in Engineering (Wayland) - www.waylandbooks.co.uk

TARGETjobs: Engineering (GTI Specialist Publishing Ltd.) - www.groupgti.com

Tomorrow's Engineers - www.tomorrowsengineers.org.uk/careers.cfm

Welsh Baccalaureate - www.wbq.org.uk

Women into Science, Engineering & Construction - www.wisecampaign.org.uk

▶Working in engineering (2010) (Babcock Lifeskills) - www.babcock-lifeskills.com/

Year in Industry (Engineering Development Trust) - www.yini.org.uk

Young Engineers - www.youngeng.org/

Addresses

BAE Systems Training College
Cwmbran Training College, Beacon House, William Brown Close, Llantarnam Park, Gwent NP44 3AB
Phone: +44 (0) 1633 835123
Web: www.cwmbrancollege.com

Engineering and Physical Sciences Research Council (EPSRC)
Polaris House North Star Avenue, Swindon, Wiltshire SN2 1ET
Phone: +44(0)1793 444 100
Web: www.epsrc.ac.uk

Engineering Council
246 High Holborn, London WC1V 7EX
Phone: +44 (0)20 3206 0500
Web: www.engc.org.uk

Engineering Development Trust (EDT)
Ridgeway, Welwyn Garden City, Hertfordshire AL7 2AA
Phone: +44 (0)1707 871520
Web: www.etrust.org.uk

Institution of Engineering and Technology (IET)
Michael Faraday House, Stevenage, Hertfordshire SG1 2AY
Phone: +44 (0)1438 313311
Web: www.theiet.org

Institution of Engineering Designers (IED)
Courtleigh, Westbury Leigh, Wiltshire BA13 3TA
Phone: +44 (0)1373 822 801
Web: www.ied.org.uk

Women into Science, Engineering & Construction (WISE)
2nd Floor Weston House, 246 High Holborn, London WC1V 7EX
Phone: +44 (0)20 3206 0408
Web: www.wisecampaign.org.uk

Similar Jobs

CAD Technician, Engineer: Automotive, Engineer: Mechanical, Ergonomist, Materials Scientist/Engineer, Naval Architect

Engineer: Electrical

also known as: Electrical Engineer

CRCI:Engineering
CLCI:RAK

Job Band: 4 to 5

Job Description

Electrical engineers are involved with the design, development, manufacture and testing of electrical generation and transmission equipment systems. These systems are used by domestic households, commercial, industrial and public sectors. They can be responsible for the installation, maintenance and control of power supplies or work in the research and design of systems for electricity generation. Engineers are increasingly challenged to work in an environmentally friendly way and in line with legal and technical regulations.

There is also work in the design, manufacture and installation of electrical equipment ranging from transformers to ventilation systems and household appliances. Some work with heavy equipment such as lifts, mining equipment and rail transport. They work as part of a multi-disciplinary team, including other engineers, those involved in production or research and after-sales staff.

Work Details

Usually work around 35-40 hrs a week, Monday to Friday, though may be required to work some weekends, or have early starts or late finishes at times. You may be based in a design laboratory using computers and sitting at a workbench. Alternatively you may be installing generators or other large pieces of equipment and need to travel to different sites. Conditions at some sites may be uncomfortable.

Qualification

• England, Wales and Northern Ireland

Band 4: For HND in electrical/electronic engineering , Diploma of Higher Education or foundation degree: 1-2 A levels, including maths and a science (preferably physics) or computing science or technology, and some GCSEs (A*-C) usually including English and maths, or equivalent.

Band 5: For degree courses in electrical engineering: 2-3 A levels, preferably including maths and physics, and some GCSEs (A*-C) usually including English, maths and sometimes physics and a foreign language, or equivalent. Exact requirements depend on the degree you take.

• Scotland

Band 4: For entry to SQA higher national award in electrical/electronic engineering and professional development awards: usually 2-3 H grades, including maths and a science (preferably physics) or computing science or technology, and some S grades (1-3), including English and maths, or similar qualifications.

Band 5: For degree courses in electrical engineering: 3-5 H grades, preferably including maths and physics, and some S grades (1-3), including English, maths and sometimes physics and a foreign language, or similar qualifications. Exact requirements depend on the degree you take.

Degree Information

A degree in electrical engineering is preferred but a degree in physics is sometimes acceptable. An MEng may give more job prospects than a BEng. There are also other Masters degrees in specific aspects of electrical engineering available.

Adult Qualifications

A degree or higher national award in electrical engineering is required. There are many Access or foundation courses for entry to engineering for those who do not meet the standard entry requirements.

Work Experience

Employers and universities may prefer candidates who have relevant work or voluntary experience. The most useful experience is with an electrical engineering firm or in any area of engineering that is relevant and demonstrates enthusiasm and commitment to the job.

Applicants to degree courses are encouraged to apply to the 'Year in Industry' scheme for a placement in industry prior to starting their studies. Students also have an opportunity to gain work experience in industry for a year between the penultimate and final years of their degree programme. This experience enhances job prospects on graduation.

The Engineering Education Scheme runs programmes in England, Scotland and Wales giving young people the chance to be involved in a real engineering project for six months. Students commit to two to three hours work a week and some time at university residents' workshops. This experience can contribute to any future university application and counts towards the Duke of Edinburgh award skills section. Check the website for details.

Similarly, Headstart offers students a chance to experience a week at university, designing, building and testing projects. As engineering careers can be diverse, a week of hands on experience can be helpful when you are trying to decide which field of engineering you want to train in. Check the website for details.

Entry and Training

A degree or BTEC/SQA higher national award is usually required. Most courses are full time and some are sandwich courses. Sponsorship for higher education courses may be possible. Relevant industrial training, initial professional development and further experience are required before becoming fully qualified. You must also commit to continuing professional development throughout your career.

Electrical engineers usually join the Institution of Engineering and Technology, and aim to become professional engineers at incorporated or chartered engineer level with the Engineering Council. This involves gaining experience and keeping detailed records of your development. Experience is followed by a professional review and an interview.

Incorporated engineers (IEng) need to be qualified to HNC/HND or BEng level, followed by a further year of learning. Another route is through an apprenticeship programme leading to S/NVQ at level 4, then to HNC/HND. Foundation degrees are available in electrical engineering or in general engineering, but need to be extended to a full degree. These can be very specific; for example, the University of Northampton offers a foundation degree in lift engineering suitable for people working in this field. The course is run through distance learning and enables you to continue working while formalising your qualification.

Chartered engineers (CEng) may qualify through an accredited course leading to an MEng degree, or a BEng (Hons) followed by an appropriate masters degree. Chartered engineers can also qualify as European engineers (EurIng) but need to be fluent in a European language.

The Tomorrow's Engineers website has lots of useful careers information including a route map and guide to engineering activities from primary school through to higher education. The Engineering Development Trust also runs a range of nationwide schemes for 11-21 year olds who may be interested in engineering as a career. See the websites for details.

A Diploma/Welsh Baccalaureate may be available in your area in engineering. The advanced level is equivalent to 3.5 A levels but for some university courses, the additional and specialist learning component of the diploma needs to include specific A levels e.g maths or physics so check entry requirements carefully. See the diplomas website for further information.

Mature applicants are usually considered but this depends on your qualifications and experience. Managerial and technological expertise is an advantage. Contact the Engineering Council for details.

The Open University (OU) runs a range of engineering courses. See the OU website for details. You may be able to receive funding for higher education from one of the larger manufacturing/engineering companies and for postgraduate study from the Engineering and Physical Science Research Council. Contact the Engineering Council UK, the Institution of Engineering and Technology or the Institute of Measurement and Control for details of all training opportunities and mature entry.

Opportunities and Pay

Major employers include the power companies but there are also jobs with rail, airports, marine and offshore industries, manufacturing and broadcasting companies, local and central government and the armed forces. Usually electrical engineers specialise in one area of work. Demand for employees is quite good and there are opportunities for promotion to general management positions.

Pay varies depending on location, type and size of employer. A graduate entrant is likely to earn around £20k a year, rising to around £25k-£35k with experience and qualifications. Some electrical engineers earn more than £50k.

Health

This job requires normal colour vision.

Skills and Qualities

able to work to deadlines, analytical skills, aptitude for figures, aptitude for teamwork, information handling skills, IT skills, practical skills, problem-solving skills, technical aptitude

Relevant Subjects

Chemistry, Design and technology, Engineering, English, ICT/Computer studies, Manufacturing, Mathematics, Physics, Science

Further Information

AGCAS: Engineering (Job Sector Briefing) (AGCAS) - www.prospects.ac.uk

Apprenticeship Schemes (National Apprenticeship Service) - www.apprenticeships.org.uk

Diplomas (Foundation, Higher and Advanced) - http://yp.direct.gov.uk/diplomas

Engineering Education Scheme - www.engineering-education.org.uk/

Engineering Education Scheme Wales - www.eesw.org.uk

Engineering Scotland (SEMTA) - www.engineeringscotland.org

Headstart Scheme - www.headstartcourses.org.uk

SEMTA - sector skills council for science, engineering and manufacturing technologies - www.semta.org.uk

So you want to work in Engineering (Wayland) - www.waylandbooks.co.uk

TARGETjobs: Engineering (GTI Specialist Publishing Ltd.) - www.groupgti.com

Tomorrow's Engineers - www.tomorrowsengineers.org.uk/careers.cfm

Welsh Baccalaureate - www.wbq.org.uk

Women into Science, Engineering & Construction - www.wisecampaign.org.uk

Year in Industry (Engineering Development Trust) - www.yini.org.uk

Addresses

Engineering and Physical Sciences Research Council (EPSRC)
Polaris House North Star Avenue, Swindon, Wiltshire SN2 1ET
Phone: +44(0)1793 444 100
Web: www.epsrc.ac.uk

Engineering Council
246 High Holborn, London WC1V 7EX
Phone: +44 (0)20 3206 0500
Web: www.engc.org.uk

Engineering Development Trust (EDT)
Ridgeway, Welwyn Garden City, Hertfordshire AL7 2AA
Phone: +44 (0)1707 871520
Web: www.etrust.org.uk

Engineering Training Council (NI)
Interpoint, 20-24 York Street, Belfast BT15 1AQ
Phone: +44 (0)28 9032 9878
Web: www.etcni.org.uk

Institution of Engineering and Technology (IET)
Michael Faraday House, Stevenage, Hertfordshire SG1 2AY
Phone: +44 (0)1438 313311
Web: www.theiet.org

University of Northampton
Park Campus Boughton Green Road, Northampton NN2 7AL
Phone: +44 (0)1604 735500
Web: www.northampton.ac.uk

Women into Science, Engineering & Construction (WISE)
2nd Floor Weston House, 246 High Holborn, London WC1V 7EX
Phone: +44 (0)20 3206 0408
Web: www.wisecampaign.org.uk

Similar Jobs

Aircraft Engineering Technician, Electrical Engineering Technician, Engineer: Broadcast, Engineer: Control & Instrumentation, Engineer: Electronics, Engineer: Telecommunications

Engineer: Electronics

also known as: Electronics Engineer, Engineer: Microelectronics

CRCI:Engineering
CLCI:RAL Job Band: 4 to 5

Job Description

Electronics engineers work on the design and production of a wide range of electronic equipment. Microelectronic engineers produce powerful microchips. Most work in research and design in specialist electronics factories. These factories produce telecommunications equipment, computers, domestic appliances, control systems and other specialised apparatus and instruments used in medicine, defence, entertainment and multimedia, etc. Others are involved in the production, testing and marketing of these products. Some use specialised knowledge in other industries such as car production, broadcasting, radar and navigation and the oil industry.

Engineers often use computer-aided design (CAD) to produce specifications and models of new products and systems. They aim to push technology forwards and to continue to improve the quality of lives through their work.

Work Details

Usually work around 35-40 hrs a week, Monday to Friday, though sometimes you may have to work longer hours. Most electronics industrial premises are clean and pleasant places. You can work in a laboratory at a workbench or on the production floor. You may make innovative use of technology and develop new techniques. Usually you work as part of a team, consulting with other engineers, and those involved with production, marketing and after sales.

Qualification

• England, Wales and Northern Ireland

Band 4: For HND in electronics, Diploma of Higher Education or foundation degree: 1-2 A levels, preferably including maths and physics, and some GCSEs (A*-C) usually including English, maths and science, or equivalent.

Band 5: For degree courses: 2-3 A levels, preferably including maths and physics, and some GCSEs (A*-C) usually including English, maths and science, or equivalent. Exact requirements depend on the degree you take.

• Scotland

Band 4: For entry to SQA higher national and professional development awards in electronics: 2-3 H grades, usually including maths and physics, and some S grades (1-3), often including English, maths and science, or similar qualifications.

Band 5: For degree courses: 3-5 H grades, preferably including maths and physics, and some S grades (1-3), including English, maths and science, or similar qualifications. Exact requirements depend on the degree you take.

Degree Information

A degree in electronic engineering is preferred but a degree in physics or systems and control engineering may be acceptable to some employers. Other engineering subjects can provide useful background knowledge, but are not usually qualifications for entry. There are several postgraduate courses if your degree is not directly relevant.

Adult Qualifications

A degree or higher national award in electronics/electronic engineering is normally required. Course entry requirements for mature applicants may be reduced, particularly if you are experienced in a relevant field. Access or foundation courses usually provide those without the required qualifications a route onto degree courses.

Work Experience

Employers and universities may prefer candidates who have relevant work or voluntary experience. The most suitable experience is with an electronics company or in any area of engineering that is relevant and demonstrates enthusiasm and commitment to the job. If you expect good A levels/H grades and intend to go to university, schemes such as 'A Year in Industry' enable you to spend a salaried year with a company to gain valuable work experience.

The Engineering Education Scheme runs programmes in England, Scotland and Wales giving young people the chance to be involved in a real engineering project for six months. Students commit to two to three hours work a week and some time at university residents' workshops. This experience can contribute to any future university application and counts towards the Duke of Edinburgh award skills section. Check the website for details.

Similarly, Headstart offers students a chance to experience a week at university, designing, building and testing projects. As engineering careers can be diverse, a week of hands on experience can be helpful when you are trying to decide which field of engineering you want to train in. Check the website for details.

Entry and Training

Training is after obtaining either a good honours degree or a BTEC/SQA higher national diploma/certificate. Courses are mainly full time but there are also some sandwich courses. There is a wide range of courses available. Sponsorship for training may be possible. Relevant industrial training, initial professional development and further experience are required before becoming fully qualified. You must also commit to continuing professional development throughout your career.

Electronics engineers usually join the Institution of Engineering and Technology, and aim to become professional engineers at incorporated or chartered engineer level with the Engineering Council. This involves gaining experience and keeping detailed records of your development. Experience is followed by a professional review and an interview.

Incorporated engineers (IEng) need to be qualified to HNC/HND or BEng level, followed by a further year of learning. Another route is through an apprenticeship programme leading to S/NVQ at level 4, then to HNC/HND. Foundation degrees are available in electronic engineering or in general engineering, but need to be topped-up to a full degree. Chartered engineers (CEng) may qualify through an accredited course leading to an MEng degree, or a BEng (Hons) followed by an appropriate masters degree. Chartered engineers can also qualify as European engineers (EurIng) but need to be fluent in a European language.

The Tomorrow's Engineers website has lots of useful careers information including a route map and guide to engineering activities from primary school through to higher education. The Engineering Development Trust also runs a range of nationwide schemes for 11-21 year olds who may be interested in engineering as a career. See the websites for details.

A Diploma/Welsh Baccalaureate may be available in your area in engineering. The advanced level is equivalent to 3.5 A levels but for some university courses, the additional and specialist learning component of the diploma needs to include specific A levels e.g maths or physics so check entry requirements carefully. See the diplomas website for further information.

Mature applicants are usually considered but this depends on your qualifications and experience. Managerial and technological expertise is an advantage. Contact the Engineering Council for details.

The Open University (OU) runs a range of engineering courses. See the OU website for details. You may be able to receive funding for higher education from one of the larger manufacturing/engineering companies and for postgraduate study from the Engineering and Physical Science Research Council. Contact the Engineering Council, the Institution of Engineering and Technology or the Institute of Measurement and Control for details of all training opportunities for mature entry.

Opportunities and Pay

Jobs are available throughout the UK and also overseas. Employment can be with a number of different organisations in manufacturing, telecommunications, broadcasting, government research establishments, airports, or the armed forces. There is a high demand for electronics engineers, and promotion opportunities to senior posts in different management roles are good. Very experienced engineers may work on a freelance basis.

Pay varies depending on location, type and size of employer. A graduate entrant is likely to earn around £20k-£25k, rising to around £35k-£45k a year with experience and qualifications. Some electronic engineers earn more than £50k.

Health
This job requires normal colour vision.

Skills and Qualities
able to take responsibility, accurate, analytical skills, aptitude for figures, aptitude for teamwork, good communication skills, IT skills, methodical, problem-solving skills, scientific approach

Relevant Subjects
Chemistry, Design and technology, Engineering, English, ICT/ Computer studies, Manufacturing, Mathematics, Physics, Science

Further Information
AGCAS: Engineering (Job Sector Briefing) (AGCAS) - www.prospects.ac.uk

Diplomas (Foundation, Higher and Advanced) - http://yp.direct.gov.uk/diplomas

Engineering Education Scheme - www.engineering-education.org.uk/

Engineering Education Scheme Wales - www.eesw.org.uk

Engineering Scotland (SEMTA) - www.engineeringscotland.org

Headstart Scheme - www.headstartcourses.org.uk

Open University - www.open.ac.uk

SEMTA - sector skills council for science, engineering and manufacturing technologies - www.semta.org.uk

TARGETjobs: Engineering (GTI Specialist Publishing Ltd.) - www.groupgti.com

Tomorrow's Engineers - www.tomorrowsengineers.org.uk/careers.cfm

Welsh Baccalaureate - www.wbq.org.uk

Women into Science, Engineering & Construction - www.wisecampaign.org.uk

Year in Industry (Engineering Development Trust) - www.yini.org.uk

Addresses
Engineering and Physical Sciences Research Council (EPSRC)
Polaris House North Star Avenue, Swindon, Wiltshire SN2 1ET
Phone: +44(0)1793 444 100
Web: www.epsrc.ac.uk

Engineering Council
246 High Holborn, London WC1V 7EX
Phone: +44 (0)20 3206 0500
Web: www.engc.org.uk

Engineering Development Trust (EDT)
Ridgeway, Welwyn Garden City, Hertfordshire AL7 2AA
Phone: +44 (0)1707 871520
Web: www.etrust.org.uk

Engineering Training Council (NI)
Interpoint, 20-24 York Street, Belfast BT15 1AQ
Phone: +44 (0)28 9032 9878
Web: www.etcni.org.uk

Institution of Engineering and Technology (IET)
Michael Faraday House, Stevenage, Hertfordshire SG1 2AY
Phone: +44 (0)1438 313311
Web: www.theiet.org

Scottish Engineering
Training Officer, 105 West George Street, Glasgow G2 1QL
Phone: +44 (0)141 221 3181
Web: www.scottishengineering.org.uk

Women into Science, Engineering & Construction (WISE)
2nd Floor Weston House, 246 High Holborn, London WC1V 7EX
Phone: +44 (0)20 3206 0408
Web: www.wisecampaign.org.uk

Similar Jobs
Electrical Engineering Technician, Engineer: Aeronautical, Engineer: Broadcast, Engineer: Control & Instrumentation, Engineer: Electrical, Engineer: Telecommunications

Engineer: Energy

also known as: Energy Technologist, Fuel & Energy Engineer

CRCI:Engineering

CLCI:RAN — Job Band: 4 to 5

Job Description
Energy engineers research and develop ways to improve the use of energy and to minimise potential environmental damage. They may work in energy production, aiming to improve quality/ economy of use and control of, for example, sulphur and nitrogen emissions. Some are employed in metal, chemical or ceramic processing, advising on the efficient use of energy. Others develop new fuels or different uses for existing fuels. Engineers may work on renewable power plants and alternative and renewable sources of energy, eg wind, solar, geothermal or wave power.

May use computer-aided design (CAD) to create 3-D models and other computer systems for design and research. They need to ensure that all UK/EU regulations that govern production and emissions are met. Some energy engineers may advise employers on energy usage and pollution control.

Work Details
Usually work a basic 35-40 hrs week, Monday to Friday, though you may be expected to work overtime and some weekends. You advise, supervise and consult with people. Key responsibilities include planning, presenting facts and efficient production. Safety standards also feature in your role. The work environment depends on the type of employment. In some places there may be a risk of contact with dangerous materials and you may need to wear overalls or protective clothing.

Qualification

- **England, Wales and Northern Ireland**

Band 4: For HND in engineering, Diploma of Higher Education or foundation degree: 1-2 A levels usually maths and physics, and some GCSEs (A*-C) usually including English, maths and science, or equivalent.

Band 5: For degree courses: 2-3 A levels, usually maths and physics, and some GCSEs (A*-C) usually including English, maths and science, or equivalent. Exact requirements depend on the degree you take.

- **Scotland**

Band 4: For entry to SQA higher national award in engineering and professional development awards: 2-3 H grades, usually including maths and physics, and some S grades (1-3), including English, maths and science, or similar qualifications.

Band 5: For degree courses: 3-5 H grades, usually including maths and physics, and some S grades (1-3), including English, maths and science, or similar qualifications. Exact requirements depend on the degree you take.

Degree Information
A first degree in energy technology or energy engineering may be preferred. However, depending on the type of employer, other engineering disciplines such as electrical or chemical engineering may be acceptable. Specialist postgraduate courses relevant to energy technology and renewable energy are available.

Adult Qualifications
A degree or higher national award is usually required. Entry to most courses for mature students is decided on an individual basis and previous education and work experience is taken into account. There are many Access or foundation courses leading to engineering degree courses for those who do not meet the standard entry criteria. Specialised postgraduate courses are available for graduates in engineering.

Work Experience
Employers and universities may prefer candidates who have relevant work or voluntary experience. The most relevant experience is within the energy industry, but something similar such as with a chemical engineering firm gives you a good basis and insight into the work. If you expect good A levels/H grades and intend to go to university, schemes such as 'A Year in Industry' enable you to spend a salaried year with a company to gain valuable work experience.

The Engineering Education Scheme runs programmes in England, Scotland and Wales giving young people the chance to be involved in a real engineering project for six months. Students commit to two to three hours work a week and some time at university residents' workshops. This experience can contribute to any future university application and counts towards the Duke of Edinburgh award skills section. Check the website for details.

Similarly, Headstart offers students a chance to experience a week at university, designing, building and testing projects. As engineering careers can be diverse, a week of hands on experience can be helpful when you are trying to decide which field of engineering you want to train in. Check the website for details.

Entry and Training
Most entrants have a degree or higher national award. Courses are usually full time and some are sandwich courses combining both study and practical work. Sponsorship for study may be possible. There is a wide range of relevant courses available but few specific courses; specialist postgraduate study is useful. Once in a job, relevant industrial training, initial professional development and further experience are required before becoming fully qualified. You must also commit to continuing professional development throughout your career.

Many entrants become members of the Energy Institute (EI), which can provide a list of accredited degree courses. The EI also runs short training courses and conferences on a range of relevant topics, such as oil and gas and energy management.

Most energy engineers aim to become professional engineers with the Engineering Council at either incorporated or chartered engineer level. Both levels involve gaining experience and keeping detailed records of your development. Experience is followed by a professional review and an interview.

Incorporated engineers (IEng) need to be qualified to HNC/HND or BEng level, followed by a further year of learning. Another route is through an apprenticeship programme leading to S/NVQ at level 4, then to HNC/HND. Foundation degrees are available in general engineering subjects and in manufacturing engineering, but need to be topped-up to a full degree. Chartered engineers (CEng) may qualify through an accredited course leading to an MEng degree, or a BEng (Hons) followed by an appropriate masters degree. Chartered engineers can also qualify as European engineers (EurIng) but need to be fluent in a European language.

The Tomorrow's Engineers website has lots of useful careers information including a route map and guide to engineering activities from primary school through to higher education. The Engineering Development Trust also runs a range of nationwide schemes for 11-21 year olds who may be interested in engineering as a career. Similarly, the Energyzone website has lots of useful information on education and training in the energy sector. Visit the websites for details.

A Diploma/Welsh Baccalaureate may be available in your area in engineering. The advanced level is equivalent to 3.5 A levels but for some university courses, the additional and specialist learning component of the diploma needs to include specific A levels eg maths or physics so check entry requirements carefully. See the diplomas website for further information.

Mature applicants are usually considered but this depends on your qualifications and experience. Managerial and technological expertise is an advantage. Contact the Engineering Council for details.

The Open University (OU) runs a range of engineering courses. See the OU website for details. There are also some distance learning courses available from the Energy Institute. You may be able to receive funding for higher education from one of the larger manufacturing/engineering companies and for postgraduate study from the Engineering and Physical Science Research Council . Contact the Engineering Council or the Institution of Engineering and Technology for details of all training opportunities for mature entry.

Opportunities and Pay
Employers include those in the gas, oil and nuclear industries that produce and distribute fuel, or manufacturing and processing industries that use fuel. Such manufacturers include chemical, steel, textiles and ceramics. Opportunities also exist with consultancies that advise on energy conservation or with manufacturers that supply power plants with generators, boilers, engines etc. Renewable energy is a growth area due to increased interest in environmental matters.

There is a good demand for qualified staff and it may be possible to work as a consultant later in your career. Promotion opportunities to senior management posts are quite good. There are increasing opportunities for freelance or contract work and opportunities to work abroad.

Pay varies depending on location, type and size of employer. As a graduate entrant you are likely to earn around £20k-£25k and with professional qualifications and experience up to £40k. Senior engineers may earn up to £60k a year.

Health
Good general fitness is needed for this work.

Skills and Qualities
able to take responsibility, analytical skills, aptitude for figures, environmental awareness, good communication skills, IT skills, problem-solving skills, scientific approach, sound judgement, technical aptitude

Relevant Subjects
Chemistry, Design and technology, Economics, Engineering, ICT/Computer studies, Mathematics, Physics, Science

Further Information
AGCAS: Engineering (Job Sector Briefing) (AGCAS) - www.prospects.ac.uk

Cogent - sector skills souncil for chemicals, pharmaceuticals, nuclear, oil & gas, petroleum & polymers - www.cogent-ssc.com

Diplomas (Foundation, Higher and Advanced) - http://yp.direct.gov.uk/diplomas

Energy Institute (Institute of Petroleum (IOP) - www.energyinst.org.uk

Energyzone - Energy Institute - www.energyzone.net

Engineering Education Scheme - www.engineering-education.org.uk/

Engineering Education Scheme Wales - www.eesw.org.uk

Engineering Scotland (SEMTA) - www.engineeringscotland.org

Headstart Scheme - www.headstartcourses.org.uk

Open University - www.open.ac.uk

SEMTA - sector skills council for science, engineering and manufacturing technologies - www.semta.org.uk

TARGETjobs: Engineering (GTI Specialist Publishing Ltd.) - www.groupgti.com

Tomorrow's Engineers - www.tomorrowsengineers.org.uk/careers.cfm

Welsh Baccalaureate - www.wbq.org.uk

Year in Industry (Engineering Development Trust) - www.yini.org.uk

Addresses

Energy Institute (EI)
61 New Cavendish Street, London W1G 7AR
Phone: +44 (0)20 7467 7100
Web: www.energyinst.org.uk

Engineering and Physical Sciences Research Council (EPSRC)
Polaris House North Star Avenue, Swindon, Wiltshire SN2 1ET
Phone: +44(0)1793 444 100
Web: www.epsrc.ac.uk

Engineering Council
246 High Holborn, London WC1V 7EX
Phone: +44 (0)20 3206 0500
Web: www.engc.org.uk

Engineering Development Trust (EDT)
Ridgeway, Welwyn Garden City, Hertfordshire AL7 2AA
Phone: +44 (0)1707 871520
Web: www.etrust.org.uk

Institution of Engineering and Technology (IET)
Michael Faraday House, Stevenage, Hertfordshire SG1 2AY
Phone: +44 (0)1438 313311
Web: www.theiet.org

Women into Science, Engineering & Construction (WISE)
2nd Floor Weston House, 246 High Holborn, London WC1V 7EX
Phone: +44 (0)20 3206 0408
Web: www.wisecampaign.org.uk

Similar Jobs

Engineer: Chemical, Engineer: Electrical, Engineer: Gas, Engineer: Mechanical, Engineer: Nuclear

Engineer: Fire

also known as: Fire Protection Engineer

CRCI:Engineering

CLCI:ROZ

Job Band: 4 to 5

Job Description

Fire protection engineers apply scientific and engineering principles and expert judgement to understand the effects of fire, and to protect people, property and the environment. They assess hazards and risks of fire, and help to mitigate their effects by making sure that buildings and transport systems are designed, built and protected appropriately. May work in various aspects of fire engineering, depending on the employer, which may be a local authority, a fire service, a specialist consultancy or a manufacturer of equipment.

Engineers may work in the design, installation and development of fire detection and control equipment, and fire-related communication systems. May direct and control equipment and manpower in the leadership and management of firefighting and rescue operations. Some engineers undertake post-fire investigations and prepare reports on what may have caused the fire. Some are involved in the development of fire safety regulations and legislation. May investigate the behaviour patterns of people faced with a fire emergency.

Work Details

Usually work around 39 hrs a week, Monday to Friday. You may have to work evenings and weekends if working with an operational fire service, or if you have to attend an urgent fire risk or post-fire investigation. The work is office based, but involves visiting industrial premises, building sites, transport systems, fire services and fire safety departments. You work with other professionals such as architects, structural engineers, firefighting services and product designers.

There may be a risk of accidents when on site, and you may need to wear special protective clothing and a helmet. You may need to travel to other premises which may mean spending nights away from home.

Qualification

- **England, Wales and Northern Ireland**

Band 4: For HND, Diploma of Higher Education or foundation degree: 1-2 A levels, usually maths and physics or chemistry, and some GCSEs (A*-C) usually including English, maths and science, or equivalent.

Band 5: For relevant degree: 2-3 A levels, preferably maths and physics or chemistry, and some GCSEs (A*-C) including English, or equivalent. Exact requirements depend on the degree you take.

- **Scotland**

Band 4: For entry to SQA higher national and professional development awards, usually 2-3 H grades, usually maths and physics or chemistry, and some S grades (1-3), including English, maths and science, or similar qualifications.

Band 5: For relevant degree: 3-5 H grades, including maths and physics or chemistry, and some S grades (1-3) including English, or similar qualifications. Exact requirements depend on the degree you take.

Degree Information

There are specific degrees available in fire engineering, structural and fire safety engineering, fire safety and risk management and fire risk engineering. However, many entrants have degrees in related subjects such as mechanical or electrical engineering, and study for fire engineering qualifications later. For accredited degrees that can lead to membership of the Institution of Fire Engineers (IFE), please see the IFE website.

Adult Qualifications

A degree or higher national award, or equivalent, is usually required. Entry requirements for mature applicants may be relaxed, particularly if you have relevant experience. Access and foundation courses may assist mature students to enter relevant degree courses.

Work Experience

Employers and universities may prefer candidates who have relevant work or voluntary experience. This is one of the more difficult direct work experiences to obtain, but spending time in a consulting engineering company demonstrates enthusiasm and commitment and gives you an insight into the work involved. Jeremy Gardner Associates Ltd (JGA) offers a scholarship fund with Edinburgh university. The scholarship is offered to two students a year who have the opportunity to work in the JGA offices in Edinburgh and gain three month's work experience. They also run a Masters placement from April to December each year in the Edinburgh, Dublin or London offices. Check the website for details.

The Engineering Education Scheme runs programmes in England, Scotland and Wales giving young people the chance to be involved in a real engineering project for six months. Students commit to 2/3 hours work a week and some time at university residents' workshops. This experience can contribute to any future university application and counts towards the Duke of Edinburgh award skills section. Check the website for details.

Similarly, Headstart offers students a chance to experience a week at university, designing, building and testing projects. As engineering careers can be diverse, a week of hands on experience can be really helpful when you are trying to decide which field of engineering you want to train in. Check the website for details.

Entry and Training

Many entrants have a fire-related HND or degree course. Some may study for another branch of engineering first and then transfer to this profession, gaining experience and further training while working in the field. Some entrants have previously been firefighters and have trained while on the job and gained qualifications and experience equivalent to a degree. Those working in research usually have a good honours degree plus a higher degree.

Most entrants join the Institution of Fire Engineers (IFE). Student membership is available if you are studying fire engineering, either full or part time. They also have details of courses accredited for full membership, including courses offered by the Fire Service College, which runs a wide range of relevant courses that can be used to build credits towards a foundation or honours degree. See the websites for full details. Relevant training, initial professional development and further responsible experience are required before becoming fully qualified. You must also commit to continuing professional development throughout your career. Grants and bursaries may be available through the Fire Service Research and Training Trust in conjunction with the IFE.

Many fire engineers also aim to become professional engineers at incorporated or chartered engineer level with the Engineering Council. This involves gaining experience and keeping detailed records of your development. Experience is followed by a professional review and an interview. For full details see the Engineering Council's website.

The Engineering Development Trust also runs a range of nationwide schemes for 11-21 year olds who may be interested in engineering as a career. A Diploma/Welsh Baccalaureate may be available in your area in engineering. The advanced level is equivalent to 3.5 A levels but for some university courses, the additional and specialist learning (ASL) component of the diploma needs to include specific A levels eg maths or physics so check entry requirements carefully. See the diplomas website for further information.

There is a mature candidate route for entry to membership of the Institution of Fire Engineers. No formal academic qualifications are required but you need to submit a technical paper to show that you have achieved a comparable level of knowledge to those with academic qualifications. Candidates must be over 35 years old and have experience of increasing responsibility in fire engineering.

Opportunities and Pay

This is a specialised area of work, but opportunities are growing and exist in a range of organisations, including fire engineering design companies, fire risk assessment units, the fire and rescue services, specialist companies that develop and manufacture fire detection and alarm systems, and consulting engineering companies. Research jobs can be in industry or with a university or college. You can also work as an independent consultant.

Pay varies depending on location, type and size of company. Starting salaries for graduate entrants are around £20k-£30k a year. Experienced fire engineers at a senior level earn around £40k-£50k or more.

Health

Good general fitness is needed for this work, especially if you want to be involved with operational fire and rescue services. Good colour vision is needed for some aspects of the work.

Skills and Qualities

analytical skills, good communication skills, good interpersonal skills, IT skills, logical, problem-solving skills, resourceful, responsible attitude, sound judgement, technical aptitude

Relevant Subjects

Chemistry, Design and technology, Engineering, ICT/Computer studies, Manufacturing, Mathematics, Physics, Science

Further Information

AGCAS: Engineering (Job Sector Briefing) (AGCAS) - www.prospects.ac.uk

Diplomas (Foundation, Higher and Advanced) - http://yp.direct.gov.uk/diplomas

Engineering Education Scheme - www.engineering-education.org.uk/

Engineering Education Scheme Wales - www.eesw.org.uk

Fire Magazine (Institution of Fire Engineers (IFE)) - www.fire-magazine.com

Fire Service College - www.fireservicecollege.ac.uk

Fire Service Research and Training Trust - www.firetrust.info

Headstart Scheme - www.headstartcourses.org.uk

Scenta - Careers Guide, Engineering, Technology and Science (Engineering Technology Board) - www.scenta.co.uk/careers.cfm

SEMTA - sector skills council for science, engineering and manufacturing technologies - www.semta.org.uk

TARGETjobs: Engineering (GTI Specialist Publishing Ltd.) - www.groupgti.com

Tomorrow's Engineers - www.tomorrowsengineers.org.uk/careers.cfm

Welsh Baccalaureate - www.wbq.org.uk

Women into Science, Engineering & Construction - www.wisecampaign.org.uk

▶Working in police, fire & security (2009) (Babcock Lifeskills) - www.babcock-lifeskills.com/

Addresses

Engineering Council
246 High Holborn, London WC1V 7EX
Phone: +44 (0)20 3206 0500
Web: www.engc.org.uk

Engineering Development Trust (EDT)
Ridgeway, Welwyn Garden City, Hertfordshire AL7 2AA
Phone: +44 (0)1707 871520
Web: www.etrust.org.uk

Engineering Training Council (NI)
Interpoint, 20-24 York Street, Belfast BT15 1AQ
Phone: +44 (0)28 9032 9878
Web: www.etcni.org.uk

Institution of Fire Engineers
London Road, Moreton-in-Marsh, Gloucestershire GL56 0RH
Phone: +44 (0)1608 812 580
Web: www.ife.org.uk

Jeremy Gardner Associates Ltd. (JGA)
22 Hanover Street, Edinburgh EH2 2EP
Phone: +44 (0)131 226 1661
Web: www.jgafire.com

Scottish Engineering
Training Officer, 105 West George Street, Glasgow G2 1QL
Phone: +44 (0)141 221 3181
Web: www.scottishengineering.org.uk

Similar Jobs

Engineer: Building Services, Engineer: Electrical, Engineer: Mechanical, Firefighter

Engineer: Gas

also known as: Gas Network Engineer

CRCI:Engineering
CLCI:RAN

Job Band: 4 to 5

Job Description

Gas engineers are concerned with the production, distribution and utilisation of natural or manufactured gas. They apply engineering skills to providing, storing and maintaining supply systems for industrial and domestic users. Some are involved with exploring and developing gas resources worldwide. Others are involved with development or manufacture of gas burning appliances, and with meeting the requirements of major consumers. Others work on pipeline design, construction and maintenance, and some work in gas utilisation so need knowledge of combustion and thermodynamics.

Engineers may use computer-aided design (CAD) technology for designing systems to improve safety, efficiency and maintenance routines. They need to have a thorough knowledge of safety legislation and procedures.

Work Details

Usually work a basic 35-40 hr week, though some weekend and irregular hours may be required. If involved with gas production and distribution you may be out on site some of the time, perhaps on a ship or rig. Key responsibilities include efficient and economic production and safety. You may also advise and inform gas users. If working for a manufacturer, you are based in an office or on industrial premises. In some jobs travel is necessary.

The work environment can be noisy and smelly and there may be a risk of accidents from equipment. You need to wear protective clothing.

Qualification

- **England, Wales and Northern Ireland**

Band 4: For HND, Diploma of Higher Education or foundation degree: 1-2 A levels, usually maths, chemistry or physics, and some GCSEs (A*-C) usually including English, maths and science, or equivalent.

Band 5: For many engineering degrees: 2-3 A levels, preferably including maths, physics and another science or technology subject, and some GCSEs (A*-C) including English and sometimes a foreign language, or equivalent qualifications. Exact requirements depend on the degree you take.

- **Scotland**

Band 4: For entry to SQA higher national and professional development awards: 2-3 H grades, usually maths and physics, and some S grades (1-3), including English, maths and science, or similar qualifications.

Band 5: For many engineering degrees: 3-5 H grades, preferably including maths and physics and another science or technology subject, and some S grades (1-3) including English and sometimes a foreign language, or similar qualifications. Exact requirements depend on the degree you take.

Degree Information

A first degree in chemical engineering, energy or fuel engineering/technology may give direct entry. Other subjects that may be acceptable to some employers include electrical engineering, mechanical engineering, production engineering or systems and control engineering. Some other engineering subjects, physics and chemistry, can also provide relevant background knowledge, but a specialist postgraduate qualification is also required.

Adult Qualifications

A degree or higher national award is usually required. Degree entry requirements are often relaxed for mature applicants, particularly if you have relevant experience. There are also many Access and foundation courses that lead to engineering qualifications. Appropriate postgraduate courses are open to engineering graduates.

Work Experience

Employers and universities may prefer candidates who have relevant work or voluntary experience, ideally within the energy industry. However something similar such as with a chemical engineering firm gives you a good basis and insight into the work. If you expect good A levels/H grades and intend to go to university, schemes such as 'A Year in Industry' enable you to spend a salaried year with a company to gain valuable work experience.

The Engineering Education Scheme runs programmes in England, Scotland and Wales giving young people the chance to be involved in a real engineering project for six months. Students commit to two to three hours work a week and some time at university residents' workshops. This experience can contribute to any future university application and counts towards the Duke of Edinburgh award skills section. Check the website for details.

Similarly, Headstart offers students a chance to experience a week at university, designing, building and testing projects. As engineering careers can be diverse, a week of hands on experience can be really helpful when you are trying to decide which field of engineering you want to train in. Check the website for details.

Entry and Training

There are few courses specific to this job and most entrants qualify with a background in a relevant engineering field often followed by a specialist postgraduate qualification. First degrees and HNDs are mainly full time but some are sandwich courses. Sponsorship for training may be possible. Relevant industrial training, initial professional development and further experience are required before becoming fully qualified. You must also commit to continuing professional development throughout your career.

Most gas engineers aim to become professional engineers with the Engineering Council at either incorporated or chartered engineer level. Applicants achieve this through membership of the Institution of Gas Engineers & Managers (IGEM). Both levels involve gaining experience and keeping detailed records of your development. Experience is followed by a professional review and an interview. Incorporated engineers (IEng) need to be qualified to HNC/HND or BEng level, followed by a further year of learning known as a Matching Section. Chartered engineers (CEng) may qualify through an accredited course leading to an MEng degree, or a BEng (Hons) followed by an appropriate masters degree. Contact IGEM for details of all routes to membership.

The Engineering Development Trust also runs a range of nationwide schemes for 11-21 year olds who may be interested in engineering as a career. Foundation degrees are available in general engineering subjects or in renewable energy technologies, but need to be extended to a full degree. Another route is through an apprenticeship programme leading to S/NVQ at level 4, then to HNC/HND.

Mature applicants are considered by employers depending on company requirements and your qualifications and experience. You may be able to qualify for incorporated/chartered engineer status if you are employed in a job at an equivalent grade to a chartered engineer (CEng) or incorporated engineer (IEng). Contact the Engineering Council or the Institution of Gas Engineers & Managers (IGEM) for details.

The Open University (OU) runs a range of engineering courses. See the OU website for details.

Opportunities and Pay

Employment can be with a division of British Gas, Transco or other gas supplier, a manufacturing or contracting company, the petroleum and chemical industries, or an industrial user. There are also good opportunities for work abroad.

Pay varies widely and depends on the company and level of responsibility, but generally a graduate entrant earns around £22k-£25k a year. With experience and professional qualifications you can earn £30k-£40k, rising to £50k or more a year.

Health
Good general fitness is needed for this work. There may be an allergy risk from fumes, pollen and dust.

Skills and Qualities
able to take responsibility, analytical skills, aptitude for maths and science, aptitude for teamwork, good organisational skills, good spoken communication, IT skills, resourceful, sound judgement, technical aptitude

Relevant Subjects
Chemistry, Design and technology, Engineering, English, ICT/ Computer studies, Manufacturing, Mathematics, Physics, Science

Further Information
AGCAS: Engineering (Job Sector Briefing) (AGCAS) - www.prospects.ac.uk

Apprenticeship Schemes (National Apprenticeship Service) - www.apprenticeships.org.uk

Cogent - sector skills souncil for chemicals, pharmaceuticals, nuclear, oil & gas, petroleum & polymers - www.cogent-ssc.com

Energy Institute (Institute of Petroleum (IOP) - www.energyinst.org.uk

Engineering Education Scheme - www.engineering-education.org.uk/

Engineering Education Scheme Wales - www.eesw.org.uk

Engineering Scotland (SEMTA) - www.engineeringscotland.org

Headstart Scheme - www.headstartcourses.org.uk

Open University - www.open.ac.uk

Scenta - Careers Guide, Engineering, Technology and Science (Engineering Technology Board) - www.scenta.co.uk/careers.cfm

SEMTA - sector skills council for science, engineering and manufacturing technologies - www.semta.org.uk

TARGETjobs: Engineering (GTI Specialist Publishing Ltd.) - www.groupgti.com

Tomorrow's Engineers - www.tomorrowsengineers.org.uk/careers.cfm

Women into Science, Engineering & Construction - www.wisecampaign.org.uk

Year in Industry (Engineering Development Trust) - www.yini.org.uk

Young Engineers - www.youngeng.org/

Addresses
Engineering Council
246 High Holborn, London WC1V 7EX
Phone: +44 (0)20 3206 0500
Web: www.engc.org.uk

Engineering Development Trust (EDT)
Ridgeway, Welwyn Garden City, Hertfordshire AL7 2AA
Phone: +44 (0)1707 871520
Web: www.etrust.org.uk

Engineering Training Council (NI)
Interpoint, 20-24 York Street, Belfast BT15 1AQ
Phone: +44 (0)28 9032 9878
Web: www.etcni.org.uk

Institution of Gas Engineers & Managers (IGEM)
IGEM House , High Street, Kegworth, Derbyshire DE74 2DA
Phone: 0844 375 4436 (UK only)
Web: www.igem.org.uk

Scottish Engineering
Training Officer, 105 West George Street, Glasgow G2 1QL
Phone: +44 (0)141 221 3181
Web: www.scottishengineering.org.uk

Similar Jobs
Engineer: Chemical, Engineer: Energy, Engineer: Marine, Engineer: Nuclear, Engineer: Petroleum, Engineer: Reservoir

Engineer: Land-based
also known as: Engineer: Agricultural, Field Engineer

CRCI:Engineering
CLCI:RAD
Job Band: 3 to 5

Job Description
Land-based engineers apply scientific and technological knowledge to a wide range of land-based industries. They may design, develop and construct machines, equipment and buildings for agriculture, horticulture, ground care or forestry. They also work with machinery such as tractors, cultivators, harvesters, or with systems to control conditions such as drying crops, milking, rearing poultry, grain silos and glasshouse technology. Engineers are increasingly involved in rural environment conservation practices such as soil conservation measures and waste management. They also apply their skills to matters involving irrigation, drainage, soil erosion and land resources.

Some land-based engineers work in developing countries abroad. They advise and use their expertise, particularly following natural disasters such as floods and earthquakes, and the aftermath of war and conflict, where there is environmental damage. Often work with other specialists, including microbiologists and geneticists as well as agronomists.

Work Details
Usually work a basic 35-40 hrs a week, Monday to Friday, though may sometimes be required to start early or work late and also work at weekends. Your place of work is an office, a laboratory or out on fieldwork. Travel may be necessary to different sites and you may need to work in isolated places. Advising, informing and consulting with people is crucial to your role.

You have to cope with some physical activity, walking on rough ground and sometimes climbing ladders. The job may require you to be outside in all weathers and you need special footwear or protective clothing. There may be a risk of accidents from equipment.

Qualification
• England, Wales and Northern Ireland
Band 4: For HND, Diploma of Higher Education or foundation degree: 1-2 A levels, preferably including maths and physics, and some GCSEs (A*-C) , usually including English and maths and science, or equivalent. Entry is often with a BTEC national award in agriculture or engineering.

Band 5: For degree courses: 2-3 A levels, usually including maths and physics, and some GCSEs (A*-C) usually including English and maths and sometimes a foreign language, or equivalent. Exact requirements depend on the degree you take.

• Scotland
Band 4: For a relevant SQA higher national and professional development awards, usually 2-3 H grades including maths and physics, and some S grades (1-3), including English, maths and science, or similar qualifications. Entry is often with an SQA national award in engineering or agriculture.

Band 5: For degree courses: 3-5 H grades, preferably including maths and physics, and some S grades (1-3), including English, maths and sometimes a foreign language, or similar qualifications. Exact requirements depend on the degree you take.

Engineer: Land-based

Degree Information
Degree subjects include agricultural or mechanical engineering, environmental engineering, off-road vehicle design and ergonomics. First degrees in agriculture, forestry, horticulture and environmental engineering/technology also provide a suitable base for a postgraduate MSc in agricultural engineering.

Adult Qualifications
A relevant higher education qualification, usually a degree or higher national award, is normally required. Adults with qualifications in other related disciplines and/or industrial experience may be eligible to join agricultural engineering courses. Access or foundation courses may also be available.

Work Experience
Employers and universities may prefer candidates who have relevant work or voluntary experience. Ideally this is with an agricultural manufacturing or engineering firm or in agricultural maintenance. If this proves difficult then any area of engineering is relevant and demonstrates enthusiasm and commitment to the job. Schemes such as 'A Year in Industry' gives those who expect good A levels/H grades and intend to go to university, the opportunity to spend a salaried year with a company to gain valuable work experience.

The Engineering Education Scheme, run by the Engineering Development Trust, offers programmes in England, Scotland and Wales for young people to be involved in a real engineering project for six months. Students commit to two to three hours work a week and some time at university residents' workshops. This valuable experience can contribute to any future university application and counts towards the Duke of Edinburgh award skills section. Check the website for details. Similarly, Headstart offers students a chance to experience a week at university, designing, building and testing projects. As engineering careers can be quite diverse, a week of hands on experience such as this can be really helpful when students are trying to decide which field of engineering they want to train in. Check the website for details.

In some areas there is a young apprenticeship (14-16) scheme that provides an extended work placement and eventual achievement of a relevant level 2 qualification whilst at school.

Entry and Training
Approved training is by practical experience after a degree or higher national award. Study can be full time or by a sandwich course. Take care to select a course that is accredited by the Engineering Council. The Tomorrow's Engineers website has lots of useful careers information including a route map and guide to engineering activities from primary school through to higher education. The Engineering Development Trust runs a range of nationwide schemes for 11-21 year olds. See the website for details.

Relevant industrial training, initial professional development and further responsible experience are required before becoming fully qualified. You must also commit to continuing professional development throughout your career. Contact the professional organisations for information.

Most agricultural engineers aim to become professional engineers at either incorporated or chartered engineer level through membership of the Institution of Agricultural Engineers (IAgrE). Both levels involve gaining experience and engineers need to keep detailed records of their development. Experience is followed by a professional review and an interview. There is no requirement for a specific period of experience; demonstration of competence and commitment are the sole criteria.

Incorporated engineers (IEng) need to be qualified to HNC/HND or BEng level, followed by a further year of learning known as a Matching Section. Another route is through an apprenticeship programme in land-based service engineering leading to S/NVQ at level 4, then to an HNC/HND. Foundation degrees are available in general engineering subjects, but need to be extended to a full degree. Chartered engineers (CEng) may qualify through an accredited course leading to an MEng degree, or a BEng (Hons) followed by an appropriate masters degree. Chartered engineers can also qualify as European engineers (EurIng) but need to be fluent in a European language.

Membership of IAgrE can be gained with a combination of academic qualifications and practical experience. Engineers whose work is concerned with environmental issues may become members of the Society for the Environment (SocEnv) and use the title of chartered environmentalist (CEnv). Existing IAgrE members can register with SocEnv.

A Diploma/Welsh Baccalaureate may be available in your area in engineering. The advanced level is equivalent to 3.5 A levels but for some university courses, the additional and specialist learning component of the diploma needs to include specific A levels eg maths or physics. Check entry requirements carefully with the individual institutions.

Mature applicants are considered, particularly if they have relevant work experience. Those wishing to receive incorporated/chartered engineer status who lack the required academic qualifications, may apply to achieve registration through the Technical Report Route. This gives applicants without post 18 academic qualifications the opportunity to demonstrate, through the writing of a technical report that they have acquired the necessary engineering knowledge. Applicants need to be employed in a job at an equivalent grade to a chartered engineer (CEng) or incorporated engineer (IEng). Contact the Engineering Council or the Institution of Agricultural Engineers for details.

The Open University (OU) runs a range of engineering courses and the Institution of Engineering Designers has accredited two OU engineering qualifications for professional registration. See the OU website for details. You may be able to receive funding for higher education from one of the larger manufacturing/engineering companies and for postgraduate study from the Engineering and Physical Sciences Research Council.

Opportunities and Pay
There are employment opportunities throughout the UK with manufacturing companies, research organisations, central government departments and agencies, conservation or environmental management, forestry, farm and estate management. There are shortages of skilled engineers, so opportunities are good at the moment. Self-employment as a consultant is possible. Work is also available abroad, mainly in developing countries.

Pay varies depending on location, type and size of company. Starting salaries for graduate entrants are generally around £18k-£24k a year and with experience £29k-£40k. Senior engineers can earn over £50k a year.

Health
There may be an allergy risk from animals, birds or pollens.

Skills and Qualities
able to work both on your own and in a team, analytical skills, flexible approach, good communication skills, good written English, information handling skills, IT skills, logical, problem-solving skills, technical aptitude

Relevant Subjects
Biology, Chemistry, Design and technology, Engineering, English, ICT/Computer studies, Land and Environment, Mathematics, Physics, Science

Further Information
Apprenticeship Schemes (National Apprenticeship Service) - www.apprenticeships.org.uk

Career Track - www.careertrack.org.uk

Diplomas (Foundation, Higher and Advanced) - http://yp.direct.gov.uk/diplomas

Engineering Education Scheme - www.engineering-education.org.uk/
Engineering Education Scheme Wales - www.eesw.org.uk
Engineering Scotland (SEMTA) - www.engineeringscotland.org
Headstart Scheme - www.headstartcourses.org.uk
Landwards (4 x year) (Institution of Agricultural Engineers) - www.iagre.org/landwards.shtml
Lantra - The Sector Skills Council for environmental & land-based sector (Lantra) http:/www.lantra.co.uk
Lantra Careers (A Future In...) (Lantra) - www.afuturein.com
Open University - www.open.ac.uk
Scenta - Careers Guide, Engineering, Technology and Science (Engineering Technology Board) - www.scenta.co.uk/careers.cfm
SEMTA - sector skills council for science, engineering and manufacturing technologies - www.semta.org.uk
TARGETjobs: Engineering (GTI Specialist Publishing Ltd.) - www.groupgti.com
Tomorrow's Engineers - www.tomorrowsengineers.org.uk/careers.cfm
Women into Science, Engineering & Construction - www.wisecampaign.org.uk
▶Working outdoors (2010) (Babcock Lifeskills) - www.babcock-lifeskills.com/
Year in Industry (Engineering Development Trust) - www.yini.org.uk
Young Engineers - www.youngeng.org/

Addresses

Agricultural Engineers Association (AEA)
Samuelson House, Forder Way, Hampton, Peterborough PE7 8JB
Phone: +44 0845 644 8748
Web: www.aea.uk.com

Engineering and Physical Sciences Research Council (EPSRC)
Polaris House North Star Avenue, Swindon, Wiltshire SN2 1ET
Phone: +44(0)1793 444 100
Web: www.epsrc.ac.uk

Engineering Council
246 High Holborn, London WC1V 7EX
Phone: +44 (0)20 3206 0500
Web: www.engc.org.uk

Engineering Development Trust (EDT)
Ridgeway, Welwyn Garden City, Hertfordshire AL7 2AA
Phone: +44 (0)1707 871520
Web: www.etrust.org.uk

Engineering Training Council (NI)
Interpoint, 20-24 York Street, Belfast BT15 1AQ
Phone: +44 (0)28 9032 9878
Web: www.etcni.org.uk

Institution of Agricultural Engineers (IAgrE)
Barton Road, Silsoe, Bedford MK45 4FU
Phone: +44 (0)1525 861 096
Web: www.iagre.org

Scottish Engineering
Training Officer, 105 West George Street, Glasgow G2 1QL
Phone: +44 (0)141 221 3181
Web: www.scottishengineering.org.uk

Society for the Environment (SocEnv)
The Old School House, 212 Long Street, Atherstone, Warwickshire CV9 1AH
Phone: +44 (0)845 337 2951
Web: www.socenv.org.uk

Similar Jobs

Agricultural Consultant/Adviser, Agricultural Research Scientist, Engineer: Manufacturing, Engineer: Mechanical, Service Technician: Land-based

Engineer: Manufacturing

also known as: Manufacturing Systems Engineer, Production Engineer

CRCI:Engineering
CLCI:RAB — Job Band: 4 to 5

Job Description

Manufacturing engineers combine engineering and managerial skills to plan and control effective manufacturing systems and components. They are involved in the organisational aspects of engineering and study production methods for the most efficient use of people, machines and materials. They work in a wide range of manufacturing and production industries and are usually involved at every stage of research and development, production of components and systems, marketing and after-sales service. May also be involved in training and managing staff and managing budgets. Work varies according to the sector or industry.

Engineers apply state-of-the-art technology to meet the needs of the company and constantly find better ways to make the products. They are competent in computer and management control systems, monitor performance, solve problems and advise on improvements and the introduction of new equipment.

Work Details

Usually work around 35-40 hrs a week, Monday to Friday. In some jobs, you may be expected to work shifts and be on call. Work may start early or finish late and can also include weekends. You collaborate with other departments such as research and development, sales and marketing. You advise and negotiate with colleagues. You are responsible for manufacturing technology and management so ensuring efficient production and high quality are key responsibilities. This job requires sound judgement and is demanding at times.

You may have to spend a lot of time in the production area, walking around and studying what is happening. The environment depends on the type of industry. You may need to wear appropriate protective clothing.

Qualification

• England, Wales and Northern Ireland

Band 4: For HND, Diploma of Higher Education or foundation degree: 1-2 A levels, usually maths and physics, and some GCSEs (A*-C) usually including English, maths and a science subject, or equivalent.

Band 5: For degree courses: 2-3 A levels, preferably including maths and physics, and some GCSEs (A*-C) usually including English and maths and sometimes a foreign language, or equivalent. Exact requirements depend on the degree you take.

• Scotland

Band 4: For entry to a relevant SQA higher national and professional development awards, usually 2-3 H grades, usually maths and physics, and some S grades (1-3), usually including English, maths and science, or similar qualifications.

Band 5: For degree courses: 3-5 H grades, including maths and preferably physics, and some S grades (1-3), usually including English and maths, or similar qualifications. Exact requirements depend on the degree you take.

Degree Information

A degree in production engineering, manufacturing systems/ engineering or mechanical/electrical engineering is preferred. Degrees in other engineering subjects and computer science may also be acceptable, particularly if followed by a specialist postgraduate course.

Adult Qualifications
A degree or higher national award is usually required. Course entry requirements for applicants with appropriate experience may be relaxed. There are also Access and foundation courses leading to engineering degrees.

Work Experience
Relevant work or voluntary experience is always useful and can improve your chances for entry to this career. Consider work within production or manufacturing engineering or in related occupations such as mechanical engineering. Applicants to degree courses are encouraged to apply to the 'Year in Industry' scheme for a placement in industry prior to starting their studies. Students also have an opportunity to gain work experience in industry for a year between the penultimate and final years of their degree programme. This experience enhances your job prospects on graduation.

In some areas there is a young apprenticeship (14-16) scheme that provides an extended work placement and eventual achievement of a relevant level 2 qualification whilst at school.

The Engineering Education Scheme runs programmes in England, Scotland and Wales giving young people the chance to be involved in a real engineering project for six months. Students commit to two to three hours work a week and some time at university residents' workshops. This valuable experience can contribute to any future university application and counts towards the Duke of Edinburgh award skills section. Check the website for details.

Similarly, Headstart offers students a chance to experience a week at university, designing, building and testing projects. As engineering careers can be diverse, a week of hands on experience can be really helpful when you are trying to decide which field of engineering you want to train in. Check the website for details.

Entry and Training
Training is after a degree or BTEC/SQA higher national award. There are few courses specific to this job and most entrants qualify with a background in a relevant engineering field followed by a specialist postgraduate qualification. Sponsorship for courses is often possible. Relevant industrial training, initial professional development and further experience are required before becoming fully qualified. You must also commit to continuing professional development throughout your career.

Tomorrow's Engineers has lots of useful careers information including a route map and guide to engineering activities from primary school through to higher education. The Engineering Development Trust also runs a range of nationwide schemes for 11-21 year olds who may be interested in engineering as a career. See the websites for details.

Most manufacturing engineers aim to become professional engineers with the Engineering Council at either incorporated or chartered engineer level. Both levels involve gaining experience and engineers need to keep detailed records of their development. Experience is followed by a professional review and an interview.

Incorporated engineers (IEng) need to be qualified to HNC/HND or BEng level, followed by a further year of learning. Another route is through an apprenticeship programme leading to S/NVQ at level 4, then to HNC/HND. Foundation degrees are available in general engineering subjects and in manufacturing engineering, but need to be topped up to a full degree. Chartered Engineers (CEng) may qualify through an accredited course leading to an MEng degree, or a BEng (Hons) followed by an appropriate masters degree. Chartered Engineers can also qualify as European Engineers (EurIng) but need to be fluent in a European language.

A Diploma/Welsh Baccalaureate may be available in your area in engineering. The advanced level is equivalent to 3.5 A levels but for some university courses, the additional and specialist learning (ASL) component of the diploma needs to include specific A levels eg maths or physics. Check entry requirements carefully with the individual institutions.

Mature applicants are usually considered but this depends on your qualifications and experience. Managerial and technological expertise is an advantage. Contact the Engineering Council for details.

The Open University (OU) runs a range of engineering courses and The Institution of Engineering Designers has accredited two OU engineering qualifications for professional registration. See the OU website for details.

Opportunities and Pay
There is a good demand for qualified production/manufacturing engineers although the recent economic downturn has had an impact on job opportunities. Jobs are with a wide variety of manufacturing companies and in all sorts of industries such as food and beverages, textiles, steel and shipbuilding, electronics, chemical and aeronautical industries, pharmaceuticals and domestic appliances. Opportunities for promotion to senior management positions are good.

Pay varies depending on location and the particular industry. Starting salaries for graduates are likely to be in the region of £20k-£25k rising to around £35-£45k with experience. Some may earn over £50k a year.

Health
This job may require good colour vision for certain areas of work.

Skills and Qualities
able to communicate effectively, able to manage people, able to work to deadlines, analytical skills, good organisational skills, information handling skills, IT skills, planning skills, problem-solving skills, technical aptitude

Relevant Subjects
Chemistry, Design and technology, Economics, Engineering, English, ICT/Computer studies, Manufacturing, Mathematics, Physics, Science

Further Information
AGCAS: Engineering (Job Sector Briefing) (AGCAS) - www.prospects.ac.uk

AGCAS: Manufacturing (Job Sector Briefing) (AGCAS) - www.prospects.ac.uk

Apprenticeship Schemes (National Apprenticeship Service) - www.apprenticeships.org.uk

Become an Engineer (IET) (Institution of Engineering and Technology (IET) - www.theiet.org/education/becomingengineer/makeyourchoice/

Diplomas (Foundation, Higher and Advanced) - http://yp.direct.gov.uk/diplomas

Engineering Connections - Apprenticeships - www.apprentices.co.uk

Engineering Education Scheme - www.engineering-education.org.uk/

Engineering Education Scheme Wales - www.eesw.org.uk

Engineering Scotland (SEMTA) - www.engineeringscotland.org

Headstart Scheme - www.headstartcourses.org.uk

Open University - www.open.ac.uk

Scenta - Careers Guide, Engineering, Technology and Science (Engineering Technology Board) - www.scenta.co.uk/careers.cfm

SEMTA - sector skills council for science, engineering and manufacturing technologies - www.semta.org.uk

Tomorrow's Engineers - www.tomorrowsengineers.org.uk/careers.cfm

Women into Science, Engineering & Construction - www.wisecampaign.org.uk

▶Working in engineering (2010) (Babcock Lifeskills) - www.babcock-lifeskills.com/

▶Working in space (2010) (Babcock Lifeskills) - www.babcock-lifeskills.com/

Year in Industry (Engineering Development Trust) - www.yini.org.uk

Young Engineers - www.youngeng.org/

Addresses

Engineering Council
246 High Holborn, London WC1V 7EX
Phone: +44 (0)20 3206 0500
Web: www.engc.org.uk

Engineering Development Trust (EDT)
Ridgeway, Welwyn Garden City, Hertfordshire AL7 2AA
Phone: +44 (0)1707 871520
Web: www.etrust.org.uk

Engineering Training Council (NI)
Interpoint, 20-24 York Street, Belfast BT15 1AQ
Phone: +44 (0)28 9032 9878
Web: www.etcni.org.uk

Institution of Engineering and Technology (IET)
Michael Faraday House, Stevenage, Hertfordshire SG1 2AY
Phone: +44 (0)1438 313311
Web: www.theiet.org

Institution of Engineering Designers (IED)
Courtleigh, Westbury Leigh, Wiltshire BA13 3TA
Phone: +44 (0)1373 822 801
Web: www.ied.org.uk

Institution of Mechanical Engineers (IMechE)
1 Birdcage Walk, Westminster, London SW1H 9JJ
Phone: +44 (0)20 7222 7899
Web: www.imeche.org.uk

Women into Science, Engineering & Construction (WISE)
2nd Floor Weston House, 246 High Holborn, London WC1V 7EX
Phone: +44 (0)20 3206 0408
Web: www.wisecampaign.org.uk

Similar Jobs

Engineer: Chemical, Engineer: Control & Instrumentation, Engineer: Design, Engineer: Mechanical, Production Manager, Quality Manager

Engineer: Marine

also known as: Maritime Engineer

CRCI:Engineering
CLCI:RAV Job Band: 4 to 5

Job Description

Marine engineers are involved in the design, construction, operation and maintenance of machinery and equipment used at sea, subsea and on offshore platforms. They usually specialise in one of three areas; shore-based shipbuilding and repair, offshore engineering including exploration of oil, gas and minerals, or service at sea as an engineering or maritime officer. They may work on a container ship, cruise liner, oil, gas or chemical carrier, submarine, oil or gas platform or in an onshore technical department. Marine engineers are concerned with the safe, efficient running of diesel engines, steam and gas turbines, hydraulics, and water and purification systems on board a ship.

They can also be involved in marine surveying, including the inspection of ships, warships, submarines and related vessels (pipe laying and survey ships) and offshore installations. Marine engineers are concerned in particular with the design and construction, safety and seaworthiness of vessels. They work in the repair and conversion of vessels and ensure that the safety precautions for crew, passengers and cargo are at a high standard and effective in all areas of work.

Work Details

Usually work a basic 35-40 hour week, Monday to Friday. However hours are flexible, especially when at sea or working to complete a project. Onshore, your place of work is an office, laboratory, workshop or construction yard. At sea, you may be on a ship or oil/gas rig. For these jobs you spend nights away from home, sometimes for long periods. You have to be able to cope with climbing ladders, with rough seas and working in close proximity to colleagues. In most jobs you advise, supervise and consult with people.

The environment can be noisy and uncomfortable and you have to put up with unpleasant weather conditions at times. There is also a risk of accidents at sea. You need to wear protective clothing.

Qualification

• England, Wales and Northern Ireland

Band 4: For HND in marine engineering, Diploma of Higher Education or foundation degree: 1-2 A levels, usually maths and physics or a technical subject, and some GCSEs (A*-C) usually including English, maths and science, or equivalent.

Band 5: For engineering degree: 2-3 A levels, including maths and physics or engineering science, and some GCSEs (A*-C) usually including English, maths and a science, or equivalent. Exact requirements depend on the degree you take.

• Scotland

Band 4: For entry to SQA higher national award in marine engineering and professional development awards: 2-3 H grades, usually maths and physics, and some S grades (1-3), including English, maths and science, or similar qualifications.

Band 5: For engineering degree courses: 3-5 H grades, including maths and physics, and some S grades (1-3), including English, maths and a science, or similar qualifications. Exact requirements depend on the degree you take.

Degree Information

A degree in marine engineering, marine technology, offshore engineering, naval architecture or mechanical engineering is ideal. Some other engineering subjects such as electrical/electronic engineering give useful background knowledge, but may not be accredited. Details of accredited courses can be obtained from the Institute of Marine Engineering, Science and Technology. There are also suitable postgraduate qualifications for engineering graduates.

Adult Qualifications

Entry with an HNC/HND is often limited to those who are sponsored by shipping companies (usually aged under 25), so a degree is usually required. Some institutions may reduce first degree entry requirements for mature students, particularly if they have relevant experience. There are also Access and foundation degree courses which can provide a route onto engineering degree courses.

Work Experience

Employers and universities may prefer candidates who have relevant work or voluntary experience. It can be difficult to obtain direct work experience, but spending time in related areas such as mechanical engineering demonstrates enthusiasm and commitment. Applicants to degree courses are encouraged to apply to the 'Year in Industry' scheme for a placement in industry prior to starting their studies. Students also have an opportunity to gain work experience in industry for a year between the penultimate and final years of their degree programme. This experience enhances job prospects on graduation.

Engineer: Marine

The Engineering Education Scheme runs programmes in England, Scotland and Wales giving young people the chance to be involved in a real engineering project for six months. Students commit to two to three hours work a week and some time at university residents' workshops. This experience can contribute to any future university application and counts towards the Duke of Edinburgh award skills section. Check the website for details.

Similarly, Headstart offers students a chance to experience a week at university, designing, building and testing projects. As engineering careers can be diverse, a week of hands on experience such as this can be helpful when you are trying to decide which field of engineering you want to train in. Check the website for details.

Entry and Training

Usually marine engineers complete a relevant engineering degree or HND before entry. There are also foundation degrees in marine engineering/science, which can lead onto an accredited degree course. Training is then on the job and is related to the requirements of the employer. Relevant industrial training, initial professional development and further experience are required before becoming fully qualified. You must also commit to continuing professional development throughout your career.

Most marine engineers join the Institute of Marine Engineering, Science and Technology (IMarEST) and aim to become professional engineers at incorporated or chartered engineer level with the Engineering Council. This involves gaining experience and keeping detailed records of your development. Experience is followed by a professional review and an interview.

Incorporated engineers (IEng) need to be qualified to HNC/HND or BEng level, followed by a further year of learning. Another route is through an apprenticeship programme leading to S/NVQ at level 4, then to HNC/HND. Foundation degrees are available in general engineering subjects, but need to be topped up to a full degree. Chartered engineers (CEng) may qualify through an accredited course leading to an MEng degree, or a BEng (Hons) followed by an appropriate masters degree. Chartered engineers can also qualify as European engineers (EurIng) but need to be fluent in a European language.

You can begin this career in the Royal Navy or Merchant Navy, where you gain national/internationally recognised qualifications that can also lead to IMarEST membership. It is also possible to enter as a marine engineering technician and with additional training and qualifications progress to engineer status.

The Tomorrow's Engineers website has lots of useful careers information including a route map and guide to engineering activities from primary school through to higher education. The Engineering Development Trust also runs a range of nationwide schemes for 11-21 year olds who may be interested in engineering as a career. See the websites for details.

A Diploma/Welsh Baccalaureate may be available in your area in engineering. The advanced level is equivalent to 3.5 A levels but for some university courses, the additional and specialist learning (ASL) component of the diploma needs to include specific A levels e.g maths or physics, so check entry requirements carefully. See the diplomas website for further information.

Mature applicants are usually considered but this depends on your qualifications and experience. Managerial and technological expertise is an advantage. There are relevant foundation degrees available as well as suitable Open University courses, and an option to qualify by taking the Engineering Council exams while in employment. Contact the Engineering Council for details. Entry to training in the Royal Navy is limited to those under 30.

Opportunities and Pay

Employment can be with marine design, construction and maintenance companies, shipping firms, the Merchant Navy/ Royal Navy, or with an engineering firm, offshore company, a shipyard or with the defence industry. There are often shortages of skilled engineers. There may be opportunities abroad.

Pay varies depending on location, type and size of employer. A graduate entrant is likely to earn around £24k a year. Experienced engineers who have gained their professional qualifications earn from around £35k and senior engineers can earn up to £50k a year.

Health

This job requires normal colour vision.

Skills and Qualities

Able to work both on your own and in a team, accurate, adaptable, analytical skills, good communication skills, good interpersonal skills, IT skills, perseverance, problem-solving skills, technical aptitude

Relevant Subjects

Chemistry, Design and technology, Engineering, English, ICT/ Computer studies, Mathematics, Physics, Science

Further Information

AGCAS: Engineering (Job Sector Briefing) (AGCAS) - www.prospects.ac.uk

Apprenticeship Schemes (National Apprenticeship Service) - www.apprenticeships.org.uk

Careers at Sea - www.careersatsea.org

Careers in the Marine Environment (IMarEST) - www.imarest.org/careers/

Diplomas (Foundation, Higher and Advanced) - http://yp.direct.gov.uk/diplomas

Engineering Education Scheme - www.engineering-education.org.uk/

Engineering Scotland (SEMTA) - www.engineeringscotland.org

Headstart Scheme - www.headstartcourses.org.uk

Marine Engineers Review (10 x year) (IMarEST) - www.imarest.org/Publications.aspx

Open University - www.open.ac.uk

Sea Your Future: A Guide to Marine Careers (IMAREST) - www.imarest.org/membership/careers

SEMTA - sector skills council for science, engineering and manufacturing technologies - www.semta.org.uk

Tomorrow's Engineers - www.tomorrowsengineers.org.uk/careers.cfm

Year in Industry (Engineering Development Trust) - www.yini.org.uk

Addresses

Engineering Council
246 High Holborn, London WC1V 7EX
Phone: +44 (0)20 3206 0500
Web: www.engc.org.uk

Engineering Development Trust (EDT)
Ridgeway, Welwyn Garden City, Hertfordshire AL7 2AA
Phone: +44 (0)1707 871520
Web: www.etrust.org.uk

Engineering Training Council (NI)
Interpoint, 20-24 York Street, Belfast BT15 1AQ
Phone: +44 (0)28 9032 9878
Web: www.etcni.org.uk

Institute of Marine Engineering, Science and Technology (IMarEST)
80 Coleman Street, London EC2R 5BJ
Phone: +44 (0)20 7382 2600
Web: www.imarest.org

Merchant Navy Training Board (MNTB)
Carthusian Court, 12 Carthusian Street, London EC1M 6EZ
Phone: +44 (0)20 7417 2800
Web: www.mntb.org.uk

Scottish Engineering
Training Officer, 105 West George Street, Glasgow G2 1QL
Phone: +44 (0)141 221 3181
Web: www.scottishengineering.org.uk

Ship Safe Training Group
The Precinct, Rochester, Kent ME1 1SR
Phone: +44 (0)1634 820 820
Web: www.sstg.org

Similar Jobs

Engineer: Mechanical, Marine Engineering Technician, Merchant Navy Deck/Navigating Officer, Merchant Navy Engineering Officer, Naval Architect, Royal Navy Officer

Engineer: Mechanical

also known as: Engineer: Mechatronics, Engineer: Robotics

CRCI:Engineering
CLCI:RAX Job Band: 4 to 5

Job Description

Mechanical engineers work on the design, planning and development, installation, operation and repair of plant, machinery and other mechanical equipment. This can be minute medical instruments or small component designs to very large vehicles, plant and machinery, including marine engines, aircraft and turbines. They may work in the biomedical or oil and gas industry, or in the research and development of mechanical body parts (such as knee joints and hearts). Others look at ways to improve the process and production of an offshore oil/gas rig. Mechanical engineers often need a knowledge of other branches of engineering, such as electronic, electrical or chemical engineering. Some work in research and development, others deal with practical problems in the operation of machinery.

Mechanical engineers help to develop, test and evaluate theoretical designs and look at the implications involving safety and reliability aspects. They are also involved in the testing of prototypes. Increasingly, engineers use computer-aided design (CAD), computer-aided manufacture (CAM) and robotics. They liaise with professional colleagues, including those from other engineering disciplines.

Work Details

Usually work around 35-40 hrs a week, Monday to Friday, though you may be required to work shifts in some industrial jobs. Sometimes you may be expected to be on call. Your place of work depends on the employing organisation but can be an office, a laboratory, industrial premises or a workshop. Depending on the product, the environment may be noisy and dirty.

There may be a risk of accidents from equipment and you need to wear special footwear, safety glasses and a helmet. You supervise, organise and consult with people, and liaise with a team. You may need to travel to other premises which may mean spending nights away from home.

Qualification

• England, Wales and Northern Ireland

Band 4: For HND, Diploma of Higher Education or foundation degree: 1-2 A levels, usually maths and physics, and some GCSEs (A*-C) usually including English, maths and science, or equivalent.

Band 5: For a degree in mechanical engineering: 2-3 A levels, preferably maths and physics or perhaps engineering, and some GCSEs (A*-C) including English, maths and sometimes a foreign language, or equivalent. Exact requirements depend on the degree you take.

• Scotland

Band 4: For entry to SQA higher national and professional development awards, usually 2-3 H grades, preferably maths and physics, and some S grades (1-3), including English, maths and science, or similar qualifications.

Band 5: For degree in mechanical engineering: 3-5 H grades, including maths and physics, and some S grades (1-3), including English, maths and sometimes a foreign language, or similar qualifications. Exact requirements depend on the degree you take.

Degree Information

A degree in mechanical engineering is preferred, but other first engineering degrees with a high mechanical engineering component, including aeronautical, computer-aided, manufacturing and agricultural engineering and engineering science, may be acceptable to some employers. Increasingly, there is an overlap between mechanical and electronic engineering and there are new courses available in manutronics and mechatronics to reflect this. Some other engineering subjects and physics can provide useful background knowledge, but not usually direct entry to this career.

Adult Qualifications

A degree or higher national award is normally required. Entry requirements for mature applicants may be relaxed, particularly if you have relevant experience. Access and foundation courses exist for mature students to enter engineering degrees.

Work Experience

Employers and universities may prefer candidates who have relevant work or voluntary experience. This can be one of the more difficult direct work experiences to obtain but spending time in related areas, such as motor vehicle maintenance, demonstrates enthusiasm and commitment and gives you an insight into the work involved. Applicants to degree courses are encouraged to apply to the 'Year in Industry' scheme for a placement in industry prior to starting their studies. Students also have an opportunity to gain work experience in industry for a year between the penultimate and final years of their degree programme. This experience enhances your job prospects following graduation.

The Engineering Education Scheme runs programmes in England, Scotland and Wales giving young people the chance to be involved in a real engineering project for six months. Students commit to 2/3 hours work a week and some time at university residents' workshops. This experience can contribute to any future university application and counts towards the Duke of Edinburgh award skills section. Check the website for details.

Similarly, Headstart offers students a chance to experience a week at university, designing, building and testing projects. As engineering careers can be diverse, a week of hands on experience can be really helpful when you are trying to decide which field of engineering you want to train in. Check the website for details.

Entry and Training

Training is by practical experience, after initial qualification with a degree or BTEC/SQA higher national diploma/certificate. Courses can be full time or part time and many are sandwich courses. Most mechanical engineers join the Institution of Mechanical Engineers. They have a Young Engineers section for student members. See the website for details. Relevant industrial training, initial professional development and further responsible experience are required before becoming fully qualified. You must also commit to continuing professional development throughout your career. Sponsorship for courses is common.

Most mechanical engineers also aim to become professional engineers at incorporated or chartered engineer level with the Engineering Council. This involves gaining experience and keeping detailed records of your development. Experience is followed by a professional review and an interview.

Incorporated engineers (IEng) need to be qualified to HNC/D or BEng level, followed by a further year of learning. Another route is through an apprenticeship programme leading to S/NVQ at level 4, then to HNC/HND. Foundation degrees are available in general engineering subjects and in chemical technology, but need to be extended to a full degree. Chartered engineers (CEng) may qualify through an accredited course leading to an MEng degree, or a BEng (Hons) followed by an appropriate masters degree. Chartered engineers can also qualify as European engineers (EurIng) but need to be fluent in a European language.

The Tomorrow's Engineers website has lots of useful careers information including a route map and a guide to engineering activities from primary school through to higher education. The Engineering Development Trust also runs a range of nationwide schemes for 11-21 year olds who may be interested in engineering as a career. See the websites for details.

A Diploma/Welsh Baccalaureate may be available in your area in engineering. The advanced level is equivalent to 3.5 A levels but for some university courses, the additional and specialist learning (ASL) component of the diploma needs to include specific A levels e.g maths or physics, so check entry requirements carefully. See the diplomas website for further information.

Mature applicants are usually considered but this depends on your qualifications and experience. Managerial and technological expertise is an advantage. Contact the Engineering Council or the Institution of Mechanical Engineers for details of mature entry routes to training and registration.

The Open University (OU) runs a range of engineering courses. See the OU website for details. You may be able to receive funding for higher education from one of the larger manufacturing/engineering companies and for postgraduate study from the Engineering and Physical Science Research Council.

Opportunities and Pay

Opportunities exist in a wide range of organisations. This includes the aerospace and automotive industries, medicine and sport engineering, oil/gas, nuclear and petrochemical industries, public sector and government agencies. There are also opportunities with the armed forces, the defence and transport industries, as well as engineering consultancies and engineering construction/manufacturing sectors.

Research jobs can be in industry or with a university or college. Opportunities for obtaining senior management positions are good and there is a steady demand for qualified engineers. You can also become an independent consultant.

Pay varies depending on location, type and size of company. Starting salaries for graduate entrants are around £20k-£25k a year. Experienced mechanical engineers at a senior level earn £35k-£50k a year.

Skills and Qualities

accurate, analytical skills, creative flair, good communication skills, good interpersonal skills, IT skills, logical, scientific approach, sound judgement, technical aptitude

Relevant Subjects

Chemistry, Design and technology, Engineering, English, ICT/Computer studies, Mathematics, Physics, Science

Further Information

AGCAS: Engineering (Job Sector Briefing) (AGCAS) - www.prospects.ac.uk

Careers in Engineering Booklets (SEMTA) - www.semta.org.uk

Diplomas (Foundation, Higher and Advanced) - http://yp.direct.gov.uk/diplomas

Engineering Education Scheme - www.engineering-education.org.uk/

Engineering Education Scheme Wales - www.eesw.org.uk

Engineering Scotland (SEMTA) - www.engineeringscotland.org

Headstart Scheme - www.headstartcourses.org.uk

Open University - www.open.ac.uk

SEMTA - sector skills council for science, engineering and manufacturing technologies - www.semta.org.uk

So you want to work in Engineering (Wayland) - www.waylandbooks.co.uk

TARGETjobs: Engineering (GTI Specialist Publishing Ltd.) - www.groupgti.com

Tomorrow's Engineers - www.tomorrowsengineers.org.uk/careers.cfm

▶Working in engineering (2010) (Babcock Lifeskills) - www.babcock-lifeskills.com/

▶Working in maths (2009) (Babcock Lifeskills) - www.babcock-lifeskills.com/

Year in Industry (Engineering Development Trust) - www.yini.org.uk

Addresses

Engineering and Physical Sciences Research Council (EPSRC)
Polaris House North Star Avenue, Swindon, Wiltshire SN2 1ET
Phone: +44(0)1793 444 100
Web: www.epsrc.ac.uk

Engineering Council
246 High Holborn, London WC1V 7EX
Phone: +44 (0)20 3206 0500
Web: www.engc.org.uk

Engineering Development Trust (EDT)
Ridgeway, Welwyn Garden City, Hertfordshire AL7 2AA
Phone: +44 (0)1707 871520
Web: www.etrust.org.uk

Engineering Training Council (NI)
Interpoint, 20-24 York Street, Belfast BT15 1AQ
Phone: +44 (0)28 9032 9878
Web: www.etcni.org.uk

Institution of Engineering and Technology (IET)
Michael Faraday House, Stevenage, Hertfordshire SG1 2AY
Phone: +44 (0)1438 313311
Web: www.theiet.org

Institution of Mechanical Engineers (IMechE)
1 Birdcage Walk, Westminster, London SW1H 9JJ
Phone: +44 (0)20 7222 7899
Web: www.imeche.org.uk

Scottish Engineering
Training Officer, 105 West George Street, Glasgow G2 1QL
Phone: +44 (0)141 221 3181
Web: www.scottishengineering.org.uk

Women into Science, Engineering & Construction (WISE)
2nd Floor Weston House, 246 High Holborn, London WC1V 7EX
Phone: +44 (0)20 3206 0408
Web: www.wisecampaign.org.uk

Similar Jobs

Engineer: Aeronautical, Engineer: Automotive, Engineer: Fire, Engineer: Manufacturing, Engineer: Traction & Rolling Stock, Mechanical Engineering Technician

Engineer: Minerals & Mining

also known as: Mining Engineer

CRCI:Engineering
CLCI:ROB
Job Band: 4 to 5

Job Description

Mining engineers assess the viability and economic potential of a new site prior to its development. They are also involved with the design, construction and operation of a mine or quarry workings.

Engineers use computer technology at the design stage, which may include computer-aided design (CAD) programs to create a three-dimensional model of the desired mine or quarry. Work also covers many aspects, including surveying, test drilling, sinking shafts, extracting ore or minerals and filling in disused shafts.

Mining engineers supervise the running of the plant, which can be for a metal, such as copper, iron or zinc, or non-metals, such as sand, clay or phosphates, or for coal. They are responsible for the overall safety of the mine, for work conditions and for any impact on the environment. Also liaises with geologists, engineers and other personnel.

Work Details

Usually work around 35-40 hrs a week, Monday to Friday, though shift work including early starts, late finishes and weekends may be required. Some engineers may also be on call at times. You work in an office and on site and are responsible for efficient production and for meeting safety and legal regulations. This job involves some physical activity including climbing ladders. The environment can be hot, dirty, dusty and uncomfortable. There may be a risk of accidents from equipment and you need to wear protective clothing and a helmet. The work may involve travel both in the UK and abroad, sometimes to very remote areas.

Qualification

- **England, Wales and Northern Ireland**

Band 4: For HND, Diploma of Higher Education or foundation degree: 1-2 A levels, usually maths and physics or chemistry, and some GCSEs (A*-C) usually including English, maths and science, or equivalent.

Band 5: For relevant degree courses: 2-3 A levels, usually chosen from maths, physics, engineering and chemistry, and some GCSEs (A*-C) usually including English and maths and sometimes a foreign language, or equivalent. Exact requirements depend on the degree you take.

- **Scotland**

Band 4: For entry to SQA higher national and professional development awards, usually 2-3 H grades, preferably maths and physics or chemistry, and some S grades (1-3), including English, maths and science, or similar qualifications.

Band 5: For relevant degree courses: 3-5 H grades, preferably including maths, physics and chemistry, and some S grades (1-3), including English, maths and sometimes a foreign language, or similar qualifications. Exact requirements depend on the degree you take.

Degree Information

There are specific first degree courses in chemical and mining/minerals engineering offered by the University of Leeds and the University of Exeter (Cornwall campus). These degrees may be preferred but degrees in civil engineering or mechanical engineering may also be acceptable. Geological sciences give relevant background knowledge. There are specialist postgraduate courses available.

Adult Qualifications

A degree or higher national award is normally required. There are relevant Access and foundation courses for adults with no formal qualifications. Course entry requirements may be relaxed for suitable mature applicants. Contact individual institutions.

Work Experience

Employers and universities may prefer candidates who have relevant work or voluntary experience. This is one of the more difficult direct work experiences to obtain, but spending time in related areas such as geology, surveying or engineering demonstrates enthusiasm and commitment and gives you an insight into some of the work involved. Applicants to degree courses are encouraged to apply to the 'Year in Industry' Scheme for a placement in industry prior to starting their studies. Students also have an opportunity to gain work experience in industry for a year between the penultimate and final years of their degree programme. This experience enhances your job prospects on graduation.

The Engineering Education Scheme, run by the Engineering Development Trust , offers programmes in England, Scotland and Wales giving young people the chance to be involved in a real engineering project for six months. Students commit to two to three hours work a week and some time at university residents' workshops. This valuable experience can contribute to any future university application and counts towards the Duke of Edinburgh award skills section. Check the website for details.

Similarly, Headstart offers students a chance to experience a week at university, designing, building and testing projects. As engineering careers can be quite diverse, a week of hands on experience such as this can be really helpful when students are trying to decide which field of engineering they want to train in.

Entry and Training

Training is usually on the job with experienced colleagues, after obtaining a relevant degree or BTEC/SQA HNC or HND. You can study full time, part time or by sandwich course and there are postgraduate courses available. It may be possible to get sponsorship for courses, either from your employer or a body such as the Engineering and Physical Sciences Research Council..

Many entrants join the Institute of Materials, Minerals and Mining (IOM3). Relevant industrial training, initial professional development and further responsible experience are required before becoming fully qualified. You must also commit to continuing professional development (CPD) throughout your career. IOM3 run a series of short courses which may support your CPD. To manage mines and other such sites, you must obtain a mine manager's certificate, known as a 'ticket', which is accepted internationally. You need to have passed an approved course prior to taking additional exams and a period of qualifying experience. Contact the IOM3 for details of all qualifying routes and approved degrees.

Most mining engineers aim to become professional engineers at incorporated or chartered engineer level with the Engineering Council (ECUK). This involves gaining experience and keeping detailed records of your development. Experience is followed by a professional review and an interview.

Incorporated engineers (IEng) need to be qualified to HNC/HND or BEng level, followed by a further year of learning known as a Matching Section. Another route is through an apprenticeship programme leading to S/NVQ at level 4, then to HNC/HND. Foundation degrees are available in general engineering subjects, but need to be topped up to a full degree. Chartered engineers (CEng) may qualify through an accredited course leading to an MEng degree, or a BEng (Hons) followed by an appropriate masters degree. Chartered engineers can also qualify as European engineers (EurIng) but need to be fluent in a European language.

The Engineering Development Trust runs a range of nationwide schemes for 11-21 year olds who are interested in engineering as a career. See the website for details. A Diploma/Welsh Baccalaureate may be available in your area in engineering. The advanced level is equivalent to 3.5 A levels but for some university courses, the additional and specialist learning component of the diploma needs to include specific A levels such as maths or physics. Check entry requirements carefully with the individual institutions. See the diplomas website for further information.

Those with considerable experience but who lack formal qualifications may be considered to qualify as a chartered/incorporated engineer. Contact the ECUK for details.

Contact professional organisations such as the Institute of Materials, Minerals and Mining (IOM3) or the ECUK, for details of mature entry routes to training and registration. Sponsorship may be available for higher education courses from the Engineering and Physical Sciences Research Council.

Opportunities and Pay
There are jobs in the UK but your career may take you to jobs based around the world, from South Africa to Australia. Many engineers join international companies and move to various different countries during their career. Employment is usually with large contractors in the extraction industries or with consultants. UK based jobs tend to be in areas that include mining consultancy, quarrying, oil and gas industry, tunnelling and mineral extraction, and also mining finance. There is generally a good demand for mining engineers.

Pay varies depending on location, type and size of company; engineers working in the oil sector generally earn more. Starting salaries for graduate entrants are around £25k a year, rising to around £60k. Some senior engineers earn more.

Health
This job requires good colour vision for certain areas of work. In some jobs there is an allergy risk from dust.

Skills and Qualities
able to make important decisions, able to work both on your own and in a team, good communication skills, IT skills, leadership qualities, problem-solving skills, project management skills, safety conscious, scientific approach, technical aptitude

Relevant Subjects
Chemistry, Design and technology, Engineering, English, Geography, ICT/Computer studies, Mathematics, Physics, Science

Further Information
AGCAS: Engineering (Job Sector Briefing) (AGCAS) - www.prospects.ac.uk

Apprenticeship Schemes (National Apprenticeship Service) - www.apprenticeships.org.uk

Careers in Engineering Booklets (SEMTA) - www.semta.org.uk

Careers in Extractives (Proskills) - www.prospect4u.co.uk

Diplomas (Foundation, Higher and Advanced) - http://yp.direct.gov.uk/diplomas

Engineering Education Scheme - www.engineering-education.org.uk/

Engineering Education Scheme Wales - www.eesw.org.uk

Headstart Scheme - www.headstartcourses.org.uk

SEMTA - sector skills council for science, engineering and manufacturing technologies - www.semta.org.uk

TARGETjobs: Engineering (GTI Specialist Publishing Ltd.) - www.groupgti.com

The Mining Journal Online - www.mining-journal.com

Welsh Baccalaureate - www.wbq.org.uk

Women into Science, Engineering & Construction - www.wisecampaign.org.uk

Year in Industry (Engineering Development Trust) - www.yini.org.uk

Addresses
Engineering and Physical Sciences Research Council (EPSRC)
Polaris House North Star Avenue, Swindon, Wiltshire SN2 1ET
Phone: +44(0)1793 444 100
Web: www.epsrc.ac.uk

Engineering Council
246 High Holborn, London WC1V 7EX
Phone: +44 (0)20 3206 0500
Web: www.engc.org.uk

Engineering Development Trust (EDT)
Ridgeway, Welwyn Garden City, Hertfordshire AL7 2AA
Phone: +44 (0)1707 871520
Web: www.etrust.org.uk

Institute of Materials, Minerals and Mining (IOM3)
1 Carlton House Terrace, London SW1Y 5DB
Phone: +44 (0)20 7451 7300
Web: www.iom3.org

Similar Jobs
Engineer: Gas, Engineer: Petroleum, Engineer: Reservoir, Geologist, Surveyor: Minerals & Waste Management

Engineer: Municipal
CRCI:Building and Construction
CLCI:UN

Job Band: 4 to 5

Job Description
Municipal engineers work for the public service branch of civil engineering in planning, design, construction and maintenance of systems such as road and traffic, water supply and the disposal of refuse and sewage. They also supervise schemes for airports, docks, bridges, land reclamation projects, coastal protection and most systems that are controlled by local and central government, and public utility companies. May be involved in the monitoring of road parking and street lighting schemes and improvements. Conducting ground surveys and producing detailed designs, often with the use of computer-aided design (CAD) software are all part of the job. Must carefully consider whether the design has an impact on the environment.

Engineers produce a contract so that engineering companies can then bid for the work, and manage the project through to completion, on budget and on time. May be required to attend public meetings to explain any new scheme or design.

Work Details
Municipal engineers usually work around 35-40 hrs a week, Monday to Friday, though some evenings and weekends may be expected. You may also have to be on call. Work is based in an office and sometimes on-site at different places. Advising and informing colleagues, supervising and organising work on site is crucial to your role. Problems must be solved quickly. You may be concerned with planning and public health issues, which sometimes require attendance at public meetings.

Work is pressurised at times and may involve making unpopular decisions. Conditions on site can be noisy and involve using ladders and scaffolding and covering rough ground. At times you are out in all sorts of weather. You need to wear protective footwear and a safety helmet. There is a risk of accidents from equipment.

Qualification

• England, Wales and Northern Ireland
Band 4: For BTEC higher national award: 1-2 A levels, preferably maths and physics, and some GCSEs (A*-C) including English, maths and science, or equivalent. There are foundation courses available for those without appropriate A levels.

Band 5: For degree courses: 2-3 A levels, preferably maths, physics or engineering science, and some GCSEs (A*-C) usually including English and a science subject, or equivalent qualifications. Exact requirements depend on the degree you take. There are foundation courses available for those without appropriate A levels.

• Scotland
Band 4: For SQA higher national award: 2-3 H grades, usually including maths and physics, and some S grades (1-3), often including English, maths and science, or similar qualifications. There are foundation courses available for those without appropriate H grades.

Band 5: For degree courses: 3-5 H grades, preferably including maths, physics/chemistry or engineering science, and some S grades (1-3) including English and a science subject, or similar qualifications. Exact requirements depend on the degree you take. There are foundation courses available for those without appropriate H grades.

Degree Information

A degree in civil/structural engineering, general engineering, and numerate subjects, including physics, maths and geology are particularly relevant. To become a chartered engineer you need an accredited MEng honours degree in civil/structural engineering, engineering science, or other accredited learning.

Adult Qualifications

Recent qualifications, such as an appropriate degree or a higher national award, are usually required. Adults applying for courses should check with individual academic institutions for details of mature entry requirements. Those with relevant qualifications and/or experience in a related area may be considered. Access or foundation courses may also be available.

Work Experience

Entry to this job can be competitive. It is important that you try to do some relevant work or voluntary experience before applying to degree courses or jobs. The types of work experience to consider are with a civil engineering or construction company. In some areas there is a young apprenticeship (14-16) scheme that provides an extended work placement and eventual achievement of a level 2 qualification whilst at school.

Other schemes, such as 'A Year in Industry' allow those who expect good A levels/H grades and intend to go to university, the opportunity to spend a salaried year with a company to gain valuable work experience. The Engineering Education Scheme in England links year 12 students with local companies to work on real engineering problems. A similar scheme operates in Wales. See the websites for details.

Entry and Training

Most municipal chartered engineers are qualified civil engineers who have trained after gaining a relevant engineering degree (MEng/BEng). Courses for these can be full time, part time, distance learning or sandwich. There are alternatives to accredited degrees, such as an Open University degree, Engineering Council examinations, cognate degrees such as maths, physics or chemistry, plus relevant experience. Relevant industrial training, initial professional development and further responsible experience are required before becoming fully qualified.

You can also apply for incorporated engineers (IEng) status through the Engineering Council UK. You need to be qualified to HNC/HND or BEng level. To become a chartered engineer (CEng) through the Institution of Civil Engineers, you must hold an MEng or accredited equivalent, plus satisfy all the requirements of the Chartered Professional Review (CPR). Chartered engineers can also qualify as European engineers (EUR ING) which is recognised in Europe. The minimum age for registration as a chartered engineer is 25, although the study and training can be completed earlier.

The 'Inspire Scholarships' scheme, offered through ConstructionSkills, the Sector Skills Council for the construction industry, offers scholarships of up to £9k to help fund a construction-related degree, such as civil engineering, architecture, surveying and construction management. Visit the bconstructive website for details. It is also possible to be sponsored by an employer.

A Diploma/Welsh Baccalaureate may be available in your area in construction and the built environment. The advanced level is equivalent to 3.5 A levels but for some university courses, the additional and specialist learning (ASL) component of the diploma needs to include specific A levels eg maths or physics. Check entry requirements carefully with the individual institutions.

Continuing professional development (CPD) is important and a key element throughout your career to keep up to date with the latest developments. The professional institutions and societies offer programmes of CPD that include workshops, conferences and short courses on a range of subjects.

Mature entrants may have difficulty in finding employment unless you have previous relevant experience. There is a Technical Report Route (TRR) offered by the Institute of Civil Engineering for those who wish to gain chartered engineer (CEng) or incorporated engineer (IEng) status, but who do not meet the required formal academic qualifications. Applicants without the appropriate qualifications are therefore expected to have had considerable relevant experience of at least 15 years; those with accredited HNC/HND (or equivalent) at least 10 years (CEng) or five years (IEng). The Open University also offers an MEng degree course and there are other options of flexible or distance-learning courses.

Opportunities and Pay

Employment is mainly with local and central government departments and agencies, engineering consultants and contractors, water and waste management companies, and public utility companies. Often organisations have a clear progression structure and opportunities are generally better in larger organisations. It helps if you are willing to move around the country to gain experience.

Starting salaries for graduate entrants are around £20k-£26k a year, rising to £26k-£40k with experience. Chartered engineers can earn up to £60k a year or more in some instances. Allowances may be given for travel costs and travelling time and a company car may be provided.

Skills and Qualities

able to follow drawings and plans, able to take responsibility, accurate, aptitude for maths and science, good spoken and written communication, methodical, planning skills, scientific approach, sound judgement, specialist IT skills

Relevant Subjects

Chemistry, Construction and built environment, Design and technology, English, ICT/Computer studies, Mathematics, Physics, Science

Further Information

AGCAS: Engineering (Job Sector Briefing) (AGCAS) - www.prospects.ac.uk

bconstructive - www.bconstructive.co.uk/

Diplomas (Foundation, Higher and Advanced) - http://yp.direct.gov.uk/diplomas

Engineering Education Scheme - www.engineering-education.org.uk/

Engineering Education Scheme Wales - www.eesw.org.uk

Open University - www.open.ac.uk

SEMTA - sector skills council for science, engineering and manufacturing technologies - www.semta.org.uk

TARGETjobs: Civil & Structural Engineering (GTI Specialist Publishing Ltd.) - www.groupgti.com

Welsh Baccalaureate - www.wbq.org.uk

▶Working in construction & the built environment (2007) (Babcock Lifeskills) - www.babcock-lifeskills.com/

Year in Industry (Engineering Development Trust) - www.yini.org.uk

Addresses

Engineering Council
246 High Holborn, London WC1V 7EX
Phone: +44 (0)20 3206 0500
Web: www.engc.org.uk

Institute of Highway Incorporated Engineers (IHIE)
De Morgan House, 58 Russell Square, London WC1B 4HS
Phone: +44 (0)20 7436 7487
Web: www.ihie.org.uk

Institution of Civil Engineers (ICE)
1 Great George Street, Westminster, London SW1P 3AA
Phone: +44 (0)20 7222 7722
Web: www.ice.org.uk

Royal Academy of Engineering
3 Carlton House Terrace, London SW1Y 5DG
Phone: +44 (0) 20 7766 0600
Web: www.raeng.org.uk

Similar Jobs

Civil Engineering Technician, Engineer: Building Services, Engineer: Civil/Structural, Surveyor: Planning & Development

Engineer: Nuclear

CRCI:Engineering
CLCI:RAN
Job Band: 4 to 5

Job Description

Nuclear engineers study the development and application of nuclear energy to produce power both economically and safely. They are concerned with design, construction, running and control of reactors and power stations and also work on the decommissioning of plants when they are no longer required. This includes work on the safe disposal of nuclear waste and protection of the workforce and public. Engineers can also develop nuclear power sources for naval submarines, or may use radiation in other areas, such as agriculture or medicine. Other areas of work include environmental monitoring and protection, nuclear research, and the design and development of power sources for spacecraft.

Work Details

Usually work around 35-40 hrs a week, Monday to Friday, though engineers working in power stations need to work shifts to cover 24 hour production. You are based in an on-site office and weekend and night work is sometimes necessary. You monitor processes and supervise other employees. You are also responsible for radiation safety, making managerial decisions and for preparing emergency plans. The work can be pressured at times.

The environment is clean and pleasant but can be enclosed. There may be a risk of exposure to radiation and accidents from equipment. You may need to wear protective clothing in certain areas of work.

Qualification

• England, Wales and Northern Ireland

Band 4: For HND in engineering: Diploma of Higher Education or foundation degree: 1-2 A levels, usually maths and physics or chemistry, and some GCSEs (A*-C) usually including English, maths and science, or equivalent.

Band 5: For degree courses: 2-3 A levels, usually including maths, physics or engineering science, and some GCSEs (A*-C) usually including English, maths and sometimes chemistry, or equivalent. Exact requirements depend on the degree you take.

• Scotland

Band 4: For entry to SQA higher national and professional development awards: at least 2-3 H grades, usually maths and physics or chemistry, and some S grades (1-3), including English, maths and science, or similar qualifications.

Band 5: For degree courses: 3-5 H grades, including English, maths and physics, and some S grades (1-3), including English, maths and sometimes chemistry, or similar qualifications. Exact requirements depend on the degree you take.

Degree Information

A degree in nuclear, mechanical or electrical engineering is usually preferred, but degrees in physics or energy technology may also be acceptable. A degree in nuclear engineering is available at the University of Lancaster in the UK and the University of Surrey runs a course in physics with nuclear astrophysics. Some other engineering subjects provide useful background, but may not meet the entry requirements. Specialist postgraduate courses are available for engineering graduates.

Adult Qualifications

A degree or higher national award is normally required. Some course entry requirements are relaxed for older applicants, particularly if you have relevant experience. There are also many Access or foundation courses for engineering. There are specialist postgraduate courses for engineering graduates.

Work Experience

Employers and universities may prefer candidates who have relevant work or voluntary experience. The most suitable experience is within the energy industry, but something similar such as work with a chemical engineering company gives you a good basis and insight into the job. If you expect good A levels/H grades and intend to go to university, schemes such as 'A Year in Industry' provide you with the opportunity to spend a salaried year with a company to gain valuable work experience.

The Engineering Education Scheme runs programmes in England, Scotland and Wales giving young people the chance to be involved in a real engineering project for six months. Students commit to two to three hours work a week and some time at university residents' workshops. This experience can contribute to any future university application and counts towards the Duke of Edinburgh award skills section. Check the website for details.

Similarly, Headstart offers students a chance to experience a week at university, designing, building and testing projects. As engineering careers can be diverse, a week of hands on experience can be helpful when you are trying to decide which field of engineering you want to train in. Check the website for details.

Information on student work placements or educational visits to UK power stations are available from companies such as British Energy Group. Check the websites for details.

Entry and Training

Training is by practical experience, after a degree or BTEC/SQA higher national award. There are few courses specific to this job and most entrants qualify with a background in a relevant engineering field, often followed by specialist postgraduate study. Initial courses are mainly full time but some are sandwich courses. Sponsorship for courses may be available. Relevant industrial training, initial professional development and further experience are required before becoming fully qualified. You must commit to continuing professional development throughout your career. Sponsorship and graduate training schemes may be available from companies such as British Energy Group.

Many entrants join the Nuclear Institute and aim to become professional engineers at incorporated or chartered engineer level with the Engineering Council. This involves gaining experience and keeping detailed records of your development. Experience is followed by a professional review and an interview.

Incorporated engineers (IEng) need to be qualified to HNC/HND or BEng level, followed by a further year of learning. Another route is through an apprenticeship programme leading to S/NVQ at level 4, then to HNC/HND. Foundation degrees are available in general engineering subjects, but need to be topped up to a full degree. Chartered engineers (CEng) may qualify through an accredited course leading to an MEng degree, or a BEng (Hons) followed by an appropriate masters degree. Chartered engineers can also qualify as European engineers (EurIng) but need to be fluent in a European language.

The Tomorrow's Engineers website has lots of useful careers information including a route map and guide to engineering activities from primary school through to higher education. The Engineering Development Trust also runs a range of nationwide schemes for 11-21 year olds who may be interested in engineering as a career. See the websites for details. Similarly, Nuclear Courses is a good source of information on education and training in this sector. Visit the websites for details.

A Diploma/Welsh Baccalaureate may be available in your area in engineering. The advanced level is equivalent to 3.5 A levels but for some university courses, the additional and specialist learning component of the diploma needs to include specific A levels e.g maths or physics so check entry requirements carefully. See the diplomas website for further information. An apprenticeship is also available in nuclear decommissioning and may provide an alternative route into this career.

Mature applicants are usually considered but this depends on your qualifications and experience. Managerial and technological expertise is an advantage. Contact the Engineering Council for details.

The Open University (OU) runs a range of engineering courses. See the OU website for details. You may be able to receive funding for higher education from one of the larger manufacturing/engineering companies and for postgraduate study from the Engineering and Physical Science Research Council. Contact the Engineering Council or the Institution of Engineering and Technology for details of all training opportunities and mature entry.

Opportunities and Pay
This is a small profession and jobs are available only in certain parts of the country. Most employment is with nuclear energy/fuel companies. There are also opportunities in technical consultancy, with organisations that oversee environmental and safety aspects of the nuclear industry, central government agencies, and with the Royal Navy. Promotion prospects may depend on future political decisions about the nuclear power industry. A good honours degree and sometimes a higher degree are required for research and development posts.

Pay varies depending on location, type and size of company. Starting salaries for graduates are around £25k a year, rising to around £35k-£45k a year. Some senior nuclear engineers earn £50k-£60k a year.

Health
This job requires normal colour vision for certain areas of work.

Skills and Qualities
able to cope under pressure, able to take responsibility, analytical skills, good communication skills, IT skills, numeracy skills, problem-solving skills, safety conscious, scientific approach, sound judgement

Relevant Subjects
Chemistry, Design and technology, Engineering, English, ICT/ Computer studies, Mathematics, Physics, Science

Further Information
AGCAS: Engineering (Job Sector Briefing) (AGCAS) - www.prospects.ac.uk
Apprenticeship Schemes (National Apprenticeship Service) - www.apprenticeships.org.uk
Cogent - sector skills souncil for chemicals, pharmaceuticals, nuclear, oil & gas, petroleum & polymers - www.cogent-ssc.com
Diplomas (Foundation, Higher and Advanced) - http://yp.direct.gov.uk/diplomas
Engineering Education Scheme - www.engineering-education.org.uk/
Engineering Education Scheme Wales - www.eesw.org.uk
Engineering Scotland (SEMTA) - www.engineeringscotland.org
Headstart Scheme - www.headstartcourses.org.uk
Nuclear Courses - www.nuclearcourses.com
Nuclear Future (bi-monthly) (BNES & INUCE) - www.nuclearinst.com/bis/Nuclear%20Institute/Journal
Nuclear Institute - www.nuclearinst.com
Nuclear Technology Engineering Consortium - www.ntec.ac.uk
Open University - www.open.ac.uk
SEMTA - sector skills council for science, engineering and manufacturing technologies - www.semta.org.uk
Steps to Engineering - www.steps.ie
Tomorrow's Engineers - www.tomorrowsengineers.org.uk/careers.cfm
Welsh Baccalaureate - www.wbq.org.uk
Women into Science, Engineering & Construction - www.wisecampaign.org.uk
Year in Industry (Engineering Development Trust) - www.yini.org.uk

Addresses
British Energy Group plc
GSO Business Park, East Kilbride G74 5PG
Phone: +44 (0)1355 846000
Web: www.british-energy.com

Engineering and Physical Sciences Research Council (EPSRC)
Polaris House North Star Avenue, Swindon, Wiltshire SN2 1ET
Phone: +44(0)1793 444 100
Web: www.epsrc.ac.uk

Engineering Council
246 High Holborn, London WC1V 7EX
Phone: +44 (0)20 3206 0500
Web: www.engc.org.uk

Engineering Development Trust (EDT)
Ridgeway, Welwyn Garden City, Hertfordshire AL7 2AA
Phone: +44 (0)1707 871520
Web: www.etrust.org.uk

Engineering Training Council (NI)
Interpoint, 20 24 York Street, Belfast BT15 1AQ
Phone: +44 (0)28 9032 9878
Web: www.etcni.org.uk

Institution of Engineering and Technology (IET)
Michael Faraday House, Stevenage, Hertfordshire SG1 2AY
Phone: +44 (0)1438 313311
Web: www.theiet.org

Lancaster University
Bailrigg, Lancaster LA1 4YW
Phone: +44 (0)1524 65201
Web: www.lancs.ac.uk

Scottish Engineering
Training Officer, 105 West George Street, Glasgow G2 1QL
Phone: +44 (0)141 221 3181
Web: www.scottishengineering.org.uk

UCAS
Customer Services Unit, PO Box 28, Cheltenham GL52 3LZ
Phone: +44 (0)871 468 0468
Web: www.ucas.com

University of Surrey
, Guildford, Surrey GU2 7XH
Phone: +44 (0)1483 300800
Web: www.surrey.ac.uk

Similar Jobs
Engineer: Chemical, Engineer: Control & Instrumentation, Engineer: Electrical, Engineer: Energy, Engineer: Gas, Engineer: Mechanical

Engineer: Petroleum
CRCI:Engineering
CLCI:SAS Job Band: 5

Job Description
Petroleum engineers use scientific and engineering principles to ensure the efficient development and production of oilfields. They integrate subsurface and topside engineering activities to bring oil

to the surface and collect and evaluate drilling and production data. Engineers use sophisticated high technology in their work. They design, install and monitor systems to extract oil reserves safely, efficiently and to maximum potential. Also manage staff at all levels, including their training, development and daily supervision. Often work in interdisciplinary teams of other professionals, including geoscientists, reservoir engineers, safety engineers, well-log analysts, and also environmental/regulatory specialists.

Work Details

Usually work 9am-5pm, Monday to Friday, when working from an office. May be expected to work shifts or unusual hours when on site or offshore. Sometimes work outdoors in all weathers. Frequent travel is required within the working day and often overnight. The work can be physically active and there may be a risk of accidents. Some of the work locations can be inhospitable and living conditions offshore are shared. Protective clothing is worn when necessary.

Qualification

• England, Wales and Northern Ireland

Band 5: For many engineering degree courses: 2-3 A levels, preferably including maths, physics and another science or technology subject, and some GCSEs (A*-C) usually including English, maths and sometimes a foreign language, or equivalent. Exact requirements depend on the degree you take.

• Scotland

Band 5: For many engineering degree courses: 3-5 H grades, preferably including maths and physics and another science or technology subject, and some S grades (1-3), including English, maths and sometimes a foreign language, or similar qualifications. Exact requirements depend on the degree you take.

Degree Information

Relevant first degrees include petroleum engineering, offshore engineering, chemistry, physics/applied physics, civil engineering, mathematics, chemical engineering, mineral and mining engineering, energy or fuel technology, and mechanical engineering. Specialist postgraduate qualifications are often required.

Adult Qualifications

A degree is normally required. Degree entry requirements are often reduced for older applicants, particularly if you have relevant experience. There are also many Access and foundation courses that lead to engineering courses. Appropriate postgraduate courses are open to engineering graduates.

Work Experience

Entry to this career is competitive, however work experience may be hard to gain as most petroleum engineering is undertaken overseas. It improves your chances at interview if you have some work experience in a related area such as chemical engineering or another area of engineering. Applicants to degree courses are encouraged to apply to the 'Year in Industry' Scheme for a placement in industry prior to starting their studies. Students also have an opportunity to gain work experience in industry for a year between the penultimate and final years of their degree programme. This experience enhances your job prospects on graduation.

The Engineering Education Scheme, run by the Engineering Development Trust, offers programmes in England, Scotland and Wales giving young people the chance to be involved in a real engineering project for six months. Students commit to two to three hours work a week and some time at university residents' workshops. This valuable experience can contribute to any future university application and counts towards the Duke of Edinburgh award skills section. Check the website for details.

Similarly, Headstart offers students a chance to experience a week at university, designing, building and testing projects. As engineering careers can be quite diverse, a week of hands on experience such as this can be really helpful when students are trying to decide which field of engineering they want to train in. Check the website for details.

Entry and Training

A good honours degree (at least a 2:1) is normally required and many entrants have a higher degree in petroleum engineering. Recruitment by major oil companies takes place annually. Training, often through a graduate training scheme, varies considerably from company to company, but generally includes formal courses to supplement practical experience.

There is a strong emphasis on attaining chartered status through the Engineering Council (ECUK). To achieve this you must become a member of one of the professional organisations, such as the Institute of Materials, Minerals and Mining (IOM3). Relevant industrial training, initial professional development and further responsible experience are required before becoming fully qualified. You must also commit to continuing professional development throughout your career. The professional organisations can help with this through relevant short training courses.

Chartered engineers (CEng) may qualify through an accredited course leading to an MEng degree, or a BEng (Hons) followed by an appropriate masters degree. Chartered engineers can also qualify as European engineers (EurIng) but need to be fluent in a European language. See the ECUK website for full details.

The Engineering Development Trust runs a range of nationwide schemes for 11-21 year olds who are interested in engineering as a career. See the website for details. A Diploma/Welsh Baccalaureate may be available in your area in engineering. The advanced level is equivalent to 3.5 A levels but for some university courses, the additional and specialist learning component of the diploma needs to include specific A levels such as maths or physics. Check entry requirements carefully with the individual institutions. See the diplomas website for further information.

The Energy Institute provides comprehensive oil, gas and energy training programmes, including introductory, intermediate and advanced levels. A number of shorter 4 day courses have been introduced to facilitate simultaneous training and working. The Offshore Petroleum Industry Training and Oil and Gas UK websites have lots of useful career information and job vacancy details. Visit the sites for full details.

The Institute of Petroleum Engineering at Heriot Watt University in Edinburgh runs a network of excellence in training. This is a joint venture with industry to ensure that courses and training meet the needs of their petrotechnical customers. The focus is on critical skills development by providing training in areas such as well design and construction. Courses are delivered through tutor led and computer based training and elearning. See the website for details.

Those with considerable experience but who lack formal qualifications may be considered for the Technical Report Route to qualify as a chartered engineer through the ECUK. This gives applicants without post 18 academic qualifications the opportunity to demonstrate, through the writing of a technical report that they have acquired the necessary engineering knowledge. Applicants need to be employed in a job at an equivalent grade to a chartered engineer (CEng) or incorporated engineer (IEng). Contact professional organisations such as the Society of Petroleum Engineers, Institute of Materials, Minerals and Mining (IOM3) or the ECUK, for details of mature entry routes to training and registration. Sponsorship may be available for higher education courses.

Opportunities and Pay
This is a worldwide business and many of the jobs are overseas. British graduates compete with graduates from many other countries and competition for jobs is fierce. Prospects for promotion to senior positions are generally good. Self employment and freelance work is possible for experienced petroleum engineers.

Pay varies depending on location and size of company. Starting salaries for graduate entrants are around £25k-£30k. Experienced and senior petroleum engineers earn around £50k-£70k.

Health
This job requires good colour vision for certain areas of work. In some jobs there is an allergy risk from dust.

Skills and Qualities
able to make important decisions, able to work both on your own and in a team, analytical skills, IT skills, methodical, problem-solving skills, resilient, resourceful, scientific approach, technical aptitude

Relevant Subjects
Chemistry, Design and technology, Engineering, English, Geography, ICT/Computer studies, Mathematics, Physics, Science

Further Information
AGCAS: Engineering (Job Sector Briefing) (AGCAS) - www.prospects.ac.uk

Britain's Offshore Oil & Gas (Oil & Gas UK) (Oil & Gas UK) - www.oilandgas.co.uk/Britains_offshore_oil_and_gas

Cogent - sector skills souncil for chemicals, pharmaceuticals, nuclear, oil & gas, petroleum & polymers - www.cogent-ssc.com

Diplomas (Foundation, Higher and Advanced) - http://yp.direct.gov.uk/diplomas

Energy Institute (Institute of Petroleum (IOP) - www.energyinst.org.uk

Engineering Education Scheme - www.engineering-education.org.uk/

Engineering Education Scheme Wales - www.eesw.org.uk

Headstart Scheme - www.headstartcourses.org.uk

Petroleum Review (monthly) (Energy Institute) - www.energyinst.org.uk/index.cfm?PageID=9

Welsh Baccalaureate - www.wbq.org.uk

Year in Industry (Engineering Development Trust) - www.yini.org.uk

Addresses
Energy Institute (EI)
61 New Cavendish Street, London W1G 7AR
Phone: +44 (0)20 7467 7100
Web: www.energyinst.org.uk

Engineering Council
246 High Holborn, London WC1V 7EX
Phone: +44 (0)20 3206 0500
Web: www.engc.org.uk

Engineering Development Trust (EDT)
Ridgeway, Welwyn Garden City, Hertfordshire AL7 2AA
Phone: +44 (0)1707 871520
Web: www.etrust.org.uk

Heriot-Watt University
Edinburgh Campus EH14 4AS
Phone: 0131 449 5111
Web: www.hw.ac.uk

Institute of Materials, Minerals and Mining (IOM3)
1 Carlton House Terrace, London SW1Y 5DB
Phone: +44 (0)20 7451 7300
Web: www.iom3.org

Offshore Petroleum Industry Training Organisation (OPITO)
Minerva House, Bruntland Road, Portlethen, Aberdeen AB12 4QL
Phone: +44 (0)1224 787800
Web: www.opito.com

Oil & Gas UK
2nd Floor, 232-242 Vauxhall Bridge Road, London SW1V 1AU
Phone: +44 (0)20 7802 2400
Web: www.oilandgas.org.uk

Society of Petroleum Engineers (SPE)
First Floor Threeways House 40-44 Clipstone Street, London W1W 5DW
Phone: +44 (0)20 7299 3300
Web: www.spe.org

UK Petroleum Industry Association (UKPIA)
Quality House, Quality Court, Chancery Lane, London WC2A 1HP
Phone: +44 (0)20 7269 7600
Web: www.ukpia.com

Similar Jobs
Engineer: Gas, Engineer: Minerals & Mining, Engineer: Reservoir, Geophysicist, Surveyor: Minerals & Waste Management

Engineer: Reservoir
CRCI:Engineering
CLCI:SAS Job Band: 5

Job Description
Reservoir engineers use scientific and engineering principles to study the characteristics and behaviour of hydrocarbon reservoirs and ensure the maximum profitable recovery of oil or gas. They use geological, seismic and well-logging data to build computer models of oil and gas fields to simulate production conditions. Data is used to make forecasts of a reservoir's yield and performance to help make informed decisions. They also liaises with geophysicists, geologists, petrophysicists and other professionals in their work, such as on development programmes and looking at methods of oil or gas recovery. Reservoir engineering is considered a part of the petroleum engineering industry.

Work Details
Usually work from 9am-5pm when working from an office. You may be expected to work shifts or unusual hours when on site or offshore. You sometimes work outdoors in all weathers. Reservoir engineers frequently travel within the working day and are often away from home overnight. Works as part of a team with other professionals. The work can be physically active and there may be a risk of accidents.

Qualification

• England, Wales and Northern Ireland
Band 5: For many engineering degree courses: 2-3 A levels, preferably including maths, physics and another science or technology subject, and some GCSEs (A*-C) usually including English, maths and sometimes a foreign language, or equivalent. Exact requirements depend on the degree you take.

• Scotland
Band 5: For many engineering degree courses: 3-5 H grades, preferably including maths and physics and another science or technology subject, and some S grades (1-3), including English, maths and sometimes a foreign language, or similar qualifications. Exact requirements depend on the degree you take.

Degree Information
A first degree in petroleum, offshore or chemical engineering, energy or fuel technology may give direct entry. Other subjects that may be acceptable to some employers include electrical

engineering or mechanical engineering. Some other engineering subjects, physics and chemistry can provide relevant background knowledge but a specialist postgraduate qualification is also required.

Adult Qualifications

A degree is normally required. Degree entry requirements are often reduced for older applicants, particularly if you have relevant experience. There are also many Access and foundation courses which can lead to engineering degree courses. Appropriate postgraduate courses are open to engineering graduates.

Work Experience

Entry to this career is competitive. Work experience may be hard to gain as most reservoir engineering is undertaken overseas. It improves your chances at interview if you have some work experience in a related area, such as chemical engineering. Applicants to degree courses are encouraged to apply to the 'Year in Industry' Scheme for a placement in industry prior to starting their studies. Students also have an opportunity to gain work experience in industry for a year between the penultimate and final years of their degree programme. This experience enhances your job prospects on graduation.

The Engineering Education Scheme, run by the Engineering Development Trust, offers programmes in England, Scotland and Wales giving young people the chance to be involved in a real engineering project for six months. Students commit to two to three hours work a week and some time at university residents' workshops. This valuable experience can contribute to any future university application and counts towards the Duke of Edinburgh award skills section. Check the website for details.

Similarly, Headstart offers students a chance to experience a week at university, designing, building and testing projects. As engineering careers can be quite diverse, a week of hands on experience such as this can be really helpful when students are trying to decide which field of engineering they want to train in. Check the website for details.

Entry and Training

A good honours degree (at least a 2:1) is normally required and many entrants have a higher degree in petroleum engineering. Recruitment by major oil companies takes place annually. Training, often through a graduate training scheme, varies considerably from company to company, but generally includes formal courses to supplement practical experience. There is a strong emphasis on attaining chartered status through the Engineering Council (ECUK). To achieve this you must become a member of one of the professional organisations, such as the Society of Petroleum Engineers or the Institute of Materials, Minerals and Mining (IOM3).

Relevant industrial training, initial professional development and further responsible experience are required before becoming fully qualified. You must also commit to continuing professional development throughout your career. The professional organisations can often help you achieve this through relevant short training courses. Chartered engineers (CEng) may qualify through an accredited course leading to an MEng degree, or a BEng (Hons) followed by an appropriate masters degree. Chartered engineers can also qualify as European engineers (EurIng) but need to be fluent in a European language. See the ECUK website for full details.

Contact organisations such as the Society of Petroleum Engineers, IOM3, and Cogent, the sector skills council for the oil/gas industry, for information on all training routes and relevant qualifications. Other useful contacts include the Energy Institute, Offshore Petroleum Industry Training and Oil and Gas UK.

The Engineering Development Trust runs a range of nationwide schemes for 11-21 year olds who are interested in engineering as a career. See the website for details. A Diploma/Welsh Baccalaureate may be available in your area in engineering. The advanced level is equivalent to 3.5 A levels but for some university courses, the additional and specialist learning component of the diploma needs to include specific A levels such as maths or physics. Check entry requirements carefully with the individual institutions.

Those with considerable experience but who lack formal qualifications may be considered for the Technical Report Route to qualify as a chartered engineer through the Engineering Council UK (ECUK). This gives applicants without post 18 academic qualifications the opportunity to demonstrate, through the writing of a technical report that they have acquired the necessary engineering knowledge. Applicants need to be employed in a job at an equivalent grade to a chartered engineer (CEng) or incorporated engineer (IEng). Contact the ECUK for details. You can also contact professional organisations such as the Society of Petroleum Engineers and the Institute of Materials, Minerals and Mining or ECUK, for details of mature entry routes to training and registration. Sponsorship may be available for higher education courses.

Opportunities and Pay

This is a worldwide business and many of the jobs are overseas. British graduates compete with graduates from many other countries and competition for jobs is fierce. Prospects for promotion to senior positions are generally good. Self employment and freelance work is possible for experienced reservoir engineers.

Pay varies depending on location and size of company. Starting salaries for graduate entrants are around £25k-£30k a year. Experienced engineers can earn around £50k-£70k and some may earn more.

Health

This job requires good colour vision for certain areas of work. In some jobs there is an allergy risk from dust.

Skills and Qualities

able to make important decisions, able to work both on your own and in a team, accurate, analytical skills, IT skills, numeracy skills, problem-solving skills, resourceful, scientific approach, technical aptitude

Relevant Subjects

Chemistry, Design and technology, Engineering, English, Geography, ICT/Computer studies, Mathematics, Physics, Science

Further Information

AGCAS: Engineering (Job Sector Briefing) (AGCAS) - www.prospects.ac.uk

Britain's Offshore Oil & Gas (Oil & Gas UK) (Oil & Gas UK) - www.oilandgas.co.uk/Britains_offshore_oil_and_gas

Cogent - sector skills souncil for chemicals, pharmaceuticals, nuclear, oil & gas, petroleum & polymers - www.cogent-ssc.com

Diplomas (Foundation, Higher and Advanced) - http://yp.direct.gov.uk/diplomas

Energy Institute (Institute of Petroleum (IOP) - www.energyinst.org.uk

Engineering Education Scheme - www.engineering-education.org.uk/

Engineering Education Scheme Wales - www.eesw.org.uk

Headstart Scheme - www.headstartcourses.org.uk

Petroleum Review (monthly) (Energy Institute) - www.energyinst.org.uk/index.cfm?PageID=9

Welsh Baccalaureate - www.wbq.org.uk

Year in Industry (Engineering Development Trust) - www.yini.org.uk

Addresses

Energy Institute (EI)
61 New Cavendish Street, London W1G 7AR
Phone: +44 (0)20 7467 7100
Web: www.energyinst.org.uk

Engineering Council
246 High Holborn, London WC1V 7EX
Phone: +44 (0)20 3206 0500
Web: www.engc.org.uk

Engineering Development Trust (EDT)
Ridgeway, Welwyn Garden City, Hertfordshire AL7 2AA
Phone: +44 (0)1707 871520
Web: www.etrust.org.uk

Institute of Materials, Minerals and Mining (IOM3)
1 Carlton House Terrace, London SW1Y 5DB
Phone: +44 (0)20 7451 7300
Web: www.iom3.org

Offshore Petroleum Industry Training Organisation (OPITO)
Minerva House, Bruntland Road, Portlethen, Aberdeen AB12 4QL
Phone: +44 (0)1224 787800
Web: www.opito.com

Oil & Gas UK
2nd Floor, 232-242 Vauxhall Bridge Road, London SW1V 1AU
Phone: +44 (0)20 7802 2400
Web: www.oilandgas.org.uk

Society of Petroleum Engineers (SPE)
First Floor Threeways House 40-44 Clipstone Street, London W1W 5DW
Phone: +44 (0)20 7299 3300
Web: www.spe.org

UK Petroleum Industry Association (UKPIA)
Quality House, Quality Court, Chancery Lane, London WC2A 1HP
Phone: +44 (0)20 7269 7600
Web: www.ukpia.com

Similar Jobs

Engineer: Gas, Engineer: Minerals & Mining, Engineer: Petroleum, Geophysicist, Surveyor: Minerals & Waste Management

Engineer: Telecommunications

also known as: Telecommunications Engineer
CRCI:Engineering
CLCI:RAL
Job Band: 4 to 5

Job Description

Telecommunications engineers work on different types of communications technology systems, including optics and fibre optics, transmission and switching technology. They research, design and develop innovative satellite and cable systems, mobile phone networks, radio and electronic networks, and multimedia systems for the Internet, intranet and email. Engineers use high technology and sophisticated equipment to test systems. May also manage and supervise a maintenance and repair programme for existing technology, providing updates and modifications. The job can involve collecting and processing remote data from satellites, aircraft and ships' radar. Engineers may also provide systems solutions for private and business clients, including setting up conferencing links and call centres, using computer telephony integration (CTI) or improving the existing technology.

Engineers work closely with clients to ensure their communications needs are met and that they remain competitive in their area of business. They ensure all new systems and equipment meet government regulations and may also need to prepare and present reports.

Work Details

Usually work a 35-40 hr week, Monday to Friday, though you may be required to start early or finish late. Some engineers are required to be on call, which can include nights and weekends, when systems can be safely tested. You often travel around to customers' premises to check systems and some may cover a large geographical area. Work is pressurised at times. A smart appearance is normally necessary.

Qualification

- **England, Wales and Northern Ireland**

Band 4: For HND in electrical/electronic engineering (communication), Diploma of Higher Education or foundation degree: 1-2 A levels, usually maths and a science, and some GCSEs (A*-C) usually including English, maths and a science, or equivalent.

Band 5: For degree courses: 2-3 A levels, usually including physics and maths, and some GCSEs (A*-C) usually including English, maths and a science, or equivalent. Exact requirements depend on the degree you take.

- **Scotland**

Band 4: For entry to SQA higher national in electronics and professional development awards, usually 2-3 H grades, including maths and a science (preferably physics), and some S grades (1-3), including English, maths and a science, or similar qualifications.

Band 5: For degree courses: 3-5 H grades, usually including physics and maths, and some S grades (1-3), including English, maths and a science, or similar qualifications. Exact requirements depend on the degree you take.

Degree Information

Degree subjects vary but include telecommunications engineering, electronic engineering, digital communications and electronics, mobile communications and internet technology, electronic and telecommunications engineering, networks and telecommunications engineering, and digital communications engineering. Other engineering subjects can provide useful background knowledge, but may not be sufficient for entry. There are several postgraduate courses if your first degree is not directly relevant.

Adult Qualifications

A degree or higher national award is usually required. Mature entrants who do not have the required entry qualifications may be able to enter higher education via an Access or foundation course. If you have relevant work experience, formal entry requirements to courses may be relaxed.

Work Experience

Employers and universities may prefer candidates who have relevant work or voluntary experience. The most useful experience is with an electronics firm or in any area of telecommunications engineering that demonstrates enthusiasm and commitment to the job. Similarly, experience involving computer systems also helps. If you expect good A levels/H grades and intend to go to university, schemes such as 'A Year in Industry', provide you with the opportunity to spend a salaried year with a company to gain valuable work experience. Check the website for details.

The Engineering Education Scheme runs programmes in England, Scotland and Wales giving young people the chance to be involved in a real engineering project for six months. Students commit to two to three hours work a week and some time at university residents' workshops. This experience can contribute to any future university application and counts towards the Duke of Edinburgh award skills section. Check the website for details.

Similarly, Headstart offers students a chance to experience a week at university, designing, building and testing projects. As engineering careers can be diverse, a week of hands on experience such as this can be really helpful when you are trying to decide which field of engineering you want to train in. Check the website for details.

Entry and Training

There are a number of specialist courses in telecommunications engineering and entrants are usually graduates or have an appropriate engineering HND. Some entrants are graduates from computer science, physics or maths courses. Many join a manufacturer's training scheme and also join the Institution of

Engineering and Technology. Relevant industrial training, initial professional development and further experience are required before becoming fully qualified. You must also commit to continuing professional development throughout your career.

Many telecommunications engineers also aim to become professional engineers with the Engineering Council at either incorporated or chartered engineer level. Both levels involve gaining experience and keeping detailed records of your development. Experience is followed by a professional review and an interview.

Incorporated engineers (IEng) need to be qualified to HNC/HND or BEng level, followed by a further year of learning. Another route is through an apprenticeship programme leading to S/NVQ at level 4, then to HNC/HND. Foundation degrees are available in general engineering subjects and in manufacturing engineering, but need to be extended to a full degree. Chartered engineers (CEng) may qualify through an accredited course leading to an MEng degree, or a BEng (Hons) followed by an appropriate masters degree. Chartered engineers can also qualify as European engineers (EurIng) but need to be fluent in a European language.

The Tomorrow's Engineers website has lots of useful careers information including a route map and guide to engineering activities from primary school through to higher education. The Engineering Development Trust also runs a range of nationwide schemes for 11-21 year olds who may be interested in engineering as a career. See the websites for details.

A diploma/Welsh Baccalaureate may be available in your area in engineering. The advanced level is equivalent to 3.5 A levels but for some university courses, the additional and specialist learning component of the diploma needs to include specific A levels e.g maths or physics. Check entry requirements carefully with the individual institutions. See the diplomas website for further information. There is also an IT and telecoms professional apprenticeship which may be available in your area and provide a route into this career.

Mature entrants must have a relevant qualification such as an BTEC/SQA higher national award or degree. Funding for relevant postgraduate study may be available from the Engineering and Physical Sciences Research Council. Mature applicants are usually considered but this depends on your qualifications and experience. Managerial and technological expertise is an advantage. Contact the Engineering Council for details.

The Open University (OU) runs a range of engineering courses. See the OU website for details.

Opportunities and Pay

Digital, multimedia communications is a rapidly developing field globally. As advances continue to be made, there is increasing demand for telecommunication engineering skills. However, job opportunities may be limited in the current economic climate. You can work for a national or international company or organisation, such as telephone companies, cable TV, cellular radio, satellite system and internet providers, and electronic communications manufacturers. There are also opportunities in research and development and in large multinational companies such as those in the oil and gas industry. Self-employment as a freelance or consultant engineer is possible.

Depending upon the type of company and level of responsibility, an engineer may earn from around £25k a year, rising to around £32k-£40k. High earners can make up to £60k a year.

Health

This job may require good colour vision for certain areas of work.

Skills and Qualities

attention to detail, enquiring mind, good concentration level, good spoken communication, good written English, IT skills, logical, methodical, problem-solving skills, technical aptitude

Relevant Subjects

Chemistry, Design and technology, Engineering, English, ICT/Computer studies, Manufacturing, Mathematics, Physics, Science

Further Information

AGCAS: Engineering (Job Sector Briefing) (AGCAS) - www.prospects.ac.uk

Apprenticeship Schemes (National Apprenticeship Service) - www.apprenticeships.org.uk

Diplomas (Foundation, Higher and Advanced) - http://yp.direct.gov.uk/diplomas

Engineering Education Scheme - www.engineering-education.org.uk/

Engineering Education Scheme Wales - www.eesw.org.uk

Engineering Scotland (SEMTA) - www.engineeringscotland.org

e-skills UK - sector skills council for business and information technology - www.e-skills.com

Headstart Scheme - www.headstartcourses.org.uk

Open University - www.open.ac.uk

SEMTA - sector skills council for science, engineering and manufacturing technologies - www.semta.org.uk

TARGETjobs: Engineering (GTI Specialist Publishing Ltd.) - www.groupgti.com

Tomorrow's Engineers - www.tomorrowsengineers.org.uk/careers.cfm

Women into Science, Engineering & Construction - www.wisecampaign.org.uk

Year in Industry (Engineering Development Trust) - www.yini.org.uk

Addresses

Engineering and Physical Sciences Research Council (EPSRC)
Polaris House North Star Avenue, Swindon, Wiltshire SN2 1ET
Phone: +44(0)1793 444 100
Web: www.epsrc.ac.uk

Engineering Council
246 High Holborn, London WC1V 7EX
Phone: +44 (0)20 3206 0500
Web: www.engc.org.uk

Engineering Development Trust (EDT)
Ridgeway, Welwyn Garden City, Hertfordshire AL7 2AA
Phone: +44 (0)1707 871520
Web: www.etrust.org.uk

Engineering Training Council (NI)
Interpoint, 20-24 York Street, Belfast BT15 1AQ
Phone: +44 (0)28 9032 9878
Web: www.etcni.org.uk

Institution of Engineering and Technology (IET)
Michael Faraday House, Stevenage, Hertfordshire SG1 2AY
Phone: +44 (0)1438 313311
Web: www.theiet.org

Scottish Engineering
Training Officer, 105 West George Street, Glasgow G2 1QL
Phone: +44 (0)141 221 3181
Web: www.scottishengineering.org.uk

Similar Jobs

Computer Hardware Engineer, Engineer: Broadcast, Engineer: Electrical, Engineer: Electronics, Network Administrator, Telecommunications Technician

Engineer: Thermal Insulation

CRCI:Building and Construction
CLCI:UJ Job Band: 1 to 3

Job Description

Thermal insulation engineers specialise in energy conservation by covering equipment such as hot pipes, vessels and boilers with insulating material to prevent heat loss. They also use insulation to keep heat out, for example in refrigeration or air-conditioning systems. Engineers utilise a variety of materials, such as wool, foam or silicate. They study plans and decide how much material is required. Duties include measuring, cutting and shaping insulating materials to fit around the pipes, vessel or boilers, and also ducting work. May cover pipes with pre-formed sections and fix the sections with clips or adhesives. The job is finished with a covering of sheet metal or other cladding material. Must be able to advise on and discuss plans for new buildings, or suggest any improvements to existing installations.

Insulation engineers work on a wide variety of projects, such as large-scale industrial projects in petrochemical works. May work in places such as oil refineries and onshore/offshore oil/gas rigs, schools and residential accommodation, power stations, office blocks and hospitals, ships, ferries and aircraft.

Work Details

Thermal insulation engineers usually work a basic 38 hour week, Monday to Friday, but may be required to work some evenings and weekends at times. Work may be indoors or outdoors and usually involves travel to different sites. This work requires the use of scaffolding and ladders and often strenuous physical activity, which involves balancing and lifting. Some workplaces can be confined or are very difficult to access, often with areas that are dirty/dusty, or with extremes of heat and cold. There may be a risk of exposure to harmful substances, and you need to wear a safety helmet, and sometimes a face mask and goggles.

Qualification

- **England, Wales and Northern Ireland**

Band 2: Although academic qualifications are not specified for this job, for an Insulation and Environmental Training Agency (IETA) apprenticeship it is an advantage to have at least 4 GCSEs (A*-C), or equivalent. Subjects such as maths, English, science and technological subjects are helpful. Those without formal qualifications usually take an entry test, providing they have a satisfactory school report.

Band 3: For BTEC national award: usually at least 4 GCSEs (A*-C) including maths, technology and a science subject, usually physics, or equivalent.

- **Scotland**

Band 2: Although academic qualifications are not specified for this job, for an Insulation & Environmental Training Agency (IETA) apprenticeship it is an advantage to have at least four S grades (1-3), or similar. Subjects such as maths, English, science and technological subjects are helpful. Those without formal qualifications usually take an entry test, providing they have a satisfactory school report.

Band 3: For SQA national award: usually at least four S grades (1-3) including maths, technology and a science subject, usually physics, or similar.

Adult Qualifications

Those with relevant work experience may be accepted for some college courses without meeting any formal entry requirements.

Work Experience

Relevant work or voluntary experience is always useful and can improve your chances when applying for entry to construction jobs and apprenticeships. Health and safety issues may mean that there are certain jobs you can't do until you are over 16. Contact your local Construction Skills office for advice.

Entry and Training

Young people aged over 16 usually enter the profession through the Insulation and Environmental Training Agency (IETA) apprenticeship scheme that lasts three years. The programme combines on-site training with experienced colleagues and training officers, together with workshop practices at IETA's approved training centre in Darlington.

A Diploma/Welsh Baccalaureate in construction and the built environment may be available in your area. Relevant S/NVQs are available. Most apprentices work towards the S/NVQ level 2 in thermal insulation through IETA/City & Guilds. Training programmes, including apprenticeship schemes, may be available in your area. Advanced apprenticeships leading to qualification at level 3 can also be a route into higher education.

Mature applicants who show evidence of good practical skills, particularly industrial or engineering skills, have a fair chance of entering training opportunities. Those who have experience of working as a heating and ventilation technician have an advantage. Refresher courses are sometimes available for those returning to work and there may be special government training schemes in some areas, including apprenticeship schemes for adults.

You can also gain recognition of previous experience through Accreditation of Prior Learning (APL) or by working towards relevant S/NVQs. Contact your local careers office, Jobcentre Plus, Next Step service or Learning and Skills Council (LSC)/Local Enterprise Company (LEC) for details of training opportunities.

Opportunities and Pay

Employers include building contractors, building services engineering firms, equipment manufacturers, or specialist insulation companies. There are opportunities throughout the UK, particularly at ports and harbours or in large commercial/industrial centres. Availability of work depends to some extent on the state of the building trade and the national economy. Currently there is a downturn in the housing market which means there may be a shortage of vacancies. However, opportunities do exist as there is still a demand for energy conservation. Promotion prospects include progression into supervisory and/or managerial roles. Work on contracts abroad in many countries is also possible. Many qualified and experienced engineers are self-employed.

Pay varies depending on area and employer. Apprentices are paid at the current industry-agreed rate and may earn £9k-£19k a year while training. A fully trained thermal insulation engineer's salary starts at around £20k a year, rising to around £25k a year with experience. Some may earn up to £30k a year. Overtime attracts additional payments. Employers usually pay travelling and subsistence expenses for any work that is required away from home.

Health

You need good physical fitness with no vertigo, claustrophobia or respiratory problems. Dust and skin irritants can cause an allergic reaction.

Skills and Qualities

able to follow drawings and plans, able to work in confined spaces, aptitude for teamwork, attention to detail, head for heights, manual dexterity, numeracy skills, safety conscious, technical aptitude

Relevant Subjects

Construction and built environment, Design and technology

Further Information

Apprenticeship Schemes (National Apprenticeship Service) - www.apprenticeships.org.uk

Building Sustainable Design (UBM) - www.bsdlive.co.uk

ConstructionSkills - sector skills council for the construction industry - www.cskills.org

Diplomas (Foundation, Higher and Advanced) http://yp.direct.gov.uk/diplomas
Summitskills - sector skills council for building services engineering - www.summitskills.org.uk
Welsh Baccalaureate - www.wbq.org.uk

Addresses

Insulation and Environmental Training Agency (IETA)
TICA House, Allington Way Yarm Road Business Park, Darlington DL1 4QB
Phone: +44 (0)1325 466 704
Web: www.tica-acad.co.uk/page/about-ieta

Thermal Insulation Contractors Association (TICA)
TICA House, Allington Way, Yarm Road Business Park, Darlington DL1 4QB
Phone: +44 (0)1325 466704
Web: www.tica-acad.co.uk/tica

Similar Jobs

Cavity Wall Insulation Technician, Ceiling Fixer, Construction Operative, Damp Proofer, Dry Liner, Heating & Ventilation Fitter/Welder, Refrigeration/Air Conditioning Technician

Engineer: Traction & Rolling Stock

also known as: Traction & Rolling Stock Engineer

CRCI:Engineering
CLCI:RAX
Job Band: 4 to 5

Job Description

Traction and rolling stock engineers manage and supervise building, maintenance and refurbishment of locomotives, carriages and goods wagons. They may design and test new trains, carriages and wagons. Engineers make sure any maintenance and repair work is carried out in the right way and to the correct standard and that strict health and safety rules are observed. They may specialise in electrical or mechanical engineering.

Engineers keep up to date with the latest techniques and materials. They advise senior managers on matters to do with engineering and make sure the team delivers everything specified in the contract and works to the budget. Also use staff and resources efficiently to get the job done and may play a part in recruiting and training technical staff.

Work Details

Normally work a 37 hr week, Monday to Friday but this may involve shift work with early, late and night shifts. You may also have to do overtime or work weekends to meet deadlines. Some engineers are on call to deal with emergencies. You divide your time between working in an office or drawing office, large engineering workshops and on the trackside. The workshops and trackside can be noisy and dirty.

You direct the work of team leaders and work with other engineers, technicians, craft workers, operatives and managers.

Qualification

- **England, Wales and Northern Ireland**

Band 4: For HND, Diploma of Higher Education or foundation degree: 1-2 A levels, usually maths and physics or computer science or technology, and some GCSEs (A*-C) usually including English, maths and science, or equivalent.

Band 5: For degree courses in mechanical engineering and electrical engineering: 2-3 A levels, preferably including maths and physics or possibly engineering, and some GCSEs (A*-C) usually including English, maths and sometimes chemistry or a foreign language, or equivalent. Exact requirements depend on the degree you take.

- **Scotland**

Band 4: For entry to SQA higher national and professional development awards, usually 2-3 H grades, usually maths and physics or computer science or technology, and some S grades (1-3), including English and maths, or similar qualifications.

Band 5: For degree courses in mechanical engineering and electrical engineering: 3-5 H grades including maths and physics or technological studies, and some S grades (1-3), usually including English, maths and sometimes chemistry or a foreign language, or similar qualifications. Exact requirements depend on the degree you take.

Degree Information

A degree in mechanical or electrical engineering is preferred. Degree courses can be full time, part time or sandwich courses. They may last 3-5 years full time. Some lead to a BEng degree and others lead to MEng at masters level. Many are accredited by the Engineering Council as partially or fully meeting the academic requirement for registration as an incorporated engineer (IEng) or a chartered engineer (CEng). Some may also be accredited by professional engineering institutions as meeting their requirements.

Adult Qualifications

Course entry requirements are usually relaxed for suitable mature applicants. If you have relevant work experience you may be accepted for some courses without needing to meet formal entry requirements. You may complete an Access or foundation course, or similar, that leads to a relevant HND or accredited degree course.

Work Experience

Employers and universities may prefer candidates with relevant work or voluntary experience who show enthusiasm and commitment to the job. Ideally this is within electrical or mechanical engineering or any other relevant area. If you expect good A levels/H grades and intend to go to university, schemes such as 'A Year in Industry' enable you to spend a salaried year with a company to gain valuable work experience.

The Engineering Education Scheme is available for Year 12 students who wish to make more informed career decisions by experiencing working on real problems. Similarly, Headstart offers students a chance to experience a week at university, designing, building and testing projects. As engineering has many areas, a week like this can be helpful when you are trying to decide which field of engineering you want to study and work in. Check the website for details.

Undergraduates on courses accredited by the IMechE or IET may be able to do a year's work experience on the Association of Train Operating Companies Professional Engineering Development Scheme.

Entry and Training

Most people enter this job with a degree in mechanical or electrical engineering. You have to do a two-day Personal Track Safety certificate course to prove that you know how to work safely in the track environment. You cannot work on or around a national railway track without a Network Rail Sentinel Track Safety card and you have to renew your certificate every two years.

Most entrants with an accredited degree join a professional institution such as the Institution of Mechanical Engineers (IMechE) or the Institution of Engineering and Technology. You then work on your professional development on the job. Members of the IMechE can follow a structured Monitored Professional Development Scheme to ensure that the necessary competence and commitment you need for the job is developed. Finally you undergo a professional review that includes an interview to become an incorporated engineer (IEng) or, with a MEng degree, a chartered engineer (CEng). You must continue to demonstrate continuing professional development throughout your career. Chartered engineers who are fluent in a foreign language can also qualify as European engineers (Eurlang).

The Association of Train Operating Companies runs a Professional Engineering Development Scheme, accredited by the IMechE and the IET. It provides comprehensive training and a fast-track route to becoming a chartered engineer for graduates employed by train operating companies.

It is possible to start out in the job as a trainee or apprentice railway fitter or railway engineering technician, gain practical knowledge, experience and qualifications at level 3, then do further training and study for an HND or a degree. Relevant foundation degrees, including a two-year foundation degree in railway engineering, may be available in some areas.

A Diploma/Welsh Baccalaureate may be available in your area in engineering. The advanced level is equivalent to 3.5 A levels but for some university courses, the additional and specialist learning (ASL) component of the diploma needs to include specific A levels, e.g maths or physics, so check entry requirements carefully. See the diplomas website for further information.

Mature applicants are usually considered by employers, depending on your qualifications and experience. Contact the Engineering Council, the Institution of Mechanical Engineers or the Institution of Engineering and Technology for details of training opportunities.

Opportunities and Pay

Use of the rail network has expanded over the last ten years with 42% growth in passenger and 52% growth in freight transport. Over the next five years there are plans to run an additional 1,700 extra passenger carriages a day and introduce light-weight trains that are more track and environmentally friendly. Keeping trains and rolling stock in service has never been more important.

Traction and rolling stock engineers find jobs with companies that build, maintain or lease trains used by operators. You may also find work with passenger and goods train companies and underground, metro and light rail operators. Promotion is likely to be into more senior engineering and management posts with responsibility for engineering issues and projects.

Earnings vary depending on the employer and the nature of the work. Salaries for graduate entrants start at about £25k. Experienced engineers earn around £30k-£40k a year, whilst senior engineers may earn £50k or more a year.

Health

Normal colour vision is required for electrical work. You may be randomly tested for drugs and alcohol at any time.

Skills and Qualities

able to work to deadlines, analytical skills, good communication skills, good interpersonal skills, IT skills, logical, numeracy skills, practical skills, safety conscious, technical aptitude

Relevant Subjects

Chemistry, Design and technology, Engineering, English, ICT/ Computer studies, Mathematics, Physics, Science

Further Information

AGCAS: Engineering (Job Sector Briefing) (AGCAS) - www.prospects.ac.uk

Diplomas (Foundation, Higher and Advanced) - http://yp.direct.gov.uk/diplomas

Engineering Education Scheme - www.engineering-education.org.uk/

Engineering Education Scheme Wales - www.eesw.org.uk

Headstart Scheme - www.headstartcourses.org.uk

Railway People (Railstaff) - www.railwaypeople.com

Railway Professional (Railway Professional) - www.railpro.co.uk

SEMTA - sector skills council for science, engineering and manufacturing technologies - www.semta.org.uk

Year in Industry (Engineering Development Trust) - www.yini.org.uk

Addresses

Association of Train Operating Companies (ATOC)
Third Floor, 40 Bernard Street, London WC1N 1BY
Phone: +44 (0)20 7841 8000
Web: www.atoc-comms.org

Engineering Council
246 High Holborn, London WC1V 7EX
Phone: +44 (0)20 3206 0500
Web: www.engc.org.uk

Engineering Training Council (NI)
Interpoint, 20-24 York Street, Belfast BT15 1AQ
Phone: +44 (0)28 9032 9878
Web: www.etcni.org.uk

Institution of Engineering and Technology (IET)
Michael Faraday House, Stevenage, Hertfordshire SG1 2AY
Phone: +44 (0)1438 313311
Web: www.theiet.org

Institution of Mechanical Engineers (IMechE)
1 Birdcage Walk, Westminster, London SW1H 9JJ
Phone: +44 (0)20 7222 7899
Web: www.imeche.org.uk

Scottish Engineering
Training Officer, 105 West George Street, Glasgow G2 1QL
Phone: +44 (0)141 221 3181
Web: www.scottishengineering.org.uk

Women into Science, Engineering & Construction (WISE)
2nd Floor Weston House, 246 High Holborn, London WC1V 7EX
Phone: +44 (0)20 3206 0408
Web: www.wisecampaign.org.uk

Women's Engineering Society
The Secretary, The IET, Michael Faraday House, Six Hills Way, Stevenage, Hertfordshire SG1 2AY
Phone: +44 (0)1438 765506
Web: www.wes.org.uk

Similar Jobs

Aircraft Engineering Technician, Engineer: Design, Engineer: Electrical, Engineer: Mechanical, Fitter: Maintenance, Rail Transport Technician

Engineering Craft Machinist

also known as: CNC Machinist

CRCI:Engineering
CLCI:RAB   Job Band: 1 to 3

Job Description

Engineering craft machinists set up and operate a wide range of engineering machines that cut, grind, bore, drill, shape and finish metal. They use instructions from engineering drawings to set up hand or computer numerically controlled (CNC) machines to make engineering parts. Machinists work to precise measurements for components and check the standard of their work, using a variety of measuring equipment, and make changes if necessary. They may set up machines for engineering machine operators. Increasingly, CNC machines are used and additional skills are needed to program and operate them.

Work Details

Usually work a basic 39 hr week that may include shifts, nights, weekends and overtime. Conditions in industrial premises depend on what is being made. Some buildings may be dirty and noisy whilst others are clean and quiet. In engineering craftwork, you have to be careful and precise. This job may require you to stand at a machine for long periods of time so you need to be physically fit. Sometimes there can be accidents with machines. You may have to wear protective clothing and items such as special shoes, safety glasses and gloves.

Qualification

• England, Wales and Northern Ireland

Band 2: For entry to jobs, no minimum qualifications are needed, but it is an advantage to have some GCSEs (A*-C) or equivalent in subjects that include maths, English and physics or another science subject, or equivalent. Technology and design are also useful subjects.

Band 3: For entry to jobs, HNC or a relevant Diploma, usually at least 4 GCSEs (A*-C) including maths, English and a science, engineering or technology subject, or equivalent.

• Scotland

Band 2: Although academic qualifications are not specified for this job, it is an advantage to have some S grades (1-3) in subjects that include maths, English and physics or another science subject, or similar. Technology and design are also useful subjects.

Band 3: For entry to jobs, usually at least four S grades (1-3) including maths, English and a science, engineering or technology subject, or similar.

Adult Qualifications

Academic qualifications are not always needed. However mechanical engineering experience is beneficial and may improve your chances for entry.

Work Experience

Relevant work or voluntary experience is always useful. It can add to your CV and improve your chances when applying for entry to jobs or apprenticeships in the engineering industry. Your personal or adult guidance adviser may be able to help you to organise work experience.

Entry and Training

Some companies have aptitude tests and entrants for training can be aged 16-17, although 18-19 year olds are also accepted. Training is on the job with experienced craft machinists, and usually, before applying for a job, with day release or block release for BTEC/City & Guilds or SQA qualifications in engineering. Alternatively, you can study for relevant qualifications, such as a BTEC/SQA national award or equivalent vocational qualifications. Craft trainees who do well can transfer to technician-level training. There are also opportunities to progress to qualified engineering technician status and register as an EngTech with the Engineering Council (ECUK). Contact ECUK for details.

S/NVQs are available at levels 1-3, including performing engineering or manufacturing operations at levels 1-2 and engineering toolmaking at level 3. The awarding body EMTA Awards Ltd offers a VRQ level 3 diploma in computer numeric control (CNC) programming/machining and in advanced manufacture techniques - CNC. Relevant training programmes, including engineering, manufacturing and metal processing apprenticeship schemes, may be available in your area. Advanced apprenticeships leading to qualification at level 3 can also be a route into higher education.

The Engineering Development Trust runs a range of nationwide schemes for 11-21 year olds who are interested in engineering as a career. See the website for details. A Diploma/Welsh Baccalaureate may be available in your area in engineering. See the diplomas website for further information.

Adults with relevant skills are welcomed. Some enter after leaving the armed forces. Government training opportunities, such as apprenticeships for adults, may be available in your area. You can also gain recognition of previous experience through Accreditation of Prior Learning or by working towards relevant S/NVQs. Contact your local careers office, Jobcentre Plus, Next Step service or Learning and Skills Council (LSC)/Local Enterprise Company (LEC) for details of training schemes.

Opportunities and Pay

You can be employed by a general mechanical engineering company or in the aircraft, motor, agricultural machinery or shipbuilding industries. You can also be employed by the armed forces. With experience it is possible to be promoted to team leader. Due to increasing automation, overall demand for machinists is decreasing.

Pay varies depending on location and employer, but bonuses and extra pay for shift work is usual. A starting salary for a trained machinist is likely to be around £18k, rising to £21k-£25k with experience.

Health

You must have normal eyesight, with or without glasses. You also have to be fit and quite strong. Some people may have problems dealing with oil and dirt, which can irritate the skin.

Skills and Qualities

able to follow drawings and plans, able to work both on your own and in a team, attention to detail, good concentration level, hand-to-eye co-ordination, IT skills, numeracy skills, precise, steady hand, technical aptitude

Relevant Subjects

Design and technology, Engineering, Mathematics, Physics, Science

Further Information

Apprenticeship Schemes (National Apprenticeship Service) - www.apprenticeships.org.uk

Apprenticeships in Scotland (Careers Info Scotland) - www.apprenticeshipsinscotland.com/about/

Diplomas (Foundation, Higher and Advanced) - http://yp.direct.gov.uk/diplomas

Engineering Connections - www.apprentices.co.uk

Engineering Scotland (SEMTA) - www.engineeringscotland.org

SEMTA - sector skills council for science, engineering and manufacturing technologies - www.semta.org.uk

Training Schemes - www.direct.gov.uk/en/educationandlearning

Addresses

Engineering Council
246 High Holborn, London WC1V 7EX
Phone: +44 (0)20 3206 0500
Web: www.engc.org.uk

Engineering Development Trust (EDT)
Ridgeway, Welwyn Garden City, Hertfordshire AL7 2AA
Phone: +44 (0)1707 871520
Web: www.etrust.org.uk

Engineering Training Council (NI)
Interpoint, 20-24 York Street, Belfast BT15 1AQ
Phone: +44 (0)28 9032 9878
Web: www.etcni.org.uk

Gauge and Toolmakers' Association (GTMA)
3 Forge House, Summerleys Road, Princes Risborough, Buckinghamshire HP27 9DT
Phone: +44 (0)1844 274 222
Web: www.gtma.co.uk

Scottish Engineering
Training Officer, 105 West George Street, Glasgow G2 1QL
Phone: +44 (0)141 221 3181
Web: www.scottishengineering.org.uk

Similar Jobs

CAD Technician, Engineering Machine Operative, Fitter: Maintenance, Sheet Metal Worker, Toolmaker, Wood Machinist

Engineering Machine Operative

CRCI:Engineering
CLCI:RAB Job Band: 1 to 2

Job Description

Engineering machine operatives are responsible for one of the many engineering machines that are pre-set to drill and cut parts. They can use a range of machines, such as lathes, grinders, borers, presses and drills, although most are specifically trained to operate one type of machine. Operatives switch the machine on and off and watch the controls when it is running. They can also load and unload the machine and check the standard of what is being made. May alter the dials and settings to maintain efficiency and with experience, they may set the machine up for use. Some machines are operated by hand and many others are controlled by computer.

Work Details

Usually work a basic 39-40 hr week, Monday to Friday, though may be required to work shifts, including evenings, nights, weekends and public holidays. You are based indoors in a modern factory or a workshop, which can be noisy. You have to stand or sit at a machine for many hours. The work can be repetitive and there may be some heavy lifting. Sometimes there can be accidents with machines. You may have to wear overalls, as work can be messy and dirty. You may also need to wear special boots, eye and ear protection.

Qualification

• England, Wales and Northern Ireland

Band 1: For entry to jobs, no minimum qualifications are needed, but you are expected to have a good level of general education and relevant experience. Some formal/vocational qualifications at any level are useful, possibly including English, maths and practical subjects.

Band 2: For entry to jobs, no minimum qualifications are needed, but it is an advantage to have some GCSEs (A*-C) or equivalent in subjects that include maths, English and physics or another science subject, or equivalent. Technology and design are useful subjects.

• Scotland

Band 1: For entry to jobs, no minimum qualifications are needed, but you are expected to have a good level of general education and relevant experience. Some formal/vocational qualifications at any level are useful, possibly including English, maths and practical subjects.

Band 2: Although academic qualifications are not always specified, many employers ask for some S grades (1-5) including maths, English and physics or another science subject, or similar. Technological studies is also useful.

Adult Qualifications

No set minimum entry qualifications are required. However, some formal qualifications such as maths, English, physics or another science subject, or equivalent, are beneficial for employment. Technology and design are also useful subjects.

Work Experience

Relevant work or voluntary experience is always useful. It can add to your CV and improve your chances when applying for entry to jobs or training schemes in the engineering industry.

Entry and Training

Most people enter this job aged 16-17, although you have to be over 18 to do some shift work. Young people usually begin training through an apprenticeship programme in industrial applications. Some companies may ask you to take an aptitude test. There may be an induction programme in a training workshop. Training is usually on the job with a skilled operative or a supervisor, or perhaps through a work-based training programme. Training usually includes safety and elementary first-aid procedures.

You may go on day or block release to a local college to work towards relevant courses/awards. Relevant S/NVQs are available at levels 1-3, such as in performing manufacturing or engineering operations at levels 1-2. When skilled and experienced you may be given further training to operate specialist machines. Relevant training programmes, including manufacturing apprenticeship schemes, may be available in your area. Advanced apprenticeships leading to qualification at level 3 can also be a route into higher education.

The Engineering Development Trust runs a range of nationwide schemes for 11-21 year olds who are interested in engineering as a career. See the website for details. A Diploma/Welsh Baccalaureate may be available in your area in engineering. See the diplomas website for further information.

Government training opportunities, such as apprenticeships for adults, may be available in your area. You can also gain recognition of previous experience through Accreditation of Prior Learning or by working towards relevant S/NVQs. Contact your local careers office, Jobcentre Plus, Next Step service or Learning and Skills Council (LSC)/Local Enterprise Company (LEC) for details of training schemes.

Opportunities and Pay

You can be employed by a general mechanical engineering company or in the aircraft, motor, agricultural machinery or shipbuilding industries. With experience you can be promoted to team leader. In general, numbers of machine operators are decreasing at the moment because of increasing automation and the recent economic downturn.

Pay depends on the employer. Starting salaries are likely to be around £12k a year, rising to £18k with experience. Skilled and experienced workers can earn more than £22k a year. Overtime and shift work can contribute to a significant proportion of pay

Health

You may have to pass a medical. For certain types of work you need good colour vision. Some of the materials used can irritate the skin and cause or aggravate allergies.

Skills and Qualities

able to follow instructions, accurate, careful, common sense, good concentration level, manual dexterity, methodical, reliable, willing to learn.

Relevant Subjects

Design and technology, Engineering, Manufacturing

Further Information

Apprenticeship Schemes (National Apprenticeship Service) - www.apprenticeships.org.uk

Apprenticeships in Scotland (Careers Info Scotland) - www.apprenticeshipsinscotland.com/about/

Diplomas (Foundation, Higher and Advanced) - http://yp.direct.gov.uk/diplomas

SEMTA - sector skills council for science, engineering and manufacturing technologies - www.semta.org.uk

Training Schemes - www.direct.gov.uk/en/educationandlearning

Addresses

Engineering Development Trust (EDT)
Ridgeway, Welwyn Garden City, Hertfordshire AL7 2AA
Phone: +44 (0)1707 871520
Web: www.etrust.org.uk

Engineering Training Council (NI)
Interpoint, 20-24 York Street, Belfast BT15 1AQ
Phone: +44 (0)28 9032 9878
Web: www.etcni.org.uk

Scottish Engineering
Training Officer, 105 West George Street, Glasgow G2 1QL
Phone: +44 (0)141 221 3181
Web: www.scottishengineering.org.uk

Similar Jobs

Assembler: Light Industry, Engineering Craft Machinist, Heat Treatment Operative, Polymer/Plastics Process Operative, Printer: Machine, Toolmaker

Engraver

CRCI:Design, Arts and Crafts
CLCI:EG
Job Band: 2 to 3

Job Description

Engravers decorate metal or glass using hand or machine tools that are increasingly computerised, to cut detailed designs and lettering. Special tools are needed to hand engrave, which is highly skilled and needs artistic ability for original designs. Glass engravers use copper wheel lathes, hand held diamond or tungsten carbon tools, acid etching or sand or grit blasting. Metal engravers use a machine, such as a pantograph, to cut lettering and decorate items by copying patterns or using a template. Engravers may use hand-held power-driven cutting tools to work on precious metals and articles of jewellery, using engine-turning engraving techniques that need a high level of skill. They may also use photo etching or bead blasting.

Objects to be decorated may be of brass, copper, aluminium, stainless steel and bronze, or a precious metal of gold or silver, or plain or crystal glass. Guns, trophies and medals, trays, jewellery, mirrors, decanters, plates and bowls are engraved. Some engravers produce their own designs.

Work Details

Usually work 37-40 hrs a week, Monday to Friday, which may include Saturdays, but you have a day off during the week to compensate. If you are self-employed you are frequently on your own unless you employ other staff. You have to be careful and accurate at all times and cope with sitting or standing for many hours. Some engraving work may be in dusty and noisy conditions so you need to wear a face mask, eye and ear protection.

Qualification

It is possible to enter this job without formal qualifications though some entrants complete art college courses first. These require higher qualifications.

- **England, Wales and Northern Ireland**

Band 2: For entry to jobs, no minimum qualifications are needed, but it is an advantage to have some GCSEs (A*-C) or equivalent in subjects that include English and maths. Sciences, art and technical subjects are also useful.

Band 3: or entry to jobs, HNC or a relevant Diploma, usually at least 4 GCSEs (A*-C) including English and maths, or equivalent.

- **Scotland**

Band 2: Although academic qualifications are not specified for this job, it is an advantage to have some S grades (1-3) in subjects that include English and maths, or similar. Sciences, art and technical subjects are also useful.

Band 3: For entry to relevant courses: usually at least four S grades (1-3) including English and maths, or equivalent.

Adult Qualifications

Good general secondary education is required. Previous qualifications or experience in art and design, craft or technical work is valuable.

Work Experience

Entry to this job is competitive and it is important that you try to do some relevant work or voluntary experience before applying. Engraving experience is hard to obtain, but any art and design, craft or technical work is valuable.

Entry and Training

There are no specific academic requirments for this job, but most entrants have a background in art and design. Training is usually on the job, often by traineeship, but posts may be difficult to obtain. There are no specific apprenticeships in jewellery, silversmithing and allied trades but these may be available in the future. Trainees are sometimes art graduates or those who have progressed through the organisation. Employers may prefer applicants with previous relevant experience and some entrants may already be trained in relevant craft skills or have practical experience obtained from a full-time design course.

There are many jewellery, silversmithing, glass and ceramics courses which give an overview of engraving. A list of full and part-time courses can be obtained from the Jewellery and Allied Industries Training Council (JAITC). There are also BTEC/SQA HND courses in subjects including gemmology, jewellery and silversmithing, horology, and art and design. A Diploma/Welsh Baccalaureate may be available in your area in creative and media and may provide a route onto higher education courses.

Glass engraving is specialist and can be studied as part of an HND, foundation degree or degree course in glass and ceramics. The International Glass Centre at Dudley College offers a one year course in glass techniques and technology and a professional development award in design (glass) at levels 2-5. It may be useful to join the Guild of Glass Engravers, the professional body which offers student and craft membership.

Mature applicants are judged on individual merit and those with relevant experience may have an advantage over school leavers, but there are few vacancies. It is useful to have previous experience in metalwork and craft design. Government training programmes may be available. Contact your local Connexions or careers office, Jobcentre Plus, Next Step service or Learning and Skills Council (LSC)/Local Enterprise Company (LEC) for details of all training opportunities and schemes, including apprenticeships for adults.

Opportunities and Pay

Engravers can work for jewellery manufacturers, silversmiths, glass manufacturers and gunsmiths or perhaps in a high street shop. Most work is to be found in London, Birmingham and Sheffield, and city or town centres throughout the UK. Jobs in metal and glass engraving are competitive and decreasing. Few are able to make a living without having a further job. However, there has been an increase in the number of self-employed engravers working in small workshops, or from home.

Pay varies considerably depending on area and type of employer. Those working in a high street shop generally earn around £15k-£17k a year, rising to around £21k with experience. An engraver working in the decorative engraving industry can expect to earn £20k-£26k a year, rising to around £30k. The gun engraving industry attracts the highest rate of pay, particularly in London.

Health

This job requires good eyesight. There may be an allergy risk from dust and skin irritants.

Skills and Qualities
able to work well on your own, attention to detail, creative flair, drawing ability, good concentration level, hand-to-eye co-ordination, patient, specialist IT skills, steady hand, technical aptitude.

Relevant Subjects
Art and Design, Design and technology

Further Information
Creative & Cultural Skills - sector skills council for advertising, crafts, cultural heritage, design, literature, music, performing & visual arts - www.ccskills.org.uk

Design Uncovered (Trotman 2009) - www.trotman.co.uk

Diplomas (Foundation, Higher and Advanced) - http://yp.direct.gov.uk/diplomas

Guild of Glass Engravers (GGE) - www.gge.org.uk/

National Association of Goldsmiths (NAG) - www.jewellers-online.org/pages/home.php

NSEAD: Careers in Art, Craft & Design (National Society for Education in Art and Design) - www.nsead.org/resources/careers.aspx

Retail Jeweller magazine (Retail Jeweller) - www.retail-jeweller.com

Your Creative Future (Design Council) (Design Council) - www.yourcreativefuture.org

Addresses
Institute of Professional Goldsmiths (IPG)
P.O. Box 668, Rickmansworth, Hertfordshire WD3 0EQ
Phone: +44 (0) 20 3004 9806
Web: www.ipgold.org.uk

International Glass Centre
Dudley College, Mons Hill Campus, 111 Wrens Hill Road, Wrens Nest Estate, West Midlands DY1 3SB
Phone: +44 (0) 1384 363101
Web: www.dudleycol.ac.uk/

Jewellery and Allied Industries Training Council (JAITC)
c/o British Jewellers' Association (BJA), Federation House, 10 Vyse Street, Birmingham B18 6LT
Web: www.jaitc.org.uk/

Similar Jobs
Artist, Ceramic Decorator, Engineering Craft Machinist, Glassmaker: Operative, Jeweller: Retail, Jewellery Designer

Entertainer
also known as: Circus Performer, Magician, Variety Performer

CRCI:Performing Arts

CLCI:GAN — Job Band: 2 to 5

Job Description
Entertainers perform on TV, radio or in theatre, variety shows and cabaret venues, films, holiday centres or in a circus. They may write a script or devise their own routines. Some specialise in verbal or visual humour such as improvisation, mime or magic. Entertainers may also dance, sing or play a musical instrument. Others may act as a comphre and direct/produce shows for holidaymakers, or specialise and become a children's entertainer using magic tricks and juggling skills. They research new performance material, write the script and may add music or dance.

Circus performers use skills such as clowning, juggling and acrobatics and aerial skills on the trapeze and high wire.

Work Details
You work irregular hours, evenings and weekends, and the work can be demanding. A lot of time is needed for rehearsing and adapting your act. Entertainers work in a variety of locations; theatres, clubs, pubs, broadcasting studios, holiday centres, the circus, or possibly film and television studios, on cruise ships or in private homes. You may have to travel extensively to get work and need to spend nights away from home, possibly for long periods.

Qualification
No particular entry qualifications are required for this job, but an exceptional talent to perform and entertain is essential. People enter with a varied level of qualifications, including higher national awards and degrees.

• England, Wales and Northern Ireland
Band 2: Although academic qualifications are not specified for this job, it is an advantage to have some GCSEs (A*-C) in subjects that include English and maths, or equivalent.

Band 3: For entry: usually at least 4 GCSEs (A*-C) including English and maths, or equivalent.

Band 4: For BTEC higher national award: 1-2 A levels and some GCSEs (A*-C) usually including English and maths, or equivalent

Band 5: For degree courses: 2-3 A levels and some GCSEs (A*-C) usually including English and maths, or equivalent. Exact requirements depend on the degree you take.

• Scotland
Band 2: Although academic qualifications are not specified for this job, it is an advantage to have some S grades (1-3) in subjects that include English and maths, or similar.

Band 3: For entry: usually at least four S grades (1-3) including English and maths, or similar.

Band 4: For SQA higher national award: usually 2-3 H grades and some S grades (1-3), often including English and maths, or similar qualifications.

Band 5: For degree courses: 3-5 H grades and some S grades (1-3), including English and maths, or similar qualifications. Exact requirements depend on the degree you take.

Degree Information
A degree in performing arts/studies, musical theatre, or music/ popular music may be helpful.

Adult Qualifications
No particular entry qualifications are required as talent, persistence and a measure of luck are all necessary for success.

Work Experience
It is essential to gain experience and build your act/performance and confidence, perhaps at school or college/university by joining a drama club. Summer jobs at a holiday centre or other place of entertainment, whether paid/unpaid, are useful.

Entry and Training
To enter this job you usually have to pass an audition. Entrants can be recruited through personal introduction and recommendation, or may become known through a talent spotting competition. Training is usually on the job developing your talent or skill into an act with audience appeal. There are courses specific to this job, and some entrants have attended a drama school. Those who work in music and dance may need to undertake formal training; check the job details for a musician and a dancer for more details. Many people begin with short acts in clubs or pubs that specialise in their type of entertainment, and progress to getting regular work.

Some enter through a degree in performing arts/studies, musical theatre, or music/popular music. Those who wish to work and learn circus skills and physical theatre, can develop their talent through courses offered by companies such as Circomedia. The

Circus Space offers a two-year foundation degree in circus arts. On successful completion of this course, students can apply for a one year BA (Hons) top up degree in circus arts. The Comedy School also offers a range of workshops and courses, along with arts centres and theatres throughout the country.

A Creative Apprenticeship Scheme is available in music entertainment. Contact Creative and Cultural Skills for details. A Diploma/Welsh Baccalaureate in creative and media may also be available in your area. Check university entry requirements carefully in case there is an additional specialist learning requirement with the diploma. See the diplomas website for further information.

Mature applicants with amateur experience may be able to progress to paid employment, though much depends on talent and an element of luck. Competition from younger entrants is fierce.

Opportunities and Pay

Jobs are available in towns and cities in theatres, nightclubs and hotels, and on cruise ships and at holiday centres. This area is highly competitive and considerable talent is required for success, as job security is limited. Most jobs are short term and for a few hours each week. If you become well known, you can expect a high standard of living, but most entertainers live a precarious life financially. Many find work through a family connection or an agent. Prospects vary according to the season, with more jobs available around Christmas and during the holiday season. The most successful entertainers often aim for radio and television.

Fees are irregular and variable in amount, so initially it is necessary to have another job or source of income. Costs include agent's fees and payment of a professional subscription to Equity, the acting union. Entertainers may earn anything from £50-£1000 a session, depending on the type of act, reputation and popularity. With regular work, you may start on £10k-£15k a year, rising to around £22k. Established entertainers can earn £30k-£60k or more.

Health

You need to be energetic for this job. If working in a circus you need to be physically fit and very agile.

Skills and Qualities

able to withstand criticism, ambitious, competitive, determined, enthusiastic, outgoing personality, self confident, sense of humour, stamina

Relevant Subjects

English, Media and communication studies, Music, Performing arts, Physical education and sport

Further Information

Apprenticeship Schemes (National Apprenticeship Service) - www.apprenticeships.org.uk

Circus Development Agency - http://circusarts.org.uk

Creative & Cultural Skills - sector skills council for advertising, crafts, cultural heritage, design, literature, music, performing & visual arts - www.ccskills.org.uk

Creative Choices - www.creative-choices.co.uk

Diplomas (Foundation, Higher and Advanced) - http://yp.direct.gov.uk/diplomas

Emerald Circus - www.emeraldcircus.com

Performers.net - online community for international variety performers - www.performers.net

Resident Entertainer - www.residententertainers.com

Skillset - sector skills council for the creative media, fashion and textiles industries - www.skillset.org

The Stage Online - www.thestage.co.uk

Welsh Baccalaureate - www.wbq.org.uk

▶Working in creative & media (2007) (Babcock Lifeskills) - www.babcock-lifeskills.com/

Addresses

Circomedia
Britannia Road, Kingswood, Bristol BS15 8DB
Phone: +44 (0)117 947 7288
Web: www.circomedia.com

Circus Space (The)
Coronet Street, London N1 6HD
Phone: +44 (020 7729 9522
Web: www.thecircusspace.co.uk

Comedy School (The)
15 Gloucester Gate, London NW1 4HG
Phone: +44(0)20 7486 1844
Web: www.thecomedyschool.com

Equity
Guild House, Upper St Martin's Lane, London WC2H 9EG
Phone: +44 (0)20 7379 6000
Web: www.equity.org.uk

National Council for Drama Training (NCDT)
249 Tooley Street, London SE1 2JX
Phone: +44 (0) 20 7407 3686
Web: www.ncdt.co.uk

Similar Jobs

Actor, Dancer, DJ, Holiday Centre Worker, Puppeteer/Puppet Maker, Singer

Environmental Health Practitioner

also known as: Environmental Health Officer, Public Health Officer

CRCI:Healthcare
CLCI:COP — Job Band: 5

Job Description

Environmental health practitioners work to improve the quality of life now and in the future, through finding ways of maintaining healthy living and working conditions in the community. They also work to prevent infectious diseases and other public health dangers. Can perform a wide variety of tasks or specialise in one area of work. They enforce legislation in many aspects of work and prosecute those who ignore the laws, standards and regulations surrounding public health and the environment. May need to appear in court to give evidence for the prosecution. Use a variety of scientific instruments and equipment to monitor and control pollution such as the atmosphere, water, noise and land pollution.

May inspect the storage and handling of food in restaurants, shops, abattoirs and food processing plants to ensure hygiene control. Also check that housing and other forms of dwelling such as boats and caravans, are of a particular standard and fit for habitation. Write and present reports and liaise with other professional colleagues.

Work Details

You usually work normal office hours of 35-39 a week, with a rota for occasional night and weekend work. Your base is an office but you spend most of your time visiting premises and meeting people. These premises can be dirty and unpleasant and you may have to wear protective clothing, special footwear or a helmet. The work involves dealing with complaints, giving people advice and sometimes making unpopular decisions. Sometimes you may encounter people who can be abusive so you must be able to deal with all kinds of reactions to your visit.

Qualification

• England, Wales and Northern Ireland

Band 5: For degree in environmental health: 2-3 A levels and some GCSEs (A*-C), or equivalent. GCSE subjects must include maths and English, and usually double science, or biology, chemistry and physics, with at least one science at A level.

- **Scotland**

Band 5: For degree in environmental health: 3-5 H grades, including chemistry, maths and preferably either physics or biology, and some S grades (1-3) including English, chemistry and maths if you do not have these subjects at H grade, or similar qualifications. Check with the University of Strathclyde for details.

Degree Information

Entrants should have a degree in environmental health, or an approved degree in a science subject followed by an accredited MSc in environmental health. A list of approved degrees can be obtained from the Chartered Institute of Environmental Health (CIEH). Preferred science degrees are environmental science, biology, food science, physics or biochemistry. Chemistry and chemical engineering provide useful background. It is also possible to study part time for an environmental health/science degree whilst in a job.

Adult Qualifications

Applicants who are suitably experienced, but who do not have the standard entry requirements for the degree in environmental health, can apply to have these requirements waived. Experience in health and hygiene or laboratory work is useful. There are flexible entry routes to BSc degrees, including a one-year science Access or a foundation degree. Graduates with a suitable BSc may be able to go straight on to a postgraduate course for a qualification in environmental health.

Work Experience

Entry to this career is highly competitive and it is essential that you have some relevant work or voluntary experience before applying. You may be able to work shadow an environmental health practitioner in local government, as some authorities are very keen to offer work experience to school students. Experience in other areas of health and hygiene, such as in a hospital, is also useful.

Entry and Training

Entry is highly competitive, but there is a steady demand for qualified staff and this is likely to increase. In England, Wales and Northern Ireland your course and training must be recognised by the Chartered Institute of Environmental Health (CIEH). You also have to complete an experiential learning portfolio (ELP) providing evidence of work-based learning and complete professional exams in order to obtain a certificate of registration. In Scotland you must have the appropriate degree from Strathclyde University and complete a minimum of 48 weeks of practical on-the-job training. You must also pass professional exams before you can achieve the Diploma in Environmental Health of the Royal Environmental Health Institute of Scotland (REHIS) and finally become an Environmental Health Officer.

Work-based practical training is an integral part of courses and can be done during or after the degree. Universities normally help students find placements. During the placement, a logbook or work record has to be completed. All CIEH/REHIS members have to undertake continuing professional development (CPD) to keep their knowledge up to date.

Several institutions offer part-time accredited degrees, often through day release, which usually takes up to 5-6 years to complete. A relevant foundation degree is also available in some areas. The CIEH/REHIS also offer a range of qualifications, including vocational qualifications. For this job, it is essential to have a driving licence.

One year science access or foundation degrees may be available for mature applicants looking to enter this profession. For those who already have a BSc in another field, postgraduate MSc courses can lead to an environmental health qualification. There may be opportunities for those studying an approved course to receive a sponsorship/training place from a local authority.

Opportunities and Pay

Many environmental health practitioners work for local authorities throughout the UK, although a growing number work for private industry, including hotel and catering organisations, housing associations, the retail industry, or for food manufacturers. There are good opportunities to work in the armed services, the NHS, central government and agencies, shipping/airline companies and holiday companies (checking hotels etc). Once qualified, you can choose to specialise in food standards, environmental pollution, housing or workplace health and safety.

There is a clear promotion route into management within local government though you may need to move jobs to increase your experience and gain further promotion. Part-time work is possible, or you can become a self-employed consultant after several years' experience in a job. You can also work abroad, where environmental health expertise is required in communities in the developing world.

Salaries vary according to the employer, but tend to be around £25k-£34k, depending on experience and qualifications. This can rise to around £35k-£60k a year with experience and managerial responsibilities. A director of public health can earn in the region of £70k a year.

Health

The work involves a risk of infection.

Skills and Qualities

able to make important decisions, enquiring mind, firm manner, good communication skills, good written English, impartial, not squeamish, responsible attitude, scientific approach, sound judgement, tactful

Relevant Subjects

Biology, Chemistry, English, Health and social care, ICT/Computer studies, Law, Mathematics, Physics, Science, Sociology

Further Information

Careers in Environmental Health (Royal Environmental Health Institute of Scotland) - www.rehis.org/about/careers-advice

Careers in Environmental Health (Chartered Institute of Environmental Health) - www.ehcareers.org

CIWM Journal for Waste and Resource Management (Chartered Institute of Waste Management) - www.ciwm.co.uk/pm/33/

Environment Agency - www.environment-agency.gov.uk

Environmental Health Careers (Chartered Institute of Environmental Health) - www.ehcareers.org

Environmental Health News (Chartered Institute of Environmental Health) - www.cieh.org/ehn

Local Government Careers (Improvement and Development Agency) - www.lgcareers.com/publications/

REHIS Journals (quarterly) (Royal Environmental Health Institute of Scotland) - www.rehis.org/documents/journals

Scottish Environment Protection Agency - www.sepa.org.uk

So you want to work in Healthcare (Wayland) - www.waylandbooks.co.uk

Addresses

Chartered Institute of Environmental Health (CIEH)
Chadwick Court, 15 Hatfields, London SE1 8DJ
Phone: +44 (0)20 7928 6006
Web: www.cieh.org

Royal Environmental Health Institute of Scotland (REHIS)
19 Torphichen Street, Edinburgh EH3 8HX
Phone: +44 (0)131 229 2968
Web: www.rehis.org

Strathclyde University
16 Richmond Street, Glasgow G1 1XQ
Phone: +44 (0)141 552 4400
Web: www.strath.ac.uk

Similar Jobs
Environmental Scientist, Forensic Scientist, Health & Safety Inspector, Health & Safety Practitioner, Health Promotion Specialist, Public Analyst, Quality Manager, Trading Standards Officer

Environmental Scientist

CRCI:Science, Mathematics and Statistics
CLCI:QOL Job Band: 4 to 5

Job Description
Environmental scientists research and advise on the effects or possible effects of human activities on the environment. They may work on projects related to pollution, waste management, flood control, energy, land use, conservation or climate change. Work activities vary, depending on the requirements of the job.

Scientists may go out and collect samples from sites or monitor plants and wildlife, or do desk research to find out about sites and their history. They analyse samples and data to test for pollutants and may use computers to work out the possible environmental impact of different scenarios. Also help to devise solutions that promote biodiversity or allow development but minimise adverse effects. They write reports and present findings and recommendations in a way that colleagues and managers can understand.

Work Details
Hours vary depending on the employer, the nature of the job and deadlines. Many work a 35-37 hr week, Monday to Friday, but may need to work additional hours at times. You divide your time between working indoors in an office and laboratory and outdoors on sites that may be cold, wet and muddy. May need to travel to sites in the UK or abroad. You form part of a small multidisciplinary team, working with technical and non-technical colleagues and managers.

Qualification
- **England, Wales and Northern Ireland**

Band 4: For HND, Diploma of Higher Education or foundation degree: 1-2 A levels and some GCSEs (A*-C) usually including English, maths and two sciences or technology, or equivalent.

Band 5: For degree courses: usually 2-3 A levels, including a science subject, and some GCSEs (A*-C) usually including English, maths and two science subjects or technology, or equivalent. Exact requirements depend on the degree you take.

- **Scotland**

Band 4: For entry to SQA higher national and professional development awards, usually 2-3 H grades and some S grades (1-3), including English, maths and a science, or similar qualifications.

Band 5: For degree courses: 3-5 H grades and some S grades (1-3), usually including English, a science and maths, or similar qualifications. Useful subjects include physics, biology, chemistry, geology and geography. Exact requirements depend on the degree you take.

Degree Information
A degree in environmental science or related subjects is particularly relevant. You can do a postgraduate course in an environmental science specialism with a degree in any science subject. Some courses may be accredited by professional institutions, such as the Institution of Environmental Sciences (IES), as wholly or partially meeting their academic requirements.

Adult Qualifications
Entry requirements may be relaxed for adults applying for higher education courses. Access or foundation courses in science provide those without the required qualifications a route onto degree courses.

Work Experience
Relevant work experience can improve your chances in the job market. Many conservation and environmental charities and local authorities offer volunteering opportunities. The national charity StudentForce for Sustainability offers work experience projects for young people and paid placements for graduates in the East Midlands. Some higher education courses include work placements or the opportunity to take part in real projects.

Entry and Training
Most people entering this field are graduates in a science or environmental science subject. Employers usually also look for people with relevant work or voluntary experience. Degree and postgraduate courses in environmental science and related subjects allow you to develop the knowledge and skills you need for this area of work.

Some people become environmental scientists after gaining experience as a technician. It may be possible to study for a Diploma in environmental and land-based studies, which offers a foundation for further study in this field.

Training is mostly on the job, but you can also attend short courses or study part time for a postgraduate qualification. You may join an appropriate professional institution such as the Chartered Institution of Water and Environmental Management (CIWEM) or the Institution of Environmental Sciences (IES). If you join a professional body that is a member of the Society for the Environment (SocEnv), you may work towards chartered environmentalist (CEnv) status. You have to fulfil academic requirements and have at least four years' professional experience, followed by a professional review interview. All environmental scientists undertake continuing professional development (CPD) to keep up to date with the latest issues and developments.

Mature entry is welcomed. For some jobs, especially consultancy roles, employers look for people with experience, voluntary or paid, of working on environmental projects.

Opportunities and Pay
Increasing environmental regulation means that many kinds of organisations need environmental scientists. There are jobs with local authorities, government agencies and voluntary sector organisations. Water, waste management, civil engineering and construction companies also employ environmental scientists. The number of environmental consultancy firms that do contract work is increasing. These used to recruit experienced staff only, but now there is a trend towards taking on junior staff and training them for this role.

You may progress into roles that involve managing whole projects or teams. Experienced staff may move into consultancy roles.

Earnings depend on where you work, the type of organisation you work for and the type of work you do. New entrants may earn £18k-£22k a year. Experienced staff earn £20k-£35k, whilst senior and principal environmental scientists can earn £35k-£50k or more.

Health
You must have a good level of fitness to undertake field work. There is an allergy risk from pollen, animals, birds and chemicals.

Skills and Qualities
able to explain clearly, analytical skills, aptitude for teamwork, good organisational skills, IT skills, logical, methodical, numeracy skills, problem-solving skills, project management skills, scientific approach.

Relevant Subjects
Biology, Chemistry, English, Geography, ICT/Computer studies, Land and Environment, Mathematics, Physics, Science

Further Information
AGCAS: Environment & Agriculture (Job Sector Briefing) (AGCAS) - www.prospects.ac.uk

Diplomas (Foundation, Higher and Advanced) - http://yp.direct.gov.uk/diplomas

Environmental Careers (Chartered Institution of Water and Environmental Management) - www.ciwem.org.uk/publications/careers/

Lantra - The Sector Skills Council for environmental & land-based sector (Lantra) http:/www.lantra.co.uk

Nature (weekly) (Nature Publishing Group) - www.nature.com/

New Scientist (weekly) (Reed) - www.newscientist.com

Student Force for Sustainability - www.studentforce.org.uk

▶Working in science (2007) (Babcock Lifeskills) - www.babcock-lifeskills.com/

▶Working with animals (2009) (Babcock Lifeskills) - www.babcock-lifeskills.com/

Addresses
British Ecological Society (BES)
Charles Darwin House 12 Roger Street, London WC1N 2JU
Phone: +44 (0)207 685 2500
Web: www.britishecologicalsociety.org

Chartered Institution of Water and Environmental Management (CIWEM)
15 John Street, London WC1N 2EB
Phone: +44 (0)20 7831 3110
Web: www.ciwem.org.uk

Environment Agency
National Customer Contact Centre, PO Box 544, Almondsbury, Rotherham S60 1BY
Phone: 08708 506 506 (UK only)
Web: www.environment-agency.gov.uk

Institution of Environmental Sciences (IES)
2nd Floor 34 Grosvenor Gardens, London SW1W 0DH
Phone: +44 (0)20 7730 5516
Web: www.ies-uk.org.uk

Scottish Environment Protection Agency
Erskine Court, Castle Business Park, Stirling FK9 4TR
Phone: +44 (0)1786 457700
Web: www.sepa.org.uk

Society for the Environment (SocEnv)
The Old School House, 212 Long Street, Atherstone, Warwickshire CV9 1AH
Phone: +44 (0)845 337 2951
Web: www.socenv.org.uk

Similar Jobs
Chemist: Analytical, Ecologist, Public Analyst, Recycling Officer, Soil Scientist, Toxicologist

Equality & Diversity Officer
also known as: Equal Opportunities Officer

CRCI:Administration, Business and Office Work
CLCI:CAG Job Band: 3 to 5

Job Description
Equality and diversity officers promote equality of opportunity within our society and work to ensure that no one experiences discrimination through gender, race, age, disability, religious belief, or sexual orientation. The exact nature of the work depends on the employing organisation. Duties may include ensuring that a workforce represents the local community in terms of ethnic origin, disability and male/female ratio of employees. May also promote equality in the promotion of existing staff and the provision of the organisation's services or products. Can also be involved in the recruitment of new employees. Officers arrange special training courses to raise awareness of the issues of equal opportunity.

They keep up to date on relevant current legislation. Also liaise with other equal opportunities professionals, community groups, local councils etc. May support victims of harassment or discrimination at hearings and tribunals.

Work Details
Work is normally office based. You usually work 35-37 hours from Monday to Friday, though some evening or weekend work may be necessary at times. You may occasionally have to travel to meetings and conferences. The work can be stressful at times and you may have to make difficult or unpopular decisions. You are likely to deal and negotiate with employers, employees and union representatives. Part-time work is possible.

Qualification
There are no formal entry qualifications, though professional training and experience in social work, youth or community work is often an advantage.

• England, Wales and Northern Ireland
Band 3: For relevant CIPD qualification, HNC or a relevant Diploma: usually 4 GCSEs (A*-C) or equivalent are preferred.

Band 4: For HND in business studies, Diploma of Higher Education or foundation degree: 1-2 A levels and some GCSEs (A*-C) usually including English and maths, or equivalent.

Band 5: For degree courses: 2-3 A levels and some GCSEs (A*-C) usually including English and maths, or equivalent. Exact requirements depend on the degree you take.

• Scotland
Band 3: For relevant CIPD qualification or an SQA national award: usually four S grades (1-3) including English and maths, or similar are preferred.

Band 4: For entry to SQA higher national and professional development awards, usually 2-3 H grades and some S grades (1-3), including English and maths, or similar qualifications.

Band 5: For degree courses: 3-5 H grades and some S grades (1-3) usually including English and maths, or similar qualifications. Exact requirements depend on the degree you take.

Degree Information
A degree in any subject is acceptable, though a degree or postgraduate qualification that includes the specific study of equality issues, such as in women's studies (ethics, sociology or social policy with women's studies etc), may give a useful background.

Adult Qualifications
There are flexible alternatives into degrees, including a one-year Access course. Mature applicants may be accepted on to a degree course without the usual entry requirements, particularly if they have relevant work experience. Professional experience and qualifications are often an advantage.

Work Experience
Employers may prefer candidates who have relevant work or voluntary experience. This can include youth, community and social work, or work in human resources/personnel sections, or working in an office environment gaining administration skills.

Entry and Training
There are no minimum qualifications to enter equal opportunities work, though this is generally a second career for those who have gained relevant experience and/or qualifications in a related area of

work. Many entrants have a proven career in human resources (HR), or possibly a background of work in the community. Knowledge of current affairs and a high level of interpersonal skills are required. Relevant experience and evidence of commitment to equality of opportunity are often considered more important than qualifications. For more senior posts, some organisations require a degree (or equivalent) or management experience, and often appropriate qualifications as a trainer.

Training may be on the job, or at a local college. In some cases, employers may support study for qualifications from the Chartered Institute of Personnel and Development (CIPD). The CIPD have a specific diversity and discrimination section which offers a range of courses. The CIPD Certificate in Employment Relations, Law and Practice is a skills based foundation level qualification equivalent to S/NVQ level 3. Successful completion leads to associate membership of the CIPD. It is also possible for more experienced HR professionals to do the Advanced Certificate in Employment Law at postgraduate level. One day courses are available in Managing Diversity, Discrimination and the Law, and Bullying and Harassment.

Relevant S/NVQs and foundation degrees may also be available. Training programmes, including personnel support apprenticeships, may be available in your area. Advanced apprenticeships leading to qualification at level 3 can also be a route into higher education.

Mature entry is common, and in particular for those with experience and/or qualifications in human resources (HR) or perhaps in community work. Some work in administrative roles in large organisations and work their way up to this role through relevant experience and acquired skills and knowledge.

Opportunities and Pay

Most opportunities occur in central and local government, including the police or military establishments. Other opportunities exist in medium to large companies or organisations, international companies, universities or colleges. Promotion may be possible to more senior posts but it may be necessary to move to another employer for promotion. Freelance or consultancy work is also possible. In a smaller company/organisation, this job may be combined with human resources/personnel duties.

Pay varies depending on the size and location of the organisation or authority, but generally starting salaries are around £18k, rising to around £26k a year with greater experience. Senior officers or managers can earn £50k a year or more.

Skills and Qualities

able to withstand criticism, able to work to a budget, efficient record keeping, fair minded, good communication skills, good interpersonal skills, good written English, persuasive, responsible attitude, self confident, tactful, trustworthy

Relevant Subjects

Business and accounting, English, Government and politics, Law, Mathematics, Psychology, Sociology

Further Information

AGCAS: Government & Public Administration (Job Sector Briefing) (AGCAS) - www.prospects.ac.uk

Local Government Careers (Improvement and Development Agency) - www.lgcareers.com/publications/

People Management Magazine (CIPD) - www.peoplemanagement.co.uk/pm

▶Working in business, administration & finance (2010) (Babcock Lifeskills) - www.babcock-lifeskills.com/

Addresses

Chartered Institute of Personnel and Development (CIPD)
151 The Broadway, London SW19 1JQ
Phone: +44 (0)20 8612 6200
Web: www.cipd.co.uk

Convention of Scottish Local Authorities (COSLA)
Rosebery House, 9 Haymarket Terrace, Edinburgh EH12 5XZ
Phone: +44 (0)131 474 9200
Web: www.cosla.gov.uk

Equality and Human Rights Commission
3 More London, Riverside Tooley Street SE1 2RG
Phone: +44 (0)20 3117 0235
Web: www.equalityhumanrights.com

Northern Ireland Local Government Association (NILGA)
Unit 5B Castlereagh Business Park, 478 Castlereagh Road, Belfast BT5 6BQ
Phone: +44(0)28 9079 8972
Web: www.nilga.org

Public and Commercial Services Union
160 Falcon Road, London SW11 2LN
Phone: +44 (0)207 924 2727
Web: www.pcs.org.uk

UNISON Learning and Organising Services (LAOS)
1 Mabledon Place, London WC1H 9AJ
Phone: 0845 355 0845 (UK only)
Web: www.unison.org.uk/laos/index.asp

Similar Jobs

Advice Worker, Community Development Worker, Community Learning & Development Officer (Scotland), Human Resources Officer/Manager, Trade Union Official, Training & Development Officer/Manager

Ergonomist

also known as: Human Factors Specialist, User-centred Designer

CRCI:Administration, Business and Office Work
CLCI:COD Job Band: 5

Job Description

Ergonomists make scientific studies of the relationship between people and their work or living/leisure environment. They aim to ensure that humans and technology work in complete harmony. Using knowledge of science and engineering techniques, they devise and design an environment that improves comfort, efficiency and safety. They investigate the limitations of the human body and analyse how equipment and machinery is used. They then make recommendations based on the results of trials and research. May also look at ways of improving working posture to reduce, for example, repetitive strain injuries or work-related upper limb disorders. Some ergonomists design working environments, including heating and lighting, to suit the needs of users and the tasks performed.

Some ergonomists specialise in specific products and others in areas that include the design of military equipment, or advise on the design of interfaces between people and computers known as HCI (human computer interaction). They work in collaboration with other professionals, including design engineers, industrial designers/physicians, computer specialists, and health and safety practitioners. Can act as an expert witness in cases of industrial injury.

Work Details

Usually work 35-40 hrs, Monday to Friday, although is expected to work extra hours at times. Those working in industry or within the armed forces work shifts. Travel within a working day is frequent and you are sometimes away from home overnight. There is occasional travel abroad.

Qualification

• England, Wales and Northern Ireland

Band 5: For degree courses: 2-3 A levels and some GCSEs (A*-C) usually including English and maths, or equivalent. Exact requirements depend on the degree you take but recommended combinations are maths, physics and biology or maths, physics and psychology.

• Scotland

Band 5: For a degree: usually 3-5 H grades and some S grades (1-3) including maths. The specific subjects depend on the degree you take, but recommended combinations are maths, physics and biology or maths, physics and psychology. A relevant SVQ 3 or similar may be acceptable for entry.

Degree Information

There are first degrees in ergonomics and in psychology with ergonomics. Related subjects, such as operational research, biological/biomedical science, product design, engineering, computer science, occupational therapy, mathematics, medicine, physiology, physics, sports science, physiotherapy or occupational psychology, often have an ergonomics option and can be followed by a postgraduate course.

Relevant postgraduate courses include ergonomics, human factors in manufacturing systems, health ergonomics, human-computer interaction with ergonomics, and ergonomics and safety at work. Contact the Ergonomics Society for details of relevant degree and postgraduate courses, including distance learning.

Adult Qualifications

Applicants with a relevant postgraduate qualification have an advantage, especially if combined with related work experience. Entry requirements may be relaxed for adults applying for higher education courses. Access or foundation courses provide those without relevant qualifications a route onto degree courses.

Work Experience

Employers and universities may prefer candidates who have relevant work or voluntary experience. The Ergonomics Society states that employers usually prefer students who have taken a gap year between school and university, and have also had some industrial experience. The Society offers its student members a work experience placement service called 'Opening Doors'. You could also contact an ergonomist to discuss their work.

Entry and Training

Most entrants are graduates with a relevant degree, though increasingly a postgraduate qualification in ergonomics or a related subject may be an advantage. Training is on the job, usually after gaining experience in other areas of work, such as psychology, engineering, design or architecture. You can also study ergonomics by taking a distance-learning course. Membership of the Ergonomics Society (ES) is achieved by obtaining a qualifying first degree with a significant ergonomics content or a degree in a relevant subject, such as psychology, engineering, biological or sports science, physics, mathematics or computer science, followed by an accepted postgraduate course of study.

Depending on the type of work you do, membership of the Institution of Occupational Safety and Health may be beneficial. It runs many short courses, including ergonomics, throughout the year. Check the website for details.

Continuing professional development (CPD) is expected of ergonomists due to ever-changing advances in their field of work. Contact the ES for further information on courses, qualifications, membership, training routes and CPD.

Mature entry is welcomed from a range of backgrounds, including those with previous work experience/qualifications in areas such as engineering, psychology, physiotherapy, and design.

Opportunities and Pay

This is a small but expanding profession and there is currently a shortage of experienced human factors and ergonomics practitioners. You might work for government departments, research laboratories, hospitals, industry or the armed forces. Ergonomists also work in academic institutions where they are involved in both research and lecturing, in addition to acting as consultants in their own specialisms. For example, the Ergonomics and Safety Research Institute, has a strong research division which feeds its consultancy programmes. Nationally and internationally, there are an increasing number of independent ergonomist consultancies and individual freelance consultants, usually with specialist areas of expertise. There are a few part-time posts.

Salaries vary depending on location, size and type of company. A qualified ergonomics graduate earns around £18k-£25k a year, rising to £26k-£40k with experience. Senior ergonomists can earn in the region of £45k a year, or more.

Skills and Qualities

analytical skills, aptitude for teamwork, good communication skills, good interpersonal skills, imaginative, IT skills, logical, perseverance, problem-solving skills, scientific approach

Relevant Subjects

Biology, Design and technology, Engineering, English, ICT/ Computer studies, Manufacturing, Mathematics, Physical education and sport, Physics, Psychology, Science

Further Information

AGCAS: Government & Public Administration (Job Sector Briefing) (AGCAS) - www.prospects.ac.uk
British Safety Council - www.britsafe.org
Ergonomics 4 Schools - www.ergonomics4schools.com
Human Factors and Ergonomics Society Careers - www.hfes.org/Web/CareerCenter/Career.aspx
Institute of Ergonomics and Human Factors (Ergonomics Society) - www.ergonomics.org.uk/
Safety and Health Practitioner (monthly) (Institution of Occupational Safety and Health (IOSH)) - www.shponline.co.uk/
The Ergonomist (monthly) (Ergonomics Society) - www.ergonomics.org.uk
Your Creative Future - www.yourcreativefuture.org.uk

Addresses

Design Council
34 Bow Street, London WC2E 7DL
Phone: +44 (0)20 7420 5200
Web: www.designcouncil.org.uk

Ergonomics and Safety Research Institute (ESRI)
Garendon Building, Holywell Park, Loughborough, Leicestershire LE11 3TU
Phone: +44 (0)1509 226900
Web: www.lboro.ac.uk/research/esri/about.htm

Ergonomics Society (ES)
Elms Court Elms Grove, Loughborough, Leicestershire LE11 1RG
Phone: +44 (0)1509 234904
Web: www.ergonomics.org.uk

Institution of Occupational Safety and Health (IOSH)
The Grange, Highfield Drive, Wigston, Leicestershire LE18 1NN
Phone: +44 (0)116 257 3100
Web: www.iosh.co.uk

Similar Jobs

Consumer Scientist, Engineer: Design, Health & Safety Practitioner, Psychologist: Occupational

Estate Agent

CRCI:Building and Construction
CLCI:UM Job Band: 2 to 5

Job Description

Estate agents arrange the marketing, buying, selling and leasing of any type of land or residential, commercial or industrial property. In some estate agencies, an agent may work across all sections of the business. However, some specialise in residential estate agency, with offices that are usually based in the high streets of villages, towns and cities. They value and sell property ranging from studio apartments to mansions with acres of land. Many agencies list their properties online in order to maximise their advertising capacity and increase the opportunity of potential sales. Some agents manage their company's website and keep it up to date.

Estate agents also deal with commercial and licensed premises, such as shops and industrial premises, pubs and hotels, or may deal specifically with lettings and property management on behalf of a property owner. Some specialise in auctioneering where a property (private or business) is valued, advertised and sold at a public auction.

Preparation of sales and advertising details, advising on price and market conditions and arranging viewing times are all part of the service. Agents may accompany buyers to view potential properties. Many offer additional services such as arranging mortgages, surveys and conveyancing and they act as an intermediary or representative between an owner and a prospective buyer. They use strong negotiation skills to secure the best possible price (or rent/lease) for a property and liaise with solicitors, banks and building societies on the legal and financial aspects of sales.

Work Details

Estate agents usually work 35-40 hrs a week from 9am to 6.30pm, Monday to Saturday, though may be required to work some evenings and Sundays on a rota basis. Works in an office and travels around to visit property. A driving licence is useful. Your clients may range from property managers of large commercial organisations to first-time home buyers. You inform, advise and help people to make decisions and need knowledge of the relevant legal technicalities. You need to have a good understanding of local facilities and knowledge of relevant law. A business-like and efficient approach is essential, even under pressure.

Qualification

Whilst academic qualifications are always helpful and applicable, personal qualities and abilities are the most important aspect of this job.

• England, Wales and Northern Ireland

Band 2: Although academic qualifications are not specified for this job, it is an advantage to have some GCSEs (A*-C) in subjects that include English and maths, or equivalent.

Band 3: For entry to some jobs: usually at least 4 GCSEs (A*-C) including English and maths, or equivalent.

Band 4: For BTEC higher national award: 1-2 A levels and some GCSEs (A*-C) usually including English and maths, or equivalent.

Band 5: For degree courses: 2-3 A levels and some GCSEs (A*-C) usually including English and maths, or equivalent. Exact requirements depend on the degree you take.

• Scotland

Band 2: Although academic qualifications are not specified for this job, it is an advantage to have some S grades in subjects that include English and maths, or similar qualifications.

Band 3: For some courses: at least four S grades (1-3) including English and maths, or similar.

Band 4: For SQA higher national award: usually 2-3 H grades and some S grades (1-3) including English, maths or similar.

Band 5: For degree: 3-5 H grades and some S grades (1-3) including English and maths. Appropriate SQA awards or similar are also considered.

Degree Information

Any degree is acceptable, but the most relevant degrees are estate agency, estate management, land and property management, property development and valuation, or a directly related subject, such as real estate (valuation and management). There are postgraduate courses for those with non-relevant degrees. Other subjects, including geography (human) or building-related disciplines, give useful backgrounds.

Adult Qualifications

Entry requirements may be relaxed for adults applying for higher education courses. Access or foundation courses give adults without qualifications a route on to degree courses. Those with relevant work experience may be accepted for some courses without needing any formal entry requirements. Entry to the BSc (Hons) in estate agency at a more advanced stage is possible for those with appropriate professional experience.

Work Experience

Employers may prefer candidates who have relevant work or voluntary experience. Relevant areas of work and skills include anything office based where you use administration skills; sales, retail, and working with the public. For adult entry you often need previous relevant employment or substantial voluntary work experience in sales, administration or surveying.

Entry and Training

Estate agency is a career that you can enter with a broad range of experience and qualifications. Professional qualifications are an advantage but not essential. You can study for a degree or diploma, then complete two years' practical training and experience. Or you can train on the job and study part time by distance learning or through a day-release course. For the full or part-time BSc in estate agency, currently offered by North East Wales Institute of HE, you do not necessarily require a high level of formal qualifications, particularly if you have relevant experience. Relevant foundation degrees are also available.

There are several membership organisations, such as the National Association of Estate Agents (NAEA). The NAEA has merged with the Association of Residential Letting Agents, the National Association of Valuers and Auctioneers, and the Institution of Commercial & Business Agents. Together they form a new awarding body, the National Federation of Property Professionals (NFOPP) which offers a range of qualifications that do not usually require formal academic qualifications.

NFOPP offers level 3 technical awards in the sale of residential property or in residential letting and property management. This is the minimum requirement for membership of the NAEA. NFOPP also offers diplomas in residential estate agency (DipREA) in lettings and management (DipRLM), or commercial property agency (DipCPA). At diploma level you should have at least three years' relevant experience. Availability of courses is subject to change so check the website carefully for details of specific registration and exam dates. Courses are by distance learning and are offered by Manchester Open Learning. See the NFOPP website for details of all available qualifications. Some local colleges also offer part-time courses that lead to NFOPP diplomas.

Alternatively you can enter this profession through a NAEA/TTC Training apprenticeship in residential estate agency. You learn on the job and may take short courses. Apprenticeships can lead to NVQs at level 2/3 and a relevant technical award. Contact Asset Skills for details of apprenticeships in your area. Advanced apprenticeships leading to qualification at level 3 can also be a route into higher education. Estate agents are sometimes valuers who are qualified through the Royal Institution of Chartered Surveyors (RICS). See separate job details (Surveyor: General Practice) for further information.

Mature applicants are often preferred by some employers, particularly those with relevant business experience. Government training opportunities, such as apprenticeships, may be available in your area. You can also gain recognition of previous experience through Accreditation of Prior Learning (APL) or by working towards relevant S/NVQs. Contact your local careers office, Jobcentre Plus, Next Step service or Learning and Skills Council (LSC) Local Enterprise Company (LEC) for details of training schemes.

Opportunities and Pay

Most people work for an estate agency, ranging from small companies to multiple agencies. There are also jobs with large international firms or real estate firms. Opportunities may depend on the property climate at the time of your application. Currently there is a downturn in the market which means there are fewer vacancies. There is often no formal career structure, so promotion depends on experience, merit and professional qualification. It is possible to specialise in land, residential, commercial or industrial property and some also work as an auctioneer. Others may move into work as a relocation agent (see job profile). Experienced estate agents may become self-employed and set up their own business.

Most estate agents' salaries are a combination of basic salary and commission, based on the percentage profit they make for the agency; the total is referred to as the 'on target earnings' (OTE). Salaries range from £13k-£30k, depending on location and experience. With commission you can earn more and some highly successful agents may make considerably more, depending on the financial property climate.

Skills and Qualities

able to manage a budget and keep records, business awareness, excellent communication skills, good interpersonal skills, good telephone manner, IT skills, negotiating skills, persuasive, self confident, understanding of legal technicalities

Relevant Subjects

Business and accounting, Economics, English, Geography, Law, Mathematics

Further Information

Apprenticeship Schemes (National Apprenticeship Service) - www.apprenticeships.org.uk

Asset Skills - sector skills council for the places where we live and work - www.assetskills.org

Estate Agency News (Estates Press Ltd) - www.estateagencynews.co.uk

Manchester Open Learning - www.mol-openlearning.co.uk

National Federation of Property Professionals (NFOPP) - www.nfopp.co.uk

The Estate Agent (10 x year) (National Association of Estate Agents) - www.naea.co.uk

Addresses

National Association of Estate Agents (NAEA)
Arbon House, 6 Tournament Court, Edgehill Drive,
Warwick CV34 6LG
Phone: +44 (0)1926 496 800
Web: www.naea.co.uk

North East Wales Institute of HE (NEWI) (Glyndwr University)
Plas Coch Campus, Mold Road, Wrexham,
Denbighshire LL11 2AW
Phone: +44 (0) 1978 290666
Web: www.newi.ac.uk/

Royal Institution of Chartered Surveyors (RICS)
RICS Contact Centre Surveyor Court Westwood Way,
Coventry CV4 8JE
Phone: +44 (0)870 333 1600
Web: www.ricscourses.org/pages/careers.aspx

Similar Jobs

Auctioneer, Domestic Energy Assessor, Property Manager, Relocation Agent, Surveyor: General Practice, Surveyor: Quantity, Surveyor: Rural Practice

European Law Solicitor

CRCI:Legal and Political Services
CLCI:LAC Job Band: 5

Job Description

Solicitors specialising in this area give skilled legal advice on matters relating to European law. They discuss legal issues with clients and handle cases on their behalf. They work in the institutions of the European Commission (EC) including the European Parliament, the Council of Ministers and the Court of Justice. Some are involved in formulating laws and implementing policies in areas such as agriculture, social affairs, transport or the environment. They may specialise in providing advice to commercial companies with European links. May also assist in resolving legal issues regarding the transportation of goods within Europe, the purchase and selling of assets, as well as the resolution of disputes.

Work Details

If working for the EC, the normal working week is 37 hrs, Monday to Friday, although you may be required to work at other times to meet deadlines. The work is office based but you may be expected to travel in Europe and sometimes live abroad.

Qualification

• England, Wales and Northern Ireland

Band 5: For degree course: three A levels (usually high grades) and some GCSEs (A*-C) including English and maths, and possibly a modern language, or equivalent qualifications. Exact requirements depend on the degree you take.

• Scotland

Band 5: For degree in Scots law: five H grades (typically AAAAB) and some S grades (1-3) or similar qualifications, usually including English and maths, and perhaps a modern language. Good H grades are required, with English preferred, preferably taken at one sitting. Exact requirements depend on the degree to be taken. Check with individual institutions.

Degree Information

Many universities offer law degrees with an option to specialise in European legal studies. In England & Wales, graduates should have either a good honours 'qualifying' degree in law or a non-law degree, such as business studies or financial management, plus the Common Professional Examination/Graduate Diploma in Law . All must complete a Legal Practice Course. Contact the Solicitor's Regulation Authority for details of all training routes.

In Northern Ireland, you must complete a law degree that is acceptable to the Law Society of Northern Ireland, followed by the Institute of Professional Legal Studies' examinations. Those with a non-law degree must also attain a satisfactory level of approved legal knowledge, such as the Bachelor of Legal Science, which is offered by Queen's University, Belfast. Contact the Law Society of Northern Ireland for details of training routes.

Adult Qualifications

Part-time and external degrees in law are available. Degree entry requirements may be relaxed for those over 23 years with legal work experience. Mature applicants can apply to take a two-year full-time or three-year part-time senior status law degree, available at various institutions in the UK. Contact the Law Society or the Solicitor's Regulation Authority for full details.

Work Experience
Entry to this job is competitive and it is important that you try to do some relevant work or voluntary experience before applying. During the last year of a degree course, applicants are recommended to obtain vacation work with a large commercial or European law firm.

Entry and Training
You must first qualify as a solicitor prior to specialising in European Law. For full details about qualifying as a solicitor, see the job profile for 'Solicitor'.

Solicitors working for the European Commission (EC) and other European Union (EU) institutions must be qualified before being recruited and the open competition recruitment process can be lengthy and complicated. Specialist temporary posts are sometimes advertised and have a more straightforward recruitment process. Some law graduates take part in the European Fast Stream of the civil service, although this is not available every year.

Solicitors wishing to practise the law of a particular European country and advise private or business clients may have to undertake additional studies or exams. This is determined by the appropriate legal body of individual countries. It is useful to gain experience by working for the Government Legal Service (GLS). The GLS offers specialist training in EU law, as well as practical language training and other relevant external training. Contact the GLS for information about training contracts and the qualified lawyer recruitment programme.

Mature applicants over the age of 25 (29 in NI), may apply to be accepted as a student of law without the usual minimum qualifications or via a senior status law degree. A standard level of education for entry applies and relevant work experience is an advantage, or may be required. There are some funding opportunities available that may help mature entrants. Contact the Law Society or the Solicitor's Regulation Authority for details.

Opportunities and Pay
If you work for the European Commission (EC) you are most likely to be based in Brussels or Luxembourg, although a small number of staff are based in European Union (EU) delegations throughout the world. You may work for individuals, law firms or business organisations with offices in Europe, as well as the UK. You may work for various departments of the Government Legal Service. There are good promotion prospects.

Pay varies considerably depending on location, size of firm and level of responsibility. Trainee solicitors earn a minimum of £16.7k when training, £18.8k if based in Central London. Solicitors earn around £25k-£70k once trained. Those working at a high level in a large commercial firm can make over £100k. Salary rates in the EU are based on the highest paid member state and are usually attractive to UK applicants.

Skills and Qualities
ability in one or more languages, analytical skills, awareness of confidentiality issues, excellent communication skills, good interpersonal skills, information handling skills, IT skills, logical, sound judgement, versatile

Relevant Subjects
Business and accounting, Economics, English, Government and politics, History, Law, Modern Foreign Languages, Psychology

Further Information
European Personnel Selection Office (EU Careers) (Office for Official Publications of the EC) - http://europa.eu/epso

Junior Lawyers (Law Society) - www.juniorlawyers.lawsociety.org.uk

Skills for Justice - sector skills council for the UK justice system - www.skillsforjustice.com

Solicitors' Regulation Authority (SRA) (SRA) - www.sra.org.uk

TARGETjobs: Law (GTI Specialist Publishing Ltd.) - www.groupgti.com

▶Working in politics & law (2010) (Babcock Lifeskills) - www.babcock-lifeskills.com/

▶Working with languages (2010) (Babcock Lifeskills) - www.babcock-lifeskills.com/

Addresses
Government Legal Service (GLS)
GLS Recruitment Team 11th Floor Lower Castle Street
Castlemead, Bristol BS1 3AG
Phone: +44 (0) 845 3000 793
Web: www.gls.gov.uk

Law Society of England & Wales
The Law Society's Hall, 113 Chancery Lane, London WC2A 1PL
Phone: +44 (0)20 7242 1222
Web: www.lawsociety.org.uk

Law Society of Northern Ireland
96 Victoria Street, Belfast BT1 3GN
Phone: +44 (0) 28 9023 1614
Web: www.lawsoc-ni.org

Law Society of Scotland
26 Drumsheugh Gardens, Edinburgh EH3 7YR
Phone: +44 (0)131 226 7411
Web: www.lawscot.org.uk

Similar Jobs
Advocate (Scotland), Barrister, Procurator Fiscal (Scotland), Solicitor

Event & Exhibition Organiser
also known as: Conference Organiser

CRCI:Marketing and Advertising
CLCI:OG — Job Band: 3 to 5

Job Description
Event and exhibition organisers plan, research, set up and organise events such as conferences/exhibitions for firms, institutions and professional organisations. They may also organise public events such as agricultural/horticultural shows, antiques and toy fairs, motor, caravan and boat shows or wedding fayres, etc. Can organise specific events such as company days, which may include team building activities. This might involve outdoor challenges in unfamiliar terrain such as orienteering, or adventure trips to destinations both inside and outside the UK.

The job involves selecting and booking a suitable venue, sending out publicity and reserving accommodation for participants. They also deal with catering, reception facilities and specialist equipment for each event such as microphones, photocopying, video and computer facilities. May also arrange speakers or delegates, media coverage and transport. Checks all details and liaises with venue staff and leaders to ensure that the event runs satisfactorily and supervises the health and safety requirements of each event. Ensures visitors can leave the event quickly and safely if necessary.

Work Details
Usually works a basic 37-39 hr week, though is expected to work unusual and long hours, including weekends and evenings. There may be a need to travel over a wide area and spend nights away from home. You advise and organise people, and consult with staff in a variety of different organisations. You are responsible for seeing that everything is efficiently organised, and need to ensure that costs are kept within an agreed budget. You usually work as part of a small team.

Work may be stressful at times as it involves working with some people who may be awkward or demanding. Most organisers spend their time at the event site walking around, so comfortable shoes are required. A smart appearance is expected and some organisers may wear a corporate uniform.

Qualification

• England, Wales and Northern Ireland

Band 3: For entry to jobs, HNC or a relevant Diploma, usually at least 4 GCSEs (A*-C) including English and maths, or equivalent. Check with colleges for information on specific course requirements.

Band 4: For HND, Diploma of Higher Education or foundation degree: 1-2 A levels and some GCSEs (A*-C) usually including English and maths, or equivalent. Check with colleges for information on specific course requirements.

Band 5: For degree courses: 2-3 A levels and some GCSEs (A*-C) usually including English,or equivalent qualifications. Exact requirements depend on the degree you take.

• Scotland

Band 3: For entry to jobs, usually at least four S grades (1-3) including English or maths, or similar.

Band 4: For entry to SQA higher national and professional development awards, usually 2-3 H grades and some S grades (1-3), including English and maths, or similar qualifications. Entry requirements vary, so check with individual colleges.

Band 5: For degree courses: 3-5 H grades and some S grades (1-3), usually including English, or similar. Exact requirements depend on the degree you take.

Degree Information

Any degree discipline is acceptable for entry to this job, but particularly useful subjects include event management, marketing, management, business-related studies, travel and tourism, communications or public relations.

Adult Qualifications

Entry requirements may be relaxed for adults applying for higher education courses. Access or foundation courses give adults without qualifications a route onto degree courses.

Work Experience

Entry to this job is competitive and it is important you try to do some relevant work or voluntary experience. The most relevant experience is anything involving sales and marketing, the use of organisation and administration skills, and working with the public. Paid or voluntary experience in helping to organise social or students events can also be useful.

Entry and Training

Most entrants to this job have had previous training and practical experience in a related area of work such as sales and marketing, or hotel and catering management. You do not need a degree for entry to this work, but many entrants are graduates and it can also be useful to be fluent in a European language and have computer skills. There are no formal graduate training schemes and most trainees learn through practical experience on the job and through external or in-house short courses. There are also foundation degrees in event management.

Some event organisers choose to become members of the Association of Event Organisers (AEO), the Association of British Professional Conference Organisers, or the Chartered Institute of Marketing, who offer relevant training courses and conferences. The AEO website details events management courses and the Society of Event Organisers runs a continuing professional development programme.

A Diploma/Welsh Baccalaureate in business, administration and finance or creative and media may be offered in your area and can be a good route into this career. There is a vocational qualification (VRQ) in event planning at levels 2-3 and EDI offers a level 3 certificate in the principles of event management.

Mature entrants are welcomed and often personality and experience are more important than academic qualifications. Some employers may ask for experience in marketing, public relations, journalism, advertising, business management and administration.

Opportunities and Pay

There are 500-600 firms of exhibition organisers in the UK, most of which are small companies. Jobs are available throughout the UK and you may be employed by an agency that organises events for different clients such as agricultural or garden societies, magazine companies, government departments or trade organisations. Alternatively you may work for a large company that has its own in-house conference/exhibition department. There are also opportunities with hotels, universities and colleges who provide event facilities. This is a growing industry with the larger venues and agencies in major cities like London, Glasgow and Manchester.

Promotion prospects vary as there is no clear promotion structure. Some event organisers move into marketing or public relations, and others become self-employed and work on a freelance basis. There are also opportunities to work abroad.

Pay depends on conditions of employment and income is variable if self-employed. Starting salaries are usually £16k-£20k a year, rising to £27k-£40k with experience. Senior managers in high profile companies can earn £50k-£70k a year. Earnings often involve commission and performance-related pay.

Skills and Qualities

able to cope under pressure, able to work to a budget, aptitude for teamwork, attention to detail, business awareness, good interpersonal skills, IT skills, planning skills, problem-solving skills, project management skills

Relevant Subjects

Business and accounting, Economics, English, Hospitality and catering, ICT/Computer studies, Leisure, travel and tourism, Mathematics, Modern Foreign Languages

Further Information

Diplomas (Foundation, Higher and Advanced) - http://yp.direct.gov.uk/diplomas

Event Magazine (quarterly) (Haymarket Marketing Publications) - www.eventmagazine.co.uk

Exhibition Bulletin (Mash Media) - www.mashmedia.net

Network for Event Organisers in Ireland (NEO Ireland) - http://new.neoireland.com/

▶ Working in business, administration & finance (2010) (Babcock Lifeskills) - www.babcock-lifeskills.com/

▶ Working in marketing, advertising & PR (2008) (Babcock Lifeskills) - www.babcock-lifeskills.com/

▶ Working in space (2010) (Babcock Lifeskills) - www.babcock-lifeskills.com/

Addresses

Association of British Professional Conference Organisers (ABPCO)
9 Wellington Park, Belfast BT9 6DJ
Phone: +44 (0)28 9038 7475
Web: www.abpco.org

Association of Event Organisers Ltd (AEO)
119 High Street, Berkhamsted, Hertfordshire HP4 2DJ
Phone: +44 (0)1442 285810
Web: www.aeo.org.uk

Chartered Institute of Marketing (CIM)
Moor Hall, Cookham, Maidenhead, Berkshire SL6 9QH
Phone: +44 (0) 1628 427120
Web: www.cim.co.uk

Society of Event Organisers
29a Market Square, Biggleswade, Bedfordshire SG18 8AQ
Phone: +44(0)1767 316255
Web: www.seoevent.co.uk

Similar Jobs

Art Exhibitions Organiser, Hotel Manager, Marketing Manager, Press Officer, Public Relations Officer, Wedding Planner

Exhibition Designer

also known as: Display Designer

CRCI:Design, Arts and Crafts
CLCI:EZ

Job Band: 4 to 5

Job Description

Exhibition designers are responsible for designing attractive and well laid out exhibitions to give information to the people viewing them. They may work on exhibitions that inform and entertain the public at places like museums, galleries, shows and events or at more specialist trade shows and conferences like air shows and flower shows.

Designers find out what the client wants, discuss the budget available and the deadlines they must meet. They use the brief and their knowledge about how crowds move and react to different material to design the exhibition. Usually sketch designs and make models for the client to approve. May use computer aided design (CAD) software to help them produce plans.

Designers organise the building of the stands, visit workshops and make sure they are delivered to the exhibition space at the right time and within budget. Also ensure that the lighting is right and there is access to things such as electrical sockets if these are needed. May help to set up displays and put up the exhibition stands ready for the event to open to the public.

Work Details

Usually work a 35-40 hour week, Monday to Friday, but may be required to work some evenings and weekends. Designers are generally based in an office or design studio, but some are home based. Some designers work alone, others work as part of a design team. You may have to travel long distances or abroad to meet clients and attend exhibitions. Increasingly client contact is carried out via email and the phone rather than face to face.

Setting up exhibitions and displays may involve some lifting and physical activity. Depending on the size of the company, you may be part of a design team or may work alone and be responsible for all aspects of the exhibition. You liaise with suppliers and other people involved in setting up the exhibition. Working to tight deadlines and receiving negative feedback from clients can be stressful.

Qualification

- **England, Wales and Northern Ireland**

Band 4: For HND, Diploma of Higher Education or foundation degree: 1-2 A levels and some GCSEs (A*-C) usually including English and maths, or equivalent.

Band 5: For degree courses: 2-3 A levels and some GCSEs (A*-C) usually including English and maths, or equivalent. Exact requirements depend on the degree you take. A diploma in creative and media may be considered as an alternative to A levels.

- **Scotland**

Band 4: For entry to SQA higher national and professional development awards, usually 2-3 H grades and some S grades (1-3), including English and maths, or similar qualifications.

Band 5: For degree courses: 3-5 H grades and some S grades (1-3), usually including English and maths, or similar qualifications. Exact requirements depend on the degree you take.

Degree Information

Relevant degree subjects include exhibition design, interior design, spatial design, interior architecture, multimedia, graphic design and 3D design. There are postgraduate courses in 3D design and exhibition design that can be taken after a first degree in an art and design subject. There are also specialist postgraduate courses in museum and heritage exhibition design.

Adult Qualifications

Entry requirements may be relaxed for adults applying for higher education courses. Access or foundation courses provide those without the required qualifications a route onto degree courses.

Work Experience

Relevant work or voluntary experience is always useful and can improve your employment prospects when applying for entry to jobs. Some courses include work placements or the opportunity to take part in real display projects. The Chartered Society of Designers (CSD) and the creative, design and advertising educational charity (D&AD) may be able to offer work placement opportunities.

Entry and Training

You may be able to enter as a junior assistant designer but employers increasingly look for graduates in design-related subjects. You need to show a portfolio of your work when applying for design courses and jobs in exhibition design. Foundation degrees are available in relevant subjects such as interior and spatial design. A Diploma/Welsh Baccalaureate may be available in your area in creative and media and may provide a route onto higher education courses.

Training may be on the job or through in-house courses or day release to colleges or other training providers. It can focus on areas such as health and safety, project management or using new computer software as well as design topics. The British Display Society (BDS) provides college-based, certificated courses, leading to recognised professional qualifications. These include a one-year course in general design and a two-year national diploma in exhibition design, retail and spatial design.

The Chartered Society of Designers (CSD) is the professional body for all types of designers and offers a continuing professional development (CPD) scheme and training for its members.

It is possible to move into this area of work from other types of design work such as interior design, graphic design or architecture. Some people progress to exhibition design after gaining experience at a junior level or in other areas of exhibition and display work, such as model making or building display stands.

Opportunities and Pay

An increase in the number of design companies across the UK in recent years and the rise in popularity of visitor attractions means that exhibition designers are often in demand. Many specialist exhibition design companies are located in London or close to other towns and cities that have large permanent exhibition centres such as Birmingham and Manchester.

However, the number of specialist exhibition design companies is small so many exhibition designers are employed by companies offering more general design and marketing services. Museums, galleries and visitor attractions may have their own in-house exhibition design teams. Some retailers also have their own display designers.

In larger companies you may be able to progress to senior designer and creative director or design manager. You may also be able to move into other areas of design work such as architecture or marketing. Many designers are self-employed as there are opportunities for freelance work for experienced exhibition designers with a network of contacts.

Depending on the size of the company, typical starting salaries are in the region of £19k-£22k, rising to around £30k-£35k a year for experienced staff. Salaries for senior staff or those running their own businesses can be as high as £60k a year.

Health

Normal colour vision is desirable as the work involves using a sense of colour.

Skills and Qualities

able to cope under pressure, able to explain clearly, able to withstand criticism, creative flair, good organisational skills, health & safety awareness, imaginative, spatial awareness, specialist IT skills.

Relevant Subjects

Art and Design, Business and accounting, Economics, English, Hospitality and catering, ICT/Computer studies, Mathematics, Media and communication studies, Psychology.

Further Information

Art & Design Directory 2010 (ISCO Publications)

Association of Event Organisers - www.aeo.org.uk

Chartered Society of Designers (Chartered Society of Designers) - www.csd.org.uk

Creative & Cultural Skills - sector skills council for advertising, crafts, cultural heritage, design, literature, music, performing & visual arts - www.ccskills.org.uk

Design Week (Design Week) - www.designweek.co.uk

Diplomas (Foundation, Higher and Advanced) - http://yp.direct.gov.uk/diplomas

Directory of Design Consultants - www.designdirectory.co.uk

New Design Partners - www.newdesignpartners.com

The Designer (Chartered Society of Designers) - www.thedesignermagazine.com

Your Creative Future (Design Council) (Design Council) - www.yourcreativefuture.org

Addresses

British Design & Art Direction (D&AD)
9 Graphite Square Vauxhall Walk, London SE11 5EE
Phone: +44 (0)20 7840 1111
Web: www.dandad.org

British Display Society (BDS)
14-18 Heralds Way, Town Centre, South Woodham Ferrers, Essex CM3 5TQ
Phone: +44 (020 8856 2030
Web: www.britishdisplaysociety.co.uk

Similar Jobs

Event & Exhibition Organiser, Film/TV & Theatre Set/Stage Designer, Graphic Designer, Interior Designer, Model Maker, Visual Merchandiser

Export Sales Manager

also known as: Exporter, International Sales Manager

CRCI:Marketing and Advertising
CLCI:OE Job Band: 3 to 5

Job Description

Export sales managers promote and sell company products to overseas customers. They handle all aspects of exporting goods though tasks can vary, depending on the type of product and the destination. This includes developing a thorough knowledge of a country's political, cultural and economic background. Export managers research and target the potential market, then plans a sales campaign. They also negotiate with customers, often in a foreign language, provide estimates of price and agree terms of the contract.

Export managers often specialise in a particular product or market, such as medical, financial or agricultural. They usually report to the sales director and are responsible for meeting sales targets. This involves setting up the financial transactions and organising the necessary documentation, including insurance. They also arrange for goods to be despatched to customers on an agreed date. May sell through agents or sales teams overseas, or sell directly by making regular trips abroad. Is also responsible for finding the right trading partners overseas and new markets.

Work Details

Usually works a basic 40 hr week, but most exporters have to work long hours, and in many posts, travel extensively. You need in-depth knowledge of the product you are selling and a good appreciation and understanding of the local environment and culture you are selling to. Keeping up to date with export and tariff controls, customs, exchange rates and other legal formalities is required. You are responsible for securing contracts, budget expenditure, solving problems quickly and dealing with extensive paperwork.

The work may be challenging and pressurised at times and can involve making difficult decisions. Fluency in a foreign language may be important for some employers.

Qualification

- **England, Wales and Northern Ireland**

Band 3: For Certificate in International Trade (CIT)/BTEC national award or for direct entry as an export assistant: usually at least 4 GCSEs (A*-C) including English and maths, or equivalent but you may be able to study for the CIT without any formal qualifications.

Band 4: For Advanced Certificate in International Trade (ACIT), the diploma in international trade or a BTEC higher national award: a CIT or 1-2 A levels and 5 GCSEs (A*-C) or equivalent. A foreign language is also useful.

Band 5: For degree courses: 2-3 A levels and some GCSEs (A*-C) usually including English and maths, or equivalent qualifications. Exact requirements depend on the degree you take. A foreign language is useful.

- **Scotland**

Band 3: For Certificate in International Trade (CIT), the diploma in international trade, BTEC national award or for direct entry as an export assistant: usually a minimum of four S grades (1-3) preferably including English and maths, or similar but you may be able to study for the CIT without any formal qualifications.

Band 4: For Advanced Certificate in International Trade (ACIT) or SQA higher national award: 2-3 H grades and five S grades (1-3) or similar. A foreign language is also useful.

Band 5: For degree courses: 3-5 H grades and some S grades (1-3), usually including English and maths, or similar qualifications. Exact requirements depend on the degree you take. A foreign language is useful.

Degree Information

Although any degree is acceptable for entry to this job, it is an advantage to have studied marketing, international trade or business studies, preferably combined with a foreign language. Some courses have options in exporting. Graduates with a technical or engineering background may be preferred for some posts. Postgraduate courses in international trade or business administration are available.

Adult Qualifications
Adult candidates with fewer than the specified qualifications may be admitted to courses. However, knowledge of languages, accounting and retailing is important.

Work Experience
Entry to this career is highly competitive and it is essential that you have some relevant work or voluntary experience before applying. Employers may prefer candidates who have relevant work or voluntary experience such as any office-based experience using administration skills, sales or retail and working with the public or in a team. Experience or knowledge of basic accounting techniques is also an advantage.

Entry and Training
Entry requirements often depend on the product or service sold. Some entrants may start as export assistants and move into senior posts after gaining experience. Others move into exporting after working in sales, marketing or a related field. However, for the export of specialist products which are technical or science based, most entrants to exporting are graduates with language skills. Some entrants train by first taking a college course leading to national or higher national BTEC/SQA award. Training for this career involves specific training in the products/services involved, general sales training and education in all aspects of exporting procedures and documentation.

The Institute of Export (IoE) offers the Young International Trader (YIT) Programme aimed at students aged 14-18 which provides an excellent basis for a career as an export sales manager. This aims to teach about the world of international business whilst students continue to study their mainstream education. Visits to ports, airports, cargo terminals or local companies involved in importing/exporting are encouraged.

Large companies usually run their own in-house training programmes and increasingly, companies require potential managers to take the IoE professional exams which start with the Certifed International Trade Advisor (CITA) or Certificate in International Trade (CIT). With three years experience, the Advanced Certificate (ACIT) and ultimately the Diploma in International Trade (DIT) are also available.

The Institute of Commercial Management (ICM) also offers a Certificate in International Trade. Check the ICM website for full details. Courses are offered by many colleges on a block, day release or evening class basis, and are also available through distance learning. The IoE also offers a range of short training courses which are relevant for continuing professional development. Contact the IoE training and development department for more information on all professional courses and training schemes. Professional bodies such as the Chartered Institute of Logistics and Transport and the British International Freight Association also offer relevant courses.

Training programmes, including apprenticeships in warehousing and storage and advanced apprenticeships in logistics operations or purchasing and supply management may be available in your area and provide a good route into this career.

Mature applicants need previous related experience, such as in sales and marketing, freight services, use of languages in business, or accountancy. This job is often a career progression for many entrants. You are usually expected to study for the Institute of Export's (IoE) professional examinations, which can also be studied through a distance-learning programme. Those who have not gained the required entrance qualifications for the advanced certificate in international trade should have at least three years' relevant experience. Contact the IoE for details.

Opportunities and Pay
The UK is a major trading nation and whilst the economic downturn has affected the demand for products and services, there are still good opportunities in this field. Areas of international marketing and sales employment include export and manufacturing companies, freight shipping and insurance companies, merchant/overseas banks and warehouse management. Opportunities in the export field are generally expanding as more companies become involved in international trading. Promotion prospects can be good for those with appropriate skills and personal qualities. Gaining professional qualifications is also important.

Rates of pay vary according to location, company size and sector. Starting salaries are around £22k-£25k a year, and with experience rise to around £30k-£45k. Senior international sales executives can earn £50k-£80k a year. Salaries may include performance or profit-related pay and a company car.

Skills and Qualities
ability in one or more languages, able to manage a budget and keep records, attention to detail, business awareness, enterprising, good communication skills, good organisational skills, information handling skills, IT skills, self-motivated

Relevant Subjects
Business and accounting, Economics, English, Geography, ICT/Computer studies, Law, Mathematics, Modern Foreign Languages, Psychology, Retail and distribution

Further Information
Apprenticeship Schemes (National Apprenticeship Service) - www.apprenticeships.org.uk

Institute of Export Development and Training Department - www.export.org.uk

Skills for Logistics - sector skills council for freight logistics industries - www.skillsforlogistics.org

Winning Edge (6 x year) (Institute of Sales & Marketing Management) - www.ismm.co.uk/magazine.php

▶Working with languages (2010) (Babcock Lifeskills) - www.babcock-lifeskills.com/

Addresses
British International Freight Association (BIFA)
Redfern House, Browells Lane, Feltham, Middlesex TW13 7EP
Phone: +44 (0)20 8844 2266
Web: www.bifa.org

Chartered Institute of Logistics and Transport (CILTUK)
Careers Manager, Logistics & Transport Centre, Earlstrees Court, Earlstrees Road, Corby NN17 4AX
Phone: +44 (0)1536 740 100
Web: www.ciltuk.org.uk

Institute of Commercial Management (ICM)
ICM House, Castleman Way, Ringwood, Hampshire BH24 3BA
Phone: +44 (0)1202 490555
Web: www.icm.ac.uk

Institute of Export (IOE)
Export House, Minerva Business Park, Lynch Wood, Peterborough PE2 6FT
Phone: +44 (0)1733 404 400
Web: www.export.org.uk

Similar Jobs
Commodity Broker, Freight Forwarder, Marketing Manager, Road Transport Manager, Sales Executive, Shipbroker/Airbroker

Facilities Manager
CRCI:Building and Construction
CLCI:UZ — Job Band: 3 to 5

Job Description
Facilities managers are responsible for an organisation's buildings and services, and making sure that the best use is made of the space and operational services. They ensure that all services are

running effectively and maintain a safe and efficient working environment. Duties are extremely varied and may include responsibilities such as the development of an organisation's property strategy and ensuring that such buildings are properly maintained. Facilities managers also advise on health and safety issues, waste management, energy efficiency and handling office moves. They control budgets and spending, and keep accounts.

Managers purchase, sell or rent property for the organisation, or may advise on relocation to another area. They use computers for all aspects of work and for writing reports. Duties may include inspecting premises to check cleanliness and security, dealing with the failure of office equipment and checking in-house catering. Must be able to respond to any problem that arises and have the ability and resources to put things right quickly. Increasingly, many organisations are contracting the running of facilities and related services to a specialist facilities management company, which is involved in making bids to run facilities for public or private sector organisations.

Work Details

Facilities managers usually work around 37-39 hrs a week, Monday to Friday, though you may be expected to work longer hours if required to deal with emergencies. Work is usually in an office though involves travelling around to visit property. A driving licence may be useful. Needs up-to-date knowledge of the relevant legal and technical requirements. Liaises with other professionals, with staff working in the building and with outside contractors.

Qualification

• England, Wales and Northern Ireland

Band 3: For entry to jobs, HNC or a relevant Diploma, usually at least 4 GCSEs (A*-C) including English and maths, or equivalent.

Band 4: For BTEC higher national award: 1-2 A levels and some GCSEs (A*-C) usually including English and maths, or equivalent.

Band 5: For degree courses: 2-3 A levels and some GCSEs (A*-C) usually including English and maths, or equivalent. Exact requirements depend on the degree you take.

• Scotland

Band 3: For entry to jobs, usually at least four S grades (1-3) including English or maths, or similar.

Band 4: For SQA higher national award: usually 2-3 H grades and some S grades (1-3) including English and maths, or similar qualifications.

Band 5: For degree courses: 3-5 H grades and some S grades (1-3), usually including English and maths, or similar qualifications. Exact requirements depend on the degree you take.

Degree Information

Any degree is acceptable but it is an advantage to have a subject such as facilities management, construction and property management, land and property management, building services engineering, business management or surveying. Postgraduate qualifications are available, such as those accredited by the British Institute of Facilities Management (BIFM) and/or the Royal Institution of Chartered Surveyors (RICS).

Adult Qualifications

Access courses to higher education are available. These courses do not require formal entry qualifications, but lead to relevant HND and degree courses. There are also specific certificates in facilities management that can lead to transferring on to an MBA programme.

Work Experience

Employers may prefer candidates who have experience in relevant work areas. The types of work experience to consider include building services engineering, surveying or work in health and safety; any business management experience is also appropriate.

Entry and Training

There is no set entry route into this job. There are a number of relevant full-time, part-time and sandwich courses leading to HNC/HNDs, foundation degrees or degrees and Asset Skills have details of the facilities management apprenticeship on their website. Often this is a second career for people and many therefore enter with a broad range of experience and qualifications in areas such as building services engineering, business management, construction or surveying.

The British Institute of Facilities Management (BIFM) offers a national qualification in facilities management (BIFM Qual). You can achieve this either by taking an accredited higher education course, by taking BIFM examinations, or by demonstrating professional competence (at least five years' facilities management experience). The Royal Institution of Chartered Surveyors (RICS) also offers membership and accredits relevant courses. Contact BIFM and RICS for details.

The BIFM also offers a range of short courses to help with continuing professional development. Those with at least eight years' experience in the industry can work towards gaining Certified Facility Manager credential through BIFM and the International Facility Management Association.

Mature entrants to this job can have a diverse range of relevant professional experience and qualifications in areas that include surveying, engineering, business management, sport and leisure management, hotel and catering, communications, property construction, health and safety, planning or environmental experience. Contact the British Institute of Facilities Management (BIFM) for details of accredited degree courses and their full range of BIFM professional qualifications. Those who have relevant work experience/qualifications may also become a chartered facilities management surveyor. Contact the Royal Institution of Chartered Surveyors (RICS) for details.

Opportunities and Pay

Opportunities are increasing in all parts of the UK. Jobs are available with a wide range of employers, including commercial and industrial companies, real estate firms, health trusts and services, central and local government, universities and colleges, as well as specialist facilities management firms. Self-employment is possible.

Pay varies according to location, size, type of employer and experience but generally, earnings tend to be initially around £20k rising to £30k a year. With further experience, managers commonly earn around £33k-£45k. Those in senior posts may earn over £55k.

Skills and Qualities

able to cope under pressure, able to manage a budget and keep records, able to prioritise work, aptitude for figures, excellent communication skills, good interpersonal skills, good organisational skills, leadership qualities, resourceful, understanding of legal technicalities

Relevant Subjects

Business and accounting, Construction and built environment, Design and technology, Economics, English, Law, Mathematics, Physics, Science

Further Information

Asset Skills - sector skills council for the places where we live and work - www.assetskills.org

FM World (fortnightly) (British Institute of Facilities Management (BIFM) - www.fm-world.co.uk

Inside Careers Guide: Management - www.insidecareers.co.uk

International Facility Management Association (IFMA) - www.ifma.org

Online resource for Facilities Professionals - www.i-fm.net

Premises & Facilities Management (Premises & Facilities Management) http:/www.pfmonthenet.net

▶ Working in construction & the built environment (2007) (Babcock Lifeskills) - www.babcock-lifeskills.com/

Addresses

British Institute of Facilities Management (BIFM)
Number One Building, The Causeway, Bishop's Stortford, Hertfordshire CM23 2ER
Phone: 0845 058 1356 (UK only)
Web: www.bifm.org.uk

Royal Institution of Chartered Surveyors (RICS)
RICS Contact Centre Surveyor Court Westwood Way, Coventry CV4 8JE
Phone: +44 (0)870 333 1600
Web: www.ricscourses.org/pages/careers.aspx

Similar Jobs

Engineer: Building Services, Health & Safety Practitioner, Property Manager, Surveyor: Building Control, Surveyor: General Practice, Surveyor: Planning & Development

Factor (Scotland)

also known as: Estate Manager (Scotland)

CRCI:Building and Construction
CLCI:UZ Job Band: 4 to 5

Job Description

Factors manage and supervise land use and property in urban and rural areas. This land and property may have forestry, residential, industrial, agricultural and commercial uses. They advise on legal and financial management, and ensure any development of the land and property is in line with current planning laws, environmental, agricultural and ecological legislation. In rural areas, factors plan crop rotation or buy and sell livestock. In industrial and commercial areas they may be responsible for lettings. Factors also take responsibility for all financial planning, the collection of estate rents from tenants, leases and tenancy agreements, and deal with investments, tax laws and farming subsidies. May be concerned with forestry, national parks, auctioneering, and also tourist attractions, including some maintenance and upkeep of drainage and estate roads.

Factors plan staffing requirements, recruit workers and supervise their training. They manage a great deal of office work, keeping records, accounts and using a computer, though usually have secretarial or clerical help.

Work Details

Hours of work vary according to the time of year and the demands of the job, and can include evening and weekends. Most factors work between 35-40 hrs a week. At some times you may be on call. Work is both in an office as well as out on the land that you manage. If you are responsible for a number of estates, farms or properties you may need to travel some distances. This may require you to spend nights away from home. You are often out in all weathers, often covering rough ground. Conditions are sometimes cold, wet, smelly and dirty. Protective clothing needs to be worn at times, including a helmet and boots.

Qualification

- **Scotland**

Band 4: For relevant SQA higher national award: usually 2-3 H grades and some S grades (1-3) often including English, maths and possibly a science subject, or similar qualifications.

Band 5: For degree courses: 3-5 H grades and some S grades (1-3), usually including English, maths and possibly a science subject, or similar qualifications. Exact requirements depend on the degree you take.

Degree Information

A Royal Institution of Chartered Surveyors (RICS) approved degree in land economy, rural enterprise and land management, agribusiness management, or rural estate management is usually preferred. Degrees in agriculture, business studies and human geography also give useful background. There are a number of relevant postgraduate qualifications, including those available for people with non-related first degrees.

Adult Qualifications

A relevant qualification, usually an SQA higher national award or a degree, is normally required. Course entry requirements may be relaxed or waived for candidates with relevant experience.

Work Experience

Entry to this job is competitive and it is important that you try to do some relevant work or voluntary experience before applying. Any experience involving management skills and administration, record and bookkeeping skills aids your application. Experience of farm work, either involving animals or crops, is also a distinct advantage in a rural environment. Seasonal work is usually available in order to gain practical experience.

Entry and Training

Most factors first qualify as members of the Royal Institution of Chartered Surveyors (RICS) in Scotland by completing an accredited degree or diploma. Other related professional qualifications are also acceptable such as those offered by the College of Estate Management (CEM), which include an entry level diploma in surveying practice that is recognised by RICS. Other courses include those at postgraduate level. You should choose your course carefully as they can vary considerably. Some factors may begin by studying part time for an accredited course whilst they are working.

All entrants continue to study by distance learning or through a day-release course for an appropriate professional qualification. The CEM offers a degree in estate management by distance learning over 4-6 years. Those already with degrees or diplomas may be exempt from some professional examinations. To be awarded a professional qualification you must usually complete a minimum of two years of practical experience. RICS members are expected to update their knowledge and skills and provide evidence of lifelong learning throughout their career. Contact RICS for further details.

Mature entrants with experience in agriculture, forestry or farming/ land management have an advantage. It is also possible for surveying technicians to undertake professional training and become a factor.

Opportunities and Pay

Employers include land-owning organisations, local government, development companies or individual farm/estate owners. There are also opportunities for employment in leisure and tourism, or you can specialise in valuation and auction work. Some factors work in private practice or are self-employed.

Pay varies depending on location, size and type of employer and whether you are self-employed. Starting salaries for graduates are around £22k, rising to over £40k with experience. Those fully experienced and qualified can earn more than £50k a year. Some employers may offer rent-free accommodation.

Health

This job requires you to be physically fit.

Skills and Qualities

able to manage a budget and keep records, aptitude for figures, business awareness, enjoy working outdoors, good communication skills, good interpersonal skills, observant, sound judgement, understanding of legal technicalities

Relevant Subjects
Biology, Business and accounting, Construction and built environment, Economics, English, Geography, Land and Environment, Law, Mathematics

Further Information
AGCAS: Environment & Agriculture (Job Sector Briefing) (AGCAS) - www.prospects.ac.uk

Scottish Farmer (weekly) (Newsquest Media) - www.thescottishfarmer.co.uk/

Addresses
College of Estate Management (CEM)
Whiteknights, Reading, Berkshire RG6 6AW
Phone: 0800 019 9697 UK only
Web: www.cem.ac.uk

Lantra in Scotland
Newlands, Scone, Perth PH2 6NL
Phone: +44(0)1738 553 311
Web: www.lantra.co.uk

Royal Institution of Chartered Surveyors (RICS) in Scotland
9 Manor Place, Edinburgh EH3 7DN
Phone: +44 (0)131 225 7078
Web: www.rics.org

Scottish Rural Property and Business Association
Stuart House, Eskmills Business Park, Musselburgh EH21 7PB
Phone: +44 (0)131 653 5400
Web: www.srpba.com

Similar Jobs
Farm Manager, Surveying Technician, Surveyor: Building Control, Surveyor: Planning & Development, Surveyor: Quantity, Surveyor: Rural Practice

Farm Manager
also known as: Agricultural Manager

CRCI:Environment, Animals and Plants
CLCI:WAB — Job Band: 3 to 5

Job Description
Farm managers are responsible for the efficient and profitable day-to-day running of a farm estate. They may be employed by a tenant farmer, commercial organisation, or single-owner farm to run the farm as a business and to maximise profit. Managers are responsible for forward planning and policy as well as making daily decisions. This may include crop rotation, stock replacement, choice and timing of fertilisers etc, depending on the type of farm. Also organise and supervises the day-to-day practical work, discussing any problems with staff.

Managers plan staffing requirements, recruit workers and supervise their training and development. They keep accurate records and accounts increasingly using computers, but may have secretarial or clerical help. Must ensure the farm complies with the regulations made by DEFRA (Department for Environment, Food & Rural Affairs). Also deal with the associated documentation and related paperwork, and apply for any relevant grants and subsidies. Usually make decisions about the buying and selling of animals or grain stock, farm produce etc.

May also manage farm activities such as the production of home products, including vegetables, butter, cheese, eggs, meat produce, such as pork, beef, chicken, wild boar, pheasants, ducks and geese, and also specialist sausages. Sometimes a farm may have an on-site shop or sell to local/national retailers, or at local farmer's markets. Other farming activities can include bed and breakfast accommodation, holiday farm cottages, caravan and camping facilities and other leisure activities.

Work Details
Farm managers work a basic 39 hr week, but are on call day and night, seven days a week and have to be prepared to work irregular and longer hours, particularly when it is the lambing season or during harvest time. They often have to work at weekends, early in the morning and late at night. Work may be indoors in an office and the rest of the time outside in all sorts of weather. The outdoor work can be strenuous with a lot of lifting and bending.

Conditions on a farm can be dirty and sometimes smelly, and the work can be highly stressful at times. On large farms, managers may spend more time working in an office, often with other staff to help them.

Qualification

- **England, Wales and Northern Ireland**

Band 4: For HND, Diploma of Higher Education or foundation degree: 1-2 A levels, including a science subject, and some GCSEs (A*-C) usually including English, maths and science, or equivalent.

Band 5: For degree: 2-3 A levels, two of which should be sciences, and some GCSEs (A*-C) including English, or equivalent qualifications. Exact requirements depend on the degree you take.

- **Scotland**

Band 4: For entry to SQA higher national and professional development awards, usually 2-3 H grades, usually including a science or maths, and some S grades (1-3), including maths, chemistry and English, or similar.

Band 5: For degree: 3-5 H grades (two of which should be sciences) and some S grades (1-3) including English and maths, or similar qualifications. Exact requirements depend on the degree you take.

Degree Information
Employers probably expect you to have a degree in one of the following subjects: agriculture, agricultural science or land and property/estate management. A professional business qualification is also very relevant. Related postgraduate qualifications are also available such as an MSc in rural land and business management or in rural estate management.

Adult Qualifications
Course entry requirements are usually relaxed for suitable mature applicants. Those without the required qualifications may complete a foundation or Access course leading to relevant HNDs or accredited degrees. Contact individual colleges or universities for details. The Studley College Trust offers funding for land-based courses. See their website for details.

Work Experience
Entry to this job is competitive and it is important that you try to do some relevant work or voluntary experience before applying. Any experience involving management skills and administration, record and bookkeeping skills will aid your application. Experience of farm work, either involving animals or crops, is usually required before securing a place on a course or a post as a trainee manager. You can gain practical farming experience during vacation time, as part of a sandwich course, or during a gap year. There may be some opportunities for experience abroad.

Entry and Training
Most farm managers have a degree, an HNC/HND, and some hold a farming-related postgraduate qualification, such as advanced farm management. There are a number of foundation degrees in agriculture and related subjects that enable progression to the third year of a degree course. Many entrants spend several years gaining experience in junior positions such as an assistant farm manager or unit manager, prior to being appointed as a farm manager. Some of the larger farm management companies such as Velcourt, Sentry Farms and Co-operative Farms offer one to two year management training schemes for graduates.

Managers are expected to continue their studies to keep up to date with agricultural and related developments. Professional development courses are available from the Open University, colleges of agriculture and other institutions, such as the Open Business School and from Lantra, the sector skills council for the environmental and land-based sector. Courses vary, but include specific areas of farming such as organic farming and the application of IT in the farming industry. Funding for some courses may be available through the Nuffield Farming Scholarships Trusts.

Training programmes, including apprenticeship schemes, may be available in your area. Advanced apprenticeships leading to qualification at level 3 can also be a route into higher education.

Mature applicants with suitable farming experience and relevant qualifications are welcomed by employers. Some may start as an assistant manager or manager of a unit, before becoming a farm manager. There are opportunities to study either full or part time for agricultural qualifications.

Opportunities and Pay

There are few vacancies for farm managers and competition for jobs is intense. Managerial posts are available throughout the UK with commercial organisations that own farms, tenant farmers and owner-occupiers. You should be prepared to move to a different part of the UK to get a job or to increase your prospects. Unless you work on a very large farm, promotion is unlikely. With experience you may be able to move into advisory work, consultancy, technical sales, teaching or work with an agricultural service industry.

Opportunities may be available abroad in central and eastern Europe and also in countries such as the USA, New Zealand and Australia for those with wide experience. Further opportunities overseas are with voluntary services overseas (VSO) or with an NGO (non-government organisation). Self-employment is possible but it is very expensive to buy land.

Earnings vary depending on the size of farm and level of responsibility. Salaries are likely to be around £20k-£26k a year, rising to £50k a year with experience.

Health

You have to be fit and healthy to do this job and you may find the work difficult if you are allergic to animals or pollen.

Skills and Qualities

able to cope under pressure, able to manage people, business awareness, efficient, good communication skills, good organisational skills, good written English, IT skills, scientific approach

Relevant Subjects

Biology, Business and accounting, Chemistry, Economics, English, ICT/Computer studies, Land and Environment, Mathematics, Science

Further Information

AGCAS: Environment & Agriculture (Job Sector Briefing) (AGCAS) - www.prospects.ac.uk

Apprenticeship Schemes (National Apprenticeship Service) - www.apprenticeships.org.uk

Co-operative Farms - www.co-operative.coop/farms

Farmer's Weekly Interactive (Reed International) - www.fwi.co.uk

Lantra - The Sector Skills Council for environmental & land-based sector (Lantra) http:/www.lantra.co.uk

Lantra Careers (A Future In...) (Lantra) - www.afuturein.com

Nuffield Farming Scholarships Trust (Nuffield Farming Scholarships Trust) - www.nuffieldscholar.org

Scottish Farmer (weekly) (Newsquest Media) - www.thescottishfarmer.co.uk/

Sentry Farms - www.sentry.co.uk

Studley College Trust - www.studleytrust.co.uk

Velcourt - www.velcourt.co.uk

▶Working with animals (2009) (Babcock Lifeskills) - www.babcock-lifeskills.com/

Addresses

Department for Environment, Food & Rural Affairs (DEFRA)
Customer Contact Unit , Eastbury House, 30 - 34 Albert Embankment, London SE1 7TL
Phone: 0845 933 5577 (UK only)
Web: www.defra.gov.uk

Department of Agriculture and Rural Development
Training & Development Dundonald House,
Upper Newtownards Road, Belfast BT4 3SB
Phone: +44 (0)28 9052 4999
Web: www.dardni.gov.uk

Institute of Agricultural Management (IAgrM)
Portway House, Sheepway, Portbury, Bristol BS20 7TE
Phone: +44 (0)1275 843 825
Web: www.iagrm.org.uk

Similar Jobs

Agricultural Consultant/Adviser, Agricultural Research Scientist, Fish Farm Manager, Forest District Manager, Forest Officer, Horticultural Manager

Farm Worker: Crops

also known as: Agricultural Worker: Crops

CRCI:Environment, Animals and Plants
CLCI:WAB Job Band: 1 to 3

Job Description

Crop workers work on an arable or mixed farm carrying out the practical tasks for the owner or farm manager. They may work on a farm that grows mostly vegetables, crops such as wheat and barley, non-food crops such as oilseed rape or energy crops that are grown as fuel. They get the soil ready for sowing seeds, plough the fields into rows and put fertiliser on the land. Then help to look after the crops through all stages of growth and check for any diseases. Finally harvest the crops when they are ready using special machinery.

Workers operate and maintain fixed plant machinery such as grain machinery. Some may drive and maintain tractors, ploughs, combine harvesters, slurry and fertiliser spreaders and other farm vehicles. Others may also help on a mixed farm with livestock such as sheep, cows, pigs or chickens. May lay, cut and trim hedges, dig ditches, put up fences and mend them. Also help repair and maintain farm buildings and machinery.

Work Details

A basic working week is usually 39 hrs, but you may have to work long and irregular hours including early mornings, evenings and weekends. Work is outdoors most of the time and in all sorts of weather. Farms can be dirty, muddy and smelly places. Physical fitness is important and you need to be able to cope with rough ground, bending down and lifting things. You may need to live on, or near, the farm and have to be very careful, especially around farm machines or near chemicals used in spraying. Sometimes, if dealing with animals on a mixed farm, you have to cope with the sight of blood. Farm workers wear boots, gloves and protective clothing for most jobs.

Qualification

• England, Wales and Northern Ireland

Band 1: No minimum qualifications are required, but you are expected to have had a good level of general education. However, some formal/vocational qualifications at any level are useful.

Band 2: Although academic qualifications are not specified for this job, it is an advantage to have some GCSEs (A*-C) in subjects that include English and maths, or equivalent.

Band 3: For course entry: usually at least 4 GCSEs (A*-C) including English and maths, or equivalent.

- **Scotland**

Band 1: No minimum qualifications are required, but you are expected to have had a good level of general education. However, some formal/vocational qualifications at any level are useful.

Band 2: Although academic qualifications are not specified for this job, it is an advantage to have some S grades (1-3) in subjects that include English and maths, or similar.

Band 3: For course entry: it is useful to have some S grades (1-3) preferably including English and maths, or similar.

Adult Qualifications

For entry to many jobs you need no qualifications, but experience of agricultural or horticultural work is useful for entry to courses.

Work Experience

Relevant work or voluntary experience is always useful and can improve your chances when applying for a job. Work experience in any aspects of farming can considerably increase your employment prospects. There are often opportunities for seasonal and holiday work in farming. Work in a garden centre, horticultural nursery, or in grounds maintenance is also useful. It is also useful to gain some carpentry/labouring skills.

Entry and Training

Most employers look for a combination of technical knowledge and practical skills. You can gain this knowledge either by taking a full time college course, by taking an apprenticeship and studying for S/NVQs or by training on the job with an experienced worker. For some full-time courses, you are expected to work on a farm for a year before you can start them. Apprenticeships enable you to earn a wage while you are learning. Most crop workers are expected to have a driving licence to enable them to drive from site to site and to drive agricultural machinery.

There are many relevant full and part-time courses offered at local colleges by BTEC and City & Guilds. Short courses are also available on specialist topics. The Lantra website has a course finder section on its website. You may need to attend specialist courses about the different machinery and vehicles used.

A Diploma/Welsh Baccalaureate may be available in your area in environment and land-based studies. S/NVQs are available in agriculture at level 1, agricultural crop production at levels 2-3, and in mixed farming at levels 2-3.

Adults may apply for government training schemes that are available in many areas of the country. You can also gain recognition of previous experience through Accreditation of Prior Learning (APL) or by working towards relevant S/NVQs. Contact your local Connexions or careers office, Jobcentre Plus, Next Step service or Learning and Skills Council (LSC)/Local Enterprise Company (LEC) for details of training schemes.

There are also distance learning courses that are offered through the Horticultural Correspondence College, including courses at various levels in mixed farming, crop technology and organic arable farming. Contact the Nuffield Farming Scholarships Trust for details on any funding and awards.

Opportunities and Pay

There are over 60,000 crop businesses in the UK, employing over 120,000 people. Increased mechanisation has steadily decreased the number of employment opportunities for crop workers. Consequently, there are more jobs for those with specialised or multi-skills and who have some relevant qualifications. There may also be more opportunities at certain times of the year, such as harvest time. On larger farms it is possible to be promoted to supervisor or unit manager. For this you need to have a lot of experience and often qualifications in agriculture.

Salaries usually range from around £12k-£14.5k a year; overtime pay can make up a significant proportion of your earnings. Salaries can rise to around £16k-£21k a year depending upon experience and responsibility. There are minimum rates of pay set out by the Agricultural Wages Board - see their website for full details. Sometimes an employer may provide an on-site farmhouse or a room for you. Usually a low rent is charged.

Health

You are likely to find this job difficult if you are allergic to animals or if you have hay fever. You have to be physically fit to do this job and have plenty of stamina.

Skills and Qualities

able to follow instructions, able to work both on your own and in a team, common sense, enjoy working outdoors, interest in growing plants, interest in new technology, manual dexterity, practical skills, reliable, strong

Relevant Subjects

Biology, Land and Environment, Science

Further Information

Agricultural Wages Board (DEFRA) (DEFRA) - www.defra.gov.uk/foodfarm/farmmanage/working/agwages/awb/index.htm

Apprenticeship Schemes (National Apprenticeship Service) - www.apprenticeships.org.uk

Diplomas (Foundation, Higher and Advanced) - http://yp.direct.gov.uk/diplomas

Lantra - The Sector Skills Council for environmental & land-based sector (Lantra) http:/www.lantra.co.uk

Lantra Careers (A Future In...) (Lantra) - www.afuturein.com

Nuffield Farming Scholarships Trust (Nuffield Farming Scholarships Trust) - www.nuffieldscholar.org

Real Life Guide to Working Outdoors (Trotman) - www.trotman.co.uk

Training Schemes - www.direct.gov.uk/en/educationandlearning

Welsh Baccalaureate - www.wbq.org.uk

►Working with animals (2009) (Babcock Lifeskills) - www.babcock-lifeskills.com/

Addresses

Department of Agriculture and Rural Development
Training & Development Dundonald House,
Upper Newtownards Road, Belfast BT4 3SB
Phone: +44 (0)28 9052 4999
Web: www.dardni.gov.uk

Horticultural Correspondence College
Fiveways House, Westwells Road, Hawthorn, Corsham SN13 9RG
Phone: +44 (0)1225 816700
Web: www.hccollege.co.uk

National Farmers Union (NFU)
Agriculture House, Stoneleigh Park, Warwickshire CV8 2TZ
Phone: +44 (0)24 7685 8500
Web: www.nfu.org.uk

NFU Scotland
Head Office, Rural Centre - West Mains, Ingliston,
Edinburgh EH28 8LT
Phone: +44 (0)131 472 4000
Web: www.nfus.org.uk

Similar Jobs

Farm Worker: Livestock, Forest Worker, Gamekeeper, Gardener, Horticultural Worker: Commercial, Shepherd

Farm Worker: Livestock

also known as: Cattle Hand, Farm Stockman/Stockwoman, Stockman/Stockwoman

CRCI:Environment, Animals and Plants
CLCI:WAB Job Band: 1 to 3

Job Description

Livestock workers are responsible for the health and welfare of livestock, such as dairy herds, beef cattle and pigs. They make up feed for the animals and give them water, clean the sheds and spread out fresh bedding. Also check the animals for diseases and look after their general wellbeing. They may need to give the animals injections, perform any minor operations, and assist the vet when required. Some work with animals that are reared for their meat, or on a dairy farm, keeping cows for milk. This involves preparing the cows for milking two or three times each day, looking after the milking machinery and ensuring hygiene standards are maintained.

Livestock workers keep accurate records or reports, often using a computer and may be required to do general farm work, such as helping with the harvest, driving tractors and slurry spreaders. They often perform general maintenance work, such as repairing fences and maintaining agricultural buildings. Some farms combine livestock with growing crops. For more information about working with sheep or poultry see the job articles for Shepherd and Farm Worker: Poultry

Work Details

A basic working week is usually 39 hrs, but you may have to work long and irregular hours, including early mornings, evenings and weekends. May often work alone with the animals. Farms can be cold, wet, dirty and smelly and you may be out in all sorts of weather. You have to cope with rough ground and the work involves strenuous effort. Farm animals and equipment can sometimes be dangerous, and you may have to cope with blood. You need to wear boots, gloves and protective clothing for most jobs.

Qualification

• England, Wales and Northern Ireland

Band 1: For entry to jobs, no minimum qualifications are needed, but you are expected to have a good level of general education and relevant experience. Some formal/vocational qualifications at any level are useful.

Band 2: For entry to jobs, no minimum qualifications are needed, but it is an advantage to have some GCSEs (A*-C) or equivalent in subjects that include English and maths.

Band 3: For entry to jobs, HNC or a relevant Diploma, usually at least 4 GCSEs (A*-C) including English and maths, or equivalent.

• Scotland

Band 1: For entry to jobs, no minimum qualifications are needed, but you are expected to have a good level of general education and relevant experience. Some formal/vocational qualifications at any level are useful.

Band 2: Although academic qualifications are not specified for this job, it is an advantage to have some S grades (1-3) in subjects that include English and maths, or similar.

Band 3: For entry to jobs, usually at least four S grades (1-3) including English and maths, or similar.

Adult Qualifications

You do not need any formal qualifications to do this job, but experience in farm work or work with animals is helpful for entry to courses.

Work Experience

Relevant work or voluntary experience is always useful and can improve your chances when applying for a job or a course. Work experience in any aspects of farming can often considerably increase your employment/course prospects. There are usually opportunities for seasonal and holiday work in farming or any area of work that includes working with, and caring for animals. It is also useful to gain some carpentry/labouring skills.

Entry and Training

Most employers look for a combination of technical knowledge and practical skills. You can gain this knowledge either by taking a full time college course, by taking an apprenticeship and studying for S/NVQs or by training on the job with an experienced worker. For some full-time courses, you are expected to work on a farm for a year before you can start them. Apprenticeships enable you to earn a wage while you are learning. Most livestock workers are expected to have a driving licence to enable them to drive from site to site.

There are many relevant full and part-time courses offered at local colleges by BTEC and City & Guilds. Short courses are also available on specialist topics. The Lantra website has a course finder section on its website.

A Diploma/Welsh Baccalaureate may be available in your area in environment and land-based studies. S/NVQs are available in agriculture at level 1, livestock production at levels 2-3, and in mixed farming at levels 2-3.

Adults may apply for government training schemes that are available in many areas of the country. You can also gain recognition of previous experience through Accreditation of Prior Learning (APL) or by working towards relevant S/NVQs. There are also various distance learning courses that are offered through the Horticultural Correspondence College, including courses at various levels in mixed farming and organic livestock farming. Contact the Nuffield Farming Scholarships Trust for details on any funding and awards.

Opportunities and Pay

Work is available on farms throughout the UK, especially in the Northern Ireland, Wales and the South West, though increased mechanisation has steadily decreased the number of workers. There are over 175,000 livestock businesses in the UK. There has been a recent increase in larger business, especially those producing pigs. There are more opportunities for seasonal and casual work, particularly for those with specialised or multi-skills.

It is possible to be promoted to supervisor on larger farms or specialised units. For this you have to have a lot of experience and often some qualifications in agriculture. The growth of farmers' markets has increased outlets for products from smaller farms.

Salaries usually range from around £12k-£14.5k a year; overtime pay can make up a significant proportion of your earnings. Salaries can rise to around £16k-£21k a year depending upon experience and responsibility. There are minimum rates of pay set out by the Agricultural Wages Board - see their website for full details. Sometimes an employer may provide an on-site farmhouse or a room for you. Usually a low rent is charged.

Health

You are likely to find it difficult to do this job if you are allergic to animals or if you have hay fever. To do this job you need to have stamina and be fit.

Skills and Qualities

able to cope with emergencies, able to keep basic records, able to work both on your own and in a team, common sense, enjoy seeing a project through to the end, good at handling animals, not squeamish, practical skills, reliable

Relevant Subjects

Biology, Land and Environment, Science

Further Information

Agricultural Wages Board (DEFRA) (DEFRA) - www.defra.gov.uk/foodfarm/farmmanage/working/agwages/awb/index.htm

Apprenticeship Schemes (National Apprenticeship Service) - www.apprenticeships.org.uk

Diplomas (Foundation, Higher and Advanced) - http://yp.direct.gov.uk/diplomas

Farmer's Weekly Interactive (Reed International) - www.fwi.co.uk

Lantra - The Sector Skills Council for environmental & land-based sector (Lantra) http:/www.lantra.co.uk

Lantra Careers (A Future In...) (Lantra) - www.afuturein.com

Nuffield Farming Scholarships Trust (Nuffield Farming Scholarships Trust) - www.nuffieldscholar.org

Real Life Guide to Working Outdoors (Trotman) - www.trotman.co.uk

Scottish Farmer (weekly) (Newsquest Media) - www.thescottishfarmer.co.uk/

Training Schemes - www.direct.gov.uk/en/educationandlearning

Welsh Baccalaureate - www.wbq.org.uk

Working with animals (2009) (Babcock Lifeskills) - www.babcock-lifeskills.com/

Addresses

Department of Agriculture and Rural Development
Training & Development Dundonald House Upper Newtownards Road, Belfast BT4 3SB
Phone: +44 (0)28 9052 4999
Web: www.dardni.gov.uk

National Farmers Union (NFU)
Agriculture House, Stoneleigh Park, Warwickshire CV8 2TZ
Phone: +44 (0)24 7685 8500
Web: www.nfu.org.uk

NFU Scotland
Head Office, Rural Centre - West Mains, Ingliston, Edinburgh EH28 8LT
Phone: +44 (0)131 472 4000
Web: www.nfus.org.uk

Similar Jobs

Farm Worker: Crops, Farm Worker: Poultry, Gamekeeper, Horse Groom, Shepherd, Stable Hand

Farm Worker: Poultry

also known as: Poultry Officer, Stockman/Stockwoman: Poultry

CRCI:Environment, Animals and Plants

CLCI:WAB — Job Band: 1 to 3

Job Description

Poultry workers look after domestic birds, such as chickens, ducks or turkeys, on a poultry farm, which may be kept for egg or meat production. Birds may be reared in free range, organic or intensive conditions. They check that the birds are being hygienically and safely reared in conditions that improve their egg production or to achieve their market weight. Workers have a knowledge of the nutritional needs of the birds and feed and give them water, usually through a carefully designed and automatic system. They also look for signs of disease or bacterial infection, nurse sick birds, and may give vitamins and medication.

Must ensure that the poultry house is well ventilated and has fresh litter, usually of chopped straw or wood shavings. Also clean out the houses and cages, sometimes by hand with a water hose or perhaps an industrial vacuum system.

Work Details

You work a basic week of 35-39 hrs, though you may be required to work shifts, and also overtime at busy periods. This means sometimes working at weekends. You work mainly indoors in large airy houses, though working with poultry can be dirty, smelly and noisy. If working with free range or organically reared birds, you may work in the open air for part of the day. You have to do some kneeling and bending down, and need to wear protective clothing usually including special shoes or boots.

Qualification

- **England, Wales and Northern Ireland**

Band 1: For entry to jobs, no minimum qualifications are needed, but you are expected to have a good level of general education and relevant experience. Some formal/vocational qualifications at any level are useful.

Band 2: For entry to jobs, no minimum qualifications are needed, but it is an advantage to have some GCSEs (A*-C) or equivalent in subjects that include English and maths.

Band 3: For entry to jobs, HNC or a relevant Diploma, usually at least 4 GCSEs (A*-C) including English, maths and science subjects.

- **Scotland**

Band 1: For entry to jobs, no minimum qualifications are needed, but you are expected to have a good level of general education and relevant experience. Some formal/vocational qualifications at any level are useful.

Band 2: Although academic qualifications are not specified for this job, it is an advantage to have some S grades (1-3) in subjects that include English, science and maths, or similar

Band 3: For entry to jobs, usually at least four S grades (1-3) including English, maths and a science subject or similar qualifications.

Adult Qualifications

For this job mature entrants do not need any qualifications, but often have to have experience of work in agriculture. Entry requirements for courses are usually relaxed for mature entrants.

Work Experience

Relevant work or voluntary experience is always useful and can improve your chances when applying for a job or a course. Work experience in any aspects of farming can often considerably increase your employment/course prospects. There are often opportunities for seasonal and holiday work in farming or any area of work that includes working with and caring for animals. It is also useful to gain some carpentry/labouring skills.

Entry and Training

To enter this job some experience of working on a farm helps, such as holiday or voluntary work, but you are provided with on-the-job training, usually with an experienced worker or supervisor. Agricultural colleges offer a wide range of short, full and part-time courses in poultry husbandry, though you often need to have some work experience before attending college. There are many options for training and certification in the poultry industry, these range from short specialist courses, to full-time courses that include an HND in poultry production.

For HND courses you usually require a higher level of qualifications. Organisations such as the British Poultry Council and Poultec Training Ltd can provide information on all aspects of the poultry industry and training.

In 2008, the British Poultry Council and the National Farmers Union (NFU) launched a new training passport scheme for employees in the poultry meat industry, which for the first time established minimum training standards. Administered by Poultec Training and Lantra, the Poultry Meat Training Initiative aims to give all workers a validated on-line training record showing all the vocational courses they have completed and when they took them.

A Diploma/Welsh Baccalaureate may be available in your area in environment and land-based studies. S/NVQs at levels 2-3 in livestock production (poultry) are available. Training programmes, including apprenticeships leading to level 2 and advanced apprenticeships leading to level 3, may be available in your area.

Adults can enter this work with a good level of relevant work experience and those who have further practical skills may have an advantage. Government training opportunities may be available in your area. Contact your local Connexions or careers office, Jobcentre Plus, Next Step service or Learning and Skills Council (LSC)/Local Enterprise Company (LEC) for details of training schemes. Also contact the British Egg Marketing Board Trust or the Nuffield Farming Scholarships Trust for details on any funding and awards.

Opportunities and Pay

Egg and poultry meat production can often be a large-scale operation, though many jobs can also be on smaller farms. Usually, all jobs are located in a rural area. You can also work for a large company that breeds the birds and then processes their meat to make different types of food. Some jobs on smaller farms may require you to collect, grade and pack the eggs ready for distribution, but in larger organisations, this job is done by an egg packer/grader. In large organisations, with experience and/or qualifications, it is possible to progress to supervisory or management posts.

Pay varies depending on area and employer, but salaries are likely to be around £7.5k-£13k a year rising to £19k a year with supervisory responsibilities. There are minimum rates of pay set out by the Agricultural Wages Board - see their website for full details. Overtime may be available, particularly at busy times.

Health

No special health requirements necessary but overall physical fitness an advantage.

Skills and Qualities

able to work both on your own and in a team, careful, hard working, methodical, not squeamish, numeracy skills, observant, practical skills

Relevant Subjects

Biology, Land and Environment

Further Information

Agricultural Wages Board (DEFRA) (DEFRA) - www.defra.gov.uk/foodfarm/farmmanage/working/agwages/awb/index.htm

Apprenticeship Schemes (National Apprenticeship Service) - www.apprenticeships.org.uk

Diplomas (Foundation, Higher and Advanced) - http://yp.direct.gov.uk/diplomas

Lantra - The Sector Skills Council for environmental & land-based sector (Lantra) http:/www.lantra.co.uk

Lantra Careers (A Future In...) (Lantra) - www.afuturein.com

Nuffield Farming Scholarships Trust (Nuffield Farming Scholarships Trust) - www.nuffieldscholar.org

Training Schemes - www.direct.gov.uk/en/educationandlearning

Welsh Baccalaureate - www.wbq.org.uk

World's Poultry Science Journal (Cambridge Journals) http:www.wpsa.com

Addresses

British Egg Marketing Board Trust
c/o 121 Station Road, Wythall, Birmingham B47 6AG
Phone: +44 (0)1564 200857
Web: www.bembtrust.org.uk

British Poultry Council (bpc)
5 -11 Lavington Street, London SE1 0NZ
Phone: 0845 302 2833 (UK only)
Web: www.poultry.uk.com

Department of Agriculture and Rural Development
Training & Development Dundonald House Upper Newtownards Road, Belfast BT4 3SB
Phone: +44 (0)28 9052 4999
Web: www.dardni.gov.uk

Poultec Training Ltd
South Green Park, Enterprise Centre , Mattishall, Dereham, Norfolk NR20 3JY
Phone: +44 (0)1362 850 983
Web: www.poultec.co.uk

Similar Jobs

Farm Worker: Crops, Farm Worker: Livestock, Gamekeeper, Shepherd, Zoo Keeper

Farrier

CRCI:Environment, Animals and Plants
CLCI:WAM — Job Band: 2 to 3

Job Description

Farriers are involved in the shoeing and related care of horses, donkeys and mules etc. They use blacksmithing skills to make and fit shoes appropriate for the individual size and type of horse, eg hunter or racehorse. Farriers work at a forge using hand tools or machines to shape metal to produce an exact and safe fit. They examine horses' hooves and remove worn or damaged shoes, then clean and trim the hoof before fitting a new shoe. The shoe may be heated before being placed on the hoof and hammered into place using special nails. The shoe is finished by filing it into the exact shape.

Farriers may fit special shoes to prevent damage to feet or legs or to correct a problem after injury. They also need to do their own administration and clerical work, such as making appointments and dealing with accounts. May also liaise with veterinary surgeons on some aspects of work.

Work Details

Farriers usually work daylight hours that vary but may include some evenings and weekends. Work is either in a forge or with travel to different sites, such as riding schools, livery stables etc. The job is physically demanding and you have to cope with hot, noisy and possibly cramped or uncomfortable conditions. You spend a lot of time bending and lifting. There may be a risk of an animal attack or injury.

Qualification

- **England, Wales and Northern Ireland**

Band 3: For entry: usually at least 4 GCSEs (A*-C) including English and maths, or equivalent. Candidates without formal educational qualifications may take a Farriery Access course. You also need a Forge Certificate that has been taken no more than three years ago.

- **Scotland**

Band 3: For entry: usually at least four S grades (1-3) including English and maths, or similar. Candidates without formal educational qualifications may take a Farriery Access course. You also need a Forge Certificate that has been taken no more than three years ago.

Adult Qualifications

Applicants over 21 years of age who do not have the required formal academic qualifications or equivalent usually take a Farriery Access course.

Work Experience

Employers or colleges may prefer candidates who have relevant work or voluntary experience. The training is long and is expensive so you should be certain of your commitment to this career. Work experience should be in some form of working with horses plus observing the work of a farrier where possible, although it is not legal to undertake any tasks of farriery. General stable work is a good substitute, as entry onto the apprenticeships asks for a background of working with horses. Working with a blacksmith is also valuable experience.

Entry and Training

By law, only farriers (not blacksmiths) are permitted to shoe horses and other equines. Candidates can enter an advanced apprenticeship at 16 and there is no upper age limit. On-the-job training and experience is given, and there are periods of off-the-job training at college. The apprenticeship lasts for four years and two months, during which time the apprentice must be employed by an Approved Training Farrier (ATF). A list of ATFs is available on the website of the Farriery Training Agency.

Block-release training currently takes place at colleges in Warwickshire, Hereford, Oatridge (in Scotland), and Myerscough College in Lancashire. Accommodation costs while attending college courses must be paid for by the apprentice who also needs to supply their own good quality tools. Those who are under 25 years on completion of the apprenticeship may be eligible for grant aid, those over 25 must finance themselves.

Farriers in the UK by law must be registered with the Farriers' Registration Council (FRC) and have passed the diploma of the Worshipful Company of Farriers (DipWCF). The WCF also offers two higher levels of qualification, associateship (AWCF) and fellowship (FWCF). Contact the FRC and WCF for details of all qualifications. It is expected that every practising farrier should consider continuing professional development (CPD) in order to keep in touch with advances in their profession.

There are various pre-farriery courses such as blacksmithing and equine studies that are useful, but do not act as entry qualifications. An S/NVQ is available at level 3 only. A Foundation degree and honours degree course in farriery is also available at Myerscough College.

Mature applicants may contact the Farriery Training Agency for details of training schemes. Experience of working with horses or working as a blacksmith, is valuable.

Opportunities and Pay

Jobs are available throughout the UK though not necessarily always in rural areas. This is a relatively small profession of around 2,500 qualified farriers in the UK and there are few vacancies, but this job can be combined with other types of business, eg blacksmithing. Currently, there is a continuing demand for farriers and farriery apprentices, and numbers are gradually increasing. However, entry is still very competitive and you may have to be prepared to live away from home to find a training place. Self-employed farriers often travel to their customers, taking their equipment with them.

Starting salaries are based on the National Minimum Wage, depending on age and year of training. Qualified farriers earn around £16k and when very experienced can earn up to £30k and more. Earnings can also be supplemented by using your blacksmithing skills in other areas of work.

Health

The work involves a possible risk of developing back problems and there is also an allergy risk from animals. This job requires good eyesight. There is usually a medical before you start work, including a test for colour blindness, although this may not necessarily exclude you.

Skills and Qualities

able to communicate effectively, able to work well on your own, accurate, business awareness, patient, strong hands, strong interest in horses, technical aptitude, willing to learn

Relevant Subjects

Biology, Design and technology, Engineering, Land and Environment

Further Information

Apprenticeship Schemes (National Apprenticeship Service) - www.apprenticeships.org.uk

Becoming an Apprentice (FRC) (Farriers Registration Council) - www.farrier-reg.gov.uk

Farriery Training Agency (FTA) - www.farrierytraining.co.uk

Forge Magazine (British Farriers and Blacksmiths Association) - www.forgemagazine.co.uk/

Lantra - The Sector Skills Council for environmental & land-based sector (Lantra) http:/www.lantra.co.uk

Lantra Careers (A Future In...) (Lantra) - www.afuturein.com

Addresses

Farriers Registration Council (FRC)
Sefton House, Adam Court, Newark Road, Peterborough PE1 5PP
Phone: +44 (0)1733 319 911
Web: www.farrier-reg.gov.uk

National Association of Farriers, Blacksmiths and Agricultural Engineers (NAFBAE)
The Bullock Building University Way, Cranfield,
Bedford MK43 0GH
Phone: +44 (0)1234 750876
Web: www.nafbae.org

Worshipful Company of Farriers
19 Queen Street, Chipperfield, Kings Langley WD4 9BT
Phone: +44 (0)1923 260 747
Web: www.wcf.org.uk

Similar Jobs

Blacksmith, Horse Groom, Riding Instructor, Stable Hand, Veterinary Nurse

Fashion Designer

also known as: Clothing Designer

CRCI:Design, Arts and Crafts

CLCI:EJ — Job Band: 3 to 5

Job Description

Fashion designers combine artistic talent with technical knowledge to create designs for clothes and accessories, usually working from a design brief. They often work as part of a team, including fashion buyers and forecasters. Must follow fashion trends closely and work out ideas by sketching by hand or using a computer-aided design (CAD) package.

Designers try out designs by draping and pinning material on a live model or dummy. They may copy and adapt other people's ideas and choose materials and colours, consider costs and adapt the design to suit pattern making and manufacturing processes. Computers are likely to be used even more in the future to make the design and production of clothing more efficient.

The three main areas of fashion are designer ready-to-wear, high street fashion, and haute couture. Designers may specialise in designs such as wedding dresses, menswear, lingerie, children's clothing or sportswear. Niche markets such as eco-fashion from sustainably sourced materials are growing. Designers visit fashion shows and trade fairs to keep up to date with new designs and fabrics. They also network with other designers and trade companies.

Work Details

Work a basic 39 hr week, Monday to Friday, though there are often longer working hours, particularly preparing for shows or releases of new collections, when you may be under pressure. You spend a lot of time working in a studio, but may also have to travel around the UK and abroad to meet clients and attend fashion shows, exhibitions and fabric houses. Sometimes your work may be criticised or rejected. You usually have to work within an agreed budget.

Fashion Designer

Qualification

• England, Wales and Northern Ireland

Band 3: For entry to jobs, HNC or a relevant Diploma, usually at least 4 GCSEs (A*-C) including English and maths, or equivalent. For foundation courses: usually at least 5 GCSEs (A*-C).

Band 4: For diploma in foundation studies in art and design: usually at least one A level and 4 GCSEs (A*-C). For BTEC higher national award: a BTEC national award, successful completion of a foundation studies course, or equivalent qualification.

Band 5: For degree courses: 2-3 A levels and some GCSEs (A*-C) usually including English and maths, or equivalent. Most students take a foundation course first. Exact requirements depend on the degree you take. A diploma in creative and media may be considered as an alternative to A levels.

• Scotland

Band 3: For entry: usually at least four S grades (1-3), including English and maths, or similar.

Band 4: For entry to SQA higher national and professional development awards, usually 2-3 H grades and some S grades (1-3), including English and maths, or similar qualifications.

Band 5: For degree courses: 3-5 H grades and some S grades (1-3), usually including English and maths, or similar. Entry requirements depend on the degree you take.

Degree Information

A degree in fashion and textile design is preferred, and there are a wide range of degrees available. It is possible to specialise during the first degree or by postgraduate study. Some courses include marketing and European languages. Graduates in any art and design subject may be acceptable, but need to gain experience and build up a portfolio of fashion work.

Adult Qualifications

Mature applicants with outstanding portfolios of work may be accepted for courses without the standard entry requirements. There are Access and foundation courses in some areas, which give adults without qualifications a route into degree courses. Check with individual colleges.

Work Experience

Entry to this job/career is highly competitive and it is essential you have some relevant work or voluntary experience before applying. Experience with an established designer or design company is ideal, but any knowledge of the manufacturing or textile side is relevant. Retail experience can also be useful. Attending relevant events such as British Graduate Fashion Week also demonstrates commitment. Some higher education courses include a work placement.

Entry and Training

Most fashion designers take full-time courses, usually to HND/degree level. These are available at a range of higher education institutions across the UK but entry to courses is highly competitive. Employers often prefer courses that combine design and technical skills. A wide-ranging portfolio of your designs is always needed, both for college and for employment to demonstrate your ability. It is also useful to take along to interview any garments that you have produced.

In England and Wales, students often take a foundation course in art and design before taking a degree course in fashion or a related subject. In Scotland, degree courses last for four years, the first year being a broad-based course before specialising in an area of fashion design in the second year. Always check course entry details with colleges. The London College of Fashion is a specialist institution which offers a range of relevant courses. Distance-learning courses are available as well as a foundation degree in fashion design. Increasingly, design is computer-based so it is important to choose a course that includes this. Foreign language skills are increasingly useful too.

A Diploma/Welsh Baccalaureate may be available in your area in creative and media and may provide a route onto higher education courses. There is also an apprenticeship in sewn products or textiles at level 2 and an advanced apprenticeship in apparel or textiles at level 3 which may be available in your area.

Once qualified, most entrants start as design assistants and work their way up to designer. Training is usually on the job, sometimes combined with attendance on short specialist courses. Skillfast is the sector skills council for fashion and textiles and a useful source of information. You can gain professional recognition and support your continuing professional development (CPD) by joining the Textile Institute.

Mature applicants with experience in art and design, fashion or sales and marketing may have an advantage, though employers also expect a portfolio of recent and wide-ranging designs that demonstrate an ability to design for the employer's target market.

Opportunities and Pay

This is a very competitive field and more than 3,000 students qualify each year. Most jobs in the UK are in London and the South East, or in larger towns in the Midlands, the North West and Scotland. Most entry level jobs as junior design assistants are in the London area, but the number of vacancies has fallen sharply inthe current economic climate. It is usually necessary to change jobs to gain experience and progress further in the fashion industry.

Mass-market designers mainly work for clothing manufacturers and mid-market designers work for consultancies or manufacturers, producing collections for particular fashion companies. Directional designers produce their own collections and are usually self-employed. Freelance designers can work from home, but have to build up contacts and a reputation. Opportunities also exist in the theatre, TV and film industry, usually on a contract basis. UK fashion design has a good reputation overseas and many new graduate designers work abroad in countries such as Italy, Germany, Spain or France to gain international experience before returning to work in the UK. There may be opportunities to move into journalism, teaching and retail buying and management.

Pay varies considerably depending on type of employer and whether you are self-employed. Newly qualified designers are likely to earn around £17k-£21k a year, rising to around £30k-£40k or more for experienced designers. Very successful designers can earn up to £60k a year, although some may earn considerably more. Freelance designer rates vary as they may charge per design or collection. Top designers are often paid for a commissioned item or a collection.

Health

Colour co-ordination may be difficult for those who do not have normal colour vision.

Skills and Qualities

artistic ability, attention to detail, business awareness, creative flair, eye for shape/colour, eye for visual effect, fashion conscious, imaginative, IT skills, technical aptitude

Relevant Subjects

Art and Design, Design and technology, ICT/Computer studies

Further Information

AGCAS: Fashion & Design (Job Sector Briefing) (AGCAS) - www.prospects.ac.uk

Behind the Scenes: Fashion (Trotman 2009) - www.trotman.co.uk

Can you Cut it? - www.canucutit.co.uk

Chartered Society of Designers (Chartered Society of Designers) - www.csd.org.uk

Design Uncovered (Trotman 2009) - www.trotman.co.uk

Diplomas (Foundation, Higher and Advanced) - http://yp.direct.gov.uk/diplomas

Drapers: Fashionnews, jobs and trends - www.drapersonline.com
Fashion & Textiles: The Essential Careers Guide (Laurence King 2010)
Future Textiles - www.futuretextiles.co.uk
Graduate Fashion Week - www.gfw.org.uk
Scottish Textiles - www.scottish-enterprise.com/textiles
What's it like to be a Fashion Designer? (A&C Black 2008)
▶Working in art & design (2009) (Babcock Lifeskills) - www.babcock-lifeskills.com/
▶Working in fashion & clothing (2008) (Babcock Lifeskills) - www.babcock-lifeskills.com/
▶Working in sport & leisure (2010) (Babcock Lifeskills) - www.babcock-lifeskills.com/

Addresses

Design Council
34 Bow Street, London WC2E 7DL
Phone: +44 (0)20 7420 5200
Web: www.designcouncil.org.uk

London College of Fashion
20 John Princes Street, London W1G 0BJ
Phone: +44 (0)20 7514 7344
Web: www.fashion.arts.ac.uk

Textile Institute
1st Floor, St James' Buildings, Oxford Street, Manchester M1 6FQ
Phone: +44 (0)161 237 1188
Web: www.textileinstitute.org

Similar Jobs

Costume Designer, Dressmaker, Film/TV & Theatre Wardrobe Supervisor, Hat Designer, Interior Designer, Tailor, Textile Designer

Fence Installer

also known as: Fencing Contractor
CRCI:Building and Construction
CLCI:UF Job Band: 1 to 2

Job Description

Fence installers install and repair different types of fences using wire, wood, concrete or metal. They use tools such as spanners, pliers, wire cutters, hammers, spades, pickaxes and sometimes heavy plant machinery. May work on basic fences, such as those around houses and gardens, or may install high-tech fences, such as around airports. Other places that need fences include schools and colleges, sports grounds, factories, fields and forests, prisons, roads, zoos and parkland. Some installers only work on one or two types of fencing. Others are experienced in many different constructions, such as light and high security fencing, panel and domestic fencing, or stock fencing.

May hang gates in some fences, including sliding gates, security gates, access barriers, automatic gates, and swing gate palisades. A number of different specialist tools, such as a hydraulic breaker for drilling through tarmac are used. May use a small plant excavator. Once the ground has been prepared and levelled, the holes for the fence posts can be dug out. The posts are then positioned and the holes are back filled with the right material to strengthen them. Wires or a support framework may be used as an additional support until any concrete has set. The fence installer then applies any preservative or protective coating that is needed.

Installers need to be aware of the surrounding area and of current planning regulations. This includes public pathways and tree preservation orders, as well as health and safety rules.

Work Details

Fence installers usually work around a 39 hr week, Monday to Friday, though some overtime and weekend work is also possible. Work is outdoors on site and in all weather conditions. Travel around a local area to different sites is common. This job involves much heavy lifting and bending down, using ladders and walking over rough ground. There is a risk of accidents from equipment so you need to wear gloves, boots, protective clothing and sometimes ear protectors. You may work alone or in a small team.

Qualification

• England, Wales and Northern Ireland

Band 1: No specific qualifications are required though you are expected to have a good level of general education. Some GCSEs at any level in maths, technology and English, or equivalent, are helpful.

Band 2: Although academic qualifications are not specified for this job, it is an advantage to have some GCSEs (A*-C) in subjects that include English, maths and technology, or equivalent.

• Scotland

Band 1: No specific qualifications are required though you are expected to have a good level of general education. Some S grades at any level in maths and English, or similar, are helpful.

Band 2: Although academic qualifications are not specified for this job, it is an advantage to have some S grades (1-3) in subjects that include English and maths, or similar.

Adult Qualifications

No particular entry requirements though you are expected to have had a good level of general education. Relevant skills and experience may be more important than specific qualifications for mature entrants.

Work Experience

Relevant work or voluntary experience is always useful and can improve your chances when applying for entry to construction jobs and apprenticeships. A local fence installer or fencing contractor may offer you the opportunity to help with general tasks or you may wish to have a Saturday/holiday job working in a construction/ gardening supplies centre to gain knowledge of fencing terms and materials. Health and safety issues may mean that there are certain jobs you can't do until you are over 16. Contact your local Construction Skills office for advice.

Entry and Training

Training is usually on the job and possibly includes a day release or short course at a local college or training centre. Aside from basic fencing, courses include areas of health and safety at work, boundary fencing basic training and boundary high security fencing training. Lantra, the Sector Skills Council for the environmental and land-based sector, operates a Fencing Industry Skills Scheme (FISS)/Construction Skills Certification Scheme (CSCS) that enables fence installers/contractors to gain S/ NVQs in fencing and aims to further develop the skills of those working within the fencing industry. FISS/CSCS training is run by training providers throughout the UK. Contact Lantra for details.

The FISS/CSCS card is recognised throughout the UK and is essential for many employers, such as the Highways Agency. This card indicates several levels of competence ranging from those who have general fencing skills (not yet a skilled fence erector) to that of a qualified supervisor at level 3.

A Diploma/ Welsh Baccalaureate in construction and the built environment may be available in your area. S/NVQs are available in fencing at levels 2-3, as well as S/NVQ at level 1 in land-based operations. There is also an NVQ in fencing business management at level 4 for those who wish to progress further. Training programmes, including apprenticeship schemes, may be available in your area for entry to this job.

Mature applicants with skills and experience in woodworking or general building may have an advantage for training. Government training opportunities may be available in your area and you can also gain recognition of previous experience through Accreditation of Prior Learning (APL) or by working towards relevant S/NVQs. Contact your local careers office, Jobcentre Plus, Next Step service or Learning and Skills Council (LSC)/Local Enterprise Company (LEC) for details of training schemes, including apprenticeships for adults.

Opportunities and Pay

The fencing industry consists of over 15,000 fencing contractors in the UK. There are also more than 47,000 multi-skilled fencing installers. Firms range from small, self-employed contractors to large commercial companies. Opportunities may increase with the growth in prison building, road networks, and emphasis on conservation.

With experience you can progress to become a supervisor, foreman/woman or estimator. Others may move to sales and marketing with a builders' merchant, or fencing firm. When experienced, self-employment is very possible. Temporary and seasonal work is common.

Pay varies depending on size and type of employer. Trainees earn around £12k a year, rising to around £15k-£17k. When experienced, earnings can reach £22k-£25k a year. Highly experienced installers leading a team may earn up to £40k. Pay can be increased by overtime work. Some successful self-employed contractors may earn more.

Health

You need to have stamina and be physically fit.

Skills and Qualities

able to follow drawings and plans, able to work both on your own and in a team, enjoy working outdoors, environmental awareness, good organisational skills, manual dexterity, practical skills, safety conscious, time management skills

Relevant Subjects

Construction and built environment

Further Information

Apprenticeship Schemes (National Apprenticeship Service) - www.apprenticeships.org.uk

ConstructionSkills - sector skills council for the construction industry - www.cskills.org

Diplomas (Foundation, Higher and Advanced)- http://yp.direct.gov.uk/diplomas

Lantra - The Sector Skills Council for environmental & land-based sector (Lantra) http:/www.lantra.co.uk

Lantra Careers (A Future In...) (Lantra) - www.afuturein.com

Training Schemes - www.direct.gov.uk/en/educationandlearning

►Working in construction & the built environment (2007) (Babcock Lifeskills) - www.babcock-lifeskills.com/

Addresses

Fencing Contractors Association (FCA)
Warren Road, Trellech, Monmouthshire NP25 4PQ
Phone: +44(0)7000 560 722
Web: www.fencingcontractors.org

Similar Jobs

Carpenter/Joiner, Construction Operative, Farm Worker: Crops, Landscape Gardener, Road Worker, Scaffolder

Film/TV & Theatre Lighting Technician

also known as: Lighting Electrician, Stage Electrician
CRCI:Performing Arts
CLCI:GAT — Job Band: 2 to 3

Job Description

Lighting technicians control the position, strength and colour of lights on stage, in a film/TV studio, on location, inside and outdoors, using a computerised desk/console. They may follow a 'lighting plot' for changes during the production. Technicians work closely with a lighting designer who decides where the lights are to be placed. They decide which lights should be used and arrange them so that the scene is lit effectively. May manage a lighting budget and arrange to hire more equipment if needed.

May use flood or spot lights, laser beams, strobes, dry-ice or smoke effects, and different filters. Technicians rig the system and ensure that wires and cables are safe. Then remove all the equipment at the end of the broadcast/production. May also work at exhibitions and conferences, concerts, fashion shows and media presentations.

Work Details

Usually work a basic 40 hr week, though may have to work unsocial hours including evenings and weekends. You work in a theatre, a studio or on location. If it is a small theatre or studio you may be in sole charge of the lighting, but a large theatre/studio needs a team of technicians to rig the lights and deal with any problems, as well as operating the lights during a performance. Work can be demanding at times. Working hours must coincide with the demands of a shooting schedule or performance. Evening shows may finish late at night and technicians may work into the early hours dismantling equipment.

You may have to climb ladders when rigging the lights and need to carry heavy equipment. Lighting control desks are often in cubicles, which can be hot, noisy and enclosed.

Qualification

- **England, Wales and Northern Ireland**

Band 2: For entry to jobs, no minimum qualifications are needed, but it is an advantage to have some GCSEs (A*-C) or equivalent in subjects that include English and maths. Craft or technology subjects may be useful but are not essential.

Band 3: For entry to jobs, HNC or a relevant Diploma, usually at least 4 GCSEs (A*-C) including English, maths or science, or equivalent.

- **Scotland**

Band 2: Although academic qualifications are not specified for this job, it is an advantage to have some S grades (1-3) in subjects that include English and maths, or similar. Craft or technology subjects may be useful, but are not essential.

Band 3: For entry to jobs, usually at least four S grades (1-3) including English, maths or science, or similar.

Adult Qualifications

Applicants should have relevant technical knowledge as an electrician and several years' practical experience.

Work Experience

Direct work experience with specialist lighting companies is most useful, but anything that is practical and creative, or uses technical/electrical equipment, is helpful. Theatres and television studios may offer voluntary work experience, including companies such as the BBC, who offer paid summer work placements. Commercial lighting companies who supply the lights, and advise on design and layout, may also be worth approaching.

Entry and Training

Most people entering this job are qualified electricians with a City & Guilds certificate in electrotechnical technology, and have obtained their skills through vocational training. You can also take a technical theatre course such as a BTEC national certificate/ diploma in production arts or an HNC/HND in performing arts (production). There are also specialist degrees in lighting design for those looking to progress to lighting design work.

The Association of British Theatre Technicians offers specialist lighting courses for stage technicians. Skillset, together with the British Film Institute produces a media and multimedia courses directory, with details of many technical lighting courses. The BBC offers a number of training schemes that cover a range of technical subjects. It may be useful to have an LGV licence for help in transporting equipment.

You can work for S/NVQs in film and television lighting at levels 3-4. Training programmes, including apprenticeship schemes, may be available in your area. Advanced apprenticeships leading to qualification at level 3 can also be a route into higher education. Once qualified, you can take specialist courses in electrical safety, inspection and pyrotechnics, or a BTEC level 5 professional diploma in concert lighting, or in light and sound.

The Association of Lighting Designers is a professional body representing lighting designers working in the live performance industry. The website has details of training courses and routes, and general industry news. The Professional Lighting and Sound Association also provides information on industry qualifications, education and training and conferences and seminars.

A Diploma/Welsh Baccalaureate in creative and media may be available in your area. Cyfle (Wales) and Scottish Screen run film and television based training courses. See the websites for further information.

Mature entrants should demonstrate evidence of an interest in the theatre, such as involvement with amateur dramatics. Government training opportunities, such as apprenticeships, may be available in your area. You can also gain recognition of previous experience through Accreditation of Prior Learning (APL) or by working towards relevant S/NVQs. Contact your local careers office, Jobcentre Plus, Next Step service or Learning and Skills Council (LSC) Local Enterprise Company (LEC) for details of training schemes, including apprenticeships for adults.

Opportunities and Pay

Jobs are available in towns and cities for film, video, theatre, specialist lighting or broadcasting companies. There are also opportunities to work freelance, when experienced/qualified. This area is highly competitive and there are few vacancies. You may be able to work your way up to senior and chief electrician (gaffer), so it is worth considering any job in this field. Some lighting technicians move into the growing area of work with special events, including outdoor music concerts/festivals, or special effects (SFX), lighting design and production. See the job profile for a SFX technician. Others become lighting directors/designers or move into television camera work.

Pay varies depending on location and employer, but starting salaries for trainees are around £10k. New entrants with some experience are likely to earn £12k-£17k, rising to £25k a year. Senior lighting technicians earn from around £35k a year. Salaries are likely to be higher in film and television.

Health

This job requires good eyesight, normal colour vision and good stamina and physical fitness.

Skills and Qualities

able to cope under pressure, aptitude for teamwork, attention to detail, eye for visual effect, good communication skills, head for heights, IT skills, quick thinking, technical aptitude

Relevant Subjects

Art and Design, Design and technology, Engineering, ICT/ Computer studies, Mathematics, Media and communication studies, Performing arts, Physics, Science

Further Information

Apprenticeship Schemes (National Apprenticeship Service) - www.apprenticeships.org.uk

BBC Recruitment Services (BBC) - www.bbc.co.uk/jobs

Behind the Scenes: Theatre (Trotman 2009) - www.trotman.co.uk

British Film Institute (BFI) - www.bfi.org.uk

Broadcast Magazine (weekly) (Emap) - www.broadcastnow.co.uk

Cyfle (Wales) - www.cyfle.co.uk

Diplomas (Foundation, Higher and Advanced) - http://yp.direct.gov.uk/diplomas

Get into Theatre - www.getintotheatre.org

Getting into Films and Television (How to books 2009)

How to get a job in Television: Build your career from Runner to Series Producer (Methuen 2009)

Media/Multimedia Courses Directory (BFI/Skillset) - www.bfi.org.uk/education/talkscourses/mediacourses/

Scottish Screen (Scottish Screen) - www.scottishscreen.com

Skillset - sector skills council for the creative media, fashion and textiles industries - www.skillset.org

The Stage Online - www.thestage.co.uk

Training Schemes - www.direct.gov.uk/en/educationandlearning

Welsh Baccalaureate - www.wbq.org.uk

Addresses

Association of British Theatre Technicians (ABTT)
55 Farringdon Road, London EC1M 3JB
Phone: +44 (0)20 7242 9200
Web: www.abtt.org.uk

Association of Lighting Designers (ALD)
PO Box 680, Oxford OX1 9DG
Phone: +44 (0)7817 060189
Web: www.ald.org.uk

BBC Recruitment Services
Recruitment BBC HR Direct, PO Box 1133, Belfast BT1 9GP
Web: www.bbc.co.uk/jobs

Professional Lighting and Sound Association (PLASA)
Redoubt House, 1 Edward Road, Eastbourne BN23 8AS
Phone: +44 (0)1323 524 120
Web: www.plasa.org

Similar Jobs

Electrician, Film/TV & Theatre Rigger, Film/TV & Theatre SFX Technician, Film/TV Camera Operator, Photographer, Roadie

Film/TV & Theatre Make-Up Artist

also known as: Make-Up Artist
CRCI:Performing Arts
CLCI:GAT — Job Band: 3 to 4

Job Description

Make-up artists apply make-up and create hairstyles for performers and personalities appearing in the theatre, or before film or TV/video cameras. They ensure continuity in hair and make-up from one day's shooting to the next. In television work, most of the make-up is to cover blemishes and to emphasise features. In drama, if special make-up is needed, the artist first studies the script and then discusses requirements with a producer or lighting manager. May need to do research into styles of a particular period. Make-up artists work out how to alter features for character parts and may use prosthetics (foam and latex) to age faces or add scars and bruises.

Often in the theatre, performers do their own make-up and hair, but the make-up artist is on hand if more complex styles are required. Also prepare beards, wigs and create special or period hair-styles.

Work Details

You work indoors but may travel to different locations. Working hours are irregular and include weekends. In TV studios, you can have contact with a large number of people, some of whom may be nervous. In specialised theatre or film make-up, you work with a regular company. This work requires creativity and imagination and like most TV, theatre and film/video jobs, can be demanding at times. Often make-up artists have to stand for long periods of time and the work can be physically demanding. You may need to wear an overall to protect you from the cosmetics used.

Qualification

• England, Wales and Northern Ireland

Band 3: For relevant courses in make-up/image styling: usually at least 4 GCSEs (A*-C) preferably including biology or science, English and maths, or equivalent.

Band 4: For foundation degree in specialist make-up/make-up design: 1-2 A levels and some GCSEs (A*-C) usually including English and maths, or equivalent. History, art and chemistry are also useful. Check individual prospectuses.

• Scotland

Band 3: For a relevant course in make-up/image styling: at least four S grades (1-3) preferably including biology or a science subject and sometimes English or similar.

Band 4: For SQA higher national award in make-up artistry: 2-3 H grades and some S grades (1-3) usually including English and maths, or similar. History, art and chemistry are also useful.

Adult Qualifications

Entry requirements may be relaxed for adults applying for higher education courses and Access or foundation courses give adults without qualifications a route into higher education.

Work Experience

Employers or colleges may prefer candidates who have relevant work or voluntary experience. This can include work with an amateur theatrical company or observation in salons, theatres or with freelance make-up artists. This may give you the opportunity to compile a portfolio of relevant experience, together with some useful contacts for possible future work.

Entry and Training

Most people enter this job after training and experience in hairdressing, make-up or beauty therapy to level 2. You usually start as a trainee and then move up to assistant make-up artist, working under the supervision of the make-up artist. Assistant make-up artists usually work with actors who make up a crowd, while personal make up artists are often assigned to one performer. With around ten years' experience you can become a make-up designer. Trainees may also have the opportunity to attend a local college or complete on-the-job training towards vocational qualifications.

There are a few specialised courses in theatrical make-up, such as the degree in Make-Up and Prosthetics for Performance at the London College of Fashion. There are relevant HNDs, foundation degrees and degree courses at a range of institutions throughout the country. There are also some private courses, but these may be expensive. Some people take specialist courses before entry. These courses are not essential, although they are becoming more popular.

The Hairdressing and Beauty Industry Authority offers careers and training advice, and the National Association of Screen Make-up Artists and Hairdressers runs short courses and is a useful source for networking and training opportunities.

A Diploma/Welsh Baccalaureate in hair and beauty may be available in your area. See the diplomas website for further information. All make-up artists are expected to own their own kit and it is essential to have a driving licence.

Mature applicants for training require formal qualifications/ experience in beauty therapy and/or hairdressing, including make-up to at least level 2. An interest and experience in theatre is an advantage. There are part-time courses in media make-up available at local colleges of further education.

Government training opportunities, such as apprenticeships, may be available in your area. You can also gain recognition of previous experience through Accreditation of Prior Learning (APL) or by working towards relevant S/NVQs. Contact your local careers office, Jobcentre Plus, Next Step service or Learning and Skills Council (LSC) Local Enterprise Company (LEC) for details of training schemes, including apprenticeships for adults.

Opportunities and Pay

You can be employed by a television, film or theatre company, producers of commercials, music or corporate videos, or companies running fashion shows. Once you have gained experience it is possible to work freelance. There are few jobs, so competition to get any job, particularly training posts, is fierce.

Many work on a freelance basis so it is difficult to summarise earnings. Some people work for little or no pay to begin with, just to get a start in the industry. However, BECTU has recommended rates for different jobs in this field. For example, the daily rate for a freelance assistant make-up artist is £178-£222. Check the website for full details.

Health

There is an allergy risk from skin irritants. This job requires normal colour vision.

Skills and Qualities

able to cope under pressure, attention to detail, creative flair, eye for visual effect, good communication skills, good interpersonal skills, good organisational skills, manual dexterity, research skills, steady hand

Relevant Subjects

Art and Design, Biology, History, Media and communication studies, Performing arts, Science

Further Information

Apprenticeship Schemes (National Apprenticeship Service) - www.apprenticeships.org.uk

BBC Recruitment Services (BBC) - www.bbc.co.uk/jobs

Behind the Scenes: Film (Trotman 2009) - www.trotman.co.uk

Behind the Scenes: Television (Trotman 2009) - www.trotman.co.uk

Broadcast Magazine (weekly) (Emap) - www.broadcastnow.co.uk

Creative Choices - www.creative-choices.co.uk

Diplomas (Foundation, Higher and Advanced) - http://yp.direct.gov.uk/diplomas

Welsh Baccalaureate - www.wbq.org.uk

► Working in hairdressing & beauty (2009) (Babcock Lifeskills) - www.babcock-lifeskills.com/

Addresses

BECTU
(Broadcasting Entertainment Cinematographic and Theatre Union)
373-377 Clapham Road, London SW9 9BT
Phone: +44 (0)207 346 0900
Web: www.bectu.org.uk

Hairdressing and Beauty Industry Authority (HABIA)
Oxford House, Sixth Avenue, Sky Business Park, Robin Hood Airport, Doncaster DN9 3EG
Phone: 0845 230 6080 (UK only)
Web: www.habia.org/

London College of Fashion
20 John Princes Street, London W1G 0BJ
Phone: +44 (0)20 7514 7344
Web: www.fashion.arts.ac.uk

National Association of Screen Make-up and Hair Artists (NASMAH)
68 Sarsfield Road, Perivale, Middlesex UB6 7AG
Phone: +44 20 8998 7494
Web: www.nasmah.co.uk

Similar Jobs
Beauty Consultant, Beauty Therapist, Costume Designer, Hairdresser, Photographic Stylist, Wig Maker

Film/TV & Theatre Rigger

CRCI:Performing Arts
CLCI:GAT Job Band: 1 to 5

Job Description
Riggers in the entertainment industry lay the power cables needed on a set, erect scaffold towers, rig-up the tracks for cameras, camera mountings, cranes and dollies. On outside broadcasts, they also run the generator vans that supply the power to the production crew. They work in theatres, television studios, and on film and broadcast sets. Some also work in stadia and festival grounds for large scale concerts and productions. Riggers attend pre-production meetings and may look at a model or mock-up of the set to see what rigging is needed.

Crane riggers need to have expertise in construction and dealing with electrics. They use plant such as fork lifts, cherry pickers, MEWPs (Mobile elevating work platforms) and other equipment that can only be used by appropriately trained operators.

A lighting rigger works as part of a team that hangs and plugs all the lanterns during the get-in, in accordance with the design plan. They also de-rig lighting at the end of production and return equipment to the correct storage area. The job may also involve checking for repairs on lanterns and cables. Several riggers are required for the first few days, to focus and colour the lanterns.

Work Details
Hours are irregular, but usually long, potentially extending to 12-hour days. You may work on touring shows or location, perhaps abroad, which may mean being away from home for variable periods of time. Awareness of health and safety issues is very important as dealing with power cables and temporary structures can be dangerous. Protective clothing may be required. For height work you need to wear harnesses. For some jobs you may be expected to hold an LGV or HGV driving licence.

Qualification
There are no set qualifications to become a rigger, as training is traditionally on the job. However, GCSEs in maths, physics, or electronics are looked upon favourably, as is a BTEC diploma in electrical engineering. There are also qualifications for working at heights and certain plant operations that you are encouraged to undertake. There may also be apprenticeships available in your area.

Adult Qualifications
There are no minimum entry requirements but it may be helpful to show that you have experience in practical or technical work, such as on a construction site. Experience in theatres or on film or television sets is also useful. You can improve your skills and qualifications by working through the Foundation Learning programme. This involves taking credit-based units and qualifications to help you progress.

Work Experience
Riggers have traditionally started out as stage hands or flymen in theatres. Experience in a theatre or on a film or television set is very useful, but may be hard to come by. Helping on school or amateur productions is also useful.

Entry and Training
Rigging has moved away from the traditional inconsistent method of becoming a rigger by working on sets and production units, learning as you go along. It is still useful to start as a stage hand, flyman or lighting or sound crew in either the theatre or music business. However, evidence of competence is now expected. There is an increasing need for an industry standard qualification, which is now being managed by PLASA. New employees need a licence. There is an apprenticeship in technical theatre - rigging, lighting and sound available at Levels 2 and 3.

A Diploma/Welsh Baccalaureate in Creative and Media may be available in your area.

Working at height courses are offered by a range of providers, but these vary according to needs of firefighters, armed forces, steeplejacks, window cleaners and so on, so make sure you choose the appropriate one for the entertainment industry.

Government training opportunities, such as apprenticeships, may be available in your area. You can also gain recognition of previous experience through Accreditation of Prior Learning or by working towards relevant S/NVQs. Contact your local careers office, Jobcentre Plus, Next Step service or Learning and Skills Council (LSC)/Local Enterprise Company (LEC) for details of all training opportunities and schemes, including apprenticeships for adults.

Opportunities and Pay
You can work in theatres, television studios, concert venues, film sets or on outdoor broadcasts. All the major television companies employ crews of riggers who work on several productions during a working week. It is also possible to find work rigging for conferences or seminars and presentations, especially where audio-visual aids are required.

There is a large pool of freelance riggers who work on short-term contracts, particularly on film sets. There may be opportunities to work abroad if you are on a film location, although some companies prefer to use local employees. Increasingly riggers are freelance or work on short-term contracts. As self-employed workers, you are responsible for your own financial administration. Alternatively, you can work for a rigging company and gain experience on a range of productions.

Apprentices can expect to earn about £12k a year. Salaries vary depending on the length of your contract and the size, location and type of employer. Freelance riggers may be paid on a daily rate, or for a contract set fee. Average earnings are around £18k a year, although experienced riggers with a good reputation can earn much more.

Health
You need to be physically fit and quite strong for this job. Some employers may request a medical certificate.

Skills and Qualities
able to follow procedures, able to work quickly, accurate, attention to detail, head for heights, responsible attitude, safety conscious, technical aptitude

Relevant Subjects
Construction and built environment, Design and technology

Further Information
Apprenticeship Schemes (National Apprenticeship Service) - www.apprenticeships.org.uk

Cyfle (Wales) - www.cyfle.co.uk

Diplomas (Foundation, Higher and Advanced) - http://yp.direct.gov.uk/diplomas

Foundation Learning (QCDA) - www.qcda.gov.uk

Get into Theatre - www.getintotheatre.org

Skillset - sector skills council for the creative media, fashion and textiles industries - www.skillset.org

Stage Jobs Pro - www.uk.stagejobspro.com

The Stage (weekly) (The Stage Newspaper Limited) - www.thestage.co.uk

Welsh Baccalaureate - www.wbq.org.uk

Addresses
Association of British Theatre Technicians (ABTT)
55 Farringdon Road, London EC1M 3JB
Phone: +44 (0)20 7242 9200
Web: www.abtt.org.uk

Association of Lighting Designers (ALD)
PO Box 680, Oxford OX1 9DG
Phone: +44 (0)7817 060189
Web: www.ald.org.uk

BECTU
(Broadcasting Entertainment Cinematographic and Theatre Union)
373-377 Clapham Road, London SW9 9BT
Phone: +44 (0)207 346 0900
Web: www.bectu.org.uk

Professional Lighting and Sound Association (PLASA)
Redoubt House, 1 Edward Road, Eastbourne BN23 8AS
Phone: +44 (0)1323 524 120
Web: www.plasa.org

Similar Jobs
Crane Operator, Electricity Distribution Worker, Film/TV & Theatre Lighting Technician, Oil & Gas Roustabout/Roughneck, Roadie, Steeplejack

Film/TV & Theatre Scenic Artist
also known as: Scenic Artist
CRCI:Design, Arts and Crafts
CLCI:EZ Job Band: 3 to 5

Job Description
Scenic artists work from the ideas of a production designer and use artistic skills to paint backdrops, murals, scenery, props (furniture etc) and other items on the sets of TV, film and theatre. They translate the production designer's vision into reality and have the ability to produce accurate cityscapes, or complex murals or paintings that are required on set. They may also work with the painting team under the direction of a set chargehand painter and often touch-up or complete the work undertaken by the painting team. May also be asked to paint complex prop pieces.

Artists are responsible for scheduling work and buying in the necessary supplies. They have a good knowledge of art history, period styles architecture and motifs as well as colour mixing, and layout and paint application skills. They are skilled in techniques such as wood graining and texturing, stippling, colour washing, and marbling and ragging and use a variety of tools, including brushes, rollers and sprays.

Artists must keep to strict health and safety guidelines and carry out all tasks in a safe working environment. They must clean up after their work, and also dispose of any waste in their specific work area.

Work Details
Usually work a basic 39 hr week that may include shifts. Hours are often long and include evenings and weekends. Most of the work is done inside in paint rooms, workshops, and in theatres. To work on different productions, travel is usually required.

Qualification
• England, Wales and Northern Ireland

Band 3: For entry to jobs, HNC or a relevant Diploma, usually at least 4 GCSEs (A*-C) including English and art, or equivalent.

Band 4: For HND, Diploma of Higher Education or foundation degree: 1-2 A levels and some GCSEs (A*-C) usually including English and art, or equivalent.

Band 5: For degree courses: 2-3 A levels and some GCSEs (A*-C) usually including English and art, or equivalent. Most students take a foundation course in art and design first. Exact requirements depend on the degree you take. A diploma in creative and media may be considered as an alternative to A levels.

• Scotland

Band 3: For entry: usually at least four S grades (1-3) including English and art, or similar qualifications.

Band 4: For entry to SQA higher national and professional development awards, usually 2-3 H grades and some S grades (1-3), including English and art, or similar qualifications.

Band 5: For degree courses: 3-5 H grades and some S grades (1-3), usually including English and art, or similar. Exact requirements depend on the degree to be taken.

Degree Information
Relevant degrees include scenic art, theatre arts, theatre design and practice, technical theatre arts, fine art, applied arts and fine art history.

Adult Qualifications
Mature applicants with experience and outstanding portfolios of work may be accepted for courses/training without the standard entry requirements. There are Access and foundation art and design courses in some areas, which give adults without qualifications a route into higher education courses. Check with individual institutions.

Work Experience
Work experience gives you an insight into what you enjoy and don't enjoy about a job or working environment, as well as the opportunity to acquire new skills. It provides valuable information to add to your CV and improves any course application and future employment prospects. Entry to this job is competitive and any practical experience in school/college or amateur plays and performances, in painting backdrops for theatre productions, or carpentry/joinery, painting/decorating or furniture making, is extremely useful. Experience working as a sign writer may also be helpful.

Entry and Training
There is no specific route into this job though most take courses to gain or improve their initial skills. Most scenic artists have formal qualifications to HNC/HND or degree level from an art school, where they gain a good understanding of art history, architecture and colour theory. However, some enter by first gaining experience in painting and decorating, art and design work, technical courses that include scenic painting, and through theatre and set design courses. A full UK driving licence is usually essential for this job.

Entry to reputable art courses is highly competitive. Talented applicants without qualifications can occasionally obtain college places, though an exceptional portfolio of work is required. Usually art students take a foundation course in art and design before taking a degree course. In Scotland, art degrees are four years long, with the first year as a foundation. Courses can be full or part time.

Most scenic artists qualify at art school, and have a good understanding of art history, architecture and colour theory. You also need knowledge of health and safety legislation when working with paints.

Specialist training organisations such as Skillset Careers (the Sector Skills Council for the Audio Visual Industries), Cyfle and Scottish Screen also offer training for those working in the film and TV industry, including apprenticeship schemes. The Central School of Speech and Drama offers a degree in theatre practice which focuses specifically on scenic art, and the Royal Academy of Dramatic Art (RADA) and the Bristol Old Vic Theatre School run specialist postgraduate courses in scenic art.

A Diploma/Welsh Baccalaureate may be available in your area in creative and media and may provide a route onto higher education courses. Training programmes, including creative and design apprenticeship schemes, may be available in your area. Advanced apprenticeships leading to qualification at level 3 can also be a route into higher education.

Mature applicants usually require some experience of set work on dramatic productions through theatre work or amateur drama. Skills gained as a painter and decorator or furniture maker are also valuable. You can gain recognition of previous experience through Accreditation of Prior Learning (APL) or by working towards relevant S/NVQs. Contact your local Connexions or careers office, Jobcentre Plus, Next Step service or Learning and Skills Council (LSC)/Local Enterprise Company (LEC) for details of all training opportunities and schemes, including apprenticeships for adults.

Opportunities and Pay

Jobs are available in all parts of the country but there are more opportunities in London and in other cities and large towns. There is strong competition for work and opportunities for full-time posts are limited. Many scenic artists are self employed although some theatres, TV, film companies and scenic workshops employ full-time scenic artists. There may be opportunities to progress to being a head of department or a production designer.

Starting salaries for a theatre residential post are around £11k-£13k rising to £14.5k a year. Some are paid around £18k-£20k depending on the level of responsibility. Freelance scenic artists negotiate their own rates. TV and film jobs usually pay higher salaries.

Health

You need knowledge of health and safety legislation when working with paints.

Skills and Qualities

able to cope under pressure, able to work quickly, aptitude for teamwork, artistic ability, attention to detail, creative flair, eye for shape/colour, eye for visual effect, head for heights, manual dexterity

Relevant Subjects

Art and Design, History, Media and communication studies, Performing arts

Further Information

Behind the Scenes: Film (Trotman 2009) - www.trotman.co.uk

Behind the Scenes: Theatre (Trotman 2009) - www.trotman.co.uk

British Film Designers Guild - www.filmdesigners.co.uk

Design Vision - www.bbc.co.uk/designvision

Diplomas (Foundation, Higher and Advanced) - http://yp.direct.gov.uk/diplomas

Performing Arts Technical Training Handbook (ABTT) (Association of British Theatre Technicians) - www.performing-arts.org.uk/

Skillset - sector skills council for the creative media, fashion and textiles industries - www.skillset.org

The Stage Online - www.thestage.co.uk

▶Working in art & design (2009) (Babcock Lifeskills) - www.babcock-lifeskills.com/

▶Working in creative & media (2007) (Babcock Lifeskills) - www.babcock-lifeskills.com/

Addresses

Association of British Theatre Technicians (ABTT)
55 Farringdon Road, London EC1M 3JB
Phone: +44 (0)20 7242 9200
Web: www.abtt.org.uk

Bristol Old Vic Theatre School
1-2 Downside Road, Bristol BS8 2XF
Phone: +44 (0) 117 973 3535
Web: www.oldvic.ac.uk

Central School of Speech and Drama
Embassy Theatre, Eton Avenue, London NW3 3HY
Phone: +44 (0)20 7722 8183
Web: www.cssd.ac.uk

Cyfle (Wales)
Galeri 13, Victoria Dock,, Caernarfon LL55 1SQ.
Phone: +44 (0) 1286 685 242
Web: www.cyfle.co.uk

Royal Academy of Dramatic Art (RADA)
62-64 Gower Street, London WC1E 6ED
Phone: +44 (0)20 7637 7076
Web: www.rada.org

Scottish Screen
249 West George Street, Glasgow G2 4QE
Phone: 0845 300 7300 (UK only)
Web: www.scottishscreen.com

Society of British Theatre Designers (SBTD)
Theatre Design Department, Rose Bruford College, Burnt Oak Lane,, Sidcup DA15 9DF
Phone: +44 (0)20 8308 2664
Web: www.theatredesign.org.uk

Similar Jobs

Artist, Film/TV & Theatre Set Craftsperson, Film/TV & Theatre Set/Stage Designer, Film/TV Producer's Assistant, Painter & Decorator

Film/TV & Theatre Set Craftsperson

CRCI:Media, Print and Publishing
CLCI:GAL
Job Band: 1 to 2

Job Description

Set craft workers construct the scenery, sets and backdrops in film, television and theatre productions. They work from a brief provided by the set designer and maintain the condition of the set during production. Use specialised construction skills, such as carpentry and joinery, fibrous plastering, or painting and decorating. May produce decorative specialist paint finishes or install glass reinforced plastic (GRP). On large film sets, they may work with materials for larger constructions, including scaffolding, metal structures, etc. They ensure each set is authentic and accurately represents the requirements of the set designer and producer. Work closely with the set designer and other members of the production team, sometimes including a scenic artist.

Work Details

May work a basic 39 hr week, but the hours are often irregular. During a production you may have to work days, evenings and weekends as needed. You may need to work outdoors, and to handle heavy equipment. There can be long periods away from home and you need to be flexible to cope with the pressure of work and to keep tight deadlines. You may work in a team with other workers, but you can work alone. Conditions can be dirty, noisy or cramped.

The job involves lifting, bending, kneeling, climbing ladders and possibly working at heights on scaffolding. There may be a risk of minor injuries and you need to wear a safety helmet and protective footwear.

Qualification

• England, Wales and Northern Ireland

Band 2: For most employers: an NVQ level 2 in a relevant construction craft. To enter training: no minimum academic qualifications, but some GCSEs (A*-C) including maths, technical subjects, science and English are useful.

• Scotland

Band 2: For most employers: an SVQ level 2 in a relevant construction craft. To enter training no minimum academic qualifications, but some S grades (1-3) including maths, technical subjects, science and English are useful.

Adult Qualifications
Employers expect mature applicants to have qualifications in a relevant construction craft.

Work Experience
Work experience gives you an idea of what you enjoy and don't enjoy about a job, as well as the chance to gain new skills. It also gives you useful information to add to your CV and improves any course application and/or your future job prospects. Entry to this job is competitive and experience in school/college or amateur plays, plus carpentry, painting/decorating or furniture making is useful.

Entry and Training
People move into set crafts from a variety of backgrounds, but all need craft skills and a proven interest in working on sets in dramatic productions. Some may have worked in the construction industry and already gained a construction award, but have an interest in applying their skills to TV, film and theatre. Others may have experience in the theatre, amateur drama or college productions and have developed good craft skills. Training is usually practical, on the job, and may be supplemented by courses from training organisations, including those offered by Skillset, the sector skills council for audio-visual industries.

S/NVQs and other vocational qualifications in a range of construction crafts are available at levels 1-3. Training programmes, including apprenticeship schemes, may be available in your area. Advanced apprenticeships leading to qualification at level 3 can also be a route into higher education.

A Diploma/Welsh Baccalaureate may be available in your area in creative and media. This can be a useful introduction to this type of career as you gain practical experience while studying. See the diplomas website or Skillset for further information.

Mature applicants require some experience of set work on dramatic productions through theatre work or amateur drama. Government training opportunities, such as apprenticeships, may be available in your area. You can also gain recognition of previous experience through Accreditation of Prior Learning (APL) or by working towards relevant S/NVQs. Contact your local careers office, Jobcentre Plus, Next Step service or Learning and Skills Council (LSC) Local Enterprise Company (LEC) for details of training schemes, including adult apprenticeships.

Opportunities and Pay
Most work is with broadcasting companies, film, theatre and other production companies. Most of those in set crafts work on a self-employed, freelance basis. There is no formal promotion route. You have to build up a good reputation within the industry to get regular work. You can go on to be a set designer. Most opportunities occur in London, with smaller numbers in some other large UK cities.

At the start of your career you may earn £14k-£20k a year. Once experienced and having built up a good reputation, you may earn £23k-£33k a year.

Health
This job requires good general fitness and normal colour vision.

Skills and Qualities
able to improvise, able to work both on your own and in a team, attention to detail, eye for shape/colour, flexible approach, good coordinator, hard working, head for heights, manual dexterity, patient

Relevant Subjects
Art and Design, Construction and built environment, Design and technology, English, History, Mathematics, Media and communication studies

Further Information
Apprenticeship Schemes (National Apprenticeship Service) - www.apprenticeships.org.uk

Behind the Scenes: Film (Trotman 2009) - www.trotman.co.uk

ConstructionSkills - sector skills council for the construction industry - www.cskills.org

Diplomas (Foundation, Higher and Advanced) - http://yp.direct.gov.uk/diplomas

Skillset - sector skills council for the creative media, fashion and textiles industries - www.skillset.org

Training Schemes - www.direct.gov.uk/en/educationandlearning

Addresses
Association of British Theatre Technicians (ABTT)
55 Farringdon Road, London EC1M 3JB
Phone: +44 (0)20 7242 9200
Web: www.abtt.org.uk

Similar Jobs
Carpenter/Joiner, Film/TV & Theatre Scenic Artist, Film/TV & Theatre Set/Stage Designer, Painter & Decorator, Plasterer, Theatre Stagehand

Film/TV & Theatre Set/Stage Designer
also known as: Art Director: TV & Film, Production Designer: Theatre/Film/Video

CRCI:Design, Arts and Crafts
CLCI:EZ — Job Band: 3 to 5

Job Description
Designers create sets for films, TV and videos, or stage settings for theatre productions such as drama, musicals, opera and ballet, and are responsible for the visual aspect of each production. They need to visually interpret the script so study it closely and take the location, background and history into account. Usually work closely with the director, production team and actors and meet with the director and producer to discuss production requirements.

Designers sketch ideas, make technical drawings by hand, or use computer-aided design (CAD). They produce a working model, a 'storyboard' of successive designs, or a digital model on-screen from which hard copies of plans, elevations, sections or perspective views can be printed out at any scale.

They may need to choose outdoor locations for some or part of a production. Also calculate the cost and work within an agreed budget. Often produce a schedule of work for the technicians and stage hands for the completion of the design. Also manage the work of the design team and those responsible for set construction. Designers are present during rehearsals and filming sessions to advise on visual presentation.

Work Details
Working hours are irregular and can include long and unsocial hours at times. During a production you have to work days, evenings and weekends as required. There may be long periods away from home, perhaps travelling abroad. You can spend a lot of time sitting at a design board in a workshop. Backstage conditions can be dusty and cramped. You have to be able to work in a team as well as on your own, and to supervise the work of others, such as technicians, set craftspeople, stage hands and prop buyers.

Qualification

- **England, Wales and Northern Ireland**

Band 3: For entry to jobs, HNC or a relevant Diploma, usually at least 4 GCSEs (A*-C) including English and maths, or equivalent. For some foundation studies courses: usually at least 5 GCSEs (A*-C).

Band 4: For a foundation course in art and design: usually at least one A level and 4 GCSEs (A*-C). For a BTEC higher national award: a BTEC national award, successful completion of a foundation studies course, or equivalent.

Band 5: For degree courses: 2-3 A levels and some GCSEs (A*-C) usually including English and maths, or equivalent. Most students take an art and design foundation course first. An advanced diploma in creative and media may be considered as an alternative to A levels. Exact requirements depend on the degree you take.

- **Scotland**

Band 3: For entry: usually at least four S grades (1-3), including English and maths, or similar.

Band 4: For entry to SQA higher national and professional development awards, usually 2-3 H grades and some S grades (1-3), including English and maths, or similar qualifications.

Band 5: For degree courses: 3-5 H grades and some S grades (1-3), usually including English and maths, or similar qualifications. Exact requirements depend on the degree you take.

Degree Information

There are a variety of relevant degrees, such as theatre design, interior design, industrial 3D design, architecture, spatial design, theatre arts and set design for stage and screen. Some applicants have a fine art degree and complete a postgraduate course in a design-related subject. There are also postgraduate courses available in theatre design.

Adult Qualifications

Mature applicants with outstanding portfolios of work may be accepted for courses without the standard entry requirements. There are Access and foundation courses in art and design in some areas, which give adults without qualifications a route onto degree courses.

Work Experience

It is important that you try to do some relevant work or voluntary experience before applying. Direct experience with a set designer is the most useful, but experience of 3D design, freehand or using computers is also helpful. Related experience of using lighting and sound equipment and of drama, are all relevant, and may help with entry to a course or degree. Television and theatre companies are good first points of contact.

Early experience can be gained by involvement in school, student or local theatre, film and music societies to gain an understanding of what is involved in staging a performance. Experience as a stage hand; working with props and set painting/constructing scenery, is valuable.

Entry and Training

This is a highly competitive area and you need to gain early experience and qualifications to succeed. Personal contacts are important as well as initiative, talent and creative flair. A portfolio of work is essential for entry to courses. Entrants usually take a full-time course in a relevant subject which may include practical placements. A range of courses are available, including national/higher national award, or a degree, including foundation degrees. A Diploma/Welsh Baccalaureate may be available in your area in creative and media and may provide a route onto higher education courses.

It may be possible for those with good creative skills to start as an art department runner and move up to design assistant and then to set/stage designer with experience. However, most entrants have a relevant degree in art, architecture, theatre/film design, interior or 3D design before applying for a job. After qualification, stage designers train on the job as assistant designers. You need to gain knowledge of many related subjects including draughtsmanship, technical drawing, colour theory, architecture, building and construction, history of design, interior design, cameras and lenses.

A careers information pack for opportunities within the broadcasting film/video industry is available from Skillset, the profession's training organisation, who also provide short on-the-job courses. Increasingly, drama schools and colleges and universities are offering stage design courses. The Society of British Theatre Designers (SBTD) produces a list of available courses and information on trainee schemes.

Mature applicants may find entry difficult, unless they have previous relevant experience. Those with professional experience in a related area, like architecture or interior design, may find a mid-career move less difficult, but contracts are usually irregular and start with a low salary. Experience of working for a design studio or design consultancy is particularly helpful.

Job prospects are improved with a relevant higher education qualification that can be studied full or part time. You need to build a portfolio of your creative work for entry to courses and for employment.

Opportunities and Pay

Only around 500 people work as set designers in the UK with theatre, ballet, opera, repertory, TV and film companies, and major employers in the West End of London and other major cities, such as Manchester and Glasgow. Many broadcasting and film companies employ talented designers direct from college as assistants. You need to build up a reputation and may have periods of unemployment and insecurity. Many designers supplement their income with other jobs, such as modelmaking, teaching or exhibition design work.

Set/stage designers have no formal promotion structure but larger theatres, consultancies and production organisations employ full-time staff who proceed to become senior production designers. Many successful designers are self-employed. Some move into teaching art and design courses, from foundation to postgraduate level, and others move into directing jobs. There are also opportunities to work abroad.

An assistant designer in the theatre may earn around £18k a year, rising to £22k for a resident designer. High earners can make £35k-£70k and a few may make considerably more, particularly in television. You may have to negotiate a daily/weekly rate for the duration of each production. Those who work on West End (London) productions may receive a percentage of box office takings. Freelance salaries can be based on guidelines from the Broadcasting Entertainment Cinematographic and Theatre Union (BECTU), but are generally between £2k-£3k per production.

Health

Good colour sense is needed. This work may be a problem for those who do not have normal colour vision.

Skills and Qualities

able to communicate effectively, able to improvise, able to work to a budget, attention to detail, creative flair, eye for shape/colour, eye for visual effect, innovative, specialist IT skills, technical aptitude

Relevant Subjects

Art and Design, Design and technology, English, History, Mathematics, Media and communication studies, Performing arts

Further Information

Behind the Scenes: Television (Trotman 2009) - www.trotman.co.uk

Behind the Scenes: Theatre (Trotman 2009) - www.trotman.co.uk

British Film Designers Guild - www.filmdesigners.co.uk

Chartered Society of Designers (Chartered Society of Designers) - www.csd.org.uk

Design Uncovered (Trotman 2009) - www.trotman.co.uk

Design Vision - www.bbc.co.uk/designvision

Diplomas (Foundation, Higher and Advanced) - http://yp.direct.gov.uk/diplomas

How to get a job in Television: Build your career from Runner to Series Producer (Methuen 2009)

Skillset - sector skills council for the creative media, fashion and textiles industries - www.skillset.org

The Stage Online - www.thestage.co.uk

▶Working in art & design (2009) (Babcock Lifeskills) - www.babcock-lifeskills.com/

▶Working in creative & media (2007) (Babcock Lifeskills) - www.babcock-lifeskills.com/

Addresses

BECTU
(Broadcasting Entertainment Cinematographic and Theatre Union)
373-377 Clapham Road, London SW9 9BT
Phone: +44 (0)207 346 0900
Web: www.bectu.org.uk

National Film and Television School
Beaconsfield Studios, Station Road HP9 1LG
Phone: +44 (0)1494 731 425
Web: www.nftsfilm-tv.ac.uk

Society of British Theatre Designers (SBTD)
Theatre Design Department, Rose Bruford College,
Burnt Oak Lane, Sidcup DA15 9DF
Phone: +44 (0)20 8308 2664
Web: www.theatredesign.org.uk

Similar Jobs

Exhibition Designer, Film/TV & Theatre Wardrobe Supervisor, Film/TV Producer, Interior Designer, Model Maker, Theatre Stage Manager, Visual Merchandiser

Film/TV & Theatre SFX Technician

also known as: Special Effects Technician

CRCI:Media, Print and Publishing
CLCI:GAL Job Band: 3 to 5

Job Description

Special effects (SFX) technicians help to create an illusion in a film, television or theatre production. They construct physical effects such as pyrotechnics (fire effects), explosions, models, collapsible furniture and specialist make-up, known as prosthetics. Use a range of skills, such as sculpting, modelmaking, electronics, joinery, metal work, chemistry and painting, to create the illusion. They tend to work in one of three areas, pyrotechnic, physical or visual effects. Work alongside TV crews, stunt coordinators, directors, including fight scene directors, and producers. Use lasers, computers and specialist software, lights and electronics, welding equipment, explosives, and a wide variety of sound equipment.

Also use specialist machines such as those that produce dry ice, fire, snow and wind. Computer-generated images (CGI) are increasingly used to create special effects.

Work Details

Usually work an eight-hour day though may need to work weekends and evenings, and be flexible within the working day, to cope with the pressure of work and tight deadlines. Television work can be particularly pressurised. You may work on set, or in a designated safety workshop. Travel may be necessary and you may need to spend nights away from home. You may be required to work outdoors, in all weathers, and need to move around heavy and complex equipment.

Qualification

• England, Wales and Northern Ireland

Band 3: For entry: usually at least 4 GCSEs (A*-C) including English and maths, or equivalent.

Band 4: For HND, Diploma of Higher Education or foundation degree: 1-2 A levels and some GCSEs (A*-C) usually including English and maths, or equivalent.

Band 5: For degree courses: 2-3 A levels and some GCSEs (A*-C) usually including English and maths or equivalent qualifications. Exact requirements depend on the degree you take.

• Scotland

Band 3: For entry to a relevant course: usually at least four S grades (1-3) or similar.

Band 4: For entry to SQA higher national and professional development awards, usually 2-3 H grades and some S grades (1-3), including English and maths, or similar qualifications.

Band 5: For degree courses: 3-5 H grades and some S grades (1-3), usually including English or similar may also be acceptable. Exact requirements depend on the degree you take.

Degree Information

Special effects encompasses many degree disciplines, including animation, visual design, 3-D design, engineering and computer science. Degrees are available in special effects, technical arts and film and visual effects, but specialist subjects are not essential. There are also relevant postgraduate qualifications.

Adult Qualifications

Those with relevant experience may not need the standard entry requirements for higher education. Access or foundation courses give adults without qualifications a route into degree courses.

Work Experience

Spending time at a television or film studio that has its own SFX department is valuable experience. It is difficult to obtain work experience at these types of organisations, so early preparation is necessary. Pinewood Film Studios have their own SFX department, but because of time constraints and insurance issues, especially for young people, they rarely take on work experience candidates. Any general work in the various aspects of TV or film work, is relevant.

Entry and Training

Training is mainly on the job supported by short courses and most begin in trainee posts. For course entry and employers, you need a portfolio of your designs, photography, art, and possibly a 'showreel' of your skills. People come into special effects from a variety of backgrounds. Many have HNDs or degrees, although it is not a formal requirement, others have engineering or computing experience. Whatever the background, good drawing skills, experience in the use of craft tools, and knowledge of electronics or photography are an asset.

You can work as a trainee. It takes around five years to qualify (two years in visual effects), and pyrotechnic special effects technicians need a licence and appropriate qualifications. Contact BECTU for full details of their Joint Industry Special Effects Training Scheme. This is a structured training programme that allows trainees to progress to technician, senior technician and supervisor. Relevant vocational qualifications at levels 3-4 may be available.

A Diploma/Welsh Baccalaureate may be available in your area in creative and media. This can be a useful introduction to this type of career as you gain practical experience while studying. See the diplomas website or Skillset for further information.

Employers expect mature applicants to have experience in relevant areas of design, engineering or handcrafts and usually look for some experience of set work on dramatic productions through, for example, theatre work or amateur drama.

Opportunities and Pay

Around 500 people are employed in SFX roles in the UK television and film industries. The large broadcasting companies employ a small number of SFX staff, but the majority work for small specialist companies, many on a freelance basis and on short-term contracts. Most opportunities occur in London, with smaller numbers in some other major UK cities.

This is a small, specialised and competitive industry. Vacancies are rarely advertised and applicants must be proactive and approach companies directly with evidence of their work, such as a portfolio or 'showreel'. The film industry is smaller so even more competitive. It is therefore important to build a good reputation. There is seldom a promotion structure, but in television, promotion to special/visual effects designer may be possible. There are roles for senior technicians and supervisors with relevant experience.

Pay varies considerably but starts at around £200-£450 a week, rising to over £1k a week with experience. Highly skilled SFX technicians earn more than £2k a week. A small number employed in major productions can earn considerably more than this.

Health
This job requires good general fitness and normal colour vision.

Skills and Qualities
able to cope under pressure, able to withstand criticism, aptitude for teamwork, creative flair, eye for visual effect, imaginative, IT skills, practical skills, resourceful, technical aptitude

Relevant Subjects
Art and Design, Chemistry, Design and technology, Engineering, ICT/Computer studies, Mathematics, Media and communication studies, Performing arts, Physics, Science

Further Information
Broadcast Magazine (weekly) (Emap) - www.broadcastnow.co.uk
Cyfle (Wales) - www.cyfle.co.uk
Diplomas (Foundation, Higher and Advanced) - http://yp.direct.gov.uk/diplomas
Scottish Screen (Scottish Screen) - www.scottishscreen.com
Skillset - sector skills council for the creative media, fashion and textiles industries - www.skillset.org

▶Working in creative & media (2007) (Babcock Lifeskills) - www.babcock-lifeskills.com/

Addresses
Association of British Theatre Technicians (ABTT)
55 Farringdon Road, London EC1M 3JB
Phone: +44 (0)20 7242 9200
Web: www.abtt.org.uk

BECTU (Broadcasting Entertainment Cinematographic and Theatre Union)
373-377 Clapham Road, London SW9 9BT
Phone: +44 (0)207 346 0900
Web: www.bectu.org.uk

Pinewood Studios
Pinewood Road, Iver Heath, Buckinghamshire SL0 0NH
Phone: +44 (0)1753 651700
Web: www.pinewoodgroup.com

Similar Jobs
Animator, Film/TV & Theatre Set Craftsperson, Film/TV & Theatre Set/Stage Designer, Film/TV/Radio & Theatre Sound Recordist

Film/TV & Theatre Wardrobe Assistant
also known as: Costume Assistant, Wardrobe Assistant

CRCI:Performing Arts
CLCI:GAT — Job Band: 1 to 2

Job Description
Wardrobe assistants work with a wardrobe supervisor/manager to make or alter costumes for film and TV productions, theatre plays, operas, ballets and musicals. They may buy or hire extra costumes if needed. Assistants look after the costumes during a performance or 'shoot', clean, iron, mend and alter clothes as required. Also look after wigs and arrange for them to be 'dressed' by the wigmaker, if necessary. They ensure that all hats, shoes, gloves, jewellery and other accessories are stored correctly and safely. May make a record of all costumes used by each actor so that they are available at the required time. This also helps to ensure that continuity is maintained. Also pack and unpack clothes needed by companies on tour.

Some wardrobe assistants also do the work of a dresser who helps one or more actors to prepare for a performance. They ensure that each item of clothing and accessory is available and help them to make quick changes, when necessary. Some assistants may do a little research to assist the costume designer at the start of a new production.

Work Details
Working hours are usually irregular and include evenings and weekends. You work in dressing rooms or workshops in a theatre, studio or on location. Travel is necessary if the company goes on tour. You help performers who may be nervous and need calming down before they appear. Sometimes you can be very busy, when there is a quick change or emergency mending or ironing to be done.

Qualification

• England, Wales and Northern Ireland
Band 1: For entry to jobs, no minimum qualifications are needed, but you are expected to have a good level of general education and relevant experience. Some formal/vocational qualifications in maths, English, art or history at any level are useful.

Band 2: For entry to jobs, no minimum qualifications are needed, but it is an advantage to have some GCSEs (A*-C) or equivalent in subjects that include English and maths.

• Scotland
Band 1: For entry to jobs, no minimum qualifications are needed, but you are expected to have a good level of general education and relevant experience. Some formal/vocational qualifications in maths, English, art or history at any level are useful.

Band 2: Although academic qualifications are not specified for this job, it is an advantage to have some S grades (1-3) in subjects that include English and maths, or similar.

Adult Qualifications
No minimum formal academic requirements are specified for entry, though qualifications in relevant practical subjects are an advantage.

Work Experience
Any practical experience in school/student productions or in other amateur plays is useful. A portfolio or show reel of your work to show employers is also helpful. Work experience with a theatrical costumier is also relevant. Contact your local theatre or amateur dramatic society for work placements or holiday jobs.

Entry and Training
It is important to have ability in sewing and an advantage to have experience in pattern cutting, drawing and drama. Employers expect evidence of your interest in dressmaking/tailoring. Training is usually on the job working with experienced wardrobe staff. Some start in this work after experience with a theatrical costumier. Some of the larger costumiers may run training schemes for wardrobe assistants.

There are a range of courses, such as those offered by City & Guilds and BTEC, run at colleges throughout the country in fashion design, tailoring and pattern cutting. These are relevant for entry to this work, but not essential. Some entrants do a degree in costume design and enter the industry first as a wardrobe assistant to gain experience and contacts. A driving licence is an advantage in this work.

S/NVQs in relevant craft subjects, are available. Training programmes, including apprenticeship schemes, may be available in your area. Advanced apprenticeships leading to qualification at level 3 can also be a route into higher education. A Diploma/Welsh Baccalaureate in creative and media may be available in your area. See the diplomas website for further information.

Entry is possible for those with dressmaking/tailoring skills, fashion design, and ideally, experience of the theatre. Government training opportunities, such as apprenticeships, may be available in your area. You can also gain recognition of previous experience through Accreditation of Prior Learning (APL) or by working towards relevant S/NVQs. Contact your local careers office, Jobcentre Plus, Next Step service or Learning and Skills Council (LSC) Local Enterprise Company (LEC) for details of training schemes, including apprenticeships for adults.

Opportunities and Pay

Jobs are found mainly in London and the South East, and in other large towns and cities. You can find work in theatre, films, television and fashion houses. With experience and more qualifications, you can progress to be a wardrobe supervisor or costume designer. Promotion prospects are better if you are willing to move jobs. Freelance work is common and there may be chances to work abroad when filming on location or touring with a theatre production. The Royal National Theatre in London has a large costume department, managing over 60,000 costumes. These are made in the theatre's workshops and they also run a hire service. They occasionally have work placement opportunities for trainees.

Pay varies greatly, but a trainee in the theatre earns around £10k-£17k, rising to around £28k a year, with experience. Pay in films and television may be higher.

Health

This job may require normal colour vision.

Skills and Qualities

able to cope under pressure, able to work quickly, attention to detail, excellent sewing skills, eye for visual effect, good interpersonal skills, good memory, good organisational skills, reliable, tactful

Relevant Subjects

Art and Design, History, Media and communication studies, Performing arts

Further Information

Apprenticeship Schemes (National Apprenticeship Service) - www.apprenticeships.org.uk

Broadcast Magazine (weekly) (Emap) - www.broadcastnow.co.uk

Costume Society - www.costumesociety.org.uk

Creative & Cultural Skills - sector skills council for advertising, crafts, cultural heritage, design, literature, music, performing & visual arts - www.ccskills.org.uk

Creative Choices - www.creative-choices.co.uk

Diplomas (Foundation, Higher and Advanced) - http://yp.direct.gov.uk/diplomas

Get into Theatre - www.getintotheatre.org

How to get a job in Television: Build your career from Runner to Series Producer (Methuen 2009)

Skillset - sector skills council for the creative media, fashion and textiles industries - www.skillset.org

The Stage Online - www.thestage.co.uk

Training Schemes - www.direct.gov.uk/en/educationandlearning

Welsh Baccalaureate - www.wbq.org.uk

Addresses

Royal National Theatre
South Bank, London SE1 9PX
Phone: +44 (0)20 7452 3400
Web: www.nationaltheatre.org.uk

Society of British Theatre Designers (SBTD)
Theatre Design Department, Rose Bruford College,
Burnt Oak Lane, Sidcup DA15 9DF
Phone: +44 (0)20 8308 2664
Web: www.theatredesign.org.uk

Similar Jobs

Clothing Alteration Hand, Costume Designer, Dressmaker, Film/TV & Theatre Wardrobe Supervisor, Sewing Machinist, Tailor

Film/TV & Theatre Wardrobe Supervisor

also known as: Wardrobe Master, Wardrobe Mistress

CRCI:Performing Arts

CLCI:GAT — Job Band: 2 to 4

Job Description

Wardrobe supervisors have overall responsibility for the management and supervision of a TV, film or theatre production's costume department and its staff. They provide individual sets of clothes, accessories and possibly wigs for the actors/contributors. May supervise a small team of workers/assistants, or for large productions, a team of up to fifty. They decide whether to make, buy, hire or alter existing costumes that are needed for theatrical performances, including film and TV productions, theatre plays, operas, ballet and musicals. During filming, wardrobe supervisors decide whether additional staff are needed to help on a particular day, and arrange their hire.

They read the script and provide a costume plot and schedule. Then measure the cast and organise the wardrobe team's workload, meeting all deadlines and budgets. Also oversee the continuity of the production, ensuring that the right costumes are available for the right scenes. Wardrobe supervisors are also responsible for purchasing fabric and sourcing other costumes and accessories such as wigs and jewellery. They often work closely with a costume designer, stage and production manager, depending on the size of the production.

Work Details

Working hours are irregular and can include evenings and weekends. You work in dressing rooms or workshops in a theatre, studio or on location. Travel is necessary if the company goes on tour. You help performers who may be nervous and need calming down before they appear. Sometimes you can be very busy, when there is a quick change to be done or you need to organise emergency mending or ironing. Your workplace may be cramped and dusty.

Qualification

Although formal qualifications are often not required, there are a range of relevant courses at all levels for those with appropriate entry qualifications.

• England, Wales and Northern Ireland

Band 3: For entry to jobs, HNC or a relevant Diploma, usually at least 4 GCSEs (A*-C) including English, maths and art or design, or equivalent.

Band 4: For HND, Diploma of Higher Education or foundation degree: 1-2 A levels and some GCSEs (A*-C) usually including English and maths, or equivalent.

• Scotland

Band 3: For entry to jobs, usually at least four S grades (1-3) including English or maths, or similar.

Band 4: For entry to SQA higher national and professional development awards, usually 2-3 H grades and some S grades (1-3), including English and maths, or similar qualifications.

Adult Qualifications

Some colleges consider adults without formal qualifications but with relevant experience.

Work Experience

Any practical experience in school/student productions or amateur plays and performances is useful. A portfolio or show reel of your work to show employers provides evidence of your experience. Contact your local theatre, amateur dramatic society or theatrical costume hire company for work placements or voluntary temporary/holiday jobs.

Entry and Training

This is not an entry level job as most entrants start this work as a wardrobe assistant, whatever their entry qualification. It is important to have sewing ability and an advantage to have experience in drama. Some wardrobe supervisors begin their career straight from school as a trainee or costume assistant in the wardrobe department of a theatre or film production company. Others start as a sewing hand where no previous theatre experience is necessary, or as a costume cutter. Skills are learned on the job. Some wardrobe supervisors may have previously worked for a maker or supplier of theatrical or fancy dress costumes (costumiers).

Some prefer to do a relevant course before entry, and there are courses available at all levels in subjects that include design, dressmaking and tailoring. Courses range from basic sewing skills to higher national diplomas and degrees. There are full or part-time foundation degrees available in subjects that include costume construction/design for stage and screen. City & Guilds offers relevant awards including tailoring and a theatre costume course, and BTEC offer a national award in costume. The London College of Fashion runs a range of relevant courses including a period costume pattern cutting course. A Diploma/Welsh Baccalaureate in creative and media may be available in your area. See the diplomas website for further information.

Mature entry is possible for those with dressmaking/tailoring skills, or fashion design. Ideally you should have experience of the theatre, film or TV productions. Knowledge of period costume may also be beneficial. Government training opportunities, such as apprenticeships, may be available in your area. You can also gain recognition of previous experience through Accreditation of Prior Learning (APL) or by working towards relevant S/NVQs. Contact your local careers office, Jobcentre Plus, Next Step service or Learning and Skills Council (LSC) Local Enterprise Company (LEC) for details of training schemes, including apprenticeships for adults.

Opportunities and Pay

Jobs are mainly available in London and the South East, and in major towns and cities. Competition is fierce for vacancies. You can find employment in theatre, including regional, fringe, children's and community theatre. The Royal National Theatre in London has a large costume department, managing over 60,000 costumes. These are made in the theatre's workshops and they also run a hire service. They occasionally have work placement opportunities for trainees.

There are also opportunities to work in touring theatre, or with ballet and opera companies, musicals, film production, and television and fashion houses. There may be opportunities to travel with a touring theatre company or film on location. Some wardrobe supervisors become freelance or move into costume design.

Pay varies greatly depending on your employer though earnings start around £20k-£25k, rising to around £30k a year. Wardrobe supervisors working on major productions may earn more.

Health

This job requires normal colour vision.

Skills and Qualities

able to work to a budget, adaptable, attention to detail, excellent sewing skills, good communication skills, good interpersonal skills, good memory, good organisational skills, tactful

Relevant Subjects

Art and Design, English, History, Media and communication studies, Performing arts

Further Information

Apprenticeship Schemes (National Apprenticeship Service) - www.apprenticeships.org.uk

Broadcast Magazine (weekly) (Emap) - www.broadcastnow.co.uk

Costume Society - www.costumesociety.org.uk

Creative & Cultural Skills - sector skills council for advertising, crafts, cultural heritage, design, literature, music, performing & visual arts - www.ccskills.org.uk

Creative Choices - www.creative-choices.co.uk

Diplomas (Foundation, Higher and Advanced) - http://yp.direct.gov.uk/diplomas

Get into Theatre - www.getintotheatre.org

Skillset - sector skills council for the creative media, fashion and textiles industries - www.skillset.org

The Stage Online - www.thestage.co.uk

Training Schemes - www.direct.gov.uk/en/educationandlearning

Welsh Baccalaureate - www.wbq.org.uk

▶ Working in art & design (2009) (Babcock Lifeskills) - www.babcock-lifeskills.com/

Addresses

Association of British Theatre Technicians (ABTT)
55 Farringdon Road, London EC1M 3JB
Phone: +44 (0)20 7242 9200
Web: www.abtt.org.uk

London College of Fashion
20 John Princes Street, London W1G 0BJ
Phone: +44 (0)20 7514 7344
Web: www.fashion.arts.ac.uk

Royal National Theatre
South Bank, London SE1 9PX
Phone: +44 (0)20 7452 3400
Web: www.nationaltheatre.org.uk

Similar Jobs

Costume Designer, Dressmaker, Fashion Designer, Film/TV & Theatre Set/Stage Designer, Film/TV & Theatre Wardrobe Assistant, Tailor

Film/TV Boom Operator

CRCI:Media, Print and Publishing
CLCI:GAL — Job Band: 3 to 5

Job Description

Boom operators are responsible for placing the boom microphone in the best place during the making of a film or a TV programme. They either hand holds the boom, which is long pole with a microphone on the end of it, or mount it on a moving platform, called a dolly. Then place it so that the sound is clearly picked up, but so that it does not get in the way of the camera operator or the actors. They are responsible for putting radio or clip microphones in the best places so that the sound mixers can capture good quality dialogue and sound effects.

Boom operators needs to ensure they are familiar with the dialogue and the script programme for each day so that they know when to move the boom. During rehearsals, they take note of lighting and camera movements so that the boom does not cast shadows. Also look after all the sound equipment, carrying out minor repairs if needed.

Work Details

Hours may be long and irregular. The boom operator arrives on set an hour before filming starts and is on set all day. Filming may take place during the day or night, and at weekends. The work may in be inside a studio or outside, often in all weathers, on location. The job may involve travelling to locations and may mean spending long periods away from home.

You work very much as a team with sound mixers and other members of the production sound department. You must also develop a good working relationship with camera operators as you need to cooperate with each other to ensure the best quality pictures and sound.

Qualification

• England, Wales and Northern Ireland

Band 3: For entry: at least 4 GCSEs (A*-C), preferably including English, maths, physics and technological studies, or equivalent.

Band 4: For HND, Diploma of Higher Education or foundation degree: 1-2 A levels and some GCSEs (A*-C) usually including English, science and maths, or equivalent.

Band 5: For degree courses: 2-3 A levels and some GCSEs (A*-C) usually including English and maths, or equivalent. Exact requirements depend on the degree you take.

• Scotland

Band 3: For entry: at least four S grades (1-3), preferably including English, maths, physics and technological studies, or similar.

Band 4: For entry to SQA higher national and professional development awards, usually 2-3 H grades and some S grades (1-3), including English, science and maths, or similar qualifications.

Band 5: For degree courses: 3-5 H grades and some S grades (1-3), usually including English and maths, or similar qualifications. Exact requirements depend on the degree you take.

Degree Information

A degree related to sound production, sound engineering, broadcasting, film production or audio technology is the most appropriate.

Adult Qualifications

Entry requirements may be relaxed for adults applying for higher education courses. Access or foundation courses provide those without the required qualifications a route onto degree courses.

Work Experience

Entry to this career is highly competitive and it is essential that you have some relevant work or voluntary experience before applying. Theatre and television companies may provide practical experience of using sound equipment. The British Film Institute (BFI) requests the help of volunteers during the BFI annual film festival in London; this type of experience is useful. Taking part in school, college/university and local amateur dramatic society productions is also valuable. Work for a hospital/community radio station is also a good way to gain experience.

Entry and Training

There are no set entry qualifications, but this is a very competitive field so any qualifications that involve learning about acoustics or sound are relevant. Many entrants have HNDs or a degree. Foundation degrees are available, including sound engineering and design, and sound and media technology. However, experience in the field of sound in the film industry often counts for more than qualifications. Many entrants start by learning about sound equipment by working for a supplier of technical equipment and services, known as a facilities house. From here you can start as a sound trainee with a film/TV production company, and move on to learn about how to operate a boom.

Most training is on the job, but there are also new entrant training schemes available from Cyfle and Scottish Screen. The National Film and Television School offers a diploma in sound recording for film and television, and there are a range of level 3 City & Guild courses available in aspects of sound. Skillset, the sector skills council for the audio visual industries, has a lot of information on its website.

Vocational training programmes, including apprenticeship schemes, may be available in your area. Advanced apprenticeships leading to qualification at level 3 can also be a route into higher education.

A Diploma/Welsh Baccalaureate may be available in your area in creative and media. This can be a useful introduction to this type of career as you gain practical experience while studying. See the diplomas website or Skillset for further information.

Adult entrants are welcomed, particularly if they have relevant experience of work involving electronics, sound or broadcasting.

Opportunities and Pay

Boom operators can work for film production companies, television broadcasters or producers of commercials. You may have to start in a job for very little pay to get a start in the industry. Vacancies can be found sometimes in trade magazines, but often you need to develop a network of contacts so that you are aware when jobs may be coming up. Much of the work is short term and many boom operators are freelance. Once experienced, you can go on to production sound mixing , sound recording or sound editing.

Starting pay as a sound trainee may be little or nothing. As a boom operator you may have to wait for payment until the film is produced, but those with a salary are likely to earn around £12k-£14k a year, rising with experience to nearer £30k. BECTU can provide details of freelance rates for this work.

Health

This job requires excellent hearing and normal colour vision. You need good general physical fitness.

Skills and Qualities

agile, aptitude for teamwork, attention to detail, flexible and adaptable, good memory, good timing, observant, safety conscious

Relevant Subjects

Design and technology, Media and communication studies, Performing arts, Physics, Science

Further Information

Apprenticeship Schemes (National Apprenticeship Service) - www.apprenticeships.org.uk

Association of Professional Recording Services (APRS) - http://www2.aprs.co.uk

Audio Media - www.audiomedia.com

British Film Institute (BFI) - www.bfi.org.uk

Diplomas (Foundation, Higher and Advanced) - http://yp.direct.gov.uk/diplomas

Film Sound - www.filmsound.org

FilmTV - www.film-tv.co.uk

How to get a job in Television: Build your career from Runner to Series Producer (Methuen 2009)

Institute of Broadcast Sound (IBS) - www.ibs.org.uk

Skillset - sector skills council for the creative media, fashion and textiles industries - www.skillset.org

► Working in creative & media (2007) (Babcock Lifeskills) - www.babcock-lifeskills.com/

Addresses

BECTU
(Broadcasting Entertainment Cinematographic and Theatre Union)
373-377 Clapham Road, London SW9 9BT
Phone: +44 (0)207 346 0900
Web: www.bectu.org.uk

Cyfle (Wales)
Galeri 13, Victoria Dock, Caernarfon LL55 1SQ.
Phone: +44 (0) 1286 685 242
Web: www.cyfle.co.uk

National Film and Television School
Beaconsfield Studios, Station Road HP9 1LG
Phone: +44 (0)1494 731 425
Web: www.nftsfilm-tv.ac.uk

Scottish Screen
249 West George Street, Glasgow G2 4QE
Phone: 0845 300 7300 (UK only)
Web: www.scottishscreen.com

Similar Jobs

Film/TV & Theatre Lighting Technician, Film/TV & Theatre SFX Technician, Film/TV Camera Operator, Film/TV Producer's Assistant, Film/TV Runner, Film/TV/Radio & Theatre Sound Recordist

Film/TV Camera Operator

CRCI:Media, Print and Publishing
CLCI:GAL Job Band: 3 to 5

Job Description

Camera operators use a camera as part of a studio or film crew and may be sent on location. They translate the ideas of a production team into visual images by setting up and using photographic equipment for making films, videos, TV programmes, and for interactive media. They work with the director of photography (DP), to ensure the right mood or atmosphere, having previously read the script and worked out suggested camera angles. Then plan the shoot to ensure that difficult shots can be finished in one take. Operators move, load and focus cameras as required by the director. Work varies and it is possible to specialise in film production, news, cartoons, features or video production.

Work Details

Work long and irregular hours that often include evenings and weekends. Shift work may be required. You can work in a studio or out on location. You may have to travel widely and stay away from home. Work may be pressurised at times and requires creativity and imagination. On outside broadcasts (OBs), and on location, you have to cope with holding cameras steady in crowds or while walking on rough ground, and sometimes working on high scaffolding. You may have to work outside in bad weather.

If you are the only camera operator, you choose your own shots and your film is edited later. If working in a team, you follow instructions received through a headset from a director. Camera crews are responsible for the health and safety of themselves and their colleagues and the public. They are often required to work in dangerous environments, including war zones.

Qualification

• England, Wales and Northern Ireland

Band 3: For BTEC national award in design (audio-visual): usually at least 4 GCSEs (A*-C) preferably including English, maths and physics, or equivalent.

Band 4: For HND, Diploma of Higher Education or foundation degree: 1-2 A levels and some GCSEs (A*-C) usually including English and maths, or equivalent. Useful subjects include both arts and sciences.

Band 5: For degree courses: 2-3 A levels and some GCSEs (A*-C) usually including English and maths, or equivalent qualifications. Exact requirements depend on the degree you take.

• Scotland

Band 3: For entry to some courses in audio-visual technology: at least four S grades (1-3) preferably including English, maths and physics.

Band 4: For entry to SQA higher national and professional development awards, usually 2-3 H grades and some S grades (1-3), including English and maths, or similar qualifications. Both arts and science subjects are useful.

Band 5: For degree courses: 3-5 H grades and some S grades (1-3), usually including English and maths, or similar. Exact requirements depend on the degree you take.

Degree Information

Graduate entrants to training schemes can be from any discipline, but a degree in media studies, performing arts, photography or media production may be an advantage. Evidence of interest in camera work and drama is important and a portfolio of student and amateur work may be required.

Adult Qualifications

Entry requirements may be relaxed for adults applying for higher education courses. Access or foundation courses give adults without qualifications a route on to degree courses.

Work Experience

Entry to this job/career is highly competitive and it essential that you have some relevant work or voluntary experience before applying. Television companies/independent camera operators, are obviously the first point of contact. Sky offers work placements for young people through their 'Reach for the Sky' programme. The BBC also offer work experience placements, but you need to apply well in advance.

There are other areas, such as still photography, or gaining knowledge and experience of lighting techniques, perhaps during full-time education or with a local amateur dramatic society. Much of the work is freelance so it is useful to build a portfolio of work/ contacts for future reference.

Entry and Training

There are no set entry requirements for this job, but as it is highly competitive as many entrants already have qualifications ranging from relevant BTEC/SQA national/higher national awards or degrees, and a portfolio of student and amateur work. Industry experience is considered to be most important. Most entrants are over 18. A driving licence and knowledge of a second language can also be helpful. Most entrants begin work as a runner/gofer, clapper/loader or camera assistant, and work their way up to camera operator, and beyond.

New entrant training schemes are available from Skillset (the sector skills council for the audio-visual industries), Scottish Screen and Cyfle (Wales), though competition for all training places is fierce. Skillset also offer information on their website about short courses in a range of relevant subjects throughout the country.

The BBC offer training courses in camera skills, and the Guild of Camera Technicians and the National Film and Television School also offer specialised short courses. Relevant foundation degrees are available, including film and television production, which includes camera work. It is important to keep up to date with new equipment and technology.

While training and working, you may be able to gain S/NVQs. Training programmes, including apprenticeship schemes, may be available in your area. Advanced apprenticeships leading to qualification at level 3 can also be a route into higher education.

A Diploma/Welsh Baccalaureate may be available in your area in creative and media. This can be a useful introduction to this type of career as you gain practical experience while studying. See the diplomas website or Skillset for further information.

Mature entrants face the same competition for training schemes. Experience of related work or completion of a relevant practical course with some technical content is useful. Adults may be able to enter this work through a government-funded training programme. Contact your local Connexions or careers office, Next Step service, Jobcentre Plus, or Learning and Skills Council (LSC)/Local Enterprise Company (LEC) for details of all training opportunities and schemes, including adult apprenticeships.

Opportunities and Pay

There are a few permanent jobs with broadcasting companies, such as the BBC and independent television and film production companies, but camera crews usually work on a freelance basis and on short-term contracts. There is stiff competition for all places and you may have to use an agent to get work as very few jobs are advertised. Most jobs are in London and the south of England.

First jobs are always at the lowest level and promotion to more senior positions is dependent on your ability and success. You can progress to camera assistant and clapperholder jobs before becoming a camera operator. Experienced camera operators may progress to lighting camera operators or directors of photography. Those with language skills can work abroad.

Pay is low whilst training and is always uncertain if you are freelance, but starting salaries are around £14k, rising to £22k-£32k a year with considerable experience. Freelance operators are likely to earn more. Freelance rates can be negotiated according to BECTU, but are usually from £300 for a ten hour day to £2k a week for a 50 hour week, depending on experience and the type of contract.

Health

This job require good general fitness, good hearing and normal colour vision.

Skills and Qualities

able to cope under pressure, aptitude for teamwork, attention to detail, creative flair, eye for visual effect, hand-to-eye co-ordination, IT skills, patient, quick thinking, steady hand, technical aptitude

Relevant Subjects

Art and Design, Design and technology, Mathematics, Media and communication studies, Performing arts, Physics, Science

Further Information

Apprenticeship Schemes (National Apprenticeship Service) - www.apprenticeships.org.uk

Broadcast Magazine (weekly) (Emap) - www.broadcastnow.co.uk

Diplomas (Foundation, Higher and Advanced) - http://yp.direct.gov.uk/diplomas

FilmTV - www.film-tv.co.uk

How to get a job in Television: Build your career from Runner to Series Producer (Methuen 2009)

Production Base - www.productionbase.co.uk

Skillset - sector skills council for the creative media, fashion and textiles industries - www.skillset.org

Techs Magazine (6 x year) (Guild of British Camera Technicians (GBCT)) - www.gbct.org/techs-magazine

Training Schemes - www.direct.gov.uk/en/educationandlearning

Work for Sky - www.workforsky.com/

▶Working in creative & media (2007) (Babcock Lifeskills) - www.babcock-lifeskills.com/

Addresses

BBC Recruitment Services
Recruitment BBC HR Direct, PO Box 1133, Belfast BT1 9GP
Web: www.bbc.co.uk/jobs

BECTU
(Broadcasting Entertainment Cinematographic and Theatre Union)
373-377 Clapham Road, London SW9 9BT
Phone: +44 (0)207 346 0900
Web: www.bectu.org.uk

Cyfle (Wales)
Galeri 13, Victoria Dock, Caernarfon LL55 1SQ.
Phone: +44 (0) 1286 685 242
Web: www.cyfle.co.uk

Guild of British Camera Technicians (GBTC)
Metropolitan Centre, Bristol Road, Greenford, Middlesex UB6 8GD
Phone: +44 (0)20 8813 1999
Web: www.gbct.org

Guild of Television Cameramen (GTC)
1 Churchill Road, Whitchurch, Tavistock, Devon PL19 9BU
Phone: +44 (0)1822 614405
Web: www.gtc.org.uk

National Film and Television School
Beaconsfield Studios, Station Road HP9 1LG
Phone: +44 (0)1494 731 425
Web: www.nftsfilm-tv.ac.uk

Scottish Screen
249 West George Street, Glasgow G2 4QE
Phone: 0845 300 7300 (UK only)
Web: www.scottishscreen.com

Similar Jobs

Film/TV & Theatre Lighting Technician, Film/TV Runner, Film/TV/Radio & Theatre Sound Recordist, Film/Video Editor, Photographer

Film/TV Director

also known as: Film Maker

CRCI:Media, Print and Publishing
CLCI:GAL Job Band: 3 to 5

Job Description

Directors use technical, creative and organisational skills to create an overall style, look and sound of a production. They work in drama, such as TV, feature films and shorts, documentaries, commercials, current affairs, light entertainment, and corporate films in a studio or on location. Directors need to understand the technical aspects of the production, as well as everyone's role in the production team. They coordinate the activities of the cast and crew to create the overall effect of a production.

Directors are responsible for casting, script editing and shot selection. They direct the camera, sound and lighting operators, actors and designers, as well as working with the film and video editors. In post-production, they are responsible for editing to create the final product. Some duties may overlap with those of the producer and increasingly the producer/director may be one person, especially on small-scale productions.

Work Details

On a shoot, you may work long and irregular hours, including evenings and weekends. You work in a studio or on location, which can be indoors or outdoors, in a range of conditions. Travel may be necessary and you may need to spend nights away from home. You constantly liaise with colleagues. The job requires you to keep to an agreed budget and work can be pressurised.

Qualification
Employers may value knowledge of the film and TV industry, coupled with enthusiasm and experience more than academic qualifications. Those with relevant degrees still need to start at a junior level and work their way up.

• England, Wales and Northern Ireland
Band 3: For entry to jobs, HNC or a relevant Diploma, usually at least 4 GCSEs (A*-C) including English and maths, or equivalent.

Band 4: For HND, Diploma of Higher Education or foundation degree: 1-2 A levels and some GCSEs (A*-C) usually including English and maths, or equivalent.

Band 5: For degree courses: 2-3 A levels and some GCSEs (A*-C) usually including English, or equivalent qualifications. Exact requirements depend on the degree you take.

• Scotland
Band 3: For some courses: four S grades (1-3) including English, or similar qualifications. Entry requirements vary, so check with colleges.

Band 4: For entry to SQA higher national and professional development awards, usually 2-3 H grades and some S grades (1-3), including English and maths, or similar qualifications.

Band 5: For degree courses: 3-5 H grades and some S grades (1-3), usually including English, or similar. Exact requirements depend on the degree you take.

Degree Information
A degree in any discipline is acceptable, but needs to be linked to production experience.

Adult Qualifications
Mature entrants need relevant experience in broadcasting or film, though may not need the standard entry requirements for higher education courses. Previous relevant experience and an ability to study at the appropriate level is desirable. Access or foundation courses give adults without qualifications a route onto degree courses.

Work Experience
Entry to this job/career is highly competitive and it is essential you have some relevant work or voluntary experience before applying. Colleges/universities may also prefer candidates with some direct practical or technical experience. Television, theatre, film companies and studios, such as Pinewood, are the first contacts to gain direct experience in a variety of aspects of film and TV work. Voluntary amateur dramatics experience is also an advantage.

Entry and Training
Directors often start in other production jobs, such as a researcher or production assistant, or develop technical skills, including camera work or editing experience. Some may even begin as a runner/gofer, an entry level job for the industry, and work towards their eventual goal as a director. Some may spend time at a film school prior to entry and develop a showreel of their work. Many have higher qualifications, including degrees, although this is not a formal requirement. Even those with degrees need to start at a junior level and work their way up.

Some relevant experience through school, college or university activities, as well as technical skills, may be useful for gaining a first post. Media-related subjects give applicants a greater understanding of the industry. Attendance at film festivals is a good way of making contacts and often offers opportunities to attend high level workshops.

Training is often practical and on the job, but some employers offer structured training programmes. Training providers for the film and TV industry include: Skillset Careers and Cyfle (Wales). Skillset have established six screen academies throughout the UK which offer postgraduate courses and also short courses for continuing professional development. Contact these organisations, and others listed in the further information section, for details on suitable courses and training programmes.

A Diploma/Welsh Baccalaureate may be available in your area in creative and media. This can be a useful introduction to this type of career as you gain practical experience while studying. See the diplomas website or Skillset for further information.

Mature applicants should be aware that this is a relatively young industry and it may be difficult to enter this career in later years, unless with considerable talent and energy. However, many ambitious film directors initiate their original projects with an aim to get them into production, though probably require independent funding. You should contact the regional screen agencies and organisations that include the UK Film Council for any funding opportunities for film projects or courses. Skillset Careers also has details of opportunities for directors.

Opportunities and Pay
Employers include terrestrial television, cable and satellite broadcasting companies or independent production companies. You can also work for well known feature film companies or independent film and video companies. Work can include advertisements, short films and documentaries. Directors may be permanent or contract employees or, increasingly, freelancers.

Many companies are based in London, although some are based elsewhere in the UK. There is a concentration of animation work in south-west England. Entry is extremely competitive, and candidates may need to move area to find work. However, opportunities are increasing for freelance work, particularly with independent film production companies and cable and satellite broadcasters.

Pay varies enormously and is hard to establish. BECTU may be able to give you information on the likely range of salaries. Many film directors agree to work at first for little, on the understanding that they receive a share of the profits, though films can often be unprofitable. Income can therefore be very variable. The most successful directors at the top of the industry can earn more than £200k a year.

Skills and Qualities
able to cope under pressure, able to get on with all kinds of people, able to motivate others, able to withstand criticism, creative flair, good communication skills, good organisational skills, health & safety awareness, imaginative, motivated, perceptive, technical aptitude

Relevant Subjects
Art and Design, English, Media and communication studies, Music, Performing arts

Further Information
Behind the Scenes: Film (Trotman 2009) - www.trotman.co.uk

British Film Institute (BFI) - www.bfi.org.uk

Broadcasting Entertainment Cinematographic and Theatre Union (BECTU) - www.bectu.org.uk

Cyfle (Wales) - www.cyfle.co.uk

Diplomas (Foundation, Higher and Advanced) http://yp.direct.gov.uk/diplomas

Film Ireland (Film Ireland Online) - www.filmireland.net

Getting into Films and Television (How to books 2009)

How to get a job in Television: Build your career from Runner to Series Producer (Methuen 2009)

Media/Multimedia Courses Directory (BFI/Skillset) - www.bfi.org.uk/education/talkscourses/mediacourses/

Northern Ireland Screen (Northern Ireland Screen) - www.northernirelandscreen.co.uk

Shooting People (Independent Filmmakers Network) (Independent Filmmakers Network) - www.shootingpeople.org

Skillset - sector skills council for the creative media, fashion and textiles industries - www.skillset.org

Addresses

Directors Guild of Great Britain (DGGB)
4 Windmill Street, London W1T 2HZ
Phone: +44 (0)20 7580 9131
Web: www.dggb.org

Pinewood Studios
Pinewood Road, Iver Heath, Buckinghamshire SL0 0NH
Phone: +44 (0)1753 651700
Web: www.pinewoodgroup.com

UK Film Council
10 Little Portland Street, London W1W 7JG
Phone: +44 (0)207 861 7861
Web: www.ukfilmcouncil.org.uk

Similar Jobs

Animator, Broadcast Researcher, Film/TV Floor Manager, Film/TV Producer, Film/TV Producer's Assistant, Theatre Stage Manager

Film/TV Floor Manager

also known as: Film/TV Assistant Director, Studio Manager: Radio

CRCI:Media, Print and Publishing
CLCI:GAL Job Band: 2 to 5

Job Description

Floor managers are responsible for coordinating activity on a studio floor for film/TV productions. They set up the studio and liaise with sound and camera crews to ensure satisfactory performance, by carrying out necessary pre-recording checks. Also arrange scenery and props, and the cueing of sound effects. May mark the floor plans for scenery and cue the actors. Also organise the people taking part, including presenters, any guests and musicians. In radio, a studio manager is responsible for controlling the sound in the studio or on location, especially for drama and music programs.

May also act as stage manager during rehearsals. If a studio audience is present, they take responsibility for their safety and their participation in the programme. May also be involved in outside broadcasts.

Work Details

Floor/studio managers have to work long and irregular hours, including evenings and weekends, to fit in with programmes and studio bookings. They pass on instructions from the director in the control room to the performers and audience in the studio and are responsible for studio discipline and everyone's safety. Sometimes you have to look after performers who may be nervous, so you need tact and patience. You are on your feet most of the time and wear headphones when in contact with the director. Working on location may mean spending time away from home.

Qualification

- **England, Wales and Northern Ireland**

Band 3: For entry to jobs, HNC or a relevant Diploma, usually at least 4 GCSEs (A*-C) including English and maths, or equivalent.

Band 4: For HND, Diploma of Higher Education or foundation degree: 1-2 A levels and some GCSEs (A*-C) usually including English and maths, or equivalent.

Band 5: For degree courses: 2-3 A levels and some GCSEs (A*-C) usually including English, or equivalent qualifications. Exact requirements depend on the degree you take.

- **Scotland**

Band 3: For entry: usually four S grades (1-3) preferably including English, or similar.

Band 4: For entry to SQA higher national and professional development awards, usually 2-3 H grades and some S grades (1-3), including English and maths, or similar qualifications.

Band 5: For degree courses: 3-5 H grades and some S grades (1-3), usually including English or similar. Exact requirements depend on the degree you take.

Degree Information

No specific degree is required, although some courses such as media studies, photography/TV/film, or drama/theatre studies, may give relevant experience and knowledge. Check course content and employment prospects before accepting a place on a course.

Adult Qualifications

Some further education and degree courses are open to mature students without qualifications, but who have relevant experience. Access or foundation courses give adults without qualifications a route onto degree courses.

Work Experience

Entry to this job/career is highly competitive and it is essential you have some relevant work or voluntary experience before applying. The BBC offers work experience placements and career information days. Colleges/universities may prefer candidates with some direct practical experience of drama and theatre. TV, theatre, film companies and studios are the most likely source of work experience in the first instance.

Entry and Training

To enter this job you need some broadcasting technical experience. People have often achieved this by starting in the industry as a runner, assistant floor manager, or in a technical role in sound and lighting. However, entrants are increasingly graduates. There are a few media courses that give you the skills to enter the industry as a trainee studio/floor manager. Training providers for the film and TV industry include: Skillset, Cyfle (together with Broadcast Training Wales) and Scottish Screen.

There are also a few special training schemes for this job run by employers, such as the BBC, but entry to these is highly competitive. The Media Courses and Multimedia Courses Directory, produced by Skillset and the British Film Institute, has details of a very wide range of film and television courses throughout the UK. After training most tend to specialise in one area of broadcasting, such as music or sports programmes. An S/NVQ in production for television is available at level 3.

A Diploma/Welsh Baccalaureate may be available in your area in creative and media. This can be a useful introduction to this type of career as you gain practical experience while studying. See the diplomas website or Skillset for further information.

The normal pattern is to start work as an assistant floor manager. Mature entry to this job is more likely for those who have previous experience in theatre stage management or broadcasting.

Opportunities and Pay

You may be employed by a film/TV or network radio company and competition for new entrants is intense. There are fewer permanent staff working for these companies now and many work on a freelance basis. Temporary short-term contracts are common. Over half of the jobs in this industry are in London and south-east England, but there are opportunities in other parts of the UK. There may be opportunities to work overseas, particularly in film. Promotion to management level from junior jobs is possible, but depends on merit and available vacancies, which are few.

Pay varies depending on type of employer and level of responsibility, but starting salaries are likely to be around £14k-£20k, rising to £25k-£40k a year, with experience. Some may earn much more. If working freelance, you can earn around £150 a day.

Health
This job requires good general fitness, good hearing and colour vision.

Skills and Qualities
able to manage people, calm, efficient, flexible and adaptable, good communication skills, problem-solving skills, quick thinking, responsible attitude, self confident, stamina, tactful, technical aptitude

Relevant Subjects
Art and Design, Design and technology, English, Media and communication studies, Music, Performing arts

Further Information
Behind the Scenes: Film (Trotman 2009) - www.trotman.co.uk

British Film Institute (BFI) - www.bfi.org.uk

Broadcast Magazine (weekly) (Emap) - www.broadcastnow.co.uk

Cyfle (Wales) - www.cyfle.co.uk

Diplomas (Foundation, Higher and Advanced) - http://yp.direct.gov.uk/diplomas

How to get a job in Television: Build your career from Runner to Series Producer (Methuen 2000)

ITV Jobs (ITV) - www.itvjobs.com

ITV Jobs (ITV) - www.itvjobs.com

Media/Multimedia Courses Directory (BFI/Skillset) - www.bfi.org.uk/education/talkscourses/mediacourses/

Skillset - sector skills council for the creative media, fashion and textiles industries - www.skillset.org

▶Working in creative & media (2007) (Babcock Lifeskills) - www.babcock-lifeskills.com/

Addresses
BBC Recruitment Services
Recruitment BBC HR Direct, PO Box 1133, Belfast BT1 9GP
Web: www.bbc.co.uk/jobs

Scottish Screen
249 West George Street, Glasgow G2 4QE
Phone: 0845 300 7300 (UK only)
Web: www.scottishscreen.com

Similar Jobs
Art Exhibitions Organiser, Event & Exhibition Organiser, Film/TV Producer, Film/TV Producer's Assistant, Theatre Producer, Theatre Stage Manager

Film/TV Producer
also known as: Radio Producer

CRCI:Media, Print and Publishing

CLCI:GAL Job Band: 4 to 5

Job Description
Producers are responsible for the content and overall quality of a production in the TV, film, radio and video industries. They are often the creator of an idea for a suitable project and oversee the production until completion. May be involved in raising funding for the project. Also coordinate and supervise all the necessary arrangements, including casting of actors, costumes, music, sets, technical effects, and all those associated with each production. Producers are also involved in marketing the project, as well as arranging the budget.

They work with a team of experts who combine their talents to create the desired effect. This includes arranging rehearsals and adapting the production/performance to suit their interpretation of the theme. Must ensure the project is completed on time and within budget.

Work Details
Hours are irregular, including evenings and weekends, often working to deadlines. Producers work closely with directors, professional and technical personnel and are supported by production assistants, managers and coordinators. Work may be pressurised at times and may involve making difficult decisions. Your casting decisions may not always be popular. Travel may be necessary, sometimes abroad, and you may need to spend nights away from home.

Qualification
- **England, Wales and Northern Ireland**

Band 4: For HND, Diploma of Higher Education or foundation degree: 1-2 A levels and some GCSEs (A*-C) usually including English and maths, or equivalent.

Band 5: For degree courses: 2-3 A levels and some GCSEs (A*-C) usually including English, or equivalent qualifications. Exact requirements depend on the degree you take.

- **Scotland**

Band 4: For entry to SQA higher national and professional development awards, usually 2-3 H grades and some S grades (1-3), including English and maths, or similar qualifications.

Band 5: For degree courses: 3-5 H grades and some S grades (1-3), usually including English, or similar. Exact requirements depend on the degree you take.

Degree Information
Any degree discipline is acceptable for entry to this job, but subjects such as media, multimedia and communication studies, broadcasting, information technology, film/television production and photography are useful.

Adult Qualifications
Entry requirements may be relaxed for adults applying for higher education courses and Access or foundation courses give adults without qualifications a route on to degree courses.

Work Experience
Entry to this career is highly competitive and it is essential you have some relevant work or voluntary experience before applying. Any experience gained in drama or broadcasting is relevant, as is time spent with a national/regional television company, or a large or independent film company. Even work for a hospital or student radio station is useful. Attendance at film festivals is a good way of making contacts and may offer the chance to attend specialist workshops.

Entry and Training
Entrants are often graduates, though employers also look for experience, ability and commitment, such as previous work gained in drama, or in broadcasting. Work experience in the creative or business side of film or programme making is useful, and you should build up a portfolio to show what you have achieved. Those with transferable skills gained in a first degree, such as media productions, finance, law or languages, should seek practical production and training experience. Most producers, even those with degrees, start in a junior post and work their way up.

Many begin their career as a runner and work their way up to the job whilst gaining valuable experience. Producers of factual programmes often start as researchers or journalists. It is important to gain as much experience as you can, in all areas of the job, including editing and directing skills. Training is often practical and on the job, but some employers offer structured training programmes, including short courses. The Media Courses and Multimedia Courses Directory produced by the British Film Institute and Skillset has a list of relevant courses in the industry.

The BBC run a training scheme, though there is fierce competition for places, and some independent TV companies also have graduate training schemes. Training providers for the film and TV industry include: Skillset, Scottish Screen, and Cyfle (Wales).

Postgraduate qualifications are not required for entry but may increase your chance of success in such a competitive industry. Choose a course carefully to ensure the content equips you with the necessary high quality technical skills and personal contacts. Appropriate S/NVQs at levels 3-4 may also be available.

A Diploma/Welsh Baccalaureate may be available in your area in creative and media. This can be a useful introduction to this type of career as you gain practical experience while studying. See the diplomas website or Skillset for further information.

Mature entry is possible for those with considerable experience in a related field.

Opportunities and Pay

18,000 people work in film and TV production in the UK. Half of the jobs in film and television production are in London, but Manchester and Edinburgh have seen growth in this sector. You may be employed by a national/regional, or independent broadcaster or smaller film company. Opportunities in the cable and satellite sector are growing but there is stiff competition for all places. Over 40% of producers are freelance, working on short-term contracts covering the period of one production. You need to approach film and television companies direct as very few vacancies are advertised. Since it is possible to work your way up, it is worth considering any job in this industry. The film industry offers a particularly structured promotion route from co-producer to line producer to associate producer, before becoming a producer.

Pay varies depending on location and the media in which you work. Trainees earn from around £14k-£16k. Producers can earn between £18k and £70k a year. Successful freelance producers can earn much more.

Skills and Qualities

able to cope under pressure, able to work to a budget, creative flair, good communication skills, good interpersonal skills, good organisational skills, motivated, negotiating skills, persuasive, project management skills, time management skills

Relevant Subjects

Art and Design, Business and accounting, English, Media and communication studies, Music, Performing arts

Further Information

Behind the Scenes: Film (Trotman 2009) - www.trotman.co.uk

British Film Institute (BFI) - www.bfi.org.uk

Broadcast Magazine (weekly) (Emap) - www.broadcastnow.co.uk

Cyfle (Wales) - www.cyfle.co.uk

Diplomas (Foundation, Higher and Advanced) - http://yp.direct.gov.uk/diplomas

How to get a job in Television: Build your career from Runner to Series Producer (Methuen 2009)

Media/Multimedia Courses Directory (BFI/Skillset) - www.bfi.org.uk/education/talkscourses/mediacourses/

Northern Ireland Screen (Northern Ireland Screen) - www.northernirelandscreen.co.uk

Skillset - sector skills council for the creative media, fashion and textiles industries - www.skillset.org

►Working in creative & media (2007) (Babcock Lifeskills) - www.babcock-lifeskills.com/

►Working in sport & leisure (2010) (Babcock Lifeskills) - www.babcock-lifeskills.com/

Addresses

BBC Recruitment Services
Recruitment BBC HR Direct, PO Box 1133, Belfast BT1 9GP
Web: www.bbc.co.uk/jobs

Producers Alliance for Cinema and Television (PACT)
3rd Floor Fitzrovia House, 153-157 Cleveland St, London W1T 6QW
Phone: +44 (0)20 7380 8230
Web: www.pact.co.uk

Production Guild
N&P Complex, Pinewood Studios, Iver Heath, Buckinghamshire SL0 0NH
Phone: +44 (0)1753 651 767
Web: www.productionguild.com

Scottish Screen
249 West George Street, Glasgow G2 4QE
Phone: 0845 300 7300 (UK only)
Web: www.scottishscreen.com

Similar Jobs

Broadcast Journalist, Film/TV Director, Film/TV Floor Manager, Film/TV Producer's Assistant, Theatre Producer, Theatre Stage Manager

Film/TV Producer's Assistant

CRCI:Media, Print and Publishing
CLCI:GAL
Job Band: 3 to 5

Job Description

Producer's assistants provides administrative support to a producer and director in the film or TV production office and on location. They work on multi-camera productions, single camera productions, outside broadcast units as well as in studio galleries, and are usually involved in the entire production process from first draft scripts to the final delivery of production paperwork and product. Duties are wide and varied, but include booking studios and technical crews, arranging meetings, word processing tasks, and circulating scripts and production schedules.

Assistants keep records of the scenes filmed and ensure good continuity. They are responsible for accurately timing the script, often to the split second, and for keeping everything up to schedule. May handle the budget for a production and deal with artist payments and expenses. Also liaise between the producer and post-production team.

Work Details

You work in a studio or out on location assisting the producer and need to travel to meetings, and make arrangements for the production. Work involves irregular and long hours. You work as part of a team including producers, researchers and technical staff. You organise technical crew, performers, guests and ancillary staff, and spend time in an office typing minutes and scripts, using a computer and phoning to make any arrangements. Work may be pressurised and demanding in a fast-paced environment.

Qualification

• England, Wales and Northern Ireland

Band 3: For entry to jobs, HNC or a relevant Diploma, usually at least 4 GCSEs (A*-C) including English and maths, or equivalent.

Band 4: For HND, Diploma of Higher Education or foundation degree: 1-2 A levels and some GCSEs (A*-C) usually including English and maths, or equivalent.

Band 5: For degree courses: 2-3 A levels and some GCSEs (A*-C) usually including English or equivalent qualifications. Exact requirements depend on the degree you take.

• Scotland

Band 3: For entry to a relevant course: usually at least four S grades (1-3) including English, or similar qualifications.

Band 4: For entry to SQA higher national and professional development awards, usually 2-3 H grades and some S grades (1-3), including English and maths, or similar qualifications.

Band 5: For degree courses: 3-5 H grades and some S grades (1-3), usually including English, or similar. Exact requirements depend on the degree you take.

Degree Information
Any degree discipline is acceptable, though film studies and English are particularly useful.

Adult Qualifications
Entry is more likely if you have good experience as a secretary, plus related media experience working in radio, TV or films/videos. Entry requirements may be relaxed for adults applying for higher education courses. Access or foundation courses give adults without qualifications a route on to degree courses.

Work Experience
Entry to this job/career is highly competitive and it is essential to have some relevant work or voluntary experience before applying. Television and theatre companies and independent camera/film production companies are the first point of contact for gaining knowledge and work experience. Many companies, from small production companies to large concerns such as the BBC and independent broadcasting companies, offer unpaid short-term placements, ranging from a few days to around four weeks. It is an advantage to have wide experience of working in local amateur productions and in student productions.

Entry and Training
A keen interest and experience in current affairs, TV, films or drama is essential. Increasingly, there is a demand for graduates, though entry without an HND/degree is possible. Those with a range of qualifications or skills, including desktop publishing, databases and spreadsheets have an advantage. Ideally, you need a good shorthand speed (100 wpm) and good typing speed (40 wpm). It may be an advantage to have experience in administration or journalism. Many develop their skills by working in a junior assistant post, gaining the required experience through a range of tasks. Others may enter as a secretary in the production office.

A course in film, video or media production may be useful. Training providers in the industry include Skillset, Scottish Screen and Cyfle (Wales). The Media Courses Directory produced by the British Film Institute and Skillset contains information on a wide range of media related courses.

A Diploma/Welsh Baccalaureate may be available in your area in creative and media. This can be a useful introduction to this type of career as you gain practical experience while studying. See the diplomas website or Skillset for further information.

Adult entry is more likely if you have good experience as a secretary, plus related media experience working in TV, films/videos, and also in radio and journalism.

Opportunities and Pay
Jobs are more likely to be based in major cities. Half of the jobs in this industry are based in London and south-east England, but there are opportunities in other major cities. This area is highly competitive, but you may be able to work your way up, so it is worth considering any job in this field. Many producer's assistant jobs are filled from within the organisation and promotion from secretarial or clerical grades is common. You are usually employed by a TV broadcasting company, an independent film or TV production company. There are opportunities with companies that produce music DVDs/videos, commercials, or corporate videos. You may work freelance and be employed on short-term contracts.

Producer's assistants can progress to more complex and costly programmes such as drama productions. In major companies you may be promoted to senior producer's assistant. Further moves may be to floor manager, researcher or vision mixer.

Pay varies depending on location and the area of your work. Trainees earn around £15k, and with experience, around £18k-£25k a year. Some may earn over £30k as a senior producer's assistant.

Skills and Qualities
calm, clear-thinking, common sense, co-operative, efficient, good communication skills, good interpersonal skills, good memory, good organisational skills, IT skills, versatile

Relevant Subjects
English, ICT/Computer studies, Media and communication studies, Performing arts

Further Information
Behind the Scenes: Film (Trotman 2009) - www.trotman.co.uk
British Film Institute (BFI) - www.bfi.org.uk

Broadcast Magazine (weekly) (Emap) - www.broadcastnow.co.uk

Cyfle (Wales) - www.cyfle.co.uk

Diplomas (Foundation, Higher and Advanced) - http://yp.direct.gov.uk/diplomas

Media/Multimedia Courses Directory (BFI/Skillset) - www.bfi.org.uk/education/talkscourses/mediacourses/

Skillset - sector skills council for the creative media, fashion and textiles industries - www.skillset.org

▶ Working in creative & media (2007) (Babcock Lifeskills) - www.babcock-lifeskills.com/

Addresses
BBC Recruitment Services
Recruitment BBC HR Direct, PO Box 1133, Belfast BT1 9GP
Web: www.bbc.co.uk/jobs

Scottish Screen
249 West George Street, Glasgow G2 4QE
Phone: 0845 300 7300 (UK only)
Web: www.scottishscreen.com

Similar Jobs
Broadcast Journalist, Broadcast Researcher, Film/TV Producer, Film/TV Runner, Film/Video Editor, Personal Assistant

Film/TV Props Manager
also known as: Film/TV Property Master, Props Manager
CRCI:Media, Print and Publishing
CLCI:GAL Job Band: 3

Job Description
Props managers work in the television or film industry and are responsible for all the items used during the production, such as furniture, documents, books, weapons, vehicles, etc., known as props. They work with the production designer, deciding what props are needed and whether these need to be hired, purchased or made specially for the production. Also organise the supply of all props needed, researching appropriate sources, and keeping costs within an agreed budget. They ensure that all props used are authentic to the style of the production. Sometimes props managers may be involved in the adaption or repair of items, so some craft skills can be an advantage.

During production, they makes sure that all props needed are in the right place at the right time, arranging transport and storage when needed. After production, they organise the return of hired props and the storage of the rest for future productions. Also maintain detailed records of props stored and of sources for specialist equipment for future reference.

Work Details
Work a basic 39-40 hr week, but hours may be irregular, especially during a production. At times it may be necessary to work evenings and weekends to complete the work of supplying the

props in time for a production to start. You liaise regularly with production designers and other members of the production team, both during the planning stages and in production. The work can be pressurised at times, particularly if dealing with requests for items at short notice. A driving licence is often needed.

You are based mainly in an office as much of the work involves research and administration. At times you may need to be on set, and there can be some physical lifting and carrying involved.

Qualification

• England, Wales and Northern Ireland

Band 3: For entry: usually at least 4 GCSEs (A*-C) including English and maths, or equivalent.

• Scotland

Band 3: For entry: usually at least four S grades (1-3) including English and maths, or similar.

Adult Qualifications

Entry requirements may be relaxed for adults applying for higher education courses. Access or foundation courses provide those without the required qualifications a route onto degree courses. A background in art and design including craft skills is useful.

Work Experience

Entry to this job is competitive. It is important that you try to do some relevant work or voluntary experience before applying. Any practical experience in school/college or amateur plays and performances, including front of house duties, or editorial production of programmes etc, is very useful.

Entry and Training

Props managers usually start as trainees in the property department of a film or television company, and it is possible to enter the industry after taking your A Levels. This is a very competitive industry and those with a background in art and design, a knowledge of craft skills and of technical drawing have an advantage. A full driving licence is usually essential.

You usually start as a props storeperson and work your way up through dressing props, standby props, assistant property master to property master. You work under the supervision of experienced property staff and learn principally on the job, although you may also attend short industry-specific courses.

Training providers for the film and TV industry include: Skillset Careers, FT2 and Cyfle (Wales). Skillset have established six screen academies throughout the UK which offer postgraduate courses and also short courses for continuing professional development (CPD). Contact these organisations, and others listed in the further information section, for details on suitable courses and training programmes.

The central school of speech and drama at the University of London run a three year degree in theatre practice covering costume and prop construction. Stage management courses may also cover props management. For example, the Academy of Live and Recorded Arts (ALRA) offer a two year stage management and technical theatre foundation degree which has a module on prop making and sourcing.

A Diploma/Welsh Baccalaureate may be available in your area in creative and media. This can be a useful introduction to this type of career as you gain practical experience while studying. See the diplomas website or Skillset for further information.

Mature entrants find it easier to enter this work if they have relevant experience in film or television, good craft skills, and also have administration and research skills.

Opportunities and Pay

Employers include terrestrial television, cable and satellite broadcasting companies, independent production companies and feature film companies. Property masters may be permanent or contract employees or, increasingly, freelance. Entry is extremely competitive, and candidates may need to move area to find work. There may be opportunities to work abroad.

Pay varies enormously and is hard to establish. Props managers are likely to earn around £40k a year.

Health

You need to be physically fit for this work as it can involve lifting and carrying large items.

Skills and Qualities

able to cope under pressure, able to work both on your own and in a team, attention to detail, creative and imaginative flair, good communication skills, good organisational skills, IT skills, leadership qualities, manual dexterity, research skills, resourceful, time management skills

Relevant Subjects

Art and Design, Design and technology, English, History, Media and communication studies, Performing arts

Further Information

Behind the Scenes: Film (Trotman 2009) - www.trotman.co.uk

British Film Institute (BFI) - www.bfi.org.uk

Diplomas (Foundation, Higher and Advanced) - http://yp.direct.gov.uk/diplomas

Kays - www.kays.co.uk

Northern Ireland Screen (Northern Ireland Screen) - www.northernirelandscreen.co.uk

Skillset - sector skills council for the creative media, fashion and textiles industries - www.skillset.org

▶Working in creative & media (2007) (Babcock Lifeskills) - www.babcock-lifeskills.com/

Addresses

Academy of Live and Recorded Arts (ALRA)
Studio One Royal Victoria Patriotic Building John Archer Way, London SW18 3SX
Phone: 00 44 (0)208 875 0789
Web: www.alra.co.uk/

Cyfle (Wales)
Galeri 13, Victoria Dock, Caernarfon LL55 1SQ.
Phone: +44 (0) 1286 685 242
Web: www.cyfle.co.uk

University of London
Information Centre Stewart House 32 Russell Square, London WC1B 5DN
Phone: +44 (0)20 7862 8360
Web: www.londonexternal.ac.uk

Similar Jobs

Film/TV & Theatre Set/Stage Designer, Film/TV Director, Film/TV Floor Manager, Film/TV Location Manager, Film/TV Runner

Film/TV Runner

also known as: Film/TV Gofer, Film/TV Production Assistant

CRCI:Media, Print and Publishing
CLCI:GAL Job Band: 4 to 5

Job Description

Runners are the most junior of a film/TV production team, and carry out a range of tasks to assist more highly skilled professionals. They work in a team of runners, in areas such as the art department, production office, on set (floor runner), as a camera and sound runner, or in the editing suite. Tasks are varied and may include doing basic research, transcribing production tapes, hiring props and helping to set up a location, taking and delivering messages, delivering packages and scripts and crowd control.

Runners also meet and greet guests, transport people between locations and studios, order lunch, and make tea and coffee throughout the working day. May do some administrative tasks such as sorting out the mail, photocopying and filing, dealing with routine correspondence, and answering the telephone.

Work Details

You may be working in a studio, on location in the UK or overseas, or in an office. When not on production, you may work normal office hours, but work often involves long hours, including nights and weekends. As broadcasting is a 24 hr operation, you may work up to six days a week at times, including public holidays. You may have to be on your feet for long periods of time, as this is a fast-moving and pressurised, though stimulating industry.

Qualification

Whilst formal qualifications are not specified for this job, realistically, entrants usually have a higher education qualification.

- **England, Wales and Northern Ireland**

Band 4: For HND, Diploma of Higher Education or foundation degree: 1-2 A levels and some GCSEs (A*-C) usually including English and maths, or equivalent.

Band 5: For degree courses: 2-3 A levels and some GCSEs (A*-C) usually including English and maths, or equivalent. Exact requirements depend on the degree you take.

- **Scotland**

Band 4: For entry to SQA higher national and professional development awards, usually 2-3 H grades and some S grades (1-3), including English and maths, or similar qualifications.

Band 5: For degree courses: 3-5 H grades and some S grades (1-3), usually including English or similar. Exact requirements depend on the degree you take.

Degree Information

Any degree discipline is acceptable, though performing arts, music, theatre/drama studies and media studies give useful background, as well as specific subjects, such as history and English (useful for research) and technical subjects.

Adult Qualifications

Entry requirements may be relaxed for adults who apply for higher education courses. Access or foundation courses give adults without qualifications a route into degree courses.

Work Experience

Some relevant experience, through school, college or university plays and performances, including front-of-house duties, as well as office skills, is useful for gaining a first post, or for entry to a higher education course. Companies such as the BBC and other major broadcasters, have work experience schemes that last for up to four weeks. Enthusiasm and motivation in a work placement can demonstrate your commitment to this area of work and may lead to a positive impression on prospective future employers.

In choosing a university or college for higher education, it is helpful if you choose one with its own television or radio station. Attendance at film festivals is often a good place to make good contacts or attend relevant specialist workshops.

Entry and Training

This work is traditionally seen as an entry level job into the production side of the broadcasting industry and also acts as a potential springboard to a media career. Whilst formal educational qualifications are seldom specified, most entrants have a degree (or a minimum of at least A levels/H grades), or even postgraduate qualifications, and are looking for an entry route into a highly competitive industry. Secretarial and IT skills are usually looked for, together with a driving licence. Catering experience and first aid qualifications may also be useful.

Training is usually practical, and is quickly acquired and applied through observation, instead of a specific on-the-job training programme. You are expected to handle your own continuing development in the area of film/TV that best suits you. Many runners see their career in areas such as editing, producing or directing, and enrol on courses to increase their specific knowledge and skills. Some large employers may give financial support towards job-specific qualifications.

Skillset works throughout the UK to promote skills in this sector. They also offer a range of short and continuing professional development courses. Check the website for details. The National Film and Television School runs masters courses and offers maintenance bursaries and scholarships depending on individual need.

A Diploma/Welsh Baccalaureate may be available in your area in creative and media. This can be a useful introduction to this type of career as you gain practical experience while studying. See the diplomas website or Skillset for further information. Cyfle (Wales) also offers a range of training courses for new entrants to the industry and professional development for those already employed.

Adult entrants to this job are rarely above the age of 30 as this is a young industry. You should be aware of the initial low salary for this job as it is regarded as a first step into the industry, regardless of qualifications and experience.

Opportunities and Pay

Around 2,000 people are employed as runners in the UK by TV, film and video production companies or post-production companies. Often the job may be combined with that of a junior researcher, which is likely to attract graduates. Competition for jobs is fierce. The majority of companies are based in London with some based in Cardiff, Manchester, Birmingham and Glasgow. Very few jobs are advertised and you need to be proactive in finding a job, sending your CV to production companies and trying to build up a network of contacts.

You usually spend two years as a runner before progressing into posts like producer's assistant or researcher. There is no guarantee of promotion or progression, but work as a runner gives an insight into the industry and provides useful contacts.

Runners are not well paid as this is a job to gain experience, so starting salaries are around £10k-£12k a year, rising to £16k. Some head runners may earn up to £20k a year, depending on additional responsibilities. A high percentage are employed on a freelance basis.

Health

This job requires good general fitness.

Skills and Qualities

able to cope under pressure, able to get on with all kinds of people, aptitude for teamwork, energetic, enthusiastic, flexible approach, good organisational skills, good spoken communication, good written English, IT skills, punctual, willing to learn

Relevant Subjects

English, ICT/Computer studies, Media and communication studies, Performing arts

Further Information

Behind the Scenes: Film (Trotman 2009) - www.trotman.co.uk

Broadcast Magazine (weekly) (Emap) - www.broadcastnow.co.uk

Cyfle (Wales) - www.cyfle.co.uk

Diplomas (Foundation, Higher and Advanced) - http://yp.direct.gov.uk/diplomas

How to get a job in Television: Build your career from Runner to Series Producer (Methuen 2009)

Media/Multimedia Courses Directory (BFI/Skillset) - www.bfi.org.uk/education/talkscourses/mediacourses/

Scottish Screen (Scottish Screen) - www.scottishscreen.com

Skillset - sector skills council for the creative media, fashion and textiles industries - www.skillset.org

So you want to work in Film & TV (Wayland) - www.waylandbooks.co.uk

Stage Management - A Career Guide (SMA) (SMA) - www.stagemanagementassociation.co.uk/pdf/2005%20Career%20Guide.pdf

The Stage Online - www.thestage.co.uk

▶Working in creative & media (2007) (Babcock Lifeskills) - www.babcock-lifeskills.com/

Addresses

BBC Recruitment Services
Recruitment BBC HR Direct, PO Box 1133, Belfast BT1 9GP
Web: www.bbc.co.uk/jobs

National Film and Television School
Beaconsfield Studios, Station Road HP9 1LG
Phone: +44 (0)1494 731 425
Web: www.nftsfilm-tv.ac.uk

Similar Jobs

Broadcast Researcher, Film/TV & Theatre Wardrobe Assistant, Film/TV Producer's Assistant, Film/Video Editor, Roadie

Film/TV Stunt Performer

also known as: Stunt Performer & Arranger

CRCI:Performing Arts
CLCI:GAB Job Band: 1 to 4

Job Description

Stunt performers are highly trained and qualified professionals who act as a stand-in/double for actors in films and TV, performing in dangerous or risky scenes. They may do a variety of stunts such as fight with weapons, fall from heights, crash cars and other vehicles, or be set on fire. Stunt performers are required to have a range of acquired skills, including acting, parachuting, driving, gymnastics, swimming and diving, martial arts and horse riding.

They carry out meticulous research to perform a stunt safely. Then duplicate as closely as possible the actor's appearance and body language so that the stunt can fit easily into the overall production. Performers are responsible for their own safety and also for that of others on the production team. They keep accurate and comprehensive records of each stunt and copies of risk assessments. Also prepare and check any equipment and safety measures before carrying out a stunt.

Work Details

Working hours are variable depending on the production, but days can be long when filming starts. You often need to be on set early for wardrobe and make-up sessions. The work may demand evenings and weekends during filming. You work in a studio or on location. Travel is necessary and you may need to spend nights away from home. There is a high risk of injury and it is important that you do not endanger other people's lives as well as your own, so safety is important. This work is dangerous and a responsible attitude to the job is essential.

Work is very physically demanding and highly pressured. You have to cope with all kinds of obstacles and use considerable physical effort. You may have to wear protective clothing, including safety harnesses and a helmet.

Qualification

There are no specific academic requirements for this job. However, you are expected to have high-level proficiency qualifications in at least six sporting and skill areas, one of which must be either boxing or martial arts.

Adult Qualifications

Adults are not required to have academic qualifications, though high-level proficiency qualifications are expected in at least six sporting and skill areas, one of which must be boxing or martial arts.

Work Experience

Entry to this job is very competitive. It is important to do some relevant work or voluntary experience before applying. Any experience of being involved in drama productions and filming helps, as does considerable background in a range of physical sports.

Entry and Training

To enter this work you must be at least 18 and meet the requirements of the Stunt Register administered by the Joint Industry Stunt Committee (JISC) of Equity, the BBC, ITV and the Producers Alliance for Cinema and TV. Entrants must provide evidence of reaching a required standard and have at least one years' experience in six or more categories from four of the five stunt groups (which are fighting, falling, riding and driving, agility and strength and water). You also need experience of drama, usually amounting to 60 days work in front of a camera.

Once on the register, you start as a probationary member, performing stunts under supervision. After a minimum of three years as a probationary member, you can become an intermediate member, and after a further two years a full member. This enables you to act as a stunt coordinator and supervise other stunts. Check the Skillset website for more details.

There are no specific training colleges or courses to prepare you for stunt work. There are some private stunt schools which offer training in certain stunts, but these are expensive and you need to ensure they meet the needs of the JISC.

A Diploma/Welsh Baccalaureate in creative and media may be available in your area. Check university entry requirements carefully in case there is an additional specialist learning requirement with the diploma. See the diplomas website for further information.

Mature entrants need exceptional skills and experience and to meet the requirements of the Stunt Register administered by the Joint Industry Stunt Committee (JISC) . This job sometimes suits ex-military personnel.

Opportunities and Pay

Around 300 people are registered as stunt performers in the UK but few are in regular work. 10-12 new entrants are admitted by the JISC to the register each year. Employers include film and television/video companies or event organisers, but this is a very small profession that is highly competitive. Employment opportunities are limited so you need to have considerable ability and talent, and a lot of luck to succeed. Employment is unlikely to be regular, so you need to have another job.

Costs are considerable and include payment of a professional subscription and insurance cover. It is worth considering any job in this field to gain experience and many stunt performers begin as actors or extras. It is anticipated that computer generated imagery (CGI) will reduce the need for stunt performers.

It is difficult to summarise earnings as each stunt carries its own price tag and is based on the ability and experience of the performer. Very few earn a considerable amount of money, most earn around £12k-£25k a year, though this is paid on a daily or job rate. However, highly skilled stunt performers can earn up to £50k and some may progress to become stunt coordinators who, if highly successful, can demand as much as £10k a week.

Health

This job requires a high standard of physical fitness and considerable stamina.

Skills and Qualities
able to work both on your own and in a team, acting ability, adaptable, adventurous, attention to detail, confident, good concentration level, good co-ordination, head for heights, quick reactions

Relevant Subjects
Leisure, travel and tourism, Media and communication studies, Performing arts, Physical education and sport

Further Information
BBC Recruitment Services (BBC) - www.bbc.co.uk/jobs

Behind the Scenes: Film (Trotman 2009) - www.trotman.co.uk

Diplomas (Foundation, Higher and Advanced) - http://yp.direct.gov.uk/diplomas

ITV Jobs (ITV) - www.itvjobs.com

Skillset - sector skills council for the creative media, fashion and textiles industries - www.skillset.org

The Stage Online - www.thestage.co.uk

Welsh Baccalaureate - www.wbq.org.uk

Addresses
Equity
Guild House, Upper St Martin's Lane, London WC2H 9EG
Phone: +44 (0)20 7379 6000
Web: www.equity.org.uk

Joint Industry Stunt Committee (JISC)
c/o Equity, Guild House, Upper St Martins Lane, London WC2H 9EG
Phone: +44 (0)20 7670 0254
Web: www.equity.org.uk

Producers Alliance for Cinema and Television (PACT)
3rd Floor Fitzrovia House, 153-157 Cleveland St, London W1T 6QW
Phone: +44 (0)20 7380 8230
Web: www.pact.co.uk

Similar Jobs
Actor, Army Soldier, Diver, Fitness Instructor, Outdoor Activities Instructor, Sports Professional

Film/TV Technical Assistant
also known as: Film/TV Tape Assistant, Film/TV Technical Runner, Video Tape (VT) Operator

CRCI:Media, Print and Publishing
CLCI:GAL
Job Band: 3 to 5

Job Description
Technical assistants set up and operate recording and editing equipment for film/TV production. They assist the film/TV editor by organising the material, keeping records and a location log, ensuring that film, sound and digitised tapes are in the correct sequence and that they meet the technical specification. Also responsible for playing back recordings for production staff and may play video clips for live transmission.

May also work in post-production helping to prepare the transmission of final versions of films/programmes. They prepare video tape machines for clients and editors and are responsible for identifying faults, quality control of output media and quality assessment reports. Assistants know how to digitise media and make copies of video and audio material. They may undertake simple editing tasks. Must have computer skills and know how to move media and machines around the building.

On a large-scale film/TV production there is more than one assistant, but on small-scale productions, the assistant may work alone and combine the work with that of an assistant editor.

Work Details
You may work in a studio, control room or editing suite overlooking a studio, using expensive and complex equipment. Work often involves long and irregular hours and is usually on a shift system. The job can be pressurised when deadlines approach. You may work on outside broadcasts.

Qualification
• England, Wales and Northern Ireland
Band 3: For course entry: usually at least 4 GCSEs (A*-C) including English or equivalent qualifications. Maths, physics and media studies may be useful.

Band 4: For HND, Diploma of Higher Education or foundation degree: 1-2 A levels and some GCSEs (A*-C) usually including English and maths, or equivalent.

Band 5: For degree courses: 2-3 A levels and some GCSEs (A*-C) usually including English and maths, or equivalent qualifications. Exact requirements depend on the degree you take.

• Scotland
Band 3: For course entry: usually four S grades (1-3) preferably including English. Maths, physics and media studies may be useful.

Band 4: For entry to SQA higher national and professional development awards, usually 2-3 H grades and some S grades (1-3), including English and maths, or similar qualifications.

Band 5: For degree courses: 3-5 H grades and some S grades (1-3), usually including English and maths, or similar. Exact requirements depend on the degree you take.

Degree Information
Any degree discipline is acceptable, though media production, technical or engineering subjects provide a good background.

Adult Qualifications
Entry requirements may be relaxed for adults applying for higher education courses. Access or foundation courses provide those without the required qualifications a route onto degree courses.

Work Experience
Entry to this job is competitive and it is important that you try to do some relevant work or voluntary experience before applying. TV, film and broadcast companies such as the BBC are the first points of contact, although there are often waiting lists of people applying for voluntary work experience. It is worth pursuing, as work experience can help to build a portfolio of work and contacts. Attendance at film festivals is also very relevant as you may have the chance to attend specialist workshops and make useful contacts.

Entry and Training
There are no set entry requirements but those who have studied a relevant course may have an advantage. Increasingly graduates in media production, digital moving image, technical or engineering subjects are entering this job. They may begin as a junior technical assistant or videotape operator, and work up to the role of technical assistant after six to eighteen months. Many now train at film school, college or university but relevant experience through school, college or film/video making workshops, is also useful for gaining a first post.

Training is usually on the job or by a specialist course. Industry-led new entrant training programmes are offered by organisations such as Skillset, Scottish Screen and Cyfle (Wales). There is strong competition for opportunities to participate in industry-based training. For example, in Scotland, Skillset work with Scottish Screen to provide structured careers advice and training bursaries. They also offer a range of short and continuing professional development courses. Check the websites for details.

Film/TV/Radio & Theatre Sound Recordist

The National Film and Television School runs masters courses and offers maintenance bursaries and scholarships depending on individual need. The National Film and Television School and British Kinematograph Sound and Television offer relevant training courses. The Media Courses Directory, produced by Skillset and the British Film Institute, holds details of all media related courses.

A Diploma/Welsh Baccalaureate may be available in your area in creative and media. This can be a useful introduction to this type of career as you gain practical experience while studying. See the diplomas website or Skillset for further information.

Employers expect mature applicants to have some relevant experience, obtained either through employment or a workshop. Practical experience in sound and camera work is useful.

Opportunities and Pay

You may be employed by a broadcasting or film/video company, but more usually by a post-production facilities house that provides editing facilities for production companies. Although the television industry is growing, competition for jobs is tough and vacancies are rarely advertised. Many companies are based in London with a few elsewhere in the UK. Progression is to editor or into sound, lighting or camera roles. There are some opportunities to work abroad.

Permanent positions are rare and most assistants are employed short term on a freelance basis. If you are in full-time employment, pay varies depending on location and type of employer, but a technical assistant usually starts on £15k-£19k a year, rising to £30k with experience. Overtime pay is usually available.

Health

This job requires good eyesight and colour vision.

Skills and Qualities

able to cope under pressure, analytical skills, attention to detail, creative flair, good communication skills, good organisational skills, IT skills, problem-solving skills, technical aptitude

Relevant Subjects

Art and Design, Design and technology, English, Media and communication studies, Music, Performing arts

Further Information

British Film Institute (BFI) - www.bfi.org.uk

Broadcast Freelancer - www.broadcastfreelancer.com

Broadcast Magazine (weekly) (Emap) - www.broadcastnow.co.uk

Cyfle (Wales) - www.cyfle.co.uk

Diplomas (Foundation, Higher and Advanced) - http://yp.direct.gov.uk/diplomas

How to get a job in Television: Build your career from Runner to Series Producer (Methuen 2009)

Image Technology (British Kinematograph, Sound and Television Society) - www.imagetechnology.info/main/

Media/Multimedia Courses Directory (BFI/Skillset) - www.bfi.org.uk/education/talkscourses/mediacourses/

Production Base - www.productionbase.co.uk

Scottish Screen (Scottish Screen) - www.scottishscreen.com

Skillset - sector skills council for the creative media, fashion and textiles industries - www.skillset.org

So you want to work in Film & TV (Wayland) - www.waylandbooks.co.uk

Televisual (monthly) (Televisual Media UK Ltd) - www.televisual.com

The Stage Online - www.thestage.co.uk

UK Screen Association - www.ukscreenassociation.co.uk

▶Working in creative & media (2007) (Babcock Lifeskills) - www.babcock-lifeskills.com/

Addresses

BBC Recruitment Services
Recruitment BBC HR Direct, PO Box 1133, Belfast BT1 9GP
Web: www.bbc.co.uk/jobs

BKSTS: The Moving Image Society
Contact via website/e-mail/telephone,
Phone: +44 (0)1753 656656
Web: https://nt12.orbital.net/bksts/about.asp

National Film and Television School
Beaconsfield Studios, Station Road HP9 1LG
Phone: +44 (0)1494 731 425
Web: www.nftsfilm-tv.ac.uk

Similar Jobs

Film/TV & Theatre SFX Technician, Film/TV Runner, Film/TV/Radio & Theatre Sound Recordist, Film/Video Editor, Theatre Stagehand

Film/TV/Radio & Theatre Sound Recordist

also known as: Engineer: Sound Recording, Sound Engineer: Recording, Sound Mixer, Studio Recording Engineer

CRCI:Media, Print and Publishing
CLCI:GAL Job Band: 2 to 5

Job Description

Sound recordists operate equipment to record music, speech and other sounds for films, CDs/DVDs, radio, television or live theatre. They position microphones and performers, and adjust volume, quality and mixture of sound to best effect. Sound recordists work in live production recording on set or on location, and maybe post-production sound to produce a final soundtrack. They watch an instrument panel during the recording in the studio and may be concerned with dubbing and special effects. Increasingly, they use digital high-tech equipment and computers. Often edit sound tracks for films or CDs/DVDs (or videos).

At the production planning stage, they usually work with a director, producer, boom operator, and perhaps the sound editor, depending on the scale of the production. May supervise the boom operator as well as the sound assistants/sound crew, and may sometimes operate the boom.

Theatre work may involve rigging equipment on stage, the auditorium and orchestra pit and recording of special sound effects for performances.

Work Details

You may be expected to work irregular and long hours, in a studio, editing suite, theatre or on location. Travel may be necessary and you may need to spend nights away from home. If out on location you need to look at the site beforehand, decide what equipment is needed, where it should be positioned and where your control centre will be. You have to move around positioning microphones in the best places for quality sound recording.

For some events, such as a large concert, you may have to climb high ladders or crawl along exposed beams to suspend microphones. All equipment has to be checked regularly, so that it does not break down during recording or production. You need to wear earphones.

Qualification

• England, Wales and Northern Ireland

Band 3: For direct entry to some employers' training schemes or for entry to a BTEC national diploma course: usually at least 4 GCSEs (A*-C) preferably including English, maths and physics, or equivalent. Check with individual colleges.

Band 4: For HND, Diploma of Higher Education or foundation degree: 1-2 A levels and some GCSEs (A*-C) usually including English, physics and maths, or equivalent.

Band 5: For degree courses: 2-3 A levels, preferably including maths and physics, and some GCSEs (A*-C) usually including English or equivalent qualifications. Exact requirements depend on the degree you take.

- **Scotland**

Band 3: For direct entry to some employers' training schemes or for entry to a relevant course: usually at least four S grades (1-3) preferably including English, maths and physics.

Band 4: For entry to SQA higher national and professional development awards, usually 2-3 H grades and some S grades (1-3), including English, physics and maths, or similar qualifications.

Band 5: For degree courses: 3-5 H grades, preferably including maths and physics, and some S grades (1-3), usually including English, or similar. Exact requirements depend on the degree you take.

Degree Information

A relevant degree in electronic or sound engineering, communication systems, media or music technology is preferred for entry to this job.

Adult Qualifications

Entry requirements may be relaxed for adults applying for higher education courses. Access or foundation courses give adults without qualifications a route on to degree courses.

Work Experience

Entry to this job/career is highly competitive, and radio stations and sound recording studios are popular places for work experience, therefore it is wise to arrange placements in advance. Theatre and television companies may provide practical experience of using sound equipment. Taking part in school, college/university and local amateur dramatic society productions is also valuable. You can work as a runner for a recording company or major broadcasting company, or work for a hospital/community radio station to gain experience.

Entry and Training

Some start as a trainee sound assistant with on-the-job training, usually after an initial qualification in sound engineering/music technology. A portfolio of your experience including a showreel, CD or DVD of your work is useful. Qualifications in sound engineering and music technology include those offered by City & Guilds, BTEC/SQA diplomas/higher national diplomas, first degrees and postgraduate qualifications. Industry-led new entrant training programmes are offered by organisations such as the Skillset Academies, Scottish Screen and Cyfle (Wales). Foundation degrees are available, including sound engineering and design, and sound and media technology.

Professional organisations, such as the Association of Professional Recording Services or the Professional Lighting & Sound Association offer further information on accredited courses. It is an advantage to have experience of working as a sound technician in amateur theatre productions or student/hospital radio, or working with turntables or mixing decks. It can be useful to be able to read music. You need to follow a programme of continuing professional development to keep up to date with the frequent advances in technology.

The National Film and Television School also runs courses in sound design and recording for film and television and offers maintenance bursaries and scholarships depending on individual need. Vocational training programmes, including apprenticeship schemes, may be available in your area. Advanced apprenticeships leading to qualification at level 3 can also be a route into higher education.

A Diploma/Welsh Baccalaureate may be available in your area in creative and media. This can be a useful introduction to this type of career as you gain practical experience while studying. See the diplomas website or Skillset for further information. Cyfle (Wales) also offer a range of training courses for new entrants to the industry and professional development for those already employed.

Previous related work or completion of a relevant practical course with technical content is appropriate. Work as a tape operator/ studio assistant can lead into jobs as a sound recordist. Adults may be able to enter this work through a government-funded training programme. Contact your local Connexions or careers office, Jobcentre Plus, Next Step service or Learning and Skills Council (LSC)/Local Enterprise Company (LEC) for details of all training opportunities and schemes, including apprenticeships for adults.

Opportunities and Pay

Work is available in broadcasting, theatres, post-production facilities and recording studios. Most of the major studios are based in London and the south of England. Many are employed freelance on short-term contracts. This area is highly competitive and currently there is limited recruitment. Promotion to sound assistant, boom operator and sound mixer may be slow and depends on previous work experience. There may be opportunities overseas.

Pay varies depending on location and employer, but day rates are on average £250. Salaries for those working full time start at around £16k, rising to £22k-£33k a year with experience. Senior sound recordists/mixers earn around £40k a year. Those who are freelance usually have to supply some of their own equipment, and this can be very expensive initially.

Health

This job requires excellent hearing and normal colour vision. You need good general physical fitness.

Skills and Qualities

aptitude for teamwork, attention to detail, good communication skills, good concentration level, good ear for music, head for heights, IT skills, patient, resourceful, stamina, technical aptitude

Relevant Subjects

Design and technology, Engineering, ICT/Computer studies, Mathematics, Media and communication studies, Music, Performing arts, Physics, Science

Further Information

Apprenticeship Schemes (National Apprenticeship Service) - www.apprenticeships.org.uk

Audio Media - www.audiomedia.com

Cyfle (Wales) - www.cyfle.co.uk

Diplomas (Foundation, Higher and Advanced) - http://yp.direct.gov.uk/diplomas

FilmTV - www.film-tv.co.uk

How to get a job in Television: Build your career from Runner to Series Producer (Methuen 2009)

Scottish Screen (Scottish Screen) - www.scottishscreen.com

Skillset - sector skills council for the creative media, fashion and textiles industries - www.skillset.org

So you want to work in Film & TV (Wayland) - www.waylandbooks.co.uk

The Stage Online - www.thestage.co.uk

▶Working in creative & media (2007) (Babcock Lifeskills) - www.babcock-lifeskills.com/

▶Working in music (2007) (Babcock Lifeskills) - www.babcock-lifeskills.com/

Addresses

Association of Professional Recording Services (APRS)
PO Box 22, Totnes, Devon TQ9 7YZ
Phone: +44 (0)1803 868 600
Web: www.aprs.co.uk

National Film and Television School
Beaconsfield Studios, Station Road HP9 1LG
Phone: +44 (0)1494 731 425
Web: www.nftsfilm-tv.ac.uk

Professional Lighting and Sound Association (PLASA)
Redoubt House, 1 Edward Road, Eastbourne BN23 8AS
Phone: +44 (0)1323 524 120
Web: www.plasa.org

Similar Jobs

DJ, Film/TV & Theatre Lighting Technician, Film/TV Boom Operator, Film/TV Camera Operator, Film/TV Floor Manager, Film/TV Technical Assistant

Film/Video Editor

also known as: Film/TV Tape Editor

CRCI:Media, Print and Publishing
CLCI:GAL Job Band: 3 to 5

Job Description

Editors work in an editing suite with the film director, arranging film/video media into a meaningful sequence for the final version of a film/TV programme. They may also work on advertisements, music videos, corporate and training programmes. During production, they check on the technical standards of the film produced.

Also work in post-production which can take longer than the filming process. Each film 'take' is marked for identification so that it can be sorted into the correct order and editors work closely with a producer and director at all stages. They use specialist software and digital technology to download editing material on to a computer. Also synchronise video and audio recordings and add captions, graphics, music, narration, and other sound or special effects. May supervise the work and training of a film/TV technical assistant.

Work Details

Usually work a basic 40 hr week, though hours can be long and irregular. You decide which frames of the tape to keep or cut and the sequence of shots for the final production. Work is in a darkened editing suite using expensive and complex equipment, including computers. The work requires creativity and imagination. You often work under pressure to meet deadlines.

Qualification

- **England, Wales and Northern Ireland**

Band 3: For entry: usually at least 4 GCSEs (A*-C) preferably including maths, physics and English, or equivalent.

Band 4: For HND, Diploma of Higher Education or foundation degree: 1-2 A levels and some GCSEs (A*-C) usually including English and maths, or equivalent.

Band 5: For degree courses: 2-3 A levels and some GCSEs (A*-C) usually including English or equivalent qualifications. Exact requirements depend on the degree you take.

- **Scotland**

Band 3: For entry: usually at least four S grades (1-3) preferably including maths, physics and English, or similar.

Band 4: For entry to SQA higher national and professional development awards, usually 2-3 H grades and some S grades (1-3), including English and maths, or similar qualifications.

Band 5: For degree courses: 3-5 H grades and some S grades (1-3), usually including English or similar. Exact requirements depend on the degree you take.

Degree Information

Graduates in any degree discipline may enter training, but communication and media studies, photography, film and television subjects, information technology and multimedia courses are the most relevant. There are specialised undergraduate and postgraduate courses in film and TV production.

Adult Qualifications

Entry requirements may be relaxed for adults applying for higher education courses and Access or foundation courses give adults without qualifications a route on to degree courses.

Work Experience

Entry to this job is very competitive and it is important that you try to do some relevant work or voluntary experience before applying. Television, film and broadcast companies are the first points of contact, although there are often waiting lists of people applying for voluntary work experience. It is worth pursuing, as work experience can help to build a portfolio of work and contacts. Previous experience of photography and drama is an advantage.

Entry and Training

This job is not one you can enter without any experience. Entrants come from a variety of backgrounds, including those on industry-based training schemes, or with HNDs, and increasingly those with degrees. Many begin as a runner or as an assistant, and work towards their eventual goal as an editor. It is useful to have a portfolio, including a showreel of your work.

Training is often practical and on the job, but some large employers such as the BBC offer structured training programmes. Training providers for the film and TV industry include the Skillset Academies, Scottish Screen, and Cyfle (Wales). Contact them for details of suitable courses and training programmes. The National Film and Television School runs a range of short courses for all grades, and the Media Courses and Multimedia Courses Directory gives information on relevant courses throughout the country. Experience in the use of editing software programs, such as Avid, Final Cut Pro and Lightworks, is essential. You must be willing to develop new skills to keep up to date with changes in technology.

It is possible to work towards an S/NVQ in production for television at level 3, and there are a range of vocational qualifications in editing. Training programmes, including apprenticeship schemes, may be available in your area. Advanced apprenticeships leading to qualification at level 3 can also be a route into higher education.

A Diploma/Welsh Baccalaureate may be available in your area in creative and media. This can be a useful introduction to this type of career as you gain practical experience while studying. See the diplomas website or Skillset for further information. Cyfle (Wales) also offers a range of training courses for new entrants to the industry and professional development for those already employed.

Mature entry is common as this is not a direct entry job. Practical experience in sound, camera or related work is essential.

Opportunities and Pay

You may be employed by a broadcasting/film company, specialist facilities house that provides editing for production companies or a computer software manufacturer. Around 11,000 people work in post-production jobs in the UK but most editors are employed on a freelance basis, which can mean periods of frantic work followed by periods of unemployment. Many jobs are in London, but there are opportunities in other cities in the UK and maybe abroad. This area is highly competitive and progress depends on a portfolio of successful contracts, personal contacts, and sheer persistence, together with determination.

Pay varies depending on the type of employer and whether you are self-employed. You may have to start on very low pay while training, with pay sometimes deferred until the film is produced. An editor may start on £18k-£26k, rising to around £30k a year with experience. Highly successful editors earn £40k-£70k a year.

Health
This job requires good eyesight and colour vision.

Skills and Qualities
able to cope under pressure, aptitude for teamwork, attention to detail, creative and imaginative flair, eye for visual effect, good communication skills, good organisational skills, IT skills, self-motivated, technical aptitude

Relevant Subjects
Art and Design, Design and technology, English, ICT/Computer studies, Media and communication studies, Music, Performing arts, Physics, Science

Further Information
Apprenticeship Schemes (National Apprenticeship Service) - www.apprenticeships.org.uk

Broadcast Magazine (weekly) (Emap) - www.broadcastnow.co.uk

Creative Review (Centaur) - www.creativereview.co.uk

Cyfle (Wales) - www.cyfle.co.uk

Diplomas (Foundation, Higher and Advanced) - http://yp.direct.gov.uk/diplomas

FilmTV - www.film-tv.co.uk

Media/Multimedia Courses Directory (BFI/Skillset) - www.bfi.org.uk/education/talkscourses/mediacourses/

Scottish Screen (Scottish Screen) - www.scottishscreen.com

Skillset - sector skills council for the creative media, fashion and textiles industries - www.skillset.org

So you want to work in Film & TV (Wayland) - www.waylandbooks.co.uk

▶Working in creative & media (2007) (Babcock Lifeskills) - www.babcock-lifeskills.com/

Addresses
BBC Recruitment Services
Recruitment BBC HR Direct, PO Box 1133, Belfast BT1 9GP
Web: www.bbc.co.uk/jobs

National Film and Television School
Beaconsfield Studios, Station Road HP9 1LG
Phone: +44 (0)1494 731 425
Web: www.nftsfilm-tv.ac.uk

Similar Jobs
Animator, Film/TV & Theatre SFX Technician, Film/TV Director, Film/TV Producer, Film/TV Technical Assistant, Film/TV/Radio & Theatre Sound Recordist

Financial Adviser/Planner
also known as: Financial Consultant, Independent Financial Adviser

CRCI:Financial Services
CLCI:NAK — Job Band: 4 to 5

Job Description
Financial advisers/planners advise people on financial matters and recommend ways to make the best use of their money. Are either 'tied' to one employer (recommending only their products), 'multi-tied' (linked to a number of product providers) or 'independent' (able to choose from the whole market for their clients). They assess the client's financial situation and provide information about appropriate products and services, such as mortgages, investments, protection policies, loans, home insurance, life assurance, savings plans and pensions. Independent financial advisers act as impartial experts for clients who may be private individuals, groups and for corporate organisations. Research and gather product information from a wide variety of specialist company databases.

Advisers are aware of changes to financial law and legislation and keep up to date on any new developments in the financial markets. They analyse information and suggest a range of options for the client.

Work Details
Working hours can be irregular and vary depending on the company. You may sometimes have to work early evenings or at weekends. Those based with one bank or company are likely to have more regular hours. The job usually involves travelling to meet clients in their homes or at their businesses. You are in contact with a wide variety of people, face to face, by telephone and by letter, and deal with personal and confidential information.

Qualification
• England, Wales and Northern Ireland
Band 4: For direct entry to training, or higher national courses before training: 1-2 A levels and some GCSEs (A*-C) or equivalent. Exact requirements depend on your employer and the course you take.

Band 5: For degree courses: 2-3 A levels and some GCSEs (A*-C) usually including English and maths, or equivalent. Exact requirements depend on the degree you take.

• Scotland
Band 4: For direct entry to training, or to higher national courses before training, you need 1-3 H grades and some S grades (1-3) or similar. Exact requirements depend on your employer and the course you take.

Band 5: For degree courses: 3-5 H grades and some S grades (1-3), usually including English and maths, or similar qualifications. Exact requirements depend on the degree you take.

Degree Information
Any degree discipline is acceptable, but financial services, or finance, accountancy, business studies/administration, economics, statistics, law, financial management and banking give an advantage.

Adult Qualifications
Many entrants are graduates or those who have professional qualifications in accountancy, banking, insurance or investment.

Work Experience
Relevant work or voluntary experience is always useful and improves your chances when applying for entry to this job. Any work experience in the finance sector is relevant and shows enthusiasm and commitment to the work. Time spent in an accountancy firm, an insurance company or even shadowing a financial adviser gives you a good insight into the profession.

Entry and Training
Many entrants are graduates, or have relevant qualifications in insurance, accountancy, law, or banking. Some entrants start work as a paraplanner, helping a financial adviser with administration, or join a bank and work their way up by studying in their own time.

On-the-job training following the Financial Services Authority (FSA) guidelines is provided by individual employers. Giving financial advice is an FSA regulated function and specific professional qualifications are required. This is the certificate in financial planning (CertFP) or an equivalent, such as the certificate for financial advisers (CeFA). These are level 3 qualifications and have no set entry requirements. You need to be licensed as an independent financial adviser with the FSA. Those with a degree in financial services, or other relevant qualifications, can apply for exemptions from certain parts of the CertFP.

Many advisers also study through the Chartered Insurance Institute for the diploma and advanced diploma in financial planning. The advanced diploma leads to chartered financial planner status. Financial planners are expected to undertake continuing professional development to keep up to date with industry changes.

A foundation degree is available in accounting and finance. An apprenticeship in advising on financial products may be available in your area. The Diploma/Welsh Baccalaureate in business, administration and finance may also be available and considered as an alternative to A levels. Most professional courses can be studied on a part-time/day-release basis or through distance learning. Relevant S/NVQs at levels 2-4 may also be available.

Mature applicants may find that there are good opportunities for older people, particularly for those with relevant experience. Distance learning is available for the certificate in financial planning (CertFP) and the certificate for financial advisers (CeFA)).

Opportunities and Pay

There are a large number of financial planners in the UK, over half of which are independent. There are opportunities throughout the UK and especially in major financial areas such as London, Manchester, Leeds, Bristol, Glasgow, Edinburgh and Cardiff. You may be employed by a firm of financial advisers, or by a building society, bank or insurance company. You can work with a group of other independent advisers, or can be self-employed and work as a consultant. Promotional opportunities depend on the organisation and in larger companies advancement to supervisory or managerial positions is possible.

Many experienced advisers become self-employed as an Independent Financial Adviser (IFA) or become a specialist in a particular product area. There is a growing need for experienced advisers to move into financial compliance.

Salaries vary depending on size and type of employer. Starting salaries are around £18k-£25k a year. Experienced advisers earn on average £30k-£40k with the most experienced and successful advisers earning around £50k-£60k a year. Some IFAs receive a basic salary plus commission, which can increase earnings.

Skills and Qualities

able to explain clearly, commercial awareness, good communication skills, good interpersonal skills, good listening skills, good organisational skills, information handling skills, IT skills, objective, trustworthy

Relevant Subjects

Business and accounting, Economics, English, ICT/Computer studies, Law, Mathematics

Further Information

AGCAS: Accountancy and Business Services (Job Sector Briefing) (AGCAS) - www.prospects.ac.uk/

Diploma in Business, Administration and Finance - www.baf-diploma.org.uk/

Financial Services Authority (FSA) - www.fsa.gov.uk/

Financial Services Skills Council - sector skills council for financial services, accountancy & finance - www.fssc.org.uk/

Insurance Careers (CII) (CII) - www.cii.co.uk/

TARGETjobs: City and Finance (GTI Specialist Publishers Ltd) - www.groupgti.com

Welsh Baccalaureate - www.wbq.org.uk

▶Working in advice & counselling (2007) (Babcock Lifeskills) - www.babcock-lifeskills.com/

▶Working in maths (2009) (Babcock Lifeskills) - www.babcock-lifeskills.com/

Addresses

Association of Independent Financial Advisers (AIFA)
2-6 Austin Friars House, Austin Friars, London EC2N 2HD
Phone: +44 (0)20 7628 1287
Web: www.aifa.net

Chartered Insurance Institute (CII)
42-48 High Road, South Woodford, London E18 2JP
Phone: +44 (0)20 8989 8464
Web: www.cii.co.uk

ifs School of Finance
IFS House, 4-9 Burgate Lane, Canterbury, Kent CT1 2XJ
Phone: +44 (0)1227 818609
Web: www.ifslearning.ac.uk

Personal Finance Society (PFS)
42-48 High Road, South Woodford, London E18 2JP
Phone: +44 (0)20 8530 0852
Web: www.thepfs.org

Similar Jobs

Bank Manager, Insurance Broker, Insurance Underwriter, Investment Analyst, Management Consultant, Stockbroker

Firefighter

CRCI:Security and Armed Forces
CLCI:MAF — Job Band: 2 to 3

Job Description

Firefighters work in a team (crew) usually of six people and respond immediately to an emergency call to a fire or accident. Fight the fire and rescue people (and animals) that are trapped. Put out fires with hoses, pumps and foam. Help in all kinds of events, such as floods, road, rail or air crashes, incidents involving explosives or biological or nuclear materials, and fuel and spillages of other dangerous substances. Supply first aid treatment to the injured until the ambulance crew arrives.

Use equipment such as axes, cutters and turntables for rescues. Must carry out regular drills and look after the appliance (fire engine) and related equipment. Give specialist advice on fire protection, prevention and safety precautions to local authorities and companies, and promote fire safety to the general public. Review building proposals and check buildings to see if there is a fire risk.

Work Details

Work an average of 42 hours a week, on a rota of shifts, including nights/weekends, but with two days off a week. There may be overtime. Team work is very important and you usually work with the same fire crew. You have to be out in all weathers and in conditions that can be dirty, extremely hot or cold, wet and dangerous. Some work requires you to be in enclosed spaces or work at heights. There is a risk from collapsing buildings, fumes and explosions. This work is very physically demanding and can also be emotionally stressful.

A specialist uniform and protective equipment is provided and you are required to carry heavy and awkward equipment at times. At the fire station, considerable time is spent on routine duties and training. Mostly, firefighters spend their on-duty time at the fire station until called out to an incident.

Some fire services have part-time (retained) firefighters, who do a set number of hours of training duty each week and are on 'standby' for emergencies. To do this, you have to be able to reach the fire station within four minutes. Retained firefighters work mostly in small towns and rural areas.

Qualification

Each fire service has its own entry standards with no minimum educational requirements, though a good general education is required.

• England, Wales and Northern Ireland

Band 2: No set qualifications, but some employers may expect specific GCSEs, such as English, science and maths or equivalent qualifications.

Band 3: For some employers: 5 GCSEs (A*-C) including maths, science and English, or equivalent qualifications, are useful.

- **Scotland**

Band 2: No set qualifications, but some employers may expect specific S grades such as English, science and maths or similar qualifications.

Band 3: For some employers: five S grades (1-3) including maths, science and English, or similar qualifications, are useful.

Adult Qualifications
There are no set minimum entry qualifications and each fire brigade sets its own standards. Applicants usually have to pass an entrance test.

Work Experience
Entry to this job is highly competitive and work experience is difficult to gain. Some fire stations may offer work experience places but this is at the discretion of the station officer. It improves your chances at interview if you have some work experience that develops your communication, decision making and team-playing skills. Experience as a part-time firefighter is also an advantage.

Entry and Training
There is very strong competition for entry and you must be over 18. Most fire services set written and practical problem-solving entry tests, and physical tests. You may have to attend an assessment centre. You attend an interview and have to supply references and undergo a medical examination. A good standard of education is required, though there are no formal entry requirements. Some entrants may have A levels/H grades or equivalent, or a degree, though there is no 'fast-track' scheme for graduates. The diploma/ welsh baccalaureate in public services may be a useful background for this career but check entry requirements carefully. 'All recruits undertake a four month basic training course, usually at a residential training centre, learning both theory and practical skills. Recruits also have to commit to a continuous training programme by attending lectures, exercises, practical training sessions and other forms of training to maintain competence levels throughout their career.

You then have up to two years as a probationer, learning on the job with experienced firefighters and being assessed throughout this period. You are also encouraged to take specialist courses, for example to get an LGV (large goods vehicle) licence. An Integrated Personal Development System (IPDS) is now in place for firefighters. This ensures that firefighters keep up to date with skills, work towards relevant qualifications, such as S/NVQs (one set at Level 2, three at Level 3, and one at level 4) in emergency fire services, and have a clear promotion structure.

Some firefighters may work towards a degree in fire science/fire risk engineering, fire safety and management, or other related qualifications, such as in public administration or management studies. Membership of the Institution of Fire Engineers is encouraged.

Retained firefighters are trained through an induction period that takes place at weekends, plus weekly drill nights and short courses. The Fire Services College in Gloucestershire provides training for those wanting promotion to supervisory ranks.

Mature entrants are welcomed though you are expected to pass a rigorous physical selection test.

Opportunities and Pay
In January 2009 the Government announced an investment of £19 million for training and equipment for firefighters in the UK. This grant is spread across the 46 Fire and Rescue Services (FRS) and allows the forces to focus on training for major incidents such as terrorism and industrial accidents. This type of training covers rescuing people from collapsed buildings, urban search and rescue and undertaking mass decontamination of the public. This is part of an £80 million three-year funding announcement made in July 2008. Therefore, job prospects look good, although not all jobs are on a full-time basis. Some can be on a retainer basis where the firefighter is paid an annual retainer and then a set rate for each callout. Check the Communities and Local Government website for more information on the development of the FRS in your area.

Fire services are located mostly in towns and cities with most firefighters working for local authority fire brigades. Some firefighters are employed by the British Airports Authority (BAA) or by individual airports. The Defence Fire Service employs firefighters for Ministry of Defence sites and other military establishments.

Experienced firefighters can apply for promotion to crew manager, watch manager, station manager and above. Promotion is based on ability, not academic qualifications, although the service actively seeks to develop all staff rather than focus on promotion opportunities alone. Some opportunities exist for transfer to HM Fire Service Inspectorate.

Salaries start at £21k for a trainee firefighter, rising to £28k a year once fully competent. Crew managers earn £29k-£31k, watch managers earn £31k-£36k and station managers earn £36k-£40k. Group managers earn £41k-£46k and area managers earn £49k-£54k. Overtime pay is also possible.

Health
You have to pass a medical and a test of strength and lung capacity. Your hearing, colour vision and eyesight in both eyes (without glasses or contact lenses) must be good. Each fire service has their own criteria so check with your local force to ensure eligibility.

Skills and Qualities
able to communicate effectively, able to cope under pressure, able to follow instructions, agile, aptitude for teamwork, determined, good stamina and physically fit, head for heights, reassuring

Relevant Subjects
Biology, Physical education and sport, Science

Further Information
AGCAS: Armed Forces & Emergency Services (Job Sector Briefing) (AGCAS) - www.prospects.ac.uk

Communities and Local Government (Local Government) - www.communities.gov.uk

Diplomas (Foundation, Higher and Advanced) - http://yp.direct.gov.uk/diplomas

Firefighter (Fire Brigades' Union) - www.fbu.org.uk/newspress/ffmag/index.php

How to Pass the UK's National Firefighter Selection Process (Kogan Page)

UK Fire Service Resources (UK Fire Service) - www.fireservice.co.uk

Welsh Baccalaureate - www.wbq.org.uk

▶Working in airports (2010) (Babcock Lifeskills) - www.babcock-lifeskills.com/

▶Working in police, fire & security (2009) (Babcock Lifeskills) - www.babcock-lifeskills.com/

Addresses
British Airports Authority (BAA)
BAA Airports Limited, The Compass Centre, Nelson Road, London Heathrow Airport, Hounslow TW6 2GW
Phone: +44 (0)20 8745 9800
Web: www.baa.com

Defence Fire Training and Development Centre
Manston, Ramsgate, Kent CT12 5BS
Phone: +44 (0)1843 823351
Web: www.dftdc.org

Institution of Fire Engineers
London Road, Moreton-in-Marsh, Gloucestershire GL56 0RH
Phone: +44 (0)1608 812 580
Web: www.ife.org.uk

Northern Ireland Fire and Rescue Service
1 Seymour Street, Lisburn, Co Antrim BT27 4SX
Phone: +44 (0)28 9266 4221
Web: www.nifrs.org

Similar Jobs
Ambulance Paramedic, Coastguard Watch Officer, Engineer: Fire, Health & Safety Practitioner, Police Officer

Fish Farm Manager

also known as: Fishery Manager, Hatchery Manager

CRCI:Environment, Animals and Plants
CLCI:WAG Job Band: 3 to 5

Job Description

Fish farm managers are responsible for the daily management and supervision of one or more fish farms and hatcheries where fish are bred and reared to be sold as food, or for sport (restocking rivers and lakes for angling), or for ornamental ponds and lakes. Species of fish are primarily rainbow trout and salmon but also other varieties, such as brown trout and carp, tench, turbot, halibut, cod, eel, Arctic char, and also shellfish, such as mussels, prawns, oysters, scallops and clams. The manager is in charge of the development of the fish or shellfish, from hatching and spawning to harvesting.

They either breed fish from eggs or buy in young fish. Also plan the workforce activities, supervise and may train the staff or arrange for them to study for relevant qualifications. Must ensure that high standards of hygiene are maintained so that the fish are kept free from disease. They also look after the day-to-day administration of the farm and are involved in marketing and selling the fish. Keep detailed records and accounts using a computer database and produce regular reports.

Also order the necessary chemicals (to keep the stock disease free) and are responsible for their safe storage and use. Some managers may also be involved in research projects. On smaller farms or fish hatcheries, they may do general tasks such as feeding and grading the fish, or checking and maintaining buildings and equipment.

Work Details

Work a basic 39 hr week, though the working hours can be long and unsocial, possibly including weekends, evenings or early mornings, and often on your own in very remote locations. The work often involves shifts as fish need to be looked after seven days a week. The work environment is damp, sometimes cold and uncomfortable, and often in unpleasant and severe weather conditions. Work requires coping with the sight of blood. Heavy lifting, carrying, standing and bending is required. Protective boots and clothing is worn.

Qualification

• England, Wales and Northern Ireland

Band 3: For entry to jobs, HNC or a relevant Diploma, usually at least 4 GCSEs (A*-C) including English and maths, or equivalent

Band 4: For HND, Diploma of Higher Education or foundation degree: 1-2 A levels and some GCSEs (A*-C) usually including English and maths, or equivalent.

Band 5: For degree courses: 2-3 A levels and some GCSEs (A*-C) usually including English and maths, or equivalent. Exact requirements depend on the degree you take.

• Scotland

Band 3: For entry to jobs, usually at least four S grades (1-3) including English and maths, or similar.

Band 4: For entry to SQA higher national and professional development awards, usually 2-3 H grades and some S grades (1-3), including English and maths, or similar qualifications.

Band 5: For degree: 3-5 H grades, often including science subjects, and some S grades (1-3) usually including English. Good H grades are required, preferably taken at one sitting. Similar qualifications may also be acceptable. Exact requirements depend on the degree to be taken.

Degree Information

Degrees in aquaculture/fisheries management, fisheries science, aquatic biology, biology, marine or freshwater biology, or environmental life science are preferred. Degrees in chemistry or other science subjects may also be acceptable. It is an advantage to do postgraduate study in a subject such as aquaculture, aquaculture/fisheries management, fisheries science, marine acquaculture, or fisheries policy/planning. Postgraduate experience in a relevant subject is particularly useful for research posts.

Adult Qualifications

Entry requirements for courses may be waived for those with relevant experience in agriculture or fish farming. At least a year's practical experience is usually needed. You can take a foundation or Access to science course to enable progress towards higher qualifications.

Work Experience

Employers or colleges/universities may prefer candidates who have relevant work or voluntary experience. This is ideally on a fish farm, with an angling society or in other areas of land-based work or agriculture. Business and IT skills are an advantage and experience of administration is also very relevant.

Entry and Training

Pre-entry experience is essential and it is useful to have knowledge and/or skills in engineering, construction and general DIY. A current driving licence is usually required. It is also an advantage to have experience in agriculture or working with animals. To enter some courses you have to have twelve months' full-time experience in fisheries work. Some entrants have a relevant degree, foundation degree in fisheries management or postgraduate qualification.

You are trained on the job and may have to enter this work as an assistant manager. It is possible to study through distance learning for qualifications such as those offered by the Institute of Fisheries Management (IFM), including the certificate in fisheries management. No particular qualifications are required, but students need to be members of the IFM. An IFM diploma course lasting two years is available for those who have completed the certificate and on completion, this can lead to an Open University degree.

Appropriate S/NVQs in fisheries management are available and BTEC offers a national award at level 3 in sports fisheries. Training programmes, including apprenticeship schemes, may be available in your area. Advanced apprenticeships leading to qualification at level 3 can also be a route into higher education.

Mature applicants with experience in fish farming, agriculture (or any work with animals), together with a practical ability in woodwork, have an advantage. The highest posts are usually for those with a relevant degree and experience. Funding for courses may be available from the Nuffield Farming Scholarships Trust. Distance learning courses are available through the Institute of Fisheries Management (IFM) leading to professional status and entry to the diploma course, which takes two years to complete.

Opportunities and Pay
There are over 1200 fish farms in the UK. Most jobs are with commercial fish farms or a water company, private estate, aquatic specialist centre, industrial firm or angling organisation. Jobs are available only in certain areas, mainly in the country or by the sea, often in remote areas. Those with a scientific/technical background may find opportunities with large organisations such as frozen-food companies or with central government, usually in research posts. Currently, around two thirds of the industry is located in Scotland, though other areas in the UK include southern and eastern England, north Yorkshire, Wales and Northern Ireland.

The industry is expanding, especially in Scotland, but most fish farms are small and operate with minimal staffing. Entry is always competitive. Some opportunities exist abroad in countries such as Iceland, France, Italy, Norway, North America and Germany, where there are well-established industries in fish farming. You can be self-employed, but it requires considerable financial investment to establish a business.

Pay varies depending on type of farm, level of responsibility and whether or not you are self-employed. Managers are likely to earn around £18k-£40k a year and some may earn more.

Health
This job requires good health and stamina. There is an allergy risk from skin irritants and chemicals.

Skills and Qualities
able to communicate effectively, able to cope under pressure, business awareness, good organisational skills, IT skills, not squeamish, observant, practical skills, scientific approach, self-motivated

Relevant Subjects
Biology, Business and accounting, Chemistry, Economics, English, Land and Environment, Mathematics, Science

Further Information
Careers in Fisheries (Institute of Fisheries Management (IFM) - www.ifm.org.uk/training/careers/

Environmental Careers (Chartered Institution of Water and Environmental Management) - www.ciwem.org.uk/publications/careers/

Fish Farmer (bi-monthly) (Oban Times Ltd) - www.fishfarmer-magazine.com

Lantra - The Sector Skills Council for environmental & land-based sector (Lantra) http:/www.lantra.co.uk

Lantra Careers (A Future In...) (Lantra) - www.afuturein.com

Nuffield Farming Scholarships Trust (Nuffield Farming Scholarships Trust) - www.nuffieldscholar.org

▶Working with animals (2009) (Babcock Lifeskills) - www.babcock-lifeskills.com/

Addresses
British Trout Association
The Rural Centre, West Mains, Ingliston, Edinburgh EH28 8NZ
Phone: +44 (0)131 472 4080
Web: www.britishtrout.co.uk

Environment Agency
National Customer Contact Centre, PO Box 544, Almondsbury, Rotherham S60 1BY
Phone: 08708 506 506 (UK only)
Web: www.environment-agency.gov.uk

Fisheries Research Services
FRS Marine Laboratory, PO Box 101, 375 Victoria Road, Aberdeen AB11 9DB
Phone: +44 (0)1224 876544
Web: www.marlab.ac.uk

Institute of Fisheries Management (IFM)
22 Rushworth Avenue, West Bridgford, Nottingham NG2 7LF
Phone: +44 (0)115 982 2317
Web: www.ifm.org.uk

Sea Fish Industry Authority (Seafish)
Training Division, Origin Way, Europarc, Grimsby DN37 9TZ
Phone: +44 (0)1472 252300
Web: www.seafish.org

Similar Jobs
Countryside Ranger, Farm Manager, Fish Farm Worker, Forest Officer, Horticultural Manager, Marine Biologist

Fish Farm Worker
also known as: Hatchery Worker

CRCI:Environment, Animals and Plants

CLCI:WAG Job Band: 1 to 3

Job Description
Fish farm workers work on a fish farm where fish are bred to be sold as food, for sport (restocking rivers and lakes for angling), or for ornamental ponds and lakes. They feed and care for rainbow trout and salmon, and other fish, such as brown trout and carp, turbot, halibut, cod, tench, eel and Arctic char, or shellfish, including mussels, prawns, oysters, scallops and clams. Must watch for signs of any disease in the fish and maintain safe and healthy conditions. Also check that the water is at the correct temperature and has the appropriate oxygen content.

Workers keep tanks clean and ensure that leaves, weeds and other debris do not get into the water. They regularly check and empty the tank filters and screens. Also apply chemicals to the water to prevent any outbreak or spread of disease. Sometimes they drain the tanks and hose them down, making sure that the process does not cause pollution to the surrounding environment.

Some fish, such as salmon, are taken from fresh water tanks and put in cages or pens in the sea. Workers may assist in harvesting the fish for sale, which involves killing the fish and packing them in ice for transportation. Some fish farms are also involved in smoking fish. Workers use power and hand tools for other general tasks and repairs such as woodwork, net repairs, plumbing and electrical work.

Work Details
A basic 39 hrs a week is usual, though longer and irregular hours are often required, particularly in spring when initial rearing takes place. You may work shifts, including weekends and evenings, as fish have to be looked after seven days a week. You may often have to work alone in an area that is quite isolated, and in all sorts of weather conditions. The work involves some heavy lifting, carrying, standing and bending. To do this sort of work you should be able to cope with the sight of blood, and you need to wear protective boots and clothing.

Qualification

• England, Wales and Northern Ireland
Band 1: For entry to jobs, no minimum qualifications are needed, but you are expected to have a good level of general education and relevant experience. Some formal/vocational qualifications at any level are useful. Practical skills and an aptitude for science, particularly biology and chemistry, may be helpful.

Band 2: For entry to jobs, no minimum qualifications are needed, but it is an advantage to have some GCSEs (A*-C) or equivalent in subjects that include English, maths and science or equivalent.

Band 3: For entry to jobs, HNC or a relevant Diploma, usually at least 4 GCSEs (A*-C) including English and maths, or equivalent. A knowledge of chemistry is often needed.

• Scotland
Band 1: For entry to jobs, no minimum qualifications are needed, but you are expected to have a good level of general education and relevant experience. Some formal/vocational qualifications at any level are useful. Practical skills and an aptitude for science, particularly biology and chemistry, may be helpful.

Band 2: Although academic qualifications are not specified for this job, it is an advantage to have some S grades (1-3) in subjects that include English, maths and science or similar.

Band 3: For entry to jobs, usually at least four S grades (1-3) including English and maths, or similar. A knowledge of chemistry is often needed.

Adult Qualifications
You do not need any qualifications to enter this job, though relevant and practical experience in agriculture is useful for entry to courses.

Work Experience
Relevant work or voluntary experience is always useful and can improve your chances when applying for entry to relevant jobs and courses. There can be opportunities for casual and seasonal work at a fish farm, or temporary/Saturday work at an aquaculture outlet that breeds and sells fish to the public. Membership of an angling club can be helpful, as can experience of practical skills such as carpentry and bricklaying.

Entry and Training
Employers usually look for a combination of technical knowledge and practical skills. Training is usually on the job though there are some college courses in fisheries studies available. It is useful if you have previous experience in farm work and working with animals, and be able to swim. It will also help you in your job if you have practical skills, such as woodwork. A certificate in fisheries management (with a fish farming option) is available as a distance-learning course from the Institute of Fisheries Management (IFM). As well as providing the knowledge and skills for fish farm workers, it also prepares you for further career progression.

A Diploma/Welsh Baccalaureate may be available in your area in environment and land-based studies. BTEC first and national awards are available in fish husbandry. Relevant training programmes, including apprenticeship schemes, may also be available in your area. Advanced apprenticeships leading to qualification at level 3 can also be a route into higher education.

Mature applicants with experience in fish farming, agriculture (or any work with animals) together with a practical ability in woodwork, have an advantage. Distance learning courses are available from the Institute of Fisheries Management (IFM).

Government training opportunities may be available in your area. You can also gain recognition of previous experience through Accreditation of Prior Learning (APL) or by working towards relevant S/NVQs. Contact your local Connexions or careers office, Jobcentre Plus, Next Step service or Learning and Skills Council (LSC)/Local Enterprise Company (LEC) for details of any training schemes.

Opportunities and Pay
Over 7,000 are employed in fish farming in the UK. Most jobs are with commercial fish farms or a water company, private estate, an industrial firm, or an angling organisation. Some opportunities exist with government departments and with the Environment Agency. Jobs are found mainly in remote rural areas or by the sea. The level of skills needed is expected to increase, creating a demand for multi-skilled workers. Currently, around two thirds of the industry is located in Scotland though other areas in the UK include southern and eastern England, north Yorkshire, Wales and Northern Ireland.

You may have to move to another part of the country to get a job. Other opportunities exist abroad in countries such as Iceland, France, Italy, Norway, North America and Germany, where there are well-established industries in fish farming.

Pay varies depending on area and type of employer, but starting salaries can be around £11k a year, rising to around £18k a year with experience.

Health
Some of the chemicals used in fish farming can irritate the skin. You must be fit to do this job.

Skills and Qualities
able to follow instructions, able to work both on your own and in a team, attention to detail, common sense, interest in fish and fishing, not squeamish, practical skills, reliable, willing to learn, willing to work in remote locations

Relevant Subjects
Biology, Chemistry, Construction and built environment, Land and Environment, Science

Further Information
Apprenticeship Schemes (National Apprenticeship Service) - www.apprenticeships.org.uk

Careers in Fisheries (Institute of Fisheries Management) (IFM) - www.ifm.org.uk/training/careers/

Diplomas (Foundation, Higher and Advanced) - http://yp.direct.gov.uk/diplomas

Environmental Careers (Chartered Institution of Water and Environmental Management) - www.ciwem.org.uk/publications/careers/

Fish Farmer (bi-monthly) (Oban Times Ltd) - www.fishfarmer-magazine.com

Lantra - The Sector Skills Council for environmental & land-based sector (Lantra) http:/www.lantra.co.uk

Lantra Careers (A Future In...) (Lantra) - www.afuturein.com

Real Life Guide to Working Outdoors (Trotman) - www.trotman.co.uk

Training Schemes - www.direct.gov.uk/en/educationandlearning

Welsh Baccalaureate - www.wbq.org.uk

Addresses
British Trout Association
The Rural Centre, West Mains, Ingliston, Edinburgh EH28 8NZ
Phone: +44 (0)131 472 4080
Web: www.britishtrout.co.uk

Environment Agency
National Customer Contact Centre, PO Box 544, Almondsbury, Rotherham S60 1BY
Phone: 08708 506 506 (UK only)
Web: www.environment-agency.gov.uk

Institute of Fisheries Management (IFM)
22 Rushworth Avenue, West Bridgford, Nottingham NG2 7LF
Phone: +44 (0)115 982 2317
Web: www.ifm.org.uk

Sea Fish Industry Authority (Seafish)
Training Division, Origin Way, Europarc, Grimsby DN37 9TZ
Phone: +44 (0)1472 252300
Web: www.seafish.org

Similar Jobs
Farm Worker: Crops, Farm Worker: Livestock, Fisherman/Fisherwoman, Gamekeeper, Horticultural Worker: Commercial, Waterway Operative

Fisherman/Fisherwoman

CRCI:Environment, Animals and Plants
CLCI:WAH
Job Band: 1 to 2

Job Description
Works at sea as part of a team that includes deckhands, a mate and a skipper, and on some vessels, an engineer. May work on deep sea trawlers, 'factory' ships, drifters, or inshore fishing boats, hunting and catching fish. Tasks vary according to experience. A

deckhand helps to load and unload nets, sort and grade the fish into different types and sizes. Guts and stores the fish in a cold place, usually on ice or in sea water tanks. Mends and maintains nets and fishing gear, either at sea or onshore. Washes the deck, and uses winches and lifting gear. Prepares meals for all of the crew and also helps with watch-keeping duties.

A mate is more experienced and has more responsibility for the vessel's equipment. Also ensures that each catch is brought safely on board and stored correctly.

The skipper is entirely responsible for the safety of a vessel, the welfare of its crew members and the catch of fish. Decides where to fish and steers the vessel to the fishing grounds and back to shore after the catch is complete. Uses electronic systems such as radio transmitters, electronic navigating systems, including global positioning systems (GPS) and fish-locating equipment, such as underwater cameras. Keeps records of each catch, and manages the business and crew.

The engineer is responsible for maintaining a fishing vessel's engine, its communications equipment and fishing gear. Every crew member follows the safety and hygiene rules of the fishing industry and is trained to act quickly in an emergency. The tasks may be shared by all of the crew, depending on the size of the vessel and experience of each crew member.

Work Details

When you are at sea, you have to work long shifts and irregular hours. You may need to stay away from home for a few days or weeks/months, or you may go to sea daily. It can be quite cramped on a fishing boat and you must always be aware of health and safety rules. You need to be able to cope with the sight of blood and the smell of fish. Energy, fitness and stamina are needed to do lifting, bending, carrying and climbing. You have to be able to put up with rough seas and be out in all sorts of extreme weather. Protective and waterproof clothing is worn, including boots and headgear.

Qualification

• England, Wales and Northern Ireland

Band 1: No minimum qualifications are required, but you are expected to have had a good level of general education.

Band 2: You do not need formal academic qualifications, but some GCSEs are an advantage, particularly for those who want to go on to become mates or skippers.

• Scotland

Band 1: Formal academic qualifications are not required for relevant training but you are expected to have a good level of general education.

Band 2: You do not need formal academic qualifications, but some S grades are an advantage, particularly for those who want to go on to become mates or skippers.

Adult Qualifications

Most employers expect adults to have relevant experience at sea and for some jobs you need to gain a required level of skills and qualifications. However, for entry to all training you do not require any formal academic qualifications, although some relevant qualifications can be an advantage.

Work Experience

Any work experience can give you skills that you can use in the future and add to your CV. Experience at sea is most useful, but any work that helps your teamwork skills and makes you more able to cope in stressful situations is also helpful. Technical skills are an advantage.

Entry and Training

Most people enter as a trainee deckhand and work up to becoming a mate and beyond to a skipper, through experience and qualifications. Some deckhands may decide to become a fishing vessel engineer and progress through the engineering route with specific qualifications. However, all new trainees must by law, complete approved basic safety training in sea survival, first aid, fire fighting, and in health and safety, before going to sea. Entrants continue their training on the job and may also go to a college and study part time, or through day release for a relevant qualification.

Contact the Seafish Industry Training Division for details of the new entrant training programme, or you can approach a skipper direct for on-the-job training, perhaps following a sea fishing apprenticeship scheme. All programmes of training are required to meet the Maritime and Coastguard Agency (MCA) requirements. There is a list of approved training providers on the Seafish Industry Authority website.

Skippers, mates and leading hands working on vessels over 16.5m long, with engine power over 750W, and operating in certain sea areas, are required to hold statutory certificates of competence. Grants may be available to help with this. The Sea Fish Authority also offer short courses in navigation, engineering, stability awareness and in GMDSS radio operation. Funding may also be available for these courses.

Appropriate S/NVQs at levels 2-4 are available in marine vessel support/operations and these qualifications are recognised by the Merchant Navy for employment.

Adults may be able to enter this work through a government-funded training programme. Contact your local Connexions or careers office, Jobcentre Plus, Next Step service or Learning and Skills Council (LSC)/Local Enterprise Company (LEC) for details of all training opportunities and schemes.

Opportunities and Pay

There are jobs on a wide range of fishing vessels and you may work for just one person or a private company. Work is found mainly off the east coasts of Scotland and England, the south west of England and the Scottish Isles, so you may have to move away from home. At the moment, there are over 6,000 fishing vessels of all sizes and types that employ around 12,000 full or part-time people, but the numbers are falling. Self-employment is quite common.

Pay varies widely depending on who you work for, but a deckhand usually earns around £10k a year, and with experience and responsibility around £15k-25k a year. Skippers earn up to around £70k a year and some earn a lot more. Money earned depends on the size and catch of the vessel, and most crew members are paid on a 'share' basis.

Health

You must be physically fit with good eyesight and hearing. Sometimes certain medical conditions, such as epilepsy and diabetes, may be a barrier to entry for this job for health and safety reasons.

Skills and Qualities

able to follow instructions, aptitude for teamwork, enjoy working outdoors, good balance, practical skills, safety conscious, strong, technical aptitude, willing to learn

Relevant Subjects

Land and Environment

Further Information

Apprenticeship Schemes (National Apprenticeship Service) - www.apprenticeships.org.uk

Lantra Careers (A Future In...) (Lantra) - www.afuturein.com

Real Life Guide to Working Outdoors (Trotman) - www.trotman.co.uk

Seafood Information Network (Seafish Information Network) http://sin.seafish.org/

Training Schemes - www.direct.gov.uk/en/educationandlearning

Addresses

Scottish Fishermen's Federation
24 Rubislaw Terrace, Aberdeen AB10 1XE
Phone: +44 (0)1224 646944
Web: www.sff.co.uk

Sea Fish Industry Authority (Seafish)
Training Division, Origin Way, Europarc, Grimsby DN37 9TZ
Phone: +44 (0)1472 252300
Web: www.seafish.org

Seafood Scotland
18 Logie Mill, Logie Green Road, Edinburgh EH7 4HS
Phone: +44 (0)131 557 9344
Web: www.seafoodscotland.org

Similar Jobs

Coastguard Watch Officer, Fish Farm Manager, Fish Farm Worker, Merchant Navy Deck Rating, Royal Navy Rating

Fitness Instructor

also known as: Aerobics Instructor, Health & Fitness Instructor, Personal Trainer, Pilates Teacher, Yoga Teacher

CRCI:Leisure, Sport and Tourism
CLCI:GAG Job Band: 1 to 4

Job Description

Fitness instructors provide exercise instruction to improve a person's fitness. They usually specialise in an area such as aerobics, keep fit, circuit training, yoga, pilates or weight training. Aerobics, step aerobics and keep-fit instructors make up their own routines and match these to music. They demonstrate exercises to classes of people who then copy them. Some fitness instructors/trainers work with individuals to test their fitness and show them how to use equipment correctly. Personal trainers and instructors may devise an individual training programme for their clients. They also ensure that their clients do not injure themselves through exercising too vigorously or incorrectly.

Work Details

Working hours vary and you may be expected to work some evenings, and at weekends. At your work you teach, advise, supervise and organise people. Usually you work with adults in a studio, gym, hall, or sometimes in clients' homes. You are active and on your feet most of the time. Exercise clothing is usually worn, such as a track suit or a leotard, and you may need to use a microphone when instructing large classes.

You have to demonstrate certain fitness exercises so you need to be supple and fit. A clear speaking voice is necessary so that you can be understood over the background music.

Qualification

An interest and ability in exercise plus the right personal qualities are often more important than qualifications for entry to courses.

Adult Qualifications

No specific qualifications are needed for entry to courses and any entry requirements may be relaxed for physically fit adults. Many people who have attended fitness classes go on to take courses to become instructors. Others are older entrants from professional or serious amateur sport.

Work Experience

Relevant work or voluntary experience is always useful and can improve your chances in application for entry to this job. The types of work experience to consider include any sort of work at a gym or leisure centre. Voluntary involvement in sport and fitness activities also demonstrates your commitment.

Entry and Training

Fitness instructors must hold recognised professional qualifications, depending on the sport/area of instruction. There are a wide range of short courses that are relevant and necessary for this job. You may have to fund any courses yourself. For courses and qualifications in all aspects of fitness, including those necessary for teaching, contact SkillsActive, tthe sector skills council for active leisure and learning.

You need to be over 18 to be eligible for public liability insurance and for entry to the Register of Exercise Professionals (REPs). There are different levels of qualification, depending on the area of work you are interested in, which are aligned with National Occupational Standards (NOS). Members of the Register are given a card and registration certificate to prove their qualification and membership. Contact REPs for details. The Keep Fit Association, Premier Training International, and YMCA Fitness Industry Training also offer a variety of recognised courses in exercise and fitness training. Check that the course you choose is acceptable to any potential employer. A degree in sports science, or in sports and exercise science, is also available. For those involved in weight and circuit training, there are British Weight Lifters' Association (BWLA) awards. Courses can be full time, part time, evening classes or modular. Contact BWLA for details.

It is important to keep up to date with new equipment and changes in the fitness industry. At work, you may be able to obtain relevant S/NVQs in subjects such as sport, recreation and allied occupations at levels 1-3, or level 2 in instructing physical activity and exercise. Active IQ also runs a level 2 diploma/certificate course in sport and recreation. Relevant training programmes, including apprenticeship schemes in instructing exercise and fitness or coaching, teaching and instructing, may be available in your area. Advanced apprenticeships leading to qualification at level 3 can be a route into higher education. A Diploma/Welsh Baccalaureate may also be available in your area in Sport & Active Leisure. Contact SkillsActive or visit the diplomas' website for further details.

The Royal Air Force (RAF) takes on recruits to train as fitness instructors. The Army and Royal Navy recruits instructors from their serving members. The armed forces also offers nationally approved awards which are the same as those recognised by civilian sporting organisations. It is an advantage to have experience in first aid for any course.

Maturity is seen as an asset and you can benefit through government training opportunities, such as apprenticeship schemes in instructing exercise and fitness, that may be available in your area. You can also gain recognition of previous experience through Accreditation of Prior Learning (APL) or by working towards relevant S/NVQs. Contact your local careers office, Jobcentre Plus, Next Step service or Learning and Skills Council (LSC) Local Enterprise Company (LEC) for details of training schemes, including adult apprenticeships.

Opportunities and Pay

Since London won the bid to host the 2012 Olympic Games, there is more focus on raising standards in sport in the UK. For those with the right qualifications and skills, employment prospects look good. Fitness training is an expanding area and jobs are available in leisure centres, private clubs, hotels or large companies, or local authority sports centres. You can also be self-employed and hire halls or studios for yourself. There are few full-time jobs so most instructors travel to several different centres to run courses. Some fitness instructors work with their clients on a one-to-one basis, often in the client's home or workplace. Others with further experience and qualifications may become lifestyle consultants.

Pay varies depending on your area and whether or not you are self-employed. Salaried staff earn from around £12k-£18k, rising to around £20k-£25k a year, depending on age, qualifications and range of responsibility. Personal trainers and commercial management posts can attract salaries of up to £30k. Self-employed personal trainers can earn around £25-£50 an hour. A successful and qualified personal trainer can build up a large client list, which can provide a lucrative income.

Health
This job requires a good standard of physical fitness.

Skills and Qualities
able to explain clearly, able to motivate others, encouraging, energetic, enthusiastic, observant, patient, physically fit, safety conscious, tactful

Relevant Subjects
Biology, Health and social care, Leisure, travel and tourism, Performing arts, Physical education and sport, Psychology, Science

Further Information
Active IQ Awarding Body - www.activeiq.co.uk

Apprenticeship Schemes (National Apprenticeship Service) - www.apprenticeships.org.uk

Apprenticeships in Scotland (Careers Info Scotland) - www.apprenticeshipsinscotland.com/about/

British Weight Lifters' Association (BWLA) - www.bwla.co.uk

Careers Information - Royal Air Force (RAF) - www.raf.mod.uk

Diplomas (Foundation, Higher and Advanced) - http://yp.direct.gov.uk/diplomas

Institute for Sport, Parks & Leisure (ISPAL) E-zine (ISPAL) - www.ispal.org.uk/ezine

Pilates - www.pilates.co.uk

Premier Training International - www.premierglobal.co.uk

Real Life Guide to Sports & Active Leisure (Trotman 2009) - www.trotman.co.uk

Register of Exercise Professionals (REPs) - www.exerciseregister.org

SkillsActive - sector skills council for active leisure, learning and well-being - www.skillsactive.com

Welsh Baccalaureate - www.wbq.org.uk

Welsh Institute of Sport - www.welsh-institute-sport.co.uk

▶Working in sport & leisure (2010) (Babcock Lifeskills) - www.babcock-lifeskills.com/

YMCA Fitness Industry Training - www.ymcafit.org.uk

Addresses
Fitness Northern Ireland
The Robinson Centre, Montgomery Road, Belfast BT6 9HS
Phone: +44 (028) 90704080
Web: www.fitnessni.org

Fitness Scotland
Airthrey Castle, University of Stirling, Bridge of Allan FK9 4LA
Phone: +44 (0)1786 466232
Web: www.fitness-scotland.com

Fitness Wales
1b Clarke Street, Ely Bridge, Cardiff CF5 5AL
Phone: +44 (0)29 2057 5155
Web: www.fitnesswales.co.uk

Keep Fit Association
1 Grove House, Foundry Lane, Horsham, West Sussex RH13 5PL
Phone: +44 (0)1403 266 000
Web: www.keepfit.org.uk

Similar Jobs
Leisure Centre Assistant, Outdoor Activities Instructor, Sports Coach, Sports Professional, Teacher: Dance, Teacher: Physical Education

Fitter: Maintenance
also known as: Engineering Maintenance Technician

CRCI:Engineering
CLCI:RAB — Job Band: 1 to 3

Job Description
Maintenance fitters diagnose and repair faults in industrial equipment, machines and instruments. They often work with complex and automated hydraulic, electrical and pneumatic machinery. Fitters track down faults with a series of checks and tests, then repair or replace the part. They can do emergency repair work and also planned maintenance work. Fitters also install and calibrate equipment. They may specialise in the control aspects of computerised machinery that have built-in electronic monitoring systems to detect faults or problems. Some supervise a team of fitters, organise schedules and liaise with production teams.

Work Details
Usually work around 39 hrs a week, Monday to Friday, though you may be required to work shifts that include nights and weekends. You can be based in industrial premises, a production site or workshop. The nature of this work may mean that you have long periods with little to do and must then cope with suddenly being very busy. You need to be able to find faults and solve problems quickly and are expected to produce a high standard of skilled work.

In this job you are usually on your feet all day and you may need to climb over machinery into awkward corners. Some premises and process plants can be noisy, dirty and oily. There is a risk of accidents from equipment and you must follow safety standards. You need to wear overalls, safety glasses and protective footwear.

Qualification
• England, Wales and Northern Ireland
Band 2: For entry to jobs, no minimum qualifications are needed, but it is an advantage to have some GCSEs (A*-C) or equivalent in subjects that include maths, English and physics or another science subject, or equivalent. Design and technology are also useful subjects.

Band 3: For entry to jobs, HNC in engineering or a relevant Diploma, usually at least 4 GCSEs (A*-C) including English, maths and physics and/or a technical/engineering subject.

• Scotland
Band 2: Although academic qualifications are not always specified for this job, many employers ask for some S grades (1-5) including maths, English and physics or another science subject, or similar. Design and technology are also useful subjects.

Band 3: For entry to jobs and for SQA national award in engineering, usually at least four S grades (1-3) including English, maths and physics and/or a technical/engineering subject.

Adult Qualifications
Some full-time college courses waive entry requirements for mature applicants.

Work Experience
Relevant work or voluntary experience is always useful. It can add to your CV and improve your chances when applying for entry to jobs or apprenticeships in the engineering industry.

Entry and Training
Training is usually through an apprenticeship scheme in industrial applications. This is generally on a modular basis after an initial period of training off the job to learn basic skills. Some companies may require you to take an aptitude test. You then learn on the job with a skilled fitter or a supervisor.

You can study for a BTEC/SQA national award through a day or block-release course while you work. You can also work towards S/NVQs in plant or engineering maintenance at levels 1-3. Some trainees enter after they have completed full time BTEC/SQA courses or national diplomas in engineering. You may start off as a maintenance fitter, but there are opportunities to progress to become a qualified engineering technician and register as an EngTech with the Engineering Council (ECUK). Contact ECUK for details. Advanced apprenticeships leading to qualification at level 3 can also be a route into higher education.

The Engineering Development Trust runs a range of nationwide schemes for 11-21 year olds who are interested in engineering as a career. See the website for details. A Diploma/Welsh Baccalaureate may be available in your area in engineering. See the diplomas website for further information.

Mature entrants often have a relevant engineering background. Experience of practical work is important and it is useful to be able to follow drawings and plans. Government training opportunities, such as apprenticeships for adults, may be available in your area. You can also gain recognition of previous experience through Accreditation of Prior Learning or by working towards relevant S/NVQs. Contact your local careers office, Jobcentre Plus, Next Step service or Learning and Skills Council (LSC)/Local Enterprise Company (LEC) for details of training schemes.

Opportunities and Pay

Most jobs are with engineering companies, manufacturing companies, public utilities, hospitals, universities and other organisations that have a large amount of technical equipment. After experience, there may be opportunities to progress to supervisory jobs or to move into other areas within the company. Opportunities exist for work abroad, perhaps on contract with a UK or multinational company. Some fitters become self-employed and look after several companies in a geographical area.

Pay varies depending on location and employer. Starting salaries are around £17k-£21k, rising to £22k-£25k a year with experience. Qualified maintenance fitters can earn £28k-£35k a year depending on experience. Shift work and overtime can make up a significant proportion of pay.

Health

This job requires good colour vision for certain areas of work and you may have to pass a colour vision test.

Skills and Qualities

able to follow drawings and plans, able to work both on your own and in a team, able to work quickly, attention to detail, good spoken communication, manual dexterity, methodical, problem-solving skills, technical aptitude

Relevant Subjects

Design and technology, Engineering, Mathematics, Physics, Science

Further Information

Apprenticeship Schemes (National Apprenticeship Service) - www.apprenticeships.org.uk

Apprenticeships in Scotland (Careers Info Scotland) - www.apprenticeshipsinscotland.com/about/

Diplomas (Foundation, Higher and Advanced) - http://yp.direct.gov.uk/diplomas

SEMTA - sector skills council for science, engineering and manufacturing technologies - www.semta.org.uk

Training Schemes - www.direct.gov.uk/en/educationandlearning

Welsh Baccalaureate - www.wbq.org.uk

Addresses

Engineering Council
246 High Holborn, London WC1V 7EX
Phone: +44 (0)20 3206 0500
Web: www.engc.org.uk

Engineering Development Trust (EDT)
Ridgeway, Welwyn Garden City, Hertfordshire AL7 2AA
Phone: +44 (0)1707 871520
Web: www.etrust.org.uk

Engineering Training Council (NI)
Interpoint, 20-24 York Street, Belfast BT15 1AQ
Phone: +44 (0)28 9032 9878
Web: www.etcni.org.uk

Scottish Engineering
Training Officer, 105 West George Street, Glasgow G2 1QL
Phone: +44 (0)141 221 3181
Web: www.scottishengineering.org.uk

Similar Jobs

Aircraft Engineering Technician, Domestic Appliance Service Technician, Electrical Engineering Technician, Gas Service Engineer, Marine Engineering Technician, Rail Transport Fitter/Electrician

Flight Operations Officer

also known as: Flight Operations Controller

CRCI:Transport and Logistics

CLCI:YAB Job Band: 3 to 5

Job Description

Flight operations officers coordinate activities to ensure that airlines operate successfully at an airport. The range of tasks varies between airlines, but may include rearranging slots for aircraft in the event of delays, forward planning to reduce disruption and monitoring aircraft to ensure that they run on time. They may have to reroute or change aircraft around. Operations officers ensure that flights have the right type of aircraft, properly maintained, in the right place with the appropriate crew. This means drawing up duty rosters and arranging cover for absences. They also arrange for maintenance and repairs to be carried out on aircraft.

Flight operations officers liaise with many different teams within an airport, including airlines, airport authorities and other internal departments working in ground services. They have to make sure that any work undertaken to prepare a flight is done to the correct standards and within set time limits. They must also deal with any unexpected problems and make sure that they are resolved as quickly and efficiently as possible.

Work Details

Staff in an operations control centre work shifts, usually of eight hours, five days a week, covering airport opening times. You are expected to work overtime if there are delays and may be on-call. It is important to live close to the airport and have access to reliable transport.

You work at a computer in the operations office of the control centre. You may also spend some time airside on the apron (where the aircraft are parked up), which can mean being outside in all weather conditions. At these times you must wear a high-visibility vest, ear defenders and safety shoes. You may be required to undergo a Criminal Records Bureau (CRB)/Disclosure Scotland check. The work can be very demanding.

Qualification

Many flight operations officers have experience in other areas of air transport, such as passenger services before entering this job. IT skills and the ability to speak a foreign language are desirable.

• England, Wales and Northern Ireland

Band 3: For entry to jobs, HNC or a relevant Diploma, usually at least 4 GCSEs (A*-C) including English and maths, or equivalent.

Band 4: For HND, Diploma of Higher Education or foundation degree: 1-2 A levels and some GCSEs (A*-C) usually including English and maths, or equivalent.

Band 5: For degree courses: 2-3 A levels and some GCSEs (A*-C) usually including English and maths, or equivalent. Exact requirements depend on the degree you take.

- **Scotland**

Band 3: For entry to jobs, usually at least four S grades (1-3) including English and maths, or similar.

Band 4: For entry to SQA higher national and professional development awards, usually 2-3 H grades and some S grades (1-3), including English and maths, or similar qualifications.

Band 5: For degree courses: 3-5 H grades and some S grades (1-3), including English and maths, or similar qualifications. Exact requirements depend on the degree you take.

Adult Qualifications
Entry requirements may be relaxed for adults applying for higher education courses. Access or foundation courses offer those without the required qualifications a route onto degree courses.

Work Experience
Relevant work experience can equip you with skills that you can use in the future or add to your CV. There are often opportunities available for voluntary work with people. A background in travel and tourism is useful and an interest in aviation may be helpful.

Entry and Training
Entrants to this job need GCSE (grades A*-C)/S (grades 1-3) including English and maths. IT skills are desirable and aptitude in a foreign language is useful.

Initial training is on the job and varies according to the organisation for which you work. If your company is a member of the United Kingdom Operations Managers Association (UKOMA), and you have been employed in flight operations for about 6 months, it may be possible to attend the one-week UKOMA operations officer training course, which combines theory and practical tuition. It aims to provide students with thorough knowledge of airline operating procedures. You may also work towards an S/NVQ in controlling aircraft operations at levels 3 and 4.

Flight operations officers have usually worked in another area of airport transport. Useful qualifications for jobs in this sector include leisure and tourism or travel and tourism courses at levels ranging from GCSE, Diploma or Welsh Baccalaureate, BTEC, S/NVQ or HNC/D and degree.

There are also BTEC awards in airline and airport operations, and apprenticeships may be available in your area.

Mature applicants with experience in other air transport jobs may have an advantage.

Government training opportunities, such as apprenticeships, may be available in your area. You can also gain recognition of previous experience through Accreditation of Prior Learning (APL) or by working towards relevant S/NVQs. Contact your local careers office, Jobcentre Plus, Next Step service or Learning and Skills Council (LSC)/Local Enterprise Company (LEC) for details of training schemes. IT skills and the ability to speak a foreign language are desirable.

Opportunities and Pay
You are employed by a passenger or cargo airline. The busiest airports are Heathrow, Gatwick, Stansted and Manchester, but there are several smaller airports throughout the UK. Contact airlines or airports directly for information about opportunities. The British Airports Authority (BAA) may also be of use.

It is possible to move on to a management or supervisory position within flight operations. There may be opportunities to work abroad.

Starting salaries are around £17k a year. Overtime allowances may be paid. Some airline companies offer concessionary travel rates and other benefits.

Health
You need good levels of stamina for this job.

Skills and Qualities
able to cope under pressure, aptitude for teamwork, commercial awareness, flexible approach, good communication skills, IT skills, logical, problem-solving skills, quick thinking

Relevant Subjects
English, ICT/Computer studies, Leisure, travel and tourism, Mathematics

Further Information
AGCAS: Transport and Logistics (Job Sector Briefing) (AGCAS) - www.prospects.ac.uk

Apprenticeship Schemes (National Apprenticeship Service) - www.apprenticeships.org.uk

Diplomas (Foundation, Higher and Advanced) - http://yp.direct.gov.uk/diplomas

GoSkills - sector skills council for passenger transport - www.goskills.org

United Kingdom Operations Managers Association (UKOMA) - www.ukoma.org

Welsh Baccalaureate - www.wbq.org.uk

▶Working in airports (2010) (Babcock Lifeskills) - www.babcock-lifeskills.com/

Addresses
British Airports Authority (BAA)
BAA Airports Limited, The Compass Centre, Nelson Road, London Heathrow Airport, Hounslow TW6 2GW
Phone: +44 (0)20 8745 9800
Web: www.baa.com

Similar Jobs
Air Traffic Controller, Airline Customer Service Agent, Airport Load Planning Officer, RAF Airman/Airwoman, RAF Officer, Transport Planner

Florist
CRCI:Retail Sales and Customer Services
CLCI:OFM Job Band: 1 to 3

Job Description
Florists display and sell a wide variety of flowers and plants from a shop. They also design and make up arrangements and displays for special occasions, such as weddings, birthdays, anniversaries, gift presentations and funerals. Materials are chosen according to the occasion, customer preference and season. Bouquets are made up in a variety of shapes, sometimes using a vase or basket, or coloured tissue and cellophane. The arrangement is finished with trimmings, such as ribbons. Florists also make wreaths of flowers using a frame with wire or tape and trimmings.

Florists receive Interflora, or similar orders, via the telephone or online and deliver these around the locality. Are usually very busy at certain times of the year, including Christmas, Easter, Valentine's Day and Mothering Sunday. Some florists may decorate local hotels, business premises, private homes and public buildings, or places used for special occasions/events. May compete in either local or national flower shows.

Work Details
Usually work from early morning until around 5-5.30pm, Monday to Saturday, but with time off during the week. Some Sunday work may be necessary at times. You usually work in a shop or workshop, and may also go out to different places to set up or deliver displays. Your job involves serving customers and giving them advice, and you need to learn a lot about the products you are

selling. There are some very busy times, eg on Saturday mornings, when there may be wedding bouquets and other arrangements to prepare and deliver.

Flowers are displayed in the pleasant surroundings of the front shop. Flower arrangements are usually made in the workshop, which can be cool and damp.

Qualification

• England, Wales and Northern Ireland

Band 1: There are no set minimum requirements to become a florist, but some employers prefer applicants to have some GCSEs, or equivalent, at any level. English, maths, and art and craft subjects are the most useful.

Band 2: For entry to BTEC first certificate and diploma in floristry: no set qualifications required though some GCSEs (A*-C) in subjects such as English, maths, art and craft, or equivalent, are useful.

Band 3: For entry to BTEC national certificate/diploma in floristry: usually 4 GCSEs (A*-C) including English, maths, art and craft subjects, or equivalent.

• Scotland

Band 1: There are no set minimum requirements to become a florist, but some employers prefer applicants to have some S grades at any level. English, maths and art and craft subjects are the most useful.

Band 2: Although academic qualifications are not specified for this job, it is an advantage to have some S grades (1-3) in subjects that include English, maths and art and design subjects, or similar.

Band 3: For some courses: usually at least four S grades (1-3) including English, maths and art and design subjects, or similar.

Adult Qualifications

There are no set minimum qualifications to enter this job. Qualifications or experience in art and craft subjects are useful.

Work Experience

Relevant work or voluntary experience is always useful and can improve your chances when applying for entry to jobs. Part-time and holiday employment in a wide range of shops is usually fairly easy to obtain, and experience of work in a florist's shop is particularly useful for finding a permanent job.

Entry and Training

New entrants can train by working with an experienced florist and learning customer service skills and shop procedures, such as handling cash, cheques and credit/debit card transactions, and also how to estimate costs. You need to be able to write messages clearly and be good at spelling. Training can lead to vocational qualifications in floristry, or you can attend a local college on a day-release or part-time basis to gain BTEC/City & Guilds awards in floristry.

There are also full-time BTEC national awards in floristry at level 3, available at some colleges. With full practical experience and a thorough knowledge of the flower industry, professional florists can take the level 4 higher diploma in floristry, developed in association with the British Florist Association. This can lead to the highest award, the master diploma in professional floristry at level 5. There are private courses in floristry, but these can be expensive.

It is possible to gain the BTEC qualifications at some colleges in Scotland. S/NVQs in floristry are available at levels 2-3. There is also an S/NVQ in floristry business management at level 4. A Diploma/Welsh Baccalaureate in retail business may be available in your area. Training programmes, including apprenticeship schemes, may also be available. Advanced apprenticeships leading to qualification at level 3 can also be a route into higher education.

Adults may be able to enter this work through a government-funded training programme. Contact your local careers office, Jobcentre Plus, Next Step service or Learning and Skills Council (LSC)/Local Enterprise Company (LEC) for details of all training opportunities and schemes, including apprenticeships for adults.

Opportunities and Pay

There are specialist florist shops in towns and cities throughout the UK, but most are small businesses, so the number of vacancies is limited. You are usually employed by a florist, who normally owns the business. There are also some jobs in large stores that have a floristry section. For some experienced florists, there is the opportunity to work abroad or perhaps teach floristry, either full or part time. Other opportunities include working in the TV/film industry, hotel chains, interior design companies and in advertising. Many florists are asked to judge competitions or to demonstrate their art at events. Due to the current economic downturn, there may be fewer opportunities for work in the retail sector.

Your pay varies depending on location and employer. A trainee might earn around £11k, rising with experience to around £13k-£16k a year. Qualified florists and managers can earn around £25k a year. Specialist florists can achieve very high earnings, depending on their success.

Health

This job is not suitable if you are allergic to pollens. You need to have normal colour vision for this work.

Skills and Qualities

able to work to deadlines, artistic ability, cash handling skills, creative flair, customer service skills, eye for shape/colour, good organisational skills, manual dexterity, numeracy skills, patient

Relevant Subjects

Art and Design, Biology, Retail and distribution, Science

Further Information

Apprenticeship Schemes (National Apprenticeship Service) - www.apprenticeships.org.uk

British Florist Association - www.britishfloristassociation.org

Diplomas (Foundation, Higher and Advanced) - http://yp.direct.gov.uk/diplomas

Florist & Wholesale Buyer (10 x year) (Wordhouse Publishing Group) - www.fandwb.com/

Lantra - The Sector Skills Council for environmental & land-based sector (Lantra) http:/www.lantra.co.uk

Lantra Careers (A Future In...) (Lantra) - www.afuturein.com

Real Life Guide to Retail (Trotman) - www.trotman.co.uk

Skillsmart Retail - sector skills council for the retail industry - www.skillsmartretail.com

Training Schemes - www.direct.gov.uk/en/educationandlearning

Welsh Baccalaureate - www.wbq.org.uk

Addresses

British Florist Association (BFA)
PO Box 5161, Dudley, West Midlands DY1 9FX
Phone: +44 (0)844 800 7299
Web: www.britishfloristassociation.org

Flowers and Plants Association (F&PA)
68 First Avenue Mortlake, London SW14 8SR
Phone: +44 (0)20 8939 6472
Web: www.flowers.org.uk

Similar Jobs

Garden Centre Assistant, Gardener, Horticultural Worker: Commercial, Market Stall Trader, Retail Assistant, Visual Merchandiser

Food Packaging Operative

also known as: Packer: Food

CRCI:Manufacturing and Production

CLCI:SAC Job Band: 1

Job Description

Food packaging operatives work for a manufacturer or a supermarket. They pack food by hand or by using a machine and this can be while sitting or standing at a conveyor belt or a work counter, perhaps with other people. May work on a production line, using a variety of packaging, such as boxes, bags and bottles. In smaller businesses, they check the food item, weigh and wrap it and may add a label indicating the weight and the price. Other jobs are in supermarkets, sometimes helping customers on the shop floor. May also be involved in packing food and other goods that have been ordered via the Internet, ready for home delivery.

Work Details

Food packaging operatives usually work a 37-40 hr week that may include shift work, evenings and weekends. Part-time work may be available. You work for a manufacturer, small business or supermarket. You stand or sit, in the same place most of the day and in some jobs you may have to do the same task over and over again. You are responsible for hygiene and the maintenance of sterile conditions. Your workplace can be noisy. There may be a risk of minor injuries and you need to wear overalls and possibly something to cover your hair.

Qualification

Employers look for an ability in basic numeracy and literacy rather than formal qualifications.

- **England, Wales and Northern Ireland**

Band 1: No minimum qualifications are required, but you are expected to have a good level of general education. However, some formal/vocational qualifications at any level are useful.

- **Scotland**

Band 1: No minimum qualifications are required, but you are expected to have a good level of general education. However, some formal/vocational qualifications at any level are useful.

Adult Qualifications

No pre-entry qualifications are usually required though some academic/vocational qualifications at any level may be an advantage. English and maths are useful subjects. You can improve your skills and qualifications by working through the Foundation Learning programme. This involves taking credit-based units and qualifications to help you progress.

Work Experience

Work or voluntary experience is always useful. This can help you when applying for jobs or apprenticeships. Your guidance counsellor or adult guidance worker should be able to advise you on how to arrange some work experience.

Entry and Training

Training is on the job, by an employer's training scheme. Topics may include company policies, health and safety rules and regulations, operation of equipment, and hygiene. You may have to sit a test to show you can work well with your hands.

S/NVQs at levels 1-2 for packaging operators or levels 1-3 in food manufacture may be available. Training programmes, including apprenticeships leading to level 2 qualifications may be available in your area. A Diploma/Welsh Baccalaureate in manufacturing and product design may also be available in your area. The food and drink section is particularly relevant for entry to this work.

PIABC is a professional awarding body operating within the Institute of Materials, Minerals and Mining. Their website has details of the certificate in packaging and NVQ Level 2 for packaging operators.

Government training opportunities, such as apprenticeships, may be available in your area. You can also gain recognition of previous experience through Accreditation of Prior Learning (APL) or by working towards relevant S/NVQs. Contact your local careers office, Jobcentre Plus, Next Step service or Learning and Skills Council (LSC) Local Enterprise Company (LEC) for details of training schemes.

Opportunities and Pay

Employment is usually with a food processing company. However, on-line supermarket services are growing in the UK and consequently packing jobs with supermarkets are increasing. With experience you can progress to supervisor or work in quality control.

Your pay varies depending on area and employer. It may start at around £10k-£12k, rising to £15k-£20k a year with experience. Overtime and shift allowances can help to increase earnings.

Health

It may be difficult to do this job if you have skin problems.

Skills and Qualities

able to work both on your own and in a team, able to work quickly, alert, manual dexterity, observant, practical skills, prepared to do repetitive tasks

Relevant Subjects

Manufacturing

Further Information

Apprenticeship Schemes (National Apprenticeship Service) - www.apprenticeships.org.uk

Careers in Food & Drink - www.careersinfoodanddrink.co.uk

Diplomas (Foundation, Higher and Advanced) - http://yp.direct.gov.uk/diplomas

Foundation Learning (QCDA) - www.qcda.gov.uk

Improve Ltd - sector skills council for food and drink manufacturing and processing - www.improveltd.co.uk

Welsh Baccalaureate - www.wbq.org.uk

▶Working in food & drink (2007) (Babcock Lifeskills) - www.babcock-lifeskills.com/

Addresses

PIABC

The Boilerhouse, Springfield Business Park, Caunt Road, Grantham, Lincolnshire NG31 7FZ

Phone: +44 (0)1476 513884

Web: www.piabc.org.uk/piabc/piabc.htm

Similar Jobs

Bottling Operative, Clothing Packer, Packer: General, Warehouse Order Picker/Assembler

Food Processing Operative

also known as: Processor: Food

CRCI:Manufacturing and Production

CLCI:SAC Job Band: 2

Job Description

Food processing operatives use a variety of techniques to convert raw ingredients into a processed product. They work in a large factory making fresh or frozen ready meals, or in a facility freezing, drying or canning one type of foodstuff e.g. vegetables. The raw material goes through a series of stages, and it is likely that you receive training in a specific role. This can range from measuring the raw materials, to manning the machinery, to packing and labelling.

Keeping the facility clean and adhering to strict hygiene regulations are an essential part of the job. Processors utilise a range of equipment such as weighing scales, knives, mixing machines, blenders, ovens and laminating packaging machines. They monitor the quality of the processed food.

Food Processing Operative

Can work for a small independent producer making more artisan products, produced by hand with a more individual finish.

Processed foods are sold in retail outlets, or may be used in fast food chains, restaurants or as airline meals. Through a process of pasteurisation, processed foods have a longer shelf life and are therefore attractive to retailers.

Work Details

Usually works a 37-40 hr week that may include shift work, evenings and weekends. Part-time work may be available. You work for a manufacturer, small business or supermarket chain. Work is normally in factory conditions with strictly controlled breaks. You may stand or sit, in the same place most of the day and in some jobs you may have to do the same task over and over again. You are responsible for hygiene and the maintenance of sterile conditions. Your workplace can be noisy. There may be a risk of minor injuries and you need to wear overalls and a hairnet/hat.

Qualification

• England, Wales and Northern Ireland

Band 2: For entry to jobs, no minimum qualifications are needed, but it is an advantage to have some GCSEs (A*-C) or equivalent in subjects that include English and maths.

• Scotland

Band 2: Although academic qualifications are not specified for this job, it is an advantage to have some S grades (1-3) in subjects that include English and maths, or similar.

Adult Qualifications

No pre-entry qualifications are usually required though some academic/vocational qualifications at any level may be an advantage. English and maths are useful subjects.

Work Experience

Work or voluntary experience is always useful. This can help you when applying for jobs or apprenticeships. Your guidance counsellor or adult guidance worker should be able to advise you on how to arrange some work experience.

Entry and Training

It is possible to enter this work without qualifications and work your way up. You can train on the job and gain qualifications while working. Improve Limiteds Proficiency Qualifications (IPQs) have replaced NVQs for on-the-job training and assessment. They focus on workforce development and raising competency standards. Improve Vocational Qualifications (IVQs) provide off-the-job learning opportunities. Options are available in food manufacture and food science and technology.

You can progress to a foundation degree in food manufacture, preparation or production. These degrees are awarded by universities and take two years to complete if studying full time or three to four years part-time. Graduates then have the option to transfer to the second or third year of an honours degree programme.

A Diploma/Welsh Baccalaureate in manufacturing and product design may be available in your area. The food and drink section is particularly relevant for entry to this work. Improve has worked on the development of this diploma by consulting with other manufacturing sector skills councils and manufacturing employers to create a qualification that meets the needs of the industry.

Improve has also worked on developing an integrated apprenticeship framework for the benefit of employers and learners. The apprenticeship in food manufacture is a good start point for those entering the industry and working in a food manufacturing environment or, depending on your current level of experience, you can apply for an advanced modern apprenticeship in food manufacture. This is a level 3 nationally recognised qualification. Bridging programmes are also in place to assist students who want to progress from further to higher education.

Improve's new food and drink IPQs and IVQs for England, Wales and Northern Ireland complement the Scottish Vocational Qualification (SVQ) in Food Manufacture and the Scottish modern apprenticeships programme.

Government training opportunities, such as apprenticeships, may be available in your area. You can also gain recognition of previous experience through Accreditation of Prior Learning (APL) or by working towards relevant S/NVQs. Contact your local careers office, Jobcentre Plus, Next Step service or Learning and Skills Council (LSC) Local Enterprise Company (LEC) for details of training schemes.

Opportunities and Pay

There are around 470,000 people employed in the food and drink manufacturing sector. This business generates a turnover of £74bn a year and is the largest manufacturing sector in the UK. Food production rates have remained fairly stable throughout the recession and some sectors have experienced growth. This is, in part, due to increasing exports, the development of new products and monitoring and responding to changes in tastes and demands from consumers.

Employment is usually with a food processing company. With experience you can progress to supervisor or work in quality control. With further training, it is possible to move into food scientist or technologist roles.

Your pay varies depending on area and employer. It may start at around £12k-£18k, rising to £20k a year with experience. Overtime and shift allowances can help to increase earnings.

Health

It may be difficult to do this job if you have skin problems.

Skills and Qualities

able to follow instructions, able to operate equipment, attention to detail, creative flair, good organisational skills, health & safety awareness, prepared to do repetitive tasks

Relevant Subjects

Manufacturing

Further Information

Apprenticeship Schemes (National Apprenticeship Service) - www.apprenticeships.org.uk

Careers in Food & Drink - www.careersinfoodanddrink.co.uk

Careers in Food Technology (Institute of Food Science and Technology) - www.foodtechcareers.org

Diplomas (Foundation, Higher and Advanced) - http://yp.direct.gov.uk/diplomas

Food and Drink Federation - www.fdf.org.uk

Food and Drink Qualifications - www.fdq.org.uk

Foundation Learning (QCDA) - www.qcda.gov.uk

Improve Ltd - sector skills council for food and drink manufacturing and processing - www.improveltd.co.uk

National Skills Academy for Food and Drink Manufacturing - http://foodanddrink.nsacademy.co.uk

Welsh Baccalaureate - www.wbq.org.uk

▶Working in food & drink (2007) (Babcock Lifeskills) - www.babcock-lifeskills.com/

Similar Jobs

Assembler: Light Industry, Baker, Brewery Worker, Food Packaging Operative, Quality Assurance Controller/Inspector

Food Scientist/Technologist

CRCI:Science, Mathematics and Statistics
CLCI:QON Job Band: 4 to 5

Job Description

Food scientists work in the food and drinks industry ensuring that products are consumer safe and of a high standard. They are experts on the chemical, biological and nutritional properties of food and drinks, and the effects of their processing and preservation. Scientists apply this knowledge and research to the efficient production and economic sale of food and drink products, ensuring that all legal and nutritional standards are satisfied. Also carry out quality control to ensure that safety and hygiene standards are met at all stages of food and drinks production.

Food technologists may be involved with the conversion of raw materials into finished products, or with the canning and freezing of perishables for storage. May work on the development of new ideas for recipes, and on the modification of existing food and drinks. They produce samples for testing and conduct experiments for new or modified products. Must follow extremely strict procedures and guidelines known as the Hazard Analysis Critical Control Points (HACCP).

Must keep up to date with changing food production legislation. Also have knowledge of the industry's market and consumer research, chemical engineering and design, food and drinks manufacturing and production planning, as well as financial management and budgetary control. They use high technology, including complex computer systems, to carry out their work.

Work Details

Usually work a basic 35-40 hr week, Monday to Friday, though if working in manufacturing, may be required to work shifts. Work with a team of scientists/technologists, liaising with other departments. The environment depends on the type of industry and your role but you usually work in a laboratory, research unit or quality control department of a food manufacturing and processing factory. A white coat or, sometimes, protective clothing is worn. Those who are vegetarians and/or have certain religious views may be limited in some areas of work.

Qualification

- **England, Wales and Northern Ireland**

Band 4: For HND, Diploma of Higher Education or foundation degree: 1-2 A levels and some GCSEs (A*-C) usually including English, science and maths, or equivalent.

Band 5: For degree courses: usually 3 A levels, including two science subjects or maths; and some GCSEs (A*-C) usually including English, maths and a science, or equivalent. Exact requirements depend on the degree you take.

- **Scotland**

Band 4: For entry to SQA higher national and professional development awards, usually 2-3 H grades and some S grades (1-3), including English, science and maths, or similar qualifications.

Band 5: For degree courses: 3-5 H grades preferably including science and maths, and some S grades (1-3) including English, or similar qualifications. Exact requirements depend on the degree you take.

Degree Information

A degree in food science/technology is preferred, but degrees in biochemistry, microbiology, nutrition, applied chemistry or life and medical science are often acceptable. Postgraduate courses in food technology are available for those with related degrees.

Adult Qualifications

Access courses to higher education as well as a foundation year prior to a degree are usually available for applicants without the traditional entry qualifications.

Work Experience

Employers or universities may prefer candidates who have relevant work or voluntary experience. Ideally, working with a food scientist or food technologist is the most useful. Related experience can be in other scientific or food-related industries, in an industrial or commercial laboratory, or with a qualified dietitian.

Entry and Training

After completing an HND/degree course in food science, food studies, food technology or a science, you continue your training by practical work experience. Those with an HND may be eligible for third year entry to a degree course. Most companies run in-house training programmes and may offer sponsorship schemes to undergraduates. It is also possible to take a postgraduate diploma in food control awarded by the Institute of Food Science and Technology (IFST). This course is designed for those working in the industry and requires academic study combined with work experience.

There are also specialised postgraduate certificates in food science and specifically one in Hazard Analysis Critical Control Points (HACCP). This is assessed by coursework only, and by using a variety of methods, including case reports, case studies and a portfolio. It is suitable for those having experience of the food industry that wish to study in more depth. At the end of the course you can proceed on to the postgraduate diploma in HACCP management.

A Diploma/Welsh Baccalaureate in manufacturing and product design may be available in your area. There are also relevant foundation degrees, including food science. There are opportunities to start your career as a laboratory assistant or food technician (see job profile) and work your way up. It is expected that you continue to update your skills and experience throughout your career and usually through short specialised courses. The IFST offer a continuing professional development (CPD) scheme for its members and the Chartered Institute of Environmental Health (CIEH) also offers courses.

Mature entrants have some opportunities for employment depending on company requirements. Direct entry to industry may be possible for those with related qualifications and/or experience in areas such as chemistry, biology, microbiology, biochemistry or nutrition.

Opportunities and Pay

The UK is the second largest producer of food and drink in the world and employs about half a million people. Jobs are available throughout the UK and sometimes abroad. You may be employed in the food processing and manufacturing industry in research, product development, analysis, production management or quality control. Some food scientists/technologists work for retail chains in purchasing, quality control, sales and marketing. There are also opportunities in some government departments, in research institutions and in consultancy work.

Currently there is a shortage of well-qualified food scientists/technologists. Consequently, the industry is keen to encourage young people onto food science and food technology degree courses. Improve, the food and drink sector skills council says that 13,000 additional food scientists and technologists will be needed by 2014. Employment prospects are very good. Self-employment or freelance work is sometimes an option.

Pay varies depending on location and employer but trainee scientists and technologists generally start at around £20k, rising to around £35k a year with experience. Those with senior managerial responsibilities can earn up to £70k a year.

Health

You require normal colour vision for certain areas of work. You also need a good sense of smell and taste. You should not be allergic to skin irritants.

Skills and Qualities

adaptable, aptitude for teamwork, attention to detail, excellent communication skills, good organisational skills, IT skills, methodical, responsible attitude, scientific approach, sound judgement, technical aptitude

Relevant Subjects

Biology, Chemistry, Design and technology, English, Hospitality and catering, ICT/Computer studies, Manufacturing, Mathematics, Physics, Science

Further Information

Careers in Food Technology (Institute of Food Science and Technology) - www.foodtechcareers.org

Diplomas (Foundation, Higher and Advanced) - http://yp.direct.gov.uk/diplomas

Food Manufacture (William Reed Business Media Ltd) - www.foodmanufacture.co.uk

Food Science & Technology (quarterly) (Institute of Food Science & Technology) - www.ifst.org/publications/fsandt/

Improve Ltd - sector skills council for food and drink manufacturing and processing - www.improveltd.co.uk

New Scientist (weekly) (Reed) - www.newscientist.com

▶Working in food & drink (2007) (Babcock Lifeskills) - www.babcock-lifeskills.com/

▶Working in science (2007) (Babcock Lifeskills) - www.babcock-lifeskills.com/

Addresses

Chartered Institute of Environmental Health (CIEH)
Chadwick Court, 15 Hatfields, London SE1 8DJ
Phone: +44 (0)20 7928 6006
Web: www.cieh.org

Department for Environment, Food & Rural Affairs (DEFRA)
Customer Contact Unit , Eastbury House, 30 - 34 Albert Embankment, London SE1 7TL
Phone: 0845 933 5577 (UK only)
Web: www.defra.gov.uk

Food and Drink Federation (FDF)
6 Catherine Street, London WC2B 5JJ
Phone: +44 (0)20 7836 2460
Web: www.fdf.org.uk

Institute of Food Science and Technology (IFST)
5 Cambridge Court, 210 Shepherd's Bush Road, London W6 7NJ
Phone: +44 (0)20 7603 6316
Web: www.ifst.org.uk

Scottish Food and Drink Federation (SFDF)
4a Torphichen Street, Edinburgh EH3 8JQ
Phone: +44 (0)131 229 9415
Web: www.sfdf.org.uk

Similar Jobs

Biotechnologist, Consumer Scientist, Dietitian, Food Technician, Microbiologist, Nutritional Therapist

Food Service Assistant

also known as: Cafi Assistant, Coffee Shop Assistant, Counter Service Assistant, Fast Food Service Assistant, Motorway Food Service Assistant, Sales Assistant: Food & Drink

CRCI:Catering and Hospitality
CLCI:IC Job Band: 1

Job Description

Food service assistants work behind a counter in a self-service restaurant, motorway services, a café, tea room or coffee shop. They may also sell snacks and take-away meals to customers in a fast-food outlet. They can work in the high street or out of town at an airport, station or shopping centre.

Assistants welcome customers, stand at a counter and take their order, sometimes through a service window to customers in their cars. They serve customers with food and beverages in fast food outlets. This may be hot food such as pizzas, burgers, chicken, fish and chips, Chinese or Indian food. They may also serve salads, rolls and sandwiches, tea, soft drinks, coffee and desserts. Assistants aim to serve customers as quickly as possible. They calculate the cost of the order, take payment of cash, credit/debit card or vouchers, and may give change to the customer using a till, which is usually computerised.

Assistants may also do simple cooking, make salads or sandwiches, and help in taking deliveries, stocking and tidying the stock rooms. They clear the work area and tidy the dining room, if there is one. They must be aware of the hygiene regulations in catering. Some food outlets do children's parties so assistants may need to oversee these. They also keep the preparation and serving areas hygienic and tidy at all times and ensure there are always clean trays, plates, glasses and cutlery available. Restocks the counter as necessary and ensures the food is attractively arranged and well presented. May also clear tables, collect trays and help to wash up or load/unload a dishwasher.

Work Details

Usually works a 37-40 hr week, which may include some evenings and weekends working shifts. You are on your feet all day and work can be busy at times. You work mainly in light and pleasant surroundings, though occasionally in hot and steamy conditions. Your job is to welcome customers and be helpful to them. Sometimes you have to cope with complaints from customers. Work can be very busy at times.

Those working at a 'drive thru' outlet may wear a headset and use a computerised touch screen ordering system. Be prepared to follow employers' rules restricting the wearing of cosmetics and jewellery. You may wear a uniform or overall, non slip shoes and something to cover your hair. In this job you are required by law to have a high standard of personal hygiene and must also follow the law surrounding health and hygiene at work.

Qualification

• England, Wales and Northern Ireland

Band 1: For entry to jobs, no minimum qualifications are needed, but you are expected to have a good level of general education and relevant experience. Some formal/vocational qualifications at any level are useful and schools and colleges may also offer basic food hygiene certificate courses.

• Scotland

Band 1: For entry to jobs, no minimum qualifications are needed, but you are expected to have a good level of general education and relevant experience. Some formal/vocational qualifications at any level are useful and schools and colleges may also offer basic food hygiene certificate courses.

Adult Qualifications
There are no formal educational requirements for mature entry, although a good standard of general education is preferable. You can improve your skills and qualifications by working through the Foundation Learning programme. This involves taking credit-based units and qualifications to help you progress.

Work Experience
Employers or colleges may prefer candidates who have relevant work or voluntary experience in food preparation, though other catering/hospitality experience is helpful. There is often plenty of paid part-time catering work available. In some areas there is a young apprenticeship (14-16) scheme that provides an extended work placement and eventual achievement of a level 2 qualification whilst at school.

Entry and Training
Employers often look for good communication skills and a welcoming personality rather than formal qualifications. The use of a foreign language is an advantage in some jobs. Some schools and colleges offer a hospitality and catering course, which may be useful prior to applying for a job. There is also a basic food hygiene certificate that can be taken whilst in full or part-time time education.

Once in a job, training is usually through working with a more experienced assistant or supervisor. Some employers may send you on a day-release course to a local college. There may be a formal in-house training programme if you work in a fast-food outlet, which has its own unique procedures. Some companies have a specific training programme of short courses covering aspects such as customer care, hygiene, and health and safety, which can lead to a nationally recognised qualification.

A Diploma/Welsh Baccalaureate may be available in your area in hospitality. Relevant S/NVQs are available, including hospitality, food and drink service, food processing and cooking and multi-skilled hospitality services at levels 1-2. Training programmes, including apprenticeships in catering and hospitality leading to level 2 and advanced apprenticeships leading to level 3, may be available in your area. The Hospitality Awarding Body (HAB) offers vocational qualifications, including customer service and quick service. There are also QCF level 2 awards in hospitality and catering principles (food and drink service). Contact People 1st for details of all relevant courses and training schemes.

Mature applicants with experience in sales, catering or customer care are usually welcomed by employers. Government training opportunities, such as apprenticeships, may be available in your area. You can also gain recognition of previous experience through Accreditation of Prior Learning (APL) or by working towards relevant S/NVQs. Contact your local careers office, Jobcentre Plus, Next Step service or Learning and Skills Council (LSC) Local Enterprise Company (LEC) for details of training schemes.

Opportunities and Pay
Most jobs are found in towns and cities throughout the UK, and out-of-town locations at airports or industrial or shopping centre complexes. Jobs are available in cafés, restaurants, hotel restaurants, business canteens, schools, colleges and universities, department stores, hospitals, airports, Eurostar, ferries and cruise ships. You can find work in a branch of a large chain of pizza, chicken or burger outlets, or in a small local fast-food shop. Jobs are also available at holiday centres, leisure/adventure parks and motorway services.

The sale of single products such as coffee, juices and health food snacks in outlets is also growing. Staff turnover is high so there are many jobs for food service assistants at the moment. Jobs can be full or part time, and there are also opportunities for seasonal work. With experience, it may be possible to be promoted to supervisor or store manager, or train for other catering jobs. Self-employment in your own food outlet may also be possible.

Pay varies considerably, but most assistants earn around the minimum wage of £5.93 an hour, rising to £6.60 an hour and with experience around £7-£8 an hour. Free or subsidised meals are usually available for staff. Your average weekly wage may also be increased by tips. Overtime pay is possible.

Health
To do this job you have to have good stamina and general fitness. People with certain skin problems may not be able to do this job.

Skills and Qualities
able to cope under pressure, able to get on with all kinds of people, able to work quickly, aptitude for teamwork, calm, friendly, hard working, numeracy skills, smart appearance

Relevant Subjects
Hospitality and catering

Further Information
Apprenticeship Schemes (National Apprenticeship Service) - www.apprenticeships.org.uk

Apprenticeships in Scotland (Careers Info Scotland) - www.apprenticeshipsinscotland.com/about/

CareerScope: Hospitality and Leisure (Springboard UK) - http://careerscope.springboarduk.net/

Diploma in Hospitality (People 1st) - www.hospitalitydiploma.co.uk

Foundation Learning (QCDA) - www.qcda.gov.uk

People 1st - sector skills council for hospitality, leisure, travel and tourism - www.people1st.co.uk

So you want to work in the Food Industry (Wayland) - www.waylandbooks.co.uk

Springboard UK (Springboard UK) - www.springboarduk.net

Springboard Wales (Springboard Wales) - http://wales.springboarduk.net/

Training Schemes - www.direct.gov.uk/en/educationandlearning

UKSP - Guide to Success in Hospitality, Leisure, Travel & Tourism - www.uksp.co.uk

▶Working in food & drink (2007) (Babcock Lifeskills) - www.babcock-lifeskills.com/

▶Working in hospitality & catering (2009) (Babcock Lifeskills) - www.babcock-lifeskills.com/

Similar Jobs
Air Cabin Crew, Bartender, Chef/Cook, Kitchen Assistant/Porter, Waiter/Waitress

Food Technician
CRCI:Science, Mathematics and Statistics
CLCI:QON — Job Band: 3

Job Description
Food technicians assist food scientists/technologists in the research and development of food production and look after the day-to-day running of a laboratory. They follow very strict guidelines called Hazard Analysis Critical Control Point (HACCP) to ensure that food and food products are safe. Technicians carry out chemical analysis, which is often automated, and check results on a computer. They test and look for any harmful micro-organisms and chemicals that could cause food poisoning. Some work on developing processing or packaging methods, others on ways of preserving food products. They use sophisticated machinery to test quality, safety, taste, and the nutritional value of processed foods.

Work Details
Usually work a basic 37-39 hr week, Monday to Friday, though if working in manufacturing may be required to work shifts. The work environment depends on the type of industry. You usually work under the supervision of a food scientist or senior technologist. You

can have responsibility for analysis and collection of results. It is important that food is processed under high standards of hygiene and you may need to wear a white coat or other protective clothing. Those who are vegetarians and/or have certain religious views may be limited in some areas of work.

Qualification

- **England, Wales and Northern Ireland**

Band 3: For entry: usually at least 4 GCSEs (A*-C) preferably including English, maths and a science, or equivalent.

- **Scotland**

Band 3: For entry: usually at least four S grades (1-3) preferably including English, maths and science, or similar.

Adult Qualifications

Some colleges may offer Access or foundation courses for those without usual entry requirements. Direct entry may be possible for those with experience in a relevant area such as chemistry, biology, microbiology, biochemistry or nutrition.

Work Experience

There are no specific requirements in terms of work experience for this job, but a scientific background is useful. Some relevant areas are in quality control in a food manufacturing company or something involving laboratory work. This enables you to get a feel of what the working environment is like.

Entry and Training

It is possible to take a full-time BTEC/SQA national award before applying for this job. Alternatively, you can go directly into a job and take a part-time BTEC/SQA certificate course through day release or evening classes. There is also on-the-job training and many firms run their own in-house training programmes. Most courses in food technology and food science offer specialist options, such as dairy products, vegetable processing, baking, meat or fish.

Relevant S/NVQs are available at levels 1-3 in food and drink manufacture or at levels 1-4 in laboratory work. Training programmes, including apprenticeship schemes, may be available in your area. Advanced apprenticeships leading to qualification at level 3 can also be a route into higher education. A Diploma/Welsh Baccalaureate in manufacturing and product design may be available in your area.

Mature entrants have opportunities for employment depending on company requirements, and the qualifications and experience of the candidate.

Opportunities and Pay

Jobs are available throughout the UK and sometimes abroad. You may be employed in the food processing and manufacturing industry, mainly in research and development. There are also jobs in the retail industry in purchasing, quality control, sales and marketing. Some food technicians are employed by government departments, universities, colleges and research institutions.

Many technicians continue their studies by taking a higher national diploma or degree course, gaining qualifications for food technologist/scientist posts.

Pay varies depending on location and employer but trainees earn in the region of £14k-£16.5k a year, rising to £20k-£25k with experience. Higher earners may make more than £30k a year with some employers.

Health

You require normal colour vision for certain areas of work. You also need a good sense of smell and taste. You should not be allergic to skin irritants.

Skills and Qualities

able to follow instructions, accurate, analytical skills, attention to detail, careful, conscientious, IT skills, observant, scientific approach, technical aptitude

Relevant Subjects

Biology, Chemistry, Design and technology, Hospitality and catering, ICT/Computer studies, Manufacturing, Mathematics, Physics, Science

Further Information

Apprenticeship Schemes (National Apprenticeship Service) - www.apprenticeships.org.uk

Diplomas (Foundation, Higher and Advanced) - http://yp.direct.gov.uk/diplomas

Improve Ltd - sector skills council for food and drink manufacturing and processing - www.improveltd.co.uk

▶Working in food & drink (2007) (Babcock Lifeskills) - www.babcock-lifeskills.com/

▶Working in science (2007) (Babcock Lifeskills) - www.babcock-lifeskills.com/

Addresses

Food and Drink Federation (FDF)
6 Catherine Street, London WC2B 5JJ
Phone: +44 (0)20 7836 2460
Web: www.fdf.org.uk

Institute of Food Science and Technology (IFST)
5 Cambridge Court, 210 Shepherd's Bush Road, London W6 7NJ
Phone: +44 (0)20 7603 6316
Web: www.ifst.org.uk

Scottish Food and Drink Federation (SFDF)
4a Torphichen Street, Edinburgh EH3 8JQ
Phone: +44 (0)131 229 9415
Web: www.sfdf.org.uk

Similar Jobs

Biochemist, Brewer: Technical, Dietitian, Food Scientist/ Technologist, Laboratory Technician: Science, Quality Assurance Controller/Inspector

Footwear Designer

also known as: Shoe Designer

CRCI:Design, Arts and Crafts
CLCI:EJ
Job Band: 4 to 5

Job Description

Footwear designers combine artistic talent with technical knowledge to create designs for footwear. They usually work as part of a team including fashion buyers. Must follow fashion trends closely and work out ideas by sketching or using computer-aided design (CAD) software. May copy and adapt other people's ideas. Usually work in one of three areas: high fashion 'one off' designs, designer ready-to-wear based on the coming season or high-street fashion.

Designers choose materials and colours, consider costs, and adapt the design to suit pattern making and manufacturing processes. They must have a good understanding of the anatomy of the foot and lower leg. May specialise in ladies', men's, children's, or sport footwear design.

Work Details

Normal working hours are from 9am to 5pm, Monday to Friday, though there are often long working hours including weekends. This is particularly when preparing for shows or releases of new collections, when you are likely to be under pressure. You spend a lot of time working in a studio, but may also have to travel around the country and abroad, to meet clients and to go to fashion shows, exhibitions and fabric houses. Sometimes your work may be criticised or rejected. You usually have to work within an agreed budget.

Qualification

• England, Wales and Northern Ireland

Band 4: For foundation degree in footwear: an art and design foundation course or national diploma in footwear, design and technology, or one A level in an art and design subject, plus 4 GCSEs at grade C or above.

Band 5: For degree in fashion design: 2-3 A levels and some GCSEs (A*-C) usually including English and maths, or equivalent. Most students take a foundation course first. Exact requirements depend on the degree you take. A diploma in creative and media may be considered as an alternative to A levels.

For a specialist degree in footwear: successful completion of an art and design foundation course or national diploma in a relevant subject, plus 2 A levels at grade C or above, including an art or design subject.

• Scotland

Band 4: For entry to SQA higher national and professional development awards, usually 2-3 H grades and some S grades (1-3), including English and maths, or similar qualifications.

Band 5: For degree courses in fashion design: 3-5 H grades and some S grades (1-3), usually including English and maths, or similar qualifications. Most students take a foundation course first. Exact requirements depend on the degree you take.

Degree Information

There is a specialist degree in footwear but other relevant subjects include fashion and textile design and art and design. Graduates in any art and design subject may be acceptable, but need to gain experience and build up a portfolio of fashion work.

Adult Qualifications

Mature applicants with outstanding portfolios of work may be accepted for courses without the standard entry requirements. There are Access and foundation courses in some areas, which give adults without qualifications a route into degree courses. Check with individual colleges.

Work Experience

The industry is very competitive so any work experience you can gain puts you at an advantage when it comes to getting a job. Skills gained as an assistant in a design studio or workshop, or in a design consultancy are useful. An understanding of the footwear industry is an advantage.

Entry and Training

Most footwear designers enter the industry after taking a degree in fashion design. Some graduates enter the industry as design assistants and progress to become a designer. A degree that includes design and technical skills is important. Often the first year is core to all art and design subjects and during years 2-4 there is the opportunity to specialise in footwear design. It is important to take a portfolio of your work along to interviews.

There are also specialist training courses in the UK and abroad. The University of Northampton and De Montfort University offer footwear design. Leicester College is an International School of Footwear with strong links with industry; it has associate schools in Turkey, India and Japan. The college offers a two-year foundation degree in footwear awarded by De Montfort University which includes work placements and visits to industry. On completion of this or the Professional Development Diploma: Footwear, you can progress to the BA (Hons) in footwear at De Montfort University. The London College of Fashion offers a diploma, a foundation degree, an honours degree or a masters in footwear. There are various colleges in Spain, Portugal and Italy offering relevant courses too.

There are specialist diplomas in manufacturing and product design or creative and media which may provide a route into footwear design. There are also apprenticeships at level 2 in footwear, textiles and sewn products and at level 3 in textiles and apparel.

On-the-job training to continue to develop your skills is important. Organisations such as the SATRA Technology Centre, the BLC Leather Technology Centre, De Montfort University and the Textile Institute run professional courses. The British Footwear Association (BFA)represents the industry in the UK and may be a useful source of information.

Entry can be difficult for mature entrants without relevant qualifications. Experience in art and design, fashion or sales and marketing is an advantage. Skills gained as an assistant in a design studio or workshop, or in a design consultancy are useful. An understanding of the footwear industry is helpful.

Opportunities and Pay

There are few opportunities for footwear designers. Employers include larger footwear manufacturers, footwear brands, design companies, or footwear retailers and agents. The job market for footwear designers is becoming an international one and the main employers are medium-sized companies with international operations.

Once you are working as a footwear designer, you can progress to become a senior designer, design director or head of department. Some decide to become freelance designers and work for companies to work on specific projects, or become self-employed.

Pay varies depending on ability, reputation and whether you are self-employed. Starting salaries for footwear designers are around £15k-£20k a year, rising to £26k-£35k with experience. Experienced designers with particular talent can earn over £60k a year.

Skills and Qualities

ambitious, artistic ability, attention to detail, creative flair, eye for shape/colour, eye for visual effect, fashion conscious, manual dexterity, specialist IT skills

Relevant Subjects

Art and Design, Design and technology, ICT/Computer studies

Further Information

BLC Leather Technology Centre - www.blcleathertech.com

British Footwear Association (BFA) (BFA) - www.britfoot.com

Can you Cut it? - www.canucutit.co.uk

Diplomas (Foundation, Higher and Advanced) - http://yp.direct.gov.uk/diplomas

Leicester International School of Footwear - www.shoeinfonet.com/schools/EU/schools_sfc_uk.htm/

SATRA Technology Centre - www.satra.co.uk

Skillfast-UK Just the Job - www.skillfast-uk.org/justthejob/

Skillsmart Retail - sector skills council for the retail industry - www.skillsmartretail.com

The Textile Institute - www.texi.org

▶Working in art & design (2009) (Babcock Lifeskills) - www.babcock-lifeskills.com/

▶Working in fashion & clothing (2008) (Babcock Lifeskills) - www.babcock-lifeskills.com/

Addresses

BLC Leather Technology Centre Ltd
Leather Trade House, Kings Park Road, Moulton Park,
Northampton NN3 6JD
Phone: +44 (0)1604 679 999
Web: www.blcleathertech.com

British Footwear Association (BFA)
3 Burystead Place, Wellingborough NN8 1AH
Phone: + 44 (0)1933 229 005
Web: www.britfoot.com

De Montfort University
The Gateway, Leicester
Phone: (0116) 255 1551
Web: www.dmu.ac.uk

London College of Fashion
20 John Princes Street, London W1G 0BJ
Phone: +44 (0)20 7514 7344
Web: www.fashion.arts.ac.uk

Similar Jobs
Costume Designer, Fashion Designer, Film/TV & Theatre Wardrobe Supervisor, Hat Designer, Textile Designer

Forecourt Assistant: Fuel Service Station

also known as: Cashier: Fuel Service Station, Petrol Station Attendant

CRCI:Retail Sales and Customer Services
CLCI:OFM Job Band: 1 to 2

Job Description
Forecourt assistants work mainly as cashiers at fuel service stations where customers pay by cash, cheque or by credit/debit card. They use a console that controls the petrol pumps and displays how much to charge each customer. Also put petrol/diesel into vehicles for customers if the station is not self-service. May help to check oil and tyres, and also monitor carwash facilities. Filling stations often sell groceries, books, cards, maps, newspapers and magazines, lottery tickets, and items for vehicles, such as antifreeze, oil and motor accessories. May also sell goods such as calor gas, flowers and hot fast-foods.

Assistants accept fuel deliveries from tankers and check meters. Sometimes have to balance till receipts and put money into a safe. They are also responsible for ordering supplies for the shop, keeping the shelves filled and the forecourt clean and tidy.

Work Details
Many petrol stations are open 24 hours a day, seven days a week. Staff usually have to work shifts on a rota basis. In a self-service station, most of the work is indoors. A small amount of time is spent outside checking meters and tidying the forecourt. Your work includes serving customers, checking on stock, and possibly helping to re-order stock.

In a non self-service station, you sometimes work outside putting fuel into vehicles. You are responsible for handling cash. Some workplaces can be smelly and dirty and you may need to wear a uniform or overalls.

Qualification

• England, Wales and Northern Ireland
Band 1: No minimum qualifications are required, but you are expected to have a good level of general education, including some ability in basic English and maths. Some formal/vocational qualifications at any level are useful.

Band 2: Some employers may require several GCSEs (A*-E) preferably including English and maths, or equivalent.

• Scotland
Band 1: No minimum qualifications are required, but you are expected to have a good level of general education, including some ability in basic English and maths. Some formal/vocational qualifications at any level are useful.

Band 2: Some employers may require several S grades (1-5) preferably including English and maths, or similar.

Adult Qualifications
Minimum qualifications are not often specified, but some ability in basic maths and English is required.

Work Experience
Relevant work or voluntary experience is always useful and can improve your chances when applying for entry to jobs in sales. It can equip you with skills that you can use in the future and add to your CV. Part-time and holiday employment is usually easy to obtain.

Entry and Training
Applicants are usually over 18, but this varies in different areas of the country. To enter this job you may have to take a basic maths test. Training is given on the job, with instruction from an experienced employee or the manager. Petrol companies sometimes offer short training seminars/courses. The Safety Pass Alliance offers training in forecourt operations.

It may be possible to work towards an S/NVQ in forecourt operations at level 2 or retail skills at levels 1-2. Other vocational qualifications are also available, such as the level 2-3 certificate in retail operations or the certificate in retail skills at levels 1-3. Training programmes, including apprenticeship schemes, may also be available. Advanced apprenticeships leading to qualification at level 3 can be a route into higher education. Contact Skillsmart Retail for details of retail apprenticeship schemes and training options. A Diploma/Welsh Baccalaureate in retail business may be available in your area.

Many employers prefer older applicants, due to the responsibility of sometimes working alone in the service station and handling large amounts of cash. It is an advantage to have some retail experience. Apprenticeship schemes for adults may be available in your area.

Opportunities and Pay
You can find jobs in most places throughout the UK, but there is often more work in towns and cities. There are regular vacancies due to a high turnover of staff. Progression into management posts is unlikely for those without any qualifications. There may be more opportunities within the wider retail industry. It is often possible to work part time.

Pay varies depending on location and employer. Most forecourt assistants earn around £10k-£13k a year, rising to around £16k a year. Some may earn around £19k, depending on experience and level of responsibility. Your basic rate of pay may be increased for working nights or at weekends. You may also receive bonus payments for shop sales.

Health
You should not be allergic to petrol or other fuels.

Skills and Qualities
able to work well on your own, cash handling skills, common sense, customer service skills, good interpersonal skills, helpful, honest, security conscious, trustworthy

Relevant Subjects
Retail and distribution

Further Information
Apprenticeship Schemes (National Apprenticeship Service) - www.apprenticeships.org.uk

Cogent - sector skills souncil for chemicals, pharmaceuticals, nuclear, oil & gas, petroleum & polymers - www.cogent-ssc.com

Diplomas (Foundation, Higher and Advanced) - http://yp.direct.gov.uk/diplomas

Foundation Learning (QCDA) - www.qcda.gov.uk
Real Life Guide to Retail (Trotman) - www.trotman.co.uk

Safety Pass Alliance (SPA) - www.safetypassports.co.uk/html/petrol.html

Skillsmart Retail - sector skills council for the retail industry - www.skillsmartretail.com

Welsh Baccalaureate - www.wbq.org.uk

▶Working in retail & customer services (2008) (Babcock Lifeskills) - www.babcock-lifeskills.com/

Addresses

Scottish Motor Trade Association
Palmerston House, 10 The Loan, South Queensferry EH30 9NS
Phone: +44 (0)131 331 5510
Web: www.smta.co.uk

Similar Jobs

Checkout Operator, Retail Assistant, Stock Control/Replenishment Assistant

Forensic Anthropologist

CRCI:Science, Mathematics and Statistics
CLCI:QOT Job Band: 5

Job Description

Forensic anthropologists are concerned with the analysis of human remains and the identification and description of remains for medico-legal purposes. They determine the identity of the deceased rather than determining the cause or manner of how the death occurred, using biological anthropology (study of humans) to understand the remains of a body's soft and hard tissue. It is critical to the successful outcome of all legal investigations to build a biological profile of the owner's life and identity and the use high technology in many aspects of the work. Forensic anthropologists seek to discover all aspects of the biological and personal identity of human remains, including racial origin, height and weight, the age at which death occurred, dental details, and any disease or trauma affecting the individual.

They assess the human bones for evidence of violence or trauma if there is suspicion of foul play and look for any scarred, broken or damaged bones, and for signs of stab wounds. Often visit the site where the remains have been discovered and helpsto exhume the body. Increasingly, a forensic anthropologist may be asked to assist in areas that identify the living, including work on the analysis of CCTV images, or to conduct research into company personnel security systems, or to help in the identification of asylum seekers.

Usually work in a multidisciplinary team of entomologists, forensic pathologists, forensic archaeologists, DNA specialists and other forensic specialists, as well as with the police and courts.

Work Details

Usually work a standard 37 hr week over five days, but are sometimes on call to deal with emergencies. You work in a laboratory/mortuary and may also make site visits, some of which may be abroad. Occasionally you appear in court to present evidence. You are responsible for conducting identification investigations carefully and accurately, and presenting detailed results clearly. The job also demands keeping up to date with technical developments.

This work involves the sight of blood, seeing distressing scenes of crime, and hearing unpleasant details discussed. A white coat or an overall, protective gloves and a face mask may be worn at times.

Qualification

• England, Wales and Northern Ireland

Band 5: For degree courses: 2-3 A levels including two sciences, usually biology and chemistry, and some GCSEs (A*-C) usually including English, maths and science, or equivalent qualifications. Exact requirements depend on the degree you take.

• Scotland

Band 5: For degree courses: 3-5 H grades including two sciences, usually biology and chemistry, and some S grades (1-3), usually including English, science and maths, or similar. Exact requirements depend on the degree you take.

Degree Information

For direct employment you need at least a 2:1 in your chosen subject followed by a postgraduate/MSc qualification. Currently, there are a few forensic anthropology first degrees, though other courses covering anatomy are most appropriate for a postgraduate course in forensic anthropology or forensic science. Other relevant postgraduate courses include subjects such as an MSc in human identification, forensic medicine, forensic archaeology and anthropology, or in forensic investigation. Check the content of each course carefully. Relevant foundation degrees in subjects such as forensic science are available at some colleges and universities, lasting between 2-4 years part time.

Adult Qualifications

Appropriate qualifications and up-to-date scientific knowledge and experience are necessary. Adults may be considered for relevant higher education courses without the usual entry requirements via Access or foundation courses.

Work Experience

Work experience gives you an insight into what you enjoy and don't enjoy about a job or working environment, as well as the opportunity to acquire new skills. It also provides valuable information to add to your CV and improves any course application and/or your future employment prospects. Experience such as hospital work or that gained in an industrial or commercial laboratory is useful. If this proves difficult to obtain, then other scientific work is attractive to employers and admissions tutors.

Entry and Training

Degree courses vary in content and you should choose your first degree very carefully if you wish to become a forensic anthropologist. It takes around seven years to become fully qualified in this profession. Postgraduate study is a requirement. Training is given on the job by experienced staff. There are usually in-house training programmes and practical casework. Specialised short courses may be provided such as those offered by suppliers of forensic science services.

You need to keep up to date with current trends in forensic science/ anthropology and its application, as well as the awareness of the investigative processes that follow evidence from a crime scene to the courtroom. You can become a member of the Forensic Science Society (FSS) or apply to join as an affiliate member when a student.

Mature applicants with recent forensic/medical laboratory work experience at technician level may have an advantage. Diplomas in specific forensic science disciplines are awarded by the Forensic Science Society (FSS).

Opportunities and Pay

This is currently a relatively small profession and therefore vacancies are scarce. However, forensic anthropology has increasingly come to play an important role in judicial investigations within the UK, and also internationally where there are issues of repatriation, war crimes and mass disasters. Consequently, there is an increasing demand for experienced and qualified specialists in this area of work.

You can work in a forensic laboratory, teach or research in a university/and or medical school or museum, or work in an industrial or central government laboratory. However, most full-time forensic anthropologists teach. A small number are employed in medical examiners' offices or by the armed forces. Others may occasionally work for non-government organisations (NGOs). Some become scenes of crime officers (SOCO) for the police.

Promotion may be limited by the small number of higher grade posts. You should be prepared to move to different laboratories if you wish to gain experience and advance your career. Fully experienced forensic anthropologists can also work freelance as private consultants. Forensic laboratories overseas recruit UK-trained staff.

Pay can vary considerably but salaries for qualified forensic anthropologists are around £28k a year, rising to around £49k a year. A daily freelance rate is around £200 to £500.

Health
It is essential to have normal colour vision and important to have no allergies to skin irritants.

Skills and Qualities
able to report accurately, analytical skills, aptitude for fieldwork, attention to detail, good communication skills, IT skills, knowledge of the criminal justice system, not squeamish, objective, resilient, sound judgement

Relevant Subjects
Biology, Chemistry, English, ICT/Computer studies, Law, Mathematics, Physics, Science

Further Information
British Association for Human Identification - www.bahid.org

Forensic Anthropology Society of Europe (FASE) (Forensic Anthropology Society of Europe) - www.labanof.unimi.it/FASE.htm

Science & Justice (quarterly) (Forensic Science Society (FSS)) - www.forensic-science-society.org.uk/publications/saj.html

▶Working in science (2007) (Babcock Lifeskills) - www.babcock-lifeskills.com/

Addresses
Forensic Science Society
Clarke House, 18A Mount Parade, Harrogate HG1 1BX
Phone: +44 (0)1423 506 068
Web: www.forensic-science-society.org.uk

International Academy of Legal Medicine (IALM)
Instituto Nacional de Medicina Legal, I.P., Largo da Se Nova, 3000-213 Ciombra
Phone: +351 239 854 220
Web: www.ialm.info

Laboratory of the Government Chemist (LGC Forensics)
Queens Road, Teddington, Middlesex TW11 0LY
Phone: +44 (0)844 2641 999
Web: www.forensic-alliance.com

University of Dundee
Nethergate, Dundee DD1 4HN
Phone: +44 1382 383 000
Web: www.dundee.ac.uk/

Similar Jobs
Forensic Scientist, Microbiologist, Pathologist, Police Scenes of Crime Officer, Public Analyst

Forensic Scientist

CRCI:Science, Mathematics and Statistics
CLCI:QOT Job Band: 4 to 5

Job Description
Forensic scientists conduct scientific examinations of material obtained from crime scenes to assist the legal process. They work closely with police and may appear in court as an expert witness though must give impartial evidence. May also accompany the police to the crime scene to give advice and to search for initial evidence, or receive such evidence from a scenes of crime police officer. Forensic scientists use a variety of techniques to identify clues, such as traces of paint, blood, other body fluids, hairs, fibres or soil. Also analyse blood samples for alcohol and drugs.

They often use complex and specialised equipment including computers and electron microscopes. Some forensic scientists specialise, for example in drugs, DNA profiling, explosives, firearms, documents or inks. Can be involved in civil law cases as well as criminal cases.

Work Details
Usually work a standard 37 hr week over 5 days, but are sometimes on call to deal with emergencies. You work in a laboratory but also make site visits and occasionally appear in court to present evidence. You are responsible for examining substances carefully and accurately, and presenting detailed results clearly.

This work involves the sight of blood, attending crime scenes, which may be distressing, and hearing unpleasant details discussed. This work also demands keeping up to date with technical developments. You may need to wear a white coat or an overall and protective gloves and a face mask.

Qualification

• England, Wales and Northern Ireland
Band 4: For entry as an assistant forensic scientist: minimum of 4 GCSEs (A*-C) including English, maths, a relevant science and preferably 1-3 A levels including a science subject, or equivalent.

Band 5: For degree courses: 2-3 A levels from maths, physics, biology, chemistry and some GCSEs (A*-C) usually including English, maths and science, or equivalent. Exact requirements depend on the degree you take.

• Scotland
Band 4: For entry to SQA higher national and professional development awards, usually 2-3 H grades and some S grades (1-3), including English, chemistry or biology and maths, or similar qualifications.

Band 5: For a degree: 3-5 H grades from maths, physics, biology, chemistry and three other S grades (1-3) including English, maths and science, or similar. Exact requirements depend on the degree you take.

Degree Information
There are some first degrees in forensic science, as well as combined subject courses. However, the Forensic Science Society (FSS) recommends a good first degree in a science subject, such as chemistry, biochemistry or biology, followed by a postgraduate/MSc qualification or direct employment. A first degree in maths or an appropriate technology subject is also useful. A relevant first degree is required for postgraduate courses in forensic science.

Adult Qualifications
Appropriate qualifications and up-to-date scientific knowledge and experience are necessary. Adults may be considered for relevant higher education courses without the usual entry requirements via

Access or foundation courses. It is also possible for those without the specified science qualifications to take a foundation year leading into the relevant degree. Check with universities.

Work Experience

Work experience gives you an insight into what you enjoy and do not enjoy about a job or working environment, as well as the opportunity to acquire new skills. It also provides valuable information to add to your CV and improves any course application and/or your future employment prospects. Relevant work or voluntary experience can be gained through hospital work, or in an industrial or commercial laboratory. If this proves difficult to secure, then other scientific work is attractive to employers and admissions tutors.

Entry and Training

Most new entrants have a relevant degree and although not specified, a postgraduate qualification may give an advantage. There are usually in-house training programmes, and specialised short courses may also be provided. For assistant scientific officers/technicians, there are day-release courses for further study to degree level. Foundation degrees in forensic science are also available at some colleges and universities, lasting between 2-4 years part time. The Forensic Science Society offers diploma courses in crime scene investigation, forensic imaging and document examination.

Entry qualifications and training are different in Scotland than in the rest of the UK, so check details carefully. Forensic scientists employed by the Home Office must meet civil service nationality requirements.

Mature applicants with recent forensic/medical laboratory work at technician level may have an advantage. Diplomas in specific forensic science disciplines are awarded by the Forensic Science Society (FSS).

Opportunities and Pay

About 5000 staff work in the UK forensic science industry. Vacancies are scarce as there are more forensic science graduates than jobs. You usually work for the Forensic Science Service (FSS), part of the Home Office, or the police in England and Wales. In Scotland, forensic science services are provided by laboratories in Aberdeen, Dundee, Edinburgh and Glasgow and are maintained by the local police force. In Northern Ireland, forensic science careers are part of the civil service. Forensic scientists can also work for independent laboratories, such as LGC Forensics, or work as private consultants. Forensic laboratories overseas recruit UK-trained staff.

Promotion may be limited by the small number of higher grade posts so it is essential to keep up to date with the latest developments in research and laboratory techniques. You should be prepared to move to different laboratories if you wish to gain experience and advance your career.

Pay can vary considerably depending on location and employer but starting salaries for trainee scientists are around £14k-£18k a year. Graduate trainees earn £20k a year. Qualified forensic scientists earn from £25k-£32k and senior scientists earn up to £50k a year. Salaries in London are usually higher.

Health

It is essential to have normal colour vision and important to have no skin allergies.

Skills and Qualities

able to report accurately, analytical skills, attention to detail, IT skills, logical, not squeamish, objective, problem-solving skills, resilient, sound judgement

Relevant Subjects

Biology, Chemistry, English, ICT/Computer studies, Law, Mathematics, Physics, Science

Further Information

Civil Service - www.civilservice.gov.uk/jobs

Science & Justice (quarterly) (Forensic Science Society (FSS)) - www.forensic-science-society.org.uk/publications/saj.html

Skills for Justice - sector skills council for the UK justice system - www.skillsforjustice.com

What's it like to be a Forensic Scientist? (A&C Black 2009)

▶Working in science (2007) (Babcock Lifeskills) - www.babcock-lifeskills.com/

Addresses

British Toxicology Society (BTS)
BTS Administrative Office PO Box 10371, Colchester, Essex CO1 9GL
Phone: +44 (0)1206 226059
Web: www.thebts.org

Forensic Science Northern Ireland (FSNI)
151 Belfast Road, Carrickfergus BT38 8PL
Phone: +44 (0) 28 9036 1888
Web: www.fsni.gov.uk

Forensic Science Service (FSS)
Trident Court, 2020 Solihull Parkway, Birmingham Business Park B37 7YN
Web: www.forensic.gov.uk

Forensic Science Society
Clarke House, 18A Mount Parade, Harrogate HG1 1BX
Phone: +44 (0)1423 506 068
Web: www.forensic-science-society.org.uk

Laboratory of the Government Chemist (LGC Forensics)
Queens Road, Teddington, Middlesex TW11 0LY
Phone: +44 (0)844 2641 999
Web: www.forensic-alliance.com

Similar Jobs

Forensic Anthropologist, Microbiologist, Pathologist, Toxicologist

Forest District Manager

CRCI:Environment, Animals and Plants
CLCI:WAF — Job Band: 5

Job Description

Forest managers oversee the development, growth and conservation of a large designated area of trees and woodlands, and are responsible for the supervision and management of the forest officers/managers, supervisors and forest craftspeople. They are also responsible for budget planning, short and long-term, and for the training and development needs of all employees. Managers plan and direct the annual programme of work, making the best use of the workforce and machinery whilst taking into account environmental issues. They are also responsible for the development and maintenance of recreational areas and facilities.

Manager ensure that fire, and health and safety regulations are observed at all times, and that regular training exercises take place. They maintain good relationships with neighbouring landowners and liaise with related professional organisations. May also be involved in environmental research and wildlife conservation projects and ensure that where possible all forest developments are sustainable.

Work Details

Usually work a basic 42 hr week, with early starts often required and with some overtime, perhaps evenings or weekends. Work is both indoors in an office and outdoors, usually travelling around from forest to forest in your allocated district, sometimes having to stay away from home overnight. The outdoor work can be cold, damp, muddy and sometimes noisy. This type of work can be very demanding both mentally and physically. You must be safety conscious as there can be a risk of accidents from equipment such as chainsaws. Protective clothing, including a hard hat and boots need to be worn at times.

Qualification

• England, Wales and Northern Ireland

Band 5: For degree courses: 2-3 A levels and some GCSEs (A*-C) usually including English and maths, or equivalent. Exact requirements depend on the degree you take.

• Scotland

Band 5: For degree courses: 3-5 H grades and some S grades (1-3), usually including English and maths, or similar qualifications. Exact requirements depend on the degree you take.

Degree Information

A degree in forestry, woodland management, forest science, environmental forestry, forestry conservation, or a related subject with a high forestry content is essential for entry to this job. It is possible to study for a postgraduate degree/diploma in forestry/ forestry and forest products.

Adult Qualifications

A forestry degree or a forestry-related subject is usually essential. Course entry requirements are usually relaxed for suitable mature applicants. Those without the required qualifications may complete a foundation or Access course leading to relevant HNDs or accredited degrees.

Work Experience

Entry to this career is competitive and it is important that you try to do some relevant work or voluntary experience before applying for jobs. To show enthusiasm and commitment to the profession it is most useful to gain experience in forestry, either with the Forestry Commission or with a private forestry company. Other related work experience is in arboriculture, horticulture or other land-based industries. Details of volunteer opportunities available can be found on the Forestry Commission's website.

Entry and Training

A good honours degree is usually needed to enter this job and a postgraduate qualification is often useful. If entering a post with the Forestry Commission, there is a management development programme available. Many entrants have worked first as a forest officer/manager and then take various forestry training schemes that are available. There is also a graduate recruitment programme available at the Forestry Commission that lasts three years and can lead to this level of responsibility.

Employers often look for district managers to have membership of the Institute of Chartered Foresters. You can join the Institute while you are studying as a student member. Most district managers are full members and are chartered foresters. To achieve this, you must have a degree or diploma in forestry or related science, pass professional exams and have two years' forestry experience.

The websites of the Institute of Chartered Foresters (ICF) and the Royal Forestry Society (RFS) provide good information on training routes and qualifications.

Mature applicants require extensive experience in forestry or arboriculture together with forestry or forestry-related qualifications such as a degree and relevant postgraduate qualification.

Opportunities and Pay

Over 31,000 people are employed in the UK in the tree and timber industries, with 3,000 being employed by the Forestry Commission. Jobs are mainly available in Wales, Scotland and northern England with employers that include the Forestry Commission, private landowners, local authorities, or private forestry or woodland estate companies. Most posts are in the countryside, sometimes in remote areas. Competition is intense for this type of work and usually there are few vacancies. Promotion prospects may depend on the organisation for which you work. Your prospects may be improved with further training and study. Those interested in scientific aspects of the work may move into the Forestry Research Agency.

Pay for a Forestry Commission district manager depends on area of responsibility and experience. Starting salaries can be around £21.5k a year, rising to around £47k a year. In the private sector, pay varies considerably but is generally less than in the Forestry Commission, except at the highest levels. You may be provided with a company vehicle.

Health

This job requires you to be physically fit and you may find this job difficult if you have hay fever.

Skills and Qualities

able to delegate, able to manage people, able to take responsibility, good communication skills, good organisational skills, IT skills, negotiating skills, planning skills, scientific approach, strong interest in the environment

Relevant Subjects

Biology, Business and accounting, Chemistry, English, Geography, Land and Environment, Science

Further Information

Forest Services Northern Ireland - www.forestserviceni.gov.uk

Forestry Journal (RFS quarterly) (Royal Forestry Society) - www.forestryjournal.co.uk

Jobs and the Natural Heritage (leaflet) (Scottish Natural Heritage) - www.snh.org.uk/

Lantra - The Sector Skills Council for environmental & land-based sector (Lantra) - http:/www.lantra.co.uk

Royal Scottish Forestry Society (RSFS) - www.rsfs.org

Addresses

British Trust for Conservation Volunteers (BTCV)
Sedum House, Mallard Way, Doncaster DN4 8DB
Phone: +44 (0)1302 388 883
Web: http://www2.btcv.org.uk

ConFor
59 George Street, Edinburgh EH2 2JG
Phone: +44 (0)131 240 1410
Web: www.confor.org.uk/

Forest Research Station
Alice Holt Lodge, Wrecclesham, Farnham, Surrey GU10 4LH
Phone: +44 (0)1420 22255
Web: www.forestry.gov.uk

Forestry Commission England
620 Bristol Business Park Coldharbour Lane BS16 1EJ
Phone: +44 (0)117 906 6000
Web: www.forestry.gov.uk

Forestry Commission Scotland
Silvan House, 231 Corstorphine Road, Edinburgh EH12 7AT
Phone: +44 (0)131 334 0303
Web: www.forestry.gov.uk

Forestry Commission Wales
Rhodfa Padarn Llanbadarn Fawr, Aberystwyth, Powys SY23 3UR
Phone: +44 (0)300 068 0300
Web: www.forestry.gov.uk

Institute of Chartered Foresters (ICF)
59 George Street, Edinburgh EH2 2JG
Phone: +44 (0)131 240 1425
Web: www.charteredforesters.org

Royal Forestry Society (RFS)
102 High Street, Tring, Hertfordshire HP23 4AF
Phone: +44 (0)1442 822 028
Web: www.rfs.org.uk

Similar Jobs

Arboriculturist, Countryside/Conservation Officer/Manager, Ecologist, Farm Manager, Forest Officer, Surveyor: Planning & Development

Forest Officer

also known as: Forester

CRCI:Environment, Animals and Plants
CLCI:WAF Job Band: 3 to 5

Job Description

Forest officers plan, organise and supervise the planting and harvesting of trees and woodland areas and negotiate the sale of timber. They are responsible for carrying out an annual care and management programme and involved in budget planning and control, including marketing. Officers may report to a forest district manager. They make decisions regarding the planting and pruning of trees and the location of roads, fences etc. Work to protect the environment from fire, pests and disease. Also responsible for health and safety standards, and must keep up to date with health and safety regulations and fire precaution practices.

Officers train forest workers in forestry aspects, including nursery work (propagation), tree planting, thinning and felling, and assist in their career development and professional qualification. They supervise daily work schedules, including the creation and maintenance of picnic and camping sites, signposts, fences and pathways, fire control areas etc.

Also liaise with the local authority, timber merchants/contractors, neighbouring landowners and countryside groups. May write reports and issue permits (for camping, caravans, sporting events etc). Increasingly, forest officers are becoming more involved with recreation and conservation aspects of their work such as the layout of nature trails, and the management of deer and other wildlife.

Work Details

A 42 hr week is standard, and usually includes early starts, evenings and weekends. Some time is spent in an office and the rest outdoors. Travel around the area is necessary. The outdoor work can be cold, damp, dirty, wet, muddy and sometimes noisy. This type of work can be very demanding both mentally and physically. You must be safety conscious as there is a risk of accidents from equipment, such as chainsaws. A hard hat, gloves, boots and protective trousers must be worn.

Qualification

• England, Wales and Northern Ireland

Band 3: For entry to jobs, HNC or a relevant Diploma, usually at least 4 GCSEs (A*-C) including English, science and maths, or equivalent.

Band 4: For HND, Diploma of Higher Education or foundation degree: 1-2 A levels and some GCSEs (A*-C) usually including English, science and maths, or equivalent.

Band 5: For degree courses: 2-3 A levels, preferably including science subjects, and some GCSEs (A*-C) usually including English and maths, or equivalent. Exact requirements depend on the degree you take.

• Scotland

Band 3: For entry to jobs, usually at least four S grades (1-3) including English, science and maths, or similar qualifications.

Band 4: For entry to SQA higher national and professional development awards, usually 2-3 H grades and some S grades (1-3), including English, science and maths, or similar qualifications.

Band 5: For degree courses: 3-5 H grades, preferably including science subjects, and some S grades (1-3), usually including English and maths, or similar qualifications. Exact requirements depend on the degree you take.

Degree Information

A degree in forestry, woodland management, forest science, environmental forestry, forestry conservation, or a related subject with a high forestry content is essential for entry to this job. It is possible to study for a postgraduate degree/diploma in forestry/forestry and forest products.

Adult Qualifications

Course entry requirements are usually relaxed for suitable mature applicants. Those without the required qualifications may complete a foundation or Access course leading to relevant HNDs or accredited degrees.

Work Experience

Entry to this job is competitive and it is important that you try to do some relevant work or voluntary experience before applying. Employers, colleges and universities may prefer some direct work experience such as forestry work, gardening, landscape gardening, work in a garden centre, a wildlife park or nature reserve. Administration and office skills are also favourably looked upon, so practical experience of this is also useful. The Forestry Commission website has details of volunteering opportunities.

Entry and Training

New entrants at forest officer level usually have at least a higher national diploma or a degree in forestry, or equivalent qualification. Many start their career at technical manager/supervisor level and all applicants must have a current full driving licence. A year's practical experience is helpful before entering degree courses and may be required before starting some courses. Details of higher education courses in forestry are available on the Institute of Chartered Foresters (ICF) website. The Royal Forestry Society website also has information about training and qualifications.

Short practical courses between two and five days are run at a range of institutions. Officers are usually required to have a chainsaw competency certificate that is awarded by the National Proficiency Tests Council (NPTC) or Scottish Skills Testing Service (SSTS). Relevant foundation degrees in forestry are also available. The Forestry Commission runs a three year graduate development programme. This includes six placements in different areas of the business.

Employers often look for forest officers to have membership of the ICF. You can join the Institute while you are studying as a student member. Most district managers are full members and are chartered foresters. To achieve this, you must have a degree or diploma in forestry or related science, pass professional exams and have two years' forestry experience.

Mature applicants usually require at least two years experience in forestry, horticulture or arboriculture. Forestry or forestry-related qualifications, such as an S/NVQ level 4 in forestry, a relevant national/higher national award or a degree, are usually required.

Opportunities and Pay

Competition is intense for this type of work and usually there are few vacancies. You may be employed by the Forestry Commission, private landowners and companies, statutory bodies and local authorities, estates, consultants and contractors, or a national company. Most posts are in rural areas that can sometimes be remote. There are also opportunities in technical management and in forest research. Promotion prospects may depend on the organisation for which you work and prospects may be improved with further training and study eg for a PhD.

Full membership of the ICF may be required by employers offering high-level posts. Self-employment as a forestry consultant may be possible. There are increasing opportunities overseas, usually on limited term contracts.

Salaries offered by the Forestry Commission depend on responsibility and experience. Starting salaries are around £18.5k, rising to around £21.5k-£28.5k a year, depending upon experience and/or qualifications. Those in senior positions earn around £30k a year. In the private sector, pay varies considerably, but is generally less than in the Forestry Commission, except at the highest levels.

Health

This job requires you to be physically fit and you may find this job difficult if you suffer from hay fever.

Skills and Qualities

able to manage people, able to motivate others, aptitude for figures, good organisational skills, good spoken communication, good written English, IT skills, planning skills, problem-solving skills, scientific approach, strong interest in the environment, technical aptitude

Relevant Subjects

Biology, Business and accounting, Chemistry, Geography, Land and Environment, Science

Further Information

AGCAS: Environment & Agriculture (Job Sector Briefing) (AGCAS) - www.prospects.ac.uk

Forest Services Northern Ireland - www.forestserviceni.gov.uk

Forestry Journal (RFS quarterly) (Royal Forestry Society) - www.forestryjournal.co.uk

Jobs and the Natural Heritage (leaflet) (Scottish Natural Heritage) - www.snh.org.uk/

Lantra - The Sector Skills Council for environmental & land-based sector (Lantra) - http:/www.lantra.co.uk

Royal Scottish Forestry Society (RSFS) - www.rsfs.org

Addresses

British Trust for Conservation Volunteers (BTCV)
Sedum House, Mallard Way, Doncaster DN4 8DB
Phone: +44 (0)1302 388 883
Web: http://www2.btcv.org.uk

ConFor
59 George Street, Edinburgh EH2 2JG
Phone: +44 (0)131 240 1410
Web: www.confor.org.uk/

Forestry Commission England
620 Bristol Business Park Coldharbour Lane BS16 1EJ
Phone: +44 (0)117 906 6000
Web: www.forestry.gov.uk

Forestry Commission Scotland
Silvan House, 231 Corstorphine Road, Edinburgh EH12 7AT
Phone: +44 (0)131 334 0303
Web: www.forestry.gov.uk

Forestry Commission Wales
Rhodfa Padarn Llanbadarn Fawr, Aberystwyth, Powys SY23 3UR
Phone: +44 (0)300 068 0300
Web: www.forestry.gov.uk

Forestry Contracting Association
PO Box 1, Lairg, Sutherland IV27 4ET
Phone: 0870 042 7999 (UK only)
Web: www.fcauk.com

Institute of Chartered Foresters (ICF)
59 George Street, Edinburgh EH2 2JG
Phone: +44 (0)131 240 1425
Web: www.charteredforesters.org

Royal Forestry Society (RFS)
102 High Street, Tring, Hertfordshire HP23 4AF
Phone: +44 (0)1442 822 028
Web: www.rfs.org.uk

Similar Jobs

Arboriculturist, Countryside/Conservation Officer/Manager, Forest District Manager, Forest Worker, Landscape Gardener, Parks Manager

Forest Worker

also known as: Forest Craftsperson

CRCI:Environment, Animals and Plants

CLCI:WAF Job Band: 1 to 3

Job Description

Forest workers use practical skills to develop, maintain and protect a forest, including planting and cutting down trees, protecting the wildlife and looking after public areas. They clear the ground, plant seedlings and young trees, and prune larger ones. Also weed and spray fertiliser to encourage growth, and cut down trees for logs. Inspect trees and may mark them for cutting down.

They use hand and power tools such as chainsaws and machines that cut down or transport the fallen tree trunks. Look after the tools and machines and undetake general maintenance and repairs. May use very large machines for tree harvesting. Also erect fences and repair or replace damaged ones. May dig drains, possibly using a machine and create pathways in the forest and keep them clear of any debris. Help to fight any outbreak of forest fires.

Forest workers are also responsible for wildlife control and conservation, and for providing a safe and welcoming environment for visitors. They protect forest and woodland areas from misuse by the general public. Also look after public facilities such as woodland trails, visitor centres, car parks, caravan/camping areas and picnic sites.

Work Details

Usually work a basic 42 hrs a week, though sometimes has to work overtime, possibly in the early mornings, evenings and weekends. The work tends to be seasonal, with busy periods in early spring and autumn. You need to walk long distances, climb ladders and lift heavy items and be prepared to be out in all sorts of weather. Forest workers must also be tactful with visitors but deal firmly with them if necessary.

The work can be dirty and dangerous. It is important to be very careful when working with machines such as chainsaws and other power tools. You need to wear protective clothing, such as boots, hard hat, ear defenders, chainsaw-proof trousers and gloves.

Qualification

- **England, Wales and Northern Ireland**

Band 1: No minimum qualifications are required, but you are expected to have a good level of general education. However, some formal/vocational qualifications at any level are useful.

Band 2: For entry to jobs, no minimum qualifications are needed, but it is an advantage to have some GCSEs (A*-C) or equivalent in subjects that include English and maths.

Band 3: For entry: usually at least 4 GCSEs (A*-C) preferably including English, science and maths, or equivalent.

- **Scotland**

Band 1: No minimum qualifications are required, but you are expected to have a good level of general education. However, some formal/vocational qualifications at any level are useful.

Band 2: Although academic qualifications are not specified for this job, it is an advantage to have some S grades (1-3) in subjects that include English and maths, or similar.

Band 3: For entry: usually at least four S grades (1-3) preferably including English, science and maths, or similar.

Adult Qualifications

For entry to many jobs you do not need academic qualifications, but experience of arboricultural or agricultural/horticultural work is useful.

Work Experience

Employers often prefer candidates who have relevant work or voluntary experience. This can include work in a garden centre, horticultural nursery, a farm, in estate grounds maintenance, or work as a volunteer with organisations that include the Woodland Trust, Volunteering England, or the British Trust for Conservation Volunteers. Such experience equips you with skills that you can use in the future and add to your CV. The Forestry Commission website has details of volunteering opportunities.

Entry and Training

No qualifications are necessary, but you are expected to gain vocational qualifications through training on the job. You may attend a local college for a relevant part-time course. It is possible to attend a one-year, full-time course for a BTEC/SQA national certificate in forestry or arboriculture (forestry), or similar qualification. For some courses you need to have a year's work experience. You usually need to have a driving licence and for some jobs an LGV (large goods vehicle) driving licence.

You are also expected to work towards the National Proficiency Tests Council (NPTC) or Scottish Skills Testing Service (SSTS) certificates of competence in areas that include chainsaw use, brush cutting operations, stump grinding, and the use of chemicals/pesticides. Forest workers often take further short practical courses to help in their work, such as chainsaw maintenance and cross cutting, pruning operations, and advanced tree climbing. The Forestry Commission may offer an apprenticeship that enables you to gain a relevant S/NVQ level 3 whilst working.

Before you enter this work you may be able to take a Diploma/ Welsh Baccalaureate in environment and land-based studies. This may be available in your area.

Mature applicants with previous experience of working in forestry/ arboricultural operations or in outdoor recreation may have an advantage. You may be able to benefit through government training opportunities, including apprenticeships, that may be available in your area. Contact your local Connexions or careers office, Jobcentre Plus, Next Step service or Learning and Skills Council (LSC)/Local Enterprise Company (LEC) for details of all training opportunities and schemes.

Opportunities and Pay

Over 10,000 forest workers are employed in the forests of the UK. You can work for the Forestry Commission, a local authority, a private forestry company or an organisation such as the National Trust, who encourage workers to develop their full potential by pursuing further training and education. Once trained, you can become self-employed as there are good opportunities for those who are prepared to undertake contract work.

Forest workers may progress to become rangers or wardens, or a fully qualified craft worker or machine operator. Supervisors generally need a level 3 qualification, such as a BTEC national certificate/diploma. With relevant qualifications, some progress to become a forest officer/manager.

Starting salaries are around £12k, rising to around £15k a year depending upon experience and/or qualifications. Supervisors can earn around £16k-£21k a year. Sometimes accommodation is provided by the employer.

Health

Forest workers have to be active and physically fit. You may find this job more difficult if you have respiratory or skin allergies such as asthma, hay fever or eczema.

Skills and Qualities

able to follow instructions, able to work both on your own and in a team, agile, enjoy working outdoors, good spoken communication, head for heights, initiative, manual dexterity, numeracy skills, practical skills, safety conscious

Relevant Subjects

Biology, Land and Environment, Science

Further Information

Apprenticeship Schemes (National Apprenticeship Service) - www.apprenticeships.org.uk

Diplomas (Foundation, Higher and Advanced) - http://yp.direct.gov.uk/diplomas

Forestry Journal (RFS quarterly) (Royal Forestry Society) - www.forestryjournal.co.uk

Jobs and the Natural Heritage (leaflet) (Scottish Natural Heritage) - www.snh.org.uk/

Lantra Careers (A Future In...) (Lantra) - www.afuturein.com

Real Life Guide to Working Outdoors (Trotman) - www.trotman.co.uk

Training Schemes - www.direct.gov.uk/en/educationandlearning

Volunteer Scotland - www.volunteerscotland.org.uk/

Woodland Trust - www.woodland-trust.org.uk

Addresses

British Trust for Conservation Volunteers (BTCV)
Sedum House, Mallard Way, Doncaster DN4 8DB
Phone: +44 (0)1302 388 883
Web: http://www2.btcv.org.uk

Forestry Commission England
620 Bristol Business Park Coldharbour Lane BS16 1EJ
Phone: +44 (0)117 906 6000
Web: www.forestry.gov.uk

Forestry Commission Scotland
Silvan House, 231 Corstorphine Road, Edinburgh EH12 7AT
Phone: +44 (0)131 334 0303
Web: www.forestry.gov.uk

Forestry Commission Wales
Rhodfa Padarn Llanbadarn Fawr, Aberystwyth, Powys SY23 3UR
Phone: +44 (0)300 068 0300
Web: www.forestry.gov.uk

National Proficiency Test Council (NPTC)
City & Guilds Land Based Services Building 500 Abbey Park, Stareton, Warwickshire CV8 2LY
Phone: +44 (0) 24 7685 7300
Web: www.nptc.org.uk

National Trust
Heelis, Kemble Drive, Swindon, Wiltshire SN2 2NA
Phone: +44 (0)1793 817400
Web: www.ntjobs.org.uk

Scottish Skills Testing Service
Young Farmers Centre, Ingliston, Edinburgh EH28 8NE
Phone: +44 (0)131 333 2040
Web: www.sayfc.org/ssts/

Volunteering England
Regents Wharf, 8 All Saints Street, London N1 9RL
Phone: 0845 305 6979 (UK only)
Web: www.volunteering.org.uk

Similar Jobs

Arboriculturist, Countryside Ranger, Farm Worker: Crops, Gardener, Greenkeeper: Golf, Groundsman/Groundswoman, Horticultural Worker: Commercial

Fork-Lift Truck Engineer

CRCI:Engineering
CLCI:RAE

Job Band: 3

Job Description

Fork-lift truck engineers routinely service and road-test fork-lift trucks. They are experts in electrical and hydraulic systems, diesel and gas powered engines. Engineers work on a wide variety of vehicles, from supermarket hand trucks to huge machines that lift and shift fully loaded containers. They inspect the truck and report on its general condition, find faults and repair or replace worn parts, checking worksheets and technical manuals. Engineers regularly use sophisticated laptop or palmtop computers to diagnose problems or to fine-tune and measure fork-lift truck performance. They may refer to computerised documentation of the technical information and drawings that were traditionally printed in paper manuals. Also use power tools, hand tools, ramps and jacks.

May work in a workshop or large garage area. Some travel around an area in a mobile workshop as most of the regular or emergency servicing work is done 'on site', visiting customers. Also responsible for making brand new fork-lifts ready for a customer by thoroughly checking and testing each machine. May work in a team with other fork-lift truck engineers.

Work Details

Usually works around 40 hrs a week, although overtime is common. There may also be shift work, including weekends. Some fork-lift truck engineers have to be on call for emergency breakdowns. The workplace may be cold and noisy. Work on lift trucks that have broken down can involve being outdoors in all weathers. You have to work quickly, sometimes under pressure, to repair or service the truck as speedily and safely as possible.

Work is often strenuous and can include some heavy lifting. You have to bend, kneel and stretch, sometimes in awkward positions. There can be accidents with equipment. Protective clothing may be needed.

Qualification

- **England, Wales and Northern Ireland**

Band 3: For entry to jobs or for a relevant BTEC national award in vehicle maintenance and repair: usually at least 3-4 GCSEs (A*-C) including English, maths and a science (preferably physics), or technology or engineering subjects, or equivalent., HNC or a relevant Diploma, usually at least 4 GCSEs (A*-C) including English and maths, or equivalent.

- **Scotland**

Band 3: For entry to jobs or for a relevant SQA national award in vehicle maintenance and repair: usually at least four S grades (1-3) including English, maths and a science (preferably physics), or technology or engineering subjects, or similar.

Adult Qualifications

Formal qualifications showing a good standard of general education may be preferred, but are not essential. Academic requirements for courses are usually relaxed for suitable mature applicants. Those without the expected minimum entry qualifications may sit a test to assess their potential for the job.

Work Experience

Any work experience can equip you with skills that you can use in the future and add to your CV. Such work can either be unpaid or voluntary, or holiday/part-time work that you have organised yourself. Experience that includes practical work with vehicles is most useful.

Entry and Training

Many trainees start on a training programme or apprenticeship at age 16-19. You train on the job, working with an experienced person, together with a local college course through either day or block release. Most work towards relevant S/NVQs. Those without the expected minimum entry qualifications may sit a test to assess their potential for the job. Employers usually expect you to have, or work towards, a level 3 qualification in fork-lift truck engineering that takes around three years to complete. You can also study full time for a relevant City & Guilds or a BTEC/SQA award, prior to employment.

Regular training is needed to keep up to date with changing technology. The National Proficiency Test Council offers a level 2 certificate of competence in fork-lift truck operations, which may provide useful experience. Short courses are available through the Fork Lift Truck Association (FLTA) such as 'Thorough Examination' which is a practical two-day course for experienced fork-lift truck engineers. Training programmes, including apprenticeship schemes, may be available in your area. Advanced apprenticeships leading to qualification at level 3 can also be a route into higher education. Contact the FLTA for details of the national apprenticeship programme for service engineers which is managed by Retail Motor Industry Training (remit), or visit their dedicated apprenticeship website where you can apply online for courses. This job requires you to have a current driving licence.

A Diploma/Welsh Baccalaureate may be available in your area in engineering. This qualification is based around work and can include an automotive specialist learning component. See the diplomas website for further information.

It is an advantage to have previous experience of electrical/ mechanical work. Mature applicants can benefit through government training opportunities, such as apprenticeships, which may be available in your area. You can also gain recognition of previous experience through Accreditation of Prior Learning (APL) or by working towards relevant S/NVQs. Contact your local careers office, Jobcentre Plus, Next Step service or Learning and Skills Council (LSC) Local Enterprise Company (LEC) for details of training schemes.

Opportunities and Pay

There is currently a shortage of qualified fork-lift truck engineers. There may be good prospects throughout the UK with opportunities from small businesses to national/international manufacturers and businesses. When fully qualified and experienced, you may work as a field service engineer with a servicing company or dealership. Some prefer to stay on the technical side and progress to management posts in parts and servicing. With further experience and qualifications you may become a qualified engineer. Others may set up their own servicing or dealership business.

As an apprentice you earn around £430 a month and receive special allowances when you attend college. Once qualified, and depending on your location and employer, a typical starting salary is around £18k-£20k a year. This rises to around £25k or more, depending on the level of responsibility.

Health

You must be in good health and have normal colour vision.

Skills and Qualities

able to follow instructions, able to work quickly, attention to detail, good communication skills, IT skills, logical, manual dexterity, problem-solving skills, safety conscious, technical aptitude

Relevant Subjects

Design and technology, Engineering, Mathematics, Physics, Science

Further Information

Apprenticeship Schemes (National Apprenticeship Service) - www.apprenticeships.org.uk

Diplomas (Foundation, Higher and Advanced) - http://yp.direct.gov.uk/diplomas

Fork Lift Truck Apprenticeships - www.fork-truck.org.uk/apprenticeships

remit - www.remit.co.uk

SEMTA - sector skills council for science, engineering and manufacturing technologies - www.semta.org.uk

Training Schemes - www.direct.gov.uk/en/educationandlearning

Addresses

Fork Lift Truck Association (FLTA)
Manor Farm Buildings, Lasham, Alton, Hampshire GU34 5SL
Phone: +44 (0)1256 381441
Web: www.fork-truck.org.uk

National Proficiency Test Council (NPTC)
City & Guilds Land Based Services Building 500 Abbey Park, Stareton, Warwickshire CV8 2LY
Phone: +44 (0) 24 7685 7300
Web: www.nptc.org.uk

Similar Jobs

Aircraft Engineering Technician, Engineer: Automotive, Fitter: Maintenance, Mechanical Engineering Technician, Vehicle Breakdown Engineer, Vehicle Mechanic/Motor Vehicle Technician

Foundry Moulder/Coremaker

CRCI:Manufacturing and Production
CLCI:SAM Job Band: 1 to 3

Job Description

Foundry moulders operate high-tech computerised machines that make moulds (or cores for hollow objects) to fill with melted metal. These are used to produce items such as parts of cookers, bells, car and aircraft parts, and other products such as metal gates and drain covers. They create a model of the finished object and pack special sand around it and inside it if it is hollow. The sand used can be green sand, sand treated with resin or chemically bonded sand. The moulder then cuts grooves in the sand so that the melted metal can run into the mould. The sand hardens and is then removed from the model. Castings are also made in 'newer' materials such as aluminium and magnesium, particularly in the automotive and aircraft industries, and in polystyrene or wax. Any necessary repairs to damaged mould shapes are carried out.

Work Details

Foundry moulders usually work a basic 37-39 hr week that can include weekends and shift work. You work in a workshop or a foundry, which traditionally was hot, dusty and noisy, but dust and fume extractors and air-conditioning now deal with this problem and have improved the work environment. The job requires you to stand for many hours, and lift and carry heavy objects, although in automated plants, heavy lifting is now done as part of the production process. This job requires a high level of skill and practical ability.

If the mould is large, you work in a moulding pit, but small moulds can be assembled on a workbench in a moulding box. You need to wear protective clothing and possibly gloves, goggles and ear defenders.

Qualification

- **England, Wales and Northern Ireland**

Band 1: No minimum qualifications are required, but you are expected to have a good level of general education. However, some formal/vocational qualifications at any level are useful.

Band 2: Although academic qualifications are not specified for this job, it is an advantage to have some GCSEs (A*-C) in subjects that include English and maths, or equivalent.

Band 3: For apprenticeships and some courses: usually at least 4 GCSEs (A*-C) including English and maths or equivalent.

- **Scotland**

Band 1: No minimum qualifications are required, but you are expected to have a good level of general education. However, some formal/vocational qualifications at any level are useful.

Band 2: Although academic qualifications are not specified for this job, it is an advantage to have some S grades (1-3) in subjects that include English and maths, or similar.

Band 3: For apprenticeships and some courses: usually at least four S grades (1-3) including English and maths, or similar.

Adult Qualifications

Generally, you are expected to have the minimum entry qualifications, which can vary, as some jobs require no formal qualifications. However, you are expected to have relevant experience.

Work Experience

Relevant work or voluntary experience is always useful and can improve your chances when applying for entry to jobs or apprenticeships in the manufacturing sector. Metals companies can offer work experience placements in engineering, production, laboratory work, design, sales and administration. Your personal or adult guidance adviser should be able to advise you about how to organise work experience with an employer.

Entry and Training

Training is usually on the job with an experienced worker or through a company training scheme that may lead to vocational qualifications. Relevant S/NVQs at levels 1-3 are available and once you have gained a level 3 qualification you can then apply for registration with the Engineering Council UK as an engineering technician (EngTech). The Institute of Cast Metals Engineers (ICME) has details on its website of a range of one-to-five day specialist courses. The main colleges running courses related to castings are Bradford College, Chesterfield College, Rotherham College of Arts and Technology and Sandwell College.

Training programmes, including engineering apprenticeship schemes, may be available in your area. Advanced apprenticeships leading to qualification at level 3 can also be a route into higher education. Metskill and Castings Technology International have information on their websites about apprenticeships in the metals industry. You can also choose to take a college course, such as BTEC first in manufacturing engineering. A Diploma/Welsh Baccalaureate may be available in your area in manufacturing and product design. This is aimed at 14-19 year olds and can be a good introduction to work in this industry.

In recent years, a foundation degree in casting technology has been launched at Bradford College to address the shortage of skilled technicians in this specialist area. The Institute of Cast Metal Engineers, the Institute of Materials, Minerals and Mining and Metallurgy & Materials have all had some input to the content of the course. These bodies also support the casting technology mentor training programme by offering work based assessment opportunities to distance learning students. Contact the college for further details.

Government training opportunities, such as an apprenticeship in specialised process operations may be available in your area. You can also gain recognition of previous experience through Accreditation of Prior Learning (APL) or by working towards relevant S/NVQs. Contact your local careers office, Jobcentre Plus, Next Step service or Learning and Skills Council (LSC) Local Enterprise Company (LEC) for details of training schemes.

Opportunities and Pay

There are 60,000 people involved in the foundry industry in the UK in about 500 companies, over 50% of which are small, employing less than 50 staff. You can be employed by a large automated foundry or a small jobbing casting company. Jobs are available mainly in industrial areas, such as the West Midlands, northern England and central Scotland. The number of foundries has declined as a result of computerisation and automation, and the move towards the use of plastics. Promotion is usually to supervisor or foreman/woman, and from there into management posts. Some move on to technician training in areas such as mechanical testing or quality control.

Pay varies depending on location but moulders are likely to earn around £15k a year, rising to £17k-£20k with experience. You may be able to increase your earnings by working shifts and overtime.

Health

This job requires good general fitness and good eyesight, and may require a medical test on entry. There is an allergy risk from dust.

Skills and Qualities

able to follow instructions, able to work both on your own and in a team, attention to detail, hard working, health & safety awareness, manual dexterity, methodical, practical skills, strong

Relevant Subjects

Design and technology, Manufacturing

Further Information

Apprenticeship Schemes (National Apprenticeship Service) - www.apprenticeships.org.uk

Diplomas (Foundation, Higher and Advanced) - http://yp.direct.gov.uk/diplomas

Foundry Trade Journal (monthly) (Institute of Cast Metals Engineers) - www.foundrytradejournal.com

Metallurgy and Materials - www.eng.bham.ac.uk/metallurgy/

Real Life Guide to Manufacturing & Product Design (Trotman 2009) - www.trotman.co.uk

Scenta - Careers Guide, Engineering, Technology and Science (Engineering Technology Board) - www.scenta.co.uk/careers.cfm

SEMTA - sector skills council for science, engineering and manufacturing technologies - www.semta.org.uk

Tomorrow's Engineers - www.tomorrowsengineers.org.uk/careers.cfm

Training Schemes - www.direct.gov.uk/en/educationandlearning

UK Centre for Materials Education - www.materials.ac.uk/

Welsh Baccalaureate - www.wbq.org.uk

Addresses

Cast Metals Federation
National Metalforming Centre, 47 Birmingham Road,
West Bromwich B70 6PY
Phone: +44 (0)121 601 6390
Web: www.castmetalsfederation.com

Castings Technology International
Advanced Manufacturing Park, Brunel Way, Rotherham,
South Yorkshire S60 5WG
Phone: +44 (0) 114 254 1144
Web: www.castingstechnology.com

Engineering Council
246 High Holborn, London WC1V 7EX
Phone: +44 (0)20 3206 0500
Web: www.engc.org.uk

Institute of Cast Metals Engineers (ICME)
National Metalforming Centre, 47 Birmingham Road,
West Bromwich, West Midlands B70 6PY
Phone: +44 (0)121 601 6979
Web: www.icme.org.uk

Institute of Materials, Minerals and Mining (IOM3)
1 Carlton House Terrace, London SW1Y 5DB
Phone: +44 (0)20 7451 7300
Web: www.iom3.org

Metskill
Units 5-6 Meadowcourt, Amos Road, Sheffield S9 1BX
Phone: +44 (0)114 244 6833
Web: www.metskill.co.uk

Similar Jobs

Blacksmith, Foundry Patternmaker, Foundry Process Operative, Mechanical Engineering Technician

Foundry Patternmaker

CRCI:Manufacturing and Production
CLCI:SAM
Job Band: 1 to 2

Job Description

Patternmakers operate full-scale, three-dimensional models as patterns for making the moulds used in casting metals. May do this using high-tech computerised machinery, plus traditional hand and machine tools to complete any intricate or complicated details of the pattern. They work from computer-aided designs (CAD) or drawings. These are produced by engineering draughtsmen/draughtswomen and designers. The patterns are created using many different materials such as wood, metal, plastic or polystyrene, wax, or a combination of these.

May first make a pattern prototype or production sample. This is then discussed with the customer and any adjustments are made. A patternmaker may also instruct foundry workers on how to use the completed patterns to make moulds.

Work Details

Patternmakers usually works a basic 37-39 hr week that can include weekends and shift work. Spends part of the time in an office working on a computer. Also works in a workshop, using automatic machinery which may be noisy and dusty. However, dust and fume extractors have improved working conditions. You may need to wear protective overalls and possibly safety glasses.

Qualification

• England, Wales and Northern Ireland

Band 2: Although academic qualifications are not specified for this job, it is an advantage to have some GCSEs (A*-C) in subjects that include English and maths, technical subjects or equivalent.

• Scotland

Band 2: Although academic qualifications are not specified for this job, it is an advantage to have some S grades (1-3) in subjects that include English and maths, technical subjects or similar.

Adult Qualifications

Generally, you are expected to have the minimum entry qualifications, which can vary, as for some jobs, no formal qualifications are required.

Work Experience

Relevant work or voluntary experience is always useful and can improve your chances when applying for entry to jobs or apprenticeships in the manufacturing sector. Metals companies can offer work experience placements in engineering, production, laboratory work, design, sales and administration. Your personal or adult guidance adviser should be able to advise you about how to organise work experience with an employer.

Entry and Training

There are several ways you can enter this work. You can start in other foundry work areas and train to become a patternmaker when you have gained some experience. You may be able to gain an apprenticeship, but for this 3-5 GCSEs/S grades (A*-G/1-5) are usually required. Metskill and Castings Technology International have information on their websites about apprenticeships in the metals industry. Some entrants choose to do a relevant course before starting work, such as a BTEC first in manufacturing engineering or City & Guilds progression award in patternmaking.

However, there are no set entry qualifications and training is usually on the job with an experienced patternmaker. There are also opportunities to gain vocational qualifications. Relevant S/NVQs in performing manufacturing operations and processing and finishing are available at levels 1-3 and once you have gained a level 3 qualification you can then apply for registration with the Engineering Council UK as an engineering technician (EngTech). The institute of Cast Metals Engineers (ICME) has details on its website of a range of one-to-five day specialist courses. The main colleges running courses related to castings are Bradford College, Chesterfield College, Rotherham College of Arts and Technology and Sandwell College.

A Diploma/Welsh Baccalaureate may be available in your area in engineering. This is aimed at 14-19 year olds and can be a good introduction to work in this area. A foundation degree in casting technology has recently been launched at Bradford College. The college also offers a mentor training programme for those completing their studies through distance learning.

Those with experience of computer-aided design or computer aided manufacture may have an advantage. Government training opportunities, such as apprenticeships, may be available in your area. You can also gain recognition of previous experience through Accreditation of Prior Learning (APL) or by working towards relevant S/NVQs. Contact your local careers office, Jobcentre Plus, Next Step service or Learning and Skills Council (LSC) Local Enterprise Company (LEC) for details of training schemes. You may be able to complete an apprenticeship in process technology.

Opportunities and Pay

There are 60,000 people involved in the foundry industry in the UK in about 500 companies, over 50% of which are small, employing less than 50 staff. You can be employed by a casting company or specialist patternmaking firm. Jobs are available mainly in industrial areas, such as the West Midlands, northern England and central Scotland. The number of foundries has declined as a result of computerisation and automation, and the move towards the use of plastics. Promotion to supervisory and management level is possible, or you may be able to move on to technician training, in quality control or mechanical testing. British qualifications in this industry are widely accepted overseas.

Pay varies depending on location and employer but trainees are likely to start at around £15k a year, rising to £18k-£25k with experience. Shift work and overtime can increase your earnings.

Health

This job requires good health and good eyesight.

Skills and Qualities

able to follow drawings and plans, accurate, aptitude for figures, attention to detail, good concentration level, hand-to-eye co-ordination, manual dexterity, patient, practical skills, precise

Relevant Subjects

Design and technology, Manufacturing, Mathematics, Physics

Further Information

Apprenticeship Schemes (National Apprenticeship Service) - www.apprenticeships.org.uk

Diplomas (Foundation, Higher and Advanced) - http://yp.direct.gov.uk/diplomas

Foundry Trade Journal (monthly) (Institute of Cast Metals Engineers) - www.foundrytradejournal.com

Real Life Guide to Manufacturing & Product Design (Trotman 2009) - www.trotman.co.uk

Scenta - Careers Guide, Engineering, Technology and Science (Engineering Technology Board) - www.scenta.co.uk/careers.cfm

SEMTA - sector skills council for science, engineering and manufacturing technologies - www.semta.org.uk

Training Schemes - www.direct.gov.uk/en/educationandlearning

UK Centre for Materials Education - www.materials.ac.uk/

Welsh Baccalaureate - www.wbq.org.uk

Addresses

Bradford College
Great Horton Road, Bradford, West Yorkshire BD7 1AY
Phone: +44 (0)1274 433333
Web: www.bradfordcollege.ac.uk/

Cast Metals Federation
National Metalforming Centre, 47 Birmingham Road, West Bromwich B70 6PY
Phone: +44 (0)121 601 6390
Web: www.castmetalsfederation.com

Castings Technology International
Advanced Manufacturing Park, Brunel Way, Rotherham, South Yorkshire S60 5WG
Phone: +44 (0) 114 254 1144
Web: www.castingstechnology.com

Engineering Council
246 High Holborn, London WC1V 7EX
Phone: +44 (0)20 3206 0500
Web: www.engc.org.uk

Institute of Cast Metals Engineers (ICME)
National Metalforming Centre, 47 Birmingham Road, West Bromwich, West Midlands B70 6PY
Phone: +44 (0)121 601 6979
Web: www.icme.org.uk

Metskill
Units 5-6 Meadowcourt, Amos Road, Sheffield S9 1BX
Phone: +44 (0)114 244 6833
Web: www.metskill.co.uk

Similar Jobs

Blacksmith, Foundry Moulder/Coremaker, Foundry Process Operative, Mechanical Engineering Technician

Foundry Process Operative

also known as: Foundry Worker

CRCI:Manufacturing and Production
CLCI:SAM Job Band: 1

Job Description

Foundry process operatives assist craftworkers such as foundry moulders or patternmakers in the metal casting industry. They carry out a range of tasks, such as sand milling operations that mix sand together to help to make the moulds into which melted metal is poured. May operate the furnace (melter/furnaceman/cupola worker). They are involved in operating machines that transport the melted metal to the moulds by pushing ladles hanging from chains (ladle man/caster). They remove the cooled metal object from the mould and grind off rough edges (grinder/fettler). Some operators drive fork lift trucks or cranes. This is necessary to transport the raw materials and castings around the foundry floor and other work departments.

Work Details

Foundry process operatives usually work a basic 37-39 hour week that can include weekends and shift work. Foundries can be dirty but are no longer the dusty places they once were due to fume and dust extractor fans and legislation governing working conditions. There is a risk of burns and a good deal of heavy lifting, although there is usually lifting equipment to help you. It may be necessary to work outside sometimes, checking that the scrap metal to be used is suitable. You need to wear protective clothing such as goggles, a face mask and possibly ear defenders.

Qualification

- **England, Wales and Northern Ireland**

Band 1: No minimum qualifications are required, but you are expected to have a good level of general education. However, some formal/vocational qualifications at any level are useful.

- **Scotland**

Band 1: No minimum qualifications are required, but you are expected to have a good level of general education. However, some formal/vocational qualifications at any level are useful.

Adult Qualifications

No formal qualifications are usually required, but you are expected to have a good level of secondary education. You can improve your skills and qualifications by working through a personalised programme of foundation learning. This involves taking credit-based units and qualifications to help you progress.

Work Experience

Work or voluntary experience is always useful. It can improve your chances when applying for jobs or apprenticeships. Metals companies can offer work experience placements in engineering and production. Opportunities may also be available in laboratory work, design, sales and administration. Your personal or adult guidance adviser should be able to give you some advice on how to get some work experience.

Entry and Training

There are no set entry qualifications and on-the-job training is usually provided with an experienced operative. Training may last from a few weeks to six months, depending on the type of task. All workers are given safety training. You may start as a general worker and then move to more complex jobs. You must be at least 18 for shift work.

There may also be opportunities to gain vocational qualifications. Relevant S/NVQs at levels 1-3 are available and once you have gained a level 3 qualification you can then apply for registration with the Engineering Council UK as an engineering technician (EngTech). The Institute of Cast Metals Engineers (ICME) has details on its website of a range of one-to-five day specialist courses. The main colleges running courses related to castings are Bradford College, Chesterfield College, Rotherham College of Arts and Technology and Sandwell College.

Training programmes, including engineering apprenticeship schemes, may be available in your area. A Diploma/Welsh Baccalaureate may also be available in your area in manufacturing and product design. This is aimed at 14-19 year olds and can be a good introduction to work in industry.

Government training opportunities, such as apprenticeships, may be available in your area. You can also gain recognition of previous experience through Accreditation of Prior Learning (APL) or by working towards relevant S/NVQs. Contact your local careers office, Jobcentre Plus, Next Step service or Learning and Skills Council (LSC) Local Enterprise Company (LEC) for details of training schemes.

Opportunities and Pay

There are 60,000 people involved in the foundry industry in the UK in about 500 companies, over 50% of which are small, employing less than 50 staff. Jobs are available mainly in UK industrial areas, such as the West Midlands and Yorkshire. Work may also be available in Humberside and central Scotland. Employers are large automated foundries or a small casting company. Promotion to specialist jobs such as patternmaker or moulder is possible. Promotion to supervisory positions is also possible. However, availability of jobs in the foundry industry has declined in recent years due to increased use of machinery and a move towards using plastics.

Pay varies depending on location and employer but trainees are likely to earn around £12k a year, rising to around £18k with experience. Income can be increased by overtime and shift allowances.

Health

This job requires good general fitness. You should be free of back and chest problems. You may have to pass a medical before entry.

Skills and Qualities

able to follow instructions, aptitude for teamwork, careful, good concentration level, hand-to-eye co-ordination, manual dexterity, safety conscious, strong

Relevant Subjects

Manufacturing

Further Information

Apprenticeship Schemes (National Apprenticeship Service) - www.apprenticeships.org.uk

Diplomas (Foundation, Higher and Advanced) - http://yp.direct.gov.uk/diplomas

Foundation Learning (QCDA) - www.qcda.gov.uk

Foundry Trade Journal (monthly) (Institute of Cast Metals Engineers) - www.foundrytradejournal.com

Real Life Guide to Manufacturing & Product Design (Trotman 2009) - www.trotman.co.uk

Scenta - Careers Guide, Engineering, Technology and Science (Engineering Technology Board) - www.scenta.co.uk/careers.cfm

SEMTA - sector skills council for science, engineering and manufacturing technologies - www.semta.org.uk

Training Schemes - www.direct.gov.uk/en/educationandlearning

UK Centre for Materials Education - www.materials.ac.uk/

Welsh Baccalaureate - www.wbq.org.uk

▶ Working in manufacturing (2010) (Babcock Lifeskills) - www.babcock-lifeskills.com/

Addresses

Bradford College
Great Horton Road, Bradford, West Yorkshire BD7 1AY
Phone: +44 (0)1274 433333
Web: www.bradfordcollege.ac.uk/

Cast Metals Federation
National Metalforming Centre, 47 Birmingham Road, West Bromwich B70 6PY
Phone: +44 (0)121 601 6390
Web: www.castmetalsfederation.com

Castings Technology International
Advanced Manufacturing Park, Brunel Way, Rotherham, South Yorkshire S60 5WG
Phone: +44 (0) 114 254 1144
Web: www.castingstechnology.com

Engineering Council
246 High Holborn, London WC1V 7EX
Phone: +44 (0)20 3206 0500
Web: www.engc.org.uk

Institute of Cast Metals Engineers (ICME)
National Metalforming Centre, 47 Birmingham Road, West Bromwich, West Midlands B70 6PY
Phone: +44 (0)121 601 6979
Web: www.icme.org.uk

Metskill
Units 5-6 Meadowcourt, Amos Road, Sheffield S9 1BX
Phone: +44 (0)114 244 6833
Web: www.metskill.co.uk

Similar Jobs
Blacksmith, Foundry Moulder/Coremaker, Foundry Patternmaker, Labourer: General, Polymer/Plastics Process Operative

Freight Forwarder
also known as: Export/Import Clerk, Shipping Clerk

CRCI:Transport and Logistics
CLCI:YAS Job Band: 3 to 5

Job Description
Freight forwarders organise the transportation of goods between countries for importers and exporters, working out which combination of sea, air, rail and road is the most suitable and economical method. They use sophisticated computer systems. Take into account cost, speed, the type of goods, safety and time requirements. Arrange for the goods to be collected and stored. They also book freight space. Freight forwarders organise packing, carriage and insurance. Work out import and export duties, deal with the necessary licences and paperwork, and apply for customs clearance for the goods.

Work Details
Usually work normal office hours, although flexibility or shift work is sometimes needed when dealing with overseas customers. Offices are generally situated close to airports, sea ports and in industrial areas. Much time is spent on the phone and you sometimes visit clients and contractors. The work involves persuading and negotiating with people and selling your service. This work is often demanding.

Qualification
• England, Wales and Northern Ireland
Band 3: For trainee entry: usually at least 4 GCSEs (A*-C) including English and maths, or equivalent.

Band 4: For BTEC higher national award: 1-2 A levels and some GCSEs (A*-C) usually including English and maths and a modern language, or equivalent.

Band 5: For degree courses: 2-3 A levels and some GCSEs (A*-C) usually including English and maths, or equivalent. Exact requirements depend on the degree you take.

• Scotland
Band 3: For trainee entry: usually at least four S grades (1-3) including English, maths and a modern language, or similar.

Band 4: For SQA higher national award: usually 2-3 H grades and some S grades (1-3), often including English, maths and a modern language, or similar qualifications.

Band 5: For degree courses: 3-5 H grades and some S grades (1-3), usually including English and maths, or similar qualifications. Exact requirements depend on the degree you take.

Degree Information
A degree in any discipline is acceptable, though there are specific degrees in logistics, transport and distribution. Business studies (especially courses including banking and insurance options), foreign languages and law, give useful background.

Adult Qualifications
Entry requirements may be relaxed for adults applying for higher education courses. Access or foundation courses give adults without qualifications a route on to degree courses.

Work Experience
Relevant work or voluntary experience is useful to employers and colleges/universities. This includes office administration, sales, marketing or accounts work. Experience of using a foreign language in work abroad is also relevant.

Entry and Training
Entrants may register as affiliates of the British International Freight Association (BIFA). Many entrants come straight from school, college or university and often begin as juniors, clerks or couriers. On-the-job training with part-time study for BIFA qualifications by day release, evening classes or a distance-learning course is usual. Membership of the Institute of Export (IOE) is awarded on the basis of a combination of work experience and qualifications. You can enter into the the certificate in international trade, offered by the Institute, from the age of 16 without formal qualifications.

There are courses in international shipping and freight run by the International Air Transport Association and the International Federation of Freight Forwarders. The Chartered Institute of Logistics and Transport (CILTUK) also offers a range of relevant professional qualifications and the IOE runs a Young Independent trader programme aimed at key stage 4 pupils and above.

You may be able to join a larger employer on a graduate training programme. There are relevant HNDs and foundation degrees, such as logistics, transport and supply chain management. The ability to speak foreign languages is useful. S/NVQs in logistics, operations management and traffic office are available at levels 2-4. Training programmes, including apprenticeship schemes in traffic office, may be available in your area. Advanced apprenticeships leading to qualification at level 3 can also be a route into higher education and cover the key principals of international trade.

Government training opportunities, such as apprenticeships, may be available in your area. You can also gain recognition of previous experience through Accreditation of Prior Learning or by working towards relevant S/NVQs. Contact your local careers office, Jobcentre Plus, Next Step service or Learning and Skills Council (LSC)/Local Enterprise Company (LEC) for details of training schemes. For direct entry, relevant experience in export, marketing or transport is essential.

Opportunities and Pay
You work for a company of freight forwarders, a major retailer, the armed forces, a warehousing or distribution company, or a manufacturing company with an export department. They are usually found in large towns and cities and near airports and ports. Some freight forwarders specialise in handling certain types of goods, in arranging particular means of transport, or in forwarding to certain countries. It is possible to be self-employed. Work is available overseas. There is a growth in opportunities, but limited vacancies for trainees. Previous work experience and qualifications are increasingly important.

Pay varies depending on area and employer. Salaries start between £12k-£15k, rising to £20k-£30k a year with experience and qualifications. Some established and experienced freight forwarders in management positions may earn £30k-£40k or more.

Skills and Qualities
attention to detail, excellent communication skills, geographical knowledge, good organisational skills, good written English, information handling skills, IT skills, logical, numeracy skills, planning skills

Relevant Subjects
Business and accounting, Economics, English, Geography, ICT/ Computer studies, Mathematics, Modern Foreign Languages, Retail and distribution

Further Information
AGCAS: Transport and Logistics (Job Sector Briefing) (AGCAS) - www.prospects.ac.uk

An International Logistics Future for You (BIFA) - www.bifa.org

Apprenticeship Schemes (National Apprenticeship Service) - www.apprenticeships.org.uk

Careers in Logistics - www.careersinlogistics.co.uk

Inside Careers Guide: Logistics & Transport Management www.insidecareers.co.uk
International Air Transport Association (IATA) - http://iata.co.uk/
International Federation of Freight Forwarders (FIATA) - www.fiata.com
International Freighting Weekly (Informa Maritime and Transport) - www.ifw-net.com/freightpubs/ifw/index.htm
Logistics and Retail Management (2009) (Kogan Page) - www.koganpage.com
Skills for Logistics - sector skills council for freight logistics industries - www.skillsforlogistics.org
Training Schemes - www.direct.gov.uk/en/educationandlearning

Addresses

British International Freight Association (BIFA)
Redfern House, Browells Lane, Feltham, Middlesex TW13 7EP
Phone: +44 (0)20 8844 2266
Web: www.bifa.org

Chartered Institute of Logistics and Transport (CILTUK)
Careers Manager, Logistics & Transport Centre, Earlstrees Court, Earlstrees Road, Corby NN17 4AX
Phone: +44 (0)1536 740 100
Web: www.ciltuk.org.uk

Institute of Export (IOE)
Export House, Minerva Business Park, Lynch Wood, Peterborough PE2 6FT
Phone: +44 (0)1733 404 400
Web: www.export.org.uk

Similar Jobs

Export Sales Manager, Road Transport Manager, Shipbroker/ Airbroker, Wholesale Manager

Funeral Director

also known as: Undertaker

CRCI:Personal and Other Services

CLCI:IP Job Band: 1 to 2

Job Description

Funeral directors make funeral arrangements and organise a burial or cremation service. They visit the relatives of the person who has died and often arrange details such as music, catering, transport, fees, notices in newspapers, and flowers. Can arrange for a minister of religion to take the service. Also help the bereaved with any forms that have to be filled in. They give advice about government grants for people who do not have much money. Collect and prepare bodies for burial or cremation. May also deal directly with members of the medical profession.

Funeral directors work closely with the cemetery or crematorium and may also help with the choice of headstone. They ensure that on the day of the funeral, everything runs smoothly and with respect. Also assist the bereaved and usually make a list of the donations.

Work Details

Usually work a basic 39 hr week, though once qualified, you have to work irregular hours. The service is on call 24 hrs a day, every day of the year. You are based in fairly large premises with comfortable reception rooms, an embalming area, cool storerooms and a garage. It is necessary to travel around the district to visit clients, arrange and attend the funeral service.

It is important that you are able to deal with people who are upset or in need of support. This work can be emotionally demanding and you need to be able to cope with some unpleasant sights. You may have to be outside in all sorts of weather and the job involves some lifting.

Qualification

- **England, Wales and Northern Ireland**

Band 1: Generally, no formal educational qualifications are required for entry into funeral directing, though applicants may find subjects such as maths, English, biology, chemistry and art very useful.

Band 2: Employers may expect some GCSEs (A*-C) including English, maths and science, or similar.

- **Scotland**

Band 1: Generally, no formal educational qualifications are required for entry into funeral directing, though applicants may find subjects such as maths, English, biology, chemistry and art very useful.

Band 2: Employers may expect some S grades (1-3) including English, maths and science, or similar.

Adult Qualifications

Generally, no formal educational qualifications are required for entry into funeral directing. Nursing qualifications can be an advantage.

Work Experience

It is difficult to obtain work experience with a funeral director, because of health and safety rules and consideration for the relatives of the dead person. Experience of working with people, especially those who are distressed or under pressure, is useful. Administrative and business skills are also useful.

Entry and Training

Entrants to this job can be as young as 17, but most are older. You need a full driving licence and driving insurance for driving a hearse which may only be available for those over 25 yrs of age. Trainees begin as a funeral operative by driving cars and carrying out routine tasks. Training is on the job under the supervision of an experienced worker. After gaining some practical experience, it is possible to study for the foundation certificate in funeral service offered by the National Association of Funeral Directors (NAFD). Those who have passed the foundation certificate may then study part time for the diploma in funeral directing. This usually takes around two years. Courses are taught by tutors from the British Institute of Funeral Directors.

A further qualification, a higher certificate in funeral service management is offered by NAFD. The Co-operative College offers a range of open or in-house short specialist courses in areas such as: understanding bereavement, monumental masonry, team leadership for the funeral service, and funeral vocational qualifications at three levels, accredited by Edexcel. The University of Bath now runs a foundation degree in funeral services, and is developing a top-up course to convert this to an honours degree.

There may also be opportunities to train as an embalmer as the jobs are often combined. Training programmes, including apprenticeship schemes, may be available in your area. Advanced apprenticeships leading to qualification at level 3 can also be a route into higher education.

Mature entry is common as experience of life is an advantage for this job. Experience in any aspect of the funeral service, or business or administration is useful. It may be possible to do an apprenticeship with a funeral director.

Opportunities and Pay

Work is available throughout the UK, mainly in towns and cities. You can be employed by a large company, a small family firm with a single office, or a company that has a number of branch offices. Promotion is more likely if you work for a large company. Work abroad is possible if you are employed by a company with branches overseas.

Pay varies depending on where you work and level of responsibility. Starting pay is likely to be around £16k a year, rising to around £30k a year with experience. A bonus payment may be given for working long hours and being at funerals.

Skills and Qualities
attention to detail, emotionally strong, good communication skills, good interpersonal skills, good organisational skills, not squeamish, patient, smart appearance, sound judgement, tactful

Relevant Subjects
Biology, Business and accounting, Religious studies, Science

Further Information
Apprenticeship Schemes (National Apprenticeship Service) - www.apprenticeships.org.uk

Funeral Service Journal (monthly) (FSJ Communications) - www.fsj.co.uk

The Journal (quarterly) (British Institute of Funeral Directors (BIFD)) - www.bifd.org.uk/journal.html

Addresses
British Institute of Funeral Directors
1 Gleneagles House, Vernon Gate, South Street, Derby DE1 1UP
Phone: 0800 032 2733 (UK only)
Web: www.bifd.org.uk

Co-operative College
Holyoake House, Hanover Street, Manchester M60 0AS
Phone: +44 (0)161 246 2926
Web: www.co-op.ac.uk

National Association of Funeral Directors (NAFD)
618 Warwick Road, Solihull, West Midlands B91 1AA
Phone: 0845 230 1343 (UK only)
Web: www.nafd.org.uk

University of Bath
Bath BA2 7AY
Phone: +44 (0)1225 388388
Web: www.bath.ac.uk

Similar Jobs
Anatomical Pathology Technician, Chauffeur/Chauffeuse, Counsellor, Crematorium Technician, Embalmer, Registrar of Births, Marriages and Deaths

Furniture Designer

CRCI:Design, Arts and Crafts
CLCI:EG
Job Band: 3 to 5

Job Description
Furniture designers create furniture items that are used in the office and at home for both the mass-produced and hand-crafted markets. They discuss requirements with the client and may research what is already in the market. Then prepare sketches for approval and then more detailed drawings or models of the item required, ensuring it can be produced to meet the client's budget. Designers may use computer-aided design (CAD) tools. The self-employed designer/craftsperson then goes on to produce the item of furniture, often using traditional methods and tools.

Work Details
You work an average of 39 hrs a week, Monday to Friday. If you are self employed the hours are more irregular and depend on the job you are doing. Late finishes and weekends may sometimes be needed to complete a project.

You may work in a design office which can be spacious and airy, but may also be expected to visit the factory or workshop where the products are made. If self employed you are likely to be based in a small workshop and work alone, or with one or two other craftspeople. If you work for a manufacturing company, you can work with a large number of designers. Furniture designers are involved in some lifting and spend a lot of the day standing and bending, using a range of hand and machine tools.

Qualification

• England, Wales and Northern Ireland
Band 3: For entry: usually at least 4 GCSEs (A*-C) including English and maths, or equivalent.

Band 4: For HND, Diploma of Higher Education or foundation degree: 1-2 A levels and some GCSEs (A*-C) usually including English and maths, or equivalent. Some take a foundation course in art and design first.

Band 5: For degree courses: 2-3 A levels and some GCSEs (A*-C) usually including English and maths, or equivalent. Exact requirements depend on the degree you take.

• Scotland
Band 3: For entry: usually at least four S grades (1-3) including English and maths, or similar.

Band 4: For entry to SQA higher national and professional development awards, usually 2-3 H grades and some S grades (1-3), including English and maths, or similar qualifications.

Band 5: For degree courses: 3-5 H grades and some S grades (1-3), usually including English and maths, or similar qualifications. Exact requirements depend on the degree you take.

Degree Information
A degree in furniture design, interior, spatial or 3D design is most useful. Course titles vary, so check propectuses carefully.

Adult Qualifications
Entry requirements may be relaxed for adults applying for higher education courses. Access or foundation courses provide those without the required qualifications a route onto degree courses.

Work Experience
Entry to this job is competitive. It is important that you try to do some relevant work or voluntary experience before applying. Relevant contacts are furniture design specialists and interior design shops. Woodworking and other practical skills are also an advantage. A business background can help with the costing and budgeting aspects of the work.

Entry and Training
The usual entry route into this job is after completing an HND or degree in furniture design, interior, spatial or 3D design. It is important that your course includes creative as well as practical elements. Some take a foundation course in art and design first. There is also a foundation degree in furniture making.

A creative apprenticeship may be an alternative route into this career. There are also entry level courses in furniture design and manufacture and furniture production and technology throughout the country and you can increase your skills by studying upholstery and furniture conservation and restoration. The Furniture Industry Research Association (FIRA) also offer relevant training courses. There are specialist diplomas in manufacturing and product design or creative and media which may provide a route into furniture design. S/NVQs are available at levels 1-3 in furniture production and in making and installing furniture at levels 2-3.

Course entry requirements vary so check carefully with colleges and universities. You need to put together a portfolio of your design work to show to prospective employers and to take to interviews for jobs and courses.

Journals such as Design Week and the arts press can help to keep you up to date with furniture designers and current trends in the industry. You can also join the Chartered Society of Designers (CSD) to gain recognition of your skills and for support with continuing professional development (CPD).

Mature applicants with experience in art and design or relevant work in carpentry and joinery may have an advantage. Employers expect a good portfolio of recent designs that demonstrate an ability to design for the employer's target market. Those with experience of computer-aided design (CAD) programs such as AutoCAD, 3D Studio or Photoshop also have an advantage. You may also require a comprehensive and up-to-date portfolio of work for entry to courses.

Opportunities and Pay

Furniture designers can work as consultants or in-house designers for manufacturing companies, furniture design companies, makers of bespoke furniture or furniture produced for the mass market. Graduates in furniture design are sought after and can also work for a design practice, an exhibition company or a firm of private designers. There are opportunities for self employment for those with strong creative and practical abilities. Manufacturers and design consultancies are found throughout the UK but mainly in London and the south east. There is also a growing furniture industry in Europe.

Opportunities to progress depend on the size of the company you work for and the size of the market they sell to. Average salaries for a qualified furniture designer are about £18k-£22k, rising to around £25k-£31k a year. Self-employed craftspeople can earn more, but usually depend on commissions from people who want one-off pieces of furniture. Salaries for those at a senior level may be £45k or more a year.

Health

Normal colour vision is needed. Those with asthma may find some of the practical aspects of the work a problem.

Skills and Qualities

artistic ability, attention to detail, awareness of production process, creative flair, eye for shape/colour, flexible approach, good communication skills, good presentation skills, manual dexterity, problem-solving skills, specialist IT skills, technical aptitude

Relevant Subjects

Art and Design, Design and technology, Manufacturing, Mathematics

Further Information

Careers in Furniture (Proskills) - www.prospect4u.co.uk

Chartered Society of Designers (Chartered Society of Designers) - www.csd.org.uk

Design Week (Design Week) - www.designweek.co.uk

Diplomas (Foundation, Higher and Advanced) - http://yp.direct.gov.uk/diplomas

Furniture Industry Research Association (FIRA) - www.fira.co.uk

NSEAD: Careers in Art, Craft & Design (National Society for Education in Art and Design) - www.nsead.org/resources/careers.aspx

▶Working in art & design (2009) (Babcock Lifeskills) - www.babcock-lifeskills.com/

Your Creative Future (Design Council) (Design Council) - www.yourcreativefuture.org

Addresses

Association of British Furniture Manufacturers (BFM)
Wycombe House 9 Amersham Hill, High Wycombe,
Buckinghamshire HP13 6NR
Phone: +44 (0)1494 523 021
Web: www.bfm.org.uk

Worshipful Company of Furniture Makers
Furniture Makers' Hall, 12 Austin Friars, London EC2N 2HE
Phone: +44 (0)20 7256 5558
Web: www.furnituremkrs.co.uk

Similar Jobs

Architect, Cabinet Maker, Conservator-Restorer, Engineer: Design, Exhibition Designer, Film/TV & Theatre Set/Stage Designer, Interior Designer

Furniture Polisher/Finisher

also known as: French Polisher

CRCI:Manufacturing and Production
CLCI:SAJ Job Band: 2 to 4

Job Description

Furniture polishers work on either new, old or antique pieces of furniture, or in buildings and private homes that have fixed timber such as wood panelling. They stain, polish and finish the item by giving it a high sheen to bring out the quality and characteristics of the wood, being careful to match the colour of stains or paint. The wooden surface is prepared by rubbing it down with sand paper, wire wool or a sanding machine, and then any holes or dents are filled. Furniture polishers mix and apply the correct stain for the type of wood. They rub in polish by hand or spray with lacquer to obtain the required finish.

Work Details

Furniture polishers/finishers usually work a basic 35-40 hr week; Monday to Friday, though may need to work additional hours at times to complete jobs. You work in a workshop/studio, industrial premises, or in buildings and private homes. Your workplace can be dusty and there is a risk of injury from toxic materials, so you need to wear gloves and possibly overalls and a face mask. You have to cope with some physical activity, including lifting, and possibly standing for many hours. The job may include travelling to work on site. You may work as part of a team, but often do this work on your own.

Qualification

- **England, Wales and Northern Ireland**

Band 2: Although academic qualifications are not specified for this job, it is an advantage for some training courses and programmes to have some GCSEs (A*-C) in subjects that include English, technical subjects and maths, or equivalent.

Band 3: Some employers may ask for 4 GCSEs (A*-C) including English, a science and maths, or equivalent.

Band 4: For relevant foundation degree: usually 1-2 A levels and some GCSEs (A*-C) usually including English and maths, or equivalent.

- **Scotland**

Band 2: Although academic qualifications are not specified for this job, it is an advantage to have some S grades (1-3) for some training programmes and courses in English, technical subjects, science and maths, or similar.

Band 3: Some employers may ask for four S grades (1-3) possibly including maths, English and a science subject or similar.

Band 4: For relevant SQA higher national award: usually 2-3 H grades and some S grades (1-3), often including English and maths, or similar qualifications.

Adult Qualifications

Qualifications may not be needed for entry to courses if the applicant has proven woodworking ability.

Work Experience

Relevant work or voluntary experience is always useful and can improve your chances when applying for entry to jobs or courses. Your personal or adult guidance adviser should be able to advise you about how to organise work experience with a relevant employer. Areas to consider include anything that develops your craft woodworking skills.

Entry and Training

There are no specific qualifications required to enter this work; some people go into the work and train on the job while others prefer to do a relevant course before they start. Many have experience of furniture making before they move on to polishing and finishing. Those who train on the job are usually under the supervision of an experienced worker and may also attend relevant courses. City & Guilds offers level 2/3 qualifications in furniture production and in making and repairing hand-crafted furniture. Foundation degrees are available in furniture making, and degrees in furniture design may include French polishing. There are also some private fee paying specialist courses in French polishing.

Training programmes, including apprenticeship schemes, may be available in your area. Advanced apprenticeships leading to qualification at level 3 can also be a route into higher education. A Diploma/Welsh Baccalaureate in manufacturing and product design may be available in your area.

Government training opportunities, such as an apprenticeship in cabinet making, may be available in your area. You can also gain recognition of previous experience through Accreditation of Prior Learning (APL) or by working towards relevant S/NVQs. Contact your local careers office, Jobcentre Plus, Next Step service or Learning and Skills Council (LSC) Local Enterprise Company (LEC) for details of training schemes.

Opportunities and Pay

Furniture polishers/finishers can find employment in most UK towns, cities and rural areas. However, vacancies are scarce and there is usually a lot of competition for jobs. You are employed either by a manufacturing company or a small firm. With experience you can specialise in restoring antique furniture, progress to a supervisory role, or become a self-employed craft worker. Some polishers/finishers may move into teaching, either at a college or by offering private short courses for groups of people.

Many polishers/finishers are self-employed and therefore earnings can vary considerably. Trainees earn around £12k a year. This rises to around £25k with experience.

Health

The work involves a risk of skin problems or chest complaints caused by skin and breathing irritants. The job requires normal colour vision.

Skills and Qualities

able to follow instructions, able to work both on your own and in a team, attention to detail, careful, eye for shape/colour, good communication skills, manual dexterity, numeracy skills, patient, practical skills

Relevant Subjects

Art and Design, Design and technology

Further Information

Apprenticeship Schemes (National Apprenticeship Service) - www.apprenticeships.org.uk
Careers in Furniture (Proskills) - www.prospect4u.co.uk
Diplomas (Foundation, Higher and Advanced) http://yp.direct.gov.uk/diplomas
Proskills UK - sector skills council for process and manufacturing industries - www.proskills.co.uk
Training Schemes - www.direct.gov.uk/en/educationandlearning
Welsh Baccalaureate - www.wbq.org.uk

Addresses

British Antique Furniture Restorers' Association (BAFRA)
The Old Rectory, Warmwell, Dorchester DT2 8HQ
Phone: +44 (0)1305 854822
Web: www.bafra.org.uk

Guild of Master Craftsmen
166 High Street, Lewes, East Sussex BN7 1XU
Phone: +44 (0)1273 478449
Web: www.guildmc.com

Timber Trade Federation
The Building Centre 26 Store Street, London WC1E 7BT
Phone: +44 (0)20 3205 0067
Web: www.ttf.co.uk

Similar Jobs

Cabinet Maker, Conservator-Restorer, Furniture Designer, Musical Instrument Technician, Picture Framer, Upholsterer

Gamekeeper

also known as: Keeper: Game

CRCI:Environment, Animals and Plants
CLCI:WAM
Job Band: 1 to 3

Job Description

Gamekeepers work on large areas of countryside called beats looking after and managing game birds, duck, deer or fish, and also protect the wildlife habitats. They breed and rear deer, duck, trout, grouse, partridge and pheasant, to ensure there are sufficient numbers. Also guard against poachers, who may try to trap and steal the game and liaise with the local police force to deal with crimes against wildlife, including badger baiting, bird egg stealing or hare coursing. Gamekeepers trap and kill natural predators such as foxes, rats, weasels, magpies and crows.

They may use chemicals to control vermin such as rats and mice and are aware of the legal restrictions on how, where and what can be controlled. Gamekeepers use a gun, work with and may train working gundogs, such as springer spaniels and labradors. They work closely with forestry workers and a manager, as well as clients. May organise shooting and fishing parties, look after the clients and organise the selling of any game after a shoot. On shoot days, they usually hire and organise the workforce of beaters. They are often required to keep records and do basic administration.

Some gamekeepers manage and protect rivers and streams that are stocked with salmon and trout. They check that fishermen have permits and regularly patrol an area, making any necessary repairs to game enclosures, buildings, game pens, fences and other equipment. Must observe the law surrounding health and safety.

Work Details

There are no set working hours for gamekeepers who need to work until all daily tasks are completed. In summer, working hours can be longer. Often works alone outdoors and in all sorts of weather, so sometimes it is cold, wet and muddy. Work varies and can include some carpentry and machinery maintenance, tree trimming, cleaning guns, skinning animals and working with gundogs.

The area covered may be large and possibly include rough ground. A vehicle is usually provided by the employer but often you are on foot. You may have to face dangerous situations, for example, dealing with poachers who are trying to steal the stock.

Qualification

- **England, Wales and Northern Ireland**

Band 1: For entry to jobs, no minimum qualifications are needed, but you are expected to have a good level of general education and relevant experience. Some formal/vocational qualifications at any level are useful.

Band 2: For entry to jobs, no minimum qualifications are needed, but it is an advantage to have some GCSEs (A*-C) or equivalent in subjects that include English and maths.

Band 3: For entry: usually at least 4 GCSEs (A* C) including English, science, design technology and maths, or equivalent.

- **Scotland**

Band 1: For entry to jobs, no minimum qualifications are needed, but you are expected to have a good level of general education and relevant experience. Some formal/vocational qualifications at any level are useful.

Band 2: Although academic qualifications are not specified for this job, it is an advantage to have some S grades (1-3) in subjects that include English, science and maths, or similar.

Band 3: For entry: usually at least four S grades (1-3) including English, science, technology and maths, or similar.

Adult Qualifications

Those with relevant work experience may be accepted for some college courses without needing any formal entry requirements.

Work Experience

Relevant work or voluntary experience such as in agriculture or forestry, with animals, or as a beater is always useful and can improve your employment prospects when applying for entry to jobs. You may be able to gain some observation experience through work shadowing a gamekeeper on a local estate. Associations such as the British Association for Shooting and Conservation (BASC) offer the experience to try out gundog handling, deer stalking, falconry and more, through 'Young Shots' days. Adults are also encouraged to try out these and other skills. Contact the BASC (and other organisations for similar opportunities) for details.

Entry and Training

Traditionally, on-the-job training was usual and though this is still common, it is now supplemented with courses leading to appropriate qualifications. Courses are available throughout the UK, such as National Proficiency Tests Council (NPTC) level 2 in gamekeeping or first/national certificates/diplomas in game or wildlife management or in countryside management (gamekeeping). It is useful to have a background and knowledge of the countryside.

Many employers expect you to have experience in agriculture or forestry before you apply for a job as a learner-keeper. There may be a minimum age of 17 years for entry to a course and you may also need to have had a year's relevant experience. It is useful to have practical ability in woodwork.

The British Association for Shooting and Conservation (BASC) and the Game Conservancy Trust offer appropriate short courses for fee-paying students. The National Gamekeepers' Association runs a meat hygiene training course. Specialist short courses are also available from the British Deer Society. Sparsholt College, Hampshire runs a range of appropriate courses, both full and part time, including an honours degree course. There are relevant foundation degree and HND subjects, including wildlife and countryside management. The National Gamekeepers' Organisation Charitable Trust can provide a list of training courses and qualifications.

A Diploma/Welsh Baccalaureate may be available in your area in environment and land-based studies. There are S/NVQs at levels 2-3 in gamekeeping and wildlife management. Training programmes, including apprenticeship schemes, may be available in your area. Advanced apprenticeships leading to qualification at level 3 can also be a route into higher education.

Mature applicants usually require experience in agriculture or forestry, work with animals or as a beater. Carpentry skills are also useful. An interest in shooting and rural pursuits over a number of years is an advantage. You should contact the local Jobcentre Plus, Next Step service, LSC/LEC, Jobcentre (NI) or ELWa (Wales) for details of possible training opportunities. The National Gamekeepers' Organisation Charitable Trust can provide a list of training courses and qualifications.

Opportunities and Pay

There are around 3,000 full-time gamekeepers working in the UK and a similar number part time. You work in the country, perhaps in remote areas and may be given free or subsidised accommodation. It can be difficult to get into this type of work. A good way is to approach existing gamekeepers for beating jobs. A clear promotion path exists from a trainee to underkeeper, second underkeeper or beatkeeper and with further experience, a single-handed keeper or senior keeper. Headkeeper jobs are few in number. Some gamekeepers move into conservation or forestry where there are a variety of related jobs.

Many gamekeepers now combine work with other jobs such as forestry or farm work. Others may specialise as fishing guides or ghillies or in deer stalking. Self-employment and part-time work is possible and there are opportunities for work overseas.

Starting salaries for an underkeeper are likely to be around £12k a year. Single-handed keepers earn around £14k-£17k and head keepers up to £25k a year. On some estates, some may earn more. Usually you receive tips from clients, and employers often supply clothing and provide other allowances, such as a vehicle and free or subsidised accommodation.

Health

To do this job you must have good stamina and physical health. You will find this job difficult if you have hay fever or if you are allergic to animals.

Skills and Qualities

able to work both on your own and in a team, enjoy working outdoors, good at handling animals, hard working, manual dexterity, not squeamish, observant, self-reliant, strong

Relevant Subjects

Biology, Design and technology, Science

Further Information

Apprenticeship Schemes (National Apprenticeship Service) - www.apprenticeships.org.uk

British Association for Shooting and Conservation - www.basc.org.uk

Lantra - The Sector Skills Council for environmental & land-based sector (Lantra) http:/www.lantra.co.uk

Lantra Careers (A Future In...) (Lantra) - www.afuturein.com

National Gamekeepers Magazine - Keeping the Balance (4 x a year) (National Gamekeepers Organisation (NGO)) - www.nationalgamekeepers.org.uk/ngo-magazine/

Scottish Gamekeepers Association - www.scottishgamekeepers.co.uk

Shooting and Conservation (bi-monthly) (British Association of Shooting and Conservation) - http:/http://www.basc.org.uk

Training Schemes - www.direct.gov.uk/en/educationandlearning

▶Working with animals (2009) (Babcock Lifeskills) - www.babcock-lifeskills.com/

Addresses

British Association for Shooting and Conservation: NI
33 Castle Street, Lisburn, Co Down BT27 4SP
Phone: +44 (0)28 9260 5050
Web: www.basc.org.uk

British Deer Society
The Walled Garden, Burgate Manor, Fordingbridge, Hampshire SP6 1EF
Phone: +44 (0)1425 655434
Web: www.bds.org.uk

Game & Wildlife Conservation Trust
Burgate Manor, Fordingbridge, Hampshire SP6 1EF
Phone: +44 (0)1425 652 381
Web: www.gct.org.uk

National Gamekeepers' Organisation (NGO)
PO Box 246, Darlington DL1 9FZ
Phone: +44 (0) 1833 660869
Web: www.nationalgamekeepers.org.uk

National Gamekeepers' Organisation Charitable Trust
PO Box 3360, Stourbridge DY7 5YG
Phone: +44 (0) 1833 660869
Web: www.gamekeeperstrust.org.uk

Sparsholt College Hampshire
Westley Lane , Sparsholt, Winchester, Hampshire SO21 2NF
Phone: +44 (0)1962 776441
Web: www.sparsholt.ac.uk

Similar Jobs

Countryside Ranger, Farm Worker: Livestock, Fish Farm Worker, Forest Worker, Shepherd

Garden Centre Assistant

also known as: Horticultural Worker: Garden Centre

CRCI:Environment, Animals and Plants

CLCI:WAD Job Band: 1 to 2

Job Description

Garden centre assistants are responsible for a variety of tasks in a garden centre, where plants, flowers, garden furniture and tools, shrubs and trees are sold. They set out displays of plants, pots and garden tools and serve customers. Also water and feed plants, prune trees and shrubs. Use liquid sprays to make sure that the plants are free from pests and diseases. In garden centres that grow their own plants, They help to prepare the soil, sow seeds, plant seedlings and small plants. Then transfer young plants to larger pots, take cuttings and use grafting techniques on good root stock plants.

Assistants put cuttings into trays or into the prepared ground and when they are large enough, puts the plants into pots ready to be sold. They label pots with price and information. Can also be responsible for a section of the centre such as aquatic plants.

Work Details

A basic 39 hr week is usual, though longer hours may be necessary during busier times, such as spring, autumn and at Christmas. Weekend work is usually required, but you are given time off during the week instead. You can work inside a superstore, shop or greenhouse, as well as outdoors. Work is usually with the public, answering questions and giving advice, taking money and giving change, or accepting cheques and credit/debit cards.

Some of the work is dirty, and you may have to cope with bending down, kneeling, standing, lifting and carrying. Protective clothing is worn when spraying plants with pesticides and also in wet weather. If working in a shop, you may be required to wear a uniform or overall.

Qualification

- **England, Wales and Northern Ireland**

Band 1: For entry to jobs, no minimum qualifications are needed, but you are expected to have a good level of general education and relevant experience. Some formal/vocational qualifications at any level are useful.

Band 2: For entry to jobs, no minimum qualifications are needed, but it is an advantage to have some GCSEs (A*-C) or equivalent in subjects that include English, science and maths.

- **Scotland**

Band 1: For entry to jobs, no minimum qualifications are needed, but you are expected to have a good level of general education and relevant experience. Some formal/vocational qualifications at any level are useful.

Band 2: Although academic qualifications are not specified for this job, it is an advantage to have some S grades (1-3) in subjects that include English, science and maths, or similar.

Adult Qualifications

You do not usually need any formal qualifications for this job though any qualification and/or experience in horticulture is useful.

Work Experience

Employers may prefer entrants who have relevant experience. A part-time or holiday job may help you to get into this work and can give you skills that you can use in the future and add to your CV. This includes weekend or seasonal work in a garden centre, a nursery, work on a farm, grounds maintenance, or with an organisation such as the Royal Horticultural Society (RHS). Any general retail experience is also very useful.

Entry and Training

Some employers look for a mix of horticultural qualifications and retail skills, but on-the-job training is usual. After about a year's experience, some entrants take a day or block-release course leading to a BTEC/SQA national certificate/diploma in horticulture horticulture or a National Proficiency Tests Council (NPTC) level 1-3 qualification. The NPTC and the Scottish Skills Testing Service (SSTS) also offer certificates of competence in areas that include garden centre skills and nursery stock production. Short courses, such as in pest control, propagation or pruning, may be provided by your employer.

You can also gain relevant qualifications through the Royal Horticultural Society (RHS), who offer nationally recognised qualifications. These include the RHS level 3 diploma and advanced certificate in horticulture. Contact the RHS for details of training opportunities and qualifications. Some RHS courses may be taken by correspondence course through the Horticultural Correspondence College, which also runs a course in garden centre work. Those interested in taking on more management responsibilities can take the RHS one year special option in plant centre management skills.

A Diploma/Welsh Baccalaureate may be available in your area in the environment and land-based studies. Relevant S/NVQs up to level 3 are available. Relevant training programmes, including apprenticeship schemes, may be available in your area. Advanced apprenticeships leading to qualification at level 3 can also be a route into higher education.

Mature applicants can benefit through government-funded training opportunities that may be available in your area. Previous experience in related outdoor work, including forestry, agriculture/horticulture, gardening, or in retail and in customer care, is an advantage. You can gain recognition of previous experience through Accreditation of Prior Learning (APL) or by working towards relevant S/NVQs. Contact your local Connexions or careers office, Jobcentre Plus, Next Step service or Learning and Skills Council (LSC)/Local Enterprise Company (LEC) for details of all training opportunities and schemes, including apprenticeships for adults.

Opportunities and Pay

Commercial horticulture is increasing, such as in large garden centres where plants are grown and sold, or in smaller garden centres or DIY stores. Larger firms tend to offer promotion for those with experience and who gain additional qualifications. After training and courses you can become a supervisor and also move into management posts. Work can be part time or casual eg at weekends, Christmas and springtime.

Pay varies depending on where you work, but starting pay is around £11k-£12k a year, rising to around £18k a year with experience. Overtime pay is usual during busy seasons.

Health

You may find this job difficult if you have hay fever. You need good stamina and to be physically fit to cope with the gardening side of the work.

Skills and Qualities
able to explain clearly, able to work both on your own and in a team, adaptable, enjoy working outdoors, friendly, helpful, honest, interest in growing plants, manual dexterity, numeracy skills, willing to learn

Relevant Subjects
Biology, Land and Environment, Science

Further Information
Apprenticeship Schemes (National Apprenticeship Service) - www.apprenticeships.org.uk

Diplomas (Foundation, Higher and Advanced) - http://yp.direct.gov.uk/diplomas

Grow - the guide to careers in horticulture - www.growcareers.info

Lantra - The Sector Skills Council for environmental & land-based sector (Lantra) - http:/www.lantra.co.uk

Lantra Careers (A Future In...) (Lantra) - www.afuturein.com

Training Schemes - www.direct.gov.uk/en/educationandlearning

Addresses
Garden Centre Association
Leafield Technical Centre Leafield, Witney, Oxfordshire OX29 9EF
Phone: +44 (0)1993 871000
Web: www.gca.org.uk

Horticultural Correspondence College
Fiveways House, Westwells Road, Hawthorn, Corsham SN13 9RG
Phone: +44 (0)1225 816700
Web: www.hccollege.co.uk

Institute of Horticulture (IoH)
Capel Manor College, Bullsmoor Lane, Enfield EN1 4RQ
Phone: +44 (0) 1992 707025
Web: www.horticulture.org.uk

National Proficiency Test Council (NPTC)
City & Guilds Land Based Services Building 500 Abbey Park, Stareton, Warwickshire CV8 2LY
Phone: +44 (0) 24 7685 7300
Web: www.nptc.org.uk

Royal Horticultural Society (RHS)
80 Vincent Square, London SW1P 2PE
Phone: 0845 260 5000 (UK only)
Web: www.rhs.org.uk

Scottish Skills Testing Service
Young Farmers Centre, Ingliston, Edinburgh EH28 8NE
Phone: +44 (0)131 333 2040
Web: www.sayfc.org/ssts/

Similar Jobs
Gardener, Greenkeeper: Golf, Groundsman/Groundswoman, Horticultural Manager, Horticultural Worker: Commercial, Retail Assistant

Gardener
also known as: Amenity Horticultural Worker, Horticultural Worker: Amenity

CRCI:Environment, Animals and Plants
CLCI:WAD Job Band: 1 to 3

Job Description
Gardeners are responsible for the care and maintenance of trees, shrubs, flower beds or fruit, in public, historic and private gardens. They may also work in public parks, on roadside verges and roundabouts, and sports fields looking after lawns, hedges and paths, and pruning trees and shrubs. Gardeners work in greenhouses as well as outdoors, looking after seedlings and taking cuttings of plants. They prepare the soil ready for planting, clear weeds, use sprays to kill bugs and diseases or apply fertilisers to improve the soil. Use hand tools, such as spades, forks, trowels and rakes. In a private garden, they may also maintain a vegetable garden to provide fresh vegetables all year round.

Gardeners use power tools, mowing machines, rotavators and hedge trimmers. Some use larger vehicles in their work, including tractors. Also undertake basic maintenance tasks on garden sheds and greenhouses, machinery and furniture, and repair walls. Some gardeners may also offer and provide a garden design service.

Work Details
Gardeners usually work a basic 37-39 hr week, though daily hours often depend on the season and on weather conditions. Weekend work is possible, and also early morning starts. Longer hours may be required in the summer months. It is important to be physically fit as there is a lot of kneeling, bending, lifting and carrying. For jobs such as pruning trees, you have to have a head for heights. Gardeners may have to travel to different places and be out in all sorts of weather.

Working in gardens is dirty and muddy. It can be hot and humid if working in a greenhouse. Gardeners use sprays, tools and machines and need to be aware of safety rules, especially when using electrical equipment and chemicals.

Qualification

- **England, Wales and Northern Ireland**

Band 1: For entry to jobs, no minimum qualifications are needed, but you are expected to have a good level of general education and relevant experience. Some formal/vocational qualifications at any level are useful.

Band 2: For entry to jobs, no minimum qualifications are needed, but it is an advantage to have some GCSEs (A*-C) or equivalent in subjects that include English and maths.

Band 3: For entry: often at least 4 GCSEs (A*-C) including English and maths, or equivalent.

- **Scotland**

Band 1: For entry to jobs, no minimum qualifications are needed, but you are expected to have a good level of general education and relevant experience. Some formal/vocational qualifications at any level are useful.

Band 2: Although academic qualifications are not specified for this job, it is an advantage to have some S grades (1-3) in subjects that include English, science and maths, or similar.

Band 3: For entry: often at least four S grades (1-3) including English and maths, or similar.

Adult Qualifications
Entry to this job can be at many different levels of qualification, and for some jobs and entry to courses, no formal qualifications are required. Course entry requirements are usually relaxed for mature entrants.

Work Experience
Employers may prefer candidates who have relevant work or voluntary experience. This can include any work in a garden centre, a horticultural nursery, on a farm or in grounds maintenance, and equips you with skills that you can use in the future and add to your CV.

Entry and Training
On-the-job training is usual, with perhaps a block or day-release course at college. Formal training may be available at your local college, which may run courses such as National Proficiency Test Council (NPTC) level 3 diplomas, BTEC national awards, S/NVQs and Royal Horticultural Society (RHS) qualifications. You may need to have worked in horticulture for a year before you can take a formal college course. Distance learning courses are available from the Horticultural Correspondence College (HCC).

Short practical courses, such as in pest control, propagation or pruning, may be provided by your employer. Other specialist courses are available, such as arboriculture (care of shrubs and trees), sports turf culture or greenkeeping. Traineeships/careerships, with a salary, are available through organisations such as the Professional Gardeners' Guild and the National Trust. Applicants should preferably have some practical experience or training in horticulture.

A Diploma/Welsh Baccalaureate may be available in your area in the environment and land-based studies. S/NVQs at levels 2-4 in amenity horticulture are available. Relevant training programmes, including apprenticeship schemes, may be available in your area. Advanced apprenticeships leading to qualification at level 3 can also be a route into higher education.

Mature applicants can benefit through government-funded training opportunities that may be available in your area. Experience of horticulture or farm work is an advantage. You can gain recognition of previous experience through Accreditation of Prior Learning (APL) or by working towards relevant S/NVQs. Contact your local Connexions or careers office, Jobcentre Plus, Next Step service or Learning and Skills Council (LSC)/Local Enterprise Company (LEC) for details of all training opportunities and schemes, including apprenticeships for adults.

Opportunities and Pay

You can work full or part time for a large employer such as a market garden or a local or national authority, caring for public parks and school grounds, or for a hospital, a landscape gardener or horticultural contractor. Other employers include organisations such as the National Trust, sports/leisure centres, theme parks or private estates. Gardeners also work for individual private households, usually on a part-time basis. Some gardeners are self-employed, running their own business and working for a variety of clients.

Jobs are also available in the royal parks, historic gardens and stately homes, at botanical gardens and horticultural society gardens. Promotion to a more senior and supervisory level usually depends upon gaining experience and qualifications. There are currently good opportunities for self-employment.

Pay can vary considerably depending on location and type of employer. Starting salaries are around £12k-£15k a year, rising to around £18k-£20k. Senior gardeners with supervisory/management responsibility may earn around £20k-£25k a year or more. Those who are self-employed usually negotiate an hourly rate, ranging from around £8-£12 or more. Gardeners offering a garden design service usually earn a higher salary.

Health

This job requires you to be physically fit and you may find this job difficult if you suffer from hay fever.

Skills and Qualities

able to work both on your own and in a team, enjoy working outdoors, hard working, interest in growing plants, manual dexterity, patient, reliable, strong

Relevant Subjects

Biology, Land and Environment, Science

Further Information

Apprenticeship Schemes (National Apprenticeship Service) - www.apprenticeships.org.uk

Diplomas (Foundation, Higher and Advanced) - http://yp.direct.gov.uk/diplomas

Grow - the guide to careers in horticulture - www.growcareers.info

Lantra - The Sector Skills Council for environmental & land-based sector (Lantra) http:/www.lantra.co.uk

Lantra Careers (A Future In...) (Lantra) - www.afuturein.com

Local Government Careers (Improvement and Development Agency) - www.lgcareers.com/publications/

Professional Gardener (Professional Gardeners Guild) (Professional Gardening Guild) - www.pgg.org.uk

Real Life Guide to Working Outdoors (Trotman) - www.trotman.co.uk

Training Schemes - www.direct.gov.uk/en/educationandlearning

Working outdoors (2010) (Babcock Lifeskills) - www.babcock-lifeskills.com/

Addresses

Horticultural Correspondence College
Fiveways House, Westwells Road, Hawthorn, Corsham SN13 9RG
Phone: +44 (0)1225 816700
Web: www.hccollege.co.uk

Institute of Horticulture (IoH)
Capel Manor College, Bullsmoor Lane, Enfield EN1 4RQ
Phone: +44 (0) 1992 707025
Web: www.horticulture.org.uk

National Proficiency Test Council (NPTC)
City & Guilds Land Based Services Building 500 Abbey Park, Stareton, Warwickshire CV8 2LY
Phone: +44 (0) 24 7685 7300
Web: www.nptc.org.uk

National Trust
Heelis, Kemble Drive, Swindon, Wiltshire SN2 2NA
Phone: +44 (0)1793 817400
Web: www.ntjobs.org.uk

Royal Horticultural Society (RHS)
80 Vincent Square, London SW1P 2PE
Phone: 0845 260 5000 (UK only)
Web: www.rhs.org.uk

Similar Jobs

Cemetery Worker, Forest Worker, Greenkeeper: Golf, Groundsman/Groundswoman, Horticultural Manager, Horticultural Worker: Commercial

Gas Distribution Worker

also known as: Gas Pipe Layer, Mains Layer: Gas, Service Layer: Gas

CRCI:Engineering
CLCI:ROZ — Job Band: 1 to 3

Job Description

Gas distribution workers lay and replace pipes that carry gas to homes and businesses and connect buildings to mains gas supplies. They follow strict health and safety rules.

The job involves being called out to gas leaks and having to deal with emergency repairs. They use plans to find gas pipes under the ground and put up barriers and signs to keep people out of danger. They dig up roads and footpaths using mechanical diggers, pneumatic drills and hand tools. They also connect new pipes, fit new parts or repair damage and make sure there are no leaks. Then, fill in holes and clear up rubble.

Gas distribution workers also visit new customers, show identification and explain what is needed and how long it will take to connect them. They use special equipment to bore a hole from the building to the gas main, feed in and connect plastic pipes and install a new gas meter. They also fill in a record of the work and clear up after the job.

Work Details

Usually work a 37-40 hr week, Monday to Friday but you may have to do paid overtime to get a job finished. Some jobs may be planned for nights or weekends. You generally take turns on a stand-by rota for call out to emergencies at night, weekends or during bank holidays. Most of the work is outdoors in all weathers. It is physically demanding and dirty work, and may involve working in tight spaces. You usually work in teams of two or three.

Health and safety is important as you are working with materials and equipment that can cause serious injuries. You wear protective clothing provided by the employer such as high-visibility jackets, fireproof trousers, thick gloves, kneepads and boots with steel toe-caps.

Qualification

• England, Wales and Northern Ireland

Band 1: For entry to jobs, no minimum qualifications are needed, but you are expected to have a good level of general education and relevant experience. Some formal/vocational qualifications at any level are useful.

Band 2: For entry to jobs, no minimum qualifications are needed, but it is an advantage to have some GCSEs (A*-C) or equivalent in subjects that include maths and English and sometimes subjects such as design and technology, ICT, science or engineering.

Band 3: For entry to jobs, HNC, advanced apprenticeship (England) or a relevant Diploma, usually at least 4 GCSEs (A*-C) including English and maths, or equivalent.

• Scotland

Band 1: For entry to jobs, no minimum qualifications are needed, but you are expected to have a good level of general education and relevant experience. Some formal/vocational qualifications at any level are useful.

Band 2: Although academic qualifications are not specified for this job, it is an advantage to have some S grades (1-3) in subjects that include maths and English and sometimes subjects such as design and technology, ICT, science or engineering.

Band 3: For entry to jobs or a modern apprenticeship: usually at least four S grades (1-3) including English and maths, or similar.

Adult Qualifications

No formal academic qualifications are required for adults. You can improve your skills and qualifications by working through the Foundation Learning programme. This involves taking credit-based units and qualifications to help you progress.

Work Experience

Work experience helps you find out what you enjoy and do not enjoy about a type of work. Paid or voluntary work outdoors, where you use machinery or do building or engineering work, may be useful.

Entry and Training

You can enter this area of work straight from school but some employers may ask you to take literacy and numeracy tests. Training is largely on the job with experienced workers and day or block release to attend courses at colleges or with training providers. You may work towards qualifications such as S/NVQ levels 1-3 in gas network operations (mains laying or service laying or craft) or S/NVQ level 3 in gas emergency service operations. Gas industry and gas network apprenticeships leading to level 2 and advanced apprenticeships leading to level 3 qualifications may be available in your area.

You must pass a one-day Utility Safety Health and Environment Awareness (Gas) course to prove that you know how to work safely. You cannot work on the gas network without an Energy & Utilities Skills Register card. This needs to be renewed every five years. See the website for details. Having a full, clean driving licence is an advantage as teams travel to sites by van.

With experience you may progress into a management role and work towards NVQ level 4 gas network engineering management.

The Energy Networks Association (ENA) has details of the Good Practise Guide for gas distributors. The ENA now represents the four British gas distribution companies in the UK and their website has useful industry information.

Employers may look for evidence of relevant skills or experience in areas such as engineering, building services engineering, plumbing or construction work.

Opportunities and Pay

You may find work with one of the gas distribution companies in the UK or the contractors they use to do the work. There are also jobs with construction companies working on new developments. Over 90% of people working in gas distribution are employed in England. There tend to be more jobs in towns and cities where more people need access to gas. Some rural areas have no gas supplies.

The Government is putting pressure on gas distribution companies to replace old gas mains more quickly. The number of jobs has been decreasing but companies still need to replace staff leaving the industry. With experience and further training, you may progress to team leader or a technical role. Some workers may go on to become managers.

Apprentice gas distribution workers earn around £11k-£15k a year and may get other benefits. Trained workers earn around £16k-£18k a year plus overtime and other payments. More experienced workers and team leaders can earn £25k-£40k a year.

Health

Good general fitness required. There may be an allergy risk from fumes, pollen and dust.

Skills and Qualities

able to communicate effectively, able to follow drawings and plans, able to work both on your own and in a team, able to work in confined spaces, attention to detail, enjoy working outdoors, manual dexterity, numeracy skills, problem-solving skills, safety conscious

Relevant Subjects

Construction and built environment, Design and technology, Science

Further Information

AGCAS: Energy & Utilities (Job Sector briefing) (AGCAS) - www.prospects.ac.uk

Apprenticeship Schemes (National Apprenticeship Service) - www.apprenticeships.org.uk

Energy & Utility Skills - sector skills council for gas, power, waste management & water industries - www.euskills.co.uk

Energy Networks Association - http://2010.energynetworks.org

National Grid - www.nationalgrid.com

Utility Week (Reed Business Info) - www.utilityweek.co.uk

Addresses

Energy Networks Association
6th Floor Dean Bradley House 52 Horseferry Road,
London SW1P 2AF
Phone: +44 (0) 20 7706 5100
Web: http://2010.energynetworks.org/

Similar Jobs

Construction Operative, Engineer: Gas, Fitter: Maintenance, Gas Service Engineer, Road Worker, Water Distribution/Sewerage Operative

Gas Service Engineer

also known as: Gas Fitter, Gas Installer

CRCI:Engineering
CLCI:ROK Job Band: 1 to 3

Job Description

Gas service engineers install, repair and maintain gas piping and all kinds of gas appliances in a customer's private or rented home or at business/industrial premises. They work with cookers, fires, meters, central heating or commercial equipment. The job involves cutting and shaping pipes, joining them together and connecting to a meter. They adjust for the correct mixture of gas and air and follow strict health and safety procedures.

Engineers check meters and test appliances and repair or replace faulty parts. They may locate gas leaks and do routine servicing. They often deal with electronic programmers and controls and may use a laptop or mobile phone to communicate with their work base. Service engineers also advise customers on different types of appliances and energy efficiency.

Work Details

Usually work around 39-40 hrs a week, involving early starts. You may need to be on call at times, particularly when dealing with emergencies. Work is in a workshop or visiting customers' premises, so travel around a geographical area is necessary. You are responsible for providing an efficient service and keenly observing regulations for safety. You deal with customers who may be anxious so must be able to reassure them. The environment can be dirty with unpleasant fumes and there may be a risk of minor injuries. You need to wear overalls and have to cope with some physical activity, including heavy lifting, bending down and kneeling in small spaces.

Qualification

• England, Wales and Northern Ireland

Band 2: For entry to jobs, no minimum qualifications are needed, but it is an advantage to have some GCSEs (A*-C) or equivalent in subjects that include maths, English and a science or technology-related subject, or equivalent.

Band 3: For apprenticeships, HNC or a relevant Diploma: usually at least 4 GCSEs (A*-C) including maths, English and a science or technology-related subject, or equivalent.

• Scotland

Band 2: Although academic qualifications are not specified for this job, it is an advantage to have some S grades (1-3) in subjects that include maths, English and a science or technology-related subject, or similar.

Band 3: For entry to jobs, usually at least four S grades (1-3) including maths, English and a science or technology-related subject, or similar qualification.

Adult Qualifications

Relevant qualifications and previous experience are usually required.

Work Experience

Relevant work or voluntary experience is always useful. It can add to your CV and improve your chances when applying for entry to jobs or apprenticeships in the engineering industry.

Entry and Training

Most entrants follow an apprenticeship programme of training, which is a combination of on-the-job experience and off-the-job training for a technical certificate. However, each gas service engineer (installer) must be assessed for competence and be registered with the Health and Safety Executive's appointed gas registration body. The Gas Safe Register has details of all registered companies and engineers qualified to work safely in the gas servicing industry and is run by Capita. See the website for full details.

Experienced engineers can complete the Nationally Accredited Certification Scheme (ACS) for entry on the register. The ACS ensures that engineers are assessed against a set of criteria based on up to date standards, best working practice and technology. Those beginning their training, have to complete S/NVQ levels 2-3 in domestic natural gas installation and maintenance. All gas service engineers, regardless of levels of experience, need evidence of their competence that is less than five years old.

Some employers support further training and allow you to gain Engineering Technician status with the Engineering Council. Advanced apprenticeships leading to qualification at level 3 can also be a route into higher education. The Institute of Domestic Heating & Environmental Engineers (IDHEE) offers a modular route to professional qualification if you have not followed a traditional course of education and training. If you are successful, you can join the IDHEE as a qualified technician and can gain full membership of the IDHEE. A driving licence is also usually a requirement for this job.

The Energy & Utility Skills website has details of training centres and employers which offer apprenticeships. The British Gas Academy and Centrica Plc also offer information on apprenticeships and other opportunities in the British Gas engineering sector (including Scottish Gas and Nwy Prydain, Wales). For example, British Gas runs an apprentice engineer scheme leading to an S/NVQ Level 3 award. The training includes a Duke of Edinburgh award for personal development. Trainees receive a training salary until qualified and then move into a qualified salary band. Further training is ongoing throughout your career. See the British Gas website for full details of the scheme.

A Diploma/Welsh Baccalaureate may be available in your area in engineering. See the diplomas website for further information.

Mature entry is common especially if you have related experience, such as plumbing, welding, heating and ventilation fitting, and in particular, armed forces experience. Due to skill shortages, adults are actively encouraged to train, and adult training schemes are often available through gas companies. You need to complete training and assessment that is recognised by the Gas Safe Register. The British Gas Academy also offers a mature student training scheme as well as opportunities for fully qualified engineers.

Government training opportunities, such as apprenticeships, may be available in your area. You can also gain recognition of previous experience through Accreditation of Prior Learning or by working towards relevant S/NVQs. Contact your local careers office, Jobcentre Plus, Next Step service or Learning and Skills Council (LSC)/Local Enterprise Company (LEC) for details of training schemes.

Opportunities and Pay

Jobs are available in most towns and cities with installation and servicing companies such as British Gas Services or the National Grid, manufacturers of domestic and industrial gas appliances, gas appliance retail outlets, and Gas Safe Register companies such as a local central heating specialist. Promotion prospects can be improved with further training. With enough experience, you can become self-employed and set up your own firm of gas service engineers.

Apprentices working for British Gas generally earn around £14k a year. Pay improves with qualification and experience but is generally around £20k-£30k. Pay is often supplemented with performance-related bonuses and overtime pay.

Health

This job requires good health and good eyesight with normal colour vision. Asthma sufferers may find this job difficult.

Skills and Qualities

able to work well on your own, aptitude for figures, careful, good communication skills, good interpersonal skills, manual dexterity, methodical, responsible attitude, safety conscious, strong

Relevant Subjects

Design and technology, Engineering, Mathematics, Physics, Science

Further Information

AGCAS: Energy & Utilities (Job Sector briefing) (AGCAS) - www.prospects.ac.uk

Apprenticeship Schemes (National Apprenticeship Service) - www.apprenticeships.org.uk

Diplomas (Foundation, Higher and Advanced) - http://yp.direct.gov.uk/diplomas

Energy & Utility Skills - sector skills council for gas, power, waste management & water industries - www.euskills.co.uk

Gas Safe Register - www.gassaferegister.co.uk

National Grid - www.nationalgrid.com

SEMTA - sector skills council for science, engineering and manufacturing technologies - www.semta.org.uk

Training Schemes - www.direct.gov.uk/en/educationandlearning

Welsh Baccalaureate - www.wbq.org.uk

Addresses

British Gas Academy
British Gas Services Recruitment Centre, Colthrop Way, Thatcham, Berkshire RG1 4AG
Web: www.britishgasacademy.co.uk

Centrica plc
Millstream, Maidenhead Road, Windsor, Berkshire SL4 5GD
Phone: +44 (0)1753 494000
Web: www.centrica.co.uk

Engineering Council
246 High Holborn, London WC1V 7EX
Phone: +44 (0)20 3206 0500
Web: www.engc.org.uk

Institute of Domestic Heating and Environmental Engineers (IDHEE)
P O Box 329, Southampton, Hampshire SO40 0BT
Phone: +44 [0] 23 80 66 89 00
Web: www.idhee.org.uk

Similar Jobs

Domestic Appliance Service Technician, Engineer: Gas, Fitter: Maintenance, Heating & Ventilation Fitter/Welder, Plumber

Genealogist

CRCI:Languages, Information and Culture
CLCI:FAG Job Band: 5

Job Description

Geneaologists carry out research into family history, to trace and chart lines of descent or family trees. They receive enquiries from clients and obtain background details. Then they locate relevant historical material from archives, libraries, courts, churches and public and military record offices, as well as private records. Original documents, such as birth certificates, census records, old court records, army and navy records, tax books and immigration records, and extracts information of interest to the client are read and interpreted. Genealogists are often employed to trace family trees, but are also involved in legal and medical work. Increasingly, they use software packages to speed up the search, and the Internet to research sites throughout the world. Compiles genealogical reports for clients and suggests further paths for research.

Work Details

Those in permanent employment usually work from 9am to 5pm, Monday to Friday. Self-employed genealogists have no set working hours. Usually your place of work is a library, records office or in your own office at home. Travel is necessary to different sites to find information. You are responsible for assessing the work to be carried out, tracking down sources, analysing details and presenting information in a written document. Skills in using computer software packages and the Internet are important.

Qualification

Although no specific qualifications are required for entry to this job, employers may prefer graduates.

• England, Wales and Northern Ireland

Band 5: For degree courses: 2-3 A levels and some GCSEs (A*-C) usually including English and maths, or equivalent. Exact requirements depend on the degree you take. History and Latin are useful subjects.

• Scotland

Band 5: For degree courses: 3-5 H grades and some S grades (1-3), including English and maths, or similar qualifications. Exact requirements depend on the degree you take. History and Latin are useful subjects.

Degree Information

Degrees can be in any subject, but a relevant discipline such as history or classics is useful. A postgraduate certificate in family and local history is available.

Adult Qualifications

Entry is possible for anyone with sufficient interest and motivation. It is important to have appropriate knowledge. History, Latin and palaeography are essential. Relevant experience, such as archive and library work, is an advantage.

Work Experience

Employers and universities may prefer candidates who have relevant work or voluntary experience, especially to ensure you are suited to such a specific career. Some experience in archiving, such as in a county or national records office or a library, in paid work, or in a voluntary capacity, is useful.

Entry and Training

Entrants are usually graduates and it is important to have a relevant degree, for example in history. It is essential to have a good knowledge of Latin and palaeography (the study of old handwriting), and to have some knowledge of legal terms. Most entrants to this career come from other professions.

Word processing and computer skills are also important. Most graduates then go on to take short full-time, part-time, residential or correspondence courses, leading to a series of qualifications from the Institute of Heraldic and Genealogical Studies (IHGS). There are several levels of qualification, of which the highest academic award is the Licentiateship of the Institute. This qualifies practitioners for membership of the Association of Genealogists and Researchers in Archives (AGRA).

Lifelong Learning UK offers a certificate at level 2 and a diploma at level 3 in libraries, archives and information services. The IHGS, the Society of Genealogists and local family history societies also run short courses in palaeography, local history, genealogy, and on different aspects of genealogical research.

There is an honours degree in family, local and community history at University Campus, Suffolk which includes genealogical research methods. The Centre for Archive & Information Studies at Dundee University offers a postgraduate certificate in family and local history.

Mature entrants should have a good knowledge of Latin and palaeography, and some knowledge of legal terms. Word processing and computer skills are also important. Contact the

Institute of Heraldic and Genealogical Studies (IHGS) or the Society of Genealogists for details on professional qualifications and relevant academic courses. This is commonly a second career for mature entrants with relevant experience.

Opportunities and Pay

This is an area of work in which interest has grown in recent years but it is still a small field of work. It is unusual to make a full-time living from this job but some work for county records offices and a few find employment in publishing or journalism. It is possible to specialise in the records of a particular area or to develop a particular skill such as transcription.

Genealogists are usually freelance and are contracted to work on different assignments by private individuals, legal firms and sometimes charitable trusts or research organisations. This job is often done from a home base. There may also be opportunities to teach and lecture in genealogy courses at further or higher education institutions.

Increasingly, genealogical information is available via the internet so there may be an opportunity to work for one of these companies.

Although there is a recommended hourly rate, fees are usually agreed when setting up contracts so pay depends on the number of clients and their background. Salaries can vary hugely, but most genealogists earn around £15-£25 an hour and this is usually a supplementary income. Those in permanent employment usually earn in the region of £15k-£25k a year but some may earn more.

Skills and Qualities

able to work well on your own, accurate, analytical skills, attention to detail, enquiring mind, imaginative, information handling skills, IT skills, methodical, research skills

Relevant Subjects

Classical studies, English, History, ICT/Computer studies

Further Information

Careers in Genealogy (Society of Genealogists (2010))

Creative & Cultural Skills - sector skills council for advertising, crafts, cultural heritage, design, literature, music, performing & visual arts - www.ccskills.org.uk

Genealogists Magazine (quarterly) (Society of Genealogy) - www.sog.org.uk/genmag/genmag.shtml

LLUK (Lifelong Learning UK) - sector skills council for the professional development of staff working in the lifelong learning sector - www.lluk.org

The Scottish Genealogist (quarterly) (SGS) - www.scotsgenealogy.com

▶Working in cultural heritage (2007) (Babcock Lifeskills) - www.babcock-lifeskills.com/

Addresses

Association of Genealogists and Researchers in Archives (AGRA)
43 Bowes Wood, New Ash Green, Longfield, Kent DA3 8QL
Web: www.agra.org.uk

Association of Scottish Genealogists and Researchers in Archives (ASGRA)
22 Marjory Place, Bathgate EH48 2TR
Phone: +44 (0)1506 653654
Web: www.asgra.co.uk

Centre for Archive & Information Studies
Tower Building, University of Dundee DD1 4HN
Phone: +44 (0)1382 385543
Web: www.dundee.ac.uk/cais

Institute of Heraldic and Genealogical Studies (IHGS)
79-82 Northgate, Canterbury, Kent CT1 1BA
Phone: +44 (0)1227 768 664
Web: www.ihgs.ac.uk

Scottish Genealogy Society
15 Victoria Terrace, Edinburgh EH1 2JL
Phone: +44 (0)131 220 3677
Web: www.scotsgenealogy.com

Society of Genealogists
14 Charterhouse Buildings, Goswell Road, London EC1M 7BA
Phone: +44 (0)20 7251 8799
Web: www.sog.org.uk

Similar Jobs

Archivist, Information Scientist, Library & Information Manager, Private Investigator, Registrar of Births, Deaths, Marriages and Civil Partnerships

Geneticist

also known as: Genetic Engineer

CRCI:Science, Mathematics and Statistics

CLCI:QOD Job Band: 5

Job Description

Geneticists study inherited characteristics in humans, animals, plants and micro-organisms. They can work in the fields of biotechnology, biomedicine, bioinformatics, the environment and agriculture, or in the context of law, archaeology or forensics. The role is often a research, teaching or clinical one, but can also involve genetic engineering. Some geneticists specialise in human genetics work, such as the Human Genome Project or medical/clinical genetics. Others specialise in animal and plant genetics.

In genetic engineering, they use specialised techniques to change the DNA (molecules which make up genetic material), which form the characteristics of organisms, perhaps to control diseases, improve crop yield or animal breeding. In biosciences and biotechnology, geneticists develop methods to extract information from genomes by data analysis and modelling. Some work on diagnosis of genetically caused disease or use genetic fingerprinting for identifying individuals. Others are concerned with population genetics, studying patterns of change in different areas.

May be responsible for managing a team of biomedical scientists and other support staff such as medical technologists, laboratory assistants and clerical assistants. May carry out research or teach, usually in a university. In this role there are often administrative tasks and you may have to write papers for conferences or publication in specialist journals.

Work Details

Usually work 9am-5pm, Monday to Friday, occasionally working outside these hours to carry out and complete experiments. You work in a laboratory, university, college, hospital or perhaps an office. Depending on your post you may have responsibility for setting up experiments, analysing results and presenting reports. In hospital work, you provide information and advice for diagnosis and treatment; this requires a high degree of accuracy.

Some work may involve having to cope with the sight of blood. In some jobs you can be monitoring quality standards, checking production schedules or supervising staff. A white coat or an overall and protective gloves is worn for some aspects of work.

Qualification

• England, Wales and Northern Ireland

Band 5: For degree courses: 2-3 A levels preferably including biology and chemistry, with physics or maths, and some GCSEs (A*-C) usually including English, maths and double science, or equivalent. Exact requirements depend on the degree you take.

- **Scotland**

Band 5: For degree: 3-5 H grades preferably including biology and chemistry, with physics or maths, and some S grades (1-3) including English, double science and maths, or similar. Exact requirements depend on the degree you take.

Degree Information

Degrees in genetics, or biology, applied biology or biochemistry are preferred by employers. Some courses offer molecular or human genetics or combine genetics with other biological sciences. Degrees in molecular biology may also be acceptable. Some other biological science degrees give a useful background. Postgraduate courses are available.

Adult Qualifications

A degree and up-to-date scientific knowledge are essential. Course requirements may be relaxed for mature applicants provided they submit evidence of previous serious study, such as a relevant Access course. Credit is given for relevant experience. It is also possible for those without the specified science qualifications to take a foundation year leading into the relevant degree. Check with individual colleges and universities for specific entry requirements.

Work Experience

Universities and employers may prefer candidates who have work or voluntary experience, in areas such as hospital work, a relevant university department, or in an industrial or commercial laboratory. If it proves difficult to gain this exact experience then similar or other scientific backgrounds are still attractive to employers and admissions tutors.

Entry and Training

Your training is by practical experience in an accredited teaching laboratory after obtaining a degree or postgraduate qualification in genetics, or a relevant biological science. Degree courses can be full time or sandwich and last for 3-4 years. A number of suitable first degree courses are available, as well as relevant postgraduate courses. For training positions within the NHS you need at least a 2:1 degree. Some employers prefer to recruit entrants with postgraduate qualifications. Membership of a professional organisation such as the Society of Biology can be attained by having a combination of academic qualifications and practical experience. Continuing professional development (CPD) is expected for scientists in career grade posts and to maintain registration with the Health Professions Council (HPC).

Mature applicants with research experience in clinical areas, including laboratory science, may have an advantage.

Opportunities and Pay

Genetics is one of the fastest moving sciences. There are opportunities in industry, medicine, agriculture or horticulture and some geneticists are employed by manufacturing companies to work on research and development, or in production. There are opportunities for clinical molecular geneticists and cytogeneticists in the NHS, but competition is intense and only a few places are offered each year. See related job articles. Others work for medical or veterinary research institutes, universities or the civil service. Organisations involved in crop production, animal breeding or pest control may employ geneticists as genetic engineers. There are opportunities to work as a consultant, particularly in agriculture and crime, or to work overseas, especially in the developing world.

Pay and promotion prospects depend largely on the type of employer, and are dependent on further training, additional responsibility and experience. The starting salary for a graduate clinical scientist trainee is around £22k a year, rising to £27k-£35k for a registered clinical scientist. Principal clinical scientists can earn up to £42k and consultants up to £73k a year. Salaries in the private sector vary, but are often higher.

Health

This job requires good colour vision for certain areas of work. There is an allergy risk from pollens or animals and the work involves a risk of infection.

Skills and Qualities

able to report accurately, accurate, analytical skills, aptitude for teamwork, attention to detail, excellent communication skills, IT skills, methodical, observant, problem-solving skills, research skills

Relevant Subjects

Biology, Chemistry, English, ICT/Computer studies, Mathematics, Physics, Science

Further Information

Advisory Council for Science Technology & Innovation - www.sciencecouncil.ie/

Genetic Engineering & Biotechnology News - www.genengnews.com

Heredity (Genetics Society) (Nature) - www.nature.com/hdy/about.html

International Forum for Genetic Engineering - www.science.anth.org.uk/ifgene/

NHS Careers (NHS Careers) - www.nhscareers.nhs.uk

▶Working in science (2007) (Babcock Lifeskills) - www.babcock-lifeskills.com/

Addresses

British Society for Human Genetics (BSHG)
Clinical Genetics Unit, Birmingham Women's Hospital B15 2TG
Phone: +44 (0)121 627 2634
Web: www.bshg.org.uk

Health Professions Council (HPC)
Park House, 184 Kennington Park Road, London SE11 4BU
Phone: +44 (0)20 7582 0866
Web: www.hpc-uk.org

Society of Biology
9 Red Lion Court, London EC4A 3EF
Phone: +44 (0)20 7936 5900
Web: http://societyofbiology.org/home

The Genetics Society (GS)
Roslin Biocentre, Wallace Building, Midlothian EH25 9PS
Phone: +44 (0)131 200 6392
Web: www.genetics.org.uk

Similar Jobs

Biologist, Biotechnologist, Clinical Molecular Geneticist, Cytogeneticist, Microbiologist

Geographical Information Systems Manager

also known as: GIS Manager, Spatial Information Systems Manager

CRCI:Languages, Information and Culture
CLCI:FAF Job Band: 4 to 5

Job Description

Geographical information systems (GIS) managers head teams of IT specialists that produce computerised mapping and geographical data systems. Managers coordinates the work of a team and oversee the production of social, economic and topographical data, which commercial organisations and local/central government use to assist in the planning of their services. This can be in diverse areas such as healthcare, crime analysis and defence, or specific tasks which range from forecasting timber production of a forest to road traffic management. Utilities also use GIS to map their cables and networks.

A GIS manager's responsibility is diverse and depends on the area of work, though usually includes project management tasks such as the control and management of project costs, the research and exploration of new applications for the use of GIS, ensuring that project deadlines are met, and solving any technical problems as they arise. Also liaises with cartographers and IT colleagues such as systems analysts, programmers and other data managers.

Work Details

Usually works a basic 39 hr week, Monday to Friday. However, the work is project based and driven by deadlines, so it can involve early starts and late finishes. Most work is office based though may also involve some travel to clients, depending on the project.

Qualification

• England, Wales and Northern Ireland

Band 4: For HND, Diploma of Higher Education or foundation degree: 1-2 A levels and some GCSEs (A*-C) usually including English and maths, or equivalent.

Band 5: For degree courses: 2-3 A levels and some GCSEs (A*-C) usually including English and maths, or equivalent. Exact requirements depend on the degree you take. Some universities require an A level in geography or computer science, depending on the course.

• Scotland

Band 4: For entry to SQA higher national and professional development awards, usually 2-3 H grades and some S grades (1-3), including English and maths, or similar qualifications.

Band 5: For degree courses: 3-5 H grades and some S grades (1-3), including English and maths, or similar qualifications. Exact requirements depend on the degree you take. Some universities require H grade in geography or computer science, depending on the course.

Degree Information

GIS management is open to all graduates, however the following subjects are particularly relevant: cartography, GIS, geography, computer science, geology, town planning, management, surveying and topography. There are also a number of postgraduate GIS courses available.

Adult Qualifications

Entry requirements may be relaxed for adults applying for higher education courses and Access or foundation courses give adults without qualifications a route on to degree courses.

Work Experience

Relevant work or voluntary experience is always useful and improves your chances in application for entry to this job. Any experience in team leading and project management is helpful. You should try to talk to those already working in GIS, perhaps in local/central government, and arrange to 'work shadow' for a few days. You can also gain valuable experience on a student internship that usually provides around four weeks' full-time work with a GIS consultancy or intelligence systems firm, or in local/central government and their appropriate agencies.

Entry and Training

Most entrants are graduates qualified in geography or computer science, but as this is a relatively new profession there are opportunities for those with degrees in other subjects. GIS and geoinformatics foundation degrees are available and can be studied full or part time. Applied geography, applied computing and computing (network systems) are useful subjects. It may be possible to enter at a more junior level with an appropriate HND. Subjects including GIS with web development, surveying, topographical studies, information technology or management are most useful. Junior posts often require strong IT skills. Education Development International (EDI) offers a vocational related qualification in GIS at Level 3.

If you have a geography or closely-related degree and have relevant postgraduate experience, you can apply to the Association for Geographic Information (AGI) to become a Chartered Geographer (GIS) - CGeog (CIS). You can also follow the non-graduate practitioner route and achieve CGeog (CIS) status if you have relevant research or industry experience. Contact the AGI or the Royal Geographical Society (RGS) for full details and for information on continuing professional development.

Most training is on the job and large companies, such as the Ordnance Survey, offer in-house training schemes. Training is useful in many areas as this is an inter-disciplinary job. Communication skills, time management, marketing and team leadership courses and experience can all support your job application or progression. Speculative applications to private consultants is a good first step into this field; they are listed in the AGI Source Book.

Mature entry is welcomed, particularly from those with relevant professional experience of managing people and projects.

Opportunities and Pay

GIS is a relatively new field of work that is still expanding and there is a wide and diverse range of employers. These include local authorities, central government (such as the Forestry Commission, Department for Transport, HM Land Registry) and their agencies, and Ordnance Survey. Other opportunities are with private consultancies, the police and emergency services, public utility companies, the telecommunications industry, and private healthcare companies. Some experienced GIS managers may work freelance or set up their own consultancy. There are some opportunities for work abroad, particularly in Europe, Australia, the USA and Canada.

Pay varies depending on the type of organisation. There is a wide range of salaries, but software design specialists and private consultants tend to pay more. Most GIS managers start on a salary ranging from £20k-£25k, rising to £30k-£40k a yr. Top level salaries may exceed £60k a year.

Skills and Qualities

able to cope under pressure, able to motivate others, analytical skills, decisive, excellent communication skills, good interpersonal skills, good organisational skills, leadership qualities, numeracy skills, self confident

Relevant Subjects

Economics, English, Geography, ICT/Computer studies, Land and Environment, Mathematics, Sociology

Further Information

AGCAS: Information Technology (Job Sector Briefing) (AGCAS) - www.prospects.ac.uk

AGI Source Book (Association for Geographic Information) (Association for Geographic Information)

Inside Careers Guide: Information Technology - www.insidecareers.co.uk

Local Government Careers (Improvement and Development Agency) - www.lgcareers.com/publications/

▶ Working in computers & IT (2010) (Babcock Lifeskills) - www.babcock-lifeskills.com/

Addresses

Association for Geographic Information (AGI)
5, St Helen's Place, Bishopsgate, London EC3A 6AU
Phone: +44 (0)20 7036 0430
Web: www.agi.org.uk

British Geological Survey (BGS)
Kingsley Dunham Centre, Keyworth, Nottingham NG12 5GG
Phone: +44 (0)115 936 3143
Web: www.bgs.ac.uk

Education Development International (EDI)
International House, Siskin Parkway East, Middlemarch Business Park, Coventry CV3 4PE
Phone: +44 (0)2476 516560
Web: www.goalonline.co.uk

Ordnance Survey
Romsey Road, Southampton, Hampshire SO16 4GU
Phone: 0845 605 0505 (UK only)
Web: www.ordnancesurvey.co.uk

Royal Geographical Society (RGS)
(with the Institute of British Geographers), 1 Kensington Gore, London SW7 2AR
Phone: +44 (0)20 7591 3000
Web: www.rgs.org

Similar Jobs

Business Analyst, Cartographer, Geophysicist, Surveyor: Geomatics/Geospatial, Surveyor: Hydrographic, Town Planner

Geological Technician

also known as: Geoscience Technician: Geological

CRCI:Science, Mathematics and Statistics

CLCI:QOL Job Band: 3 to 5

Job Description

Geological technicians are involved in gas, oil and minerals exploration, or other areas such as academic research and civil engineering. They help and support the work of geoscientists, including geologists, geochemists and geophysicists in the study of the Earth's rocks and minerals. Usually manage the day-to-day running of a laboratory and carry out tests on rock samples and fossils. May be involved with chemical analysis, cutting thin sections of rock, or operating X-ray machines and electron microscopes. Can also photograph specimens such as microfossils. Technicians make plans and diagrams for map work, log data and keep notes and records using a computer.

May prepare reports, teaching material and set up instruments. Also manage stock levels and carry out minor repairs on faulty or damaged equipment. If working at outdoor/underwater locations, they assist in surveying the designated area and the drilling/sampling programmes.

Work Details

Usually work a basic 35-40 hr week, Monday to Friday, though may be expected to work irregular hours, including evenings and weekends. Usually work in a laboratory and sometimes also on site. Travel may be required for some jobs. This work requires using computers, reading and interpreting maps and having a good knowledge of technical developments. You normally work in a team. Depending on your post, you may have responsibility for maintaining safety standards.

Some geological work can be very demanding and normally involves some physical activity; sometimes working in cold and damp or very hot conditions. There is a risk of minor injuries. Protective clothing, including a face mask, helmet and boots, is required at times.

Qualification

• England, Wales and Northern Ireland

Band 3: For entry: usually at least 4 GCSEs (A*-C) including maths, technology and a science subject, usually physics, or equivalent qualifications.

Band 4: For HND, Diploma of Higher Education or foundation degree: 1-2 A levels, preferably including chemistry and physics, and some GCSEs (A*-C) usually including English and maths, or equivalent.

Band 5: For degree courses: 2-3 A levels, preferably including maths, science and physics, and some GCSEs (A*-C) usually including English and maths, or equivalent. Exact requirements depend on the degree you take.

• Scotland

Band 3: For entry: usually four S grades (1-3) preferably including maths, technology and a science subject, usually physics, or similar qualifications.

Band 4: For entry to SQA higher national and professional development awards, 2-3 H grades, usually including chemistry and physics, and some S grades (1-3), including English and maths, or similar qualifications.

Band 5: For degree courses: 3-5 H grades, preferably including maths, science and physics, and some S grades (1-3), usually including English and maths, or similar qualifications. Exact requirements depend on the degree you take.

Degree Information

A degree in areas of geoscience such as geology, geophysics, geochemistry, mining/petroleum or engineering geology is usually required. Courses may also be combined with other subjects such as languages or computing. Specialist and conversion postgraduate courses are available for those with a relevant degree.

Adult Qualifications

Entry requirements may be relaxed for adults applying for further and higher education courses. Access or foundation courses give adults without qualifications a route onto degree courses.

Work Experience

Entry to this job is highly competitive. It is essential that you have some relevant work or voluntary experience before applying as competition for vacancies is fierce. Work or voluntary experience in a scientific field is relevant with laboratory or drawing office experience offering a distinct advantage.

Entry and Training

Entry to training posts is highly competitive and requirements can vary from those who begin as a trainee with GCSEs/S grades, A levels/H grades or equivalent, to those who have already completed a relevant higher national award or a relevant degree. On-the-job training with experienced staff is usually combined with part-time study for higher qualifications. Relevant S/NVQs are available at levels 2-4. Training programmes, including apprenticeship schemes, may be available in your area. Advanced apprenticeships leading to qualification at level 3 can also be a route into higher education.

Mature applicants require up-to-date scientific knowledge. Relevant laboratory or drawing office experience is also useful.

Opportunities and Pay

This is a small profession of about 3,500 in the UK and competition for jobs is fierce. Most jobs are with the British Geological Survey or you may be employed in the oil, gas, mining, quarrying, water or construction industries. There are also opportunities in teaching, conservation, research and museum work. The civil service employs technicians at assistant scientific officer level (ASO). Long-term surveying or civil engineering projects sometimes employ technicians; these and other jobs are often overseas. You should be prepared to be mobile if you wish to advance your career prospects.

Pay varies, but ranges from around £17k a year, rising to over £40k with experience.

Health

Normal colour vision is required for certain areas of work and no allergies to skin irritants.

Skills and Qualities

aptitude for fieldwork, aptitude for figures, attention to detail, good at writing reports, methodical, observant, problem-solving skills, scientific approach, specialist IT skills, technical aptitude

Relevant Subjects
Biology, Chemistry, Geography, ICT/Computer studies, Land and Environment, Mathematics, Physics, Science

Further Information
Apprenticeship Schemes (National Apprenticeship Service) - www.apprenticeships.org.uk

Cogent - sector skills souncil for chemicals, pharmaceuticals, nuclear, oil & gas, petroleum & polymers - www.cogent-ssc.com

Geology Today (Wiley Blackwell Publishing) - www.wiley.com/bw/journal.asp?ref=0266-6979

Planet Earth (GSI/IYPE) - www.planetearth.ie

Society for Underwater Technology (Society for Underwater Technology) - www.sut.org.uk

▶Working in science (2007) (Babcock Lifeskills) - www.babcock-lifeskills.com/

▶Working outdoors (2010) (Babcock Lifeskills) - www.babcock-lifeskills.com/

Addresses
British Geological Survey (BGS)
Kingsley Dunham Centre, Keyworth, Nottingham NG12 5GG
Phone: +44 (0)115 936 3143
Web: www.bgs.ac.uk

Energy Institute (EI)
61 New Cavendish Street, London W1G 7AR
Phone: +44 (0)20 7467 7100
Web: www.energyinst.org.uk

Geological Society (GS)
Burlington House, Piccadilly, London W1J 0BG
Phone: +44 (0)20 7434 9944
Web: www.geolsoc.org.uk

Mineral Products Qualifications Council (MPQC)
Alban Row, 27-31 Verulam Road, St Albans, Hertfordshire AL3 4DG
Phone: +44 (0)1727 817 205
Web: www.empawards.com

Natural Environment Research Council (NERC)
Polaris House North Star Avenue, Swindon, Wiltshire SN2 1EU
Phone: +44 (0)1793 411 500
Web: www.nerc.ac.uk

Similar Jobs
Geologist, Geophysicist, Laboratory Technician: Science, Oceanographer, Oil & Gas Industry Technician, Surveying Technician

Geologist
also known as: Geoscientist: Geologist

CRCI:Science, Mathematics and Statistics
CLCI:QOL Job Band: 5

Job Description
Geologists study the origin and evolution, composition and structure of the earth, its crust and its natural resources. They examine rocks, minerals and fossils from mines, wellsite and drilled samples, or open ground. Then note the occurrence of valuable deposits, thickness of strata and properties of soils. Also study volcanoes and earthquakes. They record and map observations and apply findings to the mining of natural resources, such as gas/oil exploration, and the use of land for construction, landfill sites, and other planning purposes.

May work in the water industry looking at the effects of pollution and mines on underground water. Also advise on environmental disasters and problems, including research on contaminated land, or abandoned/disused mines, such as tin and lead mines. Geologists work in a team, advising and consulting with colleagues and may supervise and organise staff.

Work Details
Usually work a basic 35-40 hr week, Monday to Friday, though may be expected to work irregular hours, sometimes away from home, including evenings and weekends. You work on site setting up equipment and carrying out surveys and also spend time working in a laboratory or office. This work requires the use of computers, reading and interpreting maps and having a good knowledge of technical developments.

Geological work can be demanding and normally involves some physical activity as well as working in cold, damp or very hot conditions. There is a risk of minor injuries and at times you need to wear protective clothing, including a helmet and boots.

Qualification

• England, Wales and Northern Ireland
Band 5: For degree courses: 2-3 A levels, including two science subjects or a science and maths, and some GCSEs (A*-C) usually including English and maths, or equivalent. Exact requirements depend on the degree you take.

• Scotland
Band 5: For degree courses: 3-5 H grades, preferably including maths and two science subjects, and some S grades (1-3), usually including English and maths, or similar qualifications. Exact requirements depend on the degree you take.

Degree Information
A degree in areas of geoscience is usually required including geology, geophysics, geochemistry, mining/petroleum or engineering geology. Courses may also be combined with other subjects such as languages or computing. Specialist and conversion postgraduate courses are available for those with a relevant degree.

Adult Qualifications
Entry requirements may be relaxed for adults applying for higher education courses and Access or foundation courses give adults without qualifications a route on to degree courses. Geology departments usually welcome applications from mature students.

Work Experience
Universities and employers may prefer candidates who have relevant work or voluntary experience. Ideally you shadow or work with somebody who is currently involved in this work, but other relevant areas for work experience are surveying or work with a mining or extraction company.

Entry and Training
Training is by practical work experience after obtaining a first degree or a postgraduate qualification in one of the geosciences. Some employers may sponsor staff on postgraduate courses. Many companies run their own in-house training programmes for new entrants and there is also ongoing training for all staff throughout their careers with larger organisations such as the British Geological Society. Membership of the professional body, the Geological Society, is awarded to applicants with appropriate qualifications and with two years' geological experience.

Mature entrants require a degree or equivalent qualification, and employers may sponsor staff on postgraduate courses. There is an Open University distance-learning degree course in natural sciences with earth sciences. You may apply to the Natural Environmental Research Council (NERC) for postgraduate study and research.

Opportunities and Pay
About 10,000 geologists and technical support staff are employed in the UK, a number that has remained stable, so there is likely to be a steady demand for qualified geologists.

Jobs are with oil, gas, mining, quarrying, water or construction companies. Geologists are also employed by the British Geological Survey that is part of the Natural Environment Research Council (NERC), which also employs geologists in some of its other research institutes such as the British Antarctic Survey. There are also some opportunities in teaching, conservation and museum work and opportunities to work abroad. You may progress to senior scientist or managerial level. Some experienced geologists become self-employed and work as consultants.

Pay varies depending on type of company, location and experience but is from around £25k a year, rising to around £40k a year with experience. Those in senior posts can earn up to £54k, and geologists working for some oil companies and consultancies can earn £70k-£100k a year.

Health

This job requires normal colour vision for certain areas of work as well as overall good health.

Skills and Qualities

able to take responsibility, adaptable, analytical skills, aptitude for fieldwork, methodical, observant, problem-solving skills, scientific approach, self-reliant, specialist IT skills

Relevant Subjects

Biology, Chemistry, English, Geography, ICT/Computer studies, Land and Environment, Mathematics, Physics, Science

Further Information

Geology Today (Wiley Blackwell Publishing) - www.wiley.com/bw/journal.asp?ref=0266-6979

Journal of the Geological Society (Geological Society Publishing House) - http://jgs.geoscienceworld.org//

Oil Careers - www.oilcareers.com

Open University - www.open.ac.uk

Society for Underwater Technology (Society for Underwater Technology) - www.sut.org.uk

Working outdoors (2010) (Babcock Lifeskills) - www.babcock-lifeskills.com/

Addresses

British Antarctic Survey (BAS)
High Cross,, Madingley Road, Cambridge CB3 0ET
Phone: +44 (0)1223 221400
Web: www.antarctica.ac.uk

British Geological Survey (BGS)
Kingsley Dunham Centre, Keyworth, Nottingham NG12 5GG
Phone: +44 (0)115 936 3143
Web: www.bgs.ac.uk

Geological Society (GS)
Burlington House, Piccadilly, London W1J 0BG
Phone: +44 (0)20 7434 9944
Web: www.geolsoc.org.uk

Geologists' Association
Burlington House, Piccadilly, London W1J 0DU
Phone: +44 (0)20 7434 9298
Web: www.geologists.org.uk

Natural Environment Research Council (NERC)
Polaris House North Star Avenue, Swindon, Wiltshire SN2 1EU
Phone: +44 (0)1793 411 500
Web: www.nerc.ac.uk

Similar Jobs

Engineer: Civil/Structural, Geological Technician, Geophysicist, Oceanographer, Surveyor: Geomatics/Geospatial, Surveyor: Minerals & Waste Management

Geophysicist

also known as: Field Seismologist, Geoscientist: Geophysicist

CRCI:Science, Mathematics and Statistics
CLCI:QOL Job Band: 5

Job Description

Geophysicists use physical techniques and sophisticated technical software to study and interpret the structure of the earth. They may be involved in exploration for oil, natural gas or mineral deposits, or archaeological surveys. They employ a variety of seismic, electrical and other methods to obtain complex data for computer analysis and examine results to show the underlying structure. Then produce reports based on the interpretation and analysis of the data and carry out tests on seismic equipment to ensure accuracy. May make adjustments or carry out repairs to equipment. May also produce geological maps and charts.

Some geophysicists carry out research into earthquakes, glaciers or volcanoes. They work closely with a small team of scientists and other earth science professionals, including those who may be working on site or offshore, and sometimes overseas. May supervise and organise staff.

Work Details

Usually work a basic 35-40 hr week, Monday to Friday, though may be expected to work irregular hours, including evenings and weekends. You work on site and also in a laboratory or office and may need to travel, perhaps overseas. This work requires using computers, reading and interpreting maps and having a good knowledge of technical developments. Depending on your post, you have responsibility for providing accurate information, making sound judgements and maintaining safety standards.

Geophysical work can be demanding and normally involves some strenuous physical activity as well as often working in cold, damp, humid or very hot conditions. There is a risk of minor injuries and you may need to wear protective clothing, including a helmet and boots.

Qualification

- **England, Wales and Northern Ireland**

Band 5: For degree courses: 2-3 A levels including two science subjects or a science and maths, and some GCSEs (A*-C) usually including English, or equivalent. Exact requirements depend on the degree you take.

- **Scotland**

Band 5: For degree courses: 3-5 H grades, preferably including maths and two science subjects, and some S grades (1-3), usually including English, or similar qualifications. Exact requirements depend on the degree you take.

Degree Information

An honours degree in geophysics/geotechnology, geology or physics is often preferred, but environmental geology, or any geoscience degree is also usually acceptable. Some relevant engineering disciplines give useful background information. Increasingly, those wishing to become a geoscientist take a postgraduate qualification such as a one-year MSc course that concentrates on a particular area of interest to employers including petroleum geology, geophysics, hydrogeology or sedimentology.

Adult Qualifications

Entry requirements may be relaxed for adults applying for higher education courses and Access or foundation courses give adults without qualifications a route on to degree courses.

Work Experience

Universities and employers may prefer candidates who have relevant work or voluntary experience. Ideally you shadow or work with somebody who currently is involved in the work, but other relevant areas for work experience are surveying, geology, archaeology, or work with a mining or extraction company. Unpaid work experience is available from some public sector organisations. Paid internships are often available with a multinational company.

Entry and Training

Training is normally by practical experience with an employer after first obtaining a degree or postgraduate qualification. Some entrants take a higher degree, particularly if their first degree is not in geoscience. Many companies run their own structured in-house training programmes covering specific technical areas such as links to engineering and petroleum geology. Some employers may sponsor staff on postgraduate courses and also welcome a second language.

It may be possible to gain a geophysical technician apprenticeship after A levels/H grades. You can then work your way into a professional post after gaining higher qualifications. Membership of a professional body is awarded to applicants with appropriate qualifications and experience. You are expected to undertake continuing professional development (CPD) throughout your career.

Mature entrants require a degree or equivalent qualification and may apply for funding to the Natural Environmental Research Council (NERC) and the Engineering and Physical Sciences Research Council (EPSRC) for postgraduate study and research.

Opportunities and Pay

A number of geophysicists are employed in the oil, water and mineral mining industries. Some work for specialist service companies who carry out seismic surveys and well logging. There are some opportunities in teaching, conservation and museum work. There are also posts with the Natural Environment Research Council (NERC) and other government-funded organisations. Long-term surveying or civil engineering projects sometimes employ geophysicists. Geophysicists must be prepared to be mobile to gain promotion as approximately 50% work on projects abroad. Traditionally, this is a small profession and opportunities reflect the economic climate. However, it is predicted that due to global issues such as radioactive waste disposal and climate change, more qualified and experienced geophysicists will be needed.

Pay and promotion depends on the type of employer and sector in which you work. Starting salaries for graduates are likely to be around £22k, rising to £25k-£45k a year with experience. Senior geophysicists working in oil exploration can earn more than £75k a year.

Health

This job will require normal colour vision for certain areas of work and good general fitness.

Skills and Qualities

able to take responsibility, accurate, aptitude for fieldwork, aptitude for maths and science, good organisational skills, methodical, problem-solving skills, scientific approach, specialist IT skills

Relevant Subjects

Biology, Chemistry, Design and technology, English, Geography, ICT/Computer studies, Mathematics, Physics, Science

Further Information

Cogent - sector skills souncil for chemicals, pharmaceuticals, nuclear, oil & gas, petroleum & polymers - www.cogent-ssc.com

Geology Today (Wiley Blackwell Publishing) - www.wiley.com/bw/journal.asp?ref=0266-6979

Oil Careers - www.oilcareers.com

Society for Underwater Technology (Society for Underwater Technology) - www.sut.org.uk

▶Working in science (2007) (Babcock Lifeskills) - www.babcock-lifeskills.com/

▶Working in space (2010) (Babcock Lifeskills) - www.babcock-lifeskills.com/

Addresses

British Geological Survey (BGS)
Kingsley Dunham Centre, Keyworth, Nottingham NG12 5GG
Phone: +44 (0)115 936 3143
Web: www.bgs.ac.uk

Energy Institute (EI)
61 New Cavendish Street, London W1G 7AR
Phone: +44 (0)20 7467 7100
Web: www.energyinst.org.uk

Engineering and Physical Sciences Research Council (EPSRC)
Polaris House North Star Avenue, Swindon, Wiltshire SN2 1ET
Phone: +44(0)1793 444 100
Web: www.epsrc.ac.uk

Geological Society (GS)
Burlington House, Piccadilly, London W1J 0BG
Phone: +44 (0)20 7434 9944
Web: www.geolsoc.org.uk

Natural Environment Research Council (NERC)
Polaris House North Star Avenue, Swindon, Wiltshire SN2 1EU
Phone: +44 (0)1793 411 500
Web: www.nerc.ac.uk

Oil & Gas UK (Scotland)
3rd Floor, The Exchange 2, 62 Market Street, Aberdeen AB11 5PJ
Phone: +44 (0)1224 577 250
Web: www.oilandgas.org.uk

Petroleum Exploration Society of GB (PESGB)
5th Floor, 9 Berkeley Street, London W1J 8DW
Phone: +44 (0)20 7408 2000
Web: www.pesgb.org.uk

Similar Jobs

Cartographer, Engineer: Minerals & Mining, Geological Technician, Geologist, Meteorologist, Oceanographer, Physicist

Glass Designer

also known as: Studio Glassware Designer

CRCI:Design, Arts and Crafts
CLCI:EG — Job Band: 3 to 5

Job Description

Glass designers usually work in stained glass, studio glass (decorative and functional), or architectural glass (manufactured) as a specialist product or craft glass designer. They pecialise as either craft or product designers.

Some may interpret and develop a product brief into a successful finished object. Others work with designing or restoring, replacing and renovating stained glass windows. This involves creating sketches and watercolours of the design and using specialist knowledge, techniques and materials to create the finished window.

Studio glassware designers create decorative and/or functional items using traditional techniques or modern technology. Architectural glass designers are involved in the mass production of items such as windows, glass panels and lighting. All designers may attend craft fairs and exhibitions, and may also give live demonstrations of the production of their work.

Work Details

Usually work a basic 39 hr week; Monday to Friday, though some employers may require early starts, late finishes and weekend work. Self-employment allows you to choose your own working hours. You work indoors, usually in a studio. Glass designers in larger companies are more likely to work in teams and with outside suppliers and clients.

The job can often be stressful and pressurised, and if self-employed, solitary at times. If you are involved in the production of your own designs, you need to wear titanium goggles and protective clothing. This can be in a hot and dusty workshop.

Qualification

• England, Wales and Northern Ireland

Band 3: For entry to jobs, HNC or a relevant Diploma, usually at least 4 GCSEs (A*-C) including English and maths, or equivalent.

Band 4: For HND, Diploma of Higher Education or foundation degree: 1-2 A levels and some GCSEs (A*-C) usually including English and maths, or equivalent.

Band 5: For degree courses: 2-3 A levels and some GCSEs (A*-C) usually including English and maths, or equivalent. Exact requirements depend on the degree you take.

• Scotland

Band 3: For entry: usually at least four S grades (1-3), including English and maths, or similar qualifications.

Band 4: For entry to SQA higher national and professional development awards, usually 2-3 H grades and some S grades (1-3), including English and maths, or similar qualifications.

Band 5: For degree courses: 3-5 H grades and some S grades (1-3), usually including English and maths, or similar qualifications. Exact requirements depend on the degree you take.

Degree Information

Some degree courses are available in glass design and architectural glass but are often linked with ceramics courses. Many design and applied arts or decorative arts and 3-D design courses have a glass option. Postgraduate courses are also available in some colleges of art.

Adult Qualifications

There are no specific qualifications for mature entrants, but a good standard of secondary education is expected. For courses in art and design, normal entry requirements may be relaxed for adults, particularly for those with relevant experience. You can also enter the profession with a degree in craft design and then a postgraduate qualification specialising in glass.

Work Experience

Relevant work or voluntary experience in design is always useful and can improve your chances when applying for entry to jobs or apprenticeships in the design sector. You may gain some experience in a design studio or workshop either as a Saturday or holiday job. As the industry is very competitive, any work experience can give you an advantage. It is worth researching companies whose products match your style, and entering competitions and exhibitions to demonstrate commitment.

Entry and Training

Many enter this job after first completing an art and design foundation course, followed by a relevant applied arts higher national diploma or degree. A foundation degree in applied arts, with glass as an option is available. An up-to-date and comprehensive portfolio of your work is required.

Formal qualifications are not essential as good design skills are more important. However, there is strong competition in the industry so degrees or HNDs in fine/visual art, decorative arts, graphic/3D design, contemporary crafts, ceramics with glass, conservation, restoration and applied design are very helpful. Glass design studios may provide weekend or summer courses, for which you may also require a portfolio of work. There are short, part-time and evening glass-making courses at some local and independent colleges. Some courses may also include the skills required to run your own business.

Dudley College offers a one-year Access course in glass techniques and technology leading to a professional development award. You can go on to study at degree level. The college also offers a BTEC intermediate/advanced course in glass techniques and technology leading to a professional development certificate/diploma at level 4 or 5. These courses are particularly aimed at those seeking employment in a glass studio or wishing to set up their own studio. The Worshipful Company of Glaziers offers competitions and awards designed to encourage undergraduates and young artists working in architectural glass design and conservation of historic glass.

Glass Training is the organisation involved in the development of training for the glass industry and the Contemporary Glass Society (CGS)publishes details of industry-relevant courses. The Crafts Council has a list of stained glass studios in the UK. Continuing professional development (CPD) is important to keep up to date with industry developments and new techniques. The National Glass Centre runs a range of relevant workshops and ongoing courses are available at a number of studios.

There is also a glass industries apprenticeship which deals with the manufacture and process of glass and related products. This includes the manufacture of mirrors and curved glass, architectural stain glass and glass blowing. S/NVQs are available in glass manufacturing and processing at level 3.

Mature applicants require an up-to-date portfolio of work for entry onto an art and design course, though formal entry qualifications may be relaxed. There is an Access to art and design course that leads to a degree. Some glass designers have developed their interest and hobby into a career through selling their individual pieces of glassware. Skills gained as an assistant in a design studio or workshop, or in a design consultancy are valued. Commercial awareness and an understanding of the glass manufacturing industry are an advantage.

Opportunities and Pay

Employers may include specialist design studios or glass product manufacturing companies. Working for larger companies offers better job security and promotion prospects, but generally allows for less artistic freedom than smaller studio work. Opportunities also arise with interior design companies and department stores. Many glass designers supplement their income with teaching and training, or with work in other areas of design.

Pay varies widely but new graduates earn around £20k-£25k a year working for a large manufacturer, rising to around £30k a year with experience. Salaries for self-employed designers vary depending on each commission.

Health

You need to be physically fit to do some aspects of this work.

Skills and Qualities

able to follow instructions, artistic ability, attention to detail, creative flair, eye for shape/colour, eye for visual effect, hand-to-eye co-ordination, patient, technical aptitude

Relevant Subjects

Art and Design, Design and technology

Further Information

Apprenticeship Schemes (National Apprenticeship Service) - www.apprenticeships.org.uk

Contemporary Glass Society - www.cgs.org.uk

Creative & Cultural Skills - sector skills council for advertising, crafts, cultural heritage, design, literature, music, performing & visual arts - www.ccskills.org.uk

Creative Choices - www.creative-choices.co.uk/

Design Uncovered (Trotman 2009) - www.trotman.co.uk

Design Week (Design Week) - www.designweek.co.uk

Journal of Stained Glass (British Society of Master Glass Painters) - www.bsmgp.org.uk/Publications/

▶Working in art & design (2009) (Babcock Lifeskills) - www.babcock-lifeskills.com/

Addresses

British Society of Master Glass Painters
PO Box 15, Minehead, Somerset TA24 8ZX
Phone: +44 (0)1643 862807
Web: www.bsmgp.org.uk

Contemporary Glass Society (CGS)
c/o Broadfield House Glass Museum Compton Drive, Kingswinford, West Midlands DY6 9NS
Phone: +44 (0)1379 741120
Web: www.cgs.org.uk

Crafts Council (CC)
44a Pentonville Road, Islington, London N1 9BY
Phone: +44 (0)20 7806 2500
Web: www.craftscouncil.org.uk

Glass Training Ltd
Suite 28 The Quadrant 99 Parkway Avenue, Parkway Business Park, Sheffield S9 4WG
Phone: 0844 809 4944
Web: www.glass-training.co.uk

National Glass Centre
Liberty Way, Sunderland SR6 0GL
Phone: +44 (0)191 515 5555
Web: www.nationalglasscentre.com

Worshipful Company of Glaziers & Painters of Glass
The Glaziers Company, 9 Montague Close, London Bridge SE1 9DD
Phone: +44 (0)20 7403 6652
Web: www.worshipfulglaziers.com

Similar Jobs

Ceramic Designer, Engraver, Glassmaker: Operative, Jewellery Designer, Product Designer

Glassmaker: Operative

also known as: Glassblower

CRCI:Manufacturing and Production
CLCI:SAD
Job Band: 1 to 2

Job Description

Glassmakers work for a manufacturer at one of the many stages in the production of glass and glass articles. This includes tasks ranging from mixing the raw materials of sand, soda ash and lime together, to inspecting the final product. Computerised equipment is used for the mixing of raw materials. It is also used for melting, moulding, cooling and shaping the glass. Work can involve the setting-up and monitoring of these machines. A range of tasks is required to make different items in glass. These include glass blowing and bending, joining pieces of glass together and decorating the finished product.

May be involved in the making of a wide variety of objects such as bottles, scientific equipment, automotive glass (windscreens/ sunroofs etc), light bulbs, crystal ware (wine glasses/giftware etc), windows, stained glass, mirrors and doors (flatware) or glass fibre.

Work Details

The hours of work are usually 39 hrs a week; Monday to Friday, and you may be expected to work shifts. You work in a factory or a studio. You may have to do the same tasks over and over again, and have to cope with some physical activity, including standing for many hours. The work environment is hot, noisy and dusty, and there may be a risk of accidents from equipment, so you need to wear protective clothing and goggles.

Qualification

• England, Wales and Northern Ireland

Band 1: No minimum qualifications are required, but you are expected to have a good level of general education. However, some formal/vocational qualifications at any level are useful. Art, design technology and science qualifications are an advantage.

Band 2: Although academic qualifications are not specified for this job, it is an advantage to have some GCSEs (A*-C) in subjects that include English and maths, science or technology or equivalent.

• Scotland

Band 1: No minimum qualifications are required, but you are expected to have a good level of general education. However, some formal/vocational qualifications at any level are useful. Art, technology and science qualifications are an advantage.

Band 2: Although academic qualifications are not specified for this job, it is an advantage to have some S grades (1-3) in subjects that include English, maths, art, science or similar.

Adult Qualifications

No pre-entry qualifications are usually required though some academic/vocational qualifications at any level may be an advantage. English, maths, art and science are useful subjects.

Work Experience

Work or voluntary experience is always useful. It can improve your chances when applying for jobs or trainee placements. Your guidance counsellor or adult guidance worker should be able to give you advice on getting some work experience.

Entry and Training

Training is on the job, usually through a training scheme, or it can be by a day-release course or evening classes. Some operatives may wish to specialise in various areas of glassmaking, including scientific glassblowing. Glass Training Ltd runs a range of courses, offering NVQs in glass manufacturing/processing and short courses in the health and safety aspects of the work.

The International Glass Centre at Dudley College runs level 2 and 3 courses in glass for students of art and design. It also runs courses for adults in hot glass and bead making. Check with the college for full details. The National Glass Centre in Sunderland also runs a range of courses aimed at those over 16.

S/NVQs in glass manufacture or glass processing are available at levels 2-3. Relevant training programmes, including apprenticeship schemes, may be available in your area. Advanced apprenticeships leading to qualification at level 3 can be a route into higher education. A Diploma/Welsh Baccalaureate in manufacturing and product design may be available in your area.

Government training opportunities, such as an apprenticeship in glass industry processes may be available in your area. You can also gain recognition of previous experience through Accreditation of Prior Learning (APL) or by working towards relevant S/NVQs. Contact your local careers office, Jobcentre Plus, Next Step service or Learning and Skills Council (LSC) Local Enterprise Company (LEC) for details of training schemes.

Opportunities and Pay

In the UK, several large companies do most of the mass glass production. Around 6,000 staff are employed. Work can be in London, the West Midlands, Yorkshire and areas in Scotland. Due to the increase in technology and automation, there are fewer opportunities for glass workers at craft and operative levels. Therefore, promotion is fairly limited. There may be opportunities in small craft facilities, often in tourist areas. Glassmakers can progress to glass designers and move to a studio/workshop.

Pay varies depending on area and employer but starts at around £10k-£12k a year. This can rise to around £14k-£30k a year. Overtime payments may be available.

Health

You must be physically fit to do this work.

Skills and Qualities

able to operate equipment, aptitude for teamwork, attention to detail, good concentration level, hand-to-eye co-ordination, health & safety awareness, manual dexterity, numeracy skills, practical skills, steady hand

Relevant Subjects
Chemistry, Design and technology, Manufacturing, Physics, Science

Further Information
Apprenticeship Schemes (National Apprenticeship Service) - www.apprenticeships.org.uk

British Glass - www.britglass.org.uk

Diplomas (Foundation, Higher and Advanced) - http://yp.direct.gov.uk/diplomas

Journal of the British Society of Scientific Glassblowers (monthly) (British Society of Scientific Glassblowers (BSSG)) - www.bssg.co.uk

Proskills UK - sector skills council for process and manufacturing industries - www.proskills.co.uk

Training Schemes - www.direct.gov.uk/en/educationandlearning

Welsh Baccalaureate - www.wbq.org.uk

▶Working in manufacturing (2010) (Babcock Lifeskills) - www.babcock-lifeskills.com/

Addresses
British Society of Scientific Glassblowers
Glassblowing Workshop, School of Chemistry, Bedson Building, University of Newcastle,, Newcastle upon Tyne. NE1 7RU
Phone: +44 (0) 191 222 7100
Web: www.bssg.co.uk

Glass Qualifications Authority (GQA)
Provincial House, Solly Street, Sheffield S1 4BA
Phone: +44 (0)114 272 0033
Web: www.glassqualificationsauthority.com

Glass Training Ltd
Suite 28 The Quadrant, 99 Parkway Avenue,
Parkway Business Park, Sheffield S9 4WG
Phone: 0844 809 4944
Web: www.glass-training.co.uk

International Glass Centre
Dudley College Mons Hill Campus, 111 Wrens Hill Road,
Wrens Nest Estate, West Midlands DY1 3SB
Phone: +44 (0) 1384 363101
Web: www.dudleycol.ac.uk/

National Glass Centre
Liberty Way, Sunderland SR6 0GL
Phone: +44 (0)191 515 5555
Web: www.nationalglasscentre.com

Similar Jobs
Ceramic Pottery Maker/Operative, Engraver, Glass Designer, Glazier, Windscreen Technician

Glazier
CRCI:Building and Construction
CLCI:UF
Job Band: 1 to 2

Job Description
Glaziers use skills to cut and fit glass in a wide range of buildings such as houses, conservatories, office blocks and shop fronts. May specialise in fitting domestic or commercial double glazing products. Others work on architectural glazing, emergency glazing, panelling, shelving or screening. Can work with glass of different types, such as plate, security, mirror, ornamental or opaque glass. May need to work with plastic, granite, marble or other glass substitutes. Special tools such as glass cutters, chisels, spirit levels, hammers and screwdrivers are used.

Glaziers measure the space, select the glass and cut it to the exact size required. They use putty, rubber strips or wooden beading to fit the glass into frameworks. Some glass is already cut to size at a manufacturer's and is delivered ready to fit. Larger glass areas require more than one glazier to fit the heavy panes of glass. They use straps or a suction pad lifting machine to hold the glass while it is being moved into place.

Glaziers often works at heights using a ladder, scaffolding or a suspended cradle. Roof glaziers bolt aluminium strips to roof beams when fitting the glass. Then they make sure the area is waterproof.

Work Details
Glaziers usually work a 37-39 hr week, Monday to Friday, though sometimes you may be on call, perhaps at weekends or in the evenings. Work is outdoors and on site, though may sometimes be indoors in a workshop. You work in a number of places, travelling to different sites. The job involves heavy lifting, bending, climbing ladders and working at heights. Conditions can be cold, wet, dirty or dusty. There is a risk of cuts or falling from heights and you need to wear a safety helmet, gloves and arm guards.

Qualification

• England, Wales and Northern Ireland
Band 1: No minimum qualifications are required, but you are expected to have a good level of general education. Entry requirements may vary.

Band 2: No minimum qualifications specified, but some GCSEs including maths, science, technical subjects and English, or equivalent, are useful for a training course, and are required by some employers.

• Scotland
Band 1: No minimum qualifications are required, but you are expected to have had a good level of general education. Entry requirements may vary.

Band 2: No minimum qualifications specified, but some S grades including maths, science, technical subjects and English, or similar, are useful for a training course, and are required by some employers.

Adult Qualifications
No formal entry requirements specified. Those with relevant work experience may be accepted for some college courses without needing any qualifications.

Work Experience
Relevant work or voluntary experience is always useful and can improve your chances when applying for entry to construction jobs and apprenticeships. A local glazing firm may offer you the opportunity to help with general tasks or you might wish to have a Saturday/holiday job working in a building supplies centre to gain knowledge of glazing terms and materials. Health and safety issues may mean that there are certain jobs you can't do until you are over 16. Contact your local Construction Skills office for advice.

Entry and Training
Most young people enter through an apprenticeship scheme. You may have to take an entrance test for some training/apprenticeship schemes, such as those approved by Construction Skills. There is a variety of methods for work-based training and qualifications including full-time training with an employer, together with attendance at a local college or Construction Skills centre on a day or block-release basis. Glass Training Ltd also helps employers set up individual employee development programmes that encourage training on the job using distance learning. They offer short training courses on all aspects of glazing.

A Diploma/Welsh Baccalaureate in construction and the built environment may be available in your area. There are relevant S/NVQs at levels 2-3, such as in glazing or fenestration installation and surveying, awarded through the Glass Qualifications Authority (GQA). Knowledge related qualifications include the technical certificate in glass related operations (glazing installation and maintenance). You can take this course through any GQA recognised centre. Contact GQA for details.

Most glaziers work towards gaining a level of competence card through the Construction Skills Certification Scheme (CSCS) to indicate your individual skill level. Training programmes, including apprenticeships leading to level 2, and advanced apprenticeships/ construction apprenticeships leading to level 3, may be available in your area. Contact ConstructionSkills for further details of all routes to training.

Mature applicants with skills and experience in, for example, woodworking or in general building may have an advantage for training. Government training opportunities may be available in your area. You can also gain recognition of previous experience through Accreditation of Prior Learning (APL) or by working towards relevant S/NVQs. Contact your local careers office, Jobcentre Plus, Next Step service or Learning and Skills Council (LSC)/Local Enterprise Company (LEC) for details of training schemes, including apprenticeships for adults.

Opportunities and Pay

Most people work for specialist glazing firms throughout the UK. These range from small companies with just a few staff to larger firms employing hundreds of people. Availability of work depends to some extent on the state of the building trade and the national economy. Currently there is a downturn in the housing market which means there may be a shortage of vacancies for glaziers.

Some firms only do certain kinds of glazing, such as glass roofing, security glass or double glazing. In larger companies there are more options to specialise. There is also more chance of promotion to become a supervisor in charge of a team. With full training and qualifications some become self-employed. Some work abroad on contracts. Temporary, casual and seasonal work is possible for those who are sub-contractors or are self-employed.

Pay varies depending on area and employer. A trainee earns around £12k a year, rising to around £16k-£20k with experience and/or qualifications. Those with more experience earn around £23k-£28k a year, and some may make up to £40k. Employers may give allowances for travel and cost of lodgings. Overtime may be available as well as incentive bonus schemes.

Health

Good general physical fitness is needed.

Skills and Qualities

able to follow drawings and plans, able to work both on your own and in a team, accurate measuring and calculating skills, head for heights, methodical, practical skills, safety conscious, steady hand, strong

Relevant Subjects

Construction and built environment, Design and technology

Further Information

Apprenticeship Schemes (National Apprenticeship Service) - www.apprenticeships.org.uk

Construction Skills Certification Scheme (CSCS) - www.cscs.uk.com

ConstructionSkills - sector skills council for the construction industry - www.cskills.org

GQA Learn - www.gqalearn.com

Training Schemes - www.direct.gov.uk/en/educationandlearning

Welsh Baccalaureate - www.wbq.org.uk

▶Working in construction & the built environment (2007) (Babcock Lifeskills) - www.babcock-lifeskills.com/

Addresses

Glass and Glazing Federation (GGF)
54 Ayres Street, London SE1 1EU
Phone: +44 (0) 20 7939 9101
Web: www.ggf.co.uk

Glass Qualifications Authority (GQA)
Provincial House, Solly Street, Sheffield S1 4BA
Phone: +44 (0)114 272 0033
Web: www.glassqualificationsauthority.com

Glass Training Ltd
Suite 28, The Quadrant, 99 Parkway Avenue, Parkway Business Park, Sheffield S9 4WG
Phone: 0844 809 4944
Web: www.glass-training.co.uk

Similar Jobs

Carpenter/Joiner, Roofer, Scaffolder, Tiler: Wall & Floor, Windscreen Technician

Golf Services Manager

also known as: Golf Course Manager

CRCI:Leisure, Sport and Tourism
CLCI:GAJ Job Band: 2 to 5

Job Description

Golf services managers are responsible for the smooth and efficient running of golf courses and golfing facilities. They work to achieve sales, profitability and service goals, in line with the golf club's business plan and guidelines. They ensure that guests and members are greeted in a pleasant manner, carry out regular checks of facilities, making sure that all equipment is in good working order and is safe and clean for customers to use. Managers liaise with the greenkeeper on all aspects of the golf course, including set up for special events and competitions and may make plans for upgrading golf facilities and equipment, if required.

Managers are also responsible for the profitable running of the golf retail shop (pro shop) on site. They may check stock levels, ensure shop security, display stock in an attractive manner and bring in new product lines. Also ensure that hire charges of equipment and 'green fees' are collected and accurately recorded. Managers prepare sales and revenue budgets for all areas of golf and report on results. They are involved in recruiting, training, supervising and developing staff that work in the golf departmen and handling any problems that may arise with staff, members or guests. Also has responsibility for marketing, or work closely with the marketing department to make sure that golf interests are represented.

Work Details

Usually work a basic 37-40 hr week, but may have to work some unsocial hours, including evenings and weekends, possibly on a rota basis. Contact is with people of all ages and you are responsible for their safety and general welfare while they use the golf course and facilities. The work is mainly office based within the golf club, hotel or resort, but you are also out and about a great deal, talking to customers and staff. The work can be challenging and you need to make difficult decisions. Depending on the type of club/resort, work can be more demanding at certain times of the year, such as during competitions.

Qualification

- **England, Wales and Northern Ireland**

Band 2: For entry to jobs, no minimum qualifications are needed, but it is an advantage to have some GCSEs (A*-C) or equivalent in subjects that include English and maths.

Band 3: For entry to jobs, HNC or a relevant Diploma, usually at least 4 GCSEs (A*-C) including English and maths, or equivalent. You may be able to follow a golf advanced apprenticeship in sporting excellence.

Band 4: For HND in golf management, Diploma of Higher Education or foundation degree: 1-2 A levels and some GCSEs (A*-C) usually including English and maths, or equivalent.

Band 5: For degree courses in golf management: 2-3 A levels and some GCSEs (A*-C) usually including English and maths, or equivalent. Exact requirements depend on the degree you take.

- **Scotland**

Band 2: Although academic qualifications are not specified for this job, it is an advantage to have some S grades (1-3) in subjects that include English and maths, or similar.

Band 3: For entry to jobs, usually at least four S grades (1-3) including English or maths, or similar.

Band 4: For entry to SQA higher national and professional development awards, usually 2-3 H grades and some S grades (1-3), including English and maths, or similar qualifications.

Band 5: For degree courses in golf management: 3-5 H grades and some S grades (1-3), including English and maths, or similar qualifications. Exact requirements depend on the degree you take.

Degree Information

Any degree is acceptable for entry to this job, but a degree in golf management or leisure or sports management is most relevant. Other subjects that give useful background for this job include hospitality management, marketing, business studies, sports and recreation, exercise and sports sciences, and sports and recreation management.

Adult Qualifications

Mature entrants already working in this area may be able to move into management but formal qualifications may be useful. There are professional courses available, such as the foundation degree or applied golf management studies course from the PGA (Professional Golfers' Association) and University of Birmingham. Entry requirements may be relaxed for adults applying for higher education courses. Access to HE or foundation courses provide those without the required qualifications a route onto degree courses.

Work Experience

Work experience gives you an insight into what you do and don't enjoy about a job or working environment, as well as the opportunity to acquire new skills. It also provides valuable information to add to your CV and improves any course application and/or your future employment prospects. This can include work in golf clubs, retail, leisure centres and catering establishments, such as restaurants or hotels.

Entry and Training

The most important requirement for any career in golf is a passion for the industry and the route into golf management can vary. It is an advantage to be able to show experience of golf, other sports or business. Some golf courses are within large hotels or leisure chains and may have structured management training programmes. More usually, training is on the job while working as an assistant manager.

Traditionally, these jobs were often filled by experienced retired business professionals and more recently by assistants with on-the-job experience and training to become a manager, or former professional golfers. While this is still possible, changes to the industry in recent years have led to increased opportunities for graduates.

Managers of some golf courses also need to coach and instruct so increasingly formal qualifications are available and may be needed. These include the BA (Hons) in Golf Management and the Applied Golf Management Studies degree from the University of Birmingham and the PGA (Professional Golfers' Association). This three-year course combines sports management with science-related golf and vocational aspects of the golf business. Male applicants need a minimum handicap of 4.4 and female applicants 6.4.

The foundation degree in Golf Performance from Myerscough College and Golf and Sports Turf Management from Bridgwater College may provide alternative routes into this career. There is also a foundation degree available in Golf Management which can be converted to a BA (Hons) with a further year of study. The PGA offers a three-year foundation degree in professional golf leading to full PGA membership.

Reid Kerr College runs an Introduction to Golf Management course which provides an understanding of what it's like to work in the golf industry, golf club procedures, etiquette and rules, tournament preparation, planning golf coaching sessions as well as first aid, communications, marketing and human resources.

Training programmes, including apprenticeship schemes in leisure management, may be available in your area. Advanced apprenticeships, leading to qualification a level 3, can also be a route into higher education. A Diploma/Welsh Baccalaureate may be available in sport and active leisure.

The English Golf Union website provides useful information online or through workshops to assist with the day to day management of golf courses.

Mature entrants with relevant experience may be preferred by some employers. It is often possible for those already working in the golfing or leisure industry to move into management.

Training programmes, including apprenticeship schemes in leisure management, may be available in your area. Advanced apprenticeships, leading to qualification at level 3, can also be a route into higher education.

Opportunities and Pay

There are over 7500 golf courses and clubs located throughout the UK and opportunities exist within large and small golf clubs. You can also work in wider commercial concerns like holiday parks/multi-leisure centres, sports centres, hotels, conference centres, and other organisations where golf may only be one part of the business. Promotion to general manager or leisure manager is possible.

Pay varies depending on location, type and size of golf course, and level of responsibility. Junior or assistant golf services managers earn around £18k-£25k a year. Managers with more experience earn around £37k or more a year. Earnings may be partly performance related. You may receive bonuses and other perks such as the use of facilities for your own leisure and recreation.

Health

A reasonable level of fitness and mobility is required as the work can be physically demanding.

Skills and Qualities

able to take responsibility, aptitude for teamwork, business awareness, enthusiastic, good communication skills, good interpersonal skills, good organisational skills, IT skills, outgoing personality, practical skills

Relevant Subjects

Business and accounting, Economics, English, Hospitality and catering, Land and Environment, Leisure, travel and tourism, Physical education and sport, Retail and distribution

Further Information

Apprenticeship Schemes (National Apprenticeship Service) - www.apprenticeships.org.uk

British Golf Industry Association (BGIA) - www.bgia.org.uk

English Golf Union - www.englishgolfunion.org

Real Life Guide to Sports & Active Leisure (Trotman 2009) - www.trotman.co.uk

SkillsActive - sector skills council for active leisure, learning and well-being - www.skillsactive.com

Addresses

British Association of Sport and Exercise Sciences (BASES)
Leeds Metropolitan University,
Carnegie Faculty of Sport and Education,
Fairfax Hall, Headingley Campus, Beckett Park LS6 3QS
Phone: +44 (0)113 812 6162
Web: www.bases.org.uk

PGA (Professional Golfers' Association)
Centenary House, The Belfry, Sutton Coldfield,
West Midlands B76 9PT
Phone: +44 (0)1675 470 333
Web: www.pga.info

Similar Jobs

Event & Exhibition Organiser, Greenkeeper: Golf, Hotel Manager, Leisure Centre Assistant, Leisure Manager, Marketing Manager

GP Practice Manager

also known as: Practice Business Manager: GP, Primary Care Manager

CRCI:Healthcare
CLCI:CAL Job Band: 2 to 3

Job Description

GP Practice managers are responsible for the efficient day-to-day running of a GP's surgery. They organise the administration and patient appointment systems. Duties vary according to the size of the practice though usually include the management and supervision of any other personnel, and the recruitment, developing and training of clerical and support staff. Managers deal with finance and the practice accounts, oversee the year-round business planning strategy, keep records, often using a computer, send invoices and pays bills.

Practice managers may see medical sales executives and administrate the purchase of medication and drugs. They liaise with local hospitals and other healthcare professionals. Also deal with any patient complaints and are responsible for the health and safety procedures of the practice.

Work Details

Work in a doctors' surgery or health centre and usually work regular office hours, though may need to work for longer hours at times. Surgery hours are usually between 8.30am and 5.30-6.00pm, although this can vary. Some evenings or Saturday work may be required but you get time off during the week. Team work is usual. Your work may involve the use of statistics, writing reports, amending patient records, drawing up plans and liaising with medical staff. A lot of work is done on a computer. You may also have to travel to meetings, conferences or for training courses.

Qualification

- **England, Wales and Northern Ireland**

Band 2: For entry to jobs, no minimum qualifications are needed, but it is an advantage to have some GCSEs (A*-C) or equivalent in subjects that include English and maths.

Band 3: For entry to jobs, HNC or a relevant Diploma, usually at least 4 GCSEs (A*-C) including English and maths, or equivalent.

- **Scotland**

Band 2: Although academic qualifications are not specified for this job, it is an advantage to have some S grades (1-3) in subjects that include English and maths, or similar.

Band 3: For entry to jobs, usually at least four S grades (1-3) including English and maths, or similar.

Adult Qualifications

Maturity is an advantage due to the personal and confidential nature of the role. Previous experience or qualifications in administration, management or a medically related job is an advantage.

Work Experience

Work experience gives you an insight into what you enjoy and don't enjoy about a job or working environment, as well as the opportunity to acquire new skills. It also provides valuable information to add to your CV and improves your employment prospects. It is useful to approach a local GP practice manager for an opportunity of work shadowing. Temporary holiday work in offices via employment agencies is helpful, particularly if you can develop good keyboard skills and a knowledge of the most popular software packages.

Entry and Training

Most people entering this job have previous relevant experience in administration and are also expected to have knowledge of computer programs. The Association of Medical Secretaries, Practice Managers, Administrators and Receptionists (AMSPAR) offers level 2-3 certificates in medical administration which are nationally recognised awards.

Some practice managers may be required to hold the level 5 diploma or certificate in primary care and health management awarded by AMSPAR. The programme is open to existing and potential managers in a health or social care environment. Candidates should be recommended by an appropriate employer and accepted by an AMSPAR-approved centre following an interview. The course is available on a part-time basis only over a 12-18 month period and covers managing ethics and medico-legal requirements, managing staff, managing processes and patient services, managing healthcare resources, and managing data and communications. You need a minimum of two years' experience within a health or social care setting and must be educated to level 3 (A level/H grade equivalent) standard.

Details of all training and qualifications are available from the AMSPAR website. The AMSPAR continuing professional development pack is available for AMSPAR members and non-members.

The Institute of Healthcare Management (IHM) awards the Management of Health and Social Care (MHSC) certificate and diploma, which are appropriate for practice managers. The IHM has also developed a fellowship scheme for practice managers.

Mature entry is usual and especially if you have previous banking, accountancy or commercial experience, management and administration skills or qualifications. This job also attracts ex-nurses and ex-armed forces personnel.

Opportunities and Pay

You are employed in a general medical practice and opportunities are available throughout the UK. Similar jobs can be found in hospitals, dental practices, with health authorities, nursing homes and other social and health service providers. Promotion is limited but may be obtained by moving to a larger practice and by taking more responsibility. Some practice managers become partners in the general practice. There are some opportunities of working overseas or occasionally, to work on a self-employed basis.

Salaries vary depending on area, size of practice and level of responsibility. A starting salary is likely to be around £21k, rising to £30k-£45k with experience. Senior managers with the most responsibility may earn up to £60k a year and those with full accountancy responsibilities may earn more in some practices.

Skills and Qualities

able to communicate effectively, aptitude for figures, customer service skills, discreet, efficient, good organisational skills, information handling skills, initiative, IT skills, resourceful

Relevant Subjects
Business and accounting, Economics, English, Health and social care, Mathematics

Further Information
AMSPAR Professional (AMSPAR) - www.amspar.com

First Practice Management - www.firstpracticemanagement.co.uk

NHS Careers (NHS Careers) - www.nhscareers.nhs.uk

NHS Careers Scotland - www.infoscotland.com/nhs

NHS Careers Wales - www.wales.nhs.uk

Addresses
Association of Medical Secretaries, Practice Managers, Administrators and Receptionists (AMSPAR)
Tavistock House North, Tavistock Square, London WC1H 9LN
Phone: +44 (0)20 7387 6005
Web: www.amspar.com

Institute of Healthcare Management (IHM)
18-21 Morley Street, London SE1 7QZ
Phone: +44 (0)20 7620 1030
Web: www.ihm.org.uk

Similar Jobs
Health Records Clerk, Health Records Clerk, Health Service Manager, Human Resources Officer/Manager, Local Government Administrator, Secretary: Medical

Graphic Design Assistant
also known as: Assistant Graphic Designer, Graphic Studio Assistant

CRCI:Design, Arts and Crafts
CLCI:ED Job Band: 3 to 5

Job Description
Graphic design assistants work with a graphic designer, helping to prepare clients' art material for print. They have thorough skills and knowledge of typography and the art and process of printing to create the required visual message. The job varies from studio to studio, and project to project, but under direction from the designer, an assistant can expect to perform background research, produce sketches and create layouts to the graphic designer's specification.

Assistants develop an idea using a variety of materials and creative methods, including photographs, drawings, lettering and patterns. They also work with oil and acrylic paints, coloured inks, crayons and pastels. Often use computer-aided design (CAD) tools.

Work Details
Usually work a basic 39 hr week; Monday to Friday. However, work is often project based and deadlines may mean working late and at weekends. The work is usually done in a studio or an office, but may involve visiting clients and printers, which can mean periods away from home. You are expected to present your ideas to senior graphic designers and clients. At times you have to work under pressure.

Qualification
• England, Wales and Northern Ireland

Band 3: For entry to jobs, HNC or a relevant Diploma, usually at least 4 GCSEs (A*-C) including English and maths, or equivalent.

Band 4: For diploma in foundation studies (art and design) or a foundation degree in graphic design: usually at least one A level and some GCSEs (A*-C), including English and maths, or equivalent qualifications. For a BTEC higher national award: successful completion of a foundation studies course or a national level programme.

Band 5: For degree courses: 2-3 A levels and some GCSEs (A*-C), usually including English and maths, or equivalent. Most students take a foundation studies course first. Exact requirements depend on the degree you take.

• Scotland

Band 3: For entry: usually at least four S grades (1-3) including English and maths, or similar.

Band 4: For entry to SQA higher national and professional development awards, usually 2-3 H grades and some S grades (1-3), including English and maths, or similar qualifications.

Band 5: For degree courses: 3-5 H grades and some S grades (1-3), usually including English and maths, or similar qualifications. Exact requirements depend on the degree you take.

Degree Information
Degrees in graphic design, art and design with a graphic design specialism, graphic communication design, illustration, 3-D design or visual art may increase your opportunities. Postgraduate courses are also available.

Adult Qualifications
Mature applicants with outstanding portfolios of work may be accepted for courses without the standard entry qualifications. There are Access and foundation courses in some areas, which give adults without qualifications a route onto degree courses. Check with individual colleges.

Work Experience
Entry to this job is competitive and it is important that you try to do some relevant work or voluntary experience before applying. This may include voluntary experience at a magazine, newspaper, private graphics company or a publicity or advertising design department of a large company. Any experience you gain at school or college such as designing posters for events looks good on a CV and helps to build your portfolio of work.

Entry and Training
Considerable talent is needed and competition for jobs is fierce. Almost all graphic design assistants take full-time courses first and there are very few opportunities for unqualified trainees, except for those with an exceptional talent. Most of those who obtain employment are graduates or hold an HND in graphics, or similar. There is a wide range of courses available with specialism in graphic design. An excellent portfolio is usually needed for employers and colleges.

On-the-job in-house training may be combined with formal training, particularly in the use of graphics software and desktop publishing packages such as Illustrator, Photoshop, Adobe Creative Suite and Quark Express. However, training can often be unstructured as many designers require their assistants to learn independently. This job is often regarded as the first step to becoming a graphic designer.

Design and Art Direction (D&AD), the British Interactive Media Association (BIMA) and the Design Business Association (DBA) offer a range of specialist training courses, workshops and events. Check their websites for details.

Mature applicants without formal entry qualifications may be accepted if they can demonstrate an enthusiasm and genuine aptitude for graphic design; usually through an excellent portfolio. Foundation degrees in graphic design can be a route onto degree courses. Part-time and distance-learning courses are also available. Experience in the art and design field and in the use of computers is an advantage. There are refresher courses that may be available for those returning to work and there may be government training schemes in some areas.

Opportunities and Pay

Entry at this level in graphic design is very competitive. Employers are throughout the UK, ranging from small design studios to large corporate companies. Opportunities are with advertising agencies, marketing and publicity departments of large companies and organisations, commercial design studios, and TV, film and audio-visual companies. With experience you can become a graphic designer, but may you need to move employers to gain promotion.

Pay varies depending on location and type of employer but you are likely to start at around £16k a year, rising to £18k-£20k. Some design assistants may earn around £25k a year.

Health

You have to be able to use colour to maximum effect and so normal colour vision is preferable.

Skills and Qualities

able to withstand criticism, adaptable, artistic ability, creative flair, drawing ability, eye for shape/colour, good communication skills, good interpersonal skills, patient, research skills, specialist IT skills

Relevant Subjects

Art and Design, Design and technology, English, ICT/Computor studies, Media and communication studies

Further Information

Creative & Cultural Skills - sector skills council for advertising, crafts, cultural heritage, design, literature, music, performing & visual arts - www.ccskills.org.uk

Design Business Association (DBA) - www.dba.org.uk

Design Week (Design Week) - www.designweek.co.uk

Diplomas (Foundation, Higher and Advanced) - http://yp.direct.gov.uk/diplomas

NSEAD: Careers in Art, Craft & Design (National Society for Education in Art and Design) - www.nsead.org/resources/careers.aspx

The Designer (Chartered Society of Designers) - www.thedesignermagazine.com

Training Schemes - www.direct.gov.uk/en/educationandlearning

▶Working in art & design (2009) (Babcock Lifeskills) - www.babcock-lifeskills.com/

▶Working in computers & IT (2010) (Babcock Lifeskills) - www.babcock-lifeskills.com/

Addresses

British Design & Art Direction (D&AD)
9 Graphite Square Vauxhall Walk, London SE11 5EE
Phone: +44 (0)20 7840 1111
Web: www.dandad.org

British Interactive Media Association (BIMA)
The Lightwell, 12-16 Laystall Street, Clerkenwel, London EC1R 4PF
Phone: +44(0)207 843 6797
Web: www.bima.co.uk

Design Council
34 Bow Street, London WC2E 7DL
Phone: +44 (0)20 7420 5200
Web: www.designcouncil.org.uk

Design Wales
University of Wales Institute, Cardiff Western Avenue CF5 2YB
Phone: +44 (0) 2920 41 7043
Web: www.designwales.org

Similar Jobs

Graphic Design: Studio Junior, Graphic Designer, Illustrator, Interactive Media Designer, Signwriter/Signmaker

Graphic Design: Studio Junior

CRCI:Design, Arts and Crafts
CLCI:ED Job Band: 2 to 3

Job Description

Studio juniors work in graphic design studios carrying out a range of daily tasks to assist graphic design assistants and graphic designers. Generally, the daily tasks include opening the post, answering the telephone, opening emails, and operating the fax machine and other office machinery. They also do other office tasks such as filing and maintaining stocks of materials. Often make the tea and coffee, and delives artwork to clients.

Juniors may sometimes operate process cameras, or assemble parts of the design produced by designers and other specialists. With experience, some may assist by using graphics software and desktop publishing programs.

Work Details

The hours are typically 9am-5pm, Monday to Friday, but you may have to work some extra hours to meet deadlines. Work is mainly in an open plan office or studio, and may involve work in front of a computer screen. You are expected to work as part of a team with other members of the design staff.

Qualification

• England, Wales and Northern Ireland

Band 2: For entry to jobs, no minimum qualifications are needed, but it is an advantage to have some GCSEs (A*-C) or equivalent in subjects that include English, maths and art, or equivalent.

Band 3: For a BTEC national diploma in art and design (graphic design): usually at least 4 GCSEs (A*-C), including English and maths, or equivalent. Students who have a very high quality portfolio of artwork and demonstrate commitment at interview may have the required formal qualifications waived by some colleges.

• Scotland

Band 2: Although academic qualifications are not specified for this job, it is an advantage to have some S grades (1-3) in subjects that include English and, maths and art, or similar.

Band 3: For entry: usually at least four S grades (1-3) including English and maths, or similar. Students who have a high quality portfolio of artwork and demonstrate commitment at interview may have the required formal qualifications waived by some colleges.

Adult Qualifications

Mature students with a high quality portfolio of artwork may have the usual required formal qualifications waived for some courses.

Work Experience

Relevant work or voluntary experience is always useful and can improve your chances in application for entry to this job. Consider any work involving the use of desktop publishing or graphics software, as well as general office jobs.

Entry and Training

This is traditionally seen as an entry-level job in graphic design with various levels of qualification. There are a few studio junior posts that offer on-the-job training for those with few qualifications. However, most employers expect a good level of education and ask for up-to-date knowledge of desktop publishing, image manipulation or graphics software packages, such as Adobe Creative Suite, Quark Express and Photoshop, or similar. Applicants to courses and jobs need to produce a portfolio of recent artwork.

A national diploma in graphic design or similar, may be asked for by some employers. A Diploma/Welsh Baccalaureate may be available in your area in creative and media and may provide a route onto higher education courses. Consider taking a part-time HNC or foundation degree in a design subject once you are employed, as this may help towards career progression. S/NVQs at level 2-3 in design may also be available.

Mature applicants are expected to have some relevant experience and specific skills obtained through various areas of employment, and therefore enter at a more senior level, such as graphic design assistant. This is very much a basic entry-level job for those with few qualifications and little work experience.

Opportunities and Pay

Opportunities occur throughout the UK, with a concentration in London and other major cities. You can be employed by a printing, reprographics, publishing, advertising or graphic design company. It may be possible to train as an assistant to a graphic designer, and with further qualification, to become a graphic designer. Some go on to become Mac Operators in desktop publishing.

Pay varies depending on location and employer. Starting salaries are around £12k-14k a year depending on your level of qualifications. Some may earn more.

Health

This job requires good eyesight and colour vision.

Skills and Qualities

able to get on with all kinds of people, adaptable, attention to detail, business awareness, common sense, co-operative, creative flair, initiative, reliable, willing to learn

Relevant Subjects

Art and Design, Design and technology, ICT/Computer studies

Further Information

Creative & Cultural Skills - sector skills council for advertising, crafts, cultural heritage, design, literature, music, performing & visual arts - www.ccskills.org.uk

Design Uncovered (Trotman 2009) - www.trotman.co.uk

Design Week (Design Week) - www.designweek.co.uk

NSEAD: Careers in Art, Craft & Design (National Society for Education in Art and Design) - www.nsead.org/resources/careers.aspx

The Designer (Chartered Society of Designers) - www.thedesignermagazine.com

▶Working in art & design (2009) (Babcock Lifeskills) - www.babcock-lifeskills.com/

▶Working in computers & IT (2010) (Babcock Lifeskills) - www.babcock-lifeskills.com/

Addresses

British Printing Industries Federation (BPIF)
Farringdon Point, 29-35 Farringdon Road, London EC1M 3JF
Phone: 0870 240 4085 (UK only)
Web: www.britishprint.com

Similar Jobs

Desktop Publishing (DTP) Operator, Graphic Design Assistant, Graphic Designer

Graphic Designer

CRCI:Design, Arts and Crafts
CLCI:ED
Job Band: 4 to 5

Job Description

Graphic designers create two or three-dimensional designs that put together images, text and colour for a variety of use including advertising, education, leisure and communication. They are also known as communication designers and use graphics software and photography to create designs for magazines and newspapers, company logos, holiday brochures, DVDs/CDs and book covers, packaging, signs and labels, websites, TV and film.

Designers use packages such as Adobe Creative Suite, Quark Express, Illustrator and Photoshop, and keep up to date with the latest developments in IT. Usually follow the client's instructions (design brief) about the type of design needed, its target audience and the cost and timescale.

Designers develop the brief through research and think creatively to produce innovative ideas for the client to consider. They prepare the layout of the design, positioning words, pictures, patterns etc, and choose the appropriate style and media to meet the business objectives of the client. Usually liaise with graphic assistants, other designers, copywriters, printers, marketing specialists and account executives.

Work Details

Usually work a basic 37-39 hr week; Monday to Friday, though may have to work extra hours, particularly when deadlines approach. The work is usually done in a studio or an office, perhaps working in a team or sometimes alone. Those who are self-employed or freelance may share office space or a studio and some may work from home. This job can be pressurised at times.

Qualification

• England, Wales and Northern Ireland

Band 4: For diploma in foundation studies (art and design) or foundation degree in graphic design: usually at least 1-2 A levels and some GCSEs (A*-C) usually including English and maths, or equivalent. For a BTEC higher national award: successful completion of a foundation studies course or a national level programme.

Band 5: For degree courses: 2-3 A levels and some GCSEs (A*-C) usually including English and maths, or equivalent. Most students take a foundation course first. Exact requirements depend on the degree you take.

• Scotland

Band 4: For entry to SQA higher national and professional development awards, usually 2-3 H grades and some S grades (1-3), including English and maths, or similar qualifications.

Band 5: For degree courses: 3-5 H grades and some S grades (1-3), usually including English and maths, or similar qualifications. Exact requirements depend on the degree you take.

Degree Information

Degrees in graphic design, art and design with a graphic design specialism, graphic communication design, illustration, 3-D design or visual art may increase your opportunities. Postgraduate courses are also available.

Adult Qualifications

Mature applicants with outstanding portfolios of work may be accepted for courses without the standard entry qualifications. There are Access and foundation courses in some areas, which give adults without qualifications a route onto degree courses. Check with individual colleges.

Work Experience

Entry to this job is very competitive and it is important that you try to do some relevant work or voluntary experience before applying. This may include voluntary experience at a magazine, newspaper or private graphics company, or a publicity or advertising design department of a large company. Any experience you can gain at school/college, such as designing posters for events, looks good on your CV and helps to build your portfolio of work.

Entry and Training

Considerable talent is needed and competition for jobs is fierce. Almost all graphic designers take full-time courses first and there are few opportunities for unqualified trainees, except for those with an exceptional talent. Most of those who obtain employment are graduates or those who hold an HND or foundation degree in graphics, or similar and begin as a graphic assistant. There are a range of courses available with specialisms in graphic design. An excellent portfolio is normally needed, both for employers and colleges.

Students usually take a diploma in foundation studies or national award course first, followed by a three-year degree course in their specialist subject. A foundation degree in graphic design is also available in some areas. In Scotland, degree courses last for four years, the first year is usually a broad-based course, before specialism in the second year. A Diploma/Welsh Baccalaureate may be available in your area in creative and media and may provide a route onto higher education courses.

Continuing professional development (CPD) is an important and key element throughout your career to keep up to date with the latest developments. A structured programme of CPD is offered by the Chartered Society of Designers (CSD) and British Design and Art Direction (BD&D) who run courses and specialist workshops. The British Interactive Media Association (BIMA) and the Design Business Association (DBA) also offer a range of training courses and events. On-the-job in-house training is usually combined with formal training, particularly in the use of graphics and animation software and desktop publishing packages such as Illustrator, Photoshop, Dreamweaver, Flash, Adobe Creative Suite and Quark Xpress.

Mature applicants without formal entry qualifications may be accepted if they can demonstrate an enthusiasm and genuine aptitude for graphic design; usually through an excellent portfolio. Part-time and distance-learning courses are also available. Experience in the art and design field and in the use of computers is an advantage. There are refresher courses that may be available for those returning to work and government training schemes in some areas.

Opportunities and Pay

There are many thousands of graphic design businesses in the UK and more vacancies arise within the field of graphic design than any other design area, but competition for jobs is intense. Jobs are available in agencies or in-house teams in major cities and towns mainly in London, the South East, Leeds and Manchester. You can work in the public and private sectors to create visual media that are used for advertising or providing information. This includes printing and publishing, TV or film work, local government, technical or scientific design, or working for a consultancy firm.

Jobs in commercial design studios allow you to work on different assignments, or specialise in an area such as packaging or magazine design. In large organisations, promotion is possible to management jobs, such as creative director or studio manager. Some move into animation or television and video graphics. Many designers work on a freelance basis and it is possible to work part time. Experienced graphic designers can work internationally with demand for their skills in countries like the USA and Japan, as well as in Europe.

Pay varies depending on location and type of employer. Starting salaries are around £18k-£23k, rising to around £26k-£35k a year with experience. High earners make around £45k and creative directors can earn around £65k a year.

Health

You have to be able to use colour to maximum effect and so normal colour vision is preferable.

Skills and Qualities

able to withstand criticism, adaptable, artistic ability, creative flair, enthusiastic, eye for shape/colour, good communication skills, good interpersonal skills, good presentation skills, imaginative, self confident, specialist IT skills

Relevant Subjects

Art and Design, Design and technology, English, ICT/Computer studies, Media and communication studies

Further Information

Chartered Society of Designers (Chartered Society of Designers) - www.csd.org.uk

Creative & Cultural Skills - sector skills council for advertising, crafts, cultural heritage, design, literature, music, performing & visual arts - www.ccskills.org.uk

Design Business Association (DBA) - www.dba.org.uk

Design Uncovered (Trotman 2009) - www.trotman.co.uk

Design Week (Design Week) - www.designweek.co.uk

Diplomas (Foundation, Higher and Advanced) http://yp.direct.gov.uk/diplomas

NSEAD: Careers in Art, Craft & Design (National Society for Education in Art and Design) - www.nsead.org/resources/careers.aspx

The Designer (Chartered Society of Designers) - www.thedesignermagazine.com

Training Schemes - www.direct.gov.uk/en/educationandlearning

▶Working in art & design (2009) (Babcock Lifeskills) - www.babcock-lifeskills.com/

▶Working in computers & IT (2010) (Babcock Lifeskills) - www.babcock-lifeskills.com/

▶Working in marketing, advertising & PR (2008) (Babcock Lifeskills) - www.babcock-lifeskills.com/

Addresses

British Design & Art Direction (D&AD)
9 Graphite Square Vauxhall Walk, London SE11 5EE
Phone: +44 (0)20 7840 1111
Web: www.dandad.org

British Design Innovation (BDI)
9 Pavilion Parade, Brighton, West Sussex BN2 1RA
Phone: +44 (0)1273 621378
Web: www.britishdesign.co.uk

British Interactive Media Association (BIMA)
The Lightwell, 12-16 Laystall Street, Clerkenwel, London EC1R 4PF
Phone: +44(0)207 843 6797
Web: www.bima.co.uk

British Interactive Media Association (BIMA)
The Lightwell, 12-16 Laystall Street, Clerkenwel, London EC1R 4PF
Phone: +44(0)207 843 6797
Web: www.bima.co.uk

Design Council
34 Bow Street, London WC2E 7DL
Phone: +44 (0)20 7420 5200
Web: www.designcouncil.org.uk

Design Wales
University of Wales Institute, Cardiff Western Avenue CF5 2YB
Phone: +44 (0) 2920 41 7043
Web: www.designwales.org

Similar Jobs

Advertising Art Director, Animator, Computer Games Animator, Interactive Media Designer, Picture Researcher, Signwriter/Signmaker, Website Designer

Greenkeeper: Golf

CRCI:Environment, Animals and Plants
CLCI:WAD Job Band: 1 to 3

Job Description

Greenkeepers are responsible for ensuring that the turf (known as the green) on a golf course is in excellent condition. They select and manage grass species to suit the soil conditions, rake and aerate the grass and use chemical fertilisers carefully to promote strong growth, and controls pests, weeds and diseases. Greenkeepers cut the grass and ensure that the land is well-drained and watered as needed. They rake bunkers, cut holes and move golf tees. Also repair any damage done to the course by golfers, or by animals, such as moles or rabbits.

May be involved in the construction of new bunkers, tees or entire golf courses. Use hand tools and machinery and are responsible for their upkeep. Greenkeepers are also expected to maintain the trees and shrubs in other parts of the grounds of a golf course. They are aware of any environmental issues, and use chemicals and water accordingly.

Work Details

Hours of work vary depending on time of year. In summer you are likely to work around 40-45 hrs a week. In winter the working week is likely to be around 30-35 hrs. Weekend work is expected, with time off in the week instead. Work is usually outside and in all types of weather. This job requires a high level of energy as there is a lot of walking, kneeling and bending. A small truck may be provided to quickly take you from one part of the golf course to another. Some of the work may be in a small team, but you are also expected to work on your own at times. Protective clothing is worn in wet weather and when spraying with pesticides and fertilisers. A uniform may be provided.

Qualification

• England, Wales and Northern Ireland

Band 1: No minimum qualifications are required, but you are expected to have had a good level of general education. However, some formal/vocational qualifications at any level are useful. Maths and science subjects are the most helpful.

Band 2: Although academic qualifications are not specified for this job, it is an advantage to have some GCSEs (A*-C) in subjects that include English, science and maths, or similar.

Band 3: For entry: usually at least 4 GCSEs (A*-C) including English and maths, or equivalent.

• Scotland

Band 1: No minimum qualifications are required, but you are expected to have had a good level of general education. However, some formal/vocational qualifications at any level are useful. Maths and science subjects are the most helpful.

Band 2: Although academic qualifications are not specified for this job, it is an advantage to have some S grades (1-3) in subjects that include English, science and maths, or similar.

Band 3: For entry: usually at least four S grades (1-3) including English and maths, or similar.

Adult Qualifications

No pre-entry qualifications are usually required though some academic/vocational qualifications at any level may be an advantage. English, science and maths are useful subjects.

Work Experience

Work experience can equip you with skills that you can use in the future and add to your CV. Employers may prefer candidates who have relevant work or voluntary experience. This can include work in a garden centre or horticultural nursery, or in grounds maintenance. An interest and some experience in playing golf is also an advantage.

Entry and Training

There are no formal entry qualifications, but an interest in golf and experience in horticulture or agriculture are useful. On-the-job training is usual and you can also study by distance learning or attend a college on a day-release course to study for S/NVQs in sports turf options at levels 2-4, or for a national certificate in sports and amenity turf maintenance, which has a specialist module in golf facilities. Most courses are offered by agricultural colleges. Contact the Greenkeepers Training Committee for details. The British and International Golf Greenkeepers Association (BIGGA) also offers training opportunities, including the master greenkeeper certificate scheme for those training in golf course management.

The Institute of Groundsmanship also runs suitable professional development awards, and there are relevant HNDs, foundation degrees, degrees and masters degrees in sports turf topics, all of which require higher entry qualifications. A Diploma/Welsh Baccalaureate may be available in your area in environment and land-based studies. Training programmes, including apprenticeship schemes, may be available in your area. Advanced apprenticeships leading to qualification at level 3 can also be a route into higher education.

Mature entrants with knowledge of golf and previous experience in horticulture, agriculture or groundsmanship have an advantage. Government training opportunities, including adult apprenticeships, may be available in your area. You can also gain recognition of previous experience through Accreditation of Prior Learning (APL) or by working towards relevant S/NVQs.

Opportunities and Pay

There are around 15,000 greenkeepers employed in the UK and employment prospects are increasing with the expansion of golf courses. There are around 3,500 golf courses in the UK and Ireland. You can work for a private golf club, a public golf course run by a local authority, a grounds maintenance contractor, or a hotel with a golf course. There are also many opportunities to work abroad, especially in Europe and the Middle East. With experience and higher qualifications it is possible to progress to head greenkeeper or to golf course superintendent/manager. Some may progress to work in turf research or development.

Pay varies depending on area and employer. Apprentices usually ear around £8.5k a year, rising to £11k-£13k a year when qualified. Some experienced greenkeepers may earn around £30k a year, and those with managerial responsibility up to £40k.

Health

This job requires you to be physically fit and may be difficult if you have an allergy such as hay fever.

Skills and Qualities

able to work well on your own, attention to detail, careful, enjoy working outdoors, environmental awareness, numeracy skills, patient, practical skills, technical aptitude

Relevant Subjects

Biology, Science

Further Information

Apprenticeship Schemes (National Apprenticeship Service) - www.apprenticeships.org.uk

Diplomas (Foundation, Higher and Advanced) - http://yp.direct.gov.uk/diplomas

Greenkeeper International (British and International Greenkeepers Association (BIGGA)) - www.bigga.org.uk/

Greenkeepers Training Committee - www.the-gtc.co.uk

Lantra - The Sector Skills Council for environmental & land-based sector (Lantra) - http:/www.lantra.co.uk

Lantra Careers (A Future In...) (Lantra) - www.afuturein.com

Real Life Guide to Working Outdoors (Trotman) - www.trotman.co.uk

The Groundsman (monthly) (Institute of Groundsmanship (IOG)) - www.thegroundsman.co.uk

Training Schemes - www.direct.gov.uk/en/educationandlearning

▶Working in sport & leisure (2010) (Babcock Lifeskills) - www.babcock-lifeskills.com/

▶Working outdoors (2010) (Babcock Lifeskills) - www.babcock-lifeskills.com/

Addresses

British and International Golf Greenkeepers Association (BIGGA)
BIGGA House, Aldwark, Alne, York YO61 1UF
Phone: +44 (0)1347 833800
Web: www.bigga.org.uk

Institute of Groundsmanship (IOG)
28 Stratford Office Village, Walker Avenue, Wolverton Mill East, Milton Keynes MK12 5TW
Phone: +44 (0)1908 312 511
Web: www.iog.org

Similar Jobs

Forest Worker, Garden Centre Assistant, Gardener, Groundsman/Groundswoman, Horticultural Worker: Commercial

Groundsman/Groundswoman

CRCI:Environment, Animals and Plants
CLCI:WAD Job Band: 1 to 3

Job Description

Groundsmen and women are responsible for ensuring that sports grounds, leisure and recreational surfaces are kept in the best possible condition. They cut the grass, weed and water, re-seeds worn patches of grass and replace damaged turf. They prepare and maintain both natural and synthetic athletics tracks, cricket and football pitches, tennis courts, bowling greens, or racetracks. This includes marking out white lines on sports pitches or courts and putting up nets and other equipment such as posts. They may have to dig ditches for drainage. Also apply fertilisers to improve soil and grass quality, and pesticides to control plant diseases.

They also look after borders, hedges, flower beds, walls, paths and public seating areas. Use hand tools such as forks, rakes and spades, as well as power tools, including hedge cutters and strimmers. Often use machinery such as rotavators and motorised mowers and sprayers. Clean and maintains equipment/machinery and do any minor repairs.

Work Details

Usually works a basic 39 hr week, though often with longer hours in the summer. Hours also often vary depending on the sport you work in. Work probably includes weekends, early mornings and late evenings. Travel to different sites may be required. This job requires a high level of energy as there is a lot of walking, kneeling, bending and possibly climbing ladders. You work outside in all sorts of weather. Protective clothing is worn in wet weather and when spraying with pesticides (chemicals) and fertilisers.

Qualification

• England, Wales and Northern Ireland

Band 1: For entry to jobs, no minimum qualifications are needed, but you are expected to have a good level of general education and relevant experience. Some formal/vocational qualifications at any level are useful. Maths and science subjects are the most helpful.

Band 2: For entry to jobs, no minimum qualifications are needed, but it is an advantage to have some GCSEs (A*-C) or equivalent in subjects that include English, science and maths.

Band 3: For entry: usually at least 4 GCSEs (A*-C) including English and maths, or equivalent.

• Scotland

Band 1: For entry to jobs, no minimum qualifications are needed, but you are expected to have a good level of general education and relevant experience. Some formal/vocational qualifications at any level are useful. Maths and science subjects are the most helpful.

Band 2: Although academic qualifications are not specified for this job, it is an advantage to have some S grades (1-3) in subjects that include English, science and maths, or similar.

Band 3: For entry: usually at least four S grades (1-3) including English and maths, or similar.

Adult Qualifications

No pre-entry qualifications are usually required though some academic/vocational qualifications at any level may be an advantage. English, science and maths are useful subjects.

Work Experience

Work experience can equip you with skills that you can use in the future and add to your CV. Employers may prefer candidates who have relevant work or voluntary experience. This can include work in a garden centre or horticultural nursery, or in grounds maintenance.

In some parts of the country, the Institute of Groundsmanship offers its National Practical Certificate award part time at a local college. This is aimed at 14-16 year olds as part of the national curriculum.

Entry and Training

No formal entry qualifications are specified, but for management positions at a later stage, it is useful to have some qualifications. On-the-job training is usual and you can also attend a college on a day-release course to study for national certificate (level 2) and advanced national certificate (level 3) courses in sports and amenity turf management.

The Institute of Groundsmanship (IOG) offers a new four-tier structure of training courses. These are short courses from foundation to management level, and are usually one to two day courses. They are available in courses that are aimed at specific sports, such as cricket, bowls, etc. The IOG also offers a distance learning option in turf culture.

Relevant HNC/HND courses are available with sports turf options, together with foundation degrees or degrees. However, for some courses you need higher qualifications. Many courses require you to have had some previous relevant practical experience.

S/NVQs in sports turf options are available at levels 2-4. A Diploma/Welsh Baccalaureate may be available in your area in environment and land-based studies. Training programmes, including apprenticeship schemes, may be available in your area. Advanced apprenticeships leading to qualification at level 3 can also be a route into higher education.

Mature entrants with previous experience in horticulture, agriculture or sport, or with an IOG qualification, have an advantage. Government training opportunities, including adult apprenticeships, may be available in your area. You can also gain recognition of previous experience through Accreditation of Prior Learning (APL) or by working towards relevant S/NVQs.

Opportunities and Pay

Employment prospects are increasing. You can work for a sports club, such as a football, tennis, golf or cricket club, or a horticultural contractor, or for schools, colleges and universities, and for hotels with sports facilities. It is also possible to find work with local authority leisure and recreation departments, though much work is done by contractors. If you gain extra qualifications you may become a head groundsman/woman, in charge of one site, or an area manager, responsible for a number of sites. Seasonal and part-time work is possible. You can be self-employed or work for a horticultural contractor. It is also possible to find work abroad where there is considerable demand for trained groundsmen/groundswomen.

Pay varies depending on area and employer. Salaries are around £11k-£14k a year rising to around £16k-£18k. Managers may earn from around £35k.

Health
This job requires you to be physically fit and may be difficult if you suffer from an allergy such as hay fever. A medical test may be required.

Skills and Qualities
able to work both on your own and in a team, attention to detail, careful, enjoy working outdoors, methodical, numeracy skills, patient, practical skills, technical aptitude

Relevant Subjects
Biology, Science

Further Information
Apprenticeship Schemes (National Apprenticeship Service) - www.apprenticeships.org.uk

Diplomas (Foundation, Higher and Advanced) - http://yp.direct.gov.uk/diplomas

Lantra - The Sector Skills Council for environmental & land-based sector (Lantra) http:/www.lantra.co.uk

Lantra Careers (A Future In...) (Lantra) - www.afuturein.com

Pitchcare - Serving the turfcare industry - www.pitchcare.com

Real Life Guide to Working Outdoors (Trotman) - www.trotman.co.uk

The Groundsman (monthly) (Institute of Groundsmanship (IOG)) - www.thegroundsman.co.uk

Training Schemes - www.direct.gov.uk/en/educationandlearning

▶Working outdoors (2010) (Babcock Lifeskills) - www.babcock-lifeskills.com/

Addresses
Institute for Sport, Parks & Leisure (ISPAL)
Abbey Business Centre, 1650 Arlington Business Park, Theale, Reading RG7 4SA
Phone: 0844 418 0077 (UK only)
Web: www.ispal.org.uk

Institute of Groundsmanship (IOG)
28 Stratford Office Village, Walker Avenue, Wolverton Mill East, Milton Keynes MK12 5TW
Phone: +44 (0)1908 312 511
Web: www.iog.org

Sports & Play Construction Association (SAPCA)
Federation House, Stoneleigh Park, , Warwickshire CV8 2RF
Phone: +44 (0)24 7641 6316
Web: www.sapca.org.uk

Similar Jobs
Farm Worker: Crops, Forest Worker, Garden Centre Assistant, Gardener, Greenkeeper: Golf, Horticultural Worker: Commercial

Guide Dog Trainer

also known as: Assistance Dog Trainer, Dog Instructor, Mobility Instructor: Guide Dogs

CRCI:Environment, Animals and Plants
CLCI:WAM Job Band: 2 to 4

Job Description
Guide dog trainers train dogs to assist people with a visual impairment (blindness or limited sight) to help them lead an independent life. They are responsible for the next stage of guide dog training following puppy walking, and before the dog meets its new owner. They begin by helping the dog to adjust to the routine of training and assessing the dog's abilities through simple walks prior to the training programme. Skills such as dealing with crowds, pavement skills and night training are also taught.

Mobility instructors take the dog through the final stages of advanced training and then match it to a compatible client. They work with this client and the guide dog for up to four weeks and help them to form their new working partnership. Also teach new owners how to handle their dogs correctly and make after-care home visits to give further help.

Trainers may specialise in working with medical assistance dogs for people with conditions, such as hypoglycaemia and similar disorders, or with seizure alert dogs that respond and warn people who are about to have an imminent epileptic seizure. Others may train and work with hearing dogs who are especially trained to assist those people who have severe hearing difficulties, and some trainers work with disability assistance dogs, which are also trained to help and support their disabled owner in their everyday life.

Work Details
Usually work 35 hrs a week, Monday to Friday, though may be expected to work some weekends and evenings, with time off on other days. There is contact with people who are in need of support and who are possibly nervous. Teaches, instructs and helps people, and is also responsible for their safety and general welfare. Work can be emotionally demanding and you need to cope with being active most of the time, including many miles of walking each day. Work is often outside and in all weathers. Warm and protective clothing is provided.

Qualification

- **England, Wales and Northern Ireland**

Band 3: For entry: usually at least 5 GCSEs (A*-C) including English, science and maths, or equivalent.

- **Scotland**

Band 3: For entry: usually at least five S grades (1-3) including English, science and maths, or similar.

Adult Qualifications
It is usually necessary to have some academic qualifications or their equivalent. English, maths and preferably a science subject are usually preferred. Contact the individual organisations for specific entry requirements. Entry requirements are often relaxed for those people who have relevant experience and skills.

Work Experience
Relevant work or voluntary experience is always useful and can improve your employment prospects when applying for entry to jobs. Any work that involves dogs, such as a Saturday job or holiday work, provides valuable experience. Contact the various organisations/societies and canine welfare charities (listed in addresses) for opportunities to gain some work and voluntary experience. Any experience of work caring for people of all ages and ability, is also extremely useful.

Entry and Training
Previous basic experience of working with dogs or other animals is usually needed. It is also an advantage to have some experience in working with people. It is an advantage, though not always specified, to have completed a course in subjects such as animal care/behaviour or a certificate in canine behaviour and psychology. The Animal Care College offers a range of these type of courses. However, all new applicants receive specific training from the relevant organisation, such as the Guide Dogs for the Blind Association (GDBA) which also offers some examinations that are validated by City & Guilds.

Training as a GDBA mobility instructor takes approximately three years, with guide dog training usually taking up to 15 months. However, you must first qualify as a guide dog trainer before applying for training as a mobility instructor. Other organisations also offer in-house and on-the-job training, usually with a training coordinator/instructor. This may take place at the employing organisation's headquarters or at a designated training centre.

The length of training depends on the employing organisation, though is usually from around ten months. With some organisations, the ability to use British Sign Language to BSL level II, is an advantage. All jobs usually require a full driving licence or the ability to show how you can cope without it.

Mature applicants with experience of working with or caring for dogs, and who also have people skills, communication and experience of working with the elderly or less able, together with the relevant entry requirements, are encouraged to apply for training posts.

Opportunities and Pay

You usually work for an organisation such as the Guide Dogs for the Blind Association (GDBA). This is a small profession and there are few vacancies. Promotion to more senior posts, such as supervisory or managerial posts, is possible after gaining experience. Similar work opportunities exist with other organisations, such as Hearing Dogs for Deaf People, Dog Aid, and Support Dogs.

Depending on the organisation, starting salary is around £14k and when qualified, rises to around £18k a year. A qualified guide dog mobility instructor for GDBA earns around £26k a year.

Health

To do this job you have to have good standard of stamina and fitness, and may find this job difficult if you are allergic to animals.

Skills and Qualities

able to inspire confidence, encouraging, good communication skills, good interpersonal skills, good organisational skills, observant, patient, perseverance, sense of humour, sympathetic

Relevant Subjects

Biology, Health and social care, Psychology

Further Information

Lantra - The Sector Skills Council for environmental & land-based sector (Lantra) - http:/www.lantra.co.uk

Lantra Careers (A Future In...) (Lantra) - www.afuturein.com

Addresses

Animal Care College
Index House High Street, Ascot, Berkshire SL5 7ET
Phone: +44 (0)1344 636436
Web: www.animalcarecollege.co.uk/

Canine Partners
Mill Lane, Heyshott, Midhurst, West Sussex GU29 0ED
Phone: 0845 658 0480 (UK only)
Web: www.caninepartners.co.uk

Dogs for the Disabled
The Frances Hay Centre, Blacklocks Hill, Banbury, Oxfordshire OX17 2BS
Phone: +44 (0) 1295 252600
Web: www.dogsforthedisabled.org

Guide Dogs for the Blind Association (GDBA)
Burghfield Common, Reading, Berkshire RG7 3YG
Phone: +44 (0)118 983 5555
Web: www.guidedogs.org.uk

Hearing Dogs for Deaf People
The Grange, Wycombe Road, Saunderton, Princes Risborough, Buckinghamshire HP27 9NS
Phone: +44 (0)1844 348 100
Web: www.hearingdogs.org.uk/

Institute for Animal Care Education
c/o Needhams Farm Uplands Road, Werneth Low, Cheshire SK14 3AG
Phone: +44 (0)161 368 4610
Web: www.iace.org.uk

Support Dogs
21 Jessops Riverside, Brightside Lane, Sheffield S9 2RX
Phone: +44 (0)114 261 7800
Web: www.support-dogs.org.uk

Similar Jobs

Animal Care Assistant, Dog Groomer, Riding Instructor, RSPCA/Scottish SPCA Inspector, Security Dog Handler/Trainer, Zoo Keeper

Gunsmith

CRCI:Engineering
CLCI:SOZ Job Band: 2

Job Description

Gunsmiths service, modify, design, repair or restore guns of any age, such as pistols, shotguns and rifles. They may carry out stock work that includes the reshaping of a pistol grip and forend, or fitting an engraved gold or silver oval/shield to the stock. Barrel work includes fitting or replacing foresights and mid-sights. Rifle work involves screw cutting, trigger tuning and re-bluing work. General servicing, cleaning or fitting/making new springs or parts is included in action work. Some gunsmiths sell guns, ammunition and sports equipment. They may also provide a valuation of a customer's gun.

Work Details

Usually work a standard 35-40 hr week, and in some jobs, this may include Saturdays. Your place of work is a shop or a workshop. You are responsible for ensuring that laws and regulations are observed. This work requires a high degree of accuracy.

Qualification

• England, Wales and Northern Ireland

Band 2: For entry to jobs, no minimum qualifications are needed, but it is an advantage to have some GCSEs (A*-C) or equivalent in subjects that include English and maths.

• Scotland

Band 2: Although academic qualifications are not specified for this job, it is an advantage to have some S grades (1-3) in subjects that include English and maths, or similar.

Adult Qualifications

No minimum academic qualifications are specified.

Work Experience

Relevant work or voluntary experience is always useful. It can add to your CV and improve your chances when applying for entry to jobs or apprenticeships in the engineering industry. Your personal or adult guidance adviser should be able to assist you on how to organise work experience.

Entry and Training

The knowledge and skills needed to become a gunsmith are learned over time. You need to learn how to handle and use a wide range of guns as well as gain knowledge of machine tool processes, metallurgy, ballistics and woodworking.

Entrants are often appointed through personal contact or direct approach. You may be taken on as an apprentice gunsmith. It can be useful to contact a firm of gunsmiths to see if there are any training opportunities. An interest in sports shooting is essential. Training is usually by practical experience, working on the job with a skilled and experienced gunsmith. Your training may include day or block release for BTEC/City & Guilds or SQA qualifications in engineering. Some may prefer to study for relevant qualifications, such as a BTEC/SQA national award or equivalent vocational qualifications, before applying for a job or apprenticeship. Short courses may be provided by gun manufacturers.

S/NVQs at level 2-3 may be available. Relevant training programmes, including apprenticeship schemes, may be available in your area. Advanced apprenticeships leading to qualification at level 3 can also be a route into higher education.

Mature applicants with retail experience, knowledge of sporting guns and any toolmaking or metalwork experience have an advantage. Related experience in the armed services is also useful. Government training opportunities, such as apprenticeships, may be available in your area. You can also gain recognition of previous experience through Accreditation of Prior Learning or by working towards relevant S/NVQs. Contact your local careers office, Jobcentre Plus, Next Step service or Learning and Skills Council (LSC)/Local Enterprise Company (LEC) for details of training schemes.

Opportunities and Pay

Jobs are only available in certain towns and major cities of the UK. Most jobs are in London, and this is also where most apprenticeships are available. Most are employed by a small firm of gunsmiths, or perhaps the armed forces. There are few vacancies in this area of work and, due to increasingly tight gun control legislation, this is likely to continue. With experience you can become self-employed. There may be opportunities to work in retail or management.

There is no standard salary range for a gunsmith. Earnings before you are fully skilled may be low. As many gunsmiths are self-employed or work for small firms, pay often depends on the amount of work completed and can vary considerably. You may earn from £8-£10 an hour in a small gunshop or £100k a year as a reputable master. Average earnings for experienced gunsmiths are around £30k-£40k a year.

Skills and Qualities

accurate, attention to detail, careful, manual dexterity, numeracy skills, patient, practical skills, problem-solving skills, responsible attitude, technical aptitude

Relevant Subjects

Design and technology, Engineering, Mathematics, Physics, Science

Further Information

Apprenticeship Schemes (National Apprenticeship Service) - www.apprenticeships.org.uk

SEMTA - sector skills council for science, engineering and manufacturing technologies - www.semta.org.uk

Training Schemes - www.direct.gov.uk/en/educationandlearning

Welsh Baccalaureate - www.wbq.org.uk

Addresses

Gun Trade Association
PO Box 43, Tewkesbury, Gloucestershire GL20 5ZE
Phone: +44 (0)1684 291 868
Web: www.guntradeassociation.com

Similar Jobs

Engineering Craft Machinist, Engineering Machine Operative, Locksmith, Toolmaker

Haematologist

CRCI:Science, Mathematics and Statistics
CLCI:QOX — Job Band: 5

Job Description

Haematologists study the types and functions of blood and blood forming tissues to identify abnormalities within blood cells. They test blood samples to count blood cells and haemoglobin levels to assess a patient's condition. Then use the tests to help doctors in the diagnosis and treatment of illnesses such as anaemia and leukaemia. Also study blood clotting, either as a check before surgery or to examine patients who have unexplained bleeding. Haematologists use a range of analysis and technical equipment, such as microscopes and computers. However, much specialised work is done manually without the use of a computer.

Work Details

Usually work 36-39 hrs a week, Monday to Friday, but hours may be flexible and unsociable as laboratory services are often available 24 hrs a day. You work in a laboratory, university, college or hospital. Depending on your employment you may have responsibility for setting up experiments, analysing results and presenting reports. In hospital work you provide information and advice for diagnosis and treatment of a patient. Your work requires a high degree of accuracy at all times.

Sometimes the work may be pressurised and intense. At a senior level, you may be required to supervise trainees and junior members of staff. A white coat or overall and protective clothing, such as gloves, are worn at times. There are administrative tasks associated with this role.

Qualification

• England, Wales and Northern Ireland

Band 5: For degree courses: 2-3 A levels in appropriate science subjects and some GCSEs (A*-C) usually including English, maths and science, or equivalent. Exact requirements depend on the degree you take.

• Scotland

Band 5: For degree courses: 3-5 H grades in appropriate science subjects and some S grades (1-3), usually including English,maths and science, or similar. Exact requirements depend on the degree you take.

Degree Information

A first or upper second class honours degree in a relevant subject is required. Most commonly acceptable are degrees in life sciences (biology, microbiology, microbiology, genetics or biochemistry). Science degrees relating to medicine such as biomedical science, may also be considered.

Adult Qualifications

Adults without the required qualifications but with relevant laboratory experience, may be considered for some courses. Check with individual universities and colleges. Access or foundation courses may be available in some areas.

Work Experience

Employers or universities may prefer candidates who have relevant work or voluntary experience in such areas as hospital work, a relevant university department, or in a laboratory engaged in haematology. Any work with a scientific background is useful.

Entry and Training

There are two entry routes into this profession. The preferred option is through a training scheme in a national training laboratory offered via the Recruitment Centre for Clinical Scientists, within the National Health Service (NHS). However, not all laboratories offer this form of training. The second, less common route, is to enter training as a Grade A associate on a two-year traineeship that is part of the laboratory's staffing quota. The award of a diploma from the Royal College of Pathologists is gained through in-service assessment of the training period and by examination. This allows associates to progress to a Grade B post. Trainees need to commit themselves to a significant amount of private study outside normal working hours.

Training and/or qualifications can lead to an MSc and provide part of the requirements for entry to the first stage of membership of the professional body, the Health Professions Council (HPC). Practical training can last up to three years. Continuing professional development (CPD) is expected for scientists in career grade posts and you must be registered with the HPC to practice as a clinical scientist.

Mature applicants to courses may be eligible for a student scholarship from the British Society for Haematology (BSH). The Deans of Medical Schools have details of any sponsorships. Applicants must be affiliated to a UK university. Contact the BSH for details of training routes and sponsorship awards.

Opportunities and Pay

This is a constantly developing specialist area of medicine, providing scope for clinical and medical experience. Most haematologists are employed by the NHS but there is also work with government departments, private laboratories, cancer research establishments, pharmaceutical firms, the national blood service and universities. Work abroad and part time is possible. Relocation may be necessary for career progression; 60% of entrants are female.

Rates of pay vary depending on employer, but for an NHS haematologist, there are three grades of pay within the career structure. Newly qualified entrants usually start on a salary scale of around £19.5k-£25k a year, rising to £23k-£32k a year. A specialist scientist can earn £28k-£37k a year.

Health

There may be a risk of allergy from skin irritants or of infection. This job requires good colour vision for certain areas of work.

Skills and Qualities

accurate, analytical skills, aptitude for teamwork, emotionally strong, IT skills, methodical, not squeamish, patient, scientific approach

Relevant Subjects

Biology, Chemistry, English, Health and social care, ICT/Computer studies, Mathematics, Physics, Science

Further Information

British Journal of Haematology (Wiley-Blackwell) - www.wiley.com/bw/journal.asp?ref=0007-1048

European Haemotology Association (European Haemotology Association) - www.ehaweb.org

National Blood Service - www.blood.co.uk

NHS Careers (NHS Careers) - www.nhscareers.nhs.uk

Scottish National Blood Transfusion Service - www.scotblood.co.uk

►Working in science (2007) (Babcock Lifeskills) - www.babcock-lifeskills.com/

Addresses

British Society for Haematology (BSH)
100 White Lion Street, London N1 9PF
Phone: +44 (0)20 7713 0990
Web: www.b-s-h.org.uk

Health Professions Council (HPC)
Park House, 184 Kennington Park Road, London SE11 4BU
Phone: +44 (0)20 7582 0866
Web: www.hpc-uk.org

Institute of Biomedical Science (IBMS)
12 Coldbath Square, London EC1R 5HL
Phone: +44 (0) 20 7713 0214
Web: www.ibms.org

Royal College of Pathologists (RCPath)
2 Carlton House Terrace, London SW1Y 5AF
Phone: +44 (0)20 7451 6700
Web: www.rcpath.org

Similar Jobs

Biochemist, Biomedical Scientist, Biotechnologist, Microbiologist, Toxicologist

Hairdresser

CRCI:Personal and Other Services
CLCI:IL Job Band: 1 to 3

Job Description

Hairdressers cut and style hair, usually in a salon, by shampooing, cutting, colouring and perming following discussion with the client. They use equipment such as scissors, razors, clippers, tongs, curlers, heated rollers, hot brushes and dryers, including infra-red lamps. May use gel, mousse, wax or spray. Hairdressers colour, perm or straighten hair using shampoos, conditioners, tints, bleaches and lotions. May trim beards and moustaches for male clients and, in some salons, may dress wigs.

Also diagnose basic hair problems and recommend treatments or improvements. They advise on hair products that may be purchased in the salon. In a small salon, may do other jobs, such as answer the phone, make appointments, prepare bills, order stock and help to keep the salon clean and tidy. Many hairdressers run their own business either from home or travelling to the homes of clients.

Work Details

Usually work a 40 hr week, including Saturdays, and sometimes salons are open late one or two evenings during the week. The salon may be closed on one weekday or you may have a day off if working a Saturday. Salons are usually well-lit, warm and pleasant environments, though you have to cope with standing for most of the time. You may need to wear light waterproof gloves and perhaps an overall to protect you from any chemicals used.

Most places work to a tight time schedule so you are constantly busy. Independent hairdressers, offering a mobile service and visiting clients' homes, need a driving licence.

Qualification

• England, Wales and Northern Ireland

Band 1: There are no minimum qualifications for this job, though employers look for a high level of motivation, smart appearance, good communication skills and personality. Some employers may prefer a few GCSEs, or equivalent.

Band 2: For course entry: colleges usually require some GCSEs, including English and maths, or equivalent. Further subjects like art and a science are useful.

Band 3: For some courses including BTEC national award/ certificate in hairdressing: usually at least 4 GCSEs (A*-C) in English, maths or science or equivalent qualifications.

• Scotland

Band 1: There are no minimum qualifications for this job, though employers look for a high level of motivation, smart appearance, good communication skills and personality. Some employers may prefer a few S grades, or similar.

Band 2: For course entry: colleges usually require some S grades, including English and maths, or similar. Further subjects like art and a science are useful.

Band 3: For some courses or a SQA national certificate: four S grades (1-3) in English, maths or science or similar.

Adult Qualifications

No minimum entry qualifications are required for direct entry. Employers look for a high level of motivation, smart appearance, good communication skills and personality. Course entry requirements may be relaxed for suitable adults.

Work Experience
It is very useful to gain some salon experience in a Saturday or holiday job. In addition, sales or reception experience can be useful, as well as other kinds of work with the public.

Entry and Training
Entry to training in the best salons is highly competitive, so some school leaving qualifications are an advantage. It is almost essential to have had hairdressing experience through Saturday or holiday work. Training routes vary. Many people enter this job aged 16-17 and follow a nationally preferred scheme of training on the job. A Diploma/Welsh Baccalaureate in hair and beauty studies may be available in your area. Other training programmes, including apprenticeship schemes, may be also available. Training may include attendance at a local college or training centre on a day-release basis, though some salons can provide in-house training, usually in the evening. Some salons also pay for and encourage their staff to attend professional training run by the larger product houses like Wella and Revlon.

The other route is a full or part-time college course before you start work that either leads to S/NVQs at levels 1-3 or BTEC national award/national certificate in hairdressing. Contact the Hairdressing and Beauty Industry Authority (HABIA) for information on all training routes and qualifications. Once qualified, you must also keep up to date with changing styles and products, sometimes by attending special short courses.

The Freelance Hair and Beauty Federation (HFBF) runs courses for freelance operators on hairdressing techniques and how to run a business.

Adults may be able to enter this work through a government-funded training programme. Contact your local Connexions or careers office, Jobcentre Plus, Next Step service or Learning and Skills Council (LSC)/Local Enterprise Company (LEC) for details of all training opportunities and schemes, including apprenticeships for adults. Experience of hairdressing or beauty work is an advantage.

Opportunities and Pay
Over 180,000 people work in 31,000 salons throughout the UK. There are also some opportunities to work in television, films, fashion, the armed forces and prison service, hospitals, and on cruise ships, but the competition for these places is fierce. If you work for a large salon or chain of hairdressers, your promotion prospects are better.

With experience, many hairdressers open their own salon or become freelance and visit clients in their own homes, or in hospitals and nursing homes. Others may move into teaching in colleges, but this usually requires further qualifications. There are foundation degrees, higher national awards and degrees in hairdressing management. There are some opportunities to work abroad, particularly at European holiday resorts.

Trainees usually earn the National Minimum Wage while training. This is £3.57 an hour aged 16-17 and £4.83 an hour aged 18-22. Once experienced, you can earn around £20k-£30k a year. A very few specialist stylists earn considerably more. Tips from clients and commission on products that are sold in the salon can supplement your income.

Health
People with sensitive skin may not be able to do this job because of the various chemicals used and because hands are in water so much during the first stage of training. You require good colour vision for certain areas of work. You are on your feet for most of the working day, so also need good levels of fitness and stamina.

Skills and Qualities
able to get on with all kinds of people, able to get on with all kinds of people, creative flair, customer service skills, eye for shape/colour, friendly, good personal grooming, manual dexterity, self confident, tactful

Relevant Subjects
Art and Design, Biology, Science

Further Information
Apprenticeship Schemes (National Apprenticeship Service) - www.apprenticeships.org.uk

Apprenticeships in Scotland (Careers Info Scotland) - www.apprenticeshipsinscotland.com/about/

Careers in Hairdressing/Barbering (HABIA) - www.habia.org/

Diplomas (Foundation, Higher and Advanced) - http://yp.direct.gov.uk/diplomas

Freelance Hair and Beauty Federation (FHBF) - www.fhbf.org.uk

Hair and Beauty Jobs - www.hairandbeautyjobs.com

Hairdressing Council - www.haircouncil.org.uk

Real Life Guide to Hairdressing (Trotman 2010) - www.trotman.co.uk

Training Schemes - www.direct.gov.uk/en/educationandlearning

Welsh Baccalaureate - www.wbq.org.uk

►Working in art & design (2009) (Babcock Lifeskills) - www.babcock-lifeskills.com/

►Working in hairdressing & beauty (2009) (Babcock Lifeskills) - www.babcock-lifeskills.com/

Addresses
Hairdressing and Beauty Industry Authority (HABIA)
Oxford House, Sixth Avenue, Sky Business Park, Robin Hood Airport, Doncaster DN9 3EG
Phone: 0845 230 6080 (UK only)
Web: www.habia.org/

Similar Jobs
Beauty Consultant, Beauty Therapist, Image Consultant, Trichologist, Wig Maker

Hat Designer
also known as: Milliner

CRCI:Design, Arts and Crafts
CLCI:EJ Job Band: 3 to 5

Job Description
Hat designers create hats by hand, working from sketches or photographs to create new shapes and designs. They may use computer-aided design (CAD) programs to help with design. Designers use materials including silk, straw, velvet and felt , have an understanding of general fashion and are aware of the forthcoming themes in fashion and colour. Some designers create hats that are based on historical designs, particularly if working on a production for a TV, film or theatre company. They ensure that all work is kept within budget, especially if working in high street ranges.

Hats are created by building up its basic shape from which an aluminium block can be made for mass manufacture. Hydraulic machinery may be used if hats are to be mass-produced. Sometimes the prototype is made by hand. Designers may work directly onto the hat by draping the fabric and pinning on trimmings such as feathers, braid, beads, ribbons or flowers, to give the desired effect. They keep up to date with design trends, colour and fabrics by attending fashion shows/exhibitions nationally and sometimes internationally. A milliner makes and/or sells hats and many hat designers are also milliners.

Work Details
Normal working hours are from 9am to 5pm; Monday to Friday, though there are often long irregular working hours to meet deadlines, particularly if you are self-employed. You may work in a studio, shop, hat boutique, fashion workshop or perhaps at home, giving advice to customers as well as being responsible for artistic

effect. Some work may take place in a factory environment. Some designers may travel to meet with clients or retail buyers or to attend fashion shows, exhibitions, production teams and fabric houses. Some designers may spend a lot of time working alone. Sometimes your work may be criticised or rejected. Overseas work is possible, particularly within Europe.

Qualification

• England, Wales and Northern Ireland

Band 3: For entry to jobs, HNC or a relevant Diploma, usually at least 4 GCSEs (A*-C) including English and maths, or equivalent. For some foundation studies courses: usually at least 5 GCSEs (A*-C) or equivalent.

Band 4: For diploma in foundation studies (art and design) or a foundation degree: usually at least one A level preferably in art, and some GCSEs (A*-C) or equivalent. For BTEC higher national award: a BTEC national award, successful completion of a foundation studies course, or equivalent.

Band 5: For degree courses: 2-3 A levels and some GCSEs (A*-C) usually including English and maths, or equivalent. Most students take a foundation studies course first. Exact requirements depend on the degree you take.

• Scotland

Band 3: For entry: usually at least four S grades (1-3) including English and maths, or similar.

Band 4: For entry to SQA higher national and professional development awards, usually 2-3 H grades and some S grades (1-3), often including English, art and maths, or similar qualifications.

Band 5: For degree courses: 3-5 H grades and some S grades (1-3), usually including English and maths, or similar qualifications. Exact requirements depend on the degree you take.

Degree Information

A degree in fashion design is preferred. It is possible to specialise either during the first degree or by postgraduate study in courses such as fashion womenswear or fashion accessories design. Some courses include marketing and European languages. Graduates in any art and design subject may be acceptable, but you have to gain experience and build up a portfolio of designs.

Adult Qualifications

Mature applicants with outstanding portfolios of work may be accepted for courses without the standard entry requirements. There are Access and foundation courses in some areas that give adults without entry qualifications a route onto degree courses. Check with individual colleges.

Work Experience

Entry to this job is competitive and it is important that you try to do some relevant work or voluntary experience before applying. Some larger companies may be willing to provide work experience. The most beneficial experience is with an established hat designer, but experience of three dimensional design, freehand work and all art and design based work, also helps with entry to a relevant course. It also gives you the opportunity to build up your portfolio of design work.

Entry and Training

Most hat designers take full-time courses, usually to HND/degree level and entry to courses is highly competitive. A portfolio of designs is needed, both for college and for employment. Students normally take a foundation studies course, before taking a relevant three-year degree course. In Scotland, degree courses last for four years, the first year is a broad based course before specialising in a design area in the second year.

Distance-learning courses are available as well as a foundation degree in fashion design and manufacture and fashion design and production in some areas. A Diploma/Welsh Baccalaureate may be available in your area in creative and media and may provide a route onto higher education courses.

HNC courses in millinery are available at Leeds College of Art and Design and Kensington and Chelsea College. Some colleges such as the London College of Fashion and Central Saint Martin's College of Art and Design offer short courses, which are suitable for non-fashion graduates. Millinery workshops are often available, including those held at Janie Lashford's School of Millinery, art and design colleges and adult education centres. City & Guilds millinery courses are available at level 2-3. Some courses may specialise in theatrical millinery. Some private courses are also available from highly experienced practising hat designers.

A diploma in manufacturing and product design is also available and may be a route into a design career. A textiles apprenticeship at levels 2-3 and an apprenticeship in apparel at level 3 may be available in your area. The Chartered Society of Designers (CSD) offers workshops and training courses as well as a membership scheme for professional designers. Attending regular fashion shows to keep ahead of fashion trends is important and continuing professional development (CPD) is necessary to maintain and update your skills.

Mature applicants with experience in art and design, fashion, or sales and marketing may have an advantage. You can gain recognition of previous experience through Accreditation of Prior Learning (APL). Foundation degrees in relevant subjects, a textiles apprenticeship at levels 2-3 or an apprenticeship in apparel at level 3 may be available in your area.

Opportunities and Pay

There are probably fewer than 1,000 hat designers and milliners in the UK, although over the last 15 years hatmaking has grown, mainly due to the wedding industry. Jobs are available in large towns and cities where you may be employed by a fashion house, chain store or hat manufacturer, or small to medium-sized hat company supplying retailers. Some work in the TV, theatre and film industry, usually under contract.

Promotion can depend on personal flair and ability. In a large fashion house, there may be the opportunity to become a senior designer. Self-employed designers/milliners may produce their own collections. Some very successful hat designers are patronised by wealthy clients. Some designers move into textile design or retail buying. There may be opportunities to work abroad.

Pay can vary considerably depending on whether you are employed, self-employed or work part time. New entrants may earn around £12k-£15k a year, rising to around £20k-£30k with experience. A successful self-employed hat designer/milliner may earn more than £35k a year, and a very few exclusive designers, much more.

Health

This job requires good eyesight and normal colour vision.

Skills and Qualities

able to work both on your own and in a team, adaptable, ambitious, attention to detail, business awareness, creative flair, eye for shape/colour, eye for visual effect, good communication skills, imaginative, manual dexterity

Relevant Subjects

Art and Design, Design and technology

Further Information

AGCAS: Fashion & Design (Job Sector Briefing) (AGCAS) - www.prospects.ac.uk

British Hat Guild - www.craftscouncil.org.uk/

Can you Cut it? - www.canucutit.co.uk

Chartered Society of Designers (Chartered Society of Designers) - www.csd.org.uk

Creative & Cultural Skills - sector skills council for advertising, crafts, cultural heritage, design, literature, music, performing & visual arts - www.ccskills.org.uk

Diplomas (Foundation, Higher and Advanced) - http://yp.direct.gov.uk/diplomas

Drapers: Fashionnews, jobs and trends - www.drapersonline.com

Future Textiles - www.futuretextiles.co.uk

Hats and That - www.hatsandthat.com/

The Hat Magazine - www.thehatmagazine.com

The Hat Site - www.thehatsite.com

▶Working in art & design (2009) (Babcock Lifeskills) - www.babcock-lifeskills.com/

▶Working in fashion & clothing (2008) (Babcock Lifeskills) - www.babcock-lifeskills.com/

Your Creative Future - www.yourcreativefuture.org.uk

Addresses

Janie Lashford's School of Millinery
1 Bowers Hill, Badsey, Evesham WR11 7HG
Phone: +44 (0)1386 832901
Web: www.themillineryschool.co.uk

London College of Fashion
20 John Princes Street, London W1G 0BJ
Phone: +44 (0)20 7514 7344
Web: www.fashion.arts.ac.uk

Similar Jobs

Costume Designer, Dressmaker, Fashion Designer, Footwear Designer, Textile Designer

Health & Safety Practitioner

also known as: Health & Safety Adviser/Consultant, Occupational Safety Officer, Safety Adviser

CRCI:Administration, Business and Office Work
CLCI:COT Job Band: 4 to 5

Job Description

Health and safety (H&S) practitioners advise on health, safety and the prevention of accidents within an organisation. They liaise with enforcing authorities, such as the Health and Safety Executive, the fire service, and relevant local authority departments, such as environmental health. They focus on risk assessment and hazard management throughout the company or organisation. Inspecting the work area and machinery to ensure that safety laws are met, is an important aspect of the job. They test safety equipment and advise on its use.

It is important that H&S practitioners work closely with departmental managers to help plan, improve, implement and monitor safe working practices. They also deal with accidents and incidents that require liaison with legal and insurance departments, or the local authority. They write reports on accidents, keep records and statistical information. Provide managers and employees with advice on how to avoid any potential accidents or hazards. May run short courses on safety training procedures and legislation. Keeping up to date with any new legislation and on all aspects of health and safety is necessary in this role.

Work Details

Usually work 9am to 5pm, Monday to Friday, though can work shifts, depending on the type of organisation. You may be on call for any accidents and emergencies and be required to work overtime at times. The job requires you to ask questions, advise workers and managers, liaise with legal and insurance departments, or regulatory bodies such as the Health and Safety Executive. This job needs a specialist knowledge of technical developments and legal regulations, and you have to keep up to date with these. Sometimes you may have to make unpopular decisions.

The job often involves physical activity and safety officers have to cope with heights and ladders, kneeling and bending down. Those working on offshore oil/gas platforms, or on construction/building sites work outdoors at times, and in all weathers. The work environment can be dirty, noisy and smelly, and you may need to wear protective clothing.

Qualification

• England, Wales and Northern Ireland

Band 4: For BTEC higher national award: 1-2 A levels and some GCSEs (A*-C) preferably including maths, science subjects and English, or equivalent.

Band 5: For degree courses: 2-3 A levels usually including one science, maths or technology subject and some GCSEs (A*-C) in other subjects, or equivalent. Exact requirements depend on the degree you take.

• Scotland

Band 4: For relevant SQA higher national award: usually 2-3 H grades and some S grades (1-3), often including English, maths and science subjects, or similar qualifications.

Band 5: For degree courses: 3-5 H grades including one science, maths or technology subject and some S grades (1-3) in other subjects, or similar qualifications. Exact requirements depend on the degree you take.

Degree Information

There are first degrees in subjects that include occupational health and safety, and health, safety and the environment. There are relevant foundation degrees available, including health and safety management, and in occupational health and safety management that can be studied full time over two years. Relevant postgraduate degrees and diplomas include occupational safety and health.

Adult Qualifications

Graduates in a related discipline are able to take a postgraduate course in occupational health and safety or in risk management. Access courses to science can lead to a relevant degree or HND course for those who have no formal qualifications. Institutions often relax entry requirements for mature applicants.

Work Experience

Experience of working at an operational level in technical or scientific industries, or work within a health and safety environment is highly relevant. An interest in law is important and also knowledge of computer applications for the analysis and preparation of reports. The Institute of Occupational Safety and Health states that good communication skills are essential for succeeding in this job. Any experience gained working with the public or in a customer service environment demonstrates skills in this area.

Entry and Training

Training is mainly on the job, usually with additional short in-house or external training courses. Entrants are increasingly graduates, though some employers may take people with BTEC/SQA higher national awards. Qualified advisers and consultants should be members of the Institute of Occupational Safety and Health (IOSH) and follow a continuing professional development (CPD) scheme to keep their professional experience up to date. Those who have an accredited degree/diploma in occupational safety and health or related discipline, an MSc/diploma in occupational safety and health, or related qualifications such as an S/NVQ at level 4 plus three years' relevant experience, can apply for membership of IOSH. Contact IOSH for details of different membership categories.

The British Safety Council (BSC) also offers a range of awards, such as a level 2 certificate in risk assessment, or a level 6 diploma in occupational safety and health. It also offers other relevant short courses that can be used towards IOSH CPD points.

Relevant S/NVQs include occupational health and safety at levels 3-4, and management of health and safety at level 5. A further level 5 S/NVQ is available in health and safety regulation. Training programmes, including apprenticeship schemes, may be available in your area. Advanced apprenticeships leading to qualification at level 3 can be a route into higher education.

Maturity is an advantage and traditionally, those with a background in engineering, management or science move into this job. Graduates with accredited degrees may be able to take a postgraduate course in occupational health and safety, or risk management, on a part or full-time basis.

Opportunities and Pay

You can work in a wide range of organisations such as large industrial, processing or manufacturing companies, the oil and gas industry, local authorities, the health sector, telecommunications, construction companies and public utilities or you can be employed by the Health & Safety Executive as a civil servant. Other opportunities include working as a health and safety S/NVQ assessor, lecturer or manager for professional bodies such as the BSC. Some advisers may work as self-employed consultants.

Experienced and qualified advisers can rise to key management positions. Those with high-level technical qualifications can progress to well-paid employment, particularly when working in hazardous environments. Part-time work and work abroad is also possible.

Salaries start at around £18k-£26k, rising to around £26k-£40k a year with greater experience and responsibility. Shift allowances and payments for unsocial hours supplement your income in some jobs. Key management posts in the oil, gas, petrochemical and nuclear industries can attract salaries in excess of £60k.

Health

You can come into contact with skin irritants or chemical that can cause allergies. The job usually requires a good level of general fitness.

Skills and Qualities

able to work to a budget, analytical skills, decisive, efficient record keeping, excellent communication skills, good presentation skills, good written English, problem-solving skills, sound judgement, technical aptitude

Relevant Subjects

Chemistry, Construction and built environment, Design and technology, Engineering, English, Law, Mathematics, Physics, Science

Further Information

AGCAS: Health (Job Sector Briefing) (AGCAS) - www.prospects.ac.uk

Apprenticeship Schemes (National Apprenticeship Service) - www.apprenticeships.org.uk

British Safety Council - www.britsafe.org

Health and Safety Executive - www.hse.gov.uk

Safety and Health Practitioner (monthly) (Institution of Occupational Safety and Health (IOSH)) - www.shponline.co.uk/

Safety Management Magazine (monthly) (British Safety Council) - www.britsafe.org/STORE/PRODUCTS/157.aspx

►Working in travel & tourism (2010) (Babcock Lifeskills) - www.babcock-lifeskills.com/

Addresses

British Safety Council (BSC)
70 Chancellors Road, London W6 9RS
Phone: +44 (0)208 741 1231
Web: www.britishsafetycouncil.co.uk

ENTO (Employment National Training Organisation)
Kimberley House, 47 Vaughan Way, Leicester LE1 4SG
Phone: +44 (0)116 251 7979
Web: www.ento.co.uk

Institution of Occupational Safety and Health (IOSH)
The Grange, Highfield Drive, Wigston, Leicestershire LE18 1NN
Phone: +44 (0)116 257 3100
Web: www.iosh.co.uk

National Examination Board for Occupational Safety & Health (NEBOSH)
Dominus Way, Meridian Business Park, Leicester LE19 1QW
Phone: +44 (0)116 263 4700
Web: www.nebosh.org.uk

Similar Jobs

Environmental Health Practitioner, Ergonomist, Health Promotion Specialist, Occupational Hygienist, Road Safety Officer

Health Promotion Specialist

also known as: Health Education Specialist

CRCI:Healthcare
CLCI:JOZ Job Band: 4 to 5

Job Description

Health promotion specialists develop partnerships with key people, communities and organisations that can affect or influence public health. They work at a number of levels from face-to-face contact with individuals, groups and communities to more strategic work such as policy development. They aim to improve public health by raising people's awareness of health issues, such as hygiene, nutrition and diet, exercise, cancer, accident prevention, mental health, HIV/Aids, drug or alcohol abuse. Also provide advice and information about all aspects of promoting and maintaining good health.

Health promotion specialists give talks, write leaflets and brochures, organise short educational courses and exhibitions, and work with the press and TV. They visit schools, community organisations, industry, office buildings, hospitals, sports and leisure centres. May also coordinate the work of other health professionals. Have to work within a set budget.

Work Details

Work is office based, Monday to Friday, but the job also involves being out of the office at times, travelling around an area. You may work in a range of locations, including health centres, hospitals, regional health authorities, business offices, community centres, and sport and fitness centres. You advise, inform and communicate with many people of all ages, concentrating on the needs and issues of individuals, their communities and cultures. The job involves public speaking.

Qualification

• England, Wales and Northern Ireland

Band 4: For some initial courses or training (eg in nursing or social work) before further training in health education: 1-2 A levels and a number of GCSEs (A*-C) or equivalent qualifications. Exact requirements depend on the qualification you take.

Band 5: For degree courses: 2-3 A levels and some GCSEs (A*-C) usually including English and maths, or equivalent. Exact requirements depend on the degree you take.

- **Scotland**

Band 4: For some initial courses or training (eg in nursing or social work) before further training in health education: 2-3 H grades and a number of S grades (1-3) or similar qualifications. Exact requirements depend on the qualification you take.

Band 5: For degree courses: 3-5 H grades and some S grades (1-3), usually including English and maths, or similar qualifications. Exact requirements depend on the degree you take.

Degree Information
Degrees in health promotion, health promotion and development, public health, health environment and society, and health studies are available. Postgraduate courses are also available in health promotion or health education. A degree or professional qualification in a relevant field such as teaching or a branch of healthcare is also acceptable.

Adult Qualifications
A degree or professional qualification is required, along with some relevant voluntary or work experience. There may be special entry standards for adults applying for degree or equivalent courses. Check with the university or organisation concerned.

Work Experience
Employers or colleges/universities may prefer candidates who have relevant work or voluntary experience. This can include shadowing a health promotion specialist, working in a similar environment such as at a youth or community centre, or working in a hospital.

Entry and Training
Entrants are usually graduates but employers may also look for relevant postgraduate qualifications. Many people enter this job with previous experience in a related field such as medicine, social work and teaching. Postgraduate courses in health promotion and health education are available at a number of institutions and can be full or part time and lead to a diploma or masters degree. Those applicants without a qualification in health education may be seconded to a postgraduate course after gaining experience. The Open University offers a certificate in promoting public health which is equivalent to that of a final year of an honours degree.

Some may enter this job without higher qualifications and train on the job with experienced staff, and gain certificates/diplomas in health promotion through short and part-time courses.

Health promotion specialists can apply to join the UK Public Health Register.

Mature entrants are often those with related experience who choose health promotion as a second career. Many move from areas such as teaching, the health service, community or social work, psychology or from other jobs that involved health promotion.

Opportunities and Pay
This is a small but expanding profession as a result of increased government focus. Employment is usually with a regional health authority but opportunities are increasing with local authorities, charities and voluntary organisations, with agencies such as the National Institute for Health and Clinical Excellence or in industry. You may also be employed as a consultant working on short-term contracts.

Pay varies depending on area, employer and experience. Starting salaries within the NHS are around £21k a year, but specialists can earn £33k-£40k. Senior managers can earn £60k or more and salaries can be higher for those who move into consultancy work.

Skills and Qualities
analytical skills, confident, encouraging, excellent communication skills, flexible approach, friendly, negotiating skills, non-judgemental, perseverance, resourceful

Relevant Subjects
Biology, Chemistry, English, Health and social care, Media and communication studies, Psychology, Science, Sociology

Further Information
AGCAS: Health (Job Sector Briefing) (AGCAS) - www.prospects.ac.uk

National Institute for Health and Clinical Excellence (NICE) - www.nice.org.uk

NHS Careers (NHS Careers) - www.nhscareers.nhs.uk

NHS Careers Scotland - www.infoscotland.com/nhs

NHS Careers Wales - www.wales.nhs.uk

Open University - www.open.ac.uk

Skills for Health - sector skills council - www.skillsforhealth.org.uk

So you want to work in Healthcare (Wayland) - www.waylandbooks.co.uk

Addresses
Faculty of Public Health
4 St Andrews Place, London NW1 4LB
Phone: +44 (0)20 7935 0243
Web: www.fphm.org.uk

Health Scotland
Woodburn House, Canaan Lane, Edinburgh EH10 4SG
Phone: +44(0)131 536 5500
Web: www.healthscotland.com

Public Health Agency
Ormeau Avenue Unit 18 Ormeau Avenue, Belfast BT2 8HS
Phone: +44 (28) 9031 1611
Web: www.publichealth.hscni.net/

Royal Society for Public Health (RSPH)
3rd Floor Market Towers, 1 Nine Elms Lane, London SW8 5NQ
Phone: +44 (0)20 3177 1600
Web: www.rsph.org.uk

Similar Jobs
Dietitian, Environmental Health Practitioner, Health Visitor, Nurse: Adult, Nutritional Therapist, Psychologist: Health

Health Records Clerk
also known as: Admissions Clerk, Clinical Record Clerk, Medical Records Clerk

CRCI:Healthcare
CLCI:CAT
Job Band: 1 to 3

Job Description
Health records clerks set up and maintain a system of keeping patients' records in hard copy files and on computer, usually in a hospital. They act as a communication link between doctors, nurses and patients. Can specialise in coding (a system of recording illnesses and treatments) and statistics, filing and administration, or work at a desk in outpatients' departments. They amend, update and store details in the correct place so that they can be found quickly and easily. Look for files when they are needed and set up files for new patients.

Can also deal with letters from GPs, make appointments, deal with emergency admissions, take patients to wards, arrange for ambulances, and answer the telephone. Keep statistics on types of illness, operations and numbers on waiting lists or beds that are available.

Work Details
Usually work a basic 37 hrs a week; Monday to Friday, and perhaps also on Saturdays. In hospitals with accident and emergency departments you may work shifts to cover evenings, weekends and bank holidays. You can work in an office, a reception area, a document filing room, or on a ward. You may have

contact with patients and medical staff, as well as other administrative staff. Papers and records have to be filed for many people and you need a methodical, systematic and efficient approach to your work.

In hospitals, some files need to be transported from place to place, clinic to ward, etc. Details of tests, operations or other information need to be correctly filed in a patient's case notes, and entered into a computer database. Coding and statistical work is done in an office environment.

Qualification

• England, Wales and Northern Ireland

Band 1: For entry to jobs, no minimum qualifications are needed, but you are expected to have a good level of general education and relevant experience. Some formal/vocational qualifications at any level are useful.

Band 2: For the Institute of Health Record Information and Management (IHRIM) certificate: usually 5 GCSEs (A*-C) including English, maths or statistics, or equivalent.

Band 3: For entry to jobs, HNC or the Institute of Health Record Information and Management (IHRIM) diploma: usually 5 GCSEs (A*-C) including English and maths, or equivalent and the IHRIM Certificate. Contact the IHRIM for details.

• Scotland

Band 1: No minimum qualifications are required, but you are expected to have a good level of general education. Hospitals may prefer those who have taken some S Grades or similar.

Band 2: For the Institute of Health Record Information and Management (IHRIM) certificate: five S grades (1-3) including English, maths or statistics, or similar.

Band 3: For the Institute of Health Record Information and Management (IHRIM) diploma: five S grades (1-3) including English, maths or statistics and usually the IHRM certificate or a similar qualification. Contact the IHRIM for details.

Adult Qualifications

The need for formal qualifications may be waived for mature applicants with relevant experience in clerical, reception or administrative work.

Work Experience

Relevant work or voluntary experience is always useful and can equip you with skills to use in the future and add to your CV. Temporary holiday work in offices via employment agencies is useful, particularly if you can develop good keyboard skills and knowledge of the most popular software packages.

Entry and Training

It is an advantage to be able to use computers and have good keyboard skills so an IT qualification is useful. Training is on the job, working with an experienced person and employers require a Criminal Records Bureau (CRB)/Disclosure Scotland check. You do not have to take the Institute of Health Record Information and Management (IHRIM) certificate, but employers usually prefer it. Most people take the course part time by distance learning, which takes 1-2 years, but you can study full time. There is also a specialised IHRIM national clinical coding qualification. The IHRIM offers certificates of technical competence (CTC) in basic medical records practice, and at supervisory level, which are assessed in the workplace.

A few colleges run full or part-time courses, or evening classes lasting a year. If you have the IHRIM certificate, or an equivalent qualification, you can take the IHRIM diploma, by day release for a year or distance learning for 1-2 years. Further information on training and qualifications is available from IHRIM.

Appropriate S/NVQs in customer care or administration are also available at levels 1-3. There is an NVQ level 2 in Support Services in Health Care. Training programmes, including apprenticeship schemes, may be available in your area. Advanced apprenticeships leading to qualification at level 3 can also be a route into higher education.

Mature applicants with relevant experience in areas such as clerical work or administration are welcomed, particularly if combined with good keyboard skills and database experience. Government training opportunities, such as apprenticeships, may be available in your area. You can also gain recognition of previous experience through Accreditation of Prior Learning or by working towards relevant S/NVQs. Contact your local careers office, Jobcentre Plus, Next Step service or Learning and Skills Council (LSC)/Local Enterprise Company (LEC) for details of all training opportunities and schemes, including apprenticeships for adults.

Opportunities and Pay

You can work throughout the UK and opportunities are generally good, particularly in the NHS where all record keeping is being transformed to be stored electronically. Most medical receptionists work for an NHS Trust in a hospital, but some work in private hospitals, medical centres, the armed forces or in GP surgeries. Promotion to supervisory and management posts is possible, especially if you have the IHRIM qualifications. With further training, you may become a medical secretary or move into work outside the health service, such as coding work for an insurance company. There are also opportunities to work abroad if you have IHRIM qualifications.

Pay depends on your employer, but in the NHS pay for clerks is around £12k £15k a year, rising to £20k for clinical coding specialists with experience and qualifications.

Skills and Qualities

able to prioritise work, able to work quickly, awareness of confidentiality issues, discreet, friendly, good communication skills, good organisational skills, helpful, IT skills, methodical

Relevant Subjects

Business and accounting, English, ICT/Computer studies, Mathematics

Further Information

Apprenticeship Schemes (National Apprenticeship Service) - www.apprenticeships.org.uk

NHS Careers (NHS Careers) - www.nhscareers.nhs.uk

NHS Careers Scotland - www.infoscotland.com/nhs

NHS Careers Wales - www.wales.nhs.uk

Training Schemes - www.direct.gov.uk/en/educationandlearning

Addresses

Association of Medical Secretaries, Practice Managers, Administrators and Receptionists (AMSPAR)
Tavistock House North, Tavistock Square, London WC1H 9LN
Phone: +44 (0)20 7387 6005
Web: www.amspar.com

Institute of Health Record and Information Management (IHRIM)
744A Manchester Road, Rochdale, Lancashire OL11 3AQ
Phone: +44 (0) 1706 868481
Web: www.ihrim.co.uk

Similar Jobs

Database Administrator, GP Practice Manager, Local Government Administrative Assistant, Receptionist, Secretary: Medical

Health Service Manager

also known as: Hospital Manager

CRCI:Healthcare

CLCI:CAL Job Band: 4 to 5

Job Description

Health service managers are responsible for the efficient delivery and commissioning of local health care, through the management of hospitals, general practitioner services and community health services. They work with clinical and non-clinical staff on a day-to-day basis. In general management, are responsible for budgets, staff welfare, information management, and discipline. Can specialise in a particular area, such as financial management (auditing, salaries, financial planning), strategic planning, purchasing and supply (stores), human resources management (recruitment, training, employee relations), management and information services (statistics, operational research, computing), or building services (catering, security, porterage, laundry or sterile services).

Managers attend committee meetings, analyse data and write reports, deal with the media and the public, give presentations, and oversee routine administration and paperwork. They also liaise with all levels of medical staff and other partnership organisations. Use computers widely in the course of the job.

Work Details

Usually work normal office hours from Monday to Friday, but may often work at home out of hours. Work is based in a hospital office, community unit (such as a day centre or sheltered home), regional or district health authority or a health trust, though you may have to travel to meetings or conferences. The work may involve using statistics, writing reports and drawing up plans, as well as liaising with senior medical and paramedical staff. You have to negotiate for resources and funds, and some of your decisions may be unpopular.

Qualification

- **England, Wales and Northern Ireland**

Band 5: For degree courses: 2-3 A levels and some GCSEs (A*-C) usually including English and maths, or equivalent. Exact requirements depend on the degree you take.

- **Scotland**

Band 5: For degree courses: 3-5 H grades and some S grades (1-3), usually including English and maths, or similar qualifications. Exact requirements depend on the degree you take.

Degree Information

A degree in any discipline is acceptable. An increasing number of universities and colleges offer degrees in health service management. Institutional management, public administration or business management subjects give useful background.

Adult Qualifications

Entry qualifications may be relaxed for adults applying for degree courses or there may be special entry routes for mature applicants, such as Access or foundation courses. Contact the universities for details.

Work Experience

Employers or universities may prefer candidates who have relevant work or voluntary experience. This can include anything in a business environment or working with a team of people especially if it gives you supervisory skills and experience. Work experience can improve the chance of successful applications to relevant degree courses. Experience of work in the health service is also an advantage.

Entry and Training

Entrants from outside the NHS are usually graduates or those who have a professional qualification in accountancy, personnel, purchasing and supply or information technology. There are four different NHS graduate training schemes that use a competency-based assessment process for entry. These two-year schemes are in general management, human resources management, finance management and infomatics management. All schemes require a 2:2 degree in any subject though applicants to the general management training scheme with a health or management-related vocational qualification (degree level equivalent), are also considered.

On-the-job training is provided together with support from a personal mentor, line manager and regional tutor for the study programme. This leads to a recognised professional qualification in management, or professional accountancy qualifications, or professional personnel and development qualification. There are a number of residential courses to gain theoretical knowledge of effective health service management and regular workshops in each locality. There are separate training schemes for the NHS in Scotland, Wales and Northern Ireland.

Some private sector companies have their own graduate training programmes. It is also possible to enter at administrative level and work your way up to apply for a junior management post. Relevant professional qualifications include those offered by the Institute of Healthcare Management, such as a certificate in managing in health and social care and the award for first line managers.

Mature entrants include those who are already working in the NHS who may apply to their local schemes office for information about the graduate management training scheme. Entrants include those in clinical practice (doctors, nurses etc) or administrators. Others from outside the health service, usually with at least a 2:2 relevant degree or degree-equivalent professional qualification, are also eligible to apply. Contact NHS Careers or the Institute of Healthcare Management for details of opportunities and courses.

Opportunities and Pay

You can work anywhere in the UK. The main employer is the national health service (NHS) but there are some opportunities for work in private healthcare or the armed forces. Promotion to senior levels is gained with experience, training and professional qualifications, but this is not automatic. Qualified and experienced managers may work overseas, such as in the Middle East.

Salaries can vary but starting salaries for graduates on the NHS training scheme are around £20k, and with experience earnings rise to between £26k-£31k a year. Senior managers, such as directors of a large health organisation earn in the region of £60k-£80k a year, and as a chief executive up to £100k.

Skills and Qualities

able to manage a budget and keep records, analytical skills, approachable, efficient, good communication skills, information handling skills, IT skills, problem-solving skills, resourceful

Relevant Subjects

Business and accounting, Economics, English, Government and politics, Health and social care, ICT/Computer studies, Law, Mathematics

Further Information

AGCAS: Government & Public Administration (Job Sector Briefing) (AGCAS) - www.prospects.ac.uk

Health Service Journal (EMAP) - www.hsj.co.uk/

Inside Careers Guide: Management - www.insidecareers.co.uk

NHS Careers (NHS Careers) - www.nhscareers.nhs.uk

NHS Careers Scotland - www.infoscotland.com/nhs

NHS Careers Wales - www.wales.nhs.uk

NHS Graduate Management Training Scheme - www.nhsgraduates.co.uk

TARGETjobs: Public Service (GTI Specialist Publishing Ltd.) - www.groupgti.com

Addresses
Central Services Agency
Human Resources, 2 Franklin Street, Belfast BT2 8DQ
Phone: +44 (0)28 9032 4431
Web: www.centralservicesagency.n-i.nhs.uk

Institute of Healthcare Management (IHM)
18-21 Morley Street, London SE1 7QZ
Phone: +44 (0)20 7620 1030
Web: www.ihm.org.uk

Similar Jobs
Accountant: Public Sector, GP Practice Manager, Health Promotion Specialist, Human Resources Officer/Manager, Local Government Administrator, Marketing Manager

Health Visitor
also known as: Nurse: Health Visitor, Nurse: Public Health
CRCI:Healthcare
CLCI:JAD Job Band: 3 to 5

Job Description
Health visitors (known as public health nurses in Scotland) are qualified registered nurses or midwives who work in the community promoting physical and mental health, social well-being, and advising on the prevention of illness. A key responsibility is for babies' welfare and development from when they leave the midwife's care until school age. They advise parents and carers on their baby or child's progress and development. Also give advice on aspects such as personal hygiene and in the home, care of young children, people with special needs, or the elderly. Health visitors also provide support and advice for those who are suffering from drug or alcohol abuse, HIV/Aids, or postnatal depression. They identify a clients' needs and arrange help.

May run clinics, such as ante/post-natal or child welfare clinics. Also liaise with social workers, local authority housing departments, Citizens' Advice Bureaux as well as other healthcare professionals. They monitor high-risk groups and plan the best way to meet local health needs. May supervise other team members, including community nursery nurses. Keep accurate records and write reports.

Work Details
Usually work a basic 37.5 hrs a week, between 9am-5pm, but may include some evening clinics and support groups. You work in a clinic and usually cover the geographical area of a GP practice so spend time visiting clients in their own home. Travel around the area is necessary. You advise and help people of all ages and abilities. There is contact with all kinds of people, often babies and pre-school children and their parents, and with people in need of support. You are responsible for health and the general welfare of people, and for organising your own workload and keeping records. Work requires coping with the sight of blood, and may be emotionally demanding.

Qualification

- **England, Wales and Northern Ireland**

Band 3: For entry to a diploma (a pre-registration programme): at least 5 GCSEs (A*-C) including English and a science subject. Relevant alternative academic and vocational qualifications are also acceptable.

Band 4: For entry to some registered nurse training courses: some colleges ask for more than the minimum 5 GCSEs (A*-C). A levels may also be required, sometimes in specific subjects, such as English and sciences. Equivalent qualifications may be accepted. Check with individual institutions.

Band 5: For a nursing degree course: 2-3 A levels and some GCSEs (A*-C) usually including English and maths, or equivalent. Exact requirements depend on the degree you take.

- **Scotland**

Band 3: For entry to a nursing diploma (a pre-registration programme): at least five S grades (1-3) including English and a science subject. Relevant alternative academic and vocational qualifications are also acceptable.

Band 4: For entry to registered nurse training: some colleges ask for more than the minimum five S grades (1-3) or similar. H grades may be required, sometimes in specific subjects such as English and sciences.

Band 5: For degree courses: 3-5 H grades and some S grades (1-3), usually including English and maths, or similar qualifications. Exact requirements depend on the degree you take.

Degree Information
A degree in nursing, nursing studies or public health leads to qualification as a registered nurse, which is followed by a post-registration course in health visiting. Some integrated nursing degree courses are available, leading to both health visitor and registered nurse qualifications. If you have a relevant first degree in natural or social science, there are a few courses providing appropriate nurse and health visitor qualifications. There are full and part-time postgraduate diplomas in Specialist Community Public Health Nursing.

Adult Qualifications
Before training as a health visitor, qualification as a registered nurse or midwife is required. Schools and colleges of nursing vary in their entry requirements for adult entry. Applicants who do not have the usual academic qualifications may be able to take an entrance test. A relevant vocational qualification at level 3 is usually acceptable. You may be able to use specific modular course credits from the Open University, or a specific Access to higher education course for entry to nursing/midwifery training. Some universities have special entry standards for mature applicants. Check with individual institutions for details.

Work Experience
The job is about rapport, communication and listening as much as the medical work. The NHS recommends that nurses wishing to move into health visiting and public health nursing spend time with a qualified practitioner to gain experience of the role, or to work as a community staff nurse. Prospective students are also recommended to read specialist journals such as Primary Health Care, which is available from the Royal College of Nursing.

Entry and Training
All applicants to health visitor training must first qualify as a registered nurse or midwife and usually need at least two years' relevant post registration experience, preferably working in obstetrics, midwifery or paediatrics. Some experience of working in community settings is also required. For full details of registered nurse training see the Nurse: Adult job article. Degree courses are available at some universities that include options for qualifying as a health visitor/public health nurse, as well as a registered nurse.

Training usually involves taking a specialist degree level course, which can be one-year full time or two years part time. The course includes information on public health, clinical supervision, and specialist options such as domestic violence and postnatal depression. Training continues on the job mentored by an experienced colleague, and appropriate short courses, such as immunisation and positive parenting. You need a driving licence for this job.

Health visitors have to renew their registration with the regulatory body, the Nursing and Midwifery Council, every three years and undertake continuing professional development of at least 35 hours of training during that period.

This job is particularly suitable for older, more experienced people. All entrants are required to be registered nurses. There are also various sources of funding for post-registration courses. 'Return to

Practice' programmes are also available for former registered nurses, midwives or health visitors wanting to return to work after a break of some years. Contact NHS Careers or your local NHS Trust for details of all training and funding opportunities.

Opportunities and Pay

You are usually employed by the NHS in rural, urban or inner city communities. Promotion can be to the management of a team of health visitors, or a manager within the NHS. There are further specialist courses on aspects of health visiting. Some go on to work in education and training. There may be opportunities to work part time and career breaks are common. Opportunities exist overseas for health visitors who have the required qualifications.

Pay can vary depending on the local health trust. Health visitors working for the NHS normally start on Band 6, earning £25k-£34k a year, rising to Band 7 (health visitor specialists) earning around £30k-£40k, or as much as £44k as a senior health visitor.

Health

This job requires a medical test on entry and good general fitness.

Skills and Qualities

able to explain clearly, able to get on with all kinds of people, able to put people at ease, able to work both on your own and in a team, calm, confident, good organisational skills, not squeamish, patient, responsible attitude

Relevant Subjects

Biology, Chemistry, English, Health and social care, Hospitality and catering, Psychology, Science, Sociology

Further Information

AGCAS: Health (Job Sector Briefing) (AGCAS) - www.prospects.ac.uk

Community Practitioner (CPHVA, monthly) (Ten Alps Publishing) - www.commprac.com/

Community Practitioners' and Health Visitors' Association - www.unitetheunion.com/cphva

NHS Careers (NHS Careers) - www.nhscareers.nhs.uk

NHS Careers Scotland - www.infoscotland.com/nhs

NHS Careers Wales - www.wales.nhs.uk

Nursing & Midwifery Uncovered (Trotman 2010) - www.trotman.co.uk

Open University - www.open.ac.uk

Public Health Nursing (6 x year) (Blackwell Publishing) - www.wiley.com/bw/subs.asp?ref=0737-1209

Royal College of Nursing Wales - www.rcn.org.uk/aboutus/wales

Skills for Health - sector skills council - www.skillsforhealth.org.uk

►Working in advice & counselling (2007) (Babcock Lifeskills) - www.babcock-lifeskills.com/

Addresses

Community Practitioners' and Health Visitors' Association (CPHVA)
Unite Transport House, 128 Theobald's Road, Holborn, London WC1X 8TN
Phone: +44 (0) 208 7611 2500
Web: www.amicus-cphva.org

Nursing and Midwifery Council (NMC)
23 Portland Place, London W1B 1PZ
Phone: +44 (0)20 7333 9333
Web: www.nmc-uk.org

Royal College of Nursing (RCN)
20 Cavendish Square, London W1G 0RN
Phone: +44 (0) 20 7409 3333
Web: www.rcn.org.uk

School of Nursing and Midwifery
Queens University Belfast, Medical Biology Centre, 97 Lisburn Road BT9 7BL
Phone: +44 (0)28 9097 2233
Web: www.qub.ac.uk/nur

Similar Jobs

Health Promotion Specialist, Midwife, Nurse: Adult, Nurse: Children, Nurse: District, Social Worker

Healthcare Assistant

also known as: Auxiliary Nurse, Clinical Support Worker, Nursing Assistant, Nursing Auxiliary

CRCI:Healthcare
CLCI:JAD'Job Band: 1 to 2

Job Description

Healthcare assistants (HCA) or auxiliary nurses (AN) work in a hospital or community clinic under the supervision of a qualified healthcare professional. The role depends on the area of employment but duties include helping qualified nurses to look after patients and assisting with a patient's overall comfort. Typical jobs include feeding, washing, toileting and dressing. Also make beds and empty bedpans, remove unclean bedlinen and towels, and replace with fresh supplies. May monitor patients by taking temperatures, pulse, respiration and weight. Control of infection is a very important part of the job.

HCAs put medical items out on trolleys for nurses and doctors to use. They accompany patients to other parts of the hospital for clinic appointments, X-ray or therapy treatments, keep the wards tidy and may also work with qualified midwives in maternity services. Some work with healthcare scientists helping them to investigate and treat disease.

Work Details

Usually work a basic 37.5 hr week over five days though may be expected to work some unsocial hours and shifts. Part-time and flexible working hours are common. You work in a hospital or a clinic and help people of all ages, including people who are in pain, upset or depressed. Work requires coping with the sight of blood, and you have to be on your feet with some lifting and bending. Work may be messy at times and you usually need to wear a uniform, except in wards for patients who are mentally ill. Protective aprons and gloves are often worn.

Qualification

- **England, Wales and Northern Ireland**

Band 1: For entry to jobs, no minimum qualifications are needed, but you are expected to have a good level of general education and relevant experience. Some formal/vocational qualifications at any level are useful.

Band 2: For entry to jobs, no minimum qualifications are needed, but it is an advantage to have some GCSEs (A*-C) or equivalent in subjects that include English and maths.

- **Scotland**

Band 1: For entry to jobs, no minimum qualifications are needed, but you are expected to have a good level of general education and relevant experience. Some formal/vocational qualifications at any level are useful.

Band 2: Although academic qualifications are not specified for this job, it is an advantage to have some S grades (1-3) in subjects that include English and maths, or similar.

Adult Qualifications

For some employers, formal qualifications may not be required for entry though you are expected to have a good standard of education. Previous experience in care work and first aid is useful.

Work Experience
Work experience gives you an insight into what you enjoy and don't enjoy about a job or working environment, as well as the opportunity to acquire new skills. It also provides valuable information to add to your CV and improves your course application and future employment prospects. There are often opportunities available for voluntary work in the NHS, which give you experience of work with people. Previous experience in a caring role is usually essential, especially if you plan to work with people who have mental health issues or learning disabilities.

Entry and Training
To enter this job you need to have a police check and may have to take an entrance test. It is an advantage to have experience in first aid and also working with people, such as shop work. Training is on the job under an experienced and qualified nurse, midwife or therapist, and possibly by short courses. It includes health and safety, hygiene, first aid, manual handling and patient skills. You may be able to gain S/NVQs level 2-3 in health and social care. Level 3 meets the minimum qualifications for entry into nurse training.

Mature entrants are particularly suited for this job. Those with experience of first aid and of working in a caring capacity or working with the public in other areas such as customer services, have an advantage. Government training opportunities, such as apprenticeships, may be available in your area. You can also gain recognition of previous experience through Accreditation of Prior Learning or by working towards relevant S/NVQs. Contact your local careers office, Jobcentre Plus, Next Step service or Learning and Skills Council (LSC)/Local Enterprise Company (LEC) for details of all training opportunities and schemes, including apprenticeships for adults.

Opportunities and Pay
You usually work for the NHS or a private residential or nursing home, a hospice or private care agency. The NHS employs over 220,000 assistants and demand is continuing to grow. With one to two years' experience as a healthcare assistant in the NHS plus an NVQ Level 3 in health, your employer may agree to second you for training as a nurse. On secondment, you receive a salary while you study. Your employer may expect you to work with them for around two years. There are also increasing opportunities to work as an assistant practitioner in the NHS.

Pay depends on who you work for and where you work but salaries generally start at around £13k a year, rising to £17k or more with experience.

Health
The work involves a risk of infection. This job may require a medical test on entry and you have to be physically fit.

Skills and Qualities
able to follow instructions, able to get on with all kinds of people, aptitude for teamwork, caring, cheerful, friendly, not squeamish, patient, practical skills, reassuring

Relevant Subjects
Biology, Health and social care, Science

Further Information
NHS Careers (NHS Careers) - www.nhscareers.nhs.uk

NHS Careers Scotland - www.infoscotland.com/nhs

NHS Careers Wales - www.wales.nhs.uk

Skills for Health - sector skills council - www.skillsforhealth.org.uk

So you want to work in Healthcare (Wayland) - www.waylandbooks.co.uk

Similar Jobs
Ambulance Care Assistant, Nurse: Adult, Occupational Therapy Assistant, Social Care Worker

Hearing Therapist
also known as: Rehabilitation Specialist: Audiology

CRCI:Healthcare

CLCI:JOD Job Band: 5

Job Description
Hearing therapists are advanced audiology practitioners who provide a comprehensive rehabilitation service for adults who have hearing impairment and/or associated difficulties and disorders, including loss or partial loss of hearing, balance problems and tinnitus. They use a variety of different techniques to work out an individual programme for each patient to improve their methods of communication in their work and socially. Give advice and counselling support to adults who have acquired a hearing loss or deficiency, or problems such as tinnitus.

Help clients to make the most of their residual hearing. This may involve giving advice about auditory equipment, including hearing aids and loop systems, and about using visual clues, such as lip reading. Also work with clients to alleviate the stress of living with hearing deficiency, and help them to cope with feelings of isolation and frustration in home, work and social environments.

Is a member of a team that works closely with ear, nose and throat (ENT) medical staff, audiological scientists, audiology technicians, speech therapists, and also liaise with statutory and non-statutory bodies such as social services, charitable organisations and patient organisations, to ensure patients' needs are met.

Work Details
Usually work a basic 37 hr week, Monday to Friday, but sometimes may need to be flexible if visiting a patient in their home. Part-time work may also be available. Your work involves meeting clients, assessing and advising them about how to improve communications with other people. You work with people in groups and individually. Your place of work may be a clinic, a hospital, medical centre or in other people's homes and you liaise with a team of medical staff and social workers.

Qualification
• England, Wales and Northern Ireland
Band 5: For degree courses in audiology: 3 A levels which should include a science subject and some GCSEs (A*-C), usually including English and maths, or equivalent. Exact requirements depend on the degree you take.

• Scotland
Band 5: For degree in audiology: 4-5 H grades including a science subject and some S grades (1-3), usually including English, maths and science subjects, or similar.

Degree Information
A BSc (Hons) degree in audiology is preferred followed by a validated MSc in rehabilitation studies. Check with the British Academy of Audiology for details of accredited degree and postgraduate courses.

Adult Qualifications
Entry requirements may be relaxed for adults applying for higher education courses. Access or foundation courses give adults without qualifications a route on to degree courses.

Work Experience
Work experience gives you an insight into what you enjoy and don't enjoy about a job or working environment, as well as the opportunity to acquire new skills. It also provides valuable information to add to your CV and improves your course application and future employment prospects. Working in a hospital environment is particularly useful. It is also useful to discuss this job with an employed audiologist/hearing therapist prior to embarking on any course of study.

Entry and Training
Maturity and relevant experience are expected, so this job is not usually available to young people. The BSc and MSc in audiology is the preferred route, but there may be a fast track route available for those with a relevant BSc in another science subject. New entrants to this profession are mainly graduates with a first degree in audiology, or are qualified and experienced audiologists. The Registration Council for Clinical Physiologists (RCCP) has a list of accredited courses.

The BSc degree in audiology takes four years, with year three spent on a full-time salaried placement in an NHS hearing clinic/department. During your degree you also complete a professional logbook that provides eligibility for registration as an audiologist with RCCP. Currently registration is voluntary, but in the future this may be one of the professions covered by the Health Professions Council and registration may be mandatory. However, registration with the HPC is required for hearing aid dispensers.

Following successful completion of the degree in audiology you must then take the vocational stage of training, which also includes studying for an MSc in audiology. You may have the opportunity to specialise in various areas of hearing therapy. Contact the British Academy of Audiology for details of all relevant training routes and accredited course information. You are expected to keep up to date through continuing professional development.

Maturity and relevant experience are needed and you are expected to have a British Academy of Audiology (BAA) accredited qualification such as a BSc (Hons) in audiology prior to entering training as a hearing therapist. Some postgraduate course entrants are experienced audiology technicians or audiologists, though those with experience/professional qualifications in related subject areas may also be considered. Contact the BAA for details of all relevant training routes and accredited course information.

Opportunities and Pay
This is a small and relatively new profession and currently there are only a few rehabilitation specialist/hearing therapist posts in the NHS. You usually work in an audiology department or at a community health centre. Some may visit patients in a residential home or in their own private homes.

A newly qualified hearing therapist working for the NHS earns from £21k-£27k a year. Specialists can earn up to £33k and senior therapists up to £45k a year.

Skills and Qualities
able to inspire confidence, able to understand other people's problems, aptitude for teamwork, clear speaking voice, emotionally strong, encouraging, good communication skills, good interpersonal skills, patient, reliable

Relevant Subjects
Business and accounting, English, Health and social care, Psychology, Science, Sociology

Further Information
Health Professions Council (HPC) - www.hpc-uk.org

NHS Careers (NHS Careers) - www.nhscareers.nhs.uk

NHS Careers Scotland - www.infoscotland.com/nhs

NHS Careers Wales - www.wales.nhs.uk

Registration Council for Clinical Physiologists (RCCP) - www.rccp.co.uk

Addresses
British Academy of Audiology (BAA)
Resources for Associations, Association House, South Park Road, Macclesfield, Cheshire SK11 6SH
Phone: +44 (0)1625 504066
Web: www.baaudiology.org

Similar Jobs
Audiological Scientist, Audiologist, Speech & Language Therapist

Heat Treatment Operative

CRCI:Engineering
CLCI:RAB Job Band: 2

Job Description
Heat treatment operatives work and oversee the furnaces used to apply heat treatments to metals to clean, temper or harden them. These metals are used to make parts for products such as cars, aircraft, tools and bicycles, etc. Operatives load and unload the furnace, using fork-lift trucks or hoists. Most furnaces are computer controlled. They also monitor the computers and products during the treatment process, setting and adjusting the temperature of the furnace. They prepare and clean the components, cool the components in salt, oil or chemical baths and test the finished parts for quality.

Operatives may also need to keep written as well as computer records. May be responsible for some of the maintenance of the furnaces and associated machinery. They work within strict health and safety guidelines and deal safely with waste materials.

Work Details
Usually work a basic 39-40 hr week that may include shifts, nights and weekends. You work in industrial premises where the environment may be hot, dirty and noisy, and there may be fumes. Much of the time is spent on your feet and you need to cope with a lot of physical activity, including lifting. There is a risk of accidents and you need to wear protective clothing.

Qualification
- **England, Wales and Northern Ireland**

Band 2: For entry to jobs, no minimum qualifications are needed, but it is an advantage to have some GCSEs (A*-C) or equivalent in subjects that include maths, English and science, or equivalent. Practical and technical subjects are also useful.

- **Scotland**

Band 2: Although academic qualifications are not specified for this job, it is an advantage to have some S grades (1-3) in subjects that include maths, English and science, or similar. Practical and technical subjects are also useful.

Adult Qualifications
Academic qualifications are not always needed, but it helps to have some formal qualifications at any level, including maths, English and a science, or relevant practical experience.

Work Experience
Relevant work or voluntary experience is always useful. It can add to your CV and improve your chances when applying for entry to jobs or apprenticeships in the engineering industry.

Entry and Training
Entrants usually start through an apprenticeship at age 16-17. However, some parts of the work may only be available to over 18s, because of health and safety issues. Some companies may require you to take an aptitude test. Training is both on the job and by day or block release to a local college to work towards relevant courses. You may work towards an S/NVQ in metal processing and allied operations at levels 2-3. Training can also be in-house under the supervision of experienced operatives and usually includes safety and elementary first-aid procedures.

Short courses are available from organisations and trade associations, such as the British Industrial Furnace Constructors Association and the Wolfson Heat Treatment Centre. Metskill is responsible for recruiting and training apprentices in South Yorkshire and the Midlands, and also looks nationally at delivering occupational standards for metal processing. Contact them for details of any available apprenticeships and vacancies in your area.

The Engineering Development Trust runs a range of nationwide schemes for 11-21 year olds who are interested in engineering as a career. See the website for details. A Diploma in engineering or manufacturing and product design may also be available in your area and provide an alternative route into this job.

Mature applicants with engineering or manufacturing experience may have an advantage. Government training opportunities, such as apprenticeships, may be available in your area. You can also gain recognition of previous experience through Accreditation of Prior Learning or by working towards relevant S/NVQs. Contact your local careers office, Jobcentre Plus, Next Step service or Learning and Skills Council (LSC)/Local Enterprise Company (LEC) for details of training schemes.

Opportunities and Pay

Work is mainly with manufacturing firms working in metals, or specialised heat treatment companies. There are also opportunities in construction, aerospace, defence, automotive and petrochemical sectors. Most firms are located in towns and cities throughout the UK. There are concentrations of this work in the Midlands, Yorkshire, the North East and South East, Belfast and parts of Scotland. There may be options for promotion to supervisory posts. The Contract Heat Treatment Association is a useful source of information for short term work.

Starting wages for apprentices are likely to be around £200 a week, rising to £28k a year with experience. The most skilled and experienced operatives can earn up to £40k a year. Overtime pay can make up a large proportion of your earnings.

Health

You have to be physically fit and have good stamina to do this job. Those who have respiratory problems may find it difficult to cope with the heat and fumes.

Skills and Qualities

able to follow instructions, good concentration level, health & safety awareness, IT skills, manual dexterity, methodical, numeracy skills, technical aptitude

Relevant Subjects

Design and technology, Engineering, Manufacturing, Mathematics, Physics, Science

Further Information

Apprenticeship Schemes (National Apprenticeship Service) - www.apprenticeships.org.uk

Contract Heat Treatment Association - www.chta.co.uk

Diplomas (Foundation, Higher and Advanced) - http://yp.direct.gov.uk/diplomas

International Heat Treatment and Surface Engineering (Maney Publishing) - www.maney.co.uk/index.php/journals/iht/

SEMTA - sector skills council for science, engineering and manufacturing technologies - www.semta.org.uk

Training Schemes - www.direct.gov.uk/en/educationandlearning

▶Working in manufacturing (2010) (Babcock Lifeskills) - www.babcock-lifeskills.com/

Addresses

British Industrial Furnace Constructors Association
National Metalforming Centre, 47 Birmingham Road, West Bromwich B70 6PY
Phone: +44 (0)121 601 6350
Web: www.bifca.org.uk

Engineering Development Trust (EDT)
Ridgeway, Welwyn Garden City, Hertfordshire AL7 2AA
Phone: +44 (0)1707 871520
Web: www.etrust.org.uk

Metskill
Units 5-6 Meadowcourt, Amos Road, Sheffield S9 1BX
Phone: +44 (0)114 244 6833
Web: www.metskill.co.uk

Wolfson Heat Treatment Centre
Federation House, 10 Vyse Street, Birmingham B18 6LT
Phone: +44 (0)121 237 1122
Web: www.sea.org.uk/whtc/

Similar Jobs

Blacksmith, Engineering Craft Machinist, Engineering Machine Operative, Foundry Moulder/Coremaker, Foundry Process Operative, Sheet Metal Worker

Heating & Ventilation Fitter/Welder

also known as: Ventilation Systems Fitter

CRCI:Building and Construction
CLCI:UJ — Job Band: 1 to 2

Job Description

Heating and ventilation fitters install, maintain and repair heating, air conditioning, ventilating and cooling systems. They work in commercial and industrial premises, such as hospitals, power stations and office blocks. Fitters use detailed drawings to assemble ducting (metal or plastic) and fittings, such as boilers, pipework, radiators and control systems. May cut pipes with flame-cutting tools. Pipes are joined by soldering or welding, pumps and valves are fitted, and checks are carried out to detect any leaks. Fitters work closely with ductwork installers.

The system is tested to make sure it is running as it should. Work can be on the sites of new buildings, or making changes or repairs to existing ones.

Work Details

Heating and ventilation fitters usually work a basic 39 hr week, Monday to Friday, though may be expected to work some evenings and at weekends to complete jobs. You may also need to be on call. The work can be in all types of building and usually involves travel to different sites. Work is mainly indoors, though may be outside at times and in all types of weather. Hand and power tools, soldering/welding equipment and saws are used in this job. You must be physically fit and able to lift heavy equipment and bend and kneel comfortably.

May need to work at heights on scaffolding or ladders. The workplace can be dirty, dusty, cold, damp and possibly cramped and enclosed as you may need to work underneath flooring. This work requires you to wear overalls and sometimes safety glasses and a protective helmet.

Qualification

• England, Wales and Northern Ireland

Band 2: Although academic qualifications are not always specified, some employers and colleges ask for 3-4 GCSEs (A*-D) in English, maths and a science or craft/technical subject, or equivalent.

• Scotland

Band 2: Although academic qualifications are not always specified, some employers and colleges ask for 3-4 S grades (1-4) in English, maths and a science or craft/technical subject, or similar.

Adult Qualifications

Those with relevant work experience may be accepted for some college courses without meeting any formal entry requirements.

Work Experience

Relevant work or voluntary experience is always useful and can improve your chances when applying for entry to construction jobs and apprenticeships. A local heating firm may offer you the opportunity to help with general tasks or you might wish to have a Saturday/holiday job working in a building supplies centre to gain knowledge of industry terms and materials. Health and safety issues may mean that there are certain jobs you cannot do until you are over 16. Contact your local Construction Skills office for advice.

Entry and Training

Most people aged 16-19 enter this work through an apprenticeship scheme, leading to a level 2/3 qualification in installation. You may have to take an entrance test in literacy and numeracy before beginning training. Training is on the job at your workplace and probably includes a day or block-release course at a local college. The Heating and Ventilating Contractors' Association has details of where you can do appropriate courses on its website. You work towards registration for an Engineering Services SKILLcard, which gives you industry-wide recognition of your skills, competence and qualifications.

A Diploma/Welsh Baccalaureate in construction and the built environment may be available in your area. S/NVQs are available at level 2-3 in mechanical engineering services (heating and ventilating installation). Relevant technical certificates are also available such as the certificate in heating and ventilating installation. Training programmes, including apprenticeships leading to level 2, and advanced apprenticeships at level 3 lead towards higher qualifications. Contact SummitSkills for details of all training routes.

Mature applicants with skills and experience in, for example, engineering, plumbing or metal work, may have an advantage for training. Government training opportunities may be available in your area. You can also gain recognition of previous experience through Accreditation of Prior Learning (APL) or by working towards relevant S/NVQs. Contact your local careers office, Jobcentre Plus, Next Step service or Learning and Skills Council (LSC)/Local Enterprise Company (LEC) for details of training schemes, including apprenticeships for adults.

Opportunities and Pay

Most fitters work for a firm of heating and ventilation engineers, a building contractor or a local authority. Some are self-employed. There is increased demand in the servicing and maintenance industry. With relevant qualifications and experience you can become a supervisor or instructor. Or you can train as a technician in building services.

Pay varies depending on area and employer. Trainees earn around £14k a year, rising to around £18k-£24k with experience. Overtime pay is possible on top of your salary.

Health

You have to be physically fit to do this job and you need normal colour vision for electrical work.

Skills and Qualities

able to follow drawings and plans, accurate measuring and calculating skills, aptitude for teamwork, head for heights, health & safety awareness, practical skills, strong, technical aptitude

Relevant Subjects

Construction and built environment, Design and technology, Mathematics, Physics, Science

Further Information

Apprenticeship Schemes (National Apprenticeship Service) - www.apprenticeships.org.uk

Careers Fact Sheets (SummitSkills) (SummitSkills) - www.summitskills.org.uk/

ConstructionSkills - sector skills council for the construction industry - www.cskills.org

Diplomas (Foundation, Higher and Advanced) - http://yp.direct.gov.uk/diplomas

Engineering Services SKILLcard - www.skillcard.org.uk

Summitskills - sector skills council for building services engineering - www.summitskills.org.uk

Training Schemes - www.direct.gov.uk/en/educationandlearning

Welsh Baccalaureate - www.wbq.org.uk

▶Working in construction & the built environment (2007) (Babcock Lifeskills) - www.babcock-lifeskills.com/

Addresses

Building Engineering Services Training
The Priory, Stomp Road, Burnham, Bucks SL1 7LW
Phone: +44 (0)1628 607800
Web: www.best-ltd.co.uk

Chartered Institution of Building Services Engineers (CIBSE)
222 Balham High Road, Balham, London SW12 9BS
Phone: +44 (0)20 8675 5211
Web: www.cibse.org

Heating and Ventilating Contractors' Association
ESCA House, 34 Palace Court, London W2 4JG
Phone: +44 (0) 020 7313 4900
Web: www.hvca.org.uk

Similar Jobs

Engineer: Building Services, Engineer: Thermal Insulation, Gas Service Engineer, Plumber, Refrigeration/Air Conditioning Technician, Welder

Helicopter Pilot: Commercial

CRCI:Transport and Logistics
CLCI:YAB — Job Band: 3 to 5

Job Description

Helicopter pilots monitor equipment and instruments enabling them to fly helicopters, and on larger helicopters direct crew members. They study the flight plan, check weather conditions and any airspace restrictions. Before take-off, they calculate fuel requirements and maximum payload. Also supervise refuelling. During the flight, they must monitor the instruments and keep watch for other aircraft. Maintaining radio contact with air traffic control during take-off and whilst in the air is very important. They are responsible for the safety and comfort of any passengers and crew.

At the end of each day helicopter pilots must complete duty hours and flight log books (logs). Work is varied and can include air ambulance work, taking critically injured or ill people to hospital, ferrying workers to and from offshore installations, work in the police force assisting those on the ground to catch criminals, or survey from the air work. Other pilots are employed in taking business people to destinations within the UK and mainland Europe, and some work for pleasure flight companies.

Work Details

Pilots fly under strict air safety rules which limit maximum flying time and 'on duty' time. Work is usually on a rota basis and you have to cope with sitting for hours in an enclosed space, which can be very noisy. You can travel worldwide and often need to spend nights away from home. There is a risk of accidents. A uniform and earphones are usually worn.

Qualification

• England, Wales and Northern Ireland

Band 3: For entry to integrated courses at an approved flight training organisation (FTO): a minimum of 5 GCSEs (A*-C) including English, maths and a physical science, preferably physics. Equivalent qualifications may also be considered.

Band 4: For direct entry: a minimum of two A levels and 5 GCSEs (A*-C) including English and maths, or equivalent. You also need to pass an aptitude test.

Band 5: For degree courses: 2-3 A levels and some GCSEs (A*-C) usually including English and maths, or equivalent. Exact requirements depend on the degree you take.

- **Scotland**

Band 3: For entry to integrated courses at an approved flight training organisation: a minimum of five S grades (1-3) in English, maths and a physical science, preferably physics, or similar.

Band 4: For entry: a minimum of three H grades and five S grades (1-3) including English and maths, or similar.

Band 5: For degree courses: 3-5 H grades and some S grades (1-3), usually including English and maths, or similar qualifications. Exact requirements depend on the degree you take.

Degree Information

Any degree is acceptable although not essential: subjects such as physics, aeronautical engineering, mathematics, computing subjects, meteorology or systems and control engineering give a useful background.

Adult Qualifications

Flying experience with the armed forces or a Private Pilot's Licence (PPL) are essential.

Work Experience

Entry to this job is highly competitive. It does improve your chances at interview if you have some work experience in anything that is related, such as airport work, particularly linked to air traffic control or meteorology. However, work experience is very hard to gain in this job.

Entry and Training

All applicants for training must be over the age of 17. You must be at least 18 to work as a helicopter pilot. Many candidates for training have degrees. Across Europe, all pilots are required to be licensed by the Joint Aviation Authority (JAA) before being able to fly or command any aircraft away from a recognised training course. In the UK, JAA licences are issued and enforced by the Civil Aviation Authority (CAA).

To work as a professional pilot you must have a Commercial Pilot's Licence (Helicopter) - CPL(H), which is only achieved via courses at an approved flight training organisation. Commercial pilots must also obtain the CAA Class One Medical Certificate. Training courses are expensive (around £45k) and include flying and ground instruction of around 100 hours. Occasionally, sponsorship may be available.

It is also possible to gain a Private Pilot's Licence (Helicopter) - PPL(H) at a cost of around £10k, which allows you to fly, but not for 'hire' or 'reward'. This can be converted to a CPL(H) through a modular professional scheme. You then need to take an annual proficiency test.

CAA-approved integrated CPL(H) courses are offered at training schools throughout the UK. A full list is available from the British Helicopter Association (BHA). Full time courses take about nine months but can also be completed part time over a longer period. It is also possible for to achieve a 'frozen' Airline Transport Pilot Licence (Helicopter) - ATPL(H) as well as a CPL(H). Pilots are awarded the full ATPL(H) when they have 1,000 hours flying experience, including 250 hours as a pilot in command. Pilots need an ATPL(H) to be able to fly on multi-pilot, multi-engine helicopters.

You can also train to fly helicopters with HM Forces. All pilots must continue training throughout their career to keep up to date with new aircraft, instruments and technology. Contact the BHA for full entry and training details.

There is no upper age limit for training to achieve the commercial pilot's licence - CPL(H). However, entrants over the age of 27 are unlikely to qualify for any sponsored training programmes and medical requirements are strict. Those who have previously trained and qualified as a helicopter pilot in the armed forces may take a bridging course for the ATPL(H).

Opportunities and Pay

There are over 1,000 professional helicopter pilots in the UK, mostly employed by helicopter operators in the south and south-east of England and east of Scotland. They may be employed to transport people or goods, or charter services flying passengers for pleasure or business trips. Many are employed to work offshore re-supplying and ferrying employees on oil or gas rigs, or are involved in the spraying of crops. Some pilots are employed by the emergency services such as police and ambulance or in the armed forces. Ex-military pilots have an advantage because of their experience.

Competition is intense but prospects for young civil pilots are improving. Self-employment and freelance work is common. There are also a few opportunities for work abroad. Currently, there is a demand for well qualified helicopter pilots but you may need to move between companies to progress. Experienced pilots can go on to become instructors. Income is variable and determined by the type of employment. Usually additional allowances are paid for overnight periods away from home or work in inhospitable areas.

Newly qualified pilots can earn around £25k a year. Experienced pilots carrying passengers, may earn around £45k-£75k a year and top captains working for large airlines may earn even more.

Health

Applicants must take a medical test and there are regular medical check-ups. This job requires a high standard of physical fitness, perfect colour vision, good hearing and eyesight.

Skills and Qualities

able to cope with emergencies, able to take responsibility, decisive, good concentration level, hand-to-eye co-ordination, information handling skills, quick reactions, sound judgement, spatial awareness, technical aptitude

Relevant Subjects

Engineering, English, Geography, ICT/Computer studies, Mathematics, Physics, Science

Further Information

A Career in Aviation (British Women Pilots' Association (BWPA)) - www.bwpa.co.uk/page7.html

AGCAS: Transport and Logistics (Job Sector Briefing) (AGCAS) - www.prospects.ac.uk

GoSkills - sector skills council for passenger transport - www.goskills.org

Joint Aviation Authorities Training Organisation (JAATO) - http://jaato.com

Starting a Career as Aircrew in Military Aviation (Air League) (Air League) - www.airleague.co.uk/scholarships.html

Addresses

Air League Educational Trust
Broadway House, Tothill Street, London SW1H 9NS
Phone: +44 (0)20 7222 8463
Web: www.airleague.co.uk

British Helicopter Association (BHA)
Graham Suite West Entrance Fairoaks Airport Chobham, Woking, Surrey GU24 8HX
Phone: +44 (0)1276 856 100
Web: www.britishhelicopterassociation.org/

British Women Pilots' Association
c/o Brooklands Museum, Brooklands Rd, Weybridge, Surrey KT13 0QN
Web: www.bwpa.co.uk/

Cabair Group of Aviation Companies
Elstree Aerodrome, Borehamwood, Hertfordshire WD6 3AQ
Phone: +44 (0)20 8236 2400
Web: www.cabair.com/

Civil Aviation Authority (CAA)
HR Department London Team Room 703 CAA House
45-59 Kingsway WC2B 6TE
Phone: +44 (0)20 7453 6040
Web: www.caa.co.uk/

Similar Jobs
Airline Pilot: Civil, Pilot: Armed Forces, RAF Officer, Royal Navy Officer

Highways Agency Traffic Officer

also known as: Traffic Officer

CRCI:Transport and Logistics
CLCI:YAD Job Band: 3

Job Description

Highways agency traffic officers patrol motorways to keep traffic moving around collisions and make road users' journeys as safe as possible. At the start of each shift they have a handover briefing from the previous shift and check over the highways vehicle. Officers keep in touch at all times with the regional control centre, which then passes relevant information on to the police. When an incident occurs, they work with the police to deal with traffic problems. In the case of a major incident, may close roads if needed. Also remove debris and abandoned vehicles from the carriageway.

Traffic officers are supported by regional control centre operators. They deal directly with the public, helping them in the event of a breakdown or a collision. May also deal with incidents where pedestrians are on the motorway, ensuring they are as safe as possible or removed if necessary.

Work Details

You work a shift pattern so that the motorways are patrolled 24 hours a day, 365 days a year. Shift patterns can either be a three shift pattern of early, late and night shifts, or a double day pattern of early and late shifts. Officers regularly work weekends and bank holidays.

Most of the shift involves driving around in a vehicle with high visibility markings. Depending on incidents, a lot of the work can also be outside in all weather conditions. You need to be able to keep calm to deal with incidents and may sometimes see unpleasant sights at the scene of accidents. The job can be stressful at times. You are provided with a uniform.

Qualification

- **England, Wales and Northern Ireland**

Band 3: For entry: usually 5 GCSEs (A*-C) including English and maths, or equivalent.

Adult Qualifications

Mature entrants are expected to have 5 GCSEs (A*-C), usually including English and maths, or equivalent qualifications.

Work Experience

Relevant work or voluntary experience is always useful and can improve your employment prospects when applying for entry to jobs. Any work experience involving driving or dealing with the public is an advantage.

Entry and Training

There is no minimum age of entry for this job, but you must have at least two years' driving experience, particularly on motorways, and no more than three points on your licence at the time of application. Experience of a customer-focused role is also important. You need to complete an application form and then have a competency-based interview that relates directly to the competencies needed for the job. You also need to live less than an hour's drive from your work location. If accepted you also have a Criminal Records Bureau (CRB) check.

Training starts with a foundation training course at the central traffic learning centre in Quinton, Birmingham. This course is usually residential and includes dealing with the public, patrolling and how to deal with a closure of the motorway. You can also take a Certificate in Traffic Management at level 3 accredited by City & Guilds. Once initial training is completed, you gain more experience and training on the job and occasionally have to attend short courses organised by the Highways Agency.

Mature applicants are welcomed, particularly those who have considerable experience of driving and dealing with the public in a customer-focused role.

Opportunities and Pay

Traffic officer jobs are with the Traffic Officer Service of the Highways Agency, which was set up to ease congestion on the English motorway network. There are regional centres in Birmingham, Nottingham, Warrington, Wakefield, Hertfordshire, Surrey and Avonmouth, and you are based in one of these. After some experience on the job it is possible to move up to a team leader position.

Starting salaries for traffic officers are around £18k a year, plus up to 20% shift allowance and an additional allowance for those based in the South East. Team leaders earn around £24k plus allowances.

Health

All entrants to this work have to have a medical. You need to be fit and have good eyesight, especially night vision.

Skills and Qualities

able to cope with emergencies, conscientious, enthusiastic, even tempered, good communication skills, good driving skills, good interpersonal skills, initiative, self-motivated

Further Information

AGCAS: Transport and Logistics (Job Sector Briefing) (AGCAS) - www.prospects.ac.uk

GoSkills - sector skills council for passenger transport - www.goskills.org
Highways Agency - www.highways.gov.uk

Similar Jobs

Driver: Lorry, Driver: Van, Police Officer

Holiday Centre Worker

CRCI:Leisure, Sport and Tourism
CLCI:GAJ Job Band: 1

Job Description

Holiday centre workers work in one of the many services that are offered for people staying at a holiday park or centre. They may work in areas such as sports, leisure, entertainments and nursery services. Some welcome new arrivals to the centre, show them to their accommodation and provide information on the holiday centre environment, activities and services. Others may arrange a programme of entertainment and activities for the guests. They may organise games, trips and competitions for people of all ages and abilities. Some workers entertain the holidaymakers by appearing in shows or other social activities, where they sing, dance or play a musical instrument.

May also help to look after swimming pools, sports and adventure playgrounds and can act as a group leader, encouraging people to join in and mix with others. Sorts out any guest problems or refers to a supervisor. May also work in guest catering, environmental or accommodation services, retail catering, shops and supermarkets, security or technical services.

Work Details

Holiday centres usually cater for families, so this job suits people who like working with children. You are expected to work unsocial hours, including evenings, weekends and possibly shifts. Most people need to live in the hotel or holiday centre where they are working. You entertain all age groups and are responsible for their safety when they take part in organised activities. You may have to deal with complaints and work is stressful at times. Coping with emergencies and with the sight of blood may be necessary if participants are injured.

Your workplace can be noisy and sometimes you may need to work outside in all kinds of weather. You have to cope with being active most of the time. A uniform is usually provided.

Qualification

• England, Wales and Northern Ireland

Band 1: For entry to jobs, no minimum qualifications are needed, but you are expected to have a good level of general education and relevant experience. Some formal/vocational qualifications at any level are useful.

• Scotland

Band 1: For entry to jobs, no minimum qualifications are needed, but you are expected to have a good level of general education and relevant experience. Some formal/vocational qualifications at any level are useful.

Adult Qualifications

No qualifications are needed, but experience of working with people is helpful. You can improve your skills and qualifications by working through the Foundation Learning programme. This involves taking credit-based units and qualifications to help you progress.

Work Experience

Any work experience can equip you with skills that you can use in the future and add to your CV. This can either be unpaid or voluntary, holiday or part-time work that you have organised yourself. Experience that demonstrates an enthusiasm for this type of work is useful, such as running a youth club or play scheme.

Entry and Training

Applicants are usually 18 or over, though minimum age requirements for this job may vary. It is an advantage to have experience in sport, music or of working with children. It is also useful to be good at speaking to groups of people. No minimum qualifications are required. However, there are a range of courses you can take that are relevant to this job, which may help you to enter and progress within the industry. Some jobs may require you to have specific qualifications, such as early years qualifications for some of the nursery and childcare jobs.

Training is on the job through an employer's in-house training scheme. You also take part in an induction programme to introduce you to the services and guest facilities. Short courses usually include health and safety and guest/customer care. Some employers offer management training schemes to workers that demonstrate an aptitude for the job. You can progress to supervisor-level training. This takes place on the job, and with an experienced employee and may be followed by further training to become head of a department/section.

Relevant qualifications include GCSE/S grades in leisure and tourism, a BTEC national certificate or diploma in sport and active leisure or travel and tourism, and relevant S/NVQs. For example, you can work for a level 2 NVQ in sport, recreation and allied occupations: activity leadership or operational services. Courses consist of core units in health and safety and session planning. There are many optional units to choose from such as developing customer relationships or supporting the development of the sport or activity.

Training programmes, including apprenticeships and advanced apprenticeships in travel and tourism services or active leisure and learning, may be available in your area. Contact the sector skills councils People 1st or SkillsActive for further details. Relevant Diplomas/Welsh Baccalaureates in travel and tourism, customer service and/or hospitality may also be available in your area.

Mature entrants are welcomed, though you must usually be physically fit and active. Those who have previously worked in the leisure industry may have an advantage. Adults may be able to enter this work through a government-funded training programme, such as an apprenticeship in travel and tourism or hospitality. Contact your local careers office, Jobcentre Plus, Next Step service or Learning and Skills Council (LSC)/Local Enterprise Company (LEC) for details of all training opportunities and schemes.

Opportunities and Pay

You work for a holiday company, such as Butlins, Center Parcs, or other similar firms. These are often located at the seaside, in the country or at other popular holiday resorts. Opportunities can be limited, but promotion to supervisor/management level from junior jobs is possible. Work abroad with international companies is also possible, including work on cruise ships.

Pay varies depending on area and employer, but most earn around £12k-£17k a year. You may be given free accommodation and food, and reduced price holidays. It may sometimes be difficult to earn a regular income as this job tends to be seasonal, with more work available in the summer.

Health

This job requires a good standard of physical fitness.

Skills and Qualities

able to cope with emergencies, able to get on with all kinds of people, energetic, enthusiastic, friendly, good organisational skills, helpful, patient, polite, sense of humour

Relevant Subjects

Leisure, travel and tourism

Further Information

Apprenticeship Schemes (National Apprenticeship Service) - www.apprenticeships.org.uk

Diplomas (Foundation, Higher and Advanced) - http://yp.direct.gov.uk/diplomas

Foundation Learning (QCDA) - www.qcda.gov.uk

Institute for Sport, Parks & Leisure (ISPAL) E-zine (ISPAL) - www.ispal.org.uk/ezine

Leisure Management Magazine (The Leisure Media Company) - www.leisuremanagement.co.uk

People 1st - sector skills council for hospitality, leisure, travel and tourism - www.people1st.co.uk

SkillsActive - sector skills council for active leisure, learning and well-being - www.skillsactive.com

Springboard UK (Springboard UK) - www.springboarduk.net

Springboard Wales (Springboard Wales) - http://wales.springboarduk.net/

UKSP - Guide to Success in Hospitality, Leisure, Travel & Tourism - www.uksp.co.uk/

▶Working in travel & tourism (2010) (Babcock Lifeskills) - www.babcock-lifeskills.com/

Addresses

Institute for Sport, Parks & Leisure (ISPAL)
Abbey Business Centre, 1650 Arlington Business Park, Theale, Reading RG7 4SA
Phone: 0844 418 0077 (UK only)
Web: www.ispal.org.uk

Institute of Sport & Recreation Management (ISRM)
and the National Association for Sports Development,
Sir John Beckwith Centre for Sport Loughborough University,
Leicestershire LE11 3TU
Phone: +44 (0)1509 226 474
Web: www.isrm.co.uk

Similar Jobs

Holiday Representative, Hotel Receptionist, Leisure Centre Assistant, Outdoor Activities Instructor, Pool Lifeguard, Theme Park Worker

Holiday Representative

also known as: Overseas Rep, Resort Representative, Travel Courier

CRCI:Leisure, Sport and Tourism
CLCI:GAX Job Band: 2 to 3

Job Description

Holiday representatives (reps) are responsible for the welfare of tourists on package holidays and ensuring that everything runs as smoothly as possible. Holiday reps stay in one place liaising between hotel staff/accommodation owners and clients to ensure the guests enjoy their holiday and that all arrangements are satisfactory. They usually meet and greet their guests at airports, arrange transfers to hotels or other accommodation and, when leaving, arrange transport back to the airport. Also advise on local facilities and tourist trips.

Holiday reps also arrange entertainment for guests either by directing or taking them to local sporting activities such as sailing, surfing, horse riding etc, or to nightclubs and restaurants. With fellow reps, may offer daily or weekly entertainment . This can include games and activities for young children, or entertainment for guests, including cabaret and karaoke nights. They may also arrange safe care for young children during the day and sell excursions and other related products such as hire cars.

Reps accompany groups on tour to visit different places, often travelling by coach. They deals with accommodation and transport, and point out places of interest. Both holiday reps and travel couriers deal with any problems that may occur such as lost travel documents, accidents and illness, disputes, travel delays and lost luggage. Also helps with language and currency problems. Must complete daily administration tasks, including paperwork, and also attend meetings with other company staff.

Work Details

Usually works unsocial and very long hours and are on call all the time you are away with a group of tourists. Travel may be necessary throughout the UK, Ireland, Europe, or worldwide, and you may need to stay away for long periods. You may be employed to work on a ship, in a hotel, or travel with a coach tour. You advise and help people, deal with complaints and cope with emergencies. Some people may be in need of support if they are ill, or need calming down if they become upset.

You are responsible for solving problems quickly, providing information on general or specific enquiries. Work can be very pressurised at times and there may be a risk of travelling accidents. You may need to wear a uniform.

Qualification

• England, Wales and Northern Ireland

Band 2: For entry to jobs, no minimum qualifications are needed, but it is an advantage to have some GCSEs (A*-C) or equivalent in subjects that include English and maths.

Band 3: For entry to jobs, HNC or a relevant Diploma, usually at least 4 GCSEs (A*-C) including English and maths and maybe a modern language, or equivalent.

• Scotland

Band 2: Although academic qualifications are not specified for this job, it is an advantage to have some S grades (1-3) in subjects that include English , maths and a modern language, or similar.

Band 3: For entry to jobs, usually at least four S grades (1-3) including English, maths, or similar.

Adult Qualifications

Relevant work experience with people is essential, such as nursing, reception, retail or travel agency work. Fluency in a foreign language is a distinct advantage.

Work Experience

Any work experience can equip you with skills that you can use in the future and add to your CV. Work experience can either be unpaid or voluntary or can be holiday or part-time work that you have organised yourself. This can be work in direct contact with the public such as retail experience, bar work, travel agency work, and any temporary or seasonal work in holiday centres both in the UK and abroad. Work with children and young adults, teamwork of any sort and administration experience are also valuable.

Entry and Training

Knowledge of a foreign language is an advantage and may be required by some employers. Some also require 6-12 months' customer service experience plus some administration experience. First aid qualifications may be expected for some jobs and experience in a related field, eg sporting activities or working with children, is an advantage. With the rise in popularity of skiing holidays, the ability to ski and/or snowboard is useful. Most tour operators also expect their resort representatives to hold a driving licence. A recognised nursery nurse qualification, such as those of the Council for Awards in Children's Care and Education (CACHE), is required for those wishing to work with children.

There are relevant vocational qualifications that you can take such as the BTEC National Award in Travel and Tourism, which may give you an advantage. You can study for the Holiday Rep Ticket Diploma which is an online training course that you can do in your spare time. The course is delivered in twelve modules and you are tested on completion of each one. There may be opportunities to gain these sorts of qualifications while on the job. A Diploma/ Welsh Baccalaureate may be available in your area in Travel and Tourism. Foundation degrees and Higher National Diplomas (HNDs) in travel and tourism are also available.

After a period of company induction and in-house training that usually lasts around 2-3 weeks, you are assigned to a resort under the supervision of experienced holiday reps. There is usually continuous on-the-job assessment by senior staff until you are considered to have sufficient experience to take more responsibility. Training programmes, including apprenticeship schemes in travel and tourism, may be available in your area. Many of the larger travel companies, e.g. Thomas Cook, offer apprenticeship schemes for 16-24 year olds, leading to a People 1st apprenticeship framework certificate in travel and tourism services. Advanced apprenticeships leading to qualification at level 3 can also be a route into higher education. Contact People 1st for further details.

Mature applicants may be preferred by some employers, especially if you have previous relevant experience in travel agency work, customer care or reception work in the hospitality and travel industries. Those with experience of living and working abroad, or with fluency in more than one language, may have an advantage. Government training opportunities, such as apprenticeships in travel and tourism, may be available in your area. You can also gain recognition of previous experience through Accreditation of Prior Learning (APL) or by working towards relevant S/NVQs. Contact your local careers office, Jobcentre Plus, Next Step service or Learning and Skills Council (LSC) Local Enterprise Company (LEC) for details of training schemes.

Opportunities and Pay

You are employed by a tour operator. This job is seasonal and you may be employed on a short-term contract. Work on a freelance basis is usually possible and opportunities abroad are generally good. There is stiff competition for places in the UK and promotion prospects are poor.

There are opportunities for resort representatives with responsibility in a specific area, for example, sporting activities, general entertainment, children, or the over 60s. Travel couriers can also specialise, for example, by working as a tour leader with trips of botanical or historical interest, or as an adventure trek leader. Some travel couriers become self-employed and work as tourist guides.

Pay varies enormously depending on the tour operator, and can be increased by tips from appreciative tourists. Trainees or newly recruited representatives are likely to earn from around £550-£650 a month. Salaries rise to around £11k-£15k a year with experience. Managers or supervisors can earn up to £25k a year. You are usually given free accommodation and perks such as subsidised travel and meals, and a percentage of any excursion sales you make.

Health
This job requires good general fitness.

Skills and Qualities
able to cope with emergencies, able to get on with all kinds of people, able to manage people, enthusiastic, friendly, good organisational skills, helpful, self confident, self-reliant, tolerant

Relevant Subjects
English, Geography, Leisure, travel and tourism, Modern Foreign Languages

Further Information
Apprenticeship Schemes (National Apprenticeship Service) - www.apprenticeships.org.uk

Career in Travel (Career in Travel) - www.careerintravel.co.uk

CareerScope: Hospitality and Leisure (Springboard UK) - http://careerscope.springboarduk.net/

Diplomas (Foundation, Higher and Advanced) - http://yp.direct.gov.uk/diplomas

Holiday Rep Ticket (Career in Travel) - www.holidayrepticket.co.uk

People 1st - sector skills council for hospitality, leisure, travel and tourism - www.people1st.co.uk

Real Life Guide to Travel and Tourism (Trotman) - www.trotman.co.uk

So you want to work in Travel & Tourism (Wayland) - www.waylandbooks.co.uk

The Diploma in Travel and Tourism - www.tandtdiploma.co.uk

Thomas Cook - www.thomascook.com

UKSP - Guide to Success in Hospitality, Leisure, Travel & Tourism - www.uksp.co.uk/

▶ Working in travel & tourism (2010) (Babcock Lifeskills) - www.babcock-lifeskills.com/

Addresses
CACHE: Council for Awards in Children's Care & Education
Apex House, 81 Camp Road, St Albans AL1 5GB
Phone: 0845 347 2123 (UK only)
Web: www.cache.org.uk

Institute of Travel and Tourism (ITT)
PO Box 217, Ware, Hertfordshire SG12 8WY
Phone: +44 (0)844 4995 653
Web: www.itt.co.uk

Similar Jobs
Air Cabin Crew, Airline Customer Service Agent, Holiday Centre Worker, Tour Operator, Tourist Guide, Tourist Information Centre Assistant

Homeopath

CRCI:Healthcare
CLCI:JOD
Job Band: 4 to 5

Job Description
Homeopaths are skilled in a complementary and holistic therapy that treats patients with small doses of natural remedies to stimulate the body's own healing powers. They obtain full personal and clinical details and undertake any necessary tests. Homeopathy use the principle that 'like cures like' to prescribe substances that would produce the patient's symptoms if they were given to a healthy person. Homeopaths prescribe natural substances, such as plants and minerals, as well as animal sources, in the form of liquids, tablets or granules that are available from the practitioner, a chemist or appropriate health company.

They treat a wide range of health conditions or emotional and psychological problems, such as asthma, toothache, digestive disorders, eczema and other skin conditions, arthritis, depression and anxiety. Also advise on exercise, diet and general lifestyle. Many homeopaths are also qualified doctors and can offer a choice of treatment. Treatment can be short or last weeks, months or years, depending on the condition.

Work Details
Usually works 9am-5pm, Monday to Friday, though may also offer evening and Saturday appointments. Many homeopaths are self-employed and therefore vary their working hours/days, and some combine this work with another job. You usually work in consulting rooms, a hospital or in your own home. You examine patients, and advise and help people. There is contact with a wide variety of clients who may be ill, in pain or distressed. You are responsible for the health and general welfare of people so work can be emotionally stressful at times.

Qualification
Homeopaths can be medically qualified with additional homeopathy training, or can specifically train. You do not need a degree or HND to train, but must usually be over 21.

• England, Wales and Northern Ireland
Band 4: For approved training courses: 1-2 A levels, usually in science subjects and particularly biology, and some GCSEs (A*-C) usually including English and maths, or equivalent.

Band 5: For a degree followed by approved training course: usually 2-3 A levels and some GCSEs (A*-C) or equivalent. Degree courses in medicine, dentistry and veterinary science require more qualifications, with specific science subjects. Exact requirements depend on the degree you take.

• Scotland
Band 4: For approved training courses: usually 2-3 H grades and some S grades (1-3) are required. H grades in science subjects are preferred, and biology is particularly useful.

Band 5: For a degree followed by approved training course : 3-5 H grades and some S grades (1-3), usually including English. Degree courses in medicine, dentistry and veterinary science require more qualifications, with specific science subjects. Exact requirements depend on the degree you take.

Degree Information
The Faculty of Homeopathy trains those with degrees in medicine, dentistry or veterinary medicine. For other courses, degrees or professional qualifications in nursing, medical sciences or other complementary medicines are an advantage. Teaching or social work courses provide a useful background.

Adult Qualifications
Mature applicants are judged on their own merits. Life and work experience is important. A science background, preferably with study to A level standard, or experience in nursing or a medical field is useful. An Access or foundation course can provide a route to higher education for those without the usual entry qualifications.

Work Experience
Relevant work or voluntary experience is always useful and can improve your chances in application for entry to this career. Consider working with the public or with people in a helping capacity. Work in a medical field such as volunteering at a hospital

is also relevant. Obviously, time spent with a qualified homeopathic practitioner is ideal, but, as with doctors, there may be issues surrounding patient confidentiality.

Entry and Training

Professional homeopathic courses are not open to school leavers. Applicants must be over the age of 21 before starting a course. There are several colleges offering training in the UK, but you need to check that the course is recognised by one of the professional organisations such as the Society of Homeopaths (SOH), and leads to professional registration. Training courses are part time over four years or full time over three years. Many applicants have relevant degrees or professional qualifications. The part-time courses are based on home study, with intensive college weekends. All courses require completion of a significant number of hours of supervised clinical experience. The SOH can supply a list of approved courses that include diplomas and degree courses.

If you are already qualified as a doctor, dentist, chiropodist/ podiatrist, pharmacist, nurse or vet, the Faculty of Homeopathy offers a short postgraduate course accredited by the British Homeopathic Association. There are accredited postgraduate level training courses in the UK, at Bristol, Glasgow, London and York. Students do not automatically receive grants for training courses and most are self-financing, so training costs can be substantial. Bursaries and loans may be available from the relevant professional associations.

The Homeopathic Medical Association (HMA) requires members to have a qualification in homeopathy, plus 100 hours of supervised practise. Applicants submit a number of case studies, have an interview with the HMA and may be observed at work. The Complementary and Natural Healthcare Council is the voluntary regulator of all complementary therapies in the UK, and once qualified, you can apply to join the CHNC Register.

A Diploma/Welsh Baccalaureate in society, health and development may be available in your area and may be relevant to this job.

Mature entrants are often those who want a career change, and it is possible to enter some courses without the required qualifications. If you have relevant work experience, including voluntary work, and can demonstrate an enthusiasm for homeopathy you may have an advantage, particularly if you do not have the required academic qualifications for entry to courses. A number of centres offer distance-learning courses in homeopathy.

Opportunities and Pay

This is a fast-growing profession and opportunities are available throughout the UK and abroad. There are around 2,000 registered homeopaths in the UK. You may set up in business for yourself or with a business partner, or you can be employed in the NHS. A small but increasing number of homeopaths work in GP surgeries. Some go on to train in another therapy as well and set up in business with other health professionals.

As most homeopaths are self-employed it is difficult to summarise earnings. Broadly speaking, you may charge between £35-£75 a session, depending on location and experience. Annual earnings tend to be from around £18k-£30k, although some may earn up to £50k a year, or more.

Health

This job requires good colour vision for certain areas of work.

Skills and Qualities

business awareness, good communication skills, good listening skills, methodical, observant, patient, reassuring, scientific approach, sound judgement, tactful

Relevant Subjects

Biology, Chemistry, English, Health and social care, Psychology, Science

Further Information

AGCAS: Health (Job Sector Briefing) (AGCAS) - www.prospects.ac.uk

British Homeopathic Association - www.britishhomeopathic.org

Complementary and Natural Healthcare Council (CNHC) - www.cnhc.org.uk

Diplomas (Foundation, Higher and Advanced) - http://yp.direct.gov.uk/diplomas

Welsh Baccalaureate - www.wbq.org.uk

Addresses

British Homeopathic Association
Hahnemann House 29 Park Street West, Luton,
Bedfordshire LU1 3BE
Phone: +44(0) 1582 408675
Web: www.trusthomeopathy.org

Homeopathic Medical Association
Administration Office 7 Darnley Road, Gravesend,
Kent DA11 0RU
Phone: +44 (0)1474 560 336
Web: www.the-hma.org

Society of Homeopaths
11 Brookfield, Duncan Close, Moulton Park,
Northampton NN3 6WL
Phone: 0845 450 6611(UK only)
Web: www.homeopathy-soh.org

Similar Jobs

Acupuncturist, Aromatherapist, Doctor: General Practitioner, Medical Herbalist, Naturopath, Reflexologist

Horse Groom

CRCI:Environment, Animals and Plants
CLCI:WAM
Job Band: 1 to 2

Job Description

Horse grooms are responsible for the good health and well-being of horses in their care. They also maintain the stables and tack (riding equipment), feed the horses with prepared feed and give them water. They groom them using specialist hand tools and check for any injury or disease. Also help to take care of sick horses and foals. Grooms give the horses exercise by riding them and may also go with others on a ride, and sometimes on foot. They may help to clean out the stables and look after the saddles and bridles using a variety of equipment.

Grooms prepare the horses for riding lessons or for competitive shows. They work closely with stable or farm managers, private owners as well as those who train the horses. May also help with training and breeding work.

Work Details

A basic working week is 40 hrs, that includes early mornings, and usually weekends and public holidays. Works inside stables and also outdoors in all sorts of weather. It can be cold, wet, smelly, dirty and dusty. Grooms need to be fit, energetic and cope with heavy lifting, eg bales of hay. Travelling around the country to attend competitions or races may be necessary. Grooms often live in to be close to the horses, so you may be offered accommodation. There is a risk of injury; you may be bitten or kicked by horses, or can fall when riding. Protective clothing is worn, such as a hard hat and body protector.

Qualification

- **England, Wales and Northern Ireland**

Band 1: For entry to jobs, no minimum qualifications are needed, but you are expected to have a good level of general education and relevant experience. Some formal/vocational qualifications at any level are useful.

Band 2: For entry to jobs, no minimum qualifications are needed, but it is an advantage to have some GCSEs (A*-C) or equivalent in subjects that include English and maths.

- **Scotland**

Band 1: For entry to jobs, no minimum qualifications are needed, but you are expected to have a good level of general education and relevant experience. Some formal/vocational qualifications at any level are useful.

Band 2: Although academic qualifications are not specified for this job, it is an advantage to have some S grades (1-3) in subjects that include English and maths, or similar. Biology is also useful.

Adult Qualifications
You do not need any formal qualifications, but experience of working with horses or other animals is essential. Entry requirements are usually relaxed for mature applicants.

Work Experience
Relevant work or voluntary experience is always useful and can improve your employment prospects when applying for entry to jobs. You can apply to local riding schools, livery yards, equestrian centres or to holiday trekking and riding centres, for paid/unpaid work or voluntary experience.

Entry and Training
Many entrants go straight into this work and train on the job. A few training opportunities are available as a 'working pupil' where entrants agree a contract, recommended by the British Horse Society (BHS), with an employer and work towards an agreed level of training and qualification.

The BHS offers a range of qualifications in horse knowledge, care and riding at levels 1-3. For entry, you do not have to be able to ride, but you usually have to have worked with, and have an interest in horses, possibly in a Saturday or a holiday job. The Association of British Riding Schools (ABRS) has practical one-day examinations, leading to the ABRS Grooms Certificate/Diploma. The British Grooms Association (BGA) has developed an Equine Skills CV in association with Lantra. This enables those working in this field to record their achievements from Foundation to Elite level.

A Diploma/Welsh Baccalaureate may be available in your area in environmental and land-based studies. Horse grooms can work for S/NVQs in horse care (levels 1-2) and horse care management (level 3). Levels 2-3 give the basic qualification for employment in the horse industry. Level 3 in horse care management can be taken by qualified people who have responsibility for others and perhaps run a small yard. Relevant training programmes, including apprenticeship schemes, may be available in your area. Advanced apprenticeships leading to qualification at level 3 can also be a route into higher education.

Mature applicants, particularly with previous experience of working with horses are welcome. However, 'working pupil' contracts are usually more appropriate for younger applicants and school leavers. You may be able to benefit from government training programmes or gain recognition of previous experience through Accreditation of Prior Learning (APL) and by working towards relevant S/NVQs.

Opportunities and Pay
This is currently an expanding industry with most jobs in England, particularly in the South East. You can work at a riding school or holiday trekking centre. Other stables focus on sports eg polo, show jumping, dressage and hunting. There are stables at agricultural/equine colleges, livery stables that care for horses, and private stables. There are a limited number of grooms employed in zoos, circuses and stud/breeding establishments, and in the armed forces.

With some employers, promotion to head groom or stable management is possible. With BHS teaching qualifications, you can go on to work as a riding instructor. There are opportunities to work abroad, for which a second language is useful. Part-time and casual work is possible.

Pay varies hugely depending on area and employer. Starting salaries are usually based on the National Minimum Wage for your age, rising to £12k-£20k a year with experience.

Health
You have to be physically fit and have plenty of stamina to do this job.

Skills and Qualities
able to work both on your own and in a team, calm, good at handling animals, good communication skills, observational skills, patient, safety conscious, strong

Relevant Subjects
Biology, Land and Environment, Physical education and sport, Science

Further Information
Apprenticeship Schemes (National Apprenticeship Service) - www.apprenticeships.org.uk

Lantra - The Sector Skills Council for environmental & land-based sector (Lantra) - http:/www.lantra.co.uk

Lantra Careers (A Future In...) (Lantra) - www.afuturein.com

So you want to work with Animals (Wayland) - www.waylandbooks.co.uk

Training Schemes - www.direct.gov.uk/en/educationandlearning

Working with animals (2009) (Babcock Lifeskills) - www.babcock-lifeskills.com/

Working with Horses (BHS) (British Horse Society) - www.bhs.org.uk/

Addresses
Association of British Riding Schools (ABRS)
Queen's Chambers, 38-40 Queen Street, Penzance TR18 4BH
Phone: +44 (0)1736 369 440
Web: www.abrs-info.org

British Grooms Association (BGA)
PO Box 592, London KT12 9ER
Phone: 0845 331 6039
Web: www.britishgrooms.org.uk

British Horse Society (BHS)
Stoneleigh Deer Park, Kenilworth, Warwickshire CV8 2XZ
Phone: 0844 848 1666 (UK only)
Web: www.bhs.org.uk

British Horse Society Ireland
Contact via website,
Phone: +44 (0)2892 683801
Web: www.bhsireland.com

Similar Jobs
Animal Care Assistant, Jockey, Riding Instructor, Stable Hand, Zoo Keeper

Horse Trainer
also known as: Trainer - Horse

CRCI:Environment, Animals and Plants

CLCI:GAG — Job Band: 2 to 5

Job Description
Horse trainers prepare thoroughbred horses for competitive events and manage breeding programmes. They are responsible for training horses for flat racing or racing over hurdles or jumps and observe the horses in training carefully, before, during and after exercise. Plans a training, diet and fitness regime for each horse. Enters horses for the races for which they are most suitable and is responsible for the completion of all racing documents. Attends race meetings to ensure that horses arrive in peak condition and assesses their performance during racing. Must understand all the rules and regulations surrounding horse racing.

Horse Trainer

Horse trainers show owners round the yard and try to attract new owners who have horses to train. Selects and buys new horses for training. Has overall responsibility for the business development of the training yard. Carries out any office work related to this and manages the staff and facilities.

Work Details

Horse trainers work very long hours with early starts and weekend work being the norm. The work is outdoors in all weather conditions. Some time is also spent indoors in an office completing paperwork and running the business. National and international travel to race meetings is common and you can be away from home for several days.

You spend a lot of time dealing with owners, some of whom may be difficult if a horse is not performing well. You also liaise with veterinary staff where there is a health issue with a particular horse. While exercising the horses, you need to wear suitable clothing, such as a hard hat, boots and body protectors. Racing yards are located in rural environments.

Qualification

• England, Wales and Northern Ireland

Band 3: For entry to jobs, HNC or a relevant Diploma, usually at least 4 GCSEs (A*-C) including English and maths, or equivalent.

Band 4: For HND, Diploma of Higher Education or foundation degree: 1-2 A levels and some GCSEs (A*-C) usually including English and maths, or equivalent.

Band 5: For degree courses: 2-3 A levels and some GCSEs (A*-C) usually including English and maths, or equivalent. Exact requirements depend on the degree you take.

• Scotland

Band 3: For entry to jobs, usually at least four S grades (1-3) including English or maths, or similar.

Band 4: For entry to SQA higher national and professional development awards, usually 2-3 H grades and some S grades (1-3), including English and maths, or similar qualifications.

Band 5: For degree courses: 3-5 H grades and some S grades (1-3), including English and maths, or similar qualifications. Exact requirements depend on the degree you take.

Degree Information

A degree in equine business and performance, equine management or equine sports performance may be useful.

Adult Qualifications

Mature entry is common to this job. There are no specific academic entry requirements, but experience with racehorses and managing a yard over a number of years is required.

Work Experience

Entry to this work is competitive. It is very important to have good experience of working with horses prior to considering moving into training. Experience of work in a racing stable is the most relevant. Any experience of business skills, including accounting and marketing is also useful. You can apply to local riding schools, livery yards, equestrian centres or to holiday trekking and riding centres, for paid/unpaid work or voluntary experience.

Entry and Training

It is possible to become a horse trainer by working your way up through a variety of jobs in the horseracing industry and building up several years' experience. Most trainers begin work as a stable hand in racing stables, working their way up to head lad or lass, or train to be a jockey and then go into horse training at the end of their riding career. For more information on training as a stable hand or a jockey, see the articles for Stable Hand and Jockey.

A Diploma/Welsh Baccalaureate may be available in your area in environmental and land-based studies and this can prove a useful background for this job. Horse grooms can work for S/NVQs in horse care (levels 1-2) and horse care management (level 3). Levels 2-3 give the basic qualification for employment in the horse industry. Level 3 in horse care management can be taken by qualified people who have responsibility for others and perhaps run a small yard. Relevant training programmes, including apprenticeship schemes, may be available in your area. Advanced apprenticeships leading to qualification at level 3 can also be a route into higher education.

It is possible to do an HND in equine performance and business, a foundation degree in equine management and horsemanship or a degree in equine sports performance. Graduates can apply for a place on the Darley Flying Start international management training programme. This two year course is for graduates who want to specialise in thoroughbred breeding and racing. Participants study horse management, business management, the thoroughbred industry, leadership and networking. There is ample opportunity for work experience. The programme takes 12 graduates a year; see their website for details.

The British Horseracing Authority also runs a graduate development programme. This consists of a two-week residential course at the British Racing School, where students are exposed to a range of speakers, get involved in field trips and are encouraged to develop networking opportunities. Students develop an appreciation of how the industry works and continue on to an eight week paid work placement. The British Horseracing Authority also runs specialist trainer courses. The assistant trainer course is a short 3 day course that focuses on the role at the stable and at racecourses, where the assistant represents the trainer in stewards enquiries. This course is suitable for head grooms with ambitions to become a trainer.

For full horse trainer qualifications, it is necessary to apply for a Licence to Train, issued by the British Horseracing Authority. To be awarded this license, candidates must complete a course that consists of 3 modules and have achieved an NVQ Level 3 in racehorse care and management. Module 1 covers horse health, nutrition, training and licensing, Module 2 deals with business, finance and law and Module 3 covers staff management. The modules are run at the British Racing School and Northern Racing College. Details of dates and application forms are available on their websites. Completion of the course does not automatically result in a license as this is a committee decision.

Mature applicants, particularly with previous experience of working with horses are welcome. You may be able to benefit from government training programmes or gain recognition of previous experience through Accreditation of Prior Learning (APL) and by working towards relevant S/NVQs or a foundation degree.

Opportunities and Pay

Most jobs are in England, particularly in the South East. You normally work at a private stables and the number of horses you train can vary greatly depending on the size of the yard. National and international travel is common and a second language can be useful. It is possible and quite common to be self employed.

Pay varies depending on area and employer. You can earn anything from £15k a year for part-time contracts to £50k if employed full time. Earnings for self employed trainers can exceed this. Leading trainers can earn a great deal if their fee structure includes a percentage of winnings.

Health

This job requires a good standard of physical fitness and stamina.

Skills and Qualities

able to manage people, able to spot potential in a horse, ambitious, business awareness, enjoy working outdoors, good communication skills, good knowledge of horses, good organisational skills, leadership qualities, safety conscious

Relevant Subjects

Biology, Business and accounting, English, Land and Environment, Mathematics, Physical education and sport, Science

Further Information

Apprenticeship Schemes (National Apprenticeship Service) - www.apprenticeships.org.uk

British Horseracing educations and standards trust - www.bhest.co.uk

British Racing School (BRS) - www.brs.org.uk

Darley Flying Start - www.darleyflyingstart.com

Diplomas (Foundation, Higher and Advanced) - http://yp.direct.gov.uk/diplomas

Lantra Careers (A Future In...) (Lantra) - www.afuturein.com

National Trainers Federation http://racehorsetrainers.org

Northern Racing College - www.northernracingcollege.co.uk/

So you want to work with Animals (Wayland) - www.waylandbooks.co.uk

Training Schemes - www.direct.gov.uk/en/educationandlearning

Welsh Baccalaureate - www.wbq.org.uk

Working with animals (2009) (Babcock Lifeskills) - www.babcock-lifeskills.com/

Working with Horses (BHS) (British Horse Society) - www.bhs.org.uk/

Addresses

Association of British Riding Schools (ABRS)
Queen's Chambers, 38-40 Queen Street, Penzance TR18 4BH
Phone: +44 (0)1736 369 440
Web: www.abrs-info.org

British Horse Society (BHS)
Stoneleigh Deer Park, Kenilworth, Warwickshire CV8 2XZ
Phone: 0044 848 1666 (UK only)
Web: www.bhs.org.uk

British Horseracing Authority (BHA)
75 High Holborn, London WC1V 6LS
Phone: +44 (0)20 7152 0000
Web: www.britishhorseracing.com/

Similar Jobs

Animal Care Assistant, Jockey, Riding Instructor, Stable Hand, Stud Manager

Horticultural Manager

CRCI:Environment, Animals and Plants
CLCI:WAD Job Band: 3 to 5

Job Description

Horticultural managers are responsible for the forward planning and day-to-day running of either a commercial or amenity horticultural enterprise, such as a fruit farm or orchard, garden centre, market garden, or a plant and shrub nursery. They manage the growing and cultivation of a wide variety of fruit, plants, bulbs, trees and ornamental trees, shrubs or vegetables. Managers organise the daily routine and discuss details with the staff. They select and order seeds, plants and bulbs, equipment and other materials such as pesticides. Plan ahead so that the crops are mature at the best time, and liaise with distribution companies to ensure that the crops are collected and delivered to customers.

They keep up-to-date records and accounts using a computer and are also responsible for budgeting, marketing, and the recruitment, supervision and training of employees. Also ensure all staff keep to the relevant health and safety regulations. Some horticultural managers may work on a private estate, theme park, national park, or for a local authority. Depending on the size of the business, managers may also be involved in the day-to-day practical tasks.

Work Details

Usually work a basic 39 hr week, Monday to Friday, but may be expected to work at weekends, sometimes in the evenings and early in the morning. The workload varies depending on the time of the year. Most time can be spent indoors in an office, but sometimes outside in all sorts of weather. Supervisory or practical tasks involve time spent in greenhouses, where it is hot and humid. Some bending and kneeling may be required. The job may involve travel, for example to visit customers or suppliers.

Qualification

• England, Wales and Northern Ireland

Band 3: For entry to jobs, HNC or a relevant Diploma, usually at least 4 GCSEs (A*-C) including English, science and maths, or equivalent

Band 4: For HND, Diploma of Higher Education or foundation degree: 1-2 A levels and some GCSEs (A*-C) usually including English and maths, or equivalent. A year of practical experience in horticulture is normally required.

Band 5: For degree courses: 2-3 A levels and some GCSEs (A*-C) usually including English and maths, or equivalent. Exact requirements depend on the degree you take.

• Scotland

Band 3: For entry: usually at least four S grades (1-3) preferably including English, science and maths, or similar.

Band 4: For entry to SQA higher national and professional development awards, usually 2-3 H grades and some S grades (1-3), including English and maths, or similar qualifications.

Band 5: For degree courses: 3-5 H grades and some S grades (1-3), usually including English and maths, or similar qualifications. Exact requirements depend on the degree you take.

Degree Information

A degree in horticulture or horticultural management may be preferred. A degree in science subjects such as biochemistry, botany, plant science, soil science or environmental science is also acceptable. It is an advantage to have a postgraduate degree or diploma in horticultural management.

Adult Qualifications

Colleges and universities offering degree, HNC/HND courses in horticulture may have special entry standards for mature applicants. Relevant foundation or Access courses may be available. Contact individual institutions for details.

Work Experience

Employers or colleges may prefer candidates who have relevant work or voluntary experience. This can include Saturday and holiday work in a garden centre, a horticultural nursery, on a farm, or in grounds maintenance and can equip you with skills that you can use in the future and add to your CV. The Institute of Horticulture (IoH) can provide a list of those organisations that offer work experience, such as the RHS.

Entry and Training

Most entrants at management level usually have a period of practical experience plus a relevant degree, foundation degree, or a higher national qualification. However, it is possible to do this job after working your way up from assistant or supervisory level, and gaining experience and qualifications. Courses are mainly full time or sandwich and can last for 1-4 years. They may combine both study and practical work. Usually, after the course, you have to take a job as a supervisor or trainee manager before getting a full management post. Some large or medium-sized companies offer management trainee schemes.

The Royal Horticultural Society (RHS) and Royal Botanical Gardens at Kew and Edinburgh offer courses and special training opportunities, including some at degree level. Those who have gained an RHS level 3 diploma (or equivalent) may apply to take the degree-level RHS master of horticulture award; MHort (RHS). Some universities offer foundation degrees in horticulture.

A Diploma/Welsh Baccalaureate may be available in your area in environment and land-based studies. Appropriate S/NVQs are available up to level 4. Training programmes, including apprenticeship schemes, may be available in your area. Advanced apprenticeships leading to qualification at level 3 can also be a route into higher education.

Mature applicants can benefit through government training opportunities that may be available in your area. Practical experience of working in a garden centre, a horticultural nursery, on a farm, in grounds maintenance, and supervisory/management and business experience is an advantage. You can gain recognition of previous experience through Accreditation of Prior Learning (APL) or by working towards relevant S/NVQs.

Also contact the horticultural professional organisations such as the Royal Horticultural Society (RHS) for information on training opportunities and qualifications, including distance learning.

Opportunities and Pay

There are around 12,800 horticultural businesses in the UK, employing over 43,000 people. This industry is currently slightly in decline, but jobs are still usually available nationwide. You can find work with a company which specialises in growing one or a variety of products, such as fruit, pot plants, vegetables, bulbs or flowers, or specialising in organic horticulture. Jobs are also with local authorities, large private estates, national and royal parks, botanical gardens, and with organisations such as the National Trust. There is always a lot of competition for management posts, so you may have to move to a different part of the UK to gain promotion. Postgraduate qualifications or MHort (RHS) may lead to academic or research posts. It is possible to become self-employed, but it can be expensive to set up your own business.

Pay varies depending on area, employer and level of responsibility. Salaries start at around £15.5k-£18k rising to £19k-£25k a year with experience. A senior manager can earn up to £40k a year.

Health

Normal colour vision is needed for some jobs. You may find this job difficult if you suffer from hay fever. To do this job you have to have good health.

Skills and Qualities

able to make important decisions, able to manage people, business awareness, good communication skills, good interpersonal skills, good organisational skills, interest in growing plants, IT skills, planning skills, scientific approach, technical aptitude

Relevant Subjects

Biology, Business and accounting, Chemistry, Economics, English, Land and Environment, Mathematics, Retail and distribution, Science

Further Information

AGCAS: Environment & Agriculture (Job Sector Briefing) (AGCAS) - www.prospects.ac.uk

Apprenticeship Schemes (National Apprenticeship Service) - www.apprenticeships.org.uk

Diplomas (Foundation, Higher and Advanced) - http://yp.direct.gov.uk/diplomas

Lantra - The Sector Skills Council for environmental & land-based sector (Lantra) http:/www.lantra.co.uk

Lantra Careers (A Future In...) (Lantra) - www.afuturein.com

Training Schemes - www.direct.gov.uk/en/educationandlearning

Addresses

Institute of Horticulture (IoH)
Capel Manor College, Bullsmoor Lane, Enfield EN1 4RQ
Phone: +44 (0) 1992 707025
Web: www.horticulture.org.uk

Royal Botanic Garden Edinburgh
20A Inverleith Row, Edinburgh EH3 5LR
Phone: +44 (0)131 552 7171
Web: www.rbge.org.uk

Royal Horticultural Society (RHS)
80 Vincent Square, London SW1P 2PE
Phone: 0845 260 5000 (UK only)
Web: www.rhs.org.uk

Similar Jobs

Arboriculturist, Countryside/Conservation Officer/Manager, Farm Manager, Horticultural Worker: Commercial, Landscape Gardener, Parks Manager

Horticultural Scientist

CRCI:Environment, Animals and Plants
CLCI:WAD Job Band: 4 to 5

Job Description

Horticultural scientists study the science and technology of cultivating vegetables, fruit, flowers and plants. They conduct research to develop new and more efficient methods of small-scale planting and production. Also investigate ways to increase yields, and to control pests and diseases. Scientists study environmental issues, including soil erosion, pollution and public health concerns, including GM (genetically modified) issues. Also seek to protect the natural habitat and wildlife. May be involved in more complex interdisciplinary studies such as genetic engineering and the molecular biology of certain fruit and vegetables. May also be concerned specifically with organic horticulture.

They work in an advisory capacity to provide information to others involved in horticulture. Also provide current information on pest control, the use of chemicals, fungicides etc and may make on-site visits to farmers and growers. May specialise in seed production, crop production, or research the development of new varieties of plants. Some horticultural scientists are involved in marketing, journalism or may teach.

Work Details

Usually work a basic 39hr week, Monday to Friday, though in some jobs is expected to work shifts or at weekends. Work is based in an office or laboratory, but can involve visiting places such as farms and horticultural nurseries, perhaps travelling over quite a wide area. You may also have to advise farmers and growers, and collect, collate and analyse information, carry out tests on soil, and prepare and present reports. The work involves meeting clients, such as seed companies or pesticide producers, and you may be involved in teaching.

Qualification

• England, Wales and Northern Ireland

Band 4: For BTEC higher national diploma courses you usually need 1-2 A levels, often including chemistry or biology, and some GCSEs (A*-C) including English and maths, or equivalent.

Band 5: For a degree: usually 2-3 A levels, including at least one science subject and some GCSEs (A*-C) that also include your A level subjects, plus English and maths, or equivalent. Chemistry and biology are often required at A level depending on the degree course.

• Scotland

Band 4: For SQA higher national award: usually 2-3 H grades, often including chemistry or biology, and some S grades (1-3) often including English and maths, or similar qualifications.

Band 5: For a degree: usually 3-5 H grades, including at least one science subject and some S grades (1-3) that also include your H grade subjects, plus English and maths, or similar. Chemistry and biology are often required at H grade depending on the degree course.

Degree Information
A degree in horticulture, biological sciences, chemistry, biotechnology, biochemistry, botany, plant science, soil science, and similar related sciences may be preferred. Relevant postgraduate qualifications, such as PhD/MSc, are usually required and are taken either before or during employment. Grants for some degree courses may be available from the Botanical Society of the British Isles.

Adult Qualifications
A degree, or perhaps an HND in a relevant subject is usually required. Entry qualifications vary for mature applicants to these courses and there may be special entry standards. Check with the university or college concerned. Foundation and Access courses may also be available.

Work Experience
Employers and universities may prefer candidates who have relevant work or voluntary experience. Experience in an industrial or commercial laboratory is ideal, but if it proves difficult to gain, then experience in other scientific and horticultural areas is relevant. Experience of work on the land, such as a plant nursery, also offers useful background experience.

Entry and Training
Entrants usually have a relevant degree and often postgraduate qualifications, eg MSc/PhD. Previous practical experience in horticulture may be needed for entry to courses. After a degree or HND, training is on the job for 1-2 years, with a programme of short courses and site visits. Those with a good honours degree can apply for a postgraduate studentship with a research organisation that allows them to work towards a higher degree whilst being employed. In some areas of the country there are foundation degrees in horticulture and in science subjects that lead onto the third year of a degree course.

Those with a relevant HND or foundation degree are likely to enter at technician level. You are expected to keep knowledge up to date through a programme of continuing personal development (CPD). The Institute of Horticulture (IoH) provides course and qualification information, as well as membership details.

Mature applicants require relevant and up-to-date experience and qualifications in horticulture or a closely related subject. Some research posts may enable progression towards a postgraduate qualification whilst working. Funding for research projects is available from organisations such as the Biotechnology and Biological Sciences Research Council (BBSRC). The Merlin Trust offers financial support for long or short-term projects for those aged 20 to 35, where enthusiasm for plants, gardens and gardening matters more than qualifications.

Opportunities and Pay
There are opportunities for work with a variety of different types of land-based employers, such as a supplier or manufacturing company, a university or college, or a research organisation such as the Biotechnology and Biological Sciences Research Council (BBSRC). Work is also available with environmental consultancies such as the Agricultural Development and Advisory Service (ADAS) or with a central government department, including the Department for the Environment, Food and Rural Affairs (DEFRA). More opportunities are being created with the expansion of genetic engineering, whilst the more 'traditional' research and development work is diminishing. Work is also available abroad.

Pay varies depending on location and type of employer. Salaries for graduates are generally around £21.5k-£26k a year, rising to £33k-£44k. Higher earners can earn up to £50k a year.

Health
This job requires good health and you may find this job difficult if you suffer from hay fever. Some posts require good colour vision.

Skills and Qualities
analytical skills, good communication skills, good organisational skills, information handling skills, IT skills, knowledge of statistics, methodical, problem-solving skills, scientific approach, technical aptitude

Relevant Subjects
Biology, Chemistry, Geography, Land and Environment, Mathematics, Science

Further Information
ADAS - Agricultural Development and Advisory Service - www.adas.co.uk

AGCAS: Environment & Agriculture (Job Sector Briefing) (AGCAS) - www.prospects.ac.uk

Lantra - The Sector Skills Council for environmental & land-based sector (Lantra) http:/www.lantra.co.uk

Addresses
Biotechnology and Biological Sciences Research Council (BBSRC)
Polaris House North Star Avenue, Swindon, Wiltshire SN2 1UH
Phone: +44 (0)1793 413 200
Web: www.bbsrc.ac.uk

Botanic Gardens Conservation International (BGCI)
Descanso House, 199 Kew Road, Richmond TW9 3BW
Phone: +44 (0)20 8332 5953
Web: www.bgci.org

Botanical Society of the British Isles (BSBI)
Botany Department, The Natural History Museum, Cromwell Road, London SW7 5BD
Web: www.bsbi.org.uk

Department for Environment, Food & Rural Affairs (DEFRA)
Customer Contact Unit , Eastbury House, 30 - 34 Albert Embankment, London SE1 7TL
Phone: 0845 933 5577 (UK only)
Web: www.defra.gov.uk

Institute of Horticulture (IoH)
Capel Manor College, Bullsmoor Lane, Enfield EN1 4RQ
Phone: +44 (0) 1992 707025
Web: www.horticulture.org.uk

Merlin Trust
Secretary, 55 Deodar Road, London SW15 2NU
Phone: +44 (0)20 8874 7636
Web: www.merlin-trust.org.uk

Natural Environment Research Council (NERC)
Polaris House North Star Avenue, Swindon, Wiltshire SN2 1EU
Phone: +44 (0)1793 411 500
Web: www.nerc.ac.uk

Royal Horticultural Society (RHS)
80 Vincent Square, London SW1P 2PE
Phone: 0845 260 5000 (UK only)
Web: www.rhs.org.uk

Society of Biology
9 Red Lion Court, London EC4A 3EF
Phone: +44 (0)20 7936 5900
Web: http://societyofbiology.org/home

Similar Jobs
Agricultural Consultant/Adviser, Agricultural Research Scientist, Biochemist, Botanist, Microbiologist, Soil Scientist

Horticultural Worker: Commercial

also known as: Greenhouse/Glasshouse Nursery Assistant, Market Garden Worker, Nursery Garden Worker

CRCI:Environment, Animals and Plants
CLCI:WAD Job Band: 1 to 3

Job Description

Commercial horticultural workers help in the cultivation of fruit, plants, trees, vegetables and flowers for large-scale commercial use. They may work outdoors in an orchard, garden or field, or in a controlled and often computerised environment, such as a greenhouse or glasshouse, where crops can include tomatoes, cucumbers, flowers, plants or fruit. Often grow new plants/crops from seed (propagation) by preparing soil beds, sowing the seeds and planting out the cuttings/grafts. Also undertake daily task each season, which include mowing lawns, watering, pruning shrubs, leaf clearing and staking plants.

Workers ensure that pests are controlled by using chemical sprays or by natural substances if growing an organic crop. They do some of the work by hand, such as planting cuttings, picking fruit or gathering in vegetables or flowers, bu use machines such as hedge trimmers, strimmers, tractors and rotavators to do other work.

Work Details

A 39-40 hr working week is usual, though may have to work at weekends and longer hours in the spring and summer months. May work in teams, or small groups of three or four, though sometimes may work alone. This job requires a lot of kneeling and bending down to look after plants, and work outside in all sorts of weather. It can be hot/cold, dirty, damp and muddy, and when working in a glasshouse or greenhouse, it can also be hot and stuffy. Plants need to be sprayed with dangerous chemicals, so protective clothing and a face mask are provided for this work. However, the rules of health and safety must always be observed.

Qualification

• England, Wales and Northern Ireland

Band 1: For entry to jobs, no minimum qualifications are needed, but you are expected to have a good level of general education and relevant experience. Some formal/vocational qualifications at any level are useful, particularly in science subjects. A qualification in horticulture is an advantage.

Band 2: For entry to jobs, no minimum qualifications are needed, but it is an advantage to have some GCSEs (A*-C) or equivalent in subjects that include English, science and maths.

Band 3: For entry: usually at least 4 GCSEs (A*-C) including English, science and maths, or equivalent.

• Scotland

Band 1: For entry to jobs, no minimum qualifications are needed, but you are expected to have a good level of general education and relevant experience. Some formal/vocational qualifications at any level are useful, particularly in science subjects. A qualification in horticulture is an advantage.

Band 2: Although academic qualifications are not specified for this job, it is an advantage to have some S grades (1-3) in subjects that include English, science and maths, or similar.

Band 3: For entry: usually at least four S grades (1-3) including English, science and maths, or similar.

Adult Qualifications

Adults may not need qualifications for entry to college courses though some practical experience in gardening, farming or forestry may be needed.

Work Experience

Employers may prefer candidates who have relevant work or voluntary experience. This can include Saturday and holiday work in a garden centre, a horticultural nursery, on a farm, or in grounds maintenance and can equip you with skills that you can use in the future and add to your CV. The IoH can provide a list of those organisations that offer work experience such as the Royal Horticultural Society.

Entry and Training

There are no formal qualifications needed to enter this work, and many people gain experience as a trainee and work alongside experienced workers. Some also gain horticultural qualifications through part-time study and on-the-job training. Employers may also provide short specialist courses, such as in tree-pruning or propagation. Any work that involves potentially dangerous tasks such as spraying with pesticides or the use of a chainsaw requires certificates of competence. Such qualifications are awarded by the National Proficiency Tests Council (NPTC), which also offer other relevant short courses.

There are also a range of full time courses you can take. The one year full-time national certificate in horticulture offered by City & Guilds/NPTC usually requires you to have a year's experience before you can start the course. They also offer an advanced national certificate for those wishing to progress to a supervisory post. There are also first certificate and national awards in horticulture from BTEC/SQA available for those who want to take a full-time course straight from school.

You can gain relevant qualifications through the Royal Horticultural Society (RHS) who offer nationally recognised qualifications that may be studied at a local college or through distance learning, including the RHS level 2 certificate in horticulture. They also offer practical training opportunities at their main gardens. Contact the RHS for details of training opportunities and qualifications. Contact Lantra or the Institute of Horticulture (IoH) for details of all relevant qualifications and where to study.

A Diploma/Welsh Baccalaureate may be available in your area in the environment and land-based studies. There are appropriate S/NVQs at levels 1-4 in this area of work. Training programmes, including apprenticeship schemes, may be available in your area. Advanced apprenticeships leading to qualification at level 3 can also be a route into higher education. A driving licence is often required.

Mature applicants can benefit through government training opportunities, including apprenticeships for adults, that may be available in your area. Any experience of gardening or related outdoor work is an advantage. There are distance-learning courses available from some colleges and organisations such as the Royal Horticultural Society. The Institute of Horticulture (IoH) also offers a range of qualifications at all stages of ability. Contact the IoH for details on training opportunities and qualifications. You can gain recognition of previous experience through Accreditation of Prior Learning (APL) or by working towards relevant S/NVQs.

Opportunities and Pay

There are around 12,800 horticultural businesses in the UK, employing over 43,000 people. This industry is currently slightly in decline, but jobs are still usually available nationwide. Commercial horticultural employers include plant nurseries, garden centres, orchards or vegetable farms, and flower/bulb growers. With experience and qualifications you can be promoted to a supervisor or a manager, although it may sometimes be necessary to change employers to reach these posts. Part-time work or contractual work such as caring for plants/displays in shops, large shopping centres, airports, hotels and offices, or as a self-employed landscape and professional gardener, is possible.

Pay varies depending on area and employer. Salaries are around £11.5k-£14k a year, rising to around £18k a year with experience. Higher earners can make around £21k a year. At busy times you may be asked to work extra hours and be given overtime pay.

Health

You have to be physically fit to do this job. You may find this job difficult if you suffer from hay fever.

Skills and Qualities
able to work both on your own and in a team, adaptable, careful, common sense, enjoy working outdoors, hard working, manual dexterity, practical skills, responsible attitude

Relevant Subjects
Biology, Land and Environment, Science

Further Information
Apprenticeship Schemes (National Apprenticeship Service) - www.apprenticeships.org.uk

Diplomas (Foundation, Higher and Advanced) - http://yp.direct.gov.uk/diplomas

Grow - the guide to careers in horticulture - www.growcareers.info

Lantra - The Sector Skills Council for environmental & land-based sector (Lantra) - http:/www.lantra.co.uk

Lantra Careers (A Future In...) (Lantra) - www.afuturein.com

Training Schemes - www.direct.gov.uk/en/educationandlearning

Addresses
Garden Centre Association
Leafield Technical Centre Leafield, Witney, Oxfordshire OX29 9EF
Phone: +44 (0)1993 871000
Web: www.gca.org.uk

Institute of Horticulture (IoH)
Capel Manor College, Bullsmoor Lane, Enfield EN1 4RQ
Phone: +44 (0) 1992 707025
Web: www.horticulture.org.uk

National Proficiency Test Council (NPTC)
City & Guilds Land Based Services Building 500 Abbey Park, Stareton, Warwickshire CV8 2LY
Phone: +44 (0) 24 7685 7300
Web: www.nptc.org.uk

Royal Horticultural Society (RHS)
80 Vincent Square, London SW1P 2PE
Phone: 0845 260 5000 (UK only)
Web: www.rhs.org.uk

Similar Jobs
Forest Worker, Garden Centre Assistant, Gardener, Greenkeeper: Golf, Groundsman/Groundswoman, Horticultural Manager

Hospital Play Specialist

CRCI:Healthcare
CLCI:JOZ — Job Band: 2 to 4

Job Description
Hospital play therapists organise play and art activities for children of all ages who are in hospital. They work as part of a multi-disciplinary health professional team and assist in the process of diagnosis, treatment and recovery of child patients. Use a dedicated hospital playroom/department or may work at a child's bedside. May organise play sessions in a clinic, ward, or elsewhere in the hospital such as outdoors, or may take children on outings. Observe the child/children at play, make notes and write reports on their progress.

Encourage children in hospital to form friendships and play together. Help them to cope with hospital routine and to understand their illness and treatment. Use play to help overcome any fears, anxieties or pain and to introduce hospital procedures such as X-rays, radiography, anaesthetics and injections.

Often work with the child, their family and friends, in particular any brothers or sisters, to provide them with support. Is keen to enable the child or children to continue their outside interests and to have fun whilst in hospital. Can also provide programmes of educational play to stimulate learning and knowledge. Organise parties and special events.

Work Details
Your hours of work are around 37 hrs in a five-day week, but may include some weekends and public holidays. You most likely work with children in a suitably equipped playroom or in areas around the hospital such as intensive care units, accident and emergency departments, outpatient clinics, hospices and in children's own homes. The work can be quite physically active and you may have to arrange and rearrange play equipment.

Qualification

• England, Wales and Northern Ireland
Band 2: For CACHE level 3 diploma in playwork: no set entry qualifications, but you must be at least 18 and most colleges prefer some GCSEs (A*-C) including English, or equivalent.

Band 3: For BTEC national diploma: at least 4 GCSEs (A*-C) or an equivalent qualification such as a BTEC first certificate.

Band 4: For BTEC level 4 professional diploma in specialised play for sick children and young people: ideally a relevant BTEC national award or CACHE level 3 diploma in child care and education, or an NVQ level 3 in children's care, learning and development is usually required for entry. Learners need to have 3 years experience of working with children and be aged 20 or over upon entry to the course. Alternative qualifications may also be acceptable.

• Scotland
Band 2: For relevant Scottish Group Award: no set entry qualifications, but most colleges ask for at least some S grades (1-3) including English, or similar.

Band 3: For relevant SQA national award: usually at least 4 S grades (1-3) or similar qualifications.

Band 4: For BTEC level 4 professional diploma in specialised play for sick children and young people: ideally a relevant BTEC/SQA national award or an SVQ level 3 in children's care, learning and development is usually required for entry. Learners need to have 3 years experience of working with children and be aged 20 or over upon entry to the course. Alternative qualifications may also be acceptable.

Adult Qualifications
For qualification and registration as a hospital play specialist within the NHS you usually require a BTEC level 4 diploma in specialised play for sick children and young people. Contact the National Association of Hospital Play Staff for information on relevant entry courses.

Work Experience
Work experience gives you an insight into what you enjoy and don't enjoy about a job or working environment, as well as the opportunity to acquire new skills. It is also provides valuable information to add to your CV and improves your course application and future employment prospects. Those with relevant work or voluntary experience in a medical or healthcare setting such as a hospital or residential care home, or of working with children have an advantage. Volunteering in a hospital play unit is ideal experience.

Entry and Training
To qualify and register with the Hospital Play Staff Education Trust (HPSET) as a hospital play specialist you need to be at least 20 years of age. All trainee hospital play specialists need a professional childcare qualification at level 3 or above, 2 years post qualifying experience working in a childcare setting, key skills at level 2 or equivalent in literacy and numeracy and to be employed in a health care setting at the time of undertaking a foundation degree course in healthcare play specialism.

Some enter with a background and/or professional qualification in areas that include nursing, drama or music therapy, psychology, social work, occupational therapy or teaching. You may be able to enter as a play assistant and study for the relevant qualifications part time whilst working. Contact the National Association of Hospital Play Staff for all routes to training, qualification and registration. You need to re-register with the HPSET every five years.

A Diploma/Welsh Baccalaureate may be available in your area in society, health and development. This can provide a useful introduction to this career. See the websites for further information.

Mature entrants may not need formal entry qualifications to do the foundation degree course in healthcare play specialism if they have experience of working in a school or nursery. Many entrants have qualifications in areas such as teaching, social work or nursing.

Opportunities and Pay

The number of professional hospital play specialists is increasing. You are usually employed by the NHS or at a private hospital, children's hospice, community centre, or in a child's own home. With experience and training there are opportunities to become a team leader or team manager.

Salaries vary from hospital to hospital. Starting salaries for assistants are around £17k-£20k a year, rising to £26k as a senior play specialist. A team manager can earn up to £33k a year. Staff working in London are paid higher salaries.

Skills and Qualities

able to stimulate learners, aptitude for teamwork, emotionally strong, friendly, good communication skills, good interpersonal skills, good organisational skills, observant, patient, reassuring

Relevant Subjects

Art and Design, English, Health and social care, Psychology

Further Information

Diplomas (Foundation, Higher and Advanced) - http://yp.direct.gov.uk/diplomas

Hospital Play Staff Education Trust (HPSET) - www.hpset.org.uk

National Association of Hospital Play Staff (NAHPS) - www.nahps.org.uk

NHS Careers (NHS Careers) - www.nhscareers.nhs.uk

NHS Careers Scotland - www.infoscotland.com/nhs

NHS Careers Wales - www.wales.nhs.uk

Skills for Care and Development - sector skills council for social care, childre, early years and young people's workforces - www.skillsforcareanddevelopment.org.uk

Welsh Baccalaureate - www.wbq.org.uk

Addresses

CACHE: Council for Awards in Children's Care & Education
Apex House, 81 Camp Road, St Albans AL1 5GB
Phone: 0845 347 2123 (UK only)
Web: www.cache.org.uk

Similar Jobs

Art Therapist, Dramatherapist, Nurse: Children, Nursery Worker, Occupational Therapist, Play Therapist

Hospital Porter

also known as: Hospital Support Worker: Porter

CRCI:Healthcare
CLCI:JOZ — Job Band: 1

Job Description

Hospital porters play a vital role in a hospital, moving frail and often very ill patients between different wards and departments in comfort and in safety. They ensure that patients, equipment and records are in the right place at the right time. Porters take patients around parts of a hospital, perhaps from the ward to the operating theatre, or for an X-ray and back again. Often they transfer the patients from ward to ward on a stretcher, in a wheelchair or on a trolley and may use special equipment that minimises lifting. May remove recently deceased people from wards or operating theatres and transport them to the hospital mortuary. Duties may be emotionally and physically demanding.

May also bring trolleys of food and drink to the wards and deliver the mail around the hospital wards and departments. Also transport complex and valuable equipment that requires expert handling around the building. They may exchange and fit medical gas cylinders, take blood samples to the labs, bring clean linen and other equipment to the wards, and take used and soiled sheets to the laundry. Work may include disposing of hazardous waste. Also move furniture, such as beds, tables and cupboards, from place to place and remove rubbish and clinical waste.

Some porters may have reception desk duties, help to monitor the hospital car parks, and assist security staff at times. They use small vehicles called 'tugs' between departments and hospital sites, and keep in touch with supervisors via radio-paging 'bleepers'.

Work Details

Usually work a 39 hr week, which may include shift work and unsocial hours, weekends, nights and public holidays. You help people, including those who are in pain, ill or upset, sometimes as a result of an accident. The job requires you to cope with heavy lifting and also a lot of walking around. Porters need to stay calm in emergencies and must be able to cope with the sight of blood. You may need to drive cars and vans, or an electric truck so some employers require a driving licence. Porters usually wear a uniform provided by their employer and may wear protective clothing for some jobs.

Qualification

• England, Wales and Northern Ireland

Band 1: For entry to jobs, no minimum qualifications are needed, but you are expected to have a good level of general education and relevant experience. Some formal/vocational qualifications at any level are useful.

• Scotland

Band 1: For entry to jobs, no minimum qualifications are needed, but you are expected to have a good level of general education and relevant experience. Some formal/vocational qualifications at any level are useful.

Adult Qualifications

No qualification entry requirements are specified, but you are expected to have a good level of education, particularly in literacy and numeracy. Some formal qualifications at any level are useful. You can improve your skills and qualifications by working through the Foundation Learning programme. This involves taking credit-based units and qualifications to help you progress.

Work Experience

Work experience gives you an insight into what you enjoy and don't enjoy about a job or working environment, as well as the opportunity to acquire new skills. It also provides valuable information to add to your CV and improves your future employment prospects. This can be either unpaid or voluntary, holiday or part-time work that you have organised yourself.

Experience of working with the public, especially in a caring role, is particularly helpful. If you do not have relevant experience, you can learn about this role by volunteering in a hospital and helping the porter.

Entry and Training

Most entrants are 18 or over, though it is possible to start work from 16 years of age. You do not need any specific qualifications but do need good written and spoken communication skills. There is no formal training programme but an induction course that introduces new porters to the hospital, its departments and wards and health and safety regulations is usual. Further on-the-job training is given under supervision of an experienced member of staff, which covers first-aid, bending and lifting techniques, use of equipment, and mortuary procedures.

There may be an opportunity to work towards S/NVQ level 2 in support services in healthcare. If working on a large site a driving licence may be required.

Mature entry is an advantage. It is useful to have work experience, working with people, or some voluntary work assisting hospital porters. It can be an advantage to have a manual handling or health and safety qualification.

Opportunities and Pay

You can work in an NHS hospital, a private hospital, clinic or for an agency providing hospital services. With experience and qualifications in supervision and management, you may be put in charge of a team of porters or work as a porter-manager. Some hospital porters move on to become healthcare assistants, sterile services technicians or work for the ambulance service. Others may train as nurses after gaining qualifications.

Pay depends on the NHS Trust or employer you work for. New entrants in the NHS start on £13k-£15k a year, rising to £17k with experience and increased responsibility. A porter team leader can earn up to £19k a year. Overtime and shift pay can increase your salary.

Health

You are expected to be physically fit and able to cope with lifting and walking considerable distances. The work may involve a risk of infection.

Skills and Qualities

able to cope under pressure, able to follow instructions, able to get on with all kinds of people, aptitude for teamwork, caring, common sense, even tempered, friendly, not squeamish, patient

Further Information

Foundation Learning (QCDA) - www.qcda.gov.uk
NHS Careers (NHS Careers) - www.nhscareers.nhs.uk
NHS Careers Scotland - www.infoscotland.com/nhs
NHS Careers Wales - www.wales.nhs.uk
Skills for Health - sector skills council - www.skillsforhealth.org.uk

Similar Jobs

Ambulance Care Assistant, Emergency Care Assistant/ Ambulance Technician, Healthcare Assistant, Hotel Porter, Sterile Services Technician

Hostel Manager

also known as: Youth Hostel Manager
CRCI:Social Work and Counselling Services
CLCI:IB Job Band: 3 to 5

Job Description

Hostel managers are responsible for the day-to-day management and administration of hostels and youth hostels. Hostels range from large city centre buildings with hundreds of beds, to small hostels in rural settings. Residential hostels are usually run by local authorities for the most vulnerable people, such as homeless, drug addicted or mentally and physically abused people. Allocate rooms according to certain criteria. Check in and out guests and residents, collect payments and issue receipts.

Hostel managers are responsible for the general welfare and behaviour of residents and handle any complaints. They keep records, including a daily log book of events, and take action when occupancy agreements are contravened. In most jobs they give general care such as simple first aid and deal with any emergencies. Ensure that the property is well maintained and in good order. Check that rooms and bathrooms are kept clean. If bed linen is provided, they make sure it is clean and changed often. If catering is provided, they organise meals or ensure any communal kitchens are up to the standard of health and safety. All managers have a range of duties that depend upon the type of accommodation they supervise. May supervise clerical, cleaning and administrative staff and are responsible for their training and development.

Work Details

Usually works a 37 hour week. In residential hostels often works shifts that include evenings, nights, early mornings and weekends. Many managers 'live in' when they are on duty, or may have permanent accommodation near to or within the hostel. Duties depend on the people for whom you are responsible. In youth hostels the work load is often heavier over holiday periods.

In a residential hostel conditions can be dirty and unpleasant at times. Sometimes clients are aggressive and violent, although there are usually security measures in place. Work is emotionally demanding and may involve making difficult decisions. Many of your clients are in need of support, so can be depressed, upset, demanding, anxious or negative.

Qualification

- **England, Wales and Northern Ireland**

Band 3: For entry: usually at least 4 GCSEs (A*-C) including English and maths, or equivalent.

Band 4: For BTEC higher national award: 1-2 A levels and some GCSEs (A*-C) usually including English and maths, or equivalent.

Band 5: For degree courses: 2-3 A levels and some GCSEs (A*-C) usually including English and maths, or equivalent. Exact requirements depend on the degree you take.

- **Scotland**

Band 3: For entry: usually at least four S grades (1-3) including English and maths, or similar.

Band 4: For SQA higher national award: usually 2-3 H grades and some S grades (1-3), often including English and maths, or similar qualifications.

Band 5: For degree courses: 3-5 H grades and some S grades (1-3), usually including English and maths, or similar qualifications. Exact requirements depend on the degree you take.

Degree Information

Any degree is acceptable for this job. However housing, psychology, sociology, social policy and administration, law, management and other business-related subjects provide the most relevant background knowledge.

Adult Qualifications

Mature applicants with practical experience in hotel work, community care work, hospitality, teaching or tourism may be accepted without higher level academic qualifications or specific vocational qualifications. Entry requirements may be relaxed for adults applying for higher education courses. Access or foundation courses provide those without the required qualifications a route onto degree courses.

Work Experience

Relevant work or voluntary experience can equip you with skills that you can use in the future and that you can add to your CV. There are often opportunities available for voluntary work that give you experience of working with people. In particular, any experience of working with vulnerable people that demonstrates your personal skills is most valued. This can include working with young people, dealing with the public in a helping capacity such as adult and community centre work, or working in the caring professions. Community Service Volunteers (CSV) have details of health and social care volunteering projects. See their website for details.

Entry and Training

This job is particularly suitable for older more experienced people. Although some enter as graduates, relevant experience is often more important than academic qualifications. You can enter this job with a good general education. For those entering work in a residential hostel for vulnerable people, experience of working in a community care setting with management skills and experience is most important. Training is mainly on the job, learning from an experienced manager.

Relevant job-related courses include S/NVQ level 4 in leadership and management for care services and S/NVQ levels 2-4 in health and social care, and housing. This includes aspects of management, budgeting, marketing and human resources, as well as issues in the social care sector. Social Care Council grants may be available and tuition fees paid for eligible students.

Managers of youth hostels and often backpackers hostels must be at least 18 years old and usually start as assistants. Those with experience in accommodation management are at an advantage. Pre-entry checks include a Criminal Records Bureau (CRB)/ Disclosure Scotland check. Training programmes, including apprenticeship schemes, may be available in your area. Advanced apprenticeships leading to qualification at level 3 can also be a route into higher education.

Adult entry is common and those with experience in community care, hospitality or social work have an advantage. Most people who become hostel managers have already worked as an assistant or deputy, so they have started some training towards or hold a relevant S/NVQ. Mature entrants are welcomed and are often considered on their relevant work/life experiences rather than on academic qualifications.

Opportunities and Pay

Hostels and youth hostels are found throughout the country. Most jobs working in hostels for vulnerable people are within the housing services department of local authorities. Work can also be found with private companies and voluntary organisations, such as rehabilitation centres, hostels or centres for the elderly or disabled. Most jobs in youth hostels are with the Youth Hostels Association (YHA)/Scottish Youth Hostels Association (SYHA). With experience, there are opportunities to work in other areas of property/care management.

Pay varies depending on location and employer. If accommodation is included, then earnings are likely to be less. Depending on experience and responsibilities, managers of youth hostels can earn in the region of £11.5k-£16k a year, rising to around £16k-£18k and up to £28k for management of the busiest hostels. Pay for those working in local authority run hostels is around £19k-£25k a year.

Skills and Qualities

able to get on with all kinds of people, able to motivate others, able to understand other people's problems, calm, caring, energetic, friendly, good organisational skills, initiative, tolerant

Relevant Subjects

Business and accounting, English, Health and social care, Hospitality and catering, Psychology, Sociology

Further Information

Apprenticeship Schemes (National Apprenticeship Service) - www.apprenticeships.org.uk

Asset Skills - sector skills council for the places where we live and work - www.assetskills.org

Association for Student Residential Accommodation - www.asra.ac.uk

Community Care (weekly) (Reed) - www.communitycare.co.uk

Community Service Volunteers - www.csv.org.uk

Hostel Management - www.hostelmanagement.com

Inside Housing - www.insidehousing.co.uk/

Local Government Careers (Improvement and Development Agency) - www.lgcareers.com/publications/

Addresses

Chartered Institute of Housing (CIH)
Octavia House Westwood Way, Coventry CV4 8JP
Phone: +44 (0)24 7685 1700
Web: www.cih.org

Convention of Scottish Local Authorities (COSLA)
Rosebery House, 9 Haymarket Terrace, Edinburgh EH12 5XZ
Phone: +44 (0)131 474 9200
Web: www.cosla.gov.uk

Institute of Hospitality
Trinity Court, 34 West Street, Sutton, Surrey SM1 1SH
Phone: +44 (0)20 8661 4900
Web: www.instituteofhospitality.org

Northern Ireland Local Government Association (NILGA)
Unit 5B Castlereagh Business Park, 478 Castlereagh Road, Belfast BT5 6BQ
Phone: +44(0)28 9079 8972
Web: www.nilga.org

Youth Hostels Association (YHA)
Trevelyan House, Dimple Road, Matlock, Derbyshire DE4 3YH
Phone: +44(0) 1629 592600
Web: www.yha.org.uk

Similar Jobs

Care Home Manager, Community Development Worker, Domestic Services Manager, Hotel Manager, Housing Officer, Social Care Worker

Hotel Manager

CRCI:Catering and Hospitality
CLCI:IB Job Band: 3 to 5

Job Description

Hotel managers plan, organise and control the efficient day-to-day running of a hotel's services and the work of its staff. They work to ensure that guests enjoy every aspect of their visit, and that the hotel makes a profit. Managers have a good working knowledge of the hotel's different areas, such as kitchen, reception, conference suite, housekeeping, health and fitness centre etc. They deal with key staff and any VIP guests, discuss arrangements with staff and deal with any problems or complaints. Managers are also involved in marketing, budgeting and financial planning, often with the use of a computer and have responsibility for the recruitment, training and development of staff.

In small hotels, they maintain stock, plan facilities, decor, menus, etc. In larger hotels this is done by a departmental head, such as a domestic services or restaurant manager, who reports directly to the hotel manager. Also writes reports and maintains financial and statistical records. Ensures that the law, rules and regulations surrounding health and safety, hygiene and licensing are applied and maintained through regular checking procedures.

Work Details

Usually works a basic 39-40 hr week, although long, irregular and unsocial hours are common, but with free time during the day. Often works on public holidays and at weekends. Holiday must be taken at times when the hotel is less busy. You need to be available during the summer, and at Christmas/New Year. This work can be very demanding and stressful at times. Any emergencies and complaints must be dealt with quickly and efficiently. At times, there is a lot of contact with guests; managers must ensure that they are happy and pleased with the hotel's accommodation and services.

Managers of small hotels often help with work in the bar, reception etc, while those in larger hotels have more administrative tasks, including the supervision of other staff. When on duty you are required to dress smartly, always be polite, and handle matters with patience and diplomacy. You may be able to live in the hotel.

Qualification

- **England, Wales and Northern Ireland**

Band 3: For entry to jobs, HNC or a relevant Diploma, usually at least 4 GCSEs (A*-C) including English and maths, or equivalent.

Band 4: For HND in hospitality, Diploma of Higher Education or foundation degree: 1-2 A levels and some GCSEs (A*-C) usually including English and maths, or equivalent.

Band 5: For degree courses in hospitality: 2-3 A levels and some GCSEs (A*-C) usually including English and maths, or equivalent. Exact requirements depend on the degree you take.

- **Scotland**

Band 3: For entry to jobs, usually at least four S grades (1-3) including English or maths, or similar.

Band 4: For entry to SQA higher national and professional development awards, usually 2-3 H grades and some S grades (1-3), including English and maths, or similar qualifications.

Band 5: For degree courses in hospitality management: 3-5 H grades and some S grades (1-3), usually including English and maths, or similar qualifications. Exact requirements depend on the degree you take.

Degree Information

Degrees such as hotel/hospitality management, international hospitality management, licensed retail management, hospitality business/management, hospitality/modern languages or travel/tourism/leisure studies are relevant to this job. For graduates with non-related degrees, there are one-year postgraduate conversion courses. Relevant postgraduate courses such as hospitality management are also available.

Adult Qualifications

Formal academic qualifications are not always necessary and entry to most courses can be gained through relevant experience in catering or in management. Entry requirements may be relaxed for adults applying for higher education courses. Access or foundation courses provide those without the required qualifications a route onto degree courses. A one-year conversion course in hotel and catering management is available to graduates who have a non-hospitality degree.

Work Experience

Entry to this job is competitive and it is important to do some relevant work or voluntary experience before applying. Any work that allows you to use or develop administration skills, sales and customer-focused work, is useful. Experience or knowledge of bookkeeping or budgeting and supervising a team is also an advantage. The Institute of Hospitality offers a placement advice service.

Entry and Training

Some people start at a lower level of responsibility and work their way up to management through experience and qualifications. Experience in catering and knowledge of a foreign language can be useful. Most entrants are graduates or have a BTEC/SQA higher national award. They usually enter directly as an assistant manager or join a management training scheme with a larger hotel or hotel chain. Some companies have fast track schemes, but most management training takes 1-2 years. Increasingly, managers are improving their business skills through an MBA (Master of Business Administration).

Entrants with fewer qualifications, such as four GCSEs/S grades or S/NVQs and relevant work experience, can work towards the business skills certificate for hospitality, leisure and tourism of the Institute of Hospitality (level 2 and 3). This can be taken by mixed mode through a college or training provider, or by self study. This can lead on to the level 4 diploma in management course. Foundation degrees in hotel and hospitality subjects are also available.

A Diploma/Welsh Baccalaureate may also be available in your area in hospitality. The advanced level is equivalent to 3.5 A levels but for some university courses, the additional and specialist learning (ASL) component of the diploma needs to include specific A levels. Check entry requirements carefully with the individual institutions. S/NVQs and BTEC National Awards in multi-skilled hospitality services and hospitality and catering principles are available at level 2. These can lead to hospitality supervision, and hospitality supervision and leadership skills at level 3 and management at level 4. Training programmes, including apprenticeship schemes in hospitality, customer service or leisure management, may be available in your area for entry to this job. Advanced apprenticeships leading to qualification at level 3 can also be a route into higher education.

Mature applicants already working in hospitality with relevant skills and experience are able to qualify for S/NVQs, which can lead to study for the Institute of Hospitality qualifications through distance-learning courses. There are open learning courses and flexible part-time courses offered by colleges and universities that lead to nationally recognised awards in hospitality and management. You can also apply to the Savoy Educational Trust for financial support to study for hospitality industry-related courses. The Trust aims to support individuals who wish to make a career in hospitality.

Opportunities and Pay

In Britain, about 50% of hotels are concentrated in south-east England, Scotland and south-west England, although hotels and guest houses can be found in most areas of the UK. The hospitality industry is struggling in the current economic climate. This may affect the number of opportunities available for hotel managers, although skilled managers may still be in demand. Competition for positions is fierce, but you can find work in large luxury hotels, small hotels, guest houses, leisure villages etc. Promotion opportunities can be good, especially if you are prepared to move around the country.

Many managers are self-employed and work in small establishments including travel lodges/motels, hotels and inns. There are good opportunities for working abroad, particularly if employed by an international hotel chain. With experience, you may be able to open your own hotel.

Pay varies depending on location, employer and level of responsibility. Trainee managers are likely to earn around £15k-£20k rising to £22k-£30k with experience. Those with the most responsibility earn up to £55k and some highly successful managers may earn more than £100k a year, depending on the size of hotel. Managers in London tend to earn more. You may be given residential use of a room or flat in the hotel and discounted hotel accommodation worldwide, particularly from large hotel chains. Additional benefits may include free or subsidised meals whilst on duty, pension and life insurance membership, a clothing allowance, and sometimes share-ownership.

Skills and Qualities

ability in one or more languages, able to cope under pressure, able to motivate others, aptitude for figures, business awareness, diplomatic, good communication skills, good interpersonal skills, IT skills, problem-solving skills, tactful

Relevant Subjects

Business and accounting, Economics, English, Hospitality and catering, Leisure, travel and tourism, Mathematics, Modern Foreign Languages

Further Information

Apprenticeship Schemes (National Apprenticeship Service) - www.apprenticeships.org.uk

British Hospitality Association (BHA) - www.bha.org.uk

CareerScope: Hospitality and Leisure (Springboard UK) - http://careerscope.springboarduk.net/

Caterer and Hotelkeeper (weekly) (Reed Business Information) - www.caterersearch.com/Home/

Diploma in Hospitality (People 1st) - www.hospitalitydiploma.co.uk

People 1st - sector skills council for hospitality, leisure, travel and tourism - www.people1st.co.uk

Real Life Guide to Hospitality & Event Management (Trotman 2010) - www.trotman.co.uk

Springboard UK (Springboard UK) - www.springboarduk.net

Springboard Wales (Springboard Wales) - http://wales.springboarduk.net/

UKSP - Guide to Success in Hospitality, Leisure, Travel & Tourism - www.uksp.co.uk

▶Working in hospitality & catering (2009) (Babcock Lifeskills) - www.babcock-lifeskills.com/

Addresses

Institute of Hospitality
Trinity Court, 34 West Street, Sutton, Surrey SM1 1SH
Phone: +44 (0)20 8661 4900
Web: www.instituteofhospitality.org

Savoy Educational Trust
Queen's House 55-56 Lincoln's Inn Fields, London WC2A 3BH
Phone: +44 (0) 207 269 9692
Web: www.savoyeducationaltrust.org.uk

Similar Jobs

Catering Manager, Domestic Services Manager, Human Resources Officer/Manager, Leisure Manager, Publican, Restaurant Manager

Hotel Porter

CRCI:Catering and Hospitality
CLCI:IC
Job Band: 1

Job Description

Hotel porters are often the first to meet guests when they arrive at a hotel; they welcome and help the guests in any way they can. They carry luggage to bedrooms and may explain how any equipment works. Porters who work during the day may help guests by looking after luggage or keys, posting items and forwarding messages.

Porters may arrange reservations for a theatre or restaurant and book taxis. They can arrange travel reservations and run personal errands. Also gives information about the hotel's services and the local area. In a fire or emergency they help to evacuate the guests safely. Night porters may serve snacks and drinks, hand out newspapers and answer the phone.

Porters may be responsible for conference facilities. These include projectors and screens, microphones and computer facilities, flipcharts and stationery. May have to move furniture and laundry around the hotel and clean the reception area. A head porter manages and supervises a team of porters.

Work Details

Usually works around 38-40 hrs a week, probably on a split shift/rota basis which includes some nights and weekends. You mainly work indoors but sometimes may have to go outside to assist guests with their luggage or open car doors. In this job you meet all kinds of people and some of them can be very demanding. It is important to remain calm and polite at all times. You need to have a good knowledge of the local area so that you can help to direct guests to different places.

The job requires you to be on your feet for most of the day and you have to do some lifting and carrying. Night porters may have times when they are able to sit down, usually by the main entrance or reception area. Most hotel porters wear uniforms provided by their employer.

Qualification

There are no formal entry qualifications for this job and employers consider personal qualities to be more important. They may ask for a good level of general education. A smart or tidy appearance and good communication skills are essential.

• England, Wales and Northern Ireland

Band 1: For entry to jobs, no minimum qualifications are needed, but you are expected to have a good level of general education and relevant experience. Some formal/vocational qualifications at any level are useful.

• Scotland

Band 1: For entry to jobs, no minimum qualifications are needed, but you are expected to have a good level of general education and relevant experience. Some formal/vocational qualifications at any level are useful.

Adult Qualifications

No pre-entry qualifications are usually required for mature entrants, though some academic/vocational qualifications at any level may be an advantage. Employers look for particular qualities and skills, including a willingness to learn. You can improve your skills and qualifications by working through the Foundation Learning programme. This involves taking credit-based units and qualifications to help you progress.

Work Experience

Any work experience can help equip you with skills to use in the future and add to your CV. There is often plenty of paid part-time work in the hospitality industry. Any work experience dealing with the public is an advantage.

Entry and Training

You are usually trained on the job by a more experienced porter over several weeks or months. Training usually covers aspects such as room service techniques, setting up and laying out of function rooms, serving drinks and snacks, health and safety, and general hotel policy. A current clean driving licence is also useful. Some hotels may first employ you at 16 as a messenger, which can lead to a job as a porter. Many employers prefer you to be over 18.

A Diploma/Welsh Baccalaureate in hospitality may be available in your area. It is possible to work towards an S/NVQ in hospitality or customer service at level 1, or in front office or multi-skilled hospitality services at level 2. An S/NVQ at level 3 is available for those wishing to progress to a supervisory post. There are also relevant BTEC awards at QCF level 2 and vocationally-related qualifications, also at level 2. Training programmes, including apprenticeshipsin customer service leading to level 2 and advanced apprenticeships leading to level 3, may be available in your area.

Mature applicants with relevant experience in customer-related occupations, security work, or work within the armed forces or other disciplined jobs, have an advantage. Government training opportunities, such as apprenticeships, may be available in your area. You can also gain recognition of previous experience through Accreditation of Prior Learning (APL) or by working towards relevant S/NVQs. Contact your local careers office, Jobcentre Plus, Next Step service or Learning and Skills Council (LSC) Local Enterprise Company (LEC) for details of training schemes.

Opportunities and Pay

There are more than 35,000 hotels and guest houses in the UK. The larger ones are most likely to employ a porter. Jobs are available throughout the country with hotels and hotel chains of all sizes. There are opportunities to progress to be a front-of-house manager, although you usually need to extend your qualifications. You are more likely to be promoted to be a concierge or head porter in a larger hotel or hotel chain. Part-time and seasonal work is common.

Pay varies depending on location and employer, but most hotel porters start on around £12k rising to £13k-£18k a year with experience. Some head porters in major UK cities earn up to £20k, or more. Basic pay can be increased by overtime pay or by generous tips from guests. Some hotel porters live-in and are given free or subsidised meals and accommodation.

Health

This job requires good general fitness.

Skills and Qualities

able to cope under pressure, able to get on with all kinds of people, diplomatic, discreet, good memory, honest, reliable, smart appearance, strong, tactful

Relevant Subjects

Hospitality and catering

Further Information

Apprenticeship Schemes (National Apprenticeship Service) - www.apprenticeships.org.uk

CareerScope: Hospitality and Leisure (Springboard UK) - http://careerscope.springboarduk.net/

Caterer and Hotelkeeper (weekly) (Reed Business Information) - www.caterersearch.com/Home/

Diploma in Hospitality (People 1st) - www.hospitalitydiploma.co.uk

Foundation Learning (QCDA) - www.qcda.gov.uk

People 1st - sector skills council for hospitality, leisure, travel and tourism - www.people1st.co.uk

Real Life Guide to Hospitality & Event Management (Trotman 2010) - www.trotman.co.uk

Springboard UK (Springboard UK) - www.springboarduk.net

Springboard Wales (Springboard Wales) - http://wales.springboarduk.net/

Training Schemes - www.direct.gov.uk/en/educationandlearning

UKSP - Guide to Success in Hospitality, Leisure, Travel & Tourism - www.uksp.co.uk

▶Working in hospitality & catering (2009) (Babcock Lifeskills) - www.babcock-lifeskills.com/

Similar Jobs

Cloakroom Attendant, Door Attendant, Hospital Porter, Hotel Receptionist, Hotel Room Attendant, Security Officer

Hotel Receptionist

CRCI:Catering and Hospitality

CLCI:IC Job Band: 2 to 3

Job Description

Hotel receptionists welcome guests, process reservations, allocate rooms, issue keys and deal with cancellations, usually operating a computer system. They deal with enquiries by telephone, email, letter, fax, or face to face at the reception desk. They also take orders for room service, newspapers, taxis and theatre tickets, receive and pass on messages and deal with enquiries and any complaints from guests. May also provide information for guests on local places of interest.

Prepares and issues invoices ensuring additional items are included. This may include use of the hotel's beauty salon facilities, meals, purchase of products, use of minibar etc. Receives payment by cash, cheque or credit/debit card, gives a receipt and keeps accurate accounts. Other tasks include general clerical work, word processing, operating the switchboard and fax machine. May exchange travellers cheques or foreign currency and keep guests' valuables in the hotel safe, or operate a security box system.

Liaises with other departments of the hotel. This may be with housekeeping staff to determine when a room is available for use, or with porters to provide assistance to guests. Helps to evacuate the building in the event of an emergency.

Work Details

Most work shifts over seven days, including early mornings, evenings and weekends. Reception areas are usually light, warm and airy with pleasant surroundings. You work behind a large counter or desk that is close to the telephone switchboard and next to a computer terminal. You need to deal with enquiries from hotel guests at all times. Work can be demanding as you often have constant interruptions.

A good knowledge of the local area is necessary. Some guests may be demanding, but you need to be able to stay calm, courteous, patient and friendly. A uniform is usually provided, or smart clothing is required.

Qualification

• England, Wales and Northern Ireland

Band 2: For entry to jobs, no minimum qualifications are needed, but it is an advantage to have some GCSEs (A*-C) or equivalent in subjects that include English and maths. Good communication skills are essential and those with additional language skills or keyboard experience may have an advantage.

Band 3: For entry to jobs, HNC or a relevant Diploma, usually at least 4 GCSEs (A*-C) including English and maths, or equivalent.

• Scotland

Band 2: Although academic qualifications are not specified for this job, it is an advantage to have some S grades (1-3) in subjects that include English and maths, or similar. Good communication skills are essential and those with additional language skills or keyboard experience may have an advantage.

Band 3: For entry to jobs, usually at least four S grades (1-3) including English or maths, or similar.

Adult Qualifications

No pre-entry qualifications are usually required for mature entrants, although some academic/vocational qualifications at any level may be an advantage. English and maths are useful subjects.

Work Experience

Relevant work experience is always useful and can improve your chances in application for entry to hotel reception work. Types of work experience to consider include office work, general receptionist work and dealing directly with customers in the hotel or leisure industries.

Entry and Training

It is very useful to have knowledge of a foreign language, good communication, word-processing and computer skills. You can study for a one or two-year qualification before entering the job, or you can go straight into employment. Appropriate courses include the BTEC level 3 certificate/diploma in front office operations, the BTEC level 3 diploma in hospitality supervision and leadership skills, or a Scottish group award in hospitality.

Even if you have professional qualifications when you start work, you still need to train on the job to learn the hotel procedures, but you may be promoted more quickly. In-house training schemes may include day or block release at a local college, possibly to work towards relevant S/NVQs. These include S/NVQs such as front office at level 2, multi-skilled hospitality services at level 2 and hospitality supervision at level 3. City & Guilds also offer a QCF level 1 award in general front office operations.

A Diploma/Welsh Baccalaureate may be available in your area in hospitality. Training programmes, including apprenticeship schemes in hospitality or customer service, may be available in your area for entry to this job. Advanced apprenticeships leading to qualification at level 3 can also be a route into higher education.

Some employers may prefer mature entrants with experience of dealing with the public, or working in administration or secretarial work. Mature applicants can take refresher courses which may be available for those returning to work and there may also be special training schemes in some areas.

Government training opportunities, such as apprenticeships in hospitality or customer service, may be available in your area. You can also gain recognition of previous experience through Accreditation of Prior Learning (APL) or by working towards relevant S/NVQs. Contact your local careers office, Jobcentre Plus, Next Step service or Learning and Skills Council (LSC) Local Enterprise Company (LEC) for details of training schemes.

Opportunities and Pay

There are around 18,000 hotel receptionists in the UK and you can find jobs in many different places. These include hotels, motels, inns, travel lodges and guest houses, though competition is fierce. Promotion prospects are better in large hotels or hotel chains, and moves into general management and central reservations departments are common for people with good reception skills and qualifications. It is possible to be promoted to a shift leader/supervisor, or head receptionist and further promotion is to front office manager or duty manager.

Some move into sales or accounts sections that can lead to other managerial posts and may achieve a qualification from the Institute of Hospitality in hotel management. Others move into personnel or training and work towards a qualification from the Chartered Institute of Personnel and Development (CIPD). Receptionists can usually find part-time work and it is possible to work abroad.

Pay varies depending on location and employer. You may start on the National Minimum Wage but most hotel receptionists earn around £12k-£18k a year, rising to around £26k a year with experience. Some reception managers in large hotels can earn up to £30k. You may be paid extra for working unsocial hours. There may also be an opportunity to live in the hotel.

Health

You are expected to be able to speak clearly.

Skills and Qualities

able to get on with all kinds of people, calm, efficient, friendly, good telephone manner, IT skills, quick thinking, smart appearance, tactful

Relevant Subjects

Business and accounting, English, Hospitality and catering, ICT/Computer studies, Leisure, travel and tourism, Modern Foreign Languages

Further Information

Apprenticeship Schemes (National Apprenticeship Service) - www.apprenticeships.org.uk

CareerScope: Hospitality and Leisure (Springboard UK) - http://careerscope.springboarduk.net/

Caterer and Hotelkeeper (weekly) (Reed Business Information) - www.caterersearch.com/Home/

Diploma in Hospitality (People 1st) - www.hospitalitydiploma.co.uk

People 1st - sector skills council for hospitality, leisure, travel and tourism - www.people1st.co.uk

Real Life Guide to Travel and Tourism (Trotman) - www.trotman.co.uk

Springboard UK (Springboard UK) - www.springboarduk.net

Springboard Wales (Springboard Wales) - http://wales.springboarduk.net/

Training Schemes - www.direct.gov.uk/en/educationandlearning

UKSP - Guide to Success in Hospitality, Leisure, Travel & Tourism - www.uksp.co.uk

▶Working in business, administration & finance (2010) (Babcock Lifeskills) - www.babcock-lifeskills.com/

▶Working in hospitality & catering (2009) (Babcock Lifeskills) - www.babcock-lifeskills.com/

Addresses

Institute of Hospitality
Trinity Court, 34 West Street, Sutton, Surrey SM1 1SH
Phone: +44 (0)20 8661 4900
Web: www.instituteofhospitality.org

Similar Jobs

Airline Customer Service Agent, Clerk: Accounts, Leisure Centre Assistant, Receptionist, Secretary, Travel Consultant

Hotel Room Attendant

also known as: Accommodation Assistant

CRCI:Catering and Hospitality
CLCI:IC Job Band: 1

Job Description

Hotel room attendants keep bedrooms and bathrooms clean and tidy in hotels/motels, guest houses and holiday centres. They change bedlinen (pillowcases, sheets and duvet covers) and make the beds. Also cleans floors, vacuums carpets and dusts furniture, empties waste paper bins and cleans the floors. Attendants see that the rooms have a well-stocked minibar, tea/coffee making facilities and small snacks. They also check there is a supply of leaflets advertising the hotel services and any local tourist information brochures.

Room attendants clean the bathrooms and replace towels, bathrobes, shampoo, soap and shower gel if required. They take away all used items from the room, including crockery, cutlery, glasses, shampoo and soap containers. Also ensures that the room is always left inviting and comfortable. Attendants liaise with reception to tell them when a room is available for new guests and sometimes help in the linen store or clean public areas of the hotel. They report to the domestic services manager if there is any damage to items in the room or if anything is not working.

Higher grade hotels require a late-duty room attendant to visit a room early in the evening to close curtains, turn down bed covers and switch on any side lights, so that the room is welcoming for returning guests. They may also arrange flowers or baskets of fruit for guests.

Work Details

Usually works 38-40 hrs a week and may need to work shifts that include evenings and weekends. Is also expected to start work early in the morning. This type of work is very energetic, involves lots of bending and stretching and you have to cope with being on your feet for much of the time.

Your workplace is usually pleasant, although some of the cleaning tasks can be messy or dusty, but you are provided with a uniform or protective clothing. You may spend a lot of your time cleaning rooms on your own, but you work as part of a team.

Qualification

• England, Wales and Northern Ireland

Band 1: For entry to jobs, no minimum qualifications are needed, but you are expected to have a good level of general education and relevant experience. Some formal/vocational qualifications at any level are useful.

• Scotland

Band 1: For entry to jobs, no minimum qualifications are needed, but you are expected to have a good level of general education and relevant experience. Some formal/vocational qualifications at any level are useful.

Adult Qualifications
No pre-entry qualifications are usually required for mature entrants, though some academic/vocational qualifications at any level may be an advantage.

Work Experience
Any work experience in cleaning and support services can help equip you with skills that you can use in the future and add to your CV. Saturday jobs and seasonal cleaning work may be available in your area at places such as hotels, shopping and leisure centres, airports, schools and colleges, or at a holiday centre village.

Entry and Training
Employers look for people who are able to cope with the physical demands of the work and who are punctual, reliable and honest. Training is on the job and usually with an experienced colleague or a housekeeper, but may sometimes include a short course to learn basic skills and the standards of the hotel. You are introduced to the hotel routine and layout, the use, care and storage of cleaning materials, health and safety procedures, and how to report accurately to the relevant personnel. Employers are increasingly keen to offer the opportunity and support for further training towards vocational qualifications, such as S/NVQs.

City & Guilds offers a QCF level 1 award in general housekeeping operations. S/NVQs are available in housekeeping at level 2 and in cleaning and support services at levels 1-2. For promotion to a supervisory or management job you usually need to achieve a higher level qualification. This may include an S/NVQ at level 3-4 in hospitality supervision, or the City & Guilds level 3 diploma in cleaning services supervision. Training programmes, including hospitality and customer service apprenticeships leading to level 2 and advanced apprenticeships leading to level 3, may be available in your area. A Diploma/Welsh Baccalaureate may also be available in your area in hospitality.

Previous cleaning experience is an advantage. Employers look for people who are able to cope with the physical demands of the work and who are punctual, reliable and honest.

Government training opportunities, such as apprenticeships in hospitality and customer service, may be available in your area. You can also gain recognition of previous experience through Accreditation of Prior Learning (APL) or by working towards relevant S/NVQs. Contact your local careers office, Jobcentre Plus, Next Step service or Learning and Skills Council (LSC) Local Enterprise Company (LEC) for details of training schemes.

Opportunities and Pay
There are many jobs available throughout the UK for room attendants, especially in towns and cities. Temporary and seasonal work is often possible and there are usually more jobs during holiday periods. It is fairly easy to find part-time work. In larger hotels it may be possible to be promoted to a supervisory or management post, such as head housekeeper. Work may also be available with an agency or contract cleaning company.

Pay varies depending on location and employer, but most room attendants earn around £5.93 (the minimum wage if you are over 21) to £7.50 an hour (around £10k-£14k a year), rising to around £15.5k a year, depending upon experience and level of responsibility. Some guests may leave you a tip. Payment is given for working shifts or overtime. Some room attendants live-in and may be given free meals and accommodation.

Health
To do this job you have to have good stamina and general fitness. If you are allergic to dust you may find this job difficult.

Skills and Qualities
able to work quickly, able to work well on your own, attention to detail, discreet, energetic, hard working, honest, methodical, neat, tactful

Relevant Subjects
Hospitality and catering

Further Information
Apprenticeship Schemes (National Apprenticeship Service) - www.apprenticeships.org.uk

CareerScope: Hospitality and Leisure (Springboard UK) - http://careerscope.springboarduk.net/

Caterer and Hotelkeeper (weekly) (Reed Business Information) - www.caterersearch.com/Home/

People 1st - sector skills council for hospitality, leisure, travel and tourism - www.people1st.co.uk

Springboard UK (Springboard UK) - www.springboarduk.net

Training Schemes - www.direct.gov.uk/en/educationandlearning

UKSP - Guide to Success in Hospitality, Leisure, Travel & Tourism - www.uksp.co.uk

▶ Working in hospitality & catering (2009) (Babcock Lifeskills) - www.babcock-lifeskills.com/

Addresses
Institute of Hospitality
Trinity Court, 34 West Street, Sutton, Surrey SM1 1SH
Phone: +44 (0)20 8661 4900
Web: www.instituteofhospitality.org

Similar Jobs
Cleaner: Domestic, Cleaner: Industrial, Domestic Services Manager, Kitchen Assistant/Porter, Laundry Assistant/Manager

House Steward
also known as: Buildings Curator, Historic Buildings Conservation Officer

CRCI:Languages, Information and Culture
CLCI:FAE Job Band: 4 to 5

Job Description
House stewards are responsible for the care and conservation of a property of historical interest. This can be a landmark building like a house, mill or castle, perhaps with gardens or on a large estate and responsibilities vary accordingly. Many properties include a visitor centre, shop and restaurant or cafi. They are usually employed by a heritage organisation or a private owner or trust.

The key areas of responsibility include preventative conservation and housekeeping, which is a practical role involving the cleaning and care of all objects within the property as well as the fabric of the building itself. Stewards recruit, train and manage a multi-skilled team of staff and volunteers to carry out these duties. They have responsibility for fire safety and security measures for the property and for ensuring that all staff are aware of procedures. Administrative duties include budgetary control, record keeping and correspondence. Maintenance varies from changing light bulbs and cutting grass to minor repairs.

An increasingly important aspect of a house steward's job is visitor care and the promotion of the property to the general public. They may also have to prepare the property for functions or filming by television and film companies. Some stewards organise educational visits for schools and may, therefore, need to have a Criminal Records Bureau (CRB)/Disclosure Scotland check.

Work Details
Working hours may depend on the season. While the property is open to the public you are expected to work bank holidays and weekends, but during the 'off' season, you work more regular hours. For functions or special events you may be expected to work unsocial hours. You may need to live on or near the site and are often on call, especially for fire and security issues. The site can be in a rural or urban location.

House Steward

Qualification

• England, Wales and Northern Ireland

Band 4: For HND, Diploma of Higher Education or foundation degree: 1-2 A levels and some GCSEs (A*-C) usually including English and maths, or equivalent.

Band 5: For degree courses: 2-3 A levels and some GCSEs (A*-C) usually including English and maths, or equivalent. Exact requirements depend on the degree you take.

• Scotland

Band 4: For degree courses: 3-5 H grades and some S grades (1-3), including English and maths, or similar qualifications. Exact requirements depend on the degree you take.

Band 5: For degree courses: 3-5 H grades and some S grades (1-3), usually including English and maths, or similar qualifications. Exact requirements depend on the degree you take.

Degree Information

Although this area of work is open to all graduates, archaeology, history, history of art, heritage or museum studies, marketing or other business-related subjects, geography or countryside management may be useful.

Adult Qualifications

Entry requirements may be relaxed for adults applying for higher education courses. Access or foundation courses provide those without the required qualifications a route onto degree courses.

Work Experience

Entry to this career is highly competitive and it is essential that you have some relevant work or voluntary experience before applying. Seasonal work as a tour guide, interpreter or visitor reception assistant, though often poorly paid, provides experience and can sometimes lead to permanent work. The National Trust offers full and part time opportunities for volunteers at most of its properties. English Heritage runs an education volunteering programme at some of its sites.

Entry and Training

New entrants are usually graduates and some may hold postgraduate qualifications. There are an increasing number of postgraduate courses in heritage management offered by a number of universities.

The Museums Association (MA) offers student, professional and institutional membership which helps to demonstrate a commitment to continuing professional development (CPD). The MA runs a database of training courses for CPD, some of which are relevant to heritage work outside museums. In Scotland, a modern apprenticeship in cultural heritage may be available.

It is possible to move between related areas within heritage management, such as events organising at a historic venue, marketing and public relations (PR), outreach, visitor services or education. You can also use your skills in a related area, such as with a funding body, tourist organisation or in facilities management.

Relevant experience is essential, even for entry-level posts, for which competition is fierce. The growing need to develop customer services means that business or financial experience in any sector is valued.

Government training opportunities, such as apprenticeships in cultural and heritage venue operation, may be available in your area. You can also gain recognition of previous experience through Accreditation of Prior Learning (APL) or by working towards relevant S/NVQs. Contact your local careers office, Jobcentre Plus, Next Step service or Learning and Skills Council (LSC) Local Enterprise Company (LEC) for details of training schemes.

Opportunities and Pay

This is a small, competitive field. The National Trust is the principal employer of house stewards in the UK, although there are some opportunities in heritage sites that are privately run by the owner family or by a trust. Opportunities are often offered on fixed-term contracts of 3-5 years. You may need to move from a small to a large site to broaden your experience. Promotion is likely to involve moving on from one historic site to another. The post may be advertised as custodian or property, heritage or general manager. There are some opportunities for part-time work or for job share.

Starting salaries range from about £13.5k- £25k a year, depending on the size of the property and the range of duties. With experience this can rise to £26k-£35k a year. There may be benefits such as free accommodation and service bills included.

Health

This job requires a good level of physical fitness and stamina.

Skills and Qualities

able to cope with emergencies, able to get on with all kinds of people, able to manage people, able to work both on your own and in a team, excellent communication skills, health & safety awareness, interest in cultural heritage, IT skills, practical skills, problem-solving skills

Relevant Subjects

Art and Design, Business and accounting, Classical studies, Construction and built environment, English, History, ICT/ Computer studies, Leisure, travel and tourism, Mathematics, Media and communication studies

Further Information

Active (The National Trust) - www.nationaltrust.org.uk/main/w-trust/w-volunteering/ w-volunteering-active_magazine.htm

Apprenticeship Schemes (National Apprenticeship Service) - www.apprenticeships.org.uk

Creative & Cultural Skills - sector skills council for advertising, crafts, cultural heritage, design, literature, music, performing & visual arts - www.ccskills.org.uk

Museums Association - www.museumsassociation.org

Addresses

Cadw
Welsh Assembly Government, Plas Carew, Unit 5/7 Cefn Coed, Parc Nantgarw, Cardiff CF15 7QQ
Phone: +44 (0)1443 33 6000
Web: www.cadw.wales.gov.uk

English Heritage
1 Waterhouse Square, 138 - 142 Holborn, London EC1N 2ST
Phone: +44 (0)20 7973 3000
Web: www.english-heritage.org.uk/

National Trust
Heelis, Kemble Drive, Swindon, Wiltshire SN2 2NA
Phone: +44 (0)1793 817400
Web: www.ntjobs.org.uk

The National Trust for Scotland
Wemyss House, 28 Charlotte Square, Edinburgh EH2 4ET
Phone: +44(0)844 493 2100
Web: www.nts.org.uk/Home/

Similar Jobs

Arts Administrator, Facilities Manager, Factor (Scotland), Leisure Manager, Museum Assistant/Technician, Museum/Art Gallery Curator

Housing Officer

CRCI:Building and Construction
CLCI:UH Job Band: 3 to 5

Job Description

Housing officers help provide and manage rented accommodation for a community or for specific groups of people, in a fixed geographical area. They usually support the principal housing officer or housing manager in looking after the day-to-day running of rented properties for the owners. The owners are normally a housing organisation, university, a local authority or a property management company.

Officers assess people's needs, keeping in mind factors such as people with physical disabilities, the homeless, students or the elderly. Housing can then be bought, built, renovated or converted to meet their needs. Organising the allocation of accommodation, dealing with the fair assessment of rents and supervising methods of collection are all part of the job. Inspecting properties and making sure that repair and maintenance work is done is important.

Generally, officers give advice on housing problems, or on appropriate sources of benefits and welfare advice. They meet with tenants' societies and may liaise with social workers, private housing associations, architects and builders. Can deal with breaches of tenancy/leasehold agreements, abandoned premises, squatters and other unauthorised occupiers. Any changes in legislative and the regulatory framework surrounding housing and related services must be adhered to.

Work Details

Housing officers work between 37 and 40 hours a week, Monday to Friday. Usually works in an office, but some time is spent visiting clients' homes and inspecting property. Flexitime and overtime is sometimes necessary. Work includes interviewing people and giving them advice, as well as dealing with enquiries and complaints. Clients can be upset, or perhaps aggressive and demanding, and in need of support. Administration, finance, keeping records and planning take up a lot of your time.

Some of the decisions that you have to make may be unpopular. When visiting property you can be out in all weathers and it may be cold, damp and perhaps dirty. Smart appearance is expected.

Qualification

- **England, Wales and Northern Ireland**

Band 3: For a relevant BTEC national course: usually at least 4 GCSEs (A*-C), or equivalent.

Band 4: For a relevant BTEC higher national award: 1-2 A levels and some GCSEs (A*-C) usually including English and maths, or equivalent.

Band 5: For degree courses: 2-3 A levels and some GCSEs (A*-C) usually including English and maths, or equivalent. Exact requirements depend on the degree you take.

- **Scotland**

Band 3: For a relevant SQA national award or modules: often at least four S grades (1-3), or similar.

Band 4: For a relevant SQA higher national award: usually 2-3 H grades and some S grades (1-3) often including English and maths, or similar qualifications.

Band 5: For degree courses: 3-5 H grades and some S grades (1-3), usually including English and maths, or similar qualifications. Exact requirements depend on the degree you take.

Degree Information

A degree in any discipline is acceptable, but degrees in housing or land and property management are particularly relevant. Town planning, urban studies, economics, facilities management, social policy, politics, government and social administration, law and business management give useful background. Foundation degrees in housing and housing studies and specific postgraduate courses are also available.

Adult Qualifications

Entry requirements may be waived for mature applicants, particularly for those with relevant experience of voluntary work or administration. Colleges and universities often have special entry schemes for adults applying for degree and higher national courses.

Work Experience

Employers or colleges may prefer candidates who have relevant work or voluntary experience. Your local authority may also offer vacation work in their housing department. Office work also provides an insight into day-to-day clerical and administration tasks that support a department.

Entry and Training

There are various routes of entry to this job and to gain membership of the Chartered Institute of Housing (CIH). Training is usually on the job, supported by study for external courses and qualifications. You need to complete the academic requirements to gain the CIH professional qualification and membership (MCIH). Graduates who do not have a degree in a housing-related subject (cognate degree) can take a one-year CIH graduate conversion course which leads to the professional diploma. Courses can be taken at a college or through distance learning. New qualifications for the sector include the Foundation Degree in Housing which is now available at the City of Bristol College in partnership with the University of Plymouth.

APEX Express is the final step to corporate membership of the CIH and involves attending a one-day course and completing a personal development plan. Those in a junior post with A levels/H grades or less may be given the opportunity to undertake an HNC in housing studies, or equivalent, either by day release at a local college or by distance learning. Conferences, seminars and short courses are also available from the CIH and include aspects such as housing management law and basic debt counselling. Contact the CIH for full details of training and membership routes.

Level 2-4 qualifications have recently been developed in housing maintenance and management by the CIH in partnership with the Chartered Institute of Building. S/NVQs in housing are available at levels 2-4. Training programmes, including apprenticeship schemes, may be available in your area for entry to this job. A new apprenticeship for housing at level 3 has been officially approved following work by Asset Skills to bring it up to date and ensure it is meeting the needs of employers. Advanced apprenticeships leading to qualification at level 3 can also be a route into higher education.

Mature applicants are often preferred by employers and this can prove to be a good second career. There are several distance-learning courses offered through the Chartered Institute of Housing (CIH) including a graduate foundation course in housing. The CIH Education Service offers a guide specifically for career changers interested in housing. Contact the CIH for information on all courses and training routes.

Opportunities and Pay

Work may be available anywhere in the UK, although most jobs are in urban areas. Most housing officers work for a variety of housing organisations as local authorities have been reducing their involvement in the housing market. Charitable bodies provide a vital part of the market, usually in the provision of short-term or emergency accommodation, whereas the larger housing organisations tend to provide long-term family housing. Jobs are also available with housing trusts, private landlords and property companies.

There is usually a clear promotion structure, to principle housing officer and management posts, but this depends on your employer. You may need to be flexible with your home location if you wish to progress to a senior level. Increasingly, there are opportunities to work abroad in countries within the Commonwealth, the EU and elsewhere, including the USA.

Pay varies depending on location, employer and level of responsibility. Generally, earnings are between £20k and £30k a year. Senior housing managers can earn in excess of £50k a year.

Skills and Qualities

able to cope under pressure, able to manage a budget and keep records, able to work both on your own and in a team, adaptable, excellent communication skills, fair minded, good interpersonal skills, good organisational skills, IT skills, problem-solving skills

Relevant Subjects

Business and accounting, Economics, English, Law, Psychology, Sociology

Further Information

A Career in Housing (The Chartered Institute of Housing (CIH)) - www.cih.org/services/careers/index.php

Asset Skills - sector skills council for the places where we live and work - www.assetskills.org

Chartered Institute of Building (CIOB) (CIOB) - www.ciob.org.uk/home

Local Government Careers (Improvement and Development Agency) - www.lgcareers.com/publications/

▶Working in business, administration & finance (2010) (Babcock Lifeskills) - www.babcock-lifeskills.com/

Addresses

Chartered Institute of Housing (CIH)
Octavia House Westwood Way, Coventry CV4 8JP
Phone: +44 (0)24 7685 1700
Web: www.cih.org

City of Bristol College
College Green Centre, St George's Road, Bristol BS1 5UA
Phone: 00 44 (0)117 312 5000
Web: www.cityofbristol.ac.uk/index.php

National Council for Voluntary Organisations
Regent's Wharf, 8 All Saints Street, London N1 9RL
Phone: +44 (0)20 7713 6161
Web: www.ncvo-vol.org.uk

Similar Jobs

Facilities Manager, Local Government Administrator, Property Manager, Social Worker, Town Planner

Human Resources Officer/Manager

also known as: Employee Relations Officer, Personnel Officer

CRCI:Administration, Business and Office Work
CLCI:CAS Job Band: 3 to 5

Job Description

Human resources (HR) officers help with the recruitment, training and development of the staff within an organisation. They are responsible for getting the best from employees and making the most efficient use of the workforce. Main areas of work include staff recruitment and selection, training and development, employee relations, employee services (health and safety, counselling, medical and social facilities), rewards (benefits, bonuses, pay, job evaluation, salary reviews), and human resources planning. They may also be involved in disciplinary matters, retirement, outplacement and pensions.

HR officers ensure that employees are treated fairly and legally within the organisation. They draw up plans and policies, write reports and attend meetings. Advise management on matters such as pay negotiations, grievance and disciplinary procedures, and employment law.

Work Details

Usually work 35-40 a week, Monday to Friday, though sometimes weekend or shift work is required. You are based in an office but may need to travel to other sites of work, depending on the size and type of employer. You have to create good communication links and liaise with line managers, trade unions, and staff in job centres and careers offices. Large companies usually have a number of human resources officers specialising in particular parts of the job.

The job may involve moving around and meeting staff in all departments. An understanding and sympathetic manner is needed when dealing with people under stress, but you also have to remain aware of your responsibilities to the company. You have to be able to work under pressure and remain calm in difficult situations.

The work involves collating and interpreting statistics, making financial calculations and gathering facts for planning, often using a computer. You sometimes have to make difficult decisions and take unpopular action, such as dealing with grievances and making people redundant.

Qualification

- **England, Wales and Northern Ireland**

Band 3: For the CIPD Certificate in Personnel Practice (CPP) and for direct entry to human resources/personnel, clerical and administrative jobs: 4 GCSEs (A*-C) or equivalent preferred, though not essential.

Band 4: For a relevant BTEC higher national award: 1-2 A levels and some GCSEs (A*-C) usually including maths and English, or equivalent.

Band 5: For degree courses: 2-3 A levels including English and some GCSEs (A*-C) usually including maths and English, or equivalent. Exact requirements depend on the degree you take.

- **Scotland**

Band 3: For the CIPD Certificate in Personnel Practice (CPP) and for direct entry to human resources/personnel, clerical or administrative jobs: four S grades (1-3) or similar preferred, though not essential.

Band 4: For an SQA higher national award: usually 2-3 H grades and some S grades (1-3), often including English and maths, or similar qualifications.

Band 5: For degree course: 3-5 H grades and some S grades (1-3), usually including English and maths, or similar qualifications. Exact requirements depend on the degree you take.

Degree Information

The degree can be in any discipline though there are first degrees in human resource management and combined subject courses, including management with human resource management, and with law, business information management, psychology and languages. These degrees and some first degrees in law, behavioural sciences and business studies may give exemptions from the Chartered Institute of Personnel and Development (CIPD) qualification scheme. Relevant foundation degrees, including human resources management and in business, are also available and may be studied either full or part time. There are postgraduate diplomas in human resource management that lead to CIPD membership.

Adult Qualifications

There are no set entry requirements. A good general education is needed with a high standard of written and spoken English and numeracy, plus a basic understanding of statistical and graphical information. There are some exemptions from CIPD qualifications for those who have been awarded a postgraduate qualification in the last ten years. Entry requirements may be relaxed for adults applying for higher education courses and Access courses give adults without qualifications a route on to degree courses.

Work Experience

Employers and/or universities may prefer candidates who have skills in administration, working with the public and in a team. You can gain such experience as a student through clubs/societies and by then taking positions of responsibility, such as helping to organise events or in a financial/administrative role. Similar voluntary or paid employment during vacations or whilst on a course placement, also provide you with relevant skills. A graduate internship scheme has been launched this year to create 5000 opportunities for graduates to gain some work experience. See the CIPD website for details. With all jobs, experience or knowledge of basic accounting or statistics is an advantage. Employers look for evidence of good interpersonal skills.

Entry and Training

Most entrants have an HND or a degree and possibly a postgraduate qualification. There is keen competition for vacancies, especially for new graduates, and membership of the Chartered Institute of Personnel Development (CIPD) is an advantage. It is usually necessary to study for the CIPD qualifications, which can be completed by following a full or part-time course, or by distance learning while working. If you are already working in HR and development, then a CIPD NVQ enables you to work towards CIPD membership. NVQs are available in personnel, learning and development and management. Assessor and verifier awards are also available. Check the CIPD website for full details.

Entry or support-level qualifications include the Certificate in Personnel Practice (CPP) and Certificate in Training Practice (CTP). The Professional Development Scheme (PDS), which has four main areas of study, is often a requirement at middle and senior management level and can be completed either by one-year full-time study, or around two to three years of part-time study that includes a number of days, evenings and block-study periods. No academic qualifications are required to enrol on a CIPD programme.

S/NVQs are available in learning and development at levels 3-5, or in personnel support, personnel management and personnel strategy at levels 3-5, which can lead to associate/licentiate level of CIPD membership. Training programmes, including apprenticeship schemes, may be available in your area. Advanced apprenticeships leading to qualification at level 3 can also be a route into higher education.

Mature entrants with experience and/or qualifications in a related area of work, such as at senior administrative or management level, or in law, may have an advantage. Distance learning and other flexible study programmes for the PDS are offered by the CIPD. Those working at a senior level and having over five years' experience, but with no formal related qualifications, may be assessed for membership of the CIPD.

Opportunities and Pay

Human resources/personnel officers work in a wide range of organisations throughout the UK, including local or central government, the NHS, industry and commerce, retail, power and water companies. Recently the number of jobs in further and higher education has increased, but entry is still competitive. Acquiring qualifications, whether S/NVQs or through the CIPD exams, is often seen as essential to promotion. It is possible to specialise in areas such as recruitment, training or industrial relations.

Promotion to human resources manager/director is dependent on personal achievement and many larger organisations have a good promotion structure. It is possible to work overseas for a multinational organisation, or set up a consultancy offering a specialised service, such as recruitment. Freelance work is also possible.

The civil service fast stream has launched an HR scheme. This enables graduates to become qualified HR professionals while working in a wide ranging job covering workforce development and change. Check the fast stream website for details.

Salaries in local authorities and in small retail organisations tend to be lower than those in large manufacturing companies and public corporations, so pay varies depending on location, size and type of company. Generally, starting salaries for graduates are likely to be in the region of £22k a year, rising to £25k-£32k with experience. Those at a more senior level can earn £35k-£60k, depending on the level of experience and responsibility. Personnel directors can earn up to £100k a year or more. Pay can vary according to your specialism. Compensation and benefits roles tend to attract higher salaries.

Skills and Qualities

able to manage people, able to work to a budget, analytical skills, approachable, discreet, efficient record keeping, excellent communication skills, flexible approach, good organisational skills, objective

Relevant Subjects

Business and accounting, Economics, English, ICT/Computer studies, Law, Mathematics, Modern Foreign Languages, Psychology, Sociology

Further Information

Civil Service Fast Stream (Civil Service) - www.civilservice.gov.uk/jobs/faststream

Human Resource Management Guide (HRM Guide Network) - www.hrmguide.co.uk/

Inside Careers Guide: Human Resources - www.insidecareers.co.uk

Local Government Careers (Improvement and Development Agency) - www.lgcareers.com/publications/

People Management Magazine (CIPD) - www.peoplemanagement.co.uk/pm

▶Working in business, administration & finance (2010) (Babcock Lifeskills) - www.babcock-lifeskills.com/

▶Working in police, fire & security (2009) (Babcock Lifeskills) - www.babcock-lifeskills.com/

Addresses

Chartered Institute of Personnel and Development (CIPD)
151 The Broadway, London SW19 1JQ
Phone: +44 (0)20 8612 6200
Web: www.cipd.co.uk

ENTO (Employment National Training Organisation)
Kimberley House, 47 Vaughan Way, Leicester LE1 4SG
Phone: +44 (0)116 251 7979
Web: www.ento.co.uk

Similar Jobs

Health Service Manager, Management Consultant, Operational Researcher, Psychologist: Occupational, Recruitment Consultant, Training & Development Officer/Manager

Hypnotherapist

CRCI:Social Work and Counselling Services
CLCI:KEZ
Job Band: 1 to 5

Job Description

Hypnotherapists use deep relaxation and suggestion to help clients change behaviour or emotions they are unhappy with. Clients may want to overcome addictions, habits, phobias, feelings or disorders that are affecting their lives.

They talk with the client to find out more about the problem and what the client wants. Ask about the client's medical history and about their daily life. Explain about hypnosis to the client and how it may help in their case. Hypnotise the client to put them into deep mental and physical relaxation. Make positive suggestions that may help the client to feel differently and change their behaviour.

Then they bring the client out of deep relaxation and ask them about their feelings during and after the session. May teach clients how to hypnotise themselves.

Hypnotherapists keep records about each client and their sessions. They prepare and distribute marketing materials. They also deal with appointments, bills, premises, insurance and general paperwork.

Work Details

Most hypnotherapists are self-employed and work part time. Hours of work vary to suit yourself and your clients. Appointments may be during the day, in the evening or at weekends. Sessions with clients usually last 60-90 minutes. May work with a client over 2-3 sessions or more, depending on the nature of the problem.

Works sitting down in a comfortable and quiet room, often in their own home or a shared practice. May travel to sessions in clients' homes, doctors' surgeries, clinics or hospitals.

Qualification

Currently there are no rules about the training you need to be a qualified hypnotherapist. The profession wants to set minimum qualifications and standards for practitioners. To practise as a hypnotherapist, you should choose a diploma (practitioner level) course accredited by professional bodies such as the UK Confederation of Hypnotherapy Organisations (UKCHO) or the General Hypnotherapy Standards Council (GHSC) or their member organisations.

Some courses are aimed specifically at healthcare professionals wishing to offer hypnotherapy to their patients. For entry to these postgraduate level courses, you need to be a fully qualified and experienced professional in your healthcare field.

Adult Qualifications

No formal qualifications are required, but training schools look for people with life experience and a mature outlook, who are able to cope with the demands of the course.

Work Experience

Work experience helps you find out what you enjoy and do not enjoy about a job. Paid or voluntary work dealing with people in a helping role is useful. Activities where you use listening skills and build a rapport with people also help. Talking to a hypnotherapist about their job gives you a valuable insight into the work. Client confidentiality means you are probably not able to watch them at work.

Entry and Training

Most hypnotherapists do a training course with a private hypnotherapy training organisation before setting up their practice. You have to pay for the course yourself. Some of the courses offered by training organisations are accredited by professional hypnotherapy bodies. Anyone wanting to go into hypnotherapy as a career should do an accredited diploma course.

As this is seen as a job where maturity and life experience is important, some providers set a minimum age for students on their courses. Courses are usually part time and often run at weekends over several months or more. They have taught, practical and self-study elements, with written assignments and practical work. Diploma courses usually cover setting up your own business as well as what you need to know about hypnotherapy.

In the future, practising hypnotherapists may have to be qualified and registered. Most hypnotherapists join one of the professional hypnotherapy bodies. Usually you need a recognised qualification and often some supervised practice. Some professional bodies maintain registers of members that the public can use to find a practitioner. The members of most of the professional bodies now appear on the National Regulatory Register for Hypnotherapy. Before long, all hypnotherapists who meet the entry criteria will be able to have an entry on this register. Hypnotherapists need to keep up to date with new ideas and techniques through workshops, courses and conferences.

People often move into hypnotherapy as a second career. Many come from areas such as education, health and social care, where they have gained valuable experience of helping people to overcome problems. Courses are often designed so that people can continue in full-time employment whilst working towards hypnotherapy qualifications.

Opportunities and Pay

Demand for all forms of complementary medicine is growing. There are over 3,800 out of an estimated 5,000 hypnotherapists on the National Regulatory Register for Hypnotherapy. Most are self-employed and a few work in private clinics. Some use hypnotherapy alongside counselling and other therapies to help people improve their daily lives. Others focus on one area of work, such as helping people to stop smoking or lose weight. Those who work for the national health service (NHS) are usually qualified medical staff. When you are well established, you may decide to offer training courses or other therapies.

Earnings vary depending on location, how much you charge and how many clients you see. Many hypnotherapists charge between £30 and £80 a session; some charge considerably more.

Skills and Qualities

able to explain clearly, able to get on with all kinds of people, able to inspire confidence, able to motivate others, able to put people at ease, awareness of confidentiality issues, business awareness, emotionally strong, good listening skills, non-judgemental

Relevant Subjects

English, Health and social care, Psychology, Sociology

Further Information

General Hypnotherapy Standards Council (GHSC) - www.ghsc.co.uk

National Regulatory Register for Hypnotherapy - www.hypnotherapyregulation.co.uk

Addresses

General Hypnotherapy Register
PO Box 204, Lymington SO41 6WP
Web: www.general-hypnotherapy-register.com

UK Confederation of Hypnotherapy Organisations (UKCHO)
Suite 404, Albany House, 324/326 Regent Street,
London W1B 3HH
Phone: +44 (0)800 952 0560
Web: www.ukcho.co.uk

Similar Jobs

Counsellor, Naturopath, Psychoanalyst, Psychologist: Counselling, Psychotherapist

Illustrator

CRCI:Design, Arts and Crafts
CLCI:ED Job Band: 3 to 5

Job Description

Illustrators design and produce illustrations for magazines and newspapers, book jackets, film animation, greetings cards and posters, packaging, education and training materials, corporate identity etc. from a brief provided by a client. They apply creative and imaginative talent with art and graphic design skills to produce an illustration that meets the requirements of the brief. This involves ongoing consultations and discussions with the client. Rough designs are initially produced to discuss with the client and they often use computer-aided design (CAD) or graphics software to create the finished piece.

Some specialise in children's book illustration or in technical, scientific or medical illustration for reference works. Illustrators produce original work for promotion purposes or for exhibitions. If working as a freelance illustrator, they need to look after their own business and keep records and accounts.

Work Details

Employed illustrators may work a basic 35-40 hr week; Monday to Friday, though may be expected to work longer hours to complete a project. May work as part of a team including authors and other designers and editors.

Self-employed illustrators usually choose the hours they work, which can be irregular as the work is often combined with other full or part-time employment. They usually work alone in a studio, often from home, and some choose to work evenings and weekends. They spend some time promoting their work to people who can sell it, such as dealers and agents and working with clients to understand their requirements.

Qualification

• England, Wales and Northern Ireland

Band 4: For diploma in foundation studies in art and design: usually at least one A level and 3-4 GCSEs (A*-C). For BTEC higher national award: a BTEC national award, successful completion of a foundation studies course, or equivalent.

Band 5: For degree courses: 2-3 A levels and some GCSEs (A*-C) usually including English and maths, or equivalent qualifications. Most students take a foundation studies course in art and design first. Exact requirements depend on the degree you take.

• Scotland

Band 4: For entry to SQA higher national and professional development awards, usually 2-3 H grades and some S grades (1-3), including English and maths, or similar qualifications.

Band 5: For degree courses: 3-5 H grades and some S grades (1-3), usually including English and maths, or similar qualifications. Exact requirements depend on the degree you take.

Degree Information

A degree in an art and design subject, such as fine art, graphic design or illustration, is most suitable. Course titles vary, so check prospectuses carefully. There are also postgraduate diplomas and degrees in fine art and illustration.

Adult Qualifications

Mature applicants with outstanding portfolios of work may be accepted for courses without the standard entry requirements. There are Access and foundation courses in some areas, which give adults without qualifications a route onto degree courses. Check with individual institutions.

Work Experience

Entry to this job/career is highly competitive and it is essential you have some relevant work or voluntary experience before applying. Most illustrators are self-employed and often self-taught so it may difficult be to gain direct relevant work experience. However any experience in a publishing company or design studio is relevant and helps to build up a good portfolio of work.

Entry and Training

Entry to reputable art courses is highly competitive. Exceptional talent is needed, and for most courses you have to provide a portfolio of work. Most illustrators take formal courses in art and design and those who obtain employment are often graduates or those with a relevant HND in illustration or an art-related subject. Talented applicants without qualifications can occasionally obtain college places. Check current course requirements carefully, because colleges accept a range of different qualifications.

Students usually take an art and design foundation studies course in art and design before taking a three-year degree course. Foundation degrees in art and design and in graphic design subjects are also available in some areas, and these can be studied full or part time. In Scotland, degree courses last for four years; the first year is general, before specialising in a particular area of art and design. A Diploma/Welsh Baccalaureate may be available in your area in creative and media and may provide a route onto higher education courses. An arts, media and publishing apprenticeship may be available in your area.

Illustrators are expected to keep up to date with the latest developments in computer technology and software packages. You can join the Association of Illustrators (AOI) or the Institute of Scientific and Technical Communicators and benefit from professional recognition and seminars and training courses. The AOI runs a one-day survival guide for students and new illustrators which provides information on all aspects of setting up a small business as a professional illustrator. Evening classes, competitions and workshops are also offered by Design & Art Direction (D&AD).

Mature applicants with experience in graphic art or in art and design may have an advantage, though entry to this work is very competitive. Part-time courses are available for mature students, but applicants must be at least 21. You need a portfolio of your work for entry to courses and for employers.

Opportunities and Pay

There is strong competition for work in art and design. Illustrators are usually freelance, receiving commissions through an art editor or agent, though they can be employed on a permanent basis by design studios or publishing companies who require onging illustration work. However, few can support themselves solely by selling their work. Career progression is limited and computer graphics programs make it increasingly possible for publishers to create their own illustrations. It can take many years, often with little income, to build up a reputation. Some may progress from freelance illustrator to art director with a firm of publishers, and a small number work as agents for other illustrators. Most have additional jobs such as teaching, community art work, art therapy and art administration.

As most illustrators work freelance, salary figures are hard to estimate. Advice about rates of pay can be found on the Association of Illustrators (AOI) website. Rates are usually per illustration and pay varies according to the state of the market. Agents' commission fees of up to 40% may be charged. Employed illustrators can earn in the range of £16k-£20k a year, rising to around £26k-£30k a year. Highly successful illustrators can earn up to £40k and a few earn more.

Skills and Qualities

artistic ability, attention to detail, creative flair, eye for shape/colour, eye for visual effect, imaginative, innovative, observational skills, technical aptitude

Relevant Subjects

Art and Design, ICT/Computer studies

Further Information

Apprenticeship Schemes (National Apprenticeship Service) - www.apprenticeships.org.uk

Artists Information Company - www.a-n.co.uk

Creative & Cultural Skills - sector skills council for advertising, crafts, cultural heritage, design, literature, music, performing & visual arts - www.ccskills.org.uk

Diplomas (Foundation, Higher and Advanced) http://yp.direct.gov.uk/diplomas

Institute of Scientific & Technical Communicators (ISTC) - www.istc.org.uk

NSEAD: Careers in Art, Craft & Design (National Society for Education in Art and Design) - www.nsead.org/resources/careers.aspx

VAROOM Journal of Illustration and Made Images (3 x year) (Association of Illustrators) - www.theaoi.com/

▶ Working in art & design (2009) (Babcock Lifeskills) - www.babcock-lifeskills.com/

▶ Working in creative & media (2007) (Babcock Lifeskills) - www.babcock-lifeskills.com/

Addresses

Association of Illustrators (AOI)
2nd Floor, Back Building, 150 Curtain Road, London EC2A 3AT
Phone: +44 (0)20 7613 4328
Web: www.theaoi.com

British Design & Art Direction (D&AD)
9 Graphite Square Vauxhall Walk, London SE11 5EE
Phone: +44 (0)20 7840 1111
Web: www.dandad.org

Similar Jobs

Artist, Graphic Designer, Illustrator: Archaeological, Illustrator: Technical/Scientific, Medical Artist, Website Designer

Illustrator: Archaeological

also known as: Surveyor: Archaeological

CRCI:Design, Arts and Crafts
CLCI:UM Job Band: 4 to 5

Job Description

Archaeological illustrators create visual representations of the past, draw or create maps, plans and illustrations of a site to be excavated, artefacts and buildings and work closely with the rest of the archaeological team. They are central to recording fieldwork, publishing results and aiding the interpretation of a site.

Illustrators first studies the site, then use sophisticated survey technologies such as systems and laser alignment or satellite positioning, to locate and plot relevant geophysical features. They produce plans and detailed drawings as the 'dig' progresses of artefacts/objects such as glass, wood, flint, antler and worked bone, bronze/iron and pottery. Also produce plans/detailed drawings of archaeological sections, as well as mapping the entire site.

They may take and develop photographs or use digital photography, microphotography, and aerial/underwater photography. During the excavation, they interpret findings and record details by cross-section plans and drawings using techniques that are closely related to architectural/engineering drawing. This requires clarity and accuracy, rather than artistic impression. May produce 3D images as well as drawings of the site, individual people, artefacts and buildings using computer software, virtual reality (VR) and geographical information systems (GIS).

Illustrators may be involved in reconstruction work for academic interpretation, education, and public presentation such as books, TV/DVD and museum displays.

Work Details

Usually work 35-40 hrs a week; Monday to Friday, sometimes in an office and also on-site, which can be outside and in all weathers. Conditions may be cold and damp. You may need to work irregular hours in an isolated place and perhaps live in a tent, hut or caravan. You advise and liaise with the project team and are responsible for analysing details and providing reports, often using sophisticated computer programs. Travel overseas may be necessary, perhaps to remote areas.

Qualification

- **England, Wales and Northern Ireland**

Band 4: For some courses: two A levels and 3-4 GCSEs (A*-C) usually including English and maths, or other equivalent qualifications.

Band 5: For degree courses: 2-3 A levels and some GCSEs (A*-C) usually including English and maths, or equivalent. Exact requirements depend on the degree you take.

- **Scotland**

Band 4: For some courses: usually 2-3 H grades and some S grades (1-3), often including English and maths, or similar qualifications.

Band 5: For degree courses: 3-5 H grades and some S grades (1-3), usually including English and maths, or similar qualifications. Exact requirements depend on the degree you take.

Degree Information

UCL Institute of Archaeology offers a course in archaeological illustration and imaging that covers both the traditional methods and modern digital methods of drawing archaeological finds. Most archaeology courses also cover illustration and survey. A degree including land surveying or a related subject is also useful. Graduates with related degrees can take a relevant postgraduate course, such as the MA in archaeological illustration also at Swindon College.

Adult Qualifications

Entry requirements may be relaxed for adults applying for higher education courses and Access or foundation courses give adults without qualifications a route into degree courses. Those with relevant work experience may be accepted for some college courses without needing any formal entry requirements. A portfolio of work is necessary for entry to art and design courses.

Work Experience

Entry to this job is competitive and it is important that you try to do some relevant work or voluntary experience before applying. Time spent with a council planning department, a land surveying practice, museum or heritage organisation, an historical society or with an archaeological illustrator/surveyor is valuable. It is advisable to look at archaeological books, reports and magazines in a library to find out as much as you can about the subject. Voluntary work on an archaeological dig shows commitment to this specialist area and also provides valuable experience.

Entry and Training

There are various routes to enter this job and as an introduction, a relevant HNC/HND course provides you with a good background in design and illustration, or in surveying. There is also a foundation degree in field archaeology. A few full-time specialist degree courses are available including postgraduate qualifications. A portfolio of your work is usually required for entry to courses and jobs. Many entrants are graduates in a related discipline who then specialise in archaeological illustration and surveying through postgraduate diplomas/degrees or through part-time, evening classes and distance-learning courses.

Many evening and short courses are run by universities and colleges throughout the UK, though the emphasis may be on traditional methods of illustration and surveying. Courses are also available in digital illustration. It is useful to have knowledge of computer-aided design (CAD) and programs such as Adobe Illustrator/Photoshop, CorelDraw, MapInfo and surveying packages, including PenMap.

The Association of Archaeological Illustrators & Surveyors (AAI&S) provides information on the profession and a range of useful links to other websites. The Institute of Field Archaeologists (IFA) has a process of personal development planning to keep archaeologists up to date. You can join the Association of Illustrators (AOI) and benefit from professional recognition and seminars and training courses.

Mature applicants with relevant experience and/or qualifications in illustration/surveying may have an advantage, though you need to be able to demonstrate your commitment and enthusiasm, as well as providing a portfolio of your work.

Opportunities and Pay

This is a small, relatively new profession, and there are few vacancies. You can work for a public organisation such as English Heritage, Historic Scotland, Cadw: Welsh Historic Monuments, and the Environment and Heritage Service (NI), or for organisations such as the National Trust and others with historic or land interests. Some illustrators find work with archaeological trusts. A few opportunities may be available with a national agency, including the Forestry Commission or a National Park.

This is not a particularly well paid job. Pay is similar to that of an archaeologist with a graduate entrant likely to earn in the region of £16k-£21k a year. Senior archaeological illustrators/surveyors with managerial responsibility or working in higher education can earn up to £30k.

Health

You need good eyesight and good colour vision for certain areas of work. Stamina and a good level of physical fitness is also necessary.

Skills and Qualities

accurate, analytical skills, aptitude for teamwork, attention to detail, drawing ability, good spoken and written communication, methodical, observant, specialist IT skills, technical aptitude

Relevant Subjects

Art and Design, Classical studies, English, Geography, History, Mathematics, Physics, Science

Further Information

Archaeological Illustration (Cambridge) - www.cambridge.org/catalogue

Artists & Illustrators (The Chelsea Magazine Co. Ltd.) - www.artistsandillustrators.co.uk/

British Archaeological Jobs Resource (BAJR) - www.bajr.org

Creative & Cultural Skills - sector skills council for advertising, crafts, cultural heritage, design, literature, music, performing & visual arts - www.ccskills.org.uk

Creative Choices - www.creative-choices.co.uk/

Current Archaeology (Current Publishing) - www.archaeology.co.uk

Graphic Archaeology News (3 x year) (Association of Archaeological Illustrators and Surveyors) - www.aais.org.uk/publications.html

Working outdoors (2010) (Babcock Lifeskills) - www.babcock-lifeskills.com/

Addresses

Association of Archaeological Illustrators & Surveyors (AAI&S)
SHES University of Reading Whiteknights PO Box 227,
Berkshire RG6 6AB
Web: www.aais.org.uk

Association of Illustrators (AOI)
2nd Floor, Back Building, 150 Curtain Road, London EC2A 3AT
Phone: +44 (0)20 7613 4328
Web: www.theaoi.com

Council for British Archaeology (CBA)
St Mary's House, 66 Bootham, York YO30 7BZ
Phone: +44 (0)1904 671 417
Web: www.britarch.ac.uk

Institute for Archaeologists (IFA)
SHES Whiteknights University of Reading PO Box 227,
Berkshire RG6 6AB
Phone: +44 (0)118 378 6446
Web: www.archaeologists.net

Similar Jobs

Archaeologist, Artist, Illustrator, Illustrator: Technical/Scientific, Medical Artist, Surveyor: Geomatics/Geospatial

Illustrator: Technical/Scientific

CRCI:Design, Arts and Crafts
CLCI:ED Job Band: 3 to 5

Job Description

Technical illustrators create detailed diagrams and drawings to aid the understanding of technical and scientific information, for textbooks or general interest publications, catalogues, instruction manuals, publicity materials and technical sales brochures. Thy usually work from instructions from a client and may prepare work for communication with the general public, specific engineers or scientists or highly skilled experts. This can also be in the form of education and training films, presentation slides, cartoon work, or natural history illustrations.

Illustrations can range from a complex aircraft, to everyday items such as cameras, calculators or televisions. Illustrators research the subject to ensure that they have all the required information. Then they examine what is to be drawn, or draw a sketch of it, for example a plan of a car gearbox or an electrical circuit, and decide on the type and function of the illustration needed. They produce a technically precise but clearly presented drawing, such as a sectional view, a cut-away drawing or an exploded view. Use various hand tools, including pencils, pens and paints, computer graphics and perhaps photographic and airbrush techniques.

Work Details

Those who are employed by a company usually work five days a week; Monday to Friday, for around 39 hours. The hours vary for self-employed illustrators, but can be long if deadlines have to be met. The work is done in a studio/office, or perhaps at home, but may involve site visits. Attention to detail and accuracy are very important.

Qualification

• England, Wales and Northern Ireland

Band 3: For entry to jobs, HNC or a relevant Diploma, usually at least 4 GCSEs (A*-C) including English and maths, or equivalent. For some foundation studies courses at least 5 GCSEs (A*-C). Equivalent qualifications may also be acceptable.

Band 4: For diploma in foundation studies (art and design): usually at least one A level and some GCSEs (A*-C). For BTEC higher national award: a BTEC national award, foundation studies course or 1-2 A levels and some GCSEs (A*-C) usually including English and maths, or equivalent.

Band 5: For degree courses: 2-3 A levels and 5 GCSEs (A*-C), usually including English and maths, or equivalent qualifications. Most students take a foundation studies course first. Exact requirements depend on the degree you take.

• Scotland

Band 3: For entry: usually at least four S grades (1-3) including English and maths, or similar.

Band 4: For entry to SQA higher national and professional development awards, usually 2-3 H grades and some S grades (1-3), including English and maths, or similar qualifications.

Band 5: For degree courses: 3-5 H grades and some S grades (1-3), usually including English and maths, or similar qualifications. Exact requirements depend on the degree you take.

Degree Information

Degrees include illustration, scientific and natural history illustration, and information illustration. Courses such as graphic design (illustration) or design and technology may provide specialist knowledge. Postgraduate courses in illustration are available for those with relevant first degrees or diplomas.

Adult Qualifications
Mature applicants with outstanding portfolios of work may be accepted for courses without the standard entry requirements. There are Access and foundation courses in some areas, which give adults without qualifications a route onto degree courses. Check with individual colleges.

Work Experience
Entry to this job is competitive and it is important that you try to do some relevant work or voluntary experience before applying. Colleges/universities may prefer candidates who have shown enthusiasm and commitment by gaining early work experience. Freelance illustrators, publishing houses and advertising firms may offer you work experience that provides the opportunity to build on your portfolio of work and develop contacts in the industry.

Entry and Training
Most technical illustrators are graduates or hold HNC/HND qualifications. Course titles and content vary, so check prospectuses carefully. A portfolio of your art work is needed for entry to courses and jobs. There are specialist courses at HND, degree and postgraduate levels, though graphic designers, or those qualified in other areas of art, may be able to become illustrators if they have good technical skills and knowledge. A degree in illustration is available at Blackpool and The Fylde College. The course has evolved out of the specialist areas of technical information illustration and scientific and natural history illustration. Most students take a foundation studies course before taking a three-year degree course.

Foundation degrees (FdAs) in art and design, illustration and animation, and in graphic design subjects are available in some areas, and these can be studied full or part time. In Scotland, degree courses last for four years; the first year is general, before specialising in a particular area of art and design.

Illustrators are expected to keep up to date with the latest developments in computer technology and software packages. The Institute of Scientific and Technical Communicators (ISTC) offers a programme of continuing professional development (CPD). You can also join the Association of Illustrators (AOI) and benefit from professional recognition and seminars and training courses.

Mature applicants with experience in graphic art or in art and design, and a technical background, may have an advantage though entry to this area of work is very competitive. Part-time art and design courses are available for mature students, but applicants must be at least 21. You need a portfolio of your work for entry to courses and for an employer.

Opportunities and Pay
Most technical illustrators are self-employed and look for projects themselves or use an agency. However, registering with an agency is highly competitive. A small number of illustrators are in full-time employment with manufacturing companies, or the automotive or aircraft industries. You can also be employed by a publisher, museum, advertising or publicity firm, government department or in industrial research. There is fierce competition for very few vacancies. Technical illustrators may specialise in a particular field such as commercials, television, or digital illustrations. There may also be opportunities to work overseas.

Pay varies depending on area and employer. Starting salaries are around £16k-£20k, rising to £25k-£30k a year with experience. High earners make over £40k a year. Agents may take up to 40% in commission.

Health
Normal colour vision is needed.

Skills and Qualities
able to work well on your own, accurate, attention to detail, drawing ability, good concentration level, meticulous, resourceful, scientific approach, specialist IT skills, technical aptitude

Relevant Subjects
Art and Design, Design and technology, Engineering, English, ICT/Computer studies, Mathematics, Physics, Science

Further Information
Communicator (ISTC, quarterly) (Institute of Scientific & Technical Communicators (ISTC)) - www.istc.org.uk/Publications/communicator.htm

Creative & Cultural Skills - sector skills council for advertising, crafts, cultural heritage, design, literature, music, performing & visual arts - www.ccskills.org.uk

VAROOM Journal of Illustration and Made Images (3 x year) (Association of Illustrators) - www.theaoi.com/

Your Creative Future (Design Council) (Design Council) - www.yourcreativefuture.org

Addresses
Association of Illustrators (AOI)
2nd Floor, Back Building, 150 Curtain Road, London EC2A 3AT
Phone: +44 (0)20 7613 4328
Web: www.theaoi.com

Institute of Scientific and Technical Communicators (ISTC)
Airport House, Purley Way, Croydon, Surrey CR0 0XZ
Phone: +44 (0)20 8253 4506
Web: www.istc.org.uk

Similar Jobs
CAD Technician, Graphic Designer, Illustrator, Illustrator: Archaeological, Medical Artist, Writer: Technical

Image Consultant

CRCI:Personal and Other Services
CLCI:IZ   Job Band: 2 to 4

Job Description
Image consultants advise clients how to make the best of their overall appearance and presentation. They are skilled and experienced in personal grooming, public speaking, colour analysis, make-up, personal shopping, wardrobe management and current fashion. Usually discuss a client's image, including personal appearance, social etiquette skills, body language and speech. Then help to assess a client's clothing needs, sort out their wardrobe and create or advise on a new style. Also help the client to understand how their appearance may affect the way others respond to them.

Having made an assessment, based on sound judgement and up-to-date knowledge, consultants provide each client with an individual programme of improvement. Clients include companies and organisations, as well as individuals and small groups.

Work Details
You need to be flexible in the hours worked and where the sessions take place, and may need to work evenings and weekends. Travel may be necessary to visit clients and this may involve time away from home. You may be invited to attend conferences and hold training sessions, often in hotel conference suites that are large and spacious. Some consultants work from home and have a set pattern of working hours, depending on their financial need. You need to have a very smart appearance.

Qualification
Image consultants enter this job with a range of qualifications and previous experience.

• England, Wales and Northern Ireland
Band 2: For entry to jobs, no minimum qualifications are needed, but it is an advantage to have some GCSEs (A*-C) or equivalent in subjects that include English and maths. For some courses: at least 3 GCSEs (A*-C) or equivalent are useful.

Band 3: For entry to jobs, HNC, professional courses or a relevant Diploma, usually at least 4 GCSEs (A*-C) including English and maths, or equivalent.

Band 4: For HND, Diploma of Higher Education or foundation degree: 1-2 A levels and some GCSEs (A*-C) usually including English and maths, or equivalent.

- **Scotland**

Band 2: For some courses: at least three S grades (1-3), including English and maths, or similar are useful.

Band 3: For SQA national certificate modules and for most professional courses: usually 3-4 S grades (1-3) or similar.

Band 4: For entry to SQA higher national and professional development awards, usually 2-3 H grades and some S grades (1-3), including English and maths, or similar qualifications.

Adult Qualifications
Some secondary qualifications, or equivalent, are usually required for entry to training courses, but many colleges welcome mature entrants over 20 and may waive academic requirements. Colleges sometimes have Access and foundation courses which require no entry qualifications.

Work Experience
Employers or colleges may prefer candidates who have relevant work or voluntary experience. Areas to consider include beauty therapy work, fashion retail or public relations. It can be useful to have experience of working in a business environment.

Entry and Training
This is usually a second career and those entering this job may have qualifications and previous experience in areas that include beauty consultancy, beauty therapy, fashion, retail, marketing or public relations. This provides a specialised area of work on which to base your future work as an image consultant. Foundation training in the core skills required for image consultancy (colour analysis, style for men and women and make-up application) is available through a wide variety of training providers. Contact The Federation of Image Consultants (TFIC) for a list of accredited and registered training providers. Courses can be expensive and may sometimes be residential.

TFIC, together with City & Guilds of London Institute, offer the joint award in image consultancy, which is only open to TFIC members. You need to have completed your foundation training, have at least one year's experience and produce an image portfolio. On successful completion of the award, you can attain Master status (MFIC) with TFIC. This qualification is not essential to practise as an image consultant, but shows clients that you have achieved a recognised standard. Seminars and workshops to keep skills up to date are also available from TFIC.

Mature entry to this job is common and often a second career following related work. This can be in areas that include beauty consultancy, beauty therapy, retail sales, fashion, marketing or public relations. Business skills are essential.

Opportunities and Pay
Image consultants are usually self-employed. This area of work is increasing and employers include private clients, such as business and professional people, including actors, singers and politicians. Clients also include corporate clients such as airlines, political parties, colleges, universities and hospitals. Any type of company may be concerned with the current commercial need to project and market a particular image and reputation.

Some consultants work with fashion retailers to train staff in methods of assessing customers more effectively. Others may run sessions at adult education centres or teach sessions at a local college. You initially need to successfully build your reputation to obtain your own consultancy.

Pay varies greatly and usually depends on your client base and success. Generally, fees can range from around £150 or more a session, for an individual or small group consultation. Corporate fees can be higher. Salaries can be around £12k-£30k a year, and those who are most successful can earn £40k a year or more.

Health
You need good colour vision to do this job.

Skills and Qualities
able to get on with all kinds of people, able to inspire confidence, excellent self presentation, eye for shape/colour, eye for visual effect, fashion conscious, good communication skills, good listening skills, good organisational skills, imaginative, tactful

Relevant Subjects
Art and Design, English, Psychology

Further Information
Become an Image Consultant (TFIC) (The Federation of Image Consultants) - www.tfic.org.uk/

Federation of Image Consultancts (TFIC) - www.tfic.org.uk

▶Working in hairdressing & beauty (2009) (Babcock Lifeskills) - www.babcock lifeskills.com/

Addresses
Hairdressing and Beauty Industry Authority (HABIA)
Oxford House, Sixth Avenue, Sky Business Park,
Robin Hood Airport, Doncaster DN9 3EG
Phone: 0845 230 6080 (UK only)
Web: www.habia.org/

Similar Jobs
Beauty Consultant, Beauty Therapist, Fashion Designer, Hairdresser, Life Coach, Personal Shopper

Immunologist
also known as: Clinical Immunologist

CRCI:Science, Mathematics and Statistics

CLCI:JAX Job Band: 5

Job Description
Immunologists study how the body defends itself against disease. They carry out tests on samples of body fluids and tissues to help diagnose, monitor and treat immune system diseases, such as asthma or HIV/AIDS. In a clinical setting, they may investigate abnormalities in a patient's immune system or measure a patient's response to tissue grafts, organ transplants and vaccinations. Immunologists are often involved in research to develop new methods of diagnosis and treatment and may also work in a university as a researcher or lecturer.

They write and deliver papers for publication or to present at conferences. May manage the work of students or other researchers and may also be involved with writing funding bids and grant applications. In industry, they are involved with product development. Immunologists in the pharmaceutical and biotechnology industries help to develop new medical products and therapies.

Usually liaise with medical and scientific colleagues and may be responsible for managing a team of biomedical scientists and other support staff such as medical technologists, laboratory assistants and clerical assistants. They are also responsible for devising experiments, analysing data and presenting reports.

Work Details
Usually work standard office hours, Monday to Friday, but may need to work early mornings, evening or weekends as laboratories can be open 24 hours a day. May also work longer hours to meet deadlines. You work in a laboratory, hospital, university, research

institute or office. This work requires a high degree of accuracy and sometimes involves having to cope with the sight of blood. You work as part of a team with other professional scientists. Protective clothing may need to be worn at times.

Qualification

• England, Wales and Northern Ireland

Band 5: For degree courses: 2-3 A levels including biology, chemistry and maths or physics and some GCSEs (A*-C) usually including English, maths and science, or equivalent. Exact requirements depend on the degree you take.

• Scotland

Band 5: For degree courses: 3-5 H grades including biology, chemistry and maths or physics and some S grades (1-3), usually including English, maths and science, or similar. Exact requirements depend on the degree you take.

Degree Information

A good honours degree in immunology or a biological science with a component in immunology is normally required. Subjects include biomedical/biological sciences, medical microbiology, biochemistry, pharmacology, physiology or genetics. An MSc in clinical immunology is an advantage.

Adult Qualifications

A formal qualification such as a degree and up-to-date scientific knowledge is essential. Course requirements may be relaxed for mature applicants provided they submit evidence of previous serious study such as a relevant Access or foundation course. Check with universities or colleges for information. Credit is given for relevant experience.

Work Experience

Universities and employers may prefer candidates who have relevant work or voluntary experience in such areas as hospital work, or in a relevant university department, or an industrial or commercial laboratory. If it proves difficult to gain this exact experience, then work in similar scientific areas is still attractive to employers and admissions tutors.

Entry and Training

The usual entry requirement is an honours degree (minimum 2:2) in immunology or a biological science with a component in immunology. Laboratory experience is a great advantage. If you want to work in industry, a four year degree course with a year in industry is useful. New entrants may follow a two-year structured training programme devised by the Clinical Scientists Training Board of the British Society for Immunology (BSI). Some health service regions operate their own training programmes outside this national scheme and employers in industry often offer their own in-house training. In academia, training for a PhD over four years is becoming more common and is usually funded by the employer. Applicants require at least a 2:1 in a relevant subject.

Mature applicants with laboratory experience may have an advantage. Contact the Clinical Scientists Training Board of the British Society for Immunology (BSI) for details of training routes for mature people.

Opportunities and Pay

This is a very small and specialised profession. Most opportunities arise in NHS hospitals, particularly the larger teaching hospitals. There is a clearly defined career structure to becoming a clinical scientist in immunology, and you can specialise in pathology or allergy. There are also some opportunities with the National Blood Service (NBS), the Health Protection Agency, private hospitals and research institutes. Promotion is possible to senior scientist or head scientist of a department. A PhD is a distinct advantage for promotion. Some immunologists move into industry, scientific writing or into research in the pharmaceutical or biotechnology industry to develop new products.

Your salary varies depending on location and particular employer. The pay also varies considerably depending on whether you work in the academic field or in industry. A newly qualified graduate working in the NHS starts at around £24k a year. Senior healthcare scientists at management level can earn up to around £62k a year. A newly qualified graduate working in industry can expect £20k-£37k a year, while those in senior positions may earn over £60k a year.

Health

You need good colour vision for some areas of work. There is a risk of allergy from skin irritants.

Skills and Qualities

able to report accurately, able to work to deadlines, accurate, adaptable, analytical skills, aptitude for teamwork, good organisational skills, information handling skills, IT skills, research skills

Relevant Subjects

Biology, Chemistry, English, Mathematics, Physics, Science

Further Information

Association of the British Pharmaceutical Industry (ABPI) - www.abpi.org.uk/education

Clinical & Experimental Immunology (British Immunology Society, monthly) (Blackwell) - www.blackwellpublishing.com/cei_enhanced/

Immunology (Wiley-Blackwell) - www.blackwellpublishing.com/imm_enhanced/

National Blood Service - www.blood.co.uk

NHS Careers (NHS Careers) - www.nhscareers.nhs.uk

Scottish National Blood Transfusion Service - www.scotblood.co.uk

► Working in science (2007) (Babcock Lifeskills) - www.babcock-lifeskills.com/

Addresses

British Society for Immunology (BSI)
Vintage House, 37 Albert Embankment, London SE1 7TL
Phone: +44 (0)20 3031 9800
Web: www.immunology.org

Health Protection Agency (HPA)
7th Floor , Holborn Gate, 330 High Holborn, London WC1V 7PP
Phone: +44 (0)20 7759 2700
Web: www.hpa.org.uk

Similar Jobs

Biochemist, Biomedical Scientist, Clinical Molecular Geneticist, Haematologist, Microbiologist, Toxicologist

Indexer

CRCI:Languages, Information and Culture
CLCI:FAD Job Band: 5

Job Description

Indexers devise methodical lists that enable readers to find information in a range of documents. Documentation includes technical manuals, books, reports or pamphlets, as well as films and digital documents, CDs, DVDs and websites.

They analyse the original document thoroughly and decide on suitable terminology for the index, then create a list or index of terms, phrases, abbreviations, or single words in alphabetical order. Writes it up in an appropriate form for publication, cross-referencing related information and ensures that it is clear and easy for readers to follow. The text is prepared for publication using specialist computer software.

Work Details

Indexers are usually self-employed and choose their own hours of work, which can be irregular and involve some evenings and weekends. Indexing is often carried out as a secondary occupation, and the indexer may work in other areas of publishing such as copy-editing, or proofreading. You have to be self-motivated, methodical and able to work under pressure to meet deadlines. You probably spend a lot of your time sitting, writing or working at a computer.

Qualification

• England, Wales and Northern Ireland

Band 5: For degree courses: 2-3 A levels and some GCSEs (A*-C) usually including English and maths, or equivalent. Exact requirements depend on the degree you take.

• Scotland

Band 5: For degree courses: 3-5 H grades and some S grades (1-3), including English and maths, or similar qualifications. Exact requirements depend on the degree you take.

Degree Information

Any degree is acceptable, however those holding degrees in subjects such as law, medicine, finance, or scientific and technological subjects are more likely to be in demand for specialist subject areas.

Adult Qualifications

Entry requirements may be relaxed for adults applying for courses. Evidence of specialist knowledge in areas such as science, medicine or law may help mature entrants.

Work Experience

Entry to this career is competitive. It is important that you try to do some relevant work or voluntary experience prior to applying for training. Experience in publishing, copy-editing, proofreading or in a technical field that may later assist with indexing is the most useful.

Entry and Training

Most entrants are experienced in a particular field of work such as publishing or librarianship. Relevant primary degrees and postgraduate courses are available and are usually full time. The Society of Indexers (SI) runs workshops and online courses for beginners which can help you to decide whether you are suited to this kind of work.

If you decide this is a job for you, you need to become accredited by the SI. This involves taking a distance-learning course through the Society. Courses can be studied at your own pace and include four assessed units of 45-50 hours of study and tests, which usually take between one and five years to complete. Book indexing personal tuition is an independent course by email, leading to a level of competence, similar to that required for accreditation, and uses tutorials as the main teaching technique. Aslib, the association for information management also runs relevant courses from time to time. After further training, experience, proven competence and accreditation, an indexer can apply to become an accredited indexer (AI) of the SI. The Society also provides opportunities for continuing professional development through workshops, conferences and local groups. Contact the SI for further information.

Mature applicants with specialist subject knowledge in another career, or those with relevant experience in publishing or librarianship, may have an advantage when applying for positions.

Opportunities and Pay

Around 1,000 people work as indexers in the UK, but only a small proportion of these work full time. You can work either for a publishing firm or for a library organising large volumes of documentation, but most indexers are self employed and work from their own homes. This is a highly competitive profession but in an increasingly digital world, indexing is growing in importance. Indexers can advertise via an 'Indexers Available' online directory, produced for and circulated to publishers by the Society of Indexers (SI). The amount of work you gain depends on your reputation, experience, areas of specialism and skills as an indexer. You can progress by specialising in a certain area, such as law, medicine, technology or finance but need a detailed knowledge and experience of your specialist subject. Part-time work is usual.

Pay can either be by the hour or by the page or sometimes a 'flat rate' for the whole job. Guidelines from the SI suggest a starting rate of around £20.50 an hour, approximately £2.30 a page or £5.25 per thousand words for an index to a straightforward text. Rates are negotiable depending on the complexity of the text and whether you have specialist subject knowledge. Experienced indexers can earn up to £30k a year.

Skills and Qualities

able to communicate effectively, able to work to deadlines, able to work well on your own, accurate, good concentration level, good spelling, IT skills, methodical, negotiating skills, self-motivated

Relevant Subjects

English, ICT/Computer studies

Further Information

Book Indexing Personal Tuition (BIPT) 07708 571548

Sidelights (Newsletter of the Society of Indexers, quarterly) (Society of Indexers) - www.indexers.org.uk/index.php?id=228

Skillset - sector skills council for the creative media, fashion and textiles industries - www.skillset.org

The Indexer: International Journal of Indexing (quarterly) (Society of Indexers) - www.theindexer.org

Thinking of becoming an Indexer (Society of Indexers (SOI))

Addresses

Aslib, The Association for Information Management
207 Davina House, 137-149 Goswell Road, London EC1V 7ET
Phone: +44 (0)20 7253 3349
Web: www.aslib.co.uk

Society of Indexers
Woodbourn Business Centre, 10 Jessell Street, Sheffield S9 3HY
Phone: +44 (0)114 244 9561
Web: www.indexers.org.uk

Similar Jobs

Archivist, Copy Editor, Editor: Publishing, Information Scientist, Library & Information Manager, Proofreader

Information Scientist

also known as: Information Specialist, Knowledge Manager, Library & Information Scientist

CRCI:Languages, Information and Culture
CLCI:FAF — Job Band: 5

Job Description

Information scientists are responsible for the efficient organisation, storage, quality and management of specialist information in sectors such as legal, technical, financial, commercial, scientific or economic. They researche and collect information from a wide variety of sources and increasingly work with electronic resources and IT systems, including the Internet. Scans publications or computerised databases to identify relevant articles, reports and books and may analyse statistical information and develop databases and content for web pages.

They also research particular topics, prepare abstracts, produce spreadsheets, catalogues and indexes material and direct it to appropriate readers. Also creates and maintains specialised databases and writes technical reports and bulletins. They may design and set up new information services and systems or manage information for a specific organisation or function.

Information Scientist

Work Details

Usually works a basic 35-39 hrs a week, Monday to Friday, but office hours may require some work in the evenings and at weekends. You study printed material, using computers for searching and for creating documents, advising and helping people, and dealing with enquiries. The work environment can vary from light, air-conditioned buildings to dusty, cramped offices. You liaise frequently with professionals in your customer base, as well as senior management. Work may be pressurised and intellectually demanding at times.

Qualification

• England, Wales and Northern Ireland

Band 5: For degree courses: 2-3 A levels and some GCSEs (A*-C) usually including English and maths, or equivalent. Exact requirements depend on the degree you take.

• Scotland

Band 5: For degree courses: 3-5 H grades and some S grades (1-3), including English and maths, or similar qualifications. Exact requirements depend on the degree you take.

Degree Information

Certain degree courses in information science management and librarianship qualifications lead to exemptions from professional exams. Many specialist libraries prefer entrants with a first degree followed by postgraduate qualification. First degree subjects in demand include business information systems, engineering, technology, science, law and some social science subjects.

Adult Qualifications

Entry requirements may be relaxed for adults applying for higher education courses and Access or foundation courses give adults without qualifications a route onto degree courses.

Work Experience

Universities may prefer candidates who have relevant work or voluntary experience to demonstrate enthusiasm and commitment to the career. Experience in a library, a records office, or similar, is taken into consideration. For those progressing to postgraduate qualification, a period of practical library experience is essential following your degree.

Entry and Training

Employers usually prefer a degree or relevant postgraduate qualification that is accredited by the Chartered Institute of Library and Information Professionals (CILIP). Specialist database and IT training is usually on the job. The ability to read journals and papers in other languages is also a considerable advantage. To become a full or chartered member of CILIP, it is usually necessary to have completed a first degree or postgraduate qualification in information science/management, and to have at least three years' approved experience in information work.

Before beginning your postgraduate course, a period of practical library experience is required and there are special graduate traineeships for this purpose. Contact CILIP for details of this and all routes to training and qualification, including a list of accredited institutions. CILIP and other professional bodies such as Aslib, the Association for Information and Management, offer short courses, seminars and conferences that cover continuing professional development, which is necessary to keep up to date throughout your career. The Society of College, National and University Libraries (SCONUL) promotes excellence in higher education and national libraries across the UK and Ireland.

Mature entrants with specialist knowledge and/or qualifications in science, engineering or law may have an advantage. Access courses may also offer a route on to higher education courses. Contact the Chartered Institute of Library and Information Professionals (CILIP) for details on course and training opportunities.

Lifelong Learning UK offers a level 2 certificate and a level 3 diploma in libraries, archives and information services or an information and library services apprenticeship which may provide an alternative route into this career.

Opportunities and Pay

Jobs are available throughout the UK, but mainly in the South East and around large cities. Employment is usually in industry, commerce, legal, financial or accountancy firms, government departments or agencies, local government, or specialist libraries (particularly academic libraries), depending upon your specialist knowledge. There are also options to be a self-employed consultant. As most departments are small, promotion prospects may be limited so willingness to move to another employer helps progress. There are a few opportunities to work overseas, particularly with the British Council. CILIP offers an international job exchange scheme (LIBEX) which enables members to exchange jobs worldwide.

Pay varies considerably depending on location and type of employer. Starting salaries are generally around £20k-£26k, rising to £30-£42k a year with experience. Senior information scientists can earn up to £60k a year or more, depending on the area of specialism.

Skills and Qualities

accurate, analytical skills, enquiring mind, good communication skills, good concentration level, good memory, information handling skills, methodical, research skills, specialist IT skills

Relevant Subjects

English, ICT/Computer studies, Modern Foreign Languages

Further Information

A Career in Information Work (CILIP) (CILIP) - www.cilip.org.uk/jobs-careers

Apprenticeship Schemes (National Apprenticeship Service) - www.apprenticeships.org.uk

British Council - www.britishcouncil.org

Library & Information Gazette (fortnightly) (CILIP) - www.cilip.org.uk/publications/gazette

LLUK (Lifelong Learning UK) - sector skills council for the professional development of staff working in the lifelong learning sector - www.lluk.org

Managing Information (monthly) (Aslib) - www.aslib.co.uk/publications/managinginformation.htm

Society of College, National and University Libraries (SCONUL) - www.sconul.ac.uk

Addresses

Aslib, The Association for Information Management
207 Davina House, 137-149 Goswell Road, London EC1V 7ET
Phone: +44 (0)20 7253 3349
Web: www.aslib.co.uk

Chartered Institute of Library and Information Professionals (CILIP)
7 Ridgmount Street, London WC1E 7AE
Phone: +44 (0)20 7255 0500
Web: www.cilip.org.uk

SLAINTE: Information and Libraries Scotland
1st Floor, Building C, Brandon Gate, Leechlee Road,
Hamilton ML3 6AU
Phone: +44 (0)1698 458 888
Web: www.slainte.org.uk

Similar Jobs

Archivist, Civil Service Operational Research Analyst, Library & Information Manager, Market Research Executive, Political/Parliamentary Researcher, Translator

Insurance Broker

CRCI:Financial Services
CLCI:NAG Job Band: 4 to 5

Job Description

Insurance brokers are independent professional advisers who act as a link between people, organisations and insurance companies, to arrange the best cover for the client at the most competitive price. A broker first identifies a client's needs, assesses the hazards they face and examines any existing policies. They offer expert and unbiased advice to the client on all insurance matters and discuss the insurance plan needed. Approach insurers to discuss risks with underwriters. Negotiate with insurance companies for the best policy. Handle policy renewals and revisions. Help clients when they need to make a claim.

Brokers keep records, chase and process accounts, collect premiums (payments) and deal with related correspondence. They are sometimes involved with marketing and acquiring new business. May specialise in a particular branch of insurance such as marine or motor insurance.

Work Details

Usually work a 35-39 hr week, Monday to Friday, and sometimes a Saturday. This is mainly an office-based job, but you may also travel to meet clients or insurance underwriters. You need to work extra hours occasionally, to finalise contracts or to attend meetings. If you work for a large company, you may need to move to another part of the country at your employer's request. Overseas travel may be involved, depending on the nature of the work. Work may be stressful as you deal with a wide range of clients and have to meet deadlines in completing projects.

Qualification

- **England, Wales and Northern Ireland**

Band 4: For training with a broking firm: usually 1-2 A levels and some GCSEs (A*-C) usually including English and maths, or equivalent.

Band 5: For degree courses: 2-3 A levels and some GCSEs (A*-C) usually including English and maths, or equivalent. Exact requirements depend on the degree you take.

- **Scotland**

Band 4: For training with a broking firm: usually 3 H grades and some S grades (1-3), often including English and maths, or similar qualifications.

Band 5: For degree courses: 3-5 H grades and some S grades (1-3), usually including English and maths, or similar qualifications. Exact requirements depend on the degree you take.

Degree Information

A degree in any discipline is acceptable, though economics, law, maths, business studies, risk management, or subjects with insurance or financial options, are preferred. Statistics and computing can provide useful background knowledge. A postgraduate degree in risk management may be an advantage.

Adult Qualifications

Insurance firms have their individual standard of entry qualifications for trainee posts. Adults without these qualifications may be accepted if they have experience in insurance, banking or other commercial work, which can be put forward as evidence of competence, through Accreditation of Prior Learning.

Work Experience

Employers or colleges/universities may prefer candidates who have relevant work or voluntary experience. This can include office-based work where you employ administration skills and gain experience of working with the public. Experience or knowledge of basic accounting techniques is also a distinct advantage.

Entry and Training

Many employers prefer applicants with A levels/H grades or equivalent, or graduates. Larger firms look for a 2.1 degree for entrants to their structured training schemes. However, personal characteristics, especially good communication skills are considered to be an advantage. On-the-job training is provided, mainly working with an experienced person. Some companies provide day release for courses, but you are also expected to do some studying in your own time. Employees of Lloyds of London also have to sit the Lloyd's and London Markets Introductory Test.

To achieve full broker status, many trainees take the exams of the Chartered Insurance Institute (CII). The CII Broker Academy is the structured progression route, and courses range from the certificate in insurance to the advanced diploma (ACII), which is the usual qualification for professional brokers. Courses can be taken face-to-face or by distance learning. It is likely to take one to two years to reach certified broker level and a further two to five years to achieve professional and then chartered status. Relevant degrees or diplomas may lead to exemption from part of the professional exams. The Faculty of Insurance Brokers has been set up by the CII to help support training. See the CII website for details.

Chartered brokers are expected to undertake continuing professional development. The ifs School of Finance also offers a range of qualifications, including a certificate in regulated general insurance, as well as a route for ACII's to gain a degree (BSc Hons) in financial services. The CII and the British Insurance Brokers Association offer specialised one day short courses for their members. Life assurance or pensions brokers need to hold a qualification in insurance or financial advice approved by the Financial Services Authority (FSA).

It is possible for a 16 year old school leaver to begin training as an insurance technician with some firms and work their way up through qualifying examinations. A Diploma/Welsh Baccalaureate in business, administration and finance may be available in your area . The advanced level is equivalent to 3.5 A levels but for some university courses, the additional and specialist learning (ASL) component of the diploma needs to include specific A levels e.g. maths. Check entry requirements carefully with the individual institutions.

Apprenticeships may also be available, or sponsorship for higher education may be possible from a large insurance company or from the Worshipful Company of Insurers. Foundation degrees in financial markets and management is offered by some higher education institutions.

Mature entrants with relevant work experience in insurance sales, underwriting or clerical/administration work may have an advantage. There are distance-learning courses for the professional qualifications of the Chartered Insurance Institute. Some of the larger insurance companies may offer sponsorship for higher education study. Past experience can also be recognised through Accreditation of Prior Learning. Contact the local Jobcentre Plus, Next Step service, LSC/LEC, Jobcentre (NI) or ELWa (Wales) for details of possible training opportunities, including apprenticeships.

Opportunities and Pay

Insurance broking companies range in size from small partnerships to large national or international companies such as Lloyd's of London, employing thousands of employees. The Greater London area has the largest employer base. It is possible to specialise in a type of insurance, such as marine or motor insurance, or you can specialise in the work you do, for example in claims work. Having the professional qualification of the Chartered Insurance Institute can improve promotion prospects and you may become a supervisor, head of department or partner. There are increasing opportunities for working abroad, particularly for those who are fluent in a European language, Japanese or Chinese.

With experience you can become self-employed. Some move on to work in insurance sectors such as underwriting and loss adjustment.

Pay varies depending on location and size of the company you work for, as well as on experience and the area of broking. Starting salaries are around £15k-£25k a year, rising to £28k-£40k with experience. Senior brokers earn between £40k-£80k, with high earners making up to £100k a year. You may be given a company car and additional benefits, such as life assurance or medical insurance.

Skills and Qualities

able to manage a budget and keep records, analytical skills, attention to detail, customer service skills, good communication skills, good interpersonal skills, IT skills, numeracy skills, self confident, trustworthy

Relevant Subjects

Business and accounting, Economics, English, ICT/Computer studies, Law, Mathematics

Further Information

AGCAS: Accountancy and Business Services (Job Sector Briefing) (AGCAS) - www.prospects.ac.uk/

Apprenticeship Schemes (National Apprenticeship Service) - www.apprenticeships.org.uk

Brokers Monthly (Insurance Publishing & Printing Co.) http:www.brokersmonthly.co.uk

CII Pathways - www.pathways.cii.co.uk

Diploma in Business, Administration and Finance - www.baf-diploma.org.uk/

Financial Services Skills Council - sector skills council for financial services, accountancy & finance www.fssc.org.uk/

Insurance Careers (CII) (CII) - www.cii.co.uk/

Lloyds of London - www.lloyds.com

The Association of British Insurers (ABI) - www.abi.org.uk

The Guide to Understanding the Insurance Industry 2008-9 by Chris Sharkey (Booksurge) (Booksurge) www.ambest.com/sales/BRGuide.asp

Welsh Baccalaureate - www.wbq.org.uk

▶Working in maths (2009) (Babcock Lifeskills) - www.babcock-lifeskills.com/

Addresses

British Insurance Brokers Association (BIBA)
8th Floor, John Stow House, 18 Bevis Marks, London EC3A 7JB
Phone: 0870 950 1790 (UK only)
Web: www.biba.org.uk

Chartered Insurance Institute (CII)
42-48 High Road, South Woodford, London E18 2JP
Phone: +44 (0)20 8989 8464
Web: www.cii.co.uk

Financial Services Authority (FSA)
Membership Department, 25 The North Colonnade, Canary Wharf, London E14 5HS
Phone: +44 (0)20 7066 1000
Web: www.fsa.gov.uk

ifs School of Finance
IFS House, 4-9 Burgate Lane, Canterbury, Kent CT1 2XJ
Phone: +44 (0)1227 818609
Web: www.ifslearning.ac.uk

Lloyd's of London
One Lime Street, London EC3M 7HA
Phone: +44 (0)20 7327 1000
Web: www.lloyds.com

Worshipful Company of Insurers (WCI)
The Insurance Hall, 20 Aldermanbury, London EC2V 7HY
Phone: +44 (0)20 7600 4006
Web: www.wci.org.uk

Similar Jobs

Compliance Officer, Insurance Business Development Manager, Insurance Loss Adjuster, Insurance Technician, Insurance Underwriter, Investment Analyst

Insurance Business Development Manager

CRCI:Financial Services
CLCI:NAG — Job Band: 3 to 4

Job Description

Insurance business development managers work for insurance companies promoting their products and key aspects to insurance brokers. They then encourage brokers to promote these products to their clients. Act as an important link between insurance brokers and the employing insurance company, and have a thorough knowledge of the company's products, such as life assurance, pensions, house cover and motor insurance. Often act as a mediator if there is a problem between a broker and insurance company.

Business development managers negotiate with underwriters as well as brokers and need to attract new business for the employing insurance company. Visit brokers regularly to advise on the company's products and provide detailed information of any new products and their suitability.

Work Details

Usually work 35-40 hrs a week, Monday to Friday. Although office based, you need to travel around a specific geographical area, visiting potential and current clients in their offices. Some rural areas are extensive and you may need to stay away from home for short periods of time. A driving licence is usually required. Many consultants increasingly work from home and are part of a team. You are expected to keep up to date with the latest company products and usually attend meetings, seminars and conferences.

Qualification

• England, Wales and Northern Ireland

Band 3: Although there are no set minimum qualifications, many companies prefer applicants to have a minimum of 4 GCSEs (A*-C) usually including maths and English, or equivalent qualifications.

Band 4: For entry to a job as a trainee: usually two A levels and some GCSEs (A*-C) including English and maths, or equivalent qualifications.

• Scotland

Band 3: Although there are no set minimum qualifications, many companies prefer applicants to have four S grades (1-3) usually including maths and English, or similar.

Band 4: For entry to a job as a trainee: usually three H grades and some S grades (1-3) including English and maths, or similar qualifications.

Adult Qualifications

Personal qualities that suit the insurance industry such as drive and self-motivation are often valued more than academic qualifications, particularly for those with relevant previous experience.

Work Experience

Employers may prefer candidates who have relevant work or voluntary experience. This can include office-based work where you employ administration skills and gain experience of working with the public. Experience or knowledge of basic accounting techniques is also a distinct advantage.

Entry and Training

Some employers may prefer applicants with previous relevant experience, for example as an insurance technician or in other sales work, but most companies ask for A levels/H grades, or equivalent, or sometimes a degree. Many large employers offer a graduate training scheme. On-the-job training is usual, working with an experienced person, perhaps also with short courses on new products or sales techniques. Some companies provide day release for courses, but you are also expected to do some studying in your own time. Relevant degrees or diplomas may lead to exemption from part of the professional exams.

Many trainees take the exams of the Chartered Insurance Institute (CII). The CII Broker Academy is the structured progression route, and courses range from the certificate in insurance to the advanced diploma (ACII), which is the usual qualification for professional brokers. Courses can be taken by face-to-face or distance learning. Relevant degrees or diplomas may lead to exemption from part of the professional exams. Contact the CII for details.

The ifs School of Finance also offers a range of qualifications, including a certificate in regulated general insurance, as well as a route for ACII's to gain a degree in financial services. The British Insurance Brokers Association also offers specialised one-day short courses for their members.

It is possible for a 16 year old school leaver to begin training as an insurance technician with some firms and work their way up through qualifying examinations. Apprenticeships may be available in your area or sponsorship for higher education may be available from a large insurance company or from the Worshipful Company of Insurers.

A Diploma/Welsh Baccalaureate in business, administration and finance may be available in your area. The advanced level is equivalent to 3.5 A levels but for some university courses, the additional and specialist learning (ASL) component of the diploma needs to include specific A levels e.g. maths. Check entry requirements carefully with the individual institutions.

Foundation degrees in financial markets and management is offered by some higher education institutions. Relevant training programmes, including apprenticeship schemes, may also be available in your area. Advanced apprenticeships leading to qualification at level 3 can be a route into higher education.

Mature entry is common and those with business experience, particularly in insurance sales or financial services, have an advantage. The Chartered Insurance Institute may award credits for prior learning which can lead to exemption from some parts of the professional exams. Contact the local Jobcentre Plus, Next Step service, LSC/LEC, Jobcentre (NI) or ELWa (Wales) for details of possible training opportunities, including apprenticeships.

Opportunities and Pay

Employers are usually major insurance companies, many based in the larger cities, where you can progress to become a sales manager, regional or area manager, and other senior roles. However, opportunities are decreasing due to the increase of information technology. You can set up your own business as a broker or in specialist fields such as marketing. There may be an opportunity to work abroad for international companies.

Pay is usually a basic salary with the rest of your income based on commission, or you may be self-employed. Earnings include various commissions and performance bonuses, and generally start at around £20k a year rising to around £25k-£30k. Senior business development managers can earn £90k or more. A company car may be provided and other benefits may include discounted general insurance, life and medical insurance.

Skills and Qualities

able to explain clearly, able to inspire confidence, aptitude for figures, excellent communication skills, good organisational skills, IT skills, negotiating skills, outgoing personality, persuasive, self-motivated

Relevant Subjects

Business and accounting, Economics, English, Mathematics, Retail and distribution

Further Information

Apprenticeship Schemes (National Apprenticeship Service) - www.apprenticeships.org.uk

Brokers Monthly (Insurance Publishing & Printing Co.) http:www.brokersmonthly.co.uk

CII Pathways - www.pathways.cii.co.uk

Diploma in Business, Administration and Finance - www.baf-diploma.org.uk/

Financial Services Skills Council - sector skills council for financial services, accountancy & finance www.fssc.org.uk/

Insurance Careers (CII) (CII) - www.cii.co.uk/

The Association of British Insurers (ABI) - www.abi.org.uk

The Guide to Understanding the Insurance Industry 2008-9 by Chris Sharkey (Booksurge) (Booksurge) - www.ambest.com/sales/BRGuide.asp

Welsh Baccalaureate - www.wbq.org.uk

▶Working in maths (2009) (Babcock Lifeskills) - www.babcock-lifeskills.com/

Addresses

British Insurance Brokers Association (BIBA)
8th Floor, John Stow House, 18 Bevis Marks, London EC3A 7JB
Phone: 0870 950 1790 (UK only)
Web: www.biba.org.uk

Chartered Insurance Institute (CII)
42-48 High Road, South Woodford, London E18 2JP
Phone: +44 (0)20 8989 8464
Web: www.cii.co.uk

Financial Services Authority (FSA)
Membership Department, 25 The North Colonnade, Canary Wharf, London E14 5HS
Phone: +44 (0)20 7066 1000
Web: www.fsa.gov.uk

ifs School of Finance
IFS House, 4-9 Burgate Lane, Canterbury, Kent CT1 2XJ
Phone: +44 (0)1227 818609
Web: www.ifslearning.ac.uk

Worshipful Company of Insurers (WCI)
The Insurance Hall, 20 Aldermanbury, London EC2V 7HY
Phone: +44 (0)20 7600 4006
Web: www.wci.org.uk

Similar Jobs

Accountant: Industry & Commerce, Accountant: Private Practice, Actuary, Insurance Broker, Insurance Technician, Pensions Adviser

Insurance Loss Adjuster

CRCI:Financial Services
CLCI:NAG — Job Band: 4 to 5

Job Description

Insurance loss adjusters are independent and impartial specialists who are appointed by an insurance company to investigate particular insurance claims and report back to the insurance company. May investigate either straightforward or large and complex insurance claims and assess the extent of the insurance company's liability. Check the claimant's policy to ensure that the loss is covered. They gather information about the incident (for example fire or theft), often by interview or a site visit, and make recommendations. Agree any necessary adjustments with the claimant and produce a report recommending a suitable payment.

Insurance Loss Adjuster

Loss adjusters may be expert in many areas, such as advising on repair techniques. They often know specialist firms in the area that can help with repairs. If required, can arrange for a salvage merchant to collect and dispose of any damaged goods. May need to further negotiate an acceptable settlement between the claimant and the insurer. They liaise with other experts, such as the police, solicitors and forensic experts, and may attend court.

Work Details

You are based in an office working around 35-40 hrs a week, Monday to Friday, but spend part of the day visiting claimants and attending meetings. It may be necessary to work in the evenings or at weekends, either visiting premises or writing reports, and you may have to be on call for emergencies. Travel overseas may be required if you are working for a company that has insured foreign property. Sound judgement and an understanding of legal technicalities are needed for this job. You may have to deal with people who are upset and in need of support, or who are being awkward or demanding.

Office work usually involves use of computers for much of the time. Assessing damage to property may mean bending, kneeling or climbing. You may need to visit scenes of accidents such as train or vehicle crashes, visit building fires or incidents on a gas or oil rig. The work can sometimes be dangerous and dirty. Scenes of accidents and disasters can also be distressing.

Qualification

• England, Wales and Northern Ireland

Band 4: For entry to Chartered Insurance Institute training: there are no entry requirements to study for these qualifications, however, it is recommended that for the diploma, entrants have the Certificate in Insurance or 5 GCSEs at grade C or equivalent.

Band 5: For degree courses: 2-3 A levels and some GCSEs (A*-C) usually including English and maths, or equivalent. Exact requirements depend on the degree you take. For entry to Chartered Insurance Institute advanced diploma training: the diploma in insurance or 3 A levels or equivalent.

• Scotland

Band 4: For entry to Chartered Insurance Institute training: there are no entry requirements to study for these qualifications, however, it is recommended that for the diploma, entrants have the Certificate in Insurance or five S grades (1-3), or similar.

Band 5: For degree courses: 3-5 H grades and some S grades (1-3), usually including English and maths, or similar qualifications. Exact requirements depend on the degree you take. For entry to Chartered Insurance Institute advanced diploma training: the diploma in insurance or 3-5 H levels or equivalent.

Degree Information

A degree in any discipline is acceptable, but some employers prefer engineering, surveying, a business subject, or law. Language and science subjects are also an advantage.

Adult Qualifications

Entry requirements may be relaxed for adults applying for higher education courses. Foundation and Access courses give adults without qualifications a route on to degree courses.

Work Experience

Relevant work or voluntary experience is always useful and improves your chances when applying for a job. Any work experience in the finance sector is relevant and shows enthusiasm and commitment to the work. Time spent in an accountancy firm, an insurance company or shadowing a loss adjuster gives you a good basis and insight into the profession.

Entry and Training

Entrants are usually those with previous experience and qualifications in an appropriate profession, such as insurance, accountancy, engineering, surveying and law, or are graduates. These entrants study for the professional qualification of the Chartered Institute of Loss Adjusters (CILA). You have to have at least two years' practice as a trainee loss adjuster before you can sit CILA's exams. To become an associate member of CILA normally needs five year's experience. Training is on the job, with study in your own time. CILA also run short courses and conferences on specialist topics.

A small number of people get into this type of work straight from school, college or university and study part time for the Chartered Insurance Institute examinations before taking CILA courses. It is possible for a 16 year old school leaver to begin training as a insurance technician with some firms and work their way up through qualifying examinations. Sponsorship for higher education may be available from a large insurance company or from the Worshipful Company of Insurers.

A Diploma/Welsh Baccalaureate in business, administration and finance may be available inyour area. The advanced level is equivalent to 3.5 A levels but for some university courses, the additional and specialist learning (ASL) component of the diploma needs to include specific A levels e.g. maths. Check entry requirements carefully with the individual institutions. Part-time foundation degrees in a range of relevant subjects are also available.

Mature entry is common since most entrants have experience and qualifications in a related profession, such as accountancy, surveying, engineering or law. You may also be able to get into loss adjusting through insurance claims assessment work. Distance-learning courses are available form the Chartered Insurance Industry for professional qualifications. Normal entry requirements may be relaxed for those over 25 years of age.

Opportunities and Pay

There are loss adjusting firms throughout the UK. You can work for one of the specialist firms of loss adjusters which range in size from small partnerships to large companies with offices nationwide and abroad. You can also work for insurance companies or risk management departments of large companies. It is also possible to be self-employed and to specialise, for example in aviation, marine or motor insurance. You may be able to gain promotion to partner in a firm, branch or area manager, or area director. This is a small profession. Work abroad is possible for British-owned companies that have offices overseas, or for foreign companies.

Despite the economic downturn, demand for financial skills is expected to increase in the medium term. Employers are currently having difficulty recruiting professionals in specific areas, including risk accounting.

A trainee loss adjuster's average earnings range from £18k-£24k rising to around £30k-£45k a year with experience, and top earners can achieve from £80k-£100k a year. Benefits may include life and medical insurance.

Health

You need a good level of general fitness.

Skills and Qualities

analytical skills, enquiring mind, good spoken communication, good written English, integrity, IT skills, methodical, objective, observational skills, time management skills

Relevant Subjects

Business and accounting, Economics, English, ICT/Computer studies, Law, Mathematics

Further Information

AGCAS: Accountancy and Business Services (Job Sector Briefing) (AGCAS) - www.prospects.ac.uk/

Diploma in Business, Administration and Finance - www.baf-diploma.org.uk/

Financial Services Skills Council - sector skills council for financial services, accountancy & finance www.fssc.org.uk/

Insurance Careers (CII) (CII) - www.cii.co.uk/

The Association of British Insurers (ABI) - www.abi.org.uk

The Guide to Understanding the Insurance Industry 2008-9 by Chris Sharkey (Booksurge) (Booksurge) - www.ambest.com/sales/BRGuide.asp

Welsh Baccalaureate - www.wbq.org.uk

▶Working in maths (2009) (Babcock Lifeskills) - www.babcock-lifeskills.com/

Addresses

Chartered Institute of Loss Adjusters (CILA)
Warwick House, 65-66 Queen Street, London EC4R 1EB
Phone: +44 (0)20 7337 9960
Web: www.cila.co.uk

Chartered Insurance Institute (CII)
42-48 High Road, South Woodford, London E18 2JP
Phone: +44 (0)20 8989 8464
Web: www.cii.co.uk

Worshipful Company of Insurers (WCI)
The Insurance Hall, 20 Aldermanbury, London EC2V 7HY
Phone: +44 (0)20 7600 4006
Web: www.wci.org.uk

Similar Jobs

Compliance Officer, Insurance Broker, Insurance Surveyor, Insurance Underwriter, Surveyor: Building Control, Surveyor: General Practice

Insurance Surveyor

also known as: Risk Analyst, Risk Surveyor

CRCI:Financial Services
CLCI:NAG Job Band: 4 to 5

Job Description

Insurance surveyors carry out a detailed analysis, especially where the risk is high or the situation is complicated, and write technical reports for an insurance underwriter. They survey industrial, commercial or other premises to assess potential hazards and insurance risk. May also assess machinery or transportation, such as ships or aeroplanes, which need to be insured.

They consider the structure of a building and its use, and examine the arrangements for safety and security relating to fire, flood, theft and so on. Recommend extra precautions, such as water sprinklers and security systems. May specialise in fire and peril, accidents, engineering or theft.

Some insurance surveyors are involved in risk management, identifying and assessing hazards and suggesting how to reduce these. Use computers for much of the work. Keeping up to date on laws relating to fire regulations, health and safety at work etc is very important in this job.

Work Details

Usually work a 35-39 hr week, Monday to Friday, though may work flexible hours, some evenings and weekends, depending on the job. Although this is an office-based job, part of the time is spent travelling and visiting sites, possibly abroad. You may often work alone, but also liaise with underwriters, brokers and health and safety officers.

Depending on the site and the type of survey, you may have to work at heights, or in conditions that are dirty or noisy. Sometimes you may need to wear protective clothing, including a safety helmet and boots. A driving licence is usually required.

Qualification

• England, Wales and Northern Ireland

Band 4: For entry to Chartered Insurance Institute training: there are no entry requirements to study for these qualifications, however, it is recommended that for the diploma, entrants have the Certificate in Insurance or 5 GCSEs at grade C or equivalent.

Band 5: For degree courses: 2-3 A levels and some GCSEs (A*-C) usually including English and maths, or equivalent. Exact requirements depend on the degree you take.

• Scotland

Band 4: For entry to Chartered Insurance Institute training: there are no entry requirements to study for these qualifications, however, it is recommended that for the diploma, entrants have the Certificate in Insurance or five S grades (1-3), or similar.

Band 5: For degree courses: 3-5 H grades and some S grades (1-3), usually including English and maths, or similar qualifications. Exact requirements depend on the degree you take. For entry to Chartered Insurance Institute advanced diploma training: the diploma in insurance or 3 H levels or equivalent.

Degree Information

A degree in any discipline is acceptable, but science, risk management, technology or engineering degrees may be preferred. Insurance surveyors are often qualified engineers. Relevant postgraduate qualifications are also available.

Adult Qualifications

Mature entrants are welcome, particularly those who already have experience and qualifications in the insurance industry, or who are qualified in a relevant specialist area, such as engineering or science. Entry qualifications for the Chartered Insurance Institute associateship examinations may be waived for those over 25 years old.

Work Experience

Employers or colleges/universities may prefer candidates who have relevant work or voluntary experience. This can include office and business administration work for a quantity surveying or engineering firm, work in insurance sales or health and safety assessment.

Entry and Training

Most entrants have experience of other areas of insurance before they start this work. Many employers recruit graduates with several year's experience of underwriting. Training is normally on the job and if you are new to the insurance industry you may follow a company training programme to familiarise yourself with different departments.

You are also expected to qualify as an Associate of the Chartered Institute of Insurance, if you have not already done so. This involves part-time study, taking a range of qualifications, culminating in the Advanced Diploma. The Institute of Risk Management offers a certificate and a diploma course, taking around four to five years to complete. Some companies provide in-house training or day release for these courses, but you are also expected to do some studying in your own time.

It is also useful to have NEBOSH (National Examination Board in Occupational Safety & Health) qualifications that provide an awareness of health and safety subject areas.

A Diploma/Welsh Baccalaureate in business, administration and finance may be available in your area. The advanced level is equivalent to 3.5 A levels but for some university courses, the additional and specialist learning (ASL) component of the diploma needs to include specific A levels e.g. maths. Check entry requirements carefully with the individual institutions.

Mature entry is common and applicants with appropriate qualifications, experience and maturity have an advantage. Those already working in the insurance industry in underwriting departments are often recruited. Applicants with experience and qualifications in areas such as architecture, engineering or science may be able to enter specialist areas of insurance surveying. However, some employers may prefer recent graduates with an engineering, science or other numerate degree for training programmes. It is possible to take distance-learning courses for the professional qualifications of the Chartered Insurance Institute and the Institute of Risk Management.

Opportunities and Pay

You can work for a large insurance company which deals with several types of insurance, specialist engineering insurance companies, or as a risk manager for a firm of insurance brokers. Experienced surveyors can become senior or chief surveyors or can move into general management. Some work as independent self-employed consultants. There are also opportunities to work overseas.

Despite the economic downturn, demand for financial skills is expected to increase in the medium term. Employers are currently having difficulty recruiting professionals in specific areas, including risk accounting.

Pay varies depending on location and size of employer. Trainees generally earn from around £21k a year, rising to around £29k-£35k. With experience, an insurance surveyor can earn £45k or more. High earners can make £70k or more a year. There may be additional benefits, such as low cost loans, medical and life insurance or a pension scheme.

Health

You need to be generally fit and able to cope with heights.

Skills and Qualities

able to inspire confidence, able to work both on your own and in a team, analytical skills, attention to detail, enquiring mind, good spoken communication, good written English, IT skills, methodical, technical aptitude

Relevant Subjects

Business and accounting, Construction and built environment, Design and technology, English, ICT/Computer studies, Mathematics, Physics, Science

Further Information

AGCAS: Accountancy and Business Services (Job Sector Briefing) (AGCAS) - www.prospects.ac.uk/

Diploma in Business, Administration and Finance - www.baf-diploma.org.uk/

Financial Services Skills Council - sector skills council for financial services, accountancy & finance - www.fssc.org.uk/

The Association of British Insurers (ABI) - www.abi.org.uk

The Guide to Understanding the Insurance Industry 2008-9 by Chris Sharkey (Booksurge) (Booksurge) - www.ambest.com/sales/BRGuide.asp

Welsh Baccalaureate - www.wbq.org.uk

▶Working in maths (2009) (Babcock Lifeskills) - www.babcock-lifeskills.com/

Addresses

Chartered Insurance Institute (CII)
42-48 High Road, South Woodford, London E18 2JP
Phone: +44 (0)20 8989 8464
Web: www.cii.co.uk

Institute of Risk Management (IRM)
6 Lloyd's Avenue, London EC3N 3AX
Phone: +44 (0)20 7709 9808
Web: www.theirm.org

National Examination Board for Occupational Safety & Health (NEBOSH)
Dominus Way, Meridian Business Park, Leicester LE19 1QW
Phone: +44 (0)116 263 4700
Web: www.nebosh.org.uk

Similar Jobs

Compliance Officer, Insurance Broker, Insurance Business Development Manager, Insurance Loss Adjuster, Insurance Underwriter

Insurance Technician

also known as: Insurance Administrative Assistant, Insurance Clerk

CRCI:Financial Services
CLCI:NAG
Job Band: 3

Job Description

Insurance technicians perform a variety of reception, clerical, administration, accounts and general office support tasks for colleagues in an insurance company. They work in all aspects of insurance, carrying out routine clerical duties, such as regularly sorting, opening and issuing of the post. Send correspondence by post, fax and email. May transfer information from forms on to computer, send out new policies and update records. Check claims to ensure that a client is fully covered by the terms of the insurance and that claim forms are fully completed. May calculate the cost of insurance premiums and give quotations for straightforward policies.

Some insurance technicians work for a broker and advise clients on suitable policies. Otheres work for an underwriter or in a claims handling department. Deal with enquiries from clients by letter and telephone, and sometimes in person. Use a computer for most of the work.

Work Details

Usually work around 35-39 hrs a week, Monday to Friday, though some technicians work on Saturdays. This is an office-based job, with a lot of time spent on the telephone or working at a computer terminal. You work as part of a team with other technicians and other insurance colleagues, though some companies have very small offices with only one or two insurance staff. The work environment is usually light and airy. Some offices are open to the public. You may have face-to-face dealings with clients or on the phone with people whose claims involve tragedy or personal loss.

Qualification

- **England, Wales and Northern Ireland**

Band 3: For entry: usually at least 4 GCSEs (A*-C) including English and maths, or equivalent.

- **Scotland**

Band 3: For entry: usually at least four S grades (1-3) including English and maths, or similar.

Adult Qualifications

Employers may consider adults without formal qualifications, but those with experience in other clerical or financial areas may have an advantage.

Work Experience

Employers or colleges/universities may prefer candidates who have relevant work or voluntary experience. This includes work which gives you the opportunity to gain skills in administration, office-based tasks such as filing, using the telephone and computers. Also relevant are customer service skills or working with numbers or money.

Entry and Training

Most companies have in-house training programmes. Some give day release to college to study for BTEC/SQA courses or the Chartered Institute of Insurance (CII) exams, such as the award in insurance, which leads on to the certificate and diploma in insurance. You can also study for the CII foundation insurance test (FIT) by distance learning which gives credits towards the award in insurance. If working for a company such as Lloyd's of London, you need to pass the Lloyds and London Markets Introductory Test (LLMIT), and this counts as an exemption to part of the CII certificate in insurance.

Relevant training programmes, including apprenticeship schemes, may be available in your area. Advanced apprenticeships leading to qualification at level 3 can be a route into higher education. The

Diploma/Welsh Baccalaureate in business, administration and finance may be useful for this type of work, and may be available in your area.

Mature applicants with experience in other clerical or financial work may have an advantage. The Chartered Insurance Institute offers distance-learning courses for the award and certificate in insurance. Contact your local careers office, Jobcentre Plus, Next Step service or Learning and Skills Council (LSC)/Local Enterprise Company (LEC) for details of training schemes.

Opportunities and Pay

Despite the economic downturn, there are some opportunities with insurance companies of varying sizes all over the UK, including broking companies and Lloyds of London. Some insurance companies deal with a range of types of insurance, others specialise, for example in life assurance. With experience, you may be promoted to supervisor, in charge of a team of technicians. Promotion usually goes to people who have Chartered Insurance Institute (CII) certificates. You can also continue to take CII courses and train as a broker, claims official, underwriter or salesperson.

Pay varies depending on area and employer. Salaries start at around £13k-£16k rising to £20k-£32k a year with experience, though some senior technicians can earn £45k or more a year. You may be given benefits such as special low mortgage rates, pension schemes, medical insurance and life assurance.

Skills and Qualities

able to explain clearly, aptitude for teamwork, excellent communication skills, good organisational skills, good telephone manner, good written English, IT skills, numeracy skills, sympathetic, tactful

Relevant Subjects

Business and accounting, Economics, English, Mathematics

Further Information

Apprenticeship Schemes (National Apprenticeship Service) - www.apprenticeships.org.uk

Diploma in Business, Administration and Finance - www.baf-diploma.org.uk/

Financial Services Skills Council - sector skills council for financial services, accountancy & finance www.fssc.org.uk/

Insurance Careers (CII) (CII) - www.cii.co.uk/

The Association of British Insurers (ABI) - www.abi.org.uk

The Guide to Understanding the Insurance Industry 2008-9 by Chris Sharkey (Booksurge) - www.ambest.com/sales/BRGuide.asp

Training Schemes - www.direct.gov.uk/en/educationandlearning

Welsh Baccalaureate - www.wbq.org.uk

▶Working in maths (2009) (Babcock Lifeskills) - www.babcock-lifeskills.com/

Addresses

Chartered Insurance Institute (CII)
42-48 High Road, South Woodford, London E18 2JP
Phone: +44 (0)20 8989 8464
Web: www.cii.co.uk

Institute of Financial Accountants (ifa)
Burford House, 44 London Road, Sevenoaks, Kent TN13 1AS
Phone: +44 (0)1732 458080
Web: www.ifa.org.uk

Similar Jobs

Accounting Technician, Bank Officer, Building Society Officer, Clerk: Accounts, Insurance Broker, Insurance Business Development Manager, Insurance Underwriter

Insurance Underwriter

CRCI:Financial Services
CLCI:NAG Job Band: 4 to 5

Job Description

Insurance underwriters assess the extent of an insurance risk, such as accident, damage to property or theft, and decide whether to accept the risk and how much to charge for the policy. Investigate background information, consulting with other professionals and experts to establish all the relevant facts. Define the terms and quote the conditions and price (premiums) of a policy, using actuarial tables or computer programs. Need to ensure that the premium is competitive, but allows the company to cover costs and make a profit. Arrange for a policy to be drawn up and check the details.

They usually specialise in one type of insurance, such as commercial lines/fleet, household, motor, life or marine. May handle risks that are simple to arrange due to well-established statistics, or more complex and high-risk insurance that can carry a value of millions of pounds.

Work Details

Usually work around 35-39 hrs a week, Monday to Friday, but may have to work longer hours at times. Although this is an office-based job, you may sometimes visit clients and insurance brokers on their own premises. Consult with insurance technicians and other professionals, such as brokers and actuaries. You need to keep up to date with changes in law and taxation, and also technological developments.

Qualification

• England, Wales and Northern Ireland

Band 4: For BTEC higher national award: 1-2 A levels and some GCSEs (A*-C) usually including English and maths, or equivalent.

Band 5: For degree courses: 2-3 A levels and some GCSEs (A*-C) usually including English and maths, or equivalent. Exact requirements depend on the degree you take.

• Scotland

Band 4: For SQA higher national award: usually 2-3 H grades and some S grades (1-3), often including English and maths, or similar qualifications.

Band 5: For degree courses: 3-5 H grades and some S grades (1-3), usually including English and maths, or similar qualifications. Exact requirements depend on the degree you take.

Degree Information

Any degree discipline is accepted, but business studies/ administration, economics, statistics, languages, law or a mathematics subject are useful. There are a few degrees in insurance, or risk management, or with insurance or financial options. These may be preferred by some employers. For some posts an engineering or science degree may be useful.

Adult Qualifications

A qualification in economics or law is an advantage. There are usually special entry standards for adults who apply for degree courses or you could take an Access or foundation level course that leads to a relevant degree. Check with the universities for details.

Work Experience

Relevant work or voluntary experience is always useful and improves your chances in application for entry into this job. Any work experience in the finance sector is relevant and shows enthusiasm and commitment to the work. Time spent in an accountancy firm, an insurance company or shadowing a commercial underwriter gives you a good basis and insight into the profession.

Entry and Training
Many employers now look to recruit entrants with a degree or a relevant HND. Graduate training schemes are available in larger companies, with on-the-job training usual, working with an experienced underwriter. Entry is usually very competitive. Most graduate schemes last around two years, followed by a further two to three years working in a specialist area of risk.

Most companies provide comprehensive in-house training, and also expect trainees to study for the Chartered Insurance Institute professional exams, such as the diploma in insurance, either through a part-time college course or by distance learning. Some companies give trainees the chance to try out different departments, including underwriting, before specialising. Continuing professional development is emphasised, with trainees encouraged to attend courses linked to relevant topics.

Underwriters working in the London Market also have to complete the Lloyd's and London Market Introductory Test (LLMIT).

Some degrees or diplomas may give exemption from part of the professional exams. A Diploma/Welsh Baccalaureate in business, administration and finance may be available in your area. Relevant part-time foundation degrees are also available in financial markets and management and financial services. It is possible to start this job at a lower entry level as an insurance technician, and work your way up by taking professional exams. Sponsorship for higher education may be available from a large insurance company or from the Worshipful Company of Insurers.

Mature entrants with relevant work experience may be accepted for some college courses without needing any formal entry requirements, and entry qualifications for the Chartered Insurance Institute examinations may be waived if you are over 25. There may be opportunities for adults who are changing careers and distance-learning courses for professional qualifications are also available. Relevant experience such as in law and finance is an advantage, but not essential. Mature entrants with work experience, for example in financial advice or investment planning, are also considered.

Opportunities and Pay
Despite the economic downturn at the moment, employers are still finding the recruitment of professional financial workers difficult. There are still opportunities to work in these sectors and some sectors, particularly in the area of underwriting are experiencing shortages of talented people.

Jobs are available throughout the UK and companies are usually located in large towns and cities. Many of the larger companies, such as Lloyd's, are based in London, but there is also a concentration of jobs in Leeds, Manchester, Bristol, Glasgow and Bournemouth. You can work for insurers, reinsurers and brokers who handle several types of insurance, or a company specialising in one type, such as life assurance or marine insurance. With experience, underwriters can be promoted to deal with greater risks and with larger sums of money, or can move into management, taking charge of a team of underwriters. You can also move into other areas of insurance, such as broking, claims work, loss adjusting or insurance surveying.

Promotion usually goes to people who have taken the Chartered Insurance Institute professional qualification. It is possible to work abroad, especially for underwriters with language skills.

Pay varies depending on location and size of employer. Graduate trainees are likely to earn around £18k-£20k a year. With experience this rises to £38k-£60k a year. Some earn as much as £100k a year. City of London salaries are usually higher and pay may be linked to performance. Lloyd's underwriters can achieve salaries of up to £300k a year. You may also be given a company car and perhaps a range of benefits, such as pension schemes, medical insurance and life assurance.

Skills and Qualities
able to make important decisions, attention to detail, enquiring mind, excellent communication skills, information handling skills, IT skills, methodical, negotiating skills, numeracy skills, sound judgement

Relevant Subjects
Business and accounting, Economics, English, ICT/Computer studies, Law, Mathematics

Further Information
AGCAS: Accountancy and Business Services (Job Sector Briefing) (AGCAS) - www.prospects.ac.uk/

Diploma in Business, Administration and Finance - www.baf-diploma.org.uk/

Financial Services Skills Council - sector skills council for financial services, accountancy & finance www.fssc.org.uk/

Insurance Careers (CII) (CII) - www.cii.co.uk/

The Association of British Insurers (ABI) - www.abi.org.uk

The Guide to Understanding the Insurance Industry 2008-9 by Chris Sharkey (Booksurge) - www.ambest.com/sales/BRGuide.asp

Welsh Baccalaureate - www.wbq.org.uk

▶Working in maths (2009) (Babcock Lifeskills) - www.babcock-lifeskills.com/

▶Working in space (2010) (Babcock Lifeskills) - www.babcock-lifeskills.com/

Addresses
Chartered Insurance Institute (CII)
42-48 High Road, South Woodford, London E18 2JP
Phone: +44 (0)20 8989 8464
Web: www.cii.co.uk

International Underwriting Association of London
London Underwriting Centre, 3 Minster Court, Mincing Lane
EC3R 7DD
Phone: +44 (0)20 7617 4444
Web: www.iua.co.uk

Lloyd's of London
One Lime Street, London EC3M 7HA
Phone: +44 (0)20 7327 1000
Web: www.lloyds.com

Worshipful Company of Insurers (WCI)
The Insurance Hall, 20 Aldermanbury, London EC2V 7HY
Phone: +44 (0)20 7600 4006
Web: www.wci.org.uk

Similar Jobs
Actuary, Compliance Officer, Financial Adviser/Planner, Insurance Broker, Insurance Loss Adjuster, Insurance Surveyor, Investment Analyst, Stockbroker

Interactive Media Designer
also known as: Multimedia Specialist

CRCI:Computers and IT
CLCI:CAV — Job Band: 3 to 5

Job Description
Interactive media designers use design and computer programming skills to combine text, data, graphics, sound, animation and other visual effects. They have knowledge of specialist interactive programming languages and use industry-standard design packages, such as Dreamweaver, Photoshop, Macromedia Flash and similar products. Designers work as part of a team producing websites, CD-ROMS, DVDs, or interactive screens. Products can be used in advertising and marketing materials, education and training resources, museum, art gallery and library publicity and collection materials, computer games and other entertainment products.

Media designers meet with clients and discuss the brief (outline of instructions), advise on what is possible and work on initial ideas using computer design packages to meet the brief. They work with other specialists, such as animators, writers and other programmers. They present the design/concept to the client for comment, and produce the final design for approval and production. Then extensively test and resolve any bugs in the program and produce the product documentation. Designers have a broad knowledge of multimedia, enabling communication with other production staff, such as graphic designers, sound engineers, film producers and photographers.

Work Details

Work 35-39 hrs a week, Monday to Friday, but additional hours may be required as deadlines approach. Work is usually desk-based in an office environment or a studio. Those working as consultants must be prepared to travel when visiting clients and to spend nights away from home. There may be frequent meetings to consult with managers and other IT and design professionals. Those working as self-employed consultants/designers usually work from home.

Qualification

• England, Wales and Northern Ireland

Band 4: For a relevant higher national award: 1-2 A levels and some GCSEs (A*-C) including English and maths, and for some courses, science, computer studies or information technology, or equivalent.

Band 5: For degree courses: 2-3 A levels including maths and science, or computer studies/information technology for some courses, and some GCSEs (A*-C) usually including English and maths, or equivalent. Exact requirements depend on the degree you take.

• Scotland

Band 4: For a relevant higher national award: 2-3 H grades and some S grades (1-3) usually including English and maths, or for some courses science, computer studies or information technology, or similar qualifications.

Band 5: For degree courses: 3-5 H grades including maths and science, or computer studies or information technology for some courses, and some S grades (1-3), often including English and maths, or similar qualifications. Exact requirements depend on the degree you take.

Degree Information

A degree in any discipline is acceptable, but a relevant subject, such as interactive multimedia, interactive media production, multimedia design, interactive and motion design, and multimedia technologies, is most useful. The Information Technology Management for Business degree (see e-skills UK) is designed in partnership with some of the biggest employers in the IT industry. Other relevant subjects include artificial intelligence, computer science, software development/engineering or information technology. Mathematics or business studies with computing is helpful for entry to training or further study.

There are vast numbers of multimedia degree courses and it is important to ensure that the course is relevant to the career you wish to pursue. There are also postgraduate courses for graduates with relevant and non-relevant degrees.

Adult Qualifications

Mature applicants may not need the standard entry requirements for higher education courses, particularly if your previous experience is relevant or you show an ability to study at the appropriate level. There are many relevant full or part-time courses available at further/higher education colleges. Access and foundation courses are available for those who have no formal qualifications but wish to pursue a relevant degree.

Work Experience

Employers or colleges/universities may prefer candidates who have relevant work or voluntary experience. This includes any role where you are working with computers and design, such as desktop publishing or graphic design. There are private firms and larger companies with design or multimedia departments who may offer you work experience of this nature. Any experience in television or film work is also an advantage.

Other schemes, such as 'The Year in Industry', enable those who expect good A levels/H grades and intend to go to university, the opportunity to spend a salaried year with a company to gain valuable work experience.

Entry and Training

This is still a young industry and those with relevant skills can progress quickly. The rapid pace of expansion in this sector in recent years means that creative talent and technical skills can be more important than formal qualifications. Large organisations with in-house training facilities may recruit applicants from other areas of computer, business or creative work who show an interest in, and aptitude for, programming. However, many entrants have a degree and relevant programming skills.

You are expected to have knowledge of industry-standard computer design packages, such as Photoshop. However you can develop further skills in the more advanced packages whilst in the job, or through online tutorials. A portfolio of creative work, including a personal website, can be a distinct advantage and short courses in programming languages such as C++ or Visual Basic, or in the use of specific products, may be helpful. There is a range of short courses available that offer training in some of the specific skills used in multimedia, such as animation, computer aided graphic design, digital photography and its manipulation for images in multimedia. Computer graphics modules and business-oriented courses on Hypertext and Java programming are useful.

Training is ongoing, both on the job and by short courses run by manufacturers to keep your skills up to date. Some employers may assist with study for professional qualifications, including those offered by the British Computer Society or the Institute for the Management of Information Systems. The Open University offers courses in computing and maths that lead to a computing degree. There are no formal entry requirements and you study through distance learning. A full or part-time foundation degree in IT is also available. A Diploma/Welsh Baccalaureate may be available in your area in IT for those aged 14-19.

An ICT higher apprenticeship is available through e-skills. This combines an apprenticeship with a foundation degree and can lead to a full honours degree. There are partnerships with colleges and universities throughout the UK. E-skills also runs a professional development programme which enables new IT professionals to fast-track their career. The programme is delivered through universities and participating employers. E-skills also offers an internship. Students are placed for a period of employment within an organisation, enabling them to develop valuable business and IT skills. Contact e-skills for details of all programmes and schemes.

Mature applicants may be expected to have relevant experience in design or IT, and experience in the use of interactive design software. There are many relevant full or part-time courses available at further/higher education colleges. Training opportunities such as Work Based Learning/Training for Work may be available in your area. Some LSCs/LECs, Jobcentres (NI) and ELWa (Wales) run specialist IT courses. You can also gain recognition of previous experience through Accreditation of Prior Learning (APL) or by working towards relevant S/NVQs.

Skillset, the sector skills council for the creative media industry, manages a range of training funds which may help to pay for relevant media courses. Contact Skillset for further details.

Opportunities and Pay

Jobs exist throughout the UK, although most vacancies are in London and the south east of England. Major employers are advertising and marketing businesses, or departments, including technical sections, in large organisations. Some media designers are employed in the IT departments of large organisations, or by companies which do a lot of Internet business. Others work in education, broadcasting, voluntary and charitable organisations, public relations, or design consultancies specialising in interactive work.

Progression to senior designer and managerial positions is possible, as well as moving to other areas of work in information and communications technology. Experienced media designers may work as self-employed consultants or set up their own company offering design services to a wide range of clients.

Pay varies depending on the location, size and type of organisation. Salaries start at around £15k-£22k a year for junior/trainee designers, rising to £22k-£32k with experience. Senior designers earn around £30k-£45k a year. High earners with specialist skills can earn more than £50k a year.

Skills and Qualities

able to get on with all kinds of people, able to work both on your own and in a team, analytical skills, attention to detail, creative flair, good communication skills, good organisational skills, imaginative, IT skills, technical aptitude

Relevant Subjects

Art and Design, Design and technology, English, ICT/Computer studies, Mathematics, Media and communication studies, Music, Physics, Science

Further Information

AGCAS: Information Technology (Job Sector Briefing) (AGCAS) - www.prospects.ac.uk

Computer Weekly (Reed Business Information) - www.computerweekly.com

Diplomas (Foundation, Higher and Advanced) - http://yp.direct.gov.uk/diplomas

e-skills UK - sector skills council for business and information technology - www.e-skills.com

Open University - www.open.ac.uk

Real Life Guide to Information & Communications Technology (Trotman) - www.trotman.co.uk

Skillset - sector skills council for the creative media, fashion and textiles industries - www.skillset.org

Welsh Baccalaureate - www.wbq.org.uk

▶Working in art & design (2009) (Babcock Lifeskills) - www.babcock-lifeskills.com/

▶Working in the Games Industry - www.workingames.co.uk

Year in Industry (Engineering Development Trust) - www.yini.org.uk

Addresses

British Computer Society (BCS)
First Floor, Block D North Star House North Star Avenue, Swindon, Wiltshire SN2 1FA
Phone: +44 (0)845 300 4417
Web: www.bcs.org

British Interactive Media Association (BIMA)
The Lightwell, 12-16 Laystall Street, Clerkenwell, London EC1R 4PF
Phone: +44(0)207 843 6797
Web: www.bima.co.uk

Institute for the Management of Information Systems (IMIS)
5 Kingfisher House, New Mill Road, Orpington, Kent BR5 3QG
Phone: +44 (0)700 002 3456
Web: www.imis.org.uk

Similar Jobs

Computer Games Animator, Computer Games Programmer, IT Applications Developer, IT Systems Developer, Website Designer, Website Developer

Interior Designer

also known as: Space Planner, Spatial Designer

CRCI:Design, Arts and Crafts

CLCI:ET — Job Band: 3 to 5

Job Description

Interior designers use design skills and techniques to make the most advantageous and appropriate use of interior space by using spatial design/planning. They design schemes for the interiors of many kinds of structures, including public buildings, shops, hotels, offices, aircraft, ships and private houses. Usually liaise with construction professionals, including architects, builders, surveyors and engineers, as well as with the client. Then research the relevant technical, architectural and scientific issues and produce a cost-effective, functional and attractive design that is relative to the interior space. Designers prepare sketches or models of the space, its colour schemes, features and furnishings.

May use computer-aided design (CAD) software when creating the designs and to present 3D images of the space. Also estimate costs, select contractors and may also supervise the project until it is complete. Then organise the various essential arts and crafts required for completion of the design project. Designers must keep up to date with innovations and trends by visiting trade fairs and exhibitions, either at home or abroad.

Work Details

Work a basic 39 hr week; Monday to Friday, but may work longer hours, including some evenings and weekends. Interior designers are studio based, but travel to clients' homes and businesses, and to project sites. The hours have to fit in with the client's needs. You may have to be away from home for short periods. In this work you have to be able to visualise ideas and communicate clearly and accurately, verbally and by drawing. You have to be able to meet deadlines and work within agreed budgets.

Qualification

- **England, Wales and Northern Ireland**

Band 3: For entry to jobs, HNC or a relevant Diploma, usually at least 4 GCSEs (A*-C) including English and maths, or equivalent.

Band 4: For foundation course in art and design: usually at least one A level and 3-4 GCSEs (A*-C) including English. For a BTEC higher national award: successful completion of a foundation studies course or a national level programme, though applicants may be accepted with an art A level and 4 GCSEs (A*-C) or equivalent. Entry requirements vary, so check with colleges.

Band 5: For degree courses: 2-3 A levels and some GCSEs (A*-C), usually including English and maths, or equivalent. Most students take a foundation studies course first. Exact requirements depend on the degree you take.

- **Scotland**

Band 3: For entry to jobs, usually at least four S grades (1-3) including English or maths, or similar.

Band 4: For entry to SQA higher national and professional development awards, usually 2-3 H grades and some S grades (1-3), including English and maths, or similar qualifications.

Band 5: For degree courses: 3-5 H grades and some S grades (1-3), usually including English and maths, or similar. Exact requirements depend on the degree you take.

Degree Information

First degrees can be in interior design, spatial design, interior design environment architectures, interior architecture and design or 3D design. There are postgraduate courses in interior and spatial design that can be taken following a first degree in an art and design subject.

Adult Qualifications
Mature applicants with outstanding portfolios of work may be accepted for courses without the standard entry requirements. There are Access and foundation courses in some areas that provide adults without qualifications a route onto degree courses. These courses may also be part time. Check with individual institutions.

Work Experience
Entry to this job is competitive and it is important that you try to do some relevant work or voluntary experience before applying. Relevant contacts are interior design shops, design services and those specialising in interior architecture. Painters and decorators can provide you with an insight into techniques and materials used. A business background can also be an advantage to help with the costing and budgeting aspects of the work.

Entry and Training
Most new entrants begin as design assistants in consultancies, or in the design departments of construction companies or an architects' practice. Many employers ask for knowledge and/or experience of computer-aided design (CAD) programs such as AutoCAD, 3D Studio or Photoshop. A Diploma/Welsh Baccalaureate may be available in your area in creative and media and may provide a route onto higher education courses.

Many entrants take an HNC/HND in 3D design, spatial design or interior design, however most are graduates. The British Interior Design Association (BIDA) can supply a list of relevant courses. A comprehensive portfolio is needed for entry to courses and for employers. Students usually take a foundation studies course before taking a three-year degree (four years in Scotland). A Professional Development Award in interior design is available in Scotland.

Foundation degrees in interior design, interior architecture and spatial design are also available from a number of colleges and universities. S/NVQs in design are available at levels 3-4. Short courses are also able on aspects such as feng shui, upholstery, paint and decorating techniques.

Once working, training is on the job, usually also with attendance on relevant short courses, such as the use of computer software packages, negotiating skills, photography, etc. It is useful to join a professional body such as BIDA or the Chartered Society of Designers (CSD) who provide opportunities for continuing professional development (CPD).

Mature applicants with experience in art and design or relevant work in kitchen, bathroom and bedroom planning may have an advantage, though employers also expect a good portfolio of recent designs to demonstrate an ability to design for the employer's target market. Those with experience of computer-aided design (CAD) programs such as AutoCAD, 3D Studio or Photoshop have an advantage. You need a comprehensive and up-to-date portfolio of your work for entry to courses.

Open and distance-learning courses in interior design are available from a range of organisations.

Opportunities and Pay
Around 7,000 people work as interior designers in the UK with opportunities concentrated in the south-east of England. Many designers begin their careers in design consultancies or design departments of building/construction-related companies. Some large businesses, such as hotel or retail organisations, have in-house designers. You can become a freelance designer, but this is a highly competitive business, so you must have good business knowledge and need to build a good professional reputation. Most television or theatre companies employ designers on a fixed-term contract basis, but this is particularly competitive.

In large companies, you can progress from design assistant to designer and there may be opportunities for promotion to management posts. Some interior designers become full-time teachers/lecturers in colleges. Others teach part time and design on a freelance basis. There may be opportunities overseas. The British Interior Design Association (BIDA) has a list of agencies on its website that specialise in interior design.

Pay varies depending on location and employer. Typical salaries start at around £20k-£25k a year for a junior designer, rising up to £30k for those with 4-5 years' experience. Senior designers can earn £35k-£70k a year.

Health
Normal colour vision is needed.

Skills and Qualities
able to work to deadlines, attention to detail, business awareness, creative and imaginative flair, eye for shape/colour, good communication skills, good interpersonal skills, IT skills, self confident, technical aptitude

Relevant Subjects
Art and Design, Design and technology, ICT/Computer studies

Further Information
Art & Design Directory 2010 (ISCO Publications)

Chartered Society of Designers (Chartered Society of Designers) - www.csd.org.uk

Creative & Cultural Skills - sector skills council for advertising, crafts, cultural heritage, design, literature, music, performing & visual arts - www.ccskills.org.uk

Design Uncovered (Trotman 2009) - www.trotman.co.uk

Design Week (Design Week) - www.designweek.co.uk

Diplomas (Foundation, Higher and Advanced) - http://yp.direct.gov.uk/diplomas

NSEAD: Careers in Art, Craft & Design (National Society for Education in Art and Design) - www.nsead.org/resources/careers.aspx

The Designer (Chartered Society of Designers) - www.thedesignermagazine.com

►Working in art & design (2009) (Babcock Lifeskills) - www.babcock-lifeskills.com/

Your Creative Future (Design Council) (Design Council) - www.yourcreativefuture.org

Addresses
British Interior Design Association (BIDA)
Units 109 111 The Chambers, Chelsea Harbour, London SW10 0XE
Phone: +44 (0) 20 7349 0800
Web: www.bida.org

Design Council
34 Bow Street, London WC2E 7DL
Phone: +44 (0)20 7420 5200
Web: www.designcouncil.org.uk

Design Wales
University of Wales Institute, Cardiff Western Avenue CF5 2YB
Phone: +44 (0) 2920 41 7043
Web: www.designwales.org

Similar Jobs
Architect, Architectural Technologist, Exhibition Designer, Film/TV & Theatre Set/Stage Designer, Furniture Designer, Graphic Designer, Visual Merchandiser

Interpreter
CRCI:Languages, Information and Culture
CLCI:FAL Job Band: 5

Job Description
Interpreters convert spoken statements from a foreign language into the mother tongue or language most usually used. They help people to communicate with each other when they do not share a common language. May also research and interpret specialised terminology.

Interpreter

There are different methods of interpreting. Simultaneous interpreting is carried out from a booth or by whispering to one or two delegates in a small group meeting or conference. Liaison interpreting is used for conversations or interviews, when the interpreter translates into and out of both languages. Consecutive interpreting is when the speaker makes breaks in a presentation to allow the interpreter, who may take notes, to relay information. Conference interpreting is where delegates speak in their own language and the interpreter, wearing headphones, immediately translates. Ad-Hoc is provided for people who are not fluent or native speakers and who need to communicate with public service providers, so that they can have access to legal, health, education or social services. This includes interpreting for the police or law courts.

Work Details

Usually works a basic 39 hr week, which may include evenings and some weekend work. Hours of work can be irregular and unsociable. Interpreters work in many different locations and need to be willing to travel anywhere at short notice.

The work requires superb concentration and can sometimes be stressful. You are responsible for accurate, unbiased interpretation of concepts, which may be complex. For some interpreting work, headphones/headsets, telephones and microphones are used. You may work a s sign language interpreter. See the Language Service Professional job profile.

Qualification

• England, Wales and Northern Ireland

Band 5: For degree courses in languages: 2-3 A levels including at least one foreign language and usually English and some GCSEs (A*-C) usually including English and maths, or equivalent. Exact requirements depend on the degree you take.

• Scotland

Band 5: For degree courses in languages: 3-5 H grades including at least one foreign language and usually English, and some S grades (1-3), including English and maths, or similar qualifications. Exact requirements depend on the degree you take.

Degree Information

First degrees in modern or applied languages that give a high level of competence in at least two foreign languages, preferably including one unusual one, give entry to postgraduate study. There are a few first degrees and several postgraduate courses in subjects, such as interpreting and translation with double honours languages, in for example, Arabic/English, French/German, French/Spanish, German/Spanish or Italian/Portuguese.

Combined degrees in languages with engineering, law or business may also be acceptable and have the advantage of providing a specialist subject area.

Adult Qualifications

It is necessary to show a high level of competence in at least two languages. Entry requirements may be relaxed for adults applying for degree courses or there may be special entry routes such as Access courses or foundation degrees. The Open University offers degrees in German, French and Spanish.

Work Experience

Employers and universities may prefer candidates who have relevant work or voluntary experience. Any experience involving use of languages, such as teaching or tourism, is relevant. Experience of public speaking or making presentations is also a distinct advantage. Consider a period of working and living in the country of each language in which you wish to specialise, to gain thorough knowledge of the institutions, culture, attitude and practices of that country.

Routes into Languages offers a work placement service for graduates to gain work experience. Check the website for details.

Entry and Training

It is necessary to be fluent in at least two foreign languages. In addition, it is an advantage to have specialist knowledge in business, law, science or technology. There are no set entry requirements but entrants are usually graduates and many have postgraduate qualifications in modern languages, or interpreting and translating. The European Commission offers training for conference interpreters. There are several further education colleges which offer courses in community interpreting with specialisms in health, law or local government.

An alternative to a degree course or postgraduate qualification is to gain qualifications through the Chartered Institute of Linguists' (IoL) examinations. The civil service may also offer training in its linguist posts, where duties include translating, as well as interpreting. For those working in public services and government-related services, the IoL also offers a diploma in public service interpreting), which is a qualifying examination for membership of the National Register of Public Service Interpreters. You can become a member of the Institute of Translation and Interpreting (ITI) when you have 200 days' experience. The ITI also supports continuing professional development . Membership of the International Association of Conference Interpreters requires 150 days' experience.

It is necessary to have a total mastery of your mother tongue. Apart from mastery of one or more other languages, you need a thorough knowledge of the institutions, culture, attitude and practices of the countries where those languages are spoken.

The Welsh Language Board has details of training courses and information about jobs using Welsh on their website e.g early years education , media and tourism and leisure. Further education institutes in Wales offer bilingual and Welsh language vocational courses. In addition, higher education courses in Welsh are available at the University of Wales: Trinity St. David, Aberystwyth University; Bangor University and Swansea University. Check the websites for details.

Mature entrants with relevant language skills and work experience in science and technology, law or business are at an advantage if they can show specialist knowledge and vocabulary.

Opportunities and Pay

Most interpreters are freelance and usually find work through agencies. There are a few full-time posts with the European Commission (EC), United Nations, NATO and international trade organisations, but there is fierce competition for these. Jobs may also be found in the public sector, working with immigration, legal, health and education, and community services. These include opportunities to support police interviews, medical consultations and court hearings as well as in specific technical, literary or business areas. There are increased opportunities for those with eastern European languages and Urdu, Punjabi and Chinese. Freelance jobs may be irregular and you may need another source of income, maybe from teaching or translating.

The National Register of Public Service Interpreters (NRPSI) has around 2000 members. Conference interpreters often work in full-time posts with international organisations in all countries. These cover all official language combinations. Some interpreters work as tourist guides. There are few promotion opportunities, though posts are available as a senior interpreter or head of department. Demand for public service and court interpreters is growing, though most are employed through agencies or are freelance interpreters. Some move into training, consultancy or management roles.

Typical starting salaries are around £19k-£26k, rising to £35k a year with experience, but there are few salaried jobs. Graduates working for the EC earn around £28k a year, rising to £32k-£50k with experience. Senior interpreters working for international organisations or with languages that are in demand can earn from £52k-£62k a year. The best paid jobs tend to be in Geneva,

Strasbourg or Luxembourg. Freelance interpreters usually earn between £200 and £700 a day, depending on the demand for the particular language and the location.

Health

Good hearing and clear speech are essential. You should also have a good level of physical stamina.

Skills and Qualities

ability in one or more languages, able to cope under pressure, awareness of confidentiality issues, clear speaking voice, clear-thinking, good communication skills, good concentration level, good memory, information handling skills, public speaking ability

Relevant Subjects

Classical studies, English, Government and politics, Modern Foreign Languages

Further Information

Careers Wales - www.careerswales.com/

CILT:The National Centre for Languages - www.cilt.org.uk

Civil Service - www.civilservice.gov.uk/jobs

European Personnel Selection Office (EU Careers) (Office for Official Publications of the EC) - http://europa.eu/epso

Institute of Translation & Interpreting (ITI) - www.iti.org.uk

Interpreters in the EU - www.europa.eu

Languages Work - www.languageswork.org.uk

Linguist Magazine (6 x a year) (Institute of Linguists) - www.iol.org.uk/linguistmagazine/default.asp

National Register of Public Service Interpreters (NRPSI) - www.nrpsi.co.uk

Routes into Languages - www.routesintolanguages.ac.uk

The Welsh Language Board - www.byig-wlb.org.uk/Pages/Hafan.aspx

▶Working in police, fire & security (2009) (Babcock Lifeskills) - www.babcock-lifeskills.com/

Working with languages (2010) (Babcock Lifeskills) - www.babcock-lifeskills.com/

Addresses

Chartered Institute of Linguists (IoL)
Saxon House, 48 Southwark Street, London SE1 1UN
Phone: +44 (0)20 7940 3100
Web: www.iol.org.uk

International Association of Conference Interpreters (AIIC)
46, avenue Blanc, CH-1202, Geneva
Phone: +41 22 908 15 40
Web: www.aiic.net

Swansea University
Singleton Park, Swansea SA2 8PP
Phone: +44 (0) 1792 205678
Web: www.swan.ac.uk/

University of Wales
King Edward VII Avenue, Cardiff CF10 3NS
Phone: +44 (0)29 2037 6999
Web: www.wales.ac.uk/en/Home.aspx

Similar Jobs

Interpreter: European Union, Language Service Professional, Secretary: Bilingual, Teacher: Community Languages, Teacher: English to Speakers of Other Languages, Translator

Interpreter: European Union

also known as: EU Interpreter

CRCI:Languages, Information and Culture
CLCI:FAL Job Band: 5

Job Description

European Union (EU) interpreters work for the Institutions of the European Commission (EC) converting spoken communications from one language to another. They may work in the European Parliament, court of auditors, European Court of Justice, or the EC services in Luxembourg. Interpreters assist people in communicating with each other when they do not share a common language. Ensures that speeches delivered in one of the official languages EU are accurately rendered into the other official languages. May need to research specialised terminology.

One of three methods of interpreting is used. Simultaneous interpreting is for conferences where delegates speak in their own language and the interpreter immediately translates. Consecutive translating is when the speaker makes breaks in a presentation to allow the interpreter to relay information. Liaison interpreting is used for conversations or interviews when the interpreter translates into and out of both languages.

Work Details

The normal working week is 37 hours; Monday to Friday, although you are expected to be available for work at other times to meet important deadlines. The work is office based, but you also spend a lot of time in language booths, particularly at the European Parliament. You are responsible for accurate, unbiased interpretation of concepts, which may be complex.

Qualification

• England, Wales and Northern Ireland

Band 5: For degree courses in languages: 2-3 A levels, including at least one foreign language and usually English and some GCSEs (A*-C) usually including English and maths, or equivalent. Exact requirements depend on the degree you take.

• Scotland

Band 5: For degree courses in languages: 3-5 H grades, including at least one foreign language and usually English, and some S grades (1-3), usually including English and maths, or similar qualifications. Exact requirements depend on the degree you take.

Degree Information

First degrees in modern or applied languages that give a high level of competence in at least two foreign languages, preferably including one unusual one give entry to postgraduate study. There are a few first degrees and several postgraduate courses in subjects, such as interpreting & translation with double honours languages, in for example, Arabic/English, French/German, French/Spanish, German/Spanish or Italian/Portuguese.

Combined degrees in languages with engineering, law or European business management may also be acceptable and have the advantage of providing a specialist subject area.

Adult Qualifications

Entry requirements may be relaxed for adults applying for degree courses, or there may be special entry routes such as Access or foundation courses. The Open University offers degrees in German, French and Spanish.

Work Experience

Entry to this career is highly competitive and it is essential that you have some relevant work or voluntary experience before applying. Any experience involving the use of languages, such as teaching or tourism, is relevant. Experience of public speaking, work (voluntary or paid) in Europe, or any experience that demonstrates your interest in the European Union is also a distinct advantage.

Entry and Training

Entrants are usually graduates, and many have postgraduate qualifications in interpreting and translating. It is necessary to be fluent in at least three working languages from the official languages of the EU, and have previous training or experience as a conference interpreter. An alternative to a degree course or postgraduate qualification is to gain qualifications through the Chartered Institute of Linguists' (IoL) examinations.

Application for interpreting posts should be made directly to the European Personnel Selection Office (EPSO). There is an open competition process of recruitment which is lengthy and complicated. Those who pass a series of tests and an interview over a period of several months, have their names published on a reserve list and can then contact departments that interest them. There is no guarantee of a job offer. Notice of the open competitions is published in the Official Journal of the European Communities and also in the national press.

To work as a freelance interpreter with the EU institutions, you must pass an inter-institutional accreditation test, and be entered into the joint EU database of accredited freelance interpreters. To be eligible for the test, you must hold a recognised university degree in conference interpreting or a degree in a subject and a postgraduate qualification in conference interpreting, and/or have documented experience in consecutive and simultaneous translating.

With a qualification in conference interpreting, you can gain a place on a European Parliament traineeship for conference interpreters. This enables you to spend time on an interpreting course at a European university giving support to other student interpreters and developing your own skills. The European Court of Justice offers a limited number of traineeships, lasting from 10-12 weeks, aimed at newly qualified conference interpreters who intend to specialise in legal interpreting. Applicants must be able to read French fluently.

The European Commission Stagiaire Scheme is a five-month training and work attachment internship for young graduates. It does not give an automatic right to a job, but provides useful insight into the Commission.

Mature entrants with experience as conference interpreters are highly regarded. Some EU grades require two or three years' relevant experience.

Opportunities and Pay

The EU is the largest employer of interpreters in the world. You are likely to be based in Brussels, Strasbourg or Luxembourg, although a small number of staff work in EU delegations throughout the world. Competition for entry is fierce but there is a shortage of well-qualified British candidates. The European Parliament, the European Commission, and the European Court of Justice each has an interpreter service, and staff and freelance interpreters are recruited jointly.

Salary rates are based on the highest of a member state and are usually attractive to UK applicants, starting at around £28k, and rising to £43k-£52k a year with experience. Salaries are also enhanced (expatriation allowance) for those working outside their own country and equal to 16% of basic salary.

Further allowances are added according to personal circumstances such as a household allowance (for officials who are the principal earner in a household, equal to 5% of basic salary), dependent children allowance (about £130 per child under 18 and an extension for those under 26 who receive formal education or vocational training), education allowance and a relocation package.

Health

Good hearing and clear speech are essential. You should also have a good level of physical stamina.

Skills and Qualities

ability in one or more languages, able to cope under pressure, awareness of confidentiality issues, clear speaking voice, good communication skills, good concentration level, good memory, information handling skills, interest in current affairs, public speaking ability

Relevant Subjects

Classical studies, English, Government and politics, Modern Foreign Languages

Further Information

CILT:The National Centre for Languages - www.cilt.org.uk

European Personnel Selection Office (EU Careers) (Office for Official Publications of the EC) - http://europa.eu/epso

Institute of Translation & Interpreting (ITI) - www.iti.org.uk

Languages Work - www.languageswork.org.uk

Linguist Magazine (6 x a year) (Institute of Linguists) - www.iol.org.uk/linguistmagazine/default.asp

Open University - www.open.ac.uk

Routes into Languages - www.routesintolanguages.ac.uk

The EU in the UK (EC) - www.ec.europa.eu/unitedkingdom

Working with languages (2010) (Babcock Lifeskills) - www.babcock-lifeskills.com/

Addresses

Chartered Institute of Linguists (IoL)
Saxon House, 48 Southwark Street, London SE1 1UN
Phone: +44 (0)20 7940 3100
Web: www.iol.org.uk

International Association of Conference Interpreters (AIIC)
46, avenue Blanc, CH-1202, Geneva
Phone: +41 22 908 15 40
Web: www.aiic.net

Similar Jobs

Civil Service Diplomatic Officer, Interpreter, Language Service Professional, Secretary: Bilingual, Teacher: English to Speakers of Other Languages, Teacher: Modern Foreign Languages, Translator

Investment Administrator

also known as: Fund Administrator
CRCI:Financial Services
CLCI:NAL
Job Band: 3 to 4

Job Description

Investment administrators are concerned with the day-to-day administration of investment trusts, supporting fund managers and analysts who help clients get the best return on their investment. Clients might include insurance policy holders, unit and investment trust holders and pension fund contributors, as well as individual investors. Duties may include processing new investment applications, updating information on a computer database, doing calculations and maintaining records. Must ensure that all fund transactions balance at the end of each working day. This can involve detailed checking.

Work on valuations, pricing administration, the analysis of fund performance, dividend unit trust and stocks and shares administration. May deal directly with the public and work with other financial specialists. Ensure that work on client accounts meets the regulations of the Financial Services Authority (FSA).

Work Details

You may work regular office hours of 9am-5pm, Monday to Friday, though sometimes you are required to work additional hours, that can include early mornings. Much of your work is done using a computer or by telephone, when contacting your clients and other professional colleagues. You often work in an open-plan environment. The work can be demanding.

Qualification

There are no set entry qualifications but most employers ask for A levels, or equivalent qualifications in subjects such as business or finance.

• England, Wales and Northern Ireland

Band 4: For entry: usually 1-2 A levels and some GCSEs (A*-C) usually including English and maths, or equivalent.

- **Scotland**

Band 4: For entry: usually usually 2-3 H grades and some S grades (1-3), often including English and maths, or similar qualifications.

Adult Qualifications
Relevant experience or a qualification in accountancy, banking, insurance or investment is an advantage.

Work Experience
Employers may prefer candidates who have relevant work or voluntary experience, such as work in finance, insurance, investment or accounts. Any business administration or IT knowledge is also an advantage.

Entry and Training
Increasingly, employers look for those with excellent A levels/H grades or a degree, ideally with some relevant work experience. Many employers have their own in-house investment administration training programme consisting of on-the-job training with experienced staff, combined with routes to professional qualifications.

The Securities & Investment Institute (SII) offers the investment administrative qualification (IAQ) for administration and operations staff, as well as specialist diplomas. Their 'Introduction to Investment foundation qualification' at level 3 is appropriate for students preparing to enter the industry (for example as part of a higher or further education programme), or for those newly recruited to the industry as part of their in-house induction programme. This qualification is recognised by the the Financial Services Skills Council (FSSC) and the Qualifications & Curriculum Authority.

Once trained, investment administrators are expected to keep up to date by doing continuing professional development. Many move on to take more advanced qualifications offered by the SII such as the diploma in investment operations. The ifs School of Finance also offers a range of professional qualifications and a foundation/intermediate certificate in personal finance aimed at both 14-16 year-olds and college students. This is delivered at schools and colleges throughout the UK.

Vocational training may also be offered by some companies. Relevant S/NVQs are available at levels 2-4 and the Diploma/Welsh Baccalaureate in business, administration and finance may also be available and useful for entry to this career. Training programmes, including FSSC apprenticeships in providing financial services may be available in your area for new and existing employees. Advanced apprenticeships leading to qualification at level 3 can also be a route into higher education.

Mature applicants may find that employers prefer those under the age of 24 for training programmes. Mature applicants can benefit through government training opportunities, such as apprenticeships, that may be available in your area. You can gain recognition of previous experience through Accreditation of Prior Learning (APL) or by working towards relevant S/NVQs. Contact your local careers office, Jobcentre Plus, Next Step service or Learning and Skills Council (LSC)/Local Enterprise Company (LEC) for details of all training opportunities and schemes.

Opportunities and Pay
Employers include investment trusts, life assurance companies, fund managers and banks. Many jobs are located in London but there are other opportunities in other major towns and cities throughout the UK. Scotland is a large and growing area for investment roles. After successful experience you are able to move into a supervisory or a more senior post. Job security is based on how well the investment industry is doing and is related to the country's economy. Despite the economic downturn and the challenges financial companies face at the moment, there are still opportunities to work in these sectors.

Salary varies depending on location and employer. A newly qualified investment administrator is most likely to start earning about £15k-£26k a year, plus bonuses. After passing the regulatory exams this can increase with experience to £35k. Higher earners with management responsibility can expect to earn up to £50k a year.

Skills and Qualities
accurate, good interpersonal skills, good organisational skills, good spoken communication, good written English, information handling skills, IT skills, numeracy skills, problem-solving skills, trustworthy

Relevant Subjects
Business and accounting, Economics, English, ICT/Computer studies, Mathematics

Further Information
Apprenticeship Schemes (National Apprenticeship Service) - www.apprenticeships.org.uk

CFA Careers Guide 2009 (CFA) (CFA Society of the UK) - www.cfauk.org

Diploma in Business, Administration and Finance - www.baf-diploma.org.uk/

eFinancialCareers - www.efinancialcareers.co.uk

Financial Services Skills Council - sector skills council for financial services, accountancy & finance - www.fssc.org.uk/

Scottish Investment Operations (SIO) - www.sio.org.uk

TARGETjobs: City and Finance (GTI Specialist Publishers Ltd) - www.groupgti.com

Training Schemes - www.direct.gov.uk/en/educationandlearning

Welsh Baccalaureate - www.wbq.org.uk

▶Working in maths (2009) (Babcock Lifeskills) - www.babcock-lifeskills.com/

Addresses
CFA Society of the UK
2nd Floor 135 Cannon Street, London EC4N 5BP
Phone: +44 (0)20 7280 9620
Web: https://secure.cfauk.org/

ifs School of Finance
IFS House, 4-9 Burgate Lane, Canterbury, Kent CT1 2XJ
Phone: +44 (0)1227 818609
Web: www.ifslearning.ac.uk

Securities & Investment Institute (SII)
8 Eastcheap, London EC3M 1AE
Phone: +44 (0)20 7645 0600
Web: www.sii.org.uk

Similar Jobs
Accounting Technician, Bank Officer, Building Society Officer, Insurance Broker, Pensions Administrator

Investment Analyst
also known as: Financial Analyst

CRCI:Financial Services

CLCI:NAL — Job Band: 4 to 5

Job Description
Investment analysts carry out detailed analysis of the future prospects of financial investments to make recommendations on what will make the most profit. They study and compare financial statements of different companies to provide information for investors, stockbrokers and fund managers, and present a written report. Consider the effect of current world affairs, including influences such as environmental factors and political changes. These include adverse weather conditions, fluctuations in oil prices and war and conflicts, which impact on the fortunes of

different industries and investments. Must be aware of stock exchange trends. Meet regularly with senior management of each potential company in which funds may be invested.

Work Details

Usually work long hours that often include early mornings and late evenings. The work is office based, but a lot of time is spent out at meetings or doing research. You may need to travel abroad. A keen interest in current affairs and economic trends is essential, as is the ability to relate to people at all levels. This work is often very demanding. Business wear is expected and is important when meeting with clients.

Qualification

Although there are no set minimum qualifications, it is rare for anyone to be accepted for training without a degree or a professional qualification, or even both.

- **England, Wales and Northern Ireland**

Band 5: For degree courses: 2-3 A levels and some GCSEs (A*-C) usually including English and maths, or equivalent. Exact requirements depend on the degree you take.

- **Scotland**

Band 5: For degree courses: 3-5 H grades and some S grades (1-3), usually including English and maths, or similar qualifications. Exact requirements depend on the degree you take.

Degree Information

Any degree discipline is acceptable, but accounting, economics, mathematics or statistics are particularly relevant. Other subjects, such as financial management, banking and business studies are also relevant, and surveying, chemistry, engineering or languages, may be useful for some specialist areas. Relevant postgraduate courses are available.

Adult Qualifications

Relevant degrees or professional qualifications and experience are usually required, for example in banking, accountancy or economics.

Work Experience

Relevant work or voluntary experience is always useful and improves your chances when applying for a job. Any work experience in the finance sector is relevant and shows motivation and commitment to the work. This includes time spent in an accountancy firm, an insurance company or even shadowing a financial adviser.

Involvement with student societies, such as business or economics, and an interest in the stock market, demonstrates enthusiasm for this area of work. Student internships with investment banks before the last year at university can help you to gain a place on a graduate training scheme.

Entry and Training

The majority of employers recruit graduates or entrants who have a related professional qualification, such as accountancy. Entry is highly competitive. Training is usually on the job combined with study for professional qualifications.

Many companies have a two or three year training programme that offers practical experience with part-time study for a qualification, such as the investment management certificate (IMC), offered by the Chartered Financial Analyst (CFA) Society of the UK. There is also a CFA graduate-level programme for investment specialists which is a self-study course. This is the accepted international professional qualification. Once you pass the three exams and meet other requirements, you earn a CFA charter. Contact the CFA Institute or CFA Society of the UK for details of all training and qualification routes.

The Association of Certified International Investment Analysts offers the Certified International Investment Analyst qualification. Full details of all appropriate training courses are available from the Financial Services Skills Council. Some masters degrees are available in finance and investment analysis. Passes in examinations from the Securities and Investment Institute and the ifs School of Finance can lead to exemptions from some parts of the IMC and the CFA qualification.

Mature applicants are welcome, but you may need a relevant degree plus professional experience in areas such as economics, banking, insurance, accountancy or actuarial work. Knowledge of City financial institutions is an important factor, and knowledge of specialist areas, such as surveying, engineering or pharmaceuticals, is also useful. A second language can also be helpful.

Opportunities and Pay

There is a lot of competition for jobs and the amount of work available depends on the economic climate. Investment analysts work for stockbrokers, life assurance companies, unit and investment trusts, fund managers, or retail and investment banks. Some may work for a large company that manages its own investment portfolio.

Many jobs are in London, although Scotland is a large and growing area for investment roles so there are also concentrated opportunities in Edinburgh and Glasgow, as well as Liverpool, Manchester and Birmingham. It is possible to work abroad, particularly in the Far East. After three years as an analyst in a bank, you may be promoted to associate level. Many investment analysts move on to become fund managers.

Pay varies depending on the type and size of employer. A graduate trainee is likely to earn around £26k-£35k rising to £45k-£80k a year. Typical salaries at senior level are in excess of £110k a year. Many analysts receive performance-related bonuses and benefits that may include medical and life insurance, low-rate mortgages and pension cover.

Skills and Qualities

ability in one or more languages, able to cope under pressure, able to report accurately, able to work both on your own and in a team, analytical skills, good at forecasting trends, IT skills, motivated, numeracy skills, sound judgement

Relevant Subjects

Business and accounting, Economics, English, Geography, Government and politics, ICT/Computer studies, Law, Mathematics

Further Information

AGCAS: Accountancy and Business Services (Job Sector Briefing) (AGCAS) - www.prospects.ac.uk/

Association of Certified International Investment Analysts (ACIIA) - www.aciia.org

CFA Careers Guide 2009 (CFA) (CFA Society of the UK) - www.cfauk.org

Financial Services Skills Council - sector skills council for financial services, accountancy & finance www.fssc.org.uk/

Professional Investor Careers magazine (March Publishing) - www.marchpublishing.co.uk/pi.html

Scottish Investment Operations (SIO) - www.sio.org.uk

TARGETjobs: City and Finance (GTI Specialist Publishers Ltd) - www.groupgti.com

Addresses

CFA Society of the UK
2nd Floor 135 Cannon Street, London EC4N 5BP
Phone: +44 (0)20 7280 9620
Web: https://secure.cfauk.org/

Chartered Financial Analyst (CFA) Institute
10th Floor, One Canada Square, Canary Wharf, London E14 5AB
Phone: 0800 1247 8132 UK only
Web: www.cfainstitute.org

ifs School of Finance
IFS House, 4-9 Burgate Lane, Canterbury, Kent CT1 2XJ
Phone: +44 (0)1227 818609
Web: www.ifslearning.ac.uk

Securities & Investment Institute (SII)
8 Eastcheap, London EC3M 1AE
Phone: +44 (0)20 7645 0600
Web: www.sii.org.uk

Similar Jobs

Commodity Broker, Economist, Financial Adviser/Planner, Investment Banker, Stock Market Trader/Market Maker, Stockbroker

Investment Banker

also known as: Corporate Finance Associate, Merchant Banker
CRCI:Financial Services
CLCI:NAD Job Band: 5

Job Description

Investment bankers provide financial services for governments, institutions and companies, advising on issues such as share issues, takeover bids, acquisitions and mergers. Provide strategic advice to clients; liaise with regulatory bodies and give investment advice and manage large funds, e.g. unit trusts and pension schemes. Arrange loans of large sums of money to companies in the UK and overseas. Deal in securities trading in equities, bonds or derivatives, and offer broking facilities. May also handle bullion dealing.

Investment bankers work within one of the three areas of an investment bank. The front area provides banking and strategic advisory services, the middle is involved with risk management and the back deals with data checking after trading, and with IT issues. Some work with lenders to support client debt and spend time researching market conditions. They also coordinate teams of professionals such as lawyers and accountants, and deal directly with entrepreneurs, chief executives and directors of companies. Must work in line with the company and Financial Services Authority (FSA) regulations.

Work Details

This can be a very demanding and pressured job, and it is often necessary to work long and irregular hours including early mornings and late evenings. The work is mainly office based, but a lot of time is spent out at meetings. You may need to travel extensively, including international visits to clients and you usually work in a team of around 5-8 people. Business wear is expected and is important when meeting clients.

An office based environment is usual and working with a team of other analysts and investment professionals is common. Extensive access to current financial information is essential.

Qualification

- **England, Wales and Northern Ireland**

Band 5: For degree courses before becoming a trainee: 2-3 A levels and some GCSEs (A*-C) usually including English and maths, or equivalent. Exact requirements depend on the degree you take.

- **Scotland**

Band 5: For entry to a degree course before becoming a trainee: 3-5 H grades and some S grades (1-3), usually including English and maths, or similar qualifications. Exact requirements depend on the degree you take.

Degree Information

A degree in any discipline is acceptable, but financial management, banking, accountancy, law, economics, business studies, mathematics, science and statistics are particularly useful. Business administration, law and marketing also give useful background knowledge. Relevant degrees may lead to exemption from some subjects in the professional exams. Postgraduate courses in investment banking are available and an MBA or a similar professional qualification may also be helpful.

Adult Qualifications

Professional experience in a related field, such as accountancy, law or finance is helpful and fluency in one or more foreign languages is an asset. Entry standards for degree courses may be relaxed for mature applicants.

Work Experience

Entry to this job is competitive and it is important that you try to do some relevant work or voluntary experience before starting on this career path. The Securities & Investment Institute offers a work experience programme. Any work experience in the finance sector is relevant and shows enthusiasm and commitment to the work. Time spent in an accountancy firm, an insurance company or even shadowing a financial adviser gives you a good basis and insight into the profession. Some investment banks offer internships for those in the penultimate year of their degree course but you need to apply early.

Entry and Training

Selection for employment is usually through tests of numeracy and reasoning, skills and competencies, together with presentations and interviews. Most investment banks recruit people with a 2:1 or first class honours degree. Increasingly, a second language is valued and entrants have relevant postgraduate degrees too. For degree students in their penultimate year of study, it is advisable to research traineeships as early as possible.

Most employers run their own company training programme for new entrants, which can include a 4-8 week induction programme, lectures, seminars and conferences, as well as practical on-the-job experience, following the standards and examinations set by the regulatory body, the Financial Services Authority.

Employers often encourage trainees to study for a professional qualification, such as those offered by the ifs School of Finance or the Securities & Investment Institute. The exact course depends on the type of work in which you wish to specialise. The CFA Society of the UK also offers relevant courses in financial analysis and the Association of Certified International Investment Analysts offers the Certified International Investment Analyst qualification. Courses are by day release, evening classes or distance learning and usually involve study in your own time. Full details of all appropriate training courses are available from the Financial Services Skills Council.

Most entrants are in their early to mid twenties so mature entry (30+) is fairly difficult without considerable relevant experience, such as in accountancy or law.

Opportunities and Pay

Most investment bankers start as investment analysts and work their way up to fund managers at associate and then vice president level. Most banks are based in London and overseas capital cities. Some of the large retail banks also have merchant banking divisions. Prospects for investment bankers are determined by the global economy. Despite the economic downturn, there are still some opportunities to work in these sectors but there is stiff competition for jobs. There are opportunities to work abroad with those banks that have international offices. Self-employment is not common.

Pay varies depending on the type and size of employer. A graduate entrant is likely to earn around £30k-£40k rising to £50k-£100k a year with experience, plus possible bonuses. Some earn more than £150k a year and increasingly, a major element of your pay may be related to performance or profits and paid as an annual bonus.

Skills and Qualities

able to manage a budget and keep records, analytical skills, business awareness, decisive, good at calculating risks, good communication skills, good interpersonal skills, information handling skills, numeracy skills, self confident

Relevant Subjects
Business and accounting, Economics, English, Government and politics, ICT/Computer studies, Law, Mathematics

Further Information
AGCAS: Accountancy and Business Services (Job Sector Briefing) (AGCAS) - www.prospects.ac.uk/

Association of Certified International Investment Analysts (ACIIA) - www.aciia.org

CFA Careers Guide 2009 (CFA) (CFA Society of the UK) - www.cfauk.org

Chartered Banker (bi-monthly) (Chartered Institute of Bankers in Scotland (CIOBS)) - www.charteredbanker.com

Financial Services Skills Council - sector skills council for financial services, accountancy & finance - www.fssc.org.uk/

Scottish Investment Operations (SIO) - www.sio.org.uk

TARGETjobs: City and Finance (GTI Specialist Publishers Ltd) - www.groupgti.com

Addresses
CFA Society of the UK
2nd Floor 135 Cannon Street, London EC4N 5BP
Phone: +44 (0)20 7280 9620
Web: https://secure.cfauk.org/

Chartered Financial Analyst (CFA) Institute
10th Floor, One Canada Square, Canary Wharf, London E14 5AB
Phone: 0800 1247 8132 UK only
Web: www.cfainstitute.org

Chartered Institute of Bankers in Scotland (CIOBS)
Drumsheugh House, 38b Drumsheugh Gardens,
Edinburgh EH3 7SW
Phone: +44 (0)131 473 7777
Web: www.charteredbanker.com

Financial Services Authority (FSA)
Membership Department, 25 The North Colonnade, Canary Wharf, London E14 5HS
Phone: +44 (0)20 7066 1000
Web: www.fsa.gov.uk

ifs School of Finance
IFS House, 4-9 Burgate Lane, Canterbury, Kent CT1 2XJ
Phone: +44 (0)1227 818609
Web: www.ifslearning.ac.uk

London Investment Banking Association (LIBA)
6 Frederick's Place, London EC2R 8BT
Phone: +44 (0)20 7796 3606
Web: www.liba.org.uk

Securities & Investment Institute (SII)
8 Eastcheap, London EC3M 1AE
Phone: +44 (0)20 7645 0600
Web: www.sii.org.uk

Similar Jobs
Accountant: Private Practice, Accountant: Public Sector, Bank Manager, Economist, Investment Analyst, Stock Market Trader/ Market Maker, Stockbroker

Investment Fund Manager
also known as: Fund Manager

CRCI:Financial Services
CLCI:NAZ
Job Band: 4 to 5

Job Description
Investment fund managers work in the financial sector managing a portfolio of investments and aim to achieve the best possible financial return on investments for their clients. Buy, sell and manage a variety of investments, including stocks and shares, unit trusts, currency, property, and government bonds. Their most important clients tend to be from larger organisations and include pension fund managers, unit and investment trusts, banks, building societies and insurance companies. May also work with individuals who have a portfolio of shares or other investments.

Have a sound knowledge of the financial investment market and are able to interpret a wide range of complex financial data. Need to exercise good financial judgement so that a client does not lose money. Keep an up-to-date knowledge of investment markets. Some fund managers may have a responsibility for the management of staff.

Work Details
Usually work long and irregular hours that include early mornings and late evenings. The job is mainly office based, though you may have to travel to some meetings. This can be a very demanding and pressurised job. Business wear is expected and is important when meeting clients.

Qualification

• England, Wales and Northern Ireland
Band 5: For entry to a degree course before becoming a trainee: 2-3 A levels and some GCSEs (A*-C) usually including English and maths, or equivalent. Exact requirements depend on the degree you take.

• Scotland
Band 5: For entry to a degree course before becoming a trainee: 3-5 H grades and some S grades (1-3), usually including English and maths, or similar qualifications. Exact requirements depend on the degree you take.

Degree Information
A degree in economics, accountancy, maths or statistics is usual, followed by a professional qualification.

Adult Qualifications
Experience in a related field, such as accountancy or finance, is helpful. Fluency in one or more foreign languages is an asset. Entry requirements may be relaxed for adults applying for higher education courses, and Access or foundation courses give adults without qualifications a route on to degree courses.

Work Experience
Entry to this career is competitive. It is important that you try to do some relevant work or voluntary experience before applying. Any work experience in the finance sector is relevant and shows commitment to the work, such as time spent in an accountancy firm, an insurance company or even shadowing a financial adviser or fund manager.

Entry and Training
Most entrants have a first degree and begin their career as an investment analyst or a trainee fund manager and progress to fund manager within two to three years, following on-the-job experience and short courses. Most fund managers have considerable financial management experience prior to appointment. All trainees must pass an exam that is recognised by the Financial Services Authority, such as the Investment Management Certificate (IMC) from the CFA Society of the UK or the Certificate in Investment Management from the Securities & Investment Institute. This is to ensure that standards are met within the industry.

The Chartered Financial Analyst (CFA) qualification is awarded to investment professionals who have passed three comprehensive and rigorous examinations over a minimum of three years, together with at least four years' professional investment experience. The CFA Society of the UK provides a programme of support to CFA candidates including workshops, web-based products and scholarships.

Passes in examinations from the Securities and Investment Institute and the ifs School of Finance can lead to exemptions from some parts of the IMC and CFA qualification.

Mature entrants require relevant professional experience and qualifications in areas such as economics, banking, accountancy, insurance or broking, and usually also have a relevant degree.

Opportunities and Pay

Competition for fund manger jobs is intense as the rewards can be extremely high. Most investment fund managers in the UK work in the City of London or other major cities, such as Edinburgh and Glasgow. Most work for life assurance companies, investment banks, stockbroking firms, pension funds and investment trusts. Others may work for large companies that manage their own investment portfolios. Prospects for investment fund managers are determined by the global economy. Despite the economic downturn, there may still be opportunities to work in this area, but there is stiff competition for jobs. There may be opportunities for self-employment for experienced managers and also chances to work overseas.

Pay depends on the size and type of employer. A graduate trainee is likely to earn around £20k-£35k and with experience £50k-£80k a year. Higher earners may make more than £100k a year. Salaries are increased by bonuses and performance-related pay. There may be other benefits including medical insurance, low-rate mortgages and good life insurance and pension cover.

Skills and Qualities

able to manage a budget and keep records, able to network and negotiate, excellent communication skills, good at calculating risks, good written English, information handling skills, integrity, IT skills, numeracy skills, sound judgement

Relevant Subjects

Business and accounting, Economics, English, Government and politics, ICT/Computer studies, Law, Mathematics

Further Information

AGCAS: Accountancy and Business Services (Job Sector Briefing) (AGCAS) - www.prospects.ac.uk/

CFA Careers Guide 2009 (CFA) (CFA Society of the UK) - www.cfauk.org

Financial Services Skills Council - sector skills council for financial services, accountancy & finance www.fssc.org.uk/

Scottish Investment Operations (SIO) - www.sio.org.uk

TARGETjobs: City and Finance (GTI Specialist Publishers Ltd) - www.groupgti.com

Addresses

CFA Society of the UK
2nd Floor 135 Cannon Street, London EC4N 5BP
Phone: +44 (0)20 7280 9620
Web: https://secure.cfauk.org/

Chartered Financial Analyst (CFA) Institute
10th Floor, One Canada Square, Canary Wharf, London E14 5AB
Phone: 0800 1247 8132 UK only
Web: www.cfainstitute.org

Financial Services Authority (FSA)
Membership Department, 25 The North Colonnade, Canary Wharf, London E14 5HS
Phone: +44 (0)20 7066 1000
Web: www.fsa.gov.uk

ifs School of Finance
IFS House, 4-9 Burgate Lane, Canterbury, Kent CT1 2XJ
Phone: +44 (0)1227 818609
Web: www.ifslearning.ac.uk

Securities & Investment Institute (SII)
8 Eastcheap, London EC3M 1AE
Phone: +44 (0)20 7645 0600
Web: www.sii.org.uk

Similar Jobs

Investment Analyst, Investment Banker, Pension Fund Manager, Pensions Adviser, Stockbroker

IT Applications Developer

also known as: Computer Applications Developer, Computer Programmer, IT Applications Programmer

CRCI:Computers and IT
CLCI:CAV Job Band: 3 to 5

Job Description

IT applications developers write/modify and test the programs that enable a computer to carry out particular tasks. They write new programs or adapt existing programs to meet the needs of a variety of business, commercial and technical users by following a specification (spec) provided by a systems analyst, which is usually in diagrammatic or written form. They are often responsible for the whole process of analysing system needs, designing the system and writing and developing programs.

Developers devise a series of logical steps and translate these to the appropriate programming language (code) upon which the computer can act. They check programs for faults (bugs) and extensively test the software using sample data. Also check that output from the program is working as expected.

Developers keep detailed records of each program, so that other maintenance programmers can adapt it later, if required. Usually work in a team with other programmers and IT professionals, and specialise in one or more code languages. May specialise in areas that include programs for the home user, or the educational microcomputer market, in business data work, or scientific applications of computing.

Work Details

Usually work 35-37 hrs a week, Monday to Friday. You sit for long periods of time in front of a screen, working on your own, even though you are part of a team. You have to be able to meet deadlines and work under pressure as deadlines approach, often doing extra hours to complete the work. The work is largely office-based, though travel within a working day and absence away from home may be required, particularly for consultancy work.

Qualification

• England, Wales and Northern Ireland

Band 4: For higher national award in computer science: 1-2 A levels and some GCSEs (A*-C) usually including English, maths and preferably computer studies, or equivalent.

Band 5: For relevant degree course: 2-3 A levels including maths, computer studies or a science and some GCSEs (A*-C) usually including English, or equivalent. Exact requirements depend on the degree you take.

• Scotland

Band 4: For higher national award in computer science: usually 2-3 H grades and some S grades (1-3) often including English, maths and preferably computer studies, or similar qualifications.

Band 5: For relevant degree courses: 3-5 H grades including maths, computer studies or a science and some S grades (1-3), usually including English, or similar qualifications. Exact requirements depend on the degree you take.

Degree Information

A degree in a relevant subject such as computer science, software engineering, information technology or artificial intelligence is usual, though mathematics or business studies with computing is helpful for entry to training or further study. The Information Technology Management for Business degree (see e-skills UK) is designed in partnership with some of the biggest employers in the IT industry. Actuarial science, operational research and statistics also give useful background. There are postgraduate courses for graduates with non-relevant degrees, such as an MSc in computer science.

Adult Qualifications

Mature applicants may not need the standard entry requirements for higher education courses, particularly if your experience is relevant or you are able to show an ability to study at the appropriate level. There are many relevant full or part-time courses available at further/higher education colleges. Access to IT/Computing and foundation courses are useful for those who have no formal qualifications but wish to pursue a relevant degree. There are a wide range of distance learning/e-learning computing courses offered by many universities, as well as private accredited IT training companies.

Work Experience

Employers or colleges and universities may prefer candidates who have relevant work or voluntary experience. This includes previous knowledge and experience of using a programming language and even writing your own new short programs, or work and voluntary experience in a company or department specialising in adapting and writing new programs.

The British Computer Society offers a work placement service through its young professional group. Other schemes, such as 'The Year in Industry', enable those who expect good grades at A level/H grade, the opportunity to spend a salaried year with a company to gain valuable work experience.

Entry and Training

Most entrants have a degree or a relevant higher national qualification and there are a wide range of courses available. Once in employment, on-the-job training is usual and you need to keep up to date with new computer languages. It is increasingly necessary to become multi-skilled so systems analysis/design skills are useful.

Professional qualifications are available through various organisations, including the British Computer Society (BCS) and the Institute for the Management of Information Systems. The Institution of Analysts and Programmers offers industry-recognised qualifications as well as up-to-date information on training options and routes. Some of the larger organisations such as IBM and the Royal Bank of Scotland offer graduate training programmes.

Several universities now offer the information technology management for business (ITMB) degree, developed by e-skills and employers to meet specific industry needs. A full or part-time foundation degree in IT is also available and a Diploma/Welsh Baccalaureate in IT may be available in your area.

An ICT higher apprenticeship is available through e-skills and there are partnerships with colleges and universities throughout the UK. This is combined with a foundation degree and can lead to a full honours degree. E-skills also offers an internship. Students are placed for a period of employment within an organisation, enabling them to develop valuable business and IT skills. E-skills also run a professional development programme which enables new IT professionals to fast-track their career. The programme is delivered through universities and participating employers. Contact e-skills for details of all programmes and schemes.

Some applications developers work towards gaining Chartered IT Professional status through the BCS. Contact them for further details.

Mature applicants with experience in computing have an advantage, though it is possible for a talented graduate to gain employment without experience. A one-year IT postgraduate conversion course is also an advantage. Employers welcome older experienced applicants, particularly those who have had experience in computer helpdesk work. Some of the larger IT companies offer sponsorship for studying IT at degree level. The Open University also offers courses in computing and maths that can lead to an appropriate computing degree. There are no formal entry requirements and you can study through distance learning.

Government training opportunities may be available in your area. Contact your local careers office, Jobcentre Plus, Next Step service or Learning and Skills Council (LSC)/Local Enterprise Company (LEC) for details of all training opportunities and schemes.

Opportunities and Pay

Applications developers are employed across all industry sectors, from finance and retail to engineering and public organisations. Employment is possible with software houses, technical and business consultancies, multinational software companies, and large computer-using organisations, such as national/international banks and insurance companies, the retail industry, travel and tourism, and the health sector. Progression to management roles and consultancy is usual, Self-employment and overseas work is possible for experienced developers.

Pay varies depending on area and employer. Typical starting salaries are around £22k-£25k a year, rising to £30k-£40k with experience. Senior posts attract salaries of up to £60k a year. Overtime pay, profit-sharing, performance-related pay or a bonus payment may be additional to your basic salary.

Skills and Qualities

able to communicate effectively, able to work both on your own and in a team, analytical skills, attention to detail, clear-thinking, good concentration level, logical, perseverance, problem-solving skills, specialist IT skills

Relevant Subjects

Business and accounting, ICT/Computer studies, Mathematics, Physics, Science

Further Information

AGCAS: Information Technology (Job Sector Briefing) (AGCAS) - www.prospects.ac.uk

Computer Weekly (Reed Business Information) - www.computerweekly.com

Diplomas (Foundation, Higher and Advanced) - http://yp.direct.gov.uk/diplomas

e-skills UK - sector skills council for business and information technology - www.e-skills.com

Inside Careers Guide: Information Technology - www.insidecareers.co.uk

Real Life Guide to Information & Communications Technology (Trotman) - www.trotman.co.uk

Skills Framework for the Information Age (SFIA) (SFIA Foundation) - www.sfia.org.uk

TARGETjobs: IT (GTI Specialist Publishing Ltd.) - www.groupgti.com

Welsh Baccalaureate - www.wbq.org.uk

▶Working in computers & IT (2010) (Babcock Lifeskills) - www.babcock-lifeskills.com/

Year in Industry (Engineering Development Trust) - www.yini.org.uk

Addresses

British Computer Society (BCS)
First Floor, Block D North Star House North Star Avenue, Swindon, Wiltshire SN2 1FA
Phone: +44 (0)845 300 4417
Web: www.bcs.org

Institute for the Management of Information Systems (IMIS)
5 Kingfisher House, New Mill Road, Orpington, Kent BR5 3QG
Phone: +44 (0)700 002 3456
Web: www.imis.org.uk

Institution of Analysts and Programmers (IAP)
Charles House, 36 Culmington Road, London W13 9NH
Phone: +44 (0)20 8567 2118
Web: www.iap.org.uk

National Computing Centre (NCC)
The Flint Glass Works 64 Jersey Street, Manchester M4 6JW
Phone: +44 (0) 845 519 1055
Web: www.ncc.co.uk

Open University (OU)
PO Box 197, Milton Keynes MK7 6BJ
Phone: +44 (0)845 300 6090
Web: http://www3.open.ac.uk

Similar Jobs

Computer Games Designer, Computer Games Programmer, Database Administrator, IT Systems Analyst/Designer, IT Systems Developer

IT Data Input Operator

also known as: Clerk: Data Entry, Computer Data Input Operator

CRCI:Computers and IT
CLCI:CAV Job Band: 1 to 2

Job Description

IT data input operators use a keyboard to type information, such as text and numbers, into a computer. They check on-screen that the data is correct and use a database and sometimes a spreadsheet to access and record data. This may include sales figures, stock lists and addresses. Some input data in a code format to create a particular output from the system. Operators may copy the data to a memory stick/CD or disk so that it can be stored and processed. They sometimes look up information and answer queries from customers, managers or other colleagues.

Data input operators often carry out other general office tasks such as filing, answering the telephone, sending emails and faxing. They may deal with general office paperwork including letters, reports and invoices.

Work Details

Usually work around 35-39 hrs a week, Monday to Friday, though some firms operate a shift system. You have to take care to enter exactly the correct information. You spend many hours sitting in one place and the work can be repetitive. Jobs may be full or part time and there are sometimes temporary/flexible work options. Work can be pressurised at times and you may have to enter data to strict deadlines.

Qualification

• England, Wales and Northern Ireland

Band 1: No minimum qualifications are required, but you are expected to have a good level of general education. Some formal/vocational qualifications at any level are useful, such as GCSEs in maths and English, or equivalent.

Band 2: For BTEC/OCR qualifications or an equivalent course: usually at least 2 GCSEs (A*-C) including English and maths, or equivalent. Some employers may expect the same.

• Scotland

Band 1: No minimum qualifications are required, but you are expected to have a good level of general education. Some formal/vocational qualifications at any level are useful, such as S grades in maths and English, or similar.

Band 2: Some courses/employers require: at least two S grades (1-3) including English and sometimes maths, or similar.

Adult Qualifications

Keyboard skills are an advantage and applicants with clerical or secretarial skills or a text processing qualification may be preferred for some jobs.

Work Experience

Relevant work or voluntary experience is always useful and can equip you with skills that you can use in the future and add to your CV. In some areas there is a young apprenticeship (14-16) scheme that provides an extended work placement and eventual achievement of a relevant level 2 qualification whilst at school. Temporary holiday work in offices via employment agencies is useful, particularly if you can develop keyboard skills and a knowledge of the most popular software packages.

Entry and Training

You may have to pass a practical test and demonstrate your keyboard skills/experience. Entry is often direct with on-the-job training in computer systems and company procedures from a supervisor or manager. You may be given the opportunity to work towards relevant qualifications through either day or block release.

There are a wide range of vocational qualifications available. These include the OCR level 1-2 certificate/diploma for IT users, the internationally recognised CLAiT/CLAiT Plus qualifications and S/NVQs for IT users at levels 1-3 or in business and administration at level 2. The new diploma for IT users (ITQ 2009) has been developed as part of a project involving a full review of the National Occupational Standards for IT users and is backed by employers.

Alternatively, you can take a relevant full or part-time course before you start work, such as a first certificate/diploma for IT practitioners or a GCSE in applied information and communication technology. The British Computer Society also offers qualifications for IT users, including the European Computer Driving Licence (ECDL) which requires no previous knowledge of IT. This is an internationally recognised qualification that enables you to demonstrate your computer skills. It is available through learning centres across the UK.

Training programmes, including IT apprenticeships leading to level 2 and advanced apprenticeships leading to level 3, may be available in your area. City & Guilds offer an ICT practitioner apprenticeship. A Diploma/Welsh Baccalaureate may be available in your area in IT for those aged 14-19.

Mature applicants can benefit through government training opportunities, such as apprenticeships, that may be available in your area. You can gain recognition of previous experience through Accreditation of Prior Learning (APL) or by working towards relevant S/NVQs. Contact your local careers office, Jobcentre Plus, Next Step service or Learning and Skills Council (LSC)/Local Enterprise Company (LEC) for details of all training opportunities and schemes.

Opportunities and Pay

Jobs are mainly located in towns and cities throughout the UK. Demand for this job is falling as most employees now have keyboard skills and do this work as part of their job. This work is often combined with other aspects of office, secretarial or customer service work. You can work for a wide range of organisations, such as mail order firms or public utilities. You can also work for local authorities and government agencies. With more experience and training you can become a computer operator or supervisor.

Pay varies depending on location and employer. Starting salaries are likely to be around £12k-£14k rising to £17k-£20k with experience. Some may earn more than this.

Health

Most of your work is at a computer screen. This is hard for anyone who suffers from eye strain or has sight problems.

Skills and Qualities
able to cope under pressure, able to work quickly, accurate, attention to detail, efficient, good concentration level, good spelling, IT skills, keyboard/typing skills, numeracy skills

Relevant Subjects
English, ICT/Computer studies

Further Information
Apprenticeship Schemes (National Apprenticeship Service) - www.apprenticeships.org.uk

Diplomas (Foundation, Higher and Advanced) - http://yp.direct.gov.uk/diplomas

e-skills UK - sector skills council for business and information technology - www.e-skills.com

Inside Careers Guide: Information Technology - www.insidecareers.co.uk

Welsh Baccalaureate - www.wbq.org.uk

▶Working in computers & IT (2010) (Babcock Lifeskills) - www.babcock-lifeskills.com/

Addresses
British Computer Society (BCS)
First Floor, Block D North Star House North Star Avenue,
Swindon, Wiltshire SN2 1FA
Phone: +44 (0)845 300 4417
Web: www.bcs.org

Similar Jobs
Administrator/Administrative Assistant, Computer Operator, Personal Assistant, Reprographics Assistant

IT Helpdesk Analyst/Operator
also known as: Computer Helpdesk Analyst/Operator, Helpdesk Professional, Technical Support Person: IT

CRCI:Computers and IT
CLCI:CAV — Job Band: 3 to 5

Job Description
Helpdesk analysts offer first-line telephone, email or web-based support to PC users who are having technical problems with computer hardware or software. They attempt to diagnose the cause of the problem and explain or email the solution to the user. Routine tasks include setting up new users, re-setting passwords and helping with the installation and configuring of software packages. Analysts may need to refer more complex problems to second-level support if problems cannot be resolved. They may work for a specific hardware/software manufacturer helping with their products, or for a company offering specialist IT support and maintenance.

Others may work for a large organisation, such as a university or hospital, central or local government or financial services company, where the analyst is part of an in-house technical support team. Can arrange for a computer support technician or field engineer to visit the client if the problem appears to be faulty hardware or software. Also log calls received and note any actions taken.

Work Details
Usually work a 35-37 hr week, Monday to Friday, though you may have early starts and late finishes, including some weekend or shift work, over seven days. You must be prepared to work overtime to solve difficult problems or to meet a deadline. You sit at a desk for many hours at a time. Those working for organisations that support home computer users, such as Internet Service Providers (ISPs), may need to work outside normal office hours.

Qualification
There are no set minimum entry qualifications for this job, though most employers expect experience of IT and computer systems and a strong aptitude for the work. Some employers may require a relevant degree or equivalent.

• England, Wales and Northern Ireland
Band 3: For most employers, or for a relevant BTEC national award: 4-5 GCSEs (A*-C) including English, maths, and preferably computer studies, information technology, or equivalent.

Band 4: For some employers or for a relevant higher national award: 1-2 A levels and some GCSEs (A*-C) usually including English, maths, and preferably science, computer studies or information technology, or equivalent.

Band 5: For degree courses: 2-3 A levels and some GCSEs (A*-C) usually including English, maths, and preferably science, computer studies or information technology, or equivalent. Computer science and software engineering courses usually specify A level maths. Exact requirements depend on the degree you take.

• Scotland
Band 3: For most employers, or for a relevant SQA national award: usually 4-5 S grades (1-3) including English, maths, and preferably computer studies or information technology, or similar.

Band 4: For some employers or for an SQA higher national award: 2-3 H grades and some S grades (1-3) including English, maths, and preferably science, computer studies or information technology, or similar qualifications.

Band 5: For degree courses: 3-5 H grades and some S grades (1-3), usually including English, maths, and preferably science, computer studies or information technology, or similar qualifications. Computer science and software engineering courses usually specify H grade maths. Exact requirements depend on the degree you take.

Degree Information
Computer science, software engineering or a computing-related degree is preferred by some employers. The Information Technology Management for Business degree (see e-skills UK) is designed in partnership with some of the biggest employers in the IT industry.

Adult Qualifications
Entry requirements may be relaxed for adults applying for higher education courses. Foundation and Access courses give adults without qualifications a route onto degree courses.

Work Experience
Entry to this job can be competitive and it is important that you try to do some relevant work or voluntary experience before applying. College courses or employers look for enthusiasm and commitment. It is useful to gain office-based experience employing administration skills and work with the public, or a team of people. Experience or knowledge of database software packages and other IT techniques is also a distinct advantage.

Entry and Training
Most employers look for knowledge of PCs and their own software/hardware. Knowledge of Windows and OS/2 is very useful. You may have to take a practical aptitude test and also need good customer service skills. Many IT helpdesks also require people with good language skills. Some employers may offer 4-6 weeks' intensive training covering in-house procedures, installations and programs. There is a wide range of computer support qualifications offered at local colleges, including those of City & Guilds (e-quals) at levels 2-4, OCR (iPRO) at levels 2-4 and BTEC awards such as the ICT practitioners national certificate/diploma. Some employers may specify a degree or higher national qualification.

Training is ongoing, both on the job and by short courses, such as those run by Microsoft and Novell. Some employers assist with study for professional qualifications, including those of the British Computer Society. Other industry recognised qualifications and e-learning programmes include those offered by the Service Desk Institute, such as the service desk analyst qualification. A popular industry-recognised entry-level qualification is the CompTIA A+

offered by the Computing Technology Industry Association which offers alternative validation paths for specific job environments. Contact CompTIA for details of the range of available qualifications.

The Open University offers courses in computing and maths that can lead to a computing degree. There are no formal entry requirements and you study through distance learning. A full or part-time foundation degree in IT is also available. E-skills runs a professional development programme which enables new IT professionals to fast-track their career. The programme is delivered through universities and participating employers. E-skills also offers an internship. Students are placed for a period of employment within an organisation, enabling them to develop valuable business and IT skills.

Relevant S/NVQs at levels 2-4 are available. The new S/NVQ for IT users (ITQ 2009) has been developed as part of a project involving a full review of the National Occupational Standards for IT users. A Diploma/Welsh Baccalaureate may be available in your area in IT and training programmes, including apprenticeship schemes, may also be a route into this job. An ICT higher apprenticeship is available through e-skills. This combines an apprenticeship with a foundation degree and can lead to a full honours degree. There are partnerships with colleges and universities throughout the UK. Contact e-skills for details of all programmes and schemes.

Mature applicants with experience in technical support, telesales, customer service, and in computer sales have an advantage. Computing qualifications are also useful. Government training opportunities may be available in your area. You can gain recognition of previous experience through Accreditation of Prior Learning (APL) or by working towards relevant S/NVQs. Contact your local careers office, Jobcentre Plus, Next Step service or Learning and Skills Council (LSC)/Local Enterprise Company (LEC) for details of all training opportunities and schemes.

Opportunities and Pay

There are increasing opportunities throughout the UK with large organisations such as banks, building societies, hospitals, the media industry, central/local government, armed forces, educational institutions, retail stores and manufacturing companies. Helpdesk analysts/operators are also employed by computer hardware/software manufacturers and Internet Service Providers (ISPs). It is possible to progress to become a senior analyst, section leader or to a managerial position. Some may progress into computer programming, IT training, or systems administration. There are also opportunities for work abroad.

Pay varies depending on area and employer. Starting salaries for trainees are likely to be around £16k-£20k a year, rising to £28k with experience. Senior operators with managerial responsibilities can earn more than £35k a year. Profit-sharing, performance-related pay or a bonus payment may be additional to your basic salary.

Skills and Qualities

able to communicate effectively, able to work both on your own and in a team, attention to detail, good listening skills, good telephone manner, helpful, IT skills, logical, patient, technical aptitude

Relevant Subjects

Design and technology, English, ICT/Computer studies, Mathematics, Science

Further Information

AGCAS: Information Technology (Job Sector Briefing) (AGCAS) - www.prospects.ac.uk

Apprenticeship Schemes (National Apprenticeship Service) - www.apprenticeships.org.uk

Computing Technology Industry Association (CompTIA) - www.comptia.org

Diplomas (Foundation, Higher and Advanced) - http://yp.direct.gov.uk/diplomas

e-skills UK - sector skills council for business and information technology - www.e-skills.com

Inside Careers Guide: Information Technology - www.insidecareers.co.uk

Open University - www.open.ac.uk

Service Desk Institute (SDI) - www.sdi-europe.com

Welsh Baccalaureate - www.wbq.org.uk

▶Working in computers & IT (2010) (Babcock Lifeskills) - www.babcock-lifeskills.com/

Addresses

British Computer Society (BCS)
First Floor, Block D North Star House North Star Avenue, Swindon, Wiltshire SN2 1FA
Phone: +44 (0)845 300 4417
Web: www.bcs.org

Similar Jobs

Computer Games Technical Support Person, Computer Operator, Database Administrator, IT Service Technician, Network Manager

IT Security Specialist

also known as: Information Security Analyst/Engineer, Network Security Specialist, Security Adminstrator

CRCI:Computers and IT

CLCI:CAV Job Band: 3 to 5

Job Description

IT security specialists design and manage an organisation's information security infrastructure, including choosing the network hardware and operating systems, securing them and then continuing to identify and resolve any weaknesses in the systems. They analyse an organisation's security risks and requirements, rate the importance of the company's products and services, and the design, implementation and maintenance of the security infrastructure to protect them.

Security specialists implement mechanisms to control users' access to the computer network through processes such as firewalls. They limit access to IT applications by passwords and take steps to deny hackers access to systems and detect unauthorised users.

The role is similar to a Network Manager (see job profile) but also involves specialist communication with management about security risks. They are also responsible for supervising and training staff, and working with operations managers to develop the company's overall security strategy.

Work Details

You work 35-37 hrs a week, Monday to Friday, though you must be prepared to work longer to meet deadlines. You usually work office hours, but you may also be required to be on call to deal with emergencies. At times, you can be called out frequently. Many hours are spent sitting at a computer. The work is normally office based, but if you are involved in a large organisation, work for a consultancy or are self-employed, you may be required to travel between sites.

Sometimes you may work on your own, but generally you work closely with other qualified security staff and must be able to communicate with staff at all levels. Due the high level of responsibility, the job can be very stressful.

Qualification

• England, Wales and Northern Ireland

Band 4: For a relevant higher national course: 1-2 A levels, preferably in maths or physics, and some GCSEs (A*-C) usually including English and maths, or equivalent. For some courses you need science, computer studies or information technology.

Band 5: For relevant degree course: 2-3 A levels including subjects such as maths, science, computer studies or information technology, and some GCSEs (A*-C) usually including English and maths, or equivalent. Exact requirements depend on the degree you take.

- **Scotland**

Band 4: For SQA higher national award: 2-3 H grades and some S grades (1-3) including English and maths, or similar qualifications. For some courses you need science, computer studies or information technology.

Band 5: For relevant degree course: 3-5 H grades in subjects such as maths, science, computer studies or information technology, and some S grades (1-3) usually including English and maths, or similar qualifications. Exact requirements depend on the degree you take.

Degree Information

The need for a degree is increasingly necessary but a technical subject is not essential and a background in business and management is particularly relevant. Many IT security specialists are graduates in computing subjects, including computer science and software engineering. Operational research, maths and electronics are also useful. Specialist degree courses are available in subjects such as information security and forensic computing, computer security and forensics, and computer security.

The Information Technology Management for Business degree (see e-skills UK) is designed in partnership with some of the biggest employers in the IT industry. There are postgraduate qualifications in information security and computer forensics that may improve your job prospects.

Adult Qualifications

Employers expect mature applicants to have relevant experience, particularly in technical areas of computing or in business and management. Mature entrants may not need the standard entry requirements for higher education courses, particularly if your previous experience is relevant and you show the ability to study at the appropriate level. Access and foundation courses give adults without qualifications a route onto degree courses. Some Jobcentre Plus offices and Jobcentres (NI) offer specialised IT courses for adults.

Work Experience

Entry to this job is competitive and it is important that you try to do some relevant work or voluntary experience before applying. Relevant skills include computer-based work such as network or IT support, programming or hardware or software specialisms. Internships and work placements are a valuable introduction to the IT industry, and enable you to make an informed career choice. The British Computer Society offers a work placement service through its young professional group.

Other schemes such as 'The Year in Industry', enable those who expect good A levels/H grades and intend to go to university, the opportunity to spend a salaried year with a company to gain valuable work experience.

Entry and Training

Entrants increasingly need a degree to start this career but this can be in a business or management area as well as technical subjects. A degree in computer science or information security is recommended. You need a good understanding of networking technologies such as TCP/IP, Windows and Unix, hardware and operating systems, and the web. An understanding of computer programming is useful and most IT security specialists are trained in risk management during their career.

Technical background is critical for working in operational security, network security, access control or information forensics, but business skills are important for roles in security management, risk analysis and project management. You can get into IT security by taking formal qualifications at degree level or higher, or by acquiring skills through workplace training. It may be difficult to obtain a job as a security specialist as a recent graduate and you may need to gain experience elsewhere in IT or business first. Many move into IT security after experience in related IT roles. Internship programmes such as the one organised through e-skills can also be a good route in.

Training is ongoing throughout your career. Some employers may assist with study for professional qualifications, including those of the British Computer Society (BCS), the Skills Framework for the Information Age and the Institute for the Management of Information Systems. A popular industry-recognised entry-level qualification is the CompTIA A+ offered by the Computing Technology Industry Association, and there is a specialist security certification, the CompTIA Security+.

The job is driven by common standards and supported by many educational opportunities and certifications. The most widely recognised certifications include CompTIA Security+, Microsoft Certified Systems Engineer (MCSE)/ Systems Administrator (MCSA) and Cisco's Certified Network Associate (CCNA) and Professional (CCNP) certifications. The Cisco Information Security Specialist (CISS) certification can be achieved by taking the CISSP (Certified Information Systems Security Professional) and achieving the skills learned in Securing Cisco Network Devices (SND).

The Information Security Specialist Group is a sub-group of the BCS, deals in all aspects of information security, has over 3000 members, and may be a useful source of information.

Several universities now offer the information technology management for business (ITMB) degree, developed by e-skills and employers to meet specific industry needs. A full or part-time foundation degree in IT networking and security is available and a Diploma/Welsh Baccalaureate in IT may also be available in your area.

Employers ask for proven experience as an IT professional with some responsibility for network security. You can also use experience in related IT roles such as systems analyst, database administrator or network engineer to move into this job. IT programming or systems operations experience is useful and a one-year IT postgraduate conversion course is an advantage for those without a relevant degree. There are many full or part-time courses available at further/higher education colleges and government training opportunities may be available in your area.

You can also gain recognition of previous experience through Accreditation of Prior Learning (APL). Contact your local careers office, Jobcentre Plus, Next Step service or Learning and Skills Council (LSC)/Local Enterprise Company (LEC) for details of all training opportunities and schemes.

Opportunities and Pay

Information security specialists are increasingly becoming an essential part of business, and information security is a top priority for IT directors. As computer networks grow and more sensitive data is stored, the need for trained, skilled computer security specialists increases. Changes in technology including the expansion of wireless networks (WiFi) and mobile technologies impact the nature of security threats so opportunities for security professionals are excellent.

There are good opportunities for graduates and those from other professions who are looking for technical and/or management roles. Employment may be with public service organisations, local authorities, government departments, financial institutions and software manufacturers. With experience, it is possible to move into network management, IT project management and security consultancy. Experienced coordinators are employed by the police, security services and specialist law firms to carry out forensic investigation of computer-based crimes. Self-employment is possible and you may be able to work overseas.

Salary depends on the location and type of company. On entry you may expect to earn between £18k-£25k a year, rising to £42k or more with experience. Senior security specialists may earn £60k or more a year. Profit-sharing, performance-related pay or a bonus payment may be additional to your basic salary.

Skills and Qualities

able to cope under pressure, able to work to deadlines, analytical skills, awareness of confidentiality issues, excellent communication skills, good interpersonal skills, project management skills, self-motivated, specialist IT skills, technical aptitude

Relevant Subjects

Business and accounting, Design and technology, English, ICT/ Computer studies, Mathematics, Physics, Science

Further Information

AGCAS: Information Technology (Job Sector Briefing) (AGCAS) - www.prospects.ac.uk

Cisco Systems Incorporated - www.cisco.com

Computing Technology Industry Association (CompTIA) - www.comptia.org

Diplomas (Foundation, Higher and Advanced) - http://yp.direct.gov.uk/diplomas

e-skills UK - sector skills council for business and information technology - www.e-skills.com

Information Security Now (ISSG)

Information Security Specialist Group (ISSG) - www.bcs-issg.org.uk

Inside Careers Guide: Information Technology - www.insidecareers.co.uk

Real Life Guide to Information & Communications Technology (Trotman) - www.trotman.co.uk

Skills Framework for the Information Age (SFIA) (SFIA Foundation) - www.sfia.org.uk

TARGETjobs: IT (GTI Specialist Publishing Ltd.) - www.groupgti.com

Welsh Baccalaureate - www.wbq.org.uk

▶Working in computers & IT (2010) (Babcock Lifeskills) - www.babcock-lifeskills.com/

Year in Industry (Engineering Development Trust) - www.yini.org.uk

Addresses

British Computer Society (BCS)
First Floor, Block D North Star House North Star Avenue, Swindon, Wiltshire SN2 1FA
Phone: +44 (0)845 300 4417
Web: www.bcs.org

Institute for the Management of Information Systems (IMIS)
5 Kingfisher House, New Mill Road, Orpington, Kent BR5 3QG
Phone: +44 (0)700 002 3456
Web: www.imis.org.uk

Similar Jobs

Database Administrator, IT Applications Developer, IT Systems Analyst/Designer, Network Administrator, Network Manager

IT Service Technician

also known as: Computer Service Technician, Network Technician

CRCI:Computers and IT
CLCI:CAV — Job Band: 2 to 4

Job Description

IT service technicians install, update and maintain computer equipment and software within companies and large organisations. Following installation of any new software/computer equipment, they carry out service tests to ensure the system is working correctly. Some technicians perform routine servicing tasks to avoid breakdowns. Others are called in to identify and repair faults as quickly as possible, usually by replacing faulty parts. May undertake tests such as checking for computer viruses or work on computer-related equipment, such as scanners, printers and digital cameras.

Service technicians install extra RAM (memory) or CD-ROM/DVD drives, soundcards, new hard disks, or specialist software for a particular user, such as a computer-aided design (CAD) program. Some service technicians deal with a network system and may be responsible for administrative tasks such as performing daily back-up programs, or issuing user passwords. They must keep up to date with advances in information technology.

Work Details

Usually work a basic 35-37 hr week, Monday to Friday, though you may need to work overtime to get the job done at times. May be required to work at weekends, be on call, or work late, when the computers are not in use. The work is normally office based. You need to travel to clients' premises, or if working for a large organisation, you may be required to travel between sites. You need to solve problems quickly and be able to take decisive action. Work may be pressurised at times.

Qualification

• England, Wales and Northern Ireland

Band 3: For BTEC national award for IT Practitioners: usually at least 4 GCSEs (A*-C) including English and maths and a science or technical subject, or equivalent.

Band 4: For BTEC higher national award in computing: 1-2 A levels and some GCSEs (A*-C) usually including English and maths and a science or technical subject, or equivalent.

• Scotland

Band 3: For SQA national award: usually at least four S grades (1-3) including English and maths and a science or technical subject, or similar.

Band 4: For SQA higher national award: usually 2-3 H grades and some S grades (1-3), often including English and maths and a science or technical subject, or similar qualifications.

Adult Qualifications

Course entry requirements are usually relaxed for suitably experienced mature applicants. There are Access, distance learning and foundation courses for those with no formal qualifications who wish to gain a relevant higher education qualification.

Work Experience

Employers or colleges/universities may prefer candidates who have relevant work or voluntary experience. This may include spending time with electronic engineering or software engineering companies, or practical experience of working on hardware and software in your own time. In some areas there is a young apprenticeship (14-16) scheme that provides an extended work placement and a level 2 qualification whilst at school.

Entry and Training

There are no set routes for entry to this job. You can start as a trainee but some employers may prefer applicants with previous relevant experience and you may have to take a practical aptitude test. BTEC/SQA, City & Guilds and OCR (iPRO) awards for IT practitioners can be studied full or part time. Most companies provide in-house training, usually after initial qualification. This job requires regular training to keep up to date with changing technology, often by attending manufacturers' courses, such as those offered by Cisco and Microsoft. A popular industry-recognised entry-level qualification is the CompTIA A+ offered by CompTIA UK. Contact CompTIA for details of the range of available qualifications.

Membership of the British Computer Society (BCS) and the Institution of Engineering and Technology can be gained with the right combination of academic qualifications and practical experience. Some technicians may wish to study further for a degree though this is not primarily a degree-entry job. A relevant foundation degree is available in some areas and there are also National Computing Centre courses leading to membership of the BCS for those without a degree.

There are relevant S/NVQs in IT or communications technology at levels 1-4. The new S/NVQ for IT users (ITQ 2009) has been developed as part of a project involving a full review of the National Occupational Standards for IT users. A Diploma/Welsh Baccalaureate in IT may be available in your area.

Training programmes, including apprenticeship schemes, may also be available. An ICT higher apprenticeship is available through e-skills. This combines an apprenticeship with a foundation degree and can lead to a full honours degree. There are partnerships with colleges and universities throughout the UK. Contact e-skills for further details.

Mature applicants with practical experience in electronics or electrical engineering are usually accepted for training by employers. Computer manufacturers, such as Microsoft and Novell, also offer accredited short courses in certified engineer programmes. You can also benefit from government training opportunities, gain recognition of previous experience through Accreditation of Prior Learning (APL), or work towards S/NVQs. Contact your local careers office, Jobcentre Plus, Next Step service or Learning and Skills Council (LSC)/Local Enterprise Company (LEC) for details of all training opportunities and schemes.

Opportunities and Pay

There are opportunities throughout the UK in industry and commerce, including the public sector, local/central government, banks and building societies, utility companies, the armed forces, and the NHS. You can also work for a computer manufacturer or specialist service firm, as computer service technicians are increasingly needed to support the home PC market. Employment is also available with companies who service and support contracts for other organisations. Opportunities are good but may be affected by the economic situation. Promotion to supervisory or senior technician positions or into allied jobs, such as marketing, is possible. Some move into jobs in computer networks. Self-employment or working as a consultant service engineer is possible.

Depending on the type of company, starting salaries are generally between £15k-£20k a year, rising to £20k-£30k with experience. Some technicians with management responsibility can earn up to £40k a year.

Health

This job requires normal colour vision. Stamina and a reasonable level of physical fitness are also required in order to be able to move and carry heavy computer equipment when necessary.

Skills and Qualities

able to work quickly, accurate, attention to detail, good communication skills, good concentration level, good interpersonal skills, logical and methodical, problem-solving skills, specialist IT skills, technical aptitude

Relevant Subjects

Design and technology, Engineering, ICT/Computer studies, Mathematics, Physics, Science

Further Information

Apprenticeship Schemes (National Apprenticeship Service) - www.apprenticeships.org.uk

Apprenticeships in Scotland (Careers Info Scotland) - www.apprenticeshipsinscotland.com/about/

CISCO Systems (UK and Ireland) - www.cisco.com/global/uk

Computer Weekly (Reed Business Information) - www.computerweekly.com

Computing Technology Industry Association (CompTIA) - www.comptia.org

Diplomas (Foundation, Higher and Advanced) - http://yp.direct.gov.uk/diplomas

e-skills UK - sector skills council for business and information technology - www.e-skills.com

Inside Careers Guide: Information Technology - www.insidecareers.co.uk

Skills Framework for the Information Age (SFIA) (SFIA Foundation) - www.sfia.org.uk

Welsh Baccalaureate - www.wbq.org.uk

▶Working in computers & IT (2010) (Babcock Lifeskills) - www.babcock-lifeskills.com/

Addresses

British Computer Society (BCS)
First Floor, Block D North Star House North Star Avenue, Swindon, Wiltshire SN2 1FA
Phone: +44 (0)845 300 4417
Web: www.bcs.org

Institution of Engineering and Technology (IET)
Michael Faraday House, Stevenage, Hertfordshire SG1 2AY
Phone: +44 (0)1438 313311
Web: www.theiet.org

National Computing Centre (NCC)
The Flint Glass Works 64 Jersey Street, Manchester M4 6JW
Phone: +44 (0) 845 519 1055
Web: www.ncc.co.uk

Similar Jobs

Computer Assembly Technician, Computer Hardware Engineer, Office Equipment Service Engineer, Retail Assistant: Computer Software, Telecommunications Technician

IT Skills Trainer

also known as: Computer Skills Trainer

CRCI:Computers and IT
CLCI:CAV
Job Band: 3 to 5

Job Description

IT skills trainers train people in a wide range of computer skills and demonstrate the varied use of computer systems. Cover a range of IT-related subjects from basic skills through to more advanced computer knowledge. May work in education at a university, college or school under the direction of a qualified teacher, or train employees in a variety of businesses and organisations. May monitor trainees' progress and be involved in assessing trainees' skills at their workplace for the award of S/NVQs. Can also be involved in Government employment training schemes. Trainees organise and plan training programmes, prepare learning materials and deliver training that can either be a single session, or a set course of training.

Can offer training in the use of major software applications, such as word processing, spreadsheets and databases, and also presentation and project management packages. Some may teach advanced skills, including program design or computer languages, and others may offer online courses of self-teaching programs (e-learning) in virtual learning environments (VLE).

Work Details

Computer/IT trainers usually work regular office hours, Monday to Friday, although some may work evenings or weekends. Work often takes place in modern office surroundings or a classroom. Those working for manufacturers or IT consultancies may need to travel to clients' premises. You usually sit at a workstation when training individuals, but are on your feet when running a training course.

Qualification

• England, Wales and Northern Ireland

Band 3: For entry: usually at least 4 GCSEs (A*-C) including English, maths, and preferably a science, computer studies, or information technology, or equivalent.

Band 4: For a relevant higher national award: 1-2 A levels and some GCSEs (A*-C) usually including English, maths, and for some courses preferably science, computer studies or information technology, or equivalent.

Band 5: For degree courses: 2-3 A levels, preferably including maths, a science, computer studies or information technology for some courses, and some GCSEs (A*-C) usually including English and maths, or equivalent. Exact requirements depend on the degree you take.

• Scotland

Band 3: For entry: usually at least four S grades (1-3) including English, maths and preferably a science, computer studies, or information technology, or similar qualifications.

Band 4: For a relevant higher national award: 2-3 H grades and some S grades (1-3) often including English and maths, and for some courses a science, computer studies or information technology, or similar qualifications.

Band 5: For degree courses: 3-5 H grades, often including maths and a science, or computer studies or information technology for some courses, and some S grades (1-3), usually including English and maths, or similar qualifications. Exact requirements depend on the degree you take.

Degree Information

Computing or business information systems/technology subjects are the most useful and there are varied postgraduate qualifications in computing. The Information Technology Management for Business (ITMB) degree is designed in partnership with some of the biggest employers in the IT industry.

Adult Qualifications

Mature entrants may not need the standard entry requirements for higher education courses, particularly if their previous experience is relevant and they show the ability to study at the appropriate level. Access and foundation courses are available for those with no formal qualifications who wish to pursue a relevant degree.

Work Experience

A high level of competence is needed for entry to this job. Some employers or college/university courses prefer candidates who have relevant work or voluntary experience. This includes any computer-based job using software or basic programming, or any experience of presenting to or helping to teach adults.

Entry and Training

There are no set qualifications to work in this field, and IT trainers either have teaching skills or a good knowledge of IT and software. Some start as IT technicians, and then learn skills in training through work experience. Others qualify as trainers or teachers, and then add IT to their specialist skills. Many entrants are graduates with computing experience, possibly in programming or systems analysis. Trainers are usually recruited for the knowledge and skills they have in the area of work in which they are instructing.

Training varies between employers but normally consists of short courses in instructing techniques. These cover demonstration skills, how and why people learn, and the use of visual aids. There are a wide range of product specific and professional qualifications, such as those developed by Microsoft, Cisco and Novell. Professional bodies, such as the British Computer Society (BCS) support certificates such as the European Computer Driving Licence (ECDL), and the Institute of IT Training (IITT) compiles a list of recognised qualifications and offers a range of relevant certificates and diplomas. The Institute Certified Training Practitioner is a trainer certificate available from the IITT and BCS which is based on assessing live training delivery.

The Open University offers courses in computing and maths that lead to a computing degree. There are no formal entry requirements and you study through distance learning. A Certificate in Training Practice (CTP) is available from the Chartered Institute of Personnel and Development and the Computing Technology Industry Association offers industry-recognised qualifications, such as the Certified Technical Trainer (CTT). A full or part-time foundation degree in various computing subjects is available in some areas or you can study for a recognised teaching qualification, including the City & Guilds teaching adult learners qualification or certificate in further education teaching.

A Diploma/Welsh Baccalaureate in information technology may be available in your area. Training programmes, including apprenticeship schemes, may be also be available. An ICT higher apprenticeship is offered through e-skills. This combines an apprenticeship with a foundation degree and can lead to a full honours degree. There are partnerships with colleges and universities throughout the UK. E-skills runs a professional development programme which enables new IT professionals to fast-track their career. The programme is delivered through universities and participating employers. E-skills also offers an internship. Students are placed for a period of employment within an organisation, enabling them to develop valuable business and IT skills. Contact e-skills for details of all programmes and schemes.

Mature entrants to IT training may need experience of work in the computing industry, either technical or non-technical, such as programming, systems analysis, or in sales and marketing. Some LSCs/LECs, Jobcentres (NI) and ELWa (Wales) run specialist IT courses. You can also gain recognition of previous experience through Accreditation of Prior Learning (APL) or by working towards relevant S/NVQs.

Opportunities and Pay

There are opportunities throughout the UK, especially in the south east of England. IT trainers work for computer hardware and software manufacturers, IT consultancies, companies with many computer-using staff, training organisations or the further educational sector. There are currently several Government initiatives aimed at raising the level of IT literacy in the UK and helping to increase demand for qualified trainers.

Career development can include promotion to lead trainer, departmental manager or area training coordinator. Other options include teaching, technical writing or working in other areas of IT. There are good opportunities for experienced trainers to work on a freelance or self-employed basis. It may be possible to work overseas.

Pay varies depending on location, employer and type of IT training. Starting salaries are likely to be around £20k-£22k a year, rising to £25k-£32k with experience. High earners with management responsibilities can earn £30k-£40k a year.

Skills and Qualities

able to explain clearly, able to stimulate learners, analytical skills, approachable, confident, encouraging, good communication skills, good interpersonal skills, logical, specialist IT skills

Relevant Subjects
Business and accounting, English, ICT/Computer studies, Mathematics, Physics, Science

Further Information
AGCAS: Information Technology (Job Sector Briefing) (AGCAS) - www.prospects.ac.uk

Chartered Institute of Personnel and Development (CIPD) - www.cipd.co.uk

Computer Weekly (Reed Business Information) - www.computerweekly.com

Computing Technology Industry Association (CompTIA) - www.comptia.org

Diplomas (Foundation, Higher and Advanced) - http://yp.direct.gov.uk/diplomas

e-skills UK - sector skills council for business and information technology - www.e-skills.com

Open University - www.open.ac.uk

Real Life Guide to Information & Communications Technology (Trotman) - www.trotman.co.uk

Skills Framework for the Information Age (SFIA) (SFIA Foundation) - www.sfia.org.uk

TARGETjobs: IT (GTI Specialist Publishing Ltd.) - www.groupgti.com

Welsh Baccalaureate - www.wbq.org.uk

▶Working in computers & IT (2010) (Babcock Lifeskills) - www.babcock-lifeskills.com/

Addresses
British Computer Society (BCS)
First Floor, Block D North Star House North Star Avenue, Swindon, Wiltshire SN2 1FA
Phone: +44 (0)845 300 4417
Web: www.bcs.org

Institute of IT Training (IITT)
Westwood House, Westwood Business Park, Coventry CV4 8HS
Phone: 0845 006 8858 (UK only)
Web: www.iitt.org.uk

Similar Jobs
IT Helpdesk Analyst/Operator, Lecturer: Further Education, Lecturer: Higher Education, Teacher: ICT, Training & Development Officer/Manager

IT Systems Analyst/Designer
also known as: Computer Systems Analyst/Designer

CRCI:Computers and IT

CLCI:CAV Job Band: 4 to 5

Job Description
IT systems analysts design and test a computer system based on the specification provided by a business analyst to meet the needs of an organisation. They draw up a detailed design document including charts and diagrams to define the components involved and use a variety of computer-assisted software engineering (CASE) tools and object-orientated programming languages, such as Visual Basic, C++ and Java.

Analysts prepare instructions for programmers and design monitoring and performance measurement processes. They ensure the system components perform to meet customer requirements and write progress reports. May oversee the implementation and testing of a system and act as a link between the user and the programmer.

In some cases the same person is responsible for both business analysis and systems design work. Some systems designers may also be involved in the development of networks and websites, or may specialise in other areas of systems design, such as research for the ongoing development of hardware and software.

Work Details
You are based in an office, but may have to travel to visit clients and spend nights away from home. Hours are usually 35-37 a week, Monday to Friday, but this varies between employers and projects. You may have to work in the evenings and at weekends. Work can be pressurised at times. You frequently consult with managers, users, analysts and programmers, and have discussions with other systems designers.

Qualification

• England, Wales and Northern Ireland
Band 4: For a relevant BTEC higher national award: 1-2 A levels and some GCSEs (A*-C) usually including English, maths and possibly other specific subjects such as physics and computer studies, or equivalent.

Band 5: For degree courses: 2-3 A levels, often including maths, and some GCSEs (A*-C) usually including English and maths, or equivalent. Exact requirements depend on the degree you take.

• Scotland
Band 4: For a relevant SQA higher national award: usually 2-3 H grades and some S grades (1-3), often including English, maths and possibly other specific subjects such as physics and computer studies, or similar qualifications.

Band 5: For degree courses: 3-5 H grades, often including maths, and some S grades (1-3) usually including English and maths, or similar qualifications. Exact requirements depend on the degree you take.

Degree Information
Most employers recruit graduates in computing subjects, such as computer science or software engineering. The Information Technology Management for Business (ITMB) degree is designed in partnership with some of the biggest employers in the IT industry. Maths, physics and other science-based and technical subjects are useful. There are relevant postgraduate courses, including a one-year IT conversion course for graduates without a computing or science background.

Adult Qualifications
Mature entrants to degree/higher national courses may not need the standard entry qualifications, or there may be a relevant Access or foundation course in your area. Contact colleges and universities for details.

Work Experience
Entry to this job is competitive and it is important that you try to do some relevant work or voluntary experience before applying. Paid work experience is usually preferred, either in general business or computing. However, internships and work placements when a student are a valuable introduction to the IT industry and enable you to make an informed career choice. Schemes, such as 'The Year in Industry', enable those who expect good A levels/H grades and intend to go to university the opportunity to spend a salaried year with a company to gain valuable work experience.

Entry and Training
Most entrants to this job are graduates. A postgraduate qualification is useful, though not essential. A degree in a computer-related subject may give you an advantage, but some employers recruit graduates with degrees in non-relevant subjects, especially business studies, and provide all the necessary IT training. It is more usual to move into this job after gaining experience in programming, business analysis or project management. Training is usually on the job, together with in-house courses for the development of business and technical skills.

Some knowledge of customer relationship management (CRM) applications, relational database management systems (RDBMS), Oracle, SQL or SAP software applications is particularly useful when applying for work. An employer may also run personal development courses dealing with presentation, team leading, communication and interpersonal skills.

There are many courses that lead to professional qualifications, such as those offered by the Institute for the Management of Information Systems, or the British Computer Society (BCS). Some universities offer an Information Technology Management for Business (ITMB) degree which has been developed by e-skills and employers to meet specific industry needs. Contact e-skills for a list of universities offering this degree. The Open University also offers courses in computing and maths, leading to a computing degree. There are no formal entry requirements and you study through distance learning. A full or part-time foundation degree in IT is also available. Graduates can also work towards job-specific S/NVQs in systems design, IT support, marketing and in project management.

E-skills also run a professional development programme which enables new IT professionals to fast-track their career. The programme is delivered through universities and participating employers. E-skills also offers an internship. Students are placed for a period of employment within an organisation, enabling them to develop valuable business and IT skills. Contact e-skills for details of all programmes and schemes. Some systems analysts/designers work towards gaining Chartered IT Professional (CITP) status through the BCS. Contact the BCS for further details.

Mature candidates are often welcomed as systems analysts/designers need some years' experience in computing, business and administration. A one-year IT postgraduate conversion course is an advantage for those without a relevant degree. Access, foundation or similar courses are available for those who have no formal qualifications but wish to pursue a relevant degree. There are many relevant full or part-time courses available at further/higher education colleges.

Some LSCs/LECs, Jobcentres (NI) and ELWa (Wales) run specialist IT courses. You can also gain recognition of previous experience through Accreditation of Prior Learning (APL) or by working towards relevant S/NVQs.

Opportunities and Pay

There are employment opportunities with software and systems houses, manufacturing companies, local/central government, and large organisations such as the NHS, utility companies, and the financial sector. There is a concentration of jobs in south-east England. One promotional route is to become a senior analyst and then progress to project manager. Experienced analysts may also use their business experience and knowledge to find work as a consultant. Promotion can lead to a number of related IT fields or you can move across sectors into lecturing or training, for example.

Self-employment is possible as a freelance consultant or working for an IT consultancy company. Work is also possible overseas.

Pay varies depending on location, size and type of employer. Recently qualified graduates start on around £20k-£24k a year and with experience, this rises to £28k-£45k. Senior level salaries for those in project management can be more than £50k a year. Salaries may also include a profit-sharing scheme, performance-related pay or a company bonus.

Skills and Qualities

able to communicate effectively, able to get on with all kinds of people, attention to detail, business awareness, information handling skills, logical, patient, persuasive, specialist IT skills, tactful

Relevant Subjects

Business and accounting, Design and technology, English, ICT/Computer studies, Mathematics, Physics, Science

Further Information

AGCAS: Information Technology (Job Sector Briefing) (AGCAS) - www.prospects.ac.uk

Computer Weekly (Reed Business Information) - www.computerweekly.com

e-skills UK - sector skills council for business and information technology - www.e-skills.com

Inside Careers Guide: Information Technology - www.insidecareers.co.uk

Open University - www.open.ac.uk

Real Life Guide to Information & Communications Technology (Trotman) - www.trotman.co.uk

Skills Framework for the Information Age (SFIA) (SFIA Foundation) - www.sfia.org.uk

▶Working in computers & IT (2010) (Babcock Lifeskills) - www.babcock-lifeskills.com/

Year in Industry (Engineering Development Trust) - www.yini.org.uk

Addresses

British Computer Society (BCS)
First Floor, Block D North Star House North Star Avenue, Swindon, Wiltshire SN2 1FA
Phone: +44 (0)845 300 4417
Web: www.bcs.org

Institute for the Management of Information Systems (IMIS)
5 Kingfisher House, New Mill Road, Orpington, Kent BR5 3QG
Phone: +44 (0)700 002 3456
Web: www.imis.org.uk

Institution of Analysts and Programmers (IAP)
Charles House, 36 Culmington Road, London W13 9NH
Phone: +44 (0)20 8567 2118
Web: www.iap.org.uk

Similar Jobs

Business Analyst, Geographical Information Systems Manager, IT Applications Developer, IT Systems Developer, Management Consultant, Network Manager

IT Systems Developer

also known as: Computer Software Developer, Computer Software Engineer, Computer Systems Developer

CRCI:Computers and IT
CLCI:CAV   Job Band: 4 to 5

Job Description

IT systems developers work on the design of the internal operations of computers and software that makes the computer function. Traditionally they work on the most complex types of software including operating systems. Increasingly, the role is used to describe the work of software analysts and applications programmers too. They work at all stages in the development of a software product. This includes writing programs to control different systems and testing codes to ensure that everything works and that the system is efficient and versatile. Developers diagnose faults as they occur and design ways to correct them. May work for specific clients to develop individual systems. Also write manuals and other documentation for the systems they develop.

Systems developers use a variety of programming languages as part of the development process; those in most demand at the moment are Visual Basic, Oracle, Java, XML and C++. Increasingly, computer-assisted software engineering (CASE) tools are used in the programming process. Also train those who need to support and maintain any new development, such as support services technicians. May support the new system once it is in place.

Work Details

Standard hours are around 39 a week, but software engineers often work longer hours to meet deadlines or diagnose and repair faults. You may sit for long periods of time in front of a screen, working on your own or as part of a team. The work is usually office based but you may have to travel to client sites to solve problems. You frequently consult with managers and other IT professionals. Work can be pressurised at times.

Qualification

• England, Wales and Northern Ireland

Band 4: For a relevant higher national award: 1-2 A levels and some GCSEs (A*-C) usually including English and maths, and for some courses science, computer studies or information technology, or equivalent.

Band 5: For degree courses: 2-3 A levels including maths and science (computer studies or information technology for some courses), and some GCSEs (A*-C) usually including English and maths, or equivalent. Exact requirements depend on the degree you take.

• Scotland

Band 4: For a relevant higher national award: usually 2-3 H grades and some S grades (1-3), often including English and maths, and for some courses science, computer studies or information technology, or similar qualifications.

Band 5: For degree courses: 3-5 H grades including maths (science, computer studies or information technology for some courses), and some S grades (1-3), usually including English and maths, or similar qualifications. Exact requirements depend on the degree you take.

Degree Information

A degree in any discipline is acceptable, but a relevant subject such as computer science, software engineering, information technology or electronics is an advantage. The Information Technology Management for Business degree (see e-skills UK) is designed in partnership with some of the biggest employers in the IT industry. Mathematics with computing is helpful for entry to training or further study. There are postgraduate courses for graduates with non-relevant degrees.

Adult Qualifications

Mature entrants may not need the standard entry requirements for higher education courses, particularly if your previous experience is relevant and you show the ability to study at the appropriate level.

Work Experience

Employers or colleges and universities may prefer candidates who have relevant work or voluntary experience. This includes direct experience or work shadowing in similar fields such as systems analysis, programming or network administration. Previous knowledge and experience of using a programming language and maybe even writing your own new short programmes is useful, or work and voluntary experience in a company specialising in adapting and writing new programmes.

Internships and work placements when a student are a valuable introduction to the IT industry and enable you to make an informed career choice. Other schemes, such as 'A Year in Industry', enable those who expect good A levels/H grades and intend to go to university the opportunity to spend a salaried year with a company to gain valuable work experience.

Entry and Training

Most entrants are graduates with a good honours degree or have a relevant HNC/HND. Some may have a postgraduate computing qualification. Some employers accept those with lesser qualifications as a trainee developer and may provide sponsorship for diploma/degree study or for professional qualifications, including those of the British Computer Society, Institution of Analysts and Programmers and the Institute of the Management of Information Systems.

Many new graduates start work as programmers and move into systems development when they have experience. While completing your initial training you are likely to be involved in testing. As you become experienced you move into writing and design work. Training is ongoing, both on the job and by short courses run by manufacturers such as Microsoft and Oracle.

Some universities offer the Information Technology Management for Business (ITMB) degree developed by e-skills and employers to meet industry needs. Contact e-skills for a list of participating universities. The Open University offers courses in computing and maths, which lead to a computing degree. There are no formal entry requirements and you study through distance learning. Full or part-time foundation degrees in IT are also available. A Diploma/ Welsh Baccalaureate may be available in your area in IT. S/NVQs for IT practitioners are available. The new S/NVQ for IT users (ITQ 2009) has been developed as part of a project involving a full review of the National Occupational Standards for IT users.

Relevant training programmes, including apprenticeship schemes, may be available in your area. An ICT higher apprenticeship is available through e-skills. This combines an apprenticeship with a foundation degree and can lead to a full honours degree. There are partnerships with colleges and universities throughout the UK.

E-skills runs a professional development programme which enables new IT professionals to fast-track their career. The programme is delivered through universities and participating employers. E-skills also offers an internship. Students are placed for a period of employment within an organisation, enabling them to develop valuable business and IT skills. Contact e-skills for details of all programmes and schemes. Some systems developers work towards gaining Chartered IT Professional (CITP) status through the British Computer Society (BCS). Contact the BCS for further details.

Mature entrants are usually expected to have experience in business or computing. Access, foundation or similar courses are available for those who have no formal qualifications but wish to pursue a relevant degree. There are many relevant full or part-time courses available at further/higher education colleges. Some LSCs/ LECs, Jobcentres (NI) and ELWa (Wales) run specialist IT courses. You can also gain recognition of previous experience through Accreditation of Prior Learning (APL) or by working towards relevant S/NVQs.

Opportunities and Pay

There are opportunities throughout the UK with employers including any organisations that use computers in their business. There are opportunities with software or systems houses, IT consultants, the electronics industry, the armed forces, local/central government, the media, educational institutions and the aerospace, instrumentation and telecommunications industry. Progress is possible to more senior developer posts or to project management. Experienced systems developers can work as self-employed consultants. Work abroad may also be available.

Pay varies depending on location, type and size of company. Starting salaries for graduate entrants are around £19k-£25k and with experience up to £45k a year. Some may earn over £50k a year. Freelance and contract work may attract higher salaries due to the specialist skills required.

Skills and Qualities

able to work both on your own and in a team, able to work in abstract terms, adaptable, analytical skills, logical and methodical, perseverance, precise, specialist IT skills, technical aptitude

Relevant Subjects

Business and accounting, Design and technology, English, ICT/ Computer studies, Mathematics, Physics, Science

Further Information

AGCAS: Information Technology (Job Sector Briefing) (AGCAS) - www.prospects.ac.uk

Apprenticeship Schemes (National Apprenticeship Service) - www.apprenticeships.org.uk

Computer Weekly (Reed Business Information) - www.computerweekly.com

Diplomas (Foundation, Higher and Advanced) - http://yp.direct.gov.uk/diplomas

e-skills UK - sector skills council for business and information technology - www.e-skills.com

Open University - www.open.ac.uk

Real Life Guide to Information & Communications Technology (Trotman) - www.trotman.co.uk

Skills Framework for the Information Age (SFIA) (SFIA Foundation) - www.sfia.org.uk

Welsh Baccalaureate - www.wbq.org.uk

▶Working in computers & IT (2010) (Babcock Lifeskills) - www.babcock-lifeskills.com/

▶Working in space (2010) (Babcock Lifeskills) - www.babcock-lifeskills.com/

Year in Industry (Engineering Development Trust) - www.yini.org.uk

Addresses

British Computer Society (BCS)
First Floor, Block D North Star House North Star Avenue, Swindon, Wiltshire SN2 1FA
Phone: +44 (0)845 300 4417
Web: www.bcs.org

Institute for the Management of Information Systems (IMIS)
5 Kingfisher House, New Mill Road, Orpington, Kent BR5 3QG
Phone: +44 (0)700 002 3456
Web: www.imis.org.uk

Institution of Analysts and Programmers (IAP)
Charles House, 36 Culmington Road, London W13 9NH
Phone: +44 (0)20 8567 2118
Web: www.iap.org.uk

Similar Jobs

Computer Games Designer, Computer Games Programmer, IT Applications Developer, IT Systems Analyst/Designer, Network Manager

IT Technical Sales Specialist

also known as: Computer Technical Sales Executive, IT Sales Manager, Software Sales Executive

CRCI:Computers and IT
CLCI:CAV Job Band: 3 to 5

Job Description

IT technical sales specialists are employed by information technology (IT) companies to sell their hardware and software products to new or existing customers. They usually work within a geographical area, such as the south east of England, a major city or a region of the world, such as Europe, the Middle East and Africa (EMEA). They visit commercial customers to discuss their computing needs to ensure that a suitable system can be recommended and supplied to suit their business requirements. Then report back to the technical and production team, who come up with proposals for the customer.

Technical sales specialists advise the customer on the available hardware/software and provide an estimate of costs. They are involved in negotiating and agreeing a contract with the customer if they decide to buy the products. They have technical knowledge about the products on offer and may demonstrate them to their best advantage and usually specialise in a particular product range or client sector. Also organise sale and delivery and, if necessary, installation and testing. Specialists source new customers and keep in contact with existing customers to update them on new technology. May arrange support for training, maintenance and consultation. Also keep records of contacts with customers and report details of requirements to the employer's sales and marketing section.

Work Details

Usually work a basic 35-40 hr week, Monday to Friday, and are based in an office. Need to travel, perhaps locally, nationally or internationally, which may involve staying away from home. The hours may be irregular and the work competitive and stressful at times. Must learn a great deal about the products, keep up to date with technical developments, and be able to communicate with people without using jargon and complex technical language.

Qualification

• England, Wales and Northern Ireland

Band 3: For a BTEC national award or entry to a job: some GCSEs (A*-C) including maths, English and preferably computer studies, or equivalent.

Band 4: For a BTEC higher national award: 1-2 A levels, preferably including maths or a science, and some GCSEs (A*-C) including maths, English and preferably computing or physics, or equivalent.

Band 5: For degree courses: 2-3 A levels, usually including maths or a science, and some GCSEs (A*-C), usually including maths and English, or equivalent. Exact requirements depend on the degree you take.

• Scotland

Band 3: For SQA national award or entry to a job: usually at least four S grades (1-3) including English and maths, and perhaps computer studies, or similar.

Band 4: For SQA higher national award: usually 2-3 H grades, preferably including maths or a science, and some S grades (1-3) including maths, English, computing or physics, or similar qualifications.

Band 5: For degree courses: 3-5 H grades, usually including maths or a science, and some S grades (1-3), usually including maths and English, or similar qualifications. Exact requirements depend on the degree you take.

Degree Information

A relevant degree is preferred in subjects such as business information systems technology, artificial intelligence, computer science, software engineering, electronic engineering or systems control engineering. The Information Technology Management for Business degree (see e-skills UK) is designed in partnership with some of the biggest employers in the IT industry. Postgraduate courses in computing are available for those with non-related degrees.

Adult Qualifications

Entry requirements may be relaxed for adults applying for higher education courses. Access or foundation courses give adults without qualifications a route onto degree courses.

Work Experience

Employers or colleges/universities may prefer candidates who have relevant work or voluntary experience. This may include other forms of sales, but it is the technical experience in hardware/software that usually helps entry to this job. Taking a relevant course may also give you an advantage.

Entry and Training

It is an advantage to have experience in computing, sales and marketing or technical work. Most entrants have a computer-related degree, or HNC/HND. Employers offer on-the-job training together with external training courses that cover customer service skills, sales, and marketing the company's products, as well as technical and product knowledge. You need to keep up to date with IT developments and you may be offered short courses by computer manufacturers for new products.

Professional qualifications are available from the British Computer Society, and the Institute of Sales and Marketing Management offers a range of courses according to your experience and expertise. The Open University offers courses in computing and maths that lead to a computing degree. There are no formal entry requirements and you study through distance learning.

A Diploma/Welsh Baccalaureate may be available in your area in IT. A full or part-time foundation degree in IT is also available. An ICT higher apprenticeship is available through e-skills. This combines an apprenticeship with a foundation degree and can lead to a full honours degree. There are partnerships with colleges and universities throughout the UK. E-skills runs a professional development programme which enables new IT professionals to fast-track their career. The programme is delivered through universities and participating employers. E-skills also offers an internship. Students are placed for a period of employment within an organisation, enabling them to develop valuable business and IT skills. Contact e-skills for details of all programmes and schemes.

This is an ideal second career if you have technical computing knowledge and qualifications. Mature applicants usually need experience in the IT industry, such as helpdesk work, computer sales, technical support or in customer services and marketing. Those applying for senior posts may benefit from a master of business administration (MBA) qualification. There are relevant distance-learning courses available, such as those offered by the Institute of Sales and Marketing Management.

Opportunities and Pay

You can work for an IT company that manufactures computers or related equipment, a dealer, a software company or a firm of consultants. Work is available throughout the UK, but concentrated in the south east of England. Promotion depends on building up a good sales record. You can progress to team leader, area management posts or a specialist technical role, or with experience you can move into IT consultancy or related areas of work such as business analysis.

Earnings vary depending on employer, the size of the company and location but generally start at around £18k-£22k a year, rising with experience to around £35k. In senior positions, some may earn more than £50k a year. Salaries usually attract various commissions and bonuses. A company car, laptop and mobile phone are likely to be part of the package.

Skills and Qualities

able to inspire confidence, business awareness, customer service skills, good communication skills, good interpersonal skills, negotiating skills, persuasive, specialist IT skills, technical aptitude, willing to train and work away from home

Relevant Subjects

Business and accounting, English, ICT/Computer studies, Mathematics, Physics, Retail and distribution, Science

Further Information

AGCAS: Information Technology (Job Sector Briefing) (AGCAS) - www.prospects.ac.uk

Computer Weekly (Reed Business Information) - www.computerweekly.com

Diplomas (Foundation, Higher and Advanced) - http://yp.direct.gov.uk/diplomas

e-skills UK - sector skills council for business and information technology - www.e-skills.com

Open University - www.open.ac.uk

Real Life Guide to Information & Communications Technology (Trotman) - www.trotman.co.uk

TARGETjobs: IT (GTI Specialist Publishing Ltd.) - www.groupgti.com

Welsh Baccalaureate - www.wbq.org.uk

▶Working in computers & IT (2010) (Babcock Lifeskills) - www.babcock-lifeskills.com/

Addresses

British Computer Society (BCS)
First Floor, Block D North Star House North Star Avenue, Swindon, Wiltshire SN2 1FA
Phone: +44 (0)845 300 4417
Web: www.bcs.org

Chartered Institute of Marketing (CIM)
Moor Hall, Cookham, Maidenhead, Berkshire SL6 9QH
Phone: +44 (0) 1628 427120
Web: www.cim.co.uk

Institute of Sales and Marketing Management (ISMM)
Harrier Court, Lower Woodside, Bedfordshire LU1 4DQ
Phone: +44 (0)1582 840 001
Web: www.ismm.co.uk

Similar Jobs

IT Systems Analyst/Designer, IT Technical Support Manager, Network Manager, Sales Executive: Technical

IT Technical Support Manager

also known as: Computer Aftersales Support Manager, Technical Support Engineer

CRCI:Computers and IT
CLCI:CAV

Job Band: 4 to 5

Job Description

Technical support managers are responsible for providing technical advice and support to computer users within their organisation. They help to resolve problems in the operation of computer systems and ensure that customers make the most effective use of their systems, and advise on the installation of computer systems and upgrades. They have a good knowledge of network operating systems and the installation of hardware and software. Are often required to write or provide user manuals for customers.

Technical support managers liaise with other staff at management level, attend meetings and write reports, particularly on the number of faults recorded and the solutions. They need to keep up to date with the latest developments in IT. May supervise a team of staff, which can include helpline operators, technicians and network administrators.

Work Details

Usually work a 35-37 hr week, Monday to Friday, though may be required to work on a 24-hour on-call system. You are based in an office but may need to travel to other sites occasionally. Many hours are spent sitting at a computer, sometimes on your own. You also communicate both in person and in writing with other colleagues and need to be able to do this without using jargon and complex technical language.

Qualification

- **England, Wales and Northern Ireland**

Band 4: For relevant BTEC higher national award: 1-2 A levels, preferably in maths or physics, and some GCSEs (A*-C) usually including English and maths, or equivalent.

Band 5: For degree courses: 2-3 A levels, with at least one in maths or physics, and some GCSEs (A*-C) usually including English and maths, or equivalent. Exact requirements depend on the degree you take.

- **Scotland**

Band 4: For relevant SQA higher national award: usually 2-3 H grades including maths or physics and some S grades (1-3), often including English and maths, or similar qualifications.

Band 5: For degree courses: 3-5 H grades with at least one in maths or physics, and some S grades (1-3), usually including English and maths, or similar qualifications. Exact requirements depend on the degree you take.

Degree Information
Subjects such as software engineering, information systems/ technology, computer science or artificial intelligence may be preferred by employers. The Information Technology Management for Business degree (see e-skills UK) is designed in partnership with some of the biggest employers in the IT industry. Systems and control engineering, physics and electronic engineering may also be acceptable. Postgraduate courses are available for science or mathematics graduates.

Adult Qualifications
Mature applicants may not need the standard entry requirements for higher education courses, particularly if your previous experience is relevant or you show an ability to study at the appropriate level. There are many relevant full or part-time courses available at further/higher education colleges. Postgraduate conversion courses are also available for those who have not studied IT at degree level and Access or foundation courses are available for those who have no formal qualifications who wish to pursue a relevant degree.

Work Experience
Employers or colleges/universities may prefer candidates who have relevant work or voluntary experience. Employers usually require experience of previous paid employment in systems analysis or network administration, or considerable voluntary experience in aspects of computing. Internships and work placements are a valuable introduction to the IT industry and enable you to make an informed choice. Other schemes, such as 'The Year in Industry', enable those who expect good grades at A level/H grade, the opportunity to spend a salaried year with a company to gain valuable work experience.

Entry and Training
Most entrants are graduates in a relevant discipline with some experience in a systems analyst or network administrator role. You may also require marketing and sales knowledge or experience. Requirements vary between employers and a degree/HND is not always necessary. Many employers provide a training programme that covers an introduction to the company, its products, customer care, sales techniques, identification of customers' needs and negotiating skills. Some technical support managers work towards gaining Chartered IT Professional (CITP) status through the British Computer Society (BCS). Contact the BCS for further details.

It is also important to keep up to date with new software and hardware developments. Training and development is ongoing which can be by via in-house training courses, attendance at college, or through short courses run by manufacturers or independent training organisations. Particularly relevant courses for this job are the Microsoft Certified Support Engineer (MCSE), Microsoft Certified IT Professional (MCITP): Enterprise Support Technician, or the Certified Novell Engineer (CNE). A popular industry-recognised entry-level qualification is the CompTIA A+ offered by CompTIA UK that has been updated to reflect changes in technology.

The Open University offers courses in computing and maths that can lead to an appropriate computing degree. There are no formal entry requirements and you study through distance learning. A full or part-time foundation degree in IT is also available. Relevant S/NVQs at levels 2-4 are available. The new S/NVQ for IT users (ITQ 2009) has been developed as part of a project involving a full review of the National Occupational Standards (NOS) for IT users. A Diploma/ Welsh Baccalaureate in IT may be available in your area.

Training programmes, including apprenticeship schemes, may be available. An ICT higher apprenticeship is available through e-skills. This combines an apprenticeship with a foundation degree and can lead to a full honours degree. There are partnerships with colleges and universities throughout the UK. E-skills also run a professional development programme which enables new IT professionals to fast-track their career. The programme is delivered through universities and participating employers. E-skills also offers an internship. Students are placed for a period of employment within an organisation, enabling them to develop valuable business and IT skills. Contact e-skills for details of all programmes and schemes.

Mature applicants with industry experience in computer sales and marketing, helpdesk work and customer service, and in particular, experience as a team leader, may have an advantage. Those looking to return to work can improve their industry-specific knowledge through short courses, run by corporate organisations. Those with an MBA (master of business administration) following at least two years' IT management experience have an advantage. Some Jobcentres/Jobcentre Plus offices, LSCs/LECs, Jobcentre (NI) and ELWa (Wales) also offer IT courses.

Opportunities and Pay
Opportunities for technical support managers are generally good because of the constant changes in technology. Jobs exist with software houses, technical and business consultancies, multinational software companies, international investment banks, public sector organisations, manufacturers of computers and related equipment, and computer dealers. Some experienced support managers can work on a freelance basis, usually on short-term contracts.

Demand is for those with the necessary technical skills, but also for those with good interpersonal skills. Promotion to senior management posts is possible and some managers become self-employed consultants. Overseas work may be available.

Pay varies depending on location and type of employer. A graduate entrant starting as first or second level support can expect to earn around £20k-£25k a year, rising to £25k-£40k with experience. Some senior managers can earn over £50k a year. Salaries may include performance-related pay, profit-sharing or company bonuses.

Skills and Qualities
able to explain clearly, able to work both on your own and in a team, analytical skills, logical, methodical, perseverance, precise, problem-solving skills, specialist IT skills, technical aptitude

Relevant Subjects
Business and accounting, Design and technology, English, ICT/ Computer studies, Mathematics, Physics, Science

Further Information
AGCAS: Information Technology (Job Sector Briefing) (AGCAS) - www.prospects.ac.uk

Computing Technology Industry Association (CompTIA) - www.comptia.org

Diplomas (Foundation, Higher and Advanced) - http://yp.direct.gov.uk/diplomas

e-skills UK - sector skills council for business and information technology - www.e-skills.com

Inside Careers Guide: Information Technology - www.insidecareers.co.uk

Open University - www.open.ac.uk

Real Life Guide to Information & Communications Technology (Trotman) - www.trotman.co.uk

Skills Framework for the Information Age (SFIA) (SFIA Foundation) - www.sfia.org.uk

TARGETjobs: IT (GTI Specialist Publishing Ltd.) - www.groupgti.com

Welsh Baccalaureate - www.wbq.org.uk

▶Working in computers & IT (2010) (Babcock Lifeskills) - www.babcock-lifeskills.com/

▶Working with languages (2010) (Babcock Lifeskills) - www.babcock-lifeskills.com/

Year in Industry (Engineering Development Trust) - www.yini.org.uk

Addresses

British Computer Society (BCS)
First Floor, Block D North Star House North Star Avenue, Swindon, Wiltshire SN2 1FA
Phone: +44 (0)845 300 4417
Web: www.bcs.org

Institute for the Management of Information Systems (IMIS)
5 Kingfisher House, New Mill Road, Orpington, Kent BR5 3QG
Phone: +44 (0)700 002 3456
Web: www.imis.org.uk

Similar Jobs

IT Applications Developer, IT Helpdesk Analyst/Operator, IT Skills Trainer, IT Systems Analyst/Designer, Network Manager

Jeweller: Retail

CRCI:Retail Sales and Customer Services
CLCI:OE Job Band: 2 to 3

Job Description

Jewellers sell jewellery, watches and silverware and may also do minor repairs. They talk to customers to find out what they would like to buy and show them suitable items or give advice about different products. May develop further skills, such as the valuation of jewellery, watches, precious gems and metals, for insurance purposes or private sale. Some shops have workshops for designing, altering and repairing rings, watches, bracelets, brooches and silver items. Precious gems, such as diamonds, can be cut, set or reset, according to the customer's wishes; necklaces restrung and items cleaned. Some assistants may develop skills in this work and divide their time between the workshop and shop counter.

Work Details

Usually work a basic 37-39 hr week, Monday to Friday. Working hours may include some Saturdays and you take a day off in lieu during the week. Some jewellers may open on a Sunday, particularly in a shopping centre or mall. You serve and give advice to customers in a shop, or can be based in a workshop, or both. In this type of work, you have to learn a great deal about the products you are selling. Repair work can be intricate.

The environment is usually comfortable, light and warm. Your work may require you to stand for most of the day at a sales counter, or sit at a workbench. You need to handle money and be responsible for security.

Qualification

- **England, Wales and Northern Ireland**

Band 2: Although academic qualifications are not specified for this job, some employers may ask for a few GCSEs (A*-C) in subjects that include English and maths, or equivalent. For some courses, GCSEs such as art and design or technical subjects are useful.

Band 3: For a BTEC national award: usually at least 4 GCSEs (A*-C) including English and maths, or equivalent. For some foundation courses in art and design: usually at least 5 GCSEs (A*-C) or equivalent.

- **Scotland**

Band 2: Although academic qualifications are not specified for this job, employers may ask for some S grades (1-3) in subjects that include English and maths, or similar. For some courses, S grades such as art and design or technical subjects are useful.

Band 3: For SQA national award: some colleges require four S grades (1-3) including English and maths, or similar.

Adult Qualifications

There are no set qualifications for this job. A good standard of general education and some ability in basic maths and English is useful and may be required.

Work Experience

Relevant work or voluntary experience is always useful and can improve your chances when applying for a job. It can equip you with skills that you can use in the future and add to your CV. Part-time and holiday employment in a wide range of shops is usually fairly easy to obtain.

Entry and Training

The training given for retail jewellery sales and manufacturing can vary depending on the employer. Training is usually on the job and possibly through a training scheme. Some employers expect their trainees to study for the jewellers' diploma of the National Association of Goldsmiths or for Gemmological Association courses. Courses include basic product and sales skills and may include a professional jewellers' valuation certificate. Study is usually by distance learning or can sometimes be via a day-release course. For those wishing to develop craft and design skills, a relevant national diploma/foundation course may be useful, but is not essential for entry.

A Diploma/Welsh Baccalaureate in retail business may be available in your area. Relevant S/NVQS are available at levels 1-3, including retail skills at levels 1-2 and jewellery manufacture at levels 2-3. There are City & Guilds awards in creative techniques in jewellery at levels 2-3. Training programmes, including apprenticeship schemes, may be available in your area. Advanced apprenticeships leading to qualification at level 3 can also be a route into higher education. See the Skillsmart Retail website for details.

Mature applicants with some experience in sales or in art and design may have an advantage.

Opportunities and Pay

You can be employed by a local independent jeweller or by a nationwide chain. Prospects of promotion to shop manager are usually better if you are employed by a large company. With experience you can become self-employed, but this requires very considerable financial investment. Due to the current economic downturn, there may be fewer opportunities for work in the retail sector.

Pay varies depending on location and type of employment. A trainee earns around £12k-£13k a year, rising with experience and responsibility to around £15k-£28k a year, with some earning more than £45k a year. Commission on sales may be paid in addition to your basic salary. You may also be given a personal discount on goods you wish to purchase.

Health

This job requires good eyesight, and normal colour vision is essential for certain areas of work.

Skills and Qualities

business awareness, confident, customer service skills, friendly, good communication skills, good interpersonal skills, patient, technical aptitude, willing to learn

Relevant Subjects

Art and Design, Business and accounting, Retail and distribution

Further Information

Apprenticeship Schemes (National Apprenticeship Service) - www.apprenticeships.org.uk

Diplomas (Foundation, Higher and Advanced) - http://yp.direct.gov.uk/diplomas

Journal of Gemmology (annual) (Gemmological Association of Great Britain) - www.gem-a.com/publications/journal-of-gemmology.aspx

Skillsmart Retail - sector skills council for the retail industry - www.skillsmartretail.com

Welsh Baccalaureate - www.wbq.org.uk

▶Working in retail & customer services (2008) (Babcock Lifeskills) - www.babcock-lifeskills.com/

Addresses

British Jewellers' Association (BJA)
Federation House, 10 Vyse Street, Birmingham B18 6LT
Web: www.bja.org.uk

Gemmological Association of Great Britain
27 Greville Street, London EC1N 8TN
Phone: +44 (0)20 7404 3334
Web: www.gem-a.info/

Jewellery and Allied Industries Training Council (JAITC)
c/o British Jewellers' Assocation (BJA), Federation House,
10 Vyse Street, Birmingham B18 6LT
Web: www.jaitc.org.uk/

National Association of Goldsmiths (NAG)
78a Luke Street, London EC2A 4XG
Phone: +44 (0)20 7613 4445
Web: www.jewellers-online.org

Similar Jobs

Engraver, Jewellery Designer, Model Maker, Retail Assistant, Watch & Clock Repairer

Jewellery Designer

also known as: Goldsmith, Silversmith

CRCI:Design, Arts and Crafts
CLCI:EG Job Band: 2 to 5

Job Description

Jewellery designers use creative skills and commercial awareness to design original items for silver and gold jewellery, and other products, such as watches, clocks and trophies. They may specialise in one area of the trade, such as the design of rings or tableware. Usually prepare detailed sketches and drawings so that a craftworker can make up the design, using traditional and hand-made methods, or the latest technology. Some items are made with a combination of both methods. Designers work closely with skilled craftworkers, including casters and engravers, diamond-mounters and other precious stone setters, pressworkers and polishers.

Many designers create and make items themselves, either for retail sale or as commissioned by an individual client. They consult closely with a client to discuss ideas, costs and timescale of production. May produce several sketches or use design-related computer software to help the client/company visualise the finished item. Must keep up to date with the latest trends and developments.

Work Details

Working hours are usually 9am to 5pm; Monday to Friday, but you may have to work extra hours to meet deadlines. You work in a studio, workshop or industrial premises. Travel may be necessary to trade fairs, craft exhibitions, retail outlets, or to an individual client's home. You need to consult with suppliers, store buyers, galleries and sometimes museums. The work can often be delicate, using very small tools. Safety glasses may be needed.

Qualification

• England, Wales and Northern Ireland

Band 3: For entry to jobs, HNC or a relevant Diploma, usually at least 4 GCSEs (A*-C) including English and maths, or equivalent.

Band 4: For foundation studies course in art and design: at least one A level or equivalent and some GCSEs (A*-C). For BTEC higher national award: a BTEC national award/Applied A level, a foundation studies diploma, or equivalent.

Band 5: For degree courses: 2-3 A levels and some GCSEs (A*-C) usually including English and maths, or equivalent. Most students take a foundation course in art and design first. Exact requirements depend on the degree you take.

• Scotland

Band 3: For entry: usually at least four S grades (1-3), including English and maths, or similar.

Band 4: For entry to SQA higher national and professional development awards, usually 2-3 H grades and some S grades (1-3), including English and maths, or similar qualifications.

Band 5: For degree courses: 3-5 H grades and some S grades (1-3), usually including English and maths, or similar qualifications. Exact requirements depend on the degree you take.

Degree Information

First degrees include: jewellery, jewellery design, silversmithing, goldsmithing, contemporary jewellery, 3-D design: metal design and jewellery and fine art/visual art. There are relevant postgraduate courses available including an MA in jewellery design at London Metropolitan University and in goldsmithing, silversmithing and metalwork and jewellery at the Royal College of Art in London.

Adult Qualifications

There are no set qualifications for this job though experience in art and design is useful. There are a variety of courses available at different levels. Mature applicants with outstanding portfolios of work may be accepted by colleges without the standard entry requirements. There are Access and foundation courses in some areas, which give adults without qualifications a route onto degree courses. Check with individual colleges.

Work Experience

Relevant work or voluntary experience is always useful and can improve your chances when applying for a job. Gold or silversmithing experience may be hard to obtain, but any art and design, craft or technical work is valuable. Work placements may be available for vacation or Saturday work in studios, museums, or in retail jewellery outlets, which provide useful insight to jewellery design, both traditional and modern.

Entry and Training

Courses are available at several levels, including foundation, BTEC/SQA higher national awards, and degree level. Most entrants are qualified to HND/degree level. A portfolio of work is usually needed for entry. A relevant foundation degree may be available in some areas of the UK such as fashion jewellery and jewellery and silversmithing design. A Diploma/Welsh Baccalaureate may be available in your area in creative and media and may provide a route onto higher education courses.

The Jewellery and Allied Industries Training Council (British Jewellers' Association) can provide a list of colleges and organisations offering jewellery courses in the UK. The Goldsmiths' Company runs a programmes for new graduates and offers awards for excellence in design as well as courses and apprenticeships. There is an NVQ available from SQA at level 2 in jewellery manufacture.

Most training is on the job, but it may be possible to attend specialist short-term courses that include gemstone cutting and carving or jewellery restoration. Colleges provide a range of part-time and evening classes in silversmithing and jewellery. Independent colleges also offer short courses in subjects from enamelling to general jewellery design. It is important to keep up to date with trends and techniques.

Mature applicants with knowledge and experience of the precious metal and jewellery industry have an advantage. Some experience in art and design is also useful. There are various routes to acquiring qualifications in art and design, including full and part-time courses, evening and distance learning courses. Funding for undergraduate/postgraduate study in silver/jewellery design may be available from organisations such as the South Square Trust.

Opportunities and Pay
This is a small profession that is highly competitive. You may work for a manufacturing company, jewellery retailer, a small firm of traditional goldsmiths/silversmiths, or be self-employed and work from home or a studio. Most employed designers are based in towns and cities throughout the UK, with the major centres of production in London, Sheffield, Birmingham and Edinburgh. Grants may be available, for example from the Crafts Council or the local LSC/LEC, ELWa (Wales), or Jobcentre (NI) for those setting up their own business.

Pay varies depending on location and type of employer. If you are employed, salaries start at around £15k-£20k a year, rising to £25k-£35k with experience. Higher earners make up to £50k a year.

Health
You need good eyesight to cope with fine and intricate work.

Skills and Qualities
able to work well on your own, artistic ability, attention to detail, business awareness, creative and imaginative flair, good communication skills, good concentration level, IT skills, manual dexterity, precise, technical aptitude

Relevant Subjects
Art and Design, Design and technology

Further Information
Chartered Society of Designers (Chartered Society of Designers) - www.csd.org.uk

Crafts Magazine (Crafts Council) - www.craftscouncil.org.uk

Creative & Cultural Skills - sector skills council for advertising, crafts, cultural heritage, design, literature, music, performing & visual arts - www.ccskills.org.uk

Design Week (Design Week) - www.designweek.co.uk

Diplomas (Foundation, Higher and Advanced) - http://yp.direct.gov.uk/diplomas

Goldsmiths' Company Directory (The Goldsmiths' Company) - www.whoswhoingoldandsilver.com

Jewellery & Allied Industries Training Council - www.jaitc.org.uk

National Association of Goldsmiths (NAG) - www.jewellers-online.org/pages/home.php

Retail Jeweller magazine (Retail Jeweller) - www.retail-jeweller.com

The Designer (Chartered Society of Designers) - www.thedesignermagazine.com

▶Working in art & design (2009) (Babcock Lifeskills) - www.babcock-lifeskills.com/

▶Working in fashion & clothing (2008) (Babcock Lifeskills) - www.babcock-lifeskills.com/

Addresses
Association for Contemporary Jewellery (ACJ)
PO Box 37807, London SE23 1XJ
Phone: +44 (0) 20 8291 4201
Web: www.acj.org.uk

British Jewellers' Association (BJA)
Federation House, 10 Vyse Street, Birmingham B18 6LT
Web: www.bja.org.uk

Contemporary British Silversmiths
PO Box 42034, London E5 9WG
Phone: +44 (0)794 478 6011
Web: www.contemporarybritishsilversmiths.org/

Crafts Council (CC)
44a Pentonville Road, Islington, London N1 9BY
Phone: +44 (0)20 7806 2500
Web: www.craftscouncil.org.uk

Goldsmiths' Company
Goldsmiths' Hall, Foster Lane, London EC2V 6BN
Phone: +44 (0)20 7606 7010
Web: www.thegoldsmiths.co.uk

Institute of Professional Goldsmiths (IPG)
P.O. Box 668, Rickmansworth, Hertfordshire WD3 0EQ
Phone: +44 (0) 20 3004 9806
Web: www.ipgold.org.uk

South Square Trust
Clerk To The Trustees, South Square Trust, P.O. Box 169, Lewes, East Sussex BN7 9FB
Phone: +44 (0)1825 872264
Web: www.southsquaretrust.org.uk/

Similar Jobs
Costume Designer, Engraver, Fashion Designer, Glass Designer, Jeweller: Retail, Model Maker

Jockey

CRCI:Leisure, Sport and Tourism
CLCI:GAG — Job Band: 1 to 2

Job Description
Jockeys rides horses for racehorse owners and trainers. The horse they ride depends on their previous race performances and weight. There are two types of competition racing: flat and jump. Most jockeys specialise in one type. Racing seasons vary, with flat races only running from March through to November, and the jump season throughout the year. Most of the time is spent exercising horses and travelling to attend races. Before a race, the horse trainer and owner talk with the jockey. Afterwards they talk about the race performance. Jockeys must be good at handling horses and be prepared to keep very fit. They must keep their weight as low as possible.

Work Details
Usually works a basic 40 hr week, though hours can be longer and include early mornings, weekends and sometimes evenings. Initially you need to 'live in' at the stables. You work in a team with other jockeys, apprentice jockeys, stable staff and a trainer, and are active most of the time, training and exercising horses. Travel over long distances may be necessary, depending on where the race meetings take place. You may have to spend nights away from home, often sleeping in with the horses. You are out in all sorts of weather which may often be cold and wet. There is a risk of accidents from falls.

Qualification

• England, Wales and Northern Ireland
Band 1: For entry to training, no minimum qualifications are needed, but you are expected to have a good level of general education and relevant experience. Some formal/vocational qualifications at any level are useful.

Band 2: For entry to training as a stable hand or jockey, no minimum qualifications are needed, but it is an advantage to have some GCSEs (A*-C) or equivalent in subjects that include English and maths.

• Scotland
Band 1: For entry to training as a stable hand or jockey, no minimum qualifications are needed, but you are expected to have a good level of general education and relevant experience. Some formal/vocational qualifications at any level are useful.

Band 2: Although academic qualifications are not specified for this job, it is an advantage to have some S grades (1-3) in subjects that include English and maths, or similar.

Adult Qualifications
No minimum qualifications are usually needed. Most start their training at around 17 yrs old.

Work Experience
Relevant work or voluntary experience is always useful. It can improve your chances when applying for entry to jobs. This type of work is popular and entry is competitive. Work experience, such as helping at stables, or caring for other animals, can often increase your employment prospects.

Entry and Training
To be considered as a jockey, it is first necessary to begin work as an apprentice. Entrants must be at least 16. Jockeys have to meet weight limits and are usually about eight stone in weight for flat racing, or nine and a half stone for jump racing. You also have to be extremely fit and in excellent health. If you are new to the industry, an S/NVQ level 1 or 2 in racehorse care from a centre approved by the British Horseracing Authority (BHA) can be a useful start. An NVQ in racehorse care and management is also available. For those under the age of 19 this is compulsory before you can get a job with a racehorse trainer.

If you already have some experience in a yard, the NVQ day release or equine industry conversion course may be more suitable. A Diploma/Welsh Baccalaureate may also be available in your area in Sport & Active Leisure. Contact SkillsActive or visit the diplomas website for further details.

Once employed by a racehorse trainer, either as an apprentice jockey (flat) or conditional jockey (jumps), a joint application is made by the trainer and the potential jockey to the Jockey Club for a licence to ride. Prior to the granting of a licence, attendance on a conditional/apprentice licence course at either the British Racing School (BRS) or the Northern Racing College is essential. Further intermediate and continuation training courses at the BRS are required as your career progresses towards riding under a full professional licence.

Apprenticeship as a jockey does not finish until you have ridden a number of winners or reached a certain age. Most apprenticeships are served between the age of 17 and 25, or 26 for jump racing. Some stable hands (see job profile) progress to become an apprentice jockey if they meet the weight/height limits and can demonstrate exceptional riding ability, together with a high level of dedication and commitment. According to the BHA many professional jockeys have entered horse racing in this way. See the Careers In Racing section of the BHA website for details of all training routes and approved courses.

There are strict age and weight limits for this job. Most apprenticeships are served between the age of 17 and 25, or 26 for jump racing. Therefore mature entrants over the age of 20 may find it difficult to be accepted for training.

Opportunities and Pay
There are less than 500 professional jockeys in the UK. Jobs are available in certain areas where racing stables are situated. This career is highly competitive and considerable talent is required for success. Once you complete your jockey apprenticeship you can become self-employed. You work through an agent or by approaching trainers directly. This can be a short career unless you can keep within the weight limits, but you can usually find employment in a related field, such as training, management or promotion work.

Pay varies depending on the stable; the larger ones pay more. Apprentice and conditional jockeys start on around £12k-£14k a year, which may include free accommodation. Once licensed, salaries rise to around £15k-£16k a year plus a fee for each race you ride in. This can rise to £22k a year with experience. Jockeys receive bonuses related to the performance of the horse they are working with, and wages are improved by prize money. Professional jockeys riding for wealthy owners have a very comfortable standard of living and can earn as much as £50k a year.

Health
You are expected to keep your weight down to required levels. There are also restrictions on height. This job requires a high standard of physical fitness and you cannot enter this job if you wear glasses. There may be an allergy risk from horses.

Skills and Qualities
ambitious, aptitude for teamwork, competitive, confident, good balance, honest, patient, physically fit, resilient, stamina

Relevant Subjects
Biology, Physical education and sport, Science

Further Information
Apprenticeship Schemes (National Apprenticeship Service) - www.apprenticeships.org.uk

British Racing School (BRS) - www.brs.org.uk

Careers in Racing (British Horseracing Authority) - www.careersinracing.com

Careers in Racing (British Horseracing Authority) - www.careersinracing.com

Diplomas (Foundation, Higher and Advanced) - http://yp.direct.gov.uk/diplomas

Jockeys Employment & Training Scheme (JETS) - www.jets-uk.org

Northern Racing College - www.northernracingcollege.co.uk/

SkillsActive - sector skills council for active leisure, learning and well-being - www.skillsactive.com

The Jockey Club - www.thejockeyclub.co.uk

Working with animals (2009) (Babcock Lifeskills) - www.babcock-lifeskills.com/

Addresses
British Horse Society (BHS)
Stoneleigh Deer Park, Kenilworth, Warwickshire CV8 2XZ
Phone: 0844 848 1666 (UK only)
Web: www.bhs.org.uk

British Horseracing Authority (BHA)
75 High Holborn, London WC1V 6LS
Phone: +44 (0)20 7152 0000
Web: www.britishhorseracing.com/

National Trainers' Federation (NTF)
9 High Street, Lambourn, Hungerford, Berkshire RG17 8XN
Phone: +44 (0)1488 71 719
Web: www.racehorsetrainers.org

Professional Jockeys Association (PJA)
39B Kingfisher Court, Hambridge Road, Newbury, Berkshire RG14 5SJ
Phone: +44 (0)1635 44102
Web: www.thepja.co.uk/Default.aspx

Similar Jobs
Horse Groom, Riding Instructor, Sports Professional, Stable Hand

Journalist
also known as: Newspaper Journalist, Reporter: Press

CRCI:Media, Print and Publishing
CLCI:FAC — Job Band: 3 to 5

Job Description
Journalists gather and report news and other articles of interest for local, regional or national newspapers. They attend events and press conferences, and interview people, by phone or in person, to get information. May use shorthand or tape machines to make notes of interviews or record their own instant observations of an event, usually investigate and write a report or story, using a computer, and submit it to the sub-editor.

Journalist

Must make sure that stories are well balanced and contain both sides of an argument. Journalists take care not to say anything in a story that may be against the law. Work is varied, but experience and knowledge are necessary for specialisation in a particular type of reporting. Must keep to tight deadlines according to whether the newspaper is a daily, weekly or evening paper.

Work Details

Journalists have to work long and irregular hours, including evenings and weekends, and those who work for national newspapers may need to work shifts. Often have to travel around a local area to cover stories, and some have to travel further afield and stay away from home overnight. A small number of journalists travel abroad. This work can be pressurised at times, particularly when you have to report a story quickly or meet publication deadlines. On some stories you may be working outdoors in all weathers.

You meet a wide range of people and need to be sensitive to their emotions. Some people may be aggressive and hostile, so you need to keep calm. You need a good knowledge and a keen interest in current affairs. Knowledge of media law and ethics is essential.

Qualification

• England, Wales and Northern Ireland

Band 4: For pre-entry training course, such as a BTEC/HND in journalism, or direct entry to a traineeship: 1-2 A levels and some GCSEs (A*-C) usually including English, or equivalent.

Band 5: For a degree, followed by traineeship or postgraduate course: 2-3 A levels and some GCSEs (A*-C) usually including English, or equivalent qualifications. Some degrees in journalism require A level English. Exact requirements depend on the degree you take.

• Scotland

Band 4: For SQA/HND course in journalism, journalism studies or direct entry to traineeship: 2-3 H grades and some S grades (1-3) usually including English, or similar.

Band 5: For a degree, followed by traineeship or postgraduate course: 3-5 H grades and some S grades (1-3), usually including English or similar. Some degrees in journalism require H grade English. Exact requirements depend on the degree you take.

Degree Information

Any degree is acceptable for entry to this job, but some employers prefer applicants with a degree in journalism. Politics, English language/literature, history, law, American studies, European studies, international relations, communication studies and media studies also give useful background knowledge for this job. There are also postgraduate courses in journalism.

Adult Qualifications

Entry requirements may be relaxed for adults applying for higher education courses. Access or foundation courses give adults without qualifications a route on to degree courses.

Work Experience

Entry to this job/career is highly competitive and it is essential to have some relevant work or voluntary experience before applying for jobs or full-time training in journalism. According to the NCTJ, relevant experience is vital for entry at any level. Working on a school/student magazine or writing for a local newspaper is appropriate.

Entry and Training

60% of people who enter this job are graduates. It is an advantage to have experience in shorthand and word processing, and also to have a driving licence. Entry to training courses is highly competitive and you usually have to submit a portfolio of your work experience. Some colleges only grant places to those who have some work experience on a newspaper, so it is helpful to keep cuttings of your work.

You can enter a training job direct from school, work under a training contract for two years and carry out your basic training on the job. Part of the training is usually spent on a registered National Council for the Training of Journalists (NCTJ) distance-learning course, followed by a block or day-release course at a local college. At the end of the training you are expected to take the NCTJ National Certificate Examination.

Alternatively, you can train on a pre-entry vocational course for both post-A level students and graduates, or a postgraduate course, before entering the job. You still have to undergo a training contract, but this usually only 18 months long. Specialist short courses are also available from the NCTJ. See their website for full details. Several foundation degrees in journalism are available.

A Diploma/Welsh Baccalaureate may be available in your area in creative and media. This can be a useful introduction to this type of career as you gain practical experience while studying. See the diplomas website or Skillset for further information.

Mature entrants with relevant experience are often considered by employers. Experts in a particular field may be able to gain some freelance work writing about their specialist subject. Distance-learning courses in journalism are available, such as those offered by the National Council for the Training of Journalists, and the London School of Journalism.

Opportunities and Pay

Around 80,000 journalists work in the UK. There are jobs for journalists throughout the UK with local, regional and national newspapers, broadcast news organisations and large industrial/commercial companies and local and central government departments that employ in-house journalists to work on publications. Jobs are concentrated in major cities. Competition for jobs is high.

Some journalists specialise in current affairs, foreign correspondence, sport, politics or entertainment. It is possible to move into magazine, broadcast or online journalism, or to become a sub-editor. Freelance work and work abroad are possible.

Pay varies depending on the employer, with national newspapers offering higher rates. Trainees with a local newspaper may earn as little as £10k a year to start with. Experienced journalists earn around £28k-£40k a year. Highly successful journalists and national newspaper editors can earn up to £80k a year. Freelance journalists can negotiate fees in line with the National Union of Journalists' guidelines.

Skills and Qualities

able to cope under pressure, able to withstand criticism, analytical skills, excellent communication skills, good listening skills, good written English, interest in current affairs, IT skills, observant, perseverance, stamina

Relevant Subjects

Business and accounting, Economics, English, Geography, Government and politics, Media and communication studies, Psychology, Sociology

Further Information

Creative Choices - www.creative-choices.co.uk

Diplomas (Foundation, Higher and Advanced) - http://yp.direct.gov.uk/diplomas

Journalism Uncovered (Trotman 2009) - www.trotman.co.uk

Media Circle - www.mediacircle.org

National Council for the Training of Journalists (NCTJ) - www.nctj.com

Press Association Training (Press Association) - www.pa-training.co.uk

Press Gazette - Journalism Today (Progressive Media International) - www.pressgazette.co.uk

Skillset - sector skills council for the creative media, fashion and textiles industries - www.skillset.org

Society of Women Writers and Journalists (SWWJ) - www.swwj.co.uk
▶Working in English (2007) (Babcock Lifeskills) - www.babcock-lifeskills.com/
▶Working in politics & law (2010) (Babcock Lifeskills) - www.babcock-lifeskills.com/
▶Working in travel & tourism (2010) (Babcock Lifeskills) - www.babcock-lifeskills.com/

Addresses

Chartered Institute of Journalists (CIoJ)
2 Dock Offices, Surrey Quays Road, London SE16 2XU
Phone: +44 (0)20 7252 1187
Web: www.cioj.co.uk

London School of Journalism
126 Shirland Road Maida Vale, London W9 2BT
Phone: +44 (0) 20 7432 8140
Web: www.home-study.com

National Union of Journalists (NUJ)
Headland House, 308-312 Grays Inn Road, London WC1X 8DP
Phone: +44 (0)20 7278 7916
Web: www.nuj.org.uk

Newspaper Society Training Dept
St Andrew's House, 18 -20 St Andrew's Street, London EC4A 3AY
Phone: +44 (0)20 7632 7400
Web: www.newspapersoc.org.uk

Similar Jobs

Broadcast Journalist, Copy Editor, Journalist: Magazine, Magazine Features Editor, Political/Parliamentary Researcher, Press Officer

Journalist: Magazine

also known as: Journalist: Periodical

CRCI:Media, Print and Publishing
CLCI:FAC Job Band: 3 to 5

Job Description

Magazine journalists research and write news and feature articles for a variety of publications, including professional journals/ periodicals and magazines, and glossy consumer/lifestyle magazines. Some journalists may write for specialist publications in business, scientific and technical fields. They use the Internet, libraries, and interviews to research and create interesting feature articles and news items ranging from past issues, current developments and future trends.

Usually write an article or news item specifically tailored to the interest of the readership. This can be in paper format, CD or audiotape, or for online viewing. May use shorthand and/or record, any interviews and their own observations. Journalists work to a deadline when the 'copy' (written text) must be submitted to the editorial team for approval. They spend time with the team, making decisions on which articles go into the next issue.

May also be involved in the production of the magazine, sub-editing and editing, deciding on layout and page design, creating headlines and picture/illustration captions, so often liaises with designers. Journalists attend relevant conferences/fairs and seminars to gain further knowledge, and to network.

Work Details

Usually work basic office hours; Monday to Friday, though late nights and weekend work are required as deadlines approach. This job is usually office based although this varies with the publication. Part-time work and career breaks are becoming more common in this industry. Travel is usually necessary during the working day and some journalists may need to travel further afield and stay away from home overnight. A small number of magazine journalists travel abroad.

This type of work can be pressurised at times, particularly when publication deadlines approach. Knowledge of media law and ethics is essential. Work dress is usually informal but smart.

Qualification

• England, Wales and Northern Ireland

Band 4: For HND, Diploma of Higher Education or foundation degree: 1-2 A levels and some GCSEs (A*-C) usually including English and maths, or equivalent.

Band 5: For degree courses: 2-3 A levels and some GCSEs (A*-C) usually including English or equivalent qualifications. Some universities require A level English. Exact requirements depend on the degree you take.

• Scotland

Band 4: For entry to SQA higher national and professional development awards, usually 2-3 H grades and some S grades (1-3), including English and maths, or similar qualifications.

Band 5: For degree courses: 3-5 H grades and some S grades (1-3), usually including English or similar. Some universities require H grade English. Exact requirements depend on the degree you take.

Degree Information

Degrees can usually be in any subject, though for specialist magazines an employer may prefer specific knowledge of the subject and/or journalism. Graduates in science, engineering and technical subjects are in particular demand for magazines that cover these areas. Relevant postgraduate qualifications are available.

Adult Qualifications

Entry requirements may be relaxed for adults applying for higher education courses. Access or foundation courses give adults without qualifications a route on to degree courses.

Work Experience

Work experience gives you an insight into what you enjoy and don't enjoy about a job or working environment, as well as the opportunity to acquire new skills. It provides valuable information to add to your CV and improves your employment prospects. Experience is essential in journalism; practical experience in writing to deadlines is very valuable to employers, whether for student newspapers and magazines, local press, or the free press. Work experience is quite difficult to obtain from magazine publishers; the Periodicals Training Council offers advice on this.

Entry and Training

There are no official entry requirements or professional qualifications for this job, although most entrants are suitably qualified graduates. There are relevant HNDs, degrees/ postgraduate degrees and/or professional qualifications available. Relevant work experience can sometimes be more important to employers than qualifications, and some enter as editorial assistants for publishing houses or trainees with a magazine with experience of newspaper journalism. You may be asked to submit a portfolio of your work to demonstrate your commitment and potential for this work.

Whilst some specialist magazine employers expect a qualification in their particular publishing field, it is the quality of your writing skills that is an employer's priority and not the qualification gained. IT skills are valuable, particularly knowledge of programs such as Quark XPress. Training is often on the job and usually informal. Larger companies sometimes offer a range of training courses.

The National Council for the Training of Journalists (NCTJ) offers relevant short courses in media law, feature writing, production and design. The NCTJ also maintains a Journalism Diversity Fund. This has been set up by those in the industry who want to support the training of journalists from ethnic and socially diverse backgrounds. You need to show commitment and potential to qualifiy. Check the website for details.

The Periodicals Training Council (PTC), the national training arm of the trade association for the magazine industry, the Periodical Publishers Association (PPA), offers a range of professional vocational qualifications, such as the diploma in publishing, the professional certificate in journalism and the editorial diploma. It also runs a range of short courses on specialist topics. Relevant foundation degrees are available in some areas, which may be taken full or part time.

A Diploma/Welsh Baccalaureate may be available in your area in creative and media. This can be a useful introduction to this type of career as you gain practical experience while studying. See the diplomas website or Skillset for further information.

Mature applicants need previous work experience in writing or journalism. Experience in journalism/secretarial work or knowledge of the book trade is an advantage and a suitable specialist background is helpful for specific trade magazines. Postgraduate qualifications in journalism can be very useful in finding employment. Relevant distance-learning courses are also available such as those offered by the London School of Journalism and the National Council for the Training of Journalists (NCTJ).

Opportunities and Pay

More than 9,000 magazines are published in the UK, mainly in London and the South East, but competition for jobs is fierce. Most jobs are not advertised, and you need to approach publishers direct to try to gain work. You can work for a large multinational and/or multi-title publishing house, on a company in-house magazine, or for a small specialist magazine with only a few staff. Typical starter jobs include editorial assistant, junior reporter and staff writer. Some may progress to senior posts, including sub-editor or magazine features editor, or move into newspaper, radio or TV journalism. A high proportion of experienced magazine journalists now work freelance for a number of publishers.

Earnings vary depending upon the location, size and success of a magazine, though are usually higher in London and south-east England. Salaries can start at £18k-£26k a year depending on the level of experience, although sometimes in order to get into this work you may have to work for a time without pay. Senior staff earn up to £35k and those who progress to become chief editor, or work for a highly successful title can earn around £60k a year or more. Freelance salaries depend upon individual success.

Skills and Qualities

able to work both on your own and in a team, able to work to deadlines, creative flair, determined, enquiring mind, good communication skills, good interpersonal skills, good written English, interest in current affairs, IT skills, research skills

Relevant Subjects

Business and accounting, Economics, English, ICT/Computer studies, Media and communication studies, Psychology, Sociology

Further Information

Creative Choices - www.creative-choices.co.uk

Diplomas (Foundation, Higher and Advanced) - http://yp.direct.gov.uk/diplomas

Journalism Uncovered (Trotman 2009) - www.trotman.co.uk

Media Week (weekly) (Haymarket Publishing Ltd) - www.haymarket.com/mediaweek/default.aspx

National Council for the Training of Journalists (NCTJ) - www.nctj.com

Press Gazette - Journalism Today (Progressive Media International) - www.pressgazette.co.uk

Skillset - sector skills council for the creative media, fashion and textiles industries - www.skillset.org

What's it like to be a Magazine Editor? (A&C Black 2009)

▶Working in creative & media (2007) (Babcock Lifeskills) - www.babcock-lifeskills.com/

▶Working in English (2007) (Babcock Lifeskills) - www.babcock-lifeskills.com/

Addresses

London School of Journalism
126 Shirland Road Maida Vale, London W9 2BT
Phone: +44 (0) 20 7432 8140
Web: www.home-study.com

Periodical Publishers' Association (PPA)
(Periodicals Training Council)
Queens House, 28 Kingsway, London WC2B 6JR
Phone: +44 (0)207 404 4166
Web: www.ppa.co.uk/

Similar Jobs

Advertising Copywriter, Broadcast Journalist, Editorial Assistant: Publishing, Journalist, Magazine Features Editor, Writer, Writer: Technical

Journalist: Scientific

CRCI:Media, Print and Publishing
CLCI:FAC　　Job Band: 4 to 5

Job Description

Scientific journalists collect and report science-based news and features for publication in specialist magazines, journals, the Internet, or the national media. They research information, conduct interviews with people, check facts and attend events. Journalists write well written articles suited to the target audience and need to be able to explain complex technical/scientific information in a clear way. They cover diverse subjects and events of national or worldwide interest. Also visit research establishments, academic conferences and attend press conferences. Then research and write a report or article, using a computer, and submit it to a sub-editor. Can also work in broadcasting or advertising.

Work Details

Usually work a basic 39 hr week, though often has to work long and irregular hours, including evenings and weekends. Those who work for national newspapers and radio/television sometimes have to work shifts. Work is office based but you may also have to travel further afield and stay away from home overnight, or for longer periods. This work can be pressurised at times, if you have to report a story quickly or meet publication deadlines.

Outdoor reporting is in all weathers and conditions. The work can be demanding and stressful, often requiring instant decision-making, and working hard and fast, though maintaining accuracy. Knowledge of media law and ethics is essential.

Qualification

• England, Wales and Northern Ireland

Band 4: For pre-entry training course, such as a BTEC/HND, or direct entry to a traineeship: 1-2 A levels and some GCSEs (A*-C) usually including English, or equivalent.

Band 5: For degree, followed by traineeship or postgraduate course: 2-3 A levels and some GCSEs (A*-C) usually including English or equivalent qualifications. Some degrees in journalism require A level English. Exact requirements depend on the degree you take.

• Scotland

Band 4: For SQA/HND course in journalism or direct entry to traineeship: 2-3 H grades and some S grades (1-3) usually including English, or similar.

Band 5: For degree, followed by traineeship or postgraduate course: 3-5 H grades and some S grades (1-3), usually including English or similar. Some degrees in journalism require H grade English. Exact requirements depend on the degree you take.

Degree Information
Any degree is acceptable for entry to this job, but most employers prefer applicants with a science-based degree. A postgraduate qualification in journalism is an advantage, such as an MSc in science communication.

Adult Qualifications
Entry requirements may be relaxed for adults applying for higher education courses. Access or foundation courses give adults without qualifications a route on to degree courses.

Work Experience
Entry to this job/career is highly competitive and it is essential to have some relevant work or voluntary experience before applying for jobs or full-time training in journalism. Work on a school/student magazine, with a local radio station or writing for a local newspaper is relevant. The Economist and Nature magazines run internships for work experience. Similarly, the New Scientist runs an editorial trainee scheme for six months and provides paid work experience and training. You need a good science degree to apply.

Entry and Training
Most people who enter this job are graduates and a science degree may be preferred. Entry to training courses is highly competitive and you usually have to submit a portfolio of your work experience. Some colleges only grant places to those with work experience on a newspaper.

You may be able to enter a job directly and carry out your basic journalist training on the job. Part of the training is usually spent on a registered National Council for the Training of Journalists (NCTJ) distance-learning course, followed by a block or day-release course at a local college. At the end of the training you are expected to take the NCTJ National Certificate Examination. You can then move over to specialist scientific journalism later.

Alternatively, you can take a degree course first and follow this by a specialist postgraduate course in science communication, before entering the job. A few larger periodical publishers run graduate training schemes. Fast-track routes and specialist courses in newspaper journalism, media and newspaper law, are also available. Contact the NCTJ, the Association of British Science Writers (ABSW), or the Periodicals Training Council (PTC), for details of accredited training and courses.

Several foundation degrees in journalism are available. It is also be an advantage to have experience in shorthand and word processing, and a driving licence. A Diploma/Welsh Baccalaureate may be available in your area in creative and media. This can be a useful introduction to this type of career as you gain practical experience while studying. See the diplomas website or Skillset for further information.

Mature entrants with relevant experience are often considered by employers, and experts in a particular field may also be able to gain some freelance work. Distance-learning courses in journalism are available, such as those offered by the National Council for the Training of Journalists, and the London School of Journalism. The Open University also runs an MSc course in Science (Communications Science/Science and the Public). Bursaries may be available from the Wellcome Trust, see the Association of British Science Writers (ABSW) website.

Opportunities and Pay
Jobs are available with specialist scientific and technical magazines, periodicals and journals and trade and professional publications. Scientific correspondents are specialised journalists who work for national newspapers, radio and television companies. The growth in digital media may increase opportunities to move into broadcast journalism as a researcher, reporter or presenter. Environmental science is a particular growth area. It is possible to work on a freelance basis and work is available abroad.

Pay varies depending on the employer, but trainees usually earn around £18k-£22k a year. With experience, salary rates are around £28k-£40k a year, and those in senior posts can earn up to £46k, depending on their responsibilities. Highly successful scientific journalists can earn much more than this. Daily freelance rates are around £100-£150.

Skills and Qualities
able to cope under pressure, able to report accurately, analytical skills, enquiring mind, excellent communication skills, friendly, good written English, IT skills, motivated, observant, perseverance, resilient

Relevant Subjects
Biology, Chemistry, English, ICT/Computer studies, Mathematics, Media and communication studies, Physics, Science

Further Information
Creative Choices - www.creative-choices.co.uk

Diplomas (Foundation, Higher and Advanced) - http://yp.direct.gov.uk/diplomas

European Medical Writers' Association - www.emwa.org

Journalism Uncovered (Trotman 2009) - www.trotman.co.uk

National Council for the Training of Journalists (NCTJ) - www.nctj.com

Nature (weekly) (Nature Publishing Group) - www.nature.com/

New Scientist (weekly) (Reed) - www.newscientist.com

Skillset - sector skills council for the creative media, fashion and textiles industries - www.skillset.org

The Economist (weekly) (Economist Newspaper Ltd) - www.economist.com/

▶Working in creative & media (2007) (Babcock Lifeskills) - www.babcock-lifeskills.com/

▶Working in science (2007) (Babcock Lifeskills) - www.babcock-lifeskills.com/

Addresses
Association of British Science Writers (ABSW)
Wellcome Wolfson Building 165 Queen's Gate, London SW7 5HD
Phone: +44 (0)870 770 3361
Web: www.absw.org.uk

London School of Journalism
126 Shirland Road Maida Vale, London W9 2BT
Phone: +44 (0) 20 7432 8140
Web: www.home-study.com

Open University (OU)
PO Box 197, Milton Keynes MK7 6BJ
Phone: +44 (0)845 300 6090
Web: http://www3.open.ac.uk

Periodical Publishers' Association (PPA) (Periodicals Training Council)
Queens House, 28 Kingsway, London WC2B 6JR
Phone: +44 (0)207 404 4166
Web: www.ppa.co.uk/

Similar Jobs
Broadcast Journalist, Broadcast Researcher, Editor: Publishing, Journalist, Writer, Writer: Technical

Judge
CRCI:Legal and Political Services
CLCI:LAF — Job Band: 5

Job Description
Judges preside over law courts and make judgements based on the evidence presented, applying current law to determine a range of disputes. These may be disputes between individuals and public bodies, issues relating to family and children, or criminal trials. Most judges work in one type of court such as High Court, Court of

Appeal, County Court and so on. They listen to the information or evidence and come to a decision based on the presented facts and existing legislation.

In a jury trail, judges instruct and advise a jury based on the evidence. They have a thorough knowledge of the law and come to fair and firm conclusions. They pass sentence on those who are found guilty.

Work Details

You work in courts and in offices. Travel is sometimes necessary with nights away from home. Courts are found in many major towns and cities. Court sessions are usually held during the day, but some can continue on into the evening. You also frequently do work at home in the evenings, reading case notes and preparing for trial.

The work involves consultation with people such as barristers, solicitors and other professionals. Details of legal cases and facts have to be quickly analysed and thoroughly understood. Discretion is important as the work is of a confidential nature. The work can be demanding and stressful at times and can involve making difficult decisions. Yous wear formal dress and have to observe the traditions and formality of the court.

Qualification

You must be a qualified and substantially experienced barrister or solicitor before being selected as a judge.

- **England, Wales and Northern Ireland**

Band 5: For degree: three A levels and 5 GCSEs (A*-C) including English and maths, or equivalent qualifications. Exact requirements depend on the degree to be taken. Check individual prospectuses.

Degree Information

In England and Wales, graduates should have either a good honours 'qualifying' degree in law or a non-law degree plus the Common Professional Examination/Graduate Diploma in Law. For admission to the Roll of Solicitors, all must complete a Legal Practice Course (LPC). Barristers follow by a one-year full-time/two-year part-time Bar Vocational Course (BVC), at the Inns of Court School of Law, London (or at a number of institutions around the country), before being called to the Bar.

Adult Qualifications

You must first qualify as a barrister or solicitor. The study and training routes are common to all entrants. Contact the Law Society for further details. For those not already qualified in law, the lengthy training time and experience required should be considered carefully.

Work Experience

The Judiciary of England and Wales runs a judicial work shadowing scheme which gives lawyers the chance to spend three days observing the work of a judge, both in and out of court, before deciding whether to apply. See the Judiciary of England and Wales website for further details.

Entry and Training

Judges are barristers or solicitors that have usually been qualified for 5 -7 years. Fellows of the Institute of Legal Executives are also eligible for appointment as district judges and tribunal chairmen. Many of the barristers who become judges have already become a Queen's Counsel (QC). Refer to the job articles on Solicitor and Barrister for full details on their training routes and qualifications.

When there is a vacancy for a judge for Her Majesty's Courts Service or the Tribunal Service, solicitors and barristers may choose to put themselves forward for possible selection. They have to complete an application form, provide references and attend interviews. From the list of candidates, the Judicial Appointments Commission (JAC) selects a candidate based on merit alone, and then recommends this candidate for the post. Contact the JAC for further details of its selection process.

Most judges start in a part-time post as a deputy judge, before acquiring a full-time position.

All entrants to the profession need substantial previous experience as a lawyer.

Opportunities and Pay

Entry is extremely competitive and considerable talent is required for success. You need to be a highly experienced and successful lawyer to be appointed as a judge. The Ministry of Justice is responsible for arranging warrants and letters of appointment for judges, once they are recommended by the JAC. Senior positions, such as Lord Chief Justice, Judges of the Court of Appeal and Master of the Rolls, are made on the recommendation of the Prime Minister.

District judges' salaries are around £102k and senior district judges earn around £128k a year. Senior circuit judges earn £138k and High Court judges earn around £173k a year. The highest position in the land, the Lord Chief Justice, earns nearly £240k a year.

Skills and Qualities

able to cope under pressure, able to explain clearly, able to inspire confidence, analytical skills, articulate, decisive, information handling skills, integrity, objective, sound judgement

Relevant Subjects

Business and accounting, Economics, English, Government and politics, History, Law, Psychology, Sociology

Further Information

Judiciary of England and Wales - www.judiciary.gov.uk

Skills for Justice - sector skills council for the UK justice system - www.skillsforjustice.com

TARGETjobs: Law (GTI Specialist Publishing Ltd.) - www.groupgti.com

Addresses

Judicial Appointments Commission (JAC)
Steel House, 11 Tothill Street, London SW1H 9LH
Phone: +44 (0)203 334 0453
Web: www.judicialappointments.gov.uk

Similar Jobs

Barrister, European Law Solicitor, Solicitor

Kinesiologist

CRCI:Healthcare
CLCI:JOD Job Band: 2

Job Description

Kinesiologists assess human movement, performance, and function by applying the sciences of biomechanics, anatomy, physiology, and motor learning. Kinesiology is also known as human kinetics. They work to rehabilitate, prevent and manage disorders to maintain or enhance movement for sport, recreation, work and exercise. They may also provide consulting services, conduct research, and develop policies for rehabilitation, ergonomics and occupational health and safety.

The technique is a blend of the principles of traditional Chinese medicine and western techniques and treats the patient in a holistic way. It is based on muscle testing to get a picture of what is happening in the patient's meridian system, and to identify the best way to deal with the stress, be it emotional, physical, environmental, nutritional or mental. It can be used to treat babies and children, the elderly, athletes and performers or those who are injured or unwell. There are various types of kinesiology.

Work Details

Many kinesiologists are self-employed and choose to work hours that suit themselves and their clients. You may have to work flexible hours and be available at weekends and some evenings. You may use a room in your own home or rent a room, sometimes at a natural health clinic, fitness or rehabilitation clinic. Newly qualified kinesiologists often work very flexible hours to build up their clientele. Those who work in health clinics or in a business workplace have more regular hours, usually Monday to Friday, though there may be some evening clinics.

You may also need to travel around a particular area. You can work alongside other health professionals such as physiotherapists and you may be required to wear a white coat or tunic or uniform.

Qualification

Anyone can train in kinesiology but you need literacy and numeracy skills to be able to follow a training course. Students generally need to be literate in English and have the ability to study at A level.

• England, Wales and Northern Ireland

Band 2: For entry to jobs, no minimum qualifications are needed, but it is an advantage to have some GCSEs (A*-C) or equivalent in subjects that include English, maths and biology.

• Scotland

Band 2: Although academic qualifications are not specified for this job, it is an advantage to have some S grades (1-3) in subjects that include English, maths and biology, or similar.

Degree Information

There are no kinesiology degrees in the UK but they are available in the US.

Adult Qualifications

Formal qualifications are not specified, however, a good standard of education, together with some formal qualifications in subjects such as English, maths and a science, or equivalent, are useful. An interest in holistic health is beneficial.

Work Experience

Relevant work or voluntary experience can equip you with skills that you can use in the future and that you can add to your CV. There are often opportunities available for voluntary work which give you experience of working with people.

Entry and Training

This is a self-regulated profession in the UK and as there are many ways that you can train, these are just a few examples of training routes. The Diploma Course in Kinesiology is available from the Classical Kinesiology Institute (CKI) to anyone wanting to train as a kinesiologist in the UK or internationally and takes two to three years of part-time study including the CKI Foundation Course.

You can also achieve professional status with the Kinesiology Federation (KF) by taking a recognised foundation training course, plus advanced kinesiology training. The core subjects include anatomy and physiology, interpersonal skills, practice management and nutrition. The KF is a professional organisation representing kinesiology practitioners, instructors and schools from the range of kinesiologies available in the UK.

The KF has over 550 members who work to an established code of conduct and so recommends that at least 50% of training should be classroom based. The federation does not develop or provide training courses, but recommends courses that meet their professional standard. Members can go on to become registered professionals and internationally registered professionals. You must meet the requirements for continuing professional development and National Occupational Standards. Whilst training under the guidance of a mentor, you can become a KF Associate.

The School of Advanced Kinesiology also offers Association of Systematic Kinesiology accredited diploma courses which also meet National Occupational Standards.

Mature applicants are welcomed by training establishments and may have an advantage as life experience is valued in this job. Previous experience is not necessary for most courses although a medically-related background or experience in counselling or beauty therapy is useful. Accredited courses are usually offered through part-time study, evenings and weekends, as well as through distance-learning courses.

Opportunities and Pay

Interest in complementary therapy is growing so this is an expanding profession. Kinesiologists work all over the country and once trained, you may be able to join an existing practice to gain experience with established practitioners. Some go on to set up their own practice, usually hiring a room in a complementary therapy centre, or working from home.

There may also be increasing opportunities to work in the health promotion industry working with individuals to enhance their health, fitness, and well-being. Kinesiologists can also be found working in fitness and personal training facilities, and increasingly in industry in a health and safety role, assessing the suitability and design of workstations and providing suggestions for improvement. There may be opportunities to study other areas of complementary medicine, or to teach.

Kinesiologists are generally self-employed and a qualified practitioner can earn between £30-£50 an hour. You are likely to earn around £30k a year working full time as a kinesiology practitioner, though some may earn more.

Health

This job requires good general fitness and your hands need to be strong.

Skills and Qualities

able to put people at ease, business awareness, caring, friendly, good communication skills, good listening skills, good sense of touch, supportive, tactful

Relevant Subjects

Biology, Health and social care

Further Information

Association of Systematic Kinesiology - www.systematic-kinesiology.co.uk

Classical Kinesiology Institute (CKI) - www.classicalkinesiology.co.uk

Complementary and Natural Healthcare Report - May 2009 (Skills for Health) - www.skillsforhealth.org.uk

Kinesiology Federation - www.kinesiologyfederation.co.uk

School of Advanced Kinesiology (SAK) - www.schoolofadvancedkinesiology.com

The Academy of Systematic Kinesiology (TASK) - www.kinesiology.co.uk

Addresses

Institute for Complementary Medicine (ICM)
Can-Mezzanine, 32-36 Loman Street, London SE1 0EH
Phone: +44 (0)207 922 7980
Web: www.i-c-m.org.uk

Similar Jobs

Acupuncturist, Aromatherapist, Massage Therapist, Medical Herbalist, Naturopath, Reflexologist

Kitchen Assistant/Porter

CRCI:Catering and Hospitality
CLCI:IC Job Band: 1

Job Description

Kitchen assistants help chefs in restaurants, hotels and other catering places by making sure that food and equipment is always in the right place. They help to prepare food, including salad preparation, making sandwiches, mixing ingredients, cleaning, peeling and slicing vegetables, skinning fish, and chopping and dicing meat. Handles sharp knives, and electronic mixing, chopping and chipping equipment. Also does other tasks for kitchen staff.

Assistants help suppliers to unload deliveries. They unpack items and store food tidily and hygienically and also clean ovens and kitchen equipment. They may also load dishes and cutlery into a dishwasher or wash them by hand and tidy up and empty bins. Also helps to ensure that the kitchen and utensils are kept to a hygienic standard and follow safe working practices.

Work Details

Usually works a 37-40 hour week that may include a split shift/rota system covering early mornings, evenings, weekends, and public holidays. You are on your feet all the time, sometimes lifting and carrying heavy things. Kitchens are usually hot, noisy and often very busy. Some equipment, cleaning fluids and sharp knives are hazardous.

You have to follow strict rules about safety and hygiene. You need to wear a protective uniform, head covering and for some tasks, hygienic gloves or waterproof boots.

Qualification

• England, Wales and Northern Ireland

Band 1: For entry to jobs, no minimum qualifications are needed, but you are expected to have a good level of general education and relevant experience. Some formal/vocational qualifications at any level are useful. Employers look for applicants that show a willingness to learn together with an interest in food and its preparation, rather than formal educational qualifications.

• Scotland

Band 1: For entry to jobs, no minimum qualifications are needed, but you are expected to have a good level of general education and relevant experience. Some formal/vocational qualifications at any level are useful. Employers look for applicants that show a willingness to learn together with an interest in food and its preparation, rather than formal educational qualifications.

Adult Qualifications

Experience of hotel and catering work may be an advantage. No pre-entry qualifications are usually required for mature entrants, though some academic/vocational qualifications at any level may be helpful. You can improve your skills and qualifications by working through the Foundation Learning programme. This involves taking credit-based units and qualifications to help you progress.

Work Experience

Any work experience can help equip you with skills that you can use in the future and add to your CV. There is often plenty of paid part-time kitchen and catering work available.

Entry and Training

Although some employers take on people as young as 16, you must be at least 18 to do certain tasks, such as using meat-slicing equipment. You are usually trained on the job by experienced staff in how to handle equipment and prepare simple meals, or through a training scheme. Off-the-job training may consist of short courses in hygiene, food safety and food preparation at a local college. Those with a keen interest and ability may be offered further training towards qualifications in catering and ultimately to chef training.

S/NVQs include food processing and cooking at level 2. Relevant vocationally-related qualifications include the City & Guilds level 1-2 international vocational qualification (IVQ) certificate/diploma in food preparation and cooking. Training programmes, including apprenticeships in catering leading to level 2 and advanced apprenticeships leading to level 3, may be available in your area. A Diploma/Welsh Baccalaureate may also be available in your area in hospitality.

Mature applicants with relevant catering experience are usually welcomed by employers. Government training opportunities, such as apprenticeships, may be available in your area. You can also gain recognition of previous experience through Accreditation of Prior Learning (APL) or by working towards relevant S/NVQs. Contact your local careers office, Jobcentre Plus, Next Step service or Learning and Skills Council (LSC) Local Enterprise Company (LEC) for details of training schemes.

Opportunities and Pay

Around 400,000 people work as kitchen assistants or kitchen porters in the UK. You can find jobs in places including hotels, restaurants, holiday centres and other leisure operations, hospitals, schools, colleges, the armed forces or business restaurants/canteens. There is usually more work in the summer and at holiday times. In some cases it may be possible to train as a chef or cook. Other options are to move into bar work, food service, fast food or banqueting provision, portering or work as a hotel room attendant.

It is possible to find part-time and temporary work, and to find work abroad in large cities and holiday resorts. There are also short-term contract jobs with event companies (holding major tournaments/ sporting events etc) or with holiday companies.

Pay varies depending on the location and employer but most kitchen assistants earn up to £7.75 an hour, and average annual incomes are £11k-£16k. You may be given free or subsidised meals.

Health

This job requires good general fitness. People with certain skin conditions may not be able to do this job.

Skills and Qualities

able to work quickly, aptitude for teamwork, common sense, co-operative, hard working, neat, reliable, stamina, willing to learn

Relevant Subjects

Hospitality and catering

Further Information

Apprenticeship Schemes (National Apprenticeship Service) - www.apprenticeships.org.uk

CareerScope: Hospitality and Leisure (Springboard UK) - http://careerscope.springboarduk.net/

Caterer and Hotelkeeper (weekly) (Reed Business Information) - www.caterersearch.com/Home/

Diploma in Hospitality (People 1st) - www.hospitalitydiploma.co.uk

Foundation Learning (QCDA) - www.qcda.gov.uk

People 1st - sector skills council for hospitality, leisure, travel and tourism - www.people1st.co.uk

So you want to work in the Food Industry (Wayland) - www.waylandbooks.co.uk

Springboard UK (Springboard UK) - www.springboarduk.net

Springboard Wales (Springboard Wales) - http://wales.springboarduk.net/

Training Schemes - www.direct.gov.uk/en/educationandlearning

UKSP - Guide to Success in Hospitality, Leisure, Travel & Tourism - www.uksp.co.uk

►Working in hospitality & catering (2009) (Babcock Lifeskills) - www.babcock-lifeskills.com/

Addresses

Institute of Hospitality
Trinity Court, 34 West Street, Sutton, Surrey SM1 1SH
Phone: +44 (0)20 8661 4900
Web: www.instituteofhospitality.org

Similar Jobs

Baker, Bartender, Chef/Cook, Food Service Assistant, Waiter/Waitress

Laboratory Assistant

CRCI:Science, Mathematics and Statistics
CLCI:QOX Job Band: 1 to 3

Job Description

Laboratory assistants carry out a variety of routine tasks, such as labelling, weighing, measuring and preparing samples, including tissue and bacteria cultures, in an educational, industrial or medical laboratory . They are responsible for completing daily tasks, such as ensuring the laboratory is kept clean and tidy,, sterilising the equipment, maintaining stock levels and ordering supplies. May carry out basic repairs, calibrate equipment, complete simple tests and keep accurate records using a computer. Also set up equipment for experiments and clear it away when completed.

Work Details

Usually work a 35-39 hr week, Monday to Friday in a laboratory, mostly under the supervision of scientists and technicians. You are on your feet most of the day and usually wear a white coat or an overall and sometimes other protective clothing. In some jobs, you may have to deal with unpleasant substances and there can be a risk of minor injuries.

Qualification

• England, Wales and Northern Ireland

Band 1: For entry to jobs, no minimum qualifications are needed, but you are expected to have a good level of general education and relevant experience. Some formal/vocational qualifications at any level are useful.

Band 2: For entry to jobs, no minimum qualifications are needed, but it is an advantage to have some GCSEs (A*-C) or equivalent in subjects that include English, science and maths.

Band 3: For entry to jobs, HNC or a relevant Diploma, usually at least 4 GCSEs (A*-C) including English, science and maths, or equivalent.

• Scotland

Band 1: For entry to jobs, no minimum qualifications are needed, but you are expected to have a good level of general education and relevant experience. Some formal/vocational qualifications at any level are useful.

Band 2: Although academic qualifications are not specified for this job, it is an advantage to have some S grades (1-3) in subjects that include English, maths and science, or similar.

Band 3: For entry to jobs, usually at least four S grades (1-3) including English, science or maths, or similar.

Adult Qualifications

Formal qualifications are not essential, but it is beneficial to have a scientific background and some laboratory experience.

Work Experience

Employers or universities may prefer candidates who have relevant work or voluntary experience in such areas as hospital work in a laboratory, a university science department or in an industrial or commercial laboratory. Any work or experience within a scientific background is an advantage.

Entry and Training

Training is on the job and through in-service training courses. You may be able to study for a BTEC/SQA award or a City & Guilds qualification at a local college. Other qualifications, such as those offered by the Institute of Science & Technology (IST), may also be available depending on the employer. The IST offers preliminary and core vocational qualifications at registered IST centres. Training can lead to S/NVQ levels 2-3 in laboratory and associated technical activities. Training programmes, including apprenticeship schemes, may be available in your area. Advanced apprenticeships leading to qualification at level 3 can also be a route into higher education.

Mature applicants who show aptitude and have a scientific background and some laboratory experience may be preferred by some employers.

Opportunities and Pay

You may be employed by local or central government, research institutions, hospitals, engineering firms, manufacturing or processing companies, schools, colleges and universities. Opportunities for applicants with mathematical, scientific and computer skills are good at the moment in a wide range of different fields. Some public analysts' laboratories recruit school leavers as junior staff, depending on the size of the laboratory. Promotion usually depends on obtaining the relevant qualifications; opportunities are generally better in larger organisations.

Pay varies depending on area and employer, but a starting salary is likely to be £12.5k-£14.5k a year, rising to £18k-£22k a year with experience. Some assistants can earn as much as £24.5k a year. Salaries can be higher in the private sector, especially in high technology areas.

Health

You need normal colour vision for some areas of work and good eyesight. There is a risk of allergy from skin irritants and restrictions on certain skin disorders.

Skills and Qualities

able to work to deadlines, accurate, aptitude for teamwork, careful, co-operative, health & safety awareness, IT skills, methodical, reliable, willing to learn

Relevant Subjects

Chemistry, Health and social care, Science

Further Information

Apprenticeship Schemes (National Apprenticeship Service) - www.apprenticeships.org.uk

▶Working in science (2007) (Babcock Lifeskills) - www.babcock-lifeskills.com/

Addresses

Association for Science Education (ASE)
College Lane, Hatfield, Hertfordshire AL10 9AA
Phone: +44 (0)1707 283 000
Web: www.ase.org.uk

Institute of Science & Technology (IST)
Kingfisher House, 90 Rockingham Street, Sheffield S1 4EB
Phone: +44 (0)114 276 3197
Web: www.istonline.org.uk

Similar Jobs

Laboratory Assistant: Medical, Laboratory Technician: Education, Laboratory Technician: Science, Operating Department Practitioner, Sterile Services Technician

Laboratory Assistant: Medical

CRCI:Science, Mathematics and Statistics
CLCI:JAX Job Band: 1 to 3

Job Description

Medical laboratory assistants work in medical pathology labs analysing samples of body tissue and fluids taken from hospital patients. They undertake daily routine tasks and support the work of biomedical scientists and technicians to help diagnose and treat patients. Work includes preparing for tests and using computers to analyse and record the data. They are responsible for labelling and sorting of tissue samples and for the disposal of chemical/biological waste. Also make up solutions of chemicals, carry out quality control on chemical stocks and keep stock control records of incoming chemicals and for ordering fresh supplies. Reports on results to superiors.

Assistants use their skills to support any aspect of pathology: clinical chemistry, haematology, transfusion science, cytopathology, histopathology, medical microbiology, immunology and tissue typing.

Work Details

Usually work a normal 9-5 week, Monday to Friday, in a hospital laboratory or outpatient's clinic. Work mostly under the supervision of scientists and technicians. You are on your feet most of the day. There is a risk of minor injuries. In some jobs, you may have to deal with unpleasant substances. Your work demands skill, attention to detail and a responsible attitude. A white coat or an overall and sometimes other protective clothing is usually worn.

Qualification

- **England, Wales and Northern Ireland**

Band 1: For entry to jobs, no minimum qualifications are needed, but you are expected to have a good level of general education and relevant experience. Some formal/vocational qualifications at any level are useful.

Band 2: For entry to jobs, no minimum qualifications are needed, but it is an advantage to have some GCSEs (A*-C) or equivalent in subjects that include English, science and maths.

Band 3: For entry to jobs, HNC or a relevant Diploma, usually at least 4 GCSEs (A*-C) including English, science and maths, or equivalent.

- **Scotland**

Band 1: For entry to jobs, no minimum qualifications are needed, but you are expected to have a good level of general education and relevant experience. Some formal/vocational qualifications at any level are useful.

Band 2: Although academic qualifications are not specified for this job, it is an advantage to have some S grades (1-3) in subjects that include English, maths and science, or similar.

Band 3: For entry: usually at least four S grades (1-3) including English, maths and a science, or similar.

Adult Qualifications

Formal qualifications are not essential, but are beneficial.

Work Experience

Employers may prefer candidates who have relevant work or voluntary experience in a medical or healthcare setting such as a hospital or residential care home. Work experience can equip you with skills that you can use in the future to add to your CV.

Entry and Training

Training is mainly on the job and begins with general safety instructions. Trainees then move onto specialised training. Certificates of competence can be awarded for the safe performance of various duties, which help if you move to similar work for another employer. You can gain preliminary and core vocational qualifications that are offered by the Institute of Science & Technology (IST). There is no central recruitment for vacancies at this level. Such vacancies are advertised locally. Contact your local general hospital or healthcare trust for vacancies and entry requirements.

Your training can lead to an S/NVQ at level 2 in clinical laboratory support or laboratory activities. Training programmes, including apprenticeship schemes, may be available in your area. Advanced apprenticeships leading to qualification at level 3 can also be a route into higher education.

Adult entry is common and mature applicants may be preferred by some employers if they show aptitude and have relevant laboratory experience. It is useful to have a scientific background.

Opportunities and Pay

You are usually employed by a hospital or NHS trust, Health Protection Agency (HPA), private clinic or laboratory. Over 3,000 medical laboratory assistants (MLAs) work in the UK, most in NHS pathology laboratories. MLAs that show particular aptitude are encouraged to become trainee biomedical scientists, though the job is not a route to qualifying as a biomedical scientist.

There is a single salary grade for all MLAs, though extra salary points may be awarded for a post that requires additional skill and responsibilities. Trainees earn around £12.5k a year, rising to nearly £21k with experience. Some specialists such as cytology screeners and phlebotomists may be paid more. There may be additional payments for weekend and evening work and for working in London.

Health

You need normal colour vision for some areas of work and good eyesight. There is a risk of allergy from skin irritants and restrictions on certain skin disorders.

Skills and Qualities

able to follow instructions, able to work to deadlines, accurate, aptitude for teamwork, good organisational skills, health & safety awareness, IT skills, methodical, not squeamish, scientific approach

Relevant Subjects

Biology, Chemistry, Health and social care, Science

Further Information

Apprenticeship Schemes (National Apprenticeship Service) - www.apprenticeships.org.uk

NHS Careers (NHS Careers) - www.nhscareers.nhs.uk

The Biomedical Scientist (monthly) (Institute of Biomedical Science (IBMS)) - www.ibms.org/

▶Working in science (2007) (Babcock Lifeskills) - www.babcock-lifeskills.com/

Addresses

Health Protection Agency (HPA)
7th Floor , Holborn Gate, 330 High Holborn, London WC1V 7PP
Phone: +44 (0)20 7759 2700
Web: www.hpa.org.uk

Institute of Science & Technology (IST)
Kingfisher House, 90 Rockingham Street, Sheffield S1 4EB
Phone: +44 (0)114 276 3197
Web: www.istonline.org.uk

Similar Jobs

Laboratory Assistant, Laboratory Technician: Education, Laboratory Technician: Science, Operating Department Practitioner, Pharmacy Technician, Sterile Services Technician

Laboratory Technician: Education

CRCI:Science, Mathematics and Statistics
CLCI:QOX Job Band: 3 to 5

Job Description

Laboratory technicians in education generally specialise in one area of science doing routine and practical tasks essential to research and development. They see that equipment and materials are ready for science experiments in class or course work. May work in a physics, chemistry or biology laboratory. Work closely with the teacher/lecturer and are responsible for setting up experiments and checking apparatus. May help the teacher/ lecturer to demonstrate and explain tasks to students.

Technicians record results, collate and prepare data for analysis. They also tidy the laboratory and ensure equipment is clean and safe according to health and safety regulations. They are responsible for the safe disposal of laboratory waste, ordering new equipment and materials and may repair damaged items.

Work Details

Usually work in a laboratory from Monday to Friday, and may be employed for around 30 hrs a week, term time only, or 35-39 hrs a week full time. This job involves a certain amount of routine work and requires a high degree of accuracy. You advise and help school students or young adults in college or university. There is sometimes a risk of exposure to harmful substances, such as unpleasant fumes or contact with dangerous materials. You may need to wear a white coat or an overall and safety glasses.

Qualification

It is common for those with higher qualifications such as A levels or equivalent, or a relevant degree, to enter this job. A number of employers may look for applicants who hold qualifications in laboratory science.

• England, Wales and Northern Ireland

Band 3: For entry to jobs, HNC or a relevant Diploma, usually at least 4 GCSEs (A*-C) including English and maths, or equivalent.

Band 4: For HND, Diploma of Higher Education or foundation degree: 1-2 A levels and some GCSEs (A*-C) usually including English, science and maths, or equivalent.

Band 5: For degree courses: 2-3 A levels preferably including chemistry, maths or physics and some GCSEs (A*-C) usually including English, maths and science, or equivalent. Exact requirements depend on the degree you take.

• Scotland

Band 3: For course entry: usually four S grades (1-3) including maths, English and two science subjects, or similar.

Band 4: For entry to SQA higher national and professional development awards, usually 2-3 H grades and some S grades (1-3), including English, science and maths, or similar qualifications.

Band 5: For degree courses: usually 3-5 H grades preferably including chemistry, maths or physics and some S grades (1-3) including English, maths and science, or similar. Exact requirements depend on the degree you take.

Degree Information

A degree in science subjects such as biology, physics or chemistry or more specialised subjects that include ecology, biomedical science, biophysics, geology and pharmacology, is relevant. A wide range of postgraduate qualifications is available.

Adult Qualifications

Entry qualifications may vary depending on experience and may be relaxed for adults applying for higher education courses. Access or foundation courses give adults without qualifications a route on to degree courses.

Work Experience

Relevant work or voluntary experience is always useful and can improve your application chances for entry to this career/job. Related laboratory work is helpful, as you need to be aware of all the equipment and chemicals used in schools, colleges and universities. Awareness or experience of the science curriculum at secondary level is a distinct advantage.

Entry and Training

Applicants must have a Criminal Records Bureau (CRB) check. Training is through practical work experience and usually, study for a relevant BTEC/SQA course, or through the Institute of Science & Technology's (ISTs) professional examinations. Most courses last for 2-3 years and include work experience. They can be part time, day or block release, or sometimes full time. Some trainees start through an apprenticeship programme and training may lead to an appropriate S/NVQ. You may be able to continue your studies for a higher qualification. In-service training courses are also available such as those offered by the Association for Science Education (ASE). Courses include specialised one-day events on a variety of subjects such as data logging, health and safety, and subject/Key Stage courses.

The ASE also offers short courses for those with little experience to management/administration level, and membership gives access to useful resources. Technician membership and relevant foundation degrees are also available. Training programmes, including apprenticeship schemes, may be available in your area. Advanced apprenticeships leading to qualification at level 3 can also be a route into higher education.

Over 90% of education laboratory technicians in schools and colleges are over 30 years of age so mature applicants with a scientific background, up-to-date knowledge and experience of laboratory work have an advantage.

Opportunities and Pay

Around 20,000 education laboratory technicians are employed in the UK. You may work for a local education authority or the governing board of an individual or independent school, a university or college. Part-time work during term time is common. Promotion is to senior technician or laboratory manager. Some train to become teachers, lecturers or research scientists. There may be competition for jobs but there is an overall shortage of experienced technicians.

Pay varies depending on area and employer, as well as your qualifications and experience. A starting salary of around £13k a year, rising to between £20k-£25k a year with experience is usual. Those in senior posts can earn around £30k-£40k a year. University salaries tend to be higher.

Health

In this job you need normal colour vision for some areas of work, good eyesight, and also a good sense of smell. There may be restrictions on certain skin conditions and you should not be allergic to any skin irritants.

Skills and Qualities

able to cope under pressure, accurate, attention to detail, efficient, good organisational skills, health & safety awareness, IT skills, numeracy skills, responsible attitude, scientific approach

Relevant Subjects

Biology, Chemistry, Mathematics, Physics, Science

Further Information

Apprenticeship Schemes (National Apprenticeship Service) - www.apprenticeships.org.uk

Education in Science (Association for Science Education) - www.ase.org.uk/htm/journals/

▶Working in schools & colleges (2007) (Babcock Lifeskills) - www.babcock-lifeskills.com/

▶Working in science (2007) (Babcock Lifeskills) - www.babcock-lifeskills.com/

Addresses

Association for Science Education (ASE)
College Lane, Hatfield, Hertfordshire AL10 9AA
Phone: +44 (0)1707 283 000
Web: www.ase.org.uk

CLEAPSS School Science Service
The Gardiner Building, Brunel Science Park, Kingston Lane, Uxbridge UB8 3PQ
Phone: +44 (0)1895 251496
Web: www.cleapss.org.uk

Institute of Science & Technology (IST)
Kingfisher House, 90 Rockingham Street, Sheffield S1 4EB
Phone: +44 (0)114 276 3197
Web: www.istonline.org.uk

Society of Biology
9 Red Lion Court, London EC4A 3EF
Phone: +44 (0)20 7936 5900
Web: http://societyofbiology.org/home

Similar Jobs

Animal Technician/Technologist, Biomedical Scientist, Civil Service Scientific Officer, Dental Technician/Technologist, Laboratory Assistant, Laboratory Technician: Science

Laboratory Technician: Science

CRCI:Science, Mathematics and Statistics
CLCI:QOX Job Band: 3 to 5

Job Description

Science laboratory technicians generally specialise in one area of science doing routine and practical tasks essential to research and development. Tasks vary depending on the scientific area such as genetics, biology, microbiology, chemistry, food science or agriculture. May include carrying out experiments and taking measurements, testing samples, preparing and analysing substances. They record results, collate and prepare data for analysis and write reports. Also take responsibility for the safe disposal of laboratory waste.

Technicians use sophisticated high-technology including computers. They also clean, calibrate and maintain equipment and check for accuracy. Also order new equipment and materials and may repair damaged items.

Work Details

Usually work a basic 35-39 hr week, Monday to Friday. If you are employed in a manufacturing or processing industry you may be expected to work shifts. This job involves a certain amount of routine work and requires a high degree of accuracy. Laboratory technicians usually work in a team, assisting senior scientists. There is sometimes a risk of exposure to harmful substances, such as unpleasant fumes, or contact with dangerous materials. You may need to wear a white coat or an overall and safety glasses.

Qualification

It is common for those with higher education qualifications, including relevant degrees or similar, to enter this job. A number of employers may look for applicants who hold qualifications in laboratory science.

• England, Wales and Northern Ireland

Band 3: For entry to jobs, HNC or a relevant Diploma, usually at least 4 GCSEs (A*-C) including maths, English and two science subjects, or equivalent.

Band 4: For HND, Diploma of Higher Education or foundation degree: 1-2 A levels and some GCSEs (A*-C) usually including maths, science and English, or equivalent.

Band 5: For degree courses: 2-3 A levels preferably including chemistry, maths or physics and some GCSEs (A*-C) usually including English, maths and science, or equivalent. Exact requirements depend on the degree you take.

• Scotland

Band 3: For entry to jobs or course entry, usually at least four S grades (1-3) including including maths, English and two science subjects, or similar.

Band 4: For entry to SQA higher national and professional development awards, usually 2-3 H grades and some S grades (1-3), including maths, science and English, or similar.

Band 5: For degree courses: 3-5 H grades preferably including chemistry, maths or physics and some S grades (1-3), usually including English, maths and science, or similar. Exact requirements depend on the degree you take.

Degree Information

A wide range of relevant degrees in science subjects such as biology, physics or chemistry or more specialised subjects including genetics, nutrition, ecology, biomedical science, analytical chemistry, biophysics, geology, meteorology and pharmacology are available.

Adult Qualifications

Entry qualifications may vary, depending on experience. Entry requirements may be relaxed for adults applying for higher education courses. Access or foundation courses give adults without qualifications a route onto degree courses.

Work Experience

Employers or universities may prefer applicants who have relevant work or voluntary experience, such as work in a hospital laboratory, a university science department or in an industrial or commercial laboratory. If this proves difficult to obtain, then any work with a scientific background is an advantage.

Entry and Training

Training is through practical experience and usually a relevant BTEC/SQA course, or the Institute of Science & Technology's (IST's) professional examinations. A wide range of courses is available covering laboratory work in medical physics, food science and other technologies, as well as the individual sciences. Courses usually last for 2-3 years, include work experience and are part time, day, block release, or full time. There are relevant foundation degrees in some areas. In-service training courses are also available.

Training may lead to relevant S/NVQs, such as laboratory and associated technical activities at levels 2-4. Training programmes, including apprenticeship schemes, may be available in your area. Advanced apprenticeships leading to qualification at level 3 can also be a route into higher education.

Mature applicants require a scientific background. Up-to-date knowledge is valuable, as is experience of laboratory work.

Opportunities and Pay

Over 80,000 laboratory technicians are employed in the UK. You can work for local or central government, research institutions, the health service, forensic science laboratories, the food industry, brewing companies, and manufacturing or processing companies. Promotion is aided by qualifications and your willingness to move around the country to gain experience. You can progress to managing a laboratory or section; such opportunities are generally better in larger organisations. Opportunities for applicants with mathematical, scientific and computer skills are generally good.

Pay varies depending on area and employer, but generally technicians start on £12k-£13k a year, rising to around £20k-£22k with experience. Those in senior posts can earn around £30k-£40k a year.

Health
You should have normal colour vision for some areas of work and good eyesight. In some jobs a good sense of smell may be necessary and there may be restrictions on certain skin conditions.

Skills and Qualities
accurate, analytical skills, aptitude for teamwork, aptitude for teamwork, health & safety awareness, IT skills, resourceful, responsible attitude, scientific approach

Relevant Subjects
Biology, Chemistry, Mathematics, Physics, Science

Further Information
Local Government Careers (Improvement and Development Agency) - www.lgcareers.com/publications/

▶Working in science (2007) (Babcock Lifeskills) - www.babcock-lifeskills.com/

Addresses
Institute of Science & Technology (IST)
Kingfisher House, 90 Rockingham Street, Sheffield S1 4EB
Phone: +44 (0)114 276 3197
Web: www.istonline.org.uk

Society of Biology
9 Red Lion Court, London EC4A 3EF
Phone: +44 (0)20 7936 5900
Web: http://societyofbiology.org/home

Similar Jobs
Animal Technician/Technologist, Biomedical Scientist, Civil Service Scientific Officer, Laboratory Assistant, Laboratory Assistant: Medical, Laboratory Technician: Education

Labourer: General

CRCI:Manufacturing and Production
CLCI:S Job Band: 1

Job Description
Labourers carry out a number of different labouring tasks in industrial premises, including a foundry, builder's yard or workshop. Some jobs are more demanding, with heavy lifting; others involve light labouring and are not as strenuous. Sometimes labourers act as 'mate' to a skilled craftworker. Daily tasks include moving materials about to where they are required or stored, and loading or stacking newly delivered goods. May help to set up and operate machines. Should be able to use work tools, trolleys and operate lifting machinery. Duties include cleaning the equipment and work area and helping in the safe removal of any waste and rubbish.

Work Details
Labourers usually work a 39 hr week and may work shifts, including a Saturday. Your place of work is an industrial premises or a workshop, and conditions can sometimes be noisy, dirty or dusty. Usually you help other workers. This is an active job and you are on your feet most of the time. You have to do heavy lifting and may climb ladders. There is a risk of minor injuries, and you may need to wear overalls or other protective clothing.

Qualification

• England, Wales and Northern Ireland
Band 1: You do not require formal qualifications to do this work though an employer may ask you to take a practical test to assess your manual dexterity. However, some formal/vocational qualifications at any level are useful.

• Scotland
Band 1: You do not require formal qualifications to do this work though an employer may ask you to take a practical test to assess your manual dexterity. However, some formal/vocational qualifications at any level are useful.

Adult Qualifications
General secondary education is expected. You can improve your skills and qualifications by working through the Foundation Learning programme. This involves taking credit-based units and qualifications to help you progress.

Work Experience
Work or voluntary experience is always useful. It can add to your CV and improve your chances when applying for jobs or apprenticeships in the manufacturing industry. Your personal or adult guidance adviser should be able to advise you about how to get some work experience.

Entry and Training
Your training is on the job, working with an experienced person or you may attend an employer's training scheme. Relevant S/NVQs in driving and machinery operations are available. Training programmes, including apprenticeships leading to level 2, may be available in your area. A Diploma/Welsh Baccalaureate in manufacturing and product design may be available in your area.

Government training opportunities, such as apprenticeships, may be available in your area. You can also gain recognition of previous experience through Accreditation of Prior Learning (APL) or by working towards relevant S/NVQs. Contact your local careers office, Jobcentre Plus, Next Step service or Learning and Skills Council (LSC) Local Enterprise Company (LEC) for details of training schemes.

Opportunities and Pay
General labouring jobs are available mainly in manufacturing companies. Job opportunities are mostly in towns and cities. With experience you can progress to supervisory level.

Pay varies depending on area and employer. Most general labourers earn between £220-£330 a week; a few higher earners make more than £400 a week. Pay can be increased significantly with overtime.

Health
You need to be in good health and have plenty of stamina to do this job.

Skills and Qualities
able to follow instructions, able to work both on your own and in a team, common sense, co-operative, hard working, practical skills, strong

Further Information
Apprenticeship Schemes (National Apprenticeship Service) - www.apprenticeships.org.uk

Diplomas (Foundation, Higher and Advanced) http://yp.direct.gov.uk/diplomas

Foundation Learning (QCDA) - www.qcda.gov.uk

Training Schemes - www.direct.gov.uk/en/educationandlearning
Welsh Baccalaureate - www.wbq.org.uk

Similar Jobs
Construction Operative, Foundry Process Operative, Oil & Gas Roustabout/Roughneck

Laminator

also known as: Boat Laminator, GRP Laminator

CRCI:Manufacturing and Production

CLCI:SAN Job Band: 1 to 2

Job Description

Laminators work with polymer-composite materials, such as glass reinforced plastics (GRP) to produce a range of items such as glass-fibre hulls (main bodies) of boats, parts for the aero industry, panels for racing cars and helmets. Boats can range from large and small leisure yachts, dinghies and jet-skis, to military vessels, including patrol boats and landing crafts. Laminators work from designs and specifications supplied by a customer. They cover the inside of a mould by heating and pressing layers of glass-fibre resin and matting and use a varied number of layers in different areas of the mould. This strengthens and waterproofs particular parts of the finished hull.

Laminators use wool or metal rollers to remove any air bubbles that are trapped between the layers of resin and matting. They need to wait until each layer is sufficiently hardened before applying the next layer of materials. In the case of large items, such as the hulls of boats, removes the mould from the completed glass-fibre hull with the use of specialised cranes. A variety of power sanders are then used to polish the hull to a fine gloss finish.

Work Details

Laminators usually work a basic 37-40 hr week; Monday to Friday, though may have to work longer to meet deadlines for a project. This job requires a lot of standing, lifting and bending. The work environment is usually in a large, warm and environmentally-controlled building that helps to harden the resins more quickly. Air-conditioning removes any smells and dust, though you are required to wear a protective face mask. You are also provided with industrial gloves and a protective overall.

Qualification

• England, Wales and Northern Ireland

Band 1: No minimum qualifications are required, but you are expected to have a good level of general education. However, some formal/vocational qualifications at any level are useful.

Band 2: Although academic qualifications are not specified for this job, it is an advantage to have some GCSEs (A*-C) in subjects that include English, maths and science or equivalent.

• Scotland

Band 1: No minimum qualifications are required, but you are expected to have a good level of general education. However, some formal/vocational qualifications at any level are useful.

Band 2: Although academic qualifications are not specified for this job, it is an advantage to have some S grades (1-3) in subjects that include English, maths and science, or similar.

Adult Qualifications

For adults, no pre-entry qualifications are usually required though some academic/vocational qualifications at any level may be an advantage. English, maths and science are useful subjects.

Work Experience

Relevant work or voluntary experience is always useful. It can improve your chances when applying for jobs or apprenticeships. Your personal or adult guidance adviser should be able to advise you about how to get some work experience. However, any experience in a manual trade is an advantage. Most important is a willingness to learn new skills and to work hard. You can gain some work experience by contacting a local boat builder or shipyard before applying for a job as a trainee.

In some areas there is a young apprenticeship (14-16) scheme that provides an extended work placement. This can lead to achievement of a relevant level 2 qualification whilst at school.

Entry and Training

Most training is on the job with an experienced laminator, though you may be able to gain job-specific qualifications through a training programme whilst working, such as S/NVQs. Or you may be offered on-the-job training together with a day or block-release course at a local college or training centre, to gain relevant qualifications in polymer/plastics. S/NVQs are available at levels 2-3 in materials processing and finishing. Training programmes, including apprenticeships leading to level 2 and advanced apprenticeships leading to level 3, may be available. See British Marine Federation for details.

A Diploma/Welsh Baccalaureate in either manufacturing and product design or engineering may be available in your area. Both of these courses are relevant for this work and can provide a good background.

Any relevant experience of operating machinery and work in manufacturing production is helpful. An ability to follow charts and diagrams is an advantage. Government training opportunities, such as apprenticeships, may be available in your area. You can also gain recognition of previous experience through Accreditation of Prior Learning (APL) or by working towards relevant S/NVQs. Contact your local careers office, Jobcentre Plus, Next Step service or Learning and Skills Council (LSC) Local Enterprise Company (LEC) for details of training schemes.

Opportunities and Pay

You can work for a specialist boat builder in a large or small shipyard. This is likely to be based on the UK coast or on a river or canal, principally on the south coast, in the South West, East Anglia, Wales, western Scotland, the Midlands and the Thames Valley. There are similar work opportunities as a laminator within the automotive and aeronautical manufacturing industries, or with a specialised laminating company that supplies products to other industries. Promotion to supervisory level is possible, especially for those with relevant qualifications.

Pay rates start at around £10k a year for apprentices, rising to around £20k-£25k with experience. Senior laminators earn up to £30k a year. Shift allowances and overtime can substantially increase your pay.

Health

A good level of stamina and physical fitness is required.

Skills and Qualities

able to follow drawings and plans, able to follow instructions, able to work quickly, accurate, aptitude for teamwork, attention to detail, manual dexterity, numeracy skills, practical skills, prepared to do repetitive tasks

Relevant Subjects

Design and technology, Manufacturing

Further Information

Apprenticeship Schemes (National Apprenticeship Service) - www.apprenticeships.org.uk

Diplomas (Foundation, Higher and Advanced) - http://yp.direct.gov.uk/diplomas

SEMTA - sector skills council for science, engineering and manufacturing technologies - www.semta.org.uk

Training Schemes - www.direct.gov.uk/en/educationandlearning

Welsh Baccalaureate - www.wbq.org.uk

Addresses

British Marine Federation (BMF)
Marine House, Thorpe Lea Road, Egham, Surrey TW20 8BF
Phone: +44 (0)1784 473 377
Web: www.britishmarine.co.uk

British Plastics Federation (BPF)
6 Bath Place, Rivington Street, London EC2A 3JE
Phone: +44 (0)20 7457 5000
Web: www.bpf.co.uk

Similar Jobs
Boatbuilder, Marine Craft Worker: Ships, Polymer/Plastics Process Operative, Polymer/Plastics Technician, Vehicle Body Repairer

Landscape Architect

CRCI:Environment, Animals and Plants
CLCI:UL Job Band: 5

Job Description
Landscape architects plan and design outdoor spaces, both urban or rural, such as the area around buildings, or land that used to be industrial, including mines and quarries. They make designs that are sustainable and at the same time aesthetically pleasing. The discipline of landscape architecture combines environment and design, art and science.

Architects work in may places, which may be anything from a new motorway, hospital or power station, to the improvement or redevelopment of an existing site. May also work on projects such as a recreation park, a private estate or a housing estate. They visit the proposed site to access its suitability and consider the scientific and technical aspects of the project before preparing drawings and plans, often using computer-aided design programs (CAD). Then estimate the project cost and prepare a contract.

Architects select contractors, monitor and supervise progress on-site and ensure that work is completed on time. May specialise in one or more areas of design, management or landscape science. They work with other professionals, including planners, surveyors, architects and civil engineers.

Work Details
Usually work a basic 37 hr five-day week, though overtime or very long hours may be expected at times. The work is office based, but you also work on-site and travel over quite a wide area. Meeting clients and advising them is central to your work, as well as negotiating and consulting with other professionals. In addition to gathering information, you are responsible for analysing details, presenting facts and writing reports. On-site conditions can be cold, muddy and damp and you may also have to cover rough ground. Protective clothing, such as a hard hat and boots, need to be worn on site visits.

Qualification

- **England, Wales and Northern Ireland**

Band 5: For degree courses: 2-3 A levels, such as geography, art and design, environmental science and biology, and some GCSEs (A*-C) usually including English and maths, or equivalent. Exact requirements depend on the degree you take.

- **Scotland**

Band 5: For degree courses: 3-5 H grades, such as geography, art and design, environmental science and biology, and some S grades (1-3), usually including English and maths, or similar qualifications. Exact requirements depend on the degree you take.

Degree Information
A degree in landscape architecture is preferred, but a good first degree in a related subject, followed by a postgraduate landscape architecture course, is also acceptable. There are a wide variety of accredited courses on offer including landscape design, environmental conservation, landscape management and restoration, and combinations with planning and ecology.

Adult Qualifications
Some academic institutions may have special entry standards for mature applicants. Those with relevant experience eg at technician level in architecture, horticulture, botany or forestry, may be exempt from normal minimum requirements for entry to courses. Check with individual universities and colleges for details.

Graduates in relevant subjects can take a postgraduate course. A list of accredited courses may be obtained from the Landscape Institute.

Work Experience
Entry to this career is highly competitive and it is essential that you try to do some relevant work or voluntary experience before applying to jobs or university courses. The most relevant experience is ideally time spent with a landscape architect, or work in an architect's office, a planning department of a local authority, or in some aspect of land and property management. Contact the Landscape Institute (LI) for further information.

Entry and Training
Most landscape architects first complete an undergraduate/postgraduate course accredited by the Landscape Institute (LI). First degree courses are studied in three or four years plus a placement year, with postgraduate courses (usually following a related first degree) taking two years full time, or longer if part time. Relevant foundation degrees are also available. For entry to courses, some institutions require you to submit a portfolio of your work in art and design.

After your accredited course, a year's practical experience and graduate diploma, you can qualify as an associate of the Landscape Institute (ALI). The next step is to undertake a two-year period of mentored experience, which is part of the 'Pathway to Chartership' (P2C). This is followed by the final stage which includes an oral examination. Successful completion of the 'Pathway' means you are eligible to become a fully qualified member of the Landscape Institute (MLI) and achieve chartered landscape architect status. When fully qualified you are expected to complete at least 20 hours a year of continuing professional development (CPD).

Mature applicants are encouraged, and those with related degrees may take full or part-time postgraduate courses. Funding for postgraduate study may be available from the Economic and Social Research Council (ESRC). Those graduates in non-related subjects who wish to re-qualify as landscape architects, may take a two year course in landscape design. See the Landscape Institute website for details of courses in colleges and universities.

Opportunities and Pay
Employment is throughout the UK, with good opportunities as the industry is rapidly expanding. Qualified chartered professionals are currently in demand due to current concerns about conservation and the quality of our environment. Around half work in private practice, but some are employed in the construction industry, forestry work, the civil service, voluntary organisations, such as the National Trust, government agencies (eg Natural England, Scottish Natural Heritage and the Countryside Council for Wales), environmental charities (eg Groundwork) or with water companies. There may be opportunities to teach in a university or college, or to work overseas, particularly in Europe, the Far East, and the Middle East.

Pay varies depending on location and employer. Salaries for graduates are likely to be around £20k, rising to £25k-£45k a year when qualified as a chartered landscape architect. Salaries are usually higher in the private sector, particularly if you become a partner.

Skills and Qualities
able to manage a budget and keep records, able to take responsibility, able to work to deadlines, aptitude for fieldwork, creative flair, drawing ability, environmental awareness, good spoken communication, good written English, IT skills, leadership qualities, planning skills

Relevant Subjects
Art and Design, Biology, Construction and built environment, Design and technology, English, Geography, Land and Environment, Mathematics, Science

Further Information

Garden Design Journal (10 x year) (Society of Garden Designers) - www.sgd.org.uk

Groundwork UK - www.groundwork.org.uk

I want to be a landscape architect (LI) (Landscape Institute (LI)) - www.iwanttobealandscapearchitect.com/

Landscape (quarterly) (Landscape Institute) - www.landscapeinstitute.org/

Lantra - The Sector Skills Council for environmental & land-based sector (Lantra) http:/www.lantra.co.uk

Lantra Careers (A Future In...) (Lantra) - www.afuturein.com

Local Government Careers (Improvement and Development Agency) - www.lgcareers.com/publications/

Planning Architecture Design Database (Queens University Belfast) - www.paddi.net

▶Working in art & design (2009) (Babcock Lifeskills) - www.babcock-lifeskills.com/

Addresses

British Association of Landscape Industries (BALI)
Landscape House, Stoneleigh Park, National Agricultural Centre, Coventry CV8 2LG
Phone: +44 (0)24 7669 0333
Web: www.bali.co.uk

Countryside Council for Wales
Maes-y-Ffynnon, Penrhosgarnedd, Bangor, Gwynedd LL57 2DW
Phone: 0845 130 6229 (UK only)
Web: www.ccw.gov.uk

Economic & Social Research Council (ESRC)
Polaris House North Star Avenue, Swindon, Wiltshire SN2 1UJ
Phone: +44 (0)1793 413 000
Web: www.esrc.ac.uk

Landscape Design Trust
PO Box 651, Redhill, Surrey RH1 9AJ
Phone: +44 (0)1737 779 257
Web: www.landscape.co.uk

Landscape Institute (LI)
33 Great Portland Street, London W1W 8QG
Phone: +44 (0)20 7299 4500
Web: www.landscapeinstitute.org

Natural England
1 East Parade, Sheffield S1 2ET
Phone: +44 (0) 845 600 3078
Web: www.naturalengland.org.uk/

Planning Architecture Design Database Ireland (PADDI)
Queen's University Belfast, AFBI Library, Newforge Lane BT9 5PX
Phone: +44 (0)28 9025 5226
Web: www.paddi.net

Scottish Natural Heritage (SNH)
Great Glen House Leachkin Road, Inverness IV3 8NW
Phone: +44 (0)1463 725000
Web: www.snh.gov.uk/

Similar Jobs

Arboriculturist, Architect, Countryside/Conservation Officer/ Manager, Landscape Gardener, Town Planner

Landscape Gardener

also known as: Garden Designer

CRCI:Environment, Animals and Plants
CLCI:WAD

Job Band: 2 to 5

Job Description

Landscape gardeners develop and maintain parks, gardens, sports or leisure centre grounds and other outdoor areas, including business parks and industrial estates. They often create or renovate gardens for private clients using their own or a customer's design. May specialise in creating features, such as rock gardens, decorative lighting, themed gardens or water features. They decide on suitable trees, shrubs and flowers, and design the layout of flowerbeds, lawns, ponds and fountains. May incorporate dry stone or brick walls and paving features into the design. They aim to make the area pleasant, attractive and in keeping with the surrounding environment.

Landscape gardeners complete a variety of tasks needed for the general upkeep of a garden, such as pruning and thinning. They may work in ornamental gardens, glasshouses, nurseries, national parks or picnic areas. Also work on other projects, such as in shopping centres and malls. Some may develop an ecological plan for a wide area, such as a forest or for a county council.

Work Details

Usually work between 37-39 hrs a week, Monday to Friday, though may also work some weekends. Early mornings and longer hours in the summer are usual. You must be physically fit to do this job as you have to do a lot of lifting, pushing wheelbarrows and bending down. Work is mainly spent outside in all weather conditions. Some work may be done indoors in an office producing designs for clients' approval. Some of the work may be under cover in offices or shopping centres. Travel to different jobs may be required.

Qualification

• England, Wales and Northern Ireland

Band 2: For entry to jobs, no minimum qualifications are needed, but it is an advantage to have some GCSEs (A*-C) or equivalent in subjects that include English and maths.

Band 3: For entry to horticulture courses: usually at least 4 GCSEs (A*-C) including English and maths, or equivalent. For some courses you may also need to have had a year's practical experience in horticulture.

Band 4: For HND, Diploma of Higher Education or foundation degree: 1-2 A levels, often including geography or biology, and some GCSEs (A*-C) usually including English and maths, or equivalent. A year's practical experience in horticulture is normally required.

Band 5: For degree courses: 2-3 A levels such as botany, art, biology, geography, environmental science, and some GCSEs (A*-C) including English and maths or science.

• Scotland

Band 2: Although academic qualifications are not specified for this job, it is an advantage to have some S grades (1-3) in subjects that include English and maths, or similar.

Band 3: For entry to horticulture courses: usually four S grades (1-3) usually including a science subject, maths and English, or similar qualifications. It is an advantage to have practical experience in horticulture.

Band 4: For entry to SQA higher national and professional development awards, usually 2-3 H grades, often geography or biology, and some S grades (1-3), including English and maths, or similar qualifications. A year's practical experience in horticulture is normally required.

Band 5: For a degree: 3-5 H grades, such as botany, art, biology, geography, environmental science, and some S grades (1-3) including English, maths or science, or similar qualifications.

Degree Information

A degree in garden design, garden art and design, landscape design and ecology, landscape planning/management, or horticulture is desirable, though related subjects include geography (physical), and biology.

Adult Qualifications
Colleges and universities offering relevant courses may have special entry standards for mature applicants. Relevant foundation and Access courses may be available: contact individual institutions for details. Experience is often taken into account, and the usual requirement of 12 months' practical experience in horticulture may be reduced for mature students.

Work Experience
Employers or colleges/universities may prefer candidates who have relevant work or voluntary experience. This can include any work in horticulture, such as in a garden centre or botanical gardens, though work in a garden design company is ideal. It may be useful to contact voluntary organisations, such as the National Trust, or environmental charities, such as Groundwork, for work experience opportunities.

Entry and Training
Many people go into this work after several years of experience of general gardening. Another route is to take a full-time course prior to entry. Courses in garden design are available through BTEC/SQA HNC/D courses, foundation degrees and degrees. Other courses are available at level 2, such as the City & Guilds course in creative techniques in garden design and the NOCN award in garden design. A driving licence is usually required for this work.

The Society of Garden Designers (SGD) runs a membership scheme for students and graduates. It also has a registered membership level for those who have been assessed and approved by the SGD.

S/NVQs at levels 2-3 in amenity horticulture with landscaping options, are available. A Diploma/Welsh Baccalaureate may be available in your area in environment and land-based studies. Training programmes, including apprenticeship schemes, may be available in your area. Advanced apprenticeships leading to qualification at level 3 can also be a route into higher education.

Mature applicants can often benefit through government training opportunities, including apprenticeships for adults, that may be available in your area. You can gain recognition of previous experience through Accreditation of Prior Learning (APL) or by working towards relevant S/NVQs. There are many relevant college/university courses that can be studied part time or through distance learning.

Opportunities and Pay
Most people in this work are self-employed. There are some organisations that may employ landscape gardeners, but entry is competitive as this is a common second career. You may be able to find work with garden centres, local authorities, private landscape companies and contractors, water companies, the National Trust and National Trust for Scotland, botanical gardens, construction companies, estates and private homes. This job can be seasonal with more work available in the summer. It is usually possible to find part-time work.

Pay varies depending on location and employer, but starting salaries for trainees are likely to be around £15k, rising to £18k-£20k with experience. Senior gardeners or those who run their own company earn around £26k-£40k a year.

Health
You have to be physically fit to do this job and may find this job more difficult if you suffer from hay fever.

Skills and Qualities
able to communicate effectively, able to work to deadlines, creative flair, eye for visual effect, good organisational skills, interest in growing plants, IT skills, patient, reliable, technical aptitude

Relevant Subjects
Art and Design, Biology, Geography, Land and Environment, Science

Further Information
Apprenticeship Schemes (National Apprenticeship Service) - www.apprenticeships.org.uk

Diplomas (Foundation, Higher and Advanced) - http://yp.direct.gov.uk/diplomas

Garden Design Journal (10 x year) (Society of Garden Designers) - www.sgd.org.uk

Groundwork UK - www.groundwork.org.uk

Grow - the guide to careers in horticulture - www.growcareers.info

I want to be a landscape architect (LI) (Landscape Institute (LI)) - www.iwanttobealandscapearchitect.com/

Lantra - The Sector Skills Council for environmental & land-based sector (Lantra) http:/www.lantra.co.uk

Lantra Careers (A Future In...) (Lantra) - www.afuturein.com

Planning Architecture Design Database (Queens University Belfast) - www.paddi.net

Professional Gardener (Professional Gardeners Guild) (Professional Gardening Guild) - www.pgg.org.uk

Real Life Guide to Working Outdoors (Trotman) - www.trotman.co.uk

Training Schemes - www.direct.gov.uk/en/educationandlearning

Addresses
Association of Landscape Contractors of Ireland (ALCI)
22 Summerhill Park, Bangor, Co Down BT20 5QQ
Phone: +44 (0)28 9127 2823
Web: www.alci.org.uk

British Association of Landscape Industries (BALI)
Landscape House, Stoneleigh Park, National Agricultural Centre, Coventry CV8 2LG
Phone: +44 (0)24 7669 0333
Web: www.bali.co.uk

Horticultural Correspondence College
Fiveways House, Westwells Road, Hawthorn, Corsham SN13 9RG
Phone: +44 (0)1225 816700
Web: www.hccollege.co.uk

Institute of Horticulture (IoH)
Capel Manor College, Bullsmoor Lane, Enfield EN1 4RQ
Phone: +44 (0) 1992 707025
Web: www.horticulture.org.uk

Landscape Institute (LI)
33 Great Portland Street, London W1W 8QG
Phone: +44 (0)20 7299 4500
Web: www.landscapeinstitute.org

Royal Horticultural Society (RHS)
80 Vincent Square, London SW1P 2PE
Phone: 0845 260 5000 (UK only)
Web: www.rhs.org.uk

Society of Garden Designers
Katepwa House, Ashfield Park Avenue, Ross-on-Wye HR9 5AX
Phone: +44 (0)1989 566695
Web: www.sgd.org.uk

Similar Jobs
Arboriculturist, Gardener, Greenkeeper: Golf, Groundsman/Groundswoman, Landscape Architect, Parks Manager

Language Service Professional

also known as: Communication Professional , Sign Language Teacher

CRCI:Languages, Information and Culture
CLCI:FAL Job Band: 3 to 5

Job Description

Language service professionals facilitate communication between deaf or deafblind and hearing people by providing live access to spoken English. There are various types of language service professionals (LSP), including British Sign Language (BSL) interpreters, lipspeakers, speech-to-text reporters (STTRs) and notetakers, both electronic and manual.

BSL/English interpreters facilitate communication between users of BSL and users of spoken English by listening carefully to or watching the message and then expressing it in the second language. Lipspeakers repeat a message to lipreaders without using their voice by producing the shape of words and the flow, rhythm, intonation and phrasing of natural speech. They also use facial expression, natural gesture and sometimes fingerspelling to help the lipreader's understanding.

Notetakers take notes from a spoken message working at speeds from 60-150 words per minute. An electronic notetaker produces a real-time summary of what is said using a laptop computer with specialised software, usually linked to a second laptop for the client to read from. STTRs use a special keyboard to type every word that is spoken by a speaker phonetically. This is then converted back into English and appears on a computer screen.

Other roles include the cued speech transliterator, who uses clear lip patterns, together with eight different hand shapes (called cues) to report what is said; the deafblind communicator guide, who helps people to take part in everyday activities; and the deafblind interpreter (manual), who uses the deafblind manual alphabet to form letters on a person's hand, spelling out what a third person is saying.

Work Details

Hours vary depending on the assignment and may include evenings and weekends. Most LSPs are self-employed and can choose their hours of work. Depending on your specialism you may need to take regular breaks so, if the assignment is longer than two hours, you may work with another LSP.

You work in a variety of settings depending on the job role. These can include further and higher educational institutions, meeting rooms and conference locations in the workplace, social service, hospital or legal environments such as police stations and the law courts or tribunals. There are also some opportunities to work in television. The work often involves travel to different locations, so a driving licence is useful.

Qualification

• England, Wales and Northern Ireland

Band 3: For entry to jobs, HNC or a relevant Diploma, usually at least 4 GCSEs (A*-C) including English and maths, or equivalent.

Band 4: For HND, Diploma of Higher Education or foundation degree: 1-2 A levels and some GCSEs (A*-C) usually including English and maths, or equivalent.

Band 5: For degree courses: 2-3 A levels and some GCSEs (A*-C) usually including English and maths, or equivalent. Exact requirements depend on the degree you take.

• Scotland

Band 3: For entry to jobs, usually at least four S grades (1-3) including English or maths, or similar.

Band 4: For entry to SQA higher national and professional development awards, usually 2-3 H grades and some S grades (1-3), including English and maths, or similar qualifications.

Band 5: For degree courses: 3-5 H grades and some S grades (1-3), including English and maths, or similar qualifications. Exact requirements depend on the degree you take.

Degree Information

A number of universities offer degree and postgraduate courses in BSL/English interpreting and/or deaf studies.

Adult Qualifications

Entry requirements may be relaxed for adults applying for higher education courses. Access or foundation courses provide those without the required qualifications a route onto degree courses. British Sign Language (BSL) courses are offered at some colleges of further education and adult learning centres.

Work Experience

Employers may prefer people who have experience of the deaf community. There may be opportunities for voluntary or paid work in community support teams, as a communication support worker, or in educational institutions.

Entry and Training

There are training courses for each of the specialist roles and a clear progression route of four levels in the Signature qualifications, which are offered in centres around the UK. At level 1 certificates are offered in British Sign Language (BSL) and developing awareness and communication with deaf and deafblind people. You can continue training in BSL to level 4. With the level 1 communication certificate you can start to specialise in areas such as notetaking, lipspeaking or speech-to-text reporting. The Signature website shows a comprehensive progression chart and has details of the centres offering qualifications. The Association of Lipspeakers, Association of Sign Language Interpreters and the Royal National Institute for Deaf People can also help you to locate course providers.

Once you are qualified you can register on the National Register of Communication Professionals Working with Deaf and Deafblind People. Registration is a means of regulating LSPs, giving the user confidence that you are committed to the highest professional standards. Consult their website for full details.

The Scottish Association of Sign Language Interpreters (SASLI) offers an apprenticeship scheme that provides an opportunity for deaf and hearing people to train as BSL/English interpreters. It offers a mix of recognised qualifications and work experience leading to registration with SASLI.

You are expected to have a good level of English language skills, and some employers require either a degree or professional experience. This is particularly important if you wish to work in television or as a BSL tutor. Experience of the deaf community is also important.

A Diploma/Welsh Baccalaureate in society, health and development may be available in your area and provide an alternative route into this career..

Mature entrants with experience in languages may have an advantage and those who have experience of the deaf community are preferred by employers.

Opportunities and Pay

Although this is a small profession, there are plenty of opportunities on a permanent or freelance basis. If you are self-employed you need to have some organisational skills and be able to manage your timetable and accounts. Your workplace depends on your specialism and can vary with each assignment. Once fully qualified and with some experience, it is possible to move into teaching, but you then need to have a teaching qualification. As a teacher you work in schools, colleges or universities. See the job profiles for Teacher: Primary school and Teacher: Secondary school for full details on how to qualify as a teacher.

Salaries range from £20k-£25k a year to more than £35k a year. However, it is common to find jobs through agencies specialising in this kind of work and be paid an hourly rate. This can range from £15-£35.

Health
Some aspects of this job require good levels of stamina.

Skills and Qualities
able to communicate effectively, able to get on with all kinds of people, awareness of confidentiality issues, discreet, good concentration level, good spelling, grammar and punctuation, impartial, IT skills, keyboard/typing skills, tactful

Relevant Subjects
English, ICT/Computer studies, Media and communication studies

Further Information
Association of Lipspeakers (ALS) (ALS) - www.lipspeaking.co.uk/training.html

Association of Notetaking Professionals (ANP) - www.anpnotetakers.co.uk

Association of Sign language Interpreters (ASLI) - www.asli.org.uk

Deafblind Scotland - www.deafblindscotland.org.uk/

Diplomas (Foundation, Higher and Advanced) - http://yp.direct.gov.uk/diplomas

Scottish Association of Sign Language Interpreters (SASLI) (SASLI) - www.sasli.co.uk/

The National Registers of Communication Professionals working with Deaf and Deafblind People (NRCPD) (NRCPD) - www.nrcpd.org.uk/index.php

▶Working in schools & colleges (2007) (Babcock Lifeskills) - www.babcock-lifeskills.com/

Working with languages (2010) (Babcock Lifeskills) - www.babcock-lifeskills.com/

Addresses
Deafblind UK
National Centre for Deafblindness John and Lucille van Geest Place
Cygnet Road Hampton, Peterborough PE7 8FD
Phone: +44 (0)1733 358 100 (Voice/Text)
Web: www.deafblind.org.uk/

Royal National Institute for Deaf People (RNID)
19-23 Featherstone Street, London EC1Y 8SL
Phone: +44 (0) 20 7296 8000
Web: www.rnid.org.uk/

Signature
Mersey House Mandale Business Park Belmont, Durham DH1 1TH
Phone: +44 (0) 191 383 1155
Web: www.signature.org.uk/

Similar Jobs
Audiologist, Interpreter, Interpreter: European Union, Secretary: Bilingual, Speech & Language Therapist, Translator

Laundry Assistant/Manager
CRCI:Personal and Other Services
CLCI:IG   Job Band: 1 to 3

Job Description
Laundry assistants or managers work in a laundry sorting clothes or other textiles, loading and operating specialised machines, and pressing, folding and packing finished items. They may check and place identification tags on each item, such as a bar code or computer chip for automatic sorting by machine. Different materials are separated, weighed and loaded into machines for washing. After they are washed, the items are dried and pressed, usually by machine. Some folding and ironing is done by hand. Repair work, such as sewing tears, may also be carried out, and finally, the laundry is packed.

Laundry managers make sure the business is profitable and runs efficiently. May process orders, invoices and keep records, train staff and deal with customer complaints.

Work Details
Usually work a basic 35-39 hr week, Monday to Friday, though you may be required to work on a shift basis, sometimes including weekends. A laundry is usually hot and steamy and some of the machines can be very noisy. In this job, you are on your feet all day and often have to lift bundles of laundry into and out of machines. Managers are less likely to work shifts, but are responsible for dealing with customers either face to face or by phone/letter, some of whom may be making complaints. They may work partly in an office, keeping records and using a computer. As a result their work may be less physically demanding.

Qualification
- **England, Wales and Northern Ireland**

Band 1: For entry to jobs, no minimum qualifications are needed, but you are expected to have a good level of general education and relevant experience. Some formal/vocational qualifications at any level are useful.

Band 2: Although academic qualifications are not always specified for this job, it is an advantage to have some GCSEs (A*-C) in subjects that include English and maths, or equivalent.

Band 3: For direct entry: usually at least 4 GCSEs (A*-C) including English or equivalent qualifications.

- **Scotland**

Band 1: For entry to jobs, no minimum qualifications are needed, but you are expected to have a good level of general education and relevant experience. Some formal/vocational qualifications at any level are useful.

Band 2: Although academic qualifications are not always specified for this job, it is an advantage to have some S grades (1-3) in subjects that include English and maths, or similar qualifications.

Band 3: For direct entry: usually at least four S grades (1-3) including English and maths, or similar qualifications.

Adult Qualifications
No formal qualifications are needed, but for entry as a manager, experience and/or qualifications in business/management are an advantage.

Work Experience
Any work experience can equip you with skills to use in the future and add to your CV. Work experience can either be unpaid or voluntary or can be holiday or part-time work that you have organised yourself. Any experience of working in a laundry, or similar environment is useful. For managers, experience of using supervisory skills or customer service is an advantage.

Entry and Training
Some employers may ask you to take a test for basic literacy and numeracy, and to operate some equipment you need to be over 18. Training for a laundry assistant is usually on the job under the supervision of a more experienced worker. Many employees also have the opportunity to take the Guild of Cleaners and Launderers (GCL) Qualification (Q) Star Scheme, through a local training provider, or other short courses, such as those offered by SATRA Fabric Care Division. SATRA provides most of the training, including short courses and seminars on specific techniques. They provide the training for the GCL Q Star qualifications, in areas such as commercial laundering, domestic laundering and ironing, and aspects of health and safety.

The Dry Cleaning and Laundry Technology Centre offers a range of courses, as does the Society of Hospital Linen Services and Laundry Managers. The website of the Textile Services Association may also offer useful information. S/NVQs at level 2 are available in laundry operations and laundry support. Training programmes, including apprenticeship schemes, may be available in your area.

With experience and training, assistants may move on to become managers. Some of the larger laundries may recruit graduates to manager posts, but this is not the normal route. Most supervisory and management jobs are filled by staff promoted from within the company.

Adults may be able to enter this work through a government-funded training programme. Contact your local Connexions or careers office, Jobcentre Plus, Next Step service or Learning and Skills Council (LSC)/Local Enterprise Company (LEC) for details of all training opportunities and schemes, including apprenticeship schemes for adults.

Opportunities and Pay

It is usually possible to find work in most towns and cities throughout the UK. You can work in a large commercial laundry or in a small laundry attached to a hospital, prison or hotel. There are many commercial laundries that handle tablecloths, sheets and household linen for hotels, and they may also provide overalls for manufacturing workers and towels for public lavatories. With experience, you can move on to a supervisor post in charge of other workers, and later move on to management.

Pay varies widely, but most entrants earn around £12.5k a year, rising to around £15k with experience. Managers of large laundries can expect to earn around £30k-£40k a year, depending on the size of the laundry.

Health

You need to have good stamina and general fitness and may need normal colour vision for certain areas of work. This job is not suitable for people with certain skin conditions or allergies.

Skills and Qualities

able to operate equipment, able to work quickly, accurate measuring and calculating skills, aptitude for teamwork, business awareness, good organisational skills, IT skills, methodical, reliable

Relevant Subjects

Hospitality and catering

Further Information

Apprenticeship Schemes (National Apprenticeship Service) - www.apprenticeships.org.uk

Cleaning Industry Handbook (BICSc) (BICSc) - www.bics.org.uk/

Laundry & Cleaning Today (LCT) - www.laundryandcleaningtoday.com

Society of Hospital Linen Services and Laundry Managers - www.linenmanager.co.uk

Training Schemes - www.direct.gov.uk/en/educationandlearning

Addresses

Dry Cleaning & Laundry Technology Centre (DTC & LTC Ltd)
Unit 10A, Drill Hall Business Centre, East Parade, Ilkley LS29 8EZ
Phone: +44 (0)1943 816545
Web: www.dtcltc.com

Guild of Cleaners & Launderers (GCL)
5 Portland Place, London , Middlesex W1B 1PW
Phone: 0845 600 1838 (UK only)
Web: www.gcl.org.uk

SATRA Fabric Care Research Division
SATRA Technology Centre, Wyndham Way, Telford Way, Kettering, Northamptonshire NN16 8SD
Phone: +44 (0)1536 410 000
Web: www.satra.co.uk

Textile Services Association (TSA)
5 Portland Place, London, Middlesex W1B 1PW
Phone: +44 (0)20 8863 7755
Web: www.tsa-uk.org

Similar Jobs

Car Valet, Cleaner: Carpet & Upholstery, Clothing Presser, Dry Cleaning Assistant/Manager, Retail Manager

Law Costs Draftsman

CRCI:Legal and Political Services
CLCI:LAG Job Band: 2 to 3

Job Description

Law costs draftsmen are concerned with all aspects of a solicitor's costs controlled by statute and common law. They deal with all areas of the law and are not restricted to certain areas, as are some solicitors and legal executives. Law costs draftsman is a generic term that includes both men and women.

They work in three main areas of costs: solicitor and client costs (those costs payable by a client to their own solicitor), public-funded (legal aid) costs (where a solicitor is representing a publicly-funded client), and those costs payable between parties (the loser of a legal case is usually ordered to pay the winner's costs). Draftsmen assess all of the charges and costs that a legal case has generated and ensure that clients are charged an appropriate fee for the work done.

Law costs draftsmen may also advise solicitors on whether it is financially realistic to pursue a case, or establish compensation resulting from litigation cases, after consulting with a specialist judge. May also sometimes represent their clients in court.

Work Details

You usually work 35-37 hrs a week, Monday to Friday, though some extra hours at times are required. You must work quickly and accurately, keeping up to date with changes in both financial and legal practices. Many law costs draftsmen are self-employed, often working from home. Team work may be required, but you also have to be able to work on your own. Discretion is important as the work is of a confidential nature. Work can be demanding at times.

Qualification

- **England, Wales and Northern Ireland**

Band 2: There are no set qualifications for entry to this job, however most employers ask for 3-5 GCSEs (A*-C) including English and maths, or equivalent.

Band 3: For membership of the Association of Law Costs Draftsmen: at least 4 GCSEs (A*-C) including English and maths, or equivalent.

Adult Qualifications

There are no set qualifications for entry. Qualifications and/or experience in business, accounting or administrative work are an advantage.

Work Experience

Work experience gives you an insight into what you enjoy and do not enjoy about a job or working environment, as well as the opportunity to acquire new skills. It also provides valuable information to add to your CV and improves any course application and/or your future employment prospects. Any work in a law or accountancy firm is useful.

Entry and Training

The usual method of entry to the profession is via a solicitor's office in a clerical or administrative post where you gain general legal knowledge.

Many entrants apply for student membership of the Association of Law Costs Draftsmen (ALCD), which is open to men and women aged 18 and over. Student members study the two-year ALCD distance-learning course, which is of a standard between A level and a university degree. Training is modular and includes general and civil costs, solicitor and client costs, special courts and tribunals, and public funding through legal aid. Certain exemptions are given for relevant academic and professional qualifications and for those with at least seven years' experience.

After completing the course and gaining five years' experience, you can apply for associate membership. A system of compulsory continuing professional development (CPD) requires all members to complete at least seven hours of training or related work each year.

Mature entrants have an advantage for this type of work, particularly if they have experience of legal, accounts or administrative work.

Opportunities and Pay

Law costs draftsmen work for firms of solicitors, for in-house legal departments of large companies, or for central and local government. The traditional starting point is in a junior position in a solicitor's office, eventually progressing to a more senior position through study for examinations. Once experienced, law costs draftsmen often work from home on a self-employed basis.

Pay varies depending on location, type of employer and employment. Starting salaries are around £15k-£20k a year for a trainee. Experienced draftsmen generally earn between £25k-£50k a year. Rates vary for self-employed draftsmen.

Skills and Qualities

accurate, analytical skills, attention to detail, good communication skills, good interpersonal skills, methodical, numeracy skills

Relevant Subjects

Business and accounting, ICT/Computer studies, Law, Mathematics

Further Information

Law Gazette (Law Society) - www.lawgazette.co.uk

Skills for Justice - sector skills council for the UK justice system - www.skillsforjustice.com

Addresses

Association of Law Costs Draftsmen (ALCD)
c/o Church Cottage, Church Lane, Stuston, Diss IP21 4AG
Phone: +44 (0)1379 741404
Web: www.alcd.org.uk

Law Society of England & Wales
The Law Society's Hall, 113 Chancery Lane, London WC2A 1PL
Phone: +44 (0)20 7242 1222
Web: www.lawsociety.org.uk

Law Society of Northern Ireland
96 Victoria Street, Belfast BT1 3GN
Phone: +44 (0) 28 9023 1614
Web: www.lawsoc-ni.org

Similar Jobs

Accounting Technician, Barristers' Clerk, Clerk: Accounts, Legal Cashier, Legal Executive, Secretary: Legal

Learning Mentor (England)

CRCI:Education and Training
CLCI:FAB
Job Band: 3 to 5

Job Description

Learning mentors work in primary and secondary schools with teaching and pastoral staff to identify, assess and work with pupils/students who need help to overcome barriers to learning, raise their confidence and improve achievement. These barriers include difficulties at home, bullying, poor study and organisational skills, poor self-esteem, bereavement, unco-operative behaviour, and those who suffer problems when transferring from primary to secondary school. They discuss these issues on a one-to-one basis with pupils and help them in setting targets to overcome such issues.

Learning mentors keep a record of sessions and are likely to discuss progress in regular meetings with senior staff. Work with, but independently from, teachers, parents, carers and counsellors, and also liaise with welfare groups, educational psychologists, educational welfare officers and social workers. May also organise school events outside of school hours, such as clubs and drop-in sessions. Some learning mentors may develop specialisms such as family liaison (known as home-school link working) or work in addressing behavioural issues.

Work Details

Most learning mentors work around 30 to 35 hrs a week, Monday to Friday, plus preparation time, and possible extra-curricular activities outside of school hours. Most of the work is indoors in schools, although visits to pupils' homes is sometimes required, which can involve travel. Some pupils can, at times, be uncooperative or aggressive, which can be emotionally demanding and stressful. Some staff work as a learning mentor part of the week, and the rest as a learning support assistant, teaching assistant (TA) or administrative worker. Sometimes you work in more than one school and need to travel between them.

Part-time or voluntary work is fairly common. Everybody working with children and vulnerable adults is required to undergo a Criminal Records Bureau (CRB) check.

Qualification

- **England, Wales and Northern Ireland**

Band 3: For entry to jobs, HNC or a relevant Diploma, usually at least 4 GCSEs (A*-C) including English and maths, or equivalent.

Band 4: For HND, Diploma of Higher Education or foundation degree: 1-2 A levels and some GCSEs (A*-C) usually including English and maths, or equivalent.

Band 5: For degree courses: 2-3 A levels and some GCSEs (A*-C) usually including English and maths, or equivalent. Exact requirements depend on the degree you take.

Degree Information

A degree in any discipline is acceptable but subjects such as psychology, social work, education, community studies, youth studies or sociology, are particularly relevant.

Adult Qualifications

Government training opportunities, such as apprenticeships, may be available in your area. You can also gain recognition of previous experience through Accreditation of Prior Learning (APL) or by working towards relevant S/NVQs. Contact your local careers office, Jobcentre Plus, Next Step service or Learning and Skills Council (LSC) Local Enterprise Company (LEC) for details of training schemes.

Work Experience

Schools or colleges usually prefer candidates who have work or voluntary experience in dealing with people, especially young people. This can include any experience in the education sector, including holiday play schemes, playcentre work or a youth club, or perhaps in a youth voluntary organisation. Some schools and colleges run volunteer mentoring schemes that provide excellent experience for those wishing to become a learning mentor. The National Mentoring Network can also provide details of a local volunteer mentoring scheme.

Entry and Training

There are no specific minimum formal qualifications but a good standard of secondary education is generally expected. The level of academic qualification required depends on the individual job and some employers may require you to have a higher level of qualifications (including qualification at degree level or professional qualifications) and relevant work experience.

There are foundation degrees available in subjects that include learning support, and supporting learning and teaching. There is also an honours degree course in learning, development and support available at Liverpool Sir John Moores University. There are no formal entry requirements for this course which runs part time on Saturdays, supported by distance learning.

All learning mentors take a Children's Workforce Development Council induction training programme. This contains five core modules and is provided centrally for delivery locally. Materials to support the programme are available online. Many schools and colleges run role-specific supervision programmes for all mentors so that they can discuss and reflect on their work. S/NVQs in learning development and support are available at levels 3-4. Learning mentors are expected to undertake continuing professional development (CPD). Many go on short courses on topics like study skills, learning styles and anger management.

Mature applicants with experience and/or qualifications in areas that include teaching, youth work, careers or counselling, human resources (personnel), social work and educational welfare, may have an advantage. However, some school and local education authorities may only require relevant life experience, together with a good general education. You are expected to understand the social factors and barriers that restrict learning and development and to be able to identify individual learning needs.

Opportunities and Pay

There are around 12,500 learning mentors employed in primary and secondary schools throughout the country, but particularly in urban areas and in areas of social deprivation. Competition for entry to this work is fierce. Promotion is possible to positions of greater responsibility or supervisory roles. Learning mentors can progress to other youth or social work or, with qualifications, move into primary or secondary teaching.

Pay depends upon your local education authority but generally, new learning mentors can expect to earn around £14k-£24k a year. With supervisory responsibility, this can rise to around £40k a year.

Skills and Qualities

able to inspire confidence, able to motivate others, assertive, awareness of confidentiality issues, good communication skills, good interpersonal skills, good listening skills, non-judgemental, patient, problem-solving skills

Relevant Subjects

English, Health and social care, Psychology, Sociology

Further Information

Good Practice Guidelines for Learning Mentors - www.standards.dfes.gov.uk/sie/documents/LMGoodPractGuide.pdf
Local Government Careers (Improvement and Development Agency) - www.lgcareers.com/publications/
Mentoring and Befriending Foundation - www.mandbf.org.uk
The Coaching and Mentoring Network - www.coachingnetwork.org.uk
▶Working in advice & counselling (2007) (Babcock Lifeskills) - www.babcock-lifeskills.com/
▶Working in schools & colleges (2007) (Babcock Lifeskills) - www.babcock-lifeskills.com/

Addresses

Children's Workforce Development Council (CWDC)
2nd Floor, City Exchange, 11 Albion Street, Leeds LS1 5ES
Phone: +44 (0)113 244 6311
Web: www.cwdcouncil.org.uk

Department for Education
Castle View House East Lane, Runcorn, Cheshire WA7 2GJ
Phone: 0870 000 2288 (UK only)
Web: www.education.gov.uk/

Similar Jobs

Education Welfare Officer (England), Personal Adviser (Connexions) (England), Social Worker, Teacher: Primary School, Teacher: Secondary School, Teaching Assistant

Leather Technologist

CRCI:Manufacturing and Production
CLCI:SAF
Job Band: 3 to 5

Job Description

Leather technologists apply scientific and technical knowledge to supervise the production of leather, analyse leather types and research into/experiment with dyes and finishes. They are concerned with production and efficiency of automated plant technology and the quality of hides. Finished products are analysed and tested in a laboratory using chemicals and dyes. Technologists are also concerned with the economic running of the tannery and are responsible for monitoring and controlling waste products safely and efficiently.

Leather tehcnologists supervise operatives and technicians, and look after the health and safety of the workforce. They use computers in much of their work and write up research work for managers. Operational reports are produced on a regular basis.

Work Details

Leather technologists usually works a 39-40 hr week, Monday to Friday, though in some jobs may be required to work weekends and shifts. Some office work is required, including writing reports on projects and management issues, but most work is done either in the laboratory or the tannery. Chemical reactions are monitored to obtain the best results for leather production and finished products are analysed to ensure that goods are of high quality. You are the intermediary between the operatives, technicians and senior management.

The tannery is smelly and noisy and you may occasionally need to wear protective clothing. As many leather production processes are also handled overseas, some travel may be necessary.

Qualification

• England, Wales and Northern Ireland

Band 3: For entry to apprenticeships: usually at least 4 GCSEs (A*-C) including English and maths, or equivalent.

Band 4: For relevant BTEC higher national diploma: 1-2 A levels, preferably in chemistry, with either physics or maths. Some GCSEs (A*-C) including science, maths and English, or equivalent.

Band 5: For degree course: 2-3 A levels, including a physical science and some GCSEs (A*-C) including maths, physics, chemistry, and English. The BTEC national award in leather technology and the certificate of achievement in leather technology may also be used for entry to the degree course.

• Scotland

Band 3: For entry: usually at least four S grades (1-3) including English and maths, or similar.

Band 4: For relevant SQA higher national award: usually 2-3 H grades, preferably including chemistry, with either physics or maths plus some S grades (1-3) including science, maths and English, or similar.

Band 5: For degree course: 3-5 H grades, including a physical science and some S grades (1-3) including maths, physics, chemistry and English. The SQA national award in textile technology may also be used for entry to the technology degree course.

Degree Information
A degree in materials technology (leather) may be preferred. Other subjects that may be acceptable, depending on the type of employer and the availability of jobs, are chemistry, textile technology or materials science. A number of leather technology postgraduate courses are available.

Adult Qualifications
Colleges may vary entry requirements for mature students with experience in industry or applied science. Access to science or engineering offer a route to higher education for those without the required entry qualifications.

Work Experience
Relevant work or voluntary experience is always useful and can improve your chances in application for entry to this job. The types of work experience to consider are in scientific laboratories, manufacturing, materials science or in quality control.

Entry and Training
Most entrants have a degree relevant to leather technology, although it is also possible to take an advanced apprenticeship and work your way up to this job via relevant training courses. The only degree in materials technology (leather) is offered by University of Northampton. The course introduces the principles and practices of leather manufacture and hide processing techniques through to the finished leather.

The University of Northampton also offers a BTEC national certificate in leather technology. It runs a range of technical short courses and a leathersellers certificate in leather studies at technician level. Northampton also offers relevant postgraduate study.

Once in post, on-the-job training is usual and in this industry a student can often progress from having few qualifications to postgraduate level. BLC Leather Technology Centre also offers a range of specialist short courses, including a five-day intensive course in leather technology.

Adults with tannery/technical experience (and who may have no formal qualifications) may apply for a one-year full-time leathersellers certificate in leather studies (technician level) at the University of Northampton. Government training opportunities, such as an apprenticeship in leather goods may be available in your area. You can also gain recognition of previous experience through Accreditation of Prior Learning (APL) or by working towards relevant S/NVQs. Contact your local careers office, Jobcentre Plus, Next Step service or Learning and Skills Council (LSC) Local Enterprise Company (LEC) for details of training schemes.

Opportunities and Pay
There are around 2,000 businesses in leather and footwear in the UK, employing around 23,000 people. Jobs are available only in certain areas such as the east Midlands, west of England and central Scotland. Most jobs are in tanneries, but some are in firms that manufacture shoes, bags, suitcases and industrial items like hydraulic seals. Promotion may be possible to production manager or technical manager, or you can move into sales. Leather production now focuses in Italy, Eastern Europe, India, Pakistan, China, Brazil, North America and Australia, so qualified technologists can also find work abroad.

Pay varies depending on location and employer but generally, trainees start on around £15k-£17k, rising to £20k-£30k with more experience.

Health
There may be an allergy risk from animal skins or irritants and there are restrictions on certain skin troubles. This job requires good colour vision for certain areas of work.

Skills and Qualities
able to take responsibility, aptitude for maths and science, attention to detail, enquiring mind, eye for shape/colour, good organisational skills, IT skills, not squeamish, problem-solving skills, technical aptitude

Relevant Subjects
Chemistry, Design and technology, Manufacturing, Mathematics, Physics, Science

Further Information
Apprenticeship Schemes (National Apprenticeship Service) - www.apprenticeships.org.uk

Journal of the Society of Leather Technologists and Chemists (Society of Leather Technologists and Chemists) - www.sltc.org/

Real Life Guide to Manufacturing & Product Design (Trotman 2009) - www.trotman.co.uk

SATRA Technology Centre - www.satra.co.uk

Society of Leather Technologists and Chemists (SLTC) - www.sltc.org

Training Schemes - www.direct.gov.uk/en/educationandlearning

Addresses
BLC Leather Technology Centre Ltd
Leather Trade House, Kings Park Road, Moulton Park,
Northampton NN3 6JD
Phone: +44 (0)1604 679 999
Web: www.blcleathertech.com

British School of Leather Technology
c/o University of Northampton Park Campus,
Boughton Green Road NN2 7AL
Phone: +44 (0)1604 735 500
Web: www.northampton.ac.uk/info/
200174/british-school-of-leather-technology

Leathersellers' Company
15 St Helen's Place, London EC3A 6DQ
Phone: +44 (0)20 7330 1444
Web: www.leathersellers.co.uk

Similar Jobs
Laboratory Technician: Science, Materials Scientist/Engineer, Saddler, Textile Colour Technologist, Textile Technologist

Leather Worker
CRCI:Manufacturing and Production
CLCI:SAF

Job Band: 1 to 2

Job Description
Leather workers use prepared animal hides (skins) to produce a wide range of leather goods such as shoes, gloves, luggage, belts and coats. They place a pattern over the leather and cut around it either with cutting shears, or by using a machine. May need to punch holes in the material in order to allow it to be stitched by a machine. Specialist or traditional leather craftworkers join together the items by hand stitching, glueing, riveting or by using a machine. Some goods require additional items, such as handles or a buckle to complete the item. Specialist tools are used for the different processes.

May decorate goods by using paints, or by 'stamping' a design on to the leather. Can specialise in items such as made-to-measure saddles.

Work Details
Most leather workers usually work a 39 hr week. This can include shift and weekend work, especially if working in a tourist area. The work environment can be an industrial premises or a smaller workshop. It can be noisy and also smelly if attached to a tannery. Some jobs include heavy lifting, while others involve sitting for long periods at a workbench. Protective clothing is usually worn.

Qualification

- **England, Wales and Northern Ireland**

Band 1: No minimum qualifications are required, but you are expected to have a good level of general education. However, some formal or vocational qualifications at any level are useful.

Band 2: Although academic qualifications are not specified for this job, some employers may require some GCSEs (A*-G) in subjects that include English and maths, or equivalent.

- **Scotland**

Band 1: No minimum qualifications are required, but you are expected to have a good level of general education. However, some formal or vocational qualifications at any level are useful.

Band 2: Although academic qualifications are not specified for this job, some employers may require some S grades (1-5) or similar in subjects that include English and maths.

Adult Qualifications

No formal qualifications are required. However, you are expected to have relevant experience.

Work Experience

Relevant work or voluntary experience is always useful. It can improve your chances when applying for jobs or apprenticeships schemes. Your personal adviser should be able to advise you about how to get some work experience.

Entry and Training

Training is usually on the job under the supervision of a more experienced worker or through an employer's training scheme. Relevant training programmes, including apprenticeship schemes, may be available in your area. Advanced apprenticeships leading to qualification at level 3 can be a route into higher education. While training you may be able to work towards S/NVQs in leather production at levels 2-3 and leather goods at level 2.

There is specialist training for those who want to work with saddlery. See the job article Saddler and the website of the Society of Master Saddlers for more information.

Mature entrants with experience of manufacturing work using sewing machines or in shoe repair have an advantage. You can benefit through government training opportunities, such as apprenticeships, which may be available in your area. You can also gain recognition of previous experience through Accreditation of Prior Learning (APL) or by working towards relevant S/NVQs. Contact your local careers office, Jobcentre Plus, Next Step service or Learning and Skills Council (LSC) Local Enterprise Company (LEC) for details of training schemes.

Opportunities and Pay

There are around 2,000 businesses in leather and footwear in the UK, employing around 23,000 people. Leather workers are employed by large UK manufacturing companies. These make mass-produced goods in industrial premises, such as shoe manufacturers. Work is also available in small companies, workshops and businesses. These make goods by using traditional craft methods. Some workers are employed as 'outworkers' working from home. They use equipment and leather that is supplied by their employer. Self-employment is possible, once experienced.

Pay depends on size and type of employer. However, employed workers can expect £10k-£12k, rising to £15k-£18k a year. Higher earners can around £20k a year. If self-employed, income depends on establishing a good reputation.

Health

There is an allergy risk from animal skins or skin irritants. This job requires a good standard of physical fitness and good sight and colour vision for some areas of work.

Skills and Qualities

able to work both on your own and in a team, attention to detail, creative flair, eye for shape/colour, good concentration level, manual dexterity, patient, practical skills, strong hands

Relevant Subjects

Art and Design, Design and technology

Further Information

Apprenticeship Schemes (National Apprenticeship Service) - www.apprenticeships.org.uk

Skillset - sector skills council for the creative media, fashion and textiles industries - www.skillset.org

Training Schemes - www.direct.gov.uk/en/educationandlearning

Addresses

Society of Master Saddlers
Green Lane Farm, Stonham, Stowmarket, Suffolk IP14 5DS
Phone: +44 (0)1449 711 642
Web: www.mastersaddlers.co.uk

Similar Jobs

Dressmaker, Leather Technologist, Saddler, Shoe Repairer, Tailor, Upholsterer

Lecturer: Further Education

also known as: College Lecturer, FE Lecturer

CRCI:Education and Training
CLCI:FAB — Job Band: 4 to 5

Job Description

Lecturers teach students over the age of 16 who are studying courses in academic, vocational or non-vocational subjects at a general/specialist college of further education (FE), a sixth form college, or a tertiary college. Associate teachers also do some teaching, but not at the same level of responsibility, and may teach using packs of materials prepared by someone else.

Courses offered are from skills for life (basic skills), GCSEs/S grades, AS/A levels/H grades through to HNC/HND, degrees and professional diplomas. It also includes vocational qualifications such as S/NVQs, or BTEC/SQA national/higher national awards, Access courses and foundation degrees. May also teach students aged 14-16 who are still at school, but take some courses, eg diplomas, at an FE college.

Non-vocational studies taught can include courses in leisure subjects such as dressmaking, car maintenance or photography, preparation for work and general life skills.

Lecturers plan syllabus, prepare lectures/lesson plans, seminars, tutorials and practical sessions. They assist in the development of new courses. Set and mark assignments, exams and tests. They also interview potential students and sometimes may need to carry out diagnostic assessments. Monitoring student progress/attendance in college and also on work placement, if appropriate, is a part of the role. May also act as a guidance or support tutor. Some administrative tasks, including students' records and examination board documentation, are also undertaken.

They attend staff, team and faculty meetings as well as in-service training days. Involvement in college open days, parents' evenings, careers and education fairs/conventions, and college course 'taster' days, is expected.

Work Details

Lecturers usually work a 37 hr week of which around 22 hrs are contact teaching hours. Some evening work may be required at times. Contract and part-time work is common. An extensive and up-to-date knowledge of your subject is required and the ability to organise your own workload. Work is challenging and often requires you to take preparation and correction work home. Your role is to teach and encourage your students and be responsible for developing their knowledge and understanding of their subject.

Mostly, the work is indoors in college lecture rooms and, depending on your subject, perhaps workshops, laboratories, or out on fieldwork. You are required to take your annual leave outside term-time.

Qualification

• England, Wales and Northern Ireland

Band 4: For HND, Diploma of Higher Education or foundation degree: 1-2 A levels and some GCSEs (A*-C) usually including English and maths, or equivalent.

Band 5: For degree courses: 2-3 A levels and some GCSEs (A*-C) usually including English and maths, or equivalent. Exact requirements depend on the degree you take.

• Scotland

Band 4: For entry to SQA higher national and professional development awards, usually 2-3 H grades and some S grades (1-3), including English and maths, or similar qualifications.

Band 5: For degree courses: 3-5 H grades and some S grades (1-3), usually including English and maths, or similar qualifications. Exact requirements depend on the degree you take.

Degree Information

Degree should be in a relevant subject followed by a course that leads to becoming a qualified further education lecturer.

Adult Qualifications

Government training opportunities, such as apprenticeships, may be available in your area. You can also gain recognition of previous experience through Accreditation of Prior Learning (APL) or by working towards relevant S/NVQs. Contact your local careers office, Jobcentre Plus, Next Step service or Learning and Skills Council (LSC) Local Enterprise Company (LEC) for details of training schemes.

Work Experience

Entry to this job can be competitive and it is important that you try to do some relevant work experience before applying for posts. Evidence of commitment to teaching as well as to the subject you will be teaching is essential. This can come in the form of working in education in a similar role or working professionally in the field in which you intend to lecture.

Entry and Training

Most new entrants are graduates, although it is also possible to enter this work with extensive experience of a particular subject and vocational qualifications. Some entrants choose to take a diploma in teaching in the lifelong learning sector before starting the work. All those working with young people are required to have a Criminal Records Bureau (CRB)/Disclosure Scotland check.

To qualify as an FE lecturer in England and Wales you are required to be fully competent in the subject you intend to teach and are also expected to be working towards the 'Qualified Teaching Learning and Skills' (QTLS), which is endorsed by Lifelong Learning UK (LLUK). This award is the equivalent of QTS (qualified teacher status) in schools and places all new entrants to teaching and training on the pathway to a professional qualification. The award is usually gained by demonstrating through professional practice.

There are several routes to QTLS for new entrants depending on your existing qualifications and experience, and whether you intend to be a full or part-time lecturer. For those already employed as a full or part-time lecturer, there are new requirements for professional recognition, including a commitment to a continuing professional development (CPD) programme. Visit the LLUK website for further information.

In Northern Ireland, a teaching qualification is not mandatory for appointment to posts in further education. However, those new entrants to full-time permanent teaching or associate lecturer posts who do not hold a BEd or postgraduate certificate in education (PGCE) must pass a postgraduate certificate/diploma in further and higher education that is awarded by the University of Ulster.

In Scotland, further education lecturers of academic subjects must be graduates and those teaching vocational subjects should have a degree or appropriate technical qualification. The teaching qualification in further education (TQ(FE)) is offered at some universities, currently Aberdeen, Dundee and Stirling. Although the TQ(FE) is currently not compulsory, these qualifications are strongly recommended for FE lecturers, and all new lecturers now require a teaching qualification. The courses may be studied part time whilst in a teaching post, with sponsorship from your employer.

Mature applicants are welcomed and those with relevant experience and academic/professional qualifications have an advantage. Many people move into this job as a second career and some may begin by teaching at an evening class and proceed to full-time lecturing. The diploma in teaching in the lifelong learning sector may be taken part time while working. This helps to prepare for the required Qualified Teaching Learning and Skills (QTLS) award.

Opportunities and Pay

Jobs are available throughout the UK in towns and cities and the number of vacancies is rising, due to the increase in student numbers at FE colleges. Competition for posts varies depending on the subject you will be teaching. Employment opportunities are with FE colleges, adult educational centres, sixth-form/tertiary colleges (not Scotland), community colleges, independent and tutorial colleges, technical colleges, the prison service and the armed forces.

Before getting a permanent position you may be employed on a short-term contract or on a sessional/visiting lecturer basis. Promotion prospects lead to senior lecturing posts, head of department, faculty head or a move into full-time college management. Some lecturers may write textbooks and course materials or move into private tuition or consultancy. There are some opportunities to do research or to work abroad with the British Council.

Salaries do vary depending on the individual colleges as each college sets its own rate of pay. Part-time lecturers are paid an hourly rate of £15-£30. Salaries for newly-qualified full-time lecturers from £22k a year; with advanced teaching and training lecturers earning up to £38k. Unqualified lecturers earn around £18k to start with. Those in leadership/management roles may earn up to around £86k.

Health

Full time posts often require a medical test before employment.

Skills and Qualities

able to explain clearly, able to motivate others, able to stimulate learners, enthusiastic, good organisational skills, IT skills, patient, sense of humour, time management skills

Relevant Subjects

English, Psychology, Sociology

Further Information

British Council - www.britishcouncil.org

LLUK (Lifelong Learning UK) - sector skills council for the professional development of staff working in the lifelong learning sector - www.lluk.org

Professional Development Forum for Scottish Lecturers - www.fepdfscotland.co.uk

Times Educational Supplement (weekly) (The Times Group) - www.tes.co.uk/

▶Working in schools & colleges (2007) (Babcock Lifeskills) - www.babcock-lifeskills.com/

▶Working in sport & leisure (2010) (Babcock Lifeskills) - www.babcock-lifeskills.com/

Addresses

Association of Teachers and Lecturers (ATL)
7 Northumberland Street, London WC2N 5RD
Phone: +44 (0)20 7930 6441
Web: www.atl.org.uk

Institute for Learning (IfL)
First Floor, 49-51 East Road, London N1 6AH
Phone: 0844 815 3202 (UK only)
Web: www.ifl.ac.uk

University and College Union (UCU)
Carlow Street, London NW1 7LH
Phone: +44 (0)20 7756 2500
Web: www.ucu.org.uk

University of Ulster
Cromore Road, Coleraine, Ulster BT52 1SA
Phone: 0870 040 0700 (UK only)
Web: www.ulster.ac.uk

Similar Jobs

Lecturer: Higher Education, NVQ/SVQ Assessor, Teacher: English to Speakers of Other Languages, Teacher: Secondary School, Training & Development Officer/Manager

Lecturer: Higher Education

also known as: HE Lecturer

CRCI:Education and Training
CLCI:FAB — Job Band: 5

Job Description

Higher education (HE) lecturers teach students aged 18 and over who are studying for first or higher degrees, foundation degrees, vocational subjects, professional or other qualifications, in universities and in some colleges of further education. They prepare course work and material for lectures, seminars and tutorials. They also assess students' coursework and supervise their research activities. Depending on the subject taught, they plan and supervise any practical work, such as laboratory work, organise field trips, or any work placements. Setting and marking exams, assignments and projects is an important aspect of this job. They often act as personal tutor and take on a pastoral role with their students.

HE lecturers usually carry out their own subject research, write papers or textbooks, attend professional conferences and seminars. They liaise with other university colleagues and also have some administrative duties. May establish links with commercial, industrial and public organisations both local and national/international.

Work Details

Works in a university/college in lecture theatres/classrooms, laboratories, studios or perhaps out on fieldwork. Contact teaching hours vary according to your contract but working hours are flexible. Sometimes you work long hours and also take work home. You are responsible for developing students' knowledge and understanding of your subject, and also need to maintain an extensive and up-to-date knowledge yourself. As well as teaching and supervising students, you are expected to do research and to make contributions to academic journals, and address conferences and meetings.

Work is with groups, with individual students and with colleagues. You should be able to relate well both to young people and to mature students. Work is challenging and you are responsible for organising your own workload.

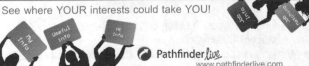

Qualification

- **England, Wales and Northern Ireland**

Band 5: For degree courses: 2-3 A levels and some GCSEs (A*-C) usually including English and maths, or equivalent. Exact requirements depend on the degree you take.

- **Scotland**

Band 5: For degree courses: 3-5 H grades and some S grades (1-3), usually including English and maths, or similar qualifications. Exact requirements depend on the degree you take.

Degree Information

New entrants require a good degree in a relevant subject and have, or be working towards, a PhD.

Adult Qualifications

Government training opportunities, such as apprenticeships, may be available in your area. You can also gain recognition of previous experience through Accreditation of Prior Learning (APL) or by working towards relevant S/NVQs. Contact your local careers office, Jobcentre Plus, Next Step service or Learning and Skills Council (LSC) Local Enterprise Company (LEC) for details of training schemes.

Work Experience

Entry to this job is competitive and it is important that you try to do some relevant work experience before applying for posts. Evidence of commitment to teaching as well as the subject is required. This can come in the form of working in education in a similar role or working professionally in the field in which you intend to lecture.

Entry and Training

Study is essential for first degree and postgraduate qualifications. Entry without a degree (usually a first or a 2.1) is not possible and applicants must have or be working towards a PhD. Applicants usually require an impressive CV (curriculum vitae) of research and publications. Many universities offer in-house courses covering personal development, IT skills, research techniques, as well as administration and management skills. Some also offer mentoring schemes for new lecturers. All those working with young people under 18 or with vulnerable adults are required to have a Criminal Records Bureau (CRB)/Disclosure Scotland check.

There are also formal postgraduate teaching qualifications for lecturers in higher education. These are now compulsory in many universities and are completed part time whilst working. They cover practical skills and theories of learning, and are accredited by the Higher Education Academy (HEA). The HEA also runs a professional development and recognition scheme, leading to membership of the Academy at three levels.

Entry to this work can be competitive unless offering a shortage subject, such as IT or engineering. There are National Teaching Fellowship Awards (England and NI) offered by the HEA for excellence in teaching that are worth £10k to lecturers or support staff in higher education.

In Scotland, you must have or work towards, a postgraduate certificate in teaching and learning in higher education that is available on a part-time basis, as well as through a distance-learning programme of study.

Mature applicants who wish to pursue a career as a lecturer in higher education and who are not graduates, face long academic training and fierce competition from younger applicants. Those with postgraduate academic qualifications, relevant experience, and for some courses, a relevant professional background, have a good chance of entry. There is a part-time postgraduate certificate in teaching and learning in higher education for those already in paid/unpaid employment. Part-time lecturing of undergraduate students, combined with research work, can lead to full-time employment.

There is also a Scottish postgraduate certificate in teaching and learning in higher education that may be studied through distance learning as well as by part-time study.

Opportunities and Pay

Employment is with a university or institute of higher education, with some teaching higher education courses in further education colleges. Specialised work opportunities are found in postgraduate institutions such as in business and law schools. There are also opportunities in the independent sector. The number of lecturers has grown over the past few years to around 130,000, due to a continuing increase in students taking HE courses. Often you may be initially employed on a short-term contract, or perhaps as a research or post-doctoral assistant.

Promotion opportunities are possible, though fiercely competitive, and can be to very senior levels, such as a reader, chair or dean, though this is heavily dependent on increasing responsibility and expertise in areas of management, administration and research. There are opportunities for part-time and freelance work, outside consultancy contracts, broadcast and conference work, writing and editing, or you may work abroad, particularly in Australia, China and Hong Kong, and the USA.

Starting salaries do vary depending on the individual institution, but are usually around £29k a year, with senior lecturers earning up to £55k. Salaries in London are usually higher.

Health

Permanent full-time jobs may require a medical test.

Skills and Qualities

able to stimulate learners, able to work both on your own and in a team, able to work to deadlines, analytical skills, capable of original thought, excellent communication skills, good organisational skills, IT skills, objective, research skills

Relevant Subjects

English, Psychology, Sociology

Further Information

LLUK (Lifelong Learning UK) - sector skills council for the professional development of staff working in the lifelong learning sector - www.lluk.org

Teaching in Higher Education (6 times a year) - www.tandf.co.uk/journals

Times Educational Supplement (weekly) (The Times Group) - www.tes.co.uk/

University Association for Lifelong Learning - www.uall.ac.uk

▶Working in English (2007) (Babcock Lifeskills) - www.babcock-lifeskills.com/

▶Working in schools & colleges (2007) (Babcock Lifeskills) - www.babcock-lifeskills.com/

Addresses

Higher Education Academy (HEA)
Innovation Way, York Science Park YO10 5BR
Phone: +44 (0)1904 717 500
Web: www.heacademy.ac.uk

University and College Union (UCU)
Carlow Street, London NW1 7LH
Phone: +44 (0)20 7756 2500
Web: www.ucu.org.uk

Similar Jobs

IT Skills Trainer, Lecturer: Further Education, Teacher: Secondary School, Training & Development Officer/Manager

Legal Cashier

also known as: Legal Accountant, Legal Administrator

CRCI:Legal and Political Services
CLCI:LAG Job Band: 2 to 3

Job Description

Legal cashiers are responsible for the accounting and finance functions in a solicitor's practice. They help to ensure that a solicitor's practice is run efficiently in line with the regulations laid down by the Law Society. They keep records of accounts and fees, ensuring that the practice is profitable. Legal cashiers provide advice to solicitors on how to invest money and deal with other financial matters such as value added tax (VAT).

Senior cashiers work closely with auditors to prepare yearly accounts and write reports for managers. They have a range of administrative duties, including marketing, personnel management, and dealing with health and safety issues.

Work Details

You usually work regular office hours, Monday to Friday, though you are expected to work extra hours at times. Quick, accurate work is required and you must keep up to date with changes in both financial and legal practice. Teamwork is usual, but you also need to work on your own. Those working on a freelance basis may need to visit their solicitor clients. Work can be demanding at times.

Qualification

• England, Wales and Northern Ireland

Band 2: There are no set entry qualifications, but some employers look for some GCSEs (A*-C) including English, maths or business studies. Equivalent qualifications such as NVQ Level 2 in business or accounting are also acceptable.

Band 3: Many employers require 5 GCSEs (A*-C), including English and maths.

Adult Qualifications

There are no set entry qualifications, those with qualifications and/or experience in business, accounting or administrative work have an advantage.

Work Experience

Work experience gives you an insight into what you enjoy and do not enjoy about a job or working environment, as well as the opportunity to acquire new skills. It also provides valuable information to add to your CV and improves any course application and future employment prospects. Experience of office and administration work, and of working with the public and giving people advice, is an advantage.

Entry and Training

Most training is on the job usually under the supervision of a senior cashier. Student membership of the Institute of Legal Cashiers and Administrators (ILCA) is open to anyone working in a solicitors' accounts department. Progression to the higher grades of membership is by ILCA qualification and experience only. The ILCA has its own structured examination scheme, which are correspondence courses with tutorial support.

The diploma is designed to cover the basic day to day work. After passing the diploma examination and with two years' experience, you can become a diploma member of the ILCA. The associate course covers accounting, financial management and legal practice and procedures. After passing the associate course and with six years' experience, you can become an associate member of ILCA.

The ILCA also runs the legal accounts training and examinations for the Institute of Legal Executives (ILEX) and a range of one and two day seminars for continuing professional development (CPD). Contact ILCA for details of all courses, qualifications and membership.

Mature entrants have an advantage, particularly if they have experience of accounts or administrative work. Because of the varied ages and backgrounds of those joining the ILCA, there are no formal requirements for embarking on the examination route.

Opportunities and Pay

Legal cashiers/accountants work for firms of solicitors, mainly in towns and cities in England, Wales and Northern Ireland. Entry to this work is competitive. The traditional starting point is a junior position in a solicitor's accounts section, eventually progressing to a more senior position through study for examinations. Completion of the Institute of Legal Cashiers and Administrators' diploma can lead to more senior positions such as practice manager. There are opportunities for legal cashiers to work on a freelance basis.

Pay varies depending on location and size of employer. Trainees earn from around £10k-£18k, rising to £20k-£30k a year with experience. Senior cashiers can earn from £35k-£42k a year.

Skills and Qualities
able to communicate effectively, accurate, analytical skills, discreet, good organisational skills, IT skills, methodical, numeracy skills, trustworthy

Relevant Subjects
Business and accounting, ICT/Computer studies, Law, Mathematics

Further Information
Law Gazette (Law Society) - www.lawgazette.co.uk

Skills for Justice - sector skills council for the UK justice system - www.skillsforjustice.com

▶Working in politics & law (2010) (Babcock Lifeskills) - www.babcock-lifeskills.com/

Addresses
Institute of Legal Cashiers and Administrators (ILCA)
2nd Floor, Marlowe House, 109 Station Road, Sidcup,
Kent DA15 7ET
Phone: +44 (0)20 8302 2867
Web: www.ilca.org.uk

Law Society of England & Wales
The Law Society's Hall, 113 Chancery Lane, London WC2A 1PL
Phone: +44 (0)20 7242 1222
Web: www.lawsociety.org.uk

Similar Jobs
Accounting Technician, Barristers' Clerk, Clerk: Accounts, Law Costs Draftsman, Legal Executive, Secretary: Legal

Legal Executive
CRCI:Legal and Political Services
CLCI:LAD Job Band: 3 to 5

Job Description
Legal executives are qualified lawyers specialising in a particular area of the law, such as family law, wills and probate, criminal cases, civil disputes, corporate and commercial, conveyancing and debt recovery. They have their own clients and can undertake representation in court where appropriate. They research and analyse legal information, such as preparing documents, looking up references and interviewing clients or witnesses.

Legal executives are often the main point of contact for clients concerning their legal affairs. Training and supervising junior staff, including clerks and secretarial staff, may be part of their job.

Work Details
You usually work normal office hours over a five-day week, but overtime is possible. The work is office based, but can involve some travel. You interview clients, explain legal language to them and give advice. You must reassure those clients who are anxious. Some of the duties involve court work. Close attention to detail is needed, when gathering information and researching cases. The work can be demanding when there are deadlines to be met.

Qualification
- **England, Wales and Northern Ireland**

Band 3: Minimum entry to ILEX exams: 4 GCSEs (A*-C) including English and three other ILEX approved academic subjects. Most entrants have A/AS levels or BTEC national awards/Applied A levels.

Band 4: Usual entry for ILEX exams: two A levels and at least one GCSE (A*-C) including English or equivalent. For HND in legal studies: at least one A level and some GCSEs (A*-C) including English and maths, or equivalent.

Band 5: For relevant degree: 2-3 A levels, or equivalent, and some GCSEs (A*-C), including English and maths, or equivalent qualifications. Exact requirements depend on the degree you take.

Degree Information
Degrees in subjects such as law, legal studies, accounting and finance, and business studies are appropriate.

Adult Qualifications
Applicants over 21 with relevant experience may be considered by the Institute of Legal Executives without formal qualifications. Trainees often transfer from legal secretarial work. Entry requirements may be relaxed for adults applying for degree and higher national courses. Check with individual colleges and universities.

Work Experience
Work experience gives you an insight into what you enjoy and do not enjoy about a job or working environment, as well as the opportunity to acquire new skills. It also provides valuable information to add to your CV and improves your employment prospects. Entry to this job is competitive. Experience of office and administration work, working with the public and giving people advice are an advantage.

Entry and Training
This job is similar to that of a solicitor, but the entry route is very different. To become a legal executive, you have to pass the examinations of the Institute of Legal Executives (ILEX) and serve a period of qualifying work experience. There are two levels of course: the professional diploma in law and practice (level 3) and the professional higher diploma in law and practice (level 6). The courses usually take two years each to complete, as most applicants are employed and study part time at one of over 100 accredited training centres. However, you can also qualify by distance learning, through the ILEX Tutorial College.

Once you have passed the exams you can become a full member of ILEX, but only after you have completed five years of qualifying experience can you become a fellow and call yourself a legal executive. Contact ILEX for further details. It is common practice for employers to assist with the cost of training as a legal executive. Once qualified you are expected to undertake continuing professional development (CPD) throughout your career.

Law graduates, with either a qualifying law degree or the graduate diploma in law are exempt from the academic part of the ILEX qualifications. They still need to take the exams in legal practice, while working in a legal environment. They are also still not eligible to become a fellow of ILEX until they have five years' experience.

Mature entrants without formal qualifications, but with previous experience and skills in areas of work that include accounting, legal secretarial, academic and commercial work, and other relevant experience, may have an advantage for training posts. It is possible to study for the ILEX examinations either part time, some weekends and evening classes, and through distance learning.

Opportunities and Pay
There are over 24,000 members of ILEX in the UK, 9000 of them are fellows. You work mainly in private practice. However, there are some opportunities in the civil service, local government, industry and in commerce. Legal executives usually specialise in litigation (disputes), conveyancing, family law, accounting, business and commercial law or probate (wills). With experience there are also prospects for promotion to head of department or to run a solicitor's branch office. As a qualified legal executive you can go on to become a partner in a law firm, train as an advocate, or decide to become a judge. You can also use the ILEX route to become a solicitor if you wish.

Pay varies depending on location and size of employer. There are opportunities for self-employment. Starting salaries for trainee legal executives are around £14k, rising to £35k a year with qualifications and experience. Senior legal executives can earn £50k-£70k a year.

Skills and Qualities
able to get on with all kinds of people, analytical skills, attention to detail, awareness of confidentiality issues, good communication skills, good concentration level, good organisational skills, IT skills, methodical, research skills

Relevant Subjects
Business and accounting, English, Law

Further Information
Law Gazette (Law Society) - www.lawgazette.co.uk

Legal Executive Journal (Institute of Legal Executives) - www.ilex.org.uk/

Skills for Justice - sector skills council for the UK justice system - www.skillsforjustice.com

▶Working in politics & law (2010) (Babcock Lifeskills) - www.babcock-lifeskills.com/

Addresses
Institute of Legal Executives (ILEX)
Kempston Manor, Bedfordshire MK42 7AB
Phone: +44 (0)1234 841 000
Web: www.ilex.org.uk

Law Society of England & Wales
The Law Society's Hall, 113 Chancery Lane, London WC2A 1PL
Phone: +44 (0)20 7242 1222
Web: www.lawsociety.org.uk

Similar Jobs
Company Secretary, Crown Prosecution Service Caseworker, Licensed Conveyancer, Magistrates' Court Legal Adviser, Paralegal, Solicitor

Leisure Centre Assistant
also known as: Sports Centre Assistant

CRCI:Leisure, Sport and Tourism
CLCI:GAJ Job Band: 1 to 3

Job Description
Leisure centre assistants carry out a range of duties and activities concerned with sport and recreation, according to the type of centre. Many centres require regular changes of equipment for different activities in the same hall, eg aerobics, badminton, children's play activities. An assistant sets up equipment and checks for safety. May supervise clients using equipment. After each session, they remove equipment and inspect for any damage. Looks after changing rooms and keeps sports areas fresh and hygienic.

May work at reception, selling tickets and making bookings, handling personal and telephone enquiries, and sometimes learning coaching skills and first aid. Can also work in the catering facilities or bar areas at sports/leisure centres.

Work Details
Usually works a basic 37-40 hr week. Shift work is common, either starting early in the day or working from mid afternoon until the centre closes in the evening. Most centres are open seven days a week so you may have to work weekends. You are responsible for the safety of participants, the cleanliness of the centre and possibly security as well. You may have to do the same task over and over again, like putting out goal posts.

Some of the equipment may be heavy to lift and set up. You may be asked to wear a company uniform and usually special footwear. You meet and work with people of all ages.

Qualification
• England, Wales and Northern Ireland
Band 1: For entry to jobs, no minimum qualifications are needed, but you are expected to have a good level of general education and relevant experience. Some formal/vocational qualifications at any level are useful.

Band 2: For entry to jobs, no minimum qualifications are needed, but it is an advantage to have some GCSEs (A*-C) or equivalent in subjects that include English and maths.

Band 3: For entry to jobs, HNC or a relevant Diploma, usually at least 4 GCSEs (A*-C) including English and maths, or equivalent.

• Scotland
Band 1: For entry to jobs, no minimum qualifications are needed, but you are expected to have a good level of general education and relevant experience. Some formal/vocational qualifications at any level are useful.

Band 2: Although academic qualifications are not specified for this job, it is an advantage to have some S grades (1-3) in subjects that include English and maths, or similar.

Band 3: For entry to jobs, usually at least four S grades (1-3) including English or maths, or similar.

Adult Qualifications
There are many different full and part-time courses that are suitable for entry to this job. Entry requirements are often relaxed for suitably experienced adults. Consult your local college for details of relevant courses.

Work Experience
Work experience gives you an insight into what you enjoy and don't enjoy about a job or working environment, as well as the opportunity to acquire new skills. It also provides valuable information to add to your CV and improves any course application and/or your future employment prospects. This can either be unpaid or voluntary, holiday or part-time work that you have organised yourself. Any experience of working in a sport/leisure environment and/or community or youth work is useful.

Entry and Training
Personal qualities such as a pleasant personality and self-motivation are generally more important than specific qualifications. There are many different full-time college courses that are suitable for entry to this job. Check with your local college for further information on City & Guilds and BTEC/SQA national awards. It is an advantage to have experience in first aid. Additional training is on the job, working with experienced staff, and by part-time or short courses to gain certain skills, such as first aid or health and safety.

The Institute for Sport, Parks and Leisure (ISPAL) and the Institute of Sport and Recreation Management (ISRM) offer a wide range of short courses that are suitable for sports and leisure assistants. This includes courses that lead to the full National Pool Plant Operators' Certificate. Further courses are available for those assistants who wish to progress to supervisory management. Check the ISPAL and ISRM websites for full course details.

At work, you may be able to obtain relevant S/NVQs in subjects such as sport, recreation and allied occupations at levels 1-3, and in leisure management at level 3. Active IQ also run a level 2 diploma/certificate course in sport and recreation. Relevant training programmes, including apprenticeship schemes in active leisure and learning, community development and/or customer service, may be available in your area. Advanced apprenticeships leading to qualification at level 3 can be a route into higher education. A Diploma/Welsh Baccalaureate may also be available in your area in Sport & Active Leisure. Contact SkillsActive for further details.

Mature entrants with relevant experience may be preferred by some employers. Some previous experience in sport and leisure or community group work is an advantage. You may be able to benefit through government training opportunities, such as apprenticeships in active leisure and learning, that may be available in your area. You can also gain recognition of previous experience through Accreditation of Prior Learning (APL) or by working towards relevant S/NVQs. Contact your local careers office, Jobcentre Plus, Next Step service or Learning and Skills Council (LSC) Local Enterprise Company (LEC) for details of training schemes, including apprenticeships for adults.

Opportunities and Pay

Since London won the bid to host the 2012 Olympic Games, there is more focus on raising standards in sport in the UK. For those with the right qualifications and skills, employment prospects look good. There are opportunities in most areas of the UK. You are employed by a local authority, a university or college, a private leisure or health and fitness centre, or a health club. It may be possible to work part time. Promotion to supervisory and management level is possible.

Pay depends on your location and employer, but is likely to be around £11k-£16k, with possible allowances and bonus payments on top of this. Further perks include the use of facilities for your own leisure and recreation.

Health

This job requires good general fitness.

Skills and Qualities

able to cope with emergencies, aptitude for teamwork, common sense, friendly, good interpersonal skills, helpful, practical skills, reliable, stamina, strong

Relevant Subjects

Biology, Health and social care, Leisure, travel and tourism, Physical education and sport, Science

Further Information

Active IQ Awarding Body - www.activeiq.co.uk

Apprenticeship Schemes (National Apprenticeship Service) - www.apprenticeships.org.uk

CareerScope: Hospitality and Leisure (Springboard UK) - http://careerscope.springboarduk.net/

Diplomas (Foundation, Higher and Advanced) - http://yp.direct.gov.uk/diplomas

Institute for Sport, Parks & Leisure (ISPAL) E-zine (ISPAL) - www.ispal.org.uk/ezine

People 1st - sector skills council for hospitality, leisure, travel and tourism - www.people1st.co.uk

Real Life Guide to Sports & Active Leisure (Trotman 2009) - www.trotman.co.uk

Recreation (10 x year) (Yudu Publishing) - www.isrm.co.uk

SkillsActive - sector skills council for active leisure, learning and well-being - www.skillsactive.com

UKSP - Guide to Success in Hospitality, Leisure, Travel & Tourism - www.uksp.co.uk/

Welsh Institute of Sport - www.welsh-institute-sport.co.uk

▶Working in sport & leisure (2010) (Babcock Lifeskills) - www.babcock-lifeskills.com/

Addresses

Fitness Northern Ireland
The Robinson Centre, Montgomery Road, Belfast BT6 9HS
Phone: +44 (028) 90704080
Web: www.fitnessni.org

Institute for Sport, Parks & Leisure (ISPAL)
Abbey Business Centre, 1650 Arlington Business Park, Theale, Reading RG7 4SA
Phone: 0844 418 0077 (UK only)
Web: www.ispal.org.uk

Institute of Sport & Recreation Management (ISRM) and the National Association for Sports Development,
Sir John Beckwith Centre for Sport Loughborough University, Leicestershire LE11 3TU
Phone: +44 (0)1509 226 474
Web: www.isrm.co.uk

Sport England
3rd Floor Victoria House, Bloomsbury Square, London WC1B 4SE
Phone: +44 (0)20 7273 1551
Web: www.sportengland.org

Sport Scotland
Doges, Templeton on the Green, 62 Templeton Street, Glasgow G40 1DA
Phone: +44 (0)141 534 6500
Web: www.sportscotland.org.uk

Sport Wales
National Sports Centre Sophia Gardens, Cardiff CF11 9SW
Phone: +44 (0)845 045 0904
Web: www.sports-council-wales.co.uk

Sports Council Northern Ireland
House of Sport, 2a Upper Malone Road, Belfast BT9 5LA
Phone: +44 (0)28 9038 1222
Web: www.sportni.net

Similar Jobs

Caretaker, Fitness Instructor, Holiday Centre Worker, Leisure Manager, Pool Lifeguard, Sports Coach

Leisure Manager

also known as: Gym Manager, Holiday Centre Manager, Recreation Manager, Sports Centre Manager

CRCI:Leisure, Sport and Tourism
CLCI:GAJ Job Band: 2 to 5

Job Description

Leisure mangers are responsible for the smooth and efficient running of leisure centres, sports centres, theme parks, bingo clubs, holiday centres, historic buildings, country parks and other recreational facilities. They plan the best use of resources and encourage people to use the facilities on offer. May organise additional activities such as sports tournaments and coaching, exhibitions, conferences and craft fairs. They are also responsible for buildings, equipment, safety of customers/visitors, finance and budgetary management, development of social/community amenities, marketing and general administration. Managers are involved in recruiting, training and supervising staff, as well as organising their daily work schedule. Also handles any problems that may arise.

Work Details

Usually works a basic 37-40 hr week, but may have to work some unsocial hours, including evenings and weekends, possibly on a rota basis. Contact is with people of all ages and you are responsible for their safety and general welfare while at the centre. The work is mainly office based but you are also out and about, talking to customers and staff. The work can be challenging and you need to make difficult decisions. Depending on the type of centre, work can be more demanding at certain times of the year.

Qualification

• England, Wales and Northern Ireland

Band 3: For entry to jobs, HNC or a relevant Diploma in business, sport, or travel and tourism, usually at least 4 GCSEs (A*-C) including English and maths, or equivalent.

Band 4: For HND, Diploma of Higher Education or foundation degree: 1-2 A levels and some GCSEs (A*-C) usually including English and maths, or equivalent.

Band 5: For degree courses: 2-3 A levels and some GCSEs (A*-C) usually including English and maths, or equivalent. Exact requirements depend on the degree you take.

• Scotland

Band 3: For direct entry or a relevant SQA national award such as leisure, business or hospitality: usually at least four S grades (1-3) preferably including English and maths, or similar.

Band 4: For entry to SQA higher national and professional development awards, usually 2-3 H grades and some S grades (1-3), including English and maths, or similar qualifications.

Band 5: For degree courses: 3-5 H grades and some S grades (1-3), including English and maths, or similar qualifications. Exact requirements depend on the degree you take.

Degree Information

Any degree is acceptable for entry to this job, but a degree in leisure or sports management may lead to exemptions from professional examinations. Subjects that give useful background information for this job include hospitality management, marketing, business studies, industrial relations, heritage management, and sports and recreation management. Postgraduate qualifications are available in leisure/sports management and related subjects.

Adult Qualifications

Entry requirements may be relaxed for adults applying for higher education courses and Access or foundation courses give adults without qualifications a route onto degree courses. Passes in English and maths are useful.

Work Experience

Work experience gives you an insight into what you do and don't enjoy about a job or working environment, as well as the opportunity to acquire new skills. It also provides valuable information to add to your CV and improves any course application and/or your future employment prospects. Useful experience includes work in retail, recreation centres, gyms and catering establishments such as restaurants or hotels.

Entry and Training

Entry to this job is possible with a range of different qualifications. However training posts are rare and competition is fierce, so some form of further or higher education is usually required. Most enter at supervisor, assistant manager or trainee manager level and progress to manager after in-house training.

During employment you may be expected to work towards professional qualification from one of the professional bodies, such as the Institute for Sport, Parks and Leisure (ISPAL) or the Institute of Sport and Recreation Management (ISRM). The certificates and diplomas from the ISRM are awarded after study by day release or evening classes or by following a correspondence course. Check the ISRM website for a full list of courses available.

ISPAL also offers tailored in-house training courses in categories such as leisure operations, leadership and management, and event management. Contact ISPAL for further details of courses, routes to membership and qualifications. Certain degree courses may give exemptions from some of these professional exams. Managers of some sports centres may also need to coach and instruct. Qualifications from the governing body of the sport may therefore also be required.

Foundation degrees are available in subjects that include sports and leisure management, tourism and leisure management, leisure and sport management, leisure services management and hospitality. Relevant training programmes, including apprenticeship schemes, BTEC awards and the NVQ in leisure management (level 3), may be available in your area. Advanced apprenticeships in leisure management and customer service leading to qualification at level 3 can be a route into higher education. Relevant Diplomas/Welsh Baccalaureates in sport and active leisure and/or hospitality may also be available in your area.

Mature entrants with relevant experience may be preferred by some employers. It is often possible for those already working in the industry to move into management. You can study for professional qualifications, such as those from the Institute of Sport and Recreation Management (ISRM), part time or via day-release courses whilst working. Adults may be able to enter this work through a government-funded training programme, such as an apprenticeship in leisure management or customer service.

You can also gain recognition of previous experience through Accreditation of Prior Learning (APL) or by working towards relevant S/NVQs. Contact your local careers office, Jobcentre Plus, Next Step service or Learning and Skills Council (LSC) Local Enterprise Company (LEC) for details of training schemes, including apprenticeship for adults.

Opportunities and Pay

Since London won the bid to host the 2012 Olympic Games, there is more focus on raising standards in sport in the UK. For those with the right qualifications and skills, employment prospects look good. There are jobs in a wide variety of organisations in towns and cities across the country. These include commercial concerns like holiday parks/multi-leisure centres, private sports clubs, or organisations where leisure may be only one part of the business, eg Forest Enterprise or the National Trust. Leisure and sports centres may also be owned by local authorities. Some organisations, such as universities or large employers, run sports centres for their own personnel.

Pay varies depending on location, type and size of project, and level of responsibility. A starting salary is likely to be around £15k-£18k, rising to £19k-£26k with experience. Managers with the most responsibility earn from around £30k-£40k, or more. Often earnings are partly performance related. Perks may include the use of facilities for your own leisure and recreation.

Skills and Qualities

able to withstand criticism, business awareness, efficient, enthusiastic, good organisational skills, initiative, IT skills, numeracy skills, outgoing personality, self confident

Relevant Subjects

Business and accounting, Economics, English, Hospitality and catering, Mathematics

Further Information

Apprenticeship Schemes (National Apprenticeship Service) - www.apprenticeships.org.uk

Diplomas (Foundation, Higher and Advanced) - http://yp.direct.gov.uk/diplomas

Institute for Sport, Parks & Leisure (ISPAL) E-zine (ISPAL) - www.ispal.org.uk/ezine

Leisure Management Magazine (The Leisure Media Company) - www.leisuremanagement.co.uk

People 1st - sector skills council for hospitality, leisure, travel and tourism - www.people1st.co.uk

Real Life Guide to Sports & Active Leisure (Trotman 2009) - www.trotman.co.uk

Recreation (10 x year) (Yudu Publishing) - www.isrm.co.uk

SkillsActive - sector skills council for active leisure, learning and well-being - www.skillsactive.com

Springboard UK (Springboard UK) - www.springboarduk.net

Springboard Wales (Springboard Wales) - http://wales.springboarduk.net/

UKSP - Guide to Success in Hospitality, Leisure, Travel & Tourism - www.uksp.co.uk/

▶Working in travel & tourism (2010) (Babcock Lifeskills) - www.babcock-lifeskills.com/

Addresses

Institute for Sport, Parks & Leisure (ISPAL)
Abbey Business Centre, 1650 Arlington Business Park, Theale, Reading RG7 4SA
Phone: 0844 418 0077 (UK only)
Web: www.ispal.org.uk

Institute of Sport & Recreation Management (ISRM) and the National Association for Sports Development,
Sir John Beckwith Centre for Sport Loughborough University, Leicestershire LE11 3TU
Phone: +44 (0)1509 226 474
Web: www.isrm.co.uk

Sport England
3rd Floor Victoria House, Bloomsbury Square, London WC1B 4SE
Phone: +44 (0)20 7273 1551
Web: www.sportengland.org

Sport Scotland
Doges, Templeton on the Green, 62 Templeton Street, Glasgow G40 1DA
Phone: +44 (0)141 534 6500
Web: www.sportscotland.org.uk

Sport Wales
National Sports Centre Sophia Gardens, Cardiff CF11 9SW
Phone: +44 (0)845 045 0904
Web: www.sports-council-wales.co.uk

Sports Council Northern Ireland
House of Sport, 2a Upper Malone Road, Belfast BT9 5LA
Phone: +44 (0)28 9038 1222
Web: www.sportni.net

Similar Jobs

Betting Shop Manager, Cinema Manager, Event & Exhibition Organiser, Hotel Manager, Marketing Manager, Sports Development Officer

Library & Information Manager

also known as: Librarian: Chartered

CRCI:Languages, Information and Culture
CLCI:FAF Job Band: 5

Job Description

Library managers organise the collection, classification, indexing and storage of information in a variety of media, including books, CDs/DVDs, newspapers, periodicals and journals, microfiche, computer software and photographs. They select, acquire, classify, catalogue and index new stock, usually with aid of a computer in an Online Public Access Catalogue (OPAC). New ways of storing and accessing information, using the Internet, web content and management systems, continue to develop. May work as part of a team who share some of the responsibilities. Helps people to easily access and use the information. Also promotes the use of the library, manages staff, develops new policies and is also responsible for budgeting and accounting, buildings, fittings, staff development and training.

Information managers are also responsible for providing library services to the community, including businesses and education, and in particular adult learners, the elderly and housebound, youth groups, schools and pre-school children, and ethnic-minority groups. Can also specialise in one field, including science, industry, art, or academic and research libraries. Use the Internet for research.

Work Details

Usually works a 36-40 hr week, Monday to Friday, though may be expected to work some evenings and on a Saturday. You advise and help people of all ages and abilities. A high standard of general knowledge is expected, together with specialist knowledge for many jobs. The work can be pressurised at times. Work environment can vary depending on the size of the library and the building.

Qualification

- **England, Wales and Northern Ireland**

Band 5: For degree courses: 2-3 A levels and some GCSEs (A*-C) usually including English and maths, or equivalent. Some courses also require a GCSE in modern languages. Exact requirements depend on the degree you take.

- **Scotland**

Band 5: For degree courses: 3-5 H grades and some S grades (1-3), including English and maths, or similar qualifications. Some courses also expect an S grade in modern languages. Exact requirements depend on the degree you take.

Degree Information

Information and library studies/management, information science/ management and information systems, can be studied as a first degree. This job can also be entered with a degree in any discipline, particularly computing, scientific/technical or business-related subjects, followed by a specialised postgraduate course in information and library management. For entry to postgraduate courses, experience in a library is required, and often a good reading knowledge of two modern languages is preferred.

Adult Qualifications

Entry requirements to degree courses in librarianship may be relaxed for mature entrants. Graduates in any degree discipline can apply for specialised postgraduate courses, which are both full and part time. Access or foundation courses to higher education are available that do not require formal entry qualifications, but lead to relevant HND and degree courses.

Work Experience

Work experience gives you an insight into what you enjoy and do not enjoy about a job or working environment, and the opportunity to acquire new skills. It also provides valuable information to add to your CV and improves any course application and/or your future employment prospects. Entry to this career is highly competitive and it is essential that you have some relevant work or voluntary experience before applying to these positions. Experience of library work, archive work or something similar, such as work in a county or national records office is expected.

Entry and Training

Employers prefer a degree or relevant postgraduate qualification that is accredited by the Chartered Institute of Library and Information Professionals (CILIP). This is the professional organisation that accredits undergraduate and postgraduate library and information courses in the UK. Before beginning a postgraduate course, a period of practical library experience is required. There are special graduate traineeships for this purpose. To become a full or chartered member of CILIP, you need to complete a first degree or postgraduate qualification in information management, and to have at least three years' approved experience in information work.

You also need to follow a programme of continuing professional development during the period of approved experience. Corporate members of CILIP with at least five years of full-time professional practice (or equivalent) can apply for the highest status of professional qualification by becoming a Fellow of CILIP. CILIP offers a range of short courses, conferences and seminars. Contact them for further details. Aslib, the Association for Information Management, also runs training courses and produces relevant publications.

Mature entrants with previous work experience in libraries or with computers, or with skills in other related fields such as languages have an advantage. An apprenticeship in information and library services may be available in your area if you have no experience at all. Lifelong Learning UK offers a level 2 certificate and a level 3 diploma in libraries, archives and information services. Check the website for details. Postgraduate courses can be studied full or part time and through distance learning.

Opportunities and Pay

You can be employed by a local authority in a public library, a hospital, a university or college in an academic library, or perhaps in industry, commerce, or by a government department or agency. Jobs are available mainly in towns and cities. There is scope to specialise, perhaps in your degree subject. Increasing opportunities are available in web content and management as alternative ways of storing information. Promotion prospects depend on your employer, but in the public sector, prospects are reduced due to spending cuts. It is possible to become self-employed and work on a consultancy basis. There may also be opportunities to work part time.

Pay varies depending on location and type of library, but salaries start at around £19k-£23k, increasing to around £29k a year. Senior librarians/information managers can earn up to £50k a year. Heads of a department or service can earn more.

Skills and Qualities

able to get on with all kinds of people, able to work to a budget, enquiring mind, good communication skills, good organisational skills, information handling skills, IT skills, literacy and numeracy skills, methodical, research skills

Relevant Subjects

Classical studies, English, ICT/Computer studies, Media and communication studies, Modern Foreign Languages

Further Information

A Career in Information Work (CILIP) (CILIP) - www.cilip.org.uk/jobs-careers

Apprenticeship Schemes (National Apprenticeship Service) - www.apprenticeships.org.uk

Library & Information Gazette (fortnightly) (CILIP) - www.cilip.org.uk/publications/gazette

LLUK (Lifelong Learning UK) - sector skills council for the professional development of staff working in the lifelong learning sector - www.lluk.org

Local Government Careers (Improvement and Development Agency) - www.lgcareers.com/publications/

Managing Information (monthly) (Aslib) - www.aslib.co.uk/publications/managinginformation.htm

▶Working in English (2007) (Babcock Lifeskills) - www.babcock-lifeskills.com/

▶Working in schools & colleges (2007) (Babcock Lifeskills) - www.babcock-lifeskills.com/

Addresses

Aslib, The Association for Information Management
207 Davina House, 137-149 Goswell Road, London EC1V 7ET
Phone: +44 (0)20 7253 3349
Web: www.aslib.co.uk

Chartered Institute of Library and Information Professionals (CILIP)
7 Ridgmount Street, London WC1E 7AE
Phone: +44 (0)20 7255 0500
Web: www.cilip.org.uk

Museums, Libraries and Archives Council (MLA)
Grosvenor House, 14 Bennetts Hill, Birmingham B2 5RS
Phone: +44 (0)121 345 7300
Web: www.mla.gov.uk

SLAINTE: Information and Libraries Scotland
1st Floor, Building C, Brandon Gate, Leechlee Road, Hamilton ML3 6AU
Phone: +44 (0)1698 458 888
Web: www.slainte.org.uk

Similar Jobs

Archivist, Information Scientist, Library Assistant, Museum/Art Gallery Curator, Patent Attorney

Library Assistant

also known as: Information Assistant

CRCI:Languages, Information and Culture
CLCI:FAF Job Band: 3

Job Description

Library assistants carry out work to support professionally qualified librarians/information managers and information scientists. Works in a public library, an academic or specialised library, such as in medical and law establishments, and for private companies. May also work in a mobile library that travels around the local area. They perform a variety of clerical/administrative tasks necessary for the day-to-day running of a library. These include issuing books, and putting data labels and barcodes on other materials, such as CDs/DVDs, and carrying out minor repairs. Library assistants also handle returned items, put books away on shelves, and complete other daily clerical work, such as dealing with the post and keeping the library tidy.

May help with the cataloguing of newly arrived material, usually on computerised systems and uses the Internet to research for specialist information. Also helps in the mounting of displays and exhibitions of a library's information material and its services, and also of local events. Answers readers queries in person and over the phone; contacts borrowers regarding overdue books and other items, usually by card or letter. Uses a central database to check the status of loans and reservations.

Work Details

Usually works a 35-40 hr week, Monday to Friday, and at times may be expected to work rotas to cover evenings and weekends. Libraries can be in old buildings or purpose built library buildings. You may work in a library department or, for some jobs, a mobile library. You give advice and help to people of all ages. Work involves some routine tasks, but can be pressurised at times. You have to cope with standing for many hours and with lifting piles of books. Work environment is usually quiet and pleasant, but can sometimes be dusty.

Qualification

• England, Wales and Northern Ireland

Band 3: For entry to jobs, HNC or a relevant Diploma, usually at least 4 GCSEs (A*-C) including English and maths, or equivalent. Qualifications in IT are also useful.

• Scotland

Band 3: For direct entry to a job or entry after a relevant course: usually at least four S grades (1-3) including English and maths, or similar. Qualifications in IT are also useful.

Adult Qualifications

Entry may be possible for adults with a good general educational background. Entry to courses is usually relaxed for mature applicants. For certain areas of library work, specialist knowledge, eg scientific/technical, can be helpful.

Work Experience
Employers or colleges may prefer candidates who have relevant work or voluntary experience. This can include anything which enables you to use administrative, computer or information handling skills. Experience of working with the public is also important, so any customer service work is relevant. In some areas there is a young apprenticeship (14-16) scheme that provides an extended work placement and eventual achievement of a relevant level 2 qualification while at school.

Entry and Training
Training is usually on the job with an experienced member of staff and you may be able to study for relevant vocational qualifications while working. The diploma/advanced diploma in applications of ICT in libraries is also a nationally recognised UK qualification that has been developed by SLAINTE: Information and Libraries Scotland and available nationwide. Lifelong Learning UK (LLUK) offers a level 2 certificate and a level 3 diploma in libraries, archives and information services. Check the website for details.

Further information on training routes and qualifications, many of which are part time or by distance learning, is available from LLUK, Aslib or the Chartered Institute of Library and Information Professionals or SLAINTE: Information and Libraries Scotland. S/NVQs are available in information and library services at levels 2-3. Apprenticeships in library and information services may also be available in your area and a Diploma in IT may be relevant for work in a public library.

There are relevant distance-learning courses available, including those offered by Aslib, The Association for Information Management. Mature applicants can benefit through government training opportunities that may be available in your area. Opportunities, such as apprenticeships, may be available in your area. You can also gain recognition of previous experience through Accreditation of Prior Learning (APL) or by working towards relevant S/NVQs. Contact your local careers office, Jobcentre Plus, Next Step service or Learning and Skills Council (LSC) Local Enterprise Company (LEC) for details of training schemes.

Opportunities and Pay
Usually you are employed by a local authority, a university or college, a hospital, prison or a government body. There are around 50,000 library assistants in the UK and most jobs are in towns and cities. There are opportunities to specialise in one particular area of library work. Promotion to senior positions usually depends on obtaining professional library qualifications. There are good opportunities to work part time and flexible hours.

Pay varies depending on location and type of library, but typical starting salaries are around £16k-£20k a year, rising with experience. Senior library assistants can earn more than this. These salaries are reflected in other types of specialist library establishments. Sectors such as the NHS and schools are likely to pay less, and assistants in public libraries may earn less than in the private sector.

Skills and Qualities
able to get on with all kinds of people, aptitude for teamwork, customer service skills, enquiring mind, good communication skills, good organisational skills, information handling skills, IT skills, methodical, patient

Relevant Subjects
English

Further Information
A Career in Information Work (CILIP) (CILIP) - www.cilip.org.uk/jobs-careers

Apprenticeship Schemes (National Apprenticeship Service) - www.apprenticeships.org.uk

Diplomas (Foundation, Higher and Advanced) - http://yp.direct.gov.uk/diplomas

Library & Information Gazette (fortnightly) (CILIP) - www.cilip.org.uk/publications/gazette

LLUK (Lifelong Learning UK) - sector skills council for the professional development of staff working in the lifelong learning sector - www.lluk.org

Local Government Careers (Improvement and Development Agency) - www.lgcareers.com/publications/

Qualifications for Library Assistants (CILIP) (CILIP) - www.cilip.org.uk/jobs-careers/qualifications

Training Schemes - www.direct.gov.uk/en/educationandlearning

▶Working in English (2007) (Babcock Lifeskills) - www.babcock-lifeskills.com/

▶Working in schools & colleges (2007) (Babcock Lifeskills) - www.babcock-lifeskills.com/

Addresses
Aslib, The Association for Information Management
207 Davina House, 137-149 Goswell Road, London EC1V 7ET
Phone: +44 (0)20 7253 3349
Web: www.aslib.co.uk

Chartered Institute of Library and Information Professionals (CILIP)
7 Ridgmount Street, London WC1E 7AE
Phone: +44 (0)20 7255 0500
Web: www.cilip.org.uk

Museums, Libraries and Archives Council (MLA)
Grosvenor House, 14 Bennetts Hill, Birmingham B2 5RS
Phone: +44 (0)121 345 7300
Web: www.mla.gov.uk

SLAINTE: Information and Libraries Scotland
1st Floor, Building C, Brandon Gate, Leechlee Road,
Hamilton ML3 6AU
Phone: +44 (0)1698 458 888
Web: www.slainte.org.uk

Similar Jobs
Administrator/Administrative Assistant, Airline Customer Service Agent, Bookshop Assistant, Customer Services Adviser, Library & Information Manager, Tourist Information Centre Assistant

Licensed Conveyancer
also known as: Property Lawyer

CRCI:Legal and Political Services
CLCI:LAZ — Job Band: 3 to 5

Job Description
Licensed conveyancers are specialist property lawyers concerned with transferring the ownership of property or land from a seller to a buyer. They work on behalf of the buyer or seller to draw up a contract for sale and see the transfer of ownership through to completion. They conduct the necessary land search enquiries with the relevant local authority, with regard to each individual property. Conveyancers obtain all the necessary documents, drafting and negotiating the contract itself, and advising their client throughout the procedure, while working to protect the client's best interests. They liaise with banks and building societies on any mortgage issues.

Conveyancers pay land tax and stamp duty relating to the properties. They keep detailed records of all payments made during the transfer of land and property. May also work on the sale and purchase of businesses. Some conveyancers undertake probate, advocacy and litigation work. Many conveyancing tasks are now done online using a computerised system.

Work Details
You usually work a basic 37 hr week, Monday to Friday, though extra weekend and evening work may be required when busy. You are based in an office, though you may have to visit clients and properties. You may spend some time working on a computer, doing research and preparing documentation. Smart clothing is normally expected.

Qualification

- **England, Wales and Northern Ireland**

Band 3: For entry to the conveyancing course approved by the Council for Licensed Conveyancers (CLC): a minimum of 4 GCSEs (A*-C) including English and maths, or equivalent.

Band 4: For entry as a trainee: some employers ask for two A levels or equivalent.

Band 5: For a degree: three A levels and some GCSEs (A*-C) including English and maths, or equivalent qualifications. Exact requirements depend on the degree you take.

Degree Information

Any degree is acceptable, but law or legal studies is the most relevant. You may also consider surveying, planning, finance/ administration or a business/management related degree.

Adult Qualifications

The Council for Licensed Conveyancers (CLC) may waive entry requirements for candidates over the age of 25.

Work Experience

Work experience gives you an insight into what you enjoy and do not enjoy about a job or working environment, as well as the opportunity to acquire new skills. It also provides valuable information to add to your CV and improves your employment prospects. Work experience with a solicitor is most appropriate, though this can be difficult to obtain as there is often considerable competition for places. Instead, you may consider working in a building society or with an estate agency firm, or anything office based where administration skills are used.

Entry and Training

In England and Wales, you are required to pass the exam set by the Council for Licensed Conveyancers (CLC), to acquire a licence. Study for the CLC course takes around two to three years on a part-time basis and is usually undertaken at the same time as a compulsory, supervised, two-year work placement scheme. This must be in qualifying employment such as a firm of licensed conveyancers, a solicitors or a building society. You can study for the CLC course through an accredited college or by CLC distance learning. Many larger law firms offer the course in-house to employees. Contact the CLC for details of all qualifying training routes.

Upon successful completion of the course, you are granted a limited licence that allows you to work as an employee of a licensed conveyancing company. After three years' experience, you may apply for the full licence, which enables you to offer conveyancing services directly to the public. You are also required to undertake 12 hours continuing professional development (CPD) each year in order to remain licensed.

Mature entrants with legal experience have an advantage. It is very useful to have experience as a legal secretary or legal executive. The examinations are available through distance learning. Contact the CLC for details on training and examinations.

Qualified solicitors and legal executives have exemption from most of the CLC examinations. See the CLC website for details.

Opportunities and Pay

At the moment there are over 1,000 licensed conveyancers, with another 3,000 working towards the licence. A downturn in the economy can result in fewer opportunities, as the housing market fluctuates. Most jobs are found in solicitors' firms and firms of licensed conveyancers. Some banks and building societies employ conveyancers, as do some councils. Licensed conveyancers can move into careers such as accountancy or the civil service, and those without full legal training can move on to starting a career in law. There are part time and job share opportunities.

Salaries for trainees usually start at around £15k a year. Once qualified, you can expect to earn £25k-£40k, depending on experience. Some earn up to £60k a year as a partner of a firm.

Skills and Qualities

attention to detail, awareness of confidentiality issues, business awareness, good at writing reports, IT skills, methodical, negotiating skills, numeracy skills, problem-solving skills, research skills

Relevant Subjects

Business and accounting, Economics, English, Law, Psychology

Further Information

CLC Chronicle (monthly) (Council for Licensed Conveyancers (CLC)) - www.conveyancer.org.uk/chronicle.asp

Law Gazette (Law Society) - www.lawgazette.co.uk

Skills for Justice - sector skills council for the UK justice system - www.skillsforjustice.com

TARGETjobs: Law (GTI Specialist Publishing Ltd.) - www.groupgti.com

▶Working in politics & law (2010) (Babcock Lifeskills) - www.babcock-lifeskills.com/

Addresses

Council for Licensed Conveyancers
16 Glebe Road, Chelmsford, Essex CM1 1QG
Phone: +44 (0)1245 349 599
Web: www.conveyancer.org.uk

Law Society of England & Wales
The Law Society's Hall, 113 Chancery Lane, London WC2A 1PL
Phone: +44 (0)20 7242 1222
Web: www.lawsociety.org.uk

Similar Jobs

Estate Agent, Legal Executive, Solicitor, Surveyor: General Practice, Town Planner

Life Coach

CRCI:Social Work and Counselling Services
CLCI:KED — Job Band: 2 to 5

Job Description

Life coaches assist individuals or groups to fulfil their potential in all areas of their lives, including relationships, careers, business, personal development and spiritual. Help clients to make progress so that they can lead more fulfilling and purposeful lives. Life coaches empower their clients to set goals for themselves and create action plans. They help their clients to achieve greater self-awareness. This is not a counselling or therapy career as progress and agenda are set by the clients themselves.

Work Details

Usually self-employed, you manage your own working hours and develop your business through networking and marketing. The work involves listening and providing motivation and support in sessions lasting from half an hour to an hour. People tell you things that are confidential and you need to have a non-judgemental attitude.

Much of the work is undertaken at home in preparing for an individual client or a client group and in reviewing sessions. The coaching is usually on business premises, in a hotel meeting room or in an individual's home. You may have to travel from client to client.

Qualification

This is generally a career for those with broad experience of life and work. There are no specific educational requirements and experience is considered to be more important. The profession is not yet regulated in the UK. However a good level of education is an advantage.

Degree Information
Any degree is acceptable, but subjects such as social studies and psychology are particularly relevant.

Adult Qualifications
There are no specific educational requirements and experience is considered to be more important. You may come to life coaching as a second career.

Work Experience
Work and life experience is essential for this job. Work involving dealing with people in a management or training capacity is especially relevant.

Entry and Training
Anyone can work as a life coach in the UK if they feel they have the right skills and qualities. However, accreditation and membership of professional bodies is an advantage and choosing a course endorsed by professional organisations is important. Check the Coaching and Mentoring Network website for information on accredited training. The Chartered Institute of Personnel and Development (CIPD) offers an Advanced Certificate in Coaching and Mentoring, which is designed for people with some experience.

As a practising life coach, you can seek accreditation by the UK International Coach Federation (ICF), which has three levels of membership, depending on your training and experience. You are eligible for Associate membership after 100 hours' practice and 60 hours' training; for Professional after 750 hours' experience and 125 hours of training and Master once you have completed 2,500 hours' practice and 200 hours' training.

Mature entrants are welcomed as broad life experience is vital for this work.

Opportunities and Pay
Life coaching is a growing field and life coaches work with both individuals and with companies. At present, as this is a relatively new field, work is based in the main cities. Most life coaches are self-employed and some have other jobs and do this work on a part-time basis.

Salaries are difficult to estimate as life coaches tend to be paid by the client and the amount of work available can be very variable. An average hourly rate for an individual client session is between £50 and £75, and for a corporate session some earn as much as £250 per hour.

Skills and Qualities
able to get on with all kinds of people, able to motivate others, able to put people at ease, awareness of confidentiality issues, clear-thinking, good communication skills, good interpersonal skills, good listening skills, non-judgemental

Relevant Subjects
Business and accounting, English, Psychology, Sociology

Further Information
Chartered Institute of Personnel and Development (CIPD) - www.cipd.co.uk

UK International Coach Federation (UKICP) - www.coachfederation.org

▶Working in advice & counselling (2007) (Babcock Lifeskills) - www.babcock-lifeskills.com/

Addresses
Association for Coaching
66 Church Road, London W7 1LB
Web: www.associationforcoaching.com

Coaching and Mentoring Network
PO Box 5551, Newbury, Berkshire RG20 7WB
Phone: +44 (0)870 733 3313
Web: www.coachingnetwork.org.uk

Similar Jobs
Advice Worker, Human Resources Officer/Manager, Image Consultant, Learning Mentor (England), Recruitment Consultant

Life Support Technician: Diving
also known as: Chamber Operator, Panel Operator

CRCI:Engineering
CLCI:RAK

Job Band: 1 to 3

Job Description
Life support technicians monitor and control surface life support equipment for divers working underwater. They work as part of a diving team and are one of the main points of surface contact. Technicians are required to respond to any abnormal condition or emergency that occurs during a dive. They use specialist control equipment to regulate the conditions in diving bells that are used at increasingly greater depths by divers in the marine construction industry.

Technicians constantly monitor data, such as atmospheric pressure and composition, fed back from instruments on the diving bell, or directly from the diver. They regularly inspect life support equipment, including helmets, oxygen masks, body armour, survival vests, night-vision devices, life rafts, and restraint harnesses. Also have a detailed knowledge of gases and conditions resulting in their interaction and act quickly in times of accident or emergency.

Technicians keep a detailed log (information record) of all actions taken during each dive. They have to keep up to date with the rapid advances in technology. If working in the armed forces, they also provide refresher combat survival training.

Work Details
Usually work a basic 37-40 hr week, though in some jobs, you may be required to work on a shift basis. The hours of work are often irregular and the work can be physically demanding. You may be based on a ship or oil/gas rig and may need to spend nights away from home or long periods at sea. Conditions can sometimes make even routine tasks difficult. You may be required to stand for long periods and need to stay alert at all times. There may be a risk of accidents from equipment or contact with dangerous materials.

Qualification

• England, Wales and Northern Ireland
Band 1: For entry to jobs, no minimum qualifications are needed, but you are expected to have a good level of general education and relevant experience. Some formal/vocational qualifications at any level are useful.

Band 2: For entry to jobs, no minimum qualifications are needed, but it is an advantage to have some GCSEs (A*-C) or equivalent in subjects that include English, maths and a science, or equivalent.

Band 3: For technician training prior to entry: usually at least 4 GCSEs (A*-C) including English, maths and a science subject, or equivalent.

• Scotland
Band 1: For entry to jobs, no minimum qualifications are needed, but you are expected to have a good level of general education and relevant experience. Some formal/vocational qualifications at any level are useful.

Band 2: Although academic qualifications are not specified for this job, it is an advantage to have some S grades (1-3) in subjects that include English, maths and a science, or similar, are useful.

Band 3: For technician training prior to entry: usually at least four S grades (1-3) including English and maths, or similar.

Adult Qualifications
There are no specific entry requirements but almost all entrants have experience in offshore work or previous technical training in an engineering-related subject. You can improve your skills and qualifications by working through the Foundation Learning programme. This involves taking credit-based units and qualifications to help you progress.

Work Experience
For jobs in diving or with the marine construction industry, employers or colleges/universities may prefer candidates who have relevant work or voluntary experience, perhaps in skilled technical areas such as welding, fitting or engineering. Although this job provides highly responsible non-diving support, any experience/qualifications in diving are a useful advantage. Many gain useful experience/qualification from working in the armed forces. Involvement with sub-aqua clubs, either local or whilst a student, or holiday dive experience, provide useful knowledge of the underwater industry.

Entry and Training
Anyone can apply for this job, though many applicants already work in the marine construction industry. This includes former divers who are retraining, or those with previous technician level training. This is not a job that is suitable for school leavers. To become an assistant life support technician (ALST) you must complete a ten-day course approved by the International Marine Contractors Association (IMCA), pass a medical test, and undergo survival training. This costs around £1000 and may be paid for by your employer.

The course includes units such as diving physics, diving physiology, plant and equipment, gas handling and toxicity and life support systems. You must then log 2,400 hours as an ALST before applying for the IMCA examination to qualify as a full life support technician. At least 50% of these hours must have been logged in the two years immediately prior to registration. Leadership training follows for those who wish to become a supervisor and have four years' work experience plus 2000 hours dive-monitoring time.

There are various funding options for the ALST course and you may be eligible for grant assistance training. Contact your local Learning and Skills Council (LSC)/Local Enterprise Company (LEC). Career Development Loans (CDLs) are also available for life support technician training.

Mature applicants with experience of living and working offshore are at an advantage. However, most life support technicians come from a variety of different backgrounds such as highly skilled technicians from other industries, qualified nurses, former divers and those specially trained for the role. There are also special training schemes for armed forces personnel, and also for some people who have been made redundant.

Contact your local careers office, Jobcentre Plus, Next Step service or Learning and Skills Council (LSC)/Local Enterprise Company (LEC) for details of training schemes.

Opportunities and Pay
There is a growth in saturation diving, with divers working at ever greater depths. However, there is still fierce competition for this work. Assistant life support technicians (ALSTs) may find it hard to get their first job as contractors tend to prefer experienced personnel. Your employer is most likely to be an offshore oil and gas company. However there are a small number of jobs with research institutes that examine different aspects of diving, including diving-related illnesses. Progression to a supervisory post is possible or you can become a trainer.

Pay varies with experience but as a newly-qualified ALST you can earn around £180 a day, rising to around £500 a day once fully qualified. Some senior North Sea saturation divers can earn £150k a year. Offshore allowances can be around £15-£20 a day on top of earnings.

Health
You must have a high standard of physical fitness and pass a strict medical. This job requires normal colour vision.

Skills and Qualities
able to work both on your own and in a team, able to work to deadlines, IT skills, practical skills, quick thinking, responsible attitude, safety conscious, technical aptitude, vigilant

Relevant Subjects
Design and technology, Engineering, Mathematics, Physical education and sport

Further Information
Diving and Undersea Vehicles (Society for Underwater Technology (SUT)) - www.sut.org.uk/

Foundation Learning (QCDA) - www.qcda.gov.uk

I want to be a Life Support Technician (IMCA) (International Marine Contractors' Association) - www.imca-int.com

Addresses
International Marine Contractors Association (IMCA)
52 Grosvenor Gardens, London SW1W 0AU
Phone: +44 (0)20 7824 5520
Web: www.imca-int.com/careers

Society for Underwater Technology (SUT)
80 Coleman Street, London EC2R 5BJ
Phone: +44 (0)20 7382 2601
Web: www.sut.org.uk

Similar Jobs
Diver, Engineer: Marine, Oceanographer, ROV Pilot

Lift Truck Operative
also known as: Fork-Lift Truck Operator
CRCI:Transport and Logistics
CLCI:YAT Job Band: 1

Job Description
Lift truck operatives move goods using a lift truck with a special lifting and carrying platform in airports, warehouses, factories, docks and builders' yards. They drive the lift truck to the goods to be carried, operate the controls so that the forks or lifting attachments are under the load and raise it, then drive to the unloading area. They stack the goods on a level or at heights. They are also responsible for carrying out minor repairs on the truck and checking oil. Also use trolleys, cranes and clamps. Lift truck operatives are aware of the rules and regulations surrounding work procedures.

Work Details
Usually work a 37-40 hr week, sometimes including shifts, evening and weekend work. Lift truck operatives work in factories, airports, warehouses, haulage depots or goods yards. You have to work carefully and follow strict safety rules. There is a risk of accidents. Safety helmets and possibly ear protectors are usually provided by employers.

Qualification

• England, Wales and Northern Ireland
Band 1: For entry to jobs, no minimum qualifications are needed, but you are expected to have a good level of general education and relevant experience. Some formal/vocational qualifications at any level are useful.

• Scotland
Band 1: For entry to jobs, no minimum qualifications are needed, but you are expected to have a good level of general education and relevant experience. Some formal/vocational qualifications at any level are useful.

Adult Qualifications
Formal qualifications are not needed. Experience of stores, warehouse or dispatch work is useful and maturity is an advantage. There are training programmes for adults in some parts of the country. You can improve your skills and qualifications by working through the Foundation Learning programme. This involves taking credit-based units and qualifications to help you progress.

Work Experience
Any work experience can equip you with skills that you can use in the future and add to your CV. Such work can either be unpaid or voluntary, or holiday/part-time work that you have organised yourself.

Entry and Training
You have to pass an approved fork lift truck training course before using a truck. You must be at least 16, but most entrants are older and many employers ask for a driving licence if the work involves driving on public roads. You then train on the job with an experienced employee. You have ongoing short training courses on aspects of the job, including maintenance and safety. All operatives must pass a Construction Plant Competence Scheme in lift truck operations. Trainers include the Fork Lift Truck Association (FLTA), which offers a wide range of courses to meet the needs of the industry. The Association of Industrial Truck Trainers monitors and accredits fork-lift truck training providers.

There are S/NVQs in forklift truck operations and plant operations at level 2. Training programmes, including apprenticeships leading to level 2 and advanced apprenticeships leading to level 3, may be available in your area. The National Proficiency Test Council offers a level 2 certificate in competence in fork-lift truck operations. There are also national opportunities to train as a fork-lift truck (service) engineer through an apprenticeship programme that lasts three years. Contact the FLTA for details.

Adults may be able to enter this work through a government-funded training programme. Government training opportunities, such as apprenticeships, may be available in your area. You can also gain recognition of previous experience through Accreditation of Prior Learning or by working towards relevant S/NVQs. Contact your local careers office, Jobcentre Plus, Next Step service or Learning and Skills Council (LSC)/Local Enterprise Company (LEC) for details of training schemes.

Opportunities and Pay
Any industry dealing with heavy goods has a demand for lift truck operatives and around 100,000 work in the UK. You can work in the building industry, warehousing and manufacturing, transport, haulage or the retail industry. Some large companies employ supervisors, or with experience you can train to become an instructor.

Pay varies depending on location and employer. Trainees can expect to earn from £12k a year, rising to £20k-£25k for experienced drivers and those who are drivers of special vehicles. Overtime and shift allowances may be available.

Health
You may have to pass a medical test.

Skills and Qualities
alert, careful, common sense, good concentration level, good co-ordination, numeracy skills, practical skills, safety conscious

Further Information
AGCAS: Transport and Logistics (Job Sector Briefing) (AGCAS) - www.prospects.ac.uk

Apprenticeship Schemes (National Apprenticeship Service) - www.apprenticeships.org.uk

Careers in Logistics - www.careersinlogistics.co.uk

Foundation Learning (QCDA) - www.qcda.gov.uk

Skills for Logistics - sector skills council for freight logistics industries - www.skillsforlogistics.org

Training Schemes - www.direct.gov.uk/en/educationandlearning

Warehouse News - www.warehousenews.co.uk

Addresses
Association of Industrial Truck Trainers (AITT)
Unit 20, The Springboard Centre, Mantle Lane, Coalville, Leicestershire LE67 3DW
Phone: +44 (0)1530 277 857
Web: www.aitt.co.uk

Fork Lift Truck Association (FLTA)
Manor Farm Buildings, Lasham, Alton, Hampshire GU34 5SL
Phone: +44 (0)1256 381441
Web: www.fork-truck.org.uk

National Proficiency Test Council (NPTC)
City & Guilds Land Based Services Building 500 Abbey Park, Stareton, Warwickshire CV8 2LY
Phone: +44 (0) 24 7685 7300
Web: www.nptc.org.uk

Road Transport Industry Training Board
Access House, Halesfield 17, Telford, Shropshire TF7 4PW
Phone: +44 (0)1952 520 200
Web: www.rtitb.co.uk

Similar Jobs
Crane Operator, Driver: Lorry, Van Driver: Sales, Warehouse Worker

Lightning Conductor Engineer
also known as: Engineer: Lightning Conductor, Lightning Protection Engineer

CRCI:Building and Construction
CLCI:RAK
Job Band: 1 to 2

Job Description
Lightning conductor engineers work at heights to install lightning conductors and electrical protection systems for a wide range of structures. These include schools, towers, power stations, flats and office blocks. A technical drawing of the system is used to plan the work schedule. Any necessary scaffolding or equipment such as ladders and work platforms are used to assist staff working at heights. A work harness is used for safety purposes.

Engineers climb or are lifted up to the place of work. They carry out the installation work and may abseil back down again. Work may also include earthing of anti-static floor systems, earthing of military equipment, and protecting historic buildings from lightning. May inspect, maintain, test or upgrade an existing installation. After finishing the work, engineers dismantle any equipment used to gain access.

Work Details
Lightning conductor engineers usually work a basic 39 hr week, though shift work or overtime may be required, including weekends. The work is outdoors on site, and in all sorts of weather conditions. This job involves climbing, lifting, balancing, kneeling and working at great heights. Travel is necessary to different sites and you may need to be away from home at times. A driving licence may be useful. There is a risk of falling from heights and accidents from equipment. A safety helmet and harness, protective footwear and outdoor wear are worn.

Qualification

• England, Wales and Northern Ireland
Band 1: No minimum qualifications are required, but you are expected to have a good level of general education. However, some formal/vocational qualifications at any level that demonstrate some mathematical and technical ability are useful.

Band 2: Although academic qualifications are not specified for this job, it is an advantage to have some GCSEs (A*-E) in subjects that include English, maths, science subjects and design and technology, or equivalent.

- **Scotland**

Band 1: No minimum qualifications are required, but you are expected to have a good level of general education. However, some formal/vocational qualifications at any level that demonstrate some mathematical and technical ability are useful.

Band 2: Although academic qualifications are not specified for this job, it is an advantage to have some S grades (1-5) in subjects that include English, maths, science subjects and design and technology, or similar.

Adult Qualifications

You do not always need qualifications, although a good basic knowledge of maths is important in this job.

Work Experience

Relevant work or voluntary experience is always useful and can improve your chances when applying for entry to construction jobs and apprenticeships. In some areas there is a young apprenticeship (14-16) scheme that provides an extended work placement and eventual achievement of a level 2 qualification whilst at school. Health and safety issues may mean that there are certain jobs you cannot do until you are over 16. Contact your local Construction Skills office for advice.

Entry and Training

A knowledge of maths for learning basic electrical theory and a good head for heights are more important than formal qualifications to enter this job. Training with an employer is usually work based, together with a day or block-release college course to achieve relevant qualifications. These include S/NVQs in accessing operations and rigging (lightning conductor engineering) at levels 2-3. You can also take a relevant one or two-year full-time course.

Various flexible training schemes are available, such as sponsored apprentice training that is offered to young people through the Steeplejack and Lightning Protection Training Group Association and Construction Skills. Trainees are sponsored by an employer and spend blocks of time each year at the National Construction College (Bircham Newton campus). There are at least 12 places a year for trainee lightning conductor engineers and you are usually offered a job at the end of the scheme.

You can enter such training schemes at 16-17 and can apply for an apprenticeship in Year 11 (January). You need to take an aptitude test involving maths, problem solving and literacy, before you start training. You also work towards gaining a level of competence card through the Construction Skills Certification Scheme (CSCS) to indicate your individual skill level. There are a range of other relevant short courses, such as mobile towers, health and safety and manual handling, available through ConstructionSkills or the Steeplejack and Lightning Protection Training Group. Contact them for details of all courses and training options.

Mature applicants can take refresher courses that are sometimes available for those returning to work and there may be special government training schemes in some areas. Employers may take older applicants who show aptitude and have previous experience. You can also gain recognition of previous experience through Accreditation of Prior Learning (APL) or by working towards relevant S/NVQs. Contact your local careers office, Jobcentre Plus, Next Step service or Learning and Skills Council (LSC)/Local Enterprise Company (LEC) for details of training schemes, including apprenticeships for adults.

Opportunities and Pay

You can work for specialist firms of lightning conductor engineers throughout the UK. Some also work for building or civil engineering firms. Many are self-employed or work on short-term contracts. Progression to supervisor or management posts is possible. Temporary, casual and seasonal work is often available. Work abroad is also possible.

Pay varies depending on area and employer. Starting salaries are around £15k a year, rising to around £20k-£23k with experience. Senior engineers can earn over £28k a year. Overtime and bonus payments may add to income.

Health

Good physical fitness, agility and stamina are needed for this job.

Skills and Qualities

able to follow drawings and plans, aptitude for teamwork, enjoy working outdoors, good balance, good organisational skills, hand-to-eye co-ordination, head for heights, health & safety awareness, numeracy skills

Relevant Subjects

Construction and built environment, Design and technology

Further Information

Apprenticeship Schemes (National Apprenticeship Service) - www.apprenticeships.org.uk

Construction Skills Certification Scheme (CSCS) (CSCS) - www.cscs.uk.com/

ConstructionSkills - sector skills council for the construction industry - www.cskills.org

▶Working in construction & the built environment (2007) (Babcock Lifeskills) - www.babcock-lifeskills.com/

Addresses

Association of Technical Lightning and Access Specialists (ATLAS)
4c St Mary's Place, The Lace Market, Nottingham NG1 1PH
Phone: +44 (0)115 955 8818
Web: www.atlas-1.org.uk

Steeplejack and Lightning Protection Training Group
105 St Peter's Street, St Albans, Hertfordshire AL1 3EJ
Phone: +44 (0)1727 896 081
Web: www.slptraininggroup.org.uk

Similar Jobs

Electrical Engineering Technician, Electrician, Roofer, Satellite Systems Technician, Scaffolder, Steeplejack

Literary Agent

also known as: Writer's Agent

CRCI:Media, Print and Publishing
CLCI:FAD Job Band: 4 to 5

Job Description

Literary agents act as an author's representative in handling the business side of publishing so that an author can concentrate on writing. They send out scripts and manuscripts and are responsible for making the best financial 'deal' and contract protection for the client with a publisher, film or television production company. Agents must be aware of the client's potential market and ensure that the client receives appropriate publicity. They advise writers on changes to their work, to make a more marketable product and needsto be able to recognise talent in new writers and decide which writers to take on the agency's books. Also attend book fairs, literary lunches/dinners, and similar events, nationally and internationally.

Agents may also act for foreign publishers who wish to bring out an English edition of a book. They usually specialise in areas of work such as fiction, non-fiction, reference books or specialist subject publishing. Must keep up to date with any legislation that may affect their clients.

Work Details

Usually work a 39 hr week; Monday to Friday, though hours and days may be variable, and you may often take work home to read. Occasional late evenings may be required when attending publicity events/book launches, or performances of their author's work. The job is mainly office based but you may be out and about meeting contacts. You give your clients advice and negotiate with publishers or producers on their behalf. Work can be very competitive and highly pressurised.

Qualification

There are no set entry requirements for this job. However, many entrants are graduates, or have previous experience in the publishing industry. Foreign languages are a particular asset for international work.

- **England, Wales and Northern Ireland**

Band 5: For degree courses: 2-3 A levels and some GCSEs (A*-C) usually including English, or equivalent qualifications. Exact requirements depend on the degree you take.

- **Scotland**

Band 5: For degree courses: 3-5 H grades and some S grades (1-3), usually including English, or similar. Exact requirements depend on the degree you take.

Degree Information

A degree in publishing is relevant but any degree discipline is acceptable for entry to this job. Degrees in English, law, languages, business or media studies provide relevant background.

Adult Qualifications

Entry requirements may be relaxed for adults applying for higher education courses. Access or foundation courses give adults without qualifications a route on to degree courses.

Work Experience

Entry to this job is highly competitive and it is important to build contacts and a reputation. Work experience such as work with a literary agency or publishing company is useful.

Entry and Training

There are no courses specific to this job and most literary agents gain experience by working for a publisher or a literary agency. It is important to have an awareness of trends in the book market, be well read and enjoy books. Entrants are often graduates, who may initially work as a rights executive, but it is also possible to begin work in a junior capacity and progress to an assistant agent, and then literary agent. Others have had previous experience in publishing, such as a rights manager or a commissioning editor. Some literary agents act for foreign publishers so knowledge of a foreign language is useful.

The Publishing Training Centre at Bookhouse runs specific courses in this sector, including basic proof-reading and copy editing which may prove useful. They also offer introductory courses in marketing management and publicity and promotion in publishing. See their website for details.

A Diploma/Welsh Baccalaureate may be available in your area in creative and media. This can be a useful introduction to this type of career as you gain practical experience while studying. See the diplomas website or Skillset for further information.

Mature entrants are welcomed and this is a often a good second career, particularly for those who have experience and/or qualifications in the publishing/broadcasting industry.

Opportunities and Pay

This area of work is difficult to enter as there is keen competition for vacancies. You may be employed by a literary agency, or with experience you can become self-employed. Success as a literary agent often depends on making contacts and building up your personal reputation. The majority of agencies are based in London and the south of England. There may be opportunities to work part time and to work from home.

The Booksellers Association of the UK and Ireland has lots of useful information on its website. This includes details on trade events, conferences and specialist book sellers. They also publish a trade directory of publishers and supply book industry information and statistics, which can be useful for tracking trends.

Salaries vary considerably as they depend on the commission percentage rate and success of your clients. Salaries with a publishing company start at around £17k a year. Assistants at a literary agency may start on a very low salary while gaining experience and contacts. The usual commission rates for a literary agent are 10%-20% of an author's earnings.

Skills and Qualities

able to manage a budget and keep records, commercial awareness, good adviser, good communication skills, good interpersonal skills, imaginative, IT skills, negotiating skills, networking skills, perceptive, sound judgement

Relevant Subjects

Business and accounting, Economics, English, Law, Mathematics, Media and communication studies, Modern Foreign Languages

Further Information

Association of Authors' Agents (AAA) - www.agentsassoc.co.uk

Diplomas (Foundation, Higher and Advanced) - http://yp.direct.gov.uk/diplomas

How to get a job in Publishing (A&C Black)

Skillset - sector skills council for the creative media, fashion and textiles industries - www.skillset.org

Society of Young Publishers - www.thesyp.org.uk/

Women In Publishing - www.wipub.org.uk

▶Working in creative & media (2007) (Babcock Lifeskills) - www.babcock-lifeskills.com/

▶Working in English (2007) (Babcock Lifeskills) - www.babcock-lifeskills.com/

Writers' & Artists' Yearbook (A&C Black) (A&C Black) - www.writersandartists.co.uk

Addresses

Booksellers Association of the United Kingdon and Ireland (BA)
Minster House 272 Vauxhall Bridge Road, London SW1V 1BA
Phone: +44 (0)20 7802 0802
Web: www.booksellers.org.uk

Publishing Training Centre at Book House
45 East Hill, Wandsworth, London SW18 2QZ
Phone: +44 (0)20 8874 2718
Web: www.train4publishing.co.uk

Similar Jobs

Editor: Publishing, Magazine Features Editor, Market Research Executive, Proofreader, Public Relations Officer

Local Government Administrative Assistant

also known as: Local Government Clerical Assistant

CRCI:Administration, Business and Office Work
CLCI:CAT Job Band: 2 to 3

Job Description

Administrative assistants work in a local council office providing clerical support for managers and other senior staff. The job includes tasks such as recording, amending, updating and storing information, usually by using a computer. May be responsible for maintaining filing systems, ensuring that important documents and archives are properly recorded and stored, and can be retrieved quickly when required. Also provide administrative support including photocopying and faxing documents, ordering stationery supplies and other office resources. May open, sort and check the incoming mail and distribute it to the relevant person or department.

Can also collect outgoing mail and use a franking machine to record payment of postage. Some assistants work at a reception or enquiry desk providing information to personal callers by telephone. May respond by email, fax, or post. In larger council offices, an administrative assistant often works in a central word-processing section, audio typing from recorded dictation or copy typing from written notes.

May be expected to work on their own initiative for large parts of the day and deal with enquiries in their manager's absence on visits to clients and sites.

Work Details

Usually work 37 hrs a week, Monday to Friday, though may sometimes be required to work overtime. Flexitime, part time and job-sharing is often possible as well as temporary or casual work. Your work has to be accurate and may be confidential. Clerical assistants often have to sit at a desk for a long time. A smart appearance is usually expected, especially when working at a public desk or information counter.

Qualification

• England, Wales and Northern Ireland

Band 2: For direct entry: most employers expect some GCSEs (A*-C) including English and maths, or equivalent.

Band 3: For entry to jobs, HNC in business or a relevant Diploma, usually at least 4 GCSEs (A*-C) including English and maths, or equivalent.

• Scotland

Band 2: For direct entry: most employers expect some S grades (1-3) including English and maths, or similar.

Band 3: For entry: usually at least four S grades (1-3) including English and maths, or similar.

Adult Qualifications

Most employers expect a good standard of secondary education, though formal entry requirements may be waived for adults with relevant skills and experience.

Work Experience

Relevant work or voluntary experience is always useful and can equip you with skills that you can use in the future and that you can add to your CV. Temporary holiday work in offices, perhaps via employment agencies, is useful, particularly if you can develop good typing/keyboard skills and knowledge of the most popular software packages. Many local authorities offer work experience for schools and colleges.

Entry and Training

Entry may be on leaving school or after a full or part-time college course to gain qualifications in business or office studies, such as S/NVQs in business administration at levels 1-4, or in office procedures at levels 1-2. Once in a job you have on-the-job training from an experienced colleague. Local authorities provide the opportunity to work towards relevant S/NVQs, or you can study part time for higher qualifications, such as BTEC national awards in business studies. Many qualifications enable entry to jobs at more senior levels. Some local authorities ask for qualifications in word-processing or keyboard skills. Those working in local authorities in Wales may be expected to speak Welsh.

A Diploma/Welsh Baccalaureate may be available in your area in business, administration and finance. The advanced level is equivalent to 3.5 A levels but for some university courses, the additional and specialist learning (ASL) component of the diploma needs to include specific A levels. Check entry requirements carefully with the individual institutions. Training programmes, including apprenticeship schemes in business administration, may also be available. Advanced apprenticeships leading to qualification at level 3 can also be a route into higher education.

Mature entrants with relevant work experience, and in particular those with office work experience, may have an advantage. Experience in the use of computer software, or in record keeping or bookkeeping, is useful. Adults may be able to enter this work through a government-funded training programme. Contact your local Connexions or careers office, Jobcentre Plus office, Next Step service or Learning and Skills Council (LSC)/Local Enterprise Company (LEC) for details of all training opportunities and schemes, including apprenticeships.

Opportunities and Pay

There is a steady demand for administrative assistants. Jobs are available throughout the UK in a local authority office or departmental section, such as planning, housing, education, social services, environmental health, finance and tourism. There are good opportunities for promotion to higher grades with experience and/or relevant qualifications.

Pay is linked to a national scale but varies depending on the local authority and level of responsibility. Starting salaries are likely to be around £13k-£15k, rising to around £15k-£22k a year for qualified and experienced staff.

Skills and Qualities

able to work both on your own and in a team, attention to detail, friendly, good organisational skills, good telephone manner, IT skills, literacy and numeracy skills, methodical

Relevant Subjects

Business and accounting, English, ICT/Computer studies

Further Information

AGCAS: Government & Public Administration (Job Sector Briefing) (AGCAS) - www.prospects.ac.uk

Apprenticeship Schemes (National Apprenticeship Service) - www.apprenticeships.org.uk

Council for Administration (CfA) - www.cfa.uk.com

Diplomas (Foundation, Higher and Advanced) - http://yp.direct.gov.uk/diplomas

Government Skills - sector skills council for central government - www.government-skills.gov.uk

Government websites - www.irlgov.ie

Institute of Professional Administrators (Institute of Professional Administrators) - www.inprad.org

Local Government Careers (Improvement and Development Agency) - www.lgcareers.com/publications/

Real Life Guide to Business & Administration (Trotman 2009) - www.trotman.co.uk

TARGETjobs: Public Service (GTI Specialist Publishing Ltd.) - www.groupgti.com

Training Schemes - www.direct.gov.uk/en/educationandlearning

▶Working in business, administration & finance (2010) Babcock Lifeskills) - www.babcock-lifeskills.com/

Addresses

Convention of Scottish Local Authorities (COSLA)
Rosebery House, 9 Haymarket Terrace, Edinburgh EH12 5XZ
Phone: +44 (0)131 474 9200
Web: www.cosla.gov.uk

Northern Ireland Local Government Association (NILGA)
Unit 5B Castlereagh Business Park, 478 Castlereagh Road, Belfast BT5 6BQ
Phone: +44(0)28 9079 8972
Web: www.nilga.org

Welsh Local Government Association
Local Government House, Drake Walk, Cardiff CF10 4LG
Phone: +44(0)29 2046 8600
Web: www.wlga.gov.uk

Similar Jobs

Administrator/Administrative Assistant, Civil Service Administrative Assistant, Clerk: Accounts, Receptionist

Local Government Administrator

CRCI:Administration, Business and Office Work
CLCI:CAG Job Band: 3 to 5

Job Description

Local government administrators provide administrative support to the professional and technical staff of a local or county council, including the elected councillors. They provide support as a committee administrator, a policy officer, a project officer or provide management and departmental support. Administrators work in council departments such as finance, housing, transport, planning, education or social services collating information, analysing statistics and producing reports. May also supervise staff carrying out any research that is required for policy decisions. Also ensure that a committee runs smoothly and supervise clerical assistants to produce reports, minutes of meetings and any other documents. They usually organise the preparation and distribution of an agenda and any papers before meetings. May be involved in writing reports on any projects undertaken.

May collect information to brief members of the committee. Then take minutes of the meeting and answer any questions. Ensure a department runs efficiently by managing staff and organising their work. May deal with financial matters, such as invoices, purchasing and budgets. Also assist in the recruitment of staff for a department, oversee their training and devise and operate an appraisal system to monitor their progress.

Work Details

Usually work normal office hours of around 35-40 hrs a week, Monday to Friday, with time off to make up for any overtime you may have to do. The work is mainly office based. You deal with a wide variety of people, such as councillors, staff in other departments and sometimes members of the public. Flexitime is normally available and it is possible to work part time or to job-share. Temporary work is usually available.

Qualification

- **England, Wales and Northern Ireland**

Band 3: For entry to some posts: usually a minimum of 4-5 GCSEs (A*-C) including English and maths, or equivalent.

Band 4: For entry to some posts: a minimum of 1-2 A levels plus some GCSEs (A*-C) usually including English and maths, or equivalent. Some local authorities ask for higher qualifications.

Band 5: For degree courses: 2-3 A levels and some GCSEs (A*-C) usually including English and maths, or equivalent. Exact requirements depend on the degree you take.

- **Scotland**

Band 3: For entry to some posts: usually a minimum of five S grades (1-3) including English and maths, or similar.

Band 4: For entry to some posts: a minimum of 2-3 H grades plus five S grades (1-3), often including English and maths, or similar qualifications. Some local authorities ask for higher qualifications.

Band 5: For degree courses: 3-5 H grades and some S grades (1-3), usually including English and maths, or similar qualifications. Exact requirements depend on the degree you take.

Degree Information

Any degree discipline is acceptable. Business administration/management and social policy and administration are particularly relevant, but business studies, politics and legal studies also give useful background. A higher degree, such as a Master of Public Administration (MPA) or postgraduate diploma, for example in social and public policy or social service planning, might be an advantage.

Adult Qualifications

A wide variety of professional qualifications is acceptable, for example in management, administration, accountancy and human resources/personnel. Entry requirements may be relaxed for adults applying for higher education courses and Access or foundation courses give adults without qualifications a route on to degree courses.

Work Experience

Relevant work or voluntary experience is always useful and can improve your chances in application for entry to this job. Employers may prefer candidates who have relevant work or voluntary experience. This can include experience of administration, secretarial work or working with the public.

Entry and Training

It is possible for clerical staff to progress through training and promotion into administrative posts. However, an increasing number of local authorities are recruiting graduates to administrative posts, and some require non-graduate entrants to have a relevant BTEC/SQA higher national award. Graduates with a 2:1 degree or above can apply for the two-year National Graduate Development Programme through the Improvement and Development Agency (IDeA). This provides graduates with a two year programme of work placements, projects and development opportunities. This also offers the opportunity to achieve the postgraduate diploma in local government management (PDLGM). This is currently delivered by the Institute of Governance and Public Management at Warwick University. The PDLGM is a bespoke academic programme, designed to develop the critical thinking skills required in senior management posts. The programme is a mix of lectures, group work, case studies, project work and individual study. Postgraduate study can also lead to gaining a relevant MBA (Master of Business Administration).

Entrants with A levels/H grades or a degree receive on-the-job training, with in-service courses in areas related to the work, such as developing leadership or using computer packages. Training and career development are encouraged. Relevant foundation degrees are also possible. Those working for local government in Wales are usually expected to be able to speak Welsh.

The Institute of Chartered Secretaries and Administrators (ICSA) offer a certificate and diploma in business practise. On successful completion of the diploma, it is possible to work towards full chartered secretary status. The Institute of Administrative Management (iam) also offers a five step training programme beginning with the introductory award in administrative management and going through to a degree programme. Consult their websites for details. In Scotland, the postgraduate diploma in public administration is a widely recognised professional qualification, and is also available for online study. The Open University offers a range of professional courses at all levels, including an MPA (Master of Public Administration) that has a flexible approach to study.

You can apply for senior posts after gaining experience and training or perhaps further qualifications, such as S/NVQs levels 2-4 in business and administration, team leading at level 2, or management at levels 3-5. From September 2009 it is possible to study for a diploma in business, administration and finance at foundation level. It is possible to progress to a higher diploma and then, an advanced level course equivalent to 3.5 A levels. See the diplomas website for details.

Mature applicants can take refresher courses that are sometimes available for those returning to work and there may be government training schemes in some areas. You can also gain recognition of previous experience through Accreditation of Prior Learning (APL) or by working towards relevant S/NVQs.

Opportunities and Pay

Local authority departments are located in towns and cities throughout the UK. There is a structured promotion route and progression is possible to management and senior management posts, particularly if you take further relevant qualifications such as an MBA, MPA, or similar.

Some administrators with the Institute of Chartered Secretaries and Administrators (ICSA) qualifications find work as a chartered/company secretary and others may move to the civil service, voluntary sector, business and commerce. Career breaks of up to three years are often available, with the employee's skills and knowledge being kept up to date with regular employer contact. This enables the employee to return to full-time employment.

Typical starting salaries are around £18k a year though those with at least two years' relevant experience may earn around £23k a year. Graduates starting the National Graduate Development Programme usually start on around £21.5k. Qualified and experienced administrators are paid from £25k-£30k. Many councils have introduced performance-related pay schemes.

Skills and Qualities

able to get on with all kinds of people, able to prioritise work, able to work to deadlines, analytical skills, attention to detail, good communication skills, good organisational skills, good written English, integrity, IT skills, project management skills

Relevant Subjects

Business and accounting, Economics, English, Government and politics, ICT/Computer studies, Law, Mathematics, Sociology

Further Information

AGCAS: Government & Public Administration (Job Sector Briefing) (AGCAS) - www.prospects.ac.uk

Council for Administration (CfA) - www.cfa.uk.com

Diplomas (Foundation, Higher and Advanced) - http://yp.direct.gov.uk/diplomas

Government Skills - sector skills council for central government - www.government-skills.gov.uk

Improvement and Development Agency (IDeA) - www.idea.gov.uk

Institute of Professional Administrators (Institute of Professional Administrators) - www.inprad.org

Local Government Careers (Improvement and Development Agency) - www.lgcareers.com/publications/

National Graduate Development Programme for Local Government - www.ngdp.co.uk

Real Life Guide to Business & Administration (Trotman 2009) - www.trotman.co.uk

TARGETjobs: Public Service (GTI Specialist Publishing Ltd.) - www.groupgti.com

Addresses

Convention of Scottish Local Authorities (COSLA)
Rosebery House, 9 Haymarket Terrace, Edinburgh EH12 5XZ
Phone: +44 (0)131 474 9200
Web: www.cosla.gov.uk

Institute of Administration Management (iam)
6 Graphite Square, Vauxhall Walk, London SE11 5EE
Phone: +44 (0)20 7091 2600
Web: www.instam.org

Institute of Chartered Secretaries and Administrators (ICSA)
16 Park Crescent, London W1B 1AH
Phone: +44 (0)20 75804741
Web: www.icsa.org.uk

Institute of Governance and Public Management (IGPM)
Warwick Business School, University of Warwick,
Coventry CV4 7AL
Phone: +44(0)24 7652 4505
Web: http://http://www2.warwick.ac.uk/fac/soc/wbs/igpm

Northern Ireland Local Government Association (NILGA)
Unit 5B Castlereagh Business Park, 478 Castlereagh Road, Belfast BT5 6BQ
Phone: +44(0)28 9079 8972
Web: www.nilga.org

Similar Jobs

Civil Service Executive Officer, Company Secretary, Education Administrator, Health Service Manager, Office Manager, School Administrator

Lock-keeper

CRCI:Transport and Logistics
CLCI:YAG Job Band: 1

Job Description

Lock-keepers operate and maintain mechanical locks that change the water level on inland canals and waterways enabling boats to travel up or down inclines. They may operate the lock mechanisms or ensure that others operate them safely and correctly. Locks vary in size and complexity. Some require a great deal of effort to raise, whereas newer hydraulic locks are almost effortless to operate, but more complex.

May help to ensure that a stretch of waterway is navigable, clear of debris and well maintained, reporting environmental issues to the relevant organisation. Lock-keepers advise boaters about the safe handling of their craft and help with breakdowns. May also advise visitors of interesting wildlife and environmental aspects of the area.

Work Details

Usually work a 42 hr week but may be expected to work evenings and weekends, especially in the summer. May work fewer hours in winter. There may be a rota to cover all duties. You work outdoors in all weathers. There is contact with the public and you are responsible for the safe operation and maintenance of the equipment. This job requires some lifting. You may need to live in a house on-site that is provided by the company.

Qualification

- **England, Wales and Northern Ireland**

Band 1: For entry to jobs, no minimum qualifications are needed, but you are expected to have a good level of general education and relevant experience. Some formal/vocational qualifications at any level are useful.

- **Scotland**

Band 1: For entry to jobs, no minimum qualifications are needed, but you are expected to have a good level of general education and relevant experience. Some formal/vocational qualifications at any level are useful.

Adult Qualifications

A general secondary education is usually required. Those without existing qualifications can work through the Foundation Learning programme by taking credit-based units and qualifications.

Work Experience

Any work experience can equip you with skills that you can use in the future and add to your CV. This can either be unpaid or voluntary or holiday/part-time work that you have organised yourself. Any previous experience related to inland waterways is an advantage, or perhaps holiday experience on a stretch of inland waterways. Any practical or mechanical experience is also useful.

Entry and Training

Almost all lock-keepers have previous experience related to inland waterways. Training is practical and on the job, usually provided by experienced colleagues. You may be able to work towards relevant S/NVQs such as a level 2 in maintaining and conserving rivers, coasts and waterways. Training programmes, including apprenticeship schemes, may be available in your area. The Association of Pleasure Craft Operators runs a competition to find the best lock-keeping team in the country each year.

Mature applicants with previous relevant working experience of paid or voluntary work on inland waterways have an advantage. Any practical or mechanical experience is also useful.

Opportunities and Pay

There are a limited number of job opportunities and they are often seasonal. The rivers Trent, Severn and some Scottish rivers offer more permanent posts. Inland waterways are mainly operated by British Waterways or the Environment Agency although some are run by other organisations such as the Norfolk Broads Authority. Many canals run through towns and cities throughout the UK as well as rural areas. Opportunities for promotion are limited but in some cases it is possible to move to supervisory posts such as a waterway supervisor or team leader with the Environment Agency. You may need to move to another part of the country to secure job improvement.

Lock-keepers generally earn around £12k-£22k a year, although pay may be increased by doing further maintenance on your stretch of water, such as hedge cutting. Accommodation may be provided by the employer.

Health

This job requires good general fitness and the ability to swim.

Skills and Qualities

able to explain clearly, able to take responsibility, able to work well on your own, common sense, enjoy working outdoors, practical skills, reliable, safety conscious, technical aptitude

Relevant Subjects

Land and Environment

Further Information

Apprenticeship Schemes (National Apprenticeship Service) - www.apprenticeships.org.uk

Broads Authority - www.broads-authority.gov.uk

Foundation Learning (QCDA) - www.qcda.gov.uk

Inland Waterways Association (IWA) (Inland Waterways Association) - www.waterways.org.uk

Skills for Logistics - sector skills council for freight logistics industries - www.skillsforlogistics.org

Addresses

Association of Inland Navigation Authorities (AINA)
Fearns Wharf, Neptune Street, Leeds LS9 8PB
Phone: +44 (0)113 243 3125
Web: www.aina.org.uk

Association of Pleasure Craft Operators (APCO)
Marine House, Thorpe Lea Road, Egham, Surrey TW20 8BF
Phone: 0844 800 9575 (UK only)
Web: http:/www.apco.org.uk

British Waterways
64 Clarendon Road, Watford WD17 1DA
Phone: +44 (()) 1923 201120
Web: www.britishwaterways.co.uk

Environment Agency
National Customer Contact Centre, PO Box 544, Almondsbury, Rotherham S60 1BY
Phone: 08708 506 506 (UK only)
Web: www.environment-agency.gov.uk

Similar Jobs

Countryside/Conservation Officer/Manager, Water Distribution/Sewerage Operative, Water/Sewerage Treatment Plant Operative, Waterway Operative

Locksmith

CRCI:Engineering
CLCI:ROZ Job Band: 1 to 2

Job Description

Locksmiths supply, fit, repair and service all types of locks and security systems. They work on private homes, cars and businesses. Work can involve key cutting, matching, repairing and servicing locks, and changing combination locks. Can also fit grilles and locks to windows and may also fit closed circuit television (CCTV) systems. Locksmiths may advise on the range of safes and security systems and the fitting of security devices in buildings such as banks and hotels. They may provide an emergency service for those who have locked themselves out, or need their locks changing for security reasons. Keys are cut by hand or by machine, often using an original as a template.

Many specialise in auto-locksmithing for cars. They often supply an emergency service for car owners who have lost their car keys or want to upgrade their car security system. Others restore, repair or replace antique keys/locks. Locksmiths may sell a range of security products.

Work Details

Usually work a basic 40 hr week that may include some Saturdays. May be on call for emergencies on a shift basis. Work is in a workshop, a shop, or out and about visiting clients' homes and customers' premises. Travel around a geographical area and in all weathers may be necessary. You deal with enquiries and are responsible for security and efficient service. A driving licence is often needed.

Qualification

- **England, Wales and Northern Ireland**

Band 2: For entry to jobs, no minimum qualifications are needed, but it is an advantage to have some GCSEs (A*-C) or equivalent in subjects that include English and maths. Technical, craft and engineering subjects are also useful.

- **Scotland**

Band 2: Although academic qualifications are not specified for this job, it is an advantage to have some S grades (1-3) in subjects that include English and maths, or similar. Technical, craft and engineering subjects are also useful.

Adult Qualifications

Employers may require a minimum of a good standard of education with some formal qualifications at any level, or their equivalent.

Work Experience

Relevant work or voluntary experience is always useful. It can add to your CV and improve your chances when applying for entry to jobs in this area. Studying woodwork or metalwork while at school or college is helpful. Any experience of working in engineering, carpentry or electronics is also very useful.

Entry and Training

Usually training is by practical experience and working alongside an experienced locksmith. Some locksmiths may offer work as an apprentice, although there are no formal apprenticeships in locksmithing. It may be useful to contact a firm of master locksmiths to see if there are any training opportunities. The British Locksmiths' Institute (BLI) runs training courses at the Master Locksmiths' Association (MLA) training centre for both newcomers and those who need more advanced training. There is a five day general locksmiths course and specialist courses dealing with electrical access control and safes.

The MLA offers a tailored City & Guilds award in basic locksmithing. The British Locksmiths and Key Cutters Association and the UK Locksmiths Association also provide training from introductory to advanced levels. Another way to gain an understanding of the industry is to attend a BLI General Locksmithing Course at MLAs Training Centre

All entrants to this work have to go through a Criminal Records Board/Disclosure Scotland check. There is a constant need for continuing professional development in this job, due to the frequency of new products being released to the market.

A Diploma/Welsh Baccalaureate may be available in your area in engineering. See diplomas website for further information.

Mature applicants with experience in areas such as the security industry, engineering, carpentry, or in electronics may have an advantage. Government training opportunities, such as apprenticeships, may be available in your area. You can also gain recognition of previous experience through Accreditation of Prior Learning or by working towards relevant S/NVQs. Contact your local careers office, Jobcentre Plus, Next Step service or Learning and Skills Council (LSC)/Local Enterprise Company (LEC) for details of training schemes.

Opportunities and Pay
Jobs can be found in most areas of the country. You can work for a local or national locksmith firm, specialist workshops, retail outlets and security manufacturers. Prospects vary depending on where you live, but there is a rising demand for qualified and experienced locksmiths. When fully experienced you can become self-employed. You may move on to work with security alarm systems.

Pay varies since there is no agreed pay scale and it depends on conditions of service. Starting wages for a trainee are £12k-£14k a year, rising to £25k with experience. Higher earners can earn £30k a year.

Skills and Qualities
attention to detail, discreet, good communication skills, good interpersonal skills, honest, logical, manual dexterity, patient, problem-solving skills, technical aptitude

Relevant Subjects
Design and technology, Engineering, Mathematics

Further Information
Diplomas (Foundation, Higher and Advanced) - http://yp.direct.gov.uk/diplomas

Institute of Certified Locksmiths http://theinstituteofcertifiedlocksmiths.org/training

Skills for Security - sector skills council for security industry - www.skillsforsecurity.org.uk/

UK Locksmiths Association - www.uklocksmithsassociation.co.uk

Welsh Baccalaureate - www.wbq.org.uk

Why Security? - A Guide to Careers in the Security Industry (Security Industry Authority) - www.the-sia.org.uk

Addresses
British Locksmiths and Keycutters Association
3 Murrow Lane, Parson Drove, Wisbech,
Cambridgeshire PE13 4JH
Phone: +44 (0)8456 445397
Web: www.blka.co.uk

Master Locksmiths' Association (MLA)
& British Locksmith's Institute, 5D Great Central Way, Woodford Halse, Daventry, Northamptonshire NN11 3PZ
Phone: +44 (0)1327 262 255
Web: www.locksmiths.co.uk

Similar Jobs
Engineering Craft Machinist, Engineering Machine Operative, Gunsmith, Security Systems Installer, Watch & Clock Repairer

Logistics Manager
also known as: Distribution Manager, Supply Chain Manager

CRCI:Transport and Logistics
CLCI:YAT — Job Band: 4 to 5

Job Description
Logistics managers are responsible for the control and movement of goods and/or raw materials held in stock for a company, retailer or manufacturer using their own transport facilities. They ensure the goods or raw materials are in the correct quantity and arrive at the required time to meet customer demand. They co-ordinate the supply chain of goods. Also monitor stock levels and track the ordering, storage and movement of goods, using a computer. Then re-order goods or materials if necessary. Analysing data and developing new systems to improve efficiency and ensure optimum profit of the company is an important aspect of the job.

Logistics managers liaise with other professionals including transport or warehouse managers, purchasing officers and also with suppliers and retail customers. Manage and supervise employees, allocating them according to changing needs, and may also be responsible for staff recruitment and development.

Work Details
You can expect to work long hours, and may be required to work some evenings and weekends. Companies running 24-hour operations may require you to work a shift system. You may also be on call to deal with any emergencies. The work can be stressful at times. Occasional travel away from home, sometimes abroad, is common.

Qualification
• England, Wales and Northern Ireland
Band 4: For direct entry to a management scheme or for BTEC higher national award: 1-2 A levels and some GCSEs (A*-C) usually including English and maths, or equivalent.

Band 5: For degree courses: 2-3 A levels and some GCSEs (A*-C) usually including English and maths. Exact requirements depend on the course you take.

• Scotland
Band 4: For direct entry to a management scheme or for SQA national award: usually 2-3 H grades and some S grades (1-3), often including English and maths, or similar qualifications.

Band 5: For degree courses: 3-5 H grades and some S grades (1-3), usually including English and maths, or similar qualifications. Exact requirements depend on the degree you take.

Degree Information
Any degree is acceptable for entry although specialist courses are available such as logistics and supply chain management. Business studies, business and finance or retail management are also appropriate. There are relevant postgraduate courses available including an MSc in transport and logistics management or in purchasing and supply chain management.

Adult Qualifications
Entry requirements may be relaxed for adults applying for higher education courses. Access or foundation courses provide those without the required qualifications a route onto degree courses.

Work Experience
Employers or universities may prefer candidates who have relevant work or voluntary experience. This can include any administrative work involving analytical and problem-solving skills, especially in a pressurised environment. Experience of using computer systems and databases is also useful.

Entry and Training
Increasingly, entrants to this job are graduates or those with a relevant diploma, though it is still possible to work your way up from a junior post to a supervisory or management position. Larger

companies may offer a management training scheme with on-the job training and part-time study or distance learning for professional qualifications, such as those offered by the Chartered Institute of Logistics and Transport (CILTUK). Those wishing to progress further in this career may choose to take one of the growing number of postgraduate courses in this subject. Courses are also offered by the Chartered Institute of Purchasing and Supply and the Institute of Operations Management.

There are relevant foundation degrees, such as logistics and transport, available for full or part-time study, or through distance learning. A Diploma/Welsh Baccalaureate in business, administration and finance may be available in your area and could be a useful route into this job. Appropriate S/NVQS are available up to level 4. Training programmes, including an apprenticeship scheme in logistics operations management, may be available in your area. Advanced apprenticeships leading to qualification at level 3 can also be a route into higher education.

Mature applicants with relevant work experience and qualifications in either retailing, or transport and distribution, have an advantage. Government training opportunities, such as apprenticeships, may be available in your area. You can also gain recognition of previous experience through Accreditation of Prior Learning or by working towards relevant S/NVQs. Contact your local careers office, Jobcentre Plus, Next Step service or Learning and Skills Council (LSC)/Local Enterprise Company (LEC) for details of training schemes.

Opportunities and Pay
Opportunities in the UK are good for logistics managers, particularly in specialised areas such as air freight distribution. Employment is available throughout the country with manufacturers, major retail companies, central and local government, charities, the armed forces or warehousing and distribution firms. You can also be employed by a company that does this work on a contractual basis for other firms and companies. There are opportunities to progress to senior roles, work overseas and for freelance work in consultancy.

Pay depends on the employer or type and size of the company. Salaries for new graduates are about £20k a year. Experienced managers earn from £45k and up to as much as £120k a year. There may be allowances for working unsociable hours and benefits such as a company car. Some companies offer performance-related pay.

Health
A medical test may be required.

Skills and Qualities
able to manage people, able to work to deadlines, business awareness, decisive, good communication skills, information handling skills, IT skills, negotiating skills, networking skills, problem-solving skills

Relevant Subjects
Business and accounting, Economics, English, Geography, Mathematics, Retail and distribution

Further Information
AGCAS: Transport and Logistics (Job Sector Briefing) (AGCAS) - www.prospects.ac.uk

Apprenticeship Schemes (National Apprenticeship Service) - www.apprenticeships.org.uk

Careers in Logistics - www.careersinlogistics.co.uk

Diplomas (Foundation, Higher and Advanced) - http://yp.direct.gov.uk/diplomas

Inside Careers Guide: Logistics & Transport Management - www.insidecareers.co.uk

Logistics and Retail Management (2009) (Kogan Page) - www.koganpage.com

Logistics and Transport Focus (monthly) (CILTUK) - www.ciltuk.org.uk/pages/ltfocus

Skills for Logistics - sector skills council for freight logistics industries - www.skillsforlogistics.org

Training Schemes - www.direct.gov.uk/en/educationandlearning

Welsh Baccalaureate - www.wbq.org.uk

Addresses
Chartered Institute of Logistics and Transport (CILTUK)
Careers Manager, Logistics & Transport Centre, Earlstrees Court, Earlstrees Road, Corby NN17 4AX
Phone: +44 (0)1536 740 100
Web: www.ciltuk.org.uk

Chartered Institute of Purchasing and Supply (CIPS)
Easton House, Easton on the Hill, Stamford, Lincolnshire PE9 3NZ
Phone: +44 (0)1780 756 777
Web: www.cips.org

Institute of Operations Management (IOM)
CILT (UK), Earlstrees Court, Earlstrees Road, Corby, Northants NN17 4AX
Phone: +44 (0)1536 740 105
Web: www.iomnet.org.uk

Institute of Transport Administration (IoTA)
The Old Studio, 25 Greenfield Road, Westoning, Bedfordshire MK45 5JD
Phone: +44 (0)1525 634940
Web: www.iota.org.uk

Similar Jobs
Freight Forwarder, Road Transport Manager, Shipbroker/Airbroker, Transport Planner, Wholesale Manager

Lottery Officer
CRCI:Administration, Business and Office Work
CLCI:COZ Job Band: 4 to 5

Job Description
Lottery officers raise funds for an organisation or group by making an application to the National Lottery or other major lottery, such as the Heritage Lottery Fund. They are aware of the basis on which lottery funds are awarded and tend to specialise in one of the lottery categories, such as the arts, education, health and environment, charities, heritage and sport. Assist in the bid process, especially with community groups within a local authority area. During the bidding process, lottery officers maintain good relationships between local groups and council members. They seek to enhance the quality and chances of success when making a bid for lottery funding. May organise a group of volunteers, hold public meetings or events and give talks. They also write letters and reports.

Lottery officers are experienced in keeping detailed records using a computer, and aware of the rules and regulations that govern lotteries. They help to decide how to award the lottery funds. They also provide information and assistance on the application procedure for lottery funding. Some have additional responsibilities in other areas, especially if working for a local authority. This may include work in leisure or culture services, sports or economic development, finance or corporate services.

Work Details
You are usually based in an office working 9am to 5pm, Monday to Friday, or you may work flexitime. Meetings or events in the evenings and weekends may involve longer hours at times. Being a lottery officer can often be a part-time job. If working full time for a local authority, you may spend less than half of your time on lottery-related work.

You meet a wide variety of people and need to contact them in writing, by telephone or email. This type of work is challenging as well as rewarding, but can be demanding when deadlines approach.

Qualification

- **England, Wales and Northern Ireland**

Band 4: For non-graduate entry or for a BTEC higher national award, or similar: 1-2 A levels and some GCSEs (A*-C) usually including English and maths, or equivalent.

Band 5: For degree courses: 2-3 A levels and some GCSEs (A*-C) usually including English and maths, or equivalent. Exact requirements depend on the degree you take.

- **Scotland**

Band 4: For non-graduate entry or SQA higher national award or similar: 2-3 H grades and some S grades (1-3) including English and maths, or similar qualifications.

Band 5: For degree courses: 3-5 H grades and some S grades (1-3) usually including English and maths, or similar qualifications. Exact requirements depend on the degree you take.

Degree Information

Any degree discipline is acceptable for entry into this type of employment. Subjects giving useful background knowledge include marketing and financial management, or similar.

Adult Qualifications

Entry requirements may be relaxed for adults applying for higher national level courses. Access or foundation courses give adults without qualifications a route into higher education.

Work Experience

Relevant work or voluntary experience is always useful and can improve your chances in application for entry to this job. The types of work experience to consider are in accountancy, industry, marketing or public relations. Work in areas that are eligible for lottery funding such as arts, education, health and environment, charities and voluntary organisations, heritage or sport, also gives useful background knowledge. The Institute of Fundraising has details of available internships on their website. Programmes such as these offer valuable work experience and are a useful addition to your CV.

Entry and Training

There are no set entry requirements though most applicants have a relevant higher-level qualification, such as a degree or equivalent professional qualification. However, it may be possible to begin work at a junior level, such as a clerical assistant or administrator with a local council, and work your way up to this job. It is an advantage to have experience in areas that include accountancy, industry and commerce, social work, marketing or public relations. Training is mainly on the job together with short development courses. In a large organisation, you may be sent on an in-house lottery funding course.

The Institute of Fundraising (IoF) offers a variety of relevant training programmes including a foundation course in fundraising practice and a certificate in fundraising management. They also offer a managing fundraising course which is delivered in a variety of formats to accommodate those in employment. It is available through the Train to Gain programme and you may qualify for a grant of up to £1000 depending on your circumstances. Check the IoF websites for details.

The Open University offers a six-month course for fundraisers called Winning Resources and Support. The course is delivered in three modules; fundraising fundamentals, fundraising techniques, and fundraising strategy which is the distance-learning route to the CiFM from the IoF. If working for a small local group, there are relevant external courses run by private agencies.

Mature entrants are particularly suitable for this job, especially those with relevant skills and experience in a business-related field such as public relations, financial management, or marketing and administration.

Opportunities and Pay

Many lottery officers are employed by a local authority, helping community groups or individuals to apply for lottery funding. You can work for a variety of small or large organisations throughout the UK that require assistance in applying for lottery funding. Some may work for a lottery organisation that provides funds to its applicants, and after gaining employment experience, perhaps in a regional role, may move to a more senior position within the organisation; designing and implementing lottery policy and procedures. Self-employment as a consultant is possible, such as assisting local community groups or schools to make bids for a lottery grant.

There are no set salaries for lottery officers and pay can vary greatly. Entrants may start at £16k-£20k, rising to around £20k-£26k with experience. Senior officers can earn more than £30k a year. Some employers operate a performance-related pay scheme. You may receive a regular salary or your income can be dependent on commission or fees.

Skills and Qualities

able to get on with all kinds of people, able to manage a budget and keep records, able to network and negotiate, able to work both on your own and in a team, able to work to deadlines, excellent communication skills, good written English, information handling skills, initiative, resourceful

Relevant Subjects

Business and accounting, Economics, English, Mathematics, Psychology, Sociology

Further Information

AGCAS: Charity & Development Work (Job Sector Briefing) (AGCAS) - www.prospects.ac.uk

Camelot Group - www.camelotgroupcareers.co.uk

Civil Service, Real Careers, Real Opportunities (Civil Service and Local Appointments Commissioners) - www.publicjobs.ie/downloads/careerinfo.pdf

Local Government Careers (Improvement and Development Agency) - www.lgcareers.com/publications/

Lotteries Council - www.lotteriescouncil.org.uk

Lottery Monitor - www.lottery-monitor.com

Open University - www.open.ac.uk

▶Working in marketing, advertising & PR (2008) (Babcock Lifeskills) - www.babcock-lifeskills.com/

Addresses

Institute of Fundraising (IoF)
Park Place 12 Lawn Lane, London SW8 1UD
Phone: +44 (0)20 7840 1000
Web: www.institute-of-fundraising.org.uk

National Lottery Commission
Human Resources, 101 Wigmore Street, London W1U 1QU
Phone: +44 (0)20 7016 3400
Web: www.natlotcomm.gov.uk

Similar Jobs

Charity Fundraiser, Civil Service Executive Officer, Local Government Administrator, Personal Assistant, Public Relations Officer

Magazine Features Editor

CRCI:Media, Print and Publishing
CLCI:FAC Job Band: 4 to 5

Job Description

Magazine features editors are responsible for a magazine's entertaining and informative content, and newsworthy articles. They usually work for the larger specialist trade magazines, or for the weekly and monthly lifestyle or consumer magazines (glossy mags). In specialist magazines, features editors maintain a full and up-to-date knowledge of the subject. If working for a 'glossy mag' they concentrate more on commissioning articles on lifestyle, health, beauty and fashion. Tasks vary depending on the magazine though they usually manage an in-house team and freelance features writers, hold regular meetings to motivate staff and generate ideas for future articles.

Editors commission a feature to be written, proofread and edit the completed article and ensure it is of sufficient quality to print. Also liaise with publishing colleagues and attend seminars, trade fairs and conferences.

Work Details

Usually work a 38-40 hr week, Monday to Friday, but occasionally late nights are required before press days. The job is usually office based although this varies with publications. Part-time work and career breaks are becoming more common in this industry. Work dress is usually informal but smart. Work can be stressful at times, especially when deadlines approach.

Qualification

• England, Wales and Northern Ireland

Band 4: For relevant BTEC higher national award: usually 1-2 A levels and some GCSEs (A*-C) including English or equivalent.

Band 5: For degree courses: 2-3 A levels and some GCSEs (A*-C) usually including English, or equivalent qualifications. Exact requirements depend on the degree you take.

• Scotland

Band 4: For SQA higher national award: usually 2-3 H grades and some S grades (1-3) including English or similar.

Band 5: For degree courses: 3-5 H grades and some S grades (1-3), usually including English, or similar. Exact requirements depend on the degree you take.

Degree Information

Some employers prefer a degree in publishing but any degree is acceptable for entry to this job. A course in English language/ literature, communication studies or media studies gives useful background knowledge. There are postgraduate courses in publishing.

Adult Qualifications

Entry requirements may be relaxed for adults applying for higher education courses and Access or foundation courses give adults without qualifications a route on to degree courses.

Work Experience

Work experience gives you an insight into what you enjoy and don't enjoy about a job or working environment, as well as the opportunity to acquire new skills. It also provides valuable information to add to your CV and improves your employment prospects. Experience is essential in journalism; practical experience writing to deadlines is valuable to employers, whether for student newspapers and magazines, local press, or free press. Work shadowing may be difficult to obtain, but it may be worth approaching the larger magazine publishers.

Entry and Training

There are no official entry requirements or qualifications for this job, although most entrants are suitably qualified graduates. Being a features editor usually requires around five years' industry experience working as a deputy features editor; most start as a junior magazine journalist. Work experience is more important to employers than qualifications but a few specialist magazines may expect a qualification in their publishing field. Training is often on the job and usually informal.

The National Council for the Training of Journalists (NCTJ) offers courses in a range of subjects, including proofreading, feature writing and subbing. The Periodicals Training Council (PTC) is the national training arm of the trade association for the magazine industry, the Periodical Publishers Association (PPA) and runs professional courses leading to a diploma in publishing or in editing. They also run short courses in topics such as writing, magazine branding and research skills. The Society for Editors and Proofreaders run courses in proofreading and copy editing. Foundation degrees are also available and may be taken full or part time.

A Diploma/Welsh Baccalaureate may be available in your area in creative and media. This can be a useful introduction to this type of career as you gain practical experience while studying. See the diplomas website or Skillset for further information.

Mature applicants need previous work experience in writing or journalism. Some experience in journalism/secretarial work or knowledge of the book trade is an advantage. A suitable specialist background is helpful for specific trade magazines. Postgraduate qualifications in journalism are useful.

Opportunities and Pay

You can work for a large multinational and/or multi-title publishing house or for a small specialist magazine with only a few staff. You may progress to the role of deputy editor or editor of the whole magazine, although there is keen competition for few posts at this level and much depends on market forces.

Earnings vary depending upon the size and subject of a magazine. Small magazines and trade publications have features editors, who generally earn around £22k-£35k a year. Those editing national 'glossy' titles can earn £40k-£60k. Deputy editors and editors can earn considerably more depending on the type and circulation of the magazine. Salaries tend to be higher for weekly than monthly magazines.

Skills and Qualities

able to withstand criticism, aptitude for teamwork, business awareness, creative and imaginative flair, decisive, enquiring mind, enthusiastic, good communication skills, good interpersonal skills, good organisational skills, IT skills

Relevant Subjects

Business and accounting, English, Media and communication studies, Psychology, Sociology

Further Information

Creative Choices - www.creative-choices.co.uk

Diplomas (Foundation, Higher and Advanced) - http://yp.direct.gov.uk/diplomas

Journalism Uncovered (Trotman 2009) - www.trotman.co.uk

Media Week (weekly) (Haymarket Publishing Ltd) - www.haymarket.com/mediaweek/default.aspx

National Council for the Training of Journalists (NCTJ) - www.nctj.com

Press Gazette - Journalism Today (Progressive Media International) - www.pressgazette.co.uk

Skillset - sector skills council for the creative media, fashion and textiles industries - www.skillset.org

What's it like to be a Magazine Editor? (A&C Black 2009)

▶Working in English (2007) (Babcock Lifeskills) - www.babcock-lifeskills.com/

Addresses

Periodical Publishers' Association (PPA)
(Periodicals Training Council)
Queens House, 28 Kingsway, London WC2B 6JR
Phone: +44 (0)207 404 4166
Web: www.ppa.co.uk/

Society for Editors and Proofreaders (SfEP)
Erico House, 93-99 Upper Richmond Road, Putney,
London SW15 2TG
Phone: +44 (0)20 8785 5617
Web: www.sfep.org.uk

Similar Jobs

Editor: Publishing, Editorial Assistant: Publishing, Journalist, Journalist: Magazine, Literary Agent, Proofreader, Writer

Magistrates' Court Legal Adviser

also known as: Assistant Justices' Clerk, Court Clerk, Legal Adviser

CRCI:Legal and Political Services
CLCI:LAB Job Band: 5

Job Description

A legal adviser is a qualified lawyer (solicitor/barrister) who provides professional advice and assists magistrates and district judges in English and Welsh courts. They make sure that all members of the court follow legal rules and advise on procedures by offering impartial guidance. They provide advice and guidance on difficult points of law and on correct sentencing for each particular offence. Legal advisers must prepare for court sessions by reading the evidence before each day's proceedings, to make sure it complies with the rules of court. They help magistrates to make decisions by carrying out legal research and identifying the key legal issues of the case.

Legal advisers also have to deal with magistrates' orders such as arranging warrants, emergency protection, legal aid, and child adoption procedures. Other work involves meeting with various lawyers, the police, prison and social workers, dealing with public enquiries, and helping with court administrative functions. They may also help justices' clerks with the training of magistrates.

Work Details

You generally work around 37 hrs a week, Monday to Friday. In emergencies you may work evenings or weekends, when special hearings take place. Some courts work on Saturdays and you may have to work on a rota basis. You are based in a magistrates' court, but may work in several around the area. There are opportunities for job-share and for part-time work. You may use a computer a lot of the time when preparing cases for court. Formal dress is required at work.

Qualification

- **England, Wales and Northern Ireland**

Band 5: For degree course: three A levels (usually high grades) and some GCSEs (A*-C) including English and maths, or equivalent qualifications. Exact requirements depend on the degree you take.

Degree Information

Graduates should have either a good honours 'qualifying' degree in law or a non-law degree, plus the Common Professional Examination/Graduate Diploma in Law.

Adult Qualifications

Degree entry requirements may be relaxed for those over 23 years with relevant legal work experience. Access or foundation courses give adults without qualifications a route on to degree courses.

Work Experience

Entry to this job is competitive and it is important that you try to do some relevant work or voluntary experience before applying. Work experience that is particularly relevant for this work is in a solicitor's office or with Citizens Advice. University students can apply for a mini-pupillage that lasts for one or two weeks. Contact the Pupillage Portal for details.

Entry and Training

Entry to this role is competitive as legal advisers are qualified solicitors or barristers. Courts require you to have at least a second class honours degree and to have passed the Legal Practice Course (LPC) or Bar Vocational Course (BVC). If you are accepted by the courts as a trainee legal adviser, the training process usually takes two years and is likely to coincide with a Law Society training contract.

On-the-job training includes an induction training programme, offered by the Judicial Studies Board, plus observing court sittings with an experienced adviser. It may also include visits to prisons and developing relationships with the Crown Prosecution Service, the National Probation Service and social service departments. Contact Her Majesty's Courts Service for further information.

Refer to entry and training details in the job articles of a solicitor or barrister for for full details of all entry and training routes to these jobs.

A standard level of education for entry applies for all entrants and relevant work experience is an advantage, or may be required. Contact the Law Society for details.

Another route to qualification is to first train as a legal executive and have at least five years' qualifying legal experience; two must be at least after successful completion of all the examinations. Contact the Institute of Legal Executives for details. This route may be particularly relevant for mature entrants as the training can be undertaken while working.

Opportunities and Pay

There are around 2000 legal advisers in England and Wales, based at over 700 magistrates' courts. There are opportunities in towns and cities where legal advisers are employed by Magistrates' Court Committees. The magistrates' courts service offers a recognised career structure for legal advisers, including a tier system which you can progress through. Legal advisers may be promoted to justice's clerk, responsible for supervising the running of a number of courts.

Salaries are dependent upon your seniority and the court(s) worked for, but generally start at around £19k-£27k for trainees, rising to around £27k-£50k a year, once qualified and/or experienced.

Skills and Qualities

able to work to deadlines, awareness of confidentiality issues, excellent communication skills, good organisational skills, IT skills, logical, objective, problem-solving skills, self confident, sound judgement

Relevant Subjects

Business and accounting, Economics, English, Government and politics, History, Law

Further Information

Judicial Studies Board - www.jsboard.co.uk

Law Gazette (Law Society) - www.lawgazette.co.uk

Pupillage Portal (ex-OLPAS) (The General Council of the Bar) - www.pupillages.com/

Skills for Justice - sector skills council for the UK justice system - www.skillsforjustice.com

TARGETjobs: Law (GTI Specialist Publishing Ltd.) - www.groupgti.com

The Role Of the Justices' Clerk and the Legal Adviser (Justices' Clerks' Society 2008) - www.jc-society.com

▶Working in politics & law (2010) (Babcock Lifeskills) - www.babcock-lifeskills.com/

Addresses

Her Majesty's Courts Service (HMCS)
Customer Service Unit, Post Post 1.40, 1st Floor, 102 Petty France, London SW1H 9AJ
Phone: 0845 4568770 (UK only)
Web: www.hmcourts-service.gov.uk

Institute of Legal Executives (ILEX)
Kempston Manor, Bedfordshire MK42 7AB
Phone: +44 (0)1234 841 000
Web: www.ilex.org.uk

Law Society of England & Wales
The Law Society's Hall, 113 Chancery Lane, London WC2A 1PL
Phone: +44 (0)20 7242 1222
Web: www.lawsociety.org.uk

Similar Jobs

Barrister, Crown Prosecution Service Caseworker, Judge, Legal Executive, Solicitor

Management Consultant

also known as: Business Change Consultant/Manager, Business Consultant, Strategy Consultant

CRCI:Administration, Business and Office Work
CLCI:CAP Job Band: 5

Job Description

Management consultants provide independent, objective advice and assistance to an organisation to improve working practices, and to increase the profits and efficiency of a business. They have particular skills in research and analysis. They look at long-term company strategy and policies, its structure and management operations. Main areas of work include advice on business strategy, manufacturing and business services, marketing, human resources, financial and management controls, IT, environmental and quality management. May use methods of study and work measurement to analyse ways of doing work and the time a job should take to do. Advice may be sought in response to increased competition, or the need to change an organisation's products, services, technology or human working practices.

Management consultants liaise with managers and other professionals, such as those in IT, accounts, marketing and human resources. They are in a position to ask relevant questions to ensure that important facts are not overlooked. They analyse the current state of the organisation/business, consider a range of possible solutions and make recommendations. May present findings as a report to the management team or board of directors, often using a computer and visual aid equipment. Need to act with great integrity to ensure that a client's interest comes first.

Some management consultants have a role in effecting change within companies, and may then hold the title of business change manager/consultant.

Work Details

Usually work normal office hours, Monday to Friday, though can often work longer hours, sometimes late into the evening, or may start early in the morning. You are normally office based, but travel to visit clients, either locally, nationally or internationally. This may involve spending some time away from home. Work can be demanding at times and you need to be able to work to deadlines. Formal business clothes are usually worn.

Qualification

- **England, Wales and Northern Ireland**

Band 5: For a relevant degree: usually 2-3 A levels and some GCSEs (A*-C) usually including English and maths, or equivalent. Exact requirements depend on the degree you take.

- **Scotland**

Band 5: For a relevant degree: usually 3-5 H grades and some S grades (1-3), usually including English and maths, or similar qualifications. Exact qualifications depend on the degree you take.

Degree Information

An honours degree (often a 2:1) is usually required and most subjects are acceptable, though business subjects, economics, maths, and behavioural sciences, such as psychology, are often preferred. It can be advantageous to have relevant postgraduate qualifications such as an MBA.

Adult Qualifications

Entrants are usually graduates and although a postgraduate qualification is not always necessary, it is certainly an advantage. Many consultants have an MBA. Mature entrants with relevant previous experience may still apply for higher education courses even if they do not meet the standard entry requirements. However, you must demonstrate ability to study at the appropriate level. For those with management experience, professional bodies, such as the Chartered Management Institute and the Institute of Business Consulting, offer a wide range of qualifications.

Work Experience

Having some work experience in any area of management or business is advantageous when applying for jobs. It may be possible to participate in summer internship programmes while still at university. Shell Step and Milkround manage such schemes and also organise graduate recruitment schemes for those who are seeking permanent employment. Check their websites for details of placements.Some large management consultancy firms have student internships during vacations, entry to which is also very competitive.

Entry and Training

Entrants usually have a degree (normally at least a 2:1) and management experience, or are sometimes those with considerable experience in an area of industry or business. Some of the larger management consultancy or accountancy firms recruit and train graduates as management/business consultants. Training is ongoing, both on the job and by short courses. A graduate often starts in a supporting role on team projects and may need to complete an MBA or MA/MSc in management consultancy, sponsored by their employer, before being promoted to a more senior role.

The Institute of Business Consulting (IBC) runs a series of courses accredited by the Chartered Management Institute (CMI). The Certificate in Management Consultancy Essentials is followed by the Diploma in Management Consultancy and experienced consultants can undertake assessment leading to the Certified Management Consultant (CMC) award through the IBC. It is also useful to become an affiliate member of the IBC prior to qualifying and practising as a consultant.

Some firms may offer training courses on consulting skills and in specific sector training, such as qualifications offered by the Chartered Institute of Personnel and Development (CIPD). Most self-employed consultants are expected to have at least 3-5 years' experience, once fully qualified. You are expected to keep up to date with new professional developments through a continuing professional development programme of study. Contact the IBC for an approved range of suitable courses, or consult the website.

The Institute of Management Services also runs training courses leading to internationally recognised qualifications. The Management Services Certificate is taught in modular format and addresses the core competencies required of a manager. The Management Services Diploma is an additional qualification for those looking to demonstrate a higher level of knowledge and skill.

The website of the Management Consultancies Association also has advice and information on a career in management consultancy.

Mature entrants with business or management experience are usually preferred by employers. Some entrants have gained work experience and/or qualifications in accountancy, particularly those who have worked for major accountancy firms.

Opportunities and Pay

There are opportunities throughout the UK, though competition for jobs is fierce. Employers include consultancy firms or departments within sizeable commercial/industrial companies, ranging from small local companies to large multinationals, many of which are based in London and the South East. Progress is possible to more senior positions and can culminate in partner status with some firms. Self-employment is an option for those with considerable experience, and work abroad is also possible.

Pay varies according to the size, location and type of employer. Starting salaries are usually around £25k-£35k a year, rising to around £35k-£75k, and up to £140k with considerable experience. Partners/directors can achieve a basic salary of up to £200k and beyond. Profit share and performance schemes may also increase your salary.

Skills and Qualities

able to cope under pressure, able to get on with all kinds of people, analytical skills, business awareness, creative flair, good communication skills, good written English, information handling skills, integrity, IT skills

Relevant Subjects

Business and accounting, Economics, English, ICT/Computer studies, Mathematics, Psychology

Further Information

Break into Biz. (CfA) (Council for Administration) - www.breakinto.biz

Chartered Institute of Personnel and Development (CIPD) - www.cipd.co.uk

Inside Careers Guide to Management Consultancy (MCA/IMC) (MCA/IMC) - www.insidecareers.co.uk/man

Inside Careers Guide: Management Consultancy - www.insidecareers.co.uk/

Management Services Journal (quarterly) (Institute of Management Services (IMS) - www.ims-productivity.com/page.cfm/content/Management-Services-Journal/

Milkround - Internships and Graduate Schemes - www.milkround.com

Step - Nurturing Talent - www.step.org.uk

TARGETjobs: Management Consulting (GTI Specialist Publishing Ltd.) - www.groupgti.com

Addresses

Chartered Management Institute (CMI)
Management House, Cottingham Road, Corby NN17 1TT
Phone: +44 (0)1536 204 222
Web: www.managers.org.uk

Institute of Business Consulting (IBC)
4th Floor, 2 Savoy Court, Strand, London WC2R 0EZ
Phone: +44 (0)20 7497 0580
Web: www.ibconsulting.org.uk

Institute of Management Services (IMS)
Brooke House, 24 Dam Street, Lichfield, Staffordshire WS13 6AA
Phone: +44 (0)1543 266909
Web: www.ims-productivity.com

Management Consultancies Association (MCA)
60 Trafalgar Square, London WC2N 5DS
Phone: +44 (0)20 7321 3990
Web: www.mca.org.uk

Similar Jobs

Accountant: Industry & Commerce, Business Analyst, Financial Adviser/Planner, Manager, Marketing Manager, Project Manager

Manager

CRCI:Administration, Business and Office Work
CLCI:C Job Band: 4 to 5

Job Description

Managers plan, direct or coordinate the work of a team of people, a department, business or organisation. They consider how company aims can best be achieved and decide what resources are needed (finance, people and equipment). They plan budgets and timescales, organise daily working practices, and keep staff informed and motivated. Many managers make decisions on the training and development of employees, and look after their welfare at work. They maintain discipline, and make firm and responsible decisions. Working towards the most efficient and productive use of human and physical resources is one of their key aims.

Managers measure progress, review strategy and adjust procedures if necessary. They interpret financial reports and accounts, and liaise with finance directors or accountants. Ensuring that relevant laws, regulations and guidelines, such as environmental management and issues of health and safety, are in place and observed also make up part of the manager's role.

Work Details

Some managers work regular office hours of 35-40 hrs a week, Monday to Friday, though others may be required to work shifts. Longer hours than other staff are usual, together with early starts and late finishes to a working day. In some jobs you may be required to work weekends and public holidays. You are usually based in an office, though you may have to travel to meetings. You may spend a lot of time working at a computer, sitting at a desk. You are responsible for the overall operation of a business. There may be involvement in monitoring the recruitment, training and organisation of staff and overseeing the budgets and targets of the management team, and the marketing of the organisation.

Travel to other offices or attendance at conferences and other events may be required, which can involve time spent away from home. The work is demanding times and may involve making difficult decisions. Overseas travel may be necessary.

Qualification

• England, Wales and Northern Ireland

Band 4: For BTEC higher national award: 1-2 A levels and some GCSEs (A*-C), usually including English and maths, or equivalent.

Band 5: For degree courses: 2-3 A levels and some GCSEs (A*-C) usually including English and maths, or equivalent. Exact requirements depend on the degree you take.

• Scotland

Band 4: For SQA higher national award: usually 2-3 H grades and some S grades (1-3), often including English and maths, or similar qualifications.

Band 5: For degree courses: 3-5 H grades and some S grades (1-3) usually including English and maths, or similar qualifications. Exact requirements depend on the degree you take.

Degree Information

A degree in any discipline is acceptable. Business studies or management degrees are particularly appropriate. Maths or statistics, business administration, marketing, economics or financial management/banking are useful for management in any sector. Foundation degrees are available in a range of relevant subjects.

Adult Qualifications

For mature entrants, a degree or higher national award is helpful but not always essential. For those with management experience, professional bodies such as the Chartered Management Institute (CMI) offer a wide range of qualifications. The Open University Business School (OUBS) offers professional distance-learning courses in management as well as an MBA (Master of Business Administration) programme. Other universities and independent business schools also offer degrees/MBAs through various options of study, including distance learning, part time, modular and evening classes.

Course entry requirements are usually relaxed for suitable mature applicants. Those without the required qualifications may complete a foundation or Access course leading to relevant HNDs or accredited degrees.

Work Experience

Relevant work or voluntary experience is always useful and can improve your chances when applying for entry to this job. The types of work experience to consider are those that involve using organisation and administration skills, sales skills, and working with the public. For adult entry you usually need previous relevant employment or substantial voluntary work experience.

Entry and Training

Most managers have considerable experience in a specific area, such as sales, marketing, technology or finance. Employers often have graduate training schemes for new entrants to the job. Qualifications may be gained through a wide range of full or part-time courses, including foundation degrees, distance learning, short courses, block or day-release schemes. Some companies also run in-service training courses. Professional organisations, such as the Chartered Management Institute (CMI), offer a wide range of qualifications, including a route to achieving chartered manager status. Courses are credit based and candidates can work their way through from a Level 2 to a Level 8 qualification. The route is in three stages and includes a continuing professional development submission. Managers with a minimum of three years' practical experience can get exemption from this. Contact the CMI for details.

There are many professional organisations that offer specialist qualifications for this area of work, such as the Institute of Administrative Management, which offers a BSc (Hons) in Business Management. All courses are available at recognised centres throughout the UK and open/distance learning options are also available. Check the website for details. A postgraduate qualification, for example an MBA or another professional qualification, is useful. The Open University Business School runs a series of courses that are suitable for continuing professional development including specialist professional development, management development and an MBA. The Institute of Leadership and Management (ILM) offers qualifications in four main categories; vocationally related, S/NVQs, international management qualifications and customised qualifications. Qualifications are available from level 2 through to level 7. Check the ILM website for details. The Institute of Operations Management offers a level 3 certificate qualification, a level 5 diploma and an advanced diploma in management. It also runs a series of short courses covering topics such as change management and master planning. Details are given on the website.

It is possible to work your way up to management level from a junior post, through gaining promotion. Some may enter junior management schemes after completing A levels/H grades, BTEC/SQA national awards, or similar qualifications. Language skills are an advantage in some posts. S/NVQs in management are available at levels 3-4 and in specialist areas of management (e.g. construction) at level 5. Training programmes, including apprenticeship schemes, may be available in your area for entry to this job. Advanced apprenticeships also lead to S/NVQs at level 3 and may provide a route into junior management.

Mature entrants may be offered specialised training courses, and relevant part-time and distance-learning courses are usually available for mature students. Employers often prefer mature people who have previous experience and/or qualifications, for their management training schemes. Sponsorship for higher education, management-related degrees may also be available from some large companies and organisations.

Opportunities and Pay

There is a steady demand for qualified and experienced staff. You can work anywhere in the UK in areas that include industry, commerce, local and central government, and the NHS. Jobs are available in all types and sizes of organisations, varying from small businesses to national/multinational companies with thousands of employees.

Pay varies considerably depending on industry and the type of business you manage. Trainee or junior managers earn around £15k-£22k (hospitality industry), £16k-£25k (manufacturing) and £20k-£28k (finance). This variation continues with experienced managers earning between £25k-£48k a year. Senior managers with high levels of responsibility can earn more than £50k in the hospitality and manufacturing industries, and more than £75k in finance.

Skills and Qualities

able to inspire confidence, able to manage people, able to take responsibility, analytical skills, decisive, good communication skills, good interpersonal skills, good presentation skills, IT skills, sound judgement

Relevant Subjects

Business and accounting, Economics, English, ICT/Computer studies, Mathematics

Further Information

AGCAS: Government & Public Administration (Job Sector Briefing) (AGCAS) - www.prospects.ac.uk

Apprenticeship Schemes (National Apprenticeship Service) - www.apprenticeships.org.uk

Break into Biz. (CfA) (Council for Administration) - www.breakinto.biz

Management Services Journal (quarterly) (Institute of Management Services (IMS)) - www.ims-productivity.com/page.cfm/content/Management-Services-Journal/

Management Today (Haymarket) (Haymarket) - www.managementtoday.co.uk/

TARGETjobs: Management Consulting (GTI Specialist Publishing Ltd.) - www.groupgti.com

Addresses

Chartered Management Institute (CMI)
Management House, Cottingham Road, Corby NN17 1TT
Phone: +44 (0)1536 204 222
Web: www.managers.org.uk

Institute of Administration Management (iam)
6 Graphite Square, Vauxhall Walk, London SE11 5EE
Phone: +44 (0)20 7091 2600
Web: www.instam.org

Institute of Leadership and Management (ILM)
Stowe House, Netherstowe, Lichfield, Staffordshire WS13 6TJ
Phone: +44 (0)1543 266 867
Web: www.i-l-m.com

Institute of Operations Management (IOM)
CILT (UK), Earlstrees Court, Earlstrees Road, Corby, Northants NN17 4AX
Phone: +44 (0)1536 740 105
Web: www.iomnet.org.uk

Open University Business School (OUBS)
PO Box 197, Milton Keynes MK7 6BJ
Phone: +44 (0)845 300 60 90
Web: http://www8.open.ac.uk/business-school/

Similar Jobs
Bank Manager, Civil Service Fast Streamer, Company Secretary, Human Resources Officer/Manager, Management Consultant, Office Manager, Production Manager

Mapping & Charting Technician
also known as: Cartographic Technician, Technical Land Surveyor

CRCI:Building and Construction
CLCI:UT Job Band: 3 to 4

Job Description
Mapping and charting technicians work in a cartographic office assisting with the production and preparation of maps and road atlases for printing and copying. They have office and some site-based duties and get involved with more basic techniques such as digitising maps, data input and other basic map work. May use Geographic Information Systems (GIS) and digital-mapping techniques to scan, analyse, process and display data on-screen. May also use computer-aided design (CAD) programs.

Can revise existing maps by adding up-to-date details of an area, including a new housing estate, a road or by-pass. May assist in the making of globes, charts, and also models of the earth. Some technicians work with historical maps.

Work Details
Mapping and charting technicians usually work a 35-40 hr week, Monday to Friday, though may be expected to have some early starts and late finishes, including weekend work. The work is mainly office based, but may involve travel to different places for site visits. A driving licence is usually preferred.

Qualification
• England, Wales and Northern Ireland
Band 3: For a relevant BTEC course or for direct entry with an employer: usually at least 4 GCSEs (A*-C) including English, maths and possibly geography, technical drawing or computer studies, or equivalent.

Band 4: For a relevant BTEC higher national award: 1-2 A levels and some GCSEs (A*-C) usually including English, maths and a science subject, or equivalent.

• Scotland
Band 3: For a relevant SQA course or for direct entry with an employer: usually four S grades (1-3) preferably including English, maths and possibly geography, technical drawing or computer studies, or similar.

Band 4: For a relevant SQA higher national award: usually 2-3 H grades and some S grades (1-3) often including English, maths and a science subject, or similar qualifications.

Adult Qualifications
Course entry requirements are usually relaxed for suitable mature applicants.

Work Experience
Relevant work or voluntary experience is always useful and can improve your employment prospects when applying for entry to jobs or colleges. Surveying, environmental work and work with computers gives you some relevant skills and experience.

Entry and Training
You can either take a full-time course or train with an employer and take a part-time course with day or block release at a college. The qualifications you need depend on your employer and level of entry. Some employers provide initial in-house training for new entrants, including digital mapping, GIS systems, topography and photogrammetry, and map design. On-the-job training towards a relevant national certificate/diploma course, such as mathematical/physical science, and land/urban studies, is usually available.

In government departments you may gain experience in several different departments before progressing to a more senior level. Technical membership (TechRICS) of the Royal Institution for Chartered Surveyors (RICS) is possible and can be gained through a variety of routes, including relevant HNC/HNDs, S/NVQ at level 4, or an assessment of technical competence (ATC) following a minimum two-year training period. From TechRICS membership there is a 'bridge' arrangement that provides a pathway to chartered surveyor status.

The Survey Association has developed a survey technician training course especially for new entrants into the geomatics industry, or for those already with experience but with no formal training. Some employers may provide this off-the-job training course, which is offered over two years in six two-week blocks of study.

Relevant S/NVQs are available at levels 3-4 in spatial data management. Relevant training programmes, including apprenticeship schemes, may be available in your area. Asset skills have details of their surveying apprenticeship on the website. Advanced apprenticeships leading to qualification at level 3 can also be a route into higher education. A Diploma/Welsh Baccalaureate may be available in your area in environment and land-based studies .

Mature applicants with a background in IT or graphic design may have an advantage. Those with knowledge of Geographic Information Systems (GIS), digital-mapping techniques and CAD systems are particularly welcomed.

Opportunities and Pay
Jobs are available mainly in Ordnance Survey offices and other central government departments, including the Hydrographic Office and the Ministry of Defence. Others work for cartographic service companies, universities, oil and public utility companies, local government planning and architect departments, the armed forces, commercial map publishers, and other specialist map-making organisations. Progression to the more senior position of cartographer is often possible, though you usually require a relevant degree to do this job.

Salaries start from around £18k and can rise to around £25k-£30k a year, though much depends on your level of responsibility and expertise.

Health
This job requires good eyesight and normal colour vision.

Skills and Qualities
accurate measuring and calculating skills, aptitude for teamwork, attention to detail, environmental awareness, good communication skills, information handling skills, methodical, spatial awareness, specialist IT skills

Relevant Subjects
Art and Design, Design and technology, Geography, ICT/Computer studies, Mathematics, Physics

Further Information
Apprenticeship Schemes (National Apprenticeship Service) - www.apprenticeships.org.uk

Asset Skills - sector skills council for the places where we live and work - www.assetskills.org

British Cartographic Society, BCS - www.cartography.org.uk

Cartographic Journal (BCS) (British Cartographic Society (BCS) - www.cartography.org.uk

Diplomas (Foundation, Higher and Advanced) - http://yp.direct.gov.uk/diplomas

Hydrographic, Meteorological & Oceanographic Training Group (HMTG) (The Royal Navy) - www.royalnavy.mod.uk/

Remote Sensing & Photogrammetry Society - www.rspsoc.org
Society of Cartographers - www.soc.org.uk
Welsh Baccalaureate - www.wbq.org.uk

Addresses

Ordnance Survey
Romsey Road, Southampton, Hampshire SO16 4GU
Phone: 0845 605 0505 (UK only)
Web: www.ordnancesurvey.co.uk

Royal Institution of Chartered Surveyors (RICS)
RICS Contact Centre Surveyor Court Westwood Way,
Coventry CV4 8JE
Phone: +44 (0)870 333 1600
Web: www.ricscourses.org/pages/careers.aspx

Survey Association (TSA), The
Northgate Business Centre, 38 Northgate,
Newark-on-Trent NG24 1EZ
Phone: +44 (0)1636 642840
Web: www.tsa-uk.org.uk

Similar Jobs

Architectural Technician, Architectural Technologist, Cartographer, Surveying Technician, Surveyor: Geomatics/Geospatial, Town Planning Support Staff

Marine Biologist

CRCI:Science, Mathematics and Statistics
CLCI:QOD Job Band: 5

Job Description

Marine biologists study micro-organisms, plant and animal life in the ocean and on the shoreline. They conduct research in the laboratory and at sea on research ships and are interested in the processes of how marine organisms develop, relate to one another, how they adapt to their environment and interact with it. They may study areas, such as the effects of pollution, nuclear power stations, coral reefs, oil refineries and industrial activity on the oceans, or the levels of stocks of particular fish species. Marine biologists analyse and interpret data from samples and remote sensing aids. They count bacteria, plankton, algae, worms, fish larvae and shrimps. May also use computer modelling to aid research.

Marine biologists rarely if ever work with large marine mammals such as whales and dolphins; such work is done by zoologists. Some marine biologists work with geologists to examine fossil marine organisms. They are responsible for devising experiments and supervising staff and can also be involved in generating project bids for funds and grants. May attend conferences, and research, write and present professional papers and reports.

Work Details

Usually work a basic 39 hr week, Monday to Friday, though sometimes hours may be longer, especially when on field trips. Much of the work is laboratory or office based, but some time may be spent on research vessels or offshore platforms at sea. This involves spending time away from home, sometimes for long periods. You work as part of a team but may need to spend periods of time working alone. This work requires a high degree of accuracy and patience.

When working offshore, you work outdoors in all weather, usually on shifts around the clock. Work can sometimes be physically demanding and there is a risk of accidents at sea. You may need to wear protective clothing at times.

Qualification

- **England, Wales and Northern Ireland**

Band 5: For degree courses: 2-3 A levels including biology and preferably chemistry, maths or physics and some GCSEs (A*-C) usually including English, science and maths, or equivalent. Exact requirements depend on the degree you take.

- **Scotland**

Band 5: For degree courses: 3-5 H grades including biology and preferably chemistry, maths or physics and some S grades (1-3), usually including English maths and science, or similar. Exact requirements depend on the degree you take.

Degree Information

There are courses leading to first degrees in marine/freshwater biology and marine science, though many marine biologists have a degree in biology or biochemistry, usually followed by a specialist higher degree.

Adult Qualifications

Entry requirements may be relaxed for mature entrants to first degree courses provided they submit evidence of previous study, such as an Access, foundation or Open University course.

Work Experience

Entry to this job is competitive and it is important that you try to do some relevant work or voluntary experience before applying to both jobs and to university. There are several Natural Environment Research Council centres around the country that may take people on work experience, such as the National Oceanography Centre, Southampton (NOCS) which also runs summer schools for final year degree students.

Entry and Training

Entrants are usually graduates who have followed a degree course lasting three or four years, either full time or sandwich. Postgraduate study is an advantage, particularly for research posts. Training continues through practical experience in the workplace together with short or residential courses. Marine biologists usually supplement their research role with specialist training such as sea survival techniques, health and safety or geographical information systems (GIS) training. There are relevant foundation degrees in subjects that include coastal conservation and marine biology, in applied biological subjects, and in biology and management of maritime and freshwater ecosystems.

Skills such as boat handling, mechanical knowledge and scuba diving are extremely useful. The Marine Biological Association (MBA) offers advanced courses on various areas of marine science. Membership of the Society of Biology can be attained by graduates with three years' relevant experience. Continuing professional development (CPD) is expected throughout your career.

Mature entrants can choose to study a BSc in natural sciences with biology through distance learning, offered by the Open University. You may be eligible for postgraduate funding and research through the Biotechnology and Biological Sciences Research Council (BBSRC).

Opportunities and Pay

Around 13,000 people in the UK work as marine biologists, employed in research, development or monitoring posts. Employers include marine laboratories, government departments or agencies such as the Department for the Environment, Food and Rural Affairs (DEFRA) or Admiralty Research Establishments, universities, fisheries and fish farms, conservation groups and some industrial concerns such as major oil companies.

Competition for research posts is fierce. Some move into consultancy or generate and manage their own contracts on a freelance basis. Others may work abroad on short or long contracts.

Pay varies depending on location and employer. A newly qualified marine biologist can earn between £17k and £20k a year, rising to £25k-£30k with experience. Those at the top of their field earn in excess of £60k a year.

Health

This job requires good general fitness and normal colour vision.

Skills and Qualities
able to live and work closely with other people, able to report accurately, analytical skills, aptitude for fieldwork, attention to detail, enjoy working outdoors, good interpersonal skills, IT skills, observant, practical skills, scientific approach

Relevant Subjects
Biology, Chemistry, English, Geography, ICT/Computer studies, Mathematics, Physics, Science

Further Information
AGCAS: Environment & Agriculture (Job Sector Briefing) (AGCAS) - www.prospects.ac.uk

Careers in the Marine Environment (IMarEST) - www.imarest.org/careers/

Journal of Experimental Marine Biology and Ecology (Science Direct) - www.sciencedirect.com/science/journal/00220981

Marine Scientist (quarterly) (ImarEST) - www.imarest.org/Publications.aspx

Oceans of Opportunity (Society for Underwater Technology (SUT)) - www.sut.org.uk/htmfoldr/oceansoop/sut_ooo.htm

Society for Underwater Technology (Society for Underwater Technology) - www.sut.org.uk

Underwater Technology (bi-annual) (SUT (Society for Underwater Technology)) - www.sut.org.uk/journal/default.htm

▶Working in science (2007) (Babcock Lifeskills) - www.babcock-lifeskills.com/

▶Working outdoors (2010) (Babcock Lifeskills) - www.babcock-lifeskills.com/

Addresses
Biotechnology and Biological Sciences Research Council (BBSRC)
Polaris House North Star Avenue, Swindon, Wiltshire SN2 1UH
Phone: +44 (0)1793 413 200
Web: www.bbsrc.ac.uk

Centre for Environment, Fisheries and Aquaculture Science
CEFAS Lowestoft Laboratory Pakefield Road, Suffolk NR33 0HT
Phone: +44 (0)1502 562 224
Web: www.cefas.co.uk

Institute of Marine Engineering, Science and Technology (IMarEST)
80 Coleman Street, London EC2R 5BJ
Phone: +44 (0)20 7382 2600
Web: www.imarest.org

Marine Biological Association (MBA)
The Laboratory, Citadel Hill, Plymouth, Devon PL1 2PB
Phone: +44 (0)1752 633 207
Web: www.mba.ac.uk

National Oceanography Centre (NOCS)
University of Southampton, Waterfront Campus, European Way SO14 3ZH
Phone: +44 (0)23 8059 6666
Web: www.noc.soton.ac.uk/

Natural Environment Research Council (NERC)
Polaris House North Star Avenue, Swindon, Wiltshire SN2 1EU
Phone: +44 (0)1793 411 500
Web: www.nerc.ac.uk

Open University (OU)
PO Box 197, Milton Keynes MK7 6BJ
Phone: +44 (0)845 300 6090
Web: http://www3.open.ac.uk

Scottish Association for Marine Science (SAMS)
Scottish Marine Institute, Oban, Argyll PA37 1QA
Phone: +44 (0)1631 559 000
Web: www.sams.ac.uk

Society of Biology
9 Red Lion Court, London EC4A 3EF
Phone: +44 (0)20 7936 5900
Web: http://societyofbiology.org/home

Similar Jobs
Biologist, Diver, Ecologist, Geologist, Oceanographer

Marine Craft Worker: Ships
also known as: Marine Craftsperson, Shipwright

CRCI:Engineering
CLCI:ROF Job Band: 2 to 3

Job Description
Marine craft workers work in a shipyard helping to build specialist vessels, particularly for the Royal Navy and the offshore industry (e.g pipe laying and survey vessels). They also repair and convert existing vessels using skills in areas of work that include welding, marking out shapes, steel cutting and bending. They make patterns for a plater to use as a cutting guide. Also position and secure sections/plates to build ships' hulls. Machine craft workers study plans, direct the crane to the correct position and then line up the sections/plates precisely by cable or brace, before securing. They also do pipe work, install engines and work on internal fittings. May also install other fittings such as hatches and decking. For repair work, they prepare the ship and set up the scaffolding for dry-dock work.

Work Details
Usually work a basic 37-40 hr week, with the possibility of overtime to complete jobs on time. You may be required to work shifts. This job covers a wide range of specialised crafts. Your place of work is in a shipyard, outdoors, and sometimes under cover. You work under supervision and also assist other people. Your work can be very busy at times and the job involves considerable physical exertion, climbing ladders and working at heights.

The environment is dirty and noisy and you often work outside, in all weather conditions. There may be a risk of accidents from equipment. You need to wear protective clothing and possibly a helmet and boots.

Qualification
• England, Wales and Northern Ireland
Band 2: For entry to jobs, no minimum qualifications are needed, but it is an advantage to have some GCSEs (A*-C), or equivalent, in subjects that include English, maths and a science. Technical and practical subjects are also useful, such as craft, design and technology.

Band 3: For some employers and entry to some courses: usually at least 4 GCSEs (A*-C) including maths, English and a science, engineering or technology subject, or equivalent qualifications.

• Scotland
Band 2: Although academic qualifications are not specified for this job, it is an advantage to have some S grades (1-3) in subjects that include English, maths and science, or similar. Technical and practical subjects are also useful.

Band 3: For entry to jobs, usually at least four S grades (1-3) including maths, English and a science, engineering or technology subject, or similar.

Adult Qualifications
Course entry requirements are usually relaxed for suitable mature applicants.

Work Experience
Relevant work or voluntary experience is always useful. It can add to your CV and improve your chances when applying for entry to jobs or apprenticeships in the engineering industry. Practical and craft experience, particularly in engineering, is extremely useful.

Entry and Training
Training is usually on the job with a skilled and experienced employee, together with part-time study through a day-release or block-release course to a college for relevant qualifications.

However, training can vary, depending on the employer. Some courses can be full time and may be taken prior to finding a job. These include BTEC/SQA national awards in subjects such as electrical, electronic and mechanical engineering, which provide a good background for entry to shipbuilding, repair and conversion. There are also vocationally related qualifications such as the City & Guilds level 2 and level 3 certificate in boatbuilding, maintenance and support.

Many trainees follow the marine craft skills apprenticeship, approved by the British Marine Federation (BMF). Shipbuilders and ship repair yards also offer apprenticeships that usually last 2-3 years and lead to S/NVQ level 2-3 and above in subjects such as marine engineering. Apprenticeships usually start with induction training in health and safety and some off-the-job training in the use of hand tools, and understanding engineering drawings and the materials used. The BMF can also offer partial training grants to students employed by specific companies who meet the registration criteria. See the website for details. The Shipbuilding & Shiprepairers' Association has a list of the main shipyards in the UK on its website.

A Diploma/Welsh Baccalaureate may be available in your area in engineering. See the diplomas website for further information.

Relevant practical and craft experience and an interest in boats is important. Craft skills such as plumbing and carpentry are an advantage when looking for work in a shipyard. There are often skill shortages in this area, so adults may find it easier to get training.

Mature applicants can benefit through training opportunities such as Work Based Learning/Training for Work that may be available in your area. You can also gain recognition of previous experience through Accreditation of Prior Learning (APL) or by working towards relevant S/NVQs. Contact your local careers office, Jobcentre Plus, Next Step service or Learning and Skills Council (LSC)/Local Enterprise Company (LEC) for details of training opportunities and schemes, including apprenticeships for adults.

Opportunities and Pay

Employment is with a shipyard; the main ones are in Cumbria, Tyneside, Plymouth and Portsmouth. Though opportunities in the shipbuilding industry were in decline, the UK still has a worldwide reputation for ship repair and conversion and is a world leader in warship production. Europe is a world leader in ship conversion, with around 40% of the global market and the UK is now one of the top three converters in Europe. Ship repair on a smaller scale is located in additional areas, at ports around the UK coast, such as Falmouth. With further qualifications, training can lead to technician level or beyond, and the skills learned are readily transferable to other engineering sectors.

Pay increases with promotion and varies depending on area and employer. Starting salaries for apprentices are likely to be around £13k a year, rising to around £18k-£23k a year once qualified. The most skilled and experienced workers can earn around £30k a year. Overtime and bonuses may be available.

Health

This job requires good general fitness and stamina. You also need good eyesight.

Skills and Qualities

able to explain clearly, able to follow drawings and plans, accurate, aptitude for teamwork, hard working, manual dexterity, numeracy skills, patient, practical skills

Relevant Subjects

Design and technology, Engineering, Mathematics, Physics, Science

Further Information

Apprenticeship Schemes (National Apprenticeship Service) - www.apprenticeships.org.uk

Diplomas (Foundation, Higher and Advanced) - http://yp.direct.gov.uk/diplomas

Engineering Scotland (SEMTA) - www.engineeringscotland.org

Sea Your Future: A Guide to Marine Careers (IMAREST) - www.imarest.org/membership/careers

SEMTA - sector skills council for science, engineering and manufacturing technologies - www.semta.org.uk

Training Schemes - www.direct.gov.uk/en/educationandlearning

Your future in the boating industry (British Marine Federation) - www.britishmarine.co.uk/upload_pub/27441_bmf_your_future41.pdf

Addresses

British Marine Federation (BMF)
Marine House, Thorpe Lea Road, Egham, Surrey TW20 8BF
Phone: +44 (0)1784 473 377
Web: www.britishmarine.co.uk

Institute of Marine Engineering, Science and Technology (IMarEST)
80 Coleman Street, London EC2R 5BJ
Phone: +44 (0)20 7382 2600
Web: www.imarest.org

Shipbuilders & Shiprepairers Association (SSA)
Marine House, Meadlake Place, Thorpe Lea Road, Egham, Surrey TW20 8BF
Phone: +44 (0)1784 223770
Web: www.ssa.org.uk

Similar Jobs

Boatbuilder, Fitter: Maintenance, Marine Engineering Technician, Mechanical Engineering Technician, Sheet Metal Worker

Marine Engineering Technician

also known as: Shipbuilding Technician

CRCI:Engineering
CLCI:RAV Job Band: 3

Job Description

Marine engineering technicians support the work of marine engineers in three main areas; marine engineering (construction and operation of propulsion machinery and associated systems), onshore (shipbuilding and repair) and offshore (fossil fuels exploration and production). Apart from the high level of engineering skills, the work varies depending upon the area in which you are employed and can include welding, mechanical, electrical and electronic engineering.

Marine engineering technicians lead teams involved in the regular servicing and maintenance of equipment and must also respond to emergency repairs as they arise. Onshore technicians working in shipyards may also supervise a team of shipbuilding craft workers and offshore technicians work on a wide variety of vessels, from passenger liners to tankers and pipe laying vessels.

Marine engineering technicians in the Royal Navy can work on a variety of vessels, including warships, submarines and aircraft carriers, anywhere in the world.

Work Details

Marine engineering technicians usually work a basic 35-40 hr week, Monday to Friday. Early starts, late finishes and some weekend work is usually required. Some technicians' work is organised into shifts. Marine technicians can spend long periods away from home, either on a ship or sea platform. Technicians must be prepared to work in oily, noisy environments and in all weather conditions when at sea.

Qualification

- **England, Wales and Northern Ireland**

Band 3: For entry to jobs, relevant HNC or Diploma: usually at least 4 GCSEs (A*-C) including English, maths and physics, or equivalent. It is also useful to have studied maths and physics at A level, or equivalent.

• **Scotland**

Band 3: For entry to jobs, usually at least four S grades (1-3) including English, maths and physics, or similar. It is also useful to have studied maths and physics at H grade, or similar.

Adult Qualifications

It is possible to enter as a trainee or an apprentice without the usual academic qualifications, particularly if you have engineering experience. Some full-time college courses waive entry requirements for mature applicants.

Work Experience

Relevant work or voluntary experience is always useful. It can add to your CV and improve your chances when applying for entry to jobs or apprenticeships in the marine engineering industry. Any practical experience in engineering or as a mechanic is useful for gaining employment in this field. Experience of working in a team is vitally important to employers.

Entry and Training

Many entrants have a qualification in engineering, such as a vocational A level or a relevant BTEC/SQA national qualification. However some enter through a 3-4 year advanced apprenticeship and gain relevant qualifications once employed, by attending college through day or block-release. Some may take BTEC/SQA awards such as an HNC/HND in marine engineering. Others work towards S/NVQs in marine engineering at levels 2-3. There are also vocationally related qualifications available. The Institute of Marine Engineering Science and Technology has a list of accredited courses on its website.

Gaining Fngineering Council technician status (EngTech) is highly regarded. To qualify as an EngTech you must do further training and assessment on the job. You are required to continue your training in the workplace through initial professional development and be committed to continuing professional development through your professional career. Technicians can also go on to register as an incorporated engineer and chartered engineer with further qualifications and training. Contact the Engineering Council for details.

The Royal Navy marine engineering technician scheme prefers entrants to be able to study at level 3 or foundation degree level. Training is initially on shore and then continues at sea. The Merchant Navy recruits technician cadets whose training leads to S/NVQs at levels 2-3 in marine vessel support/marine engineering operations.

Training programmes, including apprenticeship schemes, may be available in your area. Advanced apprenticeships leading to qualification at level 3 can also be a route into higher education. A Diploma/Welsh Baccalaureate may be available in your area in engineering. See the diplomas website for further information.

Mature entrants often have a relevant engineering background. Experience of practical work is important and it is useful to be able to follow drawings and plans. Government training opportunities, such as apprenticeships for adults, may be available in your area. You can also gain recognition of previous experience through Accreditation of Prior Learning (APL) or by working towards relevant S/NVQs. Contact your local careers office, Jobcentre Plus, Next Step service or Learning and Skills Council (LSC)/Local Enterprise Company (LEC) for details of all training opportunities and schemes, including apprenticeships for adults. For entry as a marine engineering technician, the Royal Navy currently has an upper age limit of 36.

Opportunities and Pay

Work is usually available throughout the UK. You can work for shipbuilders and in repair yards, the worldwide oil/gas industry, marine manufacturers and equipment suppliers, or the Royal Navy and Merchant Navy. There are a few opportunities for self-employment in repairing small vessels. There are good opportunities at the moment as there is a shortage of skilled technicians.

Salaries vary depending upon the type of technician you are, the company you work for and the level of responsibility you reach. Newly qualified marine engineering technicians earn around £15k a year, rising to around £20k. High earners can make around £35k a year.

Health

Working on or offshore requires a good level of physical fitness. Royal Navy and Merchant Navy entrants undertake a medical and must have good colour vision.

Skills and Qualities

able to follow drawings and plans, able to work both on your own and in a team, analytical skills, good communication skills, good interpersonal skills, IT skills, logical, methodical, problem-solving skills, technical aptitude

Relevant Subjects

Design and technology, Engineering, Mathematics, Physics, Science

Further Information

Apprenticeship Schemes (National Apprenticeship Service) - www.apprenticeships.org.uk

Careers at Sca - www.careersatsea.org

Diplomas (Foundation, Higher and Advanced) - http://yp.direct.gov.uk/diplomas

Marine Engineers Review (10 x year) (IMarEST) - www.imarest.org/Publications.aspx

Sea Your Future: A Guide to Marine Careers (IMAREST) - www.imarest.org/membership/careers

SEMTA - sector skills council for science, engineering and manufacturing technologies - www.semta.org.uk

Training Schemes - www.direct.gov.uk/en/educationandlearning

Women into Science, Engineering & Construction - www.wisecampaign.org.uk

Addresses

British Marine Federation (BMF)
Marine House, Thorpe Lea Road, Egham, Surrey TW20 8BF
Phone: +44 (0)1784 473 377
Web: www.britishmarine.co.uk

Engineering Council
246 High Holborn, London WC1V 7EX
Phone: +44 (0)20 3206 0500
Web: www.engc.org.uk

Institute of Marine Engineering, Science and Technology (IMarEST)
80 Coleman Street, London EC2R 5BJ
Phone: +44 (0)20 7382 2600
Web: www.imarest.org

Merchant Navy Training Board (MNTB)
Carthusian Court, 12 Carthusian Street, London EC1M 6EZ
Phone: +44 (0)20 7417 2800
Web: www.mntb.org.uk

Similar Jobs

Aircraft Engineering Technician, Electrical Engineering Technician, Engineer: Marine, Fitter: Maintenance, Merchant Navy Engineering Officer, Royal Navy Rating

Market Research Executive

also known as: Market Researcher

CRCI:Marketing and Advertising
CLCI:OB — Job Band: 4 to 5

Job Description

Market research executives plan and implement ways of collecting, analysing and interpreting information about the market for a product or service. They identify the information the client requires, and prepare and cost the research programme. Often use research techniques such as interviews, questionnaires, opinion polls, tests and surveys. Also supervises the work, often with a team of market research interviewers, and reports on the market information gathered.

The work may be consumer, industrial or social research and involve the use of a computer to analyse the data. Executives are usually responsible for the recruitment and training of market research interviewers and often work on more than one project at a time. They may do quantitative research involving gathering and analysing information from questionnaires or electronic surveys. May also do qualitative research which investigates attitudes, usually by interviews or focus groups. Usually specialises in one of these types.

Work Details

Usually works a basic 39 hr week, Monday to Friday, though may have to work longer hours when there are deadlines to be met. Those involved in qualitative research often work evenings and weekends as it is easier to contact people at those times.

This is an office-based job, but can involve travel throughout the UK, and perhaps overseas, to meet clients. You have to understand the needs of your client and to devise ways of finding the appropriate information. You have to present reports clearly, both face to face and in writing. You deal with a wide variety of people including the client, technical staff, managers and perhaps consumers, and supervise staff, such as interviewers.

Qualification

• England, Wales and Northern Ireland

Band 4: For HND, Diploma of Higher Education or foundation degree: 1-2 A levels and some GCSEs (A*-C) usually including English and maths, or equivalent.

Band 5: For degree courses: 2-3 A levels and some GCSEs (A*-C) usually including English and maths, or equivalent. Exact requirements depend on the degree you take.

• Scotland

Band 4: For entry to SQA higher national and professional development awards, usually 2-3 H grades and some S grades (1-3), including English and maths, or similar qualifications.

Band 5: For degree courses: 3-5 H grades and some S grades (1-3), usually including English and maths, or similar qualifications. Exact requirements depend on the degree you take.

Degree Information

It is possible to enter this job with a degree in any subject, but mathematics, statistics, psychology, economics, sociology, business studies or administration, and marketing are all useful. A degree in a science or engineering subject is normally required for industrial market research. Languages are useful for overseas posts. There are postgraduate courses in marketing with specialist market research options and social research. The Market Research Society has a list of accredited masters degrees.

Adult Qualifications

Most entrants have a degree or other higher education qualification. Entry requirements may be relaxed for adults applying for higher education courses. Access or foundation courses give adults without qualifications a route on to degree courses. For industrial market research, it is an advantage to have experience or qualifications in engineering or science.

Work Experience

Entry to this job is competitive and it is important that you try to do some relevant work or voluntary experience before applying. Direct experience with a market research agency or in marketing and public relations is useful. Any work involving interview techniques or statistical analysis is an advantage.

Entry and Training

Most entrants are graduates or hold an HND. It is usual to train on the job following a company training programme, and perhaps combined with short courses run by the Market Research Society (MRS). Some study for the MRS diploma, which may improve career prospects. Graduate entrants with some employers can join the MRS Professional Development Scheme. This is a three-year programme based on workplace training and assessment. Check the MRS website for details of all courses and training programmes.

Some companies also offer the accredited interviewer training scheme (AITS) that is run by the MRS, and equips trainers to deliver competency-based interviewer training and gain MRS trainer status. The Association for Qualitative Research offers a three-day foundation course for new researchers and the Royal Statistical Society runs regular training courses.

It is also possible to join an agency with A levels/H grades as a research assistant, and train through the MRS while working. A Diploma/Welsh Baccalaureate in business, administration and finance (BAF) may be available in your area and provide an alternative route into this job. There are also relevant foundation degrees in subjects such as marketing and business studies that are available either full or part time.

Mature applicants usually require relevant experience in advertising, sales and marketing, statistics or social/economic research. The MRS offers a range of professional courses, including online and distance-learning courses to achieve professional qualifications.

Opportunities and Pay

There is a demand for market research, particularly in the pharmaceutical industry, environmental sciences and health and social research. Market research executives work mainly for market research agencies, but some are employed in market research departments of industrial or commercial organisations, in research or planning departments of advertising agencies, in local and central government, and in research institutes. Entry is highly competitive and there are few vacancies. Most market research agencies are based in London, with a few in other large cities. Some experienced executives work on a freelance basis.

Promotion opportunities to senior research executive and director positions are good, and market research can be a route into other areas of marketing or advertising. Work is available overseas for those working for an international company.

Pay varies depending on location, type and size of company. Graduate entrants are likely to earn between £19k-£24k, and with experience £30k-£40k a year. The most successful executives can earn £45k-£80k a year. Profit-sharing and/or bonus schemes are common.

Skills and Qualities

able to work to deadlines, analytical skills, aptitude for teamwork, attention to detail, excellent communication skills, good interpersonal skills, good organisational skills, IT skills, methodical, numeracy skills

Relevant Subjects

Business and accounting, Economics, English, ICT/Computer studies, Mathematics, Psychology, Retail and distribution

Further Information

Becoming a Market Researcher (MRS) (The Market Research Society) - www.mrs.org.uk/careers/

International Journal of Market Research (6 x year) (Warc Ltd) - www.ijmr.com/

Marketing Uncovered (Trotman 2010) - www.trotman.co.uk

Marketing Week (Centaur Media Plc) - www.marketingweek.co.uk/

Social Research Association (SRA) - www.the-sra.org.uk

Welsh Baccalaureate - www.wbq.org.uk

▶Working in marketing, advertising & PR (2008) (Babcock Lifeskills) - www.babcock-lifeskills.com/

Addresses

Association for Qualitative Research (AQR)
Davey House, 31 St Neots Road, Eaton Ford PE19 7BA
Phone: +44 (0)1480 407227
Web: www.aqr.org.uk

Market Research Society (MRS)
15 Northburgh Street, London EC1V 0JR
Phone: +44 (0)20 7490 4911
Web: www.mrs.org.uk

Royal Statistical Society (RSS)
12 Errol Street, London EC1Y 8LX
Phone: +44 (0)20 7638 8998
Web: www.rss.org.uk

Similar Jobs

Advertising Account Executive, Information Scientist, Market Research Interviewer, Marketing Manager, Retail Buyer, Statistician

Market Research Interviewer

CRCI:Marketing and Advertising
CLCI:OB Job Band: 2

Job Description

Market research interviewers work for market research agencies and collect facts and opinion through interviews using a questionnaire. They collect information for businesses, advertising agencies and government. The work involves fixing times to speak to people at work or at home, to talk to people by phone, or at random in the street.

Interviewers ask questions and record the replies on a form or transfers the information to a computer. Some interviewers use computer-assisted software for recording responses and assisting with the interviewing process. Some interviewers also help market researchers prepare questions and look at the results.

Work Details

The hours are irregular and often include evenings and weekends. Much of the work is temporary and part time. You have to travel around to carry out interviews and are in contact with a wide variety of people. Most work is done by visiting people in their homes, approaching them in the street, or in public buildings and shopping malls. You may have to stand for a long time and may be out in all sorts of weather. Some market research is conducted through telephone interviewing, either from an interviewer's home or from an office.

Qualification

- **England, Wales and Northern Ireland**

Band 2: For entry to jobs, no minimum qualifications are needed, but it is an advantage to have some GCSEs (A*-C) or equivalent in subjects that include English and maths. Personal qualities are often more important than qualifications. You have to have good handwriting and computing skills to record people's answers and to write reports.

- **Scotland**

Band 2: Although academic qualifications are not specified for this job, it is an advantage to have some S grades (1-3) in subjects that include English and maths, or similar. Personal qualities are often more important than qualifications. You have to have good handwriting and computing skills to record people's answers and to write reports.

Adult Qualifications

No formal qualifications are needed for mature entrants. Personal qualities are often more important than qualifications. You have to have good handwriting and computing skills to record people's answers and to write reports.

Work Experience

Work experience gives you an insight into what you enjoy and don't enjoy about a job or working environment, as well as the opportunity to acquire new skills. It also provides valuable information to add to your CV and improves any course application and/or your future employment prospects. Voluntary work may give you experience of work with the public.

Entry and Training

There are usually no specific entry requirements, with personal qualities being more important. New entrants usually have 2-3 days of a company induction course, followed by on-the-job training and going out under supervision. This may involve completing a portfolio of your initial work experience detailing how your work has developed.

You may be able to take a recognised qualification from the Market Research Society (MRS), such as the level 2 certificate in marketing and social research. If you are working for a company that offers an Accredited Interviewer Training Scheme (AITS), you may be able to become MRS accredited and achieve the MRS certificate in interviewing skills for market and social research.

The Royal Statistical Society also runs relevant short workshops and the Association for Qualitative Research offers a three-day introductory course for new researchers. An apprenticeship in marketing and communication may be available in your area and provide a good route into this job. In some jobs, a driving licence and a car are required.

Mature applicants with previous related experience in sales and marketing may be preferred by some employers. Other experience, such as working with the public, interview work, or in customer care, is also useful. The Market Research Society (MRS) offers online courses for new entrants.

Opportunities and Pay

Most interviewers work for market research agencies and most of these are based in London, although work is available throughout the UK in towns and cities. Some interviewers work for government departments or research institutes. The Office for National Statistics is the largest employer of interviewers. Most are part-time workers, perhaps working on short-term projects and must be ready for work at short notice. There is limited job security. In large agencies, it is possible to become a supervisor or area field-work manager.

Interviewers who work full time may earn from around £11k-£20k a year and supervisors up to £25k a year. Those working for agencies can expect to earn £7-£10 an hour. Most receive a mileage allowance, fares and use of a laptop computer, on top of their daily rate of pay.

Health

This job requires good general fitness.

Skills and Qualities

able to get on with all kinds of people, able to work well on your own, attention to detail, good listening skills, good telephone manner, IT skills, objective, outgoing personality, polite, smart appearance

Relevant Subjects

English

Further Information

Apprenticeship Schemes (National Apprenticeship Service) - www.apprenticeships.org.uk

Marketing Uncovered (Trotman 2010) - www.trotman.co.uk
Office for National Statistics - www.statistics.gov.uk
Social Research Association (SRA) - www.the-sra.org.uk
▶Working in English (2007) (Babcock Lifeskills) - www.babcock-lifeskills.com/
▶Working in marketing, advertising & PR (2008) (Babcock Lifeskills) - www.babcock-lifeskills.com/

Addresses

Association for Qualitative Research (AQR)
Davey House, 31 St Neots Road, Eaton Ford PE19 7BA
Phone: +44 (0)1480 407227
Web: www.aqr.org.uk

Market Research Society (MRS)
15 Northburgh Street, London EC1V 0JR
Phone: +44 (0)20 7490 4911
Web: www.mrs.org.uk

Royal Statistical Society (RSS)
12 Errol Street, London EC1Y 8LX
Phone: +44 (0)20 7638 8998
Web: www.rss.org.uk

Similar Jobs

Contact Centre Operator, Customer Services Adviser, Market Research Executive, Recruitment Consultant, Retail Store Demonstrator, Sales Executive

Market Stall Trader

CRCI:Retail Sales and Customer Services
CLCI:OM Job Band: 1 to 2

Job Description

Market stall traders sell items such as meat, fruit and vegetables, clothes, household goods, CDs/DVDs, electrical goods, fabrics, pet food and antiques, from an indoor market or outdoor street stall. They put up a stall/stand and set out everything to be sold. May need to weigh and wrap goods. They take cash and give change, or accept cheques. At the end of the day, the money is added up and the stall is tidied away. Traders must make trips to warehouses or wholesale markets to buy goods for retail.

Some may make their own items for sale, such as craft goods, wooden furniture, paintings or clothes. Must have an awareness of the statutory legislation that surrounds market trading, including consumer legislation (Sale of Goods Act, Trade Descriptions Act) and of food hygiene, health and safety.

Work Details

Market stall traders usually work a basic 40 hr week, that may include Saturdays, Sundays and public holidays. You may have very early morning starts. May also need to spend time at home doing accounts and paperwork. Most traders have stalls in the same daily/weekly markets, or may travel around a wide area to different markets. Some work from indoor stalls in large shopping centres. You can work alone, but you meet a lot of customers during the day. Sometimes you are very busy and have to stand for many hours. If working outside you must be prepared for all types of weather.

Qualification

• England, Wales and Northern Ireland

Band 1: Although formal qualifications are not required, basic English and ability in maths are useful.

Band 2: Although academic qualifications are not specified for this job, it may be an advantage to have some GCSEs (A*-C) in subjects that include English and maths, or equivalent.

• Scotland

Band 1: Although formal qualifications are not required, basic English and ability in maths are useful.

Band 2: Although academic qualifications are not specified for this job, it may be an advantage to have some S grades (1-3) in subjects that include English and maths, or similar.

Adult Qualifications

You do not need any formal qualifications, though ability in basic maths is important.

Work Experience

Relevant work or voluntary experience is always useful and can improve your chances when applying for entry to retail jobs. It can also equip you with skills that you can use in the future and add to your CV. Part-time and holiday employment in a wide range of shops, or assisting on another market trader's stall, is usually fairly easy to arrange.

Entry and Training

You must be 18 or over if you are the sole occupier of a market stall, though it is possible to become a trader from the age of 16 if the stall is licensed to another person. Training is on the job, usually with an experienced trader. Many begin by renting a stall themselves as a casual trader. You may need to put your name on a waiting list for a vacant market site and need a special licence (public liability licence) to trade before you can set up a stall. You need to be aware of the legislation that applies to selling goods, particularly if you are selling food.

For many jobs a full driving licence and a vehicle to transport your goods is essential. It can be useful to gain some experience/training in retail sales first. The National Market Traders' Federation offers advice for those wishing to become a market trader.
Mature entrants are common and it is an advantage to have experience in selling.

Opportunities and Pay

Most outdoor/indoor markets are in towns, cities and some villages. This job is often part of a family business or you can be self-employed, in a partnership, or be employed by a stall owner. If self-employed your costs include buying a stall, stock and some kind of vehicle to transport your goods.

Your pay depends on how much you sell and its value, so income varies considerably. Traders generally start on around £12k, rising to around £15k-£18k a year. Some may earn around £26k a year, and others can earn much more.

Health

You have to be physically fit and have stamina to do this job.

Skills and Qualities

able to work well on your own, business awareness, cash handling skills, confident, friendly, good communication skills, hard working, outgoing personality, patient, practical skills

Relevant Subjects

Retail and distribution

Further Information

Foundation Learning (QCDA) - www.qcda.gov.uk
So You're Interested in Becoming a Market Trader? (NMTF) (National Market Traders' Federation) - www.nmtf.co.uk/index.php?id_cpg=7
▶Working in retail & customer services (2008) (Babcock Lifeskills) - www.babcock-lifeskills.com/

Addresses

National Market Traders' Federation
Hampton House, Hawshaw Lane, Hoyland, Barnsley S74 0HA
Phone: +44 (0)1226 749 021
Web: www.nmtf.co.uk

Similar Jobs
Antiques Dealer, Butcher: Retail, Florist, Retail Assistant: Fish, Retail Store Demonstrator, Van Driver: Sales

Marketing Manager
CRCI:Marketing and Advertising
CLCI:OB Job Band: 4 to 5

Job Description
Marketing managers plan, organise and manage how a company can provide its goods and services, at a price which suits the customers and the company. This involves discussing marketing policy with specialists such as market researchers, public relations and finance and studying competitors products and services. They look at various marketing strategies and then decide which are the best for the products/services. These strategies include advertising, websites, direct mail and attending promotional fairs.

Plans marketing campaigns, analyses how successful they were and adjusts the strategy accordingly. Produces promotional material. Writes reports, supervises the work of junior staff and oversees their training and development within the marketing department.

Work Details
Usually works a basic 39 hr week, though longer hours are usual. This is an office-based job, but involves going out to visit potential customers, or to attend exhibitions or other promotional events. You negotiate and consult with clients and colleagues and are responsible for a budget and for keeping costs within agreed limits. The work may involve a lot of travel, including overseas if you work for a company with an export market.

Qualification

• England, Wales and Northern Ireland
Band 4: For HND, Diploma of Higher Education or foundation degree: 1-2 A levels and some GCSEs (A*-C) usually including English and maths, or equivalent.

Band 5: For degree courses: 2-3 A levels and some GCSEs (A*-C) usually including English and maths, or equivalent. Exact requirements depend on the degree you take.

• Scotland
Band 4: For entry to SQA higher national and professional development awards, or for direct entry to a trainee post in marketing: usually 2-3 H grades and some S grades (1-3), including English and maths, or similar qualifications.

Band 5: For degree courses: 3-5 H grades and some S grades (1-3), including English and maths, or similar qualifications. Exact requirements depend on the degree you take.

Degree Information
Any degree is accepted though marketing or business studies are particularly relevant and may lead to exemptions from professional examinations. Some employers may prefer engineering and science for jobs in speciality marketing, and languages for export marketing. There are several postgraduate courses in marketing available, including various diplomas in management studies or export marketing, for graduates of any discipline, and MBA/MSc courses for graduates with relevant degrees.

Adult Qualifications
Entry requirements may be relaxed for adults applying for higher education courses. Access or foundation courses provide those without the required qualifications a route onto degree courses. The Chartered Institute of Marketing runs a range of professional qualifications aimed at those with relevant experience.

Work Experience
Entry to this job is competitive and it is important that you try to do some relevant work or voluntary experience before applying. Direct experience in marketing, advertising, market research, public relations or other related role is useful. The CIM career partner scheme provides a marketing work placement service aimed at final year students and recent graduates interested in a career in marketing.

Entry and Training
A career in marketing can often begin with a job in selling, either in the sales office or in the field. There are no set entry requirements, and some marketing managers have worked their way up through the marketing department, usually taking professional examinations as they learn. Creative flair and motivation are vital. However, many applicants have an HNC/HND or a degree in marketing or business studies.

Training is usually on the job, with in-house or industry-led short courses. Increasingly, trainees study part time or by distance learning for a professional qualification, such as the diploma or postgraduate professional diploma in marketing offered the Chartered Institute of Marketing (CIM), or the diploma in direct and interactive marketing offered by the Institute of Direct Marketing (IDM). The CIM and IDM also offer a range of introductory and short courses and workshops for continuing professional development.

You may need to be skilled in a foreign language if you want to work for a company with an export market, and some knowledge of languages is generally useful. It is an advantage to be confident about speaking to groups of people. You may also be encouraged to study for the Diploma in Marketing Communications offered by the Communication, Advertising and Marketing Foundation or qualifications from the Managing and Marketing Sales Association.

Those who wish to work for a specific industry or business sector, such as engineering, pharmaceuticals, agriculture/horticulture, food or textiles, may be asked for qualifications relating to that industry. Foundation degrees are available in marketing-related subjects. There are S/NVQs in marketing at levels 2-4. A Diploma/ Welsh Baccalaureate in business, administration and finance (BAF) or in creative and media for 14-19 year olds may be available in your area and provide an alternative route into this job.

Mature applicants with previous experience in a relevant field are preferred, and particularly in sales and marketing, economics, market research, advertising or statistics, including social or economic research work. The Chartered Institute of Marketing (CIM) offers relevant qualifications in marketing through distance learning.

Opportunities and Pay
Marketing managers can work for manufacturing companies, any company with a product or service to sell, charities, universities or colleges, or central/local government. You can also work for a marketing consultancy and take responsibility for a number of customer accounts. Jobs tend to be concentrated near major cities. The internet will continue to be a large part of the future of marketing so this role may continue to change as products and services are marketed online.

Promotion prospects often depend on conducting successful marketing campaigns. Opportunities for obtaining senior management or marketing director positions are good, and some experienced managers go on to set up their own marketing consultancies and work freelance.

Pay varies depending on location, type and size of company but starting salaries for recent graduates are around £23k-£25k, and £40k-£45k a year with experience. High earners can make £50k-£75k or more a year.

Skills and Qualities
able to work to deadlines, business awareness, creative flair, enterprising, excellent communication skills, good interpersonal skills, good organisational skills, IT skills, leadership qualities, self confident

Relevant Subjects
Business and accounting, Economics, English, ICT/Computer studies, Mathematics, Media and communication studies, Modern Foreign Languages, Psychology, Retail and distribution

Further Information
CIM Career Guides (Chartered Institute of Marketing (CIM)) - www.cim.co.uk/cpd/career/careerguides.aspx

Diplomas (Foundation, Higher and Advanced) - http://yp.direct.gov.uk/diplomas

Get into Marketing - www.getintomarketing.com

Inside Careers Guide: Marketing & Sales - www.insidecareers.co.uk

Marketing Week (Centaur Media Plc) - www.marketingweek.co.uk/

Welsh Baccalaureate - www.wbq.org.uk

Winning Edge (6 x year) (Institute of Sales & Marketing Management) - www.ismm.co.uk/magazine.php

▶Working in business, administration & finance (2010) (Babcock Lifeskills) - www.babcock-lifeskills.com/

▶Working in marketing, advertising & PR (2008) (Babcock Lifeskills) - www.babcock-lifeskills.com/

▶Working in travel & tourism (2010) (Babcock Lifeskills) - www.babcock-lifeskills.com/

Addresses
Chartered Institute of Marketing (CIM)
Moor Hall, Cookham, Maidenhead, Berkshire SL6 9QH
Phone: +44 (0) 1628 427120
Web: www.cim.co.uk

Communication Advertising and Marketing (CAM) Foundation Ltd
Moor Hall, Cookham, Maidenhead, Berkshire SL6 9QH
Phone: +44 (0)1628 427 120
Web: www.camfoundation.com

Institute of Direct Marketing (IDM)
1 Park Road, Teddington, Middlesex TW11 0AR
Phone: +44 (0)208 977 5705
Web: www.theidm.com

Institute of Sales and Marketing Management (ISMM)
Harrier Court, Lower Woodside, Bedfordshire LU1 4DQ
Phone: +44 (0)1582 840 001
Web: www.ismm.co.uk

Managing and Marketing Sales Association (MAMSA)
PO Box 11, Sandbach, Cheshire CW11 3GE
Phone: +44 (0)1270 526 339
Web: www.mamsasbp.com

Similar Jobs
Advertising Account Executive, Brand Manager, Market Research Executive, Press Officer, Sales Executive

Massage Therapist
CRCI:Healthcare
CLCI:JOD Job Band: 1 to 3

Job Description
Massage therapists manipulate areas of muscle and skin to make people feel more relaxed, ease pain and aid healing. They may work on the whole body or a particular area, such as the head and neck. Some focus on different types of client and massage, such as feel-good treatments or sports massage. Therapists may work through a person's clothing or directly on their skin. They ensure treatment is safe and suitable for each client.

Therapists ask clients about their medical history, lifestyle and any aches and pains they have. They make sure they are laying or seated comfortably before beginning the massage, then stroke, knead and tap areas of the body to apply and release pressure. Therapists may use oils or lotions if working directly on the skin and may ask the client for feedback on how the treatment feels. They update the client's history and treatment records after each visit.

Work Details
In health and beauty settings, massage therapists often work a 40 hr week, including some evenings and weekends. Self-employed therapists adapt their hours to suit their clients. Many work part time. The length of the session depends on the type of massage. Sessions can last from 20-90 minutes.

Usually work on your own with one client at a time in a warm and pleasant treatment room. You may use soft lighting, music and oils to scent the air. Some work from home or at a client's home or workplace. You are on your feet most of the day and spend time bending over the client. Some clients may be stressed, depressed or in pain. You usually wear a uniform or clothing that allows free movement.

Qualification
Formal qualifications are not required for entry to many courses. Subjects such as human biology, chemistry and health studies are useful. Some higher level courses require qualifications in anatomy and physiology.

• England, Wales and Northern Ireland
Band 1: For entry to jobs, no minimum qualifications are needed, but you are expected to have a good level of general education and relevant experience. Some formal/vocational qualifications at any level are useful.

Band 2: For entry to jobs, no minimum qualifications are needed, but it is an advantage to have some GCSEs (A*-C) or equivalent in subjects that include English and maths.

Band 3: For entry to jobs, HNC or a relevant Diploma, usually at least 4 GCSEs (A*-C) including English and maths, or equivalent.

• Scotland
Band 1: For entry to jobs, no minimum qualifications are needed, but you are expected to have a good level of general education and relevant experience. Some formal/vocational qualifications at any level are useful.

Band 2: Although academic qualifications are not specified for this job, it is an advantage to have some S grades (1-3) in subjects that include English and maths, or similar.

Band 3: For entry to jobs, usually at least four S grades (1-3) including English and maths, or similar.

Adult Qualifications
No formal qualifications are required, but colleges and training schools look for people able to cope with the demands of the course.

Work Experience
Work experience helps you find out what you enjoy and do not enjoy about a job. Paid or voluntary work dealing with people is useful. Experience in a care or healthcare setting is very helpful and talking to a massage therapist about their job gives you a valuable insight into the work. In some areas you can do a young apprenticeship (14-16) in health and social care. You do an extended work placement and a level 2 qualification whilst at school. For health and safety reasons there may be some jobs you cannot do until you are over 16.

Entry and Training

Currently there are no rules about the training you need to be a qualified massage therapist, but the International Therapy Examination Council (ITEC) recommends that entrants have five GCSE/S grades and the profession wants to set minimum qualifications and standards for practitioners. There are National Occupational Standards for massage therapy/bodywork, remedial massage and sports massage.

To practise as a massage therapist, you should choose a course that meets the relevant standards or the curriculum of the General Council for Massage Therapies (GCMT). Courses should take at least 6 months full time or 12 months part time. Shorter courses are suited to people with a general or leisure interest only.

You can do massage therapy courses at a college or at a private training school where you have to pay for them yourself. There are several awarding bodies, including the ITEC and the Vocational Training Charitable Trust. Once qualified, you can join one of the professional bodies and apply to go on to the registers of the GCMT and the Council for Complementary and Natural Healthcare. To join the Institute of Sport and Remedial Massage, you need a level 5 BTEC professional diploma in sport and remedial massage.

Massage therapists keep up to date with new ideas and techniques through workshops and courses. You can do courses in different types of massage such as Indian head massage, infant massage, aromatherapy massage and deep tissue massage. To stay on the practitioners' registers, you must do a certain amount of continuing professional development each year.

If you are working in a beauty or spa therapy setting, you may be able to work towards S/NVQ level 3 in beauty therapy (massage) or spa therapy. Apprenticeships in beauty therapy leading to level 2 and advanced apprenticeships in beauty therapy (massage route) and spa therapy leading to level 3 qualifications may also be available in your area.

People often move into massage therapy as a second career. Many come from a background in the health and beauty sector or with experience of other complementary therapies. Some courses are designed so that you can continue in full-time employment whilst working towards massage therapy qualifications.

Government training opportunities, such as apprenticeships, may be available in your area. You can also gain recognition of previous experience through Accreditation of Prior Learning (APL) or by working towards relevant S/NVQs. Contact your local careers office, Jobcentre Plus, Next Step service or Learning and Skills Council (LSC)/Local Enterprise Company (LEC) for details of all training opportunities and schemes, including apprenticeships for adults.

Opportunities and Pay

Demand for all forms of complementary therapies is growing. Massage treatments are no longer confined to the luxury market. They are seen by healthcare professionals as an aid to healing and promoting well-being. Beauty salons, hotels, health spas and sports and fitness centres employ massage therapists. There are also jobs in hospitals and care homes. Many have their own private practice. If you are working for an employer, you may progress to senior and management roles. If you work for yourself, you may employ others or offer other therapies such as aromatherapy or reflexology.

In a beauty or spa therapy setting, qualified massage therapists earn around £12k-£17k a year. Experienced therapists offering a range of treatments and therapies can earn up to £40k. Earnings for self-employed massage therapist vary. They depend on location, how much you charge and how many clients you see. Many massage therapists charge £20-£30 for a half hour session and £30-£50 for an hour. Some charge much more.

Health

This job requires good general fitness. There may be an allergy risk from using oils, lotions and creams. You may be at risk from repetitive strain injury to your hands or wrists.

Skills and Qualities

able to put people at ease, friendly, good communication skills, good concentration level, good listening skills, good sense of touch, good stamina and physically fit, health & safety awareness, information handling skills, observant

Relevant Subjects

Biology, Chemistry, Health and social care, Physical education and sport, Science

Further Information

Apprenticeship Schemes (National Apprenticeship Service) - www.apprenticeships.org.uk

Massage World Magazine (6 x year) (Massage World) - www.massageworld.co.uk

Skills for Health - sector skills council - www.skillsforhealth.org.uk

SkillsActive - sector skills council for active leisure, learning and well-being - www.skillsactive.com

Addresses

Complementary and Natural Healthcare Council (CNHC)
83 Victoria Street, London SW1H 0HW
Phone: +44 (0)203 178 2199
Web: www.cnhc.org.uk

General Council for Massage Therapists (GCMT)
27 Old Gloucester Street, London WC1N 3XX
Phone: 0870 850 4452 (UK only)
Web: www.gcmt.org.uk

Institute of Sport and Remedial Massage (ISRM)
28 Station Parade, Willesden Green, London NW2 4NX
Phone: +44 (0) 20 8450 5851
Web: www.theisrm.com

International Therapy Examination Council (ITEC)
2nd Floor , Chiswick Gate, 598-608 Chiswick High Road, London W4 5RT
Phone: +44 (0)20 8994 4141
Web: www.itecworld.co.uk

Vocational Training Charitable Trust (VTCT)
Eastleigh House, 3rd Floor , Upper Market Street, Hampshire SO50 9FD
Phone: +44 (0)2380 684 500
Web: www.vtct.org.uk

Similar Jobs

Acupuncturist, Aromatherapist, Beauty Therapist, Naturopath, Physiotherapist, Reflexologist, Sports Therapist

Mastic Asphalter

CRCI:Building and Construction
CLCI:UF — Job Band: 1 to 2

Job Description

Mastic asphalters spread hot mastic asphalt (a mixture of limestone and bitumen) on surfaces that need to have a seamless, waterproof and durable finish. They work on a wide variety of surfaces, such as flat roofs and decks, walls, floors and paved areas, bridge construction, car parks, sea defences and lining for landfill sites. Normally, work is team based and with a contractor. A site visit is carried out in advance of the work, the area is measured and estimates for the amount and type of asphalt required are made. Arrangements are made for the delivery of materials and equipment, such as boilers, mixers, buckets, and also hand tools or automated machinery, to smooth the finished surface.

Asphalters clean and prepare the site. They lay the asphalt to the required depth and seal the joints. Some surfaces may have a final finish, such as tiles, reflective coatings, or stone chippings. On completion of the job, all waste is cleared from the site.

Mastic Asphalter

Work Details
Mastic asphalters usually work a basic 40 hr week, Monday to Friday, though sometimes are required to work overtime, some nights, evenings and weekends to complete a job. Work is usually in a team, outdoors, and requires travel around an area to different sites. The job involves climbing ladders, working at heights on scaffolding, and bending, kneeling and balancing. Conditions are dirty and often cold, damp and wet. There is some risk of fumes and burns, or falling if working at a height. You need to wear a safety helmet, knee pads and outdoor wear or overalls.

Qualification

• England, Wales and Northern Ireland
Band 1: No minimum qualifications are required, however some formal/vocational qualifications at any level are useful.

Band 2: Although academic qualifications are not specified for this job, some GCSEs at any level including maths, English or technical subjects are useful, and may be required by some employers.

• Scotland
Band 1: No minimum qualifications are required, however some formal/vocational qualifications at any level are useful.

Band 2: Although academic qualifications are not specified for this job, some S grades at any level including maths, English or technical subjects are useful, and may be required by some employers.

Adult Qualifications
There are no formal entry requirements, but mature entry may be difficult unless you are already experienced.

Work Experience
Relevant work or voluntary experience is always useful and can improve your chances when applying for entry to construction jobs and apprenticeships. Health and safety issues may mean that there are certain jobs you cannot do until you are over 16. Contact your local ConstructionSkills office for advice.

Entry and Training
Most people enter through apprenticeship training schemes at age 16-17 and you can apply in year 11 (January). You may have to take an entrance test before you begin training. Training is usually work based together with a day or block-release college course. Various flexible training schemes are available from ConstructionSkills in conjunction with the Mastic Asphalt Council, including a three-year construction apprenticeship scheme (four years in Scotland). Polymer modified mastic asphalt can only be installed by Mastic Asphalt Council contractors. The Institute of Roofing also offers its own related qualifications.

A Diploma/Welsh Baccalaureate in construction and the built environment may be available in your area. S/NVQs are available in roofing at levels 2-3 and you need to complete these before qualifying. Training programmes, including apprenticeships leading to level 2, and advanced apprenticeships/construction apprenticeships leading to level 3, may be available in your area. There are also Construction Awards (England and Wales) available for those who are unable to gain workplace experience for NVQs. Most asphalters working on construction sites need to hold a Construction Skills Certification Scheme (CSCS) card to show their individual level of training and competence. Contact ConstructionSkills for details of the scheme.

Mature applicants who show aptitude and have relevant previous experience may be considered for training. Government training opportunities, such as apprenticeships, may be available in your area. You can also gain recognition of previous experience through Accreditation of Prior Learning or by working towards relevant S/NVQs. Contact your local careers office, Jobcentre Plus, Next Step service or Learning and Skills Council (LSC)/Local Enterprise Company (LEC) for details of all training opportunities and schemes, including apprenticeships for adults.

Opportunities and Pay
Work is available throughout the UK. Employers include roofing firms, civil engineering firms, building contractors or mastic asphalt contractors. Some asphalters are self-employed and work as contractors, or work on a 'labour only' basis using an employer's materials and tools. Some work abroad on contracts. Promotion to become a supervisor is possible, mostly in larger firms.

Mastic asphalters are mostly paid according to national industry rates, but pay can vary, depending on location and employer. Trainees usually start on around £12k a year but the rate depends on your level of qualification. Those with a level 3 qualification earn from £21k and, with experience, up to £26k a year. Bonuses and overtime pay may be available. Employers may give allowances for travel and cost of lodgings. Self-employed annual incomes can be around £25k-£30k a year, or more.

Health
Good stamina and physical fitness are required. This job is not suitable for people who have respiratory problems, or who suffer from vertigo or claustrophobia.

Skills and Qualities
able to work quickly, aptitude for teamwork, attention to detail, enjoy working outdoors, head for heights, practical skills, safety conscious

Relevant Subjects
Construction and built environment, Design and technology

Further Information
Apprenticeship Schemes (National Apprenticeship Service) - www.apprenticeships.org.uk

Careers in Construction - www.bconstructive.co.uk

Construction Skills Certification Scheme (CSCS) - www.cscs.uk.com

ConstructionSkills - sector skills council for the construction industry - www.cskills.org

Diplomas (Foundation, Higher and Advanced) - http://yp.direct.gov.uk/diplomas

Roofing Magazine online (Warners Group Publications Ltd.) - www.roofingmag.com

Welsh Baccalaureate - www.wbq.org.uk

▶Working in construction & the built environment (2007) (Babcock Lifeskills) - www.babcock-lifeskills.com/

Addresses
Institute of Roofing (IOR)
Roofing House, 31 Worship Street, London EC2A 2DX
Phone: +44 (0)20 7448 3858
Web: www.instituteofroofing.org.uk

Mastic Asphalt Council (MAC)
PO Box 77, Hastings TN35 4WL
Phone: +44 (0)1424 814 400
Web: www.masticasphaltcouncil.co.uk

Similar Jobs
Cavity Wall Insulation Technician, Construction Operative, Plasterer, Road Worker, Roofer

Materials Scientist/Engineer

also known as: Materials technologist

CRCI:Science, Mathematics and Statistics

CLCI:QOS Job Band: 5

Job Description

Materials scientists study the structure and properties of materials and develop new materials. They work with natural and manufactured materials such as glass, ceramics, plastics/ polymers or metals, natural and synthetic fibres, and sand. Many work in industry on production, analysis, design, quality control or technical sales. Some examine different uses for existing materials or test and develop new ones. They use computers in much of their work when testing and evaluating materials and create computer models of a material's internal structure and the effects/reactions displayed during experimentation. They are concerned with quality and safety testing of a product to ensure the safe use of the material.

This is a very wide field with many specialist areas that include biomedical products (artificial knee/hips), transport (aircraft/ trains) or infrastructure (bridges/tunnels). Others are involved in defence and related industries, information work, teaching or pure research.

Work Details

Work a basic 39 hr week, Monday to Friday, but may work additional hours at times, especially to complete a project on time. In production industry jobs, you may need to work shifts. You usually work in a team with other scientists, engineers, technologists and technicians in an office or industrial premises, laboratory or workshop. May travel to other sites. Depending on the post, you can be responsible for analysis and testing, product development, production schedules or quality control. You may need to wear protective clothing.

Qualification

- **England, Wales and Northern Ireland**

Band 5: For degree courses: 2-3 A levels including maths, physics and preferably chemistry and some GCSEs (A*-C) usually including English, science and maths, or equivalent. Exact requirements depend on the degree you take.

- **Scotland**

Band 5: For degree courses: 3-5 H grades including maths, physics, preferably chemistry and some S grades (1-3), usually including English, science and maths, or similar. Exact requirements depend on the degree you take.

Degree Information

A degree in materials science or materials engineering may be preferred, but degrees in closely related subjects such as metallurgy or polymer chemistry are normally acceptable. Other sciences that provide a useful background include chemistry, physics and some technology and engineering subjects. A wide choice of materials courses at postgraduate level are available.

Adult Qualifications

A formal qualification, preferably a relevant degree, is usually required. Knowledge of science and maths must be up to date. Entry requirements may be relaxed for adults applying for higher education courses. Access or foundation courses give adults without qualifications a route onto degree courses.

Work Experience

Universities and employers may prefer candidates who have relevant work or voluntary experience. Ideally you shadow or work with somebody who is currently involved in the industry. Alternatively, obtaining general experience which can help you gain or improve skills such as team working, communication and IT is also useful.

Entry and Training

Training is normally by practical work experience after obtaining a degree. First degree courses can be full time, part time or sandwich and usually last for 3-4 years. A range of courses are available and you should select one with an appropriate content for the area of materials science in which you wish to specialise. There are also relevant postgraduate courses. Most companies provide in-house training. Membership of the Institute of Materials, Minerals and Mining (IOM3) can be attained by a combination of academic qualifications and practical experience. Professional membership can also lead to registration as a chartered engineer (CEng) and/or chartered scientist (CSci) status, or incorporated engineer (IEng).

Mature applicants with experience as a technician in the ferrous/ non-ferrous metals industry may have an advantage. You may be able to study part time for some courses. The Worshipful Company of Founders may offer grants for those wishing to study metallurgy/ materials science. Professional bodies such as the Engineering and Physical Sciences Research Council (EPSRC) and the Institute of Materials, Minerals and Mining (IOM3) also offer sponsorships, scholarships or bursaries for study and research.

Opportunities and Pay

Most materials scientists work in industry and employers include the oil and gas industry, plastics and chemical manufacturers and the steel industry. Some engineers work in government departments or academic research institutions. Work is available throughout the UK and also abroad. Those with fluency in another language have an advantage for overseas work. Self-employment is possible as a consultant. Some also move into specialist journalism or technical writing, or into higher education as a lecturer.

There are around 20,000 members of the IOM3 and there is a high demand for materials scientists/engineers, particularly if you are prepared to work in production, quality control, sales or marketing.

Pay varies depending on location and employer. Starting salaries for graduates are around £20k-£25k but can be higher with a postgraduate qualification. Experienced scientists/engineers earn around £35k a year with experience. Top earners can make more than £55k a year.

Health

You need normal colour vision for certain areas of work. You may be expected to have no skin or respiratory problems.

Skills and Qualities

able to communicate effectively, analytical skills, aptitude for maths and science, initiative, IT skills, methodical, observant, problem-solving skills, project management skills, scientific approach

Relevant Subjects

Biology, Chemistry, Design and technology, Engineering, English, ICT/Computer studies, Mathematics, Physics, Science

Further Information

AGCAS: Engineering (Job Sector Briefing) (AGCAS) - www.prospects.ac.uk

Cogent - sector skills souncil for chemicals, pharmaceuticals, nuclear, oil & gas, petroleum & polymers - www.cogent-ssc.com

Materials World (monthly) (IOM) - www.iom3.org

Women into Science, Engineering & Construction - www.wisecampaign.org.uk

▶Working in science (2007) (Babcock Lifeskills) - www.babcock-lifeskills.com/

Addresses

Engineering and Physical Sciences Research Council (EPSRC)
Polaris House North Star Avenue, Swindon, Wiltshire SN2 1ET
Phone: +44(0)1793 444 100
Web: www.epsrc.ac.uk

Institute of Materials, Minerals and Mining (IOM3)
1 Carlton House Terrace, London SW1Y 5DB
Phone: +44 (0)20 7451 7300
Web: www.iom3.org

Institution of Engineering and Technology (IET)
Michael Faraday House, Stevenage, Hertfordshire SG1 2AY
Phone: +44 (0)1438 313311
Web: www.theiet.org

Scottish Engineering
Training Officer, 105 West George Street, Glasgow G2 1QL
Phone: +44 (0)141 221 3181
Web: www.scottishengineering.org.uk

Worshipful Company of Founders
Old Estate Office Fifty One, Firle, Lewes, West Sussex BN8 6LQ
Phone: +44 (0)1273 858 700
Web: www.foundersco.org.uk

Similar Jobs

Ceramic Technologist, Engineer: Civil/Structural, Engineer: Minerals & Mining, Metallurgist, NDT Technician/Engineer, Polymer/Plastics Technologist

Mechanic: Construction Plant

also known as: Construction Plant Fitter, Plant Mechanic
CRCI:Engineering
CLCI:RAE Job Band: 1 to 3

Job Description

Construction plant mechanics service, repair and look after the plant equipment and machinery used on a building site. This includes bulldozers, excavators, dump trucks, cranes and heavy trucks. They may also service air compressors, concrete mixers and electrical generators. Mechanics are responsible for the hydraulic, mechanical, electronic and electrical aspects of equipment, and may use computer testing equipment to find the fault. They use technical diagrams, drawings and manuals.

They also fix or change worn or damaged parts, test the machine and may adjust the running. Under takes routine servicing, oiling and greasing and checks the performance and safety of machinery. Also fills in the daily log sheets of completed work.

Work Details

Usually work around 37-40 hrs a week with overtime, including weekends, being common. Much of the work is done on site, so you are out in all weathers. You also work in a workshop, in dirty and oily conditions. This job is strenuous and you have to be able to bend and stretch, sometimes in awkward positions, and to lift heavy things. You may have to work at heights, for example on cranes.

This job needs to be done quickly and efficiently so that machinery is repaired as speedily as possible. Accidents with machinery can cause injuries. You sometimes need to wear a safety helmet and protective boots. You may be based on one large site or travel from site to site, usually in a specially equipped van.

Qualification

• England, Wales and Northern Ireland

Band 2: For entry to jobs, no minimum qualifications are needed, but it is an advantage to have some GCSEs (A*-C) or equivalent in subjects that include maths, English and science or technology subjects, or equivalent.

Band 3: For entry to employer training schemes, jobs, HNC or a relevant Diploma: usually at least 4 GCSEs (A*-C) including English, maths, science and technology subjects, or equivalent.

• Scotland

Band 2: Although academic qualifications are not specified for this job, it is an advantage to have some S grades (1-3) in subjects that include English and maths, or similar.

Band 3: For employer training schemes, entry to jobs and SQA national awards: usually at least four S grades (1-3) including English, maths, science and technical subjects, or similar.

Adult Qualifications

Some formal qualifications to show a good level of general education may be required.

Work Experience

Relevant work or voluntary experience is always useful as it can add to your CV and improve your chances when applying for entry to jobs or apprenticeships in the engineering industry. Health and safety issues may mean that there are certain jobs you can't do until you are over 16. Your local ConstructionSkills office can advise you on this.

Entry and Training

Most entrants train through a three to four year apprenticeship with a construction company or a plant hire firm. There are some specialist apprenticeships including one for crane operations. You may need to take an assessment test when you have an interview. Training involves on-the-job experience and block release to a college, leading to S/NVQs at level 1-3 in plant maintenance (construction). There are also vocationally related qualifications in plant maintenance at levels 1-3, including the level 3 diploma in maintaining engineering construction plant and systems. Some entrants choose to complete a BTEC/SQA or City & Guilds full-time course before starting work. The National Construction College run by ConstructionSkills offers a two-year full-time plant maintenance apprenticeship scheme. This also leads to S/NVQs at level 2-3.

Most workers on construction sites also hold a Construction Skills Certification Scheme (CSCS) Card to show their competence level. Full details are on the CSCS website. Short training courses are available to keep mechanics up to date. There are also ConstructionSkills Awards (England and Wales) available for those who are unable to gain workplace experience for NVQs. Contact ConstructionSkills or check the Careers in Construction website for details of all routes to training. You can also contact Construction Plant-hire Association for details on training courses.

A Diploma/Welsh Baccalaureate may be available in your area in engineering. This qualification is based around work and can include an automotive specialist learning component. See the diplomas website for further information.

It is an advantage for mature entrants to have relevant experience in practical or mechanical work, particularly work with agricultural equipment. The National Construction College run by ConstructionSkills offers adult courses relevant to this job, such as testing and inspection (plant). Mature applicants can benefit through government training opportunities, such as apprenticeships, that may be available in your area. You can also gain recognition of previous experience through Accreditation of Prior Learning (APL) or by working towards relevant S/NVQs. Contact your local careers office, Jobcentre Plus, Next Step service or Learning and Skills Council (LSC) Local Enterprise Company (LEC) for details of training schemes.

Opportunities and Pay

Employers include civil engineers, building contractors, plant hire companies and makers of construction machines. Work is available abroad with large civil engineering contractors. In large companies it is possible to be promoted to technician, supervisory and management levels. In small companies, promotion aspects are limited unless you move to another employer. Some plant mechanics are self-employed.

Pay can vary considerably depending on location and employer. Starting salaries for trainees are around £12k a year, rising to £16k-£25k with experience. The most skilled and experienced mechanics can earn £28k-£30k a year.

Health

You must have normal colour vision and be physically fit.

Skills and Qualities
able to work both on your own and in a team, able to work quickly, accurate, good communication skills, good concentration level, logical, methodical, practical skills, responsible attitude, safety conscious

Relevant Subjects
Design and technology, Engineering, Mathematics, Physics, Science

Further Information
Apprenticeship Schemes (National Apprenticeship Service) - www.apprenticeships.org.uk

Apprenticeships in Scotland (Careers Info Scotland) - www.apprenticeshipsinscotland.com/about/

Careers in Construction - www.bconstructive.co.uk

Construction Skills Certification Scheme (CSCS) - www.cscs.uk.com

ConstructionSkills - sector skills council for the construction industry - www.cskills.org

Diplomas (Foundation, Higher and Advanced) - http://yp.direct.gov.uk/diplomas

National Construction College (ConstructionSkills) www.cskills.org/supportbusiness/ncc

TARGETjobs: Construction & Building Services (GTI Specialist Publishers Ltd) - www.groupgti.com

Training Schemes - www.direct.gov.uk/en/educationandlearning

▶Working in construction & the built environment (2007) (Babcock Lifeskills) - www.babcock-lifeskills.com/

Addresses
Construction Plant-hire Association
27-28 Newbury Street, Barbican, London EC1A 7HU
Phone: +44 (0)20 7796 3366
Web: www.cpa.uk.net

Similar Jobs
Construction Plant Operative, Fitter: Maintenance, Fork-Lift Truck Engineer, Mechanical Engineering Technician, Rail Transport Fitter/Electrician, Service Technician: Land-based, Vehicle Mechanic/Motor Vehicle Technician

Mechanic: Motorcycle
also known as: Motorbike Mechanic, Motorcycle Technician

CRCI:Engineering
CLCI:RAE Job Band: 1 to 3

Job Description
Motorcycle mechanics service, tune, repair and test motorbikes, quad bikes, mopeds and scooters. They inspect the vehicle and report on its general condition. May also do MOT testing, routine servicing and road-testing, using sophisticated equipment and hand and power tools.

Mechanics find faults and repair or replace worn parts, checking worksheets and technical manuals. They may do diagnostic repairs on electrical or electronic systems, and alter motorbikes to suit customer needs. May refer to technical and /or computerised drawings which are used to store technical information and drawings. If working for a company that also sells new motorbikes, may unpack newly delivered bikes and assemble and test them to make sure they are working properly.

Work Details
Usually work around 39 hrs a week, but overtime is common, particularly on Saturdays. Workshops and garages can be cold and noisy. In some garages you have to be able to communicate well with customers. You have to work quickly, sometimes under pressure, to repair or service motorcycles as speedily and safely as possible.

Work is often strenuous and includes some heavy lifting. You have to bend, kneel and stretch, sometimes in awkward positions. There can be accidents with equipment. The work is oily and dirty and mechanics usually use barrier creams to protect their skin. You wear protective overalls.

Qualification
• England, Wales and Northern Ireland
Band 2: For entry to jobs and some training programmes: no minimum qualifications are needed, but it is an advantage to have some GCSEs (A*-C) or equivalent in subjects including English, maths and a science (preferably physics), or equivalent. Technology or engineering subjects are also useful.

Band 3: For entry to jobs, HNC in vehicle repair and technology or a relevant Diploma, usually at least 4 GCSEs (A*-C) including English, maths and a science (preferably physics), technology or engineering subject, or similar.

• Scotland
Band 2: Although academic qualifications are not specified for this job, for some training programmes and employers: some S grades (1-3) may be needed, including English, maths and a science (preferably physics), or similar. Technical or engineering subjects are also useful.

Band 3: For entry to jobs and for SQA national awards: usually at least four S grades (1-3) including English, maths and a science (preferably physics), or similar. Technical or engineering subjects are also useful.

Adult Qualifications
Formal qualifications showing a good standard of general education may be preferred, but are not essential. Academic requirements for courses are usually relaxed for suitable mature applicants. Specific entry requirements for courses may be relaxed for mature applicants. You can improve your skills and qualifications by working through the Foundation Learning programme. This involves taking credit-based units and qualifications to help you progress.

Work Experience
Relevant work or voluntary experience is always useful, and it can add to your CV and improve your chances when applying for entry to jobs or apprenticeships in the engineering industry. Any practical experience of motorcycle mechanics and the ability to follow diagrams is an advantage. Your personal or adult guidance adviser may be able to advise you about organising work experience.

Entry and Training
Many trainees start on a training programme or apprenticeship at age 16-19 and usually train on the job, working with an experienced person, together with day or block release to a local college. Most work towards S/NVQs in vehicle maintenance and repair at levels 2-3. You can also study full time for a City & Guilds or BTEC/SQA award, prior to employment. Some courses have specialist motorcycle routes. This job may require a driving licence and you may also have to pass a practical aptitude entrance test. National training providers of apprenticeships and motorcycle technician training include the training arm of the Retail Motor Industry Federation, ReMIT. Regular training is needed to keep up to date with changing technology.

The Institute of the Motor Industry (IMI) and City & Guilds offer nationally recognised vocationally related qualifications (VRQs) at levels 2-3 for motorcycle technician training. They also offer a level 4 qualification in other aspects of the motor industry for those who want to move on to higher education. VRQs at level 1 are also available as a pre-apprenticeship programme for school pupils aged 14-16 and provide the opportunity to 'fast track' on to higher level motor industry qualifications.

The IMI has also developed Autocity, a useful and informative website on careers in the motor industry. There is a section on motorcycle dealership that covers jobs in the workshop including; workshop control, MOTs, and master, service and diagnostic technician roles. Visit the website for more information.

Automotive Technical Accreditation (ATA) is a voluntary programme that assesses the current competence of individuals working in the retail motor trade. They assess motorcycle technicians at both technician and senior technician level. Visit the the IMI and the ATA websites for details.

A Diploma/Welsh Baccalaureate may be available in your area in engineering. This qualification is based around work and can include an automotive specialist learning component. See the diplomas website for further information.

It is an advantage to have experience of mechanical work, or servicing your own motorbike. Mature applicants can benefit through government training opportunities, such as apprenticeships, which may be available in your area. You can also gain recognition of previous experience through Accreditation of Prior Learning (APL) or by working towards relevant S/NVQs. Contact your local careers office, Jobcentre Plus, Next Step service or Learning and Skills Council (LSC) Local Enterprise Company (LEC) for details of training schemes

Opportunities and Pay

There is a steady demand for trained motorcycle mechanics and technicians throughout the UK, but entry is still competitive. Employment is usually with specialist motorcycle repairers or distributors. Some workshops specialise in particular makes of bike. In larger companies, it may be possible to gain promotion to supervisory and management jobs. Self-employment is possible, but you may have to buy your own tool kit, and the costs of setting up your own workshop can be high.

Pay varies depending on location and employer. Trainee motorcycle mechanics usually earn around £240 a week, depending on the phase of training. Qualified mechanics earn around £310-£450 a week. The highest earners can make as much as £520 a week. Pay is often increased by overtime payments and perhaps bonuses.

Health

You must be in good health and have normal colour vision.

Skills and Qualities

able to communicate effectively, able to follow drawings and plans, attention to detail, logical, manual dexterity, methodical, numeracy skills, practical skills, safety conscious, technical aptitude

Relevant Subjects

Design and technology, Engineering, Mathematics, Physics, Science

Further Information

Apprenticeship Schemes (National Apprenticeship Service) - www.apprenticeships.org.uk

Apprenticeships in Scotland (Careers Info Scotland) - www.apprenticeshipsinscotland.com/about/

Autocity (IMI) http://autocity.org.uk

Automotive Technician Accreditation (ATA) (Institute of the Motor Industry) - www.automotivetechnician.org.uk

Diplomas (Foundation, Higher and Advanced) http://yp.direct.gov.uk/diplomas

Institute of the Motor Industry (IMI) - sector skills council for the motor industry - www.motor.org.uk

Motor Industry Magazine (monthly) (Institute of the Motor Industry (IMI)) - www.motor.org.uk/magazine/index.html

remit - www.remit.co.uk

Training Schemes - www.direct.gov.uk/en/educationandlearning

What's it like to be a Motor Mechanic (A&C Black 2008)

▶Working in engineering (2010) (Babcock Lifeskills) - www.babcock-lifeskills.com/

Similar Jobs

Electrician: Auto, Engineer: Automotive, Mechanic: Construction Plant, Service Technician: Land-based, Vehicle Mechanic/Motor Vehicle Technician, Vehicle Tyre/Exhaust Fitter

Mechanical Engineering Technician

CRCI:Engineering
CLCI:RAX

Job Band: 2 to 3

Job Description

Mechanical engineering technicians are involved in the development and maintenance of all types of plant, machinery and other mechanical equipment. They work in a wide variety of fields supporting engineers, including design and development, purchasing, estimating, inspection, maintenance, repair or after-sales service. They may be responsible for installing, testing, calibrating and organising maintenance programmes. Technicians apply their knowledge in all sorts of different areas, including marine engineering, defence and aerospace, biomedical and the oil and gas industry.

Work Details

Usually work around 35-40 hrs a week; Monday to Friday, though may be required to work shifts in some industrial jobs. Sometimes you may be expected to be on call. Your place of work is on industrial premises, in a workshop, or on other sites. This work is likely to involve some physical activity, sometimes climbing ladders, bending over machines and standing. The environment depends on the type of industry but it can be noisy and dirty. Initially you work under supervision. There may be a risk of accidents with the machines. You need to wear overalls and may need to wear safety glasses, a helmet and protective footwear. You are responsible for following safety rules.

Qualification

• England, Wales and Northern Ireland

Band 3: For entry to jobs, HNC or a relevant Diploma, usually at least 4 GCSEs (A*-C) including English, maths and science, preferably physics or engineering science, or equivalent.

• Scotland

Band 3: For training on the job and some courses: usually at least four S grades (1-3) including English, maths and science, preferably physics, or similar.

Adult Qualifications

If you have relevant work experience you may be accepted for some college courses without meeting the formal entry requirements.

Work Experience

Employers or colleges may prefer candidates who have relevant work or voluntary experience. This can include the motor vehicle industry or an engineering company, even if it is not directly working in mechanical engineering. All work experience shows a degree of enthusiasm and commitment and it is useful to show an aptitude for practical work and for working with machinery and equipment.

Entry and Training

Applicants are usually aged 16-17 although some are older. Training may be by an apprenticeship lasting 3-4 years and through an employer's training scheme. Under the apprenticeship scheme, training may be tailored to each trainee so can vary. You may be trained off the job for up to a year, then on the job working with an experienced technician. You are likely to work towards S/NVQs in mechanical manufacturing engineering at levels 2-3. Advanced apprenticeships leading to qualification at level 3 can also be a route into higher education.

Some relevant full-time courses are also available, including BTEC/SQA national diplomas in mechanical engineering and City & Guilds courses that can be studied prior to gaining employment. With the right training and experience, you can qualify as an engineering technician (EngTech) with the Engineering Council. See the website and also the website of the Institution of Mechanical Engineers for details. With further study and training, you may also be able to qualify as an incorporated (IEng) or chartered engineer (CEng) with the Engineering Council.

The Tomorrow's Engineers website has lots of useful careers information including a route map and guide to engineering activities from primary school through to higher education. The Engineering Development Trust also runs a range of nationwide schemes for 11-21 year olds who may be interested in engineering as a career. See the websites for details.

A Diploma/Welsh Baccalaureate may be available in your area in engineering. See the diplomas website for further information.

Mature applicants are usually considered but this depends on your qualifications and experience. Managerial and technological expertise is an advantage. Contact the Engineering Council for details.

You can also gain recognition of previous experience through Accreditation of Prior Learning (APL) or by working towards relevant S/NVQs. Contact your local careers office, Jobcentre Plus, Next Step service or Learning and Skills Council (LSC)/Local Enterprise Company (LEC) for details of training schemes, including apprenticeships for adults. The Open University runs a range of engineering courses. See the website for details.

You may be able to receive funding for higher education from one of the larger manufacturing/engineering companies and for postgraduate study from the Engineering and Physical Science Research Council.

Opportunities and Pay

Employment can be with an engineering or manufacturing company or with a large organisation using lots of machinery. There is usually a good demand for mechanical engineering technicians. There are several ways in which you can progress, such as becoming a supervisor or moving into other areas such as sales and marketing. With further qualifications and training it may be possible to become a mechanical engineer.

Pay varies depending on location, type and size of company. Starting salaries range from around £20k a year, rising to £30k with experience. Some senior technicians can earn around £35k a year, or more.

Health

There may be an allergy risk from skin irritants.

Skills and Qualities

able to follow drawings and plans, analytical skills, aptitude for teamwork, attention to detail, good communication skills, methodical, precise, problem-solving skills, responsible attitude, technical aptitude

Relevant Subjects

Design and technology, Engineering, ICT/Computer studies, Mathematics, Physics, Science

Further Information

Apprenticeship Schemes (National Apprenticeship Service) - www.apprenticeships.org.uk

Careers in Engineering Booklets (SEMTA) - www.semta.org.uk

Diplomas (Foundation, Higher and Advanced) - http://yp.direct.gov.uk/diplomas

Open University - www.open.ac.uk

SEMTA - sector skills council for science, engineering and manufacturing technologies - www.semta.org.uk

Tomorrow's Engineers - www.tomorrowsengineers.org.uk/careers.cfm

Training Schemes - www.direct.gov.uk/en/educationandlearning

Addresses

Engineering and Physical Sciences Research Council (EPSRC)
Polaris House North Star Avenue, Swindon, Wiltshire SN2 1ET
Phone: +44(0)1793 444 100
Web: www.epsrc.ac.uk

Engineering Council
246 High Holborn, London WC1V 7EX
Phone: +44 (0)20 3206 0500
Web: www.engc.org.uk

Engineering Development Trust (EDT)
Ridgeway, Welwyn Garden City, Hertfordshire AL7 2AA
Phone: +44 (0)1707 871520
Web: www.etrust.org.uk

Engineering Training Council (NI)
Interpoint, 20-24 York Street, Belfast BT15 1AQ
Phone: +44 (0)28 9032 9878
Web: www.etcni.org.uk

Institution of Mechanical Engineers (IMechE)
1 Birdcage Walk, Westminster, London SW1H 9JJ
Phone: +44 (0)20 7222 7899
Web: www.imeche.org.uk

Similar Jobs

Aircraft Engineering Technician, CAD Technician, Engineer: Mechanical, Fitter: Maintenance, Fork-Lift Truck Engineer, Heating & Ventilation Fitter/Welder

Medical Artist

also known as: Illustrator: Medical, Medical Graphic Artist
CRCI:Design, Arts and Crafts
CLCI:ED Job Band: 3 to 5

Job Description

Medical artists use artistic and graphic techniques to produce images of the human anatomy and related medical conditions. They provide a clinical support service to those involved in patient care, education and research. May also work as an artist or graphic designer. Artists are responsible for providing visual records of medical conditions and pathological materials to help doctors in the early diagnosis or treatment of disease.

Artists offer a wide range of graphics services, including the production of audio-visual teaching and lecture material and the production of artwork for scientific posters, textbooks, brochures and medical publications. Some design three-dimensional anatomical models used for teaching medical students.

They use sophisticated software packages as well as working in traditional media and may be required to produce models, or copy X-rays and slides. Medical artists have a comprehensive knowledge of medicine and science, and work closely with a variety of healthcare professionals. They can specialise in areas that include facial reconstruction/photo-comparison, medical animation, surgical illustration, scientific research and illustration.

Work Details

Work a basic 39 hr week; Monday to Friday, though a freelance illustrator/artist can choose their own working hours. Sometimes it can be necessary to work late to meet deadlines, which may include weekends. In hospitals you are likely to be a member of a team, including photographers and audio-visual specialists, sometimes working in an operating theatre.

Medical Artist

Qualification

- **England, Wales and Northern Ireland**

Band 3: For entry to jobs, HNC or a relevant Diploma, usually at least 4 GCSEs (A*-C) including English and maths, or equivalent. For some foundation studies courses: at least 5 GCSEs (A*-C) or equivalent.

Band 4: For foundation course in art and design: usually at least one A level and some GCSEs (A*-C), or equivalent. For BTEC higher national award: a BTEC national award, successful completion of a foundation studies course, or equivalent qualification.

Band 5: For degree courses: 2-3 A levels and some GCSEs (A*-C) usually including English and maths, or equivalent qualifications. Exact requirements depend on the degree you take.

- **Scotland**

Band 3: For entry: usually at least four S grades (1-3) including English and maths, or similar.

Band 4: For entry to SQA higher national and professional development awards, usually 2-3 H grades and some S grades (1-3), including English and maths, or similar qualifications.

Band 5: For degree courses: 3-5 H grades and some S grades (1-3), usually including English and maths, or similar qualifications. Exact requirements depend on the degree you take.

Degree Information

A first degree in illustration or in graphic design, media studies or graphic art is most suitable. Course titles vary, so check prospectuses carefully. There are a few graduate programs that specifically train medical illustrators in the profession. Postgraduate qualifications are available in medical illustration from Cardiff University and in medical or forensic art from Dundee University. The Medical Artists' Education Trust (MAET) also offers a postgraduate diploma.

Adult Qualifications

Mature applicants with outstanding portfolios of work may be accepted for courses without the standard entry requirements. There are Access or foundation level courses in some areas, which give adults without qualifications a route onto degree courses. Check with individual institutions.

Work Experience

Colleges and universities may prefer candidates who have relevant work or voluntary experience. This includes all art related areas which give you the opportunity to build on your portfolio of work. Work in a hospital medical illustration department or shadowing the work of a medical artist/photographer is particularly relevant. Any experience that involves illustration or photography techniques is also useful.

Entry and Training

You usually need a media qualification in graphic design to HND or equivalent level and an understanding of scientific principles. Entrants are typically graduates in sciences or arts. However, it it possible to enter the profession and join the Institute of Medical Illustrators (IMI) as a student and undertake a three-year graduate programme. Those who already have a degree in graphic design, media studies or graphic art can enrol for a one year graduate or postgraduate programme. A Diploma/Welsh Baccalaureate may be available in your area in creative and media and may provide a route onto higher education courses.

This area of work is moving towards state registration and all practising medical artists are likely to need to complete an approved graduate or postgraduate course, and be registered with the Health Professions Council (HPC). Contact the IMI and the Committee for the Accreditation of Medical Illustration Practitioners (CAMIP) about the future plans for registration.

The Medical Artists' Education Trust (MAET) offers a postgraduate training programme. This mainly consists of self-directed study, with attendance at seminars, assessment sessions and workshops. This is aimed at those with a relevant degree or HND, and all those entering the training attend an interview.

Other training opportunities include two years' structured on-the-job training for graduates of photography to provide a knowledge and skill base to achieve a postgraduate certificate in medical illustration. A one-year distance-learning course is available from the IMI for those with a relevant degree in graphic design, photography, media studies or graphic art, already working in a medical illustration department. The IMI offers a continuing professional development (CPD) programme to its members. Contact the IMI for information on routes to qualification and a list of relevant courses. The Medical Artists' Association (MAA) also offers postgraduate qualifications, events to support CPD and may help with funding for a degree.

Mature applicants with artistic/graphic design ability and experience may be offered training, particularly those with medical or nursing qualifications. For entry to most courses, you need to have a current portfolio of work that demonstrates your skills. There are opportunities for full and part-time study for the relevant qualifications. The Medical Artists' Education Trust (MAET) offers financial assistance for some postgraduate courses.

Opportunities and Pay

Just over 1,000 people work in medical illustration in the UK. This is a little known but highly qualified profession and because of the limited number of talented medical illustrators, demand is high.

Medical artists/illustrators work as healthcare scientists in hospitals and medical schools, research organisations, and in private medicine. With experience, you can operate on a freelance basis and gain work for specialised publishers and CD-ROMs. Over 70% of medical artists are self-employed and have a wide portfolio including another specialism.

Trainee salaries are likely to be between £15k-£18k a year, rising to £25k-£31k with qualifications and experience. A very skilled medical artist may earn up to £50k a year.

Health

You must have good eyesight and normal colour vision.

Skills and Qualities

able to work both on your own and in a team, attention to detail, drawing ability, good communication skills, good concentration level, IT skills, not squeamish, observant, patient, technical aptitude

Relevant Subjects

Art and Design, Biology, Health and social care, Media and communication studies, Science

Further Information

Careers in Medical Illustration (IMI) (Institute of Medical Illustration) - www.imi.org.uk/careers/careers01.asp

Committee for the Accreditation of Medical Illustration Practitioners (CAMIP) - www.camip.org.uk

Diplomas (Foundation, Higher and Advanced) - http://yp.direct.gov.uk/diplomas

Journal of Visual Communication in Medicine (4 x year) (Informa Healthcare) - www.informahealthcare.com/

Medical Artists' Education Trust - www.maet.org.uk

NHS Careers (NHS Careers) - www.nhscareers.nhs.uk

Addresses

Health Professions Council (HPC)
Park House, 184 Kennington Park Road, London SE11 4BU
Phone: +44 (0)20 7582 0866
Web: www.hpc-uk.org

Institute of Medical Illustrators (IMI)
12 Coldbath Square, London EC1R 5HL
Phone: +44 (0) 113 233 6258
Web: www.imi.org.uk

Medical Artists Association (MAA)
Medical Illustration UK Ltd, Charing Cross Hospital,
London W6 8RF
Phone: +44 (0)20 88467165
Web: www.maa.org.uk

Similar Jobs

Artist, Graphic Designer, Illustrator, Illustrator: Technical/ Scientific, Photographer, Photographer: Clinical

Medical Herbalist

also known as: Phytotherapist

CRCI:Healthcare
CLCI:JOD Job Band: 5

Job Description

Medical herbalists use plant remedies to treat a wide range of medical conditions and diseases, and to balance the body's metabolism. They take details of the patient's lifestyle and medical history and carry out a physical examination. Then work out a treatment for the underlying causes of the symptoms, rather than for the symptoms themselves. Herbalists aim to help the body's own healing process using herbal treatment (fluid extracts and tinctures, capsules, ointments and creams) for conditions that include arthritis, high blood pressure, migraine, digestive disorders, hay fever and asthma, insomnia, psoriasis, acne, eczema and other skin problems.

Herbalists also give general advice on a client's diet and way of life, and may prescribe vitamins, minerals and other food supplements, if necessary. Sometimes they refer them to a doctor or another medical professional. In mainland Europe, herbal medicine is also known as phytotherapy. There is a growing interest in Chinese, Indian, Tibetan and Japanese traditions.

Work Details

Your place of work is usually a consulting room, either at a complementary health centre or other treatment premises, or at home. Some herbalists make home visits to their clients. You may be expected to work weekends and some evenings though the hours of work can be flexible, particularly if you are self-employed. Time is spent preparing the medicines you prescribe, as well as discussing symptoms and treatment with patients. You work with people of all ages and help those who may be ill, and perhaps in pain, anxious or depressed.

Qualification

• England, Wales and Northern Ireland

Band 5: For entry to a degree course in medicine or an approved degree course in herbal medicine: 2-3 A levels, preferably two science subjects, and some GCSEs (A*-C) usually including English and maths, or equivalent. Exact requirements depend on the degree you take.

• Scotland

Band 5: For entry to a degree course in medicine or an approved degree course in herbal medicine: 3-5 H grades, preferably two sciences and some S grades (1-3), usually including English and maths, or similar qualifications. Exact requirements depend on the degree you take.

Degree Information

For registration with the National Institute of Medical Herbalists (NIMH), a degree or postgraduate qualification in herbal medicine accredited by NIMH or the European Herbal and Traditional Medicine Practitioners Association is required. Courses can be full or part time. A degree in medicine (or possibly a qualification in another alternative therapy) is needed for entry to the postgraduate course in herbal medicine at the Scottish School of Herbal Medicine or Napier University, Edinburgh. Contact the NIMH for details.

Adult Qualifications

Entry requirements may be relaxed for adults applying for higher education courses and Access and foundation courses give adults without qualifications a route into degree courses. Evidence of your ability to cope with the course is required.

Work Experience

Relevant work or voluntary experience is always useful and can improve your chances in application for entry to the degree or postgraduate courses. Consider work which involves helping people or working with the public. Work in a medical field such as volunteering at a hospital is also relevant.

Entry and Training

The UK's main professional organisation for herbal medicine practitioners is the National Institute of Medical Herbalists (NIMH), which accredits programmes in herbal medicine. Students usually undertake a BSc degree in Herbal Medicine at an accredited institution. These can be full time or part time over varying timescales, including those offered by the universities of Middlesex, Westminster and Lincoln. The University of East London and the Scottish School of Herbal Medicine offer distance learning courses. All courses require completion of a significant number of hours of supervised clinical experience. Part-time courses involve intensive college weekend classes combined with home study. Contact NIMH or the European Herbal and Traditional Medicine Practitioners Association (EHTPA) for details of all approved courses.

It can take between 3-5 years to graduate, with further practical experience required before you can register with NIMH. There are other courses available, but these do not necessarily lead to professional registration. The EHTPA supports continuing professional development throughout your career. Once qualified, you can also register with the Institute of Complementary Medicine which oversees a mix of complementary therapies.

A Diploma/Welsh Baccalaureate may be available in society, health and development in your area and may be relevant to this job.

Mature entry to training is usual and most training centres welcome mature applicants with life experience. Some entrants take a science foundation course offered by the Open University or an Access or similar course. Other mature entrants without the normal academic qualifications may also be considered if you have some knowledge of science. Contact the individual universities as most consider applicants on their individual merit and ability to study at the level required. Some courses are available part time or through distance learning. You may be able to receive funding from the relevant professional associations.

Opportunities and Pay

This is a small but expanding profession and opportunities are likely to increase in the UK, as well as internationally. There are over 500 herbal practitioners registered with the National Institute of Medical Herbalists in the UK and Ireland. You are usually self-employed and may work in a partnership or in a centre with people practising other complementary therapies. Costs can include some financial investment if you have to equip a consulting room and keep a store of medicines and bottles for dispensing. There is an increase in the number of herbalists now being employed by pharmaceutical companies, some of which are international. Some go on to train in related areas such as homeopathy or Bach Flower Remedies, or make and sell their own products. Other medical herbalists move into publishing or journalism, or may teach as well as practise. Others work in research.

As most herbalists are self-employed it is difficult to summarise earnings. Broadly speaking, hourly rates for experienced herbalists range from £30-£75, depending on location and experience. Starting salaries can be around £15k-£20k a year. Experienced herbalists can earn £35k a year or more.

Health

This job may require good colour vision for certain areas of work.

Skills and Qualities

analytical skills, approachable, business awareness, good communication skills, patient, perceptive, reassuring, scientific approach, sound judgement, tactful

Relevant Subjects

Biology, Chemistry, English, Health and social care, Psychology, Science

Further Information

Becoming a Medical Herbalist (NIMH) - www.nimh.org.uk/about-the-nimh/training-and-accreditation/becoming-a-medical-herbalist
Complementary and Alternative Medicine Library and Information Service (CAMLIS) - www.cam.nhs.uk
Diplomas (Foundation, Higher and Advanced) - http://yp.direct.gov.uk/diplomas
Frankincense Newsletter (EHTPA) (EHTPA) - www.ehpa.eu
Journal of Contemplative Science (2 x year) (Scottish School of Herbal Medicine) - www.herbalmedicine.org.uk/Journal/journal.shtml
Open University - www.open.ac.uk
Skills for Health - sector skills council - www.skillsforhealth.org.uk
Welsh Baccalaureate - www.wbq.org.uk

Addresses

European Herbal and Traditional Medicine Practitioners Association (EHTPA)
25 Lincoln Close, Tewkesbury, Gloucestershire GL20 5TY
Phone: +44 (0) 1684 291605
Web: www.ehpa.eu

Institute for Complementary Medicine (ICM)
Can-Mezzanine, 32-36 Loman Street, London SE1 0EH
Phone: +44 (0)207 922 7980
Web: www.i-c-m.org.uk

National Institute of Medical Herbalists (NIMH)
Elm House 54 Mary Arches Street, Exeter, Devon EX4 3BA
Phone: +44 (0)1392 426 022
Web: www.nimh.org.uk

Scottish School of Herbal Medicine
Alexander Stephen House, Suites 20-22, 91 Holmfauld Road, Glasgow G51 4RY
Phone: +44 (0)141 445 2500
Web: www.herbalmedicine.org.uk

Similar Jobs

Acupuncturist, Aromatherapist, Dietitian, Homeopath, Naturopath, Reflexologist

Merchant Navy Catering Rating

CRCI:Transport and Logistics
CLCI:YAL Job Band: 2 to 3

Job Description

Catering ratings work on a seagoing ship, performing duties similar to those of a chef or cook in the catering trade. They may be based in the ship's galley (kitchen) preparing and cooking meals for the crew and also for passengers. Also wash up and clean the galley. Purchase and maintain the stores and ensure that all catering areas are kept clean and hygienic. Catering ratings also work as stewards, serving food and drink to those on board. May work in housekeeping, where they clean and look after all accommodation and public areas.

Work Details

The job may require you to stay away from home for long periods and work shifts, including weekends, evenings and public holidays. You have to cope with rough seas and there is a risk of accidents. Particular attention must be paid to hygiene rules and regulations. You are supplied with a uniform and protective clothing. Catering work is mainly indoors, except when loading stores or taking part in safety drills. Galley areas can be hot, noisy and steamy.

Qualification

- **England, Wales and Northern Ireland**

Band 2: For entry to jobs, no minimum qualifications are needed, but it is an advantage to have some GCSEs (A*-C) or equivalent in subjects that include English and maths.

Band 3: For entry to jobs, HNC or a relevant Diploma, usually at least 4 GCSEs (A*-C) including English and maths, or equivalent.

- **Scotland**

Band 2: For some vocational courses: some S grades (1-3) in subjects that include English and maths, or similar.

Band 3: For entry to jobs, usually at least four S grades (1-3) including English and maths, or similar.

Adult Qualifications

Those with catering/hospitality qualifications are preferred. Contact individual shipping companies for information on their policy.

Work Experience

Employers or colleges may prefer candidates who have relevant work or voluntary experience in food preparation, though other catering/hospitality experience can also be helpful. There is often plenty of paid part-time catering work available.

Entry and Training

You require experience and qualifications in catering work before applying for a job with a shipping company or the Royal Fleet Auxillary (RFA) which supplies the Royal Navy. Suitable courses may be studied full time at a college, or part time if you have a job. There are many relevant courses in hospitality subjects, including S/NVQs or national/higher national certificates/diplomas, specialising in food preparation and cooking. Check with local colleges for details. The RFA takes on the largest number of entrants each year. You also need to pass a medical examination.

Your training continues once you have successfully gained a post with a shipping company. Merchant Navy ratings employed by the RFA are also trained to operate defensive weapons and may have to work in emergencies, conflicts or war. With experience and qualifications, this job can lead to catering officer level.

Marine traineeships/apprenticeships are also available for entry to this job including a marine traineeship which leads to an S/NVQ in marine vessel support at level 2. Advanced apprenticeships leading to qualification at level 3 can also be a route into higher education. Contact the Merchant Navy Training Board for details of all training opportunities.

In Scotland there is an Intermediate 1 Skills for Work course in uniformed and emergency services which introduces students to careers in the Merchant Navy. Contact the Scottish Qualifications Authority for details.

Few adults over the age of 25 join the Merchant Navy but the RFA may accept applicants with shore-based catering experience.

Opportunities and Pay

Merchant Navy catering ratings work for all types of shipping companies usually on passenger and freight ferries, cargo ships, container ships and tankers. There are also jobs with the RFA.

Some may work on cruise ships, or offshore research and support vessels. There is a clear promotion structure and, with the correct certificates of competency and further training, experienced ratings can gain promotion to chief petty officer or to third officer. Ratings that spend long periods at sea have generous leave allowances.

Salaries start from £17k for a newly qualified rating, rising to over £22k with experience. Senior ratings can earn up to £30k a year. Tax-free earnings can apply on long voyages out of the country. The employer pays for food and accommodation when you are at sea, and some travel costs.

Health

You have to be fit and healthy and pass a medical. You must have almost perfect eyesight, without glasses or lenses, and normal colour vision.

Skills and Qualities

able to cope with emergencies, able to follow instructions, able to get on with all kinds of people, able to work both on your own and in a team, able to work quickly, good organisational skills, practical skills, responsible attitude, safety conscious, willing to train and work away from home

Relevant Subjects

Hospitality and catering

Further Information

Apprenticeship Schemes (National Apprenticeship Service) - www.apprenticeships.org.uk

Careers at Sea - www.careersatsea.org

Merchant Navy Careers Handbook (Beauforts Projects) - www.offshore-jobs.co.uk/sea/

Addresses

British Shipping
Carthusian Court, 12 Carthusian Street, London EC1M 6EZ
Phone: +44 (0)20 7417 2800
Web: www.british-shipping.org

Marine Society & Sea Cadets
202 Lambeth Road, London SE1 7JW
Phone: +44 (0)20 7654 7000
Web: www.ms-sc.org

Merchant Navy Training Board (MNTB)
Carthusian Court, 12 Carthusian Street, London EC1M 6EZ
Phone: +44 (0)20 7417 2800
Web: www.mntb.org.uk

Royal Navy - Royal Fleet Auxiliary (RFA) Service
Royal Fleet Auxiliary Recruitment Office, Captain Naval Recruitment HQ, Room G-13, Building 1/080, Jago Road, HMNB Portsmouth, Hampshire PO1 3LU
Phone: 0845 60 40 520 (UK only)
Web: www.royalnavy.mod.uk

Scottish Qualifications Authority (SQA)
The Optima Building 58 Robertson Street, Glasgow G2 8DQ
Phone: 0845 279 1000
Web: www.sqa.org.uk/sqa/41328.html

Similar Jobs

Caterer: Contract/Private, Chef/Cook, Royal Navy Rating, Waiter/Waitress

Merchant Navy Deck Rating

also known as: Merchant Navy Seaman/Woman

CRCI:Transport and Logistics
CLCI:YAL Job Band: 1 to 2

Job Description

Deck ratings work on commercial seagoing ships, doing cleaning, routine maintenance and repairs. They look after the deck gear, rigging and winches. They remove rust and old paint and repaint all parts of the ship. Also open and close the hatches, stow the anchor, fasten the mooring ropes and clean the deck. Deck ratings test fire and safety equipment and operate lifting gears to handle loading and unloading of cargo. They stand watch as a lookout or possibly at the helm. Help to lower the lifeboat and handle small boats to and from shore.

When in port, deck ratings assist with fire and security checks, help to moor the vessel, take stores on board as well as other cargo duties. They may be trained to operate and maintain sophisticated replenishment equipment and in the Royal Fleet Auxiliary (part of the Royal Navy), in biological, chemical and nuclear defence.

Work Details

You work watches (shifts) of 4 hours and may need to be away from home for long periods. This work is strenuous and involves climbing ladders, bending and kneeling. The work environment is noisy and can be dirty. You have to cope with rough seas and working outside in all weathers. There is a risk of accidents at sea. You wear a boiler suit or a uniform.

Qualification

- **England, Wales and Northern Ireland**

Band 1: For entry to jobs, no minimum qualifications are needed, but you are expected to have a good level of general education and relevant experience. Some formal/vocational qualifications at any level are useful.

Band 2: For many employers: no minimum qualifications are needed, but it is an advantage to have some GCSEs (A*-C) or equivalent in subjects that include English and maths.

- **Scotland**

Band 1: For entry to jobs, no minimum qualifications are needed, but you are expected to have a good level of general education and relevant experience. Some formal/vocational qualifications at any level are useful.

Band 2: For many employers: although academic qualifications are not specified for this job, it is an advantage to have some S grades (1-3) in subjects that include English, maths and a science, preferably physics, or similar.

Adult Qualifications

Entry and re-entry is possible, especially for those with direct relevant experience, such as the Royal Navy. Contact individual shipping companies for information on their policy.

Work Experience

Any relevant work or voluntary experience is useful and can improve your chances in application for entry to this career. It is rarely possible to obtain work experience on a commercial merchant ship although nautical knowledge is an advantage. Jobs involving teamwork, following and giving instructions and working under pressure provide useful experience. Membership of a sea cadet group or similar organisation indicates commitment. Fitness is important for entry to the Merchant Navy, so evidence of an interest in keeping fit is useful.

Entry and Training

You must be sponsored by a commercial shipping company before you can train and need to pass an entrance test, including a medical examination. Most employers prefer people who are aged 16-19. Training is usually combined with time at a nautical college followed by a period of practical training at sea. During training you do courses in firefighting, sea survival and first aid. The usual period of training can be up to two years. The Royal Fleet Auxiliary, which supplies the Royal Navy, takes on the largest number of entrants each year.

The Maritime and Coastguard Agency's efficient deck hand certificate and S/NVQs in marine vessel support/operations are available. Merchant Navy ratings employed by the Royal Navy are also trained to operate defensive weapons and may have to work in emergencies, conflicts or war.

Marine traineeships/apprenticeships are available for entry to this job. Advanced apprenticeships leading to qualification at level 3 can also be a route into higher education. The Merchant Navy Training Board approves the education and training framework for the merchant navy. See the website for details of all training opportunities.

In Scotland there is an Intermediate 1 Skills for Work course in uniformed and emergency services which introduces students to careers in the Merchant Navy. Contact the Scottish Qualifications Authority for details.

Mature entry after 18 years of age may be difficult except for ex-Royal Navy personnel. Others who have appropriate engineering qualifications may sometimes be offered training.

Opportunities and Pay

Most ratings are employed by cargo or container shipping companies. There are also opportunities with the Royal Fleet Auxiliary. There is a clear promotion structure and, with the correct certificates of competency and further training, experienced ratings can achieve promotion to chief petty officer, third officer, and beyond. There are opportunities for experienced ratings to work for port authorities, shipping brokers and insurance companies.

While training, allowances of between £5k-£8k a year are paid and living expenses are provided. Qualified junior deck ratings earn £20k-£22k a year, rising with experience to around £30k a year. Tax-free earnings can apply on long voyages out of the country. The employer pays for food and accommodation when you are at sea, and some travel costs. Ratings that spend long periods at sea have generous leave allowances.

Health

You have to be fit and healthy and pass a medical. You must have almost perfect eyesight, without glasses or lenses, and normal colour vision.

Skills and Qualities

able to cope with emergencies, able to follow instructions, able to work both on your own and in a team, flexible approach, hard working, manual dexterity, practical skills, reliable, willing to train and work away from home

Further Information

Apprenticeship Schemes (National Apprenticeship Service) - www.apprenticeships.org.uk

Careers at Sea - www.careersatsea.org

Chamber of Shipping: Careers (Chamber of Shipping) - www.british-shipping.org/careers/

Full Ahead Newsletter (quarterly) (The Merchant Navy Association) - www.mna.org.uk

Merchant Navy Career Opportunities - www.careersatsea.org

Merchant Navy Careers Handbook (Beauforts Projects) - www.offshore-jobs.co.uk/sea/

Addresses

British Shipping
Carthusian Court, 12 Carthusian Street, London EC1M 6EZ
Phone: +44 (0)20 7417 2800
Web: www.british-shipping.org

Marine Society & Sea Cadets
202 Lambeth Road, London SE1 7JW
Phone: +44 (0)20 7654 7000
Web: www.ms-sc.org

Maritime and Coastguard Agency (MCA)
Spring Place, 105 Commercial Road, Southampton, Hampshire SO15 1EG
Phone: +44 (0)2380 329 308
Web: www.mcga.gov.uk

Merchant Navy Association
9 Saxon Way Caistor, Market Rasen, Lincolnshire LN7 6SG
Phone: +44 (0)1472 851130
Web: www.mna.org.uk

Merchant Navy Training Board (MNTB)
Carthusian Court, 12 Carthusian Street, London EC1M 6EZ
Phone: +44 (0)20 7417 2800
Web: www.mntb.org.uk

Royal Navy - Royal Fleet Auxiliary (RFA) Service
Royal Fleet Auxiliary Recruitment Office, Captain Naval Recruitment HQ, Room G-13, Building 1/080, Jago Road, HMNB Portsmouth, Hampshire PO1 3LU
Phone: 0845 60 40 520 (UK only)
Web: www.royalnavy.mod.uk

Scottish Qualifications Authority (SQA)
The Optima Building 58 Robertson Street, Glasgow G2 8DQ
Phone: 0845 279 1000
Web: www.sqa.org.uk/sqa/41328.html

Similar Jobs

Fisherman/Fisherwoman, Merchant Navy Deck/Navigating Officer, Merchant Navy Engine-room Rating, Royal Navy Rating

Merchant Navy Deck/Navigating Officer

CRCI:Transport and Logistics
CLCI:YAL
Job Band: 3 to 5

Job Description

Navigating or deck officers control the safe navigation of a commercial ship and handling of its cargo, crew and passengers. They assist the ship's captain to plot and maintain the course using sophisticated satellite and radar equipment. Give orders to the crew, supervise the safe loading and unloading of goods and ensure that deck gear and equipment are in good working order. They also ensure that the ship's capacity and fuel use is economical. At sea, they are required to take responsibility for two watches (four-hour bridge duty periods) every 24 hours.

If working for the Royal Fleet Auxiliary supplying cargo to the Royal Navy at sea, deck officers ensure the safe transfer of cargo through inter-ship liaison, the use of sophisticated cargo handling equipment, and the control of any helicopters involved in the transfer.

Work Details

Usually work on a shift basis as ships operate 24 hrs a day, every day of the year. The work is divided into watches (shifts) that are typically four hours on watch, followed by eight hours off watch. During busier times a watch of six hours on and six hours off is usual. The amount of travel depends on the employer and the type of ship, but you may have to stay away from home for long periods, unless working on ferries. You are in charge of the safety of the crew, any passengers and the ship itself.

The job involves paperwork, such as ordering supplies, keeping records and completing paperwork for customs. You have to cope with climbing ladders and with rough seas. There is a risk of accidents at sea. The work environment can be damp, noisy and uncomfortable in bad weather. A uniform is provided.

Qualification

• England, Wales and Northern Ireland

Band 3: For entry to jobs, HNC or a relevant Diploma, usually at least 4 GCSEs (A*-C) including English, maths and either physics or a combined science, or equivalent.

Band 4: For accelerated cadetship training (three years) including onboard training: two A levels, including maths or a physical science, and four GCSEs (A*-C) including maths and science, or equivalent.

Band 5: For degree courses: 2-3 A levels and some GCSEs (A*-C) usually including English and maths, or equivalent. Exact requirements depend on the degree you take.

• Scotland

Band 3: For entry: usually at least four S grades (1-3) including English and maths, physics or a combined science, or similar qualifications.

Band 4: For accelerated cadetship training (three years) including onboard training: three H grades, including maths or a physical science, and four S grades (1-3) including maths and science, or similar qualifications.

Band 5: For degree courses: 3-5 H grades and some S grades (1-3), usually including English and maths, or similar qualifications. Exact requirements depend on the degree you take.

Degree Information

Science-based degrees are usually required. The subjects studied via a sponsored degree are currently merchant ship operations, nautical science or marine studies (merchant shipping).

Adult Qualifications

Adult entry is possible for former Royal Navy officers with experience. Graduates from all disciplines are now given consideration as well as those with other relevant qualifications and experience. Entry requirements may be relaxed for adults applying for higher education courses and Access or foundation courses give adults without qualifications a route on to degree courses.

Work Experience

Any relevant work or voluntary experience is useful and can improve your chances in application for entry to this career. Consider work experience in administration, working with technical equipment, leadership or supervisory experience. It is rarely possible to obtain work experience on a commercial merchant ship although nautical knowledge is an advantage.

Entry and Training

You must apply first to a shipping company or training group for sponsored training. You also need to pass a Maritime and Coastguard Agency medical examination, which needs to be renewed every two years.

It usually takes 3-4 years to qualify as a junior (3rd) officer including 15 months at sea. For officer cadet training you can enter with at least four good GCSEs/S grades or similar, or with A levels/H grades or equivalent. The main entry route for those wishing to become an officer and progress through the ranks is the foundation degree-based programme, which is at A level/H grade entry and includes onboard practical training. Completion of the foundation degree is combined with the professional seafaring certificates of competency. The equivalent route in Scotland is the Merchant Navy Professional Scottish Diploma, offered at Glasgow College of Nautical Studies.

Entry can also be through a sponsored three-year science-based degree course. Your fees are paid as well as an allowance for day-to-day expenses. A further year of training enables you to develop the seafaring skills that you need to complete the required sea-service for the Maritime and Coastguard Agency's (MCA) Officer of the Watch (OoW) certificate of competency. This year may also be completed during your degree if it is a sandwich course.

Graduates, usually with a science-based degree, may apply for an accelerated programme of training that leads to the highest levels of professional certification such as a Master (Captain). Merchant Navy officers employed by the Royal Fleet Auxiliary of the Royal Navy are also trained to operate defensive weapons and may have to work in emergencies, conflicts or war. Marine traineeships/ apprenticeships are also available for entry to this job. The Merchant Navy Training Board approves the education and training framework for the merchant navy. See the website for details of all training opportunities.

In Scotland there is an Intermediate 1 Skills for Work course in uniformed and emergency services which introduces students to careers in the Merchant Navy. Contact the Scottish Qualifications Authority for details.

Mature applicants should contact the Merchant Navy Training Board for all training opportunities. Scholarships for cadet training are offered by the Corporation of Trinity House in London and financial support for training may also be available from the Marine Society.

Opportunities and Pay

Around 600 trainees are employed each year. See the Merchant Navy Training Board website for sponsoring companies. You can work on many different types of ship, such as cargo vessels, container ships, tankers, marine mining vessels, oil tankers and rig supply vessels, cruise liners, freight and passenger ferries. Merchant Navy officers are also employed by the Royal Fleet Auxillary, which supplies Royal Navy ships at sea. Promotion is by merit and experience and requires appropriate certificates of competency. There is a clear promotion structure with opportunities for both men and women.

Experienced deck officers can also work ashore in administration work, for example, with shipping companies, the oil industry, harbour companies, shipping brokers and maritime insurance companies.

Pay in the Merchant Navy varies depending on employer, location and market sector. Cadet allowances are around £8k a year. The average salary for a junior officer is around £22k, rising to £27k for a 2nd officer, and around £35k for a 1st officer. A master earns around £35k-£60k a year. Tax-free earnings can apply on long voyages out of the country. The employer pays for food and accommodation when you are at sea, and some travel costs.

Health

You must have near perfect eyesight without spectacles, normal colour vision and pass an eyesight test, as well as a stringent medical test. A high standard of physical fitness is needed.

Skills and Qualities

able to communicate effectively, able to cope with emergencies, aptitude for teamwork, good organisational skills, leadership qualities, observant, problem-solving skills, sound judgement, technical aptitude, willing to train and work away from home

Relevant Subjects

Design and technology, English, Geography, Mathematics, Physics, Science

Further Information

Careers at Sea - www.careersatsea.org

Chamber of Shipping: Careers (Chamber of Shipping) - www.british-shipping.org/careers/

Merchant Navy Career Opportunities - www.careersatsea.org

Merchant Navy Careers Handbook (Beauforts Projects) - www.offshore-jobs.co.uk/sea/

Addresses

British Shipping
Carthusian Court, 12 Carthusian Street, London EC1M 6EZ
Phone: +44 (0)20 7417 2800
Web: www.british-shipping.org

Glasgow College of Nautical Studies
21 Thistle Street, Glasgow G5 9XB
Phone: +44 (0)141 565 2500
Web: www.gcns.ac.uk/

Marine Society & Sea Cadets
202 Lambeth Road, London SE1 7JW
Phone: +44 (0)20 7654 7000
Web: www.ms-sc.org

Maritime and Coastguard Agency (MCA)
Spring Place, 105 Commercial Road, Southampton,
Hampshire SO15 1EG
Phone: +44 (0)2380 329 308
Web: www.mcga.gov.uk

Merchant Navy Association
9 Saxon Way Caistor, Market Rasen, Lincolnshire LN7 6SG
Phone: +44 (0)1472 851130
Web: www.mna.org.uk

Merchant Navy Training Board (MNTB)
Carthusian Court, 12 Carthusian Street, London EC1M 6EZ
Phone: +44 (0)20 7417 2800
Web: www.mntb.org.uk

Royal Navy - Royal Fleet Auxiliary (RFA) Service
Royal Fleet Auxiliary Recruitment Office, Captain Naval Recruitment HQ, Room G-13, Building 1/080, Jago Road, HMNB Portsmouth, Hampshire PO1 3LU
Phone: 0845 60 40 520 (UK only)
Web: www.royalnavy.mod.uk

Scottish Qualifications Authority (SQA)
The Optima Building 58 Robertson Street, Glasgow G2 8DQ
Phone: 0845 279 1000
Web: www.sqa.org.uk/sqa/41328.html

Ship Safe Training Group
The Precinct, Rochester, Kent ME1 1SR
Phone: +44 (0)1634 820 820
Web: www.sstg.org

Trinity House
Trinity House Merchant Navy Scholarship Scheme c/o Chiltern Maritime Ltd Aycliffe Business Centre Archcliffe Road, Dover, Kent CT17 9EL
Phone: +44 (0)1304 212610
Web: www.trinityhouse.co.uk

Similar Jobs

Merchant Navy Deck Rating, Merchant Navy Electro-technical Officer, Merchant Navy Engineering Officer, Royal Marines Officer, Royal Navy Officer

Merchant Navy Electro-technical Officer

also known as: Merchant Navy Systems Engineer

CRCI:Transport and Logistics
CLCI:YAL Job Band: 3 to 5

Job Description

Electro-technical officers are trained engineers responsible for the vast amount of electrical and electronic equipment on board a commercial vessel. Their role arose from the invention of the global maritime distress and safety system (GMDSS) which introduced satellite communication for ships. They specialise in the maintenance and repair of a ship's navigation, communication and computer systems. Use problem-solving skills to diagnose faults or equipment breakdown and supervise the support staff that carry out the repair work. Work closely with engineering officers. Also deal with cargo or engine-room monitoring systems. They keep up to date with the latest technology.

Work Details

Seagoing work involves travel, possibly worldwide, and you may need to be away from home for long periods. You are expected to work shifts and be on call for emergencies. Work on ships requires you to cope with rough seas and bad weather at times. The work environment on a ship can be enclosed and noisy. You must be able to adapt to new equipment. There is a risk of accidents at sea.

Qualification

- **England, Wales and Northern Ireland**

Band 3: For entry to an apprenticeship: usually at least 4 GCSEs (A*-C) including English and maths, physics or a combined science, or equivalent qualifications.

Band 4: For entry: 1-2 A levels, including maths or physics or possibly both, and 4 GCSEs (A*-C), preferably including maths, English and physics (possibly double science or similar), or equivalent qualifications.

Band 5: For degree courses: 2-3 A levels, including maths and physics, and some GCSEs (A*-C) usually including English and maths. Exact requirements depend on the degree you take.

- **Scotland**

Band 3: For entry to an apprenticeship: usually at least four S grades (1-3) including English and maths, a science, preferably physics, and English or similar.

Band 4: For entry: 1-3 H grades including maths or physics, or possibly both, and four S grades (1-3), preferably including maths, English and physics (possibly double science or similar), or similar qualifications.

Band 5: For degree courses: 3-5 H grades, including maths and physics, and some S grades (1-3), usually including English and maths, or similar.

Degree Information

Degrees in electronic and communication engineering, electronic and computer systems, or similar, are most relevant.

Adult Qualifications

Civilians with relevant electronic and engineering qualifications are eligible for entry to a conversion programme. Entry requirements may be relaxed for adults applying for higher education courses. Access or foundation courses give adults without qualifications a route on to degree courses.

Work Experience

Employers or colleges may prefer candidates who have relevant work or voluntary experience. Obtaining work experience on a ship is difficult, but similar jobs and experience can first be obtained on land. Relevant areas are telecommunications and electronics and possibly work with a shore-based shipping company.

Entry and Training

Currently South Tyneside Marine College with Northumbria University offers a Foundation Degree for Electro Technical Officers, the only course of its kind in the UK. It covers a range of electronic and electrical topics including marine management, health and safety and work based learning amongst others. Otherwise. there are two routes to join as an officer cadet. With A/H levels you can join an integrated programme of education and ship board training leading to NVQ, national and higher national and professional qualifications issued by the Maritime and Coastguard Agency. Training is at one of the Merchant Navy training colleges at Southampton, Glasgow, Fleetwood or Tyneside. Alternatively, you can enter with a degree such as a BSc in merchant ship operations and qualify as a junior officer in 3-4 years, including 15 months at sea.

You can also take an HNC/HND course in maritime telecommunications, or in electronic and communications engineering (telecommunications) with marine options. Before you can go to sea you must have the Maritime Radio Communications General Certificate and the Electronic Navigational Equipment Maintenance Certificate.

Merchant Navy officers employed by the Royal Fleet Auxiliary are also trained to operate defensive weapons and may have to work in emergencies, conflicts or war. Marine traineeships/apprenticeships are also available for entry to this job. Check the Merchant Navy Training Board's website, or telephone for details on all training opportunities.

In Scotland there is an Intermediate 1 Skills for Work course in uniformed and emergency services which introduces students to careers in the Merchant Navy. Contact the Scottish Qualifications Authority for details.

Mature entrants should contact the Merchant Navy Training Board for all training opportunities. It is unusual to enter training after the age of 25. Scholarships for cadet training are offered by the Corporation of Trinity House in London and financial support for training may also be available from the Marine Society. Royal Navy officers with relevant experience or civilians with appropriate engineering qualifications, can join a conversion programme.

Opportunities and Pay

You can work for a shipping company, the armed forces, or a company that manufactures or supplies the equipment. There is little recruitment for seagoing work at present, even for experienced officers, as automated communication systems mean fewer such officers on ships. However, there are opportunities in cruise line shipping. Merchant Navy officers are also employed by the Royal Fleet Auxiliary, which supplies the Royal Navy ships at sea.

Promotion to senior rank is possible especially on large passenger vessels with large electrical plant. There are also technician opportunities in ports or power plants on-shore.

Pay in the Merchant Navy varies depending on employer, location and market sector, which means that some officers can earn as much as two to three times the salaries of others. The average starting salary is around £22k a year. This rises to £25k-£33k for a 2nd officer, £33k for a 1st officer and up to £32k-£65k a year for a chief engineer. Tax-free earnings can apply on long voyages out of the country. The employer pays for food and accommodation when you are at sea, and some travel costs.

Health

You must have perfect colour vision, good hearing and have a good standard of physical fitness. There is a medical test on entry.

Skills and Qualities

able to get on with all kinds of people, able to report accurately, able to work both on your own and in a team, adaptable, attention to detail, good concentration level, information handling skills, problem-solving skills, technical aptitude, willing to train and work away from home

Relevant Subjects

Design and technology, Engineering, English, Geography, ICT/Computer studies, Mathematics, Physics, Science

Further Information

Apprenticeship Schemes (National Apprenticeship Service) - www.apprenticeships.org.uk

Careers at Sea - www.careersatsea.org

Full Ahead Newsletter (quarterly) (The Merchant Navy Association) - www.mna.org.uk

Merchant Navy Career Opportunities - www.careersatsea.org

Merchant Navy Careers Handbook (Beauforts Projects) - www.offshore-jobs.co.uk/sea/

Addresses

British Shipping
Carthusian Court, 12 Carthusian Street, London EC1M 6EZ
Phone: +44 (0)20 7417 2800
Web: www.british-shipping.org

Marine Society & Sea Cadets
202 Lambeth Road, London SE1 7JW
Phone: +44 (0)20 7654 7000
Web: www.ms-sc.org

Maritime and Coastguard Agency (MCA)
Spring Place, 105 Commercial Road, Southampton, Hampshire SO15 1EG
Phone: +44 (0)2380 329 308
Web: www.mcga.gov.uk

Maritime Skills Alliance
1 Hillside, Beckingham, Lincoln LN5 0RQ
Web: www.maritimeskills.org

Merchant Navy Association
9 Saxon Way Caistor, Market Rasen, Lincolnshire LN7 6SG
Phone: +44 (0)1472 851130
Web: www.mna.org.uk

Merchant Navy Training Board (MNTB)
Carthusian Court, 12 Carthusian Street, London EC1M 6EZ
Phone: +44 (0)20 7417 2800
Web: www.mntb.org.uk

Scottish Qualifications Authority (SQA)
The Optima Building 58 Robertson Street, Glasgow G2 8DQ
Phone: 0845 279 1000
Web: www.sqa.org.uk/sqa/41328.html

Similar Jobs

Engineer: Electronics, Merchant Navy Deck/Navigating Officer, Merchant Navy Engineering Officer, Royal Navy Officer, Telecommunications Technician

Merchant Navy Engineering Officer

CRCI:Transport and Logistics
CLCI:YAL Job Band: 3 to 5

Job Description

Engineering officers are responsible for the maintenance and repair of a commercial ship's propulsion machinery and other equipment. They supervise the work of the engineering crew who make sure that equipment, such as the ship's engines, ventilation systems and purifiers, are working properly and efficiently. They also maintain control equipment, including computer-controlled engine management, lifts and cranes. When equipment malfunctions, they diagnose the fault and oversee the dismantling, repair and reassembly of the equipment.

May specialise in maintaining and repairing navigation, communication and computer systems and is then known as a systems engineer or electro-technical officer.

Work Details

Usually work on a shift basis as ships operate 24 hrs a day, every day of the year. Work is divided into watches (shifts) that are typically four hours on watch, followed by eight hours off watch. During busier times a watch of six hours on and six hours off is usual. The amount of travel depends on the employer and the type of ship, but often you have to stay away from home for long periods, unless working on ferries. Your time is spent mainly in the engine control room and the engine room, which may be noisy and hot.

Merchant Navy Engineering Officer

Sometimes you need to work in uncomfortable conditions, such as confined spaces or refrigerated areas. You have to cope with climbing ladders and with some rough seas, perhaps causing you sea sickness. There is a risk of accidents at sea. You wear a uniform.

Qualification

• England, Wales and Northern Ireland

Band 3: For entry to jobs, HNC or a relevant Diploma, usually at least 4 GCSEs (A*-C) including English and maths, or equivalent.

Band 4: For accelerated cadetship training (3 years): two A levels, including maths or physics, and some GCSEs (A*-C), including English and maths, or equivalent.

Band 5: For degree courses: 2-3 A levels, including maths and physics, and some GCSEs (A*-C) usually including English and maths. Exact requirements depend on the degree you take.

• Scotland

Band 3: For entry: a minimum of four S grades (1-3) including English, maths, physics or a combined science, or similar qualifications.

Band 4: For accelerated cadetship training (3 years): three H grades including maths or physics and some S grades (1-3) including English and maths, or similar.

Band 5: For degree courses: 3-5 H grades, including maths and physics, and some S grades (1-3), usually including English and maths, or similar.

Degree Information

A degree in marine engineering/technology or marine-related science is usually required for officer training.

Adult Qualifications

Adult entry is possible for those with relevant qualifications. Those with engineering qualifications can join a conversion programme. Entry requirements may be relaxed for adults applying for higher education courses. Access or foundation courses give adults without qualifications a route on to degree courses.

Work Experience

Employers or colleges may prefer candidates who have relevant work or voluntary experience. Consider work experience in any sort of engineering, technical or computing work and possibly work with a shore-based shipping company. It is very rarely possible to obtain work experience on a commercial merchant ship although nautical knowledge is an advantage.

Entry and Training

You must apply first to a shipping company or training group for sponsored training which takes 3-4 years. For officer cadet training you can enter with at least four good GCSEs/S grades or similar, or with A levels/H grades or equivalent. The main entry route for those wishing to become an officer and progress through the ranks, is the foundation degree-based programme, which is at A level/H grade entry. Completion of the foundation degree is combined with the professional seafaring certificates of competency. The equivalent route in Scotland is the Merchant Navy Professional Scottish Diploma, offered at Glasgow College of Nautical Studies.

Entry can also be through a sponsored three-year marine engineering degree course. Your fees are paid as well as an allowance for day-to-day expenses. A further year of training enables you to develop your seafaring skills and you need to complete the required sea-service for the Maritime & Coastguard Agency's Officer of the Watch (OoW) certificate of competency. This year may also be completed during your degree if it is a sandwich course.

Graduates, usually with a marine engineering or related degree, may apply for an accelerated programme of training that leads to the highest levels of professional certification such as a chief engineer. Merchant Navy officers employed by the Royal Fleet Auxiliary supporting the Royal Navy, are also trained to operate defensive weapons and may have to work in emergencies, conflicts or war.

Marine traineeships/apprenticeships are also available for entry to this job. Contact the Merchant Navy Training Board for details of all training opportunities.

In Scotland there is an Intermediate 1 Skills for Work course in uniformed and emergency services which introduces students to careers in the merchant navy. Contact the Scottish Qualifications Authority for details.

Mature entrants should contact the Merchant Navy Training Board for all training opportunities although it is unusual to enter training after the age of 25. Scholarships for cadet training are offered by the Corporation of Trinity House in London and financial support for training may also be available from the Marine Society. Royal Navy officers with relevant experience or civilians with appropriate engineering qualifications, can join a conversion programme.

Opportunities and Pay

You work on many different types of ship, such as cargo vessels, container ships, tankers, marine mining vessels, oil tankers and rig supply vessels, cruise liners, freight and passenger ferries. Merchant Navy officers are also employed by the Royal Fleet Auxiliary, which supplies Royal Navy ships at sea. Promotion is by merit and experience and requires the appropriate certificates of competency. There is a clear promotion structure with opportunities for both men and women.

Experienced engineering officers can also work ashore in production and process plants, local authorities, hospitals, hotels, shipping companies and nautical colleges.

Pay in the Merchant Navy varies hugely depending on employer, location and market sector, which means that some officers can earn as much as two to three times the salaries of others. The average starting salary is around £22k a year. A chief engineer can earn over £60k a year. Tax-free earnings can apply on long voyages out of the country. The employer pays for food and accommodation when you are at sea, and some travel costs.

Health

You have to pass a medical and an eyesight test. You must have normal colour vision and a high standard of physical fitness.

Skills and Qualities

able to cope with emergencies, able to prioritise work, aptitude for teamwork, IT skills, problem-solving skills, self-reliant, sound judgement, technical aptitude, willing to train and work away from home.

Relevant Subjects

Design and technology, Engineering, English, ICT/Computer studies, Mathematics, Physics, Science

Further Information

Careers at Sea - www.careersatsea.org

Careers in the Marine Environment (IMAREST) - www.imarest.org

Full Ahead Newsletter (quarterly) (The Merchant Navy Association) - www.mna.org.uk

Merchant Navy Career Opportunities - www.careersatsea.org

Merchant Navy Careers Handbook (Beauforts Projects) - www.offshore-jobs.co.uk/sea/

Addresses

British Shipping
Carthusian Court, 12 Carthusian Street, London EC1M 6EZ
Phone: +44 (0)20 7417 2800
Web: www.british-shipping.org

Glasgow College of Nautical Studies
21 Thistle Street, Glasgow G5 9XB
Phone: +44 (0)141 565 2500
Web: www.gcns.ac.uk/

Institute of Marine Engineering, Science and Technology (IMarEST)
80 Coleman Street, London EC2R 5BJ
Phone: +44 (0)20 7382 2600
Web: www.imarest.org

Marine Society & Sea Cadets
202 Lambeth Road, London SE1 7JW
Phone: +44 (0)20 7654 7000
Web: www.ms-sc.org

Maritime and Coastguard Agency (MCA)
Spring Place, 105 Commercial Road, Southampton, Hampshire SO15 1EG
Phone: +44 (0)2380 329 308
Web: www.mcga.gov.uk

Maritime Skills Alliance
1 Hillside, Beckingham, Lincoln LN5 0RQ
Web: www.maritimeskills.org

Merchant Navy Association
9 Saxon Way Caistor, Market Rasen, Lincolnshire LN7 6SG
Phone: +44 (0)1472 851130
Web: www.mna.org.uk

Merchant Navy Training Board (MNTB)
Carthusian Court, 12 Carthusian Street, London EC1M 6EZ
Phone: +44 (0)20 7417 2800
Web: www.mntb.org.uk

Royal Navy - Royal Fleet Auxiliary (RFA) Service
Royal Fleet Auxiliary Recruitment Office, Captain Naval Recruitment HQ, Room G-13, Building 1/080, Jago Road, HMNB Portsmouth, Hampshire PO1 3LU
Phone: 0845 60 40 520 (UK only)
Web: www.royalnavy.mod.uk

Scottish Qualifications Authority (SQA)
The Optima Building 58 Robertson Street, Glasgow G2 8DQ
Phone: 0845 279 1000
Web: www.sqa.org.uk/sqa/41328.html

Ship Safe Training Group
The Precinct, Rochester, Kent ME1 1SR
Phone: +44 (0)1634 820 820
Web: www.sstg.org

Trinity House
Trinity House Merchant Navy Scholarship Scheme c/o Chiltern Maritime Ltd Aycliffe Business Centre Archcliffe Road, Dover, Kent CT17 9EL
Phone: +44 (0)1304 212610
Web: www.trinityhouse.co.uk

Similar Jobs

Engineer: Marine, Marine Engineering Technician, Merchant Navy Electro-technical Officer, Merchant Navy Engine-room Rating, Royal Marines Officer, Royal Navy Officer

Merchant Navy Engine-room Rating

CRCI:Transport and Logistics
CLCI:YAL — Job Band: 2 to 3

Job Description

Engine-room ratings are responsible for the everyday running of the machinery in the engine room of a ship or tanker. They oil, grease and help to repair and maintain the machinery and engines. Help to take care of the electrical and safety systems, such as air-conditioning. Monitor instruments under the direction of the ship's officers and may give out engineering stores. On smaller ships, ratings take on a share of deck duties and general maintenance work.

Work Details

Life on board is a 24 hr a day operation, seven days a week, all year. Your work is divided into shifts, called watches, which are typically four hours on watch, followed by eight hours off watch. Busier times require you to work six hours on watch and six off watch. Some ratings travel worldwide and need to be away from home for long periods. Others, on ferries, travel shorter distances and are away from home less, or not at all. Leave time is usually generous.

You have to cope with rough seas and working in all weathers. Your work environment may be cramped and you have to cope with kneeling and bending down. The work is noisy and quite dirty. There is a risk of accidents at sea or with equipment. You wear a boiler suit or a uniform.

Qualification

- **England, Wales and Northern Ireland**

Band 2: For entry: some GCSEs including maths, a science subject, preferably physics, and English or equivalent qualifications.

Band 3: For some training schemes: 3-4 GCSEs (A*-D) including maths, English and a science, preferably physics, or equivalent qualifications.

- **Scotland**

Band 2: For entry: at least three S grades including maths, a science subject, preferably physics, and English or similar qualifications.

Band 3: For marine apprenticeship: at least 3-4 S grades (1-4) including maths, English and a science, preferably physics, or similar qualifications.

Adult Qualifications

Entry or re-entry is possible, especially for those with previous mechanical or electrical engineering experience or qualifications. Contact individual shipping companies for information on their policy.

Work Experience

Relevant work or voluntary experience is always useful and can improve your chances in application for entry to this career. Experience of mechanical or engineering work is very useful. Fitness is important for entry to the merchant navy, so evidence of and an interest in keeping fit is helpful.

Entry and Training

You must be sponsored by a shipping company before you can start training and take an entrance test that may include testing your practical ability. Most employers prefer entrants aged between 16-18. Training is combined with time at a nautical college followed by a period of practical training at sea. During training you take courses in firefighting, sea survival and first aid.

With seagoing experience and further training you can gain the DfT (Department for Transport) certificate of competency Class 3-4. Engine-room ratings need a special conversion course to enable them to become an engineering officer. Merchant Navy ratings employed by the Royal Fleet Auxiliary, which supplies the Royal Navy, are also trained to operate defensive weapons and may have to work in emergencies, conflicts or war. The Merchant Navy Training Board approves the education and training framework for the merchant navy. See the website for details of all training opportunities.

In Scotland there is an Intermediate 1 Skills for Work course in uniformed and emergency services which introduces students to careers the Merchant Navy. Contact the Scottish Qualifications Authority for details.

Mature entrants may have some difficulty in entering the Merchant Navy as a trainee rating, however, an exception may be made if you have technical engineering skills and experience.

Opportunities and Pay
Engine-room ratings are employed mainly by cargo or container shipping companies, ferry companies or offshore oil industry supply companies and the Royal Fleet Auxiliary. There is a clear promotion structure. With experience and certificates of competency at the correct levels, you can become a chief petty officer or a third officer.

Trainee allowances are in the range £5k-£8k a year while training but living expenses are covered. A qualified junior rating earns between £20k-£22k and the most experienced ratings can earn £25k a year. Tax-free earnings can apply on long voyages out of the country. Your employer pays for food and accommodation when you are at sea, and some travel costs. Ratings spending long periods at sea may have generous leave.

Health
You must be fit and healthy and you have to pass a medical. You must have near perfect eyesight, without glasses or lenses, and normal colour vision.

Skills and Qualities
able to get on with all kinds of people, able to work both on your own and in a team, adaptable, attention to detail, hard working, reliable, willing to train and work away from home

Relevant Subjects
Design and technology, Engineering, Mathematics, Physics

Further Information
Careers at Sea - www.careersatsea.org

Chamber of Shipping: Careers (Chamber of Shipping) - www.british-shipping.org/careers/

Full Ahead Newsletter (quarterly) (The Merchant Navy Association) - www.mna.org.uk

Merchant Navy Career Opportunities - www.careersatsea.org

Merchant Navy Careers Handbook (Beauforts Projects) - www.offshore-jobs.co.uk/sea/

Addresses
British Shipping
Carthusian Court, 12 Carthusian Street, London EC1M 6EZ
Phone: +44 (0)20 7417 2800
Web: www.british-shipping.org

Marine Society & Sea Cadets
202 Lambeth Road, London SE1 7JW
Phone: +44 (0)20 7654 7000
Web: www.ms-sc.org

Maritime and Coastguard Agency (MCA)
Spring Place, 105 Commercial Road, Southampton, Hampshire SO15 1EG
Phone: +44 (0)2380 329 308
Web: www.mcga.gov.uk

Merchant Navy Association
9 Saxon Way Caistor, Market Rasen, Lincolnshire LN7 6SG
Phone: +44 (0)1472 851130
Web: www.mna.org.uk

Merchant Navy Training Board (MNTB)
Carthusian Court, 12 Carthusian Street, London EC1M 6EZ
Phone: +44 (0)20 7417 2800
Web: www.mntb.org.uk

Scottish Qualifications Authority (SQA)
The Optima Building 58 Robertson Street, Glasgow G2 8DQ
Phone: 0845 279 1000
Web: www.sqa.org.uk/sqa/41328.html

Ship Safe Training Group
The Precinct, Rochester, Kent ME1 1SR
Phone: +44 (0)1634 820 820
Web: www.sstg.org

Similar Jobs
Merchant Navy Deck Rating, Merchant Navy Deck/Navigating Officer, Merchant Navy Engineering Officer, Royal Navy Rating

Messaging Administrator
also known as: E-Mail Administrator, Mail Server Administrator

CRCI:Computers and IT
CLCI:CAV Job Band: 3 to 5

Job Description
Messaging administrators are the communications experts who design, plan and implement servers dedicated to e-mail, instant messaging, voice mail, and other methods of communication. Administrators monitor and report on the functioning of servers as well as design and implement disaster recovery and security solutions. May also plan upgrades and the migration of data to new hardware.

Work Details
You work 37-40 hrs a week, Monday to Friday, though you must be prepared to work longer to meet deadlines. May be required to be on call to deal with emergencies. Many hours are spent sitting at a computer. The work is normally office based, but if working for a large organisation, you may be required to travel between sites. Sometimes you may work on your own, but generally you work closely with other professional colleagues.

Qualification
• England, Wales and Northern Ireland
Band 3: For entry to jobs, HNC or a relevant Diploma, usually at least 4 GCSEs (A*-C) including English and maths, and preferably ICT, or equivalent.

Band 4: For HND, Diploma of Higher Education or foundation degree: 1-2 A levels and some GCSEs (A*-C) usually including English, ICT and maths, or equivalent.

Band 5: For degree courses: 2-3 A levels, with at least one in maths or physics, and some GCSEs (A*-C) usually including English and maths, or equivalent. Exact requirements depend on the degree you take.

• Scotland
Band 3: For entry to jobs, usually at least four S grades (1-3) including English, maths and preferably ICT, or similar.

Band 4: For entry to SQA higher national and professional development awards, usually 2-3 H grades and some S grades (1-3), including English, ICT and maths, or similar qualifications.

Band 5: For entry to a degree course: 3-5 H grades, with at least one in maths or physics, and some S grades (1-3) including maths and English, or similar qualifications. Exact requirements depend on the degree you take.

Degree Information
Subjects such as network computing and related subjects, software engineering, mathematical sciences, information systems/technology, computer science or artificial intelligence may be preferred by employers. The Information Technology Management for Business degree (see e-skills UK) is designed in partnership with some of the biggest employers in the IT industry. Systems and control engineering, physics and electronic engineering may also be acceptable. Postgraduate courses are available for science or mathematics graduates.

Adult Qualifications
Mature applicants may not need the standard entry requirements for higher education courses, particularly if your previous experience is relevant or if you show ability to study at the appropriate level. Access or foundation courses give adults without qualifications a route onto degree courses.

Work Experience

Employers or colleges and universities may prefer candidates who have relevant work or voluntary experience. This can include any form of computer-based work such as network or IT support, programming or hardware or software specialisms. Any internships or work placements that you can do while studying are a valuable introduction to the IT industry and enable you to make an informed career choice.

Other schemes, such as 'A Year in Industry', enable those who expect good A levels/H grades and intend to go to university the opportunity to spend a salaried year with a company to gain valuable work experience.

Entry and Training

Entry is possible with a range of qualifications, though most employers look for knowledge and experience of using the relevant computer applications and operating systems. You may have to take a practical aptitude test and you also need good customer service skills or technical support experience for this job. Some employers offer 4-6 weeks' intensive training covering in-house procedures, installations and programs. Others may specify a degree or national/higher national qualification, such as a BTEC national certificate/diploma in computing (networking or systems support).

It is important to keep up to date with new software and hardware developments throughout your career. Training is ongoing via in-house courses, intensive online courses, attendance at a local college, or by short courses run by manufacturers or independent training organisations. Depending on the infrastructure used within the organisation, popular IT industry-recognised qualifications for this role include those relating to Microsoft Exchange Server and Active Directory, Blackberry administration or IBM Lotus Domino.

A computing entry-level qualification is the CompTIA A+ which offers alternative validation paths for specific job environments. You can also gain specific qualifications such as the Microsoft Certified Systems Engineer (MCNE). Training for these courses is typically through short courses at accredited training centres.

A Diploma/Welsh Baccalaureate in IT is available for 14-19 year olds and may be run in your area. It has been designed in partnership with universities and employers. E-skills also offers an internship. Students are placed for a period of employment within an organisation, enabling them to develop valuable business and IT skills. Contact e-skills for details. Relevant S/NVQs for ICT practitioners and professionals are available at levels 1-4 and the S/NVQ for IT users has been developed as part of a project involving a full review of the National Occupational Standards for IT users.

Training programmes, including apprenticeship schemes in IT and Telecoms, may be available in your area for entry to this job. An ICT higher apprenticeship is available through e-skills. This combines an apprenticeship with a foundation degree and can lead to a full honours degree. There are partnerships with colleges and universities throughout the UK. The Open University offers courses in computing and maths leading to a computing degree. There are no formal entry requirements and you study through distance learning. Full or part-time foundation degrees in network computing and other IT subjects are also available.

Mature applicants may encounter some difficulty unless equipped with a good level of IT training and relevant business experience. You usually need at least 2 years experience working in an IT support environment before taking on this role. There may be government training opportunities in your area and you can also gain recognition of previous experience through Accreditation of Prior Learning (APL) or by working towards relevant S/NVQs. Contact your local careers office, Jobcentre Plus, Next Step service, or Learning and Skills Council (LSC)/Local Enterprise Company (LEC) for details of all training opportunities and schemes.

Opportunities and Pay

There has been a large growth in the development of messaging over the last few years, with global communications growing in all major businesses. There are opportunities for messaging administrators across the UK in all industry sectors, including commerce, education, finance, public utilities, the health sector, armed forces, the media, or local/central government departments.

There is demand for people with the right technical skills, and good interpersonal skills. You can also work in IT training, in technical writing or work freelance for an agency. Promotion to senior or management posts, information security or systems architecture is possible and there are also opportunities to work as a self-employed consultant or contractor. Work may be available overseas.

Pay varies depending on location and type of company. A graduate entrant can earn £20k-£25k, rising to £30k-£40k with experience. Some can earn more than this. Profit-sharing, performance-related pay or a bonus payment may be additional to your basic salary.

Skills and Qualities

able to explain clearly, analytical skills, clear-thinking, good communication skills, good organisational skills, logical, perseverance, problem-solving skills, specialist IT skills, technical aptitude

Relevant Subjects

Design and technology, English, ICT/Computer studies, Mathematics, Physics, Science

Further Information

AGCAS: Information Technology (Job Sector Briefing) (AGCAS) - www.prospects.ac.uk

Computer Weekly (Reed Business Information) - www.computerweekly.com

Computing Technology Industry Association (CompTIA) - www.comptia.org

Diplomas (Foundation, Higher and Advanced) - http://yp.direct.gov.uk/diplomas

e-skills UK - sector skills council for business and information technology - www.e-skills.com

Inside Careers Guide: Information Technology - www.insidecareers.co.uk

Real Life Guide to Information & Communications Technology (Trotman) - www.trotman.co.uk

Skills Framework for the Information Age (SFIA) (SFIA Foundation) - www.sfia.org.uk

Welsh Baccalaureate - www.wbq.org.uk

▶Working in computers & IT (2010) (Babcock Lifeskills) - www.babcock-lifeskills.com/

Year in Industry (Engineering Development Trust) - www.yini.org.uk

Addresses

British Computer Society (BCS)
First Floor, Block D North Star House North Star Avenue, Swindon, Wiltshire SN2 1FA
Phone: +44 (0)845 300 4417
Web: www.bcs.org

Institute for the Management of Information Systems (IMIS)
5 Kingfisher House, New Mill Road, Orpington, Kent BR5 3QG
Phone: +44 (0)700 002 3456
Web: www.imis.org.uk

Similar Jobs

IT Applications Developer, IT Systems Developer, Network Administrator, Network Manager, Telecommunications Technician

Metallurgist

CRCI:Science, Mathematics and Statistics
CLCI:QOS Job Band: 5

Job Description

Metallurgists study the properties of metals and use this to process, produce and apply use of metals effectively. They study the alloying and treatment of metals and non-ferrous metals such as aluminium, steel, iron and nickel and are involved in their various uses in manufacturing and also in the processes of their extraction from ores. Some metallurgists develop and test new metals and alloys, others study new applications for existing ones. May be involved in the investigation of corrosion in bridges or oil/gas platforms or of suspected metallurgical failures in accidents that include aircraft, cars and trains.

Metallurgists may work with high technology equipment including sophisticated microscopes, computers and digital cameras. They are often involved in design, analysis, quality control, production or technical sales, or in information work, teaching and pure research. Also write and produce reports and documents, and may write operational or quality manuals.

Work Details

Usually work a basic 39 hr week; Monday to Friday, in an office or industrial premises, laboratory or workshop. If you are involved in a production industry you may be expected to work shifts. May use portable testing equipment outdoors in the field. You work in a team with other scientists, technologists and technicians. Depending on your post, you may be responsible for analysis and testing, product development, production schedules or quality control. Protective clothing is often worn.

Qualification

- **England, Wales and Northern Ireland**

Band 5: For degree courses: 2-3 A levels including maths, physics and preferably chemistry and some GCSEs (A*-C) usually including English, science and maths, or equivalent qualifications. Exact requirements depend on the degree you take.

- **Scotland**

Band 5: For degree courses: 3-5 H grades including maths, physics and preferably chemistry and some S grades (1-3), usually including English, science and maths, or similar. Exact entry requirements depend on the degree you take.

Degree Information

A degree in metallurgy is sometimes preferred but degrees in materials science/technology, polymer chemistry or materials engineering are usually acceptable. Subjects that provide a useful background include physics, chemistry and some engineering disciplines.

Adult Qualifications

A formal qualification, preferably a relevant degree, is usually required. Scientific and mathematical knowledge must be up to date. Entry requirements may be relaxed for adults applying for higher education courses. Relevant Open University courses are available and many colleges offer Access to science courses for mature students. A foundation year prior to the start of a science degree/ HND may be available at some HE institutions for those applicants who do not meet the traditional science entry requirements.

Work Experience

Universities and employers may prefer candidates who have relevant work or voluntary experience. Ideally you shadow or work with somebody who currently is involved in the industry but alternatively, obtaining general experience which can help you gain or improve such skills as team working, communication and IT is also useful.

Entry and Training

Usually your training is by practical experience after obtaining a degree. First degree courses can be full time, part time or sandwich and usually last 3-4 years. A range of courses are on offer and you should select one with an appropriate content for the type of area in which you wish to work. Many companies provide accredited graduate training programmes or specialised in-house training based on practical experience.

Membership of a professional body can be attained by a combination of academic qualifications and practical experience. The two main professional institutions for metallurgists are the Institute of Cast Metals Engineers (ICME) and the Institute of Materials, Minerals & Mining (IOM3). Professional membership can also lead to registration as a chartered engineer (CEng) or incorporated engineer (IEng).

Mature applicants with experience as a technician in the ferrous/ non-ferrous metals industry may have an advantage. You may be able to study part time for some courses. The Worshipful Company of Founders may offer grants for those wishing to study metallurgy/ materials science and the Engineering and Physical Sciences Research Council may also offer funding for postgraduate study and research.

Opportunities and Pay

Jobs are available throughout the UK and also abroad. Around 7,000 metallurgists are employed in the UK mainly in the metal industry by companies that manufacture iron, steel and different alloys. Some work in government departments or academic research institutions. Those with fluency in another language have an advantage in finding work overseas. Opportunities for metallurgists are currently very good, particularly if you want to work in production, quality control, sales or marketing.

Pay varies depending on location and employer. Starting salaries for graduates are around £20k rising to £30k-£35k a year with experience. Top earners with chartered engineer status can earn £37k-£50k a year.

Health

You should have normal colour vision. You may be expected to have no skin or respiratory problems.

Skills and Qualities

able to communicate effectively, accurate, analytical skills, aptitude for maths and science, logical, methodical, observant, resourceful, scientific approach, specialist IT skills

Relevant Subjects

Chemistry, Design and technology, Engineering, English, ICT/ Computer studies, Mathematics, Physics, Science

Further Information

AGCAS: Engineering (Job Sector Briefing) (AGCAS) - www.prospects.ac.uk

Foundry Trade Journal (monthly) (Institute of Cast Metals Engineers) - www.foundrytradejournal.com

Historical Metallurgy Society (2 x yr) (Historical Metallurgy Society) - www.hist-met.org

Open University - www.open.ac.uk

▶Working in science (2007) (Babcock Lifeskills) - www.babcock-lifeskills.com/

Addresses

Engineering and Physical Sciences Research Council (EPSRC)
Polaris House North Star Avenue, Swindon, Wiltshire SN2 1ET
Phone: +44(0)1793 444 100
Web: www.epsrc.ac.uk

Institute of Cast Metals Engineers (ICME)
National Metalforming Centre, 47 Birmingham Road,
West Bromwich, West Midlands B70 6PY
Phone: +44 (0)121 601 6979
Web: www.icme.org.uk

Institute of Materials, Minerals and Mining (IOM3)
1 Carlton House Terrace, London SW1Y 5DB
Phone: +44 (0)20 7451 7300
Web: www.iom3.org

Worshipful Company of Founders
Old Estate Office Fifty One, Firle, Lewes, West Sussex BN8 6LQ
Phone: +44 (0)1273 858 700
Web: www.foundersco.org.uk

Similar Jobs

Chemist: Analytical, Engineer: Minerals & Mining, Materials Scientist/Engineer, NDT Technician/Engineer, Surveyor: Minerals & Waste Management

Meteorologist

CRCI:Science, Mathematics and Statistics
CLCI:QOL Job Band: 5

Job Description

Meteorologists study all aspects of land, sea and the upper atmosphere to analyse and forecast weather conditions and climate changes. They use data collected through weather stations, radar, satellite images and remote sensors. Then analyse the information, usually running sophisticated computer models to interpret the results. They provide findings and predictions for the press, TV and radio, and organisations including the oil industry, public services, agricultural industry, defence, and air travel/transport.

Some carry out research on the dynamics, physical processes and chemical effects of the atmosphere and its impact on our environment. Also liaise with professional colleagues and clients nationally and internationally.

Work Details

Usually work a basic 37-40 hr week, though may be required to work shifts if providing weather forecasts that are required around the clock. Research work is typically nine to five, Monday to Friday though some additional hours may be required at times, including weekends.

Work in an office is common or possibly on site taking readings. Some work in remote locations or on military operations. You usually work in a team. Much of the work is carried out using computers, satellite trackers and other high-tech equipment. Depending on your post you can be responsible for gathering accurate data, presenting findings clearly, providing interpretations and giving sound advice.

Qualification

- **England, Wales and Northern Ireland**

Band 5: For degree courses: 2-3 A levels and some GCSEs (A*-C) usually including English and maths, or equivalent. Exact requirements depend on the degree you take.

- **Scotland**

Band 5: For degree courses: 3-5 H grades and some S grades (1-3), usually including English and maths, or similar qualifications. Exact requirements depend on the degree you take.

Degree Information

Relevant degrees include meteorology, meteorology with oceanography, physics with atmospheric physics, maths with meteorology, geophysical sciences, environmental earth sciences, physics/maths with ocean and climate studies, ocean science (with geography). Contact the Royal Meteorological Society for details of accredited courses. Sometimes other physical or environmental sciences may allow entry, provided applicants have a good background in maths and physics.

Postgraduate courses are available at a number of universities including Birmingham and Reading.

Adult Qualifications

Entry might be possible through an Access or foundation course or through an Open University degree. A foundation year may be available at some universities for those without the required science qualifications or equivalent.

Work Experience

Employers or colleges/universities may prefer candidates who have relevant work or voluntary experience. This can include office administration, data collection or inputting, work involving research and recording skills and jobs of a scientific background such as laboratory work. The Met Office offers a number of placements to undergraduates including one to three-month vacation summer placements. There may also be one-week work experience opportunities for pupils in Yr 10-11.

Entry and Training

Most meteorologists first complete a relevant degree or postgraduate qualification. A number of sciences are suitable and care should be taken to choose an appropriate course with a high maths and physics content. Research jobs require a postgraduate qualification in meteorology, climatology or atmospheric sciences.

Training is by practical work experience and by short courses in-house, or residential courses at the Meteorological (Met) Office College. Meteorologists employed by the Met Office must meet civil service nationality requirements. Whilst training, it may be possible to gain an S/NVQ in meteorological observing at level 3 and weather forecasting at level 4. Sponsorship may be available for meteorologists wishing to undertake an MSc/MPhil or PhD.

The Met Office has a mobile met unit (MMU) which is attached to the Royal Air Force (RAF). It is possible to enter this unit with a minimum of 2 A levels, which should include maths and/or physics. The Royal Navy also offers specialist training for officers and ratings at its hydrographic, meteorological and oceanographic training group (HMTG) in Devonport.

The Royal Meteorological Society (RMS) offers chartered status (CMet) to those who satisfy the Society as to their training, experience and competence. The RMS, together with the Society for the Environment, also offers chartered status (CEnv) to those meteorologists who have an environmental background and degree. You need to follow a programme of continuing professional development (CPD) to update your knowledge.

Mature entrants are welcome provided they have experience/qualifications in a related scientific field and up-to-date scientific knowledge. There may be opportunities for funding from the Natural Environmental Research Council (NERC) for postgraduate study and research.

Opportunities and Pay

Most meteorologists are employed by the Met Office. Others work in operational, applied or research work with some opportunities in other branches of the civil service, in universities and research councils and in the service industries supplying oil, gas, water and electricity. A few experienced meteorologists are self-employed consultants. There is a clear promotion structure in civil service posts, but less opportunity in other organisations. This is a small and highly competitive profession and you should be prepared to move to other locations or work in different areas of meteorology to advance your career.

In many jobs your pay is on a nationally agreed scale and can include an extra allowance for shift work. Salaries for graduates working for the Met Office start at £18.5k a year, with experienced meteorologists earning £32k-£46k a year. The most senior meteorologists can earn up over £70k a year.

Health

This job may require a medical test on entry.

Skills and Qualities
able to communicate effectively, accurate, analytical skills, aptitude for maths and science, good reasoning power, observant, problem-solving skills, research skills, scientific approach, specialist IT skills

Relevant Subjects
Chemistry, English, Geography, ICT/Computer studies, Mathematics, Physics, Science

Further Information
Careers in Meteorology (Royal Meteorological Society) - www.rmets.org/activities/careers/index.php

Hydrographic, Meteorological & Oceanographic Training Group (HMTG) (The Royal Navy) - www.royalnavy.mod.uk/

Mobile Met Unit (MMU) (The Met Office) - www.metoffice.gov.uk/defence/mmu.html

New Scientist (weekly) (Reed) - www.newscientist.com

Open University - www.open.ac.uk

SEMTA - sector skills council for science, engineering and manufacturing technologies - www.semta.org.uk

Weather (Royal Meteorological Society, monthly) (Wiley) - www.rmets.org/activities/publications/index.php

▶Working in science (2007) (Babcock Lifeskills) - www.babcock-lifeskills.com/

▶Working in space (2010) (Babcock Lifeskills) - www.babcock-lifeskills.com/

Addresses
Met Office
FitzRoy Road, Exeter, Devon EX1 3PB
Phone: 0870 900 0100 (UK only)
Web: www.metoffice.gov.uk

Natural Environment Research Council (NERC)
Polaris House North Star Avenue, Swindon, Wiltshire SN2 1EU
Phone: +44 (0)1793 411 500
Web: www.nerc.ac.uk

Royal Meteorological Society (RMetS)
104 Oxford Road, Reading, Berkshire RG1 7LL
Phone: +44 (0)118 956 8500
Web: www.rmets.org

Society for the Environment (SocEnv)
The Old School House, 212 Long Street, Atherstone, Warwickshire CV9 1AH
Phone: +44 (0)845 337 2951
Web: www.socenv.org.uk

Similar Jobs
Astronomer, Ecologist, Geologist, Geophysicist, Oceanographer, Physicist

Meter Reader
also known as: Electricity/Gas Meter Reader, Water Meter Reader

CRCI:Retail Sales and Customer Services
CLCI:RAK Job Band: 1 to 2

Job Description
Meter readers visit a customer's home or workplace, to collect (read) information from gas, electricity or water meters. They drive or walk around an area to read meters, at agreed intervals, in houses, shops, offices, agricultural and industrial premises. May have to check meters that are outside the building. Take readings from a meter box, checking the numbers on either a digital or dial card meter. Record the figures on special sheets, or by keying them into a hand-held computer terminal, or through a signal reading from a small radio transmitter.

Meter readers answer questions from customers relating to the meter and the energy supply. May leave a form for customers to fill in or direct customers to an enquiry line for further help. They check a meter to see that it is working correctly and has not been tampered with or damaged, and report any faults. May visit the main office at the start and end of the day to get an updated work schedule and return any completed forms. If using a hand-held computer to collect readings, work schedules are up and downloaded remotely so there is no need to visit the office each day.

Work Details
Usually work a basic 35-40 hr week, Monday to Friday, though may be required to work on a Saturday and early evenings at times. You travel around an area and spend a lot of time on your own. The job requires you to be active most of the time and involves walking and a lot of driving. Part of the job requires you to be outside in all types of weather. A uniform is usually required and a company/ personal identification badge is provided.

Qualification
- **England, Wales and Northern Ireland**

Band 1: No formal qualifications are usually needed.

Band 2: Some employers prefer applicants to have GCSEs (A*-C) including English and maths, or equivalent.

- **Scotland**

Band 1: No formal qualifications are usually needed.

Band 2: Some employers prefer applicants to have S grades (1-3) including English and maths, or similar.

Adult Qualifications
General secondary education is expected, and employers may ask for you to have basic ability in English and maths.

Work Experience
Relevant work or voluntary experience can equip you with skills that you can use in the future and add to your CV. There are often opportunities available for voluntary work which can provide experience of working with people.

Entry and Training
Most entrants are 18 or older. Training is on the job working with a more experienced colleague before working on your own. Short training courses are available that provide the specific skills needed to operate hand-held meter terminals. Training also includes record keeping, customer care issues, tariff systems and different types of meters, as well as company information and prospects. You are also made aware of any health and safety regulations that need to be observed.

This job requires you to have good references, a Criminal Records Bureau (CRB)/Disclosure Scotland check and a clean driving licence. S/NVQs are available including utilities metering operations at level 2. S/NVQs in customer service and health and safety are also relevant. Contact the CABWI Awarding Body for details of all vocational qualifications and approved training centres. Relevant training programmes, including apprenticeship schemes, may be available in your area.

Mature applicants with previous work experience in areas that include customer services, or with relevant practical/technical experience, may have an advantage.

Opportunities and Pay
Jobs are available in towns, cities and most areas throughout the UK. Your employer is usually a national energy supplier or utility company, either gas, electricity or water. Promotion to more senior posts, such as supervisor, is possible after gaining experience. Some meter readers may be employed by specialist firms that provide meters for the utility companies. Some are self-employed and work under contract to individual companies.

Pay varies depending on location and employer, but starting salaries are around £13k-£18k a year. Higher earners make around £20k a year. Performance bonus payments may be available in additional to a salary.

Health
This job requires good health and a good level of stamina.

Skills and Qualities
able to report accurately, able to work well on your own, common sense, enjoy working outdoors, friendly, good interpersonal skills, good organisational skills, prepared to do repetitive tasks, reliable, trustworthy

Further Information
AGCAS: Energy & Utilities (Job Sector briefing) (AGCAS) - www.prospects.ac.uk

Apprenticeship Schemes (National Apprenticeship Service) - www.apprenticeships.org.uk

Apprenticeships in Scotland (Careers Info Scotland) - www.apprenticeshipsinscotland.com/about/

Energy & Utility Skills - sector skills council for gas, power, waste management & water industries - www.euskills.co.uk

Scottish Water - www.scottishwater.co.uk/

Summitskills - sector skills council for building services engineering - www.summitskills.org.uk

Addresses
CABWI Awarding Body
1 Queen Anne's Gate, London SW1H 9BT
Phone: +44 (0)20 7957 4523
Web: www.cabwi.co.uk
OFWAT
Centre City Tower 7 Hill Street, Birmingham B5 4UA
Phone: +44 (0)121 644 7500
Web: www.ofwat.gov.uk

Similar Jobs
Courier, Market Research Interviewer, Postal Worker, Vending Machine Operative

Microbiologist
CRCI:Science, Mathematics and Statistics
CLCI:QOD
Job Band: 5

Job Description
Microbiologists study the biology and chemistry of micro-organisms such as viruses, bacteria, algae or fungi and their practical application. They are involved in diverse areas that include medicine and pharmaceuticals, the environment, agriculture, education and industry. May work on aspects of healthcare, researching drugs and vaccines, including devising new treatments for diabetes, cancer, malaria or HIV/Aids. Some microbiologists are involved in developing and testing new products such as antibiotics or the improvement of existing ones.

Microbiologists may work on the treatment and diagnosis of infections such as outbreaks of food poisoning. Increasingly, they are involved in genetic engineering. Some microbiologists are responsible for managing a team of biomedical scientists and other support staff such as medical technologists, laboratory assistants and clerical assistants. Some take up research or lecturing posts.

Work Details
Usually work a 35-39 hr week, Monday to Friday, in a laboratory, university, college, hospital, industrial premises or an office. Some employment may require you to begin work early or finish late. Weekend and shift work is also possible. Depending on your job you are responsible for devising experiments, analysing data, presenting reports and also supervising staff. This work normally requires a high degree of accuracy and sometimes having to cope with the sight of blood.

In some jobs you may be monitoring quality standards or checking production schedules. Conditions may sometimes be unpleasant. There is a risk of infection. A white coat/overall and protective gloves is worn for some tasks.

Qualification
- **England, Wales and Northern Ireland**

Band 5: For degree courses: 2-3 A levels including chemistry and preferably biology, maths or physics and some GCSEs (A*-C) usually including English, maths and a science, or equivalent. Exact requirements depend on the degree you take.

- **Scotland**

Band 5: For degree courses: 3-5 H grades including chemistry and preferably biology, physics or maths and some S grades (1-3), usually including English, maths and science, or similar. Exact requirements depend on the degree you take.

Degree Information
A degree in microbiology is generally preferred, but bacteriology, biology, biochemistry, cell/molecular biology, genetics and marine biology may also be acceptable subjects. Most other biological science degrees give useful background knowledge.

Adult Qualifications
A degree or equivalent qualification and up-to-date scientific knowledge are essential. Course requirements may be relaxed for mature applicants. A foundation year prior to the start of a science degree/HND may be available at some HE institutions for those applicants who do not have the traditional science qualifications. Check with universities for information. Some colleges run refresher courses for scientists wishing to return to work following a career break.

Work Experience
Universities and employers may prefer candidates who have relevant work or voluntary experience. Work experience in a hospital, a relevant university department or an industrial or commercial laboratory is ideal, but if it proves difficult to gain this exact experience, any work with a scientific background is attractive to employers and admissions tutors. Contact the appropriate professional societies for information regarding summer work placements.

Entry and Training
Training is through practical experience after obtaining a degree or postgraduate qualification in microbiology or an appropriate biological science. There are many courses available and you should choose carefully depending on the type of area in which you wish to work. Degree courses can be full time or sandwich and last 3-4 years. There may be relevant foundation degree courses that lead onto degree courses. There are also some relevant postgraduate courses that give you an advantage for some posts.

You need to keep up to date throughout your career through continuing professional development (CPD). This might be through seminars, conferences and meetings for specialised groups.

Mature applicants with experience gained in industrial work placements are welcomed by many employers. The Biotechnology and Biological Sciences Research Council (BBSRC) and Medical Research Council (MRC) may offer funding for postgraduate study and research.

Opportunities and Pay
You can be employed by a company that manufactures pharmaceuticals and agrochemicals, or the food and drink industry, to work in research and development, or in production. Some microbiologists work in the civil service, the NHS, water companies, or in environmental health. Others work in research

institutes and universities. Some specialise in areas such as molecular biology, virology or bacteriology. There is a steady demand for microbiologists in industry, around 550 bioscience companies employ 40,000 people in the UK, many of whom are microbiologists. There are also opportunities in management, marketing and teaching. Many opportunities are in south-east England.

Salaries vary depending on location, employer and experience, but average around £26k a year. Qualified microbiologists earn between £30k-£38k but high earners can make up to £62k a year.

Health
This job requires good colour vision and good eyesight.

Skills and Qualities
able to explain clearly, accurate, analytical skills, attention to detail, IT skills, methodical, observant, patient, perseverance, problem-solving skills

Relevant Subjects
Biology, Chemistry, English, ICT/Computer studies, Mathematics, Physics, Science

Further Information
International Journal of Systematic & Evolutionary Microbiology (monthly) (Society for General Microbiology (SGM)) - www.sgmjournals.org

Journal of General Virology (monthly) (Society for General Microbiology (SGM)) - http://vir.sgmjournals.org/

Journal of Medical Microbiology (monthly) (Society for General Microbiology (SGM)) - www.sgmjournals.org

Microbiology (monthly) (The Society for General Microbiology) http://mic.sgmjournals.org/

NHS Careers (NHS Careers) - www.nhscareers.nhs.uk

Women into Science, Engineering & Construction - www.wisecampaign.org.uk

▶ Working in science (2007) (Babcock Lifeskills) - www.babcock-lifeskills.com/

Addresses
Biotechnology and Biological Sciences Research Council (BBSRC)
Polaris House North Star Avenue, Swindon, Wiltshire SN2 1UH
Phone: +44 (0)1793 413 200
Web: www.bbsrc.ac.uk

Health Protection Agency (HPA)
7th Floor , Holborn Gate, 330 High Holborn, London WC1V 7PP
Phone: +44 (0)20 7759 2700
Web: www.hpa.org.uk

Health Protection Scotland
Clifton House, Clifton Place, Glasgow G3 7LN
Phone: +44 (0)141 300 1100
Web: www.hps.scot.nhs.uk

Medical Research Council (MRC)
20 Park Crescent, London W1B 1AL
Phone: +44 (0)20 7636 5422
Web: www.mrc.ac.uk

Society for General Microbiology (SGM)
Marlborough House Basingstoke Road Spencers Wood, Reading, Berkshire RG7 1AG
Phone: +44 (0)118 988 1800
Web: www.sgm.ac.uk

Society of Biology
9 Red Lion Court, London EC4A 3EF
Phone: +44 (0)20 7936 5900
Web: http://societyofbiology.org/home

Similar Jobs
Biochemist, Biologist, Biotechnologist, Chemist: Analytical, Teacher: Biological Sciences, Toxicologist

Midwife
also known as: Neonatal Nurse

CRCI:Healthcare
CLCI:JAD Job Band: 5

Job Description
Registered midwives (RMs) offer individual care and support to an expectant mother from confirmation of her pregnancy, through to birth of the baby, and for at least ten days after the baby is born (postnatal care). They monitor the health of the baby and expectant mother throughout the pregnancy and provide advice for mothers and fathers on parenting and health education. RMs deliver babies in normal births and also assist with difficult births.

RMs are experienced in offering support, counselling and advice to parents who are distressed through reasons such as a baby born with a disability, or a stillbirth. Some midwives are known as neonatal nurses and specialise in looking after babies that are born prematurely or who are unwell. Some midwives provide pre-conception advice. They work closely in a multi-disciplinary care team which includes obstetricians and other health professionals. May work in a maternity hospital or in the community. Can specialise in areas such as women's health or public health and help to run specialist services including teenage pregnancy clinics.

Work Details
Usually work a basic 37.5 hr week and are expected to work shifts and be on-call at times. You work in a hospital, clinic or local health centre and you visit patients in their homes. You need to be aware of the cultural lifestyle of an individual patient and be sensitive to their attitude to childbirth. Work can be pressurised at times and requires coping with the sight of blood. You need to be physically fit and have to cope with standing for many hours. A uniform is provided and you also wear protective clothing when necessary.

Qualification

- **England, Wales and Northern Ireland**

Band 5: For degree courses in midwifery: 2-3 A levels, usually including a science subject and some GCSEs (A*-C) usually including English and maths, or equivalent. Exact requirements depend on the degree you take.

- **Scotland**

Band 5: For degree courses in midwifery: 3-5 H grades, usually including a science subject and some S grades (1-3), usually including English and maths, or similar qualifications. Exact requirements depend on the degree you take.

Degree Information
The graduate entry route is with a degree in midwifery that does not require any previous nursing experience. Graduates with relevant degrees in biological sciences, behavioural sciences, physical sciences or health related subjects, can take shortened postgraduate training and follow this with training to qualify as a midwife.

Adult Qualifications
Universities and colleges of nursing vary in their entry requirements for adult entry. Applicants who do not have the usual academic qualifications may be able to take an entrance test. A relevant vocational qualification at level 3 is usually acceptable. Specific modular course credits from the Open University may also be used, or a specific Access to higher education course for entry to nursing/midwifery training. Some universities have special entry standards for mature applicants. Check with individual institutions for details.

Work Experience
Work experience gives you an insight into what you enjoy and do not enjoy about a job or working environment, as well as the opportunity to acquire new skills. It also provides valuable information to add to your CV and improves any course application and future employment prospects. Colleges, employers and universities may prefer candidates who show enthusiasm and commitment to the work by gaining experience of working with people in a helping capacity. This can be with babies and children or with people of all ages where communication skills can be improved.

Entry and Training
There are two routes to becoming a registered midwife. Direct entry training to registration as a midwife involves a three or four-year degree course in midwifery. Alternatively, you can complete registered adult nurse training followed by a further 18 month pre-registration midwifery programme. Contact the Health Learning and Skills advice line for details.

The degree in midwifery does not require previous nursing experience or training to enter the course. You combine academic study, including physiology, anatomy and sociology, with supervised midwifery practice in maternity services. Completion of the programme leads to registration with the Nursing and Midwifery Council (NMC) as a qualified midwife and is the preferred training route. Tuition fees are usually paid by the NHS. Check with NHS Careers for details of various schemes of training.

After registration midwives can train to specialise in areas such as family planning, teaching, research and the intensive care of newborn babies (neonatal). All midwives have a named supervisor of midwives to assist them with updating their knowledge and to ensure their practice is safe.

You need to maintain a professional portfolio throughout your career as a midwife and to notify your intention to practise with the NMC every three years. Post-registration education and practice (PREP) is the set of standards to develop your knowledge and competence and keep up to date. This includes a minimum of 35 hours' study activity every three years.

Mature entrants with life experience are welcomed for training as midwives. Registered, experienced adult nurses can take an 18 month midwifery programme. 'Return to Practice' programmes are also available for midwives wanting to return to work after a break of some years. Contact NHS Careers, the Royal College Midwives or your local NHS Trust for details.

Opportunities and Pay
There are over 40,000 midwives in the UK, most are employed by the NHS but some work for private hospitals, nursing homes, clinics or the armed forces. You can go on to become a clinical specialist in home birthing, breast feeding advice, labour ward supervision or ante-natal screening. You can also choose to go into teaching or research within a healthcare setting or a university. There are job possibilities in Europe and the developing world, with options for voluntary work, but some countries expect midwives to have the dual registered nurse/midwife qualifications. Experienced midwives can apply to become midwife consultants with the NHS. Some become self-employed and work as independent midwives.

Minimum pay levels are set nationally, but generally registered midwives working for the NHS are paid in accordance with their band. This ranges from £21k-£28k a year, rising to £34k and then up to £40k as a midwife team manager. Midwife consultants can earn up to £67k a year.

Health
This job requires a medical test on entry and good general fitness.

Skills and Qualities
able to cope with emergencies, able to inspire confidence, able to take responsibility, able to work both on your own and in a team, good communication skills, good listening skills, not squeamish, patient, perceptive, reassuring

Relevant Subjects
Biology, Chemistry, English, Health and social care, Psychology, Science

Further Information
AGCAS: Health (Job Sector Briefing) (AGCAS) - www.prospects.ac.uk

Health Learning and Skills Advice Line - http://hlas.careers-advice.org/

Independent Midwives Association - www.independentmidwives.org.uk

Midwives (bi-monthly) (Royal College of Midwives (RCM)) - www.rcm.org.uk/magazines/

NHS Careers (NHS Careers) - www.nhscareers.nhs.uk

NHS Careers Scotland - www.infoscotland.com/nhs

NHS Careers Wales - www.wales.nhs.uk

Open University - www.open.ac.uk

Royal College of Nursing Wales - www.rcn.org.uk/aboutus/wales

Addresses
Centralised Applications to Nursing and Midwifery Training House (CATCH)
Thistle House, 91 Haymarket Terrace, Edinburgh EH12 5HD
Phone: +44 (0)131 313 8000
Web: www.nes.scot.nhs.uk/

National Leadership & Innovation Agency for Healthcare (NLIAH: Wales)
Innovation House, Bridgend Road, Llanharan CF72 9RP
Phone: +44 (0)1443 233333
Web: www.wales.nhs.uk/sitesplus/829/

Nursing and Midwifery Council (NMC)
23 Portland Place, London W1B 1PZ
Phone: +44 (0)20 7333 9333
Web: www.nmc-uk.org

Royal College of Midwives
15 Mansfield Street, London W1G 9NH
Phone: +44 (0)20 7312 3535
Web: www.rcm.org.uk

School of Nursing and Midwifery
Queens University Belfast, Medical Biology Centre,
97 Lisburn Road BT9 7BL
Phone: +44 (0)28 9097 2233
Web: www.qub.ac.uk/nur

Similar Jobs
Health Visitor, Nurse: Adult, Nurse: Children, Nurse: District, Nursery Worker

Ministry of Defence Police Constable
also known as: MOD Police Constable

CRCI:Security and Armed Forces

CLCI:MAB — Job Band: 1 to 5

Job Description
Ministry of defence police constables focus on providing a major armed guarding role at defence sites requiring a high level of security, including the guarding of Britain's nuclear deterrent. They provide uniformed policing, especially at the larger Ministry of Defence (MOD) bases, ensuring that the families based there are protected. Safeguard perimeters, protect against sabotage of assets and against terrorist threats. Perform similar tasks to other police forces across the UK.

MOD police constables run several specialist units including CID, fraud squad, marine units, anti-terrorist search units, personnel protection units for VIPs, dog handling units, and special escort groups for the safe and secure transport of nuclear materials.

Work Details
You work around 40 hours each week, but this is in shifts as needed for operations. Cover needs to be available 24 hours a day, including weekends and public holidays. Overtime is sometimes required. You also have to be able to cope with emergencies and may have to deal with some distressing sights.

Work can be indoors or outside in all weather conditions. You may have to do a lot of walking or standing for many hours, and the working environment can sometimes be potentially dangerous. All officers are provided with a uniform. Depending on your duties you may also have to wear some protective clothing.

Qualification
All applicants to the MOD police service undergo selection that includes numeracy, literacy, and core skills such as communication, problem solving and decision making. Some entrants have no formal educational requirements, while others may have GCSEs, A levels or higher education qualifications.

Degree Information
A degree in any discipline is acceptable for entry, though there are many specific degrees and foundation degrees in subjects that include criminal justice, criminology and policing studies.

Adult Qualifications
There are no formal educational requirements for recruitment to the MOD police service and applications from adults are welcomed.

Work Experience
Relevant work or voluntary experience is always useful and can improve your chances in application for entry to this career/job. Any experience that provides an opportunity to work with people/the public is useful. Experience in any type of security work is also an advantage, but this is unlikely to be possible before the age of 18.

Entry and Training
There are no set entry requirements, but you have to be over 18 and pass selection tests, including one for physical fitness and the ability to handle firearms. You must also be a British citizen and have lived in the UK for over five years. Criminal convictions are not necessarily a bar to entry, but must be disclosed on application and each case is judged on its merits. There are a number of useful qualifications that you can take before applying, including S/NVQs in public services, BTEC/SQA diplomas in public services and higher education qualifications in police studies and criminology. The diploma/welsh baccalaureate in public services may be a useful background for this career but check entry requirements carefully.

Selection is in several stages and can take over six months from first application to appointment. First of all you have to complete a competency-based application form. If successful you then attend a two day assessment at Wethersfield in Essex, consisting of exercises and physical fitness checks. This is followed by references and security checks. Once appointed, the probation period is two years, 14 weeks at Wethersfield and the remainder at Aldermaston in Berkshire, where you work under the guidance of a trained constable. At this time you have the chance to visit the specialist units and must pass your firearms training.

You have to serve three years once you have completed probation. During this time you are likely to undergo further training for your choice of specialist unit, some on the job and some by attendance on a special training course.

Mature entrants with experience of work in the police force, in security or with the armed forces have an advantage.

Opportunities and Pay
There are over 3,400 officers in the Ministry of Defence police, and these are based all over the UK at one of 100 sites, from Culdrose in Cornwall to the Clyde in Scotland. The force is divided into five divisional commands, with headquarters located at York, Aldershot, Aldermaston, Foxhill and Clyde Naval Base. Entrants start as constables and can work their way through the ranks to sergeant, inspector, chief inspector and senior ranks such as chief superintendent and chief constable.

Trainees starting salary is around £22k a year, which rises to over £23k on completion of 33 weeks' training. After the full two years' probation, salary increases to over £25k a year. The top pay for a constable is £33k a year. Overtime pay is also available and there are some additional location allowances.

Health
You have to pass a medical test and a very strenuous fitness test. You have to meet certain eyesight standards, though you are allowed to wear glasses or lenses. You usually have to have normal colour vision.

Skills and Qualities
able to cope under pressure, able to stay vigilant in periods of inactivity, alert, aptitude for teamwork, good communication skills, non-judgemental, quick reactions, self confident, self-disciplined

Relevant Subjects
Law, Psychology

Further Information
AGCAS: Armed Forces & Emergency Services (Job Sector Briefing) (AGCAS) - www.prospects.ac.uk

Diplomas (Foundation, Higher and Advanced) - http://yp.direct.gov.uk/diplomas

Ministry of Defence (MoD) (MOD) - www.mod.uk

Skills for Justice - sector skills council for the UK justice system - www.skillsforjustice.com

Welsh Baccalaureate - www.wbq.org.uk

▶ Working in police, fire & security (2009) (Babcock Lifeskills) - www.babcock-lifeskills.com/

Addresses
Ministry of Defence Police Recruitment Department
Building 66 MDP Wethersfield, Braintree, Essex CM7 4AZ
Web: www.mod.police.uk

Similar Jobs
Civil Service Immigration Officer, Close Protection Officer/Bodyguard, Police Community Support Officer (England & Wales), Police Officer, Prison Officer, Private Investigator

Model
also known as: Fashion Model, Photographic Model

CRCI:Marketing and Advertising
CLCI:OT Job Band: 1 to 3

Job Description
Models work at live modelling at fashion shows, exhibitions and promotional events, such as motor trade events, or photographic modelling in a studio, or on location at home or abroad. They are photographed or filmed to promote a particular product or brand so models also do non-fashion photographic work. This may include promotion for beauty, electronics, food and drink products.

Photographic models appear in mail order catalogues, adverts in magazines, newspapers and brochures, on television, and on posters. Press advertising and editorial photographic models advertise a range of products for the face, hair or hands. The main areas of fashion modelling are 'house' or catwalk models, who display clothes to potential customers. Some models are employed by fashion houses, but most work freelance through modelling agencies.

Work Details
Modelling sessions can be in different locations, such as studios and fashion houses, at exhibitions and on location. Location work can involve some travel, and may be overseas. You may have to work long, irregular hours, spend a lot of time waiting for photographers to set up shots and must be able to cope with working in hot conditions under camera lights. Models may also have to work in cold conditions outside, filming next summer's clothes in the middle of winter, for example.

Qualification
To enter modelling, looks and personality are more important than qualifications. However, a good general education is desirable. You need to be accepted by a reputable modelling agency to enter this career.

Adult Qualifications
Without relevant experience it may be difficult to begin a modelling career as a mature person.

Work Experience
Entry to modelling is highly competitive and looks and personality are usually more important than experience. However, any work experience you can gain that helps you find out about the modelling industry is useful. As well as part-time modelling experience, work in beauty or hair salons is useful.

Entry and Training
The fashion photography industry has strict height requirements for entry. The Association of Model Agents (AMA) recommends that female models need to be at least 1.73 metres (5ft 8in) tall, though many top models are taller. Male models are usually at least 1.83 metres (6ft) tall. Most agencies also specify figure shape; the AMA gives recommendations about this on their website. Some models begin part time and at a young age although the AMA discourages this. Those wishing to pursue this career can take a training course at a private modelling college before trying to find work. However, this is not essential and these courses can be expensive.

It is helpful to build up a portfolio but portfolios of photographs are expensive and usually unnecessary when initially applying to agencies, as they are experienced enough to tell whether or not you are likely to be successful. It is essential to join a reputable agency. Contact the AMA or Alba Model Information for details. A good agency gives guidance and sometimes training on skincare, grooming, dress, exercise, health and diet. Many models learn through practical experience, and then develop a portfolio giving details and photographs of their work and experience.

Some colleges offer courses, which may be helpful for models who seek a career after modelling, such as a fashion styling, hair and make-up, or fashion styling, marketing and management. The London College of Fashion offers a range of relevant courses.

Mature entrants usually have previous and successful modelling experience, and although the industry may prefer young people, there has been a move towards the older person in some areas of marketing/advertising.

Opportunities and Pay
This is usually a short career of 10-15 years, with very few jobs for models over 30. Modelling has no career structure and is a highly competitive area of work, with limited job security. You may have to find other work to support yourself between modelling jobs. Lately, there has been an increase in the demand for male models. The majority of modelling agencies are in London, although there are a few in other major cities. Prospects of travel can vary according to the modelling contract.

Former models can work in, run or teach in modelling agencies/schools, become fashion consultants or go into fashion journalism, television presenting or acting. Modelling is not a skill that is easily transferred to any other profession so retiring models need to learn new skills to change career.

Most models work on a freelance basis, are paid for any modelling sessions they do and the agency takes around 20% of each job in commission. Some are employed by wholesale or retail fashion houses. You may not have a regular supply of work, and the amount you earn can vary a great deal so you need to manage your money well. Successful models and 'supermodels' can be very highly paid, but most models do not make a lot of money. A day on the catwalk generally earns a model anything from £100 to £3k a day.

Earnings are often very low when starting out, maybe around £50 a day but rates can be up to £500-£1k a day if you are successful. Only a few models are very successful. Working for a fashion house as a young model, you may earn £15k-£20k a year initially. Commercial photographic modelling can be more highly paid, at around £100-£250 an hour once you are experienced.

Health
You have to have a good figure for this type of work. Some agencies specify the exact measurements they require models to have. This job requires good general fitness and stamina. It is important to take care of your body and also make sure that you get enough sleep.

Skills and Qualities
able to withstand criticism, adaptable, ambitious, even tempered, fashion conscious, good personal grooming, outgoing personality, patient, punctual, stamina

Relevant Subjects
Art and Design, Performing arts

Further Information
Behind the Scenes: Fashion (Trotman 2009) - www.trotman.co.uk

Information Source for the Modeling Industry - www.e-model.net

▶Working in fashion & clothing (2008) (Babcock Lifeskills) - www.babcock-lifeskills.com/

▶Working in hairdressing & beauty (2009) (Babcock Lifeskills) - www.babcock-lifeskills.com/

Addresses
Alba Model Information
PO Box 588, Southport PR8 9BR
Web: www.albamodelinformation.com

Association of Model Agents (AMA)
11-29 Fashion Street, London E1 6PX
Phone: +44 (0)20 7422 0699
Web: www.associationofmodelagents.org/

London College of Fashion
20 John Princes Street, London W1G 0BJ
Phone: +44 (0)20 7514 7344
Web: www.fashion.arts.ac.uk

Similar Jobs
Actor, Beauty Consultant, Fashion Designer, Film/TV & Theatre Make-Up Artist, Hairdresser, Photographer

Model Maker
CRCI:Design, Arts and Crafts
CLCI:EZ — Job Band: 3 to 5

Job Description
Model makers work from instructions and drawings and use materials like wood, card, metal, plastic and plaster to 'mock up' how products or buildings might look, or to test new designs. They usually work in architectural, product or visual effects design and provide an essential link between a designer and production in a variety of work areas. They use computer-aided design (CAD) as well as 2D digital drawing and image skills, or 3D digital models and animation, to demonstrate a design.

Model Maker

Model makers in the film industry may be responsible for creating models for the visual special effects unit, props for the props master, or specific items to enhance a set and its scenery. Models are also used for testing prototypes of new products such as cars, mobile phones or for testing planes in wind tunnels, incorporating engineering and electronics. They liaise closely with production designers to provide the desired effect and appearance of the model.

Some model makers specialise in models to show how a product or development (such as a building, ship or a car) might look. They may be required to build a miniature structure to scale and fine detail, such as a nine-inch high replica of the Tower of London. Can produce models for scaled-down versions of towns, shopping centres, hotels, etc, or produce enlargements to show, for example, biological cell structure. May make models with moving parts that require basic engineering techniques or electronics.

Architects often use models to demonstrate their plans, and models are also used in TV and advertising, in museums and exhibitions, where artefacts (items of archaeological interest) are displayed, or when reproducing historical events for an exhibition. Works with other designers and professionals, including civil engineers, architects and town planners. Model makers need to have knowledge of relevant health and safety legislation and procedures.

Work Details

Usually work a basic 39 hr week; Monday to Friday in a workshop, studio or laboratory. The hours can be long and irregular, including some evenings and weekends, particularly when meeting deadlines for clients or working in film and TV. You need excellent hand skills for this intricate and painstaking work and must pay attention to fine detail. You may spend a lot of time standing.

Some of the materials used, such as adhesives, can produce fumes, and these can be dangerous and unpleasant. There can be a lot of dust. Protective clothing, including eye protection, mask and gloves, may be necessary at times.

Qualification

There are no set qualifications, but most model makers complete a relevant HND or degree. A portfolio of work is usually required.

• England, Wales and Northern Ireland

Band 3: For entry to jobs, HNC in design or a relevant Diploma, usually at least 4 GCSEs (A*-C) including English and maths, or equivalent.

Band 4: For HND in design or 3D design, Diploma of Higher Education or foundation degree: 1-2 A levels and some GCSEs (A*-C) usually including English and maths, or equivalent.

Band 5: For degree courses: 2-3 A levels and some GCSEs (A*-C) usually including English and maths, or equivalent. Exact requirements depend on the degree you take.

• Scotland

Band 3: For entry: usually at least four S grades (1-3), including English and maths, or similar.

Band 4: For entry to SQA higher national award in an art and design subject and professional development awards, usually 2-3 H grades and some S grades (1-3), including English and maths, or similar qualifications.

Band 5: For degree courses: 3-5 H grades and some S grades (1-3), usually including English and maths, or similar qualifications. Exact entry requirements depend on the degree you take.

Degree Information

Relevant first degrees include: 3D design, 3D visualisation, modelmaking, model design and model effects, animation and design, and model design and special effects.

Adult Qualifications

Mature candidates applying for courses may be accepted without the standard entry qualifications, but an outstanding portfolio is needed. Access or foundation courses are also available and may lead to entry to higher education.

Work Experience

Entry to this job is competitive and it is important that you try to do some relevant work or voluntary experience before applying. Model making as a hobby is an advantage. Consider work experience in an architect's office, or any area where two or three-dimensional products or set design is involved. Experience in engineering, electronics and carpentry can also be useful.

Entry and Training

It is possible to become a model maker without formal qualifications, and some teach themselves or take evening classes. There are ABC level 3 courses available in software skills for 3D modelling, model making and presentation and digital modelling for architectural environments. Most entrants take college courses, often a one-year foundation studies course in art and design, or a national/higher national level course, in subjects like 3D design or model making. A Diploma/Welsh Baccalaureate may be available in your area in creative and media and may provide a route onto higher education courses. You may also be able to do a design apprenticeship. A good portfolio of work is needed for entry to art and design courses.

Usually students take a foundation studies course before taking a three-year degree course. In Scotland, degree courses last for four years, the first year is general, before specialising in a particular area of art and design. The diploma in creative and media is available at foundation, higher and advanced levels and may provide a route onto higher education courses. Relevant foundation degrees in product or 3D design are available in some areas. An S/NVQ in engineering, woodworking, pattern and model making is also available at level 3.

Professional organisations such as Design and Art Direction (D&AD) provide details of ongoing training and development opportunities, offer a graduate placement scheme and run design awards. The Institution of Engineering Designers operates a membership scheme and offers workshops and events for model makers.

Mature applicants with experience in technical drawing, engineering, electronics, metalwork or woodwork, may have an advantage. You are expected to have a comprehensive portfolio of work that reflects your ability. Foundation studies courses are available in art and design to prepare mature entrants for application to higher education courses, and to help build a portfolio. You may also be able to take part in a design apprenticeship.

Opportunities and Pay

Most model makers are self-employed and gain contract work from advertising firms, museums, architects, designers, engineers, film and TV companies. A few are employed in the motor industry, aeronautical companies, central and local government, shipbuilding and civil engineering. Most opportunities are in London and the south of England. Few model makers have full-time employment and most are self employed working on a project-by-project basis. Some go on to become pattern makers making models of machine parts or work as sculptors or carpenters.

The increasing use of computer-generated imagery (CGI) for designing and cutting model parts and overseas competition is reducing the need for traditionally made models in some areas of work.

As most are self-employed, earnings vary hugely. A model maker may earn around £19k a year, rising to £23k-£30k a year with experience. The most successful can earn up to £36k.

Health

You need good eyesight, with glasses or lenses if necessary, and normal colour vision. Dust and skin irritants, such as glue and other adhesives, can cause or aggravate allergies.

Skills and Qualities
able to work well on your own, attention to detail, eye for visual effect, good communication skills, good presentation skills, manual dexterity, patient, specialist IT skills, technical aptitude

Relevant Subjects
Art and Design, Design and technology, Engineering, ICT/ Computer studies, Mathematics, Physics, Science

Further Information
Chartered Society of Designers (Chartered Society of Designers) - www.csd.org.uk

Creative & Cultural Skills - sector skills council for advertising, crafts, cultural heritage, design, literature, music, performing & visual arts - www.ccskills.org.uk

Design Uncovered (Trotman 2009) - www.trotman.co.uk

Diplomas (Foundation, Higher and Advanced) - http://yp.direct.gov.uk/diplomas

▶Working in art & design (2009) (Babcock Lifeskills) - www.babcock-lifeskills.com/

Addresses
British Design & Art Direction (D&AD)
9 Graphite Square Vauxhall Walk, London SE11 5EE
Phone: +44 (0)20 7840 1111
Web: www.dandad.org

Institution of Engineering Designers (IED)
Courtleigh, Westbury Leigh, Wiltshire BA13 3TA
Phone: +44 (0)1373 822 801
Web: www.ied.org.uk

Similar Jobs
Animator, Architectural Technologist, Carpenter/Joiner, Engineer: Design, Film/TV & Theatre Set/Stage Designer, Toymaker

Montessori Teacher

CRCI:Education and Training
CLCI:FAB Job Band: 3 to 5

Job Description
Teachers trained for this job follow the Montessori method of teaching and learning to help and encourage children mainly from 0 to 6 years old to develop at their own pace. The Montessori Method combines a philosophy with a practical approach. The main idea of this teaching is that every child should be treated with respect and given freedom to develop within the limits of a carefully structured environment. Helps children to learn everyday skills such as dressing, washing and using good manners. Also covers a wide range of subjects including mathematics, reading and writing, history, geography, science, biology, music, art, drama and literature. May also teach basic Gaelic or Welsh depending on the location of the school.

Teaches in small classes; observes and gives individual attention to each child, thereby helping them develop as an individual. Encourages children's natural desire to learn by giving them opportunities to engage in particular activities. Gives guidance, help and support to each child when needed. Teaches children to become independent and self-assured.

Work Details
Usually works a five and a half hour day, which includes classroom time and work outside in the playground, though hours may vary. Some Montessori teachers are involved in after school care from around 2-6pm. Additional time is required for preparing classes and attendance at meetings. Work is with nursery school children, or younger children and babies in a crhche. There is contact with parents/carers and with other professional colleagues.

This job requires plenty of creativity and imagination and you should be able to relate well to young children. You are responsible for supporting learners. Most jobs require you to be on your feet all day. Working with young children is very demanding but rewarding work.

Qualification
There are normally no specific entry requirements for training courses, but a good standard of education is required. Most course applicants are interviewed to assess their suitability for the work.

• England, Wales and Northern Ireland
Band 3: For entry to jobs, HNC or a relevant Diploma, usually at least 4 GCSEs (A*-C) including English and maths, or equivalent.

Band 4: For HND, Diploma of Higher Education or foundation degree: 1-2 A levels and some GCSEs (A*-C) usually including English and maths, or equivalent.

Band 5: For a degree prior to Montessori training: 2-3 A levels and some GCSEs (A*-C) usually including English and maths, or equivalent.

• Scotland
Band 3: For entry to jobs, usually at least four S grades (1-3) including English or maths, or similar.

Band 4: For entry to SQA higher national and professional development awards, usually 2-3 H grades and some S grades (1-3), including English and maths, or similar qualifications.

Band 5: For degree course prior to entry to Montessori training: 3-5 H grades and some S grades (1-3), usually including English, or similar.

Degree Information
There is no specific degree needed but many graduate entrants have a BEd degree in nursery and lower primary education.

Adult Qualifications
All entrants to the training are interviewed and assessed for suitability. A good standard of secondary education is required, but there are no specific entry requirements especially for more mature applicants with relevant experience.

Work Experience
Applicants to Montessori training courses are advised to show evidence of their interest in and commitment to teaching by having gained experience of working with children, preferably as a voluntary helper in a school. Other relevant experience could be working with young people in a youth club or other youth groups such as cubs or brownies.

Entry and Training
To teach at a Montessori school in the UK, you need to be trained in the Montessori methods and achieve the international diploma in early childhood teaching (level 4). This qualifies you to work with children from two and a half to six years old. Courses are available at the Maria Montessori Institute, the Montessori Centre International and several other centres throughout the country. Courses can be studied one year full time, two years part time and by distance learning. There is also a new foundation degree available in Montessori - Early Years Practice. All those working with children are required to have a Criminal Records Bureau (CRB)/Disclosure Scotland check.

A list of centres and courses are available on the Montessori Centre International website and on the early years and playwork qualifications database, run by the Children's Workforce Development Council. There is also a one term part-time certificate course which is aimed at teaching assistants, working with children aged two and a half to six years old run by the Maria Montessori Institute.

Two-year full-time courses cost around £7k. Some scholarships may be available from the Montessori St Nicholas Charity. In order to work in a state nursery or teach in a state primary school, a further qualification in early childhood care and education, such as that offered by CACHE, or a full teaching qualification is required. See the Nursery School Teacher and Teacher: Primary articles for full details.

Part-time and distance-learning courses are available in Montessori teaching methods, and are particularly appropriate for those with experience of nursing or teaching, or those who want to return to work after bringing up children.

Opportunities and Pay

Once trained, Montessori teachers work in one of the over 600 private Montessori schools and nurseries throughout the UK. With experience and both the early childhood and infant and toddler diplomas, it may be possible to open your own nursery or Montessori school.

Pay varies depending on location and employer. Starting salaries for those who have just completed training is around £12k-£16k a year. For those who go on to open their own school, income depends on the success of the school and the number of children attending.

Health

This job may require a medical test on entry.

Skills and Qualities

able to communicate effectively, able to motivate others, able to stimulate learners, calm, caring, creative flair, enthusiastic, good listening skills, patient, sense of humour

Relevant Subjects

Art and Design, Biology, English, Geography, History, Mathematics, Music, Performing arts, Physical education and sport, Psychology, Religious studies, Science, Sociology

Further Information

Montessori Centre International - www.montessori.org.uk

Montessori International (quarterly) (Montessori St Nicholas) - www.montessori.org.uk/magazine-and-jobs

Addresses

CACHE: Council for Awards in Children's Care & Education
Apex House, 81 Camp Road, St Albans AL1 5GB
Phone: 0845 347 2123 (UK only)
Web: www.cache.org.uk

Children's Workforce Development Council (CWDC)
2nd Floor, City Exchange, 11 Albion Street, Leeds LS1 5ES
Phone: +44 (0)113 244 6311
Web: www.cwdcouncil.org.uk

Maria Montessori Institute (MMI)
26 Lyndhurst Gardens, London NW3 5NW
Phone: +44 (0)20 7435 3646
Web: www.mariamontessori.org

Montessori Centre
18 Balderton Street, London W1K 6TG
Phone: +44 (0)20 7493 8300
Web: www.montessori.org.uk

Similar Jobs

Nursery Worker, Pre-school Supervisor/Worker, Teacher: Early Years, Teacher: Primary School, Teaching Assistant

Motorsport Professional

also known as: Racing Driver

CRCI:Leisure, Sport and Tourism
CLCI:GAG

Job Band: 1 to 4

Job Description

Motorsport professionals drive cars or ride motorbikes in competitive races and are often sponsored by industry. They usually work in a team with a manager. A special licence is needed to enter rallies or races. Before a race they must study the course and plan how to drive around it. They work closely with designers and mechanics, and help to look after the vehicle. They must also keep physically fit and active. Successful motorsport professionals may appear in media advertisements to promote the product of their sponsor. Some also give interviews to television and radio stations.

Work Details

Usually works irregular hours, often involving early starts and late finishes. You have to travel a good deal and spend nights away from home, especially if you have to race abroad. Most races are at weekends but during the week you have to spend a lot of time training or practising. You work in a team with a team manager, mechanics, sponsors and other racers. Work can be very pressurised and you are expected to be highly competitive. It is noisy at race tracks and practice circuits.

There is a risk of injury and burns if you crash, although fireproof clothing has been greatly improved and safety specifications and regulations tightened. You have to be extremely fit physically to survive long, often gruelling races.

Qualification

No specific educational qualifications are needed, though a good standard of education is helpful. You have to be extremely good at motor racing. Many professional sportsmen and women study for qualifications, including at degree level, to pursue either a related or different career when their professional competitive career is over.

Adult Qualifications

Entry is only possible for younger adults because of the training and fitness requirements.

Work Experience

Entry to this career is highly competitive. Work experience in competitive sports driving may be very hard to gain. Health and safety issues may also limit what you can do under the age of 18. It is, however, useful to gain experience in related jobs in motor sport, such as engineering work at a manufacturers or garage, help with organising races or work as a marshal.

There are opportunities for volunteering, for example the Wales Rally GB needs around 3000 volunteer officials and marshals. Volunteers in Motorsport is a Motor Sports Association (MSA) backed initiative to help more people become involved with the sport. The scheme can help you to get involved in areas such as marshalling, racing, timekeeping, technical, or other roles. Check the website for further details.

Entry and Training

There are few vacancies and this area of work is highly competitive. Most people start by joining their local motor club and gaining experience of driving and racing locally and nationally. See the Motor Sports Association (MSA) club directory to find your local club and more about getting started in racing. Amateur experience and race success is required for entry to this job. Those who demonstrate potential can enter this profession through a competitive scholarship that is offered by major motorsport racing schools.

You must be at least 16 years old to compete. Amateur racing drivers need to compete regularly and have a club membership card. A competition licence is needed to compete in more professional races. This is available at four levels: Clubman, National B, National A and International. Beginners need a National B licence. The MSA issues these licences and has overall responsibility for the profession. Before you can apply for your first race licence, you must complete a half-day MSA course for novice drivers. Courses are only run by members of the Association of Racing Drivers' Schools (ARDS). Some exemptions apply. Contact the MSA for further details. Speedway racers have to hold an Auto-Cycle Union licence to compete.

This is a short career and there is limited job security. For information on getting into all areas of motorsport, including tips from experts, see the GoMotorsport website.

Mature entrants are very unlikely to enter this job unless they have competitive and successful driving experience.

Opportunities and Pay

There are few full-time jobs in motor racing and considerable talent is required for success. Even those at the top can be on short-term contracts from the manufacturers. Some drivers find sponsors who are willing to take on the considerable costs and also provide an income. This is dependent on success in races, though if you become a top driver you can expect a very high standard of living. You may also find employment in a related field later in your career, such as coaching, management or promotional work.

In this sport it may be necessary to have another job as your income from racing may be dependent on sponsorship, appearance fees and prize money. It is very hard to summarise the average earnings of a motor sports professional, but generally it ranges from less than £22k to as much as £60k a year. Only those few professionals who are very successful achieve higher earnings.

Health

This job requires excellent fitness and stamina.

Skills and Qualities

aptitude for teamwork, competitive, determined, good concentration level, good co-ordination, quick reactions, resilient, self confident, self-disciplined

Relevant Subjects

Design and technology, Engineering, Physical education and sport, Physics, Science

Further Information

Association of Racing Drivers' Schools - www.ards.co.uk
GoMotorsport - www.gomotorsport.net
RaceTech Magazine (RaceTechMag) - www.racetechmag.com
Volunteers in Motorsport - www.volunteersinmotorsport.co.uk
▶Working in sport & leisure (2010) (Babcock Lifeskills) - www.babcock-lifeskills.com/

Addresses

British Racing Drivers' Club (BRDC)
Silverstone Circuit, Towcester, Northamptonshire NN12 8TN
Phone: +44 (0)1327 850920
Web: www.brdc.co.uk

Motor Sports Association (MSA)
Motor Sports House, Riverside Park, Colnbrook, Berkshire SL3 0HG
Phone: +44 (0)1753 765 000
Web: www.msauk.org

Motorsport Industry Association
Federation House, Stoneleigh Park, Warwickshire CV8 2RF
Phone: +44 (0)2476 692 600
Web: www.the-mia.com

Similar Jobs

Film/TV Stunt Performer, Sports Professional

Museum Assistant/Technician

CRCI:Languages, Information and Culture
CLCI:FAE Job Band: 2

Job Description

Museum assistants help with a range of tasks needed for the display, storage, cataloguing and maintenance of museum exhibits. They welcome museum visitors, provide information and answer questions. The work varies depending on the type and size of museum. May build display stands, hang paintings, move exhibits and pack objects to be sent to other exhibitions. Also help to set up special exhibitions and demonstrations and to store material in a safe, organised way. May offer customer information or give guided tours. With experience and skill, some go on to specialise in helping conservation officers look after collections.

Work Details

Usually works 35-37 hrs a week on a rota basis, that can include working on bank holidays or at the weekend. May have to work longer hours when preparing for the opening of a new exhibition. You work in a museum, usually indoors but sometimes outside, if it is an agricultural or industrial museum site. The job needs you to handle old and valuable objects with great care and responsibility. You spend most of the day on your feet and may have to lift and carry heavy objects. Some employers may ask you to undergo a Criminal Records Bureau/Disclosure Scotland check, especially if you are going to work with children. You may be provided with a uniform.

Qualification

• England, Wales and Northern Ireland

Band 2: For entry to jobs, no minimum qualifications are needed, but it is an advantage to have some GCSEs (A*-C) or equivalent in subjects that include English and maths and maybe science, technical, craft or design subjects.

• Scotland

Band 2: Although academic qualifications are not specified for this job, it is an advantage to have some S grades (1-3) or equivalent in subjects that include English and maths, and maybe science, technical, craft or design subjects.

Adult Qualifications

Some jobs may require relevant experience and qualifications in a trade, such as carpentry or engineering. Formal qualifications in science, technical, craft and design subjects, or equivalent qualifications may also be required.

Work Experience

Any work experience can equip you with skills that you can use in the future and add to your CV. Work experience can either be unpaid or voluntary, or can be holiday or part-time work that you have organised yourself. There are opportunities for voluntary work in a museum or art gallery to gain relevant experience. Check the Museums Association (MA) website for help in finding voluntary opportunities.

Entry and Training

Entrants may have some initial training in engineering or woodworking and have related City & Guilds or trade certificates. Specific museum training is on the job, working with an experienced person. Many museums also run in-service training courses, including areas such as health and safety. S/NVQ level 2 in museums, galleries and heritage and level 3 in cultural heritage operations are available. There are also levels 2 and 3 awards in cultural heritage venue operations.

Training programmes, including apprenticeship schemes in cultural and heritage venue operations, may be available in your area. There is a modern apprenticeship in museum, gallery and heritage operations in Scotland. The Museums, Libraries and

Archives Council has pledged funding for up to 50 apprenticeships in museums over the next two years. Advanced apprenticeships leading to qualification at level 3 can also be a route into higher education.

The Museums Association provides a continuing professional development scheme for those working in museums, and the Institute of Conservation offers a membership scheme.

Mature entry is welcomed particularly for those with relevant experience. Contact your local Connexions or careers office, Jobcentre Plus, Next Step service or Learning and Skills Council (LSC)/Local Enterprise Company (LEC) for details of all training opportunities.

Opportunities and Pay

There are around 2,500 museums in the UK. Jobs are available throughout the country but mainly in towns and cities. You can work for a private, national or local authority museum, or with a heritage group, such as the National Trust. Opportunities for promotion to supervisor and assistant curator are very limited and may depend on whether you are prepared to undergo training or move to another area. There are not many jobs available, but there may be a chance to do some temporary work on a part-time or seasonal short-term contract while waiting for a permanent job. Some museum assistants or technicians move into other aspects of heritage work or into conservation or tourism roles.

Pay depends on where you work and who you work for. Starting salaries are around £14k-£19k, rising with experience to £23k a year. In a senior post you may earn more.

Health

There may be an allergy risk from dust. This job requires good colour vision for certain areas of work. A good general level of fitness is also important.

Skills and Qualities

able to get on with all kinds of people, aptitude for teamwork, attention to detail, customer service skills, flexible approach, good interpersonal skills, interest in cultural heritage, IT skills, methodical, practical skills

Relevant Subjects

Art and Design, Design and technology, History, Mathematics

Further Information

Apprenticeship Schemes (National Apprenticeship Service) - www.apprenticeships.org.uk

Association of Independent Museums (AIM) (AIM) - www.aim-museums.co.uk/

Creative & Cultural Skills - sector skills council for advertising, crafts, cultural heritage, design, literature, music, performing & visual arts - www.ccskills.org.uk

Local Government Careers (Improvement and Development Agency) - www.lgcareers.com/publications/

Museum Journal (monthly) (Museums Association (MA)) - www.museumsassociation.org/mjsubscribe

Museum Practice (quarterly) (Museums Association (MA)) - www.museumsassociation.org/subscribe

Museums' Association Yearbook (Museums' Association)

Museums Galleries Scotland - www.museumsgalleriesscotland.org.uk/

▶Working in cultural heritage (2007) (Babcock Lifeskills) - www.babcock-lifeskills.com/

Addresses

Institute of Conservation (ICON)
1st Floor, Downstream Building 1 London Bridge Road SE1 9BG
Phone: +44 (0)20 7785 3807
Web: www.icon.org.uk

Museums Association (MA)
24 Calvin Street, London E1 6NW
Web: www.museumsassociation.org

Museums, Libraries and Archives Council (MLA)
Grosvenor House, 14 Bennetts Hill, Birmingham B2 5RS
Phone: +44 (0)121 345 7300
Web: www.mla.gov.uk

Northern Ireland Museums Council
6 Crescent Gardens, Belfast BT7 1NS
Phone: +44 (0)28 9055 0215
Web: www.nimc.co.uk

Scottish Museums Council
Museums Galleries Scotland 1 Papermill Wynd,
McDonald Road, Edinburgh EH7 4QL
Phone: +44 (0)131 550 4100
Web: www.museumsgalleriesscotland.org.uk/

Similar Jobs

Carpenter/Joiner, Conservator-Restorer, Library Assistant, Museum/Art Gallery Attendant, Picture Framer, Removals Operative, Taxidermist

Museum/Art Gallery Attendant

also known as: Museum Visitor Services Assistant

CRCI:Languages, Information and Culture
CLCI:FAE Job Band: 1 to 2

Job Description

Museum or art gallery attendants work in a museum or art gallery, helping visitors and making sure the display items are not harmed. Duties depend on the type of museum or art gallery. Tasks can include taking admission money and selling catalogues, postcards, books and other items. Attendants may provide information, answer questions and help people to find their way around the building and exhibition areas. Many have security duties which include checking visitors' bags and the security system. Others help to keep the museum/art gallery clean and tidy. Some attendants also help the curator to set up a display/exhibition, move around the exhibits, and help to pack/unpack items.

May wear an historical costume to represent how people dressed in the past. This is usually needed in 'working' museums that can be indoors or outdoors. Attendants have knowledge of that historical period and are able to answer visitors' questions.

Work Details

Usually works a 37-39 hr week, Monday to Friday, though may need to work on a rota to cover weekends and some evenings, and have time off during the week instead. The job involves informing and helping people and dealing with enquiries. You meet people of all ages and sometimes overseas visitors who do not speak English. Other duties include security and sometimes handling cash. You may have to stand for hours at a time but may find that you have busy and quiet periods. Attendants often wear a uniform provided by the employer.

Qualification

Many employers look for those with an outgoing and welcoming personality rather than formal qualifications.

• England, Wales and Northern Ireland

Band 1: For entry to jobs, no minimum qualifications are needed, but you are expected to have a good level of general education and relevant experience. Some formal/vocational qualifications at any level are useful.

Band 2: For entry to jobs, no minimum qualifications are needed, but it is an advantage to have some GCSEs (A*-C) or equivalent in subjects that include English and maths.

- **Scotland**

Band 1: For entry to jobs, no minimum qualifications are needed, but you are expected to have a good level of general education and relevant experience. Some formal/vocational qualifications at any level are useful.

Band 2: Although academic qualifications are not specified for this job, it is an advantage to have some S grades (1-3) in subjects that include English and maths, or similar.

Adult Qualifications
Generally, you are expected to have relevant experience. A good standard of secondary education is usually required.

Work Experience
Any work experience can equip you with skills that you can use in the future and add to your CV. Work experience can either be unpaid or voluntary or can be holiday or part-time work that you have organised yourself. Some voluntary experience in a museum, gallery or heritage site is useful.

Entry and Training
Training is usually on the job, working with an experienced colleague, learning about the museum's collections and work procedures. Some museums run short, in-service courses on customer care, security, health and safety, and other topics. S/NVQs at levels 2 and 3 in heritage care and visitor services and cultural heritage venue operations are available.

Relevant training programmes, including apprenticeship schemes in cultural and heritage operations, may be available in your area. There is a modern apprenticeship in museum gallery and heritage available in Scotland. Advanced apprenticeships leading to qualification at level 3 can be a route into higher education. The Museums, Libraries and Archives council has pledged funding for up to 50 apprenticeships in museums across England in the next two years.

Mature entrants are welcome and particularly those with related experience, such as security work or experience in tourism or customer services. Government training opportunities, such as apprenticeships, may be available in your area. You can also gain recognition of previous experience through Accreditation of Prior Learning (APL) or by working towards relevant S/NVQs. Contact your local careers office, Jobcentre Plus, Next Step service or Learning and Skills Council (LSC) Local Enterprise Company (LEC) for details of training schemes.

Opportunities and Pay
There is a range of places to work which include national and local museums, commercial galleries and museums or historic houses. Some only employ people during the summer season and it is often possible to work part-time. It can be helpful to work as a volunteer before applying for a full-time job.

Pay depends on who you work for and where you work. Starting salaries are around £15k, rising with experience to £20k a year.

Health
The job requires a good level of stamina and physical fitness.

Skills and Qualities
able to get on with all kinds of people, alert, customer service skills, firm manner, good memory, interest in cultural heritage, observant, patient, trustworthy

Relevant Subjects
History

Further Information
Apprenticeship Schemes (National Apprenticeship Service) - www.apprenticeships.org.uk

Association of Independent Museums (AIM) (AIM) - www.aim-museums.co.uk/

Careers Wales - www.careerswales.com/

Creative & Cultural Skills - sector skills council for advertising, crafts, cultural heritage, design, literature, music, performing & visual arts - www.ccskills.org.uk

Local Government Careers (Improvement and Development Agency) - www.lgcareers.com/publications/

Museum Journal (monthly) (Museums Association (MA)) - www.museumsassociation.org/mjsubscribe

Museums' Association Yearbook (Museums' Association)

Museums Galleries Scotland - www.museumsgalleriesscotland.org.uk/

National Museums and Galleries of Wales - http://nmgw.ac.uk

▶ Working in cultural heritage (2007) (Babcock Lifeskills) - www.babcock-lifeskills.com/

Addresses
Museums, Libraries and Archives Council (MLA)
Grosvenor House, 14 Bennetts Hill, Birmingham B2 5RS
Phone: +44 (0)121 345 7300
Web: www.mla.gov.uk

National Museums of Scotland
Chambers Street, Edinburgh EH1 1JF
Phone: +44 (0)0131 225 7534
Web: www.nms.ac.uk

Northern Ireland Museums Council
6 Crescent Gardens, Belfast BT7 1NS
Phone: +44 (0)28 9055 0215
Web: www.nimc.co.uk

Similar Jobs
Caretaker, Customer Services Adviser, Door Attendant, Library Assistant, Museum Assistant/Technician, Tourist Information Centre Assistant

Museum/Art Gallery Curator

CRCI:Languages, Information and Culture
CLCI:FAE Job Band: 5

Job Description
Curators acquire and manage a collection of historical or artistic objects, or those of archaeological, scientific or general interest. They are responsible for the care, restoration and development of the collections in a museum or art gallery and may have responsibility for a specific part of a collection, sometimes with the title of 'keeper'. They also arrange exhibitions and special displays, increasingly using the latest multi-media techniques. Curators identify and record items, often using a computer and organise loans and new acquisitions. They may conduct research for catalogues and arrange for conservation or restoration when necessary.

This role varies depending on the size and nature of the museum collection or art gallery. Some curators have a significant managerial role, supervising staff, such as junior curators, conservators, attendants and volunteers. May attend meetings and fundraising activities. Also, some curators may be involved in the writing of books and articles for publication, depending on their specialist area of work. They encourage visits for educational purposes, sometimes liaising with schools, and may also give lectures.

Work Details
Usually works around 37 hrs a week, though you may need to work weekends, bank holidays and additional hours at times, such as when setting up a new exhibition. Depending on the kind of post held, you may be responsible for administration, security, supervising staff and sometimes for business transactions. Art

galleries are usually spacious with subdued lighting. In museums, your work environment depends on the type of collections, and some work can be outside.

Some heavy lifting or bending and carrying may be necessary and you need to occasionally climb ladders to retrieve objects or help to hang pictures. Work can be very demanding at times. You may need to travel occasionally so a driving licence may be useful.

Qualification

• England, Wales and Northern Ireland

Band 5: For degree courses: 2-3 A levels and some GCSEs (A*-C) usually including English and maths, or equivalent. Exact requirements depend on the degree you take.

• Scotland

Band 5: For degree courses: 3-5 H grades and some S grades (1-3), including English and maths, or similar qualifications. Exact requirements depend on the degree you take.

Degree Information

A good honours degree in art history/conservation, archive and museum studies, or anthropology is usually required. The following subjects are also useful: visual/fine art, history, archaeology, biology, geology, botany, chemistry, classics, ceramics, information science/management, fashion and textile design. Degrees in heritage conservation, heritage studies or heritage management are also appropriate. Various postgraduate courses are available, including museum studies.

Adult Qualifications

A relevant degree is usually required and specialist knowledge is helpful. Mature applicants should check with individual institutions for entry requirements. Access or foundation courses to higher education may be available for those without the expected qualifications.

Work Experience

Entry to this career is highly competitive and it is essential that you have some relevant work or voluntary experience, especially for entry to a postgraduate course and for prospective employment. Contact the Museums' Association, museums, art galleries and societies for voluntary work opportunities. Evidence of commitment to the work is likely to be required.

Entry and Training

Entrants are usually graduates and many also hold a postgraduate qualification. Most postgraduate courses take 1-3 years (depending on whether they are full or part time) and also include practical experience. The Museums Association (MA) offers relevant training schemes, routes to associateship and continuing professional development. It is important to check that postgraduate courses lead to the Associateship of the Museums Association (AMA). There are a few graduate traineeships available but the competition for these is fierce. It is useful to have knowledge and expertise in a particular area. Relevant voluntary work in a museum, gallery, or a National Trust property can be valuable when applying for posts and for postgraduate study.

There is a museum, gallery and heritage modern apprenticeship available in Scotland and the Museum, Libraries and Archives Council is currently funding apprenticeships in museums across England. Many museum councils, specialist groups, the MA and other training providers, run in-service training programmes, including courses for volunteers. Short courses and S/NVQs are also available from Creative & Cultural Skills. S/NVQs are available at levels 3-5 in cultural heritage, cultural heritage venue operations and cultural heritage management. Relevant foundation degrees are also available.

Mature entrants require relevant qualifications and work experience. Many museums and galleries welcome mature applicants who have business experience, particularly in marketing, fundraising, administration, or event and exhibition management. Those with a relevant degree plus a postgraduate degree, preferably in museum studies or a related subject have an advantage. Postgraduate degrees may be studied full or part time, and through distance learning, if you have relevant work experience.

It is possible to obtain a bursary/award from organisations including the Museums Association and the Arts and Humanities Research Council for postgraduate study.

Opportunities and Pay

This area of work is highly competitive. There are museums and art galleries in large towns and cities throughout the UK, as well as in smaller towns and in rural areas. Employers include local/national museums or art galleries, universities, heritage organisations, independent museums or private commercial companies. The armed services have their own military museums that also employ professional staff. Promotion opportunities are limited, apart from the larger museums/galleries and most people move location to gain promotion. Curators may work overseas, particularly in British Commonwealth countries, Europe and the USA. There is part-time work available. Freelance and consultancy work is becoming more common as curators undertake short-term contracts to work on specific exhibitions.

Salaries are usually related to local authority or civil service rates, but private galleries have different scales often including commission on sales. The pay in museum work is often low compared with related professions. Starting salaries for assistant curators are about £15k-£19k a year. Curators earn from around £22k-£32k, and in senior posts can earn up to £40k a year.

Health

This job may require normal colour vision. It also requires a good level of stamina and physical fitness.

Skills and Qualities

able to motivate others, able to work to a budget, creative flair, excellent communication skills, good interpersonal skills, good organisational skills, information handling skills, interest in cultural heritage, IT skills

Relevant Subjects

Art and Design, Biology, Chemistry, Classical studies, English, Geography, History, Land and Environment, Leisure, travel and tourism, Science

Further Information

Arts and Humanities Research Council (AHRC) - www.ahrc.ac.uk

Association of Independent Museums (AIM) (AIM) - www.aim-museums.co.uk/

Careers Wales - www.careerswales.com/

Creative & Cultural Skills - sector skills council for advertising, crafts, cultural heritage, design, literature, music, performing & visual arts - www.ccskills.org.uk

Local Government Careers (Improvement and Development Agency) - www.lgcareers.com/publications/

Museum Journal (monthly) (Museums Association (MA)) - www.museumsassociation.org/mjsubscribe

Museum Practice (quarterly) (Museums Association (MA)) - www.museumsassociation.org/subscribe

Museums' Association Yearbook (Museums' Association)

Museums Galleries Scotland - www.museumsgalleriesscotland.org.uk/

National Museums and Galleries of Wales http://nmgw.ac.uk

► Working in cultural heritage (2007) (Babcock Lifeskills) - www.babcock-lifeskills.com/

Addresses

Museums Association (MA)
24 Calvin Street, London E1 6NW
Web: www.museumsassociation.org

Museums, Libraries and Archives Council (MLA)
Grosvenor House, 14 Bennetts Hill, Birmingham B2 5RS
Phone: +44 (0)121 345 7300
Web: www.mla.gov.uk

National Museums of Scotland
Chambers Street, Edinburgh EH1 1JF
Phone: +44 (0)131 225 7534
Web: www.nms.ac.uk

National Trust
Heelis, Kemble Drive, Swindon, Wiltshire SN2 2NA
Phone: +44 (0)1793 817400
Web: www.ntjobs.org.uk

Northern Ireland Museums Council
6 Crescent Gardens, Belfast BT7 1NS
Phone: +44 (0)28 9055 0215
Web: www.nimc.co.uk

Similar Jobs

Archaeologist, Archivist, Arts Administrator, Conservator-Restorer, House Steward, Museum Assistant/Technician

Music Composer

also known as: Songwriter

CRCI:Performing Arts
CLCI:GAD Job Band: 2 to 5

Job Description

Music composers create musical compositions, often with lyrics to be interpreted and performed by orchestras, voices, groups of musicians and soloists. They use rhythm, melody and texture and tone in a variety of ways to create a particular style of music. Music styles include classical, rock, soul, rhythm and blues, pop, jazz, funk, blues, swing, big band, country and folk. Composers of pop music are usually known as songwriters.

Music composers write for television, radio, film and theatre and increasingly for computer and hand held games, sound libraries and other media. Changing music technology has led to many new ways for composers to write, record and distribute music and many use computers and synthesizers to help with writing. Composers need to be aware of the possibilities and limitations of each instrument and the human voice. They may also work as an arranger writing musical parts for various instruments or as a singer-songwriter.

Work Details

Usually work long and irregular hours, writing, practising, rehearsing and performing. Evening and weekend work is common. You work on your own or with other composers, musicians or performers.

Composers may write at home, in schools and colleges, offices, recording studios, music venues or while travelling. The job can involve travelling around to visit publishers and artists, or to attend rehearsals and hear performances of your work.

Qualification

Experience is often more relevant than formal training routes but composers of any style of music usually have instrumental training and many are performers too.

• England, Wales and Northern Ireland

Band 2: For entry: no minimum qualifications are needed, but it is an advantage to have some GCSEs (A*-C) or equivalent in subjects that include English and maths.

Band 3: For BTEC National Diploma in music practice or popular music or a Creative and Media Diploma, usually at least 4 GCSEs (A*-C) including English and maths, or equivalent.

Band 4: For HND, Diploma of Higher Education or relevant foundation degree: 1-2 A levels and some GCSEs (A*-C) usually including English and maths, or equivalent.

Band 5: For music degree courses: 2-3 A levels, usually including music, and some GCSEs (A*-C) usually including English, or equivalent qualifications. A high standard of musical performance may be required. Exact requirements depend on the degree you take.

• Scotland

Band 2: Although academic qualifications are not specified for this job, it is an advantage to have some S grades (1-3) in subjects that include English and maths, or similar.

Band 3: For entry, usually at least four S grades (1-3) including English or maths, or similar.

Band 4: For entry to SQA higher national and professional development awards, usually 2-3 H grades and some S grades (1-3), including English and maths, or similar qualifications.

Band 5: For music degree courses: 3-5 H grades, usually including music, and some S grades (1-3), including English and maths, or similar qualifications. A high standard of musical performance may be required. Exact requirements depend on the degree you take.

Degree Information

Relevant degrees include music, music composition and professional practice and creative music technology. A wide range of postgraduate courses are also available and conservatoires now offer courses in composition.

Adult Qualifications

Adults with considerable experience, musical qualifications and preferably some training can become professional composers. Entry requirements may be relaxed for adults applying for higher education courses. Access or foundation courses give adults without qualifications a route on to degree courses.

Work Experience

Work experience gives you an insight into what you enjoy and don't enjoy about a job or working environment, as well as the opportunity to acquire new skills. It also provides valuable information to add to your CV and improves any course application and/or your future employment prospects.

It can take many years to establish a career as a music composer so it is important to be actively involved in music competitions, schemes for young artists and amateur groups where possible.

Entry and Training

Music composers usually have some form of musical training and many also have experience of working as performers, providing a good foundation for work as a composer. Classical music composers tend to need formal musical education and training, often to postgraduate level, and most have learnt to play one or more instruments from a young age. You can start at school by taking graded examinations, including the theory of music.

However, talent and the drive to write music can be more important than qualifications and experience and knowledge are valued, particularly if you want to work as a songwriter or compose for a sector such as the film or computer games industry.

There are a range of relevant courses available in composing, music and music technology at universities, music conservatoires and colleges of further education. Check UCAS for details. Conservatoires offer specific courses in composition. BTEC offers national diplomas in music practice and popular music. Foundation degrees are available in media and composition, film music and soundtrack production and music and audio production and may be an alternative route into this career.

The British Academy of Songwriters, Composers & Authors supports and protects the artistic, professional, commercial and copyright interests of songwriters, lyricists and composers of music genres and is a useful source of information.

Composers are usually members of the Musicians Union and PRS (Performing Rights Society). UK Music is a relatively new organisation which works to support the interests of the UK's commercial music industry, from artists, musicians, songwriters and composers, to major and independent record labels. The Sound and Music website is also a useful resource for aspiring composers.

Mature applicants to music schools are generally under the age of 30. Entry to music degree courses may be relaxed for applicants with relevant experience who do well at an audition. There are distance-learning courses in music, including those offered by the Open University and the Open College of the Arts. The Government also offers a New Deal for Musicians to help those that want to get into the music industry.

Opportunities and Pay

Few composers can make a living from composing alone and many combine it with other music-related work such as working as a musician, performer or conductor. Others get into composition work by teaching or arranging music. Many spend time promoting their work and by making downloads available.

Most composers are self-employed and are paid a fee for the commissions they take on. Successful composers receive commissions to write for specific occasions, ensembles, soloists, or institutions. Commission from the sales of recordings is an important source of income for composers. Alternatively composers need to interest a publisher or performer in their composition and may have to submit an initial pitch for no pay.

Pay varies greatly, few composers earn a fixed salary and income depends on building a good reputation. Commission and royalties are usually determined by the available budget of the production or programme you are composing for. As a guide, composers can earn around £300 per minute of composed music, although orchestral commissions may pay considerably more. Popular music tends to pay more in royalties than classical music.

Skills and Qualities

able to cope under pressure, able to withstand criticism, confident, creative and imaginative flair, excellent communication skills, flexible approach, good ear for music, IT skills, planning skills

Relevant Subjects

Art and Design, Business and accounting, Classical studies, English, ICT/Computer studies, Mathematics, Media and communication studies, Music, Performing arts

Further Information

British Academy of Songwriters, Composers & Authors - www.britishacademy.com

British Recorded Music Industry (BPI) - www.bpi.co.uk

Classical Music Magazine (Rhinegold)

Conservatoires Admissions Service UK - www.cukas.ac.uk

Creative & Cultural Skills - sector skills council for advertising, crafts, cultural heritage, design, literature, music, performing & visual arts - www.ccskills.org.uk

Musicians' Union - www.musiciansunion.org

Open University - www.open.ac.uk

Parents Music Room - www.bbc.co.uk/music/parents/careersguide/composing.shtml

PRS for Music - www.prsformusic.com

Sound and Music - www.soundandmusic.org

UK Music - www.ukmusic.org

▶Working in music (2007) (Babcock Lifeskills) - www.babcock-lifeskills.com/

Working in the Music Industry (How To Books) (How To Books Ltd) - www.howto.co.uk/careers/music-industry-jobs

Addresses

Open College of the Arts
Michael Young Arts Centre, Redbrook Business Park, Wilthorpe Road, Barnsley S75 1JN
Phone: 0800 731 2116 (UK only)
Web: www.oca-uk.com

UCAS
Customer Services Unit, PO Box 28, Cheltenham GL52 3LZ
Phone: +44 (0)871 468 0468
Web: www.ucas.com

Similar Jobs

Music Therapist, Musician: Classical, Musician: Pop, Singer, Teacher: Music

Music Industry Promotions Manager

also known as: Promotions Manager: Music Industry

CRCI:Performing Arts
CLCI:GAD Job Band: 1 to 5

Job Description

Promotions managers promote clients and their music-related products, represent performance artists and promote records or music venues. They are sometimes known as 'pluggers' and discuss promotions with specialists in market research, public relations, finance, etc. Also oversee the production of promotion material and advise on legal questions. They advise clients on the best and most likely dates to release their CD, and arrange for promotional/marketing features, prior to the release date. Then arrange interviews with television and radio stations and the musical press. If promoting a venue, they book suitable artists and bands, making sure that the venue is appropriate for their acts.

Promotions managers negotiate contracts, liaise with set designers, and ensure that the necessary entertainment licences are acquired, prior to any performance. They maintain administrative records including financial aspects and keep to a budgeting policy. Then assess the results and make any adjustments to the promotion strategy. Also supervise junior staff.

Work Details

This is an office-based job, but involves visiting potential customers or venues, and attending promotional events. Your hours of work are long and irregular with much of the work taking place in the evening and possibly at weekends. Some of the venues are noisy and crowded. Overseas travel is possible.

Qualification

There are no formal entry qualifications for this job. Qualifications vary from those with few or no qualifications to those with degrees and postgraduate qualifications.

Degree Information

There are specific degrees in music industry management, though any degree discipline is acceptable for entry to this job. Useful subjects include marketing, business, communications or public relations. A postgraduate diploma in marketing may also be relevant.

Adult Qualifications

Mature entrants may not need the standard entry requirements for higher education courses. Previous relevant experience and an ability to study at the appropriate level is desirable.

Work Experience

Entry to this job is very competitive and it is important to do some relevant work or voluntary experience before applying. Previous experience of promoting local bands, organising local gigs and writing reviews of gigs in student newspapers are all very relevant. Experience of work in sales, marketing, public relations and event organising is also useful.

Entry and Training
Many entrants start at a junior level in an administrative or secretarial support role with record companies, or in radio and TV. Training is usually on the job with an experienced colleague and with an in-house induction programme when you join the company. It may be useful to have studied popular music, marketing, communications, media, or to have some knowledge of accounts and contract law.

A number of relevant full-time courses for the music industry are available, including HNDs and degrees in music industry management and marketing. Relevant cultural BTEC professional diplomas are also available, including community music management at level 5, and there are foundation degrees in subjects such as music business and management.

There are also a number of relevant postgraduate courses offered by the Chartered Institute of Marketing. A full list of appropriate courses, at all levels of qualification, is available from the Music Education Directory of the British Phonographic Industry, who also run short seminars on the structure and promotion of the recording industry. You can join the Music Managers' Forum for networking opportunities and training courses.

A Diploma/Welsh Baccalaureate in creative and media may be available in your area. Check university entry requirements carefully in case there is an additional specialist learning requirement with the diploma. See the diplomas website for further information.

Mature entrants tend to be at senior levels moving from other related areas, such as marketing and sales, advertising, public relations, events management and promotion. Most of those entering the contemporary music industry tend to be younger, but older candidates with relevant experience have an advantage.

Opportunities and Pay
There is a lot of competition for jobs and most opportunities are in major cities such as London, Manchester and Leeds. Opportunities for venue management are more likely to be regionally-based throughout the UK. You can start as a junior assistant doing routine jobs and supporting the work of more senior managers, and then moving on to handling a small group of clients. Alternatively, you may manage a venue or group of venues. Few jobs are advertised, and most jobs are heard about through a network of contacts.

Some promotion managers are involved in signing and managing single artists or bands, including those who become, or who are, famous. Managers may work freelance or on contract and some set up their own company.

Starting salaries can vary but are around £15k, increasing to around £25k a year. Generally, experienced managers earn £20k-£40k a year, depending on the employer and location. However, highly successful promotion artist managers can earn salaries up to £100k. Income can also be linked to performers' success as managers usually have a percentage of performers' earnings.

Health
It is possible that prolonged exposure to high volumes of noise may affect your hearing.

Skills and Qualities
able to cope under pressure, enterprising, good interpersonal skills, good organisational skills, IT skills, knowledge of the music industry, motivated, negotiating skills, networking skills, self confident

Relevant Subjects
Business and accounting, Economics, English, Mathematics, Media and communication studies, Music, Psychology

Further Information
Concert Promoters Association (CPA) - www.concertpromotersassociation.co.uk/

Creative & Cultural Skills - sector skills council for advertising, crafts, cultural heritage, design, literature, music, performing & visual arts - www.ccskills.org.uk

Diplomas (Foundation, Higher and Advanced) - http://yp.direct.gov.uk/diplomas

Music Managers' Training Forum - www.mmf-training.com

Production Services Association (PSA) - www.psa.org.uk/

Welsh Baccalaureate - www.wbq.org.uk

▶Working in music (2007) (Babcock Lifeskills) - www.babcock-lifeskills.com/

Working in the Music Industry (How To Books) (How To Books Ltd) - www.howto.co.uk/careers/music-industry-jobs

Addresses
British Recorded Music Industry (BPI)
Riverside Building County Hall Westminster Bridge Road, London SE1 7JA
Phone: +44 (0)20 7803 1300
Web: www.bpi.co.uk

Chartered Institute of Marketing (CIM)
Moor Hall, Cookham, Maidenhead, Berkshire SL6 9QH
Phone: +44 (0) 1628 427120
Web: www.cim.co.uk

Similar Jobs
Brand Manager, Event & Exhibition Organiser, Marketing Manager, Musician: Classical, Public Relations Officer, Theatre Stage Manager

Music Therapist
CRCI:Healthcare
CLCI:JOD

Job Band: 5

Job Description
Music therapists use music and instruments creatively in a therapeutic setting, with a variety of clients, individuals or groups and of all ages and abilities. They help people with mental, physical, emotional or behavioural problems to cope with their difficulties, by listening to singing or playing music. Can help those with eating disorders, epilepsy, addictions, autism, HIV/AIDS, and stress management. Use sound therapy to stimulate or relax patients and allow them to cope with their emotions and increase their confidence and communication. Through music, they build a relationship of trust with the client or group.

Encourage the use of musical instruments so that clients can explore the sounds and actions they can create themselves, rather than being taught to sing or play an instrument. May improvise or compose music specially. Also write up case notes and produce progress reports.

Work Details
Work a basic 37 hr week that can include some weekends and evenings. Place of work varies depending on client group, and you can work in hospitals, special schools, hospices or community centres. You work with people of all ages and ability. Some have psychological, communication or emotional problems, others have learning difficulties or physical disabilities. Work is emotionally demanding at times but can be very rewarding.

Qualification

- **England, Wales and Northern Ireland**

Band 5: For degree courses prior to postgraduate qualification: 2-3 A levels usually including music, and some GCSEs (A*-C) usually including English and maths, or equivalent. Exact requirements depend on the degree you take.

- **Scotland**

Band 5: For degree courses prior to postgraduate qualification: 3-5 H grades usually including music, and some S grades (1-3), usually including English and maths, or similar qualifications. Exact requirements depend on the degree you take.

Degree Information

Three years' musical training leading to a degree or diploma from a college of music or a university is normally needed for entry to a relevant postgraduate course. In exceptional cases, a degree in another discipline such as psychology or education, together with a high level of ability in musical performance, may be acceptable. Contact the Association of Professional Music Therapists for a list of approved qualifications that are required for state registration with the Health Professions Council.

Adult Qualifications

Entry requirements may be relaxed for adults applying for higher education courses. Access or foundation courses give adults without qualifications a route on to degree courses.

Work Experience

Entry to this job is competitive. It is important that you try to do some relevant work or voluntary experience before applying for postgraduate courses. This can include teaching experience, working with the public or with people in a caring capacity, particularly those with mental health problems or learning disabilities. It may be possible to work on a voluntary basis in a hospital, a special school or day centre, or to approach a music therapist for a discussion regarding their work and some work observation.

Entry and Training

Postgraduate courses in music therapy require a high standard of musicianship, and there is tough competition for places. Courses must be recognised by the Association of Professional Music Therapists (APMT) and are offered at seven schools and universities, usually one year full time or two years part time. Check the APMT website for details. Ability in piano playing may be specified and usually three years musical training is required. An interest in working with people with learning difficulties or mental illness, preferably both, is needed. Students normally have to fund themselves through training courses, but grants and other sources of funding may be available such as that offered by the Music Therapy Charity. Applications are by post only.

All newly qualified therapists are required to undergo supervision with a state-registered music therapist, which can take up to two years. They may then apply for state registration with the APMT and the Health Professions Council. Continuing professional development is encouraged through conferences, workshops and seminars.

Mature entrants are welcome and the Health Professions Council and Association of Professional Music Therapists (APMT) recommends that applicants to the accredited postgraduate music therapy courses are aged at least 23 before embarking on such courses. It is very useful to have some experience in a related field, particularly working with those who most benefit from music therapy.

You may be required to fund your own postgraduate study, though it is possible to receive sponsorship from employers or from various related charitable bodies and trusts. Information on routes to training and sources of funding are available from the APMT and the Music Therapy Charity.

Opportunities and Pay

This is currently a small profession though numbers are increasing. Most posts are with the NHS, but jobs may also be found with a local authority, voluntary organisation and the prison service. Some specialise in work with children or those with learning disabilities or speech difficulties. Music therapy is particularly suitable for part-time work or you may be employed on a sessional basis. Some music therapists are self-employed and in private practice.

Pay depends largely on type of employer, but can be on a nationally agreed scale. A newly-qualified music therapist working for the NHS earns around £25k a year, rising to £34k-£40k with experience. A principal therapist can earn up to £46k a year. Jobs in London and south-east England attract an allowance and cost of living supplement.

Health

This job requires good hearing.

Skills and Qualities

able to inspire confidence, able to motivate others, encouraging, good communication skills, good interpersonal skills, helpful, musical creativity, patient, tactful

Relevant Subjects

English, Health and social care, Music, Performing arts, Psychology, Sociology

Further Information

Behind the Scenes: Music (Trotman 2009) - www.trotman.co.uk

British Journal of Music Therapy (BSMT/APMT) (BSMT/APMT) - www.bsmt.org/publications.htm

Health Professions Council (HPC) - www.hpc-uk.org

NHS Careers (NHS Careers) - www.nhscareers.nhs.uk

NHS Careers Scotland - www.infoscotland.com/nhs

NHS Careers Wales - www.wales.nhs.uk

Skills for Health - sector skills council - www.skillsforhealth.org.uk

▶Working in music (2007) (Babcock Lifeskills) - www.babcock-lifeskills.com/

Addresses

Association of Professional Music Therapists (APMT)
24-27 White Lion Street, London N1 9PD
Phone: +44 (0)20 7837 6100
Web: www.apmt.org

British Society for Music Therapy (BSMT)
24-27 White Lion Street, London N1 9PD
Phone: +44 (0)20 7837 6142
Web: www.bsmt.org

Music Therapy Charity
401 Shakespeare Tower, Barbican, London EC2Y 8NJ
Web: www.musictherapy.org.uk

Similar Jobs

Art Therapist, Dramatherapist, Hearing Therapist, Musician: Classical, Teacher: Music, Teacher: Special Educational Needs

Musical Instrument Technician

CRCI:Design, Arts and Crafts
CLCI:SOZ — Job Band: 2 to 4

Job Description

Musical instrument technicians use skills to design, make, repair and adjust musical instruments of all kinds. They usually specialise in one instrument or a group of instruments (eg, stringed, brass, woodwind, electronic). Technicians use a variety of hand and machine tools to cut and shape the pieces according to drawings or plans, working with metal, wood, plastic, glass fibre and other materials. They finish the work, perhaps by varnishing and cleaning. Then fine tune the instrument to ensure it is in complete working order. Also advise clients how to care for and handle their instrument.

Some may specialise in the restoration and repair of existing period instruments, or may reproduce an historical instrument to its exact measurements and shape. May also sell new and second-hand instruments and their spare parts, as well as sheet music.

Work Details

Usually work a basic 39 hr week, Monday to Friday, though if you are self-employed working hours can be irregular. It may be necessary to work late or at weekends to meet deadlines. You work in a workshop/studio, or manufacturing premises, or possibly work from home. It may be necessary to visit clients in their own homes. You are responsible for a high standard of skilled work, and must have a good ear for tuning as well as an interest in music.

Qualification

• England, Wales and Northern Ireland

Band 2: For City & Guilds courses in instrument making and repair: practical ability is required and preferably some GCSEs.

Band 3: For entry to jobs, HNC or a relevant Diploma, usually at least 4 GCSEs (A*-C) including English, physics and maths, or equivalent.

Band 4: For HND, Diploma of Higher Education or foundation degree: 1-2 A levels and some GCSEs (A*-C) usually including English, physics and maths, or equivalent.

• Scotland

Band 2: For City & Guilds courses in instrument making and repair: practical ability is required and preferably some S grades.

Band 3: For entry to jobs, usually at least four S grades (1-3) including English or maths, or similar.

Band 4: For entry to SQA higher national and professional development awards, usually 2-3 H grades and some S grades (1-3), including English, physics and maths, or similar qualifications.

Adult Qualifications

Formal qualifications or equivalent may be required for entry to some college courses, though entry requirements are usually relaxed for mature applicants. Check with individual institutions.

Work Experience

Work experience in technical musical instrument work may be hard to gain. It does, however, improve your chances at interview if you have some work experience to develop your skills in craft work, especially with wood or metal. Any experience that demonstrates your musical ear and general musical awareness is helpful. The Strad magazine offers useful information about summer schools and job opportunities for musical instrument technicians.

Entry and Training

Most people enter this career by completing a specialist college course covering instrument design, music theory, instrument history and restoration techniques, maths and acoustics. These courses are usually taught by professional musical instrument makers and repairers. It is useful to have practical ability in woodwork or metalwork, and essential to be able to follow drawings and plans, and have a good ear for tuning. It is not essential to have to play a musical instrument, but it is very useful. City & Guilds offer relevant courses in instrument making and repair at levels 1-3. Merton College offers a range of musical instrument making and repair courses for guitar, violin, woodwind and brass.

There is a foundation degree in musical instruments offered by the London Metropolitan University. A BA/BSc in musical instruments is also available. Anniesland College in Glasgow offers an HNC/NC in music making (stringed instruments) and West Dean College in Sussex runs a short course in making instruments. The Malden School of Musical Instrument Repair also runs a range of specialist courses covering most instruments. Contact the National Association of Musical Instrument Repairers (NAMIR) for details of courses.

Training is usually by practical experience after initial qualification. Some musical instrument manufacturers offer training with study via a part-time course. The Institute of Musical Instrument Technology (IMIT) has a library of specialist books and runs an accreditation scheme for musical instrument technicians, and the Music Education Directory is also a useful source of information. The British Violin Making Association website has a list of training events.

Mature applicants with practical craft skills, the ability to play an instrument, or experience in restoration/conservation work, have an advantage.

Opportunities and Pay

Work is available in most large towns and cities, and a good proportion of technicians are self-employed. You may be employed by a commercial firm of musical instrument manufacturers or repairers. Promotion prospects are limited but possible if employed by a larger, commercial company. There may be opportunities to work overseas.

Pay varies hugely depending on whether you are employed or self-employed. Generally, technicians earn around £16k-£20k rising to around£25k a year for well known repairers. Some specialist makers/repairers can earn much more.

Health

This job requires good hearing and good eyesight.

Skills and Qualities

able to work well on your own, attention to detail, business awareness, good ear for music, manual dexterity, outstanding musical ability, patient, practical skills, technical aptitude

Relevant Subjects

Art and Design, Design and technology, Music

Further Information

Behind the Scenes: Music (Trotman 2009) - www.trotman.co.uk

British Violin Making Association (BVMA) - www.bvma.org.uk

Creative & Cultural Skills - sector skills council for advertising, crafts, cultural heritage, design, literature, music, performing & visual arts - www.ccskills.org.uk

ISM Careers with Music (ISM) - www.ism.org/policy_advice/careers_with_music/

Music Education Directory - www.bpi-med.co.uk

The Intrepid Repairer (quarterly) (National Association of Musical Instrument Repairers (NAMIR)) - www.namir.org.uk/membersarea/intrepid_repairer.htm

The Journal of the Institute of Musical instrument Technology (Institute of Musical instrument Technology) - www.imit.org.uk/publications.html

The Strad - www.thestrad.com

▶Working in music (2007) (Babcock Lifeskills) - www.babcock-lifeskills.com/

Addresses

Anniesland College
19 Hatfield Drive, Glasgow G12 0YE
Phone: +44(0)141 357 3969
Web: www.anniesland.ac.uk

Institute of Musical Instrument Technology (IMIT)
Northfield House, 11 Kendal Avenue South, Sanderstead, Croydon CR2 0QR
Web: www.imit.org.uk

London Metropolitan University
Admissions: 166-220 Holloway Rd, London N7 8DB
Phone: +44 (0)20 7133 4200
Web: www.londonmet.ac.uk

Malden School of Instrument Repair
Llangunllo School, Llangunllo, Knighton, Powys
Phone: +44 (0)1547 550 622
Web: www.namir.org.uk/maldenschool.htm

National Association of Musical Instrument Repairers (NAMIR)
Contact via website,
Web: www.namir.org.uk

South Thames College Merton Campus
Morden Park London Road SM4 5QX
Phone: +44 (0)20 8408 6500
Web: www.merton.ac.uk

West Dean College
West Dean, Chichester, West Sussex PO18 0QZ
Phone: +44 (0)1243 811301
Web: www.westdean.org.uk

Similar Jobs

Cabinet Maker, Film/TV/Radio & Theatre Sound Recordist, Model Maker, Musician: Classical, Piano Tuner/Technician, Teacher: Music

Musician: Classical

also known as: Classical Musician

CRCI:Performing Arts
CLCI:GAD Job Band: 3 to 5

Job Description

Classical musicians play one or more musical instruments as a soloist, accompanist, or member of an orchestra or group to give enjoyment to an audience. This can be as part of a large orchestra or a small group, such as a string quartet. They study the score and rehearse regularly, possibly memorising music. In orchestras, classical music is directed by a conductor. Musicians can also work in a recording studio, producing music for film scores or general sale.

Some classical musicians train as music teachers and combine part-time teaching with performing duties. They may be involved in composing new material for performances. Some find full-time work in the bands of the armed forces.

Work Details

You usually work unsocial hours, evenings and weekends, and possibly long hours at a number of different venues, including theatres, concert halls and recording studios. Conditions vary, depending on where you are working. As an orchestral player, you perform regularly in large concert halls. You may have to travel on tour and spend nights away from home. You have to cope with spending a lot of time rehearsing, often in uncomfortable rehearsal rooms, which can be cold and draughty. In the summer months, you may work outdoors at open air concerts. May teach students privately or work part time at a school to supplement income.

This work calls for creativity and imagination and is very demanding. Classical musicians wear formal dress for performances. During rehearsals, dress is informal.

Qualification

• England, Wales and Northern Ireland

Band 3: For relevant BTEC national award in music and music technology: at least 4 GCSEs (A*-C), plus evidence of musical ability.

Band 4: For BTEC higher national diploma in music performance: usually 1-2 A levels or a BTEC National Certificate/Diploma in Music. Evidence of musical ability may be required.

Band 5: For degree courses: 2-3 A levels, usually including music, and some GCSEs (A*-C) usually including English, or equivalent qualifications. A high standard of musical performance is required; preferably Grade 8 in the principal instrument and Grade 5-6 in a second instrument. Check individual prospectuses.

• Scotland

Band 3: For entry to a relevant music course: usually at least four S grades (1-3) including English and maths and an audition and interview.

Band 4: For SQA higher national diploma in music: usually 2-3 H grades and some S grades (1-3), often including English and maths, or similar qualifications, plus evidence of musical ability.

Band 5: For degree courses: 3-5 H grades usually including music, and some S grades (1-3), usually including English, or similar qualifications. A high standard of musical performance is required; preferably Grade 8 in the principal instrument and Grade 5-6 in a second instrument. Check with universities.

Degree Information

Entry to this job is usually with a degree in music but is possible with a degree in any subject, together with proven musical ability. There is a wide variety of higher degrees and postgraduate diplomas in music and related subjects, including performance studies. Check content of courses carefully as some may concentrate on the purely academic side of music.

Adult Qualifications

Adults with considerable amateur experience, musical qualifications (eg Grade 8 in at least one instrument), and preferably some training can become professional musicians. Entry requirements may be relaxed for adults applying for higher education courses. Access or foundation courses give adults without qualifications a route on to degree courses.

Work Experience

Any experience with an amateur orchestra either at school, college or university is useful. It is also helpful if you have taken part in music competitions and attended auditions.

Entry and Training

Learning to play an instrument can start between the ages of five and ten, working towards the examinations of the Associated Board of the Royal Schools of Music. To enter this job, and most music courses, you need to pass an audition. Specialist music colleges known as conservatoires offer 3-4 year music diplomas, degrees and postgraduate courses. To become a classical musician, you generally specialise in one instrument and study a second as well. Check the Conservatoires Admissions Service website for details. Also visit the Association of British Orchestras for continuing professional development (CPD) courses.

The armed forces (Royal Marines, Royal Air Force and Army) offer bursaries to those who have a place on a music course studying for 3-4 years for a nationally recognised degree or diploma. Contact your local Armed Forces Careers Office for further details. A relevant foundation degree is also available at some colleges and universities lasting between 2-4 years, part time. Funding may also be available from the Musicians Benevolent Fund.

A Diploma/Welsh Baccalaureate in creative and media may be available in your area. The dance, drama and music element of the diploma has been expanded to reflect the performance and composition or technical aspects of each discipline. Check university entry requirements carefully in case there is an additional specialist learning requirement with the diploma. See the diplomas website for further information.

Once you have passed an audition for entry to a classical musician's job with an orchestra, you then go through a trial period. However, there is no guarantee of a permanent job at the end of this period. Training is continuous as you learn new pieces of music and master new styles. Scholarships may be available to help with study; check with the Worshipful Company of Musicians for details.

Mature applicants to music schools are generally under the age of 30. There are distance-learning courses in music, including those offered by the Open University and the Open College of the Arts. The Government is offering a New Deal for Musicians at the moment that assists those that want to get into the music industry.

Opportunities and Pay

There is fierce competition for all job vacancies and considerable talent is required for success. A few classical musicians have permanent contracts with orchestras but most work freelance. Many musicians supplement their income by teaching private pupils. There are permanent jobs and careers in the armed forces' military bands. Most other opportunities are in the light music field, including theatre orchestras or work on cruise ships, holiday centres, charity balls and other popular venues and events. Vacancies are seldom advertised and you need to maintain a network of contacts so you hear about upcoming vacancies. Self promotion is important.

As many musicians are self-employed, it is difficult to summarise earnings. The Musicians' Union has a range of recommended rates of pay for different types of live performers. Members of an orchestra may start on around £80-£160 a concert. Principal players in an orchestra can earn considerably more than this.

Health

You need to be in good health and have high stamina levels for this job.

Skills and Qualities

aptitude for teamwork, attention to detail, dedicated, good communication skills, outstanding musical ability, perseverance, resilient, self confident, self-disciplined, versatile

Relevant Subjects

Music, Performing arts

Further Information

Becoming an Orchestral Musician: A Guide for Aspiring Professionals (Richard Davis) (Giles de la Mare)

Behind the Scenes: Music (Trotman 2009) - www.trotman.co.uk

Conservatoires Admissions Service UK - www.cukas.ac.uk

Creative & Cultural Skills - sector skills council for advertising, crafts, cultural heritage, design, literature, music, performing & visual arts - www.ccskills.org.uk

Creative Choices - www.creative-choices.co.uk

Diplomas (Foundation, Higher and Advanced) - http://yp.direct.gov.uk/diplomas

Musicians' Benevolent Fund - www.helpmusicians.org.uk

National Association of Music Educators - www.name.org.uk

National Youth Orchestra of Ireland - www.nyoi.ie

So you want to work in Music & Dance (Wayland) - www.waylandbooks.co.uk

The Stage Online - www.thestage.co.uk

Training Schemes - www.direct.gov.uk/en/educationandlearning

Welsh Baccalaureate - www.wbq.org.uk

▶ Working in music (2007) (Babcock Lifeskills) - www.babcock-lifeskills.com/

Addresses

Associated Board of the Royal Schools of Music (ABRSM)
24 Portland Place, London W1B 1LU
Phone: +44 (0)20 7636 5400
Web: www.abrsm.org

Association of British Orchestras (ABO)
20 Rupert Street, London W1D 6DF
Phone: +44 (0)20 7287 0333
Web: www.abo.org.uk

Musicians' Union
33 Palfrey Place, London SW8 1PE
Phone: +44 (0)20 7840 5504
Web: www.musiciansunion.org.uk

Open College of the Arts
Michael Young Arts Centre, Redbrook Business Park, Wilthorpe Road, Barnsley S75 1JN
Phone: 0800 731 2116 (UK only)
Web: www.oca-uk.com

Worshipful Company of Musicians
6th Floor 2 London Wall Buildings London Wall EC2M 5PP
Phone: +44 (0)20 7496 8980
Web: www.wcom.org.uk

Similar Jobs

Entertainer, Music Therapist, Musical Instrument Technician, Royal Marines Musician/Bugler, Singer, Teacher: Music

Musician: Pop

also known as: Pop Musician

CRCI:Performing Arts

CLCI:GAD Job Band: 3 to 5

Job Description

Pop musicians play one or more musical instruments as a soloist, accompanist, or member of a band or group to give enjoyment to an audience. They improvise and make up their own arrangements, may write their own songs or perform covers of other artists' music. They choose to work in specialist areas such as hip hop, garage, jazz, rock or country and western, making music with wide commercial appeal to the general public.

May train as a teacher and combine part-time teaching work with performing. Sometimes musicians work in recording studios, producing lyrics and music for advertising or filming companies.

Work Details

You usually work unsocial hours, evenings and weekends, and possibly long hours at a number of different venues. Conditions vary, depending on the area of music in which you are involved. As a pop musician, you often perform in pubs, clubs or large concert venues. You may have to travel on tour and spend nights away from home. You have to cope with spending a lot of time rehearsing, often in uncomfortable rehearsal rooms, which can be cold and draughty.

This work calls for creativity and imagination and is very demanding. Pop musicians wear informal clothing but some follow fashion trends.

Qualification

To become a popular musician, no formal qualifications are required, although evidence of a high standard of musical ability is essential.

• England, Wales and Northern Ireland

Band 3: For entry to jobs, HNC or a relevant Diploma, usually at least 4 GCSEs (A*-C) including English and maths, or equivalent.

Band 4: For HND, Diploma of Higher Education or foundation degree: 1-2 A levels and some GCSEs (A*-C) usually including English and maths, or equivalent. Evidence of musical ability may be required.

Band 5: For degree courses: 2-3 A levels and some GCSEs (A*-C) usually including English and maths, or equivalent. Exact requirements depend on the degree you take but a high standard of musical performance is required.

• Scotland

Band 3: For entry to jobs, usually at least four S grades (1-3) including English or maths, or similar.

Band 4: For entry to SQA higher national and professional development awards, usually 2-3 H grades and some S grades (1-3), including English and maths, or similar qualifications. Evidence of musical ability may be required.

Band 5: For degree courses: 3-5 H grades and some S grades (1-3), including English and maths, or similar qualifications. Exact requirements depend on the degree you take but a high standard of musical performance is required.

Degree Information

A degree in music may be useful for this job but proven musical ability is essential. There is a wide variety of higher degrees and postgraduate diplomas in music and related subjects, including performance studies. Check content of courses carefully as some may concentrate on the purely academic side of music.

Adult Qualifications

Adults with considerable amateur experience, musical qualifications and preferably some training can become professional musicians. Entry requirements may be relaxed for adults applying for higher education courses. Access or foundation courses give adults without qualifications a route on to degree courses.

Work Experience

Any experience with an amateur band either at school, college or university is useful. It is also helpful if you have taken part in music competitions and attended auditions.

Entry and Training

Many entrants to the pop music industry are self-taught enthusiasts. If you have a talent for playing an instrument, singing or songwriting, you may not need any formal qualifications. Success in the pop music business is achieved through a combination of perseverance, determination and luck. There are, however, a number of qualification routes you can follow.

Rockschool offers popular music graded examinations in instruments such as guitar, drums, bass, vocals and popular piano. Students who want to develop performance and technical skills can take grade exams. It is also possible to work for a performance or teaching diploma if you are a grade 8 musician. Access to Music courses are available in performance, technology or professional development. Courses also cover marketing and promotion, communication and developing confidence. Students also learn how to use computers and the Internet effectively to promote their work.

The Institute of Popular Music at the University of Liverpool offers relevant degrees and postgraduate courses and has a flexible entry policy. Visit the website for specific details. It is helpful to have a CD of your work to send to music companies. A Diploma/Welsh Baccalaureate in creative and media may be available in your area. Check university entry requirements carefully in case there is an additional specialist learning requirement with the diploma. See the diplomas website for further information.

Applicants to music schools are generally under the age of 30, however, age is not a barrier to entering this business. Success is more dependent on talent and luck than qualifications and youth. The Government offers a New Deal for Musicians that helps musicians, songwriters and other performers like singers and performing DJs, pursue a professional career in music.

Opportunities and Pay

There is fierce competition for all job vacancies and considerable talent is required for success. Popular musicians tend to work on a freelance basis. Many musicians supplement their income by teaching private pupils. Most other opportunities are in the light music field, including work on cruise ships, at holiday centres, charity balls and other popular venues and events.

Vacancies are seldom advertised and you need to maintain a network of contacts so you find out when a vacancy may occur. Self promotion is important. Many pop musicians use the Internet as a route to raising their profile and try to secure gigs at local music concerts to develop a fan base. Some produce a demo disc and circulate this to record producers.

As many musicians are self-employed, it is difficult to summarise earnings. The Musicians' Union has a range of recommended rates of pay for different types of live performers. Musicians performing at pubs/clubs are likely to earn between £60-£350 a night, depending on reputation. Some popular musicians can earn considerably more than this. Selling CDs of your work at gigs can provide additional income.

Health

You need to be in good health and have stamina for this job.

Skills and Qualities

aptitude for teamwork, attention to detail, dedicated, good communication skills, musical creativity, outstanding musical ability, perseverance, resilient, self confident, self-disciplined

Relevant Subjects

Music, Performing arts

Further Information

Behind the Scenes: Music (Trotman 2009) - www.trotman.co.uk

Creative & Cultural Skills - sector skills council for advertising, crafts, cultural heritage, design, literature, music, performing & visual arts - www.ccskills.org.uk

Creative Choices - www.creative-choices.co.uk

Diplomas (Foundation, Higher and Advanced) - http://yp.direct.gov.uk/diplomas

Music Education Directory (BPI) (BPI) - www.bpi-med.co.uk

National Association of Music Educators - www.name.org.uk

PRS for Music - www.prsformusic.com

The Stage Online - www.thestage.co.uk

Training Schemes - www.direct.gov.uk/en/educationandlearning

Welsh Baccalaureate - www.wbq.org.uk

▶Working in music (2007) (Babcock Lifeskills) - www.babcock-lifeskills.com/

Addresses

Access to Music Ltd
Lionel House, 35 Millstone Lane, Leicester LE1 5JN
Phone: 0800 281842 (UK only)
Web: www.accesstomusic.co.uk

Associated Board of the Royal Schools of Music (ABRSM)
24 Portland Place, London W1B 1LU
Phone: +44 (0)20 7636 5400
Web: www.abrsm.org

Institute of Popular Music
University of Liverpool, 80-82 Bedford Street South L69 7WW
Phone: +44 (0) 151 794 3096
Web: www.liv.ac.uk/music/ipm/

Musicians' Union
33 Palfrey Place, London SW8 1PE
Phone: +44 (0)20 7840 5504
Web: www.musiciansunion.org.uk

Open College of the Arts
Michael Young Arts Centre, Redbrook Business Park,
Wilthorpe Road, Barnsley S75 1JN
Phone: 0800 731 2116 (UK only)
Web: www.oca-uk.com

Rockschool
Evergreen House 2-4 King Street, Twickenham, Surrey TW1 3RZ
Phone: 0845 460 4747 (UK only)
Web: www.rockschool.co.uk

Similar Jobs

Actor, DJ, Entertainer, Musician: Classical, Singer, Teacher: Music

Nail Technician

CRCI:Personal and Other Services
CLCI:IK Job Band: 1 to 3

Job Description

Nail technicians aim to improve the appearance and condition of the nails and skin of the hands and feet. They usually work in a high street nail bar, hairdressing or beauty salon or in spas and apply a variety of cosmetic treatments to a customer's fingers or toenails. Can provide a standard manicure and pedicure or extend the fingernails with acrylic or gel, fibre glass or silk wraps. May massage oils into the cuticle of each nail to help nourish and soften the area. Then cut, file and shape each nail into the desired style. Also apply nail polish in the colour of the client's choice or may help the client to make a choice.

Some technicians specialise in particular treatments, such as creative nail art, which involves decorating each finished nail with elaborate patterns and colours, and may apply diamante (artificial jewels) to the nails. Nail technicians also advise on a maintenance and care routine for the nails.

Work Details

Usually work around 37 hrs a week, that may include evenings and weekends. You sit at a table facing the client and may either work alone or in a salon with other technicians, beauticians, hairdressers and therapists. Health and safety is very important as you need to use and store chemicals and varnishes properly. Nail technicians often wear a white coat or salon uniform.

Qualification

There are no set qualifications to enter this job and many nail technicians have come through the traditional beauty therapy route.

• England, Wales and Northern Ireland

Band 1: For entry to jobs, no minimum qualifications are needed, but you are expected to have a good level of general education and relevant experience. Some formal/vocational qualifications at any level are useful.

Band 2: For some beauty therapy courses: at least 3 GCSEs (A*-C), or equivalent, are useful.

Band 3: For relevant BTEC national diploma: usually 3-4 GCSEs (A*-C), preferably including biology or dual science, English and maths, or equivalent.

• Scotland

Band 1: For entry to jobs, no minimum qualifications are needed, but you are expected to have a good level of general education and relevant experience. Some formal/vocational qualifications at any level are useful.

Band 2: For some beauty therapy courses: at least three S grades (1-3), or similar, are useful.

Band 3: For relevant SQA national certificate: usually 3-4 S grades preferably including biology or dual science, English and maths, or similar.

Adult Qualifications

Some secondary qualifications, or equivalent, are usually required for entry to training courses, but many colleges welcome mature entrants over 20 and may waive standard academic requirements.

Work Experience

Employers or colleges may prefer candidates who have relevant work or voluntary experience. This can be in a beauty salon, perhaps specialising in nails, although work with a hairdresser develops related skills and give the opportunity to compile a portfolio of relevant experience. Work that develops your art and design skills can be useful if you hope to practise nail art.

Entry and Training

In most areas, there are no minimum qualifications to train to be a nail technician, although some courses and employers may look for some GCSEs/S grades. A Diploma/Welsh Baccalaureate in hair and beauty studies may be available in your area. Other training programmes, including apprenticeship schemes, may laso be available. You can study courses at level 2 and 3 in nail technology, nail arts and nail treatments at local further education colleges and private colleges. Courses are awarded by the Vocational Training Charitable Trust and the International Therapy Examination Council. S/NVQs at level 2 and 3 are also available in nail services.

Some short courses are offered by various nail product distributors but do not always cover all the essential health and safety issues. On-the-job training is usually required. New nail products, techniques and fashions are constantly changing, so you should update your skills frequently.

If you want to set up a nail bar yourself, you need to have a licence from the local authority and qualifications for this vary. Some authorities accept any nationally recognised qualification, others insist on a relevant S/NVQ.

Adults may be able to enter this work through a government-funded training programme. Contact your local Connexions or careers office, Jobcentre Plus, Next Step service or Learning and Skills Council (LSC)/Local Enterprise Company (LEC) for details of all training opportunities and schemes, including apprenticeships for adults.

Opportunities and Pay

Nail extensions and nail art are very fashionable, so opportunities for nail technicians have grown rapidly. There are jobs throughout the UK in specialist nail bars, in large department stores, beauty and hairdressing salons, health clubs, at airports and in shopping malls. Many technicians aim to be self-employed. You may set up your own salon, rent a space in a beauty or hairdressing salon, or provide a mobile service, visiting clients in their own homes. Some technicians offer a service at their own house, which means that the customer visits them instead. With further training, it is possible to move into beauty or spa therapy.

Pay varies, but trainees may earn from £10k a year, rising to £18k a year with experience. Qualified and experienced nail technicians earn up to £28k a year. Tips from clients and commission on products that are sold in a salon can supplement your income.

Health

This job requires normal colour vision. There may be a risk from skin irritants.

Skills and Qualities

creative flair, eye for visual effect, good interpersonal skills, good personal grooming, health & safety awareness, manual dexterity, patient, smart appearance, tactful

Relevant Subjects

Art and Design, Biology, English, Health and social care, Science

Further Information

Apprenticeship Schemes (National Apprenticeship Service) - www.apprenticeships.org.uk

Careers in Nail Services (HABIA) - www.habia.org/

Diplomas (Foundation, Higher and Advanced) - http://yp.direct.gov.uk/diplomas

Training Schemes - www.direct.gov.uk/en/educationandlearning

Welsh Baccalaureate - www.wbq.org.uk

▶Working in hairdressing & beauty (2009) (Babcock Lifeskills) - www.babcock-lifeskills.com/

Addresses

Hairdressing and Beauty Industry Authority (HABIA)
Oxford House, Sixth Avenue, Sky Business Park, Robin Hood Airport, Doncaster DN9 3EG
Phone: 0845 230 6080 (UK only)
Web: www.habia.org/

International Therapy Examination Council (ITEC)
2nd Floor , Chiswick Gate, 598-608 Chiswick High Road, London W4 5RT
Phone: +44 (0)20 8994 4141
Web: www.itecworld.co.uk

Vocational Training Charitable Trust (VTCT)
Eastleigh House, 3rd Floor , Upper Market Street, Hampshire SO50 9FD
Phone: +44 (0)2380 684 500
Web: www.vtct.org.uk

Similar Jobs

Aromatherapist, Beauty Consultant, Beauty Therapist, Film/TV & Theatre Make-Up Artist, Podiatry/Chiropody Assistant, Spa Therapist

Nanny

CRCI:Social Work and Counselling Services
CLCI:KEB

Job Band: 2 to 3

Job Description

Nannies look after babies and children in a private home and take care of them from day to day, often because their parents are working or studying. Some work on a visiting daily basis, others live with the family. Some work short term as a maternity nanny looking after newborn babies. Discuss and plan a daily routine with the parent, carer or guardian, including the children's dietary needs, day trips and play activities. Help the baby/children with their practical needs, such as washing, dressing, eating and changing. Also help children to learn to do things for themselves.

May be expected to do domestic duties, including cooking, cleaning and tidying rooms, shopping and laundry tasks. Keep a careful watch on the children's health and safety. Report any changes in behaviour or signs of illness.

Work Details

Working hours vary according to the contract offered. You work in other people's homes and may need to live-in. Some parents expect you to work some evenings and weekends, but you are probably given time off in lieu. Ensure you have a contract with your employer. The babies or children you work with may be demanding, upset or ill. Sometimes you have to cope with emergencies, so this type of work can be emotionally demanding at times. Because you are working with children you need to be active for most of the time and your work may be noisy and messy.

You may be asked to wear a uniform and some employers require you to have a current driving licence. Nannies are increasingly being registered, in England with the Ofsted Childcare Register (OCR), in Wales with the Childcare Approval Scheme Wales. You may be asked to go on holiday with the family who employs you to continue working with the children.

Qualification

Many employers expect applicants for this job to have a qualification in early years/child care.

• England, Wales and Northern Ireland

Band 2: You can work towards a CACHE level 2 certificate in early years care and education. For some courses: some GCSEs including English language and maths are an advantage.

Band 3: For CACHE level 3 diploma in child care and education: no set entry qualifications, but most colleges prefer some GCSEs including English and maths, or equivalent.

• Scotland

Band 2: For direct entry and to work towards SVQ level 2 in early years education and childcare: some S grades, including English and maths, or similar, are an advantage.

Band 3: For Scottish Group Qualification (SGA) in early years education and childcare: no set entry qualifications, but most colleges ask for some S grades including English and maths, or similar.

Adult Qualifications

Some employers take on adults without qualifications but with experience of looking after children. Mature entrants to college courses do not always require formal qualifications. Check with individual institutions.

Work Experience

Entry to appropriate training courses is competitive and it is essential that you have some relevant work experience before applying for training or for a job as a nanny. Applicants must show evidence of their experience of working with and caring for young children such as working in a nursery school, helping at a playgroup or assisting with childminding. A driving licence is useful and you may be asked to undergo a Criminal Records Bureau (CRB)/Disclosure Scotland check.

Entry and Training

There are currently no formal entry requirements to become a nanny, but most employers/agencies prefer you to have relevant qualifications in child care and early years development. Entry to courses is highly competitive and often entrants have more than the minimum qualifications. In England, Wales and Northern Ireland, courses are validated by CACHE. In Scotland, the Scottish Social Services Council (SSSC) is responsible for regulating childcare workers.

CACHE courses, such as the certificate in childcare and education or the level 3 diploma in home-based childcare, can be studied full time over two years, or for up to five years part time. You can also take the certificate in childcare and education over one year. Candidates with this award may progress to level 3, sometimes with exemption from parts of the course. Experienced staff can complete an advanced diploma in childcare and education in 2-5 years. Check the Early Years and Playwork Qualifications Database for qualifications recognised by Ofsted. You can apply for membership of the National Childminding Association (NCMA), which has details on relevant qualifications and training routes to becoming a nanny.

In Scotland the course, currently validated by the SCCEB, is modular and lasts for two years. After the first year, students gain a national certificate and after the second year they are awarded a higher national certificate in early years care and education. Courses combine practical placements in childcare establishments with theory. Many employers expect applicants for this job to have a relevant qualification and be registered with the Scottish Social Services Council.

S/NVQs in children's care, learning and development are available at levels 2-4. Training programmes, including apprenticeship schemes, may be available in your area. Advanced apprenticeships leading to qualification at level 3 can also be a route into higher education.

There are opportunities for part-time courses and some colleges offer a flexible learning programme. Any previous child care experience is an advantage and can lead to shorter routes to qualification. There are also relevant distance-learning courses. Adults may be able to enter this work through a government-funded training programme.

Opportunities and Pay

With more parents working, the opportunities for private nannies in the UK are increasing and work is also available abroad. It is often possible to find part-time work as a nanny. You may look after the children in a family for some time, perhaps until they go to school, or it can be for a short period, perhaps when there is a new baby. There is limited job security and little opportunity for promotion. Some nannies move into nursery nursing.

Pay varies depending on area, duties, the employer, if you are employed by an agency, and whether you live-in or not. Live-in qualified nannies working full time generally earn between £12k-£22k a year, and daily qualified nannies working full time, from £18-£30k a year. Salaries are generally higher in Central London.

Health
You need to have stamina and be physically fit as there may be some lifting.

Skills and Qualities
able to cope with emergencies, calm, caring, good communication skills, good interpersonal skills, imaginative, patient, responsible attitude, sense of humour

Relevant Subjects
Biology, English, Health and social care, Hospitality and catering, Psychology

Further Information
Apprenticeship Schemes (National Apprenticeship Service) - www.apprenticeships.org.uk

Early Years and Playwork Qualifications Database - http://eypquals.cwdcouncil.org.uk/public

MNT Training - Building your future in Childcare (MNT Training) - www.mnttraining.co.uk

Scottish Childcare - www.scottishchildcare.gov.uk

Training Schemes - www.direct.gov.uk/en/educationandlearning

Addresses
Association of Nanny Agencies (ANA)
15 Church Green, Wickham Bishops, Witham, Essex CM8 3JX
Web: www.anauk.org

CACHE: Council for Awards in Children's Care & Education
Apex House, 81 Camp Road, St Albans AL1 5GB
Phone: 0845 347 2123 (UK only)
Web: www.cache.org.uk

Children's Workforce Development Council (CWDC)
2nd Floor, City Exchange, 11 Albion Street, Leeds LS1 5ES
Phone: +44 (0)113 244 6311
Web: www.cwdcouncil.org.uk

National Childminding Association of England and Wales (NCMA)
Royal Court 81 Tweedy Road, Bromley, Kent BR1 1TG
Phone: 0845 880 0044 (UK only)
Web: www.ncma.org.uk

Scottish Social Services Council (SSSC)
Compass House 11 Riverside Drive, Dundee DD1 4NY
Phone: +44 (0)845 60 30 891
Web: www.sssc.uk.com

Voice
Head Office, 2 St James' Court, Friar Gate, Derby DE1 1BT
Phone: +44 (0)1332 372 337
Web: www.voicetheunion.org.uk

Similar Jobs
Au Pair, Childminder, Nursery Worker, Pre-school Supervisor/Worker, Teaching Assistant

Nanoscientist/Nanotechnologist

CRCI:Science, Mathematics and Statistics
CLCI:QOF — Job Band: 5

Job Description
Nanoscientists design and manipulate structures at atomic and subatomic levels to create materials and devices of greater efficiency, which are measured at a billionth of a metre. They use a combination of methods from many areas of science, including physics, chemistry, biology, biosciences, material science and engineering. Nanotechnology can be used to create new products, materials, and techniques used in medicine, defence, industry (eg computers and cars) and many other fields of development and research.

Duties include proposing theories and trying to explain them through models, exploring their field through computer-aided research, and observing and measuring atomic/subatomic phenomena in the physical world. Some build specialist equipment for new types of measurement, which may not have been attempted before. May work on products for the future, for example, nanoscale filters that deactivate chemical weapons and clean the environment, or a powerful computer that is the size of a grain of sand.

Nanoscientists use sophisticated computer software to monitor and control experiments, and to analyse and display test results. They usually work in a team with other scientists, engineers and technologists, and may supervise teams of laboratory technicians.

Work Details
Usually work a 35-39 hr week; Monday to Friday, in a laboratory, an office or industrial premises. Your tasks can include advising or consulting with colleagues and supervising or organising staff. Depending on the kind of post, you may have responsibility for safety procedures, research reports, analytical data, quality standards or production schedules. This work requires a high degree of accuracy. There is a risk of minor injuries. Sometimes you may deal with unpleasant substances. You may need to wear a white coat or an overall and safety glasses.

Qualification

• England, Wales and Northern Ireland
Band 5: For degree courses: 2-3 A levels including maths or physics, and some GCSEs (A*-C) usually including English maths and science, or equivalent. Exact requirements depend on the degree you take.

• Scotland
Band 5: For degree courses: 3-5 H grades including maths or physics and some S grades (1-3), usually including English, maths and science, or similar. Exact requirements depend on the degree you take.

Degree Information
A degree in nanoscience/nanotechnology is normally preferred or combined with subjects such as microsystems, physics, chemistry, or electronic engineering. Other specific subject areas include information networks and physics, quantum and cosmological physics, materials science and particle physics. Some electrical and mechanical engineering disciplines provide useful background knowledge. Relevant postgraduate courses are available.

Adult Qualifications
A relevant qualification such as a degree/postgraduate qualification is normally required. Up-to-date scientific knowledge is essential. Course entry requirements may be relaxed for mature applicants. A foundation year prior to the start of a science degree may be available at some HE institutions for those applicants who do not have the traditional science entry qualifications or equivalent. Check with colleges or universities for specific information.

Work Experience
Employers or universities may prefer candidates who have relevant work or voluntary experience such as work in a university physics department or a physics summer school. This is ideal, as is experience in an industrial or commercial laboratory.

Entry and Training
Most entrants are graduates. Degree courses last 3-4 years and can be full time or sandwich. Postgraduate study is an advantage. Some first degree courses offer an extended year that leads to Master of Science (MSci) or MPhys. Postgraduate study also

includes MSc courses (different to MSci). A few entrants take a higher national award that lasts 2-3 years that can be full or part time. Membership of the Institute of Physics (IOP) can be attained by graduates with appropriate qualifications and 4-5 years relevant experience. You can also apply to become a chartered physicist (CPhys). Contact the IOP for details.

Training continues through practical experience in the workplace. Continuing professional development (CPD) is expected throughout your career and may be gained through professional seminars, short courses and conferences.

Mature candidates with appropriate qualifications and experience are usually preferred. Part-time study through distance learning for a BSc in natural sciences with physics is available from the Open University. The Science and Technology Facilities Council (STFC) and the Engineering and Physical Sciences Research Council (EPSRC), may offer financial support for some research and postgraduate study.

Opportunities and Pay

Nanotechnology is one of the fastest growing areas in science and engineering. Jobs arise in the cosmetics and pharmaceuticals industries, development of medical devices, computing, engineering, defence and electronics. Telecommunications, data storage and renewable energy technologies have specific applications in nanoscience. Some jobs are in pure or applied research, others are in design, development and production. Employers range from large multinational or national companies to small firms.

Salaries vary depending on area, industry and size of employer. Starting salaries for graduates are £21k-£23k a year, rising to £26k-£45k a year with experience. High earners can make more than £60k a year.

Skills and Qualities

accurate, analytical skills, good communication skills, good presentation skills, information handling skills, interest in new technology, problem-solving skills, research skills, scientific approach, specialist IT skills

Relevant Subjects

Biology, Chemistry, Design and technology, Engineering, English, ICT/Computer studies, Mathematics, Physics, Science

Further Information

Careers in Physics (Institute of Physics (IOP) - www.iop.org/activity/careers/
Nanonet Virtual Network - www.nanonet.org.uk
Nanoscale (Royal Society of Chemistry) - www.rsc.org/Publishing/Journals/NR/index.asp
Nanotechweb.org (Institute of Physics) - http://nanotechweb.org
New Scientist (weekly) (Reed) - www.newscientist.com
Open University - www.open.ac.uk
▶Working in science (2007) (Babcock Lifeskills) - www.babcock-lifeskills.com/
▶Working in space (2010) (Babcock Lifeskills) - www.babcock-lifeskills.com/

Addresses

Engineering and Physical Sciences Research Council (EPSRC)
Polaris House North Star Avenue, Swindon, Wiltshire SN2 1ET
Phone: +44(0)1793 444 100
Web: www.epsrc.ac.uk

Institute of Nanotechnology (IoN)
Suite 5/9 Scion House, Innovation Park,
University of Stirling FK9 4NF
Phone: +44 (0)1786 458 020
Web: www.nano.org.uk

Institute of Physics (IOP)
76 Portland Place, London W1B 1NT
Phone: +44 (0)20 7470 4800
Web: www.iop.org

Science and Technology Facilities Council (STFC)
Polaris House, North Star Avenue, Swindon, Wiltshire SN2 1SZ
Phone: +44 (0)1793 442 000
Web: www.scitech.ac.uk

SEMTA - Engineering Careers Information Service
14 Upton Road, Watford WD18 0JT
Phone: 0845 643 9001 (UK only)
Web: www.semta.org.uk

Similar Jobs

Chemist: Analytical, Engineer: Biomedical, Engineer: Chemical, Lecturer: Higher Education, Materials Scientist/Engineer, Physicist

Naturopath

CRCI:Healthcare
CLCI:JOD

Job Band: 5

Job Description

Naturopaths treat patients by natural methods based on the idea of wellbeing and wholeness and through the body's natural healing processes. They work to avoid the use of drugs or surgery and restore the body to its natural state of good health. They encourage belief in the body's own healing power and ensure that the body's basic needs are recognised and applied, such as safe and sufficient exposure to sunlight, appropriate daily exercise, fresh air and clean water, healthy nutrition, and rest and relaxation. Naturopaths discuss a client's health problems in detail, carry out a physical examination, look at their lifestyle and diet, and seek the cause of the symptoms. They may ask for other tests to be carried out, including blood tests.

Usually diagnose and design an individual plan of treatment for each patient and aim to remove the cause of their health problems by advising on appropriate diet and lifestyle changes, through food supplements, therapeutic massage, detoxification, hydrotherapy, psychological techniques, exercise and relaxation techniques.

May also use chiropractic or osteopathic manipulation techniques, medical herbalism, homeopathy, acupuncture and osteopathy to treat their patients. Some naturopaths liaise with doctors regarding post-surgical care.

Work Details

You may work from home, in rented consulting rooms, or visit people in their homes. The job involves helping people who may be ill, in pain or anxious. Most choose their own working hours to suit their clients, though some weekend and evening appointments may be necessary.

Qualification

- **England, Wales and Northern Ireland**

Band 5: For degree courses: 2-3 A levels including chemistry and a biological science, and some GCSEs (A*-C), usually including English and maths, or equivalent. Exact requirements depend on the degree you take.

- **Scotland**

Band 5: For degree courses: 3-5 H grades, including chemistry and a biological science, and some S grades (1-3), usually including English and maths, or similar qualifications. Exact requirements depend on the degree you take.

Degree Information

Degree and diploma courses in naturopathy are available. There is also a part-time postgraduate diploma for those who are registered in areas of osteopathy, chiropractic, medical herbalism or medicine, and other practitioners trained in anatomy, physiology, pathology, diagnosis and clinical methods to primary healthcare levels.

Adult Qualifications

Mature applicants may be considered on an individual basis. The normal academic requirements for entry to degree course may be waived if the college feels that the applicant can cope with the demands of the course. A science Access or foundation course or Open University science foundation course is useful training preparation for those without relevant qualifications. There is also a foundation year to the BSc (Hons) in health sciences (complementary therapies) course offered by the University of Westminster.

Work Experience

Relevant work or voluntary experience is always useful and can improve your chances in application for entry to this career. Consider work experience which involves helping people or working with the public. Work in a medical field such as volunteering at a hospital, is also relevant.

Entry and Training

The full-time Diploma in Naturopathy at the British College of Osteopathic Medicine and the BSc (Hons) in Osteopathic Medicine take four years. The University of Westminster BSc (Hons) in health sciences (complementary therapies) course lasts for three years full time or four years if combined with the foundation-level course. These are accredited by the General Council and Register of Naturopaths (GCRN). Contact the GCRN for details of all accredited courses.

About 40% of students have a first degree, which may give exemptions from part of the course for graduates in science or medicine. Many students are self-financing, although discretionary awards may be available. It is useful to gain experience and/or training in business related subjects, such as marketing and accounting. Many naturopaths also extend their skills and gain qualifications in other related health areas, such as homeopathy and herbal medicine.

Once qualified, you can register with the GCRN and the British Naturopathic Association. The General Naturopathic Council (GNC) defines the National Occupational Standards for naturopathy in partnership with Skills for Health and provides continuing professional development .

A Diploma/Welsh Baccalaureate in society, health and development may be available in your area and may be relevant to this job.

Mature applicants to courses without the stated entry requirements are considered on an individual basis and in all cases must be able to demonstrate evidence of study to an appropriate equivalent entry level in biology and chemistry. This is often a second career and experience of work in hospitals or with people in need of care is an advantage.

Opportunities and Pay

This is a small but growing profession. Currently, there are around 400 registered naturopaths. You can work in a private clinic, complementary health centre, in a partnership, or you can be self-employed and set up your own practice, once experienced. Training and setting-up costs may involve considerable financial investment. Some go on to teach or write books on naturopathy.

Pay may be low to begin with, so it may be necessary to have another source of income. As many naturopaths are self-employed it is difficult to summarise earnings. Broadly speaking, naturopaths earn between £30-£60 a session, depending on location and experience. Over the year, earnings may range from £20k-£50k. A few may earn around £100 a session and therefore earn considerably more over the year.

Health

This job requires good health.

Skills and Qualities

analytical skills, approachable, business awareness, encouraging, good communication skills, good listening skills, patient, perceptive, reassuring, tactful

Relevant Subjects

Biology, Chemistry, English, Health and social care, Hospitality and catering, Science

Further Information

AGCAS: Health (Job Sector Briefing) (AGCAS) - www.prospects.ac.uk

Diplomas (Foundation, Higher and Advanced) - http://yp.direct.gov.uk/diplomas

Naturopathy Online - www.naturopathyonline.com

Open University - www.open.ac.uk

Skills for Health - sector skills council - www.skillsforhealth.org.uk

Welsh Baccalaureate - www.wbq.org.uk

Addresses

Association of Naturopathic Practitioners (ANP)
Coombe Hurst, Coombe Hill Road, East Grinstead,
West Sussex RH19 4LZ
Web: www.naturopathy-anp.com

British College of Osteopathic Medicine (BCOM)
Lief House, 120-122 Finchley Road, London NW3 5HR
Phone: +44 (0)20 7435 6464
Web: www.bcom.ac.uk

British Naturopathic Association
1 Green Lane Avenue, Street, Somerset BA16 0QS
Phone: +44 (0)1458 840072
Web: www.naturopaths.org.uk

General Council & Register of Naturopaths (GCRN)
1 Green Lane Avenue, Street BA16 0QS
Phone: +44 (0) 1458 840072
Web: www.naturopathy.org.uk

General Naturopathic Council (GNC)
255A Lavender Hill, London SW11 1JD
Phone: +44 (0)20 7978 5538
Web: www.gncouncil.com

Similar Jobs

Acupuncturist, Aromatherapist, Chiropractor, Homeopath, Medical Herbalist, Osteopath

Naval Architect

CRCI:Engineering
CLCI:ROF Job Band: 4 to 5

Job Description

Naval architects are professional engineers involved in the design, development, construction and repair of sea and subsea vessels and offshore structures, which can be civilian or military. These include merchant ships and warships, recreational crafts and yachts, multihull/hovercraft and other high speed vessels, submarines and offshore oil/gas drilling rigs. They usually specialise in design, which increasingly uses computer-aided design (CAD) technology, research and development, or repair. Architects consult with the client regarding the design and specification of a vessel or structure and assess its feasibility in terms of safe, efficient and economic operation.

Naval architects take account of the impact of vessels on the marine environment. They prepares plans and check required standards, obtain materials and equipment and coordinate construction, launching and trials. Also integrate the activities of other professional engineers engaged in the project.

Work Details

Usually work a basic 35 hr week, Monday to Friday, though sometimes work evenings and weekends when deadlines approach. Work is in an office, shipyard or fabrication yard, and on boats, ships or rigs. Most yards are by the sea or a large river.

Naval Architect

You supervise and consult with people and liaise with a team. You are also responsible for monitoring progress, safety and obeying legal regulations.

The job involves some physical activity; climbing ladders and coping with rough seas. Sometimes the environment can be noisy and uncomfortable and the weather can be bad. You may need to wear protective clothing.

Qualification

• England, Wales and Northern Ireland

Band 4: For HND, Diploma of Higher Education or foundation degree: 1-2 A levels, usually maths and a science, and some GCSEs (A*-C) usually including English, maths and science, or equivalent.

Band 5: For degree courses: 2-3 A levels, usually including maths and physics or engineering science, and some GCSEs (A*-C) usually including English and maths and sometimes a foreign language, or equivalent. Exact requirements depend on the degree you take.

• Scotland

Band 4: For SQA higher national award: usually 2-3 H grades, preferably maths and a science, and some S grades (1-3) including English, maths and science, or similar qualifications.

Band 5: For degree courses: 3-5 H grades, usually including maths and physics or engineering, and some S grades (1-3) including English and sometimes a foreign language, or similar qualifications. Exact requirements depend on the degree you take.

Degree Information

A degree in naval architecture, marine engineering, ocean engineering and ship/nautical science is usually preferred. Some other engineering subjects can give relevant background knowledge but may not be suitable for direct entry. There are relevant postgraduate courses for engineering graduates.

Adult Qualifications

A degree or higher national award is normally required. Some colleges and universities may relax entry requirements for these courses for mature applicants with relevant experience. There are many Access courses for entry to engineering degrees and postgraduate courses for engineering graduates.

Work Experience

Employers or colleges/universities may prefer candidates who have relevant work or voluntary experience. This can include experience in any area of engineering as it demonstrates enthusiasm and commitment to the job. Similarly, careers involving design work, or working with machinery or computers, also helps. You can contact a shipbuilder or repair yard, or a company that specialises in building smaller sea-going vessels, and spend time with them. The Royal Institution of Naval Architects also holds details of potential work experience placements.

Applicants to degree courses are encouraged to apply to the 'Year in Industry' scheme for a placement in industry prior to starting their studies. Students also have an opportunity to gain work experience in industry for a year between the penultimate and final years of their degree programme. This experience enhances your job prospects on graduation.

The Engineering Education Scheme is for Year 12 students who wish to make more informed career decisions. There is also a well-established UK summer school programme called Headstart. It aims to give able A-level/H grade students the opportunity to learn more about degrees that lead to jobs in technology-based industries.

Entry and Training

Training is in-house by practical experience, after a degree or BTEC/SQA higher national award. Courses are usually full time but some are sandwich courses. Sponsorship may be available for certain courses. Care should be taken to select an appropriate course, because it must be accredited by the Royal Institution of Naval Architects (RINA). Contact RINA for details of all accredited academic and training courses.

Before becoming a fully qualified member of the RINA you must have held a responsible position for two years and have a total of seven years of education, training and responsible experience after reaching 18. Relevant industrial training (covering design, engineering practice and management services) and initial professional development is required. You must also commit to continuing professional development throughout your career.

Most naval architects aim to become professional engineers at incorporated or chartered engineer level with the Engineering Council. This involves gaining experience and keeping detailed records of your development. Experience is followed by a professional review and an interview.

Incorporated engineers (IEng) need to be qualified to HNC/HND or BEng level, followed by a further year of learning. Another route is through an apprenticeship programme leading to S/NVQ at level 4, then to HNC/HND. Foundation degrees are available in general engineering subjects, but need to be extended to a full degree. Chartered engineers (CEng) may qualify through an accredited course leading to an MEng degree, or a BEng (Hons) followed by an appropriate masters degree. Contact ECUK for details. Chartered engineers can also qualify as European engineers (EurIng) but need to be fluent in a European language.

A Diploma/Welsh Baccalaureate may be available in your area in engineering. The advanced level is equivalent to 3.5 A levels but for some university courses, the additional and specialist learning (ASL) component of the diploma needs to include specific A levels e.g maths or physics, so check entry requirements carefully. See the diplomas website for further information.

The Tomorrow's Engineers website has lots of useful careers information including a route map and guide to engineering activities from primary school through to higher education. The Engineering Development Trust also runs a range of nationwide schemes for 11-21 year olds who may be interested in engineering as a career. See the websites for details.

Mature applicants are usually considered but this depends on your qualifications and experience. Managerial and technological expertise is an advantage. Contact the Engineering Council for details or the Royal Institution of Naval Architects for details of mature entry routes to training and registration.

Sponsorship may be available for higher education courses from the Engineering and Physical Sciences Research Council.

Opportunities and Pay

This is a small profession and most employment is with the Ministry of Defence, large shipbuilders or repair yards, equipment manufacturers, oil rig fabricators, research and development organisations, with shipping companies, or teaching in colleges and universities. Many move into general management at a senior level or work as a consultant. Other jobs are with small craft and yacht builders. Some naval architects work as ship surveyors, ensuring that ships are safe. There are opportunities for foreign travel as many large projects are now undertaken outside Europe.

Salaries vary according to employer, location and specialisation and some naval architects are self-employed or work on a contract basis, so it is difficult to summarise earnings. A starting salary for a graduate is likely to be around £24k-£28k a year. Experienced naval architects with chartered status generally earn around £35k-£50k. High earners might earn up to £80k a year.

Skills and Qualities

analytical skills, attention to detail, creative flair, excellent communication skills, good written English, IT skills, leadership qualities, logical, problem-solving skills, spatial awareness

Relevant Subjects
Design and technology, Economics, Engineering, English, ICT/ Computer studies, Mathematics, Physics, Science

Further Information
AGCAS: Engineering (Job Sector Briefing) (AGCAS) - www.prospects.ac.uk

Careers in Naval Architecture (RINA) (Royal Institute of Naval Architects) - www.rina.org.uk

Diplomas (Foundation, Higher and Advanced) - http://yp.direct.gov.uk/diplomas

Engineering Education Scheme - www.engineering-education.org.uk/

Engineering Education Scheme Wales - www.eesw.org.uk

Headstart Scheme - www.headstartcourses.org.uk

Marine Engineers Review (10 x year) (IMarEST) - www.imarest.org/Publications.aspx

Sea Your Future: A Guide to Marine Careers (IMAREST) - www.imarest.org/membership/careers

SEMTA - sector skills council for science, engineering and manufacturing technologies - www.semta.org.uk

The Naval Architect (10 x year) (The Royal Instition of Naval Architects (RINA)) - www.rina.org.uk/tna.html

Tomorrow's Engineers - www.tomorrowsengineers.org.uk/careers.cfm

▶Working in engineering (2010) (Babcock Lifeskills) - www.babcock-lifeskills.com/

Year in Industry (Engineering Development Trust) - www.yini.org.uk

Your future in the boating industry (British Marine Federation) - www.britishmarine.co.uk/upload_pub/27441_bmf_your_future41.pdf

Addresses
Engineering and Physical Sciences Research Council (EPSRC)
Polaris House North Star Avenue, Swindon, Wiltshire SN2 1ET
Phone: +44(0)1793 444 100
Web: www.epsrc.ac.uk

Engineering Council
246 High Holborn, London WC1V 7EX
Phone: +44 (0)20 3206 0500
Web: www.engc.org.uk

Engineering Development Trust (EDT)
Ridgeway, Welwyn Garden City, Hertfordshire AL7 2AA
Phone: +44 (0)1707 871520
Web: www.etrust.org.uk

Institute of Marine Engineering, Science and Technology (IMarEST)
80 Coleman Street, London EC2R 5BJ
Phone: +44 (0)20 7382 2600
Web: www.imarest.org

Naval Architecture and Marine Engineering
Henry Dyer Building, 100 Montrose Street, Glasgow G4 0LZ
Phone: +44 (0)141 548 4094
Web: www.strath.ac.uk/na-me/

Royal Institution of Naval Architects (RINA)
10 Upper Belgrave Street, London SW1X 8BQ
Phone: +44 (0)20 7235 4622
Web: www.rina.org.uk

Women into Science, Engineering & Construction (WISE)
2nd Floor Weston House, 246 High Holborn, London WC1V 7EX
Phone: +44 (0)20 3206 0408
Web: www.wisecampaign.org.uk

Similar Jobs
CAD Technician, Engineer: Aeronautical, Engineer: Design, Engineer: Marine, Merchant Navy Engineering Officer, Royal Navy Officer

NDT Technician/Engineer
also known as: Industrial Radiographer

CRCI:Engineering
CLCI:ROZ Job Band: 3 to 5

Job Description
Non-destructive testing (NDT) technicians carry out tests and evaluate flaws in materials, without damaging the structure or material under test. NDT is a specific branch of engineering that uses a variety of testing techniques to establish the safety of machinery and metals used in different industrial settings. These may include rail, aircraft and aerospace, ships, and structures such as dams, bridges, power stations, oil/gas rigs and pipelines. Technicians use condition monitoring and diagnostic technology (CMDT) to identify and resolve developing faults before a catastrophic failure occurs, such as an aircraft engine failure at take-off.

They test for flaws such as metal fatigue or variations in structural properties including any damage or signs of weakness. They measure physical properties such as hardness and internal stress and use many techniques. These include simple techniques such as visual examination of surfaces through the well established methods of radiography, ultrasonic testing and magnetic particle crack detection, to fairly new and very specialised methods using thermography, acoustic emission and positron annihilation.

Technicians working in NDT and CMDT cooperate with designers and production staff so that they know the capabilities and limitations of NDT and CMDT. They ensure that the product can be tested and monitored satisfactorily and easily and may present their findings in a report.

Work Details
Usually work around 35-40 hrs a week, Monday to Friday, which may include some additional hours, and you may be expected to work shifts. You work in an industrial environment, workshop or a laboratory. There are safety rules to be obeyed and your key responsibility is working to a strict safety standard. Work is under supervision and you are usually part of a team. You may need to spend time away from home as some work may involve travelling to remote installations such as gas/oil rigs, or generators. Some jobs require you to wear overalls, gloves, safety glasses and perhaps something to cover your hair.

Qualification

• England, Wales and Northern Ireland
Band 3: For entry to jobs, HNC or a relevant Diploma, usually at least 4 GCSEs (A*-C) including English, maths, a science and preferably a practical/technical subject, or equivalent.

Band 4: For HND, Diploma of Higher Education or foundation degree: 1-2 A levels, including maths/science and some GCSEs (A*-C) usually including English, or equivalent.

Band 5: For relevant degree course: 2-3 A levels including maths and physics, and some GCSEs (A*-C) usually including English, or equivalent. Exact requirements depend on the degree you take.

• Scotland
Band 3: For entry to jobs, usually at least four S grades (1-3) including English, maths, a science and preferably a practical/ technical subject, or similar.

Band 4: For entry to SQA higher national and professional development awards, usually 2-3 H grades, including maths and science (preferably physics), and some S grades (1-3), including English and maths, or similar qualifications.

Band 5: For relevant degree course: 3-5 H grades including maths and physics, and some S grades (1-3), often including English, or similar qualifications. Exact requirements depend on the degree you take.

NDT Technician/Engineer

Degree Information

Relevant degrees include materials science, materials engineering, applied physics, instrumentation, metallurgy and polymer science.

Adult Qualifications

Some college courses may relax entry requirements for adults with aptitude and experience. There are specialist courses if you wish to move into NDT. For details, contact the British Institute of Non-Destructive Testing.

Work Experience

Employers or colleges/universities may prefer candidates who have relevant work or voluntary experience. Consider work in any branch of engineering, in the metal trades such as welding or in a construction company. If you expect good A levels/H grades and intend to go to university, schemes such as 'A Year in Industry' give you the opportunity to spend a salaried year with a company to gain valuable work experience.

The Engineering Education Scheme runs programmes in England, Scotland and Wales giving young people the chance to be involved in a real engineering project for six months. Students commit to two to three hours work a week and some time at university residents' workshops. This experience can contribute to any future university application and counts towards the Duke of Edinburgh award skills section.

Similarly, Headstart offers students a chance to experience a week at university, designing, building and testing projects. As engineering careers can be diverse, a week of hands on experience can be really helpful when you are trying to decide which field of engineering you want to train in. Check the websites for details.

Entry and Training

School leavers may enter this job and receive on-the-job training at technician level. Some enter through an apprenticeship scheme in related areas such as welding or engineering inspection. Entrants often have industrial experience and come from a skilled job in the metal trades or from an engineering background. Some people study at a college for national/higher national certificate/diploma in engineering, including NDT/CMDT modules, or you may be able to attend these courses on a day or block-release basis while in employment. The University of Northampton offers a foundation degree in NDT and the emphasis is on previous work experience rather than qualifications. It is a distance learning course with occasional weekend schools.

Some entrants are graduates. The Tomorrow's Engineers website has lots of useful careers information including a route map and guide to engineering activities from primary school through to higher education. The Engineering Development Trust also runs a range of nationwide schemes for 11-21 year olds who may be interested in engineering as a career. See the websites for details.

There are two main routes to professional qualification; either in-company certification or examination at a recognised test centre, leading to the Personnel Certification in NDT (PCN). Courses are accredited by the British Institute of Non-Destructive Testing (BINDT). Contact BINDT for course and qualification details. An S/NVQ in non-destructive testing is available at level 3. NDT technicians/engineers may work towards professional status with the Engineering Council UK at technician, incorporated or chartered level, depending on their qualifications.

A Diploma/Welsh Baccalaureate may be available in your area in engineering. The advanced level is equivalent to 3.5 A levels but for some university courses, the additional and specialist learning (ASL) component of the diploma needs to include specific A levels eg maths or physics. Check entry requirements carefully.

Mature applicants can benefit through government training opportunities, such as apprenticeships for adults, that may be available in your area. You can also gain recognition of previous experience through Accreditation of Prior Learning (APL) or by working towards relevant S/NVQs. Contact your local careers office, Jobcentre Plus, Next Step service or Learning and Skills Council (LSC)/Local Enterprise Company (LEC) for details of training schemes.

The Open University (OU) runs a range of engineering courses and the Institution of Engineering Designers has accredited two OU engineering qualifications for professional registration. See the OU website for details.

Opportunities and Pay

This is a fast-moving area of development in new and specialist techniques. Employers include manufacturing and construction firms, specialist NDT companies, shipbuilding and repair industry, firms operating installations such as offshore gas and oil platforms, or organisations such as airline companies who need an NDT team to test crucial equipment. There are opportunities to progress to senior levels in large companies or, with experience, the possibility of becoming a self-employed consultant. Fully qualified PCN technicians are in demand.

Pay varies depending on location and employer. Starting salaries are likely to be from around £17k, rising to £22k-£30k, with experience. Chief NDT technicians can earn up to £40k. Special payments for shift work and overtime may be offered.

Health

This job requires good eyesight and colour vision for certain areas of work.

Skills and Qualities

able to work both on your own and in a team, accurate, analytical skills, attention to detail, good communication skills, good written English, IT skills, logical, numeracy skills, problem-solving skills

Relevant Subjects

Chemistry, Design and technology, Engineering, ICT/Computer studies, Mathematics, Physics, Science

Further Information

AGCAS: Engineering (Job Sector Briefing) (AGCAS) - www.prospects.ac.uk

Apprenticeship Schemes (National Apprenticeship Service) - www.apprenticeships.org.uk

Diplomas (Foundation, Higher and Advanced) - http://yp.direct.gov.uk/diplomas

Engineering Connections - Apprenticeships - www.apprentices.co.uk

Engineering Education Scheme - www.engineering-education.org.uk/

Engineering Education Scheme Wales - www.eesw.org.uk

Engineering Scotland (SEMTA) - www.engineeringscotland.org

Headstart Scheme - www.headstartcourses.org.uk

Insight - Non-Destructive Testing and Condition Monitoring (British Institute of Non-Destructive Testing) - www.bindt.org/Publications

NDT News (BINDT) (British Institute of Non-Destructive Testing) - www.bindt.org/Publications

Open University - www.open.ac.uk

Scenta - Careers Guide, Engineering, Technology and Science (Engineering Technology Board) - www.scenta.co.uk/careers.cfm

SEMTA - sector skills council for science, engineering and manufacturing technologies - www.semta.org.uk

Tomorrow's Engineers - www.tomorrowsengineers.org.uk/careers.cfm

Women into Science, Engineering & Construction - www.wisecampaign.org.uk

Year in Industry (Engineering Development Trust) - www.yini.org.uk

Young Engineers - www.youngeng.org/

Addresses

British Institute of Non-Destructive Testing (BINDT)
1 Spencer Parade, Northampton NN1 5AA
Phone: +44 (0)1604 630124
Web: www.bindt.org

Engineering Council
246 High Holborn, London WC1V 7EX
Phone: +44 (0)20 3206 0500
Web: www.engc.org.uk

Engineering Development Trust (EDT)
Ridgeway, Welwyn Garden City, Hertfordshire AL7 2AA
Phone: +44 (0)1707 871520
Web: www.etrust.org.uk

University of Northampton
Park Campus Boughton Green Road, Northampton NN2 7AL
Phone: +44 (0)1604 735500
Web: www.northampton.ac.uk

Similar Jobs

Ceramic Technologist, Civil Engineering Technician, Laboratory Technician: Science, Materials Scientist/Engineer, Metallurgist, Quality Manager

Network Administrator

also known as: Computer Network Administrator, Network Engineer, Systems and Network Administrator

CRCI:Computers and IT
CLCI:CAV
Job Band: 3 to 5

Job Description

Network administrators install, support and maintain computer hardware and software that is connected by a network of computers and equipment. Computers are linked together to enable the exchange of common information and provide access to the Internet/Intranet. They are responsible for maintaining the network and work with IT security specialists to prevent unwanted access from 'hackers' and viruses entering or corrupting it. A network can be as small as two or three computers, a local area network (LAN), a wide area network (WAN), metropolitan area network (MAN) or a global area network (GAN) as large as the Internet, the world's largest computer network.

Network administrators need to have a good knowledge of computer software as well as hardware. They install new software and hardware and set up new user accounts and passwords. Also help to track down and resolve network problems. May provide training on new systems, discuss any hardware/software problems with users and be expected to find solutions quickly. Also carry out general administration tasks and may also work with network managers to help implement future developments of the network.

Work Details

You work 35-37 hrs a week, Monday to Friday, though you must be prepared to work longer hours on occasions to meet deadlines. May be required to be on call to deal with emergencies. Many hours are spent sitting at a computer. The work is normally office based, but if involved in a large network operation, you may be required to travel between sites. Sometimes you may work on your own, but generally you work closely with other professional colleagues and those using the network.

Qualification

• England, Wales and Northern Ireland

Band 3: For most employers, or for a relevant BTEC national award: 4-5 GCSEs (A*-C) including English, maths, and preferably ICT, or equivalent.

Band 4: For a relevant higher national award course: 1-2 A levels, preferably in maths or physics, and some GCSEs (A*-C) usually including English and maths, or equivalent.

Band 5: For relevant degree course: 2-3 A levels, preferably with at least one in maths or physics, and some GCSEs (A*-C) usually including English and maths, or equivalent. Exact requirements depend on the degree you take.

• Scotland

Band 3: For most employers, or for a relevant SQA national award: usually 4-5 S grades (1-3) including English, maths, and preferably computer studies or information technology, or similar.

Band 4: For a relevant higher national course: usually 2-3 H grades, preferably including maths or physics, and some S grades (1-3) often including English and maths, or similar qualifications.

Band 5: For relevant degree course: 3-5 H grades, preferably with at least one in maths or physics, and some S grades (1-3) usually including English and maths, or similar qualifications. Exact requirements depend on the degree you take.

Degree Information

Subjects such as network computing and related subjects, software engineering, mathematical sciences, information systems/technology, computer science or artificial intelligence may be preferred by employers. The Information Technology Management for Business degree (see e-skills UK) is designed in partnership with some of the biggest employers in the IT industry. Systems and control engineering, physics and electronic engineering may also be acceptable. Postgraduate courses are available for science or mathematics graduates.

Adult Qualifications

Mature applicants may not need the standard entry requirements for higher education courses, particularly if your previous experience is relevant or if you show ability to study at the appropriate level. Access or foundation courses give adults without qualifications a route onto degree courses.

Work Experience

Employers or colleges and universities may prefer candidates who have relevant work or voluntary experience. This can include any form of computer-based work such as network or IT support, programming or hardware or software specialisms. Internships or work placements that you can do while studying are a valuable introduction to the IT industry and enable you to make an informed career choice.

Other schemes, such as 'A Year in Industry', enable those who expect good A levels/H grades and intend to go to university the opportunity to spend a salaried year with a company to gain valuable work experience.

Entry and Training

Entry is possible with a range of qualifications, though most employers look for network knowledge and experience of using relevant computer applications and operating systems. You may have to take a practical aptitude test and you also need good customer service skills or technical support experience for this job. Some employers offer 4-6 weeks' intensive training covering in-house procedures, network installations and programs. Others may specify a degree or national/higher national qualification, such as a BTEC national certificate/diploma in computing (networking or systems support).

It is important to keep up to date with new software and hardware developments throughout your career. Training is ongoing via in-house courses, intensive online courses, attendance at a local college, or by short courses run by manufacturers or independent training organisations. A popular IT industry-recognised entry-level qualification is the CompTIA A+ which offers alternative validation paths for specific job environments. You can also gain qualifications for specific networks, eg Microsoft Certified Network Engineer (MCNE) or Certified Novell Engineer (CNE). Training for these courses is typically through short courses at accredited training centres. Cisco Systems Incorporated also offers certification at several levels for network professionals.

Network Manager

A Diploma/Welsh Baccalaureate in IT is available for 14-19 year olds and may be run in your area. It has been designed in partnership with universities and employers. E-skills also offers an internship. Students are placed for a period of employment within an organisation, enabling them to develop valuable business and IT skills. Contact e-skills for details. Relevant S/NVQs for ICT practitioners and professionals are available at levels 1-4 and the new S/NVQ for IT users (ITQ 2009) has been developed as part of a project involving a full review of the National Occupational Standards for IT users.

Training programmes, including apprenticeship schemes in IT and Telecoms, may be available in your area for entry to this job. An ICT higher apprenticeship is available through e-skills. This combines an apprenticeship with a foundation degree and can lead to a full honours degree. There are partnerships with colleges and universities throughout the UK. The Open University offers courses in computing and maths leading to a computing degree. There are no formal entry requirements and you study through distance learning. Full or part-time foundation degrees in network computing and other IT subjects are also available.

Mature applicants may need prior IT training and relevant business experience before entry to this job. There may be government training opportunities in your area and you can also gain recognition of previous experience through Accreditation of Prior Learning (APL) or by working towards relevant S/NVQs. Contact your local careers office, Jobcentre Plus, Next Step service, or Learning and Skills Council (LSC)/Local Enterprise Company (LEC) for details of all training opportunities and schemes, including apprenticeships for adults.

Opportunities and Pay

Development of computer networks over the last few years has expanded, with global communications growing in all major businesses. There are opportunities for network administrators across the UK in all industry sectors, including commerce, education, finance, public utilities, the health sector, armed forces, the media, or local/central government departments. There is a demand for people with the right technical skills, and good interpersonal skills. Promotion to network management, information security or systems architecture is possible and there are also opportunities to work as a self-employed consultant or contractor later in your career. Work may be available overseas.

Pay varies depending on location and type of company. A trainee or junior network administrator can earn between £16k-£22k a year, rising to £22k-£35k with experience. Senior network administrators/engineers can earn up to £40k a year. Profit-sharing, performance-related pay or a bonus payment may be additional to your basic salary.

Skills and Qualities

able to explain clearly, able to work both on your own and in a team, analytical skills, customer service skills, good communication skills, good organisational skills, logical and methodical, problem-solving skills, specialist IT skills, technical aptitude

Relevant Subjects

Design and technology, English, ICT/Computer studies, Mathematics, Physics, Science

Further Information

AGCAS: Information Technology (Job Sector Briefing) (AGCAS) - www.prospects.ac.uk

Cisco Systems Incorporated - www.cisco.com

Computer Weekly (Reed Business Information) - www.computerweekly.com

Computing Technology Industry Association (CompTIA) - www.comptia.org

Diplomas (Foundation, Higher and Advanced) - http://yp.direct.gov.uk/diplomas

e-skills UK - sector skills council for business and information technology - www.e-skills.com

Inside Careers Guide: Information Technology - www.insidecareers.co.uk

Open University - www.open.ac.uk

Real Life Guide to Information & Communications Technology (Trotman) - www.trotman.co.uk

Welsh Baccalaureate - www.wbq.org.uk

►Working in computers & IT (2010) (Babcock Lifeskills) - www.babcock-lifeskills.com/

Year in Industry (Engineering Development Trust) - www.yini.org.uk

Addresses

British Computer Society (BCS)
First Floor, Block D North Star House North Star Avenue, Swindon, Wiltshire SN2 1FA
Phone: +44 (0)845 300 4417
Web: www.bcs.org

Institute for the Management of Information Systems (IMIS)
5 Kingfisher House, New Mill Road, Orpington, Kent BR5 3QG
Phone: +44 (0)700 002 3456
Web: www.imis.org.uk

Similar Jobs

Computer Operator, Database Administrator, IT Helpdesk Analyst/Operator, IT Security Specialist, IT Service Technician, IT Technical Support Manager, Network Manager

Network Manager

also known as: Computer Network Manager

CRCI:Computers and IT

CLCI:CAV — Job Band: 3 to 5

Job Description

Network managers design, install, support and manage computer hardware and software that is connected by means of a network of IT equipment. Computers are linked together to enable the exchange of common information and provide access to the Internet/Intranet. Networks can be local area networks (LANs), wide area networks (WANs), metropolitan area networks (MANs) or global area networks (GANs). Have good knowledge of at least one network operating system and are capable of installing this on hardware. Work with computer network administrators and IT security specialists to track down and resolve problems in the operation and security of the software. Are also responsible for the back-up of the network.

Network managers have to possess a good knowledge of computer hardware as well as software. May supervise a team of technicians. Train network users, monitor staff workloads, and plan future staffing needs. Discuss any hardware/software problems with users and are expected to find solutions quickly. Attend meetings, and plan and implement future development of the network.

Work Details

You work 35-37 hrs a week, Monday to Friday, though you must be prepared to work longer to meet deadlines. May be required to be on call to deal with emergencies. Many hours are spent sitting at a computer. The work is normally office based, but if involved in a large network operation, you may be required to travel between sites. Sometimes you may work on your own, but generally you work closely with other professional colleagues and those using the network.

May need to have the skills required to lead a team of employees. An understanding of the business needs of the organisation is important to help you to design appropriate network systems.

Qualification

- **England, Wales and Northern Ireland**

Band 4: For a relevant higher national award course: 1-2 A levels, preferably in maths or physics, and some GCSEs (A*-C) usually including English and maths, or equivalent.

Band 5: For relevant degree course: 2-3 A levels, preferably with at least one in maths or physics, and some GCSEs (A*-C) usually including English and maths, or equivalent. Exact requirements depend on the degree you take.

- **Scotland**

Band 4: For a relevant higher national course: usually 2-3 H grades, preferably including maths or physics, and some S grades (1-3) often including English and maths, or similar qualifications.

Band 5: For relevant degree course: 3-5 H grades, preferably with at least one in maths or physics, and some S grades (1-3) usually including English and maths, or similar qualifications. Exact requirements depend on the degree you take.

Degree Information

Subjects such as network computing and related subjects, software engineering, mathematical sciences, information systems/technology, computer science or artificial intelligence may be preferred by employers. The Information Technology Management for Business degree (see e-skills UK) is designed in partnership with some of the biggest employers in the IT industry. Systems and control engineering, physics and electronic engineering may also be acceptable. Postgraduate courses are available for science or mathematics graduates.

Adult Qualifications

Mature applicants may not need the standard entry requirements for higher education courses, particularly if your previous experience is relevant or if you show ability to study at the appropriate level. Access or foundation courses give adults without qualifications a route onto degree courses.

Work Experience

Employers or colleges and universities may prefer candidates who have relevant work or voluntary experience. This can include any form of computer-based work such as network or IT support, programming or hardware or software specialisms. Any internships or work placements that you can do while studying are a valuable introduction to the IT industry and enable you to make an informed career choice.

Other schemes, such as 'A Year in Industry', enable those who expect good A levels/H grades and intend to go to university the opportunity to spend a salaried year with a company to gain valuable work experience.

Entry and Training

There is strong competition for this job and most entrants are graduates or hold an HNC/HND. It is usual to gain experience in network administration or systems analysis and progress to this job. Some employers offer the opportunity to begin as a trainee programmer and then progress to become a network manager. Others may enter through the apprenticeship route. An ICT higher apprenticeship is available through e-skills which combines an apprenticeship with a foundation degree and can lead to a full honours degree. There are partnerships with colleges and universities throughout the UK.

It is important to keep up to date with new software and hardware developments throughout your career. Training is ongoing via in-house courses, intensive online courses, attendance at a local college, or by short courses run by manufacturers or independent training organisations. A popular IT industry-recognised entry-level qualification is the CompTIA A+ which offers alternative validation paths for specific job environments. Many network managers gain qualifications for specific networks, eg Microsoft Certified Network Engineer (MCNE) or Certified Novell Engineer (CNE). Training for these courses is typically through short courses at accredited training centres. Cisco Systems Incorporated also offers certification at several levels for network professionals.

E-skills also run a professional development programme which enables new IT professionals to fast-track their career. The programme is delivered through universities and participating employers. E-skills also offers an internship in which students are placed for a period of employment within an organisation, enabling them to develop valuable business and IT skills. Contact e-skills for details of all programmes and schemes.

Some network managers work towards gaining Chartered IT Professional (CITP) status through the British Computer Society (BCS). To do this you usually need 8-10 years' IT experience plus 12 months' experience in a highly responsible IT role. Some exemptions apply. Contact the BCS for further details. Other professional qualifications include those offered by the Institute for the Management of Information Systems (IMIS).

The Open University offers courses in computing and maths leading to a computing degree. There are no formal entry requirements and you study through distance learning. Full or part-time foundation degrees in network computing and other IT subjects are also available.

Mature applicants may encounter some difficulty unless equipped with a good level of IT training and relevant business experience. There may be government training opportunities in your area and you can also gain recognition of previous experience through Accreditation of Prior Learning (APL) or by working towards relevant S/NVQs. Contact your local careers office, Jobcentre Plus, Next Step service, or Learning and Skills Council (LSC)/Local Enterprise Company (LEC) for details of all training opportunities and schemes.

Opportunities and Pay

There has been a large growth in the development of computer networks over the last few years, with global communications growing in all major businesses. There are opportunities for network managers across the UK in all industry sectors, including commerce, education, finance, public utilities, the health sector, armed forces, the media, or local/central government departments.

There is demand for people with the right technical skills, and good interpersonal skills. You can also work in IT training, in technical writing or work freelance for an agency. Promotion to senior or management posts, information security or systems architecture is possible and there are also opportunities to work as a self-employed consultant or contractor. Work may be available overseas.

Pay varies depending on location and type of company. A graduate entrant can earn £19k-£28k, rising to £35k-£48k with experience. Some can make in excess of £60k a year. Profit-sharing, performance-related pay or a bonus payment may be additional to your basic salary.

Skills and Qualities

able to explain clearly, analytical skills, clear-thinking, good communication skills, good organisational skills, logical, perseverance, problem-solving skills, specialist IT skills, technical aptitude

Relevant Subjects

Design and technology, English, ICT/Computer studies, Mathematics, Physics, Science

Further Information

AGCAS: Information Technology (Job Sector Briefing) (AGCAS) - www.prospects.ac.uk

Cisco Systems Incorporated - www.cisco.com

Computer Weekly (Reed Business Information) - www.computerweekly.com

Computing Technology Industry Association (CompTIA) - www.comptia.org

e-skills UK - sector skills council for business and information technology - www.e-skills.com

Inside Careers Guide: Information Technology - www.insidecareers.co.uk

Open University - www.open.ac.uk

Real Life Guide to Information & Communications Technology (Trotman) - www.trotman.co.uk

Skills Framework for the Information Age (SFIA) (SFIA Foundation) - www.sfia.org.uk

►Working in computers & IT (2010) (Babcock Lifeskills) - www.babcock-lifeskills.com/

Year in Industry (Engineering Development Trust) - www.yini.org.uk

Addresses

British Computer Society (BCS)
First Floor, Block D North Star House North Star Avenue, Swindon, Wiltshire SN2 1FA
Phone: +44 (0)845 300 4417
Web: www.bcs.org

Institute for the Management of Information Systems (IMIS)
5 Kingfisher House, New Mill Road, Orpington, Kent BR5 3QG
Phone: +44 (0)700 002 3456
Web: www.imis.org.uk

Similar Jobs

Database Administrator, IT Applications Developer, IT Security Specialist, IT Service Technician, IT Systems Analyst/Designer, IT Systems Developer, Network Administrator

Neurophysiologist

also known as: Clinical Neurophysiologist, Electroencephalogical Technician, Neurophysiological Technician, Physiological Measurement Technician: Neurophysiology

CRCI:Healthcare

CLCI:JOB Job Band: 3 to 5

Job Description

Neurophysiologists investigate the functions of the nervous system, measure nerve activity and neuromuscular damage. They set up and operate complex equipment to measure the activity of certain parts of the body, and help diagnose disorders and diseases, such as epilepsy, dementia, strokes, multiple sclerosis and muscular dystrophy. Prepare patients for tests and liaise with medical staff. Record the electrical activity of the brain and nervous system by attaching electrodes from an electroencephalograph (EEG) and other complex equipment to a patient. Analyse the results and report them to doctors.

Neurophysiologists usually specialise in specific areas of the profession, such as measuring hearing, heart rhythms or electrical activity in the brain. They work in a team alongside other medical staff and assist medical physicists to help develop new methods of diagnosis, care and treatment of patients.

Work Details

You usually work a 37 hr week in a hospital assisting senior colleagues, but may be required to work shifts on a rota to cover 24 hrs a day, including some weekends. Overtime work is possible. Some of the tests you perform are unpleasant or uncomfortable for the patient and you have to reassure those who are afraid, upset or in pain. You are responsible for accurate work, which can be demanding at times. You have to cope with the sight of blood. You are on your feet for much of the day. A white coat or a uniform may be provided by your employer.

Qualification

- **England, Wales and Northern Ireland**

Band 4: For employers: 2 A levels at minimum grade C in science based subjects and some GCSEs (A*-C) including science subjects, or equivalent. A foundation degree in clinical physiology can be studied two years full time or three years part time. A relevant vocational qualification may also be helpful.

Band 5: For degree courses: 2-3 A levels including at least one science subject, and some GCSEs (A*-C) usually including English, maths and two sciences. Exact requirements depend on the degree you take.

- **Scotland**

Band 4: For employers and relevant SQA higher national awards: usually 2-3 H grades in science subjects and some S grades (1-3), often including English and maths, or similar qualifications.

Band 5: For degree courses: 3-5 H grades including at least one science subject and some S grades (1-3), usually including English and maths, or similar qualifications. Exact requirements depend on the degree you take.

Degree Information

A first degree in clinical physiology is expected by most employers but other science-based degrees may be acceptable. Check with hospital neurophysical departments or the Electrophysiological Technologist's Association for details of relevant degree subjects, before embarking on a full-time degree course. Once employed, top-up courses may be available depending on your level of neurophysiological knowledge.

Adult Qualifications

Entry requirements may be relaxed for adults applying for higher education courses and Access and foundation courses give adults without qualifications a route onto degree courses. It is useful to have a good level of science qualifications or equivalent.

Work Experience

Work experience gives you an insight into what you enjoy about a job or working environment, and the opportunity to acquire new skills. It provides valuable information to add to your CV and improves your employment prospects. There is usually a waiting list for work experience in hospitals so enquire early, asking if it is possible to visit other related departments whilst you are there. Experience of working with people in a caring capacity is also an advantage.

Entry and Training

You may enter as a student practitioner with at least two science A levels/3-5 H grades (or equivalent), and train for four years towards a BSc degree in clinical physiology to become state registered with the Health Professions Council. To obtain access to a course you must find a Trust which is appointing a student and be successful in your application for the post. You receive a salary during the training period. Others enter with a first degree in a relevant science subject, including clinical physiology but it is best to check with the hospital neurophysiology department for details of relevant degree subjects before embarking on a full-time degree course.

The Electrophysiological Technologist's Association is the professional body representing neurophysiologists. It currently has over 600 members worldwide and aims to support its members and develop the profession. Continuing professional development (CPD) is an important part of the job.

Mature applicants are particularly welcomed for training though the entry requirements are the same. Contact the hospital neurophysiology department for details of training opportunities and entry requirements.

Opportunities and Pay
There are only around 500 neurophysiologists in the UK but it is a fast growing profession where high technology is used. Jobs are available, mainly in the NHS, in cities and large towns throughout the UK. You can also be employed by a local authority, in research, in private healthcare companies or in the armed forces. Promotion is often through a formal career structure leading to departmental senior officers and managers and usually requires a more advanced qualification. Some move on to work in research or for medical equipment manufacturers. There are also opportunities to work overseas.

Pay is on a nationally agreed scale and increases with promotion. Those working in the NHS follow a salary scale divided into levels of experience. Starting salaries are around £21k-£25k rising to £28k-£40k a year with experience and/or qualification, and those in senior positions working as consultants earn up to £50k or more a year.

Skills and Qualities
able to cope under pressure, able to inspire confidence, accurate, analytical skills, aptitude for teamwork, careful, good communication skills, responsible attitude, sympathetic, technical aptitude

Relevant Subjects
Biology, Design and technology, Health and social care, Mathematics, Physics, Science

Further Information
British Society for Clinical Neurophysiology - www.bscn.org.uk
European Journal of Neurology (European Federation of Neurological Studies) - www.efns.org/publications
Health Professions Council (HPC) - www.hpc-uk.org
NHS Careers (NHS Careers) - www.nhscareers.nhs.uk
NHS Careers Scotland - www.infoscotland.com/nhs
NHS Careers Wales - www.wales.nhs.uk

Addresses
Health Professions Council (HPC)
Park House, 184 Kennington Park Road, London SE11 4BU
Phone: +44 (0)20 7582 0866
Web: www.hpc-uk.org

Institute of Physics and Engineering in Medicine (IPEM)
Fairmount House, 230 Tadcaster Road, York YO24 1ES
Phone: +44 (0)1904 610 821
Web: www.ipem.ac.uk

Similar Jobs
Audiologist, Cardiac Physiologist, Clinical Scientist: Medical Physicist, Clinical Technologist, Perfusionist, Respiratory Physiologist

Nurse/Nursing Officer: Army
also known as: Queen Alexandra's Royal Army Nursing Corps: Nurse/Nursing Officer

CRCI:Security and Armed Forces
CLCI:BAF Job Band: 5

Job Description
Nurses/Nursing officers work in the Queen Alexandra's Royal Army Nursing Corps (QARANC) and are part of a multi-disciplinary medical team. Are responsible for the planning and delivery of nursing care and medical treatment to army personnel, their families and civilians. Nursing officers are involved in teaching student nurses who are undertaking the clinical component of their nurse training, and also assist in the teaching of healthcare assistants

Nursing officers are required to write reports, and carry out ward rounds with doctors and consultants. They assist ward managers with the day-to-day running of the ward and deputise in their absence.

Work Details
Once you have completed officer training you are posted to an army hospital or clinic in the UK, but later may find yourself anywhere in the world on operational duties. You are expected to work unsociable hours and shifts and help people who are ill and possibly in pain, upset or depressed. Work can sometimes be emotionally and physically tiring. You may need to enforce discipline, make some unpopular decisions and can also be expected to serve in dangerous environments where there may be a risk of injury. Nursing officers wear a uniform and sometimes protective clothing.

Qualification
The Scottish Qualifications Authority (SQA) launched a new Skills for Work course in 2008. This course introduces candidates to the uniformed and emergency services and is particularly suited to those considering a career in the Army, Royal Navy, Royal Air Force or Royal Marines. Check the website for details.

• England, Wales and Northern Ireland
Band 5: For entry to QARANC student nurse training programme: 3 A levels and 5 GCSEs (A*-C) including maths, English and a science. You need 240 UCAS points (which roughly equates to a minimum of 3 A levels at grade C or above).

• Scotland
Band 5: For entry to QARANC student nurse training programme: 4-5 H grades and some S grades (1-3) including maths, English and a science. You need 240 UCAS points at H grade.

Degree Information
A degree in nursing or nursing studies leads to registration as a nurse. Graduates with relevant first degrees such as biological sciences, behavioural sciences or health related subjects, can take a shortened postgraduate course.

Adult Qualifications
Mature applicants for nurse training who do not have the required qualifications may be able to take an entrance test. Many colleges offer Access courses for mature applicants without the standard entry requirements for higher education.

Work Experience
Employers or colleges/universities may prefer candidates who have relevant work or voluntary experience, as it demonstrates enthusiasm and commitment. This can include working with people in a helping capacity in a nursery, or in an elderly residential home as a care assistant, as a classroom assistant or in customer service. The job is about rapport, communication and listening, as much as the medical work. Work experience also prepares you for the more domestic side of the job. Many colleges say that prospective students do not always think about this part of the job and it sometimes comes as a surprise to many applicants.

Entry and Training
There are strict nationality and residence requirements for Army entry. Applicants attend a selection board that combines written examinations and physical tests designed to measure leadership potential. For entry as a nursing officer, you must be at least 23 years of age and have already completed registered nurse training (RN - adult or mental health). See the Nurse: Adult and Nurse: Mental Health job articles for full details on how to train as a nurse in civilian life.

Those with over two years' post-qualification experience enter as trainee nursing officers via a 12-week Entry Officer's Course at Keogh Barracks (Aldershot), which includes four weeks at the Royal Military Academy, Sandhurst. Qualified nurses get the opportunity to specialise by studying specific courses. Newly qualified nurses join the army training regiment at Winchester or Pirbright for soldier training that lasts 14 weeks. You can apply to join the Army and be interviewed in your last six months of nurse training. Following initial training you start work on the wards and are promoted to acting corporal.

Student nurses also begin at Winchester or Pirbright for basic military training, followed by training at the University of Central England, and practical experience that leads to qualification as a UK registered nurse. University holidays include practical experience in a variety of MOD and civilian hospitals and challenges other than nursing, such as adventure training.

The Army Health Studies Division is based in Birmingham and serves the Army, Navy and RAF. Nurses can continue their studies here up to masters level. The army provides funding and study time for those who are eligible for these courses.

Mature applicants for entry should check with their local armed forces careers office for details of upper age limits. Registered nurses who already hold a qualification in accident and emergency (A&E) or in intensive care nursing may be eligible for a 'Golden Hello' (currently £20k) upon their successful commission. Contact your local armed forces careers office or the Army Nurse Information Team for further information on entry requirements.

Opportunities and Pay

There are good opportunities for promotion and prospects are improved by taking further training. Specialist nursing courses are available and you are encouraged to continue your professional development. This job requires a great deal of personal commitment and you must complete a minimum of three years' service. Promotion is through experience and recommendation. The training and qualifications received in this job provide an excellent basis for occupations in the NHS and the private sector.

Pay varies depending on your level of qualification and/or previous nursing experience. Student nurse salaries start at £15,677 a year, registered nurses (soldiers) earn from £25,422 and nursing officers start at £29,425k a year depending on experience on entry. A bursary scheme is available for officers in training, consisting of £6,000 over three years, with a guaranteed job on completion.

Health

The work may involve the risk of infection. You take a medical test on entry and require good general fitness.

Skills and Qualities

able to give clear instructions, able to take responsibility, aptitude for teamwork, caring, decisive, efficient, leadership qualities, not squeamish, patient, reassuring

Relevant Subjects

Biology, Chemistry, English, Health and social care, Psychology, Science

Further Information

Army Careers Website - www. army.mod.uk

Careers Information - Job Explorer, Army ( ) - www.armyjobs.mod.uk/

Queen Alexandra's Royal Army Nursing Corps - www.army.mod.uk/army-medical-services/9869.aspx

Skills for Work (Scottish Qualifications Authority) - www.sqa.org.uk/sqa/31390.html

▶ Working in police, fire & security (2009) (Babcock Lifeskills) - www.babcock-lifeskills.com/

Addresses

Nursing and Midwifery Council (NMC)
23 Portland Place, London W1B 1PZ
Phone: +44 (0)20 7333 9333
Web: www.nmc-uk.org

Similar Jobs

Army Officer, Nurse/Nursing Officer: RAF, Nurse/Nursing Officer: Royal Navy, Nurse: Adult

Nurse/Nursing Officer: RAF

also known as: Princess Mary's RAF Nursing Service: Nurse/ Nursing Officer

CRCI:Security and Armed Forces
CLCI:BAL Job Band: 4 to 5

Job Description

Nurses/nursing officers work in the Princess Mary's RAF Nursing Service and are part of a multi-disciplinary medical team. Help to look after the health and fitness of everyone in the RAF, such as aircrew, ground crew and other support staff. Also provide care for entitled civilians and personnel from other services. Give medical treatment and care for patients in medical centres similar to GP surgeries, at RAF stations in the UK and overseas. Also provide nursing care at a UK based tri-service hospital or rehabilitation unit, MOD (Ministry of Defence) hospital unit or in the Princess Mary's hospital in Cyprus.

Take part in the aeromedical evacuation of casualties from overseas to hospitals in the UK for treatment. Nursing officers train and supervise the work of healthcare assistants and junior members of a nursing team. Are required to write reports and carry out ward rounds with doctors and consultants.

Work Details

Upon completion of officer training, you are posted to an RAF medical centre, health centre or hospital in the UK or abroad. You may find yourself anywhere in the world on operational duties and are expected to work unsocial hours and shifts. There is contact with people who are ill and possibly in pain, upset or depressed. Work can be emotionally demanding and physically tiring at times. You help people, working in a team, and may need to enforce discipline and make some unpopular decisions.

As a nursing officer you can be expected to serve in dangerous situations where there is a risk of injury. You wear a uniform and possibly protective clothing.

Qualification

The Scottish Qualifications Authority (SQA) launched a new Skills for Work course in 2008. This course introduces candidates to the uniformed and emergency services and is particularly suited to those considering a career in the Army, Royal Navy, Royal Air Force or Royal Marines. Check the website for details.

• England, Wales and Northern Ireland

Band 4: For entry to training with the RAF: minimum of 200 UCAS points at A level, including a science-based subject. Alternative qualifications may be considered on a case-by-case basis.

Band 5: For a degree: 2-3 A levels and a number of GCSEs (A*-C), including English, maths and a science subject. The exact requirements depend on the degree you take.

• Scotland

Band 4: For entry to training with the RAF: minimum of 200 UCAS points at H grade, including a science-based subject. Alternative qualifications may be considered on a case-by-case basis.

Band 5: For a degree: 3-5 H grades and a number of S grades (1-3) or similar, including English, maths and a science subject. Exact requirements depend on the degree you take.

Degree Information

A degree in nursing or nursing studies leads to registration as a nurse. Graduates with relevant first degrees such as biological sciences, behavioural sciences or health-related subjects can take a shortened postgraduate course.

Adult Qualifications

You must be aged 23-36 on entry and be a qualified registered nurse. Mature applicants for nurse training who do not have the required qualifications may be able to take an entrance test. Many colleges offer Access courses for mature applicants without the standard entry requirements for higher education.

Work Experience
Employers or colleges/universities may prefer candidates who have relevant work or voluntary experience, as it demonstrates enthusiasm and commitment. This can include working with people in a helping capacity in a nursery, an elderly residential home as a care assistant, as a classroom assistant or in customer service. The job is about rapport, communication and listening as much as the medical work. Work experience also prepares you for the more domestic side of the job: many colleges say that applicants do not always think about this part of the job and it sometimes comes as a surprise. Each RAF base offers its own work experience opportunities. Contact your nearest RAF base to find out what is available locally.

Entry and Training
There are strict nationality and residence requirements for RAF entry; you must be a citizen of the UK, the Commonwealth, or the Republic of Ireland since birth. Student staff nurses must be aged from 17.5 and are usually under 32. The Princess Marys Royal Air Force Nursing Service (PMRAFNS) offers a three-year training course for student nurses within the Faculty of Health and Community Care at Birmingham City University. Around half of your time is spent on clinical placements, which take place at both NHS and military establishments.

Successful graduation leads to registration as a registered nurse (adult) on the professional register of the Nursing and Midwifery Council together with the award of a BSc (Honours) in Nursing. You are then employed as a PMRAFNS staff nurse (RN). Those aged 21-33 years who have already completed professional nurse training may apply for a post as a PMRAFNS staff nurse if they are a qualified registered nurse (RN) with at least two years' post-registration experience.

The RAF also recruits psychiatric nurses who must hold RN/RMN registration and be aged 21-32. Dental nurses (minimum age of 16) are also recruited provided they have two GCSEs/S grades in English and maths (five for training a a hygienist, including English and science).

Nursing officers are encouraged to pursue further professional training in line with the Post-Registration Education and Practice of the UK Central Council. Study time is given and paid for by the RAF. Applicants attend an interview, where they undertake a series of assessments and tests designed to measure leadership potential.

Mature applicants are welcome and may apply for student staff nurse training, or enter as a staff nurse or nursing officer if they have registered nurse (RN) qualifications, together with a specified period of professional nursing experience. However, upper age limits do apply for the armed forces. You should check entry details with the local armed forces careers office.

Opportunities and Pay
There are good opportunities for promotion and prospects are improved by committing to further training. New postings are made every two or three years. This helps to keep nursing skills sharp and gives plenty of scope for further promotion. This job requires a great deal of personal commitment. The training received in this job provides an excellent basis for a variety of occupations in civilian life. An Equal Opportunities policy operates within the armed forces.

Pay increases with promotion. Student nurses after one year of training receive £24,070. Once trained, nursing officers earn £29k-£39k a year.

Health
The work may involve the risk of infection. You take a medical test on entry and require good general fitness.

Skills and Qualities
able to take responsibility, aptitude for teamwork, caring, decisive, efficient, leadership qualities, not squeamish, patient, perceptive, reassuring

Relevant Subjects
Biology, Chemistry, English, Health and social care, Psychology, Science

Further Information
Careers Information - Royal Air Force (RAF) - www.raf.mod.uk

RAF News (RAF) - www.rafnews.co.uk

Skills for Work (Scottish Qualifications Authority) - www.sqa.org.uk/sqa/31390.html

▶Working in police, fire & security (2009) (Babcock Lifeskills) - www.babcock-lifeskills.com/

Addresses
Nursing and Midwifery Council (NMC)
23 Portland Place, London W1B 1PZ
Phone: +44 (0)20 7333 9333
Web: www.nmc-uk.org

Similar Jobs
Nurse/Nursing Officer: Army, Nurse/Nursing Officer: Royal Navy, Nurse: Adult, Nurse: Children, Nurse: Mental Health, RAF Officer

Nurse/Nursing Officer: Royal Navy
also known as: Naval Nurse, Queen Alexandra's RN Nursing Service: Nurse/Nursing Officer

CRCI:Security and Armed Forces
CLCI:BAB Job Band: 4 to 5

Job Description
Nurses/nursing officers work in the Queen Alexandra's Royal Navy Nursing Service (QARNNS) and are part of a multi-disciplinary medical team. They plan, supervise and deliver nursing care to service and civilian naval personnel and their families. Look after patients and give medical treatment, usually at on-shore establishments. Are involved in teaching student nurses who are undertaking the clinical component of their nurse training and assist in the teaching of probationary medical assistants. Supervise the work of healthcare assistants and junior members of a nursing team.

Nursing officers are responsible for a group of staff, known in the Royal Navy as a 'division', both for their professional development and personal welfare. Writing reports and carrying out ward rounds with doctors and consultants are an important part of the job.

Work Details
Once you have completed officer training you are posted to a Royal Navy hospital, initially in the UK. However, you may soon find yourself anywhere in the world on operational duties working in a hospital or clinic. You are expected to work unsociable hours and shifts. There is contact with people who are ill and possibly in pain, upset or depressed. Work can sometimes be emotionally and physically tiring.

You help people and work as part of a team. Sometimes you may need to enforce discipline and make unpopular decisions. Nursing officers are liable for service at sea in times of tension or conflict and can be expected to serve in dangerous situations where there is a risk of injury. Nursing officers wear a uniform and sometimes protective clothing.

Qualification
The Scottish Qualifications Authority (SQA) launched a new Skills for Work course in 2008. This course introduces candidates to the uniformed and emergency services and is particularly suited to those considering a career in the Army, Royal Navy, Royal Air Force or Royal Marines. Check the website for details.

Nurse/Nursing Officer: Royal Navy

- **England, Wales and Northern Ireland**

Band 4: For entry to nurse training with the the Royal Navy: 240 UCAS points at A2 level or higher and a minimum of 5 GCSEs (A*-C) usually including English language, maths and a science subject, or equivalent.

Band 5: For a degree course: 2-3 A levels and 5 GCSEs (A*-C) including maths, English and a science subject. Exact requirements depend on the degree you take.

- **Scotland**

Band 4: For entry to nurse training with the Royal Navy: 240 UCAS points at H grade and some S grades (1-3) including English, maths and a science subject or equivalent.

Band 5: For a degree course: 3-5 H grades and a number of S grades (1-3) or similar qualifications. Exact requirements depend on the degree you take.

Degree Information

A degree in nursing or nursing studies leads to registration as a nurse. Graduates with relevant first degrees such as biological sciences, behavioural sciences or health related subjects, can take a shortened postgraduate course.

Adult Qualifications

Mature applicants for nurse training who do not have the required qualifications may be able to take an entrance test. Many colleges offer Access courses for mature applicants without the standard entry requirements for higher education.

Work Experience

Employers or colleges/universities may prefer candidates who have relevant work or voluntary experience, as it demonstrates enthusiasm and commitment. This can include working with people in a helping capacity in a nursery, an elderly residential home as a care assistant, as a classroom assistant, or in customer service. The job is about rapport, communication and listening as much as the medical work. Work experience also prepares you for the more domestic side of the job. Many colleges say that applicants do not always think about this part of the job and it sometimes comes as a surprise.

Entry and Training

There are strict nationality and residence requirements for entry to the Royal Navy. The Navy strongly recommends that anyone applying for service builds up their physical fitness levels. Qualified registered nurses with over two years' post-qualification experience, may enter as nursing officers if they are between the ages of 21and 38 (exceptionally up to 49). Applicants attend an Admiralty Interview Board at HMS Sultan in Gosport, Hampshire, where they undertake a series of interviews and tests designed to measure leadership potential.

After entering the Queen Alexandra's Royal Navy Nursing Service (QARNNS), the first two weeks consists of a New Entry Nursing Officer course at RH Haslar (Gosport, Hampshire). You then spend eight weeks at the Britannia Royal Naval College at Dartmouth in Devon. During your first year you also do a Combat Casualty Care Course, which lasts two weeks and a further two-week divisional officers' course. You also have regular training sessions at a 100-bed primary casualty-receiving facility. You are encouraged to move between clinical specialities in hospital and there are opportunities to work in primary care.

For entry as a naval nurse, you should be aged between 21 and 36 and have completed registered nurse training. See the Nurse: Adult and Nurse: Mental Health job articles for full details of how to train as a nurse in civilian life. After eight weeks basic training at HMS Raleigh in Cornwall, you complete a post basic qualifying course at the Defence Medical Training Centre. You then move on to courses where you learn the practical and theoretical aspects of naval leadership. This leads to promotion to acting Leading Naval Nurse and you are assigned to your first Ministry of Defence Hospital Unit or Royal Navy establishment where you begin nursing duties.

You can also enter as a student nurse (aged between 17.5 and 36) and after basic training at HMS Raleigh, you study for a three-year nursing diploma or degree. This takes place at the University of Central England in Birmingham and includes students from the Army and the RAF. University holidays include challenges other than nursing, such as adventure training as well as further general training, which involves leadership and management. When you have completed the professional qualifying courses and NMC registration, you move on to work in a Ministry of Defence Hospital Unit and enter the qualified nursing rotation programme. Each unit is supported by different training teams, allowing you to gain post qualification clinical experience.

Mature applicants for entry should check with their local armed forces careers office for details of upper age limits. Currently, men and women under 38 years with at least two years' post-registration general experience in a busy hospital, may apply to become nursing officers. You can also apply for training as a student nurse or enter as a naval nurse straight after qualification up to the age of 36. Registered nurses with specialist experience/ qualifications such as that gained in accident and emergency (A&E) departments or in an intensive care unit (ICU) may apply for a job as a nursing officer up to the age of 48.

Opportunities and Pay

As an officer, you join at the rank of sub-lieutenant depending on your nursing experience, after which you can normally expect to become a lieutenant within two years. Promotion to a more senior rank is by selection.

All nursing officers join the Service initially on a six-year Short Service Commission with the option to extend to eight years. During this period, you have the opportunity to apply for a Medium Career Commission of 18 years and subsequently apply for a Full Career Commission up to age of 55, both of which are pensionable. Training is ongoing in this job and provides an excellent basis for occupations in civilian life. Opportunities for career development include courses accredited towards a BSc or MA in military nursing. These courses are fully funded and cover specialisms such as intensive care, theatre nursing, orthopaedics, burns and plastic surgery and A & E nursing.

Basic salaries for student nurses with the Royal Navy are £16,681k a year. Qualified nurses earn £28,133-£33,832. An equal opportunities policy operates within the armed forces.

Health

The work may involve the risk of infection. You take a medical test on entry and good general fitness is required.

Skills and Qualities

able to take responsibility, aptitude for teamwork, caring, decisive, efficient, leadership qualities, not squeamish, patient, perceptive, reassuring

Relevant Subjects

Biology, Chemistry, English, Health and social care, Psychology, Science

Further Information

Careers Information package (Royal Navy) (Royal Navy) - www.royalnavy.mod.uk/

Navy News (monthly) (Royal Navy) - www.navynews.co.uk/

Queen Alexandra's Royal Army Nursing Corps - www.army.mod.uk/army-medical-services/9869.aspx

Skills for Work (Scottish Qualifications Authority) - www.sqa.org.uk/sqa/31390.html

▶Working in police, fire & security (2009) (Babcock Lifeskills) - www.babcock-lifeskills.com/

Addresses

Nursing and Midwifery Council (NMC)
23 Portland Place, London W1B 1PZ
Phone: +44 (0)20 7333 9333
Web: www.nmc-uk.org

Similar Jobs

Nurse/Nursing Officer: Army, Nurse/Nursing Officer: RAF, Nurse: Adult, Nurse: Children, Nurse: Mental Health, Royal Navy Officer

Nurse: Adult

also known as: Registered General Nurse: RGN

CRCI:Healthcare
CLCI:JAD Job Band: 3 to 5

Job Description

Adult nurses look after patients aged from 16 upwards, helping with their medical treatment. They have responsibility for the general welfare and condition of the patients, including their emotional and physical needs. Administer drugs and give injections, take blood pressure, remove stitches and help with transfusions and operations. They use sophisticated and complex technology such as kidney dialysis machines and life support equipment. Also write reports and may accompany doctors on ward rounds.

May do simpler nursing tasks too such as making beds, feeding patients, etc, but usually only for severely ill patients. Also supervise the healthcare assistants who perform the day-to-day routine tasks. Can specialise in areas such as women's health, critical care, school nursing, accident and emergency, practice nursing and cancer care.

Work Details

Usually work a basic 37.5 hr week and are expected to work unsocial hours and shifts to cover 24 hours a day. You work in a hospital, a clinic, or possibly in the community or in other people's homes, and may need to live-in for a time. There is contact with people who are ill and possibly in pain, upset or depressed. Work can be emotionally, physically and intellectually taxing. You have to deal with emergencies and be able to cope with the sight of blood. A uniform is provided by your employer and possibly protective clothing.

Qualification

• England, Wales and Northern Ireland

Band 3: Minimum entry requirements are usually at least 5 GCSEs (A*-C) including English, maths and a science subject, or equivalent.

Band 4: For entry to some registered nurse training courses: more than the minimum 5 GCSEs (A*-C) are required. A levels may be asked for, sometimes in specific subjects, such as English and sciences. Equivalent qualifications may be accepted. Check with individual institutions.

Band 5: For degree course: 2-3 A levels and some GCSEs (A*-C) usually including English, maths and a science, or equivalent. Exact requirements depend on the degree you take.

• Scotland

Band 3: Minimum entry requirements are usually at least five S grades (1-3) including English, maths and a science subject, or similar. Contact the individual institution for specific requirements.

Band 4: For entry to training courses in many colleges: more than the minimum five S grades (1-3) are required. H grades may be asked for, sometimes in specific subjects, such as English and sciences. Contact the individual institution for specific requirements.

Band 5: For degree course: 3-5 H grades and a number of S grades (1-3) usually including English, maths and science, or similar. Contact the individual institution for specific requirements.

Degree Information

A degree in nursing or nursing studies leads to registration as a qualified nurse and the majority of courses offer the specialism of adult nursing. Some courses combine nursing with another social or natural science subject and lead to two qualifications. Graduates with relevant first degrees, eg in biological sciences, behavioural sciences, physical sciences or health related subjects can take a shortened postgraduate nurse training course which takes a minimum of two years.

Adult Qualifications

Schools and colleges of nursing vary in their entry requirements for adult entry. Applicants who do not have the usual academic qualifications may be able to take an entrance test. A relevant vocational qualification at level 3 is usually acceptable or specific modular course credits from the Open University, or a specific Access to higher education course for entry to nursing training. Some universities have special entry standards for mature applicants. Check with individual institutions for details.

Work Experience

Employers or colleges/universities may prefer candidates who have relevant work or voluntary experience which demonstrates enthusiasm and commitment. This includes working with people in a helping capacity in a nursery, in an elderly residential home as a care assistant, as a classroom assistant or in customer service. The job is about rapport, communication and listening as much as the medical work. Work experience can also prepare you for the domestic side of the job. Contact the NHS trust in your area as direct work experience may be available.

Entry and Training

All nurse training involves a recognised nurse education programme; usually a 3-4 year degree programme or three-year diploma course recognised by the Nursing and Midwifery Council (NMC). Diploma courses are in the process of being phased out and from September 2013 all new full-time entrants to nursing need to study for a degree. Entry to all courses is highly competitive. You may be able to join the NHS as an apprentice or enter by taking a foundation degree. Apprenticeships last 1-4 years and involve working towards S/NVQs at level 2-3, after which you can be supported to gain your pre-nursing qualification.

In Wales, preparation to enter the nursing profession is via an NHS funded three-year Bachelor of Nursing (Hons) degree. Contact the National Leadership & Innovation Agency for Healthcare (NLIAH Wales) for details of the degree entry programme, funding information, and all training information and publications.

Elsewhere in the UK, pre-registration degrees involve spending one year on a common foundation programme (CFP), which is 50% theory and 50% practical placement in hospitals, then a further two years specialising in one of four options - adult, children, learning disability or mental health nursing. To become an adult nurse you choose this option. Once pre-registration training is completed, all nurses must register with the NMC to allow them to practise and this registration needs to be renewed every three years.

Further specialist practitioner programmes are available after registration as a qualified nurse, such as midwifery, cancer care, health visiting or school nursing. Applicants should check with NHS Careers for details of various schemes of training. All tuition fees, at degree or diploma level, are usually paid by the NHS and means-tested bursaries may also be available.

Mature entry is welcome. Various sources of funding and bursaries are available to cover full course fees and a grant to cover living expenses. The Royal College of Nursing (RCN) offers a number of post-registration awards and scholarships for qualified and experienced nurses, including some courses organised with the Open University. 'Return to Practice' programmes are also available for nurses wanting to return to work after a break of some years. Apprenticeships for adults may be an alternative route into nursing. Contact NHS Careers, the RCN or your local NHS Trust for details.

Opportunities and Pay

You are usually employed by the NHS, but there are many opportunities with private hospitals and clinics, the armed forces, and with nursing agencies. Employment prospects are usually good. Promotion can be to a specialist nurse, team leader, advanced nurse or team manager with the responsibility of running a ward, department, clinic or community nurses team. Further opportunities exist in higher management or as a nurse consultant within the hospital trust or employing hospital, or generally within the NHS. There may be opportunities to work part time, and career breaks are common.

Work is also available in Europe and in developing countries. There is scope for specialisation in areas such as cancer care, the elderly, accident and emergency and women's health, or work in specialist places such as prisons. There may be opportunities to teach or do research.

Minimum pay levels are set nationally, but generally, registered nurses working for the NHS are paid in accordance with their band. As a newly-qualified nurse (Band 5) you can earn around £21-£28k a year, rising up to £34k as a nurse team leader (Band 6). Advanced nurses at band 7 and nurse consultants can earn more. Overtime pay may also be available.

Health

The work involves a risk of infection. This job requires a medical test on entry and requires good general fitness.

Skills and Qualities

able to take responsibility, aptitude for teamwork, calm, compassionate, efficient, good communication skills, good interpersonal skills, not squeamish, patient, perceptive

Relevant Subjects

Biology, Chemistry, English, Health and social care, Psychology, Science

Further Information

AGCAS: Health (Job Sector Briefing) (AGCAS) - www.prospects.ac.uk

Apprenticeship Schemes (National Apprenticeship Service) - www.apprenticeships.org.uk

NHS Careers (NHS Careers) - www.nhscareers.nhs.uk

NHS Careers Scotland - www.infoscotland.com/nhs

NHS Careers Wales - www.wales.nhs.uk

Nursing & Midwifery Uncovered (Trotman 2010) - www.trotman.co.uk

Nursing Careers - www.nhscareers.nhs.uk/nursing

Nursing Times (Nursing Times) - www.nursingtimes.net

Royal College of Nursing Wales - www.rcn.org.uk/aboutus/wales

Addresses

National Leadership & Innovation Agency for Healthcare (NLIAH: Wales)
Innovation House, Bridgend Road, Llanharan CF72 9RP
Phone: +44 (0)1443 233333
Web: www.wales.nhs.uk/sitesplus/829/

Nursing and Midwifery Council (NMC)
23 Portland Place, London W1B 1PZ
Phone: +44 (0)20 7333 9333
Web: www.nmc-uk.org

Royal College of Nursing (RCN)
20 Cavendish Square, London W1G 0RN
Phone: +44 (0) 20 7409 3333
Web: www.rcn.org.uk

School of Nursing and Midwifery
Queens University Belfast, Medical Biology Centre,
97 Lisburn Road BT9 7BL
Phone: +44 (0)28 9097 2233
Web: www.qub.ac.uk/nur

Similar Jobs

Ambulance Paramedic, Health Promotion Specialist, Health Visitor, Nurse: Children, Nurse: District, Nurse: Mental Health

Nurse: Children

also known as: Paediatric Nurse, Registered Sick Children's Nurse: RSCN

CRCI:Healthcare
CLCI:JAD — Job Band: 3 to 5

Job Description

These specialist nurses provide medical care and treatment for babies, children and adolescents up to 18 who are chronically ill, injured or disabled. They administer drugs and injections, take out stitches, help during operations, write reports, discuss cases with doctors. They provide specialist nursing care and, wherever possible, encourage parents and family members to take part in the day-to-day needs of the child such as feeding, dressing and washing. Work very closely with the family and make sure they are fully involved in the child's care, treatment and progress.

May counsel parents and family if a child is severely ill. Also supervise healthcare assistants and nursery nurses. Can specialise in hospital and community settings including cancer care, child protection, burns and intensive care.

Work Details

Usually work a basic 37.5 hr week and are expected to work unsocial hours and shifts to cover 24 hours a day. Most posts are in hospitals but you can also work in the community at a health centre or school. Work may be emotionally demanding as patients may be upset and afraid, and it is important that you ensure that parents or guardians are directly involved. You also have to cope with your own and your colleagues' distress when dealing with seriously ill or injured, or even dying, children.

You have to cope with considerable physical exertion and with the sight of blood. The work environment can be messy and noisy and you need to wear a uniform and possibly protective clothing.

Qualification

- **England, Wales and Northern Ireland**

Band 3: Minimum entry requirements are usually at least 5 GCSEs (A*-C) including English, maths and a science subject, or equivalent.

Band 4: For entry to some registered nurse training courses: more than the minimum 5 GCSEs (A*-C) are required. A levels may be asked for, sometimes in specific subjects, such as English and sciences. Equivalent qualifications may be accepted. Check with individual institutions.

Band 5: For degree course: For degree courses: 2-3 A levels and some GCSEs (A*-C) usually including English, maths and a science, or equivalent. Exact requirements depend on the degree you take.

- **Scotland**

Band 3: Minimum entry requirements are usually at least five S grades (1-3) including English, maths and a science subject, or similar. Contact the individual institution for specific requirements.

Band 4: For entry to training courses in many colleges: more than the minimum five S grades (1-3) are required. H grades may be asked for, sometimes in specific subjects, such as English and sciences. Contact the individual institution for specific requirements.

Band 5: For degree course: 3-5 H grades and a number of S grades (1-3) usually including English, maths and a science, or similar. Contact the individual institution for specific requirements.

Degree Information

A degree in nursing or nursing studies leads to registration as a qualified nurse, but not all courses offer the child nursing specialism, so check options carefully. Some courses combine nursing with another social or natural science subject and lead to two qualifications. Graduates with relevant first degrees, eg in biological sciences, behavioural sciences, physical sciences or health related subjects can take a shortened postgraduate nurse training course which takes a minimum of two years.

Adult Qualifications

Schools and colleges of nursing vary in their entry requirements for adult entry. Applicants who do not have the usual academic qualifications may be able to take an entrance test. A relevant vocational qualification at level 3 is usually acceptable. Alternatively you may be able to take specific modular course credits from the Open University, or a specific Access to higher education course, for entry to nursing training. Some universities have special entry standards for mature applicants. Check with individual institutions for details.

Work Experience

Employers or colleges/universities may prefer candidates who have relevant work or voluntary experience which demonstrates enthusiasm and commitment. This includes working with people in a helping capacity in a nursery, as a classroom assistant or in customer service. The job is about rapport, communication and listening as much as the medical work. Work experience can also prepare you for the domestic side of the job. Contact the NHS trust in your area as direct work experience may be available.

Entry and Training

All nurse training involves a recognised nurse education programme; usually a 3-4 year degree programme or three-year diploma course recognised by the Nursing and Midwifery Council (NMC). Diploma courses are in the process of being phased out and from September 2013 all new full-time entrants to nursing need to study for a degree. Entry to all courses is highly competitive. You may be able to join the NHS as an apprentice or enter by taking a foundation degree. Apprenticeships last 1-4 years and involve working towards S/NVQs at level 2-3, after which you can be supported to gain your pre-nursing qualification.

In Wales, preparation to enter the nursing profession is via an NHS funded three-year Bachelor of Nursing (Hons) degree. Contact the National Leadership & Innovation Agency for Healthcare (NLIAH Wales) for details of the degree entry programme, funding information, and all training information and publications.

Elsewhere in the UK, pre-registration degrees involve spending one year on a common foundation programme (CFP), which is 50% theory and 50% practical placement in hospitals, then a further two years specialising in one of four options - adult, children, learning disability or mental health nursing. To become a children's adult nurse you choose this option. Once pre-registration training is completed, all nurses must register with the NMC to allow them to practise and this registration needs to be renewed every three years.

Further specialist practitioner programmes are available after registration as a qualified nurse, such as midwifery, cancer care, health visiting or school nursing. Applicants should check with NHS Careers for details of various schemes of training. All tuition fees, at degree or diploma level, are usually paid by the NHS and means-tested bursaries may also be available.

Mature entry is welcome. Various sources of funding and bursaries are available to cover full course fees and a grant to cover living expenses. The Royal College of Nursing (RCN) offers a number of post-registration awards and scholarships for qualified and experienced nurses, including some courses organised with the Open University. 'Return to Practice' programmes are also available for nurses wanting to return to work after a break of some years. Apprenticeships for adults may be an alternative route into nursing. Contact NHS Careers, the RCN or your local NHS Trust for details.

Opportunities and Pay

You are usually employed by the NHS, but there are many opportunities with private hospitals and clinics, the armed forces, and with nursing agencies. Employment prospects are usually good. Promotion can be to a specialist nurse, team leader, advanced nurse or team manager with the responsibility of running a ward, department, clinic or community paediatric nurses team. Further opportunities exist in higher management or as a nurse consultant within the hospital trust or employing hospital, or generally within the NHS. There may be opportunities to work part time, and career breaks are common.

Work is also available in Europe and in developing countries. There is scope for specialisation in areas such as cancer care, accident and emergency or work in specialist hospices where children need to be cared for. There may be opportunities to teach or do research.

Minimum pay levels are set nationally, but generally, registered nurses working for the NHS are paid in accordance with their band. As a newly qualified nurse (Band 5) you can earn around £21-£28k a year, rising up to £34k as a nurse team leader (Band 6). Advanced nurses at band 7 and nurse consultants can earn more. Overtime pay may also be available.

Health

The work involves a risk of infection. This job requires a medical test on entry and good general fitness.

Skills and Qualities

able to relate well to children and young people, alert, aptitude for teamwork, calm, compassionate, good communication skills, good interpersonal skills, not squeamish, patient, reassuring

Relevant Subjects

Biology, Chemistry, English, Health and social care, Psychology, Science, Sociology

Further Information

AGCAS: Health (Job Sector Briefing) (AGCAS) - www.prospects.ac.uk

Apprenticeship Schemes (National Apprenticeship Service) - www.apprenticeships.org.uk

NHS Careers (NHS Careers) - www.nhscareers.nhs.uk

NHS Careers Scotland - www.infoscotland.com/nhs

NHS Careers Wales - www.wales.nhs.uk

Nursing & Midwifery Uncovered (Trotman 2010) - www.trotman.co.uk

Nursing Careers - www.nhscareers.nhs.uk/nursing

Nursing Times (Nursing Times) - www.nursingtimes.net

Open University - www.open.ac.uk

Real Life Guide to Childcare (Trotman 2009) - www.trotman.co.uk

Royal College of Nursing Wales - www.rcn.org.uk/aboutus/wales

So you want to work with Children (Wayland) - www.waylandbooks.co.uk

Addresses

National Leadership & Innovation Agency for Healthcare (NLIAH: Wales)
Innovation House, Bridgend Road, Llanharan CF72 9RP
Phone: +44 (0)1443 233333
Web: www.wales.nhs.uk/sitesplus/829/

Nursing and Midwifery Council (NMC)
23 Portland Place, London W1B 1PZ
Phone: +44 (0)20 7333 9333
Web: www.nmc-uk.org

Royal College of Nursing (RCN)
20 Cavendish Square, London W1G 0RN
Phone: +44 (0) 20 7409 3333
Web: www.rcn.org.uk

School of Nursing and Midwifery
Queens University Belfast, Medical Biology Centre,
97 Lisburn Road BT9 7BL
Phone: +44 (0)28 9097 2233
Web: www.qub.ac.uk/nur

Similar Jobs

Health Visitor, Nurse: Adult, Nurse: District, Nurse: Learning Disabilities, Nurse: Mental Health, Nursery Worker

Nurse: District

also known as: Community Nurse

CRCI:Healthcare
CLCI:JAD

Job Band: 3 to 5

Job Description

District nurses provide nursing care, health education and advice to patients in their own homes, or in GPs surgeries, clinics, health centres and nursing or care homes. They assess patients, plan and manage their care, administering treatment that does not require full hospital support. May give injections and medication, check blood pressure and take blood samples, change dressings and assist a doctor in the physical examination of patients.

They visit patients, most of whom are elderly, physically disabled, have recently been discharged from hospital, have a long term illness or are terminally ill. Also maintain regular contact with other health professionals and have a teaching role, working with patients to help them care for themselves, or with family members teaching them how to care for their relatives.

Work Details

Usually work Monday to Friday, from 8am to 5pm if based at a clinic. Some provide nursing care out of hours or offer an on-call service. The work involves travelling to patients and a driving licence is therefore essential. District nurses keep detailed and up-to-date records of each patient. May work on your own or with other groups, such as social services, voluntary agencies and other NHS organisations to provide and coordinate a range of care services. Work can be emotionally, physically and intellectually taxing and you must be able to cope with some distressing sights. A uniform and protective clothing may be provided by your employer.

Qualification

• England, Wales and Northern Ireland

Band 3: Minimum entry requirements are usually at least 5 GCSEs (A*-C) including English, maths and a science subject, or equivalent.

Band 4: For entry to some registered nurse training courses: more than the minimum 5 GCSEs (A*-C) are required. A levels may be asked for, sometimes in specific subjects, such as English and sciences. Equivalent qualifications may be accepted. Check with individual institutions.

Band 5: For degree course: 2-3 A levels and some GCSEs (A*-C) usually including English, maths and a science, or equivalent. Exact requirements depend on the degree you take.

• Scotland

Band 3: Minimum entry requirements are usually at least five S grades (1-3) including English, maths and a science subject, or similar. Contact the individual institution for specific requirements.

Band 4: For entry to training courses in many colleges: more than the minimum five S grades (1-3) are required. H grades may be asked for, sometimes in specific subjects, such as English and sciences. Contact the individual institution for specific requirements.

Band 5: For degree course: 3-5 H grades and a number of S grades (1-3) including English, maths and a science, or similar. Contact the individual institution for specific requirements.

Degree Information

A degree in nursing or nursing studies leads to registration as a qualified nurse. Some courses combine nursing with another social or natural science subject and lead to two qualifications. Graduates with relevant first degrees, eg in biological sciences, behavioural sciences, physical sciences or health related subjects can take a shortened postgraduate nurse training course which takes a minimum of two years.

Adult Qualifications

Schools and colleges of nursing vary in their entry requirements for adult entry. Applicants who do not have the usual academic qualifications may be able to take an entrance test. A relevant vocational qualification at level 3 is usually acceptable. Alternatively you may be able to take specific modular course credits from the Open University, or a specific Access to higher education course, for entry to nursing training. Some universities have special entry standards for mature applicants. Check with individual institutions for details.

Work Experience

Employers or colleges/universities may prefer candidates who have relevant work or voluntary experience which demonstrates enthusiasm and commitment. This includes working with people in a helping capacity in a nursery, in an elderly residential home as a care assistant, as a classroom assistant or in customer service. The job is about rapport, communication and listening as much as the medical work. Work experience can also prepare you for the domestic side of the job.

The NHS recommends that nurses wishing to move into district nursing spend time with a qualified practitioner to gain experience of the role, or to work as a community staff nurse to gain relevant experience. Students are also recommended to read specialist journals such as Primary Nursing Care, which is available from the Royal College of Nursing (RCN). Direct work experience may be available with your local NHS trust.

Entry and Training

All applicants to district nurse training must first qualify as a registered nurse then complete a degree-level specialist practitioner programme, which usually lasts at least one academic year (or the part-time equivalent), before becoming a district nurse.

Specialist training usually involves working with elderly people, covering a range of medical and surgical nursing, and learning about social legislation. The course covers nursing practice, care and programme management and areas such as social policy, counselling and public health, and also includes placements with an experienced district nurse. It is split equally between practical experience and theory. Some experience of working in palliative care and community settings is required. For full details of registered nurse training, see the Nurse: Adult job article.

All entrants are required to be registered nurses, and mature entry is welcomed. There are various sources of funding for post-registration courses. 'Return to Practice' programmes are also available for nurses wanting to return to work after a break of some years. Contact NHS Careers, the RCN or your local NHS Trust for details.

Opportunities and Pay

District nurses are usually employed by the NHS and most are attached to one or more GP surgeries. Promotion opportunities are possible into health service management, teaching, and clinical specialisms. There are also opportunities to work abroad, particularly in developing countries.

Minimum pay levels are set nationally, but generally salaries for district nurses are around £25k-£33k a year. Registered nurses working for the NHS are paid in accordance with their band. As a newly-qualified nurse (Band 5) you can earn around £21k-£28k a year, rising up to £34k as a nurse team leader (Band 6).

Health
The job requires a medical test on entry and requires good general fitness. The work involves a risk of infection.

Skills and Qualities
able to get on with all kinds of people, able to take responsibility, adaptable, confident, good communication skills, good listening skills, good organisational skills, not squeamish, patient, reassuring

Relevant Subjects
Biology, Chemistry, Health and social care, Psychology, Science, Sociology

Further Information
AGCAS: Health (Job Sector Briefing) (AGCAS) - www.prospects.ac.uk

NHS Careers (NHS Careers) - www.nhscareers.nhs.uk

NHS Careers Scotland - www.infoscotland.com/nhs

NHS Careers Wales - www.wales.nhs.uk

Nursing & Midwifery Uncovered (Trotman 2010) - www.trotman.co.uk

Nursing Careers - www.nhscareers.nhs.uk/nursing

Nursing Times (Nursing Times) - www.nursingtimes.net

Primary Nursing Care (bi-monthly) (Community and District Nursing Association (CDNA)) - www.cdnaonline.org/

Real Life Guide to Care, Welfare & Community Work (Trotman 2010) - www.trotman.co.uk

Royal College of Nursing Wales - www.rcn.org.uk/aboutus/wales

▶Working in social care (2010) (Babcock Lifeskills) - www.babcock-lifeskills.com/

Addresses
Community and District Nursing Association
22- 24 Worple Road, Wimbledon, London SW19 4DD
Phone: +44 (0)208 971 4268 .
Web: www.cdnaonline.org

Community Practitioners' and Health Visitors' Association (CPHVA)
Unite Transport House, 128 Theobald's Road, Holborn, London WC1X 8TN
Phone: +44 (0) 208 7611 2500
Web: www.amicus-cphva.org

National Leadership & Innovation Agency for Healthcare (NLIAH: Wales)
Innovation House, Bridgend Road, Llanharan CF72 9RP
Phone: +44 (0)1443 233333
Web: www.wales.nhs.uk/sitesplus/829/

Nursing and Midwifery Council (NMC)
23 Portland Place, London W1B 1PZ
Phone: +44 (0)20 7333 9333
Web: www.nmc-uk.org

Royal College of Nursing (RCN)
20 Cavendish Square, London W1G 0RN
Phone: +44 (0) 20 7409 3333
Web: www.rcn.org.uk

School of Nursing and Midwifery
Queens University Belfast, Medical Biology Centre, 97 Lisburn Road BT9 7BL
Phone: +44 (0)28 9097 2233
Web: www.qub.ac.uk/nur

Similar Jobs
Health Promotion Specialist, Health Visitor, Midwife, Nurse: Children, Nurse: Practice, Nurse: School

Nurse: Learning Disabilities
CRCI:Healthcare
CLCI:JAD
Job Band: 3 to 5

Job Description
Learning disabilities nurses care for people with learning disabilities and help them to develop their full potential and to live independent and fulfilling lives. They help the patients to learn social skills, such as going shopping and personal hygiene, or to cope with simple tasks. Work in partnership with family carers. Nurses plan a programme of activities and work with patients in their homes and in hospitals, residential homes and day centres. They work as part of a team, along with doctors, physiotherapists, social workers, psychotherapists, teachers, occupational and speech therapists. May work with individuals who require more intensive support in hospitals, or with specialist secure units for offenders with learning disabilities.

Can also specialise in areas such as working with those who have sensory impairment or epilepsy. Also provide counselling and support for families and other carers.

Work Details
Usually work a 37.5 hr week, which may include day, evening and some weekend work. You may be expected to work shifts to help provide 24-hour care. You can work in a hospital and in the community, in a residential care home, patients' homes or medical centres. You care for people, teaching and helping them to perform everyday tasks for themselves and you work in a team. Work may be taxing and emotionally demanding. You have to cope with being active most of the time. You may need to wear a uniform.

Qualification

• England, Wales and Northern Ireland
Band 3: Minimum entry requirements are usually at least 5 GCSEs (A*-C) including English, maths and a science subject, or equivalent.

Band 4: For entry to some registered nurse training courses: more than the minimum 5 GCSEs (A*-C) are required. A levels may be asked for, sometimes in specific subjects, such as English and sciences. Equivalent qualifications may be accepted. Check with individual institutions.

Band 5: For degree course: 2-3 A levels and some GCSEs (A*-C) usually including English, maths and a science, or equivalent. Exact requirements depend on the degree you take.

• Scotland
Band 3: Minimum entry requirements are usually at least five S grades (1-3) including English, maths and a science subject, or similar. Contact the individual institution for specific requirements.

Band 4: For entry to training courses in many colleges: more than the minimum five S grades (1-3) are required. H grades may be asked for, sometimes in specific subjects, such as English and sciences. Contact the individual institution for specific requirements.

Band 5: For degree course: 3-5 H grades and a number of S grades (1-3) usually including English, maths and a science, or similar. Contact the individual institution for specific requirements.

Degree Information
A degree in nursing or nursing studies leads to registration as a qualified nurse, but not all courses offer the learning disability specialism, so check options carefully. Some courses combine nursing with another social or natural science subject and lead to two qualifications. Graduates with relevant first degrees, eg in biological sciences, behavioural sciences, physical sciences or health related subjects, can take a shortened postgraduate nurse training course which takes a minimum of two years.

Nurse: Learning Disabilities

Adult Qualifications
Schools and colleges of nursing vary in their entry requirements for adult entry. Applicants who do not have the usual academic qualifications may be able to take an entrance test. A relevant vocational qualification at level 3 is usually acceptable. Alternatively you may be able to take specific modular course credits from the Open University, or a specific Access to higher education course, for entry to nursing training. Some universities have special entry standards for mature applicants. Check with individual institutions for details.

Work Experience
Employers or colleges/universities may prefer candidates who have relevant work or voluntary experience which demonstrates enthusiasm and commitment. This includes working with people in a helping capacity in a nursery, in an elderly residential home as a care assistant, as a classroom assistant or in customer service. Any experience of working with people with a learning disability is an advantage. The job is about rapport, communication and listening as much as the medical work. Work experience can also prepare you for the domestic side of the job. Contact the NHS trust in your area as direct work experience may be available.

Entry and Training
All nurse training involves a recognised nurse education programme; usually a 3-4 year degree programme or three-year diploma course recognised by the Nursing and Midwifery Council (NMC). Diploma courses are in the process of being phased out and from September 2013 all new full-time entrants to nursing need to study for a degree. Entry to all courses is highly competitive. You may be able to join the NHS as an apprentice or enter by taking a foundation degree. Apprenticeships last 1-4 years and involve working towards S/NVQs at level 2-3, after which you can be supported to gain your pre-nursing qualification.

In Wales, preparation to enter the nursing profession is via an NHS funded three-year Bachelor of Nursing (Hons) degree. Contact the National Leadership & Innovation Agency for Healthcare (NLIAH Wales) for details of the degree entry programme, funding information, and all training information and publications.

Elsewhere in the UK, pre-registration degrees involve spending one year on a common foundation programme (CFP), which is 50% theory and 50% practical placement in hospitals, then a further two years specialising in one of four options - adult, children, learning disability or mental health nursing. To become a learning disability nurse you choose this option. Once pre-registration training is completed, all nurses must register with the NMC to allow them to practise and this registration needs to be renewed every three years.

Further specialist practitioner programmes are available after registration as a qualified nurse. Applicants should check with NHS Careers for details of various schemes of training. All tuition fees, at degree or diploma level, are usually paid by the NHS and means-tested bursaries may also be available.

Mature entry is welcome. Various sources of funding and bursaries are available to cover full course fees and a grant to cover living expenses. The Royal College of Nursing (RCN) offers a number of post-registration awards and scholarships for qualified and experienced nurses, including some courses organised with the Open University. 'Return to Practice' programmes are also available for nurses wanting to return to work after a break of some years. Apprenticeships for adults may be an alternative route into nursing. Contact NHS Careers, the RCN or your local NHS Trust for details.

Opportunities and Pay
Most learning disabilities nurses in the UK are employed by the NHS, but there are also opportunities with special schools, local authority social services departments, prisons or residential establishments. Some may progress to work as team leaders in residential establishments or become team managers of support staff. You can specialise in areas such as education, sensory disability or the management of services. There may be opportunities to work part time and career breaks are common. Work is also available in Europe and in developing countries.

Minimum pay levels are set nationally, but generally, registered nurses working for the NHS are paid in accordance with their band. As a newly-qualified nurse (Band 5) you can earn around £21k-£28k a year, rising up to £34k as a nurse team leader (Band 6). Advanced nurses at band 7 and nurse consultants can earn more. Overtime pay may also be available.

Health
This job requires good general fitness and a medical test on entry.

Skills and Qualities
able to cope with emergencies, able to explain clearly, able to get on with all kinds of people, calm, emotionally strong, encouraging, patient, resourceful, self confident

Relevant Subjects
Biology, Chemistry, English, Health and social care, Hospitality and catering, Psychology, Science

Further Information
AGCAS: Health (Job Sector Briefing) (AGCAS) - www.prospects.ac.uk

Apprenticeship Schemes (National Apprenticeship Service) - www.apprenticeships.org.uk

NHS Careers (NHS Careers) - www.nhscareers.nhs.uk

NHS Careers Scotland - www.infoscotland.com/nhs

NHS Careers Wales - www.wales.nhs.uk

Nursing & Midwifery Uncovered (Trotman 2010) - www.trotman.co.uk

Nursing Careers - www.nhscareers.nhs.uk/nursing

Nursing Times (Nursing Times) - www.nursingtimes.net

Open University - www.open.ac.uk

Royal College of Nursing Wales - www.rcn.org.uk/aboutus/wales

Addresses
National Leadership & Innovation Agency for Healthcare (NLIAH: Wales)
Innovation House, Bridgend Road, Llanharan CF72 9RP
Phone: +44 (0)1443 233333
Web: www.wales.nhs.uk/sitesplus/829/

Nursing and Midwifery Council (NMC)
23 Portland Place, London W1B 1PZ
Phone: +44 (0)20 7333 9333
Web: www.nmc-uk.org

Royal College of Nursing (RCN)
20 Cavendish Square, London W1G 0RN
Phone: +44 (0) 20 7409 3333
Web: www.rcn.org.uk

School of Nursing and Midwifery
Queens University Belfast, Medical Biology Centre,
97 Lisburn Road BT9 7BL
Phone: +44 (0)28 9097 2233
Web: www.qub.ac.uk/nur

Similar Jobs
Health Visitor, Midwife, Nurse: Mental Health, Nurse: School, Teacher: Special Educational Needs

Nurse: Macmillan

also known as: Macmillan Clinical Nurse Specialist (CNS), Macmillan Nurse

CRCI:Healthcare
CLCI:JAD Job Band: 3 to 5

Job Description

Macmillan nurses are registered nurses who specialise in cancer and palliative (pain relief) care. They provide physical, psychological, and emotional support to people who have cancer, from the point of diagnosis and throughout the patient's illness. Nurses work with a relatively small number of patients and have the time to give emotional support and information. They talk over problems with patients and their family, friends and carers.

They help a patient to make informed decisions about their medical treatment and guide them through the many different services on offer. Help them to cope with problems such as the symptoms and side-effects associated with treatment and the disease. Also give advice on the social benefits available to them, and other financial matters.

Some specialise in particular forms of cancer, such as lung or breast cancer, or in treatments like chemotherapy. Others specialise in the care and treatment of children with cancer and their families. Most are based in the community and travel to see cancer patients in their homes or in hospices. Macmillan primary care nurses are based in local GP surgeries and have cancer patients referred to them by the GP or district nurse. Others work in hospitals and see patients who have been referred by the consultant or ward sister.

Macmillan-lead cancer nurses are responsible for advising on the development of strategic services for a local cancer and palliative care nursing service. They provide a professional resource for other health professionals and give specialist advice on nursing intervention. Nurses work with local NHS Trust managers and other members of a local care management team, to review and improve cancer and palliative care in the community and hospitals.

Work Details

Usually work a basic 37.5 hr week though may be expected to work unsocial hours at times. Work is in a hospital or hospice, and often in a patient's home. There may be opportunities to work part time and career breaks are common. There is frequent contact with people who are ill and in pain and often upset or depressed. Work may be emotionally, physically and intellectually taxing. A uniform is provided by your employer.

Qualification

All Macmillan nurses are registered nurses with at least five years' experience, including two or more years in cancer or palliative care.

• England, Wales and Northern Ireland

Band 3: Minimum entry requirements are usually at least 5 GCSEs (A*-C) including English, maths and a science subject, or equivalent.

Band 4: For entry to some registered nurse training courses: more than the minimum 5 GCSEs (A*-C) are required. A levels may be asked for, sometimes in specific subjects, such as English and sciences. Equivalent qualifications may be accepted. Check with individual institutions.

Band 5: For degree course: 2-3 A levels and some GCSEs (A*-C) usually including English, maths and a science, or equivalent. Exact requirements depend on the degree you take.

• Scotland

Band 3: Minimum entry requirements are usually at least five S grades (1-3) including English, maths and a science subject, or similar. Contact the individual institution for specific requirements.

Band 4: For entry to training courses in many colleges: more than the minimum five S grades (1-3) are required. H grades may be asked for, sometimes in specific subjects, such as English and sciences. Contact the individual institution for specific requirements.

Band 5: For degree course: 3-5 H grades and a number of S grades (1-3) usually including English, maths and science, or similar. Contact the individual institution for specific requirements.

Degree Information

A degree in nursing or nursing studies leads to registration as a qualified nurse, usually with the ability to specialise in an area of nursing. Some courses combine nursing with another social or natural science subject and lead to two qualifications. Graduates with relevant first degrees, eg in biological sciences, behavioural sciences, physical sciences or health related subjects, can take a shortened postgraduate nurse training course that takes a minimum of two years. Specific degrees in palliative care and oncology may be required.

Adult Qualifications

Schools and colleges of nursing vary in their entry requirements for adult entry. Applicants who do not have the usual academic qualifications may be able to take an entrance test. A relevant vocational qualification at level 3 is usually acceptable. Alternatively you may be able to take specific modular course credits from the Open University, or a specific Access to higher education course, for entry to nursing training. Some universities have special entry standards for mature applicants. Check with individual institutions for details.

Work Experience

Employers or colleges/universities may prefer candidates who have relevant work or voluntary experience which demonstrates enthusiasm and commitment. This includes working with people in a helping capacity in a nursery, an elderly residential home as a care assistant, as a classroom assistant or in customer service. The job is about rapport, communication and listening as much as the medical work. Work experience also prepares you for the more domestic side of the job. Macmillan Cancer Support welcome volunteers in all aspects of their work. Contact their information centre for information.

Entry and Training

All Macmillan nurses are registered nurses. For full details of how to train to be a registered nurse, see the job article Nurse: Adult. Applications are filled through local NHS Trusts and advertised in the health media and journals. You need to have a minimum of five years' post-registration experience, with at least two or more years in cancer or palliative care. Increasingly a degree in palliative care or oncology is also needed.

Macmillan nurses undertake specialist training and are encouraged to gain a specialist qualification registered with the Nursing and Midwifery Council (NMC). Nurses who demonstrate a willingness to follow a degree pathway are viewed favourably. You also have to complete specialist courses in psychological and emotional support, and on managing pain and other symptoms. For this job, a UK driving licence is essential.

Other entry routes may be available for nurses who are recruited but need further training to enable them to function at a specialist level.

You need to maintain your specialist knowledge and skills throughout your careers and to be up-to-date with recent advances in research and practice development. Macmillan Cancer Support provides a number of education programmes.

Mature entry to nurse training is welcomed. Contact NHS Careers or your local NHS Trust for details. Once trained you need to have a minimum of five years' nursing experience, including at least two or more years in cancer or palliative care, and to have passed specialist courses in psychological and emotional support, and on managing pain and other symptoms.

Opportunities and Pay

There are over 4,000 Macmillan nurses employed in the UK; most work for the NHS and in the community, but are not usually associated with private health care. Posts are funded by Macmillan for a set time, usually the first three years. After this, long-term funding is taken up by the NHS or other partner organisations. Promotion can be to a lead cancer nurse in a care management role or to working as a Macmillan GP facilitator if you have the appropriate qualifications.

Macmillan nurses are paid at Band 7 on the NHS national pay scale, which is currently around £30k-£40k a year. Overtime pay may also be available.

Health

The work involves a risk of infection. This job requires a medical test on entry and good general fitness.

Skills and Qualities

able to give clear instructions, able to report accurately, able to take responsibility, committed, compassionate, emotionally strong, good communication skills, good interpersonal skills, not squeamish, perceptive

Relevant Subjects

Biology, Chemistry, Health and social care, Psychology, Science, Sociology

Further Information

AGCAS: Health (Job Sector Briefing) (AGCAS) - www.prospects.ac.uk

Macmillan Cancer Support - about us - www.macmillan.org.uk

NHS Careers (NHS Careers) - www.nhscareers.nhs.uk

NHS Careers Scotland - www.infoscotland.com/nhs

NHS Careers Wales - www.wales.nhs.uk

Nursing & Midwifery Uncovered (Trotman 2010) - www.trotman.co.uk

Nursing Careers - www.nhscareers.nhs.uk/nursing

Nursing Times (Nursing Times) - www.nursingtimes.net

Royal College of Nursing Wales - www.rcn.org.uk/aboutus/wales

Addresses

National Leadership & Innovation Agency for Healthcare (NLIAH: Wales)
Innovation House, Bridgend Road, Llanharan CF72 9RP
Phone: +44 (0)1443 233333
Web: www.wales.nhs.uk/sitesplus/829/

Nursing and Midwifery Council (NMC)
23 Portland Place, London W1B 1PZ
Phone: +44 (0)20 7333 9333
Web: www.nmc-uk.org

Royal College of Nursing (RCN)
20 Cavendish Square, London W1G 0RN
Phone: +44 (0) 20 7409 3333
Web: www.rcn.org.uk

School of Nursing and Midwifery
Queens University Belfast, Medical Biology Centre,
97 Lisburn Road BT9 7BL
Phone: +44 (0)28 9097 2233
Web: www.qub.ac.uk/nur

Similar Jobs

Health Promotion Specialist, Health Visitor, Nurse: Adult, Nurse: Children, Nurse: District, Nurse: Practice

Nurse: Mental Health

also known as: Community Psychiatric Nurse, Psychiatric Nurse, Registered Mental Nurse: RMN

CRCI:Healthcare
CLCI:JAD — Job Band: 3 to 5

Job Description

Mental health nurses help to treat patients who are suffering from some form of mental illness. This can often be brought on by a life crisis, which they cannot cope with, such as depression following a death in the family. They look after and care for those who have conditions that include neurosis, psychosis, and psychological and personality disorder. Nurses are members of a multi-disciplinary team of professionals that includes psychiatrists, GPs, health visitors, clinical psychologists and social workers. They often work with patients in the community as a community psychiatric nurse (CPN). Work to help restore patients to good health, and to regain confidence to return to, or cope with, normal everyday life.

May administer drugs and monitor their effect, and may take part in therapy sessions. In a hospital or day centre, they help with work activities and social events. May develop expertise in areas such as child and adolescent mental health, rehabilitation, substance misuse, and working with offenders.

Work Details

Most mental health care is now community-based, though you may be based in a hospital, outpatients department or day centre, a medical centre, residential home, or in specialist units, such as a drug dependency unit. You may be expected to work shifts and unsocial hours, including weekends and bank holidays, if based in a hospital, secure unit or other residential setting. In the community you can expect to work more regular hours with some on-call working at times. You work in a team and care for people in your workplace or by visiting patients at home. A driving licence is needed if you are working in the community. Your patients need emotional, as well as physical, support and they may be depressed, upset or possibly aggressive.

As well as seeing patients individually, you may work with a group of patients, eg teaching relaxation skills. There is little physical nursing but the work can be emotionally demanding. The danger of violence is a risk often associated with this branch of nursing.

Qualification

• England, Wales and Northern Ireland

Band 3: Minimum entry requirements are usually at least 5 GCSEs (A*-C) including English, maths and a science subject, or equivalent.

Band 4: For entry to some registered nurse training courses: more than the minimum 5 GCSEs (A*-C) are required. A levels may be asked for, sometimes in specific subjects, such as English and sciences. Equivalent qualifications may be accepted. Check with individual institutions.

Band 5: For degree course: 2-3 A levels and some GCSEs (A*-C) usually including English, maths and a science, or equivalent. Exact requirements depend on the degree you take.

• Scotland

Band 3: Minimum entry requirements are usually at least five S grades (1-3) including English, maths and a science subject, or similar. Contact the individual institution for specific requirements.

Band 4: For entry to training courses in many colleges: more than the minimum five S grades (1-3) are required. H grades may be asked for, sometimes in specific subjects, such as English and sciences. Contact the individual institution for specific requirements.

Band 5: For degree course: 3-5 H grades and a number of S grades (1-3) including English, maths and a science subject, or similar. Contact the individual institution for specific requirements.

Degree Information

A degree in nursing or nursing studies can lead to registration as a qualified nurse, but not all courses offer the mental health nursing specialism, so check options carefully. Some courses combine mental health nursing with social work and lead to two qualifications. Graduates with relevant first degrees, eg in biological sciences, behavioural sciences, physical sciences or health related subjects, can take a shortened postgraduate nurse training course, which takes two years minimum.

Adult Qualifications

Schools and colleges of nursing vary in their entry requirements for adult entry. Applicants who do not have the usual academic qualifications may be able to take an entrance test. A relevant vocational qualification at level 3 is usually acceptable. Alternatively you may be able to take specific modular course credits from the Open University, or a specific Access to higher education course, for entry to nursing training. Some universities have special entry standards for mature applicants. Check with individual institutions for details.

Work Experience

Employers or colleges/universities may prefer candidates who have relevant work or voluntary experience which demonstrates enthusiasm and commitment. This includes working with people in a helping capacity in a nursery, in an elderly residential home as a care assistant, as a classroom assistant or in customer service. The job is about rapport, communication and listening as much as the medical work. Work experience can also prepare you for the domestic side of the job. Contact the NHS trust in your area as direct work experience may be available.

Entry and Training

All nurse training involves a recognised nurse education programme; usually a 3-4 year degree programme or three-year diploma course recognised by the Nursing and Midwifery Council (NMC). Diploma courses are in the process of being phased out and from September 2013 all new full-time entrants to nursing need to study for a degree. Entry to all courses is highly competitive. You may also be able to join the NHS as an apprentice or enter via a foundation degree. Apprenticeships last 1-4 years and involve working towards S/NVQs at level 2-3, after which you can be supported to gain your pre-nursing qualification.

In Wales, preparation to enter the nursing profession is via an NHS funded three-year Bachelor of Nursing (Hons) degree. Contact the National Leadership & Innovation Agency for Healthcare (NLIAH Wales) for details of the degree entry programme, funding information, and all training information and publications.

Elsewhere in the UK, pre-registration degrees involve spending one year on a common foundation programme (CFP), which is 50% theory and 50% practical placement in hospitals, then a further two years specialising in one of four options - adult, children, learning disability or mental health nursing. To become a mental health nurse you choose this option. Once pre-registration training is completed, all nurses must register with the NMC to allow them to practise and this registration needs to be renewed every three years.

Further specialist practitioner programmes are available after registration as a qualified nurse. It is possible to combine training as a mental health nurse with social work. There are numerous postgraduate qualifications in mental health practice, and some which specifically develop academic and professional skills for mental health in primary care settings. All tuition fees are usually paid by the NHS and means-tested bursaries may also be available. Check with NHS Careers for details of various schemes of training.

Mature entry is welcome. Various sources of funding and bursaries are available to cover full course fees and a grant to cover living expenses. The Royal College of Nursing (RCN) offers a number of post-registration awards and scholarships for qualified and experienced nurses, including some courses organised in conjunction with the Open University. 'Return to Practice' programmes are also available for nurses wanting to return to work after a break of some years. Apprenticeships for adults may be an alternative route into nursing. Contact NHS Careers, the RCN or your local NHS Trust for details.

Opportunities and Pay

You are employed by the NHS usually in a community health care centre, day hospital, outpatients department or specialist unit. You can also work in the private health sector, in prisons and in the armed forces. There may be opportunities to work part time and career breaks are common. With experience and gaining a specialism, such as in drug or alcohol dependency, promotion to team leader or nurse consultant may be possible.

Minimum pay levels are set nationally, but generally, registered nurses working for the NHS are paid in accordance with their band. As a newly-qualified nurse (Band 5) you can earn around £21k-£28k a year, rising up to £34k as a nurse team leader (Band 6). Advanced nurses at band 7 and nurse consultants can earn more. Overtime pay may also be available.

Health

This job requires good general fitness and a medical test on entry.

Skills and Qualities

able to cope with emergencies, able to get on with all kinds of people, calm, emotionally strong, encouraging, good listening skills, non-judgemental, patient, perceptive, reassuring

Relevant Subjects

Biology, Chemistry, English, Health and social care, Psychology, Science

Further Information

AGCAS: Health (Job Sector Briefing) (AGCAS) - www.prospects.ac.uk

Apprenticeship Schemes (National Apprenticeship Service) - www.apprenticeships.org.uk

NHS Careers (NHS Careers) - www.nhscareers.nhs.uk

NHS Careers Scotland - www.infoscotland.com/nhs

NHS Careers Wales - www.wales.nhs.uk

Nursing & Midwifery Uncovered (Trotman 2010) - www.trotman.co.uk

Nursing Careers - www.nhscareers.nhs.uk/nursing

Nursing Times (Nursing Times) - www.nursingtimes.net

Royal College of Nursing Wales - www.rcn.org.uk/aboutus/wales

Addresses

Mental Health Nurses Association (MHNA)
Contact via website,
Web: www.unitetheunion.org/

National Leadership & Innovation Agency for Healthcare (NLIAH: Wales)
Innovation House, Bridgend Road, Llanharan CF72 9RP
Phone: +44 (0)1443 233333
Web: www.wales.nhs.uk/sitesplus/829/

Nursing and Midwifery Council (NMC)
23 Portland Place, London W1B 1PZ
Phone: +44 (0)20 7333 9333
Web: www.nmc-uk.org

Royal College of Nursing (RCN)
20 Cavendish Square, London W1G 0RN
Phone: +44 (0) 20 7409 3333
Web: www.rcn.org.uk

School of Nursing and Midwifery
Queens University Belfast, Medical Biology Centre,
97 Lisburn Road BT9 7BL
Phone: +44 (0)28 9097 2233
Web: www.qub.ac.uk/nur

Similar Jobs
Counsellor, Health Visitor, Nurse: Adult, Nurse: Learning Disabilities, Psychologist: Clinical, Psychotherapist

Nurse: Occupational Health
also known as: Occupational Health Nurse

CRCI:Healthcare
CLCI:JAD

Job Band: 3 to 5

Job Description
Occupational health nurses (OHNs) provide medical care for employees of a company and promote health and safety standards in the workplace. They identify potential health hazards that may exist in an employer's premises. Also deal with accidents and sudden illness and give treatments and drugs that are prescribed by a doctor. They may be involved in counselling, giving advice on personal matters and on stress management. Can work alone or as part of a larger occupational health service team, often attached to a human resources department.

OHNs provide health screening programmes for new and existing employees. They advise on accident prevention and help to monitor workers that may be exposed to health hazards such as dangerous equipment, environmental pollution and exposure to chemicals.

Work Details
Usually work between 35-40 hrs a week and may be expected to work shifts and be on call. Your place of work can be industrial premises such as a production plant, or any other business premises. You advise and care for people, examine patients and liaise with other members of a team. The work requires coping with emergencies and with the sight of blood. You need to wear a uniform, may need to wear protective clothing and have to cope with being active most of the time.

Qualification

- **England, Wales and Northern Ireland**

Band 3: Minimum entry requirements are usually at least 5 GCSEs (A*-C) including English, maths and a science subject, or equivalent.

Band 4: For entry to some registered nurse training courses: more than the minimum 5 GCSEs (A*-C) are required. A levels may be asked for, sometimes in specific subjects, such as English and sciences. Equivalent qualifications may be accepted. Check with individual institutions.

Band 5: For degree course: 2-3 A levels and some GCSEs (A*-C) usually including English, maths and a science, or equivalent. Exact requirements depend on the degree you take.

- **Scotland**

Band 3: Minimum entry requirements are at least five S grades (1-3) including English and a science subject. Relevant alternative academic and vocational qualifications are also acceptable.

Band 4: For entry to registered nurse training in many colleges: more than the minimum five S grades (1-3) or similar are required. H grades may be asked for, sometimes in specific subjects such as English and sciences.

Band 5: For degree course: 3-5 H grades and a number of S grades (1-3) including English, maths or a science subject, or similar. Exact requirements depend on the degree taken.

Degree Information
A degree in nursing or nursing studies leads to registration as a qualified nurse and the majority of courses offer the specialism of adult nursing. Some courses combine nursing with another social or natural science subject and lead to two qualifications. Graduates with relevant first degrees, eg in biological sciences, behavioural sciences, physical sciences or health related subjects, can take a shortened postgraduate nurse training course which takes a minimum of two years. There are postgraduate courses in occupational health nursing available at a number of universities throughout the country.

Adult Qualifications
Before training as an occupational health nurse, qualification as a registered nurse is usually required. It is an advantage for qualified nurses to have experience of working in accident and emergency units before going into occupational health nursing. Schools and colleges of nursing vary in their entry requirements for adult entry. Applicants who do not have the usual academic qualifications may be able to take an entrance test. A relevant vocational qualification at level 3 is usually acceptable. Alternatively you may be able to take specific modular course credits from the Open University, or a specific Access to higher education course, for entry to nursing training. Some universities have special entry standards for mature applicants. Check with individual institutions for details.

Work Experience
Employers or colleges/universities may prefer candidates who have relevant work or voluntary experience which demonstrates enthusiasm and commitment. This includes working with people in a social care environment or in customer service. The job is about rapport, communication and listening as much as the medical work.

Before entering this work, it is an advantage to learn about relevant health and safety legislation and the development of manual handling policies. Involvement in risk assessment also provides useful experience and some nurses have worked in an accident and emergency setting or practice nursing first. Performing as a Royal College of Nursing (RCN) safety representative also gives useful background to the work.

Entry and Training
You need to be a registered nurse before applying for occupational health nursing posts. For information about training as a registered nurse, see the job article Nurse: Adult.

Useful experience includes working in accident and emergency or in practice nursing. The role involves knowing about relevant health and safety legislation, the management of sickness and health promotion, ergonomics, development of manual handling policies and rehabilitation of staff with chronic conditions. There is no legal obligation to take specialist courses in occupational health nursing but most employers expect you to have completed a postgraduate or shortened degree level course to train as a specialist practitioner in occupational health nursing. Courses can be one-year full time, three years part time, or can be by distance learning. A minimum of two years' post-registration experience is required for admission to full-time courses. For part-time and distance-learning courses, students should be employed in occupational health nursing. Check with NHS Careers for details about the various schemes of training.

Mature entry is welcomed and many entrants to occupational health nursing are older, experienced nurses, particularly in emergency or general practice nursing. There are various sources of funding for post-registration courses. 'Return to Practice' programmes are also available for nurses wanting to return to work after a break of some years. Contact NHS Careers or your local NHS Trust for details of all training and funding opportunities.

Opportunities and Pay
There are around 3,500 occupational health nurses registered with the Nursing and Midwifery Council in the UK. This job exists in a wide range of organisations and you are likely to work for an industrial or commercial company, educational establishment or private consultancy. There are opportunities for part-time work and career breaks are common. With experience you can become self-employed as an occupational health consultant, or lead a team of occupational health staff.

Starting salaries in the NHS are on Band 5 which is around £21k-£27k a year. Higher earners may earn up to £40k a year.

Health
This job requires good health. The work involves a risk of infection and there is a risk of allergy from skin irritants.

Skills and Qualities
able to take responsibility, able to understand other people's problems, able to work both on your own and in a team, calm, efficient, good communication skills, not squeamish, observant, patient, responsible attitude

Relevant Subjects
Biology, Chemistry, English, Health and social care, Psychology, Science

Further Information
AGCAS: Health (Job Sector Briefing) (AGCAS) - www.prospects.ac.uk

NHS Careers (NHS Careers) - www.nhscareers.nhs.uk

NHS Careers Scotland - www.infoscotland.com/nhs

NHS Careers Wales - www.wales.nhs.uk

Nursing & Midwifery Uncovered (Trotman 2010) - www.trotman.co.uk

Nursing Careers - www.nhscareers.nhs.uk/nursing

Nursing Times (Nursing Times) - www.nursingtimes.net

Royal College of Nursing Wales - www.rcn.org.uk/aboutus/wales

SHP Magazine (monthly) (Institute of Occupational Safety & Health (IOSH)) - www.shponline.co.uk

Addresses
Institute of Occupational Safety and Health (IOSH)
The Grange, Highfield Drive, Wigston, Leicestershire LE18 1NN
Phone: +44 (0)116 257 3100
Web: www.iosh.co.uk

National Leadership & Innovation Agency for Healthcare (NLIAH: Wales)
Innovation House, Bridgend Road, Llanharan CF72 9RP
Phone: +44 (0)1443 233333
Web: www.wales.nhs.uk/sitesplus/829/

Nursing and Midwifery Council (NMC)
23 Portland Place, London W1B 1PZ
Phone: +44 (0)20 7333 9333
Web: www.nmc-uk.org

Royal College of Nursing (RCN)
20 Cavendish Square, London W1G 0RN
Phone: +44 (0) 20 7409 3333
Web: www.rcn.org.uk

School of Nursing and Midwifery
Queens University Belfast, Medical Biology Centre,
97 Lisburn Road BT9 7BL
Phone: +44 (0)28 9097 2233
Web: www.qub.ac.uk/nur

Similar Jobs
Dietitian, Health & Safety Practitioner, Health Promotion Specialist, Health Visitor, Nurse: Adult, Occupational Hygienist

Nurse: Practice
CRCI:Healthcare
CLCI:JAD — Job Band: 3 to 5

Job Description
Practice nurses are registered nurses who work at a local GP's surgery as part of a primary healthcare team that may include doctors, nurses, dietitians, and pharmacists. They are involved in almost every aspect of patient care and treatment, including health screening, family planning/sexual health advice, and the routine treatment of minor injuries. Also help with minor operations done under local anaesthetic. They offer specialist advice and information on topics such as weight control, heart conditions, travel health and blood pressure.

Practice nurses set up and manage clinics for diabetes, asthma, and well-woman/well-man clinics. They run health promotion programmes such as a planned programme against smoking and its related diseases. Also conduct seasonal vaccination programmes such as injections against flu. May be part of a team of practice nurses if employed at a large surgery. Administrative duties includes the medical restocking and maintenance of all clinical areas and consulting rooms.

Nurses keep accurate and up-to-date detailed records, often using a computer. They liaise with GPs, practice managers, office and reception staff, as well as other practice nurses and health professionals.

Work Details
Usually work a basic 37.5 hr week that may include work on a Saturday. There is contact with people who are ill and possibly in pain, upset or depressed. Work can be emotionally, physically and intellectually taxing. You have to deal with emergencies and be able to cope with the sight of blood. A uniform is provided by your employer and also protective clothing for some tasks.

Qualification

• England, Wales and Northern Ireland
Band 3: Minimum entry requirements are usually at least 5 GCSEs (A*-C) including English, maths and a science subject, or equivalent.

Band 4: For entry to some registered nurse training courses: more than the minimum 5 GCSEs (A*-C) are required. A levels may be asked for, sometimes in specific subjects, such as English and sciences. Equivalent qualifications may be accepted. Check with individual institutions.

Band 5: For degree course: For degree courses: 2-3 A levels and some GCSEs (A*-C) usually including English, maths and a science, or equivalent. Exact requirements depend on the degree you take.

• Scotland
Band 3: Minimum entry requirements are at least five S grades (1-3) including English and a science subject. Relevant alternative academic and vocational qualifications are also acceptable. Contact the individual institution for specific requirements.

Band 4: For entry to training courses in many colleges: more than the minimum five S grades (1-3) are required. H grades may be asked for, sometimes in specific subjects, such as English and sciences. Contact the individual institution for specific requirements.

Band 5: For degree course: 3-5 H grades and a number of S grades (1-3) including English, maths and a science, or similar. Contact the individual institution for specific requirements.

Degree Information
A degree in nursing or nursing studies leads to registration as a qualified nurse. Some courses combine nursing with another social or natural science subject and lead to two qualifications. Graduates with relevant first degrees, eg in biological sciences, behavioural sciences, physical sciences or health related subjects can take a shortened postgraduate nurse training course which takes a minimum of two years. There are relevant postgraduate qualifications in community specialist practice, which cover general practice nursing.

Adult Qualifications
Schools and colleges of nursing vary in their entry requirements for adult entry. Applicants who do not have the usual academic qualifications may be able to take an entrance test. A relevant vocational qualification at level 3 is usually acceptable or specific modular course credits from the Open University, or a specific Access to higher education course for entry to nursing training. Some universities have special entry standards for mature applicants. Check with individual institutions for details. There are relevant postgraduate qualifications in community specialist practice, which cover general practice nursing.

Work Experience
The job is about rapport, communication and listening as much as the medical work. The NHS recommends that those nurses wishing to move into practice nursing should spend time with a qualified practitioner to gain some experience of the role, and to also work as a community staff nurse in order to gain relevant experience. Prospective students are also recommended to read specialist journals such as Primary Health Care, which is available from the Royal College of Nursing (RCN). Contact the NHS trust in your area as direct work experience may be available.

Entry and Training
All applicants to practice nurse training must first qualify as a registered nurse and usually need at least two years' relevant post-registration experience, preferably working in adult nursing, covering a range of medical and surgical nursing. Some experience of working in community settings is also useful. For full details of how to train as a registered nurse, see the Nurse: Adult job article.

There are a few postgraduate courses that cover general practice nursing that can be taken either full or part time. Full-time courses generally take a year, part time can take from 2-5 years. A postgraduate qualification is not necessary and many general practice nurses are trained on the job, learning from more experienced colleagues, or by attending a series of short courses on specialist topics such as asthma, weight control and diabetes.

All entrants are required to be registered nurses, and mature entry is welcomed. There are also various sources of funding for post-registration courses. 'Return to Practice' programmes are also available for nurses wanting to return to work after a break of some years. Apprenticeships for adults may be an alternative route into nursing. Contact NHS Careers, the RCN or your local NHS Trust for details.

Opportunities and Pay
You are usually employed by the NHS at a GP's surgery. Promotion can be to more senior practice nurse posts, including nurse practitioner level. There may be opportunities to work part time and career breaks are common.

Practice nurses are usually paid at the NHS Band 6 specialist nurse rate of around £25k-£34k a year. Overtime pay may also be available.

Health
This job requires a good level of fitness.

Skills and Qualities
able to get on with all kinds of people, able to report accurately, able to take responsibility, calm, flexible approach, good communication skills, good interpersonal skills, good organisational skills, initiative, not squeamish

Relevant Subjects
Biology, Chemistry, Health and social care, Psychology, Science, Sociology

Further Information
AGCAS: Health (Job Sector Briefing) (AGCAS) - www.prospects.ac.uk

NHS Careers (NHS Careers) - www.nhscareers.nhs.uk

NHS Careers Scotland - www.infoscotland.com/nhs

NHS Careers Wales - www.wales.nhs.uk

Nursing & Midwifery Uncovered (Trotman 2010) - www.trotman.co.uk

Nursing Times website - www.nursingtimes.net

Practice Nursing Community - www.practicenursing.co.uk

Practice Nursing Journal (MA Healthcare Ltd) - www.practicenursing.com

Addresses
National Leadership & Innovation Agency for Healthcare (NLIAH: Wales)
Innovation House, Bridgend Road, Llanharan CF72 9RP
Phone: +44 (0)1443 233333
Web: www.wales.nhs.uk/sitesplus/829/

Nursing and Midwifery Council (NMC)
23 Portland Place, London W1B 1PZ
Phone: +44 (0)20 7333 9333
Web: www.nmc-uk.org

Practice Nurse Association
c/o Royal College of Nursing, 20 Cavendish Square, London W1G 0RN
Phone: +44 (0)20 7409 3333
Web: www.rcn.org.uk

Royal College of Nursing (RCN)
20 Cavendish Square, London W1G 0RN
Phone: +44 (0) 20 7409 3333
Web: www.rcn.org.uk

School of Nursing and Midwifery
Queens University Belfast, Medical Biology Centre,
97 Lisburn Road BT9 7BL
Phone: +44 (0)28 9097 2233
Web: www.qub.ac.uk/nur

Scottish Practice Nursing Association
25 Queen Street, Edinburgh EH2 1JX
Phone: +44 (0)131 260 6800
Web: www.spna.org.uk

Similar Jobs
Health Visitor, Nurse: Adult, Nurse: Children, Nurse: District, Nurse: Macmillan, Nurse: Mental Health

Nurse: School
also known as: Matron: School

CRCI:Healthcare

CLCI:JAD — Job Band: 3 to 5

Job Description
School nurses monitor the general health of young people in a school and have a range of key responsibilities. They may plan a health education programme and are often involved in teaching students about health-related issues. This may include sexual health and relationships, mental health problems, smoking, alcohol and drug abuse issues, dental and oral health, nutrition, or general exercise and well-being. Also check immunisation, diet, hearing, sight, personal hygiene, growth and development.

School nurses play an important role in immunisation and vaccination programmes for year groups, including TB (tuberculosis), or for emergency treatment at times of rare infection such as meningitis. They provide training for school-based staff who may need to support those in their class who have particular healthcare issues, such as diabetes, epilepsy or asthma. May provide a 'drop-in' advice and counselling service for students in secondary schools or colleges.

In some schools, such as independent boarding schools, they work as a 'matron' who may live on the school premises. School/college nurses liaise with teachers, doctors, other health professionals, and also parents/carers. School nurses increasingly work not just within schools, but also with individuals and communities as a whole.

Work Details

School nurses are usually employed by the NHS to work in schools, colleges or universities, or may work for the independent education sector. They work around 36-38 hrs a week, Monday to Friday, but jobs are often part time and term time only. If based in a boarding school, you may be on-call after hours. You have contact with school children or students who may be ill, upset, anxious or in pain.

Part of the job involves getting in touch with and talking to parents or carers. A school/college nurse must be able to relate well to young people, and be able to cope with emergencies and the sight of blood. Some school nurses cover a number of schools and need to travel between them. A driving licence is usually required.

Qualification

• England, Wales and Northern Ireland

Band 3: Minimum entry requirements are usually at least 5 GCSEs (A*-C) including English, maths and a science subject, or equivalent.

Band 4: For entry to some registered nurse training courses: more than the minimum 5 GCSEs (A*-C) are required. A levels may be asked for, sometimes in specific subjects, such as English and sciences. Equivalent qualifications may be accepted. Check with individual institutions.

Band 5: For degree course: For degree courses: 2-3 A levels and some GCSEs (A*-C) usually including English, maths and a science, or equivalent. Exact requirements depend on the degree you take.

• Scotland

Band 3: Minimum entry requirements are at least five S grades (1-3) including English and a science subject. Relevant alternative academic and vocational qualifications are also acceptable. Contact the individual institution for specific requirements.

Band 4: For entry to training courses in many colleges: more than the minimum five S grades (1-3) are required. H grades may be asked for, sometimes in specific subjects, such as English and sciences. Contact the individual institution for specific requirements.

Band 5: For degree course: 3-5 H grades and a number of S grades (1-3) including English, maths and a science, or similar. Contact the individual institution for specific requirements.

Degree Information

A degree in nursing or nursing studies leads to registration as a qualified nurse and the majority of courses offer the specialism of children's nursing. Some courses combine nursing with another social or natural science subject and lead to two qualifications. Graduates with relevant first degrees, eg in biological sciences, behavioural sciences, physical sciences or health related subjects can take a shortened postgraduate nurse training course which takes a minimum of two years.

Adult Qualifications

Schools and colleges of nursing vary in their entry requirements for adult entry. Applicants who do not have the usual academic qualifications may be able to take an entrance test. A relevant vocational qualification at level 3 is usually acceptable or specific modular course credits from the Open University, or a specific Access to higher education course for entry to nursing training. Some universities have special entry standards for mature applicants. Check with individual institutions for details.

Work Experience

Employers prefer candidates who have relevant work or voluntary experience. The job is about rapport, communication and listening as much as the medical work. It is useful to arrange to shadow an established school nurse. An understanding of health promotion, child protection, family planning, education and screening and some insight into the health needs of children and teenagers is very useful. Contact the NHS trust in your area as direct work experience may be available.

Entry and Training

School nurses are usually registered nurses who have completed a further educational programme to register as specialist community public health nurse. Employers expect applicants to have a registered nurse qualification and often prefer older, more experienced nurses. For full details of registered nurse training see the job article Nurse: Adult. Traditionally, school nurses were trained in the adult branch of nursing, but are now more likely to qualify in children's (paediatric) nursing.

With two years' experience as a registered nurse, it may be possible to start work as a school nurse without further training, particularly if you have experience of working with children, or in health promotion in the community. Knowledge of child protection, family planning, education and health screening is also an advantage. However, many employers prefer entrants to have specific training in these areas. This is by taking a degree level course for either a year full time or two years part time in community public health nursing (school nurse route). Some independent employers run short training courses for their employees, who can qualify after two years for the certificate of boarding staff through the Boarding Schools Association (BSA) and the Roehampton Institute.

As a qualified nurse you need to renew your registration with the Nursing and Midwifery Council (NMC) every three years. This includes undertaking at least 35 hours of learning in that time.

Mature entry is common in this branch of nursing. Those with experience of working with children, health promotion and work in the community, plus a knowledge of aspects of child protection, family planning, education and health screening have an advantage.

Opportunities and Pay

There are around 1,500 school nurses working for the NHS in the UK. School nurses can be employed by the local health authority, primary care trust or community trust. Opportunities also exist with schools/colleges in the independent sector. There is a steady demand for qualified staff. It is possible to work part time and promotion to supervisory posts in larger schools is possible. You can also choose to move to other work in the community such as practice nursing or health visiting.

Pay depends on your employer. School/college nurses employed by the NHS generally earn between £25k-£35k a year, rising to around £40k as a team manager. In the independent sector you may be given free or subsidised accommodation and reduced school fees for any of your school age children.

Health

This job requires good health and the work involves a risk of infection.

Skills and Qualities

able to cope with emergencies, able to explain clearly, able to take responsibility, approachable, flexible approach, good interpersonal skills, good listening skills, non-judgemental, not squeamish, reassuring

Relevant Subjects

Biology, Chemistry, English, Health and social care, Psychology, Science

Further Information

Community Practitioners' and Health Visitors' Association - www.unitetheunion.com/cphva

NHS Careers (NHS Careers) - www.nhscareers.nhs.uk

NHS Careers Scotland - www.infoscotland.com/nhs

NHS Careers Wales - www.wales.nhs.uk

Nursing Times (Nursing Times) - www.nursingtimes.net

Royal College of Nursing Wales - www.rcn.org.uk/aboutus/wales

Addresses

Boarding Schools Association (BSA)
Grosvenor Gardens House, 35-37 Grosvenor Gardens,
London SW1W 0BS
Phone: +44 (0)20 7798 1580
Web: www.boarding.org.uk

Community Practitioners' and Health Visitors' Association (CPHVA)
Unite Transport House, 128 Theobald's Road, Holborn,
London WC1X 8TN
Phone: +44 (0) 208 7611 2500
Web: www.amicus-cphva.org

National Leadership & Innovation Agency for Healthcare (NLIAH: Wales)
Innovation House, Bridgend Road, Llanharan CF72 9RP
Phone: +44 (0)1443 233333
Web: www.wales.nhs.uk/sitesplus/829/

Nursing and Midwifery Council (NMC)
23 Portland Place, London W1B 1PZ
Phone: +44 (0)20 7333 9333
Web: www.nmc-uk.org

Royal College of Nursing (RCN)
20 Cavendish Square, London W1G 0RN
Phone: +44 (0) 20 7409 3333
Web: www.rcn.org.uk

School of Nursing and Midwifery
Queens University Belfast, Medical Biology Centre,
97 Lisburn Road BT9 7BL
Phone: +44 (0)28 9097 2233
Web: www.qub.ac.uk/nur

Similar Jobs

Health Visitor, Nurse: Adult, Nurse: Children, Nurse: Occupational Health, Nurse: Practice

Nursery Worker

also known as: Early Education and Childcare Worker, Early Years Practitioner, Nursery Nurse

CRCI:Education and Training
CLCI:KEB Job Band: 1 to 3

Job Description

Nursery workers are responsible for the safety, care and education of babies and young children, usually under the age of five years old. For babies, much of the work involves physical care such as feeding, washing, changing nappies and ensuring the baby has a warm and caring environment. With toddlers, pre-school and older children, whilst still involved in some physical care, the emphasis is on developing language and social skills through play, as well as the development of educational skills, including letter and number recognition, and writing skills.

Nursery workers encourage children to experiment and use their imagination in play with a range of tactile materials, such as play dough and sand, and to enjoy play using water. They also supervise other activities, including drawing and painting, cooking, musical play, dressing up, use of building and construction toys, and using a computer. Stimulating the individual development of the children and observing their progress is a very important aspect of the job.

They keep written or word-processed records of each child and its development. Sometimes they have to liaise with social workers and other healthcare professionals, such as speech and language therapists. Most look after healthy children, in day or residential nurseries or in infant schools. Others work in hospitals, or may specialise as a community nursery nurse working under the supervision of a health visitor.

Work Details

The hours of work vary according to your contract, but are usually around 35-40 a week. Many nurseries are open from 8am to 6pm to fit in with the working lives of parents/carers. You can work in one of a number of different places such as a day nursery or workplace crhche, a hospital or residential home, a school or out in the community, or in a day care centre. Depending on where you work, you may be expected to work shifts and some evenings, weekends or irregular hours. You work with babies and young children mainly up to the age of five years old, but some nurseries offer after school and holiday care for older children. Sometimes you may work with children who are ill or have special needs.

This type of work can be emotionally demanding. Sometimes you have to cope with emergencies and deal with minor accidents. Work with children may be noisy and messy at times.

Qualification

• England, Wales and Northern Ireland

Band 1: For entry to jobs, no minimum qualifications are needed, but you are expected to have a good level of general education and relevant experience. Some formal/vocational qualifications at any level are useful.

Band 2: For entry to jobs, no minimum qualifications are needed, but it is an advantage to have some GCSEs (A*-C) or equivalent in subjects that include English and maths.

Band 3: For CACHE level 3 - diploma in child care and education (DCE): no set entry qualifications, but most colleges prefer 2-3 GCSEs (A*-C) including English and maths, or equivalent.

• Scotland

Band 1: For entry to jobs, no minimum qualifications are needed, but you are expected to have a good level of general education and relevant experience. Some formal/vocational qualifications at any level are useful.

Band 2: For SVQ level 2 in children's care, learning and development: no set entry qualifications, but some S grades including English, or similar are an advantage.

Band 3: For SVQ level 3 in children's care, learning and development: no formal qualifications stated though some S grades (1-3) including English, or similar, are useful.

Adult Qualifications

Course entry qualifications are not always needed, but this depends on the college and on the experience of the applicant.

Government training opportunities, such as apprenticeships, may be available in your area. You can also gain recognition of previous experience through Accreditation of Prior Learning (APL) or by working towards relevant S/NVQs. Contact your local careers office, Jobcentre Plus, Next Step service or Learning and Skills Council (LSC) Local Enterprise Company (LEC) for details of training schemes.

Work Experience

Relevant work or voluntary experience can equip you with skills that you can use in the future and that you can add to your CV. There are often opportunities available for voluntary work which give you experience of relevant work. Any work that involves young children and babies eg holiday projects, brownies/cubs or babysitting, provides valuable experience.

Entry and Training

You can enter this work with few qualifications and work as a nursery assistant, while training on the job. Some entrants, however, prefer to do a relevant full-time course before starting work. Entry to courses is highly competitive and often entrants have more than the minimum qualifications. In England, Wales and Northern Ireland, relevant courses are validated by the Council for Awards in Children's Care and Education (CACHE) and currently in Scotland by the Scottish Child Care & Education Board (SNNB). Check the Scottish Childcare website for further information. All entrants to this work need a Criminal Records Bureau/Disclosure Scotland check.

Nursery assistants, who work under supervision, usually take the NVQ level 2 in children's care, learning and development. They may also choose to take the certificate in child care and education (level 2), but this is one year full time and has 65 days at a work placement. Those who want to work as nursery nurses/early years practitioners usually take the level 3 diploma in child care and education, which is two years full time and has 125 work placement days. Experienced staff can complete either an NVQ level 4 in children's care, learning and development or do other CACHE professional development qualifications at level 3 and 4. See the CACHE website for full details.

There are also degrees/foundation degrees in early years studies. It is expected that nursery nurses will also work towards a new scheme of early years professional status (EYPS) as the first stage of continuing professional development (CPD). The Children's Workforce Development Council (CWDC) has details of the children's care, learning and development apprenticeship/ advanced apprenticeship. Advanced apprenticeships leading to qualification at level 3 can be a route into higher education.

In Scotland, there are SVQs at levels 2 and 3 in children's care, learning and development. These can be followed an HNC in early education and childcare. A wide range of relevant qualifications are available in early education, childcare and playwork starting at apprenticeship level. All workers in this sector need to register with the Scottish Social Services Council (SSSC).

Mature applicants are welcome and some colleges offer Accreditation of Prior Learning (APL) so that the qualification can be obtained in a shorter time. Colleges often have places allocated for mature applicants. The Open University runs distance learning courses in early years education. You may also benefit through government training opportunities that may be available in your area. Contact the local Jobcentre Plus office, Next Step service, LSC/LEC, Jobcentre (NI) or ELWa (Wales) for details of all possible training opportunities, including apprenticeships for adults.

Opportunities and Pay

At the moment there is a good demand for qualified nursery nurses/early years practitioners and job opportunities are increasing. There are over 200,000 workers in this sector. You can work for a local authority, a voluntary organisation, a company crhche, a private nursery, or an NHS Trust. Some may work on cruise ships, at holiday camps or hotels, and there may be opportunities to work abroad, either for a holiday company or private household. Once qualified, you can also work in a nursery school. Promotion opportunities are limited, but you can be self-employed and open a private nursery or playgroup.

Pay varies depending on location and employer. Salaries for nursery assistants are likely to start at around £11k-£14k rising to around £15k-£21k a year for nursery nurses. Nursery officers/ managers can earn from around £18k-£35k a year.

Health

You need to have clear speech, good general fitness and stamina to do this work.

Skills and Qualities

able to motivate others, calm, caring, creative and imaginative flair, enthusiastic, friendly, good communication skills, patient, responsible attitude, sense of humour

Relevant Subjects

Art and Design, Biology, English, Health and social care, Music, Psychology, Science

Further Information

Apprenticeship Schemes (National Apprenticeship Service) - www.apprenticeships.org.uk

Apprenticeships in Scotland (Careers Info Scotland) - www.apprenticeshipsinscotland.com/about/

Early Years Gateway - www.nurserynurseforum.com

Local Government Careers (Improvement and Development Agency) - www.lgcareers.com/publications/

Nursery World (weekly) (TSL Education Ltd) - www.tsleducation.com/nursery_world.asp

Open University - www.open.ac.uk

Scottish Childcare - www.scottishchildcare.gov.uk

So you want to work with Children (Wayland) - www.waylandbooks.co.uk

Training Schemes - www.direct.gov.uk/en/educationandlearning

► Working in social care (2010) (Babcock Lifeskills) - www.babcock-lifeskills.com/

Addresses

CACHE: Council for Awards in Children's Care & Education
Apex House, 81 Camp Road, St Albans AL1 5GB
Phone: 0845 347 2123 (UK only)
Web: www.cache.org.uk

Children's Workforce Development Council (CWDC)
2nd Floor, City Exchange, 11 Albion Street, Leeds LS1 5ES
Phone: +44 (0)113 244 6311
Web: www.cwdcouncil.org.uk

Early Years
6c Wildflower Way, Apollo Road, Belfast BT12 6TA
Phone: +44 (0)28 9066 2825
Web: www.early-years.org

National Day Nurseries Association (NDNA)
National Early Years Enterprise Centre, Longbow Close, Huddersfield HD2 1SQ
Phone: +44 (0)1484 407 7070
Web: www.ndna.org.uk

Scottish Pre-school Play Association (SPPA)
21 Granville Street, Glasgow G3 7EE
Phone: +44 (0)141 221 4148
Web: www.sppa.org.uk

Scottish Social Services Council (SSSC)
Compass House 11 Riverside Drive, Dundee DD1 4NY
Phone: +44 (0)845 60 30 891
Web: www.sssc.uk.com

Wales Pre-school Providers Association (Wales PPA)
Unit 1, The Lofts 9 Hunter Street, Cardiff Bay CF10 5GX
Phone: +44 (0)29 2045 1242
Web: www.walesppa.org

Similar Jobs

Childminder, Montessori Teacher, Nanny, Nurse: Children, Pre-school Supervisor/Worker, Teacher: Early Years

Nutritional Therapist

CRCI:Healthcare
CLCI:JOZ Job Band: 4 to 5

Job Description

Nutritional therapists apply aspects of nutrition science to promote optimum health, peak performance, disease prevention and patient care. They aim to improve the physical and mental health of a client by suggesting changes to their lifestyle and intake of food, vitamins and minerals. Clients may be suffering from conditions such as food intolerance, fatigue and depression, stress, migraine, skin disorders, hormonal imbalance or feeling generally unwell. Therapists holds one-to-one confidential consultations with clients, taking an overview of their health and lifestyle.

May advise certain changes to lifestyle and diet, or suggest nutritional supplements having clearly explained them to the client. Keep detailed notes and records, and may provide a telephone or web-based help service.

Work Details

Most nutritional therapists are self-employed, so hours are generally flexible. As a newly qualified nutritional therapist, you can expect to work a 30-40 hr week. Work is indoors and often from home, or may be based in a health clinic. You may be expected to wear smart clothes or a clinical uniform.

Qualification

- **England, Wales and Northern Ireland**

Band 4: For some nutritional therapy diploma courses: 1-2 A Levels and some GCSEs (A*-C), including English and maths with biology or chemistry.

Band 5: For a degree or some diploma courses: 2-3 A levels, usually including biology/chemistry and some GCSEs (A*-C), usually including English and maths, or equivalent. Exact requirements depend on the degree you take.

- **Scotland**

Band 4: For some nutritional therapy diploma courses: usually 2-3 H grades and some S grades (1-3), including maths and English with biology or chemistry.

Band 5: For a degree or some diploma course: 3-5 H grades, usually including biology/chemistry and some S grades (1-3), including English and maths or other similar qualifications. Exact requirements depend on the degree you take.

Degree Information

The University of Westminster offers a BSc (Hons) in health sciences/nutritional therapy and the Centre for Nutrition Education and Life Management offers a degree in nutritional therapy validated by Middlesex University. Relevant diplomas are available at a number of specialist colleges. Check with the British Association of Nutritional Therapy for accredited course information.

Adult Qualifications

Mature entry to this profession is common, and academic entry requirements to the British Association of Nutritional Therapy recognised courses may be relaxed for adult entry, particularly if you have relevant experience. There are Access and foundation courses that enable you to enter a higher education degree course.

Work Experience

Relevant work or voluntary experience is always useful and can improve your chances in application for entry to relevant courses. Types of work experience to consider are those that involve helping people or working with the public. Work in a medical field such as volunteering at a hospital is also relevant.

Entry and Training

There is no legal requirement to complete a specific course or become registered, but most nutritional therapists work towards registration with the Nutritional Therapy Council (NTC). The NTC is the regulatory body responsible for the accreditation of courses, which meet the national occupational standards (NOS) for nutritional therapy and the NTC's core curriculum.

The Complementary and Natural Healthcare Council also provides a voluntary regulation scheme for complementary healthcare professionals in the UK.

Almost all entrants have trained in nutritional therapy as a second career from a variety of backgrounds. Training courses in nutritional therapy can vary in length, content and cost, so potential students should choose carefully. Diploma courses take around 12-18 months to complete and some Nutritional Therapy diploma courses (NTDC) are available in conjunction with foundation science degrees (FdSc). Some entrants complete a degree in nutrition and a relevant postgraduate course.

Personal qualities are often deemed more important than qualifications for entry to some British Association of Nutritional Therapy (BANT) recognised courses. BANT recommends that training should include a minimum of 50 supervised hours and that all therapists also take an emergency first aid course. Membership of BANT includes acknowledgement of professional status by the NTC.

A Diploma/Welsh Baccalaureate may be available in your area in society, health and development. The advanced level is equivalent to 3.5 A levels but for some university courses, the additional and specialist learning (ASL) component of the diploma needs to include specific A levels. Check entry requirements carefully with the individual institutions. See the websites for further information.

Mature entry is common and some enter with existing professional experience and/or qualifications in areas that include nursing, midwifery, and other healthcare areas. You can also gain recognition of previous experience through Accreditation of Prior Learning (APL). Some training is available by distance learning.

Opportunities and Pay

This is a small but emerging occupation and demand for nutritional therapists in increasing. Employers include private therapy centres, but most therapists are usually self-employed and are based in London or the South East. Many experienced nutritional therapists develop a specialism in areas that include arthritis, eating disorders or preconceptual care. Some may move to teaching or lecturing posts, or establish a successful nutritional therapy business.

Since most nutritional therapists are self-employed, rates of pay vary depending on region and demand, and it is difficult to give an accurate indication of pay. Consultation fees vary from around £40-£110 a session, or from around £50 an hour. Firms employing a number of nutritional therapists may offer around £25k-£30k a year. Some therapists may earn more.

Skills and Qualities

analytical skills, business awareness, encouraging, good communication skills, good interpersonal skills, methodical, perceptive, reassuring, scientific approach, tactful

Relevant Subjects

Biology, Chemistry, English, Health and social care, Psychology, Science

Further Information

Centre for Nutrition Education and Life Management - www.cnelm.co.uk

Diplomas (Foundation, Higher and Advanced) - http://yp.direct.gov.uk/diplomas

NHS Careers (NHS Careers) - www.nhscareers.nhs.uk

NHS Careers Scotland - www.infoscotland.com/nhs

NHS Careers Wales - www.wales.nhs.uk

Register of Nutritional Therapists http://nutritionalmed.co.uk
Skills for Health - sector skills council - www.skillsforhealth.org.uk
Welsh Baccalaureate - www.wbq.org.uk

Addresses

British Association for Nutritional Therapy (BANT)
27 Old Gloucester Street, London WC1N 3XX
Phone: +44 (0)8706 061284
Web: www.bant.org.uk

Complementary and Natural Healthcare Council (CNHC)
83 Victoria Street, London SW1H 0HW
Phone: +44 (0)203 178 2199
Web: www.cnhc.org.uk

Nutritional Therapy Council (NTC)
PO Box 6114, Bournemouth, Dorset BH1 9BL
Phone: +44 (0) 1425 462507
Web: www.nutritionaltherapycouncil.org.uk

University of Westminster
309 Regent Street, London W1B 2UW
Phone: + 44 (0)20 7911 5000
Web: www.westminster.ac.uk

Similar Jobs

Dietitian, Health Promotion Specialist, Naturopath, Spa Therapist

NVQ/SVQ Assessor

CRCI:Education and Training
CLCI:FAP — Job Band: 1 to 2

Job Description

NVQ/SVQ assessors evaluate the knowledge and skills of people working towards National Vocational Qualifications (NVQs) or Scottish Vocational Qualifications (SVQs). They provide advice and support to help candidates achieve the award. They usually work with a number of candidates at the same time.

Assessors meet with new candidates to explain how the NVQ/SVQ is assessed and what they have to do. They find out what candidates already know and can do, and which areas they need to develop, then agree action plans and dates for reviewing progress. Observing candidates in their workplace is an important part of the role. They ask questions to test knowledge and see how candidates behave in different situations. They also review the evidence they collect to show that candidates have the practical skills and the knowledge they need to do their job to the standard required. The evidence may be audiotape, video, electronic or a paper-based portfolio.

Assessors keep records of each person's progress and signs off parts of the NVQ/SVQ on successful completion. They provide feedback and offer advice about areas that need further work, then forward paperwork and assessment results to the organisation that awards the NVQs/SVQs. May help to prepare an NVQ/SVQ training plan and deliver workshops. Some may have a more general training role, with NVQ/SVQ assessment as only a small part of the job.

Work Details

Usually works a 35-40 hr week, Monday to Friday. Visiting candidates during their normal working hours may mean early starts or late finishes, shift or weekend visits. It may also involve some travel. Needs to be well organised when working with several candidates based in different companies.

Often works as part of an assessment team with internal verifiers who check their work. Meets with other assessors to make sure they are all working to the same standards. Liaises with the candidates' line managers and training staff.

Qualification

- **England, Wales and Northern Ireland**

Band 1: No minimum qualifications are required, but you are expected to be competent in the area of work you are assessing. A good level of general education and some formal/vocational qualifications at any level are useful.

Band 2: Although academic qualifications are not specified for this job, it is an advantage to have some GCSEs (A*-C) in subjects that include English and maths or a level 2 vocational qualification, or equivalent.

- **Scotland**

Band 1: No minimum qualifications are required, but you are expected to be competent in the area of work you are assessing. A good level of general education and some formal/vocational qualifications at any level are useful.

Band 2: Although academic qualifications are not specified for this job, it is an advantage to have some S grades (1-3) in subjects that include English and maths, or a level 2 vocational qualification or similar.

Adult Qualifications

Government training opportunities, such as apprenticeships, may be available in your area. You can also gain recognition of previous experience through Accreditation of Prior Learning (APL) or by working towards relevant S/NVQs. Contact your local careers office, Jobcentre Plus, Next Step service or Learning and Skills Council (LSC) Local Enterprise Company (LEC) for details of training schemes.

Work Experience

Work experience helps you find out what you enjoy and don't enjoy about a type of work. For this job, you need to know about and have lots of experience of the area you are assessing. Paid or voluntary work that develops your communication or record keeping skills is useful. Teaching or training experience can improve your job prospects.

Entry and Training

You cannot do this job if you have not worked recently in the occupational area being assessed and for a long enough period to gain a good working knowledge of the job and its requirements. Formal qualifications are not required for training. However, vocational qualifications in your occupational area at level 3 or above and experience of training or teaching is useful. Some training providers require qualifications at level 2 to level 4. Others only take on people put forward by an employer.

When you train, you work towards the assessment qualifications known as A1 and A2 (both level 3). Depending on your area of work you must gain one or both of these and they take six to twelve months each to achieve. The A1 certificate assesses candidates through a range of methods, and as part of your training you are observed working with candidates. You may need to find at least two NVQ candidates to assess. You have to produce a portfolio of evidence to show that you can support and assess candidates to the standard required. Until you get your A1 certificate you cannot do formal assessments. You can then go on to take the A2 certificate in assessing candidates' performance through observation.

You can join the Institute of Assessors and Internal Verifiers (IAV) as an associate member once you have obtained your A1 or A2 certificate. After 12 months' experience you can apply for licentiate membership. Some assessors work towards training qualifications such as the Chartered Institute of Personnel and Development (CIPD) certificate in training practice. Assessors must maintain their skills in the jobs they are assessing. They must also keep themselves up to date with what is going on in their occupation area and in the fields of assessment and quality assurance of NVQ and SVQ qualifications. They may attend courses, conferences and workshops to help with this.

All those working with young people under 18 or with vulnerable adults are required to have a Criminal Records Bureau (CRB)/ Disclosure Scotland check.

Those with relevant work experience are usually accepted without any formal qualifications. Most people who get jobs as NVQ/SVQ assessors are adults because you need to have gained a good level of experience in the occupational area you are assessing.

Opportunities and Pay

There is a shortage of people with assessment skills in work-based learning and further education. NVQ/SVQ assessors work in colleges, with training providers and in organisations that train and assess their own staff. There is also freelance work for self-employed assessors.

Some assessors become internal verifiers for assessment centres. They monitor the work of assessors to make sure everyone assesses in the same way and no one is treated unfairly. Others become external verifiers for the organisations that award NVQs or SVQs. They make sure that assessment centres assess consistently and fairly. NVQ/SVQ assessors may move into teaching or training. Some may transfer their skills into other assessment roles such as childcare or education inspection or assessing organisations against 'quality mark' standards.

Salaries vary widely. Trainee assessors can earn from £15k to £22k a year. Once qualified and full time, you can earn from £18k to £30k. Freelance assessors earn around £15-£25 or may be paid by the learner. In some cases this can be around £500 each.

Skills and Qualities

able to motivate others, analytical skills, attention to detail, good communication skills, good interpersonal skills, good listening skills, good organisational skills, impartial, observant, supportive

Relevant Subjects

English, Psychology

Further Information

Excellence in Assessing (ENTO) - www.ento.co.uk/publications

LLUK (Lifelong Learning UK) - sector skills council for the professional development of staff working in the lifelong learning sector - www.lluk.org

People Management Magazine (CIPD) - www.peoplemanagement.co.uk/pm

The NVQ Assessor, Verifier and Candidate Handbook (2008) (Kogan Page) - www.koganpage.com

Addresses

Chartered Institute of Personnel and Development (CIPD)
151 The Broadway, London SW19 1JQ
Phone: +44 (0)20 8612 6200
Web: www.cipd.co.uk

ENTO (Employment National Training Organisation)
Kimberley House, 47 Vaughan Way, Leicester LE1 4SG
Phone: +44 (0)116 251 7979
Web: www.ento.co.uk

Institute of Assessors and Internal Verifiers (IAV)
PO Box 1138,, Warrington, Cheshire WA4 9GS
Phone: +44 (0)1925 485786
Web: www.iavltd.co.uk

Similar Jobs

Lecturer: Further Education, Quality Assurance Controller/ Inspector, Teacher: Secondary School, Training & Development Officer/Manager

Obstetrician/Gynaecologist

CRCI:Healthcare
CLCI:JAB Job Band: 5

Job Description

Obstetricians are medical doctors who specialise in pregnancy and childbirth and gynaecologists are doctors who work in hospitals with diseases and conditions relating to the reproductive system of women. They conduct clinics specifically for the ailments of women and give advice to women on treatments available. Perform surgical operations for women's conditions. Consult with women during pregnancy and attend at the delivery of the baby. Advise women on a range of health issues concerning pregnancy and childbirth. May work in the specialist fields of reproductive endocrinology and infertility which involve fertility drugs and assisted reproduction.

Work Details

You are expected to work irregular hours, including evenings and weekends to cover emergency care, particularly during training. You have contact with people who are ill, in pain, upset or depressed. You have to make decisions about the most appropriate treatment for their condition and maintain very accurate records. Work may be emotionally demanding, and requires coping with the sight of blood. You work in clinics, operating theatres, hospital wards and accident and emergency departments. You need to work closely as a team with other healthcare professionals, such as nurses and anaesthetists. This job is very satisfying for those wishing to work in a caring profession.

Qualification

- **England, Wales and Northern Ireland**

Band 5: For degree in medicine: usually three A levels, with good grades in chemistry and two from physics, biological sciences and maths, plus 5 GCSEs (A*-C) including English, or equivalent. Some medical schools offer a one-year pre-medical course for students with A levels in arts or mixed subjects. Check with individual schools for full details.

- **Scotland**

Band 5: For degree in medicine: usually five H grades, with good grades in chemistry and two from physics, biology and maths, plus five S grades (1-3) including English and maths, or similar. Normally science subjects not held at H grade should be offered at S grade. Some medical schools offer a one-year pre-medical course for students whose H grades do not include the required science subjects. Check with individual schools for full details.

Degree Information

A degree in medicine awarded by a university medical school and recognised by the General Medical Council is essential, followed by specialist training in obstetrics/gynaecology.

Adult Qualifications

Entry requirement standards are not normally relaxed for mature applicants, though those who consider applying should contact the individual university for advice. Graduates with a good honours degree in a related subject may obtain exemptions from certain options within the medical degree course.

Work Experience

Entry to this career is highly competitive and it is essential that you have some relevant work or voluntary experience before applying to train as a doctor so that you are able to demonstrate a long-term commitment to medicine. Evidence of this can come in the form of relevant paid or voluntary work in a healthcare setting such as work in a hospital, residential care home, or similar. You can apply for voluntary work overseas that usually has a health education or medically-related programme.

Entry and Training
Obstetricians/gynaecologists must first qualify as medical doctors by completing a medicine degree, pass the postgraduate two-year Foundation Programme and register as a doctor with the General Medical Council (GMC). For full details of medical training see the job article Doctor: Hospital.

Once you have completed the Foundation Programme, there is competition for Specialty Registrar (SpR) posts. For gynaecology and obstetrics, there is then a continuous period of training which covers 19 modules and leads to the Certificate of Completion of Training (CCT). Training is initially broader based, but then focusses on your specialty field. Progress is based on achieving competences and can take between five and seven years. Once you have achieved the CCT, you can join the specialist register of the GMC and are eligible to become a Fellow of the Royal College of Obstetricians and Gynaecologists (RCOG). You are expected to update your professional knowledge continually throughout your career. Contact the RCOG for details on all training options and courses.

Mature applicants that are suitably qualified are welcomed by medical schools of which some may have reserved places for mature/graduate entrants. There are Access courses to medicine and pre-medical foundation courses. Some Open University credits at distinction level may be accepted at some medical schools. Check with individual medical schools for details of all opportunities.

Opportunities and Pay
There are currently shortages of doctors in the UK. You usually work for an NHS hospital, a private hospital or a specialised clinic. There are some opportunities for private consultancy work or for overseas work with voluntary organisations in developing countries. Prospects may depend on willingness to move to another area to gain experience and obtain promotion. There may be opportunities to work part time or job share.

Within the NHS, junior doctors earn a basic salary and are usually paid a supplement for extra hours worked. Basic salaries are around £33k a year (including a 50% supplement for extra hours), rising to £43k-£68k (including 50% supplement) for a doctor in specialist training. A consultant can earn £73k-£174k a year. These salaries do not include on-call payments, private income or London weighting allowances. If working for a voluntary organisation abroad, your pay will be low.

Health
There is the risk of infection. You should have no allergies and a general level of general fitness.

Skills and Qualities
able to put people at ease, able to take responsibility, analytical skills, emotionally strong, good interpersonal skills, good listening skills, manual dexterity, not squeamish, scientific approach, self confident

Relevant Subjects
Biology, Chemistry, English, Health and social care, Mathematics, Physics, Psychology, Science, Sociology

Further Information
AGCAS: Health (Job Sector Briefing) (AGCAS) - www.prospects.ac.uk

BJOG: International Journal of Obstetrics and Gynaecology (Royal College of Obstetricians and Gynaecologists) - www.rcog.org.uk

Foundation Programme - www.foundationprogramme.nhs.uk

Modernising Medical Careers - www.mmc.nhs.uk

NHS Careers (NHS Careers) - www.nhscareers.nhs.uk

NHS Careers Scotland - www.infoscotland.com/nhs

NHS Careers Wales - www.wales.nhs.uk

Addresses
British Medical Association (BMA)
BMA House, Tavistock Square, London WC1H 9JP
Phone: +44 (0)20 7387 4499
Web: www.bma.org.uk

General Medical Council (GMC)
Regents Place, 350 Euston Road, London NW1 3JN
Phone: +44 (0)161 923 6602
Web: www.gmc-uk.org

Royal College of Obstetricians and Gynaecologists (RCOG) of London
27 Sussex Place, Regents Park, London NW1 4RG
Phone: +44 (0)20 7772 6200
Web: www.rcog.org.uk

Similar Jobs
Anaesthetist, Doctor: General Practitioner, Doctor: Hospital, Ophthalmologist, Surgeon

Occupational Hygienist

CRCI:Administration, Business and Office Work
CLCI:COT Job Band: 4 to 5

Job Description
An occupational hygienist anticipates, recognises, evaluates and controls health hazards at a place of work. These are mainly found in categories that are chemical (dust and vapours), physical (heat, light, radiation, noise, posture and motion), psychological (stress, bullying and violence) and biological (bacteria and viruses etc). The hygienist's primary objective is to safeguard the well-being of employees and the community at large and monitor manufacturing equipment, materials and processes. The role also involves sampling, testing then comparing the results to recognised standards and legal requirements. Evidence of risks or danger are sought. An occupational hygienist also negotiates with management, safety officers and union representatives to bring about any necessary changes.

Liaises with professional organisations, such as the Royal Society for the Prevention of Accidents (ROSPA) and the Health and Safety Executive (HSE). Coordinates staff training on health and safety issues, and aims to raise awareness of potential risks to health. May work in a team that includes safety advisers and engineers or healthcare professionals, such as doctors and occupational nurses. Keeps up to date with legal and scientific developments.

Work Details
Usually work office hours of 9am to 5pm, Monday to Friday, though may be required to work additional hours at times. May also spend time in laboratories and visiting places of work, such as manufacturing companies. The work involves arranging and taking part in meetings, writing reports and liaising with organisations, such as the HSE. Need to win the confidence of both management and workforce, and some decisions might be unpopular.

Occupational hygienists are sometimes involved in industrial disputes and may have to give evidence in court. There is a risk of exposure to harmful substances, such as solvents, chemicals, gases and radiation, so you may need to wear protective clothing.

Qualification

• England, Wales and Northern Ireland
Band 4: For a relevant BTEC higher national award: 1-2 A levels and some GCSEs (A*-C) usually including maths, science subjects and English, or equivalent.

Band 5: For degree courses: 2-3 A levels and some GCSEs (A*-C), usually including English and maths, or equivalent. Exact requirements depend on the degree you take.

• Scotland
Band 4: For relevant SQA higher national course: usually 2-3 H grades and some S grades (1-3) usually including maths, science subjects and English, or similar qualifications.

Band 5: For degree courses: 3-5 H grades and some S grades (1-3), usually including English and maths, or similar qualifications. Exact requirements depend on the degree you take.

Degree Information

There are specific degrees and foundation degrees in occupational health and safety/environmental management, and in safety management. Subjects such as chemical engineering, chemical and physical sciences, biomedical science, environmental health/ science (biological), building sciences, maths, geology or geochemistry are also relevant. Postgraduate degrees and diplomas in occupational hygiene are also available.

Adult Qualifications

Entry requirements may be relaxed for adults applying for higher education courses. Access courses to science can lead to a relevant degree or HND course. Graduates in a related discipline are able to take a postgraduate course in occupational hygiene, occupational health and safety or risk management.

Work Experience

Relevant work experience is important and improves your chances when applying for a job. Consider work within the health and safety environment, such as a department in a county council, or with an organisation such as the Health and Safety Executive. It is very useful to have gained experience in an engineering or science job.

Entry and Training

The British Occupational Hygiene Society (BOHS) has a bursary scheme for students wanting to gain a higher education qualification in Occupational Hygiene. Up to five bursaries are offered every year, each one offering up to £4,000 towards the payment of academic fees. The scheme is open to all students either already registered on, or who have been offered a place on, any UK-based postgraduate course approved by the Faculty of Occupational Hygiene.

A relevant BSc/MSc or BOHS certificate/diploma is usually required for this job. The BOHS has a list of approved university courses on their website and it is worth checking this list before embarking on a degree course as, if you have an approved degree, you are exempt from the BOHS certificate/diploma courses. You may also be eligible for a student bursary. Check the BOHS website for details. Internal promotion to this level of job is common and newly qualified graduates are in the minority. Those with relevant HNDs are likely to enter at technician level. Practical experience can be acquired during a degree or postgraduate course as well as on the job. Once in the job you need to have regular training to keep up to date with changing health and safety legislation. After one year of BOHS membership, you can apply to be included on the Institution of Occupational Safety and Health (IOSH) Register of Safety Practitioners.

Membership of the BOHS is open to all who have an interest in occupational hygiene and related topics. Those who have approved professional qualifications can become a member of the Faculty of Occupational Hygiene (FOH/BOHS). There are also courses for continuing professional development (CPD) and specialist diplomas. Contact IOSH and the BOHS (Faculty of Occupational Hygiene) for details.

Mature entrants with relevant qualifications and experience are often promoted from other scientific posts within an organisation, so maturity is an advantage. Those who have passed a course accredited by the Institution of Occupational Safety and Health (IOSH), such as the National Examination Board in Occupational Safety and Health (NEBOSH) diploma part 2 or a relevant S/NVQ at level 4, can apply for graduate membership of IOSH (Grad IOSH).

Opportunities and Pay

This is a fast-growing profession for those who have suitable experience and qualifications. Work is available in many different industries or organisations, ranging from the multinational giants of industry to small consultancies. Some may work for a local authority, government agency, the NHS, or a university or college. With experience, you can become a consultant or work for an organisation such as ROSPA or the British Safety Council. Some overseas travel is possible.

Pay varies widely depending on location, sector and employer. Starting salaries for graduates are likely to be around £18k-£32k. Experienced occupational hygienists earn between £32k-£48k. Senior hygienists working in industry earn around £50k-£80k a year.

Health

There is an allergy risk from skin irritants or dust. This job requires good general fitness.

Skills and Qualities

able to cope with emergencies, able to evaluate, able to work both on your own and in a team, analytical skills, attention to detail, good communication skills, good interpersonal skills, IT skills, methodical, scientific approach

Relevant Subjects

Biology, Chemistry, Design and technology, English, Health and social care, Mathematics, Physics, Science

Further Information

AGCAS: Health (Job Sector Briefing) (AGCAS) - www.prospects.ac.uk

Annals of Occupational Hygiene (Oxford Journals) - http://annhyg.oxfordjournals.org/current.dtl

British Safety Council - www.britsafe.org

Careers in Environmental Health (Chartered Institute of Environmental Health) - www.ehcareers.org

Health and Safety Executive - www.hse.gov.uk

Royal Society for the Prevention of Accidents (ROSPA) - www.rospa.com

Safety and Health Practitioner (monthly) (Institution of Occupational Safety and Health (IOSH)) - www.shponline.co.uk/

Addresses

British Occupational Hygiene Society (BOHS)
5/6 Melbourne Business Court , Millennium Way, Pride Park, Derby DE24 8LZ
Phone: +44 (0)1332 298101
Web: www.bohs.org

Institution of Occupational Safety and Health (IOSH)
The Grange, Highfield Drive, Wigston, Leicestershire LE18 1NN
Phone: +44 (0)116 257 3100
Web: www.iosh.co.uk

Similar Jobs

Environmental Health Practitioner, Ergonomist, Health & Safety Practitioner, Nurse: Occupational Health, Toxicologist

Occupational Therapist

CRCI:Healthcare
CLCI:JAR
Job Band: 5

Job Description

Occupational therapists (OTs) plan programmes of work and recreational activities to help people cope physically with everyday living. They aim to improve their patients' current quality of life in their social as well as working life and look at ways to boost and maximise patients' independence. OTs work as part of a team, which includes nurses, physiotherapists, consultants and social workers, to assess patients' needs and provide a programme to help develop their self reliance and independence. They develop long or short-term programmes of treatment.

May work with people with physical problems, those recovering from an accident or an operation, mental health problems, including acute anxiety, stress and depression, and those who have a disabling condition such as a stroke, motor neurone disease or muscular dystrophy. Also advise on the provision of aids and equipment designed to make everyday living easier for patients with disabilities.

May visit patients at home, particularly to help them gain confidence to return to work, or advise on any alterations to their home to improve their daily quality of life.

Work Details

Usually works 37.5 hrs a week; Monday to Friday, though may be expected to work occasional weekends, evenings or be on-call at times. You work in a hospital, clinic or in patients' homes and you may travel around a local area. You first assess your patients' physical and psychological capabilities and prepare a programme of treatment, perhaps in liaison with other professionals, to help the patient achieve maximum independence. This job involves contact with hospital patients who may be in pain, have mental problems or physical disabilities. You may need to wear a uniform.

Qualification

• England, Wales and Northern Ireland

Band 5: For degree courses: 2-3 A levels, including a science subject, preferably biology, and some GCSEs (A*-C) usually including English and maths, or equivalent. Exact requirements depend on the degree you take.

• Scotland

Band 5: For degree courses: 3-5 H grades, including English and a science subject, preferably biology, and some S grades (1-3), usually including English and maths, or similar qualifications. Exact requirements depend on the degree you take.

Degree Information

A BSc (Hons) in occupational therapy, or a relevant degree such as psychology, biology or sociology, together with a two-year postgraduate diploma in occupational therapy, is required for entry to this job. Graduates with a degree in a subject other than occupational therapy, but previous experience in health or social care, may take a postgraduate diploma course.

Adult Qualifications

Degree course entry requirements for mature applicants are assessed individually and academic requirements may be relaxed. Entry is possible through validated Access courses. Mature entrants who have qualifications in nursing or physiotherapy may be able to take the two-year postgraduate diploma.

Work Experience

Work experience gives you an insight into what you enjoy about a job or working environment, and the opportunity to acquire new skills. It provides valuable information to add to your CV and improves your course application and future employment prospects. Consider voluntary or paid experience working in a residential care home, with children, or anything involving helping and communicating with people.

Entry and Training

Training normally consists of a three or four year course leading to a BSc in occupational therapy. If you are already working as an occupational therapy support worker or a technical instructor, you may be able to study part-time but the course takes four years. Courses include specialised work in practical placements. There are also graduate entry schemes to a two year course for those who hold a recent and relevant first degree and have experience in social care or health. You can then able to apply for state registration with the Health Professions Council (HPC) which is required for professional practice in the NHS or social services in the UK.

Entry to degree courses is highly competitive and any practical experience , such as caring for the elderly or working with physically disabled people is an advantage. You need to have a Criminal Records Bureau (CRB)/Disclosure Scotland check before applying for a course. You can join the British Association of Occupational Therapists (BAOT) and the World Federation of Occupational Therapists as a student or graduate and are expected to participate in a programme of continuing professional development throughout your career. Contact the BAOT for a list of accredited courses and training routes.

A Diploma/Welsh Baccalaureate may be available in your area in society, health and development. The advanced level is equivalent to 3.5 A levels but for some university courses, the additional and specialist learning (ASL) component of the diploma needs to include specific A levels. Check entry requirements carefully with the individual institutions.

Mature entry requirements for courses may be relaxed for suitable candidates. There are a number of NHS-funded places on university courses, for which you may be eligible.

Opportunities and Pay

There are around 30,000 registered occupational therapists (OTs) in the UK. Jobs are available mainly in towns and cities and demand is strong and growing. Most OTs work for the NHS, social services or departments of health and social care. Other employers include voluntary organisations, prisons and private residential/ nursing homes. You may be able to specialise in one area of OT, working with children or the elderly, or you can opt for a rotational post to gain a range of experience. Promotion depends on experience and merit. There may be opportunities to be self-employed, move into teaching, management or research and to work part time. Opportunities exist abroad, particularly in the USA, Canada, Australia and New Zealand.

Pay is on a nationally agreed scale in the NHS. Starting salaries are around £21k-£28k, but can rise to £34k-£40 a year with experience. Consultant occupational therapists can earn around £53k a year.

Health

This job requires good general fitness.

Skills and Qualities

able to explain clearly, able to inspire confidence, encouraging, good communication skills, good interpersonal skills, manual dexterity, observant, patient, resourceful, sympathetic

Relevant Subjects

Art and Design, Biology, English, Health and social care, Hospitality and catering, Psychology, Science, Sociology

Further Information

AGCAS: Health (Job Sector Briefing) (AGCAS) - www.prospects.ac.uk

British Journal of Occupational Therapy (COT, monthly) - www.cot.co.uk/homepage/library_and_publications

Diplomas (Foundation, Higher and Advanced) - http://yp.direct.gov.uk/diplomas

Health Professions Council (HPC) - www.hpc-uk.org

NHS Careers (NHS Careers) - www.nhscareers.nhs.uk

NHS Careers Scotland - www.infoscotland.com/nhs

NHS Careers Wales - www.wales.nhs.uk

Occupational Therapy Careers Handbook 2009/10 (COT) (College of Occupational Therapy) - http://cot.org.uk

Occupational Therapy News (monthly) (College of Occupational Therapists (COT)) - www.cot.org.uk/public/publications/intro/intro.php

Welsh Baccalaureate - www.wbq.org.uk

▶Working in social care (2010) (Babcock Lifeskills) - www.babcock-lifeskills.com/

World Federation of Occupational Therapists - www.wfot.org

Addresses

British Association (BAOT)/College of Occupational Therapists (COT)
106-114 Borough High Street, Southwark, London SE1 1LB
Phone: +44 (0)20 7357 6480
Web: www.cot.co.uk

Similar Jobs

Art Therapist, Dramatherapist, Music Therapist, Speech & Language Therapist, Sports Therapist

Occupational Therapy Assistant

also known as: Clinical Support Worker: Occupational Therapy, Occupational Therapy Technician, Rehabilitation Assistant

CRCI:Healthcare
CLCI:JAR — Job Band: 1 to 3

Job Description

Occupational therapy assistants (OTAs) work with occupational therapists to help people with physical, mental and social problems to cope with everyday living and working. They find ways to help them to be independent, including ways of coping with washing and dressing, shopping and cooking and preparing to go back to work. Help to plan a programme of work for patients who may be recovering from a stroke, coping with depression, or anxious. Also help people with arthritis and those who are recovering from an operation or an accident. Can work with groups of patients.

May write reports and keep records using a computer, and do some office administration. Sometimes OTAs visit patients at home. They give advice about other services that can help. These may include voluntary organisations and charities or local authority departments, including social services.

Work Details

Usually work 37.5 hrs a week; Monday to Friday, though may be expected to work occasional weekends, evenings, or be on-call at times. You work in a hospital, day care centre, training centre or sometimes in a patient's home. You help patients who are in need of support, working under the supervision of a qualified occupational therapist. Patients may be demanding, aggressive or depressed and work can be stressful at times. You have to cope with being active most of the time and may need to wear a uniform.

Qualification

• England, Wales and Northern Ireland

Band 1: For entry to jobs, no minimum qualifications are needed, but you are expected to have a good level of general education and relevant experience. Some formal/vocational qualifications at any level are useful.

Band 2: Although academic qualifications are not specified for this job, it is an advantage to have some GCSEs (A*-C) in subjects that include English, maths, biology or another science, or equivalent.

Band 3: For entry to jobs, HNC or a relevant course, usually at least 4 GCSEs (A*-C) including English and maths, or equivalent.

• Scotland

Band 1: No minimum qualifications are required, but you are expected to have a good level of general education. Some formal/ vocational qualifications or relevant work experience at any level is useful.

Band 2: Although academic qualifications are not specified for this job, it is an advantage to have some S grades (1-3) in subjects that include English, maths, biology or another science, or similar.

Band 3: For entry to jobs, usually at least four S grades (1-3) including English and maths, or similar.

Adult Qualifications

No formal qualifications are needed although you are expected to have a good standard of education. Some employers may require a vocational award in health.

Work Experience

Work experience gives you an insight into what you enjoy about a job or working environment, and the opportunity to acquire new skills. It provides valuable information to add to your CV and improves course applications and future employment prospects. Employers may prefer candidates who have relevant work or voluntary experience in a medical or healthcare setting, such as a hospital or residential care home.

Entry and Training

You must be at least 18 and many entrants are older. It is useful to have some practical skills and experience of working with people, and it may be helpful to have an S/NVQ in support services in health care when applying for jobs. Most employers require a Criminal Records Bureau (CRB)/Disclosure Scotland check. Training is on the job through the employer's training scheme. You follow a programme that includes health and safety procedures, disability awareness, introduction to the various health aids and equipment, and how to safely move and treat a patient.

Relevant S/NVQs at level 2-3, or the higher national certificate in occupational therapy support may be available with support from your employer. Occupational therapy assistants are eligible for registration as associate members of the British Association (BAOT)/College of Occupational Therapists (COT). Experienced and able assistants can become qualified occupational therapists through an in-service four-year degree qualification programme.

Relevant foundation degrees, such as health and social care, are available in some areas of the country. Contact the BAOT/COT for information on training routes and qualifications. A Diploma/Welsh Baccalaureate may be available in your area in society, health and development. This can provide a useful introduction to this career.

Mature applicants are often preferred, particularly those who show aptitude and have previous experience. Government training opportunities, such as apprenticeships, may be available in your area. You can also gain recognition of previous experience through Accreditation of Prior Learning or by working towards relevant S/NVQs. Contact your local careers office, Jobcentre Plus, Next Step service or Learning and Skills Council (LSC)/Local Enterprise Company (LEC) for details of all training opportunities and schemes, including apprenticeships for adults.

Opportunities and Pay

Jobs are available mainly in towns and cities throughout the UK. Most assistants work for the NHS, a local authority social work department or a voluntary organisation. There are also jobs in private healthcare. Openings may be limited and voluntary work can be done to gain experience. There may be opportunities to work part time.

Pay is in line with NHS pay bands, starting at around £16k a year, rising with experience to £18k-£21k. High-cost area supplements may be offered to those working in inner/outer London.

Health

This job requires good general fitness.

Skills and Qualities

able to explain clearly, able to follow instructions, able to take responsibility, able to understand other people's problems, aptitude for teamwork, caring, encouraging, manual dexterity, patient, practical skills

Relevant Subjects

Art and Design, Biology, English, Health and social care, Hospitality and catering

Further Information

British Journal of Occupational Therapy (COT, monthly) - www.cot.co.uk/homepage/library_and_publications

Diplomas (Foundation, Higher and Advanced) - http://yp.direct.gov.uk/diplomas

NHS Careers (NHS Careers) - www.nhscareers.nhs.uk

NHS Careers Scotland - www.infoscotland.com/nhs

NHS Careers Wales - www.wales.nhs.uk

Occupational Therapy News (monthly) (College of Occupational Therapists (COT)) - www.cot.org.uk/public/publications/intro/intro.php

Training Schemes - www.direct.gov.uk/en/educationandlearning

Welsh Baccalaureate - www.wbq.org.uk

▶Working in social care (2010) (Babcock Lifeskills) - www.babcock-lifeskills.com/

Addresses

British Association (BAOT)/College of Occupational Therapists (COT)
106-114 Borough High Street, Southwark, London SE1 1LB
Phone: +44 (0)20 7357 6480
Web: www.cot.co.uk

Similar Jobs

Healthcare Assistant, Occupational Therapist, Physiotherapy Assistant, Podiatry/Chiropody Assistant, Social Care Worker, Speech & Language Therapy Assistant

Oceanographer

also known as: Marine Scientist
CRCI:Science, Mathematics and Statistics
CLCI:QOL Job Band: 5

Job Description

Oceanographers study different aspects of the oceans, such as tides, temperature, the organisms within them, or the sea floor. They use specialised and sophisticated electronic equipment, including ship-based instruments to take measurements, analyse and complete calculations, and produce sea charts. Some oceanographers are concerned with pollution of the seas and the effects of climate change. They may research the salinity and circulation of water and the effects of pollution on marine life or investigate the geological structure of the sea bed. This discipline has applications in oil and gas production or ecological developments such as wave power.

There is also an academic role in research and teaching or lecturing, usually in universities and higher education institutions. This involves writing proposals for research and papers and articles for presentation to others in the field. These are often presented at seminars and conferences wordwide. Participating in field trips is common and usually leads to data being collected for research and publication.

Work Details

Usually work a basic 37-40 hr week, though may be required to work shifts or early starts/late finishes and some weekends, often in a laboratory or office. You often spend time at sea when on fieldwork that usually involves time away from home. Shifts around the clock are usual when working offshore, but normal hours onshore. This work can be physically active. When offshore, you can be working in uncomfortable conditions and in all weathers, sometimes climbing ladders and perhaps having to cope with seasickness.

You may study the ocean bed using diving equipment or submersible vehicles and there is a risk of accidents at sea. Protective clothing is usually worn. You usually work as part of a team, often with other professional scientists.

Qualification

- **England, Wales and Northern Ireland**

Band 5: For degree courses: 2-3 A levels, including two sciences and maths, and some GCSEs (A*-C) usually including English. Exact requirements depend on the degree you take.

- **Scotland**

Band 5: For degree courses: 3-5 H grades including two sciences and maths, and some S grades (1-3), usually including English, or similar qualifications. Exact requirements depend on the degree you take.

Degree Information

A good honours degree in oceanography/marine sciences or a closely related subject may be preferred. There are few first degrees in oceanography, but there are some combined courses with an oceanography option. Degrees including physics, chemistry, geophysics, geotechnology, ecology, environmental science (biological) or geology are also acceptable. Postgraduate courses usually require a first degree in oceanography, physics, chemistry or geology. Other science subjects can provide relevant background knowledge.

Adult Qualifications

A degree or equivalent qualification is necessary. Course requirements may be relaxed if knowledge of maths and science is up to date.

Work Experience

Entry to this job is competitive and it is important that you try to do some relevant work or voluntary experience before applying to both jobs and university degrees. There are several NERC centres around the country that may take people on work experience, such as the National Oceanography Centre, Southampton (NOCS) which also runs summer schools for final year degree students. You can join a relevant society such as SUT or the Marine Biological Association (MBA).

Entry and Training

Oceanographers first complete a relevant degree or postgraduate qualification. Entry to the few first degree courses on offer is highly competitive, but there are more postgraduate courses available. Check with the Society for Underwater Technology (SUT) for suitable courses. Due to the specific areas of oceanography, you need to decide between chemical or biological oceanography, physical, geophysical or geological oceanography or marine engineering. Training is by practical work experience, in-house short courses or sometimes a residential course. Short study periods may often take place overseas.

It can be useful to have a sub-aqua/diving licence for some areas of work. You need to follow a programme of continuing professional development (CPD) to update your knowledge.

Mature applicants with a relevant first degree may apply to the Natural Environmental Research Council (NERC) for postgraduate study or for research.

Opportunities and Pay

This is a small profession and opportunities may be limited. Most oceanographers work for the National Environment Research Council (NERC) but there are also opportunities with other research organisations, universities, water companies, the Royal Navy, and some government departments. Promotion may be limited by the small number of higher grade posts and it is usual to move to other jobs in order to advance your career. An increasing number of oceanographers work for consultancies, advising on environmental issues.

Employment is often on short-term contracts, especially in research, and pay varies depending on location and employer. Starting salaries for graduates are around £19k-£28k a year, rising to £40k a year with experience. Senior oceanographers can earn up to £60k a year. Lecturers earn in the range of £25k-£35k a year, increasing to £38k-£56k a year for senior posts. Consultancy rates can be higher.

Health

This job requires normal colour vision and good general fitness.

Skills and Qualities

able to report accurately, able to work both on your own and in a team, analytical skills, aptitude for fieldwork, aptitude for maths and science, attention to detail, problem-solving skills, research skills, scientific approach, specialist IT skills, willing to train and work away from home

Relevant Subjects

Biology, Chemistry, English, Geography, ICT/Computer studies, Mathematics, Physics, Science

Further Information

Careers in the Marine Environment (IMarEST) - www.imarest.org/careers/
Oceans of Opportunity (Society for Underwater Technology (SUT)) - www.sut.org.uk/htmfoldr/oceansoop/sut_ooo.htm
Open University - www.open.ac.uk
Society for Underwater Technology
(Society for Underwater Technology) - www.sut.org.uk
▶Working outdoors (2010) (Babcock Lifeskills) - www.babcock-lifeskills.com/

Addresses

Marine Biological Association (MBA)
The Laboratory, Citadel Hill, Plymouth, Devon PL1 2PB
Phone: +44 (0)1752 633 207
Web: www.mba.ac.uk

National Oceanography Centre (NOCS)
University of Southampton, Waterfront Campus,
European Way SO14 3ZH
Phone: +44 (0)23 8059 6666
Web: www.noc.soton.ac.uk/

Natural Environment Research Council (NERC)
Polaris House North Star Avenue, Swindon, Wiltshire SN2 1EU
Phone: +44 (0)1793 411 500
Web: www.nerc.ac.uk

Similar Jobs

Engineer: Marine, Geologist, Geophysicist, Marine Biologist, Surveyor: Hydrographic

Office Equipment Service Engineer

also known as: Business Equipment Service Engineer, Field Service Engineer: Office Equipment

CRCI:Engineering
CLCI:ROK

Job Band: 1 to 4

Job Description

Office equipment service engineers install, repair and service office electrical or electronic equipment. This includes word processors, printers, scanners, photocopiers and fax machines. They routinely look after office equipment or may be called to fix a faulty machine. Following a set procedure or machine manual, engineers complete tests to locate any problems. They fix the fault by adjusting, repairing or replacing the part and checking that the machine is working. May arrange for the return of faulty equipment to a repair centre.

Service engineers may also arrange for temporary equipment to be delivered while repairs are carried out and train office staff to use new equipment correctly. The log each repair, including time, date and location, and write up reports.

Work Details

Usually work a basic 35-40 hr week, Monday to Friday, in a workshop, office, or out and about visiting customers' premises. Travel from job to job may be needed. You are responsible for fixing problems quickly and providing an efficient service. You may be expected to work on call. You have to cope with some physical activity and lifting of heavy equipment. Smart and tidy clothes are usually required.

Qualification

• England, Wales and Northern Ireland

Band 2: For entry to jobs, no minimum qualifications are needed, but it is an advantage to have some GCSEs (A*-C) or equivalent in subjects that include maths, science and English, or equivalent.

Band 3: For entry to jobs, HNC or a relevant Diploma, usually at least 4 GCSEs (A*-C) including maths, English and science, or equivalent. Practical and technical subjects are also useful.

Band 4: For HND, Diploma of Higher Education or foundation degree: 1-2 A levels and some GCSEs (A*-C) usually including English and maths, or equivalent.

• Scotland

Band 2: Although academic qualifications are not specified for this job, it is an advantage to have some S grades (1-3) in subjects that include maths, science and English, or similar.

Band 3: For entry to jobs, usually at least four S grades (1-3) including maths, English and science, or similar. Practical and technical subjects are also useful.

Band 4: For entry to SQA higher national and professional development awards, usually 2-3 H grades and some S grades (1-3), including English and maths, or similar qualifications.

Adult Qualifications

Formal educational requirements vary from company to company. Course entry requirements are usually relaxed for suitable mature applicants.

Work Experience

Relevant work or voluntary experience is always useful. It can add to your CV and improve your chances when applying for entry to jobs or apprenticeships in the engineering industry.

Entry and Training

Direct entry from school is limited as many employers prefer applicants with previous relevant experience or qualifications. Often initial training is through a relevant college course, such as a City & Guilds NVQ award in electrical/electronics servicing at levels 2-3 or a BTEC/SQA award in operations and maintenance engineering. This job requires regular training to keep up to date with different products. Equipment manufacturers run relevant short courses and refresher courses. For qualified service engineers, the training given can vary depending on the employer, but most companies provide in-house training.

Some employers may provide sponsorship for courses. Usually this job requires a driving licence. Training programmes, including apprenticeship schemes, may be available in your area. Advanced apprenticeships leading to qualification at level 3 can also be a route into higher education.

A Diploma/Welsh Baccalaureate may be available in your area in engineering. See the diplomas website for further information.

Mature applicants with recent technical, electrical or electronic experience may have an advantage. Government training opportunities, such as apprenticeships, may be available in your area. You can also gain recognition of previous experience through Accreditation of Prior Learning or by working towards relevant S/NVQs. Contact your local careers office, Jobcentre Plus, Next Step service or Learning and Skills Council (LSC)/Local Enterprise Company (LEC) for details of training schemes.

Opportunities and Pay

Jobs are available in most towns and cities. Most work is with a manufacturing company service department, an equipment hire company or a specialist service company. Increasingly, sophisticated links exist between an engineer's office and customers' equipment. This means that engineers can now service equipment all over the world. Some companies offer a consultancy or training service to clients which has resulted in engineers becoming multi-skilled.

Pay varies depending on location and employer. A new entrant might expect to earn from around £15k, rising to around £17k-£25k with experience. Highly skilled and experienced service engineers earn more than £40k a year. You may have the use of a company vehicle.

Health

This job requires good eyesight, normal colour vision and a good standard of physical fitness.

Skills and Qualities

able to cope under pressure, able to follow drawings and plans, able to work well on your own, good interpersonal skills, IT skills, manual dexterity, methodical, methodical, problem-solving skills, technical aptitude

Relevant Subjects

Design and technology, Engineering, ICT/Computer studies, Mathematics, Physics, Science

Further Information

Apprenticeship Schemes (National Apprenticeship Service) - www.apprenticeships.org.uk

Diplomas (Foundation, Higher and Advanced) - http://yp.direct.gov.uk/diplomas

e-skills UK - sector skills council for business and information technology - www.e-skills.com

SEMTA - sector skills council for science, engineering and manufacturing technologies - www.semta.org.uk

Training Schemes - www.direct.gov.uk/en/educationandlearning

Welsh Baccalaureate - www.wbq.org.uk

Addresses

Institution of Engineering and Technology (IET)
Michael Faraday House, Stevenage, Hertfordshire SG1 2AY
Phone: +44 (0)1438 313311
Web: www.theiet.org

Similar Jobs

Domestic Appliance Service Technician, Fitter: Maintenance, IT Service Technician, Mechanical Engineering Technician, Telecommunications Technician

Office Manager

CRCI:Administration, Business and Office Work
CLCI:CAP Job Band: 4 to 5

Job Description

Office managers are responsible for the efficient operation and day-to-day running of an office or an area of office work. They carry out a variety of tasks to ensure that the department or office runs smoothly. This includes supervising the daily tasks, preparing and circulating reports and documents, and setting up meetings. May also oversee IT-related work as well as administrative duties. Office managers control the office budget, and organise office maintenance and repair work. Ensure that health and safety regulations are up to standard and regularly test the procedures.

Most managers take part in policy discussions with colleagues and coordinate activities with other departments. They look after the welfare of office staff, including their training and development needs, conduct staff appraisals and keep personnel records.

Work Details

Usually work regular office hours, typically 9am to 5pm, Monday to Friday, though sometimes may be required to work outside of these hours, including early mornings or attendance at evening meetings. You organise and supervise clerical and secretarial staff, and perhaps set up office systems and procedures. The work must be completed within an agreed budget. You liaise with other staff, such as departmental managers, the company secretary and accountants. Smart, professional clothes are usually worn.

Qualification

• England, Wales and Northern Ireland

Band 4: For BTEC higher national award in a business or finance subject: 1-2 A levels and some GCSEs (A*-C) usually including English and maths, or equivalent.

Band 5: For degree courses: 2-3 A levels and some GCSEs (A*-C) usually including English and maths, or equivalent. Exact requirements depend on the degree you take.

• Scotland

Band 4: For a relevant SQA higher national award in a business or finance subject: usually 2-3 H grades and some S grades (1-3), often including English and maths, or similar qualifications.

Band 5: For degree courses: 3-5 H grades and some S grades (1-3), usually including English and maths, or similar qualifications. Exact requirements depend on the degree you take.

Degree Information

A degree in any discipline is acceptable, however it is an advantage to have a degree in business and management subjects. Degrees in information technology/systems, financial management/banking, social/public administration, economics and accountancy also give useful background. Foundation degrees are also available in relevant subjects.

Adult Qualifications

Qualifications in business studies at degree or higher national level are the most acceptable qualifications. There are Access courses in many areas that provide a route into higher education for adults without qualifications.

Work Experience

Relevant work or voluntary experience is always useful and can improve your chances when applying for jobs. Accounting and budgeting knowledge is also an advantage, as is any experience in related areas, such as legal, financial, bookkeeping, secretarial or in human resources management. Work experience in hotels and retail or customer services is relevant and, for older applicants, jobs that provide relevant management, supervisory and administrative experience are beneficial.

Entry and Training

Many entrants to office management are graduates with at least two years' related experience. It is possible to become an office manager by working in clerical and administrative jobs, gaining experience, and perhaps taking relevant part-time courses. Many entrants take full-time courses first. There is a wide range of courses available at different levels, including degrees, foundation degrees and higher national awards that can be studied either full or part time.

A wide range of professional certificates/diplomas, from introductory to advanced level, either full-time or as distance-learning programmes, are offered by organisations that include the Institute of Administrative Management, the Chartered Management Institute, and the Institute of Leadership and

Management. The Institute of Management Services also offers training courses and publishes the quarterly journal, Management Services. The Open University Business School has a wide range of courses suitable for those already working in management. You can study a short course to develop specific skills or work through a series of courses towards a particular qualification.

Following initial qualification there are often company training schemes, in-service courses on particular topics and part-time study for professional qualifications in, for example, administration, management or finance. Training programmes, including business and administration apprenticeship schemes, may be available in your area and are useful for entry to this job. Advanced apprenticeships leading to S/NVQ at level 3 are available and can often provide a route into higher education.

In any management role it is important to be aware of changes in legislation that might have an impact on decision making e.g. age discrimination laws and changes to statutory holiday entitlement and minimum wages.

Mature entrants with relevant qualifications and/or experience may have an advantage with some employers, as at least two years' relevant experience is usually required. Knowledge of programs such as Excel, PowerPoint, advanced Word and Access, is also desirable. You can gain recognition of previous experience through Accreditation of Prior Learning (APL) or by working towards relevant S/NVQs.

Professional organisations, such as the Institute of Administrative Management, the Chartered Management Institute, and the Institute of Leadership and Management offer a wide selection of qualifications at all levels of experience that can be studied either full or part time, or by distance learning.

Opportunities and Pay

Office managers are employed by employers and organisations across a very wide variety of sectors. These include commerce, education, medical and health services, the law, entertainment and leisure, transport and local/central government, and positions are available throughout the UK. Many organisations have a career structure, with promotion usually being dependent on experience and merit. Prospects are usually better in large companies or organisations.

Pay varies depending on location, size of company/organisation and level of responsibility. Starting salaries range from around £18.5k-£30k. An office manager with greater responsibility can earn around £30k-£40k a year.

Skills and Qualities

able to take responsibility, efficient, good organisational skills, good spoken communication, good written English, information handling skills, IT skills, problem-solving skills, reliable, sound judgement

Relevant Subjects

Business and accounting, Economics, English, ICT/Computer studies, Mathematics

Further Information

Apprenticeship Schemes (National Apprenticeship Service) - www.apprenticeships.org.uk

Break into Biz. (CfA) (Council for Administration) - www.breakinto.biz

Council for Administration (CfA) - www.cfa.uk.com

Management Services Journal (quarterly) (Institute of Management Services (IMS)) - www.ims-productivity.com/page.cfm/content/Management-Services-Journal/

Management Today (Haymarket) (Haymarket) - www.managementtoday.co.uk/

Addresses

Chartered Management Institute (CMI)
Management House, Cottingham Road, Corby NN17 1TT
Phone: +44 (0)1536 204 222
Web: www.managers.org.uk

Institute of Administration Management (iam)
6 Graphite Square, Vauxhall Walk, London SE11 5EE
Phone: +44 (0)20 7091 2600
Web: www.instam.org

Institute of Leadership and Management (ILM)
Stowe House, Netherstowe, Lichfield, Staffordshire WS13 6TJ
Phone: +44 (0)1543 266 867
Web: www.i-l-m.com

Institute of Management Services (IMS)
Brooke House, 24 Dam Street, Lichfield, Staffordshire WS13 6AA
Phone: +44 (0)1543 266909
Web: www.ims-productivity.com

Open University Business School (OUBS)
PO Box 197, Milton Keynes MK7 6BJ
Phone: +44 (0)845 300 60 90
Web: http://www8.open.ac.uk/business-school/

Similar Jobs

Civil Service Executive Officer, Civil Service Fast Streamer, Health Service Manager, Local Government Administrator, Manager, Personal Assistant

Off-Licence Manager

CRCI:Retail Sales and Customer Services
CLCI:OFM Job Band: 2 to 4

Job Description

Off-licence managers are responsible for the day-to-day running of an off-licence shop selling alcohol, including wines, champagnes, spirits and beers, as well as a range of other goods, such as soft drinks, mixers, crisps and other snack items. They aim to build up good retail customer relations and acquire new business to make maximum profit. On a regular basis, orders are placed with suppliers and incoming stock is checked and stored safely and securely. Managers ensure that legal requirements are met and deal with banking procedures and paperwork. May also serve in the shop, handle marketing and buying, advise customers and recruit and train staff.

Work Details

Usually work a basic 39 hr week, though off-licences can be open seven days a week, and some are open late in the evening. Therefore, staff may work shifts on a rota basis. As a manager you are responsible for organising the work of your staff. You are expected to learn point of sale (POS) systems and a great deal about the products you are selling, so that you can give advice to customers. Sometimes you may have to deal with complaints. You are also responsible for observing legal regulations, such as checking that customers are not under the age limit for purchasing alcohol.

Qualification

There are no specified minimum qualifications for this job, though employers expect a good standard of education and knowledge of maths and English. You usually need higher education qualifications to enter a management training scheme.

Adult Qualifications

Formal qualifications are not always specified, but most employers expect a good standard of education.

Work Experience
Relevant work or voluntary experience is always useful and can improve your chances when applying for entry to this type of work. It can equip you with skills that you can use in the future and add to your CV. Part-time and holiday employment in a wide range of shops is usually fairly easy to obtain.

Entry and Training
Entry requirements vary, but most enter with A levels/H grades or equivalent, depending on the employer and the area of the country. A Diploma/Welsh Baccalaureate in retail business may be available in your area. Applicants must be at least 18 with many companies preferring to recruit staff who are over 20 for their management training programmes. Some enter at assistant level and work their way up to this job, if they demonstrate management potential. Training is usually given on the job with an experienced member of staff and supported by short courses.

There are useful vocational qualifications that you can work towards, such as S/NVQs, awards, certificates and diplomas in retail skills at levels 1-2, or a QCF level 3 certificate or diploma in retail (management). You can also study full time for a BTEC higher national certificate/diploma in retail management at level 5. There is a range of specialist courses at levels 1-5 offered by the Wine & Spirit Education Trust (WSET). These start with a one-day foundation certificate in wines at level 1, which provides basic wine product knowledge and skills, to an honours diploma in wines and spirits at level 5. Contact WSET for further details.

Training programmes, including retail apprenticeship schemes, may be available in your area. Advanced apprenticeships leading to qualification at level 3 can also be a route into higher education. See the Skillsmart Retail website for details.

Mature entrants with relevant experience are welcomed and are preferred by some employers.

Opportunities and Pay
Jobs are available in most towns and cities. Many jobs are with nationwide chains of off-licence shops. There are also some privately owned independent shops, as well as jobs in supermarket off-licence sections. Career development is encouraged, particularly in larger companies, though you may need to move around the country to gain experience in different shops in order to get promotion. With experience you may be able to set up your own business, although this needs considerable financial investment. Due to the current economic downturn, there may be fewer opportunities for work in the retail sector.

Pay varies depending on location and level of responsibility. Trainee managers may earn around £16k, rising to £18.5k a year with experience. Managers with the most responsibility can earn more than £25k a year. Bonuses may be added for reaching sales targets.

Health
A good sense of smell and taste is needed for this job. You also need to be physically fit and not suffer from back problems, since the work can involve some heavy lifting.

Skills and Qualities
business awareness, cash handling skills, customer service skills, efficient, even tempered, good interpersonal skills, hard working, initiative, IT skills, trustworthy

Relevant Subjects
Business and accounting, English, Mathematics

Further Information
Apprenticeship Schemes (National Apprenticeship Service) - www.apprenticeships.org.uk

Diplomas (Foundation, Higher and Advanced) - http://yp.direct.gov.uk/diplomas

Real Life Guide to Retail (Trotman) - www.trotman.co.uk

Skillsmart Retail - sector skills council for the retail industry - www.skillsmartretail.com

TARGETjobs: Retail, Management & Sales (GTI Specialist Publishing Ltd.) - www.groupgti.com

Welsh Baccalaureate - www.wbq.org.uk

▶Working in retail & customer services (2008) (Babcock Lifeskills) - www.babcock-lifeskills.com/

Addresses
Wine & Spirit Education Trust (WSET)
International Wine & Spirit Centre, 39-45 Bermondsey Street, London SE1 3XF
Phone: +44 (0)20 7089 3800
Web: www.wset.co.uk

Similar Jobs
Catering Manager, Hotel Manager, Publican, Retail Manager, Sommelier

Oil & Gas Driller
CRCI:Engineering
CLCI:ROB — Job Band: 2 to 3

Job Description
Oil and gas drillers set up and operate various equipment on an oil rig for drilling wells in the search for oil or gas, either on or offshore. They work under supervision of a rig manager and with a derrickman up on platforms putting up the hoisting equipment (derrick). The work involves assembling drilling tools on the end of a cable and connecting sections of drill pipe. Also supervises the drilling team (roustabout, roughneck/foreman, derrickman, assistant driller) and operates controls to lower or raise the drill and regulate its speed. When a 'strike' is made, drillers operate the valves to control the flow of oil, gas or water.

Also keeps computerised records of drilling progress, analyses the performance and the factors affecting the cost and efficiency of the drilling process and makes sure that health and safety regulations are followed.

Work Details
You are expected to work regular shifts of 12 hrs on duty and 12 hrs off. Workers normally spend two or three weeks offshore followed by two or three weeks shore leave. The work sites are usually away from home and you may need to stay away for long periods which might affect your family life. This work includes supervising, giving instructions, liaising with a team of up to 20 people and arranging their training. You observe regulations and may have to cope with emergencies.

Drilling rigs are small mobile structures. The job is physically strenuous and you have to be active most of the time, with a lot of heavy lifting and working at heights. You are outside in all weathers and conditions are tough, cold, damp and noisy. There is a risk of injury and accidents from equipment and being involved in dangerous situations. You need to wear overalls, a helmet, boots, eye and ear protection and sometimes a thermal protective outfit.

Qualification
You are not able to start directly as a driller, but those who begin as a general labourer (roustabout) may progress to work as a driller with experience and related qualifications.

- **England, Wales and Northern Ireland**

Band 2: For entry to jobs, no minimum qualifications are needed, but it is an advantage to have some GCSEs (A*-C) or equivalent in subjects that include English, maths and a science subject, or equivalent.

Band 3: For entry to jobs and training courses: usually at least 4 GCSEs (A*-C) including English , maths and a science subject, or equivalent.

- **Scotland**

Band 2: Although academic qualifications are not specified for this job, it is an advantage to have some S grades (1-3) in subjects that include English, maths and a science subject, or similar.

Band 3: For entry to jobs and most training courses, usually at least four S grades (1-3) including English, maths and a science subject, or similar.

Adult Qualifications

Relevant previous employment is often more important than qualifications. You generally need to start working as a roustabout, progress to be a roughneck, derrickman and then assistant driller, before becoming a driller. You must be over 18 and at least 1.63m tall.

Work Experience

Entry to the oil and gas industry is competitive and it is important that you try to do some relevant work or voluntary experience before applying. This may be in shipbuilding or construction, or service in the armed forces. All work experience can show a degree of enthusiasm and commitment and it is useful to show an aptitude for practical work and for working with machinery and equipment.

Entry and Training

Entrants usually progress to this job after beginning as a roustabout and gaining promotion through the various jobs on the rig. This can take about 5 years. It takes around 3 years to become a roughneck, a further 2-3 years to become a derrickman and then an assistant driller. No one under 18 can work on a rig, but the usual age of entry for this job is over 25 due to the experience required. This job requires you to have good references. Offshore jobs also require a valid offshore survival certificate, often sponsored by the employer. The Energy Institute (EI) or Cogent can provide a list of centres running the course. Training is on the job through an employer's training scheme and by short courses, including some home study.

Petroleum Open Learning is part of the Offshore Petroleum Industry Training Organisation and runs a distance-learning course in oil and gas well technology at level 3. The EI also runs a comprehensive training programme for those in the oil and gas industry. Relevant training programmes, including an oil and gas extraction or an extractive and mineral processing operations apprenticeship scheme, may be available in your area. Advanced apprenticeships leading to qualification at level 3 can also be a route into higher education.

The Institute of Petroleum Engineering at Heriot Watt University in Edinburgh runs a network of excellence in training. This is a joint venture with industry to ensure that courses and training meet the needs of their petrotechnical customers. The focus is on critical skills development by providing training in areas such as well design and construction. Courses are delivered through a combination of tutor led, computer based training and elearning. See the website for details.

The Engineering Development Trust runs a range of nationwide schemes for 11-21 year olds who are interested in engineering as a career. See the website for details. A Diploma/Welsh Baccalaureate may be available in your area in engineering. This can be a useful introduction to this type of work.

Mature applicants with experience in the armed forces, Merchant Navy, or in heavy engineering, mechanical and technical work are particularly suitable for this job. Petroleum Open Learning offers a distance-learning course related to this work.

Opportunities and Pay

Work is available on mobile drilling rigs and fixed production platforms for oil and gas operation and maintenance companies, petroleum producing companies, drilling companies and drilling and well service contractors. Jobs are available onshore, often in remote areas, as well as offshore and abroad. This area is highly competitive and there is limited job security because you are employed on a contract basis and opportunities may depend on the current economic climate.

Promotion to more senior posts such as toolpusher/rig superintendent are possible after gaining experience and opportunities for this are good. Some drillers may move into managerial positions or possibly progress to drilling engineer after gaining higher education qualifications.

Derrickmen earn around £25k-£30k and drillers around £30k-£50k a year. Free accommodation and meals are usually provided. Perks may include the use of some recreational facilities and generous leave.

Health

This job requires a high standard of physical fitness, stamina, good eyesight and normal colour vision. You are expected to have no speech defects as clear communication in noisy conditions is essential. A medical test is required.

Skills and Qualities

able to live and work closely with other people, agile, alert, aptitude for teamwork, hard working, head for heights, responsible attitude, safety conscious, technical aptitude

Relevant Subjects

Design and technology, Engineering

Further Information

Apprenticeship Schemes (National Apprenticeship Service) - www.apprenticeships.org.uk

Apprenticeships in Scotland (Careers Info Scotland) - www.apprenticeshipsinscotland.com/about/

Britain's Offshore Oil & Gas (Oil & Gas UK) - www.oilandgas.co.uk/Britains_offshore_oil_and_gas

Cogent - sector skills souncil for chemicals, pharmaceuticals, nuclear, oil & gas, petroleum & polymers - www.cogent-ssc.com

Diplomas (Foundation, Higher and Advanced) - http://yp.direct.gov.uk/diplomas

Energy Institute (Institute of Petroleum (IOP) - www.energyinst.org.uk

Oil and Gas 4 U - www.oilandgas4u.com

Oil and Gas Industry Today (Einews) - www.oilandgas.einews.com

Oil and Gas Journal (Penwell Corporation) - www.ogj.com

Oil Careers - www.oilcareers.com

Petroleum Open Learning - www.petroleumopenlearning.com

Welsh Baccalaureate - www.wbq.org.uk

Addresses

Energy Institute (EI)
61 New Cavendish Street, London W1G 7AR
Phone: +44 (0)20 7467 7100
Web: www.energyinst.org.uk

Engineering Development Trust (EDT)
Ridgeway, Welwyn Garden City, Hertfordshire AL7 2AA
Phone: +44 (0)1707 871520
Web: www.etrust.org.uk

Heriot-Watt University
Edinburgh Campus EH14 4AS
Phone: 0131 449 5111
Web: www.hw.ac.uk

Offshore Petroleum Industry Training Organisation (OPITO)
Minerva House, Bruntland Road, Portlethen, Aberdeen AB12 4QL
Phone: +44 (0)1224 787800
Web: www.opito.com

Oil & Gas UK
2nd Floor, 232-242 Vauxhall Bridge Road, London SW1V 1AU
Phone: +44 (0)20 7802 2400
Web: www.oilandgas.org.uk

Similar Jobs

Engineering Craft Machinist, Engineering Machine Operative, Oil & Gas Industry Technician, Oil & Gas Roustabout/Roughneck, Quarry Operative

Oil & Gas Industry Technician

also known as: Maintenance Technician, Process Operation Technician

CRCI:Engineering
CLCI:ROB Job Band: 3 to 4

Job Description

Oil and gas technicians maintain the systems used in the oil and gas extraction industry. They either work as a process operation technician or a maintenance technician. Process operation technicians make sure all production systems for oil and gas are operating as efficiently as possible. Maintenance technicians look after the mechanical, electrical and control systems and keeps them in good repair. Some become multi-skilled in both areas.

Technicians often specialise in one of four main areas. These include instrument and control maintenance (regulating and maintaining measurement systems), mechanical maintenance (looking after valves, pumps and transmission systems), and electrical maintenance (looking after high voltage power generation and distribution systems). Those involved in process operation are responsible for starting up, controlling, monitoring and shutting down oil and gas production processes. They do this both manually and by using computerised control systems.

Work Details

Technicians either work onshore or offshore. If offshore, you are expected to work shifts, very long hours and sometimes be on call. Offshore technicians normally spend two weeks offshore, followed by two weeks shore leave. This job involves working away from home, usually staying away for several weeks at a time, which may affect your family life. The environment can be tough and often cold, wet, noisy, and possibly smelly. You are required to work in all weather conditions. There may be a risk of injury and accidents from equipment and perhaps being involved in dangerous situations. You need to wear overalls, a helmet, boots and sometimes a protective outfit.

Onshore technicians usually work 37 hrs a week, Monday to Friday, but may need to work longer hours at times to complete maintenance work.

Qualification

• England, Wales and Northern Ireland

Band 3: For entry to training on the job: usually at least 4 GCSEs (A*-C) including maths, English, and either double science, physics, chemistry or a technological subject, or equivalent. Those without science subjects at GCSE can enter with GCSE maths grade A, or A/AS level grade C plus 3 other GCSEs (A*-C) including English.

Band 4: For entry to training schemes, HND, Diploma of Higher Education or foundation degree: 1-2 A levels and some GCSEs (A*-C) usually including English, maths, and either physics, chemistry or a technological subject, or equivalent.

• Scotland

Band 3: For entry to training on the job: usually at least four S grades (1-3), including maths, English, and either physics, chemistry or technological studies, or similar. Those without science subjects at S grade can enter with S grade maths grade 1, or H grade C or above plus 3 other S grades (1-3), including English.

Band 4: For SQA higher national award or some entrants to training schemes: usually 2-3 H grades and some S grades (1-3), often including English, maths, and either physics, chemistry or technological studies, or similar qualifications.

Adult Qualifications

Standard entry qualifications are usually required by employers. Any qualifications gained in mechanical engineering or technical work are also useful.

Work Experience

Relevant work experience to undertake before applying for a technician job in the oil and gas industry may include work in shipbuilding or maintenance work in engineering. Work at an onshore installation is also helpful to give you a clearer idea of the type of work involved.

Entry and Training

Entry to this job is by an Oil and Gas Upstream Industry Technician Training Scheme. This is a four-year advanced modern apprenticeship programme which is run by the Offshore Petroleum Industry Training Organisation (OPITO) and the Engineering Construction Industry Training Board. Entry is dependent on initial testing and an interview and entrants must be at least 16 years old.

Training includes two years at college studying full time, followed by two years at an onshore or offshore oil or gas facility. If you work offshore, you have to take an offshore survival course before you start. While training you work towards S/NVQs level 2-3 in performing engineering operations and engineering maintenance or processing operations: hydrocarbons. You also study for a Higher National Certificate (HNC). Contact OPITO for further details. Petroleum Open Learning provides flexible self-learning courses for the oil and gas industry, such as the level 3 Certificate in Petroleum Processing Technology.

Once fully trained and with more experience, many technicians become an engineering technician (EngTech) with the Engineering Council UK. See their website for details.

The Engineering Development Trust runs a range of nationwide schemes for 11-21 year olds who are interested in engineering as a career. A Diploma/Welsh Baccalaureate may also be available in your area in engineering. This can be a useful introduction to this type of work.

The Energy Institute runs a range of courses in oil and gas and the Engineering Construction Industry Training Board has details of apprenticeships. See the relevant websites for details. For general oil and gas industry information, visit Oil and Gas UK.

Mature entrants with experience at technician level from other manufacturing or processing work have an advantage.

Opportunities and Pay

Employment can be with an oil operating company, a service contract company or one of the major contractors that provide maintenance services to operating companies. Jobs are available onshore, often in remote areas, as well as offshore off the east coast of England and Scotland, west of the Shetland Isles or in the Irish Sea. There is a strong demand for technicians at the moment. Once fully trained, work is also available abroad.

While training, salaries range from £12k-£20k a year and when newly qualified around £35k for offshore work. This rises up to £40k and beyond, depending on experience and responsibility. During the initial 18 months' training, a grant is available. Those who live away from home also have their accommodation and travel costs paid.

Health

This job requires a high standard of physical fitness and stamina, good eyesight and normal colour vision. You are expected to have no speech defects because clear communication while working offshore is essential. A medical test is required.

Skills and Qualities
able to follow drawings and plans, alert, good communication skills, IT skills, problem-solving skills, safety conscious, scientific approach, technical aptitude, willing to train and work away from home

Relevant Subjects
Design and technology, Engineering, Mathematics, Physics, Science

Further Information
Apprenticeship Schemes (National Apprenticeship Service) - www.apprenticeships.org.uk

Apprenticeships in Scotland (Careers Info Scotland) - www.apprenticeshipsinscotland.com/about/

Britain's Offshore Oil & Gas (Oil & Gas UK) - www.oilandgas.co.uk/Britains_offshore_oil_and_gas

Cogent - sector skills council for chemicals, pharmaceuticals, nuclear, oil & gas, petroleum & polymers - www.cogent-ssc.com

Diplomas (Foundation, Higher and Advanced) - http://yp.direct.gov.uk/diplomas

Energy Institute (Institute of Petroleum (IOP) - www.energyinst.org.uk

Energyzone - Energy Institute - www.energyzone.net

Oil and Gas 4 U - www.oilandgas4u.com

Oil and Gas Technicians - www.oilandgastechnicians.com

Oil Careers - www.oilcareers.com

Petroleum Open Learning - www.petroleumopenlearning.com

Welsh Baccalaureate - www.wbq.org.uk

Addresses
Energy Institute (EI)
61 New Cavendish Street, London W1G 7AR
Phone: +44 (0)20 7467 7100
Web: www.energyinst.org.uk

Engineering Construction Industry Training Board (ECITB)
Blue Court, Church Lane, Kings Langley, Hertfordshire WD4 8JP
Phone: +44 (0)1923 260 000
Web: www.ecitb.org.uk

Engineering Council
246 High Holborn, London WC1V 7EX
Phone: +44 (0)20 3206 0500
Web: www.engc.org.uk

Engineering Development Trust (EDT)
Ridgeway, Welwyn Garden City, Hertfordshire AL7 2AA
Phone: +44 (0)1707 871520
Web: www.etrust.org.uk

Institute of Materials, Minerals and Mining (IOM3)
1 Carlton House Terrace, London SW1Y 5DB
Phone: +44 (0)20 7451 7300
Web: www.iom3.org

Offshore Petroleum Industry Training Organisation (OPITO)
Minerva House, Bruntland Road, Portlethen, Aberdeen AB12 4QL
Phone: +44 (0)1224 787800
Web: www.opito.com

Oil & Gas UK
2nd Floor, 232-242 Vauxhall Bridge Road, London SW1V 1AU
Phone: +44 (0)20 7802 2400
Web: www.oilandgas.org.uk

Similar Jobs
Engineer: Gas, Engineer: Petroleum, Geological Technician, Mechanical Engineering Technician, Oil & Gas Driller

Oil & Gas Roustabout/Roughneck

CRCI:Engineering
CLCI:ROB — Job Band: 1 to 2

Job Description
An oil and gas roustabout works in a team that includes welders, derrickmen, roughnecks, drillers, toolpushers and crane operators. Mostly does unskilled manual labouring jobs. Works under the supervision of the driller and derrickmen. Helps to keep a drilling rig or platform working efficiently and productively. Cleans and repairs equipment and helps to maintain rigs by scraping and painting platforms. Offloads supplies and equipment from supply ships and helicopters, and moves them to storage areas. Loads and stacks equipment, including drilling pipes, and sets up machinery. Mixes and conditions drilling mud (fluid) under the direction of a mud specialist. Does general work in the pump room, such as helping to repair mud pumps.

The role of a roughneck includes making up lengths/joints of drill pipe as the drill bites deeper into the rock. Also pulls out the drill, changes the drill bit and retrieves the rock cores. Cleans equipment, such as de-silting/de-sanding machines. Keeps all drilling equipment in good condition and working order. Mostly works under the supervision of an assistant driller.

Work Details
Usually works a 12 hour shift, including meal breaks and rest periods, followed by 12 hours off duty. Workers normally spend two weeks offshore, then two weeks on shore leave. This job involves working away from home, usually staying away for several weeks at a time, and this can affect your family life. It is important to observe and follow the safety rules. You are involved in hard physical labour, climbing ladders, working on high platforms and lifting heavy pieces of drill. The environment can be noisy, wet and dirty, and there is a risk of injury.

Sometimes you may be in dangerous situations. You are out in all sorts of weather, either cold, damp and windy, or sometimes hot and dusty. Protective clothing is needed, usually overalls, a helmet, boots and gloves.

Qualification

• England, Wales and Northern Ireland
Band 1: For entry to jobs, no minimum qualifications are needed, but you are expected to have a good level of general education and relevant experience. Some formal/vocational qualifications at any level are useful.

Band 2: For entry to jobs, no minimum qualifications are needed, but it is an advantage to have some GCSEs (A*-C) or equivalent in subjects that include English and maths.

• Scotland
Band 1: For entry to jobs, no minimum qualifications are needed, but you are expected to have a good level of general education and relevant experience. Some formal/vocational qualifications at any level are useful.

Band 2: Although academic qualifications are not specified for this job, it is an advantage to have some S grades (1-3) in subjects that include English, maths and a science subject, or similar.

Adult Qualifications
Relevant previous employment is important. Any qualifications gained in mechanical engineering or technical work are particularly useful. Specific entry requirements for courses may be relaxed for mature applicants. You can improve your skills and qualifications by working through the Foundation Learning programme. This involves taking credit-based units and qualifications to help you progress.

Work Experience
Entry to this job is competitive. It is important that you try to do some relevant work or voluntary experience before applying. This may be in shipbuilding or construction, or service in the armed forces or Merchant Navy. Work at one of the offshore installation construction yards in areas such as Aberdeen and Glasgow is very relevant to this job.

In some areas there is a young apprenticeship (14-16) scheme that provides an extended work placement and eventual achievement of a relevant level 2 qualification whilst at school.

Entry and Training
The minimum age for entry is 18, but many employers prefer people between aged over 21. To get a job you need to be physically fit and have good previous work experience in a related industry such as shipbuilding, construction or the armed forces, as well as good references. New entrants usually start as a roustabout and gain promotion to the position of roughneck. This usually takes around six months.

Offshore workers new to the industry must complete Basic Offshore Safety Induction & Emergency Training, as set out by the offshore petroleum industry training organisation (OPITO). OPITO also recommends that inexperienced trainees follow this with the Offshore Oil & Gas Industry Minimum Industry Safety Training (MIST). OPITO and Cogent can provide a list of centres running this course as well as other training opportunities. You also receive a company induction through your employer. On-the-job training is then provided on the rig or platform with an experienced person. There may be additional short training courses onshore during shore leave.

Petroleum Open Learning (POL) provide flexible self-learning courses for the oil and gas industry. These can lead to qualifications such as the level 3 certificate in oil and gas well technology. Contact POL for further details. There are also Vocationally Related Qualifications, such as the City & Guilds level 2 certificate in engineering practice. Relevant training programmes, including an oil and gas industry apprenticeship scheme or an apprenticeship in extractive and mineral processing operations, may be available in your area. Advanced apprenticeships leading to qualification at level 3 can also be a route into higher education.

The Engineering Development Trust runs a range of nationwide schemes for 11-21 year olds who are interested in engineering as a career. A Diploma/Welsh Baccalaureate may be available in your area in engineering. This may provide a useful introduction to this type of work. See the diplomas website for further information.

Mature entry may not be easy unless you have relevant previous experience such as work in heavy engineering, construction, the Merchant Navy or the armed forces, particularly the Royal Navy.

Opportunities and Pay
There is a lot of competition for jobs. Most jobs in the UK are offshore. The main areas of work are located off the east coast of England and Scotland, west of the Shetland Isles and in the Irish Sea. Most work for an operating oil company, a drilling company or service contract firm. Some work for major contractors that provide maintenance and operation services to operating firms. Job opportunities depend on the demand for oil/gas and most people are employed on contracts for a few months at a time.

Promotion is possible to more senior jobs, eg assistant driller/driller or derrickman, after several years' experience. There are also opportunities to work abroad.

Pay varies depending on the company. A new roustabout earns from around £20k a year, rising to around £30k for a roughneck. Free accommodation and meals are usually provided on-site. Jobs often include generous leave and the use of some recreational facilities.

Health
You need to be very fit and have good stamina for this job. You should have good eyesight and good colour vision for certain areas of work. Also, you should have no speech defects as clear communication at times of high noise levels is essential. A medical test is required.

Skills and Qualities
aptitude for teamwork, co-operative, hard working, head for heights, practical skills, punctual, reliable, safety conscious

Further Information
Apprenticeship Schemes (National Apprenticeship Service) - www.apprenticeships.org.uk

Apprenticeships in Scotland (Careers Info Scotland) - www.apprenticeshipsinscotland.com/about/

Cogent - sector skills souncil for chemicals, pharmaceuticals, nuclear, oil & gas, petroleum & polymers - www.cogent-ssc.com

Diplomas (Foundation, Higher and Advanced) - http://yp.direct.gov.uk/diplomas

Energy Institute (Institute of Petroleum (IOP) - www.energyinst.org.uk

Energyzone - Energy Institute - www.energyzone.net

Oil and Gas 4 U - www.oilandgas4u.com

Oil Careers - www.oilcareers.com

Petroleum Open Learning - www.petroleumopenlearning.com

Welsh Baccalaureate - www.wbq.org.uk

Addresses
Energy Institute (EI)
61 New Cavendish Street, London W1G 7AR
Phone: +44 (0)20 7467 7100
Web: www.energyinst.org.uk

Engineering Development Trust (EDT)
Ridgeway, Welwyn Garden City, Hertfordshire AL7 2AA
Phone: +44 (0)1707 871520
Web: www.etrust.org.uk

Offshore Petroleum Industry Training Organisation (OPITO)
Minerva House, Bruntland Road, Portlethen, Aberdeen AB12 4QL
Phone: +44 (0)1224 787800
Web: www.opito.com

Oil & Gas UK
2nd Floor, 232-242 Vauxhall Bridge Road, London SW1V 1AU
Phone: +44 (0)20 7802 2400
Web: www.oilandgas.org.uk

Similar Jobs
Construction Operative, Construction Plant Operative, Oil & Gas Driller, Oil & Gas Industry Technician, Royal Navy Rating

Oncologist
CRCI:Healthcare
CLCI:JAB — Job Band: 5

Job Description
Oncologists are specialist medical doctors who are mainly concerned with the study, diagnosis, treatment and management of conditions such as cancer. They order diagnostic tests for patients to help find out what is wrong with them. Once the results of the tests are available, advise patients on the best method of treatment. This may be one sort of treatment or a combination of several and also includes pain management. May also help to care for patients after surgery for the removal of a cancerous tumour. May take part in research while also working in their role of looking after patients. Maintain records on patients and write reports and letters, often to the patient's general practitioner.

Oncologist

May choose to train either as a medical oncologist or a clinical oncologist. The work of a clinical oncologist is very patient orientated and deals with both radiotherapy (treating cancer using x-rays) and chemotherapy (treating cancer using chemical substances that act as a poison on living cells). Medical oncologists work mainly on treatment through the use of medication, therapy and chemotherapy; they do not use radiotherapy. They work with patients, but are also involved in research. All oncologists have to be prepared to learn new techniques on a regular basis as new treatments for different cancers are discovered.

Work Details

As a junior doctor, you are expected to work irregular and relatively long hours, but once you are working in oncology hours are more regular and usually during the day. However, days are busy, dealing with patients on the wards and in out-patients' clinics, where you are constantly making decisions and planning and prescribing treatment. You have a lot of contact with patients who are concerned about their health, ill, in pain, upset or depressed. You have to maintain detailed patient records.

Work may be emotionally demanding, especially as you are dealing with people who have very serious diseases. You need to work closely in a multidisciplinary team, including surgeons, radiologists, pathologists and specialist cancer nurses. You need to be receptive to the opinions of other specialists. This job is very satisfying for those wishing to work in a caring profession.

Qualification

• England, Wales and Northern Ireland

Band 5: For honours degree course in medicine: usually 3 A levels with good grades in chemistry and two from physics, biological sciences and maths, plus 5 GCSEs (A*-C), including English and maths, or equivalent. Some medical schools offer a one-year pre-medical course for students with A levels in Arts or mixed subjects. Check with individual schools for details.

• Scotland

Band 5: For honours degree course in medicine: usually five H grades, with good grades in chemistry and two from physics, biology and maths, plus five S grades (1-3) including English and maths, or similar. Normally science subjects not held at H grade should be offered at S grade. Some medical schools offer a one-year pre-medical course for students whose H grades do not include the required science subjects. Check with individual schools for full details.

Degree Information

A first degree in medicine awarded by a university medical school and recognised by the General Medical Council is essential, followed by specialist oncology training.

Adult Qualifications

Entry requirement standards are not normally relaxed for mature applicants, though those who consider applying should contact the individual university for advice. Graduates with a good honours degree in a related subject may obtain exemptions from certain options within the medical degree course.

Work Experience

Work experience gives you an insight into what you enjoy and don't enjoy about a job or working environment, as well as the opportunity to acquire new skills. It also provides valuable information to add to your CV and improves your course application and future employment prospects. Entry to this career is highly competitive. It is essential that you have some relevant work or voluntary experience before applying to train as a doctor. All applicants need to demonstrate a long-term commitment to medicine. Evidence of this can come in the form of relevant paid or voluntary work in a healthcare setting such as in a hospital, residential care home or similar.

Entry and Training

Oncologists must first qualify as medical doctors by completing a five year medicine degree, pass the postgraduate two-year Foundation Programme and register as a doctor with the General Medical Council (GMC). For full details of medical training see the job article Doctor: Hospital.

During the Foundation Programme, doctors decide if they want to go on to be a general practitioner or train for a specialty in a hospital. Competition for training posts is high. Those who are interested in oncology should try to obtain a rotation in oncology or palliative medicine during their Foundation Programme. They should also try to develop some knowledge of research and laboratory skills. Some entrants do an intercalated BSc to help with this. See the website of the Royal College of Physicians for more details of specialty training.

Clinical oncology training takes five years, and during the training you have to achieve the fellowship examination of the Royal College of Radiologists. Medical oncology takes four years. Training is structured and based on lectures and day-to-day clinical experience. Both types of training involve six-monthly rotations to different hospitals and clinics. They also encourage research, and some trainee oncologists take two extra years to complete a research PhD.

Once training is completed you are able to join the Specialist Register of the GMC and then apply for consultant posts. All oncologists have to undergo regular continuing professional development (CPD) to keep up to date with new developments in their field.

Mature entrants are welcomed by medical schools and especially suitably qualified mature students. Some medical schools may have reserved places for mature/graduate entrants. There are Access courses to medicine and pre-medical foundation courses. Some Open University credits at distinction level may be accepted at some medical schools. Check with individual medical schools for details of all opportunities. Once you have completed basic medical training you have to undertake the same oncology training as younger entrants.

Opportunities and Pay

There are around 320 consultant oncologists in the UK. You usually work in NHS hospitals, specialist clinics, university hospitals or research organisations. Once qualified, you may choose to specialise in one type of cancer, surgery or in particular treatments such as radiotherapy or chemotherapy. Some specialise in paediatrics and work with children and adolescents. Prospects for promotion to consultant may depend on willingness to move to another area to gain experience. Competition for consultant posts is high. There may be opportunities to work part time. There are also opportunities to work abroad.

Within the NHS, junior doctors earn a basic salary and are usually paid a supplement for extra hours worked. Basic salaries are around £33k a year (including a 50% supplement for extra hours), rising to £43k-£68k (including 50% supplement) for a doctor in specialist training. A consultant can earn £74k-£176k a year. These salaries do not include on-call payments, private income or London weighting allowances.

Health

There is a risk of infection. You should have no allergies and a good level of general fitness.

Skills and Qualities

able to cope under pressure, analytical skills, aptitude for teamwork, attention to detail, decisive, emotionally strong, excellent communication skills, good organisational skills, not squeamish, tactful

Relevant Subjects

Biology, Chemistry, English, Health and social care, Mathematics, Physics, Psychology, Science, Sociology

Further Information
AGCAS: Health (Job Sector Briefing) (AGCAS) - www.prospects.ac.uk

Clinical Oncology - www.clinicaloncologyonline.net

Modernising Medical Careers - www.mmc.nhs.uk

NHS Careers (NHS Careers) - www.nhscareers.nhs.uk

NHS Careers Scotland - www.infoscotland.com/nhs

NHS Careers Wales - www.wales.nhs.uk

Addresses
General Medical Council (GMC)
Regents Place, 350 Euston Road, London NW1 3JN
Phone: +44 (0)161 923 6602
Web: www.gmc-uk.org

Royal College of Physicians (RCP)
11 St Andrew's Place, Regent's Park, London NW1 4LE
Phone: +44 (0)207 935 1174
Web: www.rcplondon.ac.uk

Royal College of Radiologists (RCR)
38 Portland Place, London W1B 1JQ
Phone: +44 (0)20 7637 4432
Web: www.rcr.ac.uk

Similar Jobs
Doctor: General Practitioner, Doctor: Hospital, Nurse: Macmillan, Obstetrician/Gynaecologist, Radiographer: Therapeutic, Surgeon

Operating Department Practitioner
also known as: Operating Theatre Technician

CRCI:Healthcare
CLCI:JOZ Job Band: 3

Job Description
Operating department practitioners (ODPs) are members of a clinical team caring for theatre patients having surgery, also helping to care for them during recovery immediately after an operation (post-operative care). They clean and sterilise instruments and some equipment. Check stock levels of theatre supplies and keep accurate records. Prepare appropriate equipment for each operation, such as drips, drugs, swabs, dressings and also the specialised surgical instruments to be used. ODPs are trained to perform skilled duties in three main areas and work in one of these each day on a rota basis.

In the 'surgical' team, ODPs assist during operations by handing over appropriate surgical instruments and dressings. They ensure all items are accounted for at the end of each operation. As part of the 'anaesthetic' team, they reassure patients before they are anaesthetised, then help to lift them on to the operating table. They also provide assistance during the administration of a local or general anaesthetic. Work in the 'recovery' team includes taking the patient back to the recovery room after the operation and monitoring their welfare after surgery.

Work Details
Operating departments are open 24 hrs a day, 365 days a year, so you are expected to work a 37 hr week on a shift basis, which may include nights, weekends and some public holidays. As an ODP you are a skilled member of a team that helps to care for theatre patients, some of whom may be nervous or upset, immediately before their operation. ODPs also work as a member of a resuscitation team or in other departments, such as intensive care units, accident and emergency, or pain clinics. You have to cope with standing for many hours, and with some lifting.

The work requires coping with unpleasant sights and blood. Work may be pressured at times and physically demanding. Your workplace is warm and enclosed, although operating theatres are usually air conditioned. A protective outfit, including a face mask and boots is provided.

Qualification

• England, Wales and Northern Ireland
Band 3: For entry: usually at least 5 GCSEs (A*-C) including English, maths and a science subject, or equivalent. Many institutions require AS level (or equivalent) and A level qualifications.

• Scotland
Band 3: For entry: usually four S grades (1-3) preferably including English, maths and a science subject, or similar. Some institutions may require H grades or equivalent qualifications.

Adult Qualifications
Some training schools ask for formal qualifications which can vary. Applicants may be given recognition for relevant experience or be able to enter with alternative qualifications such as an appropriate Access or foundation course. Check entry requirements with individual training schools.

Work Experience
Work experience gives you an insight into what you enjoy about a job or working environment, and the opportunity to acquire new skills. It provides valuable information to add to your CV and improves your employment prospects. Relevant work or voluntary experience in a medical or healthcare setting such as a hospital or residential care home is advantageous.

Entry and Training
Applicants must be at least 18 and are subject to health and criminal record screening to protect both patients and applicants. Initial experience working in other types of hospital work, such as a healthcare assistant, can help prepare for this job.

Training is usually over two years but can take up to six years part time. It leads to a diploma in higher education (DipHE) in operating department practice to become state registered with the Health Professions Council. Some hospitals now offer training for a degree. Foundation degrees are also available. Training varies between higher education institutions, but combines practical involvement in an operating department with theory. Placements in hospital theatres, accident and emergency and intensive care units are also part of the training.

You must apply for membership of the College of Operating Department Practitioners once you are qualified and commit to continuing professional development (CPD). With experience, further training in management and technical skills may be available.

Mature entrants are welcome though you must demonstrate the ability to study for the DipHE in operating department practice or have relevant qualifications. Experience of hospital work is also an advantage. You may be eligible to apply for a means-tested bursary from the NHS for the DipHE.

Opportunities and Pay
Around 9,000 people work as ODPs in the UK and there is a growing demand. You can work for the NHS, the armed forces or a private hospital. After training and at least two years' experience, promotion to more senior grades is possible. Some ODPs become supervisors or move into research, training, education or theatre management. With qualifications and experience there are also opportunities to work abroad. Temporary work is possible through agencies.

Pay is on a nationally agreed scale and increases with promotion. Those working in the NHS follow a salary scale divided into levels of experience. An assistant practitioner earns around £18k-£22k a year. With experience and qualifications this can rise to £34k and those in senior positions can earn up to £38k a year.

Health
There is a risk of infection. This job requires good general fitness and a medical test on entry.

Skills and Qualities
able to cope with emergencies, able to follow instructions, aptitude for teamwork, attention to detail, good concentration level, IT skills, methodical, not squeamish, reassuring, responsible attitude

Relevant Subjects
Biology, Health and social care, Science

Further Information
Health Professions Council (HPC) - www.hpc-uk.org

NHS Careers (NHS Careers) - www.nhscareers.nhs.uk

NHS Careers Scotland - www.infoscotland.com/nhs

NHS Careers Wales - www.wales.nhs.uk

Addresses
College of Operating Department Practitioners (CODP)
1 Mabledon Place, London WC1H 9AJ
Phone: 0870 746 0984 (UK only)
Web: www.codp.org.uk/

Similar Jobs
Healthcare Assistant, Laboratory Assistant, Laboratory Technician: Science, Perfusionist, Sterile Services Technician

Operational Researcher
also known as: Management Scientist

CRCI:Science, Mathematics and Statistics
CLCI:COF Job Band: 5

Job Description
Operational researchers use scientific methods to help to solve organisational and management problems in commerce, government and industry. They design and introduce systems and improved methods of decision taking, often by using pilot schemes or by 'mathematical model', computer simulation or visual interactive models. May tackle problems such as planning, scheduling, stock control and the allocation of resources. They work closely with management and staff to find out how the organisation works, to agree courses of action and to review progress.

May be consulted about decisions as varied as how to estimate the profitability of a new crop on a farm, or ways to improve efficiency in a health authority.

Work Details
Usually work a basic 37-39 hr week, Monday to Friday but extra hours may be required to meet deadlines. Work is in an office and at other sites. You may need to spend some time away from home. You collect, collate and analyse information, and prepare and present reports. The work is intellectually demanding and needs sound judgement.

Qualification
- **England, Wales and Northern Ireland**

Band 5: For degree courses: 2-3 A levels and some GCSEs (A*-C) usually including English, or equivalent. Exact requirements depend on the degree you take. A good pass in maths A level is usually needed.

- **Scotland**

Band 5: For degree courses: 3-5 H grades and some S grades (1-3), usually including English, or similar qualifications. Exact requirements depend on the degree you take. A good H grade in maths is usually needed.

Degree Information
A good numerate honours degree is required. Any discipline is acceptable, though there are degrees in operational research as a single subject, or combined with other subjects. Most entrants have degrees in operational research or in other subjects requiring numeracy, such as maths, statistics, computer science, psychology, engineering, economics, business studies and sciences.

Higher degrees or diplomas in operational research, management science or management systems are available and are an advantage. The LANCS (Lancaster, Cardiff, Nottingham and Southampton universities) initiative in foundational operational research is committed to investment in this field until 2013.

Adult Qualifications
Entry requirements may be relaxed for adults applying for higher education courses. Access and foundation courses give adults without qualifications a route onto degree courses.

Work Experience
The OR (Operational Research) Society states that 'Good communication skills and business awareness are crucial, whilst literacy, numeracy and computer literacy are vital in the execution of the work'. Work experience that gives you the opportunity to gain or demonstrate these skills is the most useful. This can include the finance sector or working in a business environment.

Entry and Training
Entrants are usually honours graduates in their twenties. It is an advantage to have previous experience in computing. People with a first degree usually study for a postgraduate qualification either full time, after their first degree, or part time whilst in employment. You are trained on the job, perhaps through a graduate training scheme, with employers offering other short courses such as communication, presentation, business and management skills. The OR (Operational Research) Society offers a variety of training courses, conferences and seminars and some major international events.

A PhD in operational research is usually expected for those pursuing a research career in a university, business school, or in public/private sector senior management. The OR Society has an accreditation scheme that offers associateship to those graduates with at least two years OR experience.

Mature applicants with relevant professional experience in computing, management or statistics, may find maturity an advantage in some posts. Though most entrants are young graduates, mature applicants with a suitable degree and industrial experience may be acceptable. Postgraduate funding is available from the Engineering and Physical Sciences Research Council (EPSRC) for some courses.

Opportunities and Pay
This is an expanding profession and entry is competitive. Operational researchers can work in manufacturing industries, water companies, airlines, power companies, the retail and travel industry, telecommunications, oil and transport. Government departments and agencies such as the Defence, Science and Technology Laboratory (DSTL), the Ministry of Defence and the Government Operational Research Society (GORS) offer a structured career path. You can also work in banking, universities and consultancies. Operational research is also a good stepping stone to senior positions in general management. There are increasing opportunities to work as a consultant or for self-employment and part-time work. Work overseas is also possible.

Pay increases with experience and is high for top achievers. New entrants may start at around £19k-£30k, rising to around £45k for those with more than five years' experience. Senior operational researchers earn £80k or more a year. Those working as consultants attract a higher salary.

Skills and Qualities
able to explain clearly, analytical skills, attention to detail, excellent communication skills, good interpersonal skills, information handling skills, IT skills, logical, numeracy skills, problem-solving skills.

Relevant Subjects
Business and accounting, Design and technology, Economics, Engineering, English, ICT/Computer studies, Mathematics, Physics, Psychology, Science

Further Information
AGCAS: Accountancy and Business Services (Job Sector Briefing) (AGCAS) - www.prospects.ac.uk/

AGCAS: Government & Public Administration (Job Sector Briefing) (AGCAS) - www.prospects.ac.uk

AGCAS: Manufacturing (Job Sector Briefing) (AGCAS) - www.prospects.ac.uk

Careers in Operational Research (OR) (Operational Research Society) - www.learnabout-or.co.uk/learn/careers_home.htm

GORS (GORS) - www.operational-research.gov.uk

Management Services Journal (quarterly) (Institute of Management Services (IMS)) - www.ims-productivity.com

▶Working in maths (2009) (Babcock Lifeskills) - www.babcock-lifeskills.com/

Addresses
Defence, Science and Technology Laboratory (DSTL)
Porton Down, Salisbury, Wiltshire SP4 0JQ
Phone: +44 (0)1 9806 13000
Web: www.dstl.gov.uk

Engineering and Physical Sciences Research Council (EPSRC)
Polaris House North Star Avenue, Swindon, Wiltshire SN2 1ET
Phone: +44(0)1793 444 100
Web: www.epsrc.ac.uk

OR (Operational Research) Society
Seymour House, 12 Edward Street, Birmingham B1 2RX
Phone: +44 (0)121 233 9300
Web: www.orsoc.org.uk

Similar Jobs
Actuary, Business Analyst, Economist, Information Scientist, IT Systems Analyst/Designer, Statistician

Ophthalmologist
CRCI:Healthcare
CLCI:JAB Job Band: 5

Job Description
Ophthalmologists are medically trained doctors who have undertaken further specialist training and study in matters relating to the human eye. They work as a consultant in an eye hospital, general hospital, or a department that specialises in eyes and vision. Examine, diagnose and treat diseases and injuries to the eye. Provide both medical and surgical treatment for eye diseases, ranging from routine eye examinations to major surgery. May operate on patients with eye problems such as cataracts, or correct vision problems, such as astigmatism, nearsightedness and farsightedness.

Some ophthalmologists specialise further in different eye diseases such as retinal disease, glaucoma or in paediatric (child) ophthalmology. Work closely with optometrists, orthoptists, nurses and managers.

Work Details
If working in a hospital, you usually work a basic 37.5 hr week that may include shifts and weekends. This is not a job for those squeamish about eyes. You have contact with people of all ages who may be ill, in pain, upset or depressed. You have to make decisions about treatment and keep meticulous records. Work can be emotionally demanding and requires coping with the sight of blood.

Qualification
- **England, Wales and Northern Ireland**

Band 5: For degree in medicine: usually three A levels, with good grades in chemistry and two from physics, biological sciences and maths, plus 5 GCSEs (A*-C) including English, or equivalent. Some medical schools offer a one-year pre-medical course for students with A levels in arts or mixed subjects. Check with individual schools for full details.

- **Scotland**

Band 5: For degree in medicine: usually five H grades, with good grades in chemistry and two from physics, biology and maths, plus five S grades (1-3) including English and maths, or similar. Normally science subjects not held at H grade should be offered at S grade. Some medical schools offer a one-year pre-medical course for students whose H grades do not include the required science subjects. Check with individual schools for full details.

Degree Information
A degree in medicine awarded by a university medical school and recognised by the General Medical Council is essential.

Adult Qualifications
Entry requirement standards are not normally relaxed for mature applicants, though those who consider applying should contact the individual university for advice. Graduates with a good honours degree in a related subject may obtain exemptions from certain options within the medical degree course.

Work Experience
Entry to this career is highly competitive and it is essential that you have some relevant work or voluntary experience before applying to train as a doctor so that you are able to demonstrate a long-term commitment to medicine. Evidence of this can come in the form of relevant paid or voluntary work in a healthcare setting such as work in a hospital, residential care home, or similar. You can apply for voluntary work overseas that often has a health education or medically-related programme such as treating people for cataracts.

Entry and Training
Ophthalmologists must first qualify as medical doctors by completing a medicine degree, pass the postgraduate two-year Foundation Programme and register as a doctor with the General Medical Council (GMC). For full details of medical training see the job article Doctor: Hospital.

Once you have completed the Foundation Programme, there is competition for Specialty Registrar (SpR) posts. For ophthalmology posts, there is then a continuous period of training leading to the Certificate of Completion of Training (CCT). Training is initially broader based, but then focusses on your specialty field. Progress is based on achieving competences and can take between five and seven years in total. Once you have achieved the CCT, you can join the specialist register of the GMC and are eligible to become a Fellow of the Royal College of Ophthalmologists (FRCOphth). You are expected to update your professional knowledge continually throughout your career. Contact the RCO for details on all training options and courses.

Mature applicants that are suitably qualified are welcomed by medical schools and some may have reserved places for mature/graduate entrants. There are access courses to medicine and pre-medical foundation courses. Some Open University credits at distinction level may be accepted at some medical schools. Check with individual medical schools for details of all opportunities. Information on funding opportunities is available from the admissions and general enquiries office at University College London (Institute of Ophthalmology).

Opportunities and Pay
There are currently around 600 consultant posts in ophthalmology in the UK. You usually work for the NHS in an eye hospital, a general hospital or a specialised clinic. There are some opportunities for

private consultancy work or for overseas work with voluntary organisations in developing countries. Prospects may depend on your willingness to move to another area to gain experience and obtain promotion. Some ophthalmologists may teach or do research. There may be opportunities to work part time or job share.

Within the NHS, junior doctors earn a basic salary and are usually paid a supplement for extra hours worked. Basic salaries are around £33k a year (including a 50% supplement for extra hours), rising to £43k-£68k (including 50% supplement) for a doctor in specialist training. A consultant can earn £73k-£174k a year. These salaries do not include on-call payments, private income or London weighting allowances. If working for a voluntary organisation abroad, your pay may be low.

Health

Good colour vision is essential for this job. There is a risk of infection. You may be expected to have no allergies and a good level of general fitness.

Skills and Qualities

able to take responsibility, able to use complex equipment, analytical skills, aptitude for teamwork, emotionally strong, good communication skills, good listening skills, manual dexterity, not squeamish, scientific approach

Relevant Subjects

Biology, Chemistry, English, Mathematics, Physics, Psychology, Science, Sociology

Further Information

Becoming a Doctor (BMA) (BMA) - www.bma.org.uk/careers/becoming_doctor/index.jsp

Foundation Programme - www.foundationprogramme.nhs.uk

Insider's Guide to Medical Schools (Blackwell Books)

Modernising Medical Careers - www.mmc.nhs.uk

NHS Careers (NHS Careers) - www.nhscareers.nhs.uk

NHS Careers Scotland - www.infoscotland.com/nhs

NHS Careers Wales - www.wales.nhs.uk

Addresses

British Medical Association (BMA)
BMA House, Tavistock Square, London WC1H 9JP
Phone: +44 (0)20 7387 4499
Web: www.bma.org.uk

General Medical Council (GMC)
Regents Place, 350 Euston Road, London NW1 3JN
Phone: +44 (0)161 923 6602
Web: www.gmc-uk.org

Institute of Ophthalmology
11-43 Bath Street, London EC1V 9EL
Phone: +44 (0)207 608 6800
Web: www.ucl.ac.uk/ioo/

Royal College of Ophthalmologists
17 Cornwall Terrace, London NW1 4QW
Phone: +44 (0)207 935 0702
Web: www.rcophth.ac.uk/

Similar Jobs

Doctor: Hospital, Optometrist, Orthoptist, Physicist, Surgeon

Optical Assistant

also known as: Contact Lens Assistant, Receptionist: Optical

CRCI:Healthcare

CLCI:JAL — Job Band: 1 to 2

Job Description

Optical assistants welcome clients to an optician's shop or optical centre and help them by answering any questions and providing information. They book appointments, maintain records, order spectacle frames and prescribe lenses and contact lenses for clients. Also take messages and give out information in person and by phone. They ensure that the shop is comfortable and inviting to clients, arrange displays of frames and related goods, and may help customers to select suitable frames.

May also assist a dispensing optician with the fitting and care of a client's contact lenses. Assistants explain how to clean and care for them, plus the hygiene needed to prevent eye infections. Watch customers fit their lenses and give advice on the way to do it.

Work Details

Usually work 37 hrs a week, often including a Saturday in the front reception area of an optician's premises. Optical assistants are responsible for accurate work and for ensuring that clients are made welcome. Liaise with optometrists, opticians, as well as optical sales representatives and technicians.

Qualification

- **England, Wales and Northern Ireland**

Band 1: For entry to jobs, no minimum qualifications are needed, but you are expected to have a good level of general education and relevant experience. Some formal/vocational qualifications at any level are useful.

Band 2: For entry to jobs, no minimum qualifications are needed, but it is an advantage to have some GCSEs (A*-C) or equivalent in subjects that include English, maths and biology.

- **Scotland**

Band 1: For entry to jobs, no minimum qualifications are needed, but you are expected to have a good level of general education and relevant experience. Some formal/vocational qualifications at any level are useful.

Band 2: Although academic qualifications are not specified for this job, it is an advantage to have some S grades (1-3) in subjects that include English and maths, or similar.

Adult Qualifications

Employers expect a good level of general education particularly in literacy and numeracy.

Work Experience

Work experience gives you an insight into what you enjoy and don't enjoy about a job, as well as the chance to gain new skills. It also provides useful information to add to your CV and improves your future job prospects. Employers therefore may prefer those who have work experience in a medical or healthcare setting such as a hospital or care home.

Entry and Training

Individual employers offer on-the-job training that is supervised by experienced staff. Usually, entrants begin as a trainee and may also have off-the-job training sessions on particular topics such as customer care, health and safety, company procedures etc. The Worshipful Company of Spectacle Makers offers certificates in optical practice support at levels 2 and 3. These cover all aspects of an optical assistant's daily work, the anatomy and function of the eye, basic optics, frames and fitting, contact lenses, and can be taken by correspondence courses.

Some optical assistants with 5 GCSEs/S grades (A*-C/1-3) in English language, maths and a science, or equivalent, may progress to becoming a dispensing optician.

You may be able to obtain an S/NVQ level 2 in optical retailing or level 2-3 in customer service. Training programmes, including apprenticeship schemes, may be available in your area. Advanced apprenticeships leading to qualification at level 3 can also be a route into higher education.

Mature entrants with relevant experience may have an advantage. Relevant experience includes customer care and working with the public on a voluntary or paid basis. Medically related work or customer service experience is useful.

Opportunities and Pay
Work is available in most towns and cities. Most posts are found in private practices and you work in an optometrist or optician's shop/centre. With larger firms, promotion to supervisory level is possible. Those with at least ten years' experience in an optical field can be accepted for training as a dispensing optician without the standard entry qualifications.

As a trainee you can earn around £14k, rising to £15k-£23k with experience, depending on where you work.

Skills and Qualities
able to explain clearly, able to put people at ease, accurate, attention to detail, friendly, manual dexterity, numeracy skills, patient, precise, steady hand

Relevant Subjects
Biology, Health and social care, Mathematics, Science

Further Information
A Career in Dispensing Optics (ABDO) - www.abdo.org.uk/read.php?page=2&p=1

A Career in Vision Care (AOP) - www.assoc-optometrists.org/

Apprenticeship Schemes (National Apprenticeship Service) - www.apprenticeships.org.uk

Addresses
Association of British Dispensing Opticians (ABDO)
199 Gloucester Terrace, London W2 6LD
Phone: +44 (0)20 7298 5100
Web: www.abdo.org.uk

Worshipful Company of Spectacle Makers
Apothecaries' Hall, Black Friars Lane, London EC4V 6EL
Phone: +44 (0)20 7236 2932
Web: www.spectaclemakers.com

Similar Jobs
Optical Technician, Optician: Dispensing, Receptionist

Optical Technician
CRCI:Manufacturing and Production
CLCI:SAD — Job Band: 2

Job Description
Optical technicians prepare spectacles and contact lenses from prescriptions provided by optometrists and ophthalmologists. They make specialised lenses for spectacles or contact lenses. Simpler lenses are produced, ready finished, by a moulding process. Over 95% of lenses are now made in plastic. All products are examined for any flaws in the plastic or glass.

Computer-controlled equipment produces lenses and the optical technician needs to understand the principles behind the equipment. Takes into account aspects such as the location of optical centre, position of bifocal segments, size, thickness and strength of the lens. Also considers the type of selected frame if prescription is for spectacles. Then programs the cutting machine to produce the correct curve and buffs and polishes the lens. May apply special finishes, such as tinting, anti glare and scratch resistant coatings. May also carry out repairs to damaged lenses and spectacle frames.

Work Details
Optical technicians usually work a basic 37-40 hr week, Monday to Friday, though sometimes may be required to work overtime at busy times. In in-store laboratories attached to high street stores, you may have to work weekends on a shift basis. The work environment is light and airy, though it can be noisy at times. You are responsible for accurate and precise work, and may sit or stand for long periods.

Qualification
- **England, Wales and Northern Ireland**

Band 2: Although academic qualifications are not specified for this job, it is an advantage to have some GCSEs (A*-C) in subjects that include English and maths, technical subjects, or equivalent.

- **Scotland**

Band 2: Although academic qualifications are not specified for this job, it is an advantage to have some S grades (1-3) in subjects that include English and maths, technical subjects, or similar.

Adult Qualifications
There are no formal qualifications for this work, but a good level of secondary education is expected and it helps if you also have relevant experience.

Work Experience
Work or voluntary experience is always useful. It can improve your chances when applying for jobs or apprenticeships. Your personal or adult guidance adviser should be able to give you some advice on how to get some work experience.

Entry and Training
Individual employers offer very specific training according to the lenses they manufacture. Training can be given on the job with an experienced technician and may include a day-release or evening course. Short courses are usually offered by companies that make optical lens-cutting equipment.

The Worshipful Company of Spectacle Makers (WCSM) offers training in optical production processes at levels 2 and 3. These courses are available by correspondence course. The level 2 course is the basic training for this work; the level 3 course is aimed at senior technicians and supervisors. It is also possible to study for the optical technician's certificate - a nationally recognised qualification through the WCSM. This is available by correspondence course and leads to the qualification SMC (Tech). Holders of this award are exempt from almost all of the first year course of the Association of British Dispensing Opticians ABDO diploma.

S/NVQs in optical manufacturing are available at levels 2-3. Relevant training programmes, including optical manufacturing technician apprenticeship schemes, may be available in your area. Advanced apprenticeships leading to qualification at level 3 can be a route into higher education.

Government training opportunities, such as apprenticeships, may be available in your area. You can also gain recognition of previous experience through Accreditation of Prior Learning (APL) or by working towards relevant S/NVQs. Contact your local careers office, Jobcentre Plus, Next Step service or Learning and Skills Council (LSC) Local Enterprise Company (LEC) for details of training schemes.

Opportunities and Pay
Optical technicians are employed by manufacturers of optical instruments. Work is also available at private practices or optical laboratories throughout the UK. These companies provide a complete optical service to their customers. Some single practice opticians employ technicians and some branches of national chains have an in-house laboratory. Promotion to supervisory level is possible. Part-time work may be available. Some SMC (Tech) qualified technicians progress to become a dispensing optician. Some move into training and management.

Pay varies depending on location and employer, but most optical technicians earn between £11k-£18k a year.

Health
This job requires good eyesight.

Skills and Qualities
able to work quickly, accurate, aptitude for teamwork, attention to detail, good concentration level, hand-to-eye co-ordination, numeracy skills, practical skills, precise, steady hand

Relevant Subjects
Design and technology, Manufacturing, Mathematics, Physics, Science

Further Information
Apprenticeship Schemes (National Apprenticeship Service) - www.apprenticeships.org.uk
Training Schemes - www.direct.gov.uk/en/educationandlearning
▶Working in manufacturing (2010) (Babcock Lifeskills) - www.babcock-lifeskills.com/

Addresses
Association of British Dispensing Opticians (ABDO)
199 Gloucester Terrace, London W2 6LD
Phone: +44 (0)20 7298 5100
Web: www.abdo.org.uk

Association of Contact Lens Manufacture Ltd
PO Box 735, Devizes, Wiltshire SN10 3TQ
Phone: +44 (0)1380 860418
Web: www.aclm.org.uk

Federation of Manufacturing Opticians
199 Gloucester Terrace, London W2 6LD
Web: www.fmo.co.uk

Worshipful Company of Spectacle Makers
Apothecaries' Hall, Black Friars Lane, London EC4V 6EL
Phone: +44 (0)20 7236 2932
Web: www.spectaclemakers.com

Similar Jobs
Dental Technician/Technologist, Laboratory Technician: Science, Optical Assistant, Optician: Dispensing

Optician: Dispensing

CRCI:Healthcare
CLCI:JAL
Job Band: 3 to 5

Job Description
Dispensing opticians analyse and interpret an optical prescription provided by an optometrist (ophthalmic optician), or an ophthalmic surgeon (ophthalmologist), and supply an accurate aid to help a patient's vision. They give advice on lens type and styling of frames, and take frame, facial and lens measurements. Once glasses are ready, they use complex apparatus to measure, calculate and check lenses to ensure they meet the final ordered specification. Ensure that glasses fit well, and give advice on how to get the best results from them. May also supply and fit contact lenses and give advice on a variety of low vision aids.

Dispensing opticians do not test patients' eyes, but have an obligation to refer a patient to a doctor or optometrist if any sign of abnormality, injury or disease is spotted during a consultation. They supervise the work and training of staff including trainee opticians and non-professional staff. Also liaise with sales representatives from vision care manufacturers and keep accurate details of patients as well as business records.

Work Details
Usually work 35-40 hrs a week, which covers normal retail opening hours, perhaps including some work on a Saturday and some late finishes. You are responsible for accurate work and for providing an efficient service. You have contact with members of the public and with doctors and other opticians. You advise people about the style of frame which suits them. Business management skills are also useful.

Qualification
- **England, Wales and Northern Ireland**

Band 3: For full or part-time diploma course in ophthalmic dispensing: minimum of 5 GCSEs (A*-C) including English literature/language, maths and a science-based subject, or equivalent.

Band 4: For HND, Diploma of Higher Education or foundation degree: 2 A levels and 5 GCSEs (A*-C) usually including English, maths and preferably physics, or equivalent.

Band 5: For degree: usually at least two A levels, science subject preferred but not essential, plus some GCSEs (A*-C) including English, maths and science subjects, or equivalent qualifications. Exact requirements depend on the degree you take.

- **Scotland**

Band 3: For full or part-time diploma course in ophthalmic dispensing: minimum of five S grades (1-3) including English literature/language, maths and a science-based subject, or similar.

Band 4: For entry to SQA higher national, professional development awards or a foundation degree in England, usually 2-3 H grades and some S grades (1-3), including English, maths and science subjects, or similar qualifications.

Band 5: For degree: usually at least 3-5 H grades, science subject preferred but not essential, plus some S grades (1-3) including English, maths and science subjects, or similar qualifications. Exact requirements depend on the degree you take.

Degree Information
Degrees are available in ophthalmic dispensing and in optical management.

Adult Qualifications
Applicants with at least ten years' experience in the optical field as an optical assistant may be accepted for training courses without the standard entry qualifications. However, mature students are usually expected to have formal qualifications in English, maths and a science-based subject, or equivalent. The Association of British Dispensing Opticians runs a series of access courses in English, general science, human biology, maths and optics to help prepare mature students.

Some higher education institutions may accept applicants who have successfully completed a relevant Access to higher education course.

Work Experience
Work experience gives you an insight into what you enjoy and don't enjoy about a job or working environment, as well as the opportunity to acquire new skills. It also provides valuable information to add to your CV and improves any course application and/or your future employment prospects. Experience can include observation or work in the retail side of an optician, or general retail and work with the public.

Entry and Training
Dispensing opticians must pass the Association of British Dispensing Opticians (ABDO) examinations at level 6/7 before registering with the General Optical Council (GOC). The ABDO College is based in Kent and specialises in distance and blended learning education for the optical profession. It is the only college in the UK devoted solely to the teaching of the theoretical and practical aspects of ophthalmic dispensing. The Fellowship Dispensing Diploma training lasts for three years. A foundation degree and BSc course are also available and Access courses for those without GCSEs. Students are generally in paid employment while they study. Check with the college for full course details.

Full time and day-release courses in ophthalmic dispensing are offered at a few institutions in England. Check UCAS for details. In Scotland, Glasgow Caledonian university offers a full-time three-year degree course. A foundation degree in dispensing optics is available, both full and part time. Some employers may provide sponsorship for courses. A list of approved institutions and course information is available from the GOC.

Once qualified, some opticians take advanced part-time courses, for example in contact lens dispensing or prescribing low vision aids. Continuing education and training is compulsory for all registered dispensing opticians. Registration with the GOC must be renewed annually for as long as you practise in the UK.

Mature entrants who are qualified dispensing opticians returning to employment, may take short full-time refresher courses. Maturity is viewed as an advantage and many enter after first training as an optical assistant, or with experience as a receptionist or sales assistant in the optical profession. There are distance-learning courses for those without the required basic qualifications. Contact the Association of British Dispensing Opticians for further details on courses and training routes.

Opportunities and Pay

Around 5,500 registered dispensing opticians work throughout the UK, with most employed in private practice. Some are self-employed or in partnership, and the remainder work in hospital eye clinics, frame and lens manufacturers, prescription houses, ophthalmic instrument suppliers and manufacturers. Some work as lecturers in further/higher education. Many opticians specialise in the supply and fitting of contact lenses or low vision aids. With experience, there are good opportunities to move to assistant manager posts. There is a good demand for employees in the UK and your qualification is valid in many countries abroad.

While training, you are likely to earn £14k-£17k a year. Newly qualified dispensing opticians earn around £20k-£26k a year, rising to around £30k with 2-5 years' experience. There are no set payscales for this work and salaries vary widely.

Skills and Qualities

attention to detail, business awareness, eye for visual effect, friendly, good interpersonal skills, manual dexterity, numeracy skills, patient, precise, scientific approach

Relevant Subjects

Biology, Chemistry, English, Health and social care, Mathematics, Physics, Science

Further Information

A Career in Dispensing Optics (ABDO)- www.abdo.org.uk/read.php?page=2&p=1

A Career in Vision Care (AOP) - www.assoc-optometrists.org/

Addresses

Association of British Dispensing Opticians (ABDO)
199 Gloucester Terrace, London W2 6LD
Phone: +44 (0)20 7298 5100
Web: www.abdo.org.uk

General Optical Council (GOC)
41 Harley Street, London W1G 8DJ
Phone: +44 (0)20 7580 3898
Web: www.optical.org

UCAS
Customer Services Unit, PO Box 28, Cheltenham GL52 3LZ
Phone: +44 (0)871 468 0468
Web: www.ucas.com

Similar Jobs

Optical Assistant, Optical Technician, Optometrist, Orthoptist, Pharmacy Technician, Retail Manager

Optometrist

CRCI:Healthcare
CLCI:JAL Job Band: 5

Job Description

Optometrists examine patients' eyes, test their sight and prescribe glasses or contact lenses to correct any defects. They use precision instruments to study the condition of the eye and calculate errors in vision. Also detect any signs of disease, injury, abnormalities and any other eye defects or wider health problems. May prescribe eye drops to manage minor eye conditions. Optometrists may need to refer the patient to their GP or to an appropriate specialist. They offer advice and reassurance on vision-related matters and may also fit a patient's glasses and lenses.

May supervise the work and training of staff including trainee dispensing opticians and optometrists, and non-professional staff. Liaise with sales representatives from vision care manufacturers and keep accurate details of patients as well as business records.

Work Details

Usually work 9am-5pm, Monday to Friday, but may be required to work on a Saturday as part of the working week. Optometrists usually work flexible hours that may include some evenings. You work in a high street shop, clinic, hospital or possibly in a university or a laboratory. You advise and help people of all ages. Work is intricate and requires sound judgement. Some of the tests are conducted in a small, darkened consultation room. Most of the time the work environment is light and airy.

Qualification

• England, Wales and Northern Ireland

Band 5: For degree course: three A levels, preferably including two from biology, maths and physics, and some GCSEs (A*-C) that should include English and maths. High grades are usually required. Equivalent qualifications may be acceptable. Exact requirements depend on the degree you take.

• Scotland

Band 5: For degree course: 4-5 H grades, preferably in maths, physics, chemistry, biology, and some S grades (1-3) that should include English and maths, if not offered at H grade, or similar qualifications. High grades at H level are usually expected.

Degree Information

For entry to this job it is essential to have a degree in optometry.

Adult Qualifications

Universities vary in their requirements for mature applicants, but courses are oversubscribed and entry may be difficult. Requirements may be relaxed for those with experience as a qualified dispensing optician. Adults can take an Access course in science as a preparatory route to a degree. Check with the individual institutions for details.

Work Experience

Work experience gives you an insight into what you enjoy and don't enjoy about a job or working environment, as well as the opportunity to acquire new skills. It also provides valuable information to add to your CV and improves any course application and/or your future employment prospects. Entry to this career is competitive. It is helpful if you have arranged work shadowing of an optometrist wherever possible. Some of the larger chains may offer summer placements for students between their second and third years.

Entry and Training

To qualify as a registered optometrist, you must have an approved degree (minimum of a 2:2) in optometry from a university approved by the General Optical Council (GOC) and a certificate of clinical competence, before going on to further training. This includes a clinical pre-registration training period of around a year under the supervision of a qualified optometrist. You then need to pass the Professional Qualifying Examination (PQE) of the College of Optometrists which assesses your ability to manage patients and to practise safely. It is important to undertake continuing professional development throughout your career to ensure you keep up to date.

The optometry progression scheme is an alternative route for entrants who do not gain a degree at 2.2 or higher. This allows you to study, then take the PQE, and then move into pre-registration training. Contact the GOC for details of approved courses of study, institutions and routes to registration. Entry to training courses is highly competitive.

Higher qualifications are offered by the College of Optometrists in aspects such as orthoptics, contact lens practice and ocular conditions, including glaucoma and diabetes. Continuing education and training is now compulsory for all registered optometrists. Registration must be renewed with the GOC annually for as long as you practise in the UK.

Mature entrants are sometimes those who have qualified as dispensing opticians and wish to retrain to become optometrists. Contact the General Optical Council for details of approved courses of study and institutions, and routes to registration.

Opportunities and Pay

There are around 12,000 optometrists in the the UK and the majority work in private practice, either for a small firm, in a partnership or running their own business. Others work in the NHS, the prison service, armed forces, or for a charity. Employment and promotion opportunities are good, particularly if you study for advanced qualifications. There may be opportunities to teach, do research and to work abroad.

Starting salaries for optometrists in their pre-registration year are around £17k a year. In private practice, starting salaries once qualified are from £22k-£28k. Senior optometrists in private practice can earn £40k-£55k a year.

Skills and Qualities

able to explain clearly, able to put people at ease, able to use complex equipment, accurate, aptitude for maths and science, attention to detail, good communication skills, good interpersonal skills, manual dexterity, patient

Relevant Subjects

Biology, Chemistry, English, Health and social care, Mathematics, Physics, Psychology, Science

Further Information

A Career in Optometry (The College of Optometrists) (The College of Optometrists) - www.college-optometrists.org/

A Career in Vision Care (AOP) - www.assoc-optometrists.org/

AGCAS: Health (Job Sector Briefing) (AGCAS) - www.prospects.ac.uk

Careers in Vision Care (GOC) (General Optical Council) - www.optical.org/en/our_work/Education/index.cfm

Optometry Today (fortnightly) (Association of Optometrists) - www.optometry.co.uk/

Addresses

Association of Optometrists
61 Southwark Street, London SE1 0HL
Phone: +44 (0)20 7261 9661
Web: www.assoc-optometrists.org

College of Optometrists
42 Craven Street, London WC2N 5NG
Phone: +44 (0)20 7839 6000
Web: www.college-optometrists.org

General Optical Council (GOC)
41 Harley Street, London W1G 8DJ
Phone: +44 (0)20 7580 3898
Web: www.optical.org

Institute of Optometry
56-62 Newington Causeway, London SE1 6DS
Phone: +44 (0)20 7407 4183
Web: www.ioo.org.uk

Similar Jobs

Optician: Dispensing, Orthoptist, Pharmacist: Community

Orthodontist

CRCI:Healthcare
CLCI:JAF — Job Band: 5

Job Description

Orthodontists straighten crooked teeth to improve the look and performance of the teeth and face and correct problems with jaw growth to help people bite and chew food properly. They check the person's mouth and take photographs, x-rays and moulds of the teeth.

Orthodontists explain how they can help the patient and what the patient has to do as part of the treatment. They usually suggest a course of action that may include removing some teeth. Then they decide whether to use fixed, removable or both types of braces to straighten teeth and carry out the work. Progress is reviewed and braces adjusted in follow-up visits. Hospital orthodontists work on the most complex cases. These include those needing operations and where there are other health problems as well.

Work Details

Orthodontists in the NHS usually work a 35 hr week, Monday to Friday, and maybe Saturday mornings. In hospitals you may work irregular hours and be on call for emergencies. In general practice you choose how many hours to work depending on the size and opening hours of the practice. There are opportunities for part-time work and career breaks.

Works in a clean, comfortable, well-lit dental surgery, clinic or hospital. Patients are usually children and young people who may be in pain or upset. Wears a protective tunic or coat, mask, safety glasses and surgical gloves.

Qualification

All orthodontists are qualified and experienced dentists. For full details about how train as a dentist see the Dentist job article.

- **England, Wales and Northern Ireland**

Band 5: For entry to an orthodontics training scheme: a degree in dentistry (BDS) and relevant experience.

- **Scotland**

Band 5: For entry to an orthodontics training scheme: a degree in dentistry (BDS) and relevant experience.

Degree Information

The three-year full-time orthodontics training programme takes the form of a masters degree (MSc) or doctorate (DDS) in dental surgery/science (orthodontics). It prepares students for the examinations for membership in orthodontics (MOrth) of the Royal College of Surgeons of England (RCS), the Royal College of Physicians and Surgeons of Glasgow (RCPSG) or the Royal College of Surgeons of Edinburgh (RCSE). The programme has taught, practical and research elements. Clinical work is carried out in a hospital.

If you are a practising dentist in England in an area that doesn't have a big enough population to make a specialist practice worthwhile, you can do a three-year part-time training programme leading to a British Orthodontic Society/Faculty of General Dental

Practice UK (BOS/FGDP(UK)) diploma in primary care orthodontics RCS (Eng). It involves taught sessions, distance learning and work-based training.

Adult Qualifications
There are unlikely to be any exceptions made for adults to the entry requirements for orthodontics training programmes.

Work Experience
Entry to dentistry degrees is highly competitive, so showing relevant work or voluntary experience on your application is vital. Experience of working in a dental or orthodontics practice is ideal, but anything that involves working with the public or helping people is also relevant.

After your dentistry degree you need to spend at least two years gaining a broad experience of dental work. Talking to orthodontists working in a variety of settings may give you a clearer idea about the type of work you may like to focus on.

Entry and Training
To become a specialist in orthodontics, you need to be a qualified dentist with the British Dental Society (see the dentist job article for full details), have experience in hospital, community and/or general dental practice and be committed to continuing professional development. You can then complete a one-year vocational training scheme or two-year general practitioner training scheme to help gain some of the necessary experience.

It is advisable to study for the diploma of membership of the Joint Dental Faculties (MJDF) in England and/or the diploma of membership of the Faculty of Dental Surgeons (MFDS) in Scotland which takes 2-3 years. This is not essential to enter specialist training but the majority of applicants have this diploma.

Once you have completed your three year orthodontics training, you can work as a specialist in orthodontic practice or decide to run your own business. Some orthodontists work for the NHS.

If you want to work as a hospital orthodontics consultant, you have to train for a further two years. This is a combination of academic training at a university and clinical training in a hospital to gain a fellowship of dental surgery in orthodontics (FDS Orth). If you want to teach and do research in a university, you need a PhD degree and possibly a teaching qualification. This can involve another 3-4 years of study.

As you are likely to come into contact with children, you must pass a Criminal Records Bureau (CRB) or Disclosure Scotland check. All orthodontists have to read journals and attend courses to keep themselves up to date with the latest developments in their area of work.

Since this area of work requires considerable experience in general dentistry, all entrants are adults.

Opportunities and Pay
Orthodontists work in general and specialist practices, the community dental service and hospitals. In practices you usually have contracts with the NHS to provide orthodontics services to children and young people. You may also see patients who pay for their own treatment. With experience and further training you can become a hospital consultant or university lecturer. Many become partners in their practices or set up practices of their own.

Salary depends on your role, the type of practice and the number of patients you see. Orthodontists who work for others and carry out more orthodontic than dental work earn an average of £140k a year, and those who do more dental work than orthodontics earn around £66k a year. If you own your own practice, you earn significantly more. Orthodontic consultants in hospitals earn £73k-£173k a year. Salaried orthodontists, such as those working as specialist dentists with the community dental service, earn £67k-£77k a year.

Health
The work may involve a risk of infection. Orthodontists need good eyesight and must be able to cope with the sight of blood.

Skills and Qualities
able to explain clearly, able to inspire confidence, able to relate well to children and young people, calm, careful, creative flair, good concentration level, manual dexterity, meticulous, patient

Relevant Subjects
Biology, Chemistry, Design and technology, English, Health and social care, ICT/Computer studies, Mathematics, Physics, Science

Further Information
AGCAS: Health (Job Sector Briefing) (AGCAS) - www.prospects.ac.uk

NHS Careers (NHS Careers) - www.nhscareers.nhs.uk

NHS Careers Scotland - www.infoscotland.com/nhs

NHS Careers Wales - www.wales.nhs.uk

Royal College of Physicians and Surgeons of Glasgow - www.rcpsg.ac.uk

Royal College of Surgeons of Edinburgh - www.rcsed.ac.uk

Royal College of Surgeons of England - www.rcseng.ac.uk

Addresses
British Dental Association (BDA)
64 Wimpole Street, London W1G 8YS
Phone: +44 (0)20 7935 0875
Web: www.bda.org/

British Orthodontic Association
12 Bridewell Place, London EC4V 6AP
Phone: +44 (0)20 7353 8680
Web: www.bos.org.uk

General Dental Council (GDC)
37 Wimpole Street, London W1G 8DQ
Phone: +44 (0)20 7887 3800
Web: www.gdc-uk.org

Similar Jobs
Dental Technician/Technologist, Dentist, Prosthetist/Orthotist, Surgeon

Orthoptist
CRCI:Healthcare
CLCI:JAL Job Band: 5

Job Description
Orthoptists are involved in the investigation, diagnosis and treatment of visual defects and abnormalities of eye movement. They work with babies, children, and adults of all ages to improve their vision and quality of everyday life. This involves assessing the patient, devising and carrying out treatment or referring the patient to a specialist, such as an ophthalmic surgeon. They use complex equipment to diagnose the problem. May treat problems such as squints, lazy eye or double vision resulting from birth, disease or an accident. Orthoptists are also involved in the management of conditions such as glaucoma, retinal disease, neurological disorders, cataracts and people who have had a stroke.

They monitor progress of treatment and liaise closely with other medical and nursing staff. May supervise the clinical teaching of optometry students and other health professionals, including medical students and GPs.

Work Details
Usually work a basic 37.5 hr week, Monday to Friday. You work in a hospital, health centre clinic or a school. Travel around an area may be necessary. You examine patients, advise and help them. You are responsible for accurate work which can sometimes be

emotionally demanding. Orthoptists may need to wear a white coat, but dress code is usually at the discretion of the senior orthoptist.

Qualification

- **England, Wales and Northern Ireland**

Band 5: For degree course: usually three good A levels, preferably including biology, and 5 GCSEs (A*-C) including English, maths and a science, or equivalent qualifications. Exact requirements depend on the degree you take.

- **Scotland**

Band 5: For degree course: usually four H grades, preferably including biology, plus five S grades (1-3) including English, maths and a science subject if not offered at H grade, or similar qualifications. Exact requirements depend on the degree you take.

Degree Information

A degree in orthoptics is required for entry to this job. There are full-time degree courses at Liverpool and Sheffield universities.

Adult Qualifications

Academic institutions look at applications from adults on an individual basis. Professional qualifications and experience are considered if candidates do not have standard degree entry qualifications. Check with the university concerned.

Work Experience

Entry to degree courses is very competitive. It is recommended that you either visit your local hospital orthoptic department or arrange to work shadow an orthoptist in a clinic. Any work or voluntary experience in a caring environment, including work with children, the elderly, or with those who have physical difficulties is encouraged.

Entry and Training

You need to take a degree in orthoptics and entry to courses is highly competitive. On entering a course you need to undergo a Criminal Records Bureau/Disclosure Scotland check. Courses integrate theory with practical placements in clinical education centres in England, Scotland, Wales and Northern Ireland. After qualification, you are closely supervised by experienced orthoptists and many NHS Trusts also operate a mentoring scheme. All orthoptists must be state registered to practise, and are members of the British and Irish Orthoptic Society and the Health Professions Council. You are expected to participate in continuing professional development throughout your career.

The Department of Health provides orthoptics students with full payment of tuition fees and also a means-tested bursary towards living costs. A student loan is also available. You may wish to study for higher qualifications, particularly if you are interested in teaching or involved in research.

Mature entry to this profession is particularly welcomed, as maturity and life experience are seen as a distinct advantage. There are also good prospects for returning orthoptists. Contact NHS Careers or the British and Irish Orthoptic Society for further details of training routes and qualifications.

Opportunities and Pay

There are over 1500 registered orthoptists in the UK and most work in the NHS, but some are in private practice or with a local authority, working in schools, colleges and universities, and in clinics. Some work for a charity. Competition for training places is high, but once trained prospects are good. There is a clear promotion structure in the NHS, but prospects may be improved by willingness to move to another area of the country. Other posts in teaching, research or management are also available. Part time and locum work may be possible.

Starting salaries for graduates working for the NHS are around £21k-£27k, rising to around £25k-£35k a year with experience and increased levels of responsibility. Senior orthoptists can earn up to £64k a year. Some NHS Trusts may offer additional payments to those working in inner and outer London.

Health

This job requires good eyesight.

Skills and Qualities

able to explain clearly, able to inspire confidence, attention to detail, friendly, good communication skills, good interpersonal skills, observant, patient, scientific approach, tactful

Relevant Subjects

Biology, Chemistry, English, Health and social care, Mathematics, Physics, Science

Further Information

British and Irish Orthoptic Journal (BIOS, annual) (BIOS) - www.orthoptics.org.uk/journal
NHS Careers (NHS Careers) - www.nhscareers.nhs.uk
NHS Careers Scotland - www.infoscotland.com/nhs
NHS Careers Wales - www.wales.nhs.uk

Addresses

British and Irish Orthoptic Society (BIOS)
Tavistock House North, Tavistock Square, London WC1H 9HX
Phone: +44 (0)20 7387 7992
Web: www.orthoptics.org.uk

Health Professions Council (HPC)
Park House, 184 Kennington Park Road, London SE11 4BU
Phone: +44 (0)20 7582 0866
Web: www.hpc-uk.org

Similar Jobs

Occupational Therapist, Optician: Dispensing, Optometrist, Physiotherapist, Speech & Language Therapist

Osteopath

CRCI:Healthcare
CLCI:JOD — Job Band: 5

Job Description

Osteopaths treat people by diagnosing and treating the cause of illness and injury, rather than just the symptoms themselves. They often deal with back, neck and joint problems, as well as tension, migraine, asthma, arthritis or digestive problems. Osteopaths treat patients using their hands, rather than machines, to feel the action of muscles, joints and ligaments. They give manipulative treatment to relieve pain and correct the problem without surgery or drugs. May use deep massage techniques or direct manipulation of joints.

They usually take a patient's case history, including a full medical history, and make notes on other aspects of the patient's life, such as diet and exercise, work and leisure routines. Then perform a physical examination, check reflexes, blood pressure, and perhaps takes blood, urine tests or X-rays. May offer advice to patients on factors, such as their lifestyle, to help with long-term relief from their symptoms. Also advise patients how to prevent problems, such as improving posture.

Some osteopaths specialise in treating children, expectant mothers, those with sports-related injuries, and HIV/AIDS patients with musculoskeletal problems. They refer clients to a health specialist or GP if a condition that is not suitable for manipulation is detected and requires medical treatment.

Work Details
Many osteopaths are self-employed and choose their own hours of work. Evening and weekend work is common. You help people who are often in pain and your clients can be children, athletes or dancers, the elderly, and people of all ages who have some form of disability. In this work, if asked, you must supply information to an employer about any spent/unspent convictions, cautions, reprimands or warnings.

Qualification
• England, Wales and Northern Ireland
Band 5: For degree courses: 2-3 A levels, preferably chemistry, physics, human biology or biology, and some GCSEs (A*-C) including English, and often maths and a science subject. Exact requirements depend on the degree you take.

• Scotland
Band 5: For degree courses: 3-5 H grades, preferably chemistry, physics, human biology or biology, and some S grades (1-3), usually including English and maths and a science subject, or similar qualifications. Exact requirements depend on the degree you take.

Degree Information
A degree or a postgraduate qualification in osteopathy or osteopathic medicine is required for recognition as a registered osteopath. Degrees in subjects such as physiology, anatomy or physiotherapy may lead to exemption from part of the osteopathy degree course. Postgraduate study is available and a relevant postgraduate course is available for qualified doctors.

Adult Qualifications
Entry requirements may be relaxed for adults applying for higher education courses, and Access or foundation courses give adults without qualifications a route into degree courses.

Work Experience
Employers may prefer candidates who have relevant work or voluntary experience. This includes working in a residential care home, with children or anything involving helping and communicating with people. Ideally you should spend time with a qualified osteopath in their professional practice. Many training institutions, such as the British School of Osteopathy, have osteopaths who act as careers liaison officers. They conduct preliminary interviews in their practices of candidates for the degree course.

Entry and Training
It is illegal to practise osteopathy without being state registered, and for membership of the General Osteopathic Council (GOsC) and Register of Osteopaths, an accredited degree or postgraduate qualification in osteopathy from one of ten approved institutions is required. Most osteopaths take a full-time degree course for four/five years, but it is possible to take a part-time course. Shortened training courses are available for those with relevant qualifications. You must be 18 before you can start training.

Qualified medical doctors and physiotherapists with at least three years' experience can take a 13 month part-time course at the London College of Osteopathic Medicine. Grant assistance may be available for some courses. Short intensive science courses, designed for suitable applicants who do not have A levels/H grades or a degree in science subjects, may be available at some colleges. Training includes clinical practice beginning with many periods of observation and then progressing to work with patients. Check the GOsC website for the application process for courses as these vary between institutions.

The College of Osteopaths offers a foundation course for students who wish to enter the BSc (Hons) Osteopathy programme, but lack the necessary background in science knowledge and terminology for the degree programme. The course is held in August and November prior to the start of the degree course.

Once qualified, you undertake a mandatory programme of continuing professional development , which can include short courses and postgraduate qualifications on specialist subjects for a certain number of hours each year. Seminars and practical workshops are regularly offered by the professional organisations, such as the British Osteopathic Association.

A Diploma/Welsh Baccalaureate in society, health and development may be available in your area and may be relevant to this job.

Mature entrants are often those who wish to change their current career and there is growing interest in osteopathy from mature applicants. If you have a medically-related background you may have an advantage. There is a specific postgraduate course available to qualified doctors and for physiotherapists that have completed at least three years' experience in a qualified physiotherapy role. A science Access course or Open University science foundation course is also useful preparation for training for those without relevant qualifications. Check with individual institutions for entry requirements.

Opportunities and Pay
This is an expanding field but is still a small profession. Most osteopaths are self-employed and work in the private sector. You may work in a complementary health centre, clinic, or perhaps a sports club, dance studio or theatre. Some osteopaths work from home, with clients making an appointment, and some may work for a large company or organisation, providing care to employees. There is growing integration with the NHS so there may be opportunities to work in hospitals and GP surgeries. There is scope for specialisation in particular problems or with particular types of patients. There may also be opportunities overseas.

As most osteopaths are self-employed it is difficult to summarise earnings. Pay may be by fees and not by a regular salary. Broadly speaking, osteopaths earn between £35-£50 a session, depending on location and experience. Over the year, earnings may range from £22k to more than £35k. An established and successful osteopath may earn £35k-£65k a year.

Health
You need to be healthy and physically fit as the work can be strenuous.

Skills and Qualities
able to inspire confidence, business awareness, good listening skills, good sense of touch, observational skills, perceptive, reassuring, scientific approach, strong hands, sympathetic

Relevant Subjects
Biology, Chemistry, English, Health and social care, Physics, Psychology, Science

Further Information
AGCAS: Health (Job Sector Briefing) (AGCAS) - www.prospects.ac.uk

Diplomas (Foundation, Higher and Advanced) - http://yp.direct.gov.uk/diplomas

Forum for Osteopathic Regulation in Europe (FORE) - www.forewards.eu

Open University - www.open.ac.uk

Osteopathy Today (monthly) (British Osteopathic Assocation) - www.osteopathy.org/

The Osteopath (6 x year) (General Osteopathic Council (GOsC)) - www.osteopathy.org.uk/resources/publications/the-osteopath/

Welsh Baccalaureate - www.wbq.org.uk

Addresses
British College of Osteopathic Medicine (BCOM)
Lief House, 120-122 Finchley Road, London NW3 5HR
Phone: +44 (0)20 7435 6464
Web: www.bcom.ac.uk

British Osteopathic Association (BOA)
3 Park Terrace Manor Road, Luton, Bedfordshire LU1 3HN
Phone: +44 (0)1582 488455
Web: www.osteopathy.org

British School of Osteopathy (BSO)
275 Borough High Street, London SE1 1JE
Phone: +44 (0)20 7407 0222
Web: www.bso.ac.uk

College of Osteopaths
13 Furzehill Road, Borehamwood, Hertfordshire WD6 2DG
Phone: +44 (0)20 8905 1937
Web: www.collegeofosteopaths.ac.uk

General Osteopathic Council (GOsC)
176 Tower Bridge Road, London SE1 3LU
Phone: +44 (0)20 7357 6655
Web: www.osteopathy.org.uk

London College of Osteopathic Medicine
8-10 Boston Place, London NW1 6QH
Phone: +44 (0)207 262 5250
Web: http://lcom.org.uk

Similar Jobs

Acupuncturist, Chiropractor, Naturopath, Physiotherapist, Reflexologist, Sports Therapist

Outdoor Activities Instructor

also known as: Outdoor Development Trainer

CRCI:Leisure, Sport and Tourism
CLCI:GAG Job Band: 2 to 5

Job Description

Outdoor activities instructors work with individuals or groups, to guide and instruct them in outdoor activities/pursuits such as climbing, sailing, skiing, abseiling, orienteering, caving, cycling, canoeing and mountaineering. Instructors develop a programme according to the ability of the group and help and encourage them to learn new skills and develop confidence. May also perform exercises in survival, problem solving, leadership and teamwork skills. Some activities are often residential and can vary in length, so may require a group to camp overnight, or for a longer period of time.

Instructors often have to organise evening social activities as well as daytime instruction. They make sure that all equipment is properly maintained and safe, and need to continuously monitor the weather conditions.

Work Details

Outdoor activities instructors are expected to work very long hours, including evenings and weekends. You give instruction to people of all ages and at all levels of experience and skill. You need to make sure that course members are safe. Sometimes you need to encourage people to tackle new challenges. Work is demanding and you have to be able to remain calm in an emergency or while working under pressure.

You may have to cope with considerable physical exertion, often in bad weather conditions. You have to wear protective clothing appropriate for different sports.

Qualification

• England, Wales and Northern Ireland

Band 2: For Sports Leaders UK basic expedition leadership award: academic qualifications are not specified, but it may be an advantage to have some GCSEs (A*-C) in subjects that include English and maths, or equivalent.

Band 3: For entry to jobs, HNC or a relevant Diploma in sport or exercise science, usually at least 4 GCSEs (A*-C) including English and maths, or equivalent.

Band 4: For BTEC higher national course in sport: usually 1-2 A levels and some GCSEs (A*-C) including English and maths, or equivalent.

Band 5: For degree course: 2-3 A levels, possibly including a science, and some GCSEs (A*-C) usually including English and maths, or equivalent. Exact requirements depend on the degree you take.

• Scotland

Band 2: For Sports Leaders UK basic expedition leadership award: academic qualifications are not specified, but it may be an advantage to have some S grades (1-3) in subjects that include English and maths, or similar.

Band 3: For entry to jobs or SQA national award in sport and leisure: usually four S grades (1-3) including English and maths, or similar qualifications.

Band 4: For entry to SQA higher national course in sport and recreation or professional development awards, usually 2-3 H grades and some S grades (1-3), including English and maths, or similar qualifications.

Band 5: For degree course: 3-5 H grades, possibly including a science, and some S grades (1-3) usually including English and maths, or similar qualifications. Exact requirements depend on the degree you take.

Degree Information

There are a limited number of outdoor education and leadership development degree courses but a wide range of relevant degrees in leisure studies, sports science or physical education. Graduates in non-relevant disciplines have to show evidence of ability and experience gained in extra-mural activities. Those employed at centres run by education authorities require a teaching qualification, usually a BEd degree followed by a postgraduate certificate in education (PGCE).

Adult Qualifications

This job attracts those who already have experience as a professional or serious amateur in their sport or activity. Qualifications in relevant outdoor activities are required and experience in teaching or group work is a considerable advantage.

Work Experience

Relevant work or voluntary experience is always useful and can improve your chances in application for entry to this job. Experience, either paid or voluntary, teaching or leading groups in your chosen sport or activity is useful, as is any work involving a teaching element, especially in the leisure sector.

Entry and Training

Skill and experience together with appropriate personal qualities are often more important than academic qualifications for this job. However, for employment by a local authority, it is usually necessary to have a teaching qualification, though not necessarily in physical exercise (PE). For some jobs, specialist qualifications from the governing body of the sport involved are required. Awards in a range of sports and activities such as canoeing, climbing and mountaineering, together with considerable practical experience, are usually needed. Obtaining these qualifications can be lengthy and may be expensive as there are few grants available for courses.

All outdoor education centres in the UK must meet the licence regulations of the Adventure Activities Licensing Authority, on behalf of the Health & Safety Executive, which sets high standards for staff qualifications. Details of basic expedition leadership awards at level 2 are available from Sports Leaders UK, which offers qualification for those in the community, including youth leaders and teachers. Those who are experienced outdoor activities instructors can apply to the Institute for Outdoor Learning for professional accreditation.

You can study for BTEC/SQA awards in sport, or sport and exercise sciences. There are foundation degrees in subjects such as outdoor adventure management, outdoor education, adventure sports management and sport and adventure studies. There are also relevant degrees and postgraduate qualifications in outdoor development/education/adventure. First aid qualifications are also needed. A Diploma/Welsh Baccalaureate may be available in your area in Sport and Active Leisure. Contact SkillsActive for further details. Relevant S/NVQs at levels 2-3 are available in subjects such as sport, recreation and allied occupations: activity leadership, and in outdoor programmes. Training programmes, including apprenticeship schemes in activity leadership and coaching, leading and instructing, may also be available in your area. Advanced apprenticeships leading to qualification at level 3 can also be a route into higher education.

Maturity is an advantage, but applicants must be extremely fit. Experience and/or qualifications in sports coaching, teaching and youth work is an advantage, as well as experience gained as a physical training instructor with the armed forces. You can benefit through government training opportunities, such as apprenticeship schemes in activity leadership, that may be available in your area. You can gain recognition of previous experience through Accreditation of Prior Learning (APL) or by working towards relevant S/NVQs. Contact your local careers office, Jobcentre Plus, Next Step service or Learning and Skills Council (LSC)/Local Enterprise Company (LEC) for details of all training opportunities and schemes, including apprenticeships for adults.

Opportunities and Pay
There are jobs with outdoor education centres run by local authorities, outward bound centres, or companies offering outdoor, adventure or activity holidays. Jobs are very often seasonal contracts with more jobs in sports such as sailing available during the summer and skiing in winter. Job prospects are improved if you have coaching qualifications for a number of different sports.

Salaries depend on location and employer. Starting salaries for outdoor activity instructors can be around £10k-£12k, rising to around £12k-£19k a year with experience. Senior instructors with extra responsibilities can earn £26k a year.

Health
This job requires a high level of fitness.

Skills and Qualities
able to cope under pressure, attention to detail, confident, energetic, enthusiastic, good organisational skills, leadership qualities, patient, reassuring, safety conscious

Relevant Subjects
Biology, English, Health and social care, Leisure, travel and tourism, Physical education and sport, Psychology, Science

Further Information
Adventure Activities Licensing Authority (AALA) (Adventure Activities Licensing Authority) - www.hse.gov.uk/aala

Apprenticeship Schemes (National Apprenticeship Service) - www.apprenticeships.org.uk

Diplomas (Foundation, Higher and Advanced) - http://yp.direct.gov.uk/diplomas

SkillsActive - sector skills council for active leisure, learning and well-being - www.skillsactive.com

Sports Leaders UK - www.sportsleaders.org

Training Schemes - www.direct.gov.uk/en/educationandlearning

Welsh Institute of Sport - www.welsh-institute-sport.co.uk

▶Working in travel & tourism (2010) (Babcock Lifeskills) - www.babcock-lifeskills.com/

▶Working outdoors (2010) (Babcock Lifeskills) - www.babcock-lifeskills.com/

Addresses
Institute for Outdoor Learning
Warwick Mill Business Centre , Warwick Bridge, Carlisle, Cumbria CA4 8RR
Phone: +44 (0)1228 564580
Web: www.outdoor-learning.org

Sport England
3rd Floor Victoria House, Bloomsbury Square, London WC1B 4SE
Phone: +44 (0)20 7273 1551
Web: www.sportengland.org

Sport Scotland
Doges, Templeton on the Green, 62 Templeton Street, Glasgow G40 1DA
Phone: +44 (0)141 534 6500
Web: www.sportscotland.org.uk

Sport Wales
National Sports Centre Sophia Gardens, Cardiff CF11 9SW
Phone: +44 (0)845 045 0904
Web: www.sports-council-wales.co.uk

Sports Coach UK
114 Cardigan Road, Headingley, Leeds LS6 3BJ
Phone: +44 (0)113 274 4802
Web: www.sportscoachuk.org

Sports Council Northern Ireland
House of Sport, 2a Upper Malone Road, Belfast BT9 5LA
Phone: +44 (0)28 9038 1222
Web: www.sportni.net

Similar Jobs
Community Learning & Development Officer (Scotland), Fitness Instructor, Leisure Manager, Riding Instructor, Sports Coach, Teacher: Physical Education

Packaging Technologist

CRCI:Manufacturing and Production
CLCI:SAP — Job Band: 4 to 5

Job Description
Packaging technologists develop and design packaging that can be produced safely, and economically in bulk, to suit the type of product. They often work in industries such as the pharmaceutical and food and drink industries. Where the goods are perishable, cleanliness and avoidance of contamination are important factors. Technologists use a wide variety of materials, including paper, foil, plastic and glass to develop suitable ways of ensuring that products are safe, clean, easy to use and attractive to customers. They examine existing packaging for ways to improve quality and make packaging more environmentally friendly. All labelling and description of contents must be clear and attractive.

Work involves many industrial areas, such as supply, design, production, sales and research. Packaging technologists work closely with graphic designers on aspects that include company branding and marketing for an individual product. They ensure that the packaging is attractive and appeals to the target market.

Work Details
Packaging technologists usually work a 39 hr week, Monday to Friday, though late finishes may be expected to meet deadlines. You work in an office, industrial premises or a laboratory and you may be responsible for keeping costs within an agreed budget and for the artistic effect of the packaging. May be part of a team of packaging technologists working with scientists and technicians. In a laboratory or industrial premises, you may need to wear protective clothing.

Qualification

- **England, Wales and Northern Ireland**

Band 4: For relevant BTEC higher national award/foundation degree: 1-2 A levels and some GCSEs (A*-C), preferably including maths and English and a science subject, or equivalent.

Band 5: For degree courses: 2-3 A levels, preferably including chemistry or biology plus some GCSEs (A*-C) usually including English and maths, or equivalent. The exact requirements depend on the degree you take.

- **Scotland**

Band 4: For SQA higher national award: usually 2-3 H grades and some S grades (1-3), preferably including maths and English and a science subject or similar qualifications.

Band 5: For degree courses: 3-5 H grades, preferably including chemistry or biology, plus some S grades (1-3) preferably including English and maths, chemistry or biology (1-3), or similar qualifications. Exact requirements depend on the degree you take.

Degree Information

Degree courses in materials science, physics, chemistry, industrial design, food science, food technology, and some engineering and graphic design subjects are all relevant. A degree in polymer technology is useful. A relevant postgraduate qualification is available.

Adult Qualifications

Most employers require a degree. Course entry qualifications may be relaxed for mature applicants with work experience in quality control, packaging operations, production engineering or a related area. Access courses may give adults a route into higher education courses.

Work Experience

Relevant work or voluntary experience is always useful and can improve your chances in application for entry to this career/job. The types of work experience to consider are in packaging supply and production companies or in a science-based job, especially where the main business is materials science.

Entry and Training

Training is on the job, usually after obtaining a relevant degree. There are courses specific to this job, but quite a few others that contain packaging modules. Foundation degrees in packaging design are also available. There are also relevant part-time and distance-learning courses for those working in the industry, such as the internationally recognised certificate or diploma of the Packaging Society offered at levels 3 and 4. Short specialist courses are also available. All courses lead to qualifications awarded by the Packaging Industry Awarding Body Company (PIABC). Check the website for details.

A Diploma/Welsh Baccalaureate in manufacturing and product design may be available in your area. The advanced level is equivalent to 3.5 A levels but for some university courses, the additional and specialist learning (ASL) component of the diploma needs to include specific A levels eg maths or chemistry. Check entry requirements carefully with the individual institutions.

Mature entrants with previous practical industrial experience may have an advantage and work as an engineering technician can also lead into entry at technologist level in the packaging industry. The Packaging Society runs a corporate packaging scheme to develop training programmes for companies.

Government training opportunities, such as an apprenticeship in paper and board manufacture may be available in your area. You can also gain recognition of previous experience through Accreditation of Prior Learning (APL) or by working towards relevant S/NVQs. Contact your local careers office, Jobcentre Plus, Next Step service or Learning and Skills Council (LSC) Local Enterprise Company (LEC) for details of training schemes.

Opportunities and Pay

Job prospects for packaging technologists look good. Due to pressure from environmentalists, the packaging industry has had to adapt and respond by becoming more innovative and developing increasingly sustainable packaging options. This has resulted in skills shortages. People entering this industry should also consider that there may be a need to relocate to find work at all levels.

You can be employed by a specialist packaging producer, a materials manufacturing company or a retail company. Other opportunities are with food and drink, chemical and engineering, manufacturing and processing companies. You may also be employed as a consultant.

Pay varies depending on location and employer but entrants are likely to earn around £20k a year, rising with experience to around £30k-£35k. A senior technologist may earn more than £48k a year.

Health

This job requires good colour vision for certain areas of work.

Skills and Qualities

analytical skills, attention to detail, creative flair, eye for shape/colour, good communication skills, good organisational skills, IT skills, problem-solving skills, scientific approach, technical aptitude

Relevant Subjects

Art and Design, Biology, Chemistry, Design and technology, Economics, Engineering, ICT/Computer studies, Manufacturing, Mathematics, Physics, Science

Further Information

Diplomas (Foundation, Higher and Advanced) - http://yp.direct.gov.uk/diplomas

Packaging Futures - www.packagingfutures.com

Packaging Professional (Packaging Society (IOM3)) - www.iom3.org/content/packaging-professional

Packaging Society (Division of Institute of Materials, Minerals and Mining) - www.iom3.org/packaging

Proskills UK - sector skills council for process and manufacturing industries - www.proskills.co.uk

Welsh Baccalaureate - www.wbq.org.uk

▶Working in manufacturing (2010) (Babcock Lifeskills) - www.babcock-lifeskills.com/

Addresses

Packaging Industry Awarding Body (PIABC)
The Boilerhouse Springfield Business Park Caunt Road, Grantham NG31 7FZ
Phone: +44 (0)1476 513884
Web: www.piabc.org.uk/piabc/piabc.htm

Similar Jobs

Engineer: Design, Leather Technologist, Materials Scientist/Engineer, Paper Technologist, Polymer/Plastics Technologist

Packer: General

CRCI:Manufacturing and Production
CLCI:SAB Job Band: 1

Job Description

Packers wrap or bag a range of products to protect them during delivery, to preserve them or to display them attractively. They work on a production line packing all sorts of finished goods and use bags, boxes, trays and crates in all sizes and in a wide variety of materials. Also may use additional packing material to further protect the goods, including bubble wrap or polystyrene beads. Some packers work with goods that need a specialised packing process to preserve its contents from decaying. Can wrap boxes, label them and seal them using glue, staples, shrink-wrap etc. Sometimes weighs the package ready for distribution.

Although most packers work on a production line, some may work in places such as an airport where a company offers a service to passengers to shrink-wrap their suitcases. This protects against theft when luggage is in transit. Some may work in the removals industry.

Needs to observe health and safety regulations at all stages of the packing process, and particularly when working with hazardous materials and substances. May use special machines such as hoists or conveyor belts for large and/or heavy goods that are difficult to handle, such as electrical white goods (washing machines and fridges) or machine parts and spares for cars.

Work Details

Packers usually work a 39 hr week that may include shifts and weekends. You work in industrial premises or a shop, and you may be expected to work overtime or shifts. The work is active most of the time and involves sitting or standing for many hours. You may have to lift and carry large objects and push heavy trolleys. Skill is needed when packing fragile items, and depending on the item being packed, conditions can be sterile, dusty or hot. Overalls are usually worn as well as some sort of hair covering.

Qualification

• England, Wales and Northern Ireland

Band 1: You do not require formal qualifications to do this work but employees must be able to read, and writing skills are important if form filling is required. Any formal/vocational qualifications are useful.

• Scotland

Band 1: You do not require formal qualifications to do this work though employees must be able to read, and writing skills are important if form filling is required. Some formal/vocational qualifications at any level are useful.

Adult Qualifications

General secondary education is expected. Formal or vocational qualifications at any level are helpful. You can improve your skills and qualifications by working through the Foundation Learning programme. This involves taking credit-based units and qualifications to help you progress.

Work Experience

Work or voluntary experience is always useful. It can add to your CV and improve your chances when applying for jobs or apprenticeships in the manufacturing industry. Your personal or adult guidance adviser should be able to advise you how to get some work experience.

Entry and Training

To enter this job you may have to take a test to show that you can work well with your hands. Training is on the job with an experienced member of staff and through the employer's training scheme. Packers in the removal industry require specialist training and it is possible to complete a nationally recognised apprenticeship. Contact the British Association of Removers (BAR) for details. In some jobs you may be required to have or to gain a fork-lift certificate of competence.

Relevant S/NVQs at levels 1-2 may be available, such as those for packaging operators and in warehousing and storage. Training programmes, including apprenticeships leading to level 2, may be available in your area. A Diploma/Welsh Baccalaureate in manufacturing and product design may be available in your area. This is for 14-19 year olds and can be a relevant introduction to this work.

Government training opportunities, such as apprenticeships, may be available in your area. You can also gain recognition of previous experience through Accreditation of Prior Learning (APL) or by working towards relevant S/NVQs. Contact your local careers office, Jobcentre Plus, Next Step service or Learning and Skills Council (LSC) Local Enterprise Company (LEC) for details of training schemes.

Opportunities and Pay

Packing jobs are available in companies of all sizes throughout the UK. These range from mail order companies, shipping/forwarding agents, contract packaging firms and warehouse storage companies to airport packing services and manufacturing companies. Other employers include removals firms, retailers, export and import companies. Purchases made over the Internet have grown, leading to increased demand for packers. Promotion to supervisory level is possible.

Pay varies depending on area and employer. A starting salary for a packer is likely to be around £9k-£11k a year, rising to £18k a year with experience. Pay can be increased by overtime pay or bonuses.

Health

This job requires good general fitness.

Skills and Qualities

able to follow instructions, able to work both on your own and in a team, able to work quickly, attention to detail, careful, neat, prepared to do repetitive tasks, safety conscious, strong hands

Further Information

Apprenticeship Schemes (National Apprenticeship Service) - www.apprenticeships.org.uk

Diplomas (Foundation, Higher and Advanced) - http://yp.direct.gov.uk/diplomas

Foundation Learning (QCDA) - www.qcda.gov.uk

Packaging Professional (Packaging Society (IOM3)) - www.iom3.org/content/packaging-professional

Training Schemes - www.direct.gov.uk/en/educationandlearning

Welsh Baccalaureate - www.wbq.org.uk

Addresses

British Association of Removers (BAR)
Tangent House, 62 Exchange Road, Watford WD18 0TG
Phone: +44 (0)1923 699480
Web: www.bar.co.uk

British Contract Manufacturers and Packers Association
St Mary's Court, The Broadway, Old Amersham, Buckinghamshire HP7 0UT
Phone: +44 (0) 1494 582013
Web: www.bcmpa.org.uk

Packaging Industry Awarding Body (PIABC)
The Boilerhouse Springfield Business Park Caunt Road, Grantham NG31 7FZ
Phone: +44 (0)1476 513884
Web: www.piabc.org.uk/piabc/piabc.htm

Similar Jobs

Assembler: Light Industry, Clothing Packer, Food Packaging Operative, Removals Operative, Warehouse Worker

Paediatrician

also known as: Doctor: Paediatrician

CRCI:Healthcare
CLCI:JAB Job Band: 5

Job Description

Paediatricians focus on the healthcare needs of children. The work can range from neonatal care, intensive care work with disabled children, arranging services in the community, to one-on-one care of a child with cancer. They always work in the best interests of the child and aim to minimise the impact of illness and subsequent treatments on their quality of life.

Work as part of a multi-disciplinary team to devise a schedule of treatment for a patient. May work in a hospital, a clinic or in a community setting. Take into account physical, psychological and social factors when assessing patients so may consult with other professionals including teachers, social workers and the police.

There are opportunities to develop links with primary care providers (GPs), child psychiatry services and those dealing with specific medical conditions such as diabetes or epilepsy.

Work Details

Doctors work on a shift system, which includes nights and weekends but, in line with new legislation, the average working week for doctors should not be longer than 48 hours.

Junior hospital doctors have to live in the hospital when on call. There is contact with children who are ill or in pain, and you may spend time advising and talking to parents or guardians. You have to make decisions about treatment and keep meticulous records. Work can be emotionally demanding and requires coping with the sight of blood. Paediatricians dress informally on ward rounds and display a sense of humour in an effort to put children at ease.

Qualification

• England, Wales and Northern Ireland

Band 5: For degree in medicine: usually three A levels, with good grades in chemistry and two from physics, biological sciences and maths, plus 5 GCSEs (A*-C) including English, or equivalent. Some medical schools offer a one-year pre-medical course for students with A levels in arts or mixed subjects. Check with individual schools for full details.

• Scotland

Band 5: For degree in medicine: usually five H grades, with good grades in chemistry and two from physics, biology and maths, plus five S grades (1-3) including English and maths, or similar. Normally science subjects not held at H grade should be offered at S grade. Some medical schools offer a one-year pre-medical course for students whose H grades do not include the required science subjects. Check with individual schools for full details.

Degree Information

A degree in medicine awarded by a university medical school and recognised by the General Medical Council is essential.

Adult Qualifications

Entry requirements are not normally relaxed for mature applicants, though those who consider applying should contact the individual university for advice. Graduates with a good honours degree in a related subject may obtain exemptions from certain options within the medical degree course.

Work Experience

Entry to this career is highly competitive and it is essential that you have some relevant work or voluntary experience before applying to train as a doctor. It can be difficult to gain work experience in a hospital as you have to be over 18 and have criminal record bureau clearance. Placements may be available in volunteering roles or hospital portering.

Assisting in a youth work setting or with children with disabilities or leaning difficulties can show your commitment to working in paediatrics. There may be opportunity to help out with childrens groups such as cub scouts or after schools clubs in your local area.

Entry and Training

Paediatricians must first qualify as medical doctors by completing a five-year degree in medicine, passing the postgraduate two-year Foundation Programme and registering as a doctor with the General Medical Council (GMC). For full details of medical training see the job article Doctor: Hospital.

After registration with the GMC, you begin your paediatrics training. Level 1 Paediatrics consists of three years basic training. On completion, you are assessed by taking the membership exam for the Royal College of Paediatrics and Child Health. You also have assessments within the hospital or other workplace setting.

Level 2 lasts for two years and consists of higher specialist training in three main areas; neonatal care, community child health and acute paediatrics. Assessment is workplace based. Finally, Level 3 paediatrics is where you choose your speciality and continue to broaden your experience in general paediatrics. This stage lasts a further three years and you are qualified to apply for a consultants role on completion.

Mature applicants with suitable qualifications are welcomed by medical schools and some may have reserved places for mature/graduate entrants. There are access courses to medicine and pre-medical foundation courses. Open University credits at distinction level may be accepted at some medical schools. Check with individual medical schools for details of all opportunities.

Opportunities and Pay

The majority of paediatricians work in district hospitals looking after babies and children with short or longer term illnesses. Some work in community health with children with special needs or disabilities, or general health issues such as immunisation or allergies. Neurodisability is a growth area in paediatrics as paediatricians become involved in the management of life-long neurological problems such as cerebral palsy or brain injury. Paediatricians also work in other specialist areas including gastro-enterology, endocrinology and oncology.

Paediatricians are usually employed by the NHS, a private hospital, a research organisation or a university medical school. There are opportunities abroad with voluntary organisations in developing countries, but pay is usually lower. Prospects may depend on willingness to move to another area to gain experience and obtain promotion. Some may teach or do research. There may be opportunities to work part time or job share.

Within the NHS, junior doctors earn a basic salary and are usually paid a supplement for extra hours worked. Basic salaries are around £32k a year (including a 50% supplement for extra hours), rising to £43k-£68k (including 50% supplement) for a doctor in specialist training. A consultant can earn £73k-£174k a year. These salaries do not include on-call payments, private income or London weighting allowances.

Health

There is a risk of infection. You should have no allergies and a good level of general fitness.

Skills and Qualities

able to inspire confidence, able to take responsibility, analytical skills, aptitude for teamwork, confident, discreet, emotionally strong, good listening skills, not squeamish, sense of humour

Relevant Subjects

Biology, Chemistry, English, Health and social care, Mathematics, Physics, Psychology, Science

Further Information

AGCAS: Health (Job Sector Briefing) (AGCAS) - www.prospects.ac.uk

British Association for Community Child Health - www.bacch.org.uk/index.php

British Medical Journal (weekly) (BMJ Publishing Group Ltd) - www.bmj.com/

Money for medical students - www.money4medstudents.org/

NHS Careers (NHS Careers) - www.nhscareers.nhs.uk

NHS Careers Scotland - www.infoscotland.com/nhs

NHS Careers Wales - www.wales.nhs.uk

NHS Foundation Programme - www.foundationprogramme.nhs.uk/pages/home

So you want to be a doctor - www.wanttobeadoctor.co.uk/main.php

The Lancet (weekly) (Elsevier Ltd) - www.thelancet.com/

UK Clinical Aptitude Test - www.ukcat.ac.uk

Addresses

British Medical Association (BMA)
BMA House, Tavistock Square, London WC1H 9JP
Phone: +44 (0)20 7387 4499
Web: www.bma.org.uk

General Medical Council (GMC)
Regents Place, 350 Euston Road, London NW1 3JN
Phone: +44 (0)161 923 6602
Web: www.gmc-uk.org

Open University (OU)
PO Box 197, Milton Keynes MK7 6BJ
Phone: +44 (0)845 300 6090
Web: http://www3.open.ac.uk

Royal College of Paedriatrics and Child Health
5-11 Theobald's Road, London WC1X 8SH
Phone: 020 7092 6000
Web: www.rcpch.ac.uk/Contact-Us

Royal College of Physicians (RCP)
11 St Andrew's Place, Regent's Park, London NW1 4LE
Phone: +44 (0)207 935 1174
Web: www.rcplondon.ac.uk

Similar Jobs

Doctor: General Practitioner, Doctor: Hospital, Pharmacist: Hospital, Psychologist: Neuropsychologist

Painter & Decorator

CRCI:Building and Construction
CLCI:UF — Job Band: 1 to 2

Job Description

Painters and decorators decorate the inside and outside of buildings. May work anywhere, from private households and small offices to multi-story office blocks, stately homes and five-star hotels. Jobs can be large such as restoring an old building, or small detailed projects. They also work on oil rigs, bridges and steel structures that require heavy duty coatings.

Can specialise in one area of work or use their skills across the range of jobs required. All surfaces must be prepared in advance of any painting to ensure that the area is smooth, clean and dry with no cracks or holes. The required paint or wallpaper is applied using a variety of tools such as rollers, brushes, sponges and sprays for painting. Spray painting is popular as it reduces labour costs. For decorating, uses a pasting table and brushes, sharp scissors, and a plumb line or spirit level to make sure the wall covering hangs as it should.

May use special techniques that include marbling and graining, rag rolling, stencils, applying gold leaf, sponging and putting up borders. Wall coverings include wallpaper, hessian and cork, lining or heavy duty paper and fabrics. Healthier water-based paints are replacing oil-based paints.

Work Details

Painters and decorators usually work a 39 hr week, Monday to Friday, though may need to work some weekends. Part-time work is available. May work in a team, but sometimes you work on your own. Work can be indoors or outdoors and you may need to travel to different sites. This work involves bending down, stretching, climbing ladders and perhaps working at heights on scaffolding, or on a mobile elevated platform. There may be a risk of falling. Daily tasks include cleaning brushes and other equipment at the end of the day, and ensuring that the work area is left clean and tidy. You need to wear overalls, sometimes a face mask and goggles, and also a safety helmet, if necessary.

Qualification

- **England, Wales and Northern Ireland**

Band 2: No minimum qualifications but some GCSEs including maths, English, design and technical subjects, or equivalent, are useful and are required by some employers. Relevant vocational qualifications are also useful.

- **Scotland**

Band 2: No minimum qualifications but some S grades including maths, English, design and technical subjects or similar, are useful and are required by some employers. Relevant vocational qualifications are also useful.

Adult Qualifications

Course entry requirements are usually relaxed for suitable mature applicants.

Work Experience

Relevant work or voluntary experience is always useful and can improve your chances when applying for entry to construction jobs and apprenticeships. A local firm of painters and decorators may offer you the opportunity to help with some tasks. Health and safety issues may mean that there are certain jobs you cannot do until you are over 16. Contact your local ConstructionSkills office for advice.

Entry and Training

Most entrants begin training through an approved ConstructionSkills scheme, such as a three-year Construction Apprenticeship Scheme (four years in Scotland), which you can apply for when in year 11 (January). Other schemes include work-based training at a ConstructionSkills centre and full-time work training with an employer, usually supported by day or block release to a local college. You may have to take an entrance test before you can start training. You are expected to gain a Construction Skills Certification Scheme (CSCS) card that indicates your level of experience and qualifications.

There are also one or two-year full or part-time college courses that you can take before applying for a job. Courses include a foundation certificate (FC) in building and craft occupations that is also available in some English and Welsh schools. The FC provides a progression route to a wide range of construction NVQs and other awards, after leaving school. A Diploma/Welsh Baccalaureate in construction and the built environment may be available in your area.

Specialist training is also available for those who wish to concentrate on achieving skills in restoration and heritage work. Contact the National Heritage Training Group (NHTG) for further information. S/NVQs at levels 1-3 are available in decorative finishing and industrial painting occupations. There are also ConstructionSkills awards (England and Wales) available for those who are unable to gain workplace experience for NVQs, such as the level 1-3 diploma in painting and decorating. Contact ConstructionSkills for details of all training routes.

Mature applicants can take refresher courses that are sometimes available for those returning to work and there may be special government training schemes, such as apprenticeships, available in your area. You can also gain recognition of previous experience through Accreditation of Prior Learning or by working towards relevant S/NVQs. Contact your local careers office, Jobcentre Plus, Next Step service or Learning and Skills Council (LSC)/Local Enterprise Company (LEC) for details of all training opportunities and schemes, including apprenticeships for adults.

If you have experience without formal qualifications, you can use On-Site Assessment and Training (OSAT) or the Experienced Worker Practical Assessment (EWPA) scheme to achieve a qualification. More information is available from the ConstructionSkills website.

Opportunities and Pay
You can work for a firm of painters and decorators, a painting contractor or building firm, or for a local authority. Many are self-employed and work for private households, or work as sub-contractors. In larger firms, there may be opportunities for promotion to supervisory level. Work abroad is also possible. Temporary, casual and seasonal work is often available for those who are sub-contractors or self-employed. With the right experience, some move into interior design. Availability of work depends to some extent on the state of the building trade and the national economy. Currently there is a downturn in the housing market which means there may be a shortage of vacancies.

Pay varies depending on area and employer. A trainee earns around £13k-£15k a year, rising to £16k-£22k with experience. Some earn up to £26k a year. Those who are self-employed may earn more depending on the success of the business. Incentive bonus schemes and overtime pay are possible. Employers may also give allowances for travel and cost of lodgings.

Health
Normal colour vision is necessary and you should not be allergic to paint or chemicals. This job requires stamina and a good level of physical fitness.

Skills and Qualities
able to work both on your own and in a team, able to work to deadlines, attention to detail, eye for shape/colour, good interpersonal skills, head for heights, manual dexterity, safety conscious

Relevant Subjects
Art and Design, Construction and built environment, Design and technology

Further Information
Apprenticeship Schemes (National Apprenticeship Service) - www.apprenticeships.org.uk

Careers in Building Conservation and Restoration (NHTG) (National Heritage Training Group) - www.nhtg.org.uk/careers

Construction Skills Certification Scheme (CSCS) - www.cscs.uk.com

ConstructionSkills - sector skills council for the construction industry - www.cskills.org

Diplomas (Foundation, Higher and Advanced) - http://yp.direct.gov.uk/diplomas

Welsh Baccalaureate - www.wbq.org.uk

►Working in construction & the built environment (2007) (Babcock Lifeskills) - www.babcock-lifeskills.com/

Addresses
National Heritage Training Group (NHTG)
Carthusian Court, 12 Carthusian Street, London EC1M 6EZ
Phone: 0300 456 5517 (UK only)
Web: www.nhtg.org.uk

Painting and Decorating Association
32 Coton Road, Nuneaton CV11 5TW
Phone: +44 (0)24 7635 3776
Web: www.paintingdecoratingassociation.co.uk

Similar Jobs
Advertising Installer, Glazier, Plasterer, Signwriter/Signmaker, Tiler: Wall & Floor

See where YOUR interests could take YOU!
Pathfinder live
www.pathfinderlive.com

Paintings Conservator-Restorer
also known as: Conservator-Restorer: Paintings

CRCI:Design, Arts and Crafts
CLCI:EZ Job Band: 4 to 5

Job Description
Conservators restore, clean, conserve, repair and maintain works of fine art such as oil and watercolour paintings, religious icons, painted ceilings, wall paintings and wooden panels. They look at the extent and cause of any damage and select appropriate methods and material for the item's repair and conservation. Then choose the correct treatment to stop further deterioration or to restore the work to its original condition. They may repair holes in a canvas, or add new backing to reinforce the structure. Involves carefully removing dirt, varnishing or for older restorations using a range of tools including scalpels, microscopes, X-rays and infrared photography.

They may use materials such as solvents and adhesives, or, if solvents cannot safely be used, may clean a surface using microfriction technology. Also liaise with other professionals such as conservation scientists and other conservator-restorers and provide an opinion about the authenticity and age of paintings, icons etc. Some specialise in areas such as traditional oil paintings, modern and contemporary art, icons or Old Masters.

Work Details
Usually work around 35-37 hrs a week; Monday to Friday, though this may vary according to the pressure of work. You can often work on your own or with a small group of colleagues in a studio, lab or on-site. You may need to work at heights. The work is very intricate and requires care and a high degree of accuracy. Travel is possible throughout the UK or abroad.

Qualification
There are no set minimum entry qualifications for training with an established paintings conservator-restorer, but most entrants complete full-time training before entering work, and many enter at degree/postgraduate level. Artistic ability and scientific knowledge are essential.

• England, Wales and Northern Ireland
Band 5: For degree courses: 2-3 A levels and some GCSEs (A*-C) usually including English, art and maths, or equivalent qualifications. Most conservation degree courses require A level, or equivalent, in chemistry. Exact requirements depend on the degree you take.

• Scotland
Band 5: For degree courses: 3-5 H grades and some S grades (1-3), usually including English, art and maths, or similar qualifications. Most conservation degree courses require H grade, or equivalent in chemistry. Exact entry requirements depend on the degree you take.

Degree Information
A first degree in fine art, history of art, conservation or natural sciences is relevant both for the work and for entry to postgraduate courses. Other degrees that lend themselves to this profession include chemistry, geology and archaeology.

Adult Qualifications
Adults applying for degree courses may not need the standard entry requirements. There are also art and design Access and foundation courses in some areas, which give adults without qualifications a route into higher education. Check with individual universities.

Work Experience
Entry to this job is very competitive and it is important that you try to do some relevant work or voluntary experience before applying. College and universities may also prefer applicants who have direct observation or practical experience of the type of work involved and of the work environment.

Working as a volunteer in an art gallery or museum is particularly useful, but there are also art shops that offer restoration services and freelance restorers who may provide valuable work experience opportunities. The National Association of Decorative Fine Arts Societies (NADFAS) runs a volunteer scheme.

Entry and Training

There are two ways of entering this profession: either through completion of a relevant postgraduate course, or by becoming a trainee and learning on the job in the studio of an established conservator-restorer. Competition is fierce for all vacancies. Vacancies for traineeships are increasingly rare and most entrants are postgraduates. Restorers who work in national galleries and museums are often civil service employees and have to meet nationality and residency requirements.

Relevant postgraduate courses are available at Courtauld Institute of Art, the Hamilton Kerr Institute (part of the University of Cambridge) and Northumbria University. The City and Guilds of London Art School offers a degree in conservation studies and area museums' councils run a range of in-service courses. Details are available from the Museums, Libraries and Archives Council.

If you manage to obtain a traineeship, you may have the opportunity to study part time for a relevant qualification. Prospective trainees can send their CV to the British Association of Painting Conservator-Restorers (BAPCR) who may forward it to any Fellows of the Association who require trainees.

Student membership of the BAPCR is available for students and trainees following courses or apprenticeships in paintings conservation and restoration. Fellowship, the professional qualification of the BACPR is open to those who have completed seven years' study and practical experience, and have passed a practical examination of their ability and knowledge. Joining the Institute of Conservation (ICON), the BAPCR or the Guild of Master Craftsmen helps to develop a professional reputation. ICON's Professional Accreditation of Conservator-Restorers (PACR) Scheme is a professional membership qualification.

Mature applicants with a skill in drawing or relevant craft qualifications and experience may have an advantage. For entry to a traineeship with a qualified restorer/conservator, no formal qualifications are needed, though vacancies are very limited. Most painter conservator-restorers have studied a relevant course at postgraduate level.

Opportunities and Pay

This field of work is very small though numbers employed in the private sector have increased over the past few years. Jobs may be available in museums and galleries, though most conservators work in the private sector in partnerships, small studios, or are self-employed. Work is contracted out from auction houses, private collectors, antique dealers, the National Trust, Historic Scotland, Cadw (Wales), and similar organisations.

Some paintings conservator-restorers are employed by universities, church authorities, archaeological departments or government bodies. Others specialise in research, enter teaching or choose to become conservation scientists. Jobs are sometimes available overseas for experienced conservator-restorers in countries such as the USA, Canada and Australia.

Salaries vary depending on location and employer. In public museums and galleries, salaries follow civil service grades, whereas in the private sector they vary widely, depending on experience and competence. Entry salaries at civil service grades tend to be initially higher than those in the private sector, but at the top of the profession, larger salaries are probably earned as a private restorer. Starting salaries for graduates are around £18k and with experience £20k-£25k a year. The most skilled and experienced restorers earn more than £36k a year.

Health

Glues and other adhesives can cause or aggravate skin problems and allergies. The fumes can also be a health hazard. You must have good eyesight and good colour vision for colour matching.

Skills and Qualities

able to work well on your own, analytical skills, artistic ability, attention to detail, careful, head for heights, manual dexterity, methodical, patient, scientific approach

Relevant Subjects

Art and Design, Chemistry, Design and technology, Science

Further Information

Creative & Cultural Skills - sector skills council for advertising, crafts, cultural heritage, design, literature, music, performing & visual arts - www.ccskills.org.uk

Museums, Libraries and Archives Council - www.mla.gov.uk

The Burlington Magazine (Burlington Magazine Publications Ltd.) www.burlington.org.uk

The Picture Restorer (BAPCR) - www.thepicturerestorer.co.uk/index.html

▶Working in art & design (2009) (Babcock Lifeskills) - www.babcock-lifeskills.com/

Addresses

British Association of Paintings Conservator-Restorers (BAPCR)
PO Box 258, Blofield, Norwich NR13 4WY
Phone: +44 (0)1603 516237
Web: www.bapcr.org.uk

Guild of Master Craftsmen
166 High Street, Lewes, East Sussex BN7 1XU
Phone: +44 (0)1273 478449
Web: www.guildmc.com

Institute of Conservation (ICON)
1st Floor, Downstream Building 1 London Bridge Road SE1 9BG
Phone: +44 (0)20 7785 3807
Web: www.icon.org.uk

National Association of Decorative and Fine Arts Societies (NADFAS)
NADFAS House, 8 Guilford Street, London WC1N 1DA
Phone: +44 (0)20 7430 0730
Web: www.nadfas.org.uk

Similar Jobs

Archivist, Artist, Conservator-Restorer, Museum/Art Gallery Curator

Palaeontologist

CRCI:Science, Mathematics and Statistics
CLCI:QOL Job Band: 5

Job Description

Palaeontologists study ancient life-forms and their environments. There are four main branches of the subject. Vertebrate palaeontology is the study of fossil animals with backbones, such as fish and dinosaurs; invertebrate is of larger fossil animals without a backbone, like sponges and corals. Micropalaeontology is the study of small organisms whose shells and skeletons are found in fossils, and palaeobotany looks at plant fossils.

Participating in field trips is common and usually leads to data being collected for research and publication. Palaeontologists examine fossils from sites all over the world and note the occurrence of the properties of life-forms to establish their place in the evolutionary history of the Earth. They record, analyse, interpret and map observations and data. Then apply their findings to other related fields to enhance scientific understanding.

Palaeontologist

Usually work in a team, advising and consulting with colleagues and may supervise and organise students and staff. There is a significant academic role in research and teaching or lecturing, usually in universities. This involves writing proposals for research, and papers and articles for presentation to others in this and related fields. These are often presented at seminars and conferences worldwide. In most jobs there are administrative tasks associated with the role.

Work Details

Usually work a basic 35-40 hr week, Monday to Friday, though may be expected to work irregular hours, sometimes away from home, including evenings and weekends. You spend time working in a laboratory and office, often in a research establishment or a university. This work requires the use of computers, often using sophisticated programmes for data interpretation and modelling.

Palaeontological work often involves some physical activity as well as working in cold, damp or very hot conditions. There is a risk of minor injuries and at times you need to wear protective clothing, including a helmet and boots.

Qualification

A good level of written English is invaluable for concise presentation of ideas in scientific papers, articles and dissertations.

• England, Wales and Northern Ireland

Band 5: For degree courses: 2-3 A levels, including a science and maths, and some GCSEs (A*-C) usually including English and maths, or equivalent. Exact requirements depend on the degree you take.

• Scotland

Band 5: For degree courses: 3-5 H grades, preferably including maths and a science subjects, and some S grades (1-3), usually including English and maths, or similar qualifications. Exact requirements depend on the degree you take.

Degree Information

Geology, geoscience, chemistry, physics, biosciences, maths or computing are the most useful degree subjects. Postgraduate courses in palaeontology are available for those with a relevant degree.

Adult Qualifications

Entry requirements may be relaxed for adults applying for higher education courses and Access or foundation courses give adults without qualifications a route on to degree courses.

Work Experience

Entry to this job is very competitive and it is important that you try to do some relevant work or voluntary experience before applying to both jobs and university degrees. There are several NERC centres around the country that may take people on work experience.

Entry and Training

There is no set route to becoming a palaeontologist, and different specialist areas have different requirements. Most complete a degree in geology, but other science and geoscience degrees are acceptable, as are environmental subjects and geography. Computer sciences, maths and geoinformatics are also very useful. Botany and zoology are less common, but are also useful for some specialisations. First degree courses in palaeontology, palaeobiology, evolution and palaeoenvironments are offered at the universities of Bristol, Portsmouth and Birmingham. Swansea offers computer science and geo-informatics, which has relevance in this subject, and Plymouth offers geology with a palaeontology slant.

Postgraduate qualifications are usual. You are expected to complete original research to achieve a masters or PhD, usually under the guidance of a professional palaeontologist. Fieldwork is an essential part of this job. As palaeontology is a multidisciplinary subject, interest in related fields, for example ecology, comparative anatomy or evolution, is encouraged.

Training is by practical work experience, in-house short courses or sometimes a residential course. Short study periods may often take place overseas. You need to follow a programme of continuing professional development (CPD) to update your knowledge.

Mature entrants require a degree or equivalent qualification, and employers may sponsor staff on postgraduate courses. There is an Open University distance-learning degree course in natural sciences with earth sciences. You may apply to the Natural Environmental Research Council (NERC) for postgraduate study and research.

Opportunities and Pay

This is a very small field and posts are usually in academic institutions, in teaching or research, or in curatorial work in museums. The greatest number of non-academic job opportunities are in the fields of invertebrate palaeontology, where there is a reasonably healthy commercial market for specialists, or micropalaeontology where the study of microfossils is vital to oil exploration. Jobs are with oil, gas and mining companies. There may also be opportunities with the British Geological Survey (BGS) or the British Antarctic Survey (BAS), both part of the Natural Environment Research Council (NERC).

There are opportunities to work abroad, often on short-term contracts. You may progress to senior scientist or managerial level in a company or senior lecturer or research fellow in a university.

Pay varies depending on type of company, location and experience but is from around £25k a year, rising to around £40k a year with experience. Starting salaries for higher education lecturers do vary depending on the individual institution, but are usually around £29k a year, with senior lecturers earning up to £55k. Salaries in London are usually higher.

Health

This job requires normal colour vision for certain areas of work as well as overall good health.

Skills and Qualities

administrative skills, analytical skills, aptitude for fieldwork, aptitude for maths and science, attention to detail, good at writing reports, good communication skills, observant, problem-solving skills, research skills, specialist IT skills

Relevant Subjects

Biology, Chemistry, English, Geography, ICT/Computer studies, Land and Environment, Mathematics, Physics, Science

Further Information

Jobs in Research, Science, Academic & Related Professions - www.jobs.ac.uk

Rockwatch (Natural History Museum) - www.rockwatch.org.uk/

The Micropalaeontological Society (NHM) - www.nhm.ac.uk/

The Palaeontological Association - http://palass.com

The Palaeontological Society - http://paleosoc.org/

Addresses

British Antarctic Survey (BAS)
High Cross,, Madingley Road, Cambridge CB3 0ET
Phone: +44 (0)1223 221400
Web: www.antarctica.ac.uk

British Geological Survey (BGS)
Kingsley Dunham Centre, Keyworth, Nottingham NG12 5GG
Phone: +44 (0)115 936 3143
Web: www.bgs.ac.uk

Natural Environment Research Council (NERC)
Polaris House North Star Avenue, Swindon, Wiltshire SN2 1EU
Phone: +44 (0)1793 411 500
Web: www.nerc.ac.uk

Natural History Museum
Cromwell Road, London SW7 5BD
Phone: +44 (0)20 7942 5000
Web: www.nhm.ac.uk

Open University (OU)
PO Box 197, Milton Keynes MK7 6BJ
Phone: +44 (0)845 300 6090
Web: http://www3.open.ac.uk

Similar Jobs

Archaeologist, Geologist, Geophysicist, Lecturer: Higher Education, Museum/Art Gallery Curator, Oceanographer

Paper Manufacturing Operative

also known as: Paper Mill Worker

CRCI:Manufacturing and Production
CLCI:SAP Job Band: 1 to 2

Job Description

Paper manufacturing operatives are responsible for completing one or more of a variety of specialised tasks involved in the manufacture of paper in paper mills. They also deal with recovery and recycling plants. They work with computerised machinery that makes paper, tissue or card from wood pulp, cotton pulp, or recycled waste paper. Operatives manage computerised controls that add chemicals and water to make the paper mixture into a pulp. Machines then extract the water from the pulp to make the paper product. The reels of paper are changed using a lifting machine and specialised machines coat, polish and cut the paper.

Some workers may test the product at various stages of manufacture. Some may be involved in packing processes. Others work with the technical staff in the development of new products and improvement of existing ones. Manufacturing operatives also work closely with maintenance engineers to ensure the mill/plant runs smoothly and efficiently.

Work Details

Paper manufacturing operatives work a basic 39-40 hr week, Monday to Friday. This can include shift work, including evenings, nights and weekends. You work in a mill that usually operates over 24 hrs each day. You are responsible for safety and have to cope with working with large machines, possibly climbing ladders and some lifting. Paper mill processes are mostly controlled by computers so the work environment has seen improvements such as soundproof work rooms, but some mills can still be hot and noisy. There is a risk of accidents from equipment. You need to wear overalls and possibly safety glasses and boots.

Qualification

• England, Wales and Northern Ireland

Band 1: No minimum qualifications are required, but you are expected to have a good level of general education. However, some formal/vocational qualifications at any level are useful. Some employers may ask for aptitude in science or technology.

Band 2: Although academic qualifications are not specified for this job, it is an advantage to have some GCSEs (A*-G) in subjects that include English and maths, or equivalent.

• Scotland

Band 1: No minimum qualifications are required, but you are expected to have a good level of general education. However, some formal/vocational qualifications at any level are useful.

Band 2: Although academic qualifications are not specified for this job, it is an advantage to have some S grades (1-5) in subjects that include English and maths, or similar.

Adult Qualifications

No pre-entry qualifications are usually required though some academic/vocational qualifications at any level may be an advantage. English and maths are useful subjects.

Work Experience

Relevant work or voluntary experience is always useful and can improve your chances when applying for entry to jobs or apprenticeships in the manufacturing sector. Your personal or adult guidance adviser should be able to advise you about how to organise work experience with an employer.

Entry and Training

Training is on the job through an employer's training scheme, usually with an appropriate day-release course at a local college. Applicants must be at least 18 for shift work and for certain other tasks, although most employees are older. Apprenticeships may be available - Proskills, the sector skills council for process and manufacturing industries, runs an apprenticeship in paper and board manufacture.

There are also certificates in paper technology at levels 2 and 3 offered by the Confederation of the Paper Industry. The Institute of Paper, Printing and Publishing (IP3) offers a modular certificate course that is specifically designed as an introduction to the paper, printing and publishing sectors. On successful completion of the programme, students are awarded the IP3 Certificate.

Appropriate S/NVQs at levels 1-3 are available. A Diploma/Welsh Baccalaureate in manufacturing and product design may be available in your area. This can be taken at school and provides a good introduction to working in manufacturing.

Government training opportunities, such as an apprenticeship in paper and board manufacture may be available in your area. You can also gain recognition of previous experience through Accreditation of Prior Learning (APL) or by working towards relevant S/NVQs. Contact your local careers office, Jobcentre Plus, Next Step service or Learning and Skills Council (LSC) Local Enterprise Company (LEC) for details of training schemes.

Opportunities and Pay

In total, the paper and board industry employs over 71,000 people in over 2,000 workplaces. You can be employed by a paper mill or paper recovery/recycling plant. These are mainly located in Scotland, north-west England, Yorkshire, the East Midlands and the South East. Some jobs at operational level have decreased due to new technologies. However, others in this industry, particularly involved with recycling, have recently increased. Workers who show aptitude may progress to become a technologist. You can move into quality control, marketing and sales, engineering, supervisory or management, and other areas of work within the industry. Papermaking is an expanding and global business with opportunities at home and overseas.

Pay varies depending on location and employer but trainees are likely to start at around £12k, rising to £22k with experience and qualifications. Pay may be increased through shift work, overtime and bonuses.

Health

There is an allergy risk from skin irritants. This job may require a medical and fitness test on entry.

Skills and Qualities

able to follow instructions, able to operate equipment, aptitude for teamwork, careful, good concentration level, methodical, numeracy skills, practical skills, safety conscious

Relevant Subjects

Design and technology, Manufacturing

Further Information

Apprenticeship Schemes (National Apprenticeship Service) - www.apprenticeships.org.uk

Careers in Paper (Proskills) - www.prospect4u.co.uk

Diplomas (Foundation, Higher and Advanced) - http://yp.direct.gov.uk/diplomas

Proskills UK - sector skills council for process and manufacturing industries - www.proskills.co.uk

Training Schemes - www.direct.gov.uk/en/educationandlearning
Welsh Baccalaureate - www.wbq.org.uk

Addresses

Confederation of Paper Industries (CPI)
1 Rivenhall Road, Swindon, Wiltshire SN5 7BD
Phone: +44 (0)1793 889 600
Web: www.paper.org.uk

Institute of Paper, Printing & Publishing (IP3)
Runnymede Malthouse, off Hummer Road, Egham,
Surrey TW20 9BD
Phone: 0870 330 8625 (UK only)
Web: www.ip3.org.uk

Paper Industry Technical Association (PITA)
5 Frecheville Court, Bury, Lancashire BL9 0UF
Phone: +44 (0)161 764 5858
Web: www.pita.co.uk

Similar Jobs

Engineering Machine Operative, Polymer/Plastics Process Operative, Textile Machinery Technician

Paper Technologist

CRCI:Manufacturing and Production
CLCI:SAP Job Band: 4 to 5

Job Description

Paper technologists work in a paper mill and are involved in designing and testing equipment and processes for use in the manufacture of paper-based products. These can include tissues and corrugated board. They use raw materials such as recycled paper, wood pulp, and cotton pulp to produce a wide range of paper and boards that are used by industry. This includes products such as newspapers, magazines, packaging products, stationery, high quality art paper, lavatory paper and wallpaper.

May be involved in testing raw materials, manufacture, quality control or technical sales. Technologists coordinate trials of new products and analyse results from the trials and from laboratory tests. Some technologists carry out research on uses of new improved paper. They write technical reports for clients and production managers.

Work Details

Paper technologist usually works a 39-40 hr week and may be required to work shifts and have occasional late finishes. Those in senior positions usually work Monday to Friday, though may be required to be on call at times. You work in industrial premises, an office or a laboratory and advise, supervise and consult with people, as well as being responsible for efficient production and for keeping costs within an agreed budget. You may supervise the work of laboratory staff. You may have to cope with some physical activity, and need to wear an overall or possibly protective clothing.

Qualification

• England, Wales and Northern Ireland

Band 4: For BTEC higher national award: 1-2 A levels (including a science based subject) and some GCSEs (A*-C), preferably including maths and English and a science subject, or equivalent.

Band 5: For degree course: 2-3 A levels (preferably including at least one science subject) plus some GCSEs (A*-C), preferably including maths and English, and a science subject. The exact requirements depend on the degree to be taken.

• Scotland

Band 4: For SQA higher national award: usually 2-3 H grades (including a science-based subject) and some S grades (1-3) preferably including maths and English, and a science subject, or similar qualifications.

Band 5: For degree course: 3-5 H grades (preferably including at least one science subject) and some S grades (1-3), preferably including maths and English, and a science subject, or similar. Exact requirements depend on the degree you take.

Degree Information

Relevant degree subjects in applied science, materials science, engineering and chemistry are usual, with some courses such as chemical engineering and chemistry having a specialisation in paper science/technology. Check course contents carefully.

Adult Qualifications

Entry requirements may be relaxed for adults applying for higher education courses and Access to higher education courses give adults without qualifications a route on to degree courses.

Work Experience

Relevant work or voluntary experience is always useful and can improve your chances in application for entry to this career/job. The types of work experience to consider are in paper/packaging supply and production companies, or in a science-based job, especially where the main business is materials science.

Entry and Training

Most paper technologists take a relevant degree or HND prior to entry to the work. Once working, training is likely to be on the job, with entrants gaining experience of different areas of the work. The University of Manchester offers a postgraduate course in paper science. There are also short courses available on detailed topics available from the Confederation of Paper Industries and the Paper Industry Technical Association. Some people progress to this work after experience at a technical level in the paper making industry. They usually combine their work-based training with study for a relevant HNC/HND or degree course.

A Diploma/Welsh Baccalaureate in manufacturing and product design may be available in your area. The advanced level is equivalent to 3.5 A levels but for some university courses, the additional and specialist learning (ASL) component of the diploma needs to include specific A levels eg maths or chemistry. Check entry requirements carefully with the individual institutions.

Government training opportunities, such as an apprenticeship in paper and board manufacture may be available in your area. You can also gain recognition of previous experience through Accreditation of Prior Learning (APL) or by working towards relevant S/NVQs. Contact your local careers office, Jobcentre Plus, Next Step service or Learning and Skills Council (LSC) Local Enterprise Company (LEC) for details of training schemes.

Opportunities and Pay

There are work opportunities with paper manufacturing companies (paper mills). These are situated in certain areas of the UK, Scotland, the North West and Yorkshire, Wales, the East Midlands and South East. Other opportunities may be with a research organisation and with companies that supply machinery and chemicals to the mills. There are opportunities to work abroad. It is usually necessary to move to another employer and gain more responsibility in order to improve your employment prospects.

Pay varies depending on location, type and size of employer. Paper technologists start earning in the region of £20k-£26k rising to around £33k a year.

Health

Good physical fitness is required and you should not be allergic to dust.

Skills and Qualities

analytical skills, aptitude for maths and science, attention to detail, good communication skills, IT skills, perseverance, problem-solving skills, technical aptitude

Relevant Subjects
Chemistry, Design and technology, Engineering, English, ICT/Computer studies, Manufacturing, Mathematics, Physics, Science

Further Information
AGCAS: Manufacturing (Job Sector Briefing) (AGCAS) - www.prospects.ac.uk

Careers in Paper (Proskills) - www.prospect4u.co.uk

Diplomas (Foundation, Higher and Advanced) - http://yp.direct.gov.uk/diplomas

Training Schemes - www.direct.gov.uk/en/educationandlearning

Welsh Baccalaureate - www.wbq.org.uk

Addresses
Confederation of Paper Industries (CPI)
1 Rivenhall Road, Swindon, Wiltshire SN5 7BD
Phone: +44 (0)1793 889 600
Web: www.paper.org.uk

Institute of Paper, Printing & Publishing (IP3)
Runnymede Malthouse, off Hummer Road, Egham, Surrey TW20 9BD
Phone: 0870 330 8625 (UK only)
Web: www.ip3.org.uk

Paper Industry Technical Association (PITA)
5 Frecheville Court, Bury, Lancashire BL9 0UF
Phone: +44 (0)161 764 5858
Web: www.pita.co.uk

University of Manchester
Oxford Road, Manchester M13 9PL
Phone: +44 (0)161 306 6000
Web: www.manchester.ac.uk

Similar Jobs
Engineer: Design, Materials Scientist/Engineer, Packaging Technologist, Production Manager

Paralegal
also known as: Certified Paralegal, Legal Support Assistant

CRCI:Legal and Political Services

CLCI:LAZ — Job Band: 3 to 5

Job Description
Paralegals undertake a substantial amount of legal work, but are not qualified lawyers. They may support and assist lawyers and do a wide variety of tasks ranging from assisting solicitors in routine tasks, to more complex tasks that are similar to those performed by a trainee solicitor. Some paralegals have their own case load and have contact with clients and senior lawyers, but all the work is under the supervision of a qualified lawyer.

Most paralegals work in a wide range of organisations doing many different types of legal work. Some may work in a community legal service, such as Citizens Advice, and those who work in government analyse legal material for internal use. Experienced paralegals manage and supervise teams as well as being involved in the more complex legal work.

Work Details
You usually work regular office hours, Monday to Friday, though longer hours may be required at times. You are based in an office, but if assisting a solicitor involved in litigation, you may regularly visit a court of law. You may be required to operate office equipment, such as a photocopier or fax machine, as well as a computer. Close attention to detail is needed when gathering information and researching cases. You often have to work to tight deadlines.

Qualification
- **England, Wales and Northern Ireland**

Band 3: For entry to jobs, HNC or a relevant Diploma, usually at least 4 GCSEs (A*-C) including English and maths, or equivalent.

Band 4: For entry: many employers ask for 1-2 A levels or equivalent, plus at least 3-4 GCSEs (A*-C) including English and possibly maths, or equivalent.

Band 5: For degree in law, legal studies or similar: 2-3 A levels, usually including English and maths, and some GCSEs (A*-C), including English and possibly a modern language, or equivalent qualifications. Exact requirements depend on the degree you take.

- **Scotland**

Band 3: For entry to some jobs: usually four S grades (1-3) including English, or similar.

Band 4: For entry: many employers ask for three H grades including English, plus at least 3-4 S grades (1-3) possibly including maths, or similar qualifications.

Band 5: For degree in law, legal studies or similar: usually four H grades or similar and some S grades (1-3), or similar. English and maths are needed, possibly at H grade. Exact entry requirements depend on the course you take.

Degree Information
Degrees in subjects such as legal studies or law are the most appropriate.

Adult Qualifications
Entry requirements may be relaxed for adults applying for degree courses. Check with individual colleges and universities.

Work Experience
Work experience gives you an insight into what you enjoy and do not enjoy about a job or working environment, as well as the opportunity to acquire new skills. It also provides valuable information to add to your CV and improves your future employment prospects. Entry to this job is competitive and therefore it is important that you try to do some relevant paid or unpaid work in a law environment before applying. Experience of office and administration work, or working with the public and giving people advice, is also an advantage.

Entry and Training
There are no specific entry requirements for this work. Some entrants go straight from school with GCSEs/S grades (A*-C/1-3). Many firms prefer higher qualifications and look for A levels/H grades or BTEC/SQA awards in legal studies. Some employees favour law graduates who also may have taken either the legal practice course or the bar vocational course. These entrants may take this type of work while looking for a training contract or barrister's pupillage.

Training is usually on the job and may also include study for paralegal qualifications, such as those offered by the Institute of Paralegals, the Scottish Paralegal Association and the National Association of Licensed Paralegals. Most courses can be studied part time or through distance learning. See their websites for details. Currently, there is no nationally agreed framework for the recognition of paralegal training programmes, though this may change.

The Institute of Legal Executives (ILEX) in conjunction with City & Guilds offers vocational qualifications at levels 2-3. Contact ILEX for further details. The College of Law has recently developed courses in Legal Support Skills. Available on CD-Rom, the courses are aimed at legal secretaries and paralegals. The highest level of paralegal training is the specialist paralegal qualification, offered in association with the University of Strathclyde in Scotland and the University of the West of England in Bristol.

Adult entry is common particularly for mature entrants with previous experience of working in a legal environment. This work can be an option for law graduates who have not found training contracts and for lawyers from overseas.

Opportunities and Pay

This is a growing profession with vacancies throughout the UK. There are over 500,000 paralegals in the UK, with around 50,000 working for firms of solicitors. Other opportunities exist within the courts service, local and national government, Citizens Advice, the police and with large organisations with legal departments. Many firms now offer a career structure leading to senior paralegal and paralegal manager status. Flexible work is possible as there is a tendency for some paralegals to be employed on short-term contracts.

You may choose to work towards training as a legal executive and then a solicitor, or take professional qualifications in the area in which you work (eg trading standards).

Pay depends on the size and location of employer. Starting salaries for paralegals are around £16k-£20k a year, rising to around £30k-£40k a year, depending on the level of responsibility and experience. You also receive the full range of corporate benefits and may receive overtime payments.

Skills and Qualities

able to cope under pressure, attention to detail, awareness of confidentiality issues, good communication skills, good interpersonal skills, good organisational skills, good written English, information handling skills, IT skills, research skills

Relevant Subjects

Business and accounting, English, Law

Further Information

Citizens Advice - www.citizensadvice.org.uk
College of Law - www.college-of-law.co.uk
Law Gazette (Law Society) - www.lawgazette.co.uk
Scottish Paralegal Association - www.scottish-paralegal.org.uk
Skills for Justice - sector skills council for the UK justice system - www.skillsforjustice.com
Society of Specialist Paralegals - www.specialistparalegals.co.uk
TARGETjobs: Law (GTI Specialist Publishing Ltd.) - www.groupgti.com
TARGETjobs: Law Scotland (GTI Specialist Publishing Ltd.) - www.groupgti.com
▶Working in politics & law (2010) (Babcock Lifeskills) - www.babcock-lifeskills.com/

Addresses

ILEX Paralegal Programmes
Kempston Manor, Bedfordshire MK42 7AB
Phone: +44 (0)1234 841000
Web: www.ilexpp.co.uk

Institute of Paralegals
No.1 Poultry, London EC2R 8JR
Phone: +44 (0) 20 7099 9122
Web: www.instituteofparalegals.org

Law Society of Scotland
26 Drumsheugh Gardens, Edinburgh EH3 7YR
Phone: +44 (0)131 226 7411
Web: www.lawscot.org.uk

National Association of Licensed Paralegals
Admissions , 3.08 Canterbury Court, , Kennington Business Park , 1 - 3 Brixton Road, London SW9 6DE
Phone: +44 (0) 20 3176 0900
Web: http://national-paralegals.co.uk

Similar Jobs

Law Costs Draftsman, Legal Executive, Secretary: Legal, Solicitor

Paraplanner

also known as: Financial Services Administrator

CRCI:Financial Services
CLCI:NAK

Job Band: 3 to 4

Job Description

Paraplanners support financial advisers and planners by researching and recommending financial products that meet the clients needs. Give administrative support by writing letters, reports and proposals for the client to consider and then processing the paperwork relating to the products that the client selects.

They keep client records and help the financial adviser with client reviews of their financial portfolio. Liaise with the providers of financial products and keep the financial adviser up to date with any changes to products. Some also attend meetings with financial planners and clients to take notes.

Paraplanners are aware of the financial products that are available and any changes to financial law and legislation. They keep up to date with new developments in the financial markets and make sure that all work meets Financial Services Authority standards.

Work Details

Usually work 9am-5pm, Monday to Friday, with occasional work required beyond these hours. Most paraplanners are office based and may work within a team supporting a number of financial planners. Work can be fast-paced and may be stressful at times.

Qualification

- **England, Wales and Northern Ireland**

Band 3: For entry: usually at least 4 GCSEs (A*-C) including English and maths, or equivalent. IT skills are useful.

Band 4: For a relevant foundation degree in financial services: one A level and four GCSEs (A*-C) or equivalent.

- **Scotland**

Band 3: For entry: usually at least four S grades (1-3) including English and maths, or similar. IT skills are useful.

Band 4: For relevant SQA higher national award: usually 2-3 H grades and some S grades (1-3), often including English and maths, or similar qualifications.

Adult Qualifications

Employers expect a good standard of secondary education, an understanding of numbers and the ability to communicate well in writing. IT skills are useful.

Work Experience

Relevant work or voluntary experience is always useful and can improve your employment prospects when applying for entry to jobs. Working in an office, particularly in a financial environment using administration skills or working with numbers is useful. Experience of basic accounting skills is also an advantage.

Entry and Training

Employers look for personality and communication skills as well as the basic academic qualifications. Entrants are expected to have a good understanding of numbers and excellent written communication skills. Paraplanners are usually trained on the job and encouraged by employers to study for examinations.

There are a range of professional customer service and administration qualifications available. These include the Chartered Insurance Institute certificate in financial administration and the Chartered Institute of Bankers in Scotland certificate in sales and service. The ifs School of Finance also offers relevant customer service qualifications and has recently introduced a specific level 4 qualification for paraplanners which focuses on researching the market on behalf of financial advisers.

The Institute of Financial Planning also offers the Certificate in Paraplanning and exam workshops. Check the websites for details.

Foundation degrees in financial services can be a useful route into this job. Relevant training programmes, including apprenticeship schemes in advising on financial products may also be available in your area. Advanced apprenticeships leading to qualification at level 3 can be a route into higher education. A Diploma/Welsh Bacclaureate in business, adminstration and finance may also be available in your area, and may provide a useful start to this career.

Mature entrants with relevant experience, or who are looking to change career, can find opportunities to work as a paraplanner.

Opportunities and Pay

There are around 35,000 paraplanners in the UK and there are opportunities to work in towns and cities nationwide. Ongoing changes to the financial services industry may increase opportunities to advise the public on financial products in the future. Employers include insurance brokers, firms of independent financial advisers, life assurance, investment and pensions companies, banks, building societies and accountants.

It is possible to progress to supervisory positions by taking further professional qualifications. Some paraplanners move on to become mortgage or financial advisers.

New entrants are likely to earn around £15k-£20k a year, rising to £22k-£40k with experience. Senior paraplanners can earn more than this. Bonuses may also be paid as a percentage of sales of the team or the individual financial adviser you work for.

Skills and Qualities

attention to detail, confident, customer service skills, good telephone manner, good written English, IT skills, numeracy skills, research skills, time management skills, trustworthy

Relevant Subjects

Business and accounting, Economics, English, ICT/Computer studies, Law, Mathematics

Further Information

Apprenticeship Schemes (National Apprenticeship Service) - www.apprenticeships.org.uk
CII Pathways - www.pathways.cii.co.uk
Diploma in Business, Administration and Finance - www.baf-diploma.org.uk/
Financial Services Skills Council - sector skills council for financial services, accountancy & finance www.fssc.org.uk/
Inside Careers Guide: Banking, Securities & Investments - www.insidecareers.co.uk
Institute of Financial Planning - www.financialplanning.org.uk/planners/ifp.cfm
TARGETjobs: City and Finance (GTI Specialist Publishers Ltd) - www.groupgti.com
The Paraplanner - www.the paraplanner.com
Welsh Baccalaureate - www.wbq.org.uk
▶Working in business, administration & finance (2010) (Babcock Lifeskills) - www.babcock-lifeskills.com/
▶Working in maths (2009) (Babcock Lifeskills) - www.babcock-lifeskills.com/

Addresses

Association of Independent Financial Advisers (AIFA)
2-6 Austin Friars House, Austin Friars, London EC2N 2HD
Phone: +44 (0)20 7628 1287
Web: www.aifa.net

Chartered Institute of Bankers in Scotland (CIOBS)
Drumsheugh House, 38b Drumsheugh Gardens, Edinburgh EH3 7SW
Phone: +44 (0)131 473 7777
Web: www.charteredbanker.com

Chartered Insurance Institute (CII)
42-48 High Road, South Woodford, London E18 2JP
Phone: +44 (0)20 8989 8464
Web: www.cii.co.uk

ifs School of Finance
IFS House, 4-9 Burgate Lane, Canterbury, Kent CT1 2XJ
Phone: +44 (0)1227 818609
Web: www.ifslearning.ac.uk

Personal Finance Society (PFS)
42-48 High Road, South Woodford, London E18 2JP
Phone: +44 (0)20 8530 0852
Web: www.thepfs.org

Securities & Investment Institute (SII)
8 Eastcheap, London EC3M 1AE
Phone: +44 (0)20 7645 0600
Web: www.sii.org.uk

Similar Jobs

Accounting Technician, Administrator/Administrative Assistant, Financial Adviser/Planner, Insurance Broker, Insurance Technician, Pensions Administrator

Park Warden

also known as: Park Constable

CRCI:Environment, Animals and Plants
CLCI:WAR
Job Band: 1

Job Description

Park wardens patrol around a park or sports ground, sometimes with a dog, to make sure that people are not doing any damage and checking that the area is a suitable environment for public use. They check equipment such as swings, slides, climbing frames and other equipment. Some park wardens take bookings for people who want to use putting greens, boating lakes and tennis courts. They take fees from customers, give out tickets and keep records. Others work with school and local community groups during educational visits to the park.

When the park is busy, wardens may direct drivers to car parks. Duties may also include some gardening tasks and general ground maintenance. They may have to pick up any litter, keep shelters clean and tidy and may open and close security gates at various times during the day and evening. Park wardens may be required to supervise more than one park in an area.

Work Details

Usually work a basic 39 hr week, though may be expected to work weekends and longer evenings in the summer. You may work on a rota basis with other wardens. This is an active job and you may have to deal with the unexpected. There may be rough ground and a lot of walking around required. You have contact with a wide variety of people, some of whom may be awkward and you may need to deal with threatening behaviour. The work is mainly outdoors and in all weathers and you need to wear a uniform.

Qualification

Personal qualities and fitness are often more important than qualifications.

• England, Wales and Northern Ireland

Band 1: For entry to jobs, no minimum qualifications are needed, but you are expected to have a good level of general education and relevant experience. Some formal/vocational qualifications at any level are useful.

• Scotland

Band 1: For entry to jobs, no minimum qualifications are needed, but you are expected to have a good level of general education and relevant experience. Some formal/vocational qualifications at any level are useful.

Adult Qualifications
You do not usually need any qualifications though experience in the armed forces or security work is useful. Employers often prefer older people. Those without existing qualifications can work through the Foundation Learning programme by taking credit-based units and qualifications.

Work Experience
Employers may prefer candidates who have relevant experience. This can include work in a garden centre, nursery, on a farm or in grounds maintenance. Work experience can give you skills that you can use in the future and add to your CV.

Entry and Training
On-the-job training, working alongside a more experienced employee is usual. You are expected to learn gardening techniques, health and safety regulations, customer care aspects, as well as how to use any new machinery and equipment. It may be useful to have a driving licence and a first aid certificate.

S/NVQs at levels 2-4 are available in subjects such as amenity horticulture. A Diploma/Welsh Baccalaureate may be available in your area in environment and land-based studies. Training programmes, including apprenticeship schemes, may be available in your area. Advanced apprenticeships leading to qualification at level 3 can also be a route into higher education.

Mature applicants with a background in outdoor work such as conservation or amenity work, groundsmanship duties or work with the public have an advantage. Government training opportunities may be available in your area. You can also gain recognition of previous experience through Accreditation of Prior Learning (APL) or by working towards relevant S/NVQs. Contact your local Connexions or careers office, Jobcentre Plus, Next Step service or Learning and Skills Council (LSC)/Local Enterprise Company (LEC) for details of training schemes, including apprenticeships for adults.

Opportunities and Pay
Jobs can be found mainly in towns and cities. Jobs with some local authorities are less frequent at the moment as some work may now be carried out by a private company rather than by council workers. Some district councils and the Royal Parks may employ park wardens or park constables for similar work. Promotion opportunities are limited but you may progress to a supervisory post as a senior park warden or parks officer.

Pay varies on where you work and who you work for, but most park wardens earn around £8-£8.50 an hour. In some areas you may be given help with accommodation within the park.

Health
You may find this job difficult if you suffer from hay fever. To do this job you must be in good health and have plenty of stamina.

Skills and Qualities
able to work well on your own, alert, approachable, common sense, enjoy working outdoors, firm manner, good spoken communication, helpful

Relevant Subjects
Land and Environment

Further Information
Apprenticeship Schemes (National Apprenticeship Service) - www.apprenticeships.org.uk
Diplomas (Foundation, Higher and Advanced) - http://yp.direct.gov.uk/diplomas
Foundation Learning (QCDA) - www.qcda.gov.uk
Local Government Careers (Improvement and Development Agency) - www.lgcareers.com/publications/
Real Life Guide to Working Outdoors (Trotman) - www.trotman.co.uk
Training Schemes - www.direct.gov.uk/en/educationandlearning
▶Working in cultural heritage (2007) (Babcock Lifeskills) - www.babcock-lifeskills.com/

Addresses
Convention of Scottish Local Authorities (COSLA)
Rosebery House, 9 Haymarket Terrace, Edinburgh EH12 5XZ
Phone: +44 (0)131 474 9200
Web: www.cosla.gov.uk

Northern Ireland Local Government Association (NILGA)
Unit 5B Castlereagh Business Park, 478 Castlereagh Road, Belfast BT5 6BQ
Phone: +44(0)28 9079 8972
Web: www.nilga.org

Similar Jobs
Countryside Ranger, Garden Centre Assistant, Gardener, Groundsman/Groundswoman, Parks Officer, Security Officer

Parking Attendant
also known as: Car Park Attendant, Parking Enforcement Officer, Traffic Warden

CRCI:Security and Armed Forces
CLCI:IJ
Job Band: 1 to 2

Job Description
Parking attendants are taking over the role of traffic wardens, as an increasing number of local authorities are taking on the responsibility for traffic control. Work in a controlled on-street parking area to ensure that parking regulations are being observed. Issue fixed penalty notices (parking tickets) if they are not. Help to maintain order in roads and streets that are constantly used. This includes main shopping areas, residential areas, streets and roads surrounding hospitals and schools, and leisure facilities. Arrange for illegally parked vehicles to be wheel-clamped and removed.

Some attendants supervise an outdoor car park, usually in a city or busy town. They collect the parking fee from each customer as they arrive. May direct a customer to the most convenient available space. Ensure that the cars are safe and watch the entrances and exits. In a 'pay and display' car park, check that cars are displaying a valid parking ticket. In multi-storey and large car parks, the attendant may check tickets at the exit. They calculate the fee to be charged. Also check season tickets to ensure that they are valid.

In 'pay and display' car parks, attendants usually empty the cash machines. They also check the supply of tickets and issue fixed penalty notices (parking tickets) if they discover that a vehicle does not have a valid parking ticket. May also be required to look after a closed-circuit television (CCTV) security system in some multi-storey or surface car parks. Deal with any problems such as lost tickets, car keys, etc.

Work Details
Usually work a 39 hr week that may include evenings and weekends. Early starts are common and sometimes you are asked to do shift work. You are on your own for a lot of the time, but you also interact with members of the public. Sometimes you may have to deal with people who are being awkward and abusive. Work is often quiet, though it can get very busy at times. May use a hand held computer to issue tickets and a mobile phone or two-way radio to keep in touch with the control room.

In some jobs you work indoors in a small ticket office, checking tickets and taking money. In other jobs you are out in all sorts of weather, walking around checking cars. Some parking attendants wear uniforms.

Parking attendants may have to appear at a court hearing if a person objects to their parking ticket. The attendant has to explain why the ticket was issued and present records.

Qualification

• England, Wales and Northern Ireland

Band 1: No qualifications are needed though employers may require basic numeracy and literacy skills.

Band 2: Some employers may ask for a few GCSEs (A*-C) including English and maths, or similar qualifications.

• Scotland

Band 1: No qualifications are needed though employers may require basic numeracy and literacy skills.

Band 2: Some employers may ask for a few S grades (1-3) including English and maths, or similar qualifications.

Adult Qualifications

No formal qualifications are needed, though employers expect basic skills in numeracy and literacy.

Work Experience

Any work experience can equip you with skills that you can use in the future and add to your CV. This can be unpaid or voluntary work, or holiday or part-time work that you have organised yourself.

Entry and Training

Initial training is on the job with an experienced attendant. Some large employers run induction courses and offer short training courses. It is useful to have a driving licence. You may be offered the opportunity to work towards job-related qualifications. Parking attendants can find themselves in situations where members of the public are abusive to them. For this reason, the industry has become more regulated. There is now more of a focus on training staff in conflict management.

The diploma/welsh baccalaureate in public services may be a useful background for this career but check entry requirements carefully. You can work for a City and Guilds level 2 award for Civil Enforcement Officers (Parking). This course uses scenario-based training and is assessed by a 40-question multiple choice exam. You can build on this qualification by completing a level 2 NVQ in Controlling Parking Areas. It is also possible to gain a level 2 BTEC award in vehicle immobilisation. This is a two part course. Part one covers the use of vehicle immobilisation equipment (clamps). Part two deals with communication and conflict management. You need to keep up to date with national traffic laws and local parking regulations. Check the British Parking Association's website for full details on all training courses.

Mature applicants with experience in customer care, handling money, or other security work may have an advantage. Employers expect you to have the ability to read, count, and calculate quickly. Mature applicants are particularly welcome.

Opportunities and Pay

There are jobs in most towns and cities, though many large car parks are now automated requiring less staff. Most available jobs are with operators of city car parks. These are usually private companies or local authorities. Check the Local Government Careers website for jobs. There are also some jobs with large office blocks, colleges and universities, hotels, industrial premises and hospitals. Jobs also exist at long-term car parks at airports and sea terminals.

It is often possible to work part time covering periods when the car park is busiest. This is usually at the end of the afternoon when shops and offices close. Often there are more jobs in the summer or at busy times such as Christmas.

Depending on experience and responsibility attendants are likely to start at around £12k a year, rising to around £13k-£19k a year. Overtime pay can increase this significantly.

Health

You need good stamina and should be physically fit to do this job.

Skills and Qualities

able to work both on your own and in a team, alert, calm, efficient, numeracy skills, polite, safety conscious, security conscious, trustworthy

Further Information

Apprenticeship Schemes (National Apprenticeship Service) - www.apprenticeships.org.uk

Diplomas (Foundation, Higher and Advanced) - http://yp.direct.gov.uk/diplomas

Foundation Learning (QCDA) - www.qcda.gov.uk

Local Government Careers (Improvement and Development Agency) - www.lgcareers.com/publications/

Professional Security Magazine - www.professionalsecurity.co.uk

Skills for Security - sector skills council for security industry - www.skillsforsecurity.org.uk/

Welsh Baccalaureate - www.wbq.org.uk

▶Working outdoors (2010) (Babcock Lifeskills) - www.babcock-lifeskills.com/

Addresses

British Parking Association
Stuart House, 41-43 Perrymount Road, Haywards Heath, West Sussex RH16 3BN
Phone: +44 (0)1444 447 300
Web: www.britishparking.co.uk

Similar Jobs

Park Warden, Police Community Support Officer (England & Wales), Rail Transport Train Guard, Security Officer

Parks Manager

CRCI:Environment, Animals and Plants
CLCI:WAD Job Band: 3 to 5

Job Description

Parks managers work to ensure parks and other open spaces in cities and towns are well maintained. They coordinates the work of other horticulturists, landscape architects/gardeners, parks officers, wardens and other park workers. The job involved planning and developing the park acreage to its full potential, in horticultural, educational and entertainment areas. Some parks contain herds of animals, such as deer, and these also need to be well managed and cared for. Managers may introduce nature education trails to inform people of the parks natural or introduced trees, plants and animals, or devise healthy walks of varying degrees of ability. They establish links with local schools/colleges, volunteer and community groups. May also plan and oversee park events such as music concerts, including orchestral and jazz concerts, and popular music bands and performers.

Some park managers are responsible for the growth and provision of any floral displays in their local town or city throughout the year, and for the displays and plants within council-owned buildings. They coordinate publicity, work within a set budget and are responsible for detailed reports. Also spend time on cost estimates and finance, health and safety matters, and are responsible for recruitment, training and development of staff.

Work Details

Usually work a standard 37 hour week, Monday to Friday, though sometimes may be required to attend meetings or events in the evenings and at weekends. You are based in council offices or outside in the park itself. Travel is therefore necessary around an area to visit different locations during the working day. For some park visits you need to wear protective clothing, such as boots, hard hat, ear defenders and gloves.

Parks Manager

Qualification

• England, Wales and Northern Ireland

Band 3: For entry: usually at least 5 GCSEs (A*-C) including English and maths and a science subject, or equivalent. Practical experience in horticulture may be needed.

Band 4: For HND, Diploma of Higher Education or foundation degree: 1-2 A levels and some GCSEs (A*-C) usually including English, science and maths, or equivalent.

Band 5: For degree courses: 2-3 A levels and some GCSEs (A*-C) usually including English, maths and a science, or equivalent. Exact requirements depend on the degree you take.

• Scotland

Band 3: For entry: usually at least five S grades (1-3) including English, maths and a science, or similar. It is also an advantage to have practical experience in horticulture.

Band 4: For entry to SQA higher national and professional development awards, usually 2-3 H grades and some S grades (1-3), including English, science and maths, or similar qualifications.

Band 5: For degree courses: 3-5 H grades and some S grades (1-3), usually including English, maths and a science, or similar qualifications. Exact requirements depend on the degree you take. Good H grades are required, preferably taken at one sitting.

Degree Information

A degree in horticulture or horticultural management is preferred. Degrees in related subjects with an element of horticulture, including agriculture, botany or forestry may also be acceptable. It is an advantage to have a postgraduate degree or diploma in horticultural management.

Adult Qualifications

Colleges and universities offering degree, HNC/HND courses in horticulture may have special entry standards for mature applicants. Relevant foundation or Access courses may be available. Contact individual institutions for details.

Work Experience

Work experience gives you an insight into what you enjoy and do not enjoy about a job or working environment, as well as the opportunity to acquire new skills. It also provides valuable information to add to your CV and improves your employment prospects. Previous work or voluntary experience in a horticultural job, a garden nursery, a commercial garden, or with local or national parks and gardens is valuable. You may be able to gain a work placement whilst on some horticultural courses. Work that has used management skills is also desirable to employers.

Entry and Training

There is no standard entry route to becoming a parks manager, but all entrants are expected to have gained extensive practical and/or professional knowledge of horticulture, business and managerial/ supervisory experience. Employers may ask for a relevant higher national diploma or a Royal Horticultural Society (RHS) qualification. Some park managers enter as suitably experienced graduates with qualifications in botany, landscape gardening or horticulture. Others may have been promoted from a position such as a parks officer. Training is on the job and may include time off for further study. A full, valid driving licence is usually required.

There are relevant full or part-time courses in horticulture available, including degrees and foundation degrees, BTEC/SQA higher national certificates/diplomas, and those offered by the professional bodies. Distance learning courses are also available. Contact the Royal Horticultural Society (RHS) for a complete list of qualifications and training information. The Institute for Sport, Parks and Leisure (ISPAL) offer a professional qualifications scheme, a continuing professional development (CPD) programme, and an annual national parks conference.

A Diploma/Welsh Baccalaureate in environment and land-based studies may be available in your area.

Mature entry is welcomed to this profession, provided applicants can show they have relevant professional experience. Practical experience of working in a garden centre, a horticultural nursery, in grounds maintenance, and supervisory/management and business experience is an advantage. The Royal Horticultural Society offers a general examination in horticulture for those without any relevant qualifications.

Government training opportunities may be available in your area. You can also gain recognition of previous experience through Accreditation of Prior Learning (APL) or by working towards relevant S/NVQs.

Opportunities and Pay

You are most likely to work for a city or local council, although there are some opportunities with national parks and charitable organisations. There are other opportunities to specialise in areas such as arboricultural park management, or botanical gardens, or to work for organisations such as the Royal Parks Agency. Promotion prospects can include posts as an area or district manager, or a director of parks.

Pay varies depending on location and employer, but starting salaries for those with management experience can be around £27k-£30k a year, rising to around £40k a year, although a few may earn more.

Health

A good level of health may be needed for this job.

Skills and Qualities

able to take responsibility, able to work to a budget, decisive, efficient, environmental awareness, good spoken communication, good written English, planning skills, sound judgement

Relevant Subjects

Biology, Business and accounting, Chemistry, Economics, English, Land and Environment, Mathematics, Science

Further Information

A Career in Sport, Parks & Leisure (ispal) (ISPAL) - www.ispal.org.uk

AGCAS: Government & Public Administration (Job Sector Briefing) - (AGCAS) - www.prospects.ac.uk

Diplomas (Foundation, Higher and Advanced) - http://yp.direct.gov.uk/diplomas

Local Government Careers (Improvement and Development Agency) - www.lgcareers.com/publications/

Training Schemes - www.direct.gov.uk/en/educationandlearning

Addresses

Convention of Scottish Local Authorities (COSLA)
Rosebery House, 9 Haymarket Terrace, Edinburgh EH12 5XZ
Phone: +44 (0)131 474 9200
Web: www.cosla.gov.uk

Institute for Sport, Parks & Leisure (ISPAL)
Abbey Business Centre, 1650 Arlington Business Park, Theale, Reading RG7 4SA
Phone: 0844 418 0077 (UK only)
Web: www.ispal.org.uk

Institute of Horticulture (IoH)
Capel Manor College, Bullsmoor Lane, Enfield EN1 4RQ
Phone: +44 (0) 1992 707025
Web: www.horticulture.org.uk

Northern Ireland Local Government Association (NILGA)
Unit 5B Castlereagh Business Park, 478 Castlereagh Road, Belfast BT5 6BQ
Phone: +44(0)28 9079 8972
Web: www.nilga.org

Royal Horticultural Society (RHS)
80 Vincent Square, London SW1P 2PE
Phone: 0845 260 5000 (UK only)
Web: www.rhs.org.uk

Similar Jobs

Arboriculturist, Forest Officer, Horticultural Manager, Landscape Gardener, Park Warden, Parks Officer

Parks Officer

CRCI:Environment, Animals and Plants
CLCI:WAD Job Band: 1 to 3

Job Description

Parks officers supervise a team of gardeners and park wardens who look after public parks and open spaces. They plan and maintain the cultivation of parks, outdoor recreation centres, sports pitches, open spaces in residential areas and on school/college premises. May supervise groups of up to 20 gardeners/wardens and are responsible for the organisation and routine of their work, often under the direction of the parks manager. They plan year-round work, according to each season and current ground conditions and change work timetable if the weather is not as expected.

They monitor the quality and progress of the team and ensure that machinery and equipment is maintained. They also spend time with their employer (usually local or county council) and departmental colleagues, on cost estimates and finance, health and safety matters, as well as the recruitment and training of employees.

Work Details

Parks officers usually work a flexible five-day week, working a basic 37-39 hr week, though sometimes has to work overtime, possibly in the evenings and at weekends. You spend part of your time in an office and the rest of the time outdoors, in all weather conditions. The outdoor work can sometimes be cold, damp, dirty, wet and muddy. Travel may be necessary around an area to visit different locations during the working day. For some work, you need to wear protective clothing, such as boots, hard hat, ear defenders and gloves.

Qualification

- **England, Wales and Northern Ireland**

Band 1: No minimum qualifications are required, but you are expected to have a good level of general education. However, some qualifications at any level are useful.

Band 2: Although academic qualifications are not specified for this job, it is an advantage to have some GCSEs (A*-C) in subjects that include English and maths, or equivalent. Science subjects are useful.

Band 3: For entry: usually at least 5 GCSEs (A*-C) including English and maths, or equivalent. Practical experience in horticulture and landscape work is usually required.

- **Scotland**

Band 1: No minimum qualifications are required, but you are expected to have a good level of general education. However, some qualifications at any level are useful.

Band 2: Although academic qualifications are not specified for this job, it is an advantage to have some S grades (1-3) in subjects that include English and maths, or similar. Science subjects are useful.

Band 3: For entry: usually at least five S grades (1-3) including English and maths, or similar. Practical experience in horticulture and landscape work is usually required.

Adult Qualifications

For entry to many jobs you need no qualifications, but experience of horticultural work is useful.

Work Experience

Employers may prefer candidates who have relevant work or voluntary experience. This can include work in a garden centre, a horticultural nursery, on a farm or in grounds maintenance. This can equip you with skills that you can use in the future and add to your CV.

Entry and Training

Many parks officers begin their career as a gardener or park warden and complete S/NVQ at levels 1-2 in amenity horticulture as part of their training. They gain a practical knowledge of horticulture at a college of further education and at their place of work. Further training is expected, usually to gain S/NVQs in amenity horticulture and training in supervisory skills at levels 3-4. Employers usually offer relevant training in supervisory skills, health and safety, first aid and specific horticultural techniques.

At a more senior level of work, some councils may ask for a relevant City & Guilds award, BTEC/SQA national certificate/diploma or a Royal Horticultural Society (RHS) qualification. The Institute for Sport, Parks and Leisure (ISPAL) offer a professional qualifications scheme, a continuing professional development (CPD) programme, and an annual national parks conference. Relevant training is also offered by the Institute of Groundsmanship who have a membership scheme and offer conferences and events. A full, valid driving licence is also usually required.

A Diploma/Welsh Baccalaureate may be available in your area in environment and land-based studies. Training programmes, including apprenticeship schemes, may be available in your area. Advanced apprenticeships leading to qualification at level 3 can also be a route into higher education.

Mature applicants with a background in outdoor work such as conservation or amenity work, groundsmanship duties or work with the public have an advantage. Government training opportunities, including apprenticeships for adults, may be available in your area. You can also gain recognition of previous experience through Accreditation of Prior Learning (APL) or by working towards relevant S/NVQs.

Opportunities and Pay

Parks officers may be employed by a local or county council, or by a private company that manages the park for a council on a contractual basis. When experienced, some parks officers can progress into management within the parks division/department or other divisions/departments within the council.

Pay depends on the employer, but starting pay can range from around £17k-£20k a year. With experience you may earn up to £25k-£30k a year, and more for a managerial post.

Health

To do this job you have to be physically fit. This job is more difficult if you have respiratory or skin allergies such as asthma, hay fever or eczema.

Skills and Qualities

able to manage people, able to motivate others, able to work to a budget, able to work to deadlines, aptitude for teamwork, enthusiastic, good communication skills, good organisational skills, IT skills, planning skills, practical skills

Relevant Subjects

Biology, Land and Environment, Mathematics, Science

Further Information

A Career in Sport, Parks & Leisure (ispal) (ISPAL) - www.ispal.org.uk

Apprenticeship Schemes (National Apprenticeship Service) - www.apprenticeships.org.uk

Diplomas (Foundation, Higher and Advanced) - http://yp.direct.gov.uk/diplomas

Lantra - The Sector Skills Council for environmental & land-based sector (Lantra) http:/www.lantra.co.uk

Local Government Careers (Improvement and Development Agency) - www.lgcareers.com/publications/

Professional Gardener (Professional Gardeners Guild) (Professional Gardening Guild) www.pgg.org.uk

Training Schemes - www.direct.gov.uk/en/educationandlearning

Addresses

Convention of Scottish Local Authorities (COSLA)
Rosebery House, 9 Haymarket Terrace, Edinburgh EH12 5XZ
Phone: +44 (0)131 474 9200
Web: www.cosla.gov.uk

Institute for Sport, Parks & Leisure (ISPAL)
Abbey Business Centre, 1650 Arlington Business Park, Theale, Reading RG7 4SA
Phone: 0844 418 0077 (UK only)
Web: www.ispal.org.uk

Institute of Groundsmanship (IOG)
28 Stratford Office Village, Walker Avenue, Wolverton Mill East, Milton Keynes MK12 5TW
Phone: +44 (0)1908 312 511
Web: www.iog.org

Northern Ireland Local Government Association (NILGA)
Unit 5B Castlereagh Business Park, 478 Castlereagh Road, Belfast BT5 6BQ
Phone: +44(0)28 9079 8972
Web: www.nilga.org

Royal Horticultural Society (RHS)
80 Vincent Square, London SW1P 2PE
Phone: 0845 260 5000 (UK only)
Web: www.rhs.org.uk

Similar Jobs

Countryside Ranger, Gardener, Groundsman/Groundswoman, Horticultural Worker: Commercial, Landscape Gardener, Parks Manager

Patent Attorney

also known as: Patent Agent

CRCI:Legal and Political Services

CLCI:LAK Job Band: 5

Job Description

Patent attorneys give specialist legal and technical advice to clients, either individuals or a company, on matters relating to patent law, or to those who wish to obtain patents. A patent gives the owner the right to stop other others using their invention for a certain period of time. Patent attorneys are trained and experienced in the art of drafting, obtaining and enforcing patents and have detailed knowledge of intellectual property law. They check that the invention is a new one, write a detailed description of the invention in legal terms and then prepare specifications for the patent office. They also negotiate the application and represent the client before the examiner.

When disputes occur, for example, on patent validity, they offer advice. May now also act as advocates in the Patents County Court or the European Patents Office. Some patent attorneys become heavily involved in litigation in UK and possibly European courts. Some specialise in trade marks, industrial designs or electronics.

Work Details

A standard week is around 37 hrs, Monday to Friday, but you may work longer hours at times to meet deadlines. Patent attorneys are office based, but the job involves some travel in the UK and perhaps to the European patent offices in Munich and The Hague. Clients can be single inventors or large companies. You have to analyse complex details, give sound advice and present information clearly both in person and in writing. Securing a patent and enforcing it is often a very long and difficult process. You may work for more than one client at a time, which can be demanding.

Qualification

- **England, Wales and Northern Ireland**

Band 5: For a degree: 2-3 A levels and some GCSEs (A*-C) are required, usually including English, science, maths, engineering, or equivalent qualifications. Exact requirements depend on the degree you take. Knowledge of French and German is preferred.

- **Scotland**

Band 5: For a degree: 3-5 H grades and some S grades (1-3) or similar are required, usually including English, science, maths, engineering, or similar. Knowledge of French and German is required. Exact entry requirements depend on the course you take.

Degree Information

Usually a first or upper second class honours degree in a science, engineering or technical subject. Postgraduate qualifications include a relevant MSc or a postgraduate certificate in intellectual property law.

Adult Qualifications

Relevant qualifications and experience in science, maths, technology or engineering are essential, especially in research and development. A reasonable working knowledge of French and German is preferred. Entry requirements may be relaxed for adults applying for higher education courses and Access or foundation courses give adults without qualifications a route on to degree courses.

Work Experience

Employers prefer candidates who have relevant work or voluntary experience. This includes experience in the UK Intellectual Property Office or European Patent Office. Other relevant experience can be in a law firm or in a more technical environment such as engineering.

Entry and Training

This is a graduate profession, and requires an eligible scientific, technical or engineering degree, plus good English skills. Most patent attorneys enter the profession as a trainee, known as a technical assistant, and gain skills through in-house training in a patent agent's office or a company's patent department. Entry to training posts is very competitive.

While training you need to study for the examinations set by the Chartered Institute of Patent Attorneys (CIPA). This may take between 4-5 years, or less if you are exempt from parts of the exam, and you must already be working in the profession to qualify. Some companies sponsor employees through academic training, such as certificate and masters courses in intellectual property. These are available at several universities, some of which give exemptions from the CIPA foundation papers. Successful completion of the examinations gives entry to the Register of Patent Agents, following at least two years in the profession.

You can also qualify by working as a solicitor in a firm with an intellectual property department. Some of these companies train recruits to qualify as registered patent attorneys. Contact CIPA for details of all routes to qualifying.

Most patent attorneys also become European patent attorneys by taking the European qualifying examination. This broadens your opportunities considerably as most patents are now international. A working knowledge of French and German is therefore also required. Contact the European Patent Office for further details.

Mature entrants with considerable related experience in industrial research and development may sometimes move into patent work. Those with a scientific research and development background also be able to transfer their professional knowledge to patent work. You need to qualify with the Chartered Institute of Patent Attorneys to be able to join the Register of Patent Agents.

Opportunities and Pay
There are around 1730 registered patent attorneys in the UK and around half work in private practice, mostly in large cities. Some large industrial companies and government organisations employ patent attorneys to handle their inventions. Over 75% of all attorneys are based in London and the South East. In private practice experienced attorneys can become partners. Some move to executive or management posts, others choose to qualify as a patent examiner or move to work in the UK Intellectual Property Office. There are good opportunities for working abroad.

Pay varies depending on location and employer. Graduate trainees are generally paid £22k-£32k a year. Those who are newly qualified can earn around £55k-£60k. Some department heads and partners in a private firm can earn £80k-£300k a year.

Skills and Qualities
ability in one or more languages, able to work to deadlines, analytical skills, attention to detail, excellent communication skills, good written English, information handling skills, IT skills, scientific approach, technical aptitude

Relevant Subjects
Business and accounting, Chemistry, Design and technology, Engineering, English, Law, Mathematics, Modern Foreign Languages, Physics, Science

Further Information
Patent Attorney as a Career (CIPA) (Chartered Institute of Patent Agents) - www.cipa.org.uk/pages/about-careers

▶Working in engineering (2010) (Babcock Lifeskills) - www.babcock-lifeskills.com/

▶Working in science (2007) (Babcock Lifeskills) - www.babcock-lifeskills.com/

Addresses
Chartered Institute of Patent Attorneys (CIPA)
95 Chancery Lane, London WC2A 1DT
Phone: +44 (0)20 7405 9450
Web: www.cipa.org.uk

European Patent Office (EPO)
Erhardtstrasse 27 80469, Munich
Phone: +49 89 2399-0
Web: www.epo.org/

UK Intellectual Property Office (UK IPO)
Concept House, Cardiff Road, Newport NP10 8QQ
Phone: 0845 950 0505 (UK only)
Web: www.ipo.gov.uk

Similar Jobs
Information Scientist, Library & Information Manager, Patent Examiner, Solicitor, Trade Mark Attorney, Writer: Technical

Patent Examiner
CRCI:Legal and Political Services
CLCI:LAK — Job Band: 5

Job Description
Patent examiners check patent applications submitted to the UK Intellectual Property Office or European Patent Office (EPO) by patent attorneys and others for a new invention, trademark, or a design. They usually specialise in one subject area, working in one of around twenty-six specialist groups. They conduct a search to check the originality of each application and look at the specification in detail to ensure that it is clear and legally acceptable. Examiners write a report and may discuss suggested changes with the inventor or patent attorney. They then either grant or refuse the patent. If there is a dispute, patent examiners can act for the UK Intellectual Property Office or EPO.

Work Details
You usually work regular office hours of around 37 hrs a week, Monday to Friday. The work is almost entirely office based. You have to analyse complex information, make sound decisions, and be a competent negotiator. Report writing requires the ability to communicate clearly in writing. The work is intellectually demanding and involves making decisions with which people may not agree. You may work on your own for some of the time.

Qualification
• England, Wales and Northern Ireland
Band 5: For degree course: 2-3 A levels and some GCSEs (A*-C), usually including English and maths, or equivalent qualifications. Exact requirements depend on the degree you take.

• Scotland
Band 5: For degree course: 3-5 H grades and some S grades (1-3), usually including English and maths, or similar qualifications. Exact requirements depend on the degree you take.

Degree Information
A good honours degree in science, engineering, maths or computer technology is usually required, or equivalent industrial experience at that level. Knowledge of French and German is normally needed, although there are opportunities to improve language skills on the job.

Adult Qualifications
An appropriate degree is required; usually science, engineering, maths, computer technology, or equivalent industrial experience at that level. Entry requirements may be relaxed for adults applying for higher education courses and Access or foundation courses give adults without qualifications a route on to degree courses.

Work Experience
Employers and universities may prefer candidates who have relevant work or voluntary experience. This includes experience with the UK Patent Office or European Patent Office. Other relevant experience can be in a law firm or a more technical environment such as engineering or science.

The World Intellectual Property Organization offers summer internships for students approaching the end of their degree course.

Entry and Training
You need a first or upper second class honours degree in science, engineering, a mathematical subject or computer technology for entry. You also have to meet the civil service's nationality and residency requirements and must have an interest in law as well as in science and technology, and technical developments. The UK Intellectual Property Office (IPO) provides an induction programme followed by in-house training on aspects of intellectual property law and on the basic skills required for the job. Trainees are encouraged to study for a postgraduate diploma in intellectual property law. Foreign language tuition may also be provided. Assistant examiners work closely with a senior examiner for a year. You continue to be supervised until you are promoted to examiner.

Entrants to the European Patents Office (EPO) need a similar degree, plus an extensive knowledge of either English, French or German, and the ability to understand the other two languages. The EPO offers similar training that lasts two years, covering all aspects of patent examination and including additional language training in French and German. All UK IPO and EPO staff are encouraged to undertake specific personal development.

Mature entry is possible, usually for those qualified in law, mathematics, engineering, computer technology or science. Those who have worked in scientific research and development may also transfer their professional knowledge to patent work.

Opportunities and Pay
Most opportunities are with the UK Intellectual Property Office in Newport, South Wales, where over 300 patent examiners currently work. A few examiners work in London. There is a formal promotion structure. Patent examiners trained in the UK can also work for the European Patent Office (EPO). The EPO is rapidly expanding and needs examiners, particularly engineering and science graduates, to staff their offices based in The Hague, Munich and Berlin.

Assistant examiners can be promoted to examiner after two-four years' experience, with possible further promotion to senior examiner after five-nine years. Many patent examiners progress to become patent attorneys, or further specialise as trade mark attorneys.

Starting salaries for associate patent examiners working for the UK Intellectual Property Office are £22k-£26k a year. Experienced examiners earn between £26k-£51k a year. More senior posts are paid at senior civil service rates. European Patent Office salaries are competitive and include allowances.

Skills and Qualities
analytical skills, attention to detail, excellent communication skills, good written English, information handling skills, IT skills, negotiating skills, scientific approach, sound judgement, understanding of legal technicalities

Relevant Subjects
Chemistry, Design and technology, Engineering, English, Law, Mathematics, Modern Foreign Languages, Physics, Science

Further Information
World Intellectual Property Organization (WIPO) (WIPO) - http://www/wipo.int/

Addresses
European Patent Office (EPO)
Erhardtstrasse 27 80469, Munich
Phone: +49 89 2399-0
Web: www.epo.org/

UK Intellectual Property Office (UK IPO)
Concept House, Cardiff Road, Newport NP10 8QQ
Phone: 0845 950 0505 (UK only)
Web: www.ipo.gov.uk

Similar Jobs
Information Scientist, Patent Attorney, Trade Mark Attorney, Writer: Technical

Pathologist

CRCI:Healthcare
CLCI:JAB Job Band: 5

Job Description
Pathologists investigate the cause and effect of disease and may also carry out autopsy/post-mortem examinations to determine the cause of death of those who die without an obvious cause. They work in a laboratory supervising the work of other laboratory staff such as scientists and technicians. A medical pathologist, working in a hospital, may also be responsible for the care of patients such as those with anaemia, immune and metabolic disorders. As a consultant, you have a staff of around 50 or more depending on the size of hospital, including trainee and qualified doctors as well as biomedical and clinical scientists who provide technical expertise.

Pathologists work across different areas of medicine including genetics, anatomy and biochemistry. Can specialise in clinical pathology (study of chemical changes in the body due to disease), haematology (study of blood and its disorders), histopathology (examination of body tissue), forensic pathology (applied use of pathology for legal purposes), immunology (study of the immune system) or medical microbiology (diagnosis and control of infection).

Work Details
Whilst initially training as a doctor you are expected to work very long and irregular hours, including evenings, weekends and on-call duties. When specialising in pathology you are usually based in a laboratory of a hospital, medical school or research institute and work more regular hours. Some pathologists have contact with people who are ill and upset. Work can be emotionally demanding and requires coping with the sight of blood. The work carries a risk of infection especially when dealing with deaths from infectious diseases such as HIV/Aids and hepatitis. You may need to wear a white coat or protective clothes, including a face mask and gloves.

Qualification

• England, Wales and Northern Ireland
Band 5: For degree in medicine: usually three A levels, with good grades in chemistry and two from physics, biological sciences and maths, plus 5 GCSEs (A*-C) including English, or equivalent. Some medical schools offer a one-year pre-medical course for students with A levels in arts or mixed subjects. Check with individual schools for full details.

• Scotland
Band 5: For degree in medicine: usually five H grades, with good grades in chemistry and two from physics, biology and maths, plus five S grades (1-3) including English and maths, or similar. Normally science subjects not held at H grade should be offered at S grade. Some medical schools offer a one-year pre-medical course for students whose H grades do not include the required science subjects. Check with individual schools for full details.

Degree Information
A degree in medicine awarded by a university medical school and recognised by the General Medical Council is essential, followed by additional specialist study. Other graduate scientists working in a pathology laboratory may have first degrees in subjects such as biomedical science or microbiology.

Adult Qualifications
Entry requirement standards are not normally relaxed for mature applicants, though those who consider applying should contact the individual university for advice. Graduates with a good honours degree in a related subject may obtain exemptions from certain options within the medical degree course.

Work Experience
Entry to this career is highly competitive and it is essential that you have some relevant work or voluntary experience before applying to train as a doctor so that you are able to demonstrate a long-term commitment to medicine. Evidence of this can come in the form of relevant paid or voluntary work in a healthcare setting such as work in a hospital, residential care home, or similar. You can also apply for voluntary work overseas that usually has a health education or medically-related programme.

Entry and Training
Pathologists must first qualify as medical doctors by completing a medicine degree which takes five years, then pass the postgraduate two-year Foundation Programme and register as a doctor with the General Medical Council (GMC). For full details of medical training see the job article Doctor: Hospital.

Once you have completed the Foundation Programme, there is competition for specialty registrar posts, under the Modernising Medical Careers initiative. For pathology posts, there is then a continuous period of training leading to the Certificate of Completion of Training (CCT). Training is initially broader based, but then narrows down to focus on your specialty field. You must decide which area of pathology you want so specialise in, for example chemical, histopathology, haematology etc. Progress is based on achieving competences and can take between five and seven years. Once you have achieved the CCT and become a member of the Royal College of Pathologists (RCPath), you can join the specialist register of the GMC. You are expected to update your professional knowledge continually throughout your career. Contact the RCPath for details of courses, bursaries and training routes.

Mature applicants that are suitably qualified are welcomed by medical schools and some may have reserved places for mature graduate entrants. Check with individual medical schools. There are access courses to medicine and pre-medical foundation courses. Some Open University credits at distinction level may be accepted at some medical schools. Check with individual medical schools for details of all opportunities.

Opportunities and Pay
Pathologists work mainly for the NHS or research laboratories although there are some opportunities within privately run hospitals. Consultant posts may be easier to obtain than in some of the more popular medical specialisms, such as general medicine or surgery, and may be more numerous in inner city rather than rural areas. Some pathologists specialise in computer forensics. Forensic pathologists are employed by the Home Office, Metropolitan Police and Procurators Fiscal (Scotland).

Within the NHS, junior doctors earn a basic salary and are usually paid a supplement for extra hours worked. Basic salaries are around £33k a year (including a 50% supplement for extra hours), rising to £43k-£68k (including 50% supplement) for a doctor in specialist training. A consultant can earn £73k-£174k a year. These salaries do not include on-call payments, private income or London weighting allowances.

Health
There is a risk of infection especially when dealing with deaths from infectious diseases such as HIV/AIDS and hepatitis. This job requires good general fitness.

Skills and Qualities
able to take responsibility, analytical skills, emotionally strong, good communication skills, good concentration level, IT skills, not squeamish, observant, patient, scientific approach

Relevant Subjects
Biology, Chemistry, English, Mathematics, Physics, Science

Further Information
Becoming a Doctor (BMA) - www.bma.org.uk/careers/becoming_doctor/index.jsp
British Medical Journal (weekly) (BMJ Publishing Group Ltd) - www.bmj.com/
Foundation Programme - www.foundationprogramme.nhs.uk
Insider's Guide to Medical Schools (Blackwell Books)
Journal of Clinical Pathology (BMJ Publishing Group) - http://jcp.bmj.com/
Journal of Pathology (Pathological Society of Great Britain and Ireland) (John Wiley & Sons Ltd) - http://www3.interscience.wiley.com/journal/1130/home
Modernising Medical Careers - www.mmc.nhs.uk
NHS Careers (NHS Careers) - www.nhscareers.nhs.uk
NHS Careers Scotland - www.infoscotland.com/nhs
NHS Careers Wales - www.wales.nhs.uk
Open University - www.open.ac.uk
Pathological Society http://wwwpathsoc.org
The Lancet (weekly) (Elsevier Ltd) - www.thelancet.com/
UK Clinical Aptitude Test - www.ukcat.ac.uk

Addresses
Association of Clinical Pathologists
189 Dyke Road, Hove, East Sussex BN3 1TL
Phone: +44 (0)1273 775700
Web: www.pathologists.org.uk

British Medical Association (BMA)
BMA House, Tavistock Square, London WC1H 9JP
Phone: +44 (0)20 7387 4499
Web: www.bma.org.uk

Forensic Science Society
Clarke House, 18A Mount Parade, Harrogate HG1 1BX
Phone: +44 (0)1423 506 068
Web: www.forensic-science-society.org.uk

General Medical Council (GMC)
Regents Place, 350 Euston Road, London NW1 3JN
Phone: +44 (0)161 923 6602
Web: www.gmc-uk.org

Royal College of Pathologists (RCPath)
2 Carlton House Terrace, London SW1Y 5AF
Phone: +44 (0)20 7451 6700
Web: www.rcpath.org

Similar Jobs
Clinical Research Associate, Doctor: Hospital, Forensic Scientist, Immunologist, Microbiologist

Payroll Officer
also known as: Wages Clerk

CRCI:Financial Services
CLCI:CAT
Job Band: 2 to 3

Job Description
Payroll officers calculate the salaries and wages of company employees, deduct tax and national insurance, and keep records of what has been paid. Calculate bonus payments and overtime pay. Most work is done with the use of computers, spreadsheets and calculators. Must take account of changes in employees' circumstances, such as promotion, general pay increases, maternity leave and sick pay. Must also keep accurate records to make sure employees are paid correctly.

Payroll officers answer any queries employees have about their wage, salary or contributions. May manage a team of payroll clerks or assistants. In many offices, they also carry out other general office duties such as filing, photocopying and answering the telephone.

Work Details
Usually work a basic 35-39 hrs a week, from 9am-5pm, Monday to Friday. This job is mainly office based. You may have to spend a lot of time using computers and speaking to people on the phone. The work has to be done neatly and accurately and you need to be able to handle many tasks at the same time. There are many legal rules and regulations to learn, which must be followed. You must always use discretion in your work as you are working with personal and sensitive information. Flexitime and part-time working opportunities are possible.

Qualification

- **England, Wales and Northern Ireland**

Band 2: Although academic qualifications are not specified for this job, it is an advantage to have some GCSEs (A*-C) in subjects that include English and maths, or equivalent.

Band 3: For entry: usually at least 4 GCSEs (A*-C) including English and maths, or equivalent.

- **Scotland**

Band 2: Although academic qualifications are not specified for this job, it is an advantage to have some S grades (1-3) in subjects that include English and maths, or similar.

Band 3: For entry: usually at least four S grades (1-3) including English and maths, or similar.

Adult Qualifications
There are no set entry requirements, but some relevant experience of office work or work with figures is an advantage. Some employers may prefer mature applicants.

Work Experience
Relevant work or voluntary experience is always useful and can equip you with skills that you can use in the future and add to your CV. Temporary holiday work in offices via employment agencies is useful, particularly if you can develop good keyboard skills and knowledge of the most popular accounting or payroll software packages.

Entry and Training
You can enter this job straight after leaving school or after completing a relevant course. Training is usually a mixture of on-the-job training and relevant courses. Some companies run their own in-house training programmes or you may take a part-time college course in subjects such as accounting, business studies or business and finance.

The Institute of Payroll Professionals (IPP) offers a range of courses, including many short courses on legislative issues and an introductory course in three parts leading to a national payroll certificate, which gives a unit 3 exemption for the IPP diploma in payroll management. The International Association of Bookkeepers (IAB) also offers several qualifications in payroll, and these can be studied face-to-face or by distance learning. The Institute of Certified Bookkeepers also offers a level 3 diploma in payroll management.

S/NVQs are available in payroll administration at levels 2 and 3 in association with the Association of Accounting Technicians (AAT). Candidates that complete these are granted exemptions from certain parts of the AAT accounting qualification, including the S/NVQ and diploma pathway. Training programmes, including apprenticeship schemes and the Diploma/Welsh Baccalaureate in business, administration and finance may also be available in your area. The Financial Services Skills Council (FSSC) offer apprenticeships for both new and existing employees. The apprenticeship is made up of a technical certificate which represents a professional qualification, an NVQ/SVQ and the opportunity to obtain, key, core and essential skills. Contact the FSSC for further details.

There are opportunities for adults who are changing careers in this profession and for those who are looking to re-enter the labour market after a career break. Payroll provides an opportunity for people to step up from general bookkeeping or accountancy roles and specialise in a particular field.

Mature entry is therefore common. There are many payroll, accounting and bookkeeping courses which can be studied part time or by distance learning. Mature applicants can benefit through government training opportunities that may be available in your area. You can gain recognition of previous experience through Accreditation of Prior Learning (APL) or by working towards relevant S/NVQs.

Opportunities and Pay
Over 60,000 people are employed in payroll departments throughout the UK. Larger organisations may have their own payroll department. Payroll officers work in many different organisations, including private companies, financial institutions such as banks, insurance companies and building societies, educational institutions and in local government. They may also work in payroll bureaux that provide payroll services to smaller companies.

With experience officers can move on to supervisory or management positions. Promotion prospects are usually better for those who take courses in payroll accounting. Officers often move from one organisation to another to gain experience and promotion.

Pay varies depending on location and employer. Starting salaries are likely to be around £16k a year rising to around £20k-£30k with experience.

Skills and Qualities
able to cope under pressure, aptitude for figures, attention to detail, diplomatic, discreet, efficient record keeping, good communication skills, IT skills, methodical

Relevant Subjects
Business and accounting, Economics, ICT/Computer studies, Mathematics

Further Information
Apprenticeship Schemes (National Apprenticeship Service) - www.apprenticeships.org.uk

Diploma in Business, Administration and Finance - www.baf-diploma.org.uk/

Financial Services Skills Council - sector skills council for financial services, accountancy & finance - www.fssc.org.uk/

Payroll World (Payroll World) - www.payrollworld.com

Training Schemes - www.direct.gov.uk/en/educationandlearning

Welsh Baccalaureate - www.wbq.org.uk

Addresses
Association of Accounting Technicians (AAT)
140 Aldersgate Street, London EC1A 4HY
Phone: +44 (0)20 7397 3000
Web: www.aat.org.uk

Institute of Certified Bookkeepers
1 Northumberland Avenue, Trafalgar Square, London WC2N 5BW
Phone: 0845 060 2345 (UK only)
Web: www.book-keepers.org

Institute of Payroll Professionals (IPP)
Shelly House, Farmhouse Way, Monkspath, Solihull B90 4EH
Phone: +44 (0)121 712 1000
Web: www.payrollprofession.org

International Association of Bookkeepers (IAB)
Suite 30 , 40 Churchill Square Kings Hil, West Malling,
Kent ME19 4YU
Phone: 0844 330 3527 (UK only)
Web: www.iab.org.uk

Similar Jobs
Accounting Technician, Bank Officer, Building Society Officer, Clerk: Accounts, Pensions Administrator

Pension Fund Manager
also known as: Pension Scheme Manager, Pensions Manager

CRCI:Financial Services
CLCI:NAN Job Band: 4 to 5

Job Description
Pension fund managers are responsible for the management and effective operation of a pension scheme for employees. They ensure that pension contributions are collected and that the money is efficiently invested. Answer enquiries from members of pension schemes and their financial advisers. May contribute to annual and financial reports.

They update records, provide regular statements and ensure that people get the pension benefits that are due to them. Liaise with investment managers, trade union officials, stockbrokers, lawyers and officials of the Department of Work and Pensions to ensure compliance with pensions administration regulations. Some give presentations on pension matters. Ensuring that all staff and products meet the standards set by the Financial Services Authority is also part of this job.

Work Details
You are normally office based and work regular office hours, Monday to Friday, though you should be prepared to work extra hours at times and sometimes away from home. As a manager, you need to be able to manage clerical staff. Team work is usual but you also have to be able to work on your own. Much of the work is done with the use of a computer and you may need to contact people by telephone or email.

Qualification

- **England, Wales and Northern Ireland**

Band 4: There are no set minimum entry requirements for student registration with the Pensions Management Institute, but it is recommended that potential students have at least 5 GCSEs (A*-C) including maths and English, plus two A levels, or equivalent qualifications.

Band 5: For degree courses: 2-3 A levels and some GCSEs (A*-C) usually including English and maths, or equivalent. Exact requirements depend on the degree you take.

- **Scotland**

Band 4: There are no set minimum entry requirements for student registration with the Pensions Management Institute, but it is recommended that potential students have at least five S grades (1-3) including maths and English, plus three H grades, or similar qualifications.

Band 5: For degree courses: 3-5 H grades and some S grades (1-3), usually including English and maths, or similar qualifications. Exact requirements depend on the degree you take.

Degree Information
Any degree discipline is acceptable, but accountancy, business studies/administration, mathematics, economics, statistics, law and financial management/banking are generally more advantageous.

Adult Qualifications
Course entry requirements are usually relaxed for suitable mature applicants. Those without the required qualifications may complete a foundation or Access course leading to relevant HNDs or accredited degrees.

Work Experience
Relevant work or voluntary experience is always useful and can improve your chances when applying for this job. Any experience in the finance sector is relevant, and time spent in an accountancy firm, an insurance company or shadowing a pensions adviser gives you a good basis and insight into the profession. Some employers offer summer vacation work experience placements. The Pensions Management Institute website gives details of summer internships and industrial placements.

Entry and Training
Most entrants to pension fund management have a degree, although there are no set entry requirements for this work. It is possible to start as a pensions administrator, gain experience and professional qualifications and progress to management posts. For those with a degree, postgraduate study is not essential, but studying for the professional exams of the Pensions Management Institute (PMI) may improve your chances of career development.

Training usually takes around three years of part-time study and includes practical on-the-job experience. Study can be through distance-learning courses or by evening classes at a college. Trainees usually gain experience in several different departments during the first 12-18 months of their training. Successful completion of the Advanced Diploma in Retirement Provision of the PMI, together with three years' practical experience, leads to associate membership of the PMI (APMI).

Students must be at least 18 years old to register with the PMI; graduates and others with relevant professional qualifications may be exempt from some examinations. Professional qualifications from the Chartered Insurance Institute, the Institute of Payroll Professionals, the ifs School of Finance and the Institute of Chartered Secretaries and Administrators are also useful.

Appropriate S/NVQs in financial advice are available at levels 3-4. The Financial Services Skills Council (FSSC) offer apprenticeships for both new and existing employees. The apprenticeship is made up of a technical certificate which represents a professional qualification, an NVQ/SVQ and the opportunity to obtain, key, core and essential skills. Contact the FSSC for further details as there may also be relevant apprenticeships in retail financial services available in your area. A Diploma/Welsh Bacclaureate in business, adminstration and finance may also be available in your area, and may provide a useful start to this career.

Pensions managers are expected to do continuing professional development. The PMI runs a structured development programme.

Mature entrants are welcome, particularly those with experience of work in pensions. Experience of accounts, insurance or administrative work together with maturity can also be an advantage.

Opportunities and Pay
The government is reducing its commitment to the state pension and has introduced changes to the legal regulation of the pensions industry in recent years, so the role of the pension scheme manager is becoming increasingly important. The UK pensions industry is one of the largest in the world; typical employers include large companies which manage their own pension schemes, public sector pension providers, or insurance or life assurance firms and consultancies that manage a scheme on behalf of a company.

Opportunities are increasing, with jobs available throughout the UK, though competition for jobs is fierce. Many jobs are based in the London area, but there is also a concentration of employment in Edinburgh and Glasgow. Promotion can be to pension fund manager of a larger company or into general management. There are also opportunities for experienced pension fund managers to work as self-employed consultants. Work abroad is possible if you work for a multinational company.

Pay varies depending on the location and size of company. Starting salaries for graduates are around £20k a year, rising to £35k-£45k with experience. Some senior managers working for large companies can earn salaries as high as £85k a year. Performance-related bonuses are often available.

Skills and Qualities
able to motivate others, analytical skills, attention to detail, decisive, good communication skills, good interpersonal skills, good organisational skills, information handling skills, IT skills, numeracy skills

Relevant Subjects
Business and accounting, Economics, English, ICT/Computer studies, Law, Mathematics

Further Information
AGCAS: Accountancy and Business Services (Job Sector Briefing) (AGCAS) - www.prospects.ac.uk/

Apprenticeship Schemes (National Apprenticeship Service) - www.apprenticeships.org.uk

Diploma in Business, Administration and Finance - www.baf-diploma.org.uk/

Financial Services Skills Council - sector skills council for financial services, accountancy & finance - www.fssc.org.uk/

Inside Careers Guide: Pensions - www.insidecareers.co.uk

Pensions Management - www.pensions-management.co.uk
PMI Careers Guide to Pensions (PMI) - www.insidecareers.co.uk/pen
Welsh Baccalaureate - www.wbq.org.uk

Addresses

Chartered Insurance Institute (CII)
42-48 High Road, South Woodford, London E18 2JP
Phone: +44 (0)20 8989 8464
Web: www.cii.co.uk

Financial Services Authority (FSA)
Membership Department, 25 The North Colonnade, Canary Wharf, London E14 5HS
Phone: +44 (0)20 7066 1000
Web: www.fsa.gov.uk

ifs School of Finance
IFS House, 4-9 Burgate Lane, Canterbury, Kent CT1 2XJ
Phone: +44 (0)1227 818609
Web: www.ifslearning.ac.uk

Institute of Chartered Secretaries and Administrators (ICSA)
16 Park Crescent, London W1B 1AH
Phone: +44 (0)20 75804741
Web: www.icsa.org.uk

Institute of Payroll Professionals (IPP)
Shelly House, Farmhouse Way, Monkspath, Solihull B90 4EH
Phone: +44 (0)121 712 1000
Web: www.payrollprofession.org

National Association of Pension Funds (NAPF)
NIOC House, 4 Victoria Street, London SW1H 0NX
Phone: +44 (0)20 7808 1300
Web: www.napf.co.uk

Pensions Management Institute (PMI)
PMI House 4-10 Artillery Lane, London E1 7LS
Phone: +44 (0)20 7392 7410
Web: www.pensions-pmi.org.uk

Similar Jobs

Accountant: Industry & Commerce, Actuary, Financial Adviser/ Planner, Investment Analyst, Pensions Administrator, Pensions Adviser

Pensions Administrator

CRCI:Financial Services
CLCI:NAN

Job Band: 3

Job Description

Pensions administrators are concerned with the day-to-day administration of pension schemes. Undertake a wide range of duties which may include updating contributions information on a computer database, doing straightforward calculations and maintaining accurate records of the details of scheme members. May deal directly with the public, giving advice on entitlement to a pension and on contribution rates that need to be paid. They need to keep up-to-date with the legal implications that govern income tax, social security and pensions.

Pensions administrators deal with enquiries from scheme members, trustees, employers, independent financial advisers and the Department of Work and Pensions in writing and by telephone. Look up information, check details and calculate entitlements.

Work Details

You are usually office based and may be based in a large contact centre. Regular working hours of 35 hrs a week are normal, Monday to Friday, though you should be prepared to work extra hours at times. Pensions administrators working in contact centres may be required to work shifts to cover evenings and weekends.

Part time work and job sharing is widely available. Face-to-face contact with customers is rare and you work with clients online or using the telephone. Team work is usual and much work is done with the use of a computer.

Qualification

- **England, Wales and Northern Ireland**

Band 3: For entry: usually at least 4 GCSEs (A*-C) including English and maths, or equivalent.

- **Scotland**

Band 3: For entry: usually at least four S grades (1-3) including English and maths, or similar.

Adult Qualifications

Employers expect a good standard of secondary education.

Work Experience

Relevant work or voluntary experience is always useful and can improve your chances in application for entry to this job. Working in an office environment using administration skills or working with numbers is useful and helps you to decide whether this career is right for you. Experience of basic accounting skills is also an advantage.

Entry and Training

Employers look for personality and communication skills as well as the basic academic qualifications. Many administrators are now required to take examinations to assess working practice and competence. Pensions administrators can take relevant examinations through the Pensions Management Institute (PMI), such as the Qualification in Pensions Administration (QPA), the Diploma in Pensions Calculations (DPC) and the Qualification in Public Sector Pensions Administration.

The QPA is an S/NVQ level 4 work-based qualification for pensions administrators and consists of eight units that are assessed by evidence collected during work, and case study examinations. There are no entry requirements and students complete the course at their own pace, but it generally takes between two and four years to complete. After qualifying there is an opportunity to apply for ordinary membership of the PMI.

Some entrants study for the DPC through the PMI. This is also a level 4 qualification divided into five units, but it is a vocational-related qualification (VRQ) rather than an S/NVQ. The National Association of Pensions Funds and the Chartered Insurance Institute also offers a range of relevant training courses. Details of all approved qualifications are available from the Financial Services Authority.

Training programmes, including apprenticeship schemes in providing financial services, may be available in your area. In Scotland specific apprenticeship pathways in pensions administration and pensions advice are available. Advanced apprenticeships leading to qualification at level 3 can also be a route into higher education. A Diploma/Welsh Baccalaureate in business, administration and finance may be available in your area, and may be a useful introduction to this career.

Mature applicants are welcomed but you are required to pass the same exams as those people who enter from school or college. There are opportunities for adults who are changing careers or looking to re-enter the labour market after a career break.

Previous experience in a related area such as accountancy or insurance is an advantage. You can gain recognition of previous experience through Accreditation of Prior Learning (APL), or by working towards relevant S/NVQs. Contact your local careers office, Jobcentre Plus, Next Step service or Learning and Skills Council (LSC)/Local Enterprise Company (LEC) for details of all training opportunities and schemes, including apprenticeships.

Opportunities and Pay

The Government is reducing its commitment to the state pension and has introduced changes to the legal regulation of the pensions industry in recent years, so the role of pension scheme employees is becoming increasingly important. The UK pensions industry is one of the largest in the world; employers include the pensions department or section of an organisation which runs its own pension scheme, an insurance company, large trade unions or with firms of consultants or actuaries.

Promotion to senior pensions administrator/supervisor or team leader, and progression to pensions management is possible. With further qualifications you may also become a pensions adviser. It is also possible to diversify into other roles in the financial sector, including paraplanning, financial advice or consultancy.

Pay varies depending on location and employer. Trainees start at around £15k-£20k rising to £30k a year with experience. Senior administrators with more than five years' experience can earn up to £40k a year.

Skills and Qualities

accurate, aptitude for teamwork, attention to detail, efficient record keeping, excellent communication skills, good telephone manner, information handling skills, IT skills, numeracy skills, trustworthy

Relevant Subjects

Business and accounting, Economics, English, ICT/Computer studies, Law, Mathematics

Further Information

Apprenticeship Schemes (National Apprenticeship Service) - www.apprenticeships.org.uk

Diploma in Business, Administration and Finance - www.baf-diploma.org.uk/

Financial Services Skills Council - sector skills council for financial services, accountancy & finance - www.fssc.org.uk/

Inside Careers Guide: Pensions - www.insidecareers.co.uk

PMI Careers Guide to Pensions (PMI) - www.insidecareers.co.uk/pen

Training Schemes - www.direct.gov.uk/en/educationandlearning

Welsh Baccalaureate - www.wbq.org.uk

Addresses

Chartered Insurance Institute (CII)
42-48 High Road, South Woodford, London E18 2JP
Phone: +44 (0)20 8989 8464
Web: www.cii.co.uk

Financial Services Authority (FSA)
Membership Department, 25 The North Colonnade, Canary Wharf, London E14 5HS
Phone: +44 (0)20 7066 1000
Web: www.fsa.gov.uk

National Association of Pension Funds (NAPF)
NIOC House, 4 Victoria Street, London SW1H 0NX
Phone: +44 (0)20 7808 1300
Web: www.napf.co.uk

Pensions Management Institute (PMI)
PMI House 4-10 Artillery Lane, London E1 7LS
Phone: +44 (0)20 7392 7410
Web: www.pensions-pmi.org.uk

Similar Jobs

Accounting Technician, Bank Officer, Insurance Broker, Insurance Technician, Paraplanner, Pensions Adviser

Pensions Adviser

also known as: Retirement Benefits Consultant

CRCI:Financial Services
CLCI:NAN — Job Band: 4 to 5

Job Description

Pensions advisers advise private clients, either companies or individual clients, on the options and merits of various pension products and help them to choose the most appropriate pension for their retirement. Explain the risks involved with each scheme and may be involved in the scheme design, valuations and calculation of transfer values. Make mathematical calculations and apply taxation rules. Liaise with the pension fund's solicitors, HM Revenue and Customs and employee's representatives.

They also help a client to consider alternative schemes or make adjustments to an existing scheme should their circumstances change. Use a computer in much of the work. Keep up to date with all the rules and regulations for pension contributions and tax. Following rules and guidelines from the Financial Services Authority is an important aspect of this job.

Work Details

Usually work office hours, Monday to Friday, if working for an insurance or pensions company, but need to be flexible if an independent adviser. Some work from home. Work independently or as part of a small team, and are supported by pensions administrators. The work usually involves a lot of travel, meeting clients in their own homes or businesses. You may need to work evenings and weekends and also spend short periods away from home. You are in contact with a wide variety of people, face to face, by telephone and by letter/email. Work can be stressful because it may be very competitive.

Qualification

• England, Wales and Northern Ireland

Band 4: For BTEC higher national award: 1-2 A levels and some GCSEs (A*-C) usually including English and maths, or equivalent.

Band 5: For degree courses: 2-3 A levels and some GCSEs (A*-C) usually including English and maths, or equivalent. Exact requirements depend on the degree you take.

• Scotland

Band 4: For SQA higher national award: usually 2-3 H grades and some S grades (1-3), often including English and maths, or similar qualifications.

Band 5: For degree courses: 3-5 H grades and some S grades (1-3), usually including English and maths, or similar qualifications. Exact requirements depend on the degree you take.

Degree Information

Any degree discipline is acceptable, but accountancy, business studies/administration, mathematics, economics, statistics, law and financial management/banking give useful background knowledge.

Adult Qualifications

Relevant professional qualifications may provide some exemption from the Pensions Management Institute examinations. Entry requirements may be relaxed for adults applying for higher education courses. Foundation and Access courses give adults without qualifications a route on to degree courses.

Work Experience

Relevant work or voluntary experience is always useful and improves your chances in application for entry into this job. Any work experience in the finance sector is relevant and shows enthusiasm and commitment to the work, such as time spent in an accountancy firm, an insurance company or even shadowing a pensions adviser. The Pensions Management Institute website gives details of summer internships and industrial placements.

Entry and Training
There are no set entry requirements, but most people who enter this job have a degree, HND, BTEC/SQA award, or a relevant initial qualification in accountancy, insurance or banking. Some of the larger companies offer graduate training programmes, but usually ask for a 2.1 degree.

The Pensions Management Institute offers a training programme based on a credit system. This means that entrants can start the programme from different points depending on their qualifications, and choose the route they take. Most pensions advisers are likely to be encouraged to work towards the advanced diploma in retirement provision, which, after three years' experience, leads to associate membership of the Institute.

Advisers who want to be involved in more general financial advice need to take a Financial Services Authority recognised qualification, such as the certificate in financial planning (Cert FP) awarded by the Chartered Insurance Institute. There are no educational requirements for those wishing to take the Cert FP. Some exemptions are available for those students holding other financial, investment or accounting qualifications.

Other approved qualifications include those offered by the ifs School of Finance, Chartered Institute of Bankers in Scotland, and the Securities & Investment Institute. Study is possible through distance learning, including computer-based training, or residential courses. Continuing professional development is expected throughout your career.

An apprenticeship in advising on financial products or a Diploma/ Welsh Baccalaureate in business, administration and finance may be available in your area, and may be a useful start to this career. Appropriate S/NVQs at levels 2-4 may also be available.

Mature entry is an advantage for this job and relevant professional qualifications such as insurance, legal or actuarial, may grant exemptions from some of the qualifying exams. It is advantageous to have some experience of working with the general public. Many pensions administrators and also those who have worked in a supporting role to financial advisers, may move into this job.

You can gain recognition of previous experience through Accreditation of Prior Learning (APL) or by working towards relevant S/NVQs. Contact your local careers office, Jobcentre Plus, Next Step service or Learning and Skills Council (LSC)/Local Enterprise Company (LEC) for details of all training opportunities and schemes, including apprenticeships.

Opportunities and Pay
The government is reducing its commitment to the state pension and has introduced changes to the legal regulation of the pensions industry in recent years, so the role of the pensions advisers is becoming increasingly important. The UK pensions industry is one of the largest in the world. Pensions advisers are employed by insurance companies, banks and financial institutions, as well as pension companies and large organisations, including accountancy firms and trade unions.

Promotion prospects depend on the organisation you work for, but advancement to senior adviser or investment manager is possible. There may be opportunities to move into general management or training. It is also possible to work abroad advising British people overseas. An adviser may be self-employed or work for a group of independent advisers.

Earnings for pension advisers, including various commissions and bonuses, are likely to start at around £22k-£30k a year, rising to £40k with experience. The most experienced and successful advisers and those taking on managerial roles can earn more than £70k a year.

Skills and Qualities
able to explain clearly, analytical skills, attention to detail, good interpersonal skills, good listening skills, good spoken communication, good written English, IT skills, numeracy skills, sound judgement

Relevant Subjects
Business and accounting, Economics, English, ICT/Computer studies, Law, Mathematics

Further Information
Apprenticeship Schemes (National Apprenticeship Service) - www.apprenticeships.org.uk

Diploma in Business, Administration and Finance - www.baf-diploma.org.uk/

Financial Services Skills Council - sector skills council for financial services, accountancy & finance www.fssc.org.uk/

Inside Careers Guide: Pensions - www.insidecareers.co.uk

PMI Careers Guide to Pensions (PMI) - www.insidecareers.co.uk/pen

TARGETjobs: City and Finance (GTI Specialist Publishers Ltd) - www.groupgti.com

Training Schemes - www.direct.gov.uk/en/educationandlearning

Welsh Baccalaureate - www.wbq.org.uk

Addresses
Chartered Institute of Bankers in Scotland (CIOBS)
Drumsheugh House, 38b Drumsheugh Gardens,
Edinburgh EH3 7SW
Phone: +44 (0)131 473 7777
Web: www.charteredbanker.com

Chartered Insurance Institute (CII)
42-48 High Road, South Woodford, London E18 2JP
Phone: +44 (0)20 8989 8464
Web: www.cii.co.uk

Financial Services Authority (FSA)
Membership Department, 25 The North Colonnade, Canary Wharf, London E14 5HS
Phone: +44 (0)20 7066 1000
Web: www.fsa.gov.uk

ifs School of Finance
IFS House, 4-9 Burgate Lane, Canterbury, Kent CT1 2XJ
Phone: +44 (0)1227 818609
Web: www.ifslearning.ac.uk

Pensions Management Institute (PMI)
PMI House 4-10 Artillery Lane, London E1 7LS
Phone: +44 (0)20 7392 7410
Web: www.pensions-pmi.org.uk

Securities & Investment Institute (SII)
8 Eastcheap, London EC3M 1AE
Phone: +44 (0)20 7645 0600
Web: www.sii.org.uk

Similar Jobs
Actuary, Financial Adviser/Planner, Insurance Broker, Investment Analyst, Paraplanner, Pension Fund Manager, Pensions Administrator

Perfusionist
also known as: Clinical Perfusion Scientist

CRCI:Healthcare
CLCI:JOB Job Band: 5

Job Description
Perfusionists are key members of the cardiac surgical team, operating complex medical equipment that keeps a patient's heart and lungs working during heart surgery and other major organ transplants. They monitor readings and the patient's condition as the operation takes place to keep the patient alive during, for example, open-heart surgery or a liver transplant. Control the activity of machines that pump blood around the patient's body replacing carbon dioxide with oxygen in the patient's bloodstream. Administer blood transfusions. Work with surgeons, anaesthetists, theatre nurses and other support staff.

Perfusionists have additional key responsibility in intensive care units where they operate and manage other vital equipment to support the circulation of critically ill patients. May also be involved in research.

Work Details

You usually work a 37 hr week in a hospital assisting senior colleagues, but may be required to work shifts on a rota to cover 24 hrs a day, including some weekends. Overtime work is possible. You work in a hospital operating theatre with other specialists such as surgeons, anaesthetists and theatre nurses. Work can be pressured at times. You help people and work closely in a team. You need to cope with the sight of blood, and are expected to wear a uniform and protective clothing.

Qualification

• England, Wales and Northern Ireland

Band 5: For degree courses: 2-3 A levels and some GCSEs (A*-C) usually including English, science and maths, or equivalent. Exact requirements depend on the degree you take.

• Scotland

Band 5: For degree courses: 3-5 H grades and some S grades (1-3), usually including English, science and maths, or similar qualifications. Exact requirements depend on the degree you take.

Degree Information

A degree in a biological or clinical science subject is needed for this job. Many science degrees are not considered sufficient grounding and may make finding a trainee perfusion position difficult. Check the content of the first degree you choose carefully. A postgraduate diploma in clinical perfusion sciences is available at North East Surrey College of Technology (NESCOT) for trainees working in a clinical cardiac unit. There is also an MSc in clinical perfusion science.

Adult Qualifications

Employers expect relevant qualifications to enable you to cope with the level of academic training required but entry requirements may be relaxed for adults applying for higher education courses. Access and foundation courses give adults without qualifications a route on to degree courses.

Work Experience

Work experience gives you an insight into what you enjoy about a job or working environment, and the opportunity to acquire new skills. It provides valuable information to add to your CV and improves your employment prospects. Consider working with people, either in a team or in a helping capacity. Experience of working in a hospital environment is always useful. A list of the forty or so NHS hospitals and those in the private sector with perfusion units can be obtained from the Society of Clinical Perfusion Scientists.

Entry and Training

You need a relevant BSc degree in a science subject and to obtain a training post in a hospital with a perfusion unit. Perfusion is a very small profession and only four or five vacancies occur each year for students who want to train. Trainee posts are in hospitals that carry out major open-heart surgery and organ transplants and many of these are located in London. There may also be training opportunities through London Perfusion Science. Consult the website for details.

Training consists of practical on-the-job experience under supervision, and formal academic study leading to a PgCert, a PgDip, and with later study, an MSc in Perfusion Science. North East Surrey College of Technology (NESCOT) is the only qualifying MSc course in the country. On completion of the diploma and with experience of 150 clinical procedures, perfusionists are then eligible to take the professional examination, the certificate of accreditation in basic clinical perfusion sciences, and to practise as an independent, fully competent clinical perfusionist. Students who successfully complete this course receive professional registration and accreditation from the Society of Clinical Perfusion Scientists of Great Britain and Ireland.

A foundation degree is available in clinical physiology that includes a module in perfusion and can be studied either full or part time.

Mature applicants are particularly welcome though you usually require an accredited degree/postgraduate degree for direct entry.

Opportunities and Pay

Around 350 people work as qualified perfusionists in the UK. This is a very small and specialised profession that is continuing to grow. Opportunities are in one of the 40 NHS hospitals with perfusion units or in private hospitals. Most vacancies are in London or other major cities in the UK. Promotion prospects are reasonably good and usually through a formal structure, requiring experience and advanced qualifications. You may need to move between hospitals to develop your career. Some move into research or education and training. Progress to senior positions depends on the advanced qualifications you take and the level of your involvement in clinical research. British qualifications are well regarded in other parts of the world and opportunities exist, particularly in the Middle East, USA and the rest of Europe.

Pay is on a nationally agreed scale and increases with promotion. Those working in the NHS follow a salary scale divided into levels of experience and are graded as either medical technical officers or clinical scientists. Trainee clinical perfusionists start earning around £20k a year, rising to around £25k on qualifying, then £35k-£45k with experience. Department managers can earn around £53k-£79k a year.

Health

There is a risk of infection. You require good general fitness.

Skills and Qualities

able to communicate effectively, able to follow procedures, able to put people at ease, able to take responsibility, accurate, aptitude for teamwork, calm, IT skills, not squeamish, technical aptitude

Relevant Subjects

Biology, Chemistry, Health and social care, ICT/Computer studies, Mathematics, Physics, Science

Further Information

AGCAS: Health (Job Sector Briefing) (AGCAS) - www.prospects.ac.uk

NHS Careers (NHS Careers) - www.nhscareers.nhs.uk

NHS Careers Scotland - www.infoscotland.com/nhs

NHS Careers Wales - www.wales.nhs.uk

Perfusionist Journal (bi-monthly) (Soc of Clinical Perfusion Scientists of GB) - www.sopgbi.org/

Addresses

London Perfusion Science (LPS)
5 Great College Street, London SW1P 3SJ
Phone: 07703 182420 (UK only)
Web: www.londonperfusionscience.com

North East Surrey College of Technology (NESCOT)
Reigate Road, Ewell, Epsom, Surrey KT17 3DS
Phone: +44 (0)20 8394 1731
Web: www.nescot.ac.uk

Society of Clinical Perfusion Scientists of GB & Ireland
The Royal College of Surgeons 35-43 Lincoln's Inn Field, London WC2A 3PN
Phone: +44 (0)207 869 6891
Web: www.scps.org.uk/

Similar Jobs

Cardiac Physiologist, Clinical Scientist: Medical Physicist, Clinical Technologist, Operating Department Practitioner, Respiratory Physiologist

Personal Adviser (Connexions) (England)

CRCI:Social Work and Counselling Services
CLCI:KED Job Band: 4 to 5

Job Description

Personal advisers work with young people to help them make a successful move into further education, training or employment. Aim to help young people between the ages of 13-19, and those with a disability or learning difficulty up to 25, to achieve their full potential and overcome any barriers to their learning. They offer support, guidance, advice and information on their options and act as a mentor, giving support on a one-to-one basis. They assess what extra help is needed, such as help with housing. May work with students in the last few years of their compulsory education, or with those who have recently left school or college.

Work with agencies such as social services, the probation service and housing, as well as employers, parents/carers and training organisations. They promote links with the local community, give talks and do administration tasks which include record keeping.

Work Details

Personal advisers work in one or more of a school/college, a Connexions centre or a one-stop shop. They work variable hours from Monday to Friday, though sometimes you may be required to work in the evening and at weekends. Some advisers work through community-based projects that provide an outreach service to young people. It is necessary to travel around a local area and sometimes further afield, particularly in rural areas. You work with secondary school students, young adults and parents/carers. Sometimes you may need to visit young people and their parents/carers in their own homes.

Your duties include interviewing and advising young people as well as liaison with teachers, social workers and other professionals. Some personal advisers work with those who have special needs. Work can be pressurised at times and you may need to deal with a crisis that can occur in the life of a young person.

Qualification

- **England, Wales and Northern Ireland**

Band 4: For entry to courses: 1-2 A levels and some GCSEs (A*-C), usually including English and maths, or equivalent.

Band 5: For degree courses: 2-3 A levels and some GCSEs (A*-C) usually including English and maths, or equivalent. Exact requirements depend on the degree you take.

Degree Information

A degree in any discipline is acceptable but subjects such as psychology, social work, education, community studies, youth studies or sociology, are particularly relevant.

Adult Qualifications

Qualifications and experience in teaching, social work, careers guidance, youth or probation work, are an advantage.

Work Experience

Entry to this job is competitive and it is important that you do some relevant work or voluntary experience before applying. Relevant work includes anything involving dealing with young people and the public in a helping capacity, such as at youth and community centre work. Areas which involve listening skills and any observation or direct experience in the caring professions are useful.

Entry and Training

You can become a personal adviser by taking a Qualification in Careers Guidance (QCG) or through on-the-job training. The QCG is a one-year full-time or two-year part-time course which combines academic study with work-based learning. Most people entering this course have a degree, but you may also be accepted with relevant experience, so you should check with course providers. See the Institute of Career Guidance (ICG) website for details of colleges and universities providing the QCG.

Alternatively a new work-based training route is available, which will replace NVQ levels 3-4 in advice and guidance in 2011. These include the level 4 Diploma in Career Information and Advice and the level 6 Diploma in Career Guidance and Development. Contact Lifelong Learning UK for details of the new qualifications and ICG for details of all routes to qualifying. The work-based route means you may be able to start as a trainee personal adviser and work towards the required qualifications. Experience of working with young people may be required, and it is useful to have a background in a relevant area like youth work, social work, careers advice or education.

As part of your training, you also complete other Connexions training courses that cover specific areas, such as counselling, drugs awareness, health and safety issues, child protection and equal opportunities. Entrants are also trained in the framework for assessment, planning, implementation and review (APIR), a scheme for working with young people. Until fully qualified, you work under supervision.

The National Open College Network offers awards and certificates in information, advice or guidance at NQF levels 1-3. The minimum age for entry to courses is 18. Contact your local Open College Network for further information. You need Criminal Records Bureau (CRB) clearance to make sure you are suitable to work with young people. You may find it useful to have a driving licence, as you need to travel within the local area.

Maturity and experience are essential for this job. An Access course is available for those with relevant experience and aptitude. You can also gain recognition of previous experience through Accreditation of Prior Learning (APL), or by working towards relevant NVQs. Those with qualifications in careers advice (QCG - Qualification in Careers Guidance), social work (social work degree or diploma), or in youth work (National Youth Agency's professional certification), can train to become personal advisers (Connexions).

Opportunities and Pay

Personal advisers (PAs) are employed directly by local authorities. Children's trusts have been set up in each local authority area with responsibility to plan and commission integrated youth services. It is uncertain how Connexions services and the PA role will change in the future as the Coalition Government are currently reviewing how young people receive advice and guidance services. Check with the Department for Education for the most up-to-date information.

PAs may be employed to work in one main location or a variety of locations. For example, they may work in careers or Connexions centres, or as an outreach service and work in a number of locations in the community. Others are based in, and employed by, schools or further education colleges. The Connexions Service also employs advisers to advise and support young people over the phone and online.

Promotion to a senior or management post is possible after gaining experience and it is also possible to move into related areas such as education welfare and training, youth work and the care sector. There are opportunities for part time, flexi-time, job-sharing and work during school term time only.

Pay varies depending on location and employer, but is likely to be around £15k-£22k for a trainee, progressing to £23k-£29k a year as a qualified adviser. With experience a personal adviser can earn up to £35k a year.

Skills and Qualities

able to inspire confidence, administrative skills, awareness of confidentiality issues, excellent communication skills, fair minded, friendly, good organisational skills, information handling skills, IT skills, non-judgemental.

Relevant Subjects
English, Psychology, Sociology

Further Information
Careers Guidance Today (quarterly) (Institute of Careers Guidance (ICG) - www.icg-uk.org/career_guidance_today.html

Connexions Direct (Connexions) - www.connexions-direct.com

LLUK (Lifelong Learning UK) - sector skills council for the professional development of staff working in the lifelong learning sector - www.lluk.org

National Open College Network - www.nocn.org.uk

▶Working in advice & counselling (2007) (Babcock Lifeskills) - www.babcock-lifeskills.com/

▶Working in schools & colleges (2007) (Babcock Lifeskills) - www.babcock-lifeskills.com/

Addresses
Department for Education
Castle View House East Lane, Runcorn, Cheshire WA7 2GJ
Phone: 0870 000 2288 (UK only)
Web: www.education.gov.uk/

Institute of Career Guidance (ICG)
Ground Floor Copthall House 1 New Road, Stourbridge, West Midlands DY8 1PH
Phone: +44 (0)1384 376 464
Web: www.icg-uk.org

Similar Jobs
Careers Adviser, Counsellor, Learning Mentor (England), Probation Officer, Social Worker, Teacher: Secondary School

Personal Assistant
also known as: Executive Assistant, Executive Secretary, PA

CRCI:Administration, Business and Office Work
CLCI:CAT Job Band: 3 to 5

Job Description
Personal assistants (PAs) work closely with a senior manager or business executive, supporting them, their team and department. PAs are usually the first point of contact with people from inside/outside the organisation. They screen mail and phone calls, making decisions about what to deal with and what to pass on, organise the work, deal with correspondence and keep an office diary. Also prepare agendas and take minutes, schedule travel and conference arrangements, handle enquiries and possibly supervise other office staff.

PAs collect and compile information for any reports the executive may have to write. May be responsible for recruiting, training and organising the work of other staff. Use word processing software and a networked/personal computer. Executive assistants (EAs) have the additional responsibility of organising an individual's personal life as well as supporting their business work.

Work Details
Usually work 37-40 hrs a week, Monday to Friday, but extra hours may be required. This largely depends on the working hours of your boss. You work from a desk in an office, attend meetings if required and may need to travel on occasions. PAs/EAs deal with confidential information, so need to be discreet and tactful. You come into contact with many people, depending on the company, such as other members of the office team, executives and directors, and representatives of other organisations.

You usually work for people who have very demanding jobs and whose work is often pressurised. Some businesses have flexitime, part-time work and job-share opportunities.

Qualification
• England, Wales and Northern Ireland
Band 3: For entry: usually at least 4 GCSEs (A*-C) including English and possibly maths, or equivalent. A foreign language, IT or business subject is particularly useful for courses and/or employment.

Band 4: For HND, Diploma of Higher Education or foundation degree: 1-2 A levels and some GCSEs (A*-C) usually including English and maths, or equivalent.

Band 5: For degree courses: 2-3 A levels and some GCSEs (A*-C) usually including English and maths, or equivalent. Exact requirements depend on the degree you take.

• Scotland
Band 3: For direct entry you usually need at least four S grades (1-3) including English and possibly maths, or similar qualifications. A foreign language, IT or business subject is particularly useful for courses and/or employment.

Band 4: For entry to SQA higher national and professional development awards, usually 2-3 H grades and some S grades (1-3), including English and maths, or similar qualifications.

Band 5: For degree courses: 3-5 H grades and some S grades (1-3), usually including English and maths, or similar qualifications. Exact entry requirements depend on the degree you take.

Degree Information
Any degree discipline is acceptable, though business-related degrees and subjects are particularly useful, as well as those combined with a modern foreign language.

Adult Qualifications
There may be special entry standards for adults applying for secretarial or related courses, or Access or foundation courses for mature applicants to gain entry to degree courses. Contact universities and colleges for details.

Work Experience
Entry to this job is competitive and it is important that you try to do some relevant work or voluntary experience before applying. Experience or an employed background in related areas such as legal, financial, bookkeeping, in-house events management, secretarial work and human resources are all relevant. Experience or knowledge of basic accounting techniques are also a distinct advantage.

Entry and Training
Increasingly, there is a demand for graduates and for those with a range of qualifications and skills in desktop publishing, databases and spreadsheets. You need excellent shorthand and typing/keyboard skills. There is a wide range of full and part-time courses for personal assistants/executive secretaries, including those courses offered by OCR, LCCI, BTEC/SQA. Courses include the level 3 diploma in administration (OCR) and the level 3 private secretary's diploma (LCCI). Check entry requirements with individual colleges as entry can be flexible. Relevant postgraduate courses are also available and continuing professional development (CPD) is encouraged. Some private colleges also offer short, intensive courses.

On-the-job training is provided by employers and you might be able to work towards S/NVQs in business and administration at levels 3-4 or the European Computer Driving Licence (ECDL), to improve your IT skills. Fully qualified PAs have the opportunity to join a professional organisation, such as the Institute of Professional Administrators (IPA) or the professional body of the sector in which they are working, such as the Chartered Institute of Personnel and Development (CIPD), if working in human resources. Visit the Council for Administration (CFA) website for details of training routes.

Entry without a degree/HND is possible. You can start work at junior secretarial level and become a PA or executive secretary by gaining secretarial experience and qualifications. Advanced apprenticeships leading to qualification at level 3 can also be a route into higher education.

A Diploma/Welsh Baccalaureate may be available in your area in business, administration and finance. The advanced level is equivalent to 3.5 A levels. See the diplomas website for further information.

Mature applicants with relevant experience may be preferred by some employers. Adults may be able to enter this work through a government-funded training programme. Contact your local Connexions or careers office, Jobcentre Plus, Next Step service or Learning and Skills Council (LSC)/Local Enterprise Company (LEC) for details of all training opportunities and schemes, including apprenticeships.

Opportunities and Pay

Companies that employ personal assistants (PAs) or executive assistants (EAs) tend to be based in towns and cities. Competition can be fierce and additional skills such as foreign languages improve employment prospects. You can work in business, industry, local or central government, the media, or for an individual, such as an author or a politician. It is possible to work for an agency obtaining temporary contracts with different firms. There is no clear promotion structure, though the most senior PAs or EAs work for managing directors, company presidents and chief executives.

Pay varies depending on location and company, but starting salaries are around £18k, rising to £20k-£25k a year with experience. Senior PAs/EAs earn from around £25k to more than £35k a year. EAs usually attract a higher salary due to the additional responsibility and often longer working hours.

Skills and Qualities

able to prioritise work, attention to detail, calm, discreet, flexible approach, good communication skills, good organisational skills, good spelling, grammar and punctuation, good telephone manner, initiative, IT skills, reliable, tactful

Relevant Subjects

Business and accounting, English, ICT/Computer studies

Further Information

AGCAS: Government & Public Administration (Job Sector Briefing) (AGCAS) - www.prospects.ac.uk

Council for Administration (CfA) - www.cfa.uk.com

Diplomas (Foundation, Higher and Advanced) - http://yp.direct.gov.uk/diplomas

Institute of Professional Administrators (Institute of Professional Administrators) - www.inprad.org

Real Life Guide to Business & Administration (Trotman 2009) - www.trotman.co.uk

The Definitive Personal Assistant and Secretarial Handbook (2009) (Kogan Page)

Training Schemes - www.direct.gov.uk/en/educationandlearning

▶Working in business, administration & finance (2010) (Babcock Lifeskills) - www.babcock-lifeskills.com/

▶Working in English (2007) (Babcock Lifeskills) - www.babcock-lifeskills.com/

Addresses

Chartered Institute of Personnel and Development (CIPD)
151 The Broadway, London SW19 1JQ
Phone: +44 (0)20 8612 6200
Web: www.cipd.co.uk

Institute of Professional Administrators
6 Graphite Square, Vauxhall Walk, London SE11 5EE
Phone: +44 (0) 20 7091 7340
Web: www.inprad.org/index.html

Similar Jobs

Office Manager, Rural Business Administrator, School Administrator, Secretary, Secretary: Legal, Secretary: Medical

Personal Shopper

also known as: Fashion Adviser, Styling Consultant

CRCI:Retail Sales and Customer Services
CLCI:OE
Job Band: 1 to 2

Job Description

Personal shoppers help people to buy items that suit their lifestyle, appearance, personality and budget. Often specialise in fashion, beauty and accessories. May shop for gifts for clients to give to others or to provide everything needed for an event. May be based in a single store or design house. Help customers find what they want and spend money in the store. May work independently for clients and shop in a range of stores, shopping malls and airports.

Make appointments with clients and find out what they need help with. Spend time learning about their lifestyle, image, likes and dislikes. Look at body size and shape, colouring and skin tone to decide the styles and colours that suit the client best. May go round the store(s) with the client or bring items to them for the client to try on or inspect. Use knowledge of stock, fashion, the client and their budget to find accessories to complement the main item. Offer an honest opinion on whether items look right. If working in-store, promotes the store's loyalty card, credit cards and other deals.

Personal shoppers also set up and update client records. Keep track of what is in stock and anything new. May notify clients when new items that may be of interest come in. If self-employed, prepare and distribute marketing materials. Deal with appointments, bills, premises, insurance and general paperwork.

Work Details

Hours of work vary, depending on clients' needs. May include evening and weekend work, or shifts in places such as airports. You may work part time or be self-employed. May meet clients in a smart and comfortable VIP area with rooms where they can try on clothing. Most work with members of the public, but some work with celebrities, events organisers and film, TV or theatre wardrobe assistants and stylists. You need to be of smart appearance and may wear a uniform supplied by the employer.

Qualification

- **England, Wales and Northern Ireland**

Band 1: No minimum qualifications are required, but you are expected to have a good level of general education. However, some formal/vocational qualifications at any level are useful.

Band 2: Although academic qualifications are not specified for this job, it is an advantage to have some GCSEs (A*-C) in subjects that include English and maths, or equivalent.

- **Scotland**

Band 1: No minimum qualifications are required, but you are expected to have a good level of general education. However, some formal/vocational qualifications at any level are useful.

Band 2: Although academic qualifications are not specified for this job, it is an advantage to have some S grades (1-3) in subjects that include English and maths, or similar.

Adult Qualifications

There are no formal entry requirements for this job.

Work Experience

Paid or voluntary work experience in retail or customer care is useful. You can build up your fashion knowledge by reading magazines. Trend spotting on the high street and helping friends and family to shop allows you to improve your skills. Work shadowing a personal shopper can give you a valuable insight into the job.

In some areas you can do a young apprenticeship (14-16) in retail. You do an extended work placement and a level 2 qualification whilst at school. A Diploma/Welsh Baccalaureate in retail business may also be available in your area. For health and safety reasons there may be some jobs you cannot do until you are over 16.

Entry and Training

You do not need any particular qualifications for this job. Employers look for people with retail and customer care skills and experience. People entering this area of work may well have beauty therapy, retail or customer care qualifications. Training is on the job. You can work towards relevant qualifications such as S/NVQ level 2/3 in customer service and an ABC level 3 diploma in fashion retailing, if appropriate.

For self-employed personal shoppers, foundation training in core skills such as colour analysis and style assessment for men and women is available through a wide variety of training providers. Contact the Federation of Image Consultants, the professional body for image consultants, stylists and personal shoppers, for a list of accredited and registered training providers. Courses can be expensive. Personal shoppers need to keep up to date with the latest lifestyle and fashion trends and brands.

Adults often enter this area of work. It is common for stores to employ people who have been retail assistants (often in the same store), beauty consultants or worked in the fashion industry. Self-employed personal shoppers often develop their network of contacts and potential clients in a former job role.

Opportunities and Pay

Exclusive design houses, boutiques and large stores in major cities employ personal shoppers. There are also jobs in airports and shopping malls. Independent personal shoppers are often based in or near large shopping centres. In-store workers can progress to become supervisors or managers. You may go on to set up your own business using your network of contacts. Some become personal assistants or stylists to celebrities.

Personal shoppers in stores or shopping centres earn around £14k-£20k. Experienced staff may earn up to £30k a year. Some staff get bonuses and commission on top of their basic salary. Depending on the employer, those managing teams can earn £30k-£70k a year. Earnings for self-employed personal shoppers vary. They depend on what services you offer, how many clients you see and how much you charge. Prices for a half-day's consultation and shopping can range from £90-£300.

Health

For jobs in retail, employers expect normal eyesight (with or without glasses/lenses) and hearing. You need to have normal colour vision and be able to speak clearly.

Skills and Qualities

able to get on with all kinds of people, able to put people at ease, creative flair, customer service skills, good listening skills, good memory, good organisational skills, patient, perceptive, tactful

Relevant Subjects

English, Retail and distribution

Further Information

Apprenticeship Schemes (National Apprenticeship Service) - www.apprenticeships.org.uk

Behind the Scenes: Fashion (Trotman 2009) - www.trotman.co.uk

Diplomas (Foundation, Higher and Advanced) - http://yp.direct.gov.uk/diplomas

Federation of Image Consultancts (TFIC) - www.tfic.org.uk

Foundation Learning (QCDA) - www.qcda.gov.uk

How to get ahead in retail (Raintree Publishers) (Raintree Publishers)

Real Life Guide to Retail (Trotman) - www.trotman.co.uk

Skillsmart Retail - sector skills council for the retail industry - www.skillsmartretail.com

Welsh Baccalaureate - www.wbq.org.uk

▶Working in hairdressing & beauty (2009) (Babcock Lifeskills) - www.babcock-lifeskills.com/

▶Working in retail & customer services (2008) (Babcock Lifeskills) - www.babcock-lifeskills.com/

Addresses

Institute of Customer Service (ICS)
2 Castle Court, St Peter's Street, Colchester, Essex CO1 1EW
Phone: +44 (0)1206 571716
Web: www.instituteofcustomerservice.com

Similar Jobs

Beauty Consultant, Image Consultant, Retail Assistant, Retail Buyer

Pest Control Technician

also known as: Local Government Pest Control Officer
CRCI:Personal and Other Services
CLCI:IJ Job Band: 1 to 2

Job Description

Pest controllers use chemicals or traps to get rid of pests and vermin that are a danger to health, cause damage to crops or spoil food stocks. Pests include rats, fleas, cockroaches, rabbits, moles and wasps. They may also deal with birds, such as starlings and pigeons, that can damage buildings and be a danger to public health. They visit people's homes, warehouses, offices, schools, hospitals, shops and outdoor areas, inspect the problem, identify the cause, and carry out the treatment needed. Methods include trapping, shooting, laying poison, spraying an area with liquid insecticide, or using gas fumigation.

Some premises may require action to prevent further pest problems, such as metal spikes on window sills and roofs to stop birds from landing, or sealing rat holes to prevent further access. Pest controllers follow rules to dispose of dead or captured animals. They record details of each treatment that has been carried out, including location, date and time of visit, and store the information on a database.

Work Details

Usually work 37-39 hrs a week, Monday to Friday, though may have to work occasional evenings or weekends. Travels around an area to different sites in a company car or van. For much of the time, you work on your own. Depending on the pest hazard, you may have to cope with working in cold, damp, dirty, cramped places, and often outdoors in all sorts of weather. Some jobs require you to climb ladders.

Pest control technicians usually wear protective clothing, including gloves, a face mask and eye goggles, to protect against bites, stings, and dust, and from the chemicals used. There is a risk of direct exposure to skin irritants and infections. You may also have to cope with the sight of blood.

Qualification

- **England, Wales and Northern Ireland**

Band 1: For entry to jobs, no minimum qualifications are needed, but you are expected to have a good level of general education and relevant experience. Some formal/vocational qualifications at any level are useful.

Band 2: For some jobs: 3-4 GCSEs (A*-C) including science, maths and English, or equivalent, are an advantage.

- **Scotland**

Band 1: For entry to jobs, no minimum qualifications are needed, but you are expected to have a good level of general education and relevant experience. Some formal/vocational qualifications at any level are useful.

Band 2: For some jobs: 3-4 S grades (1-3) including science, maths and English, or similar qualifications, are an advantage.

Adult Qualifications
No entry qualifications are needed, but experience of the building trade or the use of chemicals is useful.

Work Experience
Any work experience can equip you with skills that you can use in the future and add to your CV. This can either be unpaid, or holiday/part-time work that you have sorted out yourself. You may be able to spend some time with a pest control officer that works for a local council, perhaps work shadowing.

Entry and Training
This job is not often open to school leavers, due to insurance requirements. Training is usually on the job and organised by your employer. Many technicians gain the British Pest Control Association (BPCA)/Royal Society for Public Health (RSPH) level 2 certificate in pest control. This usually takes five days full time. You then can take more advanced qualifications, such as certificate of proficiency in fumigation and the certificated surveyor in pest control. Contact the BPCA or the RSPH for details on qualifications and training routes.

The National Pest Technicians Association offers an advanced diploma in pest management and training seminars covering a variety of topics. Many technicians join the Professional Pest Technician Registration Scheme, administered by DATAS. This provides them with a credit-type card, showing details of their professional qualifications. Contact DATAS for further details. A driving licence is usually essential for this job.

Mature applicants to this job are usually preferred by employers and most pest control technicians (pest control officers in local government) are over the age of 25. Contact the British Pest Control Association (BPCA) or the Royal Society for Public Health (RSPH) for details on qualifications and training routes. The BPCA offers many of its training schemes by online learning.

Opportunities and Pay
Jobs are mainly based in towns and cities throughout the UK. You may be employed by a private pest control contractor, a local council, or be self-employed. Often there is more work in the summer when there are more pests. With experience, you can be promoted to supervisory roles, depending on the size of the organisation you work for.

Pay varies widely, but trainees start on around £13k a year, rising to about £22k when you are a registered professional. Supervisors may earn around £20k-£30k a year. Overtime payments and bonus schemes may boost your salary.

Health
The work involves a risk of infection, and there may also be a risk from skin irritants, chemicals, animals, birds and from insect stings. This job requires good health and physical fitness, good eyesight, and you should not suffer from any allergies or asthma.

Skills and Qualities
able to work well on your own, emotionally strong, enquiring mind, good communication skills, health & safety awareness, not squeamish, numeracy skills, practical skills, problem-solving skills, responsible attitude

Relevant Subjects
Biology, Chemistry, Land and Environment, Science

Further Information
Asset Skills - sector skills council for the places where we live and work - www.assetskills.org

Local Government Careers (Improvement and Development Agency) - www.lgcareers.com/publications/

Pest Control Portal - www.pestcontrolportal.com/

Professional Pest Controller (quarterly) (British Pest Control Association (BPCA)) - www.bpca.org.uk/ppc/ppconline.asp

Today's Technician (quarterly) (National Pest Technicians Association) - www.npta.org.uk/assets/pages/todaystechnician.html

Addresses
British Pest Control Association (BPCA)
Ground Floor, 1 Gleneagles House, Vernongate, South Street, Derby DE1 1UP
Phone: +44 (0)1332 294288
Web: www.bpca.org.uk

DATAS Associates Ltd
Queen Street Close, March, Cambridgeshire PE15 8SP
Phone: +44 (0)1354 659061
Web: www.datas.co.uk

National Pest Technicians Association (NPTA)
NPTA House, Hall Lane, Kinoulton, Nottingham NG12 3EF
Phone: +44 (0)1949 81133
Web: www.npta.org.uk

Royal Society for Public Health (RSPH)
3rd Floor Market Towers, 1 Nine Elms Lane, London SW8 5NQ
Phone: +44 (0)20 3177 1600
Web: www.rsph.org.uk

Similar Jobs
Cleaner: Industrial, Environmental Health Practitioner, Gamekeeper, Refuse Collector, RSPCA/Scottish SPCA Inspector

Pet Behaviour Counsellor
also known as: Clinical Animal Behaviourist, Pet Psychologist

CRCI:Environment, Animals and Plants
CLCI:WAL Job Band: 4 to 5

Job Description
Pet behaviour counsellors help people to deal with problem behaviour in companion animals. They advise an owner whose animal has developed inappropriate behaviour, such as aggression towards people, dogs or other animals, or toileting problems, destructiveness etc. Counsellors aim to help clients to improve their relationship with companion animals by preparing a treatment programme that also takes into account the physical and emotional circumstances of the owner. They usually take referrals from veterinary surgeons and also work closely with them.

Counsellors are aware of the influence that some animal medical conditions have on a pet's behaviour. They may give talks or lectures and may also write articles for the press, books and booklets. Must keep up to date with the latest developments in the field of animal behavioural therapy.

Work Details
A working week varies according to the number of appointments, though you may also be expected to work some evenings and weekends if the animal owners are not available during the working day. Some pet behaviour counsellors are able to use accommodation at a veterinary practice. A reasonable amount of travelling to different clinics and owners' premises is necessary. There may be risk of attack by aggressive or nervous animals and you may be working with people who are upset and in need of support. Your work involves listening and providing encouragement.

Qualification

- **England, Wales and Northern Ireland**

Band 4: For HND, Diploma of Higher Education or foundation degree: 1-2 A levels and some GCSEs (A*-C) usually including English, science and maths, or equivalent.

Band 5: For degree courses: 2-3 A levels and some GCSEs (A*-C), or equivalent. Subjects such as English, maths, chemistry, physics, biology may be preferred. Exact requirements depend on the degree you take.

- **Scotland**

Band 4: For entry to SQA higher national and professional development awards, usually 2-3 H grades and some S grades (1-3), including English, science and maths, or similar qualifications.

Band 5: For degree courses: 3-5 H grades and some S grades (1-3), or similar. Subjects such as English, maths, chemistry, physics, biology may be preferred. Exact requirements depend on the degree you take.

Degree Information

A degree in animal behaviour, animal sciences, behavioural studies, veterinary science, psychology, or one of the biological sciences provides the best background. There is an increasing number of specialist postgraduate courses on applied animal behaviour and animal behaviour counselling.

Adult Qualifications

Mature applicants for undergraduate courses are often considered with a variety of entry qualifications such as Open University credits, university extramural courses, academic qualifications, foundation or Access courses, or equivalent. Check with individual institutions because entry requirements vary.

Work Experience

Experience of work, especially with companion animals, over a period of several years is very important. This can be gained by voluntary work at places such as dog kennels, catteries, vet practices, animal welfare/rescue centres and livery stables.

Entry and Training

In order to get into this work you need a mixture of skills and experience in handling animals and a good knowledge of the theory of animal behaviour. There are no set entry requirements for this job, as anyone can call themselves a pet behaviour counsellor. However, the Association for the Study of Animal Behaviour (ASAB) and the Association of Pet Behaviour Counsellors (APBC) recommend a degree or postgraduate qualification in animal behaviour/science. Information on training courses is available from the APBC.

Experience is important as well as qualifications. You are required to have practical handling skills and experience, together with empathy and an ability to communicate and motivate owners. You also require the skills to run a professional, financially sound and accountable practice. Those who have an honours degree or higher in a behavioural or biological science and a minimum of three years' regular clinical experience, may apply to the ASAB for registration as a clinical animal behaviourist. They can also become a full member of the APBC. You are expected to keep your skills up to date by attending seminars and workshops.

There are foundation degrees available in animal behaviour and these can be used for entry to a full honours degree course. The Animal Care College also offers relevant short courses.

Mature applicants with a broad understanding of the factors that affect peoples' lives have an advantage for this job. It would suit those who understand how people/families interact with different types of companion animals, such as dogs, cats and horses. You may be able to obtain a grant for relevant study or travel from the Association for the Study of Animal Behaviour (ASAB). Some foundation degrees in animal behaviour, such as that at Bishop Burton College, are available partly by distance learning.

Opportunities and Pay

Currently, there are limited career opportunities, though there has been a slight increase in jobs becoming available with larger welfare charities, such as Blue Cross, and rescue centres. However, most pet behaviour counsellors work on a self-employed basis. You need to build up a client-base which may involve taking referrals from vets or from organisations that use working animals. There are opportunities to work with sporting animals, particularly horses. Some counsellors are invited to give talks and lectures in the UK, and sometimes abroad.

Counsellors charge between £85-£250 (and over) for a session depending on the type of treatment involved and whether it takes place in a clinic/centre or at the client's home. Those working with sporting animals generally earn higher fees.

Health

The job involves a risk of infection and there is an allergy risk from animals.

Skills and Qualities

able to communicate effectively, able to inspire confidence, able to motivate others, emotionally strong, friendly, good at handling animals, good listening skills, patient, perceptive, reassuring

Relevant Subjects

Biology, Chemistry, Health and social care, Mathematics, Physics, Psychology, Science, Sociology

Further Information

Association for the Study of Animal Behaviour - http://asab.nottingham.ac.uk

Becoming a Pet Counsellor (APBC) - www.apbc.org.uk/

Careers in Animal Behaviour (Blue Cross) - www.bluecross.org.uk/

Working with Horses (BHS) (British Horse Society) - www.bhs.org.uk/

Addresses

Animal Care College
Index House High Street, Ascot, Berkshire SL5 7ET
Phone: +44 (0)1344 636436
Web: www.animalcarecollege.co.uk/

Association of Pet Behaviour Counsellors (APBC)
PO Box 46, Worcester WR8 9YS
Phone: +44 (0)1386 751 151
Web: www.apbc.org.uk

Bishop Burton College
York Road, Bishop Burton, Beverley HU17 8QG
Phone: +44 (0)1964 553101
Web: www.bishopb-college.ac.uk

Similar Jobs

Guide Dog Trainer, Psychologist, RSPCA/Scottish SPCA Inspector, Veterinary Nurse, Veterinary Surgeon, Zoo Keeper

Pet Shop Assistant

also known as: Retail Assistant: Pet Shop

CRCI:Retail Sales and Customer Services
CLCI:WAM Job Band: 1 to 2

Job Description

Pet shop assistants work in a pet shop, or pet superstore and aquatic centre, looking after and selling small animals, reptiles, fish, birds and insects. They also sell pet food and pet health care goods, such as worming and flea treatments, animal shampoos etc, and equipment such as bedding and cages, tanks and toys. May serve customers and take payment for goods, giving change or handling credit/debit card transactions. Can also be involved in feeding the animals and cleaning out cages and tanks.

Assistants regularly check the health and condition of animals and check for any signs of disease. They advise customers on animal/fish care and answer any queries. In some jobs, may be required to measure and weigh pet food in bags for sale and check the shelves and replace stock when necessary.

Work Details

Usually work a basic 35-39 hr week, and may need to work Saturdays and possibly Sundays. Your workplace may be warm, though sometimes may be smelly, dirty and messy. You have to cope with being on your feet all day. Sometimes animals or birds may bite or scratch.

Qualification

• England, Wales and Northern Ireland

Band 1: No minimum qualifications are required, but you are expected to have a good level of general education. However, some formal/vocational qualifications at any level are useful.

Band 2: Although academic qualifications are not specified for this job, it may be an advantage to have some GCSEs (A*-C) in subjects that include English and maths, or equivalent.

• Scotland

Band 1: No minimum qualifications are required, but you are expected to have a good level of general education. However, some formal/vocational qualifications at any level are useful.

Band 2: Although academic qualifications are not specified for this job, it may be an advantage to have some S grades (1-3) in subjects that include English and maths, or similar.

Adult Qualifications

Although no formal qualifications are needed, an interest in animals is essential. Those with some academic/vocational qualifications may have an advantage. English and maths are useful subjects.

Work Experience

Relevant work or voluntary experience is always useful and can improve your chances when applying for entry to jobs in sales. It can equip you with skills that you can use in the future and add to your CV. Some experience of working with animals or in a shop is useful, perhaps through a Saturday or holiday job. Experience of dealing with money transactions is also an advantage.

Entry and Training

You can enter this job with few academic qualifications if you have a keen interest in animals. You are trained on the job with an experienced member of staff. You can study for the City & Guilds advanced Level 3 certificate in the principles of pet retail management, developed by the Pet Care Trust. The course is appropriate for all staff and can be taken through day release at a local further education college or via the Pet Care Trust's correspondence course. Assessment is through examination.

A Diploma/Welsh baccalaureate in retail business may be available in your area. Some colleges offer full-time courses in animal care that can be useful for pet shop work. Relevant S/NVQs are available in animal care (pet care and retail) at levels 1-3, or in retail skills at levels 1-2. There are also relevant vocationally-related qualifications (VRQs) you can do at levels 2-3. These include a level 3 award and certificate in small animal care. Training programmes, including apprenticeship schemes, may be available in your area. Advanced apprenticeships leading to qualification at level 3 can also be a route into higher education. See the Skillsmart Retail website for details of retail apprenticeship schemes and training options.

Adults may be able to enter this work through a government-funded training programme. Contact your local careers office, Jobcentre Plus, Next Step service or Learning and Skills Council (LSC)/Local Enterprise Company (LEC) for details of all training opportunities and schemes, including apprenticeships for adults. Some experience of working in a shop or with animals is useful.

Opportunities and Pay

Jobs are mainly in towns and cities throughout the UK. Due to a steady growth in pet ownership, pet superstores and pet shop chains are on the increase. You can also work in a garden centre that has a pet and aquatic centre, or in an independent pet shop. With experience you can progress to supervisory or management posts.

Pay varies depending on location and employer. Most pet shop assistants earn around £10k-£12k, rising to around £14k a year.

Health

You may find this job difficult if you have certain allergies.

Skills and Qualities

able to get on with all kinds of people, careful, cash handling skills, common sense, customer service skills, good at handling animals, not squeamish, patient

Relevant Subjects

Biology, Retail and distribution

Further Information

Apprenticeship Schemes (National Apprenticeship Service) - www.apprenticeships.org.uk

Diplomas (Foundation, Higher and Advanced) - http://yp.direct.gov.uk/diplomas

Foundation Learning (QCDA) - www.qcda.gov.uk

Lantra - The Sector Skills Council for environmental & land-based sector (Lantra) http:/www.lantra.co.uk

Skillsmart Retail - sector skills council for the retail industry - www.skillsmartretail.com

Training Schemes - www.direct.gov.uk/en/educationandlearning

Welsh Baccalaureate - www.wbq.org.uk

▶Working in retail & customer services (2008) (Babcock Lifeskills) - www.babcock-lifeskills.com/

▶Working with animals (2009) (Babcock Lifeskills) - www.babcock-lifeskills.com/

Addresses

Pet Care Trust/Dog Groomers' Association
Bedford Business Centre, 170 Mile Road MK42 9TW
Phone: +44 (0)1234 273933
Web: www.petcare.org.uk

Similar Jobs

Animal Care Assistant, Garden Centre Assistant, Retail Assistant, Retail Assistant: Health Foods, Veterinary Nurse, Zoo Keeper

Pharmacist: Community

also known as: Retail Chemist, Retail Pharmacist

CRCI:Healthcare
CLCI:JAG Job Band: 5

Job Description

Community pharmacists supply drugs and medicines to the general public from a high street or supermarket pharmacy. They ensure that patients get the best results from their medicines and dispense ready-made products or make up prescriptions issued by a doctor. They are responsible for the safe and correct storage of substances and for keeping a register of controlled drugs. May advise on the use and side effects of medicines and drugs.

Can offer advice on minor ailments such as viruses, sports injuries, allergies and skin conditions, general aches and pains, baby and children's problems, or women's health, often acting as a link between the customer and the doctor. Also help with the prevention of illnesses such as providing the right medicine and preparations for those travelling abroad, advice on giving up smoking and on general healthy living. May offer blood pressure and cholesterol level checks.

Also supervise and train pharmacy technicians and sales assistants. Keep detailed and accurate records of all transactions, using a computerised system.

Work Details

Usually work a 39 hr week that may include some evenings and weekends. You work in a chemist's high street shop, large supermarket, a health centre or rural pharmacy. Tasks include informing, advising and helping people. You are responsible for giving sound advice, drug security, keeping records and for checking the legality and accuracy of prescriptions.

Community pharmacists are usually also responsible for handling money and running a business efficiently. Work can be pressurised at times and may occasionally require coping with the sight of blood. There may be a risk of exposure to harmful substances.

Qualification

• England, Wales and Northern Ireland

Band 5: For degree course: A level in chemistry, plus two more A levels in maths, physics or a biological science, and some GCSEs (A*-C), including English and maths if not offered at A level, or equivalent qualifications.

• Scotland

Band 5: For degree course: four H grades including chemistry and English, plus two from maths, physics and biology, and some S grades (1-3) including English and maths, or similar qualifications.

Degree Information

An approved masters degree in pharmacy (MPharm) is essential to register with the General Pharmaceutical Council (GPhC)/ Pharmaceutical Society of Northern Ireland (PSNI). Postgraduate courses on specialist topics are offered at many universities throughout the UK. These are useful for those who want to go into research or teaching.

Adult Qualifications

Some universities may modify the normal degree course entry requirements for mature applicants. Due to the highly scientific nature of the course, acceptance is unlikely without some of the required science entry subjects and chemistry is particularly important. Check with individual schools of pharmacy for details. Graduates in related disciplines, such as chemistry, biochemistry or pharmacology, and health care workers, such as doctors, nurses or dispensing technicians, must still take a degree in pharmacy.

Work Experience

Entry to this career is competitive and universities/employers may prefer candidates who have relevant work or voluntary experience. It may be important to show evidence of commitment to, and understanding of the work involved, such as work in a retail pharmacy/chemist's shop. Other relevant areas are in hospital pharmacy or other medically-related work.

Entry and Training

Training is by a four-year masters degree in pharmacy (five year sandwich) course approved by the General Pharmaecutical Council (GPhC). These courses cover the origin and chemistry of drugs, preparation of medicines, action and uses of medicines, and pharmacy practice. This is followed by a pre-registration year of practical training in a community pharmacy. Five year sandwich degree courses have the pre-registration year integrated into the course.

During the pre-registration year you follow a varied programme gaining experience in dispensary work, inpatient and outpatient pharmacies. You also discuss drug treatment with staff and patients and are supervised closely by an experienced pharmacist. Following the satisfactory completion of the pre-registration year, you then need to take the GPhC Registration exam, prior to joining the register of the General Pharmaceutical Council (GPhC)/Pharmaceutical Society of Northern Ireland (PSNI). Check the website for details. Continuing professional development is mandatory.

Mature entrants may find that some employers prefer to recruit younger applicants. Contact the professional pharmaceutical societies for further details on training routes and qualifications.

Opportunities and Pay

This is the largest branch of pharmacy as most pharmacists are employed in community pharmacies and there is a continuing demand for employees. Employment can be in a small pharmacy or with a large retail company owning a number of pharmacy shops, outlets or supermarkets. Increasingly, some pharmacists are now based within GP practices and employed by the NHS Primary Care Trusts. If buying your own pharmacy/chemist business your costs involve considerable financial investment.

Newly qualified community pharmacists earn around £21k-£28k a year depending on the employer. This can rise with experience to around £34k-£40k, with some senior community pharmacists earning much more.

Health

This job requires normal colour vision.

Skills and Qualities

accurate, business awareness, good communication skills, good concentration level, good interpersonal skills, IT skills, methodical, patient, responsible attitude, scientific approach

Relevant Subjects

Biology, Business and accounting, Chemistry, English, Health and social care, Mathematics, Physics, Retail and distribution, Science

Further Information

AGCAS: Health (Job Sector Briefing) (AGCAS) - www.prospects.ac.uk

Careers in Pharmacy (Commitment to Pharmacy) (Royal Pharmaceutical Society of Great Britain) - www.rpharms.com/about-pharmacy/careers-in-pharmacy.asp

Chemist & Druggist Education (UBM Medica) - www.chemistanddruggist.co.uk/education

General Pharmaceutical Council (GPhC) - www.pharmacyregulation.org

Interested in Pharmacy - careers leaflets (Royal Pharmaceutical Society of Great Britain) - www.rpsgb.org.uk/acareerinpharmacy/

NHS Careers (NHS Careers) - www.nhscareers.nhs.uk

NHS Careers Scotland - www.infoscotland.com/nhs

NHS Careers Wales - www.wales.nhs.uk

Pharmaceutical Journal (weekly) (Pharmaceutical Press) - www.pjonline.com/

Addresses

National Pharmacy Association (NPA)
Mallinson House 38-42 St Peter's Street, St Albans, Hertfordshire AL1 3NP
Phone: +44 (0)1727 858687
Web: www.npa.co.uk

Pharmaceutical Society of Northern Ireland (PSNI)
73 University Street, Belfast BT7 1HL
Phone: +44 (0)28 9032 6927
Web: www.psni.org.uk

Royal Pharmaceutical Society of Great Britain (RPSGB)
1 Lambeth High Street, London SE1 7JN
Phone: +44 (0)20 7735 9141
Web: www.rpharms.com

Similar Jobs
Biochemist, Chemist, Pharmacist: Hospital, Pharmacist: Industrial, Pharmacologist

Pharmacist: Hospital

CRCI:Healthcare
CLCI:JAG

Job Band: 5

Job Description
Hospital pharmacists are responsible for the ordering, safety and secure storage, and distribution of drugs and medicines used in a hospital. They see that all drugs and medicines are stored correctly and in accordance with legal requirements. Also organise the delivery of drugs or sterile products to wards and departments, and supplies to outpatients. Must ensure that all medication is accurately dispensed for inpatients and outpatients, and in the correct form and dose. This is usually in the form of capsules and tablets, liquids, creams and injections.

Pharmacists regularly attend ward rounds, and are increasingly involved with selecting treatments for patients. They advise on the use and side effects of drugs or may participate in research. May counsel patients on their drug treatments, particularly those on complex drug therapy. Also liaise with physicians, nurses and other health care professionals. They supervise and check the work of less qualified and experienced staff.

Pharmacists usually manage a budget and provide detailed information to individual wards on their drug expenditure. If working in a teaching hospital, they may lecture clinical staff on various aspects of drugs, their application and side effects.

Work Details
Usually work from 9am-5pm, which can involve some evenings or weekends. Your place of work is a hospital and you are expected to work on a rota basis and possibly have on-call duties. Tasks include informing, advising and consulting with people and you can also be involved in teaching. You are responsible for health, safety and legal regulations. Work can be pressurised at times and perhaps with exposure to the sight of blood. You may have to cope with standing for many hours. There may be a risk of exposure to harmful substances and you may need to wear protective clothing.

Qualification

• England, Wales and Northern Ireland
Band 5: For degree course: A level in chemistry, plus two more A levels in maths, physics or a biological science, and some GCSEs (A*-C), including English and maths if not offered at A level, or equivalent qualifications.

• Scotland
Band 5: For degree course: four H grades including chemistry and English, plus two from maths, physics and biology, and some S grades (1-3) including English and maths, or similar qualifications.

Degree Information
An approved masters degree in pharmacy (MPharm) is essential to register with the General Pharmaceutical Council (GPhC)/ Pharmaceutical Society of Northern Ireland (PSNI). Postgraduate courses on specialist topics are offered at many universities throughout the UK. These are useful for those who want to go into research or teaching.

Adult Qualifications
Some universities may modify the normal degree course entry requirements for mature applicants. Due to the highly scientific nature of the course, acceptance is unlikely without some of the required science subjects and chemistry is particularly important. Check with individual schools of pharmacy for details. Graduates in related disciplines, such as chemistry, biochemistry or pharmacology, and health care workers, such as doctors, nurses or dispensing technicians, must still take a degree in pharmacy. Access or foundation courses give adults without qualifications a route on to degree courses.

Work Experience
Entry to this career is competitive and universities and employers may prefer candidates who have relevant work or voluntary experience. Ideally you work shadow a person in the job, but if it proves difficult to gain this type of placement, then other relevant experience in a retail or industrial pharmacy, in a medical laboratory or other medically-related work is useful.

Entry and Training
Training is by a four-year masters degree in pharmacy (five year sandwich) course approved by the General Pharmaceutical Council (GPhC). These courses cover the origin and chemistry of drugs, preparation of medicines, action and uses of medicines, and pharmacy practice. This is followed by a pre-registration year of practical training in a community pharmacy. Five-year sandwich degree courses have the pre-registration year integrated into the course.

During the pre-registration year you follow a varied programme gaining experience in dispensary work, inpatient and outpatient pharmacies. You also discuss drug treatment with staff and patients and are supervised closely by an experienced pharmacist. Following the satisfactory completion of the pre-registration year, you then need to take the GPhC Registration exam, prior to joining the register of the General Pharmaceutical Council (GPhC)/ Pharmaceutical Society of Northern Ireland (PSNI). Check the website for details. After several years' experience following registration, you are expected to specialise in an area of pharmacology practice such as paediatric care, haematology, radiopharmacy or quality control. You can also study for a specialist master's degree or a PhD. Continuing professional development is mandatory.

Mature entrants may find that some employers prefer to recruit younger applicants. Contact the professional pharmaceutical societies/associations for further details on training routes and qualifications.

Opportunities and Pay
Over 7,500 hospital pharmacists are employed by NHS Trusts, private hospitals or health centres. There may be opportunities to teach or undertake research. Some are employed by pharmaceutical agencies. Promotion to more senior posts is possible after gaining experience and higher qualifications. There is a clear promotion structure in the NHS.

The salary for pre-registration graduates starts at around £21k a year. Qualified hospital pharmacists earn £28k-£40k and pharmacist advanced/ consultants can earn up to £80k a year. NHS Trusts offer additional payments to those working in inner and outer London.

Health
This job requires normal colour vision.

Skills and Qualities
accurate, analytical skills, good communication skills, good concentration level, good interpersonal skills, IT skills, methodical, responsible attitude, scientific approach

Relevant Subjects
Biology, Chemistry, English, Health and social care, Mathematics, Physics, Science

Further Information
AGCAS: Health (Job Sector Briefing) (AGCAS) - www.prospects.ac.uk

Careers in Pharmacy (Commitment to Pharmacy) (Royal Pharmaceutical Society of Great Britain) - www.rpharms.com/about-pharmacy/careers-in-pharmacy.asp

Chemist & Druggist Education (UBM Medica) - www.chemistanddruggist.co.uk/education

Clinical Pharmacist (RPSGB, 11 issues a year) (Pharmaceutical Press) - www.pjonline.com/

General Pharmaceutical Council (GPhC) - www.pharmacyregulation.org

Interested in Pharmacy - careers leaflets (Royal Pharmaceutical Society of Great Britain) - www.rpsgb.org.uk/acareerinpharmacy/

NHS Careers (NHS Careers) - www.nhscareers.nhs.uk

NHS Careers Scotland - www.infoscotland.com/nhs

NHS Careers Wales - www.wales.nhs.uk

Pharmaceutical Journal (weekly) (Pharmaceutical Press) - www.pjonline.com/

Addresses

National Pharmacy Association (NPA)
Mallinson House 38-42 St Peter's Street, St Albans, Hertfordshire AL1 3NP
Phone: +44 (0)1727 858687
Web: www.npa.co.uk

Pharmaceutical Society of Northern Ireland (PSNI)
73 University Street, Belfast BT7 1HL
Phone: +44 (0)28 9032 6927
Web: www.psni.org.uk

Royal Pharmaceutical Society of Great Britain (RPSGB)
1 Lambeth High Street, London SE1 7JN
Phone: +44 (0)20 7735 9141
Web: www.rpharms.com

Similar Jobs

Biochemist, Chemist, Pharmacist: Community, Pharmacist: Industrial, Pharmacologist

Pharmacist: Industrial

CRCI:Manufacturing and Production
CLCI:SAV Job Band: 5

Job Description

Industrial pharmacists are involved in the research, development or production of safe drugs and medicines. They decide on the safest form in which to produce the drug or medicine while also considering the safest and most effective way of delivery to a human body or animal. Work involves liaising with other experts in the pharmaceutical industry, including pharmacologists, microbiologists and specialist chemists. May decide between products such as a tablet or capsule, liquid or gel, injection, or creams and ointments. Industrial pharmacists also work on the improvement of existing drugs and medicines or may develop new forms of drugs to improve their efficiency. May be involved in clinical trials to assess the safety and effectiveness of new drugs or in obtaining licences for their use once trials are completed.

Can specialise in, for example, testing drugs for safety and effectiveness, manufacturing and production, research work, quality assurance or marketing. Can also work in technical information, administration, marketing and sales. Some industrial pharmacists may use their specialist knowledge to train medical representatives.

Work Details

Industrial pharmacists usually work a 37-39 hr week; Monday to Friday, though may be expected to work shifts. There may be some opportunities for part-time work. Your place of work is most likely to be a laboratory, industrial premises or sometimes an office. Tasks include supervising and organising others, eg lab technicians, and you have responsibility for efficient production, monitoring work progress and quality control. The work environment can be noisy and smelly, and there may be a risk of exposure to harmful substances. You may need to wear overalls or other protective clothing.

Qualification

- **England, Wales and Northern Ireland**

Band 5: For degree course: A level chemistry, plus two more A levels in maths, physics or a biological science, and at least 5 GCSEs (A*-C) including English, maths and double science. Equivalent qualifications are also acceptable; check with individual institutions.

- **Scotland**

Band 5: For degree course: 3-5 H grades including chemistry and English, plus maths, physics or biology, and some S grades (1-3) or similar. Exact requirements depend on the degree you take.

Degree Information

An approved degree in pharmacy is essential to register with the Royal Pharmaceutical Society of Great Britain (RPSGB). Relevant postgraduate courses are also available.

Adult Qualifications

Some universities may modify the normal degree course entry requirements for mature applicants. However, because of the highly scientific nature of the course, acceptance is unlikely without some of the required science entry subjects; chemistry is particularly important. Check with individual schools of pharmacy for details. Graduates in related disciplines, such as chemistry, biochemistry or pharmacology, and health care workers, such as doctors, nurses or dispensing technicians, must still take a degree in pharmacy. Access or foundation courses give adults without qualifications a route on to degree courses.

Work Experience

Entry to this career is competitive and universities/employers may prefer candidates who have relevant work or voluntary experience. Ideally you volunteer or work shadow in the industry, but time spent in a hospital or retail pharmacy, or in laboratory work is also useful. The Industrial Pharmacists Group (RPSGB) holds details of holiday placements.

Entry and Training

Training is by a four-year degree in pharmacy that is accredited by the Royal Pharmaceutical Society of Great Britain (RPSGB), followed by a pre-registration year of examined work experience. This leads to professional registration. The General Pharmaceutical Council (GPhC) replaces the RPSGB in 2010 as the regulator for pharmacists, pharmacy technicians and pharmacy premises. Check the website for details. Many pre-registration schemes combine six months of the year in industry with six months in either a hospital or retail pharmacy. Sandwich course degrees usually incorporate this pre-registration training as part of the course.

Often industrial pharmacists work as an entry pharmacist for 2-3 years before studying to complete a PhD/MSc. Pharmacists working in research often require a postgraduate qualification. On-the-job training in research areas may be provided by an employer to graduates who demonstrate a keen interest and ability.

An industrial pharmacist who also wishes to become a QP (a qualified person who is named on the product licence) must have specific knowledge of the physical and chemical properties of materials and their effects, the law relating to the manufacture, sale and supply of medicinal products, process technologies, microbiology and pharmacology, and the clinical implications of process and material variation. All industrial pharmacists are expected to undertake continuing professional development (CPD) to keep up to date with new developments.

Mature entrants may find that some employers prefer to recruit younger applicants. Contact the professional pharmaceutical societies/associations for further details on training routes and qualifications for mature entrants.

Opportunities and Pay
There are over 2,000 industrial pharmacists working in the UK. You can be employed by a major pharmaceutical company, manufacturing company or a research organisation, including those involved in the production of veterinary and agricultural products. There is a rising demand for trained industrial pharmacists both in the UK and abroad. Promotion to senior posts is possible after gaining experience. Some move into consultancy work in areas that include design management, research project laboratory management, or project management.

Industrial pharmacists' salaries start at around £25k (£28k with an MSc, £31k with a PhD), with experience this may rise to around £38k and senior pharmacists can earn over £70k a year.

Health
This job requires normal colour vision. There may be an allergy risk from skin irritants. For certain posts you may have to take a health test before entry.

Skills and Qualities
able to take responsibility, analytical skills, aptitude for teamwork, attention to detail, good communication skills, good reasoning power, good written English, methodical, observant, scientific approach

Relevant Subjects
Biology, Chemistry, English, Health and social care, ICT/Computer studies, Manufacturing, Mathematics, Physics, Science

Further Information
A Healthy Scotland (Royal Pharmaceutical Society in Scotland) (RPSGB) - www.rpsgb.org.uk/scotland/pdfs/scotrepahs.pdf

Association of the British Pharmaceutical Industry (ABPI) - www.abpi.org.uk/education

Careers in Pharmacy (Commitment to Pharmacy) (Royal Pharmaceutical Society of Great Britain) - www.rpharms.com/about-pharmacy/careers-in-pharmacy.asp

Chemist & Druggist Education (UBM Medica) - www.chemistanddruggist.co.uk/education

Chemistry and Industry (SCI) - www.soci.org/Chemistry-and-Industry/Cnl-Data/2009/19

General Pharmaceutical Council (GPhC) - www.pharmacyregulation.org

Interested in Pharmacy - careers leaflets (Royal Pharmaceutical Society of Great Britain) - www.rpsgb.org.uk/acareerinpharmacy/

Pharmaceutical Journal (weekly) (Pharmaceutical Press) - www.pjonline.com/

SEMTA - sector skills council for science, engineering and manufacturing technologies - www.semta.org.uk

▶Working in manufacturing (2010) (Babcock Lifeskills) - www.babcock-lifeskills.com/

Your Society (RPSGB - Industrial Pharmacists Group) (Royal Pharmaceutical Society of Great Britain) - www.rpsgb.org/societyfunctions/aboutthesociety/

Addresses
Royal Pharmaceutical Society of Great Britain (RPSGB)
1 Lambeth High Street, London SE1 7JN
Phone: +44 (0)20 7735 9141
Web: www.rpharms.com

Similar Jobs
Biochemist, Biotechnologist, Pharmacist: Community, Pharmacist: Hospital, Pharmacologist, Toxicologist

Pharmacologist
CRCI:Science, Mathematics and Statistics
CLCI:QOB Job Band: 5

Job Description
Pharmacologists study the effects of medicines, drugs and chemicals on humans and animals. They carry out experiments to improve and develop drugs for use in prevention, treatment or cure of diseases. Also work on drugs to improve their effectiveness in the treatment of diseases such as cancer, heart and lung disease, HIV/Aids, or malaria. They use sophisticated technology, including computers in their research and assess drug effectiveness using laboratory tests. May help with clinical trials, standardising dosages or methods of drug production. Some pharmacologists specialise in poison detection (toxicology).

Work Details
Usually work a 35-39 hr week, Monday to Friday, in a laboratory at a college, university, hospital, research institute or industrial premises, as well as some time in an office. Depending on the type of post, you can have responsibility for analysing results, monitoring safety standards and supervising the work of others. You often share data and results with other professionals or with customers. This may involve writing reports or articles for publication, and attending conferences and meetings. Some specialise in research or teaching and some work with animals. This work requires a high degree of accuracy and can involve the sight of blood. You often work in sterile conditions. You may need to wear a white coat/overall and possibly protective gloves.

Qualification
- **England, Wales and Northern Ireland**

Band 5: For degree courses: 2-3 A levels including chemistry and physics and/or biology and 5 GCSEs (A*-C) usually including English, maths and a science, or equivalent. Exact requirements depend on the degree you take.

- **Scotland**

Band 5: For degree courses: 3-5 H grades including chemistry and physics and/or biology and five S grades (1-3), usually including English, maths and science, or similar. Exact requirements depend on the degree you take.

Degree Information
A degree in pharmacology is normally preferred. Degrees in a related field, such as biochemistry, physiology, pharmacy, immunology, microbiology, biology or chemistry, may give entry to an appropriate postgraduate course.

Adult Qualifications
A relevant degree and up-to-date scientific knowledge are essential. Course entry requirements may be relaxed for mature applicants, but academic standards in maths and science are expected. A foundation year prior to the start of a science degree may be available at some HE institutions for those applicants who do not have the traditional science qualifications.

Work Experience
Universities and employers may prefer candidates who have relevant work or voluntary experience. Work experience in a hospital, a relevant university department or an industrial or commercial laboratory is ideal but, if it proves difficult to gain this exact experience, any work with a scientific background is attractive to employers and admissions tutors. Contact the appropriate professional societies for information regarding summer work placements.

Entry and Training
Training is through practical work experience after obtaining a degree or postgraduate qualification. Those with an HND in pharmacology usually enter at technician level and may be able to

study for a degree, but most entrants are graduates/postgraduates. Degree courses can be full time or sandwich and last 3-4 years. There are a number of relevant first degree courses and there are also postgraduate courses which are necessary if you want to work in research.

Training continues via short courses, such as those offered by The British Pharmacological Society (BPS) and the Association of the British Pharmaceutical Industry (ABPI). The BPS offers a programme of continuing professional development (CPD). Membership of the society can be attained by having a combination of academic qualifications and practical experience.

Mature applicants with experience gained in industrial work placements are welcomed by many employers. Part-time study for a postgraduate MSc course in pharmacology is available. Pharmaceutical companies, charities and the Medical Research Council (MRC) may offer funding for postgraduate study and research.

Opportunities and Pay
This is a small profession and the work is highly specialised. However, there is a demand for trained and qualified staff. You can be employed by a manufacturing, pharmaceutical or biotechnology company, research organisation such as the Medical Research Council (MRC), university, local government or the civil service. Promotion prospects depend on the organisation for which you work. Some move into medical sales and marketing, patent work and medical writing. There are a concentration of jobs in London and the south east and opportunities to work overseas.

Pay varies depending on location and employer, but starting salaries for graduates are around £26k a year in industry and £21.5k a year in universities, rising to about £28k. Senior pharmacologists can earn up to £70k a year.

Health
Normal colour vision is required for some areas of work. There is an allergy risk from skin irritants or animals.

Skills and Qualities
able to report accurately, accurate, analytical skills, aptitude for teamwork, attention to detail, good communication skills, project management skills, resourceful, responsible attitude, specialist IT skills

Relevant Subjects
Biology, Chemistry, English, Health and social care, ICT/Computer studies, Mathematics, Physics, Science

Further Information
Association of the British Pharmaceutical Industry (ABPI) - www.abpi.org.uk/education

British Journal of Clinical Pharmacology (Blackwell Publishing/BPS) - www.bjcp-journal.com/

Careers in the Pharmaceutical Industry (ABPI) (Association of British Pharmaceutical Industry (ABPI)) - www.abpi.org.uk/education/careers.asp

Civil Service - www.civilservice.gov.uk/jobs

E-Journal of the British Pharmacological Society (British Pharmacological Society) - www.pa2online.org

▶Working in science (2007) (Babcock Lifeskills) - www.babcock-lifeskills.com/

Addresses
British Pharmacological Society (BPS)
16 Angel Gate City Road, London EC1V 2PT
Phone: +44 (0) 131 718 4457
Web: www.bps.ac.uk

Medical Research Council (MRC)
20 Park Crescent, London W1B 1AL
Phone: +44 (0)20 7636 5422
Web: www.mrc.ac.uk

Similar Jobs
Biochemist, Biotechnologist, Microbiologist, Pharmacist: Industrial, Sales Executive: Medical, Toxicologist

Pharmacy Technician
also known as: Dispensary Assistant, Medicine Counter Assistant

CRCI:Healthcare
CLCI:JAG Job Band: 2 to 3

Job Description
Pharmacy technicians work under the supervision of a pharmacist in a hospital, laboratory or chemist's shop, helping to prepare, dispense and store medicines and drugs. They make up prescriptions, measure liquids, count tablets, etc and check stock and keep it in good order. Also do clerical work, such as invoicing and ordering. In community pharmacies, they deal with the public and may also sell other products such as cosmetics and toiletries. Explain to patients how to take or apply their medication and discuss any possible side-effects.

In a hospital, a technician also transports pharmacy supplies to the wards and ensures they have an adequate supply of drugs for each patient. They work closely with ward staff, particularly when a patient arrives at or leaves the hospital. Some technicians may specialise in areas, such as paediatric care, haematology, radiopharmacy or quality control.

In an industrial setting a technician assists pharmacists in the research and development of new drugs and medicines. They also see to the day-to-day running of the laboratory, stock control, record keeping, quality control and assist in clinical trials. Use a computer to monitor stock levels and order new supplies.

Work Details
Usually work a basic 37-39 hr week; Monday to Friday, though in some jobs you may be expected to work Saturdays and possibly evenings or shifts. Depending on the type of employment, your place of work is a shop, a hospital, or an industrial or research laboratory. You work under supervision and if you work in a shop, have regular contact with the public and have to handle money. In a hospital you have some contact with patients who may be in some distress or pain.

Work can be pressurised at times and can occasionally require coping with the sight of blood. You may have to cope with standing for many hours. There may be a risk of exposure to harmful substances and you need to wear protective clothing.

Qualification
• England, Wales and Northern Ireland
Band 3: For entry to jobs, HNC or a relevant Diploma, usually at least 4 GCSEs (A*-C) including English, maths and science, or equivalent.

• Scotland
Band 3: For entry to jobs, usually at least four S grades (1-3) including English and maths and science, or similar.

Adult Qualifications
Entry requirements for mature applicants vary, depending on the employer.

Work Experience
Work experience gives you an insight into what you enjoy and don't enjoy about a job or working environment, as well as the opportunity to acquire new skills. It also provides valuable information to add to your CV and improves any course application and/or your future employment prospects. Employers may therefore prefer candidates who have relevant work or voluntary experience in a medical or healthcare setting such as a hospital or a high street pharmacy.

Entry and Training
Entrants are usually 16-18 and have on-the-job training with an experienced technician or supervisor. A two-year college-based or distance-learning course is available for trainee technicians that leads to S/NVQ level 3 in pharmacy services. Registration with the General Pharmaceutical Council (GPhC) will be mandatory from July 2011 and to register you need to have the S/NVQ. Check the GPhC website for details.

The National Pharmacy Association offers training for dispensary assistants and medicine counter assistants. These are self-study courses and many then go on to train as pharmacy technicians. Some entrants may also study for BTEC/SQA national awards in science. Training programmes, including apprenticeship schemes, may be available in your area. Advanced apprenticeships leading to qualification at level 3 can also be a route into higher education.

Mature entrants with relevant skills and experience may be offered a training post. There are distance learning and other self-study courses available from organisations such as the National Pharmacy Association (NPA). Contact the professional pharmaceutical societies/associations for further details on training routes and qualifications.

Opportunities and Pay
You can be employed by an NHS Trust, a private hospital, a manufacturing company, a research organisation or by a retail pharmacist. The number of pharmacy technicians is increasing and there may be shortages of staff in some areas. There may also be opportunities to work part time.

Pay depends largely on type of employer, but starting salaries in the community and industry are around £15k-£19k a year. A pharmacy technician working for the NHS follows the salary scale for healthcare scientists. Starting salaries are around £18k-£22k a year, rising to around £34k for specialist posts.

Health
This job requires normal colour vision.

Skills and Qualities
able to cope under pressure, able to explain clearly, able to get on with all kinds of people, good concentration level, good organisational skills, methodical, reliable, scientific approach, self confident, tactful

Relevant Subjects
Biology, Chemistry, English, Health and social care, Mathematics, Retail and distribution, Science

Further Information
Apprenticeship Schemes (National Apprenticeship Service) - www.apprenticeships.org.uk

General Pharmaceutical Council (GPhC) - www.pharmacyregulation.org

NHS Careers (NHS Careers) - www.nhscareers.nhs.uk

NHS Careers Scotland - www.infoscotland.com/nhs

NHS Careers Wales - www.wales.nhs.uk

▶Working in science (2007) (Babcock Lifeskills) - www.babcock-lifeskills.com/

Addresses
Association of Pharmacy Technicians UK (APTUK)
4th Floor, 1 Mabledon Place, London WC1H 9AJ
Phone: +44 (0)20 7551 1551
Web: www.aptuk.org

National Pharmacy Association (NPA)
Mallinson House 38-42 St Peter's Street, St Albans, Hertfordshire AL1 3NP
Phone: +44 (0)1727 858687
Web: www.npa.co.uk

Royal Pharmaceutical Society of Great Britain (RPSGB)
1 Lambeth High Street, London SE1 7JN
Phone: +44 (0)20 7735 9141
Web: www.rpharms.com

Similar Jobs
Clinical Technologist, Laboratory Technician: Education, Laboratory Technician: Science, Pharmacist: Community, Pharmacist: Hospital, Retail Assistant

Phlebotomist
CRCI:Healthcare
CLCI:JOZ
Job Band: 1 to 3

Job Description
Phlebotomists work in a hospital or health centre as a clinical support worker specialising in the taking, transporting and storage of blood samples. They collect blood from a patient for examination in a laboratory to provide information to help medical staff diagnose and treat illness. Need to extract the sample without harming the patient or disturbing the nursing care they are receiving. Ensure that the blood is taken correctly and hygienically, so that the specimen is not contaminated in any way.

Phlebotomists are responsible for ensuring that each sample is accurately labelled and transported to the correct laboratory in the required time. May combine this job with other, more general clinical support duties.

Work Details
You work around 37 hours a week, Monday to Friday, in a hospital outpatient clinic or on the wards, or in a GP health centre. You also work in a laboratory, usually under the supervision of scientists and technicians. You are on your feet most of the day and wear a white coat or an overall, and sometimes other protective clothing. You have to cope with the sight of blood. There is a risk of minor injuries.

Your work demands skill, attention to detail and a responsible attitude. You work with babies, adults and older people with a wide range of conditions. You need to follow the appropriate procedure for each type of patient you work with.

Qualification
- **England, Wales and Northern Ireland**

Band 2: Minimum entry requirements are at least two GCSEs, or equivalent at any level.

Band 3: For entry: usually at least 4 GCSEs (A*-C) including English and maths, or equivalent.

- **Scotland**

Band 2: Minimum entry requirements are at least two S grades, or similar at any level.

Band 3: For entry: usually at least four S grades (1-3) including English and maths, or similar.

Adult Qualifications
Formal qualifications are not essential, but it is useful to have a scientific background and some laboratory experience.

Work Experience
Work experience gives you an insight into what you enjoy about a job or working environment, and the opportunity to acquire new skills. It provides valuable information to add to your CV and improves your employment prospects. Relevant work or voluntary experience in a medical or healthcare setting such as a hospital or residential care home is extremely useful.

Entry and Training
Training is mainly on the job, lasts about six months and begins with general health and safety instructions. Trainees then move on to specialised individual training which includes formal theoretical training and supervised practice in various settings, leading to the successful completion of National Occupational Standards. Certificates of competence are awarded for the safe performance of various duties, which help if you move to similar work for another employer. There is no central recruitment for vacancies at this level, you need to apply for a trainee post within a hospital and vacancies are advertised locally. If you are interested in a career in phlebotomy, contact your local Hospital or Primary Care Trust (PCT) to enquire about trainee posts.

The National Association of Phlebotomists (NAP) offers a variety of short professional courses for phlebotomists and trainees. These cover infection control, anatomy and physiology, paediatrics and child protection. Contact the NAP for information on all courses and workshops. Be very careful when selecting courses as other courses offering phlebotomy training for non-medically trained students (who are not already in a phlebotomy job), may not meet the eligibility criteria of the NAP. A hospital or PCT can support your professional training programme. You can also work towards S/NVQs in health care.

Mature applicants who show aptitude and who have relevant previous experience may be considered by employers for training.

Opportunities and Pay
Around 10,000 people work as phlebotomists in the UK. Most work for the NHS and are employed by a hospital or NHS trust. Others work in a GP practice, health centre or private laboratory. As increased levels of health screening are introduced, growing opportunities are available throughout the country in towns and cities. It is also possible to work part time. With experience you can become a team leader or manager. If you show particular aptitude, you may be encouraged to train as a biomedical scientist. It is also possible to train for another biomedical science job, for example in cervical screening, haematology or immunology.

The starting salary for a phlebotomist is around £13k-£16k a year. With experience this may rise to around £20k a year. Managers may earn more.

Health
You need normal colour vision for some areas of work and good eyesight. There is a risk of allergy from skin irritants and restrictions on certain skin disorders.

Skills and Qualities
able to work both on your own and in a team, able to work to deadlines, accurate, good communication skills, good interpersonal skills, manual dexterity, methodical, not squeamish, scientific approach

Relevant Subjects
Biology, Health and social care, Science

Further Information
NHS Careers (NHS Careers) - www.nhscareers.nhs.uk

NHS Careers Scotland - www.infoscotland.com/nhs

NHS Careers Wales - www.wales.nhs.uk

Addresses
Institute of Biomedical Science (IBMS)
12 Coldbath Square, London EC1R 5HL
Phone: +44 (0) 20 7713 0214
Web: www.ibms.org

National Association of Phlebotomists (NAP)
12 Coldbath Square, London EC1R 5HL
Phone: +44 (0)20 7833 8784
Web: www.phlebotomy.org

Similar Jobs
Laboratory Assistant, Laboratory Assistant: Medical, Laboratory Technician: Science

Photographer
CRCI:Media, Print and Publishing
CLCI:EV Job Band: 2 to 5

Job Description
Photographers use film or a digital camera to take photographs of events, people, places or objects for artistic purposes, or to illustrate/record and sell them, usually for a living. They usually work to a brief (instructions) set by the employer or client. Tasks include arranging the subject, checking the lighting and working out the best place for the shots. They develop and print photographs and may make enlargements. The growth in digital photography has led to much of the work involving image manipulation using computers.

Most are involved in general practice photography, including weddings and family portraits, and the rest specialise in areas such as press, police, industrial, scientific, fashion, magazine and advertising, or medical photography.

Work Details
Some photographers work standard office hours of around 37 a week; Monday to Friday, with some work on a Saturday. For others, the hours are irregular and can be long. Your base is a studio with time spent in darkrooms or working at a computer. Your actual place of work varies, depending on the type of photography and the particular task. You may need to travel and spend time away from home, on location. Police photographers are expected to work shifts. Most photographers have to communicate easily with people and be able to put them at ease. Press photographers need quick reactions and may sometimes work in areas of conflict.

Some shots have to be taken from heights, which may involve working on scaffolding or ladders. There may be some lifting and carrying of heavy equipment. Dangerous chemicals are used in traditional developing, but the use of digital photography and related computer programs is becoming more common.

Qualification
No set entry qualifications for this job but a good standard of secondary education is expected by employers. You need an up-to-date portfolio of your work for employers and colleges. Some courses may require you to have academic qualifications.

• England, Wales and Northern Ireland
Band 2: For entry as a photographic assistant, leading to training as a photographer: some GCSEs (A*-C) are an advantage.

Band 3: For entry to jobs, HNC or a relevant Diploma, usually at least 4 GCSEs (A*-C) including English and maths, or equivalent.

Band 4: For HND, Diploma of Higher Education or foundation degree: 1-2 A levels and some GCSEs (A*-C) usually including English and maths, or equivalent.

Band 5: For degree courses: 2-3 A levels and some GCSEs (A*-C) usually including English, or equivalent qualifications. Exact requirements depend on the degree you take.

• Scotland
Band 2: For entry as a photographic assistant, leading to training as a photographer: some S grades (1-3) are an advantage.

Band 3: For entry to an appropriate course: usually at least four S grades (1-3) or similar.

Band 4: For entry to SQA higher national and professional development awards, usually 2-3 H grades and some S grades (1-3), including English and maths, or similar qualifications.

Photographer

Band 5: For degree courses: 3-5 H grades and some S grades (1-3), usually including English, or similar. Exact requirements depend on the degree you take.

Degree Information

A degree in photography, or an art and design subject with a photography specialism, is preferred. Courses in visual communication, communication media, electronic imaging, and graphics, are useful. There are a few postgraduate courses for those with relevant first degrees.

Adult Qualifications

Mature applicants with outstanding portfolios of work may be accepted for courses without the standard entry requirements. There are Access and foundation courses in some areas; these give adults without qualifications a route on to degree courses.

Work Experience

Entry to this job is competitive and it is important to do some relevant work or voluntary experience before applying. Work in a photographic studio is ideal, but any work to develop your art and design skills is useful. It is important to build up a portfolio of your work, perhaps through amateur photography.

Entry and Training

It is possible to start by becoming a photography assistant and train with a photographer, perhaps taking a part-time course. There are also many full-time courses in art and design or photography at national, higher national and degree level. Several degree courses incorporate the British Institute of Professional Photography's (BIPP) Professional Qualifying Exam (PQE), which is highly regarded by the industry. See the Skillset website for details. BIPP also offers professional photography qualifications at licentiateship, associateship and fellowship levels, as well as short courses. Professional recognition can also be attained from the Royal Photographic Society.

Press photographers or photojournalists can train by working on a provincial newspaper and by following the training scheme of the National Council for the Training of Journalists (NCTJ), which involves practical experience and block-release study at college.

A number of relevant foundation degrees are available at some colleges and universities, lasting between two and four years, depending on whether they are part or full time. There are vocational qualifications in photography and photo imaging at levels 2-4 or you can work for a BTEC HNC/HND in photography. Training programmes, including apprenticeship schemes, may be available in your area. Advanced apprenticeships leading to qualification at level 3 can also be a route into higher education.

A Diploma/Welsh Baccalaureate may be available in your area in creative and media. This can be a useful introduction to this type of career as you gain practical experience while studying. See the diplomas website or Skillset for further information.

Many adult entrants already have amateur photography experience, and set up their own general practices. Adults may be able to enter this work through a government-funded training programme. Contact your local Connexions or careers office, Jobcentre Plus, Next Step service or Learning and Skills Council (LSC)/Local Enterprise Company (LEC) for details of all training opportunities and schemes, including apprenticeships for adults.

Opportunities and Pay

There are around 25,000 professional photographers in the UK, of which very many are self employed. Many photographers work in general practice, which includes portrait, wedding photography and publicity work for local businesses. Most photography businesses are small, with only 1-5 employees. Employment can be with the media, industrial firms, civil service, police, the armed forces (particularly the RAF), hospital and medical schools, and universities. Some photographers work in graphic design departments.

Photography is highly competitive and to be successful you have to build up a reputation and contacts. Some specialisms are even more difficult than others to get into, such as fashion, advertising and magazine work. Most of this work is done in London. Part-time work in photography is possible and freelancing is common. Some use a photographic agent to find work. Freelance photographers are paid a fee for each job which may range between £150-£600 a day.

Pay varies greatly; trainees earn around £12k a year, rising to £15k-£50k a year. Highly successful photographers can earn a lot more than this. Average salaries tend to be around £20k.

Health

You must have normal colour vision and good eyesight. The work involves the use of chemicals which can cause allergic reaction.

Skills and Qualities

artistic ability, attention to detail, creative flair, eye for visual effect, good communication skills, good interpersonal skills, good organisational skills, hand-to-eye co-ordination, head for heights, observant, patient, self confident, technical aptitude

Relevant Subjects

Art and Design, Chemistry, ICT/Computer studies, Media and communication studies, Physics, Science

Further Information

Apprenticeship Schemes (National Apprenticeship Service) - www.apprenticeships.org.uk

Association of Photographers (AOP) (AOP) - www.aop.org

Beyond The Lens (Association of Photographers (AOP)) - www.beyond-the-lens.com

British Journal of Photography (weekly) (Incisive Photographic Ltd) - www.bjp-online.com

Diplomas (Foundation, Higher and Advanced) - http://yp.direct.gov.uk/diplomas

National Council for the Training of Journalists (NCTJ) - www.nctj.com

Photo Imaging (Skillset) (Skillset) - www.skillset.org/photo/careers/

Professional Photographer - www.professionalphotographer.co.uk

Professional Photographers Association of Northern Ireland - www.ppani.co.uk

Skillset - sector skills council for the creative media, fashion and textiles industries - www.skillset.org

Training Schemes - www.direct.gov.uk/en/educationandlearning

▶Working in creative & media (2007) (Babcock Lifeskills) - www.babcock-lifeskills.com/

Addresses

British Institute of Professional Photography (BIPP)
1 Prebendal Court Oxford Road, Aylesbury,
Buckinghamshire HP19 8EY
Phone: +44 (0)1296 718530
Web: www.bipp.com

Royal Photographic Society
Fenton House , 122 Wells Road, Bath, Somerset BA2 3AH
Phone: +44 (0)1225 325 733
Web: www.rps.org

Similar Jobs

Film/TV & Theatre Lighting Technician, Film/TV Camera Operator, Graphic Designer, Photographer: Clinical, Photographic Laboratory Machine Print Operative, Photographic Stylist

Photographer: Clinical

also known as: Medical Videographer, Photographer: Medical

CRCI:Healthcare

CLCI:JOZ Job Band: 4 to 5

Job Description

Clinical photographers take photographs or films to record operations and other medical procedures for educational and scientific purposes, or to assist in diagnosis. They may take photos of internal parts of the body or slides of tissue cultures or sections. Also take photographs or make videos/CDs or DVDs of patients to show the progress of a disease and treatment. May also photograph bodies during a postmortem. Clinical photographers are involved in specialised photo imaging techniques, such as the use of thermal imaging, micro and macro-photography and endoscopy to photograph internal organs. They use a high degree of technical skill and some medical knowledge.

Photographers also provide a range of graphic design services to employees in medical and paramedical roles. This includes the production of audio-visual teaching and lecture material and the production of artwork for scientific posters, brochures and medical publications. They may specialise in forensic photography, working with a pathologist, or in photography during surgery.

Work Details

Usually work in a hospital in a medical illustrating department. A working week of 9am-5pm, Monday to Friday, is usual, but you may have to work shifts or be on call. You have to be able to communicate with patients and make them feel at ease. You also work closely with other healthcare professionals and audio-visual technicians. The work requires a high degree of accuracy, even when working under pressure. You have to be able to cope with the sight of blood.

Qualification

• England, Wales and Northern Ireland

Band 4: For HND, Diploma of Higher Education or relevant foundation degree: 1-2 A levels and some GCSEs (A*-C) usually including English, maths and a science, or equivalent, and proven photographic ability. Entry requirements vary, so check with colleges.

Band 5: For degree courses: 2-3 A levels and some GCSEs (A*-C) usually including English, maths and a science, or equivalent qualifications. Exact requirements depend on the degree you take.

• Scotland

Band 4: For entry to SQA higher national and professional development awards, usually 2-3 H grades and some S grades (1-3), including English, maths and a science, or similar, and proven photographic ability. Entry requirements vary, so check with colleges.

Band 5: For degree courses: 3-5 H grades and some S grades (1-3), including English, maths or a science, or similar. Exact requirements depend on the degree you take.

Degree Information

A degree in clinical photography or a degree in science/medicine, followed by a qualification in clinical photography, is preferred for entry to clinical photography training.

Adult Qualifications

Entry requirements may be relaxed for mature applicants with experience in photography, or specialist knowledge in art or medicine. There are Access and foundation courses in some areas, which give adults without qualifications a route on to degree courses.

Work Experience

Employers or colleges/universities may prefer candidates who have relevant work or voluntary experience. Work experience in general photography is relevant and helps to build a portfolio of work. Work in a hospital, work shadowing a clinical photographer, or discussing the job, is particularly useful, though some aspects of their work are not available, because of patient confidentiality.

Entry and Training

There are a few entry routes to clinical photography, but all require an academic qualification in photography. You need a degree in clinical photography to qualify but may take a photography degree, find a training position and study for a one-year graduate or postgraduate certificate in clinical photography while you are working.

Alternatively, you can take a full-time degree or postgraduate course in medical illustration/clinical photography and then look for work. Courses include anatomy, physiology and study of diseases. Because of the important effect this job has on people's health, many entrants to this work have a degree level medicine or science qualification, a formal photography qualification and a specialist clinical photography qualification. For entry to a photography degree, an up-to-date portfolio of work is needed as entry is very competitive. The University of Westminster offers a degree in clinical photography. Specialist postgraduate qualifications are available from Cardiff and Staffordshire Universities. The Institute of Medical Illustrators offers a range of training courses and the British Institute of Professional Photography is also a useful source of information.

Qualified clinical photographers need to be registered with the Health Professions Council. Contact the Committee for the Accreditation of Medical Illustration Practitioners for details. Once you are registered you need to undergo continuous professional development to keep up to date.

Entry to this work is extremely competitive, and mature entrants need a relevant educational background to HND or degree level, plus a portfolio and the specialist training needed for clinical photography.

Opportunities and Pay

Clinical photographers are usually employed by the NHS, research, medical departments in universities or colleges or work freelance for medical publishers. These are mainly located in cities throughout the UK.

Pay varies depending on the individual NHS Trust and is on a similar level to medical technical officers. As a guide, once experienced you are likely to earn £20k-£26k. Senior clinical photographers usually earn in the region of £33k-£39k a year.

Health

Normal colour vision and good eyesight are needed.

Skills and Qualities

able to follow instructions, able to put people at ease, aptitude for teamwork, attention to detail, careful, IT skills, not squeamish, scientific approach, tactful, technical aptitude

Relevant Subjects

Art and Design, Biology, Chemistry, ICT/Computer studies, Media and communication studies, Physics, Science

Further Information

British Journal of Photography (weekly)
(Incisive Photographic Ltd) - www.bjp-online.com

Careers in Medical Illustration (IMI) (Institute of Medical Illustration) - www.imi.org.uk/careers/careers01.asp

Committee for the Accreditation of Medical Illustration Practitioners (CAMIP) - www.camip.org.uk

Journal of Visual Communication in Medicine (4 x year)
(Informa Healthcare) - www.informahealthcare.com/

Medical Artists' Education Trust - www.maet.org.uk

NHS Careers (NHS Careers) - www.nhscareers.nhs.uk

Photo Imaging (Skillset) (Skillset) -
www.skillset.org/photo/careers/

Skills for Health - sector skills council - www.skillsforhealth.org.uk

▶ Working in art & design (2009) (Babcock Lifeskills) -
www.babcock-lifeskills.com/

Addresses

British Institute of Professional Photography (BIPP)
1 Prebendal Court Oxford Road, Aylesbury,
Buckinghamshire HP19 8EY
Phone: +44 (0)1296 718530
Web: www.bipp.com

Health Professions Council (HPC)
Park House, 184 Kennington Park Road, London SE11 4BU
Phone: +44 (0)20 7582 0866
Web: www.hpc-uk.org

Institute of Medical Illustrators (IMI)
12 Coldbath Square, London EC1R 5HL
Phone: +44 (0) 113 233 6258
Web: www.imi.org.uk

Similar Jobs

Graphic Designer, Medical Artist, Photographer, Radiographer: Diagnostic

Photographic Laboratory Machine Print Operative

also known as: Digital Imaging Technician, Mini-Lab Technician

CRCI:Media, Print and Publishing
CLCI:EV

Job Band: 2 to 3

Job Description

Photographic print operatives work in a photographic laboratory, where traditional photographic processing and printing skills are combined with the operation of sophisticated laboratory equipment, mini-labs and imaging equipment. They may also provide a specialist developing and printing service for professional photographers. Tasks include setting, monitoring and adjusting machinery, and refilling as needed with paper, ink and chemicals.

May do retouching to remove blemishes or to produce special effects. May use computerised digital imaging to adjust processes and manipulate images, such as merging two or more photographs. May be involved with producing large format prints, such as posters, fine art canvases, banners and exhibition stands.

Work Details

The hours are usually around 38-40 a week, Monday to Friday, though overtime and weekend work is possible. Some large companies may have a shift system. You usually work in a fast-paced computerised laboratory, which is clean and brightly lit. You may spend long hours sitting at a computer. The work requires attention to detail and a high degree of accuracy. You wear protective clothing, including goggles and gloves, when dealing with chemicals.

Qualification

Specific qualifications are not always needed but increasing use of digital imaging technology means that experience of computing and associated photographic software is helpful.

• England, Wales and Northern Ireland

Band 2: For direct entry as a trainee: qualifications are not always needed, but some employers ask for some GCSEs (A*-C), or equivalent. Useful subjects are science, maths, art and English.

Band 3: For entry to jobs, HNC in photography or a relevant Diploma, usually at least 4 GCSEs (A*-C) including English, science and maths, or equivalent, and a portfolio of photographic work.

• Scotland

Band 2: For direct entry as a trainee: qualifications are not always needed, but some employers ask for some S grades (1-3), or similar. Useful subjects are science, maths, art and English.

Band 3: For SQA national award in photography and photographic laboratory practice: usually at least four S grades (1-3), preferably including maths, English and a science, or similar, and a portfolio of photographic work.

Adult Qualifications

There are no set entry qualifications but a knowledge of basic science, IT and some artistic ability is useful.

Work Experience

Employers or colleges may prefer candidates with relevant work or voluntary experience. This is ideally in a photographic laboratory. Work that develops your computer skills, especially working with digital images, and experience in amateur photography is very useful.

Entry and Training

There are no set entry qualifications, but some experience or knowledge of photography is useful. Entrants are also usually expected to have good computing skills and a working knowledge of image manipulation software, such as Photoshop, Quark XPress, Illustrator or InDesign. You usually train on the job, working with experienced staff and perhaps taking short courses run by product and equipment manufacturers.

It is possible to take a full-time course first at a college, though entry to these courses is highly competitive. The Open College of the Arts offers digital photography courses, and there is a foundation degree in photography and digital imaging. Specific City & Guilds courses are also available at levels 2-4 in photo imaging and photo image printing or you can work for a BTEC HNC/HND in photography. Training programmes, including apprenticeship schemes, may be available in your area. Advanced apprenticeships leading to qualification at level 3 can also be a route into higher education.

The British Association of Picture Libraries and Agencies (BAPLA) has news of technological developments in printing and details of short courses. Registered members can also participate in the discussion forums and receive the BAPLA newsletter.

A Diploma/Welsh Baccalaureate may be available in your area in creative and media. This can be a useful introduction to this type of career as you gain practical experience while studying. See the diplomas website or Skillset for further information.

Adults with previous experience in traditional film processing or operating a mini-lab in a retail outlet may have an advantage. You may be able to enter this work through a government-funded training programme. Contact your local Connexions or careers office, Jobcentre Plus, Next Step service or Learning and Skills Council (LSC)/Local Enterprise Company (LEC) for details of all training opportunities and schemes, including apprenticeships for adults.

Opportunities and Pay

Most operators work in photofinishing and professional processing labs. Some may be employed in hospitals, research establishments, broadcasting companies, universities, colleges, digital picture libraries and in the armed forces. There has been a rapid expansion of laboratories over the past 15-20 years.

This is an industry of around 15,000 people. There is currently a good demand for skilled operators, especially in London and south-east England, though the rapid growth in downloading digital photographs directly to a PC may impact on future employment opportunities. High levels of computer skills are increasingly required. Many photographic laboratories are diversifying and producing large scale products such as posters and exhibition materials.

Operators can gain promotion to higher grade posts in companies with a formal promotion structure. Some specialise in digital image manipulation. Part-time work and self-employment are possible.

Pay varies depending on location and employer, but a trainee is likely to earn around £12k-£15k, rising to £25k a year, with experience. Highly skilled and experienced digital technicians can earn up to £38k a year.

Health

You must have normal colour vision and good eyesight. The chemicals used can cause allergic reaction.

Skills and Qualities

attention to detail, eye for shape/colour, eye for visual effect, good concentration level, hand-to-eye co-ordination, IT skills, numeracy skills, technical aptitude

Relevant Subjects

Art and Design, Chemistry, ICT/Computer studies, Media and communication studies, Physics, Science

Further Information

Apprenticeship Schemes (National Apprenticeship Service) - www.apprenticeships.org.uk

Beyond The Lens (Association of Photographers (AOP)) - www.beyond-the-lens.com

British Journal of Photography (weekly) (Incisive Photographic Ltd) - www.bjp-online.com

Diplomas (Foundation, Higher and Advanced) - http://yp.direct.gov.uk/diplomas

Photo Imaging (Skillset) (Skillset) - www.skillset.org/photo/careers/

Skillset - sector skills council for the creative media, fashion and textiles industries - www.skillset.org

▶Working in creative & media (2007) (Babcock Lifeskills) - www.babcock-lifeskills.com/

Addresses

Association of Photographers (AOP)
81 Leonard Street, London EC2A 4QS
Phone: +44 (0)20 7739 6669
Web: www.the-aop.org

British Association of Picture Libraries and Agencies (BAPLA)
18 Vine Hill, London EC1R 5DZ
Phone: +44 (0)20 7713 1780
Web: www.bapla.org

Open College of the Arts
Michael Young Arts Centre, Redbrook Business Park,
Wilthorpe Road, Barnsley S75 1JN
Phone: 0800 731 2116 (UK only)
Web: www.oca-uk.com

Similar Jobs

Digital Imaging Specialist, Laboratory Technician: Education, Laboratory Technician: Science, Photographer, Photographic Stylist, Print Finisher, Textile Colour Technologist

Photographic Stylist

also known as: Media Stylist

CRCI:Media, Print and Publishing
CLCI:EV Job Band: 2 to 4

Job Description

Photographic stylists are responsible for setting the scene of each photograph or shoot (set of photographs) so that a photographer captures the desired mood and style. They work mainly in fashion and advertising in editorial photography, and with lighting technicians and set/prop builders. Stylists need to understand both the image that is being created, and the needs and interests of the potential audience. They discuss the audience, style and other requirements with the photographer, choose appropriate clothing for the models and use props (movable objects) to achieve the desired effect.

Stylists may need to source, hire or purchase individual props. They build good relationships with specialist and antique dealers to enable the desired items to be borrowed for the duration of a shoot. Photographic styling of food is a specialist area and stylists may need to supply or even prepare the food. They may also work with special equipment such as cotton buds and tweezers to ensure the food looks just right.

Work Details

If working for a large company, you are more likely to have regular working hours, though you may be required to work longer hours to meet deadlines. You need to be flexible to meet the needs of clients and to ensure that the best use is made of models or hired equipment. If self-employed, your hours of work are determined by a combination of your own needs and that of the client.

Stylists work in a photographer's studio, a stage or set, an office, or perhaps from home. On location, you may travel around and spend time away from home. Work can take place outdoors. Some lifting and bending is necessary when moving props around, and you may have to climb ladders if helping to arrange a set or stage. Working with paints and glues may require protective clothing, including a face mask.

Qualification

There are no set entry qualifications for this job. Many photographic stylists have an art and design background, and some have an HND/degree, or equivalent.

• England, Wales and Northern Ireland

Band 2: For entry as a photographic assistant: some GCSEs (A*-C), or equivalent, are an advantage.

Band 3: For entry to jobs, HNC or a relevant Diploma, usually at least 4 GCSEs (A*-C) including English and maths, or equivalent.

Band 4: For foundation degree in fashion styling and photography: 1-2 A levels in art at level C or above, and 4 GCSEs (A*-C) usually including English and maths, or equivalent qualifications.

• Scotland

Band 2: For entry as a photographic assistant: some S grades (1-3) in subjects including English and maths or similar, are an advantage.

Band 3: For entry to a relevant course: usually at least four S grades (1-3) including English and maths, or similar.

Band 4: For SQA higher national award and professional development awards: 2-3 H grades and some S grades (1-3) usually including English and maths, or similar qualifications.

Adult Qualifications

Mature applicants with outstanding portfolios of work may be accepted for courses without the standard entry requirements. There are Access and foundation courses in some areas; these give adults without qualifications a route onto higher education courses.

Work Experience

Entry to this job is competitive and it is important to do some relevant work or gain voluntary experience before applying. This may be in a photographic studio or with a fashion designer, but any area of work that increases your awareness of visual design is useful. Experience in amateur photography can also help, and you should try to build up a portfolio of your work.

Entry and Training

There are many routes into this job and entry levels vary, but you usually need good artistic training. Knowledge and an interest in photography is desirable and experience of working in a photographic studio is useful. You need to demonstrate an interest in fashion, lifestyle and popular culture. Some stylists may begin their career as a fashion model and transfer their knowledge and skills to the photographic side of the industry.

It is possible to enter by becoming a photography assistant and training with a photographer, perhaps taking a part-time course at a local college. There are a wide range of courses dealing with art and design, both full and part time, and at many different levels. The British Institute of Professional Photography (BIPP) runs a range of training courses, provides support for professional photographers and produces The Photographer. See their website for details. The British Display Society runs a one year certificate and a two year diploma in display design. They also run a selection of short courses in styling and merchandising. The London College of Fashion offers a foundation degree, an honours degree and a masters in fashion photography. Check with colleges of further education for information on the complete range of part-time/full-time courses.

The Chartered Society of Designers and the Picture Research Association also have useful information on their websites. There are guidelines on exhibition design and fashion design and photolibrary links for members.

Useful S/NVQs include those in design, graphic design and photo imaging. Training programmes, including an apprenticeship via Creative and Cultural Skills, may be available in your area. Advanced apprenticeships leading to qualification at level 3 can also be a route into higher education.

Mature candidates may find that some design studios and agencies prefer younger applicants, unless you can demonstrate extraordinary talent for the job. Experience in amateur photography and in art and design is useful. An up-to-date portfolio of your work is essential.

Opportunities and Pay

This is a small but growing profession, due to a current demand for lifestyle magazines and a growth in the advertising and media industry, particularly in the areas of fashion, interior design and cookery. There is fierce competition for jobs, particularly for junior posts. It may be possible to work for a magazine, media, publishing or design company, or in the marketing department of a large company. Most stylists are self-employed and work closely with other, usually self-employed, photographers. Contacts in the industry and focused networking are therefore important, as most stylists get their work through personal recommendation.

Promotion depends not only on your reputation, but also on the size and type of employer. It may be necessary to frequently change your job to enable progression to head stylist. Some may move into design, work in marketing and sales, or in exhibition work. Some stylists work from home on a freelance basis.

Pay varies greatly, but trainees can earn around £14k, rising to around £35k a year for those with considerable experience and success. Income for those who are self-employed depends on the hours worked and contracts achieved, but rates can range from £200-£400 a day.

Health

You must have normal colour vision and good eyesight.

Skills and Qualities

able to work quickly, aptitude for teamwork, attention to detail, business awareness, creative flair, excellent communication skills, eye for shape/colour, eye for visual effect, good organisational skills, networking skills, observant, practical skills

Relevant Subjects

Art and Design, Chemistry, Media and communication studies, Physics, Science

Further Information

AGCAS: Media (Job Sector Briefing) (AGCAS) - www.prospects.ac.uk

Apprenticeship Schemes (National Apprenticeship Service) - www.apprenticeships.org.uk

Beyond The Lens (Association of Photographers (AOP)) - www.beyond-the-lens.com

Chartered Society of Designers (Chartered Society of Designers) - www.csd.org.uk

Creative & Cultural Skills - sector skills council for advertising, crafts, cultural heritage, design, literature, music, performing & visual arts - www.ccskills.org.uk

Getting Into Art and Design (Trotman)

Picture Research Association (PRA) - www.picture-research.org.uk

▶Working in art & design (2009) (Babcock Lifeskills) - www.babcock-lifeskills.com/

▶Working in fashion & clothing (2008) (Babcock Lifeskills) - www.babcock-lifeskills.com/

Addresses

Association of Photographers (AOP)
81 Leonard Street, London EC2A 4QS
Phone: +44 (0)20 7739 6669
Web: www.the-aop.org

British Display Society (BDS)
14-18 Heralds Way, Town Centre, South Woodham Ferrers, Essex CM3 5TQ
Phone: +44 (020 8856 2030
Web: www.britishdisplaysociety.co.uk

British Institute of Professional Photography (BIPP)
1 Prebendal Court Oxford Road, Aylesbury, Buckinghamshire HP19 8EY
Phone: +44 (0)1296 718530
Web: www.bipp.com

London College of Fashion
20 John Princes Street, London W1G 0BJ
Phone: +44 (0)20 7514 7344
Web: www.fashion.arts.ac.uk

Similar Jobs

Costume Designer, Fashion Designer, Film/TV & Theatre Set/Stage Designer, Interior Designer, Photographer, Visual Merchandiser

Physician Assistant

CRCI:Healthcare
CLCI:JAB Job Band: 5

Job Description

Physicians assistants (PAs) support doctors in the diagnosis and management of patients in hospitals and GP surgeries. They are trained to perform a number of roles, including taking medical histories, performing medical examinations, diagnosing illnesses and analysing test results, all under the direct supervision of a doctor. They are mid-level practitioners and part of a group of healthcare workers which includes staff such as nurse practitioners and extended scope practitioners.

PAs can provide care to a wide variety of patients, permitting the provision of extra capacity for doctors to deliver their services. They enhance the quality and continuity of care for patients by performing a number of medical roles. They work mainly in general medicine but specialisms are being introduced in areas such as anaesthesia, so it is possible to practise under the supervision of a named doctor in any medical specialty.

Work Details
You are expected to work long hours, which may include nights and weekends. You work in consulting rooms or wards, GP surgeries, accident and emergency departments and out of hours clinics. Some work in academic roles in universities and hospitals. The work can involve standing for long periods. You have to make decisions about treatment and keep meticulous records. Work can be emotionally demanding, and requires coping with the sight of blood. This job is very satisfying for those wishing to work in a caring profession.

Qualification
• England, Wales and Northern Ireland
Band 5: For degree in life or health sciences followed by a postgraduate diploma in physician assistant studies: usually three A levels, with good grades in chemistry and two from physics, biological sciences and maths, plus 5 GCSEs (A*-C) including English, or equivalent. Some medical schools offer a one-year pre-medical course for students with A levels in arts or mixed subjects. Check with individual schools for full details.

• Scotland
Band 5: For degree in life or health sciences followed by a postgraduate diploma in physician assistant studies: usually five H grades, with good grades in chemistry and two from physics, biology and maths, plus five S grades (1-3) including English and maths, or similar. Normally science subjects not held at H grade should be offered at S grade. Some medical schools offer a one-year pre-medical course for students whose H grades do not include the required science subjects. Check with individual schools for full details.

Degree Information
An honours degree in a health-related or life science awarded by a university medical school and recognised by the General Medical Council is essential, followed by specialist training. Life sciences include subjects such as biology, biochemistry, medical sciences, nursing and physiotherapy. The postgraduate diploma in physician assistant studies is open to graduates in life sciences or health-related subjects.

Adult Qualifications
Entry requirement standards are not normally relaxed for mature applicants, though those who consider applying should contact the individual university for advice.

Work Experience
Entry to this career is competitive and it is essential that you have some relevant work or voluntary experience before applying to train to demonstrate a long-term commitment to medicine. You must be able to demonstrate experience of working with the public, an interest in health or social care and excellent communication skills. Evidence of this can come in the form of relevant paid or voluntary work in a healthcare setting such as work in a hospital, residential care home, or similar. You can also apply for voluntary work overseas that usually has a health education or medically-related programme.

Entry and Training
Entry requirements to physician assistant (PA) postgraduate programmes vary but most students have a healthcare or life science undergraduate degree and some healthcare experience. Healthcare staff who have a qualification in, for example, nursing, physiotherapy or working as a paramedic, may also apply to universities to become a PA. Increasing numbers of students continue their studies directly from their primary degree.

PAs have to meet a nationally approved standard of training and practice. Training is provided by the University of Hertfordshire, Birmingham University, Wolverhampton University and St Georges Medical School at the University of London. The postgraduate diploma in PA studies involves intensive training over two years, with students studying for 46 weeks each year. Courses cover many elements of the standard four or five-year medical programme that doctors study but focus on general medicine in general practice and hospital settings, rather than speciality care. However, Birmingham University, with the Royal College of Anaesthetists (RCoA), also offers a specific physician assistant (anaesthesia) postgraduate diploma. In Scotland the University of Edinburgh supervises this course.

PA courses are made up of 50% theoretical learning in the key areas of medicine, plus 50% clinical training in a range of settings including general hospital medicine and mental health. Trainee practitioners receive instruction and clinical support from a medical supervisor to gain experience in GP practices and hospital-based areas, such as accident and emergency, paediatrics, mental health and gynaecology departments. There is progress towards making this a registered profession.

Suitably qualified mature applicants are welcomed by medical schools. The role offers new and attractive opportunities for people to switch to a health-oriented career later in their working lives. If you have professional medical experience and training, you can gain recognition of previous experience through Accreditation of Prior Learning (APL). Healthcare staff who have a qualification in, for example, nursing, physiotherapy or working as a paramedic may also apply to universities providing physician assistant courses. There are also access courses to medicine and pre-medical foundation courses. Check with individual medical schools for details of all opportunities.

Opportunities and Pay
The role of physician assistant is relatively new in healthcare in the UK, but it is a growing area of employment supported by the NHS and the Department of Health. PAs are employed by the NHS and there are opportunities to work in many areas of healthcare. You can go on to teach, supervise or make contributions to research. There are also opportunities for international placements in the USA.

Salaries for qualified physician assistants range between £22.5k-£32k a year, depending on experience.

Skills and Qualities
able to put people at ease, able to take responsibility, analytical skills, aptitude for teamwork, emotionally strong, good communication skills, not squeamish, scientific approach, self confident

Relevant Subjects
Biology, Chemistry, English, Health and social care, Physics, Psychology, Science, Sociology

Further Information
British Medical Journal (weekly) (BMJ Publishing Group Ltd) - www.bmj.com/

NHS Careers (NHS Careers) - www.nhscareers.nhs.uk

NHS Careers Scotland - www.infoscotland.com/nhs

NHS Careers Wales - www.wales.nhs.uk

The Lancet (weekly) (Elsevier Ltd) - www.thelancet.com/

Addresses
British Medical Association (BMA)
BMA House, Tavistock Square, London WC1H 9JP
Phone: +44 (0)20 7387 4499
Web: www.bma.org.uk

General Medical Council (GMC)
Regents Place, 350 Euston Road, London NW1 3JN
Phone: +44 (0)161 923 6602
Web: www.gmc-uk.org

Royal College of Anaesthetists (RCoA)
Churchill House, 35 Red Lion Square, London WC1R 4SG
Phone: +44 (0)20 7092 1500
Web: www.rcoa.ac.uk

Royal College of Physicians (RCP)
11 St Andrew's Place, Regent's Park, London NW1 4LE
Phone: +44 (0)207 935 1174
Web: www.rcplondon.ac.uk

UK Association of Physician Assistants (UKAPA)
UKAPA Ltd, 34 George Street, Woburn, Bedfordshire MK17 9PY
Web: www.ukapa.co.uk

Similar Jobs
Ambulance Paramedic, Anaesthetist, Doctor: General Practitioner, Doctor: Hospital, Nurse: Adult

Physicist

CRCI:Science, Mathematics and Statistics
CLCI:QOF Job Band: 5

Job Description
Physicists study the Earth and the universe, and analyse all forms of matter and energy. The work is either in experimental research or theoretical analysis, and covers a wide variety of areas, including optics, mechanics, acoustics, power sources, space exploration, and electromagnetism. Other areas include artificial intelligence, nanotechnology, robotics, electronics, climate forecasting, and nuclear physics. Some physicists work on product design or production of a variety of everyday appliances and specialist equipment. Others carry out pure or applied research in areas such as medicine, information technology, energy, or the environment.

They use computer software to monitor and control experiments and to analyse and display test results. Usually work in a team with other scientists and engineers and often supervise laboratory technicians.

Work Details
Usually work a 35-39 hr week, Monday to Friday, in a laboratory, an office or industrial premises. Tasks can include advising or consulting with colleagues and supervising or organising staff. Depending on the kind of post, you may have responsibility for safety procedures, research reports, analytical data, quality standards or production schedules. This work requires a high degree of accuracy. There is a risk of minor injuries. Sometimes you deal with unpleasant or hazardous substances. You may need to wear protective clothing and safety glasses.

Qualification

• England, Wales and Northern Ireland
Band 5: For degree courses: 2-3 A levels including physics and preferably maths or chemistry and some GCSEs (A*-C) usually including English, maths and science, or equivalent. Exact requirements depend on the degree you take.

• Scotland
Band 5: For degree courses: 3-5 H grades including physics and maths or chemistry and some S grades (1-3), usually including English, maths and science, or similar. Exact requirements depend on the degree you take.

Degree Information
A degree in physics is normally preferred, but astronomy, astrophysics, medical physics or geophysics may also be acceptable. Other specific subject areas include computational physics, biomedical physics, particle physics, space science, environmental physics and laser physics. Some of the engineering disciplines provide useful background knowledge.

Adult Qualifications
A relevant qualification such as a degree is required. Up-to-date scientific knowledge is essential. Course entry requirements may be relaxed for mature applicants. A foundation year prior to the start of a science degree may be available at some HE institutions for those applicants who do not have the traditional science entry qualifications or equivalent. Check with colleges or universities for specific information.

Work Experience
Employers or universities may prefer candidates who have relevant work or voluntary experience, such as work in a university physics department or a physics pre-degree summer school. This is ideal, as is experience in an industrial or commercial laboratory.

Entry and Training
Most entrants are graduates. You should choose your course carefully depending on the area in which you wish to work. Degree courses last 3-4 years and can be full time or sandwich. Postgraduate study is an advantage. Some first degree courses offer an extended year that leads to Master of Science (MSci) or MPhys. Postgraduate study also includes MSc courses (different to MSci). A few entrants take a higher national award that lasts 2-3 years and can be full or part time.

Membership of the Institute of Physics can be attained by graduates with appropriate qualifications and 4-5 years relevant experience. You can also apply to become a chartered physicist (CPhys) or chartered scientist (CSci). Contact the IOP for details. There is a foundation degree in physics that allows you to progress to a BSc and relevant postgraduate course.

Training continues through practical experience in the workplace. Continuing professional development (CPD) is expected throughout your career and may be gained through professional seminars, short courses and conferences.

Mature candidates with appropriate qualifications and experience are usually preferred. Part-time study through distance learning for a BSc in natural sciences with physics is available from the Open University (OU). The Science and Technology Facilities Council (STFC) and the Engineering & Physical Sciences Research Council (EPSRC) may offer financial support for some research and postgraduate study.

Opportunities and Pay
There are opportunities for physicists in many areas of technology, manufacturing and engineering. These include oil production, electronics, aerospace, optics, medicine, computing, nuclear power, transport, engineering, forensic science and in the chemical industry. Some are employed in pure or applied research, others in design, development and production, marketing and teaching. Employers range from large multinational or national companies to small firms. Posts are also available in the civil service or research councils and in the NHS.

There is good demand for trained and qualified physicists and there is plenty of scope for specialisation. Relocation may be necessary for career progression.

Salaries vary depending on area, industry and size of employer. Starting salaries for graduates are around £21k-£25k rising to around £35k with experience and further qualifications, such as a PhD. Consultant physicists can earn over £50k a year and senior medical physicists more then £65k.

Skills and Qualities
able to communicate effectively, accurate, analytical skills, aptitude for maths and science, flexible approach, good concentration level, IT skills, problem-solving skills, technical aptitude

Relevant Subjects
Chemistry, Design and technology, Engineering, English, ICT/ Computer studies, Mathematics, Physics, Science

Further Information

Careers in Engineering Booklets (SEMTA) - www.semta.org.uk

Careers in Physics (Institute of Physics (IOP) - www.iop.org/activity/careers/

Institute of Physics; Electronic Journals (Institute of Physics (IoP)) http://iopscience.iop.org.journals

New Scientist (weekly) (Reed) - www.newscientist.com

NHS Careers (NHS Careers) - www.nhscareers.nhs.uk

Open University - www.open.ac.uk

▶Working in science (2007) (Babcock Lifeskills) - www.babcock-lifeskills.com/

▶Working in space (2010) (Babcock Lifeskills) - www.babcock-lifeskills.com/

Addresses

Engineering and Physical Sciences Research Council (EPSRC)
Polaris House North Star Avenue, Swindon, Wiltshire SN2 1ET
Phone: +44(0)1793 444 100
Web: www.epsrc.ac.uk

Institute of Physics (IOP)
76 Portland Place, London W1B 1NT
Phone: +44 (0)20 7470 4800
Web: www.iop.org

Institute of Physics and Engineering in Medicine (IPEM)
Fairmount House, 230 Tadcaster Road, York YO24 1ES
Phone: +44 (0)1904 610 821
Web: www.ipem.ac.uk

Science and Technology Facilities Council (STFC)
Polaris House, North Star Avenue, Swindon, Wiltshire SN2 1SZ
Phone: +44 (0)1793 442 000
Web: www.scitech.ac.uk

Similar Jobs

Acoustics Physicist, Astronomer, Clinical Scientist: Medical Physicist, Engineer: Nuclear, Geophysicist, Meteorologist, Teacher: Physical Sciences

Physiological Scientist

also known as: Clinical Physiologist, Physiologist
CRCI:Science, Mathematics and Statistics
CLCI:QOD Job Band: 5

Job Description

Physiological scientists measure, evaluate and record the capacity of various parts of the body to function normally. They use complex and high-tech equipment and methods to measure the function of vital organs, such as the heart, lungs and brain, in patients who have long-term health problems or those who are seriously ill. These results are used to assess patient health and to help to manage disease and disability. May also test and adjust equipment and teach patients how to use it. Rehabilitation and counselling are an important part of the work.

Some specialise in human, animal or plant physiology. Others work in scientific journalism or publishing, sports physiology, patent law or science communication. Many teach and train or supervise staff. It is possible to progress to medical/veterinary science and subjects allied to medicine, including optometry, radiotherapy or speech science. Those that work in the NHS as a clinical physiological scientist usually specialise in audiology, cardiology, gastroenterology, neurophysiology or respiratory physiology.

Work Details

Usually work a 37hr week, Monday to Friday, mostly in a laboratory in a hospital or community clinic. You may have to work shifts to give 24hr cover in some departments. Others work in a university, college, research institute or a manufacturing company. You also spend time working in an office. Depending on your post you may have responsibility for setting up experiments, analysing results and presenting reports. In hospital work, you provide information and advice for diagnosis and treatment; this requires a high degree of accuracy. You are part of a multidisciplinary team. In some jobs you can be monitoring quality standards, checking production schedules or supervising staff. There is a risk of infection and you usually wear a white coat and some protective clothing.

Qualification

• England, Wales and Northern Ireland

Band 5: For degree courses: 2-3 A levels including chemistry, biology and preferably maths or physics and some GCSEs (A*-C) usually including English, maths and a science, or equivalent. Exact requirements depend on the degree you take.

• Scotland

Band 5: For degree courses: 3-5 H grades including chemistry, biology and preferably physics or maths and some S grades (1-3), usually including English, maths and science, or similar. Exact requirements depend on the degree you take.

Degree Information

A degree in physiology is preferred but degrees in botany, zoology, biochemistry or biology may also be acceptable. Most other biological science subjects provide useful background.

Adult Qualifications

A degree or equivalent qualification and up-to-date scientific knowledge are essential.

Work Experience

Universities and employers may prefer candidates who have relevant work or voluntary experience, in such areas as hospital work or in a relevant university department or an industrial or commercial laboratory. If it proves difficult to gain this exact experience, any work with a scientific background is attractive to employers and admissions tutors.

Entry and Training

Training is usually by practical experience after obtaining a degree or taking a postgraduate qualification in physiology or a relevant biological science. Degree courses can be full time or sandwich and last for three or four years. A number of first degree courses are available and some courses include a physiology option as part of a biological sciences course. There are also some relevant postgraduate courses. Entry into medicine or veterinary science is becoming more common for physiology graduates.

Another option is to become a clinical physiological scientist through obtaining a training post within an NHS hospital providing you hold the appropriate A levels/H grades or equivalent for the area of specialism. You receive on-the-job training and study part time for a BSc in clinical physiology in your chosen field. However, those wishing to specialise in audiology must undertake a full-time degree programme at a university. Completion of the degree leads to state registration with the Health Professions Council. Contact the NHS for details.

Continuing professional development (CPD) is expected throughout your career and may be gained through professional seminars, short courses and conferences.

Access or foundation courses give adults without qualifications a route onto degree courses. Mature entry is unlikely unless you have relevant experience and qualifications.

Opportunities and Pay

There are varied opportunities in medicine, agriculture or horticulture. Some physiologists work for research institutes, universities, the civil service or armed forces. In the NHS they are known as clinical physiologists or physiological scientists. Some may work in space research or sports science. There are employment opportunities with pharmaceutical companies to work on research and development, or in production. Some physiological scientists/physiologists may move into management, marketing or sales posts and the media.

Pay varies depending on location and employer, but starting salaries for graduates are generally around £21k-£27k. Experienced physiologists earn up to £36.5k in the NHS. Additional allowances are usually paid for working in London.

Health

You need normal colour vision for some areas of work. There is an allergy risk from pollens or animals.

Skills and Qualities

able to put people at ease, able to use complex equipment, accurate, analytical skills, aptitude for teamwork, good communication skills, initiative, IT skills, methodical, scientific approach

Relevant Subjects

Biology, Chemistry, English, Health and social care, ICT/Computer studies, Mathematics, Physics, Science

Further Information

Journal of Physiology (2 x month) (The Physiological Society) - www.physoc.org

NHS Careers (NHS Careers) - www.nhscareers.nhs.uk

Physiology News (quarterly.) (The Physiological Society) - www.physoc.org/site/cms/

▶Working in science (2007) (Babcock Lifeskills) - www.babcock-lifeskills.com/

▶Working in space (2010) (Babcock Lifeskills) - www.babcock-lifeskills.com/

▶Working in sport & leisure (2010) (Babcock Lifeskills) - www.babcock-lifeskills.com/

Addresses

Health Professions Council (HPC)
Park House, 184 Kennington Park Road, London SE11 4BU
Phone: +44 (0)20 7582 0866
Web: www.hpc-uk.org

Physiological Society
Peer House, Verulam Street, London WC1X 8LZ
Phone: +44 (0)20 7269 5710
Web: www.physoc.org

Registration Council for Clinical Physiologists
RCCP Administration c/o EBS City Wharf Davidson Road, Lichfield WS14 9DZ
Phone: 0845 226 3064 (UK only)
Web: www.rccp.co.uk

Similar Jobs

Audiological Scientist, Cardiac Physiologist, Laboratory Technician: Science, Neurophysiologist, Perfusionist, Zoological Scientist

Physiotherapist

CRCI:Healthcare
CLCI:JAN Job Band: 5

Job Description

Physiotherapists use techniques such as therapeutic exercises, manual therapy (massage) and heat treatment, to help patients recover from an accident, injury or disease. They aim to restore muscles, improve movement and encourage independence. Usually discuss and plan treatment with medical staff, then give massage to relieve pain. May use a gym, water in the form of hydrotherapy or electrical therapy and devices to treat patients. Also teach people to do exercises and give help and encouragement. They are aware of the psychological, cultural and social factors which may influence a client and affect their rate of recovery. Keep notes on progress and meets with other team members and healthcare professionals.

May specialise in an out-patients department of a hospital, treating spinal and joint problems, accidents and sports injuries. Can specialise in care of the elderly, terminally ill, women's health, orthopaedics or paediatrics.

Work Details

Usually work 37 hrs a week, Monday to Friday in a hospital, but may be in the community, perhaps attached to a GPs surgery. You may work some evenings and weekends. You work in a fitness centre, sports clinic, voluntary organisation (who offer support for those suffering from medical conditions such as multiple sclerosis), occupational healthcare department in an industrial organisation or large company, or education and health promotion. Some physiotherapists run sessions in different centres or companies, and some visit patients' homes. It is also possible to work in animal therapy.

There is contact with people of all ages, including patients in hospital, people with special needs and people who are ill or in pain. This work is very demanding and requires coping with the sight of blood. You have to be prepared for considerable physical exertion and sometimes heavy lifting. A white coat or a uniform is usually worn.

Qualification

- **England, Wales and Northern Ireland**

Band 5: For degree courses: 2-3 A levels, including a biological science, and some GCSEs (A*-C) usually including English, maths and a science. Exact requirements depend on the degree you take.

- **Scotland**

Band 5: For degree courses: 3-5 H grades, including a biological science, and some S grades (1-3), usually including English, maths and a science. Exact requirements depend on the degree you take.

Degree Information

An approved degree course in physiotherapy is required. There are a number of accelerated postgraduate courses for those with a good honours degree in psychology, biology or sports science subjects.

Adult Qualifications

Applications are welcomed from mature people who can show evidence of recent study at an appropriate level, or an appropriate Access course. Experience of working as a physiotherapy helper or a care worker is an advantage.

Work Experience

Entry to this career is competitive and it is important that you gain some relevant work or voluntary experience before applying for a job or degree course. It can be difficult to organise work experience in physiotherapy because of the training pressures on physiotherapy departments. Work experience in any aspect of healthcare is useful. Admissions tutors want to ensure that you are able to communicate well with all ages and sections of the community, and can cope with illness and disability.

Entry and Training

Applicants must usually be 18 (17 in Scotland) before they can begin training. As physiotherapists work with children and other vulnerable people, a Criminal Records Bureau (CRB)/Disclosure Scotland check is also required before you start your training. A degree in physiotherapy combines academic study in anatomy, physiology, physics and pathology, with clinical practice. Degree courses last for 3-4 years and lead to membership of the Chartered Society of Physiotherapy (CSP) and state registration with the Health Professions Council. Part-time programmes are available.

Universities have a number of NHS-funded places for degree-level students. Not all courses are approved by the CSP so contact them for a full list of accredited courses. It is an advantage to have experience in sporting activities and to be able to swim. Students with a visual impairment can train on mainstream physiotherapy programmes with support from the RNIB Physiotherapy Support Service. Once qualified, it is important to follow a programme of continuing professional development . Contact the CSP for details of post-qualifying courses.

A Diploma/Welsh Baccalaureate may be available in your area in society, health and development. The advanced level is equivalent to 3.5 A levels but for some university courses, the additional and specialist learning (ASL) component of the diploma needs to include specific A levels. Check entry requirements carefully with the individual institutions.

Mature entrants with experience of working as a physiotherapy assistant or care worker may have an advantage. The number of mature entrants for training is increasing. There are a number of NHS-funded places on university courses and you may also be eligible for a non-means-tested student loan. Completion of a foundation degree may allow entry to the second year of a physiotherapy degree course.

Opportunities and Pay

There are around 50,000 registered physiotherapists in the UK. Most work in the NHS, but some run their own private practices. As the importance of therapies is recognised, there are growing opportunities in GP practices, sports clubs and health farms, but also in large firms, residential homes, schools, universities and the armed forces. The CSP recommends two-years experience and further training before going into private practice. After training and experience you can specialise in one area such as orthopaedics, obstetrics, sports therapy or working with the elderly. Some physiotherapists do preventative work, helping people to keep fit and prevent injury. It is possible to gain promotion to higher grades, with teaching, research or health service management responsibilities. There are also opportunities to work overseas.

Pay varies depending on location and employer. A newly qualified physiotherapist can earn around £21k-£28k a year in the NHS, rising to a maximum of £34k-£40k as a specialist physiotherapist. Consultants can earn up to £64k. Those in the private sector can earn considerably more depending on experience and reputation.

Health

This job requires good general fitness and a medical assessment on entry.

Skills and Qualities

able to explain clearly, able to inspire confidence, emotionally strong, encouraging, enthusiastic, manual dexterity, patient, reassuring, sympathetic, trustworthy

Relevant Subjects

Biology, Chemistry, English, Health and social care, Physical education and sport, Physics, Psychology, Science, Sociology

Further Information

AGCAS: Health (Job Sector Briefing) (AGCAS) - www.prospects.ac.uk

Diplomas (Foundation, Higher and Advanced) - http://yp.direct.gov.uk/diplomas

Frontline (fortnightly) (Chartered Society of Physiotherapy) - www.csp.org.uk/director/newsandevents/frontline.cfm

Health Professions Council (HPC) - www.hpc-uk.org

NHS Careers (NHS Careers) - www.nhscareers.nhs.uk

NHS Careers Scotland - www.infoscotland.com/nhs

NHS Careers Wales - www.wales.nhs.uk

Physiotherapy Journal (Elsevier Science) - www.physiotherapyjournal.com

SkillsActive - sector skills council for active leisure, learning and well-being - www.skillsactive.com

Welsh Baccalaureate - www.wbq.org.uk

Addresses

Chartered Society of Physiotherapy (CSP)
14 Bedford Row, London WC1R 4ED
Phone: +44 (0)20 7306 6666
Web: www.csp.org.uk

RNIB Physiotherapy Support Service
RNIB Resource Centre, University of East London,
Romford Road E15 4LZ
Phone: +44 (0)20 8223 4950
Web: www.uel.ac.uk/rnib/pss/pss.htm

Similar Jobs

Chiropractor, Osteopath, Podiatrist/Chiropodist, Sport & Exercise Scientist, Sports Therapist

Physiotherapy Assistant

also known as: Clinical Support Worker: Physiotherapy

CRCI:Healthcare

CLCI:JAN Job Band: 1 to 3

Job Description

Physiotherapy assistants help to look after patients being treated by a registered physiotherapist. They get equipment ready for different types of therapy, greet and look after patients as they arrive and prepare them for treatment. May help the patient through the basic exercise programme, according to the physiotherapist's instructions. May also monitor a patient during an exercise programme, or if receiving treatment from heat and massage machines or hydrotherapy and ice treatment equipment. They clear up after each treatment, put the equipment away, and may also clean the work area.

Assistants measure a client for mobility aids such as walking sticks, crutches and wheelchairs and show them how to use an aid safely. Also keep records, often using a computer, book future appointments and may also do general clerical and administrative tasks in the office and reception area of some clinics.

Work Details

Usually work 37 hrs a week, Monday to Friday, in a hospital or out in the community. You help people who are in need of support, and possibly in pain or distress. Work requires coping with the sight of blood and can be physically demanding. You have to be physically fit because you need to lift patients and equipment. This job needs you to be active most of the time and you have to wear a uniform.

Qualification

• England, Wales and Northern Ireland

Band 1: For entry to jobs, no minimum qualifications are needed, but you are expected to have a good level of general education and relevant experience. Some formal/vocational qualifications at any level are useful.

Band 2: For entry to jobs, no minimum qualifications are needed, but it is an advantage to have some GCSEs (A*-C) or equivalent in subjects that include English and maths. Some employers may require biology or another science.

Band 3: For entry to jobs, HNC or a relevant Diploma, usually at least 4 GCSEs (A*-C) including English, maths and a science or equivalent qualifications.

• Scotland

Band 1: For entry to jobs, no minimum qualifications are needed, but you are expected to have a good level of general education and relevant experience. Some formal/vocational qualifications at any level are useful.

Band 2: Although academic qualifications are not specified for this job, it is an advantage to have some S grades (1-3) in subjects that include English, biology or another science. Similar qualifications may be acceptable.

Band 3: For entry to jobs, usually at least four S grades (1-3) including English, maths or a science, or similar qualifications.

Adult Qualifications
No qualifications are usually needed, but experience in care work, such as in a hospital or residential care, is an advantage.

Work Experience
Work experience gives you an insight into what you enjoy about a job or working environment, and the opportunity to acquire new skills. It provides valuable information to add to your CV and improves any course application and future employment prospects. Employers may prefer candidates who have relevant work or voluntary experience in a medical or healthcare setting, such as a hospital or residential care home.

Entry and Training
Entrants aged 18 and over are preferred. You are trained on the job and supervised by an experienced member of staff. Assistants can join the Chartered Society of Physiotherapy (CSP), which provides support for education and networking opportunities.

Assistant practitioners in the NHS work in a broad range of health areas including physiotherapy. Some hospital trusts may offer an apprenticeship, or a scheme leading to the start of a physiotherapy degree. Experienced physiotherapy assistants can also become qualified physiotherapists through a part-time qualification programme, set up for those who wish to train as a state registered chartered physiotherapist. Contact the CSP for details. Relevant S/NVQs at level 2-3 in health and social care may be available.

Foundation degrees can help you to qualify as an assistant practitioner within the NHS, and may be available in your area. A Diploma/Welsh Baccalaureate may be available in your area in society, health and development. This can provide useful background for this career.

Mature applicants are often preferred and employers may take older applicants who show aptitude and have previous experience. Relevant work refresher courses are sometimes available for those returning to work, and there may be special training schemes in some areas.

Opportunities and Pay
Jobs are mainly in towns and cities throughout the UK. Most assistants work for the NHS in hospital physiotherapy departments, but there may also opportunities in health centres and sports clubs. You can also work in private practice. Opportunities in this field may be limited so evidence of experience through voluntary work is beneficial. Job-share, flexitime and part-time work are possible.

Pay is usually according to NHS pay bands, starting at around £14k-£16k a year, rising to around £19k a year with experience. A physiotherapy assistant practitioner earns around £21k a year.

Health
This job requires good general fitness.

Skills and Qualities
able to follow instructions, able to inspire confidence, aptitude for teamwork, dedicated, encouraging, friendly, patient, reassuring, reliable, trustworthy

Relevant Subjects
Biology, English, Health and social care, Physical education and sport, Science

Further Information
Apprenticeship Schemes (National Apprenticeship Service) - www.apprenticeships.org.uk

Diplomas (Foundation, Higher and Advanced) - http://yp.direct.gov.uk/diplomas

Health Service Journal (HSJ) - www.hsj.co.uk

NHS Careers (NHS Careers) - www.nhscareers.nhs.uk

NHS Careers Scotland - www.infoscotland.com/nhs

NHS Careers Wales - www.wales.nhs.uk

Physiotherapy Journal (Elsevier Science) - www.physiotherapyjournal.com

SkillsActive - sector skills council for active leisure, learning and well-being - www.skillsactive.com

Training Schemes - www.direct.gov.uk/en/educationandlearning

Welsh Baccalaureate - www.wbq.org.uk

Addresses
Chartered Society of Physiotherapy (CSP)
14 Bedford Row, London WC1R 4ED
Phone: +44 (0)20 7306 6666
Web: www.csp.org.uk

Similar Jobs
Healthcare Assistant, Occupational Therapy Assistant, Operating Department Practitioner, Physiotherapist, Podiatry/Chiropody Assistant

Piano Tuner/Technician

CRCI:Design, Arts and Crafts
CLCI:SOZ Job Band: 2

Job Description
Piano tuners/technicians adjust piano strings to the correct pitch so that the precise notes can be played. They work in different locations, including people's homes, schools, colleges and universities, concert halls, restaurants and pubs, theatres and other public places. Usually work on upright and grand pianos, and often tune pianos specifically for individual concerts or a sound recording performance. They use a tuning fork and special hand tools (wedges and cranks) to get the correct pitch by adjusting the tension of the strings. Then find and correct any faults.

Piano tuners listen to make sure that the sound is exactly right for each note played. They repair damaged or worn strings, tuning pins, hammers, etc, and may also repair the piano case. Some may specialise in other stringed keyboard instruments such as harpsichords.

Work Details
Work is usually during the day from Monday to Friday, though you may have to work evenings and occasional weekends to suit the needs of customers. Tuners may stand or sit while tuning, whichever they prefer. Travel may be necessary to tune pianos in people's homes and other locations, such as schools, concert halls and recording studios. It is essential to have an ear for music.

Qualification
Qualifications are not always required, but to do this job effectively, you need to have had some basic training, or to have gained experience in a reputable workshop.

• England, Wales and Northern Ireland
Band 2: Formal qualifications are not required for basic training as a piano tuner, but it is an advantage to have some GCSEs (A*-C) or equivalent in subjects that include English and maths. A musical background is an obvious advantage.

• Scotland

Band 2: Formal qualifications are not required for basic training as a piano tuner but some S grades or similar may be useful. A musical background is an obvious advantage.

Adult Qualifications

Most basic courses do not require formal qualifications or musical background, though practical skills and an interest in music are desirable.

Work Experience

Work experience in piano tuning may be hard to gain. It does, however, improve your chances at interview if you have some work experience to develop your musical ear or your skills in craft work. Contact piano tuners in your area for work-shadowing experience.

Entry and Training

Training is usually on the job, often in a piano shop. Some trainees spend a period abroad with piano manufacturers to learn this skill. There are specialist courses available such as the piano tuning and repair programme at Newark College in Nottinghamshire. There are no specific entry requirements, except an interest in music. It is not essential to be able to play the piano, although it does help with the work. There is also a foundation degree in musical instruments available at London Metropolitan University. Entrants to this need 1 A level/H grade and 3 GCSEs/S grades (A*-C/1-3) including English. Contact the Pianoforte Tuners' Association (PTA) for details of all full and part-time courses.

Those who have relevant qualifications may wish to progress to a degree in music technology. Membership of the PTA is awarded to those who have completed at least five years' experience from the start of training, which must include two years' training and two years' working as a piano tuner. The Association has around 240 members. It is possible, although expensive, to take private lessons in piano tuning. Kemble & Company Limited, the UK's only piano manufacturer, may provide in-house training.

Blind or partially-sighted tuners may be able to enter the Home Workers' Scheme, which provides support to those wishing to set up and run their own business from home. The Association of Blind Piano Tuners (ABPT) serves the professional needs of blind and partially-sighted piano tuners throughout the world.

Mature applicants with practical skills such as woodworking and DIY, as well as having an ear for music, may have an advantage for training and employment. Evening classes in piano tuning may be available in some areas.

Opportunities and Pay

The European piano building industry is in decline as countries such as Japan, Korea, Indonesia and China are now leaders in production. This shift in manufacturing to Asia has left many piano builders from Europe looking for work in the industry.

Jobs are available throughout the UK, particularly in the south of England, but most tuners are likely be self-employed. You may work for a piano manufacturing company, piano dealership, or a small craft workshop. There are good opportunities to work part time. Some may move into restoration work. Funding to start your own business may be available by contacting organisations such as The Prince's Trust.

Pay varies depending on whether you are employed/self-employed, full or part time. Fees for an initial piano fine-tuning session range from £40-£60 but can be more for a successful and specialist tuner/technician. Small pitch adjustment is around £50-£60 and for a semitone pitch adjustment, fees can be around £100+ a session. Those who are employed may earn around £17k-£20k a year after two years' experience, rising to £25k with more experience. Highly successful piano tuners/technicians may earn up to £45k, particularly those who move into piano restoration.

Health

It is essential to have good hearing.

Skills and Qualities

able to work well on your own, attention to detail, business awareness, good communication skills, good ear for music, manual dexterity, patient, reliable, self-motivated

Relevant Subjects

Music

Further Information

International Piano (Orpheus Publications) - www.rhinegold.co.uk/magazines/international_piano

Piano Tuners Quarterly (RNIB vocational magazine) (Royal National Institute for the Blind) - www.rnib.org.uk/

The Princes's Trust - www.princes-trust.org.uk

▶Working in music (2007) (Babcock Lifeskills) - www.babcock-lifeskills.com/

Addresses

Association of Blind Piano Tuners (ABPT)
31 Wyre Crescent, Lynwood, Darwen, Lancashire BB3 0JG
Phone: 0844 736 1976 (UK only)
Web: www.uk-piano.org

Kemble and Company Ltd
Yamaha Music UK Ltd Sherbourne Drive Tilbrook,
Milton Keynes MK7 8BL
Phone: +44 (0) 870 4445575
Web: www.kemble-pianos.co.uk

London Metropolitan University
Admissions: 166-220 Holloway Rd, London N7 8DB
Phone: +44 (0)20 7133 4200
Web: www.londonmet.ac.uk

Newark College
Friary Road, Newark, Nottinghamshire NG24 1BP
Phone: 01636 680 680
Web: www.lincolncollege.ac.uk

Pianoforte Tuners' Association
The PTA Secretary, P O Box 1312, Lightwater, Woking,
Surrey GU18 5UB
Phone: 0845 602 8796 (UK only)
Web: www.pianotuner.org.uk

Royal National College for the Blind
College Road, Hereford HR1 1EB
Phone: +44 (0)1432 265 725
Web: www.rncb.ac.uk

Similar Jobs

Musical Instrument Technician, Musician: Classical, Teacher: Music

Picture Framer

CRCI:Design, Arts and Crafts
CLCI:SAJ — Job Band: 1 to 2

Job Description

Picture framers make frames to display pictures and other items in the best way and to protect them from damage. This may be caused by airborne pollution, humidity and damp, UV light, insects and mould. They may frame paintings, medals, tapestries, sports trophies, old manuscripts, certificates, maps and photographs. Framers help the customer to choose framing materials and the frame shape, then prepare the artwork by pasting, taping or pressing on to aboard. They prepare canvas or tapestries by stretching them over a frame.

Picture Framer

Framers cut the mounting board for the border using a special machine and use a hand saw or machine to make the frame. They cut glass to size and assemble the frame, mounting and artwork. Then pin and tape the backing into place and fix any hooks or other method of displaying the framed item. Some picture framers may also sell prints, greetings cards, paintings or perhaps artists' materials.

Work Details

Usually work in a shop, gallery or workshop. Full-time staff mostly work a basic 37-40 hr week, which may include a Saturday and a day off during the week. May be able to choose the daily working hours, especially if self-employed. The work area varies, but is usually light, airy and pleasant. Work is detailed and requires a lot of concentration. You must be able to take responsibility for a high standard of skilled work, organising the work load and possibly running a business efficiently.

Many customers expect to have advice in choosing a frame. It is important to keep up to date with design trends. Protective clothing and a face mask are worn when cutting glass/wood or using glues. For some specialist or valuable work, special gloves are required.

Qualification

• England, Wales and Northern Ireland

Band 1: For entry to jobs, no minimum qualifications are needed, but you are expected to have a good level of general education and relevant experience. Some formal/vocational qualifications at any level are useful.

Band 2: For entry to jobs, no minimum qualifications are needed, but it is an advantage to have some GCSEs (A*-C) or equivalent in subjects that include English, maths and art and design or design technology.

• Scotland

Band 1: For entry to jobs, no minimum qualifications are needed, but you are expected to have a good level of general education and relevant experience. Some formal/vocational qualifications at any level are useful.

Band 2: Although academic qualifications are not specified for this job, it is an advantage to have some S grades (1-3) in subjects that include English, maths, art and craft and design technology, or similar.

Adult Qualifications

Formal qualifications are not usually needed for mature entrants, but any level of qualification in art and craft or design and technology subjects is an advantage.

Work Experience

Relevant work or voluntary experience is always useful and can improve your chances when applying for jobs. Any work that involves picture framing or woodworking skills, such as a Saturday job or holiday work, is very helpful.

Entry and Training

Training may mean working with a skilled person or taking a course at a local college or adult education centre. Some courses can be short, including weekend courses, others can last 8-10 weeks, and some up to a year part time. In many areas, there may be only private fee-paying courses. Training programmes, including relevant apprenticeship schemes, may be available in your area. Advanced apprenticeships leading to qualification at level 3 can also lead into higher education.

You can take tests to qualify for the Guild Commended Framer (GCF) qualification of the Fine Art Trade Guild. An advanced programme is also available in textiles, in mount design and function, and in conservation framing, but you must gain your GCF first. The Guild also offers a list of trainers throughout the country. It is important to go on short refresher courses to learn new methods and to keep up to date with changes in equipment and frame designs.

Mature applicants often find this is a good second career and entry is therefore common. Entry to this job is easier if you have experience in art or woodwork. Previous sales or business experience is also a valuable asset. Contact the local Jobcentre/ Jobcentre Plus office, LSC/LEC, Next Step service, Jobcentre (NI) or ELWa (Wales) for details of possible training opportunities.

Opportunities and Pay

Work is mainly found in towns and cities, and may be with a contract framer, a specialist frame shop, an art gallery or museum, a photographers or gift shop. Organisations such as the National Trust or Historic Scotland may employ picture framers. This job can be done from home on a part-time basis and many people are self-employed, when experienced. Costs include buying your own equipment, but there may be grants for those setting up their own business. Prospects depend on your own ability.

Pay varies depending on where you work. Those who work full time as a trainee can expect around £12k a year, rising to around £20k with experience. A specialist framer in a gallery or museum may earn more than £25k a year. Earnings for self-employed framers depend on the success of the business.

Health

This job requires normal colour vision.

Skills and Qualities

able to work well on your own, attention to detail, business awareness, creative flair, eye for visual effect, manual dexterity, numeracy skills, safety conscious, technical aptitude

Relevant Subjects

Art and Design, Design and technology, Mathematics

Further Information

Apprenticeship Schemes (National Apprenticeship Service) - www.apprenticeships.org.uk

Art Business Today (5 x year) (Fine Art Trade Guild) - www.fineart.co.uk

Creative & Cultural Skills - sector skills council for advertising, crafts, cultural heritage, design, literature, music, performing & visual arts - www.ccskills.org.uk

The GCF Study Guide (Fine Art Trade Guild) - www.fineart.co.uk

Training Schemes - www.direct.gov.uk/en/educationandlearning

▶Working in art & design (2009) (Babcock Lifeskills) - www.babcock-lifeskills.com/

Addresses

Fine Art Trade Guild (FATG)
16-18 Empress Place, London SW6 1TT
Phone: +44 (0)20 7381 6616
Web: www.fineart.co.uk

Historic Scotland
Longmore House, Salisbury Place, Edinburgh EH9 1SH
Phone: +44 (0)131 668 8600
Web: www.historic-scotland.gov.uk

National Trust
Heelis, Kemble Drive, Swindon, Wiltshire SN2 2NA
Phone: +44 (0)1793 817400
Web: www.ntjobs.org.uk

Similar Jobs

Cabinet Maker, Carpenter/Joiner, Graphic Design Assistant, Graphic Design: Studio Junior, Visual Merchandiser, Wood Machinist

Picture Researcher

CRCI:Media, Print and Publishing
CLCI:FAD Job Band: 4 to 5

Job Description

Picture researchers find and licence appropriate images, usually photographic, for a client. They liaise with clients and negotiate the terms, conditions and fees for the contract. They work from a client's brief, using archives, picture libraries and search engines to source images that meet the client's needs. The images sought range from a place, person or event to a conceptual theme like happiness or liberty. Although most of the work is carried out online, there are still occasions when a smaller specialist may only be able to offer transparencies or CD-ROMs. The researcher must consider the eventual use and location of the image; the size, colour, available space and format and the audience it is aimed at; as well as the budget available and where it is to be distributed.

It may be that the images required have to come from a variety of sources, possibly incurring charges. It is the researcher's responsibility to ensure that copyright is not infringed and that licences are acquired. Researchers also carry out administrative tasks, such as keeping records. IT skills are important as they have to edit, manipulate and store images. They may also commission photographers to make new images.

Work Details

You usually work a basic 39 hour week, Monday to Friday. However, late finishes and weekend work may be required if deadlines need to be met. You are usually office based, but may need to travel to small collections with no online resources. You use a computer most of the time.

Qualification

• England, Wales and Northern Ireland

Band 4: For HND, Diploma of Higher Education or foundation degree: 1-2 A levels and some GCSEs (A*-C) usually including English and maths, or equivalent.

Band 5: For degree courses: 2-3 A levels and some GCSEs (A*-C) usually including English and maths, or equivalent. Exact requirements depend on the degree you take.

• Scotland

Band 4: For entry to SQA higher national and professional development awards, usually 2-3 H grades and some S grades (1-3), including English and maths, or similar qualifications.

Band 5: For entry to a degree course: 3-5 H grades and some S grades (1-3) including maths and English, or similar qualifications. Exact requirements depend on the degree you take.

Degree Information

Your degree subject is not important, although anthropology, art history, botany, history, languages, photography or science are all viewed favourably.

Adult Qualifications

Most picture libraries look for researchers with a degree in a subject relevant to their collection, or someone with a keen interest in a certain type of photography. A good level of general knowledge is considered an asset.

Work Experience

Picture libraries and agencies often ask that candidates have some prior experience of this kind of work or a related area, such as graphic design or photography. It is therefore common for new entrants to undertake some unpaid work to show their aptitude and improve their CV. The Skillset website has up to date information on work experience.

Entry and Training

Most new entrants are graduates. Publishing or visual arts qualifications are also useful. However, most picture libraries look for well-educated researchers with a degree relevant to their collection or part of it. The Picture Research Association lists picture research courses on its website, including one-day, distance learning and occasional courses. Some of these are offered by the Publishing Training Centre (PTC) at Book House.

Two postgraduate diplomas/MAs in publishing at Oxford Brookes, and publishing and book production at the University of Plymouth, offer modules on picture research.

The Skillset website describes the national occupational standards (NOS) for photo imaging and jobs related to it. These give a detailed breakdown of the knowledge, skills and training needed for the job.

The British Association of Picture Libraries and Agencies (BAPLA) is the biggest online resource for posts within the picture industry. It endorses picture research courses at the London School of Publishing, the London College of Communication and the PTC.

There is no specific entry route for this job, but skills acquired with experience in graphic design, IT, publishing, museum and art gallery work, work in picture libraries or photography are useful.

Government training opportunities, such as apprenticeships, may be available in your area. You can also gain recognition of previous experience through Accreditation of Prior Learning or by working towards relevant S/NVQs. Contact your local careers office, Jobcentre Plus, Next Step service or Learning and Skills Council (LSC)/Local Enterprise Company (LEC) for details of all training opportunities and schemes, including apprenticeships for adults.

Opportunities and Pay

Employers include publishers, broadcast media such as film and television, advertising agencies, and multimedia companies undertaking web-based work. You can also work for picture agencies, picture libraries, art galleries or museums. There is strong competition for posts. Freelance opportunities are increasingly common.

Picture researchers earn in the range of £18k-£25k a year, rising to around £34k. Picture editors can make £36k-£38k a year. Freelance rates vary from £125-£190 a day. The National Union of Journalists website has a useful guide to freelance rates.

Health

Normal colour vision is expected in this job.

Skills and Qualities

administrative skills, creative flair, eye for visual effect, good communication skills, good organisational skills, good telephone manner, IT skills, methodical, negotiating skills, research skills

Relevant Subjects

Art and Design, Design and technology, English, ICT/Computer studies

Further Information

Association of Photographers (AOP) (AOP) - www.aop.org

Picture Research Association (PRA) - www.picture-research.org.uk

Skillset - sector skills council for the creative media, fashion and textiles industries - www.skillset.org

Addresses

British Association of Picture Libraries and Agencies (BAPLA)
18 Vine Hill, London EC1R 5DZ
Phone: +44 (0)20 7713 1780
Web: www.bapla.org

British Institute of Professional Photography (BIPP)
1 Prebendal Court Oxford Road, Aylesbury,
Buckinghamshire HP19 8EY
Phone: +44 (0)1296 718530
Web: www.bipp.com

National Union of Journalists (NUJ)
Headland House, 308-312 Grays Inn Road, London WC1X 8DP
Phone: +44 (0)20 7278 7916
Web: www.nuj.org.uk

Similar Jobs

Broadcast Researcher, Editorial Assistant: Publishing, Graphic Designer, Photographer, Political/Parliamentary Researcher

Pilot: Armed Forces

also known as: Army Pilot, Helicopter Pilot: Armed Forces, RAF Pilot, Royal Marines Pilot, Royal Navy Pilot

CRCI:Security and Armed Forces
CLCI:B

Job Band: 4 to 5

Job Description

Pilots in the armed forces fly aeroplanes or helicopters for one of the specialist flight divisions of the Army, Royal Navy, Royal Marines or the Royal Air Force (RAF). They command, train and discipline their aircrew, as well as looking after their welfare and career development. Directly instruct new pilots when more experienced and monitor flight equipment and instruments. Are trained in management and administration.

If serving in the Flying Branch of the RAF, pilots safeguard the UK from the air, protect NATO airspace and are involved in humanitarian and military aid. Fly a wide variety of aircraft, but usually specialise in one specific type that is designed for a particular role. May fly a Sea King helicopter that is used for reconnaissance, or for search and rescue (SAR) missions, or a Hercules transport aircraft, used for ferrying troops and equipment into combat zones, and for transporting people and supplies between bases. May fly combat aircraft, such as the Eurofighter Typhoon used in reconnaissance, air defence and 'strike' roles. Are also trained to operate weapons.

Royal Navy or Royal Marine officers, serving in the Fleet Air Arm, pilot either helicopters or aircraft, including the Lynx, Sea King and Merlin helicopters, or vertical landing aircraft and fast-jet (short) take-off aircraft. Work includes carrying troops to destinations throughout the world, anti-submarine work, or attacking enemy surface vessels. In addition, the Fleet Air Arm also provide SAR along sections of the UK coastline and some hazardous parts of the country, including isolated offshore islands.

Army officer pilots serve in the Army Air Corps and are mainly trained to operate helicopters and fixed wing aircraft in battle conditions. Perform reconnaissance missions and also direct artillery fire from the air.

Work Details

You may find yourself anywhere in the world on operational duties and are expected to work unsocial hours and shifts. Pilots have to cope with sitting for hours in an enclosed space which can be very noisy. You have to be able to work under pressure, enforce discipline if necessary and sometimes make unpopular decisions. There is a risk of accidents and you can be expected to serve in dangerous situations, where there is a risk of injury or of being killed. The job requires you to wear a uniform and possibly protective clothing.

Qualification

The Scottish Qualifications Authority (SQA) launched a new Skills for Work course in 2008. This course introduces candidates to the uniformed and emergency services and is particularly suited to those considering a career in the Army, Royal Navy, Royal Air Force or Royal Marines. Check the website for details.

- **England, Wales and Northern Ireland**

Band 4: For entry: a minimum of two A levels and 5 GCSEs (A*-C) including English and maths are needed. Equivalent qualifications, such as a BTEC national award, may also be acceptable.

Band 5: For degree course leading to graduate entry: 2-3 A levels and some GCSEs (A*-C) including English and maths. Check individual prospectuses.

- **Scotland**

Band 4: For entry: a minimum of three H grades and five S grades (1-3) including English and maths are needed. Other qualifications such as SQA qualifications or similar may also be acceptable.

Band 5: For degree course leading to graduate entry: 3-5 H grades and some S grades (1-3) including English and maths. Exact requirements depend on the degree you take. Qualifications such as an SQA or similar may also be acceptable for entry to some courses. Check with universities for specific course requirements.

Degree Information

Any degree is acceptable for officer entry. Subjects such as physics, aeronautical engineering, mathematics, computing subjects, meteorology or systems and control engineering give a useful background.

Adult Qualifications

Standard entry requirements apply to applicants of any age. Entry requirements may be relaxed for adults applying for higher education courses and Access or foundation courses give adults without qualifications a route on to degree courses.

Work Experience

Entry to this career is highly competitive. Work experience may be hard to gain because of the nature of the work. However, it improves your chances at interview if you have some work experience that can develop your skills in leadership and in areas that enable you to demonstrate your initiative and responsibility. As a young person, getting involved in groups such as a local cadet organisation, or the scouts/guides helps to show enthusiasm and commitment. Often you can gain valuable experience from a school's Air Training Corp (ATC) or university air squadron. The Air League Educational Trust also has details of flying scholarships on their website. Check for full details.

Entry and Training

There are nationality and residence requirements for entry as an armed forces pilot. Entry is very competitive and selection is based on aptitude, character and personality. RAF applicants should be aged 17.5-25 yrs old; Royal Navy applicants 17-26 years old and, for Army applicants, 17-28. Many new entrants are graduates. Fixed wing and advanced helicopter training is carried out jointly with the Fleet Air Arm (RN), Army Air Corps and the RAF Flying Branch. After basic training (10 months), pilots can specialise in a particular type of aircraft or helicopter. For example, fighter pilot training involves a further 6 months basic flying training, 9 months fixed wing training, 9 months fast jet training, 9 months air combat training and front line squadron training. Officers are expected to keep training throughout their careers.

There are various forms of scholarship, sponsorship and bursary schemes available. The RAF offers sponsorship schemes including sixth form scholarships and university bursaries for degree course students. RAF flying scholarships are not necessarily linked to entry and there is no compulsion to join, following successful completion. The Royal Navy also offer sponsorship for both A levels/H grades and degree courses. Check the individual forces websites for full details of all funded training opportunities.

The Army requires 44-week initial training at Sandhurst in leadership, Army organisation, and in the battle skills required by all officers and soldiers.

Mature entrants are usually graduates and entry to the armed forces is the same for all applicants. Previous flying or aircraft experience is very useful.

Opportunities and Pay

Promotion is competitive and prospects are improved by taking further training. This job requires a great deal of personal commitment and you are on a Short Service, Medium or Permanent Commission, with a minimum commitment of 7-12 years, depending on the branch of Service. Opportunities exist for experienced officers for training and employment as flying instructors and test pilots. The training received in this job provides an excellent basis for occupations in civilian life.

Pilots in the armed forces are paid according to their rank (see Army/RAF/Navy jobs). For example, pay for a pilot after one year in the RAF is £34,670 a year. If you are still in the RAF after four years and have not given notice to leave the Service, you can expect to get a bonus of £3,750, or £5,500 after five years. You may have to commit to a further minimum period of service to receive a bonus. If you spend between 12 and 18 years in the RAF, you will get a grant when you leave to help you settle back into civilian life.

Health

Applicants must pass a strict medical test before being accepted and there are regular medical check-ups. This job requires a high standard of physical fitness, perfect colour vision, good hearing and eyesight.

Skills and Qualities

able to cope with emergencies, able to work in confined spaces, alert, good concentration level, good co-ordination, information handling skills, initiative, leadership qualities, quick reactions, self confident

Relevant Subjects

Design and technology, Engineering, English, Geography, Government and politics, Mathematics, Physical education and sport, Physics, Psychology, Science

Further Information

AGCAS: Armed Forces & Emergency Services (Job Sector Briefing) (AGCAS) - www.prospects.ac.uk

Army Careers Website - www. army.mod.uk

Careers Information - Job Explorer, Army - www.armyjobs.mod.uk/

Careers Information - Royal Air Force (RAF) - www.raf.mod.uk

Careers Information package (Royal Navy) (Royal Navy) - www.royalnavy.mod.uk/

Real Life Guide to Armed Forces (Trotman 2009) - www.trotman.co.uk

Skills for Work (Scottish Qualifications Authority) - www.sqa.org.uk/sqa/31390.html

Starting a Career as Aircrew in Military Aviation (Air League) (Air League) - www.airleague.co.uk/scholarships.html

▶Working in police, fire & security (2009) (Babcock Lifeskills) - www.babcock-lifeskills.com/

Addresses

Air League Educational Trust
Broadway House, Tothill Street, London SW1H 9NS
Phone: +44 (0)20 7222 8463
Web: www.airleague.co.uk

Similar Jobs

Airline Pilot: Civil, Helicopter Pilot: Commercial, RAF Airman/Airwoman, RAF Officer, Royal Marines Officer, Royal Navy Officer

Plaster Technician

also known as: Orthopaedic Technician

CRCI:Healthcare
CLCI:JOZ — Job Band: 1 to 2

Job Description

Plaster or orthopaedic technicians apply and remove casts that hold parts of the body still to allow them to heal, usually after a fracture. They also fit equipment to support injuries and help mobility, such as air cast boots, slings, fabric supports and crutches.

It is important to follow the doctor's instructions on the type of cast to apply. Plaster technicians put the part of the body in the right position. May then apply splints or braces. They use plaster of Paris, a range of resin-covered materials on fibreglass, polypropylene and polyester bases, or special bandages that set hard when wet to make up the cast. Advise the patient on how to look after the cast and what to do if they have any problems with it. Remove casts using cutting equipment, looking out for any signs of infection. Updating patient records and keeping the plaster room tidy and well stocked with materials and equipment is also part of the job. With experience, they may train staff from their own and other departments in cast-making techniques.

Work Details

In the NHS you work a 37.5 hr week. May work shift rotas to cover evenings, weekends and bank holidays. You may be able to work part time.

You are mostly in hospital plaster rooms. Sometimes work in accident and emergency (A&E) units, operating theatres or clinics. You are part of a team with consultants, doctors, other plaster technicians and healthcare staff. The work calls for a lot of standing and some bending. Using plaster of paris and wet bandages can be messy. You need to wear a uniform, latex gloves and protective coverings supplied by the employer.

Qualification

• England, Wales and Northern Ireland

Band 1: No minimum qualifications are required, but you are expected to have a good level of general education and practical skills. Some formal/vocational qualifications at any level are useful.

Band 2: Although academic qualifications are not specified for this job, it is an advantage to have some GCSEs (A*-C) in subjects that include English and maths, or equivalent.

• Scotland

Band 1: No minimum qualifications are required, but you are expected to have a good level of general education and practical skills. Some formal/vocational qualifications at any level are useful.

Band 2: Although academic qualifications are not specified for this job, it is an advantage to have some S grades (1-3) in subjects that include English and maths, or similar.

Adult Qualifications

No formal qualifications are required.

Work Experience

Work experience helps you find out what you enjoy and do not enjoy about a job. Paid or voluntary work experience in a healthcare setting improves your job prospects. Usually employers look for people already working in a hospital. Working with people with disabilities may also be useful.

In some areas you can do a young apprenticeship (14-16) in health and social care. You do an extended work placement and a level 2 qualification whilst at school. For health and safety reasons there may be some jobs you cannot do until you are over 16.

Entry and Training
Employers look for people with experience of healthcare work. In particular they value fracture clinic experience. Usually an orthopaedic consultant recommends you for training. You need to pass a medical and, as you are likely to come into contact with children, have a Criminal Records Bureau (CRB/Disclosure Scotland check.

You learn on the job with experienced plaster technicians. When you have at least six months' experience in the job, you can attend a five-week full-time residential course or a twenty-week day release course in casting techniques. Only six UK hospitals offer this course (Newport, Belfast, Bradford, Crewe, Dundee and Glasgow). Passing the final exam leads to a certificate in casting techniques known as the British casting certificate. You must renew your certificate every three years by providing evidence of over 150 hours of casting work and 35 hours of continuing professional development (CPD) during that period. CPD activities include attending courses, study days or conferences, private study and research work.

You can join the Association of Orthopaedic Technicians as an unqualified associate or as a certificate member.

Adults with relevant experience are welcomed in this job.

Opportunities and Pay
There are jobs for plaster technicians in NHS and private hospitals all over the UK. Some work for agencies that provide cover when regular staff are away. You can go on to become a senior and then a lead plaster technician. Some take on training roles or move into technical sales with companies selling to hospital fracture clinics.

Pay for new entrants starts at about £17k and rises to around £20k a year. Experienced staff in more senior roles earn £23k-£26k and some may earn up to £32k a year.

Health
This job may require a medical test on entry and good general fitness.

Skills and Qualities
able to explain clearly, able to get on with all kinds of people, able to put people at ease, able to work both on your own and in a team, calm, manual dexterity, not squeamish, practical skills

Relevant Subjects
Biology, Health and social care, Science

Further Information
Apprenticeship Schemes (National Apprenticeship Service) - www.apprenticeships.org.uk
Association of Orthopaedic Technicians (AOT) - www.aot-uk.com
NHS Careers (NHS Careers) - www.nhscareers.nhs.uk
Skills for Health - sector skills council - www.skillsforhealth.org.uk

Similar Jobs
Emergency Care Assistant/Ambulance Technician, Healthcare Assistant, Occupational Therapy Assistant, Prosthetic/Orthotic Technician, Radiography Assistant

Plasterer

CRCI:Building and Construction
CLCI:UF — Job Band: 1 to 2

Job Description
Plasterers repair and plaster walls, ceilings and floors for the building trade. They work on a range of projects, from houses to state-of-the-art buildings, including airport terminals, stately homes, sports stadia, offices and hotels. Two main areas of work are solid and fibrous plastering. A solid plasterer gets the area ready and puts the plaster mix on in layers. Uses a wet brush and trowel to get a smooth, flat finish for painters and decorators to work on. May work on the outside walls of buildings (rendering) or floors (screeding).

A fibrous plasterer makes decorative plasterwork moulds such as cornices, centre pieces and panelling. May work from architects' designs or copy a design from a photo or artist's drawing. Sometimes does restoration work using historical designs. The mouldings are made in a workshop and the finished piece is fixed on-site. Plasterers often work with electricians, painters, plumbers, and heating and ventilating engineers.

Work Details
Plasterers usually work a 38 hr week, Monday to Friday, though may include some overtime and work on Saturdays. You may work at different sites or be based mainly in a workshop. You may need to travel to different sites. The job involves lifting, bending, kneeling and working at heights on scaffolding and ladders. You use tools such as trowels, straight edges and levels. Working both outdoors and indoors, the conditions can be dirty, messy, dusty, and perhaps wet or damp.

There is a risk of falling from heights. You may at times need to wear a safety helmet, overalls and sometimes gloves, a face mask and safety glasses.

Qualification
• England, Wales and Northern Ireland
Band 2: Although academic qualifications are not specified for this job, it is an advantage to have some GCSEs (A*-C) in subjects that include English, maths, science or technical subjects, or equivalent.

• Scotland
Band 2: Although academic qualifications are not specified for this job, it is an advantage to have some S grades (1-3) in subjects that include English, maths, science or technical subjects, or similar.

Adult Qualifications
There are no minimum qualifications specified for this job. Course entry requirements are usually relaxed for suitable mature applicants.

Work Experience
Relevant work or voluntary experience is always useful and can improve your chances when applying for entry to construction jobs and apprenticeships. Health and safety issues may mean that there are certain jobs you cannot do until you are over 16. Contact your local ConstructionSkills office for advice.

Entry and Training
Most entrants begin training through an approved ConstructionSkills scheme such as a three-year construction apprenticeship scheme (four years in Scotland), which you can apply for when in year 11 (January). Other schemes include work-based training at a ConstructionSkills centre and full-time work training with an employer, usually supported by day or block release to a local college. You may have to take an entrance test before you can start training. There are also one or two-year full-time college courses. You work towards gaining a level of competence card through a Construction Skills Certification Scheme (CSCS) to indicate your individual skill level.

The Federation of Plastering and Drywall Contractors offers short courses, often 1-2 days, on specialised areas of work, including CSCS introduction and update. Specialist training is also available for those who wish to concentrate on achieving skills in restoration and heritage work. Contact the National Heritage Training Group for further information. Other courses are available from organisations such as the Society for the Protection of Ancient Buildings that offers specialised courses on working with lime.

A Diploma/Welsh Baccalaureate in construction and the built environment may be available in your area. There is an entry-level certificate in preparation for employment in plastering, which requires no prior experience. You may be able to work towards S/NVQs in plastering at levels 1-3 while you work. Training programmes, including plastering apprenticeships leading to level 2 and advanced apprenticeships/construction apprenticeships leading to level 3, may be available in your area. There are also Construction Awards (England and Wales) available for those who are unable to gain workplace experience for NVQs. These include the new level 1-3 diploma in plastering. Contact ConstructionSkills for further details.

Mature applicants can take refresher courses that are sometimes available for those returning to work. There may be special government training schemes, such as apprenticeships, in some areas. If you have experience without formal qualifications, you can use On-Site Assessment and Training (OSAT) or the Experienced Worker Practical Assessment (EWPA) scheme to achieve a qualification. More information is available from the ConstructionSkills website.

Opportunities and Pay

Most work for a firm of plasterers or a building contractor. Promotion to supervisory level is possible, mainly in larger firms. Many are self-employed. Seasonal and short-term work is often available for sub-contractors and the self-employed. You may be able to work abroad. Availability of work depends on the state of the building trade and the national economy. Currently there is a downturn in the housing market which means there may be a shortage of vacancies.

Pay varies depending on area and employer. A trainee plasterer earns around £14k a year; when skilled this rises to around £18k-£24k. The most skilled and experienced workers, including the self-employed, can earn up to £28k a year. Employers may give allowances for travel and cost of lodgings. Overtime and bonus payments can add to income.

Health

You should not be allergic to dust. Plasterers need to have stamina and be physically fit.

Skills and Qualities

able to work both on your own and in a team, able to work quickly, agile, eye for visual effect, head for heights, health & safety awareness, manual dexterity

Relevant Subjects

Art and Design, Construction and built environment, Design and technology

Further Information

Apprenticeship Schemes (National Apprenticeship Service) - www.apprenticeships.org.uk

Construction Awards
http://gbca.com/events/construction-awards

Construction Skills Certification Scheme (CSCS) - www.cscs.uk.com

ConstructionSkills - sector skills council for the construction industry - www.cskills.org

Diplomas (Foundation, Higher and Advanced)-
http://yp.direct.gov.uk/diplomas

Specialist Building Finishes (bi-monthly) (FPDC) - www.fpdc.org/Specialist-Building-Finishes-Magazine.aspx

Training Schemes - www.direct.gov.uk/en/educationandlearning

Welsh Baccalaureate - www.wbq.org.uk

▶Working in construction & the built environment (2007) (Babcock Lifeskills) - www.babcock-lifeskills.com/

▶Working in cultural heritage (2007) (Babcock Lifeskills) - www.babcock-lifeskills.com/

Addresses

Federation of Plastering and Drywall Contractors (FPDC)
4th Floor 61 Cheapside, London EC2V 6AX
Phone: +44 (0)20 7634 9480
Web: www.fpdc.org

Gypsum Products Development Association
PO Box 35084, London NW1 4XE
Phone: +44 (0)20 7935 8532
Web: www.gpda.com

National Heritage Training Group (NHTG)
Carthusian Court, 12 Carthusian Street, London EC1M 6EZ
Phone: 0300 456 5517 (UK only)
Web: www.nhtg.org.uk

Society for the Protection of Ancient Buildings (SPAB)
37 Spital Square, London E1 6DY
Phone: +44 (0)20 7377 1644
Web: www.spab.org.uk

Similar Jobs

Bricklayer, Ceiling Fixer, Dry Liner, Glazier, Painter & Decorator, Tiler: Wall & Floor

Plastic Surgeon

also known as: Doctor: Plastic Surgeon

CRCI:Healthcare
CLCI:JAB — Job Band: 5

Job Description

Plastic surgeons use specialist medical knowledge and skill to care for patients who may need or want plastic surgery. Patients may need reconstructive plastic surgery to restore function and appearance after an illness or accident. They may want cosmetic surgery to alter their appearance. Most plastic surgeons specialise in a particular area which can include trauma, congenital abnormalities or cancer care.

Works in a hospital, and examines and talks to patients in a ward as part of the ward round. May also work in outpatient clinics and have emergency duties. Carries out, or refers the patient for tests such as X-rays or blood tests, and arranges surgery. Cares for and monitors the patient after surgery.

Works as part of a team including nurses and other health professionals. Supports the work of other surgeons dealing with restorative surgery after a major operation, deals with serious burns cases, skin grafts and microsurgery.

Work Details

You are expected to work long hours, which may include nights and weekends. You work in consulting rooms, wards and operating theatres. The work can involve standing and bending for long periods. You have to make decisions about treatment and keep meticulous records. Work can be emotionally demanding, and requires coping with the sight of blood. This job can be very satisfying for those wishing to work in a caring profession.

Qualification

- **England, Wales and Northern Ireland**

Band 5: For degree in medicine: usually three A levels, with good grades in chemistry and two from physics, biological sciences and maths, plus 5 GCSEs (A*-C) including English, or equivalent. Some medical schools offer a one-year pre-medical course for students with A levels in arts or mixed subjects. Check with individual schools for full details.

- **Scotland**

Band 5: For degree in medicine: usually five H grades, with good grades in chemistry and at least two from physics, biology and maths, plus five S grades (1-3) including English and maths, or similar. Normally science subjects not held at H grade should be offered at S grade. Some medical schools offer a one-year pre-medical course for students whose H grades do not include the required science subjects. Check with individual schools for full details.

Plastic Surgeon

Degree Information

A degree in medicine awarded by a university medical school and recognised by the General Medical Council is essential, followed by specialist training.

Adult Qualifications

Entry requirement standards are not normally relaxed for mature applicants, though those considering applying should contact the individual university for advice. Graduates with a good honours degree in a related subject may obtain exemptions from certain options within the medical degree course.

Work Experience

Entry to this career is highly competitive and it is essential that you have some relevant work or voluntary experience before applying to train as a doctor so that you are able to demonstrate a long-term commitment to medicine. Evidence of this can come in the form of relevant paid or voluntary work in a healthcare setting such as work in a hospital, residential care home, or similar. You can apply for voluntary work overseas that usually has a health education or medically-related programme.

It can be hard to find clinical work experience but it is a useful addition to your application and can help you decide if you are suited to surgery, and what areas are of most interest. You need to be at least 16, possibly older, to find a work placement in a hospital. Contact the work placement co-ordinator or human resources staff at your local hospital to find out whether they accept work experience students.

Entry and Training

Training to become a surgeon takes time, is very competitive and not everyone who starts the process will finish. Surgeons must first qualify as medical doctors by completing a 5 year medical degree, pass the postgraduate two-year Foundation Programme and register as a doctor with the General Medical Council (GMC). For full details of medical training see the job article Doctor: Hospital.

Once you have completed the Foundation Programme, there is competition for entry to two year core surgical training, under the Modernising Medical Careers initiative. This covers all aspects of surgery. After core training, you then have to apply for posts for specialty training on one of eight specialist surgery training programmes. This can take approximately six years to complete. Progress is based on achieving competences, and leads to the Certificate of Completion of Specialist Training (CCST) and Fellowship of the Royal College of Surgeons (FRCS).

Once you have achieved the CCST, you can join the specialist register of the GMC and apply for a post as a consultant. You are expected to update your professional knowledge continually throughout your career. Contact the Royal College of Surgeons (RCS) for details of courses, bursaries and training routes. The RSC also runs surgical careers afternoons for medical students at the College in London twice a year. These sessions are free to attend and all participants are provided with a certificate of attendance for their portfolios.

The British Association of Plastic, Reconstructive and Aesthetic Surgeons offers a series of advanced educational courses and an e-Learning programme in partnership with the Department of Health. Their website also has details of awards, grants and funds and fellowships available to support educational and professional development. Similarly, the British Burns Association has details of grants and specialist courses.

The British Association of Aesthetic Plastic Surgeons promotes advancement in plastic surgery by supporting specialist training and liaising with other professional organisations internationally.

For students under the age of 25, the armed forces sometimes offers medical cadetships. Contact your nearest armed forces careers office for details.

The Medical Womens Federation awards and oversees a variety of grants and prizes throughout the year. See their website for further details. Medical students may qualify for an NHS bursary to cover some of their fees.

Mature applicants that are suitably qualified are welcomed by medical schools and some may have reserved places for mature/graduate entrants. There are access courses to medicine and pre-medical foundation courses. Open University credits in specific courses at distinction level may be accepted at some medical schools. Check with individual medical schools for details of all opportunities.

Opportunities and Pay

Surgeons are usually employed by the NHS, a private hospital or the armed forces. There are also opportunities abroad with voluntary organisations in developing countries, but pay is usually low. Plastic surgery is considered to be one of the more competitive areas of surgery, with limited training opportunities. Prospects may depend on willingness to move to another area to gain experience and obtain promotion. There may be opportunities to work part time or job share.

Within the NHS, junior doctors earn a basic salary and are usually paid a supplement for extra hours worked. Basic salaries are around £33k a year (including a 50% supplement for extra hours), rising to £43k-£68k (including 50% supplement) for a doctor in specialist training. A consultant can earn £73k-£174k a year. These salaries do not include on-call payments, private income or London weighting allowances.

Health

There is a risk of infection. You should have no allergies and a good level of general fitness.

Skills and Qualities

analytical skills, aptitude for teamwork, confident, emotionally strong, good communication skills, manual dexterity, not squeamish, problem-solving skills, responsible attitude, scientific approach

Relevant Subjects

Biology, Chemistry, English, Health and social care, Mathematics, Physics, Psychology, Science

Further Information

Army Careers Website - www. army.mod.uk

Becoming a Doctor (BMA) (BMA) - www.bma.org.uk/careers/becoming_doctor/index.jsp

Becoming a Doctor: Is Medicine really the career for you? (Matt Green & Tom Nolan, 2008) (Apply2 Ltd)

British Association of Aesthetic Plastic Surgeons - www.baaps.org.uk/

British Association of Plastic, Reconstructive and Aesthetic Surgeons - www.bapras.org.uk/

British Burns Association - www.britishburnsassociation.org/

Medical Women's Federation - www.medicalwomensfederation.org.uk/

NHS Careers (NHS Careers) - www.nhscareers.nhs.uk

NHS Careers Scotland - www.infoscotland.com/nhs

NHS Careers Wales - www.wales.nhs.uk

So you want to be a doctor - www.wanttobeadoctor.co.uk/main.php

Surgical Specialities http://surgicalcareers.rcseng.ac.uk/documents/Surgical%20Specialties%20booklet.pdf

The Surgeon (6 x year) (Royal College of Surgeons of Edinburgh and Ireland) - www.thesurgeon.net

UK Clinical Aptitude Test - www.ukcat.ac.uk

Women in Surgery http://surgicalcareers.rcseng.ac.uk/wins

Addresses
British Medical Association (BMA)
BMA House, Tavistock Square, London WC1H 9JP
Phone: +44 (0)20 7387 4499
Web: www.bma.org.uk

General Medical Council (GMC)
Regents Place, 350 Euston Road, London NW1 3JN
Phone: +44 (0)161 923 6602
Web: www.gmc-uk.org

Open University (OU)
PO Box 197, Milton Keynes MK7 6BJ
Phone: +44 (0)845 300 6090
Web: http://www3.open.ac.uk

Royal College of Surgeons of England
35-43 Lincolns Inn Fields, London WC2A 3PE
Phone: +44 (0)20 7405 3474
Web: www.rcseng.ac.uk

Similar Jobs
Anaesthetist, Cardiologist, Doctor: Hospital, Ophthalmologist, Pathologist, Surgeon

Play Therapist

CRCI:Social Work and Counselling Services
CLCI:JOZ Job Band: 5

Job Description

Play therapists help children and young people, usually aged 3-12 years, or adolescents up to the age of 16, to express their feelings and explore their difficulties through play. They work with a child/ young person who can be suffering from a range of psychological difficulties, such as anxiety, depression, aggression, attention deficit hyperactivity disorder or those with complex life experiences. These can include family breakdown, grief, abuse, domestic violence and trauma. Usually work on a one-to-one basis, but can also work with groups.

Help them to face and overcome their problems. With young children, may use toys during a session. Also provide art and play materials, such as paints, crayons, water and sand, to get the young person to express their feelings. Use techniques, such as observation and listening to what is being said or done by the child/ young person. May plan a session to tackle a particular problem or issue that seriously affects their everyday life, often using puppets to represent friends or family characters.

Play therapists make detailed notes and produce a written report on each session. They are regularly supervised by clinical experts and liaise with other professionals, including social workers and doctors, psychiatrists, psychologists, psychotherapists, psychiatric nurses and/or occupational therapists. Also work closely with parents/carers. They are aware of the legal requirements that govern work with children and young people.

Work Details

Sessions are usually held during the day, Monday to Friday, though some may be held after school, up to 6.30pm or 7.00pm. Many therapists work part time and combine this work with their professional job, such as a social worker or teacher. Work can be in a separate room that is equipped for play, or you may need to travel to the client's home or school. This requires you to take any necessary equipment with you, such as puppets and painting/ drawing materials.

Sometimes you may have to attend a court and perhaps present a report. This work can sometimes be stressful and emotional, so you must be able to cope.

Qualification

• England, Wales and Northern Ireland

Band 5: For degree courses: 2-3 A levels and some GCSEs (A*-C) usually including English, maths and sometimes a science subject, or other equivalent qualifications. Exact requirements depend on the degree you take.

• Scotland

Band 5: For degree courses: 3-5 H grades and some S grades (1-3), usually including English, maths and sometimes a science subject, or similar qualifications.

Degree Information

A degree or professional qualification is required, such as in social work, teaching, psychology, occupational therapy, speech therapy, psychiatry or psychiatric nursing. This is followed by a specialised postgraduate course in play therapy that is validated by the British Association of Play Therapists (BAPT). Contact the BAPT for course details.

Adult Qualifications

Degree entry requirements may be relaxed for adults but evidence of academic ability and recent study is usually needed. Check with individual universities and colleges for details. Access or foundation courses give adults without qualifications a route on to degree courses.

Work Experience

Employers or universities may prefer candidates who have relevant work or voluntary experience as it demonstrates enthusiasm and commitment. Any work with children or young people, especially in a play or leisure setting such as a nursery, holiday play scheme, or in a youth and community centre is useful.

Entry and Training

This is usually a second career for those who have a specific degree and/or a professional qualification and experience of working with children for a minimum of two years. You also need to have a Criminal Record Bureau (CRB)/Disclosure Scotland check. British Association of Play Therapists (BAPT) validated postgraduate courses in play therapy are available for those with a relevant degree and experience in areas such as teaching, social work or occupational therapy. Personal therapy and supervised practice are essential elements of the training. If you have accrued enough supervised clinical practice throughout the course, you can then register as a practitioner with full membership of BAPT once your course is complete. However, criteria for full membership is currently under review. Contact BAPT for details.

A range of courses are available. Play Therapy (UK) and the Academy of Play and Child Psychotherapy also have full information on accredited courses. Training includes on-the-job experience under the supervision of a qualified play therapist and continues throughout your career as continuing professional development (CPD). You must also keep up to date with developments in research. A driving licence is useful.

Mature entry is usual as many have first qualified in areas that include teaching, social work, counselling, psychology or nursing. Maturity and life experience are essential for this work. Many entrants have work experience or a background of working with emotionally stressed children, within education, health or social services. Often such work has included the study of psychology. The average age of a play therapy student is between 30 and 45 yrs.

Opportunities and Pay

Jobs are available mainly in towns and cities and but the majority of opportunities are in south-east England. The need for qualified play therapists is growing, but there are few full-time posts available. Most play therapists work part time for a number of organisations. Some work on a freelance basis. Jobs are available in schools, with social services and voluntary organisations, and in private practice. Some work for charities such as the NSPCC and Barnardo's.

Work may be combined with other employment, including teaching, mental health and child nursing, or in social work. The specialised career as a play therapist is growing, therefore promotion and future prospects will improve.

Pay depends on the number of sessions worked, your location and experience. Generally, a 50-minute session (BAPT recommended) attracts a fee of £35-£70. You can charge additional fees for travel time, attendance at meetings, report writing and for court attendances. A full-time post, if available, attracts an annual salary of around £26k-£32k a year, depending on experience. Those working in London may earn more.

Health
Good mental health is important for this job and you must be able to cope with undergoing personal therapy or counselling.

Skills and Qualities
able to put people at ease, able to report accurately, able to understand other people's problems, emotionally strong, encouraging, good listening skills, observant, perceptive, sensitive, tactful.

Relevant Subjects
English, Health and social care, Psychology, Sociology

Further Information
British Journal of Play Therapy (British Association of Play Therapists) - www.bapt.info/journalofplaytherapy.htm

Play Therapy (The UK Society for Play & Creative Arts Therapies Ltd. (PTUK)) - www.playtherapy.org.uk/

Play Therapy Careers (BAPT) - www.playtherapycareers.org.uk

Play Therapy Careers (BAPT) (BAPT) - www.bapt.info/playtherapycareers.htm

The Guide to Play Therapy (BAPT) (BAPT) - www.bapt.info/publications.htm

What is Play Therapy? (BAPT) (BAPT) - www.bapt.info/publications.htm

►Working in social care (2010) (Babcock Lifeskills) - www.babcock-lifeskills.com/

Addresses
Academy of Play and Child Psychotherapy (APAC)
The Coach House, Belmont Road, Uckfield, East Sussex TN22 1BP
Phone: +44 (0) 1825 761143
Web: www.apac.org.uk

British Association of Play Therapists (BAPT)
1 Beacon Mews, South Road, Weybridge, Surrey KT13 9DZ
Phone: +44 (0)1932 828638
Web: www.bapt.info

Play Therapy UK (PTUK)
The Coach House, Belmont Road, Uckfield, East Sussex TN22 1BP
Phone: +44 (0)1825 761143
Web: www.playtherapy.org.uk/

Similar Jobs
Counsellor, Dramatherapist, Hospital Play Specialist, Occupational Therapist, Psychologist, Psychotherapist

Plumber

CRCI:Building and Construction
CLCI:UF
Job Band: 1 to 3

Job Description
Plumbers install and repair hot and cold water supplies, sanitary systems and heating systems. They fit and repair soil, gas and waste pipes, and also air-conditioning, ventilation and extraction systems. Plumbers provide a skilled and essential service for individual households, businesses and industrial premises. May work on new buildings or the extension and maintenance of existing buildings and systems. They make sure all work complies with building regulations.

Piping and different materials, including copper, steel, brass or plastic are used. These are cut, shaped and then joined in position by clipping them together, or by welding or soldering. Fixing leaks and drainpipes, clearing drains, and making roofs watertight and weatherproof are all part of the job.

Work Details
Plumbers usually work a 37-40 hr week, Monday to Friday, though may need to work on a Saturday, and also be on-call for emergencies. Work is in a variety of different places, such as building sites, private houses, offices, hospitals, shops and industrial premises. Travel is necessary around an area or possibly to sites away from home, depending on the job. Work can be indoors or outdoors. This job is very active and involves kneeling, bending, climbing ladders and sometimes working at heights on scaffolding.

You often work in damp, dirty, smelly, uncomfortable and cramped conditions and you may need to wear protective overalls. Sometimes safety glasses and a helmet must be worn.

Qualification
- **England, Wales and Northern Ireland**

Band 2: No minimum entry qualifications, but most employers ask for some GCSEs including maths, English, science, technical subjects, or equivalent.

Band 3: Some courses may require you to have at least 4 GCSEs (A*-D) in subjects such as English, maths, science, design and technology, or equivalent.

- **Scotland**

Band 2: No minimum entry qualifications, but most employers ask for some S grades including maths, English, science, technical subjects, or similar.

Band 3: Some courses may require you to have at least four S grades (1-4) in subjects such as English, maths, science, design and technology, or similar.

Adult Qualifications
Formal educational entry requirements are not always required. Any relevant existing qualifications you have are an advantage and may count towards workplace awards.

Work Experience
Relevant work or voluntary experience is always useful and can improve your chances when applying for entry to construction jobs and apprenticeships. Health and safety issues may mean that there are certain jobs you cannot do until you are over 16. Contact your local ConstructionSkills office for advice.

Entry and Training
There is a clear training and qualification route to becoming a professional plumber. Many aged 16 to 19 begin as apprentices and work towards qualification as a skilled operative and progress with further experience and qualifications. Membership of a professional body can help further your career. Training is an

important and continuous part of a plumbing career, as the rate of technological advancement is rapid. The ConstructionSkills scheme offers a three-year construction apprenticeship scheme (four years in Scotland). You can apply for apprenticeship schemes when in Year 11 (January).

Other schemes include work-based training at an approved centre and full-time work training with an employer, usually supported by day or block release to a local college. There are also relevant one or two-year full-time college courses that you can take before applying for a job and working towards S/NVQs. The British Plumbing Employers Council is one of the professional training organisations for the industry and offers a range of learning support modules that provide help with gaining S/NVQs.

The Chartered Institute of Plumbing and Heating Engineering, SummitSkills Ltd and other organisations (see addresses) also offer advice on training and qualifications within the industry. Plumbers need to apply for a Construction Skills Certificate Scheme (CSCS) registration card of the Joint Industry Board (JIB). The JIB for Plumbing, Mechanical Engineering Services (JIB-PMES) scheme is the standard measure of skills, knowledge and competency for the UK plumbing industry. A JIB-PMES card can only be obtained with relevant work-based qualifications, plus evidence of experience in the industry.

A Diploma/Welsh Baccalaureate in construction and the built environment may be available in your area. S/NVQs in plumbing are available at levels 2-3. The industry recommends all plumbers reach a minimum of level 3. The S/NVQ level 3 also includes assessment on water regulations, unvented hot water systems and ACS gas safety. Relevant technical certificates and construction awards in plumbing are also available.

Mature applicants can take refresher courses that are sometimes available for those returning to work and there may be special government training schemes or apprenticeships for adults in some areas. Contact your local careers office, Jobcentre Plus, Next Step service or Learning and Skills Council (LSC)/Local Enterprise Company (LEC) for details of training schemes. The Chartered Institute of Plumbing and Heating Engineering (CIPHE) offers a Master Plumber Certificate Scheme for those with at least ten years' plumbing experience, including training. Contact the CIPHE for information on the minimum requirements and conditions, which include membership of the CIPHE, registered plumber (RP) status, or registration as an engineering technician (Eng Tech).

City & Guilds senior awards are also available for those who have achieved a relevant S/NVQ at level 3 (or similar) and have a minimum of five years' professional experience.

Opportunities and Pay

There are approximately 28,000 plumbers in the UK working mainly for a plumbing contractor or maintenance firm, though many are self-employed, particularly in the domestic sector. Employers include firms of heating engineers, plumbing or building contractors, gas companies or the chemical industry. Most employers have a Joint Industry Board grading system through which a plumber progresses as they gain more qualifications and experience. Some work towards technician or supervisory roles, or specialise in a specific area of expertise. Temporary, casual and seasonal work is often available for those who are sub-contractors or are self-employed. Opportunities may exist for work abroad.

Pay varies depending on area and employer. Apprentices in the first year of training start on around £5k-£7k a year. Qualified plumbers earn around £17k-£21k a year, rising to around £22k-£30k with experience. Those with supervisory experience can earn around £35k a year, and some may earn more. Employers may operate bonus schemes and overtime is common.

Health

You need a good level of general fitness and stamina. You should not be allergic to dust.

Skills and Qualities

able to follow drawings and plans, able to work both on your own and in a team, aptitude for maths and science, good interpersonal skills, good organisational skills, manual dexterity, practical skills, safety conscious

Relevant Subjects

Construction and built environment, Design and technology

Further Information

Apprenticeship Schemes (National Apprenticeship Service) - www.apprenticeships.org.uk

Apprenticeships in Scotland (Careers Info Scotland) - www.apprenticeshipsinscotland.com/about/

Careers Fact Sheets (SummitSkills) (SummitSkills) - www.summitskills.org.uk/

ConstructionSkills - sector skills council for the construction industry - www.cskills.org

Diplomas (Foundation, Higher and Advanced) - http://yp.direct.gov.uk/diplomas

Plumbing - A Career with a Future (IPHE) (Chartered Institute of Plumbers and Heating Engineers (CIPHE)) - www.ciphe.org.uk

Real Life Guide to Plumbing (Trotman 2010) - www.trotman.co.uk

Summitskills - sector skills council for building services engineering - www.summitskills.org.uk

Welsh Baccalaureate - www.wbq.org.uk

▶Working in construction & the built environment (2007) (Babcock Lifeskills) - www.babcock-lifeskills.com/

Addresses

Association of Plumbing and Heating Contractors
12 The Pavilions, Cranmore Drive, Solihull B90 4SB
Phone: +44 (0)121 711 5030
Web: www.competentpersonsscheme.co.uk

British Plumbing Employers Council Training (BPEC)
2 Mallard Way , Pride Park, Derby DE24 8GX
Phone: 0845 644 6558 (UK only)
Web: www.bpec.org.uk

Chartered Institute of Plumbing and Heating Engineering (CIPHE)
64 Station Lane, Hornchurch, Essex RM12 6NB
Phone: +44 (0)1708 472 791
Web: www.iphe.org.uk

Joint Industry Board for Plumbing Mechanical Engineering Services in England and Wales
JIB-PMES, PO Box 267, PE19 9DN
Phone: +44 (0)1480 476925
Web: www.jib-pmes.org.uk

Scottish and Northern Ireland Plumbers Employers Federation
2 Walker Street, Edinburgh EH3 7LB
Phone: +44 (0)131 225 2255
Web: www.snipef.org

Similar Jobs

Domestic Appliance Service Technician, Electrician, Engineer: Building Services, Gas Service Engineer, Heating & Ventilation Fitter/Welder, Refrigeration/Air Conditioning Technician

Podiatrist/Chiropodist

CRCI:Healthcare
CLCI:JAT — Job Band: 5

Job Description

Podiatrists/chiropodists deal with the assessment, diagnosis and treatment of the lower limb and foot. They treat patients who may be elderly, those with foot injuries or having laser treatment or nail surgery, and people with diabetes. Work with people of all ages, but play an important role in helping those who are older to stay mobile and maintain their independence. Also diagnose and treat diseases, injuries or abnormalities of the foot such as corns, skin infections or structural problems. Advise patients about keeping their feet in a healthy condition.

May recommend foot exercises, or treat the condition with drugs, chemicals, ultrasound, hydrotherapy, massage, etc. They use a scalpel to cut away hardened skin and corns, or an electric drill to treat some nail conditions. Refer major problems to medically qualified specialists. Apply dressings and sometimes perform minor surgery or fit appliances, such as orthotic insoles to realign the foot. Also advise patients on footwear. Some senior podiatrists may set fractures and perform surgery too. They work closely with other health professionals including doctors, health visitors, district nurses and diabetic and orthopaedic specialists. Health promotion is an important aspect of the work.

Work Details

You work in a clinic, hospital, health centre, residential home, school, or in a patient's home. Travel may be necessary to visit your patients. If you are employed by the NHS, your working week is usually 37.5 hours over five days. Some chiropodists are expected to work Saturdays and possibly evenings, particularly in the private sector. Your workplace can also be your own home and you are able to choose the hours you wish to work. This may include evening appointments for those who are unable to visit during the day.

You advise and help people of all ages who are sometimes upset and in pain. Occasionally you may have to deal with feet that are dirty or neglected.

Qualification

- **England, Wales and Northern Ireland**

Band 5: For degree courses: 2-3 A levels and some GCSEs (A*-C) usually including English and maths and preferably two science subjects, or equivalent. Exact requirements depend on the degree you take.

- **Scotland**

Band 5: For degree courses: 3-5 H grades and some S grades (1-3), usually including English and maths and preferably two science subjects, or similar qualifications. Exact requirements depend on the degree you take.

Degree Information

A degree in podiatry or podiatric medicine is required for entry to this job.

Adult Qualifications

Entry requirements for degree courses may be relaxed for those with relevant experience. There is an Access to science course that provides a route into higher education for applicants without the required academic qualifications.

Work Experience

Work experience gives you an insight into what you enjoy about a job or working environment, and the opportunity to acquire new skills. It provides valuable information to add to your CV and improves your employment prospects. The Society of Chiropodists and Podiatrists states that universities look for clues that you have a real understanding of podiatry. Most course tutors are also keen to see evidence of work shadowing a podiatrist. This can be with NHS or private state-registered practitioners, and organising a visit is fairly easy. They also look for evidence of activities requiring good interpersonal skills.

Entry and Training

If working for the NHS, you must be state registered with a degree in podiatry approved by the Health Professions Council, and a member of the Society of Chiropodists and Podiatrists (SCP). Degree courses combine theoretical study in biological studies, pathology, dermatology, therapeutic sciences, anatomy and pharmacology, with practical clinical training. Podiatry students have to undertake 1,000 clinical hours before they can graduate. This degree is offered at 13 schools of podiatry and each year the number of places is limited. The NHS funds places on an approved course and students can apply for a bursary. New entrants must also pass a Criminal Records Bureau (CRB)/Disclosure Scotland check.

You may be able to gain examination exemptions for part of the chiropody course if you already hold a degree in a subject such as physiology, biology, nursing, physiotherapy or zoology. Postgraduate study and training is possible and you can specialise in working with children or podiatric surgery. A fellowship in podiatric surgery enables you to operate on bone and joint problems. Contact the SCP for information on recognised courses. Continuing professional development is important throughout your career.

A Diploma/Welsh Baccalaureate may be available in your area in society, health and development. The advanced level is equivalent to 3.5 A levels but for some university courses, the additional and specialist learning (ASL) component of the diploma needs to include specific A levels. Check entry requirements carefully with the individual institutions.

Mature students are encouraged to apply and make up a large proportion of the intake at most schools. Entry requirements vary but you are usually required to have undertaken recent academic study and to have a formal qualification focused around biology, usually to A level or equivalent. There are a number of NHS-funded places on relevant university courses and you may also be eligible for a bursary or student loan. The Society of Chiropodists and Podiatrists offers a distance-learning course.

Opportunities and Pay

Around 10,000 podiatrists are registered in the UK and there are opportunities to work in GP practices, health centres and hospitals throughout the country. Most are employed by the NHS when they first qualify providing assessment, evaluation and foot care for a wide range of patients. but may move into private work with experience and have their own practice. You can specialise in particular areas such as biomechanics, podiatric surgery, forensic podiatry or working with children. Many combine private work with doing some sessions with the NHS. There is a formal promotion structure in the NHS, but few senior posts are available. Employment prospects are good and there are also opportunities to work with some large firms, the armed forces, or overseas. Some podiatrists/chiropodists move into surgery, teaching, research or a combination of both. Flexible and part-time work are possible.

Pay is on a nationally agreed scale in the NHS and tends to be considerably more in the private sector. A community podiatrist working for the NHS can earn around £21k-£28k, rising to around £34k-£40k a year with experience. Advanced podiatrists with specialist knowledge such as a diabetic clinical podiatrist can earn around £30k-£43k a year and consultants up to £73k. In private practice podiatrists/chiropodists can earn around £40-£50 a session.

Health

This job requires good eyesight.

Skills and Qualities

able to get on with all kinds of people, able to put people at ease, good communication skills, good interpersonal skills, not squeamish, patient, scientific approach, steady hand, sympathetic, tactful

Relevant Subjects

Biology, Chemistry, English, Health and social care, Science

Further Information

AGCAS: Health (Job Sector Briefing) (AGCAS) - www.prospects.ac.uk

Alliance of Private Sector Practitioners - www.thealliancepsp.com
Careers in Chiropody/Podiatry (SCP)
(Society of Chiropodists and Podiatrists) - www.feetforlife.org/podiatrychiropodycareers/index.html
Diplomas (Foundation, Higher and Advanced)- http://yp.direct.gov.uk/diplomas
Health Professions Council (HPC) - www.hpc-uk.org
NHS Careers (NHS Careers) - www.nhscareers.nhs.uk
NHS Careers Scotland - www.infoscotland.com/nhs
NHS Careers Wales - www.wales.nhs.uk
Podiatry Now (Society of Chiropodists and Podiatrists) - www.feetforlife.org/
Welsh Baccalaureate - www.wbq.org.uk

Addresses

Institute of Chiropodists and Podiatrists
27 Wright Street, Southport, Merseyside PR9 0TL
Phone: +44 (0)1704 546 141
Web: www.iocp.org.uk

Society of Chiropodists and Podiatrists (SCP)
1 Fellmonger's Path, Tower Bridge Road, London SE1 3LY
Phone: +44 (0)20 7234 8620
Web: www.feetforlife.org

Similar Jobs

Nurse: Adult, Occupational Therapist, Physiotherapist, Prosthetist/Orthotist, Reflexologist

Podiatry/Chiropody Assistant

also known as: Clinical Support Worker: Podiatry Assistant, Footcare Assistant

CRCI:Healthcare
CLCI:JAT Job Band: 1 to 2

Job Description

Podiatry/chiropody assistants perform a range of tasks to help podiatrists/chiropodists in their treatment of a patient's lower limb or foot. Helps to treat patients who may be elderly, have foot injuries, diabetes, or who are having laser treatment or nail surgery. Once the patient has been assessed by the podiatrist/chiropodist, an assistant may prepare and apply a dressing, cut toe nails, and also write up the patient's notes. They look after and order any necessary equipment. Some assistants assess patients before referring them to the podiatrist/chiropodist.

With experience, assistants may help a podiatrist in the operating theatre, by setting up for an operation and preparing and sterilising instruments.

Work Details

Working hours are usually 36.5 hrs a week; Monday to Friday. You are likely to be based in a hospital or clinic, in the public or private sector. There may be opportunities to work part time. Some jobs require you to be mobile and visit various clinics within a local area. There is daily contact with patients of all ages and abilities, particularly children and elderly people who may be in pain or upset. All staff are responsible for adopting and maintaining safe and hygienic working practices.

Work can involve coping with unpleasant sights at times. Occasionally, you may have to deal with feet that are dirty and neglected, so you need to have a mature approach and be tactful.

Qualification

- **England, Wales and Northern Ireland**

Band 1: For entry to jobs, no minimum qualifications are needed, but you are expected to have a good level of general education and relevant experience. Some formal/vocational qualifications at any level are useful.

Band 2: For entry to jobs, no minimum qualifications are needed, but it is an advantage to have some GCSEs (A*-C) or equivalent in subjects that include English and maths. A science subject such as biology is useful.

- **Scotland**

Band 1: For entry to jobs, no minimum qualifications are needed, but you are expected to have a good level of general education and relevant experience. Some formal/vocational qualifications at any level are useful.

Band 2: Although academic qualifications are not specified for this job, it is an advantage to have some S grades (1-3) in subjects that include English and maths, or similar. A science subject such as biology is useful.

Adult Qualifications

No qualifications are required for some posts, but experience in care work, such as in a hospital or in residential care, is an advantage.

Work Experience

Employers may prefer candidates who have work or voluntary experience in a medical or healthcare setting such as a hospital or residential care home. Work experience can equip you with skills that you can use in the future and add to your CV.

Entry and Training

Training begins once you are employed and involves a combination of formal instruction and work shadowing. You need to complete a minimum of 500 clinical hours plus practical, theoretical and oral assessments. Trainees study a variety of topics including skin and nail pathology, microbiology, inflammation, anatomy, circulation, podiatric conditions and nail operations. Entry to the NHS is through the normal healthcare assistant route.

There is no central recruitment or training programme and most vacancies are advertised locally by Hospital Trusts, or by private, independent podiatrists/chiropodists. The Society of Chiropodists and Podiatrists runs relevant courses. You can also take a diploma in foot health practice and join the voluntary register of foot health practitioners.

It is not possible to progress directly to qualification as a podiatrist/chiropodist. Please look at the podiatrist/chiropodist job details for entry and training information. However, some employers may support you to take a part-time degree course whilst you continue to work, though you need to have higher qualifications to enter the course.

A Diploma/Welsh Baccalaureate may be available in your area in society, health and development and can provide a useful introduction to this career. See the diplomas website for further information.

Mature applicants are welcomed and may be able to benefit through training opportunities such as Work Based Learning/Training for Work that may be available in your area. You can gain recognition of previous experience through Accreditation of Prior Learning (APL) or by working towards relevant S/NVQs in health or health care.

Opportunities and Pay

You may work for the NHS, in private practice, or possibly the armed forces. Some podiatry assistants are also employed in the retail footwear industry. You can work as a self-employed foot health practitioner delivering routine footcare to the public.

Starting salaries for a podiatry/chiropody assistant working for the NHS are around £15k-£18k a year. With experience and qualifications, this may rise to around £21k a year.

Health

This job requires good eyesight.

Skills and Qualities
able to inspire confidence, careful, friendly, good organisational skills, not squeamish, patient, scientific approach, strong hands, sympathetic, tactful

Relevant Subjects
Biology, Health and social care, Science

Further Information
Alliance of Private Sector Practitioners - www.thealliancepsp.com
Diplomas (Foundation, Higher and Advanced) - http://yp.direct.gov.uk/diplomas
NHS Careers (NHS Careers) - www.nhscareers.nhs.uk
NHS Careers Scotland - www.infoscotland.com/nhs
NHS Careers Wales - www.wales.nhs.uk
Podiatry Now (Society of Chiropodists and Podiatrists) - www.feetforlife.org/
Training Schemes - www.direct.gov.uk/en/educationandlearning
Welsh Baccalaureate - www.wbq.org.uk
Working as a Podiatry Assistant (SCP) www.feetforlife.org/careers/assistant.html

Addresses
Institute of Chiropodists and Podiatrists
27 Wright Street, Southport, Merseyside PR9 0TL
Phone: +44 (0)1704 546 141
Web: www.iocp.org.uk

Society of Chiropodists and Podiatrists (SCP)
1 Fellmonger's Path, Tower Bridge Road, London SE1 3LY
Phone: +44 (0)20 7234 8620
Web: www.feetforlife.org

Similar Jobs
Occupational Therapy Assistant, Physiotherapy Assistant, Podiatrist/Chiropodist, Radiography Assistant, Reflexologist

Police Community Support Officer (England & Wales)

CRCI:Security and Armed Forces
CLCI:MAB Job Band: 1 to 2

Job Description
Police community support officers (PCSOs) work alongside police officers in a supporting role. This provides a visible and accessible presence in a local community. Work in a small team or in pairs under the direction of a police supervisory officer. Patrol an area to help deter criminal activity. Reassure all members of that community. Report back any concerns of the community or an individual, so that action can be taken to assist the community. Daily tasks vary according to the area and the officer in charge, but PCSOs usually deal with minor incidents that do not require full police powers. Have the authority to issue fixed penalty notices for offences such as dropping litter or for riding on the footpath. At times are given the authority to direct traffic.

Give support at ceremonial and special events. Help police officers during public demonstrations or at major sporting events, such as controlling football crowds. Respond to major incidents and security alerts. Play an important part in tackling antisocial behaviour, graffiti and environmental issues. Aim to make a community a happier and more comfortable place in which to live.

Work Details
Usually work a 37-40 hr week, in a shift system, usually between the hours of 8am and midnight, including weekends and bank holidays. Some forces have shifts covering 24 hours a day, every day. There are opportunities to work part time and flexible working may also be available. You are based at a police station, but most time is spent on foot patrol in all weathers. A uniform, similar to that worn by police officers, distinctive headwear and a communication radio are provided.

Qualification
Applicants can enter with a wide range of qualifications and/or experience.

- **England, Wales and Northern Ireland**

Band 1: There are no minimum academic qualifications required for this job but a good standard of literacy is needed for writing up reports.

Band 2: For some forces: some GCSEs (A*-C) including maths and English or a qualification in public services are useful.

Adult Qualifications
There are no formal educational requirements for recruitment and applications from adults are especially welcome.

Work Experience
Relevant work or voluntary experience is always useful. It can improve your chances when applying for this career. Any experience that provides an opportunity to work with people is useful. Direct experience may be difficult to arrange, but anything that shows you are community spirited and a team player is useful. Some professional experience with a security firm may be helpful.

Entry and Training
Entry requirements depend on the individual police force though there are no minimum qualifications required. Selection is usually by application form, an assessment and an interview. There are also medical and fitness requirements and a security check on your background. Applicants who have studied a course in public service, such as an NVQ level 2, a BTEC qualification or a foundation degree in public services, may have an advantage. The diploma/welsh baccalaureate in public services may be a useful background for this career but check entry requirements carefully.

Training for PCSOs is organised by individual police forces. It is less intensive than that of police officers and special constables. The Wider Policing Learning Development Programme (WPLDP) delivers training to a consistent standard across the UK and arranges training packages to be delivered at further education institutes, supports training for PCSO supervisors and develops tools and skills for tackling anti-social behaviour.

Length of training varies but can last from three weeks to four months, depending on the employing police force. Training includes classroom study on issues such as incident management, relevant areas of the law and using the police computer. It also covers radio procedures, first aid and personal safety. Training after this is on the beat, for specific tasks and under supervision of police officers. You continue to develop your skills and train whilst employed.

Mature entry is welcome in this profession as long as you can pass the health and fitness tests. Some employers may look for those applicants with experience of community service, either paid or voluntary.

Opportunities and Pay
Community support officers are employed by the individual 43 police forces in England and Wales and the British Transport Police, and, though numbers are growing in this new profession, entry may be competitive. You can move into the supervision and management of PCSOs, use skills to tutor new recruits, or progress to full police officer status if you pass the entry requirements.

Pay varies according to the police force and area. Starting salaries for PCSOs are around £16k a year. With experience, this rises to £19k-£21k a year. There are additional allowances for working shifts and overtime pay.

Health
Applicants are often required to pass a medical and fitness test.

Skills and Qualities
able to cope under pressure, approachable, aptitude for teamwork, calm, confident, decisive, good communication skills, non-judgemental, observant

Relevant Subjects
Law, Psychology

Further Information
Diplomas (Foundation, Higher and Advanced) - http://yp.direct.gov.uk/diplomas

Foundation Learning (QCDA) - www.qcda.gov.uk

How to Pass the Police Selection System (2010) (Kogan Page) - www.koganpage.com

National PCSO's Website - www.national-pcsos.co.uk

Passing the Police and PCSO Recruit Assessment Process (Law Matters) (Law Matters) - www.learningmatters.co.uk/index.asp

Real Life Guide to the Police Service (Trotman 2009) - www.trotman.co.uk

Skills for Justice - sector skills council for the UK justice system - www.skillsforjustice.com

Welsh Baccalaureate - www.wbq.org.uk

▶Working in police, fire & security (2009) (Babcock Lifeskills) - www.babcock-lifeskills.com/

Addresses
British Transport Police
HR Business Centre Recruitment Department 7th Floor,
The Axis,10 Holiday Street, Birmingham B1 1TF
Phone: +44 (0) 121 634 5630
Web: www.btp.police.uk

Similar Jobs
Anti-Social Behaviour Officer, Community Development Worker, Ministry of Defence Police Constable, Police Front Office Staff, Police Officer, Social Worker

Police Family Liaison Officer

CRCI:Security and Armed Forces
CLCI:MAB — Job Band: 2 to 5

Job Description
Police family liaison officers act as a link between families affected by a serious incident and the investigating police officers. Maintain regular contact with a caseload of families. Are part of the investigating team when someone has been murdered or has died in suspicious circumstances. May act as a police adviser on issues such as the family appearing at a press conference. Also coordinate a multi-agency approach to the investigation, including victim support, social services and whether counselling or child care is required. Source the appropriate advice should there be issues relating to the culture or religion of a family or victim.

Work Details
Usually work a basic 40 hr week that may include eight-hour shifts, weekends, evenings and public holidays. There is often overtime, sometimes involving staying with a distressed family overnight, for which you are given additional pay or time off. Your time is divided between office work at your station and time visiting families. You meet people of all ages and deal with many who are upset and grieving. Many family liaison officers work part time in this role and the rest of the time on general police duties.

Qualification
You must first train as a police officer. All applicants to the police service undergo a recruitment test that includes numeracy, literacy, and core skills such as communication, problem solving and decision making. Some entrants have no formal educational requirements, while others may have GCSEs, A levels or higher education qualifications.

Degree Information
A degree in any discipline is acceptable for entry, though there are many specific degrees in subjects that include criminal justice, criminology and policing studies.

Adult Qualifications
There are no formal educational requirements for recruitment to the police service and applications from adults are welcomed. Entry requirements may be relaxed for adults applying for higher education courses and Access or foundation courses give adults without qualifications a route on to degree courses.

Work Experience
Relevant work or voluntary experience is always useful and can improve your chances in application for entry to this career. Any experience that provides an opportunity to work with people/the public is useful. Experience as a volunteer special constable provides useful background.

Entry and Training
You must first train as a police officer (see Police Officer job article) before applying to become a family liaison officer (FLO). The diploma/welsh baccalaureate in public services may be a useful background for this career but check entry requirements carefully.

Family liaison officers come from all branches of a police force and usually have to complete an intensive training course of approximately seven days, followed by related in-service training. The course modules include understanding the factors affecting a grieving family and those factors affecting crime victims themselves, developing an awareness of the needs of ethnic minority families, and understanding the role of support agencies. You need to update your knowledge throughout your work as a FLO.

You must first train as a police officer. Mature applicants should bear in mind that the normal retirement age of police constables/sergeants is 60 and that all new recruits must undertake a two-year probationary period. Check with individual police forces. Maturity is seen as an asset and many join after a period in the armed forces or merchant navy. A special resettlement course is offered by the army for those who wish to pursue a police career after army service.

Experience as a volunteer special constable provides useful background, though this is not a formal route to recruitment as a police officer. However, you can also gain valuable experience as a police community support officer (see job article) and take the entrance test to become a police officer.

Opportunities and Pay
There is a rising interest in this role and its status has improved within the police force. This has resulted in increased competition for posts within some forces. To be promoted to sergeant, inspector and beyond, you must pass the relevant promotion exams.

Family liaison officers are on normal police pay scales and conditions of employment. Pay increases with promotion. As a student police officer or constable, you earn around £23k, rising to £27k on completion of the training period. Constables earn up to £36K depending on experience. Sergeants earn around £36k-£41k a year. Senior police officers such as chief constables can earn more than £100k a year. You are supplied with a uniform or possibly a clothes allowance. Accommodation may be provided or an accommodation allowance paid. There are extra allowances for working in London.

Health
You have to pass a medical test and a very strenuous fitness test. There are certain eyesight standards, though many forces allow the wearing of glasses or lenses. You usually have to have normal colour vision. There are no minimum height requirements, but your height must be in proportion to your weight.

Skills and Qualities
able to cope with emergencies, able to inspire confidence, able to understand other people's problems, good communication skills, good interpersonal skills, good listening skills, observant, perceptive, resilient, tactful

Relevant Subjects
English, Law, Psychology, Sociology

Further Information
Could you? Police (Home Office) - www.policecouldyou.co.uk/

Diplomas (Foundation, Higher and Advanced) - http://yp.direct.gov.uk/diplomas

How to Pass the Police Recruitment Tests (How To books)

How to Pass the Police Selection System (2010) (Kogan Page) - www.koganpage.com

National Policing Improvement Agency (NPIA) - www.npia.police.uk

Passing the Police and PCSO Recruit Assessment Process (Law Matters) - www.learningmatters.co.uk/index.asp

Police Information - www.police-information.co.uk

Police Recruitment (Scotland) - www.scottish.police.uk

Skills for Justice - sector skills council for the UK justice system - www.skillsforjustice.com

TARGETjobs: Public Service (GTI Specialist Publishing Ltd.) - www.groupgti.com

Welsh Baccalaureate - www.wbq.org.uk

▶Working in police, fire & security (2009) (Babcock Lifeskills) - www.babcock-lifeskills.com/

Addresses
Police Service of Northern Ireland
Police Headquarters, Brooklyn, 65 Knock Road, Belfast BT5 6LE
Web: www.psni.police.uk

Similar Jobs
Counsellor, Police Community Support Officer (England & Wales), Police Officer, Police Scenes of Crime Officer, Prison Officer, Social Worker

Police Financial Investigator

CRCI:Security and Armed Forces
CLCI:MAB Job Band: 2 to 5

Job Description
Police financial investigators use accountancy and financial skills to investigate financial offences to ensure that criminals do not get away with financial crimes. Identify assets that may have been obtained as a result of a crime and prepare paperwork to document how the crime has been committed. Analyse and profile defendants to provide information to help on-going criminal investigations. Obtain information from financial institutions such as banks to assist with investigations. Help fight against money laundering and improve detective rates for financial crimes, such as fraud. Use specialist computer databases and software to help with their work.

May have to interview suspected criminals and search the homes of offenders for detailed financial information. May also have to give evidence in court.

Work Details
Usually work 35-40 hrs a week, although this may include evenings and weekends if you need to deal with cash seizures or interviews. Work is mainly office based in a police station, dealing with a large amount of paperwork and doing research, often on a computer. May have to travel to suspects' homes or to courts to give evidence and obtain permission to access financial information about a suspect. Liaises regularly with other police colleagues while working on an investigation.

Police officers doing this work may wear police uniforms, but civilians do not.

Qualification
Entrants to this work may be police officers or civilians. Some entrants to the police have no formal educational qualifications, while others may have GCSEs, A levels or higher education qualifications. Civilians usually have a higher education or relevant professional qualification.

Degree Information
A degree in any discipline is acceptable for entry to the police, but for this work a degree that includes computing, accounting, law or criminology is particularly relevant.

Adult Qualifications
There are no formal educational requirements for recruitment to the police service and applications from adults are welcomed. Entry requirements may be relaxed for adults applying for higher education courses and Access or foundation courses give adults without qualifications a route on to degree courses.

Work Experience
Relevant work or voluntary experience is always useful and can improve your chances in application for entry to this career. Any experience in research or investigation is useful, particularly if this is combined with experience of working with computer databases and the Internet. Working in an accounts office and dealing with the public, particularly if this involves interviewing, also provides useful background.

Entry and Training
Most financial investigators come into this work after training as police officers. The diploma/welsh baccalaureate in public services may be a useful background for this career but check entry requirements carefully. Police basic training takes two years, and after this police officers can choose to go into an area of specialisation. For full details of police training see the Police Officer job article. Civilians are increasingly being used. Experience of research and investigation is important, and professional qualifications in accounting, law or similar provide useful background.

Training for this role is the job of National Policing Improvement Agency (NPIA) and they have set up a structured training programme for accreditation. The NPIA is recognised under the Proceeds of Crime Act. Training starts with pre-course online study leading to an access exam. Successful completion of the exam leads on the modular skills based courses which take around 13-15 weeks to complete, and lead to temporary accreditation. After the courses you have to complete a personal development portfolio within 12 months to achieve full accreditation. In order to maintain accreditation, you must enter into a programme of continuing professional development.

Accreditation leads to a BTEC professional development certificate in financial investigation. To achieve the diploma course you need to take additional courses in confiscation and either money laundering or enhanced financial investigation. The University of Teesside offers an MA in financial investigation and financial crime for those who want to build on their professional knowledge.

Mature entrants are welcomed as more civilians are coming into this work. Those with a background in research or investigating are particularly useful. Qualifications in accounting are not essential, but experience in finance and accounts is an asset.

Opportunities and Pay

There are over 3,000 financial investigators working in the UK, and this number is growing. Work is available mainly with police forces throughout the country. The Serious Fraud Office, Serious Organised Crime Agency, HM Revenue and Customs and other Government departments also employ financial investigators.

With experience you may be able to develop a specialist role in particular areas of this work, for example money laundering. Financial investigators who are also serving police officers may move on to more senior roles in the police service.

Starting salaries are around £23k-£24k a year. Senior investigators can expect to earn around £32k a year.

Health

Police officers have to pass a medical test and a very strenuous fitness test. It is necessary to have normal colour vision and good eyesight, though many forces allow the wearing of glasses or lenses. There are no minimum height requirements, but your height must be in proportion to your weight. Civilian entrants need to be in good health but are not likely to go through the same stringent medical.

Skills and Qualities

able to work both on your own and in a team, analytical skills, attention to detail, decisive, good interviewing skills, integrity, problem-solving skills, research skills, resourceful, sense of humour.

Relevant Subjects

Business and accounting, Economics, English, ICT/Computer studies, Law, Mathematics, Psychology

Further Information

Could you? Police (Home Office) - www.policecouldyou.co.uk/

Diplomas (Foundation, Higher and Advanced) - http://yp.direct.gov.uk/diplomas

HM Revenue & Customs (HMRC) (HM Revenue & Customs) - www.hmrc.gov.uk

How to Pass the Police Recruitment Tests (How to Books)

National Policing Improvement Agency (NPIA) - www.npia.police.uk

Police Recruitment (Scotland) - www.scottish.police.uk

Serious Fraud Office - www.sfo.gov.uk

Serious Organised Crime Agency (SOCA) - www.soca.gov.uk

Skills for Justice - sector skills council for the UK justice system - www.skillsforjustice.com

Welsh Baccalaureate - www.wbq.org.uk

▶Working in police, fire & security (2009) (Babcock Lifeskills) - www.babcock-lifeskills.com/

Addresses

Police Service of Northern Ireland
Police Headquarters, Brooklyn, 65 Knock Road, Belfast BT5 6LE
Web: www.psni.police.uk

Similar Jobs

Accountant: Industry & Commerce, Accountant: Private Practice, Accountant: Public Sector, Police Officer, Police Scenes of Crime Officer, Private Investigator

Police Front Office Staff

also known as: Enquiry Desk Operator: Police

CRCI:Security and Armed Forces
CLCI:MAB Job Band: 2 to 4

Job Description

Police front office staff deal with enquiries and give advice to people calling in at the police station. They either sort out the problem or quickly pass the details on to others who can. Make sure no one goes into the main building without their knowledge. Undertake office tasks such as filing and updating records. May provide emergency first aid.

Front office staff handle payments and paperwork for fines, licences and permits. They accept and keep records of items that are being handed in, such as lost property and weapons. Take down the details of crimes, missing persons and vehicle accidents. Compile reports and add information to files and computer databases. Make sure victims of crime and witnesses are looked after. May take routine statements and answer questions in court.

Work Details

Usually work a 37 hr week including weekends and bank holidays. Often work shifts to provide cover until midnight or later. Part-time work may be available. Work at a desk or counter in a police station. The work can be stressful. Deal with members of the public who may be angry, frightened or upset. Some may be aggressive. Liaise with professionals such as police officers, solicitors, victim support staff and social workers. A uniform is provided.

Qualification

Qualifications in IT or public services may be useful. A first aid qualification may be an advantage.

• England, Wales and Northern Ireland

Band 2: Although academic qualifications are not specified for this job, you need reading and writing skills. It is an advantage to have some GCSEs (A*-C) in subjects that include English and maths, or a BTEC first award in public services, or equivalent.

Band 3: For direct entry or entry to a BTEC national award in uniformed public services: at least 4 GCSEs (A*-C) including English and maths, or equivalent.

Band 4: For some jobs: 1-2 A levels, BTEC national award in uniformed public services or equivalent plus some GCSEs (A*-C) including English and maths, or equivalent.

• Scotland

Band 2: Although academic qualifications are not specified for this job, you need reading and writing skills. It is an advantage to have some S grades (1-3) in subjects that include English and maths, or similar.

Band 3: For entry: usually four S grades (1-3) including English and maths, or SVQ level 2 in public services, or similar.

Band 4: For some jobs: three H grades plus some S grades (1-3) including English and maths, or similar.

Adult Qualifications

Employers look for people with the knowledge and skills that come from a good level of secondary education.

Work Experience

Experience of working with the public or people who are upset or stressed is useful. Being able to show that you have used clerical and data inputting skills can be an advantage. Paid or voluntary work experience in a community or customer service setting is also valued. You may be able to get experience of this type of work in a volunteer police support staff role. Contact your local police force to see if there is a scheme in your area.

Entry and Training

Employers look for people with reasonable IT and keyboard skills. In some areas, being able to speak a second language is an advantage. You have to pass a Criminal Records Bureau (CRB)/ Disclosure Scotland and background check, plus a medical.

Training is mostly on the job with experienced staff. You may also do some training courses in-house or at a police training centre. As well as learning about police procedures, using ICT systems and treating everyone fairly, you also learn first aid, self-defence and how to handle difficult situations. HNC/HND and foundation degree courses in public services may be available in your area. A Diploma/Welsh Baccalaureate in public services may be available in your area.

Mature applicants are welcome. A background in a public, customer or uniformed service setting is an advantage.

Opportunities and Pay

There are 52 police forces in the UK and most of them employ front counter staff. In the Metropolitan police, this job is done by station police community service officers. It may be hard to progress in this role, as there are not many supervisory posts. You can move into other support roles, such as administration or answering 999 or 112 calls. There are also helpdesk or non-emergency call handling jobs. Some front counter staff decide to train as police officers.

New entrants earn around £14k-£17k a year. Experienced staff earn around £17k-£20k.

Skills and Qualities

able to cope under pressure, able to get on with all kinds of people, aptitude for teamwork, assertive, awareness of confidentiality issues, excellent communication skills, good listening skills, information handling skills, keyboard/typing skills, non-judgemental

Relevant Subjects

Business and accounting, English, ICT/Computer studies, Law, Psychology

Further Information

Could you? Police (Home Office) - www.policecouldyou.co.uk/

Diplomas (Foundation, Higher and Advanced) - http://yp.direct.gov.uk/diplomas

Police Oracle (Police Oracle) - www.policeoracle.com/

Scottish Police (Scottish Police) - www.scottish.police.uk/

Skills for Justice - sector skills council for the UK justice system - www.skillsforjustice.com

Welsh Baccalaureate - www.wbq.org.uk

►Working in police, fire & security (2009) (Babcock Lifeskills) - www.babcock-lifeskills.com/

Addresses

Police Service of Northern Ireland
Police Headquarters, Brooklyn, 65 Knock Road, Belfast BT5 6LE
Web: www.psni.police.uk

Similar Jobs

Court Usher, Emergency Services Control Room Operator, Police Community Support Officer (England & Wales), Police Officer, Receptionist

Police Officer

also known as: PC, WPC

CRCI:Security and Armed Forces

CLCI:MAB — Job Band: 2 to 5

Job Description

Police officers are responsible for maintaining law and order, and aim to detect and prevent crime. Help to protect people and their property. The work is extremely varied and depends upon the branch of the force you wish to work for. May patrol the streets on foot or by car, control traffic and crowds, deal with accidents, investigate crimes, arrest and interview suspects. May work at the police station in the communications room or at reception answering enquiries. They are assigned to incidents by control room staff, but also spend time forging links with communities. Write notes and reports, and may give evidence in court. Use a computer to store, research and record information.

Depending on the police force, officers can specialise in areas such as special operations (surveillance), child protection, dog handling or mounted police, fraud, drugs, nationality (immigration), criminal investigation department (CID), underwater search unit and river police, and traffic section.

Work Details

Usually work a basic 40 hr week that may include eight-hour shifts, weekends, evenings and public holidays. There is often overtime, for which you are given additional pay or have time off. You meet people of all ages and have to deal with people who are upset, aggressive or are suspected of breaking the law. You also have to cope with emergencies and the sight of blood, and cope with some distressing sights, such as victims of murder, suicide or traffic accidents. The job may require you to inform people of bad news such as the injury or death of a relative.

Based at a police station, you may have to do a lot of walking, driving or standing for many hours, and there is risk of assault. You need to wear a uniform, protective clothing and may be given special equipment.

Qualification

All applicants to the police service undergo a recruitment test that includes numeracy, literacy, and core skills such as communication, problem solving and decision making. Some entrants have no formal educational qualifications, while others may have GCSEs, A levels or higher education qualifications.

- **England, Wales and Northern Ireland**

Band 2: Although academic qualifications are not specified for this job, it is an advantage to have some GCSEs (A*-C) in subjects that include English and maths, or equivalent.

Band 3: For entry: usually at least 4 GCSEs (A*-C) including English and maths, or equivalent.

Band 4: For BTEC higher national award: 1-2 A levels and some GCSEs (A*-C) usually including English and maths, or equivalent.

Band 5: For degree courses: 2-3 A levels and some GCSEs (A*-C) usually including English and maths, or equivalent. Exact requirements depend on the degree you take.

- **Scotland**

Band 2: Although academic qualifications are not specified for this job, it is an advantage to have some S grades (1-3) in subjects that include English and maths, or similar.

Band 3: For entry: usually at least four S grades (1-3) including English and maths, or similar.

Band 4: For SQA higher national award: usually 2-3 H grades and some S grades (1-3), often including English and maths, or similar qualifications.

Band 5: For degree courses: 3-5 H grades and some S grades (1-3), usually including English and maths, or similar qualifications. Exact requirements depend on the degree you take.

Degree Information

A degree in any discipline is acceptable for entry, though there are many specific degrees in subjects that include criminal justice, criminology and policing studies.

Adult Qualifications

There are no formal educational requirements for recruitment to the police service and applications from adults are welcomed. Entry requirements may be relaxed for adults applying for higher education courses and Access or foundation courses give adults without qualifications a route on to degree courses.

Work Experience

Relevant work or voluntary experience is always useful and can improve your chances in application for entry to this career. Any experience that provides an opportunity to work with people/the public is useful. Experience as a volunteer special constable provides useful background.

Entry and Training

There are currently 52 police forces in England, Wales, Scotland and Northern Ireland. Nationality and residency requirements exist for this job and you must also be at least eighteen when you apply (18.5 yrs actual recruitment age) and be able or in the process of learning to drive. There are no minimum or maximum height restrictions. Your background is checked for security reasons, though a criminal record is not always a bar to employment. Applicants must, however, declare any previous convictions including juvenile offences. For those under 18, there are relevant college courses such as the BTEC first and national diplomas/Welsh baccalaureates in public services or a higher national diploma in criminology. Foundation degrees are also available in subjects that include public services, criminal justice and police studies.

All recruits must pass the Initial Recruitment Test, including a medical and physical fitness assessment. Once accepted, student police officers train through the national Initial Police Learning and Development Programme. Each individual police force is responsible for its local implementation and delivery, usually on a flexible basis. The programme lasts for two years and is in four phases. Phase one is the introductory phase and lasts between one and three weeks. Phase two is a two week course dealing with community engagement. Phase three is split into two sections: section A deals with procedures and guidelines and section B deals with supervised control. Each section lasts twelve weeks.

The final phase of this training deals with independent control. This covers critical incident training for one week, foot patrol for four weeks, a driving course for three weeks and protected independence for six weeks. By the end of the two year probationary period, trainees can have achieved an NVQ Level 3 and 4 in policing.

After basic training, it is possible to specialise, for example in working with dogs or in the CID. All applicants for police recruitment can choose to be selected for the High Potential Development Scheme (HPDS), which is a fast-track to senior positions in the police service. Graduate or postgraduate study forms part of this scheme. In Scotland, there is an Accelerated Career Path for graduate entrants.

Mature applicants should bear in mind that the normal retirement age of police constables/sergeants is 60 yrs and that all new recruits must undertake a two-year probationary period. Check with individual police forces as some have a cut off point of 55 yrs. Maturity is seen as an asset and many join after a period in the armed forces or merchant navy. A special resettlement course is offered by the army for those who wish to pursue a police career after army service.

Experience as a volunteer special constable provides useful background, though this is not a formal route to recruitment as a police officer. However, you can also gain valuable experience as a police community support officer (see job article) and take the entrance test to become a police officer.

Opportunities and Pay

To be promoted to sergeant or inspector and beyond, you must pass the relevant promotion exams. Officers who show exceptional potential may gain accelerated promotion, even if they have not come through the High Potential Development Scheme. Opportunities also exist in other separate police organisations such as the British Transport Police, MOD and Civil Nuclear Constabulary. Part-time work and job sharing are possible.

Pay increases with promotion. As a student police officer or constable, you earn around £23k, rising to £27k on completion of the training period. Constables can earn up to £36k depending on experience and sergeants earn around £36k-£41k. Inspectors can earn £46k-£50k a year and chief inspectors and superintendents earn £54k-£70k. Chief superintendents and chief constables can earn considerably more. You are supplied with a uniform or possibly a clothes allowance. Accommodation may be provided or an accommodation allowance paid. There are extra allowances for working in London.

Health

You have to pass a medical test and a very strenuous fitness test. You have to meet certain eyesight standards, though many forces allow the wearing of glasses or lenses. You usually have to have normal colour vision. There are no minimum height requirements, but your height must be in proportion to your weight.

Skills and Qualities

able to cope with emergencies, aptitude for teamwork, firm manner, good communication skills, honest, impartial, IT skills, observant, quick reactions, tactful

Relevant Subjects

English, Law, Psychology, Sociology

Further Information

AGCAS: Armed Forces & Emergency Services (Job Sector Briefing) (AGCAS) - www.prospects.ac.uk

Could you? Police (Home Office) - www.policecouldyou.co.uk/

Diplomas (Foundation, Higher and Advanced) - http://yp.direct.gov.uk/diplomas

How to Pass the Police Recruitment Tests (How to Books)

How to Pass the Police Selection System (2010) (Kogan Page) - www.koganpage.com

National Policing Improvement Agency (NPIA) - www.npia.police.uk

Passing the Police and PCSO Recruit Assessment Process (Law Matters) - www.learningmatters.co.uk/index.asp

Police Recruitment (Scotland) - www.scottish.police.uk

Real Life Guide to the Police Service (Trotman 2009) - www.trotman.co.uk

Skills for Justice - sector skills council for the UK justice system - www.skillsforjustice.com

TARGETjobs: Public Service (GTI Specialist Publishing Ltd.) - www.groupgti.com

Welsh Baccalaureate - www.wbq.org.uk

▶ Working in police, fire & security (2009) (Babcock Lifeskills) - www.babcock-lifeskills.com/

Addresses

British Transport Police
HR Business Centre Recruitment Department 7th Floor, The Axis10 Holiday Street, Birmingham B1 1TF
Phone: +44 (0) 121 634 5630
Web: www.btp.police.uk

Civil Nuclear Constabulary
Culham Science Centre, Abingdon, Oxfordshire OX14 3DB
Phone: +44 (0)1235 466 666
Web: www.cnc.police.uk

Ministry of Defence Police Recruitment Department
Building 66 MDP Wethersfield, Braintree, Essex CM7 4AZ
Web: www.mod.police.uk

Police Scenes of Crime Officer

Police Service of Northern Ireland
Police Headquarters, Brooklyn, 65 Knock Road, Belfast BT5 6LE
Web: www.psni.police.uk

Similar Jobs

Ministry of Defence Police Constable, Police Community Support Officer (England & Wales), Police Front Office Staff, Police Scenes of Crime Officer, Prison Officer, Private Investigator

Police Scenes of Crime Officer

also known as: CSI, Police Crime Scene Investigator/Examiner, SOCO

CRCI:Security and Armed Forces
CLCI:MAB

Job Band: 2 to 5

Job Description

Scenes of crime officers (SOCOs) known in some forces as crime scene investigators (CSIs) or examiners, collect and record physical evidence to help the police in criminal investigations. They work as part of a police investigation team and may advise on the need to get specialist assistance such as a forensic scientist. Visit crime scenes, including road accidents, murder scenes, fires, and also attend post mortems. Protect the crime scene from contamination. Make a detailed search of the area, collecting samples such as blood, paint, body fluid stains and fibres.

Use high tech equipment and computers for forensic and intelligence gathering. Some SOCOs/CSIs are also trained in a number of related specialist roles, including E-fit training that creates computer graphic images of a suspect based on eyewitness accounts. Biological, chemical, or radiological training enables SOCOs/CSIs to gather evidence in hostile environments such as biologically or chemically contaminated areas.

Other training may cover major incidents/disasters where there have been fatalities. They maintain accurate records of their work, usually on a computer; write reports and may give evidence in court.

Work Details

Usually work a 37-40 hr week that may include shifts, weekends and public holidays. May also take part in a standby rota, that includes being on call at any time of the day or night. Based at a police station, you drive to crime scenes in the area. A driving licence is usually essential. Your work may be indoors or outdoors and in all types of weather. Conditions are often difficult, unpleasant and sometimes dangerous. At times you may be required to wear a white coat, overall, protective mask and gloves.

Qualification

There are no set qualifications required for entry to this job as requirements vary greatly between police forces.

- **England, Wales and Northern Ireland**

Band 2: Some forces require a minimum of 3 GCSEs (A*-C) usually including English, maths and science subjects, or equivalent qualifications.

Band 3: For some forces: 5 GCSEs (A*-C) including maths, science and English, or equivalent qualifications are useful.

Band 4: For some forces: A levels and some GCSEs (A*-C) or equivalent qualifications are useful.

Band 5: For degree: 2-3 A levels and several GCSEs (A*-C). The exact requirements depend on the degree you take.

- **Scotland**

Band 2: Some forces require a minimum of three S grades (1-3) usually including English, maths and science subjects, or similar qualifications.

Band 3: For some employers: five S grades (1-3) including maths, science and English, or similar qualifications, are useful.

Band 4: For some employers: H grades and some S grades (1-3) or similar qualifications, are useful.

Band 5: For degree: 3-5 H grades and several S grades (1-3) or similar qualifications.

Degree Information

A degree in forensic science or forensic investigation is useful, though not essential. Degrees and postgraduate courses in various aspects of criminology are available.

Adult Qualifications

Entry requirements vary greatly between police forces and may be relaxed for adults applying for higher education courses. Access or foundation courses give adults without qualifications a route onto degree courses.

Work Experience

Relevant work or voluntary experience is always useful and can improve your chances in application for entry to this career. Any work that provides an opportunity to work with people/the public is useful. For this job, some previous work in a related area such as laboratory work or photography, is desirable.

Entry and Training

There is no minimum age limit but school or college leavers do not normally have enough experience of life for this job. Crime scene investigators (CSIs) are usually recruited from outside the police force in their early twenties and above. Each police force sets its own entry level of education and qualifications required, so you must contact the human resources section of the police force you wish to work for. All entrants go through a security check and a medical.

A training (CSI) programme is available at the National Police Improvement Agency (NPIA) residential centre in Durham. Module one consists of pre course learning for 6-8 weeks, followed by a five week residential course and the completion of a professional development portfolio, completed in the work place over six months. Module 2 also consists of three parts; pre course work involves the preparation of a case study and written assignment of 2,000 words, a four week residential course and a professional development portfolio completed in the workplace over a period of six months. Crime scene investigator development and managers' courses are also available. Check the NPIA website for full details on all courses.

Following the courses, training continues on the job for around 1-2 years, including visits to crime scenes within the employing police force, together with a formally organised visit to a forensic laboratory. There is also a development CSI course to increase skills in specialised areas of work, including scenes where explosives and/or firearms have been used, and the investigation of suspicious fires. Successful completion of full CSI training provides entry onto the Durham University undergraduate diploma in crime scene examination. Durham also runs a course in fingerprint examination; see the website for details.

A foundation degree in fingerprint identification has also been developed by the NPIA in conjunction with the University of Teeside. Specialist courses are also available in crime scene management, development crime scene investigation, footwear marks coding and intelligence and digital photography. Contact the NPIA for details on all courses.

Mature entrants are normally preferred to younger applicants, particularly those used to dealing with the public. Scientific experience such as working in a laboratory is an advantage.

Opportunities and Pay

There are around 2000 CSIs working in police forces throughout the UK, many for the Metropolitan Police. Competition for vacancies is fierce. In some cases, the work is done both by civilian and uniformed police officers, but in many forces the work is undertaken entirely by civilian staff. There may be opportunities for promotion to senior or principal crime scene examiner with management responsibilities. Some may move into the British Transport or Ministry of Defence police and others into training.

Starting salaries for CSIs are around £16k a year, with fully trained CSIs generally earning around £24k-£25k a year. Senior officers earn up to £35k a year.

Health
It is essential to have normal colour vision (lenses and spectacles accepted) and no allergies to skin irritants.

Skills and Qualities
able to work both on your own and in a team, attention to detail, firm manner, good communication skills, IT skills, methodical, not squeamish, objective, observational skills, scientific approach

Relevant Subjects
Biology, Chemistry, English, Law, Mathematics, Physics, Science

Further Information
Could you? Police (Home Office) - www.policecouldyou.co.uk/

Forensic Science Society - www.forensic-science-society.org.uk

How to Pass the Police Recruitment Tests (How to Books)

How to Pass the Police Selection System (2010) (Kogan Page) - www.koganpage.com

National Policing Improvement Agency (NPIA) - www.npia.police.uk

Police Recruitment (Scotland) - www.scottish.police.uk

Real Life Guide to the Police Service (Irotman 2009) - www.trotman.co.uk

Skills for Justice - sector skills council for the UK justice system - www.skillsforjustice.com

▶Working in police, fire & security (2009) (Babcock Lifeskills) - www.babcock-lifeskills.com/

▶Working in science (2007) (Babcock Lifeskills) - www.babcock-lifeskills.com/

Addresses
Police Service of Northern Ireland
Police Headquarters, Brooklyn, 65 Knock Road, Belfast BT5 6LE
Web: www.psni.police.uk

Similar Jobs
Anatomical Pathology Technician, Forensic Scientist, Laboratory Technician: Science, Photographer: Clinical, Police Officer, Public Analyst

Political/Constituency Organiser

CRCI:Legal and Political Services
CLCI:COB Job Band: 4 to 5

Job Description
Political, or Constituency, organisers work for a political party or Member of Parliament (MP), organising and running the work of the constituency (electoral area). They act as secretary to the local office, analyse the local electoral register, handle membership and recruitment, oversee fund raising and voluntary help. The also act as a point of contact for local party members and constituents.

Organisers arrange surgeries and meetings, handle public relations and may deal with problems on behalf of the MP or constituency. They promote the party and its elected members. They take part in charity events and other social functions, and may give interviews to journalists. May research the background of any issues that occur in the constituency.

Constituency organisers liaise between the local party and its members of parliaments in England (MP), Scotland (MSP) and in Europe (MEP) and Assembly members in Wales. They must be well prepared for a local/national election and run the campaign efficiently. They also have a detailed knowledge and understanding of electoral law and procedures.

Work Details
The hours are irregular, often involving evenings and weekends at times of party conferences or elections. You are based in an office and are out and about in different places. You organise and persuade people, and deal with enquiries. The work involves meeting a wide variety of people, including colleagues and members of the local community. You are responsible for the office administration and must have up-to-date knowledge of legal regulations.

At times the work is demanding and you may need to take work home. You need to show genuine enthusiasm for the political party concerned, have a keen interest in current affairs, and a good knowledge of local facilities. This job requires a great deal of personal commitment.

Qualification

• England, Wales and Northern Ireland
Band 4: For HND, Diploma of Higher Education or foundation degree: 1-2 A levels and some GCSEs (A*-C) usually including English and maths, or equivalent.

Band 5: For degree: 2-3 A levels and some GCSEs (A*-C) are required, usually including English and maths, or equivalent qualifications. Exact requirements depend on the degree you take.

• Scotland
Band 4: For entry to SQA higher national awards, usually 2-3 H grades and some S grades (1-3), including English and maths, or similar qualifications.

Band 5: For degree courses: 3-5 H grades and some S grades (1-3), usually including English and maths, or similar. Exact requirements depend on the degree you take.

Degree Information
Any degree is suitable for entry to this job. There are advantages in having studied subjects such as politics, economics, social policy, industrial relations, law, public relations or marketing.

Adult Qualifications
Specific academic qualifications are not always required for mature entrants with relevant experience and the right personality.

Work Experience
Entry to this job is competitive and it is important that you try to do some relevant work or voluntary experience before applying. Relevant areas are public relations or marketing, legal areas or administration, ideally in local government departments. Work involving a trade union is useful and voluntary experience of political or charity campaigning at a local level also provides excellent experience. Becoming a member of the UK Youth Parliament, which is open to those aged 11-18 inclusive, or of the Scottish Youth Parliament (14-25), provides an insight into the workings of politics and governance in the UK.

Entry and Training
Whilst there are no set minimum educational requirements, most applicants are graduates. You usually also need extensive experience, such as voluntary work or an internship with the party concerned, before applying for a job as an organiser. The selection process varies but can be an interview with both written and oral tests.

Most training is on the job, working alongside more experienced members of the team. Training depends on the individual political party, and the larger ones usually have their own training programmes. You are expected to keep up to date by attending workshops, seminars and conferences. Contact the local offices of the political party in which you are interested for further information. See the House of Commons website for information about how to look for a job working for an MP or in a politics-related setting.

Mature entrants with extensive experience of voluntary work or an internship with the party concerned, strong administrative and organisational skills, together with an ability to communicate with people of diverse backgrounds, are particularly welcomed.

Opportunities and Pay

There are around 3,500 constituency organisers in the UK, mainly working for the larger political parties. Some smaller parties only employ organisers for election campaigns. There are few opportunities for full-time permanent posts and competition for these is fierce. There are more opportunities if you are willing to work in a voluntary capacity.

Some experienced organisers may take on regional or national posts with the party, while others move into commerce or industry. It is useful to have had experience of this work if you intend to put yourself forward to become a local councillor or Member of Parliament.

Political/constituency organisers earn from £19k to more than £30k a year, depending on experience and level of responsibility. A car may also be provided.

Health

This job requires good health.

Skills and Qualities

able to get on with all kinds of people, administrative skills, enthusiastic, excellent communication skills, flexible approach, good organisational skills, interest in current affairs, IT skills, self confident, self-motivated, understanding of political processes

Relevant Subjects

Business and accounting, Economics, English, Government and politics, History, Law, Media and communication studies, Sociology

Further Information

Electus UK: Your Doorway to a Career in Politics - www.electus-start.com

House of Commons: How to Get a Job Working for an MP (House of Commons) - www.w4mp.org

The House Magazine (Dods Parliamentary Communications Limited) - www.epolitix.com/house-magazine/house-about

▶Working in politics & law (2010) (Babcock Lifeskills) - www.babcock-lifeskills.com/

Addresses

Scottish Youth Parliament
Rosebery House, 9 Haymarket Terrace, Edinburgh EH12 5EZ
Phone: +44 (0)131 313 2488
Web: www.syp.org.uk

UK Youth Parliament
15 Clerkenwell Green, London EC1R 0DP
Phone: +44 (020 7553 9890
Web: www.ukyouthparliament.org.uk/

Similar Jobs

Political/Parliamentary Researcher, Politician, Public Affairs Executive/Consultant, Public Relations Officer, Trade Union Official

Political/Parliamentary Researcher

CRCI:Legal and Political Services
CLCI:COB

Job Band: 5

Job Description

Political or parliamentary researchers carry out research on the country's changing social, political and economic trends for a UK political party. Political parties may be represented in the UK Parliament, the National Assembly for Wales, or the Scottish or European Parliaments. Researchers analyse issues in depth and report on the possible outcomes of a political party's planned policies. They visit the House of Commons library in order to conduct research and also use the Parliamentary intranet, the Internet and computer databases to search for information.

Researchers monitor daily news sources and reports of the day's proceedings in Parliament in order to rapidly identify emerging political issues. They are also required to provide facts for defending or attacking existing policies. They draft and write articles, briefings for debates and speeches for politicians, including the preparation and drafting of parliamentary questions and answers. They help Members of Parliament (MPs) to prepare papers for select committees.

Researchers also undertake basic administrative duties, including arranging meetings, preparing agendas and minutes for the meetings. They answer questions from members of the public on political party issues. May also work for a local councillor, senior party officials, and regional elected bodies. Some researchers deal with MPs' phone calls and manage their diaries.

Work Details

You usually work about 37 hrs a week, though the job can involve working long and unsocial hours, including early mornings and late nights, in order to respond quickly to the latest news. The work is office-based. You often work to tight deadlines and under pressure, as you are in direct competition with the other political parties and bodies. There may be some travel to party conferences, seminars, specialist conferences and similar events. You may travel abroad regularly if you have a Foreign Office brief.

Qualification

• England, Wales and Northern Ireland

Band 5: For a degree: 2-3 A levels and some GCSEs (A*-C), usually including English and maths, or equivalent qualifications. Exact requirements depend on the degree you take.

• Scotland

Band 5: For a degree: 3-5 H grades and some 2-3 S grades (1-3) or similar are required, usually including English and maths. Exact requirements depend on the degree you take.

Degree Information

This work is open to all graduates, though in practice, a good honours degree is normally required. Many entrants have a higher degree, particularly if the first degree was not in a relevant subject such as politics and government, social policy, law, public administration, history, economics, or sociology. Postgraduate qualifications are very useful in what is often a very competitive profession.

Adult Qualifications

The same minimum level of qualification is usually expected from mature entrants as from younger people.

Work Experience

Work experience gives you an insight into what you enjoy and do not enjoy about a job or working environment, as well as the opportunity to acquire new skills. It also provides valuable information to add to your CV and improve your employment prospects. Entry to this career is highly competitive, and it is essential that you have some relevant work or voluntary experience in academic or social research before applying for a job. You can apply for an internship as an MP's assistant, or similar political role, during university vacations.

Any political work for a students' union is also very helpful. Party membership, although not essential, is very useful in showing commitment to your future employer and can keep you up to date on various aspects of the party's work.

Entry and Training
As yet, there is no recognised professional qualification for political researchers. People are generally employed due to their high level of expertise in a particular field, gained either academically or professionally. Most entrants have a good honours degree (at least a 2.1) in a relevant subject and entry is rarely possible with an HND or pass degree. Many posts also require a reasonable understanding of statistics.

It may be beneficial to do an internship or a more junior paid post at first, perhaps as a research assistant or similar, to gain experience. When applying for a research job with a Member of Parliament (MP), it is important to know the background of the MP and details about his/her constituency. There is very little by the way of organised on-the-job training except for short, in-house induction courses or perhaps further IT training. Researchers are expected to be responsible for their own skills and professional development.

Mature entrants with experience and a proven record in corporate/ market or academic research or other relevant professions, particularly if combined with strong administrative and organisational skills, may have an advantage. An ability to communicate with people of diverse backgrounds is also helpful. Most entrants, however, are under 40 years old due to the intense pace of the work. A diploma in politics and government is available through distance learning from the Open University and foundation degrees can lead to completion of a first degree.

Opportunities and Pay
You work for a political party in the UK, the National Assembly for Wales, or the Scottish or European Parliaments, or for local authorities, senior party officials, and regional elected bodies. Competition is intense for advertised posts.

Opportunities for progression are limited as there are few management positions. Many researchers, therefore, become political analysts or journalists, lobbyists, think-tank members, academics, or elected politicians. Others may move into the civil service. Self-employment or freelance work is occasionally possible once firmly established and trusted.

Most researchers start with a salary of around £23k a year, which can rise with experience and responsibility to around £34k a year. Some senior researchers can earn up to £50k a year. Internships are not always paid.

Health
For this job you should have stamina and be physically fit, as you often work under pressure.

Skills and Qualities
analytical skills, confident, enquiring mind, excellent communication skills, good organisational skills, information handling skills, IT skills, perseverance, research skills, understanding of political processes

Relevant Subjects
Business and accounting, Economics, English, Government and politics, History, Law, Mathematics, Media and communication studies, Sociology

Further Information
Electus UK: Your Doorway to a Career in Politics - www.electus-start.com

The House Magazine (Dods Parliamentary Communications Limited) - www.epolitix.com/house-magazine/house-about

Working for an MP Homepage - www.w4mp.org

▶Working in politics & law (2010) (Babcock Lifeskills) - www.babcock-lifeskills.com/

Addresses
Conservative Party
Conservative Campaign Headquarters, 30 Millbank, London SW1P 4DP
Phone: +44 (0)20 7222 9000
Web: www.conservatives.com

Labour Party
Eldon House, Regent Centre, Newcastle upon Tyne NE3 3PW
Phone: +44 (0)8705 900200
Web: www.labour.org.uk

Liberal Democrats
4 Cowley Street, London SW1P 3NB
Phone: +44 (0)20 7222 7999
Web: www.libdems.org.uk

Open University (OU)
PO Box 197, Milton Keynes MK7 6BJ
Phone: +44 (0)845 300 6090
Web: http://www3.open.ac.uk

Similar Jobs
Information Scientist, Journalist, Market Research Executive, Political/Constituency Organiser, Politician, Public Affairs Executive/Consultant

Politician
also known as: Member of Parliament, MP

CRCI:Legal and Political Services
CLCI:COB Job Band: 2 to 5

Job Description
Politicians are democratically elected to represent the views, ideas and concerns of people in a constituency, at either national or local level, or for the European Union. They join committees, attend meetings and take part in debates. They may specialise in a particular subject such as health, the environment or education. Looking into matters of concern for their constituents is an important part of a politician's job. They hold constituency 'surgeries' (open sessions) to offer help and give advice to members of the public. Some hold a governmental post (such as a minister) if their party is in power. If not, they are described as members of the opposition. They may give interviews and appear on television and radio.

Politicians attend local, national and international functions, including party conferences, charity events and other social functions. They work closely with representatives of the local community, local authority and police force. At local level, councillors are elected to serve the county, district, borough or parish, usually in which they live.

Work Details
The hours can be very long at times and usually involve working late into the evening, as well as at weekends. National politicians' offices are in their constituency, though you may also work in either London, Edinburgh, Belfast, Cardiff or Strasbourg/Brussels, depending on the parliament or assembly you are elected to. You often need to travel to other parts of the country and sometimes abroad. You represent many different people, giving them advice and information.

The work is often demanding and involves making difficult or unpopular decisions. You have to do a lot of background reading and research. Politicians have to be strongly motivated, need to challenge people in other parties and have the ability to take part in debates. In a Parliament there are many rules and traditions that politicians need to follow.

Politician

Qualification
Active involvement in the political party is more important than qualifications. It is possible to become a politician with few or no formal qualifications at any level, though many have a degree or other qualifications from previous education, training or employment. Graduates have any degree, but subjects such as politics, law economics, industrial relations, international relations, and social policy and administration give useful background.

Adult Qualifications
No minimum qualifications are specified, but it is very important to be experienced in local politics, perhaps as a councillor, or in trade union work before standing for election. Qualifications or experience in business, law or economics are useful.

Work Experience
Entry to this career is very competitive and it is important that you try to do some relevant work or gain voluntary experience before applying. It is particularly important to demonstrate your commitment to political activity and to your chosen party, perhaps through party political groups for young people or at university. You should try to gain some experience of public speaking and debating. Involvement with the UK or Scottish Youth Parliament can be very helpful.

Any committee experience is also very useful. It may be possible to get work experience with a member of a parliament, often as a researcher. You can also apply for a paid/unpaid parliamentary internship to gain valuable experience of a working parliament. Visit the House of Commons, 'working for an MP' website to look for a job working for an MP, or in a politics-related setting.

Entry and Training
There is no particular route to becoming a politician. Most have had successful careers in other areas of work, often in business, the law and education, and have achieved their goals through interest, ambition and determination. You need to gain support of local members, and therefore experience of campaigning and some background within the party are often more important than qualifications. It is also advisable to have had relevant experience, perhaps in local politics, trade union work or as a political researcher. Many begin working for a political party on a voluntary basis or through an internship. Contact the local office of the political party that interests you for further details of opportunities.

To become a member of parliament (MP), you have to be at least 18 and a member of the political party for which you want to be a candidate. There are UK nationality requirements, and people in certain occupations are not eligible to stand for election. Candidates must undergo a series of selection interviews before they can be 'adopted' by their political party and the constituency. Although you may be elected, you can lose your job if your party is voted out at the next election. In some political parties, training is offered in communication skills, speech writing, and in handling the media. The UK Parliament offers work placements over a whole academic year for some university sandwich courses. See the UK Parliament website for details.

In Parliament, MPs are supported and advised by party whips (members who are appointed to encourage attendance at important debates and issues), and from more experienced MPs.

Maturity is usual for this occupation and many entrants have had considerable experience in another career. Some may have worked as a political researcher or perhaps as an elected party official, or have served as a local councillor. Others have held senior posts in public services or in the business sector, or have had a career in law. You may also get sponsorship from a trade union or from a local party constituency association.

Opportunities and Pay
There are 650 MPs representing constituencies in the UK and 72 MEPs representing UK constituencies at the European Parliament. Scotland has its own Parliament to deal with Scottish domestic affairs only. This is based in Edinburgh where its 129 members are elected as MSPs (Members of the Scottish Parliament). Elected members of the Welsh Assembly at Cardiff similarly deal with domestic affairs only. Scottish MPs deal with national affairs in the House of Commons, London. The Northern Ireland Assembly meets at Stormont, near Belfast, and has 108 elected members, six from each of the 18 Westminster constituencies.

This job requires a great deal of personal commitment, though some MPs have another job as well. There is limited job security because you have to be re-elected when there is a local, general or European election.

The basic salary for MPs in the House of Commons is £65k a year, plus allowances to cover expenses such as staffing. You can earn more, depending on your level of responsibility. For example, a whip receives £91k a year. The Prime Minister is currently paid £142k a year. Local authority councillors receive no salary, but are eligible for certain allowances including attendance at meetings and travel expenses.

Health
You have to be fit enough to cope with the stress and lifestyle which go with this job.

Skills and Qualities
able to cope under pressure, able to motivate others, analytical skills, determined, good debating skills, information handling skills, integrity, project management skills, self-motivated, understanding of political processes

Relevant Subjects
Business and accounting, Economics, English, Geography, Government and politics, History, Law, Mathematics, Media and communication studies, Performing arts, Sociology

Further Information
Electus UK: Your Doorway to a Career in Politics - www.electus-start.com

House of Commons: How to Get a Job Working for an MP - www.w4mp.org

The House Magazine (Dods Parliamentary Communications Limited) - www.epolitix.com/house-magazine/house-about

▶Working in politics & law (2010) (Babcock Lifeskills) - www.babcock-lifeskills.com/

Addresses
European Parliament UK Office
2 Queen Anne's Gate, London SW1H 9AA
Phone: +44 (0)20 7227 4300
Web: www.europarl.org.uk

House of Commons
Information Office, House of Commons, London SW1A 0AA
Phone: +44 (0)20 7219 4272
Web: www.parliament.uk

Northern Ireland Assembly
Communications Office Northern Ireland Assembly Parliament Buildings Ballymiscaw Stormont, Belfast BT4 3XX
Phone: +44 (0)28 9052 1333
Web: www.niassembly.gov.uk

Scottish Parliament
Edinburgh EH99 1SP
Phone: +44 (0)131 348 5000
Web: www.scottish.parliament.uk

Scottish Youth Parliament
Rosebery House, 9 Haymarket Terrace, Edinburgh EH12 5EZ
Phone: +44 (0)131 313 2488
Web: www.syp.org.uk

UK Youth Parliament
15 Clerkenwell Green, London EC1R 0DP
Phone: +44 (020 7553 9890
Web: www.ukyouthparliament.org.uk/

Welsh Assembly Government
Cathays Park, Cardiff CF10 3NQ
Phone: 0845 010 3300 (UK only)
Web: www.wales.gov.uk

Similar Jobs
Civil Service Executive Officer, Political/Constituency Organiser, Political/Parliamentary Researcher, Public Affairs Executive/ Consultant, Trade Union Official

Polymer/Plastics Process Operative

CRCI:Manufacturing and Production
CLCI:SAN
Job Band: 1 to 2

Job Description
Plastics process operatives monitor machines, such as injection or extrusion moulding machines, used to make plastic and rubber products within the plastics processing industry. May be responsible for a number of machines. They regularly check the speed, temperature and pressure gauges and ensure that the goods are produced at the speed required. Quality checks are carried out on the product (eg CDs/DVDs, vehicle tyres, TV cases and computer parts) to find and rectify any faults or flaws.

Process operatives monitor the size, colour and weight of a sample. May be required to remove and help to pack the finished product. Some process workers may finish items, such as plastic bottles, by trimming off any extra pieces of plastic. They report any mechanical faults to a supervisor and close down the machines in an emergency.

Work Details
Most operatives work a basic 37-40 hr week and it may be necessary to work shifts, possibly in the evenings and at weekends. You work in manufacturing premises. These are usually well lit and well ventilated, but may be warm, noisy and dusty, and you may also have to cope with unpleasant fumes. The job requires you to follow safety procedures at all times and observe health and safety regulations. Most of the time you are on your feet and may have to lift heavy objects. You need to wear overalls and perhaps a face mask or gloves.

Qualification

• England, Wales and Northern Ireland
Band 1: No minimum qualifications are required, but you are expected to have a good level of general education. However, some formal/vocational qualifications at any level are useful.

Band 2: Although academic qualifications are not specified for this job, it is an advantage to have some GCSEs (A*-C) in subjects that include English, maths and science or equivalent.

• Scotland
Band 1: No minimum qualifications are required, but you are expected to have a good level of general education. However, some formal/vocational qualifications at any level are useful.

Band 2: Although academic qualifications are not specified for this job, it is an advantage to have some S grades (1-3) in subjects that include English, maths and science, or similar.

Adult Qualifications
For adults, no pre-entry qualifications are usually required, though some academic/vocational qualifications at any level may be an advantage. English, maths and science are useful subjects.

Work Experience
Relevant work or voluntary experience is always useful. It can improve your chances when applying for jobs or apprenticeships. Your personal or adult guidance adviser should be able to advise you about how to get some work experience.

Entry and Training
Applicants must be at least 18 for shift work. Training is mainly on the job with supervision and assessment by an experienced work colleague, and perhaps with the opportunity to work towards a range of vocational courses in polymer and composite-based process support. Learnplastics.com offers online courses such as injection moulding and extrusion.

S/NVQs at levels 1-3 in polymer processing and related operations are available. Relevant training programmes, including apprenticeship schemes, may be available in your area. Advanced apprenticeships leading to qualification at level 3 can be a route into higher education. A Diploma/Welsh Baccalaureate may be available in your area in manufacturing and product design. This would give good background for entry to this type of work.

Government training opportunities, such as an apprenticeship in polymer processing and related operations may be available in your area. You can also gain recognition of previous experience through Accreditation of Prior Learning (APL) or by working towards relevant S/NVQs. Contact your local careers office, Jobcentre Plus, Next Step service or Learning and Skills Council (LSC) Local Enterprise Company (LEC) for details of training schemes.

Opportunities and Pay
Opportunities in plastics and rubber processing are growing. Employers throughout the UK range from either a small extrusion company to a large manufacturer. Promotion to supervisory level is possible, especially for those with relevant qualifications. Some operatives move to machine moulding or setting. Job opportunities are fewer at the moment, due to the current economic downturn, but are likely to be good when the situation improves, particularly for those who are willing to work towards the appropriate qualifications.

Pay can vary considerably depending on location and employer but is likely to start at around £11k-£13k a year, rising to £19k with experience. Skilled workers and team leaders can make more than £25k a year. You can increase your pay by working extra shifts and overtime.

Health
There is an allergy risk from skin irritants. This job requires good general fitness.

Skills and Qualities
able to follow instructions, able to work quickly, attention to detail, good concentration level, numeracy skills, practical skills, prepared to do repetitive tasks, responsible attitude, safety conscious

Relevant Subjects
Chemistry, Manufacturing

Further Information
All-Island Polymer and Plastics Network (All-Island Polymer and Plastics Network) - www.polymernetwork.com

Apprenticeship Schemes (National Apprenticeship Service) - www.apprenticeships.org.uk

Cogent - sector skills souncil for chemicals, pharmaceuticals, nuclear, oil & gas, petroleum & polymers - www.cogent-ssc.com

Diplomas (Foundation, Higher and Advanced) - http://yp.direct.gov.uk/diplomas

learnplastics - www.learnplastics.com

National Skills Academy Process Industries - www.process.nsacademy.co.uk

Plastics and Rubber Weekly (PRW) - www.prw.com/advertising/print.html

Training Schemes - www.direct.gov.uk/en/educationandlearning

Welsh Baccalaureate - www.wbq.org.uk

▶Working in manufacturing (2010) (Babcock Lifeskills) - www.babcock-lifeskills.com/

Addresses

British Plastics Federation (BPF)
6 Bath Place, Rivington Street, London EC2A 3JE
Phone: +44 (0)20 7457 5000
Web: www.bpf.co.uk

Institute of Materials, Minerals and Mining (IOM3)
1 Carlton House Terrace, London SW1Y 5DB
Phone: +44 (0)20 7451 7300
Web: www.iom3.org

Similar Jobs

Engineering Machine Operative, Foundry Process Operative, Laminator, Polymer/Plastics Technician, Polymer/Plastics Technologist

Polymer/Plastics Technician

also known as: Rubber Technician

CRCI:Manufacturing and Production
CLCI:SAN
Job Band: 3

Job Description

Polymer technicians work with a team which is responsible for the efficient production in the plastics, composites and rubber industries. They produce a vast array of products that are used in our everyday lives. These can include leisure, business or household items through to the automotive, aircraft, medical, marine and space industry. May work in product development under the supervision of a technologist. May be involved in introducing new materials, tooling and process techniques.

Technicians help to make sure that the manufacturing process is effective. They test new products before they go on the market, help to solve problems that arise and monitor the materials that are used. May be involved in working directly with the machines involved in the processes, such as extrusion and injection moulding machines. Specialist equipment is used to test the durability, flexibility, size and strength of polymers. Technicians perform quality checks on the chemicals used and also the finished product. Some may supervise machine operators or other staff or work in sales and marketing.

Work Details

Polymer/plastics technicians usually work a 37-40 hr week, Monday to Friday, though may be required to work shifts that include weekends and evenings. You work in industrial premises, an office or a laboratory, and can be advising, supervising and consulting with people. You may have to cope with some physical activity and need to wear an overall or possibly protective clothing.

Qualification

- **England, Wales and Northern Ireland**

Band 3: For entry to an advanced apprenticeship or an appropriate course: usually at least 5 GCSEs (A*-C) including English, maths and science, or equivalent.

- **Scotland**

Band 3: For entry to an apprenticeship or relevant course: usually at least five S grades (1-3) including English, maths or science, or similar.

Adult Qualifications

Mature entrants may not need the usual academic qualifications if they have relevant experience.

Work Experience

Relevant work or voluntary experience is always useful and can improve your chances when applying for entry to jobs or apprenticeships in the manufacturing sector. Your personal or adult guidance adviser should be able to advise you about how to organise work experience with an employer.

Entry and Training

Most new entrants follow a structured technician apprenticeship training programme, which usually includes day release at a college for appropriate qualifications, such as a BTEC/SQA national certificate/diploma. Some entrants may complete a full-time BTEC or SQA national award before entry.

In Northern Ireland a collaborative venture between the South Eastern Regional College, the Polymer Processing Research Centre and Queen's University Belfast has resulted in the Polymer Apprenticeship Programme. This apprenticeship provides the necessary training to prepare students for work in the industry. Check the All-Island Polymer and Plastics Network website for details.

S/NVQs at levels 2-3 in process operations or process engineering machine maintenance are available. Advanced apprenticeships leading to qualification at level 3 can be a route into higher education. A Diploma/Welsh Baccalaureate in manufacturing and product design may be available in your area. This can be a good introduction to this type of work.

Adults with appropriate operative training in the plastics, composites or rubber industries may be acceptable for technician level training. Government training opportunities, such as an apprenticeship in polymer processing and related operations may be available in your area. You can also gain recognition of previous experience through Accreditation of Prior Learning (APL) or by working towards relevant S/NVQs. Contact your local careers office, Jobcentre Plus, Next Step service or Learning and Skills Council (LSC) Local Enterprise Company (LEC) for details of training schemes.

Opportunities and Pay

There are over 13,500 companies involved in this type of work in the UK, employing over 270,000 people. You may be employed by a small injection moulding company, a multi-national polymer/plastics manufacturing company, or possibly a research organisation. The multi-national companies are mainly based in the Midlands, the north of England or Scotland. Jobs are increasing especially for qualified technicians. Promotion prospects can be improved by further training and qualification.

Pay varies depending on area and employer, but starts at around £14k (less if on an apprenticeship), rising to £18k-£28k a year. Overtime pay is possible.

Health

There may be an allergy risk from skin irritants. This job requires good colour vision for certain areas of work.

Skills and Qualities

able to manage people, able to take responsibility, aptitude for teamwork, good communication skills, good organisational skills, IT skills, numeracy skills, practical skills, problem-solving skills, technical aptitude

Relevant Subjects

Chemistry, Design and technology, Engineering, Science

Further Information

All-Island Polymer and Plastics Network (All-Island Polymer and Plastics Network) - www.polymernetwork.com

Apprenticeship Schemes (National Apprenticeship Service) - www.apprenticeships.org.uk

Careers in Coatings (Proskills) - www.prospect4u.co.uk

Cogent - sector skills souncil for chemicals, pharmaceuticals, nuclear, oil & gas, petroleum & polymers - www.cogent-ssc.com

Composites UK - www.composites-proc-assoc.co.uk

Diplomas (Foundation, Higher and Advanced) - http://yp.direct.gov.uk/diplomas

National Skills Academy Process Industries - www.process.nsacademy.co.uk

Plastics and Rubber Weekly (PRW) - www.prw.com/advertising/print.html

Training Schemes - www.direct.gov.uk/en/educationandlearning

Welsh Baccalaureate - www.wbq.org.uk

▶Working in manufacturing (2010) (Babcock Lifeskills) - www.babcock-lifeskills.com/

Addresses

British Plastics Federation (BPF)
6 Bath Place, Rivington Street, London EC2A 3JE
Phone: +44 (0)20 7457 5000
Web: www.bpf.co.uk

British Rubber and Polyurethane Products Association
5 Berewyk Hall Court, White Colne,, Colchester, Essex EC2A 3JE
Phone: +44 (0)1787 226995
Web: www.brppa.co.uk/

Institute of Materials, Minerals and Mining (IOM3)
1 Carlton House Terrace, London SW1Y 5DB
Phone: +44 (0)20 7451 7300
Web: www.iom3.org

Similar Jobs

Laboratory Technician: Science, Laminator, Marine Engineering Technician, Polymer/Plastics Process Operative, Polymer/Plastics Technologist, Quality Assurance Controller/Inspector

Polymer/Plastics Technologist

also known as: Plastics/Polymer Technologist

CRCI:Manufacturing and Production

CLCI:SAN Job Band: 4 to 5

Job Description

Polymer technologists work in the manufacture of products made from polymers (includes rubber, plastics, adhesives, resins and fibres). They are concerned with production and development processes for products used in a wide range of industries, such as packaging and motor industries. Duties can include working on complex problems that may arise for the company or for customers. May specify new materials, products and processes. May be involved in testing raw materials, manufacture of goods, quality control or technical sales and marketing. Some carry out research on uses of new improved materials and processes and may also supervise laboratory staff. Liaising with engineers, technicians and operatives, as well as other scientists is an important part of the job.

Work Details

Usually works a 35-40 hr week, Monday to Friday, though may be required to work overtime to meet deadlines. You work in industrial premises, an office or a laboratory and advise, supervise and consult with people as well as being responsible for efficient production. You may have to cope with some physical activity, and need to wear an overall, or possibly protective clothing.

Qualification

• England, Wales and Northern Ireland

Band 4: For BTEC higher national award: 1-2 A levels preferably from chemistry, physics or maths and some GCSEs (A*-C), or a BTEC national award in polymer processing and materials technology, or equivalent.

Band 5: For degree courses: 2-3 A levels, preferably in chemistry, physics or maths, and some GCSEs (A*-C) including English. The exact requirements depend on the degree to be taken.

• Scotland

Band 4: For SQA higher national award: usually 2-3 H grades, preferably in chemistry, physics or maths and some S grades (1-3), often including English and maths or similar.

Band 5: For degree courses: 3-5 H grades, including chemistry and two from biology, physics and maths, and some S grades (1-3) usually including English and maths, or similar qualifications. Exact requirements depend on the degree you take.

Degree Information

A degree in polymer science is preferred but employers may also accept degrees in chemistry or materials science/technology and some engineering degrees, including materials/aerospace/ biomaterials engineering. There are opportunities for postgraduate study.

Adult Qualifications

A relevant higher education qualification is normally required for entry to this job at a professional level. However, entry requirements may be relaxed for adults applying for higher education courses. Access or foundation courses provide those without the required qualifications a route onto degree courses.

Work Experience

Employers or colleges/universities may prefer candidates who have relevant work or voluntary experience. This includes experience of working with chemicals or materials, or in a laboratory. In some areas there is a young apprenticeship (14-16) scheme that provides an extended work placement, leading to achievement of a relevant level 2 qualification whilst at school.

Schemes such as 'A Year in Industry' enable those who expect good A levels/H grades and intend to go to university the opportunity to spend a salaried year with a company in order to gain valuable work experience.

Entry and Training

Most entrants have a relevant HND/foundation degree or degree in a subject including polymer science/technology. The website of the Institute of Materials, Minerals and Mining (IOM3) has details of degree courses accredited by them. See their website for details. Graduates have to undertake further training whilst in employment. Some of this may be on the job, some is by attendance on short courses to update particular skills. For example, Cranfield University runs a series of short continuing professional development (CPD) courses including topics such as composites performance, composite structures in motorsport and materials selection. It is also possible to enter at technician level and progress into this job.

A Diploma/Welsh Baccalaureate in manufacturing and product design may be available in your area. The advanced level is equivalent to 3.5 A levels but for some university courses, the additional and specialist learning (ASL) component of the diploma needs to include specific A levels eg maths or chemistry. Check entry requirements carefully with the individual institutions.

Adults with appropriate experience as a polymer/plastics technician may be able to move into this role, but they may need to study for further qualifications.

Government training opportunities, such as an apprenticeship in polymer processing and related operations may be available in your area. You can also gain recognition of previous experience through Accreditation of Prior Learning (APL) or by working towards relevant S/NVQs. Contact your local careers office, Jobcentre Plus, Next Step service or Learning and Skills Council (LSC) Local Enterprise Company (LEC) for details of training schemes.

Opportunities and Pay
There are over 13,500 companies involved in polymer processing in the UK, employing over 270,000 people. You are employed by one of the many multi-national manufacturing companies involved in plastics processing or possibly a research organisation. Promotion opportunities are good for those with appropriate experience and qualifications. With experience you may move into equipment development, product design or technical sales.

Pay varies depending on location, type and size of employer but a graduate entrant is likely to start on around £22k-£26k, rising to around £35k a year.

Health
There may be an allergy risk from skin irritants. This job requires good colour vision for certain areas of work.

Skills and Qualities
analytical skills, aptitude for maths and science, aptitude for teamwork, good communication skills, good interpersonal skills, IT skills, problem-solving skills, resourceful, sound judgement, technical aptitude

Relevant Subjects
Chemistry, Design and technology, Engineering, ICT/Computer studies, Manufacturing, Mathematics, Physics, Science

Further Information
AGCAS: Engineering (Job Sector Briefing) (AGCAS) - www.prospects.ac.uk

AGCAS: Manufacturing (Job Sector Briefing) (AGCAS) - www.prospects.ac.uk

All-Island Polymer and Plastics Network - www.polymernetwork.com

Careers in Coatings (Proskills) - www.prospect4u.co.uk

Cogent - sector skills souncil for chemicals, pharmaceuticals, nuclear, oil & gas, petroleum & polymers - www.cogent-ssc.com

Composites UK - www.composites-proc-assoc.co.uk

Diplomas (Foundation, Higher and Advanced) - http://yp.direct.gov.uk/diplomas

Plastics and Rubber Weekly (PRW) - www.prw.com/advertising/print.html

Polymer Innovation Newtwork (Polymer Innovation Network) http:www.polymerinnovate.com

Real Life Guide to Manufacturing & Product Design (Trotman 2009) - www.trotman.co.uk

Welsh Baccalaureate - www.wbq.org.uk

Year in Industry (Engineering Development Trust) - www.yini.org.uk

Addresses
British Plastics Federation (BPF)
6 Bath Place, Rivington Street, London EC2A 3JE
Phone: +44 (0)20 7457 5000
Web: www.bpf.co.uk

British Rubber and Polyurethane Products Association
5 Berewyk Hall Court, White Colne, Colchester, Essex EC2A 3JE
Phone: +44 (0)1787 226995
Web: www.brppa.co.uk/

Cranfield University
College Road, Cranfield, Bedfordshire MK43 0AL
Phone: +44 (0) 1234 750111
Web: www.cranfield.ac.uk/

Institute of Materials, Minerals and Mining (IOM3)
1 Carlton House Terrace, London SW1Y 5DB
Phone: +44 (0)20 7451 7300
Web: www.iom3.org

Similar Jobs
Ceramic Technologist, Engineer: Chemical, Leather Technologist, Materials Scientist/Engineer, Packaging Technologist, Polymer/ Plastics Technician

Pool Lifeguard
also known as: Lifeguard: Pool

CRCI:Leisure, Sport and Tourism
CLCI:GAJ — Job Band: 1 to 3

Job Description
Pool lifeguards keep a close watch on swimmers using a swimming pool, especially beginners and children. They walk around the pool, or sit in a raised observation chair watching swimmers, and closely supervise the use of chutes, flumes and diving boards. Lifeguards interrupt bad behaviour and make sure that swimmers are safe. They also help people in trouble and give immediate first aid, including artificial resuscitation if necessary. Monitors state of the water and checks filters and pumps and may also be responsible for the hygienic operation of the pool and surrounding area. Looks after changing rooms and can also be responsible for other facilities such as jacuzzis, chutes, slides, showers and spa pools. Lifeguards must be able to swim well and be competent in lifesaving techniques.

Work Details
Usually works a basic 37 hr week, which is likely to involve unsocial hours and shifts, including weekends. Much of the work is seasonal and part time. You are responsible for the swimmers' safety and need to be alert at all times in case of accidents. You have to be able to cope with the sight of blood as swimmers often fall on the hard pool surround or injure themselves on equipment. Monitoring the hygiene of the water and checking the filter and chemicals requires great care. Conditions at the pool are humid and noisy.

Qualification
For most lifeguard courses, strict swimming entry criteria usually exist.

• England, Wales and Northern Ireland
Band 1: No minimum qualifications are required, but you are expected to have a good level of general education and relevant experience. Some formal/vocational qualifications at any level are useful.

Band 2: For entry to jobs, no minimum qualifications are needed, but it is an advantage to have some GCSEs (A*-C) or equivalent in subjects that include English and maths.

Band 3: For entry to jobs and some courses: usually at least 4 GCSEs (A*-C) including English and maths, or equivalent.

• Scotland
Band 1: No minimum qualifications are required, but you are expected to have a good level of general education. However, some formal/vocational qualifications at any level are useful.

Band 2: Although academic qualifications are not specified for this job, it is an advantage to have some S grades (1-3) in subjects that include English and maths, or similar.

Band 3: For entry to jobs and some courses: four S grades (1-3) including English and maths, or similar, may be required.

Adult Qualifications
No particular academic qualifications are needed but employers may look for a good standard of English and maths. For most lifeguard courses, strict swimming entry criteria usually exist.

Work Experience
Any work experience can equip you with skills that you can use in the future and add to your CV. This can either be unpaid or voluntary, holiday or part-time work that you have organised yourself. Any experience you can gain in a sports or leisure centre is relevant.

Entry and Training
To become a pool lifeguard, you must be at least 16 years of age, be able to swim well and hold a current life-saving certificate. Most have either the Lifesavers Royal Life Saving Society UK's (RLSS) National Pool Lifeguard Qualification (NPLQ), or the STA Level 2 Certificate for Pool Lifeguards offered by the National Rescue Standard (NaRS). RLSS courses are managed and awarded by the Institute of Qualified Lifeguards. Contact them for further details about courses and training. Both RLSS and STA courses are available from approved training centres in the UK and have strict swimming entry criteria. RLSS require you to swim 50 metres in less than 60 seconds, dive into deep water, swim 100 metres continuously on front and back, tread water for 30 seconds, surface dive to the floor of the pool and climb out unaided without a ladder/steps. Contact RLSS/NaRS for full details.

Some employers may offer RLSS/NaRS training while you are working on other jobs away from the poolside. It is an advantage to have a qualification in first aid. There is usually specific on-the-job training and also short courses. For attendants whose responsibility includes pool plant and water quality maintenance, the Institute of Sport & Recreation Management (ISRM) offers a foundation and operators certificate, leading to the Level 3 Certificate in Pool Plant Operations, which is valid for five years and can be upgraded by attending a seminar.

You may be able to obtain S/NVQs in sport, recreation and allied occupations at levels 1-3. A Diploma/Welsh Baccalaureate may also be available in your area in Sport & Active Leisure. Contact SkillsActive for further details. Relevant training programmes, including apprenticeship schemes, may be available in your area. Advanced apprenticeships leading to qualification at level 3 can be a route into higher education.

Mature entrants are required to have the Royal Life Saving Society UK's (RLSS) National Pool Lifeguard Certificate or the Pool Lifeguard Certificate offered by the National Rescue Standard (NaRS). You need to be a strong swimmer and physically fit. It is an advantage to have experience and/or qualifications/awards in sports and also first aid. Adults can also gain recognition of skills and previous experience via APL (Accreditation of Prior Learning) and by taking relevant S/NVQs.

Opportunities and Pay
There are jobs throughout the UK but mainly in towns and cities. Jobs are mainly in local authority swimming pools, leisure/sports centres, clubs, hotels and holiday centres. Promotion to supervisory level is possible.

Pay varies depending on region and employer, but most pool lifeguards working full time earn around £11k-£15k a year. A supervisor can earn around £16k-£20k a year. There are good opportunities to work overtime and with allowances for certain shifts, you are able to earn extra money. Perks may include free use of the pool and other leisure facilities.

Health
This job requires good general fitness. In some pools chemicals may be used which can affect those with chest and skin problems.

Skills and Qualities
able to cope with emergencies, alert, encouraging, firm manner, friendly, responsible attitude, stamina, strong, tolerant

Relevant Subjects
Biology, Health and social care, Leisure, travel and tourism, Physical education and sport, Science

Further Information
Apprenticeship Schemes (National Apprenticeship Service) - www.apprenticeships.org.uk
Diplomas (Foundation, Higher and Advanced) http://yp.direct.gov.uk/diplomas
Institute for Sport, Parks & Leisure (ISPAL) E-zine (ISPAL) - www.ispal.org.uk/ezine
Institute of Qualified Lifeguards (IQL) - www.iql.org.uk
Local Government Careers (Improvement and Development Agency) - www.lgcareers.com/publications/
Real Life Guide to Sports & Active Leisure (Trotman 2009) - www.trotman.co.uk
SkillsActive - sector skills council for active leisure, learning and well-being - www.skillsactive.com
▶Working in sport & leisure (2010) (Babcock Lifeskills) - www.babcock-lifeskills.com/

Addresses
Institute of Sport & Recreation Management (ISRM)
and the National Association for Sports Development Sir John Beckwith Centre for Sport Loughborough University,
Leicestershire LE11 3TU
Phone: +44 (0)1509 226 474
Web: www.isrm.co.uk

Lifesavers: Royal Life Saving Society UK (RLSS)
River House, High Street, Broom, Warwickshire B50 4HN
Phone: +44 (0)1789 773 994
Web: www.lifesavers.org.uk

Swimming Teachers' Association (STA)
Anchor House, Birch Street, Walsall, West Midlands WS2 8HZ
Phone: +44 (0)1922 645 097
Web: www.sta.co.uk

Similar Jobs
Fitness Instructor, Holiday Centre Worker, Leisure Centre Assistant, Outdoor Activities Instructor, Sports Coach

Pool Plant Operator
also known as: Swimming Pool Technician
CRCI:Engineering
CLCI:ROK — Job Band: 2 to 3

Job Description
Pool plant operators monitor the water quality in a swimming pool, spa or hot tub. They test and correct the pH levels as necessary to achieve the correct water chemistry. They are responsible for managing stocks of all chemicals and making sure they are safely locked away after use. A log is kept of any adjustments made to the water.

They maintain the filtration system in the pool and monitor the heating and dehumidification systems to ensure a comfortable environment for pool users. Also carries out checks for any damage or repairs needed to ladders, disabled hoists or diving boards. Looks out for general deterioration in the tiles and grout, which may lead to leaks.

If working with an outdoor pool, they are responsible for draining and cleaning it during the winter months. When the season starts again, prepares the pool for use by checking all of the equipment and filling it with chemically balanced water.

Work Details
Normally works a 35-40 hour week which can include weekends and early starts. May be based at a leisure centre or health club, or work for a local authority or pool equipment supplier. Alternatively, may work for a contract services organisation, driving to different sites and carrying out maintenance duties. May wear protective gloves when handling chemicals.

Pool Plant Operator

Qualification

- **England, Wales and Northern Ireland**

Band 2: For entry to jobs, no minimum qualifications are needed, but it is an advantage to have some GCSEs (A*-C) or equivalent in subjects that include English and maths.

Equivalent qualifications which may be acceptable include the Foundation Diploma, functional skills level 1, vocational qualifications at level 1 and Welsh Baccalaureate (foundation diploma level). Check with individual employers. You may be able to follow an apprenticeship scheme.

Band 3: For entry to jobs, HNC or a relevant Diploma, usually at least 4 GCSEs (A*-C) including English and maths, or equivalent.

Equivalent qualifications which may be acceptable include the Higher Diploma, functional skills level 2, vocational qualifications at level 2 and Welsh Baccalaureate (intermediate diploma level). Check with individual institutions/employers. You may be available to follow an advanced apprenticeship scheme.

- **Scotland**

Band 2: Although academic qualifications are not specified for this job, it is an advantage to have some S grades (1-3) in subjects that include English and maths, or similar.

Other qualifications which may be acceptable include SVQ levels 1 and 2, Skills for Work courses, and intermediate levels of National awards and certificates. Check with individual employers.

Band 3: For entry to jobs, usually at least four S grades (1-3) including English or maths, or similar.

Other qualifications which may be acceptable include SVQ levels 1 and 2, Skills for Work courses, and intermediate levels of National awards and certificates. Check with individual employers.

Adult Qualifications

No academic qualifications are specified but qualifications/ experience in maintenance work are useful.

Work Experience

Any work experience can give you skills to use in the future and add to your CV. This can either be unpaid or holiday/part-time work that you have arranged yourself. Experience that shows your practical skills in maintenance work is most useful.

Entry and Training

People with practical work experience and skills can enter this role without qualifications and receive on-the-job training. Knowledge of basic maths and writing ability is usually required as you have to calculate the quantities of chemicals and write reports. Those working in schools need a Criminal Records Bureau (CRB)/ Disclosure Scotland check.

A Diploma/Welsh Baccalaureate in sport and active leisure may be available in your area and can be a useful introduction to this job. The Qualifications and Credit Framework run a number of vocational qualifications in swimming pool management. For example, you can work for a level 2 qualification in the principles and practise of swimming pool water testing or swimming pool and spa water treatment.

The Institute of Swimming Pool Engineers (IPSE) runs a home study course leading to certified technician status. This can be followed by an IPSE diploma and a programme of workshops. Similarly, the Institute of Sport and Recreation Management run a pool plant operators certificate at levels 2 and 3.

The Safety Training Awards (STA) revised their foundation and certificate level qualifications in February 2010. The Foundation Certificate course is designed to provide the skills necessary to competently test and maintain swimming pool and spa water quality. Candidates must be 16 years of age to undertake the basic 5 hour taught programme. No prior knowledge is required.

The STA Certificate in Swimming Pool and Spa Water treatment has been designed for training in the management and operation of swimming pool and spa water treatment equipment. Candidates must be 18 years of age or older to undertake the 12 hour taught programme and have successfully completed the Foundation Certificate (or equivalent qualification). Those who achieve these qualifications and have the requisite amount of work experience can become tutors themselves.

Asset Skills runs a cleaning and support services apprenticeship covering all aspects of cleaning including dealing with hazardous chemicals and large machinery.

Control of Substances Hazardous to Health (COSHH) regulations demand that employers control substances that may be harmful to employees, and as chemicals can aggravate asthma and dermatitis, pool plant operators may have to carry out assessments of their workplace. They may also need Gas Safe Register membership if they work with gas on site.

The Swimming Pool and Allied Trades Association runs a health and safety executive approved course for pool plant operators. This training allows them to dive and work to a maximum of 4 metres and carry out any maintenance work that requires hand tools only.

A driving licence may be necessary if you work for a contract services organisation.

Mature applicants with experience in maintenance work or handling hazardous chemicals may have an advantage. If working in a school, you need to have a Criminal Records Bureau (CRB)/Disclosure Scotland check.

Government training opportunities, such as apprenticeships, may be available in your area. You can also gain recognition of previous experience through Accreditation of Prior Learning (APL) or by working towards relevant S/NVQs. Contact your local careers office, Jobcentre Plus, Next Step service or Learning and Skills Council (LSC) Local Enterprise Company (LEC) for details of training schemes.

Opportunities and Pay

Jobs are available throughout the UK. You can work for a leisure centre or health club, a local authority or pool equipment supplier. Alternatively, you may work for a contract services organisation and drive to various locations carrying out maintenance work. With experience, and additional qualifications, there may be chances for promotion. This can include supervising other staff. You may need to move jobs to gain promotion. Some operators move into training roles.

Salaries range from £15k to £20k a year but can be higher for those with additional managerial responsibilities.

Health

You need to be physically fit to carry out some of the duties involved in this job. Handling chemicals may prove difficult for allergy sufferers.

Skills and Qualities

able to work both on your own and in a team, accurate measuring and calculating skills, good at writing reports, good organisational skills, health & safety awareness, problem-solving skills, responsible attitude

Relevant Subjects

Biology, Chemistry, Construction and built environment, English, Leisure, travel and tourism, Mathematics, Science

Further Information

Apprenticeship Schemes (National Apprenticeship Service) - www.apprenticeships.org.uk

Asset Skills - sector skills council for the places where we live and work - www.assetskills.org

Diplomas (Foundation, Higher and Advanced) - http://yp.direct.gov.uk/diplomas

Gas Safe Register - www.gassaferegister.co.uk

Leisure Jobs UK - www.leisurejobs.com

Pool Water Treatment Advisory Group - www.pwtag.org

Safety Training Awards - www.sta.co.uk/

Swimming Pool and Allied Trades Association - www.spata.co.uk

Welsh Baccalaureate - www.wbq.org.uk

Addresses

Institute of Sport & Recreation Management (ISRM) and the National Association for Sports Development, Sir John Beckwith Centre for Sport, Loughborough University, Leicestershire LE11 3TU
Phone: +44 (0)1509 226 474
Web: www.isrm.co.uk

Institute of Swimming Pool Engineers (ISPE)
PO Box 3083, Norwich, Norfolk NR6 7YL
Web: www.ispe.co.uk/

Similar Jobs

Caretaker, Gas Service Engineer, Heating & Ventilation Fitter/Welder, Leisure Manager

Port Operative

also known as: Docker, Marine Operative, Stevedore

CRCI:Transport and Logistics

CLCI:YAG Job Band: 1

Job Description

Port operatives work in three main areas: stevedoring, passenger operations and marine operations. As stevedores, they load and unload cargo from ships and dock storage areas and transport it within the port. They use a variety of equipment including fork-lift trucks, cranes and hoists to lift and remove the ship's goods or to load them into the ship's hold. Also fasten/unfasten the cargo to appropriate lifting gear when working in the hold. Stevedores drive vehicles that tow or carry cargo when working with roll-on/roll-off ferries. If vehicles are being transported, they drive them on or off the ship. May work on container ships and use dockside cranes and hoists on the ship to load/unload the containers. May also transport dry bulk cargo such as grain, loaded by elevator, or liquid cargo such as oil, loaded by pipeline. They ensure all types of cargo are safely transported, stacked and stored. Stevedores are required to maintain lifting equipment and report any faults.

Passenger operatives normally work in ports with ferry services or a cruise terminal. Work and conditions vary and are dependent on the type of passenger service the port offers. Passenger ferries are used for short river crossings or longer sailings to Europe and between the UK and Ireland, whilst cruise ships sail all over the world. Working in a passenger terminal, operatives may provide travel information, check documentation, answer individual enquiries and ensure passengers travel through the terminal safely and efficiently. Dealing with passengers in vehicles, operatives work outdoors, in vehicle holding areas or by the ship's loading ramps. They may be required to check travel documentation, answer general queries and also direct traffic to and from the vessel ensuring they follow designated routes and do not stray into restricted areas. May be required to maintain security in their area and to liaise closely with Immigration, Customs & Excise and the police.

Marine operatives deal with the "wet side" of port work, which means working from, or crewing, small harbour craft. The type used depends on the traffic the port handles, but can include transporting passengers and crew to ships moored off shore and shipping pilots to vessels entering port. May also carry out operational tasks such as tying up larger vessels, cleaning up after a pollution incident, placing and maintenance of marker buoys in the harbour entrance and sometimes in rescuing people from the water. The size and speed of these craft varies, from small unpowered rowing boats to fast, well equipped pilot launches. Working under supervision, a marine operative may be required to navigate the craft, ensure it is kept clean and well maintained and operate VHF radio and radar equipment.

Work Details

Usually work a 40 hr week that includes 8 hour shifts in a 24 hr period over seven days. Ships must be unloaded on schedule so you need to be flexible. At times the work is very busy and you have to work quickly. Work is mainly outdoors in all weathers, but some time is spent in the holds of ships, which can be hot, cramped and smelly. You need to have a good head for heights as you may be operating large cranes and climbing ladders. If in a passenger terminal, you may wear a uniform. On dockside or on vessels, you are required to wear high visibility jackets and other protective clothing.

Qualification

- **England, Wales and Northern Ireland**

Band 1: No minimum qualifications are required, but you are expected to have a good level of general education. However, some formal/vocational qualifications at any level are useful.

- **Scotland**

Band 1: No minimum qualifications are required, but you are expected to have a good level of general education. However, some formal/vocational qualifications at any level are useful.

Adult Qualifications

Though formal academic qualifications are not needed, employers expect applicants to have a good standard of reading, be able to write clearly and do basic number work. You can improve your skills and qualifications by working through the Foundation Learning programme. This involves taking credit-based units and qualifications to help you progress.

Work Experience

Any work experience can equip you with skills that you can use in the future and add to your CV. For stevedoring work, experience of driving cranes, fork lift trucks or lorries can be an advantage, and engineering skills are also useful for carrying out basic maintenance. Passenger operatives in international ports may find a second language useful. Marine operatives benefit from previous experience with sailing small craft.

Entry and Training

Entry is usually over the age of 21, although some ports recruit passenger operatives from the age of 17. You need to pass a medical examination. Most companies require a driving licence. For a stevedore, training is on the job with a supervisor or experienced stevedore and usually begins with cargo handling techniques, lasting two weeks. This includes operating lifting machinery such as forklift trucks or cranes, signalling instructions and health and safety training. You are shown the correct ways of lifting, bending and methods of safe loading/unloading. There may be short courses offered by your employer on new or different types of cargo and equipment.

Similar programmes exist for marine and passenger operatives. S/NVQs at level 2 in port operations, marine operations (ports) and stevedoring are available. Supervision of port operations at level 3 is also available. There may also be funding for apprenticeships in port operations for 16-24 year olds. Marine operatives are normally required to achieve sea survival, fire fighting and boat handling certificates.

Mature applicants need to be physically fit for this job and have plenty of stamina. Mechanical skills and experience of driving LGVs, cranes and lift-trucks, is particularly welcomed.

Government training opportunities, such as apprenticeships, may be available in your area. You can also gain recognition of previous experience through Accreditation of Prior Learning or by working towards relevant S/NVQs. Contact your local careers office, Jobcentre Plus, Next Step service or Learning and Skills Council (LSC)/Local Enterprise Company (LEC) for details of training schemes.

Opportunities and Pay

The UK commercial ports industry is the largest in Europe with over 120 ports. Most are in the south-east and east of England. As ports have become more mechanised, there is an increased demand for crane operators and forklift truck drivers. Port operatives are employed by port authorities or private cargo handling companies. It is possible to progress to become a foreman/woman, supervisor and into management areas. There are lists of major port employers on the websites of the British Ports Association and Associated British Ports.

Pay varies according to location and employer, but starting salaries for stevedores are likely to be around £12k a year, rising to over £18k with skills and experience. You may earn as much as £35k a year with bonuses and overtime pay. You receive a skills allowance payment for operating equipment such as large cranes.

Health

You need to be physically fit for this job and employers usually require you to have a medical test. Normal colour vision is required.

Skills and Qualities

ability in one or more languages, able to follow instructions, aptitude for teamwork, enjoy working outdoors, head for heights, honest, methodical, reliable, safety conscious

Relevant Subjects

Retail and distribution

Further Information

AGCAS: Transport and Logistics (Job Sector Briefing) (AGCAS) - www.prospects.ac.uk

Apprenticeship Schemes (National Apprenticeship Service) - www.apprenticeships.org.uk

Associated British Ports - www.abports.co.uk

British Ports Association - www.britishports.org.uk

Foundation Learning (QCDA) - www.qcda.gov.uk

Port Skills & Safety (Port Skills and Safety) - www.portskillsandsafety.co.uk

Skills for Logistics - sector skills council for freight logistics industries - www.skillsforlogistics.org

Addresses

Port Skills and Safety
4th Floor Carthusian Court, 12 Carthusian Street,
London EC1M 6EZ
Phone: +44 (0)20 7260 1790
Web: www.portskillsandsafety.co.uk

UK Major Ports Group (UKMPG)
4th Floor, Carthusian Court, 12 Carthusian Street,
London EC1M 6EZ
Phone: +44 (0)20 7260 1785
Web: www.ukmajorports.org.uk

Similar Jobs

Construction Plant Operative, Crane Operator, Lift Truck Operative, Merchant Navy Deck Rating, Rail Transport Station Operative, Warehouse Worker

Post Office Counter Clerk

also known as: Post Office Customer Service Adviser

CRCI:Retail Sales and Customer Services
CLCI:CAM — Job Band: 1 to 2

Job Description

Post office counter clerks work at a counter in a post office outlet offering help and advice to customers on the products and services offered by the Royal Mail Group. Daily tasks may include dealing with pension and benefit payments, sales of stamps and postal orders, TV licences and renewals. Also deal with passport applications, savings accounts, vehicle tax disc renewals and over-the-counter banking services, such as cash withdrawals and payment of cheques. Other services include foreign exchange transactions, health and travel insurance, selling and payments of national lottery tickets, and processing of customer payments for electricity, telephone, gas and water.

Also weigh letters and parcels and assist people with the completion of forms, such as passport applications and road tax. Keep accurate records, using a computerised system, and make sure the cash balances at the end of the day.

Work Details

Work a five-day week, Monday to Friday, and a Saturday morning on a rota basis. You usually sit or stand behind a counter which is screened for security. You meet and serve members of the public. Sometimes the post office is very busy and you have to be able to work quickly without making mistakes. There is paperwork to complete and money to be counted and checked.

Qualification

• England, Wales and Northern Ireland

Band 1: No specific formal qualifications are required, but applicants must pass an aptitude test covering basic numeracy skills and a selection interview, which assesses communication skills. However, some GCSEs (A-D grades) are useful, especially maths and English, or equivalent.

Band 2: Some GCSEs (A*-C) such as English and maths or equivalent, are often preferred.

• Scotland

Band 1: No specific formal qualifications are required, but applicants must pass an aptitude test covering basic numeracy skills and a selection interview, which assesses communication skills. However, some S grades at any level are useful, especially maths and English, or similar.

Band 2: Some S grades (1-3) such as English and maths or similar, are often preferred.

Adult Qualifications

Formal qualifications are not usually required, though you need to pass an aptitude test, covering basic numeracy skills, and a selection interview, which assesses communication skills.

Work Experience

Relevant work or voluntary experience can equip you with skills that you can use in the future and add to your CV. There are often opportunities available for voluntary work which provide experience of working with people. Any retail experience such as Saturday or holiday employment is also relevant.

Entry and Training

Applicants for this job need to pass an aptitude test covering basic numeracy skills and attend a selection interview, which assesses communication skills. You can also become a counter clerk after working as a retail assistant in a Post Shop. Training is on the job and at a local training centre. Initial training lasts for four weeks, two of which are spent as a trainee in a post office. Background training includes the use of a computer, accounting, benefits payments, customer care, and the issuing of legal documents, such as licences and passports. You learn about the many products and services the Royal Mail Group offers to its customers. Short courses are also available to update skills when systems change.

S/NVQs are available at level 3 in customer service and level 2 in retail skills. Relevant training programmes, including apprenticeship schemes, may be available in your area. There is a specific apprenticeship in mail services that covers the collection, processing and delivery of mail. Advanced apprenticeships leading to qualification at level 3 can be a route into higher education. A Diploma/Welsh Baccalaureate in retail business may also be available in your area.

Mature applicants with relevant previous experience are welcome. Some retail, office or financial work experience is an advantage.

Opportunities and Pay

The Post Office is part of the Royal Mail Group that operates post offices all over the UK. Some post offices are run by small business owners who run it as a franchise. Vacancies are usually advertised locally and on the Post Office website, and vary from region to region. Job opportunities are expected to decrease over the next few years due to the closure of many smaller offices and the increasing automation of services. However, there is still a need for computer-literate staff. Part-time and seasonal opportunities may arise.

Once you have experience you can apply for promotion to assistant branch manager, supervisor, manager, or other jobs in administration at regional headquarters. Those with management potential may have the opportunity to study for accountancy or management qualifications.

Pay varies depending on location. However, salaries range from £12k-£19k a year.

Skills and Qualities

able to get on with all kinds of people, accurate, cash handling skills, customer service skills, good communication skills, good written English, honest, IT skills, methodical, numeracy skills

Relevant Subjects

Business and accounting, Mathematics

Further Information

Diplomas (Foundation, Higher and Advanced) - http://yp.direct.gov.uk/diplomas

Post Office Ltd - www.postoffice.co.uk

Royal Mail Group plc - www.royalmailgroup.com

Skillsmart Retail - www.skillsmartretail.com/SR/Careers/Home/default.aspx

Welsh Baccalaureate - www.wbq.org.uk

▶Working in retail & customer services (2008) (Babcock Lifeskills) - www.babcock-lifeskills.com/

Similar Jobs

Bank Officer, Building Society Officer, Customer Services Adviser, Postal Worker, Retail Assistant

Postal Worker

also known as: Postal Delivery Worker, Postman/Postwoman

CRCI:Transport and Logistics

CLCI:YAT — Job Band: 1 to 2

Job Description

Postal workers are responsible for the collection, sorting and daily delivery of mail to homes, shops, business premises etc, within a certain area. They collect the mail from post offices, post boxes and places of work at various times of the day. They take it to the sorting office where it is handled by automated machines called IMPs (Integrated Mail Processors). Some items may require sorting and coding by hand. May help to load the sorted mail on to vans or lorries, where it is transported by road and air to its destination. Usually travel around in a van or on a bicycle, but may do a lot of the round on foot. They ensure mail is delivered on schedule.

Work Details

Usually work a basic 40 hours a week. Shift work is normal, including early mornings, weekends and nights. You work at a depot and outdoors, and need to work in all weathers. You have to do a lot of lifting and carrying. Sorting office workers may have to spend a lot of time sitting. Delivery workers expect to walk a 'round' of at least 2-3 miles a day. A uniform and footwear are provided for all seasons. Subsidised meals are also provided.

Qualification

• England, Wales and Northern Ireland

Band 1: No minimum qualifications are required, but you are expected to have a good level of general education. However, some formal/vocational qualifications at any level are useful. Selection is by an aptitude test and interview.

Band 2: Although academic qualifications are not specified for this job, it is an advantage to have some GCSEs (A*-C) in subjects that include English and maths, or equivalent.

• Scotland

Band 1: No minimum qualifications are required, but you are expected to have a good level of general education. However, some formal/vocational qualifications at any level are useful. Selection is by an aptitude test and interview.

Band 2: Although academic qualifications are not specified for this job, it is an advantage to have some S grades (1-3) in subjects that include English and maths, or similar.

Adult Qualifications

Generally, you are expected to have the minimum entry qualifications, which can vary, though for some jobs, no formal qualifications are required. However, you are expected to have relevant experience. All applicants must pass an aptitude test and an interview.

Work Experience

Any work experience can equip you with skills that you can use in the future and add to your CV. This can either be unpaid or voluntary or holiday/part-time work that you have organised yourself.

Entry and Training

Royal Mail offers training, including an 18-month apprenticeship programme for 16-24 year olds which includes the NVQ in mail services at level 2. All entrants have to pass a written aptitude test and an interview. Trainees of all ages spend some time at a Royal Mail Training Centre to learn the delivery and sorting process, how other mail operations work, and have on-the-job training before progressing to a job as a postal worker. Training may involve short courses. Parcelforce Worldwide has similar training schemes for their parcel handlers, sorters and drivers. The Royal Mail and Parcelforce Worldwide provide driver training for many employees. A driving licence is useful.

Several bulk mail companies in the private sector may also offer similar training opportunities. Training programmes, including apprenticeship schemes, may be available in your area. Advanced apprenticeships leading to qualification at level 3 can also be a route into higher education. An S/NVQ in mail services is available at level 2.

Mature entry is welcome and previous experience in working with the general public or driving, delivery or warehouse work, is an advantage. You may have to pass a medical examination and the upper age limit for employment by Royal Mail is currently 65. It is also important to have good reading skills and to be physically fit. Previous relevant experience can be put forward as evidence of competence through the Accreditation of Prior Learning scheme.

Opportunities and Pay

Royal Mail Group Ltd employs over 200,000 staff in its 3 branches, Post Office Ltd., Parcelforce Worldwide and Royal Mail. There are opportunities throughout the country including apprenticeships, and recruitment is usually via local sorting offices. There are often more applicants than vacancies but staff turnover is high so the Royal Mail are always recruiting, particularly for part time and temporary employees. Check with local Royal Mail or Parcelforce Worldwide for details of vacancies.

After a probationary period of six months, you can gain promotion to a higher grade and after one year of satisfactory service, it is possible to apply for promotion as a supervisor or manager. There are opportunities to move into parcel delivery, courier work and post office counter work. Similar opportunities exist in private sector business postal services that handle bulk mail. Temporary seasonal work is usually available at Christmas.

Pay varies, depending on the employer and location. As a guide, post room assistants earn around £15k a year, rising with experience to around £20k a year. Overtime pay is normal and there are extra payments for unsociable hours, driving duties and weekend work. Other benefits include paid holiday and subsidised meals.

Health

You must have a good standard of general fitness.

Skills and Qualities

able to get on with all kinds of people, able to work both on your own and in a team, good memory, health & safety awareness, honest, literacy and numeracy skills, reliable, responsible attitude, time management skills

Relevant Subjects

English

Further Information

Royal Mail Group (Royal Mail Group plc) - www.royalmailgroup.com

Skills for Logistics - sector skills council for freight logistics industries - www.skillsforlogistics.org

Similar Jobs

Courier, Meter Reader, Post Office Counter Clerk, Van Driver: Sales, Warehouse Worker

Pre-school Supervisor/Worker

also known as: Early Years Worker, Nursery Assistant, Pre-school Leader

CRCI:Social Work and Counselling Services

CLCI:KEB Job Band: 1 to 2

Job Description

Pre-school supervisors/workers look after groups of children, usually aged from three to five years old, at a pre-school group or day nursery. Aim to provide a stimulating learning environment and play activities to develop children's skills and how they express themselves. Set up safe and creative indoor and outdoor play areas, as well as areas for story telling and 'quiet' times. Encourage them to join in planned activities such as music, singing, games, and story telling.

They set out different materials for the children to use, such as sand, paints, paper and toys. Help them to recognise letters, figures and basic words. Through educational play, they help children to learn how to mix with others, how to listen and follow instructions, and to do practical tasks, including the safe use of scissors, or perhaps dressing themselves in outdoor clothing. Deal with any emergencies that arise and reports any accidents or injury to a parent, carer or guardian.

They help prepare the child for primary school, write reports on their progress and attend team meetings to plan the development of those in their care. Some day nurseries care for babies and toddlers too.

Work Details

Playgroups can be set up in all sorts of places such as community centres, church halls or schools and sometimes you take the children outdoors to play. Pre-school workers often have assistants to help them. You may also work with children who have special needs. Work with children may be noisy and messy as you are looking after, teaching and organising them, and making sure they are safe. Part of your job is talking to parents about their children.

Qualification

- **England, Wales and Northern Ireland**

Band 1: No qualifications are needed, but some GCSEs or equivalent are helpful.

Band 2: Some employers may ask for a few GCSEs or equivalent.

- **Scotland**

Band 1: No qualifications are needed, but some S grades or similar are helpful.

Band 2: Some employers may ask for a few S grades or similar.

Adult Qualifications

No minimum qualifications are specified but voluntary work with children to gain experience can be helpful.

Work Experience

Relevant work or voluntary experience can equip you with skills to use in the future and add to your CV. There are often opportunities available for voluntary work that provide experience of work with early years children.

Entry and Training

You must be at least 18 to train as a pre-school supervisor/worker. All staff are encouraged to gain relevant qualifications. Many applicants have previous experience in working with children. You need to have an enhanced Criminal Records Bureau (CRB)/ Disclosure Scotland check. Knowledge of first aid is helpful. The Pre-school Learning Alliance awards qualifications at a number of colleges and education centres throughout the country. Courses are usually part time, but there are also some full-time courses and distance-learning programmes.

Qualifications such as CACHE level 1 - getting started in a pre-school setting, CACHE level 2 - certificate in pre-school practice (CPP) and CACHE level 3 - diploma in pre-school practice (DPP), are available. Vocational qualifications in children's care, learning and development at levels 2-4 and playwork at levels 2-4 are also available.

Mature applicants are welcome and many have previous experience and/or qualifications of work with young children. Relevant courses are usually part time, but there are also some full-time courses and distance-learning programmes.

Opportunities and Pay

Pre-schools are found in most places in the UK. You can be employed by a private or state run pre-school, nursery or playgroup, a voluntary organisation, or a local authority. There are opportunities to work part time. Promotion is possible in larger organisations and the experience is useful for those hoping to train for other work with children. With experience and qualifications you can also set up your own playgroup, pre-school or nursery and be self-employed.

Pay varies depending on location and employer. Supervisors/ leaders can earn between £14k-£20k a year, but most pre-school workers are paid an hourly rate, starting at the National Minimum Wage.

Health
You have to be fit to do this job.

Skills and Qualities
calm, creative flair, energetic, enthusiastic, friendly, good organisational skills, imaginative, patient, reliable

Relevant Subjects
English, Health and social care, Psychology

Further Information
First and Foremost (Pre-school Learning Alliance) (Pre-school Learning Alliance) - www.pre-school.org.uk

Looking at Learning Together (Pre-school Learning Alliance) (Pre-school Learning Alliance) - www.pre-school.org.uk

Practical Pre-School - www.practicalpreschool.com

▶Working in social care (2010) (Babcock Lifeskills) - www.babcock-lifeskills.com/

Working in the Childcare Sector - how to progress your career (PSLA) (PSLA) - www.pre-school.org.uk/documents/207

Addresses
CACHE: Council for Awards in Children's Care & Education
Apex House, 81 Camp Road, St Albans AL1 5GB
Phone: 0845 347 2123 (UK only)
Web: www.cache.org.uk

Early Years
6c Wildflower Way, Apollo Road, Belfast BT12 6TA
Phone: +44 (0)28 9066 2825
Web: www.early-years.org

Pre-school Learning Alliance
The Fitzpatrick Building, 188 York Way, London N7 9AD
Phone: +44 (0)20 7697 2500
Web: www.pre-school.org.uk

Scottish Pre-school Play Association (SPPA)
21 Granville Street, Glasgow G3 7EE
Phone: +44 (0)141 221 4148
Web: www.sppa.org.uk

Wales Pre-school Providers Association (Wales PPA)
Unit 1, The Lofts 9 Hunter Street,, Cardiff Bay CF10 5GX
Phone: +44 (0)29 2045 1242
Web: www.walesppa.org

Similar Jobs
Au Pair, Childminder, Montessori Teacher, Nursery Worker, School Lunchtime Supervisor, Teaching Assistant

Presenter: Radio & TV
also known as: Broadcast Presenter, Radio Presenter

CRCI:Media, Print and Publishing

CLCI:GAL Job Band: 3 to 5

Job Description
Presenters inform or entertain listeners and viewers on any television or radio network and, increasingly, online. They work on live or pre-recorded programmes and introduce and host on national or regional radio and TV, interviewing guests, reading news bulletins, and linking items between programmes. Presenters work in areas such as chat shows, travel, music, weather, sport, light entertainment, documentaries or quiz programmes. Some may specialise in a particular type, such as current affairs.

Usually discuss the planned programme with a producer. Some presenters may write their own script having researched and rehearsed the item. They work closely with the production team and are responsible for keeping to the planned programme when on air. If working in smaller regional or independent radio stations, they may be required to operate the recording and playback equipment.

Work Details
You work in a studio or out on location. Hours of work may be long and irregular, including early mornings, evenings and weekends. You must enjoy meeting a range of people from all walks of life. When conducting interviews, you have to be able to put people at ease, as some may be nervous, and to react quickly to unplanned events if necessary. You aim to provide information and present facts clearly and concisely, so that they are easy to understand.

Presenters must be able to engage their audience in all circumstances, have the ability to handle stress, and to make quick decisions under pressure. Presenters in radio broadcasting need to have knowledge of technical equipment.

Qualification
• England, Wales and Northern Ireland
Band 4: For HND, Diploma of Higher Education or foundation degree: 1-2 A levels and some GCSEs (A*-C) usually including English and maths, or equivalent.

Band 5: For degree courses: 2-3 A levels and some GCSEs (A*-C) usually including English or equivalent qualifications. Exact requirements depend on the degree you take.

• Scotland
Band 4: For entry to SQA higher national and professional development awards, usually 2-3 H grades and some S grades (1-3), including English and maths, or similar qualifications. Exact subjects depend on the course to be studied.

Band 5: For degree courses: 3-5 H grades and some S grades (1-3), usually including English or similar. Exact requirements depend on the degree you take.

Degree Information
There are limited specific degrees in broadcast journalism, but degrees in subjects such as communication studies, media studies, journalism, politics, international relations and drama/theatre studies are useful. Postgraduate courses are also available.

Adult Qualifications
Entry requirements may be relaxed for adults applying for higher education courses. Access or foundation courses give adults without qualifications a route onto degree courses.

Work Experience
Entry to this career is highly competitive and it is essential that you have some relevant work or voluntary experience before applying. Time spent with a national or regional television company, a large or independent film company, or in hospital or student radio is an advantage. Check the Hospital Broadcasting Association and Community Media Association websites for information.

Entry and Training
There are no formal entry routes and there is much emphasis on having the right personality, work experience and skills. Many presenters come from a journalism background, while others start their career as an actor, musician or DJ, or have extensive knowledge of a specific area such as sport or natural history. Some have gained experience as a runner in the broadcast industry and worked their way into the job. There is stiff competition for places and it is difficult for anyone to enter who does not have relevant practical experience. A showreel or DVD of your work is useful.

Most entrants have an HND or degree. To follow a broadcast journalist route, there is a wide variety of degree/postgraduate training accredited by the Broadcast Journalism Training Council (BJTC). The BBC offers training schemes for broadcast journalists, which provide useful background and experience. Drama school training is useful preparation though for most, training is on the job.

There are also many specialist courses available from private trainers, but these can be very expensive and you need to be sure they cover your training needs. Contact Skillset, the sector skills council for audio-visual industries, for information on training routes and courses.

A Diploma/Welsh Baccalaureate may be available in your area in creative and media. This can be a useful introduction to this type of career as you gain practical experience while studying. See the diplomas website or Skillset for further information. Cyfle (Wales) also offers a range of training courses for new entrants to the industry and professional development for those already employed.

Mature entrants are often those who have had previous and successful careers as journalists, politicians, sports personalities or celebrities. It is difficult to get into this job without some experience in other areas of radio or television work and younger presenters may be preferred for training and for young people's and children's programmes. A broadcasting background in any capacity, including work as a researcher/assistant producer, is an advantage.

Opportunities and Pay
This is one of the most sought-after jobs in broadcasting. Opportunities are increasing with the growth in cable and satellite channels but jobs are rarely advertised, and posts are given through internal promotion, or to those persistent enough to keep contacting employers and sending their demo tapes. You may have a permanent contract with a broadcasting company, but many people work freelance, on short-term contracts. There is stiff competition for places and limited job security. Jobs are available mainly in London and the South East, but there are opportunities in local/national radio and TV stations, satellite channels and independent companies in the larger cities throughout the UK.

Work may also be available in the non-broadcast sector, such as training and corporate productions. Many presenters in this sector have been well known in another field, such as journalism, cookery, research, politics, sport, the performing arts, or specialist areas such as science.

Starting salaries for presenters working for the local media range are around £15k a year. With training this can rise to £25k. The most popular and successful presenters can earn much more than £100k a year. Freelance rates can be negotiated in line with the Broadcasting, Entertainment, Cinematographic and Theatre Union (BECTU) guidelines.

Skills and Qualities
able to cope under pressure, aptitude for teamwork, clear speaking voice, good communication skills, good concentration level, good memory, good written English, information handling skills, quick thinking, research skills, self confident, smart appearance

Relevant Subjects
English, Government and politics, Media and communication studies, Performing arts

Further Information
Careers Wales - www.careerswales.com/
Channel 4 - www.channel4.com

Community Media Association (CMA) - www.commedia.org.uk

Cyfle (Wales) - www.cyfle.co.uk

Diplomas (Foundation, Higher and Advanced) - http://yp.direct.gov.uk/diplomas

Hospital Broadcasting Association - www.hbauk.com
Media Circle - www.mediacircle.org

Media Week (weekly) (Haymarket Publishing Ltd) - www.haymarket.com/mediaweek/default.aspx

Skillset - sector skills council for the creative media, fashion and textiles industries - www.skillset.org

Welsh Baccalaureate - www.wbq.org.uk

▶Working in creative & media (2007) (Babcock Lifeskills) - www.babcock-lifeskills.com/

▶Working in English (2007) (Babcock Lifeskills) - www.babcock-lifeskills.com/

▶Working in music (2007) (Babcock Lifeskills) - www.babcock-lifeskills.com/

Addresses
BBC Recruitment Services
Recruitment BBC HR Direct, PO Box 1133, Belfast BT1 9GP
Web: www.bbc.co.uk/jobs

BECTU
(Broadcasting Entertainment Cinematographic and Theatre Union)
373-377 Clapham Road, London SW9 9BT
Phone: +44 (0)207 346 0900
Web: www.bectu.org.uk

Broadcast Journalism Training Council (BJTC)
18 Miller's Close, Rippingale, Nr. Bourne, Lincolnshire PE10 0TH
Phone: +44 (0)1778 440 025
Web: www.bjtc.org.uk

Similar Jobs
Actor, Broadcast Journalist, Broadcast Researcher, DJ, Journalist

Press Officer
also known as: Media Officer

CRCI:Marketing and Advertising
CLCI:OG Job Band: 4 to 5

Job Description
Press officers are responsible for representing a public or private organisation to the media. They usually work in a busy public sector organisation, charity or large corporate company.- and the job involves answering questions from journalists. They write and edit press releases and news articles and deal with telephone or face-to-face enquiries from newspapers, television or magazines. Using knowledge of the employer's operations and communication skills, they provide accurate information and promote the employer's desired image to the media.

Press officers may arrange interviews and encourage media interest for company events such as product launches. They often accompany senior staff to interviews or on official visits. In the private sector they undertake a broader range of activities, such as organising press conferences and large promotional events.

Work Details
Within smaller firms, you are likely to work standard office hours, Monday to Friday, with additional weekend and evening work as required. Hours may be longer with larger firms and more senior press officers may be required to be on call for extended periods. You are probably based primarily in an office, though may need to travel for press conferences and presentations in various locations. You are likely to spend a lot of time on the phone.

Personal presentation is important, particularly when dealing with the public or in television. This job may be pressurised at times, and you need to remain calm and assured. May work in a team, especially if handling large promotional events such as trade fairs or exhibitions.

Qualification
- **England, Wales and Northern Ireland**

Band 4: For HND, Diploma of Higher Education or foundation degree: 1-2 A levels and some GCSEs (A*-C) usually including English and maths, or equivalent.

Band 5: For degree courses: 2-3 A levels and some GCSEs (A*-C) usually including English and maths, or equivalent. Exact requirements depend on the degree you take.

• Scotland

Band 4: For entry to SQA higher national and professional development awards, usually 2-3 H grades and some S grades (1-3), including English and maths, or similar qualifications.

Band 5: For degree courses: 3-5 H grades and some S grades (1-3), including English and maths, or similar qualifications. Exact requirements depend on the degree you take.

Degree Information

Any degree is usually acceptable for this job, but a degree involving communication, such as English, journalism, public relations or media studies is most useful. Postgraduate courses in media-related subjects are available.

Adult Qualifications

Entry requirements may be relaxed for adults applying for higher education courses. Access or foundation courses provide those without the required qualifications a route onto degree courses.

Work Experience

Entry to this job is competitive and it is important that you try to do some relevant work or voluntary experience before applying. Direct experience with public relations or journalism, or advertising and marketing is ideal. Experience of dealing with the public in a busy working environment is also useful. Contact your local council and the Government Communication Network for work placement opportunities.

Entry and Training

Many press officers come from careers in public relations (PR) and entry to these posts is competitive. A degree is an advantage and it is often necessary to have a recognised professional qualification in public relations, journalism or media relations, and relevant IT training. A qualification in a second language can also be an advantage. The Government Communication Network within the Cabinet Office is a network of around 4,000 professional communicators who work in government. These are civil service positions, so you need to pass written assessments and a formal interview, as well as meet the civil service's nationality requirements.

In the private sector, press officers are usually employed by larger organisations and charities that have a public face. Training is on the job, under the supervision of an experienced press officer. Much of the initial training involves learning details about the organisation and how it operates. A position as a press officer may also form part of a journalist's career route towards editorship.

Mature applicants with relevant experience, including public relations or media, have an advantage.

Opportunities and Pay

Most positions are based in large towns and cities. The Government Communication Network (GCN) and local and central government are the largest employers of press officers, and entry is very competitive. Large commercial and industrial companies, charities and colleges and universities often employ press officers, or in some cases teams of press officers. You can progress from small to larger companies or from local to national government. You may progress to senior press officer and be put in charge of a team of officers. Within the GCN you can be promoted to senior government communication posts, with considerable responsibility. You can also progress to become a newspaper or media environment editor.

Pay varies depending on the size of the employer and the region, but starting salaries are around £20k, rising to around £25k-£32k a year with experience. Senior press officers may earn up to £50k a year.

Skills and Qualities

able to get on with all kinds of people, able to withstand criticism, analytical skills, calm, excellent communication skills, good interpersonal skills, good written English, information handling skills, IT skills, negotiating skills

Relevant Subjects

Business and accounting, Economics, English, Media and communication studies, Psychology, Sociology

Further Information

AGCAS: Media (Job Sector Briefing) (AGCAS) - www.prospects.ac.uk

Civil Service - www.civilservice.gov.uk/jobs

Government Communications Network (GCN) - www.civilservice.gov.uk/my-civil-service/networks/professional

Local Government Careers (Improvement and Development Agency) - www.lgcareers.com/publications/

▶Working in creative & media (2007) (Babcock Lifeskills) - www.babcock-lifeskills.com/

▶Working in English (2007) (Babcock Lifeskills) - www.babcock-lifeskills.com/

▶Working in marketing, advertising & PR (2008) (Babcock Lifeskills) - www.babcock-lifeskills.com/

Addresses

Chartered Institute of Public Relations (CIPR)
52-53 Russell Square, London WC1B 4HP
Phone: +44 (0)20 7631 6900
Web: www.cipr.co.uk

Similar Jobs

Advertising Copywriter, Event & Exhibition Organiser, Journalist, Marketing Manager, Public Relations Officer

Print Finisher

also known as: Bookbinder

CRCI:Media, Print and Publishing
CLCI:SAR — Job Band: 1 to 2

Job Description

Print finishers work in the printing industry and operate the machines that sort and trim printed materials and turn them into books, labels, brochures, or cartons. They use a variety of machines that cut, collate, glue, stitch, staple, bind or wrap the finished item. Some machines are automatic or operated by computer. Machines are also used for creasing, indexing, round cornering, numbering and making holes in the pages. They set up or programme the machine, load it with the printed pages and check that the job runs accurately.

May use special machines that create the hard, outer covers for books. Then cover them with cloth fabric and finally fix the pages. May have to drive a forklift truck to move bulky items around.

Work Details

Usually work a 37-39 hr week that may include shifts and some weekend work. You may have to operate a wide variety of different machines and complete a number of different tasks. You work in a printing workshop, where the machines can be noisy and there is a good deal of dust. However, workshop conditions vary and most firms have efficient dust extractors.

You are on your feet most of the day and may have to lift heavy piles of books and papers. There may be a risk of accidents from the machinery. Protective overalls and ear protectors may need to be worn at times.

Qualification

• England, Wales and Northern Ireland

Band 1: No minimum qualifications are required, but you are expected to have a good level of general education. However, some formal/vocational qualifications at any level are useful. Computer studies is also relevant.

Band 2: Employers may expect you to have some GCSEs (A*-C) preferably in English, maths, a science subject, technical subject or equivalent. Computer studies is also useful.

- **Scotland**

Band 1: No minimum qualifications are required but you are expected to have a good level of general education. However, some formal/vocational qualifications at any level are useful. Computer studies is also relevant.

Band 2: Employers may expect you to have some S grades (1-3) preferably in English, maths, a science subject, technical subject or similar. Computer studies is also useful.

Adult Qualifications

Entry requirements vary according to employer but formal qualifications are not always necessary.

Work Experience

Relevant work experience is always useful and can help your chances when applying for jobs or apprenticeships in printing. It can equip you with skills that you can use in the future and add to your CV. Temporary summer jobs may lead to jobs or training places.

Entry and Training

On-the-job training may lead towards work-related qualifications, or training may be combined with day or block-release courses for a BTEC/SQA national award in media production or an ABC diploma in print production. Some courses may be taken prior to employment. Regulations do not allow people under 18 to operate machinery, but you may start training at 16.

A Diploma/Welsh Baccalaureate may be available in your area in creative and media. This can be a useful introduction to this type of career as you gain practical experience while studying. See the diplomas website or Skillset for further information.

The Institute of Paper, Printing and Publishing runs an introductory IP3 certificate course. This is delivered in modular format so students can attend training one day a week, while continuing to work. This course is an introduction to the paper, printing and publishing sector and successful completion earns you an industry recognised qualification.

The British Printing Industries Federation offers short courses in print estimating, processes and technology. Leicester College is the national centre of vocational excellence in print skills and offers a range of courses at NVQ level 2 and 3 and advanced apprenticeship. Print finishers must keep up to date with developments in print technology.

S/NVQs in mechanised print finishing and binding are available at levels 2-3. Training programmes, including apprenticeship schemes, may be available in your area. Advanced apprenticeships leading to qualification at level 3 can be a route into higher education.

The Skills4Print website has comprehensive details of careers in print ranging from technical certificates, NVQs and apprenticeships to print trainee vacancies. They also offer team leader and supervisor training to support career progression. View the Print Careers article for an overview of jobs in this sector.

Mature applicants may be given preference if they work in other parts of the printing industry and wish to retrain.

Opportunities and Pay

Proskills UK is working in collaboration with PrintIT! to improve young people's knowledge and experience of printing in the UK through schools based competitions. The focus is on Year 9 and 10 students studying graphics and product design for their GCSEs. It is also relevant to the creative and media diploma students. See the PrintIT! website for details of the competitions.

The printing industry in the UK employs more than 160,000 people. These jobs are spread over 12,000 companies as employment can be with a small firm producing business cards or letterheads, a medium sized book producer or a large company printing weekly magazines. Jobs are found mainly in towns and cities throughout the country. Promotion to supervisor is possible with larger firms. It helps to become multi-skilled in the different areas of printing as small firms often want one worker to be capable of working on a variety of tasks.

Pay varies but a trainee usually earns around £13k-£16k, rising to £30k a year. This can be increased a lot by shift work and overtime.

Health

This job requires good colour vision for certain areas of work and good eyesight. You need to be physically fit as the job may involve the moving of materials. There may be an allergy risk from glue and other adhesives.

Skills and Qualities

able to follow instructions, able to work both on your own and in a team, attention to detail, health & safety awareness, IT skills, manual dexterity, methodical, meticulous, reliable, technical aptitude

Relevant Subjects

Design and technology, Manufacturing

Further Information

Apprenticeship Schemes (National Apprenticeship Service) - www.apprenticeships.org.uk

Careers in Print (Proskills) - www.prospect4u.co.uk

Diplomas (Foundation, Higher and Advanced)- http://yp.direct.gov.uk/diplomas

Institute of Bookbinding and Allied Trades - www.ibat.org.uk

Jobs in Print - www.jobsinprint.com

Print Week (weekly) (Haymarket) - www.printweek.com/

PrintIT! - www.printit.org.uk

Proskills UK - sector skills council for process and manufacturing industries - www.proskills.co.uk

Skills4Print - www.skills4print.com/

Skillset - sector skills council for the creative media, fashion and textiles industries - www.skillset.org

Addresses

British Printing Industries Federation (BPIF)
Farringdon Point, 29-35 Farringdon Road, London EC1M 3JF
Phone: 0870 240 4085 (UK only)
Web: www.britishprint.com

Institute of Paper, Printing & Publishing (IP3)
Runnymede Malthouse, off Hummer Road, Egham, Surrey TW20 9BD
Phone: 0870 330 8625 (UK only)
Web: www.ip3.org.uk

Leicester College
Freeman Park Campus, Aylestone Road, Leicester, Leicestershire LE2 7 LW
Phone: +44 (0)116 224 2240
Web: www.leicestercollege.ac.uk

Similar Jobs

Bookbinder: Handcraft, Engineering Machine Operative, Engraver, Printer: Machine, Reprographics Assistant

Printer: Machine

also known as: Machine Printer, Print Minder

CRCI:Media, Print and Publishing
CLCI:SAR Job Band: 1 to 2

Job Description

Machine printers set up and work the presses that print words and pictures onto paper, plastic, metal and other materials. They receive plates or blocks with the printed material on them and are told how many copies to make, what colour they should be, etc. Also restock the machine with the correct ink, place the paper or other material to be printed into the press and select the speed, pressure and ink flow, using controls. May take trial copies and adjust the machine if necessary. Then start the printing, controlling the process from a computer and checking constantly for quality.

Also unload the printed material, stack and forward it to the print finisher. Then clean the press for the next job. Printers are responsible for the routine maintenance of the presses.

Work Details

Usually work a 37-39 hr week, possibly doing shifts and some weekend work. You may have to operate different machines and print using various techniques, including lithographic and digital printing. Most modern printing machines are computerised.

You work in a printing workshop, where the machines can be noisy and there is a good deal of dust. Workshop conditions vary and most firms now have efficient dust extractors. You are on your feet most of the day and may have to lift heavy piles of books and papers. There may be a risk of accidents from the machinery. You may need to wear overalls and ear protectors.

Qualification

- **England, Wales and Northern Ireland**

Band 2: For entry to jobs, no minimum qualifications are needed, but it is an advantage to have some GCSEs (A*-C) or equivalent in subjects that include English, maths and science, computing or a technical subject.

- **Scotland**

Band 2: Although academic qualifications are not specified for this job, it is an advantage to have some S grades (1-3) or equivalent in subjects that include English and maths, or science and a technical or computer subject.

Adult Qualifications

Adults with no formal qualifications, but with some experience of the printing industry, may be accepted by some employers.

Work Experience

Relevant work experience is useful and can help your chances when applying for jobs or apprenticeships in the print industry. It can give you skills that you can use in the future and add to your CV. Temporary summer jobs may lead to jobs and training places.

Entry and Training

Applicants must be at least 18 for shift work but you may be able to start your training earlier. Training can be via a full-time diploma in printing, prior to employment, which gives an introduction to all aspects of the print industry. On-the-job training can last up to three years, and usually includes study by day or a block release for an appropriate City & Guilds qualification/S/NVQ at levels 2/3 in machine printing. A relevant BTEC/SQA national award is available which can be taken full or part time. Training programmes, including apprenticeship schemes, may be available in your area. Advanced apprenticeships leading to qualification at level 3 can also be a route into higher education.

A Diploma/Welsh Baccalaureate may be available in your area in creative and media. This can be a useful introduction to this type of career as you gain practical experience while studying. See the diplomas website or Skillset for further information.

The Institute of Paper, Printing and Publishing runs an introductory IP3 certificate course. This is delivered in modular format so students can attend training one day a week, while continuing to work. This course is an introduction to the paper, printing and publishing sector and successful completion earns you an industry recognised qualification.

The British Printing Industries Federation offers short courses in print estimating, processes and technology. Leicester College is the national centre of vocational excellence in print skills and offers a range of courses at NVQ level 2-3 and an advanced apprenticeship. Printers must keep up to date with changes in printing techniques.

The Skills4Print website has comprehensive details of careers in print ranging from technical certificates, NVQs and apprenticeships to print trainee vacancies. They also offer team leader and supervisor training to support career progression. View the Print Careers article for an overview of jobs in this sector.

Previous experience of operating machinery, particularly within the printing industry, is an advantage. Adults may be able to enter this work through a government-funded training programme. Contact your local Connexions or careers office, Jobcentre Plus, Next Step service or Learning and Skills Council (LSC)/Local Enterprise Company (LEC) for details of all training opportunities and schemes, including adult apprenticeships.

Opportunities and Pay

Proskills are working in collaboration with PrintIT! to improve young people's knowledge and experience of printing in the UK through schools based competitions. The focus is on Year 9 and 10 students studying graphics and product design for their GCSEs. It is also relevant to the creative and media diploma students. See the PrintIT! website for details of the competitions.

The printing industry in the UK employs more than 160,000 people. These jobs are spread over 12,000 companies as employment can be with a small firm producing business cards or letterheads, a medium sized book producer or a large company printing weekly magazines. Jobs are mainly in towns and cities in London and the South East, Birmingham, Bristol, Glasgow, Manchester and Leeds. It helps if you become multi-skilled in the different areas of printing as small firms often want one worker to be capable of working on a variety of tasks. Promotion to supervisor is possible and there are opportunities for part-time work. There are good chances to work abroad.

Pay can vary, but trainees usually earn around £15k-£16k a year, rising to £18k-£25k with experience. Many skilled and experienced printers can earn up to £40k a year with overtime and bonuses.

Health

This job requires normal colour vision and good eyesight.

Skills and Qualities

able to work both on your own and in a team, able to work to deadlines, attention to detail, eye for shape/colour, good concentration level, health & safety awareness, IT skills, manual dexterity, meticulous, practical skills, technical aptitude

Relevant Subjects

Design and technology, Manufacturing

Further Information

Apprenticeship Schemes (National Apprenticeship Service) - www.apprenticeships.org.uk

Careers in Print (Proskills) - www.prospect4u.co.uk

Diplomas (Foundation, Higher and Advanced)- http://yp.direct.gov.uk/diplomas

Jobs in Print - www.jobsinprint.com
Print Week (weekly) (Haymarket) - www.printweek.com/
PrintIT! - www.printit.org.uk
Proskills UK - sector skills council for process and manufacturing industries - www.proskills.co.uk
Skills4Print - www.skills4print.com/
Skillset - sector skills council for the creative media, fashion and textiles industries - www.skillset.org
Training Schemes - www.direct.gov.uk/en/educationandlearning

Addresses

British Printing Industries Federation (BPIF)
Farringdon Point, 29-35 Farringdon Road, London EC1M 3JF
Phone: 0870 240 4085 (UK only)
Web: www.britishprint.com

Institute of Paper, Printing & Publishing (IP3)
Runnymede Malthouse, off Hummer Road, Egham, Surrey TW20 9BD
Phone: 0870 330 8625 (UK only)
Web: www.ip3.org.uk

Leicester College
Freeman Park Campus, Aylestone Road, Leicester, Leicestershire LE2 7 LW
Phone: +44 (0)116 224 2240
Web: www.leicestercollege.ac.uk

Similar Jobs

Engineering Machine Operative, Print Finisher, Printing Administrator, Reprographics Assistant

Printing Administrator

also known as: Production Planner - Printing

CRCI:Media, Print and Publishing
CLCI:SAR

Job Band: 3 to 4

Job Description

Printing administrators are responsible for organising the various aspects of printing, as well as specialist administration of a printing company, whether in manufacturing processes or in a copy shop. Tasks can include scheduling workloads, quality control, estimating or buying, or marketing and sales. Depending on the size and type of organisation, additional elements of the role can include checking product specifications and making necessary adjustments, liaising with other departments and customers and attending meetings. May negotiate with suppliers of all materials used in the printing process. May also deal with technical difficulties that occur with the printing techniques and processes.

Administrators analyse problems, provide solutions to improve efficiency, and are involved in development of new business opportunities. They may be responsible for in-house training, including work-based training towards qualifications for new staff, and the continuing development and training of existing staff.

Work Details

Usually work a 37-40 hr week that may include shifts and weekend work. You work in an office, and in industrial premises or a workshop, where conditions can be noisy and dusty, though computerisation and high technology have improved work environments. Work can be pressurised as, with improvements in technology and printing processes, deadlines may be tighter.

Qualification

• England, Wales and Northern Ireland

Band 3: For entry: at least 4 GCSEs (A*-C) usually including maths, English, art/science and a technical subject, or equivalent. Subjects may vary according to the job.

Band 4: For HND, Diploma of Higher Education or foundation degree: 1-2 A levels and some GCSEs (A*-C) usually including English, maths and science, or equivalent qualification. Check individual prospectuses.

• Scotland

Band 3: For entry: usually at least four S grades (1-3) usually including maths, English, art/science and a technical subject, or similar. Subjects may vary according to the job.

Band 4: For entry to SQA higher national and professional development awards, usually 2-3 H grades and some S grades (1-3), including English, maths and science, or similar qualifications. Entry requirements vary so check prospectuses carefully.

Adult Qualifications

Adults with relevant experience may have entry requirements waived. Check with individual institutions.

Work Experience

Relevant work or voluntary experience is useful and improves your chances in application for entry to this job. Direct experience in the printing industry, work on a local newspaper or in free press production is helpful. Work involving accounts and purchasing is also useful.

Entry and Training

Some may enter this work following experience in printing production as a print operator in machine printing, origination or print finishing. Some may choose to do a relevant full-time courses prior to entry. There are relevant qualifications including S/NVQs, City & Guilds and full or part-time HNC/HNDs. The University of the Arts, London (London College of Communication) offers a range of relevant courses in printing, including the ABC diploma in print production. Leeds City College and Leicester College are national centres of vocational excellence in print skills and offer a range of courses.

A Diploma/Welsh Baccalaureate may be available in your area in creative and media. This can be a useful introduction to this type of career as you gain practical experience while studying. See the diplomas website or Skillset for further information.

The Institute of Paper, Printing and Publishing (IP3) offers an industry accredited foundation certificate covering basic knowledge of the industry. Successful completion of the certificate provides automatic membership of the Institute. The British Printing Industries Federation also offers short courses, part time and distance-learning courses.

Relevant foundation degrees are available in printing and publishing production, or in print media. These offer a bridge to a final year of an appropriate degree. An S/NVQ is available in print administration at level 3. This covers estimating, production, purchasing, health and safety and customer accounts. Training programmes, including apprenticeship schemes, may be available in your area. Advanced apprenticeships leading to qualification at level 3 can also be a route into higher education.

The Independent Print Industries Association (iPIA) has details of upcoming seminars and exhibitions on their website. They also offer training courses on integrating digital printing methods, covering areas such as technology, marketing and sales. Visit the website for details. Similarly, the YMP runs training weekends and conferences to support the development of those already working in the industry.

The Skills4Print website has comprehensive details of careers in print ranging from technical certificates, NVQs and apprenticeships to print trainee vacancies. They also offer team leader and supervisor training to support career progression. View the Print Careers article for an overview of jobs in this sector.

Mature entrants with either experience of the printing production process or of supervising and estimating in another industry may have an advantage.

Opportunities and Pay
The printing industry in the UK employs more than 160,000 people. These jobs are spread over 12,000 companies as employment can be with a small firm producing business cards or letterheads, a medium sized book producer or a large company printing weekly magazines. Jobs are available in larger towns and cities, mainly concentrated in London and the South East, Nottingham, Leeds, Birmingham, Glasgow, Manchester and Bristol. Administrators form a small percentage of the industry. Promotion to departmental/general management is possible, particularly with further training and qualifications.

Proskills UK is working in collaboration with PrintIT! to improve young people's knowledge and experience of printing in the UK through schools based competitions. The focus is on Year 9 and 10 students studying graphics and product design for their GCSEs. It is also relevant to the creative and media diploma students. See the PrintIT! website for details of the competitions.

Pay varies depending on location and type/size of employer though trainees may start at around £19k-£25k a year. With experience and increased responsibility, salaries can be as much as £50k a year.

Health
There may be a risk of allergy from skin irritants and this job requires normal colour vision.

Skills and Qualities
able to manage a budget and keep records, able to take responsibility, good communication skills, good interpersonal skills, good organisational skills, imaginative, IT skills, leadership qualities, numeracy skills, problem-solving skills, technical aptitude

Relevant Subjects
Art and Design, Chemistry, Design and technology, English, ICT/ Computer studies, Manufacturing, Mathematics, Media and communication studies, Physics, Science

Further Information
Apprenticeship Schemes (National Apprenticeship Service) - www.apprenticeships.org.uk

Careers in Print (Proskills) - www.prospect4u.co.uk

Diplomas (Foundation, Higher and Advanced) - http://yp.direct.gov.uk/diplomas

Independent Print Industries Association (IPIA) - www.ipia.org.uk

Jobs in Print - www.jobsinprint.com

Print Week (weekly) (Haymarket) - www.printweek.com/

PrintIT! - www.printit.org.uk

Proskills UK - sector skills council for process and manufacturing industries - www.proskills.co.uk

Skillset - sector skills council for the creative media, fashion and textiles industries - www.skillset.org

YMP (Print industry) - www.ymp.org.uk

Addresses
British Printing Industries Federation (BPIF)
Farringdon Point, 29-35 Farringdon Road, London EC1M 3JF
Phone: 0870 240 4085 (UK only)
Web: www.britishprint.com

Institute of Paper, Printing & Publishing (IP3)
Runnymede Malthouse, off Hummer Road, Egham, Surrey TW20 9BD
Phone: 0870 330 8625 (UK only)
Web: www.ip3.org.uk

Leeds City College
Cookridge Street, Leeds, West Yorkshire LS2 8BL
Phone: +44 (0)113 297 6300
Web: www.leedscitycollege.ac.uk

Leicester College
Freeman Park Campus, Aylestone Road, Leicester, Leicestershire LE2 7 LW
Phone: +44 (0)116 224 2240
Web: www.leicestercollege.ac.uk

University of the Arts - London College of Communication
Elephant & Castle, London SE1 6SB
Phone: +44 (0)20 7514 6569
Web: www.lcc.arts.ac.uk

Similar Jobs
Print Finisher, Printer: Machine, Production Manager, Quality Assurance Controller/Inspector

Prison Governor
CRCI:Security and Armed Forces
CLCI:MAD Job Band: 2 to 5

Job Description
Prison governors are involved in the administration and management of a prison service or unit (such as a young offender institution) overseeing both staff and inmates. Duties vary depending on the grade of governor/manager but main responsibilities include security, welfare, development and rehabilitation of prisoners. May organise the training and supervision of staff. Keep records of prisoners' behaviour and progress, and organise educational, leisure and work activities, counselling and parole.

Must be sensitive to the needs of staff and offenders and be able to control unrest. Carry out risk assessment on all categories of prisoner. Liaise with other professionals such as social workers, chaplains, forensic psychologists, probation officers, doctors and other medical staff.

Work Details
Usually work a basic 39 hr week (37 in Scotland) on a shift basis, including evenings, weekends and public holidays. May work in a prison, an open prison, a young offenders' institution or a remand centre. Mainly sit at a desk in an office. Also spend time walking around the prison to maintain frequent contact with the prisoners and ensuring that everything is running smoothly. There are times when some prisoners may become abusive, aggressive or violent so you need to be able to cope with such situations.

You must be sensitive to the everyday needs of staff and inmates and make responsible decisions. Governors are not uniformed officers and wear everyday business clothes.

Qualification
• England, Wales and Northern Ireland
Band 3: For management training after entry and experience as a prison officer: no set entry requirements, but at least 4 GCSEs including English and maths are useful.

Band 4: For management training after entry and experience as a prison officer: 1-2 A levels, a BTEC national award or equivalent is an advantage.

Band 5: For degree: usually 2-3 A levels and some GCSEs (A*-C). The exact requirements depend on the degree you take.

• Scotland
Band 3: For management training after entry and experience as a prison officer: no set entry requirements, but at least four S grades including English and maths are useful.

Band 4: For management training after entry and experience as a prison officer: 2-3 H grades and/or an SQA national award or similar are an advantage.

Band 5: For degree: usually 3-5 H grades and some S grades (1-3) depending on the degree taken.

Prison Governor

Degree Information
An honours degree in any discipline is acceptable, though criminology, psychology, social policy and administration, public services, social work, youth and community studies, law, sociology and business administration give a useful background.

Adult Qualifications
Graduates of any discipline and with at least three years' management experience may apply for entry to the prison service as unit managers. Entry requirements may be relaxed for adults applying for higher education courses. Access or foundation courses give adults without qualifications a route on to degree courses.

Work Experience
Employers may prefer candidates who have relevant work or voluntary experience such as social work, community work or time spent with a youth offending team or in a youth centre. Hospital volunteering can also provide relevant experience. This demonstrates an interest in helping people.

Entry and Training
Entry to governor grades is either through the intensive development scheme (IDS) for graduates. The diploma/welsh baccalaureate in public services may be a useful background for this career but check additional and specialist learning requirements carefully. It is also possible to enter through the two-year senior prison manager programme for those with four or more years' experience at senior prison officer level, who demonstrate management potential and ability. See the job article: Prison Officer, for full details of general entry requirements to the Prison Service.

A graduate that joins the IDS is first required to undertake training as a prison officer and then work as a uniformed prison officer for up to 12 months. Then, as a senior prison officer, you are responsible for a group of staff and become a trainee operations manager. At each stage of your training, you are supported by the leadership and management development programme, with on and off-the-job mentors. Within two and a half to three years of joining the IDS, you can become the head of a busy unit or function within a prison or offenders' institution. At all stages of promotion you need to attend a job simulation assessment centre.

In Scotland there are two similar ways to become a prison governor; promotion through the ranks after joining as a prison officer, or through direct entry, which usually requires a degree and substantial management experience. Direct entry requires you to follow a two-year programme in which you work in a prison as a unit manager whilst training. Governors work at different levels of responsibility, ranging from Governor Grade 5 to Governor Grade 1, which is the most senior grade. Your work involves training and supervising staff, and arranging work and leisure activities for prisoners. A Governor Grade 5 might work in all parts of the prison and have a lot of contact with prisoners. Governor Grade 4 staff have additional responsibilities, while those at Governor Grade 3 may have overall responsibility for a small prison. Governors in larger establishments are at Grade 2 or 1.

Northern Ireland has its own requirements and is also reducing its staffing levels. See the NI Prison Service website for further information. The contract companies that run private prison establishments have a direct entry route for their management level staff and their own entry requirements.

Mature entrants are required to pass the standard entry tests and medical examinations. Prison officers can become governors through experience and promotion through the grades. Entrants are also welcomed from the police, civil service, or the armed forces, and others who have relevant managerial experience. There are also opportunities for specialists, including psychologists and instructors.

Opportunities and Pay
The National Offender Management System (NOMS) graduate programme offers you the opportunity to progress and develop leadership qualities within the prison service. Within a three year period you can develop leadership qualities and operational expertise needed for working in a challenging prison environment.

Prison governors are traditionally employed by a Home Office Agency, though some prisons have 'contracted out' and are run by private companies. Approximately 1000 prison governors/managers work in 157 prisons and units throughout the UK. These are located in both rural and urban locations all over the UK. A few governors work in administration at Prison Service Headquarters or in training at Prison Service colleges. Promotion is based on merit and governors must be prepared to move to any establishment within the Prison Service. Experienced governors may choose to work as an area manager or operational director with responsibility for several establishments.

Prison governors are paid on a scale of seven increments that reflects their experience and level of responsibility. Managers (governors) start earning from £23k-£43k a year. Senior managers (governors) are paid £44k-£78k a year. There are additional payments for 'required hours' and for locality payments.

Health
You have to pass a medical test and have good hearing and good eyesight. Glasses or lenses may be acceptable.

Skills and Qualities
able to cope under pressure, able to inspire confidence, able to manage people, able to understand other people's problems, good communication skills, good organisational skills, IT skills, leadership qualities, perceptive, sound judgement

Relevant Subjects
English, Law, Psychology, Sociology

Further Information
Becoming a Prison Officer (HM Prison Service) (HM Prison Service) - www.hmprisons.gov.uk/

Diplomas (Foundation, Higher and Advanced) http://yp.direct.gov.uk/diplomas

Northern Ireland Prison Service - www.niprisonservice.co.uk

Prison Service News (Magazine, HMPS) (HM Prison Service) - www.hmprisonservice.gov.uk/prisoninformation/prisonservice-magazine

Scottish Prison Service Recruitment (Scottish Prison Service) - www.sps.gov.uk/

Skills for Justice - sector skills council for the UK justice system - www.skillsforjustice.com

Welsh Baccalaureate - www.wbq.org.uk

►Working in police, fire & security (2009) (Babcock Lifeskills) - www.babcock-lifeskills.com/

Addresses
HM Prison Service HQ
Cleland House, Page Street, London SW1P 4LN
Web: www.hmprisonservice.gov.uk

Prison Officers' Association
Cronin House, 245 Church Street, London N9 9HW
Phone: +44 (0)20 8803 0255
Web: www.poauk.org.uk

Scottish Prison Service
Communication Branch Room, 338 Calton House,
5 Redheughs Rigg, Edinburgh EH12 9HW
Phone: +44 (0)131 244 8745
Web: www.sps.gov.uk

Similar Jobs
Army Officer, Police Officer, Prison Officer, Royal Marines Officer, Royal Navy Officer

Prison Officer

CRCI:Security and Armed Forces
CLCI:MAD Job Band: 2 to 3

Job Description

Prison officers are responsible for the secure custody, welfare and development of people in prison, a detention centre and other secure units where people are detained. Keep order and enforce regulations. Patrol buildings and grounds, to ensure a secure environment and carry out searches of cells if required. Meet prisoners when they first arrive and provide them with clothing and details of prison policy. Help with any paperwork such as form filling. Work to reform and rehabilitate offenders back into society.

May help prisoners/offenders to sort out their personal problems, and provide appropriate care and support for those at risk of self harm. Escort prisoners, both inside and outside the prison and supervise them at work, and at leisure. Assist prisoners to learn practical skills, such as horticulture, IT, hairdressing, catering and motor mechanics, or to arrange formal academic study, including distance-learning courses.

May have additional responsibilities as a higher grade prison officer and may supervise other prison officers and oversee their training and development. Liaise with professionals, including doctors, forensic psychologists and social workers.

Work Details

Usually work a basic 39 hr week (37 in Scotland) over a shift cycle, including nights, weekends and public holidays. The work is mostly indoors with occasional outdoor work and you work as part of a team. On some shifts there are long periods when it is very quiet and at other times you are very busy. The work can be stressful and there may be emergencies that require you to act quickly and decisively. You have to cope with a fair amount of verbal abuse and aggression.

People in prisons can be difficult and sometimes dangerous, and aspects of the work can be very unpleasant. You also work with people who are depressed or in need of support.

Qualification

There are no specific entry requirements in England and Wales, but all prison officers have to sit entry tests and assessments. Those with a higher academic entry level, such as a degree, may join the National Offender Management System graduate programme (NOMS). See the Prison Governor job article for details.

• England, Wales and Northern Ireland

Band 2: For entry as a prison officer: no specific entry requirements, but some GCSEs (A*-C), including English and maths are useful.

Band 3: It is an advantage to have at least 4 GCSEs (A*-C) including maths and English or equivalent qualifications.

• Scotland

Band 3: Usually five S grades (1-3) including maths and English or similar qualifications.

Adult Qualifications

There are no specific entry requirements. Those with some experience of engineering, construction or other vocational subjects may specialise as prison instructors.

Work Experience

Relevant work or voluntary experience is always useful and can improve your chances in application for entry to this career. Anything that provides the opportunity to work with the public is always useful.

Entry and Training

You must be aged at least 18 yrs old and up to 62 years in England and Wales, 18-63 in Scotland. In Northern Ireland, there is no recruitment at the moment. There are some nationality and residency requirements, you must not be an undischarged bankrupt.

The diploma/welsh baccalaureate in public services may be a useful background for this career. In England and Wales, there are no specific entry qualifications, but all applicants sit the prison officer selection tests in numeracy and language, and if successful attend a job simulation assessment centre, followed by a medical, and fitness and criminal records check. New officers have eight weeks' basic training. This comprises an initial induction week followed by classroom based learning, practical training, team building exercises and practising realistic prison-based scenarios. During your probationary year working on the job, you are expected to complete work towards NVQ level 3 in custodial care.

In Scotland, five S grades are required for entry. You have one week's induction, followed by a two year training period. Year one is the Officer Foundation Programme which incorporates six weeks college based learning and competence-based training. Year two is the Officer Placement Programme. This covers work-based learning and opportunities to work towards SVQs. You are contractually required to achieve an SVQ in custodial care level 3 by the end of this two year training period. Failure to do so may result in dismissal from the Scottish prison service.

Prison officers also receive in-service training throughout their careers. Special training is available in equality and diversity, anti-bullying and suicide prevention. Once experienced at a senior officer level, there is a chance to undergo management training for governor posts. Those who enter the Prison Service with a degree may follow an intensive development scheme.

Mature applicants are welcomed and particularly those with experience in the armed forces, probation service, police and security work. It is also useful to have practical skills or training in physical education, building trades, engineering, nursing, or similar.

Opportunities and Pay

Currently, there are 157 prisons and units that are located in both rural and urban locations all over the UK. Promotion is through ability and by completing a training programme through the grades of officer to manager/senior manager and governor. Officers must be prepared to be posted to any area of the country. Some prisons have 'contracted out' and are run by private companies who provide their own recruitment methods, grades, promotion and training.

Pay can vary depending on the area of the country in which you work. Depending on entry level, prison officers generally earn from £17k-£25k (£15k-£20k in Scotland), with senior officers earning from £31k a year.

Health

You must have a high standard of physical fitness, good hearing and good eyesight, though glasses or lenses may be acceptable. You have to pass a medical and fitness test.

Skills and Qualities

able to discipline, able to understand other people's problems, alert, aptitude for teamwork, good communication skills, patient, responsible attitude, sense of humour, tolerant, trustworthy

Relevant Subjects

English, Law, Psychology, Sociology

Further Information

Becoming a Prison Officer (HM Prison Service) - www.hmprisons.gov.uk/

Diplomas (Foundation, Higher and Advanced) - http://yp.direct.gov.uk/diplomas

Prison Service News (Magazine, HMPS) (HM Prison Service) - www.hmprisonservice.gov.uk/prisoninformation/

Scottish Prison Service Recruitment (Scottish Prison Service) - www.sps.gov.uk/

Skills for Justice - sector skills council for the UK justice system - www.skillsforjustice.com

Welsh Baccalaureate - www.wbq.org.uk

►Working in police, fire & security (2009) (Babcock Lifeskills) - www.babcock-lifeskills.com/

Addresses

HM Prison Service HQ
Cleland House, Page Street, London SW1P 4LN
Web: www.hmprisonservice.gov.uk

Prison Officers' Association
Cronin House, 245 Church Street, London N9 9HW
Phone: +44 (0)20 8803 0255
Web: www.poauk.org.uk

Scottish Prison Service
Communication Branch Room 338 Calton House
5 Redheughs Rigg, Edinburgh EH12 9HW
Phone: +44 (0)131 244 8745
Web: www.sps.gov.uk

Similar Jobs

Army Soldier, Drug/Alcohol Advice Worker, Ministry of Defence Police Constable, Police Officer, Prison Governor, Security Officer

Private Investigator

CRCI:Security and Armed Forces
CLCI:MAG Job Band: 2 to 5

Job Description

Private investigators carry out investigations for people and for companies. Look into theft, business or insurance fraud, and computer fraud. Give advice to companies on how to make sure that their industrial secrets are not stolen. Carry out checks for firms on staff, clients and job applicants. Provide reports on people's finances and possessions, to show their ability to pay debts. Trace missing persons for parents and other relatives, or search for friends who have lost touch, and also for debtors. Collect photographic and video evidence in personal and matrimonial matters. May have to attend court hearings to present findings.

Research and maintain information on a computer database. May do some administration such as own accounts and tax returns.

Work Details

Working hours are usually irregular, often involving night and weekend work, and you have to spend long hours walking around or sitting. You may need to spend nights away from home. Some work is office based but most of your work is out and about, driving or on foot. You can spend days sitting in a cramped van or be out in all weathers. A driving licence is usually needed. Clients can include industrial companies, lawyers, insurance companies and private individuals.

Duties may include interviewing people and taking statements, and you can come into contact with people who are distressed or angry, aggressive or threatening.

Qualification

There are no set qualifications for this job, though a good standard of education is required. Entrants vary from those with few formal qualifications to those with higher education qualifications, including degrees/postgraduate diplomas, and/or professional qualifications.

Adult Qualifications

There are no set qualifications, though a good standard of education is required. Entrants are from many backgrounds and have a variety of qualifications and/or professional experience.

Work Experience

Relevant work or voluntary experience is always useful and can improve your chances for entry to this career. It may sometimes be possible to do work experience with a private investigator, but other areas to consider include the legal profession and anything involving dealing with the public, particularly in administration and information management.

Entry and Training

Most entrants are mature adults and it is very uncommon for school or college leavers to enter directly. Training is mostly on the job with in-service courses in, for example, surveillance and using technological equipment. The Association of British Investigators and the Institute of Private Investigators run a range of one-day courses on specialist topics. There are also two-day foundation courses for beginners. The Academy of Professional Investigation offers a 12 module level 3 distance-learning course in private investigation (accredited by Edexcel), that covers a wide variety of topics as well as the laws surrounding aspects of the work. Successful completion of the course can earn a Level 3 and Level 4 NVQ in investigation.

There are also relevant courses at national certificate/diploma, foundation degree, degree, and postgraduate level. S/NVQs in intelligence analysis are available at level 3. These cover information evaluation, methodology and intelligence analysis applied to decision making. The Security Industry Authority (SIA) is intending to bring in licensing for private investigators in the near future. See the SIA website for details.

Mature applicants have an advantage for this job and it is often a second career. Employers usually look for people with relevant experience, such as with the police and prison service, armed forces, security, immigration or legal work.

Opportunities and Pay

Private investigators are usually self-employed or work for an agency. Most agencies are found in cities or large towns. There are around 10,000 investigators in the UK, and opportunities are increasing since agencies now take on some work that used to be the responsibility of the police service. Larger agencies have opportunities for experienced investigators to be promoted to senior investigator or team supervisor. It is possible to specialise, including business fraud, fingerprints or industrial counter espionage.

Self-employment is possible or, with experience, you may set up your own agency, though this is initially a costly process due to the purchase of sophisticated equipment or regularly used items such as cameras, camcorders and binoculars. It is possible to work abroad.

It is very difficult to summarise private investigators' earnings, which vary from around £15k-£22k a year, to more than £30k a year depending on whether you work for an agency or are self-employed. Once established, you may earn more than £70k a year. Regional differences apply. Some agencies supply a car or give a car allowance.

Health

You need to fit and healthy as this is a physically active job.

Skills and Qualities

able to report accurately, able to work well on your own, analytical skills, attention to detail, information handling skills, integrity, methodical, numeracy skills, observant, tactful & discreet

Relevant Subjects

Business and accounting, English, ICT/Computer studies, Law, Psychology

Further Information

Academy Newsletter for Private Investigators (API) (API) - www.pi-academy.com

Apprenticeship Schemes (National Apprenticeship Service) - www.apprenticeships.org.uk

British Agents - www.britishagents.com

Private Investigator Magazine (PI Magazine and PImagazine) - www.pimagazine.com

Skills for Security - sector skills council for security industry - www.skillsforsecurity.org.uk/

Why Security? - A Guide to Careers in the Security Industry (Security Industry Authority) - www.the-sia.org.uk

▶Working in police, fire & security (2009) (Babcock Lifeskills) - www.babcock-lifeskills.com/

Addresses

Academy of Professional Investigation (API)
The Priory Syresham Gardens, Haywards Heath, West Sussex RH16 3LB
Phone: +44 (0)1444 441 111
Web: www.pi-academy.com/

Association of British Investigators (ABI)
295/297 Church Street, Blackpool FY1 3PJ
Phone: +44 (0) 1253 297502
Web: www.theabi.org.uk

Institute of Professional Investigators
Claremont House 70-72 Alma Road, Windsor, Surrey SL4 3EZ
Phone: 0870 330 8622 (UK only)
Web: www.ipi.org.uk

Security Industry Authority (SIA)
PO Box 1293, Liverpool L69 1AX
Phone: 0844 892 1025 (UK only)
Web: http://sia.homeoffice.gov.uk/Pages/home.aspx

TASK International Limited
Inkerman House, 3-4 Elwick Road, Ashford, Kent TN23 1PF
Phone: +44 (0)1223 614796
Web: www.task-int.com

World Association of Professional Investigators (WAPI)
212 Piccadilly, London W1J 9HG
Phone: +44 (0)87 09099970
Web: www.wapi.com

Similar Jobs

Civil Service Immigration Officer, Police Financial Investigator, Police Officer, Police Scenes of Crime Officer, Security Officer, Store Detective

Probation Officer

also known as: Criminal Justice Social Worker (Scotland)

CRCI:Social Work and Counselling Services
CLCI:KEB Job Band: 5

Job Description

Probation officers work closely with offenders and offenders' families to challenge and reduce offending behaviour. They work in close co-operation with the law courts, the prison service, police and youth offending teams and other statutory agencies, as well as other voluntary and community organisations. Provide community service, anti-offending behaviour programmes and specialist support services to both adult and young offenders, which aim to stop them committing further offences.

Often attend courts to give independent advice and information of a client's background. Provide reports on people charged with an offence, to help magistrates and judges decide on the sentence they pass in court. Are usually required to provide a pre-sentence report outlining the offence, the personal background details of the accused, the possible risk of re-offending, and if appropriate, the most suitable non-prison sentence.

Probation officers supervise offenders who have been given a community order (community service order in Scotland), a community rehabilitation order (probation order in Scotland), a combined community punishment and rehabilitation order, or a drug treatment and testing order. Suggest suitable ways of dealing with offenders, visit prisoners and their families and supervise those on probation to help solve problems and make changes in their lives.

Work Details

Usually works a basic 37-39 hr week, and may be expected to work irregular hours, including evenings and weekends, though is usually given time off at other times to make up for this. This work is usually based in an office, but you have to travel quite extensively within an agreed area to visit your clients. Your work involves interviewing, observing and assessing people and situations, investigating people's backgrounds, writing reports and providing information to the Courts.

Clients may be aggressive, anxious, negative, resentful, and sometimes there may be a risk of assault. This sort of work is emotionally demanding and often involves making difficult decisions.

Qualification

• England, Wales and Northern Ireland

Band 5: For degree courses and the diploma in probation studies (DipPS): 2-3 A levels and some GCSEs (A*-C) usually including English and maths, or equivalent qualifications. Exact requirements depend on the degree you take.

• Scotland

Band 5: For degree courses: 3-5 H grades and some S grades (1-3), usually including English and maths, or similar qualifications.

Degree Information

Degrees in criminal and community justice or social work are available. Degrees in psychology, sociology, social policy and administration, law, and youth and community studies, give relevant background knowledge, but provide no training advantage. Some social work degree courses include the diploma award and there are relevant postgraduate degrees. It is advisable to contact the appropriate government probation service for details of training routes before embarking on a course.

Adult Qualifications

Some institutions may give exemption from the stated entry qualifications to applicants over 25. Access or foundation courses give adults without qualifications a route on to degree courses. The Open University currently offers social work qualifications, and an extended DipSW programme for candidates with family commitments.

Work Experience

Relevant work or voluntary experience is always useful and improves your chances in application for entry to this job. Consider opportunities to deal with young people, the public in a helping capacity such as youth and community centres, or in the caring professions. Although work experience is not an essential requirement, it demonstrates enthusiasm and commitment. There is often a voluntary work programme coordinated through the prison service. This provides an insight into the work of the prison and probation service.

Entry and Training

Training for probation work differs within the UK. In England and Wales the training of probation officers is currently under review. At present, to become a qualified probation officer you must complete an in-service two-year training programme to gain the

Diploma in Probation Studies (DipPS) awarded by Skills for Justice. Selection for training is by regional probation committees. Candidates must be at least 20, complete a series of rigorous tests, exercises and interviews and pass a Criminal Records Bureau (CRB) check. Emphasis is placed on wider experience and talents, combining on-the-job training with study for the DipPS. The programme combines a BA honours degree in community justice, and an NVQ in community justice at level 4. Some three-year degree courses in social work are combined with the diploma. Check the National Probation Service website for changes to the current training requirements.

In Scotland, probation work is carried out by social workers that are specialists in criminal justice. All trainees are required to hold an honours or postgraduate degree in social work. Students undertaking the degree are required to register with the Scottish Social Services Council and need to have a Disclosure Scotland check. Those wishing to become a probation officer in Northern Ireland follow a similar social work degree programme and must be qualified social workers. Contact the Probation Board for Northern Ireland.

A distance-learning programme is also available. Contact Skills for Justice for local details on the training and qualification programme. There are regional offices throughout the UK. The Open University also offers relevant courses that provide a route into social work training. In England and Wales, the National Offender Management Service (NOMS) brings together the work of the Prison and National Probation Services as a single service to oversee the end-to-end management of offenders. Continuing professional development (CPD) is encouraged throughout your career.

It may be possible to enter as a probation service officer at the age of 20 and work your way up, and there may be apprenticeship schemes in your area involving the NVQ in community justice at level 3. Details are available from Skills for Justice.

Adult entry is encouraged and there is no upper age limit for training. Life experience and maturity are an advantage in probation work. The qualifications required are for all age groups; however, in England & Wales, those who already hold the Diploma in Social Work (DipSW) or the Certificate of Qualification in Social Work (CQSW) may be given the opportunity to study for the Diploma in Probation Studies (DipPS).

Opportunities and Pay

In England and Wales you are employed by the National Probation Service (NPS) which is split into 42 local areas. In Northern Ireland probation work is carried out by the Probation Board for Northern Ireland. In Scotland your employer is a local authority social work department. Promotion to senior posts is possible after gaining experience, but prospects may be limited as there are a small number of higher grade posts. There may be opportunities to teach students in educational establishments or voluntary organisations.

Trainees earn £17k-£19k and when fully qualified, £26k rising to £35k a year. There is an allowance paid for working in or around London.

Skills and Qualities

able to inspire confidence, able to work to deadlines, aptitude for teamwork, emotionally strong, excellent communication skills, good organisational skills, knowledge of the criminal justice system, planning skills, problem-solving skills, sound judgement

Relevant Subjects

English, Law, Psychology, Sociology

Further Information

Careers in Probation (National Probation Service) - www.probation.homeoffice.gov.uk

Criminal Justice System (CJS) - www.cjsonline.gov.uk

National Offender Management Service - www.justice.gov.uk/about/noms.htm

Probation Bulletin (Shaw & Sons) - www.probationbulletin.co.uk

Skills for Justice - sector skills council for the UK justice system - www.skillsforjustice.com

▶Working in advice & counselling (2007) (Babcock Lifeskills) - www.babcock-lifeskills.com/

▶Working in police, fire & security (2009) (Babcock Lifeskills) - www.babcock-lifeskills.com/

Addresses

National Association of Probation Officers (NAPO)
4 Chivalry Road, London SW11 1HT
Phone: +44 (0)20 7223 4887
Web: www.napo.org.uk

National Probation Service
1st Floor Abell House, John Islip Street, London SW1P 4LH
Web: www.probation.homeoffice.gov.uk

Open University (OU)
PO Box 197, Milton Keynes MK7 6BJ
Phone: +44 (0)845 300 6090
Web: http://www3.open.ac.uk

Probation Board for Northern Ireland
80-90 North Street, Belfast BT1 1LD
Phone: +44 (0)28 9026 2400
Web: www.pbni.org.uk

Scottish Social Services Council (SSSC)
Compass House 11 Riverside Drive, Dundee DD1 4NY
Phone: +44 (0)845 60 30 891
Web: www.sssc.uk.com

Similar Jobs

Community Development Worker, Counsellor, Police Officer, Prison Governor, Prison Officer, Probation Service Officer (England & Wales), Social Worker

Probation Service Officer (England & Wales)

also known as: Probation Assistant

CRCI:Social Work and Counselling Services
CLCI:KEB — Job Band: 2 to 3

Job Description

Probation service officers (PSOs) assist and support a probation officer in the criminal justice system, to supervise low risk criminal offenders, before and after they are sentenced. PSOs offer support to offenders so that they can work towards making lifestyle changes. They assist probation officers during court procedures, making sure the pre-sentence reports (PSRs) are available. Help to produce the PSR, which outlines the offence, personal background details of the accused, the possibility of re-offending, and if appropriate, the most suitable non-prison sentence.

May work as part of a specialist team, such as training and education support or victim support. Also maintain case files, supervise low risk offenders, and deliver offending behaviour programmes, including skills for life or drug rehabilitation programmes. Work as the sessional supervisor of volunteers, supporting those who are ordered to work on community service activities. PSOs also help to support the victims of crime and regularly visit prisoners (those with over a 12 month sentence) and their families.

Work in close co-operation with the prison service, police, local authorities and voluntary agencies, youth offending teams, health services, substance misuse/drug services, and the law courts.

Work Details

Usually works a basic 37 hr week that may include shifts that cover evenings and weekends. This work is usually based in an office, but you may have to travel quite extensively within an agreed area to visit your clients, and also to prisons, hostels, courts and day centres. Your work involves assisting at interviews, investigating people's backgrounds, writing reports and providing information.

Clients may be indifferent, aggressive, anxious, negative, resentful, and sometimes there may be a risk of assault. This sort of work is emotionally demanding and often involves making difficult decisions.

Qualification

• England, Wales and Northern Ireland

Band 2: Some employers ask for 5 GCSEs at any level, usually including English and maths, or equivalent qualifications. Relevant work experience is also accepted if an applicant does not have formal educational qualifications. Contact the individual probation service for details.

Band 3: Some employers ask for a minimum of 5 GCSEs (A*-C) usually including English and maths or equivalent qualifications. Relevant work experience is also accepted if an applicant does not have formal educational qualifications. Contact the individual probation service for details.

Adult Qualifications

Those without the minimum educational qualifications may be accepted if they can demonstrate relevant work experience.

Work Experience

Work experience gives you an insight into what you enjoy and don't enjoy about a job or working environment, as well as the opportunity to acquire new skills. It also provides valuable information to add to your CV and improves any future course application and/or your employment prospects. Care work and youth work schemes as a volunteer or paid worker is very useful.

Entry and Training

Entry is usually by application to one of the nine consortia areas of the National Probation Service (NPS). The application process involves interviews, including a short test of an applicant's thinking ability, and a short presentation to reflect a problem-solving exercise. Applicants must declare any spent or unspent convictions, reprimands, warnings, or cautions to an employer if asked. A full UK driving licence is essential. New recruits to the NPS undergo a six week induction training programme. Further training is on the job within the probation consortia that you work for. Ongoing regular in-house training is required to keep up to date with new technology advances or changes in the legal system.

Probation service officers (PSOs) work towards an NVQ level 3 in community justice. There are a range of relevant NVQs at levels 3-4 in community justice, and there may be advanced apprenticeships in community and youth justice in your area. Information is available on the Skills for Justice website. With experience and higher qualifications, it is possible to progress to become a probation officer.

In Northern Ireland, there is no equivalent to this role, although regional probation officers have support staff. Contact the Probation Board for Northern Ireland for details.

Many entrants are adults and applications are welcome due to their life and work experience. It is useful, though not essential, to have worked in areas such as youth work, care work and any work involving people management.

Opportunities and Pay

Probation service officers (PSOs) are employed by the National Probation Service, part of the National Offender Management Service (NOMS) in England and Wales. Around 6,300 people work as PSOs and demand is likely to grow. Some PSOs may progress to become qualified probation officers via the trainee probation officer programme, or move into the police service.

Pay varies between different areas, although salaries are usually around £20k a year, rising to £23k-£26k with experience. There may be a shift allowance and overtime pay. Those working in London receive an additional allowance.

Skills and Qualities

able to inspire confidence, able to withstand criticism, emotionally strong, firm manner, good communication skills, good interpersonal skills, good listening skills, perseverance, persuasive

Relevant Subjects

Law, Psychology, Sociology

Further Information

Apprenticeship Schemes (National Apprenticeship Service) - www.apprenticeships.org.uk

Careers in Probation (National Probation Service) - www.probation.homeoffice.gov.uk

National Offender Management Service - www.justice.gov.uk/about/noms.htm

Probation Bulletin (Shaw & Sons) - www.probationbulletin.co.uk

Skills for Justice - sector skills council for the UK justice system - www.skillsforjustice.com

▶Working in social care (2010) (Babcock Lifeskills) - www.babcock-lifeskills.com/

Addresses

National Association of Probation Officers (NAPO)
4 Chivalry Road, London SW11 1HT
Phone: +44 (0)20 7223 4887
Web: www.napo.org.uk

National Probation Service
1st Floor Abell House, John Islip Street, London SW1P 4LH
Web: www.probation.homeoffice.gov.uk

Probation Board for Northern Ireland
80-90 North Street, Belfast BT1 1LD
Phone: +44 (0)28 9026 2400
Web: www.pbni.org.uk

Similar Jobs

Counsellor, Learning Mentor (England), Police Officer, Prison Officer, Probation Officer, Social Worker

Procurator Fiscal (Scotland)

CRCI:Legal and Political Services
CLCI:LAB — Job Band: 5

Job Description

A procurator fiscal Is a legally qualified civil servant who is responsible for investigating crime and initiating court proceedings in criminal cases, on behalf of the Crown throughout Scotland. They work under the direction of the Lord Advocate. They receive reports from the police and law enforcement bodies. In cases which are considered by a jury, the procurator fiscal interviews witnesses, gathers and reviews forensic and other evidence. They consider the details and decide if prosecution is necessary. They also ensure that court cases are heard within strict time limits. They conduct jury trials in the Sheriff Court and prepare cases for Crown Counsel in the High Court.

The procurator fiscal investigates sudden or suspicious deaths, often attending the scene of a murder. They also investigate accidents and inquire into the cause of fires. They investigate any complaints against the police. May take direct control of police work, usually on fairly serious crimes.

Work Details

Officially the working week is 37 hours, but extra hours are normally necessary. The work is office based, with court work, but also involves going out to visit, for example, the scenes of crimes or prisons. Procurators fiscal also operate an 'on call' rota over weekends and evenings. Good organisational skills are needed, since the work requires the handling of several cases at once, all at different stages of investigation and proceedings. Logical thought, analytical ability and sound judgement are essential. The ability to work with, and communicate with a wide range of people is necessary, including people who are being investigated, bereaved families, and agencies, such as the police, social services and Customs & Excise.

The amount and nature of the work requires the ability to work under pressure. Attending scenes of crime may be unpleasant. An official gown is worn for court appearances.

Qualification

• Scotland

Band 5: For law degree: five H grades, usually including English, maths, a science subject, perhaps a modern language, and some S grades (1-3). Good H grades are needed (AAAAB) preferably taken at one sitting. Similar qualifications may also be acceptable. Check with universities.

Degree Information

The degree must be in law from a Scottish university. It is possible to combine study for a law degree with study of another discipline. Graduates in other disciplines may be able to complete an LLB (Bachelor of Laws) in two years.

Adult Qualifications

You must first qualify as a solicitor or advocate in Scotland.

Work Experience

Entry to this job is competitive and is only available to solicitors or advocates who qualify in Scotland. Practical experience in an advocate's chambers, in a solicitor's office or with the police, is an advantage. Attendance at court to observe a variety of court cases also helps.

Entry and Training

This job is only open to solicitors or advocates who have qualified in Scotland. There are nationality and residency requirements for this job. Entry is very competitive, since there is a limited number of posts. You must have an LLB degree in Scottish law, or complete three years' pre-diploma training and pass the exams of the Law Society of Scotland. You must also complete a traineeship to qualify as a solicitor, or undergo a period of pupillage or training known as 'devilling' to qualify as an advocate. For full details of how to train as an advocate or solicitor, read the articles on these jobs.

Qualified solicitors and advocates join the service as a procurator fiscal depute and work shadow experienced staff to gain knowledge of the work. Once in the job, you also need to take short courses throughout your career to keep up to date with changes in the law and for special topics. The Royal Faculty of Procurators provides a programme of continuing professional development (CPD) seminars available for lawyers.

A small number of two-year legal traineeships are available with the Crown Office and Procurator Fiscal Service (COPFS). The first year is spent in the specialised units of the Crown Office. The second year is based in a district office. See the website of the COPFS for details.

Mature entrants need to qualify using the standard routes to professional qualification. However, maturity is an advantage in this job.

Opportunities and Pay

Procurators fiscal are civil servants appointed by the Lord Advocate. They are linked to the 11 prosecutorial areas in Scotland. There is a formal graded promotion structure and promotion to senior posts is by competition, when vacancies arise. A procurator fiscal can also move into other civil service posts.

Generally, fiscal depute salaries start at around £27k-£33k depending upon experience, rising to around £56k for senior posts.

Skills and Qualities

able to cope under pressure, analytical skills, attention to detail, aware of legal and ethical considerations, decisive, good communication skills, good organisational skills, public speaking ability, sound judgement

Relevant Subjects

English, History, Law, Performing arts

Further Information

Skills for Justice - sector skills council for the UK justice system - www.skillsforjustice.com

TARGETjobs: Law Scotland (GTI Specialist Publishing Ltd.) - www.groupgti.com

The Journal
(Law Society of Scotland) - www.journalonline.co.uk

▶Working in politics & law (2010) (Babcock Lifeskills) - www.babcock-lifeskills.com/

Addresses

Crown Office & Procurator Fiscal Service (COPFS)
The Crown Office 25 Chambers Street, Edinburgh EH1 1LA
Phone: +44 (0)131 226 2626
Web: www.crownoffice.gov.uk

Law Society of Scotland
26 Drumsheugh Gardens, Edinburgh EH3 7YR
Phone: +44 (0)131 226 7411
Web: www.lawscot.org.uk

Royal Faculty of Procurators in Glasgow
12 Nelson Mandela Place, Glasgow G2 1BT
Phone: +44 (0)141 331 0533
Web: www.rfpg.org

Similar Jobs

Advocate (Scotland), European Law Solicitor, Sheriff (Scotland), Solicitor

Product Designer

CRCI:Design, Arts and Crafts
CLCI:ROZ — Job Band: 3 to 5

Job Description

Product designers design almost anything we use in our daily lives, ranging from household goods to specialised items such as computers or cars. They also investigate how existing designs can be manufactured more cost effectively. Some work in the medical field designing tools and devices. Designers have to be aware that products must have a commercial advantage over competitors so must consider costings in their work. They work with a team of people, such as design engineers, computer aided design technicians or model makers discussing design and effectiveness in the development process. Also liaise with sales and marketing staff on pricing and market appeal.

Designers need to understand the different stages of development in the manufacturing process, from research, to sketching designs, producing a model and creating a presentation board for client viewing. They use drawings, 3D models and computer designs to communicate their ideas. Most work for manufacturing companies or design consultancies.

Work Details

Usually work around 37 hours a week from Monday to Friday. You may have to work longer hours to finish a design brief to meet a deadline. Work is normally based in a clean, light studio or office. You may also spend time in production areas which can be noisy, dusty or dirty. Contract or freelance work is common but you may need a driving licence if visiting clients at their premises. If your company designs for the international market, you may have to travel overseas.

Qualification

• England, Wales and Northern Ireland

Band 3: For entry to jobs, HNC or a relevant Diploma, usually at least 4 GCSEs (A*-C) including English and maths, or equivalent.

Band 4: For HND, Diploma of Higher Education or foundation degree: 1-2 A levels and some GCSEs (A*-C) usually including English and maths and an art or technology subject, or equivalent.

Band 5: For degree courses: 2-3 A levels and some GCSEs (A*-C) usually including English, maths, physics and an art or technology subject, or equivalent. Exact requirements depend on the degree you take.

• Scotland

Band 3: For entry to jobs, usually at least four S grades (1-3) including English or maths, or similar.

Band 4: For entry to SQA higher national and professional development awards, usually 2-3 H grades and some S grades (1-3), including English and maths and an art or technology subject, or equivalent.

Band 5: For degree courses: 3-5 H grades and some S grades (1-3), usually including English, maths, physics and an art or technology subject, or equivalent. Exact requirements depend on the degree you take.

Degree Information

Relevant courses include product design engineering and product design technology. There are relevant postgraduate courses available in product design, plastics product design, sustainable product design and plastic product design with management. Choose your course carefully and check requirements as you may need maths and physics for some courses and art and design, or design and technology are often stipulated.

Adult Qualifications

Course entry requirements are usually relaxed for suitable mature applicants. Those without the required qualifications may complete a foundation or Access course leading to relevant HNDs or accredited degress. You may need a portfolio of your work to demonstrate your artistic and technological ability.

Work Experience

Entry to this job is competitive and it is important that you try to do some relevant work or voluntary experience before applying. Work using CAD software or assisting in a design company is particularly useful. Some degree courses include a work placement.

If you expect good A levels and intend to go to university, schemes such as 'A Year in Industry' give you the opportunity to spend a salaried year with a company to gain valuable work experience.

The Engineering Education Scheme runs programmes in England, Scotland and Wales giving young people the chance to be involved in a real design project for six months. Students commit to two to three hours work a week and some time at university residents' workshops. This experience can contribute to any future university application and counts towards the Duke of Edinburgh award skills section. Similarly, Headstart offers students a chance to experience a week at university, designing, building and testing projects. Check the relevant websites for details.

Entry and Training

It is very difficult to get into work as a product designer without a relevant HNC/HND, and most entrants are graduates. Course titles and content vary, so check prospectuses carefully to ensure that the course is relevant to the particular area of work you wish to specialise in. Specialist courses, or courses with an industrial design option, are available at BTEC/SQA higher national level, and at degree level. These include a level 2/3 BTEC certificate and diploma in art and design and a level 4 BTEC foundation diploma in art and design. It is useful to choose a course that offers an industrial placement. Foundation degrees are also available.

Postgraduate qualifications may offer an advantage in some areas of work. Contact the Chartered Society of Designers for routes to qualification and a list of accredited courses. The Design Business Association also offers a range of industry specific training courses, membership services, and member events. See the website for details.

Training is mainly on the job with in-house courses that may include product knowledge or enhancement of CAD (computer-aided design) training in the design packages used within the company. You need to keep your knowledge up to date throughout your career by undergoing a programme of continuing professional development (CPD). The Design Council runs a range of CPD courses including brand strategy and making good project proposals. They also operate the 'Your Creative Future' website which has lots of useful information for those considering a career in design.

A Diploma/Welsh Baccalaureate may be available in your area in manufacturing and product design. The advanced level is equivalent to 3.5 A levels but for some university courses, the additional and specialist learning (ASL) component of the diploma needs to include specific A levels eg art and design, design technology, maths or physics. Check entry requirements carefully.

Government training opportunities, such as apprenticeships for adults, may be available in your area. You can also gain recognition of previous experience through Accreditation of Prior Learning (APL) or by working towards relevant S/NVQs. Contact your local careers office, Jobcentre Plus, Next Step service or Learning and Skills Council (LSC) Local Enterprise Company (LEC) for details of training schemes.

Opportunities and Pay

Around 3 million people work in product design, carrying out a variety of different jobs throughout the UK. There is steady demand for product designers in all areas, but in particular, looking at new ways of designing products more cost effectively. Increasingly, product designers also have to consider how existing products can be adapted to be more environmentally friendly or manufactured in a more sustainable way.

There is strong competition for jobs but experienced designers with a thorough understanding of technology have an advantage. Employers include manufacturing companies and design consultancies. There are good prospects for promotion to senior designer or team leader roles. More experienced designers may also move into project management. Work abroad is possible, especially if you are employed by a multinational company. Vacancies are advertised on the websites of professional bodies for designers, such as the Chartered Society of Designers, by specialist recruitment agencies, and in specialist publications. There are also opportunities for self-employment.

The Sorrell Foundation is an organisation dedicated to inspiring young people in the field of design in the UK. The Foundation runs a number of programmes, including the 'Young Design' Programme. This programme brings designers of all ages together, including school and university students. See the website for details.

Pay varies depending on location and the particular industry. Starting salaries for graduates are likely to be in the region of £16k-£20k rising to around £35-£45k with experience. Some may earn over £50k a year.

Health

Normal colour vision is required.

Skills and Qualities

able to work both on your own and in a team, attention to detail, commercial awareness, creative and imaginative flair, design ability, good at forecasting trends, good communication skills, inventive, project management skills, technical aptitude

Relevant Subjects

Art and Design, Business and accounting, Design and technology, Engineering, ICT/Computer studies, Manufacturing, Mathematics, Physics, Science

Further Information

Apprenticeship Schemes (National Apprenticeship Service) - www.apprenticeships.org.uk

Chartered Society of Designers - www.csd.org.uk

Creative & Cultural Skills - sector skills council for advertising, crafts, cultural heritage, design, literature, music, performing & visual arts - www.ccskills.org.uk

Design Business Association (DBA) - www.dba.org.uk

Diplomas (Foundation, Higher and Advanced) - http://yp.direct.gov.uk/diplomas

Engineering Education Scheme - www.engineering-education.org.uk/

Engineering Education Scheme Wales - www.eesw.org.uk

Headstart Scheme - www.headstartcourses.org.uk

SEMTA - sector skills council for science, engineering and manufacturing technologies - www.semta.org.uk

The Sorrell Foundation - www.thesorrellfoundation.com/

Tomorrow's Engineers - www.tomorrowsengineers.org.uk/careers.cfm

Welsh Baccalaureate - www.wbq.org.uk

Year in Industry (Engineering Development Trust) - www.yini.org.uk

Your Creative Future (Design Council) - www.yourcreativefuture.org

Addresses

Design & Technology Association (D&TA)
16 Wellesbourne House, Walton Road, Warwickshire CV35 9JB
Phone: +44 (0)1789 470 007
Web: www.data.org.uk

Design Council
34 Bow Street, London WC2E 7DL
Phone: +44 (0)20 7420 5200
Web: www.designcouncil.org.uk

Similar Jobs

CAD Technician, Computer Games Designer, Engineer: Design, Ergonomist, Exhibition Designer, Model Maker, Toymaker

Production Manager

also known as: Manufacturing Production Manager, Operations Manager

CRCI:Manufacturing and Production
CLCI:SAB

Job Band: 4 to 5

Job Description

Production managers ensure the production department of a manufacturing company runs smoothly and efficiently. They are responsible for production of goods at the right quality, quantity and price. Goods have to be produced within given timeframes. Managers ensure the workforce and equipment are employed efficiently. May draw up production schedules and be involved in selecting the equipment and layout of the factory or plant. Can work in any manufacturing industry such as paper, textiles, chemicals and plastics, clothing, food or electronics.

Production managers act as a link between managers and operators, discussing requirements and problems with both, and building up good relationships between workers, colleagues and senior managers. They ensure that health and safety guidelines are followed.

Work Details

Production managers usually work a basic 37-40 hr week that may include shifts and weekends. You are based on the shop floor and in an office, usually in industrial premises. You supervise and organise people and are responsible for monitoring progress, maintaining efficient production and high quality control. You require a knowledge of any new legal regulations. Your work is pressurised at times.

The environment depends on the type of industry. There is a risk of accidents from equipment and you may need to wear appropriate protective clothing.

Qualification

- **England, Wales and Northern Ireland**

Band 4: For BTEC higher national award: 1-2 A levels and some GCSEs (A*-C) usually including English, maths and science, or equivalent.

Band 5: For degree courses: 2-3 A levels and some GCSEs (A*-C) usually including English and maths, or equivalent. Exact requirements depend on the degree you take.

- **Scotland**

Band 4: For SQA higher national award: usually 2-3 H grades and some S grades (1-3), often including English, maths and science, or similar qualifications.

Band 5: For degree courses: 3-5 H grades and some S grades (1-3), usually including English, maths and science, or similar qualifications. Exact requirements depend on the degree you take.

Degree Information

Graduate management training schemes usually accept graduates of any degree discipline but this depends on the industry. Some employers prefer applicants to have studied a degree, such as engineering, technology, mathematics, computer science or a science, particularly those with a sandwich placement in industry. There are a number of degrees available in manufacturing management and manufacturing systems. Relevant postgraduate degrees are also available.

Adult Qualifications

A relevant qualification, usually a higher national diploma or a degree, is normally required. However, entry requirements may be relaxed for adults applying for higher education courses. Access or foundation courses provide a route onto degree courses for those without the required qualifications.

Work Experience

Relevant work or voluntary experience is always useful and can improve your chances in application for entry to this job. This can be in manufacturing and industry, working as part of a team and building communication and administration skills. Applicants to degree courses are encouraged to apply to the 'Year in Industry' Scheme for a placement in industry prior to starting their studies. Students may also have an opportunity to gain work experience in industry for a year between the penultimate and final years of their degree programme. This experience enhances their job prospects on graduation.

Entry and Training

Entry to management training schemes usually requires a degree or equivalent qualification. Courses are available at universities and colleges throughout the UK. You may also be able to study for professional qualifications in management by part-time study or distance learning. Foundation degrees are available in manufacturing management and business studies.

Training is by practical experience on the job with an experienced person, usually following induction training in the business processes of the company. Although entrants are often graduates, it is possible to be promoted to this work from junior production posts. Training given varies according to the specific needs of the employer. The Institute of Operations Management is the professional body for those working in production management and offers short courses and certificates/diplomas at different levels. The Chartered Management Institute also runs a range of specialist management training courses.

A Diploma/Welsh Baccalaureate may be available in your area in manufacturing and product design. The advanced level is equivalent to 3.5 A levels but for some university courses, the additional and specialist learning (ASL) component of the diploma needs to include specific A levels eg maths or physics. Check entry requirements carefully with the individual institutions.

Adults with sufficient experience in engineering, manufacturing or other kinds of industry or production process work may have an advantage. You may be able to study for professional qualifications in management by part-time study or distance learning whilst already in a job. The Open University offers a range of business and management qualifications including degrees, diplomas and certificates.

Opportunities and Pay

Employment is with a manufacturing company and jobs exist in a wide range of organisations and can be known by different titles. Entrants are sometimes appointed to this job from within the organisation. Opportunities for technically qualified production managers are good. Promotion depends on your experience and merit. There may also be opportunities abroad for experienced production managers.

Pay varies depending on location and type of organisation, but starting salaries tend to be from £20k-£24k a year, and with experience can rise to £38k. Senior managers can earn more than £60k a year.

Skills and Qualities

able to cope under pressure, able to motivate others, able to take responsibility, attention to detail, decisive, good communication skills, good organisational skills, IT skills, planning skills, problem-solving skills

Relevant Subjects

Chemistry, Design and technology, Engineering, English, ICT/ Computer studies, Manufacturing, Mathematics, Physics, Science

Further Information

AGCAS: Manufacturing (Job Sector Briefing) (AGCAS) - www.prospects.ac.uk

Diplomas (Foundation, Higher and Advanced) - http://yp.direct.gov.uk/diplomas

Manufacturing Institute - www.manufacturinginstitute.co.uk

Open University - www.open.ac.uk

Operations Management (Institute of Operations Management) - www.iomnet.org.uk/control-and-news/default.aspx

Real Life Guide to Manufacturing & Product Design (Trotman 2009) - www.trotman.co.uk

Welsh Baccalaureate - www.wbq.org.uk

Women into Science, Engineering & Construction - www.wisecampaign.org.uk

▶Working in manufacturing (2010) (Babcock Lifeskills) - www.babcock-lifeskills.com/

Year in Industry (Engineering Development Trust) - www.yini.org.uk

Addresses

Chartered Management Institute (CMI)
Management House, Cottingham Road, Corby NN17 1TT
Phone: +44 (0)1536 204 222
Web: www.managers.org.uk

Institute of Operations Management (IOM)
CILT (UK), Earlstrees Court, Earlstrees Road, Corby, Northants NN17 4AX
Phone: +44 (0)1536 740 105
Web: www.iomnet.org.uk

Similar Jobs

Engineer: Manufacturing, Management Consultant, Manager, Quality Assurance Controller/Inspector, Road Transport Manager

Project Manager

CRCI:Administration, Business and Office Work
CLCI:CAP Job Band: 5

Job Description

Project managers are responsible for successfully initiating, planning, carrying out and concluding a project. They work in one or a variety of sectors, including the construction industry, architecture, information technology (IT) and other areas which are involved with the development of a product or service.

The roles and responsibilities of a project manager vary, but include planning activities and resources, drawing up schedules and time estimates, developing a budget or cost estimates, implementing quality controls and risk analysis, team building, training and management, customer liaison and strategic development. These roles vary depending on the nature of the project being managed.

Work Details

Usually work normal office hours, Monday to Friday, though can often work longer hours, sometimes late into the evening, or may start early in the morning. You are normally office based, but may travel to visit clients, either locally, nationally or internationally. This may involve spending some time away from home.

Depending on the nature of the project or the company, project managers may need to visit sites outdoors, which may require wearing protective clothing such as a hard hat or goggles. Work can be demanding at times and you need to be able to work to deadlines. Formal business clothes are usually worn.

Qualification

- **England, Wales and Northern Ireland**

Band 5: For degree courses: 2-3 A levels and some GCSEs (A*-C) usually including English and maths, or equivalent. Exact requirements depend on the degree you take.

- **Scotland**

Band 5: For degree courses: 3-5 H grades and some S grades (1-3), including English and maths, or similar qualifications. Exact requirements depend on the degree you take.

Degree Information

Project managers come from a variety of different backgrounds, including scientific and technological. Therefore a degree in any subject may be acceptable. There are increasingly degrees and foundation degrees offered in project management, but it is more usually offered as part of a degree in business or management. Masters degrees in project management are available at Aberdeen and Liverpool universities.

Adult Qualifications
Entrants are usually graduates. Although a postgraduate qualification is not necessary, it is an advantage. Mature applicants with relevant previous experience may still apply for higher education courses even if they do not meet the standard entry requirements. For those with experience in many industries, the Association of Project Management offers a range of training opportunities and courses, some of which incur a cost. The PRINCE2 qualification is seen as an industry standard for project management.

Work Experience
Having some work experience in industry, management, finance or IT is advantageous when applying for jobs. Experience of co-ordinating projects in any sector, paid or voluntary, is useful.

Entry and Training
Project management can take you in many different directions in a variety of industries. Projects may be short term, involving key skills, or full-time longer term opportunities. Project management jobs can be open to new graduates, although most project management opportunities are available to candidates with considerable experience in a range of sectors.

The Association of Project Management (APM) offers membership and training to those interested in entering this career. Student membership is open to graduates who undertake the introductory certificate in project management. It is possible to become an associate while undertaking this qualification as a way of entering the profession. Relevant work experience is required for non-graduates. Associate membership is also available to those with two or more years experience while studying for the APMP, an internationally recognised qualification which incorporates your technical project management and leadership skills. With five or more years experience, you can become a full member while taking the practitioner qualification. Finally, with ten or more years experience, you can become a fellow and undertake the certificated project manager qualification.

PRINCE2 (PRojects IN Controlled Environments) is a process-based method for effective project management. It is used extensively by the UK Government and is widely recognised and used in the private sector, both in the UK and internationally. It is accredited by the Office of Government Commerce.

The APM has introduced a new route to APMP for PRINCE2 registered practitioners, offering benefits that equip professionals with the skills to effectively manage projects. It includes some topics that are not available in PRINCE2, such as budgeting and cost management, conflict management, communication, earned value management, leadership, negotiation, procurement, sponsorship and teamwork.

The National Centre for Project Management at Middlesex University offers training courses in project management skills and competencies. These are available in-house or at a training venue. There is a cost associated, which may be paid by your employer.

This career is most usually open to mature candidates with a background in industry, science, education, IT or retail. You may have experience in project co-ordination which enables you to develop a range of skills that you can then use in managing a project.

Opportunities and Pay
There are opportunities throughout the UK in commercial, IT and retail companies; public service sectors, such as the NHS or government departments; and construction and energy facilities. You may start out involved in a short-term project co-ordination role and build a portfolio of experience. It is possible to work across a range of industries as many of the skills used are not sector related. You may also be part of a business change project, working with management consultants and contractors. Consultancy and freelance opportunities exist, and there are opportunities to work abroad.

Pay varies according to the size, location and type of employer. However, the average salary in the UK for project managers is around £45k a year, with the typical range being £34k-£58k a year. Positions in IT often pay more, and salaries in London and south-east England are also usually higher.

Skills and Qualities
able to cope under pressure, able to delegate, able to motivate others, aptitude for teamwork, enthusiastic, excellent communication skills, integrity, leadership qualities, problem-solving skills.

Relevant Subjects
Business and accounting, Economics, English, ICT/Computer studies, Mathematics

Further Information
Office of Government Commerce (OGC) (OGC) - http:// www.ogc.gov.uk

PRINCE2 (OGC) - www.prince2.com

Addresses
Association for Project Management (APM)
Ibis House, Regent Park, Princes Risborough,
Buckinghamshire HP27 9LE
Phone: +44 (0)845 458 1944
Web: www.apm.org.uk/

National Centre for Project Management, Middlesex University
College House, Trent Park, Bramley Road, London N14 4YZ
Phone: +44 (0)20 8411 2299
Web: www.eis.mdx.ac.uk/ncpm/

Similar Jobs
Art Exhibitions Organiser, Business Analyst, Human Resources Officer/Manager, Management Consultant, Quality Manager

Proofreader
CRCI:Media, Print and Publishing
CLCI:FAD — Job Band: 3 to 5

Job Description
Proofreaders check the quality of written text before it is printed or published, and mark any mistakes in spelling, punctuation and grammar, using standard symbols that indicate the type of correction required. May work on books, magazines, brochures, and marketing and advertising literature. May correct content and ensure that any house style is followed and that text is consistent throughout. They check page numbering, layout and contents pages. Work on printed proofs or on screen. Proofreaders use dictionaries, reference books and other sources of information in their work. Increasingly, proofreading skills are applied to websites.

Work Details
Hours of work vary depending on the quantity of work received. Many proofreaders are self-employed and work from home. Whether employed full time or freelance, you may need to work some evenings and weekends, to meet publishers' deadlines. Proofreading involves sitting for many hours and is a solitary job, so you may not have contact with many people. Work can be demanding at times and requires a high degree of accuracy.

Qualification
There are no specified minimum academic requirements for this job, although an excellent knowledge of English grammar and spelling is expected. A good degree in English language (or English with literature) is preferred, and other areas of specialist subject knowledge, including other languages, is an advantage.

Adult Qualifications
Entry requirements vary depending on the type of work. Some publishers may not require particular qualifications, but increasingly, they employ graduates.

Work Experience
Entry to this job is highly competitive and work experience with a proofreader is hard to gain because this is typically a freelance job. You can offer to proofread publicity materials or documents, letters etc for a local charity or business, to gain valuable experience to add to your CV. It also improves your chances if you can get some work experience in publishing. Proofreading may also form a part of more general jobs for companies that publish their own advertising or training literature.

Entry and Training
Some enter this job with experience in publishing or journalism. There are short, private courses available in proofreading and editorial skills. These can be full time, part time or by distance learning. You need a comprehensive understanding and appreciation of the nuances of English grammar, spelling and punctuation. For most jobs you need to be familiar with the British Standard Printer's marks. Contact the Publishing Training Centre, the Society for Editors and Proofreaders (SfEP), and Chapterhouse, for details of courses and costs. Similarly, Publishing Scotland offers a range of courses in copy editing and proofreading. Many courses are offered online.

The Open University (OU) offers distance learning, continuing professional development (CPD) courses and the Publishers Association has negotiated with the OU for its members to receive a discount on the continuous flexible online professional development course fees. The Publishers Association also runs a series of courses suitable for proofreaders.

You can visit the Society of Young Publishers website for comprehensive details on getting started in this career. Opportunities to network can develop through speaker meetings and conferences and the members area can be a useful route to employment and contract work.

You can choose to become a member of the SfEP. Once you have completed a basic training course, you are eligible for mentoring by an experienced proofreader. Your mentor provides you with a copy of an existing or past job for proofreading. They then review your work, give feedback and advice and answer any questions. You can also register to enter your name on the SfEP Directory of Editorial Services. You need to keep up to date with developments in publishing, particularly those linked to online publishing.

Mature entrants are often those with previous experience in publishing or a related area of work. Contact the Publishing Training Centre, the Society of Editors and Proofreaders, and Chapterhouse, for details of courses, costs and membership and costs. Distance learning courses are available. Book Careers also has useful information on their website about setting up as a freelancer.

Opportunities and Pay
Most proofreaders are self-employed, though there are some opportunities to work for a printing, graphic design or publishing company, or an agency. Competition for work is fierce and opportunities can be limited, especially if you have no previous experience in publishing. However, opportunities are increasing with the growth in the number of websites and corporate publications. Location is not important and you can work from home.

Pay is usually on an hourly basis. The SfEP recommends a minimum rate of £19.25 an hour for experienced proofreaders. Highly paid specialist work can attract over £30 an hour. Full-time employed proofreaders start at around £17k a year. Some clients may pay more than this for a highly experienced proofreader

Health
This job requires good eyesight.

Skills and Qualities
able to read quickly, able to use proofreading marks, able to work well on your own, accurate, attention to detail, good concentration level, good spelling, grammar and punctuation, IT skills, methodical, observant

Relevant Subjects
English

Further Information
Book Careers - www.bookcareers.com
Careers in Book Publishing (The Publishers Association) - www.publishers.org.uk/
Editing Matters (bi-monthly) (Society for Editors & Proofreaders (SFEP)) - www.sfep.org.uk/pub/mag/magazine.asp
Society of Young Publishers - www.thesyp.org.uk/
Women In Publishing - www.wipub.org.uk
► Working in English (2007) (Babcock Lifeskills) - www.babcock-lifeskills.com/

Addresses
Chapterhouse
The Glebe House Whitestone, Exeter EX4 2LF
Phone: +44 (0)1392 811642
Web: www.chapterhousepublishing.co.uk

Open University (OU)
PO Box 197, Milton Keynes MK7 6BJ
Phone: +44 (0)845 300 6090
Web: http://www3.open.ac.uk

Publishing Scotland
Scottish Book Centre, 137 Dundee Street, Edinburgh EH11 1BG
Phone: +44 (0)131 228 6866
Web: www.publishingscotland.co.uk/

Publishing Training Centre at Book House
45 East Hill, Wandsworth, London SW18 2QZ
Phone: +44 (0)20 8874 2718
Web: www.train4publishing.co.uk

Society for Editors and Proofreaders (SfEP)
Erico House, 93-99 Upper Richmond Road, Putney, London SW15 2TG
Phone: +44 (0)20 8785 5617
Web: www.sfep.org.uk

Similar Jobs
Copy Editor, Desktop Publishing (DTP) Operator, Editor: Publishing, Editorial Assistant: Publishing, Secretary: Legal, Writer: Technical

Property Manager
CRCI:Building and Construction
CLCI:UH — Job Band: 3 to 5

Job Description
Property managers look after leasehold properties on behalf of private owners or commercial organisations. They are usually responsible for a portfolio of properties, possibly specialising in either commercial premises or accommodation. They have primary responsibility to the owner and secondary to the tenant/ lessee. Managers carry out the owner's instructions regarding the

property, control costs of services and maintenance, and aim to maximise revenue on the property by making improvements that will increase its market value.

Property managers assure the tenant's use and enjoyment of the premises without unnecessary interference from the landlord. They also ensure that all services are running effectively and maintain a safe and efficient living or working environment. Duties may include the development of an organisation's property strategy. May offer advice on health and safety issues, waste management and energy efficiency and ensure that budgets, spending and accounts are kept under control.

Property managers use computers for all aspects of work and for writing reports. Duties may include inspecting premises to check cleanliness and security, dealing with the failure of service or office equipment. Must be able to respond to any problem that arises and have the ability and resources to put things right quickly.

Work Details

Property managers usually work around 37-39 hrs a week, Monday to Friday, though may be expected to work longer hours if required to deal with emergencies. Work is usually office based although some travel is necessary to visit property. A driving licence is usually required. May need to travel throughout the UK, which can require nights away from home. Needs up-to-date knowledge of the relevant legal and technical requirements. Liaises with other professionals, like surveyors, with staff working in the building and with outside contractors.

Qualification

• England, Wales and Northern Ireland

Band 3: For entry: usually at least 4 GCSEs (A*-C) including English and maths, or equivalent.

Band 4: For BTEC higher national award: 1-2 A levels and some GCSEs (A*-C) usually including English and maths, or equivalent.

Band 5: For degree courses: 2-3 A levels and some GCSEs (A*-C) usually including English and maths, or equivalent. Exact requirements depend on the degree you take.

• Scotland

Band 3: For entry: usually at least four S grades (1-3) including English and maths, or similar.

Band 4: For SQA higher national award: usually 2-3 H grades and some S grades (1-3), often including English and maths, or similar qualifications.

Band 5: For degree courses: 3-5 H grades and some S grades (1-3), usually including English and maths, or similar qualifications. Exact requirements depend on the degree you take.

Degree Information

Any degree is acceptable but it may be an advantage to have a subject such as construction and property management, land and property management, business management or surveying.

Adult Qualifications

Entry requirements may be relaxed for adults applying for higher education courses. Access or foundation courses provide those without the required qualifications a route onto degree courses.

Work Experience

Employers may prefer candidates who have experience in relevant work areas. The types of work experience to consider include estate agency, leasehold management, surveying, business management, communications, property construction or planning.

Entry and Training

Property management is a career that you can enter with a broad range of experience and qualifications. You can study for a degree or diploma, then complete professional examinations offered by the Institute of Residential Property Management (IRPM). Or you can train on the job and study part time by distance learning or through a day-release course.

Part 1 of the professional examination is based on an open learning course in England and Wales or a distance learning pack in Scotland, which is available for anyone to purchase. The part 2 examination is supported by more advanced and intensive training organised by the Association of Residential Managing Agents, some of which are offered in conjunction with Southampton Solent University. Passing these examinations can lead to membership of the IRPM. The Chartered Institute of Housing has produced student guides which incorporate the examination regulations, which vary between England/Wales and Scotland, due to differences in legal structure.

The Royal Institution of Chartered Sureveyors (RICS) Associate qualification (AssocRICS) is a new grade of membership that can be achieved by work experience to demonstrate that you meet the standards. There are no minimum requirements to start on the Associate qualification.

There is a full, sandwich or part-time BSc in building surveying and property management currently offered by the University of Bolton. You do not necessarily require a high level of formal qualifications, particularly if you have relevant experience. Relevant foundation degrees are also available.

There are several membership organisations, such as the Association of Residential Letting Agents (ARLA). ARLA has merged with other professional bodies, such as the National Association of Estate Agents (NAEA), to form an awarding body, the National Federation of Property Professionals (NFOPP), which offers a range of qualifications that do not usually require formal academic qualifications. Courses are by distance learning and are offered through Manchester Open Learning. See the NFOPP website for details of all available qualifications. Some local colleges also offer part-time courses that lead to NFOPP diplomas.

Mature entrants to this job can have a diverse range of relevant professional experience and qualifications in areas that include estate agency, leasehold management, surveying, business management, communications, property construction or planning.

Opportunities and Pay

Opportunities are increasing in all parts of the UK. Jobs are available with a wide range of employers, including commercial and industrial companies, real estate firms, health trusts and services, central and local government, universities and colleges, as well as specialist property management firms. In areas where the government housing policy is enhancing opportunities, there are promotion prospects within larger property management companies, housing departments of local government and estate agency. There may be some opportunities to work abroad.

Pay varies according to location, size, type of employer and experience but generally graduate property managers earn between £18k-£25k a year, rising to over £30k a year. Benefits and bonuses are common and can enhance earnings.

Skills and Qualities

able to get on with all kinds of people, able to work to a budget, aptitude for teamwork, good interpersonal skills, good organisational skills, good telephone manner, IT skills, negotiating skills, problem-solving skills, understanding of legal technicalities

Relevant Subjects

Business and accounting, Construction and built environment, Economics, English, Law, Mathematics

Further Information

Asset Skills - sector skills council for the places where we live and work - www.assetskills.org

National Federation of Property Professionals (NFOPP) - www.nfopp.co.uk

Tenant Services Authority - www.tenantservicesauthority.org/

Addresses

Association of Residential Managing Agents (ARMA)
178 Battersea Park Road, London SW11 4ND
Phone: +44 (0)20 7978 2607
Web: www.arma.org.uk

Chartered Institute of Housing (CIH)
Octavia House Westwood Way, Coventry CV4 8JP
Phone: +44 (0)24 7685 1700
Web: www.cih.org

Chartered Institute of Housing (Scotland)
6 Palmerston Place, Edinburgh EH12 5AA
Phone: +44 (0)131 225 4544
Web: www.cih.org

Institute of Residential Property Management (IRPM)
178 Battersea Park Road, London SW11 4ND
Phone: +44 (0)20 7622 5092
Web: www.irpm.org.uk

Royal Institution of Chartered Surveyors (RICS)
RICS Contact Centre Surveyor Court Westwood Way, Coventry CV4 8JE
Phone: +44 (0)870 333 1600
Web: www.ricscourses.org/pages/careers.aspx

Similar Jobs

Estate Agent, Facilities Manager, Housing Officer, Relocation Agent

Prosthetic/Orthotic Technician

CRCI:Healthcare
CLCI:JOL Job Band: 3

Job Description

Prosthetic technicians manufacture and maintain the various types of prosthetic devices (prostheses) that replace all or part of a patient's missing limb or body part. This may be as a result of an accident, through disease such as breast cancer, or perhaps being born with a limb or part of a limb missing. Orthotic technicians create and maintain a supporting splint or brace, and footwear (orthoses) for the limbs or spine, which help a patient to keep mobile, prevents physical problems from escalating, or to relieve pain. The aim of technicians in both fields is to give each patient the best way to lead an independent life.

You work closely with prosthetists, orthotists and podiatrists and are a member of the rehabilitation team that works with affected people. Use a variety of materials such as metals, leather, carbon fibre, plastics, and composite materials, to construct the required device from plaster casts, measurements and drawings. You are frequently involved in the design stage, as many of the prostheses/orthoses are made to measure and designed specifically for each patient.

Duties also include assisting in the casting process, maintenance of products, scheduling patients for department staff, and if necessary, educating the patients about the process. Your exact role varies depending on the organisation.

Work Details

Usually work a 37 hr week, Monday to Friday, though may be expected to work early starts or late finishes, including some weekend work. Much of the work takes place within the rehabilitation technology workshop unit of a hospital or private manufacturer's workshop. You need to be aware of any health risks during the manufacturing process, such as fumes or dangerous machinery.

Qualification

- **England, Wales and Northern Ireland**

Band 3: For course entry: usually at least 5 GCSEs (A*-C) including English, maths and a science, design technology or engineering subject, or equivalent.

- **Scotland**

Band 3: For course entry: usually at least five S grades (1-3) including English, maths and a science, technological education or engineering subject, or similar.

Adult Qualifications

Generally, you are expected to have the minimum entry qualifications to undertake the necessary training. Craft qualifications such as metalwork, leatherwork and plastic fabrication subjects may be an advantage.

Work Experience

Work experience, voluntary or paid, gives you an insight into what you enjoy about a job or working environment, and the opportunity to acquire new skills. It provides valuable information to add to your CV and improves any course application and/or your future employment prospects. There are currently few qualified prosthetics/orthotic technicians so it may be difficult to gain direct experience shadowing or observing them. Consider shadowing someone who works in physiotherapy, podiatry, occupational therapy or other medical related work with people with physical disabilities.

Entry and Training

Trainee prosthetic/orthotic technicians are usually employed in a laboratory or workshop and receive on-the-job-training together with off-site attendance for a relevant course to support their work, such as a BTEC national certificate in engineering. You can take a relevant course prior to applying for a job, which may be full or part time at a local college. Employers look for all-round skills in craft subjects such as leatherwork, metalwork and plastic fabrication.

Currently, trainees in hospitals and manufacturing companies are employed through an apprenticeship scheme and study for work-related qualifications. Prosthetic/orthotic technicians may apply to the British Association of Prosthetists and Orthotists (BAPO) to become an affiliated technician member.

There are National Occupational Standards for prosthetic/orthotic technicians and a national training programme is in the process of development. Prosthetic/orthotic technicians are currently not required to be state registered with the Health Professions Council, but this may change in the future.

With experience and skills, prosthetic/orthotic technicians can go on to study for a degree in prosthetics/orthotics and qualify as a prosthetist/orthotist. Contact BAPO for details on training routes and qualification. Organisations such as the Orthotic Education and Training Trust fund short courses which are approved by BAPO.

Mature entrants with the relevant skills required for this job have an advantage. Previous experience includes any gained in the engineering/manufacturing industry or craft-related work with metals, leather and plastic fabrication. Government training opportunities, including apprenticeships for adults, may be available in your area. You can also gain recognition of previous experience through Accreditation of Prior Learning (APL), or by working towards relevant S/NVQs.

Opportunities and Pay

Employment is mainly with hospitals or specialist manufacturing companies. Experience can lead to senior and management positions, or to qualification as a prosthetist/orthotist. British companies with bases overseas may provide opportunities to work abroad.

Salaries start at around £13k-£18k depending on experience and may rise to around £24k a year.

Health
This job requires good general fitness.

Skills and Qualities
able to work both on your own and in a team, attention to detail, good communication skills, manual dexterity, perseverance, practical skills, precise, technical aptitude

Relevant Subjects
Art and Design, Biology, Design and technology, Engineering, Health and social care, Manufacturing, Mathematics, Physics, Science

Further Information
Apprenticeship Schemes (National Apprenticeship Service) - www.apprenticeships.org.uk

BAPOmag (British Association of Prosthetists and Orthotists) - www.bapo.com/site/

Health Professions Council (HPC) - www.hpc-uk.org

NHS Careers (NHS Careers) - www.nhscareers.nhs.uk

NHS Careers Scotland - www.infoscotland.com/nhs

NHS Careers Wales - www.wales.nhs.uk

Orthotic Education and Training Trust (OETT) - www.oett.org.uk

Addresses
British Association of Prosthetists and Orthotists (BAPO)
Sir James Clark Building, Abbey Mill Business Centre,
Paisley PA1 1TJ
Phone: 0845 166 8490 (UK only)
Web: www.bapo.com/site/

Directorate of Prosthetics and Orthotics
University of Salford , School of Health Care Professions,
Allerton Building, Frederick Road Campus M6 6PU
Phone: 0845 2340184 (UK only)
Web: www.healthcare.salford.ac.uk/prosthetic

National Centre for Training & Education in Prosthetics and Orthotics
University of Strathclyde, Curran Building, 131 St James Road,
Glasgow G4 0LS
Phone: +44 (0)141 548 3433
Web: www.strath.ac.uk/prosthetics

Similar Jobs
Dental Technician/Technologist, Engineer: Biomedical, Laboratory Assistant: Medical, Plaster Technician, Podiatrist/Chiropodist, Prosthetist/Orthotist

Prosthetist/Orthotist

CRCI:Healthcare
CLCI:JOL
Job Band: 5

Job Description
Prosthetists/Orthotists work with other healthcare professionals such as doctors, physiotherapists and occupational therapists in hospitals, providing callipers, splints, supports and artificial limbs for people who may need them permanently or temporarily. A prosthetist works with patients who have all or part of a limb missing, fitting a replacement (prosthesis). Many people may have been born with a limb missing or have been in an accident. Others have had a limb or body part removed through a disease such as cancer. An orthotist works with people who have a disabling condition of the spine or limbs, fitting a brace, neck collar or splint (orthoses).

Both take casts or measurements from the patient, decide what materials to use and design the article. Some prostheses and orthoses are ready-made by specialised manufacturers, others by prosthetic/orthotic technicians. Then they fit and adjust the new attachment and help the patient to use it.

Work Details
You mostly work a 35-40 hr week, Monday to Friday, in a hospital, clinic, or a workshop. You may be expected to work occasional evenings or Saturdays. You may work in a number of locations, with people of all ages and if you work for a manufacturing or service company you may need to travel to visit patients. You help people with disability or those who have suffered trauma, and you need to be sensitive to their difficulties. Work can be emotionally and physically demanding. You have to keep up to date with new technical developments. Usually work with a team of nurses and physiotherapists.

Qualification

- **England, Wales and Northern Ireland**

Band 5: For degree courses: 3 A levels at good grades, usually including including maths and physics or technical studies, and preferably biology or chemistry, and 5 GCSEs (A*-C), including English and maths, or equivalent. If maths is not offered at A level, other evidence of mathematical ability is required.

- **Scotland**

Band 5: For degree courses: 3-5 H grades, usually including maths and physics or technical studies, and preferably biology or chemistry, and five S grades (1-3), usually including English. If maths is not offered at H level, other evidence of mathematical ability is required.

Degree Information
A degree in prosthetics and orthotics approved by the British Association of Prosthetists and Orthotists and the Health Professions Council is essential for this job. Four-year degree courses are offered by the universities of Strathclyde and Salford. The fourth year is usually spent working in clinical practice.

Adult Qualifications
Entry requirements for degree courses are flexible for mature applicants, though adults without standard entry qualifications have to satisfy the universities of their ability to complete the course. Appropriate Access or foundation courses may be acceptable. Contact universities for details.

Work Experience
Work experience gives you an insight into what you enjoy about a job or working environment, and the opportunity to acquire new skills. It provides valuable information to add to your CV and improves your employment prospects. There are currently few qualified prosthetists/orthotists so it may be difficult to gain direct experience shadowing or observing them. Consider observing physiotherapy, podiatry, occupational therapy or other medical related work with people with physical disabilities.

Entry and Training
The Universities of Salford and Strathclyde offer degrees, which include studies in anatomy, physiology, pathology, biomechanics, material science and orthotic/prosthetic science. The courses also provide clinical experience in assessing patients and fitting prosthetic and orthotic devices. The final year involves two six-month placements, one orthotic and the other prosthetic. Entry to the courses is highly competitive and you must have a Criminal Records Bureau (CRB)/Disclosure Scotland check before starting your course. Completion of the degree course leads to state registration with the Health Professions Council (HPC).

You can specialise in either orthotics or prosthetics though you may choose to work in both areas. The University of Strathclyde offers a range of postgraduate courses and research degrees. Once qualified you are expected to keep your knowledge up to date and maintain your registration with the HPC through a programme of continuing professional development (CPD). Organisations such as the Orthotic Education and Training Trust fund short courses which are approved by the British Association of Prosthetists and Orthotists.

Mature entrants with relevant experience, including nursing or engineering, have an advantage. Voluntary work in a hospital or rehabilitation centre is useful. You may apply for an NHS funded place at a university though competition for places is fierce. An NHS means-tested bursary scheme or a non-means-tested student loan may be available. Contact NHS Careers for details.

Opportunities and Pay

This is a small and specialised profession with no formal career structure, but there is a national and international shortage of trained and experienced prosthetists/orthotists. Career prospects are excellent throughout the UK and the rest of the world, and in particular the USA. Around 800 prosthetists/orthotists work in the UK for private clinics or manufacturing and servicing companies, but there are increasing opportunities in the NHS. Most prosthetic and orthotic graduates begin their careers working for commercial companies who work for NHS hospitals. As you become more experienced, you may specialise in a particular area of clinical work or move into management, teaching or research.

The UK training programme is internationally recognised and many opportunities exist for graduates to work abroad. There are excellent opportunities with British companies who have offices abroad, or with overseas companies and health or voluntary organisations, such as the Red Cross. Increasingly, prosthetic/orthotic work is important in areas of the world where there are communities that have been traumatised by conflict, war or natural disaster.

A graduate can expect to earn around £21k-£28k a year, and with experience this may rise to £40k if you have management responsibilities. Senior consultant prosthetists/orthotists can earn up to £64k a year.

Health

This job requires good general fitness.

Skills and Qualities

able to get on with all kinds of people, caring, encouraging, manual dexterity, observant, perseverance, scientific approach, sympathetic, tactful

Relevant Subjects

Biology, Design and technology, Engineering, English, Health and social care, ICT/Computer studies, Mathematics, Physics, Psychology, Science

Further Information

BAPOmag (British Association of Prosthetists and Orthotists) - www.bapo.com/site/

Health Professions Council (HPC) - www.hpc-uk.org

NHS Careers (NHS Careers) - www.nhscareers.nhs.uk

NHS Careers Scotland - www.infoscotland.com/nhs

NHS Careers Wales - www.wales.nhs.uk

Orthotic Education and Training Trust (OETT) - www.oett.org.uk

The Role of the Orthotist and Prosthetist (British Association of Prosthetists & Orthotists) - www.bapo.org/site/content/view/49/82/

▶Working in science (2007) (Babcock Lifeskills) - www.babcock-lifeskills.com/

Addresses

British Association of Prosthetists and Orthotists (BAPO)
Sir James Clark Building, Abbey Mill Business Centre,
Paisley PA1 1TJ
Phone: 0845 166 8490 (UK only)
Web: www.bapo.com/site/

National Centre for Training & Education in Prosthetics and Orthotics
University of Strathclyde, Curran Building, 131 St James Road,
Glasgow G4 0LS
Phone: +44 (0)141 548 3433
Web: www.strath.ac.uk/prosthetics

Strathclyde University
16 Richmond Street, Glasgow G1 1XQ
Phone: +44 (0)141 552 4400
Web: www.strath.ac.uk

University of Salford - School of Health Care Professions
Allerton Building, Frederick Road Campus,
University of Salford M6 6PU
Phone: +44 (0)845 234 0184
Web: www.healthcare.salford.ac.uk/prosthetic/

Similar Jobs

Dental Technician/Technologist, Engineer: Biomedical, Occupational Therapist, Orthodontist, Physiotherapist, Podiatrist/Chiropodist

Psychiatrist

CRCI:Healthcare
CLCI:JAB Job Band: 5

Job Description

Psychiatrists are qualified doctors specialising in work with people with mental health problems and illnesses, such as depression, drug or alcohol dependency, Alzheimer's disease, anorexia or schizophrenia. They apply medical knowledge to the prevention, diagnosis and treatment of illnesses, diseases and disorders. Assess each patient's condition and diagnose and treat using a combination of measures, including drugs, psychological counselling, and occasionally, physical treatment such as electroconvulsive therapy (ECT). May use 'talking treatments', including cognitive behavioural therapy instead of medication, to help people cope with their immediate situation in a positive way and work towards a long-term goal.

Psychiatrists can specialise and work in areas such as adult, old age, children and adolescent, mental health and learning disabilities and psychotherapy. Can also be involved in forensic work with prisoners and other offenders. Work with a wide range of health professionals, including clinical and counselling psychologists, social workers, psychiatric nurses and occupational therapists.

Work Details

Doctors initially work long, irregular hours whilst training, but when qualified as a psychiatrist, you are usually able to confine your workload to a more regular timetable, although sometimes you may be on call. There is contact with people who are disturbed, upset or depressed. You have to make decisions about treatment and keep records. Work can be emotionally demanding. This job is very satisfying for those wishing to work in a caring profession.

Qualification

• England, Wales and Northern Ireland

Band 5: For degree in medicine: usually three A levels, with good grades in chemistry and two from physics, biological sciences and maths, plus 5 GCSEs (A*-C) including English, or equivalent. Some medical schools offer a one-year pre-medical course for students with A levels in arts or mixed subjects. Check with individual schools for full details.

• Scotland

Band 5: For degree in medicine: usually five H grades, with good grades in chemistry and two from physics, biology and maths, plus five S grades (1-3) including English and maths, or similar. Normally science subjects not held at H grade should be offered at S grade. Some medical schools offer a one-year pre-medical course for students whose H grades do not include the required science subjects. Check with individual schools for full details.

Degree Information
A first degree in medicine awarded by a university medical school and recognised by the General Medical Council is essential, followed by specialist psychiatric training.

Adult Qualifications
Entry requirement standards are not normally relaxed for mature applicants, though those who consider applying should contact the individual university for advice. Graduates with a good honours degree in a related subject may obtain exemptions from certain options within the medical degree course.

Work Experience
Entry to this career is competitive. It is important that you try to do some relevant work or voluntary experience before applying. This can be in any healthcare setting such as a hospital or care home, though areas that use listening skills and observation, or direct experience in the caring professions, are also useful. It is an advantage to talk to a psychiatrist about the work, but direct observation is unlikely to be possible because of client confidentiality issues.

Entry and Training
Psychiatrists must first qualify as medical doctors by completing a medicine degree which takes five years, then pass the postgraduate two-year Foundation Programme and register as a doctor with the General Medical Council (GMC). For full details of medical training see the job article Doctor: Hospital.

Once you have completed the Foundation Programme, there is competition for Specialty Registrar (SpR) posts, under the Modernising Medical Careers initiative. This covers all aspects of psychiatry. After core training, you then have to apply for posts for a further three years' specialty training, where you concentrate on one branch of psychiatry eg. general, adult, child, adolescent, forensic, addiction etc. Progress is based on achieving competences and leads to the Certificate of Completion of Training (CCT). Once you have achieved the CCT, you can join the specialist register of the GMC and apply for a post as a consultant. You are expected to update your professional knowledge continually throughout your career. Contact the Royal College of Psychiatrists for details of courses, bursaries and training routes.

Mature entrants are welcomed by medical schools and particularly suitably qualified mature students. Some medical schools may have reserved places for mature graduate entrants. There are access courses to medicine and pre-medical foundation courses. Some Open University credits at distinction level may be accepted at some medical schools. Check with individual medical schools for details of all opportunities.

Opportunities and Pay
There is a shortage of psychiatrists in the UK and training provision for new staff has been increased. Psychiatrists are usually employed by the NHS, private hospitals, a research organisation, the armed forces or a university medical school. Some specialise in research into genetic or biochemical reasons for mental health diseases. Prospects for promotion may depend on your willingness to move to another area to gain experience and obtain promotion. There are some opportunities for work abroad with voluntary organisations in developing countries. There may be opportunities to work part time or job share.

Within the NHS, junior doctors earn a basic salary and are usually paid a supplement for extra hours worked. Basic salaries are around £33k a year (including a 50% supplement for extra hours), rising to £43k-£68k (including 50% supplement) for a doctor in specialist training. A consultant can earn £73k-£174k a year. These salaries do not include on-call payments, private income or London weighting allowances. If working for a voluntary organisation abroad, your pay may be low.

Health
This job requires good general fitness and while training as a doctor the work carries a risk of infection.

Skills and Qualities
able to put people at ease, analytical skills, aptitude for teamwork, attention to detail, awareness of confidentiality issues, emotionally strong, good interpersonal skills, good listening skills, objective, perceptive

Relevant Subjects
Biology, Chemistry, English, Health and social care, Mathematics, Physics, Psychology, Science, Sociology

Further Information
Becoming a Doctor (BMA) (BMA) - www.bma.org.uk/careers/becoming_doctor/index.jsp

British Journal of Psychiatry (Royal College of Psychiatrists, monthly) (High Wire Press (for RCP)) - www.rcpsych.ac.uk/publications/journals/bjpinfo1.aspx

Foundation Programme - www.foundationprogramme.nhs.uk

Insider's Guide to Medical Schools (Blackwell Books)

Modernising Medical Careers - www.mmc.nhs.uk

NHS Careers (NHS Careers) - www.nhscareers.nhs.uk

NHS Careers Scotland - www.infoscotland.com/nhs

NHS Careers Wales - www.wales.nhs.uk

Open University - www.open.ac.uk

Psychiatric Bulletin (monthly) (Royal College of Psychiatrists) http://pb.rcpsych.org/

Addresses
British Medical Association (BMA)
BMA House, Tavistock Square, London WC1H 9JP
Phone: +44 (0)20 7387 4499
Web: www.bma.org.uk

General Medical Council (GMC)
Regents Place, 350 Euston Road, London NW1 3JN
Phone: +44 (0)161 923 6602
Web: www.gmc-uk.org

Royal College of Psychiatrists
National HQ, 17 Belgrave Square, London SW1X 8PG
Phone: +44 (0)20 7235 2351
Web: www.rcpsych.ac.uk

Similar Jobs
Nurse: Mental Health, Psychoanalyst, Psychologist: Clinical, Psychologist: Neuropsychologist, Psychotherapist

Psychoanalyst
also known as: Psychotherapist: Psychoanalytic

CRCI:Social Work and Counselling Services
CLCI:KEL Job Band: 5

Job Description
Psychoanalysts talk with patients to help them see what is causing their unwanted feelings and behaviours. Patients may want to overcome obsessions, phobias, feelings or behaviours that are affecting their lives. May specialise in working with children, young people or adults.

Psychoanalysts have one-to-one sessions with the patient. Aim to build trust and encourage the patient to talk freely about very personal issues. They listen to what the patient is saying and guide the conversation. Also watch them closely for non-verbal reactions. Encourage them to explore thoughts and feelings they may not be aware of having. They go over events in the patient's life to find out what first caused them to feel or behave in this way. May use hypnotherapy or analyse dreams to look for clues. Help patients to see what is behind their problem and work out ways of dealing with it. Make notes after the session, when the patient has left.

Work Details

Most psychoanalysts are self-employed. Hours of work vary to suit yourself and your patients. Appointments may be during the day, in the evening or at weekends. Sessions with patients usually last 50 mins. Sees each patient several times a week, often over several months or more, depending on the nature of the problem.

Works sitting down in a comfortable and quiet office in a private practice, clinic or hospital. Patients may be worried, angry or upset.

Qualification

Currently there are no rules about the training you need to be a qualified psychoanalyst. The profession wants to set minimum qualifications and standards for practitioners. To practise as a psychoanalyst, you should choose a course accredited by a professional body such as the British Psychoanalytic Council (BPC) or the International Psychoanalytical Association (IPA) or their member organisations. To be accepted onto a course, usually you must be qualified at least to degree level and specialise in a field related to mental health.

• England, Wales and Northern Ireland

Band 5: For degree courses: 2-3 A levels and some GCSEs (A*-C) usually including English and maths, or equivalent. Exact requirements depend on the degree you take.

• Scotland

Band 5: For degree courses: 3-5 H grades and some S grades (1-3), usually including English and maths, or similar qualifications. Exact requirements depend on the degree you take.

Degree Information

To be accepted onto many psychoanalytic psychotherapy training courses, it is an advantage to have a degree in medicine, nursing, psychology or social work and preferably a postgraduate qualification or experience in the field of mental health. Some universities offer postgraduate courses in subjects related to psychoanalysis.

Adult Qualifications

Higher education course entry requirements may be relaxed for adults. Access or foundation courses provide those without the required qualifications a route onto degree courses. Each body offering psychoanalytic psychotherapy training sets its own entry requirements.

Work Experience

Most course providers value experience of treating patients with mental health problems. Training organisations may help you to arrange a work placement if you do not have this kind of experience.

Experiencing psychoanalysis yourself can help you to decide whether psychoanalytic training is the right choice for you. It can also be an advantage in the application process. Using an analyst approved by the training body means you should be able to stay with the same analyst when you start training.

Entry and Training

Several organisations offer training in areas such as psychoanalysis, analytical psychology and psychoanalytic psychotherapy. The selection process involves several interviews to assess your suitability. Most people accepted onto courses are qualified medical practitioners, psychologists or social workers. All courses are part time and last for at least four years. You have to undergo psychoanalysis with an approved analyst three or more times a week, depending on the course, for the whole of the training period. After the first year you take part in seminars, do theory work and carry out supervised sessions with the same patients over one or more years. You have to pay for the psychoanalysis course and sessions, which are expensive.

If you complete a course accredited by the British Psychoanalytic Council (BPC) or the International Psychoanalytical Association (IPA) and join one of their member bodies, your name can be added to the BPC Register of Psychoanalysts. Members of the public and medical staff can use this to find qualified practitioners. Broader psychotherapy organisations, such as the UK Council for Psychotherapy (UKCP), also maintain registers that include qualified psychoanalysts. Qualifications accredited by the IPA are recognised internationally.

Psychoanalysts keep up to date with new ideas and techniques through lectures, presentations to colleagues and courses. To stay on the practitioners' register, you must do a certain amount of continuing professional development (CPD) each year.

Since this area of work requires considerable experience in the field of mental health, all entrants are adults. People may move into psychoanalytic psychotherapy from careers in medicine, psychology and social work, where they have gained valuable experience of helping people to overcome psychological problems. Courses are usually designed so that people can continue in full-time employment whilst working towards psychoanalytic psychotherapy qualifications.

Opportunities and Pay

There are around 1,300 psychoanalytical therapists registered with the British Psychoanalytic Council (BPC). Psychoanalysts work in the private, public and voluntary sectors. Many work in private practices, especially around London. Others work in hospitals or clinics. Some may combine this work with other jobs, for example in psychiatry or psychotherapy. With experience, you may train others or provide psychoanalysis to people who are being trained.

In private practice, earnings vary depending on location, how much you charge and how many patients you see. Many psychoanalysts charge from £35-£75 for a 50 minute session; some charge considerably more. Trainee psychoanalysts may charge much less. Full-time salaries may be in the region of £20k-£27k a year for newly qualified psychoanalysts, to £38k or more for experienced analysts.

In the national health service (NHS), trainee psychoanalytical psychotherapists start on around £20k, rising to £24k-£33.5k a year once qualified and experienced. Principal psychotherapists can earn up to £45.6k a year.

Skills and Qualities

able to inspire confidence, able to put people at ease, awareness of confidentiality issues, business awareness, emotionally strong, good communication skills, good listening skills, logical, non-judgemental, observant

Relevant Subjects

Biology, English, Health and social care, Psychology, Science, Sociology

Further Information

British Journal of Psychotherapy (British Association of Psychotherapists) - www.bap-psychotherapy.org

Making Sense of Psychotherapy and Psychoanalysis (Mind) - www.mind.org.uk/help/medical_and_alternative_care

Psychoanalytic Psychotherapy (BPC) (British Psychoanalytical Council) - www.psychoanalytic-council.org/

Addresses

British Association of Psychotherapists (BAP)
37 Mapesbury Road, London NW2 4HJ
Phone: +44 (0)20 8452 9823
Web: www.bap-psychotherapy.org

British Psychoanalytic Council (BPC)
Unit 7 , 19-23 Wedmore Street,, London N19 4RU.
Phone: +44 (0)20 7561 9240
Web: www.bcp.org.uk

Institute of Psychoanalysis
Byron House, 112a Shirland Road, Maida Vale, London W9 2EQ
Phone: +44 (0)20 7563 5000
Web: www.psychoanalysis.org.uk

International Psychoanalytic Association (IPA)
Broomhills, Woodside Lane, London N12 8UD
Phone: +44 (0)20 8446 8324
Web: www.ipa.org.uk

UK Council for Psychotherapy (UKCP)
2nd Floor Edward House , 2 Wakley Street, London EC1V 7LT
Phone: +44 (0)20 7014 9955
Web: www.psychotherapy.org.uk

Similar Jobs

Counsellor, Hypnotherapist, Psychiatrist, Psychologist, Psychotherapist

Psychologist

CRCI:Social Work and Counselling Services
CLCI:KEL Job Band: 5

Job Description

Psychologists are concerned with the scientific study of the mind (thoughts and feelings) and human behaviour. Psychologists examine various aspects of human experience and behaviour and apply their understanding of people in a variety of professional areas, such as clinical, counselling, educational, forensic, health, occupational, sport psychology and neuropsychology. They also often work in academic settings as teachers or in research.

Psychologists are not usually medically qualified and only a small proportion of people studying psychology degrees go on to work with patients. New areas such as environmental and consumer psychology are developing. All psychologists use a range of resources and techniques, which include computers, video and audio recording, and other specialised equipment for experimental work.

Work Details

Usually works a basic 37 hr week, though may need to work out-of-office hours in some jobs. Depending on your branch of psychology, you work with a variety of people, including children of all ages, parents, elderly people, those with special needs, and those in special institutions. Work settings include hospitals, health services, child guidance clinics, assessment centres, offices, community homes, schools, colleges, universities, medical centres, prisons and in industry. You also work with a range of other professionals.

This job can be emotionally demanding. Duties involve teaching, counselling, advising, interviewing people, carrying out tests and observing and assessing people and situations.

Qualification

• England, Wales and Northern Ireland

Band 5: For degree courses in psychology: 2-3 A levels and some GCSEs (A*-C) usually including English, maths and sometimes science subjects, or equivalent. Psychology is not required for entry to degree courses, but students may find that study at this level helps them to decide if they are suited to studying psychology at degree level. Exact requirements depend on the degree you take.

• Scotland

Band 5: For degree courses in psychology: 3-5 H grades and some S grades (1-3), usually including English, maths and sometimes science subjects, or similar qualifications. Psychology is not required for entry to degree courses, but students may find that study at this level helps them to decide if they are suited to studying psychology at degree level.

Degree Information

A good honours degree in psychology, approved by the British Psychological Society (BPS), provides the Graduate Basis for Registration (GBR) and is required for all postgraduate training courses. A conversion course can also lead to BPS approval. This is followed by a postgraduate training course in your chosen field. Some first degree courses are more relevant than others for BPS accreditation, so applicants must carefully consider their future career choice.

Adult Qualifications

Applicants without the normal entry qualifications should contact academic institutions for mature entry standards, which may be relaxed. The Open University has a scheme that offers top-up courses for graduates, or psychology credits that provide eligibility for registration with the British Psychological Society (BPS).

Work Experience

Entry to this job is competitive and it is important that you do some relevant work or voluntary experience before applying for degree courses. Relevant work includes anything involving dealing with people in a helping capacity. It is an advantage to have relevant experience in areas such as education, hospital work or working with people. Areas that involve listening skills and any observation or direct experience in the caring professions is also useful.

It is helpful to arrange time to talk directly to a psychologist about the work, but direct observation may not be possible because of client confidentiality.

Entry and Training

You should ensure that your first degree course is relevant for the branch of psychology you plan to follow. The Health Professions Council (HPC) is now the regulator of practitioner psychologists in the UK and is responsible for approving all qualifications. To be registered with the HPC you need to complete accredited postgraduate training in your chosen branch of psychology.

To register as a chartered psychologist, you must obtain the Graduate Basis for Chartered Membership (GBC) from the British Psychological Society (BPS) by completing an accredited qualification in psychology (1-4 yrs), and then an accredited postgraduate training course in your chosen branch of psychology. Chartered status is not a legal requirement but many employers prefer psychologists who are members of the BPS. Graduates with a non-related degree may be able to take a conversion course but all qualifications must be approved by the BPS/HPC.

Following your academic training, most psychologists undertake a period of supervised practice, although the length and type of this training depends on your branch of psychology. Chartered psychologists need to take part in a programme of continuing professional development (CPD), including attendance at conferences and post-qualification courses, or undertaking topical research. You may be required to undertake a further ten days of training a year in your particular area of specialism. Contact the BPS or HPC for information on all training routes and approved qualifications.

Mature entrants with a degree and/or relevant postgraduate degree may have an advantage for training posts. The Open University offers a British Psychological Society (BPS) accredited BSc degree in psychology and a postgraduate conversion diploma. There are also BPS accredited conversion courses for those with degrees in other subjects.

Opportunities and Pay

This is a wide ranging profession with many applications. The British Psychological Society (BPS) has over 48,000 members and professional psychologists are employed by local authorities, the civil service, the prison service, armed forces and the NHS. There are also posts in the private sector working in human resource management or market research. Alternatively you can be self-employed and work as a consultant on a freelance basis.

There may also be opportunities for research and teaching. Part-time work or job sharing is possible. Career pathways for chartered psychologists are generally well defined and promotion opportunities are good.

Pay varies depending on the area of psychology in which you work. Generally, starting salaries for graduates are around £20k-£26k, rising to £28k-£42k a year with experience. Senior psychologists earn from around £44k to more than £70k a year.

Skills and Qualities

able to put people at ease, analytical skills, awareness of confidentiality issues, good communication skills, good interpersonal skills, objective, perceptive, problem-solving skills, scientific approach, tactful

Relevant Subjects

Biology, English, Health and social care, Mathematics, Psychology, Science, Sociology

Further Information

British Journal of Mathematical & Statistical Psychology (BPS, 3 pa) (British Psychological Society) - www.bpsjournals.co.uk/journals/bjmsp

British Journal of Psychology (BPS, quarterly) - www.bpsjournals.co.uk/journals/bjp

British Journal of Social Psychology (BPS, quarterly) - www.bpsjournals.co.uk/journals/bjsp

Careers in Psychology (British Psychological Society) - www.bps.org.uk/careers/

NHS Careers (NHS Careers) - www.nhscareers.nhs.uk

Psychologist Appointments (BPS) (BPS) - www.psychapp.co.uk

Psychology Uncovered (Trotman 2010) - www.trotman.co.uk

The Psychologist (monthly) (BPS) - www.thepsychologist.org.uk

▶Working in advice & counselling (2007) (Babcock Lifeskills) - www.babcock-lifeskills.com/

Addresses

British Psychological Society (BPS)
St Andrews House, 48 Princess Road East, Leicester LE1 7DR
Phone: +44 (0)116 254 9568
Web: www.bps.org.uk

Health Professions Council (HPC)
Park House, 184 Kennington Park Road, London SE11 4BU
Phone: +44 (0)20 7582 0866
Web: www.hpc-uk.org

Open University (OU)
PO Box 197, Milton Keynes MK7 6BJ
Phone: +44 (0)845 300 6090
Web: http://www3.open.ac.uk

Similar Jobs

Counsellor, Psychoanalyst, Psychologist: Clinical, Psychologist: Educational, Psychologist: Sport & Exercise, Psychotherapist, Social Worker

Psychologist: Clinical

CRCI:Social Work and Counselling Services
CLCI:KEL — Job Band: 5

Job Description

Clinical psychologists are concerned with the application of psychological theories, models and research to a range of psychological, psychiatric, mental health and developmental problems. Provide a variety of services including assessment, therapy, and consultancy services. Work primarily with children and adults who have health problems or a range of emotional, behavioural, psychiatric or development difficulties, to improve their everyday lives. Clinical psychologists also use scientific knowledge, counselling and therapy to help them resolve or cope with their difficulties. Clients may suffer from anxieties, obsessions, HIV/AIDS, addictions or other social or behavioural problems. They work with the elderly and people with physical disabilities. They assess clients, using interviews, tests and observation, to decide on the appropriate help.

Clinical psychologists also work with clients' families and other psychologists, medical staff and professionals such as social workers. They write reports, carry out research and attend meetings and case conferences.

Work Details

Usually works a basic 37 hr week though may need to work some evenings and weekends. You work in a hospital, health centres, clinic, residential home, or remand centre, with all kinds of people in need of support. Patients may be in institutions, mentally ill, depressed or have learning difficulties. Clients can be anxious, nervous, aggressive or negative and your work is emotionally demanding. You consult with professionals such as medical staff, social workers and occupational therapists. With experience you may produce legal reports or act as a witness in court. You may need to travel to meetings and to visit clients, so a driving licence is an asset.

Qualification

• England, Wales and Northern Ireland

Band 5: For degree courses in psychology: 2-3 A levels and some GCSEs (A*-C) usually including English, maths and sometimes science subjects. Psychology is not required for entry to degree courses, but students may find that study at this level helps them to decide if they are suited to studying psychology at degree level. Exact requirements depend on the degree you take.

• Scotland

Band 5: For degree courses in psychology: 3-5 H grades and some S grades (1-3), usually including English, maths and sometimes science subjects. Psychology is not required for entry to degree courses, but students may find that study at this level helps them to decide if they are suited to studying psychology at degree level.

Degree Information

A good honours degree in psychology, approved by the British Psychological Society (BPS), provides the Graduate Basis for Registration (GBR) and is required for all postgraduate training courses. A conversion course can also lead to BPS approval. Some first degree courses are more relevant than others for BPS accreditation, so applicants must carefully consider their future career choice.

Adult Qualifications

Applicants without the normal entry qualifications should contact academic institutions for entry standards for mature applicants, which may be relaxed. The Open University offers top-up credit courses leading to Graduate Basis for Registration (GBR) with the British Psychological Society (BPS).

Work Experience

Relevant work experience includes dealing with people in a helping capacity but clinical work experience is the most useful. Listening skills and any observation or direct experience in the caring professions is also useful. It is an advantage if you are able to talk to a psychologist about the work but direct observation may not be possible because of client confidentiality issues. Some experience in nursing, hospital work or residential care work is usually expected and this, and research experience is usually part of your undergraduate study.

Entry and Training
You should choose your first degree course carefully, checking that it is relevant for clinical psychology. The Health Professions Council (HPC) is now the regulator of practitioner psychologists in the UK and is responsible for approving all qualifications. To be registered with the HPC you need to complete accredited postgraduate training in clinical psychology.

To register as a chartered clinical psychologist (which many employers prefer), you need to obtain the Graduate Basis for Chartered Membership (GBC) by completing an accredited qualification in psychology (1-4 yrs) and then the three-year doctorate course in clinical psychology. Competition for places on the postgraduate course is fierce with only 30% of applicants being accepted each year. Graduates with a non-related degree are able to take a conversion course, but all qualifications must be approved by the BPS/HPC. On completing the doctorate you are eligible to apply to the BPS for chartered status.

Chartered psychologists need to take part in a programme of continuing professional development (CPD), including attendance at conferences and post-qualification courses, or undertaking topical research. You may be required to undertake a further ten days of training a year in your particular area of specialism. Contact the BPS or HPC for information on all training routes and approved qualifications.

The NHS offers postgraduate training posts to selected psychology graduates who have relevant clinical work experience, such as working as a nurse or care assistant, or as a research/psychology assistant. The Clearing House for Postgraduate Courses in Clinical Psychology handles all applications for clinical psychology training courses.

Mature applicants should note that the training period is lengthy and it may be difficult for some applicants to undertake. Mature entrants with a degree and/or relevant postgraduate degree may have an advantage for training posts. The Open University offers a British Psychological Society (BPS) accredited BSc degree in psychology and a postgraduate conversion diploma. There are also BPS accredited conversion courses for those with degrees in other subjects.

Opportunities and Pay
This is the largest specialisation in psychology and opportunities are increasing. Most work for the NHS but some are employed by a university, college or the civil service, and some are in private practice, working in legal or corporate areas. The civil service has opportunities to work in departments such as the prison service, Ministry of Defence (MOD) and the Department for Children, Schools and Families (DCSF). Local authorities offer employment in social services or education departments, working in community homes, assessment or child guidance centres.

Many organisations have clear career paths and promotion to senior posts is possible after gaining experience, although a move to another geographical area may be necessary. There may be opportunities for part-time work.

Pay is usually on a nationally agreed scale but in private practice it varies according to your employer. A trainee clinical psychologist working in the NHS earns from £24.8k a year, and once fully qualified earns £29k-£39k a year. A consultant clinical psychologist can earn up to £79k a year.

Skills and Qualities
able to work both on your own and in a team, awareness of confidentiality issues, emotionally strong, good communication skills, good interpersonal skills, IT skills, methodical, objective, patient, problem-solving skills

Relevant Subjects
Biology, Chemistry, English, Health and social care, Mathematics, Psychology, Science, Sociology

Further Information
AGCAS: Health (Job Sector Briefing) (AGCAS) - www.prospects.ac.uk

British Journal of Clinical Psychology (BPS, quarterly) - www.bpsjournals.co.uk/journals/bjcp

Careers in Psychology (British Psychological Society) - www.bps.org.uk/careers/

NHS Careers (NHS Careers) - www.nhscareers.nhs.uk

Psychologist Appointments (BPS) (BPS) - www.psychapp.co.uk

Psychology Uncovered (Trotman 2010) - www.trotman.co.uk

▶Working in advice & counselling (2007) (Babcock Lifeskills) - www.babcock-lifeskills.com/

Addresses
British Psychological Society (BPS)
St Andrews House, 48 Princess Road East, Leicester LE1 7DR
Phone: +44 (0)116 254 9568
Web: www.bps.org.uk

Clearing House for Postgraduate Courses in Clinical Psychology
Fairbairn House , 71-75 Clarenden Road, Leeds LS2 9PL
Phone: +44 (0)113 343 2737
Web: www.leeds.ac.uk/chpccp

Health Professions Council (HPC)
Park House, 184 Kennington Park Road, London SE11 4BU
Phone: +44 (0)20 7582 0866
Web: www.hpc-uk.org

Similar Jobs
Counsellor, Nurse: Mental Health, Psychologist, Psychologist: Neuropsychologist, Psychotherapist, Social Worker

Psychologist: Counselling
CRCI:Social Work and Counselling Services
CLCI:KEL Job Band: 5

Job Description
Counselling psychologists are concerned with helping people to resolve their problems or cope with any stress, illness or difficulty that is affecting their everyday life. They work with people who have physical and mental health issues, assessing them to define their difficulties through discussion, observation and using a range of psychometric tests. An individual programme of treatment such as one-to-one or group therapy, counselling or advice is then delivered.

It is important to monitor clients' progress and keep written records. They usually work with a particular client group, such as adults with mental health conditions, children and families, or older adults. Are part of a professional team including doctors, nurses, social workers, occupational therapists and physiotherapists. May also teach and carry out research. Counselling psychologists tend to focus on less severe issues than clinical psychologists.

Work Details
Usually works a basic 37 hr week, Monday to Friday, though may need to work some evenings and weekends. Travel within a working day may be required. May work with a wide variety of people including children of all ages, parents, the elderly, people with special needs, patients in hospital, prisoners, etc. Work includes contact with other professionals. You may work in private practice, a child guidance clinic, assessment centre, a university or college, a prison or in industrial premises. Duties involve teaching, counselling, advising, interviewing people, carrying out tests, observing and assessing people.

If self-employed, you may have a suitable consulting area at home or in rented premises. Clients can be anxious, nervous, aggressive or negative, so your work may be emotionally demanding at times. Local travel may be involved so a driving licence is an asset.

Qualification

- **England, Wales and Northern Ireland**

Band 5: For degree courses in psychology: 2-3 A levels and some GCSEs (A*-C) usually including English, maths and sometimes science subjects. Psychology is not required for entry to degree courses, but students may find that study at this level helps them to decide if they are suited to studying psychology at degree level. Exact requirements depend on the degree you take.

- **Scotland**

Band 5: For degree courses in psychology: 3-5 H grades and some S grades (1-3), usually including English, maths and sometimes science subjects. Psychology is not required for entry to degree courses, but students may find that study at this level helps them to decide if they are suited to studying psychology at degree level.

Degree Information

A good honours degree in psychology, approved by the British Psychological Society (BPS), provides the Graduate Basis for Registration (GBR) and is required for all postgraduate training courses. A conversion course can also lead to BPS approval. Some first degree courses are more relevant than others for BPS accreditation, so applicants must carefully consider their future career choice.

Adult Qualifications

Applicants without the normal entry qualifications should contact academic institutions for entry standards for mature applicants, which may be relaxed. The Open University offers top-up credit courses leading to Graduate Basis for Registration (GBR) with the British Psychological Society (BPS).

Work Experience

Relevant work experience includes anything dealing with people in a helping capacity, using listening skills and any observation or direct experience in the caring professions. It is useful to talk to a counselling psychologist about the work, but direct observation may not be possible because of client confidentiality issues.

Entry and Training

You should choose your first degree course carefully, checking that it is relevant for counselling psychology. It is often necessary to have completed a basic course in counselling skills. The Health Professions Council (HPC) is now the regulator of practitioner psychologists in the UK and is responsible for approving all qualifications. To be registered with the HPC you need to complete accredited postgraduate training in counselling psychology.

Check for relevant course details with the British Psychological Society (BPS). To register as a chartered counselling psychologist (which many employers prefer), it is necessary to obtain the Graduate Basis for Chartered Membership (GBC) by completing a BPS accredited qualification in psychology (1-4 yrs) and then the three-year doctorate course in counselling psychology.

Graduates with a non-related degree are able to take a conversion course, but all qualifications must be approved by the BPS/HPC. On completing the doctorate you are eligible to apply to the BPS for chartered status. The BPS has a mandatory requirement for chartered psychologists, who are practising, to undertake and maintain a record of their continuing professional development (CPD).

Mature applicants should note that the training period is lengthy. Entrants with a degree and/or relevant postgraduate degree may have an advantage for training posts. The Open University offers a British Psychological Society (BPS) accredited BSc degree in psychology and a postgraduate conversion diploma. There are also BPS accredited conversion courses for those with degrees in other subjects.

Opportunities and Pay

Jobs are available throughout the UK. Counselling psychologists are employed by different organisations such as local authorities and the civil service, the NHS, prison and probation service, voluntary organisations, student counselling services, and in private hospitals. Opportunities in the private sector include running employee assistance programmes in human resource management. You can be self-employed and work as a consultant on a freelance basis.

There may be opportunities to do research or teach. Career pathways for chartered psychologists are generally well defined and promotion opportunities are good. Part-time work or job sharing is possible.

Depending on the employer or whether self-employed, starting salaries for graduates are in the region of £23k-£30k a year, rising to around £28k-£42k a year with experience. Senior psychologists can earn a salary of more than £70k a year.

Skills and Qualities

able to understand other people's problems, awareness of confidentiality issues, emotionally strong, good communication skills, good interpersonal skills, IT skills, non-judgemental, perceptive, reassuring, scientific approach

Relevant Subjects

Biology, English, Health and social care, Mathematics, Psychology, Science, Sociology

Further Information

AGCAS: Health (Job Sector Briefing) (AGCAS) - www.prospects.ac.uk

British Journal of Social Psychology (BPS, quarterly) - www.bpsjournals.co.uk/journals/bjsp

Careers in Psychology (British Psychological Society) - www.bps.org.uk/careers/

Division of Counselling Psychology (BPS) - www.counsellingpsychology.org.uk

NHS Careers (NHS Careers) - www.nhscareers.nhs.uk

Psychologist Appointments (BPS) (BPS) - www.psychapp.co.uk

Psychology Uncovered (Trotman 2010) - www.trotman.co.uk

▶ Working in advice & counselling (2007) (Babcock Lifeskills) - www.babcock-lifeskills.com/

Addresses

British Association for Counselling and Psychotherapy (BACP)
BACP House, 15 St John's Business Park, Lutterworth, Leicestershire LE17 4HB
Phone: +44 (0)1455 883300
Web: www.bacp.co.uk

British Psychological Society (BPS)
St Andrews House, 48 Princess Road East, Leicester LE1 7DR
Phone: +44 (0)116 254 9568
Web: www.bps.org.uk

Health Professions Council (HPC)
Park House, 184 Kennington Park Road, London SE11 4BU
Phone: +44 (0)20 7582 0866
Web: www.hpc-uk.org

Similar Jobs

Counsellor, Psychologist: Clinical, Psychologist: Educational, Psychologist: Health, Psychotherapist, Social Worker

Psychologist: Educational

CRCI:Social Work and Counselling Services
CLCI:KEL Job Band: 5

Job Description

Educational psychologists are concerned with children and young people's learning and development. They work mainly in schools, assisting teachers and parents. Deal with social and emotional problems, such as disruptive behaviour, or assisting children and young adults with physical and mental difficulties, the disadvantaged, and also gifted children. Use assessment techniques and decide on the most suitable course of treatment, which may include a learning programme, counselling or family therapy.

Educational psychologists liaise with school staff, the family, social workers and medical experts. Provide training such as behaviour management for those dealing with young people. Attend case conferences and meetings, conduct research and write reports.

Work Details

Usually works a basic 37 hr week, Monday to Friday, though may need to work some evenings and weekends. Your work usually takes place in an office or a child guidance clinic, but you may also visit clients' homes, or work in a nursery, primary or secondary school, special schools/units, or in medical centres.

You work mainly with children and young adults up to age 19, who may be aggressive, depressed, anxious or negative about their learning and future. Your clients can also be children with special needs, school refusers or exceptionally gifted children. You also work with parents, teachers, social workers and other medical staff.

Qualification

• England, Wales and Northern Ireland

Band 5: For degree courses in psychology: 2-3 A levels and some GCSEs (A*-C) usually including English, maths and sometimes science subjects. Psychology is not required for entry to degree courses, but students may find that study at this level helps them to decide if they are suited to studying psychology at degree level. Exact requirements depend on the degree you take.

• Scotland

Band 5: For degree courses in psychology: 3-5 H grades and some S grades (1-3), usually including English, maths and sometimes science subjects. Psychology is not required for entry to degree courses, but students may find that study at this level helps them to decide if they are suited to studying psychology at degree level.

Degree Information

Qualifications in both teaching and psychology are usually required and postgraduate training in educational psychology is also necessary. A good honours degree in psychology approved by the British Psychological Society that qualifies for the Graduate Basis for Registration (GBR) is required for all postgraduate training courses.

Adult Qualifications

Applicants without the normal entry qualifications should contact academic institutions for entry standards for mature applicants, which may be relaxed. The Open University offers top-up credit courses leading to Graduate Basis for Registration (GBR) with the British Psychological Society.

Work Experience

Relevant work experience includes dealing with people in a helping capacity, or work with children in or out of education. It is also useful to talk directly to an educational psychologist about the work, but direct observation may not be possible because of client confidentiality issues.

Entry and Training

Entry to training courses is highly competitive and you need a good and approved honours degree to gain a place on an educational psychology postgraduate course. The Health Professions Council (HPC) is now the regulator of practitioner psychologists in the UK and is responsible for approving all qualifications. To be registered with the HPC you need to complete accredited postgraduate training in your chosen branch of psychology. To register as a chartered psychologist, you must obtain the Graduate Basis for Chartered Membership (GBC) from the British Psychological Society (BPS) by completing an accredited qualification in psychology (1-4 yrs), and then an accredited postgraduate training course in educational psychology. Graduates with a non-related degree may be able to take a conversion course but all qualifications must be approved by the BPS/HPC.

To become an educational psychologist in England, Wales and Northern Ireland, you need to complete a three-year educational psychology doctorate training programme that is accredited by the BPS/HPC. You also need experience of working with children in an educational, childcare or community setting. The course includes 300 days of professional placement work under supervision. Qualified teachers may be given exemptions from some parts of the doctorate.

The application process for funded educational psychology training places involves submitting an application form, equal opportunities form and completed check list to the Children's Workforce Development Council. On completing the doctorate in educational psychology you are eligible to apply to the BPS for chartered status. The BPS has a mandatory requirement for chartered psychologists, who are practising, to undertake and maintain a record of their continuing professional development (CPD).

In Scotland, you also need the BPS GBC plus experience of working directly with children to apply for the two-year MSc in educational psychology. This is followed by a year of supervised practice. Usually a UK degree in psychology, or the completion of a BPS accredited graduate conversion course, is acceptable for entry.

Mature applicants should note that the training period is lengthy. However, age and life experience are considered an advantage. Previous experience as a qualified teacher is very relevant. Those without the usual entry requirements should contact institutions for information on courses, which need to be BPS-approved. Those with a non-relevant degree should contact the British Psychological Society (BPS) for details of accredited conversion courses. The Open University offers a BPS accredited BSc degree in psychology and a postgraduate conversion diploma.

Opportunities and Pay

The demand for educational psychologists is increasing. You are usually employed by the psychological services of local education or social services departments, or by health authorities. You can work anywhere in the UK. Some educational psychologists work in private practice. Promotion to more senior posts, particularly in local authority children's services departments, is possible after gaining experience. However, prospects are limited by the small number of higher grade posts. There are opportunities for self employment or freelance work.

Qualified and experienced educational psychologists working in local government earn between £32k-£49k a year. Senior and principal educational psychologists are on a separate salary scale, starting at £42k a year.

Skills and Qualities

able to put people at ease, able to work both on your own and in a team, awareness of confidentiality issues, efficient record keeping, flexible approach, good at writing reports, good communication skills, good interpersonal skills, good listening skills, sound judgement

Relevant Subjects

Biology, English, Health and social care, Mathematics, Psychology, Science, Sociology

Further Information

British Journal of Educational Psychology (BPS, quarterly) - www.bpsjournals.co.uk/journals/bjep

Careers in Psychology (British Psychological Society) - www.bps.org.uk/careers/

Children's Workforce Development Council (CWDC) - www.cwdcouncil.org.uk

Local Government Careers (Improvement and Development Agency) - www.lgcareers.com/publications/
Psychologist Appointments (BPS) (BPS) - www.psychapp.co.uk
Psychology Uncovered (Trotman 2010) - www.trotman.co.uk
▶Working in advice & counselling (2007) (Babcock Lifeskills) - www.babcock-lifeskills.com/
▶Working in social care (2010) (Babcock Lifeskills) - www.babcock-lifeskills.com/

Addresses

Association of Educational Psychologists (AEP)
4 The Riverside Centre, Frankland Lane, Durham DH1 5TA
Phone: +44 (0)191 384 9512
Web: www.aep.org.uk

British Psychological Society (BPS)
St Andrews House, 48 Princess Road East, Leicester LE1 7DR
Phone: +44 (0)116 254 9568
Web: www.bps.org.uk

Health Professions Council (HPC)
Park House, 184 Kennington Park Road, London SE11 4BU
Phone: +44 (0)20 7582 0866
Web: www.hpc-uk.org

Open University (OU)
PO Box 197, Milton Keynes MK7 6BJ
Phone: +44 (0)845 300 6090
Web: http://www3.open.ac.uk

Similar Jobs

Counsellor, Psychologist, Psychologist: Occupational, Psychologist: Sport & Exercise, Psychotherapist, Social Worker, Teacher: Special Educational Needs

Psychologist: Forensic

CRCI:Social Work and Counselling Services
CLCI:KEL Job Band: 5

Job Description

Forensic psychologists use expertise based on psychological theory and research to develop treatment programmes. They provide advice on offending behaviour to those in the criminal justice system. Work mainly with offenders in prisons and under supervision of the probation service. Focus on therapy techniques and one-to-one assessments to determine, for example, the risk of re-offending.

Forensic psychologists work closely with hospital staff, prison officers, the police, social workers, probation officers, psychiatrists, university staff and representatives of the judicial and legal systems. May undertake research projects and oversee the training and development of staff. Can work in teaching, training and applied research.

They use a variety of techniques including the use of computers, video and audio recording, and other specialised equipment for experimental work.

Work Details

Usually works a basic 37 hr week, Monday to Friday, though may need to work some evenings and weekends. Travel within a working day may be required, sometimes to locations with difficult access, so a driving licence is an asset. You spend time in prisons where you experience some noise, smells and security lock-up procedures, and in police stations and courts. Category A institutions impose camera observation and entry searches. Duties may involve teaching, counselling, advising, interviewing people, carrying out tests, observing and assessing people. You may also attend court to provide expert witness testimony. Clients can be anxious, nervous, aggressive or negative, so your work may be emotionally demanding at times.

Qualification

• England, Wales and Northern Ireland

Band 5: For degree courses in psychology: 2-3 A levels and some GCSEs (A*-C) usually including English, maths and sometimes science subjects, or equivalent. Psychology is not required for entry to degree courses, but students may find that study at this level helps them to decide if they are suited to studying psychology at degree level. Exact requirements depend on the degree you take.

• Scotland

Band 5: For degree courses in psychology: 3-5 H grades and some S grades (1-3), usually including English, maths and sometimes science subjects. Psychology is not required for entry to degree courses, but students may find that study at this level helps them to decide if they are suited to studying psychology at degree level.

Degree Information

An honours degree (NFQ Level 8) course in psychology approved by the Psychological Society of Ireland (PSI) is required, followed by a professional postgraduate qualification in forensic psychology.

Some first degree courses are more relevant than others for PSI membership, so applicants should ensure that their chosen undergraduate degrees are accredited by the PSI or the British Psychological Society.

Adult Qualifications

You usually need the standard academic entry requirements for a degree, but mature applicants without these should contact academic institutions. Some universities reserve places each year for mature students.

Work Experience

Relevant work experience includes anything dealing with people in a helping capacity, using listening skills and any observation or direct experience in the caring professions. Voluntary work experience may be available with organisations such as the National Association for the Care and Resettlement of Offenders (NACRO). It is useful to talk to a forensic psychologist about the work, but direct observation may not be possible because of confidentiality issues.

Entry and Training

You should choose your first degree course carefully, checking that it is relevant for forensic psychology. The Health Professions Council (HPC) is now the regulator of practitioner psychologists in the UK and is responsible for approving all qualifications. You need to be registered with the HPC to become a forensic psychologist and for this you need to complete accredited postgraduate training.

To register as a chartered forensic psychologist, it is necessary to gain the Graduate Basis for Chartered Membership (GBC) by completing an appropriate British Psychological Society (BPS) accredited qualification in psychology (1-4 yrs) and then an accredited MSc in forensic psychology, or stage 1 of the BPS diploma in forensic psychology. Stage 2 of the diploma involves a minimum of two years' practical experience under the supervision of a chartered forensic psychologist. Some universities offer a Doctorate programme that covers both stage 1 and 2 of the diploma in forensic psychology.

Graduates with a non-related degree are able to take a conversion course but all qualifications must be approved by the BPS/HPC. The prison and probation services and the NHS offer supervision for achievement of BPS chartered status, which takes a minimum of three years. In Scotland criminal justice social work (probation work) is carried out by social work departments.

Continuing professional development (CPD) is a career-long process that psychologists undertake in order to keep up to date and to maintain and enhance their professional skills. The BPS has a mandatory requirement for chartered psychologists, who are practising, to undertake and maintain a record of their CPD.

Mature applicants should note that the training period is lengthy. However, age and life experience are considered an advantage. Those without the usual entry requirements should contact institutions for information on courses, which need to be BPS-approved. Those with a non-relevant degree should contact the British Psychological Society (BPS) for details of accredited conversion courses. Mature applicants find it useful to have previous related work experience. The Open University offers a BPS accredited BSc degree in psychology and a postgraduate conversion diploma.

Opportunities and Pay

Forensic psychology is one of the fastest growing areas of employment for psychology graduates. Around 800 chartered forensic psychologists work in the UK, mainly for the prison and probation services but also with academic institutions, the NHS, local and central government departments. Alternatively, you can be self-employed and work as a consultant on a freelance basis.

There may be opportunities to do research or teach. Career pathways for chartered psychologists are generally well defined and promotion opportunities are good.

Depending on the employer, starting salaries for graduates range from about £20k a year, rising to around £28k-£42k a year with experience. Senior psychologists can earn a salary of more than £60k a year.

Skills and Qualities

able to understand other people's problems, able to work both on your own and in a team, awareness of confidentiality issues, awareness of confidentiality issues, emotionally strong, excellent communication skills, good listening skills, non-judgemental, perceptive, scientific approach

Relevant Subjects

Biology, Chemistry, English, Health and social care, Mathematics, Psychology, Science, Sociology

Further Information

Careers in Psychology (British Psychological Society) - www.bps.org.uk/careers/

Legal and Criminological Psychology (BPS, bi-annual) - www.bpsjournals.co.uk/journals/lcp/

NACRO (National Association for the Care and Resettlement of Offenders) - www.nacro.org.uk

Open University - www.open.ac.uk

Psychologist Appointments (BPS) (BPS) - www.psychapp.co.uk

Psychology Uncovered (Trotman 2010) - www.trotman.co.uk

▶ Working in advice & counselling (2007) (Babcock Lifeskills) - www.babcock-lifeskills.com/

Addresses

British Psychological Society (BPS)
St Andrews House, 48 Princess Road East, Leicester LE1 7DR
Phone: +44 (0)116 254 9568
Web: www.bps.org.uk

Health Professions Council (HPC)
Park House, 184 Kennington Park Road, London SE11 4BU
Phone: +44 (0)20 7582 0866
Web: www.hpc-uk.org

HM Prison Service HQ
Cleland House, Page Street, London SW1P 4LN
Web: www.hmprisonservice.gov.uk

National Probation Service
1st Floor Abell House, John Islip Street, London SW1P 4LH
Web: www.probation.homeoffice.gov.uk

Northern Ireland Prison Service
Prison Service HQ, Dundonald House, Upper Newtownards Road, Belfast BT4 3SU
Phone: +44 (0)28 9052 5065
Web: www.niprisonservice.gov.uk

Probation Board for Northern Ireland
80-90 North Street, Belfast BT1 1LD
Phone: +44 (0)28 9026 2400
Web: www.pbni.org.uk

Scottish Prison Service
Communication Branch Room 338 Calton House
5 Redheughs Rigg, Edinburgh EH12 9HW
Phone: +44 (0)131 244 8745
Web: www.sps.gov.uk

Similar Jobs

Counsellor, Probation Officer, Psychologist: Clinical, Psychologist: Educational, Psychologist: Occupational, Psychotherapist

Psychologist: Health

also known as: Health Psychologist
CRCI:Social Work and Counselling Services
CLCI:KEL
Job Band: 5

Job Description

Health psychologists apply psychological research and methods to improve a person's physical health and to prevent physical health problems. This may include helping people adapt to chronic illnesses, reducing stress in those with heart problems, resolving psychological problems related to diet, drug abuse or smoking, and looking at their medication and treatment. They encourage the use of exercise, healthy dietary choice, teeth brushing, health checks, self-examination and other positive behaviour. Also work on identifying the psychological factors that contribute to physical illness.

Some also work on the improvement of healthcare systems or on the formulation of healthcare policy. Work is often as part of a multi-disciplinary treatment team, or it may be in research, or education, teaching the skills to other health staff.

Work Details

Usually works a basic 35-40 hr week though sometimes extra hours may be needed. You work with people with mental and physical health issues in need of support, and their families. You may also work as part of a multi-disciplinary team with other healthcare professionals and social workers. Clients can be anxious, nervous, aggressive or negative, and work is sometimes emotionally demanding. There are some opportunities for part-time or freelance work.

Qualification

• England, Wales and Northern Ireland

Band 5: For degree courses in psychology: 2-3 A levels and some GCSEs (A*-C) usually including English, maths and sometimes science subjects. Psychology is not required for entry to degree courses, but students may find that study at this level helps them to decide if they are suited to studying psychology at degree level. Exact requirements depend on the degree you take.

• Scotland

Band 5: For degree courses in psychology: 3-5 H grades and some S grades (1-3), usually including English, maths and sometimes science subjects. Psychology is not required for entry to degree courses, but students may find that study at this level helps them to decide if they are suited to studying psychology at degree level.

Degree Information

A good honours degree in psychology approved by the British Psychological Society (BPS) that qualifies for the Graduate Basis for Registration (GBR) is required for all postgraduate training courses. A conversion course can also lead to BPS approval or you can sit the BPS qualifiying exam. Some first degree courses are more relevant than others for BPS accreditation, so applicants should carefully consider future career choice.

Adult Qualifications
The correct academic qualifications are essential for this job; mature applicants without the standard requirements should contact academic institutions, which may relax entry conditions. The Open University offers top-up courses leading to graduate basis for registration (GBR) with the British Psychological Society.

Work Experience
Relevant work experience includes anything dealing with people in a helping capacity, using listening skills and any observation or direct experience in the caring professions. It is useful to talk to a health psychologist about the work, but direct observation may not be possible because of client confidentiality issues.

Entry and Training
You should choose your first degree course carefully, checking that it is relevant for health psychology. The Health Professions Council (HPC) is now the regulator of practitioner psychologists in the UK and is responsible for approving all qualifications. You need to be registered with the HPC to become a health psychologist and for this you need to complete accredited postgraduate training.

To become a chartered health psychologist, it is necessary to gain the Graduate Basis for Chartered Membership (GBC) by completing an appropriate British Psychological Society (BPS) accredited qualification in psychology (1-4 yrs) and then a postgraduate qualification in health psychology. Finally you need two years' supervised experience. The postgraduate course may be an approved MSc or stage 1 of the BPS qualification in health psychology. Some universities offer a Doctorate programme that covers both stages of the society's qualification in health psychology.

Graduates with a non-related degree are able to take a conversion course, but all qualifications must be approved by the BPS/HPC. Continuing professional development (CPD) is a career-long process that psychologists undertake in order to keep up to date and to maintain and enhance their professional skills. The BPS has a mandatory requirement for chartered psychologists, who are practising, to undertake and maintain a record of their CPD.

Mature applicants should note that the training period is lengthy. However, age and life experience are considered an advantage. Those without the usual entry requirements should contact institutions for information on courses, which need to be British Psychological Society (BPS)-approved. Those with a non-relevant degree should contact the BPS for details of accredited conversion courses. Mature applicants find it useful to have previous related work experience. The Open University offers a BPS accredited BSc degree in psychology and a postgraduate conversion diploma.

Opportunities and Pay
There are around 500 health psychologists in the UK. This is a rapidly evolving area of work, and job opportunities are increasing in many areas, particularly in teaching and research. You can work in a variety of settings, for the NHS in clinics or hospitals, university departments, academic health research units, health promotion, schools or in industry.

If you work for the NHS, pay is usually on a nationally agreed scale. Private health psychologists can earn considerably more than NHS workers but opportunities are currently more limited. Salaries for newly qualified health psychologists are around £26k-£30k a year, and for senior posts can be over £50k a year.

Skills and Qualities
able to understand other people's problems, able to work both on your own and in a team, awareness of confidentiality issues, emotionally strong, good communication skills, good interpersonal skills, good listening skills, IT skills, patient, scientific approach

Relevant Subjects
Biology, Chemistry, English, Health and social care, Mathematics, Psychology, Science, Sociology

Further Information
British Journal of Health Psychology (BPS, quarterly) - www.bpsjournals.co.uk/journals/bjhp

Careers in Psychology (British Psychological Society) - www.bps.org.uk/careers/

Division of Health Psychology - www.health-psychology.org.uk

Health Psychology Update (DHP, quarterly) (DHP) - www.health-psychology.org.uk

NHS Careers (NHS Careers) - www.nhscareers.nhs.uk

Psychologist Appointments (BPS) - www.psychapp.co.uk

Psychology Uncovered (Trotman 2010) - www.trotman.co.uk

Skills for Care and Development - sector skills council for social care, childre, early years and young people's workforces - www.skillsforcareanddevelopment.org.uk

▶Working in advice & counselling (2007) (Babcock Lifeskills) - www.babcock-lifeskills.com/

Addresses
British Association of Sport and Exercise Sciences (BASES)
Leeds Metropolitan University,
Carnegie Faculty of Sport and Education,
Fairfax Hall, Headingley Campus, Beckett Park LS6 3QS
Phone: +44 (0)113 812 6162
Web: www.bases.org.uk

Division of Health Psychology
British Psychological Society, St Andrews House,
48 Princess Road East, Leicester LE1 7DR
Phone: +44 (0)116 254 9568
Web: www.health-psychology.org.uk

Health Professions Council (HPC)
Park House, 184 Kennington Park Road, London SE11 4BU
Phone: +44 (0)20 7582 0866
Web: www.hpc-uk.org

Similar Jobs
Counsellor, Psychologist, Psychologist: Clinical, Psychologist: Occupational, Psychologist: Sport & Exercise, Psychotherapist, Social Worker

Psychologist: Neuropsychologist
also known as: Clinical Neuropsychologist, Neuropsychologist

CRCI:Social Work and Counselling Services
CLCI:KEL Job Band: 5

Job Description
Neuropsychologists work as qualified psychologists specialising in the link between the human brain and behaviour. Some specialise in research, whereas others treat patients directly. Both involve conducting tests and assessments to identify and improve treatment of various disorders. Neuropsychologists commonly work in three areas; acute, rehabilitation and in the community. They write reports, carry out research, and attend meetings and case conferences. Experienced neuropsychologists also commonly act as expert witnesses for the courts. Research is an important aspect of neuropsychological practice.

In acute settings they work alongside neurosurgeons and neurologists, usually in a regional neurosciences centre. Are concerned with the early effects of trauma, neurosurgery and neurological disease. In rehabilitation centres, they provide post-acute assessment, training and support for people who have sustained brain injury, or who have other neurological problems. Apply knowledge of anatomy, physiology and pathology of the nervous system to help people with brain injuries. Play a central role in the multi-disciplinary team, which aim to maximise recovery, minimise disability, and prepare the client for return to the community or a residential placement.

If working in community services, neuropsychologists perform a similar role, but support those who have returned to community living. Also work with patients' families and liaise with, for example, other psychologists, medical staff and other professionals such as social workers.

Work Details

Usually works a basic 37 hr week though may need to work some evenings and weekends. You work in a hospital or clinic, rehabilitation centre, in a university or research establishment, or in private practice. You work with people who are in need of support, usually due to brain damage or trauma. Patients or clients can be anxious, nervous, aggressive or negative, and your work can be emotionally demanding. You consult with other health professionals, including medical staff, social workers and health therapists. Part-time work is possible.

Qualification

• England, Wales and Northern Ireland

Band 5: For degree courses in psychology: 2-3 A levels and some GCSEs (A*-C) usually including English, maths and sometimes science subjects. Psychology is not required for entry to degree courses, but students may find that study at this level helps them to decide if they are suited to studying psychology at degree level. Exact requirements depend on the degree you take.

• Scotland

Band 5: For degree courses in psychology: 3-5 H grades and some S grades (1-3), usually including English, maths and sometimes science subjects. Psychology is not required for entry to degree courses, but students may find that study at this level helps them to decide if they are suited to studying psychology at degree level.

Degree Information

A good honours degree in psychology approved by the British Psychological Society (BPS) that qualifies for the Graduate Basis for Registration (GBR) is required for all postgraduate training courses. A conversion course can also lead to BPS approval or you can sit the BPS qualifiying exam. Some first degree courses are more relevant than others for BPS accreditation, so applicants should carefully consider future career choice.

Adult Qualifications

Applicants without the normal entry qualifications should contact academic institutions for mature entry standards, which may be relaxed. The Open University has a scheme that offers top-up courses for graduates, or to gain sufficient psychology credits that provide eligibility for registration with the British Psychological Society.

Work Experience

Work experience gives you an insight into what you enjoy about a job or working environment, and the opportunity to acquire new skills. It provides valuable information to add to your CV, and improves your degree course entry and employment prospects. Relevant work includes anything dealing with people in a helping or caring capacity. Some experience with a neuropsychologist practice is useful but may be difficult to arrange because of client confidentiality.

Entry and Training

To become a neuropsychologist you must be eligible for the British Psychological Society (BPS)'s Graduate Basis for Chartered Membership (GBC), usually by taking a BPS-accredited honours degree before specialising in neuropsychology. To become a practitioner member of the BPS's Division of Neuropsychology, entrants must first establish their professional competence in either clinical or educational psychology, and be registered with the Health Professions Council (HPC).

You then need to complete an additional BPS Practitioner Full Membership Qualification (PFMQ) in adult or paediatric clinical neuropsychology. Applicants submit case studies and reports and pass four examinations in areas of neuropsychology. If your first degree course is not accredited, or your degree is not in psychology, then you can gain GBC by taking a BPS accredited conversion course, which converts your degree to the equivalent of an honours degree with psychology as the main subject. Contact the BPS for further details of all qualifying routes.

Continuing professional development (CPD) is a career-long process that psychologists undertake in order to keep up to date and to maintain and enhance their professional skills. The BPS has a mandatory requirement for chartered psychologists, who are practising, to undertake and maintain a record of their CPD.

Mature applicants should note that the training period is lengthy. However, age and life experience are considered an advantage. Those without the usual entry requirements should contact institutions for information on courses, which need to be British Psychological Society (BPS)-approved. Those with a non-relevant degree should contact the BPS for details of accredited conversion courses. Mature applicants find it useful to have previous related work experience. The Open University offers a BPS accredited BSc degree in psychology and a postgraduate conversion diploma.

Opportunities and Pay

Most work is for the NHS in a regional neurosciences centre, a rehabilitation centre, and in community services. Some neuropsychologists are employed by a university or by the independent sector within both private and not-for-profit charitable organisations. There is a clear promotion structure within the NHS.

Pay for neuropsychologists in the NHS is on the same national scale as clinical psychologists, but in private practice it varies according to your employer. A trainee clinical psychologist working in the NHS earns from £24.8k a year, and once fully qualified earns £29k-£39k a year. A consultant psychologist can earn up to £79k a year. Many senior neuropsychologists substantially supplement their income by undertaking private medico-legal consultancy as expert witnesses in personal injury cases.

Skills and Qualities

able to work both on your own and in a team, analytical skills, awareness of confidentiality issues, emotionally strong, good communication skills, good interpersonal skills, good listening skills, IT skills, logical, objective

Relevant Subjects

Biology, Chemistry, English, Health and social care, Mathematics, Psychology, Science, Sociology

Further Information

AGCAS: Health (Job Sector Briefing) (AGCAS) - www.prospects.ac.uk

British Journal of Psychology (BPS, quarterly) - www.bpsjournals.co.uk/journals/bjp

Careers in Psychology (British Psychological Society) - www.bps.org.uk/careers/

Division of Neuropsychology (DoN) (BPS) - www.bps.org.uk/don

NHS Careers (NHS Careers) - www.nhscareers.nhs.uk

Psychologist Appointments (BPS) - www.psychapp.co.uk

Psychology Uncovered (Trotman 2010) - www.trotman.co.uk

The Clinical Neuropsychologist (8 x year) (Psychology Press) - www.neuropsychologyarena.com/journals/Clinical-Neuropsychologist-1385-4046

The Psychologist (monthly) (BPS) - www.thepsychologist.org.uk

▶Working in advice & counselling (2007) (Babcock Lifeskills) - www.babcock-lifeskills.com/

Addresses

British Psychological Society (BPS)
St Andrews House, 48 Princess Road East, Leicester LE1 7DR
Phone: +44 (0)116 254 9568
Web: www.bps.org.uk

Health Professions Council (HPC)
Park House, 184 Kennington Park Road, London SE11 4BU
Phone: +44 (0)20 7582 0866
Web: www.hpc-uk.org

Open University (OU)
PO Box 197, Milton Keynes MK7 6BJ
Phone: +44 (0)845 300 6090
Web: http://www3.open.ac.uk

Similar Jobs

Nurse: Mental Health, Psychiatrist, Psychologist, Psychologist: Clinical, Psychotherapist, Social Worker

Psychologist: Occupational

also known as: Psychologist: Organisational

CRCI:Social Work and Counselling Services
CLCI:KEL Job Band: 5

Job Description

Occupational psychologists are concerned with the performance of people at work and in training. They look at how organisations function and how individuals and small groups behave at work. They study factors affecting people at work to help maximise job satisfaction and increase the effectiveness of an organisation or group. May be involved with selection and/or vocational guidance, personnel management, time management and counselling. Can develop and use psychometric tests. Some psychologists study work environments to improve health and safety and efficiency.

Occupational psychologists are often involved in redundancy procedures or pre-retirement counselling. They work closely with other professionals such as ergonomists and engineers in the design of a building or redesign of the work environment.

Work Details

Usually works a basic 37 hr week, though may need to work out-of-office hours in some jobs. Work involves observing, assessing and interviewing people, carrying out tests, persuading people, negotiating, advising and counselling. Duties are likely to include preparing and presenting reports and you may also be responsible for health and safety, recruitment of staff, and staff training and development.

Qualification

• England, Wales and Northern Ireland

Band 5: For degree courses in psychology: 2-3 A levels and some GCSEs (A*-C) usually including English, maths and sometimes science subjects. Psychology is not required for entry to degree courses, but students may find that study at this level helps them to decide if they are suited to studying psychology at degree level. Exact requirements depend on the degree you take.

• Scotland

Band 5: For degree courses in psychology: 3-5 H grades and some S grades (1-3), usually including English, maths and sometimes science subjects. Psychology is not required for entry to degree courses, but students may find that study at this level helps them to decide if they are suited to studying psychology at degree level.

Degree Information

A good honours degree in psychology approved by the British Psychological Society (BPS) that qualifies for the Graduate Basis for Registration (GBR) is required for all postgraduate training courses. A conversion course can also lead to BPS approval or you can sit the BPS qualifiying exam. Some first degree courses are more relevant than others for BPS accreditation, so applicants should carefully consider future career choice.

Adult Qualifications

Applicants without the normal entry qualifications should contact academic institutions for mature entry standards, which may be relaxed. The Open University has a scheme that offers top-up courses for graduates, or to gain sufficient psychology credits that provide eligibility for registration with the British Psychological Society.

Work Experience

Entry to this job is competitive and it is important that you do some relevant work or voluntary experience before applying to degree courses. It is an advantage to have relevant experience in industry or working with people in a helping capacity. The use of listening skills, observation or direct experience in the caring professions is also helpful. It is useful to talk to an occupational psychologist about the work, but direct observation may not be possible because of client confidentiality issues.

Entry and Training

You should choose your first degree course carefully, checking that it is relevant for occupational psychology. The Health Professions Council (HPC) is now the regulator of practitioner psychologists in the UK and is responsible for approving all qualifications. To be registered as an occupational psychologist with the HPC you need to complete accredited postgraduate training (see below).

To register as a chartered occupational psychologist you need to obtain the Graduate Basis for Chartered Membership (GBC) by completing an appropriate British Psychological Society (BPS) accredited degree in psychology (1-4 yrs). Graduates with a non-related degree are able to take a conversion course but all qualifications must be approved by the BPS/HPC. You then complete an accredited postgraduate masters course in occupational psychology, or stage 1 of the Society's Qualification in Occupational Psychology. This is followed by two years' approved supervised practice as an occupational psychologist (stage 2 of the Society's Qualification in Occupational Psychology).

Continuing professional development (CPD) is a career-long process that psychologists undertake in order to keep up to date and to maintain and enhance their professional skills. The BPS has a mandatory requirement for chartered psychologists, who are practising, to undertake and maintain a record of their CPD.

Mature applicants should note that the training period is lengthy. However, age and life experience are considered an advantage. Those without the usual entry requirements should contact institutions for information on courses, which need to be British Psychological Society (BPS)-approved. Those with a non-relevant degree should contact the BPS for details of accredited conversion courses. Mature applicants find it useful to have previous related work experience. The Open University offers a BPS accredited BSc degree in psychology and a postgraduate conversion diploma.

Opportunities and Pay

This area of psychology is highly competitive. However it is a growing field and there are a wide range of applications. You may be employed by industry, commerce, a university or research organisation. The civil service is a large employer of occupational psychologists and there are opportunities with the prison service, home office and ministry of defence. Some are employed as consultants and there may be opportunities for part-time work. Many organisations now employ occupational psychologists to work in human resources management and market research, especially in the private sector.

Most companies have clearly defined career paths and promotion to more senior posts is possible after gaining experience. A move to another area of the UK may be necessary for those seeking promotion.

Pay varies depending on location, sector and employer. Graduate trainee psychologists start earning around £20k-£26k a year, rising to £28k-£42k with experience and full qualifications. Senior psychologists earn from around £42k to over £70k a year. Salaries in the private sector and as a consultant tend to be higher, and may rise to more than £100k a year.

Skills and Qualities

able to get on with all kinds of people, able to prioritise work, analytical skills, good communication skills, good interpersonal skills, good listening skills, good presentation skills, objective, perceptive

Relevant Subjects

Biology, English, Health and social care, Mathematics, Psychology, Sociology

Further Information

Careers in Psychology (British Psychological Society) - www.bps.org.uk/careers/

Civil Service - www.civilservice.gov.uk/jobs

Journal of Occupational & Organizational Psychology (BPS, quarterly) (British Psychological Society) - www.bpsjournals.co.uk/journals/joop/

NHS Careers (NHS Careers) - www.nhscareers.nhs.uk

Psychologist Appointments (BPS) - www.psychapp.co.uk

Psychology Uncovered (Trotman 2010) - www.trotman.co.uk

▶Working in advice & counselling (2007) (Babcock Lifeskills) - www.babcock-lifeskills.com/

Addresses

Association of Business Psychologists (ABP)
211/212 Piccadilly, London W1J 9HG
Phone: +44 (0)207 917 1733
Web: www.theabp.org.uk/

Division of Occupational Psychology
British Psychological Society, St Andrews House,
48 Princes Road East, Leicester, Leicestershire LE1 7DR
Phone: +44 (0)116 254 9568
Web: www.bps.org.uk/dop

Health Professions Council (HPC)
Park House, 184 Kennington Park Road, London SE11 4BU
Phone: +44 (0)20 7582 0866
Web: www.hpc-uk.org

Open University (OU)
PO Box 197, Milton Keynes MK7 6BJ
Phone: +44 (0)845 300 6090
Web: http://www3.open.ac.uk

Similar Jobs

Careers Adviser, Ergonomist, Human Resources Officer/Manager, Psychologist, Psychologist: Educational, Psychologist: Health

Psychologist: Sport & Exercise

CRCI:Social Work and Counselling Services
CLCI:KEL Job Band: 5

Job Description

Sport and exercise psychologists study the psychological factors associated with participation in exercise and sport. They usually practice either as a sport psychologist, working with sports participants over a range of sports, or as an exercise psychologist, helping the general public to become more active. May practice as both, but this is less common.

Sports psychologists help prepare athletes to perform better and deal with the demands of training. May counsel referees on how to deal with the stressful parts of their work. May attend coaching sessions and advise coaches on how to build cohesion within their team. May use psychology to help an athlete to cope with the effects of an injury. They help athletes at the end of their career to deal with the transition to another type of work.

Exercise psychologists look at how they can use psychology to motivate people to do more exercise. May do research into why some groups of people exercise more than others. May be involved in explaining the benefits of exercise, particularly for those who may have some psychological disorders. Help individuals and groups to implement target setting in exercise regimes.

Work Details

Working hours are likely to be irregular and may involve working evenings, early mornings and weekends. Some time may be spent office based, doing research, some lecturing or teaching, and the rest in consultancy working with a team or an individual. When working directly with those involved in sport or exercise, you may be in team premises, a gym, on a sports field, working in a GP practice or maybe even a prison. Clients can be anxious or under stress, and the work can be emotionally demanding. You spend a lot of time consulting with other professionals and need to write reports. You may need to travel to work with different clients.

Qualification

Sport and exercise psychology is a relatively new field. There are two main routes for qualification at the moment, either via the British Psychological Society to become a chartered psychologist or via the British Association of Sport and Exercise Sciences to become accredited.

• England, Wales and Northern Ireland

Band 5: For relevant degree course: 2-3 A levels and some GCSEs (A*-C) usually including English, maths and sometimes science subjects. Psychology is not required for entry to psychology degree courses, but students may find that study at this level helps them to decide if they are suited to studying psychology at degree level. Exact requirements depend on the degree you take.

• Scotland

Band 5: For relevant degree course: 3-5 H grades and some S grades (1-3), usually including English, maths and sometimes science subjects. Psychology is not required for entry to psychology degree courses, but students may find that study at this level helps them to decide if they are suited to studying psychology at degree level. Exact requirements depend on the degree you take.

Degree Information

A good honours degree in psychology approved by the British Psychological Society (BPS) that qualifies for the Graduate Basis for Registration (GBR) is required for all postgraduate training courses accredited by BPS. A conversion course can also lead to BPS approval, or you can sit the BPS qualifying exam. A degree in sport and exercise science is relevant for the accreditation route via British Association of Sport and Exercise Sciences.

Adult Qualifications

Applicants without the normal entry qualifications should contact academic institutions for entry standards for mature applicants, which may be relaxed. The Open University offers top-up credit courses leading to Graduate Basis for Registration (GBR) with the British Psychological Society.

Work Experience

Relevant work experience includes dealing with people, helping them with sport, perhaps in a coaching role. Listening skills and any observation or direct experience in the caring professions is also useful. It is an advantage if you are able to talk to a psychologist about the work; direct observation may not be possible because of client confidentiality issues.

Entry and Training

Sports and exercise psychologists at the moment have two main routes for training. You can choose to take a first degree in sport and exercise science, followed by an MSc in sport and exercise psychology. After three years' experience under the supervision of a British Association of Sport and Exercise Sciences (BASES) accredited practitioner, you can apply to be accredited by BASES.

Alternatively you can choose to follow the psychology route, with the British Psychological Society (BPS). You should choose your first degree course carefully, checking that it is relevant for sport and exercise psychology. To register as a chartered psychologist (which many employers prefer), you need to obtain the Graduate Basis for Chartered Membership (GBC) by completing a BPS accredited degree in psychology (1-4 yrs) or conversion course. You then need a BPS accredited MSc in sport and exercise psychology, or stage 1 of the society's qualification in sport and exercise psychology. This is followed by the society's stage 2 qualification in sport and exercise psychology, which involves two years' supervised practice. Completion of this leads to chartered psychologist status.

The BPS website (see the Division of Sport and Exercise Psychology section) has full details of the entry route and of those courses that are accredited by them at both undergraduate and postgraduate level. The BPS has a mandatory requirement for chartered psychologists, who are practising, to undertake and maintain a record of their continuing professional development (CPD).

You also need to be registered with the Health Professions Council (HPC) to use the title sport and exercise psychologist. This involves completing stage 2 of the BPS qualification in sport and exercise psychology, or equivalent HPC approved qualification. Contact the HPC for further registration details.

Mature applicants should note that the training period is lengthy and it may be difficult for some applicants to undertake. Mature entrants with a degree and/or relevant postgraduate degree may have an advantage for training posts. The Open University offers a British Psychological Society (BPS) accredited BSc degree in psychology and a postgraduate conversion diploma. There are also BPS accredited conversion courses for those with degrees in other subjects. There are transition arrangements in place for those entrants who are already British Association of Sport and Exercise Sciences accredited. See the BPS website for details.

Opportunities and Pay

This is a relatively new branch of psychology, and at the moment only very few work full time in this work. Most sport and exercise psychologists combine consultancy with lecturing or research work. However, this is a growing field, particularly with the 2012 Olympics approaching and with the Government's wish to make us a more healthy society by doing more exercise and eating more sensibly. Work may be available with professional sports teams or national governing bodies, such as Sport England, the British Olympic Association and the National Sports Medicine Institute. There is fierce competition for all jobs.

Salaries vary depending on whether you are freelance or employed. The average salary for a lecturer in sport and exercise psychology is around £35k-£40k a year. Those who do find full-time posts with a professional sports team are usually paid more.

Skills and Qualities

able to motivate others, able to work both on your own and in a team, efficient record keeping, good at writing reports, good communication skills, good interpersonal skills, good listening skills, good presentation skills, objective, perceptive, scientific approach

Relevant Subjects

Biology, English, Health and social care, Mathematics, Physical education and sport, Psychology, Science, Sociology

Further Information

British Journal of Psychology (BPS, quarterly) - www.bpsjournals.co.uk/journals/bjp

Careers in Psychology (British Psychological Society) - www.bps.org.uk/careers/

Open University - www.open.ac.uk

Psychologist Appointments (BPS) - www.psychapp.co.uk

Psychology Uncovered (Trotman 2010) - www.trotman.co.uk

The Psychologist (monthly) (BPS) - www.thepsychologist.org.uk

▶Working in advice & counselling (2007) (Babcock Lifeskills) - www.babcock-lifeskills.com/

Addresses

British Association of Sport and Exercise Sciences (BASES)
Leeds Metropolitan University,
Carnegie Faculty of Sport and Education, Fairfax Hall,
Headingley Campus, Beckett Park LS6 3QS
Phone: +44 (0)113 812 6162
Web: www.bases.org.uk

British Olympic Association
60 Charlotte Street,, London W1T 2NU
Phone: +44 (0) 207 842 5700
Web: www.olympics.org.uk

British Psychological Society (BPS)
St Andrews House, 48 Princess Road East, Leicester LE1 7DR
Phone: +44 (0)116 254 9568
Web: www.bps.org.uk

Health Professions Council (HPC)
Park House, 184 Kennington Park Road, London SE11 4BU
Phone: +44 (0)20 7582 0866
Web: www.hpc-uk.org

Sport England
3rd Floor Victoria House, Bloomsbury Square, London WC1B 4SE
Phone: +44 (0)20 7273 1551
Web: www.sportengland.org

Sport Scotland
Doges, Templeton on the Green, 62 Templeton Street,
Glasgow G40 1DA
Phone: +44 (0)141 534 6500
Web: www.sportscotland.org.uk

Sport Wales
National Sports Centre Sophia Gardens, Cardiff CF11 9SW
Phone: +44 (0)845 045 0904
Web: www.sports-council-wales.co.uk

Sports Council Northern Ireland
House of Sport, 2a Upper Malone Road, Belfast BT9 5LA
Phone: +44 (0)28 9038 1222
Web: www.sportni.net

Similar Jobs

Psychologist, Psychologist: Counselling, Psychologist: Health, Sport & Exercise Scientist, Sports Coach, Sports Development Officer

Psychotherapist

CRCI:Social Work and Counselling Services
CLCI:KEL — Job Band: 5

Job Description

Psychotherapists work with people suffering from psychological or emotional problems. They help distressed clients by getting them to understand their inner conflicts and they help clients to find ways to deal with them. Psychotherapists carry out treatment, either with an individual or groups of clients, families or couples, and with children, as well as adults. Explore the clients' feelings during discussion sessions, but sometimes advise on the use of medication (prescribed by a medical practitioner) or use hypnotherapy. Group treatment can consist of acting out problems (role play) and exploring hidden emotions.

Psychotherapists can be grouped into areas based on their different therapeutic approaches: these include constructivist therapy, couple, sexual and family therapy, humanistic and integrative therapy, psychoanalytical therapy and cognitive behavioural therapy.

Work Details

Working hours vary widely depending on the number of clients seen each day. An extended working day is common in private practice as clients may sometimes come before or after work. Many in private practice work from their own homes or rent a consulting room. If employed in a residential setting, you may be required to work shifts.

Some of your clients may be anxious, nervous, aggressive or negative and your work may be emotionally demanding. It is also solitary. There are strict codes of practice and ethics to protect both therapists and clients.

Qualification

• England, Wales and Northern Ireland

Band 5: For degree courses: 2-3 A levels and some GCSEs (A*-C) usually including English and maths, or equivalent. Exact requirements depend on the degree you take.

• Scotland

Band 5: For degree courses: 3-5 H grades and some S grades (1-3), usually including English, maths or similar qualifications. Exact requirements depend on the degree you take.

Degree Information

A degree in any discipline is acceptable, but subjects such as psychology, medicine, nursing, social work or sociology may be particularly relevant. Some training courses in psychotherapy may ask for a first degree in psychology or a related discipline.

Adult Qualifications

Entry requirements may be relaxed for adults applying for higher education courses. Access or foundation courses give adults without qualifications a route on to degree courses.

Work Experience

Employers or colleges/universities may prefer candidates who have relevant work or voluntary experience. This includes anything dealing with people in a helping capacity. Areas that involve listening skills and any observation or direct experience in the caring professions are useful. It is an advantage if you are able to talk directly to a psychotherapist about the work. Direct observation is not usually possible because of client confidentiality issues. You also need experience of working with the client group you intend to specialise in, for example, adults or children.

Entry and Training

This is not a job that is open to school leavers as maturity and life experiences are essential. Few of those under age 30 are considered for entry. Most entrants to training in psychotherapy have a degree in psychology or are qualified in a related area such as psychiatric nursing, medicine or social work, and have already gained experience of working with people who have problems relating to mental health.

Training is expensive and courses, which are usually part time, can last 4-6 years and include theory, supervised clinical work and seminars. The NHS offers a limited number of training posts in child and adult psychotherapy and offer some financial support towards training costs. For information about child and adolescent psychotherapists in the NHS, contact the Association of Child Psychotherapists.

Currently, in private practice, there is no registration or licensing of psychotherapists in the UK. Therefore no specific certificates or diplomas are (in theory) required. However, there are plans to introduce statutory regulation of psychotherapists through the Health Professions Council (HPC). Also, for a recognised position with a public institution, training must meet the standards set by the UK Council for Psychotherapy (UKCP) and the British Psychoanalytic Council (BPC). For a list of accredited courses in Scotland, contact the professional body, Counselling & Psychotherapy in Scotland.

It may be useful to join a voluntary regulatory body such as the UKCP, BPC, British Association for Counselling and Psychotherapy or the British Association of Psychotherapists.

Mature entry is common and is an advantage, though those over 45 may find entry to some courses difficult. Few applicants under the age of 25 have the necessary maturity and life experience. For child psychotherapy, previous experience with children is essential. This job is often a second career for those with relevant previous experience or qualifications. Experience and qualifications in nursing (particularly mental health), counselling, social work, medicine, psychiatry and psychology are an advantage for this job.

Opportunities and Pay

Many psychotherapists work in private practice, though some work in the NHS in child guidance clinics, schools for emotionally disturbed children, student or family health centres, voluntary organisations or psychoanalytical institutes. Most opportunities exist in large towns and cities throughout the UK. Within the NHS there is a formal career structure and, with extensive experience, it is possible to become a training therapist or supervisor.

A trainee psychotherapist working in the NHS is likely to earn around £20k-£27k a year, rising to £33.4k with qualifications and experience. Principal psychotherapists can earn up to £45.6k a year.

Skills and Qualities

able to communicate effectively, able to inspire confidence, awareness of confidentiality issues, emotionally strong, good listening skills, non-judgemental, objective, observant, patient, self-motivated

Relevant Subjects

Biology, English, Health and social care, Psychology, Science, Sociology

Further Information

AGCAS: Health (Job Sector Briefing) (AGCAS) - www.prospects.ac.uk

British Journal of Psychotherapy (British Association of Psychotherapists) - www.bap-psychotherapy.org

NHS Careers (NHS Careers) - www.nhscareers.nhs.uk

Psychoanalytic Psychotherapy (BPC) - www.psychoanalytic-council.org/

The Psychotherapist (quarterly) (UK Council for Psychotherapy (UKCP)) - www.psychotherapy.org.uk/thepsychotherapist.html

Training in Counselling & Psychotherapy Directory (BACP) (British Association for Counselling & Psychotherapy) - www.bacp.co.uk/information/education

► Working in advice & counselling (2007) (Babcock Lifeskills) - www.babcock-lifeskills.com/

Addresses

Association of Child Psychotherapists (ACP)
120 West Heath Road, London NW3 7TU
Phone: +44 (0)20 8458 1609
Web: www.childpsychotherapy.org.uk/

Association of Independent Psychotherapists
PO Box 1194, London N6 5PW
Phone: +44 (0)207 700 1911
Web: www.aip.org.uk

British Association for Counselling and Psychotherapy (BACP)
BACP House, 15 St John's Business Park, Lutterworth, Leicestershire LE17 4HB
Phone: +44 (0)1455 883300
Web: www.bacp.co.uk

British Association of Psychotherapists (BAP)
37 Mapesbury Road, London NW2 4HJ
Phone: +44 (0)20 8452 9823
Web: www.bap-psychotherapy.org

British Psychoanalytic Council (BPC)
Unit 7 , 19-23 Wedmore Street,, London N19 4RU.
Phone: +44 (0)20 7561 9240
Web: www.bcp.org.uk

Counselling & Psychotherapy in Scotland (COSCA)
16 Melville Terrace, Stirling FK8 2NE
Phone: +44 (0)1786 475 140
Web: www.cosca.org.uk

Guild of Psychotherapists
47 Nelson Square, Blackfriars Road, London SE1 0QA
Phone: +44 (0)207 401 3260
Web: www.guildofpsychotherapists.org.uk

UK Council for Psychotherapy (UKCP)
2nd Floor Edward House , 2 Wakley Street, London EC1V 7LT
Phone: +44 (0)20 7014 9955
Web: www.psychotherapy.org.uk

Similar Jobs

Counsellor, Hypnotherapist, Nurse: Mental Health, Psychiatrist, Psychoanalyst, Psychologist: Health

Public Affairs Executive/Consultant

also known as: Lobbyist

CRCI:Legal and Political Services
CLCI:COB Job Band: 5

Job Description

Public affairs executives provide policy advice based on close analysis of the political system, promoting the interests of their clients within this structure by knowing the key decision-makers and presenting cases to them. Clients include non-profit organisations, private sector companies and sometimes overseas governments. They monitor the work of government, non-governmental organisations (NGOs) and other political institutions, and relay it to their clients. They also monitor information sources such as Hansard and the European Commission. Liaising regularly with civil servants, politicians, local authority staff and other regulatory bodies is an important part of the job.

Public affairs executives attend events such as party conferences and select committee hearings. They conduct detailed research, write briefings, press releases and campaign material on behalf of their client. Must keep up to date with political developments so that they can advise clients appropriately.

Work Details

You usually work regular hours of around 35-40 hrs a week, though this job can also involve working some unsocial hours, including early mornings and late nights to enable you to respond quickly to the latest news. You may find yourself working to tight deadlines, often under pressure. You may have to travel to meetings and to visit clients. Smart clothes are usually expected.

Qualification

- **England, Wales and Northern Ireland**

Band 5: For degree courses: 2-3 A levels and some GCSEs (A*-C) usually including English and maths, or equivalent qualifications. Exact requirements depend on the degree you take.

- **Scotland**

Band 5: For degree courses: 3-5 H grades and some S grades (1-3) usually including English and maths, or similar. Exact requirements depend on the degree you take.

Degree Information

A good honours degree is normally required, preferably in a related subject such as politics and government, social policy, law, business/management, economics, or public relations. Many entrants have a higher degree, particularly if the first degree is not in a relevant subject. Relevant postgraduate courses include an MSc in public affairs and lobbying. Modern European languages are also helpful.

Adult Qualifications

The same minimum level of qualification is usually expected from mature entrants as from younger people. Entry requirements may be relaxed for adults applying for higher education courses, and Access or foundation courses give adults without qualifications a route on to degree courses. Those with experience and a proven record in corporate consultancy work or other relevant professions have an advantage.

Work Experience

Relevant work or voluntary experience is essential for this job to demonstrate a passion and good understanding for politics. This can be gained through work placements with political bodies, a trade union, internships, student politics, or campaign work for a pressure group or charity. It may be possible to find work experience with a member of a parliament, often as a temporary researcher, or a work placement with the European Commission.

Entry and Training

There are various routes into public affairs consultancy. Some join the industry straight from university, others join from a related profession later on in their career. Competition for posts is intense; few posts are advertised and so you may need to make speculative applications to consultancies. Most entrants have a good honours degree in a relevant subject. Postgraduate qualifications are useful in giving you an advantage in what is a very competitive profession.

It is important to back up academic qualifications with work placements or internships, as most consultancies require some experience. Most placements are not advertised publicly so you need to approach companies directly.

Training is often on the job, complemented by external courses covering areas such as parliamentary procedure and policy-making. The Hansard Society, Dods Parliamentary Communications and Parli-training offer these courses. Graduates often start by doing research for more experienced consultants.

Larger consultancies have graduate training programs lasting between six and twelve months, and arrange work experience placements in outside organisations. Some employers encourage their consultants to obtain the Chartered Institute of Public Relations advanced certificate and/or diploma, as lobbying now requires fuller use of PR. The Public Affairs network offers free membership to those involved with government affairs, including students. Members can receive details of job vacancies, training courses and industry events, such as free regular networking gatherings in Westminster. Consult the website for more details.

Maturity is usual for this occupation and many entrants have considerable experience in a related career. With the right experience, mature entrants can enter at a more senior level and bypass the initial training.

Opportunities and Pay

You may work in house for an organisation such as a charity or professional association, or for a consultancy that looks after several clients. Most firms are fairly small and are usually in London or Brussels, with some consultants working in major UK regional centres such as Edinburgh, Belfast and Cardiff. There are opportunities for freelance work and self-employment once firmly established and trusted. To gain more senior posts, where you are responsible for a group of clients, you may have to be prepared to move company.

Salaries vary according to the size of consultancy and level of experience. Most consultants start with a salary of around £18k-£22k, which can rise with experience and responsibility to around £25k-£30k a year.

Health
As this is a demanding job it is important that you are in good health.

Skills and Qualities
able to cope under pressure, able to inspire confidence, analytical skills, excellent communication skills, information handling skills, IT skills, project management skills, research skills, understanding of political processes

Relevant Subjects
Business and accounting, Economics, English, Government and politics, History, Law, Media and communication studies, Sociology

Further Information
Dods Parliamentary Communications - www.dodsparlicom.com

Electus UK: Your Doorway to a Career in Politics - www.electus-start.com

Hansard Society - www.hansardsociety.org.uk

Inside Careers Guide: Management Consultancy - www.insidecareers.co.uk/

Jobs in Public Affairs - www.publicaffairsjobs.com

Parli-training - www.parli-training.org.uk

Public Affairs Network - www.publicaffairsnetworking.com

Public Affairs News online - www.publicaffairsnews.com

Addresses
Association of Professional Political Consultants (APPC)
c/o College of Public Policy, 1st Floor, The Registry,
Royal Mint Court, London EC3N 4QN
Web: www.appc.org.uk

Chartered Institute of Public Relations (CIPR)
52-53 Russell Square, London WC1B 4HP
Phone: +44 (0)20 7631 6900
Web: www.cipr.co.uk

Public Relations Consultants Association (PRCA)
Willow House 17-23 Willow Place, London SW1P 1JH
Phone: +44 (0)20 7233 6026
Web: www.prca.org.uk

Similar Jobs
Civil Service Fast Streamer, Journalist, Political/Constituency Organiser, Political/Parliamentary Researcher, Politician, Public Relations Officer

Public Analyst

CRCI:Science, Mathematics and Statistics
CLCI:COP Job Band: 5

Job Description
Public analysts provide scientific expertise for local authorities to ensure that community health is protected and that the authority is able to enforce regulations in areas of public health and safety. They examine a diverse range of household items and food in the interests of consumer safety, including tinned foods, toys, cosmetics, baby foods etc. May analyse substances for pollution and poisons or check foodstuffs for quantities of additives and contamination. Also test the quality of household goods and materials to ensure they comply with health and safety regulations. May test the atmosphere for gas emissions and ensure that water is safe to use.

Analysts advise on waste disposal, chemical spillage and fire risk. They look at safety at work by monitoring the level of fumes, noise, asbestos contamination etc. Duties include completing surveys, interpreting data and writing reports, referring to current legislation. May be required to appear in a court of law as an expert witness. Also liaise with departments such as trading standards, food standards agencies and environmental health.

Work Details
The hours are usually regular, Monday to Friday, but you can be on call at times. You work in a laboratory or sometimes out on fieldwork. Knowledge of technical developments and any new legal regulations is essential. You have to analyse unpleasant, perhaps smelly and sometimes harmful substances. Protective clothing is worn for some areas of work. For travel between sites, a driving licence may be useful.

Qualification

• England, Wales and Northern Ireland
Band 5: For degree courses: 2-3 A levels including chemistry, physics and preferably maths and some GCSEs (A*-C) usually including English, maths and science, or equivalent. Exact requirements depend on the degree you take.

• Scotland
Band 5: For degree courses: 3-5 H grades including chemistry, physics and preferably maths and some S grades (1-3), usually including English, maths and science, or similar. Exact requirements depend on the degree you take.

Degree Information
Most public analysts have a degree in chemistry, though environmental science, forensic science, biochemistry, microbiology or food science may also be acceptable. It is an advantage to have a relevant MSc or PhD.

Adult Qualifications
Most entrants need a degree or an equivalent qualification. Adults applying for degree courses may not need the standard entry requirements and Access and foundation courses may be available.

Work Experience
Employers or colleges/universities may prefer candidates who have relevant work or voluntary experience. This can include work in a laboratory or in chemical related industries in the public or private sector.

Entry and Training
To be a public analyst and to practise as a food examiner, the law requires you to hold the Mastership in Chemical Analysis (MChemA) from the Royal Society of Chemistry (RSC). Study for this qualification can take up to five years' part-time after graduating. The RSC works closely with the Association of Public Analysts (APA) to ensure candidates have the skills and experience to qualify, but you must be in relevant employment and have several years' experience in a working laboratory. An MSc in food safety, either part time or through distance learning is also available.

There is an S/NVQ at level 5 in analytical chemistry that is the principal route onto the Analytical Chemists Register. Successful completion of the award also leads to exemption from Part A of the Mastership in Chemical Analysis (MChemA) examination. Holders of the level 5 S/NVQ are entitled to use the designation 'Registered Analytical Chemist'.

On-the-job training is offered by the employer and you are expected to update your knowledge throughout your career through continuing professional development (CPD).

Mature candidates with appropriate qualifications and experience are usually preferred. A foundation year prior to the start of a science degree may be available at some HE institutions for those applicants who do not have the traditional science A levels/H grades or equivalent.

Opportunities and Pay

There are currently 26 public analysts' laboratories throughout the UK. Local authorities own around two-thirds of these and the remaining third are privately owned. Usually they carry out work on a consultancy basis for clients that include industrial and water companies. This is a small, though elite, profession with very few, fully qualified public analysts in the UK. However, there are graduate (or equivalent) scientists working in the Public Analyst Service.

A public analyst typically earns around £18k-£30k a year, rising to around £50k a year with experience, though some may earn more, particularly in the private sector.

Health

This work involves a risk of infection. Skin irritants and chemicals can cause allergies. This job also requires good colour vision for certain areas of work.

Skills and Qualities

able to report accurately, accurate, analytical skills, aptitude for teamwork, conscientious, good written English, health & safety awareness, IT skills, scientific approach, sound judgement

Relevant Subjects

Biology, Chemistry, English, Health and social care, ICT/Computer studies, Law, Mathematics, Physics, Science

Further Information

AGCAS: Government & Public Administration (Job Sector Briefing) (AGCAS) - www.prospects.ac.uk

►Working in science (2007) (Babcock Lifeskills) - www.babcock-lifeskills.com/

Addresses

Association of Public Analysts (APA)
c/o Edinburgh Scientific Services 4 Marine Esplanade EH6 7LU
Web: www.publicanalyst.com

Royal Society of Chemistry (RSC)
Education Department, Burlington House, Piccadilly,
London W1J 0BA
Phone: +44 (0)20 7437 8656
Web: www.rsc.org

Similar Jobs

Biochemist, Chemist: Analytical, Environmental Health Practitioner, Forensic Scientist, Health & Safety Practitioner, Toxicologist, Trading Standards Officer

Public Relations Officer

also known as: Corporate Communications Officer, Media Affairs Officer

CRCI:Marketing and Advertising
CLCI:OG

Job Band: 4 to 5

Job Description

Public relations officers manage and maintain the reputation and standing of an organisation using many forms of media communication. They operate in two distinct areas: 'in-house' public relations department or externally as a consultancy, providing a service. Public relations officers provide information and ideas to create a good and favourable attitude towards an organisation's policies, image, services and products. They write press releases, newsletters and other publications, produces videos and organises events.

Uses online media, press, radio, TV, exhibitions, lectures and brochures to communicate and also assesses public opinion and informs the employer. They may speak in public at press conferences, meetings and on radio or TV. Can work for a large organisation or for a public relations agency.

Work Details

Usually works a basic 35-40 hr week, though you are often expected to work long hours and travel around the country or overseas to meet with clients. The job brings you into contact with a wide variety of people, including organisation executives at a high level. You are responsible for providing an efficient service for your clients and keeping to agreed financial budgets. The work may be pressurised at times.

Qualification

- **England, Wales and Northern Ireland**

Band 4: For HND, Diploma of Higher Education or foundation degree in a relevant subject such as business studies: 1-2 A levels and some GCSEs (A*-C) usually including English and maths, or equivalent.

Band 5: For degree courses: 2-3 A levels and some GCSEs (A*-C) usually including English and maths, or equivalent. Exact requirements depend on the degree you take.

- **Scotland**

Band 4: For entry to SQA higher national and professional development awards in a relevant subject such as business studies: usually 2-3 H grades and some S grades (1-3), including English and maths, or similar qualifications.

Band 5: For degree courses: 3-5 H grades and some S grades (1-3), including English and maths, or similar qualifications. Exact requirements depend on the degree you take.

Degree Information

There are degree courses available in public relations but any degree is acceptable for entry to this job. Subjects which give useful background knowledge include communication studies, journalism, English, media studies, business studies, marketing and psychology. There are also a number of postgraduate courses in PR. The Chartered Institute of Public Relations (CIPR) can provide a list of approved first degrees and postgraduate courses.

Adult Qualifications

Many entrants to public relations move into this career after working in advertising, the media, marketing, journalism or business. Entry requirements may be relaxed for adults applying for higher education courses. Access or foundation courses provide those without the required qualifications a route onto degree courses.

Work Experience

Entry to this job is very competitive. It is important that you try to do some relevant work or gain voluntary experience before applying. Direct experience or work shadowing with a public relations firm or in journalism, advertising or marketing is ideal. Voluntary work with a charity or in helping to promote university events is also relevant. The Chartered Institute of Public Relations offers help with work placement to its student members.

Entry and Training

The majority of entrants are graduates and it is an advantage to have a postgraduate degree or diploma and relevant experience. Training is on the job, often through an in-house training scheme supplemented by seminars, short courses and conferences organised by the Chartered Institute of Public Relations (CIPR). Larger agencies may offer a graduate training scheme.

For professional training, the CIPR offers an advanced certificate for graduates in any subject who would like to go into PR or are in the first few years of their PR career. Entry to the higher level CIPR diploma is relevant if you want to take on a more strategic role. The Internal Communication Certificate is ideal for those working in internal communication.

It is possible to join a PR agency as an administrator or publicity assistant and gain promotion to PR officer. The Foundation Award in Public Relations is a new qualification from the CIPR which is at A/H level standard and may help those considering PR as a career option. Trainees in employment may also be encouraged to study for the diploma in marketing communications offered by the Communication, Advertising and Marketing (CAM) Foundation. This consists of five modules, one in public relations, which can be studied part time, or by intensive or distance learning.

The Public Relations Consultants Association (PRCA) also offers a range of online and distance-learning courses and a three-tier qualifications programme. Check the website for details. The CIPR and the PRCA support continuing professional development (CPD) in the form of workshops, seminars and courses for their members.

Mature entrants are welcomed and those with a background in areas that include advertising, journalism, marketing and publicity, may have an advantage. There are distance-learning courses in PR, such as those available from the Chartered Institute of Public Relations.

Opportunities and Pay

This is a very popular career and entry is competitive, despite the fact that it is a growing area. Most are employed in-house by organisations including central government and local authorities, commercial companies and professional associations, charity organisations and the police. The Government Communications Network is a very large employer of public relations officers.

Others work for consultancies ranging from large multinational organisations to small agencies with one or two people. Some of the largest agencies are in London and the surrounding area. Most entrants start as a junior account executive, move up to account executive after one to two years and then on to account manager after around three years. Promotion usually depends on moving from company to company to broaden your experience or to move into a more specialist role. Some opportunities exist for experienced public relations officers to work abroad for multinational companies and organisations. You may also be self-employed and work as a consultant.

Pay varies depending on location, size and type of organisation. Starting salaries are around £16k-£22k, rising to £25k-£40k a year for experienced PR managers. PR directors can earn £60k-£80k or more a year.

Skills and Qualities

able to cope under pressure, analytical skills, confident, good communication skills, good interpersonal skills, good organisational skills, good written English, imaginative, interest in current affairs, IT skills

Relevant Subjects

Business and accounting, Economics, English, Media and communication studies, Psychology, Retail and distribution, Sociology

Further Information

AGCAS: Media (Job Sector Briefing) (AGCAS) - www.prospects.ac.uk

Government Communications Network (GCN) - www.civilservice.gov.uk/my-civil-service/networks/professional

International Correspondence Schools - www.icslearn.co.uk

PR Week (Haymarket) - www.prweek.com/uk/

▶Working in creative & media (2007) (Babcock Lifeskills) - www.babcock-lifeskills.com/

▶Working in English (2007) (Babcock Lifeskills) - www.babcock-lifeskills.com/

▶Working in marketing, advertising & PR (2008) (Babcock Lifeskills) - www.babcock-lifeskills.com/

Addresses

Chartered Institute of Public Relations (CIPR)
52-53 Russell Square, London WC1B 4HP
Phone: +44 (0)20 7631 6900
Web: www.cipr.co.uk

Communication Advertising and Marketing (CAM) Foundation Ltd
Moor Hall, Cookham, Maidenhead, Berkshire SL6 9QH
Phone: +44 (0)1628 427 120
Web: www.camfoundation.com

Public Relations Consultants Association (PRCA)
Willow House 17-23 Willow Place, London SW1P 1JH
Phone: +44 (0)20 7233 6026
Web: www.prca.org.uk

Similar Jobs

Advertising Copywriter, Event & Exhibition Organiser, Journalist, Market Research Executive, Marketing Manager, Press Officer

Publican

also known as: Bar/Pub Manager, Licensee: Pub

CRCI:Catering and Hospitality
CLCI:IB Job Band: 3 to 5

Job Description

Publicans plan and organise the running of a licensed public house, inn, wine or cafi bar, or other licensed premises. They usually rent or manage a pub owned by a brewery, but some are freehold (independent). Publicans are responsible for hiring and training staff, keeping accounts, paying wages and ordering cellar stock. They also supervise stock deliveries, check the condition of barrelled beer, and make sure that bar shelves are filled. Often organises and provides meals and bar snacks, and perhaps entertainment and accommodation. Is responsible for the health, safety and security of the premises, staff and customers.

Publicans may be required to provide regular progress and financial reports to the employing brewery, company or landlord. They keep the premises well maintained and aim to give good customer service and make a profit. They must also observe the laws that govern the selling of intoxicating liquor.

Work Details

Publicans/licensees and pub and bar managers usually work long, unsocial hours, including evenings, weekends and public holidays, and often have few holidays. The Licensing Act of 2003 came into force in 2005 and introduced flexible opening hours for licensed premises and some pubs and bars are open 24 hours a day, 7 days a week.

Some managers live in the pub or bar they run. You need good business sense to develop the potential of the pub/bar. You are responsible for keeping accounts and maintaining high standards of hygiene and safety. You need to be outgoing as you meet many different types of people. Some customers can be awkward or aggressive, so you need to keep calm. Pubs are often noisy and are very busy at times. You are on your feet for most of the time and often have to change heavy beer and lager barrels.

Qualification

No minimum academic qualifications are needed to become a free-house owner or a tenant of a public house, though a good education is necessary, particularly in maths and English. You need to have good business sense and be able to work on accounts and other administrative tasks.

- **England, Wales and Northern Ireland**

Band 3: For entry to jobs, HNC or a relevant Diploma, usually at least 4 GCSEs (A*-C) including English and maths, or equivalent.

Band 4: For HND, Diploma of Higher Education or foundation degree: 1-2 A levels and some GCSEs (A*-C) usually including English and maths, or equivalent.

Band 5: For degree courses: 2-3 A levels and some GCSEs (A*-C) usually including English and maths, or equivalent. Exact requirements depend on the degree you take.

- **Scotland**

Band 3: For entry to jobs, usually at least four S grades (1-3) including English or maths, or similar.

Band 4: For entry to SQA higher national and professional development awards, usually 2-3 H grades and some S grades (1-3), including English and maths, or similar qualifications.

Band 5: For degree courses: 3-5 H grades and some S grades (1-3), usually including English and maths, or similar qualifications. Exact requirements depend on the degree you take.

Degree Information

Any degree discipline is acceptable for entry to this job, but degrees in hospitality, brewing, licensed retail management and hospitality management (licensed premises) are most useful. Foundation degrees are available in licensed retail management and hospitality management.

Adult Qualifications

Entry requirements may be relaxed for adults applying for higher education courses. Access or foundation courses provide those without the required qualifications a route onto degree courses.

Work Experience

Entry to this job is competitive and it is important that you do some relevant work or voluntary experience before applying. This includes work in retail, customer service, restaurants, hotels and other jobs that involve working with the public.

Entry and Training

Entry to this job is very competitive and selection is based on aptitude, motivation, character and personality. Many pubs and bars are now owned and run by national and international groups who run formal training programmes so they may prefer applicants with qualifications. However, it is also possible to train on the job, follow a structured career path and achieve relevant qualifications. In England and Wales, 16-17 year olds are only allowed to work behind a bar as part of an apprenticeship programme.

To work as a publican, you must obtain both a national certificate for licensees at level 2 from the British Institute of Innkeeping (BII), and a premises license from the local authority which details opening hours etc. The BIIAB (awarding body) offers a wide range of qualifications for new and existing publicans and managers up to Foundation degree level, including the Scottish Licensees Certificate which acknowledges the legal differences between working in England and Scotland. These include a level 1 award in responsible alcohol retailing, and a level 2 national certificate for personal licence holders. They also offer advanced qualifications in skills that include cellar and beer quality management.

Relevant courses are also run by the Wine & Spirit Education Trust at levels 1-5. S/NVQs in catering, multi-skilled hospitality services and hospitality supervision are available at levels 1-3. BIIAB runs level 3 diplomas and advanced certificates in licensed hospitality. There are other vocationally-related qualifications you can do. Training programmes, including apprenticeship schemes in hospitality or customer service, may be available in your area. Advanced apprenticeships leading to qualification at level 3 can also be a route into higher education.

A Diploma/Welsh Baccalaureate may be available in your area in hospitality. The advanced level is equivalent to 3.5 A levels but for some university courses, the additional and specialist learning (ASL) component of the diploma needs to include specific A levels. Check entry requirements carefully with the individual institutions.

Mature entry is common and applicants with previous business or catering experience, including running their own business, have an advantage. Personal qualities and motivation are considered of prime importance. Relevant qualifications, including professional qualifications, are available through full or part-time courses and by distance learning.

Government training opportunities, such as apprenticeships, may be available in your area. You can also gain recognition of previous experience through Accreditation of Prior Learning (APL) or by working towards relevant S/NVQs. Contact your local careers office, Jobcentre Plus, Next Step service or Learning and Skills Council (LSC) Local Enterprise Company (LEC) for details of training schemes

Opportunities and Pay

There are around 60,000 pubs in the UK. The hospitality industry and pubs in general are struggling in the current economic climate. This may affect the number of opportunities available for publicans. You can be employed as a manager by a brewery or property company and paid a salary plus profit-related bonuses. Tenants or licensees are self-employed; they buy their own stock and pay wages to their staff. If you buy a tenancy or leasehold then this requires an investment of capital and you must also sell alcohol from the brewer involved. However, tenancies are declining at the moment. The most expensive option is to buy the freehold of a pub which lets you sell beer from any brewery you choose and your income then depends on how well you develop the pub.

There are good opportunities for managers who work for one of the larger national or international groups who can use their experience and qualifications to move within the organisation to larger establishments and other areas. You can progress to be a 'mobile manager' that moves to each new outlet as the organisation expands, or an area manager. You may also have a room or flat to live in on the premises and there may be opportunities to work abroad.

Pay varies depending on location and turnover of the public house. Trainee managers earn around £16k-£20k a year. Employed publicans generally earn around £25k-£30k a year, rising to £40k in some areas. Independent publicans earn from as little as £12k a year to more than £50k a year. Many employers offer a competitive pay and benefits package, which may include free accommodation, meals while on duty and use of a car.

Health

You need to be physically fit for this job.

Skills and Qualities

able to get on with all kinds of people, able to manage people, business awareness, energetic, enterprising, good communication skills, good organisational skills, hard working, honest, outgoing personality

Relevant Subjects

Business and accounting, English, Hospitality and catering, Mathematics

Further Information

Apprenticeship Schemes (National Apprenticeship Service) - www.apprenticeships.org.uk

Barkeeper-A Resource for Hospitality Businesses - www.barkeeper.co.uk

BII - Professional body for the Licensed Retail Sector (British Institute of Innkeepers) - www.bii.org/home

British Beer and Pub Association (BBPA) - www.beerandpub.com

CareerScope: Pubs & Bars Magazine (Springboard UK) - http://careerscope.springboarduk.net
Diploma in Hospitality (People 1st) - www.hospitalitydiploma.co.uk
People 1st - sector skills council for hospitality, leisure, travel and tourism - www.people1st.co.uk
Publican's Industry Handbook (The Publican) - www.thepublican.com/
Springboard UK - www.springboarduk.net
Springboard Wales - http://wales.springboarduk.net/
The Publican online - www.thepublican.com
UKSP - Guide to Success in Hospitality, Leisure, Travel & Tourism - www.uksp.co.uk
▶Working in food & drink (2007) (Babcock Lifeskills) - www.babcock-lifeskills.com/
▶Working in hospitality & catering (2009) (Babcock Lifeskills) - www.babcock-lifeskills.com/

Addresses

Wine & Spirit Education Trust (WSET)
International Wine & Spirit Centre, 39-45 Bermondsey Street, London SE1 3XF
Phone: +44 (0)20 7089 3800
Web: www.wset.co.uk

Similar Jobs

Bartender, Catering Manager, Hotel Manager, Off-Licence Manager, Restaurant Manager

Puppeteer/Puppet Maker

CRCI:Performing Arts
CLCI:EZ
Job Band: 1 to 4

Job Description

Puppeteers operate puppets and puppet makers make movable models of a person or animal for a live performance in front of an audience, and for TV, film and video. They may make or operate a variety of puppets, including glove and rod puppets, marionettes (those operated by strings) and body puppets. Some puppeteers may make their own puppets, as well as performing with them. Some puppet makers specialise in creating one type of puppet and can also be involved in the design of a stage or set. They use specially designed tools and may also create the clothing.

Puppeteers often write the words (a script) for a puppet or for the whole puppet show. They may operate the puppets in an educational setting, often in a mainstream or special educational needs school, and sometimes to entertain those in a hospital.

Work Details

Puppeteers' performing hours are likely to be more irregular than those of a puppet maker. If on tour or based in a theatre you may have rehearsals during the day to prepare for performances, which can be during the daytime as well as evenings and weekends. In the film/TV industry, hours may also be irregular and the work can be pressurised to meet deadlines.

You may need to travel around an area or abroad and some productions may require you to be away from home, sometimes for long periods. Some shows are performed outdoors. You may need to help move equipment, so there can be some bending, lifting and carrying. This job involves a lot of physical activity at times.

Puppet makers work mainly in a workshop and usually have a standard working week, with regular hours. Overtime and evening work may be necessary when tight deadlines need to be met. You need to wear protective clothing or a mask, when working with certain substances and materials.

Qualification

There are no formal qualifications for entering this area of work. Interest, aptitude and experience are more important. Entrants range from those without any educational qualifications, to those with higher education qualifications, or a degree.

Degree Information

Degree courses in puppetry are available.

Adult Qualifications

There are no minimum qualifications for entry to this job.

Work Experience

It is useful to have some voluntary experience with a puppeteer or puppet maker, and often a direct approach to those in the industry can be successful.

Entry and Training

There is no set route into puppetry. People who make and/or operate puppets may have worked in the arts or theatre, in amateur drama productions, including those at school or college. Some have experience in costume making or toy and model-making, and others have been to drama school. To enter this job as a puppeteer, you need to pass an audition. It is helpful to have an up-to-date portfolio of your work, particularly for entry to some courses.

There are short courses in some areas, such as with the British Puppet and Model Theatre Guild, and also some specialist longer courses in puppetry. The London School of Puppetry, based in London and Yorkshire, runs short courses, summer workshops and a two year diploma course and the Puppet Centre Trust runs a range of short courses. The Central School of Speech and Drama at the University of London runs a three year honours degree in puppetry. Staffordshire University offers a degree course in stop-motion animation and puppetry.

Some puppet theatre companies and enthusiasts, such as the Little Angel Theatre and the Norwich Puppet Theatre, advertise workshops and training sessions, from basic puppetry to work on specialised techniques.

A Diploma/Welsh Baccalaureate in creative and media may be available in your area, providing an introduction to this type of work. See the diplomas website for further information.

Mature entrants need amateur experience in the relevant area of puppetry. It is an advantage to have experience in drama or music, and for puppet making, skills in handicrafts, together with an artistic flair. For entry to some higher level courses, it is helpful to have an up-to-date portfolio of your work, as often entry requirements may be relaxed for mature applicants. Contact the individual college/university for details.

Opportunities and Pay

There are opportunities in all parts of the country, but many companies that work in film and TV are clustered around south-east England, where much of the industry is based. Employment can be with a puppet touring company or resident theatre company. Some jobs are available with production companies that produce work for the film and TV industries. Most puppeteers/ puppet makers are self-employed.

Pay varies greatly depending on your employer, or whether you are self-employed. Often, touring companies rely on grants from organisations such as the Arts Council and therefore the rate of pay is low. Higher earnings that may be in the region of £750 a week, are usually achieved in companies that have an established record of working in the film and TV industry.

Health

This job requires good general fitness and normal colour vision.

Skills and Qualities
able to communicate effectively, able to improvise, able to withstand criticism, attention to detail, enthusiastic, eye for shape/colour, good co-ordination, innovative, manual dexterity, self confident

Relevant Subjects
Art and Design, Design and technology, English, Media and communication studies, Music, Performing arts

Further Information
Arts Council - www.artscouncil.org.uk

British Puppet and Model Theatre Guild - www.puppetguild.org.uk/

British UNIMA (Union Internationale de la Marionette - www.unima.org.uk

Creative & Cultural Skills - sector skills council for advertising, crafts, cultural heritage, design, literature, music, performing & visual arts - www.ccskills.org.uk

Diplomas (Foundation, Higher and Advanced) - http://yp.direct.gov.uk/diplomas

Little Angel Theatre - www.littleangeltheatre.com

Norwich Puppet Theatre http://puppettheatre.co.uk

The Puppet Master (BPMTG) - www.puppetguild.org.uk/pubsmu.htm

Welsh Baccalaureate - www.wbq.org.uk

Addresses
British Toymakers Guild (BTG)
PO Box 240, Uckfield TN22 9AS
Phone: +44 (0) 1225 442 440
Web: www.toymakersguild.co.uk

Central School of Speech and Drama
Embassy Theatre, Eton Avenue, London NW3 3HY
Phone: +44 (0)20 7722 8183
Web: www.cssd.ac.uk

London School of Puppetry
2 Legard Road, London N5 1DE
Phone: 0845 409 5906 (UK only)
Web: www.londonschoolofpuppetry.com

Puppet Centre Trust
Battersea Arts Centre, Lavender Hill, London SW11 5TN
Phone: +44 (0)20 7228 5335
Web: www.puppetcentre.org.uk

Similar Jobs
Actor, Animator, Costume Designer, Entertainer, Model Maker, Toymaker

Purchasing/Procurement Officer
also known as: Buyer, Purchase & Supplies Officer

CRCI:Transport and Logistics
CLCI:OP Job Band: 3 to 5

Job Description
Purchasing or procurement officers purchase goods, equipment, raw materials or services for an organisation, aiming for the best value in cost and quality. They find the most suitable sources of supply. Negotiate price and agree on delivery arrangements, using judgement about quality and amount, and draw up a contract with the supplier. Purchasing officers provide a link between different departments within the organisation and suppliers. May be responsible for checking the standard of goods when they are delivered, or overseeing the provision of services that the company has purchased.

Work Details
Usually work regular office hours, Monday to Friday, though may be required to work evenings and weekends at times. You are normally based in an office but also visit suppliers, so you may be away from home overnight. In some jobs it is necessary to travel abroad. The work involves negotiating with suppliers, and you need to collect, collate and analyse information. You are responsible for keeping costs within an agreed budget, and for meeting deadlines.

Qualification
• England, Wales and Northern Ireland
Band 4: For HND, Diploma of Higher Education or foundation degree: 1-2 A levels and some GCSEs (A*-C) usually including English and maths, or equivalent.

Band 5: For degree courses: 2-3 A levels and some GCSEs (A*-C) usually including English and maths, or equivalent. Exact requirements depend on the degree you take.

• Scotland
Band 4: For entry to SQA higher national and professional development awards, usually 2-3 H grades and some S grades (1-3), including English and maths, or similar qualifications.

Band 5: For degree courses: 3-5 H grades and some S grades (1-3), usually including English and maths, or similar qualifications. Exact requirements depend on the degree you take.

Degree Information
A degree in any subject is acceptable, but business studies and marketing give useful background knowledge, and may provide exemption from all or part of the foundation stage of the Chartered Institute of Purchasing and Supply (CIPS) professional examinations. Postgraduate courses in purchasing and supply are also available.

Adult Qualifications
There are opportunities for adults already working in a commercial or business environment, with entry routes to the Chartered Institute of Purchasing and Supply (CIPS) requiring no academic qualifications. A degree, higher national qualification or relevant experience can lead to exemption from some of the CIPS examinations. Entry requirements may be relaxed for adults applying for higher education courses. Access or foundation courses give adults without qualifications a route on to degree courses.

Work Experience
Entry to this job is competitive and it is important that you try to do some relevant work or voluntary experience before applying. Buying, selling or marketing experience and skills in business administration is the most relevant.

Entry and Training
Training is usually on the job through a company training scheme. Entrants often attend part-time college courses leading to the Chartered Institute of Purchasing and Supply (CIPS) professional exams. The level at which you begin depends on the qualifications you have, but most employers prefer at least A levels/H grades or equivalent, and many are graduates or have a foundation degree, often in business studies. However, there are no formal qualifications required to study for the CIPS advanced certificate.

Relevant experience or qualifications may provide exemption from all or part of the foundation stage of the CIPS qualification. A graduate diploma is also available. For some jobs it is useful to have some knowledge of foreign languages. An S/NVQ in supply chain management at level 4 is also available and accredited by CIPS. It is important to keep up to date with changes throughout your career so continuing professional development is important.

Maturity, relevant experience such as purchasing, work as a sales manager or retail/wholesale manager and selling or marketing experience is valued by employers. The Chartered Institute of

Purchasing and Supply (CIPS) offers full membership through the Personal Development Plan (PDP) to senior practitioners who are not able to study but have at least 5 years' experience.

Opportunities and Pay
This profession is expanding with a demand for new entrants, but competition is strong. Employment is available in a range of organisations, including the retail industry, manufacturing, public utilities (gas, water and electricity), gas and oil industry, the armed forces, commerce, local and national government, or the NHS. Opportunities for promotion are generally better in larger organisations. You can also go on to become a self-employed consultant.

Salaries vary depending on the location and the size of the company. A new entrant can expect around £18k-£25k, rising to £35k-£45k a year with experience. The most successful purchasing officers can earn more than £50k a year.

Health
Normal colour vision may be required for certain areas of work.

Skills and Qualities
able to manage a budget and keep records, able to work to deadlines, aptitude for teamwork, attention to detail, business awareness, good communication skills, good organisational skills, IT skills, negotiating skills, networking skills

Relevant Subjects
Business and accounting, Economics, English, ICT/Computer studies, Mathematics, Modern Foreign Languages, Retail and distribution

Further Information
Improve Ltd - sector skills council for food and drink manufacturing and processing - www.improveltd.co.uk

Inside Careers Guide: Purchasing & Supply - www.insidecareers.co.uk

Skills for Logistics - sector skills council for freight logistics industries - www.skillsforlogistics.org

Skillsmart Retail - sector skills council for the retail industry - www.skillsmartretail.com

▶Working in business, administration & finance (2010) (Babcock Lifeskills) - www.babcock-lifeskills.com/

▶Working in fashion & clothing (2008) (Babcock Lifeskills) - www.babcock-lifeskills.com/

Addresses
Chartered Institute of Purchasing and Supply (CIPS)
Easton House, Easton on the Hill, Stamford, Lincolnshire PE9 3NZ
Phone: +44 (0)1780 756 777
Web: www.cips.org

Similar Jobs
Advertising Media Buyer, Commodity Broker, Export Sales Manager, Logistics Manager, Retail Buyer, Retail Merchandiser

Quality Assurance Controller/Inspector

CRCI:Manufacturing and Production
CLCI:SAB
Job Band: 2 to 3

Job Description
Quality assurance controllers carry out special tests to ensure a manufactured product meets the required standard to go on to the next stage of production or to be passed to the customer. Some samples require simple visual inspection to find holes, cracks, and impurities; for others, it may be necessary to use a microscope. Other products, especially food, need to be test-weighed and checked to ensure high standards. May use special instruments to measure and weigh products. Can use automated machinery to rapidly test thousands of samples. Controllers keep accurate records, including charts and statistics, and analyse the results. May need to write and present a report.

Quality assurance controllers can work in industry in the production of items that are either complicated or subject to careful analysis such as chemicals, pharmaceuticals, computers, food, glass products, machinery or vehicles. Quality control may be the responsibility of a technician who is also involved in other work.

Work Details
Quality assurance controllers usually work a basic 35-40 hr week that may include shifts and weekends. You work in a laboratory or industrial premises and are responsible for maintaining standards, monitoring work progress and possibly hygiene and legal regulations. This work requires a high degree of accuracy. You may have to cope with some physical activity. The work environment depends on the type of industry and in some cases there is a risk of exposure to harmful substances. If so, you need to wear protective clothing, and perhaps gloves and safety glasses.

Qualification
- **England, Wales and Northern Ireland**

Band 2: Although academic qualifications are not specified for this job, it is an advantage to have some GCSEs (A*-C) in subjects that include English and maths, or equivalent

Band 3: For entry: usually at least 4 GCSEs (A*-C) including English, maths and a science or equivalent. A practical or technical subject is also useful.

- **Scotland**

Band 2: Although academic qualifications are not specified for this job, it is an advantage to have some S grades (1-3) in subjects that include English and maths, or similar.

Band 3: For entry: usually at least four S grades (1-3) including English, a science and maths, or similar. A practical or technical subject is also useful.

Adult Qualifications
For direct entry, employers may prefer candidates with an appropriate level of qualification and experience of the industry.

Work Experience
Employers or colleges/universities may prefer candidates who have relevant work or voluntary experience. This can include experience of working in a laboratory or a background in manufacturing. In some areas there is a young apprenticeship (14-16) scheme that provides an extended work placement and eventual achievement of a relevant level 2 qualification whilst at school.

Entry and Training
Most entrants are those who are already experienced production line or shop floor workers. For some jobs in more specialised and technical industries, employers may prefer applicants with a higher level of qualification such as A levels/H grades, HNDs or a degree. Training is on the job and may include a day or a block-release course.

There are BTEC/SQA courses in manufacturing engineering, and the Chartered Quality Institute (CQI) also offers a level 3 certificate and level 5 diploma course in quality leading to membership of the CQI. The certifcate course is for those new to quality assurance, while the diploma course is aimed at those already in a quality oriented role. Both are offered as block release, evening or correspondence courses. The CQI encourages continuing professional development (CPD) and also runs a range of short courses. See their website for full details.

Relevant S/NVQs up to level 4 are available. Training programmes, including apprenticeship schemes, may be available in your area. Advanced apprenticeships leading to qualification at level 3 can also be a route into higher education. A Diploma/Welsh Baccalaureate in engineering or in manufacturing and product design may be available in your area. These courses are relevant for entry to this work and may be taken from the age of 14-19.

Adult entry is common as many employers recruit those who have experience of work on the shop floor, or of making production decisions, particularly in the manufacturing sector. Distance-learning courses are available from the Chartered Quality Institute (CQI). Government training opportunities, such as apprenticeships, may be available in your area. You can also gain recognition of previous experience through Accreditation of Prior Learning (APL) or by working towards relevant S/NVQs. Contact your local careers office, Jobcentre Plus, Next Step service or Learning and Skills Council (LSC) Local Enterprise Company (LEC) for details of training schemes.

Opportunities and Pay

Employment is with a manufacturing company in areas that include pharmaceuticals, engineering and electronics, textiles, paper and glass, or food and drink. There is scope for specialisation. It is possible to progress to a management post. This job exists in a wide range of organisations though increasingly more complex technology has led to some decline in numbers and entrants having higher qualifications.

Pay varies depending on location and employer, but trainees are likely start at around £14k-£19k, rising to £20k-£25k a year with experience. Some earn more than £35k-£40k a year. Overtime and shift work may add to income.

Health

This job requires good eyesight and good colour vision for some areas of work. There may be an allergy risk from skin irritants.

Skills and Qualities

able to report accurately, accurate, alert, analytical skills, aptitude for teamwork, attention to detail, IT skills, methodical, numeracy skills, responsible attitude, scientific approach

Relevant Subjects

Biology, Chemistry, Design and technology, ICT/Computer studies, Manufacturing, Mathematics, Physics, Science

Further Information

AGCAS: Engineering (Job Sector Briefing) (AGCAS) - www.prospects.ac.uk

AGCAS: Manufacturing (Job Sector Briefing) (AGCAS) - www.prospects.ac.uk

Apprenticeship Schemes (National Apprenticeship Service) - www.apprenticeships.org.uk

Diplomas (Foundation, Higher and Advanced) - http://yp.direct.gov.uk/diplomas

Improve Ltd - sector skills council for food and drink manufacturing and processing - www.improveltd.co.uk

Quality Manufacturing Today - www.qualitymanufacturingtoday.com

Qualityworld (monthly) (Chartered Quality Institute) - www.thecqi.org/qualityworld/

SEMTA - sector skills council for science, engineering and manufacturing technologies - www.semta.org.uk

Training Schemes - www.direct.gov.uk/en/educationandlearning

Welsh Baccalaureate - www.wbq.org.uk

▶Working in manufacturing (2010) (Babcock Lifeskills) - www.babcock-lifeskills.com/

Addresses

British Quality Foundation (BQF)
32-34 Great Peter Street, London SW1P 2QX
Phone: +44 (0)20 7654 50000
Web: www.quality-foundation.co.uk

Chartered Quality Institute (CQI)
12 Grosvenor Crescent, London SW1X 7EE
Phone: +44 (0)20 7245 6722
Web: www.thecqi.org

Similar Jobs

Cloth/Garment Examiner, Laboratory Technician: Science, NDT Technician/Engineer, Production Manager, Quality Manager, Trading Standards Officer

Quality Manager

also known as: Quality Assurance Manager

CRCI:Administration, Business and Office Work
CLCI:COD Job Band: 4 to 5

Job Description

Quality managers are responsible for ensuring that organisations meet quality standards for the products they make or the services they provide. They put systems in place to ensure that working practices are up to standard and consistent. Analyse business and production statistics and publish reports on how well a system is performing against set targets, called benchmarks. They initiate schemes such as total quality management (TQM) and Six Sigma to improve quality and methods of production, by helping to change attitudes and behaviour of employees.

May use ISO 9000, a family of standards for quality management systems, and liaise with other managers and staff to ensure quality systems are working effectively. May also have additional managerial duties, including the management of a team. Quality managers are required to be up to date on national and international legal standards, health and safety regulations and ensure that products and systems comply with any requirements.

Work Details

Usually work a 37-40 hr week, Monday to Friday, for a company or organisation that provides all types of goods or services. Some jobs require you to be on call, work weekends and be available for shifts. Some jobs are office based, but you may also work in a laboratory supervising staff, as well as on site in the design and production sections. Your key responsibility is to ensure that the rules are obeyed and high standards are upheld. You may need to travel to meetings and to other sites.

Qualification

• England, Wales and Northern Ireland

Band 4: For a relevant BTEC higher national award: usually 1-2 A levels and some GCSEs (A*-C) usually including English, maths, and a science, or equivalent.

Band 5: For degree courses: 2-3 A levels and some GCSEs (A*-C) usually including English, maths and a science, or equivalent. Exact requirements depend on the degree you take.

• Scotland

Band 4: For SQA higher national award: usually 2-3 H grades and some S grades (1-3), often including maths, English and a science, or similar.

Band 5: For degree courses: usually 3-5 H grades and some S grades (1-3), usually including English, maths and science, or similar qualifications.

Degree Information

Subjects such as business, engineering and management, mathematical, physical and applied science are relevant. A one-year full-time BSc in quality management (top-up) is available that can also be studied on a part-time basis. A number of postgraduate courses are also available.

Adult Qualifications
Course entry requirements are usually relaxed for suitable mature applicants. Those without the required qualifications may complete a foundation or Access course leading to relevant HNDs or accredited degrees.

Work Experience
Entry to this job may be competitive and it is important that you try to do some relevant work or voluntary experience before applying. Work in a company that operates a quality management system is relevant, as is work shadowing a quality manager. Work placements during a degree course give useful experience to add to your CV.

Entry and Training
Entry requirements vary considerably between industries and employers, but most entrants have a relevant higher national award or degree. Some employers particularly look for a qualification in science, engineering or business. Training is usually on the job, learning the QA systems of the organisation, but many employers offer a graduate training programme. During training, you may also be required to take professional qualifications.

A level 3 certificate in quality that provides the required underpinning knowledge is available from the Chartered Quality Institute (CQI) as well as the eligibility to apply for associate membership. There is also a level 5 diploma in quality that meets the academic requirement for the qualification route to CQI membership, and which is nationally recognised by industry and government. The CQI now offers a route to Chartered Quality Professional status for those with member or fellow status of the CQI. Short courses in aspects of quality assurance, and continuing professional development (CPD) are also offered by the CQI. Contact the institute for further details of membership and courses offered.

A level 4 diploma in quality management is available from the Chartered Management Institute (CMI). A certificate in management, or equivalent, and/or quality management experience is usually required before you can work for the diploma. Contact CMI for details of training providers. There are also foundation degrees in many relevant subjects. Entry is sometimes possible without an HND/degree and you may have the opportunity to work your way up to management level, though some employers may require higher qualifications for progression to management posts.

Mature candidates with background experience in industry or management and the right aptitude may be preferred, and may be promoted to manager through a company's in-house management training programme. The Chartered Quality Institute certificate in quality (level 3) is available part time and by distance learning. It can be taken over a period of one, two and three years depending on how quickly you want to complete it. After completing this course, it is possible to go on to the Level 5 qualification which is equivalent to a diploma.

Opportunities and Pay
Employment is with both large multinational companies and small organisations in the commercial and service sectors and in manufacturing. There is scope for specialisation in larger companies, but QA work in small organisations is likely to be more varied.

Career development possibilities are good as there has been an increasing emphasis on quality assurance over recent years and this continues to expand. With experience and qualifications, self-employment or freelance work as a consultant is possible. Some managers move into other areas, such as production, health and safety and technical sales.

Pay varies depending on location, type and size of organisation, but starting salaries are likely to be around £20k-£25k a year, rising to £25k-£48k a year with experience. Senior managers may earn over £50k a year. However, salaries in industries such as oil and gas can be significantly higher.

Skills and Qualities
analytical skills, attention to detail, diplomatic, good communication skills, good interpersonal skills, IT skills, knowledge of statistics, observant, persuasive, problem-solving skills.

Relevant Subjects
Manufacturing

Further Information
Quality Management and Training - www.qmt.co.uk
Qualityworld (monthly) (Chartered Quality Institute) - www.thecqi.org/qualityworld/
UK Excellence (bi-monthly) (British Quality Foundation (BQF)) - www.quality-foundation.co.uk

Addresses
British Quality Foundation (BQF)
32-34 Great Peter Street, London SW1P 2QX
Phone: +44 (0)20 7654 50000
Web: www.quality-foundation.co.uk

Chartered Management Institute (CMI)
Management House, Cottingham Road, Corby NN17 1TT
Phone: +44 (0)1536 204 222
Web: www.managers.org.uk

Chartered Quality Institute (CQI)
12 Grosvenor Crescent, London SW1X 7EE
Phone: +44 (0)20 7245 6722
Web: www.thecqi.org

Quality Management and Training
PO Box 172, Guildford, Surrey GU2 7FN
Phone: +44 (0)1483 453 511
Web: www.qmt.co.uk

Similar Jobs
Manager, NDT Technician/Engineer, Operational Researcher, Production Manager, Quality Assurance Controller/Inspector, Statistician

Quarry Operative
CRCI:Engineering
CLCI:ROB — Job Band: 1 to 2

Job Description
A quarry operative does a range of jobs to quarry minerals and materials, including limestone, granite, chalk, slate, gravel, sandstone and clay. At gravel pits, they may drive heavy plant machinery such as excavators and draglines. May also work the machines that do the washing and grading. Quarry operatives often work in a team, under the supervision of the quarry manager.

In stone quarries, explosives are used for blasting and machines for crushing rock. Other jobs include operating ready-mixed concrete plant, driving trucks and delivering materials to customers. Some quarry workers carry out repairs and maintain machinery and other quarrying equipment.

Work Details
Usually works around 39-40 hrs a week but you may be expected to work shifts. You work outdoors on site and start work under supervision. Working conditions may be difficult. When blasting you have to be very careful and follow regulations and safety standards so that nobody is injured. This work involves physical activity such as walking over rough ground and climbing ladders.

The environment is noisy, dirty, dusty and sometimes muddy. You are out in all sorts of weather. There is a risk of minor injuries or accidents from equipment. You need to wear overalls, a safety helmet, protective footwear and sometimes ear protectors and a face mask.

Qualification

• England, Wales and Northern Ireland

Band 1: For entry to jobs, no minimum qualifications are needed, but you are expected to have a good level of general education and relevant experience. Some formal/vocational qualifications at any level are useful.

Band 2: For entry to jobs, no minimum qualifications are needed, but it is an advantage to have some GCSEs (A*-C) or equivalent in subjects that include maths, English, science and technology, or equivalent.

• Scotland

Band 1: For entry to jobs, no minimum qualifications are needed, but you are expected to have a good level of general education and relevant experience. Some formal/vocational qualifications at any level are useful.

Band 2: Although academic qualifications are not specified for this job, it is an advantage to have some S grades (1-3) in subjects that include English and maths, or similar.

Adult Qualifications

Although formal qualifications are not always specified, a good secondary education and experience of work in the construction industry are helpful. Specific entry requirements for courses may be relaxed for mature applicants. You can improve your skills and qualifications by working through the Foundation Learning Tier. This involves taking credit-based units and qualifications to help you progress.

Work Experience

Entry to this job may be competitive. Relevant work or voluntary experience, perhaps in construction or other heavy work, is always useful and can improve your chances when applying for entry to jobs. Health and safety issues may mean that there are certain jobs you can't do until you are over 16.

Entry and Training

Applicants aged over 18 may be preferred. Training is on the job through an employer's training scheme and by short courses, covering areas such as blasting techniques, shotfiring, welding, plant operations, and health and safety. Some operatives may work towards S/NVQs at level 2 in plant operations (extractives) and at level 1-3 in process operations. There is also an S/NVQ in blasting operations at level 3. Contact the awarding body, the Mineral Products Qualifications Council (MPQC), for details of relevant S/NVQs and other qualifications. The MPQC provides and approves a range of training courses designed to meet the needs of the extraction and mineral processing industries. These include the plant operator scheme for those with a minimum of 3 months' operational experience.

Those working with explosives as shotfirers need a Shotfiring Certificate to work on a quarry. Certificate courses are run by approved MPQC trainers. This job may require an LGV (large goods vehicle) driving licence. Training programmes, including apprenticeships in extracting and mineral processing operations, leading to level 2 and advanced apprenticeships leading to level 3, may be available in your area.

The Mineral Products Association website has details of the various roles in quarrying. See their website for details.

A Diploma/Welsh Baccalaureate may be available in your area in engineering. See the diplomas website for further information.

There are good opportunities for mature entry, particularly for those with relevant experience such as work in the building/construction or mining industries.

Government training opportunities, such as apprenticeships, may be available in your area. You can also gain recognition of previous experience through Accreditation of Prior Learning (APL) or by working towards relevant S/NVQs. Contact your local careers office, Jobcentre Plus, Next Step service or Learning and Skills Council (LSC) Local Enterprise Company (LEC) for details of training schemes, including apprenticeships for adults.

Opportunities and Pay

Jobs are mostly found in rural areas. There are fewer opportunities in this area due to developments in technology. Employment can be with either a large contractor or a small firm. Promotion to more senior jobs, such as chargehand or supervisor, is possible after gaining experience.

Pay varies depending on your area and employer. A starting wage is likely to be around £13k a year. Pay increases with promotion and can be up to £30k. More can be earned if overtime is worked.

Health

There is an allergy risk from dust. This job requires good stamina and physical fitness.

Skills and Qualities

able to follow instructions, aptitude for teamwork, common sense, co-operative, efficient, numeracy skills, practical skills, responsible attitude, safety conscious

Further Information

Apprenticeship Schemes (National Apprenticeship Service) - www.apprenticeships.org.uk

Careers in Quarrying - www.careersinquarrying.co.uk/

Diplomas (Foundation, Higher and Advanced) - http://yp.direct.gov.uk/diplomas

Proskills UK - sector skills council for process and manufacturing industries - www.proskills.co.uk

Quarry Management (monthly) (QMJ Publishing Ltd) - www.quarrymanagement.com/

The Mining Journal Online - www.mining-journal.com

Training Schemes - www.direct.gov.uk/en/educationandlearning

Welsh Baccalaureate - www.wbq.org.uk

Addresses

Institute of Quarrying
7 Regent Street, Nottingham NG1 5BS
Phone: +44 (0)115 945 3880
Web: www.quarrying.org

Mineral Products Association
Gillingham House, 38 - 44 Gillingham Street, London SW1V 1HU
Phone: +44 (0) 20 7 963 8000
Web: www.mineralproducts.org

Mineral Products Qualifications Council (MPQC)
Alban Row, 27-31 Verulam Road, St Albans, Hertfordshire AL3 4DG
Phone: +44 (0)1727 817 205
Web: www.empawards.com

Similar Jobs

Construction Operative, Construction Plant Operative, Crane Operator, Demolition Operative, Engineering Machine Operative, Road Worker

Radiographer: Diagnostic

CRCI:Healthcare
CLCI:JAP Job Band: 5

Job Description

Diagnostic radiographers use radiation and high-tech computerised equipment to treat people who are injured or ill. They have considerable knowledge of anatomy, physiology, pathology and technology. Radiographers screen for abnormalities, produce and interpret high quality images of organs, limbs and other parts of the body to allow doctors to diagnose different diseases, monitor body processes and investigate injuries. They use a range of techniques, including magnetic resonance imaging (MRI), computed tomography (CT) scanning, ultrasound, fluoroscopy, angiography, or X-rays.

May be involved in surgical procedures such as biopsies, the removal of kidney stones or the insertion of a stent into the body to widen blood vessels. Must ensure that the patient is only exposed to the absolute and safe minimum amount of radiation necessary to produce an exact and clear image.

Work Details

Usually work a 35-37 hr week in a hospital or clinic, though may take part in an on-call rota that involves weekends, nights and evenings, and public holidays. The work involves understanding and using complex equipment and working as part of a medical team. There is daily contact with patients and you look after people of all ages, some of whom may be in pain or upset. You generally only see each patient once or twice until a diagnosis is made. You are responsible for safety and a high level of accuracy.

Work requires coping with unpleasant sights and can be emotionally demanding. You may need to be on your feet for many hours and have to help lift people or move equipment. You need to wear a uniform and protective clothing.

Qualification

- **England, Wales and Northern Ireland**

Band 5: For degree courses: 2-3 A levels and some GCSEs (A*-C) usually including English, maths or physics and another science subject, or equivalent. Exact requirements depend on the degree you take.

- **Scotland**

Band 5: For degree courses: 3-5 H grades and some S grades (1-3), usually including English, maths or physics and another science subject, or similar. Exact requirements depend on the degree you take.

Degree Information

A degree in diagnostic radiography is required for entry to this job. It is then possible to specialise by taking a postgraduate course in an area such as medical ultrasound, CT scanning, or paediatric imaging.

Adult Qualifications

Mature entrants may be accepted on to degree courses without the standard academic qualifications. Check with the institution for details. Entry is also possible through validated Access and foundation courses. Many radiography education centres welcome mature candidates.

Work Experience

Colleges and universities may prefer candidates who have relevant work or voluntary experience. Although not essential, work experience is recommended before applying for a radiography degree to make sure you are choosing the right profession. Ideally, experience with a radiographer is most useful but if this proves difficult to arrange, experience working with people in a healthcare or hospital environment is helpful.

Entry and Training

You need to complete a degree in diagnostic radiography approved by the Health Professions Council (HPC), at one of 23 universities in the UK. A lot of work is computer-based so you also need computer and keyboard skills. Most radiography courses take three years, there are also some part-time study routes. State registration with the HPC is essential to gain employment in the NHS. Courses combine academic study with clinical experience in hospital departments. Once qualified and in employment you can choose to specialise in areas of diagnostic radiotherapy such as magnetic resonance or ultrasound, and take relevant postgraduate qualifications.

Continuing professional development (CPD) is important. Additional qualifications and state registration are gained through postgraduate courses, which are available for those with experience. Contact the Society of Radiographers for details on all accredited courses and training.

Mature applicants are welcome. If you have a first degree, you can qualify as a radiographer by taking a postgraduate diploma. Funding for first degrees and postgraduate courses is usually available through bursaries from the Department of Health.

Opportunities and Pay

There is a shortage of radiographers, particularly in London and south-east England, and an increasing demand nationwide. Most are employed by the NHS but there are also jobs in private practice, or possibly in the armed forces or a sports club. There is a formal career structure for radiographers within the NHS. Promotion depends on experience and is based on interview and merit. Postgraduate qualifications are an advantage. Qualified and experienced radiographers have the opportunity to become consultant radiographers.

Some radiographers move into research or university education. Manufacturers also employ diagnostic radiographers as application specialists. Some go on to train as sonographers or ultrasonographers. There is a demand for radiographers overseas, particularly in Australia, New Zealand, Canada, the Netherlands and Saudi Arabia.

Pay is on a nationally agreed scale if employed by the NHS, but varies in the private sector. Starting salaries for newly qualified radiographers working for the NHS are around £21k a year, with radiographer specialists earning up to £35k Advanced radiographers/team managers earn in excess of £38k and consultants can earn up to £60k. Rates in London are higher.

Health

This job requires good health and a medical test on entry.

Skills and Qualities

able to inspire confidence, able to use complex equipment, accurate, aptitude for teamwork, attention to detail, good interpersonal skills, IT skills, not squeamish, responsible attitude, scientific approach

Relevant Subjects

Biology, Chemistry, English, Health and social care, Mathematics, Physics, Psychology, Science

Further Information

AGCAS: Health (Job Sector Briefing) (AGCAS) - www.prospects.ac.uk

Health Professions Council (HPC) - www.hpc-uk.org

NHS Careers (NHS Careers) - www.nhscareers.nhs.uk

NHS Careers Scotland - www.infoscotland.com/nhs

NHS Careers Wales - www.wales.nhs.uk

Radiography Careers - www.radiographycareers.co.uk/

Radiography Careers Information (Society of Radiographers) - www.sor.org/public/careerinfo/careers.htm

Synergy Magazine (monthly) (Society of Radiographers) - www.synergymagazine.co.uk/

Addresses

Society of Radiographers (SOR)
207 Providence Square , Mill Street, London SE1 2EW
Phone: +44 (0)20 7740 7200
Web: www.sor.org

Similar Jobs

Clinical Technologist, Neurophysiologist, Photographer: Clinical, Radiographer: Therapeutic, Respiratory Physiologist

Radiographer: Therapeutic

also known as: Radiotherapy Radiographer

CRCI:Healthcare
CLCI:JAP Job Band: 5

Job Description

Therapeutic radiographers use controlled amounts of radiation and high-tech computerised equipment to treat people who have cancer. They have considerable knowledge of anatomy, physiology, pathology and technology. Plan and deliver prescribed treatments using X-radiation and other radioactive sources to treat cancer. Localise the areas for treatment and set up the radiation equipment so that the right dosage of radiation is used for the right amount of time, exposing the targeted tissue to as much as possible while minimising the effect on the rest of the body.

Radiographers are involved in the care of patients from the initial referral clinic stage, where pre-treatment information is given, through the planning process, treatment and follow-up stages. Work in a multi-disciplinary team, often under the direction of a clinical oncologist and with other health professionals who look after patients requiring a range of treatments, including chemotherapy and surgery. This includes providing the patient with information, support and perhaps counselling.

Work Details

Usually work a 35-37 hr week in a hospital or clinic, though may take part in an on-call rota that involves weekends, nights and evenings, and public holidays. The work involves understanding and using complex equipment and working as part of a medical team. There is daily contact with patients and you look after people of all ages, who may be in pain or upset. You are involved in treating people over long periods of time. You are responsible for safety and a high level of accuracy.

Work requires coping with unpleasant sights and can be emotionally demanding. You may need to be on your feet for many hours and have to help lift people or move equipment. You need to wear a uniform and protective clothing.

Qualification

• England, Wales and Northern Ireland

Band 5: For degree courses: 2-3 A levels and some GCSEs (A*-C) usually including English, maths or physics and another science subject, or equivalent. Exact requirements depend on the degree you take.

• Scotland

Band 5: For degree courses: 3-5 H grades and some S grades (1-3), usually including English, maths or physics and another science subject, or similar. Exact requirements depend on the degree you take.

Degree Information

A degree in radiography or therapeutic radiography is required for entry to this job. It is possible then to specialise in areas such as treatment planning, palliative care or therapy aspects of nuclear medicine. Foundation degrees in diagnostic imaging and radiography can be a route to a full time degree.

Adult Qualifications

Mature entrants may be accepted on to degree courses without the standard academic qualifications. Check with the institution concerned. Entry is also possible through validated Access or foundation courses. Many radiography education centres welcome mature candidates.

Work Experience

Colleges and universities may prefer candidates who have relevant work or voluntary experience. Although not essential, work experience is recommended before applying for a radiography degree to make sure you are choosing the right profession. Experience with a radiographer is most useful but if this proves difficult to arrange then experience working with people in a healthcare or hospital environment is helpful.

Entry and Training

You need to complete a degree in radiography or therapeutic radiography approved by the Health Professions Council, at one of 14 universities in the UK. A lot of work is computer-based so you also need computer and keyboard skills. Most radiography courses take three years, there are also some part-time study routes. State registration is essential to gain employment in the NHS. Courses combine academic study with clinical experience in hospital departments. Once qualified and in employment you can choose to specialise in areas of therapeutic radiotherapy such as patient care or treatment planning.

Continuing professional development (CPD) is important. Additional qualifications and state registration are gained through postgraduate courses, which are available for those with experience. Contact the Society of Radiographers for details on all accredited courses and training.

Mature applicants are welcomed. If you have a first degree, you can qualify as a radiographer by taking a postgraduate diploma. Funding for first degrees and postgraduate courses is usually available through bursaries from the Department of Health.

Opportunities and Pay

There is a shortage of radiographers, particularly in London and south-east England, and an increasing demand nationwide. Most are employed by the NHS but there are also jobs in private practice in special radiotherapy or oncology centres, or possibly in the armed forces. There is a formal career structure for radiographers within the NHS. Promotion depends on experience and is based on interview and merit; postgraduate qualifications are an advantage. Qualified and experienced radiographers have the opportunity to become consultant radiographers.

Some radiographers move into research or teaching. Some go on to train as sonographers or ultrasonographers. There is a demand for radiographers overseas, particularly in Australia, New Zealand, Canada, the Netherlands and Saudi Arabia.

Pay is on a nationally agreed scale if employed by the NHS, but varies in the private sector. Starting salaries for newly qualified radiographers working for the NHS are around £21k a year, with radiographer specialists earning up to £35k Advanced radiographers/team managers earn in excess of £38k and consultants can earn up to £60k. Rates in London are higher.

Skills and Qualities

able to inspire confidence, able to use complex equipment, accurate, aptitude for teamwork, attention to detail, good interpersonal skills, IT skills, not squeamish, responsible attitude, scientific approach

Relevant Subjects

Biology, Chemistry, English, Health and social care, Mathematics, Physics, Psychology, Science

Further Information

AGCAS: Health (Job Sector Briefing) (AGCAS) - www.prospects.ac.uk

Health Professions Council (HPC) - www.hpc-uk.org

NHS Careers (NHS Careers) - www.nhscareers.nhs.uk

NHS Careers Scotland - www.infoscotland.com/nhs

NHS Careers Wales - www.wales.nhs.uk

Radiography Careers - www.radiographycareers.co.uk/

Radiography Careers Information (Society of Radiographers) - www.sor.org/public/careerinfo/careers.htm

Synergy Magazine (monthly) (Society of Radiographers) - www.synergymagazine.co.uk/

▶Working in maths (2009) (Babcock Lifeskills) - www.babcock-lifeskills.com/

Addresses
Society of Radiographers (SOR)
207 Providence Square , Mill Street, London SE1 2EW
Phone: +44 (0)20 7740 7200
Web: www.sor.org

Similar Jobs
Cardiac Physiologist, Clinical Scientist: Medical Physicist, Clinical Technologist, Neurophysiologist, Radiographer: Diagnostic, Respiratory Physiologist

Radiography Assistant

also known as: Clinical Support Worker: Imaging Support Workers, Imaging Support Worker

CRCI:Healthcare
CLCI:JAP Job Band: 1 to 2

Job Description
Radiography assistants work in a healthcare professional team that uses X-ray and radiation equipment, and assist the work of qualified diagnostic and therapeutic radiographers. They help to prepare specialised equipment and look after the preparation and reproduction of film images. Ensure there is a clean and hygienic working environment. Identifying equipment failure and reporting faults immediately is an essential part of the job. May undertake basic maintenance of equipment. Also undertake some routine procedures when working with a qualified radiographer, such as radiography of certain areas of the body, or assisting with specialised procedures, such as biopsies.

Radiography assistants acquire a basic knowledge of anatomy, physiology, pathology and technology to assist the radiographer in more advanced areas of their work. Support patients prior to, during and after imaging procedures.

Work Details
Working hours are usually 37 hours a week, Monday to Friday, though you may be required to work on a shift basis including some evenings and weekends. You work as part of a team in a hospital or clinic, in either the public or private sector. There is daily contact with patients of all ages and abilities, who may be in pain or upset. All staff are responsible for adopting and maintaining safe and accurate working practices.

Work requires coping with unpleasant sights at times and can be emotionally demanding. You may need to be on your feet for many hours. This work requires a good standard of physical fitness, because you may have to help lift patients or move equipment.

Qualification

• England, Wales and Northern Ireland
Band 1: No minimum qualifications are required, but you are expected to have a good level of general education. However, some formal/vocational qualifications at any level are useful.

Band 2: Although academic qualifications are not specified for this job, it is an advantage to have some GCSEs (A*-C) in subjects that include English, maths and a science subject, or equivalent.

• Scotland
Band 1: No minimum qualifications are required, but you are expected to have a good level of general education. However, some formal/vocational qualifications at any level are useful.

Band 2: Although academic qualifications are not specified for this job, it is an advantage to have some S grades (1-3) in subjects that include English, maths and a science subject, or similar.

Adult Qualifications
No minimum qualifications are usually needed but entry requirements may vary. Some formal qualifications or their equivalent may be required to qualify for more advanced work.

Work Experience
Work experience gives you an insight into what you enjoy about a job or working environment, and the opportunity to acquire new skills. It provides valuable information to add to your CV and improves your employment prospects. Relevant work or voluntary experience in a medical or healthcare setting such as a hospital or residential care home is an advantage.

Entry and Training
Most training is on the job under the supervision of a qualified radiographer. Training is mostly work based, but may include off-site short courses, seminars and lectures. You may have the opportunity to take a certificate in assistant radiographic practice, such as the one offered by Cardiff University, or a BTEC professional development certificate for assistant practitioners in imaging offered by the University of Derby. There is also a two-year part time certificate of higher education in service course at Robert Gordon University in Aberdeen. Contact the Society of Radiographers (SOR) for details of all courses.

The number of assistant practitioners is increasing within the NHS and you may also be able to study for a distance-learning foundation degree in radiography and oncology, which is work based and studied over two years. This enables you to take on an increased range of tasks. There is no central recruitment and most vacancies are advertised locally by individual hospital trusts.

The SOR has introduced a career progression framework for the radiography profession. Coupled with changes to career development structures within the NHS, this has led to the need for assistants to be accredited as assistant practitioners and for their qualifications and practice in radiography to be recognised within the NHS. There are also S/NVQs at level 2-4 in radiation protection.

Mature applicants are welcome and experience in care work, such as in a hospital or in residential care, is an advantage.

Opportunities and Pay
You can be employed by the NHS, in private practice or the armed forces. There may also be opportunities to work part time or job share. You can progress to become an assistant practitioner and study to become a qualified radiographer with support from your employer.

Pay for experienced radiography assistant practitioners working for the NHS is around £17k-£21k a year.

Health
This job requires good health and a medical test on entry.

Skills and Qualities
able to get on with all kinds of people, accurate, aptitude for teamwork, attention to detail, good communication skills, health & safety awareness, not squeamish, patient, responsible attitude, scientific approach

Relevant Subjects
Biology, Health and social care, Physics, Science

Further Information
Foundation Learning (QCDA) - www.qcda.gov.uk

NHS Careers (NHS Careers) - www.nhscareers.nhs.uk

NHS Careers Scotland - www.infoscotland.com/nhs

NHS Careers Wales - www.wales.nhs.uk

Radiography Careers Information (Society of Radiographers) - www.sor.org/public/careerinfo/careers.htm

Synergy Magazine (monthly) (Society of Radiographers) - www.synergymagazine.co.uk/

Addresses
Society of Radiographers (SOR)
207 Providence Square , Mill Street, London SE1 2EW
Phone: +44 (0)20 7740 7200
Web: www.sor.org

Similar Jobs
Clinical Technologist, Healthcare Assistant, Photographer: Clinical, Physiotherapy Assistant, Plaster Technician, Radiographer: Diagnostic

RAF Airman/Airwoman
also known as: Royal Air Force Airman/Airwoman

CRCI:Security and Armed Forces
CLCI:BAL Job Band: 1 to 3

Job Description
RAF airmen/airwomen work in one of the many specialist ground trades such as telecommunications, catering and engineering, or as aircrew (non-commissioned officer, NCO). A wide range of trades and professions are available, depending on aptitude and personal choice including firefighters, police, cartographers, sports and fitness instructors, assistant air traffic controllers, caterers, musicians, transport drivers and technicians, photographers, electrical or weapons technicians, medical and dental assistants. Some work in air/helicopter crews on patrol missions.

All airmen and airwomen carry out other military duties that include taking part in military exercises, training sessions and guarding RAF bases. The aim is to keep the RAF efficient and flying at all times and to maintain security of UK/NATO airspace.

Work Details
Hours of work vary depending on the operational requirements of the job and you can be expected to work irregular hours, possibly shifts and flexible hours according to the needs of the RAF. Airmen/airwomen work in a wide range of different trades so your workplace depends on the job but can be a workshop, an office, laboratory, a machine room or outdoors. Aircrew (NCOs) fly on-board multi-engine aircraft and on helicopters. You may be away from home for several months when on detachment.

Work is usually under supervision and you are required to accept discipline. You need to wear a uniform and perhaps headphones or protective clothing.

Qualification
The majority of jobs require no formal qualifications, though all entrants must pass a series of aptitude tests.

• England, Wales and Northern Ireland
Band 1: For some trades: qualifications are not needed, but a number of GCSEs or equivalent qualifications at any level are useful.

Band 2: For some trades a minimum of 2-3 GCSEs (A*-E) including maths, English, physics or a physics-based science subject, or equivalent qualifications are needed.

Band 3: For some trades at least 5 GCSEs (A*-C) are required. Subjects needed may include maths, English, physics or other suitable science subject, or equivalent qualifications.

• Scotland
Band 1: For most jobs: qualifications are not needed though a number of S grades or similar at any level are useful.

Band 2: For some trades a minimum of 2-3 S grades (1-5) including maths, English, physics or a physics-based science subject, or similar qualifications are needed.

Band 3: For some trades at least five S grades (1-3) are required. Subjects needed may include English, maths, physics or other suitable science subject, or similar qualifications.

Adult Qualifications
Certain jobs in the RAF may require some formal/vocational qualifications, but for many at this level there are no specific formal entry requirements.

Work Experience
Relevant work or voluntary experience is always useful and can improve your chances when applying for entry to the armed forces. Fitness is a requirement for the armed forces, so evidence of an interest in keeping physically fit is useful. The RAF offers the opportunity of work experience at some of its bases. Contact a base near you for further details.

Entry and Training
Some specialist jobs require specific entry qualifications that are mainly described in terms of GCSEs/S grades or technical/vocational qualifications such as BTEC/SQA national awards, or equivalent. These are mainly needed for jobs as nurses, radiographers and dental technicians, engineering technicians and aircrew. Check with the local armed forces careers office for the exact minimum qualifications required for each trade. Entrants are usually aged 16-29, but for some jobs, such as student nurses and RAF police, the minimum age is 17.5. There are nationality and residence requirements for entry. All entrants take an aptitude test and have a medical.

All recruits complete nine weeks' basic military training through a recruiting training course (RTC) before joining their own trade group. If joining an RAF trade, you are stationed at RAF Halton in Buckinghamshire and if training as an RAF Regiment Gunner, you train at RAF Honington in Suffolk. Aircrew (NCOs) spend ten weeks at RAF Cranwell and need to complete the Airman Aircrew Initial Training Course (AAITC). You are promoted to acting sergeant when successful. Specialist training is given on the job and by short courses.

The length of training can vary from a few weeks for certain trades and up to eighteen months for others. Trainees are also encouraged to work for nationally recognised qualifications such as City & Guilds, BTEC/SQA awards and for S/NVQs.

Mature applicants should be aware that the upper age limit for most trades is 29, though some trades specify different age limits, such as staff nurses and weapon systems operator (under 36). Check current regulations carefully as age limits are subject to review. Relevant work experience is an advantage.

Opportunities and Pay
There are over 30,000 non-commissioned personnel in the RAF. Vacancies in some trades are more competitive than others. See the RAF website for trades in need of recruits. You can be stationed anywhere in the UK or sent to serve anywhere in the world when needed. Prospects for promotion are good for airmen/women who do well in their trade training, with chances of promotion improved by further training. You must complete a minimum length of service. This can sometimes be a short career but the training given and nationally recognised qualifications earned can be extremely useful in civilian work.

Rate of pay depends on rank and trade and increase with promotion. For instance, a new recruit earns £13,377k a year during training. This rises to £16,681k as a senior aircraftman/woman but can rise up to £36,204k for sergeant positions. Pay can also be increased by bonuses for length of service. If you have still not given notice after 7 year's service, you are eligible for a bonus of £5,500 in return for committing to two more years of service. Flying pay is also added to basic salary for aircrew. You are usually given an overseas living allowance when working abroad.

An Equal Opportunities policy operates within the armed forces, though as an exception, females are not currently able to train as a gunner.

Health
Applicants must pass a strict medical before being accepted into the RAF. There are also regular medical check ups. For some jobs there are specific requirements relating to height, wearing glasses or contact lenses, colour vision and hearing. Check with the local Armed Forces Careers Office for detailed information on current health regulations.

Skills and Qualities
able to cope under pressure, able to follow instructions, aptitude for teamwork, efficient, good communication skills, good stamina and physically fit, prepared to go into combat, quick reactions, self-disciplined, willing to learn

Relevant Subjects
Design and technology, Engineering, Mathematics, Physical education and sport, Physics, Science

Further Information
Careers Information - Royal Air Force (RAF) - www.raf.mod.uk

RAF News (RAF) - www.rafnews.co.uk

Skills for Work (Scottish Qualifications Authority) - www.sqa.org.uk/sqa/31390.html

Starting a Career as Aircrew in Military Aviation (Air League) (Air League) - www.airleague.co.uk/scholarships.html

▶Working in police, fire & security (2009) (Babcock Lifeskills) - www.babcock-lifeskills.com/

Addresses
Air League Educational Trust
Broadway House, Tothill Street, London SW1H 9NS
Phone: +44 (0)20 7222 8463
Web: www.airleague.co.uk

Welbeck - Defence Sixth Form College
Forest Road, Woodhouse, Loughborough,
Leicestershire LE12 8WD
Web: www.dsfc.ac.uk/

Similar Jobs
Aircraft Engineering Technician, Army Soldier, Engineer: Electronics, Engineer: Mechanical, Mechanical Engineering Technician, Royal Navy Rating

RAF Officer
also known as: Royal Air Force Officer

CRCI:Security and Armed Forces

CLCI:BAL Job Band: 4 to 5

Job Description
A Royal Air Force (RAF) officer manages, motivates and leads a trained team of airmen/airwomen under their command and is also responsible for their welfare and career development. Works as a specialist in a particular branch of the service such as aircrew, engineering, air traffic control, intelligence, supply and security. Others work as physical education officers, training and development officers, and in administration. There are also opportunities for qualified professional specialists such as doctors, nurses, dentists, lawyers and chaplains.

Work Details
This job requires a great deal of personal commitment. Working hours vary according to operational requirements but may be irregular, including weekends and shift duty. You must be available for duty at all times. Although some of the work involves routine tasks, you also have to be able to work under pressure. You are responsible for overseeing other ranks and must be able to deal with their work-related and personal problems. The work environment varies depending on the type of job you are doing, but many jobs involve working in noisy conditions.

When on active duty you may be at risk of being injured or killed. You may need to wear protective clothing, headphones or ear protectors. On detachment, you may be away from home for several months.

Qualification
There are different qualifications needed for various branches of the service. Check with the local Armed Forces Careers Office for information on the specific qualification requirements for each branch.

- **England, Wales and Northern Ireland**

Band 4: For many branches of the service: a minimum of two A levels and 5 GCSEs (A*-C) including English and maths are needed. Equivalent qualifications, such as a BTEC national award may also be acceptable.

Band 5: For degree course leading to graduate entry: 2-3 A levels and some GCSEs (A*-C) including English and maths. Check individual prospectuses.

- **Scotland**

Band 4: For many branches of the service: a minimum of three H grades and five S grades (1-3) including English and maths are needed. An SQA award or similar qualification may also be acceptable.

Band 5: For degree course leading to graduate entry: 3-5 H grades and some S grades (1-3) including English and maths. Exact requirements depend on the degree you take. Alternative qualifications such as SQAs may also be acceptable for entry to some courses. Check with universities for specific course requirements.

Degree Information
Any degree discipline is acceptable for officer entry. Some branches of the service require science or engineering degrees. Specialist areas require appropriate professional qualifications, including catering, physical education, medicine, dentistry, law, and nursing.

Adult Qualifications
Formal secondary education qualifications and a degree (or equivalent qualifications) are required, depending on the commission. Entry requirements may be relaxed for adults applying for higher education courses and Access or foundation courses give adults without qualifications a route onto degree courses.

Work Experience
Relevant work or voluntary experience is always useful and can improve your chances in application for entry to this career. The type of work experience to consider is in areas that develop your skills in leadership and enable you to demonstrate your initiative and responsibility. As a young person, getting involved in groups such as a local cadet organisation, or the Scouts/Guides, helps to show enthusiasm and commitment. Often you can gain valuable experience from a school's Air Training Corp (ATC) or university air squadron.

The RAF offers work experience at some of its bases, including a 12-month placement for engineering undergraduates.

Entry and Training
Many entrants are graduates (although displaying the right character is as important) and a degree or recognised equivalent qualification is required for certain areas of work such as engineering, as well as for professionally qualified entrants such as doctors, nurses or lawyers. There are nationality and residence requirements. Selection is based on aptitude, character and personality. Selection testing takes place at RAF Cranwell in Lincolnshire, lasts four days and includes interviews, aptitude tests, a medical and fitness tests. The interview panel are looking for leadership potential.

Applicants must be at least 17 years and 6 months, but upper age limits depend on the branch of the service and the level of entry. For most branches the upper age limit for entry is 36. There is a 30-week Initial Officer Training (IAT) course at RAF Cranwell for most officer entry, or a shorter course for certain selected specialist areas such as the medical branch. After initial training, you then go on to specialist training in your chosen area. Training is by practical experience, classroom work and specialist courses.

The armed forces have their own sixth form residential college. Science and technology-based A level courses at Welbeck College last for two years and successful students may go on to a degree course at university or straight to the officer training programme at RAF Cranwell. University bursaries may be available of up to £4k a year.

Mature applicants should be aware that the usual age of entry is between 17 years and 6 months and and 36 yrs; the precise age limit varies depending on the profession. There is usually a delay between acceptance and training, therefore candidates should apply a year in advance of age limits. Check current regulations carefully as age limits are subject to review. There may be financial support for adults, including university sponsorship for those who have gained a place, or a definite offer for a UK recognised degree.

There is also an engineering sponsorship scheme that is available through the Defence Technical Undergraduate Scheme which comes with a bursary of £4k a year. Contact your local armed forces careers office for information.

Opportunities and Pay

There are over 600 RAF officers recruited each year, and competition for entry to some specialisms is fierce. Promotion can be achieved with further training and is usually faster for graduates. You must complete a minimum length of service, the exact length of which depends on the chosen branch of service. Most officers join for an initial six years, but many extend their service beyond this. When you leave the RAF, you are able to transfer to civilian work as the training you receive provides an excellent basis for other jobs.

The starting salary for pilot officers (non-graduate entry) is £24k a year. Flying officers (graduate entry) earn £29k-£32k, flight lieutenants earn £37k-£44k, and squadron leaders earn £48k-£56k. Flying pay is added to basic salary for aircrew. An Equal Opportunities policy operates within the armed forces though as an exception, females are currently not able to join the RAF Regiment, but can apply for all other RAF officer positions.

Health

Applicants must pass a strict medical before being accepted into the RAF. There are also regular medical check ups. For some jobs there are specific requirements relating to height, wearing glasses or contact lenses, colour vision and hearing. Check with RAF Careers Information Offices for detailed information on current health regulations.

Skills and Qualities

able to inspire confidence, able to take responsibility, decisive, information handling skills, initiative, IT skills, leadership qualities, prepared to go into combat, quick thinking, self confident

Relevant Subjects

Design and technology, Engineering, English, Geography, Government and politics, Mathematics, Physical education and sport, Physics, Psychology, Science

Further Information

Careers Information - Royal Air Force (RAF) - www.raf.mod.uk

RAF News (RAF) - www.rafnews.co.uk

Real Life Guide to Armed Forces (Trotman 2009) - www.trotman.co.uk

Skills for Work (Scottish Qualifications Authority) - www.sqa.org.uk/sqa/31390.html

Starting a Career as Aircrew in Military Aviation (Air League) (Air League) - www.airleague.co.uk/scholarships.html

TARGETjobs: Public Service (GTI Specialist Publishing Ltd.) - www.groupgti.com

▶Working in police, fire & security (2009) (Babcock Lifeskills) - www.babcock-lifeskills.com/

Addresses

Air League Educational Trust
Broadway House, Tothill Street, London SW1H 9NS
Phone: +44 (0)20 7222 8463
Web: www.airleague.co.uk

Welbeck - Defence Sixth Form College
Forest Road, Woodhouse, Loughborough,
Leicestershire LE12 8WD
Web: www.dsfc.ac.uk/

Similar Jobs

Air Traffic Controller, Airline Pilot: Civil, Army Officer, Pilot: Armed Forces, Royal Marines Officer, Royal Navy Officer

Rail Track Maintenance Worker

also known as: Track Worker

CRCI:Transport and Logistics

CLCI:YAF Job Band: 1 to 3

Job Description

Track maintenance workers check, repair and keep railway tracks and the area around them in good order. They work on tracks, bridges, tunnels, fences and level crossings. Clear anything on or blocking the track such as fallen rocks and trees, snow and leaves. Look out for anything that may be a hazard in the future. May renew worn or damaged sections of track. Reporting problems, accidents and incidents, and attending briefing meetings, are part of the job.

Maintenance workers use hand tools, machinery and specialist equipment to measure and lay tracks and level the stones around the rails. May have to break up ground and mix and lay concrete. They follow strict health and safety procedures. Some work in gangs that patrol different sections of track on foot, checking them for wear or damage. May act as a lookout to warn other workers about approaching trains or danger, and direct trains using hand signals.

Work Details

Normally work shifts based on a 35 hr week. Shifts can be early, late or at night, including weekends and bank holidays. A lot of repair work takes place at night and at weekends. You may also be on call for emergencies. Sometimes you may need to work away from home. You work outdoors in all weathers. It is physically demanding and often dirty and noisy work.

Usually you work with other track maintenance workers in small teams or gangs. You wear high-visibility clothing, protective boots and other safety gear provided by the employer.

Qualification

• England, Wales and Northern Ireland

Band 1: For entry to jobs, no minimum qualifications are needed, but you are expected to have a good level of general education and relevant experience. Some formal/vocational qualifications at any level are useful.

Band 2: For entry to jobs, no minimum qualifications are needed, but it is an advantage to have some GCSEs (A*-C) or equivalent in subjects that include English and maths.

Band 3: For entry to jobs, HNC, a relevant Diploma or advanced apprenticeships, usually at least 4 GCSEs (A*-C) including English and maths, or equivalent.

• Scotland

Band 1: For entry to jobs, no minimum qualifications are needed, but you are expected to have a good level of general education and relevant experience. Some formal/vocational qualifications at any level are useful.

Band 2: Although academic qualifications are not specified for this job, it is an advantage to have some S grades (1-3) in subjects that include English and maths, or similar.

Band 3: For entry to apprenticeships: usually at least four S grades (1-3) including English, maths and science, or similar.

Adult Qualifications
Adults can enter this area of work without formal qualifications, but some academic/vocational qualifications at any level may be an advantage. English and maths are useful subjects.

Work Experience
Work experience helps you find out what you enjoy and do not enjoy about a type of work. Paid or voluntary work that involves labouring or working outdoors is useful.

In some areas you can do a young apprenticeship (14-16) in engineering or construction. You do an extended work placement and a level 2 qualification whilst at school. For health and safety reasons there may be some jobs you cannot do until you are over 16.

Entry and Training
Unless you are in an apprenticeship you usually have to be 18 or over to go into this job. Employers look for people who are physically fit and used to outdoor work. You have to pass a medical that tests your fitness, eyesight and hearing. You are also tested for alcohol and drugs. While you are working you may be tested for these at any time.

Training is on the job with experienced track maintenance workers and through in-house or external courses. For Network Rail you have to take a two-day personal track safety (PTS) certificate course to prove that you know how to work safely in the track environment, and to renew your certificate every two years. You may work towards NVQs at levels 2-3 in railway engineering.

A rail transport engineering apprenticeship may be available in your area. Advanced apprenticeships with Network Rail take three years, training is a mix of learning on the job with experienced staff and going to college or a specialist residential training centre. You spend all of the first year at the training centre in Gosport, and then go back for courses during your second and third years. You work towards NVQ level 2 in rail track engineering maintenance, NVQ level 3 in railway engineering and a technical certificate such as a BTEC national award in engineering. Advanced apprenticeships with companies that do contract work for London Underground can lead to qualifications in engineering and civil engineering.

Some jobs require a full clean driving licence as they involve driving road vehicles to sites.

Employers look for evidence of relevant skills or experience of outdoor work in areas such as construction or civil engineering.

Opportunities and Pay
Network Rail is responsible for 22,000 miles of track in the UK and is the main employer in this area of work. Only Network Rail staff can work on national railway tracks. Long-term plans for track renewal work and more trains on the network has led to a demand for track workers. Companies that have track maintenance contracts with London Underground and other light rail operators also need track workers.

Network Rail track workers may progress to become leading track workers and help to run a track-work team. Others specialise in machine operation, welding or track inspections. You may go on to become a track chargeworker and run a small team of track workers. With further training, track workers may become technicians. Some may become trainers and run courses for track maintenance workers. It is even possible to become an engineer or manager.

Salaries for apprentices start at £8k-£13k a year, rising to £14k-£18k by the final year. Starting salaries for track workers are around £16k a year, whilst leading track workers earn around £20k. Supervisory roles earn up to £30k a year. Depending on the job, you may also get shift supplements, overtime, a geographical allowance and free or cheap rail travel.

Health
You need to be physically fit, have good hearing and eyesight and normal colour vision. You may be randomly tested for drugs and alcohol at any time.

Skills and Qualities
able to communicate effectively, able to cope under pressure, able to work both on your own and in a team, enjoy working outdoors, health & safety awareness, manual dexterity, practical skills, technical aptitude, willing to work shifts

Relevant Subjects
Construction and built environment, Design and technology, Engineering, Physics, Science

Further Information
AGCAS: Transport and Logistics (Job Sector Briefing) (AGCAS) - www.prospects.ac.uk

Apprenticeship Schemes (National Apprenticeship Service) - www.apprenticeships.org.uk

Association of Train Operating Companies (ATOC) - www.atoc.org

GoSkills - sector skills council for passenger transport - www.goskills.org

Network Rail Advanced Apprenticeship Scheme (Network Rail) http://careers.networkrail.co.uk/apprentices

Network Rail Careers (Network Rail) - www.networkrail.co.uk/aspx/1063.aspx

Railway People (Railstaff) - www.railwaypeople.com

▶Working outdoors (2010) (Babcock Lifeskills) - www.babcock-lifeskills.com/

Addresses
Transport for London
Palestra 4th Floor (Green Zone) 197 Blackfriars Road,
London SE1 8N
Phone: 0845 602 7000 (UK only)
Web: www.tfl.gov.uk/

Tubelines
15 Westferry Circus, Canary Wharf, London E14 4HD
Phone: +44 (0)845 660 5466
Web: www.tubelines.com

Similar Jobs
Construction Plant Operative, Fitter: Maintenance, Rail Transport Fitter/Electrician, Rail Transport Technician, Road Worker, Welder

Rail Transport Fitter/Electrician

CRCI:Engineering
CLCI:RAK — Job Band: 3

Job Description
Rail transport fitters look after and repair locomotives, carriages and goods wagons. They also keep other machinery used to work on trains in good repair. Some may work on building new locomotives and carriages.

Fitters use plans, manuals, hand and power tools to do routine servicing and repair faults. They clean and replace parts to keep engines, carriages and machinery running smoothly. Also put in and look after electrical wiring, checking and adjusting instruments to make sure they are giving the right readings. Fitters have to observe strict health and safety rules.

Work Details
Normally work shifts based on a 37 hr week. Shifts can be early, late or night work, including weekends and bank holidays. You may also be on call for emergencies. Usually work inside a heated depot

or workshop. Sometimes you have to work outside at the side of the railway track in poor weather or at night. Some fitters work at stations to do immediate repairs so trains and equipment can remain in service. You wear overalls, protective boots and other safety gear provided by the employer. It is often a dirty, oily and noisy job. The work usually involves bending, kneeling and lifting.

You work as part of a team and follow instructions from senior technicians and engineers. Usually work alongside craftspeople such as upholsterers, painters and metal workers.

Qualification

• England, Wales and Northern Ireland

Band 3: For entry to jobs, HNC or a relevant Diploma, usually at least 4 GCSEs (A*-C) including English, maths and science, or equivalent. Some employers may ask for grade B or above. Engineering and technology subjects are also useful.

• Scotland

Band 3: For entry to jobs, usually at least four S grades (1-3) including English, maths and science, or similar. Some employers may ask for grade 2 or above. Engineering and technology subjects are also useful.

Adult Qualifications

Adults can enter this area of work with qualifications and experience related to mechanical and electrical maintenance roles or similar craft trades.

Work Experience

Work experience gives you an insight into what you do and don't enjoy about a job or working environment, as well as the opportunity to acquire new skills. It also provides valuable information to add to your CV and improves any course application and/or your future employment prospects. Paid or voluntary work that uses engineering skills may be useful.

In some areas you can do a young apprenticeship (14-16) scheme in engineering. You do an extended work placement and a level 2 qualification whilst at school. For health and safety reasons there may be some jobs you cannot do until you are over 16.

Entry and Training

You can go into this area of work straight from school. You have to pass a medical that tests your fitness, eyesight and hearing and are also tested for alcohol and drugs. While you are working, you may also be tested for these at any time. You may have to do an aptitude test to see if you are suited to this type of work.

Training is a mix of learning on the job with experienced staff and going to college or a training centre. Some training courses may be residential. On apprenticeships you work towards NVQ level 2 in rail transport engineering. On advanced apprenticeships you work towards NVQ level 3 in railway engineering and a technical certificate such as BTEC national certificate or diploma. Depending on your employer, you may work towards other qualifications too.

You also have to do a two-day personal track safety certificate course to prove that you know how to work safely in a track environment. You cannot work on or around the track without a Network Rail Sentinel Track Safety card showing this. You have to renew your certificate every two years.

A Diploma/Welsh Baccalaureate may be available in your area in engineering. See the diplomas website for further information.

Employers look for people who have been fitters or electricians in other areas of work. Experience of maintaining machinery or doing electrical work in any craft job role is useful.

Government training opportunities, such as apprenticeships for adults, may be available in your area. You can also gain recognition of previous experience through Accreditation of Prior Learning or by working towards relevant S/NVQs. Contact your local careers office, Jobcentre Plus, Next Step service or Learning and Skills Council (LSC)/Local Enterprise Company (LEC) for details of training schemes.

Opportunities and Pay

Use of the rail network has increased over the last ten years. Keeping trains and rolling stock in service has never been more important. Railway fitters/electricians work for firms that build, maintain or lease trains used by operators. They may also work directly for passenger and goods train companies and underground, metro and light rail operators.

Apprentices earn around £13k-£15k a year. Pay for qualified staff varies depending on the employer, the nature of the work and shift patterns. Newly qualified staff may earn up to £18k, whilst those with more experience earn up to £25k a year. Some earn up to and over £30k a year. You may get other benefits such as free or reduced price rail travel.

Health

You need to have good stamina and be physically fit, have good hearing and eyesight and normal colour vision. You may be randomly tested for drugs and alcohol at any time.

Skills and Qualities

able to follow drawings and plans, able to work both on your own and in a team, attention to detail, literacy and numeracy skills, logical, manual dexterity, methodical, problem-solving skills, safety conscious, willing to work shifts

Relevant Subjects

Design and technology, Engineering, Mathematics, Physics, Science

Further Information

Apprenticeship Schemes (National Apprenticeship Service) - www.apprenticeships.org.uk

Diplomas (Foundation, Higher and Advanced) - http://yp.direct.gov.uk/diplomas

GoSkills - sector skills council for passenger transport - www.goskills.org

Personal Track Safety - http:www.ptscourse.co.uk

Railway People (Railstaff) - www.railwaypeople.com
Welsh Baccalaureate - www.wbq.org.uk

Addresses

Association of Train Operating Companies (ATOC)
Third Floor, 40 Bernard Street, London WC1N 1BY
Phone: +44 (0)20 7841 8000
Web: www.atoc-comms.org

Similar Jobs

Aircraft Engineering Technician, Electrical Engineering Technician, Fitter: Maintenance, Mechanic: Construction Plant, Rail Track Maintenance Worker, Rail Transport Technician, Vehicle Mechanic/Motor Vehicle Technician

Rail Transport Station Operative

also known as: Railway Station Assistant

CRCI:Transport and Logistics
CLCI:YAF Job Band: 1 to 2

Job Description

Station operatives assist rail passengers and undertake several platform duties, which may include selling tickets and railcards, meeting and greeting customers and generally providing a high level of customer service. Duties may include helping at the ticket barrier to validate tickets, answering passenger enquiries, using the public address and CCTV systems. Some station operatives load, unload and move luggage, goods and parcels, using small trucks and lifts. Can assist in the tanking and shunting of trains, and may also have some cleaning duties.

Work Details

Usually work a basic 37-40 hr week, which includes shifts, weekends and public holidays. The job requires you to meet the public, answer enquiries and deal with complaints from passengers. It is important to be both polite and helpful. You are always on your feet and there may be some heavy lifting involved. There is both indoor and outdoor work, and you have to be out in all weathers. A uniform is provided by your employer.

Qualification

• England, Wales and Northern Ireland

Band 1: No minimum qualifications are required, but you are expected to have a good level of general education. However, some formal/vocational qualifications at any level are useful and employers expect good basic numeracy and communication skills.

Band 2: Although academic qualifications are not specified for this job, it is an advantage to have some GCSEs (A*-C) in subjects that include English and maths, or equivalent.

• Scotland

Band 1: No minimum qualifications are required, but you are expected to have a good level of general education. However, some formal/vocational qualifications at any level are useful and employers expect good basic numeracy and communication skills.

Band 2: Although academic qualifications are not specified for this job, it is an advantage to have some S grades (1-3) in subjects that include English and maths, or similar.

Adult Qualifications

No pre-entry qualifications are usually required though some academic/vocational qualifications at any level may be an advantage. English and maths are useful subjects and you are expected to have good basic numeracy and communication skills.

Work Experience

Any work experience can equip you with skills that you can use in the future and add to your CV. Work experience can either be unpaid or voluntary or can be holiday or part-time work that you have organised yourself.

Entry and Training

You can apply to one of the 27 train operating companies (TOCs) in the UK or to Network Rail. You have to take an entrance test, pass a medical examination and must be at least 18. There may be short courses at your employer's training centre and you also train on the job with experienced workers and the station manager.

Employers may offer S/NVQs at level 2 in rail transport operations or levels 2-4 in customer service. Details are available from your local train operating company. Training programmes, including apprenticeship schemes such as the rail transport operations apprenticeship, may be available in your area. Advanced apprenticeships leading to qualification at level 3 can also be a route into higher education.

Mature applicants may find it useful to have some previous experience in working with people in a customer-focused role. Government training opportunities, such as apprenticeships, may be available in your area. You can also gain recognition of previous experience through Accreditation of Prior Learning or by working towards relevant S/NVQs. Contact your local careers office, Jobcentre Plus, Next Step service or Learning and Skills Council (LSC)/Local Enterprise Company (LEC) for details of training schemes.

Opportunities and Pay

There are over 2,500 rail stations in the UK and passenger journeys by train are increasing so many companies are actively recruiting. You work for a train operating company, Network Rail or one of the light rail companies or metro systems like London Underground. Jobs are usually in towns and cities and duties may vary depending on the employer. You can progress to become an assistant ticket inspector, ticket inspector or move into on-board services. There are also opportunities for promotion to supervisory and managerial posts for those who show aptitude. You may be recommended for driver training.

Income varies depending on location, train company and when you work but generally, salaries start at around £13k, rising to £14k-£18k a year. Those with supervisory responsibilities can earn £21k a year. Free or reduced price travel is sometimes offered as a benefit.

Health

You have to pass a medical test. You must have good hearing and eyesight and normal colour vision. It is important to speak clearly. Rail employees have to undergo random drug and alcohol testing throughout their working lives.

Skills and Qualities

able to get on with all kinds of people, customer service skills, good memory, good organisational skills, health & safety awareness, helpful, IT skills, polite, smart appearance

Further Information

AGCAS: Transport and Logistics (Job Sector Briefing) (AGCAS) - www.prospects.ac.uk

Apprenticeship Schemes (National Apprenticeship Service) - www.apprenticeships.org.uk

Association of Train Operating Companies (ATOC) - www.atoc.org

GoSkills - sector skills council for passenger transport - www.goskills.org

Light Rail Transit Association - www.lrta.org

Rail Technology Magazine (Cognitive Publishing Ltd) - www.railtechnologymagazine.com

Training Schemes - www.direct.gov.uk/en/educationandlearning

Transport for London http:/www.tfl.gov.uk

Addresses

Network Rail
Kings Place, 90 York Way, London N1 9AG
Phone: 08457 11 41 41 (UK only)
Web: www.networkrailcareers.co.uk

Similar Jobs

Airline Customer Service Agent, Customer Services Adviser, Port Operative, Rail Transport Train Driver

Rail Transport Technician

also known as: Engineering Maintenance Technician: Railways
CRCI:Transport and Logistics
CLCI:YAF Job Band: 3

Job Description

Transport technicians work with telecommunications equipment or with the signalling equipment to control the movement of trains. If working as signals specialists, they install and maintain the electronic, electrical and mechanical systems needed for signals, points machines and track circuits. If working in telecommunications, they install telephone/computer links and keep them operating efficiently. Also work with communication systems such as TV monitors, radio and information display systems.

Work Details

Usually work a basic 37-40 hr week, which includes shifts, weekends and public holidays. Travel is necessary to different sites and some technicians have to travel long distances. Signal technicians work mostly outdoors in all weathers and often work at heights. Telecommunications technicians can work outdoors, indoors or underground. Protective clothing may be needed.

Qualification

- **England, Wales and Northern Ireland**

Band 3: For entry to jobs, HNC or a relevant Diploma, usually at least 4 GCSEs (A*-C) including English and maths, or equivalent.

- **Scotland**

Band 3: For entry to jobs, usually at least four S grades (1-3) including English and maths, or similar.

Adult Qualifications

Mature entry is possible if applicants have suitable qualifications or experience in electrical work or electronics.

Work Experience

Employers or colleges may prefer candidates who have relevant work or voluntary experience. Some related areas are electronics, working with electrical and mechanical systems, telecommunications or general engineering.

Entry and Training

You must be at least 16 to enter a training apprenticeship with Network Rail, and pass an entrance test in English and numeracy. You train in one of four fields; track, signalling, electrification and plant or telecoms. Training usually lasts for three years and is a mixture of on-the-job training with experienced staff, and off-the-job training at a rail transport training centre, with day release or block release to a college. You must attend Personal Track Safety (PTS) training before you are awarded a safety card allowing you to work.

Courses lead to BTEC/SQA awards in telecommunications or electronic engineering and to relevant S/NVQs at level 2-3. It may also be possible to study for a foundation degree at the end of the course. Training programmes, including apprenticeship schemes such as the rail transport operations apprenticeship, may be available in your area. Advanced apprenticeships leading to qualification at level 3 can also be a route into higher education. A Diploma/Welsh Baccalaureate in engineering may also be available in your area.

Mature entry is common, particularly for those who are experienced and qualified in electrical work or electronics. Those who have previous experience of similar jobs, including the armed forces, may have an advantage. If unqualified, you may be able to enter this work through a government-funded training programme. Contact your local Connexions or careers office, Jobcentre Plus, Next Step service or Learning and Skills Council (LSC)/Local Enterprise Company (LEC) for details of all training opportunities and schemes, including apprenticeships.

Opportunities and Pay

Network Rail has introduced a new system which provides a single, national system of train driver to signaller communication. This is to be rolled out nationwide by 2013 and along with modernisation, sophisticated technical systems and safety improvement programmes will result in an increase in the number of technician jobs. 4-500 signal specialists alone are employed each year. Railway signal and telecommunications technicians can also be employed by contract companies working on behalf of Network Rail. With experience you can become a senior technician or move to a supervisory or management position.

Pay for a qualified technician working for Network Rail starts at around £17k, rising to around £28k a year with experience. Highly skilled and experienced workers, particularly in signalling can earn more than £30k a year. Overtime pay is common. Benefits for workers and their immediate family include free or subsidised rail travel.

Health

You have to pass a medical test, which includes tests for alcohol and drugs. You must have good eyesight, with glasses if necessary, good hearing and normal colour vision.

Skills and Qualities

able to work both on your own and in a team, able to work to deadlines, attention to detail, health & safety awareness, IT skills, technical aptitude

Relevant Subjects

Design and technology, Engineering, ICT/Computer studies, Mathematics, Physics, Science

Further Information

AGCAS: Transport and Logistics (Job Sector Briefing) (AGCAS) - www.prospects.ac.uk

Apprenticeship Schemes (National Apprenticeship Service) - www.apprenticeships.org.uk

Association of Train Operating Companies (ATOC) - www.atoc.org

Diplomas (Foundation, Higher and Advanced) - http://yp.direct.gov.uk/diplomas

GoSkills - sector skills council for passenger transport - www.goskills.org

Light Rail Transit Association - www.lrta.org

Rail Technology Magazine (Cognitive Publishing Ltd) - www.railtechnologymagazine.com

Training Schemes - www.direct.gov.uk/en/educationandlearning

Welsh Baccalaureate - www.wbq.org.uk

Working outdoors (2010) (Babcock Lifeskills) - www.babcock-lifeskills.com/

Addresses

Institution of Railway Signal Engineers (IRSE)
4th Floor, 1 Birdcage Walk, London SW1H 9JJ
Phone: +44 (0)20 7808 1180
Web: www.irse.org

Network Rail
Kings Place, 90 York Way, London N1 9AG
Phone: 08457 11 41 41 (UK only)
Web: www.networkrailcareers.co.uk

Similar Jobs

Engineer: Traction & Rolling Stock, Marine Engineering Technician, Merchant Navy Electro-technical Officer, Rail Track Maintenance Worker, Rail Transport Fitter/Electrician, Telecommunications Technician

Rail Transport Train Driver

CRCI:Transport and Logistics
CLCI:YAF Job Band: 1 to 2

Job Description

Train drivers drive diesel or electric trains, carrying passengers or goods. They have detailed knowledge of the route, track layout, speed limits and the timetable. Start the train using sophisticated high-tech controls, monitor the speed so that the journey is smooth and safe. Must strictly follow the rules of signalling and safety. Drivers carry out safety-related checks before every journey and write up a report at the end. They stop the train for passengers to get on and off and for goods to be loaded and unloaded. May also control the doors and make announcements as many trains now are driver only, especially on short routes.

Work Details

Usually work a 35 hr week, which includes weekends, evenings and public holidays on a shift basis. You spend long periods of time sitting in a small cab, which is noisy. Much of the time you are on your own. A uniform is provided.

Qualification

- **England, Wales and Northern Ireland**

Band 1: No minimum qualifications are required, but you are expected to have a good level of general education. However, some formal/vocational qualifications at any level are useful.

Band 2: Although academic qualifications are not specified for this job, it is an advantage to have some GCSEs (A*-C) in subjects that include English and maths, or equivalent.

- **Scotland**

Band 1: No minimum qualifications are required, but you are expected to have a good level of general education. However, some formal/vocational qualifications at any level are useful.

Band 2: Although academic qualifications are not specified for this job, it is an advantage to have some S grades (1-3) in subjects that include English and maths, or similar.

Adult Qualifications

No pre-entry qualifications are usually required though some academic/vocational qualifications at any level may be an advantage. English and maths are useful subjects.

Work Experience

Employers may prefer candidates who have relevant work or voluntary experience. Some train operating companies provide work experience placements, but if you cannot gain railway work experience, then any work that develops your mechanical knowledge is useful.

Entry and Training

Mechanical knowledge or experience of mechanical work is an advantage. Applicants go through a selection process at a train crew assessment centre. You must be aged at least 21 when you start driver training. Between 16 and 18, you work in the railway yards and depots, from 18 you may work on a train.

Training takes 9-18 months, with classroom sessions and practice with an instructor. If you apply to drive high-speed trains you have more training courses, aptitude tests and assessments. You must also complete a personal track safety (PTS) certificate. Eurostar drivers must have at least five years' experience of driving high-speed mainline trains, and then take a further one-year classroom course, together with high level French and train simulator experience. You can transfer to driving if you train first as a conductor or guard. Training programmes, including apprenticeship schemes such as the rail transport operations apprenticeship, may be available in your area. You may be able to work towards S/NVQ level 2 in rail transport operations (driving).

Mature applicants are welcomed and particularly those with related experience. Companies currently set training upper age limits of 45-50. Eurostar applicants must have at least five years' experience of driving high-speed mainline trains, and an aptitude for learning French. French speakers have an advantage.

Opportunities and Pay

Rail passenger services are run by Train Operating Companies (TOCs) covering different parts of the country, together with freight companies, underground and light rail companies, Eurostar and Eurotunnel. You can apply to drive high-speed trains or move into supervisory and management jobs, after you have built up some experience. An increase in passenger and freight transport by train has created a demand for train drivers, particularly in London and the south-east of England.

The pay depends on your employer, with larger firms generally paying more. A trainee driver earns around £18.5k-£24k a year, rising to between £26k-£40k on completion of training. Overtime pay is common. Eurostar drivers can earn from £38k-£44k a year. Benefits for workers and their immediate family include free or subsidised rail travel. You may be paid extra for overtime and unsociable hours.

Health

You have to pass a medical test, including tests for alcohol and drugs, and must have normal colour vision, good eyesight and good hearing. There will be random drug and alcohol testing throughout your working life.

Skills and Qualities

able to work well on your own, good concentration level, good memory, observant, quick reactions, responsible attitude, safety conscious, sound judgement, technical aptitude

Further Information

AGCAS: Transport and Logistics (Job Sector Briefing) (AGCAS) - www.prospects.ac.uk

Apprenticeship Schemes (National Apprenticeship Service) - www.apprenticeships.org.uk

GoSkills - sector skills council for passenger transport - www.goskills.org

Light Rail Transit Association - www.lrta.org

Rail Technology Magazine (Cognitive Publishing Ltd) - www.railtechnologymagazine.com

Addresses

Association of Train Operating Companies (ATOC)
Third Floor, 40 Bernard Street, London WC1N 1BY
Phone: +44 (0)20 7841 8000
Web: www.atoc-comms.org

Similar Jobs

Driver: Lorry, Driver: Tram, Rail Transport Station Operative, Rail Transport Train Guard

Rail Transport Train Guard

also known as: Train Conductor

CRCI:Transport and Logistics
CLCI:YAF Job Band: 1 to 2

Job Description

Train guards are responsible for safety checks on trains and signal to the driver to start the train at the right time. On passenger trains, they check and sell tickets on board, make announcements, answer passengers' questions, and on some trains, may control the opening and closing of the doors. Check heating, lighting, toilets and other equipment and report any faults. On freight trains guards they make sure that wagons are properly and safely loaded and couplings are secure.

Work Details

You can work on local or longer distance services, or with Eurostar/ Eurotunnel, on a rota of shifts, including weekends, evenings, nights and public holidays. On passenger trains you meet many people including those who may be impatient, awkward or aggressive. The safety of all passengers is a main responsibility. You are on your feet a lot of the time, walking up and down the train and there can be some lifting involved. A uniform and protective clothing is provided by the company.

Qualification

Many employers look for personal qualities and a good general education together with a reasonable standard of spoken English and basic arithmetic skills, rather than formal qualifications.

- **England, Wales and Northern Ireland**

Band 1: For entry to jobs, no minimum qualifications are needed, but you are expected to have a good level of general education and relevant experience. Some formal/vocational qualifications at any level are useful.

Band 2: Although academic qualifications are not specified for this job, it is an advantage to have some GCSEs (A*-C) in subjects that include English and maths, or equivalent. A knowledge of French is required for Channel Tunnel services.

- **Scotland**

Band 1: For entry to jobs, no minimum qualifications are needed, but you are expected to have a good level of general education and relevant experience. Some formal/vocational qualifications at any level are useful.

Band 2: A few S grades including maths and English or similar may be useful. A knowledge of French is required for Channel Tunnel services.

Adult Qualifications

Train operating companies (TOCs) look for the ability to write and speak clearly in English and to work with numbers. A knowledge of French is required for Channel Tunnel services.

Work Experience

Any work experience can equip you with skills that you can use in the future and add to your CV. This can either be paid or voluntary or holiday/part-time work that you have organised yourself.

Entry and Training

You have to take an entrance test and a medical, and be aged at least 18 to start training as a rail guard. Mechanical aptitude or experience is useful. Train operating companies (TOCs) usually provide in-house training programmes that include on the job training with an experienced guard. With experience you can train to become a train driver. S/NVQs at level 2 in rail transport operations (passenger services) or at levels 2-3 in customer service are available. Training programmes, including apprenticeship schemes such as the one in rail transport operations, may be available in your area. Advanced apprenticeships leading to qualification at level 3 can also be a route into higher education.

Adults with previous experience of working with the public, especially in customer services or handling cash, have an advantage. Training programmes, including apprenticeship schemes such as the one in rail transport operations, may be available in your area.

Opportunities and Pay

Many trains are now driver only so there are fewer jobs for guards, particularly on shorter routes. Rail guards are employed by UK TOCs. Eurostar/Eurotunnel operate a service through the Channel Tunnel and their applicants are required to have a knowledge of French. There are opportunities for promotion to supervisory and managerial posts or, for those who show aptitude, to be recommended for driver training.

Income varies depending on location, train company and when you work. Salaries start at around £13k, rising to around £25k a year. With overtime, you may earn more. You may also be paid extra for unsociable hours. Benefits for workers and their immediate family include free or subsidised rail travel.

Health

You have to pass a medical test, which includes testing for alcohol and drugs. You must be generally fit and healthy and have normal colour vision, good hearing and good eyesight, and be able to speak clearly. You have to undergo random drug and alcohol testing throughout your working life.

Skills and Qualities

able to cope with emergencies, able to get on with all kinds of people, able to work well on your own, cash handling skills, even tempered, good communication skills, honest, observant, responsible attitude, safety conscious

Further Information

AGCAS: Transport and Logistics (Job Sector Briefing) (AGCAS) - www.prospects.ac.uk

Apprenticeship Schemes (National Apprenticeship Service) - www.apprenticeships.org.uk

Association of Train Operating Companies (ATOC) - www.atoc.org

GoSkills - sector skills council for passenger transport - www.goskills.org

Light Rail Transit Association - www.lrta.org

Northern Ireland Railways - www.translink.co.uk/nir.asp

Rail Technology Magazine (Cognitive Publishing Ltd) - www.railtechnologymagazine.com

Addresses

Network Rail
Kings Place, 90 York Way, London N1 9AG
Phone: 08457 11 41 41 (UK only)
Web: www.networkrailcareers.co.uk

Similar Jobs

Rail Transport Station Operative, Rail Transport Technician, Rail Transport Train Driver

Receptionist

CRCI:Administration, Business and Office Work
CLCI:CAT Job Band: 2 to 3

Job Description

Receptionists welcome and help guests, customers, clients, patients or visitors when they arrive. They usually sit at a desk or workstation in a public area and answer any questions, provide information and direct people to the correct place. Also take messages and give out information in person and by phone. May work on a telephone switchboard and do clerical work as well, mostly on a computer. May make up bills and deal with cash, credit cards and cheques. They keep the reception area tidy and well organised and may provide refreshments and printed information. The receptionist is also responsible for seeing that a 'visitors' book is kept. They request information such as the name of visitor, who they are meeting, time of arrival/departure and car registration and details.

At a hotel reception desk, the receptionist registers the guests and gives them the keys or swipe cards to their room. Medical and dental receptionists make a note of a patient's name as they arrive and informs staff of their arrival. Then they call out the patient's name when it is their turn to see the doctor/dentist. Also book future appointments if required.

Work Details

Usually work 39 hrs a week, Monday to Friday. In places such as hotels and hairdressing salons works in the evenings, at night and at weekends. This may be on a rota or shift basis. Full and part-time work and job-sharing are also possible. Your role is to make a good first impression on visitors. You are under pressure sometimes, dealing with several visitors and phone calls at once. Some of the people you meet are friendly and pleasant. Some can be rude, impatient or angry and you need to deal with them calmly and politely.

Qualification

- **England, Wales and Northern Ireland**

Band 2: There are no minimum qualifications. However, for some courses you may need some GCSEs (A*-C) including English language, or equivalent qualifications such as in business administration or hospitality.

- **Scotland**

Band 2: There are no minimum qualifications. However, for some courses you may need some S grades (1-3) including English language, or similar qualifications such as in business administration or hospitality.

Adult Qualifications
Colleges often accept mature applicants without qualifications, especially if they have relevant experience.

Work Experience
Relevant work or voluntary experience is always useful and can equip you with skills that you can use in the future and that you can add to your CV. Temporary holiday work in offices via employment agencies is useful, particularly if you can develop good keyboard skills and a knowledge of using a switchboard. In some areas there is a young apprenticeship (14-16) scheme in business administration that provides an extended work placement and eventual achievement of a level 2 qualification whilst at school.

Entry and Training
Experience of office practice, typing/keyboard skills, use of fax/ copier machines or dealing with the public, is an advantage. An ability in a foreign language is useful for some jobs such as hotel reception work. There are many courses that you can take before going into a job, including secretarial and office-practice courses, as well as specialist courses, for example in hotel or medical reception (hospital or general practice). Once employed you have on-the-job training with an experienced person. Employment-based training can lead to relevant certificates and diplomas, eg the level 2 certificate for veterinary practice receptionists.

S/NVQs are available in reception at levels 1-2, administration at 1-4 and customer service at 1-4. For example, the NVQ Level 2 in Front Office offers training in how to deal with customers, payments and bookings and diverse areas such as maintaining hygiene standards in the environment, providing foreign exchange facilities and tourist information. Training programmes, including apprenticeship schemes, may be available in your area. Advanced apprenticeships leading to qualification at level 3 can also be a route into higher education.

From September 2009 it is possible to study for a diploma in hospitality. On successful completion of the foundation level, you can move on to the higher and then advanced levels, equivalent to 3.5 A levels. Check the website for details.

Mature applicants with relevant experience may be preferred by some employers. Adults may be able to enter this work through a government-funded training programme. Contact your local Connexions or careers office, Jobcentre Plus, Next Step service or Learning and Skills Council (LSC)/Local Enterprise Company (LEC) for details of all training opportunities and schemes, including apprenticeships.

Opportunities and Pay
Many companies have receptionists. For example, hairdressing and beauty salons, hotels, garages, and the surgeries of doctors, dentists and vets. You can also work in banking, insurance, or for schools, colleges, local councils and so on. Promotion prospects depend on the company you work for. You can apply for jobs in larger companies to gain more experience. Such jobs are often better paid.

Pay varies depending on location and employer. Most earn around £11k-£17k a year. A senior receptionist can earn around £18k-£22k a year. Higher paid receptionists can earn around £22k-£25k a year.

Health
You need good hearing and clear speech in this job.

Skills and Qualities
calm, confident, efficient, firm manner, friendly, good communication skills, good interpersonal skills, good memory, good telephone manner, IT skills, responsible attitude

Relevant Subjects
English, Hospitality and catering, ICT/Computer studies

Further Information
Apprenticeship Schemes (National Apprenticeship Service) - www.apprenticeships.org.uk

Apprenticeships in Scotland (Careers Info Scotland) - www.apprenticeshipsinscotland.com/about/

Break into Biz. (CfA) (Council for Administration) - www.breakinto.biz

Diplomas (Foundation, Higher and Advanced) - http://yp.direct.gov.uk/diplomas

Institute of Professional Administrators (Institute of Professional Administrators) - www.inprad.org

People 1st - sector skills council for hospitality, leisure, travel and tourism - www.people1st.co.uk

Training Schemes - www.direct.gov.uk/en/educationandlearning

▶Working in retail & customer services (2008) (Babcock Lifeskills) - www.babcock-lifeskills.com/

Addresses
Association of Medical Secretaries, Practice Managers, Administrators and Receptionists (AMSPAR)
Tavistock House North, Tavistock Square, London WC1H 9LN
Phone: +44 (0)20 7387 6005
Web: www.amspar.com

Institute of Customer Service (ICS)
2 Castle Court, St Peter's Street, Colchester, Essex CO1 1EW
Phone: +44 (0)1206 571716
Web: www.instituteofcustomerservice.com

Similar Jobs
Health Records Clerk, Hotel Receptionist, Local Government Administrative Assistant, Police Front Office Staff, Secretary, Switchboard Operator, Travel Consultant

Recruitment Consultant
also known as: Employment Agency Consultant, Job Agency Consultant

CRCI:Administration, Business and Office Work
CLCI:KED Job Band: 2 to 5

Job Description
Recruitment consultants provide a link between employers and people looking for jobs, by matching vacancies to job seekers. They contact employers to obtain details of available jobs, follow up interviews for feedback, keep records on employers, candidates and job details. Screening the job-seeker's qualifications, skills, experience, and general suitability for the job is an important part of this role. They also give advice, including any recommendations for further training, and arrange suitable job interviews. Some recruitment consultants negotiate salary or terms and conditions. They attract new business by phone or through advertisements in newspapers and magazines.

Work Details
Usually work normal office hours, Monday to Friday, but there is occasional evening or Saturday morning work. Some specialist agencies have variable opening hours. For most of the time you work in an office, interviewing and advising people. You come into contact with a wide variety of people including employers and probably have to spend a lot of time on the phone, including 'cold calling'. You may travel to meet clients and conduct interviews. Some jobs are with international agencies and require you to travel overseas.

Qualification

- **England, Wales and Northern Ireland**

Band 3: For entry to jobs, HNC or a relevant Diploma, usually at least 4 GCSEs (A*-C) including English and maths, or equivalent.

Band 4: For HND, Diploma of Higher Education or foundation degree: 1-2 A levels and some GCSEs (A*-C) usually including English and maths, or equivalent.

Band 5: For degree courses: usually 2-3 A levels and some GCSEs (A*-C), including English and maths, or equivalent. Exact requirements depend on the degree you take.

- **Scotland**

Band 3: For entry to jobs, usually at least four S grades (1-3) including English and maths, or similar.

Band 4: No specific entry requirement, but entrants usually have 2-3 H grades and some S grades (1-3), often including English and maths, or similar qualifications.

Band 5: For degree courses: usually 3-5 H grades and some S grades (1-3), including English and maths, or similar qualifications. Exact requirements depend on the degree you take.

Degree Information

There is a degree in recruitment practice though any subject is acceptable. Those who have gained the Recruitment and Employment Confederation's diploma in recruitment practice can enter the degree in recruitment practice in year two.

Adult Qualifications

Entry requirements may be relaxed for adults applying for higher education courses. Access or foundation courses give adults without qualifications a route on to degree courses.

Work Experience

Relevant work or voluntary experience is always useful and can improve your chances in application for entry to this job. Consider working with the public or in a communication or customer service environment. Employment agencies say that 'they look for people who have a strong sales and/or marketing background'. Work experience in these areas is therefore extremely useful.

Entry and Training

Those entering this job are usually aged 21-25, although there are no fixed age limits. Larger agencies run induction training programmes, which include on-the-job training. The Recruitment and Employment Confederation (REC) is the trade association for the industry and offers a certificate in recruitment practice (CertRP). This is aimed at those who wish to join the industry or who are in their first two years of working in the job. The certificate is relevant for those wishing to set up their own employment agency. After experience on the job or in a related field, the REC offers the diploma in recruitment practice (DipRP), which provides access to a degree in recruitment practice in year two, currently validated by Middlesex University Business School. The diploma can also be taken by those with less experience but with A levels/H grades, a degree or equivalent qualifications.

The certificate/diploma is available through a distance-learning programme, combined with workshops throughout the duration of each course. There is also a foundation (FdA)/BA (Hons) degree in recruitment practice at Middlesex University Business School. Other relevant professional qualifications include the certificate in recruitment and selection offered by the Chartered Institute of Personnel and Development (CIPD). The REC and CIPD also offer a range of short courses to help with continuing professional development (CPD).

A Diploma/Welsh Baccalaureate may be available in business, administration and finance in your area. Check the websites for details.

Mature applicants do not always require formal qualifications as relevant experience in customer services, sales or marketing, and personality are highly valued by employers. However, the average age for the industry tends to be between 22 and 35.

Government training opportunities, such as apprenticeships, may be available in your area. You can also gain recognition of previous experience through Accreditation of Prior Learning or by working towards relevant S/NVQs. Contact your local careers office, Jobcentre Plus, Next Step service or Learning and Skills Council (LSC)/Local Enterprise Company (LEC) for details of training schemes.

Opportunities and Pay

Around 100,000 people work in the recruitment industry and the sector is growing. Over 6,000 agencies are members of the Recruitment and Employment Federation. It is possible to start work in a secretarial or clerical job and be promoted to the position of consultant. You can work anywhere in the UK but jobs are available mainly in towns and cities and tend to be concentrated in London and south-east England. Promotion to more senior posts is possible after gaining experience, and opportunities are generally better in larger organisations. Agencies are usually general, but some specialise in specific sectors such as computing, finance, healthcare, or teaching. Many experienced consultants are self-employed and run their own agency. It is possible to work part time, or to work abroad.

The Association of Graduate Recruiters supports employers in all aspects of recruitment. Its website has useful labour market information and publications.

Pay is usually a basic salary plus commission and benefits and can vary considerably depending on the sector of recruitment. Salaries start at around £15k-£20k a year, rising to around £24k. Higher earners in managerial positions or in international executive recruitment can make around £30k-£50k or more a year and senior consultants dealing with executive search and selection can earn in excess of £100k.

Skills and Qualities

able to cope under pressure, able to put people at ease, customer service skills, good communication skills, good interpersonal skills, good telephone manner, initiative, IT skills, negotiating skills, networking skills

Relevant Subjects

Business and accounting, English, Psychology

Further Information

Agency Central Recruit2Recruit Jobs resources - www.agencycentral.co.uk/jobsites/recruitment.htm

Diplomas (Foundation, Higher and Advanced) - http://yp.direct.gov.uk/diplomas

Inside Careers Guide: Human Resources - www.insidecareers.co.uk

Middlesex University Business School - www.mdx.ac.uk/bs/

People Focus Magazine (CIPD Ireland) - www.cipd.co.uk/branch/Ireland/resources

People Management Magazine (CIPD) - www.peoplemanagement.co.uk/pm

Recruiter - www.recruitermagazine.co.uk

Training Schemes - www.direct.gov.uk/en/educationandlearning

Welsh Baccalaureate - www.wbq.org.uk

▶ Working in business, administration & finance (2010) (Babcock Lifeskills) - www.babcock-lifeskills.com/

Addresses

Association of Graduate Recruiters (AGR)
Innovation Centre, Warwick Technology Park,
Gallows Hill CV34 6UW
Phone: +44 (0)1926 623236
Web: www.agr.org.uk

Chartered Institute of Personnel and Development (CIPD)
151 The Broadway, London SW19 1JQ
Phone: +44 (0)20 8612 6200
Web: www.cipd.co.uk

Recruitment and Employment Confederation (REC)
15 Welbeck Street, London W1G 9XT
Phone: +44 (0)20 7009 2100
Web: www.rec.uk.com

Similar Jobs

Adult Guidance Worker, Advice Worker, Human Resources Officer/Manager, Sales Executive, Training & Development Officer/Manager

Recycling Officer

also known as: Environmental Officer, Waste Management Officer

CRCI:Personal and Other Services
CLCI:IJ Job Band: 4 to 5

Job Description

Recycling officers are responsible for a local authority's environmental policy on reducing waste and planning the re-use and recovery of a wide range of waste materials, such as glass, paper and cans. They work to improve established recycling strategies and develop new systems to collect and recycle waste to meet national targets. May be responsible for negotiating outside contracts for the safe disposal of waste or recycling schemes. Also give advice on waste management such as advising local businesses on their waste disposal methods.

Often help to promote recycling by giving presentations and writing articles. May give talks to children in local schools and other groups, including members of community organisations. Also publicise the council's recycling initiatives by talking to local newspapers, writing press releases, and being interviewed on local radio. May be involved in the production of posters, leaflets and recycling guides, and for providing information for a council's website.

Recycling officers answer queries from members of the public and deal with any complaints, for example, if a recycling site is overflowing or has a problem with vermin, such as rats. They oversee the local area distribution of bags, and recycling boxes or bins. Must keep up to date on European policy and legislation, attend conferences and meetings, and undertake research. Also draft reports, compile statistics, prepare budgets, deal with contracts and supervise staff.

Work Details

Mostly work 35-37 hrs a week, Monday to Friday, though some evening and weekend duties may be required. Work is partly office based, but also involves some outdoor work, travelling around an area to check on existing recycling facilities, visiting companies, as well as looking for new sites. A driving licence is useful. The work involves dealing with the public and the local media, and can be pressurised at times.

Qualification

• England, Wales and Northern Ireland

Band 4: For relevant courses: usually 1-2 A levels and some GCSEs (A*-C), including English, maths and science, or equivalent qualifications. Exact subjects required depend on the course you take.

Band 5: For relevant degree: usually 2-3 A levels and some GCSEs (A*-C), including English, maths and science, or equivalent qualifications. Exact subjects depend on the degree you take.

• Scotland

Band 4: For relevant courses: usually three H grades and some S grades (1-3), including English, maths and science, or similar qualifications. Exact subjects depend on the degree you take.

Band 5: For relevant degree: usually 3-5 H grades and some S grades (1-3), including English, maths and science, or equivalent qualifications. Exact subjects depend on the degree you take.

Degree Information

A wide range of degree subjects are acceptable, but degrees in environmental science, environmental management, earth sciences, materials science/technology, wastes management, biology, chemistry, surveying, geology and civil or structural engineering degrees are particularly relevant. There are also relevant postgraduate qualifications. A list of appropriate postgraduate courses are available from the Chartered Institution of Wastes Management.

Adult Qualifications

Course requirements may be relaxed for mature applicants provided they submit evidence of previous serious study, such as a relevant foundation or Access course. Check with universities or colleges for information. Credit is given for relevant experience.

Work Experience

Entry to this job can be competitive and it is important that you try to do some relevant work or voluntary experience before applying to study for a degree or for a job. The most relevant experience is within a council's waste management department or with a contract company used by a council. However, any voluntary experience in environmentally-related issues is also relevant, including work for a community recycling organisation.

Entry and Training

Although there are no formal minimum entry requirements for this work, almost all entrants are graduates or those who have considerable relevant work experience. However, it is sometimes possible to start in a technical support role and then move into waste management/recycling. The Wastes & Resources Action Programme runs three day recycling managers training courses, specifically for local authority recycling/waste management officers with three years' experience.

Training is mainly on the job, combined with courses available through the Chartered Institution of Wastes Management (CIWM) or Waste Management Industry Training and Advisory Board. A basic introduction course in the management of waste is available from the CIWM, as well as a wide range of specialist short courses. Relevant S/NVQs are available at levels 3-4 in management of recycling operations. VRQs (vocationally related qualifications) are available at level 3, such as the principles and practices of sustainable waste management, and at level 4 in waste treatment technologies. A foundation degree in waste management is available.

Members of the CIWM can gain recognition as chartered environmentalists (CEnv). Contact the Society for the Environment or the CIWM for further information. Membership of the CIWM requires you to take part in a continuing professional development (CPD) scheme throughout your career.

Mature applicants with relevant skills and experience with a local authority or private waste disposal contractors may have an advantage. It is useful to be able to demonstrate knowledge of current environmental issues, European and worldwide. The Wastes & Resources Action Programme runs three day recycling managers training courses, specifically for local authority recycling/waste management officers with three years' experience.

Opportunities and Pay

Opportunities are rapidly increasing, in both the public and private sector, but competition for jobs is keen. Employment can be with local authorities, central government agencies or private sector companies. Promotion may be possible to more senior positions with a greater policy-making role. It is sometimes possible to move into consultancy work. You may specialise in one aspect of the work. There are also opportunities to work for a regulatory body such as the Environment Agency.

Pay varies depending on location and employer. Starting salaries in councils are around £16k-£20k a year, rising to around £25k-£40k a year, after considerable experience. Pay may be higher in private sector jobs.

Health

This job requires good general fitness. You may find this job difficult if you suffer from hay fever.

Skills and Qualities

able to report accurately, able to work both on your own and in a team, aptitude for fieldwork, good communication skills, good interpersonal skills, good organisational skills, IT skills, problem solving skills, resourceful, scientific approach

Relevant Subjects

Biology, Chemistry, Engineering, Geography, Land and Environment, Mathematics, Physics, Science

Further Information

AGCAS: Environment & Agriculture (Job Sector Briefing) (AGCAS) - www.prospects.ac.uk

Community Recycling Network - www.crn.org.uk

Energy & Utility Skills - sector skills council for gas, power, waste management & water industries - www.euskills.co.uk

Local Government Careers (Improvement and Development Agency) - www.lgcareers.com/publications/

Materials Recycling Week (EMAP Construct) - www.mrw.co.uk

The Journal for Waste & Resource Management Professionals (Chartered Institution of Wastes Management (CIWM)) - www.ciwm.co.uk/pm/33

▶Working outdoors (2010) (Babcock Lifeskills) - www.babcock-lifeskills.com/

Addresses

Chartered Institution of Wastes Management (CIWM)
9 Saxon Court, St Peter's Gardens, Marefair,
Northampton NN1 1SX
Phone: +44 (0)1604 620 426
Web: www.ciwm.co.uk

Environment Agency
National Customer Contact Centre, PO Box 544, Almondsbury, Rotherham S60 1BY
Phone: 08708 506 506 (UK only)
Web: www.environment-agency.gov.uk

Society for the Environment (SocEnv)
The Old School House, 212 Long Street, Atherstone,
Warwickshire CV9 1AH
Phone: +44 (0)845 337 2951
Web: www.socenv.org.uk

Waste Management Industry Training and Advisory Board (WAMITAB)
Peterbridge House, 3 The Lakes, Northampton NN4 7HE
Phone: +44 (0)1604 231 950
Web: www.wamitab.org.uk

Wastes & Resources Action Programme (WRAP)
The Old Academy 21 Horse Fair, Banbury, Oxfordshire OX16 0AH
Phone: 0808 100 2040 (UK only)
Web: www.wrap.org.uk

Similar Jobs

Countryside/Conservation Officer/Manager, Ecologist, Engineer: Civil/Structural, Environmental Health Practitioner, Environmental Scientist, Town Planner

Reflexologist

CRCI:Healthcare
CLCI:JOD
Job Band: 2

Job Description

Reflexologists treat health problems by using manually controlled pressure on particular points of the feet and hands. They help to release tensions in the body by stimulating the reflexes to release blockages in the body's energy pathways. This improves circulation and restores energy flow to restore the body to good health. Reflexologists treat many problems, including backache, migraine, sinus problems and other breathing difficulties, hormonal imbalance and stress-related disorders, and digestive problems.

Reflexology does not claim to cure, but to help the body's own healing processes, and to produce a relaxing effect. Reflexologists talk to the client about their problem or illness, including the things that can affect lifestyle, such as diet, exercise and working practices.

Work Details

Many reflexologists are self-employed and choose to work hours that suit themselves and their clients. You may have to work flexible hours and be available at weekends and some evenings. You may use a room in your own home or rent a room, sometimes at a natural health clinic. Newly qualified reflexologists often work very flexible hours to build up their clientele. If you work in a clinic, health centre, hospice, hospital or care homes you have more regular hours, usually Monday to Friday, though there may be some evening clinics. Reflexologists usually sit to give treatment which generally lasts around an hour. You may be required to wear a white coat or uniform.

Qualification

• England, Wales and Northern Ireland

Band 2: For entry to jobs, no minimum qualifications are needed, but it is an advantage to have some GCSEs (A*-C) or equivalent in subjects that include English, maths and biology, or equivalent.

• Scotland

Band 2: Although academic qualifications are not specified for this job, it is an advantage to have some S grades (1-3) in subjects that include English, maths and biology, or similar.

Adult Qualifications

Formal qualifications are not specified, however, a good standard of education, together with some formal qualifications in subjects such as English, maths and a science, or equivalent, are useful. An interest in holistic health is beneficial.

Work Experience

Relevant work or voluntary experience can equip you with skills that you can use in the future and that you can add to your CV. There are often opportunities available for voluntary work which give you experience of working with people.

Entry and Training

There is no single nationally recognised qualification in reflexology. However, the Association of Reflexologists (AoR) has a register of training schools and offers membership to those who have either trained on an accredited course, or undertaken additional training to reach accredited standards. Full membership of the AoR can be achieved after a year in professional practice following successful completion of a course. Members can then use the letters MAR (Member of the Association of Reflexologists). Other schools and colleges offering reflexology training issue their own certificates or diplomas. Distance-learning courses include those offered by the International Institute of Reflexology (IIR). The AoR and the Scottish Institute of Reflexology also support continuing professional development through a wide range of courses and seminars.

The British Register of Complementary Practitioners (Reflexology Division) is maintained by the Institute for Complementary Medicine and accepts those who have completed courses which meet similar requirements to the AoR, along with one year of supervised practice. Courses are part time and last at least nine months of an academic year. Most courses are held at weekends or evenings and include home study and practice.

There are full or part-time foundation degrees in complementary approaches to health-aromatherapy and reflexology, and a number of vocationally related diplomas and qualifications in reflexology available. Degree courses in reflexology are currently offered by Napier University in Edinburgh, but these courses require higher education qualifications. Contact the universities for individual admission details. Foundation degrees in complementary health are also available.

Mature applicants are welcomed by training establishments. Previous experience is not necessary for most courses although a medically-related background or experience in counselling or beauty therapy is useful. Accredited courses are usually offered through part-time study, evenings and weekends, as well as through distance-learning courses. This is often a second career and there are sources of funding, including loans and bursaries, which may be available from the professional bodies.

Opportunities and Pay

The Association of Reflexologists estimates that there are around 32,000 reflexologists in the UK. Interest in complementary therapy is continuing to grow so this is an expanding profession and there is a demand for reflexology. Reflexologists work all over the country and once trained, you may be able to join an existing practice to gain experience with established practitioners. Many reflexologists set up their own practice, usually hiring a room in a complementary therapy centre, or working from home.

Most reflexologists are self-employed, but you can also work for the NHS, large companies, hospices and care homes, private clinics or sports and leisure centres. NHS Nurses and healthcare workers are also adding reflexology to their skills. There may be opportunities to study other areas of complementary medicine, or to teach reflexology.

Salaries depend on how much you work and whether you are employed or work for yourself. Most reflexologists charge £25-£35 a session, but this can be £30-£60 in London. Income therefore depends on where you work and your experience. Salaried reflexologists earn around £20k-£40k a year, though some may earn more.

Health

This job requires good general fitness and your hands need to be strong and flexible.

Skills and Qualities

able to put people at ease, business awareness, caring, friendly, good communication skills, good listening skills, good sense of touch, strong hands, supportive, tactful

Relevant Subjects

Biology, Health and social care, Science

Further Information

Careers in Reflexology (AoR) (AoR) - www.aor.org.uk/careers
Skills for Health - sector skills council - www.skillsforhealth.org.uk

Addresses

Association of Reflexologists (AoR)
5 Fore Street, Taunton, Somerset TA1 1HX
Phone: 01823 351010
Web: www.aor.org.uk

British Reflexology Association
Monks Orchard, Whitbourne, Worcester WR6 5RB
Phone: +44 (0)1886 821207
Web: www.britreflex.co.uk

Institute for Complementary Medicine (ICM)
Can-Mezzanine, 32-36 Loman Street, London SE1 0EH
Phone: +44 (0)207 922 7980
Web: www.i-c-m.org.uk

International Institute of Reflexology (IIR)
146 Upperthorpe, Walkley, Sheffield S6 3NF
Phone: +44 (0)1142 812 100
Web: www.reflexology-uk.co.uk

Reflexology Forum
Dalton House, 60 Windsor Avenue, London SW19 2RR
Phone: 0800 037 0130 (UK only)
Web: www.reflexologyforum.org

Similar Jobs

Aromatherapist, Massage Therapist, Medical Herbalist, Naturopath, Podiatrist/Chiropodist, Spa Therapist

Refrigeration/Air Conditioning Technician

also known as: Building Services Technician

CRCI:Building and Construction
CLCI:UJ Job Band: 3

Job Description

Refrigeration/air conditioning technicians are responsible for producing the design (technical specification and drawings) and installing the units that control air quality, humidity and temperature, in retail, domestic and industrial/office environments. They often use computer-aided design (CAD) software. Projects may include systems for hospitals, office blocks, power stations, and manufacturing sectors, such as food production, storage and distribution, or road/rail and sea transportation, storage and distribution systems. Some jobs are office based and more involved with estimating, preparing work schedules, drawing plans and designing layout. Others are on site, supervising the installation, testing and operation of systems.

On large projects, technicians work as part of a team under the direction of a qualified engineer. On smaller projects, they supervise the work through to completion, organising the workforce, planning work schedules, and overseeing the delivery and storage of materials. Some technicians work in sales and surveying. All technicians need to keep up to date with national/European law surrounding refrigerants.

Work Details

Refrigeration/air conditioning technicians usually work a 37-39 hr week, though may be required to work additional hours in order to meet deadlines. The work can be in an office or on site and you may need to travel between sites. You are in contact with architects, surveyors, builders and fitters, estimators and suppliers. You carry out tests using instruments and measuring equipment. Sometimes you have to climb ladders and walk over rough ground. When on site, conditions can be cramped, cold, dirty and you need to wear boots, a safety helmet and overalls.

Qualification

• England, Wales and Northern Ireland

Band 3: For entry: usually at least 4 GCSEs (A*-C) including maths, technology and a science subject (preferably physics), or equivalent.

• Scotland

Band 3: For entry: usually at least four S grades (1-3) including maths, technology and a science subject (preferably physics), or similar.

Adult Qualifications

Those with relevant work experience may be accepted for some college courses without meeting any formal entry requirements.

Work Experience

Relevant work or voluntary experience is always useful and can improve your chances in application for entry to this job. Training or apprenticeship providers may prefer those who have a good awareness of what is involved in the job or some experience of practical tasks. The areas to consider for work experience are those in the construction trades that also relate to engineering, using machinery, equipment and technology.

Entry and Training

Most enter this work through an apprenticeship scheme to become a technician at age 16-19, learning on the job in the workplace and attending a local college for a relevant day or block-release course, such as those offered by BTEC/SQA and City & Guilds. Other routes include a full-time course for a national diploma or Scottish group award, before applying to an employer for a trainee technician post. If handling ozone depleting substances (ODS) in your work, you must, by law, also obtain a specialist qualification, such as the City & Guilds (2078) handling refrigerants, or a safe handling certificate from ConstructionSkills. You also work towards eligibility for registration for an Engineering Services SKILLcard, which gives you industry-wide recognition of your skills, competence and qualifications.

Technicians can aim for EngTech registration from the Engineering Council after relevant work experience and an approved qualification such as S/NVQ level 3 or a national certificate/ diploma. A vocationally-related qualification (VRC) in maintenance of refrigeration systems, level 3 diploma, is awarded by Emta Awards Ltd. Further study and experience can lead to becoming a qualified engineer. There are relevant foundation degrees available that may be studied full or part time. Contact the Air Conditioning and Refrigeration Industry Board, SummitSkills, or the Chartered Institution of Building Services Engineers (CIBSE) for further details on training routes and relevant qualifications.

A Diplom/Welsh Baccalaureate in construction and the built environment may be available in your area. S/NVQs are available in mechanical engineering services - refrigeration and air conditioning at levels 2 and 3.

Mature applicants can take refresher courses that are sometimes available for those returning to work and there may be special government training schemes or apprenticeships for adults in some areas. You can also gain recognition of previous experience through Accreditation of Prior Learning (APL) or by working towards relevant S/NVQs. Contact your local careers office, Jobcentre Plus, Next Step service or Learning and Skills Council (LSC)/Local Enterprise Company (LEC) for details of all training opportunities and schemes, including apprenticeships for adults.

Opportunities and Pay

Jobs are available in most towns and cities, and most work for a firm of heating and ventilating engineers or a large building contractor. The demand for air conditioning systems has increased both domestically and internationally, so work may be available locally or abroad. Some technicians may progress to become chartered engineers through further qualification and experience.

Pay varies depending on area and employer but starting salaries are likely to be around £17k for a trained technician. With experience, earnings can increase to around £20k-£28k a year and the highest paid technicians can earn up to £35k.

Health

You have to have good colour vision for any electrical work and should not be allergic to dust or skin irritants.

Skills and Qualities

able to estimate, able to explain clearly, able to follow drawings and plans, aptitude for teamwork, attention to detail, good interpersonal skills, health & safety awareness, numeracy skills, planning skills, specialist IT skills

Relevant Subjects

Construction and built environment, Design and technology, Engineering, Mathematics, Physics

Further Information

Apprenticeship Schemes (National Apprenticeship Service) - www.apprenticeships.org.uk

Apprenticeships in Scotland (Careers Info Scotland) - www.apprenticeshipsinscotland.com/about/

Careers Fact Sheets (SummitSkills) (SummitSkills) - www.summitskills.org.uk/

ConstructionSkills - sector skills council for the construction industry - www.cskills.org

Diplomas (Foundation, Higher and Advanced) - http://yp.direct.gov.uk/diplomas

Engineering Services SKILLcard - www.skillcard.org.uk

My Career (HVCA) (Heating and Ventilating Contractors' Association (HVCA)) - www.hvca.org.uk

Summitskills - sector skills council for building services engineering - www.summitskills.org.uk

Welsh Baccalaureate - www.wbq.org.uk

Addresses

Air Conditioning and Refrigeration Industry Board (ACRIB)
Kelvin House, 76 Mill Lane, Carshalton, Surrey SM5 2JR
Phone: +44 (0)20 8254 7842
Web: www.acrib.org.uk

Building Engineering Services Training
The Priory, Stomp Road, Burnham, Bucks SL1 7LW
Phone: +44 (0)1628 607800
Web: www.best-ltd.co.uk

Chartered Institution of Building Services Engineers (CIBSE)
222 Balham High Road, Balham, London SW12 9BS
Phone: +44 (0)20 8675 5211
Web: www.cibse.org

Emta Awards Ltd (EAL)
Head Office, 14 Upton Road, Watford, Hertfordshire WD18 0JT
Phone: +44 (0)1923 652400
Web: www.eal.org.uk

Engineering Council
246 High Holborn, London WC1V 7EX
Phone: +44 (0)20 3206 0500
Web: www.engc.org.uk

Heating and Ventilating Contractors' Association
ESCA House, 34 Palace Court, London W2 4JG
Phone: +44 (0) 020 7313 4900
Web: www.hvca.org.uk

Similar Jobs

Engineer: Building Services, Engineer: Thermal Insulation, Heating & Ventilation Fitter/Welder, Plumber

Refuse Collector

also known as: Dustman/Dustwoman, Refuse Operative, Waste Collection Operative

CRCI:Personal and Other Services
CLCI:IJ Job Band: 1

Job Description

Refuse collectors collect waste, load it on to a special lorry and take it to an official rubbish tip, such as a landfill site or a waste transfer station. They work in a team calling at houses, offices, shops and other buildings, to empty bins or remove plastic sacks of waste. May throw sacks into the lorry or empty bins using an automatic lift. May also supply new plastic bags or bins to houses. Sometimes they collect larger items that people have thrown out, such as furniture or electrical white goods.

Some operators sort rubbish and do labouring work at tips. Can specialise in removing waste that is hazardous or a danger to health such as hospital waste or chemicals. May also collect recyclable waste, such as paper, garden clippings, newspapers, plastic and glass, which is sorted separately. Drivers act as team leaders. They check the vehicle before each shift and ensure it is driven safely. Must be able to manoeuvre the vehicle, sometimes in narrow roads.

Work Details

Usually work 37-39 hrs a week, starting early, about 7am, and possibly including weekends and some public holidays. There may be shifts or rotas. You work outside in all weathers and travel around an area, probably on a regular route. Workloads are heavier during Christmas and Easter, and you may have to work longer hours. You have to be able to lift heavy bins, boxes, plastic bags and other items. This sort of work is often dirty, dusty and smelly.

There is a risk of minor injuries from things like broken glass. You are also working with machinery, often in busy streets, so you must be careful. Protective overalls, high visibility jackets, double thickness trousers, footwear and gloves are provided.

Qualification

- **England, Wales and Northern Ireland**

Band 1: For entry to jobs, no minimum qualifications are needed, but you are expected to have a good level of general education and relevant experience. Some formal/vocational qualifications at any level are useful.

- **Scotland**

Band 1: For entry to jobs, no minimum qualifications are needed, but you are expected to have a good level of general education and relevant experience. Some formal/vocational qualifications at any level are useful.

Adult Qualifications

No qualifications are needed. You can improve your skills and qualifications by working through the Foundation Learning programme. This involves taking credit-based units and qualifications to help you progress.

Work Experience

Any manual work experience can equip you with skills to use in the future and add to your CV. This can either be unpaid or holiday/part-time work that you have sorted out yourself.

Entry and Training

You must be at least 18 to apply for a job as a loader and drivers must be over 21. There are no formal entry requirements, but drivers need an LGV (large goods vehicle) licence. You may take a course to introduce you to the work that includes manual handling, operation of the equipment, customer service and health and safety aspects. You are then trained on the job by an experienced crew member.

You may work towards work-based qualifications offered by the Waste Management Industry Training and Advisory Board (WAMITAB) or City & Guilds. You can also gain certificates of competence at levels 1-3 and certificates of technical competence at levels 3-4 through WAMITAB. S/NVQs in waste management operations are available at levels 1-4. The Chartered Institution of Wastes Management also provides relevant training courses.

Mature applicants with experience of manual work may have an advantage.

Opportunities and Pay

Jobs can be found throughout the country and most are with local authorities. There are some jobs with companies that clear demolition sites or collect paper or food waste. Jobs such as depot superintendent or inspector may be available for those with additional training and suitable experience.

Pay varies depending on where you work. Average pay is likely to be from £12k-£25k a year. Your normal weekly wage may be increased by overtime pay and bonuses.

Health

To do this job you need to be fit and strong. The dusty work is not suitable for people who have asthma.

Skills and Qualities

aptitude for teamwork, not squeamish, reliable, responsible attitude, safety conscious, strong

Further Information

Energy & Utility Skills - sector skills council for gas, power, waste management & water industries - www.euskills.co.uk
Foundation Learning (QCDA) - www.qcda.gov.uk
Local Government Careers (Improvement and Development Agency) - www.lgcareers.com/publications/

Addresses

Chartered Institution of Wastes Management (CIWM)
9 Saxon Court, St Peter's Gardens, Marefair,
Northampton NN1 1SX
Phone: +44 (0)1604 620 426
Web: www.ciwm.co.uk

Waste Management Industry Training and Advisory Board (WAMITAB)
Peterbridge House, 3 The Lakes, Northampton NN4 7HE
Phone: +44 (0)1604 231 950
Web: www.wamitab.org.uk

Similar Jobs

Cleaner: Street, Construction Operative, Driver: Lorry, Groundsman/Groundswoman, Recycling Officer, Removals Operative

Registrar of Births, Deaths, Marriages and Civil Partnerships

CRCI:Legal and Political Services
CLCI:LAZ Job Band: 2

Job Description

Registrars are responsible for recording all births (including stillbirths), deaths, marriages and civil partnerships within their district. They collect and record information according to UK law. They interview those who are about to get married and make sure that all the legal requirements are met before issuing registration forms and certificates. Registrars also handle fees that must be paid for the certificates. They attend some religious marriages to complete the registration process and, as a superintendent registrar, also conduct civil marriage/partnership ceremonies. May also officiate at renewal of vows ceremonies and at citizenship celebrations.

Registrars interview a parent (or parents) after the birth of a baby, record the details on a register and provide a copy of the birth certificate. They also interview relatives after a death or stillbirth, take details and issue a death certificate. Registrars inform a coroner or a procurator fiscal (Scotland) if they are think a death is suspicious. They are also responsible for keeping historical records dating back to 1837, and if asked, issue a copy of a record for legal and family research purposes.

They use a computer to record all work details and deal with other paperwork, including statistical data that needs to be sent to the General Register Office, General Register Office for Scotland or General Register Office Northern Ireland.

Work Details

You usually work 36-38 hrs a week, which includes weekends and public holidays. Some religions require a funeral to take place on the day of a person's death, so you may also be on call outside normal working hours. You work mainly in an office within the local council offices, but you may conduct marriage or civil partnership ceremonies at different places in your area. The work is usually by appointment only, though in remote areas of Scotland you can be based in your own home or at a local post office.

Civil marriage and partnership ceremonies now take place in a many locations, including hotels, castles and stately homes, in hospitals or prisons, as well as in civic buildings. Registrars need to be able to cope with people who can be emotional or distressed at times.

Qualification

- **England, Wales and Northern Ireland**

Band 2: Although no minimum qualifications are specified, a good standard of education is required. Several GCSEs including English (and Welsh in Wales) and maths are desirable.

- **Scotland**

Band 2: For entry: three S grades (1-3), including English and maths, are required, or similar qualifications.

Adult Qualifications

There are no minimum qualifications required, though a good standard of general secondary education is desirable.

Work Experience

Work experience gives you an insight into what you enjoy and do not enjoy about a job, as well as the chance to gain new skills. It also gives you information to add to your CV and improves job prospects. Work experience can either be unpaid, or can be holiday or part-time work that you have arranged yourself. Experience of administration work within a local council is useful. It may also be possible to work shadow a local registrar to find out more about the job.

Entry and Training

In England, Wales and Northern Ireland, no specific minimum qualifications are required other than a good standard of general education. However, it is essential to be computer-literate, to be able to operate specialist software programs, and use email. All applicants need previous experience of dealing with a wide range of people. Training is on the job and includes gaining knowledge and understanding of the laws surrounding registration.

In Scotland all registry staff to work towards the certificate of proficiency in the law and practice of registration. This is a professional qualification, recognised by the General Register Office in Scotland. Study is through distance learning and on-the-job training under the supervision of a registrar.

As registrars usually need to travel around, it is useful to have a full, clean driving licence and access to a car.

There is no upper age limit for starting this work and maturity, combined with evidence of working with a wide range of people is an asset. Those with previous experience in administration have an advantage. Those who have certain previous occupations are not allowed to become registrars, including funeral directors, doctors and midwives, ministers of religion, and those who have previously worked in the life assurance industry.

Opportunities and Pay

Registrars are employed by local authorities. There are about 1750 registrars in England and Wales and about 500 in Scotland. Promotion depends on the size of the council, but it is possible to be promoted from assistant registrar, to registrar and superintendent. In larger councils it may be possible to specialise in different aspects of work. Scotland has two grades, assistant registrar and registrar.

With further training there may be chances to move into other areas of work with the council, eg administration manager or legal executive.

Actual rates of pay vary, but starting pay for assistant registrars is around £17k rising to over £32k for those in senior posts.

Health

You may be required to have a medical examination.

Skills and Qualities

able to put people at ease, able to work both on your own and in a team, discreet, efficient record keeping, good interpersonal skills, good organisational skills, IT skills, public speaking ability, understanding of legal technicalities

Relevant Subjects

English, Law

Further Information

Local Government Careers (Improvement and Development Agency) - www.lgcareers.com/publications/

Addresses

Association of Registrars of Scotland (AROS)
Municipal Buildings College Street, Dumbarton G82 1NR
Web: www.aros.org.uk

General Register Office (GRO)
PO Box 2, Southport PR8 2JD
Phone: (0)845 603 7788
Web: www.direct.gov.uk/en/Governmentcitizensandrights/Registeringlifeevents/index.htm

General Register Office for Scotland (GROS)
New Register House 3 West Register Street, Edinburgh EH1 3YT
Phone: +44 (0)131 334 0380
Web: www.gro-scotland.gov.uk

General Register Office Northern Ireland
General Register Office, Oxford House, 49-55 Chichester Street, Belfast BT1 4HL
Phone: +44 (0) 28 90 252000
Web: www.groni.gov.uk

Similar Jobs

Civil Service Administrative Assistant, Civil Service Administrative Officer, Legal Executive, Local Government Administrator, Secretary: Legal

Rehabilitation Officer: Visually Impaired

also known as: Community Resource Worker: Visual Impairment, Community Support Worker for the Visually Impaired

CRCI:Social Work and Counselling Services
CLCI:KEB Job Band: 4 to 5

Job Description

Rehabilitation officers provide a range of services to people with vision impairments to help restore their independence. They visit people in their homes and assess their needs, by talking with them and their family. Explore the impact of the sight problems both on a practical and emotional level. Offer an information service regarding activities and services in the local area and assist them to make contact as required. May provide information and advice on eye conditions, government benefits and entitlements and aids and appliances.

Rehabilitation officers give training in independent living skills, which cover a range of skills including personal care, tasks about the house, such as cooking and cleaning, and mobility training. They may also teach Braille. Some rehabilitation officers work with local authorities and service providers to ensure that the environment is as accessible as possible to people with sight problems. This includes physical access, such as audible signals at traffic lights, well marked steps and kerb edges, and access to information in appropriate formats. May need to write reports and work with other professionals and eye specialists.

Work Details

Usually work a basic 37-39 hr week, but this may include evenings and weekends to allow visits to people in their homes at suitable times. Work is mainly indoors, in an office and in people's homes, but usually involves a fair amount of travelling. A driving licence is usually required. You may deal with people who are upset or possibly angry over their sight problems, and you need to be concerned, but practical in the ways you can help them. Work may be emotionally demanding. You also need to liaise with other support workers in the community, local authorities and other organisations to ensure that the best help possible is available for your clients.

Qualification

A degree level education is not always required, though preferred. It is very important to have the right personality, and a background in social or community work is a great advantage.

• England, Wales and Northern Ireland

Band 4: For HND, Diploma of Higher Education or foundation degree: 1-2 A levels and some GCSEs (A*-C) usually including English and maths, or equivalent.

Band 5: For degree courses: 2-3 A levels and some GCSEs (A*-C) usually including English and maths, or equivalent. Exact requirements depend on the degree you take.

• Scotland

Band 4: For entry to SQA higher national and professional development awards, usually 2-3 H grades and some S grades (1-3), including English and maths, or similar qualifications.

Band 5: For entry to a degree course: 3-5 H grades and some S grades (1-3) including maths and English, or similar qualifications. Exact requirements depend on the degree you take.

Degree Information

Any degree may be acceptable, although a degree in rehabilitation work, visual impairment or social care is the most relevant.

Adult Qualifications

Entry requirements may be relaxed for adults applying for higher education courses. Access to HE or foundation courses provide those without the required qualifications a route onto degree courses.

Work Experience

Entry to this work is competitive, so any work, either paid or voluntary, that involves working with people in a caring capacity is an advantage. Any work experience you can gain as a volunteer working with people who are vision impaired is also very useful. Charities such as the RNIB, Action for Blind People or Vision-Aid are a useful starting point.

Entry and Training

There are no set formal entry requirements for this work, but most entrants have a qualification in rehabilitation and experience of some type of community or social work. Training is usually on the job under the supervision of experienced workers, with possible day release to professional courses. There is a BTEC Professional Diploma in rehabilitation studies (visual impairment) at levels 4 and 5.

The Royal National Institute of the Blind (RNIB), with Birmingham City University (BCU), offers a foundation degree in rehabilitation work (visual impairment). You can then progress to a two-year BSc or BSc Hons top-up degree, through part-time study. Contact BCU for further details. Canterbury Christ Church University also offers a foundation degree in health and social care (visual impairment rehabilitation).

RNIB Scotland has an Employment and Learning Centre based on the campus of Jewel and Esk Valley College in Edinburgh. The Centre offers rehabilitation courses for people who have lost their sight as adults, or whose sight has deteriorated and wish to stay in their present jobs or find new employment.

Training programmes, including apprenticeship schemes, may be available in your area. Advanced apprenticeships in health and social care, leading to qualification at level 3, can also be a route into higher education. You need to have Criminal Records Bureau (CRB)/Disclosure Scotland clearance and be registered with the Independent Safeguarding Authority to do this job.

Mature entrants without formal qualifications may be able to enter this work if you have considerable experience of working with people in a social care field or in rehabilitation work.

Government training opportunities, such as apprenticeships, may be available in your area. You can also gain recognition of previous experience through Accreditation of Prior Learning or by working towards relevant S/NVQs. Contact your local careers office, Jobcentre Plus, Next Step service or Learning and Skills Council (LSC)/Local Enterprise Company (LEC) for details of training schemes.

Opportunities and Pay

Most entrants to this work are employed by local authority social services departments, or national and international charities. With qualifications and experience, there are opportunities for promotion to senior or supervisory rehabilitation roles. Some may even lecture in rehabilitation studies. You may need to be prepared to move to another area of the country to gain promotion.

Salaries are usually in the range of £16k-£28k a year. Senior rehabilitation officers can earn up to £35k a year.

Skills and Qualities

able to get on with all kinds of people, able to motivate others, able to report accurately, able to work both on your own and in a team, good communication skills, IT skills, patient, problem-solving skills, tactful

Relevant Subjects

Health and social care, Psychology, Sociology

Further Information

Action for Blind People - www.actionforblindpeople.org.uk/

Local Government Jobs - www.localgovernmentjobs.ie

NB Magazine (RNIB) - www.rnib.org.uk/professionals/healthsocialcare/eyecareprofessionals/nbmagazine/Pages/nb_magazine.aspx

RNIB - www.rnib.org.uk

Vision-Aid - www.visionaid.org/

Addresses

Birmingham City University
Perry Barr, Birmingham B42 2SU
Phone: +44 (0)121 331 5595;
Web: www.bcu.ac.uk/

Similar Jobs
Advice Worker, Community Development Worker, Occupational Therapist, Social Worker, Social Worker: Medical

Religious Leader
CRCI:Social Work and Counselling Services
CLCI:FAM Job Band: 4 to 5

Job Description
Religious leaders conduct religious services and rituals of a particular faith and play a prominent role in the welfare of a community. They explain and promote a code of beliefs, lead acts of worship and preach publicly at a place of worship. They officiate at funerals, weddings, baptisms, bar mitzvahs, festivals and other events of celebration. Encourage their community to live by religious principles and practice. Give help, spiritual guidance, and support in times of stress to individuals and families.

Some religious leaders may also work in community centres, hospitals, prisons, and in schools, colleges and universities. Some combine their work with academic teaching, though not necessarily religious studies, or write articles for religious or community publications. Financial and administrative duties may also come under a leader's governance.

Some religious leaders liaise with leaders of other faiths to look at ways to help their shared community and promote understanding and tolerance. May become involved in social welfare and human rights issues. Need to have current knowledge of how their faith views potentially contentious issues such as HIV/Aids, contraception, abortion, euthanasia, and homosexual relationships.

Work Details
There are no set hours of work as this is a vocation and leaders need to be prepared to work each day of the year. Hours are irregular although some ceremonies must take place at set times of the day or week. You hold services, prayer meetings, and advise, teach and help people. Religious leaders have contact with a large number of people, often including those who are upset and in need of support.

Although you have an office, perhaps at your home, you go out and about to attend meetings or work in the community. Travel around an area is necessary to visit people in their homes or in other places such as a hospital. Work can be very demanding at times. Some religions may require you to wear formal dress on certain occasions.

Qualification
Entry requirements vary across the major world religions now practised in Britain. Many religious leaders experience a vocational calling and a strong belief in their faith, commitment, and active participation and observance of its rules and regulations are paramount.

• England, Wales and Northern Ireland
Band 4: For entry to training: usually two A levels and some GCSEs (A*-C). Useful subjects include English, history, religious studies, or equivalent.

Band 5: For degree course in theology: 2-3 A levels and some GCSEs (A*-C) including English and maths, or equivalent qualifications. Exact requirements depend on the degree you take.

• Scotland
Band 4: For entry to training: usually three H grades and some S grades (1-3). Useful subjects include English, history, religious studies, or similar.

Band 5: For degree course in theology: 3-5 H grades and some S Grades (1-3) including English and maths, or similar qualifications. Exact requirements depend on the degree you take.

Degree Information
Any degree is acceptable, though for some denominations, a degree in theology and religious studies usually leads to shortened vocational training. Postgraduate study and training also depends on the denomination.

Adult Qualifications
Maturity is an advantage due to knowledge and life experience. If formal entry qualifications are required for training, these are usually relaxed.

Work Experience
As maturity or life experience is often an entry requirement, some useful work or voluntary experience may be welfare or community-based jobs such as youth work, work in residential care homes, social work or nursing.

Entry and Training
There are more than 170 faiths or belief systems in the UK, but those with the most followers include Christianity, Judaism, Islam, Hinduism, Buddhism and Sikhism. Religious leaders are subject to the differing laws of faith, so there is no set standard entry route. Some selection procedures can be lengthy and require evidence of commitment and practical experience. In some denominations, women are excluded from leadership or ministry. Marital status is also a restricting factor in some faiths.

If formal training is required, theology and divinity courses are available at non-graduate, undergraduate and postgraduate levels. Applicants must be at least 18 before a course can be started, though most entrants are older. Training is by specialist course and by practical experience, often after an initial degree. Usually professional status is gained after a probationary period and this may include a ceremony to be ordained. Priests attend a seminary (training college) and rabbis are required to attend a yeshiva (Orthodox Jewish college or seminary).

Long periods of reflection, meditation and study of the particular faith are usual. For some, this may involve spending time at a monastery or retreat.

Adult entry is common as this job is particularly suitable for older, more experienced people. The training period is often shorter for older entrants, though usually requires periods of time spent away from home. Formal training can be full or part time, or by distance learning, weekend (or longer) residential courses, and summer schools. Some theological colleges and institutes offer a variety of training programmes, including postgraduate study. A degree in religious studies is also available from the Open University.

Opportunities and Pay
This work requires a great deal of personal commitment to the chosen faith. Most work is within a local area but there are also opportunities in hospitals, universities/colleges, schools, prisons, and in the armed forces. Teaching posts may also require a teaching qualification. In some faiths there is work in missions overseas and opportunities to meet religious leaders and visit holy places worldwide. There may be opportunities to teach, work in counselling or interfaith relations, as well as charity or humanitarian work.

In Britain, most religious groups are registered voluntary charitable organisations and are governed by requirements, which include annual accountable meetings. Payments to a religious leader depend upon the financial resources of each faith and some give their expertise and services free.

If a salary is paid, this is usually modest, but you may be given accommodation and paid extra allowances to cover essential expenses. Some religious leaders may receive an annual salary of around £16k-£20k rising to around £30k a year. In some faiths, certain services such as weddings and funerals attract payment. Starting salaries for Chaplains in the armed forces are £38k-£42k a year.

Health
You need to be physically and emotionally strong for this job.

Skills and Qualities
able to inspire confidence, able to set an example, able to understand other people's problems, approachable, belief & commitment, integrity, leadership qualities, patient, perseverance, public speaking ability, supportive

Relevant Subjects
Classical studies, English, History, Psychology, Religious studies, Sociology

Further Information
Ministry in the Church of England - www.cofe-ministry.org.uk

Open University - www.open.ac.uk

UK Priest - www.ukpriest.org

Addresses
Board of Deputies of British Jews
6 Bloomsbury Square, London WC1A 2LP
Phone: +44 (0)20 7543 5400
Web: www.boardofdeputies.org.uk/index.php

Buddhist Society
58 Eccleston Square, London SW1V 1PH
Phone: +44 (0)20 7834 5858
Web: www.thebuddhistsociety.org

Catholic Church in England & Wales
39 Eccleston Square, London SW1V 1BX
Phone: +44 (0)20 7630 8220
Web: www.catholic-ew.org.uk

Christian Education Movement
1020 Bristol Road, Selly Oak, Birmingham B29 0LB
Phone: +44 (0)121 472 4242
Web: www.christianeducation.org.uk

Church of England (CofE)
Church House, Great Smith Street, London SW1P 3AZ
Phone: +44 (0)20 7898 1000
Web: www.cofe.anglican.org

Church of Scotland
121 George Street, Edinburgh EH2 4YN
Phone: +44 (0)131 225 5722
Web: www.churchofscotland.org.uk

Churches Together in Britain & Ireland
39 Eccleston Square, London SW1V 1BX
Phone: +44 (0) 845 680 6851
Web: www.ctbi.org.uk

Hindu Council UK
Community Hall, Shri Venkateswara (Balaji) Temple,
Dudley Road East, Birmingham B69 3DU
Phone: +(44/0) 121 552 354
Web: www.hinducounciluk.org

Inter Faith Network for the UK
8A Lower Grosvenor Place, London SW1W 0EN
Phone: +44 (0)20 7931 7766
Web: www.interfaith.org.uk

Muslim Council of Britain (MCB)
PO Box 57330, London E1 2WJ
Phone: 0845 262 6786 (UK only)
Web: www.mcb.org.uk

Network of Sikh Organisations UK
Suite 405 Highland House, 165 The Broadway, Wimbledon,
London SW19 1NE
Phone: +44 (0)208 544 8037
Web: www.nsouk.co.uk

Similar Jobs
Community Development Worker, Community Learning & Development Officer (Scotland), Counsellor, Social Worker

Relocation Agent
also known as: Search Consultant

CRCI:Building and Construction
CLCI:UM
Job Band: 3 to 5

Job Description
Relocation agents assist an individual person or company, often from abroad, through all stages of buying or renting a house or changing business premises. They work on behalf of the client to save them time and money, and to make the change of location easier. They advise the client on market availability, find a selection of suitable properties in a specified area/region and arrange viewings. May advise the client on matters that include raising appropriate finance and deal with all paperwork and help negotiate the final agreement transaction, whether for purchase or rent.

Increasingly, agents work for a client wishing to purchase or rent a property abroad. They undertake visa and immigration services, arrange transportation of household goods, carry out school/college searches and area orientation. They also provide any other facilities or information that is required.

Work Details
Relocation agents usually work a basic 39 hr week, Monday to Friday, but may be required to work some evenings and weekends. Work is in an office but involves travelling around to visit property, perhaps a considerable distance from the office. The type of clients you deal with depend on your firm. They may range from property managers of large commercial organisations and companies wishing to relocate employees, to independent people looking to move to a new region of the country or relocate from abroad.

You inform, advise and help people to make decisions. You need knowledge of the relevant legal technicalities and need to have a good understanding of facilities in various areas of the UK and abroad. You are likely to need good research skills to do this job. A businesslike and efficient approach is essential, even under pressure.

Qualification
- **England, Wales and Northern Ireland**

Band 3: For BTEC national award: usually at least 4 GCSEs (A*-C) including English and maths, or equivalent.

Band 4: For BTEC higher national award: 1-2 A levels and some GCSEs (A*-C) usually including English and maths, or equivalent.

Band 5: For degree courses: 2-3 A levels and some GCSEs (A*-C) usually including English, maths and possibly a science subject, or equivalent. Exact requirements depend on the degree you take.

- **Scotland**

Band 3: For SQA national award: at least four S grades (1-3) or similar.

Band 4: For SQA higher national award: a minimum of two H grades and some S grades (1-3) or similar.

Band 5: For relevant degree: 3-5 H grades and some S grades (1-3) or similar.

Degree Information
Any degree is acceptable, but it is an advantage to have studied land and property management/surveying or a directly related subject. There are postgraduate courses for those with non-relevant degrees. Other subjects, such as geography (human) or building-related disciplines give useful backgrounds.

Adult Qualifications
Entry requirements may be relaxed for adults applying for higher education courses and Access courses give adults without qualifications a route onto degree courses. Those with relevant work experience may be accepted for some college courses without needing any formal entry requirements.

Work Experience
Employers may prefer candidates who have relevant work or voluntary experience such as office-based work, where you gain skills in administration, sales, retail and dealing with the public. For adult entry you usually need relevant experience or substantial voluntary work experience in estate agency, sales, administration or surveying.

Entry and Training
The majority of relocation agents/search consultants begin their careers as estate agents (see separate job details) or in related professions such as surveying. Professional qualifications are an advantage for entering estate agency, but currently are not essential. You can study for a degree or diploma and then complete two years of practical training and experience. Other routes include training on the job together with part-time study by distance learning or a day-release course. Relevant foundation degrees are also available. You can also become a relocation agent by gaining qualifications or professional experience in marketing or human resources.

There is a specific professional qualification for this job that is offered by the Association of Relocation Professionals (ARP) together with the European Academy of Relocation Professionals (EARP). There are three levels of certification and those with experience in the relocation industry can apply for exemption points at level one. You qualify by attending training seminars through the ARP, such as the fundamentals of relocation and the legal training programme. Level three acts as the final stage of professional qualification and is also part of an ongoing professional development programme. Upon successful completion, trainees are awarded the designation of Certified European Relocation Professional (CERP 3). Contact the ARP for details of all training and membership routes.

Mature entry is common, as employers usually look for those with relevant experience and/or relevant qualifications such as work as an estate agent, sales and marketing experience or in land and property surveying. Some relocation agents/search consultants are expatriates with personal experience of relocation. This experience, combined with qualifications can be very useful.

Opportunities and Pay
Many relocation agents are self-employed, having moved on from more senior estate agency posts to set up their own business. There are many small firms that may deal with regional or local relocation, but there are also large UK companies concerned with the international relocation of companies and expatriates. Opportunities may depend on the property climate at the time of your application. Currently there is a downturn in the market which means there may be fewer vacancies.

Most relocation agents' salaries are a combination of basic salary and commission. This is based on a percentage of the price (or rental) of the property found, at the end of the transaction. An average figure tends to be in the region of 1-1.5% of the purchase price (+VAT), or 10% of the annual rental figure. Relocation agents start earning around £20k-£29k, rising to around £35k-£55k a year and over. Some very successful agents working in corporate relocation can earn up to and over £55k-£70k a year. A car may be provided, and commission and/or bonus payments depend upon your success in the job.

Skills and Qualities
able to communicate effectively, able to manage a budget and keep records, able to report accurately, good interpersonal skills, good organisational skills, IT skills, problem-solving skills, quick thinking, research skills

Relevant Subjects
Business and accounting, Economics, English, Geography, Law, Mathematics, Modern Foreign Languages

Further Information
ARP Quarterly Newsletter (Association of Relocation Professionals) - www.relocationagents.com

Association of Relocation Professionals - http://arp-relocation.com

The Estate Agent (10 x year) (National Association of Estate Agents) - www.naea.co.uk

Addresses
European Academy of Relocation Professionals (EARP)
PO Box 189, Diss, Norfolk IP22 1NS
Phone: +44 (0)1379 651 671
Web: www.earp.eu.com

National Association of Estate Agents (NAEA)
Arbon House, 6 Tournament Court, Edgehill Drive,
Warwick CV34 6LG
Phone: +44 (0)1926 496 800
Web: www.naea.co.uk

Similar Jobs
Estate Agent, Facilities Manager, Relocation Agent, Surveyor: General Practice, Surveyor: Quantity

Removals Operative
also known as: Furniture Remover

CRCI:Transport and Logistics

CLCI:YAT — Job Band: 1

Job Description
Removals operatives are part of a team that moves household and office furniture or personal belongings from one place to another. They pack china, glass, books, linen, and the contents of wardrobes and cupboards into boxes or cartons. Take apart large items, such as beds and wardrobes, lift carpets and take down curtains. They pack everything tidily and secure it safely in a van. Travel with the van and unload it. Removal operatives unpack boxes and put the furniture/equipment in the right place. Reassemble the beds, wardrobes and other dismantled items. Most large firms also operate a storage service for items that are not immediately required.

Some firms operate a European service and drive the household goods to destinations abroad. Others pack goods for overseas travel, placing them in a purpose built container. Some firms specialise in the packaging, removal and storage of objects such as art works or office equipment.

Work Details
Usually work a basic 40 hr week though sometimes the hours can be long and irregular, and you may be required to work at weekends. You work in customers' homes or offices and are expected to get on well with people. You may spend a lot of time driving or in a lorry cab. Some firms specialise in long-distance removals so you have to travel all over the UK or perhaps abroad, which involves spending nights away from home. You work in a team and make sure that things are carried and stored safely. There is a lot of heavy lifting. There may be some paperwork. This work can be dusty.

Qualification

- **England, Wales and Northern Ireland**

Band 1: No minimum qualifications are required, but you are expected to have a good level of general education, especially in English and maths. However, some formal/vocational qualifications at any level are useful.

- **Scotland**

Band 1: For entry to jobs, no minimum qualifications are needed, but you are expected to have a good level of general education and relevant experience. Some formal/vocational qualifications at any level are useful.

Adult Qualifications

Formal qualifications are not required, though some at any level are useful, especially in English and maths. Those without existing qualifications can work through the Foundation Learning programme by taking credit-based units and qualifications.

Work Experience

Any work experience can equip you with skills that you can use in the future and add to your CV. This can either be unpaid, voluntary or holiday/part-time work that you have organised yourself.

Entry and Training

Training is usually on the job, learning from an experienced worker. You learn removal techniques such as lifting and loading, packing/unpacking and how to handle antiques and other valuable items. The British Association of Removers runs short courses, ranging from basic skills to the BTEC awards in removals management and practical estimating. There are also short courses on manual handling, health and safety and safe loading and packaging. You need a LGV driving licence to be a driver.

It is possible to gain S/NVQs in driving goods vehicles and distribution, warehousing and storage operations at levels 1-3. The Packaging Society also runs a range of courses at all levels. Check the website for details. Training programmes, including apprenticeship schemes, may be available in your area. Advanced apprenticeships leading to qualification at level 3 can also be a route into higher education.

Government training opportunities, such as apprenticeships, may be available in your area. You can also gain recognition of previous experience through Accreditation of Prior Learning or by working towards relevant S/NVQs. Contact your local careers office, Jobcentre Plus, Next Step service or Learning and Skills Council (LSC)/Local Enterprise Company (LEC) for details of training schemes. Employers look for those who are physically fit and strong.

Opportunities and Pay

Around 30,000 people work as removals operatives in the UK and the sector in growing due to increased numbers of people relocating. You work for a removal firm or are self-employed and there may be opportunities for travel overseas. Furniture removal companies are found in most towns and cities. You can progress to foreperson, driver or an estimator providing quotations for customers. You can also, with experience, set up your own business.

Pay varies depending on location and employer. Starting salaries are around £10k-£14k a year, rising to £18k-£20k. Senior staff and drivers may earn up to £30k a year. Overtime may be available and you may be given tips by customers. When you have to spend time away from home, you are paid a living allowance.

Health

You have to be fit to do this job. There is a risk of back injuries.

Skills and Qualities

aptitude for teamwork, careful, customer service skills, good interpersonal skills, hard working, health & safety awareness, honest, practical skills, resourceful, trustworthy

Further Information

Apprenticeship Schemes (National Apprenticeship Service) - www.apprenticeships.org.uk
Careers in Logistics - www.careersinlogistics.co.uk
Foundation Learning (QCDA) - www.qcda.gov.uk
Skills for Logistics - sector skills council for freight logistics industries - www.skillsforlogistics.org
Training Schemes - www.direct.gov.uk/en/educationandlearning

Addresses

British Association of Removers (BAR)
Tangent House, 62 Exchange Road, Watford WD18 0TG
Phone: +44 (0)1923 699480
Web: www.bar.co.uk

Packaging Society
Institute of Materials, Minerals and Mining, 1 Carlton House Terrace, London SW1Y 5DB
Phone: +44 (0)20 7451 7300
Web: www.iom3.org/packaging/

Similar Jobs

Airport Baggage Handler, Lift Truck Operative, Packer: General, Roadie, Theatre Stagehand, Warehouse Worker

Reprographics Assistant

also known as: Photocopying Assistant, Print Room Assistant
CRCI:Media, Print and Publishing
CLCI:SAR Job Band: 1 to 2

Job Description

Reprographics assistants photocopy and print pages of text for an organisation or for the public. They mainly use photocopiers, but sometimes various print-finishing machines. They photocopy the number of copies needed and then sorts them, using other machines to collate, fold and staple the pages. They usually copy and bind in bulk. Most are fully automated digital copiers that receive copy direct from a computer. Must accurately cost the job and package the work when finished.

Assistants make sure the machines are clean, safe, and that health and safety regulations are followed. They deal with any problems, such as paper getting stuck in the machine, or contact an engineer. Also clean and maintain the copier and replace paper, ink and toner.

Work Details

Working hours are usually around 9am-5pm; Monday to Friday, and may include a Saturday. Some companies have flexitime and you may have to work overtime, when there are large orders to be completed. Other tasks include keeping records of the customer, the number of copies required and when they are needed. You may also have to order paper, ink and toner.

Often copying has to be done quickly, so you need to work under pressure to get things done on time. You must learn to use new machines. You are on your feet all day and also have to lift heavy boxes of paper.

Qualification

- **England, Wales and Northern Ireland**

Band 1: For many employers, formal qualifications are not required, although a good standard of education is usually expected.

Band 2: Although academic qualifications are not specified for this job, it is an advantage to have some GCSEs (A*-C) or equivalent in subjects that include English, maths and an IT/craft subject.

- **Scotland**

Band 1: For many employers, formal qualifications are not required, although a good standard of education is usually expected.

Band 2: Although academic qualifications are not specified for this job, it is an advantage to have some S grades (1-3) in subjects that include English, maths and an IT/craft subject.

Adult Qualifications
Qualifications are not usually needed.

Work Experience
Any work experience can equip you with skills that you can use in the future and add to your CV. This can either be unpaid or voluntary, or can be holiday or part-time work that you have organised yourself.

Entry and Training
Reprographics assistants often go straight into the job and have on-the-job training. Representatives from the manufacturers of the equipment may visit the company to do specific product training. Assistants that also use printing machines can take a full-time course first, or a part-time course during employment. Courses include a relevant BTEC award in media production (print based) or a City & Guilds award in printing and graphic communications at levels 2-3. A range of vocational related qualifications are available at level 2-3. Training programmes, including apprenticeship schemes, may be available in your area. Advanced apprenticeships leading to qualification at level 3 can also be a route into higher education.

The British Printing Industries Federation (BPIF) has details of courses on its website. They also have special interest sections, including one on in house print finishing departments where members can discuss any technological challenges they experience. Similarly, the Institute of Paper, Print and Packaging offers a certificate course as an introduction to the paper, printing and publishing sectors. It is suitable for newcomers and those already working in the industry. On successful completion of the programme, students are awarded the IP3 Certificate and can gain automatic entry to IP3 at AIP3 grade. This qualification is recognised throughout all three industry sectors.

Mature entrants with experience in printing, graphics or general office work may have an advantage.

Opportunities and Pay
Around 20,000 reprographics assistants are employed in the UK and there are good opportunities with printing firms of all sizes. You can work for any organisation that has a reprographics or print section, such as central and local government, a hospital, university, college or a school. You can also work in a shop that does fast printing and photocopying for the public. In a large company, you may be able to gain promotion to supervisor, or become a print shop manager.

Pay varies depending on area and employer, but a starting pay is likely to be around £10k, rising to around £15k a year with experience. Supervisors can earn up to £21k a year. Overtime pay may be available.

Health
There may be an allergy risk as chemcials are used in this job. It is an advantage if you have good colour vision.

Skills and Qualities
able to follow instructions, able to prioritise work, able to work quickly, friendly, good organisational skills, IT skills, methodical, numeracy skills, practical skills

Further Information
Apprenticeship Schemes (National Apprenticeship Service) - www.apprenticeships.org.uk
Print Week (weekly) (Haymarket) - www.printweek.com/
Proskills UK - sector skills council for process and manufacturing industries - www.proskills.co.uk

Addresses
British Printing Industries Federation (BPIF)
Farringdon Point, 29-35 Farringdon Road, London EC1M 3JF
Phone: 0870 240 4085 (UK only)
Web: www.britishprint.com

Institute of Paper, Printing & Publishing (IP3)
Runnymede Malthouse, off Hummer Road, Egham, Surrey TW20 9BD
Phone: 0870 330 8625 (UK only)
Web: www.ip3.org.uk

Similar Jobs
Engineering Machine Operative, IT Data Input Operator, Local Government Administrative Assistant, Print Finisher, Printer: Machine, Printing Administrator

Respiratory Physiologist
also known as: Clinical Respiratory Physiologist, Respiratory Physiology Technician

CRCI:Healthcare
CLCI:JOB Job Band: 3 to 5

Job Description
Respiratory physiologists work in hospitals and clinics and are highly skilled practitioners who perform a wide range of diagnostic tests to assess all aspects of lung function. They work with patients who have respiratory problems, and use a variety of highly specialised equipment (often linked to computers) and techniques to measure and monitor a patient's breathing function. The tests can calculate levels of carbon dioxide and oxygen in patients' breathing systems or analyse blood gases, test for allergies, or lung capacity. May also test a patient's response to exercise or their breathing during sleep.

Provide doctors with the test results, which assist with the full diagnosis and establish how a patient may react to a particular treatment. May also supervise therapy for patients with lung disorders, particularly bronchitis, asthma and emphysema. Work in partnership with doctors, nurses and other healthcare professionals.

Work Details
Usually work a basic 37 hr week, Monday to Friday. Some hospital-based physiologists may be required to work shifts on a rota system to cover 24 hrs a day. There is contact with people of all ages and abilities. You are responsible for a high standard of skilled work. Part-time work is possible. A uniform or white coat is provided by your employer.

Qualification

- **England, Wales and Northern Ireland**

Band 4: For BTEC higher national award: 2 A levels including a science and some GCSEs (A*-C), usually including English and maths. Equivalent qualifications may also be acceptable. Check individual prospectuses.

Band 5: For degree courses: 2-3 A levels with at least two science subjects (biology, chemistry, physics or maths), and some GCSEs (A*-C) usually including English and maths, or equivalent. Exact requirements depend on the degree you take.

- **Scotland**

Band 4: For SQA higher national award: usually 2-3 H grades and some S grades (1-3), often including English and maths, or similar qualifications.

Band 5: For degree courses: 3-5 H grades with at least 2-3 in science subjects (biology, chemistry, physics or maths), and some S grades (1-3), usually including English and maths, or similar qualifications. Exact requirements depend on the degree you take.

Degree Information
A degree in clinical physiology is required for state registration with the Health Professions Council.

Adult Qualifications
Entry requirements may be relaxed for adults applying for higher education courses and relevant Access and foundation courses, including a one-year Access to clinical physiology course, give adults without qualifications a route on to degree courses.

Work Experience
Employers and colleges may prefer candidates who have good knowledge and awareness gained through practical work experience. There is often a waiting list for work experience in hospitals so enquire early, asking if it is possible to visit other related departments whilst you are there. Experience of working with people in a caring capacity is also an advantage.

Entry and Training
Entry and training routes vary but most employers now prefer applicants to enter with at least A levels/H grades or equivalent. You need to find employment as a trainee physiological scientist and then train on the job through a four-year part-time programme of study for a BSc degree in clinical physiology. This leads to state registration with the Health Professions Council. You can study by block release or day release and if you already have relevant qualifications at HNC/HND or a related degree, you can complete the BSc in a shorter time. The course has a specialist option in respiratory physiology in year four of the programme, and also incorporates the professional qualifications of competence from the Association of Respiratory Technology and Physiology (ARTP).

NHS funding may be available to assist students in full-time university-based training. Once qualified you are expected to continue updating your knowledge through a programme of continuing professional development (CPD). The ARTP holds a voluntary register for clinical physiologists who have followed an approved training programme.

Mature entry is welcomed in this profession but relevant qualifications or evidence of academic ability to train part time for the BSc in clinical physiology, are important. Adults who already have relevant experience in a clinical support role may also apply for training if they can demonstrate the ability to achieve the degree. NHS funding may be available to assist students in full-time university-based training.

Opportunities and Pay
There are around 1,300 respiratory physiologists in the UK working mainly in hospitals in towns and cities. You can be employed by the NHS, governmental departments, the private sector, or the armed forces. Prospects are good as there is a shortage of qualified experts. Promotion is often through a formal career structure leading to departmental senior officers and managers. The armed forces also have a clear career progression structure. One expanding area of the respiratory physiologist's role is the assessment and management of sleep-related breathing disorders. Some may go on to become clinical scientists; others may move into university research or education, or work overseas.

Pay is on a nationally agreed scale and increases with promotion. Newly qualified respiratory physiologists earn around £21k-£28k a year, rising with experience. Salaries can be as high as £50k for those in management positions. Those working in inner London receive an additional living allowance.

Skills and Qualities
accurate, analytical skills, aptitude for teamwork, careful, decisive, good interpersonal skills, IT skills, responsible attitude, sympathetic, technical aptitude

Relevant Subjects
Biology, Chemistry, English, Health and social care, ICT/Computer studies, Mathematics, Physics, Science

Further Information
A Career in Respiratory Physiology (ARTP) - www.artpweb2.f9.co.uk

Health Professions Council (HPC) - www.hpc-uk.org

NHS Careers (NHS Careers) - www.nhscareers.nhs.uk

NHS Careers Scotland - www.infoscotland.com/nhs

NHS Careers Wales - www.wales.nhs.uk

Addresses
Association for Respiratory Technology & Physiology (ARTP)
Executive Business Supprt Ltd, City Wharf, Davidson Road, Lichfield WS14 9DZ
Phone: 0845 226 3062
Web: www.artp.org.uk

Physiological Society
Peer House, Verulam Street, London WC1X 8LZ
Phone: +44 (0)20 7269 5710
Web: www.physoc.org

Similar Jobs
Audiologist, Cardiac Physiologist, Clinical Technologist, Neurophysiologist, Perfusionist

Restaurant Manager

CRCI:Catering and Hospitality
CLCI:IB Job Band: 3 to 5

Job Description
Restaurant managers plan and supervise the efficient and profitable running of a restaurant, cafi or food outlet. They ensure that the quality of food and service are of a consistently high standard and is also responsible for recruitment and dismissal of staff, their work rotas, development and training. They plan menus and purchase supplies of food or discuss these with the head chef. May welcome customers to the restaurant and organise table reservations.

Also deals with budgets, stock control and accounts, using a computer. Ensures that hygiene and health and safety regulations are met at all times and deals with any complaints.

Work Details
Usually works 38-40 hrs a week, though hours are often irregular and sometimes very long, including public holidays, evenings and weekends. In some jobs it may be necessary for you to cover at other restaurants, so a willingness to travel is important. This work can be busy and pressurised at times, so you must be able to remain calm. It is important that your clients and customers are pleased and satisfied with the food and environment.

The job is generally indoors in warm and pleasant surroundings, though sometimes conditions may be cramped, hot and noisy. A formal dress code is usually required, or a uniform may be provided by the employer.

Qualification
Previous experience in a customer service environment can be more important to some employers than formal qualifications. However, formal management recruitment schemes may ask for a degree or equivalent level of qualification for entry. Language skills are not essential but may be an advantage.

• England, Wales and Northern Ireland
Band 3: For entry to jobs, HNC or a relevant Diploma, usually at least 4 GCSEs (A*-C) including English and maths, or equivalent.

Band 4: For HND, Diploma of Higher Education or foundation degree: 1-2 A levels and some GCSEs (A*-C) usually including English and maths, or equivalent.

Band 5: For degree courses: 2-3 A levels and some GCSEs (A*-C) usually including English and maths, or equivalent. Exact requirements depend on the degree you take.

- **Scotland**

Band 3: For entry to jobs, usually at least four S grades (1-3) including English or maths, or similar.

Band 4: For entry to SQA higher national and professional development awards, usually 2-3 H grades and some S grades (1-3), including English and maths, or similar qualifications.

Band 5: For degree courses n hospitality management: 3-5 H grades and some S grades (1-3), including English and maths, or similar qualifications. Exact requirements depend on the degree you take.

Degree Information

Degrees in hotel/restaurant management, hospitality management and culinary arts management are relevant for entry to this job, though not necessarily essential. Alternative courses may include consumer studies, food science, nutrition or dietetics. Relevant postgraduate qualifications are beneficial, particularly for those without an appropriate first degree.

Adult Qualifications

Entry requirements may be relaxed for adults with relevant work experience applying for higher education courses. Access or foundation courses provide those without the required qualifications a route onto degree courses.

Work Experience

Relevant work or voluntary experience is always useful and improves your chances in application for entry to this career. Types of work experience to consider include work in hotels, retail, customer service, or anything that gives you relevant management or supervisory experience. Accounting and budgeting knowledge is also an advantage. In some areas there is a young apprenticeship (14-16) scheme that provides an extended work placement and eventual achievement of a relevant level 2 qualification whilst at school.

Entry and Training

There are many routes into restaurant management. Some go into full-time training at a catering college, others work to gain experience and study part time, and some join apprenticeship schemes. It is possible to work your way up to management level but formal recruitment schemes may ask for a degree or equivalent level of qualification for entry. Entrants to management training schemes, which usually last 12-18 months, are often graduates or those who have a relevant professional qualification. These schemes usually include courses in financial management, sales and marketing, food safety and customer service. Entrants usually join as a trainee at assistant manager level.

Many courses in hospitality management can be studied part time whilst in employment. Training routes and nationally recognised qualifications are offered by professional organisations. This includes the Institute of Hospitality, which offers a level 3 certificate or level 4 diploma in management for hospitality, leisure and tourism. Continuing professional development is also available and encouraged. Relevant foundation degrees are available and can be studied full or part time. There are relevant BTEC national and higher national awards in hospitality management at level 3 and 5. A basic food hygiene certificate may also be helpful. S/NVQs at levels 1-3 are available in hospitality, multi-skilled hospitality services and hospitality supervision.

A Diploma/Welsh Baccalaureate may also be available in your area in hospitality. The advanced level is equivalent to 3.5 A levels but for some university courses, the additional and specialist learning (ASL) component of the diploma needs to include specific A levels. Check entry requirements carefully with the individual institutions. Training programmes, including hospitality and catering or customer service apprenticeship schemes, may be available in your area for entry to this job. Advanced apprenticeships leading to qualification at level 3 can also be a route into higher education.

Mature applicants need relevant experience in catering and managerial work. Government training opportunities, such as apprenticeships, may be available in your area. You can also gain recognition of previous experience through Accreditation of Prior Learning (APL) or by working towards relevant S/NVQs. Contact your local careers office, Jobcentre Plus, Next Step service or Learning and Skills Council (LSC) Local Enterprise Company (LEC) for details of training schemes.

You can also apply to the Savoy Educational Trust for financial support to study for hospitality industry-related courses. The Trust aims to support individuals who wish to make a career in hospitality.

Opportunities and Pay

The hospitality industry, and in particular the restaurant business, has struggled during the recent economic downturn which may affect the number of opportunities available for restaurant managers, although skilled managers may still be in demand. Restaurant managers can be employed to work in private restaurants, hotels, pubs, pizza restaurants, tapas bars, bistros, wine bars, etc.

Promotion to manage more than one restaurant is possible and regional or area management opportunities exist for those working in chain restaurants. You can also progress to hotel or pub management. If you are seeking promotion you need to be prepared to move around the country. Many skilled and experienced managers are also self-employed and run their own restaurants. It is possible to find part-time work and work abroad.

Pay can vary considerably depending on location, size of restaurant and level of responsibility. Assistant managers may earn £16k-£25k, and up to £35k a year with experience. Senior managers of successful restaurants can earn £35k-£70k a year. Salaries are higher in London and large cities. Some restaurant managers are provided with accommodation.

Skills and Qualities

able to cope under pressure, able to get on with all kinds of people, able to manage a budget and keep records, able to motivate others, attention to detail, business awareness, energetic, good communication skills, good organisational skills, quick thinking

Relevant Subjects

Business and accounting, Economics, English, Hospitality and catering, ICT/Computer studies, Leisure, travel and tourism, Mathematics, Modern Foreign Languages

Further Information

Apprenticeship Schemes (National Apprenticeship Service) - www.apprenticeships.org.uk

British Hospitality Association (BHA) - www.bha.org.uk

Diploma in Hospitality (People 1st) - www.hospitalitydiploma.co.uk

People 1st - sector skills council for hospitality, leisure, travel and tourism - www.people1st.co.uk

Restaurant Magazine (William Reed Business Media) - www.bighospitality.co.uk

Springboard UK - www.springboarduk.net

Springboard Wales - http://wales.springboarduk.net/

Training Schemes - www.direct.gov.uk/en/educationandlearning

UKSP - Guide to Success in Hospitality, Leisure, Travel & Tourism - www.uksp.co.uk

▶Working in food & drink (2007) (Babcock Lifeskills) - www.babcock-lifeskills.com/

▶Working in hospitality & catering (2009) (Babcock Lifeskills) - www.babcock-lifeskills.com/

Addresses
British Hospitality Association (BHA)
Queens House, 55-56 Lincoln's Inn Fields, London WC2A 3BH
Phone: +44 (0)207 404 7744
Web: www.bha.org.uk

Institute of Hospitality
Trinity Court, 34 West Street, Sutton, Surrey SM1 1SH
Phone: +44 (0)20 8661 4900
Web: www.instituteofhospitality.org

Savoy Educational Trust
Queen's House 55-56 Lincoln's Inn Fields, London WC2A 3BH
Phone: +44 (0) 207 269 9692
Web: www.savoyeducationaltrust.org.uk

Wine & Spirit Education Trust (WSET)
International Wine & Spirit Centre, 39-45 Bermondsey Street, London SE1 3XF
Phone: +44 (0)20 7089 3800
Web: www.wset.co.uk

Similar Jobs
Caterer: Contract/Private, Catering Manager, Chef/Cook, Hotel Manager, Publican, Sommelier

Retail Assistant
also known as: Sales Assistant

CRCI:Retail Sales and Customer Services
CLCI:OE

Job Band: 1 to 2

Job Description
Retail assistants work in high street stores, shops and supermarkets/superstores, serving customers who wish to buy goods. They accept payment in cash, by cheque or by credit/debit card and use a computerised till, product database, barcode reader, or security tagging system. Some goods may need to weighed and packed, or be gift-wrapped. In some shops, assistants keep sales area and shelves full, clean and tidy. May set up displays, price goods with a hand-held label/barcode machine, and check stock quantities. Some retail assistants answer customers' queries or complaints, or refer them to a supervisor.

Work Details
Usually work a basic 35-39 hr week, though the hours of work vary depending on the type of shop or store. In many companies you have to work some evenings and also on Saturdays and possibly Sundays. You get time off during the week instead. You may have to deal with customer complaints and sometimes cope with people who are being awkward. There may be a need to learn about the product you are selling, so that you can properly advise customers. You must handle payments and give the correct change for cash purchases. You may need to handle discount cards/vouchers or loyalty cards.

Qualification

- **England, Wales and Northern Ireland**

Band 1: No minimum qualifications are required, but you are expected to have a good level of general education. However, some formal/vocational qualifications at any level are useful and may be required by some employers.

Band 2: Employers may ask for some GCSEs (A*-C) preferably including English and maths, or equivalent. These qualifications may also be required for entry to some courses.

- **Scotland**

Band 1: No minimum qualifications are required, but you are expected to have a good level of general education. However, some formal/vocational qualifications at any level are useful and may be required by employers.

Band 2: Employers may ask for some S grades (1-3) preferably including English and maths, or similar. These qualifications may also be required for entry to some courses.

Adult Qualifications
Although formal qualifications are not always required, those with some academic/vocational qualifications may have an advantage. Ability in basic maths is important.

Work Experience
Relevant work or voluntary experience is always useful and can improve your chances when applying for entry to jobs in sales. It can equip you with skills that you can use in the future and add to your CV. Part-time and holiday employment in a wide range of shops is usually fairly easy to obtain.

Entry and Training
Training is normally given on the job, although many employers also run off-the-job training courses for new employees. These courses can cover topics such as handling cash, cheque and credit/debit card payments, customer services, health and safety, and how to cope with customer complaints. At other times there may be short training courses to learn about new products. The exact amount of training can vary depending on your employer. For those in the fashion retail sector, the Fashion Retail Academy, offers a range of courses from level 2 to foundation degrees. Check the website for details.

A Diploma/Welsh Baccalaureate in retail business may be available in your area. There are also some part-time college courses leading to relevant qualifications or appropriate S/NVQs at levels 1-3 in retail skills, retail sales and customer service. Training programmes, including apprenticeship schemes, may be also available. Advanced apprenticeships leading to qualification at level 3 can also be a route into higher education. See the Skillsmart Retail website for details.

Mature entrants are often actively recruited by employers, such as supermarkets and chain stores, who seek those over 50 for specific jobs. Experience of working with the public is an advantage. You may be able to enter this work through a government-funded training programme. Contact your local careers office, Jobcentre Plus, Next Step service or Learning and Skills Council (LSC)/Local Enterprise Company (LEC) for details of all training opportunities and schemes, including apprenticeships for adults.

Opportunities and Pay
Jobs in high street stores/shops are mostly in urban areas. You can also work in out-of-town shopping centres or supermarkets. It may be possible to move from assistant to supervisor and to management level jobs. Opportunities for promotion are often better with larger firms. There are options to work on a part-time, casual or seasonal basis. Due to the current economic downturn, there may be fewer opportunities in the retail sector at present.

Rates of pay depend on your employer. Most start on around £9k-£11k, rising to £15k-£18k a year with experience. Some companies operate a bonus scheme and many give staff the option to buy goods at reduced prices.

Health
You need good general fitness for this job and you also have to speak clearly. Employers also expect normal eyesight (with or without glasses/lenses) and hearing.

Skills and Qualities
able to get on with all kinds of people, cash handling skills, common sense, customer service skills, excellent communication skills, good memory, honest, IT skills, numeracy skills, punctual

Relevant Subjects
Retail and distribution

Further Information

Apprenticeship Schemes (National Apprenticeship Service) - www.apprenticeships.org.uk

Apprenticeships in Scotland (Careers Info Scotland) - www.apprenticeshipsinscotland.com/about/

Diplomas (Foundation, Higher and Advanced) - http://yp.direct.gov.uk/diplomas

Foundation Learning (QCDA) - www.qcda.gov.uk

Inside Careers Guide: Marketing & Sales - www.insidecareers.co.uk

Real Life Guide to Retail (Trotman) - www.trotman.co.uk

Skillsmart Retail - sector skills council for the retail industry - www.skillsmartretail.com

Training Schemes - www.direct.gov.uk/en/educationandlearning

Welsh Baccalaureate - www.wbq.org.uk

▶Working in retail & customer services (2008) (Babcock Lifeskills) - www.babcock-lifeskills.com/

▶Working in sport & leisure (2010) (Babcock Lifeskills) - www.babcock-lifeskills.com/

Addresses

British Shops and Stores Association (BSSA)
Middleton House 2 Main Road Middleton Cheney, Banbury, Oxfordshire OX17 2TN
Phone: +44 (0)1295 712 277
Web: www.british-shops.co.uk

Fashion Retail Academy
15 Gresse Street, London W1T 1QL
Phone: +44 (0)20 7307 2345
Web: www.fashionretailacademy.ac.uk

Similar Jobs

Bookshop Assistant, Checkout Operator, Retail Assistant: Computer Software, Retail Assistant: Health Foods, Retail Store Demonstrator, Vehicle Parts Operative

Retail Assistant: Computer Software

CRCI:Retail Sales and Customer Services
CLCI:OFM — Job Band: 1 to 2

Job Description

Computer software retail assistants advise customers about the computer hardware and software that best suits their needs, and sells it to them. They work for a computer/software retail firm and usually have in-depth knowledge of the products on sale. This includes computers (PCs or desktops/notebooks), printers and scanners, and software such as games programs. They also sell accessories and consumables such as cables, paper, toner cartridges and books on computing. May be required to demonstrate the hardware/software, set up the displays of products, and deal with returned goods and customer complaints.

Many sales assistants also process a loan application for some customers to buy their chosen goods, deal with cash and debit/credit transactions and provide a detailed receipt and guarantee details to customers.

Work Details

Usually work a basic 35-39 hr week. You may work shifts and some evenings and weekends. Many stores also have mail and web-order services. This may require giving customers technical advice and taking orders over the telephone or by email. You need to be physically fit as you may be required to lift and handle heavy items. Some firms may provide a uniform. Casual business wear may also be acceptable.

Qualification

• England, Wales and Northern Ireland

Band 1: No formal educational qualifications are specified for entry to this job, though basic maths skills are important.

Band 2: Some employers may ask for some GCSEs (A*-C) preferably including English and maths, or equivalent. Applied ICT qualifications are often also acceptable to employers.

• Scotland

Band 1: No formal educational qualifications are specified for entry to this job, though basic maths skills are important.

Band 2: Employers may ask for some S grades (1-3) preferably including English and Maths, or similar. ICT qualifications are often also acceptable to employers.

Adult Qualifications

A good standard of general education is required and knowledge of IT and practical skills is an advantage. Ability in basic maths is important.

Work Experience

Relevant work or voluntary experience is always useful and can improve your employment prospects when applying for entry to jobs. Any work that involves sales, dealing with the public, or customer care, such as a Saturday job or holiday work, provides valuable experience. Work that gives you an up-to-date knowledge of information technology is also advantageous.

Entry and Training

Employers look for a reasonable technical ability, as well as up-to-date knowledge of information technology. An induction course together with on-the-job training is normally given. Some larger employers also provide training courses that deal with specific roles, such as customer care, handling complaints and dealing with payments. The exact amount of training given varies depending on your employer. Computer manufacturers also provide short courses on their hardware/software products.

A Diploma/Welsh Baccalaureate in retail business may be available in your area. Relevant S/NVQs at levels 1-2 are available in retail skills. Other vocational qualifications are also available, such as the level 2-3 certificate in retail operations. Training programmes, including retail apprenticeship schemes, may also be available. Advanced apprenticeships leading to qualification at level 3 can also be a route into higher education. See the Skillsmart Retail website for details.

Mature entrants are welcomed, particularly those with previous retail experience or skills in customer care and in dealing with the public. Knowledge and/or experience of information technology is an advantage. Government training opportunities may be available in your area. Contact your local careers office, Jobcentre Plus, Next Step service or Learning and Skills Council (LSC)/Local Enterprise Company (LEC) for details of any training schemes, including apprenticeships for adults.

Opportunities and Pay

You can work in outlets ranging from small computer shops to large chain stores and office suppliers. In larger firms, it may be possible to move from sales assistant to supervisor and management level jobs. There are options to work part time and to work extra hours during the Christmas and sales period. However, due to the current economic downturn, there may be fewer opportunities in the retail sector at present.

Most earn in the range of £170-£210, rising to £250-£300 a week. Higher earners can make around £430-£460 a week. Many firms give staff the option to buy goods at reduced prices.

Health

A reasonable level of fitness is required as sales staff are often on their feet for much of the day. Some lifting of heavy boxes may also be required.

Skills and Qualities
able to explain clearly, aptitude for teamwork, customer service skills, good communication skills, good listening skills, initiative, IT skills, self confident, technical aptitude

Relevant Subjects
ICT/Computer studies, Retail and distribution

Further Information
Apprenticeship Schemes (National Apprenticeship Service) - www.apprenticeships.org.uk

Diplomas (Foundation, Higher and Advanced) - http://yp.direct.gov.uk/diplomas

Foundation Learning (QCDA) - www.qcda.gov.uk

Skillsmart Retail - sector skills council for the retail industry - www.skillsmartretail.com

TARGETjobs: Retail, Management & Sales (GTI Specialist Publishing Ltd.) - www.groupgti.com

Welsh Baccalaureate - www.wbq.org.uk

▶Working in computers & IT (2010) (Babcock Lifeskills) - www.babcock-lifeskills.com/

▶Working in retail & customer services (2008) (Babcock Lifeskills) - www.babcock-lifeskills.com/

Similar Jobs
IT Service Technician, IT Technical Sales Specialist, Retail Assistant, Retail Store Demonstrator, Sales Executive

Retail Assistant: Fish
also known as: Fish Sales Assistant, Fishmonger, Sales Assistant: Fish

CRCI:Retail Sales and Customer Services
CLCI:OFM Job Band: 1 to 2

Job Description
A fish retail assistant prepares fish and seafood for sale and serves customers at a fish counter. Usually works in a large supermarket, fresh fish shop or a market. Unpacks pre-prepared fish for display or may fillet, skin and cut up whole fish. May also be required to shell prawns and prepare cooked crabs. Arranges all the fish and seafood on crushed ice for the counter display. Keeps work and display areas hygienic. Helps customers choose fish and may also give advice on cooking methods.

If working for a small business, may visit a market to buy fish daily or take deliveries of fish from a supplier or supermarket warehouse. May also organise delivery of fish to local hotels, restaurants and catering firms.

Work Details
Usually work a basic 35-39 hr week, though the hours of work can vary depending on the size of shop or supermarket. With some firms you may have to work evenings and also on Saturdays, or possibly Sundays, with time off during the week instead. You may have to deal with customers' complaints and occasionally cope with people who are being awkward. There may be a need to learn about the product you are selling so that you can properly advise customers. The job requires you to handle money and you may also be responsible for keeping accounts. You need to be aware of hygiene and health regulations.

You are on your feet for many hours and need to cope with some lifting. The job may also require you to gut and skin fish, so there is a risk of minor injuries from knives. You need to wear a protective overall and possibly something to cover your hair. Your workplace may be cold and wet and you need to cope with the smell of fish.

Qualification
- **England, Wales and Northern Ireland**

Band 1: No minimum qualifications are required, but some formal/vocational qualifications at any level are useful. Maths and English are the most useful subjects.

Band 2: Employers may ask for some GCSEs (A*-C) preferably including English and maths, or equivalent. These qualifications may also be required for entry to some courses.

- **Scotland**

Band 1: No minimum qualifications are required, but some formal/vocational qualifications at any level are useful. Maths and English are the most useful subjects.

Band 2: Employers may ask for some S grades (1-3) preferably including English and maths, or similar. These qualifications may also be required for entry to some courses.

Adult Qualifications
Although formal qualifications are not always required, those with some academic/vocational qualifications may have an advantage. Ability in basic maths is important.

Work Experience
Relevant work or voluntary experience is always useful and can improve your chances when applying for entry to jobs in sales. It can equip you with skills that you can use in the future and add to your CV. Part-time and holiday employment in a wide range of shops is usually fairly easy to obtain.

Entry and Training
Training is normally given on the job, although many employers also run off-the-job training courses for new employees. These courses can cover topics such as handling cash, cheque and credit/debit card payments, customer services, health and safety, food hygiene and how to cope with customer complaints. It is useful to work towards a food hygiene certificate and your employer may arrange this for you. The exact amount of training varies depending on your employer.

The Sea Fish Industry Authority (Seafish) offers a range of courses, including a one-day introductory fishmongering course which is suitable for those keen to start a career in the seafood retail industry. The course covers topics such as knife skills, hygiene and customer service. They also offer a health and safety in the seafood industry course, available as a one-day course or as an open learning module. Contact Seafish for details.

There are also some part-time college courses leading to relevant qualifications or appropriate S/NVQs at levels 1-3 in retail skills, retail sales and customer service. A Diploma/Welsh Baccalaureate in retail business may be available in your area. Training programmes, including apprenticeship schemes, may be available. Advanced apprenticeships leading to qualification at level 3 can also be a route into higher education. See the Skillsmart Retail website for details of retail apprenticeship schemes and training options.

Mature entrants are sometimes actively recruited by employers, such as supermarkets. Experience in sales work is an advantage. You may be able to enter this work through a government-funded training programme. Contact your local careers office, Jobcentre Plus, Next Step service or Learning and Skills Council (LSC)/Local Enterprise Company (LEC) for details of all training opportunities and schemes, including apprenticeships for adults.

Opportunities and Pay
Most jobs are with large supermarkets. You can also work for a small firm which is often a family business. In a supermarket it may be possible to move from assistant to supervisor and to management level jobs. You may be able to move into fish wholesaling and contract buying. You can become self-employed as a fishmonger in a small shop or in a market. Some have a mobile van business and

travel to locations around towns and villages, selling fish to households, hotels and restaurants. Set-up costs may be expensive and your income heavily depends on your success.

Rates of pay vary but are generally around £9k-£11k, rising to £15k-£18k a year. Some firms operate a bonus scheme and many give staff the option of buying goods at reduced prices.

Health
Certain skin troubles may be irritated by this work and make entry to the job unsuitable.

Skills and Qualities
able to get on with all kinds of people, careful, excellent communication skills, friendly, not squeamish, numeracy skills, polite, punctual, steady hand

Relevant Subjects
Hospitality and catering, Retail and distribution

Further Information
Apprenticeship Schemes (National Apprenticeship Service) - www.apprenticeships.org.uk
Apprenticeships in Scotland (Careers Info Scotland) - www.apprenticeshipsinscotland.com/about/
Diplomas (Foundation, Higher and Advanced) - http://yp.direct.gov.uk/diplomas
Foundation Learning (QCDA) - www.qcda.gov.uk
Real Life Guide to Retail (Trotman) - www.trotman.co.uk
Seafood Scotland Newsletter, NEWSnet (Seafood Scotland) www.seafoodscotland.org
Skillsmart Retail - sector skills council for the retail industry - www.skillsmartretail.com
The Seafood Training Academy - www.seafoodacademy.org
Training Schemes - www.direct.gov.uk/en/educationandlearning
Welsh Baccalaureate - www.wbq.org.uk
▶Working in retail & customer services (2008) (Babcock Lifeskills) - www.babcock-lifeskills.com/

Addresses
Sea Fish Industry Authority (Seafish)
Training Division, Origin Way, Europarc, Grimsby DN37 9TZ
Phone: +44 (0)1472 252300
Web: www.seafish.org

Seafood Scotland
18 Logie Mill, Logie Green Road, Edinburgh EH7 4HS
Phone: +44 (0)131 557 9344
Web: www.seafoodscotland.org

Similar Jobs
Butcher: Retail, Butcher: Wholesale, Retail Assistant, Retail Assistant: Health Foods

Retail Assistant: Health Foods
also known as: Sales Assistant: Health Foods
CRCI:Retail Sales and Customer Services
CLCI:OFM Job Band: 1 to 2

Job Description
Retail assistants in health food stores sell a range of natural and organic foods. May also sell health-related books, homeopathic and herbal remedies. May give advice on the health and lifestyle benefits of food and supplement items on sale. They serve customers, sometimes weighing the items, and accept cash, cheques and credit/debit cards in payment. They have to regularly check stock since foodstuffs have a limited shelf life. Food is re-ordered as required. Assistants also keep the shop clean and tidy and arrange attractive displays of the items for sale.

Work Details
Usually work a basic 35-39 hr week. You may be expected to work at weekends but have other days off during the week instead. Days of work vary depending on the shop. Some may open six or seven days a week. In this type of work you need to learn a lot about the products you sell, so that you can give reliable advice to customers. You have to cope with being on your feet most of the day and may also need to wear an overall.

Qualification
- **England, Wales and Northern Ireland**

Band 1: No minimum qualifications are required, but you are expected to have a good level of general education. However, some formal/vocational qualifications at any level are useful.

Band 2: Employers may ask for some GCSEs (A*-C) preferably including English and maths, or equivalent. These qualifications may also be required for entry to some work related courses.

- **Scotland**

Band 1: No minimum qualifications are required, but you are expected to have a good level of general education. However, some formal/vocational qualifications at any level are useful.

Band 2: Employers may ask for some S grades (1-3) preferably including English and maths, or similar. These qualifications may also be required for entry to some courses.

Adult Qualifications
No pre-entry qualifications are usually required, though some academic/vocational qualifications at any level may be an advantage. English and maths are useful subjects.

Work Experience
Relevant work or voluntary experience is always useful and can improve your chances when applying for entry to jobs in sales. It can equip you with skills that you can use in the future and add to your CV. Part-time and holiday employment in a wide range of shops is usually available.

Entry and Training
On-the-job training is usually provided by a manager or experienced member of staff, though many employers also run off-the-job training courses for new employees. These courses can cover topics such as handling cash, cheque and credit/debit card payments, or how to cope with customer complaints. There may also be short training courses to learn more about the products. The exact amount of training varies depending on your employer. The Health Food Institute offers a short induction course and a certificate/diploma in health food retailing available through distance learning.

There are also some part-time college courses leading to relevant qualifications or appropriate S/NVQs at levels 1-3 in retail skills, retail sales and customer service. A Diploma/Welsh Baccalaureate in retail business may be available in your area. Training programmes, including apprenticeship schemes, may also be available. Advanced apprenticeships leading to qualification at level 3 can also be a route into higher education. See the Skillsmart Retail website for details.

Adults may be able to enter this work through a government-funded training programme. Contact your local careers office, Jobcentre Plus, Next Step service or Learning and Skills Council (LSC)/Local Enterprise Company (LEC) for details of all training opportunities and schemes, including apprenticeships for adults. Relevant experience in selling, running a small business or in dealing with health products is helpful. Experience of working with the public is an advantage.

Opportunities and Pay
There are jobs available in most parts of the UK. You can be employed by the owner of the shop or large national chain, or you can perhaps work in a co-operative, where everyone shares in the shop's profits. Self-employment is possible, if you have enough money to stock a shop. There are options to work on a part-time basis. Due to the current economic downturn, there may be fewer opportunities in the retail sector at present.

Rates of pay vary, but are mostly around £9k-£11k, rising to £15k-£18k a year. Some firms operate a bonus scheme and many give staff the option to buy goods at reduced prices.

Skills and Qualities
able to work well on your own, business awareness, cash handling skills, customer service skills, friendly, IT skills, numeracy skills, practical skills

Relevant Subjects
Hospitality and catering, Retail and distribution

Further Information
Apprenticeship Schemes (National Apprenticeship Service) - www.apprenticeships.org.uk

Apprenticeships in Scotland (Careers Info Scotland) - www.apprenticeshipsinscotland.com/about/

Diplomas (Foundation, Higher and Advanced) - http://yp.direct.gov.uk/diplomas

Foundation Learning (QCDA) - www.qcda.gov.uk

Real Life Guide to Retail (Trotman) - www.trotman.co.uk

Skillsmart Retail - sector skills council for the retail industry - www.skillsmartretail.com

Training Schemes - www.direct.gov.uk/en/educationandlearning

Welsh Baccalaureate - www.wbq.org.uk

▶Working in retail & customer services (2008) (Babcock Lifeskills) - www.babcock-lifeskills.com/

Addresses
Health Food Institute
Gothic House, Barker Gate, Nottingham NG1 1JU
Phone: +44 (0)115 941 4188
Web: www.healthfoodinstitute.org.uk

Similar Jobs
Bookshop Assistant, Pet Shop Assistant, Retail Assistant, Retail Assistant: Fish

Retail Buyer
CRCI:Retail Sales and Customer Services
CLCI:OE
Job Band: 4 to 5

Job Description
Retail buyers choose and buy items to make up a product range to sell in shops at a profit. They usually focus on one product area such as books, clothing or food. Must analyse sales, trends and economic forecast data to see what consumers want and how much they will pay. Buyers review which products are selling well and which are less successful and often visit stores to gain feedback from staff and customers. They need to keep an eye on what competitors are doing. Anticipating future demand and planning a range accordingly, as well as writing reports on findings are all part of the job.

Buyers go to trade shows and exhibitions, see sales representatives and use the internet to find out what is new. They build good working relationships with new and existing suppliers. They identify new products and look at samples to assess quality. Buyers assess costs and profit margins, decide on quantities, negotiate the best deals, place orders and arrange for delivery. They present ranges to retail managers. May work on layouts and local and national promotions with visual merchandisers and marketing staff and move stock between stores to meet demand.

Work Details
Usually work a 37 hr week, Monday to Friday. Often have to work extra hours to meet deadlines. Part time and freelance work may be possible, but is not common. Work activities may vary according to the season.

Are usually based at the retail chain's head office. Spend time travelling and away from home when visiting stores, sourcing goods or meeting suppliers. May make short visits abroad. Liaise with in-house marketing, merchandising, senior management and shop staff. Work with manufacturers, wholesalers and importers. The job is high-pressured and carries a lot of responsibility. Working to targets and deadlines can be stressful.

Qualification
- **England, Wales and Northern Ireland**

Band 4: For BTEC higher national award in a business, retailing or marketing subject: 1-2 A levels and some GCSEs (A*-C), or a relevant BTEC national award.

Band 5: For degree courses: 2-3 A levels and some GCSEs (A*-C) usually including English and maths, or equivalent. Exact requirements depend on the degree you take.

- **Scotland**

Band 4: For SQA higher national award in a business, retailing or marketing subject: usually 2-3 H grades and some S grades (1-3), or similar qualifications.

Band 5: For degree courses: 3-5 H grades and some S grades (1-3), usually including English and maths, or similar qualifications. Exact requirements depend on the degree you take.

Degree Information
Any degree is accepted, although subjects such as retail and distribution and business studies are particularly relevant and help to develop your commercial awareness. Some retail courses, especially those related to fashion, cover buying. You may be able to do a sandwich course where you spend a year on a work placement.

Adult Qualifications
Entry requirements may be relaxed for adults applying for higher education courses. Access or foundation courses give adults without qualifications a route onto degree courses.

Work Experience
Entry to this area of work is competitive, and work experience can give you an advantage. Employers look for people with retail experience and a strong interest in their retail area. Paid or voluntary work experience in a retail setting is an advantage. Leisure or other activities that show your interest in a particular field may be useful. Some higher education courses include work placements or the opportunity to take part in real projects.

Entry and Training
Entry is very competitive and many entrants have an HNC/HND or a degree. You usually need a qualification in fashion if you want to be a fashion buyer. Training is often through an employer's general management training scheme offering a mix of both on and off-the-job training. Management training schemes usually involve working in different departments, including the buying department, and in-store to gain overall experience. After this, you may be offered a post as a buyer and train for this role on the job with experienced staff. Some fashion retailers run training schemes just for buyers. In smaller organisations, training is likely to be on the job.

The British Shops & Stores Association offers a summer school and masters training programme. See their website for details. Larger retailers may offer continuing professional development schemes and in-house courses. Buyers may study part time or by distance learning for professional qualifications from bodies such as the Chartered Institute of Marketing and the Chartered Institute of Purchasing and Supply. It is also important to watch out for external factors that influence consumer behaviour by keeping up with fashions, media, arts and current affairs. You may also be able to work towards S/NVQs at levels 2-5 in supply chain management. The Institute of Grocery Distribution offers a range of courses relevant to the food and drink retail sector.

If you do not have higher education qualifications, you may be able to join the organisation as a purchase administrator or as a buyer's assistant. In this role you can learn the skills and gain the experience you need to apply for a trainee or junior buyer post. A relevant foundation degree may be available in some areas. Apprenticeships in retailing leading to level 2 and advanced apprenticeships leading to level 3 qualifications may be available in your area.

In some areas you can do a young apprenticeship (14-16) in retail. You do an extended work placement and a level 2 qualification whilst at school. A Diploma/Welsh Baccalaureate in retail business may be available in your area. For health and safety reasons there may be some jobs you cannot do until you are over 16.

Adults with experience in areas such as retail, business or stock control are welcome in this area of work.

Opportunities and Pay
Buying departments employ relatively few staff, so competition for jobs is fierce. Retail buyers work for independent and chain stores, mail order, internet and TV-based retailers. Jobs are often based in London and the south east of England, where many large retail chains have their head offices. In smaller outlets, the role may be combined with other roles such as management and merchandising (deciding buying policies). In larger organisations you can progress from junior to assistant to senior buyer posts. You may move on into management roles such as trading manager or buying controller. Buyers may also move into marketing, merchandising, store and product management roles.

Earnings depend on the size of the organisation, location, type of products and bonuses for meeting targets. Many employers offer staff discounts and good benefits packages. Junior and assistant buyers earn from £18k-£30k a year, sometimes more. Buyers earn around £25k-£50k a year, and senior buyers earn £40-£80k or more.

Health
This job requires good health. In some roles, normal colour vision is needed.

Skills and Qualities
able to make important decisions, able to work to deadlines, analytical skills, business awareness, good communication skills, good interpersonal skills, good organisational skills, literacy and numeracy skills, negotiating skills, networking skills

Relevant Subjects
Business and accounting, Economics, English, ICT/Computer studies, Mathematics, Psychology, Retail and distribution

Further Information
AGCAS: Retail (Job Sector Briefing) (AGCAS) - www.prospects.ac.uk

Apprenticeship Schemes (National Apprenticeship Service) - www.apprenticeships.org.uk

Diplomas (Foundation, Higher and Advanced) - http://yp.direct.gov.uk/diplomas

Inside Careers Guide: Purchasing & Supply - www.insidecareers.co.uk

Real Life Guide to Retail (Trotman) - www.trotman.co.uk

Skillsmart Retail - sector skills council for the retail industry - www.skillsmartretail.com

Welsh Baccalaureate - www.wbq.org.uk

▶Working in retail & customer services (2008) (Babcock Lifeskills) - www.babcock-lifeskills.com/

Addresses
British Shops and Stores Association (BSSA)
Middleton House 2 Main Road Middleton Cheney, Banbury, Oxfordshire OX17 2TN
Phone: +44 (0)1295 712 277
Web: www.british-shops.co.uk

Chartered Institute of Marketing (CIM)
Moor Hall, Cookham, Maidenhead, Berkshire SL6 9QH
Phone: +44 (0) 1628 427120
Web: www.cim.co.uk

Chartered Institute of Purchasing and Supply (CIPS)
Easton House, Easton on the Hill, Stamford, Lincolnshire PE9 3NZ
Phone: +44 (0)1780 756 777
Web: www.cips.org

Institute of Grocery Distribution (IGD)
Careers Information Service, Grange Lane, Letchmore Heath, Watford, Hertfordshire WD25 8GD
Phone: +44 (0)1923 857141
Web: www.igd.com

Similar Jobs
Advertising Media Buyer, Commodity Broker, Market Research Executive, Purchasing/Procurement Officer, Retail Manager, Retail Merchandiser

Retail Manager
CRCI:Retail Sales and Customer Services
CLCI:OE Job Band: 3 to 5

Job Description
Retail managers are responsible for the commercial success and efficient day-to-day running of a supermarket, retail store or department. They aim to increase sales and maximise profits, while minimising wastage and costs. Also arrange special promotional events, displays and advertising to meet sales targets. Managers oversee stock control and arrange re-ordering. They select, train and supervise sales and support staff. Are also responsible for seeing that safety and hygiene standards are maintained and for the security of the premises. Dealing with customer complaints is an important element of the job.

Work Details
Usually work a basic 35-39 hr week, though most managers have to work long hours, including some evenings, Saturdays and possibly Sundays. You are responsible for running the business efficiently and for solving problems quickly. The work is challenging and demanding at times and can involve making difficult decisions when dealing with staff. You have to cope with being on your feet and being active most of the time.

Qualification
• England, Wales and Northern Ireland
Band 4: For BTEC higher national certificate/diploma in retail management, which is needed to enter some management training schemes: a minimum of 1-2 A levels and some GCSEs (A*-C), or equivalent.

Band 5: For degree courses: 2-3 A levels and some GCSEs (A*-C) preferably including English and maths, or equivalent. Exact requirements depend on the degree you take.

• Scotland
Band 4: For SQA higher national award, which is needed to enter some management training schemes: 2-3 H grades and some S grades (1-3), or similar.

Band 5: For degree courses: 3-5 H grades and some S grades (1-3) preferably including English and maths, or similar qualifications. Exact requirements depend on the degree you take.

Degree Information

Any degree is acceptable, though it may be an advantage to have studied retail management or marketing. Business studies or business administration also give useful background knowledge. Alternatively, it is possible to take a postgraduate qualification, eg a master of business administration (MBA), or an MSc/Diploma in marketing, with options in retail management.

Adult Qualifications

Adult candidates with fewer than the specified qualifications may be admitted to courses. For those over 21, it is also possible to enter higher education through an Access or foundation course that leads to a relevant HND/degree course.

Work Experience

Employers or colleges/universities may prefer candidates who have relevant work or voluntary experience. It can be useful to have some experience in shop work, through a Saturday or holiday job. This can be in various areas of retail, the leisure industry, catering establishments, such as restaurants or hotels, and other related work. This gives you the opportunity to gain some business administration skills and the chance to work with the public.

Entry and Training

Entry to management training schemes with retail stores or supermarkets is very competitive and many trainees are graduates, have A levels/H grades, or a higher national award. Management training schemes usually include spending time working in different departments to gain overall experience. Some existing staff, with no or few qualifications may also attend management training courses, which can either be run in-house or at a college, and can gain relevant national/higher national BTEC/ SQA awards. Foundation degrees in retail management are also available.

There are also some part-time college courses leading to relevant qualifications, such as a QCF level 3 certificate/diploma in retail (management), or appropriate S/NVQs at levels 1-4 in retail or sales. Training programmes, including apprenticeship schemes, may be available in your area. Advanced apprenticeships leading to qualification at level 3 can also be a route into higher education. See the Skillsmart Retail website for details.

A Diploma/Welsh Baccalaureate in retail business may be available in your area.

Mature entrants with previous management, sales or supervisory experience may have an advantage. However, recruitment to employer training programmes varies widely, unless it is a specified graduate training programme. Adults may be able to enter this work through a government-funded training programme. Contact your local careers office, Jobcentre Plus, Next Step service or Learning and Skills Council (LSC)/Local Enterprise Company (LEC) for details of all training opportunities and schemes, including apprenticeships for adults.

Opportunities and Pay

Employment is with a retail company or possibly a nationwide chain, in towns, cities and out-of-town sites, such as airports or retail/industrial parks. Retail managers may run a store that is part of a major chain, or manage/own a single, independent store. In large stores, retail managers often have a team of senior managers specialising in areas such as customer services, individual departments, personnel, systems or administration. Opportunities for promotion and overall prospects can be better in larger companies. However, to gain promotion, it is often necessary to work at a store in another part of the country.

Rates of pay vary and depend on the employer and size of retail operation. New entrants earn in the region of £14k-£20k, rising to around £23k-£30k a year. High earners make from £30k-£60k a year, and more in larger retail operations. Bonuses can increase salaries.

Health

A good level of general fitness is needed for this job.

Skills and Qualities

business awareness, decisive, energetic, good communication skills, good interpersonal skills, initiative, IT skills, leadership qualities, negotiating skills, quick thinking

Relevant Subjects

Business and accounting, Economics, English, ICT/Computer studies, Mathematics, Psychology, Retail and distribution

Further Information

AGCAS: Retail (Job Sector Briefing) (AGCAS) - www.prospects.ac.uk

Apprenticeship Schemes (National Apprenticeship Service) - www.apprenticeships.org.uk

Diplomas (Foundation, Higher and Advanced) - http://yp.direct.gov.uk/diplomas

Inside Careers Guide: Management - www.insidecareers.co.uk

Logistics and Retail Management (2009) (Kogan Page) - www.koganpage.com

Real Life Guide to Retail (Trotman) - www.trotman.co.uk

Skillsmart Retail - sector skills council for the retail industry - www.skillsmartretail.com

Welsh Baccalaureate - www.wbq.org.uk

▶Working in retail & customer services (2008) (Babcock Lifeskills) - www.babcock-lifeskills.com/

Addresses

Institute of Grocery Distribution (IGD)
Careers Information Service, Grange Lane, Letchmore Heath, Watford, Hertfordshire WD25 8GD
Phone: +44 (0)1923 857141
Web: www.igd.com

Similar Jobs

Export Sales Manager, Human Resources Officer/Manager, Marketing Manager, Off-Licence Manager, Purchasing/ Procurement Officer, Retail Buyer

Retail Merchandiser

CRCI:Retail Sales and Customer Services
CLCI:OM — Job Band: 3 to 5

Job Description

Retail merchandisers supervise the buying policy for retail stores or supermarkets, including planning, pricing and distribution. They gather and analyse sales information from branch and department managers. Also, forecast sales and plan stock levels, in order to maximise profits. Use information technology, including electronic point of sale systems (EPOS) to access and analyse sales information from individual or from all of the company's branches.

Merchandisers also advise buyers on policy guidelines and may visit suppliers. May also design layout and organise stock control systems for new stores. Responsibilities vary greatly in different retail companies.

Work Details

Usually work a basic 35-39 hr week, from Monday to Friday, though longer hours are necessary at times. You may have to travel throughout the country or sometimes overseas to visit suppliers. This work involves collecting, collating and analysing information, often using a computer, and you are responsible for keeping costs within an agreed budget. You also spend time meeting with suppliers and with other staff in the company. This type of work can be challenging.

Qualification

• England, Wales and Northern Ireland

Band 4: For some management training schemes or for relevant BTEC higher national award: 1-2 A levels and some GCSEs (A*-C), usually including English and maths, or equivalent.

Band 5: For degree courses: 2-3 A levels and some GCSEs (A*-C) usually including English and maths, or equivalent. Exact requirements depend on the degree you take.

• Scotland

Band 4: For some management training schemes or for relevant SQA higher national course in a business, retailing or marketing subject: 2-3 H grades and some S grades (1-3), often including English and maths, or similar qualifications.

Band 5: For degree courses: 3-5 H grades and some S grades (1-3), usually including English and maths, or similar qualifications. Exact requirements depend on the degree you take.

Degree Information

A degree in any subject is acceptable, though there are a few specific courses in subjects that include fashion management (with buying and merchandising), and in fashion merchandising management. It is also an advantage to have studied retail management/marketing as an option in a first degree or as a relevant postgraduate course. A degree in business studies/administration also gives useful background knowledge.

Adult Qualifications

Adult candidates with fewer than the specified qualifications may be admitted to courses. For those over 21, it is also possible to enter higher education through an Access or foundation course that leads to a relevant HND/degree course.

Work Experience

Employers or colleges/universities may prefer candidates who have relevant work or voluntary experience. It can be useful to have some experience of working in a shop, through a Saturday or holiday job. Work can be in various areas of retail, the leisure industry, catering establishments, such as restaurants or hotels, and other related work. This gives you the opportunity to gain some business administration skills and the chance to work directly with the public.

Entry and Training

Training is usually through an employer's general management training programme that can include a mixture of both on and off-the-job training. Entry is very competitive and many trainees are graduates, have A levels/H grades, or a higher national award. Management training schemes usually include spending time working in different departments, including merchandising, to gain overall experience. You then learn more about merchandising with an experienced employee/manager.

You can study for the professional qualifications of the Chartered Institute of Purchasing and Supply, such as the foundation diploma at level 4 or the advanced diploma at level 5. The level 3 certificate in purchasing and supply is an entry-level qualification for those that are new to the profession. Courses can either be taken part time at a local college or through a distance-learning course. Relevant foundation degrees are available, including retail management and retail technology.

There are also some part-time college courses leading to relevant qualifications, such as a QCF level 3 certificate/diploma in retail (management), or appropriate S/NVQs at levels 1-3 in retail skills. Training programmes, including apprenticeship schemes, may be available in your area. Advanced apprenticeships leading to qualification at level 3 can also be a route into higher education. See the Skillsmart Retail website for details.

A Diploma/Welsh Baccalaureate in retail business may be available in your area.

Mature entrants require business experience, preferably in buying or marketing. It is possible to transfer to this job from other areas of retailing. However, recruitment to employer training programmes varies widely, unless it is a specified graduate training programme. Adults may be able to enter this work through a government-funded training programme. Contact your local careers office, Jobcentre Plus,Next Step service or Learning and Skills Council (LSC)/Local Enterprise Company (LEC) for details of all training opportunities and schemes, including apprenticeships for adults.

Opportunities and Pay

Employers include independent retailers, nationwide retail organisations, mail order or internet companies, manufacturers and wholesalers. Most jobs are based at head offices which are located mostly in London and the south of England. Opportunities for promotion depend largely on the type of company, but prospects can be better in larger organisations. However, you may be expected to work at stores in different parts of the country.

Pay varies depending on area, type and size of company. Starting salaries are likely to be around £15k-£18k a year. Experienced merchandising managers earn from £20k-£40k a year. Senior managers may earn more than £50k a year.

Health

This job requires good health.

Skills and Qualities

able to communicate effectively, able to work to a budget, analytical skills, business awareness, decisive, good at forecasting trends, IT skills, negotiating skills, planning skills, sound judgement

Relevant Subjects

Business and accounting, Economics, English, ICT/Computer studies, Mathematics, Psychology, Retail and distribution

Further Information

AGCAS: Retail (Job Sector Briefing) (AGCAS) - www.prospects.ac.uk

Apprenticeship Schemes (National Apprenticeship Service) - www.apprenticeships.org.uk

Diplomas (Foundation, Higher and Advanced) - http://yp.direct.gov.uk/diplomas

Inside Careers Guide: Purchasing & Supply - www.insidecareers.co.uk

Real Life Guide to Retail (Trotman) - www.trotman.co.uk

Skillsmart Retail - sector skills council for the retail industry - www.skillsmartretail.com

Welsh Baccalaureate - www.wbq.org.uk

▶Working in retail & customer services (2008) (Babcock Lifeskills) - www.babcock-lifeskills.com/

Addresses

Chartered Institute of Marketing (CIM)
Moor Hall, Cookham, Maidenhead, Berkshire SL6 9QH
Phone: +44 (0) 1628 427120
Web: www.cim.co.uk

Chartered Institute of Purchasing and Supply (CIPS)
Easton House, Easton on the Hill, Stamford, Lincolnshire PE9 3NZ
Phone: +44 (0)1780 756 777
Web: www.cips.org

Institute of Grocery Distribution (IGD)
Careers Information Service, Grange Lane, Letchmore Heath, Watford, Hertfordshire WD25 8GD
Phone: +44 (0)1923 857141
Web: www.igd.com

Similar Jobs
Marketing Manager, Purchasing/Procurement Officer, Retail Assistant, Retail Buyer, Retail Manager

Retail Store Demonstrator
also known as: In-store Demonstrator, Product Demonstrator

CRCI:Retail Sales and Customer Services
CLCI:OE Job Band: 1 to 2

Job Description
Retail store demonstrators demonstrate and promote products to encourage people to buy them. Products may include items such as make-up, wine, food, toys and electrical goods. They set up demonstrations in shops, shopping centres and large stores, at trade fairs or exhibitions or sometimes work in customers' homes. They display the product and attract interest by talking about its advantages to possible customers.

Demonstrators offer free samples, leaflets, stickers, badges, or money-off vouchers, in order to increase sales. They make sure there is enough stock and keep accurate records of orders/sales.

Work Details
Usually work around eight hours a day during busy shopping periods. This may include weekends and evenings. Employment can be on a casual contract for only a day or two at a time, although some contracts are longer and more regular. You work on your own, but meet a large number of people at work. The work involves informing and advising people about the product you are promoting and trying to persuade them to buy it. The job requires you to stand for many hours. Sometimes you may need to wear a uniform.

Qualification
- **England, Wales and Northern Ireland**

Band 1: There are no set entry qualifications for this job. However, some formal/vocational qualifications at any level are useful.

Band 2: Although academic qualifications are not specified for this job, it may be an advantage to have some GCSEs (A*-C) in subjects that include English and maths, or equivalent.

- **Scotland**

Band 1: There are no set entry qualifications for this job. However, some formal/vocational qualifications at any level are useful.

Band 2: Although academic qualifications are not specified for this job, it may be an advantage to have some S grades (1-3) in subjects that include English and maths, or similar.

Adult Qualifications
There are no set entry requirements, although some academic/vocational qualifications at any level may be an advantage.

Work Experience
Relevant work or voluntary experience is always useful and can improve your chances when applying for entry to jobs in sales. It can equip you with skills that you can use in the future and add to your CV. Part time and holiday employment in a wide range of shops is usually fairly easy to obtain.

Entry and Training
Most demonstrators work on a freelance basis and register with marketing or employment agencies for work. These agencies may run short training courses in selling techniques. Manufacturers may also give some training on the product that the demonstrator is to promote. Employers look for a smart, tidy appearance with a clear speaking voice. This job may require a driving licence.

Practical qualifications, such as certificates in first aid and hygiene, may be helpful. Experience in certain types of work, including catering, food handling, sales and marketing, are also useful. There are some part-time college courses leading to relevant qualifications or appropriate S/NVQs at levels 1-3 in retail skills, retail sales and customer service. A Diploma/Welsh Baccalaureate in retail business may be available in your area.

It is an advantage to have experience in sales work. Employers are generally looking for people with a smart, tidy appearance and a clear speaking voice.

Opportunities and Pay
Jobs are mainly in towns and cities. You can work for a wide range of firms, including promotion agencies, manufacturers, or in store for shops or retail outlets. Most people are employed on a freelance or per session basis. There are often opportunities to work on a part-time or seasonal basis, such as at Christmas and New Year. Promotion prospects are limited, but with experience, you may progress to a supervisory role. You may be able to move into a related area of work, such as mail order or marketing and product promotion for party planning firms.

Pay varies hugely depending on the employer and the work you are doing. Most earn in the region of £13k, rising to £16k a year. Those demonstrating certain products, such as cosmetics, are likely to be paid commission on the products they sell.

Health
This job requires good general fitness.

Skills and Qualities
able to explain clearly, calm, customer service skills, enthusiastic, friendly, perseverance, persuasive, reliable, self confident, smart appearance

Relevant Subjects
English, Retail and distribution

Further Information
Diplomas (Foundation, Higher and Advanced) - http://yp.direct.gov.uk/diplomas

Foundation Learning (QCDA) - www.qcda.gov.uk

Real Life Guide to Retail (Trotman) - www.trotman.co.uk

Skillsmart Retail - sector skills council for the retail industry - www.skillsmartretail.com

TARGETjobs: Retail, Management & Sales (GTI Specialist Publishing Ltd.) - www.groupgti.com

Welsh Baccalaureate - www.wbq.org.uk

►Working in retail & customer services (2008) (Babcock Lifeskills) - www.babcock-lifeskills.com/

Addresses
Institute of Sales and Marketing Management (ISMM)
Harrier Court, Lower Woodside, Bedfordshire LU1 4DQ
Phone: +44 (0)1582 840 001
Web: www.ismm.co.uk

Similar Jobs
Beauty Consultant, Market Stall Trader, Retail Assistant, Sales Executive

Riding Instructor
also known as: Horse Riding Instructor

CRCI:Leisure, Sport and Tourism
CLCI:WAM Job Band: 1 to 3

Job Description
Riding instructors teach riding techniques to all kinds of people, from beginners to experts, including horse care and stable management as well as riding. They work with people one at a time or in groups and develop a training programme that suits individual needs and improves riding ability. Can also work with

people who have special educational needs. Instructors may teach riders who take part in competitions and horse show, or may teach flat riding or jumping. The job also includes training and exercising horses.

Assists in cleaning out stables and tack, and changes the bedding. Some instructors also do paperwork, such as ordering equipment and feed, or handling accounts and writing reports.

Work Details

Usually works long hours, including early starts and late finishes, and some evenings and weekends. Many of your pupils are children, although you can teach people of all ages and abilities. You need to cope with some lifting, and work is mainly outdoors in all sorts of weather. Sometimes you work in an indoor training centre, but this can still be cold. There is a risk of injury; you can be bitten or kicked by horses, or may fall when riding. Protective clothing is worn such as a hard hat and body protector.

Qualification

• England, Wales and Northern Ireland

Band 1: No minimum qualifications are required, but you are expected to have a good level of general education. However, some formal/vocational qualifications at any level are useful.

Band 2: Although academic qualifications are not specified for this job, it is an advantage to have some GCSEs (A*-C) or equivalent in subjects that include English and maths.

Band 3: For entry to jobs and some courses if you are under 18: usually at least 4 GCSEs (A*-C) including English and maths, or equivalent, plus a basic knowledge of horsemanship.

• Scotland

Band 1: No minimum qualifications are required, but you are expected to have a good level of general education. However, some formal/vocational qualifications at any level are useful.

Band 2: Although academic qualifications are not specified for this job, it is an advantage to have some S grades (1-3) in subjects that include English and maths, or similar, plus a basic knowledge of horsemanship.

Band 3: For entry to jobs and some college courses if you are under 18: usually at least four S grades (1-3) including English or maths, or similar.

Adult Qualifications

Those aged over 18 do not usually require formal academic qualifications for entry to courses.

Work Experience

Work experience gives you an insight into what you enjoy and don't enjoy about a job or working environment, as well as the opportunity to acquire new skills. It also provides valuable information to add to your CV and improves any course application and/or your future employment prospects. Any work that involves horses, such as a Saturday job or holiday work at stables, provides valuable experience.

Entry and Training

Most employers expect instructors to have gained qualifications from the British Horse Society (BHS) or from the Association of British Riding Schools (ABRS). The BHS offers a series of exams leading to qualification as a riding instructor. Qualifications are awarded on behalf of the BHS through the awarding body Equestrian Qualifications Limited (EQL). There is a clearly defined route starting with a preliminary teaching test. This is available to gold or junior gold members of the society who have attained horse knowledge, care and riding stage 2 and are at least 18 years old. After the preliminary teaching test, candidates work through the grades of assistant instructor and intermediate instructor, before finally gaining the full qualification of Instructor BHSI. Check their website for complete course details. EQL also awards level 1-3 equine coaching certificates on behalf of the British Equestrian Federation. See the EQL website for full details of qualifications.

The ABRS also offers a clear progression route for becoming a fully qualified riding instructor. Their programme starts with an initial teaching award. Applicants must be at least 17 and a half years old, hold a first aid certificate, a child protection certificate and a riding and road safety certificate. This initial qualification is followed by a teaching certificate and an advanced teaching diploma. Check the ABRS website for full details on all courses. The Coaching Ireland website also has some useful information about becoming a sports coach.

S/NVQs are available at levels 1-3 through EQL in horse care/horse care and management. A Diploma/Welsh Baccalaureate may also be available in your area in Sport & Active Leisure. Contact SkillsActive for further details. Training programmes, including apprenticeship schemes in coaching, teaching and instructing or activity leadership, may be available in your area. Advanced apprenticeships leading to qualification at level 3 can also be a route into higher education.

Mature entrants with relevant experience may be exempt from some parts of the British Horse Society (BHS) or from the Association of British Riding Schools (ABRS) examinations. Experience of working with horses or with other animals, and experience of working with children, for example teaching, is an advantage.

Opportunities and Pay

Riding is becoming increasingly popular and there is a need for well-qualified instructors. Opportunities exist in riding schools or equestrian centres such as private stables, competition yards, agricultural/equine colleges, trekking centres, polo yards, livery stables, stud yards, or riding holiday hotels. You may be given a room or flat to live in on the premises. This job can be seasonal, with more work in summer than in winter. Work with the police or armed forces is possible, but training usually takes place whilst in service.

Good riding instructors may also become judges for competitions in show jumping or dressage, or be selected to become British Horse Society (BHS) examiners. There may be an opportunity to work abroad or work part time. You can be self-employed and have your own stables, or work on a freelance basis.

Pay varies depending on location and employer, and whether accommodation, meals and livery are provided. Starting salaries for BHS preliminary teachers are in the region of £12k a year. BHS assistant instructors earn up to £15k, intermediate instructors earn £16k-£20k, a fully qualified instructor earns £20k-£25k, and a fellow of the BHS can earn upwards of £25k a year.

Health

You have to be fit, healthy and free from allergies to animals to do this job.

Skills and Qualities

able to explain clearly, agile, dedicated, energetic, enthusiastic, firm manner, friendly, patient, responsible attitude, tactful

Relevant Subjects

Biology, English, Leisure, travel and tourism, Physical education and sport, Science

Further Information

Apprenticeship Schemes (National Apprenticeship Service) - www.apprenticeships.org.uk

Association of British Riding Schools, Online Fact Sheets - www.abrs-info.org

Diplomas (Foundation, Higher and Advanced) - http://yp.direct.gov.uk/diplomas

Equestrian Qualifications Limited (EQL) - www.equestrian-qualifications.org.uk

Lantra - The Sector Skills Council for environmental & land-based sector (Lantra) - http:/www.lantra.co.uk
Real Life Guide to Working with Animals & Wildlife (Trotman) - www.trotman.co.uk
SkillsActive - sector skills council for active leisure, learning and well-being - www.skillsactive.com
▶Working in sport & leisure (2010) (Babcock Lifeskills) - www.babcock-lifeskills.com/
Working with Horses (BHS) (British Horse Society) - www.bhs.org.uk/

Addresses

Association of British Riding Schools (ABRS)
Queen's Chambers, 38-40 Queen Street, Penzance TR18 4BH
Phone: +44 (0)1736 369 440
Web: www.abrs-info.org

British Horse Society (BHS)
Stoneleigh Deer Park, Kenilworth, Warwickshire CV8 2XZ
Phone: 0844 848 1666 (UK only)
Web: www.bhs.org.uk

Similar Jobs

Farrier, Guide Dog Trainer, Horse Groom, Jockey, Sports Coach

Road Safety Officer

CRCI:Transport and Logistics
CLCI:YAD Job Band: 3 to 5

Job Description

Road safety officers encourage the safe use of public roads through education, training and publicity. They give advice and organise ways to promote road safety, including exhibitions. Visit places, such as schools and colleges to give talks and film shows, and distribute leaflets and posters. Organise training schemes for cyclists or drivers and also publicity campaigns, for example about drinking and driving. May arrange and manage road safety campaign exhibitions and rallies.

Road safety officers liaise and work with a wide range of people and groups, including community and voluntary groups, schools, colleges and playgroups, the police, employers, and local authority highways departments, such as road engineers and surveyors. May assist the police in accident investigations.

Work Details

Usually work a basic 37 hr week, based in an office but you travel to different places, such as exhibitions or schools. Road safety officers relate well to people of all ages, giving talks to groups, which can be in the evening, and possibly some Saturdays. Your work involves meeting with a wide range of people, including children in playgroups and schools, people in community groups, the police, local councillors, road engineers and surveyors. You have to keep up to date with legal regulations.

Qualification

This job is not open to school leavers. Experience and personal qualities are as important as academic qualifications and the following are given as a guide only.

- **England, Wales and Northern Ireland**

Band 3: For entry to jobs, HNC or a relevant Diploma, usually at least 4 GCSEs (A*-C) including English and maths, or equivalent.

Band 4: For HND, Diploma of Higher Education or foundation degree: 1-2 A levels and some GCSEs (A*-C) usually including English and maths, or equivalent.

Band 5: For degree courses: 2-3 A levels and some GCSEs (A*-C) usually including English and maths, or equivalent. Exact requirements depend on the degree you take.

- **Scotland**

Band 3: For entry to jobs, usually at least four S grades (1-3) including English and maths, or similar.

Band 4: For entry to SQA higher national and professional development awards, usually 2-3 H grades and some S grades (1-3), including English and maths, or similar qualifications.

Band 5: For degree courses: 3-5 H grades and some S grades (1-3), including English and maths, or similar qualifications. Exact requirements depend on the degree you take.

Degree Information

Any degree is acceptable and exact entry requirements depend on the course.

Adult Qualifications

There are no fixed educational qualifications but entrants have to be able to cope with courses that are equivalent to higher national awards. Relevant work experience is essential. Entry requirements may be relaxed for adults applying for higher education courses. Access or foundation courses give adults without qualifications a route onto degree courses.

Work Experience

Entry to this job is usually for candidates who have had previous employment in a variety of work areas. Employers may look for voluntary work experience or a background in education and training, working with children of different ages or with the public.

Entry and Training

Entry to this job as an assistant can be with some GCSEs/S grades or equivalent. However, some local authorities may prefer entrants to have studied to degree level. Training is mainly on the job with an experienced colleague, and you need to keep up to date with the law surrounding road safety. There are relevant certificates and diplomas in road safety studies, including a BTEC professional diploma in accident and safety management. This course and others are available by distance-learning programmes. A driving licence is needed. The Institute of Road Safety Officers provides a programme of continuing professional development.

Mature applicants are welcomed as this job is particularly suitable for more experienced people. Experience in teaching, driving, police work or perhaps engineering is an advantage.

Opportunities and Pay

Road safety officers usually work for local authorities. In some authorities the road safety education and engineering departments are combined and, in future, staff may have to be able to cope with both aspects of the work. Some road safety officers specialise in areas such as publicity or working with schools. Promotion to senior posts is possible, but may require moving to another area of the country.

Trainee road safety officers working for county councils earn around £14k-£22k a year. Road safety officers earn around £19k-£26k a year. Senior officers taking on a managerial role can earn up to £36k.

Skills and Qualities

able to work both on your own and in a team, approachable, creative and imaginative flair, energetic, good communication skills, good coordinator, good presentation skills, persuasive, resilient, self confident

Relevant Subjects

English, Psychology, Sociology

Further Information

InRoads (IRSO journal, 3 issues a year) (IRSO) - www.irso.org.uk
Local Authority Road Safety Officers' Association (Road Safety GB) - www.larsoa.org.uk

'THINK' Magazine: Official Road Safety Campaign Magazine (Department for Transport) (UK Department for Transport) - www.thinkroadsafety.gov.uk/think

Addresses

Association of Industrial Road Safety Officers (AIRSO)
68 The Boulevard, Worthing BN13 1LA
Phone: +44 (0)1903 506095
Web: www.airso.org.uk

Institute of Road Safety Officers (IRSO)
Head Office, Pin Point, Rosslyn Crescent, Harrow, Middlesex HA1 2SU
Phone: 0870 010 4442
Web: www.irso.org.uk

Royal Society for the Prevention of Accidents (RoSPA)
RoSPA House, Edgbaston Park, 353 Bristol Road, Edgbaston, Birmingham B5 7ST
Phone: +44 (0)121 248 2000
Web: www.rospa.com

Similar Jobs

Driving Examiner, Driving Instructor, Health & Safety Practitioner, Public Relations Officer, Teacher: Primary School, Teacher: Secondary School

Road Transport Manager

CRCI:Transport and Logistics
CLCI:YAD Job Band: 3 to 5

Job Description

Road transport managers plan and organise the efficient movement by road, of goods or people. They cost the routes and plan the work schedules of drivers and vehicles to ensure optimum profits of a company. Study traffic surveys to revise timetables and rates. Supervise maintenance staff and drivers including the allocation of vehicles to drivers and making emergency plans, for example in case of vehicle breakdown. May be involved in employee recruitment and training. Investigate and deal with customer complaints.

Road transport managers need up-to-date knowledge of the UK/EU laws and regulations relating to the transportation of goods and services. This includes driver hours and environmental issues surrounding fuel emissions and traffic congestion. They ensure that company vehicles are safe, meet legal requirements and customs legislation.

Work Details

You are based in an office, though you may travel to depots and meetings. Shift work is common and you may be expected to work irregular hours and be on call as transport operates 24 hrs a day. You spend a lot of time on the phone, liaising with customers and employees, sometimes dealing with complaints. The work can be demanding at times and involve difficult decisions. Those working for an international company may be required to travel abroad.

The work involves monitoring the attendance and performance of staff, staff appraisal and discipline, administration, planning, safety and legal regulations.

Qualification

Qualifications in business studies or similar subjects are useful, but are not essential. However an increasing number of entrants are graduates.

• England, Wales and Northern Ireland

Band 4: For direct entry to a management training scheme, or for BTEC higher national award: 1-2 A levels, preferably at least one should be economics or geography, and some GCSEs (A*-C) usually including English and maths, or equivalent. For the CILTUK level 5 operational management qualification, an A/AS level in economics or geography is recommended. Equivalent qualifications may be considered.

Band 5: For degree courses: 2-3 A levels preferably including economics and/or geography, and some GCSEs (A*-C) usually including English and maths. Exact requirements depend on the degree you take.

• Scotland

Band 4: For direct entry to a management training scheme or for SQA higher national award: 2-3 H grades, preferably at least one should be economics or geography, and some S grades (1-3) including English and maths, or similar. For the CILTUK level 5 operational management qualification, an H grade in economics or geography, or similar, is recommended.

Band 5: For degree courses: 3-5 H grades preferably including economics and/or geography, and some S grades (1-3), usually including English and maths, or similar.

Degree Information

Any degree is acceptable for entry to this job though transport management/administration, logistics, business studies or transport planning are the most directly related and may give exemption from some of the Chartered Institute of Logistics and Transport (CILTUK) exams. A list of recognised courses is available from the institute. Business studies, industrial relations, economics and human geography degrees also give useful background. Postgraduate qualifications in transportation management are also available.

Adult Qualifications

There may be special entry requirements for adults applying for degree or higher national courses. Contact the universities or colleges for details.

Work Experience

Relevant work or voluntary experience is always useful and can improve your chances in application for entry to this job. Consider work experience in any company dealing with transport or the movement of goods. This can be a road haulage company, a wholesale or retail organisation, or a bus or coach operator.

Entry and Training

Some transport managers start as drivers, administrators, clerical assistants or warehouse operatives and work up to management or supervisory posts, although increasingly entrants are graduates. On-the-job training with part-time study or distance learning for the professional qualifications of the Chartered Institute of Logistics and Transport (CILTUK) is usual. Large transport companies have management training schemes.

You need to have a certificate of professional competence (CPC) in road transport, an award that can be gained at many centres throughout the UK. Those with appropriate qualifications such as those offered by CILTUK are exempt from the CPC. Contact CILTUK for details of courses. A LGV (large goods vehicle) or PCV (passenger carrying vehicle) driving licence may be needed.

Academic qualifications in transport and logistics management range from HNDs, foundation degrees, degrees and postgraduate degrees. VRQs (vocationally related qualifications) are available in national road haulage operations, and relevant S/NVQs such as managing road passenger transport at level 3 and transportation for professionals working in transport at a strategic level are available at level 4.

Mature applicants who are experienced drivers may move into management without requiring formal qualifications. Relevant experience of other jobs in the transport industry or other forms of management are an advantage. There are distance-learning courses available from CILTUK and a number of centres throughout the UK offer the certificate of professional competence (CPC) in road transport through full time, part time or distance learning.

Opportunities and Pay
Road transport accounts for 55% of all freight movement in the UK and opportunities are expected to increase in this industry in the next few years. Road transport managers are employed by road haulage companies, wholesale or retail organisations, local authorities, vehicle rental companies and bus and coach operators. In large companies, promotion is possible to area manager, superintendent or general management. Some experienced managers become transport planners, freelance consultants or set up their own companies. There are opportunities to move between companies and specialise in other modes of transport. Contract haulage has increased in recent years due to larger companies contracting out these services.

Pay depends on the employer or size of company. Starting salaries are around £15k-£20k a year, rising to £25k-£45k with experience. Senior managers earn from around £32k to more than £50k a year. Some may reach as much as £80k. There may be allowances for working unsociable hours, benefits such as a company car and performance-related pay schemes.

Health
You may have to take a medical test.

Skills and Qualities
able to manage people, analytical skills, business awareness, decisive, geographical knowledge, good communication skills, good organisational skills, IT skills, logical, understanding of legal technicalities

Relevant Subjects
Business and accounting, Economics, English, Geography, Mathematics, Retail and distribution

Further Information
AGCAS: Transport and Logistics (Job Sector Briefing) (AGCAS) - www.prospects.ac.uk

Careers in Logistics - www.careersinlogistics.co.uk

Inside Careers Guide: Logistics & Transport Management - www.insidecareers.co.uk

Local Transport Today (fortnightly) (Landor Publishing) - www.transportxtra.com/magazines/local_transport_today/

Logistics and Retail Management (2009) (Kogan Page) - www.koganpage.com

Skills for Logistics - sector skills council for freight logistics industries - www.skillsforlogistics.org

Transport Manager's & Operator's Handbook (2010) (Kogan Page) - www.koganpage.com

Addresses
Chartered Institute of Logistics and Transport (CILTUK)
Careers Manager, Logistics & Transport Centre, Earlstrees Court, Earlstrees Road, Corby NN17 4AX
Phone: +44 (0)1536 740 100
Web: www.ciltuk.org.uk

Institute of Transport Administration (IoTA)
The Old Studio, 25 Greenfield Road, Westoning, Bedfordshire MK45 5JD
Phone: +44 (0)1525 634940
Web: www.iota.org.uk

Similar Jobs
Freight Forwarder, Logistics Manager, Shipbroker/Airbroker, Wholesale Manager

Road Worker

also known as: Highways Maintenance Operative

CRCI:Building and Construction
CLCI:UN Job Band: 1 to 2

Job Description
Road workers build, improve, repair and maintain public roads and pavements. May widen roads, build dual carriageways or carry out resurfacing work. They repair potholes and wide cracks in a road or footpath surface. Duties include laying kerbs and slabs, digging access trenches for pipes/cables and drains, and using digging machines, pneumatic drills, 360-degree excavators, picks, rakes and spades. They spread concrete or tarmac and flatten it with a roller. Roads are painted using an automatic paint-distributing machine and road signs are put up and taken down as and when needed.

Road workers also plant and maintain grass, hedges and landscaped areas around roads. They put up and repair roadside fences, central reservations and barriers. Some road workers spread a mixture of sand/grit and salt on to main road surfaces during icy weather. May also be involved in snow clearance.

Work Details
Road workers usually work a 37-39 hr week, Monday to Friday, though may be required to work some evenings and weekends. They often start early in the morning and may also have to work overtime, or be on call. Road workers work in gangs where each person may have a specialised task. They need to travel around on different contracts and may spend time away from home. The job also involves walking, sometimes on rough ground, bending, and lifting heavy items. Working on the roads can be dusty and sometimes cold and damp. Workers are out in all sorts of weather and need to wear protective clothing and equipment, including ear defenders, hard hats, gloves and boots.

Qualification

• England, Wales and Northern Ireland
Band 1: No minimum qualifications are required, but you are expected to have had a good level of general education. However, some formal/vocational qualifications at any level are useful.

Band 2: No minimum entry qualifications, but it is useful to have some GCSEs, including maths, English, science and technical subjects, or equivalent.

• Scotland
Band 1: No minimum qualifications are required, but you are expected to have had a good level of general education. However, some formal/vocational qualifications at any level are useful.

Band 2: No minimum entry qualifications, but it is useful to have some S grades, including maths, English, science and technical subjects, or similar.

Adult Qualifications
No formal entry qualifications are required. Relevant experience is often more important.

Work Experience
Relevant work or voluntary experience is always useful and can improve your chances when applying for entry to construction jobs and apprenticeships. In some areas there is a young apprenticeship (14-16) scheme that provides an extended work placement and eventual achievement of a level 2 qualification whilst at school. Health and safety issues may mean that there are certain jobs you cannot do until you are over 16. Contact your local ConstructionSkills office for advice.

Entry and Training
Most road workers start as a construction operative. Training is on the job and you learn basic skills and can be assessed in topics such as excavation on the highway, reinstatement of bituminous

material, slabs and footways, and health and safety at work. Relevant S/NVQs are available, such as roadbuilding (construction) at levels 1-2 and highways maintenance at level 2.

On site at least one person must be a trained and qualified operative. To qualify you need either a City & Guilds or CABWI awarding body qualification in street works excavation and reinstatement, or a Scottish Qualifications Authority (SQA) national award in excavation and reinstatement. Qualified operatives and supervisors must apply for a Streetworks registration card, which currently needs to be renewed every five years. Contact Streetworks for information about registration requirements and details of all suitable courses and qualifications.

A Diploma/Welsh Baccalaureate in construction and the built environment may be available in your area. You may also take short courses or day-release courses at a local college or training centre for relevant qualifications to improve your ability and knowledge. Training programmes, including apprenticeships leading to level 2, may be available in your area. Contact ConstructionSkills for details.

Mature applicants can take refresher courses that are sometimes available for those returning to work, and there may be special government training schemes or apprenticeships for adults in some areas. Those with existing experience in the building and construction industry have a good chance of training opportunities. You can also gain recognition of previous experience through Accreditation of Prior Learning (APL) or by working towards relevant S/NVQs. Contact your local careers office, Jobcentre Plus, Next Step service or Learning and Skills Council (LSC)/Local Enterprise Company (LEC) for details of all training opportunities and schemes, including apprenticeships for adults.

Opportunities and Pay

Jobs are available throughout the UK with road repair contractors and civil engineering firms. Many local authorities now use contractors for this work. With experience and practical qualifications you can become a supervisor (or ganger). Some train to work on plant machines. Temporary, casual and seasonal work is often available for those who are sub-contractors or are self-employed.

Pay varies depending on area and employer. Most new entrants start on around £12k-£14k a year; after training this rises to around £15k. A supervisor may earn £17k-£20k a year. Overtime and bonus payments may be available.

Health

You must have stamina and be physically fit to do this job. Upper body strength is important. You should not be allergic to pollens or dust.

Skills and Qualities

able to work both on your own and in a team, common sense, enjoy working outdoors, hard working, manual dexterity, safety conscious

Relevant Subjects

Construction and built environment

Further Information

Apprenticeship Schemes (National Apprenticeship Service) - www.apprenticeships.org.uk

Apprenticeships in Scotland (Careers Info Scotland) - www.apprenticeshipsinscotland.com/about/

ConstructionSkills - sector skills council for the construction industry - www.cskills.org

Diplomas (Foundation, Higher and Advanced) - http://yp.direct.gov.uk/diplomas

Streetworks Qualification Register - www.skillstrainingcentre.co.uk

Training Schemes - www.direct.gov.uk/en/educationandlearning

Welsh Baccalaureate - www.wbq.org.uk

▶ Working in construction & the built environment (2007) (Babcock Lifeskills) - www.babcock-lifeskills.com/

Addresses

CABWI Awarding Body
1 Queen Anne's Gate, London SW1H 9BT
Phone: +44 (0)20 7957 4523
Web: www.cabwi.co.uk

Similar Jobs

Bricklayer, Construction Operative, Construction Plant Operative, Demolition Operative, Mastic Asphalter, Rail Track Maintenance Worker

Roadie

also known as: Road Crew

CRCI:Performing Arts

CLCI:GAD Job Band: 1 to 3

Job Description

Roadies provide technical support when touring with bands, or other musical groups. They assist musicians before and after a live concert or recording, by setting up and dismantling their equipment on stage. Usually load a van, lifting and carrying instruments and equipment. They work with all kinds of sound equipment, including drum sets and guitars, and may also tune some instruments prior to the performance.

Roadies set up and control lighting effects. They use fork-lift trucks and hydraulic lifting equipment to position the lighting and sound equipment. Also set up the stage for rehearsals and concerts, and make sure that the equipment is working. Some specialise, perhaps in sophisticated and complex lighting or special effects (SFX), such as lasers or fireworks (pyrotechnics).

Others may be involved in administrative tasks, such as arranging backstage passes for journalists, friends, relatives, etc. May book hotel/airline tickets and arrange catering facilities. Some roadies drive the truck or van that carries the technical and music equipment.

Work Details

Depending upon the contract, you can work long hours, from early in the morning until very late at night, seven days a week. You need to travel in the UK and possibly abroad and may be away from home for long periods. You have to cope with heavy lifting and carrying, and the work is a mixture of busy and quiet times. Often you need to cope with heights, especially if working with lighting, in concert halls or at outdoor events.

When on tour you may need to spend long hours in a cramped and crowded van or truck. Some roadies may have to sleep and eat their meals in a van or truck.

Qualification

Formal academic qualifications are not needed. Roadies who specialise in working with electrical and electronic equipment may have qualifications in these trades, but often this is not the case.

Adult Qualifications

Formal academic qualifications are not needed but any experience/qualifications in electrical/electronics are useful.

Work Experience

Many enter this industry helping musical friends to move and set up their instruments for an amateur performance, and travelling with them when on tour. You can gain valuable experience with a local theatre or amateur dramatic society assisting in the stage set-up and dismantling processes.

Entry and Training

Most entrants are over 18 and often have friends in the business. You may have to do unpaid work with a loading crew before going on tour. Training is on the job through practical experience and with skilled roadies. Those who specialise in electrical/technical work can take a City & Guilds or SQA course part or full time, maybe as part of an electrical/technical apprenticeship. A Diploma/Welsh Baccalaureate in creative and media may be available in your area. See the diplomas website for further information.

Roadies who specialise in pyrotechnics, lighting effects, sound production and rigging, require technical qualifications. These can usually be obtained by taking short specialist courses. A list of suitable courses is available from the Production Services Association, the British Recorded Music Industry and the Association of British Theatre Technicians. A driving licence is required, particularly an LGV (large goods vehicle) driving licence, or perhaps a PSV (passenger service vehicle) licence. A first aid or health and safety certificate, and skill in other languages may also be useful. The Professional Lighting and Sound Association has useful information on continuing professional development and seminars on its website.

Mature applicants must be able to cope with the physical nature of the job and the strenuous lifestyle. Experience in electronics or electrical work is an advantage.

Opportunities and Pay

You work for a touring musical band/group or a haulage firm specialising in moving bands and their equipment, a music promoter, equipment hire company or music venue. Most roadies are self-employed. Often, you can be employed on short contracts and be without work for some of the time. Vacancies are found advertised in the music press or on the Internet. Often the best way to find work is to hear about opportunities through a network of contacts. With experience you can become a road manager or a band manager.

Pay varies depending on area and employer, but as a guide, an unskilled roadie earns around £50 a concert if employed full time or £12k a year. Those skilled in lighting, audio or other technical areas earn around £20k-£32k. Living expenses are sometimes paid.

Health

You need to have good stamina and be physically fit and healthy. You need good colour vision for certain areas of work.

Skills and Qualities

able to cope under pressure, able to follow instructions, able to get on with all kinds of people, aptitude for teamwork, head for heights, manual dexterity, reliable, safety conscious, strong

Relevant Subjects

Design and technology, Engineering, Mathematics, Music, Physics, Science

Further Information

Diplomas (Foundation, Higher and Advanced) - http://yp.direct.gov.uk/diplomas

Music Tech (Plum Digital Media) - www.musictechmag.co.uk
Music Week (UBM Information Ltd.) - www.musicweek.com

Welsh Baccalaureate - www.wbq.org.uk

▶Working in music (2007) (Babcock Lifeskills) - www.babcock-lifeskills.com/

Addresses

Association of British Theatre Technicians (ABTT)
55 Farringdon Road, London EC1M 3JB
Phone: +44 (0)20 7242 9200
Web: www.abtt.org.uk

British Recorded Music Industry (BPI)
Riverside Building County Hall Westminster Bridge Road, London SE1 7JA
Phone: +44 (0)20 7803 1300
Web: www.bpi.co.uk

Production Services Association
PO Box 2709, Bath, Avon BA1 3YS
Phone: +44 (0)1225 332 668
Web: www.psa.org.uk

Professional Lighting and Sound Association (PLASA)
Redoubt House, 1 Edward Road, Eastbourne BN23 8AS
Phone: +44 (0)1323 524 120
Web: www.plasa.org

Similar Jobs

Driver: Lorry, Film/TV & Theatre Lighting Technician, Film/TV & Theatre SFX Technician, Film/TV/Radio & Theatre Sound Recordist, Removals Operative, Theatre Stagehand

Roofer

CRCI:Building and Construction
CLCI:UF — Job Band: 1 to 2

Job Description

Roofers build, maintain and repair roofs on domestic, public and industrial structures, using a range of materials such as tiles, slate, felt and sheeting. They work on flat or pitched (sloped) roofs, ensuring that they are fully waterproof. May need to strip out old materials and prepare surface for repair or new roof. They measure the area to be covered and calculate the materials needed, then cut them to size.

May specialise in one aspect of roofing, such as laying felt, slates and tiles or cladding and sheeting. A felt roofer puts down layers of felt to make roofs weatherproof and prevent leaks. Usually uses 'torch-on' felts that are laid by applying heat directly to the underside of the felt roll to melt the bitumen. May need to fit insulation board before laying felt. Seals the joints between each sheet to ensure that the covering is weatherproof.

A roofer working with slates and tiles works from the bottom of the roof upwards, laying slates or tiles in horizontal rows and nailing them to battens, ensuring that they overlap. Makes accurate cuts to fit corners and gable ends. Cements ridge tiles to fix securely and seals joints. Uses lead sheet for weatherproof flashings on a range of buildings, including church spires and other unusual shapes.

A sheeter works with aluminium, plastic, fibre-cement, steel and galvanised steel, or glass-reinforced plastic. Some also specialise in fitting wall cladding. May lay fibreglass insulation and/or fit roof lights and waterproof flashings, some of which are made of lead.

Work Details

Roofers usually work a basic 37-39 hr week, though sometimes are required to work overtime, evenings and weekends to complete a job. You work longer hours over the summer months. Work is outdoors and you travel to different sites. You may work in a team of roofers or on your own. The job involves climbing ladders, working at heights on scaffolding, bending, kneeling, lifting and balancing. You may need to operate lifts to work on some roofs. Conditions may be cramped, dirty and often cold, damp and wet. There is a risk of falling and you need to wear a safety helmet, knee pads, outdoor wear or overalls.

Qualification

- **England, Wales and Northern Ireland**

Band 1: No minimum qualifications are required, but you are expected to have had a good level of general education. However, some formal/vocational qualifications at any level are useful.

Band 2: Although academic qualifications are not specified for this job, it is an advantage to have some GCSEs (A*-C) in subjects that include English and maths, or equivalent.

- **Scotland**

Band 1: No minimum qualifications are required, but you are expected to have had a good level of general education. However, some formal/vocational qualifications at any level are useful.

Band 2: Although academic qualifications are not specified for this job, it is an advantage to have some S grades (1-3) in subjects that include English and maths, or similar.

Adult Qualifications
No formal entry requirements, but it may be difficult for adults to find employment without relevant experience.

Work Experience
Relevant work or voluntary experience is always useful and can improve your chances when applying for entry to construction jobs and apprenticeships. In some areas there is a young apprenticeship (14-16) scheme that provides an extended work placement and eventual achievement of a level 2 qualification whilst at school. Health and safety issues may mean that there are certain jobs you cannot do until you are over 16. Contact your local ConstructionSkills office for advice.

Entry and Training
Training is usually work based together with a day or block-release college course. Various flexible training schemes are available from ConstructionSkills and City & Guilds. Most people enter this job through a three-year construction apprenticeship scheme (four years in Scotland), which you can apply for in Year 11 (January). You may have to take an entrance test before you start training. You work towards gaining a level of competence card through a Construction Skills Certification Scheme (CSCS) to indicate your individual skill level. The Institute of Roofing offers its own professional qualifications and can also offer advice on the development of skills within the industry.

A Diploma/Welsh Baccalaureate in construction and the built environment may be available in your area. S/NVQs are available in roofing occupations at levels 2-3, applied waterproof membranes at level 1, roof sheeting and cladding, and slating and tiling, also at at levels 2-3. Training programmes, including apprenticeships leading to level 2, and advanced apprenticeships/construction apprenticeships leading to level 3, may be available in your area. There are also Construction Awards (England and Wales) available for those who are unable to gain workplace experience for NVQs.

Specialist training is also available for those who wish to concentrate on achieving skills in restoration and heritage work. Contact the National Heritage Training Group (NHTG) for further information.

Those with a minimum of four GCSEs (A*-C)/S grades (1-3) and S/NVQ level 2 in roofing may train as roofing technicians and become more involved in estimating and planning.

Mature applicants can take refresher courses that are sometimes available for those returning to work and there may be special government training schemes or apprenticeships for adults in some areas. Employers may take older applicants who show aptitude and have previous experience. You can also gain recognition of previous experience through Accreditation of Prior Learning (APL) or by working towards relevant S/NVQs. Contact your local careers office, Jobcentre Plus, Next Step service or Learning and Skills Council (LSC)/Local Enterprise Company (LEC) for details of training schemes.

Opportunities and Pay
Work is located throughout the UK with employers such as roofing firms, building contractors and local authorities. Availability of work depends to some extent on the state of the building trade and the national economy. Currently there is a downturn in the housing market which means there may be a shortage of vacancies. Some roofers are self-employed and work as contractors. Others work on a 'labour only' basis using an employer's roofing materials. Some work abroad on contracts. Promotion to become a supervisor is possible, mostly in larger firms. Progression to technician level and then to construction management is also possible.

Pay varies depending on location and employer. Trainees usually earn around £12k a year; with skill and experience this can rise to around £15k-£20k. Some earn around £20k-£25k a year. Overtime and bonus payments may be available.

Health
Good physical fitness, agility and stamina is needed, and you should not be allergic to dust.

Skills and Qualities
able to estimate, able to follow drawings and plans, able to follow instructions, aptitude for figures, aptitude for teamwork, attention to detail, enjoy working outdoors, head for heights, practical skills, safety conscious

Relevant Subjects
Construction and built environment, Design and technology

Further Information
Apprenticeship Schemes (National Apprenticeship Service) - www.apprenticeships.org.uk

Construction Awards - http://gbca.com/events/construction-awards

ConstructionSkills - sector skills council for the construction industry - www.cskills.org

Diplomas (Foundation, Higher and Advanced) - http://yp.direct.gov.uk/diplomas

Institute of Roofing - www.institute of roofing.org

Roofing Magazine online (Warners Group Publications Ltd.) - www.roofingmag.com

Training Schemes - www.direct.gov.uk/en/educationandlearning

Welsh Baccalaureate - www.wbq.org.uk

▶Working in construction & the built environment (2007) (Babcock Lifeskills) - www.babcock-lifeskills.com/

Addresses
Institute of Roofing (IOR)
Roofing House, 31 Worship Street, London EC2A 2DX
Phone: +44 (0)20 7448 3858
Web: www.instituteofroofing.org.uk

National Federation of Roofing Contractors
Roofing House, 31 Worship Street, London EC2A 2DY
Phone: +44 (0)20 7638 7663
Web: www.nfrc.co.uk

National Heritage Training Group (NHTG)
Carthusian Court, 12 Carthusian Street, London EC1M 6EZ
Phone: 0300 456 5517 (UK only)
Web: www.nhtg.org.uk

Similar Jobs
Carpenter/Joiner, Ceiling Fixer, Scaffolder, Steeplejack, Thatcher

ROV Pilot
also known as: Remote Operated Vehicle Pilot, ROV Technician

CRCI:Engineering
CLCI:ROB Job Band: 4 to 5

Job Description
ROV pilots use a remote operated vehicle (ROV) to perform a range of underwater tasks, often at depths that divers cannot operate. The ROV is usually piloted from and connected to a ship or offshore platform. Pilots use ROVs to inspect and monitor existing structures or equipment, such as oil and gas platforms, for health and safety purposes. They also assist with marine

construction projects, such as the laying of cables on the sea bed, or pipelines. Other uses of ROVs include operating and maintaining valves on subsea manifolds, and observing divers by video.

ROV pilots keep a log (activity record) for each operation. They move the ROV in and out of the water with the use of a crane. Also undertake routine maintenance and solve technical problems. They work mainly in the oil and gas industry and for marine construction companies.

Work Details

You are most likely to work shifts that cover 24 hrs. You often work outdoors in poor weather. This is highly responsible work as the lives of fellow workers can depend on assessments of the construction project, using ROVs. You usually work as part of a team with other ROV pilots, headed by a supervisor, sometimes known as an offshore party chief. A significant amount of time can be spent away from home, particularly when working offshore. Travelling to and from the oil and gas platforms can be quite dangerous. The work is not as seasonal as conventional diving.

Qualification

To work in this area there are no set educational qualifications, though most ROV pilots are educated to HND or degree level in a technical subject.

• England, Wales and Northern Ireland

Band 4: For HND in electrical and electronic engineering, Diploma of Higher Education or foundation degree: 1-2 A levels including maths and a science (preferably physics), or computing science or technology, plus some GCSEs (A*-C) including English, or equivalent.

Band 5: For relevant degree courses: usually 2-3 A levels, preferably including maths and physics, and some GCSEs (A*-C) including English, and sometimes chemistry and a modern language, or equivalent. Exact requirements depend on the degree you take.

• Scotland

Band 4: For entry to SQA higher national in electrical and electronic engineering and professional development awards, usually 2-3 H grades, including maths and a science (preferably physics), or computing science or technology, plus some S grades (1-3) including English, or similar qualifications.

Band 5: For relevant degree: usually 3-5 H grades, preferably including maths and physics, and some S grades (1-3) including English, and sometimes chemistry and a modern language, or similar qualifications. Exact requirements depend on the degree you take.

Degree Information

Degrees in engineering that include the study of electronics, hydraulics, pneumatics, plant maintenance or electrical engineering, are most useful.

Adult Qualifications

A degree or higher national award in electrical engineering, or similar, may be preferred. There are many Access or foundation courses suitable for entry to engineering. Entry requirements may be relaxed for suitable adults applying for higher education courses.

Work Experience

Employers or colleges/universities may prefer candidates who have relevant work or voluntary experience. This may include work in any area of engineering or electronics, particularly in the marine construction industry. Schemes such as 'A Year in Industry' give those who expect good A levels/H grades and intend to go to university the opportunity to spend a salaried year with a company to gain valuable work experience.

The Engineering Education Scheme, run by the Engineering Development Trust, offers programmes in England, Scotland and Wales giving young people the chance to be involved in a real engineering project for six months. Students commit to two to three hours work a week and some time at university residents' workshops. This valuable experience can contribute to any future university application and counts towards the Duke of Edinburgh award skills section. Check the website for details.

Similarly, Headstart offers students a chance to experience a week at university, designing, building and testing projects. As engineering careers can be quite diverse, a week of hands on experience such as this can be really helpful when students are trying to decide which field of engineering they want to train in.

Entry and Training

This area of work is not suitable for school leavers due to lack of experience. Mature applicants with relevant qualifications and experience are preferred, especially those who have completed a period of relevant technical employment or training, together with a good background in electronics or hydraulics. Some of the larger ROV contractors train personnel in house. There are also courses in ROV training that are approved by the International Marine Contractors Association (IMCA) and run by training agencies. These include courses in entry level requirements for new remote operated vehicle personnel, hydraulics and health and safety management. It is an advantage but not essential to study these courses.

Training may take place in an onshore glass-walled training pool with dive sites that simulate offshore conditions, as well as a range of underwater structures of concrete and steel, shipwrecks etc. You then progress to real work and wreck sites. The Underwater Centre offers several course modules ranging from beginners to courses for experienced ROV pilot technicians, with extensive electronic engineering experience. The website has comprehensive information on the IMCA guidlines for ROV personnel. Relevant S/NVQs are available in electronics/ engineering subjects. If working offshore, all entrants also need to take a basic offshore safety induction and emergency training (BOSIET) course. BOSIET courses vary in length between providers - usually 2.5 to 3 days, and with the advent of e-learning some providers allow the theory parts to be completed via the internet.

A Diploma/Welsh Baccalaureate may be available in your area in engineering. The advanced level is equivalent to 3.5 A levels but for some university courses, the additional and specialist learning component of the diploma needs to include specific A levels eg maths or physics. Check entry requirements carefully with the individual institutions. See the diplomas website for further information.

Mature applicants are preferred, usually having completed a period of relevant technical employment or training, together with a good background in electronics or hydraulics. Experience with pneumatics, plant maintenance or electrical engineering are also of interest to employers.

Opportunities and Pay

Currently, there is a skills shortage of experienced ROV pilots. You usually start as a junior ROV technician and work your way up. Jobs are mainly in the oil and gas industry, either directly with marine construction companies or with specialist employment agencies. Increasingly, ROVs are being used in marine archaeology, the investigation of shipwrecks, environmental science surveys, in civil engineering and in defence and security. It may also be possible to do inland work, or harbour surveys. Some ROV pilots move into supervisory and management positions, particularly with contracting companies or in the wider marine construction industry. Most ROV contracting companies operate throughout the world, so there are good opportunities for travel.

You often earn a daily contract rate but some are employed on an annual salary of around £30k-£40k. Daily rates vary from around £180-£450 a day, depending on qualifications and experience. The highest salaries are usually in the oil and gas industry and can be around £60k a year. Allowances are usually paid for time spent offshore.

Health

To work offshore in any capacity, it is necessary to undergo and pass a special medical examination. This job requires normal colour vision.

Skills and Qualities

able to cope under pressure, able to work both on your own and in a team, good co-ordination, IT skills, quick thinking, responsible attitude, safety conscious, spatial awareness, technical aptitude, vigilant

Relevant Subjects

Design and technology, Engineering, ICT/Computer studies, Mathematics, Physics, Science

Further Information

Cogent - sector skills souncil for chemicals, pharmaceuticals, nuclear, oil & gas, petroleum & polymers - www.cogent-ssc.com

Diplomas (Foundation, Higher and Advanced) - http://yp.direct.gov.uk/diplomas

Diving and Undersea Vehicles
(Society for Underwater Technology (SUT)) - www.sut.org.uk/

Engineering Education Scheme - www.engineering-education.org.uk/

Engineering Education Scheme Wales - www.eesw.org.uk

Headstart Scheme - www.headstartcourses.org.uk

I want to be a ROV Pilot/Technician (IMCA factsheet) (IMCA) - www.imca-int.com/documents/careers/

ROV Exchange - www.rovexchange.com

SEMTA - sector skills council for science, engineering and manufacturing technologies - www.semta.org.uk

Serpent - www.serpentproject.com

Year in Industry (Engineering Development Trust) - www.yini.org.uk

Addresses

Engineering Development Trust (EDT)
Ridgeway, Welwyn Garden City, Hertfordshire AL7 2AA
Phone: +44 (0)1707 871520
Web: www.etrust.org.uk

International Marine Contractors Association (IMCA)
52 Grosvenor Gardens, London SW1W 0AU
Phone: +44 (0)20 7824 5520
Web: www.imca-int.com/careers

Society for Underwater Technology (SUT)
80 Coleman Street, London EC2R 5BJ
Phone: +44 (0)20 7382 2601
Web: www.sut.org.uk

Underwater Centre
Marine Walk Carmichael Way, Fort William,
Invernesshire PH33 6FF
Phone: +44 (0)1397 703786
Web: www.theunderwatercentre.co.uk

Similar Jobs

Diver, Engineer: Aeronautical, Engineer: Electronics, Engineer: Marine, Engineer: Mechanical

Royal Marines Commando

CRCI:Security and Armed Forces
CLCI:BAB Job Band: 1 to 2

Job Description

Royal marine commandos serve in the frontline strike force of the Royal Navy in commando units and on ships of the Fleet. Are primarily trained for special combat on land or sea. Commando units include air and special boat squadrons. Train to a very high level of physical combat fitness to operate successfully in any environment throughout the world. Are highly trained in a wide range of skills, such as mountaineering and climbing, skiing, parachuting, and survival skills. Also learn multi-weapons handling and map reading. Can be involved in mountain, arctic and jungle operations. Assist in natural disasters, such as floods and earthquakes, in any area of the world.

Most commandos initially serve as riflemen, but can also specialise in one of a wide range of trades or roles, such as engineers, mechanics, chefs, and mountain leaders. Others serve as clerical workers, communications technicians, physical training instructors, drivers, vehicle mechanics, and in weapons and signals.

Work Details

Commandos usually work eight-hour shifts but are on call at all times. You can be posted to serve wherever needed around the world, and sometimes be in dangerous situations. This is a physically active job and much of the time is spent working and training outdoors. You are expected to work long and irregular hours when on operations and exercises, respond to supervision and accept discipline. The work can be very demanding and requires coping with the sight of blood.

Your work environment can often be tough and uncomfortable. You have to cope with considerable physical exertion. When on active service you may be in danger of being injured or killed. You need to wear a uniform and protective clothing.

Qualification

You are not required to have educational qualifications though all applicants must pass a selection test (which covers reasoning, literacy, numeracy and mechanical comprehension), an interview, a medical examination and the three-day Potential Royal Marines Course (PRMC).

- **England, Wales and Northern Ireland**

Band 1: Although no qualifications are needed some GCSEs are useful, especially in English and maths or equivalent.

Band 2: For certain areas of work: some GCSEs (A*-C) including English and maths or equivalent qualifications may be required.

- **Scotland**

Band 1: Although no qualifications are needed some S grades are useful, especially in English and maths or similar.

Band 2: For certain areas of work: some S grades (1-3) including English and maths, or similar qualifications.

Adult Qualifications

You are not required to have formal educational qualifications though all applicants must pass a selection test.

Work Experience

Relevant work or voluntary experience is always useful and can improve your chances when applying for entry to the armed forces. It can help you to decide which trade or branch of the armed services is most appropriate for you. As a young person, getting involved in groups such as a local cadet organisation, or the scouts/guides, helps to show enthusiasm and commitment. Often you can gain valuable experience from a school's Combined Cadet Force (CCF). Fitness is a requirement for the armed forces, so evidence of an interest in keeping fit is useful.

Entry and Training

There are nationality and residency requirements. Entry is very competitive and selection is based on aptitude, character and personality. Applicants must be at least 151.5 cm (5 ft) tall with the minimum weight requirement being 60 kg. You must be at least 16 yrs old, and under 33. However, no commando is deployed on operational duties before the age of 18. This occupation is exempt from the Sex Discrimination Act and currently only male entrants are accepted.

Basic commando training of 32 weeks takes place at the Commando Training Centre at Lympstone, Devon. It includes one week of amphibious warfare skills training in Dorset, some classroom work, as well as tough physical training. The final three-day exercise on Dartmoor uses all your skills and training to achieve the prestigious Green Beret, and to become a commando. After basic training, marines can work towards gaining civilian national qualifications, awards and diplomas. These can range from apprenticeships to leadership and management qualifications or degrees. These qualifications prove valuable when returning to civilian life.

Mature applicants are welcome and some work experience related to the type of trade applied for is helpful. The current upper age limit is 26. Check regulations carefully.

Opportunities and Pay

There are 7,200 commandos in the Royal Marines at present, and currently there is a shortage. Nevertheless entry is very competitive. You must complete a minimum length of service. All commandos are offered a full career from age 18-40. It may be possible to extend this depending on personnel requirements at the time. You must serve a minimum of three years from when you join or from 18, whichever is the later. Promotion to the rank of corporal or sergeant is possible for marines who have a good record in work and training. Promotion to commissioned officer level is also possible. When you leave the Marines, the skills and nationally recognised qualifications gained can be used to transfer to civilian work.

Pay on entry is currently £13k; trained commandos earn £16k-£28k a year. Warrant Officer 1 earns up to £45k. Extra allowances are given for family separation and special service. Certain specialists, such as qualified divers and those working on submarines, receive additional pay.

Health

Applicants must pass a very strict medical test. Good eyesight is required and normal colour vision is needed for certain areas of work. There are regular medical check ups. You are expected to reach a high level of physical fitness. Ask your local armed forces careers office for full details.

Skills and Qualities

able to follow orders, able to live and work closely with other people, aptitude for teamwork, determined, good stamina and physically fit, head for heights, prepared to go into combat, quick reactions, self-reliant, technical aptitude

Relevant Subjects

Design and technology, Geography, Physical education and sport

Further Information

Careers Information package (Royal Navy) - www.royalnavy.mod.uk/

Navy News (monthly) (Royal Navy) - www.navynews.co.uk/

Royal Marines - www.royalmarines.mod.uk/careers

Skills for Work (Scottish Qualifications Authority) - www.sqa.org.uk/sqa/31390.html

▶Working in police, fire & security (2009) (Babcock Lifeskills) - www.babcock-lifeskills.com/

Similar Jobs

Army Officer, Army Soldier, Diver, Royal Marines Officer, Royal Navy Diver, Royal Navy Rating

Royal Marines Musician/Bugler

CRCI:Security and Armed Forces
CLCI:BAB

Job Band: 1 to 2

Job Description

Royal marine musicians/buglers provide musical support for the Royal Navy/Royal Marines Band Service (RMBS) on every type of occasion. They are universally recognised as one of the finest musical bodies worldwide. Perform in an orchestra/band and play music ranging from marching music to classical and pop standards. Certain musicians may be required to play two instruments; for instance clarinet/cornet players may also perform on the violin. Buglers play the bugle, snare drum and E flat herald trumpet, and have a different rank structure and uniform.

In addition to music-making, musicians/buglers are also trained as part of the Royal Navy Medical Branch, and may serve as casualty handlers on hospital ships.

Work Details

The work can be strenuous and you need to maintain fitness throughout your career. You perform every variety of music in a vast array of venues that include official ceremonial events, television, recording and radio work. During busy periods there is a constant stream of performances, sometimes two each day, including rehearsals when the time allows. The job involves a lot of unsociable hours and travelling from place to place, including overseas.

You work under supervision and are required to accept discipline. In times of conflict you carry out medical duties. When on active service you can be in danger of being injured or killed. This job requires you to wear a uniform.

Qualification

The Scottish Qualifications Authority (SQA) launched a new Skills for Work course in 2008. This course introduces candidates to the uniformed and emergency services and is particularly suited to those considering a career in the Army, Royal Navy, Royal Air Force or Royal Marines. Check the website for details.

• England, Wales and Northern Ireland

Band 1: No formal qualifications are required. Personal qualities, musical ability and good motivation are considered important.

Band 2: Although formal qualifications are not needed, some GCSEs or equivalent at any level are helpful. Personal qualities, musical ability and good motivation are important.

• Scotland

Band 1: Formal qualifications are not needed. Personal qualities, musical ability and good motivation are important.

Band 2: Although formal qualifications are not needed, some S grades or similar at any level are helpful. Personal qualities, musical ability and good motivation are important.

Adult Qualifications

No formal educational qualifications are required for entry though you have to pass a selection test.

Work Experience

Relevant work or voluntary experience is always useful and can improve your chances when applying for entry to the armed forces. Membership of a school/youth orchestra, or a marching band like the Sea Cadets or Boys' Brigade, is an advantage. Fitness is a requirement for the armed forces, so evidence of an interest in keeping fit is useful.

Entry and Training

Entry is very competitive and selection is based on aptitude, character and personality. There are strict nationality and residency requirements for entry to the RMBS. Applicants must be aged between 16 and 33, and of 151.5 cm (5 ft) minimum height. For entry you need to pass the Royal Naval Recruitment Test, that includes literacy, numeracy and mechanical comprehension, and attend 5 days of musical auditions at the Royal Marines School of Music.

The ability to play an instrument well is important. If there are no vacancies in your instrument category, you may have to learn one or even two new instruments. Many players have to be 'double-handed' because of the range of music (orchestral, dance and military) performed by the Band Service. Bugle players are required to play at a level comparable to Grade 8 due to the number of high profile engagements the Royal Marines Band Service undertake each year.

The first 16 weeks of training covers physical fitness, infantry and medical skills. You then start specialist qualification study. This is 2 years and 8 months for Musicians and 2 years for Buglers. You have individual lessons on each instrument. There are also classes in the elements of music, aural (hearing) training, orchestral instrumental practice, band instrumental practice training, band (marching and playing) and choir practice. Students are trained in all aspects of military music. All musicians studying at the School have the opportunity to commence study on a BMus (Hons) Degree Course validated by an external exam board.

At the end of your training period you are ready to join your first marine band as a Royal Marines Musician. There are five bands in the Service but you may not get to play in the one you choose in the first instance.

Mature applicants should note that currently, the upper age limit for entry is usually under 33 years. Some relevant musical experience is useful such as membership of a marching band. Personal qualities and good motivation are considered important.

Opportunities and Pay

There are around 350 members of the RMBS at present. This job requires a great deal of personal commitment and you must complete a minimum length of service. The length of your career is flexible. After you complete initial training you can serve up to 32 years, earning a pension and a lump sum. As a musician/bugler or an NCO you can serve to the age of 40 or even 50, providing you maintain your full fitness and ability. Those with both musical and leadership qualities can be selected for a command course leading to promotion to band corporal or sergeant. Further promotion to bandmaster is also possible. All officers in the RMBS are promoted from the ranks.

Buglers may be promoted to colour sergeant bugler and warrant officer and require no further musical qualifications. However, educational examinations have to be passed for advancement to warrant officer. Buglers can then be selected for training as drum majors or bugle majors. The training/qualifications received in this job provide a good basis for occupations in civilian life.

Musicians start on a salary of £13k. Once trained, musicians can earn up to £28k a year.

Health

Applicants must pass a medical test. There are regular medical checkups. You are expected to reach a high level of physical fitness. Check with your local armed forces careers information offices for detailed information on current health regulations.

Skills and Qualities

able to live and work closely with other people, adventurous, dedicated, good co-ordination, outstanding musical ability, practical skills, self confident, self-disciplined, smart appearance, versatile.

Relevant Subjects

Media and communication studies, Music, Physical education and sport

Further Information

Careers Information package (Royal Navy) - www.royalnavy.mod.uk/

Navy News (monthly) (Royal Navy) - www.navynews.co.uk/

Royal Marines - www.royalmarines.mod.uk/careers

Skills for Work (Scottish Qualifications Authority) - www.sqa.org.uk/sqa/31390.html

▶Working in music (2007) (Babcock Lifeskills) - www.babcock-lifeskills.com/

▶Working in police, fire & security (2009) (Babcock Lifeskills) - www.babcock-lifeskills.com/

Addresses

Royal Marines Band Service HQ
Walcheren Building Whale Island, Portsmouth,
Hampshire PO2 8ER
Web: www.royalmarinesbands.co.uk/pages/index1.htm

Similar Jobs

Army Soldier, Merchant Navy Deck Rating, Musician: Classical, RAF Airman/Airwoman, Royal Marines Commando, Royal Navy Rating

Royal Marines Officer

also known as: Marines Officer

CRCI:Security and Armed Forces

CLCI:BAB Job Band: 4 to 5

Job Description

A Royal Marines officer is trained to lead elitist commando troops for frontline strike operations on land, sea and air, or wherever they are needed around the world, both within and outside NATO. May be responsible for troops involved in arctic, desert, mountain or jungle warfare, or on duty in areas of conflict or disaster. Is highly trained in a wide range of skills, such as mountaineering and climbing, skiing, parachuting, and survival skills.

Some serve in the Special Boat Squadron or detachments with the Royal Navy. Others specialise in intelligence, signals, landing craft, motor transport or weapons and there are opportunities to train as helicopter pilots or mountain leaders.

Work Details

You are expected to work unusual hours, including shifts (usually eight hours), and are always on call. You are responsible for the safety and welfare of those under your command. Officers plan and organise the work and are expected to solve problems quickly and act decisively. RM officers work on land or sea, and can be on active duty anywhere worldwide. The work is often physically demanding and can also be emotionally stressful at times.

You must be able to cope with working at heights, carrying weights, and in extremes of heat and cold. When on active duty you may be in dangerous situations, where you can be at risk of being injured or killed. A uniform and protective clothing is necessary.

Qualification

The Scottish Qualifications Authority (SQA) launched a new Skills for Work course in 2008. This course introduces candidates to the uniformed and emergency services and is particularly suited to those considering a career in the Army, Royal Navy, Royal Air Force or Royal Marines. Check the website for details.

- **England, Wales and Northern Ireland**

Band 4: The minimum entry requirements are five GCSEs (A*-C) including English language, mathematics and two A levels. Applicants with alternative qualifications are considered on their individual merits.

Band 5: For degree courses leading to graduate entry (full/short service commission): 2-3 A levels and some GCSEs (A*-C) including maths and English. The exact requirements depend on the degree you take.

- **Scotland**

Band 4: The minimum entry requirements are five S grades (1-3) including English language and mathematics and three H grades. Applicants with alternative qualifications are considered on their individual merits.

Band 5: For degree courses leading to graduate entry (full/short service commission): 3-5 H grades and some S grades (1-3) including maths and English, or similar qualifications. Check individual requirements.

Degree Information

Direct graduate entrants must have a UK degree and English and maths at GCSE (A*-C) or equivalent qualifications.

Adult Qualifications

Formal academic secondary education qualifications and a degree (or equivalent qualifications) are needed, depending on the type of commission and the experience of the applicant. Direct entrants should be between 17 and 26 on the first day of the month of entry. Maximum age limits vary depending on the specialism but late entry is rare.

Work Experience

Entry to this job is competitive and it is important that you try to do some relevant work or voluntary experience before applying. Direct experience with the marines is not possible but work experience that enables you to develop your skills in leadership and in areas that enable you to demonstrate your initiative and responsibility, may help your application. As a young person, getting involved in groups such as a local cadet organisation or the scouts/guides, helps to show enthusiasm and commitment. Often you can gain valuable experience from a school's Combined Cadet Force (CCF).

Entry and Training

Entry is extremely competitive and selection is based on aptitude, character and personality. There are nationality and residency requirements. Applicants must be at least 17 and usually up to age 26, but the maximum age for officer entry varies according to specialism. This occupation is exempt from the Sex Discrimination Act and currently only male entrants are accepted. Candidates attend a Potential Officers Course (POC) and, if considered suitable, they are invited to attend an Admiralty Interview Board (AIB). Both the POC and the AIB combine physical and academic tests designed to assess leadership potential.

Training is extremely demanding, with the first 60 weeks (Phase One) spent at the Commando Training Centre at Lympstone in Devon. It consists of periods of distinct training (initial, military, amphibious and commando), lasting a total of 32 weeks leading to the award of the Marines' Green Beret. Phase One is structured to develop the Young Officer's skills to a level where they can work in a unit as soon as they pass out. This is followed by Phase Two training which consists of a 12 month probationary period in one of the Units in the Royal Marines Command.

You are expected to keep training throughout your career. The Royal Marines award bursaries for university study, and scholarships for students at school taking A levels/H grades. Check the website for full details.

Mature applicants should note that currently there are age restrictions for certain routes of entry, the usual maximum age being 26. There may be financial support for adults, including a university cadetship for those who have gained a place, or a definite offer, for a UK recognised degree. Contact your local armed forces careers office for information.

Opportunities and Pay

Though the Royal Marines is a relatively small force there is always a demand for suitable applicants. This is a very demanding job that requires a great deal of personal commitment. Marines officers usually start with a short term commission of twelve years, of which you are required to serve at least 3-5 years after completing phase two training. Skills and training gained in the Marines can provide a good basis for occupations in civilian life. The promotion structure for full career officers is clearly defined, but beyond certain ranks is based on selection.

Pay increases with promotion. Second lieutenants earn from £23k-£31k a year. Captains earn £36k-£43k and senior colonels £92k-£96k a year. Extra allowances are given for family separation, flying duties and special service. Certain specialists such as qualified divers and those working on submarines, receive additional pay. Perks may include generous leave, a travel allowance and the use of recreational facilities.

Health

Applicants must pass a very strict medical test. Good eyesight is required and normal colour vision is needed for certain areas of work. There are regular medical check ups. You are expected to reach a high level of physical fitness. Ask your local armed forces careers office for full details.

Skills and Qualities

able to discipline, able to live and work closely with other people, aptitude for teamwork, good spoken and written communication, information handling skills, initiative, leadership qualities, prepared to go into combat, quick reactions

Relevant Subjects

Design and technology, Engineering, English, Geography, Government and politics, Mathematics, Physical education and sport, Physics, Psychology, Science

Further Information

Careers Information package (Royal Navy) - www.royalnavy.mod.uk/

Navy News (monthly) (Royal Navy) - www.navynews.co.uk/

Skills for Work (Scottish Qualifications Authority) - www.sqa.org.uk/sqa/31390.html

TARGETjobs: Public Service (GTI Specialist Publishing Ltd.) - www.groupgti.com

▶Working in police, fire & security (2009) (Babcock Lifeskills) - www.babcock-lifeskills.com/

Similar Jobs

Army Officer, Merchant Navy Deck/Navigating Officer, Merchant Navy Engineering Officer, RAF Officer, Royal Marines Commando, Royal Navy Officer

Royal Navy Diver

CRCI:Security and Armed Forces
CLCI:BAB

Job Band: 1 to 2

Job Description

Royal navy divers undertake a wide range of diving tasks, either based on shore or on Royal Navy (RN) vessels. Primary tasks involve underwater mine and explosive ordnance disposal, and a diver is deployed once a ship has found a target using its mine-hunting sonar. Provide advice to those in command of any threats surrounding explosive ordnance disposal. Use highly specialised, state of the art diving equipment. Usually work in a team of 5-6 divers based on board a ship, or are part of a shore-based team that performs extensive underwater tasks on a vessel.

Also conduct a range of surveying operations and large engineering tasks, including propeller blade removal. Take part in national and multinational naval exercises.

Work Details

Ratings can be posted to serve at sea or shore establishments and are expected to work eight-hour shifts that can include weekends and public holidays. There is opportunity to travel worldwide and you can be away from home for long periods of time. You work under supervision, usually in teams, and are required to accept discipline. The work may be very demanding and teamwork is essential. You may have to cope with rough weather at sea, be expected to climb ladders, and generally cope with life aboard a ship or submarine.

Your work environment can be cold, damp and confined. When on active duty, there is a risk of being injured or killed. You need to wear a uniform.

Qualification

All applicants must pass selection tests in literacy, numeracy, reasoning and mechanical comprehension. Check with your local armed forces careers office for details.

• England, Wales and Northern Ireland

Band 1: No formal qualifications are needed though GCSEs or equivalent at any level are useful.

Band 2: Some GCSEs (A*-C) including English, maths, and a suitable science subject or equivalent qualifications are desirable, but not essential.

• Scotland

Band 1: No formal qualifications are needed though S Grades or similar at any level are useful.

Band 2: Some S grades (1-3), such as English, maths, and a suitable science subject or similar qualifications are desirable, but not essential.

Adult Qualifications

Fitness is more important than formal qualifications. However, entrants to the armed forces have to meet specific entry requirements.

Work Experience

Relevant work or voluntary experience is always useful and can improve your chances in application for entry to this career. Areas to consider are those that develop your skills in leadership, as well as areas that enable you to demonstrate your initiative and responsibility. As a young person, getting involved in groups such as a local cadet organisation, or the scouts/guides, shows enthusiasm and commitment. Developing your skills in swimming and sports diving is also very helpful.

Entry and Training

There are nationality and residency requirements for entry. The minimum age for joining is 18 and the current upper age limit is up to 33. Preference is given to those with previous diving experience, either commercial or sub-aqua. This occupation is exempt from the Sex Discrimination Act and currently only male entrants are accepted. All rating entrants spend nine weeks of basic training at HMS Raleigh at Torpoint (Plymouth) and then must pass a one week aptitude course at the Defence Diving School in Portsmouth. Divers then go on to professional training (20 weeks), which includes diving theory, open-water search techniques, basic mine warfare training, mine clearance dive techniques, underwater engineering techniques and deep-water diving up to a depth of 60 metres.

You are then posted to a ship based at Portsmouth or Faslane in Scotland to consolidate your training. Depending on service requirements at the time, you may be posted to front line service for a period of 12-24 months. On completion of training, you are awarded the Health & Safety Executive (HSE) accredited diver certificate. Apart from specialised diver training, it is also possible to study for national educational qualifications at all levels, including degrees.

Mature applicants should note that the upper age limit for entry is currently up to 33. Preference is given to those with previous diving experience. Those with mechanical/civil engineering experience or construction also have an advantage. Check current regulations carefully.

Opportunities and Pay

There are opportunities for advancement in the Royal Navy with around 25% of ratings becoming officers. You must complete a minimum length of service. You can give twelve month's notice two and half years after you have completed your initial professional training. This can sometimes be a short career but your skills, training and qualifications can be used to transfer to civilian work.

Pay on entry is currently £13k a year; able ratings earn £16k-£28k; leading ratings £27k-£32k; petty officers earn £28k-£36k; chief petty officers £32k-£42k and warrant officers earn £37k-£45k. Pay increases with promotion and you receive a travel allowance, free uniform and accommodation allowance if required, plus additional pay for family separations, and bonuses after completing a specified length of service. The specialism attracts cash bonuses according to skill and responsibility levels.

Health

Applicants must pass a strict medical test, and there are regular medical check ups at times during your career. You are expected to reach a high level of physical fitness. All applicants must also pass a series of strength tests and a fitness test that requires you to be able to run 1.5 km in your best time.

Skills and Qualities

able to work in confined spaces, adaptable, alert, aptitude for teamwork, attention to detail, good concentration level, good stamina and physically fit, loyal, technical aptitude, willing to learn

Relevant Subjects

Engineering, Physical education and sport

Further Information

Careers Information package (Royal Navy) - www.royalnavy.mod.uk/

Health and Safety Executive - www.hse.gov.uk

Navy News (monthly) (Royal Navy) - www.navynews.co.uk/

Skills for Work (Scottish Qualifications Authority) - www.sqa.org.uk/sqa/31390.html

▶Working in police, fire & security (2009) (Babcock Lifeskills) - www.babcock-lifeskills.com/

Similar Jobs

Army Soldier, Diver, Merchant Navy Deck Rating, RAF Airman/Airwoman, Royal Marines Commando, Royal Navy Rating

Royal Navy Officer

CRCI:Security and Armed Forces
CLCI:BAB — Job Band: 4 to 5

Job Description

Royal navy officers command, motivate and lead the many personnel that make up the Royal Navy (RN). There are several specialist roles within the Royal Navy; these include warfare officer, training management officer, air traffic controller, engineering officer, logistics officer, medical, dental and nursing officers and naval chaplains. The Royal Navy operates warships, submarines, ship-borne aircraft, as well as many support vessels and shore stations.

Royal Navy Officer

Lead those working to keep ships, weapons systems, communications and all other equipment at peak performance. Serve to protect our country (and others worldwide) from attack. Also guard our coastline and offshore interests, such as oil, gas and fisheries. Play an important role for our allies of the North Atlantic Treaty Organisation (NATO).

Naval ships are on constant alert against drug traffickers, illegal immigrants and terrorists. May be required to assist following environmental disasters, such as floods and oil spills, or carry out search and rescue operations on land and on sea. Officers are also responsible for the general day-to-day welfare and discipline of the ratings (sailors) under their command.

Work Details

You are expected to work shifts and irregular hours though an eight-hour duty shift is usual, which can include weekends and public holidays. Longer hours are necessary during operational missions on board ship and during military exercises. On shore-based stations, hours can be more regular. It is necessary to be away from home for long periods of time when serving at sea, and you must be prepared to move at any time within the UK or overseas. At sea, you are expected to share living quarters with colleagues. Some postings can be in dangerous conditions.

This can be a very demanding and pressurised job, which requires sound judgement and the ability to relate well to your serving colleagues. The work environment varies depending on the type of job you are doing. However, when at sea you must be able to cope with rough weather.

Qualification

The Scottish Qualifications Authority (SQA) launched a new Skills for Work course in 2008. This course introduces candidates to the uniformed and emergency services and is particularly suited to those considering a career in the Army, Royal Navy, Royal Air Force or Royal Marines. Check the website for details.

• England, Wales and Northern Ireland

Band 4: For entry: two A levels and 5 GCSEs (A*-C) including English and maths. Equivalent qualifications are considered on individual merit. Check with the armed forces careers office.

Band 5: For degree course leading to graduate entry: 2-3 A levels (180 UCAS points) and some some GCSEs (A*-C) including English and maths. Check individual prospectuses.

• Scotland

Band 4: For entry: three H grades and five S grades (1-3) including English and maths. Similar qualifications are considered on individual merit. Check with the armed forces careers office.

Band 5: For degree course leading to graduate entry: 3-5 H grades (180 UCAS points) and five S grades (1-3) including English and maths. Similar qualifications such as an SQA award may be acceptable for entry to some courses. Check with universities for information on specific course requirements.

Degree Information

Any degree discipline is acceptable for officer entry. Graduate entrants to engineer officer posts must have an accredited engineering degree. Medical and dental officers require appropriate medical and dental qualifications.

Adult Qualifications

Formal secondary education qualifications and a degree (or equivalent qualifications) are required, depending on the commission. Entry requirements may be relaxed for adults applying for higher education courses and Access or foundation courses give adults without qualifications a route on to degree courses.

Work Experience

Relevant work or voluntary experience is always useful and can improve your chances in application for entry to this career. Consider areas that develop your skills in leadership and those that enable you to demonstrate your initiative and responsibility. As a young person, getting involved in groups such as a local cadet organisation, or the scouts/guides, helps to show enthusiasm and commitment. Often you can gain valuable experience from a school's Combined Cadet Force (CCF).

Entry and Training

Applicants must be British, Irish or Commonwealth citizens and between 17 and up to 26-46 yrs old, depending on specialisation. Check current regulations carefully. Your weight should be in proportion to your height. If you cannot swim, then try to learn as soon as possible. Most jobs are open to both men and women except for a small number of areas currently unavailable to women, such as the Royal Marines, submarine service and mine clearance diving.

Entry is very competitive. All applicants attend a two-day Admiralty Interview Board where they take a series of written tests and a physical test and participate in a discussion group exercise, all of which are designed to measure leadership potential. Finally there is an individual interview. Selection is based on aptitude, character and personality.

There are several entry routes: Naval College Entry (NCE), Direct Graduate Entry (DGE), and entry via one of several sponsorship schemes. It is also possible to gain promotion from the ranks. Many officer entrants are graduates with a degree or recognised equivalent qualification in certain areas of work, such as dentistry or engineering. Officer entry through NCE may be with Scholarships/Reserved Place Schemes that are available for students at school, who are studying for A levels/H grades.

Bursaries can be awarded for study at university, such as the Defence Technical Undergraduate Scheme for applicants entering higher education to study for an engineering degree at selected universities. This Scheme offers sponsorship to a limited number of students commencing or part way through an approved science or engineering degree at Aston, Loughborough, Newcastle, Northumbria or Southampton universities.

The armed forces also have their own sixth form residential college. Welbeck teaches a science and technology based A-level curriculum designed to prepare students for a technical degree at a leading UK university. This gives a head start into training for a career as an officer within the armed forces.

New officers begin training at the Britannia Royal Naval College in Dartmouth. Training is through practical experience, classroom work and specialist courses and falls into three phases; militarisation, initial sea training and academic training and education. After initial training you then receive further training in your chosen specialism. Officers are encouraged to update their training throughout their careers. In some specialisations, it may be possible to study for professional qualifications.

Mature applicants should note that upper age limits vary according to the job or professional specialism. There may be financial support for adults, including university bursaries for those who have gained a place, or a definite offer for a UK recognised degree. There is also an engineering sponsorship scheme that is available through the Defence Technical Undergraduate Scheme. Contact your local armed forces careers office for information.

Opportunities and Pay

This job requires a great deal of personal commitment and the length of career depends on the type of commission held. Around 500 officers are recruited by the RN each year. During training, those who show exceptional potential and leadership can be offered key college (Dartmouth) and divisional appointments that carry prestige and responsibility. Promotion prospects are improved by taking further training. There are usually good opportunities for former officers who transfer to civilian work as their training and management skills provide an excellent basis for a wide range of jobs.

Income depends on age on entry and rank. On appointment a midshipman (non-graduate entry) earns from £15k a year, and a sub lieutenant from £29k-£32k a year. A lieutenant/captain earns £37k-£44k; lieutenant commander/major earns £46k-£56k; commander/lt colonel earns £65k-£76k and captain/colonel earns £79k-£87k. Extra allowances are given for family separation and for length of service. Certain specialists such as qualified divers and those working on submarines receive additional pay. There are separate pay scales for other specialisms including medical and dental officers.

Health

Applicants must pass a strict medical test. Normal colour vision is needed for certain areas of work. There are regular medical check ups and compulsory drugs testing. You are expected to reach a high level of physical fitness.

Skills and Qualities

able to discipline, able to live and work closely with other people, aptitude for teamwork, decisive, good communication skills, good stamina and physically fit, information handling skills, leadership qualities, responsible attitude, self confident

Relevant Subjects

Design and technology, Engineering, English, Geography, Government and politics, Mathematics, Physical education and sport, Physics, Psychology, Science

Further Information

Careers Information package (Royal Navy) - www.royalnavy.mod.uk/

Navy News (monthly) (Royal Navy) - www.navynews.co.uk/

Real Life Guide to Armed Forces (Trotman 2009) - www.trotman.co.uk

Royal Navy Handbook (Ministry of Defence)

Skills for Work (Scottish Qualifications Authority) - www.sqa.org.uk/sqa/31390.html

TARGETjobs: Public Service (GTI Specialist Publishing Ltd.) - www.groupgti.com

▶Working in police, fire & security (2009) (Babcock Lifeskills) - www.babcock-lifeskills.com/

Addresses

Welbeck - Defence Sixth Form College
Forest Road, Woodhouse, Loughborough,
Leicestershire LE12 8WD
Web: www.dsfc.ac.uk/

Similar Jobs

Army Officer, Merchant Navy Deck/Navigating Officer, Merchant Navy Electro-technical Officer, Nurse/Nursing Officer: Royal Navy, RAF Officer, Royal Marines Officer

Royal Navy Rating

also known as: Navy Rating, Sailor: Royal Navy

CRCI:Security and Armed Forces
CLCI:BAB Job Band: 1 to 3

Job Description

Royal navy ratings serve on ships, submarines or onshore supporting the sea-going fleet and personnel in any one of the six branches of the Royal Navy; Warfare (weapons and electronic systems), Fleet Air Arm, Medical, Engineering, Logistics (administration, accounting, stores and catering) and the Submarine Service. Are part of a team working to keep ships, weapons systems, communications and all other equipment at peak performance. Have a skill or trade essential to ensure an efficient Naval service, and serve to protect our country (and others worldwide) from attack. Also guard our coastline and offshore interests, such as oil, gas and fisheries. Play an important role for our allies of the North Atlantic Treaty Organisation (NATO).

Naval ships are on constant alert against drug traffickers, illegal immigrants and terrorists. May be required to help following environmental disasters, such as floods and oil spills, or carry out search and rescue operations on land and on sea.

Work Details

Ratings (sailors) can be posted to serve at sea or shore establishments and are expected to work eight-hour shifts that can include weekends and public holidays. There is opportunity to travel worldwide and you can be away from home for long periods of time. You work under supervision usually in teams and are required to accept discipline. The work can be very demanding. You may have to cope with rough weather at sea, be expected to climb ladders and generally cope with life aboard a ship or submarine. At sea, you are expected to share living quarters with colleagues.

Your work environment can be cold, damp and confined. When on active duty you may be at risk of being injured or killed. You need to wear a uniform.

Qualification

For many jobs there are no formal entry qualifications, though all applicants must pass selection tests in literacy, numeracy, reasoning and mechanical comprehension. There are specific qualifications needed for certain trades. Check with your local armed forces careers office for details. It is strongly recommended that all applicants build up their fitness levels before applying.

- **England, Wales and Northern Ireland**

Band 1: For many jobs: no qualifications are required. However, GCSEs or equivalent at any level are useful.

Band 2: For certain trades: some GCSEs (A*-C) including English, maths, geography, physics, or a suitable science subject, or equivalent qualifications, are needed.

Band 3: For certain areas of work: 4-5 GCSEs (A*-C) including subjects such as English, maths, geography, physics, or a suitable science subject, or equivalent qualifications, depending on the trade chosen.

- **Scotland**

Band 1: For many jobs: no qualifications are required. However, some S grades or similar at any level are useful.

Band 2: For certain trades: some S grades (1-3) including English, maths, geography, physics or a suitable science subject, or similar qualifications, are needed.

Band 3: For certain areas of work: five S grades (1-3) including subjects such as English, maths, geography, physics or a suitable science subject, or similar qualifications, depending on the trade chosen.

Adult Qualifications

There are no minimum educational requirements, though some trades may require some secondary qualifications. Check with the armed forces careers office for details.

Work Experience

Relevant work or voluntary experience is always useful and can improve your chances when applying for entry to the armed forces. It can help you to decide which trade or branch of the armed services is most appropriate for you. Fitness is a requirement for the armed forces so evidence of an interest in keeping fit is also useful.

Entry and Training

Entrants must be British, Irish or Commonwealth citizens and over 151.5 cm (5 ft) tall, with weight in proportion to height. The minimum age of entry is 16 yrs and the maximum is 36 years. However, for some areas of work such as divers, medical assistants, student naval nurses and dental hygienists, entrants must be aged 17-18. Check with your local armed forces careers office for current regulations. If you cannot swim, then try to learn as soon as possible. Selection tests take place at armed forces careers offices. At a later date you are required to attend an interview, medical and fitness test.

There is a wide range of trades available depending on skill and personal choice. All entrants spend nine weeks on basic training at HMS Raleigh at Torpoint (Plymouth) then go on to professional training in the area of work or trade they have chosen. This takes place at naval establishments around the country, and is normally given on the job and through short courses. You are then posted to a ship or shore base. It is possible to study for national educational qualifications at all levels, including S/NVQs, BTEC/City & Guilds awards, degrees, and professional qualifications.

Most jobs (trades) are open to both men and women except for a small number of areas currently unavailable to women, such as the Royal Marines, submarine service and mine clearance diving.

Mature applicants are welcomed, usually up to your 37th birthday. Nurses have an upper age limit of 33. Check current regulations carefully. All necessary trades training is funded by the Royal Navy.

Opportunities and Pay

The RN provides plenty of opportunities and a variety of jobs, though the recruitment numbers can vary between specialist areas. In total the Royal Navy recruits over 4,000 ratings a year. Promotion prospects are improved with further training and for special skills and service, in submarines for example. Around 25% of ratings also become officers. Most ratings join for 18 years or up to the age of 40, whichever is the later, but you can leave 2.5 years after completion of your initial professional training. Skills, training and qualifications gained can be used for transfer to civilian work.

Pay on entry is currently £13k a year; able ratings earn £16k-£28k, leading ratings earn £27k-£32k, petty officers £32k-£36k, chief petty officers £32k-£42k, and warrant officers £37k-£45k. Pay increases with promotion and you receive a travel allowance, free uniform and accommodation allowance if required, plus additional pay for family separations and bonuses after completing a specified length of service. Additional pay is also given to mine clearance divers, submariners and ratings in the Survey Service.

Health

Applicants must pass a very strict medical test. Normal colour vision is needed for certain areas of work. There are regular medical check ups and you are expected to reach a high level of physical fitness.

Skills and Qualities

able to follow orders, able to live and work closely with other people, aptitude for teamwork, good stamina and physically fit, practical skills, prepared to go into combat, self-disciplined, technical aptitude, willing to learn

Relevant Subjects

Design and technology, Engineering, Mathematics, Physical education and sport, Physics, Science

Further Information

Careers Information package (Royal Navy) (Royal Navy) - www.royalnavy.mod.uk/

Navy News (monthly) (Royal Navy) - www.navynews.co.uk/

Real Life Guide to Armed Forces (Trotman 2009) - www.trotman.co.uk

Royal Navy Handbook (MOD) (Ministry of Defence)

Skills for Work (Scottish Qualifications Authority) - www.sqa.org.uk/sqa/31390.html

▶Working in computers & IT (2010) (Babcock Lifeskills) - www.babcock-lifeskills.com/

▶Working in police, fire & security (2009) (Babcock Lifeskills) - www.babcock-lifeskills.com/

Similar Jobs

Army Soldier, Marine Engineering Technician, Merchant Navy Deck Rating, Merchant Navy Engine-room Rating, RAF Airman/Airwoman, Royal Marines Commando

RSPCA Animal Collection Officer

also known as: Animal Collection Officer: RSPCA

CRCI:Environment, Animals and Plants

CLCI:WAL

Job Band: 1

Job Description

Collection officers work for the Royal Society for the Prevention of Cruelty to Animals (RSPCA) and deal with all kinds of animals, including pets. They collect, secure and move animals that are injured, sick or need to be taken from a dangerous location. Then transport them safely and carefully to an RSPCA clinic, or other safe place. May be required to kill them without pain when necessary. May also take part in animal rescues, and be on hand to retrieve the animal and take it to a safe place, or for treatment by a vet.

Work Details

Usually work shifts that involve weekends and bank holidays. In addition, may need to travel/drive long distances to collect animals. This work can be very physical and may involve the use of ropes, ladders or boats, in order to rescue animals. You regularly meet people who may be very upset, abusive, or may attempt to stop your work. Some animals may try to harm or attack you, particularly when in pain or frightened.

Where you work can sometimes be dirty, muddy, wet or smelly, and you are outdoors in all sorts of weather. A uniform and protective clothing is provided.

Qualification

- **England, Wales and Northern Ireland**

Band 1: For entry to jobs, no minimum qualifications are needed, but you are expected to have a good level of general education and relevant experience. Some formal/vocational qualifications at any level are useful.

Adult Qualifications

A good general education is required. You can improve your skills and qualifications by working through the Foundation Learning programme. This involves taking credit-based units and qualifications to help you progress.

Work Experience

Relevant work experience is useful and can improve your job prospects. Any work that involves animals, such as a Saturday job or holiday work, is useful. Volunteers are also welcome by the RSPCA. Some volunteers help to feed and clean out where the animals live or assist in exercising and re-training rescued animals. Others may help in reception and in answering the phone. Contact your local branch for details.

Entry and Training

It is an advantage to have worked with animals, and those that have an S/NVQ level 2 in animal care have an advantage. Applicants to this job need to pass an interview and a medical test. They also have to have a Criminal Records Bureau check. Preference is given to those who have proven experience of work in communicating with people from all aspects and areas of life. You also need to be able to demonstrate that you can successfully work under pressure.

A current, clean driving licence that has been held for at least three years, is essential. You must also be able to swim for 50 metres, fully clothed. Experience of driving different types of vehicles, such as four wheel drive (4WD) is desirable.

All new trainees undergo three weeks of basic training, which includes the use of ropes, ladders and boats that are used in the rescue and recovery of animals. They are also trained in euthanasia methods to use on dying animals. There may be opportunities to undergo personal development and take relevant NVQs at levels 1-3, though this is not a requirement of the job. Most animal collection officers undergo annual refresher training.

Mature applicants with relevant experience of working with animals, or work with the public, perhaps in the police or armed forces, are looked on favourably. You must have a valid driving licence.

Opportunities and Pay

You work for the Royal Society for the Prevention of Cruelty to Animals (RSPCA). Jobs are available throughout the UK, though there are usually few vacancies, so entry is very competitive. Jobs are advertised in the local press and the RSPCA does not accept any written or email enquiries for these jobs. However, you can telephone the local office to ask whether there are such jobs available, and how and when they are advertised.

Progress to inspector grade is possible. All animal collection officers wishing to become inspectors need to apply for a place on the student inspector training programme that is also open to applicants from outside the RSPCA. There is a lot of competition for places on the training programme.

Pay for an animal collection officer ranges from £14k a year, including a 6% unsocial hours allowance. There is an extra allowance for those working in and around London.

Health

Robust physical health and good stamina is required.

Skills and Qualities

able to cope under pressure, able to work well on your own, firm manner, good at handling animals, initiative, not squeamish, sound judgement, tactful

Relevant Subjects

Biology, Land and Environment, Science

Further Information

Foundation Learning (QCDA) - www.qcda.gov.uk

Real Life Guide to Working with Animals & Wildlife (Trotman) - www.trotman.co.uk

▶Working with animals (2009) (Babcock Lifeskills) - www.babcock-lifeskills.com/

Addresses

RSPCA
Wilberforce Way, Southwater, Horsham, West Sussex RH13 9RS
Phone: 0300 1234 555 (UK only)
Web: www.rspca.org.uk

Similar Jobs

Guide Dog Trainer, RSPCA/Scottish SPCA Inspector, Security Dog Handler/Trainer, Zoo Keeper

RSPCA/Scottish SPCA Inspector

CRCI:Environment, Animals and Plants
CLCI:WAL
Job Band: 3

Job Description

Inspectors work for the Royal Society/Scottish Society and Ulster Society for the Prevention of Cruelty to Animals, providing 24-hr cover for animals in need. They carry out rescues, investigate complaints of cruelty and ill-treatment of animals and household pets, and regularly check on their welfare, environment and accommodation. Inspectors encourage kindness to animals in their handling and treatment, deal with sick and injured animals, and may rescue trapped animals. They follow up cases of cruelty and neglect, advising or instructing animal owners on the care and treatment of their animals. May need to caution owners on possible prosecution. The main emphasis of the work is on work with people to help animals, rather than directly with the animals themselves.

Also write reports and give advice to the police, vets and to the public. May be required to give evidence in court. They inspect places, such as cattle markets, abattoirs, riding stables, pet shops, kennels and docks. Inspectors work closely with other professionals, including the police, coastguards, fire brigades, and organisations such as the British Divers Marine Life Rescue service.

Work Details

Usually work from 8.30-9am to 5-6pm, Monday to Friday, though are expected to be on emergency call outside of these hours, at night and at weekends. Travel is necessary, possibly over quite a wide area. In investigating cruelty allegations, you have to deal with unpleasant sights, people who are upset or aggressive, and also those who have broken the law. You are involved in educating the public, giving advice, and collecting evidence for court cases. Work can involve strenuous activity, including climbing ladders or down cliffs, or clambering over rough ground. Your environment can be dirty and smelly and you may be out in all sorts of weather.

There is a risk of attack from animals and being confronted with threatening behaviour. Some inspectors do undercover work involving illegal activities, such as badger baiting or dog fighting. Others volunteer for international rescue and emergency work, helping after a flood, earthquake or oil spillage etc. This work can be dangerous at times. You wear a uniform and further protective clothing when necessary.

Qualification

- **England, Wales and Northern Ireland**

Band 3: For entry: a minimum of 5 GCSEs (A*-C) is specified, preferably including English and a science subject (biology), or equivalent qualifications.

- **Scotland**

Band 3: For entry: a minimum of five S grades (1-3), including English and a science subject (biology) or similar qualifications.

Adult Qualifications

A good general education is required with some formal qualifications such as English language and a science subject, preferably biology, or equivalent qualifications.

Work Experience

Relevant work or voluntary experience is always useful and can improve your employment prospects when applying for entry to jobs. Volunteers are welcome at RSPCA, Scottish SPCA and Ulster SSPCA centres. Some volunteers help to feed and clean out the animals' accommodation or assist in exercising and in the socialisation of rescued animals. Others may help in reception and in answering the phone. Contact your local branch for details.

Entry and Training

This job is not open to school leavers as applicants need to be more mature to cope with this work. You must have a clean UK driving licence, and the RSPCA also requires you to be able to swim for 50 metres, fully clothed. It is an advantage to have completed a course in animal husbandry. For the RSPCA it is not essential to have worked with animals, though this is an advantage. Preference is given to those who have proven experience of work in communicating with people, from all areas of life, and those who can demonstrate that they have worked successfully under pressure.

You have to pass an interview and a medical test. In England and Wales, the initial training takes twelve months. In Scotland, probationary inspectors are based at the Scottish SPCA

Headquarters in Edinburgh for training. The Scottish SPCA requires practical experience of work with animals, preferably farm animals, or a veterinary background.

RSPCA/SSPCA training cover animal welfare legislation and training in court work, investigation skills and interview techniques, mountain and boat rescue techniques, media and public speaking, and basic veterinary skills and animal-handling techniques. Appropriate S/NVQs may be available at levels 1-3.

Mature applicants with relevant work experience, such as working with animals, or work with the public, perhaps in the police or armed forces, have an advantage.

Opportunities and Pay
You are employed by the RSPCA/Scottish SPCA/ Ulster SSCPA, which are registered charities. There are few vacancies and entry is highly competitive. Promotion to more senior posts is possible after gaining experience. Qualified inspectors must be prepared to serve in any part of the country.

Student RSPCA inspectors earn around £22k rising to around £24k-£27k a year when fully qualified.

Health
You need to have good general health and are given a medical test when you enter the job. There may be an allergy risk from animal fur.

Skills and Qualities
able to report accurately, able to work well on your own, fair minded, firm manner, good at handling animals, good communication skills, good interpersonal skills, not squeamish, sound judgement

Relevant Subjects
Biology, English, Land and Environment, Law, Science

Further Information
Careers Profile: RSPCA inspector (RSPCA) - www.rspca.org.uk/

Lantra Careers (A Future In...) (Lantra) - www.afuturein.com

▶Working with animals (2009) (Babcock Lifeskills) - www.babcock-lifeskills.com/

Addresses
RSPCA
Wilberforce Way, Southwater, Horsham, West Sussex RH13 9RS
Phone: 0300 1234 555 (UK only)
Web: www.rspca.org.uk

Scottish SPCA
Kingseat Road, Halbeath, Dunfermline KY11 8RY
Phone: +44 (0)3000 999 999
Web: www.scottishspca.org

Ulster SPCA
13 Clogharevan Road, Bessbrook, Belfast, Co Armagh BT35 7BH
Phone: +44 (0)28 3083 0631
Web: www.uspca.co.uk

Similar Jobs
Countryside Ranger, Guide Dog Trainer, Police Officer, RSPCA Animal Collection Officer, Veterinary Nurse, Zoo Keeper

Rural Business Administrator
also known as: Farm Secretary

CRCI:Administration, Business and Office Work
CLCI:CAT — Job Band: 2 to 3

Job Description
Rural business administrators provide the office services needed to run a farm or other agricultural business efficiently. They have specialist knowledge of rural and agricultural business and work closely with the farmer, estate manager or other employer. They keep records of livestock and crops, usually on a database, do the bookkeeping and accounts, prepare wages and calculate VAT, fill in official forms and complete orders. May prepare and complete forms and other documentation for central government departments, such as the Department for Environment, Food and Rural Affairs (DEFRA). This may involve dealing with subsidies, grants, the annual census, and agricultural law.

Also deal with mail, type letters and reports, and answer telephones. Liaise with bank managers, accountants, government officers and agricultural and environmental consultants.

Work Details
Resident administrators/farm secretaries work for one business only, whilst others travel around an area making regular visits to farms and businesses. Administrators are usually based in a countryside office on a farm or other agricultural business, but may have to do some outdoor tasks, such as recording data, whatever the weather. A working week of around 35 to 39 hours is expected, but this can be irregular, sometimes longer and with weekend and evening work. Part-time work is possible. You are often on your own, but also have to liaise with people such as the farm or estate manager, other employees, bank managers, accountants and visitors, including those from DEFRA or HM Revenue & Customs.

The work needs some understanding of the technical side of farming and of relevant legal matters. You have to keep your knowledge of regulations, the law, technical information and computer packages up to date.

Qualification
• England, Wales and Northern Ireland
Band 2: No minimum entry qualifications but many employers prefer some GCSEs, for example, English and maths. Basic keyboard and computer skills may be required.

Band 3: For course entry or direct entry to the job: usually a minimum of 4 GCSEs (A*-C). Some basic keyboard and computer skills may be required.

• Scotland
Band 2: For some courses: a minimum of three S grades (1-3) possibly including maths and English, or similar. Basic keyboard and computer skills may be required.

Band 3: For some specialist courses: a minimum of 3-4 S grades (1-3) including English language and preferably maths or similar. Some basic keyboard and computer skills may be required.

Adult Qualifications
Mature applicants may be accepted for courses without any academic qualifications, particularly if they have relevant experience, such as bookkeeping or computer skills. Some knowledge of the agricultural industry is also helpful.

Work Experience
Relevant work or voluntary experience is always useful and can equip you with skills that you can use in the future and that you can add to your CV. Temporary holiday work in offices, perhaps via employment agencies, is useful. Experience of farm work, either involving animals or crops, is also a distinct advantage. In some areas there is a young apprenticeship (14-16) scheme in business administration that provides an extended work placement and eventual achievement of a level 2 qualification whilst at school.

Entry and Training
Courses specifically for rural business administrators/farm secretaries are available at some agricultural colleges either part time or through distance learning. For example, Bridgwater College in Somerset offers a distance learning course leading to a Certificate in Rural Business Administration. The course covers bookeeping, employment and livestock and crop record keeping.

Contact the college directly for further details. Those with relevant qualifications can apply for membership of the Institute of Agricultural Secretaries and Administrators (IAgSA), which offers a programme of continuing professional development (CPD). Other appropriate courses include the City & Guilds diploma in business and administration, including a bookkeeping and accounts vocational award, and relevant BTEC/Applied A levels in agriculture or business administration. In Scotland, general secretarial SQA awards may be adapted to meet the specific duties of a rural business administrator/farm secretary.

Once employed, you are trained on the job and may be able to gain a level 3 certificate in rural business administration from the National Proficiency Tests Council (NPTC) or S/NVQs levels 3-4 in administration. Training programmes, including apprenticeship schemes, may be available in your area. Advanced apprenticeships leading to qualification at level 3 can also be a route into higher education.

Mature entrants may be preferred by some employers and most agricultural colleges also welcome mature students. Those currently working in the farming industry do not usually require formal entry qualifications to relevant courses, but need to have the ability to study and an aptitude to learn. There may be training schemes in your area for suitably qualified unemployed adults. Contact your local Connexions or careers office, Jobcentre Plus, Next Step service or Learning and Skills Council (LSC)/Local Enterprise Company (LEC) for details of all training opportunities and schemes, including apprenticeships.

Opportunities and Pay

Jobs are usually in rural areas, but some administrators/ secretaries work in related organisations based in towns, such as agricultural consultants or land agencies. There is no formal promotion structure, but you can move to a larger farm or estate to get more responsibility. Currently, the changes in agricultural legislation and technology have increased the demand for experienced or suitably qualified rural business administrators/ farm secretaries. There is a lot of competition for vacancies.

Resident administrators live on or near to the farm or rural business premises and may be provided with accommodation. You may be able to have free or cheaper farm produce and be offered facilities such as horse riding. Many mobile administrators/secretaries who visit a group of farms are self-employed.

Salaries vary depending on the area and size of business. Initially you are likely to earn around £12k-£16k a year. When experienced you can earn up to £26k a year.

Health

This job can be unsuitable for people with allergies to pollens, animals or poultry.

Skills and Qualities

accurate, adaptable, good communication skills, good organisational skills, initiative, IT skills, numeracy skills, reliable, self-reliant, trustworthy

Relevant Subjects

Biology, Business and accounting, English, ICT/Computer studies, Land and Environment, Mathematics

Further Information

AGCAS: Environment & Agriculture (Job Sector Briefing) (AGCAS) - www.prospects.ac.uk

Apprenticeship Schemes (National Apprenticeship Service) - www.apprenticeships.org.uk

Farmer's Weekly Interactive (Reed International) - www.fwi.co.uk

Lantra - The Sector Skills Council for environmental & land-based sector (Lantra) - http:/www.lantra.co.uk

National Proficiency Test Council (NPTC) - www.nptc.org.uk

Real Life Guide to Business & Administration (Trotman 2009) - www.trotman.co.uk

Scottish Farmer (weekly) (Newsquest Media) - www.thescottishfarmer.co.uk/

Training Schemes - www.direct.gov.uk/en/educationandlearning

Addresses

Bridgwater College
Bath Road, Bridgwater, Somerset TA6 4PZ
Phone: 00 44 (0)1278 455464
Web: www.bridgwater.ac.uk/default.php

Department for Environment, Food & Rural Affairs (DEFRA)
Customer Contact Unit , Eastbury House, 30 - 34 Albert Embankment, London SE1 7TL
Phone: 0845 933 5577 (UK only)
Web: www.defra.gov.uk

Institute of Agricultural Secretaries and Administrators (IAgSA)
National Agricultural Centre, Stoneleigh Park, Kenilworth CV8 2LG
Phone: +44 (0)24 7669 6592
Web: www.iagsa.co.uk

Institute of Professional Administrators
6 Graphite Square, Vauxhall Walk, London SE11 5EE
Phone: +44 (0) 20 7091 7340
Web: www.inprad.org/index.html

Similar Jobs

Clerk: Accounts, Farm Manager, Personal Assistant, Secretary, Secretary: Legal

Saddler

CRCI:Manufacturing and Production
CLCI:SAW Job Band: 2

Job Description

Saddlers make saddles and harnesses from leather and other materials, sometimes doing all the work by hand and sometimes using machines for more off-the-peg saddles. They make the basic frame (tree), from metal or wood, then cut the pieces of leather to the right shape and fits them together using tacks, glue and hand stitching. Saddles are packed with flocking, polished and sometimes decorated using stamps or punches. Some saddlers specialise in a particular type of saddle, eg racing saddles. Others mainly make items such as bridles and harnesses.

The use of cutting and sewing machines has increased in this industry, but hand-made saddles, harnesses or other articles are still in demand. Most saddlers offer a saddle fitting service to ensure the saddle fits the horse and rider as well as possible.

Work Details

Saddlers usually work a basic 37-39 hr week, but may work longer hours to complete a job. You work in industrial premises or workshops and studios. You have to cope with some physical activity and some lifting. You may also spend a lot of time sitting and bending over your work, and need to get used to the smell of glue and polishes.

Qualification

- **England, Wales and Northern Ireland**

Band 2: Although academic qualifications are not specified for this job, some college courses and employers may require some GCSEs (A*-C) that include English and maths or equivalent.

- **Scotland**

Band 2: Although academic qualifications are not specified for this job, some employers/college courses may require some S grades (1-3) in subjects that include English and maths or similar.

Adult Qualifications
Employers/colleges may waive entry requirements for adults with experience in the leather industry.

Work Experience
Relevant work or voluntary experience is always useful. It can improve your chances when applying for jobs or apprenticeships. Your personal or adult guidance adviser should be able to advise you about how to get some work experience. In some areas, there is a young apprenticeship (14-16) scheme. This provides an extended work placement. It can lead to a relevant level 2 qualification whilst at school.

Entry and Training
Usually training is by an apprenticeship scheme, with on-the-job instruction. The Society of Master Saddlers in conjunction with the Worshipful Company of Saddlers run such a scheme. It is up to you to find a training place with a master saddler - a list of these can be found on the website of the Society of Master Saddlers. There is a lot of competition for apprenticeships and it may help if you can provide evidence of practical ability, eg samples of work you have done.

Saddlery apprenticeships usually last four years. After six months on-the-job training you may attend the Saddlery Training Centre and take 16 one-week modules. This can lead to a City & Guilds qualification in Saddlery Skills Assessment at three levels. During your apprenticeship you are visited by a representative of the Society to ensure your training is progressing well. S/NVQs are available in leather goods at level 2 and at level 2-3 in footwear and leather products manufacture.

You may also choose to do your training through a full time course through Capel Manor College. They offer a two-year full-time course leading to a level 3 advanced certificate in saddlery and the Cordwainer's Diploma. You need 4 GCSEs/S grades (A*-C/1-3) or a BTEC first diploma to enter this course. There are also a number of private colleges running courses. Details are on the Society of Master Saddlers' website.

Government training opportunities, such as an apprenticeship in saddlery may be available in your area. You can also gain recognition of previous experience through Accreditation of Prior Learning (APL) or by working towards relevant S/NVQs. Contact your local careers office, Jobcentre Plus, Next Step service or Learning and Skills Council (LSC) Local Enterprise Company (LEC) for details of training schemes.

Opportunities and Pay
There are over 700 saddlery businesses in the UK. The majority are small, based in rural areas and deal with providing bespoke saddles. The main large manufacturers are in Walsall in the West Midlands. Although there is demand for saddlers, there are more applicants than places on apprenticeship schemes. It may be difficult to find training but when experienced, you can become self-employed.

As many saddlers are either self-employed or work part time, it is difficult to summarise their earnings. A trainee saddler generally earns around £10k a year. Most experienced saddlers generally earn around £15k-£20k.

Health
You need to have very good eyesight.

Skills and Qualities
able to work both on your own and in a team, attention to detail, creative flair, good concentration level, manual dexterity, patient, strong hands

Relevant Subjects
Art and Design, Design and technology

Further Information
Apprenticeship Schemes (National Apprenticeship Service) - www.apprenticeships.org.uk

Training Schemes - www.direct.gov.uk/en/educationandlearning

Addresses
Capel Manor College
Bullsmoor Lane, Enfield, Middlesex EN1 4RQ
Phone: +44 (0)8456 122 122
Web: www.capel.ac.uk

Saddlery Training Centre
3H Stanley Court Glenmore Business Park Telford Road
Churchfields, Salisbury, Wiltshire SP2 7GH
Phone: +44 (0)1722 341144
Web: www.saddlerytraining.com

Society of Master Saddlers
Green Lane Farm, Stonham, Stowmarket, Suffolk IP14 5DS
Phone: +44 (0)1449 711 642
Web: www.mastersaddlers.co.uk

Worshipful Company of Saddlers
Saddlers' Hall , 40 Gutter Lane, London EC2V 6BR
Phone: +44 (0)207 726 8661
Web: www.saddlersco.co.uk

Similar Jobs
Leather Worker, Sewing Machinist, Shoe Repairer, Upholsterer

Sales Executive
also known as: Sales Representative

CRCI:Marketing and Advertising
CLCI:OM Job Band: 3 to 5

Job Description
Sales executives promote and sells a company's goods or services to retailers or manufacturers and may sometimes sell directly to customers. They must learn all about the products or services being sold and try to show or describe them, to their best advantage. The job involves visiting or telephoning clients regularly to get orders, promote sales, answer queries and give information about prices and new products. They may negotiate variations in prices, accept payment and arrange for delivery of goods. Also keeps records of contacts with customers and reports details of customer requirements to the employer's sales section.

Sales executives may be responsible for a sales team, for organising their workload by product or region, and monitoring and reporting on sales figures in line with the agreed budget. May also be involved in agreeing the company's sales strategy.

Work Details
Works a basic 39-40 hr week, Monday to Friday, though additional and sometimes long hours are often necessary to meet targets. This job involves a good deal of travelling around to visit customers. If you are responsible for a large sales region you may have to stay away from home overnight, or longer. You organise your own workload and maybe that of others.

Sales executives have considerable paperwork to do in the evenings or at weekends and may also keep accounts. You have regular contact with your customers and sometimes have to deal with complaints. You may be expected to represent the company at trade shows or promotional events. You are expected to dress smartly.

Qualification

- **England, Wales and Northern Ireland**

Band 4: For HND, Diploma of Higher Education or foundation degree: 1-2 A levels and some GCSEs (A*-C) usually including English and maths, or equivalent.

Band 5: For degree courses: 2-3 A levels and some GCSEs (A*-C) usually including English and maths, or equivalent. Exact requirements depend on the degree you take.

- **Scotland**

Band 4: For entry to SQA higher national and professional development awards, usually 2-3 H grades and some S grades (1-3), including English and maths, or similar qualifications.

Band 5: For degree courses: 3-5 H grades and some S grades (1-3), including English and maths, or similar qualifications. Exact requirements depend on the degree you take.

Degree Information

A degree in any discipline is acceptable for entry to this job but subjects such as business or management, marketing, technology, computing or a modern language are useful.

Adult Qualifications

No standard entry requirements, but this varies according to the product or service being sold. Entry requirements may be relaxed for adults applying for higher education courses. Entry requirements may be relaxed for adults applying for higher education courses. Access or foundation courses give adults without qualifications a route on to degree courses.

Work Experience

Relevant work or voluntary experience is always useful and can improve your chances when applying for entry to jobs. Any work or business experience is an advantage, particularly if this is in a sales or marketing environment. Any work with people, such as in retail or telesales, is also relevant.

Entry and Training

There are no set entry requirements for entry to this work, but employers expect a good standard of education and look for people with good communications skills and business awareness. Entrants are usually in their twenties and increasingly are those with qualifications, including HNC/HNDs or degrees in relevant subjects and with professional skills and experience.

Training can vary depending on the employer, but is often on the job working with an experienced person until you are familiar with the area and the products or services. Larger companies may offer graduate training schemes, particularly for specialist products or services. Some employers may encourage staff to take professional exams, such as those offered by the Institute of Sales and Marketing Management, Managing and Marketing Sales Association or the Chartered Institute of Marketing (CIM). Courses range from basic sales skills to advanced level skills, such as the intensive diploma in strategic sales practice available from the CIM, for those with at least five years' sales experience.

Short courses are also available to improve skills in specific areas, such as closing a sale. There are S/NVQs in sales at levels 2-4. A Diploma/Welsh Baccalaureate may be available in your area in business, administration and finance (BAF) which can provide a useful background to this job and there are also relevant foundation degrees in marketing, management and business. Overseas sales executives may require fluency in a foreign language. A full driving licence is usually essential.

Mature entrants with relevant experience and qualifications may be preferred by some employers. There are relevant distance-learning courses available, such as those offered by the Institute of Sales and Marketing Management.

Opportunities and Pay

Jobs are available throughout the UK, working for wholesale distributors and manufacturers in all sectors. Promotion usually depends on building up a good sales record and successful executives can move rapidly on to become area/regional managers. Opportunities are generally better in larger organisations. Some executives may move into export sales. Opportunities are also available overseas.

Starting salaries depend on the product or service and the employer but are generally around £15k-£35k a year, rising to around £50k or more for those with over three years' experience. Earnings can be over £100k for successful executives with managerial responsibilities. Most sales staff are given a basic salary plus commission on sales, or are paid bonuses for achieving or exceeding sales targets. You are usually given a company car or paid an allowance for travel costs and travelling time.

Health

This job requires good health.

Skills and Qualities

able to work both on your own and in a team, business awareness, determined, excellent communication skills, good interpersonal skills, hard working, IT skills, perseverance, self confident, self-motivated

Relevant Subjects

Business and accounting, English, Mathematics, Retail and distribution

Further Information

Diplomas (Foundation, Higher and Advanced) - http://yp.direct.gov.uk/diplomas

Inside Careers Guide: Marketing & Sales - www.insidecareers.co.uk

TARGETjobs: Retail, Management & Sales (GTI Specialist Publishing Ltd.) - www.groupgti.com

Winning Edge (6 x year) (Institute of Sales & Marketing Management) - www.ismm.co.uk/magazine.php

▶Working in marketing, advertising & PR (2008) (Babcock Lifeskills) - www.babcock-lifeskills.com/

Addresses

Chartered Institute of Marketing (CIM)
Moor Hall, Cookham, Maidenhead, Berkshire SL6 9QH
Phone: +44 (0) 1628 427120
Web: www.cim.co.uk

Institute of Sales and Marketing Management (ISMM)
Harrier Court, Lower Woodside, Bedfordshire LU1 4DQ
Phone: +44 (0)1582 840 001
Web: www.ismm.co.uk

Managing and Marketing Sales Association (MAMSA)
PO Box 11, Sandbach, Cheshire CW11 3GE
Phone: +44 (0)1270 526 339
Web: www.mamsasbp.com

Similar Jobs

Insurance Business Development Manager, Marketing Manager, Retail Assistant: Computer Software, Retail Manager, Sales Executive: Medical, Sales Executive: Technical

Sales Executive: Medical

also known as: Medical Sales Executive, Medical Sales Representative

CRCI:Marketing and Advertising
CLCI:OM Job Band: 4 to 5

Job Description

Medial sales executives are employed by pharmaceutical companies to promote the sale of prescription drugs, medicines and medical products to family doctors, hospital doctors and pharmacists, and retail pharmacists. They work within a geographical area of the UK and visits hospitals, GP surgeries, health centres and pharmacies to inform them about the range of products that are available. The job includes explaining the benefits, doses and correct use of the products and encourages clients to buy them or prescribe them for their patients. They may specialise in a specific area of therapy, such as gynaecology, paediatrics or oncology.

Sales Executive: Medical

This job combines an interest in science with a business role. Sales executives keep doctors informed about new developments and obtain feedback about medicines in use. They also attend medical conferences and seminars, and make presentations to groups of healthcare professionals.

Work Details

Usually works a basic 39-40 hr week, Monday to Friday, though additional hours are often necessary, including spending time at home on paperwork and travelling. You spend a lot of time driving around to visit clients and may need to spend nights away from home. The job is a mix of formal appointments and speculative calls to healthcare employees. Your work also involves entertaining clients. This is a very competitive job, you may have to be persistent to get appointments to meet people so the job can be demanding. You are expected to dress smartly.

Qualification

• England, Wales and Northern Ireland

Band 4: For HND, Diploma of Higher Education, foundation degree or relevant training: 1-2 A levels and some GCSEs (A*-C) usually including English and maths, or equivalent.

Band 5: For degree courses: 2-3 A levels, including a science subject, and some GCSEs (A*-C) usually including English and maths, or equivalent. Exact requirements depend on the degree you take.

• Scotland

Band 4: For entry to SQA higher national, professional development awards or relevant training: usually 2-3 H grades and some S grades (1-3) often including a science subject and English and maths, or similar qualifications.

Band 5: For degree courses: 3-5 H grades, including a science subject, and some S grades (1-3), usually including English and maths, or similar qualifications. Exact requirements depend on the degree you take.

Degree Information

A degree in a medical or a life sciences subject is often preferred because of its specialist content. Other acceptable subjects may include chemistry, some biological sciences, and paramedical subjects. A business-related degree can also be relevant.

Adult Qualifications

Relevant experience and personality can be more important than formal qualifications for some employers. Entry requirements may be relaxed for adults applying for higher education courses. Access or foundation courses give adults without qualifications a route on to degree courses.

Work Experience

Employers may prefer candidates who have relevant work or voluntary experience. This may include previous experience in sales, customer services, retail or administration. Work within the health sector is an advantage, particularly in an area where you can gain some medical background. Shadowing an existing medical sales executive can give you a clear idea of what the job involves.

Entry and Training

Although this area of work is open to all graduates, a medical or life science background may be preferred. In fact over 50% of medical sales executives have a science degree. For non-graduate entry, qualifications and experience in related work, such as nursing, pharmaceutical, biological or medical laboratory work or in ethical sales and marketing, are usually required.

Companies provide induction training about the products and how to promote them for new entrants. This is intense and can take up to six months. After this training you may accompany an experienced executive before you are given an area of your own. All staff attend regular short courses to learn about new products.

All medical sales executives are required to take the Prescription Medicines Code of Practice Authority (PMCPA) examinations within the first two years of employment. The PMCPA administer the code of practice for the Association of the British Pharmaceutical Industry.

Some entrants may also choose to work towards general sales qualifications, such as those offered by the Managing and Marketing Sales Association, the Institute of Sales and Marketing Management and the Chartered Institute of Marketing. Continuing professional development to keep up to date with new products and research developments is crucial for this job. A full driving licence is essential.

Mature applicants with related experience in the field and in particular, sales experience, are usually preferred. Various backgrounds are acceptable for entry to this job including life science graduates, nurses, pharmacists, paramedics and medical technicians.

Opportunities and Pay

There are around 10,000 medical sales executives in the UK. Employers are usually pharmaceutical and healthcare companies that produce medical goods, equipment and drugs. There are opportunities to specialise once you have experience.

Promotion depends on building up a good sales record, but opportunities for successful sales staff are good. Pharmaceuticals is an international industry and some of the main employers are multinational companies, so there may also be opportunities to work overseas. With experience, you may be able to move into sales training, area management or product management.

Starting salaries are around £18k-£24k a year, rising to £25k-£40k with experience. At senior level you can earn £40-£60k a year. You may be given a company car or paid an allowance for travel costs and travelling time. Sales executives are often paid a basic salary plus commission on sales or bonuses for meeting or exceeding sales targets.

Health

This job requires good health.

Skills and Qualities

able to work both on your own and in a team, business awareness, confident, excellent communication skills, good organisational skills, IT skills, networking skills, outgoing personality, planning skills, resilient

Relevant Subjects

Biology, Chemistry, English, Health and social care, Mathematics, Physics, Retail and distribution, Science

Further Information

All about Medical Sales - www.allaboutmedicalsales.com

Association of the British Pharmaceutical Industry (ABPI) - www.abpi.org.uk/education

Careers in the Pharmaceutical Industry (ABPI) (Association of British Pharmaceutical Industry) - www.abpi.org.uk/education/careers.asp

Prescription Medicines Code of Practice Authority (PMCPA) - www.pmcpa.org.uk

The Magazine for Medical Sales Professionals (PF Pharmaceutical Field) - www.pharmafield.co.uk

Winning Edge (6 x year) (Institute of Sales & Marketing Management) - www.ismm.co.uk/magazine.php

▶Working in science (2007) (Babcock Lifeskills) - www.babcock-lifeskills.com/

Addresses

Chartered Institute of Marketing (CIM)
Moor Hall, Cookham, Maidenhead, Berkshire SL6 9QH
Phone: +44 (0) 1628 427120
Web: www.cim.co.uk

Institute of Sales and Marketing Management (ISMM)
Harrier Court, Lower Woodside, Bedfordshire LU1 4DQ
Phone: +44 (0)1582 840 001
Web: www.ismm.co.uk

Managing and Marketing Sales Association (MAMSA)
PO Box 11, Sandbach, Cheshire CW11 3GE
Phone: +44 (0)1270 526 339
Web: www.mamsasbp.com

Similar Jobs

Marketing Manager, Pharmacologist, Purchasing/Procurement Officer, Sales Executive, Sales Executive: Technical

Sales Executive: Technical

also known as: Technical Sales Representative
CRCI:Marketing and Advertising
CLCI:OM Job Band: 4 to 5

Job Description

Technical sales executives sell specialised equipment, parts and machinery to industrial and commercial users. May sell items such as electronics, IT equipment, chemicals and engineering equipment and tools. They establish the needs of customers and recommend the most suitable products. Explaining and discussing details of the product and referring complex queries to technical service support colleagues is part of the role. Also records sales and order information and forwards details on a daily basis to the sales department.

They maintain contact with customers to check that they are satisfied with the goods supplied and may attend trade fairs, exhibitions and demonstrations. Also researches and establishes new and prospective buyers.

Work Details

Usually works a basic 39-40 hr week, though may have to work long hours, including spending time at home on paper work. This job involves a good deal of travelling around to visit customers. If you are responsible for a large sales region, you may need to be away from home overnight or for several days. You are responsible for organising your own workload. Sometimes you may deal with complaints from customers. You are expected to give advice and information about your products.

Qualification

The subjects and qualifications that are most appropriate depend on the company or product.

• England, Wales and Northern Ireland

Band 4: For HND, Diploma of Higher Education or foundation degree: 1-2 A levels and some GCSEs (A*-C) usually including English and maths, or equivalent.

Band 5: For degree courses: 2-3 A levels and some GCSEs (A*-C) usually including English and maths, or equivalent. Exact requirements depend on the degree you take.

• Scotland

Band 4: For entry to SQA higher national and professional development awards, usually 2-3 H grades and some S grades (1-3), including English and maths, or similar qualifications.

Band 5: For degree courses: 3-5 H grades and some S grades (1-3), including English and maths, or similar qualifications. Exact requirements depend on the degree you take.

Degree Information

It is possible to enter this job with a degree in any subject. Depending on the product to be sold, the following subjects give useful background knowledge: physics, chemistry, materials science, engineering, technology, agriculture, horticulture, food science/technology, computing science, information systems and technology or software engineering.

Adult Qualifications

Degree or further education qualifications are an advantage. Entry requirements may be relaxed for adults applying for higher education courses. Access or foundation course give adults without qualifications a route onto degree courses.

Work Experience

Employers may prefer candidates who have relevant work or voluntary experience such as previous experience in sales, retail or administration, as well as time spent in a scientific or technological environment.

Entry and Training

For selling high technology and specialised products you are likely to need a degree or HNC/HND in a relevant subject. Professional skills and experience can also be important. Training is usually on the job through a graduate training programme organised by your employer. This can include intensive courses to learn about the product and courses in sales techniques. You may also attend regular training courses to keep up to date with new developments and products.

Some employers encourage staff to take professional exams, such as those offered by the Institute of Sales and Marketing Management, Managing and Marketing Sales Association, or the Chartered Institute of Marketing (CIM). Courses range from basic sales skills to advanced level training, such as the diploma in strategic sales available from CIM for those with at least five years' sales experience. There are also S/NVQs in sales at levels 2-4. A full driving licence is usually essential.

Mature entrants with relevant experience and qualifications may be preferred by some employers. Employers may recruit people with experience in technical marketing or technical product development. There are relevant distance-learning courses available, such as those offered by the Institute of Sales and Marketing Management.

Opportunities and Pay

Jobs are available throughout the UK, most being with manufacturing companies or distribution companies that deal with high technology products. Promotion, perhaps to area or regional manager, depends on building up a good sales record. There are opportunities to move into training or recruitment within a company.

Starting salaries are around £20k-£25k a year, rising to £35k, with experience. The most experienced and successful sales executives earn around £40k-£50k a year, often higher for those with managerial responsibilities. Sales executives are usually paid a basic salary plus commission on sales or bonuses for meeting or exceeding sales targets. You are usually given a company car, or may be paid an allowance for travel costs and travelling time.

Health

This job requires good general health.

Skills and Qualities

able to work well on your own, business awareness, determined, excellent communication skills, good interpersonal skills, IT skills, outgoing personality, persuasive, self-motivated, technical aptitude

Relevant Subjects

Chemistry, Design and technology, Engineering, English, ICT/Computer studies, Mathematics, Physics, Retail and distribution, Science

Further Information

AGCAS: Manufacturing (Job Sector Briefing) (AGCAS) - www.prospects.ac.uk

Diplomas (Foundation, Higher and Advanced) - http://yp.direct.gov.uk/diplomas

TARGETjobs: Retail, Management & Sales (GTI Specialist Publishing Ltd.) - www.groupgti.com

Winning Edge (6 x year) (Institute of Sales & Marketing Management) - www.ismm.co.uk/magazine.php

▶Working in marketing, advertising & PR (2008) (Babcock Lifeskills) - www.babcock-lifeskills.com/

Addresses

Chartered Institute of Marketing (CIM)
Moor Hall, Cookham, Maidenhead, Berkshire SL6 9QH
Phone: +44 (0) 1628 427120
Web: www.cim.co.uk

Institute of Sales and Marketing Management (ISMM)
Harrier Court, Lower Woodside, Bedfordshire LU1 4DQ
Phone: +44 (0)1582 840 001
Web: www.ismm.co.uk

Managing and Marketing Sales Association (MAMSA)
PO Box 11, Sandbach, Cheshire CW11 3GE
Phone: +44 (0)1270 526 339
Web: www.mamsasbp.com

Similar Jobs

IT Technical Sales Specialist, Sales Executive, Sales Executive: Medical, Vehicle Sales Executive

Sales/Marketing Assistant

CRCI:Marketing and Advertising
CLCI:OB Job Band: 3 to 5

Job Description

Sales and marketing assistants provide support to sales and marketing departments by coordinating and helping to run all sales and marketing activities and events. They create and compile marketing material, such as presentations, brochures and letters and also help to analyse market opportunities and gather customer data, usually in a database. May help to set up and attend marketing events such as conferences and exhibitions.

May provide administrative support to the sales and marketing manager and other members of the team. This may include screening calls and correspondence, diary management and making travel arrangements.

Work Details

Usually works a basic 39 hr week, Monday to Friday, though longer hours may be necessary at times. This is an office-based job, but may also involve going out to visit potential customers or to attend exhibitions or other promotional events. The work may also involve quite a lot of travel, including overseas travel if you work for a company with an export market.

Qualification

- **England, Wales and Northern Ireland**

Band 3: For entry to jobs, HNC or a relevant Diploma, usually at least 4 GCSEs (A*-C) including English and maths, or equivalent.

Band 4: For HND, Diploma of Higher Education or foundation degree: 1-2 A levels and some GCSEs (A*-C) usually including English and maths, or equivalent.

Band 5: For degree courses: 2-3 A levels and some GCSEs (A*-C) usually including English and maths, or equivalent. Exact requirements depend on the degree you take.

- **Scotland**

Band 3: For entry to jobs, usually at least four S grades (1-3) including English or maths, or similar.

Band 4: For entry to SQA higher national and professional development awards, usually 2-3 H grades and some S grades (1-3), including English and maths, or similar qualifications.

Band 5: For degree courses: 3-5 H grades and some S grades (1-3), including English and maths, or similar qualifications. Exact requirements depend on the degree you take.

Degree Information

Any degree is accepted, though marketing and business studies are most relevant and may lead to exemptions from professional examinations. Some employers may prefer engineering and science subjects for jobs in specialist marketing areas, and languages for export marketing.

Adult Qualifications

Entry requirements may be relaxed for adults applying for higher education courses. Access or similar courses provide those without the required qualifications a route onto degree courses. The Chartered Institute of Marketing offers a range of professional qualifications aimed at those with relevant experience.

Work Experience

Entry to this job is popular and competitive and it is important that you try to do some relevant work or voluntary experience before applying. Direct experience in marketing, advertising, market research or public relations is extremely useful. Any work dealing with people and using communication skills is also very relevant.

Entry and Training

A career in marketing can often begin with a job in selling, either in the sales office or in the field. Some companies may recruit sales and marketing assistants with previous advertising, public relations or market research experience, or industrial production companies may recruit from their technical staff. However, formal qualifications are becoming increasingly important. Many universities offer marketing degrees and a range of other courses with marketing as a central component. Some companies may prefer to recruit graduates and you may need to be skilled in a foreign language if you want to work for a company with an export market.

Training is usually on the job, with in-house or industry-led short courses. Increasingly, trainees study part time or by distance learning for a professional qualification, such as the diploma or postgraduate professional diploma in marketing offered the Chartered Institute of Marketing (CIM), or the diploma in direct and interactive marketing offered by the Institute of Direct Marketing (IDM). The CIM and IDM also offer a range of introductory and short courses and workshops for continuing professional development.

To work in a specific industry or business sector, such as engineering, pharmaceuticals, agriculture/horticulture, food or textiles, you may be asked for qualifications relating to that industry. Foundation degrees are available in marketing-related subjects and there are S/NVQs in marketing at levels 2-4. A Diploma/Welsh Baccalaureate in business, administration and finance (BAF) or in creative and media for 14-19 year olds may be available in your area and provide an alternative route into this job.

Mature entrants can study relevant qualifications in marketing through distance learning. Adults may be able to enter this work through a government-funded training programme, such as an apprenticeship in marketing and communications or sales and telesales. Contact your local careers office, Jobcentre Plus, Next Step service or Learning and Skills Council (LSC)/Local Enterprise Company (LEC) for details of all training opportunities and schemes.

Opportunities and Pay

Sales and marketing assistants can work in a wide variety of industry sectors throughout the country. Most manufacturing companies and service organisations have a sales and marketing department. There are also opportunities within universities or colleges, marketing agencies, or central/local government. Promotion prospects to positions such as marketing manager are possible, depending on individual performance and gaining appropriate qualifications.

There are links to other areas of work such as market research, advertising, public relations and certain areas of journalism. Some people move between these disciplines to gain further experience and develop their careers.

Pay varies widely depending on the size and type of company and the range of responsibilities. Starting salaries for sales and marketing assistants are around £18k-£26k a year; graduate entrants usually earn around £20k. This can rise with experience to £30-£35k a year.

Skills and Qualities
analytical skills, business awareness, creative and imaginative flair, good communication skills, good coordinator, good interpersonal skills, good organisational skills, IT skills, self confident, self-motivated

Relevant Subjects
Business and accounting, Economics, English, ICT/Computer studies, Mathematics, Media and communication studies, Psychology, Retail and distribution

Further Information
Apprenticeship Schemes (National Apprenticeship Service) - www.apprenticeships.org.uk

Apprenticeships in Scotland (Careers Info Scotland) - www.apprenticeshipsinscotland.com/about/

CIM Career Guides (Chartered Institute of Marketing (CIM)) - www.cim.co.uk/cpd/career/careerguides.aspx

Diplomas (Foundation, Higher and Advanced) - http://yp.direct.gov.uk/diplomas

Get into Marketing - www.getintomarketing.com

Inside Careers Guide: Marketing & Sales - www.insidecareers.co.uk

Welsh Baccalaureate - www.wbq.org.uk

▶Working in marketing, advertising & PR (2008) (Babcock Lifeskills) - www.babcock-lifeskills.com/

Addresses
Chartered Institute of Marketing (CIM)
Moor Hall, Cookham, Maidenhead, Berkshire SL6 9QH
Phone: +44 (0) 1628 427120
Web: www.cim.co.uk

Institute of Direct Marketing (IDM)
1 Park Road, Teddington, Middlesex TW11 0AR
Phone: +44 (0)208 977 5705
Web: www.theidm.com

Institute of Sales and Marketing Management (ISMM)
Harrier Court, Lower Woodside, Bedfordshire LU1 4DQ
Phone: +44 (0)1582 840 001
Web: www.ismm.co.uk

Similar Jobs
Advertising Account Executive, Export Sales Manager, Market Research Executive, Marketing Manager, Public Relations Officer, Sales Executive

Satellite Operator
also known as: Operator - Satellites

CRCI:Engineering
CLCI:RAL Job Band: 4 to 5

Job Description
Satellite operators work as part of a team supporting the operation, maintenance and ongoing development of satellites. Satellites are used for observing civilian and military activity on earth, communications, navigation, weather monitoring and research. Jobs are classified as downstream and split into communications, broadcasting or navigation service provision. Satellites are also used to make new discoveries about our solar system, study pollution on earth or to connect the worlds remotest communities and help aid agencies reach a disaster zone.

Satellites are usually controlled by computer and these are manned by operators. Most operators have a background in engineering or telecommunications technology. May work on power generation, telemetry or heat, orbit or altitude control. May also be involved in working on a new satellite or developing technology to map a distant planet.

Work Details
Usually works a basic 40 hour week but weekend and shift work may be required to complete a project. Time is spent monitoring the performance of the satellites and dealing with any necessary repairs or adjustments to instrumentation or computers. The work is largely office based but if working in a consultative role, you may spend time travelling to other offices or international events on development. You work as part of a larger team, responsible for the design, launch and maintenance of a satellite.

Qualification
- **England, Wales and Northern Ireland**

Band 4: For HND, Diploma of Higher Education or foundation degree: 1-2 A levels and some GCSEs (A*-C) usually including English and maths, or equivalent.

Band 5: For degree courses: 2-3 A levels and some GCSEs (A*-C) usually including English and maths, or equivalent. Exact requirements depend on the degree you take.

- **Scotland**

Band 4: For entry to SQA higher national and professional development awards, usually 2-3 H grades and some S grades (1-3), including English and maths, or similar qualifications.

Band 5: For degree courses: 3-5 H grades and some S grades (1-3), including English and maths, or similar qualifications. Exact requirements depend on the degree you take.

Degree Information
A university degree or equivalent in a space-related engineering discipline, computer science, or related subject.

Adult Qualifications
A relevant higher education qualification, usually a degree, is normally required. Entry requirements may be relaxed for adults applying for higher education courses and Access or foundation courses give adults without qualifications a route onto degree courses.

Work Experience
Employers or universities may prefer candidates who have relevant work or voluntary experience. Applicants to degree courses can apply to the Year in Industry scheme for a placement in industry prior to starting their studies. This scheme is run by the Engineering Development Trust (EDT) to encourage people to consider careers in engineering and science. Visit their website for details on other schemes such as Headstart and the Engineering Education Scheme (England and Scotland). All schemes provide students with valuable experience which can contribute to a university application and/or enhance job prospects.

Entry and Training
Entry is usually with a good degree in electronic engineering, computer engineering or a related subject. Courses are mainly full time but there are sandwich courses and sponsorship for training may be possible through the Science and Technologies Engineering Council. Foundation degrees are available in general engineering and computing subjects.

Training programmes including engineering apprenticeships may be available in your area. Apprenticeship programmes can lead to S/NVQ at level 4, then to HNC/HND. Chartered engineers (CEng) may qualify through an accredited course leading to an MEng degree, or a BEng (Hons) followed by an appropriate masters degree. Chartered engineers can also qualify as European engineers (EurIng) but need to be fluent in a European language.

A Diploma/Welsh Baccalaureate may be available in your area in engineering. The advanced level is equivalent to 3.5 A levels but for some university courses, the additional and specialist learning component of the diploma needs to include specific A levels e.g. maths and physics. Check entry requirements carefully with the individual institutions.

Incorporated engineers (IEng) need to be qualified to HNC/HND or BEng level, followed by a further year of learning known as the Matching Section. Specific graduate development programme (GDP) opportunities exist with companies such as Astrium. Their GDP programme runs for two years and is open to graduates with limited post graduate work experience. Similarly, the European Space Agency (ESA) offers a one year training contract to help young graduates gain valuable work experience. See the ESA website for details.

Astrium also runs an apprenticeship scheme for those seeking to enter the industry without a degree. Apprentices spend the first year of their training at full-time college and the next two years gaining hands-on work experience. They also attend college in three separate blocks over the two year period. Disciplines covered include design, manufacturing and assembly, quality assurance and cost engineering. At the end of the three years, students gain an HNC qualification which covers both mechanical and electrical elements, as well as a Modern Apprenticeship which includes NVQ 3 in engineering.

The International Space School Educational Trust runs courses for teachers to help bring space science into the classroom. Check their website for details of upcoming courses and developments in the space industry in the United States.

Depending on the company requirements as well as the qualifications and experience of the candidate, mature applicants may be considered by employers Experience in spacecraft hardware, software or operations is advantageous. Candidates should have good computer skills

Those wishing to gain incorporated/chartered engineer status and who lack the required academic qualifications, may apply to achieve registration through the Technical Report Route. This gives applicants without post 18 academic qualifications the opportunity to demonstrate, through the writing of a technical report, that they have acquired the necessary engineering knowledge. Contact the Engineering Council for details.

Opportunities and Pay

Satellites are an essential part of our daily lives. They allow us to send and receive messages almost instantly, transmit television signals, monitor weather and find our way when lost through global positioning (GPS). With the development of broadband, digital broadcasting and 3G phone technologies, the sector is experiencing even faster growth. Weather forecasting, pollution monitoring and mapping are also growth areas.

British companies manufacture satellites used in navigation, communications and research. They can provide expertise in computers, control systems and broadcasting.

Pay varies depending on location and size of company. A graduate entrant can expect to earn around £20k-£25k rising to about £35k-£40k a year with experience. Those with managerial responsibilities can earn more.

Health

This job requires normal colour vision.

Skills and Qualities

analytical skills, aptitude for maths and science, attention to detail, good communication skills, IT skills, planning skills, practical skills, problem-solving skills, technical aptitude

Relevant Subjects

Chemistry, Design and technology, Engineering, ICT/Computer studies, Mathematics, Physics, Science

Further Information

Apprenticeship Schemes (National Apprenticeship Service) - www.apprenticeships.org.uk

Astrium - www.astrium.eads.net/

Diplomas (Foundation, Higher and Advanced) - http://yp.direct.gov.uk/diplomas

Engineering Development Trust - www.go4set.org.uk/EDT.html

European Satellite Operators Association - www.esoa.net

European Space Agency (European Space Agency) - www.esa.int

NASA (National Aeronautics and Space Administration) - www.nasa.gov

National Space Centre Online - www.spacecentre.co.uk/Page.aspx/

Science and Technologies Engineering Council http:www.scitech.ac.uk

Scottish Wider Access Programme (SWAP) - www.scottishwideraccess.org/

SEMTA - sector skills council for science, engineering and manufacturing technologies - www.semta.org.uk

Space Careers - www.space-careers.com

Space School UK http://spaceschool.co.uk/

UK Space Agency - www.ukspaceagency.bis.gov.uk/

Welsh Baccalaureate - www.wbq.org.uk

Women into Science, Engineering & Construction - www.wisecampaign.org.uk

Year in Industry (Engineering Development Trust) - www.yini.org.uk

Addresses

British National Space Centre (BNSC)
Polaris House North Star Avenue, Swindon, Wiltshire SN2 1SZ
Phone: +44 (0)20 7215 5000
Web: http://bnsc.gov.uk

Engineering Council
246 High Holborn, London WC1V 7EX
Phone: +44 (0)20 3206 0500
Web: www.engc.org.uk

International Space School Educational Trust (ISSET)
5 Herbert Terrace, Penarth CF64 2AH
Phone: +44 (0) 2920 710295
Web: www.isset.org/

Scottish Engineering
Training Officer, 105 West George Street, Glasgow G2 1QL
Phone: +44 (0)141 221 3181
Web: www.scottishengineering.org.uk

Similar Jobs

Astronaut, Electrical Engineering Technician, Engineer: Aeronautical, IT Applications Developer, IT Applications Developer, IT Systems Developer, Telecommunications Technician

Satellite Systems Technician

also known as: Aerial Rigger, Television Aerial Erector

CRCI:Engineering
CLCI:RAL

Job Band: 1 to 3

Job Description

Satellite system technicians put up television aerials, satellite and digital dishes and fit them to premises in the commercial, educational and healthcare sectors and in domestic homes.

They may design and fit a brand new system, upgrade an existing system, or realign/repair one that has been damaged, possibly through bad weather conditions.

Technicians carry out a site survey to quote for the job. They select a good receiver for the area and discuss the positioning of the system with the customer. Then they assemble the mast or dish array, connect the cable to it and join it to a junction box or TV top decoder using tools, wire, brackets, etc. to fix firmly. Technicians are also responsible for running the cable to sockets inside buildings, changing position for the best reception, tuning the receiver, testing equipment and dealing with any faults. May also work on cable installation working from detailed plans.

Work Details

Usually work a basic 40 hr week, Monday to Friday. Weekend and shift work may be required by some employers. Time is spent outside working on rooftops, where there is a risk of falling. You also work indoors in clients' homes. Travel around an area is necessary and you have to cope with considerable physical exertion as well as climbing ladders and working at heights in all weather conditions. Occasionally you have to work in a confined space. You may need to wear overalls and a safety helmet. You are responsible for safety.

Qualification

• England, Wales and Northern Ireland

Band 1: For entry to jobs, no minimum qualifications are needed, but you are expected to have a good level of general education and relevant experience. Some formal/vocational qualifications at any level are useful.

Band 2: For entry to jobs, no minimum qualifications are needed, but it is an advantage to have some GCSEs (A*-C) or equivalent in subjects that include English, maths and a science or technical subject, or equivalent.

Band 3: For entry to jobs, HNC or a relevant Diploma, usually at least 4 GCSEs (A*-C) including English, maths and a science or technical subject, or equivalent.

• Scotland

Band 1: For entry to jobs, no minimum qualifications are needed, but you are expected to have a good level of general education and relevant experience. Some formal/vocational qualifications at any level are useful.

Band 2: Although academic qualifications are not specified for this job, it is an advantage to have some S grades (1-3) in subjects that include English, maths and a science or technical subject, or similar.

Band 3: For entry to jobs, usually at least four S grades (1-3) including English, maths and a science or technical subject, or similar.

Adult Qualifications

There are no minimum entry requirements but it may be helpful to show that you have experience in practical or technical work, such as electronics. You can improve your skills and qualifications by working through the Foundation Learning programme. This involves taking credit-based units and qualifications to help you progress.

Work Experience

Relevant work or voluntary experience is always useful and can improve your chances in application for entry to this job. The type of work experience to consider includes electronics, electrical engineering, communications, some branches of mechanical engineering, or any sort of practical or technical work.

Entry and Training

Most enter as a trainee installer and train on the job and by day release, short course or by distance learning. The Confederation of Aerial Industries provides formal training in all aspects of aerial and dish installation through a range of short courses. Study for a City & Guilds certificate in electrical and electronic servicing or in digital TV aerial installation can also be helpful. You are expected to keep training throughout your career to learn new procedures and to keep up to date with developments in equipment.

S/NVQs are available at levels 2-4 in communication technologies practitioners/professionals. Training programmes, including apprenticeships leading to level 2 and advanced apprenticeships leading to level 3, may be available in your area. Once trained to level 3, you may wish to study for a BTEC HNC/HND in electrical/electronic engineering, through either a part or full-time course at a local college, and become a fully qualified telecoms technician.

A Diploma/Welsh Baccalaureate may be available in engineering your area. See the diplomas website for further information.

Applicants over 21 may be preferred by some employers due to the high cost of motor insurance for young drivers. Previous experience in electronics, electrical engineering, communications, or sometimes mechanical engineering, is an advantage.

Government training opportunities, such as apprenticeships for adults, may be available in your area. You can also gain recognition of previous experience through Accreditation of Prior Learning or by working towards relevant S/NVQs. Contact your local careers office, Jobcentre Plus, Next Step service or Learning and Skills Council (LSC)/Local Enterprise Company (LEC) for details of training schemes

Opportunities and Pay

Jobs are available throughout the country due to new digital technology. In the UK, the digital switchover of all televisions from the analogue system has already started and is due for completion in 2012. This is creating demand for people with the right training. Such is this demand that the Confederation of Aerial Industries (CAI) is in the process of designing and implementing a new apprenticeship scheme in signal reception for those wanting to enter this career. The scheme has not been finalised yet but you can track its progress on the CAI website. The Registered Digital Installers Licensing Board has details of training schemes on its website and companies like BSkyB and BT also run apprenticeship schemes. Check the websites for details.

Employment is with a specialist contracting firm for major telecommunications and cable companies, TV and broadcast companies, mobile phone companies, central government, such as the Ministry of Defence, or the armed forces. Some qualified technicians are self-employed. Others become fully qualified telecommunication technicians and progress to engineering technician status.

Pay rises with experience and varies depending on location and employer. Technicians start at around £14k a year, rising to around £20k-£30k with experience and senior responsibilities. Overtime may be available.

Health

You need to have good stamina and be physically fit. This job requires good eyesight with normal colour vision and good general fitness.

Skills and Qualities

able to work well on your own, agile, good communication skills, good interpersonal skills, head for heights, health & safety awareness, IT skills, practical skills, technical aptitude

Relevant Subjects

Design and technology, Engineering, Mathematics, Physics, Science

Further Information

Apprenticeship Schemes (National Apprenticeship Service) - www.apprenticeships.org.uk

Diplomas (Foundation, Higher and Advanced) - http://yp.direct.gov.uk/diplomas
Foundation Learning (QCDA) - www.qcda.gov.uk
Registered Digital Installers Licensing Board - www.rdi-lb.tv
SEMTA - sector skills council for science, engineering and manufacturing technologies - www.semta.org.uk
Training Schemes - www.direct.gov.uk/en/educationandlearning
Welsh Baccalaureate - www.wbq.org.uk
Work for Sky - www.workforsky.com/

Addresses

Confederation of Aerial Industries (CAI)
Communications House, 41a Market Street, Watford, Hertfordshire WD18 0PN
Phone: +44 (0)1923 803030
Web: www.cai.org.uk

Similar Jobs

Electrical Engineering Technician, Fitter: Maintenance, Lightning Conductor Engineer, Rail Transport Technician, Security Systems Installer, Telecommunications Technician

Saw Doctor

CRCI:Manufacturing and Production
CLCI:ROZ
Job Band: 1 to 2

Job Description

Saw doctors work in a sawmill or a specialised tool cutting and grinding company, keeping saws in good working order. They sharpen blades by grinding or filing (by hand or machine) and reset saw teeth by bending to correct angle for cutting. Blades are examined for cracks or faults and any damaged parts are welded. They join broken ends by brazing. Repairs and maintenance of various types of saw, eg circular saw or bandsaw are the responsibility of the saw doctor.

Work Details

Saw doctors usually work a basic 39 hr week, Monday to Friday. In some jobs you may need to work on a Saturday. You work in a sawmill, workshop or manufacturing premises. You are responsible for a high standard of skilled work. The environment is noisy and perhaps uncomfortable because of sawdust. There is a risk of injury and accidents from equipment, so you may need to wear overalls and possibly safety glasses.

Qualification

- **England, Wales and Northern Ireland**

Band 1: No minimum qualifications are required, but you are expected to have a good level of general education. However, some formal/vocational qualifications at any level are useful.

Band 2: Although academic qualifications are not specified for this job, it is an advantage to have some GCSEs (A*-C) in subjects that include English and maths, or equivalent.

- **Scotland**

Band 1: No minimum qualifications are required, but you are expected to have a good level of general education. However, some formal/vocational qualifications at any level are useful.

Band 2: Although academic qualifications are not specified for this job, it is an advantage to have some S grades (1-3) in subjects that include English and maths, or similar.

Adult Qualifications

No minimum academic qualifications are required. Those with relevant experience have an advantage.

Work Experience

Relevant work or voluntary experience is always useful. It can improve your chances when looking for jobs or apprenticeships. Your personal or adult guidance adviser should be able to advise you about how to get some work experience.

Entry and Training

Often people enter this job after some experience of general work in a sawmill or in the timber industry. Training is by practical experience on the job. Applicants over 18 may be preferred as regulations do not allow people under 18 to operate machinery. S/NVQs in woodmachining (construction/sawmilling extrusion) are available at levels 2 and 3. At level 2, option B has two suitable modules; produce and maintain wood machine tooling and machinery and equipment maintenance. At S/NVQ Level 3, you also learn how to resolve wood machining problems.

The Saw Doctors' Association (SDA) runs regular 1-3 day training modules covering all aspects of saw and tool grinding. Contact the SDA for full details.

Mature entrants with related experience in sawmill work or relevant engineering skills are preferred. The Saw Doctors' Association (SDA) runs regular 1-3 day training modules in all aspects of saw and tool grinding. The SDA is planning to produce the modules as distance-learning materials.

Opportunities and Pay

Employment is with a sawmill or tool hire company. You can be self-employed. There are few vacancies because sawmills are becoming increasingly mechanised.

Pay varies depending on area and employer, but as a guide, a trainee earns between £200-£250 a week. This can rise up to £350 when highly skilled. Overtime pay may be available.

Health

There is an allergy risk from dust.

Skills and Qualities

able to work well on your own, attention to detail, careful, patient, practical skills, responsible attitude, safety conscious, steady hand.

Relevant Subjects

Design and technology

Further Information

Lantra - The Sector Skills Council for environmental & land-based sector (Lantra) http:/www.lantra.co.uk
The Wood Technology Society - www.iom3.org/content/wood-technology
Wood Focus (3 x year) (Institute of Wood Science) - www.iom3.org/content/wood-technology

Addresses

Saw Doctors' Association (SDA)
Unit 1, Queen Street, Darlaston, West Midlands WS10 8JF
Phone: 07779 148871
Web: www.sdauk.co.uk

Similar Jobs

Forest Worker, Sawmilling Operative, Wood Machinist

Sawmilling Operative

CRCI:Manufacturing and Production
CLCI:SAJ
Job Band: 1

Job Description

Sawmilling operatives work with felled timber logs of all sizes to produce manageable planks for the timber/wood manufacturing industry. They set up and use a variety of power saws in a sawmill.

Bark from the logs is stripped and they are sawed into rough planks. Can also cut these planks into smaller pieces. Operatives use lifting equipment or a conveyor belt to move the wood. They choose the best blade for cutting each type of wood and fit it to a circular or a band saw. Machinery is operated from a control panel and wood is checked for flaws or faults. Sawmilling operatives also clean and maintain the equipment. Increasingly sawmill equipment is becoming more computerised.

Work Details
Sawmilling operatives are expected to work shifts and stand for hours at a time. You have to be very active and physically fit as tyou often have to lift heavy pieces of wood. The workplace is usually noisy, dusty and often cold. There is a risk of accidents from equipment. You need to wear overalls, goggles, a face mask and ear protectors.

Qualification
- **England, Wales and Northern Ireland**

Band 1: No minimum qualifications are required, but you are expected to have a good level of general education. However, some formal/vocational qualifications at any level are useful.

- **Scotland**

Band 1: No minimum qualifications are required, but you are expected to have a good level of general education. However, some formal/vocational qualifications at any level are useful.

Adult Qualifications
No minimum formal qualifications are needed. You can improve your skills and qualifications by working through the Foundation Learning programme. This involves taking credit-based units and qualifications to help you progress.

Work Experience
Relevant work or voluntary experience is always useful. It can improve your chances when applying for jobs or apprenticeships. Your personal or adult guidance adviser should be able to advise you about how to get some work experience.

Entry and Training
Training is usually on the job with an experienced worker. It is useful to have practical ability in woodwork. You may be able to work for S/NVQ levels 2-3 in woodmachining (construction/ sawmilling extrusion). These S/NVQs have units that deal with workplace safety and organisational methods. There are also more specialised units that cover wood machining and equipment maintenance. Training programmes, including apprenticeships leading to level 2 and advanced apprenticeships leading to level 3, may be available in your area.

A Diploma/Welsh Baccalaureate in manufacturing and product design may be available in your area.

Government training opportunities, such as apprenticeships, may be available in your area. You can also gain recognition of previous experience through Accreditation of Prior Learning (APL) or by working towards relevant S/NVQs. Contact your local careers office, Jobcentre Plus, Next Step service or Learning and Skills Council (LSC) Local Enterprise Company (LEC) for details of training schemes.

Opportunities and Pay
There is increased competition in this industry as cheaper timber is imported from eastern Europe. However, there is growth in the UK industry as more sustainable building products are sought to meet the demand for environmentally friendly development. Carbon dioxide emissions from wood are lower than from other building products. Also greater use of wood helps the government reach targets on environmental and social commitments. Although increased mechanisation reduces the need for manual labour, overall growth predictions mean job prospects look good. You may have to relocate to find work.

You are employed by a sawmill or wood yard. Jobs are available only in certain areas of the UK. With experience, you can move to other jobs such as a wood machinist, who cuts and shapes wood for the furniture, timber and construction trades.

Pay varies depending on area and employer but a trainee earns between £200-£250 a week, rising to £350 with experience. Overtime pay may be available.

Health
You need to be fit and in good health to do this job. There may be a risk of chest complaints due to exposure to wood dust.

Skills and Qualities
able to follow instructions, able to work both on your own and in a team, attention to detail, common sense, good concentration level, hard working, numeracy skills, practical skills, safety conscious, strong.

Relevant Subjects
Design and technology

Further Information
Apprenticeship Schemes (National Apprenticeship Service) - www.apprenticeships.org.uk

Diplomas (Foundation, Higher and Advanced) - http://yp.direct.gov.uk/diplomas

Foundation Learning (QCDA) - www.qcda.gov.uk

Lantra - The Sector Skills Council for environmental & land-based sector (Lantra) - http:/www.lantra.co.uk

Welsh Baccalaureate - www.wbq.org.uk

Wood Focus (3 x year) (Institute of Wood Science) - www.iom3.org/content/wood-technology

Addresses
Institute of Wood Science
TThe Institute of Materials, Minerals and Mining,
1 Carlton House Terrace, London SW1Y 5DB
Phone: +44 (0)20 7451 7300
Web: www.iom3.org/content/wood-technology

Timber Trade Federation
The Building Centre 26 Store Street, London WC1E 7BT
Phone: +44 (0)20 3205 0067
Web: www.ttf.co.uk

Similar Jobs
Forest Worker, Saw Doctor, Wood Machinist

Scaffolder
CRCI:Building and Construction
CLCI:UF — Job Band: 1 to 2

Job Description
Scaffolders put up scaffolding by fitting together metal tubes and connectors, and fixing fittings and wooden or metal platforms. This allows construction workers to reach high levels on a wide range of buildings, bridges and other structures. They also put up scaffolding inside buildings to support working platforms for bricklayers, or for painting and decorating jobs. Base plates and poles are erected, then levels are checked and joins are secured with couplings. Scaffolding is removed when projects are finished. Being safety conscious is an important part of the job as those working on or below the scaffold must be protected. A variety of hand tools such as pulleys and winches, spanners, plumb lines and spirit levels are all used. Base plates and poles are erected, then levels are checked and joins are secured with couplings.

Scaffolders fix wooden platforms, guard rails, ladders, hoists and safety nets. Can set up framework scaffolding to support buildings or structures that are still being built until the cement sets hard. This is known as 'falsework'. They also erect stands for public events, such as outdoor concerts and sports events.

Scaffolder

Work Details

Scaffolders usually work a basic 37-39 hr week, though sometimes are required to work overtime, evenings and weekends to complete a job. Work can be outdoors or indoors using hoists, ladders and winches. They travel around an area to different sites and may need to spend time away from home on some contracts. A driving licence may be useful. Scaffolders work in a team at heights with much bending, lifting, kneeling and balancing. Conditions may be dirty and often cold, damp and wet.

There is a risk of falling so you need to wear a safety helmet, protective clothing and a safety harness for some jobs. They need to be aware of safety for all site workers and any visitors or passers-by.

Qualification

• England, Wales and Northern Ireland

Band 1: No minimum qualifications are required, but you are expected to have had a good level of general education. However, some formal/vocational qualifications at any level are useful.

Band 2: Although qualifications are not specified for this job, GCSEs in maths, English or a technical subject are helpful. Equivalent vocational qualifications are also useful.

• Scotland

Band 1: No minimum qualifications are required, but you are expected to have had a good level of general education. However, some formal/vocational qualifications at any level are useful.

Band 2: Although qualifications are not specified for this job, S grades in maths, English or a technical subject are helpful. Similar vocational qualifications are also useful.

Adult Qualifications

Mature entrants do not always require qualifications for this type of work, though a good standard of education is usually required.

Work Experience

Relevant work or voluntary experience is always useful and can improve your chances when applying for entry to construction jobs and apprenticeships. Health and safety issues may mean that there are certain jobs you cannot do until you are over 16. Contact your local ConstructionSkills office for advice.

Entry and Training

Most people start training with an employer and follow the Construction Industry Scaffolders' Record Scheme (CISRS). There are four types of card available, depending on your position, level of training and experience. Training is mainly on the job, with off site instruction at approved centres (11-12 weeks total). This leads to S/NVQ at level 2 in accessing operations and rigging. After at least two years' work experience you can qualify for a basic scaffolders' record card. Or you can do a 42-week full-time course at the National Construction College, including on-site work experience. This qualifies you for the CISRS basic and advanced card on completion of S/NVQs at levels 2 and 3.

Alternatively, five years' practical experience, a one-week assessment and completion of S/NVQ at level 2 also leads to qualification for the relevant scaffolders' card. Contact ConstructionSkills or the National Access & Scaffolding Confederation for details of training schemes and a list of approved CISRS training providers

A Diploma/Welsh Baccalaureate in construction and the built environment may be available in your area. Training programmes, including apprenticeships leading to level 2 and advanced apprenticeships/construction apprenticeships leading to level 3, may be available in your area. There are also Construction Awards (England and Wales) available for those who are unable to gain workplace experience for NVQs.

Employers may take older applicants who show aptitude and have previous relevant experience. Those with experience of building labouring work may have an advantage. You can also gain recognition of previous experience through Accreditation of Prior Learning (APL) or by working towards relevant S/NVQs. Contact your local careers office, Jobcentre Plus, Next Step service or Learning and Skills Council (LSC)/Local Enterprise Company (LEC) for details of all training schemes, including apprenticeships for adults. The National Construction College (ConstructionSkills) offers scaffolding and access course for adults.

Opportunities and Pay

Some scaffolders work for specialist scaffolding contractors, building contractors or a large company, such as an oil or power supply firm. Availability of work depends on the state of the building trade and the national economy. Currently there is a downturn in the housing market which means there may be a shortage of vacancies. You may be employed on a short-term contract. It is also possible to be self-employed. Temporary, casual and seasonal work is often available for those who are sub-contractors or are self-employed. Work abroad is also possible.

Pay varies depending on area and employer. Apprentices start on around £5k-£10k a year. Once trained, pay is around £16k-£20k a year, rising to £20k-£26k a year with experience. Overtime and bonus payments may boost your income. You may be given an allowance for travel costs and time, or a subsistence allowance when working away from home.

Health

Good physical fitness, agility and stamina are needed for this job.

Skills and Qualities

able to follow drawings and plans, able to work quickly, accurate measuring and calculating skills, agile, aptitude for teamwork, enjoy working outdoors, good balance, head for heights, health & safety awareness, responsible attitude

Relevant Subjects

Construction and built environment, Design and technology

Further Information

Apprenticeship Schemes (National Apprenticeship Service) - www.apprenticeships.org.uk

Construction Awards - http://gbca.com/events/construction-awards

Construction Industry Scaffolders Record Scheme (CISRS) - www.cisrs.org.uk/

ConstructionSkills - sector skills council for the construction industry - www.cskills.org

Diplomas (Foundation, Higher and Advanced) -http://yp.direct.gov.uk/diplomas

Training Schemes - www.direct.gov.uk/en/educationandlearning

Welsh Baccalaureate - www.wbq.org.uk

► Working in construction & the built environment (2007) (Babcock Lifeskills) - www.babcock-lifeskills.com/

Addresses

National Access & Scaffolding Confederation
4th Floor, 12 Bridewell Place, London EC4V 6AP
Phone: +44 (0) 20 7822 7400
Web: www.nasc.org.uk

Similar Jobs

Demolition Operative, Film/TV & Theatre Rigger, Lightning Conductor Engineer, Roofer, Satellite Systems Technician, Steeplejack

School Administrator

also known as: Secretary: School

CRCI:Administration, Business and Office Work
CLCI:CAT Job Band: 2 to 3

Job Description

School administrators carry out a range of office tasks that help to keep the school running smoothly. Duties vary depending on the size of the school. They are often the first point of contact people have with the school so welcomes people in and make sure they sign in and are taken to the person they need to visit. Also answer the phone, deal with enquiries and pass on messages.

Administrators usually do office tasks such as photocopying, printing, filing and sorting the post as well. May check and order stationery, pay invoices and make sure equipment is maintained and repaired. May also produce letters and other documents, take notes at meetings and send and check emails. Many keep staff and student records up to date. Some pull together statistical information to send to the Government and provide support to senior staff.

May check up on absent students, handle lost property and take charge of the first aid room and health and safety issues. Often deal with petty cash and collect dinner money and payments for trips and clubs.

Work Details

Usually work a 37 hour week, Monday to Friday, during term time. In smaller schools the post may be part time, ranging from six to fifteen hours a week. In many secondary and independent schools the job is full time, all year round. You are expected to take your annual leave during school holidays.

Administrators sit at a desk or workstation for much of the day. May work alone or as part of an administrative team. They come into contact with students, parents and carers, governors, teachers, senior staff and other professionals, such as social workers. May work closely with the head teacher. Smart/professional or smart-casual dress code is usually expected.

Qualification

There are no standard entry requirements for this job, but employers look for people with a good grasp of maths, English and ICT. Qualifications in administration, word processing, computer or secretarial skills are an advantage.

• England, Wales and Northern Ireland

Band 2: For entry to some posts: although academic qualifications may not be specified for this job, it is an advantage to have some GCSEs (A*-C) in subjects that include English and maths, or equivalent.

Band 3: For most jobs: usually at least 4 GCSEs (A*-C) including English and maths, or equivalent.

• Scotland

Band 2: Although academic qualifications are not specified for this job, it is an advantage to have some S grades (1-3) in subjects that include English and maths, or similar.

Band 3: For most jobs: usually at least four S grades (1-3) including English and maths, or similar.

Adult Qualifications

Generally you are expected to have the minimum entry qualifications, which can vary, although for some jobs no formal qualifications are required if you have relevant experience.

Work Experience

Work experience helps you find out what you enjoy and don't enjoy about a job or type of work. Paid or voluntary work that develops your administration and ICT skills is always useful. Working in an office and in educational settings can improve your job prospects.

Entry and Training

Most employers look for people with experience of office work. You also need to pass a Criminal Records Bureau (CRB) or Disclosure Scotland check. Some people enter this area of work as a school clerical or administrative assistant. They learn the skills and gain the experience they need to apply for jobs as school administrators.

Training is largely on the job, although you may do external short courses to update your skills in using certain computer software. The school or the local authority train you to use special school software such as the Schools Information Management System (SIMS).

The School of Education Administration (SEA) runs a two-month distance-learning course, covering the key areas of time management, stress management and dealing with visitors. There is an additional introduction to the school administration module for those who are not already working as school administrators. For people working in this job, SEA also offers a one-year, level 3 distance-learning course leading to an Institute of Administrative Management (iam) Certificate in Educational Administration. This certificate is accepted as an administration technical certificate for the business and administration apprenticeship/advanced apprenticeship. It can also be used as a stepping stone to the Certificate of School Business Management run by the National College of School Leadership (NCSL).

The iam offers a range of qualifications in administration management along with a continuing professional development (CPD) scheme for members. Full-time or part-time foundation degrees in relevant subjects may be available in some areas. You may work towards S/NVQs in Business and Administration at levels 1 to 4 or a qualification in support work in schools at level 2/3. Relevant training programmes, including apprenticeships in Business Administration leading to level 2, and advanced apprenticeships leading to level 3, may be available in your area.

Those with relevant work experience may be taken on without any formal qualifications. Many of the people who get jobs as school administrators are adults with several years' experience of office work. A significant number are graduates. You can gain recognition of previous experience through Accreditation of Prior Learning (APL) or by working towards relevant S/NVQs.

Opportunities and Pay

The number of school administrators has been rising over the last few years. Most schools in the UK, including independent schools have at least one. However, entry to this job is very competitive as many people want jobs that fit in with school hours and holidays.

For promotion, you may need to look for posts in larger schools or ones where the role has more responsibility. Some school administrators become school bursars or business managers. School administrators have the skills to move into many administration jobs outside of education. Some move into teaching or learning support assistant roles.

Salaries vary depending on the size of the school and what the role involves. Starting salaries in state schools can be around £14k-£16k a year. With experience you can earn around £20k and in senior posts up to £40k a year.

Skills and Qualities

able to cope under pressure, able to work both on your own and in a team, able to work to deadlines, calm, discreet, good communication skills, good interpersonal skills, good organisational skills, good written English, IT skills, numeracy skills, patient, trustworthy

Relevant Subjects

Business and accounting, Economics, English, ICT/Computer studies, Mathematics

Further Information

Local Government Careers (Improvement and Development Agency) - www.lgcareers.com/publications/

Skills4schools - www.skills4schools.co.uk

Support staff (Training and Development Agency for Schools) - www.tda.gov.uk/support.aspx

▶Working in business, administration & finance (2010) (Babcock Lifeskills) - www.babcock-lifeskills.com/

▶Working in schools & colleges (2007) (Babcock Lifeskills) - www.babcock-lifeskills.com/

Addresses

Institute of Administration Management (iam)
6 Graphite Square, Vauxhall Walk, London SE11 5EE
Phone: +44 (0)20 7091 2600
Web: www.instam.org

National College for Leadership of Schools and Children's Services, Triumph Road, Nottingham NG8 1DH
Phone: 0845 609 0009 (UK only)
Web: www.nationalcollege.org.uk/

School of Educational Administration (SEA)
Earlstrees Court Earlstrees Road, Corby, Northamptonshire NN17 4HH
Phone: +44 (0)1536 399007
Web: www.admin.org.uk

Similar Jobs

Civil Service Administrative Officer, Education Administrator, Local Government Administrator, Office Manager, Personal Assistant, School Business Manager/Bursar

School Business Manager/Bursar

CRCI:Education and Training
CLCI:CAT Job Band: 4 to 5

Job Description

School business managers/bursars provide professional leadership and management to ensure the effectiveness, efficiency and success of all support services in a school, college or university. They ensure that income, staff and the facilities are used to the best possible advantage. The job can vary widely, but generally ensures that the school runs efficiently and smoothly, and that costs are kept within a budget. They advise the head teacher and governing body on investment and financial policy.

Business managers are responsible for the purchasing of all goods and services for the school. They handle income, invoices, and orders supplies. Arranging the maintenance and development of buildings and grounds; as well as keeping accounts and dealing with salaries, pensions and wages, are very important aspects of the job. May oversee catering, which can be contracted out, to ensure that the premises meet hygiene and food safety regulations.

May have other responsibilities such as staff management and recruitment, the development of the school's admissions and appeals policy, or the training and development of support staff. A bursar may also be required to bid and secure additional funds and grants, or oversee the marketing strategy. Some bursars work in hospitals and residential homes.

Work Details

Usually works a 37 hr week, Monday to Friday, though may work longer than average office hours. Evening and weekend work is sometimes necessary due to parents' and governors' meetings, as well as other events that take place during the academic year. The work is mainly office based, but you need to move around the school and its grounds to manage the buildings, oversee the facilities, and to support staff. Employment in a school may require work in term-time only. Part-time work and job sharing is possible.

Qualification

There are no standard entry qualifications for this job but most school business managers/bursars have degree level or professional qualifications.

- **England, Wales and Northern Ireland**

Band 5: For degree courses: 2-3 A levels and some GCSEs (A*-C) usually including English and maths, or equivalent. Exact requirements depend on the degree you take.

- **Scotland**

Band 5: For degree courses: 3-5 H grades and some S grades (1-3), usually including English and maths, or similar qualifications. Exact requirements depend on the degree you take.

Degree Information

Any degree discipline is acceptable for entry to this job. However, a degree in accountancy, business management, human resources, or in public administration, is usually an advantage. There are several relevant postgraduate courses.

Adult Qualifications

Entry requirements may be relaxed for adults applying for higher education courses. Access or foundation courses provide those without the required qualifications a route onto degree courses.

Government training opportunities, such as apprenticeships, may be available in your area. You can also gain recognition of previous experience through Accreditation of Prior Learning (APL) or by working towards relevant S/NVQs. Contact your local careers office, Jobcentre Plus, Next Step service or Learning and Skills Council (LSC) Local Enterprise Company (LEC) for details of training schemes.

Work Experience

Entry to this job is competitive and it is important that you try to do some relevant work or voluntary experience before applying. Experience of administration/secretarial work, handling finances, particularly in the education sector, and working with people in a team or with the public, is an advantage.

Entry and Training

Many people apply for this job as a second career and have a wide range of qualifications and experience. Previous management experience may include banking, teaching, financial services, the armed services, human resources, accountancy, manufacturing, administrative or hospitality management. In the independent school sector, approximately 40% of entrants are former armed forces personnel, with chartered accountants being the next largest group. Other school business managers/bursars have achieved promotion from working in school administration and gaining relevant qualifications. Computer literacy is an essential skill. Accountancy experience is not essential, but is very helpful.

The National College for Leadership of Schools and Children's Services offers a bursar development programme including a certificate/diploma in school business management using a mix of school-based distance learning and residential courses with tutor support. The certificate is for new entrants and those who aspire to become a bursar, and the diploma is for experienced bursars who wish to extend their skills. Both awards are accredited by the Institute of Administration Management. There is also a part-time BA (Hons) in school business management that is offered by Manchester Metropolitan University. The course is intended as a 'top up' degree for graduates of the National College for Leadership of Schools and Children's Services, and can be studied over two years.

The National Association of School Business Management offers a range of courses, from one-day induction programmes to an MSc in education leadership. It also encourages continuing professional development and offers a short related courses. The Independent Schools' Bursars Association offers a bursar course for those already in post.

Appropriate S/NVQs (such as administration, finance or management) may be gained through college-based or work-based training. S/NVQs at levels 4-5 in management are most relevant.

Mature applicants, often those pursuing a second career, are particularly valued and especially those with accountancy/financial, and relevant managerial and organisational experience. Contact organisations such as the National Association of School Business Management, the Independent Schools' Bursars Association, or the National College for Leadership of Schools and Children's Services for details on school business management/bursar development programmes and vacancy information. The armed forces run a relevant two week course, two to three times a year in Aldershot for retiring services personnel.

Opportunities and Pay

There are opportunities for work as a school business manager/bursar in educational establishments throughout the UK and there is always keen competition for posts that become available. The job title of bursar is more usual in independent schools, and colleges and universities, whereas in many state schools the job title varies, such as finance officer, business director, school business manager or deputy head (resources). Sometimes in colleges/university the job title may include that of a finance and administration manager.

Progression to larger organisations is more likely through the successful attainment of a relevant postgraduate qualification. Opportunities exist in British schools overseas.

There are no set salary scales for bursars. Pay varies with the employer and depends on experience, size of the establishment and level of responsibility. Starting salaries are around £24k-£40k a year, rising to around £30-£60k, though a bursar at some independent schools can earn upto £100k a year. Some independent schools may provide accommodation, a car and other benefits.

Skills and Qualities

able to cope under pressure, able to prioritise work, aptitude for figures, discreet, efficient, good communication skills, good interpersonal skills, IT skills, motivated, project management skills

Relevant Subjects

Business and accounting, Economics, English, ICT/Computer studies, Law, Mathematics

Further Information

How to become a Bursar (Independant Schools' Bursers Association) - www.theisba.org.uk
Local Government Careers (Improvement and Development Agency) - www.lgcareers.com/publications/
Teachernet: Bursar Development Programme (Department for Education) - www.teachernet.gov.uk/whole school/remodelling/bursars/
▶Working in business, administration & finance (2010) (Babcock Lifeskills) - www.babcock-lifeskills.com/
▶Working in schools & colleges (2007) (Babcock Lifeskills) - www.babcock-lifeskills.com/

Addresses

Association of School and College Leaders (ASCL)
130 Regent Road, Leicester LE1 7PG
Phone: +44 (0)116 299 1122
Web: www.ascl.org.uk

Independent Schools' Bursars Association (ISBA)
Unit 11-12, Manor Farm, Cliddesden, Basingstoke, Hampshire RG25 2JB
Phone: +44 (0)1256 330 369
Web: www.theisba.org.uk

Institute of Administration Management (iam)
6 Graphite Square, Vauxhall Walk, London SE11 5EE
Phone: +44 (0)20 7091 2600
Web: www.instam.org

National Association of School Business Management (NASBM)
First Floor Offices, 140 Wood Street, Rugby CV21 2SP
Phone: +44 (0)1788 573 300
Web: www.nasbm.org.uk

National College for Leadership of Schools and Children's Services
Triumph Road, Nottingham NG8 1DH
Phone: 0845 609 0009 (UK only)
Web: www.nationalcollege.org.uk/

Similar Jobs

Accountant: Public Sector, Company Secretary, Education Administrator, Human Resources Officer/Manager, Local Government Administrator, School Administrator

School Lunchtime Supervisor

also known as: Midday Supervisor
CRCI:Education and Training
CLCI:FAB — Job Band: 1

Job Description

Lunchtime supervisors make sure that children eat lunch, stay safe and obey school rules during lunch breaks at school. A small number of jobs may involve running play activities. During lunch, they look out for children who need help with carrying or cutting food or opening packaging, encouraging good table manners and healthy eating. They clear up after accidents, including spills and sickness. May help to set up and clear dining tables.

In the playground or inside in bad weather, they supervise pupils, making sure they do not leave the grounds, talk to strangers or go where they are not allowed. They break up fights and arguments and comfort children who are upset. They take anyone who is injured or ill to get first aid and reports more serious accidents. Knowing what treatment to give children with allergies or medical conditions in their care is an important part of the job. Also help young children to use the toilets, wash their hands and sometimes change clothes.

Supervisors report any problems they cannot sort out to the duty teacher. They are aware of child protection issues and pass on any concerns about possible abuse to a senior member of staff.

Work Details

You work part time, term time only for 5-7 hours a week. Hours worked fall between 12 noon and 2pm, Monday to Friday. Most work in primary schools. Some work in special schools or with younger year groups in secondary schools.

You usually work with one class or year group. Most of the time you are on your feet. You spend some of the time outdoors, which can be cold. School lunchtimes can be lively and noisy.

Qualification

You do not need qualifications for this job. Experience of dealing with children and knowledge of first aid are useful. If the job involves doing lunchtime play activities, a playwork qualification or experience can be an advantage.

• England, Wales and Northern Ireland

Band 1: For entry to jobs, no minimum qualifications are needed, but you are expected to have a good level of general education and relevant experience. Some formal/vocational qualifications at any level are useful.

- **Scotland**

Band 1: For entry to jobs, no minimum qualifications are needed, but you are expected to have a good level of general education and relevant experience. Some formal/vocational qualifications at any level are useful.

Adult Qualifications

There are no formal entry requirements for this job. In England and Wales, you can improve your skills and qualifications by working through the Foundation Learning programme. This involves taking credit-based units and qualifications to help you progress.

Work Experience

Work experience helps you find out what you enjoy and do not enjoy about a job or type of work. Paid or voluntary work that gives you experience of working with children or first aid skills can improve your job prospects. Volunteering in school helps school staff to get to know you, which can be an advantage.

Entry and Training

As the job involves working with children, you need to pass a Criminal Records Bureau (CRB) or Disclosure Scotland check. For many jobs you need to be aged 18 or over. The head teacher or a member of staff trains you on the job. The local authority may run training for groups of new lunchtime supervisors. Usually you have to do a first aid course. You may get a qualification such as the first aid qualification (FAQ) level 2 certificate in paediatric first aid or the EDI level 2 certificate in first aid for those caring for children.

You may be able to do further training such as a level 2 or level 3 qualification in support work in schools or a City & Guilds level 2 or level 3 award in safeguarding children and young people.

Maturity and experience of caring for children is valued. Schools often like to employ people known to the school, such as parents.

Opportunities and Pay

You may be employed by the school or by the local authority. There are more than 17,000 primary schools in England, 2,100 in Scotland, 1,500 in Wales and 800 in Northern Ireland. Many have a lunchtime supervisor for each year group or class. Competition for jobs depends on the popularity of the school.

With experience you may become a senior supervisor. In this job you sort out problems and help staff work together to make sure things run smoothly. Some lunchtime supervisors have other jobs in or outside of school. In school they may be clerical, classroom or learning support assistants. Some employers may ask for formal qualifications for these job roles.

Lunchtime supervisors are usually paid an hourly rate of around £6-£8 an hour. Senior supervisors earn around £7-£10 an hour.

Health

This job requires stamina and good eyesight and hearing.

Skills and Qualities

able to relate well to children and young people, able to work both on your own and in a team, calm, health & safety awareness, observant, responsible attitude, sense of humour

Further Information

Local Government Careers (Improvement and Development Agency) - www.lgcareers.com/publications/

Skills4schools - www.skills4schools.co.uk

Support staff (Training and Development Agency for Schools) - www.tda.gov.uk/support.aspx

Training & Development Agency (TDA) - www.tda.gov.uk

▶Working in schools & colleges (2007) (Babcock Lifeskills) - www.babcock-lifeskills.com/

Similar Jobs

Childminder, Nursery Worker, Pre-school Supervisor/Worker, Teaching Assistant

Screenwriter

also known as: Scriptwriter

CRCI:Media, Print and Publishing

CLCI:GAL Job Band: 5

Job Description

Screenwriters create scripts for TV or film, for the games market or for corporate production companies. They may work on comedy or children's programmes, drama serials/series, feature films and animation, adaptations or documentaries. Screenwriters may develop and work on an original idea, or for a commissioned work. They research the background material, plan and draft scripts before submitting them to producers or a production company. Once accepted, considerable time is spent rewriting the script to satisfy all parties in the production.

Work Details

Working hours vary according to the professional relationship between a screenwriter, the material, and the producer/broadcaster. You may work indoors and often work from home, which enables you to choose your own working hours. This work requires strong motivation and self-discipline. Often work is found through personal contacts and networking, therefore self-publicising is important. You need to be able to cope with having your work criticised or rejected. Sometimes screenwriters have to keep to a schedule and attend meetings with agents and producers; others, particularly once established, are left to their own devices.

Qualification

There are no formally defined qualifications for becoming a screenwriter. Talent, creativity and luck are as important as academic ability. However, most screenwriters have degrees. A portfolio demonstrating writing talent may be as valuable as formal qualifications for entry to some courses.

- **England, Wales and Northern Ireland**

Band 5: For degree courses: 2-3 A levels and some GCSEs (A*-C) usually including English, or equivalent qualifications. Exact requirements depend on the degree you take.

- **Scotland**

Band 5: For degree courses: 3-5 H grades and some S grades (1-3), usually including English or similar. Exact requirements depend on the degree you take.

Degree Information

Useful first degree subjects include English, writing, scriptwriting, journalism, and a variety of film/media studies. There are full-time, part-time and distance-learning postgraduate courses in screenwriting, offered by many universities.

Adult Qualifications

Talent, creativity and luck are as important as academic qualifications. Entry requirements may be relaxed for adults applying for higher education courses. Access or foundation courses give adults without qualifications a route on to degree courses.

Work Experience

Employers or universities may prefer candidates who have relevant work or voluntary experience. Skills in journalism, in particular writing to deadlines, are useful. It is also useful to get involved in drama through school, college/university, amateur dramatics or youth theatre, to develop your skills and talent. Further experience, including front of house duties, directing, lighting, or editorial production of programmes is useful.

Entry and Training

There is no set entry route or formal entry requirements. Production companies are sent unsolicited scripts from thousands of aspiring screenwriters, yet most fall short of the required standards. Companies usually expect them to be in standard Mastershot format. However, there are national schemes, competitions and initiatives designed to discover new talent. Details of these are available from Skillset, the sector skills council for the audio-visual industries. It may be helpful to join organisations such as the Screenwriters' Workshop (Euroscript), the Script Factory, TAPS and the New Producer's Alliance, as they offer a range of services and help for aspiring screenwriters to refine their ideas.

Some screenwriters are graduates in English, screenwriting, creative writing, journalism, or film/media studies. Writing courses are offered at many further education colleges and at adult education centres. There are also full and part-time courses at film and television schools that give prospective screenwriters the opportunity to work with directors, actors and other specialists in the industry. There is a Diploma in advanced screenwriting available through the London Film School.

The Skillset Screen Academy Network across England, Wales and Scotland offer screenwriting courses and summer schools, short courses, master classes, work placements and bursaries. Contact Skillset for further details. Grants and awards may be available for some projects or professional development from such organisations as the UK Film Council, the Arts Council and local development agencies.

The UK Film Council has some funding available for the development of scripts and the Writers Bureau offers a range of writing courses and support materials.

A Diploma/Welsh Baccalaureate may be available in your area in creative and media. This can be a useful introduction to this type of career as you gain practical experience while studying. See the diplomas website or Skillset for further information. Cyfle (Wales) also offers a range of training courses for new entrants to the industry and professional development for those already employed.

Mature applicants already working in other sectors (eg literature, theatre, journalism, publishing and advertising) who wish to enter the screen industry may combine their work with study through a distance-learning, evening class or on-line screenwriting course. Contact Skillset for information on all education, bursaries and training options. You need a portfolio of work that demonstrates your writing talent. Experience in word processing is an advantage.

Opportunities and Pay

This job is highly competitive and few people are successful at earning a living from their writing alone. For some this is a part-time occupation in addition to a full-time job.

It is hard to summarise earnings for screenwriters as writers work freelance and are paid piece by piece or through royalties. The Writers' Guild of Great Britain displays recommended pay rates for screenwriters on its website. Earnings are tied to the commercial success of the work, and the rates at which projects are completed vary hugely. Screenwriters working for the BBC tend to be paid by the minute or by the episode.

Skills and Qualities

able to withstand criticism, able to work well on your own, creative flair, creative writing ability, good organisational skills, imaginative, IT skills, perseverance, self-disciplined, self-motivated

Relevant Subjects

English, Media and communication studies

Further Information

BBC Writers Room - www.bbc.co.uk/writersroom

Cool Careers - a different way to find your perfect job by Carolyn Boyes (2008) (Collins)

Cyfle (Wales) - www.cyfle.co.uk

Diplomas (Foundation, Higher and Advanced) - http://yp.direct.gov.uk/diplomas

Euroscript (Euroscript) - www.lsw.org.uk

Script Factory - www.scriptfactory.co.uk

Skillset - sector skills council for the creative media, fashion and textiles industries - www.skillset.org

TAPS: developing scriptwriters - www.tapsnet.org

The New Writer Magazine (6 x year) (New Writer) - www.thenewwriter.com/

The Writer's Handbook 2010 (Macmillan) - www.thewritershandbook.com/

Writers' Guild of Great Britain - www.writersguild.org.uk

Writersnet - www.writers.net

Addresses

Arts Council of England
National Service Centre, The Hive, 49 Lever Street, Manchester M1 1FN
Phone: 0845 300 6200 (UK only)
Web: www.artscouncil.org.uk

Arts Council of Northern Ireland
77 Malone Road, Belfast BT9 6AQ
Phone: +44 (0)28 9038 5200
Web: www.artscouncil-ni.org

Arts Council of Wales
Bute Place, Cardiff CF10 5AL
Phone: 0845 8734 900 (UK only)
Web: www.artswales.org

London Film School
24 Shelton Street, London WC2H 9UB
Phone: +44 (020 7836 9642
Web: www.lfs.org.uk

Scottish Arts Council
12 Manor Place, Edinburgh EH3 7DD
Phone: +44 (0)131 226 6051
Web: www.scottisharts.org.uk

UK Film Council
10 Little Portland Street, London W1W 7JG
Phone: +44 (0)207 861 7861
Web: www.ukfilmcouncil.org.uk

Writers Bureau
Sevendale House, 7 Dale Street, Manchester M1 1JB
Phone: 0845 345 5995
Web: www.writersbureau.com

Similar Jobs

Advertising Copywriter, Broadcast Researcher, Journalist, Journalist: Magazine, Writer

Sculptor

CRCI:Design, Arts and Crafts
CLCI:EB — Job Band: 3 to 5

Job Description

Sculptors create original forms or designs in three dimensions by carving, modelling or welding materials such as stone, metal, wood, clay, resin, ice or plastic. They sketch and plan the design and select suitable material. May use an existing object to make a sculpture. Sculptors use a variety of tools such as drills, knives and chisels, to carve and shape the desired effect. Sometimes makes an original from which a mould is made for casting in metal.

Some specialise, for example, in creating ice sculptures for special occasions such as a wedding reception, or may weld metal to create small or large objects to place in a garden or other landscape site. Others specialise in heraldic carving or statues, or work on restoration projects. Sculptors may have to promote their own work and negotiate with people who commission or exhibit their sculptures. Some sculptors may also take up a 'residency', running classes in a school or hospital, and others may teach privately.

Work Details

Sculptors are usually based in studios or workshops, but also travel to exhibitions. Depending on the materials used, the environment can be dusty or noisy, and you may have to lift and move heavy objects. Hours are irregular, since the work is often combined with other full-time or part-time jobs. You are likely to have to work in the evenings and at weekends and may have to work alone for long periods. At times you may be under pressure to meet deadlines.

Qualification

• England, Wales and Northern Ireland

Band 3: or entry to jobs, HNC or a relevant Diploma, usually at least 4 GCSEs (A*-C) including English and maths, or equivalent. For some foundation studies courses: usually at least 5 GCSEs (A*-C), or equivalent.

Band 4: For foundation studies course in art and design: usually at least one A level and some GCSEs (A*-C). For BTEC higher national award: a BTEC national award, successful completion of a foundation studies course, or equivalent qualification.

Band 5: For degree courses: 2-3 A levels and some GCSEs (A*-C) usually including English, maths and art or equivalent qualifications, together with a portfolio of work. Exact requirements depend on the degree you take.

• Scotland

Band 3: For entry: usually at least four S grades (1-3), including English, maths and art, or similar.

Band 4: For entry to SQA higher national and professional development awards, usually 2-3 H grades and some S grades (1-3), including English, maths and art, or similar qualifications.

Band 5: For degree courses: 3-5H grades and some S grades (1-3), usually including English, maths and art, or similar, together with a portfolio of work. Exact entry requirements depend on the degree you take.

Degree Information

Degrees can be in fine art sculpture or an art and design subject with a sculpture specialism. There are several postgraduate diplomas and degrees available.

Adult Qualifications

Mature applicants with outstanding portfolios of work may be accepted for courses without the standard entry requirements. There are Access or foundation courses in some areas, which give adults without qualifications a route into degree courses; check with individual colleges.

Work Experience

Entry to this job is competitive and it is important that you try to do some relevant work or voluntary experience before applying. Much of the work is freelance, so it is not easy to gain work experience with an established sculptor. Practical experience is needed to build up a suitable portfolio of work. Work experience in an art gallery or museum is useful.

Entry and Training

Although there are no formal entry requirements, most sculptors take formal courses, usually at degree level and entry to these is highly competitive. A good portfolio of recent work is required by almost all colleges and universities, and to demonstrate your work to potential clients and employers. Check current course requirements carefully because colleges accept a range of different qualifications. Talented applicants without qualifications can occasionally achieve course entry.

Students usually take a foundation studies course in art and design before progressing to a three-year degree course that specialises in sculpture. A full-time foundation degree may be available. In Scotland, degree courses last for four years, the first year usually being a general course, before specialism in the second year. A Diploma/Welsh Baccalaureate may be available in your area in creative and media and may provide a route onto higher education courses.

Some successful sculptors are self-taught and others begin their career by taking evening courses at a local education centre. The Royal British Society of Sculptors provides awards and bursaries to newly emerging sculptors, and runs professional development seminars.

There are part-time courses available for mature students over 21. Distance learning in sculpture is also available, such as the qualifications offered by the Open College of the Arts. Some private courses may be costly so you should choose carefully. There are also a wide range of courses available at adult education centres and colleges that offer day/evening art and design courses.

Opportunities and Pay

This area is highly competitive. Most sculptors work on a freelance basis, perhaps commissioned to produce sculptures for individuals or organisations. However, few can support themselves solely by selling their work. It can take many years, often with very little income, to build a reputation. The Crafts Council runs the 'Next Move' scheme which helps sculptors, who are about to set up a practice, to rent free studio space at a college, and provide access to equipment and a maintenance grant for two years. There may be opportunities to work abroad if you have a strong portfolio.

Pay depends on your reputation and how much work you do, but is generally low until you get established. Many sculptors have other sources of income such as teaching, art therapy, art administration, or community art. Generally, earnings can be around £20k-£25k a year. Sculptors in-residence at a school, hospital or prison can earn around £26k a year for teaching and mentoring. Highly successful sculptors can earn considerably more.

Health

Certain materials, such as plaster or wood, can create a fair amount of dust. This can cause allergies or may give you problems if you have asthma, for example.

Skills and Qualities

able to withstand criticism, able to work well on your own, creative flair, eye for shape/colour, good co-ordination, manual dexterity, self-motivated, stamina, technical aptitude

Relevant Subjects

Art and Design, Design and technology

Further Information

Artists Information Company - www.a-n.co.uk

Artist's Magazine (F&W Media Inc.) - www.artistsnetwork.com/artistsmagazine/

Creative & Cultural Skills - sector skills council for advertising, crafts, cultural heritage, design, literature, music, performing & visual arts - www.ccskills.org.uk

Society of Portrait Sculptors - www.portrait-sculpture.org

▶Working in art & design (2009) (Babcock Lifeskills) - www.babcock-lifeskills.com/

Addresses

Arts Council of England
National Service Centre, The Hive, 49 Lever Street,
Manchester M1 1FN
Phone: 0845 300 6200 (UK only)
Web: www.artscouncil.org.uk

Arts Council of Northern Ireland
77 Malone Road, Belfast BT9 6AQ
Phone: +44 (0)28 9038 5200
Web: www.artscouncil-ni.org

Arts Council of Wales
Bute Place, Cardiff CF10 5AL
Phone: 0845 8734 900 (UK only)
Web: www.artswales.org

Crafts Council (CC)
44a Pentonville Road, Islington, London N1 9BY
Phone: +44 (0)20 7806 2500
Web: www.craftscouncil.org.uk

National Society for Education in Art and Design (NSEAD)
3 Masons Wharf Potley Lane, Corsham, Wiltshire SN13 9FY
Phone: +44 (0)1225 810134
Web: www.nsead.org

Open College of the Arts
Michael Young Arts Centre, Redbrook Business Park,
Wilthorpe Road, Barnsley S75 1JN
Phone: 0800 731 2116 (UK only)
Web: www.oca-uk.com

Royal British Society of Sculptors
108 Old Brompton Road, London SW7 3RA
Phone: +44 (0) 20 7373 8615
Web: www.rbs.org.uk

Scottish Arts Council
12 Manor Place, Edinburgh EH3 7DD
Phone: +44 (0)131 226 6051
Web: www.scottisharts.org.uk

Similar Jobs
Art Therapist, Artist, Ceramic Designer, Model Maker, Stonemason: Banker, Teacher: Art, Toymaker

Secretary
CRCI:Administration, Business and Office Work
CLCI:CAT Job Band: 2 to 3

Job Description
Secretaries provide comprehensive clerical and administrative support for either one manager or for a team of people or managers. They deal with correspondence and documents, answer the telephone and welcome visitors. May keep a business diary, check e-mails, set up appointments, note cancellations, and make travel arrangements for a manager or executive. Also open and sort the mail ensuring it is circulated to the correct place or person. Often produce letters and reports dictated by managers, using shorthand, or by audio-typing, and usually using word processing software.

Secretaries may prepare and send out the agenda for meetings, take minutes and type them up afterwards. May be required to administrate an office petty cash system, noting any income and expenditure, and do some bookkeeping. A junior secretary often manages filing and record keeping and uses office equipment, such as fax machines and photocopiers.

Work Details
Usually work from 9am to 5pm, Monday to Friday, although sometimes overtime is necessary. Work is based in an office and you spend a lot of time at a desk or computer. You have contact with a wide range of people, such as senior staff, visitors from other organisations and perhaps members of the public. Your work may involve training and supervising junior staff and sometimes you may have to work under pressure. Part-time work or job-sharing is possible.

Qualification
There are no set minimum qualifications to enter this job and there are opportunities at all levels of qualification.

- **England, Wales and Northern Ireland**

Band 2: For some courses and employers: some GCSEs (A*-C) usually including maths and English, or equivalent. Basic keyboard and computer skills are required.

Band 3: For some full-time courses: usually at least 4 GCSEs (A*-C) preferably including English and maths, or equivalent qualifications. Requirements vary from college to college.

- **Scotland**

Band 2: For some courses and employers: some S grades (1-3) usually including maths and English, or similar. Basic keyboard and computer skills are required.

Band 3: For some full-time courses: usually at least four S grades (1-3) preferably including English and maths, or similar qualifications. Requirements vary from college to college.

Adult Qualifications
Some colleges accept adults without qualifications, but may use entry tests for some courses.

Work Experience
Employers or colleges may prefer candidates who have relevant work or voluntary experience such as work as an administrative assistant, using a range of office and computer skills. Work shadowing an experienced secretary is extremely useful so that you can appreciate the range of extra tasks undertaken. If you can gain experience in a variety of different types of office, then this is also an advantage. In some areas there is a young apprenticeship (14-16) scheme that provides an extended work placement and eventual achievement of a level 2 qualification whilst at school.

Entry and Training
You can start work as an administrator, doing on-the-job training and attending part-time courses for secretarial qualifications. There are also full-time courses, which you can take before going into a job. There are a wide range of courses leading to BTEC/SQA, OCR or London Chamber of Commerce & Industry (LCCI) qualifications, such as the OCR certificate or diploma in text processing at levels 1-3. S/NVQs relevant to secretarial work are available at levels 1-4, such as business and administration at levels 2-4. Check the Council for Administration (CFA) website for details of training courses.

In some jobs a knowledge of foreign languages or the ability to use a wider variety of computer packages (Excel, Dreamweaver, PowerPoint etc) is useful. The European Computer Driving Licence (ECDL) is a popular qualification for demonstrating your ability in using a wide range of computer packages. Training programmes, including apprenticeship schemes, may be available in your area for entry to this job. Advanced apprenticeships leading to qualification at level 3 can also be a route into higher education. Contact the Institute of Professional Administrators for details of different routes to qualification and membership.

From September 2009 you can work for a diploma in business, administration and finance. On successful completion of the foundation level, you can progress to higher, progression or advanced levels. The advanced diploma is equivalent ot 3.5 A levels and is a good foundation for any secretarial career. Visit the diploma website for full details.

Mature entrants may take refresher courses, which are sometimes available for those returning to work, and there may be special government training schemes in some areas. Contact your local Connexions or careers office, Jobcentre Plus, Next Step service or Learning and Skills Council (LSC)/Local Enterprise Company (LEC) for details of all training opportunities and schemes, including apprenticeships. You can gain recognition of previous experience through Accreditation of Prior Learning (APL) or by working towards relevant S/NVQs.

Opportunities and Pay

Secretaries can work in a very wide range of organisations, from small businesses to large multinational companies, voluntary organisations, central and local government. There is a steady demand for qualified staff. Temporary work is often available through agencies. You can become a senior secretary or an executive secretary/personal assistant after gaining experience. Some also become medical, bilingual or legal secretaries, or rural business administrators after taking specialised qualifications. Look at the Association of Medical Secretaries, Practice Managers and Administrators' (AMSPAR) and the Institue of Legal Secretaries' websites for further information on training.

Pay varies depending on location and employer. Starting salaries are likely to be around £14k-£18k, rising to around £18k-£24k a year with experience. Senior secretaries can earn up to £26k a year and more.

Health

This job requires good hearing and clear speech.

Skills and Qualities

able to work to deadlines, accurate, discreet, friendly, good organisational skills, good spoken and written communication, good telephone manner, good written English, IT skills, keyboard/typing skills

Relevant Subjects

English, ICT/Computer studies

Further Information

Apprenticeship Schemes (National Apprenticeship Service) - www.apprenticeships.org.uk

Diplomas (Foundation, Higher and Advanced) - http://yp.direct.gov.uk/diplomas

Institute of Professional Administrators (Institute of Professional Administrators) - www.inprad.org

Local Government Careers (Improvement and Development Agency) - www.lgcareers.com/publications/

Training Schemes - www.direct.gov.uk/en/educationandlearning

▶Working in English (2007) (Babcock Lifeskills) - www.babcock-lifeskills.com/

Addresses

Association of Medical Secretaries, Practice Managers, Administrators and Receptionists (AMSPAR)
Tavistock House North, Tavistock Square, London WC1H 9LN
Phone: +44 (0)20 7387 6005
Web: www.amspar.com

Council for Administration (CFA)
6 Graphite Square, Vauxhall Walk, London SE11 5EE
Phone: +44 (0)20 7091 9620
Web: www.cfa.uk.com

Institute of Legal Secretaries and PAs
3.08 Canterbury Court, Kennington Business Park
1 3 Brixton Road, London SW9 6DE
Phone: 0845 643 4974 (UK only)
Web: www.institutelegalsecretaries.com

Institute of Professional Administrators
6 Graphite Square, Vauxhall Walk, London SE11 5EE
Phone: +44 (0) 20 7091 7340
Web: www.inprad.org/index.html

Similar Jobs

Court Reporter, Personal Assistant, Rural Business Administrator, Secretary: Bilingual, Secretary: Legal, Secretary: Medical

Secretary: Bilingual

also known as: Bilingual PA, Secretarial Linguist

CRCI:Administration, Business and Office Work
CLCI:CAT
Job Band: 3 to 5

Job Description

Bilingual secretaries carry out a wide range of office-based tasks using one or more foreign languages. They combine fluent language skills with secretarial experience to communicate through accurate translation and interpretation of information. European languages are the most commonly used, though there is increasing demand for specific languages, such as Japanese, Mandarin/Cantonese, or Arabic. Duties include translating and word processing documents, letters and reports, dealing with mail, answering phones, and setting up meetings and appointments. Also make travel arrangements and contact foreign organisations.

May be required to interpret at meetings, organise conferences or participate in social or cultural occasions for overseas visitors. Some bilingual secretaries perform a personal assistant (PA) role, which may also involve office management.

Work Details

Usually work normal office hours of 9am to 5pm, Monday to Friday, but may be asked to work at other times due to the time differences between other countries. May be required to travel around the country or abroad. Part-time work is possible for this job. There is a lot of contact with clients, suppliers and representatives of foreign organisations. This type of work can be pressured and you have to work efficiently and quickly.

Qualification

There are no set entry requirements. However, a high level of fluency in one or more foreign languages combined with secretarial skills is essential for this job.

• England, Wales and Northern Ireland

Band 3: For some secretarial courses and entry to some jobs: at least 4 GCSEs (A*-C) including English, or equivalent.

Band 4: For HND, Diploma of Higher Education or foundation degree: 1-2 A levels and some GCSEs (A*-C) usually including English and maths, or equivalent.

Band 5: For a language degree course: 2-3 A levels, including one or more modern languages, and some GCSEs (A*-C) including English, or equivalent. Exact requirements depend on the degree you take.

• Scotland

Band 3: For some secretarial courses and entry to some jobs: at least four S grades (1-3) including English, or similar.

Band 4: For entry to SQA higher national and professional development awards, usually 2-3 H grades and some S grades (1-3), including English and maths, or similar qualifications.

Band 5: For a language degree course: 3-5 H grades, including one or more modern languages, and some S grades (1-3) including English, or similar qualifications. Exact requirements depend on the degree you take.

Degree Information

A degree in one or more foreign languages is preferred. Currently, languages that are in most demand in the UK include French, German, Spanish, Italian and Dutch. There is an increasing demand for Arabic, Japanese, Mandarin/Cantonese, Portuguese and Russian. In the UK public sector British Sign Language, Hindi, Swahili, Turkish, Urdu and Welsh are needed to serve some local communities effectively.

Business studies, business administration and office systems management also provide useful background, though graduates in these or other subjects should have proven language ability.

Adult Qualifications
Entry requirements may be relaxed for adults applying for higher education courses. Access and foundation courses give adults without qualifications a route on to degree courses.

Work Experience
Employers or colleges/universities may prefer candidates who have relevant work or voluntary experience. Any work experience that involves the use of a foreign language is an advantage. Work shadowing an experienced bilingual secretary is extremely useful so that you can appreciate the range of extra tasks undertaken. Work experience in different office environments is also useful. In some areas there is a young apprenticeship (14-16) scheme that provides an extended work placement and eventual achievement of a level 2 qualification whilst at school.

Entry and Training
You must be able to write and speak fluently in one or more foreign languages and have good typing/shorthand skills and a knowledge of the culture, economics and politics of the relevant countries. Bilingual secretaries gain their language skills through a degree course or by living and working in another country. Some learn multiple languages and develop mother tongue fluency from a young age.

A range of secretarial and language courses are available at different levels. These are mainly full time, though some are part time for 1-2 years, with postgraduate courses usually lasting a year. Specific bilingual secretarial courses are no longer available and it is usual for entrants to have gained their language skills first and then go on to learn secretarial skills. Once employed you have on-the-job training. Short courses, some customised, may be available in languages for business which can help provide terminology related to specific sectors.

Relevant S/NVQs are available in administration and also in language units at levels 1-4. Training programmes, including apprenticeship schemes, may be available in your area. Advanced apprenticeships leading to qualification at level 3 can also be a route into higher education.

From September 2011 it will be possible to study for a diploma in languages and international communications in England. Diplomas are at foundation, higher, progression and advanced level. The advanced level is equivalent to 3.5 A levels and this early specialism in languages may prove advantageous when applying for university language courses.

Mature entrants may take refresher courses, which are sometimes available for those returning to work, and there may be special government training schemes in some areas. Contact your local Connexions or careers office, Jobcentre Plus, Next Step service or Learning and Skills Council (LSC)/Local Enterprise Company (LEC) for details of all training opportunities and schemes, including apprenticeships. You can gain recognition of previous experience through Accreditation of Prior Learning (APL) or by working towards relevant S/NVQs.

Opportunities and Pay
You can work in this country or abroad, for a foreign company based in the UK or for an international company with offices overseas. The jobs are usually in large cities and there is a lot of competition for vacancies. You can also work for an import/export company, the Foreign and Commonwealth Office, European Union, or for the United Nations. Some local authorities also have links with Europe. You may also choose to work in universities and colleges, British and foreign banks, international law firms, insurance companies, and in the travel and tourism industries.

Bilingual/multilingual secretaries often use their job as an entry point to a particular industry or type of work in which they are interested. They may move into translating, sales, human resources or even stockbroking.

Pay can vary considerably depending on the location and type of employer. Starting salaries are likely to be around £16k-£20k a year, rising to around £25k a year with experience. Those who are highly experienced and qualified may earn up to around £35k a year. Languages such as Russian, Mandarin/Cantonese and Japanese, combined with high level computer skills, command even higher salaries.

Health
Clear speech is an important requirement of this role.

Skills and Qualities
ability in one or more languages, attention to detail, discreet, efficient, friendly, good communication skills, good telephone manner, good written English, initiative, IT skills

Relevant Subjects
Business and accounting, English, ICT/Computer studies, Modern Foreign Languages

Further Information
Apprenticeship Schemes (National Apprenticeship Service) - www.apprenticeships.org.uk

Diplomas (Foundation, Higher and Advanced) - http://yp.direct.gov.uk/diplomas

Institute of Professional Administrators - www.inprad.org

Local Government Careers (Improvement and Development Agency) - www.lgcareers.com/publications/

Real Life Guide to Business & Administration (Trotman 2009) - www.trotman.co.uk

Training Schemes - www.direct.gov.uk/en/educationandlearning

Addresses
Institute of Professional Administrators
6 Graphite Square, Vauxhall Walk, London SE11 5EE
Phone: +44 (0) 20 7091 7340
Web: www.inprad.org/index.html

National Centre for Languages
3rd Floor, 111 Westminster Bridge Road, London SE1 7HR
Phone: 08456 12 5885 (UK only)
Web: www.cilt.org.uk

Similar Jobs
Civil Service EU Administrator, Personal Assistant, Secretary, Secretary: Legal, Teacher: Modern Foreign Languages, Translator

Secretary: Legal
CRCI:Administration, Business and Office Work
CLCI:CAT — Job Band: 2 to 4

Job Description
Legal secretaries provide secretarial and administrative support to professional staff in legal offices. Duties include dealing with correspondence, legal documents and records, as well as general office duties. They meet visitors, answer the phones and keep clients informed about their business. Also organise lawyers' diaries, making appointments for clients. Usually work from dictation, using audiotapes. Also prepare and proofread contracts, licences, wills, leases etc, using the correct/standard terminology and layout.

Legal secretaries deal with highly confidential and sensitive information. They file case notes and keep records of costs, accounts and office petty cash. With experience, they may attend court hearings or visit custody cells to take notes.

Secretary: Legal

Work Details

Usually work normal office hours, though some offices have flexitime, and you may also be asked to work extra hours at busy times. Part-time work is possible. Most of the time you work in the office but the job can sometimes require attendance at court hearings or visits to property. Legal work often has to be done urgently, perhaps to meet court deadlines, so your work may be pressurised at times.

Qualification

There are no set academic entry requirements, but for entry to training courses some qualifications may be necessary.

• England, Wales and Northern Ireland

Band 2: Employers may expect some GCSEs (A*-C) including English, or equivalent. The Institute of Legal Executives (ILEX) prefer applicants to have English at GCSE (A*-C) for the certificate/ diploma course.

Band 3: For some courses: usually at least 4 GCSEs (A*-C) usually including English, or equivalent.

Band 4: For HND, Diploma of Higher Education or foundation degree: 1-2 A levels and some GCSEs (A*-C) usually including English and maths, or equivalent.

• Scotland

Band 2: Employers may expect some S grades (1-3) including English, or similar. The Institute of Legal Executives (ILEX) prefer applicants to have English at GCSE (A*-C) for the certificate/ diploma course.

Band 3: For some courses: at least four S grades (1-3) including English, or similar.

Band 4: For entry to SQA higher national and professional development awards, usually 2-3 H grades and some S grades (1-3), including English and maths, or similar qualifications.

Adult Qualifications

Entry requirements for college courses vary for mature applicants and may be waived; check with local institutions or the professional organisations. Relevant diploma courses are offered by professional organisations, such as the Institute of Legal Secretaries and PAs and the Institute of Legal Executives (ILEX). Courses can be taken through distance learning.

Work Experience

Employers or colleges may prefer candidates who have relevant work or voluntary experience such as work as an office junior, using a range of office and computer skills. Work shadowing an experienced secretary is extremely useful so that you can appreciate the range of extra tasks undertaken. Experience in a law office is a distinct advantage.

Entry and Training

Legal secretaries must have very good typing, word-processing and audio-typing skills. Shorthand is also useful. It is usual to take a secretarial course before getting into a job, though it is also possible to enter as an office junior and work your way up. General secretarial courses can lead to BTEC/SQA, OCR or London Chamber of Commerce & Industry (LCCI) qualifications, such as the OCR certificate or diploma in text processing at levels 1-3. S/ NVQs relevant to secretarial work are available at levels 1-4, such as business and administration at levels 2-4.

Once you have secretarial skills, you may go on to take a course such as the legal secretaries diploma, offered by the Institute of Legal Secretaries and PAs. This can be studied at an evening class or through distance learning. The Institute of Legal Executives (ILEX) offers a level 2 certificate for legal secretaries and a level 2/ level 3 award in legal information processing. Courses can be followed at any workplace or college that is registered as an ILEX Approved Centre. There is a distance learning option with the ILEX Tutorial College.

Some colleges offer 1-2 year full-time legal secretary courses leading to awards from other various bodies, including OCR. With the HNC/HND in legal services, you can do paralegal work in law offices, for example buying and selling property on behalf of clients or preparing court papers. In Scotland, you can take the SQA higher national diploma in legal studies. Training programmes, including apprenticeship schemes, may be available in your area. Advanced apprenticeships leading to qualification at level 3 can also be a route into higher education.

From September 2009 it is possible to work for a diploma in business, administration and finance. The diploma is a new qualification for 14-19 year olds available at foundation, higher, progression and advanced levels. The advanced diploma is equivalent to 3.5 A levels. Check the diplomas website for details.

Mature applicants can take refresher courses that are sometimes available for those returning to work and there may be special government training schemes in some areas. You can also gain recognition of previous experience through Accreditation of Prior Learning (APL) or by working towards relevant S/NVQs.

Opportunities and Pay

Legal secretaries work for firms of solicitors/advocates, in barristers' chambers and law courts, as well as in legal departments of government, the local council and large industrial and financial organisations. Promotion prospects are normally good in this job as there are a variety of options available, although there may be some slowdown in availability of opportunities due to the depressed property market. With experience you can apply for senior secretarial jobs, office management or legal administration. In England and Wales, legal secretaries can also take additional training to become legal executives, paralegals or licensed conveyancers. Some may take a degree or further qualifications from the Institute of Legal Executives (ILEX) to qualify as a solicitor or barrister.

Although the legal system in Scotland is separate from the English system, those secretaries with sufficient training and experience can move between countries. If you have suitable language skills it is possible to work abroad, for the European Court of Justice, or at overseas offices of solicitors.

Pay varies depending on location and size of employer. Salaries for legal secretaries start at around £14k-£17k, rising to around £20k a year with experience. Senior secretaries can earn around £22k-£32k a year and more in cities such as Edinburgh, Leeds, London and Manchester.

Skills and Qualities

able to work to deadlines, accurate, discreet, efficient, good memory, good organisational skills, good written English, IT skills, methodical, trustworthy

Relevant Subjects

English, ICT/Computer studies, Law

Further Information

Apprenticeship Schemes (National Apprenticeship Service) - www.apprenticeships.org.uk

Diplomas (Foundation, Higher and Advanced) - http://yp.direct.gov.uk/diplomas

Institute of Professional Administrators (Institute of Professional Administrators) - www.inprad.org

Law Gazette (Law Society) - www.lawgazette.co.uk

Law Uncovered (Trotman 2009) - www.trotman.co.uk

Local Government Careers (Improvement and Development Agency) - www.lgcareers.com/publications/

Real Life Guide to Business & Administration (Trotman 2009) - www.trotman.co.uk

Skills for Justice - sector skills council for the UK justice system - www.skillsforjustice.com

TARGETjobs: Law (GTI Specialist Publishing Ltd.) - www.groupgti.com

TARGETjobs: Law Scotland (GTI Specialist Publishing Ltd.) - www.groupgti.com

▶Working in politics & law (2010) (Babcock Lifeskills) - www.babcock-lifeskills.com/

Addresses

Institute of Legal Executives (ILEX)
Kempston Manor, Bedfordshire MK42 7AB
Phone: +44 (0)1234 841 000
Web: www.ilex.org.uk

Institute of Legal Secretaries and PAs
3.08 Canterbury Court Kennington Business Park
1 3 Brixton Road, London SW9 6DE
Phone: 0845 643 4974 (UK only)
Web: www.institutelegalsecretaries.com

National Association of Licensed Paralegals
Admissions , 3.08 Canterbury Court, , Kennington Business Park ,
1 - 3 Brixton Road, London SW9 6DE
Phone: +44 (0) 20 3176 0900
Web: http://national-paralegals.co.uk

Similar Jobs

Court Reporter, Law Costs Draftsman, Legal Cashier, Legal Executive, Paralegal, Secretary

Secretary: Medical

also known as: Medical Secretary

CRCI:Administration, Business and Office Work
CLCI:CAT Job Band: 2 to 4

Job Description

Medical secretaries provide secretarial support for health professionals in a range of settings, such as a hospital or GP surgery. They may work for a consultant or group of consultants, or for a doctor or several doctors in a practice. Some medical secretaries work in health centres, pharmaceutical companies, in a university medical school or research department. They arrange appointments, answer the telephone and keep track of health records and files, both manually and with the use of a computer. May attend meetings, arrange diaries and organise travel for senior consultants. Also liaise with other healthcare professionals.

Secretaries make notes during a clinic session and produce documents such as letters, reports for patients' records and minutes of meetings. May receive tape recorded dictation and audio type the information into patients' records, letters etc. May also work from handwritten notes. May be required to arrange transport for patients.

Work Details

Usually work around 35-39 hrs a week, Monday to Friday, although may sometimes have to work on a Saturday or in the evening. Part-time work, flexitime and job-sharing are possible. Medical secretaries are office based and much of the work is done sitting at a desk. If working in the NHS, there is significant contact with GPs, patients and other healthcare staff. In some jobs you may have to help people who are unwell, anxious or upset and you must be able to put people at ease. The work involves writing up confidential patients' notes, which may contain unpleasant medical details.

Qualification

There are no minimum entry qualifications, though a good standard of education and solid secretarial skills are required.

• England, Wales and Northern Ireland

Band 2: For some secretarial courses: it is an advantage to have some GCSEs (A*-C) usually including maths and English, or equivalent. Basic keyboard and computer skills are usually required.

Band 3: For the AMSPAR advanced diploma for medical secretaries: preferably a minimum of 4 GCSEs (A*-C) including English, or equivalent.

Band 4: For some courses: 1-2 A levels and some GCSEs (A*-C), or equivalent.

• Scotland

Band 2: For some secretarial courses it is an advantage to have some S grades (1-3) usually including English and maths, or similar. Basic keyboard and computer skills are usually required.

Band 3: For SQA national certificate in office administration (including optional medical modules) or the AMSPAR advanced diploma for medical secretaries: preferably a minimum of four S grades (1-3) including English, or similar qualifications.

Band 4: For some courses: usually 2-3 H grades and some S grades (1-3), or similar qualifications.

Adult Qualifications

For entry to courses it is an advantage to have experience of either a medical background, such as nursing, or some office experience. Adults may be accepted for college courses without academic qualifications if they have relevant experience. Applicants for the Association of Medical Secretaries, Practice Managers, Administrators & Receptionists (AMSPAR) or the British Society of Medical Secretaries (BSMS) qualifications may be exempt from formal entry requirements if they have sufficient experience of administration in a healthcare environment.

Work Experience

Entry to this job/career is fairly competitive, because employed medical secretaries tend to stay with this career path longer, and vacancies are therefore less common. Practical work experience may be hard to gain because there is a lot of confidential and private information that only employed practice staff may access. It may however be possible to talk to a medical secretary to find out about the work, and observe or work shadow for a short while. Any experience of work in an office or with the public in a healthcare capacity is an advantage.

Entry and Training

You need to have accurate typing/keyboard skills, shorthand and a knowledge of medical terminology. It is usual to take an Association of Medical Secretaries, Practice Managers, Administrators & Receptionists (AMSPAR) or British Society of Medical Secretaries (BSMS) course, or relevant SQA course, before going into employment. Courses usually cover such areas as medical shorthand/terminology, medical audio typing/word-processing, administration, legal aspects and communications.

There may also be a period of work experience involved in some college courses. Some courses are part time or through distance learning, whilst in a job. Once employed you have on-the-job training. The BSMS also provides training suitable for continuing professional development (CPD). The SQA professional development award (PDA) in medical administration is aimed principally at those already employed in this work who want to gain a relevant qualification.

S/NVQs at levels 2-4 in business and administration are available. Training programmes, including apprenticeship schemes, may be available in your area for entry to this job. Advanced apprenticeships leading to qualification at level 3 can also be a route into higher education.

From September 2009 it is possible to work for a diploma in business, administration and finance. The diploma is a new qualification for 14-19 year olds and is available at foundation, higher, progression and advanced levels. The advanced diploma is equivalent to 3.5 A levels. Check the website for full details.

Mature applicants with relevant secretarial/reception skills experience, particularly using medical terminology, have an advantage. A background knowledge in human biology is also helpful. You can also gain recognition of previous experience through Accreditation of Prior Learning (APL) or by working towards relevant S/NVQs.

Opportunities and Pay

Medical secretaries work in hospitals, in general practice, the private hospital sector and also for medical and holistic centres, medical research organisations, private clinics and in the armed forces. There are now more opportunities to work in general practice owing to the increasing amount of administration involved. There is work in medical schools supporting consultants, professors and other academic staff, and for drug companies. With experience you can become, for example, a personal assistant either in healthcare or in industry and commerce, or work as a general practice manager. There are opportunities for medical secretaries to work overseas, particularly in the Middle East.

Pay varies depending on the individual employer though is around £15k-£18k a year, rising to around £22k. Senior secretaries earn around £22k-£26k a year. Pay is higher in London and in the private sector.

Skills and Qualities

accurate, attention to detail, discreet, efficient, good communication skills, good interpersonal skills, good organisational skills, helpful, IT skills, reliable, tactful

Relevant Subjects

Biology, English, ICT/Computer studies, Science

Further Information

AMSPAR Professional (AMSPAR) - www.amspar.com

Diplomas (Foundation, Higher and Advanced) - http://yp.direct.gov.uk/diplomas

Institute of Professional Administrators - www.inprad.org

NHS Careers (NHS Careers) - www.nhscareers.nhs.uk

Real Life Guide to Business & Administration (Trotman 2009) - www.trotman.co.uk

The Journal of Medical Secretaries and Administrators (British Society of Medical Secretaries and Administrators) - www.bsmsa.org.uk/

Addresses

Association of Medical Secretaries, Practice Managers, Administrators and Receptionists (AMSPAR)
Tavistock House North, Tavistock Square, London WC1H 9LN
Phone: +44 (0)20 7387 6005
Web: www.amspar.com

British Society of Medical Secretaries (BSMS)
132 Mayfield Road, Edinburgh EH9 3AH
Phone: +44 (0)131 466 0682
Web: www.bsmsa.org.uk/

Similar Jobs

GP Practice Manager, Health Records Clerk, Personal Assistant, Receptionist, Secretary, Secretary: Legal

Security Dog Handler/Trainer

also known as: Dog Handler

CRCI:Security and Armed Forces

CLCI:MAZ Job Band: 1

Job Description

Dog handlers control and work closely with a dog on a variety of security premises. These can include industrial and business premises, recreational centres or ports and airports. Can work in crime prevention and detection roles. The dog usually lives and trains with their handler to build a good working relationship. Handlers train and work with a dog to take advantage of their sharp senses, particularly that of smell. They use the dog to find substances, such as drugs or explosives. Also track down and find people such as criminals or people who have had an accident while mountain climbing. Can be employed to detect and capture those attempting to enter the country illegally.

Handlers and their dogs may be used to protect property, including airfields, private property or military premises. When working with the police, they also help to control crime and to detect firearms and other weapons.

Work Details

The hours can sometimes be long and variable but you normally work on a shift or rota basis that covers 24 hrs, seven days a week. Some jobs require you to be on call for emergencies. In HM Revenue & Customs, you work at ports and airports. You may check an aircraft, passengers, their luggage, an aircraft's cargo or the land surrounding an airport. You may also check cars and other vehicles, freight, passengers and their luggage, ferry terminals, or patrol the area surrounding a ferry port or the Channel Tunnel Link. You are on your feet, walking most of the time, so you must be physically fit. Much of the work is outside in all weathers and terrains.

Qualification

For most jobs you first need to join the organisation of your choice, such as the police, fire service, HM Revenue & Customs, private security organisation or the armed forces.

- **England, Wales and Northern Ireland**

Band 1: For most jobs: no academic qualifications are needed but a number of GCSEs or equivalent at any level are helpful.

- **Scotland**

Band 1: For most jobs: no academic qualifications are needed but a number of S grades or similar at any level are helpful.

Adult Qualifications

No specific qualifications required. Those without existing qualifications can work through the Foundation Learning programme by taking credit-based units and qualifications.

Work Experience

Any work experience can equip you with skills that you can use in the future and add to your CV. This can include work that is unpaid or voluntary. It can be holiday experience, or part-time work. Any work with animals, especially dogs and with the public is useful. Many animal sanctuaries welcome voluntary assistance. You could approach your local veterinary practice for work experience.

Entry and Training

In many private sector jobs, there are no formal entry requirements. It is an advantage to have a good knowledge and/or experience of dogs prior to training. You should also really enjoy working with dogs. For some organisations, applicants may be required to take a basic recruitment test. This can include numeracy, information checking, use of English, reasoning and observation. Those who wish to enter the armed forces or police/fire service as a dog handler need to satisfy the general entry requirements, and gain entry first. Basic training is then required, which can be a period of up to two years. You may be required to undertake an assessment course to ensure you are suitable for training as a dog handler.

Courses can be very demanding for both handler and dog. Trainee dog handlers learn to understand the principles of dog training, use of protective equipment, verbal and visual training commands, methods of search procedures, and the health and welfare of the dog. They also include the law surrounding dogs and their use in security work. Details of courses such as general purpose security dog handling, drug detection and safety techniques are available on the websites of the National Association of Security Dog Users and the National Training Inspectorate for Professional Dog Users. The British Institute of Professional Dog Trainers now also offers courses specifically aimed at the security industry.

Those employed as a security guard are required to hold a Security Industry Authority (SIA) licence under the Private Security Industry Act. Contact the SIA for details. The ASET Level 2 National Award for General Purpose Security Dog Handlers is aimed at those with security guarding experience and an SIA licence.

This role is suitable for mature people with experience of working with dogs. It is important to be physically fit and agile. Those with military training or experience of handling dogs are especially sought after by security firms.

Opportunities and Pay

There is a lot of competition for this type of employment, but at the moment more experienced handlers are needed, particularly in private security work. Employers include the police, armed forces, fire service, HM Revenue and Customs, private security firms, or in mountain rescue. Promotion in the services depends on your service record, experience and qualifications. Many involved in private security are self-employed.

Salaries for dog handlers depend very much on the type of employer. Generally, starting salaries in private security are around £15k, and as an experienced handler in all areas of employment, you can expect to earn £20k a year. Senior positions and those requiring specialist knowledge can earn up to £30k.

Health

You must be physically fit and agile for this job. There are specific fitness tests for entry to basic training with the armed services and the police.

Skills and Qualities

agile, assertive, energetic, good at handling animals, hard working, patient, quick reactions, responsible attitude

Relevant Subjects

Physical education and sport

Further Information

Could you? Police (Home Office) - www.policecouldyou.co.uk/

Foundation Learning (QCDA) - www.qcda.gov.uk

Police Service of Northern Ireland - www.psni.police.uk

Skills for Security - sector skills council for security industry - www.skillsforsecurity.org.uk/

▶Working in police, fire & security (2009) (Babcock Lifeskills) - www.babcock-lifeskills.com/

Addresses

British Institute of Professional Dog Trainers (BIPDT)
PO Box 5894, Milton Keynes MK10 1FJ
Phone: +44 (0) 1908 526856
Web: www.bipdt.org.uk

National Association of Security Dog Users (NASDU)
Unit 11 Boundary Business Centre, Boundary Way, Woking, Surrey GU21 5DH
Phone: +44 (0)1483 888588
Web: www.nasdu.co.uk

National Training Inspectorate for Professional Dog Users (NTIPDU)
New House, Cefn Vaynor, Berriew, Welshpool SY21 8PP
Phone: +44 (0)1686 640781
Web: www.ntipdu.org

Security Industry Authority (SIA)
PO Box 1293, Liverpool L69 1AX
Phone: 0844 892 1025 (UK only)
Web: http://sia.homeoffice.gov.uk/Pages/home.aspx

Similar Jobs

Civil Service Customs Officer, Guide Dog Trainer, Police Officer, RSPCA/Scottish SPCA Inspector, Security Officer

Security Officer

also known as: Security Guard

CRCI:Security and Armed Forces

CLCI:MAG — Job Band: 1 to 3

Job Description

Security officers ensure people, buildings and property are secure and safe from theft, vandalism, damage by fire, flood or attacks. Patrol a designated area looking for fires, or potential burglars/shoplifters. May use cameras and CCTV, sophisticated electronic systems and two-way radios. Some use dogs in their work. May control a security gate, do reception work, check deliveries or spot credit card fraud. A mobile guard does similar work using a van to patrol several places.

A cash-in-transit guard travels in an armoured van to protect items like money and jewellery, which are being taken from one place to another. May be required to write brief reports and give evidence to the police and law courts.

Work Details

Security officers usually work a basic 39-42 hour week, though may have to work unsocial hours. Shift work is possible and can include nights, weekends and public holidays. Some officers only work night shifts, whilst others, such as cash-in-transit guards and some static guards, work during the day. Overtime is common. Some officers work mainly indoors, while others work both outdoors and indoors and can be out in all weather conditions. You may have to protect industrial premises, an office block, building site, an area of docks, airport or a shop, or perhaps deal with the public at a security gate or on reception.

Static and mobile guards usually work alone but may have to approach people whom they suspect. Cash-in-transit guards normally work in teams of 4-6. There is a risk of danger and of being attacked, though you are trained not to put yourself at risk. You need to wear a uniform and perhaps a helmet.

Qualification

• England, Wales and Northern Ireland

Band 1: Although no formal qualifications are needed, some GCSEs are useful, especially in English and maths, or equivalent.

Band 2: No set minimum educational entry requirements, though some GCSE passes including English, or equivalent, are useful.

• Scotland

Band 1: Although no formal qualifications are needed, some S grades are useful, especially in English and maths, or similar.

Band 2: No set minimum educational entry requirements, though some S grade passes including English and maths, or similar, are useful.

Adult Qualifications

Personal qualities and physical fitness are often more important than formal qualifications.

Work Experience

Any relevant work experience can equip you with skills that you can use in the future and add to your CV. This can either be unpaid/voluntary, or holiday/part-time work that you have organised yourself.

Entry and Training

Security officers are now required to hold a Security Industry Authority (SIA) licence under the Private Security Industry Act 2001. If the job requires dealing with CCTV, an SIA public space surveillance (CCTV) licence may also be needed. The licence costs £245 and lasts for three years.

To obtain a licence, you must be over 18 and have an identity and Criminal Records Bureau/Disclosure Scotland check. Those with a criminal record are not necessarily excluded from obtaining a licence as the SIA looks at the seriousness and relevance of the offence. You must have passed certain courses before you are eligible to apply for a licence. These include a level 2 BTEC award in security operations and a level 2 certificate for security guards. Check the SIA website for a comprehensive course listing.

Front line security staff also have to undertake specific training to obtain a licence. This training is delivered as a two part course covering the role and responsibilities of a security officer and communication skills and conflict management. The course can be delivered over four days or during evening and/or weekend sessions. You have to pass two exams to complete the course. Training varies widely depending on the employer. Most companies have short induction courses that cover topics such as legal powers and aspects of the work. Most officers also have on-the-job training with experienced workers or supervisors. Large companies often have formal training programmes, both on and off the job. You may need a clean current driving licence.

Through the International Professional Security Association (IPSA), you can take a range of short specialist training courses and supervisory and management correspondence courses. There are also other relevant courses available at foundation, degree and postgraduate level in risk and security management. Check the IPSA website for details.

Training programmes, including apprenticeship schemes, may be available in your area. Advanced apprenticeships leading to qualification at level 3 can also be a route into higher education.

Adult entry is common, particularly for those with previous experience of the police, fire or prison services or the armed forces. You may be able to enter this work through a Government funded training programme.

Opportunities and Pay

The demand for security officers is growing and vacancies are advertised regularly. You can work for an organisation or a private security company which provides a security service to banks and building societies, universities, colleges and schools, hotels, ships, airports or shopping centres. It is possible to become a supervisor, to specialise or perhaps to move into management. Promotion prospects are better in large organisations and there may be a chance to work abroad. Self-employment is possible and with experience you can set up your own security company.

Pay varies depending on location and employer. New entrants start at around £12k-£15k a year, rising to £20k with experience. Some security guards can earn up to £30k a year.

Health

You have to be fit and healthy and pass a medical. There may be height restrictions.

Skills and Qualities

able to report accurately, alert, common sense, firm manner, honest, observant, quick reactions, responsible attitude, security conscious, trustworthy.

Further Information

Apprenticeship Schemes (National Apprenticeship Service) - www.apprenticeships.org.uk

Foundation Learning (QCDA) - www.qcda.gov.uk

International Professional Security Association (IPSA) (IPSA) - www.ipsa.org.uk/

Professional Security Magazine - www.professionalsecurity.co.uk

Skills for Security - sector skills council for security industry - www.skillsforsecurity.org.uk/

Training Schemes - www.direct.gov.uk/en/educationandlearning

Why Security? - A Guide to Careers in the Security Industry (Security Industry Authority) - www.the-sia.org.uk

►Working in airports (2010) (Babcock Lifeskills) - www.babcock-lifeskills.com/

►Working in police, fire & security (2009) (Babcock Lifeskills) - www.babcock-lifeskills.com/

►Working in retail & customer services (2008) (Babcock Lifeskills) - www.babcock-lifeskills.com/

Addresses

British Security Industry Association (BSIA)
Kirkham House, John Comyn Drive, Worcester WR3 7NS
Phone: +44 (0)845 389 3889
Web: www.bsia.co.uk

Security Industry Authority (SIA)
PO Box 1293, Liverpool L69 1AX
Phone: 0844 892 1025 (UK only)
Web: http://sia.homeoffice.gov.uk/Pages/home.aspx

Security Institute
1 The Courtyard, Caldecote CV10 0AS
Phone: 08453 707 717
Web: www.security-institute.org

Similar Jobs

Close Protection Officer/Bodyguard, Door Supervisor, Police Officer, Private Investigator, Security Dog Handler/Trainer, Store Detective

Security Systems Installer

also known as: Alarm Fitter: Security Systems

CRCI:Engineering
CLCI:ROZ
Job Band: 1 to 2

Job Description

Security systems installers install and maintain security and emergency alarm systems that control building or site access and detect intruders. These can be for industry and commerce, or for private homes. They work out what is needed or follow a plan drafted by a security systems designer. Installers fit electronic equipment to buildings to protect against intruders or fire and flood. They use hand and power tools and follow complex wiring circuits.

Installers may fit a radio-linked system or use a wire-free, infrared or fibre optic system. Some systems can include closed circuit television (CCTV), Intercom or gate automation. They may also service existing systems, and detect and repair faults. The job includes filling out system and customer documents, demonstrating how the system works and training clients how to use their system.

Work Details

Usually work around 39 hrs a week that may include a Saturday. You may need to work overtime, be on call or work a 24 hr rota. Your place of work is in clients' homes, business premises and many other indoor and outdoor locations. Travel around an area or further afield is necessary. The job involves some physical activity, including climbing ladders and working at heights, and some kneeling or bending. Some locations may be dusty and cramped. You may need to wear overalls. The work also requires knowledge of technical developments. You are mostly responsible for security, safety and for giving sound advice.

Qualification

• England, Wales and Northern Ireland

Band 1: For entry to jobs, no minimum qualifications are needed, but you are expected to have a good level of general education and relevant experience. Some formal/vocational qualifications at any level are useful.

Band 2: For entry to jobs, no minimum qualifications are needed, but it is an advantage to have some GCSEs (A*-C) or equivalent in subjects that include English and maths.

• Scotland

Band 1: For entry to jobs, no minimum qualifications are needed, but you are expected to have a good level of general education and relevant experience. Some formal/vocational qualifications at any level are useful.

Band 2: Although academic qualifications are not specified for this job, it is an advantage to have some S grades (1-3) in subjects that include English and maths, or similar.

Adult Qualifications

A good standard of secondary education is expected. You can improve your skills and qualifications by working through the Foundation Learning programme. This involves taking credit-based units and qualifications to help you progress.

Work Experience

Relevant work or voluntary experience is always useful. It can add to your CV and improve your chances when applying for entry to jobs or apprenticeships in the engineering industry.

Entry and Training

For this job integrity and honesty can be more important than academic qualifications and applicants' backgrounds are thoroughly checked. A driving licence may be required and good colour vision is a requirement. Training programmes, including apprenticeships leading to level 2 and advanced apprenticeships leading to level 3, may be available in your area. Training is on the job under the supervision of experienced colleagues. You may attend a day-release course, possibly working towards S/NVQs levels 2-3 in providing security, emergency and alarm systems. Short specialised courses are also available.

Skills for Security accredits courses for installers including apprenticeship standards. The framework covers specific training in security systems. Scotland has introduced modern apprenticeships in security systems at levels 2 and 3. Visit the Skills for Security website for details.

The Security Systems & Alarms Inspection Board runs a certification scheme for companies who install intruder alarms, CCTV systems and access control systems. The website has details of certified companies.

A Diploma/Welsh Baccalaureate may be available in your area in engineering. See the diplomas website for further information.

If you have previous experience in electrical work you may have an advantage with some employers. Government training opportunities, such as apprenticeships for adults, may be available in your area. You can also gain recognition of previous experience through Accreditation of Prior Learning or by working towards relevant S/NVQs. Contact your local careers office, Jobcentre Plus, Next Step service or Learning and Skills Council (LSC)/Local Enterprise Company (LEC) for details of training schemes.

Opportunities and Pay

According to the British Security Industry Association, even in the current economic downturn, there is a need for skilled systems engineers. Due to significant technological developments in security systems, there is good demand for security systems installers. The apprenticeships system in this area is developing as more skilled apprentices will be needed to meet the growing demands of the industry.

Employment is often with a small specialist service. You can be self-employed once you have experience. Some specialise, for instance in intruder alarms or CCTV. Promotion prospects can be improved with further training. You may have the use of a company van.

Pay varies according to employer and location. Staring salaries may be up to £15k. Most installers earn around £20k-£25k a year, rising to £40k with experience. Salary depends on experience and the complexity of the work.

Health

There may be an allergy risk from dust. Normal colour vision and a good standard of physical fitness is required.

Skills and Qualities

able to explain clearly, able to follow drawings and plans, able to work both on your own and in a team, honest, IT skills, manual dexterity, problem-solving skills, security conscious, technical aptitude, trustworthy

Relevant Subjects

Design and technology, Engineering, Mathematics, Physics, Science

Further Information

Apprenticeship Schemes (National Apprenticeship Service) - www.apprenticeships.org.uk

Diplomas (Foundation, Higher and Advanced) -http://yp.direct.gov.uk/diplomas

Foundation Learning (QCDA) - www.qcda.gov.uk

National Security Inspectorate - www.nsi.org.uk

Skills for Security - sector skills council for security industry - www.skillsforsecurity.org.uk/

Training Schemes - www.direct.gov.uk/en/educationandlearning

Welsh Baccalaureate - www.wbq.org.uk

Addresses

British Security Industry Association (BSIA)
Kirkham House, John Comyn Drive, Worcester WR3 7NS
Phone: +44 (0)845 389 3889
Web: www.bsia.co.uk

Security Systems & Alarms Inspection Board
The Smoke House, Cliffords Fort, North Shields,
Tyne & Wear NE30 1JE
Phone: +44 (0)191 2963242
Web: www.ssaib.org

Similar Jobs

Electrician, Engineer: Electronics, Locksmith, Satellite Systems Technician, Telecommunications Technician

Service Technician: Land-based

also known as: Farm Machinery Mechanic, Mechanic: Agricultural, Technician: Land-based

CRCI:Engineering
CLCI:RAD — Job Band: 1 to 3

Job Description

Land-based service technicians repair, test and service agricultural plant or horticultural machinery in a workshop or on site. They find the fault, repair or replace broken parts, and check/change the oil and brake fluid. May also adjust and test the machinery using a technical manual and following the manufacturer's recommended procedures. Technicians may need to make new parts using machine or hand tools, and often use welding equipment. They work on large farm vehicles such as cultivators, harvesters and all terrain vehicle-quads, or small items, such as lawnmowers and chain saws.

Technicians may use computerised testing equipment and a computer to keep records on a database. Some help to prepare customers' estimates. May also be responsible for stock management and replacing spare parts when new stocks are required.

Work Details

Usually work 37-40 hrs a week and in some seasons, such as harvest time, may have to work longer hours including evenings and weekends. Sometimes you may be on call and have to work unsocial hours. Your place of work is in a workshop or outdoors on site, or you may have to travel around an area to do repairs. When repairing broken machinery, you have to be able to find the problem and fix it quickly. A high level of skill is expected.

You need to climb in and out of machines and to work underneath them. There may be a risk of accidents from equipment. Sometimes you are out in bad weather and may be working in oily, muddy, smelly or uncomfortable places. You need to wear overalls and sometimes safety glasses.

Qualification

• England, Wales and Northern Ireland

Band 2: For entry to jobs, no minimum qualifications are needed, but it is an advantage to have some GCSEs (A*-C) or equivalent in subjects that include English, maths and science or technical subjects.

Band 3: For entry to jobs, HNC in land-based technology or a relevant Diploma, usually at least 4 GCSEs (A*-C) including English, maths and science or technical subjects, or equivalent.

• Scotland

Band 2: Although academic qualifications are not specified for this job, it is an advantage to have some S grades (1-3) including maths, English and science or technical subjects, or similar.

Band 3: For SQA national award and for apprenticeships: usually at least four S grades (1-3) including maths, English and science or technical subjects, or similar qualifications.

Adult Qualifications

Course entry requirements are usually relaxed for mature applicants.

Work Experience

Relevant work or voluntary experience is always useful and it can add to your CV and improve your chances when applying for entry to jobs or apprenticeships in the engineering industry. Career Track have a list of companies that offer relevant work experience on the apprenticeship section of their website.

Entry and Training

Training is usually through a 3-4 year land-based service engineering apprenticeship programme. You may have to take an entrance test to enter and most applicants are 16-17. Apprenticeships are available through the larger manufacturers. The British Agricultural and Garden Machinery Association (BAGMA) also organise apprenticeships. Contact BAGMA or see the Career Track website for details. Completion of an accredited apprenticeship programme qualifies entry into the Institution of Agricultural Engineers at associate member grade (AMIAgrE) or you can join the Landbased Technician Accreditation Scheme. There are four categories of registration which measure and assess your competence at technician level. Contact IAgrE for details.

The Engineering Development Trust runs a range of nationwide schemes for 11-21 year olds. See the website for details. There are also college courses that are also approved by BAGMA and Lantra, including City & Guilds certificates and BTEC/SQA first and national diplomas in subjects that include land-based technology. The national diploma in land-based technology is a three year sandwich course, with the second year based in industry. S/NVQs at levels 2-3 are available in land-based service engineering. The Tomorrow's Engineers website has lots of useful careers information including a route map and qualifications structure in engineering. Visit the website for further details.

Courses can be day release or block release. After initial qualification you may be able to do further study and transfer to a higher course, including a higher national award. Progression to qualification as a registered engineering technician (EngTech) with the Engineering Council is possible, and with further experience and qualification, you can qualify as an incorporated/chartered engineer. On-going training is important because of the constant advances in technology. This job may require a driving licence.

A Diploma/Welsh Baccalaureate may be available in your area in engineering and this gives good background knowledge for entry to this work.

Experience in mechanical engineering or vehicle repair is often expected for direct entry to jobs. Mature applicants can benefit through government training opportunities, such as apprenticeships, that may be available in your area. You can also gain recognition of previous experience through Accreditation of Prior Learning or by working towards relevant S/NVQs. Contact your local careers office, Jobcentre Plus, Next Step service or Learning and Skills Council (LSC) Local Enterprise Company (LEC) for details of training schemes.

Opportunities and Pay

Over 20,000 technicians are employed in this type of work and job prospects are normally good, although most sectors have been affected by the recent economic downturn. Most are employed by specialist machinery companies, manufacturers and distributors, though there are also some jobs with large farms, private estates and local authority parks departments. Prospects vary depending on where you live. Sometimes people specialise in one particular type of machinery. You may have to buy your own tool kit.

Pay varies depending on the location and employer. Following an apprenticeship, salaries start at around £15k-£20k a year. Experienced technicians can earn up to £30k a year. Top diagnostic technicians can earn £30k-£40k a year.

Health

This job requires good eyesight and normal colour vision, as well as good general fitness.

Skills and Qualities

able to work quickly, careful, conscientious, manual dexterity, methodical, perseverance, practical skills, problem-solving skills, reliable, safety conscious

Relevant Subjects

Design and technology, Engineering, Mathematics, Physics, Science

Further Information

Apprenticeship Schemes (National Apprenticeship Service) - www.apprenticeships.org.uk

Career Track - www.careertrack.org.uk

Diplomas (Foundation, Higher and Advanced) - http://yp.direct.gov.uk/diplomas

Engineering Connections - Apprenticeships - www.apprentices.co.uk

Landwards (4 x year) (Institution of Agricultural Engineers) - www.iagre.org/landwards.shtml

Lantra - The Sector Skills Council for environmental & land-based sector (Lantra) http:/www.lantra.co.uk

SEMTA - sector skills council for science, engineering and manufacturing technologies - www.semta.org.uk

Tomorrow's Engineers - www.tomorrowsengineers.org.uk/careers.cfm

Training Schemes - www.direct.gov.uk/en/educationandlearning
Women into Science, Engineering & Construction - www.wisecampaign.org.uk

Addresses

British Agricultural & Garden Machinery Association (BAGMA)
Middleton House 2 Main Road Middleton Cheney, Banbury, Oxfordshire OX17 2TN
Phone: +44 (0) 1295 713344
Web: www.bagma.com

Engineering Development Trust (EDT)
Ridgeway, Welwyn Garden City, Hertfordshire AL7 2AA
Phone: +44 (0)1707 871520
Web: www.etrust.org.uk

Institution of Agricultural Engineers (IAgrE)
Barton Road, Silsoe, Bedford MK45 4FU
Phone: +44 (0)1525 861 096
Web: www.iagre.org

Similar Jobs

Engineer: Land-based, Mechanic: Construction Plant, Vehicle Breakdown Engineer, Vehicle Mechanic/Motor Vehicle Technician

Sewing Machinist

CRCI:Manufacturing and Production
CLCI:SAH Job Band: 1 to 2

Job Description

Sewing machinists use a wide variety of machines to stitch together different items for the clothing and textile industry, such as shirts, skirts, trousers, bridal wear and dresses. They also work on specialist goods such as car seat covers, outdoor clothing and tents. May sew household goods such as curtains, bedding and upholstery covers. Can specialise in garments and equipment for a sport, such as climbing, sailing and windsurfing, or horse riding. Machinists use the latest technology to complete the work quickly and accurately. They put together the pieces of material and guide them quickly through the machine. Some complicated processes are computerised. Most of the work involves high speed machines.

Machinists often work in a team to complete a garment. Others may finish a whole item by themselves. Some of the work can be repetitive. May have to oil and clean the machine, change the needles and tidy the surrounding work area.

Work Details

Sewing machinists usually work a 37-40 hr week. May be expected to work shifts. Part-time work is often available. You work under supervision. Work is usually in industrial premises or a workshop. It can be noisy and dusty. Some machinists may also work at home. Most of the work involves sitting for long periods and can be repetitive.

Qualification

- **England, Wales and Northern Ireland**

Band 1: Formal qualifications are not usually required.

Band 2: For some employers and courses: 3-4 GCSEs or equivalent are useful.

- **Scotland**

Band 1: Formal qualifications are not usually required.

Band 2: For some employers and courses: 3-4 S grades or similar are useful.

Adult Qualifications

General secondary education is required.

Work Experience

Work or voluntary experience is always useful. It can improve your chances when applying for jobs or apprenticeships. Your personal or adult guidance adviser is able to advise you how to get some work experience. Knowledge of working with a sewing machine is very useful.

Entry and Training

Most employers require applicants to complete a practical aptitude test to assess their skills and they may also be given an eyesight test. It is useful to have some experience of sewing. Training is by an employer's training scheme and possibly, by day or block-release course. Multi-skilling is very important so training is likely to cover different areas. There are a range of qualifications available including relevant S/NVQs levels 1-3. City & Guilds and ABC also offer other courses, including courses on sewing, textiles and garment manufacture.

Training programmes, including apprenticeship schemes, may be available in your area. Advanced apprenticeships leading to qualification at level 3 can also be a route into higher education.

Government training opportunities, such as apprenticeships, may be available in your area. You can also gain recognition of previous experience through Accreditation of Prior Learning (APL) or by working towards relevant S/NVQs. Contact your local careers office, Jobcentre Plus, Next Step service or Learning and Skills Council (LSC) Local Enterprise Company (LEC) for details of training schemes.

Opportunities and Pay

Due to large scale production moving overseas, the industry is in decline and, during the current economic downturn, vacancies in the clothing and textile industries have been down by 30%. You can work for a textile or garment manufacturing company. Most opportunities exist in the East Midlands, north-west Yorkshire and some parts of Scotland and Northern Ireland.

With experience you can become a sample machinist and work for a clothing designer, or you can become a supervisor or instructor. It may be possible for you to work from home.

Salaries start at around £11k-£13k a year. With experience this can rise to £14k-£18k. You may earn a bonus and overtime might be available. There may be opportunities to buy products at reduced prices.

Health

This job requires good eyesight, and perhaps an eyesight test or a medical test on entry. It may also require good colour vision for some areas of work.

Skills and Qualities

able to cope under pressure, able to follow instructions, able to work quickly, accurate, aptitude for teamwork, attention to detail, eye for visual effect, good concentration level, manual dexterity

Relevant Subjects

Manufacturing

Further Information

ABC Awards - www.abcawards.co.uk

Apprenticeship Schemes (National Apprenticeship Service) - www.apprenticeships.org.uk

Skillset - sector skills council for the creative media, fashion and textiles industries - www.skillset.org

Training Schemes - www.direct.gov.uk/en/educationandlearning

▶ Working in fashion & clothing (2008) (Babcock Lifeskills) - www.babcock-lifeskills.com/

Similar Jobs

Clothing Alteration Hand, Dressmaker, Film/TV & Theatre Wardrobe Assistant, Tailor, Upholsterer

Sheet Metal Plater

also known as: Fabricator: Sheet Metal

CRCI:Manufacturing and Production

CLCI:RON Job Band: 2 to 3

Job Description

Sheet metal platers use heavy sheet metal (more than 3mm thick) to make items for industry such as those used in building construction, boilers, chemical plant and large vehicles. They study drawings and mark out the plate for cutting by using a template or by measuring. Material is cut to shape with machines, oxy-acetylene equipment and powerful guillotines or saws, which may also fold, bend or drill holes in metal. Sheet metal platers move plates into position with cranes and hoists, and assemble parts using bolts, rivets or welds. Rough edges are filed and the finished item is polished.

Metal platers help to make, modify or repair machines and products, such as those in the construction, chemical, oil/gas and agricultural industries, or in the shipbuilding and aircraft industries. Some of the work is automated and computer controlled.

Work Details

Sheet metal platers usually work a basic 39-40 hr week that may include shifts and weekend work, either in a large workshop or a construction site. You have to cope with some physical activity including some lifting. The environment depends on the type of industry, but is often noisy and dirty. You may have to work at height, be willing to live away from home and work in all weather conditions. There may be a risk of accidents from equipment and you should be safety aware at all times. You may work on your own, or in a team. You need to wear overalls, safety glasses and possibly a face mask and ear defenders.

Qualification

- **England, Wales and Northern Ireland**

Band 2: Although academic qualifications are not specified for this job, it is an advantage to have some GCSEs (A*-C) in subjects that include English and maths or equivalent. Practical and technical subjects are also useful.

Band 3: For BTEC national award or apprenticeship training: usually 4 GCSEs (A*-C) including English, maths, science and technical or equivalent practical qualifications.

- **Scotland**

Band 2: Although academic qualifications are not specified for this job, it is an advantage to have some S grades (1-3) in subjects that include English and maths, or similar. Practical and technical subjects are useful.

Band 3: For entry to a course or apprenticeship training: usually at least four S grades (1-3) including English, maths, science and technical, or similar practical qualifications. College entry requirements may vary.

Adult Qualifications

Generally, you are expected to have the minimum entry qualifications, which can vary, as for some jobs no formal qualifications are required. However, you are expected to have relevant experience.

Work Experience

Relevant work or voluntary experience is always useful and can improve your chances when applying for entry to jobs or apprenticeships in the manufacturing sector. Your personal or adult guidance adviser should be able to advise you about how to organise work experience with an employer.

Entry and Training

Entry may be through a full-time college course or work-based training scheme. Useful courses prior to entry include BTEC/SQA national award in engineering. If applying for work-based training, you may have to attend an interview and take an aptitude test. There are various apprenticeship schemes, including those offered by the Engineering Construction Industry Training Board (ECITB). The Engineering Training Council has details of apprenticeships in Northern Ireland and Scottish Engineering has details for Scotland. Applicants for training schemes are usually age 16-17. The Welding Institute (TWI) also runs many relevant courses. Check their website for details. Training is normally on the job with part-time study at college or at a company training centre.

You may be able to work towards relevant S/NVQs at levels 2-3. Advanced apprenticeships leading to qualification at level 3 (NVQ in fabrication and welding) can be a route into higher education. A Diploma/Welsh Baccalaureate may be available in your area in engineering. This is for 14-19 year olds and is relevant for entry to this work.

Government training opportunities, such as apprenticeships, may be available in your area. You can also gain recognition of previous experience through Accreditation of Prior Learning (APL) or by working towards relevant S/NVQs. Contact your local careers office, Jobcentre Plus, Next Step service or Learning and Skills Council (LSC) Local Enterprise Company (LEC) for details of training schemes.

The Engineering Construction Industry Training Board (ECITB) runs two training programmes leading to skills and safety cards to ensure competence in the workplace.

Opportunities and Pay

Employment can be with a company that requires fabrication of large metal structures, such as a petrochemical plant, a shipyard, a firm of civil engineers or an oil refinery. Prospects vary depending on where you live. Promotion to supervisory level is possible and may depend on further qualifications and training.

Pay varies depending on area and employer but generally, a trainee earns around £14k-£16k a year, rising to £17k-£22k with experience. The most skilled and experienced workers can earn around £27k. Salaries may be more if overtime or shifts are worked.

Health

This job requires good general fitness and also good eyesight and normal colour vision.

Skills and Qualities

accurate, good concentration level, manual dexterity, numeracy skills, practical skills, safety conscious, steady hand, strong, technical aptitude.

Relevant Subjects

Design and technology, Engineering, Manufacturing, Mathematics

Further Information

Apprenticeship Schemes (National Apprenticeship Service) - www.apprenticeships.org.uk

Diplomas (Foundation, Higher and Advanced) - http://yp.direct.gov.uk/diplomas

Scenta - Careers Guide, Engineering, Technology and Science (Engineering Technology Board) - www.scenta.co.uk/careers.cfm

SEMTA - sector skills council for science, engineering and manufacturing technologies - www.semta.org.uk

Training Schemes - www.direct.gov.uk/en/educationandlearning

Welsh Baccalaureate - www.wbq.org.uk

Addresses

Engineering Construction Industry Training Board (ECITB)
Blue Court, Church Lane, Kings Langley, Hertfordshire WD4 8JP
Phone: +44 (0)1923 260 000
Web: www.ecitb.org.uk

Engineering Training Council (NI)
Interpoint, 20-24 York Street, Belfast BT15 1AQ
Phone: +44 (0)28 9032 9878
Web: www.etcni.org.uk

Scottish Engineering
Training Officer, 105 West George Street, Glasgow G2 1QL
Phone: +44 (0)141 221 3181
Web: www.scottishengineering.org.uk

Welding Institute (TWI), The
Granta Park, Great Abington, Cambridge CB21 6AL
Phone: +44 (0)1223 899 000
Web: www.twi.co.uk

Similar Jobs

Heat Treatment Operative, Marine Craft Worker: Ships, Sheet Metal Worker, Vehicle Body Repairer, Welder

Sheet Metal Worker

CRCI:Manufacturing and Production
CLCI:RON Job Band: 1 to 3

Job Description

Sheet metal workers use thin sheet metal (up to 3mm thick) to make products such as vehicle body panels, storage systems, drinks cans and domestic appliances. They use mild steel, galvanised steel, stainless steel, aluminium or copper. Engineering drawings are used to mark the plate for cutting by using a template or by measuring. Any cutting to shape is done with snips or a saw, and the sheets are folded or bent into shape with presses. A variety of methods are employed including manual and CNC machinery, roller and hammers, or drills. Workers assemble parts using rivets or welds and file rough edges. May finish by polishing. Many processes are computer controlled.

Work Details

Sheet metal workers usually work a basic 37-40 hr week that can include shifts and weekend work. Works mainly for the aerospace and vehicle industries, a light engineering firm or a specialised sheet metal manufacturer. You have to cope with some physical activity including some lifting. The environment depends on the type of industry and is often noisy and dirty. There may be a risk of accidents from equipment and you are responsible for safety. Protective clothing such as overalls, safety glasses, a face mask and ear defenders are worn. May work on your own or as part of a small team.

Qualification

- **England, Wales and Northern Ireland**

Band 2: Although academic qualifications are not specified for this job, it is an advantage to have some GCSEs, including maths, English and science. Practical and technical subjects are also useful.

Band 3: For BTEC national award and advanced apprenticeships: usually at least 4 GCSEs (A*-C) including English, maths and science. Technical or practical subjects are also useful.

- **Scotland**

Band 2: Although academic qualifications are not specified for this job, it is an advantage to have some S grades (1-3), in subjects that include English, maths and science. Practical and technical subjects are also useful.

Band 3: For entry to apprenticeships: usually at least four S grades (1-3) including English, maths and science. Technical or similar qualifications are also useful.

Adult Qualifications

Generally, you are expected to have the minimum entry qualifications, which can vary as for some jobs, no formal qualifications are required. However, you are expected to have relevant experience.

Work Experience

Relevant work or voluntary experience is always useful and can improve your chances when applying for entry to jobs or apprenticeships in the manufacturing sector. Your personal or adult guidance adviser should be able to advise you about how to organise work experience with an employer.

Entry and Training

Entry may be through a full-time college course or a work-based training scheme. Useful courses that may be taken prior to entry include relevant BTEC/SQA national awards or City & Guilds certificate in engineering. Check with local colleges. If applying for work-based training, you may have to attend an interview and take an aptitude test.

There are various apprenticeship schemes, including that offered by the Engineering Construction Industry Training Board (ECITB). The Engineering Training Council has details of apprenticeships in Northern Ireland and Scottish Engineering has details for Scotland. Applicants for training schemes are usually age 16-17. The Welding Institute (TWI) also runs many relevant courses. Check their websites for details.

Training is normally on the job with part-time study at college or at a company training centre. You may be able to work towards S/NVQs in fabrication and welding at levels 2-3. Advanced apprenticeships leading to qualification at level 3 can also be a route into higher education. A Diploma/Welsh Baccalaureate may be available in your area in engineering. This is for 14-19 year olds and is relevant for entry to this type of work.

Mature applicants can benefit through government training opportunities that may be available in your area. You can gain recognition of previous experience through Accreditation of Prior Learning (APL) or by working towards relevant S/NVQs. Contact your local Connexions or careers office, Jobcentre Plus, Next Step service or Learning and Skills Council (LSC)/Local Enterprise Company (LEC) for details of all training opportunities and schemes, including apprenticeships for adults.

The Engineering Construction Industry Training Board (ECITB) runs two training programmes leading to skills and safety cards to ensure competence in the workplace.

Opportunities and Pay

Employment can be with a manufacturing company, light engineering firm, in the car and aerospace industry, or with a firm of civil engineers. Prospects vary depending on where you live. Promotion to supervisory level is possible and may depend on further qualifications and training.

Pay varies depending on area and employer but generally a trainee earns around £14k a year, rising to £17.5k-£22k with experience. The most skilled and experienced workers can earn around £27k a year. Pay can be more if overtime or shifts are worked.

Health

This job requires good general fitness and also good eyesight and normal colour vision.

Skills and Qualities

able to follow drawings and plans, able to work both on your own and in a team, accurate, good concentration level, manual dexterity, numeracy skills, practical skills, safety conscious, steady hand, strong, technical aptitude

Relevant Subjects

Design and technology, Engineering, Manufacturing, Mathematics

Further Information

Apprenticeship Schemes (National Apprenticeship Service) - www.apprenticeships.org.uk

Diplomas (Foundation, Higher and Advanced) - http://yp.direct.gov.uk/diplomas

Scenta - Careers Guide, Engineering, Technology and Science (Engineering Technology Board) - www.scenta.co.uk/careers.cfm

SEMTA - sector skills council for science, engineering and manufacturing technologies - www.semta.org.uk

Training Schemes - www.direct.gov.uk/en/educationandlearning

Welsh Baccalaureate - www.wbq.org.uk

Addresses

Engineering Construction Industry Training Board (ECITB)
Blue Court, Church Lane, Kings Langley, Hertfordshire WD4 8JP
Phone: +44 (0)1923 260 000
Web: www.ecitb.org.uk

Engineering Training Council (NI)
Interpoint, 20-24 York Street, Belfast BT15 1AQ
Phone: +44 (0)28 9032 9878
Web: www.etcni.org.uk

Scottish Engineering
Training Officer, 105 West George Street, Glasgow G2 1QL
Phone: +44 (0)141 221 3181
Web: www.scottishengineering.org.uk

Welding Institute (TWI), The
Granta Park, Great Abington, Cambridge CB21 6AL
Phone: +44 (0)1223 899 000
Web: www.twi.co.uk

Similar Jobs

Heat Treatment Operative, Marine Craft Worker: Ships, Sheet Metal Plater, Vehicle Body Repairer, Welder

Shepherd

CRCI:Environment, Animals and Plants
CLCI:WAB Job Band: 1 to 3

Job Description

Shepherds are responsible for the health and welfare of a flock of sheep, either on a lowland farm or estate, or on hills and moors. They make sure that they have sufficient food and water. Also dip sheep to keep their fleece and skin free from bugs, check that there is no disease in the flock and give them injections if required. Shepherds look after sheep and lambs during the lambing season and in summer, they organise the shearing of the sheep. May have a sheepdog to help control the flock so is responsible for training and looking after it.

May use a rough terrain vehicle to get about the land and hillsides. May also do other jobs on the farm or estate, such as erecting and repairing fences and walls, and maintaining buildings and hedges.

Work Details

Usually work a basic 39 hr week, though have to work irregular hours, such as early mornings, evenings, weekends and at night. Work is mainly outdoors and in all sorts of weather. Most shepherds train and work with a sheepdog. In spring, when the lambs are born, you have to work very long hours and may need to bring the ewes into a large and airy shed. Some shepherds live in a house or cottage on (or near to) the farm. Usually you work on your own for a lot of time, but may work in a team for some jobs, such as dipping or shearing the sheep.

The job requires a good degree of physical fitness and the ability to cope with rough ground and lifting. Health and safety procedures must be followed at all times. You need to deal with the sight of blood and sometimes wear protective clothing, including gloves and boots.

Qualification

- **England, Wales and Northern Ireland**

Band 1: For entry to jobs, no minimum qualifications are needed, but you are expected to have a good level of general education and relevant experience. Some formal/vocational qualifications at any level are useful.

Band 2: For entry to jobs, no minimum qualifications are needed, but it is an advantage to have some GCSEs (A*-C) or equivalent in subjects that include English and maths.

Band 3: For entry to jobs, HNC or a relevant Diploma, usually at least 4 GCSEs (A*-C) including English and maths, or equivalent.

- **Scotland**

Band 1: For entry to jobs, no minimum qualifications are needed, but you are expected to have a good level of general education and relevant experience. Some formal/vocational qualifications at any level are useful.

Band 2: Although academic qualifications are not specified for this job, it is an advantage to have some S grades (1-3) in subjects that include English and maths, or similar.

Band 3: For entry to jobs, usually at least four S grades (1-3) including English and maths, or similar.

Adult Qualifications

Mature entrants do not usually need any formal qualifications but experience in farm work is helpful. Employers expect a good level of general education. Course entry requirements are usually relaxed for mature entrants.

Work Experience

Relevant work or voluntary experience is always useful and can improve your chances when applying for jobs. Any experience of farm work or working with animals, especially sheep, is an advantage. You can gain useful experience through holiday work or a weekend job.

Entry and Training

Most employers look for a combination of technical knowledge and practical skills. You can gain this knowledge either by taking a full time college course, by taking an apprenticeship and studying for S/NVQs or by training on the job with an experienced worker. For some full-time courses, you are expected to work on a farm for a year before you can start the course. Apprenticeships enable you to earn a wage while you are learning. Most shepherds are expected to have a driving licence to enable them to drive from site to site.

There are many relevant full and part-time courses offered at local colleges by BTEC and City & Guilds. Short courses are also available on specialist topics, such as sheep dipping, sheep shearing and flock management. The Lantra website has a course finder section on its website. You can also contact the National Sheep Association (NSA) for information on the UK sheep industry.

A Diploma/Welsh Baccalaureate may be available in your area in environment and land-based studies. S/NVQs are available in agriculture at level 1, livestock production at levels 2-3, and in mixed farming at levels 2-3.

Adults can enter this work with a good level of relevant work experience and those who have further practical skills may have an advantage. Contact your local Connexions or careers office, Jobcentre Plus, Next Step service or Learning and Skills Council (LSC)/Local Enterprise Company (LEC) for details of training schemes. Funding for some courses may be available through the Nuffield Farming Scholarships Trusts.

Opportunities and Pay

The UK is one of the EU's largest producers of sheep, with over 35 million sheep and lambs in the country. Jobs are found mainly in rural areas throughout the UK and you may have to live in a place far from a town or city. Fewer shepherds are now employed and prospects are poor, although on a large estate you may manage a flock and several staff, if sufficiently experienced and qualified. The job may be combined with other general farm skills, or as a livestock worker, looking after cattle or pigs, as well as sheep. Some shepherds are self-employed and look after several flocks in an area through contract work.

Salaries usually range from around £12k-£14.5k a year; overtime pay can make up a significant proportion of your earnings. Salaries can rise to around £16k-£19k a year depending upon experience and responsibility. There are minimum rates of pay set out by the Agricultural Wages Board - see their website for full details. You may be given free or low rent accommodation on the farm or estate where you work.

Health
No special health requirements are necessary but overall physical fitness an advantage.

Skills and Qualities
able to cope with emergencies, able to work both on your own and in a team, common sense, good at handling animals, not squeamish, practical skills, reliable, strong

Relevant Subjects
Biology, Land and Environment, Science

Further Information
Agricultural Wages Board (DEFRA) - www.defra.gov.uk/foodfarm/farmmanage/working/agwages/awb/index.htm

Apprenticeship Schemes (National Apprenticeship Service) - www.apprenticeships.org.uk

Diplomas (Foundation, Higher and Advanced) - http://yp.direct.gov.uk/diplomas

Farmer's Weekly Interactive (Reed International) - www.fwi.co.uk

Lantra - The Sector Skills Council for environmental & land-based sector (Lantra) http:/www.lantra.co.uk

Lantra Careers (A Future In...) (Lantra) - www.afuturein.com

Nuffield Farming Scholarships Trust (Nuffield Farming Scholarships Trust) - www.nuffieldscholar.org

Real Life Guide to Working Outdoors (Trotman) - www.trotman.co.uk

Scottish Farmer (weekly) (Newsquest Media) - www.thescottishfarmer.co.uk/

Training Schemes - www.direct.gov.uk/en/educationandlearning

Welsh Baccalaureate - www.wbq.org.uk

Addresses
Department of Agriculture and Rural Development
Training & Development Dundonald House,
Upper Newtownards Road, Belfast BT4 3SB
Phone: +44 (0)28 9052 4999
Web: www.dardni.gov.uk

National Association of Agricultural Contractors
The Old Cart Shed, Easton Lodge Farm, Old Oundle Road,
Wansford, Peterborough PE8 6NP
Phone: 08456 448750 (UK only)
Web: www.naac.co.uk

National Farmers Union (NFU)
Agriculture House, Stoneleigh Park, Warwickshire CV8 2TZ
Phone: +44 (0)24 7685 8500
Web: www.nfu.org.uk

National Sheep Association
The Sheep Centre, Malvern, Worcestershire WR13 6PH
Phone: +44 (0)1684 892 661
Web: www.nationalsheep.org.uk

NFU Scotland
Head Office, Rural Centre - West Mains, Ingliston,
Edinburgh EH28 8LT
Phone: +44 (0)131 472 4000
Web: www.nfus.org.uk

Similar Jobs
Farm Worker: Crops, Farm Worker: Livestock, Forest Worker, Gamekeeper, Zoo Keeper

Sheriff (Scotland)

CRCI:Legal and Political Services
CLCI:LAF Job Band: 5

Job Description
Sheriffs preside over law courts and make judgements based on the evidence presented, applying current law to determine a range of disputes. These may be disputes between individuals and public bodies, issues relating to family and children, or criminal trials. Most work in Sheriff Courts, though more senior sheriffs preside over the Court of Session, the Court of Appeal or the High Court of the Justiciary. They listen to the presented information or evidence and come to a decision based on existing legislation.

In a jury trial, sheriffs instruct and advise the jury, based on the evidence. They have a thorough knowledge of the law and come to fair and firm conclusions. They pass sentence on those found guilty.

Work Details
The work is usually Monday to Friday, although occasionally courts work on Saturdays. You are in court from 10am until around 5pm, but also work earlier in the mornings and in the evenings to prepare relevant case papers and witness statements. You may be called on at short notice for urgent applications of warrants and child protection orders.

You work in courts and in an office, which are located in many major towns and cities. Travel is sometimes necessary with nights away from home, as some sheriffs work in more than one court, especially in rural areas. The work involves consultation with people such as advocates, solicitors and other professionals.

Details of legal cases and facts have to be quickly analysed and thoroughly understood. Discretion is important as the work is of a confidential nature. The work can be demanding and stressful at times, and involves making difficult decisions. You wear formal dress and have to observe the traditions and formality of the court.

Qualification

- **Scotland**

Band 5: For degree: five H grades, including English (maths/science and perhaps a modern language depending on the qualification taken) and some S grades (1-3) or similar qualifications. Good H grades are needed, preferably taken at one sitting. Similar qualifications may also be acceptable.

Degree Information
A good honours degree (or ordinary degree with distinction) in Scottish law from a Scottish university (currently Aberdeen, Dundee, Edinburgh, Glasgow and Strathclyde), is required for training. Alternatively a good honours degree in another subject from a UK university, followed by an ordinary degree (second class or above) in Scottish law from a Scottish university is acceptable. This must be followed by a diploma in legal practice.

Adult Qualifications
You must first qualify as an advocate or solicitor, and then have at least 10 years' experience. The study and training routes are common to all entrants, though certain exemptions may apply.

Work Experience
Prior to embarking on a career in law, it is advisable to gain practical experience of court attendance, or of work with an advocate or solicitor. As entry to a career in law is competitive, it is useful to seek work experience with general law firms. Towards the end of a degree, you can try to obtain vacation work with a large commercial law firm.

Entry and Training
Sheriffs are either experienced advocates or solicitors (see job articles for solicitor and advocate for full entry end training details). Advocates or solicitors, with at least 10 years' experience and usually either a Queen's Counsel (QC) or with considerable court experience, may apply to become a sheriff, preferably having already served as a temporary or part-time sheriff. Recruitment and appointments are dealt with by the Judicial Appointments Board for Scotland. It advertises posts, interviews candidates and makes recommendations for appointment to the First Minister.

Training for members of the judiciary is provided by the Judicial Studies Committee (JSC). Where possible new sheriffs attend an induction course of around five days and then spend a further five days with an experienced sheriff before sitting alone. They continue to attend courses offered by the JSC on a variety of topics. They are expected to keep up to date with every aspect of the law of the UK and Scotland, as well as the European Court of Human Rights.

Maturity is common as most sheriffs require substantial experience as a lawyer (advocate/solicitor). The study and training routes are common to all entrants, although certain exemptions may apply for mature applicants wishing to train. For those not already qualified in law, the lengthy training time should be considered carefully. Sheriffs are able to work up to the age of 70.

Opportunities and Pay
There are 49 Sheriff Courts in Scotland. Some are presided over by one sheriff, while those in the larger cities have several. In rural districts, one sheriff may serve several courts. Entry is extremely competitive and considerable talent is required for success. All sheriffs in Scotland are appointed by the Queen on the advice of the First Minister, having been recommended by the independent Judicial Appointments Board.

Progression to more senior posts, such as Lord President and Lord Justice Clerk, are made on recommendation of the Prime Minister.

Salaries for sheriffs are around £128k a year.

Skills and Qualities
able to inspire confidence, analytical skills, articulate, awareness of confidentiality issues, good listening skills, information handling skills, logical, patient, sound judgement

Relevant Subjects
Business and accounting, Economics, English, Government and politics, History, Law, Psychology, Sociology

Further Information
Judicial Studies Committee - www.judicialstudies-scotland.org.uk

TARGETjobs: Law Scotland (GTI Specialist Publishing Ltd.) - www.groupgti.com

▶ Working in politics & law (2010) (Babcock Lifeskills) - www.babcock-lifeskills.com/

Addresses
Judicial Appointments Board for Scotland
38-39 Drumsheugh Gardens, Edinburgh EH3 7SW
Phone: +44 (0) 131 528 5101
Web: www.judicialappointmentsscotland.gov.uk

Law Society of Scotland
26 Drumsheugh Gardens, Edinburgh EH3 7YR
Phone: +44 (0)131 226 7411
Web: www.lawscot.org.uk

Scottish Courts Service (SCS)
Saughton House Broomhouse Drive, Edinburgh EH11 3XD
Phone: +44 (0)131 444 3300
Web: www.scotcourts.gov.uk

Similar Jobs
Advocate (Scotland), European Law Solicitor, Procurator Fiscal (Scotland), Solicitor

Sheriff Officer (Scotland)
also known as: Messenger-at-Arms (Scotland)
CRCI:Legal and Political Services
CLCI:LAZ

Job Band: 3

Job Description
Sheriff officers work for courts in Scotland enforcing court orders against people who owe sums of money. They deliver legal documents, such as summonses to debtors, and deal with certain types of debt recovery. They write letters to debtors, visit them at home and as a last resort, are legally authorised to repossess property or remove goods. They also offer money management advice to debtors and negotiate payment by instalments.

Sheriff officers work in the regional civil courts and messengers-at-arms work in the court of sessions. Both are referred to as officers of the court and have the power to force entry to both domestic and commercially owned premises. Messengers-at-arms travel anywhere in Scotland to enforce orders of the court. Sheriff officers hold a 'commission' for work in a particular geographical area of the country.

Work Details
You usually work around 37-40 hrs a week, but you need to be flexible as you are often likely to work weekends and evenings. You are based in an office, but spend most of the time travelling and visiting debtors. Time may be spent away from home, overnight or for several nights at a time. Some heavy lifting may be required, especially if removing furniture or equipment from debtors' premises.

You have to deal with people who can be angry, upset or destructive. Many officers/messengers-at-arms combine this work with another job. Part-time work and self-employment is possible.

Qualification

- **Scotland**

Band 3: For Society of Messengers-at-Arms and Sheriff Officers' exams: minimum of five S grades (1-3) including English and maths. Other qualifications may be acceptable - check with the Society for details.

Adult Qualifications
Entry requirements may be waived for mature entrants with relevant experience. Check with the Society of Messengers-at-Arms and Sheriff Officers for details.

Work Experience
Relevant work or voluntary experience is always useful and can improve your chances for entry to this job. The types of work experience to consider are working with the public, administration and finance based work.

Entry and Training
There are nationality requirements and age restrictions, and your background may be checked for security reasons. You need to prove that you have no criminal or debt record. The minimum age of application to become an officer is 20, but it is possible to begin training before this age. You usually start as an assistant, or 'witness', to a sheriff officer. Training with an experienced officer is on the job and lasts for three years. After this training period, you

must pass the examinations of the Society of Messengers-at-Arms and Sheriff Officers (SMASO) in order to gain a commission as a sheriff officer.

To become a messenger-at-arms you must have at least two years' experience as a sheriff officer, and pass an additional examination before applying for a commission. The SMASO offers its members a programme of continuing professional development (CPD). A full clean driving licence and use of a car are usually needed.

Maturity is definitely an advantage and applicants without the required educational qualifications can take the sheriff officers' examination if they have relevant previous experience. It is an advantage to have experience and qualifications in related areas, such as the law, police and the armed forces.

Opportunities and Pay

There are over 200 sheriff officers and about 130 of these are also messengers-at-arms. Employers are usually commercial firms but officers are commissioned by the courts.

Starting salaries are around £17k a year rising to around £21k a year. The highest salaries are £25k-£29k a year. Many firms pay a basic salary, plus a form of commission or incentive payments.

Health

You may need to pass a medical and fitness assessment, as a good general level of fitness is required .

Skills and Qualities

able to cope under pressure, able to get on with all kinds of people, able to work both on your own and in a team, assertive, determined, numeracy skills, sound judgement, tactful, understanding of legal technicalities

Relevant Subjects

English

Addresses

Law Society of Scotland
26 Drumsheugh Gardens, Edinburgh EH3 7YR
Phone: +44 (0)131 226 7411
Web: www.lawscot.org.uk

Scottish Courts Service (SCS)
Saughton House Broomhouse Drive, Edinburgh EH11 3XD
Phone: +44 (0)131 444 3300
Web: www.scotcourts.gov.uk

Society of Messengers-at-Arms and Sheriff Officers (SMASO)
11 Alva Street, Edinburgh EH2 4PH
Phone: +44 (0)131 225 9110
Web: www.smaso.org

Similar Jobs

Court Administrative Officer/Assistant, Credit Manager, Debt Counsellor

Shipbroker/Airbroker

CRCI:Transport and Logistics
CLCI:YAS Job Band: 4 to 5

Job Description

Shipbrokers arrange the transportation of goods and commodities by sea for a client. They employ a vessel, or buy and sell ships on behalf of their client. Act as a link between people who hold cargo space on ships and aircraft and those who have goods to be moved. They buy and sell freight space on behalf of clients, sometimes chartering ships or aircraft to carry the cargo. In shipbroking, can act as a ship owner's agent in a port, dealing with customs and excise, paperwork for loading cargo, and the arrangements for crew.

Airbrokers play a similar role in finding suitable aircraft for passenger charters and for cargo, and may also deal in selling planes and spare parts. Building a worldwide network of contacts in the shipping or air industry is an important part of the job.

Work Details

You are based in an office, but are likely to travel abroad frequently. A lot of time is spent on the phone, calling all over the world. This means that the hours are very long and irregular. You have to be able to negotiate good terms for your clients. You must be able to work under pressure, to meet tight deadlines, sometimes (especially in airbroking) in emergency situations.

Qualification

There are no specific academic qualifications needed though a good general education is required. The majority of entrants hold a degree level qualification.

• England, Wales and Northern Ireland

Band 4: For BTEC higher national award: 1-2 A levels and some GCSEs (A*-C) usually including English and maths, or equivalent.

Band 5: For degree courses: 2-3 A levels and some GCSEs (A*-C) usually including English and maths, or equivalent. Exact requirements depend on the degree you take.

• Scotland

Band 4: For SQA higher national award: usually 2-3 H grades and some S grades (1-3), often including English and maths, or similar qualifications.

Band 5: For degree courses: 3-5 H grades and some S grades (1-3), usually including English and maths, or similar qualifications. Exact requirements depend on the degree you take.

Degree Information

A degree in any discipline is acceptable though subjects such as maritime business, shipping, business studies, geography, accountancy, economics, transport, logistics and distribution, and foreign languages are particularly useful. Maritime and shipping logistics degrees are available at a couple of universities in the UK. There is a masters degree course in international maritime studies run by Southampton Solent University.

Adult Qualifications

Entry to this job is with a wide range of formal and vocational qualifications at all levels. Entry requirements may be relaxed for adults applying for higher education courses and Access or foundation courses give adults without qualifications a route on to degree courses.

Work Experience

Entry to this job is competitive and it is important to try to do some relevant work or voluntary experience before applying. Relevant experience can be gained with an export or freight firm or in a transport office. Business, commercial and administration work is also relevant.

Entry and Training

Most entrants are graduates, though it is possible to enter this job with qualifications ranging from S/NVQs, to foundation degrees and degrees. Some on-the-job graduate training programmes are offered by larger companies and training is with experienced brokers. The largest ship/air brokers, the Baltic Exchange, runs a series of specialist shipping courses and workshops.

Membership of the Institute of Chartered Shipbrokers (ICS) can be attained by obtaining on-the-job experience and the Institute's professional qualifications, which are studied through distance-learning courses. The ICS offers a comprehensive range of day and short courses, including vocational qualifications. A foundation diploma for new entrants to the profession is also available. There are relevant HNDs and foundation degrees, such as logistics and transport, or logistics and supply chain. Contact the ICS for details on all qualifications and routes to training.

Mature entry is possible for those with related experience in industry or commerce, and most entrants are graduates. Previous experience at sea, or airline or freight forwarding work is particularly useful.

Opportunities and Pay

There are around 2,000 firms working in this area, which can be local, national or international. Most jobs are in London at the Baltic Exchange, the centre of the chartering market in the UK, which covers the world. It keeps a register of those looking for employment, but competition is fierce and there are few vacancies. Improvements in communication technology are leading to the development of emerging markets in other locations.

There are no set salaries so it is difficult to summarise earnings. Pay varies considerably depending on qualifications, experience and reputation, but is usually based on a low to medium basic rate with bonuses for good performance.

Skills and Qualities

able to cope under pressure, able to manage a budget and keep records, business awareness, good coordinator, good telephone manner, IT skills, methodical, negotiating skills, networking skills, resourceful

Relevant Subjects

Business and accounting, Economics, English, Geography, ICT/ Computer studies, Law, Mathematics, Modern Foreign Languages, Retail and distribution

Further Information

AGCAS: Transport and Logistics (Job Sector Briefing) (AGCAS) - www.prospects.ac.uk

Fairplay (International Shipping Weekly) - www.fairplay.co.uk

Inside Careers Guide: Logistics & Transport Management - www.insidecareers.co.uk

▶Working in business, administration & finance (2010) (Babcock Lifeskills) - www.babcock-lifeskills.com/

Addresses

Baltic Exchange Ltd
38 St Mary Axe, London EC3A 8BH
Phone: +44 (0)20 7623 5501
Web: www.balticexchange.com

Institute of Chartered Shipbrokers (ICS)
Coracle Online Ltd, Browns Farm, Belchamp St Paul, Sudbury, Suffolk CO10 7DQ
Phone: +44 (0) 1787 278 013
Web: www.ics.org.uk

Southampton Solent University
East Park Terrace, Southampton, Hampshire SO14 0YN
Phone: +44 (0)23 8031 9000
Web: www.solent.ac.uk/contactus/contact_home.aspx

Similar Jobs

Export Sales Manager, Freight Forwarder, Logistics Manager, Road Transport Manager

Shoe Repairer

also known as: Cobbler, Heel Bar Operator

CRCI:Retail Sales and Customer Services
CLCI:OFZ Job Band: 1 to 2

Job Description

Shoe repairers repair worn or damaged footwear at a specialised shoe repair shop or a heel bar in a high street or shopping centre. They strip off worn heels and soles, and cut, shape and fit replacements by nailing, sewing or glueing. They carry out other repair work, such as replacing zips on handbags or stitching leather goods, such as bags, belts or suitcases. Repairers use specialist machinery, as well as hand tools. More difficult repair work is done by craft workers who have a longer training period. Some shops/ heel bars provide a key cutting, engraving or shoe dyeing service. May also sell shoe polishes, laces, shoe dyes and some larger shops sell handbags and luggage items.

Work Details

Usually work a 40 hr week, in a shop, a workshop, or possibly a factory. You may be expected to work at weekends, but have time off during the week instead. Work can be very busy at times. You may have to stand for many hours. Your workplace can be dusty and noisy with unpleasant fumes and you may need to wear an overall and sometimes a facemask. There is a risk of minor injuries from machines.

Qualification

• England, Wales and Northern Ireland

Band 1: Pre-entry qualifications are not specified, though GCSEs in English, maths and craft subjects are useful, or equivalent.

Band 2: Some employers may ask for GCSEs (A*-C) in subjects that include English and maths, or equivalent.

• Scotland

Band 1: Pre-entry qualifications are not specified, though S grades in English, maths and craft subjects, or similar, are useful.

Band 2: Some employers may ask for S grades (1-3) in subjects that include English and maths, or similar.

Adult Qualifications

No qualifications are needed, but a good standard of education is useful.

Work Experience

Relevant work or voluntary experience is always useful and can improve your chances when applying for entry to jobs in sales. It can equip you with skills that you can use in the future and add to your CV. Part-time and holiday employment in a wide range of shops is usually fairly easy to obtain.

Entry and Training

Applicants to this job may need to pass an aptitude test that includes basic English, arithmetic and practical skill application. Employers may look for applicants with related experience in areas such as leatherwork. Other retail or customer service experience is also useful. Some employers offer an on-the-job training programme where you learn with an experienced employee. Many entrants are recruited through work-based training schemes. Training includes practical aspects of shoe repair, use of specialist machinery and possibly key cutting and engraving.

It is possible to work towards S/NVQ levels 2-3 in footwear repair whilst working. Training programmes, including apprenticeship schemes, may be available in your area. Advanced apprenticeships leading to qualification at level 3 can also be a route into higher education.

Adults may be able to enter this work through a government-funded training programme. Contact your local careers office, Jobcentre Plus, Next Step service or Learning and Skills Council (LSC)/Local Enterprise Company (LEC) for details of all training opportunities and schemes, including apprenticeships for adults. Those with previous work experience of retail work, handling cash or credit/debit cards, or who have a level of craft skills, may have an advantage.

Opportunities and Pay

You work for a small firm or a nationwide chain mostly in towns and cities. However, many repair shops are small, so there are very few opportunities. Some jobs are available with shoe manufacturers. Promotion to supervisor is more likely in larger firms. With experience, you can become self-employed and either offer a general repair service or specialise in repairing one type of footwear, such as sports or dance shoes.

Pay varies depending on location and employer, but most shoe repairers earn from around £11k, with shop managers making £21k a year. Some employers run a bonus payment scheme.

Health
You should not be allergic to glue or other adhesives. Normal colour vision is needed for dyeing work.

Skills and Qualities
able to operate equipment, attention to detail, cash handling skills, customer service skills, manual dexterity, practical skills, safety conscious

Relevant Subjects
Design and technology

Further Information
Apprenticeship Schemes (National Apprenticeship Service) - www.apprenticeships.org.uk

Foundation Learning (QCDA) - www.qcda.gov.uk

Real Life Guide to Retail (Trotman) - www.trotman.co.uk

Shoe Repairers Information - www.shoerepairer.info

Training Schemes - www.direct.gov.uk/en/educationandlearning

Similar Jobs
Locksmith, Saddler, Sewing Machinist, Upholsterer

Shopfitter
CRCI:Building and Construction
CLCI:SAJ Job Band: 1 to 3

Job Description
Shopfitters design, build and install interiors for shops, offices and hotels. May refurbish existing shops and other premises, such as restaurants, offices and art galleries. They make a variety of articles including counters, worktops, partitions, cupboards and shelves. They also build and fit shop fronts, doorways and entrances. Different types of wood and other materials such as glass, metal and plastic are used. Some can be inexpensive materials which are mainly used for basic construction; some are expensive hardwoods which can be used for decorative features.

Shopfitters survey and measure the area of work and may prepare drawings for the client. They study drawings, make calculations, choose materials and cut to size. A range of hand tools, power tools and cutting machines, including chisels, planes, mortise machines and saws are used. They also make and fix objects and fittings by nailing, jointing or glueing.

Work Details
Shopfitters usually work a basic 39 hr week, though sometimes need to work long and irregular hours, including overtime, evenings and weekends to complete jobs. Work can be on different sites or in a workshop. You may need to travel and sometimes stay away from home. The job involves physical activity such as lifting, bending, kneeling, climbing ladders and working at heights on scaffolding. You can work in a team with other workers including bricklayers, painters and plasterers, but sometimes you may work on your own. The work environment can be dirty, noisy and dusty.

There is a risk of minor injuries so you need to wear a safety helmet, goggles, ear protectors and protective footwear.

Qualification
• England, Wales and Northern Ireland
Band 1: Minimum qualifications are not always required, but you are expected to have had a good level of general education. However, some formal/vocational qualifications at any level are useful.

Band 2: Although academic qualifications are not specified for this job, it is an advantage to have some GCSEs (A*-C) in subjects that include English, maths, design and technology and a science, or equivalent.

Band 3: For entry to some training schemes or courses: usually at least 4 GCSEs (A*-C) including English, maths, design and technology and a science, or equivalent.

• Scotland
Band 1: Minimum qualifications are not always required, but you are expected to have had a good level of general education. However, some formal/vocational qualifications at any level are useful.

Band 2: Although academic qualifications are not specified for this job, it is an advantage to have some S grades (1-3) in subjects that include English, maths, design and technology and a science, or similar.

Band 3: For entry to some training schemes or courses: usually at least four S grades (1-3) including English, maths, design and technology and a science, or similar.

Adult Qualifications
Formal qualifications are not always required. Entry requirements for some courses and training may be relaxed for adults with relevant experience.

Work Experience
Relevant work or voluntary experience is always useful and can improve your chances when applying for entry to construction jobs and apprenticeships. It is useful to work shadow an experienced shopfitter or carpenter/joiner that is involved in construction, building or restoration work. For work experience, health and safety issues may mean that there are certain jobs you cannot do until you are over 16. Contact your local ConstructionSkills office for advice.

Entry and Training
Most shopfitters start by working in one of the construction trades, the most relevant being carpentry and joinery (see separate job profile). Many begin training at 16-17 through specific schemes, such as those offered by ConstructionSkills. Some shopfitting or general building firms offer apprenticeship schemes. To enter a training scheme you may have to pass an entrance test, usually called an initial assessment. Training can be on the job, with day or block-release for relevant courses.

Introductory vocational courses include basic carpentry and joinery skills offered by City & Guilds and the ConstructionSkills level 2 and 3 diploma in shopfitting bench joinery. Various colleges may also offer one or two-year full-time courses. There are also various levels of qualifications in carpentry and joinery that are offered by the Institute of Carpenters (IOC), including the master certificate scheme (Master Carpenter/Master Joiner). Both the IOC and the National Association of Shopfitters offer membership and training schemes relevant to shopfitters.

A Diploma/Welsh Baccalaureate in construction and the built environment may be available in your area. S/NVQs in wood occupations (shopfitting benchwork or shopfitting sitework) are available at levels 2-3. Training programmes, including apprenticeships leading to level 2 and advanced apprenticeships/construction apprenticeships leading to level 3, may be available in your area. Contact ConstructionSkills and the IOC for details of all training schemes.

Mature applicants with relevant work experience in woodworking or the building and construction trades have a reasonable chance of training opportunities. Government training schemes may be available in your area. Contact your local careers office, Jobcentre Plus, Next Step service or Learning and Skills Council (LSC)/Local Enterprise Company (LEC) for details of training opportunities, including apprenticeships for adults. The Carpenters' Company offers funding for wood-related courses undertaken in the UK through their Charitable Trust.

Opportunities and Pay

You can be employed by a small firm of shopfitters, joiners or builders, a large building contractor or a local authority, or you can be self-employed. The work may be seasonal and short-term contracts are often offered. You may be promoted to foreman or supervisor. Some shopfitters specialise in fitting shops or offices. Others may focus on types of shop, such as pharmacy design and fitting.

Pay depends on where you work and who you work for. Starting salaries are around £13k-£16k a year. With experience and qualifications you can earn £23k a year. Supervisors earn £25k-£30k or more. Employers may give allowances for travel and cost of lodgings. Overtime and bonus payments may boost your income.

Health

This job requires good stamina and physical fitness. There may be an allergy risk from dust.

Skills and Qualities

able to cope under pressure, able to follow drawings and plans, able to work both on your own and in a team, accurate measuring and calculating skills, attention to detail, creative and imaginative flair, good concentration level, manual dexterity, numeracy skills, practical skills

Relevant Subjects

Construction and built environment, Design and technology

Further Information

Apprenticeship Schemes (National Apprenticeship Service) - www.apprenticeships.org.uk

ConstructionSkills - sector skills council for the construction industry - www.cskills.org

Diplomas (Foundation, Higher and Advanced) - http://yp.direct.gov.uk/diplomas

Real Life Guide to Carpentry and Cabinet Making (Trotman) - www.trotman.co.uk

Welsh Baccalaureate - www.wbq.org.uk

►Working in construction & the built environment (2007) (Babcock Lifeskills) - www.babcock-lifeskills.com/

Addresses

Carpenters' Company
Carpenters' Hall, Throgmorton Avenue, London EC2N 2JJ
Phone: +44 (0)20 7588 7001
Web: www.carpentersco.com

Institute of Carpenters (IOC)
Third Floor D , Carpenters' Hall, 1 Throgmorton Avenue, London EC2N 2BY
Phone: +44 (0)20 7256 2700
Web: www.instituteofcarpenters.com

National Association of Shopfitters (NAS)
NAS House, 411 Limpsfield Road, Warlingham, Surrey CR6 9HA
Phone: +44 (0)1883 624 961
Web: www.shopfitters.org

Scottish Building Apprenticeship & Training Council (SBATC)
Crichton House, 4 Crichtons Close, Holyrood, Edinburgh EH8 8DT
Phone: +44 (0)131 556 8866
Web: www.sbatc.co.uk

Similar Jobs

Cabinet Maker, Carpenter/Joiner, Ceiling Fixer, Construction Operative, Wood Machinist

Signwriter/Signmaker

CRCI:Design, Arts and Crafts
CLCI:ET

Job Band: 2 to 4

Job Description

Signmakers design and produce signs for a wide variety of uses including office buildings and shops, pubs, banks, petrol stations, lorries, vans and road signs. They may meet clients to discuss their needs and quote a price for the job. Traditional methods are still sometimes used, which involve painting/enamelling by hand or by silk screen printing. Signs are often on wood and typically used for traditional pub signs and signs for narrow boats.

Modern methods use computer-aided design (CAD) and digital cameras and technology. Signmakers select the size and type of font and produce the agreed text by microprocessing. Graphics can be included and images, such as company logos, scanned in. They use a variety of materials such as vinyl, metal, glass, plastic or perspex and glass signs can be electronic or illuminated. Can also engrave text and designs onto metal or plastic, using a machine or by hand.

Work Details

Usually work a 35-40 hr week from Monday to Friday, with the possibility of overtime in the evenings and at weekends. You may work for a manufacturing company, studio or workshop and perhaps on-site where the signs are being installed. Some travel may therefore be involved. Signmaking is more computerised and technical today. As well as traditional signs, you may work on electrical installations which involves climbing ladders, working at heights in all weathers, and heavy lifting. A knowledge of current planning law is needed.

Qualification

• England, Wales and Northern Ireland

Band 2: Although academic qualifications are not specified for this job, it is an advantage to have some GCSEs (A*-C) in subjects that include art, design and technology, English and maths, or equivalent.

Band 3: For entry to jobs, HNC in graphic design or a relevant Diploma, usually at least 4 GCSEs (A*-C) including art, design and technology, English and maths, or equivalent.

Band 4: For HND, Diploma of Higher Education or foundation degree: 1-2 A levels and some GCSEs (A*-C) usually including English, art and maths, or equivalent qualifications.

• Scotland

Band 2: Although academic qualifications are not specified for this job, it is an advantage to have some S grades (1-3) in subjects that include art, design and technology, English and maths, or similar.

Band 3: For entry: usually at least four S grades (1-3) including art, design and technology, English and maths, or similar.

Band 4: For entry to SQA higher national and professional development awards, usually 2-3 H grades and some S grades (1-3), including English and maths, or similar qualifications.

Adult Qualifications

Entry requirements may be relaxed for adults applying for courses, and Access or foundation courses give adults without qualifications a route into higher education courses.

Work Experience

Employers or colleges may prefer candidates who have relevant work or voluntary experience. This may be in a signmaking business, or in other areas involving design, such as the print industry. This can equip you with skills that you can use in the future and add to your CV.

Entry and Training
There are no set qualifications to become a signwriter/signmaker. It is possible to work full time and train on the job, with training at a college and through distance learning. S/NVQs in sign making are available at levels 2-3. Training programmes, including apprenticeship schemes in signmaking and polymer processing may be available in your area for entry to this job. Foundation and Advanced apprenticeships may be available through the British Sign and Graphics Association (BSGA), leading to an S/NVQ at level 3 in signmaking.

Signwork and typography are also included in some interior, multimedia or graphic design courses, as an optional module. Some entrants specialise in signmaking after an HNC/D in graphic design or graphic communication. A Diploma/Welsh Baccalaureate may be available in your area in creative and media and may provide a route onto higher education courses.

You may need to work towards gaining a level of competence card through a Construction Skills Certification Scheme (CSCS) to indicate your individual skill level of sign installation (illuminated or non-illuminated). Increasingly, these are likely to be demanded before sign installers are allowed to work on construction sites. You may also need to have training in working safely at heights.

Mature applicants with some art training in calligraphy, interior/graphic design, or work experience as a painter and decorator, may have an advantage. Training programmes, including apprenticeship schemes in signmaking and polymer processing may be available in your area for entry to this job. A good portfolio of recent creative work is an advantage.

Opportunities and Pay
This is a highly skilled and specialised market. Companies range from small self-employed signwriters/signmakers to large firms with a multi-million pound turnover. Signmaking businesses are located in all parts of the UK, though they are most often found in industrial estates in towns and cities. Employment is also with engraving companies or high street print/design firms.

You can start work as a screen printer and then progress to learn how to engrave and typeset. Larger firms usually have a promotion structure, with opportunities to progress to supervisory and management jobs. There are opportunities to specialise in working as an estimator, process planner or quality technician. Some opportunities exist abroad with international companies, especially in Europe.

Pay varies depending on location, employer and whether you are self-employed. An apprentice with a signmaking company is likely to earn around £12k a year, rising to £17k-£23k with experience. Those with management responsibility and skills in sales and design may earn £25k or more a year.

Health
This job requires good eyesight and normal colour vision. Working with paint can cause problems for people with allergies.

Skills and Qualities
able to follow instructions, able to work well on your own, accurate, creative and imaginative flair, drawing ability, eye for visual effect, specialist IT skills, steady hand, technical aptitude

Relevant Subjects
Art and Design, Design and technology, English

Further Information
Apprenticeship Schemes (National Apprenticeship Service) - www.apprenticeships.org.uk

Cogent - sector skills souncil for chemicals, pharmaceuticals, nuclear, oil & gas, petroleum & polymers - www.cogent-ssc.com

Creative & Cultural Skills - sector skills council for advertising, crafts, cultural heritage, design, literature, music, performing & visual arts - www.ccskills.org.uk

Creative Choices - www.creative-choices.co.uk/

Sign Directions (8 x year) (Visage communications) - www.bsga.co.uk/sd_web/sd_index.html

▶ Working in art & design (2009) (Babcock Lifeskills) - www.babcock-lifeskills.com/

Addresses
British Sign and Graphics Association (BSGA)
5 Orton Enterprise Centre, Bakewell Road, Orton Southgate, Peterborough PE2 6XU
Phone: +44 (0)1733 230 033
Web: www.bsga.co.uk

Similar Jobs
Desktop Publishing (DTP) Operator, Graphic Design Assistant, Graphic Designer, Picture Framer, Printer: Machine, Visual Merchandiser

Singer
also known as: Pop Star: Singer, Rock Star: Singer, Soloist
CRCI:Performing Arts
CLCI:GAD Job Band: 2 to 5

Job Description
Singers can sing as a soloist or a member of a professional choir, vocal group or band, to entertain an audience. They study and rehearse songs to be performed. May play their own accompaniment, such as a piano or guitar. Most singers specialise in opera, light music, jazz or popular music. Classical singers may be a member of a choir that is part of an opera company.

Some singers spend their time in a music recording studio working on recordings for TV, film, radio and for CDs. Successful singers appear in their own promotional videos and some work demands acting and dance ability as well.

Work Details
You are usually expected to work unsocial hours including evenings and weekends. To get work you may have to travel a good deal and live away from home for long periods. Working conditions vary, depending on which area of music you are involved in. If you sing classical music or you are a theatre singer you may be performing in large concert halls and theatres, but if you are a pop/rock/folk singer, you may sometimes sing in pubs/clubs that can be noisy, crowded and hot. Some performances may be in the open air, such as at pop festivals or in the garden of a stately home.

Performing requires creativity and imagination and the job can be very demanding. You have to cope with standing for many hours rehearsing. Rehearsal rooms are often uncomfortable and cold. Dress is usually informal except for those involved in classical music.

Qualification
To become a singer, no formal qualifications are required, although considerable talent and evidence of a high standard of musical ability is essential. People enter the profession from a variety of backgrounds, ranging from few or no qualifications to a degree or performers' diploma. However, qualifications are no guarantee of work.

Adult Qualifications
As intensive classical voice training does not usually take place until after the age of 22, entry is possible for adults with considerable amateur experience. Entry is by audition and academic entry requirements may be negotiable.

Work Experience
Any singing opportunity in school or as a student, or in amateur plays and performances, is valuable experience. It is very useful to join a choir or a chorus for a touring music company. Entering singing competitions is another good way to gain relevant experience.

Entry and Training
Entry to training courses at a music conservatoire, academy or drama college is highly competitive. To enter this career, and most music courses, you need to pass an audition. Applicants are usually in their early twenties before intensive voice training can begin but general musical training can be started at an earlier age. Many begin their singing career in a choir school, often from the age of eight, and combine this with academic education as well as musical training.

There are seven music conservatoires in the UK that run a range of courses for vocal training including a postgraduate course in vocal performance. For courses at conservatoires, you need to apply through the Conservatoires UK Admissions Service. There are many other courses in music, but you need to check contents carefully as some are more academic than performance related.

In popular music there is no clear training route and many begin their professional career as a lead vocalist with a band, and may become a soloist at a later date. Others attend a drama college and are taught singing, alongside other performance subjects, such as dance and acting. There are a few higher education college courses in contemporary singing, such as the honours degree in Voice - Music Performance and Production offered by the London College of Contemporary Music. Most singers need to continue to have professional private fee-paying lessons throughout their career.

A Diploma/Welsh Baccalaureate in creative and media may be available in your area. Check university entry requirements carefully in case there is an additional specialist learning requirement with the diploma. See the diplomas website for further information.

Mature entrants have more opportunities when their voice matures, though it is more difficult to break into the pop/rock industry. Some may begin as a songwriter and move into performing their original music. Music schools/colleges usually relax their entry requirements for those with considerable talent and performing experience. The Government is offering a New Deal for Musicians that offers help for those wanting to get into the music business.

Opportunities and Pay
Singing is a very competitive business and very few are able to find full-time work. The jobs that are available are mainly in towns and cities, usually in broadcasting, theatre, cabaret, the music recording industry and in films. There is limited job security and considerable talent is required for success. Most singers are freelance but may have contracts for regular work with choirs. There are more opportunities in light music than in classical. Some singers work on cruise ships, or at a holiday centre, and others work as backing artists to other singers. Many people have teaching jobs to supplement their performance earnings.

Pay can be comparatively low and irregular, but the few who succeed can expect a high standard of living. Salaries are rarely fixed and most singers are paid on a per gig or concert basis. To begin with you may earn anything from no fee at all to £30 an hour but singers can earn from £50-£500 a night. Rates for West End performers start at around £450 a week. The Musicians Union has information of the latest rates offered in the industry.

Health
This job requires normal hearing and good stamina and physical fitness.

Skills and Qualities
able to withstand criticism, able to work well with others, belief & commitment, determined, hard working, outstanding musical ability, resilient, self confident, self-disciplined

Relevant Subjects
Modern Foreign Languages, Music

Further Information
British Academy of Singwriters, Composers and Authors - www.britishacademy.com

Conservatoires Admissions Service UK - www.cukas.ac.uk

Diplomas (Foundation, Higher and Advanced) - http://yp.direct.gov.uk/diplomas

Incorporated Society of Musicians - www.ism.org

The Singer (bi-monthly) (Rhinegold Publishing) - www.rhinegold.co.uk/magazines

Training Schemes - www.direct.gov.uk/en/educationandlearning

Vocalist - www.vocalist.org.uk

Welsh Baccalaureate - www.wbq.org.uk

► Working in music (2007) (Babcock Lifeskills) - www.babcock-lifeskills.com/

Addresses
London Centre of Contemporary Music
50-52 Union Street Southwark, London SE1 1TD
Phone: +44 (0)20 7378 7458
Web: www.lccm.org.uk

Musicians' Union
33 Palfrey Place, London SW8 1PE
Phone: +44 (0)20 7840 5504
Web: www.musiciansunion.org.uk

Similar Jobs
Actor, Dancer, Music Composer, Music Therapist, Musician: Classical, Teacher: Music

Social Care Worker
also known as: Care Assistant, Homecare Assistant, Residential Care Worker, Social Care Worker: Home

CRCI:Social Work and Counselling Services
CLCI:KEB — Job Band: 1 to 3

Job Description
Social care workers provide personal and practical day-to-day care for people in their own home or in a residential care home. They help people such as the elderly, the young or those with physical or mental disability or illness. Listen and talks to their clients about any worries or concerns, and give support and reassurance. Help people with personal care such as washing, dressing, toileting, and feeding.

If working in someone's home, may care for blind and partially sighted people or those affected by progressive illnesses, such as Alzheimer's or Parkinson's disease, as well as the terminally ill. Also look after people who have been in hospital and require short-term help until they are able to cope with their everyday life. Social care workers prepare meals and do housework and laundry, go shopping, collect pensions and pay bills.

In a residential home, they also escort clients to other places, eg young people to college, and organise recreational activities. Attend meetings and training courses with other colleagues and may be a 'key worker' for some clients.

Work Details
In a day centre, you usually work a 37 hr week, Monday to Friday, but in residential homes you may live-in all of the time or on a rota basis. You may work shifts including weekends and nights.

Home care service is generally available from 7am to 10.30pm for seven days a week, 365 days a year. Hours are flexible, anything from 10 to 37 hrs a week, and shift work, early starts and late finishes, are common. You travel around a district, sometimes caring for up to eight people a day. This job supports those who, without such care, might be in hospital or residential care.

Your work is very energetic and involves some bending down and lifting. You are trained in the correct way to lift and handle a person. You may be on your feet for most of the time. Some jobs are messy and unpleasant. Sometimes you work with difficult clients, so your work can be stressful. Because of health and safety risks, special equipment and protective clothing may be issued.

Qualification
• England, Wales and Northern Ireland
Band 1: For training schemes: no qualifications are needed but some GCSEs, or equivalent at any level, are useful.

Band 2: Although academic qualifications are not specified for this job, it is an advantage to have some GCSEs (A*-C) in subjects that include English and maths, or equivalent.

Band 3: For entry: usually at least 4 GCSEs (A*-C) including English and maths, or equivalent.

• Scotland
Band 1: For training schemes: no qualifications are needed but some S grades, or similar at any level, are useful.

Band 2: Although academic qualifications are not specified for this job, it is an advantage to have some S grades (1-3) in subjects that include English and maths, or similar.

Band 3: For entry: usually at least four S grades (1-3) including English and maths, or similar.

Adult Qualifications
No pre-entry qualifications are usually required though some academic/vocational qualifications at any level may be an advantage. English and maths are useful subjects.

Work Experience
Relevant work or voluntary experience can equip you with skills to use in the future and that you can add to your CV. There are often opportunities available for voluntary work which give you experience of working with people. It is an advantage to have some experience in community service; this could be through the Red Cross, scouting/guiding or similar activities. In some areas there is a young apprenticeship (14-16) scheme that provides an extended work placement and achievement of a relevant level 2 qualification whilst at school. A first aid certificate, such as those offered by St John Ambulance or the Red Cross, is useful.

Entry and Training
This job is not normally open to school leavers other than those on a training programme, as experience of work and life is greatly valued. It is helpful to take a course in youth work, childcare or health and social care. In the past, social care workers have not required specific qualifications. However, staff are now often expected to obtain a relevant qualification for the work they do, and there is a qualifications framework for staff who wish to make a career in social care. This enables you to work your way to become a care manager or a social worker. You can also train to become a health worker or a nurse by starting in social care.

On-the-job training schemes last for 1-2 years and may include day release to a local college. Pre-entry courses include a BTEC diploma/certificate/SQA national award in health and social care, usually taken over one-year full time. BTEC national award courses are two years full time. A City & Guilds progression award in care is also available at various colleges; no formal entry qualifications are required. A driving licence may be necessary. Pre-employment checks include a Criminal Records Bureau (CRB)/Disclosure Scotland check, and some jobs require you to be registered with the General Social Care Council (GSCC). The GSCC holds a register of social care workers in England.

Most employers offer training to S/NVQ level 2 in health and social care, with opportunities for progression to levels 3-4. Training programmes, including apprenticeship schemes, may be available in your area. Advanced apprenticeships leading to qualification at level 3 can also be a route into higher education.

Some employers prefer older applicants as maturity and experience are important for this type of job. You may be able to enter this work through a government-funded training programme. Contact your local Connexions or careers office, Jobcentre Plus, Next Step service, or Learning and Skills Council (LSC)/Local Enterprise Company (LEC) for details of all training opportunities and schemes, including apprenticeships.

Opportunities and Pay
Around 1.2 million people work in social care and jobs are available throughout the UK. You can be employed by social services departments, health authorities, voluntary or private organisations. For suitably experienced care assistants, usually over 21 years of age, there may be opportunities to train as social workers and obtain a professional qualification. Promotion is gained through experience and qualifications. Some care assistants move into nursing, set up their own agency or become managers of care homes. Flexitime, part-time and temporary work is possible.

Pay varies depending on area and employer but salaries for inexperienced workers are likely to be around £11k, rising to £18k a year with experience and some qualifications. Senior care assistants earn up to £22k, and team leaders around £28k. If you don't work for a local authority, your rate of pay may be at an hourly rate that varies widely, depending on experience and qualifications.

Health
This job requires good general fitness.

Skills and Qualities
able to get on with all kinds of people, able to put people at ease, able to work both on your own and in a team, caring, emotionally strong, good listening skills, not squeamish, patient, reliable, trustworthy

Relevant Subjects
Health and social care, Hospitality and catering

Further Information
Apprenticeship Schemes (National Apprenticeship Service) - www.apprenticeships.org.uk

Community Care (weekly) (Reed) - www.communitycare.co.uk

Compass: Complete Guide to Social Work and Social Care - www.compassjobsfair.com

Jobs in Social Care (Department of Health) - www.socialcarecareers.co.uk/

Local Government Careers (Improvement and Development Agency) - www.lgcareers.com/publications/

Real Life Guide to Care, Welfare & Community Work (Trotman 2010) - www.trotman.co.uk

Real Life Guide to Care, Welfare & Community Work (Trotman 2010) - www.trotman.co.uk

Skills for Care and Development - sector skills council for social care, childre, early years and young people's workforces - www.skillsforcareanddevelopment.org.uk

Social Care and Social Work Careers - www.socialworkandcare.co.uk

Training Schemes - www.direct.gov.uk/en/educationandlearning
▶ Working in social care (2010) (Babcock Lifeskills) - www.babcock-lifeskills.com/

Addresses

Care Council for Wales
South Gate House, Wood Street, Cardiff CF10 1EW
Phone: +44 (0)29 2022 6257
Web: www.ccwales.org.uk

General Social Care Council (GSCC)
Goldings House, 2 Hay's Lane, London SE1 2HB
Phone: +44 (0)20 7397 5100
Web: www.gscc.org.uk

Northern Ireland Social Care Council
7th Floor, Millennium House, 19-25 Great Victoria Street, Belfast BT2 7AQ
Phone: +44 (0)28 9041 7600
Web: www.niscc.info

Scottish Social Services Council (SSSC)
Compass House 11 Riverside Drive, Dundee DD1 4NY
Phone: +44 (0)845 60 30 891
Web: www.sssc.uk.com

Social Care Association
350 West Barnes Lane, Motspur Park, Surrey KT3 6NB
Phone: +44 (0)20 8949 5837
Web: www.socialcaring.co.uk

Similar Jobs

Healthcare Assistant, Nurse: Mental Health, Nurse: Occupational Health, Nursery Worker, Occupational Therapy Assistant

Social Worker

also known as: Field Social Worker

CRCI:Social Work and Counselling Services
CLCI:KEB
Job Band: 5

Job Description

Social workers give advice, practical help and emotional support to vulnerable people with problems or disadvantages, so that they can try to overcome their difficulties. Aim to help people make constructive changes to their current lifestyle, or learn to live with what cannot be changed. They work as part of a team that cover a local geographical area and they specialise in social issues. These may include child protection, school exclusions, help for groups such as the sick or elderly, or those of all ages with physical or learning difficulties. May specialise in one particular area of work such as people with HIV/Aids, or those who have mental health problems.

Social workers look at the needs of the client, they interview the client and develop a relationship of confidence. Arrange suitable assistance from relevant agencies and authorities, follow clients' progress, and write reports. Liaise with other health professionals, including medical staff, the police and probation officers. They attend regular team meetings and professional conferences.

Work Details

Usually works around 37 hrs a week, Monday to Friday, though may be required to work on a rota basis to cover evenings and weekends. For most of the time you are in an office, but you also have to travel around the district to clients' homes, hospitals and courts. Your work involves advising and helping people and part of your job requires you to keep records and maintain confidentiality. You work in a team, liaising with other agencies. This job is emotionally demanding and stressful and can involve making unpopular decisions. Sometimes you may be involved in fairly dangerous situations, perhaps being confronted with threatening behaviour or assault.

Qualification

- **England, Wales and Northern Ireland**

Band 5: For degree courses: 2-3 A levels and some GCSEs (A*-C) usually including English and maths, or equivalent. Exact requirements depend on the degree you take.

- **Scotland**

Band 5: For degree courses: 3-5 H grades and some S grades (1-3), usually including English and maths, or similar qualifications. Exact requirements depend on the degree you take.

Degree Information

A BSc Hons in social work approved by the General Social Care Council (GSCC) is required; postgraduate diplomas and MAs, MPhil and DPhil are also available. Degrees in psychology, sociology, social policy and administration, law, and youth and community studies provide relevant background knowledge for this job but give no training advantage. However, you can qualify in social work if you undertake a relevant postgraduate qualification such as a diploma or masters degree.

Adult Qualifications

For those without the degree entry requirements there are Access and foundation courses to social work that lead to further study at degree level. Those with a degree can qualify by taking a relevant postgraduate course.

Work Experience

Relevant work or voluntary experience is always useful and can improve your chances in application for entry to this job. Consider experience that gives you the opportunity of dealing with young people in a helping capacity such as at youth and community centres, or in the caring professions. Although work experience is not an essential requirement it demonstrates enthusiasm and commitment. Check the Social Work and Care Careers website or contact Community Service Volunteers.

Entry and Training

A Diploma/ Welsh Baccalaureate in society, health and development may be available in your area. From 2011, humanities and social science may also be available.

Entry is by a General Social Care Council approved degree programme in social work that lasts at least three years (four in Scotland) and can be studied full or part time, and through distance learning. The course offers a balance between practical and academic study, and includes 200 days of practical placement. You may be eligible for a social work bursary to help with fees, contact the NHS Business Services Authority for details. Postgraduate research degrees are also available in social work and social care. Most training courses require applicants to have a period of relevant practical experience in a social work or a social care setting.

Pre-entry checks include a Criminal Records Bureau (CRB)/ Disclosure Scotland check and a medical examination. All social workers need to be registered with the GSCC to demonstrate that they have completed the required social work training, and conduct and competence requirements. Social workers then follow a programme of continuing professional development (CPD), including studying for post-qualifying awards.

Details of all courses, current training routes and registration are available from the professional organisations listed in further information. Contact your local authority or social services human resources section for training/qualification opportunities.

Mature people, who are already in relevant employment, may have an opportunity to work towards a degree in social work on a part-time basis. For those within social services departments, funding is normally available and bursaries may be awarded to those who are not employer funded.

Opportunities and Pay
There are over 100,000 social workers in the UK, but there is still a shortage, and jobs are more widely available in urban areas. Most field social workers are employed by local authorities but there are also opportunities with the NHS, the armed forces, charities and voluntary organisations and independent social work agencies. Some experienced social workers are employed by the Department of Health as inspectors and advisers.

There are opportunities for promotion to team leader or service manager and it is increasingly common to specialise in one area of social work, such as in adult social care, children, young people and their families and carers, or mental health. Medical or residential (home care management) work offers further opportunities. There are opportunities to work part time or to job share.

Pay varies depending on the employer, but in a local authority it is on a nationally agreed scale and usually increased by allowances for unsociable hours. In the private sector it depends largely on the type of employer. Pay can also be increased by additional payments for working in deprived areas. Newly qualified social workers generally earn around £20k-£28k, rising to £28k-£35k a year and beyond, with further experience and responsibilities.

Skills and Qualities
able to cope under pressure, able to inspire confidence, able to understand other people's problems, awareness of confidentiality issues, efficient record keeping, emotionally strong, good at writing reports, good communication skills, good interpersonal skills, good listening skills, resilient

Relevant Subjects
English, Government and politics, Health and social care, Law, Psychology, Sociology

Further Information
Become a Social Worker (GSCC) - www.gscc.org.uk

Community Service Volunteers - www.csv.org.uk

Compass: Complete Guide to Social Work and Social Care - www.compassjobsfair.com

Diplomas (Foundation, Higher and Advanced) - http://yp.direct.gov.uk/diplomas

Local Government Careers (Improvement and Development Agency) - www.lgcareers.com/publications/

NHS Business Services Authority - Social Work Bursary - www.nhsbsa.nhs.uk/

Skills for Care and Development - sector skills council for social care, childre, early years and young people's workforces - www.skillsforcareanddevelopment.org.uk

Social Care and Social Work Careers - www.socialworkandcare.co.uk

Social Work Careers (Department of Health) - www.socialworkcareers.co.uk/socialwork/

Welsh Baccalaureate - www.wbq.org.uk

▶Working in social care (2010) (Babcock Lifeskills) - www.babcock-lifeskills.com/

Addresses
British Association of Social Workers (BASW)
16 Kent Street, Birmingham B5 6RD
Phone: +44 (0)121 622 3911
Web: www.basw.co.uk

Care Council for Wales
South Gate House, Wood Street, Cardiff CF10 1EW
Phone: +44 (0)29 2022 6257
Web: www.ccwales.org.uk

General Social Care Council (GSCC)
Goldings House, 2 Hay's Lane, London SE1 2HB
Phone: +44 (0)20 7397 5100
Web: www.gscc.org.uk

Northern Ireland Social Care Council
7th Floor, Millennium House, 19-25 Great Victoria Street, Belfast BT2 7AQ
Phone: +44 (0)28 9041 7600
Web: www.niscc.info

Scottish Social Services Council (SSSC)
Compass House 11 Riverside Drive, Dundee DD1 4NY
Phone: +44 (0)845 60 30 891
Web: www.sssc.uk.com

Similar Jobs
Care Home Manager, Community Development Worker, Community Learning & Development Officer (Scotland), Counsellor, Health Promotion Specialist, Probation Officer, Social Worker: Medical

Social Worker: Medical
also known as: Almoner (Scotland), Medical Social Worker, Social Worker: Healthcare

CRCI:Social Work and Counselling Services
CLCI:KEB Job Band: 5

Job Description
Medical social workers support patients and their families in a hospital or hospice setting. They help them to resolve or cope with problems resulting from illness or disability, or from the social conditions in which they live. Work with medical colleagues to assess the patient's needs in the medical environment and on the patient's return home. Give practical help, such as advising on social benefits, or taking steps to provide immediate aid, including the care of children or other dependant relatives. Also assist with aftercare and rehabilitation, such as the fitting of special aids to assist in daily life in the home, or the delivery of meals, and regular visits from home care assistants. May counsel people with cancer, HIV/Aids, people who have suffered abuse, or people who have been involved in trauma or bereavement.

Those based in a hospital work in an assessment team of healthcare professionals, including occupational therapists, physiotherapists, nurses and consultants. Medical social workers ensure the aftercare is in place when the patient leaves hospital. Those in a hospice assist families with not only their grief, but with critical arrangements and paperwork.

Work Details
Usually works around 37 hrs a week, Monday to Friday, though may be required to work on a rota basis. Some evening and weekend work may be required. Work can be in a hospital, hospice, a clinic, GP practice or accident and emergency unit and sometimes you need to go into clients' homes. You work with all kinds of people, including people who are in pain, upset or depressed and in need of support. The work is very demanding and can be stressful at times, and it may involve making difficult decisions. You liaise with a team, including medical staff, and your work involves keeping confidential records.

Qualification
- **England, Wales and Northern Ireland**

Band 5: For degree courses: 2-3 A levels and some GCSEs (A*-C) usually including English and maths, or equivalent. Exact requirements depend on the degree you take.

- **Scotland**

Band 5: For degree courses: 3-5 H grades and some S grades (1-3), usually including English and maths, or similar qualifications. Exact requirements depend on the degree you take.

Degree Information
A BSc Hons in social work approved by the General Social Care Council (GSCC) is required; postgraduate diplomas and MAs, MPhil and DPhil are also available. Degrees in psychology,

sociology, social policy and administration, law, and youth and community studies provide relevant background knowledge for this job but give no training advantage. However, you can qualify in social work if you undertake a relevant postgraduate qualification such as a diploma or masters degree.

Adult Qualifications
For those without the degree entry requirements, there are Access and foundation courses to social work that lead to further study at degree level. Those with a degree can qualify by taking a relevant postgraduate course.

Work Experience
Relevant work or voluntary experience is always useful and can improve your chances in application for entry to this job. Consider experience that gives you the opportunity of dealing with young people in a helping capacity such as at youth and community centres, or in the caring professions. Although work experience is not an essential requirement it demonstrates enthusiasm and commitment. Check the Social Work and Care Careers website or contact Community Service Volunteers.

Entry and Training
A Diploma/ Welsh Baccalaureate in society, health and development may be available in your area. From 2011, humanities and social science may also be available.

Entry is by a General Social Care Council (GSCC) approved degree in social work that lasts at least three years (four in Scotland) and can be studied full or part time, and through distance learning. The course offers a balance between practical and academic study, and includes 200 days of practical placement. You may be eligible for a social work bursary to help with fees. Contact the NHS Business Services Authority for details. Postgraduate research degrees are also available in social work and social care. Most training courses require applicants to have a period of relevant practical experience in a social work or a social care setting.

Pre-entry checks include a Criminal Records Bureau (CRB) or Disclosure Scotland check and a medical examination. All social workers need to be registered with the GSCC to demonstrate that they have completed the required social work training, and conduct and competence requirements. Social workers then follow a programme of continuing professional development (CPD), including studying for post-qualifying awards.

Details of all courses, current training routes and registration are available from the professional organisations listed in further information. Contact your local authority or social services human resources section for training/qualification opportunities.

Mature people who are already in relevant employment, may have an opportunity to work towards a degree in social work on a part-time basis. For those within social services departments, funding is normally available and bursaries may be awarded to those who are not employer funded.

Opportunities and Pay
Most medical social workers are employed by the NHS and based in hospitals or other medical premises. Some experienced medical social workers are employed by the Department of Health as inspectors and advisers. There are opportunities for promotion to team leader or service manager. There may be opportunities to work part time or to job share.

Pay varies depending on the employer, but in the NHS it is on a nationally agreed scale and usually increased by allowances for unsociable hours. Newly qualified social workers generally earn around £20k-£28k, rising to £28k-£35k a year and more, with further experience and responsibilities.

Skills and Qualities
able to cope under pressure, able to inspire confidence, able to understand other people's problems, emotionally strong, good communication skills, good interpersonal skills, good listening skills, good organisational skills, non-judgemental, resilient.

Relevant Subjects
Business and accounting, English, Health and social care, Law, Psychology, Science, Sociology

Further Information
Become a Social Worker (GSCC) (GSCC) - www.gscc.org.uk

British Journal of Healthcare Management (Wiley-Blackwell) - www.bjhcm.co.uk

Community Service Volunteers - www.csv.org.uk

Compass: Complete Guide to Social Work and Social Care - www.compassjobsfair.com

Diplomas (Foundation, Higher and Advanced) - http://yp.direct.gov.uk/diplomas

Local Government Careers (Improvement and Development Agency) - www.lgcareers.com/publications/

NHS Business Services Authority - Social Work Bursary - www.nhsbsa.nhs.uk/

Skills for Care and Development - sector skills council for social care, childre, early years and young people's workforces - www.skillsforcareanddevelopment.org.uk

So you want to work in Healthcare (Wayland) - www.waylandbooks.co.uk

Social Care and Social Work Careers - www.socialworkandcare.co.uk

Social Work Careers (Department of Health) - www.socialworkcareers.co.uk/socialwork/

Welsh Baccalaureate - www.wbq.org.uk

Addresses
British Association of Social Workers (BASW)
16 Kent Street, Birmingham B5 6RD
Phone: +44 (0)121 622 3911
Web: www.basw.co.uk

Care Council for Wales
South Gate House, Wood Street, Cardiff CF10 1EW
Phone: +44 (0)29 2022 6257
Web: www.ccwales.org.uk

General Social Care Council (GSCC)
Goldings House, 2 Hay's Lane, London SE1 2HB
Phone: +44 (0)20 7397 5100
Web: www.gscc.org.uk

Northern Ireland Social Care Council
7th Floor, Millennium House, 19-25 Great Victoria Street, Belfast BT2 7AQ
Phone: +44 (0)28 9041 7600
Web: www.niscc.info

Scottish Social Services Council (SSSC)
Compass House 11 Riverside Drive, Dundee DD1 4NY
Phone: +44 (0)845 60 30 891
Web: www.sssc.uk.com

Similar Jobs
Care Home Manager, Counsellor, Nurse: Occupational Health, Social Worker

Software Tester
also known as: Computer Software Tester, Computer Systems Acceptance Tester, IT Systems Acceptance Tester, Quality Assurance Tester, Software Testing Engineer, User Acceptance Tester

CRCI:Computers and IT
CLCI:CAV — Job Band: 3 to 4

Job Description
Software testers test the quality and useability of software before it is released for use in a business or home environment. They work out all the ways in which the software is likely to be used and

create a test plan to test it over and over again during its development phase. Testers follow the test plan/script which includes negative tests to try and 'break' the system. They identify the possible risks with the software when it is being used and whether it is easy for a user to understand. Also evaluate the product and locate any problems with the software. Testers often work on a specific part of the program to check that each detail works properly. They act as the software's first audience and identify and report on any aspects that need to be improved.

Testers can be involved in testing all sorts of computer software, from individual programs to whole applications or products (a series of programs that store and process information to do a specific task). They may help with the development of a new program, test a new version, or simply carry out a routine check of existing software. Testing usually includes the use of screens and how to print information from the application, as well as how data is processed. Testers usually work in a team. Once the software goes into a live environment, they may help the customer support team with quality assurance issues.

Work Details

Work a basic 37 hr week, Monday to Friday, although you may need to work extra hours to meet deadlines. You are normally based at a desk or workstation and need to concentrate for long periods of time. Software testing is very much a team effort and you need to consult regularly with colleagues.

Qualification

• England, Wales and Northern Ireland

Band 3: For most employers, or for a relevant BTEC national award: usually at least 4 GCSEs (A*-C) including English, maths and preferably computer studies, information technology, or equivalent.

Band 4: For some employers and BTEC higher national award: 1-2 A levels and some GCSEs (A*-C) usually including English, maths and preferably science, computer studies or information technology, or equivalent.

• Scotland

Band 3: For most employers, or a relevant SQA national award: usually at least four S grades (1-3) including English, maths and preferably computer studies or information technology, or similar.

Band 4: For some employers and SQA higher national award: 2-3 H grades and some S grades (1-3) often including English, maths and preferably science, computer studies or information technology, or similar qualifications.

Adult Qualifications

Mature entrants may not need to meet the standard entry requirements for higher education courses, particularly if your previous experience is relevant and you show the ability to study at the appropriate level.

Work Experience

Entry to this job is highly competitive and it is important that you try to do some relevant work or voluntary experience in aspects of the computing industry before applying. College courses or employers look for enthusiasm and commitment. Relevant work experience with computers can demonstrate this and helps to improve your chances on application. A successful work experience placement can be an effective way into the job.

Entry and Training

You need to have a good knowledge of ICT and most testers have a relevant qualification in a computing or business-related subject. Some have a degree and some programming knowledge or experience is desirable. You also need to be able to document findings and communicate them to colleagues. The Information Systems Examination Board, a division of the British Computer Society (BCS), offers the Foundation Certificate in Software Testing. Check the BCS website for details. Training is usually on the job and ongoing, as technology changes rapidly. You need to keep up with technology throughout your career so continuing professional development is important.

A Diploma/Welsh Baccalaureate may also be available in your area in IT and foundation degrees are available in computing subjects. S/NVQs are available in a range of IT subjects at levels 2-4. The new S/NVQ for IT users (ITQ 2009) has been developed as part of a project involving a full review of the National Occupational Standards for IT users. Training programmes, including IT apprenticeship schemes, may be available in your area for entry to this job. Advanced apprenticeships leading to qualification at level 3 can also be a route into higher education.

The Open University offers courses in computing and maths that can lead to a computing degree. There are no formal entry requirements and you study through distance learning. Foundation degrees in IT, in game production or in animation and games, are also available.

Mature applicants with knowledge or experience in testing and report writing have a fair chance of entry. There are many full or part-time courses available at further/higher education colleges for careers that do not require degree level entry. Some LSCs/LECs, Jobcentres (NI) and ELWa (Wales) run high technology courses. You can also gain recognition of previous experience through Accreditation of Prior Learning (APL) or by working towards relevant S/NVQs.

Opportunities and Pay

Software testers work for computer manufacturers and software houses, software consultancies and electronics companies, or any business using computer software. There may also be employment opportunities with large specialist software testing and quality assurance companies. Progression to quality assurance (QA) team leader or QA manager is possible and there are opportunities to move into software design and development, business or systems analysis or project management. There may also be opportunities for experienced testers to work as self-employed consultants and work abroad may be available.

Depending on the size and location of company, salaries are in the range of £21k-£27k a year, rising to around £33k. Higher earners can earn around £42k a year. Profit-sharing, performance-related pay or a bonus payment may be additional to your basic salary.

Skills and Qualities

able to communicate effectively, able to cope under pressure, able to work both on your own and in a team, able to work to deadlines, attention to detail, good at writing reports, logical, methodical, planning skills, specialist IT skills

Relevant Subjects

Art and Design, Design and technology, ICT/Computer studies, Mathematics, Physics, Science

Further Information

AGCAS: Information Technology (Job Sector Briefing) (AGCAS) - www.prospects.ac.uk

Computer Weekly (Reed Business Information) - www.computerweekly.com

Diplomas (Foundation, Higher and Advanced) - http://yp.direct.gov.uk/diplomas

e-skills UK - sector skills council for business and information technology - www.e-skills.com

Information Systems Exam Board (ISEB) - www.bcs.org/iseb

Inside Careers Guide: Information Technology - www.insidecareers.co.uk

Open University - www.open.ac.uk

Skills Framework for the Information Age (SFIA Foundation) - www.sfia.org.uk

Soil Scientist

TARGETjobs: IT (GTI Specialist Publishing Ltd.) - www.groupgti.com

Welsh Baccalaureate - www.wbq.org.uk

▶Working in computers & IT (2010) (Babcock Lifeskills) - www.babcock-lifeskills.com/

Addresses

British Computer Society (BCS)
First Floor, Block D North Star House North Star Avenue, Swindon, Wiltshire SN2 1FA
Phone: +44 (0)845 300 4417
Web: www.bcs.org

Similar Jobs

Business Analyst, Computer Games Playtester, IT Helpdesk Analyst/Operator, IT Systems Developer, Quality Assurance Controller/Inspector

Soil Scientist

CRCI:Science, Mathematics and Statistics
CLCI:QOL Job Band: 5

Job Description

Soil scientists collect and analyse data relating to the properties of soils and investigate influences such as climate, environment, land use and biodiversity, on them. they examine soil samples in the field and laboratory. Then produce maps of soil types and their distribution. Also provide information and advice to those in agriculture, industry, construction, local and central government, and other scientists dealing with environmental problems.

Some carry out research for the private and public sectors. Others work in an academic setting, usually a university, carrying out research or teaching. Attendance and participation at conferences and seminars nationally and internationally is common. Writing reports and articles for publication and papers for presentation is an important part of this job.

Can specialise in areas such as soil surveying, involving land capability studies and land evaluation work, landscape design, or in archaeological excavation work.

Work Details

Usually work a basic 40 hr week, but may have to work longer hours and some weekends. You are usually based in an office or laboratory but may have to visit sites such as farms and nurseries, perhaps travelling over a wide area. Laboratory and fieldwork can frequently involve weekend working. Most scientists work in small, interdisciplinary teams. Overseas work is common, especially for research and fieldwork. Overnight absences from home are common.

Career breaks are possible, but part-time work is unusual and most commonly found only in laboratory work. Self-employed soil scientists usually offer a consultancy role, but this comes with considerable experience in the field.

Qualification

- **England, Wales and Northern Ireland**

Band 5: For degree courses: 2-3 A levels including science subjects and some GCSEs (A*-C) including maths, or equivalent. Chemistry and biology are often required at A level, depending on the course you take.

- **Scotland**

Band 5: For a degree: 3-5 H grades, including science subjects and some S grades (1-3) including maths, or similar qualifications. Chemistry and biology are often required at H grade, depending on the course you take.

Degree Information

A degree in soil science or at least a significant course content of soil science is required. Relevant degree subjects include physical/ mathematical/applied sciences, urban and land studies. Degrees in agricultural/horticultural science, archaeology, ecology, crop and soil science, environmental science (biological), geochemistry, geography, geology, biology, botany/plant science and zoology, may increase your opportunities. Aberdeen is the only UK university to offer an undergraduate course in plant and soil science.

A good honours and postgraduate degree are essential. It is not possible to enter this profession with an HND only; a pre-entry postgraduate qualification, such as an MSc in soil science, or similar, is essential for most posts involving field and/or laboratory work.

Adult Qualifications

A good honours and postgraduate degree are almost essential. Entry qualifications vary for mature applicants to these courses and there may be special entry standards. Check with the individual university or college.

Work Experience

Universities and employers may prefer candidates who have relevant work or voluntary experience. Ideally you may shadow or work with somebody who is currently involved in the work, but alternatively it is relevant to undertake work involving geology. Obtaining general experience, which can help you gain or improve such skills as team working, communication and IT, is also an advantage.

Entry and Training

Experience in agriculture or horticulture may be needed for entry to some courses. It is an advantage to have gained experience through course work, voluntary and vacation work and overseas experience. Those lacking experience often study for an MSc in soil or environmental sciences. Some jobs may require you to have experience or postgraduate qualifications. Training is on the job for 1-2 years, together with a programme of short courses and site visits. Industry-recognised qualifications may also be required by your employer, such as environmental science, engineering, and geology, amongst many others. There are some opportunities for higher degree study when in employment.

You are expected to follow a programme of continuing professional development (CPD) throughout your career to expand your skills and knowledge. Soil scientists working on several sites need to have a valid driving licence.

Maturity is an advantage for consultancy and overseas posts when combined with relevant previous experience and strong personal qualities.

Opportunities and Pay

Typical employers include local and central government, environmental consultancies, universities, industrial companies and the National Soil Resources Institute at Cranfield University. Some jobs are in restricted locations and include specialist research centres such as the Natural Environmental Research Council (NERC) and Biotechnology and Biological Sciences Research Council (BBSRC) stations. It is possible to work in a technical role to a senior level or to move into project management. Promotion is based largely on experience, scientific publication and performance.

Consultancy opportunities are available for those with a great deal of experience. It is also possible to obtain contract work for specific, usually short-term, projects. There are British nationality requirements for jobs in the civil service.

Pay varies depending on location, level of entry and type of employer. Starting salaries are generally £19k-£24k a year, rising to £30k-£40k a year, with experience. Some soil scientists earn around £50k a year. Salaries with voluntary organisations are low, with the highest pay in industrial companies or consultancy. Work abroad is often better paid and may include accommodation costs. Lecturers earn in the range of £25k-£35k a year, increasing to £38k-£56k a year for senior posts.

Health

Must be physically fit and not prone to back problems. You may find this job difficult if suffering from an allergy such as hay fever. Some posts require good colour vision.

Skills and Qualities

adaptable, aptitude for fieldwork, aptitude for teamwork, good communication skills, information handling skills, problem-solving skills, research skills, scientific approach, specialist IT skills, technical aptitude

Relevant Subjects

Biology, Chemistry, English, Geography, ICT/Computer studies, Land and Environment, Mathematics, Science

Further Information

AGCAS: Environment & Agriculture (Job Sector Briefing) (AGCAS) - www.prospects.ac.uk

European Journal of Soil Science (BSSS, 6 x year) (Blackwell) - www.soils.org.uk/pages/european-journal-soil-science

Addresses

Biotechnology and Biological Sciences Research Council (BBSRC)
Polaris House North Star Avenue, Swindon, Wiltshire SN2 1UH
Phone: +44 (0)1793 413 200
Web: www.bbsrc.ac.uk

British Society of Soil Science (BSSS)
BSSS Administrative Centre, Cranfield University,
Building 53 MK43 0AL
Phone: +44 (0)1234 752983
Web: www.soils.org.uk

Institute of Biological, Environmental & Rural Sciences (IBERS)
Aberystwyth University Penglais SY23 3DA
Phone: +44 (0)1970 621904
Web: www.aber.ac.uk/en/ibers/about-us/

Institute of Professional Soil Scientists (IPSS)
The British Society of Soil Science Building 53
Cranfield University MK43 0AL
Phone: +44 (0)1234 752 983
Web: www.soilscientist.org

National Soil Resources Institute
Cranfield University, Bedfordshire MK43 0AL
Phone: +44 (0) 1234 754086
Web: www.cranfield.ac.uk/sas/nsri/index.jsp

Natural Environment Research Council (NERC)
Polaris House North Star Avenue, Swindon, Wiltshire SN2 1EU
Phone: +44 (0)1793 411 500
Web: www.nerc.ac.uk

Similar Jobs

Agricultural Research Scientist, Archaeologist, Chemist: Analytical, Countryside/Conservation Officer/Manager, Ecologist, Environmental Scientist, Geologist

Solicitor

also known as: Lawyer: Solicitor

CRCI:Legal and Political Services

CLCI:LAB Job Band: 5

Job Description

Solicitors provide clients with specialist legal advice and act for them on a variety of personal and business matters. They work directly with clients to establish the facts of a case, and form an opinion using extensive legal knowledge. They handle details on the client's behalf and complete relevant paperwork, such as letters or extensive contracts. They may be consulted on, for example, purchase and sale of property, legal aid, criminal cases, divorce and custody of children, taxation, or in the preparation of contracts and wills.

When necessary, solicitors represent the client in court or instruct barristers/advocates to do so. May specialise in areas such as litigation, insurance, international law or company and commercial law.

Work Details

Your hours are officially 9am-5pm, Monday to Friday, but extra hours are common, including taking work home. You are based in an office and, depending on your specialism, may also spend time in court. You give advice to private and business/corporate clients and explain complicated issues clearly. You must be able to analyse information and solve problems quickly. The work can be demanding at times and you may have to make difficult decisions.

Qualification

• England, Wales and Northern Ireland

Band 5: For degree course: three A levels (usually high grades) and some GCSEs (A*-C) including English and maths or equivalent qualifications. Exact requirements depend on the degree you take.

• Scotland

Band 5: For degree in Scots law: five H grades (typically AAAAB), and some S grades (1-3), usually including English and maths, or similar. Exact requirements depend on the degree you take.

Degree Information

In England and Wales, graduates should have either a good honours qualifying degree in law or a non-law degree plus the Common Professional Examination (CPE)/Graduate Diploma in Law (GDL). For admission to the Roll of Solicitors, all must complete a Legal Practice Course (LPC). Contact the Solicitors' Regulation Authority for details of all degree courses.

In Northern Ireland, a law degree that is acceptable to the Law Society of Northern Ireland must first be gained, followed by successful completion of the Institute of Professional Legal Studies' examinations. Those with a non-law degree must also attain a satisfactory level of approved legal knowledge, such as the Bachelor of Legal Science, offered by Queen's University, Belfast. Contact the Law Society of Northern Ireland for details of all training routes.

Adult Qualifications

Part-time and external degrees in law are available. Degree entry requirements may be relaxed for those over 23 years with legal work experience. Mature applicants can apply to take a two-year full time or three-year part time senior-status law degree, available at various institutions in the UK. Contact the Law Society or the Solicitors' Regulation Authority for further details.

Work Experience

Entry to this job is competitive and it is important that you do some relevant work or voluntary experience before applying. The College of Law suggests that applicants for postgraduate courses should seek work experience at every opportunity with general law firms. During the last year of a degree course, applicants should seek vacation work with two or three types of law firm. Large firms are the main providers of placements, but smaller firms are worth trying, as is the Government Legal Service. University students can apply for a mini-pupillage that lasts for one or two weeks. Contact the Pupillage Portal (formerly OLPAS) for details.

Entry and Training

A qualifying law degree covers the required foundations of legal knowledge and develops legal research skills and knowledge of the English legal system. Non-law graduates can apply to take the Common Professional Examination (CPE)/Graduate Diploma in Law (GDL).

After completing a law degree, or equivalent, all trainees must take the Legal Practice Course (LPC, England and Wales), or the Diploma in Legal Practice (Scotland), on a full or part-time basis. Following the postgraduate LPC, trainee solicitors must complete a training contract lasting two-years full time or four-years part time. The training contract must be taken within a Law Society authorised training establishment which is usually a firm of solicitors or in-house legal department. Entry to training contracts is fiercely competitive.

An alternative route is to achieve a post as a legal executive and by examination, become a Fellow of the Institute of Legal Executives (ILEX). This enables you to apply for the LPC or CPE/GDL courses. After completion, the two-year training contract is normally waived due to previous experience as a practising legal executive. There are several similar routes of qualification open to those in Northern Ireland and intending students should contact the Law Society of Northern Ireland for specific details.

The Diploma in Legal Practice in Scotland is a 26-week, full-time postgraduate course and is currently available at seven universities in Scotland. Following completion of the diploma, trainees must complete a two-year training contract with a practising solicitor in Scotland. The traineeship includes a Professional Competence Course (PCC) lasting several weeks. You may also qualify in Scotland through pre-diploma training for non-graduates, who are already employed by a firm of solicitors in another capacity and have achieved a set standard of academic education.

There is also a foundation degree in law, available in England and Wales, that enables access to a law degree. Contact the law societies for details of all qualifying training routes.

Mature applicants over the age of 25 (29 in NI) may apply to be accepted as a student of law without the usual minimum qualifications, or via a senior-status law degree. A standard level of education for entry applies and relevant work experience is an advantage, or may be required. Contact the Law Society for details.

Another route to qualification (England and Wales), is to first train as a legal executive and have at least five years' qualifying legal experience; at least two must be after successful completion of all the examinations. Contact the Institute of Legal Executives for details. The Law Society of Northern Ireland and the Law Society of Scotland also offer alternative training routes. Contact the individual societies for details of alternative training routes and qualifications.

Opportunities and Pay

Most solicitors work in private practice, ranging from small, independent high street solicitors practices to large city firms that can be national/international. Others work for local authorities or the civil service, Crown Prosecution Service, the Government Legal Service, the armed forces, the Magistrates' Court Service, and in industry or commerce. There is stiff competition for places. Solicitors work all over the UK and can also work abroad. Specialisation is usual, for example, in criminal work, commercial work or compensation. Self-employment and part-time work is possible.

Pay varies considerably depending on location, the size and type of firm. As a trainee, you can expect up to £19k a year in London and a minimum of £16k a year elsewhere. Newly qualified solicitors earn around £20k (£30k in London). Experienced solicitors in private practice earn in the range of £30k-£70k a year. Those in local government earn £35k-£50k a year. A partner, depending on the area of law and size of the firm, may earn up to £150k a year.

Skills and Qualities

aware of legal and ethical considerations, awareness of confidentiality issues, excellent communication skills, good memory, information handling skills, IT skills, problem-solving skills, sound judgement, time management skills, versatile

Relevant Subjects

Business and accounting, Economics, English, History, Law, Psychology

Further Information

Junior Lawyers (Law Society) - www.juniorlawyers.lawsociety.org.uk

Pupillage Portal (ex-OLPAS) (The General Council of the Bar) - www.pupillages.com/

Solicitors' Regulation Authority (SRA) - www.sra.org.uk

TARGETjobs: Law (GTI Specialist Publishing Ltd.) - www.groupgti.com

TARGETjobs: Law Scotland (GTI Specialist Publishing Ltd.) - www.groupgti.com

▶Working in advice & counselling (2007) (Babcock Lifeskills) - www.babcock-lifeskills.com/

▶Working in politics & law (2010) (Babcock Lifeskills) - www.babcock-lifeskills.com/

Addresses

Institute of Legal Executives (ILEX)
Kempston Manor, Bedfordshire MK42 7AB
Phone: +44 (0)1234 841 000
Web: www.ilex.org.uk

Law Society of England & Wales
The Law Society's Hall, 113 Chancery Lane, London WC2A 1PL
Phone: +44 (0)20 7242 1222
Web: www.lawsociety.org.uk

Law Society of Northern Ireland
96 Victoria Street, Belfast BT1 3GN
Phone: +44 (0) 28 9023 1614
Web: www.lawsoc-ni.org

Law Society of Scotland
26 Drumsheugh Gardens, Edinburgh EH3 7YR
Phone: +44 (0)131 226 7411
Web: www.lawscot.org.uk

Similar Jobs

Advocate (Scotland), Barrister, Coroner, Crown Prosecution Service Caseworker, European Law Solicitor, Legal Executive, Procurator Fiscal (Scotland), Sheriff (Scotland)

Sommelier

also known as: Cellarmaster, Wine Waiter

CRCI:Catering and Hospitality
CLCI:IC   Job Band: 1 to 3

Job Description

Sommeliers are trained wine professionals who specialise in buying, storing, selling and serving wine and other drinks. They manage the wine service in licensed fine restaurants, clubs, wine bars and hotels. They also develop the wine list and train other restaurant staff. Increasingly, sommeliers may also be specialists in beers, spirits, soft-drinks, cocktails, mineral waters and tobaccos. Works closely with restaurant management to make sure that the selection of wines and other drinks complements the restaurant menu. Meets with wine suppliers to source new wines and attends wine tastings. Ensures that the wines for large functions are in stock.

They greet customers once they are seated at the restaurant table and show them the wine list. Customers may ask about the wines. The sommelier answers their questions and gives advice on which wine goes best with the food they have ordered. They take orders for wines and drinks and take the orders to the bar/cellar. The sommelier uncorks the bottles and takes them to the table for the customer to try. If the customer is happy with the wine, the sommelier serves all the guests at the table.

Work Details
You normally work a 39-40 hr week on a shift basis. You may work in the evenings, at weekends and on public holidays. There may be long days. Work can begin early in the morning, unloading the latest wine delivery and checking stock levels, until late at night in the restaurant. You work mainly in the restaurant and look after all sorts of people. You must be able to cope with difficult customers and complaints, and remain efficient and courteous.

In this job you are on your feet for most of the time. There are times when you are very busy so you need to work quickly. Busy restaurants and bars can be hot, crowded and noisy. You need to follow the rules and regulations that govern health and safety, hygiene and alcohol provision. A uniform may be required and provided by the employer, or they may specify a basic style, such as a black skirt/trousers and white or coloured shirt.

Qualification
Employers look for those who have the ability to communicate well and have a welcoming personality. The use of a foreign language is an advantage in some jobs.

• England, Wales and Northern Ireland
Band 1: No minimum qualifications are required, but you are expected to have a good level of general education. Some formal/vocational qualifications at any level are useful.

Band 2: Although academic qualifications are not specified for this job, it is an advantage to have some GCSEs (A*-C) in subjects that include English and maths, or equivalent.

Band 3: For entry: usually at least 4 GCSEs (A*-C) including English and maths, or equivalent.

• Scotland
Band 1: No minimum qualifications are required, but you are expected to have a good level of general education. Some formal/vocational qualifications at any level are useful.

Band 2: Although academic qualifications are not specified for this job, it is an advantage to have some S grades (1-3) in subjects that include English and maths, or similar.

Band 3: For entry: usually at least four S grades (1-3) including English and maths, or similar.

Adult Qualifications
No pre-entry qualifications are usually required for mature entrants, although some academic/vocational qualifications at any level may be an advantage. English and maths are useful subjects.

Work Experience
Any work experience can equip you with skills that you can use in the future and add to your CV. There is often plenty of paid part-time bar and restaurant work available, including Saturday and seasonal jobs. Any sales work or other work with the public is also useful.

Entry and Training
You are likely to start work as a waiter or wine waiter and work your way up to sommelier through experience and relevant qualifications. Knowledge of a foreign language can be useful if you want to work overseas or on a cruise ship. A passion for and a desire to develop knowledge of wine and food is important. There are numerous wine appreciation courses available. You may be able to train while you work and be supported by your employer.

Some employers ask for certificates in wine knowledge such as those offered by the Wine & Spirit Education Trust (WSET). WSET offers specialist training in wines and spirits that range from a one-day foundation course in wines at level 1, to the Honours Diploma at level 5, which can lead to the ultimate qualification, a Master of Wine. WSET is approved by the UK government as a national awarding body for vocational qualifications. Courses can be taken at a range of venues throughout the UK or overseas. Contact WSET for further details.

Specialist courses in the study of wine and spirits are also offered by the Court of Master Sommeliers; these range from an introductory sommelier certificate course to the Master Sommelier Diploma. Apart from the introductory course, you must be employed in wine service to join these courses. The Institute of Masters of Wine offers an education programme which is mainly based on self study, leading to the internationally recognised qualification, Master of Wine. The European Wine Academy offers a certificate in Sommeliership and Restaurant Management, made up of forty lectures. They also offer a practical sommelier training and wine tasting programme, which can be studied via e-learning.

It is possible to take full-time courses, including BTEC awards/first diplomas or SQA national certificate modules in hospitality. The University of Brighton offers a foundation degree in wine business. Relevant S/NVQs are available, including food and drink service and multi-skilled hospitality services at level 2, or in catering and hospitality. Training programmes, including apprenticeships in hospitality or customer service leading to level 2 and advanced apprenticeships leading to level 3, may be available in your area. A Diploma/Welsh Baccalaureate may also be available in your area in hospitality.

Continuing professional development is important as you must keep up to date with what is happening in wine regions around the world. Trips to vineyards and wine fairs are valuable.

Mature applicants with experience either as a waiter/waitress, or in catering or customer care, are usually welcomed by employers. Most sommeliers are adults who have worked in hospitality and specifically trained for this role.

Adults may be able to enter this work through a government-funded training programme, such as an apprenticeship. You can gain recognition of previous experience through Accreditation of Prior Learning (APL) or by working towards relevant S/NVQs. Contact your local Connexions or careers office, Jobcentre Plus, Next Step service or Learning and Skills Council (LSC)/Local Enterprise Company (LEC) for details of all training opportunities and schemes.

Opportunities and Pay
Jobs are available throughout the UK. You can work in restaurants, pubs and hotels. There may also be opportunities to work on cruise ships and in bistros and tapas bars etc. There are increasingly more female sommeliers too. Work abroad is possible, particularly if you speak the host language.

Promotion opportunities may be better if you have specialist sommelier or wine appreciation training. You can progress to be a hotel, bar or restaurant manager, or work for a wine importer or manufacturer.

Pay varies, but sommeliers can earn £14k-£18k a year in the leisure industry, rising to £20k-£40k in hotels and restaurants, with experience and qualifications. Your pay may be increased if customers leave you tips. Some restaurants add a service charge to the bill and share this between staff. You are probably given free or subsidised meals while on duty.

Health
People with certain skin conditions may not be able to do this job. For this job you need to have good general fitness.

Skills and Qualities
able to work quickly, alert, clear speaking voice, energetic, friendly, good memory, numeracy skills, polite, smart appearance, steady hand

Relevant Subjects
Hospitality and catering

Further Information

Apprenticeship Schemes (National Apprenticeship Service) - www.apprenticeships.org.uk
CareerScope: Hospitality and Leisure (Springboard UK) - http://careerscope.springboarduk.net/
Court of Master Sommeliers - www.courtofmastersommeliers.org
Decanter (IPC Media) - www.decanter.com
Diploma in Hospitality (People 1st) - www.hospitalitydiploma.co.uk
European Wine Academy - www.europeanwineacademy.org
People 1st - sector skills council for hospitality, leisure, travel and tourism - www.people1st.co.uk
Sommelier Jobs - www.sommelierjobs.com
Springboard UK - www.springboarduk.net
Springboard Wales - http://wales.springboarduk.net/
Training Schemes - www.direct.gov.uk/en/educationandlearning
UKSP - Guide to Success in Hospitality, Leisure, Travel & Tourism - www.uksp.co.uk
Wine & Spirit Magazine (William Reed Business Media Ltd) - www.wine-spirit.com
▶Working in hospitality & catering (2009) (Babcock Lifeskills) - www.babcock-lifeskills.com/

Addresses

Institute of Masters of Wine
Mapre House, 2-3 Philpot Lane, London EC3M 8AN
Phone: +44 (0)20 7621 2830
Web: www.mastersofwine.org

Wine & Spirit Education Trust (WSET)
International Wine & Spirit Centre, 39-45 Bermondsey Street, London SE1 3XF
Phone: +44 (0)20 7089 3800
Web: www.wset.co.uk

Similar Jobs

Bartender, Catering Manager, Restaurant Manager, Waiter/Waitress, Wine Producer

Spa Therapist

CRCI:Personal and Other Services
CLCI:IK Job Band: 3

Job Description

Spa therapists use therapy techniques and treatments to improve a client's appearance and enhance their overall sense of well-being. They also work to reduce stress levels. At the first visit the therapist asks a client to answer some questions about their health and looks at their lifestyle. A programme of treatment is then produced for each client. They may offer treatments and therapies such as massage, body scrubs, body wraps, therapeutic baths, facials, manicures, pedicures and aromatherapy. A client may receive a slimming/nutrition plan and look at ways of body detoxification. Spa products are also offered to a client for purchase and use at home.

Therapists have a range of duties, such as ensuring there are sufficient supplies of spa products, and helping to maintain hygiene and cleanliness in all areas of the spa environment. Most therapists work in a team alongside other specialists such as nutritionists and medical professionals.

Work Details

Generally work 37-40 hrs a week, often including weekends and some evening work. There are opportunities to work flexible hours and many work part time. You work in a treatment room or a wet room with an individual client. There are long periods of standing and bending, the work can be quite physically demanding. The work environment is warm, pleasant and usually fragrant from the spa products. You are required to wear a smart uniform.

Qualification

• England, Wales and Northern Ireland

Band 3: For an NVQ level 3 in spa therapy or equivalent: usually 4 GCSEs (A*-C) or an NVQ at level 2 in beauty therapy. English, maths and a science are useful subjects.

• Scotland

Band 3: For an SVQ level 3 in spa therapy or equivalent: usually four S grades (1-3) or an SVQ at level 2 in beauty therapy. English, maths and a science are useful subjects.

Adult Qualifications

Some formal academic qualifications (or equivalent) are usually required for entry to training courses, but many colleges welcome mature entrants over 20, and may waive entry requirements.

Work Experience

Entry to this job is competitive and it is important that you try to do some relevant work or voluntary experience before applying. This is typically Saturday or holiday work in a spa, beauty or hairdressing salon. In addition, any sales or reception experience may be useful, as well as other kinds of work with the public.

The Vocational Training Charitable Trust (VTCT) runs diploma courses in schools at three levels in beauty therapy and hairdressing. These are aimed at 14-19 year olds and provide relevant background to this work.

Entry and Training

A Diploma/Welsh Baccalaureate in hair and beauty studies may be available in your area. Spa therapists need to hold or be working towards an S/NVQ in spa therapy at level 3 (or equivalent). You may begin your training by assisting qualified staff, whilst initially working towards a relevant S/NVQ at level 2, but to become fully qualified you must hold a relevant qualification at level 3. Edexcel, the Vocational Training Charitable Trust and City & Guilds all award this qualification.

The International Therapy Examination Council also offers a level 3 diploma in spa treatments. There are details on the website of where you can take this course. A range of specialised courses in subjects such as aromatherapy, Indian head massage, reflexology, Reiki and holistic massage, sports massage and lymphatic drainage are also available.

Higher level qualifications are not needed but can be useful if you want to move later into spa management. Foundation degrees are available in beauty and spa service, spa therapies and spa management. There is also a degree in spa management with hospitality at University College Birmingham.

Private training schools also offer related courses, some of which can be very expensive and which may not provide a qualified career pathway. The quality of these courses can vary so it is important to make sure that these qualifications are acceptable, in order to get professional insurance cover.

It is essential to keep up-to-date with new therapies, products and techniques. The Hairdressing and Beauty Industry Authority offers a continuing professional development (CPD) programme. Training programmes, including apprenticeship schemes, may be available in your area. Advanced apprenticeships leading to qualification at level 3 can also be a route into higher education.

Maturity is an asset and it is useful to have experience and/or qualifications in the beauty/spa industry. Work in customer services is also an advantage. You may be able to enter this work through a government training programme, including an apprenticeship for adults.

Opportunities and Pay

Employment opportunities include hotels, fitness and health centres/farms, holiday resorts, medical, residential and day spas, high street spas and product suppliers, and on cruise ships. The spa business is a growing industry and qualified spa therapists are currently in great demand, so it is vital that you achieve nationally recognised training and qualifications.

There are usually good opportunities to move into supervisory and management work. Spa therapists may also move into training or, with further qualification, may teach their subject. There are good opportunities for working overseas.

Pay varies, depending on the employer, the area in which you work and the number of treatments you are qualified to offer. Newly qualified spa therapists earn around £12k a year, rising to £16k-£19k a year with experience. Some therapists with managerial duties earn around £20k-£34k a year or more. Tips from clients and commission for sales of services and products can supplement your salary.

Health

There is an allergy risk from skin irritants. You need to be physically fit to do this work.

Skills and Qualities

able to get on with all kinds of people, able to work both on your own and in a team, discreet, friendly, good interpersonal skills, good listening skills, good personal grooming, manual dexterity, outgoing personality

Relevant Subjects

Art and Design, Biology, Chemistry, English, Health and social care, Leisure, travel and tourism, Science

Further Information

Apprenticeship Schemes (National Apprenticeship Service) - www.apprenticeships.org.uk

Careers in Spa Therapy (HABIA) - www.habia.org/uploads/Spa_Leaflet.pdf

Diplomas (Foundation, Higher and Advanced) - http://yp.direct.gov.uk/diplomas

Federation of Holistic Therapists - www.fht.org.uk

Hair and Beauty Jobs - www.hairandbeautyjobs.com

Spa Business Assocation Ltd - www.spabusinessassociation.co.uk/

Training Schemes - www.direct.gov.uk/en/educationandlearning

Welsh Baccalaureate - www.wbq.org.uk

▶Working in hairdressing & beauty (2009) (Babcock Lifeskills) - www.babcock-lifeskills.com/

Addresses

Hairdressing and Beauty Industry Authority (HABIA)
Oxford House, Sixth Avenue, Sky Business Park,
Robin Hood Airport, Doncaster DN9 3EG
Phone: 0845 230 6080 (UK only)
Web: www.habia.org/

International Therapy Examination Council (ITEC)
2nd Floor , Chiswick Gate, 598-608 Chiswick High Road,
London W4 5RT
Phone: +44 (0)20 8994 4141
Web: www.itecworld.co.uk

Vocational Training Charitable Trust (VTCT)
Eastleigh House, 3rd Floor, Upper Market Street,
Hampshire SO50 9FD
Phone: +44 (0)2380 684 500
Web: www.vtct.org.uk

Similar Jobs

Aromatherapist, Beauty Consultant, Beauty Therapist, Nail Technician, Nutritional Therapist, Reflexologist

Space Scientist

also known as: Research Scientist: Space

CRCI:Science, Mathematics and Statistics

CLCI:QOF Job Band: 5

Job Description

A space scientist observes and interprets natural and experimental conditions in the field of space research. May be involved in building instruments and robotics for use in space. Others work in research posts, investigating the galaxy and managing radio transmission of data from distant points in space to an investigator at a ground laboratory.

Uses computer simulations and data sets to monitor and understand changes in the earths make-up and forecast future events. Uses satellites to take pictures and microwaves to measure depth. Also uses radar pulse, directed to earth from space to examine surfaces. Findings are interpreted using calibrating instruments, logging data and analysing results. This work is important for studying and understanding climate change and other natural changes, but it can also be experimental when artificial conditions are created and the consequences observed.

Most space science is conducted by unmanned, automated spacecraft but some flights have human flight crews carrying out hands-on manipulation of equipment.

Work Details

Usually works a 35-40 hour week that may include unusual hours, depending on projects. You are based in an office or laboratory and have to collate and analyse data and use computer simulations to combine observations. Prepares and presents reports on findings and publishes professional papers. The work is detailed and can be mentally challenging when solutions are sought. Often works as part of a group, nationally and internationally.

Qualification

- **England, Wales and Northern Ireland**

Band 5: For degree courses: 2-3 A levels and some GCSEs (A*-C) usually including English and maths, or equivalent. Exact requirements depend on the degree you take.

- **Scotland**

Band 5: For degree courses: 3-5 H grades and some S grades (1-3), including English and maths, or similar qualifications. Exact requirements depend on the degree you take.

Degree Information

A university degree or equivalent in astrophysics, physics, maths, geophysics or geology is preferred, but combined degrees including astronomy are also acceptable. Computer science and electronic/software engineering are also useful.

Adult Qualifications

A relevant higher education qualification, usually a degree, is normally required together with a postgraduate qualification. A relevant PhD is required to undertake research. Entry requirements may be relaxed for adults applying for higher education courses and Access or foundation courses give adults without qualifications a route onto degree courses.

Work Experience

Entry to this career is competitive. Any work experience, particularly in the field of physics or design technology, is beneficial and can improve your chances at interview for university degree courses. Any experience that develops your skills in IT or computer modelling is very helpful.

Entry and Training

Training starts after having gained a good undergraduate honours degree in a physics-related subject. This is normally followed by a PhD. During your three year PhD, you are supervised by an experienced scientist and work towards the writing of your thesis. On completion of your PhD, you may work as a post-doctoral research fellow before securing a permanent appointment at a university.

You may start at university as a lecturer then move to senior lecturer, reader and professor if you pursue an academic career. Work involves teaching as well as research, and you may have particular management responsibilities as you become more senior. Some scientists choose to leave academia after their PhD and go to work in industry, government research organisations, the European Space Agency or NASA.

The University of Leicester hosts Space School UK (SSUK) each year. This residential programme is run for different age groups and the senior course is particularly suitable for A level students considering studying space science, astronomy or technology. Students who attend the programme benefit from the research facilities developed to study astronomy, planetary science and earth observation, while also having the National Space Centre close by for a visit.

It is possible for those with backgrounds in mathematics, computer science, or some branches of chemistry or engineering to move into this work, but mature entry as a space scientist is almost impossible without a postgraduate qualification. Graduates with a relevant first degree may be able to receive financial support from the Science and Technology Facilities Council (STFC).

Opportunities and Pay

With the launch of the UK Space Agency, there is currently a lot of excitement and optimism around the space industry. Space science and research contributes more than £6.5 billion a year to the economy and employs nearly 19,000 highly qualified people. In recent years, British scientists have been involved with missions to Mars, Venus, Saturn and Mercury and have had success with discovering a frozen sea on Mars and landing on Saturns moon.

Jobs are available in research through university-based groups or in spin-off companies that deal with satellite technology and communications. There may be opportunities to work abroad and to work on a contract basis. Promotion prospects are improved in larger organisations and may involve moving into different areas of work and widening your skill set.

University College London runs the Mullard Space Science Laboratory (MSSL), the largest university space research group in the UK. Their work includes research into fields ranging from the Earth's climate to the most distant galaxies in the known Universe, using innovative space instruments. Since 1966, they have been involved in over 35 satellite missions and 200 rocket experiments. The MSSL website has details of their outreach programme where they visit schools and run demonstrations up to A level stage.

The Nuffield Foundation offers funding for students aged 16 and above to work alongside scientists. This is available through their Science Bursaries for Schools and Colleges scheme. Similarly, the European Space Agency offers internships for undergraduate level students and one-year training contracts for graduate students.

The International Space School Educational Trust runs courses for teachers to bring space science into the classroom. Check their website for details of upcoming courses and developments in the space industry in the United States.

Pay varies depending on location and the particular industry/ employer. Starting salaries for graduates are likely to be in the region of £20k-£25k, rising to around £35k-£45k a year with experience. A space scientist employed by a university earns up to £30k, but senior researchers and lecturers can earn up to £57k a year.

Skills and Qualities

able to work both on your own and in a team, able to work in abstract terms, analytical skills, aptitude for maths and science, attention to detail, good presentation skills, problem-solving skills, research skills, specialist IT skills, technical aptitude

Relevant Subjects

Chemistry, Design and technology, Engineering, English, Geography, ICT/Computer studies, Mathematics, Physics, Science

Further Information

European Space Agency (European Space Agency) - www.esa.int

NASA (National Aeronautics and Space Administration) - www.nasa.gov

National Space Centre Online - www.spacecentre.co.uk/Page.aspx/

Nuffield Foundation - www.nuffieldfoundation.org/

Scottish Wider Access Programme (SWAP) - www.scottishwideraccess.org/

SEMTA - sector skills council for science, engineering and manufacturing technologies - www.semta.org.uk

Space Careers - www.space-careers.com

Space School UK - http://spaceschool.co.uk/

UCL Mullard Space Science Laboratory - www.mssl.ucl.ac.uk/

UK Space Agency - www.ukspaceagency.bis.gov.uk/default.aspx

Women into Science, Engineering & Construction - www.wisecampaign.org.uk

▶Working in science (2007) (Babcock Lifeskills) - www.babcock-lifeskills.com/

▶Working in space (2010) (Babcock Lifeskills) - www.babcock-lifeskills.com/

Addresses

British National Space Centre (BNSC)
Polaris House North Star Avenue, Swindon, Wiltshire SN2 1SZ
Phone: +44 (0)20 7215 5000
Web: http://bnsc.gov.uk

International Space School Educational Trust (ISSET)
5 Herbert Terrace, Penarth CF64 2AH
Phone: +44 (0) 2920 710295
Web: www.isset.org/

Science and Technology Facilities Council (STFC)
Polaris House, North Star Avenue, Swindon, Wiltshire SN2 1SZ
Phone: +44 (0)1793 442 000
Web: www.scitech.ac.uk

Similar Jobs

Astronaut, Astronomer, Engineer: Aeronautical, Geophysicist, Meteorologist, Nanoscientist/Nanotechnologist

Speech & Language Therapist

CRCI:Healthcare
CLCI:JAS Job Band: 5

Job Description

Speech and language therapists help people who have disorders of the voice, speech and language, to cope and overcome their communication difficulties. They work mostly with people of all ages including children and the elderly but also those with learning difficulties. May treat people who have a stammer, or those with a lack of understanding and of using language, or who have difficulty in swallowing. Also help with psychiatric disorders, people who are recovering from a head injury, those who are learning to cope with a degenerative disease, such as Parkinson's disease, and people who have developed cancer of the mouth or throat.

Therapists decide on the best method of treatment and way of supporting a client through their treatment. This includes teaching muscle control by exercises and may use special devices to train the patient to produce fluent and intelligible sounds. They build a trusting relationship with a client to inspire confidence and motivation and maintain contact with other medical professionals who are involved with the patient. Also involve family members in the patient's care, treatment and progress, and may also need to counsel them.

Work Details

If working in the NHS you usually work 37.5 hrs a week, Monday to Friday, in hospitals, clinics and day centres. Some therapists work in education or in private practice. Travel around a local area may be involved when you need to visit a patient in their own home. You teach and help people and work with those who are in need of support, possibly hospital patients, or people of all ages with disabilities. Your work involves liaising with medical staff, teachers, social workers and psychologists. You are responsible for thorough work and for organising your own work load. Work can be emotionally demanding at times.

Qualification

• England, Wales and Northern Ireland

Band 5: For degree courses: 2-3 A levels including biology and sometimes a modern language, and some GCSEs (A*-C), usually including English, a biological science, and preferably maths and a modern language or equivalent. Exact requirements depend on the degree you take.

• Scotland

Band 5: For degree courses: 3-5 H grades, including biology and sometimes a modern language, and some S grades (1-3), usually including English and a biological science, and preferably maths and a modern language, or similar qualifications. Exact requirements depend on the degree you take.

Degree Information

A specialist degree in speech and language therapy or in clinical language sciences, speech pathology or human communication is essential and available at a number of universities and colleges. There are also some two-year postgraduate courses; usually a degree in a related subject such as psychology, linguistics or biological sciences is expected.

Adult Qualifications

Degree entry requirements may be relaxed for adults, but evidence of academic ability and recent study is usually needed. Those without the required qualifications may complete a foundation or Access course leading to relevant HNDs or accredited degrees. Check with individual universities and colleges for details.

Work Experience

Work experience gives you an insight into what you enjoy about a job or working environment, and the opportunity to acquire new skills. It provides valuable information to add to your CV and improves your course application and future employment prospects. This includes voluntary or paid experience of working in a residential care home, work with children, or anything involving helping and communicating with people.

Entry and Training

This job is a graduate entry only profession and entry to both first degree and postgraduate training courses is highly competitive. Training consists of a 3-4 year degree course that combines theoretical study in anatomy, linguistics, psychology or physiology, with clinical practice in hospitals, health centres or schools. All courses must be accredited by the Royal College of Speech and Language Therapists (RCSLT) and these are run at eighteen colleges and universities in the UK. It is possible to study part time. After completing the course you apply for membership of the RCSLT and state registration with the Health Professions Council (HPC).

A year of supervised practical experience in employment is normally required before you are professionally qualified. It is illegal to practise under the protected title of speech and language therapist if you are not registered with the HPC. Each individual is responsible for maintaining their own registration. Further study and training can lead to specialising in working with people with hearing impairment, pre-school children or those with learning disabilities.

Continuing professional development is important throughout your career, and to maintain your registration. Contact the RCSLT for a list of post-registration accredited courses and routes to training and qualification.

A Diploma/Welsh Baccalaureate may be available in your area in society, health and development. The advanced level is equivalent to 3.5 A levels but for some university courses, the additional and specialist learning (ASL) component of the diploma needs to include specific A levels. Check entry requirements carefully with the individual institutions.

Mature entrants with relevant experience, including work as a speech and language therapy assistant have an advantage. Graduates with a related background such as linguistics or psychology may enter the degree course in speech therapy or the accredited two-year postgraduate course. Graduates of other disciplines may also be able to enter the postgraduate course. Check with the individual universities for course entry requirements. There are a number of NHS-funded places on university courses and you may also be eligible for a non-means-tested student loan.

Opportunities and Pay

There are around 11,500 registered therapists in the UK and a shortage of qualified professionals. Jobs are available mainly in towns and cities and most are with the NHS in hospitals and outpatients clinics. There are also opportunities in education, in private practice, or with prisons and charitable and voluntary organisations. Promotion depends on experience and merit. There may be opportunities to teach or do research and study for a higher degree. Part-time work is possible and job-share and career breaks are common. You can become a self-employed speech and language therapist. Check the Association of Speech and Language Therapists in Independent Practice website for details.

A newly qualified speech and language therapist working for the NHS earns around £18k-£22k a year, and with experience a specialist speech therapist can earn up to £40k. A principal or consultant therapist up to £64k a year.

Health

You are expected to have clear speech and good hearing.

Skills and Qualities

able to explain clearly, able to inspire confidence, encouraging, good listening skills, initiative, patient, perseverance, scientific approach, sympathetic, tactful

Relevant Subjects

Biology, English, Health and social care, Modern Foreign Languages, Psychology, Science, Sociology

Further Information

A Career in Speech and Language Therapy (RCSLT) (Royal College of Speech and Language Therapists (RCSLT)) - www.rcslt.org/speech_and_language_therapy

Afasic: Unlocking Speech and Language - www.afasic.org.uk

Association of Speech and Language Therapists in Independent Practice, ASLTIP - www.helpwithtalking.com

Diplomas (Foundation, Higher and Advanced) - http://yp.direct.gov.uk/diplomas

Health Professions Council (HPC) - www.hpc-uk.org

NHS Careers (NHS Careers) - www.nhscareers.nhs.uk

NHS Careers Scotland - www.infoscotland.com/nhs

NHS Careers Wales - www.wales.nhs.uk

Welsh Baccalaureate - www.wbq.org.uk

Addresses
Royal College of Speech and Language Therapists (RCSLT)
2 White Hart Yard, London SE1 1NX
Phone: +44 (0)20 7378 3012
Web: www.rcslt.org

Similar Jobs
Audiologist, Dramatherapist, Hearing Therapist, Play Therapist, Speech & Language Therapy Assistant, Teacher: Special Educational Needs

Speech & Language Therapy Assistant
also known as: Bilingual Co-worker: Speech & Language Therapy, Clinical Support Worker: Speech & Language Therapy

CRCI:Healthcare
CLCI:JAS Job Band: 1 to 2

Job Description
Speech and language therapy assistants work in a team and support the work of a registered speech and language therapist (SLT) by helping patients to develop communication skills. Assistants work with a variety of patients, mostly children, but also elderly people and adults with mental and learning disabilities. They usually work with patients on a one-to-one basis, but are also involved in group therapy. They liaise with the speech and language therapist on a client's treatment programme and make any necessary changes. Also prepare rooms and equipment.

Assistants greet each patient and provide personal assistance, such as help with their mobility. Also perform some clerical and administrative duties. Some specialise as bilingual co-workers who work with clients in a language of their choice and act as an interpreter between the patient or carer and the speech and language therapist.

Work Details
Usually work a basic 37.5 hr week that may include shifts and weekends, although part-time work and job sharing is available. Assistants are normally employed at a community health centre, hospital, assessment unit, special school or a private clinic. You work with people who are in need of support, possibly hospital patients, children and people of all ages who may have physical or mental learning disabilities. Work can be emotionally demanding.

Qualification

- **England, Wales and Northern Ireland**

Band 1: For entry to jobs, no minimum qualifications are needed, but you are expected to have a good level of general education and relevant experience. Some formal/vocational qualifications at any level are useful.

Band 2: For entry to jobs, no minimum qualifications are needed, but it is an advantage to have some GCSEs (A*-C) or equivalent in subjects that include English and maths. Language skills are useful.

- **Scotland**

Band 1: For entry to jobs, no minimum qualifications are needed, but you are expected to have a good level of general education and relevant experience. Some formal/vocational qualifications at any level are useful.

Band 2: Although academic qualifications are not specified for this job, it is an advantage to have some S grades (1-3) in subjects that include English and maths, or similar. Language skills are useful.

Adult Qualifications
There are no formal educational requirements but relevant experience and language skills are useful.

Work Experience
Relevant work or voluntary experience in a caring role/childcare is always useful and can improve your chances when applying for jobs and training. Work shadowing with a speech and language therapist is very helpful. Contact your local NHS Trust for opportunities.

Entry and Training
Induction and in-service training is offered in most jobs. A variety of learning and development opportunities are available to speech and language therapy (SLT) assistants. These include in-service education, informal learning such as work shadowing and portfolio keeping, short courses, accredited vocational education, and access to the SLT qualifying courses. S/NVQs and Council for Awards in Children's Care and Education qualifications in childcare and education can also be very useful.

There is a demand for bilingual co-workers so knowledge of another language and/or culture is particularly useful. Assistants/bilingual co-workers who support the work of speech and language therapists can join the Royal College of Speech and Language Therapists as associate members. With qualifications and experience you can progress on to a degree course and qualification as a SLT.

A Diploma/Welsh Baccalaureate may be available in your area in society, health and development and can be a useful introduction to this career. See the diplomas website for further information.

Mature entry is welcomed in this profession, although previous experience in a caring profession is expected. Most employers offer training to S/NVQ level 3 in health or social care. You can gain recognition of previous experience through Accreditation of Prior Learning (APL) or by working towards relevant S/NVQs.

Opportunities and Pay
Jobs are available mainly in towns and cities throughout the UK. Most assistants are employed by NHS Trusts, others find work in the private sector, education services and charities. There is strong competition for jobs. Many jobs are part time or term time only and some are on a fixed-term contract. With experience and qualifications you can progress to qualify as a speech and language therapist.

Assistants' pay is in accordance with NHS pay bands, starting at around £15k-£18k a year, rising to around £22k with experience.

Health
You must have clear speech and good hearing.

Skills and Qualities
able to put people at ease, aptitude for teamwork, emotionally strong, encouraging, good communication skills, good interpersonal skills, patient, perseverance, sympathetic, tactful

Relevant Subjects
Biology, Health and social care, Modern Foreign Languages, Psychology, Sociology

Further Information
A Career in Speech and Language Therapy (RCSLT) (Royal College of Speech and Language Therapists (RCSLT)) - www.rcslt.org/speech_and_language_therapy

Diplomas (Foundation, Higher and Advanced) - http://yp.direct.gov.uk/diplomas

NHS Careers (NHS Careers) - www.nhscareers.nhs.uk

NHS Careers Scotland - www.infoscotland.com/nhs

NHS Careers Wales - www.wales.nhs.uk

Welsh Baccalaureate - www.wbq.org.uk

Addresses
CACHE: Council for Awards in Children's Care & Education
Apex House, 81 Camp Road, St Albans AL1 5GB
Phone: 0845 347 2123 (UK only)
Web: www.cache.org.uk

Royal College of Speech and Language Therapists (RCSLT)
2 White Hart Yard, London SE1 1NX
Phone: +44 (0)20 7378 3012
Web: www.rcslt.org

Similar Jobs
Healthcare Assistant, Nurse: Learning Disabilities, Nursery Worker, Occupational Therapy Assistant, Physiotherapy Assistant, Speech & Language Therapist

Sport & Exercise Scientist
CRCI:Leisure, Sport and Tourism
CLCI:GAG Job Band: 5

Job Description
Sport and exercise scientists study and research scientific aspects that influence sport and exercise, including human performance, capability and endurance. They give specialist advice, based on research and analysis, to improve an individual's or team's sporting performance. This may involve designing and administering a training programme that enables the client to achieve a personal or team goal, or to improve their general level of physical fitness. They look at factors influencing health, particularly stress and diet. and may measure blood pressure, heart recovery rate, body fat percentage, joint flexibility and lung capacity. May also develop and maintain diagnostic and testing equipment and monitor the client's progress through record keeping.

Scientists may be required to devise a programme for people who are recovering from surgery or from a range of medical conditions or a sports injury. They also consult with other professionals including doctors, physiotherapists, psychologists and sports coaches.

Work Details
Usually works a basic 40 hr week, though actual working hours depend on the type and location of employment. Weekend and evening work is quite possible. Those in research or teaching establishments usually work regular office hours. You mainly work indoors in a laboratory, classroom/lecture hall, treatment room or sometimes outdoors in a sports stadium dressing room, or on the pitch or track.

Some work as sports and fitness consultants at a gymnasium or sports and fitness club. Others may work in a sports medicine centre providing consultation on sports injuries and giving advice on treatment.

Qualification
• England, Wales and Northern Ireland
Band 5: For relevant degree courses: 2-3 A levels, preferably including biology and either chemistry, maths or bio-mechanics, and some GCSEs (A*-C) usually including English and maths, or equivalent. Exact requirements depend on the degree you take.

• Scotland
Band 5: For a relevant degree: 3-5 H grades, preferably including biology and either chemistry, maths or bio-mechanics and some S grades (1-3) in subjects that include English and maths, or similar qualifications. Exact requirements depend on the degree you take.

Degree Information
Relevant first degrees are available in sports science and there are a wide variety of combined degrees, including sports science with biosciences, psychology, exercise science, sport development and management, and social sciences. There are also postgraduate courses available in sports science, including related courses such as cardiovascular rehabilitation.

Adult Qualifications
Mature entry to sports science courses may be possible through a suitable access programme such as Access to science. Check with the individual institution for mature entry requirements.

Work Experience
Entry to this career is highly competitive and it is essential that you have some relevant work or voluntary experience before applying. Specialised experience in sports and exercise science is usually gained during an undergraduate or higher degree course, but any work within sport, especially teaching or leading groups, is helpful. Graduates may be interested in applying for the British Association of Sport and Exercise Sciences (BASES) Supervised Experience (SE) scheme. Contact BASES for further details.

Entry and Training
This is usually a graduate profession with entrants requiring a first degree in sports science and/or a postgraduate degree, or teaching/coaching qualifications. Applicants with a related degree such as physiology or physical education usually require a further degree in sports science. For those with a biology-related subject, there are postgraduate courses available. A relevant foundation degree may also be acceptable for entry. Most degrees should cover physiology, biomechanics and psychology and entrants to the profession usually require knowledge of all three. Many then choose to specialise in one of these areas. Check course details carefully to find the right course for your chosen career. Some entrants start at assistant level and progress from there once experienced.

The British Association of Sport and Exercise Sciences (BASES) is the professional body for sport and exercise science in the UK. Many employers require individuals to have BASES accreditation for entry to jobs. BASES also offer a Supervised Experience (SE) scheme, which helps to develop the competencies required for accreditation, as well as a programme of continuing professional development (CPD). On this scheme you work with a BASES accredited sport and exercise scientist to gain appropriate experience. Contact BASES for further information. Other related professional organisations include the British Psychological Society and the Register of Exercise Professionals.

A Diploma/Welsh Baccalaureate may be available in your area in Sport & Active Leisure. The advanced level is equivalent to 3.5 A levels but for some university courses, the additional and specialist learning (ASL) component of the diploma needs to include specific A levels eg maths or biology. Check entry requirements carefully with the individual institutions.

This is a graduate profession, so mature entry is unlikely without the relevant qualifications. However, much depends on your experience and level of ability. Government training opportunities, such as apprenticeships, may be available in your area. You can also gain recognition of previous experience through Accreditation of Prior Learning (APL) or by working towards relevant S/NVQs. Contact your local careers office, Jobcentre Plus, Next Step service or Learning and Skills Council (LSC) Local Enterprise Company (LEC) for details of training schemes.

Opportunities and Pay
This is a relatively new profession that is still fairly small. As a result of this, there is often lots of competition for vacancies. However, since London won the bid to host the 2012 Olympic Games, there is more focus on raising standards in sport in the UK. For those with the right qualifications and skills, employment prospects are encouraging.

Employment exists in universities, colleges of higher education and with sporting organisations, such as the national governing bodies of sport, the British Olympic Association, the Sports Council, National Sports Medicine Institute and commercial sports performance centres. Some sports scientists may move into sports and leisure management, sports coaching, clinical exercise therapy or become a physical education teacher. There are opportunities for experienced and well-qualified sports scientists to be self-employed consultants.

Pay depends on the employer and your area of specialism but a sports scientist generally earns in the region of £20k-£26k rising to around £27k-£34k with experience. High earners can make £36k-

£60k a year. Those who teach/lecture earn the usual annual salary for qualified teachers/lecturers, which ranges from around £24k-£44k a year. Self-employed consultants may charge £25-£50 an hour with a daily rate of £130-£450.

Skills and Qualities
able to explain clearly, able to inspire confidence, able to report accurately, encouraging, IT skills, observant, patient, scientific approach, tactful

Relevant Subjects
Biology, Chemistry, English, Health and social care, ICT/Computer studies, Leisure, travel and tourism, Mathematics, Physical education and sport, Physics, Psychology, Science

Further Information
Careers in Sport and Exercise Sciences (BASES) - www.bases.org.uk/careers

Diplomas (Foundation, Higher and Advanced) - http://yp.direct.gov.uk/diplomas

Real Life Guide to Sports & Active Leisure (Trotman 2009) - www.trotman.co.uk

SkillsActive - sector skills council for active leisure, learning and well-being - www.skillsactive.com

Welsh Baccalaureate - www.wbq.org.uk

Welsh Institute of Sport - www.welsh-institute-sport.co.uk

▶ Working in sport & leisure (2010) (Babcock Lifeskills) - www.babcock-lifeskills.com/

Addresses
British Association of Sport and Exercise Sciences (BASES)
Leeds Metropolitan University,
Carnegie Faculty of Sport and Education,
Fairfax Hall, Headingley Campus, Beckett Park LS6 3QS
Phone: +44 (0)113 812 6162
Web: www.bases.org.uk

British Olympic Association
60 Charlotte Street, London W1T 2NU
Phone: +44 (0) 207 842 5700
Web: www.olympics.org.uk

British Psychological Society (BPS)
St Andrews House, 48 Princess Road East, Leicester LE1 7DR
Phone: +44 (0)116 254 9568
Web: www.bps.org.uk

National Sports Medicine Institute of the UK
32 Devonshire Street, London W1G 6PX
Phone: +44 (0)20 7908 3636

Register of Exercise Professionals (REPs)
3rd Floor, 8-10 Crown Hill, Croydon, Surrey CR0 1RZ
Phone: +44 (0)20 8686 6464
Web: www.exerciseregister.org

Sport England
3rd Floor Victoria House, Bloomsbury Square, London WC1B 4SE
Phone: +44 (0)20 7273 1551
Web: www.sportengland.org

Sport Scotland
Doges, Templeton on the Green, 62 Templeton Street,
Glasgow G40 1DA
Phone: +44 (0)141 534 6500
Web: www.sportscotland.org.uk

Sport Wales
National Sports Centre Sophia Gardens, Cardiff CF11 9SW
Phone: +44 (0)845 045 0904
Web: www.sports-council-wales.co.uk

Sports Council Northern Ireland
House of Sport, 2a Upper Malone Road, Belfast BT9 5LA
Phone: +44 (0)28 9038 1222
Web: www.sportni.net

Similar Jobs
Physiotherapist, Psychologist: Sport & Exercise, Sports Coach, Sports Professional, Sports Therapist, Teacher: Physical Education

Sports Coach
also known as: Sports Instructor

CRCI:Leisure, Sport and Tourism
CLCI:GAG
Job Band: 2 to 5

Job Description
Sports coaches teach skills and correct techniques for particular sports to those who participate regularly in sport. They work with all levels of ability and standards, from beginner to expert, aiming to increase trainees' confidence, ability and enjoyment, and to develop their talent. Coaches arrange training programmes, correct errors, give advice and encouragement, and attend competitions. Most teach one sport or a range of related sports. Some combine competing, or administrative and development work with coaching.

Work Details
Usually works unsocial and irregular hours, including weekends and evenings. Travel may be necessary to attend competitions or to use good training facilities. You may need to spend nights away from home, especially if you have to travel abroad. You are responsible for the safety and welfare of your trainees and for instructing them in the rules and regulations of your particular sport. A flexible, sensitive approach is required when dealing with competitors who may be anxious or nervous.

You need to cope with being active at times, but often standing around for long periods at other times. You can be out in all sorts of weather for outdoor sports, which means you may get cold and wet. Work can be pressurised and can be more demanding at certain times of the year. Good up-to-date knowledge of your particular sport is essential.

Qualification
Professional coaching usually requires a certificate/diploma recognised by the governing body of the sport, rather than academic qualifications.

• England, Wales and Northern Ireland
Band 2: For entry to jobs, no minimum qualifications are needed, but it is an advantage to have some GCSEs (A*-C) or equivalent in subjects that include English and maths.

Band 3: For entry to jobs, HNC or a relevant diploma in sport coaching, usually at least 4 GCSEs (A*-C) including English and maths, or equivalent.

Band 4: For HND in sport and exercise sciences, Diploma of Higher Education or foundation degree: 1-2 A levels and some GCSEs (A*-C) usually including English and maths, or equivalent. Colleges may request a science subject at A level, preferably biology.

Band 5: For degree courses in sports science: 2-3 A levels, preferably including a science/sport subject, and some GCSEs (A*-C) usually including English and maths, or equivalent. Exact requirements depend on the degree you take.

• Scotland
Band 2: Although academic qualifications are not specified for this job, it is an advantage to have some S grades (1-3) in subjects that include English and maths, or similar.

Band 3: For entry to jobs or SQA national award in sport (coaching): usually at least four S grades (1-3) including English or maths, or similar. Entry to courses in by an interview and evidence of your ability in sport.

Band 4: For entry to SQA higher national course in sport and exercise science (coaching): at least 2-3 H grades and some S grades (1-3) often including English and maths, or similar qualifications. Colleges may request a science subject at H grade, preferably biology.

Band 5: For degree course in sports science: 3-5 H grades, preferably including a science, and some S grades (1-3) usually including English and maths, or similar qualifications. Exact requirements depend on the degree you take.

Degree Information

A degree course in physical education, movement studies, sports and exercise science/studies, or sports coaching/coaching science, usually provides the required coaching qualifications. It is also possible to enter this job with any degree if you have the required level of sporting expertise. Many universities have excellent sports facilities and some offer sports scholarships. There are some postgraduate courses in sports coaching.

Adult Qualifications

Employers usually expect a valid certificate/diploma recognised by the governing body of the sport. This is often more important than academic qualifications.

Work Experience

Relevant work or voluntary experience is always useful and can improve your chances in application for entry to this job. This includes any sort of work at a sports facility, such as a gym or leisure centre, or work with a teaching element, as well as work teaching or leading groups in your chosen sport. Experience of helping with sports at club level may also give you an advantage.

Entry and Training

There are a number of different ways to train as a sports coach, but you usually need to gain qualifications from the National Governing Body (NGB) of your sport. There are full-time college courses in sport, such as BTEC national/higher national courses in sport (coaching). There are also a variety of short courses run by further education colleges and the NGBs of different sports. Contact the governing body of your chosen sport via the national sports council websites for details of required qualifications.

Coaching qualifications are also available through Sports Coach UK, such as the UK Coaching Certificate (UKCC), which endorses level 1-3 coaching qualifications in a wide range of sports. Some colleges/universities offer courses at degree or postgraduate level, including a relevant foundation degree in sports coaching. Sports Leaders UK also runs training courses in a variety of disciplines, leading to various sports leadership awards at level 1-3. Check the website for details.

While employed, you can also work towards an S/NVQ at levels 2 and 3 in sport and recreation (coaching, teaching and instructing), or level 2 and 3 in exercise and fitness instructing. The awarding body, NCFE, also offer an introductory level 2 vocationally-related qualification (VRQ) in sports coaching. A Diploma/Welsh Baccalaureate may be available in your area in Sport & Active Leisure. The advanced level is equivalent to 3.5 A levels but for some university courses, the additional and specialist learning (ASL) component of the diploma needs to include specific A levels. Check entry requirements carefully with the individual institutions.

Relevant training programmes, including apprenticeship schemes in coaching, teaching and instructing or instructing exercise and fitness, may be available in your area. Advanced apprenticeships leading to qualification at level 3 can be a route into higher education. For courses and qualifications in all aspects of sports coaching, contact SkillsActive, the sector skills council for active leisure and learning.

Mature candidates with appropriate qualifications, experience and maturity are preferred. You may benefit from government training opportunities, such as apprenticeships in coaching, teaching and instructing or instructing exercise and fitness, that may be available in your area. You can gain recognition of previous experience through Accreditation of Prior Learning (APL) or by working towards relevant S/NVQs. Contact your local careers office, Jobcentre Plus, Next Step service or Learning and Skills Council (LSC)/Local Enterprise Company (LEC) for details of all training opportunities and schemes, including apprenticeships for adults.

Opportunities and Pay

This area of work is highly competitive, there are few full-time jobs and considerable talent is required for success. Opportunities depend upon which sport you choose; for example there are a large number of golf instructors in full-time jobs, but few hockey coaches. There will be an increase in coaching opportunities leading up to the Olympic Games in 2012. The Department for Culture, Media and Sport is also encouraging more children to exercise regularly through their Every Child Matters Campaign, again, creating demand for coaches to implement programmes. There are opportunities for jobs with local authorities, or universities and colleges, leisure centres, large hotels, holiday camps and centres, outward bound schools, and with commercial sports clubs such as football and rugby clubs. Opportunities also exist within most of the armed forces for suitable recruits to train as physical training instructors.

Private sports clubs usually employ part-time instructors, often to work in the evenings and at weekends, so you may be employed on a sessional or seasonal basis. Your success and therefore progression is likely to depend on the success of the person or team you coach.

Due to the nature of employment in this job it is hard to summarise earnings. Most coaches work part time and often in a voluntary capacity. Coaches working freelance earn from £15-£30 an hour. Most salaried coaches earn around £15k-£20k rising to around £30k a year. Some may earn around £35k a year and top class coaches can earn considerably more than this.

Health

This job requires good general fitness and good health.

Skills and Qualities

able to explain clearly, able to inspire confidence, able to manage people, calm, encouraging, enthusiastic, hard working, observant, perseverance, resilient

Relevant Subjects

Biology, English, Health and social care, Leisure, travel and tourism, Physical education and sport, Psychology, Science

Further Information

Apprenticeship Schemes (National Apprenticeship Service) - www.apprenticeships.org.uk

Central Council of Physical Recreation (CCPR) (Central Council of Physical Recreation (CCPR)) - www.ccpr.org.uk

Department for Culture, Media and Sport - www.culture.gov.uk

Diplomas (Foundation, Higher and Advanced) - http://yp.direct.gov.uk/diplomas

Real Life Guide to Sports & Active Leisure (Trotman 2009) - www.trotman.co.uk

SkillsActive - sector skills council for active leisure, learning and well-being - www.skillsactive.com

Sports Leaders UK - www.sportsleaders.org

Welsh Institute of Sport - www.welsh-institute-sport.co.uk

What's it like to be a Sports Trainer? (A&C Black 2008)

▶Working in sport & leisure (2010) (Babcock Lifeskills) - www.babcock-lifeskills.com/

Addresses

Sport England
3rd Floor Victoria House, Bloomsbury Square, London WC1B 4SE
Phone: +44 (0)20 7273 1551
Web: www.sportengland.org

Sport Scotland
Doges, Templeton on the Green, 62 Templeton Street, Glasgow G40 1DA
Phone: +44 (0)141 534 6500
Web: www.sportscotland.org.uk

Sport Wales
National Sports Centre Sophia Gardens, Cardiff CF11 9SW
Phone: +44 (0)845 045 0904
Web: www.sports-council-wales.co.uk

Sports Coach UK
114 Cardigan Road, Headingley, Leeds LS6 3BJ
Phone: +44 (0)113 274 4802
Web: www.sportscoachuk.org

Sports Council Northern Ireland
House of Sport, 2a Upper Malone Road, Belfast BT9 5LA
Phone: +44 (0)28 9038 1222
Web: www.sportni.net

Similar Jobs

Fitness Instructor, Outdoor Activities Instructor, Riding Instructor, Sports Professional, Sports Therapist, Teacher: Physical Education

Sports Development Officer

CRCI:Leisure, Sport and Tourism
CLCI:GAG Job Band: 4 to 5

Job Description

Sports development officers are responsible for encouraging participation in sport and for ensuring that opportunities are available for all ages and abilities. They usually work as a member of a sports development team. They may set up and deliver training courses for teachers, volunteers, coaches and officials, to promote sport and organise competitions, holiday activities and leagues for children. They also establish links between schools, sports clubs and sports governing bodies and may work in the community with adult groups, youth organisations and local sports councils. They attend local, regional and national meetings, as well as sports seminars, conferences and other related events.

Work Details

Usually works a 35-37 hr week that may include weekend work. Your work involves organising people, providing encouragement and support, taking part in in-service training for teachers or other professionals and liaising with a team. You are office-based but you may also need to travel over quite a wide area, and are expected to sit on committees and attend meetings, of which many are in the evening. Sometimes you may also have to organise courses that are held in the evening or at weekends.

Occasionally you may be expected to coach or supervise your own particular sport. If you are in direct contact with participants, you need to be able to relate well to young people.

Qualification

- **England, Wales and Northern Ireland**

Band 4: For entry to BTEC higher national course in sport and leisure management (sports development & coaching) or a Diploma of Higher Education or foundation degree: 1-2 A levels and some GCSEs (A*-C) usually including English and maths, or equivalent. Colleges often request a science subject at A level, preferably biology.

Band 5: For degree course in sports science: 2-3 A levels and some GCSEs (A*-C) usually including English and maths, or equivalent. Many courses require a science subject at A level. Exact requirements depend on the degree you take.

- **Scotland**

Band 4: For entry to SQA higher national course in sport and leisure management (sports development & coaching): usually 2-3 H grades and some S grades (1-3) often including English and maths, or similar qualifications. Colleges often request a science subject at H grade, preferably biology.

Band 5: For degree course in sports science: 3-5 H grades and some S grades (1-3) usually including English and maths, or similar qualifications. Many degree courses require a science subject at H grade. Exact requirements depend on the degree you take.

Degree Information

Usually a degree in a sports-related subject is required, such as sports studies, sports science or sports technology, but high achievers in specific sports may be accepted with any degree. Sports subjects studied with recreation management, administration and coaching, or social policy are particularly relevant. Postgraduate courses are available for those with a non-relevant degree.

Adult Qualifications

Most applicants have a degree and some have postgraduate qualifications too. Entry to degree courses depends on college policy, and some run Access courses for adults without the required educational qualifications. Those with a teaching qualification, especially in PE, are regarded favourably.

Work Experience

Work experience gives you an insight into what you do and don't enjoy about a job or working environment, as well as the opportunity to acquire new skills. It also provides valuable information to add to your CV and improves any course application and/or your future employment prospects. This can include experience of playing or teaching sport, working with young people in sport, including holiday jobs, or being involved with a leisure, youth or community centre.

Entry and Training

Increasingly, sports development is becoming a graduate profession, though even with a degree it can be a difficult industry to get into. Some enter with an HNC/D in sport and leisure management (sports development and coaching) at level 5. The Institute for Sport and Recreation Management (ISRM) and City & Guilds offer a Higher Professional Diploma (HPD) in sports management. Courses are available at a range of local colleges or via distance learning. Contact ISRM for further details. Foundation degrees are available in relevant subjects such as sports and leisure management. Once employed by a local authority or organisation you may be offered an in-house training programme.

You need to demonstrate your commitment and interest in sport and sports development. Relevant training courses, workshops, seminars or conferences are offered by the various sporting regional bodies such as Sports England/Scotland/Wales and Northern Ireland. The professional body for the leisure industry is now the Institute for Sport, Parks and Leisure (ISPAL). ISPAL also runs short courses, events and workshops, such as the two-day, level 1 foundation workshop for those new to sports development, and the National Sports Development Seminar for those already working in sports development. Contact ISPAL, Sportscoach UK and Sports Leaders UK for details on all training courses and continuing professional development programmes.

A Diploma/Welsh Baccalaureate may be available in your area in Sport & Active Leisure. The advanced level is equivalent to 3.5 A levels but for some university courses, the additional and specialist learning (ASL) component of the diploma needs to include specific A levels eg biology. Check entry requirements with the individual institutions. Relevant S/NVQs are available at level 3 in sports development and at level 4 in managing sport and active leisure.

Mature entrants with knowledge of sport and also experience in human resource management, finance and marketing have an advantage. Former sportsmen and women, including coaches, may be accepted for development posts, provided that they have relevant experience in administration. High achievers in their chosen sport may also be preferred.

Opportunities and Pay

There has been a recent rise in the level of government support for programmes encouraging exercise, particularly for young people. For example, Scotland has introduced a 'Fit for Girls' (FfG) programme aimed at schoolgirls aged 11-16 to encourage a more active lifestyle. Similarly, the 'Every Child Matters' campaign in England looks to increase overall wellbeing for children. This drive to create a healthier nation, coupled with an increased focus on sport in the run up to the 2012 Olympics means employment prospects in this sector look good.

Employment can be with a local authority, a Sports Council, university, a voluntary organisation, or a sport's national governing body. There is no fixed career progression in this area of employment so prospects may depend on your willingness to move to another area.

Pay depends largely on the type of employer and varies according to seniority. Qualified sports development officers earn around £18k-£28k, and those with increased managerial responsibilities earn around £30k to more than £35k a year. You may be given an allowance for travel costs and travelling time.

Health

Good general fitness is usually required.

Skills and Qualities

able to take responsibility, aptitude for teamwork, calm, enthusiastic, friendly, good communication skills, good organisational skills, initiative, self confident

Relevant Subjects

Biology, Business and accounting, English, Leisure, travel and tourism, Physical education and sport, Psychology, Science

Further Information

Diplomas (Foundation, Higher and Advanced) - http://yp.direct.gov.uk/diplomas

Institute for Sport, Parks & Leisure (ISPAL) E-zine (ISPAL) - www.ispal.org.uk/ezine

Local Government Careers (Improvement and Development Agency) - www.lgcareers.com/publications/

SkillsActive - sector skills council for active leisure, learning and well-being - www.skillsactive.com

Sports Leaders UK - www.sportsleaders.org

Welsh Institute of Sport - www.welsh-institute-sport.co.uk

► Working in sport & leisure (2010) (Babcock Lifeskills) - www.babcock-lifeskills.com/

Addresses

Institute for Sport, Parks & Leisure (ISPAL)
Abbey Business Centre, 1650 Arlington Business Park, Theale, Reading RG7 4SA
Phone: 0844 418 0077 (UK only)
Web: www.ispal.org.uk

Institute of Sport & Recreation Management (ISRM) and the National Association for Sports Development Sir John Beckwith Centre for Sport, Loughborough University, Leicestershire LE11 3TU
Phone: +44 (0)1509 226 474
Web: www.isrm.co.uk

Sport England
3rd Floor Victoria House, Bloomsbury Square, London WC1B 4SE
Phone: +44 (0)20 7273 1551
Web: www.sportengland.org

Sport Scotland
Doges, Templeton on the Green, 62 Templeton Street, Glasgow G40 1DA
Phone: +44 (0)141 534 6500
Web: www.sportscotland.org.uk

Sport Wales
National Sports Centre Sophia Gardens, Cardiff CF11 9SW
Phone: +44 (0)845 045 0904
Web: www.sports-council-wales.co.uk

Sports Coach UK
114 Cardigan Road, Headingley, Leeds LS6 3BJ
Phone: +44 (0)113 274 4802
Web: www.sportscoachuk.org

Sports Council Northern Ireland
House of Sport, 2a Upper Malone Road, Belfast BT9 5LA
Phone: +44 (0)28 9038 1222
Web: www.sportni.net

UK Sport
40 Bernard Street, London WC1N 1ST
Phone: +44 (0)20 7211 5100
Web: www.uksport.gov.uk

Similar Jobs

Leisure Manager, Outdoor Activities Instructor, Psychologist: Sport & Exercise, Sports Coach, Teacher: Physical Education

Sports Professional

CRCI:Leisure, Sport and Tourism
CLCI:GAG Job Band: 1 to 5

Job Description

Sports professionals compete in professional games and sports, such as football, rugby, cricket, tennis, golf, darts, snooker, boxing, horse racing and equestrian sports. They work with a coach, a team of coaches or a trainer to reach a high standard of expertise, training regularly to improve fitness, strength and stamina and to improve skill in a chosen sport. They follow the rules and regulations of the relevant governing sports body, look after any personal sports equipment. and often help to train or teach others. May also work as a sports referee or umpire.

Work Details

Usually works irregular hours often with early starts and late finishes, including some weekends and possibly evenings. Travel is necessary to take part in competitions or to attend special training facilities. You need to spend nights away from home, especially if you have to go abroad. The life of a sports professional is very disciplined, spending a great deal of time in fitness training and rigorous coaching sessions for your particular sport and perhaps following a special diet and lifestyle.

You require strong motivation to compete in what can be a highly pressurised job. There is always the risk that injury might end your sporting career suddenly.

Qualification

Entrants are not required to have any specific academic qualifications, though for most sports, a good education is extremely useful. It is essential that you are very good at your chosen sport.

Adult Qualifications

Success in amateur sport is essential before you can become professional. However, opportunities to become a professional in most sports tend to diminish rapidly from around your mid 20s.

Sports Professional

Work Experience
Entry to a sports career is highly competitive. Extensive experience in your chosen sport is required. However, it may also be helpful to find out more about your sport and its place in society by gaining experience in coaching or administration, perhaps at a local leisure centre.

Entry and Training
This area of work is highly competitive and extensive talent is required for success. Most sports people turn professional after achieving considerable success in amateur competition. The training opportunities vary according to the sport. Team sports, such as football, rugby and cricket, have training programmes for school leavers who have been spotted by talent scouts. Some sports, such as golf, have options for training while employed in the sport. Contact the national governing body (NGB) of your chosen sport via the national sports council websites for details of training opportunities and any specific entry requirements.

Whilst there are no specified academic qualifications required for most sports, to qualify as a golf professional through the Professional Golfers' Association (PGA), you need to become a registered assistant at a PGA recognised golf facility and complete a three-year foundation degree in professional golf studies. To enter this course you need a minimum of four GCSEs/S grades. As the career of a sports professional may be fairly short-lived, having a degree or equivalent qualification may be a useful back up when embarking on a second career. Most universities have excellent sports facilities, which all undergraduates can use.

A career as a sports referee usually develops from amateur status in your sport. In football, you can take a basic referees course and then work your way up to referee at national or international level. However, the Football Association only has ten international referees so it is very competitive. Contact the Referees Association for full details.

Although graduates of any discipline may become involved in professional sport, study of a sport-related subject might be more appropriate. Some universities offer sports scholarships. Many individual sports require considerable personal financial investment to reach professional level, eg tennis or ice skating. In some sports there may be government-funded apprenticeship schemes, such as the Advanced Apprenticeship in Sporting Excellence (AASE) which is aimed at 16-18 year olds with serious potential. This scheme encompasses a variety of sports including football, athletics, rugby, swimming, tennis and cricket. SkillsActive aim to roll it out across all Olympic sports by the end of 2010. It is run at 12 academies throughout the UK and attached to major sporting clubs, with over 2500 athletes taking part in the scheme. It takes around two years to complete. Contact SkillsActive for available entry categories and details of all training schemes.

A Diploma/Welsh Baccalaureate may be available in your area in Sport & Active Leisure. The advanced level is equivalent to 3.5 A levels but for some university courses, the additional and specialist learning (ASL) component of the diploma needs to include specific A levels. Check entry requirements carefully with the individual institutions. There are also sports related S/NVQs such as the NVQ level 3 in Achieving Excellence in Sports Performance.

Mature entry to most sports is usually only possible for young adults because of training and fitness requirements. Contact the national governing body of your chosen sport for details.

Opportunities and Pay
Prospects vary according to your particular sport but there is always limited job security. Many careers are over by the age of 35, though in some sports, the opportunity to become a professional rapidly declines during your mid 20s. A great deal depends on luck and remaining free from injury. Sporting careers can end suddenly due to injury so some professionals go on to become referees or umpires.

The Department for Culture, Media and Sport is encouraging more children to exercise regularly through their Every Child Matters Campaign. This drive to create a healthier nation, coupled with an increased focus on sport in the run up to the 2012 Olympics means funding and employment prospects in this sector look good.

Some sports professionals may have annual contracts or are self-employed in their sporting capacity and have other jobs to further support themselves. Later in your career, you may be employed in a related field, such as coaching, management, sports development, journalism/photography, broadcasting, selling or promotional work.

Later in your career, you may be employed in a related field, such as coaching, management, sports development, journalism/ photography, broadcasting, selling or promotional work.

Your income from sport may be dependent on sponsorship, appearance fees and prize money. It is very hard to summarise the earnings of a sports professional, but it is fair to say that most earn in the range of £20k-£28k a year, and only a very few are able to make considerable earnings. Expenses for some sports can be very high. These may include accommodation, entry fees, equipment and travel expenses.

Health
This job requires a very high standard of physical fitness. 100% vision, with or without glasses/lenses is preferred, and maintaining a well proportioned body is essential.

Skills and Qualities
ambitious, aptitude for teamwork, competitive, dedicated, determined, resilient, resourceful, self confident, self-disciplined, stamina

Relevant Subjects
Biology, Physical education and sport, Science

Further Information
Apprenticeship Schemes (National Apprenticeship Service) - www.apprenticeships.org.uk

Diplomas (Foundation, Higher and Advanced) - http://yp.direct.gov.uk/diplomas

Institute for Sport, Parks & Leisure (ISPAL) E-zine (ISPAL) - www.ispal.org.uk/ezine

Professional Golfers' Association (PGA) - www.pga.info

Referees Association - www.footballreferee.org

SkillsActive - sector skills council for active leisure, learning and well-being - www.skillsactive.com

Welsh Institute of Sport - www.welsh-institute-sport.co.uk

▶Working in sport & leisure (2010) (Babcock Lifeskills) - www.babcock-lifeskills.com/

Addresses
Central Council of Physical Recreation (CCPR)
Burwood House, 14 -16 Caxton Street, London SW1H 0QT
Phone: +44 (0)20 7976 3900
Web: www.ccpr.org.uk

Institute for Sport, Parks & Leisure (ISPAL)
Abbey Business Centre, 1650 Arlington Business Park, Theale, Reading RG7 4SA
Phone: 0844 418 0077 (UK only)
Web: www.ispal.org.uk

Sport England
3rd Floor Victoria House, Bloomsbury Square, London WC1B 4SE
Phone: +44 (0)20 7273 1551
Web: www.sportengland.org

Sport Scotland
Doges, Templeton on the Green, 62 Templeton Street, Glasgow G40 1DA
Phone: +44 (0)141 534 6500
Web: www.sportscotland.org.uk

Sport Wales
National Sports Centre Sophia Gardens, Cardiff CF11 9SW
Phone: +44 (0)845 045 0904
Web: www.sports-council-wales.co.uk

Sports Coach UK
114 Cardigan Road, Headingley, Leeds LS6 3BJ
Phone: +44 (0)113 274 4802
Web: www.sportscoachuk.org

Sports Council Northern Ireland
House of Sport, 2a Upper Malone Road, Belfast BT9 5LA
Phone: +44 (0)28 9038 1222
Web: www.sportni.net

Similar Jobs

Fitness Instructor, Jockey, Motorsport Professional, Outdoor Activities Instructor, Sports Coach, Teacher: Physical Education

Sports Therapist

CRCI:Healthcare
CLCI:JOD Job Band: 4 to 5

Job Description

Sports therapists give advice and treatment to sports enthusiasts, athletes and others who wish to improve their level of fitness, overcome or prevent injury and improve their performance. They are also trained to carry out first aid. Therapists use movement and manipulation techniques to identify and treat muscle and joint injuries. Also use massage techniques, saunas, hydrotherapy baths, dance exercise, weighted exercise equipment and electronic muscle-exercisers. They calculate the level, frequency and duration of treatments and follow health and safety rules.

Therapists check the progress of each client, explain treatment, advise on diet and may help clients manage pain. Some specialise in one sport such as football or athletics, or just one aspect of the work, whereas others use a range of techniques.

Work Details

The hours of work may need to be flexible and you can be expected to work evenings and weekends. You usually work in treatment rooms, a clinic, hospital, gym, fitness centre or sports club, or outdoors at sporting events, or in a swimming or hydrotherapy pool. You have to be prepared for considerable physical exertion and sometimes heavy lifting. Smart/casual or tracksuit-style clothing is usually worn.

Qualification

• England, Wales and Northern Ireland

Band 4: For HND, Diploma of Higher Education or foundation degree: 1-2 A levels and some GCSEs (A*-C) usually including English and maths, or equivalent.

Band 5: For degree courses: 2-3 A levels and some GCSEs (A*-C) usually including English, maths and a science, or equivalent. Exact requirements depend on the degree you take.

• Scotland

Band 4: For entry to SQA higher national and professional development awards, usually 2-3 H grades and some S grades (1-3), including English, maths and a science, or similar qualifications.

Band 5: For degree courses: 3-5 H grades, including a biological science, and some S grades (1-3), usually including English, maths and a science, or similar qualifications. Exact requirements depend on the degree you take.

Degree Information

Many sports therapists have a degree in physiotherapy and a postgraduate degree in sports therapy or sports medicine. Some may have alternative qualifications such as a degree in sports science or sports rehabilitation.

Adult Qualifications

Many sports therapists are physiotherapists who have chosen to specialise after experience of general physiotherapy. Applications for physiotherapy degrees are welcomed from mature people, who can show evidence of recent study at an appropriate level. Previous experience is not necessary, but some health-related experience is useful.

Work Experience

Entry to this career is competitive and it is important that you try to gain some relevant work or voluntary experience before applying for a job or degree course. Work experience in any aspect of healthcare is useful. If you take the physiotherapy route it is competitive, so it is important to gain some relevant experience if you can. It can be difficult to organise work experience specifically in physiotherapy because of the current training pressures on physiotherapy departments. A discussion with a practising sports therapist is useful and demonstrates initiative.

Entry and Training

Sports therapy is not currently a state-registered profession. You may enter with an HND or degree in sports therapy, though many sports therapists train in physiotherapy first, taking an approved degree that is acceptable for membership of the Chartered Society of Physiotherapy. The Society of Sports Therapists (SST) is working with the British Association of Sports Rehabilitators and Trainers and the Health Professions Council (HPC) to establish sports therapy as a registered career by 2012. Currently, sports therapists must hold accredited qualifications if they wish to voluntarily register with the HPC.

There are relevant full-time courses at HND, foundation degree and degree level in sports science, sports studies and sports rehabilitation. Some therapists have a background in gymnastics or in an area of complementary medicine such as osteopathy or chiropractic. The SST has details of nationally approved qualifications, including diplomas in sports therapy, the treatment and management of injuries, an advanced diploma in clinical sports therapy and other specialised courses.

SkillsActive, the sector skill organisation for sporting activities, also has details of approved courses, including those offered by the International Institute of Sports Therapy. All these qualifications are based on skills assessment and have no set educational requirements for entry. Continuing professional development is important. If you are a member of the SST, this amounts to a set number of training hours each year and a valid first aid certificate.

A Diploma/Welsh Baccalaureate may be available in your area in sport and active leisure and/or society, health and development. The advanced level is equivalent to 3.5 A levels but for some university courses, the additional and specialist learning (ASL) component of the diploma needs to include specific A levels. Check entry requirements carefully with the individual institutions.

Mature entry is common and is viewed as an asset. Those who have skills or professional experience and qualifications in physiotherapy or related disciplines have an advantage. You need to be physically fit and active for this work, as well as having a thorough knowledge of sport.

Opportunities and Pay

This is a relatively new career and there is an increasing demand for specialist sports therapists. Many work in sports and health clubs as well as for professional football, rugby and basketball clubs and private hospitals. Some work in specialist sports clinics attached to NHS hospitals or GP surgeries. Promotion may be to supervisory positions. Others work in their own private clinic and build their client base according to their reputation. Some move into research and lecturing, or become specialists in certain areas of work. There are opportunities to work part-time and to work or travel nationally and internationally, particularly with a sports team.

Most newly qualified sports therapists earn around £18k-£28k a year. Experienced therapists working privately or with a professional team can earn around £35k a year or more. Pay in the private sector varies depending on employer, reputation and location. Self-employed therapists may charge around £40-£50 an hour.

Health
This job requires a very good level of stamina and general fitness.

Skills and Qualities
able to motivate others, able to understand other people's problems, firm manner, good communication skills, good interpersonal skills, manual dexterity, patient, perseverance, problem-solving skills, sympathetic

Relevant Subjects
Biology, Chemistry, English, Health and social care, Physical education and sport, Physics, Psychology, Science, Sociology

Further Information
AGCAS: Health (Job Sector Briefing) (AGCAS) - www.prospects.ac.uk

British Association of Sports Rehabilitators and Trainers - www.basrat.org

Diplomas (Foundation, Higher and Advanced) - http://yp.direct.gov.uk/diplomas

Health Professions Council (HPC) - www.hpc-uk.org

Physical Therapy in Sport (4 x year) (Elsevier) - www.elsevier.com/wps/find/journaldescription.cws_home/623067/description

Physiotherapy Journal (Elsevier Science) - www.physiotherapyjournal.com

SkillsActive - sector skills council for active leisure, learning and well-being - www.skillsactive.com

Society of Sports Therapists (SST) - www.society-of-sports-therapists.org

Welsh Baccalaureate - www.wbq.org.uk

Addresses
Chartered Society of Physiotherapy (CSP)
14 Bedford Row, London WC1R 4ED
Phone: +44 (0)20 7306 6666
Web: www.csp.org.uk

National Sports Medicine Institute of the UK
32 Devonshire Street, London W1G 6PX
Phone: +44 (0)20 7908 3636

Similar Jobs
Chiropractor, Nutritional Therapist, Osteopath, Physiotherapist, Sports Coach

Stable Hand
also known as: Stable Lad/Lass

CRCI:Environment, Animals and Plants
CLCI:GAG

Job Band: 1 to 2

Job Description
Stable hands work at a racing stable and are an important member of a team that is responsible for the general well-being of horses in their care. They work hard each day on tasks such as mucking out the stables, and keeping them clean and dry for the horses. Includes putting down fresh bedding and making sure there is enough water, hay and other feed. They carefully measure the feed and give each horse any required supplements. also clean the tack, such as bridles and saddles, and sweep out the yard. Stable hands also check the horses for any signs of illness, such as colic, or infections, such as mud fever. They report any changes in a horse's condition to the head lad/lass, or to the trainer.

Also exercise and care for two or three horses every day as well as doing the normal yard duties. Head lads/lasses are in charge of the stable staff team. Stable hands and travelling head lads/lasses go with their horses to race meetings all over the UK, and sometimes, all over the world. It is their responsibility to make sure that the horses are in peak condition to race when they arrive at the racecourse. May work in a stud or breeding yard, looking after stallions, mares and foals.

Work Details
Usually work a basic 40 hr week, spread over 5.5 days, though hours are often longer and include early mornings, some weekends and evenings, which are worked on a rota basis. Overtime is common. You work in a team with other stable hands, apprentice jockeys, head lads/lasses, jockeys and a trainer. Much of the work is outdoors and in all sorts of weather, which may often be cold and wet. Stables can also be dusty. The work involves bending, lifting and carrying feed and sometimes heavy equipment. Travel over long distances may be necessary, depending on where the race meetings take place, and there are often nights away from home. There is a risk of accidents from falls. A driving licence is useful.

Qualification

- **England, Wales and Northern Ireland**

Band 1: No formal qualifications are required, but you are expected to have a reasonable level of general education.

Band 2: Although formal qualifications are not specified for this job, it is useful, though not necessary for entry, to have riding and equine care skills to NVQ level 2 standard.

- **Scotland**

Band 1: No formal qualifications are required, but you are expected to have a reasonable level of general education.

Band 2: Although formal qualifications are not specified for this job, it is useful, though not necessary for entry, to have riding and equine care skills to SVQ level 2 standard.

Adult Qualifications
Most entrants are aged between 16 and 19 years old, but more mature entrants with relevant experience stand a good chance of entry.

Work Experience
This type of work is popular and entry is very competitive. Work experience, such as helping at a stable, can often improve your chances in getting a job. Caring for other types of animals is also useful. You can get good experience by working with horses during school holidays and through regular weekend work. Farm work is also useful.

An equine industry conversion course is available free to those with good horse care and riding skills who want to find out more about the horseracing industry. See the website of the British Horseracing Authority for details.

Entry and Training
Although there are no set entry qualifications, some work with horses is useful, though riding experience is not necessary. Those who are under 19 years old have to do a foundation course prior to entry to training. During this course you learn to ride as well as gaining the skills needed for work in a racing yard. The British Racing School (BRS) in Newmarket and the Northern Racing College (NRC) in Doncaster are two main training centres in England. There is also a training centre at Oatridge College in West Lothian, Scotland. Courses last nine to twelve weeks.

At the end of the course there are apprenticeship opportunities with a racehorse trainer. Apprenticeships lead to an S/NVQ at level 2 in racehorse care and usually take a further nine to twelve months. It is also possible to gain an S/NVQ at level 3 in horse care and management, or in racehorse care and management. The NRC and BRS also offer other training courses, such as equine transport courses at both certificate and advanced certificate level (NRC) and two day courses specially aimed at head lads/lasses to provide supervisory skills (BRS).

Working in a racing yard with a stable full of thoroughbred horses is very hard work but you gain valuable experience and follow a clear career path. With further experience you can move to become head lad/lass when it is useful to have already gained a level 3 course in racehorse care and management. This shows that you have the necessary skills for the job.

With further experience it is possible to become an assistant trainer or trainer. Some stable hands can train to be a jockey (see job article) by first becoming an apprentice jockey. However, they must meet the weight/height limits and be able to ride to a very high standard. They must also show that they have the desire to work hard in order to become a jockey. The British Horseracing Authority (BHA) says that many professional jockeys have entered horse racing in this way.

Foundation courses at accredited training schools are available to mature applicants too, although most entrants to this career are aged 16 to 19.

Opportunities and Pay

Jobs are available in racing stables throughout the UK though only in certain areas, usually the countryside. There are over 650 licensed racehorse trainers' yards and currently there is a shortage of stable staff. When experienced, you can become a travelling head lad/lass, assistant head lad/lass, and a head lad/lass. Some become an assistant trainer or trainer.

In the racing industry there is a clear pay scale and career path. Pay rates are agreed by the National Association of Stable Staff (NAOSS) according to the level of qualification and experience. 16-17 year olds with S/NVQ level 1 earn £142.80 for a 40 hr week, those with S/NVQ level 2 earn £168. Stable staff with more than seven years' experience or 5 years experience and an S/NVQ level 3 earn £264 a week. These are all minimum rates. Some employers offer a room at the stables in which to live. There is also a share of any pooled prize money. Stable staff receive a further payment for work on a Sunday and an overnight allowance for work away from the yard.

Health

There may be an allergy risk from horses. You need to be physically fit and have plenty of stamina to do this job.

Skills and Qualities

aptitude for teamwork, confident, enjoy working outdoors, hard working, observant, patient, strong interest in horses, willing to train and work away from home

Relevant Subjects

Biology, Land and Environment, Physical education and sport

Further Information

Apprenticeship Schemes (National Apprenticeship Service) - www.apprenticeships.org.uk

Careers in Racing (British Horseracing Authority) - www.careersinracing.com

Lantra - The Sector Skills Council for environmental & land-based sector (Lantra) http:/www.lantra.co.uk

Stable Staff (BRS) - www.brs.org.uk/Careers/Stable_Staff/

▶Working with animals (2009) (Babcock Lifeskills) - www.babcock-lifeskills.com/

Addresses

British Horseracing Authority (BHA)
75 High Holborn, London WC1V 6LS
Phone: +44 (0)20 7152 0000
Web: www.britishhorseracing.com/

British Horseracing Education & Standards Trust (BHEST)
Suite 16, Unit 8 Kings Court, Willie Snaith Road, Newmarket, Suffolk CB8 7SG
Phone: +44 (0)1638 560743
Web: www.bhest.co.uk

British Racing School (BRS)
Snailwell Road, Newmarket, Suffolk CB8 7NU
Phone: +44 (0)1638 665 103
Web: www.brs.org.uk

National Association of Stable Staff (NAOSS)
74a High Street, Swadlincote, Derbyshire DE11 8HS
Phone: +44 (0)1283 211522
Web: www.naoss.co.uk

Northern Racing College (NRC)
The Stables, Rossington Hall, Great North Road, Doncaster DN11 0HN
Phone: +44 (0)1302 861 000
Web: www.northernracingcollege.co.uk

Oatridge College
Ecclesmachan, Broxburn, West Lothian EH52 6NH
Phone: +44 (0)1506 864800
Web: www.oatridge.ac.uk

Similar Jobs

Farrier, Horse Groom, Jockey, Riding Instructor

Statistician

CRCI:Science, Mathematics and Statistics
CLCI:QOJ Job Band: 5

Job Description

Statisticians collect, analyse and interpret quantitative information in areas that include education and government, industry, health and market research, and present it clearly in numerical form. They decide if, and how, statistical methods can be applied to a problem by collecting relevant data and producing meaningful figures, graphs, tables or written reports. Then present their results using computing and communication skills. May use data to forecast or predict outcomes, such as the effect of changes in the birth rate on future pupil numbers. Also check quality control standards in industry, or monitor and review the efficiency of procedures within bodies such as the police authorities or national health service.

Can work in a variety of industries for example, in pharmaceuticals, to help to research and develop medicines and drugs; or as an economist studying trends that have an impact on the economy.

Work Details

Usually work a basic 37-39 hr week, Monday to Friday, but may work additional hours at times. Part-time work is possible and flexible working patterns are common. Work is office based, but usually requires travel for regular meetings with clients or to attend regional, national and international conferences. Statisticians often work in a team, informing, consulting and liaising with colleagues. You have responsibility for accurate analysis of the data collected, interpretation of your findings and clear presentation of your results. Much of the work is done using computers.

Qualification

- **England, Wales and Northern Ireland**

Band 5: For degree courses: 2-3 A levels, including a maths subject, and some GCSEs (A*-C) usually including English and maths, or equivalent. Subjects such as science, computing and economics are also useful. Exact requirements depend on the degree you take.

- **Scotland**

Band 5: For degree courses: 3-5 H grades, including a maths subject, and some S grades (1-3) usually including English, or similar qualifications. Subjects such as science, computing and economics are also useful. Exact requirements depend on the degree you take.

Degree Information

A degree course in statistics or applied statistics is usually preferred but degrees in subjects such as economics, operational research, mathematics, life/medical sciences and business-related subjects are also acceptable. Degrees which make considerable use of statistical methods or those which include computing, management or languages, are sometimes useful. Postgraduate MSc/diploma courses in statistics are available for those with relevant first degrees.

Adult Qualifications

Formal qualifications such as a degree are normally required. Those with fewer qualifications or relevant work experience can take the Royal Statistical Society (RSS) exams leading to entry to the graduate diploma, or to a degree course. Those with non-relevant first degrees may be able to take postgraduate degrees in statistics.

Work Experience

Relevant work or voluntary experience is always useful and can improve your chances in application for entry into this job. Any work experience in the finance sector is relevant and demonstrates enthusiasm and commitment to the work. Time spent in an actuarial or accountancy firm, an insurance company or shadowing a statistician gives you a good basis and insight into the profession. Details of three-month Summer placements and one-year student placements are available at the civil service jobs online website.

Entry and Training

Training is by practical work experience. It may be possible to join as a statistical assistant but most entrants are graduates with a degree that has a quantitative component such as statistics, mathematics, operational research, life or medical science, economics or business-related subjects. Some employers offer sponsorship for sandwich courses or support part-time study for an MSc in statistics. Membership of the Royal Statistical Society (RSS) and chartered statistician (CStat) status can be attained with appropriate qualifications and relevant experience. Ordinary/higher certificate/graduate diploma examinations are offered by the RSS, but these are mainly part-time and distance-learning courses, for those already in employment.

There is a fast-stream assistant statistician (AS) recruitment scheme operated by Government Statistical Service (GSS) recruitment, which is open to graduates with a numerate subject honours degree. You can also apply for direct entry as a statistical officer (StO) with the same entry requirements as for the fast stream, though the selection procedure is different. Those without degrees can also apply as an StO if they have at least two years' relevant work experience.

The GSS also recruits temporary statistical officers (TSOs) separately in order to fill urgent vacancies for departments. These posts are available for periods of up to 12 months, with the possibility of extension or permanent employment. Minimum entry qualifications are the same as for an StO.

An MSc in medical statistics may be an advantage to those seeking employment for medical statistician posts and jobs in the pharmaceutical industry. Holders of PhD degrees are also in great demand. It is an advantage to have experience in computing, particularly statistical software packages such as SPSS (Statistical Package for Social Sciences).

Mature entry is difficult for those without relevant qualifications, and some experience gained previously in a relevant field, such as commercial, financial or business, is preferred. You may prefer to take the ordinary/higher certificate/graduate diploma examinations that are offered by the Royal Statistical Society (RSS); the graduate diploma is equivalent to an honours degree in statistics. These are mainly part-time and distance-learning courses, for those already in employment. You may be able to receive funding for relevant postgraduate study or research from the Engineering and Physical Sciences Research Council (EPSRC). The Open University (OU) provides learning materials recommended by the RSS.

Opportunities and Pay

This is a small but emerging profession and opportunities for statisticians are good at the moment. Jobs are available throughout the UK with a concentration in London and other major cities. The Government Statistical Service (GSS) is the largest employer in the UK and most statisticians work for the civil service, or in the pharmaceutical industry.

You can be employed by an industrial firm, research organisation, higher education institution, market research organisation or financial institution. Some are self-employed and work as part of management consultancy groups. Home working and career breaks are often possible. Pharmaceutical companies may provide work abroad and some international secondments are open to government statisticians.

Pay varies depending on location and type of employer. Starting salaries for graduates are around £18k (£21k in London) a year, rising to £25k-£45k with experience. Higher salaries of £60k plus a year may be achieved through promotion. Performance bonuses are common in this field. Generally, salaries are higher in business, particularly in the pharmaceutical industry.

Skills and Qualities

able to explain clearly, accurate, attention to detail, flexible approach, good at forecasting trends, impartial, information handling skills, IT skills, logical, numeracy skills, sound judgement

Relevant Subjects

Economics, English, ICT/Computer studies, Mathematics

Further Information

Careers for Statisticians and Statistical Programmers within the Pharmaceutical Industry (Statisticians in the Pharmaceutical Industry (PSI)) - www.psiweb.org/newcareers

Civil Service Jobs online - www.civilservice.gov.uk/jobs/

Government Statistical Service (GSS) (Office of National Statistics (ONS)) - www.ons.gov.uk/jobs/

Open University - www.open.ac.uk

►Working in maths (2009) (Babcock Lifeskills) - www.babcock-lifeskills.com/

►Working in science (2007) (Babcock Lifeskills) - www.babcock-lifeskills.com/

Addresses

Engineering and Physical Sciences Research Council (EPSRC)
Polaris House North Star Avenue, Swindon, Wiltshire SN2 1ET
Phone: +44(0)1793 444 100
Web: www.epsrc.ac.uk

Institute of Mathematics and its Applications (IMA)
Catherine Richards House 16 Nelson Street,
Southend-on-Sea SS1 1EF
Phone: +44 (0)1702 354 020
Web: www.ima.org.uk

Royal Statistical Society (RSS)
12 Errol Street, London EC1Y 8LX
Phone: +44 (0)20 7638 8998
Web: www.rss.org.uk

Statisticians in the Pharmaceutical Industry Ltd (PSI)
PSI Executive office, Kingston Smith Association Management, Association House, South Park Road, Macclesfield SK11 6SH
Phone: +44 (0)1625 267882
Web: www.psiweb.org

UK Statistics Authority
Statistics House Tredegar Park, Newport NP10 8XG
Phone: +44 (0)845 604 1857
Web: www.statisticsauthority.gov.uk

Similar Jobs
Actuary, Economist, Market Research Executive, Operational Researcher, Quality Manager, Teacher: Mathematics

Steeplejack
CRCI:Building and Construction
CLCI:UF Job Band: 1 to 2

Job Description
Steeplejacks work at heights to build, inspect, repair, clean, and sometimes demolish very tall buildings and structures. They install basic lightning protection systems and aircraft warning lights. May work on church spires, oil refineries, large chimneys, stately homes and castles, bridges, monuments and cooling towers. Steeplejacks plan work, put up special scaffolding, access ladders, cradles (work platforms) and fix safety harnesses. May need to abseil to reach some areas of work. They replace damaged stonework, brickwork, roof tiles or glass, and may weld metal or paint surfaces. All equipment is dismantled once the job is done.

Work Details
Steeplejacks usually work a basic 39 hr week, though shift work or overtime may be required, including weekends. The work is outdoors on site, and in all sorts of weather conditions. This job involves climbing, lifting, balancing, kneeling and working at great heights. Travel is necessary to different sites and you may need to be away from home at times. A driving licence may be useful. There is a risk of falling from heights and accidents from equipment. A safety helmet and harness, protective footwear and outdoor wear are worn.

Qualification
- **England, Wales and Northern Ireland**

Band 1: No minimum academic qualifications are required for this work.

Band 2: Although academic qualifications are not specified for this job, GCSEs in maths, English, science or a technical subject are helpful for the calculations, measurements and theory. Equivalent vocational qualifications are also useful.

- **Scotland**

Band 1: No minimum academic qualifications are required for this work.

Band 2: Although academic qualifications are not specified for this job, S grades in maths, English, science or a technical subject are helpful for the calculations, measurements and theory. Similar vocational qualifications are also useful.

Adult Qualifications
Mature entrants do not always require qualifications for this type of work, although a good standard of education is useful.

Work Experience
Relevant work or voluntary experience is always useful and can improve your chances when applying for entry to construction jobs and apprenticeships. In some areas there is a young apprenticeship (14-16) scheme that provides an extended work placement and eventual achievement of a level 2 qualification whilst at school. Health and safety issues may mean that there are certain jobs you cannot do until you are over 16. Contact your local ConstructionSkills office for advice.

Entry and Training
Training with an employer is open to all age groups and is usually work based, together with a day or block-release college course to achieve relevant qualifications. Courses can also be run over one or two years, full time. Various flexible training schemes are available, such as sponsored apprentice training that is offered to young people through the Steeplejack and Lightning Protection Training Group and ConstructionSkills. This scheme guarantees a job after successful completion of the three-year training period. Trainees are sponsored by an employer and spend blocks of time each year at the National Construction College (Bircham Newton campus).

You can enter such training schemes at 16-17 and can apply for an apprenticeship in Year 11 (January). You may need to take an aptitude test before you start training. You also work towards gaining a level of competence card through a Construction Skills Certification Scheme (CSCS) to indicate your individual skill level. There are a range of other relevant short courses, such as mobile towers, health and safety and manual handling, available through ConstructionSkills or the Steeplejack and Lightning Protection Training Group. Contact them for details.

A Diploma/Welsh Baccalaureate in construction and the built environment may be available in your area. S/NVQs are available in accessing operations and rigging (steeplejacking) at levels 2-3. Training programmes, including apprenticeships leading to level 2, and advanced apprenticeships/construction apprenticeships leading to level 3 may be available in your area. There are also Construction Awards (England and Wales) available for those who are unable to gain workplace experience for NVQs.

Mature applicants can take refresher courses that may be available for those returning to work and there may be special government training schemes in some areas. Employers may take older applicants who show aptitude and have previous experience. You can also gain recognition of previous experience through Accreditation of Prior Learning (APL) or by working towards relevant S/NVQs. Contact your local careers office, Jobcentre Plus, Next Step service or Learning and Skills Council (LSC)/Local Enterprise Company (LEC) for details of training schemes, including apprenticeships for adults.

Opportunities and Pay
There are jobs with large building or civil engineering firms, chimney builders or steeplejack contractors. Many are self-employed or work on short-term contracts. Progression to supervisor posts is possible. Temporary, casual and seasonal work is often available. Work abroad is also possible.

Pay varies depending on area and employer. Starting salaries are around £15k a year, rising to around £20k-£25k with experience. Top earners can make around £32k a year. Overtime and bonus payment may add to your income.

Health
Good physical fitness, agility and stamina is needed, and you should not be allergic to dust.

Skills and Qualities
aptitude for teamwork, careful, enjoy working outdoors, good at calculating risks, good balance, good organisational skills, hand-to-eye co-ordination, head for heights, health & safety awareness, manual dexterity

Relevant Subjects
Construction and built environment, Design and technology, Physical education and sport.

Further Information

Apprenticeship Schemes (National Apprenticeship Service) - www.apprenticeships.org.uk

Construction Awards - http://gbca.com/events/construction-awards

ConstructionSkills - sector skills council for the construction industry - www.cskills.org

Training Schemes - www.direct.gov.uk/en/educationandlearning

Welsh Baccalaureate - www.wbq.org.uk

▶Working in construction & the built environment (2007) (Babcock Lifeskills) - www.babcock-lifeskills.com/

Addresses

Association of Technical Lightning and Access Specialists (ATLAS)
4c St Mary's Place, The Lace Market, Nottingham NG1 1PH
Phone: +44 (0)115 955 8818
Web: www.atlas-1.org.uk

Steeplejack and Lightning Protection Training Group
105 St Peter's Street, St Albans, Hertfordshire AL1 3EJ
Phone: +44 (0)1727 896 081
Web: www.slptraininggroup.org.uk

Similar Jobs

Demolition Operative, Lightning Conductor Engineer, Roofer, Satellite Systems Technician, Scaffolder

Sterile Services Technician

also known as: Hospital Sterile Services Technician

CRCI:Healthcare
CLCI:JOZ Job Band: 1 to 2

Job Description

Sterile services technicians work in a hospital's sterile services department, processing reusable medical devices from operating theatres, accident and emergency departments, wards and clinics. Many devices have to be taken apart, decontaminated, reassembled and examined under a microscope or magnifier, before being sterilised. They make sure that the quality of the service meets nationally recognised standards and that the equipment is safe to use on patients.

Prepare medical equipment and supplies for use using automated machines. Receive instructions on which items are needed and make up packs of the items for wards and operating theatres. They inspect the equipment to make sure that nothing is missing or defective. Clean and sterilise the reusable instruments and larger pieces of equipment using a specialised wash machine, a decontaminating machine, and a sterilising machine. Inspect, label and date the items, keeping accurate records so items can be traced.

Technicians test the wash cycle daily, decontaminating and sterilising equipment to make sure the machines are working correctly and efficiently. Keep supplies in a secure store room and as required, take them around the hospital by trolley to wards, operating theatres and departments. May work in a team of around 20 people.

Work Details

Usually work 37 hours a week, Monday to Friday, though may also work on a shift basis and be on-call at times. Early morning starts are common, around 7.30am-8am. The work is strenuous and you are on your feet for most of the day. You need to cope with items that are dirty, messy and smelly, as well as the sight of blood. Your workplace is hot and humid, but may be air-conditioned. You need to wear protective clothing, and sometimes gloves, a face mask and a gown.

Qualification

- **England, Wales and Northern Ireland**

Band 1: No minimum qualifications are required, but you are expected to have a good level of general education. Some formal/vocational qualifications at any level are useful.

Band 2: Although academic qualifications are not specified for this job, some employers prefer some GCSEs (A*-C) in subjects that include English and maths and a science subject, or equivalent.

- **Scotland**

Band 1: No minimum qualifications are required, but you are expected to have a good level of general education. Some formal/vocational qualifications at any level are useful.

Band 2: Although academic qualifications are not specified for this job, some employers prefer some S grades (1-3) in subjects that include English and maths and a science subject, or equivalent.

Adult Qualifications

Employers usually require you to have a good general education with formal qualifications in English language, maths and a science subject, or equivalent qualifications.

Work Experience

Work experience gives you an insight into what you enjoy about a job or working environment, as well as the opportunity to acquire new skills. It provides valuable information to add to your CV and improves your employment prospects. Experience can either be unpaid or voluntary, or holiday/part-time work that you have organised yourself.

Entry and Training

Training is on the job with an experienced member of staff and following a training programme that leads to technician membership of the Institute of Decontamination Sciences (IDSc). Training usually covers record keeping, theatre procedures, health and safety, emergency procedures, and safe storage requirements of sterile instruments and equipment. There is a range of vocationally-related qualifications in infection prevention at level 2. The IDSc is currently working with the UK Department of Health, the Health Care Commission and other government agencies to develop a new range of career-based educational programmes and qualifications in decontamination.

Those wishing to progress to supervisory or management posts also need to gain a separate qualification at level 3 from the Institute of Leadership and Management or take supervisory management training within an NHS Trust training school.

Mature entrants may be preferred by some employers and particularly those with previous technical experience. You may be able to take refresher courses that are sometimes available for those returning to work, and there may be special training schemes in some areas. You can also gain recognition of previous experience through Accreditation of Prior Learning (APL).

Opportunities and Pay

Around 2,500 people work as sterile services technicians and opportunities are good. Jobs are mainly in towns and cities throughout the UK working for an NHS Trust in the sterile supplies department of a hospital. Other jobs are with private hospitals, the armed forces, or independent theatre units that provide sterile services for operating theatres. With experience and qualification as a technician you can become a supervisor or manager. There are also opportunities to work in hospitals abroad.

Pay depends on who you work for, but generally trainees are paid around £13k rising to around £16k a year with experience and technical qualifications. Senior technicians in supervisory positions can earn £17k-£27k a year.

Health
There is a risk of allergy from skin irritants and a risk of infection. You are required to have a good level of fitness for this job.

Skills and Qualities
able to follow instructions, aptitude for teamwork, attention to detail, careful, flexible approach, health & safety awareness, not squeamish

Relevant Subjects
Health and social care

Further Information
Foundation Learning (QCDA) - www.qcda.gov.uk

Institute of Decontamination Sciences (IDSc) - www.idsc-uk.co.uk

NHS Careers (NHS Careers) - www.nhscareers.nhs.uk

NHS Careers Scotland - www.infoscotland.com/nhs

NHS Careers Wales - www.wales.nhs.uk

Training Schemes - www.direct.gov.uk/en/educationandlearning

Addresses
Institute of Leadership and Management (ILM)
Stowe House, Netherstowe, Lichfield, Staffordshire WS13 6TJ
Phone: +44 (0)1543 266 867
Web: www.i-l-m.com

Similar Jobs
Healthcare Assistant, Hospital Porter, Laboratory Assistant, Laboratory Assistant: Medical, Operating Department Practitioner

Stock Control/Replenishment Assistant
also known as: Shelf Filler, Supermarket Shelf Filler

CRCI:Retail Sales and Customer Services
CLCI:OE Job Band: 1

Job Description
Stock control/replenishment assistants put goods on shelves, in refrigerators or on display stands, usually in a supermarket or other self-service store. They check shelves for gaps and take note of what has been sold. They collect replacement items from a stockroom or warehouse using a trolley. Goods are arranged neatly and safely on a shelf or display counter. Reduced items are labelled for a quick sale. Assistants check existing stock for out-of-date items and remove them. They keep shelves clean and tidy and may help customers to find items or work at the checkout tills.

Work Details
Usually work a 37-40 hr week, and although staff work during the day to keep the shelves well stocked during opening hours, much of the main work is done late in the evening or at night, when the store is closed. This can mean working shifts, including nights and weekends. You are on your feet for most of the time and need to be able to climb ladders in order to collect goods from the warehouse. Some heavy lifting and bending is required. Shelf fillers often have to wear an overall or a uniform.

Qualification

- **England, Wales and Northern Ireland**

Band 1: No qualifications are needed, but some employers may give a test in basic maths.

- **Scotland**

Band 1: No qualifications are needed, but some employers may give a test in basic maths.

Adult Qualifications
No special qualifications are needed for this job. You can improve your skills and qualifications by working through the Foundation Learning programme. This involves taking credit-based units and qualifications to help you progress.

Work Experience
Relevant work or voluntary experience is always useful and can improve your chances when applying for entry to retail jobs. It can equip you with skills that you can use in the future and add to your CV. Part-time and holiday employment in a wide range of shops is usually fairly easy to obtain.

Entry and Training
Training is usually on the job working alongside an experienced worker and often with some off-the-job training to learn about stock control, stock rotation, pricing and health and safety. With experience, you may be offered training as a checkout operator (see job profile) or learn about customer service. A Diploma/Welsh Baccalaureate in retail business may be available in your area. You may be able to gain an S/NVQ in retail skills at level 1-2. Other vocational qualifications are also available, such as the level 2 certificate in retail operations. Training programmes, including retail apprenticeship schemes, may also be available in your area.

Mature applicants are increasingly being employed for this job, particularly if they have previous experience in similar work, such as retail sales or warehouse work.

Opportunities and Pay
Stock control assistants work in supermarkets, hypermarkets, large stores and warehouses in towns and cities, or at out-of-town shopping centres. There are good opportunities for part-time, casual and seasonal work. In larger stores you can become leader/ supervisor of a particular section. There may be opportunities to work as a checkout operator or retail assistant.

Pay varies depending on location and employer. Most shelf fillers earn in the range of £10k-£18k a year. Overtime may be available. Many companies allow staff to buy goods at reduced prices.

Health
You have to be generally fit for this type of work, and because the job involves lifting, you should not suffer from back problems.

Skills and Qualities
able to get on with all kinds of people, able to work both on your own and in a team, co-operative, customer service skills, health & safety awareness, honest, methodical, punctual, reliable

Further Information
Apprenticeship Schemes (National Apprenticeship Service) - www.apprenticeships.org.uk

Diplomas (Foundation, Higher and Advanced) - http://yp.direct.gov.uk/diplomas

Foundation Learning (QCDA) - www.qcda.gov.uk

Real Life Guide to Retail (Trotman) - www.trotman.co.uk

Skillsmart Retail - sector skills council for the retail industry - www.skillsmartretail.com

Welsh Baccalaureate - www.wbq.org.uk

▶Working in retail & customer services (2008) (Babcock Lifeskills) - www.babcock-lifeskills.com/

Similar Jobs
Checkout Operator, Retail Assistant, Vehicle Parts Operative, Warehouse Order Picker/Assembler, Warehouse Worker

Stock Market Trader/Market Maker
also known as: Dealer/Trader: Stock Exchange, Stock Exchange Trader/Market Maker

CRCI:Financial Services
CLCI:NAL Job Band: 5

Job Description
Stock market traders buy and sell stocks and shares (securities) each day on the City of London Stock Exchange, making profits for clients. Most clients are company investors such as insurance companies. They give quotes for buying and selling prices, and

may deal in futures and options (derivatives), commodities or foreign exchange (FX). May specialise in UK shares, the gilt-edged market, fixed interest securities or international equities. Decide on prices for dealing, depending on market supply and demand. Monitor trends and keep prices under constant review by telephone and by electronic dealing online. A keen interest in social, economic, and current affairs is useful in this job.

As prices change very quickly, traders need to use computerised information databases to keep up to date on the latest financial news. Inform stockbrokers and other traders through Stock Exchange Trading Services (SETS) and the Stock Exchange Automated Quotations System.

Work Details

The hours are very long, usually 7am to 5.30pm or later, to take advantage of foreign markets in different time zones. The work is done in a dealing room, which can be large and very noisy. You sit at a dealing desk using a microphone, telephone and computer screens constantly, though meeting with other colleagues (traders) is also important. This is a very demanding, highly pressured and stressful job, and the work is highly competitive.

Qualification

There are no formal entry requirements but most firms look for recent graduates, especially those with a keen interest in the financial market and how it operates.

• England, Wales and Northern Ireland

Band 5: For degree courses before training: 2-3 A levels and some GCSEs (A*-C) usually including English and maths, or equivalent. Exact requirements depend on the degree you take.

• Scotland

Band 5: For degree courses before training: 3-5 H grades and some S grades (1-3), usually including English and maths, or similar qualifications. Exact requirements depend on the degree you take.

Degree Information

Usually a 2:1 minimum in any degree discipline is accepted, though subjects such as finance, politics, economics, maths and business studies may give an advantage.

Adult Qualifications

There are often special entry standards for adults applying for degree courses. Check with universities for details. However, mature applicants who begin a degree course may struggle to find employment.

Work Experience

Entry to this job is extremely competitive and any relevant vacation work or internship in the financial sector provides a marked advantage and demonstrates enthusiasm and commitment to the work. Many banks offer work experience placements and internships to penultimate-year degree students during the summer vacation period. You should keep up to date by reading the financial press.

Entry and Training

It can be difficult to find trainee posts and most firms have a policy of only recruiting recent graduates. Entrants usually need a 2.1 and often have to go though interviews and psychometric tests. Foreign language skills can be a great advantage. Most companies have their own comprehensive in-house training programmes supplemented by lectures, seminars and conferences. Training usually takes up to two years, working in all departments of the firm, watching experienced colleagues at their work and familiarising themselves with the day-to-day business, technology and terminology.

All traders must qualify to earn a place on the Stock Exchange's list of eligible traders, before they can trade. This requires passing an appropriate examination recognised by the Financial Services Skills Council (FSSC). Check the FSSC website for details of examinations. Language training is often provided for those wishing to specialise in trading stocks of a particular foreign country. The Securities & Investment Institute offers relevant qualifications for this work and the Investment Management Certificate from the Chartered Financial Analyst Society of the UK is also relevant. Traders are expected to undertake continuing professional development to keep up to date with what is happening in the financial world. Short courses are available for this, including those run by the London Metal Exchange.

Mature applicants may find that firms consider only recently qualified young graduates. However, those with a solid knowledge and experience of the securities industry, banking, insurance or economics may have an advantage.

Opportunities and Pay

This is a small profession, with most jobs being in London. There are also good opportunities in other cities including Glasgow and Edinburgh. Competition for jobs is intense and this is a career dominated by younger people. There are only a small number of market-making firms, but other organisations, such as investment banks and stockbroking firms employ market makers/traders. Promotion is based on merit and performance and routes are generally structured from trader, senior trader, associate, through to a managing director, although job titles vary. Opportunities exist for work abroad, especially in the Far East.

A graduate entrant is likely to earn around £30k a year, rising to around £37k with experience, although some earn substantially more. With experience, this rises to around £80k and a successful trader can earn £140k or more a year. Registered market makers/traders can earn very high salaries. Sign-on bonuses and shares in the company are usual and annual salary is also increased by performance-related bonuses. Additional benefits include mortgage subsidies and non-contributory pension schemes.

Health

This is a demanding and pressurised job and you need good physical and mental stamina.

Skills and Qualities

able to cope under pressure, analytical skills, confident, excellent communication skills, good at calculating risks, good at forecasting trends, good concentration level, integrity, IT skills, quick thinking.

Relevant Subjects

Business and accounting, Economics, English, ICT/Computer studies, Law, Mathematics

Further Information

AGCAS: Accountancy and Business Services (Job Sector Briefing) (AGCAS) - www.prospects.ac.uk/

Financial Services Skills Council - sector skills council for financial services, accountancy & finance - www.fssc.org.uk/

Inside Careers Guide: Banking, Securities & Investments - www.insidecareers.co.uk

TARGETjobs: City and Finance (GTI Specialist Publishers Ltd) - www.groupgti.com

▶Working in maths (2009) (Babcock Lifeskills) - www.babcock-lifeskills.com/

Addresses

CFA Society of the UK
2nd Floor 135 Cannon Street, London EC4N 5BP
Phone: +44 (0)20 7280 9620
Web: https://secure.cfauk.org/

Chartered Financial Analyst (CFA) Institute
10th Floor, One Canada Square, Canary Wharf, London E14 5AB
Phone: 0800 1247 8132 UK only
Web: www.cfainstitute.org

Financial Services Authority (FSA)
Membership Department, 25 The North Colonnade, Canary Wharf, London E14 5HS
Phone: +44 (0)20 7066 1000
Web: www.fsa.gov.uk

London Metal Exchange (LME)
56 Leadenhall Street, London EC3A 2DX
Phone: +44 (0)20 7264 5555
Web: www.lme.co.uk

London Stock Exchange
10 Paternoster Square, London , EC4M 7LS
Web: www.londonstockexchange.com

Securities & Investment Institute (SII)
8 Eastcheap, London EC3M 1AE
Phone: +44 (0)20 7645 0600
Web: www.sii.org.uk

Similar Jobs
Actuary, Commodity Broker, Investment Analyst, Investment Fund Manager, Pension Fund Manager, Stockbroker

Stockbroker
also known as: Private Client Stockbroker, Wealth Manager
CRCI:Financial Services
CLCI:NAL Job Band: 5

Job Description
Stockbrokers advise private, corporate or institutional clients on investments, and buy and sell shares (known as securities) on the Stock Exchange, for a profit on their behalf. Trade on the Internet and by telephone. Study and research information, including investment analysts' reports about the financial state of companies, and watch market trends. Absorbing information regarding the market in domestic and foreign equities, government stocks and securities, is a key to success in this job.

They discuss the types of securities most suited to the client and may manage and review their investments (portfolio). Negotiate with market makers/traders to get the best price for sale or purchase. Some specialise in investing in certain markets, such as technology, or in specific regions, such as the Far East. Have more direct contact with clients than traders. In a large firm, may specialise in certain services, industries or regional markets.

Work Details
This is a very demanding job and the work can be highly competitive. It involves making difficult decisions and can be stressful at times. The working day starts at 7am and lasts for at least 12 hours. You usually work in a large dealing room, spending a lot of time using the telephone and computers. Dealing rooms can be busy and noisy.

Qualification
There are no formal entry requirements, but most firms look for graduates with at least a 2:1 degree.

- **England, Wales and Northern Ireland**

Band 5: For degree courses: 2-3 A levels and some GCSEs (A*-C) usually including English and maths, or equivalent. Exact requirements depend on the degree you take. A second language is also useful.

- **Scotland**

Band 5: For degree courses: 3-5 H grades and some S grades (1-3), usually including English and maths, or similar qualifications. Exact requirements depend on the degree you take. A second language is also useful.

Degree Information
Any degree discipline is acceptable, but business studies/ administration and economics are particularly useful. Accountancy, politics, statistics, law or financial management/ banking can also provide relevant background knowledge.

Adult Qualifications
Entry requirements may be relaxed for adults applying for higher education courses. Foundation and Access courses give adults without qualifications a route on to degree courses.

Work Experience
Entry to this job is very competitive. It is important that you try to do some relevant work or voluntary experience before starting on this career path. Any work experience in the finance sector is relevant and shows enthusiasm and commitment to the work. Time spent in an accountancy firm, an insurance company or shadowing a financial adviser gives you a good basis and insight into the profession. Summer internships at investment banks may be available, and are particularly valuable in the summer before the last year at university.

Entry and Training
The majority of entrants are graduates, usually with a good honours degree in a relevant subject, such as economics, law, business or accountancy. Interviews may often include psychometric testing and aptitude tests. Increasingly, entrants also have postgraduate qualifications such as an MBA/MSc. Only a small number of firms take on non-graduates. Most firms have comprehensive in-house training for new entrants. To become a registered stockbroker you need to pass an appropriate Financial Services Authority qualifying examination such as the certificates offered by the Securities & Investment Institute (SII). Language skills, especially in German, French, Japanese and Russian, are advantageous for those working in overseas markets.

Many firms also require trainees to take the SII diploma, which can take up to three years to complete. Other relevant professional distance-learning qualifications include those offered by the CFA Society of the UK and the ifs School of Finance. A list of qualifications is available from the Financial Services Skills website.

A Diploma/Welsh Baccalaureate in business, administration and finance may be available in your area, and is a useful route onto higher education courses.

Mature entry can be difficult over the age of 25 unless already qualified in accountancy, actuarial work, banking or another relevant field. Applicants who have passed securities and futures exams may be considered.

Opportunities and Pay
You can work for a firm of stockbrokers or another financial institution with a stockbroking division, such as an investment bank. Most stockbroking firms are in London, although there are also opportunities in other large UK cities and smaller regional offices. It is a career that is dominated by younger people; there is fierce competition for jobs and limited vacancies. Promotion is very much based on performance although experienced stockbrokers may set up their own firm. It is also possible to work abroad, particularly in the Far East. This is a fast-moving industry where there is no guarantee of job security but the financial rewards are high for those in work.

Pay varies depending on the type and size of employer. A graduate/ trainee entrant is likely to earn around £25k-£35k and with experience may rise to around £50k-£80k a year. Some earn in excess of £100k a year. Many brokers receive performance-related bonuses in addition to their salary.

Health
This is a demanding job and you need good physical and mental stamina.

Skills and Qualities
able to cope under pressure, analytical skills, decisive, good at calculating risks, good communication skills, good interpersonal skills, integrity, IT skills, numeracy skills, quick thinking

Relevant Subjects
Business and accounting, Economics, English, ICT/Computer studies, Law, Mathematics

Further Information
AGCAS: Accountancy and Business Services (Job Sector Briefing) (AGCAS) - www.prospects.ac.uk/

Diploma in Business, Administration and Finance - www.baf-diploma.org.uk/

Financial Services Skills Council - sector skills council for financial services, accountancy & finance - www.fssc.org.uk/

Professional Investor Careers magazine (March Publishing) - www.marchpublishing.co.uk/pi.html

TARGETjobs: City and Finance (GTI Specialist Publishers Ltd) - www.groupgti.com

Welsh Baccalaureate - www.wbq.org.uk

Addresses
Association of Private Client Investment Managers and Stockbrokers (APCIMS)
22 City Road , Finsbury Square, London EC1Y 2AJ
Phone: +44 (0) 20 7448 7100
Web: www.apcims.co.uk

CFA Society of the UK
2nd Floor 135 Cannon Street, London EC4N 5BP
Phone: +44 (0)20 7280 9620
Web: https://secure.cfauk.org/

Financial Services Authority (FSA)
Membership Department, 25 The North Colonnade, Canary Wharf, London E14 5HS
Phone: +44 (0)20 7066 1000
Web: www.fsa.gov.uk

ifs School of Finance
IFS House, 4-9 Burgate Lane, Canterbury, Kent CT1 2XJ
Phone: +44 (0)1227 818609
Web: www.ifslearning.ac.uk

London Investment Banking Association (LIBA)
6 Frederick's Place, London EC2R 8BT
Phone: +44 (0)20 7796 3606
Web: www.liba.org.uk

London Stock Exchange
10 Paternoster Square, London , EC4M 7LS
Web: www.londonstockexchange.com

Securities & Investment Institute (SII)
8 Eastcheap, London EC3M 1AE
Phone: +44 (0)20 7645 0600
Web: www.sii.org.uk

Similar Jobs
Commodity Broker, Economist, Insurance Broker, Investment Analyst, Investment Banker, Stock Market Trader/Market Maker

Stone & Brick Restorer/Cleaner
CRCI:Building and Construction
CLCI:UX Job Band: 1

Job Description
Stone and brick restorers/cleaners clean, restore and care for the outside walls of buildings and monuments. They use wire brushes and blasting equipment to remove layers of dirt and stains. The stonework is washed with substances such as acid, or the surface is sprayed with very strong jets of steam or water. Restorers may use high-tech laser cleaning equipment, especially for conservation projects. Damaged brick or stonework is pointed or sealed, using mortar or other fillers. May insert wire to make the stonework stronger.

Work Details
Stone and brick restorers/cleaners usually work a basic 39 hr week, though may be required to work additional hours to finish a job on time. The work is outdoors on a wide variety of buildings and requires travel around an area. A driving licence may be useful. You have to manage lifting, balancing, working at heights on scaffolding and ladders, and being on your feet all day. Conditions are often dusty and possibly cold, damp and noisy. There may be a risk of falling or injury and you need to wear protective clothing, goggles, gloves, and possibly a face mask and ear protectors.

Qualification
• England, Wales and Northern Ireland
Band 1: No minimum formal qualifications are required. However, some formal/vocational qualifications at any level may give you an advantage.

• Scotland
Band 1: No minimum formal qualifications are required. However, some formal/vocational qualifications at any level may give you an advantage.

Adult Qualifications
Mature entrants do not usually require qualifications for this type of work, although a good standard of education may give you an advantage. You can improve your skills and qualifications by working through the Foundation Learning programme. This involves taking credit-based units and qualifications to help you progress.

Work Experience
Relevant work or voluntary experience is always useful and can improve your chances when applying for entry to work. In some areas there is a young apprenticeship (14-16) scheme that provides an extended work placement and eventual achievement of a level 2 qualification whilst at school. Health and safety issues may mean that there are certain jobs you cannot do until you are over 16.

Entry and Training
Training is on the job with an experienced worker together with short courses on the various techniques used and the cleaning products available. These may be offered by the manufacturers of products and equipment.

Training is available nationally (in collaboration with ConstructionSkills) in both cleaning and surface repair. Details are available from the training officer at Stone Federation Great Britain.

A Diploma/Welsh Baccalaureate in construction and the built environment may be available in your area. It may be possible to gain relevant S/NVQs. There is a level 1 certificate in preparation for employment in the construction industries through Open College North West. This gives an introduction to the skills and occupational areas within the construction industry. Training programmes, including construction apprenticeships leading to level 2 and advanced apprenticeships leading to level 3, may be available in your area. Contact ConstructionSkills for details.

Mature applicants can take refresher courses that are sometimes available for those returning to work and there may be special training schemes in some areas. Work based learning, Training for Work or New Deal training opportunities may be available. You can also gain recognition of previous experience through Accreditation of Prior Learning (APL) or by working towards relevant S/NVQs.

Contact your local careers office, Jobcentre Plus, Next Step service or Learning and Skills Council (LSC)/Local Enterprise Company (LEC) for details of training schemes, including apprenticeships for adults.

Opportunities and Pay

Work is mostly for building exterior cleaning companies, mainly in towns and cities where stone or brick has been used for building. Work is increasing in the restoration and conservation sector. With experience, some people become self-employed, but it requires a large investment to start your own company. There may be opportunities to work abroad.

Pay varies depending on area and employer. As a guide, for cleaning work starting salaries start from £13k a year. Restoration salaries range from £10k to £30k a year.

Health

You have to be physically fit. You should not be allergic to dust or chemicals.

Skills and Qualities

agile, careful, creative flair, enjoy working outdoors, head for heights, practical skills, safety conscious, strong hands

Relevant Subjects

Construction and built environment

Further Information

Apprenticeship Schemes (National Apprenticeship Service) - www.apprenticeships.org.uk

Asset Skills - sector skills council for the places where we live and work - www.assetskills.org

Cleaning Industry Handbook (BICSc) (BICSc) - www.bics.org.uk/

ConstructionSkills - sector skills council for the construction industry - www.cskills.org

Diplomas (Foundation, Higher and Advanced) - http://yp.direct.gov.uk/diplomas

Foundation Learning (QCDA) - www.qcda.gov.uk

Training Schemes - www.direct.gov.uk/en/educationandlearning

Welsh Baccalaureate - www.wbq.org.uk

▶Working in construction & the built environment (2007) (Babcock Lifeskills) - www.babcock-lifeskills.com/

Addresses

Stone Federation Great Britain (SFGB)
Channel Business Centre, Ingles Manor, Castle Hill Avenue, Folkestone, Kent CT20 2RD
Phone: +44 (0)1303 856123
Web: www.stone-federationgb.org.uk

Similar Jobs

Bricklayer, Engraver, Steeplejack, Stonemason: Banker, Stonemason: Fixer

Stonemason: Banker

also known as: Banker Mason

CRCI:Building and Construction
CLCI:UF Job Band: 1 to 2

Job Description

Banker stonemasons cut and shape rough stone blocks, either for new buildings or to repair and restore existing buildings. May work on stone clad modern buildings, private houses, stately homes, ancient monuments and castles. They provide stonework for all uses, including walls, fireplaces, arches, staircases, and for graves and monuments. Material is prepared by first cutting the design or geometric pattern onto the stone from a template or pattern provided. The shape is measured and marked out. Power driven tools are then used to cut the stone. The stonemason checks that all angles are accurate and smooths and finishes the block, making stone ready for 'fixing'.

Special shapes, such as figures, letters or columns, are carved into the stone, sometimes by hand. Traditional tools such as mallets, levels, trowels and chisels are used. May also specialise in working with marble, granite or limestone.

Work Details

Banker stonemasons usually work a 39 hr week, Monday to Friday, though may be required to work on a Saturday at times to complete jobs. Part-time work is also available. They are based in a workshop where the job involves bending, stretching, lifting and standing for many hours. Skilled use of manual tools such as mallets, chisels, cutting tools, drills and trowels is necessary. It is usually very dusty and there may be a risk of minor injuries. Uses safety equipment such as overalls, goggles and sometimes a face mask. In small firms, banker masons may also fix stone; see job article Stonemason: Fixer.

Qualification

• England, Wales and Northern Ireland

Band 1: No minimum qualifications are required but employers expect you to have a good general education and a natural talent for stonemasonry.

Band 2: Although academic qualifications are not specified for this job, it is an advantage to have some GCSEs in maths, English, science or technical subjects, or equivalent.

• Scotland

Band 1: No formal qualifications required but employers expect you to have a good general education and a natural talent for stonemasonry.

Band 2: Although academic qualifications are not specified for this job, it is an advantage to have some S grades in maths, English, science or technical subjects, or equivalent.

Adult Qualifications

Entry requirements are usually relaxed for mature students, though you are expected to have a good standard of general education. A natural talent for stonemasonry is essential.

Work Experience

Relevant work or voluntary experience is always useful and can improve your chances when applying for entry to construction jobs and apprenticeships. In some areas there is a young apprenticeship (14-16) scheme that provides an extended work placement and eventual achievement of a level 2 qualification whilst at school. Health and safety issues may mean that there are certain jobs you cannot do until you are over 16. Contact your local ConstructionSkills office for advice.

Entry and Training

Most people enter this work through a flexible, work-based training scheme offered by ConstructionSkills/City & Guilds. Routes for training include full-time work with an employer and attendance on day or block release courses at a college; a one or two-year full-time college course, or a work-based training programme at a ConstructionSkills centre. You also work towards gaining a level of competence card through a Construction Skills Certification Scheme (CSCS) to indicate your individual skill level.

Many people enter training schemes at 16-17 and you can apply for an apprenticeship in Year 11 (January). You may have to take an ability test before you can start training. Courses are also available from the Building Crafts College, including the City & Guilds Diploma in advanced stonemasonry and City & Guilds multiskills course. They also run a range of short courses and specialised evening classes.

Specialist training is also available for those who wish to concentrate on achieving skills in restoration and heritage work. Contact the National Heritage Training Group for further information.

A Diploma/Welsh Baccalaureate in construction and the built environment may be available in your area. S/NVQs in stonemasonry are available at levels 1-3. Training programmes, including apprenticeships leading to level 2 and advanced apprenticeships/construction apprenticeships leading to level 3, may be available in your area. There are also Construction Awards (England and Wales) available for those who are unable to gain workplace experience for NVQs.

Mature applicants with aptitude and related experience are often welcomed by employers. Government training opportunities, such as apprenticeships, may be available in your area. You can also gain recognition of previous experience through Accreditation of Prior Learning or by working towards relevant S/NVQs. Contact your local careers office, Jobcentre Plus, Next Step service or Learning and Skills Council (LSC)/Local Enterprise Company (LEC) for details of all training opportunities and schemes, including apprenticeships for adults.

Opportunities and Pay

Availability of work depends to some extent on the state of the building trade and the national economy. Currently there is a downturn in the housing market which means there may be a shortage of vacancies. However, there is an increased demand for skilled stonemasons for restoring and conserving old buildings. Work is possible with building contractors, stonemasonry firms, national heritage organisations, or a firm specialising in stone repair and restoration. Short-term, casual and seasonal work is often possible for those who are sub-contractors or self-employed. There may also be opportunities abroad.

Pay varies depending on area and employer. New entrants earn around £12k-£14k a year. With experience this rises to around £18k-£23k a year. Senior or self-employed stonemasons can earn around £30k or more a year. Overtime and bonus payments may be paid on top of your income.

Health

This job requires stamina and physical fitness, and you should not be allergic to dust.

Skills and Qualities

able to follow drawings and plans, attention to detail, creative flair, enjoy working outdoors, eye for shape/colour, eye for visual effect, manual dexterity, numeracy skills, practical skills, strong

Relevant Subjects

Art and Design, Construction and built environment, Design and technology

Further Information

Apprenticeship Schemes (National Apprenticeship Service) - www.apprenticeships.org.uk

Building Conservation Courses (Cathedral Communications Limited) - www.buildingconservation.com

Construction Awards - http://gbca.com/events/construction-awards

Construction Skills Certification Scheme (CSCS) - www.cscs.uk.com

ConstructionSkills - sector skills council for the construction industry - www.cskills.org

Creative & Cultural Skills - sector skills council for advertising, crafts, cultural heritage, design, literature, music, performing & visual arts - www.ccskills.org.uk

Diplomas (Foundation, Higher and Advanced) - http://yp.direct.gov.uk/diplomas

Training Schemes - www.direct.gov.uk/en/educationandlearning

Welsh Baccalaureate - www.wbq.org.uk

Addresses

Building Crafts College
Kennard Road, Stratford, London E15 1AH
Phone: +44 (0)20 8522 1705
Web: www.thebcc.ac.uk

National Association of Memorial Masons (NAMM)
1 Castle Mews, Rugby CV21 2XL
Phone: +44 (0)1788 542 264
Web: www.namm.org.uk

National Heritage Training Group (NHTG)
Carthusian Court, 12 Carthusian Street, London EC1M 6EZ
Phone: 0300 456 5517 (UK only)
Web: www.nhtg.org.uk

Scottish Stone Liaison Group (SSLG)
16 Rocks Road, Charlestown, Dunfermline KY11 3EN
Phone: +44 (0) 1383 872006
Web: www.sslg.co.uk

Stone Federation Great Britain (SFGB)
Channel Business Centre, Ingles Manor, Castle Hill Avenue, Folkestone, Kent CT20 2RD
Phone: +44 (0)1303 856123
Web: www.stone-federationgb.org.uk

Similar Jobs

Bricklayer, Carpenter/Joiner, Engraver, Signwriter/Signmaker, Stone & Brick Restorer/Cleaner, Stonemason: Fixer

Stonemason: Fixer

also known as: Fixer Mason
CRCI:Building and Construction
CLCI:UF

Job Band: 1 to 2

Job Description

Fixer stonemasons use dressed stone to build and repair masonry structures on site. Structures include walls, arches, memorial stones and tombs. Selects material which has been prepared by a banker mason and checks architects' plans for required size and shape. Prepares a bed of mortar on which to lay stones. Checks level and fills in joints. Uses specialised winches and lifting equipment to put heavy stones in place. Fixes facing stone onto brick or steel frames using wire or metal bolts. Repairs existing stonework and may be involved in historic building conservation.

Work Details

Fixer stonemasons usually work a 39 hr week, though you may have to work late or some weekends at times to complete a project. You may be expected to work overtime and possibly longer hours in the summer. Work is outdoors and you travel to different sites. This job involves heavy lifting, rough ground, bending down and working at heights on scaffolding and ladders. The work is dirty and dusty and it is often cold and damp.

There is a risk of minor injuries or possibly falling from heights, and safety equipment such as overalls, a safety helmet, protective footwear and sometimes goggles are used. In small firms, masons may also cut and shape stone, as well as fixing; see article on Stonemason: Banker.

Qualification

- **England, Wales and Northern Ireland**

Band 1: No minimum qualifications are required, but you are expected to have a good level of general education.

Band 2: Although academic qualifications are not specified for this job, it is an advantage to have some GCSEs (A*-D) including maths, English, science or technical subjects, or equivalent qualifications.

- **Scotland**

Band 1: No minimum qualifications are required, but you are expected to have a good level of general education.

Band 2: Although academic qualifications are not specified for this job, it is an advantage to have some S grades (1-4) in subjects that include English, maths, science or technical subjects, or similar qualifications.

Adult Qualifications
Entry requirements are usually relaxed for mature students, though you are expected to have a good standard of general education. A natural talent for stonemasonry is essential.

Work Experience
Relevant work or voluntary experience is always useful and can improve your chances when applying for entry to construction jobs and apprenticeships. In some areas there is a young apprenticeship (14-16) scheme that provides an extended work placement and eventual achievement of a level 2 qualification whilst at school. Health and safety issues may mean that there are certain jobs you cannot do until you are over 16. Contact your local ConstructionSkills office for advice.

Entry and Training
Most people enter this work through a flexible, work-based training scheme offered by ConstructionSkills/City & Guilds. Routes for training include full-time work with an employer and attendance on day or block release to a college, a one or two-year full-time college course, or a work-based training programme at a ConstructionSkills centre. You also work towards gaining a level of competence card through a Construction Skills Certification Scheme (CSCS) to indicate your individual skill level.

Many people enter training schemes at 16-17 and you can apply for an apprenticeship in Year 11 (January). You may have to take an ability test before you can start training. Courses are also available from the Building Crafts College, including the City & Guilds Diploma in advanced stonemasonry and City & Guilds multiskills course. They also run a range of short courses and specialised evening classes.

Specialist training is also available for those who wish to concentrate on achieving skills in restoration and heritage work. Contact the National Heritage Training Group for further information.

A Diploma/Welsh Baccalaureate in construction and the built environment may be available in your area. S/NVQs in stonemasonry are available at levels 1-3. Training programmes, including apprenticeships leading to level 2 and advanced apprenticeships/construction apprenticeships leading to level 3, may be available in your area. There are also Construction Awards (England and Wales) available for those who are unable to gain workplace experience for NVQs.

Mature applicants with aptitude and related experience are often welcomed by employers. Government training opportunities, such as apprenticeships, may be available in your area. You can also gain recognition of previous experience through Accreditation of Prior Learning or by working towards relevant S/NVQs. Contact your local careers office, Jobcentre Plus, Next Step service or Learning and Skills Council (LSC)/Local Enterprise Company (LEC) for details of all training opportunities and schemes, including apprenticeships for adults.

Opportunities and Pay
Availability of work depends to some extent on the state of the building trade and the national economy. However, there is an increased demand for skilled stonemasons for restoring and conserving old buildings. Work is possible with building contractors, stonemasonry firms, a national historic organisation, or a firm specialising in stone repair and restoration. Short-term, casual and seasonal work is often possible for those who are sub-contractors or self-employed. There are opportunities to work abroad.

Pay varies depending on area and employer. New entrants earn around £12k-£14k a year. With experience this rises to around £18k-£23k a year. Senior or self-employed stonemasons can earn around £30k or more a year. Overtime and bonus payments may be paid on top of your income.

Health
This job requires stamina and physical fitness, and you should not be allergic to dust.

Skills and Qualities
able to work both on your own and in a team, accurate, attention to detail, enjoy working outdoors, eye for visual effect, head for heights, manual dexterity, numeracy skills, safety conscious, strong.

Relevant Subjects
Construction and built environment, Design and technology

Further Information
Apprenticeship Schemes (National Apprenticeship Service) - www.apprenticeships.org.uk

Building Conservation Courses (Cathedral Communications Limited) - www.buildingconservation.com

Construction Awards - http://gbca.com/events/construction-awards

ConstructionSkills - sector skills council for the construction industry - www.cskills.org

Creative & Cultural Skills - sector skills council for advertising, crafts, cultural heritage, design, literature, music, performing & visual arts - www.ccskills.org.uk

Diplomas (Foundation, Higher and Advanced) - http://yp.direct.gov.uk/diplomas

Training Schemes - www.direct.gov.uk/en/educationandlearning
Welsh Baccalaureate - www.wbq.org.uk

Addresses
Building Crafts College
Kennard Road, Stratford, London E15 1AH
Phone: +44 (0)20 8522 1705
Web: www.thebcc.ac.uk

National Association of Memorial Masons (NAMM)
1 Castle Mews, Rugby CV21 2XL
Phone: +44 (0)1788 542 264
Web: www.namm.org.uk

National Heritage Training Group (NHTG)
Carthusian Court, 12 Carthusian Street, London EC1M 6EZ
Phone: 0300 456 5517 (UK only)
Web: www.nhtg.org.uk

Stone Federation Great Britain (SFGB)
Channel Business Centre, Ingles Manor, Castle Hill Avenue, Folkestone, Kent CT20 2RD
Phone: +44 (0)1303 856123
Web: www.stone-federationgb.org.uk

Similar Jobs
Bricklayer, Carpenter/Joiner, Engraver, Signwriter/Signmaker, Stone & Brick Restorer/Cleaner, Stonemason: Banker

Store Detective

CRCI:Security and Armed Forces
CLCI:MAG Job Band: 1 to 3

Job Description
Store detectives are employed to detect and prevent theft from shops and stores. They patrol the store watching customers and looking out for signs of anyone trying to steal items. Carefully follow or observe people who are behaving suspiciously. Use a variety of

technological aids to help prevent theft, such as electronic tags on goods, loop alarms, mirrors, CCTV equipment and two-way radio. Deal with people who are attempting to use a stolen credit card to purchase goods. If someone is observed stealing an item, may make a citizen's arrest before calling the police.

Store detectives write reports of incidents and may have to give evidence in court. May also deal with any emergencies, including a bomb/fire alert, or assist a customer who has had an accident or become ill.

Work Details

Usually work a 40 hr week, Monday to Saturday, and work shifts with early starts and late finishes. A working week may include Sundays, and also some overtime hours. Store detectives work in shops and stores, usually indoors but with some security checks outdoors. You need to dress in a similar way to the store's customers, so that you are not noticed. Spend most of the day walking around, or watching a screen that shows the people who are shopping, and deal with the public on a regular basis. Often work in a team that covers the whole store or shop.

Qualification

• England, Wales and Northern Ireland

Band 1: Formal qualifications are not needed for this job, though employers expect a good level of education and basic skills in maths and English. Written and verbal communication skills are important.

Band 2: No set minimum educational entry requirements though some GCSE passes including English and maths or equivalent, are useful.

• Scotland

Band 1: Formal qualifications are not needed for this job, though employers expect a good level of education and basic skills in maths and English. Written and verbal communication skills are important.

Band 2: No set minimum educational entry requirements though some S grades including English or maths or similar, are useful.

Adult Qualifications

There are no minimum qualifications for this job though written and verbal communication skills are important.

Work Experience

Any relevant work experience can equip you with skills that you can use in the future and add to your CV. It can either be unpaid/ voluntary, or holiday/part-time work that you have organised yourself. You can gain some valuable experience by working in a shop or store as a sales assistant, either as a Saturday or holiday job.

Entry and Training

Most entrants are over 21 yrs old and training varies depending on the employer. Larger companies usually run their own training programmes. Smaller companies concentrate on more personal instruction from supervisors or experienced workers. Most companies have an induction course. This covers topics such as legal powers and the company's policy on crime. Preparing accurate reports is a major aspect of training, as these may be used in court.

Many members of the security industry now have to be licensed by the Security Industry Authority (SIA) under the Private Security Industry Act. This includes store detectives who work for agencies, who are self-employed or under contract. The licence costs £245 and lasts for three years. Those monitoring a public area CCTV are also required to hold an SIA public space surveillance (CCTV) licence. Those who are employed 'in-house' may also be required to hold a licence. Contact the SIA for full details on how to obtain the licence.

Short courses on specialist topics are offered by organisations such as the International Professional Security Association. You can work for an S/NVQ Level 2 in providing security services. This course consists of core units on: producing documents, making sure your actions reduce risks to health and safety, communicating effectively and efficiently in the workplace, controlling security incidents and giving customers a positive impression of yourself and your organisation. You then choose from optional units to suit your particular specialism, eg maintaining CCTV recording media libraries and preserving potential evidence, or providing covert security in retail environments.

Mature applicants with previous work experience in a uniformed service such as the police, fire service or the armed forces, usually have an advantage. You may be able to enter this work through a government-funded training programme.

Opportunities and Pay

Opportunities exist in all major towns and cities throughout the UK. Most department stores, supermarkets and chain stores employ store detectives. Demand for them is growing. Some are employed by security firms that provide a service to stores on a contract basis. Progression is possible to a supervisory position or as a security manager. Promotion prospects are better in large organisations. Part time and seasonal temporary work, such as at Christmas, is possible.

Pay varies depending on location and employer, but starting salaries are likely to be around £14k a year, rising to £18k-£29k, with experience.

Health

You need to be fit and healthy and pass a medical.

Skills and Qualities

able to get on with all kinds of people, able to work both on your own and in a team, confident, discreet, firm manner, good communication skills, observant, quick reactions, resourceful, vigilant

Relevant Subjects

Law

Further Information

Apprenticeship Schemes (National Apprenticeship Service) - www.apprenticeships.org.uk

Foundation Learning (QCDA) - www.qcda.gov.uk

International Professional Security Association (IPSA) - www.ipsa.org.uk/

Professional Security Magazine - www.professionalsecurity.co.uk

Skills for Security - sector skills council for security industry - www.skillsforsecurity.org.uk/

Training Schemes - www.direct.gov.uk/en/educationandlearning

Why Security? - A Guide to Careers in the Security Industry (Security Industry Authority) - www.the-sia.org.uk

▶Working in police, fire & security (2009) (Babcock Lifeskills) - www.babcock-lifeskills.com/

Addresses

British Security Industry Association (BSIA)
Kirkham House, John Comyn Drive, Worcester WR3 7NS
Phone: +44 (0)845 389 3889
Web: www.bsia.co.uk

Security Industry Authority (SIA)
PO Box 1293, Liverpool L69 1AX
Phone: 0844 892 1025 (UK only)
Web: http://sia.homeoffice.gov.uk/Pages/home.aspx

Security Institute
1 The Courtyard, Caldecote CV10 0AS
Phone: 08453 707 717
Web: www.security-institute.org

Similar Jobs

Police Community Support Officer (England & Wales), Police Officer, Prison Officer, Private Investigator, Security Officer

Street Lighting Inspector

also known as: Electrical Inspector

CRCI:Engineering
CLCI:RAK
Job Band: 2 to 3

Job Description

Street lighting inspectors are responsible for ensuring that lighting in public areas is functional and safe. They look at problems with street lights, traffic lights, pedestrian crossings, lighting columns (metal and concrete) or illuminated bollards. Inspectors work with a team of lighting technicians and inspectors for county, unitary and metropolitan councils. They follow an annual planned programme of inspection and maintenance work, and also make site visits in response to any emergency.

May also visit an area to speak with local residents for their opinions on the quality of their public lighting. They answer requests from the public with regard to lamp replacement and deal with complaints such as poor lighting in a busy street, or when lighting and equipment have been vandalised. Inspectors make regular visits to sites where contractors have been employed to carry out maintenance or repairs and to check the progress and quality of the work. Also write technical reports, and liaise with other council officials, electricity supply companies, and contractors.

Work Details

Usually work a 37 hr week, Monday to Friday, but sometimes work unsocial hours for emergency repairs. Most working hours are spent on site visits, checking street lighting in all weather conditions. Time is also spent in an office environment planning a policy of repairs and maintenance within an agreed budget, and organising visits and taking repair requests by telephone. Some on-site tests are in awkward to reach places. The environments can be messy, noisy or dangerous. Rubber gloves, goggles and safety clothing are worn when checking lights. These are provided by your employer.

Qualification

• England, Wales and Northern Ireland

Band 2: For entry to jobs and training: no minimum qualifications are needed, but it is an advantage to have some GCSEs (A*-C) or equivalent in subjects that include English, maths, and a science, or equivalent. Craft or technology subjects are useful but not essential.

Band 3: For entry to jobs and training, HNC or a relevant Diploma, usually at least 4 GCSEs (A*-C) including English, maths and science, or equivalent.

• Scotland

Band 2: Although academic qualifications are not specified for this job, it is an advantage to have some S grades (1-3) in subjects that include English, maths and a science, or similar. Craft or technology subjects are useful but not essential.

Band 3: For entry to jobs, usually at least four S grades (1-3) including English, maths and science, or similar.

Adult Qualifications

Some formal qualifications are helpful for entry to training courses. If you have relevant work experience and electrical knowledge you may be accepted for some college courses without meeting the formal entry requirements.

Work Experience

Relevant work or voluntary experience is always useful. It can add to your CV and improve your chances when applying for entry to jobs or apprenticeships. Some councils may offer work experience opportunities; contact them individually. Knowledge of first aid is also helpful for entry to this work. Health and safety issues may mean that there are certain jobs you can't do until you are over 16.

Entry and Training

You must be a qualified electrician before you can work as a street lighting inspector. Most employers also expect a few years' experience as an electrician after qualification. Once recruited, entrants must take further short courses run by individual electricity supply companies, together with on-the-job training. Inspectors are also sent on specialised courses, including those covering the Electricity at Work Act and health and safety regulations.

The popular route to qualifying as an electrician is usually through an apprenticeship when you are 16-19, with a contractor, engineering firm or supply company. Training is by practical experience, on the job and through college courses. Study for the City & Guilds certificate in electrotechnical technology at levels 2-3 is usually part of your apprenticeship. You can study by day-release or block-release course whilst working for an employer. The Electrical Contractors' Association (ECA) has details of available funding for ECA members and non members. Check the website to see if you might be eligible for a grant towards an agreed training programme.

You may also work towards an S/NVQ at level 2-3 in electrotechnical services, which enables you to meet the requirements of the Electrotechnical Certification Scheme (ECS). The ECS card scheme is administered by the Joint Industry Board/ Scottish Joint Industry Board for the Electrical Contracting Industry. You can receive an 'apprentice' ECS card whilst undertaking an Advanced Apprenticeship. Contact the Joint Industry Board/Scottish Joint Industry Board for details.

The Institution of Lighting Engineers has details of specialist training programmes including an exterior lighting diploma. They have also formed a new Young Lighting Professionals group for lighting professionals aged under 30. Check the website for details. The Highway Electrical Academy (HEA) operates a sector scheme for highway electrical works. This requires that employees working in the highway electrical industry are assessed for competence by their employers and issued with a competence certificate. The HEA runs specific training courses aimed at meeting the requirements of the sector scheme. See the HEA website for details.

The Scottish Electrical Charitable Training Trust and the Electrical Training Trust also have details of training schemes and apprenticeships in Scotland and Northern Ireland respectively. Visit their websites for details. A Diploma/Welsh Baccalaureate may be available in your area in engineering. See the diplomas website for further information.

Mature entry is common as experience as an electrician is required before you can become a street lighting inspector. Adult electricians can be assessed through the Crediting Electrotechnical Competence scheme that leads to S/NVQ at level 3 and meets the requirements for an ECS card. Manchester Open Learning offers electrical installation courses through distance learning.

Joint Industry Board approved courses may be available through government sponsored training, such as work-based learning schemes. Many employers train adults due to a shortage of school leaver trainees. Contact your local careers office, Jobcentre Plus, Next Step service or Learning and Skills Council (LSC)/Local Enterprise Company (LEC) for details of training schemes, including apprenticeships for adults.

Opportunities and Pay

Employment is with specialist street lighting, communications or civil engineering contractors who compete for local authority external contracts. There are more opportunities with larger authorities and they usually have a clearer promotion structure. Internal promotion prospects are therefore limited with smaller authorities. Some inspectors may become road lighting engineers.

Pay varies depending on area and employer. As an apprentice electrician you can earn around £12k and, once qualified, from around £17k a year. With a few years' experience you can earn £20k-£25k a year and those with specific street lighting qualifications and management responsibilities can earn more.

Health

A reasonable level of physical fitness is needed for this role.

Skills and Qualities

able to work in confined spaces, aptitude for teamwork, common sense, good communication skills, good interpersonal skills, good organisational skills, health & safety awareness, manual dexterity, responsible attitude, technical aptitude

Relevant Subjects

Design and technology, Engineering, Mathematics, Physics, Science

Further Information

Apprenticeship Schemes (National Apprenticeship Service) - www.apprenticeships.org.uk

Careers in Engineering Booklets (SEMTA) - www.semta.org.uk

Diplomas (Foundation, Higher and Advanced) - http://yp.direct.gov.uk/diplomas

Electrical Contractors' Association - www.eca.co.uk

Energy & Utility Skills - sector skills council for gas, power, waste management & water industries - www.euskills.co.uk

Highway Electrical News (bi-monthly) (Highlec Publishing) - www.highwayelectrical.org.uk/

Lighting Journal (bi-monthly) (Institution of Lighting Professionals) - www.theilp.org.uk/

Local Government Careers (Improvement and Development Agency) - www.lgcareers.com/publications/

Manchester Open Learning - www.mol-openlearning.co.uk

Summitskills - sector skills council for building services engineering - www.summitskills.org.uk

Training Schemes - www.direct.gov.uk/en/educationandlearning

Welsh Baccalaureate - www.wbq.org.uk

Addresses

Electrical Training Trust (ETT)
Units 57-59 Ballymena Business Development Centre
62 Fenaghy Road BT42 1FL
Phone: +44 (0)28 2565 0750
Web: www.ett-ni.org/

Highway Electrical Academy/ASLEC
Bowden House, 1 Church Street, Henfield, West Sussex BN5 9NS
Phone: +44 (0)1273 491145
Web: www.highwayelectrical.org.uk/

Institution of Lighting Engineers (ILE)
Regent House, Regent Place, Rugby, Warwickshire CV21 2PN
Phone: +44 (0)1788 576492
Web: www.ile.org.uk

Joint Industry Board (JIB) for the Electrical Contracting Industry
Kingswood House 47-51 Sidcup Hill, Kent DA14 6HP
Phone: +44 (0)20 8302 0031
Web: www.jib.org.uk

Scottish Electrical Charitable Training Trust (SECTT)
The Walled Garden, Bush Estate, , Midlothian EH26 0SE
Phone: +44 (0)131 445 5659
Web: www.sectt.org.uk

Scottish Joint Industry Board for the Electrical Contracting Industry
The Walled Garden, Bush Estate, Midlothian EH26 0SB
Phone: +44(0)131 445 9216
Web: www.sjib.org.uk

Similar Jobs

Electrical Engineering Technician, Electrician, Engineer: Building Services, Engineer: Electrical, Street Lighting Operative

Street Lighting Operative

CRCI:Engineering
CLCI:RAK Job Band: 1 to 3

Job Description

Street lighting operatives work in a team that carries out routine maintenance and an emergency response service for street lighting and other illuminated units. They work in many locations, including rural areas, town centres and on high volume motorways. Operatives carry out street lighting improvement and installation schemes and the job includes checking lighting, beacons, traffic signs and signals, bollards and pelican crossings. They also maintain motorway telephones, closed circuit television (CCTV), incident detection systems and variable message signs, checking for faults and defects and any danger to road users.

Operatives keep covers, shades and signs clean and replace sodium lamps or lighting elements. They often work from an automated ladder mounted on a vehicle. May also use GIS (Geographical Information Systems) computer software to complete inventories of street lighting units and to store information on defects and repairs.

Work Details

Usually work a basic 37 hr week, Monday to Friday, though you may need to work weekends at times. Inspections often take place at night so you may work irregular hours. Your place of work is outdoors and travel around an area is necessary. You are responsible for thorough work and have to cope with working at heights and some lifting. The work environment may be dirty and possibly cold, damp and noisy. There is a risk of falling or minor injuries and you need to wear overalls and a helmet. You are required to know and observe rules governing health and safety.

Qualification

• England, Wales and Northern Ireland

Band 1: For entry to jobs, no minimum qualifications are needed, but you are expected to have a good level of general education and relevant experience. Some formal/vocational qualifications at any level are useful.

Band 2: For entry to jobs, no minimum qualifications are needed, but it is an advantage to have some GCSEs (A*-C) or equivalent in subjects that include English, maths and science plus a practical subject, or equivalent. Craft or technology subjects are useful but not essential.

Band 3: For entry to jobs, HNC or a relevant Diploma, usually at least 4 GCSEs (A*-C) including English, maths and science, or equivalent.

• Scotland

Band 1: For entry to jobs, no minimum qualifications are needed, but you are expected to have a good level of general education and relevant experience. Some formal/vocational qualifications at any level are useful.

Band 2: Although academic qualifications are not specified for this job, it is an advantage to have some S grades (1-3) in subjects that include English, maths and science plus a practical subject, or similar. Craft or technology subjects are useful, but not essential.

Band 3: For entry to jobs and some courses: usually at least four S grades (1-3) including English, maths and science, or similar.

Adult Qualifications

Some formal qualifications are helpful for entry to training courses. If you have relevant work experience and electrical knowledge you may be accepted for some college courses without meeting the formal entry requirements. You can improve your skills and qualifications by working through the Foundation Learning programme. This involves taking credit-based units and qualifications to help you progress.

Work Experience

Relevant work or voluntary experience is always useful. It can add to your CV and improve your chances when applying for entry to jobs or apprenticeships in the engineering industry.

Entry and Training

Many join this job through an apprenticeship scheme. Most applicants take a selection test and have an interview. Training is by practical experience, learning on the job through an experienced person, after an initial period learning basic skills. You also receive health and safety induction training and may do external courses at college through day or block release. All street lighting operatives are now required to be registered and must be assessed by their employers as being competent to carry out the level of work required. You work towards S/NVQs that enable you to meet the requirements of the Electrotechnical Certification Scheme (ECS). The ECS card scheme is administered by the Joint Industry Board/ Scottish Joint Industry Board for the Electrical Contracting Industry.

Operatives work towards an S/NVQ at level 2 in installing highway electrical systems and level 3 in electrotechnical services. Relevant training programmes, including apprenticeship schemes, may be available in your area. Advanced apprenticeships leading to qualification at level 3 can also be a route into higher education.

The Highway Electrical Academy (HEA) operates a registration scheme for those who work specifically on highway electrical work. Entrants to this work start on a trainee card and work towards their S/NVQ achieving skilled card status once training is complete. The card has to be renewed every three years. Contact HEA for details.

The Institution of Lighting Engineers has details of specialist training programmes including an exterior lighting diploma. They have also formed a new Young Lighting Professionals group for lighting professionals aged under 30. Check the website for details. The Scottish Electrical Charitable Training Trust and the Electrical Training Trust also have details of training schemes and apprenticeships in Scotland and Northern Ireland respectively. Visit their websites for details. A Diploma/Welsh Baccalaureate may be available in your area in engineering. See the diplomas website for further information.

Qualified electricians are welcomed by employers. Mature applicants can benefit through training opportunities such as Work Based Learning, Training for Work or New Deal that may be available in your area. You can also gain recognition of previous experience through Accreditation of Prior Learning or by working towards relevant S/NVQs. Contact your local careers office, Jobcentre Plus, Next Step service or Learning and Skills Council (LSC)/Local Enterprise Company (LEC) for details of training schemes, including apprenticeships for adults.

Opportunities and Pay

Employment is with specialist street lighting, communications or civil engineering contractors who compete for local authority external contracts. A similar job is a street lighting inspector (see job article) who is employed by a local authority. Promotion prospects can be improved with further training and qualifications. You may progress to become a street lighting technician or into supervisory/management posts with higher qualifications.

Pay depends on your employer and location, but most start on around £13k a year, rising to around £17k. Fully qualified electricians with specialist qualifications can earn more.

Health

There may be an allergy risk from dust. This job requires good health and physical fitness.

Skills and Qualities

able to communicate effectively, able to operate equipment, aptitude for teamwork, careful, common sense, co-operative, good co-ordination, head for heights, health & safety awareness, IT skills

Further Information

Apprenticeship Schemes (National Apprenticeship Service) - www.apprenticeships.org.uk

Diplomas (Foundation, Higher and Advanced) - http://yp.direct.gov.uk/diplomas

Electrical Contractors' Association - www.eca.co.uk

Energy & Utility Skills - sector skills council for gas, power, waste management & water industries - www.euskills.co.uk

Highway Electrical News (bi-monthly) (Highlec Publishing) - www.highwayelectrical.org.uk/

Lighting Journal (bi-monthly) (Institution of Lighting Professionals) - www.theilp.org.uk/

Local Government Careers (Improvement and Development Agency) - www.lgcareers.com/publications/

Training Schemes - www.direct.gov.uk/en/educationandlearning

Welsh Baccalaureate - www.wbq.org.uk

Addresses

Electrical Training Trust (ETT)
Units 57-59 Ballymena Business Development Centre
62 Fenaghy Road BT42 1FL
Phone: +44 (0)28 2565 0750
Web: www.ett-ni.org/

Highway Electrical Academy/ASLEC
Bowden House, 1 Church Street, Henfield, West Sussex BN5 9NS
Phone: +44 (0)1273 491145
Web: www.highwayelectrical.org.uk/

Institution of Lighting Engineers (ILE)
Regent House, Regent Place, Rugby, Warwickshire CV21 2PN
Phone: +44 (0)1788 576492
Web: www.ile.org.uk

Joint Industry Board (JIB) for the Electrical Contracting Industry
Kingswood House 47-51 Sidcup Hill, Kent DA14 6HP
Phone: +44 (0)20 8302 0031
Web: www.jib.org.uk

Scottish Electrical Charitable Training Trust (SECTT)
The Walled Garden, Bush Estate, Midlothian EH26 0SE
Phone: +44 (0)131 445 5659
Web: www.sectt.org.uk

Scottish Joint Industry Board for the Electrical Contracting Industry
The Walled Garden, Bush Estate, Midlothian EH26 0SB
Phone: +44(0)131 445 9216
Web: www.sjib.org.uk

Similar Jobs

Construction Operative, Electrical Engineering Technician, Electrician, Street Lighting Inspector

Surgeon

also known as: Doctor: Surgeon

CRCI:Healthcare

CLCI:JAB Job Band: 5

Job Description

Surgeons use specialist medical knowledge and skill to care for patients who may need surgery. Diagnose problems and operate on parts of the body to address specific injuries, diseases or conditions. They work in a hospital, and examine and talk to patients in a ward as part of the ward round. May also work in outpatient clinics and have emergency duties. Carry out, or refer the patient for tests such as X-rays or blood tests, and arrange surgery or suitable alternative treatment. Also care for and monitor the patient after surgery. Surgeons are supported by a team including nurses and other health professionals.

Surgeon

They usually specialise in a particular branch of surgery, for example neurosurgery (skull, brain and spinal cord), ear nose and throat (ENT), paediatric (children up to 14-16), cardiothoracic (heart and chest), orthopaedic (bones and joints), or plastic and reconstructive surgery.

Work Details

You are expected to work long hours, which may include nights and weekends. You work in consulting rooms, wards and operating theatres. The work can involve standing and bending for long periods. You have to make decisions about treatment and keep meticulous records. Work can be emotionally demanding, and requires coping with the sight of blood. This job is very satisfying for those wishing to work in a caring profession.

Qualification

• England, Wales and Northern Ireland

Band 5: For degree in medicine: usually three A levels, with good grades in chemistry and two from physics, biological sciences and maths, plus 5 GCSEs (A*-C) including English, or equivalent. Some medical schools offer a one-year pre-medical course for students with A levels in arts or mixed subjects. Check with individual schools for full details.

• Scotland

Band 5: For degree in medicine: usually five H grades, with good grades in chemistry and two from physics, biology and maths, plus five S grades (1-3) including English and maths, or similar. Normally science subjects not held at H grade should be offered at S grade. Some medical schools offer a one-year pre-medical course for students whose H grades do not include the required science subjects. Check with individual schools for full details.

Degree Information

A degree in medicine awarded by a university medical school and recognised by the General Medical Council is essential, followed by specialist training.

Adult Qualifications

Entry requirement standards are not normally relaxed for mature applicants, though those who consider applying should contact the individual university for advice. Graduates with a good honours degree in a related subject may obtain exemptions from certain options within the medical degree course.

Work Experience

Entry to this career is highly competitive and it is essential that you have some relevant work or voluntary experience before applying to train as a doctor so that you are able to demonstrate a long-term commitment to medicine. Evidence of this can come in the form of relevant paid or voluntary work in a healthcare setting such as work in a hospital, residential care home, or similar. You can apply for voluntary work overseas that usually has a health education or medically-related programme.

Entry and Training

Surgeons must first qualify as medical doctors by completing a medicine degree, pass the postgraduate two-year Foundation Programme and register as a doctor with the General Medical Council (GMC). For full details of medical training see the job article Doctor: Hospital.

Once you have completed the Foundation Programme, there is competition for entry to two year core surgical training. This covers all aspects of surgery. After core training, you then have to apply for posts for specialty training on one of eight specialist surgery training programmes. This can take five to six years. Progress is based on achieving competences, and leads to the Certificate of Completion of Specialist Training (CCST) and Fellowship of the Royal College of Surgeons (FRCS). Once you have achieved the CCST, you can join the specialist register of the GMC and apply for a post as a consultant. You are expected to update your professional knowledge continually throughout your career. Contact the Royal College of Surgeons for details of courses, bursaries and training routes.

For students under the age of 25, the armed forces sometimes offer medical cadetships. Contact your nearest armed forces careers office for details.

Mature applicants that are suitably qualified are welcomed by medical schools and some may have reserved places for mature/ graduate entrants. There are access courses to medicine and pre-medical foundation courses. Some Open University credits at distinction level may be accepted at some medical schools. Check with individual medical schools for details of all opportunities.

Opportunities and Pay

There are around 5,000 consultant surgeons in the UK at the moment. Surgeons are usually employed by the NHS, a private hospital or the armed forces. There are also opportunities abroad with voluntary organisations in developing countries, but pay is usually low. Prospects may depend on your willingness to move to another area to gain experience and obtain promotion. There may be opportunities to work part time or job share.

Within the NHS, junior doctors earn a basic salary and are usually paid a supplement for extra hours worked. Basic salaries are around £33k a year (including a 50% supplement for extra hours), rising to £43k-£68k (including 50% supplement) for a doctor in specialist training. A consultant can earn £73k-£174k a year. These salaries do not include on-call payments, private income or London weighting allowances.

Health

There is a risk of infection. You should have no allergies and a good level of general fitness.

Skills and Qualities

able to put people at ease, able to take responsibility, analytical skills, aptitude for teamwork, emotionally strong, good communication skills, manual dexterity, not squeamish, scientific approach, self confident

Relevant Subjects

Biology, Chemistry, English, Health and social care, Mathematics, Physics, Psychology, Science, Sociology

Further Information

Becoming a Doctor (BMA) (BMA) - www.bma.org.uk/careers/becoming_doctor/index.jsp

Becoming a Doctor: Is Medicine really the career for you? (Matt Green & Tom Nolan, 2008) (Apply2 Ltd)

British Medical Journal (weekly) (BMJ Publishing Group Ltd) - www.bmj.com/

Foundation Programme - www.foundationprogramme.nhs.uk

Medicine Uncovered (Trotman 2009) - www.trotman.co.uk

Modernising Medical Careers - www.mmc.nhs.uk

NHS Careers (NHS Careers) - www.nhscareers.nhs.uk

NHS Careers Scotland - www.infoscotland.com/nhs

NHS Careers Wales - www.wales.nhs.uk

Open University - www.open.ac.uk

The Lancet (weekly) (Elsevier Ltd) - www.thelancet.com/

The Surgeon (6 x year) (Royal College of Surgeons of Edinburgh and Ireland) - www.thesurgeon.net

UK Clinical Aptitude Test - www.ukcat.ac.uk

Addresses

British Medical Association (BMA)
BMA House, Tavistock Square, London WC1H 9JP
Phone: +44 (0)20 7387 4499
Web: www.bma.org.uk

General Medical Council (GMC)
Regents Place, 350 Euston Road, London NW1 3JN
Phone: +44 (0)161 923 6602
Web: www.gmc-uk.org

Royal College of Surgeons of England
35-43 Lincolns Inn Fields, London WC2A 3PE
Phone: +44 (0)20 7405 3474
Web: www.rcseng.ac.uk

Similar Jobs

Anaesthetist, Doctor: General Practitioner, Doctor: Hospital, Obstetrician/Gynaecologist, Ophthalmologist, Pathologist

Surveying Technician

also known as: Surveyor: Technical

CRCI:Building and Construction
CLCI:UM Job Band: 3 to 4

Job Description

Surveying technicians support chartered surveyors across a range of surveying specialisms. They offer advice and specialist knowledge in areas such as land and property management and valuation, mineral surveying and in estate agencies. Technicians work in a surveying team and are involved in costing for building projects, negotiating payments to sub-contractors, collecting and analysing technical data. They use architects' drawings to work out what materials and labour are needed and the likely costs.

Duties include monitoring site work so that payment can be made to building contractors. Surveying technicians are normally accomplished in specific IT applications and in delivering on specific tasks to a high standard. May use technical equipment for surveying on site and liasing with a wide range of professional colleagues is essential.

Work Details

Surveying technicians usually work a basic 35-40 hr week, Monday to Friday, though may be expected to have early starts and late finishes, including some weekend work. The work is mainly office based, but involves travel to different places for site visits. A driving licence is useful. You advise and negotiate with architects, engineers and builders, as well as clients. Helping with the planning and design stages of a project and assisting with overall cost control is key to your role. You need to be able to handle complex calculations and work to deadlines.

On-site inspection involves some physical activity, such as climbing ladders and scaffolding, so you may need to wear a protective helmet. You may be working outside in all weathers.

Qualification

- **England, Wales and Northern Ireland**

Band 3: For BTEC national course: usually 4 GCSEs (A*-C) including maths, a science subject and English, or equivalent.

Band 4: For BTEC higher national award: 1-2 A levels and some GCSEs (A*-C) usually including English, maths and possibly a science subject, or equivalent.

- **Scotland**

Band 3: For an SQA national course: usually four S grades (1-3) including maths, a science subject and English, or similar.

Band 4: For SQA higher national award: usually 2-3 H grades, preferably maths and physics, and some S grades (1-3) often including English, maths and a science subject, or similar qualifications.

Adult Qualifications

Entry requirements for training with an employer vary but relevant national awards are helpful. Course entry requirements are usually relaxed for suitable mature applicants. Those without the required qualifications may complete a foundation or Access course leading to relevant HNDs.

Work Experience

Relevant work or voluntary experience is always useful and can improve your chances in application to this job or to a college course. The types of work experience to consider include work in a surveyor's office or a related area, such as jobs in the construction industry, an architect's office or local government. In some areas there is a young apprenticeship (14-16) scheme that provides an extended work placement and eventual achievement of a level 2 qualification whilst at school. A Diploma/Welsh Baccalaureate in construction and the built environment may be available in your area.

Entry and Training

You can take a full-time course or train with an employer and take a part-time course with day or block release at a college. Technical membership (TechRICS) of the Royal Institution for Chartered Surveyors (RICS) can be gained through a variety of routes through a points system, including relevant HNC/HNDs, S/NVQs at level 3-4, or an assessment of technical competence (ATC) following a training period. You need at least 100 points to be eligible for final assessment. From TechRICS membership there is a 'bridge' arrangement that provides a pathway to chartered surveyor status.

A distance-learning course, the diploma in surveying practice (DipSP), is available from the College of Estate Management that allows those in relevant employment to study in their own time and at their own pace. The diploma meets RICS academic requirements for TechRICS membership. Contact RICS for further information on membership, training routes and relevant courses.

The Chartered Surveyors Training Trust offers a programme that allows entry at different levels, depending on your qualifications, but with a minimum of 4 GCSEs (A*-C). Help with job seeking or course finding is also available. This programme is based on the apprenticeship and is available at present in Greater London.

Relevant S/NVQs are available at levels 3-4, such as in surveying, property and maintenance. Training programmes, including apprenticeship schemes, may be available in your area for entry to this job. Advanced apprenticeships leading to qualification at level 3 can also be a route into higher education.

Mature applicants with experience in the building industry may have an advantage. Refresher courses are sometimes available for those returning to work and there may be special government training schemes in some areas, including apprenticeships for adults. You can gain recognition of previous experience through Accreditation of Prior Learning (APL) or by working towards relevant S/NVQs.

Opportunities and Pay

Jobs are available throughout the UK with a wide range of employers, mainly in larger cities. You can work for a building contractor, a civil engineering firm, construction and property companies, estate agents, insurance companies, banks and building societies, auction houses, a rural estate, antique and art dealerships, a local council or a government department. For those working in property surveying, availability of work may depend on the state of the building trade and the national economy. Currently there is a downturn in the housing market which means there may be a shortage of vacancies.

There are usually opportunities for further training, often offered in-house, and you may be able to work towards becoming a qualified surveyor with chartered status. Opportunities exist abroad for certain specialisms in Europe and elsewhere.

Pay varies depending on location and employer. Starting salaries are likely to be around £18k rising to £25k-£30k with experience.

Health

You should be physically fit.

Skills and Qualities

able to communicate effectively, able to get on with all kinds of people, analytical skills, aptitude for teamwork, attention to detail, good organisational skills, methodical, numeracy skills, problem-solving skills, specialist IT skills

Relevant Subjects

Construction and built environment, Design and technology, Geography, ICT/Computer studies, Mathematics, Physics

Further Information

Apprenticeship Schemes (National Apprenticeship Service) - www.apprenticeships.org.uk

Asset Skills - sector skills council for the places where we live and work - www.assetskills.org

Diplomas (Foundation, Higher and Advanced) - http://yp.direct.gov.uk/diplomas

The Survey Association - www.tsa-uk.org.uk

Training Schemes - www.direct.gov.uk/en/educationandlearning

Welsh Baccalaureate - www.wbq.org.uk

▶Working in construction & the built environment (2007) (Babcock Lifeskills) - www.babcock-lifeskills.com/

Addresses

Chartered Institute of Building (CIOB)
Englemere King's Ride, Ascot, Berkshire SL5 7TB
Phone: +44 (0)1344 630 700
Web: www.ciob.org.uk

Chartered Surveyors Training Trust (CSTT)
16th Floor The Tower Building 11 York Road, London SE1 7NX
Phone: +44 (0)207 871 0454
Web: www.cstt.org.uk

College of Estate Management (CEM)
Whiteknights, Reading, Berkshire RG6 6AW
Phone: 0800 019 9697 UK only
Web: www.cem.ac.uk

Royal Institution of Chartered Surveyors (RICS)
RICS Contact Centre Surveyor Court Westwood Way, Coventry CV4 8JE
Phone: +44 (0)870 333 1600
Web: www.ricscourses.org/pages/careers.aspx

Similar Jobs

Architectural Technologist, Clerk of Works/Site Inspector, Construction Estimator, Surveyor: Quantity, Town Planning Support Staff

Surveyor: Building

CRCI:Building and Construction
CLCI:UM — Job Band: 4 to 5

Job Description

Building surveyors provide advice on the structure of all types and sizes of property and construction. They assess the condition of a property before purchase, sale, alteration or repair and organise structural surveys for new properties and the restoration of old buildings. May provide advice on health and safety regulations, planning law and building regulations. Surveyors are concerned with environmental issues, such as energy efficiency. They write reports, provide valuations, and work out estimates of costs but also draw up plans and specifications. May put contracts out to tender, and supervise a contractor's work, including checking the accounts.

Building surveyors deal with fire precautions and insurance claims. May need to attend court to give evidence where there are construction disputes, or if building regulations have not been followed. Can specialise in maintenance, repair, design or contract work. Some work on the restoration and maintenance of historic buildings and monuments.

Work Details

Building surveyors usually work a 35-39 hr week, Monday to Friday, but may be required to work longer hours at times, including weekends. Some projects require early starts and late finishes. Work is based both in an office and on site, sometimes with travel to different sites. A driving licence is essential. The job includes advising clients, analysing details and presenting facts. Surveyors also have responsibility for observing the relevant laws and building regulations, carrying out site supervision and monitoring progress. Work may involve making unpopular decisions.

Conditions on site may be damp, dirty or cramped, so you need to be physically active, and may sometimes have to climb ladders or scaffolding. You need to wear protective equipment such as a safety helmet and boots when on site.

Qualification

• England, Wales and Northern Ireland

Band 4: For BTEC higher national award: 1-2 A levels and some GCSEs (A*-C) usually including English, maths and possibly a science subject, or equivalent.

Band 5: For degree courses: 2-3 A levels and some GCSEs (A*-C) usually including English, maths and possibly a science subject, or equivalent. Exact requirements depend on the degree you take.

• Scotland

Band 4: For SQA higher national award: usually 2-3 H grades and some S grades (1-3), often including English, maths and possibly a science subject, or similar qualifications.

Band 5: For degree courses: at least 3-5 H grades and some S grades (1-3), usually including English, maths and possibly a science subject, or similar qualifications. Exact requirements depend on the degree you take.

Degree Information

A Royal Institute of Chartered Surveyors (RICS) accredited degree in building surveying is usually preferred for entry to this job. Degrees in building, architecture or civil engineering may also be acceptable, especially if followed by an appropriate postgraduate qualification.

Graduates with non-accredited degrees may undertake a conversion course (modules from an accredited degree) often through distance learning, whilst in a job.

Adult Qualifications

A relevant qualification, usually a degree or a higher national award, is normally required. Entry requirements may be relaxed for adults applying for higher education courses and Access or foundation courses give adults without qualifications a route on to degree courses. Those with experience and/or qualifications in other related disciplines may be accepted by the professional bodies for further training.

Details of special entry standards for adults can be obtained from the university, college or professional organisation concerned. Graduates without an accredited degree may take a one-year conversion course in surveying.

Work Experience
Employers or universities may prefer candidates who have relevant work or voluntary experience. Ideally, time spent with a building surveying firm or practitioner is the most relevant, but related experience, such as work in an architectural practice or civil engineering firm, is also useful. Student membership of RICS or a related professional organisation shows commitment to the profession.

Entry and Training
Most building surveyors qualify as members of the Royal Institution of Chartered Surveyors (RICS) by completing an accredited degree or diploma, but there are other professional organisations that accredit courses and offer membership, which may also be acceptable. These include the Chartered Institute of Building (CIOB) and the Association of Building Engineers (ABE). You should choose your course carefully, because they vary considerably.

Most people first take a three-year full-time or four-year sandwich course for a degree or diploma, but some begin by studying part time for an accredited course whilst working. The Chartered Surveyors Training Trust (CSTT) provides advanced apprenticeships mainly in London and the South East for people aged 16-24. All trainees of the CSTT follow a work-based learning programme, with four days a week spent with an employer and one day at college. Contact CSTT for further details.

All entrants continue to study by distance learning or a day-release course for an appropriate professional qualification. There are professional examination exemptions for holders of relevant degrees and diplomas. For those with non-related degrees there are conversion courses. Professional qualification to chartered status usually requires at least two years' practical experience after training, followed by a final assessment called the APC (Assessment of Professional Competence). You are expected to follow agreed levels of continuing professional development throughout your career.

Some building surveyors first qualify as surveying technicians (see separate job details). Those with an HND enter at technical surveyor level. There are foundation degree courses in surveying/engineering, but before embarking on any course of study you should check with RICS or a related professional organisation for details of accredited qualifications.

Mature applicants with experience in the construction industry or planning may have an advantage. Professional surveying institutions accept mature applicants through various routes of entry. Progression routes can also include S/NVQs, full-time, part-time, distance learning, and foundation degree courses. Technical membership of RICS (Tech RICS) can also provide a progression route to chartered status.

Opportunities and Pay
Typical employers include specialised private practices, such as property consultancies, surveying firms and construction companies, or local/central government departments and agencies. Jobs are also available with housing associations, loss adjusters, leisure groups and retail organisations. Availability of work depends on the state of the building trade and the national economy. Currently there is a downturn in the housing market which means there may be a shortage of vacancies.

Promotion opportunities, including project management positions, are generally better in larger organisations. Further promotion can lead to becoming a partner in a private firm, or head of department in local or central government. Many experienced building surveyors set up their own practices. Work abroad may be possible.

Salaries vary considerably and your age, qualifications and experience, as well as geographical location, can affect your pay. A graduate entrant can expect a starting salary in the region of £18k-£22k a year, and when chartered around £29k-£41k. A partner in a firm can earn up to £70k a year. Some may earn more.

Health
You need good general fitness to do this job.

Skills and Qualities
able to follow drawings and plans, analytical skills, aptitude for maths and science, aptitude for teamwork, attention to detail, environmental awareness, good spoken and written communication, negotiating skills, observational skills, specialist IT skills

Relevant Subjects
Business and accounting, Construction and built environment, Design and technology, Engineering, English, Mathematics, Physics, Science

Further Information
ConstructionSkills - sector skills council for the construction industry - www.cskills.org

TARGETjobs: Construction & Building Services (GTI Specialist Publishers Ltd) - www.groupgti.com

TARGETjobs: Property (GTI Specialist Publishers Ltd) - www.groupgti.com

TARGETjobs: Quantity Surveying & Building Surveying (GTI Specialist Publishing Ltd) http:/www.groupgti.com

▶ Working in construction & the built environment (2007) (Babcock Lifeskills) - www.babcock-lifeskills.com/

Addresses
Association of Building Engineers (ABE)
Lutyens House, Billing Brook Road, Weston Favell, Northampton NN3 8NW
Phone: +44 (0)845 126 1058
Web: www.abe.org.uk

Chartered Institute of Building (CIOB)
Englemere King's Ride, Ascot, Berkshire SL5 7TB
Phone: +44 (0)1344 630 700
Web: www.ciob.org.uk

Chartered Surveyors Training Trust (CSTT)
16th Floor The Tower Building 11 York Road, London SE1 7NX
Phone: +44 (0)207 871 0454
Web: www.cstt.org.uk

Royal Institution of Chartered Surveyors (RICS)
RICS Contact Centre Surveyor Court Westwood Way, Coventry CV4 8JE
Phone: +44 (0)870 333 1600
Web: www.ricscourses.org/pages/careers.aspx

Similar Jobs
Architect, Facilities Manager, Surveyor: Building Control, Surveyor: General Practice, Surveyor: Planning & Development, Town Planner

Surveyor: Building Control
CRCI:Building and Construction
CLCI:UM Job Band: 3 to 5

Job Description
Building control surveyors play an important role in ensuring that all residential and commercial buildings are safe places in which to live and work. They first check the applicants' plans and drawings to make sure they follow the building regulations. Construction site visits are an important part of the job. Building control surveyors make sure that government building regulations are observed at the construction stages of any new building. They also give advice on health and safety regulations, conservation and energy issues, access for the less able, public health, and planning law. They provide a written report explaining any suggestions for alteration to the building, and may draw up plans and specifications to support

any changes. May be involved in the pre-application stage of a new building or conversion/restoration of an old one, and offer advice on any design issues.

Building control surveyors maintain accurate records of each visit and issue a completion certificate after the final satisfactory inspection. They take legal action if the work is not up to standard, or is not built to the agreed specification. May be required to give evidence in court where there has been a breach of building control regulations. Surveyors working for local authorities may be involved in approving demolitions and surveying potentially dangerous buildings. They calculate the fee to be charged to a client for building control services.

Work Details

Building control surveyors usually work a 35-39 hr week, Monday to Friday, though may be required to work longer hours at times, including weekends. Some projects require early starts and late finishes. Work is based both in an office and frequently on site, sometimes with travel to different sites. A driving licence is essential. The job includes advising, analysing details and presenting facts. You are also responsible for observing building control regulations and monitoring progress. Work may involve making unpopular decisions.

Conditions on site can be damp, dirty or cramped. You need to be physically active and sometimes have to climb ladders or scaffolding. Protective clothing or a safety helmet is worn when on site.

Qualification

• England, Wales and Northern Ireland

Band 3: For direct entry: usually at least 5 GCSEs (A*-C) including English, maths and a science subject, or equivalent.

Band 4: For BTEC higher national award: 1-2 A levels and some GCSEs (A*-C) usually including English, maths, and possibly a science subject, or equivalent.

Band 5: For degree courses: 2-3 A levels and some GCSEs (A*-C) usually including English, maths, and possibly a science subject, or equivalent. Exact requirements depend on the degree you take.

• Scotland

Band 3: For direct entry: usually at least five S grades (1-3) including English, maths and a science subject, or similar.

Band 4: For SQA higher national award: usually 2-3 H grades and some S grades (1-3), often including English, maths and possibly a science subject, or similar.

Band 5: For degree courses: at least 3-5 H grades and some S grades (1-3), usually including English, maths and possibly a science subject, or similar qualifications. Exact requirements depend on the degree you take.

Degree Information

Degrees in building surveying, building/construction studies or civil/structural engineering are acceptable for this job. You should first check with the Royal Institution of Chartered Surveyors (RICS) and the Association of Building Engineers (ABE) for a list of accredited courses before embarking on your degree. Postgraduate courses are also available though are not required for entry.

Graduates with non-accredited degrees may undertake a conversion course (modules from an accredited degree), often through distance learning whilst in a job.

Adult Qualifications

Entry requirements may be relaxed for adults applying for higher education courses and Access or foundation courses give adults without qualifications a route on to degree courses. Those with experience and/or qualifications in other related disciplines may be accepted by the professional bodies for further training. Details of special entry standards for adults can be obtained from the university, college or professional organisation concerned. Graduates without an accredited degree may take a one-year conversion course.

Work Experience

Employers or universities may prefer candidates who have relevant work or voluntary experience. Ideally, time spent with a building surveying firm or practitioner is the most relevant, but related experience such as work in an architectural practice or civil engineering firm is also useful. Student membership of the Royal Institution of Chartered Surveyors or a related professional organisation shows commitment to the profession.

Entry and Training

Many people take a three-year full-time or four-year sandwich course for a degree or diploma, though some begin by studying part time for an accredited course whilst working. Relevant courses include a BTEC/SQA national certificate/diploma and the HNC/HND in building studies. It is possible to enter a job (particularly in local government) at assistant building control surveyor level after gaining building craft training and experience, and then study part time for relevant qualifications.

Most building control surveyors qualify as members of the Royal Institution of Chartered Surveyors (RICS) or the Association of Building Engineers (ABE) by completing an accredited degree or diploma. You should choose your course carefully, because they vary considerably. There are professional examination exemptions for holders of relevant degrees and diplomas. Professional qualification for chartered status of RICS usually requires at least two years' practical experience after training, followed by a final assessment called the APC (Assessment of Professional Competence). The ABE also offers corporate membership to graduates with a minimum of one year's professional experience, and associate membership to those with a relevant diploma and at least two years' relevant experience. You are expected to follow agreed levels of continuing professional development throughout your career.

Some building control surveyors first qualify as surveying technicians (see separate job details). Appropriate foundation degrees are available and can be studied full or part time. Advanced apprenticeships may be available in your area. The Chartered Surveyors Training Trust (CSTT) provides advanced apprenticeships mainly in London and the South East for people aged 16-24. All trainees of the CSTT follow a work-based learning programme, with four days a week spent with an employer and one day at college. Contact CSTT for further details.

Mature applicants with experience in the construction industry or planning may have an advantage. Professional surveying institutions accept mature applicants through various routes of entry. Progression routes also include S/NVQs, full-time, part-time, distance learning, and foundation degree courses. Technical membership of the Royal Institution of Chartered Surveyors (Tech RICS) also provides a progression route to chartered status.

Opportunities and Pay

Jobs are located throughout the UK. The majority of building control surveyors are employed by local authorities, due to the statutory nature of the job. There are opportunities for work in the private sector with a consultancy practice as an approved site inspector. Availability of work depends to some extent on the state of the building trade and the national economy. Currently there is a downturn in the housing market which means there may be a shortage of vacancies. Promotion opportunities, including project management positions, are generally better in larger organisations. Those with relevant qualifications and experience may work as an independent and self-employed building control approved inspector. There may be opportunities for work abroad.

Salaries can vary considerably though usually start at around £15k-£20k a year, rising to around £22k-£30k with experience. Senior surveyors can earn around £40k a year, or more.

Health
You need good general fitness to do this job.

Skills and Qualities
able to manage a budget and keep records, able to take responsibility, aptitude for maths and science, attention to detail, good communication skills, good presentation skills, logical, specialist IT skills, technical aptitude

Relevant Subjects
Business and accounting, Construction and built environment, Design and technology, Engineering, English, Mathematics, Physics, Science

Further Information
Building Engineer (monthly) (Association of Building Engineers) - www.abe.org.uk/publications/buildingengineer

ConstructionSkills - sector skills council for the construction industry - www.cskills.org

Local Government Careers (Improvement and Development Agency) - www.lgcareers.com/publications/

TARGETjobs: Construction & Building Services (GTI Specialist Publishers Ltd) - www.groupgti.com

► Working in construction & the built environment (2007) (Babcock Lifeskills) - www.babcock-lifeskills.com/

Addresses
Association of Building Engineers (ABE)
Lutyens House, Billing Brook Road, Weston Favell, Northampton NN3 8NW
Phone: +44 (0)845 126 1058
Web: www.abe.org.uk

Chartered Institute of Building (CIOB)
Englemere King's Ride, Ascot, Berkshire SL5 7TB
Phone: +44 (0)1344 630 700
Web: www.ciob.org.uk

Chartered Surveyors Training Trust (CSTT)
16th Floor The Tower Building 11 York Road, London SE1 7NX
Phone: +44 (0)207 871 0454
Web: www.cstt.org.uk

Royal Institution of Chartered Surveyors (RICS)
RICS Contact Centre Surveyor Court Westwood Way, Coventry CV4 8JE
Phone: +44 (0)870 333 1600
Web: www.ricscourses.org/pages/careers.aspx

Similar Jobs
Architect, Engineer: Building Services, Engineer: Municipal, Surveyor: Building, Surveyor: Planning & Development, Surveyor: Quantity

Surveyor: General Practice
also known as: Estimator: Property, Property Surveyor, Valuation Surveyor, Valuer

CRCI:Building and Construction
CLCI:UM Job Band: 4 to 5

Job Description
Surveyors use expert knowledge to estimate the value of commercial and residential property, land or other goods for tax, investment, insurance, sales and marketing purposes. Work is available in the private and public sectors. Surveyors measure sites and premises accurately and consider the known facts about the item to be valued. Current trends, future developments, supply and demand the local economy are all taken into consideration when carrying out a valuation. Can deal with various branches of valuation, including garages, hotels, works of art, house contents, livestock, farms, or industrial plant and machinery.

May be involved in negotiating deals connected with buying, selling and renting property. General practice surveyors often combine work with related areas, such as agricultural auctioning and surveying, or estate management.

Work Details
Surveyors usually work a 35-40 hr week, Monday to Friday, though may be expected at times to have early starts and late finishes, including some weekend work. You work in an office, or sometimes a salesroom or other locations, and need to travel to different sites to visit clients and other colleagues. Overnight stays away from home may be required. A driving licence is usually required. The work environment varies according to the type of survey. In some locations you may have to climb ladders and walk over rough ground. You are expected to dress smartly, even on a site, and may need to wear protective clothing.

You advise and consult with a wide range of people and require knowledge of tax matters and an understanding of legal technicalities. This work can be very demanding and involve making difficult decisions.

Qualification
• England, Wales and Northern Ireland
Band 4: For BTEC higher national award: 1-2 A levels and some GCSEs (A*-C), or equivalent. English, maths, science subjects, geography or economics are preferred subjects.

Band 5: For degree courses: 2-3 A levels and some GCSEs (A*-C) including English, maths and preferably a science subject, or equivalent. Exact requirements depend on the degree you take.

• Scotland
Band 4: For SQA higher national award: usually 2-3 H grades and some S grades (1-3), or similar qualifications. English, maths, science subjects, geography or economics are preferred subjects.

Band 5: For degree courses: 3-5 H grades and some S grades (1-3) including English, maths and preferably a science subject, or similar qualifications. Exact requirements depend on the degree you take.

Degree Information
Any degree is acceptable, but it is an advantage to have studied estate management, surveying, land and property management, or a directly related subject, such as planning and architecture. Other subjects, such as fine art, economics and geography, give useful background for some areas of valuation work. The Royal Institution of Chartered Surveyors (RICS) website has details of accredited degree courses. Graduates without an accredited degree may take a one-year conversion course in surveying.

Adult Qualifications
A relevant qualification, usually a degree, is normally required. Those with a relevant HND, such as land and property, are normally required to top this up to a preferred degree. Those with experience and/or qualifications in a related area may be accepted by the professional bodies for further training. Course entry requirements are usually relaxed for suitable mature applicants. Those without the required qualifications may complete a foundation/Access course leading to a relevant HND or accredited degree.

Work Experience
Employers or colleges/universities may prefer candidates who have relevant work or voluntary experience. This includes direct experience with a valuation office/department, or similar. This can be at a surveyor's office, a property management company, or an auction house. Experience in clerical and sales work within an estate agency is also very helpful.

Entry and Training
Most people complete a full-time degree first. You may have exemptions from the professional exams if your degree is in a relevant subject. It is usual to join a professional organisation such

as the Royal Institution of Chartered Surveyors (RICS) or the Institute of Revenues, Ratings and Valuation (IRRV) and achieve professional qualification. Those who do not have the exemptions may study part time whilst working, through day release/distance learning or evening classes. There are intensive postgraduate conversion courses available for those without an accredited degree. Professional qualification to chartered status usually requires at least two years' practical experience after training, followed by a final assessment called the APC (Assessment of Professional Competence).

Some general practice surveyors first qualify as surveying technicians (see separate job details). Those with an HND enter at technician level. Relevant S/NVQs are available, such as in surveying, property and maintenance at level 3-4. Advanced apprenticeships leading to qualification at level 3 can also be a route into higher education. Appropriate foundation degrees are also available that can be studied full or part time. The Chartered Surveyors Training Trust provides advanced apprenticeships mainly in London and the South East.

Mature applicants with experience in the construction industry or planning may have an advantage and it is useful to have experience in building, architecture, administration, law or marketing. Professional surveying institutions accept mature applicants through various routes of entry. Progression routes can also include S/NVQs, full time, part time, distance learning, and foundation degree courses. Technical membership (Tech RICS) of the Royal Institution of Chartered Surveyors (RICS) can also provide a progression route to chartered status.

Opportunities and Pay

Work is possible with a variety of employers throughout the UK, including property developers, estate agents, banks or building societies, local and central government, private practice and public utility companies. Work may be available overseas for those with foreign language skills. For those working in property surveying, opportunities may depend on the housing market at the time of entry. Currently there is a downturn in the housing market which means there may be fewer vacancies for surveyors. There is often no formal career structure in the private sector and promotion depends on merit and available vacancies.

Pay varies depending on area and type of company. A graduate entrant is likely to earn around £20k-£25k rising to £28k-£35k with experience and once fully qualified. Senior surveyors earn around £52k, while partners can earn £60k-£110k a year. Your pay may increase with commission and bonuses.

Health

Normal colour vision is needed for certain areas of work.

Skills and Qualities

accurate measuring and calculating skills, analytical skills, aptitude for teamwork, excellent communication skills, good interpersonal skills, initiative, negotiating skills, networking skills, self confident, understanding of legal technicalities

Relevant Subjects

Art and Design, Business and accounting, Economics, English, Geography, Law, Mathematics

Further Information

Apprenticeship Schemes (National Apprenticeship Service) - www.apprenticeships.org.uk

Asset Skills - sector skills council for the places where we live and work - www.assetskills.org

Chartered Institute of Building (CIOB) - www.ciob.org.uk/home

Local Government Careers (Improvement and Development Agency) - www.lgcareers.com/publications/

TARGETjobs: Property (GTI Specialist Publishers Ltd) - www.groupgti.com

Addresses

Chartered Surveyors Training Trust (CSTT)
16th Floor The Tower Building 11 York Road, London SE1 7NX
Phone: +44 (0)207 871 0454
Web: www.cstt.org.uk

Institute of Revenues Rating and Valuation (IRRV)
41 Doughty Street, London WC1N 2LF
Phone: +44 (0)20 7831 3505
Web: www.irrv.org.uk

Royal Institution of Chartered Surveyors (RICS)
RICS Contact Centre Surveyor Court Westwood Way, Coventry CV4 8JE
Phone: +44 (0)870 333 1600
Web: www.ricscourses.org/pages/careers.aspx

Women into Science, Engineering & Construction (WISE)
2nd Floor Weston House, 246 High Holborn, London WC1V 7EX
Phone: +44 (0)20 3206 0408
Web: www.wisecampaign.org.uk

Similar Jobs

Auctioneer, Construction Estimator, Estate Agent, Surveyor: Building Control, Surveyor: Planning & Development, Surveyor: Rural Practice

Surveyor: Geomatics/Geospatial

also known as: Engineer: Geomatics/Geospatial, Land Surveyor

CRCI:Building and Construction

CLCI:UM — Job Band: 4 to 5

Job Description

Geomatic/geospatial surveyors carry out surveys and collect data on specific areas of land, using precise measurements and mapping of the built environment. They measure and plot the physical and man-made features of the earth, for construction work, digital mapping (cartography), or to establish and record property boundaries. Can use instruments such as theodolites to measure and record distances, angles and elevations of roads, rivers and mountains. May also use aerial photography, electronic and laser beam measuring equipment, and satellites. Coastal surveys involve instruments to measure and plot shorelines, high and low water marks, tides, currents and navigational channels.

Surveyors use computer-aided design (CAD) to produce virtual 3D models of surveys, and other IT software to interpret data and produce reports. They provide detailed information for analysis by engineers, planners and architects, and advice for a wide range of clients.

Work Details

Geomatics/geospatial surveyors usually work a basic 35-40 hr week, Monday to Friday, but may be required to work some evenings and weekends at times. Spends much of their time on fieldwork, living and working on site, and sometimes in isolated places for long spells with poor accommodation facilities. You may be expected to work unusual hours and spend long periods away from home. You need to travel to sites, possibly sometimes abroad. A driving licence is useful. The work can be technically and physically demanding, and takes place in all weather conditions.

Qualification

- **England, Wales and Northern Ireland**

Band 4: For BTEC higher national award: 1-2 A levels and some GCSEs (A*-C) usually including English, maths and possibly geography or a science subject, or equivalent qualifications.

Band 5: For degree courses: 2-3 A levels and some GCSEs (A*-C) usually including English, maths and possibly a science subject, or equivalent. Exact requirements depend on the degree you take.

- **Scotland**

Band 4: For SQA higher national award: usually 2-3 H grades and some S grades (1-3) often including English, maths and possibly geography or a science subject, or similar qualifications.

Band 5: For degree courses: 3-5 H grades and some S grades (1-3) usually including English, maths and possibly a science subject, or similar qualifications. Exact requirements depend on the degree you take.

Degree Information

Preferred degree subjects include geographic information science, surveying and mapping science, earth science, or land/estate surveying. Subjects such as geography (physical), maths, geology, geophysics, civil engineering surveying are also useful. Graduates without an accredited degree may take a one-year conversion course in surveying. Relevant postgraduate degrees in surveying or in specialist topics such as geographical information science or geodetic surveying are also available.

Adult Qualifications

A relevant degree or a higher national award is required. Those with experience and/or qualifications in other related disciplines may be accepted by the professional bodies for further training. Details of special entry standards for adults can be obtained from the university, college or professional organisation concerned.

Work Experience

Employers or universities may prefer candidates who have relevant work or voluntary experience. Health and safety regulations often make it difficult to gain direct site experience of surveying, but it may be possible to obtain work experience in a surveyors' or cartographic office. Student membership of the Royal Institution of Chartered Surveyors (RICS), or a related professional organisation, shows commitment to the profession.

For those who expect good A levels/H grades and intend to go to university the opportunity to spend a salaried year with a company is invaluable. Schemes such as 'A Year in Industry' provide such an opportunity.

Entry and Training

Most geomatics/geospatial surveyors qualify as members of the Royal Institution of Chartered Surveyors (RICS) by completing an accredited degree, but there are other professional qualifications that are also acceptable. Contact RICS and the Institution of Civil Engineering Surveyors for details of the various training routes and qualifications.

You should choose your course carefully as they vary considerably. Most people first take a three-year full-time or four-year sandwich course for a degree, but some start by studying part time for an accredited course while working. There are also foundation courses in surveying/engineering.

All entrants continue to study, usually by distance learning, for an appropriate professional qualification. There are some professional exam exemptions for holders of relevant degrees. Check with professional bodies for further details. For those with non-related degrees there are some appropriate and intensive postgraduate conversion courses available. Professional qualification to chartered status usually requires at least two years' practical experience after training, followed by a final assessment called the APC (Assessment of Professional Competence). You must also commit to continuing professional development throughout your career.

You could choose to qualify as a chartered surveyor by first qualifying as a surveying technician (see separate job details). Those with an HND enter at technician level. Advanced apprenticeships leading to qualification at level 3 may be available in your area and can also be a route into higher education. Appropriate foundation degrees are also available; these can be studied full or part time.

Mature applicants with experience in the construction industry or planning may have an advantage. Professional surveying institutions accept mature applicants through a variety of training schemes. Progression routes can also include S/NVQs, full-time, part-time, distance-learning, and foundation degree courses. Technical membership (Tech RICS) of the Royal Institution of Chartered Surveyors (RICS) can also provide a progression route to chartered status.

Opportunities and Pay

Most work for local and central government, specialist surveying practices and on special surveying projects for large construction firms. Others work for consulting engineers, utilities companies (gas, water, electricity) cartographic publishers, Ordnance Survey (OS), and mapping companies. Some move into archaeological surveying. Work is available abroad and particularly in relatively unmapped areas, including the Caribbean, Africa and the Middle East.

Pay varies depending on area and type of company. A graduate entrant is likely to earn around £20k-£25k rising to £28k-£35k with experience and once fully qualified. Senior surveyors earn around £52k, while partners can earn between £60k-£110k a year. Your pay may increase with commission and bonuses.

Health

This job requires good general fitness, good eyesight (with or without glasses) and normal colour vision for some areas of work.

Skills and Qualities

able to work both on your own and in a team, accurate, analytical skills, aptitude for fieldwork, attention to detail, excellent communication skills, numeracy skills, problem-solving skills, safety conscious, specialist IT skills

Relevant Subjects

Design and technology, English, Geography, Mathematics, Physics, Science

Further Information

Apprenticeship Schemes (National Apprenticeship Service) - www.apprenticeships.org.uk

Geomatics World (6 x year) (PV Publications Ltd/RICS) - www.pvpubs.com

▶Working outdoors (2010) (Babcock Lifeskills) - www.babcock-lifeskills.com/

Year in Industry (Engineering Development Trust) - www.yini.org.uk

Addresses

Institution of Civil Engineering Surveyors (ICES)
Dominion House, Sibson Road, Sale, Cheshire M33 7PP
Phone: +44 (0)161 972 3100
Web: www.ices.org.uk

Royal Institution of Chartered Surveyors (RICS)
RICS Contact Centre Surveyor Court Westwood Way, Coventry CV4 8JE
Phone: +44 (0)870 333 1600
Web: www.ricscourses.org/pages/careers.aspx

Women into Science, Engineering & Construction (WISE)
2nd Floor Weston House, 246 High Holborn, London WC1V 7EX
Phone: +44 (0)20 3206 0408
Web: www.wisecampaign.org.uk

Similar Jobs

Cartographer, Geological Technician, Illustrator: Archaeological, Surveyor: Building, Surveyor: Hydrographic, Surveyor: Planning & Development

Surveyor: Hydrographic

CRCI:Building and Construction
CLCI:UM Job Band: 4 to 5

Job Description

Hydrographic surveyors measure and map the world's underwater surfaces and study the shape of the seabed using satellite navigation. They carry out surveys of oceans, ports, harbours, inland waterways and rivers and find out the depth of water, measure tides and currents. Can be involved with offshore surveys to help in the location of gas and oil, for sea mining projects and to locate wrecks. Rivers and coastal areas are surveyed to advise on dredging and flood protection and investigate the location of offshore wind turbines and subsea cables.

The surveyor uses survey information to produce and update marine and navigation charts. Uses specialised technical software, global positioning systems (GPS), echo sounders and sonar to provide information for the production of nautical charts and maps. In deep oceans may use remotely operated vehicles (ROVs). Needs an understanding of and consideration for environmental issues. Assesses the environmental impact of a project, such as whether animals may be disturbed.

Work Details

Hydrographic surveyors' working hours can be irregular and unsocial and are often determined by tides and daylight. Much of the work is offshore and this can mean spending long periods of time away from home, with long periods of leave. When offshore you may be living in cramped conditions, and working alongside other surveyors. The work is often outdoors in cold and wet conditions. When working on site, safety regulations have to be adhered to and protective clothing, such as a hard hat and waterproofs, is often needed.

When onshore, hours are likely to be more regular, but may involve on call duties at weekends. Overseas work is common.

Qualification

- **England, Wales and Northern Ireland**

Band 4: For BTEC higher national award: 1-2 A levels and some GCSEs (A*-C) usually including English, maths and geography or a science subject, or equivalent.

Band 5: For degree courses: 2-3 A levels and some GCSEs (A*-C) usually including English, maths and a science subject, or equivalent. Exact requirements depend on the degree you take.

- **Scotland**

Band 4: For SQA higher national award: usually 2-3 H grades and some S grades (1-3) often including English, maths and a science subject, or similar qualifications.

Band 5: For degree courses: 3-5 H grades and some S grades (1-3), usually including English, maths and a science subject, or similar qualifications. Exact requirements depend on the degree you take.

Degree Information

Preferred degree subjects include geographic information science, surveying and mapping science, earth science, marine science or land/estate surveying. Subjects such as geography (physical), engineering, maths, geology, geophysics and civil engineering surveying are also useful. Graduates without an accredited degree may take a one-year conversion course in surveying. Relevant postgraduate degrees in hydrography, geomatics and hydrographic surveying are also available.

Adult Qualifications

A relevant degree or a higher national award is required. Those with experience and/or qualifications in other related disciplines may be accepted by the professional bodies for further training. Details of special entry standards for adults can be obtained from the university, college or professional organisation concerned.

Work Experience

Employers or universities may prefer candidates who have relevant work or voluntary experience. Health and safety regulations often exclude direct site experience of surveying, but it may be possible to obtain work experience in a surveyor's or in a cartographic office. Relevant vacation work, especially in the summer before a final university year, can be an advantage. Any experience of navigation or work with global positioning systems is helpful.

Schemes such as 'A Year in Industry' provides an opportunity to gain valuable work experience.

Entry and Training

A relevant HND or degree is required for entry, often followed by a postgraduate qualification in hydrographic surveying, particularly for those with a non-relevant HE qualification. There are intensive postgraduate conversion courses available for those without an accredited degree. Entry to this job is competitive and personal qualities are very important, because of the nature of the work at sea. Knowledge of global positioning, navigation and geographical information systems is an advantage. You are normally also expected to have a driving licence.

Training is usually in house, including induction training, information about company procedures and offshore survival and safety. Many entrants work towards chartered status with the Royal Institution of Chartered Surveyors (RICS) and this usually requires an initial accredited degree, at least two years' practical experience after training, followed by a final assessment called the APC (Assessment of Professional Competence). You must also commit to continuing professional development (CPD) throughout your career.

Depending on initial entry qualifications, some entrants choose to work towards chartered marine scientist or technologist status with the Institute of Marine Engineering, Science and Technology (IMarEST). See the websites of RICS and IMarEST for full details of training routes. In the Royal Navy you can train to become a hydrographic surveyor at HMS Raleigh in Cornwall.

Another route towards qualification as a chartered surveyor is by first qualifying as a surveying technician (see separate job details). Those with an HND enter at technician level. Advanced apprenticeships leading to qualification at level 3 may be available in your area and can also provide a route into higher education. Appropriate foundation degrees are also available that can be studied full or part time.

Mature applicants with experience in other surveying work or navigation may have an advantage. Professional surveying institutions accept mature applicants through various routes of entry. Progression routes can also include S/NVQs, full-time, part-time, distance-learning, and foundation degree courses. Technical membership (Tech RICS) of the Royal Institution of Chartered Surveyors (RICS) can also provide a progression route to chartered status.

Royal Navy training at the hydrographic training facility may provide an advantage.

Opportunities and Pay

Hydrographic surveying is a comparatively small profession, with only a few thousand working in this field all over the world. Opportunities exist in the UK and overseas, particularly in the Middle and Far East, in South America and the USA. You can work for national charting agencies, port and harbour authorities, contract survey companies, oil companies, land reclamation companies, coastal protection agencies, pipe and cable laying firms, construction firms, or the Royal Navy. With four or five years' experience, chartered surveyors may be able to do self-employed contract surveyor work.

Pay varies depending on area and type of company. Starting salaries for graduates are around £20k-£25k a year, plus a daily offshore allowance. Most hydrographic surveyors spend around

150 days a year offshore. Once fully qualified, salaries rise to £30k-£35k with experience. Senior surveyors earn around £39k-£48k, with additional pay for those working offshore.

Health

You need to be physically fit to cope with the demands of the job.

Skills and Qualities

able to live and work closely with other people, adaptable, aptitude for maths and science, enjoy working outdoors, environmental awareness, good concentration level, logical, patient, problem-solving skills, specialist IT skills

Relevant Subjects

Design and technology, English, Geography, ICT/Computer studies, Mathematics, Physics, Science

Further Information

Apprenticeship Schemes (National Apprenticeship Service) - www.apprenticeships.org.uk

Hydrographic Journal (International Federation of Hydrographic Surveyors) - www.hydrographicsociety.org/Publications/welcome.html

Sea Your Future: A Guide to Marine Careers (IMAREST) - www.imarest.org/membership/careers

Year in Industry (Engineering Development Trust) - www.yini.org.uk

Addresses

Institute of Marine Engineering, Science and Technology (IMarEST)
80 Coleman Street, London EC2R 5BJ
Phone: +44 (0)20 7382 2600
Web: www.imarest.org

International Federation of Hydrographic Surveyors
PO Box 103, Plymouth PL4 7YP
Phone: +44 (0)1752 223512
Web: www.hydrographicsociety.org

Royal Institution of Chartered Surveyors (RICS)
RICS Contact Centre Surveyor Court Westwood Way, Coventry CV4 8JE
Phone: +44 (0)870 333 1600
Web: www.ricscourses.org/pages/careers.aspx

Women into Science, Engineering & Construction (WISE)
2nd Floor Weston House, 246 High Holborn, London WC1V 7EX
Phone: +44 (0)20 3206 0408
Web: www.wisecampaign.org.uk

Similar Jobs

Cartographer, Geographical Information Systems Manager, Geophysicist, Oceanographer, Surveyor: Geomatics/Geospatial

Surveyor: Minerals & Waste Management

CRCI:Building and Construction
CLCI:UM Job Band: 4 to 5

Job Description

Mineral and mining surveyors carry out surface and underground surveys for mining and waste management purposes. They identify potential mineral resources, design the process for extracting minerals and secure planning permission to mine. They have legal responsibility for up to date and accurate plans of mines, quarries and the surrounding area and make use of high-tech electronic and computerised equipment, including computer-aided design (CAD). Must be able to negotiate legal matters such as subsidence and compensation. Duties include calculating the amount of minerals from measurements taken, and plotting gradients, levels and geological faults. May forecast the possible environmental effects of mining, including air pollution.

Mineral and mining surveyors work as part of a multi-disciplinary team to explore sites for minerals and other deposits. They provide valuations of mineral deposits and write or prepare planning applications. Can give advice on restoring the site to its previous existence when the mine/quarry is exhausted. Also, may suggest ideas for site development. Surveyors prepare plans to deal with any waste and decides where it needs to go.

Work Details

Mineral and mining surveyors may work a basic 35-40 hr week, Monday to Friday, but hours can vary and you may need to work some evenings and weekends at times. Work is based in an office, but is sometimes on site or even underground. You liaise with a team of other professionals, such as geologists and engineers to ensure safe and legal operation of the mine. Conditions on site can be dirty, dusty, dark and enclosed and sometimes hot and noisy. There is rough ground, ladders to climb and the job involves bending down. There is a risk of minor injuries and you need to wear a hard hat on site and underground.

Qualification

• England, Wales and Northern Ireland

Band 4: For BTEC higher national award: 1-2 A levels and some GCSEs (A*-C) usually including English, maths and possibly a science subject, or equivalent.

Band 5: For degree courses: 2-3 A levels and some GCSEs (A*-C) usually including English, maths and possibly a science subject, or equivalent. Geography and geology are also useful subjects. Exact requirements depend on the degree you take.

• Scotland

Band 4: For SQA higher national award: usually 2-3 H grades and some S grades (1-3), often including English, maths and possibly geography or a science subject, or similar qualifications.

Band 5: For degree courses: 3-5 H grades and some S grades (1-3), usually including English, maths and possibly a science subject, or similar qualifications. Geography and geology are also useful subjects. Exact requirements depend on the degree you take.

Degree Information

Currently there are no RICS approved degrees in minerals/mining surveying. Degrees in minerals/mining engineering, oceanography, geophysics or geology may be acceptable. There is a one-year conversion course in surveying. There are approved postgraduate courses in environmental management and technology.

Adult Qualifications

A relevant qualification, usually a degree or a higher national award, is normally required. Those with experience and/or qualifications in a related area may be accepted by the professional bodies for further training. Course entry requirements are usually relaxed for suitable mature applicants. Those without the required qualifications may complete a foundation or Access course leading to relevant HNDs or accredited degrees.

Work Experience

Employers or colleges/universities may prefer candidates who have relevant work or voluntary experience. This can include work in a surveyor's planning office, a mining engineering firm or with a private geologist or geophysics firm. They may only offer observational work as there may be health and safety issues attached to obtaining practical work experience in this area. Student membership of the Royal Institution of Chartered Surveyors (RICS), or a related professional organisation, shows commitment to the profession.

Other schemes, such as 'A Year in Industry', enable those who expect good A levels/H grades and intend to go to university the opportunity to spend a salaried year with a company in order to gain valuable work experience.

Entry and Training

Most minerals and waste management surveyors qualify as members of the Royal Institution of Chartered Surveyors (RICS) by completing an accredited degree or diploma in another type of surveying, but there are other professional qualifications that are also acceptable. Contact RICS and the Institution of Civil Engineering Surveyors for details of the various training routes and qualifications. You should choose your course carefully as they vary considerably.

Most people first take a three-year full-time or four-year sandwich course for a degree or diploma. Others start by studying part time for an accredited course while working. There are also foundation degrees in surveying/engineering. Details of approved courses can be obtained from the relevant professional body. All entrants continue to study, usually by distance learning, for an appropriate professional qualification. There are some professional exam exemptions for holders of relevant degrees and diplomas. For those with non-related degrees there are some appropriate postgraduate courses.

Professional qualification to chartered status usually requires at least two years' practical experience after training, followed by a final assessment called the APC (Assessment of Professional Competence). You must also commit to continuing professional development throughout your career. A number of professionals go on to gain further qualifications such as those available through the Chartered Institution of Wastes Management.

You can qualify as a surveying technician first and then move on to the full surveyor qualification. (see separate job details). Advanced apprenticeships leading to qualification at level 3 may be available in your area and can also be a route into higher education. Appropriate foundation degrees are also available that can be studied full or part time.

Mature applicants with experience in the construction industry or planning may have an advantage. Professional surveying institutions accept mature applicants through various routes of entry. Progression routes can also include S/NVQs, full-time, part-time, distance-learning, and foundation degree courses. Technical membership (Tech RICS) of the Royal Institution of Chartered Surveyors (RICS) can also provide a progression route to chartered status.

Opportunities and Pay

You can work for a mining or quarrying company, the valuations office agency (VOA) (part of HM Revenue & Customs), for a local authority, or as a consultant in private practice. This is a growing surveying specialisation due to the increasing emphasis on environmental issues and waste management. There may be good opportunities for jobs in the UK and overseas.

Pay varies depending on area and type of company. A graduate entrant is likely to earn around £18k-£25k rising to £30k-£35k with experience and once fully qualified. Senior surveyors earn around £35k-£49k, while partners can earn over £74k a year.

Health

You need to have good general fitness and no dust allergies.

Skills and Qualities

able to take responsibility, analytical skills, aptitude for maths and science, aptitude for teamwork, excellent communication skills, good interpersonal skills, good organisational skills, information handling skills, safety conscious, specialist IT skills

Relevant Subjects

Design and technology, English, Geography, Mathematics, Physics, Science

Further Information

Apprenticeship Schemes (National Apprenticeship Service) - www.apprenticeships.org.uk

Careers in Extractives (Proskills) - www.prospect4u.co.uk

Geomatics World (6 x year) (PV Publications Ltd/RICS) - www.pvpubs.com

Year in Industry (Engineering Development Trust) - www.yini.org.uk

Addresses

Chartered Institution of Wastes Management (CIWM)
9 Saxon Court, St Peter's Gardens, Marefair,
Northampton NN1 1SX
Phone: +44 (0)1604 620 426
Web: www.ciwm.co.uk

Institute of Materials, Minerals and Mining (IOM3)
1 Carlton House Terrace, London SW1Y 5DB
Phone: +44 (0)20 7451 7300
Web: www.iom3.org

Institution of Civil Engineering Surveyors (ICES)
Dominion House, Sibson Road, Sale, Cheshire M33 7PP
Phone: +44 (0)161 972 3100
Web: www.ices.org.uk

Royal Institution of Chartered Surveyors (RICS)
RICS Contact Centre Surveyor Court Westwood Way,
Coventry CV4 8JE
Phone: +44 (0)870 333 1600
Web: www.ricscourses.org/pages/careers.aspx

Women into Science, Engineering & Construction (WISE)
2nd Floor Weston House, 246 High Holborn, London WC1V 7EX
Phone: +44 (0)20 3206 0408
Web: www.wisecampaign.org.uk

Similar Jobs

Engineer: Minerals & Mining, Geological Technician, Geologist, Metallurgist, Surveyor: Geomatics/Geospatial, Surveyor: Planning & Development

Surveyor: Planning & Development

CRCI:Building and Construction
CLCI:UM Job Band: 4 to 5

Job Description

Planning and development surveyors specialise in all aspects of urban and rural planning. They develop land, roads and property from the initial planning stage to completion of the project. They research facts and figures of local economic, geographic and social trends and interpret statistics, studies plans/maps, assesses transport and infrastructure requirements. This is followed up with a written report on the potential of land and property projects. Planning surveyors look at the financial aspects of the project and other aspects including protection of the immediate environment and any historical buildings or sites. They discuss proposals with other professionals, check regulations and assess conflicting views whilst all the time complying with planning regulations.

The planning part of the role is often in the public sector and the development role in the private sector. May take plans through legal stages. May also have to raise the necessary finance for projects from financial institutions and investors.

Work Details

Planning and development surveyors usually work a 35-40 hr week, Monday to Friday, though may be expected to have some early starts and late finishes, including some weekend work. The work is office and desk based but includes travel to different sites at times. You consult and liaise with a team which includes other surveyors, planners, engineers and architects. In the private sector you also work with clients. Analysing details, presenting facts, providing information and giving sound advice are your core responsibilities.

You need to be aware of legal regulations and be interested in social and economic trends. Work may involve making difficult decisions. On-site inspection involves some physical activity.

Qualification

• England, Wales and Northern Ireland

Band 4: For BTEC higher national award: 1-2 A levels and some GCSEs (A*-C) usually including English, maths and possibly geography or a science subject, or equivalent qualifications.

Band 5: For degree courses: 2-3 A levels and some GCSEs (A*-C) usually including English, maths and possibly geography or a science subject, or equivalent qualifications. Exact requirements depend on the degree you take.

• Scotland

Band 4: For SQA higher national award: usually 2-3 H grades and some S grades (1-3), often including English, maths and possibly geography or a science subject, or similar qualifications.

Band 5: For degree courses: 3-5 H grades and some S grades (1-3), often including English, maths and possibly geography or a science subject, or similar qualifications. Exact requirements depend on the degree you take.

Degree Information

Approved degrees for entry to training include urban land economics, planning and development surveying, or land management. Degrees in town planning, economics, geography (human) and landscape architecture are also acceptable and provide useful background knowledge. You can follow these degrees with an appropriate postgraduate conversion course in surveying.

Adult Qualifications

A relevant qualification, usually a degree or a higher national award, is normally required. Those with experience and/or qualifications in a related area may be accepted by the professional bodies for further training. Course entry requirements are usually relaxed for suitable mature applicants. Those without the required qualifications may complete a foundation or Access course leading to relevant HNDs or accredited degrees. Graduates without an accredited degree may take a one-year conversion course in surveying.

Work Experience

Employers, colleges and universities may prefer candidates who have relevant work or voluntary experience. This includes experience in a surveyor's practice or a surveying department of a local or county council. Student membership of the Royal Institution of Chartered Surveyors (RICS), or a related professional organisation, shows commitment to the profession.

Other schemes, such as 'A Year in Industry', enable those who expect good A levels/H grades and intend to go to university the opportunity to spend a salaried year with a company in order to gain valuable work experience.

Entry and Training

Most planning and development surveyors qualify as members of the Royal Institution of Chartered Surveyors (RICS) by completing an accredited degree or diploma. There are other professional training routes that are also widely recognised, such as through the Institution of Civil Engineering Surveyors (ICES) or the Chartered Institute of Building. Contact the professional organisations for details.

You should choose your course carefully as they vary considerably. Most people first take a three-year full-time or four-year sandwich course for a degree or diploma. Some start by studying part time for an accredited course while working. Details of approved courses can be obtained from the relevant professional body.

All entrants continue to study, usually by distance learning, for an appropriate professional qualification. There are some professional exam exemptions for holders of relevant degrees and diplomas; check with professional bodies for further details. For those with non-related degrees there are some approved postgraduate courses. Professional qualification to chartered status usually requires at least two years' practical experience after training, followed by a final assessment called the APC (Assessment of Professional Competence). You must also commit to continuing professional development (CPD) throughout your career. Senior surveyors also often hold additional qualifications such as those of the Royal Town Planning Institute.

You can also qualify as a chartered surveyor by first qualifying as a surveying technician (see separate job details). Advanced apprenticeships leading to qualification at level 3 can also be a route into higher education. Appropriate foundation degrees are also available that can be studied full or part time.

Mature applicants with experience in the construction industry or planning may have an advantage. Professional surveying institutions accept mature applicants through various routes of entry. Progression routes can also include S/NVQs, full-time, part-time, distance-learning, and foundation degree courses. Technical membership (Tech RICS) of the Royal Institution of Chartered Surveyors (RICS) can also provide a progression route to chartered status.

Opportunities and Pay

You can work for a firm of surveyors, a planning consultant or a property developer. Some planning and development surveyors are in private practice or are self-employed as consultants. Others are employed by the civil service or a local authority to work on environmental planning at national or local level. Promotion opportunities are generally better in larger organisations. Availability of work depends to some extent on the state of the building trade and the national economy. Currently there is a downturn in the housing market which means there may be a shortage of vacancies. There are increasing opportunities for work in European countries.

Pay varies depending on area and type of company. A graduate entrant is likely to earn around £20k-£23k rising to £30k-£35k with experience and once fully qualified. Senior planning and development surveyors earn on average around £50k a year.

Skills and Qualities

analytical skills, aptitude for maths and science, excellent communication skills, good at writing reports, good presentation skills, information handling skills, IT skills, negotiating skills, problem-solving skills, understanding of legal technicalities

Relevant Subjects

Business and accounting, Construction and built environment, Design and technology, Economics, English, Geography, Land and Environment, Mathematics, Science

Further Information

Apprenticeship Schemes (National Apprenticeship Service) - www.apprenticeships.org.uk

TARGETjobs: Property (GTI Specialist Publishers Ltd) - www.groupgti.com

Why Become a Chartered Planning and Development Surveyor (RICS) - www.rics.org/careers

Year in Industry (Engineering Development Trust) - www.yini.org.uk

Addresses

Chartered Institute of Building (CIOB)
Englemere King's Ride, Ascot, Berkshire SL5 7TB
Phone: +44 (0)1344 630 700
Web: www.ciob.org.uk

Institution of Civil Engineering Surveyors (ICES)
Dominion House, Sibson Road, Sale, Cheshire M33 7PP
Phone: +44 (0)161 972 3100
Web: www.ices.org.uk

Royal Institution of Chartered Surveyors (RICS)
RICS Contact Centre Surveyor Court Westwood Way, Coventry CV4 8JE
Phone: +44 (0)870 333 1600
Web: www.ricscourses.org/pages/careers.aspx

Royal Town Planning Institute (RTPI)
41 Botolph Lane, London EC3R 8DL
Phone: +44 (0)20 7929 9494
Web: www.rtpi.org.uk

Women into Science, Engineering & Construction (WISE)
2nd Floor Weston House, 246 High Holborn, London WC1V 7EX
Phone: +44 (0)20 3206 0408
Web: www.wisecampaign.org.uk

Similar Jobs

Architect, Surveyor: General Practice, Surveyor: Geomatics/Geospatial, Surveyor: Quantity, Town Planner

Surveyor: Quantity

also known as: Commercial Manager, Construction Cost Consultant

CRCI:Building and Construction
CLCI:UM Job Band: 4 to 5

Job Description

Quantity surveyors use architects' and engineers' plans to make an initial estimate of the cost of a building or engineering project. They advise on total costs and prepare detailed lists of materials, taxes, labour and maintenance required, known as the 'bill of quantities'. They examine tenders received from contractors and advise the client on the best one to choose.

Quantity surveyors prepare the contract, work schedules and payment arrangements. They check the work that is in progress on site, monitor expenditure and arrange part and final payments, and ensure the project follows the agreed budget. Must be able to follow up on any variations from the contract as agreed by all parties. Through negotiation and careful monitoring, ensures the efficient completion of the project.

Work Details

Quantity surveyors usually work a 35-40 hr week, Monday to Friday, though may be expected to have some early starts and late finishes, including some weekend work. Works for the developer who is financing the project or the contractor who is carrying out the work. May work on several projects and as part of a team.

Work is mainly office based, but also includes travel to different places for site inspections. You advise and negotiate with architects, engineers and builders, as well as clients. Participation in the planning and design stages of a project is crucial and you are responsible for overall cost control. You need to be able to handle complex calculations and work to deadlines. On-site inspection involves some physical activity.

Qualification

- **England, Wales and Northern Ireland**

Band 4: For BTEC higher national award: 1-2 A levels and some GCSEs (A*-C) usually including English, maths and possibly a science subject, or equivalent.

Band 5: For degree courses: 2-3 A levels and some GCSEs (A*-C) usually including English, maths and possibly a science subject, or equivalent. Exact requirements depend on the degree you take.

- **Scotland**

Band 4: For SQA higher national award: usually 2-3 H grades and some S grades (1-3), often including English, maths and possibly a science subject, or similar qualifications.

Band 5: For degree courses: 3-5 H grades and some S grades (1-3), usually including English, maths and possibly a science subject, or similar qualifications. Exact requirements depend on the degree you take.

Degree Information

A relevant degree in quantity surveying is preferred, although degrees in construction cost management, architecture, building or civil engineering may also be acceptable, especially if followed by an appropriate postgraduate qualification. Other related subjects may also be considered; details of approved degrees can be obtained from the Royal Institution of Chartered Surveyors (RICS), the Chartered Institute of Building and the Institution of Civil Engineering Surveyors.

Adult Qualifications

A relevant qualification, usually a degree or a higher national award, is normally required. Those with experience and/or qualifications in a related area may be accepted by the professional bodies for further training. Course entry requirements are usually relaxed for suitable mature applicants. Those without the required qualifications may complete a foundation or Access course leading to relevant HNDs or accredited degrees. Graduates without an accredited degree may take a one-year conversion course in surveying.

Work Experience

Employers or colleges/universities may prefer candidates who have relevant work or voluntary experience. This includes work in a surveyor's office or department within a local or county council, an architectural practice or a civil engineering firm. Student membership of the Royal Institute of Chartered Surveyors (RICS), or a related professional organisation, shows commitment to the profession.

Other schemes, such as 'A Year in Industry', enable those who expect good A levels/H grades and intend to go to university the opportunity to spend a salaried year with a company in order to gain valuable work experience.

Entry and Training

Most quantity surveyors qualify as members of the Royal Institute of Chartered Surveyors (RICS) by first completing an accredited degree or diploma. There are other professional qualifications that are also acceptable, such as through the Institution of Civil Engineering Surveyors or the Chartered Institute of Building. Contact the professional organisations for details. There are some professional exam exemptions for holders of relevant degrees and diplomas.

Most people first take a three-year full-time or four-year sandwich course for a degree/diploma. Some start by studying part time for an accredited course while working. All entrants continue to study by distance learning or day release for an appropriate professional qualification. A BSc in quantity surveying is available from the University of Reading, as a distance-learning course that meets the requirements for full membership of RICS. You should choose your training route carefully as they vary considerably. Contact RICS for further information on membership, training routes and courses.

To qualify as a chartered surveyor, graduates must complete the assessment of professional competence (APC) after two years' practical training while in employment, and must pass a final professional assessment interview. You must also commit to continuing professional development throughout your career.

Some quantity surveyors qualify as a surveying technician first (see separate job details) and then undertake further training. The Chartered Surveyors Training Trust provides advanced apprenticeships mainly in London and the South East. This can lead to qualification at level 3 and can also be a route into higher education. Appropriate foundation degrees are also available that can be studied full or part time. The CIOB also has a professional development programme which takes three years and is based on skills and competence requirements.

Mature applicants with experience in the construction industry or planning may have an advantage. Professional surveying institutions accept mature applicants through various routes of entry. Progression routes can also include S/NVQs, full-time, part-time, distance-learning, and foundation degree courses. Technical membership of the Royal Institute of Chartered Surveyors (RICS) can also provide a progression route to chartered status.

Opportunities and Pay

There are around 40,000 quantity surveyors in the UK. You can work in private practice, for a building contractor, a civil engineering firm/consultancy, or central or local government. Some are self-employed. Availability of work may depend on the state of the building trade and the national economy. Currently there is a downturn in the housing market which means there may be a shortage of vacancies. Promotion opportunities are generally better in larger organisations and management prospects may depend on a willingness to move to another office or area. Some become partners in a private practice. There are opportunities to work abroad.

Pay varies depending on area and type of company. A graduate entrant is likely to earn around £18k-£21k rising to £30k-£35k with experience and once fully qualified. Senior surveyors earn around £35k-£50k, while partners can earn in excess of £70k a year. Your pay may increase with commission and bonuses.

Health

This job requires good general fitness.

Skills and Qualities

aptitude for figures, aptitude for teamwork, attention to detail, business awareness, excellent communication skills, good presentation skills, information handling skills, IT skills, methodical, negotiating skills

Relevant Subjects

Business and accounting, Construction and built environment, Design and technology, Economics, English, Geography, ICT/Computer studies, Mathematics, Physics

Further Information

AGCAS: Engineering (Job Sector Briefing) (AGCAS) - www.prospects.ac.uk

Inside Careers Guide: Management - www.insidecareers.co.uk

TARGETjobs: Property (GTI Specialist Publishers Ltd) - www.groupgti.com

TARGETjobs: Quantity Surveying & Building Surveying (GTI Specialist Publishing Ltd) http:/www.groupgti.com

▶Working in construction & the built environment (2007) (Babcock Lifeskills) - www.babcock-lifeskills.com/

▶Working in maths (2009) (Babcock Lifeskills) - www.babcock-lifeskills.com/

Year in Industry (Engineering Development Trust) - www.yini.org.uk

Addresses

Chartered Institute of Building (CIOB)
Englemere King's Ride, Ascot, Berkshire SL5 7TB
Phone: +44 (0)1344 630 700
Web: www.ciob.org.uk

Chartered Surveyors Training Trust (CSTT)
16th Floor The Tower Building 11 York Road, London SE1 7NX
Phone: +44 (0)207 871 0454
Web: www.cstt.org.uk

Institution of Civil Engineering Surveyors (ICES)
Dominion House, Sibson Road, Sale, Cheshire M33 7PP
Phone: +44 (0)161 972 3100
Web: www.ices.org.uk

Royal Institution of Chartered Surveyors (RICS)
RICS Contact Centre, Surveyor Court, Westwood Way, Coventry CV4 8JE
Phone: +44 (0)870 333 1600
Web: www.ricscourses.org/pages/careers.aspx

Women into Science, Engineering & Construction (WISE)
2nd Floor Weston House, 246 High Holborn, London WC1V 7EX
Phone: +44 (0)20 3206 0408
Web: www.wisecampaign.org.uk

Similar Jobs

Clerk of Works/Site Inspector, Engineer: Building Services, Engineer: Civil/Structural, Surveying Technician, Surveyor: Building Control, Surveyor: General Practice

Surveyor: Rural Practice

also known as: Land Agent, Surveyor: Agricultural

CRCI:Building and Construction
CLCI:UM Job Band: 4 to 5

Job Description

Rural practiice surveyors provide specialist advice to the rural community about their agricultural land and buildings. They are concerned with every aspect of the management of agricultural land, rural estates and areas of forest. Thye value, buy and sell land for clients or large companies. Usually, they specialise in estate management (responsible for staff, stock and land) or in valuation work (valuing land, stock, timber, buildings and agricultural plant).

Surveyors give advice to farmers and landowners on how to unlock the value of their assets by diversification. May include selling livestock at auction, changing land use and rural management, without damaging the long-term value of their businesses.

Dealing with investments, tax laws and farming subsidies are all part of the specialist knowledge required for the job. May advise on rural planning such as alternative uses of land for camping and caravan sites, country parks, nature trails and reserves, or long-distance footpaths. Can be involved in national parks and also in auctions.

Work Details

May work a basic 35-40 hr week; Monday to Friday, but hours are more likely to be variable to fit in with clients. Works in an office as well as out on the land that you are managing. If you are responsible for a number of estates or properties you have to travel and this may include nights away from home. Running the estate efficiently and dealing with any complaints is your key responsibility.

Work requires sound judgement, knowledge of tax matters and familiarity with EU regulations. You can be out in all weathers covering rough ground, and conditions can be cold, wet and sometimes dirty and smelly.

Surveyor: Rural Practice

Qualification

- **England, Wales and Northern Ireland**

Band 4: For BTEC higher national award: 1-2 A levels and some GCSEs (A*-C) usually including English, maths, geography and possibly a science subject, or equivalent.

Band 5: For degree courses: 2-3 A levels and some GCSEs (A*-C) usually including English and maths, or equivalent. Other useful subjects include geography, geology, physical science, economics, law, IT and business studies. Exact requirements depend on the degree you take.

- **Scotland**

Band 4: For SQA higher national award: usually 2-3 H grades and some S grades (1-3), often including English, maths, geography and possibly a science subject, or similar qualifications.

Band 5: For degree courses: 3-5 H grades and some S grades (1-3), usually including English and maths, or similar qualifications. Other useful subjects include geography, geology, physical science, economics, law, IT and business studies. Exact requirements depend on the degree you take.

Degree Information

An approved degree in rural planning, rural resource planning, land economy, surveying or land/estate surveying, rural enterprise and land management or estate/property management is preferred. Degrees in agriculture, business studies, forestry and geography (human) give useful background knowledge. Postgraduate courses are available for those with non-related degrees. Details of approved degrees can be obtained from the Royal Institution of Chartered Surveyors (RICS) or the Central Association of Agricultural Valuers (CAAV).

Adult Qualifications

A relevant qualification, usually a degree, is normally required and those with a relevant HND, such as land and property, are normally required to top this up to a preferred degree. Those with experience and/or qualifications in a related area may be accepted by the professional bodies for further training. Course entry requirements are usually relaxed for suitable mature applicants. Those without the required qualifications may complete a foundation/Access course leading to relevant HNDs or accredited degrees. Graduates without an accredited degree may take a one-year conversion course in surveying.

Work Experience

Employers or colleges/universities may prefer candidates who have relevant work or voluntary experience. This includes experience in a surveyor's practice or a surveying department of a local or county council. Experience of work on a farm or on the land is also very important. Student membership of the Royal Institute of Chartered Surveyors (RICS), or a related professional organisation, shows commitment to the profession.

Other schemes, such as 'A Year in Industry', offer those who expect good A levels/H grades and intend to go to university, the opportunity to spend a salaried year with a company in order to gain valuable work experience.

Entry and Training

Most rural surveyors qualify as members of the Royal Institute of Chartered Surveyors (RICS) by first completing an accredited degree or diploma. There are other professional qualifications that are also acceptable, such as those through the Central Association of Agricultural Valuers (CAAV). There are some professional exam exemptions for holders of relevant degrees and diplomas.

Most people first take a three-year full-time or four-year sandwich course for a degree/diploma, but some start by studying part time for an accredited course while working. For those with non-related degrees there are some appropriate postgraduate conversion courses. All entrants continue to study by distance learning or day release for an appropriate professional qualification. The College of Estate Management offers distance-learning courses for those currently working in the profession, including a BSc in estate management and a diploma in surveying practice that meets RICS requirements. You should choose your course carefully as they vary considerably. Contact RICS or CAAV for further information on membership, training routes and courses.

To qualify as a chartered surveyor, graduates must complete the assessment of professional competence (APC) after two years' practical training and must pass a final professional assessment interview. You must also commit to continuing professional development throughout your career.

Another route towards becoming a chartered surveyor is by first qualifying as a surveying technician (see separate job details). Some may choose to study by distance learning to gain the RICS diploma in valuation, rather than gain chartered surveyor status. Advanced apprenticeships leading to qualification at level 3 may be available in your area and can also be a route into higher education. S/NVQs are available at levels 3-4 in surveying, property and maintenance. Appropriate foundation degrees are also available and can be studied full or part time.

Mature applicants with experience in agriculture, construction or planning may have an advantage. Professional surveying institutions accept mature applicants through various routes of entry. Progression routes can also include S/NVQs, full-time, part-time, distance-learning, and foundation degree courses. Technical membership (Tech RICS) of the Royal Institute of Chartered Surveyors (RICS) can also provide a progression route to chartered status.

Opportunities and Pay

Most rural surveyors work for private firms of chartered surveyors or for a firm of agricultural surveyors, central or local government, or other land-owning organisations, such as the National Trust. There are opportunities for employment in leisure and tourism, with charities or utility companies, or with property developers. Some may also specialise in valuation and auction work. There are a few opportunities to work as a lecturer at an agricultural college or with other universities. Some become self-employed.

Pay varies depending on area and type of company. A graduate entrant is likely to earn around £20k-£25k. The average salary for an experienced surveyor is about £36k a year. Your pay may increase with commission, bonuses and other benefits.

Health

This job requires good general fitness.

Skills and Qualities

aptitude for maths and science, attention to detail, business awareness, diplomatic, discreet, good communication skills, good interpersonal skills, information handling skills, negotiating skills, understanding of legal technicalities

Relevant Subjects

Business and accounting, Construction and built environment, Economics, English, Geography, Land and Environment, Mathematics

Further Information

Apprenticeship Schemes (National Apprenticeship Service) - www.apprenticeships.org.uk

CAAV Newsletter (quarterly) (Central Association of Agricultural Valuers (CAAV)) - www.caav.org.uk

Farmer's Weekly Interactive (Reed International) - www.fwi.co.uk

TARGETjobs: Property (GTI Specialist Publishers Ltd) - www.groupgti.com

▶Working in construction & the built environment (2007) (Babcock Lifeskills) - www.babcock-lifeskills.com/

Year in Industry (Engineering Development Trust) - www.yini.org.uk

Addresses

Central Association of Agricultural Valuers (CAAV)
Market Chambers, 35 Market Place, Coleford,
Gloucestershire GL16 8AA
Phone: +44 (0)1594 832 979
Web: www.caav.org.uk

College of Estate Management (CEM)
Whiteknights, Reading, Berkshire RG6 6AW
Phone: 0800 019 9697 UK only
Web: www.cem.ac.uk

Royal Institution of Chartered Surveyors (RICS)
RICS Contact Centre, Surveyor Court, Westwood Way,
Coventry CV4 8JE
Phone: +44 (0)870 333 1600
Web: www.ricscourses.org/pages/careers.aspx

Women into Science, Engineering & Construction (WISE)
2nd Floor Weston House, 246 High Holborn, London WC1V 7EX
Phone: +44 (0)20 3206 0408
Web: www.wisecampaign.org.uk

Similar Jobs

Agricultural Consultant/Adviser, Estate Agent, Factor (Scotland), Farm Manager, Surveyor: General Practice

Switchboard Operator

also known as: Telephonist

CRCI:Administration, Business and Office Work
CLCI:CAI Job Band: 1 to 2

Job Description

Switchboard operators operate a telephone switchboard for a large or small business. They quickly answer incoming calls and pass them through to the correct person. Operators mainly answer enquiries and take messages. May direct a call to an automatic 'voice mail' service when employees cannot take the call. Some work for a telephone-operating company where the work includes dealing with directory enquiries. Others may receive customer queries or complaints and pass these on to the relevant person. Some work at an emergency call centre, putting callers through to the emergency services. You usually work in front of a computer screen with access to a database.

The job is often combined with reception/front of house duties where operators welcome visitors, answer enquiries and may show visitors to a waiting area. Other duties may include daily office tasks, such as maintaining a visitors' book, handing out the mail, and faxing documents.

Work Details

Usually work around 35-39 hrs a week, Monday to Friday, and during daytime hours. However, may be required to work a rota of shifts to cover organisations that operate over 24 hours a day. This can include night shifts and weekends. Some jobs are part time or on a job-share basis. Short-term contract and casual work is also possible, usually through an agency. You have to spend a long time sitting at switchboard or a VDU, usually wearing a headset.

Sometimes you have to deal with several calls at once. Some of the callers may be annoyed, so you need to remain polite and helpful at all times.

Qualification

• England, Wales and Northern Ireland

Band 1: For many jobs you do not need any formal qualifications. However, you are expected to have a good level of general education. Good written and verbal communication, computer skills and accuracy are an advantage. Some formal/vocational qualifications at any level are useful.

Band 2: For direct entry to the job: no minimum qualifications, though employers prefer some GCSEs (A*-C) including English, or equivalent. Subjects such as maths and IT may also be useful. Good written and verbal communication, computer skills and accuracy are often requested.

• Scotland

Band 1: For many jobs you do not need any formal qualifications. However, you are expected to have a good level of general education. Good written and verbal communication, computer skills and accuracy are an advantage. Some formal/vocational qualifications at any level are useful.

Band 2: For direct entry to the job: no minimum qualifications, though it is an advantage to have some S grades (1-3) including English, or similar. Subjects such as maths and IT may also be useful. Good written and verbal communication, computer skills and accuracy are often requested.

Adult Qualifications

There are no set qualifications for entry though many employers require you to have a good standard of spoken English.

Work Experience

Relevant work or voluntary experience is always useful and can equip you with skills that you can use in the future and that you can add to your CV. Temporary holiday work in offices or call centres via employment agencies is useful, particularly if you can develop good keyboard and telephone skills and experience of dealing with people.

Entry and Training

You may have to take an aptitude test to get into this job. Training is on the job with an experienced operator and includes learning about the switchboard, VDU and keyboard. Short courses on telephone techniques may sometimes be offered at a local college or training organisation, or may be included in business studies and secretarial courses. If you can speak a foreign language, you may be able to work on calls to and from other countries.

S/NVQs are available at levels 1-4 in customer service and at levels 1-2 in contact centre operations. Training programmes, including apprenticeship schemes, may be available in your area for entry to this job.

Mature entrants require no minimum entry requirements though a good general education is expected. Those with a relevant background in customer care, telesales, or call centre experience may have an advantage.

Opportunities and Pay

Jobs are available throughout the UK. You can work for a telephone company, hotel or hospital. Jobs are also available in local/central government, finance services, large shops and stores, and colleges. In some companies you can become a manager, looking after a number of telephonists and training new employees. Modern telephone systems have reduced the number of jobs, as most employees can now dial and receive their own calls. The job may be combined with other duties, such as reception/front of house.

Pay varies depending on location and employer. Most operators earn around £12k-£17k a year. This can rise to around £18k-£21k a year with experience.

Health

You need good hearing and clear speech in this job.

Skills and Qualities

able to cope under pressure, able to work quickly, clear speaking voice, customer service skills, even tempered, good communication skills, good interpersonal skills, good memory, IT skills, polite

Relevant Subjects
English

Further Information
Apprenticeship Schemes (National Apprenticeship Service) - www.apprenticeships.org.uk

Real Life Guide to Business & Administration (Trotman 2009) - www.trotman.co.uk

▶Working in retail & customer services (2008) (Babcock Lifeskills) - www.babcock-lifeskills.com/

Addresses
Council for Administration (CFA)
6 Graphite Square, Vauxhall Walk, London SE11 5EE
Phone: +44 (0)20 7091 9620
Web: www.cfa.uk.com

Institute of Customer Service (ICS)
2 Castle Court, St Peter's Street, Colchester, Essex CO1 1EW
Phone: +44 (0)1206 571716
Web: www.instituteofcustomerservice.com

Similar Jobs
Contact Centre Operator, Emergency Services Control Room Operator, Hotel Receptionist, Local Government Administrative Assistant, Receptionist

Tailor
also known as: Bespoke Tailor, Handcraft Tailor

CRCI:Manufacturing and Production

CLCI:SAH — Job Band: 2 to 3

Job Description
Tailors make made-to-measure (bespoke) handmade garments such as coats and suits to fit individual customers. They usually work with a team of assistants who do simpler sewing tasks, but may sometimes work alone. Discussions about the style of the clothes, the fabric required and taking customers' measurements are all part of the service. The customer receives a quote detailing the cost of material and estimated time to make the garment, and if accepted, the style is converted to a pattern. The pattern is used to cut the cloth, matching and marking it carefully.

The tailor then loosely stitches (bastes) the garment for fitting, makes adjustments and sews it together by hand and machine. Some tailors make a garment entirely by hand for exclusive customers. May specialise in suits, kilts or military uniforms. May spend some time researching and getting design ideas from brochures, pattern books and exhibitions.

Work Details
Waged tailors usually work a standard five-day 40 hr week, though overtime is common. You may need to be prepared to work some evenings and weekends for customer fittings. You work in a workshop, a shop, which is usually warm and well lit, or possibly at home. You give advice to customers and need to be aware of current fashion trends. The work can be close and intricate, although some jobs can be repetitive. You may have deadlines to meet, which put you under pressure.

Qualification

• England, Wales and Northern Ireland
Band 2: Formal qualifications are not always essential, but some employers prefer GCSEs, including English, maths, art and design, or equivalent.

Band 3: For some courses: usually at least 4 GCSEs (A*-C) including English and maths, art and design or equivalent. For those with fewer qualifications, a good portfolio of work may help you to get on a course.

• Scotland
Band 2: Formal qualifications are not always essential, but some employers prefer some S grades, including English, maths, art and design, or similar.

Band 3: For some courses: usually at least four S grades (1-3) including English and maths, art and design or similar. For those with fewer qualifications, a good portfolio of work may help you to get on a course.

Adult Qualifications
A good standard of secondary education is expected. Some colleges consider adults without formal qualifications but with relevant experience.

Work Experience
Work or voluntary experience is always useful. It can improve your chances when applying for jobs or apprenticeships. Your personal or adult guidance adviser should be able to advise you how to get work experience.

Entry and Training
Training can often be through an apprenticeship with on-the-job training and day or block release to a college to gain qualifications. This can take up to five years to complete. Newham College in conjunction with Savile Row offer a four-year apprenticeship in bespoke tailoring; there is fierce competition for places. Some entrants may choose to do courses to develop their skills before entering this work. Suitable courses include ABC level 3 diploma in handcraft tailoring, ABC level 3 in pattern cutting and construction techniques and City & Guilds certificate in design and craft at levels 1-3.

The London College of Fashion runs a BA (Hons) in bespoke tailoring. Tailoring courses are available at other institutions throughout the UK. Check the UCAS website for details.

Once trained, tailors are likely to continue to perfect their techniques by learning new skills from other experienced tailors.

Government training opportunities, such as apprenticeships, may be available in your area. You can also gain recognition of previous experience through Accreditation of Prior Learning (APL) or by working towards relevant S/NVQs. Contact your local careers office, Jobcentre Plus, Next Step service or Learning and Skills Council (LSC) Local Enterprise Company (LEC) for details of training schemes.

Opportunities and Pay
Most large bespoke tailoring houses are in major cities, particularly London. There is still a demand for made-to-measure garments from those who value hand-crafted clothes. However, there is a decline in bespoke tailoring in the UK due to competition from abroad. The popularity of off-the-peg suits has also had an adverse impact on the industry.

You can be employed by a manufacturing company, a firm of bespoke tailors, a shop, or large retail store. Promotion to supervisory and management level is possible. You may be able to become self-employed after training. There are often opportunities to travel abroad for those at the top of their profession.

Pay varies depending on location and employer. Once trained, salaries start at around £10.5k-£13k a year, rising to £18k with experience. High class tailors such as those on Savile Row (London) and successful self-employed tailors, earn up to £50k. Tailors may be paid a set amount for each garment they produce (piece work). The amount you earn very much depends on your skill, ability and pace of work.

Health
This job requires good eyesight and good colour vision for certain areas of work.

Skills and Qualities
accurate, attention to detail, excellent sewing skills, eye for shape/colour, eye for visual effect, good communication skills, good concentration level, manual dexterity, numeracy skills, smart appearance

Relevant Subjects
Art and Design

Further Information
ABC Awards - www.abcawards.co.uk

Apprenticeship Schemes (National Apprenticeship Service) - www.apprenticeships.org.uk

Savile Row Bespoke Association - www.savilerowbespoke.com

Skillset - sector skills council for the creative media, fashion and textiles industries - www.skillset.org

Training Schemes - www.direct.gov.uk/en/educationandlearning

▶Working in fashion & clothing (2008) (Babcock Lifeskills) - www.babcock-lifeskills.com/

Addresses
London College of Fashion
20 John Princes Street, London W1G 0BJ
Phone: +44 (0)20 7514 7344
Web: www.fashion.arts.ac.uk

Newham College of Further Education
East Ham Campus, High Street South, London E6 6ER
Phone: +44 (0)29 8257 4000
Web: www.newham.ac.uk

Similar Jobs
Clothing Alteration Hand, Clothing Pattern Cutter/Grader, Costume Designer, Dressmaker, Film/TV & Theatre Wardrobe Assistant, Upholsterer

Tattooist
also known as: Body Artist
CRCI:Personal and Other Services
CLCI:IZ Job Band: 1 to 5

Job Description
Tattooists use technical and artistic skills to decorate a client's body with designs, words and pictures, by injecting tiny amounts of coloured ink into the top layer of skin. They discuss the design with clients and ensure they understand that a tattoo is permanent. Then draw the design or apply a transfer onto the customer's skin. They use a special machine with electrically operated inkjet needles to create tiny holes in the skin, and traces the outline of the shape. The holes are filled with pigments (colours) and blended to create the final design.

Some tattooists may specialise in a design (called a 'flash'), such as Aboriginal tribal armbands, Egyptian and Viking designs, or Chinese symbols. May also create new designs and sell them. Some tattooists combine their work with body piercing.

Work Details
Usually work 5-6 days a week, including some evenings and on Saturdays. Work is in a shop or studio, which may be attached to a beauty salon or other cosmetic service, such as body piercing. Studios are normally light, warm and hygienic. The work takes place in a private cubicle or room. You spend most of the time seated or standing, whilst concentrating on a small area of a client's skin.

You need to wear protective gloves and maintain high standards of hygiene and safety. You also must be able to cope with the sight of blood. Sometimes you may have to cope with clients who are nervous or who are unhappy with their tattoos.

Qualification
Tattooists can range from those with little or no formal educational qualifications, to those who may have already had a background in fine arts or graphics, perhaps up to degree level, or similar.

Adult Qualifications
No specific educational qualifications are needed for entry to this job, although you may be asked for a portfolio of artistic work

Work Experience
Experience in a tattoo studio on a short-term basis may be very difficult to gain. Other relevant areas to consider are cosmetic services or beauty therapy or any work that allows you to develop your artistic and design skills. It is very helpful to build up a portfolio of work.

Entry and Training
Entrants can range from talented school/college leavers to graduates, often with an art and design background. Artistic flair is essential. Applicants often need an up-to-date portfolio of their work, showing their design skills and artistic talent. There are no formal courses leading to qualification as a tattooist. Entry is usually via a traineeship with a registered and skilled tattooist that normally lasts around two to three years. You receive on-the-job training and learn technical skills, health and safety, how to run a business, as well as customer care skills. However, training opportunities are rare and most trainees are over 18.

Tattooists have to be registered with the local environmental health department and follow strict guidelines on maintaining hygienic premises and equipment. Failure to do this can result in the equipment being confiscated, fines imposed and the premises shut down. You may be expected to purchase and maintain your own equipment, which can cost in the region of £5k.

Mature entrants with a background or qualifications in art and design have an advantage. Areas such as graphic arts and fashion, or in beauty therapy and cosmetics, provide valuable experience for this type of work.

Opportunities and Pay
Almost all fully trained tattooists are self-employed. The demand for tattoos has increased in recent years and there are opportunities to work throughout the country. However, it may be difficult to find a studio that will take on a trainee, and you may need to travel to a different area to secure training. There are some opportunities for work abroad.

Trainees are sometimes required to pay for their on-the-job training, which can cost from £5k-£10k, until fully trained. A newly trained tattooist earns around £6 an hour (around £10k a year for full-time work). Experienced tattooists charge for each piece of work or tattoo, the inks used and the complexity of the design. Tattoos can cost from around £30-£100 each. Generally, full time and established tattooists can earn from £23k-£38k a year, or more. Earnings depend on the reputation of your work and studio location.

Health
This job requires normal colour vision.

Skills and Qualities
able to put people at ease, attention to detail, business awareness, creative flair, eye for shape/colour, eye for visual effect, good communication skills, health & safety awareness, not squeamish, steady hand

Relevant Subjects
Art and Design, Biology, Health and social care, Science

Addresses
British Tattoo Artists Federation
389 Cowley Road, Oxford OX4 2BS
Phone: +44 (0)1865 716 877
Web: www.tattoo.co.uk

Similar Jobs
Artist, Beauty Consultant, Film/TV & Theatre Make-Up Artist, Graphic Design: Studio Junior, Graphic Designer, Nail Technician

Tax Adviser
also known as: Financial Consultant: Tax, Tax Practitioner, Tax Technician

CRCI:Financial Services
CLCI:NAK
Job Band: 3 to 5

Job Description
Tax advisers use a combination of law, administration and accountancy to provide tax advice to companies and individual clients. Need to understand tax legislation and to be able to explain it to clients in simple language that they can understand. Keeping up to date with changes in tax legislation is very important in this job.

They review the client's financial circumstances and work out the amount of tax that they need to pay and when it is due. Prepare tax returns and may deal with HM Revenue and Customs on their behalf. Advise on ways to reduce tax bills and audit tax records. Some tax advisers offer other financial services and produce reports for clients.

Help with tax planning by analysing the client's financial accounts and giving advice on the tax implications of future business plans and transactions. May also work with companies that trade overseas and assess international tax. May specialise in a particular area of tax, such as VAT or personal tax.

Work Details
Usually work a 37 hr week, Monday to Friday. Depending on the employer, you may do some evening or weekend work, particularly at the end of the financial year. Self employment is quite common for experienced tax advisers. You work in an office and use a computer, but also spend time travelling to meet clients. This can be a challenging environment to work in as it is constantly changing. The work may be stressful at times.

Qualification

• England, Wales and Northern Ireland
Band 3: For entry and to register as a student with the Association of Taxation Technicians (ATT): usually at least 4 GCSEs (A*-C) including English and maths, or equivalent.

Band 4: For BTEC higher national award: 1-2 A levels and some GCSEs (A*-C) usually including English and maths, or equivalent.

Band 5: For degree courses: 2-3 A levels and some GCSEs (A*-C) usually including English and maths, or equivalent. Exact requirements depend on the degree you take.

• Scotland
Band 3: For entry and to register as a student with the Association of Taxation Technicians (ATT): usually at least four S grades (1-3) including English and maths, or equivalent.

Band 4: For SQA higher national award: usually 2-3 H grades and some S grades (1-3), often including English and maths, or similar qualifications.

Band 5: For degree courses: 3-5 H grades and some S grades (1-3), usually including English and maths, or similar qualifications. Exact requirements depend on the degree you take.

Degree Information
Subjects such as economics, management and business or finance are useful. Law and maths are also relevant. There are specialist degrees in law and taxation or accounting and taxation.

Adult Qualifications
Entry requirements may be relaxed for adults applying for higher education courses. Access or foundation courses provide those without the required qualifications a route onto degree courses. Adults who are qualified solicitors or accountants are exempt from some of the professional exams and can register directly with the Chartered Institute of Taxation.

Work Experience
Relevant work or voluntary experience is always useful and can improve your employment prospects when applying for entry to jobs. Try to obtain vacation work, attend relevant workshops and arrange to meet or shadow tax practitioners if possible.

Entry and Training
Most entrants are graduates or have obtained a further qualification after leaving school. They often find employment and start work as a tax trainee for a tax company. However, it is also possible to get a trainee position directly after leaving school. There are two main areas to work in as a tax adviser. You can either work for the government or in private practice or industry as a tax practitioner. Her Majesty's Revenue and Customs has a structured career and training path. Check the website for full details.

Two main bodies award tax qualifications in the UK, the Association of Taxation Technicians (ATT) and the Chartered Institute of Taxation (CIOT). To become a tax technician, you need to pass the ATT exams in four certificates of competency. These include subjects such as personal taxation, business taxation and accounting principles. With two years' experience, it is then possible to move on to take the CIOT exams to become a Chartered Tax Adviser (CTA). The CTA qualification can be studied part time and through distance learning. Qualified accountants and lawyers are exempt from the ATT exams and can specialise in tax by directly taking the CIOT exams.

Continuing professional development (CPD) is an important and key element throughout your career to keep up to date with the latest developments. Tax is an ever changing area and the ATT and the CIOT support members by offering a range of courses and seminars to provide CPD. The CIOT offers the advanced diploma in international taxation for those who want to specialise in this area.

Foundation degrees in financial services are available. A Diploma/ Welsh Baccalaureate in business, administration and finance may be available in your area and may be relevant for entry to this career. The advanced level is equivalent to 3.5 A levels but for some university courses, the additional and specialist learning (ASL) component of the diploma needs to include specific A levels Check entry requirements carefully with individual institutions.

There are opportunities for qualified lawyers and accountants to specialise in tax and move into this career. Distance learning courses to study for the Association of Taxation Technicians or the Chartered Institute of Taxation exams are available.

Opportunities and Pay
The tax environment changes according to the economy, government and changes to legislation so opportunities vary from year to year. However, if you are well qualified and obtain experience this can be a stable and well-paid career. Jobs are available in cities and towns throughout the UK with accountants, solicitors and tax consultancy companies, as well as HM Revenue and Customs. Large companies also employ tax advisers.

Those with the relevant experience and qualifications can go on to become senior professional practice tax managers or to work in commercial management. Some become self employed tax consultants and run consultancy businesses. There are also opportunities to work overseas.

Starting salaries for tax trainees can be around £19k-£25k a year, rising to £35k for part-qualified tax advisers Qualified chartered tax advisers earn £35k-£50k a year. Senior tax advisers can earn up to £60k and those with director or partner status can earn £120k.

Skills and Qualities
good communication skills, good interpersonal skills, good listening skills, good organisational skills, information handling skills, IT skills, numeracy skills, objective, problem-solving skills, trustworthy.

Relevant Subjects
Business and accounting, Economics, English, ICT/Computer studies, Law, Mathematics.

Further Information
AGCAS: Accountancy and Business Services (Job Sector Briefing) (AGCAS) - www.prospects.ac.uk/

Diploma in Business, Administration and Finance - www.baf-diploma.org.uk/

Financial Services Skills Council - sector skills council for financial services, accountancy & finance - www.fssc.org.uk/

HM Revenue & Customs (HMRC) - www.hmrc.gov.uk

Inside Careers Guide: Chartered Tax Advisers - www.insidecareers.co.uk

TARGETjobs: City and Finance (GTI Specialist Publishers Ltd) - www.groupgti.com

Tax Working - www.taxworking.org

Taxation Magazine (Reed Elsevier Limited) - www.taxation.co.uk

Welsh Baccalaureate - www.wbq.org.uk

▶Working in advice & counselling (2007) (Babcock Lifeskills) - www.babcock-lifeskills.com/

▶Working in business, administration & finance (2010) (Babcock Lifeskills) - www.babcock-lifeskills.com/

▶Working in maths (2009) (Babcock Lifeskills) - www.babcock-lifeskills.com/

Addresses
Association of Taxation Technicians (ATT)
1st Floor, Artillery House, 11-19 Artillery Row, London SW1P 1RT
Phone: 0844 251 0830 (UK only)
Web: www.att.org.uk

Chartered Institute of Taxation (CIOT)
First Floor, 11-19 Artillery Row, London SW1P 1RT
Phone: +44 (0)20 7340 0550
Web: www.tax.org.uk

Personal Finance Society (PFS)
42-48 High Road, South Woodford, London E18 2JP
Phone: +44 (0)20 8530 0852
Web: www.thepfs.org

Similar Jobs
Accountant: Private Practice, Civil Service Tax Inspector, Compliance Officer, Debt Counsellor, Financial Adviser/Planner, Pensions Adviser

Taxidermist

CRCI:Environment, Animals and Plants
CLCI:WAZ Job Band: 2 to 3

Job Description
Taxidermists specialise in the art and craft of preserving animals, birds and fish so that they look lifelike. They make models of the original body using an artificial framework and natural hide, skin or feathers. This involves studying how the animal stands and building the model using materials such as steel rods, fibreglass, wood, and papier-machi. They skin the animal and then tan (soak in a chemical) the skin before fitting it to the framework. Then put the eyes (usually acrylic or glass), teeth, claws and other parts into place. If working on a display, for example in a museum, they create a natural background and put the specimen in a natural position.

Sometimes taxidermists specialise in animal victims of road accidents or in game species. They keep detailed records of how the creature was obtained, understand any legal aspects of taxidermy, and keep to a strict code of practice.

Work Details
Work regular office hours in a workshop of a museum, or if self-employed, perhaps in your own home with flexible working hours. Some taxidermists may work alone, meeting very few people. Work is intricate and can require coping with unpleasant sights. You need to wear protective clothing and eye goggles, particularly when working with chemicals.

Qualification
Artistic ability, manual skills and an interest in wildlife are often seen as more important than qualifications.

• England, Wales and Northern Ireland
Band 3: For a junior post in a museum it is an advantage to have 3-5 GCSEs (A*-C) usually including maths, English, art, chemistry and biology, or equivalent qualifications.

• Scotland
Band 3: For a junior post in a museum it is an advantage to have 3-5 S grades (1-3) usually including maths, English, art, chemistry and biology, or similar qualifications.

Adult Qualifications
Evidence of artistic ability and manual dexterity are important. Qualifications may not be needed, depending on the employer. Experience in modelmaking or craft skills are an advantage.

Work Experience
Relevant work or voluntary experience is always useful and can improve your chances in application for entry to this job as this is a shrinking profession, and a very specialised job. Voluntary work experience may be possible in museums, where some aspects of taxidermy may be covered. It can also be useful to directly approach a qualified taxidermist for work experience.

Entry and Training
There are no national recognised qualifications for this work. Many taxidermists are self taught, but some may find on-the-job training alongside a more experienced taxidermist. An interest in natural history eg bird watching or collecting animal bones and skulls, is useful. The Guild of Taxidermists runs short courses in certain aspects of taxidermy, including one-day seminars and a two-day annual conference. It has a qualification system to credit members' work. They have levels such as 'specialist' and 'master' for those with a lot of experience and skill.

Mature applicants may find that younger people may be preferred for training posts, though much depends on the dedication and artistic ability of each applicant.

Opportunities and Pay
This is a small profession and few vacancies arise. You can work for a local authority, national or independent museum, or for a commercial taxidermy firm. Success may depend on contacts and personal reputation. This can be a satisfying career and one which is of benefit to science, for those who have an interest in nature and a general aptitude for intricate work. For senior posts in museums, professional membership of the Guild of Taxidermists is needed. There are opportunities to work part time or you can be self employed.

For those who are self-employed earnings are generally low and most have an alternative source of income. Taxidermists employed by a museum earn around £12k-£30k a year or more, if taking on a managerial role. There may be the opportunity to earn up to £50k a year.

Health
This job requires good eyesight and normal colour vision for many areas of work. Working with some of the chemicals used can be difficult for those with allergies or asthma.

Skills and Qualities
able to work well on your own, attention to detail, eye for shape/ colour, imaginative, manual dexterity, not squeamish, observant, patient, practical skills, scientific approach

Relevant Subjects
Art and Design, Biology, Chemistry, Design and technology, Science

Further Information
Creative & Cultural Skills - sector skills council for advertising, crafts, cultural heritage, design, literature, music, performing & visual arts - www.ccskills.org.uk
Guild of Taxidermists Journal (annual) - www.taxidermy.org.uk
Real Life Guide to Working with Animals & Wildlife (Trotman) - www.trotman.co.uk

Addresses
Guild of Taxidermists
c/o Lancashire County Museums Stanley Street, Preston PR1 4YP
Web: www.taxidermy.org.uk

Museums Association (MA)
24 Calvin Street, London E1 6NW
Web: www.museumsassociation.org

Similar Jobs
Anatomical Pathology Technician, Embalmer, Museum Assistant/ Technician

Teacher: Art
CRCI:Education and Training
CLCI:FAB Job Band: 5

Job Description
Art teachers motivate and encourage the imagination and creativity of students through the teaching of art, design and crafts in schools and colleges. They prepare and deliver structured learning programmes, plan lessons and use a variety of resources, such as textbooks, the internet, audio-visual materials, worksheets as well as practical work. May teach a range of art and design disciplines, such as painting and drawing, printing, ceramics, photography, modelmaking and computer aided design (CAD), or may specialise in one discipline only, such as ceramics. They set projects, oversee and correct students' practical work and help to develop their individual talent. Also organise exhibitions of students' work.

Some teachers prepare students for national examinations. They set and mark internal assessments and exams. They also record the progress of each pupil and give individual advice and guidance. Attending meetings including parents' evenings and help to organise school or group outings, such as a visit to an art gallery or exhibition, is also part of the job.

Work Details
You work in a school, a sixth form college or possibly tutoring at home; teaching, supervising and advising students. Mostly work 39 weeks a year in a school, with contact teaching time between 9am-3.30pm, Monday to Friday. In some schools, usually in the independent sector, work fewer weeks a year, but often including a Saturday during term-time. This job is very satisfying if you wish to work with young people. Talent, creativity and imagination is required. You also have contact with other professional colleagues, as well as parents/carers.

You should be able to relate well to young people and are responsible for supporting learners to reach required learning targets. The job involves undertaking out-of-hours duties and working at home, for example on lesson preparation and writing reports. Most jobs require you to be on your feet all day. Teaching is a demanding but very rewarding profession.

Qualification
- **England, Wales and Northern Ireland**

Band 5: For degree courses: 2-3 A levels, possibly including art, and some GCSEs (A*-C) usually including English and maths, or equivalent. A good portfolio of art work is required. Exact requirements depend on the degree you take.

- **Scotland**

Band 5: For degree course in an art and design subject: 3-5 H grades, including art and design or product design and preferably English, and some S grades, including maths, or similar qualifications. A good portfolio of your art work is required.

Degree Information
The degree should be in an art and design subject followed by a postgraduate certificate in education course (PGCE). BEd degrees can only be used to teach art in primary schools.

Adult Qualifications
Mature applicants with outstanding portfolios of work may be accepted for art and design degree courses without the standard requirements. In some areas there are Access and foundation courses, which give adults without qualifications a route onto degree courses. Check with individual colleges.

Work Experience
Entry to this job is competitive and it is important that you do some relevant work experience before applying to teacher training. You should work towards building a portfolio of your artistic talent and any art experience gained. Visits to art galleries and museums are valuable. Applicants are also advised to show evidence of their interest in and commitment to teaching by working with young people, such as being a voluntary helper in a school, a youth club, sports group, or holiday play activity/sports scheme.

Entry and Training
Most art/art and design teachers have an art and design degree. A portfolio of work is needed for entry to all art and design courses. All those working with young people are required to have a Criminal Records Bureau (CRB)/Disclosure Scotland check.

In England and Wales, to teach in a mainstream or special school, you need qualified teacher status (QTS) achieved by taking an undergraduate or postgraduate certificate in education course (PGCE) or through an employment-based route into teaching, and train on the job.

In Scotland, the quickest and most popular way to qualify as an art teacher is to have a degree in an art related subject and then do a one-year professional graduate diploma in education (PGDE).

For full details on the entry route to teaching throughout the UK, please read the article Teacher: Secondary School.

Mature applicants are encouraged and there are many options for training and qualification, including distance-learning courses.

For further details on all teacher training routes throughout the UK, please read the article Teacher: Secondary School.

Opportunities and Pay

Teachers are mainly employed in state schools and the numbers are steadily increasing. Work is also available in independent schools, colleges and academies, adult learning centres, pupil referral units, secure training units or young offenders' institutions, and the armed forces. There are opportunities for promotion, for example to head of department and beyond, though your prospects may depend on willingness to move to another area. Part-time work, private tuition, supply teaching and job-sharing is possible. Work abroad is also available.

A newly qualified teacher (NQT) earns from around £21k a year. A career changer or mature entrant may, depending on previous experience, start at a higher level in the scale.

Additional responsibilities in a school can attract a higher salary. Advanced Skills Teachers (ASTs) earn from around £36k-£55k a year. Teachers in the independent sector can usually expect to earn a higher salary with additional perks, such as subsidised accommodation and school fees.

There is an allowance for working in London. You are advised to contact your local education department or other employer for full salary scale/grade details.

Health

You have to pass a health check to get into teaching.

Skills and Qualities

able to discipline, able to explain clearly, able to stimulate learners, artistic ability, fair minded, good communication skills, good organisational skills, IT skills, self confident, tactful

Relevant Subjects

Art and Design, Design and technology, English, ICT/Computer studies, Psychology, Sociology

Further Information

Open University - www.open.ac.uk

Scottish Government - Education and Training - www.scotland.gov.uk/Topics/Education

Teach First - www.teachfirst.org.uk

Teachernet (Dept for Education) - www.teachernet.gov.uk

Teaching Scotland Magazine (GTCS magazine) - www.gtcs.org.uk

Teaching Training Wales - www.educationcymru.org

Training & Development Agency (TDA) - www.tda.gov.uk

▶Working in art & design (2009) (Babcock Lifeskills) - www.babcock-lifeskills.com/

▶Working in schools & colleges (2007) (Babcock Lifeskills) - www.babcock-lifeskills.com/

Addresses

Department of Education NI (DENI)
Rathgael House, Balloo Road, Bangor BT19 7PR
Phone: +44 (0)28 9127 9279
Web: www.deni.gov.uk

General Teaching Council for England (GTC)
Whittington House, 19-30 Alfred Place, London WC1E 7EA
Phone: 0370 001 0308 (UK only)
Web: www.gtce.org.uk

General Teaching Council for Northern Ireland (GTCNI)
4th Floor, Albany House, 73-75 Great Victoria Street, Belfast BT2 7AF
Phone: +44 (0)28 9033 3390
Web: www.gtcni.org.uk

General Teaching Council for Scotland (GTC Scotland)
Clerwood House, 96 Clermiston Road, Edinburgh EH12 6UT
Phone: +44 (0)131 314 6000
Web: www.gtcs.org.uk

General Teaching Council for Wales (GTCW)
4th Floor, Southgate House, Wood Street, Cardiff CF10 1EW
Phone: +44 (0)29 2055 0350
Web: www.gtcw.org.uk

Graduate Teacher Training Registry (GTTR)
Rosehill, New Barn Lane, Cheltenham GL52 3LZ
Phone: +44 (0) 1242 222444
Web: www.gttr.ac.uk

Similar Jobs

Art Therapist, Artist, Teacher: Design Technology, Teacher: Primary School, Teacher: Secondary School, Teacher: Technological Education

Teacher: Biological Sciences

CRCI:Education and Training
CLCI:FAB Job Band: 5

Job Description

Prepare and deliver structured learning programmes in biological subjects for students aged 11-19 (12-18 in Scotland) in secondary education or at a college. Teachers in this subject area play a vital role in helping young people achieve their potential, both educationally and personally. They prepare classroom materials and illustrate lessons with plant and animal specimens. Also use a variety of resources, such as textbooks, the internet, audio-visual materials, worksheets, as well as practical work. They may prepare students for national academic and vocational examinations. Most teachers follow a syllabus, but some organise own teaching schedule. They set assignments and internal exams, correct written work and record progress of each individual student.

Some biology teachers also help with school administration, pastoral care, educational events, field trips, school clubs and societies, and sporting events. Attending staff meetings, training and development days, and parents'/carers' evenings is part of the job. They may also supervise the work of a teaching/classroom assistant and help them to develop their skills.

Work Details

You usually work 39 weeks a year with contact teaching time between 9am-3.30pm, Monday to Friday. Contact teaching time is generally decreasing to allow more time for administration and teacher development. In some schools, usually in the independent sector, you work fewer weeks a year, but may work on a Saturday. You should be able to relate well to young people and are responsible for supporting learners to reach required learning targets. The job can involve undertaking out-of-hours duties and also working at home, for example on lesson preparation and writing reports. You have contact with other professionals as well as parents and carers.

Teaching requires you to spend each day sitting, standing, carrying/moving learning materials (often equipment), and walking around, depending on the teaching activity. A teaching career is very demanding and requires creativity and imagination. However, it is a very rewarding profession.

Qualification

• England, Wales and Northern Ireland

Band 5: For degree courses: 2-3 A levels, including biology and another science, preferably chemistry, plus some GCSEs (A*-C) including English, maths and physics. Exact requirements depend on the degree you take.

• Scotland

Band 5: For degree courses: 3-5 H grades, including biology, English and another science, preferably chemistry, plus two S grades (1-3) including physics, and also maths if not at H grade, or similar qualifications. Exact subjects required depend on the degree course taken.

Teacher: Biological Sciences

Degree Information
A degree in biology or a related subject is required, followed by a postgraduate certificate in education (PGCE). In England and Wales it is possible to take a BEd or a BA/BSc that combines degree studies and teacher training, leading to qualified teacher status (QTS).

Adult Qualifications
Graduates in biology or a related subject can take a one-year postgraduate certificate in education. Routes to a first degree are available for adults without the necessary formal qualifications through Open University and Access courses.

Work Experience
Entry to this job is competitive and it is important that you do some relevant work experience before applying to teacher training. Applicants are also advised to show evidence of their interest in and commitment to teaching by working with young people, such as a being a voluntary helper in a school, a youth club, sports group, or holiday play activity/sports scheme.

Entry and Training
In England and Wales, to teach in a mainstream or special school, you need qualified teacher status (QTS) achieved by taking an undergraduate or postgraduate certificate in education course (PGCE) or through an employment-based route into teaching, and train on the job. All those working with children and young people are required to have a Criminal Records Bureau (CRB)/Disclosure Scotland check.

For full details on the entry route to teaching throughout the UK, please read the article Teacher: Secondary School.

The Association for Science Education offers the chance for experienced and highly skilled science teachers to gain Chartered Science Teacher status.

Mature applicants are encouraged and there are many options for training and qualification. For full details on all teacher training routes, qualifications and funding, please read the article Teacher: Secondary School.

Opportunities and Pay
Teachers are mainly employed in state schools and the numbers are steadily increasing. Work is also available in independent schools, colleges and academies, adult learning centres, pupil referral units, secure training units or young offenders' institutions, and the armed forces. There are opportunities for promotion, for example to head of department and beyond, though your prospects may depend on willingness to move to another area. Part-time work, private tuition, supply teaching and job-sharing is possible. Work abroad is also available.

A newly qualified teacher (NQT) earns from around £21k a year. A career changer or mature entrant may, depending on previous experience, start at a higher level in the scale.

Additional responsibilities in a school can attract a higher salary. Advanced Skills Teachers (ASTs) earn from around £36k-£55k a year. Teachers in the independent sector can usually expect to earn a higher salary with additional perks, such as subsidised accommodation and school fees.

There is an allowance for working in London. You are advised to contact your local education department or other employer for full salary scale/grade details.

Health
This job requires a health check on entry and normal colour vision for certain areas of work. There is an allergy risk from pollens and skin irritants.

Skills and Qualities
able to discipline, able to explain clearly, able to stimulate learners, enthusiastic, good communication skills, good interpersonal skills, good organisational skills, IT skills, patient, scientific approach

Relevant Subjects
Biology, Chemistry, English, Land and Environment, Mathematics, Psychology, Science, Sociology

Further Information
Journal of Biological Education (quarterly) (Society of Biology) - www.societyofbiology.org.home

Open University - www.open.ac.uk

Scottish Government - Education and Training - www.scotland.gov.uk/Topics/Education

Teach First - www.teachfirst.org.uk

Teach in Scotland (Scottish Government Education Department) - www.teachinginscotland.com

Teachernet (Dept for Education) - www.teachernet.gov.uk

Teaching Scotland Magazine (GTCS magazine) - www.gtcs.org.uk

Teaching Training Wales - www.educationcymru.org

Training & Development Agency (TDA) - www.tda.gov.uk

▶Working in schools & colleges (2007) (Babcock Lifeskills) - www.babcock-lifeskills.com/

Addresses
Association for Science Education (ASE)
College Lane, Hatfield, Hertfordshire AL10 9AA
Phone: +44 (0)1707 283 000
Web: www.ase.org.uk

Department of Education NI (DENI)
Rathgael House, Balloo Road, Bangor BT19 7PR
Phone: +44 (0)28 9127 9279
Web: www.deni.gov.uk

General Teaching Council for England (GTC)
Whittington House, 19-30 Alfred Place, London WC1E 7EA
Phone: 0370 001 0308 (UK only)
Web: www.gtce.org.uk

General Teaching Council for Northern Ireland (GTCNI)
4th Floor, Albany House, 73-75 Great Victoria Street, Belfast BT2 7AF
Phone: +44 (0)28 9033 3390
Web: www.gtcni.org.uk

General Teaching Council for Scotland (GTC Scotland)
Clerwood House, 96 Clermiston Road, Edinburgh EH12 6UT
Phone: +44 (0)131 314 6000
Web: www.gtcs.org.uk

General Teaching Council for Wales (GTCW)
4th Floor, Southgate House, Wood Street, Cardiff CF10 1EW
Phone: +44 (0)29 2055 0350
Web: www.gtcw.org.uk

Graduate Teacher Training Registry (GTTR)
Rosehill, New Barn Lane, Cheltenham GL52 3LZ
Phone: +44 (0) 1242 222444
Web: www.gttr.ac.uk

Society of Biology
9 Red Lion Court, London EC4A 3EF
Phone: +44 (0)20 7936 5900
Web: http://societyofbiology.org/home

Similar Jobs
Biochemist, Biologist, Microbiologist, Teacher: Secondary School, Zoological Scientist

Teacher: Business Studies & Economics

CRCI:Education and Training
CLCI:FAB Job Band: 5

Job Description

Business studies teachers offer a range of topics, including accounting, commerce, economics, office and information studies in secondary schools and colleges, or may specialise in one of the areas. They plan suitable courses in line with the curriculum. They prepare individual lessons using a variety of resources, including textbooks, the internet, audio-visual materials, and worksheets. Also help pupils/students to understand business and economic theory and gain experience in practical work. Some teachers prepare students for national academic and vocational examinations. They set assignments and internal exams, correct written work and record progress of individual students.

Business studies teachers supervise project work, assess the progress of students and mark exams. Some teachers are involved with managing work experience programmes or assisting with career choices and student applications to higher education. Attending staff meetings, training and development days and parents'/carers' evenings is part of the job. Some also have administration duties, pastoral work and assist in some after-school activities.

Work Details

You usually work 39 weeks a year with contact teaching time between 9am-3.30pm, Monday to Friday. Contact teaching time is generally decreasing to allow more time for administration and teacher development. In some schools, usually in the independent sector, you work fewer weeks a year, but often work on a Saturday. You should be able to relate well to young people and are responsible for supporting learners to reach required learning targets. The job can involve undertaking out-of-hours duties and also working at home, for example on lesson preparation and writing reports. You have contact with other professionals as well as parents and carers.

Teaching requires you to spend each day sitting, standing, carrying/moving learning materials (often equipment), and walking around, depending on the teaching activity. A teaching career is very demanding and requires creativity and imagination. However, it is a very rewarding profession.

Qualification

- **England, Wales and Northern Ireland**

Band 5: For a degree course in a related discipline: 2-3 A levels and some GCSEs (A*-C) including English and maths, or equivalent.

- **Scotland**

Band 5: For a degree course in a related discipline: 3-5 H grades and some S grades (1-3), or similar. English and maths are usually required but exact requirements depend on the degree you take.

Degree Information

To teach this subject, a degree in business and economics or a related subject and a postgraduate certificate in education (PGCE) is needed.

Adult Qualifications

Graduates in business studies, economics or a related subject can take a one-year postgraduate course in education. Routes to a first degree are available for adults without the necessary formal qualifications through Open University, foundation and Access courses.

Work Experience

Entry to this job is competitive and it is important that you do some relevant work experience before applying to teacher training. Applicants are also advised to show evidence of their interest in and commitment to teaching by working with young people, such as being a voluntary helper in a school, a youth club, sports group, or holiday play activity/sports scheme.

Entry and Training

In England and Wales, to teach in a mainstream or special school, you need qualified teacher status (QTS) achieved by taking an undergraduate or postgraduate certificate in education course (PGCE) or through an employment-based route into teaching, and train on the job. All those working with children and young people are required to have a Criminal Records Bureau (CRB)/Disclosure Scotland check.

For full details of the entry routes to teaching throughout the UK, please read the article Teacher: Secondary School.

Mature applicants are encouraged and there are many options for training and qualification, including distance-learning courses. For full details of the entry routes to teaching please read the article Teacher: Secondary School.

Opportunities and Pay

Teachers are mainly employed in state schools and the numbers are steadily increasing. Work is also available in independent schools, colleges and academies, adult learning centres, pupil referral units, secure training units or young offenders' institutions, and the armed forces. There are opportunities for promotion, for example to head of department and beyond, though your prospects may depend on willingness to move to another area. Part-time work, private tuition, supply teaching and job-sharing is possible. Work abroad is also available.

A newly qualified teacher (NQT) earns from around £21k a year. A career changer or mature entrant may, depending on previous experience, start at a higher level in the scale.

Additional responsibilities in a school can attract a higher salary. Advanced Skills Teachers (ASTs) earn from around £36k-£55k a year. Teachers in the independent sector can usually expect to earn a higher salary with additional perks, such as subsidised accommodation and school fees.

There is an allowance for working in London. You are advised to contact your local education department or other employer for full salary scale/grade details.

Health

You have to have a health check to get into teaching.

Skills and Qualities

able to discipline, able to explain clearly, able to stimulate learners, enthusiastic, fair minded, good communication skills, good interpersonal skills, good organisational skills, IT skills, patient

Relevant Subjects

Business and accounting, Economics, English, ICT/Computer studies, Law, Mathematics, Psychology, Sociology

Further Information

Economics & Business Education Association (EBEA) - www.ebea.org.uk

Open University - www.open.ac.uk

Scottish Government - Education and Training - www.scotland.gov.uk/Topics/Education

Teach First - www.teachfirst.org.uk

Teach in Scotland (Scottish Government Education Department) - www.teachinginscotland.com

Teachernet (Dept for Education) - www.teachernet.gov.uk

Teaching Business & Economics (termly) (Economics & Business Education Association) - www.ebea.org.uk/publications/magazines_20102011/

Teaching Scotland Magazine (GTCS magazine) - www.gtcs.org.uk

Teaching Training Wales - www.educationcymru.org

Training & Development Agency (TDA) - www.tda.gov.uk

▶Working in business, administration & finance (2010) (Babcock Lifeskills) - www.babcock-lifeskills.com/

▶Working in schools & colleges (2007) (Babcock Lifeskills) - www.babcock-lifeskills.com/

Addresses

Department of Education NI (DENI)
Rathgael House, Balloo Road, Bangor BT19 7PR
Phone: +44 (0)28 9127 9279
Web: www.deni.gov.uk

General Teaching Council for England (GTC)
Whittington House, 19-30 Alfred Place, London WC1E 7EA
Phone: 0370 001 0308 (UK only)
Web: www.gtce.org.uk

General Teaching Council for Northern Ireland (GTCNI)
4th Floor, Albany House, 73-75 Great Victoria Street, Belfast BT2 7AF
Phone: +44 (0)28 9033 3390
Web: www.gtcni.org.uk

General Teaching Council for Scotland (GTC Scotland)
Clerwood House, 96 Clermiston Road, Edinburgh EH12 6UT
Phone: +44 (0)131 314 6000
Web: www.gtcs.org.uk

General Teaching Council for Wales (GTCW)
4th Floor, Southgate House, Wood Street, Cardiff CF10 1EW
Phone: +44 (0)29 2055 0350
Web: www.gtcw.org.uk

Graduate Teacher Training Registry (GTTR)
Rosehill, New Barn Lane, Cheltenham GL52 3LZ
Phone: +44 (0) 1242 222444
Web: www.gttr.ac.uk

Similar Jobs

Accountant: Industry & Commerce, Lecturer: Further Education, Lecturer: Higher Education, Teacher: Mathematics, Teacher: Secondary School

Teacher: Classics

CRCI:Education and Training
CLCI:FAB
Job Band: 5

Job Description

Classics teachers prepare and deliver lessons at secondary school level in Latin and Ancient Greek or in classical civilisation studies. They follow a syllabus designed to improve pupils' comprehension of the chosen language, and also to widen their understanding of classical life, literature, art and history. They plan individual lessons and use a variety of resources, such as textbooks, the internet, audio-visual materials, and worksheets. Some teachers prepare students for national examinations. They set assignments and internal exams, correct written work and record progress of each individual student. Some may teach another subject.

Many teachers help with school administration, pastoral care, educational events, field trips, school clubs and societies, and sporting events. Attending staff meetings, training and development days, and parents'/carers' evenings is also part of the job.

Work Details

You usually work 39 weeks a year with contact teaching time between 9am-3.30pm, Monday to Friday. Contact teaching time is generally decreasing to allow more time for administration and teacher development. In some schools, usually in the independent sector, you work fewer weeks a year, but often work on a Saturday. You should be able to relate well to young people and are responsible for supporting learners to reach required learning targets. The job involves undertaking out-of-hours duties and working at home, for example on lesson preparation and writing reports. You have contact with other professionals as well as parents and carers.

Teaching requires you to spend each day sitting, standing, carrying/moving learning materials (often equipment), and walking around, depending on the teaching activity. A teaching career is very demanding and requires creativity and imagination. However, it is a very rewarding profession.

Qualification

- **England, Wales and Northern Ireland**

Band 5: For degree course: 2-3 A levels including classics and some GCSEs (A*-C) including English and maths, or equivalent. The exact requirements depend on the degree you take.

- **Scotland**

Band 5: For degree course: 3-5 H grades, including English and classics, and some S grades (1-3) including maths, or similar qualifications.

Degree Information

A good degree, preferably in classics, classical civilisation or ancient history, together with a postgraduate certificate in education (PGCE), is required for entry to this job. Currently Kings College London and the University of Cambridge offer a PGCE in classics.

Adult Qualifications

Access and foundation courses are available for those who do not have the standard entry requirements for a degree course, but may not be available in subjects such as Latin and Ancient Greek.

Work Experience

Entry to this job is competitive and it is important that you do some relevant work experience before applying to teacher training. Applicants are also advised to show evidence of their interest in and commitment to teaching by working with young people, such as being a voluntary helper in a school, a youth club, sports group, or holiday play activity/sports scheme.

Entry and Training

In England and Wales, to teach in a mainstream or special school, you need qualified teacher status (QTS) achieved by taking an undergraduate or postgraduate certificate in education course (PGCE) or through an employment-based route into teaching, and train on the job. All those working with children and young people are required to have a Criminal Records Bureau (CRB)/Disclosure Scotland check.

In Scotland, the quickest and most popular way to qualify as a secondary school teacher of classics is to have a degree in a classics related subject and then do a one-year professional graduate diploma in education (PGDE).

For full details of the entry routes to teaching throughout the UK, please read the article Teacher: Secondary School.

Mature applicants are encouraged and there are many options for training and qualification, including distance-learning courses.

For further details on all teacher training routes throughout the UK, please read the article Teacher: Secondary School.

Opportunities and Pay

There are fewer opportunities for teachers of classics and you may have to be able to teach another subject as well. Employment is likely to diminish in state schools, but there are still good opportunities to teach in independent schools. Your prospects may depend on willingness to move to another area. Classics teachers trained in Scotland may teach in England, Wales and NI, but not vice versa. Part-time work, private tuition, supply teaching and job-sharing may be possible. Work abroad is also available.

A newly qualified teacher (NQT) earns from around £21k a year. A career changer or mature entrant may, depending on previous experience, start at a higher level in the scale.

Additional responsibilities in a school can attract a higher salary. Advanced Skills Teachers (ASTs) earn from around £36k-£55k a year. Teachers in the independent sector can usually expect to earn a higher salary with additional perks, such as subsidised accommodation and school fees.

There is an allowance for working in London. You are advised to contact your local education department or other employer for full salary scale/grade details.

Health

This job requires a health check on entry.

Skills and Qualities

able to explain clearly, able to stimulate learners, encouraging, enthusiastic, fair minded, firm manner, good communication skills, good interpersonal skills, good organisational skills, patient

Relevant Subjects

Classical studies, English, History, Psychology, Sociology

Further Information

Iris Project (The Iris Project) - www.irismagazine.org

Journal of Classics Teaching (3 x year) (JACT) - www.jact.org

Scottish Government - Education and Training - www.scotland.gov.uk/Topics/Education

Teach First - www.teachfirst.org.uk

Teach in Scotland (Scottish Government Education Department) - www.teachinginscotland.com

Teachernet (Dept for Education) - www.teachernet.gov.uk

Teaching Training Wales - www.educationcymru.org

Training & Development Agency (TDA) - www.tda.gov.uk

▶Working in schools & colleges (2007) (Babcock Lifeskills) - www.babcock-lifeskills.com/

Addresses

Department of Education NI (DENI)
Rathgael House, Balloo Road, Bangor BT19 7PR
Phone: +44 (0)28 9127 9279
Web: www.deni.gov.uk

General Teaching Council for England (GTC)
Whittington House, 19-30 Alfred Place, London WC1E 7EA
Phone: 0370 001 0308 (UK only)
Web: www.gtce.org.uk

General Teaching Council for Northern Ireland (GTCNI)
4th Floor, Albany House, 73-75 Great Victoria Street,
Belfast BT2 7AF
Phone: +44 (0)28 9033 3390
Web: www.gtcni.org.uk

General Teaching Council for Scotland (GTC Scotland)
Clerwood House, 96 Clermiston Road, Edinburgh EH12 6UT
Phone: +44 (0)131 314 6000
Web: www.gtcs.org.uk

General Teaching Council for Wales (GTCW)
4th Floor, Southgate House, Wood Street, Cardiff CF10 1EW
Phone: +44 (0)29 2055 0350
Web: www.gtcw.org.uk

Graduate Teacher Training Registry (GTTR)
Rosehill, New Barn Lane, Cheltenham GL52 3LZ
Phone: +44 (0) 1242 222444
Web: www.gttr.ac.uk

Joint Association of Classical Teachers (JACT)
Senate House, Malet Street, London WC1E 7HU
Phone: +44 (0)20 7862 8719
Web: www.jact.org

Similar Jobs

Lecturer: Further Education, Lecturer: Higher Education, Teacher: History, Teacher: Modern Foreign Languages, Teacher: Secondary School

Teacher: Community Languages

CRCI:Education and Training
CLCI:FAB Job Band: 5

Job Description

Teachers of community languages prepare and give lessons in a language such as Arabic, Bengali, Gaelic, Japanese, Punjabi, Mandarin Chinese, Turkish, Urdu or Welsh, usually in a state secondary school. They may also teach another language such as French, German or Spanish. The lessons usually cover communication skills, grammar, literature and culture. They may use a language laboratory to improve students' fluency and pronunciation skills. In some schools teachers may prepare students for national academic/vocational examinations. They respond to pupils' diverse learning needs, and set suitable and achievable learning challenges.

Community language teachers develop a learning plan and strategy for each pupil/student, and keep relevant and informative records, often using a computer. Some teachers also help with school administration, pastoral care, school outings, clubs and societies. They attend staff meetings, training and development days and parents'/carers' evenings.

Work Details

You usually work 39 weeks a year with contact teaching time mainly between 9am-3.30pm, Monday to Friday. Contact teaching time is generally decreasing to allow more time for administration and teacher development. In some schools, usually independent schools, you work fewer weeks a year, but often work on a Saturday. You should be able to relate well to young people and are responsible for supporting learners and reaching required learning targets.

The job can involve undertaking out-of-hours duties and also working at home, for example on lesson preparation and writing reports. You may also work in a community centre or similar, offering twilight or evening sessions.

You have contact with other professionals as well as parents and carers. Teaching requires you to spend each day sitting, standing, carrying/moving learning materials (often equipment), and walking around, depending on the teaching activity. A teaching career is very demanding, and it also requires creativity and imagination. However, it is a very rewarding profession.

Qualification

• England, Wales and Northern Ireland

Band 5: For degree course: 2-3 A levels and some GCSEs (A*-C) in other subjects, including English and maths, or equivalent. The exact requirements depend on the degree you take.

• Scotland

Band 5: For degree courses: 3-5 H grades and some S grades (1-3) usually including English, or similar.

Degree Information

A degree with one or more languages and a postgraduate certificate in education (PGCE) is usually required for this job. However, many teachers of community languages are native speakers, so a degree in the relevant language may not be as important as one in education. There is limited provision for courses in community languages although opportunities are increasing. Check with the teaching authority to ensure your degree meets the requirements for entry to teacher training.

Teacher: Community Languages

Adult Qualifications

Adults aged 23 or over may enter degree courses with a variety of qualifications or via Access or foundation courses. For graduates there are some part-time postgraduate courses in education courses available.

Work Experience

Entry to teaching is competitive and it is important that you try to do some relevant work experience before applying to teacher training. Applicants are advised to show evidence of their interest in and commitment to working with young people, preferably as a voluntary helper in a school, a youth club, sports group, or holiday play activity/sports scheme.

The Student Associate Scheme (England) gives registered students in full or part-time higher education, on courses not leading to qualified teacher status, the opportunity to work in a school alongside experienced teachers. Contact the Training and Development Agency (TDA) for details. The TDA can also provide details for prospective teachers to gain knowledge of a classroom environment through 'taster' days, short courses, or a discussion with a qualified, practising teacher. For details of similar opportunities in Scotland, contact the Scottish Government - Education and Training Department, or for Northern Ireland, the Department of Education in Northern Ireland (DENI).

Entry and Training

Community languages are within the teaching area of modern foreign languages (see separate job profile). However, it is important to state that those wishing to gain QTS are not required to have a degree in the community language itself, provided there is sufficient knowledge of that subject, ie native speakers of the language.

Those wishing to train as a community language teacher have a better chance of gaining a place on teacher training courses if they are able to offer a second language such as French, German or Spanish, currently the most commonly taught languages in state secondary schools. For prospective community language teachers who cannot offer a second language, there are free courses in French and German (modern languages extension course) that enhance employability. Those wishing to teach in a primary school are advised to take a primary PGCE with a language specialism option. Contact CILT, the national centre for languages for their leaflet 'Qualify to teach community languages', or contact the Training and Development Agency (TDA) for details.

In Scotland, for the PGDE in Gaelic applicants must be fluent in Gaelic, with good reading and writing skills in the language.

For details on all teacher training routes, qualifications and funding, contact the TDA for schools (England & Wales), the Department of Education Northern Ireland (DENI), or the the Scottish Government - Education and Training Department. See also the articles Teacher: Secondary and Teacher: Primary.

CILT, the National Centre for Languages, also has details regarding language teaching and research, training and professional development. See the website for information. All those working with children and young people are required to have a Criminal Records Bureau (CRB)/Disclosure Scotland check.

Mature applicants are encouraged and there are many options for training and qualification, including distance-learning courses. Some two-year part-time PGCE (PGDE in Scotland) courses are available and there are also appropriate Open University courses for both a relevant UK degree and PGCE/PGDE. Full details are given in the article Teacher: Secondary School.

Opportunities and Pay

In some community language subjects, this is a relatively new area of teaching. Community language teachers are mainly employed in state schools, some in independent schools, and opportunities are steadily increasing. Your prospects may depend on willingness to move to another area of the country. Part-time work, private tuition, supply teaching and job-sharing is possible. Work abroad is also available, particularly with organisations such as Voluntary Services Overseas (VSO) and with the British Council.

A newly qualified teacher (NQT) earns from around £21k a year. A career changer or mature entrant may, depending on previous experience, start at a higher level in the scale. 'Golden hellos' (or teaching grants in Wales) ranging from around £2.5k-£5k are available to newly qualified teachers who teach in an eligible (usually shortage) subject. In Scotland you can apply for a preference waiver payment of £6k if you are prepared to work anywhere in Scotland during your probationary year. Advanced Skills Teachers (ASTs) earn from around £36k-£55k a year.

These salaries are representative throughout the UK (except for London, which attracts a further allowance) but you are advised to contact your local education department or other employer for full salary scale/grade details.

Health

This job requires a health check on entry and usually requires normal hearing ability.

Skills and Qualities

ability in one or more languages, able to explain clearly, approachable, good communication skills, good organisational skills, good presentation skills, patient, perceptive, self confident

Relevant Subjects

English, Modern Foreign Languages, Psychology, Sociology

Further Information

British Council - www.britishcouncil.org

Qualify to Teach Community Languages (CILT: The National Centre for Languages) - www.cilt.org.uk/commlangs/pathways.htm

Scottish Government - Education and Training - www.scotland.gov.uk/Topics/Education

Teach in Scotland (Scottish Government Education Department) - www.teachinginscotland.com

Teachernet (Dept for Education) - www.teachernet.gov.uk

Teaching Scotland Magazine (GTCS magazine) - www.gtcs.org.uk

Teaching Training Wales - www.educationcymru.org

Teaching Wales (quarterly) (General Teaching Council for Wales) - www.gtcw.org.uk/

Training & Development Agency (TDA) - www.tda.gov.uk

Voluntary Service Overseas (VSO) - www.vso.org.uk

Working with languages (2010) (Babcock Lifeskills) - www.babcock-lifeskills.com/

Addresses

Chartered Institute of Linguists (IoL)
Saxon House, 48 Southwark Street, London SE1 1UN
Phone: +44 (0)20 7940 3100
Web: www.iol.org.uk

CILT, the National Centre for Languages
3rd Floor, 111 Westminster Bridge Road, London SE1 7HR
Phone: 08456 12 5885 (UK only)
Web: www.cilt.org.uk

Department of Education NI (DENI)
Rathgael House, Balloo Road, Bangor BT19 7PR
Phone: +44 (0)28 9127 9279
Web: www.deni.gov.uk

General Teaching Council for England (GTC)
Whittington House, 19-30 Alfred Place, London WC1E 7EA
Phone: 0370 001 0308 (UK only)
Web: www.gtce.org.uk

General Teaching Council for Northern Ireland (GTCNI)
4th Floor, Albany House, 73-75 Great Victoria Street,
Belfast BT2 7AF
Phone: +44 (0)28 9033 3390
Web: www.gtcni.org.uk

General Teaching Council for Scotland (GTC Scotland)
Clerwood House, 96 Clermiston Road, Edinburgh EH12 6UT
Phone: +44 (0)131 314 6000
Web: www.gtcs.org.uk

General Teaching Council for Wales (GTCW)
4th Floor, Southgate House, Wood Street, Cardiff CF10 1EW
Phone: +44 (0)29 2055 0350
Web: www.gtcw.org.uk

Graduate Teacher Training Registry (GTTR)
Rosehill, New Barn Lane, Cheltenham GL52 3LZ
Phone: +44 (0) 1242 222444
Web: www.gttr.ac.uk

National Association for Language Development in the Curriculum (NALDIC)
Building L46, University of Reading, London Road, Berkshire RG1 5AQ
Phone: +44 (0) 118 986 9040
Web: www.naldic.org.uk

Open University (OU)
PO Box 197, Milton Keynes MK7 6BJ
Phone: +44 (0)845 300 6090
Web: http://www3.open.ac.uk

Similar Jobs

Interpreter, Lecturer: Further Education, Teacher: English to Speakers of Other Languages, Teacher: Modern Foreign Languages, Teacher: Primary School, Teacher: Secondary School

Teacher: Dance

also known as: Dance Instructor
CRCI:Education and Training
CLCI:FAB Job Band: 2 to 5

Job Description

Dance teachers help groups and individuals of varying ages and abilities to learn and improve their dance skills. Some work mainly with people who want to do dance as a leisure or keep-fit activity. Others coach people who want to take dance exams, do dance competitions or pursue a career in the performing arts. May teach a range of dance styles or focus on a particular dance form such as tap, ballroom or ballet.

They plan lessons, choose music and work out dance routines. Show pupils how to perform moves and reduce risk of injury. Also provide feedback to help people improve. May teach theory if required. Some teachers may need to keep records and make sure people working towards exams cover all they need to know. They may also organise or assist with shows and workshops.

Private dance teachers may need to prepare and distribute marketing materials, as well as deal with bills, premises, licences, insurance and general paperwork. Those working in a school or college, supervise and advise students and may have other duties. In secondary schools they often teach other subjects as well. In primary schools the class teacher usually teaches dance.

Work Details

Hours of work vary as private dance teachers put on classes when their customers are available. This may be during the day, after school, in the evening or at weekends. Dance teachers in schools mostly work 39 weeks a year, with contact teaching time between 9am-3.30pm, Monday to Friday. You may be involved in putting on after school activities or rehearsals for performances.

Most of the work takes place in a dance studio, hall or sports hall. Private dance teachers may hold classes in different locations and have to travel between them. Some venues may be very basic and lack comfort and equipment. You are on your feet most of the day and classes can be noisy and physically demanding. You need to wear suitable footwear and clothing that allows you to move freely, such as a tracksuit and trainers, so you can demonstrate dance moves.

Qualification

To become a private dance teacher you do not need formal qualifications, but a good standard of performance is required. People enter the profession from a variety of backgrounds. Many come to dance teaching after a career as a performer. Some have no or few qualifications; others have a dance qualification, a dance teaching qualification or a degree plus a postgraduate teaching qualification. Check all course entry requirements carefully.

Adult Qualifications

You can become a private dance teacher without formal qualifications. Entry requirements for higher education courses may be relaxed for adults. Access or foundation courses give adults without qualifications a route onto degree courses.

Work Experience

Work experience helps you find out what you enjoy and do not enjoy about a job. Paid or voluntary work with children or young people or where you teach or coach others may be useful. Helping a local dance or drama group with dance related activities or with school or college shows may give you an insight into this type of work.

Entry and Training

Most dance teachers work in the private sector, but some prefer to teach in state schools. A degree in dance or a related subject followed by a postgraduate certificate (England and Wales) or diploma (Scotland) in education (PGCE or PGDE) or a BEd degree is required for teaching dance in state schools. A PGCE specialising in dance is available from the Royal Academy of Dance. For full details of teacher training routes see the article Teacher: Secondary School.

Teachers in private dance schools need to perform dance styles to a high standard. You do not need qualified teacher status (QTS), but many teachers have qualifications to teach specific dance styles from one or more dance awarding bodies. The Council for Dance Education and Training (CDET) is the national standards body for the professional dance industry. They have registered and accredited four awarding bodies for dance teaching in the UK. These are the Royal Academy of Dance, the British Ballet Organisation, the British Theatre Dance Association and the Imperial Society of Teachers of Dance. Dance teachers who have been trained by these organisations can go on the CDET UK directory of registered dance teachers. Only teachers registered with the appropriate dance awarding body can enter students for its exams.

Many entrants start training as dancers in an established dance school. After passing the graded exams of one or more of the dance awarding bodies, you can then follow a teacher training programme. This leads to teaching qualifications at different levels. Those qualified to associate level often still teach under supervision. Dance schools and awarding bodies each have their own teaching methods. Courses may be full time, part time or by distance learning.

All dance teachers dealing with children or young people have to undergo a Criminal Records Bureau (CRB)/Disclosure Scotland check.

Dance teaching is a popular career move for people who have been professional dancers. Dancers' Career Development provides practical help and funding for professional dancers who wish to retrain after a career in dance performance.

Mature applicants to teaching in state schools are encouraged. There are many options for training and qualification, including distance-learning courses and on-the-job training. See the Training and Development Agency for Schools (TDA) and Teach in Scotland websites for more information.

Opportunities and Pay

Most private dance teachers are self-employed. Many run private dance schools or give lessons in premises like leisure and community centres. Others do freelance work for dance schools or fitness centres owned by other people. Some mix teaching dance with other jobs like running exercise classes or offering massage. Some dance teachers move into other areas that use their dance and teaching skills, like choreography or dance therapy. Jobs in these areas are limited and may mean further training.

Opportunities for dance teachers in state schools are increasing. Dancers without qualified teacher status sometimes teach in state schools, assisting a qualified teacher to offer dance as part of the curriculum.

Rates of pay for teachers in private dance schools vary. They range from £10-£20 or more an hour for teaching group classes. Experienced teachers working with people who want to perform or dance competitively are likely to earn more. Earnings for self-employed dance teachers depend on the location, style of dance taught, size and type of class and the experience of the teacher. Fees for private lessons range from £8-£15 for leisure classes to £50-£100 an hour for private tuition. Newly qualified teachers in state schools earn around £21k a year.

Health

This job requires good general fitness and stamina. To work in a state school you may need to have a health check.

Skills and Qualities

able to motivate others, attention to detail, business awareness, creative flair, dance skills, excellent communication skills, good interpersonal skills, good organisational skills, observant, patient

Relevant Subjects

Media and communication studies, Music, Performing arts, Physical education and sport, Psychology

Further Information

Dance Matters (National Dance Teachers Association) (National Dance Teachers Association) - www.ndta.org.uk

Dancing Times (Dancing Times Ltd) - www.dancing-times.co.uk

Foundation for Community Dance - www.communitydance.org.uk

So you want to work in Music & Dance (Wayland) - www.waylandbooks.co.uk

Teach in Scotland (Scottish Government Education Department) - www.teachinginscotland.com

Training & Development Agency (TDA) - www.tda.gov.uk

▶Working in schools & colleges (2007) (Babcock Lifeskills) - www.babcock-lifeskills.com/

Addresses

British Ballet Organisation (BBO)
Woolborough House, 39 Lonsdale Road, Barnes, London SW13 9JP
Phone: +44 (0)20 8748 1241
Web: www.bbo.org.uk

British Theatre Dance Association
The International Arts Centre, Garden Street, Leicester LE1 3UA
Phone: 0845 166 2179 (UK only)
Web: www.btda.org.uk

Council for Dance Education and Training (CDET)
Old Brewer's Yard, 17 - 19 Neal Street, Covent Garden, London WC2H 9UY
Phone: +44 (0)207 240 5703
Web: www.cdet.org.uk

Dancers' Career Development
19-20 Hatton Place, London EC1N 8RU
Phone: +44 (0)20 7831 1449
Web: www.thedcd.org.uk

Imperial Society of Teachers of Dancing (ISTD)
22-26 Paul Street, London EC2A 4QE
Phone: +44 (0)20 7377 1577
Web: http://istd.org

National Dance Teachers Association (NDTA)
PO Box 4099, Lichfield, Staffordshire WS13 6WX
Phone: +44 (0)1543 308618
Web: www.ndta.org.uk

Royal Academy of Dance (RAD)
36 Battersea Square, London SW11 3RA
Phone: +44 (0)20 7326 8000
Web: www.rad.org.uk

Similar Jobs

Choreographer, Dancer, Dramatherapist, Fitness Instructor, Teacher: Secondary School

Teacher: Design Technology

CRCI:Education and Training
CLCI:FAB
Job Band: 5

Job Description

Design technology (DT) specialists teach students in secondary schools and colleges the design and production of objects that have a practical use. They use a variety of resources, such as textbooks, the internet, audio-visual materials, worksheets, as well as practical work. Some teachers prepare students for national examinations. They follow a syllabus, but may organise own teaching schedule. Set assignments and internal exams, correct written work and record progress of each individual student. They cover the handling of different materials, such as plastics, metals and wood. Teach courses that cover, for example, engineering, microelectronics, product design, technical graphics, and computer-aided design (CAD) techniques.

DT teachers encourage pupils to design creatively, help them to study practical problems and choose appropriate solutions. Oversee the process of turning an idea into a real product. Some DT teachers may develop local business links in order to place students on work experience opportunities. Attending staff meetings, training and development days, and parents'/carers' evenings is part of the job. They may also supervise classroom/ teaching assistants and support them in developing their skills.

Work Details

You usually work 39 weeks a year with contact teaching time between 9am-3.30pm, Monday to Friday. Contact teaching time is generally decreasing to allow more time for administration and teacher development. In some schools, usually in the independent sector, you work fewer weeks a year, but often work on a Saturday. You should be able to relate well to young people and are responsible for supporting learners to reach required learning targets. The job involves out-of-hours duties and working at home, for example on lesson preparation and writing reports. You have contact with other professionals as well as parents and carers.

Teaching requires you to spend each day sitting, standing, carrying/moving learning materials (often equipment), and walking around, depending on the teaching activity. Part-time work, private tuition, supply teaching and job-sharing is possible. A teaching career is very demanding and requires creativity and imagination. However, it is a very rewarding profession.

This job is only available in England, Wales and Northern Ireland. A similar job, teacher of technological education (see job profile), is available in Scotland, but the entry requirements differ.

Qualification

- **England, Wales and Northern Ireland**

Band 5: For degree course: at least two A levels and some GCSEs (A*-C) including English and maths, or equivalent. Exact requirements depend on the degree you take, but may include art, science or technology subjects.

Degree Information

The degree should be in design technology, industrial design, an appropriate art and design course, architecture, technology or an engineering subject, followed by a postgraduate certificate of education (PGCE).

Adult Qualifications

Adults with relevant experience may be accepted for degree courses without the standard entry requirements. In some areas there are Access courses to teaching, which give adults without qualifications a route into degree courses. Check with individual colleges or universities. Teaching technology is often a second career for people with appropriate technical qualifications and experience in industry, engineering or art and design.

Work Experience

Entry to this job is competitive and it is important that you do some relevant work experience before applying to teacher training. Applicants are advised to show evidence of their interest in and commitment to teaching by working with young people, preferably as a voluntary helper in a school, a youth club, sports group, or holiday play activity/sports scheme.

Entry and Training

In England and Wales, to teach in a mainstream or special school, you need qualified teacher status (QTS) achieved by taking an undergraduate or postgraduate certificate in education (PGCE), or through an employment-based route into teaching and train on the job. All those working with children and young people are required to have a Criminal Records Bureau (CRB) check.

First degrees should be appropriate to the subject to be taught. It is recommended that you have two specialisms in the following areas: electronics and communications technology, food technology, materials technology or textiles technology. You should always choose any course carefully to ensure that your first degree enables entry to a PGCE. There is additional funding of £9k a year for those training to teach design technology.

For full details of the entry routes into teaching, please read the article Teacher: Secondary School.

Mature applicants are encouraged and there are many options for training and qualification, including distance-learning courses.

For further details on all teacher training routes, please read the article Teacher: Secondary School.

Opportunities and Pay

Design and technology teachers are in strong demand, particularly in state schools. Work is also available in independent schools, colleges and academies, pupil referral units, secure training units or young offenders' institutions, and the armed forces. There are opportunities for promotion, for example to head of department and beyond. Your prospects may depend on willingness to move to another area. Work abroad may be available.

A newly qualified teacher (NQT) earns from around £21k a year. A career changer or mature entrant may, depending on previous experience, start at a higher level in the scale.

Additional responsibilities in a school can attract a higher salary. Advanced Skills Teachers (ASTs) earn from around £36k-£55k a year. Teachers in the independent sector can usually expect to earn a higher salary with additional perks, such as subsidised accommodation and school fees.

There is an allowance for working in London. You are advised to contact your local education department or other employer for full salary scale/grade details.

Health

You have to pass a health check to enter teaching.

Skills and Qualities

able to discipline, able to stimulate learners, eye for shape/colour, good communication skills, good organisational skills, inventive, IT skills, self confident, technical aptitude

Relevant Subjects

Art and Design, Construction and built environment, Design and technology, Engineering, English, ICT/Computer studies, Mathematics, Physics, Psychology, Science, Sociology

Further Information

Design and Technology on the Web - www.design-technology.info

Teach First - www.teachfirst.org.uk

Teachernet (Dept for Education) - www.teachernet.gov.uk

Teaching Training Wales - www.educationcymru.org

Training & Development Agency (TDA) - www.tda.gov.uk

▶Working in schools & colleges (2007) (Babcock Lifeskills) - www.babcock-lifeskills.com/

Addresses

Design & Technology Association (D&TA)
16 Wellesbourne House, Walton Road, Warwickshire CV35 9JB
Phone: +44 (0)1789 470 007
Web: www.data.org.uk

General Teaching Council for England (GTC)
Whittington House, 19-30 Alfred Place, London WC1E 7EA
Phone: 0370 001 0308 (UK only)
Web: www.gtce.org.uk

General Teaching Council for Northern Ireland (GTCNI)
4th Floor, Albany House, 73-75 Great Victoria Street,
Belfast BT2 7AF
Phone: +44 (0)28 9033 3390
Web: www.gtcni.org.uk

General Teaching Council for Wales (GTCW)
4th Floor, Southgate House, Wood Street, Cardiff CF10 1EW
Phone: +44 (0)29 2055 0350
Web: www.gtcw.org.uk

Graduate Teacher Training Registry (GTTR)
Rosehill, New Barn Lane, Cheltenham GL52 3LZ
Phone: +44 (0) 1242 222444
Web: www.gttr.ac.uk

Similar Jobs

Film/TV & Theatre Set/Stage Designer, Graphic Designer, Model Maker, Teacher: Art, Teacher: Secondary School

Teacher: Drama

CRCI:Education and Training
CLCI:FAB — Job Band: 5

Job Description

Drama specialists teach the dramatic arts, including acting, movement and mime, usually in a secondary school. They plan courses, aiming to help pupils develop imagination and self-expression. They also encourage fluency of speech and extension of vocabulary, directing classes so that new skills and confidence are gained. May also direct and produce plays and other performances. Some teachers prepare students for national examinations. Attending staff meetings, training and development days and parents'/carers' evenings is part of the job. They may also supervise the work of a teaching/classroom assistant.

Teacher: Drama

Most drama teachers also teach another subject as well; drama is often part of the English department. May also help with some school administration, pastoral care, educational events, field trips, school clubs and societies, and other events. Can specialise in areas such as working with those who are disadvantaged, with less able students, or with youth groups.

Work Details

You usually work 39 weeks a year with contact teaching time between 9am-3.30pm, Monday to Friday. Contact teaching time is generally decreasing to allow more time for administration and teacher development. In some schools, usually in the independent sector, you work fewer weeks a year, but often work on a Saturday. You should be able to relate well to young people and are responsible for supporting learners and reaching required learning targets. The job involves out-of-hours duties and working at home, for example on lesson preparation and writing reports. You have contact with other professionals as well as parents and carers.

Teaching requires you to spend each day sitting, standing, carrying/moving learning materials (often equipment), and walking around, depending on the teaching activity. A teaching career is very demanding and requires creativity and imagination. However, it is a very rewarding profession.

Qualification

- **England, Wales and Northern Ireland**

Band 5: For degree course in drama or theatre studies: 2-3 A levels, preferably including English and some GCSEs (A*-C) including English and maths, or equivalent. The exact requirements depend on the degree you take.

- **Scotland**

Band 5: For degree course in drama or theatre studies: 3-5 H grades including English and some S grades (1-3) including English and maths, or similar qualifications. Exact requirements depend on the degree you take.

Degree Information

A degree in drama/theatre studies, education studies with English or drama, or a related subject, together with a postgraduate certificate in education (PGCE), is required for entry to this job.

Adult Qualifications

Entry requirements for BEd courses in the UK vary according to different colleges. Some welcome mature entrants via Access or foundation courses. For graduates there are a few part-time postgraduate courses in education available.

Work Experience

Entry to this job is competitive and it is important that you do some relevant work experience before applying to teacher training. Applicants are advised to show evidence of their interest in and commitment to teaching by working with young people, preferably as a voluntary helper in a school. Experience of working in a local dramatic society, or with a school, college/university drama club in any capacity, is extremely valuable. Other relevant experience can be working with young people in a youth club, sports group, or holiday play activity/sports scheme.

Entry and Training

To enter drama courses you may have to pass an audition, and it is an advantage to have experience in drama and music. In England and Wales, to teach drama in a maintained or special school, you need qualified teacher status (QTS) achieved by taking an undergraduate or postgraduate certificate in education course (PGCE) or through an employment-based route into teaching, and train on the job. All those working with children and young people are required to have a Criminal Records Bureau (CRB)/Disclosure Scotland check.

In Scotland, the quickest and most popular way to qualify as a secondary school teacher of drama is to have a degree in drama or theatre studies and then do a one-year professional graduate diploma in education (PGDE).

For full details on the entry route to teaching throughout the UK, please read the article Teacher: Secondary School.

Mature applicants are encouraged and there are many options for training and qualification, including distance-learning courses.

For further details on all teacher training routes throughout the UK, please read the article Teacher: Secondary School.

Opportunities and Pay

Teachers are mainly employed in state schools and opportunities are steadily increasing. Work is also available in independent schools, colleges and academies, pupil referral units, secure training units, young offenders' institutions, and also the armed forces. There are opportunities for promotion, for example to head of department and beyond. Your prospects may depend on willingness to move to another area. Part-time work, private tuition, supply teaching and job-sharing is possible. Work abroad is also available, particularly with organisations such as Voluntary Service Overseas and with the British Council.

A newly qualified teacher (NQT) earns from around £21k a year. A career changer or mature entrant may, depending on previous experience, start at a higher level in the scale.

Additional responsibilities in a school can attract a higher salary. Advanced Skills Teachers (ASTs) earn from around £36k-£55k a year. Teachers in the independent sector can usually expect to earn a higher salary with additional perks, such as subsidised accommodation and school fees.

There is an allowance for working in London. You are advised to contact your local education department or other employer for full salary scale/grade details.

Health

This job requires a health check on entry.

Skills and Qualities

able to discipline, able to stimulate learners, clear speaking voice, energetic, enthusiastic, good communication skills, good organisational skills, imaginative, self confident, sense of humour

Relevant Subjects

Classical studies, English, History, Media and communication studies, Music, Performing arts, Psychology, Sociology

Further Information

British Council - www.britishcouncil.org

Scottish Government - Education and Training - www.scotland.gov.uk/Topics/Education

Teach First - www.teachfirst.org.uk

Teach in Scotland (Scottish Government Education Department) - www.teachinginscotland.com

Teachernet (Dept for Education) - www.teachernet.gov.uk

Teaching Training Wales - www.educationcymru.org

Training & Development Agency (TDA) - www.tda.gov.uk

Voluntary Service Overseas (VSO) - www.vso.org.uk

▶Working in schools & colleges (2007) (Babcock Lifeskills) - www.babcock-lifeskills.com/

Addresses

Department of Education NI (DENI)
Rathgael House, Balloo Road, Bangor BT19 7PR
Phone: +44 (0)28 9127 9279
Web: www.deni.gov.uk

General Teaching Council for England (GTC)
Whittington House, 19-30 Alfred Place, London WC1E 7EA
Phone: 0370 001 0308 (UK only)
Web: www.gtce.org.uk

General Teaching Council for Northern Ireland (GTCNI)
4th Floor, Albany House, 73-75 Great Victoria Street,
Belfast BT2 7AF
Phone: +44 (0)28 9033 3390
Web: www.gtcni.org.uk

General Teaching Council for Scotland (GTC Scotland)
Clerwood House, 96 Clermiston Road, Edinburgh EH12 6UT
Phone: +44 (0)131 314 6000
Web: www.gtcs.org.uk

General Teaching Council for Wales (GTCW)
4th Floor, Southgate House, Wood Street, Cardiff CF10 1EW
Phone: +44 (0)29 2055 0350
Web: www.gtcw.org.uk

Graduate Teacher Training Registry (GTTR)
Rosehill, New Barn Lane, Cheltenham GL52 3LZ
Phone: +44 (0) 1242 222444
Web: www.gttr.ac.uk

National Council for Drama Training (NCDT)
249 Tooley Street, London SE1 2JX
Phone: +44 (0) 20 7407 3686
Web: www.ncdt.co.uk

Similar Jobs

Actor, Dramatherapist, Film/TV Director, Lecturer: Further Education, Teacher: Secondary School, Theatre Stage Manager

Teacher: Early Years

also known as: Nursery School Teacher

CRCI:Education and Training
CLCI:FAB Job Band: 5

Job Description

Early years or nursery teachers plan and organise structured, creative and free play for children aged between three and five years old, designed to encourage their social, personal and emotional development and prepare them for primary school. They stimulate interest and increase children's understanding of life by helping them to take part in a variety of activities, such as painting and craftwork, music, dance and singing, cooking, dressing-up, role play and stories, nature activities, water and sand play. They organise games and outings, encourage good behaviour and friendliness.

Early years/nursery teachers help children to become more independent. They read to children and encourage them to talk. Introduce stories, songs, rhymes and games as a way of teaching numbers and counting to young children. Also teach basic self-help skills such as putting on coats, washing hands and tying shoelaces. In England and Wales, nursery school teachers also teach the national curriculum (foundation stage) in accordance with early learning goals criteria. In Scotland they work within the 3-5 curriculum framework.

They write reports, keep records and profiles of each child. May liaise with speech therapists, social workers and other health workers. Supervise assistant staff such as parent volunteers, student nursery nurses and sessional workers.

Work Details

Place of work is a nursery school, which is usually friendly and attractive but can also be noisy and messy. School hours are often 8.30am to 3.30pm, Monday to Friday, for around 39 weeks each year, or less in the independent sector. Work can be very demanding and requires creativity and imagination. You have to cope with being on your feet for most of the day, usually in a classroom, but with some outside activities. The job can be full or part time, or by supply teaching when permanent teachers are temporarily away from their school.

Qualification

• England, Wales and Northern Ireland

Band 5: For BEd degree courses: at least two A levels and some GCSEs (A*-C) including English, maths and a science subject, or equivalent qualifications. Exact requirements depend on the degree you take. A CACHE diploma in childcare and education may also be acceptable for course entry.

• Scotland

Band 5: For BEd degree courses: at least three H grades, including English, and some S grades (1-3) including maths and often a science. Similar qualifications may be acceptable.

Degree Information

Most entrants to this job qualify by studying for three or four years for a BEd degree in primary education 3-7 or primary education (foundation stage/key stage 1). You can also enter this job with a postgraduate certificate in education (PGCE) that specialises in early years.

There are also foundation degrees in early years that can be topped up to a full honours degree in early years care and education. This then needs to be followed by a relevant PGCE.

Adult Qualifications

Contact specific institutions for entry requirements, as some accept alternative entry qualifications for BEd courses. Entry via Access or foundation courses is often available. Most courses prefer applicants with experience in working with young children.

Work Experience

Entry to this job is competitive and it is important that you do relevant work experience before applying for teacher training. Applicants are advised to show evidence of their interest in and commitment to teaching by work experience with children, such as a regular voluntary helper in a school or assisting at a holiday activity club.

The Student Associate Scheme (England) gives registered students in full or part-time higher education, on courses not leading to qualified teacher status, the opportunity to work in a school alongside experienced teachers. You are paid (tax free) for each day you work for at least ten days or more. Contact the Training and Development Agency (TDA) for details. The TDA can also provide details for intending teachers to gain knowledge of a classroom environment through 'taster' days, short courses, or perhaps a discussion with a qualified and practising teacher. For details of similar opportunities in Scotland, contact Scottish Government - Education and Training, or for Northern Ireland, the Department of Education in Northern Ireland (DENI).

Entry and Training

For teaching in a state nursery school or nursery class in a primary school, it is essential that the course followed results in Qualified Teacher Status (QTS). Applicants for degree-level courses must be at least 18 and should be able to relate well to small children. Entry to training courses is often highly competitive and requires evidence of experience of working with pre-school children. It is useful to be able to play a musical instrument and have a range of relevant skills. All those working with children are required to have a Criminal Records Bureau (CRB)/Disclosure Scotland check.

Training is usually full time with a mixture of theory and practical experience. All newly qualified teachers (NQTs) must then successfully complete a one-year induction period and register with the General Teaching Council in England, Wales or Northern Ireland. All entrants must also pass a QTS skills test (England only) in literacy, numeracy, and in information and communications technology (ICT). The Training and Development Agency for

Schools (England and Wales) and the Department of Education of Education Northern Ireland websites have information on all aspects of teacher training and development.

In Scotland, you must achieve qualified status (TQ) by first taking a relevant degree followed by a one-year college-based PGDE course, or a four-year course at a teacher education institution (TEI) leading to a BEd. Qualified teachers have to register with the General Teaching Council for Scotland before teaching in a Scottish state-funded school. A one-year probationary period is required before full registration. The Scottish Executive Education Department's website websites has information on all aspects of teacher training and development.

Independent nursery schools may also prefer their nursery teachers to have QTS or TQ status.

All UK teaching staff are encouraged to regularly take short, specialised courses on the various aspects of child behaviour and development, and follow a programme of continuing professional development (CPD).

Mature entry is encouraged and often this job in the independent sector attracts teachers retiring from the maintained sector. Some two-year part-time PGCE (in Scotland PGDE) courses are available and there are appropriate Open University and other distance-learning courses for both a degree and PGCE (in Scotland PGDE).

In England and Wales there are training routes particularly suitable for adults as you can work while training. For example, entrants to the Registered Teacher Programme (England and Wales only) leading to qualified teacher status (QTS) must be over 24 and have completed two years in higher education (or part-time equivalent). It is also essential to have maths and English at a standard equivalent to at least GCSE (A*-C). Funding, student loans and bursaries are available.

Opportunities and Pay

Currently, there are good job opportunities due to the increasing number of nursery schools. Employment is with a local authority nursery/primary school or with an independent nursery school. In Scotland, you may also be employed to work in a nursery run by a social work department of a local authority. Promotion to more senior posts is possible after gaining experience. Some qualified and experienced teachers move into school inspection work, teacher training, education administration, or run their own playgroup, nursery or private school.

Salaries vary according to location and employer. Starting salaries for a qualified state nursery school teacher are around £21k a year and rise to around £42k for a nursery head teacher. Teachers in London may receive an additional allowance. These salaries are representative throughout the UK, but contact your local area education department or other employer for full salary scale/grade details.

Health

This job sometimes requires a medical test on entry. You need to have plenty of stamina to deal with a group of young, lively children.

Skills and Qualities

able to relate well to children and young people, able to stimulate learners, creative and imaginative flair, energetic, excellent communication skills, good listening skills, good organisational skills, patient, sense of humour

Relevant Subjects

Art and Design, English, Music, Psychology, Sociology

Further Information

Open University - www.open.ac.uk

Scottish Government - Education and Training - www.scotland.gov.uk/Topics/Education

TARGETjobs: Teaching (GTI Specialist Publishers Ltd) - www.groupgti.com

Teachernet (Dept for Education) - www.teachernet.gov.uk

Teaching Scotland Magazine (GTCS magazine) - www.gtcs.org.uk

Training & Development Agency (TDA) - www.tda.gov.uk

Addresses

British Association for Early Childhood Education (BAECE)
136 Cavell Street, London E1 2JA
Phone: +44 (0)20 7539 5400
Web: www.early-education.org.uk

CACHE: Council for Awards in Children's Care & Education
Apex House, 81 Camp Road, St Albans AL1 5GB
Phone: 0845 347 2123 (UK only)
Web: www.cache.org.uk

Department of Education NI (DENI)
Rathgael House, Balloo Road, Bangor BT19 7PR
Phone: +44 (0)28 9127 9279
Web: www.deni.gov.uk

General Teaching Council for England (GTC)
Whittington House, 19-30 Alfred Place, London WC1E 7EA
Phone: 0370 001 0308 (UK only)
Web: www.gtce.org.uk

General Teaching Council for Northern Ireland (GTCNI)
4th Floor, Albany House, 73-75 Great Victoria Street,
Belfast BT2 7AF
Phone: +44 (0)28 9033 3390
Web: www.gtcni.org.uk

General Teaching Council for Scotland (GTC Scotland)
Clerwood House, 96 Clermiston Road, Edinburgh EH12 6UT
Phone: +44 (0)131 314 6000
Web: www.gtcs.org.uk

General Teaching Council for Wales (GTCW)
4th Floor, Southgate House, Wood Street, Cardiff CF10 1EW
Phone: +44 (0)29 2055 0350
Web: www.gtcw.org.uk

Similar Jobs

Montessori Teacher, Nursery Worker, Pre-school Supervisor/Worker, Teacher: Primary School, Teacher: Special Educational Needs, Teaching Assistant

Teacher: English

CRCI:Education and Training
CLCI:FAB — Job Band: 5

Job Description

English teachers prepare and deliver a structured learning programme of English language and literature at secondary school level. They follow a syllabus and aim to widen pupils' knowledge and understanding of the subject, paying particular attention to grammar and spelling. They plan individual lessons and use a variety of resources, such as textbooks, the internet, audio-visual materials, worksheets and practical work. Some teachers prepare students for national examinations. They set assignments and exams, correct written work and record progress of each individual student.

English teachers lead and encourage discussion and individual thought, giving help where necessary. In some schools, may also teach drama. Teachers help with school administration, pastoral care, school clubs and societies. May also supervise a classroom/teaching assistant and assist them to further develop their skills.

Work Details

You usually work 39 weeks a year with contact teaching time between 9am-3.30pm, Monday to Friday. Contact teaching time is generally decreasing to allow more time for administration and teacher development. In some schools, usually in the independent sector, you work fewer weeks a year, but often work on a Saturday. You should be able to relate well to young people and are responsible for supporting learners to reach required learning targets. The job involves undertaking out-of-hours duties and working at home, for example on lesson preparation and writing reports. You have contact with other professionals as well as parents and carers.

Teaching requires you to spend each day sitting, standing, carrying/moving learning materials (often equipment), and walking around, depending on the teaching activity. A teaching career is very demanding and also requires creativity and imagination. However, it is a very rewarding profession.

Qualification

• England, Wales and Northern Ireland

Band 5: For degree course: 2-3 A levels including English and some GCSEs (A*-C) including maths or equivalent. The exact requirements depend on the degree you take.

• Scotland

Band 5: For degree course: 3-5 H grades including English and some S grades (1-3) including maths, or similar. The exact requirements depend on the degree you take.

Degree Information

A degree in English together with a postgraduate certificate in education (PGCE) is usually required for entry to this job.

Adult Qualifications

University entry requirements for mature entrants can vary and Access or foundation courses are often available. In England and Wales there are a few part-time postgraduate training courses and the Open University runs an 18 month distance learning course in some subjects.

Work Experience

Entry to this job is competitive and it is important that you do some relevant work experience before applying to teacher training. Applicants are also advised to show evidence of their interest in and commitment to teaching by having working with young people, such as being a voluntary helper in a school, a youth club, sports group, or holiday play activity/sports scheme.

Entry and Training

In England and Wales, to teach in a mainstream or special school, you need qualified teacher status (QTS) achieved by taking an undergraduate or postgraduate certificate in education course (PGCE) or through an employment-based route into teaching, and train on the job. All those working with children and young people are required to have a Criminal Records Bureau (CRB)/Disclosure Scotland check.

In Scotland, the most popular way to qualify as a secondary school teacher in English is to have a degree in English language or English literature and then do a one-year professional graduate diploma in education (PGDE).

For full details on the entry route to teaching throughout the UK, please read the article Teacher: Secondary School.

The National Association for the Teaching of English (NATE) is the professional body supporting those working in English education.

Mature applicants are encouraged and there are many options for training and qualification, including distance-learning courses. For further details on all teacher training routes throughout the UK, please read the article Teacher: Secondary School.

Opportunities and Pay

Teachers are mainly employed in state schools and opportunities are steadily increasing. Work is also available in independent schools, colleges and academies, pupil referral units, secure training units, young offenders' institutions, and also the armed forces. There are opportunities for promotion, for example to head of department and beyond. Your prospects may depend on willingness to move to another area. Part-time work, private tuition, supply teaching and job-sharing is possible. Work abroad is also available, particularly with organisations such as Voluntary Services Overseas and with the British Council.

A newly qualified teacher (NQT) earns from around £21k a year. A career changer or mature entrant may, depending on previous experience, start at a higher level in the scale.

Additional responsibilities in a school can attract a higher salary. Advanced Skills Teachers (ASTs) earn from around £36k-£55k a year. Teachers in the independent sector can usually expect to earn a higher salary with additional perks, such as subsidised accommodation and school fees.

There is an allowance for working in London. You are advised to contact your local education department or other employer for full salary scale/grade details.

Health

This job requires a health check on entry.

Skills and Qualities

able to discipline, able to stimulate learners, enthusiastic, excellent communication skills, fair minded, good written English, IT skills, patient, self confident, sense of humour

Relevant Subjects

English, Psychology, Sociology

Further Information

English in Education (3 x year) (National Association for the Teaching of English) - www.wiley.com/bw/journal.asp?ref=0425-049425-0494

Modern English Teacher (Pavilion - OLM Group) - www.onlineMET.com

Open University - www.open.ac.uk

Scottish Government - Education and Training - www.scotland.gov.uk/Topics/Education

Teach First - www.teachfirst.org.uk

Teach in Scotland (Scottish Government Education Department) - www.teachinginscotland.com

Teachernet (Dept for Education) - www.teachernet.gov.uk

Teaching English (British Council) - www.teachingenglish.org.uk

Teaching Scotland Magazine (GTCS magazine) - www.gtcs.org.uk

Teaching Training Wales - www.educationcymru.org

Training & Development Agency (TDA) - www.tda.gov.uk

▶Working in English (2007) (Babcock Lifeskills) - www.babcock-lifeskills.com/

▶Working in schools & colleges (2007) (Babcock Lifeskills) - www.babcock-lifeskills.com/

Addresses

Department of Education NI (DENI)
Rathgael House, Balloo Road, Bangor BT19 7PR
Phone: +44 (0)28 9127 9279
Web: www.deni.gov.uk

General Teaching Council for England (GTC)
Whittington House, 19-30 Alfred Place, London WC1E 7EA
Phone: 0370 001 0308 (UK only)
Web: www.gtce.org.uk

General Teaching Council for Northern Ireland (GTCNI)
4th Floor, Albany House, 73-75 Great Victoria Street,
Belfast BT2 7AF
Phone: +44 (0)28 9033 3390
Web: www.gtcni.org.uk

General Teaching Council for Scotland (GTC Scotland)
Clerwood House, 96 Clermiston Road, Edinburgh EH12 6UT
Phone: +44 (0)131 314 6000
Web: www.gtcs.org.uk

General Teaching Council for Wales (GTCW)
4th Floor, Southgate House, Wood Street, Cardiff CF10 1EW
Phone: +44 (0)29 2055 0350
Web: www.gtcw.org.uk

National Association for the Teaching of English (NATE)
50 Broadfield Road, Sheffield S8 0XJ
Phone: +44 (0)114 255 5419
Web: www.nate.org.uk

Similar Jobs

Lecturer: Further Education, Lecturer: Higher Education, Teacher: Drama, Teacher: English to Speakers of Other Languages, Teacher: Secondary School

Teacher: English to Speakers of Other Languages

also known as: Teacher of English as a Foreign Language, TEFL Teacher

CRCI:Education and Training
CLCI:FAB

Job Band: 4 to 5

Job Description

Called ESOL or EFL teachers, they teach people for whom English is not their first language, either in the UK or overseas. Prepare and give lessons in English to small groups of students. Aim to improve the four basic language skills; reading and writing, listening and speaking, by using a variety of resources, activities and techniques. Also cover national culture and way of life. May use textbooks, pictures and flash cards, question and answer sessions, audio tapes, mime, games, computers, role-play or video. Must be prepared to teach a range of ages, backgrounds and abilities. Encourage the students to interact and communicate with each other using the skills learned in each lesson.

ESOL/EFL teachers mark and give constructive feedback on the students' oral and written work. May be expected to take students on short trips to cities including places or buildings of local or historical interest, in order to broaden their knowledge and improve conversation and vocabulary. Can also spend time organising social or sports activities.

Work Details

You work variable hours depending on the appointment and often may be expected to work some evenings and possibly weekends. Place of work is a school, college, a university, or possibly in people's homes. Students can be of all ages and have a variety of language learning needs. In residential language schools you may have to get involved in sports and social events with your students. You may work with small or large groups, or you may give individual tuition. You are responsible for creative and imaginative work that requires many hours in the preparation of lessons and teaching materials.

Work is mainly in a classroom or perhaps outdoors, when taking students on an outing or playing sport. The work involves sitting/ standing, and can be quite active. Overseas, teaching hours can sometimes be long and irregular, in the early morning and evenings. Adult education classes often take place in the evening.

Qualification

- **England, Wales and Northern Ireland**

Band 4: For HND, Diploma of Higher Education or foundation degree: 1-2 A levels and some GCSEs (A*-C) usually including English and maths, or equivalent.

Band 5: For degree courses: 2-3 A levels and some GCSEs (A*-C) usually including English and maths, or equivalent. Exact requirements depend on the degree you take.

- **Scotland**

Band 4: For entry to SQA higher national and professional development awards, usually 2-3 H grades and some S grades (1-3), including English and maths, or similar qualifications.

Band 5: For degree courses: 3-5 H grades and some S grades (1-3), usually including English and maths, or similar qualifications. Exact requirements depend on the degree you take.

Degree Information

Any degree discipline is acceptable for entry to this job. However, the most useful subjects include English, modern European/non-European languages, or linguistics. An MA degree in TESOL is available.

Adult Qualifications

A degree in modern languages or in English is an advantage but is not essential. Entry requirements vary for mature entrants to colleges of education and language schools. Experience in teaching is valuable and qualifications in appropriate languages, especially unusual ones, are most useful.

Work Experience

Entry to this job is competitive and it is important that you try to do some relevant work experience before applying for training and for jobs. Experience of teaching, knowledge and wide use of foreign languages, particularly the more unusual ones, is a distinct advantage. Work experience in areas where you communicate with people of all ages is also helpful.

Entry and Training

Most entrants to this job are graduates. The umbrella term TESOL (Teaching English to Speakers of Other Languages) is used to incorporate TEFL and TESL. Teaching English as a Foreign Language (TEFL) is mostly used in the UK for those people for whom English is a foreign language and who need to use English for short-term study, work or leisure purposes. Teaching people who intend to settle in the UK or for whom English is a second language in their home country is usually done by Teachers of English as a Second Language, known as TESL or TE2L.

Training can be by full or part-time course, or by distance learning. The most widely recognised and approved qualifications are from Cambridge ESOL and Trinity College London. To teach ESOL in the private sector, the minimum qualifications are the CertTESOL (Trinity College London), which involves four weeks full time up to nine months part time training, involving a minimum of 130 timetabled hours, or the University of Cambridge's CELTA (Cambridge Certificate in English Language Teaching to Adults) qualification that lasts four to five weeks full time or from 16 weeks to one year part time. These courses usually require at least two A levels/H grades or equivalent, but need little or no teaching experience.

A certificate to specialise in English Language Teaching for Young Learners (CELTYL) is also available from Cambridge ESOL. Trinity College London also offers a higher qualification, the DipTESOL. These higher qualifications require an ESOL certificate and teaching experience. There are also a wide number of private colleges offering TEFL courses for those who particularly want to work teaching English overseas. Care should be taken to select an appropriate course as they can vary enormously and should be recognised by the British Council. Most are private fee-paying courses.

Teaching in state schools (UK) requires a degree plus qualified teacher status (QTS). Those wanting to teach adults in the public sector need the Diploma in Teaching English in the Lifelong Learning Sector (DTLLS ESOL). Training can be full or part time. All new entrants to teaching in further education institutions have to register with the Institute for Learning. With the DTLLS and some experience, you can apply for Qualified Teacher Learning and Skills (QTLS) status.

All those working with young people under 18 and vulnerable adults are required to have a Criminal Records Bureau (CRB)/ Disclosure Scotland check.

Mature entry is an advantage for this job with applicants bringing experience and qualifications from a wide variety of work, or from living and working abroad. Many enter this work as a second career. Some specialist certificate courses can be full time (typically 4-5 weeks) or part time (usually from a few months to over a year). For more details contact the individual organisations in the address section that offer professional qualifications.

Opportunities and Pay

Opportunities are increasing for ESOL (English to speakers of other languages) teachers. In the UK, jobs are mainly with commercial language schools teaching overseas students on short courses, often during the summer period. Jobs in language schools tend to be concentrated in London, Oxford, Cambridge, and on the south coast of England. There are some jobs with local authorities teaching immigrant/asylum seeker groups, work in foreign embassies, in industry, and in cultural institutes. Some ESOL teachers are employed by UK universities and colleges. After some work experience you can be self-employed as a freelance teacher. There is keen competition for vacancies and promotion opportunities are limited.

There are some full-time jobs, but there are good opportunities for temporary, seasonal or part-time work. Experienced and highly qualified ESOL teachers may move into management positions or write ESOL books and teaching materials. Good opportunities do exist to work abroad for employers such as the British Council, independent schools, language schools, government departments, industrial concerns and voluntary organisations. Work is available in several countries.

Starting salaries for those teaching in the UK are likely to be £12k-£14k in the private sector and around £20k a year in further education. You may be paid at an hourly rate. With experience you can earn up to £30k a year. Pay for those working overseas varies considerably depending not only on your qualifications and experience, but also the cost of living in each individual country. You may also receive an accommodation allowance.

Skills and Qualities

able to explain clearly, able to get on with all kinds of people, clear speaking voice, confident, encouraging, good communication skills, good interpersonal skills, outgoing personality, patient, sense of humour

Relevant Subjects

English, Modern Foreign Languages, Psychology, Sociology

Further Information

CILT:The National Centre for Languages - www.cilt.org.uk

English Teaching Professional (Keyways Publishing Ltd.) - www.etprofessional.com

LLUK (Lifelong Learning UK) - sector skills council for the professional development of staff working in the lifelong learning sector - www.lluk.org

Modern English Teacher (Pavilion - OLM Group) - www.onlineMET.com

NALDIC Quarterly (Nat Assoc for Lang Development in the Curriculum) - www.naldic.org.uk/docs/publications/index.cfm

Scottish Association for TEFL - www.satefl.org.uk/index.html

Teaching English Abroad (Crimson 2009)

►Working in English (2007) (Babcock Lifeskills) - www.babcock-lifeskills.com/

►Working with languages (2010) (Babcock Lifeskills) - www.babcock-lifeskills.com/

Addresses

British Council
10 Spring Gardens, London SW1A 2BN
Phone: +44 (0)20 7930 8466
Web: www.britishcouncil.org

English UK
219 St John Street, London EC1V 4LY
Phone: +44 (0)20 7608 7960
Web: www.englishuk.com

Institute for Learning (IfL)
First Floor, 49-51 East Road, London N1 6AH
Phone: 0844 815 3202 (UK only)
Web: www.ifl.ac.uk

International Association of Teachers of English as a Foreign Language (IATEFL)
Darwin College University of Kent, Canterbury CT2 7NY
Phone: +44 (0)1227 824 430
Web: www.iatefl.org

National Association for Teaching English and other Community Languages to Adults (NATECLA)
National Centre, South Birmingham College, Room HA205, Hall Green Campus, Cole Bank Road B28 8ES
Phone: +44 (0)121 688 8121
Web: www.natecla.org.uk

National Association for the Teaching of English (NATE)
50 Broadfield Road, Sheffield S8 0XJ
Phone: +44 (0)114 255 5419
Web: www.nate.org.uk

Trinity College London
89 Albert Embankment, London SE1 7TP
Phone: +44 (0)20 7820 6100
Web: www.trinitycollege.co.uk

University of Cambridge - ESOL
ESOL Examinations, 1 Hills Road, Cambridge CB1 2EU
Web: www.cambridge-efl.org

Similar Jobs

Interpreter, Lecturer: Further Education, Teacher: Community Languages, Teacher: English, Teacher: Modern Foreign Languages

Teacher: Food Technology

also known as: Teacher: D&T Food Technology, Teacher: Home Economics

CRCI:Education and Training
CLCI:FAB — Job Band: 5

Job Description

Food technology teachers offer the skills required for the efficient management of the home including the choice and purchase of a house, suitable furnishing, wise buying and budgeting, hygiene and nutrition. They help students to plan, cost and cook nutritious meals. They explain and demonstrate the correct use of domestic appliances and equipment. They also inform students about services available for the consumer and how to budget. Some teachers prepare students for national examinations. They set assignments and exams, correct written work and record progress.

Some teachers may help with school administration, pastoral care, school outings, clubs and societies. Attending staff meetings, training and development days and parents'/carers' evenings is part of the job. They may also supervise the work of a teaching/ classroom assistant or technician.

Teacher: Food Technology

Work Details

You usually work 39 weeks a year with contact teaching time between 9am-3.30pm, Monday to Friday. Contact teaching time is generally decreasing to allow more time for administration and teacher development. In some schools, usually in the independent sector, you work fewer weeks a year, but often work on a Saturday. You should be able to relate well to young people and are responsible for supporting learners to reach required learning targets. The job involves out-of-hours duties and working at home, for example, on lesson preparation and writing reports. You have contact with other professionals as well as parents and carers.

Teaching requires you to spend each day sitting, standing, carrying/moving learning materials (often equipment), and walking around, depending on the teaching activity. A teaching career is very demanding, and it also requires creativity and imagination. However, it is a very rewarding profession.

Qualification

• England, Wales and Northern Ireland

Band 5: For degree courses: 2-3 A levels and some GCSEs (A*-C) usually including English and maths, or equivalent. Exact requirements depend on the degree you take.

• Scotland

Band 5: For degree courses: 3-5 H grades and some S grades (1-3), usually including English and maths, or similar qualifications. Exact requirements depend on the degree you take.

Degree Information

It is expected that your degree has a food focus such as food science, food technology, food product development, nutrition, hospitality, or consumer science/studies, together with a postgraduate certificate in education (PGCE).

Adult Qualifications

Applicants without academic entry requirements may gain entry to relevant university courses by first taking an Access or foundation course. Check with individual institutions.

Work Experience

Entry to this job is competitive and it is important that you do some relevant work experience before applying to teacher training. Applicants are advised to show evidence of their interest in and commitment to teaching by working with young people, preferably as a voluntary helper in a school, a youth club, sports group, or holiday play activity/sports scheme.

Entry and Training

In England and Wales, to teach in a mainstream or special school, you need qualified teacher status (QTS) achieved by taking an undergraduate or postgraduate certificate in education course (PGCE) or through an employment-based route into teaching, and train on the job. All those working with children and young people are required to have a Criminal Records Bureau (CRB)/Disclosure Scotland check.

In Scotland, the quickest and most popular way to qualify as a secondary school teacher of food technology is to have a degree in a food related subject and then do a one-year professional graduate diploma in education (PGDE).

For full details on the entry route to teaching throughout the UK, please read the article Teacher: Secondary School.

Mature applicants are encouraged and there are many options for training and qualification, including distance-learning courses.

For further details on all teacher training routes throughout the UK, please read the article Teacher: Secondary School.

Opportunities and Pay

The requirements for compulsory food education (not Scotland) means that opportunities for qualified food technology teachers are increasing. Teachers are mainly employed in state schools and work is also available in independent schools, colleges and academies, adult learning centres, pupil referral units, secure training units or young offenders' institutions, and the armed forces. There are opportunities for promotion, for example to head of department and beyond, though your prospects may depend on willingness to move to another area. Part-time work, private tuition, supply teaching and job-sharing is possible. Work abroad is also available.

A newly qualified teacher (NQT) earns from around £21k a year. A career changer or mature entrant may, depending on previous experience, start at a higher level in the scale.

Additional responsibilities in a school can attract a higher salary. Advanced Skills Teachers (ASTs) earn from around £36k-£55k a year. Teachers in the independent sector can usually expect to earn a higher salary with additional perks, such as subsidised accommodation and school fees.

There is an allowance for working in London. You are advised to contact your local education department or other employer for full salary scale/grade details.

Health

People with certain skin conditions are not able to do this job. All potential teachers have to undergo a health check.

Skills and Qualities

able to discipline, able to explain clearly, enthusiastic, even tempered, eye for visual effect, good organisational skills, good sense of taste and smell, manual dexterity, patient, self confident

Relevant Subjects

Art and Design, Biology, Business and accounting, Chemistry, Economics, English, Hospitality and catering, Psychology, Science, Sociology

Further Information

Scottish Government - Education and Training - www.scotland.gov.uk/Topics/Education

Teach First - www.teachfirst.org.uk

Teach in Scotland (Scottish Government Education Department) - www.teachinginscotland.com

Teachernet (Dept for Education) - www.teachernet.gov.uk

Teaching Scotland Magazine (GTCS magazine) - www.gtcs.org.uk

Teaching Training Wales - www.educationcymru.org

Training & Development Agency (TDA) - www.tda.gov.uk

▶Working in schools & colleges (2007) (Babcock Lifeskills) - www.babcock-lifeskills.com/

Addresses

Department of Education NI (DENI)
Rathgael House, Balloo Road, Bangor BT19 7PR
Phone: +44 (0)28 9127 9279
Web: www.deni.gov.uk

Design & Technology Association (D&TA)
16 Wellesbourne House, Walton Road, Warwickshire CV35 9JB
Phone: +44 (0)1789 470 007
Web: www.data.org.uk

General Teaching Council for England (GTC)
Whittington House, 19-30 Alfred Place, London WC1E 7EA
Phone: 0370 001 0308 (UK only)
Web: www.gtce.org.uk

General Teaching Council for Northern Ireland (GTCNI)
4th Floor, Albany House, 73-75 Great Victoria Street,
Belfast BT2 7AF
Phone: +44 (0)28 9033 3390
Web: www.gtcni.org.uk

General Teaching Council for Scotland (GTC Scotland)
Clerwood House, 96 Clermiston Road, Edinburgh EH12 6UT
Phone: +44 (0)131 314 6000
Web: www.gtcs.org.uk

General Teaching Council for Wales (GTCW)
4th Floor, Southgate House, Wood Street, Cardiff CF10 1EW
Phone: +44 (0)29 2055 0350
Web: www.gtcw.org.uk

Similar Jobs

Consumer Scientist, Food Scientist/Technologist, Lecturer: Further Education, Teacher: Secondary School

Teacher: Geography

CRCI:Education and Training
CLCI:FAB Job Band: 5

Job Description

Geography teachers prepare and deliver a structured learning programme through the study of the Earth's natural features and of mankind's responses to them. They follow a syllabus designed to increase pupils' knowledge and interpretation of geography. They plan individual lessons and use a variety of resources, such as textbooks, the internet, audio-visual materials, worksheets and practical work. Some teachers prepare students for national examinations. Often take students on field trips to collect samples and do map work of an area. They encourage discussion and set project work.

Teachers set homework and exams, correct written work and record progress of each individual student. Many have school administration responsibilities and assist in pastoral work, school clubs and societies. Attending staff meetings, training and development days and parents'/carers' evenings is part of the job. They may also supervise the work of a teaching/classroom assistant.

Work Details

You usually work 39 weeks a year with contact teaching time between 9am-3.30pm, Monday to Friday. Contact teaching time is generally decreasing to allow more time for administration and teacher development. In some schools, usually in the independent sector, you work fewer weeks a year, but often work on a Saturday. You should be able to relate well to young people and are responsible for supporting learners to reach required learning targets. The job involves undertaking out-of-hours duties and working at home, for example on lesson preparation and writing reports. You have contact with other professionals as well as parents and carers.

Teaching requires you to spend each day sitting, standing, carrying/moving learning materials (often equipment), and walking around, depending on the teaching activity. A teaching career is very demanding, and it also requires creativity and imagination. However, it is a very rewarding profession.

Qualification

- **England, Wales and Northern Ireland**

Band 5: For degree courses: 2-3 A levels and some GCSEs (A*-C) usually including English and maths, or equivalent. Exact requirements depend on the degree you take. Some courses require A levels in geography, maths or a science.

- **Scotland**

Band 5: For degree courses: 3-5 H grades and some S grades (1-3), usually including English and maths, or similar qualifications. Exact requirements depend on the degree you take. Some courses require H grades in geography, maths or a science.

Degree Information

A degree in geography or a closely related subject is required, followed by a postgraduate certificate in education (PGCE). In England and Wales it is possible to qualify with a BEd or a BA/BSc degree with Qualified Teacher Status (QTS).

Adult Qualifications

Graduates in geography or a closely related subject can take a one-year postgraduate course in education. Routes to a first degree are available for adults without the necessary formal qualifications through Open University and Access or foundation courses.

Work Experience

Entry to this job is competitive and it is important that you do some relevant work experience before applying to teacher training. Applicants are advised to show evidence of their interest in and commitment to teaching by working with young people, preferably as a voluntary helper in a school, a youth club, sports group, or holiday play activity/sports scheme.

Entry and Training

In England and Wales, to teach in a mainstream or special school, you need qualified teacher status (QTS) achieved by taking an undergraduate or postgraduate certificate in education course (PGCE) or through an employment-based route into teaching, and train on the job. All those working with children and young people are required to have a Criminal Records Bureau (CRB)/Disclosure Scotland check.

In Scotland, the quickest and most popular way to qualify as a secondary school teacher of geography is to have a degree in a geography related subject and then do a one-year professional graduate diploma in education (PGDE). Or you could study some PGDE courses through part time or distance learning.

For full details on the entry routes to teaching throughout the UK, please read the article Teacher: Secondary School.

Qualified and experienced geography teachers may apply to the Royal Geographical Society (RGS) to become a chartered geographer (CGeog). Contact the RGS for details.

Mature applicants are encouraged and there are many options for training and qualification, including distance-learning courses. For further details on all teacher training routes throughout the UK, please read the article Teacher: Secondary School.

Opportunities and Pay

Teachers are mainly employed in state schools and the numbers are steadily increasing. Work is also available in independent schools, colleges and academies, adult learning centres, pupil referral units, secure training units or young offenders' institutions, and the armed forces. There are opportunities for promotion, for example head of department and beyond, though your prospects may depend on willingness to move to another area. Part-time work, private tuition, supply teaching and job-sharing is possible. Work abroad is also available.

A newly qualified teacher (NQT) earns from around £21k a year. A career changer or mature entrant may, depending on previous experience, start at a higher level in the scale.

Additional responsibilities in a school can attract a higher salary. Advanced Skills Teachers (ASTs) earn from around £36k-£55k a year. Teachers in the independent sector can usually expect to earn a higher salary with additional perks, such as subsidised accommodation and school fees.

There is an allowance for working in London. You are advised to contact your local education department or other employer for full salary scale/grade details.

Health

This job requires a health check on entry.

Skills and Qualities

able to discipline, able to stimulate learners, analytical skills, energetic, enthusiastic, environmental awareness, excellent communication skills, fair minded, IT skills, patient

Relevant Subjects

English, Geography, Government and politics, Land and Environment, Leisure, travel and tourism, Psychology, Sociology

Further Information

Open University - www.open.ac.uk

Scottish Government - Education and Training - www.scotland.gov.uk/Topics/Education

Teach First - www.teachfirst.org.uk

Teach in Scotland (Scottish Government Education Department) - www.teachinginscotland.com

Teachernet (Dept for Education) - www.teachernet.gov.uk

Teaching Scotland Magazine (GTCS magazine) - www.gtcs.org.uk

Teaching Training Wales - www.educationcymru.org

Training & Development Agency (TDA) - www.tda.gov.uk

▶Working in schools & colleges (2007) (Babcock Lifeskills) - www.babcock-lifeskills.com/

Addresses

Department of Education NI (DENI)
Rathgael House, Balloo Road, Bangor BT19 7PR
Phone: +44 (0)28 9127 9279
Web: www.deni.gov.uk

General Teaching Council for England (GTC)
Whittington House, 19-30 Alfred Place, London WC1E 7EA
Phone: 0370 001 0308 (UK only)
Web: www.gtce.org.uk

General Teaching Council for Northern Ireland (GTCNI)
4th Floor, Albany House, 73-75 Great Victoria Street, Belfast BT2 7AF
Phone: +44 (0)28 9033 3390
Web: www.gtcni.org.uk

General Teaching Council for Scotland (GTC Scotland)
Clerwood House, 96 Clermiston Road, Edinburgh EH12 6UT
Phone: +44 (0)131 314 6000
Web: www.gtcs.org.uk

General Teaching Council for Wales (GTCW)
4th Floor, Southgate House, Wood Street, Cardiff CF10 1EW
Phone: +44 (0)29 2055 0350
Web: www.gtcw.org.uk

Royal Geographical Society (RGS)
(with the Institute of British Geographers), 1 Kensington Gore, London SW7 2AR
Phone: +44 (0)20 7591 3000
Web: www.rgs.org

Similar Jobs

Geologist, Geophysicist, Lecturer: Further Education, Lecturer: Higher Education, Teacher: Secondary School, Town Planner

Teacher: History

CRCI:Education and Training
CLCI:FAB — Job Band: 5

Job Description

History teachers specialise in teaching students about past events and help them to understand people, their country and culture today. They follow a structured syllabus, aiming to widen pupils' knowledge and understanding of the subject. They plan individual lessons and use a variety of resources, such as textbooks, the internet, audio-visual materials and worksheets. Some teachers prepare students for national examinations. They set assignments and exams, correct written work and record progress of individual students. Sometimes they organise trips to historical sites, including places abroad.

History teachers lead and encourage discussion and promote individual thought, giving help where necessary. Carry out some administrative tasks and may assist in pastoral work, or with school clubs and societies. Attending staff meetings, training and development days and parents'/carers' evenings is also part of the job. They may supervise the work of a teaching/classroom assistant.

Work Details

You usually work 39 weeks a year with contact teaching time between 9am-3.30pm, Monday to Friday. Contact teaching time is generally decreasing to allow more time for administration and teacher development. In some schools, usually in the independent sector, you work fewer weeks a year, but often work on a Saturday. You should be able to relate well to young people and are responsible for supporting learners to reach required learning targets. The job involves undertaking out-of-hours duties and working at home, for example on lesson preparation and writing reports. You have contact with other professionals as well as parents and carers.

Teaching requires you to spend each day sitting, standing, carrying/moving learning materials (often equipment), and walking around, depending on the teaching activity. A teaching career is very demanding, and it also requires creativity and imagination. However, it is a very rewarding profession.

Qualification

• England, Wales and Northern Ireland

Band 5: For degree courses: 2-3 A levels usually including English and history, and some GCSEs (A*-C) usually including English and maths, or equivalent. Exact requirements depend on the degree you take.

• Scotland

Band 5: For degree courses: 3-5 H grades including English and/or history and some S grades (1-3), usually including English and maths, or similar qualifications. Exact requirements depend on the degree you take.

Degree Information

A degree in history, together with a postgraduate certificate in education (PGCE) is usually required for entry to this job.

Adult Qualifications

Adults aged 23 or over may enter degree courses with a variety of qualifications or via Access or foundation courses. For graduates there are part-time postgraduate courses in education available. The Open University also runs an 18 month distance-learning course for some subjects.

Work Experience

Entry to this job is competitive and it is important that you do some relevant work experience before applying to teacher training. Applicants are advised to show evidence of their interest in and commitment to teaching by working with young people, preferably as a voluntary helper in a school, a youth club, sports group, or holiday play activity/sports scheme.

Entry and Training

In England and Wales, to teach in a mainstream or special school, you need qualified teacher status (QTS) achieved by taking an undergraduate or postgraduate certificate in education course (PGCE) or through an employment-based route into teaching, and train on the job. All those working with children and young people are required to have a Criminal Records Bureau (CRB)/Disclosure Scotland check.

In Scotland, the quickest and most popular way to qualify as a secondary school teacher of history is to have a degree in history and then do a one-year professional graduate diploma in education (PGDE).

For full details of the entry routes into teaching throughout the UK, please read the article Teacher: Secondary School.

Mature applicants are encouraged and there are many options for training and qualification, including distance-learning courses. For further details on all teacher training routes, please read the article Teacher: Secondary School.

Opportunities and Pay

Teachers are mainly employed in state schools and the numbers are steadily increasing. Work is also available in independent schools, colleges and academies, adult learning centres, pupil referral units, secure training units or young offenders' institutions, and the armed forces. There are opportunities for promotion, for example to head of department and beyond, though your prospects may depend on willingness to move to another area. Part-time work, private tuition, supply teaching and job-sharing is possible. Work abroad is also available.

A newly qualified teacher (NQT) earns from around £21k a year. A career changer or mature entrant may, depending on previous experience, start at a higher level in the scale.

Additional responsibilities in a school can attract a higher salary. Advanced Skills Teachers (ASTs) earn from around £36k-£55k a year. Teachers in the independent sector can usually expect to earn a higher salary with additional perks, such as subsidised accommodation and school fees.

There is an allowance for working in London. You are advised to contact your local education department or other employer for full salary scale/grade details.

Health

This job requires a health check on entry.

Skills and Qualities

able to discipline, able to inspire confidence, able to stimulate learners, enthusiastic, fair minded, good interpersonal skills, good spoken communication, good written English, patient, self confident.

Relevant Subjects

Classical studies, English, Government and politics, History, Psychology, Sociology

Further Information

Open University - www.open.ac.uk

Scottish Government - Education and Training - www.scotland.gov.uk/Topics/Education

Teach First - www.teachfirst.org.uk

Teach in Scotland (Scottish Government Education Department) - www.teachinginscotland.com

Teachernet (Dept for Education) - www.teachernet.gov.uk

Teaching Scotland Magazine (GTCS magazine) - www.gtcs.org.uk

Teaching Training Wales - www.educationcymru.org

Training & Development Agency (TDA) - www.tda.gov.uk

▶Working in schools & colleges (2007) (Babcock Lifeskills) - www.babcock-lifeskills.com/

Addresses

Department of Education NI (DENI)
Rathgael House, Balloo Road, Bangor BT19 7PR
Phone: +44 (0)28 9127 9279
Web: www.deni.gov.uk

General Teaching Council for England (GTC)
Whittington House, 19-30 Alfred Place, London WC1E 7EA
Phone: 0370 001 0308 (UK only)
Web: www.gtce.org.uk

General Teaching Council for Northern Ireland (GTCNI)
4th Floor, Albany House, 73-75 Great Victoria Street, Belfast BT2 7AF
Phone: +44 (0)28 9033 3390
Web: www.gtcni.org.uk

General Teaching Council for Scotland (GTC Scotland)
Clerwood House, 96 Clermiston Road, Edinburgh EH12 6UT
Phone: +44 (0)131 314 6000
Web: www.gtcs.org.uk

General Teaching Council for Wales (GTCW)
4th Floor, Southgate House, Wood Street, Cardiff CF10 1EW
Phone: +44 (0)29 2055 0350
Web: www.gtcw.org.uk

Similar Jobs

Archaeologist, Lecturer: Further Education, Lecturer: Higher Education, Museum/Art Gallery Curator, Teacher: Classics, Teacher: Secondary School

Teacher: ICT

CRCI:Education and Training
CLCI:FAB Job Band: 5

Job Description

ICT teachers specialise in teaching young people at secondary school about computers and information technology. They help them to develop ICT (information and communication technology) skills using computers and programs, including keyboarding skills, databases and spreadsheets. Advise students on the use of the internet and other systems, giving pupils individual help when necessary. Some teachers prepare students for national academic and vocational examinations. They set assignments and exams, correct written work and record progress of individual students.

Teachers do some administration, pastoral work, or help with school clubs and societies. Attending staff meetings, training and development days and parents'/carers' evenings are part of the job. They may also supervise the work of a technician.

Work Details

You usually work 39 weeks a year with contact teaching time between 9am-3.30pm, Monday to Friday. Contact teaching time is generally decreasing to allow more time for administration and teacher development. In some schools, usually in the independent sector, you work fewer weeks a year, but often work on a Saturday. You should be able to relate well to young people and are responsible for supporting learners to reach required learning targets. The job involves undertaking out-of-hours duties and working at home, for example on lesson preparation and writing reports. You have contact with other professionals as well as parents and carers.

Teaching requires you to spend each day sitting, standing, carrying/moving learning materials (often equipment), and walking around, depending on the teaching activity. A teaching career is very demanding, and it also requires creativity and imagination. However, it is a very rewarding profession.

Qualification

• England, Wales and Northern Ireland

Band 5: For degree courses: 2-3 A levels including maths, and some GCSEs (A*-C) usually including English and maths, or equivalent. Exact requirements depend on the degree you take.

• Scotland

Band 5: For degree courses: 3-5 H grades and some S grades (1-3), usually including English and maths, or similar qualifications. Exact requirements depend on the degree you take.

Degree Information
A degree in computer science or a closely related subject is required, followed by a postgraduate certificate in education (PGCE).

Adult Qualifications
Graduates in computing disciplines can take a one-year postgraduate course in education. For those with a non-relevant degree, but at least a year of mathematical higher education, there are some two-year conversion courses. For adults without the necessary formal qualifications, routes to a first degree are available through Open University and Access or foundation courses.

Work Experience
Entry to this job is competitive and it is important that you do some relevant work experience before applying to teacher training. Applicants are advised to show evidence of their interest in and commitment to teaching by working with young people, preferably as a voluntary helper in a school, a youth club, sports group, or holiday play activity/sports scheme.

Entry and Training
In England and Wales, to teach in a mainstream or special school, you need qualified teacher status (QTS) achieved by taking an undergraduate or postgraduate certificate in education course (PGCE) or through an employment-based route into teaching, and train on the job. All those working with children and young people are required to have a Criminal Records Bureau (CRB)/Disclosure Scotland check.

In Scotland, the quickest and most popular way to qualify as a secondary school teacher of ICT is to have a degree in a computer based subject and then do a one-year professional graduate diploma in education (PGDE).

For full details on the entry routes into teaching throughout the UK, please read the article Teacher: Secondary School.

Mature applicants are encouraged and there are many options for training and qualification, including distance-learning courses.

For further details on all teacher training routes, please read the article Teacher: Secondary School.

Opportunities and Pay
Teachers are mainly employed in state schools and the numbers are steadily increasing. Work is also available in independent schools, colleges and academies, adult learning centres, pupil referral units, secure training units or young offenders' institutions, and the armed forces. There are opportunities for promotion, for example to head of department and beyond, though your prospects may depend on willingness to move to another area. Part-time work, private tuition, supply teaching and job-sharing is possible. Work abroad is also available.

A newly qualified teacher (NQT) earns from around £21k a year. A career changer or mature entrant may, depending on previous experience, start at a higher level in the scale.

Additional responsibilities in a school can attract a higher salary. Advanced Skills Teachers (ASTs) earn from around £36k-£55k a year. Teachers in the independent sector can usually expect to earn a higher salary with additional perks, such as subsidised accommodation and school fees.

There is an allowance for working in London. You are advised to contact your local education department or other employer for full salary scale/grade details.

Health
This job requires a health check on entry.

Skills and Qualities
able to discipline, able to explain clearly, able to stimulate learners, fair minded, good organisational skills, observant, patient, self confident, specialist IT skills, technical aptitude

Relevant Subjects
English, ICT/Computer studies, Mathematics, Physics, Psychology, Science, Sociology

Further Information
ICT Teacher's website - www.icteachers.co.uk
Open University - www.open.ac.uk
Scottish Government - Education and Training - www.scotland.gov.uk/Topics/Education
Teach First - www.teachfirst.org.uk
Teach in Scotland (Scottish Government Education Department) - www.teachinginscotland.com
Teachernet (Dept for Education) - www.teachernet.gov.uk
Teaching Scotland Magazine (GTCS magazine) - www.gtcs.org.uk
Teaching Training Wales - www.educationcymru.org
Training & Development Agency (TDA) - www.tda.gov.uk
►Working in schools & colleges (2007) (Babcock Lifeskills) - www.babcock-lifeskills.com/

Addresses
British Educational Communications and Technology Agency (BECTA)
Millburn Hill Road, Science Park, Coventry CV4 7JJ
Phone: +44 (0)24 7641 6994
Web: www.becta.org.uk

Department of Education NI (DENI)
Rathgael House, Balloo Road, Bangor BT19 7PR
Phone: +44 (0)28 9127 9279
Web: www.deni.gov.uk

General Teaching Council for England (GTC)
Whittington House, 19-30 Alfred Place, London WC1E 7EA
Phone: 0370 001 0308 (UK only)
Web: www.gtce.org.uk

General Teaching Council for Northern Ireland (GTCNI)
4th Floor, Albany House, 73-75 Great Victoria Street, Belfast BT2 7AF
Phone: +44 (0)28 9033 3390
Web: www.gtcni.org.uk

General Teaching Council for Scotland (GTC Scotland)
Clerwood House, 96 Clermiston Road, Edinburgh EH12 6UT
Phone: +44 (0)131 314 6000
Web: www.gtcs.org.uk

General Teaching Council for Wales (GTCW)
4th Floor, Southgate House, Wood Street, Cardiff CF10 1EW
Phone: +44 (0)29 2055 0350
Web: www.gtcw.org.uk

Similar Jobs
IT Applications Developer, IT Skills Trainer, Lecturer: Further Education, Lecturer: Higher Education, Teacher: Secondary School

Teacher: Mathematics

CRCI:Education and Training
CLCI:FAB Job Band: 5

Job Description
Maths teachers prepare and deliver a structured learning programme in mathematical subjects at secondary schools. They may also teach computing subjects. They plan individual lessons and use a variety of resources, such as textbooks, the internet, audio-visual materials, worksheets and practical work.

Some maths teachers prepare students for national academic and vocational examinations. They set assignments and exams, correct written work and record progress of individual students.

Attending staff meetings, training and development days and parents'/carers' evenings is part of the job. They may also supervise the work of a teaching/classroom assistant. Some teachers help with school administration, pastoral care, school outings, clubs and societies.

Work Details

You usually work 39 weeks a year with contact teaching time between 9am-3.30pm, Monday to Friday. Contact teaching time is generally decreasing to allow more time for administration and teacher development. In some schools, usually in the independent sector, you work fewer weeks a year, but often work on a Saturday. You should be able to relate well to young people and are responsible for supporting learners to reach required learning targets. The job involves undertaking out-of-hours duties and working at home, for example on lesson preparation and writing reports. You have contact with other professionals as well as parents and carers.

Teaching requires you to spend each day sitting, standing, carrying/moving learning materials (often equipment), and walking around, depending on the teaching activity. A teaching career is very demanding, and it also requires creativity and imagination. However, it is a very rewarding profession.

Qualification

• England, Wales and Northern Ireland

Band 5: For degree courses: 2-3 A levels, including maths, and some GCSEs (A*-C) usually including English and physics, or equivalent. Exact requirements depend on the degree you take.

• Scotland

Band 5: For degree courses: 3-5 H grades, including maths and English, and some S grades (1-3) including physics, or similar qualifications. Exact requirements depend on the degree you take.

Degree Information

A degree in maths, computer science or a closely related subject is required, followed by a postgraduate certificate in education (PGCE).

Adult Qualifications

Graduates in mathematical or computing disciplines can take a one-year postgraduate course in education. For those with a non-relevant degree, but at least a year of mathematical higher education, there are some two-year conversion courses. For those without the necessary formal qualifications, routes to a first degree are available through Open University and Access or foundation courses.

Work Experience

Entry to this job is competitive and it is important that you do some relevant work experience before applying to teacher training. Applicants are advised to show evidence of their interest in and commitment to teaching by working with young people, preferably as a voluntary helper in a school, a youth club, sports group, or holiday play activity/sports scheme.

Entry and Training

In England and Wales, to teach in a mainstream or special school, you need qualified teacher status (QTS) achieved by taking an undergraduate or postgraduate certificate in education course (PGCE) or through an employment-based route into teaching, and train on the job. All those working with children and young people are required to have a Criminal Records Bureau (CRB)/Disclosure Scotland check.

In Scotland, the quickest and most popular way to qualify as a secondary school teacher of maths is to have a degree in a maths-based subject and then do a one-year professional graduate diploma in education (PGDE).

For full details on the entry route to teaching throughout the UK, please read the article Teacher: Secondary School.

Chartered mathematics teacher status may be gained through the Institute of Mathematics and its Applications. The Association of Teachers of Mathematics and the Mathematics Association also provide information and support.

Mature applicants are encouraged and there are many options for training and qualification, including distance-learning courses. For further details on all teacher training routes throughout the UK, please read the article Teacher: Secondary School.

Opportunities and Pay

Teachers are mainly employed in state schools and the numbers are steadily increasing. Work is also available in independent schools, colleges and academies, adult learning centres, pupil referral units, secure training units or young offenders' institutions, and the armed forces. There are opportunities for promotion, for example to assistant headteacher, head of department and beyond, though your prospects may depend on willingness to move to another area. Part-time work, private tuition, supply teaching and job-sharing is possible. Work abroad is also available.

A newly qualified teacher (NQT) earns from around £21k a year. A career changer or mature entrant may, depending on previous experience, start at a higher level in the scale.

Additional responsibilities in a school can attract a higher salary. Advanced Skills Teachers (ASTs) earn from around £36k-£55k a year. Teachers in the independent sector can usually expect to earn a higher salary with additional perks, such as subsidised accommodation and school fees.

There is an allowance for working in London. You are advised to contact your local education department or other employer for full salary scale/grade details.

Health

This job requires a health check on entry.

Skills and Qualities

able to discipline, able to explain clearly, able to stimulate learners, analytical skills, good communication skills, good interpersonal skills, IT skills, numeracy skills, patient, self confident

Relevant Subjects

English, ICT/Computer studies, Mathematics, Physics, Psychology, Science, Sociology

Further Information

Open University - www.open.ac.uk

Scottish Government - Education and Training - www.scotland.gov.uk/Topics/Education

Teach First - www.teachfirst.org.uk

Teach in Scotland (Scottish Government Education Department) - www.teachinginscotland.com

Teachernet (Dept for Education) - www.teachernet.gov.uk

Teaching Scotland Magazine (GTCS magazine) - www.gtcs.org.uk

Teaching Training Wales - www.educationcymru.org

Training & Development Agency (TDA) - www.tda.gov.uk

▶Working in maths (2009) (Babcock Lifeskills) - www.babcock-lifeskills.com/

▶Working in schools & colleges (2007) (Babcock Lifeskills) - www.babcock-lifeskills.com/

Addresses

Association of Teachers of Mathematics (ATM)
Unit 7 Prime Industrial Park, Shaftesbury Street, Derby DE23 8YB
Phone: +44 (0)1332 346599
Web: www.atm.org.uk

Department of Education NI (DENI)
Rathgael House, Balloo Road, Bangor BT19 7PR
Phone: +44 (0)28 9127 9279
Web: www.deni.gov.uk

General Teaching Council for England (GTC)
Whittington House, 19-30 Alfred Place, London WC1E 7EA
Phone: 0370 001 0308 (UK only)
Web: www.gtce.org.uk

General Teaching Council for Northern Ireland (GTCNI)
4th Floor, Albany House, 73-75 Great Victoria Street, Belfast BT2 7AF
Phone: +44 (0)28 9033 3390
Web: www.gtcni.org.uk

General Teaching Council for Scotland (GTC Scotland)
Clerwood House, 96 Clermiston Road, Edinburgh EH12 6UT
Phone: +44 (0)131 314 6000
Web: www.gtcs.org.uk

General Teaching Council for Wales (GTCW)
4th Floor, Southgate House, Wood Street, Cardiff CF10 1EW
Phone: +44 (0)29 2055 0350
Web: www.gtcw.org.uk

Institute of Mathematics and its Applications (IMA)
Catherine Richards House 16 Nelson Street, Southend-on-Sea SS1 1EF
Phone: +44 (0)1702 354 020
Web: www.ima.org.uk

Mathematical Association
259 London Road, Leicester LE2 3BE
Phone: +44 (0)116 221 0013
Web: www.m-a.org.uk

Similar Jobs

Lecturer: Further Education, Lecturer: Higher Education, Statistician, Teacher: Secondary School

Teacher: Modern Foreign Languages

also known as: MFL Teacher
CRCI:Education and Training
CLCI:FAB Job Band: 5

Job Description

Language teachers prepare and give lessons at secondary school level in one or two modern languages, most often French, German, Italian, Spanish or Russian. Courses cover communication skills, grammar, culture and literature, using a range of texts and resources. They may use a language laboratory to improve students' fluency and pronunciation. They set exams, correct work and record progress. Many language teachers also encourage students to learn about the relevant country by arranging visits and exchanges. Usually teachers are expected to teach two foreign languages. May also prepare students for national examinations.

Some teachers help with school administration, pastoral care, school outings, clubs and societies. Attending staff meetings, training and development days and parents'/carers' evenings is part of the job May also supervise the work of a teaching/ classroom assistant.

Work Details

You usually work 39 weeks a year with contact teaching time between 9am-3.30pm, Monday to Friday. Contact teaching time is generally decreasing to allow more time for administration and teacher development. In some schools, usually in the independent sector, you work fewer weeks a year, but often work on a Saturday. You should be able to relate well to young people and are responsible for supporting learners to reach required learning targets. The job involves undertaking out-of-hours duties and also working at home, for example on lesson preparation and writing reports. You have contact with other professionals as well as parents and carers.

Teaching requires you to spend each day sitting, standing, carrying/moving learning materials (often equipment), and walking around, depending on the teaching activity. A teaching career is very demanding, and it also requires creativity and imagination. However, it is a very rewarding profession.

Qualification

- **England, Wales and Northern Ireland**

Band 5: For degree courses: 2-3 A levels, including at least one modern language and sometimes English, and some GCSEs (A*-C) including English and maths, or equivalent. Exact requirements depend on the degree you take.

- **Scotland**

Band 5: For degree courses: 3-5 H grades, including at least one modern language and English, and some S grades (1-3), usually including maths, or similar qualifications. Exact requirements depend on the degree you take.

Degree Information

A degree with one or more languages and a postgraduate certificate in education (PGCE) is usually required for this job. Check with teaching authorities to ensure your degree meets the requirements for entry to teacher training.

Adult Qualifications

Adults aged 23 or over may enter degree courses with a variety of qualifications or via Access or foundation courses. Entry requirements may be more flexible for subjects where there are teacher shortages. For graduates there are part-time postgraduate courses in education available. The Open University also offers a flexible distance-learning postgraduate course in modern foreign language teaching (Spanish, French or German).

Work Experience

Applicants to courses are advised to show evidence of their interest in and commitment to teaching by working with young people, preferably as a voluntary helper in a school, a youth club, sports group, or holiday play activity/sports scheme. Work experience to improve your language skills is gained in several ways, including taking a gap year work placement abroad, or through an educational exchange programme whilst at school or university. Some language courses offer a period of residence abroad as part of your first degree. Contact CILT, the National Centre for Languages for information on work experience.

Entry and Training

In England and Wales, to teach in a mainstream or special school, you need qualified teacher status (QTS) achieved by taking an undergraduate or postgraduate certificate in education course (PGCE) or through an employment-based route into teaching, and train on the job. All those working with children and young people are required to have a Criminal Records Bureau (CRB)/Disclosure Scotland check.

In Scotland, the quickest and most popular way to qualify as a secondary school teacher of languages is to have a degree in modern foreign language taught in secondary schools, and then do a one-year professional graduate diploma in education (PGDE).

For full details on the entry route to teaching throughout the UK, please read the article Teacher: Secondary School.

Mature applicants are encouraged and there are many options for training and qualification, including distance-learning courses.

For further details on all teacher training routes throughout the UK, please read the article Teacher: Secondary School.

Opportunities and Pay

Teachers are mainly employed in state schools and the numbers are steadily increasing. Work is also available in independent schools, colleges and academies, adult learning centres, pupil referral units, secure training units or young offenders' institutions, and the armed forces. There are opportunities for promotion, for example to head of department and beyond, though your prospects may depend on willingness to move to another area. Part-time work, private tuition, supply teaching and job-sharing is possible. Work abroad is also available.

A newly qualified teacher (NQT) earns from around £21k a year. A career changer or mature entrant may, depending on previous experience, start at a higher level in the scale.

Additional responsibilities in a school can attract a higher salary. Advanced Skills Teachers (ASTs) earn from around £36k-£55k a year. Teachers in the independent sector can usually expect to earn a higher salary with additional perks, such as subsidised accommodation and school fees.

There is an allowance for working in London. You are advised to contact your local education department or other employer for full salary scale/grade details.

Health

This job requires a health check on entry and usually requires normal hearing.

Skills and Qualities

ability in one or more languages, able to discipline, able to explain clearly, encouraging, good communication skills, good interpersonal skills, good organisational skills, patient, self confident, sense of humour

Relevant Subjects

Classical studies, English, Modern Foreign Languages, Psychology, Sociology

Further Information

Open University - www.open.ac.uk

Scottish Government - Education and Training - www.scotland.gov.uk/Topics/Education

TARGETjobs: Teaching (GTI Specialist Publishers Ltd) - www.groupgti.com

Teach First - www.teachfirst.org.uk

Teach in Scotland (Scottish Government Education Department) - www.teachinginscotland.com

Teachernet (Dept for Education) - www.teachernet.gov.uk

Teaching Scotland Magazine (GTCS magazine) - www.gtcs.org.uk

Teaching Training Wales - www.educationcymru.org

Training & Development Agency (TDA) - www.tda.gov.uk

Working with languages (2010) (Babcock Lifeskills) - www.babcock-lifeskills.com/

Addresses

CILT, the National Centre for Languages
3rd Floor, 111 Westminster Bridge Road, London SE1 7HR
Phone: 08456 12 5885 (UK only)
Web: www.cilt.org.uk

Department of Education NI (DENI)
Rathgael House, Balloo Road, Bangor BT19 7PR
Phone: +44 (0)28 9127 9279
Web: www.deni.gov.uk

General Teaching Council for England (GTC)
Whittington House, 19-30 Alfred Place, London WC1E 7EA
Phone: 0370 001 0308 (UK only)
Web: www.gtce.org.uk

General Teaching Council for Northern Ireland (GTCNI)
4th Floor, Albany House, 73-75 Great Victoria Street, Belfast BT2 7AF
Phone: +44 (0)28 9033 3390
Web: www.gtcni.org.uk

General Teaching Council for Scotland (GTC Scotland)
Clerwood House, 96 Clermiston Road, Edinburgh EH12 6UT
Phone: +44 (0)131 314 6000
Web: www.gtcs.org.uk

General Teaching Council for Wales (GTCW)
4th Floor, Southgate House, Wood Street, Cardiff CF10 1EW
Phone: +44 (0)29 2055 0350
Web: www.gtcw.org.uk

Similar Jobs

Interpreter, Secretary: Bilingual, Teacher: Community Languages, Teacher: English to Speakers of Other Languages, Teacher: Secondary School, Translator

Teacher: Music

also known as: Peripatetic Music Teacher

CRCI:Education and Training

CLCI:FAB — Job Band: 5

Job Description

Music teachers prepare lessons and give instruction, either to individuals or classes and groups, in music (instruments, singing and theory) to students of all ages. May either work in a secondary or primary school, a music conservatoire or do private tuition.

In school this involves teaching the history, theory and appreciation of many different types and styles of music. Increasingly, they are involved in the use of music technology and the use of specialist programs to help a student with their own composition. Choose courses to stimulate interest and enthusiasm for music and to develop individual talents. May prepare students for music exams, including national examinations. Often organise an orchestra/choir, and direct and produce concerts etc.

Private teachers offer instrumental or singing teaching to individuals or groups. They plan lessons and prepare pupils for graded exams. Also organise the marketing and running of their business.

Work Details

If teaching in schools, you usually work 39 weeks a year with contact teaching time between 9am-3.30pm, Monday to Friday. In some schools you work fewer weeks a year, but often work on a Saturday. You should be able to relate well to young people and are responsible for supporting learners and reaching required learning targets. The job requires you to spend time on lesson preparation and writing reports. Most music teachers are involved with a lot of after school work, such as rehearsals for orchestras, concerts and musicals.

You have contact with other professionals as well as parents and carers. Teaching requires you to spend each day sitting, standing, carrying/moving learning materials (often equipment), and walking around, depending on the teaching activity. A teaching career is very demanding, and it also requires creativity and imagination. However, it is a very rewarding profession.

Private music teachers work with individuals in their own or their pupil's home. Hours are more flexible, but are likely to include evenings and weekends. Visiting (peripatetic) teachers go into schools and work with pupils to develop their singing or ability on a particular instrument. Lessons usually take place before or after school or in the lunch hour.

Teacher: Music

Qualification

• England, Wales and Northern Ireland

Band 5: For music degree: two A levels including music and some GCSEs (A*-C) including English and maths, plus an audition and interview. Applicants usually require a Grade 8 on main instrument and Grade 6 on second instrument. Equivalent qualifications may be acceptable for entry to courses.

• Scotland

Band 5: For music degree: minimum of three H grades, including English and preferably music, and some S grades (1-3) including maths, plus an audition and interview. Applicants usually require a Grade 8 on main instrument and Grade 6 on second instrument. Similar qualifications may be acceptable for entry to courses.

Degree Information

A degree in music, together with a postgraduate certificate in education (PGCE) or a BEd degree in music is required for entry to this job in state schools.

Adult Qualifications

Adults may enter courses that lead to BEd/BA and qualified teacher status (QTS) with a variety of qualifications. Some colleges run Access or foundation courses for those adults without the required academic qualifications. Minimum requirements may be waived for mature entrants with considerable musical talent. Shortened two-year BEd courses may be available for those with advanced qualifications in music. The Open University also runs a flexible PGCE for music for those in England, Wales and Northern Ireland.

Work Experience

Work experience helps you find out what you enjoy and do not enjoy about a job. For those who want to train to teach music in a state school, it is important to have some relevant work experience. Applicants are advised to show evidence of their interest in and commitment to teaching by working with young people, preferably as a voluntary helper in a school, a youth club or holiday play scheme. Experience of an orchestra/choral society when at school/university, or with a local music/choral society is an advantage.

Entry and Training

To enter most music courses you have to pass an audition and need to be able to play two instruments, possibly including the piano. All music teachers dealing with children or young people have to undergo a Criminal Records Bureau (CRB)/Disclosure Scotland check.

In order to teach music in a secondary school in the UK, you need qualified teacher status (QTS) (England and Wales) or attain a Teaching Qualification - secondary education (TQ) (Scotland). For primary school teaching, you usually train to teach all subjects at primary level, but specialise in music. See the articles: Teacher : Secondary School and Teaching: Primary School for full details of all training routes to mainstream teaching. For further details on all qualifications and funding, also contact the Training and Development Agency (TDA) for schools (England and Wales), the Department of Education Northern Ireland (DENI), or Scottish Government - Education and Training.

To teach in a music conservatoire, you usually need a postgraduate qualification in music.

Those with exceptional music skills may be able to teach privately without any qualifications, but most professional private music teachers have a formal qualification in music, such as a teaching or performing degree or diploma from a recognised music college. They are specialists in their instrument (including singing and voice production) and they have good performing skills. With a minimum of four hours teaching a week for at least a year, and a recognised music qualification, you can be registered as a music teacher with the Incorporated Society of Musicians (ISM).

Qualified teachers who want to extend their skills can take the Music Teaching in Professional Practice distance learning programme. This is offered by the ISM in conjunction with the University of Reading, and takes between two and three years. The Associated Board of the Royal Schools of Music also provides a programme of professional development for instrument and vocal teachers.

Mature applicants to teaching in state schools are encouraged. There are many options for training and qualification, including distance-learning courses and on-the-job training. For further details on all teacher training routes, qualifications and funding, contact the Training and Development Agency (TDA) for schools (England & Wales), the Department of Education Northern Ireland (DENI), or Scottish Government - Education and Training.

Music teaching is also a popular career move for people who have been professional musicians and want to move into teaching others a musical skill.

Opportunities and Pay

Currently, there is a shortage of music teachers in state schools. You can be employed by a local authority, college or an independent school. Newly qualified teachers may find themselves on temporary contracts. Private tuition, part-time work, supply teaching and job-sharing is possible. Work overseas is also available.

A newly qualified teacher (NQT) earns from around £21k a year. A career changer or mature entrant may, depending on previous experience, start at a higher level in the scale. Contact your local education department or other employer for full salary scale/grade details.

Teachers in the independent sector can usually expect to earn a higher salary with additional perks, such as subsidised accommodation and school fees. Private music teachers working with individual pupils normally charge an hourly rate. The current average is between £25 and £35 an hour.

Health

This job requires good hearing. You may be required to have a health check in order to teach in state schools.

Skills and Qualities

able to explain clearly, able to stimulate learners, able to work both on your own and in a team, enthusiastic, good communication skills, good interpersonal skills, good organisational skills, outstanding musical ability, patient, sense of humour

Relevant Subjects

English, Music, Performing arts, Psychology, Sociology

Further Information

Behind the Scenes: Music (Trotman 2009) - www.trotman.co.uk

British & International Music Yearbook (Rhinegold Directories) - www.rhinegold.co.uk

Open University - www.open.ac.uk

Routes into Teaching Music (Dept for Education) - http://publications.teachernet.gov.uk/default.aspx

Scottish Government - Education and Training - www.scotland.gov.uk/Topics/Education

So you want to work in Music & Dance (Wayland) - www.waylandbooks.co.uk

Teach in Scotland (Scottish Government Education Department) - www.teachinginscotland.com

Training & Development Agency (TDA) - www.tda.gov.uk

▶Working in music (2007) (Babcock Lifeskills) - www.babcock-lifeskills.com/

Addresses

Associated Board of the Royal Schools of Music (ABRSM)
24 Portland Place, London W1B 1LU
Phone: +44 (0)20 7636 5400
Web: www.abrsm.org

Department of Education NI (DENI)
Rathgael House, Balloo Road, Bangor BT19 7PR
Phone: +44 (0)28 9127 9279
Web: www.deni.gov.uk

Incorporated Society of Musicians (ISM)
10 Stratford Place, London W1C 1AA
Phone: +44 (0)20 7629 4413
Web: www.ism.org

Music Education Council (MEC)
54 Elm Road Hale, Altrincham, Cheshire WA15 9QP
Phone: +44 (0)161 928 3085
Web: www.mec.org.uk

National Association of Music Educators (NAME)
Gordon Lodge Snitterton Road, Matlock, Derbyshire DE4 3LZ
Phone: +44 (0)1629 760791
Web: www.name.org.uk/

Similar Jobs

Arts Administrator, Lecturer: Further Education, Music Therapist, Musician: Classical, Teacher: Primary School, Teacher: Secondary School

Teacher: Physical Education

also known as: PE Teacher, Sports Teacher

CRCI:Education and Training
CLCI:FAB Job Band: 5

Job Description

PE staff teach a wide range of physical education (PE) activities and sports to young people of all abilities, in a gym, and also outdoors on playing fields, track and courts. They stimulate and motivate interest in sport and PE, and help develop pupils' sporting talents. They give instruction in apparatus work, exercises, posture and in a wide variety of sports, which may include orienteering, sailing and canoeing. PE teachers organise and supervise indoor and outdoor games and sporting events, giving coaching to groups and to individuals. Plan competitions, matches and other recreational activities, including taking groups to an outdoor activity centre, and accompanying school teams to matches at other schools.

Some PE teachers prepare pupils for national exams. Give individual advice and guidance to students and may refer them to another professional, such as a careers adviser or counsellor. Some PE teachers may also teach another subject. Attending staff meetings, training and development days, and parents'/carers' evenings is part of the job. May also help with school administration, pastoral care, clubs and societies.

Work Details

You usually work 39 weeks a year with contact teaching time between 9am-3.30pm, Monday to Friday. Contact teaching time is generally decreasing to allow more time for administration and teacher development. PE teachers may have to work outside normal school hours as competitions are often on Saturday mornings or late afternoons. You should be able to relate well to young people and are responsible for supporting learners to reach required learning targets.

The job also involves working at home, for example on activity preparation and writing reports. You have contact with other professionals as well as parents and carers. A teaching career is very demanding, and it also requires creativity and imagination. However, it is a very rewarding profession.

Your responsibilities include the health and safety of those you teach and you have to cope with any emergencies that may occur. You are physically active and on your feet for hours at a time. There is a risk of minor injuries and, like anyone involved in sport, you can suffer long term physical damage to vulnerable areas like your back and knees. You wear sportswear most of the day.

Qualification

• England, Wales and Northern Ireland

Band 5: For degree courses: 2-3 A levels, possibly including PE or sports studies, and some GCSEs (A*-C) usually including English and maths, or equivalent. Exact requirements depend on the degree you take.

• Scotland

Band 5: For degree course: 3-5 H grades including English, and some S grades (1-3) including maths, or similar. Exact requirements depend on the degree you take.

Degree Information

A degree in physical education (PE) or sports science or similar, together with a postgraduate certificate in education (PGCE), or a BEd degree in PE, or BA in physical education with ITT/QTS (secondary) is required for entry to this job.

Adult Qualifications

Adults aged 23 or over may enter BEd courses with a variety of qualifications or via Access or foundation courses. For graduates there are part-time postgraduate courses in education available.

Work Experience

Entry to this job is competitive and it is important that you do some relevant work experience before applying to teacher training. Applicants are advised to show evidence of their interest in and commitment to teaching by working with young people, preferably as a voluntary helper in a school, a youth club, sports group, or holiday play activity/sports scheme.

Entry and Training

In England and Wales, to teach in a mainstream or special school, you need qualified teacher status (QTS) achieved by taking an undergraduate or postgraduate certificate in education (PGCE), or through an employment-based route into teaching and train on the job. Entry to training courses is highly competitive, so you have to provide evidence that you have a particular ability in PE. All those working with children and young people are required to have a Criminal Records Bureau (CRB)/Disclosure Scotland check.

In Scotland, the quickest and most popular way to qualify as a secondary school teacher in physical education is to take a four-year degree course in physical education at either Edinburgh or Stirling University.

For full details on the entry route to teaching throughout the UK, please read the article Teacher: Secondary School.

Mature applicants are encouraged and there are many options for training and qualification, including distance-learning courses.

For further details on all teacher training routes throughout the UK, please read the article Teacher: Secondary School.

Opportunities and Pay

Teachers are mainly employed in state schools and opportunities are steadily increasing. Work is also available in independent schools, colleges and academies, pupil referral units, secure training units, young offenders' institutions, and also the armed forces. There are opportunities for promotion, for example to head of department and beyond. Your prospects may depend on willingness to move to another area. Part-time work, private tuition, supply teaching and job-sharing is possible.

A newly qualified teacher (NQT) earns from around £21k a year. A career changer or mature entrant may, depending on previous experience, start at a higher level in the scale.

Additional responsibilities in a school can attract a higher salary. Advanced Skills Teachers (ASTs) earn from around £36k-£55k a year. Teachers in the independent sector can usually expect to earn a higher salary with additional perks, such as subsidised accommodation and school fees.

There is an allowance for working in London. You are advised to contact your local education department or other employer for full salary scale/grade details.

Health
This job requires a health check on entry and good general fitness and stamina.

Skills and Qualities
able to discipline, able to explain clearly, able to stimulate learners, able to take responsibility, enthusiastic, good communication skills, good organisational skills, health & safety awareness, patient, supportive

Relevant Subjects
Biology, English, Leisure, travel and tourism, Physical education and sport, Psychology, Science, Sociology

Further Information
Open University - www.open.ac.uk

Physical Education and Sport Pedagogy (4 x year) (Association for Physical Education (afPE)) - www.afpe.org.uk/public/member_journals.htm

Scottish Government - Education and Training - www.scotland.gov.uk/Topics/Education

TARGETjobs: Teaching (GTI Specialist Publishers Ltd) - www.groupgti.com

Teach in Scotland (Scottish Government Education Department) - www.teachinginscotland.com

Teachernet (Dept for Education) - www.teachernet.gov.uk

Teaching Scotland Magazine (GTCS magazine) - www.gtcs.org.uk

Teaching Training Wales - www.educationcymru.org

Training & Development Agency (TDA) - www.tda.gov.uk

What's it like to be a Sports Trainer? (A&C Black 2008)

►Working in schools & colleges (2007) (Babcock Lifeskills) - www.babcock-lifeskills.com/

►Working in sport & leisure (2010) (Babcock Lifeskills) - www.babcock-lifeskills.com/

Addresses
Association for Physical Education (afPE)
Room 117, Bredon, University of Worcester,
Henwick Grove, WR2 6AJ
Phone: +44 (0)1905 855584
Web: www.afpe.org.uk

Department of Education NI (DENI)
Rathgael House, Balloo Road, Bangor BT19 7PR
Phone: +44 (0)28 9127 9279
Web: www.deni.gov.uk

General Teaching Council for England (GTC)
Whittington House, 19-30 Alfred Place, London WC1E 7EA
Phone: 0370 001 0308 (UK only)
Web: www.gtce.org.uk

General Teaching Council for Northern Ireland (GTCNI)
4th Floor, Albany House, 73-75 Great Victoria Street,
Belfast BT2 7AF
Phone: +44 (0)28 9033 3390
Web: www.gtcni.org.uk

General Teaching Council for Scotland (GTC Scotland)
Clerwood House, 96 Clermiston Road, Edinburgh EH12 6UT
Phone: +44 (0)131 314 6000
Web: www.gtcs.org.uk

General Teaching Council for Wales (GTCW)
4th Floor, Southgate House, Wood Street, Cardiff CF10 1EW
Phone: +44 (0)29 2055 0350
Web: www.gtcw.org.uk

Similar Jobs
Fitness Instructor, Outdoor Activities Instructor, Sport & Exercise Scientist, Sports Coach, Sports Development Officer, Sports Therapist

Teacher: Physical Sciences
also known as: Chemistry Teacher, Physics Teacher, Science Teacher

CRCI:Education and Training
CLCI:FAB Job Band: 5

Job Description
Science teachers prepare and deliver a structured learning programme in physics or chemistry at secondary school level to students aged 11-19 (12-18 in Scotland). They follow a syllabus and illustrate lessons with practical experiments, demonstrations and visual aids. Plan individual lessons and use a variety of resources, such as textbooks, the internet, audio-visual materials and worksheets. Science teachers give pupils individual help when necessary. Some prepare students for national examinations. They set assignments and internal exams, correct written work and record each student's progress.

Teachers may also have school administration or pastoral care duties, and help with school outings, clubs and societies. May also supervise a classroom/teaching assistant or laboratory technician, supporting them to increase their knowledge and ability.

Work Details
You usually work 39 weeks a year with contact teaching time between 9am-3.30pm, Monday to Friday. Contact teaching time is generally decreasing to allow more time for administration and teacher development. In some schools, usually independent schools, you work fewer weeks a year, but often work on a Saturday. You should be able to relate well to young people and are responsible for supporting learners to reach required learning targets. The job involves undertaking out-of-hours duties and working at home, for example on lesson preparation and writing reports. You have contact with other professionals as well as parents and carers.

Teaching requires you to spend each day sitting, standing, carrying/moving learning materials (often equipment), and walking around, depending on the teaching activity. A teaching career is very demanding, and it also requires creativity and imagination. However, it is a very rewarding profession.

Qualification
- **England, Wales and Northern Ireland**

Band 5: For degree courses: 2-3 A levels including physics or chemistry, and some GCSEs (A*-C) usually including English and maths, or equivalent. Exact requirements depend on the degree you take.

- **Scotland**

Band 5: For degree courses: 3-5 H grades including physics or chemistry and English, and some S grades (1-3) including maths, or similar qualifications. Exact requirements depend on the degree you take.

Degree Information
A degree in physics, chemistry or a related subject is required, followed by a postgraduate certificate in education (PGCE).

Adult Qualifications
Adults aged 23 or over may enter BEd courses with a variety of qualifications or via Access or foundation courses. Entry requirements may be more flexible for subjects where there are teacher shortages. For graduates there are part-time postgraduate courses in education available.

Work Experience
Entry to this job is competitive and it is important that you do some relevant work experience before applying to teacher training. Applicants are advised to show evidence of their interest in and commitment to teaching by working with young people, preferably as a voluntary helper in a school, a youth club, sports group, or holiday play activity/sports scheme.

Entry and Training
In England and Wales, to teach in a mainstream or special school, you need qualified teacher status (QTS) achieved by taking an undergraduate or postgraduate certificate in education course (PGCE) or through an employment-based route into teaching, and train on the job. All those working with children and young people are required to have a Criminal Records Bureau (CRB)/Disclosure Scotland check.

In Scotland, the quickest and most popular way to qualify as a secondary school teacher of physical sciences is to have a degree in either physics or chemistry and then do a one-year professional graduate diploma in education (PGDE).

For full details on the entry route to teaching throughout the UK, please read the article Teacher: Secondary School.

The Association for Science Education offers the chance for experienced and highly skilled science teachers to gain Chartered Science Teacher status.

Mature applicants are encouraged and there are many options for training and qualification, including distance-learning courses.

For further details on all teacher training routes throughout the UK, please read the article Teacher: Secondary School.

Opportunities and Pay
Teachers are mainly employed in state schools and the numbers are steadily increasing. Work is also available in independent schools, colleges and academies, adult learning centres, pupil referral units, secure training units or young offenders' institutions, and the armed forces. There are opportunities for promotion, for example to head of department and beyond, though your prospects may depend on willingness to move to another area. Part-time work, private tuition, supply teaching and job-sharing is possible. Work abroad is also available.

A newly qualified teacher (NQT) earns from around £21k a year. A career changer or mature entrant may, depending on previous experience, start at a higher level in the scale.

Additional responsibilities in a school can attract a higher salary. Advanced Skills Teachers (ASTs) earn from around £36k-£55k a year. Teachers in the independent sector can usually expect to earn a higher salary with additional perks, such as subsidised accommodation and school fees.

There is an allowance for working in London. You are advised to contact your local education department or other employer for full salary scale/grade details.

Health
This job requires a health check on entry.

Skills and Qualities
able to discipline, able to explain clearly, able to stimulate learners, good communication skills, good interpersonal skills, good organisational skills, IT skills, patient, scientific approach, self confident

Relevant Subjects
Chemistry, Design and technology, English, ICT/Computer studies, Mathematics, Physics, Psychology, Science, Sociology

Further Information
Open University - www.open.ac.uk

Scottish Government - Education and Training - www.scotland.gov.uk/Topics/Education

TARGETjobs: Teaching (GTI Specialist Publishers Ltd) - www.groupgti.com

Teach First - www.teachfirst.org.uk

Teach in Scotland (Scottish Government Education Department) - www.teachinginscotland.com

Teachernet (Dept for Education) - www.teachernet.gov.uk

Teaching Scotland Magazine (GTCS magazine) - www.gtcs.org.uk

Teaching Training Wales - www.educationcymru.org

Training & Development Agency (TDA) - www.tda.gov.uk

▶Working in schools & colleges (2007) (Babcock Lifeskills) - www.babcock-lifeskills.com/

Addresses
Association for Science Education (ASE)
College Lane, Hatfield, Hertfordshire AL10 9AA
Phone: +44 (0)1707 283 000
Web: www.ase.org.uk

Department of Education NI (DENI)
Rathgael House, Balloo Road, Bangor BT19 7PR
Phone: +44 (0)28 9127 9279
Web: www.deni.gov.uk

General Teaching Council for England (GTC)
Whittington House, 19-30 Alfred Place, London WC1E 7EA
Phone: 0370 001 0308 (UK only)
Web: www.gtce.org.uk

General Teaching Council for Northern Ireland (GTCNI)
4th Floor, Albany House, 73-75 Great Victoria Street, Belfast BT2 7AF
Phone: +44 (0)28 9033 3390
Web: www.gtcni.org.uk

General Teaching Council for Scotland (GTC Scotland)
Clerwood House, 96 Clermiston Road, Edinburgh EH12 6UT
Phone: +44 (0)131 314 6000
Web: www.gtcs.org.uk

General Teaching Council for Wales (GTCW)
4th Floor, Southgate House, Wood Street, Cardiff CF10 1EW
Phone: +44 (0)29 2055 0350
Web: www.gtcw.org.uk

Institute of Physics (IOP)
76 Portland Place, London W1B 1NT
Phone: +44 (0)20 7470 4800
Web: www.iop.org

Royal Society of Chemistry (RSC)
Education Department, Burlington House, Piccadilly, London W1J 0BA
Phone: +44 (0)20 7437 8656
Web: www.rsc.org

Similar Jobs
Chemist, Lecturer: Further Education, Physicist, Teacher: Biological Sciences, Teacher: Secondary School

Teacher: Primary School

also known as: Primary Teacher

CRCI:Education and Training

CLCI:FAB

Job Band: 5

Job Description

Teachers in primary schools play a vital role in helping children aged 3 to 11 years old in their educational learning and development, to achieve their potential and in preparation for secondary education. In Scotland the age band is 4.5 to 12. They also help develop a child's character, independence and social skills through structured learning and play activities. Prepare and deliver learning programmes in a variety of subjects. Teach a class of pupils in most subjects, including PE, geography, history and science, as well as literacy and numeracy. May also teach their specialist subject to other classes in the school. They use a variety of resources, including audio-visual aids and computers, and apply a variety of teaching techniques.

Sometimes called Key Stage (KS) 1 or 2 teachers, they organise projects and may prepare pupils for statutory national tests (commonly known as SATS). Monitoring and recording the work and progress of each pupil is a significant part of the job. They write reports and attend staff meetings and parents' evenings. Often also supervise the work of a classroom/teaching assistant. May take children out to places of interest. May also specialise as a special educational needs coordinator (SENCO).

Work Details

As a teacher, you usually work 39 weeks a year in a school, with contact teaching time worked between 9am-3.30pm, Monday to Friday. In some schools, usually independent preparatory schools, you work fewer weeks a year, but may work on a Saturday. You should be able to relate well to young children and are responsible for supporting learners to meet nationally required learning targets. The job can involve undertaking out-of-hours duties and also working at home, for example on lesson preparation, marking work and writing reports.

Most jobs require you to be on your feet for much of the day. You have contact with primary school children and their parents/carers, and also with other professional colleagues. Some administrative work is necessary. A teaching career is very demanding and requires creativity and imagination. However, it is a very rewarding profession.

Qualification

- **England, Wales and Northern Ireland**

Band 5: For BEd in primary education with qualified teacher status (QTS): 2-3 A levels and some GCSEs (A*-C) usually including English, maths and a science, or equivalent. Exact requirements depend on the degree you take.

- **Scotland**

Band 5: For BEd in primary education: at least three H grades, including English, and five S grades (1-3); must include maths at 1-2 or H grade maths, or similar qualifications. Exact requirements depend on the degree you take.

Degree Information

The majority of primary school teachers qualify by studying for a four-year BEd degree at university. You can also enter this job with a degree in any subject relevant to the primary curriculum followed by a postgraduate certificate in education (PGCE).

Adult Qualifications

Institutions vary in the entry requirements they demand from mature students for the BEd course. Entry is often possible via an Access or foundation course. Most colleges prefer adults who have experience in working with young children. The Open University offers an 18 month, part-time postgraduate certificate in education.

Work Experience

Entry to this job is competitive and it is important that you try to do some relevant work experience before applying to teacher training. Applicants are advised to show evidence of their interest in and commitment to teaching by working with children, preferably as a voluntary helper in a school, a youth club, sports group, or holiday play activity/sports scheme.

The Training & Development Agency (TDA) can provide details for prospective teachers to gain knowledge of a classroom environment through 'taster' days, short courses, or a discussion with a qualified, practising teacher. For details of similar opportunities in Scotland, contact Scottish Government - Education and Training, or for Northern Ireland, the Department of Education in Northern Ireland (DENI).

Entry and Training

In England and Wales, to teach in a mainstream state or special school you need qualified teacher status (QTS) achieved by taking an undergraduate or postgraduate course (PGCE) or through an employment-based route into teaching, and train on the job. For more information about teaching three to five year olds, see also the article Teacher: Early Years. All teachers in training have to undergo a Criminal Records Bureau (CRB)/Disclosure Scotland check.

For initial teacher training (ITT) for primary teaching, you need GCSEs (or equivalent) in English, mathematics and science at grade C or above. It is an advantage to have experience in the use of computers, and also useful to be able to read music and play a musical instrument. You are also required to pass numeracy, literacy and ICT (information and communications technology) skills tests to teach in England.

You should always choose any course carefully to ensure that your first degree enables entry to a PGCE course, which may last one year full time or two years part time. Primary teacher training includes instruction in teaching all the subjects in the primary national curriculum. In Wales primary teachers are also taught how to teach Welsh. Newly qualified teachers (NQTs) follow a probation programme over three terms and must register with the General Teaching Council for England/Wales.

There is also a Fast Track teaching programme (England/Wales) that provides accelerated leadership development for existing QTS teachers in the early stages of their career. Contact the National College for Leadership of Schools and Children's Services for details.

In order to be qualified to teach in Northern Ireland, a teacher must have either a recognised teaching degree after completing an approved teacher training course (normally four years) at a UK university or college of higher education, or a recognised degree or equivalent qualification plus a PGCE, awarded after completing a one-year full-time course at a UK university or college of higher education. Contact the Department of Education Northern Ireland (DENI) for information on teacher training routes and further professional development. You must register as a teacher with the General Teaching Council for Northern Ireland.

In Scotland, to qualify as a teacher you have to complete a programme of Initial Teacher Education (ITE). You can either follow a four-year BEd degree course in primary education or take a relevant first degree followed by a one-year professional graduate diploma in education (PGDE). You can study some PGDE courses through part time or distance learning. State school teachers are required to have a TQ (Teaching Qualification - primary education). Newly qualified teachers follow an induction year programme in order to achieve full registration with the General Teaching Council for Scotland.

Qualified, registered and experienced teachers who do not wish to move into management posts may apply for chartered teacher status. This is achieved through a programme of continual assessment and when completed, you are awarded a masters degree and, through the GTC Scotland, the professional award of chartered teacher.

All teachers must keep up to date with new ideas and methods and are expected to do continuing professional development (CPD). For further details on all teacher training routes, qualifications and funding, contact the Training & Development Agency (TDA) for schools (England & Wales), the Department of Education Northern Ireland (DENI), or Scottish Government - Education and Training.

Mature applicants are encouraged and there are many options for training and qualification, including distance-learning courses. Course entry qualifications for older people may be relaxed for suitable applicants. Some two-year part-time PGCE (PGDE in Scotland) courses are available and there are appropriate Open University courses for both a degree and PGCE/PGDE. Courses can be offered on a flexible learning basis that includes training at weekends, evenings or through distance learning.

Graduates may also be able to qualify through the school centred initial teacher training (SCITT) programme run by groups of local schools. Other routes to teaching include on-the-job training for those over 24 (England & Wales) who can qualify through the Registered Teacher Programme. You must have GCSE or equivalent in English and maths and have successfully completed two years' full-time higher education (or part-time equivalent). Graduates are often preferred and can qualify through the Graduate Teacher Programme (not NI). Trainees on either of these programmes are paid a salary whilst they are training.

A 'Return to Teaching' programme is also available to non-serving (QTS) teachers who have not taught for a minimum period of seven years. Participants on all such courses are eligible for training bursaries and childcare support. In Scotland, some Higher Education Institutions (HEIs) may offer a short course (usually one day a week for around ten weeks) for those wishing to return to teaching. Contact the individual universities for details. There is also a Fast Track teaching programme (England/Wales) that provides accelerated leadership development for existing QTS teachers in the early stages of their career. Contact the National College for Leadership of Schools and Children's Services for details.

Contact the Training & Development Agency (TDA) for schools (England & Wales), the Department of Education Northern Ireland (DENI), or Scottish Government - Education and Training, for details on all teacher training routes and qualifications.

Opportunities and Pay

Employment is with a local authority or an individual school. Prospects vary depending on where you live and may depend on willingness to move to another area. Promotion to headteacher or deputy/assistant headteacher is possible after gaining experience. Part-time work, supply teaching and job-sharing is possible. There is a good demand for Welsh speakers in Wales and Gaelic speakers in Scotland. There are some opportunities for private tuition, or perhaps work in a hospital. Work overseas is also available.

A newly qualified teacher (NQT) earns a minimum of £21k a year. A career changer or mature entrant may, depending on previous experience, start at a higher level in the scale. 'Golden hellos' (teaching grants in Wales) ranging from around £2.5k to £5k are available to newly qualified teachers who teach in an eligible (usually shortage) subject.

Additional responsibilities in a school can attract a higher salary. Advanced Skills Teachers (ASTs) earn from around £36k to £55k a year. If you take on a leadership role, such as an assistant headteacher, a deputy (depute in Scotland), principal or headteacher, the scale ranges from £36k to £102k. The larger and more challenging the school, the higher up the pay scale a headteacher's salary is. Teachers in the independent sector can usually expect to earn a higher salary with additional perks, such as subsidised accommodation and school fees.

These salaries are representative throughout the UK (except for London, which attracts a further allowance) but you are advised to contact your local education department or other employer for full salary scale/grade details.

Health

This job requires a health check on entry.

Skills and Qualities

able to cope under pressure, able to discipline, able to relate well to children and young people, able to stimulate learners, creative and imaginative flair, good communication skills, good organisational skills, IT skills, patient, sense of humour

Relevant Subjects

Art and Design, Biology, English, Geography, History, Mathematics, Music, Performing arts, Psychology, Religious studies, Science, Sociology

Further Information

Association of Teachers' Education Centres in Ireland - www.atcci.ie

Open University - www.open.ac.uk

Scottish Government - Education and Training - www.scotland.gov.uk/Topics/Education

So you want to work with Children (Wayland) - www.waylandbooks.co.uk

TARGETjobs: Teaching (GTI Specialist Publishers Ltd) - www.groupgti.com

Teach in Scotland (Scottish Government Education Department) - www.teachinginscotland.com

Teachernet (Dept for Education) - www.teachernet.gov.uk

Teaching Scotland Magazine (GTCS magazine) - www.gtcs.org.uk

Training & Development Agency (TDA) - www.tda.gov.uk

▶ Working in schools & colleges (2007) (Babcock Lifeskills) - www.babcock-lifeskills.com/

Addresses

Department of Education NI (DENI)
Rathgael House, Balloo Road, Bangor BT19 7PR
Phone: +44 (0)28 9127 9279
Web: www.deni.gov.uk

General Teaching Council for England (GTC)
Whittington House, 19-30 Alfred Place, London WC1E 7EA
Phone: 0370 001 0308 (UK only)
Web: www.gtce.org.uk

General Teaching Council for Northern Ireland (GTCNI)
4th Floor, Albany House, 73-75 Great Victoria Street, Belfast BT2 7AF
Phone: +44 (0)28 9033 3390
Web: www.gtcni.org.uk

General Teaching Council for Scotland (GTC Scotland)
Clerwood House, 96 Clermiston Road, Edinburgh EH12 6UT
Phone: +44 (0)131 314 6000
Web: www.gtcs.org.uk

General Teaching Council for Wales (GTCW)
4th Floor, Southgate House, Wood Street, Cardiff CF10 1EW
Phone: +44 (0)29 2055 0350
Web: www.gtcw.org.uk

Graduate Teacher Training Registry (GTTR)
Rosehill, New Barn Lane, Cheltenham GL52 3LZ
Phone: +44 (0) 1242 222444
Web: www.gttr.ac.uk

Independent Schools Council (ISC)
St Vincent House, 30 Orange Street, London WC2H 7HH
Phone: +44 (0)20 7766 7070
Web: www.isc.co.uk

Learning and Teaching Scotland (LTS)
The Optima, 58 Robertson Street, Glasgow G2 8DU
Phone: +44 (0)141 282 5000
Web: www.ltscotland.org.uk

National College for Leadership of Schools and Children's Services
Triumph Road, Nottingham NG8 1DH
Phone: 0845 609 0009 (UK only)
Web: www.nationalcollege.org.uk/

Scottish Council of Independent Schools (SCIS)
21 Melville Street, Edinburgh EH3 7PE
Phone: +44 (0)131 220 2106
Web: www.scis.org.uk

Similar Jobs

Montessori Teacher, Nursery Worker, Teacher: Early Years, Teacher: Secondary School, Teacher: Special Educational Needs, Teaching Assistant

Teacher: Religious Education

also known as: RE Teacher

CRCI:Education and Training
CLCI:FAB

Job Band: 5

Job Description

Teach religious education (RE) to pupils in a single or multi-faith school, and also play a vital role in helping children and young people achieve their potential, both educationally and personally. RE teachers aim to widen pupils' knowledge and understanding of the subject. They research and plan individual lessons, and use a variety of resources, such as textbooks, the internet, audio-visual materials and worksheets. Introduce topics that allows the pupils to explore an individual faith (or faiths) in depth. They may use varied artefacts (objects) to teach RE, including art materials, and religious paintings, or music for spiritual development, and CDs/DVDs and videos on related topics.

RE teachers lead and encourage discussion and promote individual thought and confidence, giving help where necessary. Some teachers prepare students for national examinations, and set assignments and exams. Correct any written work and record progress of individual pupil/students. They may help with a school assembly, do some administration work, pastoral work, and in some schools, help to run school clubs and societies.

Attending staff meetings, training and development days and parents'/carers' evenings is part of the job. They may also supervise the work of a teaching/classroom assistant.

Work Details

You usually work 39 weeks a year with contact teaching time between 9am-3.30pm, Monday to Friday. Contact teaching time is generally decreasing to allow more time for administration and teacher development. In some schools, usually in the independent sector, you work fewer weeks a year, but often work on a Saturday. You should be able to relate well to young people and are responsible for supporting all level of learners.

The job involves out-of-hours duties and working at home, for example on lesson preparation and writing reports. You have contact with other professionals as well as parents and carers. Teaching requires you to spend each day sitting, standing, carrying/moving learning materials (often equipment), and walking around, depending on the teaching activity. A teaching career is very demanding, and it also requires creativity and imagination. However, it is a very rewarding profession.

Qualification

- **England, Wales and Northern Ireland**

Band 5: For degree courses: 2-3 A levels and some GCSEs (A*-C) usually including English and maths, or equivalent. Exact requirements depend on the degree you take.

- **Scotland**

Band 5: For degree courses: 3-5 H grades and some S grades (1-3), usually including English and maths, or similar qualifications. Exact requirements depend on the degree you take.

Degree Information

A degree containing study of the subject(s) to be taught is essential, together with a postgraduate certificate in education (PGCE). However, it is not a requirement to have studied theology/religious studies, though this is helpful. Other useful subjects include philosophy, sociology/social studies and some combined studies.

Adult Qualifications

Adults aged 23 or over may enter degree courses with a variety of qualifications or via Access or foundation courses. Entry requirements may be more flexible for subjects where there are teacher shortages. For graduates there are part-time postgraduate courses in education available. The Open University also runs an 18-month distance-learning postgraduate course in some subjects.

Work Experience

Entry to this job is competitive and it is important that you do some relevant work experience before applying to teacher training. Applicants are advised to show evidence of their interest in and commitment to teaching by working with young people, preferably as a voluntary helper in a school, a youth club, sports group, or holiday play activity/sports scheme.

Entry and Training

Religious education in the UK is a subject that teaches children and young people about faith(s) and what it means to be religious. You do not necessarily need to be religious yourself to teach RE, and most RE teachers come from a wide and diverse background. In some schools you may teach other subjects along with RE, though you need to have had the required training. At the moment, RE has shortage subject status, but more people are now applying to teach it, so this may go soon. All those working with children and young people are required to have a Criminal Records Bureau (CRB)/Disclosure Scotland check.

In England and Wales, to teach in a mainstream or special school, you need qualified teacher status (QTS) achieved by taking an undergraduate or postgraduate certificate in education course (PGCE) or through an employment-based route into teaching, and train on the job.

In Scotland, the quickest and most popular way to qualify as a secondary school teacher of RE is to have a degree in a related subject and then do a one-year professional graduate diploma in education (PGDE).

For full details on the entry route to teaching throughout the UK, please read the article Teacher: Secondary School.

Mature applicants are encouraged and there are many options for training and qualification, including distance-learning courses. Some two-year part-time PGCE (PGDE in Scotland) courses are available and there are also appropriate Open University courses.

For further details on all teacher training routes throughout the UK, please read the article Teacher: Secondary School.

Opportunities and Pay

Teachers are mainly employed in state schools and the numbers are steadily increasing. Work is also available in independent schools, colleges and academies, adult learning centres, pupil referral units, secure training units or young offenders' institutions, and the armed forces. There are opportunities for promotion, for example to a head of department and beyond, though your prospects may depend on willingness to move to another area. Part-time work, private tuition, supply teaching and job-sharing is possible. Work abroad is also available.

A newly qualified teacher (NQT) earns from around £21k a year. A career changer or mature entrant may, depending on previous experience, start at a higher level in the scale.

Additional responsibilities in a school can attract a higher salary. Advanced Skills Teachers (ASTs) earn from around £36k-£55k a year. Teachers in the independent sector can usually expect to earn a higher salary with additional perks, such as subsidised accommodation and school fees.

There is an allowance for working in London. You are advised to contact your local education department or other employer for full salary scale/grade details.

Health
This job requires a health check on entry and usually requires normal hearing ability.

Skills and Qualities
able to discipline, able to explain clearly, able to inspire confidence, able to stimulate learners, fair minded, good communication skills, good interpersonal skills, good organisational skills, good presentation skills, patient

Relevant Subjects
Classical studies, English, Geography, History, Psychology, Religious studies, Sociology

Further Information
Open University - www.open.ac.uk

Scottish Government - Education and Training - www.scotland.gov.uk/Topics/Education

Teach in Scotland (Scottish Government Education Department) - www.teachinginscotland.com

Teach RE (The Culham Institute) - www.teachre.com

Teachernet (Dept for Education) - www.teachernet.gov.uk

Teaching Training Wales - www.educationcymru.org

Training & Development Agency (TDA) - www.tda.gov.uk

▶Working in schools & colleges (2007) (Babcock Lifeskills) - www.babcock-lifeskills.com/

Addresses
Department of Education NI (DENI)
Rathgael House, Balloo Road, Bangor BT19 7PR
Phone: +44 (0)28 9127 9279
Web: www.deni.gov.uk

General Teaching Council for England (GTC)
Whittington House, 19-30 Alfred Place, London WC1E 7EA
Phone: 0370 001 0308 (UK only)
Web: www.gtce.org.uk

General Teaching Council for Northern Ireland (GTCNI)
4th Floor, Albany House, 73-75 Great Victoria Street,
Belfast BT2 7AF
Phone: +44 (0)28 9033 3390
Web: www.gtcni.org.uk

General Teaching Council for Scotland (GTC Scotland)
Clerwood House, 96 Clermiston Road, Edinburgh EH12 6UT
Phone: +44 (0)131 314 6000
Web: www.gtcs.org.uk

General Teaching Council for Wales (GTCW)
4th Floor, Southgate House, Wood Street, Cardiff CF10 1EW
Phone: +44 (0)29 2055 0350
Web: www.gtcw.org.uk

Graduate Teacher Training Registry (GTTR)
Rosehill, New Barn Lane, Cheltenham GL52 3LZ
Phone: +44 (0) 1242 222444
Web: www.gttr.ac.uk

Similar Jobs
Community Development Worker, Community Learning & Development Officer (Scotland), Lecturer: Further Education, Religious Leader, Teacher: History, Teacher: Primary School, Teacher: Secondary School

Teacher: Secondary School
also known as: Secondary School Teacher

CRCI:Education and Training
CLCI:FAB Job Band: 5

Job Description
Teachers in a secondary school prepare and deliver structured learning programmes, usually in a specific subject area, for students aged 11-18 (12-18 in Scotland). They usually teach one or more National Curriculum subjects, or one of an increasing number of vocational subjects. Play a vital role in helping young people achieve their potential, both educationally and personally. They plan individual lessons and use a variety of resources, such as textbooks, the internet, audio-visual materials, worksheets and practical work. May prepare students for national academic and vocational examinations. Set assignments and exams, correct written work and record progress of each individual student.

If they are form teachers, they give individual advice and guidance to students and may refer them to another professional, such as a personal/careers adviser or health adviser. May also help with school administration, pastoral care, educational events, field trips, school clubs and societies, and sporting events. Some teachers may be involved with managing work experience programmes or assisting with career choices and student applications to higher education.

Teachers attend staff meetings, training and development days and parents'/carers' evenings, and may also supervise the work of a teaching/classroom assistant.

Work Details
Usually work 39 weeks a year with contact teaching time between 9am and 3.30pm, Monday to Friday. Contact teaching time is generally decreasing to allow more time for administration and teacher development. In some schools, usually independent schools, you work fewer weeks a year, but often work on a Saturday. You should be able to relate well to young people and are responsible for supporting learners to reach required learning targets. The job can involve undertaking out-of-hours duties and also working at home, for example on lesson preparation and writing reports. You have contact with other professionals as well as parents and carers.

Teaching requires you to spend each day sitting, standing, carrying/moving learning materials (often equipment), and walking around, depending on the teaching activity. A teaching career is very demanding, and it also requires creativity and imagination. However, it is a very rewarding profession.

Qualification

• England, Wales and Northern Ireland
Band 5: For degree courses: 2-3 A levels and some GCSEs (A*-C) usually including English and maths, or equivalent. Exact requirements depend on the degree you take.

• Scotland
Band 5: For degree courses: 3-5 H grades and some S grades (1-3), usually including English and maths, or similar qualifications. Exact requirements depend on the degree you take.

Teacher: Secondary School

Degree Information

A degree including study of the subject(s) to be taught is usual, together with a postgraduate certificate in education (PGCE). It is also possible to qualify to teach some secondary school subjects by studying for a four year concurrent BEd/BA degree, which includes teaching practice.

Adult Qualifications

Adults (aged 23 or over) may enter degree courses with a variety of qualifications or via Access or foundation courses. Entry requirements may be more flexible for subjects where there are teacher shortages. For graduates there are part-time postgraduate courses in education available. The Open University also runs a distance-learning postgraduate certificate of education course in some subjects.

Work Experience

Entry to this job is competitive and it is important that you do relevant work experience before applying to teacher training. Applicants are advised to show evidence of their interest in and commitment to teaching by working with young people, preferably as a voluntary helper in a school, in a youth club, sports group, or holiday play activity/sports scheme.

The Student Associate Scheme (England) gives registered students in full or part-time higher education, on courses not leading to qualified teacher status, the opportunity to work in a school alongside experienced teachers. You are paid (tax free) for each day you work for at least ten days or more. Contact the Training and Development Agency (TDA) for details. The TDA can also provide details for prospective teachers to gain knowledge of a classroom environment through 'taster' days, short courses, or a discussion with a qualified and practising teacher. For details of similar opportunities in Scotland, contact Scottish Government - Education and Training, or for Northern Ireland, the Department of Education in Northern Ireland (DENI).

Entry and Training

In England and Wales, to teach in a mainstream state school, you need qualified teacher status (QTS) achieved by taking an undergraduate or postgraduate certificate in education course (PGCE) or through an employment-based route into teaching, and train on the job. For initial teacher training (ITT) you require a UK degree or equivalent, plus GCSEs (or equivalent) in English/ mathematics at grade C or above. You also require a science at GCSE (A*-C) if you want to teach at key stage 2/3. In Wales, you do not need to be able to speak Welsh unless you are teaching in a Welsh-speaking school. All teachers in training have to undergo a Criminal Records Bureau (CRB)/Disclosure Scotland check.

First degrees should be relevant to the subject you want to teach. You should always choose any course carefully to ensure that your first degree enables entry to a PGCE. Courses last one-year full time or two years part time, or through distance learning. High flying graduates may train to teach under the Teach First scheme. This takes two years, spent in challenging schools while qualifying as a teacher. Newly qualified teachers (NQTs) follow a probation programme over three terms and must register with the General Teaching Council for England/Wales.

In England and Wales, those applying for a first headship are required to have achieved the national professional qualification for headship (NPQH). Contact the National College for Leadership of Schools and Children's Services for details.

In order to be qualified to teach in Northern Ireland, a teacher must have either a recognised teaching degree after completing an approved teacher training course (normally four years) at a UK university or college of higher education, or a recognised degree or equivalent qualification plus a PGCE, awarded after completing a one-year full-time course at a UK university or college of higher education. You must also register as a teacher with the General Teaching Council for Northern Ireland.

To qualify as a secondary school teacher in Scotland you need to have a degree in the subject you wish to teach and then do a one-year professional graduate diploma in education (PGDE). You can study some PGDE courses through part time or distance learning. There are eight universities in Scotland that offer programmes of Initial Teacher Education (ITE) - see the General Teaching Council for Scotland (GTC Scotland) website for full details. Newly qualified teachers follow an induction programme in order to achieve full registration with GTC Scotland.

Qualified, registered and experienced teachers who do not wish to move into management posts may apply for chartered teacher status. This is achieved through a programme of continual assessment and when completed, you are awarded a masters degree and, through the GTC Scotland, the professional award of chartered teacher.

All teachers must keep up to date with new ideas and methods and are expected to do continuing professional development (CPD). For further details on all teacher training routes, qualifications and funding, contact the Training and Development Agency (TDA) for schools (England & Wales), the Department of Education Northern Ireland (DENI), or Scottish Government - Education and Training.

Mature applicants are encouraged and there are many options for training and qualification, including distance-learning courses. Some two-year part-time PGCE (PGDE in Scotland) courses are available and there are also appropriate Open University courses. Graduates with subjects that are not in the National Curriculum may take a subject knowledge enhancement course that takes up to 36 weeks, prior to doing a PGCE.

Graduates may also be able to qualify through the school-centred initial teacher training (SCITT) programme run by and based in groups of local schools (England only). All SCITT courses last one year and lead to QTS and many, not all, award the PGCE. However, places are limited.

Other routes to teaching include on-the-job training for those over 24 (England & Wales) who can qualify through the Registered Teacher Programme (RTP). You must have GCSE or equivalent in English and maths and have successfully completed two years full-time higher education, such as an HND/Dip HE (or part-time equivalent). You first need to be working in a school as an unqualified teacher. The RTP takes 1-2 years, depending on your teaching experience. Graduates can qualify through the Graduate Teacher Programme (GTP), though not in Northern Ireland. Trainees on either of these programmes are paid a salary whilst they are training.

A Return to Teaching (RTT) programme is also available to non-serving (QTS) teachers who have not taught for a minimum period of seven years. Participants on all such courses are eligible for training bursaries and childcare support. In Scotland, some Higher Education Institutions may offer a short course (usually one day a week for around ten weeks) for those qualified teachers who wish to return to teaching. Contact the individual universities for details. A 'Fast Track' Teaching programme (England) is a professional development programme that provides those with the appropriate skills and knowledge to become leaders in education. The programme focuses on providing leadership development for existing qualified teachers.

For further details on all teacher training routes, qualifications and funding, contact the Training and Development Agency (TDA) for schools (England & Wales), the Department of Education Northern Ireland (DENI), or Scottish Government - Education and Training.

Opportunities and Pay

Teachers are mainly employed in state schools and the numbers are steadily increasing. Work is also available in independent schools, colleges and academies, adult learning centres, pupil referral units, secure training units or young offenders' institutions, and the armed forces. There are opportunities for promotion, for example to head of department and beyond, though your prospects may depend on willingness to move to another area. Part-time work, private tuition, supply teaching and job-sharing is possible. Work abroad is also available.

A newly qualified teacher (NQT) earns from around £21k a year. A career changer or mature entrant may, depending on previous experience, start at a higher level in the scale. 'Golden hellos' (or teaching grants in Wales) ranging from around £2.5k-£5k are available to newly qualified teachers who teach in an eligible (usually shortage) subject. In Scotland you can apply for a preference waiver payment of £6k if you are prepared to work anywhere in Scotland during your probationary year.

Additional responsibilities in a school can attract higher salaries. Advanced Skills Teachers (ASTs) earn from around £36k-£55k a year. If you take on a leadership role, such as an assistant headteacher, a deputy (depute in Scotland), principal or headteacher, the scale ranges from £36k-£102k. The larger and more challenging the school, the higher up the pay scale a head teacher's salary will be. Teachers in the independent sector can usually expect to earn a higher salary with additional perks, such as subsidised accommodation and school fees. Contact your local education department or other employer for full salary scale/grade details.

Health

All applicants for teaching posts complete a medical fitness questionnaire and may be asked to consent to a medical examination.

Skills and Qualities

able to cope under pressure, able to discipline, able to explain clearly, able to inspire confidence, able to stimulate learners, even tempered, good communication skills, good interpersonal skills, good organisational skills, IT skills, reliable

Relevant Subjects

English, Psychology, Sociology

Further Information

Careers Wales - www.careerswales.com/

Scottish Government - Education and Training - www.scotland.gov.uk/Topics/Education

So you want to work with Children (Wayland) - www.waylandbooks.co.uk

TARGETjobs: Teaching (GTI Specialist Publishers Ltd) - www.groupgti.com

Teach First - www.teachfirst.org.uk

Teach in Scotland (Scottish Government Education Department) - www.teachinginscotland.com

Teachernet (Dept for Education) - www.teachernet.gov.uk

Teaching Scotland Magazine (GTCS magazine) - www.gtcs.org.uk

Teaching Training Wales - www.educationcymru.org

Teaching Wales (quarterly) (General Teaching Council for Wales) - www.gtcw.org.uk/gtcw/index.php/en/publications/teaching-wales

Training & Development Agency (TDA) - www.tda.gov.uk

▶Working in schools & colleges (2007) (Babcock Lifeskills) - www.babcock-lifeskills.com/

Addresses

Department of Education NI (DENI)
Rathgael House, Balloo Road, Bangor BT19 7PR
Phone: +44 (0)28 9127 9279
Web: www.deni.gov.uk

General Teaching Council for England (GTC)
Whittington House, 19-30 Alfred Place, London WC1E 7EA
Phone: 0370 001 0308 (UK only)
Web: www.gtce.org.uk

General Teaching Council for Northern Ireland (GTCNI)
4th Floor, Albany House, 73-75 Great Victoria Street, Belfast BT2 7AF
Phone: +44 (0)28 9033 3390
Web: www.gtcni.org.uk

General Teaching Council for Scotland (GTC Scotland)
Clerwood House, 96 Clermiston Road, Edinburgh EH12 6UT
Phone: +44 (0)131 314 6000
Web: www.gtcs.org.uk

General Teaching Council for Wales (GTCW)
4th Floor, Southgate House, Wood Street, Cardiff CF10 1EW
Phone: +44 (0)29 2055 0350
Web: www.gtcw.org.uk

Graduate Teacher Training Registry (GTTR)
Rosehill, New Barn Lane, Cheltenham GL52 3LZ
Phone: +44 (0) 1242 222444
Web: www.gttr.ac.uk

Independent Schools Council (ISC)
St Vincent House, 30 Orange Street, London WC2H 7HH
Phone: +44 (0)20 7766 7070
Web: www.isc.co.uk

Learning and Teaching Scotland (LTS)
The Optima, 58 Robertson Street, Glasgow G2 8DU
Phone: +44 (0)141 282 5000
Web: www.ltscotland.org.uk

National College for Leadership of Schools and Children's Services
Triumph Road, Nottingham NG8 1DH
Phone: 0845 609 0009 (UK only)
Web: www.nationalcollege.org.uk/

Scottish Council of Independent Schools (SCIS)
21 Melville Street, Edinburgh EH3 7PE
Phone: +44 (0)131 220 2106
Web: www.scis.org.uk

Similar Jobs

Community Development Worker, Community Learning & Development Officer (Scotland), Lecturer: Further Education, Lecturer: Higher Education, Teacher: Primary School, Teacher: Special Educational Needs

Teacher: Special Educational Needs

also known as: SEN Teacher

CRCI:Education and Training

CLCI:FAB Job Band: 5

Job Description

Teach children and young people who either have greater learning difficulties than others of the same age or are gifted pupils, all of whom therefore have special educational needs (SEN). Issues arise from medical and physical conditions, or emotional, behavioural and social problems. They usually work in small groups or with individual pupils of all ages, either within or outside the class. They can cover the full range of curriculum subjects. They aim to develop a pupil's potential and increase their confidence.

SEN teachers plan work and activities to meet the needs of pupils, which for some may include the use of special or adapted equipment and facilities. They use a variety of teaching strategies and skills, including specialist skills when necessary such as the use of Braille (written language for those with visual impairment) and sign language for those pupils with hearing difficulties. They also help to support pupils with behavioural problems in school and develop methods to improve their behaviour, such as anger management strategies and counselling sessions.

Teacher: Special Educational Needs

Some work with pupils with mild learning difficulties, such as those who have fallen behind the majority of their class and who are expected only to need extra help for a short period of time. They help them in skill areas of reading, writing, spelling, language and maths. They work with other members of school staff to identify each pupil's individual special needs and writes a development plan for each pupil/student. Devise and deliver in-service training to mainstream teachers and other SEN staff.

SEN teachers hold discussions with parents/carers and liaise with other agencies such as educational psychologists, speech and language therapists, social workers, and medical professionals. May combine the post of a special educational needs teacher with other mainstream teaching responsibilities. Attend staff meetings, training and development days and parents'/carers' evenings, and may also supervise the work of a teaching/classroom assistant.

Work Details

Usually work 39 weeks a year with contact teaching time usually worked between 9am and 3.30pm, Monday to Friday. Contact teaching time is generally decreasing to allow more time for administration and teacher development. In some schools, usually independent schools, you work fewer weeks a year, but often work on a Saturday. You should be able to relate well to young people and are responsible for supporting learners and reaching required learning targets.

The job can involve undertaking out-of-hours duties and also working at home, for example on lesson preparation and writing reports. You have contact with other professionals as well as parents and carers. In some jobs, travelling around an area may be necessary. Some special schools are residential, where staff may work long irregular hours. You work with students who are in need of support and some may be aggressive.

This job requires you to spend each day sitting, standing, carrying/moving learning materials (often equipment), and walking around, depending on the teaching activity. Work requires creativity and imagination and can often be taxing and emotionally demanding. However, this is a very rewarding profession.

Qualification

• England, Wales and Northern Ireland

Band 5: For degree courses: 2-3 A levels and some GCSEs (A*-C) usually including English, maths and a science subject, or equivalent. Exact requirements depend on the degree you take.

• Scotland

Band 5: For degree courses: 3-5 H grades and some S grades (1-3), usually including English and maths, or similar qualifications. Exact requirements depend on the degree you take.

Degree Information

Entrants to this job are usually qualified teachers with several years' work experience. Initial qualifications can be either BEd degree or any degree (relevant to the curriculum) followed by a postgraduate certificate in education (PGCE).

Adult Qualifications

Entrants to most specialist courses require at least two years' teaching in ordinary schools. This is after either a BEd degree, or a postgraduate course in education, following a first degree. There are a variety of routes to gaining qualified teacher status (QTS), such as part-time and distance courses (Open University), or by school-based learning, as well as many college courses.

Work Experience

Entry to this job is competitive and it is important that you try to do some relevant work experience before applying to teacher training. Applicants are advised to show evidence of their interest in and commitment to teaching by working with young people, preferably as a voluntary helper in a school, youth club, sports group, or holiday play activity/sports scheme.

Entry and Training

Experience of teaching in mainstream schools is usually required, followed by specialist training, although some entrants do come into this work as a first teaching post. All teacher training includes aspects of dealing with those with special educational needs, but there are also specialist and more advanced courses available. All those working with children and young people are required to have a Criminal Records Bureau (CRB)/Disclosure Scotland check.

Those dealing with vision, hearing or multi-sensory impaired children must take further qualifications within three years of taking up a post. More general training can be by part-time or full-time graduate diploma courses. Funding may be available through the Training & Development Authority postgraduate professional development programme. There are also in-service training courses that are held throughout the UK, often organised by local authorities for schools in their area. Nasen also runs specialist courses. See the websites for details.

In England and Wales, to teach in a maintained or special school, you need qualified teacher status (QTS) achieved by taking an undergraduate or postgraduate certificate in education course (PGCE) or through an employment-based route into teaching, and train on the job.

For full details of the entry route for teaching, read the Teacher: Secondary School and Teacher: Primary School articles.

Mature entry is common as most SEN teachers have at least two years' experience before taking additional specialist SEN training and qualification. There are many options for initial teacher training and qualification, including distance-learning courses. Some two-year part-time PGCE (PGDE in Scotland) courses are available and there are also appropriate Open University courses for both a relevant UK degree and PGCE/PGDE.

For full details of the entry route for teaching, read the Teacher: Secondary School and Teacher: Primary School articles.

Opportunities and Pay

There are over 15,000 special educational needs (SEN) teachers employed by local authorities in special and mainstream schools, and in a variety of settings, including pupil referral units, youth custody centres or community homes. Other opportunities are in special schools run by voluntary organisations such as the Royal National Institute for the Blind, Barnado's, and in the NHS. The number of teachers required in mainstream schools is continuing to increase. With at least two years' experience it is possible to progress to the role of a special educational needs coordinator (SENCO) or to a specialist or advanced skills teacher.

Opportunities also include work in a local education authority (LEA) as a special needs officer/assessment officer. Part-time work, supply teaching and job-sharing is possible. Some SEN teachers are employed as private tutors. Work overseas is also available.

Starting salaries for teachers outside London are usually £21k a year. Those working in SEN have additional allowances of from around £2k-£3k a year. With experience you can earn up to £35k a year.

Health

Teacher training courses require a medical test on entry.

Skills and Qualities

able to explain clearly, able to stimulate learners, flexible approach, good interpersonal skills, good organisational skills, patient, perceptive, perseverance, problem-solving skills, sense of humour

Relevant Subjects

Art and Design, Biology, English, Geography, History, Mathematics, Psychology, Sociology

Further Information

Open University - www.open.ac.uk

Scottish Government - Education and Training - www.scotland.gov.uk/Topics/Education

Special (2 x year) (nasen) - www.nasen.org.uk/special/

Teach in Scotland (Scottish Government Education Department) - www.teachinginscotland.com

Teachernet (Dept for Education) - www.teachernet.gov.uk

Teaching Scotland Magazine (GTCS magazine) - www.gtcs.org.uk

Training & Development Agency (TDA) - www.tda.gov.uk

▶Working in schools & colleges (2007) (Babcock Lifeskills) - www.babcock-lifeskills.com/

Addresses

Department of Education NI (DENI)
Rathgael House, Balloo Road, Bangor BT19 7PR
Phone: +44 (0)28 9127 9279
Web: www.deni.gov.uk

General Teaching Council for England (GTC)
Whittington House, 19-30 Alfred Place, London WC1E 7EA
Phone: 0370 001 0308 (UK only)
Web: www.gtce.org.uk

General Teaching Council for Northern Ireland (GTCNI)
4th Floor, Albany House, 73-75 Great Victoria Street, Belfast BT2 7AF
Phone: +44 (0)28 9033 3390
Web: www.gtcni.org.uk

General Teaching Council for Scotland (GTC Scotland)
Clerwood House, 96 Clermiston Road, Edinburgh EH12 6UT
Phone: +44 (0)131 314 6000
Web: www.gtcs.org.uk

General Teaching Council for Wales (GTCW)
4th Floor, Southgate House, Wood Street, Cardiff CF10 1EW
Phone: +44 (0)29 2055 0350
Web: www.gtcw.org.uk

nasen
nasen House, 4-5 Amber Business Village, Amber Close, Amington, Tamworth B77 4RP
Phone: +44 (0)1827 311500
Web: www.nasen.org.uk

Similar Jobs

Dramatherapist, Nurse: Learning Disabilities, Psychologist: Educational, Teacher: Early Years, Teacher: Primary School, Teacher: Secondary School

Teacher: Technological Education

CRCI:Education and Training
CLCI:FAB Job Band: 5

Job Description

Technical education teachers prepare and deliver a structured learning programme, usually for students aged 12-18, in craft and design/product design, graphic communication, practical craft skills, and technological studies. They provide an interesting range of activities and opportunities that contribute significantly to pupils' growing awareness and appreciation of technological applications in their environment. For example, craft and design focuses on developing pupils' abilities in investigating, creating, organising and problem-solving, in addition to the acquisition of technical skills.

Graphic communication introduces some of the graphic skills employed in modern industry and commerce. Also gives pupils knowledge and experience of modern manual and computer-aided drawing methods. Technological studies develops pupils' knowledge and understanding of electronics, mechanisms, manufacturing, and the pneumatics and control systems used in modern industry.

Technical education teachers prepare courses according to a syllabus and needs of the pupils. Record progress of each student and develop their individual talent. They supervise practical work, set and mark assignments and internal exams. May become involved in school clubs and extra-curricular events. Attending staff meetings, training and development days and parents'/carers' evenings are part of the job. They may also supervise the work of a classroom assistant or technician.

Work Details

You usually work 39 weeks a year with contact teaching time between 9am-3.30pm, Monday to Friday. Contact teaching time is generally decreasing to allow more time for administration and teacher development. In some schools, usually in the independent sector, you work fewer weeks a year, but often work on a Saturday. You should be able to relate well to young people and are responsible for supporting learners to reach required learning targets.

The job involves out-of-hours duties and working at home, for example on lesson preparation and writing reports. You have contact with other professionals as well as parents and carers. Workshops may be noisy and perhaps dusty. You are responsible for ensuring safety as there is a risk of accidents from equipment. Overalls and safety eye wear may be worn for some tasks.

Teaching requires you to spend each day sitting, standing, carrying/moving learning materials (often equipment), and walking around, depending on the teaching activity. A teaching career is very demanding, and it also requires creativity and imagination. However, it is a very rewarding profession.

Qualification

• Scotland

Band 5: For BEd degree: 3-5 H grades, including maths and English and preferably technological studies or physics, and usually five S grades (1-3) or similar. Exact requirements depend on the degree you take.

Degree Information

The more direct route is the four-year BEd course, but an alternative way into the job is the professional graduate diploma in education (PGDE) course. This usually requires a first degree in design and technology, science, engineering or physics.

Adult Qualifications

Entry requirements for BEd degree courses may be reduced for mature applicants and Access courses are acceptable. Relevant industrial experience is an advantage for this job. A technical qualification, such as a higher national award, may give entry to a shortened two or three-year BEd course; contact specific institutions for information. You usually need H grade English (or similar) for entry to a course. Some Open University arts courses may be accepted in place of the H grade.

Work Experience

Entry to this job is competitive and it is important that you do some relevant work experience before applying to teacher training. Applicants are advised to show evidence of their interest in and commitment to teaching by working with young people, preferably as a voluntary helper in a school, a youth club, sports group, or holiday play activity/sports scheme. Contact Scottish Government - Education and Training for details of opportunities that are available for intending teachers, such as taster days, work shadowing etc.

Entry and Training

To qualify as a teacher of technological education you can complete a degree with qualified teacher status in technological education at Glasgow University, in design and technology at Edinburgh University or in technology with education at Aberdeen University. All those working with children and young people are required to have a Disclosure Scotland check.

You can also gain a degree in a related subject and then complete a one-year professional graduate diploma in education (PGDE). For those with a related degree/HND you can join year three of the degree course in technology with education at Aberdeen. State school teachers are required to have a TQ (Teaching Qualification - secondary education). Newly qualified teachers follow an induction programme in order to achieve full registration with the General Teaching Council for Scotland.

All teachers must keep up to date with new ideas and methods and are expected to do continuing professional development (CPD). For further details of all training routes, qualifications and funding, contact Scottish Government - Education and Training. See also the article Teacher: Secondary.

This particular job is only available in Scottish schools though a similar job, teacher of design technology, is available in the rest of the UK.

Mature applicants are encouraged and there are increased options for teacher training and qualification. Contact Scottish Government - Education and Training for details of all training opportunities. Relevant industrial experience is also an advantage for this job.

Opportunities and Pay

There is a steady demand for qualified staff, due to teacher shortages in this subject. Teachers are mainly employed in state schools and the numbers are steadily increasing. Work is also available in independent schools, colleges and academies, adult learning centres, pupil referral units, secure training units or young offenders' institutions, and the armed forces. There are opportunities for promotion, for example to head of department and beyond, though your prospects may depend on willingness to move to another area. Part-time work, private tuition, supply teaching and job-sharing is possible.

Teachers are employed on a six-point scale starting at around £21k a year and rising at point 6 to £34k. Mature entrants who have relevant experience enter at a higher point on the scale. You can apply for a preference waiver payment of £6k if you are prepared to work anywhere in Scotland during your probationary year. You are advised to contact your local area education department or other employer for full salary scale/grade details.

Health

Entry to teacher training courses requires a health check.

Skills and Qualities

able to discipline, able to explain clearly, able to stimulate learners, creative flair, eye for shape/colour, good communication skills, good interpersonal skills, good organisational skills, responsible attitude, technical aptitude

Relevant Subjects

Art and Design, Construction and built environment, Design and technology, Engineering, English, ICT/Computer studies, Mathematics, Physics, Psychology, Science, Sociology

Further Information

Open University - www.open.ac.uk

Scottish Government - Education and Training - www.scotland.gov.uk/Topics/Education

Scottish Technology Teachers' Association - www.scottish-tta.org.uk

Teach in Scotland (Scottish Government Education Department) - www.teachinginscotland.com

Teaching Scotland Magazine (GTCS magazine) - www.gtcs.org.uk

Addresses

General Teaching Council for Scotland (GTC Scotland)
Clerwood House, 96 Clermiston Road, Edinburgh EH12 6UT
Phone: +44 (0)131 314 6000
Web: www.gtcs.org.uk

Learning and Teaching Scotland (LTS)
The Optima, 58 Robertson Street, Glasgow G2 8DU
Phone: +44 (0)141 282 5000
Web: www.ltscotland.org.uk

Scottish Council of Independent Schools (SCIS)
21 Melville Street, Edinburgh EH3 7PE
Phone: +44 (0)131 220 2106
Web: www.scis.org.uk

Students Award Agency for Scotland (SAAS)
Gyleview House 3 Redheughs Rigg, Edinburgh EH12 9HH
Phone: 0845 111 1711 (UK only)
Web: www.student-support-saas.gov.uk

Similar Jobs

IT Skills Trainer, Lecturer: Further Education, Teacher: Secondary School, Training & Development Officer/Manager

Teaching Assistant

also known as: Bilingual Support Assistant, Classroom Assistant, Learning Support Assistant, Non-Teaching Assistant, Support Assistant: School

CRCI:Education and Training
CLCI:FAB Job Band: 1 to 3

Job Description

Teaching assistants work under the supervision of a qualified teacher with classroom activities and programmes of learning, usually in nursery, primary or secondary schools, special schools, and independent schools. The role and job title can vary depending on the particular job and the age of the pupils/students. Some teaching assistants (TAs)/classroom assistants (CAs) may work with a whole class, whilst others may be appointed to provide support to a small group, or to work solely with one pupil/student. Generally, those working in primary schools are likely to have a variety of tasks, such as handing out the work materials (paper, books, paints and crayons etc) and tidying away at the end of each classroom session. They assist the class teacher in the display of art and craft work.

Can help pupils with activities such as reading and writing and with practical sessions, such as painting. If working with very young children, may help them to get undressed/dressed for activities such as PE and games, or may look after those who are unwell, or who have had a minor accident. Some TAs may listen to children reading aloud, and also read stories to them. May also supervise the pupils at break times/lunch times, or on class outings and at sports events. Helps to encourage appropriate, social and safe behaviour and seeks to encourage learning through play activities.

TAs also provide learning support to those pupils who have special educational needs, including those with severe learning, behavioural or physical difficulties. Depending upon the age of the pupil and the type and severity of difficulty, the TA works under supervision of a teacher to help pupils achieve their individual learning goals. May work with pupils who are autistic, or who have visual/auditory impairments. Also assists with appropriate therapy sessions and works to improve pupils' independent living skills.

Some TAs help those pupils/students with emotional/physical problems to achieve their potential whilst in education, usually on a one-to-one basis. Others are appointed as bilingual support assistants who focus on those pupils for whom English is an additional language. In England, a higher level teaching assistant (HLTA) takes on more responsibility, such as assisting a teacher to record the progress and achievements of each pupil/student, help in the production of lesson plans, worksheets, plans etc, and in the delivery of learning activities within an agreed system of supervision.

All teaching/classroom assistants are involved in a team approach to learning and developing an educational development plan for each pupil/student. They may also work with other professionals who assist the teacher, such as educational psychologists, social workers and speech/art therapists. TAs also liaise with other teachers as well as building relationships with parents and carers.

Work Details

Usually works school hours, Monday to Friday, term time only, though may be required to work at other times, such as parent-teacher evenings and for staff training days. Many assistants work part time. Some jobs are specifically for work with those who are less able either physically or emotionally. Work is very demanding and you have to cope with always being on your feet and also being physically active.

Sometimes you have to cope with the sight of blood if there is an accident. The workplace is noisy and sometimes messy. Protective clothing is required for practical sessions, such as arts and craft sessions.

Qualification

Some employers may require formal qualifications such as nursery nursing or other early years/child care qualification. There are no set minimum qualifications, but increased competition for places has meant that employers can select candidates with a range of skills and qualifications.

• England, Wales and Northern Ireland

Band 1: No minimum qualifications are required, but you are expected to have a good level of general education, especially in literacy and numeracy. However, some formal/vocational qualifications at any level are useful.

Band 2: Some employers prefer a number of GCSEs (A*-C) including English and maths. Higher level teaching assistants (HLTAs) in England require excellent numeracy and literacy skills equivalent to NVQ level 2 in maths and English. Specialist skills/training in curriculum areas such as ICT and languages, including sign language, is an advantage.

Band 3: For entry to jobs, HNC or a relevant Diploma, usually at least 4 GCSEs (A*-C) including English and maths, or equivalent.

• Scotland

Band 1: No minimum qualifications are required, but you are expected to have had a good level of general education, especially in literacy and numeracy. However, some formal/vocational qualifications at any level are useful.

Band 2: Although academic qualifications are not specified for this job, it is an advantage to have some S grades (1-3) in subjects that include English and maths, or similar.

Band 3: For entry to jobs, usually at least four S grades (1-3) including English or maths, or similar.

Adult Qualifications

Maturity is an advantage and previous experience of working with children is essential. For jobs with younger children a qualification in nursery nursing or similar, is an advantage.

Government training opportunities, such as apprenticeships, may be available in your area. You can also gain recognition of previous experience through Accreditation of Prior Learning (APL) or by working towards relevant S/NVQs. Contact your local careers office, Jobcentre Plus, Next Step service or Learning and Skills Council (LSC) Local Enterprise Company (LEC) for details of training schemes.

Work Experience

Relevant work or voluntary experience can equip you with skills that you can use in the future and that you can add to your CV. There are often opportunities available for voluntary work, particularly in a school, which give you experience of working with young people. Other opportunities exist in the care and education of children, such as childminding, helping at a nursery school, in a hospital, or with a group such as guides/scouts.

Entry and Training

Applicants must be at least 18 but most entrants are older. To enter this work it is important to be able to show that you have experience in working with children or young people. All entrants have to go through a Criminal Records Bureau (CRB)/Disclosure Scotland check. You are usually trained on the job when you are in employment, possibly with some in-service courses. There is a range of suitable vocational qualifications that require no formal qualifications and which are suitable for those teaching assistants with little experience. These include an Open University level 1 certificate in supporting learning in primary schools.

Most local authorities run a four-day induction programme for new TAs, using materials provided by the Training & Development Agency (TDA) for Schools. During 2010, the TDA plans to develop a new introductory qualification. TAs are encouraged to gain qualifications while working. Support Work in Schools (SWiS) qualifications are available at levels 2-3 and are designed to provide training that is relevant to the TA's work in school as they are flexible and individually tailored. NVQs level 2-3 in supporting teaching and learning in schools and SVQs level 2-4 in children's care, learning and development are also available. Some schools may also require a TA to gain training and qualifications in specific areas, including sign language for those working with auditory impaired pupils, or training in visual awareness, including Braille.

TAs with experience can move on to become higher level teaching assistants (HLTAs). Training for this is on the job, and in order to train you need the support of the school and the funding to complete the preparation for assessment. This assessment identifies an individual TA's training needs and then defines their programme of learning. At the moment there are specialist HLTAs in secondary science and maths. In 2011 there are likely to be specialists in food technology. Full details HLTS training can be found on the TDA website.

Specific foundation degrees for teaching assistants can lead to initial teacher training (ITT) and are available at some colleges and universities, with courses lasting 2-4 years part time. However, to enter any ITT programme (not Scotland), a teaching assistant should have GCSEs (or equivalent) in English and maths (A*-C) and if born on or after 1 September 1979, must also have GCSE (or equivalent) in a science subject (A*-C).

Some colleges also offer other relevant qualifications, including CACHE/BTEC certificates and diplomas in areas of child care and education, early years care and education at levels 2-4, which may be studied full or part time. Contact the Training & Development Agency (TDA) for Schools for further information on the range of qualifications and progression routes for teaching assistants. The main qualification in Scotland is currently the PDA for learning support assistants.

Apprenticeships programmes for teaching/classroom assistants, may be available in your area for entry to this job. Advanced apprenticeships leading to qualification at level 3 can also be a route into higher education.

Mature applicants with qualifications and/or experience of working with children and young people are welcomed and may have an advantage. Previous experience, paid or voluntary work, in areas such as nursery nursing, youth work and play work is useful. This job (and qualification) is also useful for those who wish to work in other areas, including social work and child care, where further study is required. See the entry and training section for details of training routes and relevant qualifications.

Opportunities and Pay

You are employed by a local education authority or an individual school and jobs are available throughout the UK. This job is particularly suitable for part-time work and some may do this job on a voluntary basis before applying for a salaried post. There are increasing opportunities for teaching assistants but also increased competition for jobs. Some places on teacher training courses are being reserved for those TAs who wish to progress into fully qualified teaching posts.

Depending on location and type of employer; starting salaries are around £14k-£16k a year. Higher level teaching assistants can earn around £19k a year. Part-time posts are paid pro-rata.

Health

You need good general health and stamina to do this work.

Skills and Qualities

able to discipline, able to follow instructions, able to relate well to children and young people, alert, calm, good communication skills, good interpersonal skills, good organisational skills, patient, sense of humour

Relevant Subjects

English, Health and social care, Psychology

Further Information

Apprenticeship Schemes (National Apprenticeship Service) - www.apprenticeships.org.uk

Learning Support (6 x year) (Brightday Publishing) - www.learningsupport.co.uk

Open University - www.open.ac.uk

Scottish Government - Education and Training - www.scotland.gov.uk/Topics/Education

Skills4schools - www.skills4schools.co.uk

Training & Development Agency (TDA) - www.tda.gov.uk

▶Working in schools & colleges (2007) (Babcock Lifeskills) - www.babcock-lifeskills.com/

Addresses

CACHE: Council for Awards in Children's Care & Education
Apex House, 81 Camp Road, St Albans AL1 5GB
Phone: 0845 347 2123 (UK only)
Web: www.cache.org.uk

Department of Education NI (DENI)
Rathgael House, Balloo Road, Bangor BT19 7PR
Phone: +44 (0)28 9127 9279
Web: www.deni.gov.uk

Similar Jobs

Montessori Teacher, Pre-school Supervisor/Worker, School Lunchtime Supervisor, Teacher: Early Years, Teacher: Primary School, Teacher: Special Educational Needs

Telecommunications Technician

also known as: Communications Technician, Installation Technician, Phone Technician, Telecoms Technician

CRCI:Engineering

CLCI:RAL — Job Band: 2 to 4

Job Description

Telecoms technicians install and maintain complex electronic equipment for communication systems such as telephones, computer networks and fax machines. They also work with digital or satellite systems, radio networks and mobile telephone networks. Technicians put in new systems, take wires to a home, office or other building from poles or underground cables and install sockets and exchanges. They examine systems and equipment for faults using test equipment at a base or in customers' premises, and carry out repairs. Some technicians lay and joint cables underground or overhead. Others may be involved in the design and development areas of work.

Work Details

Usually work 37-40 hrs a week, Monday to Friday, but may be expected to work occasional weekends and sometimes be on call. Most technicians travel around an area to exchanges, business premises, clients' homes and other work sites such as new buildings. You are responsible for a high standard of accurate work.

Maintenance technicians deal with complaints and are responsible for quickly finding and sorting problems. You need to cope with some physical activity, such as lifting and bending, sometimes working at heights and carrying heavy test equipment. You may be out on site in all sorts of weather. Technicians working with manufacturers usually work indoors in industrial premises or a workshop, but may also visit customers' premises. You may need to wear protective overalls and sometimes a safety helmet and safety glasses.

Qualification

• England, Wales and Northern Ireland

Band 2: For entry to jobs, no minimum qualifications are needed, but it is an advantage to have some GCSEs (A*-C) or equivalent in subjects that include maths, English and a science or technical subject, or equivalent.

Band 3: For entry to jobs, technical training, HNC in communications technology or a relevant Diploma, usually at least 4 GCSEs (A*-C) including English, science (preferably physics) and a technical subject, or equivalent.

Band 4: For relevant HND, Diploma of Higher Education or foundation degree: 1-2 A levels in maths and a science plus some GCSEs (A*-C), or equivalent.

• Scotland

Band 2: Although academic qualifications are not specified for this job, it is an advantage to have some S grades (1-3) in maths, English and a science or technical subject, or similar.

Band 3: For entry to jobs, technical training and relevant SQA national award: usually at least four S grades (1-3) including maths, English, science (preferably physics) and a technical subject, or similar.

Band 4: For entry to SQA higher national award in electronics and professional development awards: usually 2-3 H grades including maths and a science (preferably physics), and some S grades (1-3), including English and maths, or similar qualifications.

Adult Qualifications

If you have relevant work experience you may be accepted for some college courses without meeting the formal entry requirements.

Work Experience

Relevant work or voluntary experience is always useful. It can add to your CV and improve your chances when applying for entry to jobs or apprenticeships in the communications or engineering industry. Any experience of working with computers or telephone systems is also useful.

Entry and Training

To enter this job directly you have to take a maths test and pass a practical aptitude test. Training depends on entry level but is often through an employer's training scheme. Relevant S/NVQs at levels 1-4 are available. Training programmes, including apprenticeship schemes, may be available in your area. Advanced apprenticeships leading to qualification at level 3 can also be a route into higher education. Training lasts for approximately 3-4 years. Entrants can also choose to study either full or part time for BTEC/SQA national/higher national awards, such as the level 3 National Certificate in communications technology, and then begin on-the-job training. There is frequently sponsorship for courses.

Following completion of an S/NVQ level 3 or a national award, you can apply for Engineering Technician (EngTech) status with the Engineering Council. To do this you need to go through a professional review that assesses commitment to and competence in the work. You are expected to do continuing professional development to keep up to date with new technologies. Some technicians may progress to becoming a chartered or incorporated engineer. Contact the Engineering Council for details.

Foundation degrees are available in electronic engineering or in general engineering. The Tomorrow's Engineers website has lots of useful careers information including a route map and guide to engineering activities from primary school through to higher education. The Engineering Development Trust also runs a range of nationwide schemes for 11-21 year olds who may be interested in engineering as a career. See the websites for details.

A Diploma/Welsh Baccalaureate may be available in your area in engineering. This can be a useful entry to this type of work. See the diplomas website for further information.

Mature applicants with previous experience in electronics, electrical, communications or sometimes mechanical engineering have an advantage. There are good opportunities if you have been employed in relevant work, such as signals, in the Merchant Navy or in the armed forces. Training opportunities such as New Deal/Training for Work may be available. You can also gain recognition of previous experience through Accreditation of Prior Learning (APL) or by working towards relevant S/NVQs.

Opportunities and Pay
Jobs are available with companies such as British Telecom, Orange, Vodaphone and NTL. There are also opportunities with other organisations involved in communications, including broadcasting, cable TV and phone companies, software companies, equipment manufacturers, railway traffic control and the armed forces. There is a good demand for skilled workers in this rapidly changing environment. Job opportunities are spread throughout the country. Promotion to management level from junior jobs is possible.

Pay varies depending on area, size and type of company. Apprentice technicians earn around £13k-£18k, rising to £25k-£30k a year with experience and additional qualifications.

Health
This job requires good eyesight and normal colour vision. There may be a medical test for entry to this job.

Skills and Qualities
able to follow drawings and plans, able to work both on your own and in a team, attention to detail, good communication skills, health & safety awareness, IT skills, manual dexterity, methodical, problem-solving skills, technical aptitude

Relevant Subjects
Design and technology, Engineering, ICT/Computer studies, Manufacturing, Physics, Science

Further Information
AGCAS: Energy & Utilities (Job Sector briefing) (AGCAS) - www.prospects.ac.uk

Apprenticeship Schemes (National Apprenticeship Service) - www.apprenticeships.org.uk

Diplomas (Foundation, Higher and Advanced) - http://yp.direct.gov.uk/diplomas

Engineering Connections - www.apprentices.co.uk

e-skills UK - sector skills council for business and information technology - www.e-skills.com

SEMTA - sector skills council for science, engineering and manufacturing technologies - www.semta.org.uk

Telecoms Careers - www.careers.telecoms.com

Tomorrow's Engineers - www.tomorrowsengineers.org.uk/careers.cfm

Training Schemes - www.direct.gov.uk/en/educationandlearning

Women into Science, Engineering & Construction - www.wisecampaign.org.uk

Addresses
Engineering Council
246 High Holborn, London WC1V 7EX
Phone: +44 (0)20 3206 0500
Web: www.engc.org.uk

Engineering Development Trust (EDT)
Ridgeway, Welwyn Garden City, Hertfordshire AL7 2AA
Phone: +44 (0)1707 871520
Web: www.etrust.org.uk

Engineering Training Council (NI)
Interpoint, 20-24 York Street, Belfast BT15 1AQ
Phone: +44 (0)28 9032 9878
Web: www.etcni.org.uk

Institution of Engineering and Technology (IET)
Michael Faraday House, Stevenage, Hertfordshire SG1 2AY
Phone: +44 (0)1438 313311
Web: www.theiet.org

Scottish Engineering
Training Officer, 105 West George Street, Glasgow G2 1QL
Phone: +44 (0)141 221 3181
Web: www.scottishengineering.org.uk

Similar Jobs
Electrical Engineering Technician, Engineer: Broadcast, Engineer: Telecommunications, IT Service Technician, Merchant Navy Electro-technical Officer

Textile Colour Technologist
also known as: Colour Technologist: Textiles, Textile Technician: Dyeing

CRCI:Manufacturing and Production
CLCI:SAV Job Band: 3 to 5

Job Description
Textile colour technologists source and produce new pigments and dyes, checking them for colour fastness. They forecast trends in the development of colour and investigate cheap and environmentally-friendly dyes. They use technical and chemical knowledge to produce a dye 'recipe' for colouring a wide variety of fibres, yarns and fabrics that are used in the textile industry. Technologists keep extremely detailed records of dye recipes and processes, which are also electronically or computer controlled. May choose and purchase the dye and chemical supply. Particular dyes are selected for different fabrics, using laboratory tests and calculations.

If working in production, textile colour technologists take into account any fabric processes/finishes such as bleaching or waterproofing, which can affect the dyeing process. They determine correct mix, supervise machine settings and monitor the process, making adjustments when necessary. Technologists check finished product for quality control and check that the dye is colour fast. Liaising with maintenance staff and the design team is an important part of the job.

Textile Colour Technologist

Work Details
Textile colour technologists usually work a 39 hr week that may require working shifts and weekends if working in production. You work either in a textile mill or a dye works, which might be hot and humid, or in a specialist dyeing laboratory. Many working environments are light and airy with extractors for removing the fumes and steam. Your role may include the supervision of textile operatives. A key responsibility is quality control, as well as testing for colour fastness and match, using chemical and physical tests. Needs to wear protective clothing such as an overall and footwear in the dyeing area.

Qualification

• England, Wales and Northern Ireland
Band 3: For relevant BTEC national certificate: at least 4 GCSEs (A*-C) usually including chemistry, maths and English, or equivalent.

Band 4: For relevant BTEC higher national award/foundation degree: 1-2 A levels, chemistry preferred, and some GCSEs (A*-C) including maths and English or equivalent qualifications.

Band 5: For degree courses: 2-3 A levels and some GCSEs (A*C) usually including English, chemistry and maths or equivalent qualifications. The exact requirements depend on the degree you take.

• Scotland
Band 3: For entry: usually at least four S grades (1-3) usually including chemistry, maths and English, or similar.

Band 4: For relevant SQA higher national award: usually 2-3 H grades, including chemistry and some S grades (1-3) including maths and English, or similar qualifications.

Band 5: For degree courses: 3-5 H grades and some S grades (1-3), usually including English, chemistry and maths, or similar. Exact requirements depend on the degree you take.

Degree Information
There are relevant degree courses in some colleges and universities in subjects such as chemistry with colour science, design and colour technology, or in textile science, textile technology, textile management or textile production. Check course details carefully as some modules of the textile courses are on dyeing and colouring.

Adult Qualifications
Some colleges may consider adults without qualifications but with previous work experience in an engineering or technical field. Entry requirements may be relaxed for adults applying for higher education courses and Access courses give adults without qualifications a route on to degree courses. Check with individual institutions.

Work Experience
Relevant work or voluntary experience is always useful and can improve your chances when applying for entry to technical jobs in the manufacturing sector. Your personal or adult guidance adviser should be able to advise you about how to organise work experience with an employer. The most relevant work experience is in a chemical laboratory or in the textile industry.

Entry and Training
There are various entry routes into this work, but as it has a high scientific content most entrants have taken a degree course prior to entry. Other relevant qualifications that may be taken prior to applying for a job include certificate/diplomas at national/higher national level offered by BTEC/SQA, and also progression awards/ certificates offered by City & Guilds, which are usually available at local colleges, either full or part time. Once iworking, training can be on the job with an experienced or senior technician, and may include study for specialist qualifications.

The degree level associateship of the Society of Dyers and Colourists is awarded to those who have at least two years' practical experience, have an honours degree or equivalent, and who pass the professional exams. Entrants to the graduate diploma can be exempt from some, if not all, of the exams providing they pass an interview, hold an appropriate degree and have industrial experience. These professional qualifications allow the holder to use the title Chartered Colourists. There are a range of short courses and courses for continuing professional development (CPD) also available. Check the SDC website for full details.

Training programmes, including apprenticeship schemes, may be available in your area. Advanced apprenticeships leading to qualification at level 3 can also be a route into higher education. The Textile Centre of Excellence has details of apprenticeship schemes. A Diploma/Welsh Baccalaureate in manufacturing and product design may be available in your area. The advanced level is equivalent to 3.5 A levels but for some university courses, the additional and specialist learning (ASL) component of the diploma needs to include specific A levels eg chemistry. Check entry requirements carefully with the individual institutions.

Mature applicants with previous experience in textiles and clothing, or in a related industry such as chemicals, may have an advantage. The Society of Dyers and Colourists (SDC) has six distance learning modules on dyeing. These are suitable for those already working in the industry or those wishing to take the society's licentiate and associate examinations.

Opportunities and Pay
You are employed by a textile manufacturing company/laboratory or with a specialist dyeing and finishing firm. Jobs are available mainly in areas where this industry is concentrated, including Lancashire, west Yorkshire, the Midlands, the Scottish Borders and central Scotland and Northern Ireland. Usually there is a steady demand for trainees and skilled workers, but this is less the case at the moment as, due to the current economic downturn, there are more applicants for fewer places.

Promotion prospects are improved by studying to obtain professional qualification and can lead to work in research and development, sales, marketing and management, either in the UK or abroad.

Pay varies depending on location and employer but most technologists earn from around £17k a year, rising to £20k-£22k with experience. Senior technicians earn in the region of £30k-£35k.

Health
There may be an allergy risk from skin irritants and fumes. This job requires good eyesight and normal colour vision.

Skills and Qualities
able to work both on your own and in a team, analytical skills, attention to detail, good communication skills, good organisational skills, health & safety awareness, IT skills, practical skills, problem-solving skills, scientific approach

Relevant Subjects
Chemistry, Design and technology, Manufacturing, Mathematics, Science

Further Information
AGCAS: Manufacturing (Job Sector Briefing) (AGCAS) - www.prospects.ac.uk

Apprenticeship Schemes (National Apprenticeship Service) - www.apprenticeships.org.uk

Coloration Technology (6x a year) (Society of Dyers and Colourists (SDC)) http://sdc.org.uk/publications/publ.htm

Diplomas (Foundation, Higher and Advanced) - http://yp.direct.gov.uk/diplomas

International Dyer (World Textile Information Network (WTiN)) http://internationaldyer.com/

Skillset - sector skills council for the creative media, fashion and textiles industries - www.skillset.org

Welsh Baccalaureate - www.wbq.org.uk

▶Working in fashion & clothing (2008) (Babcock Lifeskills) - www.babcock-lifeskills.com/

Addresses

British Textile Technology Group
Unit 14, Wheel Forge Way, Trafford Park, Manchester M17 1EH
Phone: +44 (0)161 873 6543
Web: www.bttg.co.uk

East Midlands Textiles Association (EMTEX)
69 - 73 Lower Parliament Street, Sutton in Ashfield, Nottinghamshire NG1 3BB
Phone: + 44 (0) 115 911 5339
Web: www.emtex.org.uk

Performance Textiles Association
MUTA c/o Luther Pendragon Priory Court, Pilgrim Street, London EC4V 6DR
Phone: +44 (0) 207 618 9196
Web: www.performancetextiles.org.uk

Scottish Enterprise
Scottish Textiles Apex House 99 Haymarket Terrace, Edinburgh EH12 5DH
Phone: +44 (0) 131 313 6243
Web: https://www.scottish-enterprise.com/your-sector/textiles.aspx

Society of Dyers and Colourists (SDC)
PO Box 244 Perkin House 82 Grattan Road, Bradford BD1 2LU
Phone: +44 (0)1274 725 138
Web: www.sdc.org.uk

Textile Centre of Excellence
Textile House, , Red Doles Lane, Huddersfield HD2 1YF
Phone: +44 (0)1484 346 500
Web: www.textilehouse.co.uk

Textile Institute
1st Floor, St James' Buildings, Oxford Street, Manchester M1 6FQ
Phone: +44 (0)161 237 1188
Web: www.textileinstitute.org

Similar Jobs

Chemist, Laboratory Technician: Science, Textile Designer, Textile Machinery Technician, Textile Technologist

Textile Designer

CRCI:Design, Arts and Crafts
CLCI:EP
Job Band: 3 to 5

Job Description

Textile designers produce creative designs for knitted, woven and printed textiles, used to make clothing, interior furnishings and other textile products. They may specialise in one area such as children's clothing or furnishing fabrics. Designers produce sketches using either traditional design tools, such as paper, pens/pencils and paints, or by computer-aided design (CAD). Samples are made and shown to design companies or to individual clients. Then the appropriate quality of yarn and dyes for woven material and the number of separate screens needed for different colours when printing are selected, as these decisions affect the cost.

Usually work with fashion designers and buyers to anticipate future trends in fashionable colours and fabrics. They keep up to date with developments in manufacturing technology. Also work to an agreed budget and liaise with customers, marketing, technical and buying staff as well as design colleagues. Some designers make their own items for sale direct to the public or through craft shops, exhibitions and fairs.

Work Details

Usually work a 9am to 5pm day, Monday to Friday, though sometimes extra hours and/or weekend work is necessary if there are deadlines to meet. The work is based in a studio/office, often in front of a computer screen, but you may have to visit customers at times. Attendance at trade fairs often requires time away from home, especially if you want to sell your work abroad. Freelance designers work hours to suit themselves, but must keep to a deadline.

Qualification

• England, Wales and Northern Ireland

Band 3: For entry to jobs, HNC or a relevant Diploma, usually at least 4 GCSEs (A*-C) including English and maths, or equivalent. For some foundation studies courses: usually at least 5 GCSEs (A*-C).

Band 4: For diploma in foundation studies (art and design): usually at least one A level and some GCSEs (A*-C). For BTEC higher national award: a BTEC national award, successful completion of a foundation studies course, or equivalent qualification.

Band 5: For degree courses: 2-3 A levels and some GCSEs (A*-C); useful subjects are maths, technology, art, design, history, history of art and English, or equivalent. Most students take a foundation studies course first. Exact requirements depend on the degree you take.

• Scotland

Band 3: For entry: usually at least four S grades (1-3) including English and maths, or similar.

Band 4: For entry to SQA higher national and professional development awards, usually 2-3 H grades and some S grades (1-3), including English and maths, or similar qualifications.

Band 5: For degree courses: 3-5 H grades including art, and some S grades (1-3), usually including English and maths, or similar. Exact entry requirements depend on the degree you take.

Degree Information

Degree should be in textile design, textile and fashion design, printed textiles and surface pattern design, or art and design with a textile specialism. Postgraduate courses are available including textile design, textile design with clothing manufacture, and textile design with fashion and management.

Adult Qualifications

Adult candidates for courses may be accepted with few or no qualifications provided that they present a good portfolio of work. There are Access and foundation level courses in some areas, which give adults without qualifications a route into degree courses. Check with individual institutions.

Work Experience

Entry to this job/career is highly competitive and it is essential that you have some relevant work or voluntary experience before applying. It may be possible to gain work experience with a textile design or manufacturing company. Work with fashion or costumes is also helpful.

Entry and Training

Most people enter this work through an HNC/HND or a degree in textile or fashion design that covers printed, woven, knitted and embroidered textiles. Foundation studies courses in art and design and a good portfolio of work are usually essential for entry to degree courses. Foundation degrees are also available in textiles, textile design, and textile design and practice. In Scotland, degree courses last for four years, the first year is general, before specialising in a particular area of art and design. Pre-entry postgraduate courses are not essential, but can be helpful. A

Diploma/Welsh Baccalaureate may be available in your area in creative and media and may provide a route onto higher education courses.

Training is usually on the job and the length depends on prior experience. Specialist courses are available at all levels, for example in constructed textiles and carpet design. The Chartered Society of Designers (CSD) runs seminars as part of their continuing professional development (CPD) scheme, and the Textile Institute offers a range of courses and membership levels dependent on qualifications.

Some people begin as a machinist or cutter and progress to textile designer. City & Guilds offer courses at level 3 in design and crafts. It is then possible to go on to a relevant higher education course. Relevant S/NVQs at levels 1-3 are available in design subjects, apparel manufacturing and manufacturing textiles.

There are part-time courses available for mature students over 21. Distance learning in art and design is also available at various levels of qualification, including those offered by the Open College of the Arts or the London Art College. There is a wide range of courses available at adult education centres and colleges that offer day/evening art and design courses. Some private courses may be costly and you should choose carefully.

Opportunities and Pay

There are around 12,000 textile designers in the UK with a higher concentration in London, the North West, the East Midlands and Scotland. You may be employed by a textile manufacturer or specialist design company/studio to design fabrics for clothes or furnishings, carpets, embroidery, lace, wallpaper or tiles. Competition for jobs is fierce and most company design departments or design studios are small. Opportunities are good for designers wishing to work abroad, particularly in countries such as France, Italy and the USA.

It is possible to set up a small craft business in the UK, designing and selling your own work, once you have gained some experience. Freelance work is also possible. Some designers may work as a textile or fashion buyer.

Pay varies depending on location, employer and whether you work freelance. Starting salaries for newly qualified designers are around £12k, rising to £25k a year with three to four years' experience. Freelance designer rates vary as they may charge per design or collection and agents can take up to 30% commission. Design directors may earn £28k-£40k a year.

Health

This job requires good eyesight and good colour vision.

Skills and Qualities

able to work to deadlines, aptitude for teamwork, artistic ability, attention to detail, creative and imaginative flair, eye for shape/colour, eye for visual effect, good communication skills, good presentation skills, specialist IT skills

Relevant Subjects

Art and Design, Design and technology, ICT/Computer studies, Manufacturing

Further Information

AGCAS: Fashion & Design (Job Sector Briefing) (AGCAS) - www.prospects.ac.uk

Chartered Society of Designers (Chartered Society of Designers) - www.csd.org.uk

Design Uncovered (Trotman 2009) - www.trotman.co.uk

Drapers: Fashionnews, jobs and trends - www.drapersonline.com

Future Textiles - www.futuretextiles.co.uk

Textiles (quarterly) (Textile Institute) - www.textileinstitute.org/PublicationsMags.asp

The Designer (Chartered Society of Designers) - www.thedesignermagazine.com

The Textile Institute - www.texi.org

▶Working in art & design (2009) (Babcock Lifeskills) - www.babcock-lifeskills.com/

▶Working in creative & media (2007) (Babcock Lifeskills) - www.babcock-lifeskills.com/

▶Working in fashion & clothing (2008) (Babcock Lifeskills) - www.babcock-lifeskills.com/

Addresses

Crafts Council (CC)
44a Pentonville Road, Islington, London N1 9BY
Phone: +44 (0)20 7806 2500
Web: www.craftscouncil.org.uk

Design Council
34 Bow Street, London WC2E 7DL
Phone: +44 (0)20 7420 5200
Web: www.designcouncil.org.uk

Design Wales
University of Wales Institute, Cardiff Western Avenue CF5 2YB
Phone: +44 (0) 2920 41 7043
Web: www.designwales.org

London Art College
PO Box 22, Milnthorpe LA7 7WY
Phone: 0800 3280 465 (UK only)
Web: www.londonartcollege.co.uk

Open College of the Arts
Michael Young Arts Centre, Redbrook Business Park, Wilthorpe Road, Barnsley S75 1JN
Phone: 0800 731 2116 (UK only)
Web: www.oca-uk.com

Scottish Enterprise
Atrium Court 50 Waterloo Street, Glasgow G2 6HQ
Phone: +44 (0)141 248 2700
Web: www.scottish-enterprise.com

Textile Institute
1st Floor, St James' Buildings, Oxford Street, Manchester M1 6FQ
Phone: +44 (0)161 237 1188
Web: www.textileinstitute.org

Similar Jobs

Fashion Designer, Footwear Designer, Graphic Designer, Interior Designer, Textile Machinery Technician

Textile Machinery Technician

CRCI:Manufacturing and Production
CLCI:SAG Job Band: 2 to 3

Job Description

Textile machinery technicians install, maintain and repair the machinery used in the textile industry in the production of yarn or cloth. They see that production runs smoothly and efficiently and carry out routine cleaning, oiling and process supervision to avoid breakdowns or delays in production. Technicians are responsible for seeing that the work environment is safe for staff. They diagnose minor problems, often with the use of computers, and put them right before they cause any major difficulties. May have to strip the machine, replace any faulty or damaged parts, then carry out tests to ensure the machine is fully operational. With the growth in the use of more technologically advanced equipment, technicians usually need detailed knowledge of electrical as well as mechanical industries.

Technicians show textile operators how to operate machines. May organise workloads, supervise staff and write reports. They work on machines in all stages of production, including dyeing, printing or finishing, and may be involved with quality control. All technicians must record their daily work tasks in detail and accurately.

Work Details

Textile machinery technicians usually work a 37-40 hr week that may require working shifts and weekends. You work in industrial premises or a workshop, which may be warm, noisy and dusty, although many working environments are now light and airy with extractors for removing the dust. Work can be pressurised at times, especially if the machinery breaks down. You are responsible for instructing the machine operatives in the safe use of the machinery. This job requires you to stand for many hours at a time.

Qualification

• England, Wales and Northern Ireland

Band 3: For direct entry to training or a relevant course: at least 4 GCSEs (A*-C), usually including maths, a science subject and English. Students with lower grades can take a preliminary BTEC first qualification in engineering or science.

• Scotland

Band 3: For entry: usually at least four S grades (1-3) including English, maths and a science/technological subject, or similar.

Adult Qualifications

Some colleges may consider adults without qualifications but with previous work experience in an engineering or technical field.

Work Experience

Employers or colleges/universities may prefer candidates who have relevant work or voluntary experience. This can include observation and shadowing of a textile machinery technician or experience in related areas where you work with machinery. Jobs in mechanical engineering or in manufacturing are relevant.

Entry and Training

It is usual to enter this job as a textile, electrical, or mechanical engineering technician apprentice. Training can be on the job with an experienced or senior technician, and may include study for work-based qualifications. Other relevant qualifications include national certificate/diplomas offered by BTEC/SQA and progression awards/certificates offered by City & Guilds, which are usually available at local colleges, either full or part time.

There are opportunities for professional development to gain EngTech status when suitably experienced and qualified. Contact the Engineering Council for details. Associateship of the Textile Institute is awarded to those who have at least two years' practical experience, have a relevant higher national award, or equivalent, and who pass the professional exams. The Textile Centre of Excellence also has details of apprenticeship schemes. Check their website for details.

Relevant S/NVQs up to level 3 are available. Training programmes, including apprenticeship schemes, may be available in your area. Advanced apprenticeships leading to qualification at level 3 can also be a route into higher education. A Diploma/Welsh Baccalaureate in manufacturing and product design may be available in your area. This is available for 14-19 year olds and can form a good introduction to this type of work.

Mature applicants with previous experience in textiles and clothing, or in a related industry such as engineering or chemicals, may have an advantage. Government training opportunities, such as apprenticeships, may be available in your area. You can also gain recognition of previous experience through Accreditation of Prior Learning (APL) or by working towards relevant S/NVQs. Contact your local careers office, Jobcentre Plus, Next Step service or Learning and Skills Council (LSC) Local Enterprise Company (LEC) for details of training schemes.

Opportunities and Pay

There are around 6,000 textile companies in the UK employing 2,000 machinery technicians. Jobs are mostly available in certain areas where this industry is concentrated such as west Yorkshire, Lancashire the Scottish Borders, Northern Ireland, and the Midlands, However, demand for technicians in some industries is declining as a result of the introduction of high-tech machinery with better electronics. There is also competition from textile firms based abroad and vacancies have decreased further in the UK, due to the current economic downturn.

Pay varies depending on location and employer but most trained technicians earn from around £18k-£20k a year. With experience this can rise to £25k.

Health

There may be an allergy risk from dust. This job requires good eyesight and good colour vision for certain areas of work.

Skills and Qualities

able to cope under pressure, able to work both on your own and in a team, attention to detail, health & safety awareness, IT skills, manual dexterity, numeracy skills, perseverance, problem-solving skills, technical aptitude

Relevant Subjects

Design and technology, Engineering, Manufacturing, Mathematics, Physics, Science

Further Information

Apprenticeship Schemes (National Apprenticeship Service) - www.apprenticeships.org.uk

Diplomas (Foundation, Higher and Advanced) - http://yp.direct.gov.uk/diplomas

Skillset - sector skills council for the creative media, fashion and textiles industries - www.skillset.org

Training Schemes - www.direct.gov.uk/en/educationandlearning

Welsh Baccalaureate - www.wbq.org.uk

Addresses

British Textile Technology Group
Unit 14, Wheel Forge Way, Trafford Park, Manchester M17 1EH
Phone: +44 (0)161 873 6543
Web: www.bttg.co.uk

East Midlands Textiles Association (EMTEX)
69 - 73 Lower Parliament Street, Sutton in Ashfield, Nottinghamshire NG1 3BB
Phone: + 44 (0) 115 911 5339
Web: www.emtex.org.uk

Engineering Council
246 High Holborn, London WC1V 7EX
Phone: +44 (0)20 3206 0500
Web: www.engc.org.uk

Performance Textiles Association
MUTA c/o Luther Pendragon Priory Court, Pilgrim Street, London EC4V 6DR
Phone: +44 (0) 207 618 9196
Web: www.performancetextiles.org.uk

Scottish Enterprise
Scottish Textiles Apex House 99 Haymarket Terrace, Edinburgh EH12 5DH
Phone: +44 (0) 131 313 6243
Web: https://www.scottish-enterprise.com/your-sector/textiles.aspx

Textile Centre of Excellence
Textile House, , Red Doles Lane, Huddersfield HD2 1YF
Phone: +44 (0)1484 346 500
Web: www.textilehouse.co.uk

Textile Institute
1st Floor, St James' Buildings, Oxford Street, Manchester M1 6FQ
Phone: +44 (0)161 237 1188
Web: www.textileinstitute.org

Similar Jobs

Electrical Engineering Technician, Fitter: Maintenance, Mechanical Engineering Technician, Textile Colour Technologist, Textile Operative

Textile Operative

CRCI:Manufacturing and Production
CLCI:SAG

Job Band: 1 to 2

Job Description

Textile operatives carry out a variety of different tasks in a textile manufacturing company. They control and monitor the computerised and electronic machinery that turns raw fibre into a finished product. Any faults or mechanical failures, are reported to a technician, though most operatives usually carry out minor repairs. May stop a loom if the yarn breaks, then joins the broken ends together again. Also makes sure that the shuttles and bobbins are kept full of thread, or may clean the dye off the rollers between batches of work.

Most operatives specialise in a particular area of textile production, such as cotton, wool, lace, carpet and rug production. All operatives have to keep their work area clean and tidy.

Work Details

Textile operatives usually work a 37-40 hr week that may require working shifts and weekends. This job covers work with a wide variety of different machines. You work in industrial premises or a workshop, which may be warm, noisy and dusty, although many working environments are now light and airy with extractors for removing the dust. This job may require you to do the same task over and over again. Operatives have to be fairly active, standing for many hours and lifting heavy objects. Overalls and ear protectors are usually supplied by your employer.

Qualification

• England, Wales and Northern Ireland

Band 1: No minimum qualifications are required, but you are expected to have a good level of general education. However, some formal/vocational qualifications at any level are useful.

Band 2: Although academic qualifications are not specified for this job, it is an advantage to have some GCSEs (A*-C) in subjects that include English and maths, or equivalent.

• Scotland

Band 1: No minimum qualifications are required, but you are expected to have a good level of general education. However, some formal/vocational qualifications at any level are useful.

Band 2: Although academic qualifications are not specified for this job, it is an advantage to have some S grades (1-3) in subjects that include English and maths, or similar.

Adult Qualifications

No pre-entry qualifications are usually required though some academic/vocational qualifications at any level may be an advantage. English and maths are useful subjects.

Work Experience

Relevant work or voluntary experience is always useful and can improve your chances when applying for entry to jobs or apprenticeships in the manufacturing sector. Your personal or adult guidance adviser should be able to advise you about how to organise work experience with an employer.

Entry and Training

Training is mainly on the job, usually through an employer's training scheme or may involve some off-the-job training at a college or training centre. After you have some experience, you may be able to do craft/technician training. You can train to be multi-skilled in a wide range of jobs or specialise in a particular area of work within the company. Relevant courses include ABC awards at levels 1-3 in fashion and textiles and level 1-2 in sewing and textiles.

S/NVQs levels 1-3 are available in manufacturing textiles, and training programmes, including apprenticeship schemes, may be available in your area. A Diploma/Welsh Baccalaureate in manufacturing and product design may be available in your area.

Government training opportunities, such as an apprenticeship in textiles may be available in your area. You can also gain recognition of previous experience through Accreditation of Prior Learning (APL) or by working towards relevant S/NVQs. Contact your local careers office, Jobcentre Plus, Next Step service or Learning and Skills Council (LSC) Local Enterprise Company (LEC) for details of training schemes.

Opportunities and Pay

You work for a manufacturing company and jobs are usually only available in certain areas, such as west Yorkshire, Lancashire, the Scottish Borders, Northern Ireland, and the Midlands where this industry is concentrated. However, there is a trend for production processes to be transferred overseas with the more technical roles currently remaining in the UK. Therefore, with experience and additional training you can progress to other jobs that are more technical/technological, or move into sales and marketing, and other areas in this industry. During the current economic downturn, there are fewer vacancies generally in the textile industry.

Pay varies depending on location and employer. Starting salaries are around £11k-£13k a year rising to around £15k-£17k with experience. Those working at senior operative level may earn around £20k a year. Income may be increased by overtime payments.

Health

There is an allergy risk from dust. This job requires good health and perfect colour vision for some areas of work.

Skills and Qualities

able to work both on your own and in a team, able to work quickly, good concentration level, health & safety awareness, manual dexterity, methodical, observant, practical skills

Relevant Subjects

Manufacturing

Further Information

Apprenticeship Schemes (National Apprenticeship Service) - www.apprenticeships.org.uk

Diplomas (Foundation, Higher and Advanced) - http://yp.direct.gov.uk/diplomas

Skillset - sector skills council for the creative media, fashion and textiles industries - www.skillset.org

Training Schemes - www.direct.gov.uk/en/educationandlearning

Welsh Baccalaureate - www.wbq.org.uk

Addresses

East Midlands Textiles Association (EMTEX)
69 - 73 Lower Parliament Street, Sutton in Ashfield, Nottinghamshire NG1 3BB
Phone: + 44 (0) 115 911 5339
Web: www.emtex.org.uk

Scottish Enterprise
Scottish Textiles Apex House 99 Haymarket Terrace, Edinburgh EH12 5DH
Phone: +44 (0) 131 313 6243
Web: https://www.scottish-enterprise.com/your-sector/textiles.aspx

Similar Jobs
Cloth/Garment Examiner, Sewing Machinist, Textile Designer, Textile Machinery Technician

Textile Technologist
CRCI:Manufacturing and Production
CLCI:SAG Job Band: 4 to 5

Job Description
Textile technologists use scientific and technical knowledge of textile production processes to solve problems in the manufacture of yarn, fibres and fabric. Most textile technologists work in one of the specialised areas of either engineering, research and development, production, quality control, or in marketing, buying and selling, and management. They work with both natural and man-made fibres and maintain technical control of production processes, developing new and improved techniques. Some technologists study and analyse new fibres and design ideas. They may develop materials that are more resistant to fire or more water repellent. Developing new technical textiles, such as those used in medicine or industry, is a growth area.

In quality control, samples are tested and causes of weaknesses and faults in product are diagnosed. Supervision of a team of textile technicians and operatives in manufacturing and production may be necessary. Textile technologists provide technical support to buyers, designers and merchandisers. May have to write and present reports on their work to colleagues.

Work Details
Usually works a 39-40 hr week that may require working early mornings or late evenings at times. You are likely to be based in an office, but visit production processing areas or laboratories. Industrial premises may be warm, noisy and dusty. However, many working environments are now light and airy with extractors for removing the dust. Travel may be required in the UK and occasionally overseas.

Fashion markets are constantly changing, so technologists have to be able to respond appropriately. Computer controlled machinery is now used in most factories.

Qualification
• England, Wales and Northern Ireland
Band 4: For BTEC higher national award/foundation degree: 1-2 A levels and some GCSEs (A*-C) usually including maths, a physical science and English, or equivalent.

Band 5: For degree course: 2-3 A levels usually including maths, physics and chemistry and some GCSEs (A*-C). The exact requirements depend on the degree you take.

• Scotland
Band 4: For SQA higher national award: usually 2-3 H grades and some S grades (1-3) including sciences, maths and English, or similar.

Band 5: For degree course: 3-5 H grades usually including maths, physics and chemistry and some S grades (1-3), usually including English and maths, or similar qualifications. Exact requirements depend on the degree you take.

Degree Information
A degree course in textile technology/manufacturing is preferred by employers because of its specialist knowledge content, but production engineering, physics and chemistry may also be acceptable. Postgraduate courses in textile technology are available for graduates in physical sciences and other related subjects.

Adult Qualifications
Mature applicants are usually science graduates. Entry qualifications for degree courses may be relaxed for mature applicants and Access courses may be available.

Work Experience
Relevant work or voluntary experience is always useful and can improve your chances in application for entry to this job. Direct experience in the textile industry, or in other areas of science, technology and manufacturing is an advantage. Joining the Textile Institute as a student member can be useful.

Entry and Training
Those who have an HNC/HND are likely to be employed initially as a textile technician, and with experience, gain promotion to the role of a technologist. However, most entrants are graduates with a relevant degree. Training is usually through practical experience after obtaining a degree, or after completing a postgraduate course. There are full-time, part-time or sandwich courses at first degree level. A foundation degree is available in textiles.

In-house training and development usually consists of company-specific production processes, management skills courses, health and safety awareness, and quality control and cost structure. Some of the larger employers offer a formal and structured training programme of specific assignments that aim to build on your existing academic and technical knowledge. The Textile Institute has professional qualifications at fellowship, associateship and licenciateship levels for applicants who meet their requirements. The Textile Centre of Excellence offers training in a number of areas including leadership and management and technical textiles. Check their website for full details.

A Diploma/Welsh Baccalaureate in manufacturing and product design may be available in your area. The advanced level is equivalent to 3.5 A levels but for some university courses, the additional and specialist learning (ASL) component of the diploma needs to include specific A levels eg chemistry or physics. Check entry requirements carefully with the individual institutions.

Mature applicants with previous practical work experience may have an advantage though still need the required academic qualifications. Those already in a textile technician role may be able to progress to entry as a technologist.

Government training opportunities, such as an apprenticeship in textiles may be available in your area. You can also gain recognition of previous experience through Accreditation of Prior Learning (APL) or by working towards relevant S/NVQs. Contact your local careers office, Jobcentre Plus, Next Step service or Learning and Skills Council (LSC) Local Enterprise Company (LEC) for details of training schemes.

Opportunities and Pay
You are employed by a textile manufacturing company, a research organisation or a university or college. Jobs are usually available only in certain areas that include the Scottish Borders, west Yorkshire, Lancashire, the East Midlands, and Northern Ireland. There are currently around 1,000 textile technologists in the UK. Usually there are good opportunities for well qualified technologists, some of whom go into buying, selling and marketing. However, during the economic downturn there are less vacancies in this field. There may be opportunities to travel and work abroad once you are experienced.

Pay varies depending on location and employer but trainees are likely to start on around £21k, rising to £25k-£35k a year with experience. Higher earners make around £45k a year.

Health
This job requires good eyesight and good colour vision. There is an allergy risk from skin irritants.

Skills and Qualities
analytical skills, aptitude for teamwork, flexible approach, good communication skills, good organisational skills, IT skills, leadership qualities, observant, perseverance, scientific approach

Relevant Subjects
Chemistry, Design and technology, Manufacturing, Mathematics, Physics, Science

Further Information
AGCAS: Manufacturing (Job Sector Briefing) (AGCAS) - www.prospects.ac.uk

Diplomas (Foundation, Higher and Advanced) - http://yp.direct.gov.uk/diplomas

Real Life Guide to Manufacturing & Product Design (Trotman 2009) - www.trotman.co.uk

Skillset - sector skills council for the creative media, fashion and textiles industries - www.skillset.org

Welsh Baccalaureate - www.wbq.org.uk

► Working in fashion & clothing (2008) (Babcock Lifeskills) - www.babcock-lifeskills.com/

Addresses
Performance Textiles Association
MUTA c/o Luther Pendragon Priory Court, Pilgrim Street, London EC4V 6DR
Phone: +44 (0) 207 618 9196
Web: www.performancetextiles.org.uk

Textile Centre of Excellence
Textile House, , Red Doles Lane, Huddersfield HD2 1YF
Phone: +44 (0)1484 346 500
Web: www.textilehouse.co.uk

Textile Institute
1st Floor, St James' Buildings, Oxford Street, Manchester M1 6FQ
Phone: +44 (0)161 237 1188
Web: www.textileinstitute.org

Similar Jobs
Leather Technologist, Materials Scientist/Engineer, Textile Colour Technologist, Textile Designer, Textile Machinery Technician

Thatcher
CRCI:Building and Construction
CLCI:SAW — Job Band: 1 to 2

Job Description
Thatchers cover the roofs of buildings with reeds or straw to make them weatherproof. They work on buildings such as houses, pubs, barns, dovecotes or summer houses. One of three types of thatching material is commonly used: water reed (Norfolk reed), long straw (Midlands, Hampshire and East Anglia) and combed wheat straw (mainly Devon). May also use imported thatching material. Traditional specialist hand tools are used in this job. These include cutting and fixing tools, such as eave-knives, hooks, hammers and mallets, long needles, and shearing hooks.

May have to erect scaffolding or prepare ladders. Old or damaged thatch is removed and roof timbers are checked for damage or rot. The thatching material is pegged to the roof in overlapping layers. The thatch is fixed into position with horizontal hazelwood strips or steel spars (sways). The edges are cut away and often, part of the roof is decorated with patterns or shapes; traditionally a pheasant or fox, though modern designs can include aeroplanes, pigs or dragons. Thatchers beat and brush the thatch until it is smooth and often cover it with protective wire netting to keep out birds and pests.

If self employed, thatchers have to calculate costs and timescales for each job. Many thatched buildings are in conservation areas and have to be finished to strict standards.

Work Details
There are no set hours for this job and each roof takes several weeks or months to complete. The work involves travelling around an area to different sites and sometimes you may need to work away from home. You work longer hours in the summer to take advantage of the daylight. You mostly work on your own and may not meet many people. The roofs are dusty and you are out in all sorts of weather. You have to cope with ladders or scaffolding and there is a risk of falling or injury.

This job requires much kneeling, balancing and possibly lifting. You may need to wear a face mask at times when conditions are dusty, and most thatchers wear protective leather or rubber kneepads.

Qualification
- **England, Wales and Northern Ireland**

Band 1: No formal qualifications are needed.

Band 2: For some training courses: 3-4 GCSEs (A*-C) or equivalent may be required.

- **Scotland**

Band 1: No formal qualifications are needed.

Band 2: For some training courses: 3-4 S grades (1-3) or similar may be required.

Adult Qualifications
Academic qualifications are not usually necessary for mature entrants but it is important that you have good hand skills.

Work Experience
Relevant work or voluntary experience is always useful and can improve your chances when applying for entry to this job. Health and safety issues may mean that there are certain jobs you cannot do until you are over 16. Contact your local ConstructionSkills office for advice.

Entry and Training
Training is usually on the job with a master thatcher and can be supplemented by a short residential or day-release course. Training can take up to five years and may also be supported by short training events and seminars held by the National Society of Master Thatchers (NSMT). Subjects can cover all aspects of thatching, including health and safety awareness. A list of master thatchers, or of short courses and seminars, is available from the NSMT. The society may also be able to offer help to those seeking an apprenticeship.

Specialist training is also available for those who wish to concentrate on achieving skills in restoration and heritage work. Contact the National Heritage Training Group for further information.

An NVQ in roof occupations (thatching) is available at level 2-3. Training programmes, including apprenticeships leading to level 2 and advanced apprenticeships/construction apprenticeships leading to level 3, may be available in your area.

Government training opportunities, such as apprenticeships, may be available in your area. You can also gain recognition of previous experience through Accreditation of Prior Learning or by working towards relevant S/NVQs. Contact your local careers office, Jobcentre Plus, Next Step service or Learning and Skills Council (LSC)/Local Enterprise Company (LEC) for details of all training opportunities and schemes, including apprenticeships for adults. You can also contact a master thatcher. A list of master thatchers and their location is available from the National Society of Master Thatchers.

Opportunities and Pay
Jobs are mainly available in the Midlands, East Anglia, south/south-east England and a few in areas of Scotland, Wales and Northern Ireland. Competition for jobs is fierce. It is becoming more fashionable to return roofs to thatch, particularly as newly thatched

roofs can be made to withstand fire. Most thatchers are self-employed and this job is often part of a family business. Some master thatchers may find contract work abroad.

As most thatchers are self-employed, earnings depend on how many hours you work. You are likely to earn around £14k-£16k, but experienced and self-employed thatchers can earn around £23k-£35k a year.

Health
This job requires good general fitness and there is a risk of allergies from pollens and dust.

Skills and Qualities
able to work both on your own and in a team, agile, enjoy working outdoors, good balance, good organisational skills, head for heights, manual dexterity, numeracy skills, safety conscious

Relevant Subjects
Construction and built environment

Further Information
Apprenticeship Schemes (National Apprenticeship Service) - www.apprenticeships.org.uk

Building Conservation Courses (Cathedral Communications Limited) - www.buildingconservation.com

ConstructionSkills - sector skills council for the construction industry - www.cskills.org

Guild of Straw Craftsmen - www.strawcraftsmen.co.uk

Lantra - The Sector Skills Council for environmental & land-based sector (Lantra) http:/www.lantra.co.uk

►Working outdoors (2010) (Babcock Lifeskills) - www.babcock-lifeskills.com/

Addresses
National Heritage Training Group (NHTG)
Carthusian Court, 12 Carthusian Street, London EC1M 6EZ
Phone: 0300 456 5517 (UK only)
Web: www.nhtg.org.uk

National Society of Master Thatchers (NSMT)
13 Parkers Hill Tetsworth, Thame, Oxfordshire OX9 7AQ
Phone: +44 (0)1844 281208
Web: www.nsmtltd.co.uk

Thatching Information Service
Thatchers Rest , Levens Green, Old Hall Green, Ware, Hertfordshire SG11 1HD
Phone: +44 (0)1920 438710
Web: www.buildingconservation.com/directory/ad318.htm

Similar Jobs
Carpenter/Joiner, Fence Installer, Forest Worker, Roofer, Scaffolder, Steeplejack

Theatre Producer

CRCI:Performing Arts
CLCI:GAB — Job Band: 4 to 5

Job Description
Theatre producers are responsible for making arrangements for every aspect of the production to prepare it for presentation to the public on stage. They choose which productions to put on., arrange the financing and publicity, and selects a creative team that includes a director, performers and technicians. Producers deal with any problems, as they arise. When a production is on tour, the producer is responsible for booking venues in advance, and making all the arrangements for publicity and transport. They support the production throughout and ensure everything runs smoothly, on time and to budget.

In commercial theatre, they aim to make a profit to cover all expenses, including the salaries of all performers and production staff, and to satisfy the investors. In a subsidised production, without investors, producers are known as production managers, they work within a given budget and have full responsibility and control of all financial aspects.

Work Details
Usually work a basic 39 hr week, which includes additional unsocial hours at weekends and in the evening. This work is emotionally and physically demanding. Not all theatres have comfortable areas backstage, so your work environment can be gloomy and hot. Often rehearsals for a new production are alongside a current production, so performers and other staff have heavy workloads. Teamwork is essential.

Qualification

• England, Wales and Northern Ireland
Band 4: For HND, Diploma of Higher Education or foundation degree: 1-2 A levels and some GCSEs (A*-C) usually including English and maths, or equivalent.

Band 5: For degree courses: 2-3 A levels and some GCSEs (A*-C) usually including English and maths, or equivalent. Subjects such as communication and media may be useful. Exact requirements depend on the degree you take.

• Scotland
Band 4: For entry to SQA higher national and professional development awards, usually 2-3 H grades and some S grades (1 3), including English and maths, or similar qualifications.

Band 5: For degree courses: 3-5 H grades and some S grades (1-3), usually including English and maths, or similar. Subjects such as communication and media may be useful. Exact requirements depend on the degree you take.

Degree Information
Any degree discipline is acceptable, although theatrical production, performing arts, media production, music, theatre/drama studies, business or communications, are particularly useful. A pre-entry postgraduate qualification can be an advantage, particularly if you have a non-relevant degree.

Adult Qualifications
Entry is possible, especially if you have good business experience, plus related media experience in radio, TV or films/videos. You are likely to start as a production assistant.

Work Experience
Entry to this job/career is highly competitive and it is essential to have some relevant work or voluntary experience before applying. Television and theatre companies, independent camera/film production companies are the first point of contact. Many companies, from small production companies to large concerns, such as the BBC and independent broadcasting companies, offer unpaid short-term placements, ranging from a few days to four weeks. Experience of coordinating an amateur production, particularly using sound, lighting and props, demonstrates your skills.

Entry and Training
Increasingly, there is a demand for graduates though entry without an HND/degree is possible. Choose a course carefully to ensure the content equips you with good technical skills and offers the opportunity to make good contacts. Those with a range of qualifications and/or practical theatre skills, including sound, lighting and props experience, have an advantage. Foundation degrees are available in theatre production, technical theatre and in performance and events production. Relevant postgraduate qualifications are not required for entry but may increase your chance of success in a competitive industry.

Many develop their skills by working in a junior post and gaining the required experience as they work. Others transfer their skills gained in related areas that include writing and acting. There are also relevant short courses available. The Conference of Drama Schools can provide a list of training providers. The Creative and Cultural Skills website is also a useful source of information.

The Theatrical Management Association offers a range of services to those involved in all aspects of theatrical production. It offers relevant seminars and courses on topics such as working with the media, dealing with finance, fundraising and resolving disputes. Stage One offers bursaries and runs workshops for new producers.

A Diploma/Welsh Baccalaureate in creative and media may be available in your area. Check university entry requirements carefully in case there is an additional specialist learning requirement with the diploma. See the diplomas website for further information.

Although there are no formal age barriers for this job, producers rarely transfer from other industries and must have a solid foundation in media to gain contracts and posts.

Opportunities and Pay

Jobs are likely to be based in major UK cities, concentrated in London and south-east England, or with a touring theatre company. There are further opportunities with fringe theatre, regional companies, and educational theatre, children's theatre, HM prisons, or with a local community. This area is highly competitive, but you may be able to work your way up, so it is worth considering any job in this field. Networking and contacts are vital to success, as well as your competency in the job. You may be employed by a theatre company or if working freelance, employed on short-term contracts.

Pay varies depending on location and the area of your work. Average starting salaries are around £18k a year, rising to £20k-£31k a year. Some may earn up to £65k a year. Highly successful freelance producers can earn much more.

Health

You need to be physically fit with good stamina for this job.

Skills and Qualities

able to manage a budget and keep records, adaptable, assertive, attention to detail, good interpersonal skills, good organisational skills, persuasive, planning skills, problem-solving skills, resourceful

Relevant Subjects

Business and accounting, Economics, English, Mathematics, Media and communication studies, Performing arts

Further Information

AZ Theatre - http://aztheatre.org.uk

BBC Recruitment Services (BBC) - www.bbc.co.uk/jobs

Behind the Scenes: Theatre (Trotman 2009) - www.trotman.co.uk

Creative & Cultural Skills - sector skills council for advertising, crafts, cultural heritage, design, literature, music, performing & visual arts - www.ccskills.org.uk

Diplomas (Foundation, Higher and Advanced) - http://yp.direct.gov.uk/diplomas

Prompt (quarterly) (Theatrical Management Association (TMA)) - www.tmauk.org/Prompt/

Society of London Theatre (SOLT) - www.solt.co.uk

Stage One - www.stageone.uk.com

The Stage (weekly) (The Stage Newspaper Limited) - www.thestage.co.uk

Welsh Baccalaureate - www.wbq.org.uk

Addresses

BECTU
(Broadcasting Entertainment Cinematographic and Theatre Union)
373-377 Clapham Road, London SW9 9BT
Phone: +44 (0)207 346 0900
Web: www.bectu.org.uk

Conference of Drama Schools (CDS)
PO Box 34252, London NW5 1XJ
Web: www.drama.ac.uk

Theatrical Management Association (TMA)
32 Rose Street, London WC2E 9ET
Phone: +44 (0)207 557 6700
Web: www.tmauk.org

Similar Jobs

Actor, Film/TV & Theatre Lighting Technician, Film/TV & Theatre Set/Stage Designer, Film/TV Floor Manager, Film/TV Producer, Theatre Stage Manager

Theatre Stage Manager

also known as: Stage Manager
CRCI:Performing Arts
CLCI:GAB
Job Band: 3 to 5

Job Description

Stage managers are responsible for the smooth running of theatre performances, sometimes under the direction of a producer. They bridge the gap between the artists and the technical side of a performance. Also plan and coordinate rehearsals and performances, and act as a 'prompt' during these. Managers make notes on the performance, cues, and script changes. They liaise between the director and technical staff and supervise a team that may include a deputy stage manager and one or more assistant managers. Also buy or hire scenery, properties and costumes, or have these made. They need technical skill to supervise lighting, scene changes and sound effects.

Small productions often run with only a stage manager so all areas of the production need to be looked after. When the performance run begins, stage managers take full responsibility for the production, supervising scene changes, cueing sound and lighting operators, and actors. They are responsible for supervising the setting up of all equipment before a production (called getting in) and for taking it all down at the end (called getting out).

Work Details

Work irregular hours, including evenings, weekends, and possibly long hours during a production. Travel is necessary if you are with a touring company and you need to spend time away from home. You are responsible for coordinating the different people involved in a theatrical production. Some of these may be difficult to handle, including some actors who may be unpredictable, so you have to be tactful and patient. You are on your feet most of the time and required to deal with many different problems simultaneously. Behind the scenes at a theatre can be hot, dusty and rather gloomy.

Qualification

- **England, Wales and Northern Ireland**

Band 3: For entry to jobs, a drama school stage management course, HNC or a relevant Diploma, usually at least 4 GCSEs (A*-C) including English and maths, or equivalent.

Band 4: For HND in performing arts (stage management) or technical theatre and production arts, Diploma of Higher Education or foundation degree: 1-2 A levels and some GCSEs (A*-C) usually including English and maths, or equivalent.

Band 5: For degree courses: 2-3 A levels and some GCSEs (A*-C) usually including English and maths or equivalent qualifications. Exact requirements depend on the degree you take.

- **Scotland**

Band 3: For entry to jobs or to a drama school stage management course, usually at least four S grades (1-3) including English and maths, or similar.

Band 4: For entry to SQA higher national ward in technical stage management and professional development awards, usually 2-3 H grades and some S grades (1-3), including English and maths, or similar qualifications.

Band 5: For degree courses: 3-5 H grades and some S grades (1-3), usually including English and maths or similar. Exact requirements depend on the degree you take.

Degree Information

Degree subjects include stage management, theatre production, theatre and performance technology and theatre design. A degree in drama or theatre studies is useful, particularly if it is possible to include options covering technical skills. It is possible to enter with any degree but a wide experience of theatrical work is essential.

Adult Qualifications

There are fast track schemes for more mature students. Entry requirements to higher education may be relaxed for adults and Access or foundation courses give adults without qualifications a route on to degree courses.

Work Experience

It is essential to have experience in theatre work before training and to continue to gain experience perhaps with student productions and/or casual work in theatres. Gaining knowledge and experience of lighting and other techniques can also help your application. Voluntary work with an amateur dramatic company is helpful.

Entry and Training

Entry is possible with a range of different qualifications, but it is essential to have practical experience of performance-related work. New entrants often gain valuable experience in practical jobs within the industry, such as a lighting technician, sound recordist, set/stage designer etc. Entry is often as an assistant stage manager where you can train whilst working with an experienced stage management team.

Applicants may have completed a drama school/college course, a degree in stage management or a relevant degree in drama/theatre studies, or perhaps in music. It is important to make sure that any course you choose is accredited by the National Council for Drama Training. Foundation degrees are available in technical theatre, production, performance and events production. The websites of Creative & Cultural Skills and the Conference of Drama Schools provide useful sources of information.

The Stage Management Association is the professional body representing stage management in the UK and offers short courses for those wishing to upgrade or enhance their skills. A full driving licence is a great asset, particularly if you are working for a touring company.

A Diploma/Welsh Baccalaureate in creative and media may be available in your area. Check university entry requirements carefully in case there is an additional specialist learning requirement with the diploma. See the diplomas website for further information.

Mature entrants need to have a relevant background/experience. It is essential to have amateur dramatic experience and to be able to show that you have good organisational skills.

Opportunities and Pay

Around 2,000 people work as theatre stage managers in the UK. You are usually employed by a theatre, ballet or opera company, ranging from a small touring company to medium-sized local repertory company, or a large-scale theatre that is located in the West End (London), or in another major city. The number of theatres and touring companies has declined, so competition for jobs is fierce. Vacancies are rarely advertised and you need to build up a good network of contacts so that you find out when work is available.

Considerable talent is required for success and it may be necessary to move locations to improve your chances of promotion. You can progress to theatre producer or director of a theatre, move to similar jobs in film or broadcasting, or become freelance.

Pay varies depending on the location and the particular employer. An assistant stage manager is likely to earn £17k, rising to £22k-£24k as a stage manager. An experienced stage manager working on a major production can earn £40k a year. Those working freelance can earn more, particularly in the West End.

Health

You need stamina and need to be physically fit for this work.

Skills and Qualities

able to cope under pressure, attention to detail, calm, good communication skills, good interpersonal skills, good organisational skills, observant, problem-solving skills, resourceful, tactful

Relevant Subjects

Art and Design, Design and technology, English, Media and communication studies, Performing arts

Further Information

Behind the Scenes: Theatre (Trotman 2009) - www.trotman.co.uk

CDS Guide to Careers Backstage (Conference of Drama Schools) - www.drama.ac.uk/

Creative & Cultural Skills - sector skills council for advertising, crafts, cultural heritage, design, literature, music, performing & visual arts - www.ccskills.org.uk

Creative Choices - www.creative-choices.co.uk

Dance and Drama Awards - www.direct.gov.uk/en/EducationAndLearning

Diplomas (Foundation, Higher and Advanced) - http://yp.direct.gov.uk/diplomas

Get into Theatre - www.getintotheatre.org

Prompt (quarterly) (Theatrical Management Association) (TMA) - www.tmauk.org/Prompt/

Stage Management - A Career Guide (SMA) - www.stagemanagementassociation.co.uk/pdf/2005%20Career%20Guide.pdf

The Stage Online - www.thestage.co.uk

Welsh Baccalaureate - www.wbq.org.uk

Addresses

Conference of Drama Schools (CDS)
PO Box 34252, London NW5 1XJ
Web: www.drama.ac.uk

National Council for Drama Training (NCDT)
249 Tooley Street, London SE1 2JX
Phone: +44 (0) 20 7407 3686
Web: www.ncdt.co.uk

Stage Management Association (SMA)
First Floor 89 Borough High Street, London SE1 1NL
Phone: +44 (0) 20 7403 7999
Web: www.stagemanagementassociation.co.uk

Similar Jobs

Actor, Film/TV & Theatre Set/Stage Designer, Film/TV Floor Manager, Film/TV Producer, Theatre Producer, Theatre Stagehand

Theatre Stagehand

also known as: Stage Crew, Stagehand

CRCI:Performing Arts

CLCI:GAT Job Band: 1 to 3

Job Description

Stagehands move scenery, furniture and props that are needed for a theatrical performance, including plays and musicals, ballet and opera. They prepare the stage for each show and carry out the instructions of the stage manager. Then make sure that everything is in the right place for each scene. They set up scenery, props and furniture and may move all, or some, around during an interval.

Stagehands may help to build and paint the stage sets, as well as ensure that all equipment is kept in a clean, safe and usable state. They clear the stage after the play has finished and store all items in a backstage location, or at a special warehouse.

Work Details

Usually work a basic 40 hr week, though the hours can be longer at times. They are likely to include evening and weekend work. The busiest times are at the beginning and end of a show and between scenes, when changing scenery, furniture and props. You usually work in a team with other technicians, and have to cope with climbing ladders and with heavy lifting, when moving and putting up scenery. If working for a touring company, you may need to spend time away from home. You may need to wear overalls.

Qualification

There are no formal entry qualifications for this job as people come from a variety of backgrounds, and with a range of different academic and practical qualifications. Practical skills in carpentry and joinery are useful.

• England, Wales and Northern Ireland

Band 1: For entry to jobs, no minimum qualifications are needed, but you are expected to have a good level of general education and relevant experience. Some formal/vocational qualifications at any level are useful.

Band 2: For entry to jobs, no minimum qualifications are needed, but it is an advantage to have some GCSEs (A*-C) or equivalent in subjects that include English and maths.

Band 3: For entry to jobs, HNC or a relevant Diploma, usually at least 4 GCSEs (A*-C) including English and maths, or equivalent.

• Scotland

Band 1: For entry to jobs, no minimum qualifications are needed, but you are expected to have a good level of general education and relevant experience. Some formal/vocational qualifications at any level are useful.

Band 2: Although academic qualifications are not specified for this job, it is an advantage to have some S grades (1-3) in subjects that include English and maths, or similar.

Band 3: For entry to jobs, usually at least four S grades (1-3) including English and maths, or similar.

Adult Qualifications

No formal qualifications are specified, but those with experience of carpentry or joinery and an interest in the theatre, are more likely to obtain jobs.

Work Experience

Any practical experience in school/college or amateur plays and performances, including front-of-house duties, or editorial production of programmes etc, is useful. Relevant work experience, including joinery, metalwork or painting, may be an advantage.

Entry and Training

Applicants are normally over 18 and usually have some work experience before entering this job. Training is on the job, working with an experienced team, but there are also relevant BTEC certificates and diplomas in performing arts (production) which can be useful, particularly if you want to move into stage management later. A Diploma/Welsh Baccalaureate in creative and media may be available in your area. See the diplomas website for further information.

The Association of British Theatre Technicians runs relevant short courses. For instance, their bronze award covers such subjects as health and safety, manual handling, electrical installation and testing, rigging and pyrotechnics. Training programmes, including apprenticeship schemes, may be available in your area. Advanced apprenticeships leading to qualification at level 3 can also be a route into higher education.

Mature entrants with experience of working in amateur dramatics or school/student productions may have an advantage. Practical experience in lifting and carrying heavy items such as furniture, goods delivery, or of painting and decorating and woodworking is useful.

Opportunities and Pay

Jobs are mainly in towns or cities with a theatre, opera and ballet company, or with a large scale touring company. It may be possible to find temporary work when theatres are busy at Christmas. Promotion opportunities are limited unless you work in a large team, where you can progress to be stage technician, team leader or stage/tour manager. Some experienced stagehands work on a self-employed, freelance basis.

Salaries vary depending on the location and type of production, but starting salaries for stagehands are around £14k a year, rising to around £20k with experience. Those with technical skills can earn up to £30k a year.

Health

This job requires good stamina and physical fitness for moving scenery and props.

Skills and Qualities

able to work quickly, aptitude for teamwork, attention to detail, co-operative, flexible approach, head for heights, patient, practical skills, reliable, safety conscious

Relevant Subjects

Construction and built environment, Design and technology, Media and communication studies, Performing arts

Further Information

Apprenticeship Schemes (National Apprenticeship Service) - www.apprenticeships.org.uk

Behind the Scenes: Theatre (Trotman 2009) - www.trotman.co.uk

CDS Guide to Careers Backstage (Conference of Drama Schools) - www.drama.ac.uk/

Creative Choices - www.creative-choices.co.uk

Diplomas (Foundation, Higher and Advanced) - http://yp.direct.gov.uk/diplomas

Get into Theatre - www.getintotheatre.org

Sightline (quarterly) (Association of British Theatre Technicians) - www.abtt.org.uk

Skillset - sector skills council for the creative media, fashion and textiles industries - www.skillset.org

Stage Jobs Pro - www.uk.stagejobspro.com

The Stage Online - www.thestage.co.uk

Welsh Baccalaureate - www.wbq.org.uk

Addresses
Association of British Theatre Technicians (ABTT)
55 Farringdon Road, London EC1M 3JB
Phone: +44 (0)20 7242 9200
Web: www.abtt.org.uk

Stage Management Association (SMA)
First Floor 89 Borough High Street, London SE1 1NL
Phone: +44 (0) 20 7403 7999
Web: www.stagemanagementassociation.co.uk

Similar Jobs
Film/TV & Theatre Lighting Technician, Film/TV & Theatre Set/Stage Designer, Film/TV/Radio & Theatre Sound Recordist, Removals Operative, Roadie, Warehouse Worker

Theatrical Agent
also known as: Entertainment Agent

CRCI:Media, Print and Publishing
CLCI:GAB Job Band: 2 to 5

Job Description
Theatrical agents organise the careers of clients in the performing arts, usually actors, dancers,singers or musicians. They use knowledge and experience of the entertainment and performing arts business, to keep clients in work and satisfied with the progress of their career. Usually check casting lists and organise auditions for clients. May also organise tours, book venues and arrange publicity.

Some clients form long-lasting professional relationships with their agents, while others may change agents regularly. Agents liaise regularly with casting directors to gain roles/jobs for clients and to negotiate fees. They use administrative and IT skills to manage their business and keep up-to-date records.

Work Details
You usually work in an office, keeping standard office hours; Monday to Friday, though may often have to see clients in plays and shows in the evening and at weekends. You may spend a lot of your day on the telephone, talking to clients and to casting directors. You may have to deal with clients who are despondent if out of work, or need to decide between offers. The work may be stressful at times as there is a lot of competition between agencies.

Qualification
No specific academic qualifications are required, but a good standard of education is expected. Employers may look for qualifications in relevant areas, such as performing arts or public relations.

• England, Wales and Northern Ireland
Band 2: For entry to jobs, no minimum qualifications are needed, but it is an advantage to have some GCSEs (A*-C) or equivalent in subjects that include English and maths.

Band 3: For entry to jobs, HNC or a relevant Diploma, usually at least 4 GCSEs (A*-C) including English and maths, or equivalent.

Band 4: For HND in performing arts, Diploma of Higher Education or foundation degree: 1-2 A levels and some GCSEs (A*-C) usually including English and maths, or equivalent. Useful subjects are theatre studies, English literature, history and modern languages.

Band 5: For degree courses: 2-3 A levels and some GCSEs (A*-C) usually including English or equivalent qualifications. Exact requirements depend on the degree you take.

• Scotland
Band 2: Although academic qualifications are not specified for this job, it is an advantage to have some S grades (1-3) in subjects that include English and maths, or similar.

Band 3: For entry: usually at least four S grades (1-3) are preferred. Useful subjects include English, history and modern languages.

Band 4: For entry to SQA higher national and professional development awards, usually 2-3 H grades and some S grades (1-3), including English and maths, or similar qualifications. Useful subjects include theatre studies, drama, English literature, history and modern languages.

Band 5: For degree courses in theatre studies: 3-5 H grades and some S grades (1-3), usually including English or similar. Exact requirements depend on the degree you take.

Degree Information
It is possible to enter this job with a degree in any subject, but agencies look for those trained in areas such as law, drama/performing arts, public relations and accountancy. Business and management are also relevant.

Adult Qualifications
Entry requirements may be relaxed for adults applying for higher education courses and Access or foundation courses give adults without qualifications a route on to degree courses.

Work Experience
Knowledge and experience in performing arts, especially production, is helpful. Experience in school/college or amateur plays and performances, including front of house duties, or editorial production of programmes is useful. You may be able to find work experience in an agent's office, which allows you to see how the industry works and also build up valuable contacts.

Entry and Training
There are various routes into this job, but it is useful to have knowledge and experience of the entertainment industry, as well as skills or qualifications involving people management. Most begin their career following relevant experience as a trainee/assistant with an established theatrical agent and receive training on the job. Prior to the job you can attend drama school, perhaps on a production course, or work in an area such as personnel or marketing. Involvement in entertainment and theatre at an amateur level is useful for gaining experience of the industry and for building contacts.

Some agents start in this work following experience in performing arts as an actor, singer or dancer. They may initially do some work to help friends and colleagues, using their own network of contacts, and move on to full time work later.

A Diploma/Welsh Baccalaureate may be available in your area in creative and media. This can be a useful introduction to this type of career as you gain practical experience while studying. See the diplomas website or Skillset for further information. Cyfle (Wales) also offers a range of training courses for new entrants to the industry and professional development for those already employed.

Previous experience in marketing, personnel, law, accountancy, public relations, or the entertainment/performing arts industries, is useful for mature entrants.

Opportunities and Pay
Jobs are based in major towns and cities in the UK, with a good proportion in London and south-east England. Successful agents may become self-employed and set up their own business. It is possible to progress to other careers in the entertainment industry, such as casting direction or production work.

Pay for the self-employed is based upon a percentage of the fees your clients earn. Salaries for those employed with an agency are generally around £12k, rising to £30k a year with experience. Top agents can earn as much as £250k a year as their pay is based on commission from their performers' work.

Skills and Qualities
able to cope under pressure, business awareness, confident, encouraging, good communication skills, good organisational skills, good telephone manner, good written English, initiative, IT skills, negotiating skills, networking skills

Relevant Subjects
Business and accounting, Economics, English, Media and communication studies, Music, Performing arts, Psychology

Further Information
Cyfle (Wales) - www.cyfle.co.uk

Diplomas (Foundation, Higher and Advanced) - http://yp.direct.gov.uk/diplomas

Media Week (weekly) (Haymarket Publishing Ltd) - www.haymarket.com/mediaweek/default.aspx

National Entertainment Agents Council (NEAC) - www.neac.org.uk

Performers.net - online community for international variety performers - www.performers.net

Skillset - sector skills council for the creative media, fashion and textiles industries - www.skillset.org

Stage Jobs Pro - www.uk.stagejobspro.com

Stage Management - A Career Guide (SMA) - www.stagemanagementassociation.co.uk/pdf/2005%20Career%20Guide.pdf

The Acting Website - www.theactingwebsite.com

The Stage Online - www.thestage.co.uk

▶Working in creative & media (2007) (Babcock Lifeskills) - www.babcock-lifeskills.com/

Addresses
Agents' Association (Great Britain)
54 Keyes House, Dolphin Square, London SW1V 3NA
Phone: +44 (0)20 7834 0515
Web: www.agents-uk.com

Equity
Guild House, Upper St Martin's Lane, London WC2H 9EG
Phone: +44 (0)20 7379 6000
Web: www.equity.org.uk

Similar Jobs
Music Industry Promotions Manager, Public Relations Officer, Recruitment Consultant, Theatre Stage Manager

Theme Park Worker
also known as: Arcade Worker, Fairground Worker

CRCI:Leisure, Sport and Tourism
CLCI:GAZ   Job Band: 1

Job Description
Theme park workers work in a theme park, fairground or amusement park looking after the 'rides' and helping people on and off them. They make sure that the ride cars/seats are loaded properly and that people act safely. Sometimes they are responsible for collecting money and giving out tickets to the customers and may also operate the machinery. A fairground worker moves with the fair to a new location and helps to dismantle the rides and assemble them at the new site. Theme park workers also work in food and beverage at catering outlets throughout the site, or selling souvenirs and other items in various shops. They may also work in the park hotels.

Work Details
You are expected to work very long hours, especially during the evening and at weekends. Fairgrounds and theme parks may be open until 10 or 11 pm. Some sites are permanent, particularly at popular holiday and seaside resorts, and you may be able to live at home. However, some fairs travel around an area and possibly throughout the UK, or Europe. You have to stay with the fair wherever it pitches camp. The fairground or parks are often noisy and crowded. There may be a risk of accidents from equipment.

Qualification

• England, Wales and Northern Ireland
Band 1: Employers look for personality and good customer contact skills rather than educational qualifications. For entry to jobs, no minimum qualifications are needed, but you are expected to have a good level of general education and relevant experience. Some formal/vocational qualifications at any level are useful.

• Scotland
Band 1: Employers look for personality and good customer contact skills rather than educational qualifications. For entry to jobs, no minimum qualifications are needed, but you are expected to have a good level of general education and relevant experience. Some formal/vocational qualifications at any level are useful.

Adult Qualifications
No formal qualifications are required but you are expected to be good at basic arithmetic. You can improve your skills and qualifications by working through the Foundation Learning programme. This involves taking credit-based units and qualifications to help you progress.

Work Experience
Any work experience can equip you with skills that you can use in the future and add to your CV. This can either be unpaid or voluntary, holiday or part-time work that you have organised yourself. You may be able to gain some casual or seasonal work at a theme park, or to gain experience of work in catering and hospitality with a food or hotel chain.

Entry and Training
Most entrants are aged 18 or over as regulations do not allow those under the age of 18 to operate machinery. It is useful to be good at speaking to groups of people and to be good at basic arithmetic. Training is on the job with an experienced worker. You should also receive training in health and safety. This job may require a large goods vehicle (LGV) driving licence.

A Diploma/Welsh Baccalaureate may be available in your area in hospitality and/or travel and tourism. It may be possible to work towards an S/NVQ at level 1-3 in sport, recreation & allied occupations: operational services, or at level 1-2 in customer service. Apprenticeships in customer service and/or leisure management may also be relevant. Contact SkillsActive or People 1st for details of relevant qualifications.

Employers may prefer mature applicants with an outgoing personality and experience of dealing with people. Government training opportunities, such as apprenticeships in customer service and/or leisure management, may be available in your area. You can also gain recognition of previous experience through Accreditation of Prior Learning (APL) or by working towards relevant S/NVQs. Contact your local careers office, Jobcentre Plus, Next Step service or Learning and Skills Council (LSC) Local Enterprise Company (LEC) for details of training schemes, including apprenticeships for adults.

Opportunities and Pay
Some theme park workers are self-employed, particularly those that work for a family business at a travelling fairground. There are permanent static fairs located at seasides, holiday resorts and indoor family entertainment centres. There are opportunities to work part time, though this job is mainly seasonal. Promotion to supervisor level is possible.

Pay varies depending on location and employer. Most fairground workers earn in the range of £9.5k-£13.5k a year, though some supervisors may earn around £15k or more. You are likely to be given free or reduced price tickets and perhaps accommodation.

Health
This job requires good general fitness.

Skills and Qualities
able to get on with all kinds of people, alert, aptitude for teamwork, calm, friendly, hard working, manual dexterity, numeracy skills, safety conscious, stamina

Relevant Subjects
Leisure, travel and tourism

Further Information
Diplomas (Foundation, Higher and Advanced) - http://yp.direct.gov.uk/diplomas

Foundation Learning (QCDA) - www.qcda.gov.uk

People 1st - sector skills council for hospitality, leisure, travel and tourism - www.people1st.co.uk

Real Life Guide to Sports & Active Leisure (Trotman 2009) - www.trotman.co.uk

SkillsActive - sector skills council for active leisure, learning and well-being - www.skillsactive.com

Springboard UK - www.springboarduk.net

Springboard Wales - http://wales.springboarduk.net/

Training Schemes - www.direct.gov.uk/en/educationandlearning

Addresses
Association of Leading Visitor Attractions
4 Westminster Palace Gardens, Artillery Row, London SW1P 1RL
Web: www.alva.org.uk/information

British Association of Leisure Parks, Piers and Attractions (BALPPA)
Suite 12, 37 Tanner Street, London SE1 3LF
Phone: +44 (0)20 7403 4455
Web: www.balppa.org

Similar Jobs
Customer Services Adviser, Fitter: Maintenance, Holiday Centre Worker, Holiday Representative, Leisure Centre Assistant, Roadie

Tiler: Wall & Floor
also known as: Tile Fixer

CRCI:Building and Construction

CLCI:UF — Job Band: 1 to 3

Job Description
Tilers lay tiles on interior or exterior surfaces, such as the floors and walls of buildings. May work in hospitals, shopping centres, industrial premises, swimming pools, or bathrooms, kitchens and conservatories in houses/flats. They usually work with ceramic, terracotta, stone, marble and other materials. The surface to be tiled is measured and the volume of tiles required is calculated. Tilers study a plan and mark the area carefully. They also check that the surface to be covered is clean, dry, level and straight.

Sheets of hardboard, including moisture resistant (marine) plywood, may be used and cut to size, before laying the tiles. Then, mixed cement or adhesive is spread onto the surface with a trowel. Specialist tools are used to trim the tiles to the correct shape, press them into position and seal the joints with grout. The area is then cleaned and polished once the grout has hardened. May also lay laminate tiles, stone, mosaic or terrazzo flooring and do decorative work, including murals.

Work Details
Tilers usually work a basic 39 hr week, Monday to Friday, but may be required to work some evenings and weekends at times. The work is normally indoors in different types of building and you need to travel to different sites. You may need to work away from home for some contracts. You have to cope with kneeling, bending down and perhaps working at heights on scaffolding or ladders. Skilled use of manual tools such as cutters, trowels and levels is necessary. Working conditions are often dirty and can be cramped.

There is a chance of sustaining minor injuries, such as cuts, and you may have to cope with fumes at times. You have to wear protective clothing, knee pads and sometimes a face mask and goggles.

Qualification
• England, Wales and Northern Ireland
Band 2: For entry as a trainee craftsperson: although no set entry requirements are specified, some GCSEs including maths, English and a science/technical subject, or equivalent qualifications, are usually needed and are required by some employers.

Band 3: For some courses: usually 4 GCSEs (A*-E) including maths, English and a science/technical subject, or equivalent.

• Scotland
Band 2: For entry as a trainee craftsperson: although no set entry requirements are specified, some S grades, including maths, English and a science/technical subject, or similar qualifications, are usually required by some employers.

Band 3: For some courses: usually four S grades (1-5) including maths, English and a science/technical subject, or similar.

Adult Qualifications
Those with relevant work experience may be accepted for some college courses without meeting any formal entry requirements.

Work Experience
Relevant work or voluntary experience is always useful and can improve your chances in application for entry to this job. In some areas there is a young apprenticeship (14-16) scheme that provides an extended work placement and eventual achievement of a level 2 qualification whilst at school. Health and safety issues may mean that there are certain jobs you cannot do until you are over 16. Contact your local ConstructionSkills office for advice. The foundation certificate in building & craft occupations is available in some schools in England and Wales.

Entry and Training
Most entrants follow a training programme through The Tile Association /ConstructionSkills which combines on-site training with more formal training at a local college or training centre. There is a three-year construction apprenticeship scheme (four years in Scotland) that involves hands-on work with an experienced employee together with a day or block-release course at a local college or training centre. There are also 1-2 year full-time college courses.

Many people enter training schemes at 16-17 and you can apply for an apprenticeship in Year 11 (January). You may have to take an entrance test before you start training. You work towards gaining a level of competence card through a Construction Skills Certification Scheme (CSCS) to indicate your individual skill level.

A Diploma/Welsh Baccalaureate in construction and the built environment may also be available in your area. Most people work towards S/NVQs in wall and floor tiling at levels 2-3. Specialist training is also available for those who wish to concentrate on achieving skills in restoration and heritage work. Contact the National Heritage Training Group for further information. There are also Construction Awards (England and Wales) available for those who are unable to gain workplace experience for NVQs.

Mature applicants who show aptitude and have previous experience may have an advantage. There may be government training schemes in your area. You can also gain recognition of previous experience through Accreditation of Prior Learning (APL) or by working towards relevant S/NVQs. Contact your local careers office, Jobcentre Plus, Next Step service or Learning and Skills Council (LSC)/Local Enterprise Company (LEC) for details of training schemes, including apprenticeships for adults.

Opportunities and Pay

Availability of work depends on the state of the building trade and the national economy. Currently there is a downturn in the housing market which means there may be a shortage of vacancies. Many tilers are self-employed or work for building contractors or specialist tiling firms. Some tilers and tiling companies specialise in artistic work. When experienced and qualified you can progress to technician level or to a supervisory/management post. Temporary, casual and seasonal work is often available for those who are sub-contractors or are self-employed. There are also job opportunities to work abroad on contracts.

Pay varies depending on area and employer. Salaries range from around £18k a year. The most skilled and experienced workers earn up to £40k a year. Overtime and bonus payments may be available. Those who are self employed may earn more.

Health

You need to be physically fit and have stamina for this job. You need normal colour vision and should not be allergic to dust, glue and other adhesives.

Skills and Qualities

able to follow drawings and plans, accurate measuring and calculating skills, aptitude for teamwork, attention to detail, creative flair, eye for shape/colour, manual dexterity, planning skills, practical skills, safety conscious

Relevant Subjects

Construction and built environment, Design and technology

Further Information

Apprenticeship Schemes (National Apprenticeship Service) - www.apprenticeships.org.uk

Carpet and Flooring Review (Gearing Media Group) - www.cfr-magazine.com

Construction Awards - http://gbca.com/events/construction-awards

ConstructionSkills - sector skills council for the construction industry - www.cskills.org

Diplomas (Foundation, Higher and Advanced) - http://yp.direct.gov.uk/diplomas

Training Schemes - www.direct.gov.uk/en/educationandlearning

Welsh Baccalaureate - www.wbq.org.uk

▶Working in construction & the built environment (2007) (Babcock Lifeskills) - www.babcock-lifeskills.com/

Addresses

National Heritage Training Group (NHTG)
Carthusian Court, 12 Carthusian Street, London EC1M 6EZ
Phone: 0300 456 5517 (UK only)
Web: www.nhtg.org.uk

Tile Association (TTA), The
Forum Court, 83 Copers Cope Road, Beckenham, Kent BR3 1NR
Phone: +44 (0)20 8663 0946
Web: www.tiles.org.uk

Similar Jobs

Carpenter/Joiner, Carpet & Flooring Fitter, Damp Proofer, Glazier, Plasterer, Roofer

Timber Frame Erector

CRCI:Building and Construction
CLCI:UF Job Band: 1 to 3

Job Description

Timber frame erectors assemble and erect timber-framed buildings, such as houses and hotels, according to the plans and specifications given by the manufacturer. They follow instructions from the site agent on the work required and study drawings and plans. Carpentry tools and other more specialist tools such as nail guns and circular saws are used in this line of work. Timber frame erectors work with a team of other carpenters on site to join and fix pieces of timber together to make the building frame.

If a crane is used, they are involved in the set up and may give instructions to the crane driver. They ensure that the crane is de-rigged and taken safely off site at the end of the job.

Work Details

Timber frame erectors usually work a basic 39 hr week, possibly including some Saturdays to meet deadlines. Travel is necessary and sometimes you may need to stay away from home. The job involves physical activity such as lifting, bending, kneeling, climbing ladders and working at heights on scaffolding. Work is mostly outdoors in all weather.

You usually work on different building sites, as part of a team with carpenters/joiners and site workers. The work environment may be dirty, noisy, dusty and possibly cold, hot, damp or muddy. There is a risk of minor injuries and you need to wear a safety helmet and protective footwear.

Qualification

• England, Wales and Northern Ireland

Band 2: No minimum educational qualifications for courses, but some GCSEs including maths, technical subjects, science and English, or equivalent, are helpful for some training programmes and courses.

Band 3: For direct entry: employers may require you to have 3-5 GCSEs (A*-E) in subjects such as English, maths, science and technology, or equivalent qualifications.

• Scotland

Band 2: No minimum educational qualifications for courses, but S grades including maths, technical subjects, science and English, or similar, are useful for some training programmes and courses.

Band 3: Some courses may require you to have 3-5 S grades (1-5) in subjects such as English, maths, science and technology, or similar qualifications.

Adult Qualifications

Entry requirements for some courses and training may be relaxed for adults with relevant experience.

Work Experience

Relevant work or voluntary experience is always useful and can improve your chances when applying for entry to construction jobs and apprenticeships. Health and safety issues may mean that there are certain jobs you cannot do until you are over 16. Contact your local ConstructionSkills office for advice.

Entry and Training

Most entrants to this work are qualified carpenters and begin by completing a carpentry or general construction apprenticeship, either with a firm of timber erectors or a firm of carpenters/joiners. You can also take qualifications through the UK Timber Frame Association (UKTFA) who have developed an open learning training and accreditation scheme for timber frame erectors, in conjunction with City & Guilds, which is recognised by many industry manufacturers. The approved certification scheme is available at three levels, bronze, silver and gold, and ranges from an induction for new entrants to supervisory level training. Contact UKTFA for details.

Training is usually on the job, learning with an experienced employee, and by a day or block-release course to a local college/ training centre. Introductory vocational courses include basic carpentry and joinery skills offered by City & Guilds. Various colleges also offer one or two-year full-time courses, such as carpentry and joinery courses offered by the Building Crafts College. The Institute of Carpenters also offers various levels of qualification in carpentry and joinery, including the master certificate scheme (Master Carpenter/Master Joiner). Once you have done your basic training, you can work towards gaining a level of competence card through the Construction Skills Certification Scheme (CSCS) to indicate your individual skill level.

A Diploma/Welsh Baccalaureate in construction and the built environment may be available in your area. S/NVQs in wood occupations (heavy structural timber framing and site carpentry) are available at levels 1-3. Training programmes, including apprenticeships leading to level 2 and advanced apprenticeships/construction apprenticeships leading to level 3, may also be available in your area. There are also Construction Awards (England and Wales) available for those who are unable to gain workplace experience for NVQs.

Mature applicants with relevant work experience in the building and construction trades stand a reasonable chance of securing training opportunities. Government training schemes, such as apprenticeships, may be available in your area. You can also gain recognition of previous experience through Accreditation of Prior Learning or by working towards relevant S/NVQs. Contact your local careers office, Jobcentre Plus, Next Step service or Learning and Skills Council (LSC)/Local Enterprise Company (LEC) for details of all training opportunities and schemes, including apprenticeships for adults. The Carpenters' Company offers funding for wood-related courses undertaken in the UK through their Charitable Trust.

Opportunities and Pay

There are opportunities with timber building firms, carpentry firms and construction companies throughout the UK. Some timber frame erectors are carpenters and joiners who are self-employed and work independently on short or long-term contracts. Availability of work depends to some extent on the state of the building trade and the national economy. Although there is a downturn in the housing market at the moment, timber-framed buildings are still popular. This means that there are opportunities in some areas for carpenters and joiners with the right skills. Once qualified and experienced, you can progress to supervisory posts such as gang leader.

Pay varies according to employer and level of skill. Generally, an inexperienced worker may initially earn around £12k a year and, when skilled, this can rise to £14k-£19k a year. Some work may be on short term contracts at a daily rate of around £130 a day. Employers may give allowances for travel and cost of lodgings. Overtime and bonus payments may boost your income.

Health

You need a good general level of fitness. There may be an allergy risk from dust.

Skills and Qualities

able to follow drawings and plans, able to work both on your own and in a team, attention to detail, enjoy working outdoors, hard working, head for heights, health & safety awareness, manual dexterity, numeracy skills

Relevant Subjects

Construction and built environment, Design and technology

Further Information

Apprenticeship Schemes (National Apprenticeship Service) - www.apprenticeships.org.uk

Construction Awards - http://gbca.com/events/construction-awards

ConstructionSkills - sector skills council for the construction industry - www.cskills.org

Diplomas (Foundation, Higher and Advanced) - http://yp.direct.gov.uk/diplomas

Real Life Guide to Carpentry and Cabinet Making (Trotman) - www.trotman.co.uk

Timber Trades Journal (fortnightly) (The Timber Trade Industry) - www.ttjonline.com

Welsh Baccalaureate - www.wbq.org.uk

▶ Working in construction & the built environment (2007) (Babcock Lifeskills) - www.babcock-lifeskills.com/

Addresses

British Woodworking Federation (BWF)
Royal London House, 22-25 Finsbury Square, EC2A 1DX
Phone: +44 (0) 844 209 2610
Web: www.bwf.org.uk

Building Crafts College
Kennard Road, Stratford, London E15 1AH
Phone: +44 (0)20 8522 1705
Web: www.thebcc.ac.uk

Carpenters' Company
Carpenters' Hall, Throgmorton Avenue, London EC2N 2JJ
Phone: +44 (0)20 7588 7001
Web: www.carpentersco.com

Institute of Carpenters (IOC)
Third Floor D , Carpenters' Hall, 1 Throgmorton Avenue, London EC2N 2BY
Phone: +44 (0)20 7256 2700
Web: www.instituteofcarpenters.com

Timber Trade Federation
The Building Centre, 26 Store Street, London WC1E 7BT
Phone: +44 (0)20 3205 0067
Web: www.ttf.co.uk

UK Timber Frame Association
The e-Centre, Cooperage Way Business Village, Alloa FK10 3LP
Phone: +44 (0)1259 272 140
Web: www.timber-frame.org

Similar Jobs

Carpenter/Joiner, Crane Operator, Fence Installer, Roofer, Scaffolder, Wood Machinist

Toolmaker

also known as: Engineering Craft Machinist: Toolmaker

CRCI:Engineering
CLCI:RAX — Job Band: 1 to 3

Job Description

Toolmakers work from technical drawings in a range of manufacturing industries and make special tools to a high specification. Tools include jigs, gauges and moulds used in production work to cut, shape and form metal, alloys and other materials. Toolmakers operate specialised engineering machines such as lathes and grinders and precision cutters. Modern technology, such as wire erosion, computer numerically controlled (CNC) machines and computer aided manufacture (CAM), is increasingly used. Depending on the toolroom, they may specialise in a certain area. Also check the accuracy of the finished item by fitting it onto the production machine, running tests and making adjustments as needed. May also repair tools.

Toolmaker

Work Details

Usually work a basic 39 hr week that may include shifts, nights, weekends and overtime. Toolmakers work in toolrooms that are usually quieter than production floors. Conditions depend on the type of industry; some toolrooms can be clean and quiet, while others are noisy and dirty. You are likely to be standing for long periods. This is a highly-skilled job and you have to be able to adapt to different specialised machines. There can be accidents with equipment and you may have to wear protective clothing such as overalls, special shoes or safety glasses.

Qualification

• England, Wales and Northern Ireland

Band 2: For entry to jobs, no minimum qualifications are needed, but it is an advantage to have some GCSEs (A*-C) or equivalent in subjects that include English, maths and physics or another science subject, or equivalent. Technology and design are also useful subjects.

Band 3: For an advanced apprenticeship in engineering: 4 GCSEs (A*-C), usually including maths, English, physics and another science subject or design technology, or equivalent.

• Scotland

Band 2: Although academic qualifications are not specified for this job, it is an advantage to have some S grades (1-3) in subjects that include maths, English and physics or another science subject, or similar. Technological studies is also useful.

Band 3: For a modern apprenticeship: usually four S grades (1-3), including English, maths, physics and another science or technology subject, or similar.

Adult Qualifications

Most entrants are school leavers. Colleges often relax academic course entry requirements for adults, particularly if you have relevant experience.

Work Experience

Relevant work or voluntary experience is always useful. It can add to your CV and improve your chances when applying for entry to jobs or apprenticeships in the engineering industry.

Entry and Training

Most entrants do an apprenticeship, either as a craft machinist or in engineering multi-skilling. Many companies have aptitude tests and most entrants are 16-17, although 18-19 year olds are also accepted. Training usually starts with a period of several months away from the workplace, learning engineering workshop skills at a training centre. This is followed by 2-3 years' work on the shopfloor with day or block release for BTEC/SQA or City & Guilds qualifications in engineering. S/NVQs are available at levels 1-3 in performing engineering operations, engineering toolmaking and mechanical manufacturing engineering.

Some entrants choose to do a full-time engineering course prior to entry as an apprentice. The most skilled apprentices specialise in toolmaking and some may go on to register as an Engineering Technician (EngTech) with the Engineering Council (ECUK). Contact ECUK for details. The Gauge and Toolmakers' Association runs courses in advanced toolmaking. Relevant training programmes, including apprenticeship schemes in toolmaking, precision engineering or metal processing, may be available in your area. Advanced apprenticeships leading to qualification at level 3 can also be a route into higher education.

The Engineering Development Trust runs a range of nationwide schemes for 11-21 year olds who are interested in engineering as a career. See the website for details. A Diploma/Welsh Baccalaureate may be available in your area in engineering. See the diplomas website for further information.

Mature applicants usually require relevant previous experience, for example as a craft machinist or in other mechanical engineering work. There are special training courses for adults in some areas. Government training opportunities, such as apprenticeships, may be available in your area. You can also gain recognition of previous experience through Accreditation of Prior Learning or by working towards relevant S/NVQs. Contact your local careers office, Jobcentre Plus, Next Step service or Learning and Skills Council (LSC)/Local Enterprise Company (LEC) for details of training schemes.

Opportunities and Pay

Employers include engineering companies or manufacturing companies which make, for example, planes, ships or household equipment. Work is concentrated in the West Midlands, the North West, London, the South East and parts of Scotland. The number of jobs available is falling because of the increase in the use of computer controlled machines. With experience, you can become a supervisor.

Pay varies depending on location and employer. Starting salaries are around £16k-£22k a year. Average salaries once qualified are around £25k. Shift work and overtime can make up a significant proportion of pay.

Health

Good eyesight is needed, with glasses or lenses if necessary. You have to be fit. In this type of work you can come into contact with substances which irritate the skin and may cause allergies.

Skills and Qualities

able to follow drawings and plans, accurate, attention to detail, good concentration level, hand-to-eye co-ordination, numeracy skills, precise, steady hand, technical aptitude

Relevant Subjects

Design and technology, Engineering, Manufacturing, Mathematics, Physics, Science

Further Information

Apprenticeship Schemes (National Apprenticeship Service) - www.apprenticeships.org.uk

Diplomas (Foundation, Higher and Advanced) - http://yp.direct.gov.uk/diplomas

Engineering Connections - www.apprentices.co.uk

Engineering Scotland (SEMTA) - www.engineeringscotland.org

SEMTA - sector skills council for science, engineering and manufacturing technologies - www.semta.org.uk

Tomorrow's Engineers - www.tomorrowsengineers.org.uk/careers.cfm

Training Schemes - www.direct.gov.uk/en/educationandlearning

Welsh Baccalaureate - www.wbq.org.uk

Women into Science, Engineering & Construction - www.wisecampaign.org.uk

▶Working in manufacturing (2010) (Babcock Lifeskills) - www.babcock-lifeskills.com/

Addresses

Engineering Council
246 High Holborn, London WC1V 7EX
Phone: +44 (0)20 3206 0500
Web: www.engc.org.uk

Engineering Development Trust (EDT)
Ridgeway, Welwyn Garden City, Hertfordshire AL7 2AA
Phone: +44 (0)1707 871520
Web: www.etrust.org.uk

Engineering Training Council (NI)
Interpoint, 20-24 York Street, Belfast BT15 1AQ
Phone: +44 (0)28 9032 9878
Web: www.etcni.org.uk

Gauge and Toolmakers' Association (GTMA)
3 Forge House, Summerleys Road, Princes Risborough, Buckinghamshire HP27 9DT
Phone: +44 (0)1844 274 222
Web: www.gtma.co.uk

Scottish Engineering
Training Officer, 105 West George Street, Glasgow G2 1QL
Phone: +44 (0)141 221 3181
Web: www.scottishengineering.org.uk

Similar Jobs
Engineering Craft Machinist, Engineering Machine Operative, Fitter: Maintenance, Gunsmith, Locksmith

Tour Operator

CRCI:Leisure, Sport and Tourism
CLCI:GAX Job Band: 2 to 5

Job Description
Tour operators plan and organise the travel and accommodation for package holidays. They are responsible for careful planning and buying of transport services for rail, air, boat and coach travel. Operators negotiate terms with hotel managers for the best accommodation possible. May also design, write, produce and distribute brochures or take bookings, keep accounts and handle complaints. A few travel abroad to inspect locations and evaluate the facilities offered, such as accommodation, restaurants and bars, beaches and other attractions of an area.

Tour operators may organise tour excursions. Some operators provide specialist trips such as adventure holidays, language courses, trekking holidays or visits to historical sites. Others may specialise in organising business conferences.

Work Details
Most operators work a basic 39 hr week, but the start and finish times of a day can vary. You may be expected to work longer than average office hours. Some weekend work, including public holidays, may be required. Most of the time you work in an office. Travel may be necessary, possibly overseas within Europe or worldwide, but some operators have contract managers who do this. Costs must be kept within an agreed budget. Work can be pressurised at times and may be more demanding at certain times of the year.

Qualification

• England, Wales and Northern Ireland
Band 3: For direct entry as a trainee: usually at least 4 GCSEs (A*-C) are required, preferably including English, maths, geography and a foreign language, or equivalent.

Band 4: For HND, Diploma of Higher Education or foundation degree: 1-2 A levels and some GCSEs (A*-C) usually including English and preferably maths, geography and a foreign language.

Band 5: For degree courses: 2-3 A levels and some GCSEs (A*-C) usually including English and maths, or equivalent. Exact requirements depend on the degree you take.

• Scotland
Band 3: For direct entry as a trainee: usually at least four S grades (1-3) are preferred. Useful subjects are English, maths, geography and a foreign language, or similar.

Band 4: For entry to SQA higher national and professional development awards, usually 2-3 H grades and some S grades (1-3), including English and preferably maths, geography and a foreign language, or similar.

Band 5: For a degree: 3-5 H grades and some S grades (1-3) usually including English and maths, or similar qualifications. Exact requirements depend on the degree you take.

Degree Information
Graduates in any discipline may enter, but degrees in travel and tourism or marketing may be preferred. Subjects such as administration, business studies, geography, leisure studies and any foreign language provide a useful background for this job. It is possible to study for a postgraduate diploma in tourism management.

Adult Qualifications
Entry requirements may be relaxed for adults applying for higher education courses and Access or foundation courses give adults without qualifications a route on to degree courses.

Work Experience
Employers or colleges/universities may prefer candidates who have relevant work or voluntary experience. This can include office administration, events management, hospitality and catering and travel agency work. Working for a travel company as a travel representative abroad is also relevant.

Entry and Training
Entry is competitive and it can be difficult to enter this work without relevant experience. Most people start in other travel and tourism roles and work their way up to the role of a tour operator. There are no set entry and training requirements, though knowledge of one or more foreign languages is useful. Many larger travel companies offer in-house training for their tour operators. A programme of continuous professional development called the Accredited Travel Professional (ATP) scheme has been created by ABTA, in association with People 1st and the Institute of Travel and Tourism. There are three levels of membership, depending on your experience and qualifications in the industry.

There are relevant vocational qualifications that you can take such as the BTEC National Award in Travel and Tourism, which may give you an advantage. A Diploma/Welsh Baccalaureate may be available in your area in Travel and Tourism. Foundation degrees and Higher National Diplomas (HNDs) in travel and tourism are also available.

Training programmes, including apprenticeship schemes in travel and tourism, may be available in your area. Many of the larger travel companies, e.g. First Choice, offers apprenticeship schemes for 16-24 year olds, leading to a People 1st apprenticeship framework certificate in travel and tourism services. Advanced apprenticeships leading to qualification at level 3 can also be a route into higher education. Contact People 1st for further details.

Mature applicants are welcomed and especially those with previous experience in related work areas such as customer care, business and retail sales. Government training opportunities, such as apprenticeships in travel and tourism, may be available in your area. You can also gain recognition of previous experience through Accreditation of Prior Learning (APL) or by working towards relevant S/NVQs. Contact your local careers office, Jobcentre Plus, Next Step service or Learning and Skills Council (LSC) Local Enterprise Company (LEC) for details of training schemes.

Opportunities and Pay
You work for a tour company. There are a wide range of tasks within tour operations and in smaller companies you can gain experience by being involved in a broad range of work. In larger companies you may be able to gain experience by working in product development, marketing or reservations, and there may be more opportunities for promotion. However, some companies are reducing staff numbers due to the steady rise in independent travel that is booked through the Internet.

Pay can vary considerably depending on the type and size of organisation and whether or not you are self-employed. Salaries start from around £17k-£23k a year, rising to £25k-£40k a year with experience. Some very successful tour operators can earn over £50k a year. Tour operating companies may offer holidays at favourable rates to their staff.

Skills and Qualities
able to cope under pressure, able to work to a budget, attention to detail, business awareness, co-operative, efficient, good communication skills, IT skills, planning skills, quick thinking

Relevant Subjects
Business and accounting, Economics, English, Geography, ICT/ Computer studies, Leisure, travel and tourism, Mathematics, Modern Foreign Languages

Further Information
ABTA Magazine (Absolute Publishing Ltd.) - www.abtamagazine.co.uk

AGCAS: Tourism (Job Sector Briefing) (AGCAS) - www.prospects.ac.uk

Apprenticeship Schemes (National Apprenticeship Service) - www.apprenticeships.org.uk

Diplomas (Foundation, Higher and Advanced) - http://yp.direct.gov.uk/diplomas

GoSkills - sector skills council for passenger transport - www.goskills.org

International Association of Tour Managers (International Association of Tour Managers) - www.iatm.co.uk

People 1st - sector skills council for hospitality, leisure, travel and tourism - www.people1st.co.uk

So you want to work in Travel & Tourism (Wayland) - www.waylandbooks.co.uk

Training Schemes - www.direct.gov.uk/en/educationandlearning

UKSP - Guide to Success in Hospitality, Leisure, Travel & Tourism - www.uksp.co.uk/

▶Working in travel & tourism (2010) (Babcock Lifeskills) - www.babcock-lifeskills.com/

Addresses
Accredited Travel Professional (ATP)
ATP Training Limited, 3rd Floor, 30 Park Street, London SE1 9EQ
Web: www.a-t-p.org.uk

Association of British Travel Agents (ABTA)
30 Park Street, London SE1 9EQ
Web: www.abta.com

First Choice Holidays
HR Direct, Jetset House, Lowfield Heath, Crawley,
West Sussex RH11 0PQ
Phone: 0800 169 5692 (UK only)
Web: www.firstchoice4jobs.co.uk

Institute of Travel and Tourism (ITT)
PO Box 217, Ware, Hertfordshire SG12 8WY
Phone: +44 (0)844 4995 653
Web: www.itt.co.uk

Similar Jobs
Holiday Representative, Sales Executive, Tourist Guide, Tourist Information Centre Assistant, Travel Agency Manager, Travel Consultant

Tourist Guide
CRCI:Leisure, Sport and Tourism
CLCI:GAX Job Band: 2 to 5

Job Description
Tourist guides escort visitors around cities and towns, historic and tourist sites and give detailed information on features of interest, particularly where related to British life, both past and present. They may be employed as a guide for attractions such as local craftwork, a stately home, castle, city, garden, cathedral or an area of countryside. Takes groups on foot or by coach. Points out details and describes origin, history, current facts etc, and answers questions. Can specialise, for example, in foreign or youth parties or in 'theme' tours.

Work Details
You do not need to travel far if you are employed to show people around a country house or a city, but many tour guides have to travel widely, both in the UK and abroad. You are expected to work irregular hours, perhaps some evenings and weekends, and usually longer hours in the summer. Tourist guides need to be aware of the cultural mix of the groups they work with and be enthusiastic about their work.

You may sometimes have to cope with emergencies, especially if someone is taken ill on tour. It may be necessary to walk around a good deal, showing people the sights. You should have a clear speaking voice which can be easily heard.

Qualification

- **England, Wales and Northern Ireland**

Band 2: For entry to jobs, no minimum qualifications are needed, but it is an advantage to have some GCSEs (A*-C) or equivalent in subjects that include English, maths and geography.

Band 3: For entry to jobs, HNC or a relevant Diploma, usually at least 4 GCSEs (A*-C) including English, maths, geography and a foreign language, or equivalent.

Band 4: For relevant HND, Diploma of Higher Education or foundation degree: 1-2 A levels and some GCSEs (A*-C). Useful subjects include English and preferably maths, geography and a foreign language, or equivalent qualifications.

Band 5: For a degree: 2-3 A levels and some GCSEs (A*-C) usually including English and maths, or equivalent. Exact requirements depend on the degree you take.

- **Scotland**

Band 2: Although academic qualifications are not specified for this job, it is an advantage to have some S grades (1-3) in subjects that include English, maths and geography, or similar.

Band 3: For entry to jobs, usually at least four S grades (1-3) including English or maths, geography and a foreign language, or similar.

Band 4: For entry to SQA higher national and professional development awards, usually 2-3 H grades and some S grades (1-3), including English and preferably maths, geography and a foreign language, or similar qualifications.

Band 5: For a degree: 3-5 H grades and some S grades (1-3) usually including English and maths, or similar qualifications. Exact requirements depend on the degree you take.

Degree Information
Any degree discipline is acceptable, but there are a wide range of degrees in tourism, including tourism studies/management, European tourism and global tourism. Subjects which also give useful knowledge related to this job include any foreign language, history, archaeology, geography, history of art, European studies or American studies.

Adult Qualifications
Good general knowledge and wide interests are often more important than formal qualifications. Entry requirements may be relaxed for adults applying for higher education courses. Access or foundation courses provide those without the required qualifications a route onto degree courses.

Work Experience
Employers or colleges/universities may prefer candidates who have relevant work or voluntary experience. This can include work in a museum, an art gallery, or working with the public in a variety of areas such as customer service or retail.

Entry and Training
You need to have a real interest and knowledge of a particular location/area and must enjoy speaking to groups of people. Relevant knowledge of a foreign language, or in history, art, archaeology, music or architecture, is useful. Formal qualifications are an advantage, but are not essential. Good verbal communication skills, a pleasant personality and self confidence are often more important. Training varies, but is usually by practical experience and specialist courses. Most regional tourist boards run part-time courses that lead to a registered guide qualification, such as the award of the Blue or Green Badge certificate in tour guiding. Owners of sites and visitor attractions usually provide their own in-house training for guides.

The Institute of Tourist Guiding (ITG) is a qualifications body that accredits courses and runs examinations at educational levels 2-4. All Institute accredited training programmes and qualifications in tourist guide/commentary and heritage interpretation are area specific, such as the St Paul's Cathedral Guide course or the Northern Ireland Blue Badge course. Once qualified, you are expected to extend your level of knowledge and skills through further development courses. ITG accredited Blue Badge Guides can now do a top-up course to progress to a BA (Hons) in Tourist Guiding. Contact the ITG or the Scottish Tourist Guides Association for details of the Blue Badge or other levels of qualification.

There are relevant vocational qualifications that you can take such as the BTEC National Award in Travel and Tourism, which may give you an advantage. A Diploma/Welsh Baccalaureate may be available in your area in Travel and Tourism. You may be able to work towards S/NVQs levels 2-3 in travel and tourism services. Foundation degrees and Higher National Diplomas (HNDs) in travel and tourism are also available.

Training programmes, including apprenticeship schemes in travel and tourism, may be available in your area. Many of the larger organisations offer apprenticeship schemes for 16-24 year olds, leading to a People 1st apprenticeship framework certificate in travel and tourism services. Advanced apprenticeships leading to qualification at level 3 can also be a route into higher education. Contact People 1st for further details.

Mature applicants are welcomed and any relevant work experience is an advantage. Knowledge of local history is helpful and fluency in at least one foreign language is an advantage for entry to courses.

Opportunities and Pay
Tourist guides often work on a freelance basis, but you can be employed by a tour or coach operator, or by organisations, such as the National Trust, or a local authority. If you are successful, you may be able to obtain a full-time post. Some tourist guides move on to become tour managers, accompanying a tour group who are visiting different places. Seasonal work is common and some part-time opportunities are available.

It may be difficult to earn a regular income, especially as the work is often seasonal/part time and depends upon the fluctuating travel market. Pay varies depending on area and level of expertise. The Association of Professional Tourist Guides recommends that Blue Badge guides earn £122-£190 per half day in London. You can earn more if you guide in a foreign language. Experienced tourist guides working full time can earn £12k-£20k a year, rising to £25k with experience, but this depends on your specialist knowledge and skills. You may be able to supplement your pay with tips and payment from other work.

Health
A clear speaking voice is required.

Skills and Qualities
able to cope with emergencies, able to get on with all kinds of people, clear speaking voice, confident, good communication skills, good interpersonal skills, good memory, patient, physically fit, stamina

Relevant Subjects
English, Geography, History, Leisure, travel and tourism, Modern Foreign Languages, Performing arts

Further Information
AGCAS: Government & Public Administration (Job Sector Briefing) (AGCAS) - www.prospects.ac.uk

Apprenticeship Schemes (National Apprenticeship Service) - www.apprenticeships.org.uk

Association of Professional Tourist Guides (APTG) - www.touristguides.org.uk

Careers Wales - www.careerswales.com/

Diplomas (Foundation, Higher and Advanced) - http://yp.direct.gov.uk/diplomas

People 1st - sector skills council for hospitality, leisure, travel and tourism - www.people1st.co.uk

Real Life Guide to Travel and Tourism (Trotman) - www.trotman.co.uk

The Diploma in Travel and Tourism - www.tandtdiploma.co.uk

Visit Britain - www.visitbritain.com

Visit Scotland - www.visitscotland.com

Visit Wales - www.visitwales.co.uk

Welsh Baccalaureate - www.wbq.org.uk

▶ Working in cultural heritage (2007) (Babcock Lifeskills) - www.babcock-lifeskills.com/

▶ Working in travel & tourism (2010) (Babcock Lifeskills) - www.babcock-lifeskills.com/

Addresses
Guild of Registered Tourist Guides
52d Borough High Street, London SE1 1XN
Phone: +44 (0)207 403 1115
Web: www.blue-badge-guides.com

Institute of Tourist Guiding (ITG)
Coppergate House, 16 Brune Street, London E1 7NJ
Phone: +44 (0)20 7953 8397
Web: www.itg.org.uk

Institute of Travel and Tourism (ITT)
PO Box 217, Ware, Hertfordshire SG12 8WY
Phone: +44 (0)844 4995 653
Web: www.itt.co.uk

National Trust
Heelis, Kemble Drive, Swindon, Wiltshire SN2 2NA
Phone: +44 (0)1793 817400
Web: www.ntjobs.org.uk

Scottish Tourist Guides Association (STGA)
Norrie's House, 18b Broad Street, Stirling FK8 1EF
Phone: +44 (0)1786 451953
Web: http://stga.co.uk

Similar Jobs
Event & Exhibition Organiser, Holiday Centre Worker, Holiday Representative, Museum/Art Gallery Attendant, Tour Operator, Tourist Information Centre Assistant

Tourist Information Centre Assistant

CRCI:Leisure, Sport and Tourism
CLCI:GAX Job Band: 2

Job Description

Tourist information centre assistants work at an information centre handing out leaflets, maps, etc to visitors. They provide travel information and answers enquiries from tourists and encourage people to spend time and money in a particular area by promoting local facilities. They advise on places of interest and travel routes and make reservations for sightseeing tours, sporting events, theatre trips, etc. May also arrange hotel and bed and breakfast accommodation locally and liaise with other centres to book accommodation further afield.

Assistants answer the telephone and written enquiries and use a computer in much of the work. May sell goods such as maps, guidebooks and souvenirs. They gather information for centre use and also to give to customers and keeps publicity information up to date. Consult timetables and reference books on a regular basis.

Work Details

Usually works a basic 35-39 hr week, with irregular hours, including weekends and often longer hours in the summer. Some busy centres operate shift work. You need to acquire a good knowledge of local facilities so that you are able to advise tourists on the best places to visit. Most assistants see a large number of people, including visitors from overseas. Work can be hectic at times and may require spending a lot of time on the phone.

You need to write letters and answer queries which arrive through the post. Certain times of the year may be quieter than others and some centres may close during the winter months. A uniform is often provided by the employer.

Qualification

• England, Wales and Northern Ireland

Band 2: For entry to jobs, no minimum qualifications are needed, but it is an advantage to have some GCSEs (A*-C) or equivalent in subjects that include English, maths, geography and a modern language, or equivalent.

• Scotland

Band 2: Although academic qualifications are not specified for this job, it is an advantage to have some S grades (1-3) in subjects that include English, maths, geography and a modern language, or similar.

Adult Qualifications

There are no set minimum entry requirements, though adults may be expected to have a good level of general education. In some areas, fluency in one or two foreign languages may be required.

Work Experience

Any work experience can equip you with skills that you can use in the future and add to your CV. This can either be unpaid or voluntary, holiday or part-time work that you have organised yourself. Any seasonal or voluntary work at a tourist information centre, or experience of working with customers, is useful.

Entry and Training

There are no set minimum entry requirements but applicants are expected to have a good general education. The right sort of personality for the job is often regarded as equally important. It is an advantage to have experience of working with people. For some posts, you may need to be fluent in a European language. Many entrants are over 21. Some follow a relevant college course first, such as a BTEC National Award in Travel and Tourism, which may give you an advantage. Once employed, your employer usually offers an induction course. Training is then carried out on the job by employers and regional tourist boards, and perhaps by day-release course or evening classes. See the Britain Express website for a list of tourist information centres.

Tourist information centre assistants may be expected to work for S/NVQs in travel and tourism services at levels 2-3. A Diploma/ Welsh Baccalaureate may be available in your area in Travel and Tourism. Foundation degrees and Higher National Diplomas (HNDs) in travel and tourism are also available. Training programmes, including apprenticeship schemes in travel and tourism, may be available in your area. Many of the larger organisations offer apprenticeship schemes for 16-24 year olds, leading to a People 1st apprenticeship framework certificate in travel and tourism services. Advanced apprenticeships leading to qualification at level 3 can also be a route into higher education. Contact People 1st for further details.

Mature applicants with experience of information handling, such as clerical work, or working with people, may have an advantage. Government training opportunities, such as apprenticeships in travel and tourism, may be available in your area. You can also gain recognition of previous experience through Accreditation of Prior Learning (APL) or by working towards relevant S/NVQs. Contact your local careers office, Jobcentre Plus, Next Step service or Learning and Skills Council (LSC) Local Enterprise Company (LEC) for details of training schemes.

Opportunities and Pay

You work for a local authority, regional tourist board or environmental organisation throughout the UK. There are around 500 tourist information centres located throughout England. There are 80 in Wales and 30 in Northern Ireland. About a fifth open only between Easter and September each year. In Scotland, the area tourist boards (around 150 centres) employ tourist information assistants mainly on a seasonal basis, though approximately 60 centres are open all year round.

Promotion prospects are limited but the training can lead to work in travel agency or tour operating fields. Part-time and seasonal work is more plentiful than permanent posts.

Pay varies depending on location and employer but, as a guide, full-time salaries for trainees start at around £10k, with experienced workers generally earning up to £19k a year.

Skills and Qualities

able to get on with all kinds of people, approachable, efficient, enthusiastic, good communication skills, good memory, good telephone manner, IT skills, patient, smart appearance

Relevant Subjects

English, Geography, History, Leisure, travel and tourism, Modern Foreign Languages

Further Information

Apprenticeship Schemes (National Apprenticeship Service) - www.apprenticeships.org.uk

Britain Express - www.britainexpress.com/TIC/index.htm

Careers Wales - www.careerswales.com/

Diplomas (Foundation, Higher and Advanced) - http://yp.direct.gov.uk/diplomas

Local Government Careers (Improvement and Development Agency) - www.lgcareers.com/publications/

People 1st - sector skills council for hospitality, leisure, travel and tourism - www.people1st.co.uk

So you want to work in Travel & Tourism (Wayland) - www.waylandbooks.co.uk

The Diploma in Travel and Tourism - www.tandtdiploma.co.uk

UKSP - Guide to Success in Hospitality, Leisure, Travel & Tourism - www.uksp.co.uk/

Visit Britain - www.visitbritain.com

Visit Scotland - www.visitscotland.com

Visit Wales - www.visitwales.co.uk

Welsh Baccalaureate - www.wbq.org.uk

▶ Working in cultural heritage (2007) (Babcock Lifeskills) - www.babcock-lifeskills.com/

▶ Working in travel & tourism (2010) (Babcock Lifeskills) - www.babcock-lifeskills.com/

Addresses

Institute of Travel and Tourism (ITT)
PO Box 217, Ware, Hertfordshire SG12 8WY
Phone: +44 (0)844 4995 653
Web: www.itt.co.uk

Similar Jobs

Airline Customer Service Agent, Hotel Receptionist, Library & Information Manager, Tourist Guide, Travel Consultant

Town Planner

CRCI:Building and Construction
CLCI:US Job Band: 5

Job Description

Town planners manage the development of towns, cities and countryside for the current and future benefit of society. They help to create more affordable housing and are concerned with residential, commercial, recreational, transport and civic land. Planners aim to understand the needs of the local environment, economy and population to make the best social and economic use of available land. They encourage development for the purpose of economic growth, but at the same time must protect the environment and architectural heritage. Duties include researching and collecting information relevant to proposed plans. May consult with other experts to create policies for managing traffic and providing sustainable solutions to transport needs and works to engage communities in having a say in how their environment is developed.

Town planners make policies and implement them. They attend public meetings about planning issues and the impact of development proposals on the local environment. Must be able to write reports and consult with other professionals, including engineers, environmentalists, architects and surveyors. Planners manage teams of planning support staff that include technicians, enforcement officers and administration officers.

Work Details

Town planners usually work a 35-40 hr week, Monday to Friday, though may be expected to work outside office hours and some evenings or Saturdays for public meetings. You usually work in an office, but spend some of your time travelling to meetings and making site visits. Works with a team that includes architects, landscape architects, surveyors and statisticians, construction managers and civil engineers. A proportion of your job is to research and analyse complex information, present facts and produce detailed reports.

Up-to-date knowledge of current laws and regulations that surround planning and the environment is crucial. Work can be very demanding and involve making unpopular decisions, especially when budgetary limitations mean that compromises have to be made.

Qualification

- **England, Wales and Northern Ireland**

Band 5: For degree courses: 2-3 A levels and some GCSEs including English, maths and preferably geography, economics or a foreign language, or equivalent qualifications. Exact requirements depend on the degree you take.

- **Scotland**

Band 5: For degree courses: 3-5 H grades and some S grades (1-3) including English, maths and preferably geography, economics or a foreign language, or similar qualifications. Exact requirements depend on the degree you take.

Degree Information

An approved specialist first degree in town planning meets the academic requirements for professional qualification and is usually completed in four years (five if a sandwich course). You can also take a three-year BA degree and a one-year postgraduate qualification. There are a range of postgraduate planning courses. Most courses require a minimum of a 2:1 for entry. The following first degree subjects may provide an advantage; architecture, building, economics, geology, geography, ecology, surveying, sociology, transportation, environmental science (biological/physical), statistics or landscape architecture/design.

Adult Qualifications

Entry requirements may be relaxed for adults applying for higher education courses and foundation/Access courses give adults without qualifications a route onto degree courses. Those with a planning-related degree may take an intensive (12 months) postgraduate conversion course or other 2-3 year postgraduate distance-learning course that leads to Royal Town Planning Institute (RTPI) accreditation.

Work Experience

Employers or colleges/universities may prefer candidates who have relevant work or voluntary experience. This may include work with a private practice dealing with town planning, but is more likely to be with a local authority planning department. Other areas to consider include environmental organisations or building/ construction companies.

Entry and Training

To become a chartered town planner (essential for work in this country and overseas as a town planner) you need to gain a Royal Town Planning Institute (RTPI) accredited academic qualification that includes both specialist and spatial planning. You also need two years' spatial planning experience before you undertake the assessment of professional competence (APC) and gain Membership of the RTPI (MRTPI).

Most study for a degree and/or postgraduate qualification in planning. Entry to courses is highly competitive. First degree courses are full time or sandwich. Postgraduate courses can be full/part time or through distance learning and entry usually requires a good relevant first degree in planning or a planning-related subject. There is a postgraduate programme that has a one-year intensive course as well as combined MA/MPlan distance-learning courses that take between 36 and 39 months to complete.

The Joint Distance Learning Consortium is run by a consortium of four planning schools. They offer an MA in town and country planning through distance learning. There may be a relevant foundation degree available in your area. Contact the RTPI for details of accredited courses and training routes to professional qualification. RTPI members are expected to update their knowledge and skills through continuing professional development.

Mature applicants with relevant experience such as in civil engineering, architecture or chartered surveying may become associate members of the Royal Town Planning Institute (RTPI) and take an accredited postgraduate qualification. A structured programme of progression from associate to chartered membership is being developed. Funding may be available for postgraduate study through the Economic and Social Research Council.

Opportunities and Pay
Jobs are available throughout the UK, traditionally in the public sector. There are opportunities in urban development corporations, health authorities, tourist boards and environmental organisations, as well as local and central government departments and agencies. Some town planners work in private practice or are self-employed as consultants, where there are increasing opportunities. There may be opportunities to work overseas, particularly for those with fluency in a foreign language.

Pay varies depending on location and whether you work in the public or private sector. A starting salary for a newly qualified planner can range from £14k-£27k. Senior town planners can earn around £25k-£34k a year and top earners can expect in excess of £55k.

Skills and Qualities
able to follow drawings and plans, able to report accurately, able to work to deadlines, analytical skills, excellent communication skills, imaginative, information handling skills, IT skills, negotiating skills, objective

Relevant Subjects
Business and accounting, Construction and built environment, Economics, English, Geography, History, Law, Mathematics, Sociology

Further Information
AGCAS: Government & Public Administration (Job Sector Briefing) (AGCAS) - www.prospects.ac.uk

Careers in Planning (Royal Town Planning Institute) - www.rtpi.org.uk/

Economic and Social Research Council - www.esrc.ac.uk

Joint Distance Learning Consortium - www.uwe.ac.uk/fbe/courses/pg/tcpjdl

Local Government Careers (Improvement and Development Agency) - www.lgcareers.com/publications/

Planning (weekly) (Royal Town Planning Institute, Haymarket) - www.planningresource.co.uk

Scottish Planner (bi-monthly) (Royal Town Planning Institute in Scotland) - www.scotland.rtpi.org.uk/newsletters

▶Working in cultural heritage (2007) (Babcock Lifeskills) - www.babcock-lifeskills.com/

Addresses
Convention of Scottish Local Authorities (COSLA)
Rosebery House, 9 Haymarket Terrace, Edinburgh EH12 5XZ
Phone: +44 (0)131 474 9200
Web: www.cosla.gov.uk

Planning Service
Millennium House, 17-25 Great Victoria Street, Belfast BT2 7BN
Phone: +44 (0)28 9041 6700
Web: www.planningni.gov.uk

Royal Town Planning Institute (RTPI)
41 Botolph Lane, London EC3R 8DL
Phone: +44 (0)20 7929 9494
Web: www.rtpi.org.uk

Similar Jobs
Architect, Engineer: Municipal, Geographical Information Systems Manager, Surveyor: Planning & Development, Town Planning Support Staff

Town Planning Support Staff
also known as: Administration Officer: Planning, Enforcement Officer: Planning, Planning Support Assistant, Town Planning Technician

CRCI:Building and Construction
CLCI:US

Job Band: 3 to 4

Job Description
Town planning support staff are the administrators, enforcement officers, and planning technicians in a planning department. They do a great deal of the basic planning work. They provide technical and practical assistance for town planners in planning the layout and development of town or country areas. The work can include specialist and general administration, graphic design and cartography, plan preparation and survey work, enforcement and inspection, development control, and IT systems. Support staff analyse data and update and store records. They check regulations and prepare reports. Some handle the administration of planning and development proposals that are submitted for committee approval. May revise maps, set up exhibitions and produce leaflets and drawings for public consultation.

Many support staff are skilled in desktop publishing and computer-aided design (CAD), and in geographical information systems (GIS). Some may also provide advice on planning matters to members of the public. Duties include liaising with a team that includes town planners, engineers and architects, as well as other support staff.

Work Details
Town planning support staff usually work a 35-40 hr week, Monday to Friday, though may be expected to work outside normal office hours, including some evenings. Work is mainly in an office, which may also be open to the public. Some support staff go out on site, or to meetings, so travel around an area may be necessary. A driving licence may be useful. You organise surveys, collect information, collate and analyse the results, and produce reports. The work may also include consulting with people, such as developers and members of the public.

Qualification
• England, Wales and Northern Ireland
Band 3: For entry: minimum of 4 GCSEs (A*-C) including maths and English, or equivalent. Useful subjects include geography, science or statistics, history, geography or economics.

Band 4: For BTEC higher national award: 1-2 A levels and some GCSEs (A*-C) usually including English and maths, or equivalent. Useful subjects include geography, science or statistics, history, geography or economics.

• Scotland
Band 3: For entry: minimum of four S grades (1-3) including maths and English, or similar. Useful subjects include geography, science or statistics, history, geography, economics or modern studies.

Band 4: For SQA higher national award: 2-3 H grades and some S grades (1-3) usually including English and maths, or similar qualifications. Useful subjects include geography, science or statistics, history, geography, economics or modern studies.

Adult Qualifications
Course entry requirements are usually relaxed for suitable mature applicants. Contact individual course providers.

Work Experience
Relevant work or voluntary experience is always useful and can improve your chances in application for entry to this job. Useful work includes working with information, using office and administration skills or gaining experience of working with the public. Local and central government offices may offer work

experience opportunities. Useful areas of government work include planning, architecture, surveying or environmental offices. Work in the construction industry may also be relevant.

Entry and Training

It is useful to have an interest in environmental matters, using computers and drawing skills. A Diploma/Welsh Baccalaureate in construction and the built environment may be available in your area. Some full-time courses may be studied before entry to a job, but support staff can enter work without relevant previous training. Study for courses depends partly on any qualifications already achieved. Training is usually in the workplace combined with part-time study for an appropriate BTEC/SQA award, such as an HNC/HND in planning or towards an S/NVQ level 3-4 in built environment development and control.

Once you have enough relevant spatial planning experience and a recognised qualification, you can gain technical membership (TechRTPI) of the Royal Town Planning Institute (RTPI). Those without a recognised academic qualification can gain membership with at least 10 years' relevant experience in an enforcement, administrative or technical role. Contact the RTPI for details of all courses, membership and study options. Training programmes, including apprenticeship schemes, may be available in your area for entry to this job. Advanced apprenticeships leading to qualification at level 3 can also be a route into higher education.

Mature applicants with relevant experience in administration, surveying, statistics, cartography or graphic design may have an advantage. Some move into this work from other roles in related departments. Entrants without recognised academic qualifications, but who have at least 10 years' experience in an enforcement, technical or administration role can become technical members (TechRTPI) of the Royal Town Planning Institute (RTPI).

Opportunities and Pay

Most work for a local or central government planning department, but there are opportunities with organisations that include environmental agencies, regional development and tourist authorities, enterprise agencies, national health trusts and in the voluntary sector. A few experienced support staff are employed in the private sector with consulting firms. In local/central government there is a clear promotion structure to senior level.

Pay varies depending on location and whether you work in the public or private sector. Starting salaries are around £13k-£17k a year, rising to around £27k with experience.

Health

This job requires good colour vision for certain areas of work.

Skills and Qualities

able to follow drawings and plans, able to work both on your own and in a team, able to work to deadlines, drawing ability, environmental awareness, excellent communication skills, good written English, IT skills, methodical, numeracy skills

Relevant Subjects

Art and Design, Construction and built environment, Geography, ICT/Computer studies, Mathematics

Further Information

Apprenticeship Schemes (National Apprenticeship Service) - www.apprenticeships.org.uk

Asset Skills - sector skills council for the places where we live and work - www.assetskills.org

Careers in Planning (Royal Town Planning Institute) - www.rtpi.org.uk/

Diplomas (Foundation, Higher and Advanced) - http://yp.direct.gov.uk/diplomas

Local Government Careers (Improvement and Development Agency) - www.lgcareers.com/publications/

Planning (weekly) (Royal Town Planning Institute, Haymarket) - www.planningresource.co.uk

Scottish Planner (bi-monthly) (Royal Town Planning Institute in Scotland) - www.scotland.rtpi.org.uk/newsletters

Addresses

Northern Ireland Local Government Association (NILGA)
Unit 5B Castlereagh Business Park, 478 Castlereagh Road, Belfast BT5 6BQ
Phone: +44(0)28 9079 8972
Web: www.nilga.org

Planning Service
Millennium House, 17-25 Great Victoria Street, Belfast BT2 7BN
Phone: +44 (0)28 9041 6700
Web: www.planningni.gov.uk

Royal Town Planning Institute (RTPI)
41 Botolph Lane, London EC3R 8DL
Phone: +44 (0)20 7929 9494
Web: www.rtpi.org.uk

Similar Jobs

Architectural Technician, Architectural Technologist, CAD Technician, Facilities Manager, Surveying Technician, Surveyor: Building Control, Town Planner

Toxicologist

also known as: Clinical Toxicologist

CRCI:Science, Mathematics and Statistics

CLCI:QOD — Job Band: 5

Job Description

Toxicologists undertake laboratory and field studies to identify any harmful effects of chemicals, biological materials and radiation on animals, plants, humans and the environment. They develop safe products including food and drink, household goods, cosmetics, pesticides, medicines and drugs. Tasks include isolating, identifying and measuring the level of toxic (poisonous) substances in biological materials. They conduct experiments, evaluate statistical data and write reports. May deal with the effects that toxic substances have on human health.

Also advise other medical professionals on the treatment and management of a patient who has become affected by a harmful chemical or drug. An ecotoxicologist specialises in the protection of our environment from the harmful effects of chemicals and pollution.

Work Details

Usually work a basic 35-39 hr week, Monday to Friday, but occasionally work outside these hours to conduct or complete experiments. In some employment you may be required to work weekends or shifts. If working with the NHS you may need to be available 'on call'. Your work is usually based in a laboratory as part of a mulitdisciplinary team. This job may involve travel, occasionally overseas.

Qualification

• England, Wales and Northern Ireland

Band 5: For degree courses: 2-3 A levels usually including chemistry, biology, maths or physics and some GCSEs (A*-C) usually including English, maths and science, or equivalent. Exact requirements depend on the degree you take.

• Scotland

Band 5: For degree courses: 3-5 H grades including chemistry and also biology and physics or maths and some S grades (1-3), usually including English, maths and science, or similar. Exact requirements depend on the degree you take.

Degree Information
Degrees in toxicology, environmental toxicology or immunology and toxicology are available. Other relevant degree subjects include biochemical sciences, biological sciences, applied life sciences, biomedical science, food sciences, medical laboratory science, medical and veterinary sciences, crop and soil sciences, forensic science, or chemical, environmental and physical sciences. A relevant first degree can also be followed by a specialist higher degree.

Adult Qualifications
Course entry requirements to first degree subjects may be relaxed for mature applicants provided they submit evidence of previous serious study such as an Access or Open University course. A foundation year prior to the start of a science degree may be available at some HE institutions for applicants who do not have the traditional science qualifications. Check with universities for details.

Work Experience
Universities and employers may prefer candidates who have relevant work or voluntary experience in a hospital, a relevant university department, or an industrial or commercial laboratory. If it proves difficult to gain this exact experience, any work with a scientific background is attractive to employers and admissions tutors.

Entry and Training
Entry to toxicology is via a relevant degree, and initial training is practical and laboratory based. In-house training may include good laboratory practice (GLP), court reporting and report writing, project management and data interpretation. Toxicology is normally studied as part of an undergraduate course in a related subject such as biochemistry. A higher degree (PhD or MSc/MPhil) may be taken in-house with an employer. After several years' experience, toxicologists can gain professional qualifications awarded by the Society of Biology and the Royal College of Pathologists (RCPath). Specialist diplomas or higher degrees in subjects that include waste management, pesticide or pollution science, are available to those working in ecotoxicology and the environment.

Membership of the British Toxicology Society (BTS) can be attained after five years' experience and evidence of continuing professional development. This allows automatic membership of the Federation of European Toxicologists and the European Societies of Toxicology (EUROTOX). Clinical toxicologists are first medically trained as doctors and then go on to specialise as a toxicologist. You are expected to follow a programme of continuing professional development (CPD) through your career.

Mature candidates with appropriate qualifications and experience are usually preferred. Funding from the Medical Research Council (MRC), or from pharmaceutical companies, utilities companies, or government departments and agencies, may be available for postgraduate study and research.

Opportunities and Pay
This is a growing profession due to the expansion of chemical products. Toxicologists work in a range of environments. Many work in chemical, pharmaceutical, cosmetic, food, agrochemical and water companies. Research is also conducted in universities and there are a small number of teaching opportunities. Analytical, medical, clinical and forensic toxicology is carried out in some larger hospitals, as well as in specialist regional toxicology units in the NHS or Forensic Science Service. Ecotoxicology and environmental toxicology is a growing area. Various other government departments and agencies also employ toxicologists and there are increasing numbers of jobs available for experienced toxicologists in consultancy firms.

Pay varies depending on location and employer, but generally, starting salaries for graduates are around £21.5k-£26.5k a year, rising to around £28k-£30k a year. Specialist scientists earn around £40k a year with experience.

Health
This job requires good general fitness. The work involves a risk of infection and an allergy risk from skin irritants. You need good colour vision for some areas of work.

Skills and Qualities
able to explain clearly, able to report accurately, accurate, analytical skills, aptitude for teamwork, attention to detail, IT skills, methodical, problem-solving skills, safety conscious

Relevant Subjects
Biology, Chemistry, English, Health and social care, ICT/Computer studies, Land and Environment, Mathematics, Physics, Science

Further Information
Association of the British Pharmaceutical Industry (ABPI) - www.abpi.org.uk/education

Federation of European Toxicologists and European Societies of Toxicology (EUROTOX) - www.eurotox.com

MRC Network (bi-monthly) (Medical Research Council (MRC)) - www.mrc.ac.uk/Newspublications/Publications/Network/index.htm

NHS Careers (NHS Careers) - www.nhscareers.nhs.uk

Open University - www.open.ac.uk

►Working in science (2007) (Babcock Lifeskills) - www.babcock-lifeskills.com/

Addresses
British Toxicology Society (BTS)
BTS Administrative Office PO Box 10371, Colchester, Essex CO1 9GL
Phone: +44 (0)1206 226059
Web: www.thebts.org

Forensic Science Service (FSS)
Trident Court, 2920 Solihull Parkway, Birmingham Business Park B37 7YN
Web: www.forensic.gov.uk

Medical Research Council (MRC)
20 Park Crescent, London W1B 1AL
Phone: +44 (0)20 7636 5422
Web: www.mrc.ac.uk

Royal College of Pathologists (RCPath)
2 Carlton House Terrace, London SW1Y 5AF
Phone: +44 (0)20 7451 6700
Web: www.rcpath.org

Society of Biology
9 Red Lion Court, London EC4A 3EF
Phone: +44 (0)20 7936 5900
Web: http://societyofbiology.org/home

Similar Jobs
Chemist: Analytical, Food Scientist/Technologist, Forensic Scientist, Immunologist, Pharmacologist, Public Analyst

Toymaker
CRCI:Design, Arts and Crafts
CLCI:EG Job Band: 3 to 5

Job Description
Toymakers make individual craft toys by hand or design toys for a larger manufacturer to mass produce. They produce items such as puppets, teddy bears, dolls houses and dolls, nursery and educational toys, board games and jigsaws, hobby and rocking horses, model-making kits, toy soldiers, hanging mobiles and moving/mechanical toys. They work with different materials such as textiles, card, wood, plastic and metal. Also use design skills, drawing by hand and using computer-aided design (CAD). May

use carving, sewing, engineering and painting skills too. They must ensure that all toys are designed/made to meeting strict safety requirements.

Some toymakers create designs for manufacturers, or design and produce goods independently for sale at craft fairs, exhibitions, the Internet, shops and galleries. Many toymakers specialise in one area of work.

Work Details

If employed by a company, usually work Monday to Friday from 9am to 5pm with other members of an in-house design team. If working freelance or self-employed, you are able to choose your own hours. Longer hours may be necessary at times to meet deadlines or for busy times of the year, such as at Christmas. Work in a comfortable office environment with access to a studio/ workshop. Self-employed toymakers usually have their own workshop that may be rented or in their own home.

You may need to travel to see customers, visit shops, craft fairs, markets and exhibitions. Some may set up a website and sell through the Internet. The work requires creative talent and imagination as well as an awareness of market trends.

Qualification

There are no set minimum academic requirements for entry, but many toymakers take a design course and then specialise in this area of work.

• England, Wales and Northern Ireland

Band 3: For entry to jobs, HNC or a relevant Diploma, usually at least 4 GCSEs (A*-C) including English, maths and art and design, or equivalent. For some foundation studies courses: usually at least 5 GCSEs (A*-C).

Band 4: For diploma in foundation studies (art and design): usually at least one A level and some GCSEs (A*-C), including English, art and maths. For BTEC higher national award you need a BTEC national award, successful completion of a foundation studies course, or equivalent qualification.

Band 5: For degree courses: 2-3 A levels and some GCSEs (A*-C) usually including English and maths, or equivalent. Most students take a foundation studies course first. Exact requirements depend on the degree you take.

• Scotland

Band 3: For entry: usually at least four S grades (1-3) including English and maths, or similar.

Band 4: For entry to SQA higher national and professional development awards, usually 2-3 H grades and some S grades (1-3), including English and maths, or similar qualifications.

Band 5: For degree courses: 3-5 H grades and some S grades (1-3), usually including English and maths, or similar. Exact requirements depend on the degree to be taken.

Degree Information

A degree in art and design, craft studies or product design is an advantage, with specialism in a relevant area, such as 3D design, woodwork or textiles.

Adult Qualifications

You can do this job without formal qualifications, but many craftspeople have taken specialised courses. Mature applicants with outstanding portfolios of work may be accepted for courses without the standard entry requirements. There are Access and foundation level courses in some areas, which give adults without qualifications a route onto degree courses. Check with individual colleges and universities.

Work Experience

Entry to this job is competitive and it is important that you try to do some relevant work or voluntary experience before applying. Any work experience that involves design or craft work in a variety of materials is relevant and helps to prepare a portfolio of work. Any practical experience in school/college, such as developing sewing skills in costume making, carpentry/joinery, painting/decorating or furniture making is useful. Art and craft courses, including evening classes at a local college are also helpful.

Entry and Training

Many entrants take courses in craft or design subjects and a portfolio is needed for entry to colleges and universities. Course titles vary, so check prospectuses carefully. Other useful qualifications include those offered by City & Guilds in a range of creative crafts and design subjects. Art and design foundation degrees are also available in subjects that include 3D design, model making, and creative arts and crafts. Courses are usually two-years full time. There are numerous part-time and evening courses in toymaking throughout the country. The Crafts Council provides information on short courses and runs a funding scheme for self-employed toymakers.

Organisations including the British Toy and Hobby Association (BTHA) and the British Toymakers Guild (BTG) offer advice and guidance on the rules and regulations surrounding toy design safety and on marketing your designs.

S/NVQs at levels 1-4 are available in aspects of craft skills, design and business skills. Training programmes, including apprenticeship schemes, may be available in your area for entry to this job. Advanced apprenticeships leading to qualification at level 3 can also be a route into higher education.

Mature entrants are often those who turn a skill or hobby into a business idea. Some experience in the art and design area is useful, as is practical craft work with textiles, wood and ceramics. Business skills are useful for those who become self-employed.

Opportunities and Pay

This is a very limited field as most mass production of toys is done abroad. Success depends on market trends as well as your creative ability. It may not be possible to make a living entirely from toy making or designing, so you may have to have another job. You may work for a toy manufacturer, but are more likely to work freelance or be self-employed. Grants may be available, for example from the Crafts Council or from the local LSC/LEC, Jobcentre and ELWa, to set up in business.

The British Toy and Hobby Association (BTHA) and the British Toymakers Guild (BTG) both have around 150 members. The BTHA represents the interests of large and small manufacturers in the UK, while the BTG specialises in craft toymakers.

Generally, you may start earning between £10k-£15k a year, rising with experience. Working for a large manufacturer, you may earn up to around £35k a year. A successful designer of a popular toy may earn over £45k.

Health

If working with colours, for example in paints or fabrics, you may have difficulty if you do not have normal colour vision.

Skills and Qualities

able to work both on your own and in a team, attention to detail, creative and imaginative flair, eye for shape/colour, hand-to-eye co-ordination, initiative, safety conscious, self-motivated, specialist IT skills, technical aptitude

Relevant Subjects

Art and Design, Design and technology, Mathematics

Further Information

Apprenticeship Schemes (National Apprenticeship Service) - www.apprenticeships.org.uk

BTG Guide to Toy Safety - www.toymakersguild.co.uk

BTG Marketing Traditional Toys (British Toymakers Guild) - www.toymakersguild.co.uk/

Creative & Cultural Skills - sector skills council for advertising, crafts, cultural heritage, design, literature, music, performing & visual arts - www.ccskills.org.uk

Design Week (Design Week) - www.designweek.co.uk

Toy News (monthly) (Intent Media) - www.toynewsmag.com

Toys 'n' Playthings (Lema Publishing Ltd) - www.toysnplaythings.co.uk

►Working in art & design (2009) (Babcock Lifeskills) - www.babcock-lifeskills.com/

Your Creative Future (Design Council) (Design Council) - www.yourcreativefuture.org

Addresses

British Toy and Hobby Association (BTHA)
80 Camberwell Rd, London SE5 0EG
Phone: +44 (0)20 7701 7271
Web: www.btha.co.uk

British Toymakers Guild (BTG)
PO Box 240, Uckfield TN22 9AS
Phone: +44 (0) 1225 442 440
Web: www.toymakersguild.co.uk

Crafts Council (CC)
44a Pentonville Road, Islington, London N1 9BY
Phone: +44 (0)20 7806 2500
Web: www.craftscouncil.org.uk

Design Wales
University of Wales Institute, Cardiff Western Avenue CF5 2YB
Phone: +44 (0) 2920 41 7043
Web: www.designwales.org

Similar Jobs

Engineer: Design, Jewellery Designer, Model Maker, Product Designer, Textile Designer

Trade Mark Attorney

CRCI:Legal and Political Services
CLCI:LAK
Job Band: 4 to 5

Job Description

Trade mark attorneys are specialist legal professionals who are qualified to advise clients about trade marks and related issues. Trade marks (TM) are distinctive names, symbols, logos or mottos used to identify a company, product or service. Trade mark attorneys represents clients' interests with registration bodies in the UK, the EU and worldwide. They advise clients, who use a TM to distinguish their company from a competitor, on their proposed or existing TM. They have in-depth knowledge of TMs and the law relating to them. They also have a working knowledge of related issues such as copyright, industrial designs, and unfair competition.

Trade mark attorneys inform clients on the correct and legal use of a TM in advertising and on other intellectual property issues. They advise on matters of TM infringement and help to resolve conflict. If the case goes to court, they provide support to the solicitors and barristers conducting the case. They research new TMs and oversee all procedural details of its registration. Attorneys manage a portfolio of UK and overseas brands. They also handle renewals of TMs, which is every ten years in the UK.

Work Details

The hours are officially 9am-5pm, Monday to Friday, but extra hours are common, including working at home. You are based in an office and can spend some time in court. The work is often demanding and difficult decisions are sometimes required. Travel around the UK and overseas may also be required.

Qualification

- **England, Wales and Northern Ireland**

Band 4: Minimum entry requirements to the profession: two A levels and 5 GCSEs (A*-C) in approved subjects, usually including English and maths, or equivalent.

Band 5: For degree: at least two A levels and 5 GCSEs (A*-C), including English and maths, or equivalent qualifications. Exact requirements depend on the degree you take.

- **Scotland**

Band 4: Minimum entry requirements to the profession: 2-3 H grades and five S grades (1-3), in approved subjects, usually including English and maths, or similar.

Band 5: For degree courses: 3-5 H grades and five S grades (1-3), usually including English and maths, or similar. Exact requirements depend on the degree you take.

Degree Information

You may enter this job with a degree in any subject, though employers usually prefer subjects such as English, law, modern European languages and non-European languages.

Adult Qualifications

Entry requirements may be relaxed for adults applying for higher education courses. Access or foundation courses give adults without qualifications a route on to relevant degree courses.

Work Experience

Entry to this job is competitive. It is important that you do some relevant work experience before applying. It is useful to have experience in areas such as the legal profession or business. Any experience of applying research skills is important. Some large firms of trade mark attorneys offer work placements.

Entry and Training

Most trade mark attorney are registered on the Register of Trade Mark Agents, which requires passing the professional exams of the Institute of Trade Mark Agents (ITMA), plus a period of experience. You therefore have to already be working in the profession to qualify. There are three components - a certificate course provided by Queen Mary and Westfield College or Manchester University; the professional qualification course provided by Nottingham Law School, and an experience requirement regulated by ITMA and the Intellectual Property Regulation Board (IPREG). The courses are a mixture of intensive short courses, spread in total over two years. The experience requirement is around three years, with exemptions for relevant experience gained elsewhere. See the ITMA website for full details.

Those with specific qualifications or training such as a law degree and ITMA approved professional qualifications, may be eligible for exemption from some or all of the foundation papers of the qualifying examination. Such candidates usually find it easier to find a job as a trainee. It is a professional requirement that you continue to update your knowledge through a programme of continuing professional development (CPD), throughout your career as a trade mark attorney. Contact the ITMA for details of all routes into the profession and of the various membership grades.

Mature entrants with relevant qualifications and training, such as law, have an advantage. Part-time degrees in law are available. Qualified legal executives also have an advantage.

Opportunities and Pay

This is currently a small but expanding profession, with over 800 registered trade mark attorneys in the UK. Most are based in London or the South East. The majority of work is in private practice, either in trade mark companies or in a firm of patent agents with a department specialising in trade mark work. Many firms of solicitors are developing trade mark departments. Further opportunities are with large companies with specialist trade mark departments.

With experience you can progress to more senior levels, including the opportunity to become a partner in a company. Some qualified and experienced trade mark attorneys may form their own company.

Salaries depend on an individual employer, but starting salaries range from £20k-£25k a year and increase as you pass your examinations. Once fully qualified, you can expect to earn around £40k a year. Senior trade mark attorneys can earn £50-£100k a year.

Skills and Qualities

analytical skills, attention to detail, business awareness, clear-thinking, excellent communication skills, good interpersonal skills, information handling skills, IT skills, precise, self-motivated

Relevant Subjects

Business and accounting, Design and technology, English, Law

Further Information

Intellectual Property Regulation Board (IPReg) - www.ipreg.org.uk
International Trademark Association (INTA) - www.inta.org

Addresses

Institute of Trade Mark Attorneys
5th Floor Outer Temple 222 -225 Strand, London WC2R 1BA
Phone: +44 (0)20 7101 6090
Web: www.itma.org.uk

UK Intellectual Property Office (UK IPO)
Concept House, Cardiff Road, Newport NP10 8QQ
Phone: 0845 950 0505 (UK only)
Web: www.ipo.gov.uk

World Intellectual Property Organization
34, chemin des Colombettes, CH-1211, Geneva 20
Phone: +44 22 338 9111
Web: www.wipo.int

Similar Jobs

Legal Executive, Patent Attorney, Patent Examiner, Solicitor

Trade Union Official

CRCI:Social Work and Counselling Services
CLCI:CAS — Job Band: 3 to 5

Job Description

Trade union officials represent the interests of trades union members in discussions with an employer for a variety of matters. These may include pay and working conditions, education and training programmes, equal opportunities, employment contracts, health and safety in the workplace, and redundancy procedures. They circulate information, write reports and recruit new members. Deal with any legal requirements, disputes and unfair dismissal claims.

Trade union officials represent members in difficulty, for example, in cases of personal injury. They deal with the press and media on union matters. May represent the union at regional/national level, or may be employed at a head office.

Work Details

You are usually based in an office working a basic week of around 35-40 hrs, but have to travel to members' workplaces and to meetings and conferences. The hours can be long and may include evening and weekend work. You negotiate with employers or their representatives, give shop stewards and union representatives advice on matters such as pensions, contracts and employees' rights and deal with problems and complaints. The work can be stressful at times and you may have to make difficult or unpopular decisions.

Qualification

There are no specific entry qualifications, though an increasing number of trade union officials have degrees or equivalent vocational qualifications.

• England, Wales and Northern Ireland

Band 3: For entry: usually at least 4 GCSEs (A*-C) including English and maths, or equivalent.

Band 4: For BTEC higher national award: 1-2 A levels and some GCSEs (A*-C) usually including English and maths, or equivalent.

Band 5: For degree courses: 2-3 A levels and some GCSEs (A*-C) usually including English and maths, or equivalent. Exact requirements depend on the degree you take.

• Scotland

Band 3: For entry: usually at least four S grades (1-3) including English and maths, or similar.

Band 4: For SQA higher national award: usually 2-3 H grades and some S grades (1-3), often including English and maths, or similar qualifications.

Band 5: For degree courses: 3-5 H grades and some S grades (1-3), usually including English, maths or similar qualifications. Exact requirements depend on the degree you take.

Degree Information

A degree in any subject is acceptable, but trade union studies or industrial relations and human resources management, are particularly useful. Some subjects, including politics, law, social policy and administration, sociology, social history and economics, business and management also provide useful background knowledge.

Adult Qualifications

Previous working experience in a relevant field is essential together with direct experience of union work.

Work Experience

Employers or colleges may prefer candidates who have relevant work experience. This includes administration work, customer services, advocacy work such as at the Citizens Advice Bureau and any experience of legal matters. Almost all entrants have completed a period of voluntary work in a trade union, maybe as a shop steward.

Entry and Training

This job is not suitable for school leavers and most entrants are 21 or over. There are two main routes into this job, either via a branch/regional office, or head office employment. Applicants often have professional qualifications such as legal, teaching, journalism or accountancy. An increasing number of applicants are graduates and it is possible to obtain sponsorship from the Trades Union Congress (TUC).

Relevant experience is usually needed, possibly as a shop steward or union committee member. Selection is conducted by an interview, perhaps by a panel of executive or committee members, though sometimes there is a ballot. Training is on the job, with short courses. The TUC has a professional development programme of short courses in relevant topics through unionlearn. These include collective bargaining, equality, occupational health and safety, employment law, and developing representative skills. Check the Employment National Training Organisation website for trade union training standards.

Mature entry is usual for this job and especially for those with significant voluntary union work. Some enter with professional qualifications in subjects that include law, and media-related subjects. There are relevant short training courses that are offered by the Trades Union Congress (TUC) and also distance-learning courses available, including those offered through an independent union (eg UNISON Open College). There may be financial support from the TUC, the General Federation of Trades Unions Educational Trust or from an independent union.

Opportunities and Pay

Jobs are based in union offices throughout the UK at local, regional or national level. You work for a Trade Union, or the TUC. Currently, there are not many salaried full-time union officials and the chances of getting into this type of work are decreasing, with fewer unions altogether and smaller unions being amalgamated. A lot of union work is done on an unpaid voluntary basis. There may be opportunities to be a union learning representative if you have an adult education or training background. A few officials can work for an international trade union abroad. Chances of progression are limited, although promotion to regional or national posts is possible. Some trade union officials move into politics at local/ national level, or into personnel work.

New officials start on salaries of around £20k a year, rising to £22k-£30k a year with experience. Some officials and those in senior management may earn around £32k-£50k a year, or more. As a general secretary, you may earn up to £80k a year.

Skills and Qualities

able to withstand criticism, fair minded, good communication skills, good interpersonal skills, good organisational skills, interest in current affairs, IT skills, negotiating skills, networking skills, problem-solving skills

Relevant Subjects

Business and accounting, Economics, English, Government and politics, Law, Mathematics, Sociology

Further Information

ENTO (Employment National Training Organisation) (Employment National Training Organisation)) - www.ento.co.uk

In TOUCH (monthly e-bulletin,TUC) - www.tuc.org.uk/the_tuc/index.cfm?mins=267

Union Learn (TUC) - www.unionlearn.org.uk

▶Working in advice & counselling (2007) (Babcock Lifeskills) - www.babcock-lifeskills.com/

Addresses

General Federation of Trade Unions (GFTU)
Headland House 308-312 Grays Inn Road, London WC1X 8DP
Phone: +44 (0)207 520 8340
Web: www.gftu.org/content/

Irish Congress of Trade Unions (Northern Ireland Committee)
4-6 Donegall Street Place, Belfast BT1 2FN
Phone: +44 (0)28 9024 7940
Web: www.ictuni.org

Scottish Trades Union Congress (STUC)
333 Woodlands Road, Glasgow G3 6NG
Phone: +44 (0)141 337 8100
Web: www.stuc.org.uk

Trades Union Congress (TUC)
Congress House, Great Russell Street, London WC1B 3LS
Phone: +44 (0)20 7636 4030
Web: www.tuc.org.uk

UNISON Learning and Organising Services (LAOS)
1 Mabledon Place, London WC1H 9AJ
Phone: 0845 355 0845 (UK only)
Web: www.unison.org.uk/laos/index.asp

Wales Trades Union Congress
Transport House 1 Cathedral Road, Cardiff CF11 9SD
Phone: +44 (0)29 2034 7010
Web: www.tuc.org.uk/tuc/regions_info_wales.cfm

Similar Jobs

Equality & Diversity Officer, Health & Safety Practitioner, Human Resources Officer/Manager, Political/Constituency Organiser, Training & Development Officer/Manager

Trading Standards Officer

also known as: Consumer Adviser, Enforcement Officer: Trading Standards

CRCI:Retail Sales and Customer Services
CLCI:COP Job Band: 4 to 5

Job Description

Trading standards officers (TSOs) are legally qualified officers who safeguard the public by ensuring that traders and businesses comply with a broad range of consumer laws. These include trades descriptions, weights and measures, consumer protection, food and drugs, under-age sales, consumer credit and animal welfare. They check the accuracy of equipment for weighing and measuring, including such things as petrol pumps, bar measures and scales. Products are sampled and safety checks are carried out routinely. Pricing structures and advertising literature are checked for accuracy. Routine monitoring, investigating complaints from the public on property/services misdecsriptions and checking the legality of imported goods are all part of the job.

Officers advise traders on how to correct any problem and monitor their progress. They keep records, write reports and occasionally prepare evidence for court cases. All businesses and industries are covered, including dairies, street markets, factories, garages, night clubs, petrol stations, shops, rural enterprises, and many others. Some TSOs specialise in a particular area of trading standards work.

Work Details

Usually work a basic 37 hr week from Monday to Friday, with occasional weekend work or early mornings. Are office-based but may have to visit premises that are dirty and unpleasant, so protective clothing may be needed. You may meet some aggressive and abusive people, so you need to remain calm but assertive.

Qualification

- **England, Wales and Northern Ireland**

Band 4: For direct entry to some posts: 1-2 A levels and some GCSEs (A*-C) usually including English, maths and a science, or equivalent.

Band 5: For a degree: 2-3 A levels and some GCSEs (A*-C). Passes in maths, physics or a double science, and English may be needed for entry to the professional qualifications of the Trading Standards Institute. Exact requirements depend on the degree you take.

- **Scotland**

Band 4: For direct entry to some posts: 2-3 H grades and some S grades (1-3) usually including English, maths and a science, or similar.

Band 5: For a degree: 3-5 H grades and some S grades (1-3) or similar. The exact requirements depend on the degree you take, but passes in maths, physics or a double science, and English may be needed for entry to the professional qualifications of the Trading Standards Institute.

Degree Information

The Trading Standards Institute approves the following BA/BSc degrees: consumer protection, consumer affairs, trading standards, law and trading standards, or forensic investigation and consumer law. For those applying to enter this job under the Accreditation of Prior Experience and Learning (APEL) scheme, subjects such as law, physical sciences, engineering and technology are useful.

Adult Qualifications
Entry requirements may be relaxed for adults applying for higher education courses. Access or foundation courses give adults without qualifications a route onto degree courses.

Work Experience
Relevant work or voluntary experience is an advantage, especially in quality assurance and manufacturing. This can include experience in local government, dealing with the public or with a team of people. Taking part in the Young Consumers of the Year competition, coordinated through the Trading Standards Institute, demonstrates a strong interest in this type of work.

Entry and Training
You can enter this work through the traditional graduate entry route, with a Trading Standards Institute (TSI) accredited consumer protection degree, followed by TSI professional qualifications. Alternatively you can enter a more junior role from the age of 18 and progress through the TSI qualifications framework whilst working. The level of qualification you need depends on your job and your area of specialism. The TSI has a trading standards qualifications framework which includes the foundation certificate in consumer affairs and trading standards, the diploma in consumer affairs and trading standards and the higher diploma. You can enter the framework at different levels and gain credits via the Accreditation of Prior Experience and Learning (APEL) scheme.

Manchester Metropolitan University offers a BSc in trading standards and an accredited one-year graduate diploma in trading standards, suitable for graduates without a TSI accredited degree. It may be possible to seek support and sponsorship whilst studying. Employers expect officers to continue updating their skills and knowledge, and may provide a programme of continuing professional development. The TSI also operates a continuous professional and personal development scheme. A driving licence is essential.

There are good opportunities for mature applicants. A possible route for mature applicants already employed in trading standards is through the Accreditation of Prior Experience and Learning Scheme (APEL). Those already working in consumer affairs, consumer protection, citizens advice bureau, other statutory or voluntary consumer organisations, or customer service departments in the private sector can also train to become a trading standards officer. Contact the Trading Standards Institute for details on routes to training and qualification.

Opportunities and Pay
Trading standards officers usually work for local authorities, but there are some opportunities to work in private industry, in an advisory capacity or in quality control. There is a steady demand for qualified staff and it is possible to specialise in consumer affairs or other areas. There is a formal promotion structure in local government and opportunities to move into more senior roles and general management. Some qualified and experienced officers may set up a consultancy giving specialist advice.

Pay varies depending on the local authority, but ranges from £24k-£34k. Senior officers can earn over £40k a year.

Health
This job requires good health.

Skills and Qualities
able to work both on your own and in a team, assertive, diplomatic, enquiring mind, good at writing reports, good communication skills, good interpersonal skills, information handling skills, IT skills, sound judgement

Relevant Subjects
English, Law, Mathematics, Physics, Retail and distribution, Science

Further Information
A Career in Trading Standards (TSI) - www.tradingstandards.gov.uk/

AGCAS: Government & Public Administration (Job Sector Briefing) (AGCAS) - www.prospects.ac.uk

Local Government Careers (Improvement and Development Agency) - www.lgcareers.com/publications/

ts today (Trading Standards Institute, monthly) (Cambridge Publishers) - www.tradingstandards.gov.uk/products/publications.cfm

▶Working in retail & customer services (2008) (Babcock Lifeskills) - www.babcock-lifeskills.com/

Addresses
Convention of Scottish Local Authorities (COSLA)
Rosebery House, 9 Haymarket Terrace, Edinburgh EH12 5XZ
Phone: +44 (0)131 474 9200
Web: www.cosla.gov.uk

Manchester Metropolitan University (MMU)
All Saints Building, Manchester M15 6BH
Phone: +44 (0)161 247 2000
Web: www.mmu.ac.uk

Northern Ireland Local Government Association (NILGA)
Unit 5B Castlereagh Business Park, 478 Castlereagh Road, Belfast BT5 6BQ
Phone: +44(0)28 9079 8972
Web: www.nilga.org

Trading Standards Institute (TSI)
1 Sylvan Court, Sylvan Way, Southfields Business Park, Basildon, Essex SS15 6TH
Phone: 0845 608 9400 (UK only)
Web: www.tradingstandards.gov.uk/

Trading Standards Service
Dept of Enterprise, Trade & Investment Netherleigh Massey Avenue, Belfast BT4 2JP
Phone: +44 (0)28 9052 9900
Web: www.detini.gov.uk

Similar Jobs
Environmental Health Practitioner, Health & Safety Practitioner, Quality Manager

Training & Development Officer/ Manager

CRCI:Education and Training
CLCI:FAP — Job Band: 3 to 5

Job Description
Training officers Identify, develop and organise appropriate staff training programmes for employees of an organisation. They consider the staff training needs of individual employees using methods such as appraisal schemes, job analysis, or through consultation with managers as well as staff. They then estimate the costs involved and decide the best way to provide training, including the use of training providers. They also set up and administer a range of appropriate schemes, aiming to develop relevant skills. Must cater for both new and experienced workers at all levels in the organisation. Evaluating training programmes on their completion is also part of this job.

Officers produce training materials for in-house courses. May also deliver training personally. May set up a graduate training programme or a management training scheme for existing employees. They monitor progress, assess the effectiveness of the programme and review the training policy.

Training & Development Officer/Manager

Work Details

Usually work around 35-40 hrs a week, Monday to Friday, though sometimes you may need to run courses at weekends or in the evening. The work is office based, perhaps with time spent in a training centre or classroom. There may be some travel involved, for example when negotiating with other organisations (eg colleges/training provider centres). You may work with management to help to devise a training and development programme, and also contribute to the employee performance appraisal process.

You may have to address groups of people and need to be able to control and manipulate group situations, as well as stimulate enthusiasm.

Qualification

• England, Wales and Northern Ireland

Band 4: For HND, Diploma of Higher Education or foundation degree: 1-2 A levels and some GCSEs (A*-C) usually including English and maths, or equivalent.

Band 5: For degree courses: 2-3 A levels and some GCSEs (A*-C) usually including English and maths, or equivalent. Exact requirements depend on the degree you take.

• Scotland

Band 4: For entry to SQA higher national and professional development awards, usually 2-3 H grades and some S grades (1-3), including English and maths, or similar qualifications.

Band 5: For degree courses: 3-5 H grades and some S grades (1-3), including English and maths, or similar qualifications. Exact requirements depend on the degree you take.

Degree Information

The degree can be in any discipline, though psychology, business and related areas, IT, and human resources management give useful background. Some first degrees and postgraduate qualifications lead to exemptions from the Chartered Institute of Personnel and Development (CIPD) Professional Qualification Scheme (contact CIPD for list). Relevant postgraduate diplomas/ MSc degrees are available in subjects that include training management/development which can be studied part time or through distance learning.

Adult Qualifications

A good general education, with a high standard of written and spoken English, numeracy and a basic understanding of statistical and graphical information is needed. A degree/postgraduate or professional qualification in a subject such as business studies, human resource management, personnel, and related subjects is useful, though not essential.

Work Experience

Employers or colleges may prefer candidates who have relevant work or voluntary experience. This includes work in administration or with people where you can develop your communication skills, particularly in a training or human resources department of a large company. Work-shadowing a training officer is an excellent way to find out more about the job.

Entry and Training

Many people entering this career at management level have a degree/postgraduate qualification and relevant experience, though it is possible to start as a trainee or at assistant level in a personnel or training department and first become a training officer and then gain professional qualifications. Specialist or technical knowledge is needed for some posts. Training is by on-the-job experience and relevant courses, such as the Chartered Institute of Personnel and Development (CIPD) Certificate in Training Practice. This is a skills-based modular course that usually takes around one year and leads to associate membership of the CIPD.

Employers look on membership of the CIPD as an asset. The CIPD's flexible Professional Development Scheme includes modules appropriate to training specialists and involves assignments, a project and examinations, as well as work experience. Successful completion of all four modules leads to graduate membership of the CIPD. There are also more advanced courses, such as the Advanced Certificate in Managing Organisational Learning, and a wide range of short courses on specialist topics also available from the CIPD.

Relevant foundation degrees are available that can be studied either full or part time. On-the-job S/NVQs are available in learning and development at levels 3-5. S/NVQs in personnel at levels 3-5 may also be available.

Mature applicants are welcomed especially those with relevant work experience. Knowledge of business organisation, office procedures and accounting practices is an advantage. This is often a second career, following, for example, teaching (especially in further education), personnel work, work in industry or administration. A good general education, with a high standard of written and spoken English, numeracy and a basic understanding of statistical and graphical information, is needed.

There are relevant flexible learning courses that are offered by organisations such as the Chartered Institute of Personnel and Development (CIPD). The CIPD Professional Development Scheme is a postgraduate programme, however there are no formal entry requirements, and extra support is available if you are new to study, or returning after a break.

Opportunities and Pay

Training officers/managers can work in any organisation that trains their own staff, including the national health service, central and local government, financial organisations, retail companies and manufacturing companies. There are also national training bodies and commercial training providers. There is a steady increase in the number of jobs in this type of work. British-trained officers/ managers have opportunities to work abroad, particularly those who have previous experience of the country in which they wish to work. Freelance training and consultancy work is also possible and such opportunities are increasing.

Pay varies depending on location, size and type of company. Salaries at start at around £18k-£28k. Training officers/managers with around ten years' experience can earn around £35k- £60k a year.

Skills and Qualities

able to manage a budget and keep records, able to motivate others, confident, good communication skills, good interpersonal skills, good organisational skills, good presentation skills, innovative, IT skills, problem-solving skills

Relevant Subjects

Business and accounting, Economics, English, Psychology

Further Information

LLUK (Lifelong Learning UK) - sector skills council for the professional development of staff working in the lifelong learning sector - www.lluk.org

People Management Magazine (CIPD) - www.peoplemanagement.co.uk/pm

Addresses

Chartered Institute of Personnel and Development (CIPD)
151 The Broadway, London SW19 1JQ
Phone: +44 (0)20 8612 6200
Web: www.cipd.co.uk

ENTO (Employment National Training Organisation)
Kimberley House, 47 Vaughan Way, Leicester LE1 4SG
Phone: +44 (0)116 251 7979
Web: www.ento.co.uk

Similar Jobs
Human Resources Officer/Manager, IT Skills Trainer, Lecturer: Further Education, NVQ/SVQ Assessor, Psychologist: Occupational, Teacher: Secondary School

Translator

CRCI:Languages, Information and Culture
CLCI:FAL Job Band: 5

Job Description
Translators convert written text from a foreign language into the mother tongue or language of use, ensuring that the meaning of the original text is retained. They read textbooks/manuscripts and other related resources to gain specialist knowledge. Researches a wide range of terminology and language specific phrases and reads through original documents to produce a verbal summary. They check words using dictionaries and thesauruses and may check difficult points with the client before preparing final drafts. Most translators work from at least two foreign languages, including common European languages to more specialist ones of Africa, eastern Europe or Asia.

Translators usually work in one subject area based on a good knowledge of the required specialist vocabulary. The main demand is for technical and scientific translation, business reports, private letters and documents, literature, and for the legal, medical and pharmaceutical professions. Some work involves editing computer-translated documents.

Work Details
Employed, in-house translators usually work from 9am-5pm in an office, though many translators work from home and choose their own working hours. Freelance work can involve irregular and sometimes very long hours. The work is very intensive and can be pressurised at times, particularly when working to a deadline. Use of email and the Internet can feature prominently through every stage of the work. Normally you work on your own. You are responsible for accurate work and for conveying the exact meaning of the documents you are translating.

Qualification

- **England, Wales and Northern Ireland**

Band 5: For degree courses: 2-3 A levels and some GCSEs (A*-C) usually including English, a modern language and maths, or equivalent. Exact requirements depend on the degree you take.

- **Scotland**

Band 5: For degree courses: 3-5 H grades and some S grades (1-3), usually including English, a modern language and maths, or similar qualifications. Exact requirements depend on the degree you take.

Degree Information
You need to show a high level of competence in at least two modern languages, as well as in English. There are a few first degrees and several postgraduate courses in interpreting and translating. Modern European (and non-European) languages are useful or combined degrees such as languages with business, law or science which give the required specialist knowledge.

There is an increasing demand for Arabic, Japanese, Mandarin/Cantonese, Portuguese, and Russian as well as eastern European languages. In the UK public sector, British Sign Language, Hindi, Swahili, Turkish, Urdu and Welsh are needed to serve some local communities effectively. There is a postgraduate degree in translation, which can enhance your qualifications.

Adult Qualifications
Maturity is an advantage. A high level of linguistic competence is essential and specialist knowledge is usually required, eg accountancy, law or engineering.

Work Experience
Employers and universities may prefer candidates who have relevant work or voluntary experience. Relevant experience includes other work with languages such as teaching English as a foreign language, tutoring or working time spent abroad. Routes into Languages offers a placement scheme to help graduates gain work experience. Check the website for details.

Entry and Training
Employers require evidence of competence in modern European and non-European languages, together with a high standard of written English. Entrants are usually, but not always, graduates. Many have postgraduate degrees or the Chartered Institute of Linguists (IoL) diploma in translation (Dip Trans). The IoL also offers a certificate in bilingual studies and an international diploma in bilingual communication. The six official languages are English, French, Russian, Spanish, Chinese and Arabic, though other languages that are asked for include German, Italian, east European and Scandinavian languages.

As well as offering two foreign languages (preferably including one unusual one), it is important to have some knowledge of the institutions, culture and attitudes of the countries where your specialist languages are spoken. Training can be during a first degree or postgraduate course, or by specialist distance-learning or part-time college courses for an IoL diploma. Some employers, such as the civil service or the European Union, have their own training schemes, which are highly competitive. It is an advantage to have experience in word processing.

The Institute of Translation and Interpreting (ITI) offers training short courses, workshops and a number of publications that aim to further develop a translator's skill through continuing professional development (CPD). Becoming a member of ITI is seen as an advantage and is accepted recognition of translator status.

Translation services can be required on a more local level e.g. organisations such as The Welsh Language Board provide support to those who use Welsh for work. Their website has details of training courses and further education institutes in Wales offering bilingual and Welsh language vocational courses. Higher education courses in Welsh are available at the University of Wales: Trinity St. David, Aberystwyth University; Bangor University and Swansea University. Check the websites for details.

Mature entrants with experience in languages combined with expertise in areas such as law, finance, science and engineering, have an advantage, especially for freelance work. Experience of any job using languages is helpful. It is also important to have some knowledge of the institutions, culture and attitudes of the countries where your specialist languages are spoken, possibly achieved through living abroad.

Routes into Languages offers a placement scheme to help graduates gain work experience. Check the website for details.

Opportunities and Pay
Jobs are widely available throughout the UK and translation agencies are located in most UK major cities. There are increasing opportunities in the civil service, armed forces, multinational companies, the BBC, NATO, the European Union (EU) and the United Nations. Considerable talent is required for success in this job. There has been an increased demand for Asian and eastern European language translators, both within the civil service and commercial firms. There are good opportunities to work overseas. Many translators are self-employed and work on a freelance basis. This means that income can be irregular, so it may be necessary to have another job such as part-time teaching.

Starting salaries for translators are from £18k a year, rising to £25k-£30k a year with experience. Senior translators, or translators with a particular specialism can earn from £30k-£35k a year, or more. Freelance translators can earn from around £75-£180 per 1000 words or Chinese/Japanese characters, depending on their ability and experience.

Skills and Qualities
ability in one or more languages, able to cope under pressure, able to work well on your own, awareness of confidentiality issues, good concentration level, good written English, information handling skills, IT skills, networking skills, self-disciplined

Relevant Subjects
Classical studies, Engineering, English, Government and politics, Modern Foreign Languages, Science

Further Information
Careers Wales - www.careerswales.com/

CILT:The National Centre for Languages - www.cilt.org.uk

European Personnel Selection Office (EU Careers) (Office for Official Publications of the EC) - http://europa.eu/epso

Institute of Translation & Interpreting (ITI) - www.iti.org.uk

Linguist Magazine (6 x a year) (Institute of Linguists) - www.iol.org.uk/linguistmagazine/default.asp

Routes into Languages - www.routesintolanguages.ac.uk

The Welsh Language Board - www.byig-wlb.org.uk/Pages/Hafan.aspx

▶Working with languages (2010) (Babcock Lifeskills) - www.babcock-lifeskills.com/

Addresses
Chartered Institute of Linguists (IoL)
Saxon House, 48 Southwark Street, London SE1 1UN
Phone: +44 (0)20 7940 3100
Web: www.iol.org.uk

Institute of Translation and Interpreting (ITI)
Fortuna House South Fifth Street, Milton Keynes MK9 2PQ
Phone: +44 (0)1908 325 250
Web: www.iti.org.uk

Swansea University
Singleton Park, Swansea SA2 8PP
Phone: +44 (0) 1792 205678
Web: www.swan.ac.uk/

University of Wales
King Edward VII Avenue, Cardiff CF10 3NS
Phone: +44 (0)29 2037 6999
Web: www.wales.ac.uk/en/Home.aspx

Similar Jobs
Interpreter, Language Service Professional, Secretary: Bilingual, Teacher: Community Languages, Teacher: Modern Foreign Languages, Writer: Technical

Transport Planner
also known as: Transportation Planner

CRCI:Transport and Logistics

CLCI:YAD — Job Band: 5

Job Description
Transport planners prepare strategic road transport plans, surveys and reports for local and central government, large engineering companies and transport services. They work with a team of developers, surveyors and statisticians and are closely involved in providing information and instruction for decision makers and communities. Take into account the social and environmental effects of road transport and its infrastructure (access roads and junctions, car and cycle parking, bus interchange facilities etc).

Transport planners research and write reports, present travel and transport surveys, and write project funding bids. They use mathematical models, statistical analysis, computerised simulation models, travel surveys, and forecasting techniques. Understand the existing transport network, its strengths and weaknesses, and work to improve road transport function for the future, balancing environmental, economic and political factors in the process.

They usually participate in public consultations and may act as a witness at planning appeals and at public inquiries. Negotiate and liaise with councillors and politicians, planning and highways authorities, transport providers, engineers, developers, and also resident groups.

Work Details
Officially work a basic 40 hr week, Monday to Friday, but extra hours are commonly needed as deadlines approach. Usually you are office based, but there may be travel within the UK and abroad on site visits or to meetings. Occasional evening work may be required such as attendance at some council meetings or resident group meetings. Analysing details, presenting facts and writing reports is essential to this job. Sometimes you need to make unpopular decisions, which can be stressful.

Qualification
- **England, Wales and Northern Ireland**

Band 5: For degree courses: 2-3 A levels and some GCSEs (A*-C) usually including English and maths, or equivalent. Exact requirements depend on the degree you take.

- **Scotland**

Band 5: For degree courses: 3-5 H grades and some S grades (1-3), including English and maths, or similar qualifications. Exact requirements depend on the degree you take.

Degree Information
Any degree is acceptable for entry to this job though subjects such as transport management, urban planning, geography, environmental science, civil/structural engineering, maths, business studies, economics, social science, and geographical information systems, are usually preferred. A postgraduate qualification in transport planning is viewed favourably by many employers. Contact the Universities Transport Partnership for details.

Adult Qualifications
Some academic institutions have reduced entry requirements for mature applicants, check with individual universities/colleges for details. Most postgraduate courses are offered part time, lasting for up to five years.

Work Experience
Relevant voluntary work, previous paid or unpaid employment, or work shadowing in a planning department or highways authority, or a road transport consultancy, demonstrates your commitment to a prospective employer. Summer placement schemes of paid employment for 6-8 weeks are often available for undergraduates. The Transport Planning Society is able to offer advice on suitable work experience opportunities.

Entry and Training
Most enter with a first degree from a broad range of subjects, but employment prospects are increased with a specialist postgraduate degree in transport planning. First degree courses are full time or sandwich for four or five years. There are also relevant foundation degree courses that lead to a BSc/BA degree. Some local authorities and larger consultancies offer a graduate training programme that lasts around two years. Other employers offer on-the-job training covering a similar programme.

Most employers offer financial assistance for gaining a post-entry Masters qualification and time off to attend a day-release course. You can also work towards a professional qualification with chartered status from a relevant professional body, including the Royal Town Planning Institute, Chartered Institute of Logistics & Transport, Institution of Highways & Transportation (IHT), and the Institution of Civil Engineers. The Transport Planning Society (TPS) and IHT offer a transport planning professional (TPP) qualification and the TPS, with GoSkills, also offers work-based qualifications for alternative routes to incorporated or chartered status via S/NVQs in transport planning at levels 3 and 4.

Continuing professional development (CPD) is important for keeping up to date with the latest developments. The professional institutions and societies offer programmes of CPD that include workshops, conferences and short courses.

Experience in transport, town planning, urban design, logistics, engineering or environmental matters can be helpful. However, those who have gained chartered status from a relevant professional body or a Masters in transport planning, have an advantage. You may be able to receive funding (loans/bursaries) for postgraduate study from relevant professional associations.

Opportunities and Pay

Around 10,000 transport planners are employed throughout the UK in both public and private sectors, with larger consultancies, organisations and professional bodies tending to be based in major cities. The TPS is promoting opportunities to attract new people, as there is currently a shortage of qualified personnel to deal with the introduction of local transport plans. Opportunities are with local authorities, professional consulting planners and engineers, freight companies, regional transport executives, and central government and its agencies. There is also employment with universities and research organisations, strategic rail, maritime and aviation bodies, and with bus and train operating companies.

Promotion prospects are good but it may be necessary to move to a post in a different part of the country, unless working for a large organisation or consultancy. There may be opportunities to work on contracts abroad with some areas of employment.

Most start on a salary of around £20k a year, £23k for holders of a Masters degree. With experience, salaries can rise to around £60k, but senior transport planners can earn over £100k a year. Salaries tend to be higher in consultancies.

Skills and Qualities

aptitude for teamwork, good communication skills, good interpersonal skills, good presentation skills, IT skills, negotiating skills, objective, problem-solving skills, project management skills

Relevant Subjects

Business and accounting, Construction and built environment, Economics, English, Geography, Land and Environment, Mathematics, Science, Sociology

Further Information

AGCAS: Transport and Logistics (Job Sector Briefing) (AGCAS) - www.prospects.ac.uk

GoSkills - sector skills council for passenger transport - www.goskills.org

Local Transport Today (fortnightly) (Landor Publishing) - www.transportxtra.com/magazines/local_transport_today/

Logistics and Retail Management (2009) (Kogan Page) - www.koganpage.com

Skills for Logistics - sector skills council for freight logistics industries - www.skillsforlogistics.org

Transport Planning Opportunities - www.transportationopportunities.org.uk

Universities Transport Partnership (UTP) - www.utp.org.uk

Addresses

Chartered Institute of Logistics and Transport (CILTUK)
Careers Manager, Logistics & Transport Centre, Earlstrees Court, Earlstrees Road, Corby NN17 4AX
Phone: +44 (0)1536 740 100
Web: www.ciltuk.org.uk

Institute of Highway Incorporated Engineers (IHIE)
De Morgan House, 58 Russell Square, London WC1B 4HS
Phone: +44 (0)20 7436 7487
Web: www.ihie.org.uk

Institution of Civil Engineers (ICE)
1 Great George Street, Westminster, London SW1P 3AA
Phone: +44 (0)20 7222 7722
Web: www.ice.org.uk

Institution of Highways & Transportation
119 Britannia Walk, London N1 7JE
Phone: +44 (0)20 7336 1555
Web: www.iht.org

Royal Town Planning Institute (RTPI)
41 Botolph Lane, London EC3R 8DL
Phone: +44 (0)20 7929 9494
Web: www.rtpi.org.uk

Transport Planning Society (TPS)
1 Great George Street, London SW1P 3AA
Phone: +44 (0)20 7665 2238
Web: www.tps.org.uk

Similar Jobs

Engineer: Civil/Structural, Engineer: Municipal, Logistics Manager, Road Transport Manager, Surveyor: Planning & Development, Town Planner

Travel Agency Manager

CRCI:Leisure, Sport and Tourism
CLCI:GAX Job Band: 3 to 5

Job Description

Travel agency managers are responsible for the smooth and efficient running of an office for a travel group company, tour operator or an independent travel agent. Most planning is done from an office and only a few managers travel to check resorts and hotels. They arrange work rotas for agency staff and are responsible for their individual training and development. Managers have overall responsibility for the sale of tickets, reservations, finance and administration, and deal with any complaints. They may arrange specialist or individual itineraries, business travel or package holidays and can organise insurance, visas and foreign currency exchange. They work to achieve company sales targets, compile accounts and sales figures, and provide regular reports for head office management.

Work Details

Usually works a basic 37-39 hr week, either in an office/call centre or in a high-street travel agency. If working in leisure travel you may work Saturdays, but have time off during the week instead. If you work in a call centre you may work shifts that include evenings and weekends. In some posts, travel may occasionally be necessary to other countries. You advise customers about the best type of holiday for their needs, so you need to have a sound knowledge of what is available each year. If you are in corporate or group travel you may have to organise complicated itineraries to fit in with work schedules.

Work is often pressurised and may be more demanding at certain times of the year. You spend a lot of time on the phone, and use computer links to providers of the services that you require.

Qualification

- **England, Wales and Northern Ireland**

Band 3: For entry to jobs, HNC or a relevant Diploma, some employers require at least 4 GCSEs (A*-C), or equivalent. Useful subjects are English, maths, geography and a foreign language.

Band 4: For HND, Diploma of Higher Education or foundation degree: 1-2 A levels and some GCSEs (A*-C) usually including English and preferably maths, geography and a modern language, or equivalent.

Band 5: For degree courses: 2-3 A levels and some GCSEs (A*-C) preferably including English, maths and a modern language, or equivalent. Exact requirements depend on the degree you take.

- **Scotland**

Band 3: For entry to jobs, usually at least four S grades (1-3). including English or maths, or similar. Useful subjects are English, maths, geography and a foreign language.

Band 4: For entry to SQA higher national and professional development awards, usually 2-3 H grades and some S grades (1-3), including English and preferably maths, geography and a modern language, or similar.

Band 5: For degree courses: 3-5 H grades and some S grades (1-3) preferably including English, maths and a modern language, or similar qualifications. Exact requirements depend on the degree you take.

Degree Information

Graduates in any discipline may enter, but degrees in business, tourism/travel studies, or marketing may be preferred. Subjects that give useful background knowledge for this job include administration and leisure studies. It is possible to study for a postgraduate diploma in tourism.

Adult Qualifications

Entry requirements for courses may vary for adults. Direct entry to this job requires experience in business or retail management.

Work Experience

Employers may prefer candidates who have relevant work or voluntary experience. This can include retail experience, administration roles and different roles within the tourism or travel industry. Personal experience of travel is also a great advantage.

Entry and Training

Competition for places is keen and practical skills in business and management can often be considered more important than academic qualifications. Some travel agencies recruit graduates with retail experience and some large agencies have special training schemes for those with degrees or HND level qualifications. Many managers start as travel agents/consultants and gain promotion after experience.

Training is usually in-house and may lead to relevant S/NVQs at level 3 (supervisory) and 4 (management). Large companies run their own S/NVQ programmes. Other short external courses are available, such as those through the Institute of Travel and Tourism (ITT). A programme of continuous professional development (CPD) called the Accredited Travel Professional (ATP) scheme has been created by ABTA, in association with People 1st and the Institute for Travel and Tourism (ITT). There are three levels of membership, depending on your experience and qualifications in the industry. See the ATP website for further details.

There are relevant vocational qualifications that you can take such as the BTEC National Award in Travel and Tourism, which may give you an advantage. A Diploma/Welsh Baccalaureate may be available in your area in Travel and Tourism. Foundation degrees and Higher National Diplomas (HNDs) in travel and tourism are also available. Training programmes, including apprenticeship schemes in travel and tourism, may be available in your area. Many of the larger travel companies, e.g. First Choice, offer apprenticeship schemes for 16-24 year olds, leading to a People 1st apprenticeship framework certificate in travel and tourism services. Advanced apprenticeships leading to qualification at level 3 can also be a route into higher education. Contact People 1st for further details.

Mature applicants with relevant experience in customer care, retail sales, travel and business may be preferred by some agencies. Government training opportunities, such as apprenticeships in travel and tourism, may be available in your area. You can also gain recognition of previous experience through Accreditation of Prior Learning (APL) or by working towards relevant S/NVQs. Contact your local careers office, Jobcentre Plus, Next Step service or Learning and Skills Council (LSC) Local Enterprise Company (LEC) for details of training schemes.

Opportunities and Pay

Travel agencies are based in towns and cities throughout the UK. You are employed by a small independent firm or a high-street/nationwide chain. Business travel arrangements are generally made by phone, while leisure travel tends to be face to face with clients. Some organisations specialise in business or another type of travel, some sell holidays to the general public and some do both.

There is a decline in the number of high-street travel agencies due to the growth of online bookings. Most towns and cities have at least one travel agent. Many are small branches of large nationwide chains, with three or four agents/consultants and a manager. Promotion opportunities are generally better with larger organisations, but smaller companies may be able to offer a wide range of experience.

Pay varies according to the individual employer and depends on the amount of responsibility and experience that you have. Salaries are from £18k a year, rising to around £26k a year. Senior managers can earn up to £40k a year. Some companies pay commission and perks may include subsidised travel.

Skills and Qualities

able to cope under pressure, able to get on with all kinds of people, able to take responsibility, business awareness, friendly, good memory, IT skills, methodical, planning skills, self confident

Relevant Subjects

Business and accounting, Economics, English, Geography, ICT/Computer studies, Leisure, travel and tourism, Mathematics, Modern Foreign Languages

Further Information

ABTA Magazine (Absolute Publishing Ltd.) - www.abtamagazine.co.uk

Accredited Travel Professional (ATP) - www.a-t-p.org.uk

AGCAS: Tourism (Job Sector Briefing) (AGCAS) - www.prospects.ac.uk

Apprenticeship Schemes (National Apprenticeship Service) - www.apprenticeships.org.uk

Diplomas (Foundation, Higher and Advanced) - http://yp.direct.gov.uk/diplomas

People 1st - sector skills council for hospitality, leisure, travel and tourism - www.people1st.co.uk

The Diploma in Travel and Tourism - www.tandtdiploma.co.uk

UKSP - Guide to Success in Hospitality, Leisure, Travel & Tourism - www.uksp.co.uk/

Addresses

Association of British Travel Agents (ABTA)
30 Park Street, London SE1 9EQ
Web: www.abta.com

First Choice Holidays
HR Direct, Jetset House, Lowfield Heath, Crawley,
West Sussex RH11 0PQ
Phone: 0800 169 5692 (UK only)
Web: www.firstchoice4jobs.co.uk

Guild of Travel Management Companies
GTMC Euston Fitzrovia 85 Tottenham Court Road,
London W1T 4TQ
Phone: +44 (0)20 7268 3540
Web: www.gtmc.org

Institute of Travel and Tourism (ITT)
PO Box 217, Ware, Hertfordshire SG12 8WY
Phone: +44 (0)844 4995 653
Web: www.itt.co.uk

Similar Jobs

Manager, Retail Manager, Tour Operator, Travel Consultant

Travel Consultant

CRCI:Leisure, Sport and Tourism
CLCI:GAX   Job Band: 2 to 3

Job Description

Travel consultants advise customers and make arrangements for holidays, or for specialist or business travel. Work may involve selling holidays at a shop counter, processing bookings behind the scenes, or both. They give information, quote fares and suggest routes, tours, etc. Consultants check availability of flights and hotel bookings using a computer. Also advise customers on health requirements such as vaccinations, and give information on passports, visas and insurance schemes.

Some agents work face-to-face with customers in an agency. Others work in an office or call centre and make travel arrangements or give advice over the telephone. Consultants also handle correspondence, and issue tickets and documents. May also provide foreign currency and travellers cheques. In business travel, complicated schedules to fit in with meetings in different destinations have to be arranged.

Work Details

Most travel consultants work a basic 39 hr week, either in an office/call centre or in a high-street travel agency. If working in leisure travel, you are expected to work Saturdays, but have time off during the week instead. If you work in a call centre you work shifts that include evenings and weekends. You need a sound knowledge of the different types of holiday available each year, as you are asked for advice by your customers.

Most consultants now use computers and you need to be careful to enter the correct information when taking bookings. You may also handle money and credit/debit card transactions. Work involves spending a lot of time on the phone and can be hectic. Part-time work is possible. You may need to wear a uniform.

Qualification

• England, Wales and Northern Ireland

Band 2: For entry to jobs, no minimum qualifications are needed, but it is an advantage to have some GCSEs (A*-C) or equivalent in subjects that include English, maths and geography.

Band 3: For entry to jobs, HNC or a relevant Diploma, usually at least 4 GCSEs are expected. Useful subjects are English, maths, geography and a foreign language, or equivalent.

• Scotland

Band 2: Although academic qualifications are not specified for this job, it is an advantage to have some S grades (1-3) in subjects that include English, maths and geography.

Band 3: For entry to jobs, usually at least four S grades (1-3). Useful subjects are English, maths, geography and a foreign language.

Adult Qualifications

Most employees begin their careers in this industry as young junior clerks, but there are still some opportunities for adults. Experience of office work or sales is an advantage. Adults are often accepted onto travel and tourism courses without the usual minimum qualifications.

Work Experience

Any work experience can equip you with skills that you can use in the future and add to your CV. Work experience can either be unpaid or voluntary, or can be holiday or part-time work that you have organised yourself. This includes retail experience, administration and customer service. Wide experience of personal travel is also a great advantage.

Entry and Training

There are no set entry and training requirements. It is an advantage to have experience of using computers, or in reception or secretarial work. It is also useful to have some knowledge of foreign languages and travel. Travel agencies provide in-house training, which may involve taking short external courses, such as those through the Institute of Travel and Tourism (ITT). Large companies run their own S/NVQ programmes such as in travel and tourism services at levels 2-3.

A Diploma/Welsh Baccalaureate may be available in your area in Travel and Tourism. Foundation degrees and Higher National Diplomas (HNDs) in travel and tourism are also available. Training programmes, including apprenticeship schemes in travel and tourism, may be available in your area. Many of the larger organisations, e.g. First Choice, offer apprenticeship schemes for 16-24 year olds, leading to a People 1st apprenticeship framework certificate in travel and tourism services. Advanced apprenticeships leading to qualification at level 3 can also be a route into higher education. Contact People 1st for further details.

The ITT, ABTA and People 1st jointly run a scheme of continuing professional development (CPD) called the Accredited Travel Professional Scheme (ATP). See the ATP website for details. Relevant self-study courses are available through the International Air Transport Association (IATA), such as the IATA Global Distribution Systems Fares and Ticketing Course. IATA also run a travel and tourism training programme for consultants, leading to a Diploma in Travel and Tourism Consulting. Check the IATA website for details.

Mature applicants with relevant experience in travel, customer care, retail sales and in business, may be preferred by some agencies. You may benefit through government training opportunities such as apprenticeship schemes that may be available in your area. Government training opportunities, such as apprenticeships in travel and tourism, may be available in your area. You can also gain recognition of previous experience through Accreditation of Prior Learning (APL) or by working towards relevant S/NVQs. Contact your local careers office, Jobcentre Plus, Next Step service or Learning and Skills Council (LSC) Local Enterprise Company (LEC) for details of training schemes.

Opportunities and Pay

Travel agencies are based in towns and cities throughout the UK. You are employed by a small independent firm or a high-street/nationwide chain. Some organisations specialise in business or another type of travel, some sell holidays to the general public and some do both. There is a decline in the number of high-street travel agencies. This is due to increased Internet use and direct bookings. There may be opportunities to work from home, liaising with specific clients to arrange bespoke itineraries.

Promotion to management level from junior jobs is possible and depends on experience, qualifications and merit; opportunities are generally better in larger organisations. It is possible to move to different areas of work within the travel and tourism industry, such as work as a travel courier, resort representative, or work in a tourist information centre.

Your pay varies according to the individual employer. As a junior consultant you are likely to earn around £11k-£16k a year rising to around £20k a year. Some may earn around £25k, depending on the level of responsibility. It is not unusual for consultants to be paid commission and receive bonuses for achieving targets. Perks may also include subsidised travel.

Skills and Qualities
attention to detail, conscientious, efficient, good communication skills, good memory, good telephone manner, helpful, IT skills, patient, responsible attitude

Relevant Subjects
Business and accounting, English, Geography, ICT/Computer studies, Leisure, travel and tourism, Modern Foreign Languages

Further Information
ABTA Magazine (Absolute Publishing Ltd.) - www.abtamagazine.co.uk

Accredited Travel Professional (ATP) (Accredited Travel Professional) - www.a-t-p.org.uk

Apprenticeship Schemes (National Apprenticeship Service) - www.apprenticeships.org.uk

Diplomas (Foundation, Higher and Advanced) - http://yp.direct.gov.uk/diplomas

International Air Transport Association (IATA) - http://iata.co.uk/

People 1st - sector skills council for hospitality, leisure, travel and tourism - www.people1st.co.uk

The Diploma in Travel and Tourism - www.tandtdiploma.co.uk

Training Schemes - www.direct.gov.uk/en/educationandlearning

▶Working in retail & customer services (2008) (Babcock Lifeskills) - www.babcock-lifeskills.com/

▶Working in travel & tourism (2010) (Babcock Lifeskills) - www.babcock-lifeskills.com/

Addresses
Association of British Travel Agents (ABTA)
30 Park Street, London SE1 9EQ
Web: www.abta.com

First Choice Holidays
HR Direct, Jetset House, Lowfield Heath, Crawley, West Sussex RH11 0PQ
Phone: 0800 169 5692 (UK only)
Web: www.firstchoice4jobs.co.uk

Institute of Travel and Tourism (ITT)
PO Box 217, Ware, Hertfordshire SG12 8WY
Phone: +44 (0)844 4995 653
Web: www.itt.co.uk

Similar Jobs
Airport Information Assistant, Customer Services Adviser, Tour Operator, Tourist Information Centre Assistant, Travel Agency Manager

Tree Surgeon
also known as: Arboricultural Worker, Arborist Craftsperson

CRCI:Environment, Animals and Plants

CLCI:WAF Job Band: 1 to 2

Job Description
Tree surgeons inspect, diagnose, treat and care for established trees as well as removing damaged trees. They examine a tree to assess its condition and determine appropriate treatment. May remove damaged or diseased trees or sections. Also use chemical sprays to control any disease or pests and prune trees to improve appearance and reduce hazards eg branches over a road. Tree surgeons develop tree care and maintenance programmes. They may work in public parks and gardens, private gardens and also in the agricultural sector caring for commercial trees, such as fruit trees. Can also operate as a climber or ground staff.

Those working at ground level must clear the area as quickly as possible and also ensure the climber is working safely, out of the way of overhead power lines and keeping the ropes away from the chainsaw. Tree surgeons are aware of the laws surrounding their working practice, such as observing tree preservation orders, and health and safety.

Work Details
Working hours are around 35-40 a week, but are variable depending on your employer, contract and the location of the job. You are likely to work from 7.30-8.00am to 4.30-5pm; Monday to Friday, with some weekend working. Travelling a long distance is not uncommon whether you are self-employed or not, so your day may start early and finish late. Emergency work, such as dealing with dangerous, fallen trees during and after stormy weather or those causing road blockages, may involve out-of-hours work, at night and at weekends.

Work is done mostly in parks, woods, public and private gardens, at the roadside or in forests. You climb trees with the use of a safety harness to prune them and also work with a chainsaw. Good mobility and agility is an important factor with most of the work. It can be physically demanding and noisy work depending on the nature of the task, especially for junior/trainee positions. Safety regulations must be observed at all times. The work can sometimes be hazardous and you must be aware of falling branches/trees. A hard hat, gloves and protective clothing are usually provided.

Qualification
• England, Wales and Northern Ireland
Band 1: For entry to jobs, no minimum qualifications are needed, but you are expected to have a good level of general education and relevant experience. Some formal/vocational qualifications at any level are useful.

Band 2: For entry to jobs, no minimum qualifications are needed, but it is an advantage to have some GCSEs (A*-C) or equivalent in subjects that include English and maths.

• Scotland
Band 1: For entry to jobs, no minimum qualifications are needed, but you are expected to have a good level of general education and relevant experience. Some formal/vocational qualifications at any level are useful.

Band 2: Although academic qualifications are not specified for this job, it is an advantage to have some S grades (1-3) in subjects that include English and maths, or similar.

Adult Qualifications
For entry to many jobs at this level, no formal qualifications are required. Subjects such as English, maths and biology or practical subjects are useful, though not usually specified.

Work Experience
Employers may prefer candidates who have relevant work or voluntary experience, such as practical work in a garden centre, a horticultural nursery, on a farm, or in grounds maintenance. It is sometimes difficult to gain practical experience with a professional arboriculturalist because of the nature of some tasks and the implications for health and safety, but observation is still useful. However, climbing and rope skills are an advantage.

Entry and Training
It is possible to begin working as a tree surgeon without formal qualifications, usually assisting qualified professionals. However, a National Proficiency Tests Council (NPTC)/Scottish Skills Testing Service (SSTS) certificate of competence is required by law to be able to use a chainsaw and other tree equipment. Courses, such as

tree climbing, tree pruning and felling are also available. Many tree surgeons also train as general horticulturists and at some stage may decide to specialise. There is a growing range of qualifications at various levels available to people wanting to start (and progress) a career in arboriculture (for more details see job article: Arboriculturist).

Appropriate part and full-time BTEC/SQA courses are available at a number of colleges. There are only a few specialist arboriculture courses, but a number of agriculture, horticulture and forestry courses have options in arboriculture. In addition to college-based courses, the Royal Horticultural Society (RHS) also offers a number of short courses, the Arboricultural Association awards a technician's certificate (level 3) and the Royal Forestry Society offers a certificate in arboriculture..

Appropriate S/NVQs are available at levels 1-3 in subjects that include arboriculture and in forestry. A Diploma/Welsh Baccalaureate may be available in your area in environment and land-based studies. Relevant training programmes, including apprenticeship schemes, may be available in your area. Advanced apprenticeships leading to qualification at level 3 can also be a route into higher education.

Climbing and rope skills are an advantage for this job. Mature applicants can benefit through government training opportunities that may be available in your area. You can gain recognition of previous experience through Accreditation of Prior Learning (APL) or by working towards relevant S/NVQs. Contact your local Connexions or careers office, Jobcentre Plus, Next Step service or Learning and Skills Council (LSC)/Local Enterprise Company (LEC) for details of all training opportunities and schemes, including apprenticeships for adults.

Opportunities and Pay

This is an expanding industry throughout the UK, but competition for posts is keen. There is a great demand for people who specialise in climbing. Most tree surgeons work for specialist contractors who carry out work for local authorities, utility companies or public bodies. There are some opportunities with large landscape and garden centres, national parks, private estates and woodland contractors. In Scotland, the job is usually combined with forestry and landscaping. With experience and/or higher qualifications, some may progress to supervisory or management posts with larger employers, or may qualify as a professional arboriculturist.

Some experienced tree surgeons become self-employed and set up their own company or consultancy. Overseas opportunities for trained tree surgeons occur in countries such as Germany, America, Australia and New Zealand.

Salaries start at around £11k-£13k and with experience can rise to around £14k-£18k a year. A person in a senior position can earn around £25k-£26k a year.

Health

Fitness and mobility are important for this job and you must have a good head for heights and not suffer from vertigo.

Skills and Qualities

agile, aptitude for teamwork, enjoy working outdoors, good co-ordination, good spoken communication, head for heights, methodical, practical skills, quick reactions, safety conscious

Relevant Subjects

Biology, Land and Environment, Science

Further Information

Arboricultural Journal (Aboricultural Association) - www.trees.org.uk

Diplomas (Foundation, Higher and Advanced) - http://yp.direct.gov.uk/diplomas

Jobs and the Natural Heritage (leaflet) (Scottish Natural Heritage) - www.snh.org.uk/

Lantra - The Sector Skills Council for environmental & land-based sector - http:/www.lantra.co.uk

Lantra Careers (A Future In...) - www.afuturein.com

Real Life Guide to Working Outdoors (Trotman) - www.trotman.co.uk

Treeline (International Society of Arboriculture) - www.isa-arboriculture.org

Addresses

Arboricultural Association
Ullenwood Court, Ullenwood, Cheltenham GL53 9QS
Phone: +44 (0)1242 522152
Web: www.trees.org.uk

National Proficiency Test Council (NPTC)
City & Guilds Land Based Services Building 500 Abbey Park, Stareton, Warwickshire CV8 2LY
Phone: +44 (0) 24 7685 7300
Web: www.nptc.org.uk

Royal Forestry Society (RFS)
102 High Street, Tring, Hertfordshire HP23 4AF
Phone: +44 (0)1442 822 028
Web: www.rfs.org.uk

Royal Horticultural Society (RHS)
80 Vincent Square, London SW1P 2PE
Phone: 0845 260 5000 (UK only)
Web: www.rhs.org.uk

Scottish Skills Testing Service
Young Farmers Centre, Ingliston, Edinburgh EH28 8NE
Phone: +44 (0)131 333 2040
Web: www.sayfc.org/ssts/

Similar Jobs

Arboriculturist, Countryside Ranger, Forest Worker, Gardener, Groundsman/Groundswoman, Horticultural Worker: Commercial

Trichologist

CRCI:Healthcare
CLCI:IL Job Band: 2 to 4

Job Description

Trichologists use scientific techniques to diagnose disorders and diseases of the hair or scalp, such as damaged or thinning hair, skin irritations, infections and diseases. Examine a client's hair and scalp. They discuss hair care, medical history, medication and diet. Commonly request blood tests either directly or through a client's GP. If appropriate, trichologists prescribe treatment, which involves applying lotions, head massage, or sometimes electrical/light treatment. May advise clients on the type of shampoo to use or make recommendations about changes to their diet. A client may require only one consultation or treatment over a longer period.

Work Details

You mostly work a standard week of 9am-5pm, Monday to Friday, but this can be flexible. As well as working in clinics, trichologists also work in research laboratories, or teach on trichology courses. Some may have a consulting room in their home, and be self-employed. You help people who may be upset and who need support and guidance. Sometimes you examine skin diseases, which can be contagious. Protective gloves may be worn during an examination.

Qualification

- **England, Wales and Northern Ireland**

Band 2: Although academic qualifications are not specified for this job, it is an advantage to have some GCSEs (A*-C) in subjects that include English, maths and a science, or equivalent. Chemistry, physics, human biology, or equivalent, are an advantage as trichology courses have scientific modules.

Band 3: For entry to courses: usually at least 4 GCSEs (A*-C) including English, maths and a science, or equivalent.

Band 4: For entry to relevant higher education courses: 1-2 A levels and some GCSEs (A*-C) usually including maths, English, and a science, such as chemistry, physics, human biology, or equivalent.

- **Scotland**

Band 2: Although academic qualifications are not specified for this job, it is an advantage to have some S grades (1-3) in subjects that include maths, English and a science. Chemistry, physics, human biology, or similar, are an advantage as trichology courses have scientific modules.

Band 3: For entry to courses: usually at least four S grades (1-3) in subjects such as maths, English, and a science. Chemistry, physics, human biology, or similar, are an advantage due to the scientific content of many trichology course modules.

Band 4: For entry to relevant higher education courses: two H grades or similar and a minimum of four S grades (1-3) including maths, English, and a science, such as chemistry, physics, human biology, or similar.

Adult Qualifications

Mature applicants without appropriate academic qualifications are usually required to supply a curriculum vitae (CV) and provide evidence of an ability to complete the course. Useful relevant qualifications include those from medical-related professions (particularly nursing or the caring professions). Sometimes it may also be necessary to attend an interview.

Work Experience

Work experience gives you an insight into what you enjoy about a job or working environment, and the opportunity to acquire new skills. It provides valuable information to add to your CV and improves your employment prospects. Work experience with a trichologist is usually very hard to gain, due to the confidential nature of the work. It improves your chances at interview if you have some relevant work experience that can develop your skills in biological science, or your awareness of healthcare and beauty issues. Work in hairdressing can also be helpful. It may be useful to contact a professional trichologist to discuss their role and career route.

Entry and Training

The main training and qualifying body for aspiring professional trichologists in the UK, and the professional association for qualified trichologists, is the Institute of Trichologists. The Institute offers a two-year distance-learning course leading to associate membership. The course is accompanied by compulsory clinical training in college one day a month and progression is through examinations and assignments. A further two years of both practice (under mentor guidance), study and a thesis, is required to obtain full membership. Whilst there is generally no exemption from the full course, exception is given for scientific researchers or medical professionals who have specialised in the hair and scalp.

The Institute also operates a code of professional practice and ethics for its members and holds a list of qualified professionals in the UK and worldwide.

The Trichological Society also offers professional qualification through distance learning that takes two to four years, though this can be extended. High proportions of students already have a medical/scientific first degree and usually take less time to qualify. Successful students are awarded the Society's diploma in pure trichology after a period of examination, practical study (24 working days), observation (minimum ten hours) and a final year dissertation.

You are expected to follow a programme of continuing professional development (CPD) throughout your career.

Mature entrants are welcomed though this profession is still quite small and there are few vacancies for training. A medical/science background is an advantage.

Opportunities and Pay

This is a very small profession and there are not many jobs available. You can work for a clinic attached to a hairdressing salon, but most trichologists are self-employed in private practice. This means that you have to be responsible for the administration of your own business. There are a few research jobs for manufacturers of hair products.

Initial earnings are likely to be low. During the time it takes to build up a client list, most trichologists have to do other work to support themselves. Salaries depend on the location of the practice, demand and promotion. A trichologist with five years' experience and an established patient list earns around £35k a year. Successful and self-employed trichologists can earn significantly more than this.

Health

There is a risk of allergy from skin irritants.

Skills and Qualities

able to put people at ease, friendly, good listening skills, observant, patient, scientific approach, smart appearance, sympathetic, tactful

Relevant Subjects

Biology, Chemistry, Physics, Science

Addresses

Institute of Trichologists
Ground Floor, Office 24, Langroyd Road, London SW17 7PL
Phone: +44 (0) 845 604 4657
Web: www.trichologists.org.uk

Trichological Society
1 Kings Mews, Bloomsbury, London WC1N 2JA
Phone: +44 (0)870 7666 996
Web: www.hairscientists.org

Similar Jobs

Beauty Therapist, Hairdresser, Wig Maker

Upholsterer

CRCI:Manufacturing and Production
CLCI:SAJ　　Job Band: 1 to 2

Job Description

Upholsterers cover furniture frames such as chairs, sofas or bed heads with padding and fabric. There are two types of upholsterer - a production upholsterer and a craft upholsterer. In production, may work with new furniture using pre-cut materials, and concentrate on a particular task, such as working on the arms. Can also work to complete the whole item. Craft upholsterers are highly skilled and may work on new, old and antique furniture, using a variety of specialist tools and materials.

Craft upholsterers make detailed notes/diagrams of the item and sometimes take photographs of the original piece to ensure that the refurbished item matches the original style and shape. They prepare the pattern and select and cut the material to be used. They fix springs, webbing and wadding pads to the frame, using hand or power tools, such as staple guns, glue guns, cutters and upholstery needles.

Lining and top material is attached by stitching, tacking and glueing. May add castors, trimmings, etc. Sometimes repairs are carried out, which involves stripping off old upholstery first. May also give advice, including the selection of a fabric, or be required to provide an estimate of the cost of a job.

Work Details
Upholsterers usually work a 35-40 hr week; Monday to Friday. The working hours may vary and some evening or weekend work may be required. Work is in industrial premises, a traditional craft workshop/studio, or possibly at home. The work requires a high degree of accuracy. Some environments may be noisy and dusty. You have to cope with some physical activity, including kneeling and lifting. You are likely to wear protective clothing such as overalls, a mask and gloves. If you are self-employed you may need to travel around an area and need a driving licence.

Qualification
- **England, Wales and Northern Ireland**

Band 1: No minimum qualifications are required, but you are expected to have a good level of general education. However, some formal/vocational qualifications at any level are useful.

Band 2: Although academic qualifications are not specified for this job, it is an advantage to have some GCSEs (A*-C) in subjects that include English, design technology and maths, or equivalent.

- **Scotland**

Band 1: No minimum qualifications are required, but you are expected to have a good level of general education. However, some formal/vocational qualifications at any level are useful.

Band 2: Although academic qualifications are not specified for this job, it is an advantage to have some S grades (1-3) in subjects that include English, technology and maths, or similar.

Adult Qualifications
No minimum educational qualifications are required though you may be asked to take a practical test. Some level of formal qualifications is an advantage. There are furniture restoration courses specifically designed for adults.

Work Experience
Relevant work or voluntary experience is always useful. It can improve your chances when applying for jobs or apprenticeships. Your personal or adult guidance adviser should be able to advise you about how to get some work experience.

Entry and Training
To enter this job you may have to demonstrate practical ability. Training is usually on the job with an experienced upholsterer. This can be combined with a college day-release course. City & Guilds offers a range of courses in creative techniques in upholstery at levels 1-3. You can also complete NVQs in making and installing furniture (level 2), and NVQ level 3 in making and installing production furniture and in making and repairing hand-crafted furniture and furnishings. These NVQs include upholstery modules.

The Association of Master Upholsterers & Soft Furnishers runs training courses for professionals, leading to qualifications that they have developed in association with Proskills, the sector skills council.

Training programmes, including apprenticeship schemes, may be available in your area. Advanced apprenticeships leading to qualification at level 3 can also be a route into higher education. A Diploma/Welsh Baccalaureate in manufacturing and product design may be available in your area. This may be relevant for entry to this work.

Government training opportunities, such as apprenticeships, may be available in your area. You can also gain recognition of previous experience through Accreditation of Prior Learning (APL) or by working towards relevant S/NVQs. Contact your local careers office, Jobcentre Plus, Next Step service or Learning and Skills Council (LSC) Local Enterprise Company (LEC) for details of training schemes.

Opportunities and Pay
There are opportunities throughout the UK with furniture manufacturers or a traditional craft workshop/studio. Many upholsterers work for, or in partnership with, antique dealers, furniture restorers, or interior decorators. With experience you can specialise in one type of furniture, such as antique furniture. You can become self-employed once you are fully trained. There is a shortage of skilled upholsterers. This job can be done from home and there are some opportunities for part-time work.

A trainee is likely to start on around £12k a year, rising to around £20k with experience. Some may earn around £30k, and the most skilled and successful upholsterers can earn more. Your income may be increased with overtime payments and bonuses.

Health
This job requires good general fitness. There may be an allergy risk from dust. Normal colour vision is required.

Skills and Qualities
able to work quickly, accurate, attention to detail, eye for shape/colour, good concentration level, manual dexterity, neat, numeracy skills, patient, strong

Relevant Subjects
Art and Design, Design and technology

Further Information
Apprenticeship Schemes (National Apprenticeship Service) - www.apprenticeships.org.uk

Diplomas (Foundation, Higher and Advanced) - http://yp.direct.gov.uk/diplomas

Proskills UK - sector skills council for process and manufacturing industries - www.proskills.co.uk

The Strippers and Stuffers Gazette (annual) (Guild of Traditional Upholsterers) - www.gtu.org.uk/publications.html

Training Schemes - www.direct.gov.uk/en/educationandlearning

Welsh Baccalaureate - www.wbq.org.uk

Addresses
Association of Master Upholsterers & Soft Furnishers
Francis Vaughan House, Q1 Capital Point Business Centre,
Capital Business Park Parkway, Cardiff CF3 2PU
Phone: +44 (0)292 077 8918
Web: www.upholsterers.co.uk

Guild of Traditional Upholsterers
Feathers Barn, Cox Park, Gunnislake, Cornwall PL18 9BB
Web: www.gtu.org.uk

Similar Jobs
Clothing Pattern Cutter/Grader, Conservator-Restorer, Furniture Polisher/Finisher, Interior Designer, Leather Worker, Saddler, Sewing Machinist

Van Driver: Sales
CRCI:Retail Sales and Customer Services
CLCI:OM Job Band: 1 to 2

Job Description
Sales van drivers drive a van around an area to sell and deliver goods, stopping at certain places so that customers can buy items such as milk, fish, groceries, fruit and vegetables or meat. This is an essential service in rural and remote areas and also for people who are unable to get to shops easily. Van drivers also work in fast food, delivering burgers, kebabs, hot dogs, ice-cream or fish and chips. They often tour housing estates or stop in a lay-by near to a major road. May have a regular pitch where they park and sell from, or a regular round. May also attend events, such as open-air concerts and festivals.

Drivers stock the van, take orders and collect money. They need to keep accounts and make out bills. They also keep a note of everything that has been sold and maintain stock control. May be responsible for cleaning and maintaining the van.

Work Details

Usually work a basic 40 hr week, but may need to work irregular hours, involving early starts, evenings and weekends. Legal limits of no more than ten driving hours a day apply to van drivers. In some jobs, such as milk delivery, you have to start work very early in the morning. Some employers may operate a piecework system of working, so that drivers can finish work when all their deliveries are completed. You need to spend some time at home completing accounts and paperwork. This job requires you to be out in all sorts of weather. There may be some heavy lifting. You may need to wear an overall or a uniform.

Qualification

• England, Wales and Northern Ireland

Band 1: You do not need qualifications, though some employers may give a test in basic maths and English.

Band 2: Employers may ask for some GCSEs (A*-C) preferably including English and maths, or equivalent. These qualifications may also be required for entry to some courses.

• Scotland

Band 1: You do not need qualifications, though some employers may give a test in basic maths and English.

Band 2: Employers may ask for some S grades (1-3) preferably including English and maths, or similar. These qualifications may also be required for entry to some courses.

Adult Qualifications

You do not need formal qualifications for this job, though employers may expect a good standard of education and an ability in English and maths.

Work Experience

Relevant work or voluntary experience is always useful and can improve your chances when applying for entry to jobs in sales. It can equip you with skills that you can use in the future and add to your CV. Part-time and holiday employment in a wide range of shops is usually fairly easy to obtain.

Entry and Training

It helps your chances of entry if you are competent at driving and have experience of selling goods. Most van drivers receive on-the-job training, working with an experienced driver. You must have a clean driving licence and be at least 18 to sit a test for a Category C1 licence to drive light goods vehicles (LGV). Because of the high cost of insurance, most employers prefer people over 21, or even 25. The Young LGV Driver Scheme, managed by Skills for Logistics, allows a young person to obtain a full Category C driving licence at the age of 18 instead of 21, and a Category C+E licence before the age of 21. You must also pass the Driver Certificate of Professional Competence (CPC), designed to improve the knowledge and skills of professional LGV drivers.

Appropriate S/NVQs are available at levels 1-3, such as driving goods vehicles at levels 2 & 3, or carry and deliver goods at level 2. Training programmes, including apprenticeships leading to level 2 and advanced apprenticeships leading to level 3, may be available in your area. Contact Skills for Logistics for details of all relevant training opportunities.

Mature applicants over the age of 25 may be preferred because insurance premiums are lower. Any sort of driving experience, or experience in sales or in running a small business is useful.

Opportunities and Pay

Jobs that involve a lot of selling may pay more than delivery work. You can have your own van and be self-employed. Some companies ask drivers to take out a franchise, which requires you to put some money in the business, possibly several thousands of pounds. You might also have to buy your own van or equipment. Some drivers move into related areas of transport or retail and others may progress to administrative, supervisory and management posts.

For most drivers, pay varies depending on how much you sell and if working full time. A starting salary is around £10k-£15k, rising to around £18k a year. High earners can make around £22k a year.

Health

You have to be quite fit for this job.

Skills and Qualities

able to work well on your own, basic understanding of vehicle maintenance, business awareness, cash handling skills, efficient record keeping, health & safety awareness, reliable, self-motivated, trustworthy

Relevant Subjects

Retail and distribution

Further Information

Apprenticeship Schemes (National Apprenticeship Service) - www.apprenticeships.org.uk

Foundation Learning (QCDA) - www.qcda.gov.uk

Skills for Logistics - sector skills council for freight logistics industries - www.skillsforlogistics.org

▶Working in retail & customer services (2008) (Babcock Lifeskills) - www.babcock-lifeskills.com/

Similar Jobs

Driver: Bus, Driver: Lorry, Driver: Van, Market Stall Trader, Postal Worker

Vehicle Body Refinisher

also known as: Car Spray Painter, Paint Technician: Vehicles

CRCI:Engineering

CLCI:RON Job Band: 1 to 2

Job Description

Vehicle body refinishers apply a paint finish to damaged vehicles, such as car body panels, and then apply a protective material or varnish. They work on vehicles that have been first repaired by a vehicle body repairer by preparing the surface, masking areas not to be sprayed and mixing paint to match. Refinishers may use a computerised system to mix and match the exact colour of paint required. Then they spray the object using a machine or hand-held spray gun.

They also smooth and polish the surfaces between coats of paint and clean and adjust equipment. Also touch up paintwork after machine spraying and apply trims and replace fittings.

Work Details

Usually work a basic 39 hour week, though may also work shifts and some Saturday mornings. You work in a workshop, sometimes in a ventilated paint spraying booth and may need to cope with standing for many hours with some lifting, kneeling, bending down and possibly climbing ladders. You are responsible for careful work. The workplace can be smelly with unpleasant fumes, so you need to wear a face mask, overalls and possibly gloves and goggles.

Qualification

• England, Wales and Northern Ireland

Band 1: For entry to jobs, no minimum qualifications are needed, but you are expected to have a good level of general education and relevant experience. Some formal/vocational qualifications at any level in maths, sciences and technical subjects are an advantage.

Band 2: For entry to jobs, no minimum qualifications are needed, but it is an advantage to have some GCSEs (A*-C) or equivalent in subjects that include English and maths, and a science, technology or engineering subject, or equivalent.

• Scotland

Band 1: For entry to jobs, no minimum qualifications are needed, but you are expected to have a good level of general education and relevant experience. Some formal/vocational qualifications at any level are useful.

Band 2: Although no formal entry requirements are specified, many employers prefer applicants to have some S grades (1-3) in English and maths, and a science, technical or engineering subject, or similar.

Adult Qualifications

Good secondary education is often expected and some relevant practical experience, particularly in the motor trade, is useful. Specific entry requirements for courses may be relaxed for mature applicants. You can improve your skills and qualifications by working through the Foundation Learning programme. This involves taking credit-based units and qualifications to help you progress.

Work Experience

Relevant work or voluntary experience is always useful. It can add to your CV and improve your chances when applying for entry to jobs or apprenticeships in the engineering industry. Any practical experience in the motor industry gives you an advantage.

Entry and Training

Many trainees start at age 16-19 on a training programme or apprenticeship in vehicle body and paint operations. You usually train on the job, working with an experienced person, together with day or block release to a local college. Most work towards S/NVQs in vehicle body and paint operations at levels 2-3. You can also study full time for a relevant BTEC/SQA award prior to employment. This job may require a driving licence and you may have to pass a practical aptitude entrance test. National training providers of apprenticeships, and automotive training and qualifications include the training arm of the Retail Motor Industry Federation, ReMIT, and Thatcham. See their websites for details.

The Institute of the Motor Industry (IMI) also offers nationally recognised vocationally related qualifications (VRQs) at levels 2-3 for those wishing to progress to technician level and beyond to higher education. VRQs at level 1 are also available as a pre-apprenticeship programme for school pupils aged 14-16 and provides the opportunity to 'fast track' onto higher level motor industry qualifications.

The IMI has also developed Autocity, a useful and informative website on careers in the motor industry. There is a section on body repair that covers the roles of paint technician and senior paint technician. Information is provided on qualifications, progression routes and industry links. Visit the website for more information.

Thatcham is a leading provider in skills training for crash repairs and now offers specific apprenticeships through the Thatcham Apprentice Programme. The vehicle body paint technician apprenticeship lasts for three years and consists of twelve modules. Thatcham has an online jobshop facility for candidates looking to secure an apprenticeship. Jobshop registration is free and applicant details are made available to hundreds of bodyshops and repair centres across the UK.

Automotive Technical Accreditation (ATA) is a voluntary programme that assesses the current competence of individuals working in the retail motor trade. They assess paint technicians at both technician and senior technician level. Check the IMI or the ATA websites for details. The Vehicle Builders and Repairers Association also has details of training courses and industry news on their website.

Mature applicants can take refresher courses that may be available for those returning to work and there may be special training schemes in some areas. Employers may take older applicants who show aptitude and have previous related experience. Government training opportunities, such as apprenticeships, may be available in your area. You can also gain recognition of previous experience through Accreditation of Prior Learning (APL) or by working towards relevant S/NVQs. Contact your local careers office, Jobcentre Plus, Next Step service or Learning and Skills Council (LSC) Local Enterprise Company (LEC) for details of training schemes, including apprenticeships for adults.

Opportunities and Pay

Jobs are located throughout the UK and mainly in towns and cities. Employment is with motor vehicle retail dealers, a local garage or coachbuilder. Other employers include a wide range of firms with fleet vehicles. These can include public utilities, local and central government, road hauliers, supermarket chains and coach and bus service operators. With experience you can progress to supervisor level jobs.

Pay varies depending on area and employer. A trainee paint technician earns between £7k-£13k a year; when skilled/qualified this rises to around £19k a year. The most skilled and experienced workers can earn up to £30k a year. Overtime may be available.

Health

You should have no skin problems and no breathing problems as there may be a risk of allergic reaction. Normal colour vision is required as is good stamina and physical fitness.

Skills and Qualities

able to work well on your own, attention to detail, careful, good concentration level, good co-ordination, patient, steady hand, strong hands

Further Information

Apprenticeship Schemes (National Apprenticeship Service) - www.apprenticeships.org.uk

Autocity (IMI) - http://autocity.org.uk

Automotive Technician Accreditation (ATA) (Institute of the Motor Industry) - www.automotivetechnician.org.uk

BODY (monthly) (Vehicle Body Repairer's Association (VBRA)) - www.bodymag.co.uk/

Institute of the Motor Industry (IMI) - sector skills council for the motor industry - www.motor.org.uk

Motor Industry Magazine (monthly) (Institute of the Motor Industry (IMI)) - www.motor.org.uk/magazine/index.html

remit - www.remit.co.uk

Thatcham - www.thatcham.org

Training Schemes - www.direct.gov.uk/en/educationandlearning

Addresses

Vehicle Builders & Repairers Association
Belmont House, Gildersome, Leeds LS27 7TW
Phone: +44 (0)113 253 8333
Web: www.vbra.co.uk

Similar Jobs
Mechanical Engineering Technician, Painter & Decorator, Vehicle Body Repairer, Vehicle Mechanic/Motor Vehicle Technician

Vehicle Body Repairer
also known as: Car Body Repairer, Motor Vehicle Body Repairer, Panel Beater

CRCI:Engineering
CLCI:RON Job Band: 1 to 3

Job Description
Panel beaters repair or replace vehicle body panels damaged by metal corrosion or accidents. They clean vehicles with solvents, sand down panels and restore the damaged area to its original condition using both hand and machine tools. May also beat out any dents and recreate shape with filler. Panels may need to be replaced from stock or sheet metal, cut and shaped, then welded or riveted in place. They order any replacement parts and may need to fit a replacement bonnet, door, windscreen or bumper. Also straightens bent chassis and may need to carry out spray-paint repair to match the original.

Work Details
Usually work a basic 39 hr week, Monday to Friday, though sometimes this may include working evenings or on a Saturday. Some employers may require you to work overtime or shifts. Computerised and electronic equipment is increasingly used. Repair work usually takes place in an indoor workshop or ventilated paint spraying booth, where the environment can be cold, noisy and cramped. You need a high level of skill and work may be pressurised at times. You have to cope with being active most of the time, as well as kneeling, bending down and lifting. There may be a risk of minor injuries from equipment. You need to wear overalls and possibly safety glasses and a face mask.

Qualification
- **England, Wales and Northern Ireland**

Band 2: For entry to jobs, no minimum qualifications are needed, but it is an advantage to have some GCSEs (A*-C) or equivalent in subjects that include maths, English and a science-based subject, or equivalent.

Band 3: For entry to jobs, HNC or a relevant Diploma, usually at least 4 GCSEs (A*-C) including English, maths and a science-based subject, or equivalent, particularly for technician training. Engineering or craft subjects are also helpful.

- **Scotland**

Band 2: Although academic qualifications are not specified for this job, it is an advantage to have some S grades (1-3) in subjects that include maths, English and a science-based subject, or similar.

Band 3: For entry to jobs, usually at least four S grades (1-3) in English, maths and a science-based subject, or similar, particularly for technician training. Engineering or craft subjects are also helpful.

Adult Qualifications
Formal qualifications are not always necessary and course requirements are usually relaxed for mature entrants.

Work Experience
Relevant work or voluntary experience is always useful. It can add to your CV and improve your chances when applying for entry to jobs or apprenticeships in the motor industry.

Entry and Training
Many trainees start on a training programme or apprenticeship at age 16-19. You usually train on the job, working with an experienced person, together with a local college course through either day or block release. Most work towards S/NVQs in vehicle body and paint operations at levels 2-3. You can also study full time for a BTEC/SQA award prior to employment. City & Guilds runs an entry-level award in vehicle systems and body paint maintenance, which gives 14-19 year olds some experience of working in this sector. This job may require a driving licence and you may have to pass a practical aptitude entrance test. There are national training providers of apprenticeships and automotive training, such as Thatcham. See the website for details.

The Institute of the Motor Industry is the sector skills council for the retail motor industry. They offer nationally recognised vocationally related qualifications (VRQs) in vehicle body and paint operations at levels 2-4, for those wishing to progress to technician level and onto higher education. VRQs at level 1 are also available as a pre-apprenticeship programme for school pupils aged 14-16. These provide the opportunity to 'fast track' onto higher level motor industry qualifications.

Automotive Technician Accreditation (ATA) is a voluntary programme that assesses the current competence of individuals working in the retail motor trade. They assess panel technicians and paint technicians at both technician and senior technician level. Check the websites for details.

Mature applicants can take refresher courses that are sometimes available for those returning to work and there may be special training schemes in some areas. Employers may take older applicants who show aptitude and have previous related experience. Government training opportunities, such as apprenticeships, may be available in your area. You can also gain recognition of previous experience through Accreditation of Prior Learning (APL) or by working towards relevant S/NVQs. Contact your local careers office, Jobcentre Plus, Next Step service or Learning and Skills Council (LSC) Local Enterprise Company (LEC) for details of training schemes.

Opportunities and Pay
Jobs are available in almost every town and city and there is a steady demand for experienced repairers. Employment is with a garage or body repair shop, motor retail outlet, customised bodyshop or fleet vehicle firms such as bus/coach companies, haulage firms, public utility companies, the armed services or rail transport. Promotion opportunities are generally better in larger organisations and prospects can be improved with further training. With experience, you can become self-employed.

Pay varies depending on location and employer. Trainees earn around £10k-£12k a year. Once qualified, this may rise to around £15k-£19k a year. Some highly skilled workers can earn up to £30k a year. Overtime may be available.

Health
This job requires good health and you are expected to have strength, stamina and physical fitness. There may be an allergy risk from dust and paint. For some tasks good colour vision is required.

Skills and Qualities
able to work both on your own and in a team, attention to detail, eye for shape/colour, good communication skills, good interpersonal skills, health & safety awareness, manual dexterity, patient, practical skills

Relevant Subjects
Design and technology, Engineering, Physics, Science

Further Information
Apprenticeship Schemes (National Apprenticeship Service) - www.apprenticeships.org.uk

Apprenticeships in Scotland (Careers Info Scotland) - www.apprenticeshipsinscotland.com/about/

Automotive Technician Accreditation (ATA) (Institute of the Motor Industry) - www.automotivetechnician.org.uk

BODY (monthly) (Vehicle Body Repairer's Association (VBRA)) - www.bodymag.co.uk/
Institute of the Motor Industry (IMI) - sector skills council for the motor industry - www.motor.org.uk
Motor Industry Magazine (monthly) (Institute of the Motor Industry (IMI)) - www.motor.org.uk/magazine/index.html
Thatcham - www.thatcham.org
Training Schemes - www.direct.gov.uk/en/educationandlearning
Women into Science, Engineering & Construction - www.wisecampaign.org.uk

Addresses

Vehicle Builders & Repairers Association
Belmont House, Gildersome, Leeds LS27 7TW
Phone: +44 (0)113 253 8333
Web: www.vbra.co.uk

Similar Jobs

Laminator, Sheet Metal Worker, Vehicle Body Refinisher, Vehicle Mechanic/Motor Vehicle Technician, Welder

Vehicle Breakdown Engineer

also known as: Patrol Mechanic, Roadside Assistance Technician, Vehicle Service Patroller

CRCI:Engineering
CLCI:RAE — Job Band: 1 to 3

Job Description

Vehicle breakdown engineers provide a roadside repair service for motorists whose vehicle has broken down or been damaged in an accident. They fix the vehicle quickly at the roadside, or if the fault cannot be repaired, arrange for the vehicle to be taken to a local garage or place of safety. They may tow or transport it to the driver's home, using a pick-up truck or transporter. Breakdown engineers receive messages from a control centre on a mobile phone or radio link and use a computerised system to record each visit and the work carried out.

They carry spare parts such as batteries, handle cheques for spare parts and give a receipt. Usually travel around a geographical area, including rural areas, motorways and town and city centres.

Work Details

Usually work a basic 39-40 hr week, though shift work and weekend work is quite common. You drive in all sorts of weather and it can be dark and cold. The work can be oily and dirty, and you work on your own. There may be a risk of road accidents. This job involves dealing with a wide variety of people who are sometimes upset or perhaps demanding.

You are responsible for solving problems quickly and remaining calm when under pressure. Sometimes you have to cope with waiting around. A uniform is usually required and provided by the employer.

Qualification

Before applying to become a breakdown engineer it is essential to be a qualified motor vehicle technician with several years' experience.

• England, Wales and Northern Ireland

Band 2: For entry to jobs, no minimum qualifications are needed, but it is an advantage to have some GCSEs (A*-C) or equivalent in subjects that include English and maths and a science, or equivalent. Practical and technical subjects are also useful.

Band 3: For entry to jobs, HNC or a relevant Diploma, usually at least 4 GCSEs (A*-C) including English and maths, science and technical or practical subjects, or equivalent.

• Scotland

Band 2: Although academic qualifications are not specified for this job, for some training programmes to become a motor vehicle technician it is an advantage to have some S grades (1-3) in subjects that include English, maths and a science, or similar. Practical and technical subjects are also useful.

Band 3: For entry to jobs, usually at least four S grades (1-3) including English, maths, science and technical or practical subjects, or similar.

Adult Qualifications

Only qualified and experienced motor vehicle technicians are considered for employment. Course entry requirements may be relaxed for suitable mature applicants.

Work Experience

Entrants to this work have to be experienced motor vehicle technicians. Those who also have work experience in dealing with breakdowns or accidents have an advantage. Experience of dealing with the public in difficult situations is also helpful.

Entry and Training

Entrants to this work are expected to have qualified as a motor vehicle technician at S/NVQ level 3 or equivalent and most have at least five years' post-qualification experience. To become a qualified technician, most do an apprenticeship. A specialist roadside assistance and recovery apprenticeship is available. See the Motor Vehicle Technician job article for full details of initial training. A clean driving licence is preferred. To enter this job you may need to pass a selection interview, a driving assessment, written tests and show practical ability in technical skill.

Initial training for breakdown engineers in customer care and practical skills is by a short course organised by your employer. This job requires regular training to keep up to date with new developments in the trade. S/NVQs are available at levels 2-3 in roadside assistance and recovery. The Institute of the Motor Industry (IMI) and City & Guilds also run vocationally related qualifications at levels 2-3 in roadside assistance and recovery. You can then progress to a range of further education and professional body awards at level 4 and above. Contact IMI for details of all routes to training.

The IMI has also developed Autocity, a useful and informative website on careers in the motor industry. There is a section on mobile/specialist roles including recovery drivers, mobile technicians and roadside assistance as well as information on qualification routes, career progression and industry links. Visit the website for more information.

The Institute of Vehicle Recovery offers training courses in heavy vehicle, light vehicle, and bus and coach recovery. Courses on roadside safety awareness and evidence preservation are also offered. See their website for details. The Automative Technician Accreditation (ATA) is a voluntary programme that assesses the current competence of individuals working in the retail motor trade. They assess roadside assistance technicians at diagnostic and master technician level. Check the ATA website for details.

A Diploma/Welsh Baccalaureate may be available in your area in engineering. This qualification is based around work and can include an automative specialist learning component. See the diplomas website for further information.

Most entrants to this work are at least 21, because of the requirements of experience and qualifications.

Opportunities and Pay

There are over 7,000 vehicle breakdown engineers in the UK and jobs are available throughout the country. You may be employed by the AA/RAC, which directly employ their own engineers. You can also work for a local garage who are contracted with other organisations that offer a breakdown service, such as Green Flag. With experience you can progress to a supervisory role.

Salaries usually start at around £25k a year and may rise to £30k-£40k with more experience. Your pay may depend on the number of cars you manage to repair.

Health
This job requires a good standard of physical fitness, good eyesight and normal colour vision. A medical test on entry is required.

Skills and Qualities
able to cope under pressure, able to explain clearly, able to work quickly, able to work well on your own, attention to detail, common sense, good interpersonal skills, manual dexterity, methodical, technical aptitude

Relevant Subjects
Design and technology, Engineering, Mathematics, Physics, Science

Further Information
Autocity (IMI) http://autocity.org.uk

Automobile Association (AA) - www.theaa.com

Automotive Technician Accreditation (ATA) (Institute of the Motor Industry) - www.automotivetechnician.org.uk

Diplomas (Foundation, Higher and Advanced) - http://yp.direct.gov.uk/diplomas

Green Flag - www.greenflag.com

Institute of the Motor Industry (IMI) - sector skills council for the motor industry - www.motor.org.uk

Motor Industry Magazine (monthly) (Institute of the Motor Industry (IMI)) - www.motor.org.uk/magazine/index.html

RAC - www.rac.co.uk

Recovery Operator (Association of Vehicle Recovery Operators (AVRO)) - www.avrouk.com

What's it like to be a Motor Mechanic (A&C Black 2008)

Addresses
Institute of Vehicle Recovery (IVR)
Top Floor, Bignell House, Horton Road, West Drayton, Middlesex UB7 8EJ
Phone: +44 (0)1895 436 426
Web: www.theivr.com

Similar Jobs
Electrician: Auto, Fitter: Maintenance, Mechanic: Motorcycle, Vehicle Body Repairer, Vehicle Mechanic/Motor Vehicle Technician, Vehicle Tyre/Exhaust Fitter

Vehicle Mechanic/Motor Vehicle Technician

also known as: Auto Mechanic, Bus/Coach Mechanic, Car Mechanic, Lorry Mechanic, Mechanic: Light/Heavy Vehicle

CRCI:Engineering
CLCI:RAE Job Band: 1 to 3

Job Description
Motor vehicle technicians repair, test, tune and service cars, vans, motorcycles, buses, coaches or lorries. They inspect the vehicle and report on its general condition and complete routine servicing and road-testing. Technicians find faults and repair or replace worn parts, checking worksheets and technical manuals, and using sophisticated equipment, as well as hand and power tools, ramps and jacks. They may use technology such as a laptop or hand-held computer to diagnose electronic faults and to measure performance. May also may refer to computerised technical information and drawings that were traditionally printed in paper manuals.

Technicians may fit accessories, recover broken-down vehicles and complete roadside repairs. They may become an MOT tester once sufficiently experienced. Semi-skilled fitters replace parts such as tyres, often in fast-fit centres. Technicians may do skilled diagnostic work, including work on electronic and computer systems.

Work Details
Usually work around 40 hrs a week, although overtime is common. There may also be shift work, including weekends. Some technicians have to be on call. Workshops and garages can be cold and noisy. Work on vehicles that have broken down involves being outdoors in all weathers. In some garages you have to be able to communicate well with customers. You have to work quickly, sometimes under pressure, to repair or service vehicles as speedily and safely as possible.

Work is often strenuous and includes some heavy lifting. You have to bend, kneel and stretch, sometimes in awkward positions. There may be a risk of accidents with equipment. Protective clothing may be needed. The work is oily and dirty and technicians often use barrier creams to protect their skin.

Qualification

• England, Wales and Northern Ireland
Band 2: For entry to jobs and some training programmes and employers: no minimum qualifications are needed, but it is an advantage to have some GCSEs (A*-C) or equivalent in subjects that include English, maths and science (preferably physics), technology or engineering subject, or equivalent.

Band 3: For entry to jobs, HNC in vehicle repair and technology or a relevant Diploma: usually at least 4 GCSEs (A*-C) including English, maths and a science (preferably physics), technology or engineering subject, or equivalent.

• Scotland
Band 2: Although academic qualifications are not specified for this job, for some training programmes and employers: it is an advantage to have some S grades (1-3) in subjects that include English, maths and science (preferably physics) or technical/engineering subjects, or similar.

Band 3: For entry to jobs, usually at least four S grades (1-3) including English or maths, and science, preferably physics, or technical/engineering subjects, or similar.

Adult Qualifications
Formal qualifications showing a good standard of general education may be preferred, but are not essential. Academic requirements for courses are usually relaxed for suitable mature applicants.

Work Experience
Relevant work or voluntary experience is always useful, and it can add to your CV and improve your chances when applying for entry to jobs or apprenticeships in the engineering industry. Any practical experience of car mechanics and the ability to follow diagrams is an advantage.

Entry and Training
Many trainees start on a training programme or vehicle maintenance and repair apprenticeship at age 16-19. You usually train on the job, working with an experienced person, together with day or block release to a local college course. Most work towards S/NVQs in vehicle maintenance and repair at levels 2-3. You can also study full time for a City & Guilds or a BTEC/SQA award, prior to employment. This job may require a driving licence and you may have to pass a practical aptitude entrance test. Regular training is needed to keep up to date with changing technology. National training providers of apprenticeships and automotive training include the training arm of the Retail Motor Industry Federation, ReMIT. See their website for details.

Thatcham has been a leading provider in skills training for crash repairs for a long time and now offers specific apprenticeships through the Thatcham Apprentice Programme. Thatcham has an online jobshop facility for candidates looking to secure an apprenticeship. Jobshop registration is free and applicant details are made available to hundreds of bodyshops and repair centres across the UK.

The Institute of the Motor Industry (IMI) and City & Guilds also offer nationally recognised vocationally related qualifications (VRQs) at levels 2-4 for those reaching technician level and possibly onto higher education. VRQs at level 1 are also available as a pre-apprenticeship programme for school pupils aged 14-16 and provide the opportunity to 'fast track' onto higher level motor industry qualifications. The Automotive Technician Accreditation (ATA) is a voluntary programme that assesses the current competence of individuals working in the retail motor trade. They assess light vehicle technicians at both technician and senior technician level. Visit the IMI or the ATA websites for details.

The IMI has also developed Autocity, a useful and informative website on careers in the motor industry. Information on qualification routes, career progression and industry links is available. Visit the website for further details.

Transport Training Services (TTS) also run a series of programme led apprenticeships. The Department for Employment and Learning has introduced programme-led apprenticeships for young people who have not been able to secure employment in their chosen field. Under this scheme at TTS, you work towards a NVQ Level 2 in either vehicle maintenance and repair or vehicle refinishing. See their website for further details.

A Diploma/Welsh Baccalaureate may be available in your area in engineering. This qualification is based around work and can include an automotive specialist learning component. See the diplomas website for further information.

It is an advantage to have experience of mechanical work. Evidence of practical skill such as servicing your own car is helpful. Mature applicants can benefit through government training opportunities, such as apprenticeships, that may be available in your area. You can also gain recognition of previous experience through Accreditation of Prior Learning (APL) or by working towards relevant S/NVQs. Contact your local careers office, Jobcentre Plus, Next Step service or Learning and Skills Council (LSC) Local Enterprise Company (LEC) for details of training schemes, including apprentceships for adults.

Opportunities and Pay

There is a steady demand for trained mechanics and technicians throughout the UK. Employment is usually with garages, transport companies, road haulage companies or large organisations with a lot of fleet vehicles, such as the police and utility companies. You can either work on cars or on heavy vehicles such as lorries and coaches. Some garages specialise in particular makes of car. In larger companies, it is usually possible to gain promotion to supervisory and management jobs. Opportunities also exist in the armed forces (who have an established training scheme) and with road assistance organisations such as the RAC/AA and others. Self-employment is possible.

Pay varies depending on location and employer. Trainee technicians usually earn between £11k-£20k a year depending on phase of training. Qualified technicians earn around £22k-£26k and those who reach master technician level (often sports car technicians) can earn up to £45k a year. Pay is often increased by overtime payments and perhaps bonuses.

Health

You must be in good health and have normal colour vision.

Skills and Qualities

able to follow instructions, able to work quickly, attention to detail, good communication skills, IT skills, manual dexterity, methodical, numeracy skills, safety conscious, technical aptitude

Relevant Subjects

Design and technology, Engineering, Mathematics, Physics, Science

Further Information

Apprenticeship Schemes (National Apprenticeship Service) - www.apprenticeships.org.uk

Autocity (IMI) http://autocity.org.uk

Automotive Technician Accreditation (ATA) (Institute of the Motor Industry) - www.automotivetechnician.org.uk

Diplomas (Foundation, Higher and Advanced) - http://yp.direct.gov.uk/diplomas

Institute of the Motor Industry (IMI) - sector skills council for the motor industry - www.motor.org.uk

Motor Industry Magazine (monthly) (Institute of the Motor Industry (IMI)) - www.motor.org.uk/magazine/index.html

remit - www.remit.co.uk

Thatcham - www.thatcham.org

Training Schemes - www.direct.gov.uk/en/educationandlearning

What's it like to be a Motor Mechanic (A&C Black 2008)

▶Working in airports (2010) (Babcock Lifeskills) - www.babcock-lifeskills.com/

Addresses

Transport Training Services (TTS)
15 Dundrod Road, Nutts Corner, Crumlin, Co Antrim BT29 4SS
Phone: +44 (0)28 9082 5653
Web: www.transport-training.co.uk

Similar Jobs

Electrician: Auto, Mechanic: Construction Plant, Mechanic: Motorcycle, Service Technician: Land-based, Vehicle Breakdown Engineer, Vehicle Tyre/Exhaust Fitter

Vehicle Parts Operative

also known as: Salesperson: Vehicle Parts

CRCI:Retail Sales and Customer Services

CLCI:YAT Job Band: 1 to 2

Job Description

Vehicle parts operatives advise customers on vehicle parts and accessories and make direct sales. Customers may be members of the public, garages that fix or service vehicles or mechanics. They sell parts for light vehicles such as cars and motorbikes or for heavy vehicles such as buses or lorries.

Operatives deal with customers on the phone, face to face and by email. Use knowledge of motor vehicles to help people work out exactly what they want. May suggest possible solutions to customers' problems. Use computer software, the Internet, catalogues and microfiche to identify the right part for the vehicle's age and make. Find the parts from stock or order them from suppliers. Let customers know when parts arrive or arrange or make deliveries. Prepare invoices and take payments.

Stock control is an important part of the job and may be computer based. Operatives check actual stock against stock records. They tidy stock on display and in the stockroom. Make sure parts are in the right place and easy to find. Order more stock if levels are running low. Check deliveries, pay invoices, update records and put new stock away. Follow health and safety rules and pay attention to security issues.

Work Details

Usually work a 39-40 hr week, which may include shifts, evenings and some weekends. Deal with customers for front counter parts sales and sometimes back counter sales to the service department. Stock areas/warehouses can be light, spacious and airy, though sometimes also cold. At times you may be very busy and have to work quickly. You can be on your feet for long periods of time. Some unloading, lifting and carrying of heavy goods may be required and you may need to climb ladders.

You must follow safety regulations, for example, to make sure that there are no accidents because of items being stacked badly. A uniform may be provided by the employer. Catalogues, computers and microfiche are used regularly to find information on parts.

Qualification

• England, Wales and Northern Ireland

Band 1: No minimum qualifications are required, but you are expected to have a good level of general education. However, some formal/vocational qualifications at any level are useful.

Band 2: Although academic qualifications are not specified for this job, some employers ask for some GCSEs (A*-C) in subjects that may include English, maths, ICT, science or technology, or equivalent.

• Scotland

Band 1: No minimum qualifications are required, but you are expected to have a good level of general education. However, some formal/vocational qualifications at any level are useful.

Band 2: Although academic qualifications are not specified for this job, some employers ask for some S grades (1-3) in subjects that may include English, maths, ICT, science or technology, or similar.

Adult Qualifications

No formal qualifications are required. Employers may look for ability in basic maths.

Work Experience

Work experience helps you find out what you enjoy and do not enjoy about a type of work. Paid or voluntary work where you meet or sell items to members of the public may be useful. Experience of working with cars or a good level of knowledge about them may help you stand out.

In some areas you can do a young apprenticeship (14-16) scheme in the motor industry. You do an extended work placement and a level 2 qualification whilst at school. For health and safety reasons there may be some jobs you cannot do until you are over 16.

Entry and Training

Employers favour applicants with good people skills, who are interested in motor vehicles. Training is mostly on the job. There may be opportunities to do short courses in-house or at colleges or training centres. You may be able to work towards S/NVQ levels 2-3 in vehicle parts operations or study for a technical certificate such as an Institute of the Motor Industry Awards Ltd level 2 or level 3 certificate in vehicle parts operations. Apprenticeships leading to level 2 and advanced apprenticeships leading to level 3 qualifications may be available in your area. You may have to pass an entry test.

If the job involves making deliveries, you need a full driving licence.

Adults can enter this area of work and train on the job. Employers look for people with experience of the motor industry, warehouse or retail work and good practical knowledge of motor vehicles.

Opportunities and Pay

There are around 8,000 firms in the UK that sell motor vehicle parts. They employ around 89,000 staff. There are jobs for parts operatives with car dealerships, garages, parts shops and wholesalers. You may be able to move on to posts where you supervise others or become a parts manager. Within the sector you can become a parts sales representative and sell parts to the trade. With the skills you acquire, you can move into jobs in retail in other sectors as well.

Whilst training, you are likely to earn around £6k-£8k a year. Qualified vehicle parts operatives earn between £10k and £15k, and in a senior role you may earn up to £20k or more. Parts managers earn around £30k-£33k a year.

Health

You need good general fitness for this job. It is important to be able to speak clearly and to have normal levels of vision and hearing with glasses/contact lenses or hearing or other aids if necessary.

Skills and Qualities

able to get on with all kinds of people, basic understanding of vehicle maintenance, cash handling skills, customer service skills, good organisational skills, good telephone manner, IT skills, methodical, numeracy skills, problem-solving skills

Relevant Subjects

Design and technology

Further Information

Apprenticeship Schemes (National Apprenticeship Service) - www.apprenticeships.org.uk
Autocity (IMI) http://autocity.org.uk
Foundation Learning (QCDA) - www.qcda.gov.uk

Addresses

Institute of the Motor Industry (IMI)
Fanshaws Brickenden, Hertford, Hertfordshire SG13 8PQ
Phone: +44 (0)1992 511 521
Web: www.motor.org.uk

Similar Jobs

Builders' Merchant, Retail Assistant, Stock Control/Replenishment Assistant, Vehicle Mechanic/Motor Vehicle Technician, Vehicle Sales Executive, Warehouse Worker

Vehicle Sales Executive

also known as: Car Salesperson, Sales Executive: Car
CRCI:Retail Sales and Customer Services
CLCI:OFM Job Band: 2 to 3

Job Description

Vehicle sales executives work in a car dealership selling new or used vehicles from one particular manufacturer, or for a used-car dealer who handles different makes. They advise customers on the range of new and used vehicles and help them to make a choice. Sales executives assess a buyer's needs, show and discuss the advantages of different vehicles and arrange test drives. May advise large companies about 'fleet' vehicles. They negotiate individual and 'fleet' deals, and arrange purchase or hire terms. May also trade-in or buy cars, sometimes from vehicle auctions and help with sales promotions and publicity.

Work Details

Usually work a basic 40 hr week, though the job may require you to work some evenings, Saturdays and possibly Sundays, but there is time off during the week instead. You work inside a showroom or outside where cars are also displayed on a forecourt. There is also some office work that usually includes dealing with telephone enquiries. You have contact with a large number of people and are responsible for business transactions. The work can be pressurised at times and requires learning a great deal about the product you are selling.

Qualification

• England, Wales and Northern Ireland

Band 2: There are no specified minimum qualifications, though an employer may require you to have some GCSEs (A*-C), usually including maths and English, or equivalent.

Band 3: For some training schemes employers require a minimum of 4 GCSEs (A*-C) preferably including maths and English, or equivalent.

- **Scotland**

Band 2: There are no specified minimum qualifications, though an employer may require you to have some S grades (1-3), usually including maths and English, or similar.

Band 3: For some management training schemes employers require a minimum of four S grades (1-3) preferably including maths and English or similar.

Adult Qualifications
No minimum qualifications specified, though a good standard of education is required.

Work Experience
Relevant work or voluntary experience is always useful and can improve your chances when applying for entry to jobs in sales. It can equip you with skills that you can use in the future and add to your CV. Part-time and holiday retail employment is usually easy to obtain and provides valuable experience.

Entry and Training
You need to have a driving licence and it is useful to have some knowledge of vehicle maintenance. Training is on the job and possibly by short specialised courses. The Institute of the Motor Industry (IMI) offers a certificate/diploma at levels 2-3 in vehicle sales, covering the main skills needed in the showroom and all aspects of vehicle retailing. These qualifications lead to licentiate membership and associate membership of the IMI.

Due to the high cost of motor insurance for young drivers, most sales staff are over 21, but training in this type of work can be started at an earlier age, through an apprenticeship scheme. It may be useful to enhance your career, when experienced, by obtaining an automotive retail management certificate or diploma that is offered jointly through the IMI and the Chartered Management Institute.

S/NVQs in vehicle sales are available at levels 2-3. Training programmes, including apprenticeship schemes, may be available in your area. Advanced apprenticeships leading to qualification at level 3 can be a route into higher education. A Diploma/Welsh Baccalaureate in retail business may also be available in your area.

Mature applicants are preferred by some employers, and it is an advantage to have experience in retail, working with the public, and ideally some previous motor trade industry experience.

Opportunities and Pay
Jobs are available with new and used car sales dealerships mainly in towns and cities, although the current economic downturn may reduce opportunities. Promotion depends on building a good sales record and opportunities are generally better in larger organisations. With experience, you can be self-employed, but setting up your own business requires considerable financial investment.

On top of a basic salary, car sales executives receive commission on each vehicle they sell, therefore earnings vary enormously. Most earn in the region of £10k-£22k, increasing to around £25k-£34k a year, with experience. The most successful sales executives can earn up to around £50k a year. Those with managerial responsibility earn up to £60k-£70k a year. Many dealerships also provide a car for personal use.

Skills and Qualities
aptitude for figures, basic understanding of vehicle maintenance, business awareness, customer service skills, good interpersonal skills, IT skills, motivated, negotiating skills, persuasive, self confident

Relevant Subjects
Business and accounting, Retail and distribution

Further Information
Apprenticeship Schemes (National Apprenticeship Service) - www.apprenticeships.org.uk

Diplomas (Foundation, Higher and Advanced) - http://yp.direct.gov.uk/diplomas

Welsh Baccalaureate - www.wbq.org.uk

▶Working in retail & customer services (2008) (Babcock Lifeskills) - www.babcock-lifeskills.com/

Addresses
Chartered Management Institute (CMI)
Management House, Cottingham Road, Corby NN17 1TT
Phone: +44 (0)1536 204 222
Web: www.managers.org.uk

Institute of the Motor Industry (IMI)
Fanshaws Brickenden, Hertford, Hertfordshire SG13 8PQ
Phone: +44 (0)1992 511 521
Web: www.motor.org.uk

Similar Jobs
Car Rental Agent, Retail Assistant, Sales Executive: Technical, Vehicle Parts Operative

Vehicle Tyre/Exhaust Fitter
also known as: Fast-Fit Technician, Tyre Fitting Technician

CRCI:Engineering
CLCI:RAE Job Band: 1 to 2

Job Description
Vehicle fitters check a vehicle's tyres and exhaust and fit new ones, if required. They give customers advice on which tyres or parts of the exhaust need replacing. May work on certain types of vehicles such as light vehicles, including cars and vans. May also work on heavy vehicles such as lorries, buses and coaches. Fitters need to check the vehicle according to all the legal requirements.

To fit tyres, they lift the car on a hydraulic jack and use power and hand tools to remove the worn tyre. They fit the new tyre, fill it with air to the correct pressure and check for leaks. Also balance and align wheels using special equipment. To fit exhausts, fitters lift the car on a ramp, unbolt and replace the whole exhaust or parts of it. They may also replace brakes and shock absorbers.

Work Details
Usually work around 39 hrs a week, often with some Saturdays required. The hours can be long and involve shifts, because fitting centres are often open late and at weekends. You usually work in a workshop. Some fitters travel, especially those who work on farm vehicles or on lorries. Fitters often deal with customers and some have to take payment and provide a customer receipt.

The work involves heavy lifting, kneeling and bending down, so you have to be fit and strong. Workshops can be quite dirty and sometimes noisy and you may have to work in cramped spaces. There can be accidents with equipment.

Qualification

- **England, Wales and Northern Ireland**

Band 1: For entry to jobs, no minimum qualifications are needed, but you are expected to have a good level of general education and relevant experience. Some formal/vocational qualifications at any level are useful.

Band 2: For entry to jobs, no minimum qualifications are needed, but it is an advantage to have some GCSEs (A*-C) or equivalent in subjects that include English, technology and maths, or equivalent. Employers expect a good standard of literacy and numeracy.

- **Scotland**

Band 1: For entry to jobs, no minimum qualifications are needed, but you are expected to have a good level of general education and relevant experience. Some formal/vocational qualifications at any level are useful.

Band 2: Although academic qualifications are not specified for this job, it is an advantage to have some S grades (1-3) in subjects that include technical subjects, English and maths, or similar. Employers expect a good standard of literacy and numeracy.

Adult Qualifications

Formal educational qualifications are not always needed for adults, although employers expect a good standard of literacy and numeracy. Specific entry requirements for courses may be relaxed for mature applicants. You can improve your skills and qualifications by working through the Foundation Learning programme. This involves taking credit-based units and qualifications to help you progress.

Work Experience

Relevant work or voluntary experience is always useful. It can add to your CV and improve your chances when applying for entry to jobs or apprenticeships in the motor vehicle industry. In some areas there is a young apprenticeship (14-16) scheme that provides an extended work placement and eventual achievement of a relevant level 1 or 2 qualification whilst at school.

Entry and Training

There are no set entry requirements for this job and a genuine interest in motor vehicles is more important. Many trainees start at age 16-19 and usually train on the job, working with an experienced person. Most then do a local college course, through either day or block release. Some employers have practical aptitude tests. You usually need to have a driving licence or must be willing to learn to drive. Basic training often takes around six weeks, but it can take up to two years to be fully trained.

Some major employers offer two-year apprenticeship schemes in vehicle fitting. Contact the Institute of the Motor Industry (IMI) for details of all apprenticeships in the retail motor industry. Trainees can often work towards S/NVQs at levels 1-2 in vehicle fitting operations. The IMI and City & Guilds run vocationally-related qualifications (VRQs) at levels 1-2 in vehicle fitting operations. The level 3 VRQ is aimed at technicians in tyre/exhaust and vehicle fitting. Level 1 is also available as a pre-apprenticeship programme for school pupils aged 14-16.

The IMI has developed Autocity, a useful and informative website on careers in the motor industry. Information on qualification routes, career progression and industry links is available. Visit the website for more information.

Thatcham has been a leading provider in skills training for crash repairs for a long time and now offers specific apprenticeships through the Thatcham Apprentice Programme. Thatcham has an online jobshop facility for candidates looking to secure an apprenticeship. Jobshop registration is free and applicant details are made available to hundreds of bodyshops and repair centres across the UK.

Automotive Technical Accreditation (ATA) is a voluntary programme that assesses the current competence of individuals working in the retail motor trade. Governed by the IMI, ATA registered technicians sign and are bound by a special code of conduct. They are issued with a photo identity card and their details are included on the ATA web site. Visit the the IMI and the ATA websites for details.

A Diploma/Welsh Baccalaureate may be available in your area in engineering. This qualification is based around work and can include an automotive specialist learning component. See the diplomas website for further information.

Adult entry is possible. Employers may take older applicants who show aptitude and have previous related experience. Any experience with motor vehicles or industrial work gives you an advantage. Some tyre and exhaust franchisers or manufacturers may provide training courses for those wishing to set up their own business.

Mature applicants can take refresher courses that may be available for those returning to work and there may be special training schemes in some areas. Government training opportunities, such as apprenticeships, may be available in your area. You can also gain recognition of previous experience through Accreditation of Prior Learning (APL) or by working towards relevant S/NVQs. Contact your local careers office, Jobcentre Plus, Next Step service or Learning and Skills Council (LSC) Local Enterprise Company (LEC) for details of training schemes, including adult apprenticeships.

Opportunities and Pay

Fitters mostly work in tyre and exhaust centres and these can either be small local firms or large nationwide chains. Some work in garages or for transport companies. These companies can be found all over the UK, but are usually in towns and cities. There are more people applying for jobs than there are vacancies for fitters. In large companies it is possible to become a supervisor or a manager.

Starting wages for trainee tyre/exhaust fitters are likely to be around £6k-£9k a year. Qualified fitters can earn £11k and £15k a year and those with experience can earn up to £20k a year.

Health

You have to be very fit to do this job.

Skills and Qualities

able to explain clearly, able to work both on your own and in a team, able to work quickly, attention to detail, hard working, manual dexterity, methodical, numeracy skills, polite, practical skills

Relevant Subjects

Design and technology

Further Information

Apprenticeship Schemes (National Apprenticeship Service) - www.apprenticeships.org.uk

Apprenticeships in Scotland (Careers Info Scotland) - www.apprenticeshipsinscotland.com/about/

Autocity (IMI) http://autocity.org.uk

Automotive Technician Accreditation (ATA) (Institute of the Motor Industry) - www.automotivetechnician.org.uk

Diplomas (Foundation, Higher and Advanced) - http://yp.direct.gov.uk/diplomas

Institute of the Motor Industry (IMI) - sector skills council for the motor industry - www.motor.org.uk

Motor Industry Magazine (monthly) (Institute of the Motor Industry (IMI)) - www.motor.org.uk/magazine/index.html

Thatcham - www.thatcham.org

Training Schemes - www.direct.gov.uk/en/educationandlearning

Similar Jobs

Mechanic: Motorcycle, Vehicle Body Refinisher, Vehicle Body Repairer, Vehicle Mechanic/Motor Vehicle Technician, Windscreen Technician

Vending Machine Operative

also known as: Van Driver: Vending Machines

CRCI:Retail Sales and Customer Services
CLCI:OFZ Job Band: 1 to 2

Job Description

Vending machine operatives travel around an area to clean, maintain and restock vending machines. They visit a number of locations, such as offices, schools, colleges and universities, hotels, leisure centres and shopping centres, each day. Must ensure that the machines are fully stocked and are working properly and collect cash from the machine and take it to the vending company's office or may make payments to the company at a bank. Servicing the machines and carrying out any small repairs are also part of the job. Any major faults are reported to a supervisor or to a company service engineer.

Work Details

Usually work a 35-40 hr week, Monday to Friday but this can be on shifts and on call in case a machine needs to be repaired urgently. You work in different places, often travelling around in a van, usually supplied by your employer. There is some lifting and bending in this job. You work on your own and may need to wear a corporate uniform.

Qualification

- **England, Wales and Northern Ireland**

Band 1: No formal academic qualifications are needed, but employers prefer a good standard of education and a basic ability in maths and English.

Band 2: Employers may ask for some GCSEs (A*-C) including English and maths, or equivalent.

- **Scotland**

Band 1: No formal academic qualifications are needed but employers prefer a good standard of education and a basic ability in maths and English.

Band 2: Employers may ask for some S grades (1-3) including English and maths, or similar.

Adult Qualifications

You do not need formal qualifications for this job, though employers expect a good standard of education and ability in English and maths.

Work Experience

Any work experience can equip you with skills that you can use in the future and add to your CV. Work experience can either be unpaid or voluntary or can be holiday or part-time work that you have organised yourself.

Entry and Training

To enter this job you may need to take a basic maths and literacy test. Most vending machine operatives are in their twenties and on-the-job training is usual, working with an experienced member of staff. It includes instruction on the vending machines used, health and safety and stock control. Appropriate S/NVQs are available at levels 1-3. Training programmes, including apprenticeships may be available in your area.

You must have a clean driving licence and be at least 18 to sit a test for a Category C1 licence to drive light goods vehicles (LGV). Because of the high cost of insurance, most employers prefer people over 21, or even 25. The Young LGV Driver Scheme, managed by Skills for Logistics, allows a young person to obtain a full Category C driving licence at the age of 18 instead of 21, and a Category C+E licence before the age of 21. You must also pass the Driver Certificate of Professional Competence (CPC), designed to improve the knowledge and skills of professional LGV drivers.

The Automatic Vending Association offers its members information and advice regarding training and continuing professional development in areas that include health and safety, cleaning, and marketing vending products. There is a Level 3 S/NVQ in drinks dispense systems (installation and maintenance).

Mature applicants over the age of 25 may be preferred because insurance premiums are lower. Any sort of driving experience, or experience in sales or in running a small business is useful. Government training opportunities may be available in your area. You can also gain recognition of previous experience through Accreditation of Prior Learning (APL) or by working towards relevant S/NVQs. Contact your local careers office, Jobcentre Plus, Next Step service or Learning and Skills Council (LSC)/Local Enterprise Company (LEC) for details of training schemes, including apprenticeships for adults.

Opportunities and Pay

Jobs are found in most towns and cities with a local firm or a large company that has vending machines throughout the UK. With experience you can be promoted to supervisor and management posts, though this is more likely in a larger company.

Pay varies depending on location and employer. Salaries range from £11k-£19k a year depending on experience and responsibility.

Health

It is useful to be generally fit for this job.

Skills and Qualities

able to work well on your own, attention to detail, efficient record keeping, numeracy skills, practical skills, reliable, security conscious, smart appearance, trustworthy

Relevant Subjects

Retail and distribution

Further Information

Apprenticeship Schemes (National Apprenticeship Service) - www.apprenticeships.org.uk
Foundation Learning (QCDA) - www.qcda.gov.uk
Skills for Logistics - sector skills council for freight logistics industries - www.skillsforlogistics.org
Training Schemes - www.direct.gov.uk/en/educationandlearning

Addresses

Automatic Vending Association (AVA)
1 Villiers Court, 40 Upper Mulgrave Road, Cheam, Surrey SM2 7AJ
Phone: +44 (0)20 8661 1112
Web: www.ava-vending.co.uk/

Transport Training Services (TTS)
15 Dundrod Road, Nutts Corner, Crumlin, Co Antrim BT29 4SS
Phone: +44 (0)28 9082 5653
Web: www.transport-training.co.uk

Similar Jobs

Driver: Bus, Driver: Lorry, Driver: Van, Meter Reader, Postal Worker

Veterinary Animal Nursing Assistant

also known as: Animal Nursing Assistant

CRCI:Environment, Animals and Plants
CLCI:WAL Job Band: 1 to 2

Job Description

Veterinary animal nursing assistants (ANAs) care for animals in a vet's practice, feeding, grooming and cleaning them. They also prepare treatment areas and assist vets and nurses (VNs) throughout the practice. ANAs work mostly with small animals, but in some vets' practices they can assist in work with farm animals, horses, and species such as snakes. In some practices, there may also be duties, such as keeping records, and booking appointments.

Work Details

Usually work a basic 35-40 hr week that may include shifts and weekends. Work is mainly indoors and employers usually provide uniforms and protective clothing. You need to cope with blood when cleaning wounds and assisting with emergencies. The work may be messy and smelly, and your workplace can often be noisy. You work with animals that are experiencing pain and there may be a risk of attack by nervous or aggressive animals.

Qualification

• England, Wales and Northern Ireland

Band 1: No formal qualifications are required, though applicants are expected to have a good level of general education and a keen interest in animals. However, some formal/vocational qualifications at any level are useful.

Band 2: Although academic qualifications are not specified for this job, it is an advantage to have some GCSEs (A*-C) in subjects that include English and maths, or equivalent.

• Scotland

Band 1: No formal qualifications are required, though applicants are expected to have a good level of general education and a keen interest in animals. However, some formal/vocational qualifications at any level are useful.

Band 2: Although academic qualifications are not specified for this job, it is an advantage to have some S grades (1-3) in subjects that include English and maths, or similar.

Adult Qualifications

No formal academic qualifications required at this level and mature entry is possible. Experience with animals is necessary.

Work Experience

This type of work is popular and entry is competitive. Relevant work or voluntary experience is always useful and can improve your employment prospects when applying for entry to jobs. Any work that involves animals, such as a Saturday job or holiday work at a cattery or kennels, or on a farm, provides valuable experience.

Entry and Training

The British Veterinary Nursing Association (BVNA) offers a level 2 certificate for those wishing to become a qualified animal nursing assistant (ANA). This can be a day-release course or distance learning course that lasts around one year for those already employed within a practice. Applicants must work full time (at least 35 hrs a week) or part time (at least 20 hrs a week) within a veterinary practice and be over 16 yrs old. You must also be enrolled with the BVNA.

Key topics of the course include animal management, animal science, basic veterinary nursing and veterinary reception and administration. Candidates need to be working in all areas of the practice: reception, consulting rooms, operating theatre and kennels, in order to gain the necessary work experience.

A qualified member of staff in the practice usually acts as a mentor and assists in the compilation of a case log of your work. Successful completion of the ANA certificate can mean that you can register as a student veterinary nurse on the Royal College of Veterinary Surgeons (RCVS) veterinary nursing scheme. In order to do this you also have to have Key Skills level 2 in communication and application of number.

Mature applicants for training often have previous experience of working with animals. You need to be employed in a veterinary practice in order to train as an animal nursing assistant (ANA). Successful completion of the ANA enables you to register as a student veterinary nurse on the Royal College of Veterinary Surgeons (RCVS) veterinary nursing scheme. Contact the British Veterinary Nursing Association (BVNA) for details.

Opportunities and Pay

Most jobs are in private practices, but assistants also work at animal welfare societies, animal hospitals, universities and zoos. With further training it is possible to become a qualified vet's nurse, and then specialise in a particular area, such as with horses.

Starting pay is around £9k a year if under 18 years of age.

Health

You need to have good health and stamina for this work. This job may involve a risk of infection or allergic reaction to the animals.

Skills and Qualities

calm, emotionally strong, good at handling animals, methodical, not squeamish, observant, patient

Relevant Subjects

Biology, Science

Further Information

Lantra - The Sector Skills Council for environmental & land-based sector (Lantra) http:/www.lantra.co.uk

VNJ (monthly) (BVNA) - www.bvna.org.uk

►Working with animals (2009) (Babcock Lifeskills) - www.babcock-lifeskills.com/

Addresses

British Veterinary Nursing Association (BVNA)
82 Greenway Business Centre Harlow Business Park,
Essex CM19 5QE
Phone: +44 (0)1279 408 644
Web: www.bvna.org.uk

Royal College of Veterinary Surgeons (RCVS)
Belgravia House, 62-64 Horseferry Road, London SW1P 2AF
Phone: +44 (0)20 7222 2001
Web: www.rcvs.org.uk

Similar Jobs

Animal Care Assistant, Animal Technician/Technologist, Horse Groom, Veterinary Nurse, Zoo Keeper

Veterinary Nurse

CRCI:Environment, Animals and Plants
CLCI:WAL Job Band: 3 to 5

Job Description

Veterinary nurses (VNs) work alongside a vet (veterinary surgeon) providing medical treatment and a high standard of care to animals, including cats, dogs, rabbits, birds, hamsters and other domestic pets. Although VNs work mostly with small animals, in some vets' practices they may work with farm animals, horses and exotic species, such as snakes. They work mainly in the surgery, but may sometimes go on site visits. Tasks include developing X-rays and helping the vet during operations. They get the animal ready, perhaps by shaving part of its coat, then sterilise the instruments, prepare medicines and obtain samples for commercial laboratories. Also take specimens from animals and carry out simple laboratory tests.

VNs clean the animal and look after it while it is recovering and also groom and exercise animals in their care. They keep the work area tidy and may do reception work, such as answering the phone, filing and keeping records. Also book appointments for clients and give advice to owners on such matters as vaccination, general animal welfare and training.

Work Details

Working hours are usually around 38 hrs a week, though you are likely to be expected to work weekends, irregular hours and possibly on-call duties that may include nights. You need to cope with the sight of blood eg cleaning wounds and helping with operations. The work can be messy and smelly, and the workplace can be noisy. You work with animals in pain and there may be a risk of attack by aggressive or nervous animals. A uniform and protective clothing is provided by employers.

Qualification

• England, Wales and Northern Ireland

Band 3: For entry: a minimum of 5 GCSEs (A*-C) including English, maths and one science subject, or equivalent. Alternatively, the animal nursing assistant (ANA) certificate together with Key Skills level 2 in communication and application of number, is acceptable for entry.

Band 4: For HND, Diploma of Higher Education or foundation degree in veterinary nursing: 1-2 A levels and some GCSEs (A*-C) usually including English, science and maths, or equivalent.

Band 5: For degree courses: minimum two A levels and five GCSEs including English, maths and one science subject, or equivalent. RCVS qualifications are also considered.

• Scotland

Band 3: For entry: a minimum of five S grades (1-3) including English language, maths and one science subject, or similar. Alternatively, the animal nursing assistant (ANA) certificate, together with Core Skills in numeracy and in communication, is also acceptable for entry.

Band 4: For entry to SQA higher national and professional development awards, usually 2-3 H grades and some S grades (1-3), including English, science and maths, or similar qualifications.

Band 5: For degree courses: 3-5 H grades, including English and biology, though chemistry/physics may also be considered and five S grades (1-3) including English, maths and one science subject, or similar. RCVS qualifications are also considered.

Degree Information

BSc (Hons) in veterinary nursing or veterinary nursing and practice management degrees are available.

Adult Qualifications

If over 21, it is possible to enter the degree course without formal qualifications provided you show high levels of ability and experience. Veterinary nurses (VNs) who already hold the RCVS VN certificate may top-up to degree level through such courses as the BSc (Hons) Veterinary Nursing (top-up) offered by Middlesex University. An Access to science course is also another option towards higher education.

Work Experience

This type of work is popular and entry is competitive, particularly entry to training places. Relevant work or voluntary experience is always useful and can improve your employment prospects when applying for entry to jobs, or for entry to courses. Any work that involves animals, such as experience at a vets, a Saturday job or holiday work, perhaps at a cattery or kennels, or on a farm, provides valuable experience. You can also gain valuable work experience as a voluntary helper for organisations that include the RSPCA/Scottish SPCA, Ulster SPCA, the People's Dispensary for Sick Animals (PDSA) and animal rescue centres.

Entry and Training

Entrants to the Royal College of Veterinary Surgeons (RCVS) training must be employed at a veterinary nurse approved centre (VNAC) or at an RCVS registered training practice (TP) before beginning the two-year. The RCVS website has details of VNACs and TPs. You need to contact the RCVS to register as a student veterinary nurse (VN) before starting your training. You work under supervision at a vets and usually have day or block-release to college to work towards NVQ level 2/3.

You can also choose to train through a full-time degree course. Courses are usually four years long. Those who wish to train by this route must satisfy the entry requirements in either academic or equivalent qualifications, or with British Veterinary Nursing Association (BVNA) qualifications. There are also HNDs and foundation degrees available in veterinary nursing. All courses combine study and practical work.

Qualified veterinary nurses working in approved training centres are eligible to go on to study for a two-year diploma in advanced veterinary nursing (surgical). This is a modular course and can be taken on a very flexible basis. If you are specifically interested in nursing horses, there is an RCVS certificate in equine veterinary nursing. All VNs are required to keep up to date by undertaking continuing professional development (CPD).

It is possible to begin work in a vet's surgery without academic qualifications, as an animal nursing assistant. Applicants who are unable to meet the educational RCVS requirements may take a one-year animal nursing assistant (ANA) certificate, which provides a direct entry route to VN training and qualification. See the Veterinary Animal Nursing Assistant job article for full details.

Training programmes, including apprenticeship schemes, may be available in your area. Advanced apprenticeships leading to qualification at level 3 can also be a route into higher education.

Mature applicants for training often have previous experience of working with animals and those without the required minimum qualifications for training can begin as an animal nursing assistant. However, those without formal qualifications, but can show high levels of ability and experience may also apply for VN training.

Opportunities and Pay

Career prospects are improving and there is an increasing demand for more specialised nursing. Many veterinary nurses (VNs) work in a vet's practice, but posts are also available with the RSPCA/ Scottish SPCA, Ulster SPCA, the PDSA, Blue Cross, university veterinary schools, zoos, kennels/catteries, central government departments and research establishments. You can be promoted to senior/head nurse or become a practice manager. Some veterinary nurses become involved in teaching and increasingly are moving into related careers, such as marketing posts within pharmaceutical companies.

Some boarding/breeding establishments often employ VNs as managers. Jobs may be available for trained nurses abroad in countries including New Zealand and Australia.

Salaries vary from practice to practice and may also depend on the area in which you work. Generally, trainee VNs earn around £11k-£12k and when fully qualified £15k-£18k a year. Senior/head nurses earn around £19k-£24k a year, depending on experience and on the size of practice. Sometimes accommodation may be provided.

Health

The work may involve a risk of infection and there is an allergy risk from animals. You need to be physically fit and have plenty of stamina.

Skills and Qualities

able to work well on your own, calm, good at handling animals, IT skills, not squeamish, observant, patient, reassuring, scientific approach

Relevant Subjects

Biology, Chemistry, Land and Environment, Science

Further Information

A Career as a Veterinary Nurse (Royal College of Veterinary Surgeons) - www.rcvs.org.uk/veterinarynurses

A Career in Veterinary Nursing (British Veterinary Nursing Association (BVNA)) www.bvna.org.uk/smartweb/careers

Lantra - The Sector Skills Council for environmental & land-based sector (Lantra) - http:/www.lantra.co.uk

Real Life Guide to Working with Animals & Wildlife (Trotman) - www.trotman.co.uk

VETNNET - www.vetnnet.com

VNJ (monthly) (BVNA) - www.bvna.org.uk

Working with animals (2009) (Babcock Lifeskills) - www.babcock-lifeskills.com/

Addresses

British Equine Veterinary Association (BEVA)
Mulberry House , 31 Market Street , Fordham, Ely CB7 5LQ
Phone: +44 (0)1638 723 555
Web: www.beva.org.uk

British Veterinary Nursing Association (BVNA)
82 Greenway Business Centre Harlow Business Park,
Essex CM19 5QE
Phone: +44 (0)1279 408 644
Web: www.bvna.org.uk

Royal College of Veterinary Surgeons (RCVS)
Belgravia House, 62-64 Horseferry Road, London SW1P 2AF
Phone: +44 (0)20 7222 2001
Web: www.rcvs.org.uk

Royal Veterinary College (RVC)
Royal College Street, London NW1 0TU
Phone: +44 (0)20 7468 5000
Web: www.rvc.ac.uk

Similar Jobs

Animal Care Assistant, Animal Technician/Technologist, Horse Groom, Veterinary Animal Nursing Assistant, Veterinary Surgeon

Veterinary Pathologist

CRCI:Environment, Animals and Plants
CLCI:WAL

Job Band: 5

Job Description

Veterinary pathologists investigate the cause and effects of disease and illness in animals, such as cancer or viral/bacterial infection. They also carry out an autopsy/post-mortem on a dead animal's body to determine the cause of death or the extent of disease.

Pathologists work in a laboratory and supervise the work of other laboratory staff, such as scientists and technicians. They usually work with a particular group of animals, such as birds (including wild or exotic birds), chicken and pheasant, or with small/large domestic animals, including cats and dogs, cattle and horses. Some veterinary pathologists may specialise in working with species of fish or with laboratory animals, including mice and rabbits.

The job involves looking at and examining in detail samples of an animal's blood, tissue and urine and carrying out tests to analyse the type of disease and its cause. They write reports of their findings and provide precise analytical details. Some veterinary pathologists work in veterinary research and areas of development. This can be new or improved medicines/ treatments, national disease surveillance in livestock, or vaccination trials.

Work Details

Usually work a basic 35-40hr week, Monday to Friday, which may need to include some evening and weekend work at times. Travel may be necessary at times to various sites, such as farms, stables, a vet's practice, clinics, or to zoos and wild animal reserves. However, most work is done indoors in a laboratory that is clean and hygienic, quiet and well-lit. Specific protective clothing is usually worn during tests and examinations, including overalls, gloves and a facemask.

Qualification

- **England, Wales and Northern Ireland**

Band 5: For degree course: high grades usually required in at least three A levels, to include chemistry and two others from physics, maths and a biological science; some GCSEs (A*-C) including English, biology, maths, physics (or combined science, double), or equivalent qualifications. A non-science subject for the third A level is acceptable at some veterinary schools, and GCSE double science is usually acceptable in place of separate science subjects.

- **Scotland**

Band 5: For degree course: high grades in five H grades, usually to include chemistry and two from physics, biology or maths; some S grades (1-3) including English, biology, maths, physics (or combined science, double). Many universities also accept similar qualifications.

Degree Information

Either a degree in veterinary science/medicine followed by a postgraduate qualification, or a degree in veterinary pathology taken as an additional part of a veterinary medicine degree.

Adult Qualifications

Qualification as a veterinary surgeon is usually required for entry.

Work Experience

Entry to this career is highly competitive and it is essential that you have gained some relevant work or voluntary experience before applying for first degree courses. According to the RCVS, all applicants need to show evidence of their interest and commitment by having gained work experience in a veterinary practice, including the handling of animals and livestock. Work on a farm, in kennels/catteries, a wildlife sanctuary/animal welfare society, or similar, also demonstrates enthusiasm. Generally, you must complete at least 4-6 weeks' (preferably more) work experience for entry to courses.

Entry and Training

Most veterinary pathologists first train and qualify as veterinary surgeons before training in this specialism. For those working in diagnostic pathology this is essential. Those in research posts may not absolutely need a qualification in veterinary medicine, but without it may find career progression difficult.

Upon graduation there are two basic types of postgraduate education: on-the-job training and residency programmes. You gain on-the-job experience working as a junior veterinary pathologist or as an assistant in a laboratory. Some employers provide time for study and training. There are some residency training opportunities in university veterinary medicine schools. See the Royal College of Veterinary Surgeons website for more details.

Once fully qualified as a veterinary pathologist, you are expected to follow a programme of continuing professional development (CPD) throughout your career in order to maintain up-to-date knowledge and skills. The Royal College of Veterinary Surgeons (RCVS) provides information on CPD and the Royal College of Pathologists (RCP) offers a membership scheme that requires you to take the RCP veterinary pathology examination to qualify as a member.

There is also a BSc/BA (Hons) course in veterinary pathology (intercalated) at Cambridge University and the University of London, which lasts one year and is usually completed between the second and third year of the five or six years veterinary degree course. This means that the time taken to complete vet training is extended by a year, but does form a good introduction to the work, although it is not a full professional training in veterinary pathology.

There is also a degree course in veterinary pathogenesis (BSc Hons) offered by the University of Bristol, though this must be followed by a veterinary medicine degree course that is validated by the Royal Veterinary College (RVC) to be able to practise as a veterinary pathologist. Postgraduate qualifications are usual and include an advanced certificate in veterinary practice (veterinary pathology).

Most adults enter this profession after qualifying as a veterinary surgeon (see job article). Funds for training are few and fiercely contested, but may be available from pharmaceutical companies, commercial diagnostic laboratories, the Royal College of Veterinary Surgeons (RCVS) Trust Fund, and the Biotechnology and Biological Sciences Research Council (BBSRC). Contact the RCVS for information on available courses and sources of funding.

Opportunities and Pay

There are opportunities in industry, government laboratories, universities, diagnostic laboratories and research institutes. Promotion prospects are possible from assistant/junior posts to veterinary pathologist status leading to senior positions, consultant and head of department. Some veterinary pathologists may work in other countries such as the USA or within the European Union (EU) and others may work as a freelance consultant.

Salaries vary depending on employer, though for an assistant/junior veterinary pathologist post usually start at around £15k a year, rising to around £33k-£48k with experience and promotion. Senior and consultant posts can attract a salary up to and over £65k.

Health

The work involves a risk of infection.

Skills and Qualities

able to work both on your own and in a team, analytical skills, attention to detail, good at handling animals, good spoken communication, good written English, health & safety awareness, IT skills, methodical, problem-solving skills, scientific approach.

Relevant Subjects

Biology, Chemistry, English, Land and Environment, Mathematics, Physics, Science

Further Information

European College of Veterinary Pathologists - www.ecvpath.org

Veterinary Record (weekly journal) (British Veterinary Association) - http://veterinaryrecord.bvapublications.com

VetPathCareers - www.vetpathcareers.com

Working with animals (2009) (Babcock Lifeskills) - www.babcock-lifeskills.com/

Addresses

Biotechnology and Biological Sciences Research Council (BBSRC)
Polaris House North Star Avenue, Swindon, Wiltshire SN2 1UH
Phone: +44 (0)1793 413 200
Web: www.bbsrc.ac.uk

British Veterinary Association (BVA)
7 Mansfield Street, London W1G 9NQ
Phone: +44 (0)20 7636 6541
Web: www.bva.co.uk

Royal College of Pathologists (RCPath)
2 Carlton House Terrace, London SW1Y 5AF
Phone: +44 (0)20 7451 6700
Web: www.rcpath.org

Royal College of Veterinary Surgeons (RCVS)
Belgravia House, 62-64 Horseferry Road, London SW1P 2AF
Phone: +44 (0)20 7222 2001
Web: www.rcvs.org.uk

Royal Veterinary College (RVC)
Royal College Street, London NW1 0TU
Phone: +44 (0)20 7468 5000
Web: www.rvc.ac.uk

Veterinary Laboratories Agency
New Haw, Addlestone, Surrey KT15 3NB
Phone: +44 (0)1932 341111
Web: www.defra.gov.uk/vla/

Similar Jobs

Animal Physiotherapist, Animal Technician/Technologist, Forensic Scientist, Pathologist, Veterinary Surgeon

Veterinary Surgeon

CRCI:Environment, Animals and Plants
CLCI:WAL — Job Band: 5

Job Description

Veterinary surgeons (vets) combine practical surgical skills with their knowledge of animal physiology, medicine and nutrition. They aim to prevent disease in animals and diagnoses, treat and care for sick and injured animals. Usually treat animals with drugs through tablets or injections, give anaesthetics, perform operations and take X-rays, assisted by veterinary nurses (VNs). They give advice on the general health, breeding and disease control of both large and small animals.

Vets also give general and healthcare advice to owners about caring for and feeding their animals. They check livestock to prevent outbreaks of disease and deal with nutritional or genetic problems. Also liaise with other professionals, and supervise and train veterinary staff. May specialise in caring for particular types of animals, such as horses, or may move into research or disease prevention.

Many vets carry out inspection duties for central and local government, including testing for notifiable diseases, such as bovine brucellosis, rabies and tuberculosis, or looking at the living conditions of animals in zoos, cattle markets, laboratories, riding stables, kennels or in pet shops.

Work Details

Veterinary surgeons who work for a practice rarely work a standard 9-5 day. A vet is required to provide 24 hrs a day emergency cover, so usually works a shift/rota system with other members of the practice. Work is usually in consulting rooms of a private veterinary practice, but also visits people's homes or travels to farms, stables etc within a local area.

Vets are responsible for animal welfare and health, giving sound advice and observing legal regulations. The work can be very demanding and requires coping with the sight of blood. Some aspects of the work may be upsetting, such as the need to humanely kill badly injured or diseased animals to prevent them suffering excessively.

Physical fitness and stamina is essential due to some heavy lifting, kneeling, bending down and walking on rough ground. The work environment can sometimes be dirty, smelly, cold or wet. There is a risk of attack from distressed animals. Protective clothing is usually necessary.

Qualification

- **England, Wales and Northern Ireland**

Band 5: For degree course: high grades usually required in at least three A levels, to include chemistry and biology and either physics or maths, plus some GCSEs (A*-C) including English, biology, maths, physics (or combined science, double), or equivalent qualifications. A non-science subject for the third A level is acceptable at some veterinary schools, and GCSE double science is usually acceptable in place of separate science subjects.

• **Scotland**

Band 5: For degree course: high grades in five H grades (AAABB), usually to include chemistry and two from physics, biology or maths; some S grades (1-3) including English, biology, maths, physics (or combined science, double). Many universities also accept similar qualifications.

Degree Information

A Royal College of Veterinary Surgeons (RCVS) approved degree in veterinary science/medicine is required for entry to this job. Courses are available at Bristol, Cambridge, Edinburgh, Glasgow, Liverpool and London (Royal Veterinary College). Nottingham University also offers degrees/postgraduate qualifications (currently awaiting RCVS validation), including a non-science students' veterinary course.

Adult Qualifications

Most successful mature applicants to degree courses in veterinary sciences/medicine have a first or upper second class honours degree in a related subject, such as zoology or biochemistry. Some universitiies offer degrees for no-science students. All potential mature applicants should contact the vet schools for advice.

Work Experience

Entry to this career is highly competitive and it is essential that you have some relevant work or voluntary experience before applying to veterinary schools. According to the RCVS, all applicants need to show evidence of their interest and commitment by having gained work experience in a veterinary practice, including the handling of animals and livestock. Work on a farm, in kennels/catteries, a wildlife sanctuary/animal welfare society, or similar, also demonstrates enthusiasm. You must complete at least 4-6 weeks' (preferably more) work experience for entry to courses.

Entry and Training

Vets must be registered with the RCVS to practise in the UK or the European Union (EU). This is achieved by successful completion of a veterinary science/medicine degree course from a UK university, or equivalent qualification awarded by a member state of the EU, or another overseas qualification that is recognised by the RCVS. Entry to training courses, which last for five years (six at Cambridge) is highly competitive. Before training, some related practical experience is required by veterinary schools in a veterinary practice or on a farm, at kennels/catteries or stables.

A BVetMed graduate accelerated programme that lasts four years, is available for students with a degree in a biological science discipline. Contact the RCVS for details of all training/qualification options.

Graduates usually start as an assistant vet in a private practice and gain experience on the job from a senior vet. After experience they may choose to study further for specialist courses in subjects like cardiology and ophthalmology through the RCVS. This can lead to specialist status.

All RCVS registered vets have to undertake continuing professional development (CPD) each year. At the moment this requirement is 105 hours over a three year period. Short courses and seminars are available through the RCVS, the British Veterinary Association (BVA), the British Equine Veterinary Association (BEVA) and the British Small Animal Veterinary Association (BSAVA).

Mature applicants to veterinary science/medicine courses require the same level of qualifications as a young person, and also need work experience in handling animals. However, there are very few training places available for mature entrants. Applications from graduates with a first or upper second class honours degree in a related subject, such as biochemistry or zoology, are more likely to be considered. Contact the RCVS for information on all available training opportunities.

Opportunities and Pay

In the UK there are over 20,000 vets registered with the RCVS. Currently, employment prospects are good and the number of vacancies still outweighs the number of available qualified vets. Most vets are in private general practice, but you can also work in a university, local government, the Royal Army Veterinary Corps, an animal welfare society or charity, including the RSPCA/Scottish SPCA, Ulster SPCA or PDSA. Jobs are also available in safari parks and zoos, and in the public sector, including the Meat Hygiene Service, Veterinary Medicines Directorate, Veterinary Laboratories Agency and the Overseas Development Administration.

Other opportunities are in industry and commerce, such as pharmaceutical companies and international/overseas organisations. There are opportunities for research and in lecturing at veterinary schools. You may be self-employed or work part time, and there are opportunities to work as a locum (temporary appointment).

Pay depends upon the size and location of the practice. Entrants are likely to earn around £30k a year, which may be enhanced by allowances for accommodation, travel expenses, professional membership fees and for continuing professional development (CPD). With over 5 years' experience, earnings can be around £48k a year. A senior partner in a practice can earn in the region of £70k-£100k a year.

Health

Good physical fitness is essential. The work involves a risk of infection.

Skills and Qualities

able to inspire confidence, assertive, good at handling animals, good communication skills, IT skills, manual dexterity, not squeamish, observant, problem-solving skills, scientific approach, tactful

Relevant Subjects

Biology, Chemistry, English, Land and Environment, Mathematics, Physics, Science

Further Information

Career as a Veterinary Surgeon (Royal College of Veterinary Surgeons) - www.rcvs.org.uk

Government Veterinary Service (DEFRA) - www.defra.gov.uk/gvs

Lantra Careers (A Future In...) (Lantra) - www.afuturein.com

Real Life Guide to Working with Animals & Wildlife (Trotman) - www.trotman.co.uk

Veterinary Record (weekly journal) (British Veterinary Association) - http://veterinaryrecord.bvapublications.com

▶Working with animals (2009) (Babcock Lifeskills) - www.babcock-lifeskills.com/

Addresses

British Equine Veterinary Association (BEVA)
Mulberry House , 31 Market Street , Fordham, Ely CB7 5LQ
Phone: +44 (0)1638 723 555
Web: www.beva.org.uk

British Small Animal Veterinary Association (BSAVA)
Woodrow House, 1 Telford Way, Waterwells Business Park, Quedgley, Gloucestershire GL2 2AB
Phone: +44 (0)1452 726 700
Web: www.bsava.com

British Veterinary Association (BVA)
7 Mansfield Street, London W1G 9NQ
Phone: +44 (0)20 7636 6541
Web: www.bva.co.uk

Royal Army Veterinary Corps
Contact via website,
Phone: 0845 730 0111 (UK only)
Web: www.army.mod.uk/army-medical-services/5320.aspx

Royal College of Veterinary Surgeons (RCVS)
Belgravia House, 62-64 Horseferry Road, London SW1P 2AF
Phone: +44 (0)20 7222 2001
Web: www.rcvs.org.uk

Royal Veterinary College (RVC)
Royal College Street, London NW1 0TU
Phone: +44 (0)20 7468 5000
Web: www.rvc.ac.uk

Similar Jobs

Animal Physiotherapist, Biologist, RSPCA/Scottish SPCA Inspector, Veterinary Nurse, Veterinary Pathologist, Zoological Scientist

Visual Merchandiser

also known as: Retail Display Assistant, Window Dresser

CRCI:Design, Arts and Crafts
CLCI:ET Job Band: 2 to 4

Job Description

Visual merchandisers design, plan and create window displays of goods and products for a retail store or outlet and floor/counter displays inside a store/shop. They arrange products in a store according to a particular display design and policy of a chain store or manufacturer and are responsible for reflecting the 'look' or image of a product or company. They use creative skills to reflect current trends and encourage customers to buy the products. May create themed displays for a group of stores, or for individual seasons such as Spring, Christmas and holiday themes.

Visual merchandisers research lifestyle concepts and trends and follow a plan or scale drawing to create the display, often using computer-aided design (CAD) packages. They usually work with others in a team, which may include graphic artists and fashion designers. In smaller shops, this work may be the responsibility of a sales assistant or manager.

Work Details

Full-time display staff normally work around a 39 hour week; five days a week, including evenings and possibly weekends. The work involves keeping up to date with current trends and fashions. Team work is usually involved. You may remain in one place or need to travel around to different places. The work involves bending down, kneeling, lifting and carrying. Sometimes the area for the display can be small and cramped. You may also have to climb ladders.

Qualification

• England, Wales and Northern Ireland

Band 2: For entry to jobs, no minimum qualifications are needed, but it is an advantage to have some GCSEs (A*-C) or equivalent in subjects that include English and maths.

Band 3: For entry to jobs, HNC or a relevant Diploma, usually at least 4 GCSEs (A*-C) including art and English, or equivalent. A portfolio of work is required.

Band 4: For HND, Diploma of Higher Education or foundation degree: 1-2 A levels and some GCSEs (A*-C) usually including English and maths, or equivalent.

• Scotland

Band 2: Although academic qualifications are not specified for this job, it is an advantage to have some S grades (1-3) in subjects that include English and maths, or similar.

Band 3: For entry: usually at least four S grades (1-3) including English and maths, or similar. A portfolio of work may be required.

Band 4: For entry to SQA higher national and professional development awards, usually 2-3 H grades and some S grades (1-3), including English and maths, or similar qualifications.

Adult Qualifications

Formal qualifications are not essential, but are useful for some college courses. Entry requirements may be relaxed for mature applicants who have relevant experience. There are Access and foundation level courses in some areas, which give adults without qualifications a route onto higher education courses. Check with individual institutions.

Work Experience

Employers or colleges/universities may prefer candidates who have relevant work or voluntary experience. This includes work in a shop or any work area, such as advertising, that increases your awareness of visual design.

Entry and Training

There are no set entry qualifications, but most entrants have a relevant qualification in an art and design subject. A portfolio of art work is usually needed for college entry and for employment. Many entrants take a British Display Society (BDS) course or a BTEC/SQA course prior to employment. The BDS offers national diplomas in retail and design and point of sale design. There are full and part-time courses available, including a City & Guilds course in visual merchandising, and also some distance learning, day-release and evening classes. The courses usually include work experience and can last between one and three years, depending on the level of course you take. It is also possible for retail/sales assistants to move into display work, training on the job and following a recognised course of study.

Courses offered by the BDS includes the general certificate and general certificate higher level, both one year full time, and the national diploma in retail display design, which is two years part time. Their website has full details, including information on colleges that run the courses. The Fashion Retail Academy also runs a level 4 one year full-time diploma in visual merchandising, plus a range of short courses. The Chartered Society of Designers runs a continuing professional development (CPD) scheme.

A Diploma/Welsh Baccalaureate may be available in your area in creative and media and may provide a route onto higher education courses. Foundation degrees are available in visual design communication, visual merchandising and promotional design. Training programmes, including apprenticeship schemes, may be available in your area for entry to this job. Advanced apprenticeships leading to qualification at level 3 can also be a route into higher education.

For mature entrants, previous experience in design or retail is an advantage and a good portfolio of work can be very useful for employers and courses. You can benefit through government training opportunities that may be available in your area. You can also gain recognition of previous experience through Accreditation of Prior Learning (APL)or by working towards relevant S/NVQs. Contact your local Connexions or careers office, Jobcentre Plus, Next Step service or Learning and Skills Council (LSC)/Local Enterprise Company (LEC) for details of all training opportunities and schemes, inlcuding apprenticeships for adults.

Opportunities and Pay

There is usually strong competition for jobs, with employment in independent shops, chain stores, supermarkets and department stores, airports, hotels and cruise liners, film and TV, airports and seaports. Some manufacturing companies have staff who set up displays in shops or at exhibitions. It is also possible to obtain work with design companies that supply displays for small stores. Further opportunities for display work exist with museums, art galleries, theme parks, historic and stately homes. In some companies there are prospects for promotion to jobs such as supervisor, display manager or merchandiser. Freelance work is possible.

Pay can vary considerably but generally, salaries start at around £14k, rising to around £23k-£24k a year with experience. High earners can expect up to £35k a year and some may earn more.

Health
This job requires stamina and good general fitness. Normal colour vision is desirable, since the work involves using a sense of colour.

Skills and Qualities
able to work both on your own and in a team, adaptable, creative and imaginative flair, eye for shape/colour, eye for visual effect, good communication skills, good interpersonal skills, manual dexterity, specialist IT skills

Relevant Subjects
Art and Design, Design and technology, Retail and distribution

Further Information
AGCAS: Fashion & Design (Job Sector Briefing) (AGCAS) - www.prospects.ac.uk

Apprenticeship Schemes (National Apprenticeship Service) - www.apprenticeships.org.uk

Chartered Society of Designers (Chartered Society of Designers) - www.csd.org.uk

Design Week (Design Week) - www.designweek.co.uk

Drapers: Fashionnews, jobs and trends - www.drapersonline.com

Real Life Guide to Retail (Trotman) - www.trotman.co.uk

Skillsmart Retail - sector skills council for the retail industry - www.skillsmartretail.com

The Designer (Chartered Society of Designers) - www.thedesignermagazine.com

Training Schemes - www.direct.gov.uk/en/educationandlearning

▶Working in art & design (2009) (Babcock Lifeskills) - www.babcock-lifeskills.com/

▶Working in fashion & clothing (2008) (Babcock Lifeskills) - www.babcock-lifeskills.com/

▶Working in retail & customer services (2008) (Babcock Lifeskills) - www.babcock-lifeskills.com/

Addresses
British Display Society (BDS)
14-18 Heralds Way, Town Centre, South Woodham Ferrers, Essex CM3 5TQ
Phone: +44 (020 8856 2030
Web: www.britishdisplaysociety.co.uk

Design Council
34 Bow Street, London WC2E 7DL
Phone: +44 (0)20 7420 5200
Web: www.designcouncil.org.uk

Design Wales
University of Wales Institute, Cardiff Western Avenue CF5 2YB
Phone: +44 (0) 2920 41 7043
Web: www.designwales.org

Fashion Retail Academy
15 Gresse Street, London W1T 1QL
Phone: +44 (0)20 7307 2345
Web: www.fashionretailacademy.ac.uk

Similar Jobs
Exhibition Designer, Film/TV & Theatre Set/Stage Designer, Interior Designer, Photographic Stylist, Retail Assistant, Retail Manager

Volunteer Manager
also known as: Volunteer Coordinator, Volunteer Organiser

CRCI:Social Work and Counselling Services
CLCI:KEM — Job Band: 3 to 5

Job Description
Volunteer managers recruit, train and coordinate groups of volunteers for 'not for profit' organisations, either for their own charity or on behalf of clients. Look for and arrange volunteer work and manage and design volunteer projects. Supervise and support volunteers during their work, and provide them with necessary information. Often publicises volunteer projects, perhaps giving presentations locally, and writing articles or reports on them.

Volunteer managers take care of some of the organisation's administrative affairs, which include maintaining accounts and general administration, grant applications, working with fundraisers, as well as information and database management. May be in charge of running a charity shop.

Work Details
Usually works a basic 39 hr week, Monday to Friday, though may be required to work occasional extra hours at evenings and weekends, depending on workload. Some employers offer flexitime. You normally work from an office, but may be required to visit the community, perhaps giving presentations in schools or community centres, for which your own means of transport is helpful. You are likely to come into contact with a wide range of people and often need to be persuasive and diplomatic.

Qualification
No specific qualifications are required but employers expect a good standard of secondary education. A qualification in marketing or a subject such as social care is particularly useful.

• England, Wales and Northern Ireland
Band 3: For entry: usually at least 4 GCSEs (A*-C) including English and maths, or equivalent.

Band 4: For BTEC higher national award: 1-2 A levels and some GCSEs (A*-C) usually including English and maths, or equivalent.

• Scotland
Band 3: For entry: 3-4 S grades (1-3) including English and maths, or similar.

Band 4: For SQA higher national award: usually 2-3 H grades and some S grades (1-3), often including English and maths, or similar qualifications.

Adult Qualifications
Any qualifications in a relevant subject, such as marketing or social care are useful, but not usually specified. Experience in voluntary work is the most important factor for entry, though employers expect a good standard of secondary education.

Work Experience
There can be considerable competition for this job, so extensive experience in volunteer work can be a great advantage, as can work experience in people management or in sales and marketing.

Entry and Training
Volunteer managers/coordinators come from a variety of backgrounds and with a wide range of qualifications. Some large organisations may prefer graduates, preferably in social sciences, but enthusiasm, experience and commitment to the job are the most important factors for entry. You can study for a marketing, personnel management, or social care course before applying, while maintaining an interest in voluntary work. A criminal record bureau (CRB)/Disclosure Scotland check is required if working with vulnerable groups such as children or the elderly.

Training is on the job and usually ongoing, often with additional courses run by the employer. Some of the larger charities run graduate training programmes. Websites such as Volunteering England and Volunteering Wales have details of opportunities in volunteering.

The Award Scheme Development Accreditation Network (ASDAN) awards Community Volunteering Qualifications (CVQ) at levels 1-3. Working for a Charity runs relevant short courses and Volunteering England runs an excellence in volunteer management programme. Some coordinators choose to study for the Chartered Institute of Marketing's certificate and diploma. Some postgraduate courses are also available, such as an MSc in voluntary sector organisation. There are also NVQs in the management of volunteers at levels 3-5.

Mature entry is common and this can be a second career for those with experience in a related area, such as business and administration, marketing and finance, or public relations. Some may begin as a volunteer worker and apply for this job when experienced.

Opportunities and Pay

Large companies, political parties, hospitals and large charity organisations, are increasingly employing their own volunteer managers; these charities may be national or international and require coordinators in various parts of the country and overseas. Volunteer organiser agencies working on behalf of clients are likely to be small organisations probably working at a local level. With professional experience and qualifications, you can move into the marketing and publicity sector, or into social work or charity fundraising.

Salaries vary widely but tend to be around £18k-£24k a year, and up to £40k with experience. Many posts are part time so pro-rata rates apply. Larger organisations may pay more to those volunteer organisers/coordinators in managerial roles.

Skills and Qualities

able to delegate, committed, good communication skills, good interpersonal skills, good presentation skills, IT skills, negotiating skills, outgoing personality, patient, persuasive

Relevant Subjects

Business and accounting, Economics, English, Mathematics, Psychology, Sociology

Further Information

AGCAS: Charity & Development Work (Job Sector Briefing) (AGCAS) - www.prospects.ac.uk

Association of Volunteer Managers - www.volunteermanagers.org.uk

Careers Wales - www.careerswales.com/

Volunteering England - www.volunteering.org.uk

Volunteering Wales - www.volunteering-wales.net/

Wales Council for Voluntary Action (WCVA) - www.wcva.org.uk

Addresses

Award Scheme Development Accreditation Network (ASDAN)
Wainbrook House, Hudds Vale Road, St George, Bristol BS5 7HY
Phone: +44 (0)117 941 1126
Web: www.asdan.co.uk

Chartered Institute of Marketing (CIM)
Moor Hall, Cookham, Maidenhead, Berkshire SL6 9QH
Phone: +44 (0) 1628 427120
Web: www.cim.co.uk

Volunteer Development Agency
129 Ormeau Road, Belfast BT7 1SH
Phone: +44 (0)28 9023 6100
Web: www.volunteering-ni.org

Volunteer Development Scotland
Jubilee House, Forthside Way, Stirling FK8 1QZ
Phone: +44 (0)1786 479593
Web: www.vds.org.uk

Working for a Charity
NCVO, Regent's Wharf, 8 All Saints Street, London N1 9RL
Web: www.wfac.org.uk

Similar Jobs

Aid Worker, Charity Fundraiser, Community Development Worker, Social Worker

Waiter/Waitress

CRCI:Catering and Hospitality
CLCI:IC Job Band: 1

Job Description

Waiters and waitresses serve food and drinks to customers at dining tables in cafis, restaurants, pubs, hotels and other catering places. They welcome people, show them to a table, hand out the menu and take their orders. They need to have knowledge of the food being served and may advise customers what to choose. Waiting staff take the customers' orders to the kitchen staff for preparation, collect orders from the kitchen when the food is ready and served onto a plate, and deliver it to customers. This is known as 'plate service'. They may be trained to deliver prepared food from the kitchen and serve it to customers at the table. This is called 'silver service'. A 'gueridon' service may be offered at some restaurants when the food is cooked and served at the customer's table.

Also prepares bills, takes payment by cash, giving change if required, and takes payments by cheque, credit/debit card, and gives a receipt. Clears and lays tables for the next customers. Ensures that linen, cutlery, china and glassware are clean and correctly placed on tables.

Work Details

A 39-40 hr week is normally worked on a shift basis. You often work in the evenings, at weekends and on public holidays. Sometimes you start work in the early morning and may not finish until late evening, but you have time off during the afternoon instead. You look after all sorts of people. You must be able to cope with difficult customers and complaints, and remain calm and courteous. Work varies depending upon the type of restaurant. In this job you are on your feet most of the time and have to carry trays, which can be heavy. There are times when you are very busy so you need to work quickly. Work in the kitchen can be noisy, hot and steamy.

You need to follow the rules and regulations that govern health and safety, hygiene and alcohol provision. A uniform may be required. This may be provided by the employer or they may specify a basic style, such as a black skirt/trousers and a white or coloured shirt.

Qualification

There are no formal requirements for entry but a good standard of general education is preferable. Employers look for those who have the ability to communicate well and have a welcoming personality. The use of a foreign language is an advantage in some jobs.

- **England, Wales and Northern Ireland**

Band 1: No minimum qualifications are required, but you are expected to have a good level of general education. Some formal/ vocational qualifications at any level are useful.

- **Scotland**

Band 1: No minimum qualifications are required, but you are expected to have a good level of general education. Some formal/ vocational qualifications at any level are useful.

Adult Qualifications

No pre-entry qualifications are usually required for mature entrants, although some academic/vocational qualifications at any level may be an advantage. English and maths are useful subjects. You can improve your skills and qualifications by working through the Foundation Learning programme. This involves taking credit-based units and qualifications to help you progress.

Work Experience

Any work experience can equip you with skills that you can use in the future and add to your CV. There is often plenty of paid part-time catering work available, including Saturday and seasonal jobs. Any sales work or other work with the public is also useful.

Entry and Training
Training schemes often combine on-the-job training with block-release or day-release study at a local college. It is also possible to take full-time courses, including BTEC first diplomas/SQA national certificate modules in hospitality. There are also specialist courses available in subjects such as preparing food at a table, hygiene and health and safety. Relevant S/NVQs are available, including food and drink service and multi-skilled hospitality services at level 2, or in catering and hospitality. Training programmes, including apprenticeships in hospitality or customer service leading to level 2 and advanced apprenticeships leading to level 3, may be available in your area. A Diploma/Welsh Baccalaureate may also be available in your area in hospitality.

For those wishing to specialise in wines and spirits, the Wine and Spirits Education Trust (WSET) offer relevant qualifications, such as the foundation certificate in wines at level 1. See the Sommelier job article for further details. Promotion opportunities may be better if you have specialist training in silver service or wine appreciation, for example. Knowledge of a foreign language can be useful if you want to work overseas or on a cruise ship.

Mature applicants with experience in sales, catering or customer care are usually welcomed by employers. Government-funded training schemes, such as apprenticeships, may be available in your area. You can also gain recognition of previous experience through Accreditation of Prior Learning (APL) or by working towards relevant S/NVQs. Contact your local careers office, Jobcentre Plus, Next Step service or Learning and Skills Council (LSC)/Local Enterprise Company (LEC) for details of all training opportunities and schemes.

Opportunities and Pay
Jobs are available throughout the UK in restaurants and pubs, hotels, cafis, roadside and motorway outlets, leisure and holiday centres, Eurostar, ferries and cruise ships, airports, bistros, tapas bars and coffee shops etc. More than 150,000 people work as waiters/waitresses. There is often more work in the summer and during the Christmas and New Year period when restaurants are busier. It is fairly easy to find temporary and part-time work as staff turnover is high.

Experience can lead to extra responsibility. This can include looking after a group of tables and supervising junior staff. You can progress to head waiter ('maitre d') or manager. Work abroad is possible, particularly if you speak the host language.

Pay varies, but most waiters/waitresses earn from the minimum wage to £7.00 an hour and some earn more. A head waiter can earn around £10.50 an hour. Your pay can be increased if customers leave you tips. Some restaurants add a service charge to the bill and share this between staff. You are probably given free or subsidised meals while on duty.

Health
People with certain skin conditions may not be able to do this job. For this job you need to have good general fitness.

Skills and Qualities
able to work quickly, alert, clear speaking voice, energetic, friendly, good memory, numeracy skills, polite, smart appearance, steady hand

Relevant Subjects
Hospitality and catering

Further Information
Apprenticeship Schemes (National Apprenticeship Service) - www.apprenticeships.org.uk

CareerScope: Hospitality and Leisure (Springboard UK) - http://careerscope.springboarduk.net/

Caterer and Hotelkeeper (weekly) (Reed Business Information) - www.caterersearch.com/Home/

Diploma in Hospitality (People 1st) - www.hospitalitydiploma.co.uk

Foundation Learning (QCDA) - www.qcda.gov.uk

People 1st - sector skills council for hospitality, leisure, travel and tourism - www.people1st.co.uk

So you want to work in the Food Industry (Wayland) - www.waylandbooks.co.uk

Springboard UK - www.springboarduk.net

Springboard Wales - http://wales.springboarduk.net/

Training Schemes - www.direct.gov.uk/en/educationandlearning

UKSP - Guide to Success in Hospitality, Leisure, Travel & Tourism - www.uksp.co.uk

► Working in food & drink (2007) (Babcock Lifeskills) - www.babcock-lifeskills.com/

► Working in hospitality & catering (2009) (Babcock Lifeskills) - www.babcock-lifeskills.com/

Addresses
British Hospitality Association (BHA)
Queens House, 55-56 Lincoln's Inn Fields, London WC2A 3BH
Phone: +44 (0)207 404 7744
Web: www.bha.org.uk

Wine & Spirit Education Trust (WSET)
International Wine & Spirit Centre, 39-45 Bermondsey Street, London SE1 3XF
Phone: +44 (0)20 7089 3800
Web: www.wset.co.uk

Similar Jobs
Air Cabin Crew, Bartender, Food Service Assistant, Kitchen Assistant/Porter, Restaurant Manager, Sommelier

Warden: Sheltered Housing
also known as: Scheme Warden, Sheltered Housing Warden, Supported Housing Warden

CRCI:Social Work and Counselling Services
CLCI:KEZ Job Band: 2 to 3

Job Description
Wardens are responsible for the day-to-day management and administration of warden controlled sheltered housing and the welfare of tenants. They support tenants and help them to live independently in their home. They help the sheltered housing scheme to run smoothly, deal with any problems that arise and manage any communal facilities on site. Wardens carry out regular health and safety checks and reports any repair or maintenance issues.

They offer a rapid response when a community alarm system is activated and deal with any emergencies. May give simple first aid. Wardens maintain face-to-face contact with tenants to identify individual needs, and are aware of changes in their medical or social circumstances. Arrange appropriate support for tenants from voluntary and statutory agencies, handle any complaints and encourage participation in leisure and community-based activities. All wardens have a range of duties that depend upon the type of accommodation they supervise. May supervise clerical, cleaning and administrative staff and are responsible for their training and development.

Work Details
Hours of work are often 9am to 5pm, Monday to Friday, with an emergency service operating at other times. May work unsociable hours, including evenings and weekends. You may be on call at all times of the day and night. Most wardens 'live in' when they are on duty, or may have permanent accommodation near to or within the sheltered housing. Duties depend on the people for whom you are responsible.

You may have to deal with distressed, ill or lonely residents.

Qualification

• England, Wales and Northern Ireland

Band 2: Although academic qualifications are not specified for this job, it is an advantage to have some GCSEs (A*-C) in any subject, or equivalent.

Band 3: For entry to some courses and jobs: at least 4 GCSEs (A*-C) including English and maths, or equivalent.

• Scotland

Band 2: Although academic qualifications are not specified for this job, it is an advantage to have some S grades (1-3) in any subject, or similar qualifications.

Band 3: For entry to some courses and jobs: at least four S grades (1-3) including English and maths, or similar qualifications.

Adult Qualifications

Formal qualifications are not always required for this job. Practical experience in care work, nursing, or social work are often more important than any specific vocational qualifications.

Work Experience

Relevant work or voluntary experience can equip you with skills that you can use in the future and that you can add to your CV. There are often opportunities available for voluntary work that give you experience of working with people. In particular, any experience of working with vulnerable people that demonstrates your personal skills is most valued. Community Service Volunteers (CSV) has details of health and social care volunteering projects.

Entry and Training

This job is particularly suitable for older, more experienced people. Although no minimum qualifications are specified, those with experience of working in a care setting or in accommodation management are at an advantage. Training is mainly on the job, learning from an experienced warden, combined with short courses in topics such as health and safety. Pre-entry checks include a Criminal Records Bureau (CRB)/Disclosure Scotland check.

There are job-related qualifications that you can do, including vocationally related qualifications. The Chartered Institute of Housing (CIH) has devised a level 2-4 certificate in housing with a housing support pathway (levels 3-4 only) which is applicable to wardens. The Centre for Housing and Support (CHS) offers the full range of CIH qualifications as well as a foundation degree in housing with support. This is a three-year part-time course which is validated by the University of Plymouth. CHS also offers a range of short courses for people working in sheltered housing which can contribute to your continuing professional development (CPD). Topics include conflict and dispute in sheltered housing and lone working. Contact the CIH or CHS for details of all available courses.

The Sheltered Housing Network (SHN) also offers a range of sheltered/supported housing qualifications at levels 2-4, including a national certificate and diploma. Contact SHN for details. Relevant S/NVQs in health and social care and housing are available at levels 2-4. Training programmes, including apprenticeship schemes, may be available in your area. A new advanced modern apprenticeship in housing is available through the sector skills council Asset Skills and the CIH. Contact Asset Skills for details. Advanced apprenticeships leading to qualification at level 3 can also be a route into higher education.

Adult entry is common and those with experience in social work, nursing, or care work have an advantage. You can study through distance learning for the Chartered Institute of Housing certificate in housing at levels 2-4.

Opportunities and Pay

Sheltered accommodation is found throughout the country. Most jobs are with local authorities, housing associations, privately owned sheltered housing or almshouses. With experience you can move into housing officer work or management of sheltered housing. With additional qualifications it may be possible to move into other related areas, such as social work or counselling.

Pay varies depending on location and employer. If accommodation is included, earnings are likely to be less. Depending on experience and responsibilities, wardens of sheltered housing can earn in the region of £12.5k-£16k a year, rising to around £20k-£26k with more experience and up to £30k for management roles. You may receive shift allowances and overtime on top of your basic salary.

Skills and Qualities

able to cope under pressure, able to cope with emergencies, able to live and work closely with other people, approachable, caring, energetic, friendly, good communication skills, good organisational skills, health & safety awareness, tolerant

Relevant Subjects

English, Health and social care, Psychology, Sociology

Further Information

Apprenticeship Schemes (National Apprenticeship Service) - www.apprenticeships.org.uk

Asset Skills - sector skills council for the places where we live and work - www.assetskills.org

Community Care (weekly) (Reed) - www.communitycare.co.uk

Community Service Volunteers - www.csv.org.uk

Inside Housing - www.insidehousing.co.uk/

Local Government Careers (Improvement and Development Agency) - www.lgcareers.com/publications/

Qualifications for Housing (Chartered Institute of Housing, CIH) - www.cih.org/education/

Sheltered Housing Leaflets (ERoSH) (ERoSH) - www.shelteredhousing.org/information

▶Working in social care (2010) (Babcock Lifeskills) - www.babcock-lifeskills.com/

Addresses

Centre for Housing and Support (CHS)
1st Floor, Elgar House, Shrub Hill Road, Worcester WR4 9EE
Phone: +44 (0)1905 727272
Web: www.chs.ac.uk

Chartered Institute of Housing (CIH)
Octavia House Westwood Way, Coventry CV4 8JP
Phone: +44 (0)24 7685 1700
Web: www.cih.org

ERoSH, the Essential Role of Sheltered Housing
PO Box 2616, Chippenham, Wiltshire SN15 1WZ
Phone: +44 (0)1249 654249
Web: www.shelteredhousing.org

Irish Council for Social Housing (ICSH)
50 Merrion Square East, Dublin 2
Phone: +353 (0)1 661 8334
Web: www.icsh.ie

National Wardens Association
Katepwa House, Ashfield Park Avenue, Ross-on-Wye HR9 5AX
Phone: +44 (0)1989 566699
Web: www.shelteredhousingmanagers.co.uk

Sheltered Housing Network (SHN)
8 Station Road, Thurnscoe, Rotherham S63 0JR
Phone: 0845 680 9015 (UK only)
Web: www.shn.org.uk

Similar Jobs

Care Home Manager, Community Development Worker, Domestic Services Manager, Hostel Manager, Housing Officer, Social Care Worker

Warehouse Manager

CRCI:Transport and Logistics
CLCI:YAT Job Band: 2 to 5

Job Description

Warehouse managers organise the efficient arrival, storage and dispatch of goods and commodities in a warehouse. They keep records and monitor stock, usually using computer systems. Ensure that stock levels are maintained so that goods are available, but that stock levels are not so high as to be uneconomical. Some stock, such as food or chemicals and medicines, may have special requirements to consider, such as temperature, fragility, date.

Warehouse managers take into account health and safety considerations, including security, fire, and equipment maintenance procedures. They have supervisory and training responsibilities for warehouse staff. Some managers meet with customers to monitor quality. Ensure that Government and EU regulations are met.

Work Details

You work around 39 hrs a week. This is usually during the day, but can also be in the evenings and at weekends. Some managers are on call to deal with emergencies. There may also be seasonal demands for some goods.

You work part of the time in the warehouse, which can be light, spacious and airy, but also cold. The rest of the time is spent in an office dealing with paperwork, often working on a computerised system. In a smaller company, you may have a more 'hands-on' role.

Qualification

It is possible to enter this job without a degree or HND, but increasingly employers look for higher level qualifications.

- **England, Wales and Northern Ireland**

Band 2: For entry to jobs, no minimum qualifications are needed, but it is an advantage to have some GCSEs (A*-C) or equivalent in subjects that include English and maths.

Band 3: For entry to jobs, HNC or a relevant Diploma, usually at least 4 GCSEs (A*-C) including English and maths, or equivalent.

Band 4: For HND, Diploma of Higher Education or foundation degree: 1-2 A levels and some GCSEs (A*-C) usually including English and maths, or equivalent.

Band 5: For degree courses: 2-3 A levels and some GCSEs (A*-C) usually including English and maths, or equivalent. Exact requirements depend on the degree you take.

- **Scotland**

Band 2: Although academic qualifications are not specified for this job, it is an advantage to have some S grades (1-3) in subjects that include English and maths, or similar.

Band 3: For entry to jobs, usually at least four S grades (1-3) including English and maths, or similar.

Band 4: For entry to SQA higher national and professional development awards, usually 2-3 H grades and some S grades (1-3), including English and maths, or similar qualifications.

Band 5: For degree courses: 3-5 H grades and some S grades (1-3), including English and maths, or similar qualifications. Exact requirements depend on the degree you take.

Degree Information

Although there are opportunities for graduates in any subject, a degree in transport and logistics, business management, retail management, business information systems or business with a foreign language, may be useful.

Adult Qualifications

Entry requirements may be relaxed for adults applying for higher education courses. Access to HE or foundation courses provide those without the required qualifications a route onto degree courses.

Work Experience

Relevant work or voluntary experience is always useful and can improve your chances in application for entry to this career. Consider work experience in any company dealing with the movement or storage of goods, such as a transport or large distribution company.

Entry and Training

It is possible to enter this job after some years of general warehouse work. Advanced apprenticeships leading to qualification at level 3 can be a route into higher education. However, most warehouse managers start training with a post-school qualification in supply chain management, or increasingly a degree in a business-related subject. Foundation degrees and HNDs are available. Some warehouse managers move to this specialised role after some years of general management experience.

Training is often on the job and takes about two to three years. The Chartered Institute of Logistics and Transport offers those in post a range of qualifications from introductory certificates to diplomas and post-graduate qualifications. Large logistics companies may also run graduate training schemes.

This is often a second career following experience in the industry. Adults may be able to enter warehouse management if they have experience of general management or logistics, distribution or transport management. Working as a warehouse worker or supervisor can also lead to trainee management positions.

Opportunities and Pay

Warehouse managers work in many different types of company and all over the country. You can work in a supermarket or other large shop, or with a mail order company, cash and carry company, a manufacturing or distribution company. Other jobs exist in the health service and government departments. Many companies are located close to airports, ports and motorways. With experience you can go on to supervise a chain of warehouses.

Pay varies with location and employer but is likely to start between £17k-£25k a year, rising to £35k-£60k a year for those in senior positions. Some employers offer benefits that can enhance your salary.

Health

Good general health is needed for this job.

Skills and Qualities

able to manage people, able to motivate others, analytical skills, aptitude for figures, aptitude for teamwork, good communication skills, health & safety awareness, IT skills, planning skills, problem-solving skills

Relevant Subjects

English, ICT/Computer studies, Mathematics, Retail and distribution

Further Information

AGCAS: Transport and Logistics (Job Sector Briefing) (AGCAS) - www.prospects.ac.uk

Apprenticeship Schemes (National Apprenticeship Service) - www.apprenticeships.org.uk

Logistics and Retail Management (2009) (Kogan Page) - www.koganpage.com

Skills for Logistics - sector skills council for freight logistics industries - www.skillsforlogistics.org

UK Warehousing Association (UKWA) - www.ukwa.org.uk

Addresses

Chartered Institute of Logistics and Transport (CILTUK)
Careers Manager, Logistics & Transport Centre, Earlstrees Court, Earlstrees Road, Corby NN17 4AX
Phone: +44 (0)1536 740 100
Web: www.ciltuk.org.uk

Similar Jobs

Freight Forwarder, Logistics Manager, Purchasing/Procurement Officer, Road Transport Manager, Warehouse Order Picker/ Assembler, Warehouse Worker

Warehouse Order Picker/Assembler

CRCI:Transport and Logistics
CLCI:YAT Job Band: 1

Job Description

Order assemblers work in a warehouse or large store collecting and assembling ordered goods together before they are packed. They read order sheets and go around the warehouse collecting the goods on the list. They make up the order and take it to a supervisor to be checked. The goods are then brought together in a specific area, ready for collection or to be passed on to the packers. May decide to send other goods if what is ordered is out of stock. They record levels of stock. Learning where to find the items and how to read computer coded numbers, is part of the job

Work Details

Usually work a 37-40 hr week that may include shift work, evenings, weekends and public holidays. The work is normally in a warehouse, which may be large and airy, but cold. You spend a lot of time on your feet and there is some lifting and carrying. It may be necessary to climb ladders to collect goods. Safety shoes are usually provided.

Qualification

- **England, Wales and Northern Ireland**

Band 1: No minimum qualifications are required, but you are expected to have a good level of general education and to be competent in simple arithmetic, writing and verbal skills. Some formal/vocational qualifications at any level are useful.

- **Scotland**

Band 1: No minimum qualifications are required, but you are expected to have a good level of general education and to be competent in simple arithmetic, writing and verbal skills. Some formal/vocational qualifications at any level are useful.

Adult Qualifications

Employers look for people who can read and write clearly, and can do basic maths. Those without existing qualifications can work through the Foundation Learning programme by taking credit-based units and qualifications.

Work Experience

Any work experience can equip you with skills that you can use in the future and add to your CV. This can either be unpaid, voluntary or holiday/part-time work that you have organised yourself.

Entry and Training

Training is on the job, working with experienced employees. It helps if you can use a computer or are willing to adapt to new technology. It is possible to gain S/NVQs in distribution, warehousing and storage at levels 1-3. You may also take a course offered by the Chartered Institute of Logistics and Transport (CILTUK). Training programmes, including apprenticeship schemes, may be available in your area. Advanced apprenticeships leading to qualification at level 3 can also be a route into higher education.

Mature applicants may sometimes be preferred by employers.

Opportunities and Pay

You can work for a company that makes and sells products as well as distributing goods. An increase in internet shopping has resulted in a growth of online and mail order companies in many areas of the country. There are also more opportunities with the growth of home deliveries by supermarkets. Once you have experience you can become a supervisor, or with relevant qualifications move into warehouse management.

Wages are often paid on an hourly rate. The weekly rate varies from £220-£440, depending on experience. Overtime and shift work can make up a significant proportion of your earnings. You may be able to buy goods at reduced prices.

Health

In some warehouses the goods are colour coded, so you may need normal colour vision. You have to have stamina and be physically fit.

Skills and Qualities

able to work quickly, able to work well on your own, attention to detail, good memory, honest, IT skills, methodical, trustworthy

Relevant Subjects

Retail and distribution

Further Information

Apprenticeship Schemes (National Apprenticeship Service) - www.apprenticeships.org.uk

Careers in Logistics - www.careersinlogistics.co.uk

Foundation Learning (QCDA) - www.qcda.gov.uk

Improve Ltd - sector skills council for food and drink manufacturing and processing - www.improveltd.co.uk

Skillsmart Retail - sector skills council for the retail industry - www.skillsmartretail.com

UK Warehousing Association (UKWA) - www.ukwa.org.uk

Addresses

Chartered Institute of Logistics and Transport (CILTUK)
Careers Manager, Logistics & Transport Centre, Earlstrees Court, Earlstrees Road, Corby NN17 4AX
Phone: +44 (0)1536 740 100
Web: www.ciltuk.org.uk

United Kingdom Warehousing Association (UKWA)
Walter House, 418-422 Strand, London WC2R 0PT
Phone: +44 (0)207 836 5522
Web: www.ukwa.org.uk

Similar Jobs

Builders' Yard Assistant, Lift Truck Operative, Stock Control/ Replenishment Assistant, Warehouse Worker

Warehouse Worker

CRCI:Transport and Logistics
CLCI:YAT Job Band: 1 to 2

Job Description

Warehouse workers are employed in a warehouse, receiving, storing and sending out goods and commodities. They are responsible for checking a consignment of goods as it arrives and ensuring that the correct goods and quantity have been delivered. Also check for broken, damaged or faulty goods. They sign forms to confirm receipt of the delivery, store the goods correctly and update records, often using a computer.

Warehouse workers may use a lift truck or trolley to put the goods in the right space in the warehouse. They carry out stock checks to ensure that the quantities of goods tallies with stock records.

Report any mistakes to a team leader or supervisor. Order more supplies when the stocks are getting low. Ensure goods leave the warehouse in perfect condition and in the right quantity, for dispatch to customers.

Some workers may be required to sell goods directly to customers and tradespeople from the warehouse. May help the lorry driver to load the goods.

Work Details

You usually work 37-40 hrs a week. Many employers operate a 24 hr shift basis and you may be required to work at weekends. Warehouses can be light, spacious and airy, though sometimes can be cold. At times you may be very busy and have to work quickly. You can be on your feet for long periods of time. Some lifting and carrying of heavy goods may be required and you may need to climb ladders.

You must follow safety regulations, for example, to make sure that there are no accidents because of items being stacked badly. There are opportunities for part time and temporary work.

Qualification

• England, Wales and Northern Ireland

Band 1: No minimum qualifications are required, but you are expected to have a good level of general education. However, some formal/vocational qualifications at any level are useful. Most employers expect applicants to be able to read and write clearly and be able to do some basic figure work.

Band 2: Although academic qualifications are not specified for this job, it is an advantage to have some GCSEs (A*-C) in subjects that include English and maths, or equivalent.

• Scotland

Band 1: No minimum qualifications are required, but you are expected to have a good level of general education. However, some formal/vocational qualifications at any level are useful. Most employers expect applicants to be able to read and write clearly and be able to do some basic figure work.

Band 2: Although academic qualifications are not specified for this job, it is an advantage to have some S grades (1-3) in subjects that include English and maths, or similar.

Adult Qualifications

No pre-entry qualifications are usually required though some academic/vocational qualifications at any level may be an advantage. English and maths are useful subjects. The ability to read, write and work with figures is needed.

Work Experience

Any work experience can equip you with skills that you can use in the future and add to your CV. This can either be unpaid, voluntary or holiday/part-time work that you have organised yourself.

Entry and Training

You are trained on the job by a supervisor or experienced worker and there may also be day release or block-release courses available at a local college in carrying and handling techniques, health and safety issues and record keeping. It is an advantage to be able to use a computer. For some posts it is useful to have experience of working with cash or dealing with cheques or credit/debit cards. Some workers over the age of 18 may be required to drive a lift truck. The Chartered Institute of Logistics and Transport (CILTUK) offers a relevant warehouse management introductory course for supervisors.

S/NVQs levels 2-3 are available in distribution, warehousing and storage operations. Training programmes, including apprenticeship schemes, may be available in your area. Advanced apprenticeships leading to qualification at level 3 can also be a route into higher education.

Mature applicants for this job find it an advantage to have specialist knowledge of the type of goods being stored by the company. Government training opportunities, such as apprenticeships, may be available in your area. You can also gain recognition of previous experience through Accreditation of Prior Learning or by working towards relevant S/NVQs. Contact your local careers office, Jobcentre Plus, Next Step service or Learning and Skills Council (LSC)/Local Enterprise Company (LEC) for details of training schemes.

Opportunities and Pay

Over 400,000 warehouse workers work in many different types of company and all over the country. You can work in a supermarket or other large shop, or with a mail order company, cash and carry company, a manufacturing or distribution company. Other jobs exist in the armed forces, the health service and government departments. With ability and experience you can become a team leader, a supervisor, or move into warehouse management. Promotion chances are increased if you gain some relevant qualifications.

Pay varies depending on the size and location of the company. Salaries may be paid at an hourly rate, coming to around £13k, rising to between £14k-£17k or more with experience and responsibility. Team leaders can earn up to £22k a year. Overtime pay is possible at busy times.

Health

You have to be fit to do this job. Some employers have a colour coding system, so you may require normal colour vision.

Skills and Qualities

able to work well on your own, careful, good memory, health & safety awareness, honest, IT skills, methodical, reliable, trustworthy.

Relevant Subjects

Retail and distribution

Further Information

Apprenticeship Schemes (National Apprenticeship Service) - www.apprenticeships.org.uk

Careers in Logistics - www.careersinlogistics.co.uk

Improve Ltd - sector skills council for food and drink manufacturing and processing - www.improveltd.co.uk

Skillsmart Retail - sector skills council for the retail industry - www.skillsmartretail.com

Training Schemes - www.direct.gov.uk/en/educationandlearning

UK Warehousing Association (UKWA) - www.ukwa.org.uk

Addresses

Chartered Institute of Logistics and Transport (CILTUK)
Careers Manager, Logistics & Transport Centre, Earlstrees Court, Earlstrees Road, Corby NN17 4AX
Phone: +44 (0)1536 740 100
Web: www.ciltuk.org.uk

United Kingdom Warehousing Association (UKWA)
Walter House, 418-422 Strand, London WC2R 0PT
Phone: +44 (0)207 836 5522
Web: www.ukwa.org.uk

Similar Jobs

Builders' Merchant, Builders' Yard Assistant, Lift Truck Operative, Stock Control/Replenishment Assistant, Vehicle Parts Operative, Warehouse Order Picker/Assembler

Watch & Clock Repairer

also known as: Horologist

CRCI:Engineering
CLCI:ROZ Job Band: 1 to 4

Job Description

Watch and clock repairers service, repair or restore mechanical and electronic watches, clocks and chronometers. This usually involves removing the mechanism from its casing, examining it for faults, taking out any damaged parts and repairing or replacing them using specialist hand/machine tools. Then they clean, oil and reassemble the item, before testing and adjusting it if necessary. The work is precise and delicate requiring traditional craft and modern tools. Also advises customers and, if in a shop, may sell jewellery and precision instruments.

Some repairers may specialise in restoring antique clocks, including long case and wall clocks, watches and other timepieces. Others specialise in the servicing, restoration and repair of public clocks. This may include clocks on churches, in airports, road and rail transport public areas, outside shops and department stores, local and central government buildings, town and city squares and other public places.

Work Details

Usually work a basic 39 hr week, Monday to Friday, though some employers may require you to work on a Saturday. You work in a shop, workshop or perhaps from home. This work is very skilled, intricate and time consuming, and can involve sitting for long periods. Your work environment is usually quiet and dust free. You give advice to customers and sometimes need to deal with complaints. May need a good head for heights if working on tall buildings.

Qualification

• England, Wales and Northern Ireland

Band 1: For entry to jobs, no minimum qualifications are needed, but you are expected to have a good level of general education and relevant experience. Some formal/vocational qualifications at any level are useful.

Band 2: For entry to train on the job, no minimum qualifications are needed, but it is an advantage to have some GCSEs (A*-C) or equivalent in subjects that include English, maths and preferably a science or technical/engineering subject, or equivalent.

Band 3: For entry to jobs, HNC or a relevant Diploma, usually at least 4 GCSEs (A*-C) including English, maths and preferably a science or technical/engineering subject, or equivalent.

Band 4: For a relevant HND, Diploma of Higher Education or foundation degree: 1-2 A levels and some GCSEs (A*-C) usually including English and maths, or equivalent.

• Scotland

Band 1: For entry to jobs, no minimum qualifications are needed, but you are expected to have a good level of general education and relevant experience. Some formal/vocational qualifications at any level are useful.

Band 2: Although academic qualifications are not specified for this job, it is an advantage to have some S grades (1-3) in subjects that include English, maths and preferably a science or technical/engineering subject, or similar.

Band 3: For entry to jobs, usually at least four S grades (1-3) including English, maths and preferably a science or technical/engineering subject, or similar.

Band 4: For entry to a relevant SQA higher national and professional development awards, usually 2-3 H grades and some S grades (1-3), including English and maths, or similar qualifications.

Adult Qualifications

A good standard of secondary education is required, though entry requirements are usually relaxed for mature applicants. You can improve your skills and qualifications by working through the Foundation Learning programme. This involves taking credit-based units and qualifications to help you progress.

Work Experience

Relevant work or voluntary experience is always useful. It can add to your CV and improve your chances when applying for entry to jobs or apprenticeships in this area. Retail work, such as a Saturday or holiday job in a jewellers, or any experience in a watch and clock repair workshop, provides a helpful introduction to this profession.

Entry and Training

Training is usually through a specialist course and by practical experience. Apprenticeships may be available. You may be required to take a practical skills test for entry. Study is important for professional qualification and most entrants qualify with the British Horological Institute (BHI) or through the Watchmakers of Switzerland Training and Education Programme (WOSTEP). Courses are available at some local colleges for the BHI examinations and they cover all aspects of clock and watch repair. For those already working in the industry, the BHI also offers distance-learning courses leading to professional qualification as well as seminars and residential short courses, such as antique clock repair.

The British School of Watchmaking in Manchester offers training under the WOSTEP programme and West Dean College runs a diploma course in the conservation and restoration of antique clocks. Entry to this course is with a degree, or alternative qualifications plus appropriate experience in horology.

A two-year HND in Horology is offered at Birmingham City University and the course includes completion of the BHI's professional examinations. Birmingham City University also offer the BHI preliminary certificate on a flexible attendance basis, with one day of theory each academic week. Successful completion of this certificate is an entry requirement for level 1 of the HND in Horology.

Epping Forest Horology Club has offered workshop facilities with tutor guidance for a number of years and also offers a course of theory lessons. The course lasts 15 weeks and uses the theory part of the BHI distance learning year 1 material. This is to support members working towards the BHI qualification. Check the club's website for further details.

A Diploma/Welsh Baccalaureate may be available in your area in engineering. See the diplomas website for further information. For general information on watch and clock repair, visit the websites of The Worshipful Company of Clockmakers and Watchuseek.

Mature applicants are usually welcomed by employers for training, particularly those with experience in making precision tools and instruments. Short courses and distance-learning courses are available from the British Horological Institute (BHI). Bursaries for training may be available from the Worshipful Company of Clockmakers. There are sometimes introductory evening classes at local adult education centres and also short courses run by the private sector.

Government training opportunities, such as apprenticeships, may be available in your area. You can also gain recognition of previous experience through Accreditation of Prior Learning or by working towards relevant S/NVQs. Contact your local careers office, Jobcentre Plus, Next Step service or Learning and Skills Council (LSC)/Local Enterprise Company (LEC) for details of training schemes.

Opportunities and Pay

This is a small profession but the growth in the use of mechanical watches has led to a worldwide shortage of skilled horologists. Jobs are available in most towns and cities and may be available overseas, mainly in Europe. Employment can be with a small firm, a large jewellery retail company or possibly a private company. It is possible to specialise in restoration work and there are good opportunities in the antiques trade or with a museum. Qualified watch repairers may be able to find additional work adjusting instruments or in surgical instrument manufacture or repair. There are also good opportunities to become self-employed.

Pay depends largely on the type of employer and can be variable if you are self-employed. If you are employed with a small firm you are likely to earn between £15k-£20k a year. Self-employed repairers may earn up to £30k a year. Specialist repairers/restorers may earn up to £50k.

Health

Good eyesight is essential.

Skills and Qualities

able to work well on your own, accurate measuring and calculating skills, good communication skills, good concentration level, good interpersonal skills, manual dexterity, patient, precise, steady hand, technical aptitude

Relevant Subjects

Design and technology, Mathematics, Physics

Further Information

Apprenticeship Schemes (National Apprenticeship Service) - www.apprenticeships.org.uk

Birmingham City University - www.bcu.ac.uk

Diplomas (Foundation, Higher and Advanced) - http://yp.direct.gov.uk/diplomas

Epping Forest Horology Club - www.efhc.org.uk

Horological Journal (monthly) (British Horological Institute) - www.bhi.co.uk/

Training Schemes - www.direct.gov.uk/en/educationandlearning

Watchuseek - http://watchuseek.com

Welsh Baccalaureate - www.wbq.org.uk

West Dean College - www.westdean.org.uk

Addresses

British Horological Institute (BHI)
Upton Hall Upton, Newark NG23 5TE
Phone: +44 (0)1636 813 795
Web: www.bhi.co.uk

British School of Watchmaking
Units 5 & 6 Crossford Court Dane Road Sale, Manchester M33 7BZ
Web: www.britishschoolofwatchmaking.co.uk/

Watchmakers of Switzerland Training and Education Programme
Rue des Saars 99, 2000 Neuchatel
Web: http://wostep.ch

Worshipful Company of Clockmakers
Salters' Hall, Fore Street, London EC2Y 5DE
Phone: +44 (0)20 7638 5500
Web: www.clockmakers.org

Similar Jobs

Computer Assembly Technician, Engineering Craft Machinist, Jeweller: Retail, Locksmith, Toolmaker

Water Distribution/Sewerage Operative

also known as: Public Utilities Water Mains/Services Layer

CRCI:Building and Construction
CLCI:UN

Job Band: 1 to 3

Job Description

Water distribution/sewerage operatives install, maintain and repair the water distribution, pumping, sewage and drainage systems. They do this in people's homes and for businesses. A range of specialist tools such as high pressure water jets, pneumatic drills and lifting equipment are used in this work. They also use high-tech closed circuit TV, to find leaks from the mains and any sewage blockages in pipes and drains. Operatives lay and repair water mains and waste services, including hydrants and stopcocks. They take out and replace any faulty sections of pipe. When working, operatives are careful not to cut through any gas pipes and electricity cables.

Water distribution/sewerage operatives also carry out routine minor repairs of tools and equipment, and clean tools and machinery. May also install water meters and hydrants. Duties can include responding to emergencies such as major leaks, burst pipes and damage to pipes and drains. They follow safety procedures in all aspects of work.

Work Details

Water distribution/sewerage operatives usually work around 37 hrs a week, Monday to Friday, during daytime hours. You may need to work on call at times for emergency work outside normal working hours. Shift work is also possible. You may need to travel to different sites, therefore a driving licence is sometimes required. You often work on your own but sometimes may work in a team, particularly if the job requires heavy machinery or equipment. Work is outdoors in all sorts of weather, and it can be cold and wet. Some of the work may take place inside large water and sewerage systems.

There is a risk of exposure to harmful substances, including sewage and other waste products, so you need to wear protective clothing and often use breathing apparatus.

Qualification

- **England, Wales and Northern Ireland**

Band 1: Minimum qualifications are not always required, but you are expected to have a good level of general education. However, some formal/vocational qualifications at any level are useful.

Band 2: Although academic qualifications are not always specified for this job, it is an advantage to have some GCSEs (A*-C) in subjects that include English and maths, science and technology, or equivalent.

Band 3: For entry to apprenticeship schemes: some employers require at least 4 GCSEs (A*-C) preferably including English and maths, science/technology, or equivalent.

- **Scotland**

Band 1: Minimum qualifications are not always required, but you are expected to have a good level of general education. However, some formal/vocational qualifications at any level are useful.

Band 2: Although academic qualifications are not always specified for this job, it is an advantage to have some S grades (1-3) in subjects that include English and maths, science and technology, or similar.

Band 3: For entry to training schemes: some employers require at least four S grades (1-3) including English and maths, science/technology, or similar.

Adult Qualifications

Formal qualifications are not always required.

Work Experience
Any work experience can equip you with skills that you can use in the future and add to your CV. Work experience can either be unpaid or voluntary or can be holiday or part-time work that you have organised yourself. Health and safety issues may mean that there are certain jobs you cannot do until you are over 16.

Entry and Training
Some companies offer training schemes for junior operatives such as an apprenticeship. Training is usually on the job through practical experience, most likely with an experienced person. This follows an initial induction period to learn about the industry. Areas of work covered usually include water technology and supply, health and safety regulations, environmental aspects, customer care and the water distribution system.

All new entrants to the water industry are required to join the National Water Hygiene Scheme, managed by Energy & Utility Skills (EU Skills). Once you have successfully completed all three elements of the scheme (health screening questionnaire, awareness training and a water hygiene test), you are issued with a National Water Hygiene Card. This is valid for three years. Contact EU Skills for further details.

Day release to a local college for a course such as the City & Guilds level 2 certificate in water engineering is often available. Apprentices often work towards relevant S/NVQs at levels 1-3, such as network construction operations (water) or operating process plant. Check with Energy & Utility Skills or contact your local water company for details of training programmes in your area, including apprenticeships leading to level 2 and advanced apprenticeships leading to level 3.

A Diploma/Welsh Baccalaureate may be available in your area. Useful subject areas are Construction and the Built Environment or Engineering. The Diploma in Environmental and Landbased Studies may also be of use.

Mature entrants usually require some experience in the water or construction industry, or other relevant experience. Government training opportunities may be available in your area. You can also gain recognition of previous experience through Accreditation of Prior Learning (APL) or by working towards relevant S/NVQs. Contact your local careers office, Jobcentre Plus, Next Step service or Learning and Skills Council (LSC)/Local Enterprise Company (LEC) for details of training schemes, including apprenticeships for adults.

Opportunities and Pay
Employment is with a water company (England and Wales), Scottish Water or the Northern Ireland Water Service. There are usually good opportunities within the water industry and you may be able to progress to a supervisory post after gaining experience and relevant qualifications. Some operatives may progress to study for engineering qualifications at technician or degree level.

Pay can vary considerably depending on location and employer. A starting salary is likely to be around £13k a year rising to £17k with experience. Average pay can be around £18k rising to around £25k (including overtime/shift pay) when fully experienced.

Health
You need a good level of general fitness in this job.

Skills and Qualities
able to follow instructions, able to work in confined spaces, able to work well on your own, enjoy working outdoors, health & safety awareness, not squeamish, observant, practical skills

Relevant Subjects
Construction and built environment, Design and technology

Further Information
AGCAS: Energy & Utilities (Job Sector briefing) (AGCAS) - www.prospects.ac.uk

Apprenticeship Schemes (National Apprenticeship Service) - www.apprenticeships.org.uk

Diplomas (Foundation, Higher and Advanced) - http://yp.direct.gov.uk/diplomas

Energy & Utility Skills - sector skills council for gas, power, waste management & water industries - www.euskills.co.uk

Scottish Water - www.scottishwater.co.uk/portal/page/portal/SWE_PGP_HOME/SWE_PGE_HOME

Training Schemes - www.direct.gov.uk/en/educationandlearning

Utility Week (Reed Business Info) - www.utilityweek.co.uk

Welsh Baccalaureate - www.wbq.org.uk

Addresses
Northern Ireland Water (NIW)
PO Box 1026, Belfast BT1 9DJ
Web: www.niwater.com

OFWAT
Centre City Tower 7 Hill Street, Birmingham B5 4UA
Phone: +44 (0)121 644 7500
Web: www.ofwat.gov.uk

Water UK
1 Queen Anne's Gate, London SW1H 9BT
Phone: +44 (0)20 7344 1844
Web: www.water.org.uk

Similar Jobs
Construction Operative, Construction Plant Operative, Plumber, Road Worker, Water/Sewerage Treatment Plant Operative, Waterway Operative

Water Keeper/Bailiff

CRCI:Environment, Animals and Plants
CLCI:WAR Job Band: 1 to 3

Job Description
Water keepers/bailiffs monitor lakes and stretches of waterways/rivers that are popular with recreational users and they protect river fish. They check the banks of the canal, river or reservoir for erosion or damage, and arrange for reconstruction if necessary. Ensures that anglers have licences to fish when needed and arranges prosecution proceedings when they cant produce an up to date licence. Conducts surveys of insect life and protected species of fish and monitors the waterways for pollution levels, wildlife and numbers of fish types.

Takes notes of water levels. Also checks how fast the water is flowing. May work with scientists, farmers, landowners and fisherman. Assesses any damage caused by pollution. Offers advice on the proper handling and treatment of sewage and industrial waste disposed into rivers, lakes and waterways.

In Scotland, water bailiffs have similar powers to gamekeepers as they have the authority to arrest lawbreakers. They may also produce witness statements and act as a prosecution witness in court. Water bailiffs in England need to have a warrant from the Environment Agency to exercise similar duties.

Work Details
Usually works around 37-39 hrs per week, but water keepers/bailiffs often work shifts, including nights and weekends. The work involves working outdoors, usually patrolling the area on foot, often in all sorts of weather. Depending on the employer, water keepers/bailiffs may live in a house provided as part of the employment package. A full driving license is required.

Water keepers/bailiffs often work alone and on occasions may have to do quite heavy work. Waterproof clothing and waders are provided as the work may involve wading in cold flowing water.

Qualification

• England, Wales and Northern Ireland

Band 1: For entry to jobs, no minimum qualifications are needed, but you are expected to have a good level of general education and relevant experience. Some formal/vocational qualifications at any level are useful.

Band 2: For entry to jobs, no minimum qualifications are needed, but it is an advantage to have some GCSEs (A*-C) or equivalent in subjects that include English and maths.

• Scotland

Band 1: For entry to jobs, no minimum qualifications are needed, but you are expected to have a good level of general education and relevant experience. Some formal/vocational qualifications at any level are useful.

Band 2: Although academic qualifications are not specified for this job, it is an advantage to have some S grades (1-3) in subjects that include English and maths, or similar.

Adult Qualifications

Mature entry is common with employers preferring candidates who demonstrate relevant work experience, for example game keeping or farm work.

Work Experience

Relevant work or voluntary experience is always useful and can improve your employment prospects when applying for entry to jobs. Membership of an angling club shows a strong interest in fishing, and any experience of working with animals or the environment is helpful.

Entry and Training

Those who enter this work without experience are trained on the job by an experienced bailiff. Applicants have to pass a medical examination. Some enter this career by doing voluntary work for local fishing clubs or landowners. Some prefer to gain a relevant qualification before entry.

The Institute of Fisheries Management runs a certificate course in fisheries management. It is modular based and includes the study of freshwater biology, fisheries laws and bailiff/keeper duties. This can be followed with a diploma course. The diploma course is aimed at managers, lasts two years and is at a more advanced level. Modules cover areas such as fishery laws and administration and water quality and recreational amenity. Both courses can be taken on a correspondence basis.

It is possible to work for a BTEC Entry Level Award in Land-based Studies as part of the Foundation Learning curriculum. BTEC also offers a first certificate and diploma in fish husbandry. A Diploma/ Welsh Baccalaureate may be available in your area in environment and land based studies and can provide good background for this career.

The Association of Salmon Fishery Boards (ASFB) in Scotland runs a bailiff training course every spring. The ASFB states that individuals who have not completed the course and passed the exam should not be issued with a warrant card. They stipulate that bailiffs should have passed this exam regardless of whether they are employed on a full-time, part-time, seasonal or voluntary basis. See also the British Trout Association website for a listing of all courses in the UK.

Adults can enter this work with a good level of relevant work experience and those who have practical skills may have an advantage. Government training opportunities, such as apprenticeships, may be available in your area. You can also gain recognition of previous experience through Accreditation of Prior Learning (APL) or by working towards relevant S/NVQs. Contact your local careers office, Jobcentre Plus, Next Step service or Learning and Skills Council (LSC) Local Enterprise Company (LEC) for details of training schemes.

Opportunities and Pay

Jobs are mainly based in the country, usually in remote areas. Water keepers/bailiffs are mainly employed by the central/regional fisheries boards, water companies, or private landowners.

LANTRA runs a Women and Work programme to encourage women to gain qualifications in traditionally male dominated occupations. Aquaculture, environmental conservation and fisheries management are included in this scheme. Check the website for details on opportunities in your area.

Pay varies depending on area and employer. Salaries for water keepers/bailiffs are generally £15k-£30k a year.

Health

This job require good general fitness.

Skills and Qualities

able to work well on your own, alert, enjoy working outdoors, environmental awareness, firm manner, observant, practical skills, reliable, strong

Further Information

Association of Salmon Fishery Boards - www.asfb.org.uk/asfb/asfb.asp

Countryside Jobs Service - www.countryside-jobs.com

Diplomas (Foundation, Higher and Advanced) - http://yp.direct.gov.uk/diplomas

FISH - www.ifm.org.uk/publications/fish/

Lantra - The Sector Skills Council for environmental & land-based sector (Lantra) http:/www.lantra.co.uk

Real Life Guide to Working Outdoors (Trotman) - www.trotman.co.uk

Welsh Baccalaureate - www.wbq.org.uk

Women and Work Programme - www.lantra.co.uk/businesses/england/womenandwork/

▶Working in police, fire & security (2009) (Babcock Lifeskills) - www.babcock-lifeskills.com/

Addresses

British Trout Association
The Rural Centre, West Mains, Ingliston, Edinburgh EH28 8NZ
Phone: +44 (0)131 472 4080
Web: www.britishtrout.co.uk

Environment Agency
National Customer Contact Centre, PO Box 544, Almondsbury, Rotherham S60 1BY
Phone: 08708 506 506 (UK only)
Web: www.environment-agency.gov.uk

Institute of Fisheries Management (IFM)
22 Rushworth Avenue, West Bridgford, Nottingham NG2 7LF
Phone: +44 (0)115 982 2317
Web: www.ifm.org.uk

Similar Jobs

Countryside Ranger, Fish Farm Manager, Fish Farm Worker, Gamekeeper, Water/Sewerage Treatment Plant Operative

Water/Sewerage Treatment Plant Operative

also known as: Production Operative: Water/Sewerage, Waste Treatment Plant Operative, Waste Water Process Plant Operator

CRCI:Building and Construction
CLCI:UN Job Band: 1 to 3

Job Description

Water/sewerage treatment plant operatives work at a wastewater/sewerage treatment plant. They work to prevent contaminated water and sewage going into our streams, rivers and the sea, and the public water supply. Operatives make sure that all work is done in line with industry regulations. Duties include operation of the machines and equipment that treat, pump and recycle water to make it clean and safe for customers.

Water/sewerage treatment plant operatives monitor the automatic and computerised processes that filter, purify and analyse water, sewage or industrial waste. They check the condition of plant equipment, including pipes and fittings and carry out routine maintenance tasks, such as washing and replacing filters. Operatives check that water levels are correct and may add chemicals and microbes to the supply. The chemical containers are changed using overhead cranes and hoists to lift and move them into place. Regular inspections of the reservoir and flow outlets are necessary. May also check rainfall and weather changes. Operatives sometimes unload and store deliveries of supplies.

Work Details

Water/sewerage treatment plant operatives work a basic 37-39 hr week, Monday to Friday. However you may need to work shifts, including evenings/weekends, and be on call for emergencies. The work requires you to be active most of the time and you may have to use ladders. Contact with unpleasant and smelly substances is part of the job. You are often outside in all weather conditions. There is a risk of exposure to harmful substances and you need to wear protective clothing.

Qualification

• England, Wales and Northern Ireland

Band 1: Minimum qualifications are not always required, but you are expected to have a good level of general education. However, some formal/vocational qualifications at any level are useful.

Band 2: Although academic qualifications are not always specified for this job, it is an advantage to have some GCSEs (A*-C) in subjects that include English and maths, science and technology, or equivalent.

Band 3: For entry to apprenticeship schemes: some employers require at least 4 GCSEs (A*-C) preferably including English and maths, science/technology, or equivalent.

• Scotland

Band 1: Minimum qualifications are not always required, but you are expected to have a good level of general education. However, some formal/vocational qualifications at any level are useful.

Band 2: Although academic qualifications are not always specified for this job, it is an advantage to have some S grades (1-3) in subjects that include English and maths, science and technology, or similar.

Band 3: For entry to training schemes: some employers require at least four S grades (1-3) including English and maths, science/technology, or similar.

Adult Qualifications

Qualifications are not always needed, though a good standard of education is important.

Work Experience

Any work experience can equip you with skills that you can use in the future and add to your CV. Work experience can either be unpaid or voluntary or can be holiday or part-time work that you have organised yourself. Any experience of working with machinery, especially with computer-operated machinery, is useful.

Entry and Training

Some companies offer training schemes for junior operatives such as a water industry (process operations) apprenticeship scheme. Training is usually on the job with an experienced person. This follows an initial induction period during which you learn about the industry. Your training may also include day release or short courses at a local college, or through the company's own training and development scheme. You cover subjects such as water technology and supply, health and safety regulations, environmental aspects, science and computing. Entrants to the water industry are required to join the National Water Hygiene Scheme, managed by Energy & Utility Skills (EU Skills). Once you have successfully completed all three elements of the scheme (health screening questionnaire, awareness training and a water hygiene test), you are issued with a National Water Hygiene Card. This is valid for three years. Contact EU Skills for further details.

Relevant S/NVQs are available at level 2, such as S/NVQ in operating process plant and NVQ in utilities control centre operations. City and Guilds also run a level 2 certificate and level 3 diploma in water engineering. Check with Energy & Utility Skills or contact your local water company for details of training programmes in your area, including apprenticeships leading to level 2 and advanced apprenticeships leading to level 3. ACS Distance Education runs a flexible environmental waste management course which covers water quality and treatment.

A Diploma/Welsh Baccalaureate may be available in your area. Useful subject areas are Construction and the Built Environment or Engineering.

Mature applicants, particularly those with a knowledge of mechanical engineering, are usually considered by employers for training. It is also an advantage to have relevant experience in the water or construction industry. Government training opportunities may be available in your area. You can also gain recognition of previous experience through Accreditation of Prior Learning (APL) or by working towards relevant S/NVQs. Contact your local careers office, Jobcentre Plus, Next Step service or Learning and Skills Council (LSC)/Local Enterprise Company (LEC) for details of training schemes, including apprenticeships for adults.

Opportunities and Pay

Water treatment and sewerage works are mostly located in or close to towns and cities throughout the UK, with some sited in remote locations. Employment is with a water company (England/ Wales), Scottish Water or the Northern Ireland Water Council. There are usually good opportunities within the water industry and you may be able to progress to a supervisory post after gaining experience. Occasionally there are opportunities to progress further as an inspector, area superintendent, controller, or to management positions with some companies.

Pay varies depending on area and employer but generally starts at around £9k-£12k a year, rising to £15k with experience. Those who are fully experienced and have managerial responsibilities can earn around £35k a year.

Health

This job requires stamina and good physical fitness. There is an allergy risk from chemicals and skin irritants.

Skills and Qualities

able to work both on your own and in a team, environmental awareness, health & safety awareness, methodical, observational skills, practical skills, reliable, responsible attitude

Relevant Subjects
Construction and built environment, Design and technology, Land and Environment

Further Information
Apprenticeship Schemes (National Apprenticeship Service) - www.apprenticeships.org.uk

Chartered Institute of Water and Environmental Management (CIWEM) (CIWEM) - www.environmentalcareers.org.uk/careers/job/water_treatment_operator.asp

Diplomas (Foundation, Higher and Advanced) - http://yp.direct.gov.uk/diplomas

Energy & Utility Skills - sector skills council for gas, power, waste management & water industries - www.euskills.co.uk

Scottish Water - www.scottishwater.co.uk/portal/page/portal/SWE_PGP_HOME/SWE_PGE_HOME

Training Schemes - www.direct.gov.uk/en/educationandlearning

Welsh Baccalaureate - www.wbq.org.uk

Addresses
ACS Distance Education
PO Box Box 4171, Stourbridge, West Midlands DY8 2WZ
Phone: +44 (0)800 328 4723
Web: www.acsedu.co.uk

Northern Ireland Water (NIW)
PO Box 1026, Belfast BT1 9DJ
Web: www.niwater.com

OFWAT
Centre City Tower 7 Hill Street, Birmingham B5 4UA
Phone: +44 (0)121 644 7500
Web: www.ofwat.gov.uk

Water UK
1 Queen Anne's Gate, London SW1H 9BT
Phone: +44 (0)20 7344 1844
Web: www.water.org.uk

Similar Jobs
Construction Plant Operative, Water Distribution/Sewerage Operative, Waterway Operative

Waterway Operative
also known as: Reservoir Operative

CRCI:Building and Construction
CLCI:UN — Job Band: 1

Job Description
Waterway operatives look after a reservoir or stretch of waterway such as a canal or river. They check the banks on either side of the canal, river, or around the reservoir to ensure safety regulations are being followed. A wide range of tools and equipment, including mowers, hedge trimmers, strimmers, and power saws are used. Operatives trim or remove any branches or trees that threaten the flow of water. Rubbish is cleared away to prevent the water being blocked or getting dirty and contaminated. Fences and walls are repaired and filter beds, valves and water/lock gates are cleaned regularly. Water levels are monitored and operatives also check how fast the water is flowing and whether there is any contamination. Any major faults are reported to a supervisor.

Work Details
Waterway operatives usually work a basic 39 hr week, Monday to Friday, but may be required to work some evenings/weekends and be on call at times. You work outdoors in all weather conditions and it may be cold and wet at times. You have to manage walking over rough ground and being continually on your feet. In this job you may not meet many people.

Qualification
- **England, Wales and Northern Ireland**

Band 1: No minimum qualifications are required, but some formal/vocational qualifications at any level are useful.

- **Scotland**

Band 1: No minimum qualifications are required, but some formal/vocational qualifications at any level are useful.

Adult Qualifications
No minimum qualifications are required, but a good level of general education is useful. You can improve your skills and qualifications by working through the Foundation Learning programme. This involves taking credit-based units and qualifications to help you progress.

Work Experience
Any work experience can equip you with skills that you can use in the future and add to your CV. Work experience can either be unpaid or voluntary or holiday/part-time work that you have organised yourself. Many waterway societies and organisations welcome voluntary help, where you can gain local knowledge of a stretch of waterway/canal. There may also be paid seasonal work in the summer, when you can gain valuable practical experience.

Entry and Training
Some companies offer training schemes for junior operatives, such as a water industry apprenticeship scheme. Training is mainly on the job with an experienced operative or supervisor. This is after an initial induction period where you learn about the industry. You may also receive structured water industry related training. Day release to a local college for relevant short courses, such as a relevant technical certificate, is often available.

All new entrants to the water industry are required to join the National Water Hygiene Scheme, managed by Energy & Utility Skills (EU Skills). Once you have successfully completed all three elements of the scheme (health screening questionnaire, awareness training and a water hygiene test), you are issued with a National Water Hygiene Card. This is valid for three years. Contact EU Skills for further details.

A Diploma/Welsh Baccalaureate in Environmental and Landbased Studies may be available in your area. Relevant S/NVQs may be available at levels 1-2, including the S/NVQ in network construction operations (operative) at level 1. Check with Energy & Utility Skills or contact your local water company for details of training programmes in your area, including apprenticeships leading to level 2 and advanced apprenticeships leading to level 3. You may need a driving licence for this job.

Mature applicants with a background and/or qualifications in construction work, particularly with brick, wood and metalworking skills, as well as agricultural skills, are welcomed by employers. Boat craft and mechanical skills are also an advantage with some employers.

Government training opportunities, such as apprenticeships, may be available in your area. You can also gain recognition of previous experience through Accreditation of Prior Learning or by working towards relevant S/NVQs. Contact your local careers office, Jobcentre Plus, Next Step service or Learning and Skills Council (LSC)/Local Enterprise Company (LEC) for details of all training opportunities and schemes, including apprenticeships for adults.

Opportunities and Pay
There are good opportunities within the water/waterways industry. Jobs are based throughout the country where there are stretches of water. Some jobs are in remote areas. Employment is mainly with a water company (England/Wales), Scottish Water or the Northern Ireland Water Council. Jobs are also possible with organisations that include British Waterways, and Waterways Ireland. You may be able to progress to team leader and management posts after gaining experience and/or relevant qualifications.

Pay varies depending on area and employer, but is generally around £11k to £13k a year. Overtime and bonus payments increase earnings.

Health
This job requires a good level of fitness.

Skills and Qualities
able to work well on your own, common sense, enjoy working outdoors, hard working, observant, practical skills, reliable, safety conscious

Relevant Subjects
Construction and built environment, Land and Environment

Further Information
Apprenticeship Schemes (National Apprenticeship Service) - www.apprenticeships.org.uk

Chartered Institute of Water and Environmental Management (CIWEM) (CIWEM) - www.environmentalcareers.org.uk/careers/

Diplomas (Foundation, Higher and Advanced) - http://yp.direct.gov.uk/diplomas

Energy & Utlility Skills - sector skills council for gas, power, waste management & water industries - www.euskills.co.uk

Foundation Learning (QCDA) - www.qcda.gov.uk

Scottish Water - www.scottishwater.co.uk

Training Schemes - www.direct.gov.uk/en/educationandlearning

Welsh Baccalaureate - www.wbq.org.uk

Addresses
British Waterways
64 Clarendon Road, Watford WD17 1DA
Phone: +44 (()) 1923 201120
Web: www.britishwaterways.co.uk

British Waterways - Scotland Office
Canal House, Applecross Street, Glasgow G4 9SP
Phone: +44 (0)141 332 6936
Web: www.britishwaterways.co.uk

Northern Ireland Water (NIW)
PO Box 1026, Belfast BT1 9DJ
Web: www.niwater.com

OFWAT
Centre City Tower 7 Hill Street, Birmingham B5 4UA
Phone: +44 (0)121 644 7500
Web: www.ofwat.gov.uk

Water UK
1 Queen Anne's Gate, London SW1H 9BT
Phone: +44 (0)20 7344 1844
Web: www.water.org.uk

Waterways Ireland
2 Sligo Road, Enniskillen, Co Fermanagh BT74 7JY
Phone: +44 (0)28 6632 3004
Web: www.waterwaysireland.org

Similar Jobs
Construction Operative, Construction Plant Operative, Water Distribution/Sewerage Operative, Water/Sewerage Treatment Plant Operative.

Website Author/Editor
also known as: Web Content Manager, Web Editorial Officer, Webmaster, Website Manager

CRCI:Computers and IT
CLCI:CAV Job Band: 3 to 5

Job Description
Website authors are responsible for planning and overseeing the continuous management of a website and its publication content. They set up and run websites on the internet and advise on what can be included. Also ensure the information is current and accurate, and that new information follows the webpage editorial style, as well as the structure, design and layout. The role is journalistic but also demands technical skills in multimedia.

Website authors have a knowledge and understanding of the business needs of a company, and select the hardware/software required for businesses wishing to trade over the internet (e-commerce). The web editor may use a content management system to maintain the site, or manually build/edit web pages using hypertext markup language (HTML) and Javascript.

They monitor the website's use and produce statistics for marketing purposes. Also liaise with colleagues who have an interest in the website, such as marketing and sales departments, communications and public relations sections. The team may consist of artists, researchers, multimedia specialists and writers. May supervise those who design and program the pages that make up the website, but in a small company the developer, designer and webmaster is often one person.

Some manage an Intranet (closed network) service that is accessed and used within a single organisation or company. May be responsible for website security and ensure that it complies with the legal issues that govern each website, such as data protection, libel and obscenity, and copyright.

Work Details
Work a basic 35-39 hrs a week, Monday to Friday, although may need to work extra hours at times to meet deadlines. You are normally based at a desk/workstation and sit in front of a computer for long periods of time. You must be prepared to travel to visit clients and spend nights away from home. You may be responsible for other members of staff such as assistant editors or freelancers and frequently consult with other managers and employees.

Qualification
- **England, Wales and Northern Ireland**

Band 4: For a relevant higher national award: 1-2 A levels and some GCSEs (A*-C) including English and maths, and for some courses preferably science, computer studies or information technology, or equivalent.

Band 5: For degree courses: 2-3 A levels including maths and science, or computer studies/information technology for some courses, and some GCSEs (A*-C) usually including English and maths, or equivalent. Exact requirements depend on the degree you take.

- **Scotland**

Band 4: For a relevant higher national award: 2-3 H grades and some S grades (1-3) usually including English and maths, or for some courses science, computer studies or information technology, or similar qualifications.

Band 5: For degree courses: 3-5 H grades including maths and science, with computer studies or information technology for some courses, and some S grades (1-3), often including English and maths, or similar qualifications. Exact requirements depend on the degree you take.

Website Author/Editor

Degree Information

There are many web, internet, digital media, e-business and e-commerce degrees available, but course content varies so check carefully. However, specialist subjects are not always essential. The Information Technology Management for Business degree (see e-skills UK) is designed in partnership with some of the biggest employers in the IT industry. There are also one-year top-up courses in subjects that include internet applications. Postgraduate degrees/diplomas are available in a variety of relevant subjects.

Adult Qualifications

Mature applicants may not need the standard entry requirements for higher education courses, particularly if your previous experience is relevant or you show an ability to study at the appropriate level. There are many relevant full or part-time courses available at further/higher education colleges. Access and foundation courses are available for those who have no formal qualifications but want to pursue a relevant degree.

Work Experience

Entry to this job is competitive and it is important that you try to do some relevant work or voluntary experience before applying. Any work experience with business computing, graphic design and multimedia is particularly relevant. Writing, editing, or journalism experience is also useful.

Entry and Training

There is no set route into this career and the speed and pace of expansion in this sector means that skills are often more important than formal qualifications. It is useful to build a portfolio of your work as this is a young industry and those with relevant skills can progress rapidly. Web editors may have a background in journalism, proofreading or marketing, though many jobs require technical skills or a particular knowledge of the sector, such as sport or education.

Many entrants have a degree and relevant experience in website development or design. It is important to have a knowledge of search engine techniques, information architecture and to keep up to date with online trends. Training is ongoing, both on the job and by short courses including research methods and copyright laws run by manufacturers.

The Society for Editors and Proofreaders and the National Union of Journalists offer relevant courses in web writing and editing. The World Wide Web Consortium (W3C) is a useful source of information on web accessibility and standards and the UK Web Design Association offers free membership for web professionals. Some employers may assist with study for professional qualifications, including those of the British Computer Society and the HTML Writers' Guild. The Certified Internet Webmaster course certifies skills for new entrants and IT professionals. The Open University offers courses in computing and maths, which can lead to a computing degree. There are no formal entry requirements and you study through distance learning. Various full or part-time foundation degrees in relevant IT subjects are also available.

A Diploma/Welsh Baccalaureate may be available in your area in IT and an ICT higher apprenticeship is available through e-skills. This combines an apprenticeship with a foundation degree and can lead to a full honours degree. There are partnerships with colleges and universities throughout the UK. E-skills runs a professional development programme which enables new IT professionals to fast-track their career. The programme is delivered through universities and participating employers. E-skills also offers an internship. Students are placed for a period of employment within an organisation, enabling them to develop valuable business and IT skills. Contact e-skills for details of all programmes and schemes.

Mature entrants are expected to have relevant experience in business computing, website development or design. Some editors have a background in journalism, publishing or marketing, though the job may demand technical skills. There are many relevant full or part-time courses available at further/higher education colleges, or you can study through distance learning, or online.

Opportunities and Pay

Opportunities occur throughout the UK with employers in all areas of industry and commerce, including the public sector, local/central government, the retail industry, charity organisations, advertising companies and broadcasting companies. Most organisations have websites and need a web editor to write and manage web content. Some are employed in the IT departments of large organisations or companies who do a lot of business via the internet. Others work as self-employed web design consultants in editorial team management, technical writing and website training for a number of companies. It may also be possible to work abroad.

Pay varies depending on the location, size and type of organisation. Salaries start at around £20k-£25k a year. Experienced editors/webmasters can earn around £28k-£35k a year, with high earners making up to £45k a year.

Skills and Qualities

able to cope under pressure, analytical skills, creative flair, excellent communication skills, good spelling, grammar and punctuation, imaginative, leadership qualities, logical, specialist IT skills, technical aptitude

Relevant Subjects

Art and Design, Business and accounting, Design and technology, English, ICT/Computer studies, Mathematics, Media and communication studies, Physics, Science

Further Information

AGCAS: Information Technology (Job Sector Briefing) (AGCAS) - www.prospects.ac.uk

Certified Internet Webmaster (CIW) - www.ciwcertified.com

Diplomas (Foundation, Higher and Advanced) - http://yp.direct.gov.uk/diplomas

e-skills UK - sector skills council for business and information technology - www.e-skills.com

HTML Writers Guild - www.hwg.org

New Media Age (NMA) - www.nma.co.uk

Open University - www.open.ac.uk

Real Life Guide to Information & Communications Technology (Trotman) - www.trotman.co.uk

Skillset - sector skills council for the creative media, fashion and textiles industries - www.skillset.org

Society for Editors and Proofreaders - www.sfep.org.uk

The Internet Uncovered (Trotman 2009) - www.trotman.co.uk

UK Web Design Association - www.ukwda.org

Welsh Baccalaureate - www.wbq.org.uk

►Working in computers & IT (2010) (Babcock Lifeskills) - www.babcock-lifeskills.com/

►Working in creative & media (2007) (Babcock Lifeskills) - www.babcock-lifeskills.com/

World Wide Web Consortium - www.w3.org

Addresses

British Computer Society (BCS)
First Floor, Block D North Star House North Star Avenue, Swindon, Wiltshire SN2 1FA
Phone: +44 (0)845 300 4417
Web: www.bcs.org

British Interactive Media Association (BIMA)
The Lightwell, 12-16 Laystall Street, Clerkenwel, London EC1R 4PF
Phone: +44(0)207 843 6797
Web: www.bima.co.uk

National Union of Journalists (NUJ)
Headland House, 308-312 Grays Inn Road, London WC1X 8DP
Phone: +44 (0)20 7278 7916
Web: www.nuj.org.uk

Similar Jobs

Database Administrator, IT Applications Developer, IT Systems Analyst/Designer, IT Systems Developer, Website Designer, Website Developer

Website Designer

also known as: Internet Engineer, Multimedia Architect

CRCI:Computers and IT
CLCI:CAV Job Band: 3 to 5

Job Description

Website designers create internet web pages for clients, using text, graphics and special features such as interactive buttons and animations. They are responsible for the design, layout and coding of each individual web page. Work is similar to that of a website developer using interactive programming languages such as HTML and Javascript and computer-generated imagery (CGI). Key skills are in the design and the use of specialist website design software such as Frontpage. Designers liaise with writers, other designers, systems administrators/specialists and other IT professionals to ensure the website fulfils its purpose. Some designers pass designs onto website programmers/developers to produce the end product.

Designers need to achieve a balance between a site that is attractive and interesting to look at, and one that is interactive, easy to use and user-friendly. They ensure the website is designed to be accessed from many different devices, including mobile phones, digital TVs and PDAs (personal digital assistants). Also decide on font style, size of text, colours, backgrounds, animation, appropriate and eye catching graphics and button icons, and any audio and video sequences. They check all spelling, grammar and punctuation, and ensure that the site works accurately and properly before uploading onto the internet.

Work Details

Usually work a basic 35-39 hr week, Monday to Friday, although you may have to work extra hours when deadlines approach. Therefore the work environment can sometimes be stressful. This job is normally office or studio based. You must be prepared to travel locally, nationally and sometimes internationally to visit clients and spend nights away from home. You frequently consult with managers and other IT professionals.

Qualification

No set entry requirements but most employers/customers wish to see evidence of design for successful sites or relevant experience.

• England, Wales and Northern Ireland

Band 3: For some employers or for a BTEC national award and some foundation courses: 4-5 GCSEs (A*-C) preferably including English and maths, or equivalent.

Band 4: For BTEC higher national award: 1-2 A levels and some GCSEs (A*-C) usually including English and maths, and for some courses preferably science, computer studies or information technology, or equivalent.

Band 5: For degree courses: 2-3 A levels including maths and science, or computer studies/information technology for some courses, and some GCSEs (A*-C) usually including English and maths, or equivalent. Exact requirements depend on the degree you take.

• Scotland

Band 3: For entry or a relevant SQA national award: usually at least four S grades (1-3) including English and maths, or similar.

Band 4: For SQA higher national award: usually 2-3 H grades and some S grades (1-3), often including English and maths, or similar qualifications.

Band 5: For degree courses: 3-5 H grades and some S grades (1-3), usually including English and maths, or similar qualifications. Exact requirements depend on the degree you take.

Degree Information

There are a number of degree courses that combine design and computing, such as multimedia, digital media and computing, interactive media, new media, multimedia design and multimedia computing. The Information Technology Management for Business degree (see e-skills UK) is designed in partnership with some of the biggest employers in the IT industry. Other relevant subjects include artificial intelligence, computer science, software engineering and information technology.

Computer graphics modules and business courses in Hypertext and Java programming are also useful. There are a number of relevant postgraduate courses, including those for graduates with non-relevant degrees.

Adult Qualifications

Mature applicants may not need to meet the standard entry requirements for higher education courses, particularly if your previous experience is relevant or you show an ability to study at the appropriate level. There are many relevant full or part-time courses available at further/higher education colleges. Access and foundation courses are available for those who have no formal qualifications but wish to pursue a relevant degree.

Work Experience

Entry to this job is competitive and it is important that you try to do some relevant work or voluntary experience before applying. Multimedia, animation, computer programming experience, or work with computer graphics are all useful for this job. Where possible, try to build up a portfolio of your work in the form of a CD, DVD or 'live' website.

Entry and Training

There is no set route into this job and it is really a job for a designer with IT skills, rather than purely a technical IT job. Most employers/customers wish to see evidence of successful websites or relevant experience. Some employers may provide IT training for those who have a background in art and design. Training is ongoing, both on the job and by short courses run by manufacturers. Many website designers have a graphic design degree and familiarity with the internet and interactive design. However, like many other internet jobs, it is possible for those with relevant skills and flair to find employment without formal qualifications.

You can enter this job without an art and design background, but with excellent skills in copying or cloning graphics, and then working on the functional aspects of integrating all the IT. Experience of design packages such as Photoshop, Flash and Dreamweaver is particularly useful. Entry to degree courses is competitive and an excellent portfolio of relevant work is normally needed. In some cases talented applicants without formal qualifications can obtain college places.

The Certified Internet Webmaster course certifies skills for new entrants and IT professionals, and Adobe offer various certification levels for their own products. Some employers may assist with study for professional qualifications, including those of the British Computer Society and the HTML Writers Guild. The UK Web Design Association offers free membership to web professionals. The Open University offers courses in computing and maths, which lead to a computing degree. There are no formal entry requirements and you study through distance learning. It is important to keep up to date with web technology.

Various full or part-time foundation degrees in subjects such as web design, graphic design, multimedia or interactive media, are available. A Diploma/Welsh Baccalaureate may be available in your area in IT. Relevant S/NVQs at levels 1-4 are available in IT practitioner subjects. The new S/NVQ for IT users (ITQ 2009) has been developed as part of a project involving a full review of the National Occupational Standards for IT users.

Training programmes, including apprenticeship schemes, may be available for entry to this job. An ICT higher apprenticeship is available through e-skills. This combines an apprenticeship with a foundation degree and can lead to a full honours degree. There are partnerships with colleges and universities throughout the UK. E-skills runs a professional development programme which enables new IT professionals to fast-track their career. The programme is delivered through universities and participating employers. E-skills also offers an internship. Students are placed for a period of employment within an organisation, enabling them to develop valuable business and IT skills. Contact e-skills for details of all programmes and schemes.

Mature applicants may be expected to have relevant experience in design or IT, and experience in the use of interactive design software. Access and foundation or similar courses are available for those who have no formal qualifications but wish to pursue a relevant degree.

There are many relevant full or part-time courses available at further/higher education colleges. Training opportunities such as Work Based Learning/Training for Work may be available in your area. Some LSCs/LECs, Jobcentres (NI) and ELWa (Wales) run specialist IT courses. You can also gain recognition of previous experience through Accreditation of Prior Learning (APL) or by working towards relevant S/NVQs.

Opportunities and Pay

The rapid expansion of the business use of the internet/intranet has increased opportunities throughout the UK, but concentrated in the south east of England. Some designers are employed in the IT departments of large organisations, or companies which do a lot of business via the internet. Many website designers work in the new media design teams of established design consultancies, with internet service providers (ISPs), advertising agencies, the public sector, local/central government and charity organisations. In large organisations, progress may be possible to design team or web content management jobs. Experienced designers may work as self-employed consultants or as technical writers. There are opportunities to work overseas.

Pay varies depending on the location, size and type of organisation. Salaries start at around £20k-£25k a year for graduates, rising to £30k with experience. High earners with specialist skills can earn up to £45k a year, although some earn considerably more.

Skills and Qualities

able to work both on your own and in a team, analytical skills, artistic ability, creative and imaginative flair, design ability, enthusiastic, eye for shape/colour, logical, specialist IT skills, technical aptitude

Relevant Subjects

Art and Design, Design and technology, English, ICT/Computer studies, Mathematics, Media and communication studies, Physics, Science

Further Information

AGCAS: Information Technology (Job Sector Briefing) (AGCAS) - www.prospects.ac.uk

Certified Internet Webmaster (CIW) - www.ciwcertified.com

Diplomas (Foundation, Higher and Advanced) - http://yp.direct.gov.uk/diplomas

e-skills UK - sector skills council for business and information technology - www.e-skills.com

HTML Writers Guild - www.hwg.org

New Media Age (NMA) - www.nma.co.uk

Open University - www.open.ac.uk

Real Life Guide to Information & Communications Technology (Trotman) - www.trotman.co.uk

Skillset - sector skills council for the creative media, fashion and textiles industries - www.skillset.org

The Internet Uncovered (Trotman 2009) - www.trotman.co.uk

UK Web Design Association - www.ukwda.org

Welsh Baccalaureate - www.wbq.org.uk

▶Working in computers & IT (2010) (Babcock Lifeskills) - www.babcock-lifeskills.com/

▶Working in creative & media (2007) (Babcock Lifeskills) - www.babcock-lifeskills.com/

World Wide Web Consortium - www.w3.org

Addresses

British Computer Society (BCS)
First Floor, Block D North Star House North Star Avenue, Swindon, Wiltshire SN2 1FA
Phone: +44 (0)845 300 4417
Web: www.bcs.org

British Interactive Media Association (BIMA)
The Lightwell, 12-16 Laystall Street, Clerkenwel, London EC1R 4PF
Phone: +44(0)207 843 6797
Web: www.bima.co.uk

Similar Jobs

Advertising Art Director, Computer Games Designer, Graphic Designer, Interactive Media Designer, Website Author/Editor, Website Developer

Website Developer

also known as: IT Web Developer

CRCI:Computers and IT
CLCI:CAV — Job Band: 4 to 5

Job Description

Website developers use computer programming skills to combine text, data, graphics, sound and animation, and other visual effects, into internet websites. They have knowledge of specialist interactive programming languages as well as more widely used computer languages. Developers write the programming code and also test and deal with any bugs in the written programs. There is not always a clear-cut distinction between a website developer and website designer, but a developer's expertise is in the relevant program languages such as HTML and Javascript, rather than design skills. They work as part of a team that is made up of individuals with expertise in IT, creative design and business.

Website developers upload the website onto the server and register it with search engines to maximise the numbers of visitors to the site. Also ensure that the website can be accessed from many different devices, including mobile phones, digital TVs and PDAs (personal digital assistants). May update and maintain existing websites. Can also use skills in the production of CD-ROMs and DVDs.

Work Details

Work regular hours of 35-39 a week, although you may have to work extra hours when deadlines approach. You are normally office or studio based. Those working freelance must be prepared to travel to visit clients and spend nights away from home. You frequently consult with managers and IT professionals. Most of your time is spent sitting in front of a computer.

Qualification

• England, Wales and Northern Ireland

Band 4: For a relevant BTEC higher national award: 1-2 A levels and some GCSEs (A*-C) usually including English and maths, and for some courses science, computer studies or information technology, or equivalent.

Band 5: For degree courses: 2-3 A levels and some GCSEs (A*-C) preferably including maths or science, and computer studies or information technology for some courses, and some GCSEs (A*-C) usually including English and maths, or equivalent. Exact requirements depend on the degree you take.

- **Scotland**

Band 4: For a relevant SQA higher national award: usually 2-3 H grades and some S grades (1-3), often including English and maths, and for some courses science, computer studies or information technology, or similar qualifications.

Band 5: For degree courses: 3-5 H grades preferably including maths or science, and computer studies or information technology for some courses, and some S grades (1-3), usually including English and maths, or similar qualifications. Exact requirements depend on the degree you take.

Degree Information

Specific degrees such as internet application development, internet engineering, web management, and web design and development are available. The Information Technology Management for Business degree (see e-skills UK) is designed in partnership with some of the biggest employers in the IT industry.

Specialist subjects are not essential and subjects such as computer science, digital media and computing, artificial intelligence or software engineering are also acceptable. Computer graphics modules and business oriented courses on Hypertext and Java programming are also useful. There are postgraduate courses for graduates with non-relevant degrees.

Adult Qualifications

Mature entrants may not need the standard entry requirements for higher education courses, particularly if your previous experience is relevant and you show the ability to study at the appropriate level. Access and foundation or similar courses are available for those who have no formal qualifications but wish to pursue a relevant degree.

Work Experience

Entry to this job is competitive and it is important that you try to do some relevant work or voluntary experience before applying. Multimedia, animation, computer programming experience, or work with computer graphics are all useful for this job. Where possible, try to build up a portfolio of your work in the form of a CD, DVD or 'live' website.

Entry and Training

Rapid expansion in this sector in recent years means that skills are generally more important than qualifications. However, entrants usually have a degree and relevant programming skills in HTML, Javascript, ASP, Visual Basic, XML or C++. This is still a young industry and those with appropriate skills can progress rapidly. Training is ongoing, both on the job and by short courses run by manufacturers. Most graduates start work either as a programmer or in testing or maintaining existing websites. Once suitably experienced there is progress into work dealing with client consultancy. Some employers may assist with study for professional qualifications, including those of the British Computer Society and the HTML Writers Guild.

The Open University offers courses in computing and maths, which lead to a computing degree. There are no formal entry requirements and you study through distance learning. S/NVQs at levels 2-4 are available in relevant IT subject areas. The new S/NVQ for IT users (ITQ 2009) has been developed as part of a project involving a full review of the National Occupational Standards for IT users. The Certified Internet Webmaster course certifies skills for new entrants and IT professionals, and Adobe offers various certification levels for their own products. The UK Web Design Association offers free membership to web professionals.

A Diploma/Welsh Baccalaureate may be available in your area in IT. Various full or part-time foundation degrees are available in IT subjects. An ICT higher apprenticeship is available through e-skills. This combines an apprenticeship with a foundation degree and can lead to a full honours degree. There are partnerships with colleges and universities throughout the UK. E-skills runs a professional development programme which enables new IT professionals to fast-track their career. The programme is delivered through universities and participating employers. E-skills also offers an internship. Students are placed for a period of employment within an organisation, enabling them to develop valuable business and IT skills. Contact e-skills for details of all programmes and schemes.

Mature applicants may be expected to have relevant experience in IT and the use of interactive design software. Some of the larger IT companies offer sponsorship for studying IT at degree level. There are many relevant full or part-time courses available at further/higher education colleges.

Training opportunities such as Work Based Learning/Training for Work may be available in your area. Some LSCs/LECs, Jobcentres (NI) and ELWa (Wales) run specialist IT courses. You can also gain recognition of previous experience through Accreditation of Prior Learning (APL) or by working towards relevant S/NVQs.

Opportunities and Pay

Opportunities are available throughout the UK and with the rapid expansion of business, and individual use of the Internet, CD-ROMs and DVDs, job opportunities exist. IT expansion is likely to continue in the areas of online service provision and web hosting so opportunities in this area are good. Some developers are employed in the IT departments of large organisations or companies which do a lot of business via the Internet. Others work in marketing or public relations, or design consultancies specialising in interactive work.

Experienced developers can work as self-employed consultants or set up their own company offering development services to a wide range of clients. There are opportunities to travel and work overseas.

Pay varies depending on the location, size and type of organisation. Salaries start at around £18k-£25k a year and with experience rise to £25k-£40k. High earners with specialist skills can earn more.

Skills and Qualities

able to communicate effectively, able to work both on your own and in a team, analytical skills, attention to detail, imaginative, logical, methodical, problem-solving skills, specialist IT skills, technical aptitude

Relevant Subjects

Art and Design, Business and accounting, Design and technology, English, ICT/Computer studies, Mathematics, Media and communication studies, Physics, Science

Further Information

AGCAS: Information Technology (Job Sector Briefing) (AGCAS) - www.prospects.ac.uk

Certified Internet Webmaster (CIW) - www.ciwcertified.com

Diplomas (Foundation, Higher and Advanced) - http://yp.direct.gov.uk/diplomas

e-skills UK - sector skills council for business and information technology - www.e-skills.com

HTML Writers Guild - www.hwg.org

New Media Age (NMA) - www.nma.co.uk

Open University - www.open.ac.uk

Skillset - sector skills council for the creative media, fashion and textiles industries - www.skillset.org

The Internet Uncovered (Trotman 2009) - www.trotman.co.uk

UK Web Design Association - www.ukwda.org

Welsh Baccalaureate - www.wbq.org.uk

▶Working in computers & IT (2010) (Babcock Lifeskills) - www.babcock-lifeskills.com/

▶Working in creative & media (2007) (Babcock Lifeskills) - www.babcock-lifeskills.com/

World Wide Web Consortium - www.w3.org

Addresses

British Computer Society (BCS)
First Floor, Block D North Star House North Star Avenue, Swindon, Wiltshire SN2 1FA
Phone: +44 (0)845 300 4417
Web: www.bcs.org

British Interactive Media Association (BIMA)
The Lightwell, 12-16 Laystall Street, Clerkenwel, London EC1R 4PF
Phone: +44(0)207 843 6797
Web: www.bima.co.uk

Institution of Analysts and Programmers (IAP)
Charles House, 36 Culmington Road, London W13 9NH
Phone: +44 (0)20 8567 2118
Web: www.iap.org.uk

Similar Jobs

Computer Games Programmer, Interactive Media Designer, IT Applications Developer, IT Systems Developer, Website Author/ Editor, Website Designer

Wedding Planner

also known as: Bridal Consultant, Wedding Coordinator

CRCI:Personal and Other Services

CLCI:IZ Job Band: 2 to 4

Job Description

Wedding planners help couples to plan their wedding and organise either all the details or just one aspect of the event. They meet the couple to discuss what they want and find out the budget they have available. Then suggest ideas, being creative if the couple want a wedding that is different. They may be involved in organising the venue, photography, transport, accommodation, seating plan, music, outfits, hair, makeup and any other aspect of the event. May negotiate prices with suppliers and organise payments. Usually attend the wedding to ensure that it runs smoothly.

Must research potential suppliers of services, equipment and venues for weddings and keep detailed records. Usually maintain a portfolio of weddings that have been organised for use in future marketing. Also attend bridal fairs and conferences to keep up to date with new ideas.

Work Details

Hours can be irregular and on occasions you may have work long days, including often working evenings and weekends. You are usually office or home based, but need to travel regularly to visit clients, venues and suppliers. You may work alone or as part of a small team, but also have regular contacts with clients, often acting as liaison between the family of the bride and groom. You may be organising more than one wedding at a time and on occasions the work may be stressful to ensure all is completed on time.

Qualification

There are no set entry qualifications, with personal qualities often being more important.

- **England, Wales and Northern Ireland**

Band 2: Although academic qualifications are not specified for this job, it is an advantage to have some GCSEs (A*-C) in subjects that include English and maths, or equivalent.

Band 3: For entry: employers usually look for at least 4 GCSEs (A*-C) including English and maths, or equivalent.

Band 4: For HND, Diploma of Higher Education or foundation degree: 1-2 A levels and some GCSEs (A*-C) usually including English and maths, or equivalent.

- **Scotland**

Band 2: Although academic qualifications are not specified for this job, it is an advantage to have some S grades in subjects that include English and maths, or similar.

Band 3: For entry: most employers usually look for at least four S grades (1-3) including English and maths, or similar.

Band 4: For entry to SQA higher national and professional development awards, usually 2-3 H grades and some S grades (1-3), including English and maths, or similar qualifications.

Adult Qualifications

Mature entrants should have a good standard of secondary education, but experience is often of more value than specific qualifications.

Work Experience

Relevant work or voluntary experience is always useful and can improve your chances in application for entry to this job. Any experience of working with people or planning events is relevant. Organising social events for your college or university is also useful.

Entry and Training

There are no specific entry qualifications for this work and many entrants have previous experience in event management, catering, marketing or public relations. Some enter this work after the experience of planning their own wedding. Qualifications in event management or hospitality and catering may be an advantage. There is a foundation degree available in event management and S/ NVQs in events at level 2-4.

You may find it helpful to take a specialist course in wedding planning available from private organisations. A level 4 diploma in wedding planning is available from the Institute of Professional Wedding Planners. This is accredited by ASET and available by distance learning. The National Association of Professional Wedding Services also offers a distance learning course through Absolute Perfection Wedding Consultancy. Two day courses are available from the UK Alliance of Wedding Planners.

Mature entrants with experience in events management, catering management or public relations may have an advantage.

Opportunities and Pay

On average around 26% of weddings in the UK now have the help of a wedding planner. This is growing in popularity as couples find they do not have the time to plan their weddings in the detail they would like. Wedding planners are employed by specialist wedding planning firms, hotels and conference centres, venues that specialise in weddings and event organising agencies. Entry to jobs is very competitive. Once experienced, many wedding planners become self-employed.

If employed, starting salaries are around £16k-£20k a year, rising to £25k-£35k with experience. Those who are self-employed, usually earn a fee based on a percentage of the cost of the wedding. This can range from 10-20% depending on experience, with the average wedding costing around £20k.

Skills and Qualities

attention to detail, business awareness, confident, creative flair, diplomatic, good communication skills, good interpersonal skills, good organisational skills, imaginative, networking skills, problem-solving skills

Relevant Subjects

Business and accounting, Economics, English, Hospitality and catering, ICT/Computer studies, Leisure, travel and tourism, Mathematics

Further Information

UK Alliance of Wedding Planners (UKAWP) - www.ukawp.com

▶Working in hospitality & catering (2009) (Babcock Lifeskills) - www.babcock-lifeskills.com/

Addresses

Institute of Professional Wedding Planners
Overbrook Business Centre, Poolbridge Road, Blackford, Wedmore, Somerset BS28 4PA
Phone: 0800 781 1715
Web: www.inst.org/wedding-planner-courses/become.htm

National Association of Professional Wedding Services (NAPWS)
The Wedding Association, London SW19 1DB
Phone: +44 (0) 208 090 1921
Web: www.theweddingassociation.co.uk

Similar Jobs

Catering Manager, Charity Fundraiser, Event & Exhibition Organiser, Personal Assistant, Public Relations Officer, Restaurant Manager

Welder

also known as: Welder Fabricator

CRCI:Engineering
CLCI:RON Job Band: 1 to 3

Job Description

Welders join metal or strong plastic by using extreme heat to melt the parts together. This involves checking that the pieces for joining are clean and in the correct shape/position. They may use a jig to hold the pieces in position. Some pieces may already be in position and tack welded together by a pipe fitter or a sheet metal worker/plater. The job requires skill in the timing and judging of colour changes of the material involved as welders have to hold an electrode or gas torch at the join. May also follow work instructions from technical drawings.

Some welding processes are done by machine which the welder then operates (including electron beam and laser welding), or through computer programmable robots as used in large scale manufacturing, such as the ship and automotive industries. Welders usually specialise in one type of welding.

Work Details

Usually work a basic 39 hr week, Monday to Friday, though some shift work and overtime may be expected. Place of work can be industrial premises, a workshop or on site and may be either indoors or outdoors. You have to cope with some physical activity including kneeling and bending down, climbing ladders and possibly heavy lifting. The work environment may be hot, noisy and sometimes cramped or enclosed. There may be a risk of burns or accidents from equipment, so you may need to wear goggles or a face mask, gloves, overalls and possibly a helmet. In some situations you may also need breathing equipment.

Qualification

• England, Wales and Northern Ireland

Band 2: For entry to jobs, no minimum qualifications are needed, but it is an advantage to have some GCSEs (A*-C) or equivalent in subjects that include English, maths and a science. Practical and technical subjects are also useful.

Band 3: For entry to jobs, HNC or a relevant Diploma, usually at least 4 GCSEs (A*-C) including English, maths, science (preferably physics) and a technical, design or engineering subject, or equivalent.

• Scotland

Band 2: Although academic qualifications are not specified for this job, it is an advantage to have some S grades (1-3) in subjects that include maths, English and a science (preferably physics), or similar. Practical and technical subjects are also useful.

Band 3: For entry to jobs, usually at least four S grades (1-3) including English or maths, science (preferably physics) and a technical, design or engineering subject, or similar.

Adult Qualifications

Formal qualifications may not be required, but some related experience in mechanical engineering or metal working is helpful. Course entry requirements are usually relaxed for mature students.

Work Experience

Relevant work or voluntary experience is always useful. It can add to your CV and improve your chances when applying for entry to jobs or apprenticeships in the engineering industry.

Entry and Training

Most people enter this work via an apprenticeship in fabrication and welding. Others may do a full-time course first such as a BTEC/SQA national award in manufacturing engineering (fabrication and welding), an S/NVQ at levels 2-3 in fabrication and welding engineering or a vocationally related qualification at levels 1-3. You can then enter an advanced apprenticeship. Others may train on the job under the supervision of experienced welders, with day release for appropriate courses. You may have to take an aptitude test. The Engineering Construction Industry Training Board runs apprenticeship programmes at craft and technician level and many of their courses are covered by grants. Visit the website for full details.

The Welding Institute runs a range of training courses in welding, including the International Institute of Welding/European Welding Federation Diploma. Most welders also do a welding approval test to gain a Welder Approval Certificate, which is the industry-recognised qualification.

A Diploma/Welsh Baccalaureate in engineering may be available in your area. See the diplomas website for further information.

Mature entry is possible, especially for those with skills in metalwork and technical drawing, and there may be special training opportunities for adults in some areas via the Welding Institute or the Engineering Construction Industry Training Board. On-the-job training programmes may be open to adults with relevant work experience after an initial period off the job to learn basic skills. Training opportunities such as Work Based Learning/Training for Work may be available in your area. You can also gain recognition of previous experience through Accreditation of Prior Learning or by working towards relevant S/NVQs.

Contact your local Jobcentre Plus, Next Step service or Learning and Skills Council (LSC)/Local Enterprise Company (LEC) for details of training schemes, including apprenticeships for adults.

Opportunities and Pay

Employment can be with a manufacturing or construction company, shipyard, civil engineering company, the Ministry of Defence, or there may be opportunities to become self-employed. Prospects vary depending on where you live and may depend on your willingness to move to another area.

Pay varies depending on area and employer, but salaries are likely to be around £200-£230 a week while training, rising to around £380 with experience. The most skilled and experienced workers can earn more than £700 a week. Pay is variable if a piece work rate is paid, but can be more if overtime is worked.

Health

This job requires good general fitness, stamina and also normal colour vision, good hearing and good eyesight. There is an allergy risk from skin irritants.

Skills and Qualities
able to follow drawings and plans, able to work in confined spaces, able to work well on your own, accurate, good concentration level, hand-to-eye co-ordination, patient, perseverance, safety conscious, steady hand

Relevant Subjects
Design and technology, Engineering, Mathematics, Physics, Science

Further Information
Apprenticeship Schemes (National Apprenticeship Service) - www.apprenticeships.org.uk

Diplomas (Foundation, Higher and Advanced) - http://yp.direct.gov.uk/diplomas

SEMTA - sector skills council for science, engineering and manufacturing technologies - www.semta.org.uk

Training Schemes - www.direct.gov.uk/en/educationandlearning

TWI Training & Examination Services - www.twitraining.com

Welsh Baccalaureate - www.wbq.org.uk

Addresses
Engineering Construction Industry Training Board (ECITB)
Blue Court, Church Lane, Kings Langley, Hertfordshire WD4 8JP
Phone: +44 (0)1923 260 000
Web: www.ecitb.org.uk

Welding Institute (TWI), The
Granta Park, Great Abington, Cambridge CB21 6AL
Phone: +44 (0)1223 899 000
Web: www.twi.co.uk

Similar Jobs
Engineering Craft Machinist, Rail Track Maintenance Worker, Sheet Metal Plater, Sheet Metal Worker, Toolmaker, Vehicle Body Repairer

Welfare Benefits Adviser
also known as: Benefits Adviser, Welfare Rights Adviser

CRCI:Social Work and Counselling Services

CLCI:KEK Job Band: 2 to 4

Job Description
Welfare benefits advisers work with the public to advise them on matters relating to welfare and benefits, such as housing benefits, tax credits, maternity benefits, employment rights, disability living allowance, pensions and social security. They interview the client, either face-to-face, by telephone or email, and assess the client's situation. Explain how different benefits and legislation work and help the client to claim their full entitlement. This may involve helping clients to fill in forms, writing letters or making phone calls on their behalf.

Must keep up to date with welfare and benefits policies and legislation as entitlements change frequently. Welfare benefits advisers research relevant information, often using a computer, write reports and keep confidential records. They work with other benefits agencies and organisations. Help clients to appeal against any negative benefit decisions made. Those working at a more senior level, such as welfare caseworkers, also represent clients at appeal tribunals.

Work Details
Usually works a 37 hr week, Monday to Friday. Depending on the employer, you may do some evening or weekend work. Part-time work or job sharing is quite common. You are based in an advice centre or office where the public can visit, but may need to travel to a client's home, or attend tribunals. Deals with clients face to face in an interview room, or over the phone.

Work involves listening and asking questions, informing and advising, providing encouragement and support, and dealing with confidential information. The job can be emotionally challenging and stressful at times. You work with a wide range of people who are members of the local community, some of whom may be upset or demanding. Occasionally, you may be confronted with threatening behaviour. Work is on a one-to-one basis with clients, but you also liaise with other advisers and external organisations.

Qualification
Employers look for at least basic English language and numeracy skills. Qualifications held by people entering this area of work vary widely and relevant knowledge and experience are often more important than specific qualifications. Good communication skills are essential. Useful and relevant subjects include law, English, sociology and social science.

Adult Qualifications
Employers look for people with the right personal qualities, level of maturity and experience, rather than those with specific qualifications.

Work Experience
Usually you need some paid or voluntary experience in advice work if you want to work as a welfare benefits adviser. Organisations such as the Citizens Advice Bureau accept volunteers from the age of 16 and some actively encourage student volunteers. Experience of work that involves using listening skills and helping people is useful. Many colleges and adult education services offer courses that provide an introduction to counselling for people interested in developing these skills.

Entry and Training
Relevant knowledge and experience are often more important than specific qualifications for entry to this job. However, you do need good English and basic maths skills as a minimum. Usually people move into benefits advising from general advice work, such as debt, housing or employment. Once you have experience and knowledge, you then specialise in giving welfare and benefits advice. Most paid advice workers start out as volunteers. In some areas being able to speak a second language is an advantage. Due to the nature of the work, you need to undergo a Criminal Records Bureau (CRB)/Disclosure Scotland check.

Many advice organisations run their own training schemes that include initial training and short specialised courses on topics related to benefits advice. Courses and training programmes are based on the national occupational standards for legal advice. You gain practical knowledge and skills on the job, supervised or mentored by experienced staff. Relevant S/NVQs include advice and guidance at levels 2-4, supporting legal advice provision at level 2, and legal advice at levels 3-4. Ongoing training and continuing professional development (CPD) is an important aspect of this work. You need to keep up to date with the latest legislation and changes to taxes and benefits.

All advisers doing voluntary or paid work with the Citizens Advice Bureau (CAB) undertake a set training programme. In England and Wales this leads to a CAB certificate in generalist advice work, equivalent to NVQ level 3. A Diploma/Welsh Baccalaureate in society, health and development may be available in your area, and from 2011, also one in humanities and social science.

Adult entry is common as people usually choose to specialise in benefits advising after working as paid or voluntary general advice workers. Often adults can offer a mature outlook and life experience that is an advantage in this area of work. A background in law, welfare rights, consumer advice or counselling may be particularly helpful.

Opportunities and Pay

Welfare benefits advisers work mostly in the voluntary sector and for local authorities. Employers include charitable organisations, advice centres, law centres, health services and housing associations. There are also opportunities with colleges, universities and trade unions. Work is available across the UK, but mostly in urban areas. Some jobs are fixed-term contracts which may or may not be renewed. Due to the current economic downturn, opportunities for advisers are good. With experience you may take on more complex cases and can be promoted to welfare rights caseworker. You can also supervise others or go into management.

Trainee advisers earn around £12k-£18k a year. Starting salaries for trained welfare benefits advisers are around £18k-£22k a year, rising to £25k with experience. Welfare rights caseworkers, or those in supervisory or management roles, may earn around £24k-£30k a year.

Skills and Qualities

able to explain clearly, able to put people at ease, awareness of confidentiality issues, good communication skills, good interviewing skills, good listening skills, IT skills, negotiating skills, non-judgemental, understanding of legal technicalities

Relevant Subjects

Business and accounting, Economics, English, Health and social care, Law, Mathematics, Psychology, Sociology

Further Information

Adviser Magazine (bi-monthly) (Citizens Advice Bureau) - www.citizensadvice.org.uk/index/adviser_resources

AGCAS: Charity & Development Work (Job Sector Briefing) (AGCAS) - www.prospects.ac.uk

Citizens Advice Northern Ireland - www.citizensadvice.co.uk

Citizens Advice Scotland - www.cas.org.uk

Diplomas (Foundation, Higher and Advanced) - http://yp.direct.gov.uk/diplomas

rightsnet - Welfare Rights website for Advisers - www.rightsnet.org.uk/

Welsh Baccalaureate - www.wbq.org.uk

▶Working in advice & counselling (2007) (Babcock Lifeskills) - www.babcock-lifeskills.com/

Working with languages (2010) (Babcock Lifeskills) - www.babcock-lifeskills.com/

Addresses

AdviceUK
6th Floor, 63 St Mary Axe, London EC3A 8AA
Phone: +44 (0)20 7469 5700
Web: www.adviceuk.org.uk

Citizens Advice
Myddleton House, 115-123 Pentonville Rd, London N1 9LZ
Phone: +44 (0)20 7833 2181
Web: www.citizensadvice.org.uk

National Association for Voluntary Community Action (NAVCA)
The Tower, 2 Furnival Square, Sheffield S1 4QL
Phone: +44 (0)114 278 6636
Web: www.navca.org.uk

Similar Jobs

Adult Guidance Worker, Advice Worker, Careers Adviser, Community Development Worker, Community Learning & Development Officer (Scotland), Counsellor, Debt Counsellor

Wholesale Manager

CRCI:Retail Sales and Customer Services
CLCI:OK Job Band: 3 to 5

Job Description

Wholesale managers plan and direct the efficient movement of goods from the manufacturer to retailers and consumers. Also plan budgets and timescales for the distribution of goods. They may negotiate the purchase of goods, control stocks, arrange storage and transport and can be responsible for the marketing of goods. Some managers specialise in particular types of goods, such as groceries or electrical goods. They receive them in bulk from manufacturers and distribute them in smaller packaged quantities to outlets, such as shops and stores. Are sometimes responsible for the supervision, training and development of staff.

Work Details

Usually work a basic 39 hr week, Monday to Friday, but may be required to work weekends, evenings or early mornings. The work is office-based, though you may have to travel to meetings. You can be involved in monitoring the recruitment, training and organisation of staff, overseeing the budgets and targets of the management team, and the marketing of the organisation. The work is demanding at times and can involve making difficult decisions.

Qualification

• England, Wales and Northern Ireland

Band 4: For most BTEC higher national awards: 1-2 A levels and some GCSEs (A*-C) including English and maths, or equivalent. The exact subjects depend on the course you take.

Band 5: For a degree course: usually 2-3 A levels plus some GCSEs (A*-C). Exact requirements depend on the degree you take.

• Scotland

Band 4: For an SQA higher national award: 2-3 H grades and some S grades (1-3) including English and maths, or similar. The exact subjects depend on the course you choose.

Band 5: For a degree course: usually 3-5 H grades and some S grades (1-3), or similar. The specific subjects depend on the degree you take.

Degree Information

A degree in any discipline is acceptable. Business studies degrees are particularly appropriate, and maths or statistics, business administration, marketing, economics or financial management are useful.

Adult Qualifications

A degree or higher national award is helpful, but may not be essential. However, entry requirements may be relaxed for adults applying for higher education courses. Access or foundation courses give adults without qualifications a route on to degree courses.

Work Experience

Employers may prefer candidates who have relevant work or voluntary experience. This can include previous experience in sales, retail, administration or warehousing.

Entry and Training

Some employers run in-house training schemes, usually aimed at existing staff who demonstrate potential. You may also be taken on as a management trainee if you have a degree, BTEC/SQA higher national awards, or sometimes with A levels/H grades, or equivalent. In-house training in larger organisations may include placements in sales and support departments, as well as courses in management skills, communication and technology. Some companies may offer work-related qualifications, including S/NVQs, such as distribution, warehousing and storage operations at levels 2-3.

Alternatively you can train through the Chartered Institute of Logistics and Transport, which offers certificate, diploma and advanced diploma level qualifications. There are foundation degrees available in many relevant subjects. For some jobs you may need a fork-lift truck licence.

Mature entrants with previous relevant experience in warehouse distribution and transport, or other management experience, may have an advantage, though some employers may prefer younger applicants for training programmes. Adults may be able to enter this work through a government-funded training programme. Contact your local careers office, Jobcentre Plus, Next Step service or Learning and Skills Council (LSC)/Local Enterprise Company (LEC) for details of all training opportunities and schemes, including apprenticeships for adults.

Opportunities and Pay

You may work for a wholesale or retail organisation or with a manufacturer who offers a wholesaling service, with jobs available throughout the UK. Wholesalers may specialise in a particular range of products or supply a single, large-scale retailer. In larger companies, it is possible to progress to more senior management jobs.

Pay rates vary, but wholesale managers earn in the region of £20k, rising with experience to £25k-£30k a year. Senior wholesale managers earn from around £40k to more than £50k a year. Bonus payments may be paid, but depend on the size of the company and its location.

Skills and Qualities

able to motivate others, able to take responsibility, able to work to deadlines, decisive, efficient, good organisational skills, information handling skills, IT skills, leadership qualities, planning skills

Relevant Subjects

Business and accounting, Economics, English, ICT/Computer studies, Mathematics, Retail and distribution

Further Information

Skills for Logistics - sector skills council for freight logistics industries - www.skillsforlogistics.org

Training Schemes - www.direct.gov.uk/en/educationandlearning

Addresses

Chartered Institute of Logistics and Transport (CILTUK)
Careers Manager, Logistics & Transport Centre, Earlstrees Court, Earlstrees Road, Corby NN17 4AX
Phone: +44 (0)1536 740 100
Web: www.ciltuk.org.uk

Institute of Grocery Distribution (IGD)
Careers Information Service, Grange Lane, Letchmore Heath, Watford, Hertfordshire WD25 8GD
Phone: +44 (0)1923 857141
Web: www.igd.com

Similar Jobs

Freight Forwarder, Purchasing/Procurement Officer, Retail Manager, Road Transport Manager

Wig Maker

CRCI:Personal and Other Services
CLCI:IL Job Band: 1 to 2

Job Description

Wig makers create wigs and hairpieces for people who wear them either for fashion, therapeutic reasons, or when working in the performing arts. They also make the wigs worn by barristers and judges in courts of law. First, they make a fabric mount of the correct size and shape from measurements of the client's head. Then weave or knot strands of natural hair or artificial hair into the base or net, arranging lengths and colour to give the desired effect and to look natural. The wig is then cut and styled. Some wig makers personally fit wigs for customers and give advice on how to look after them. Also clean and dress wigs and carry out repairs.

Wig makers may work closely with other specialists, such as make-up artists and SFX (special effects) technicians in the TV, film and theatre industry. May also work with medical staff whose patients require wigs due to injury and illness, or the side effects of some treatments, such as chemotherapy. Some wigs are now made by specialised machinery.

Work Details

Depending on your job, you may work in a theatre or a studio/workshop. Most are small, but some may now use specialised machines, and these can be noisy. You work 5-6 days a week, possibly including some weekends. Some jobs may require long and unsocial hours. It may also be necessary to visit clients at home. If your employer provides wigs for the health service, you may have to deal with people who are ill and in need of support.

Qualification

- **England, Wales and Northern Ireland**

Band 1: No formal qualifications are required but you are expected to have a good level of general education and relevant experience. Some formal/vocational qualifications at any level are useful.

Band 2: Entry requirements vary, but for some jobs and for courses: a number of GCSEs including English, maths, art and science, are preferred.

- **Scotland**

Band 1: No formal qualifications are required but you are expected to have a good level of general education and relevant experience. Some formal/vocational qualifications at any level are useful.

Band 2: Entry requirements vary, but for some jobs and courses: a number of S grades including English, maths, art and science, are preferred.

Adult Qualifications

Experience and qualifications in hairdressing are an advantage, although non-experienced applicants, who have the dexterity and skill required for this work, may be considered suitable.

Work Experience

It may be possible to gain work experience with a theatrical or cosmetic wig maker, but any work to do with hairdressing or beauty is very useful. Practical experience in make-up for school/college or amateur plays also helps.

Entry and Training

You may be trained on the job, working with an experienced wig maker, but there are few openings. Modules in wig making may also be included as part of hairdressing, theatrical make-up or beauty therapy courses. There are some specialist courses in wig making available, such as those offered by the Wig Academy, that concentrates on courses for film, TV and theatre. Fees can be expensive. Experience in hairdressing is very useful for this job.

You can also study for the City & Guilds certificate in wig making at level 2. This covers health and hygiene, weaving and knotting, cutting and styling and sales techniques. The Edexcel level 3 course in performing arts also has a module on period hair design and wig making.

Those working using specialised wig making machines are trained to use the equipment. This may take two to three months.

Mature entrants with experience, and or qualifications in hairdressing/beauty therapy may have an advantage. Those who have life experience and maturity are also at an advantage when dealing with sensitive situations, such as clients who may have had full or partial hair loss through illness or medical treatments.

Opportunities and Pay

There are jobs with small wig making companies and manufacturing workshops. You may also work in the theatre, film or television industry, or with wax model makers. There are a few jobs making legal wigs that involve different techniques using horsehair. There are, however, limited opportunities. When experienced you may become self-employed. This job is suitable for part-time work and it is also possible to do this work at home.

Pay varies, but trainees generally earn around £10k-£13k a year, rising to around £18k a year, with experience. High earners can make around £25k a year, and some, working in theatre and film, can earn more.

Health

This job requires good eyesight and normal colour vision.

Skills and Qualities

able to work both on your own and in a team, attention to detail, creative flair, eye for shape/colour, good concentration level, manual dexterity, methodical, patient, reassuring, tactful

Relevant Subjects

Art and Design

Further Information

The Wig Academy - www.thewigacademy.co.uk

▶Working in hairdressing & beauty (2009) (Babcock Lifeskills) - www.babcock-lifeskills.com/

Addresses

Hairboo
Contact via website, Barnsley S71 1AQ
Phone: +44 (0)1226 786 555
Web: www.hairboo.com/

Similar Jobs

Film/TV & Theatre Make-Up Artist, Hairdresser, Sewing Machinist, Trichologist

Windscreen Technician

also known as: Automotive Glazier, Vehicle Glazing Technician

CRCI:Engineering
CLCI:RAE — Job Band: 1 to 2

Job Description

Windscreen technicians replace and repair damaged windscreens and windows in all sorts of vehicles. Most work on cars and light vans. Some work on large vehicles such as lorries, tractors, buses and trains.

They assess the job to see what is required, disconnect any electrical parts and remove any wipers, trims and interior mirrors. Then they cut out and remove the old glass and adhesive before checking the new window or windscreen is the right size and type for the vehicle and is not damaged. They clean the edges of the glass and the opening it is going into, apply the adhesive and carefully stick the glass in place. Then clean off any excess adhesive and refit any parts that have been removed. Those working on large commercial vehicles may have to cut glass to size using special equipment.

Some technicians meet customers to discuss the job with them. They may have to arrange to bring vehicles to a garage or workshop. Sometimes technicians repair glass by filling a chip or crack with a clear resin and polishing the whole area. They ensure that any work done meets the vehicle manufacturer's safety requirements. Also follow health and safety procedures and complete job sheets and other paperwork.

Work Details

Usually work a 40 hr week, Monday to Friday. Some may work shifts, including weekends, to cover call-outs at any time of the day. Often works alone without supervision. Meets members of the public. Works alongside other windscreen technicians and vehicle mechanics.

May be mobile, garage or depot-based or work in a vehicle assembly factory. Mobile technicians drive from job to job in specially fitted out vans. Works at the roadside and outside people's homes and workplaces in all weathers. Garages and factories can be noisy and hot or cool. Wears overalls or a uniform, protective boots and other safety gear provided by the employer. The work often involves lifting and handling chemicals.

Qualification

• England, Wales and Northern Ireland

Band 1: For entry to jobs, no minimum qualifications are needed, but you are expected to have a good level of general education and relevant experience. Some formal/vocational qualifications at any level are useful.

Band 2: For entry to jobs, no minimum qualifications are needed, but it is an advantage to have some GCSEs (A*-C) or equivalent in subjects that include English and maths.

• Scotland

Band 1: For entry to jobs, no minimum qualifications are needed, but you are expected to have a good level of general education and relevant experience. Some formal/vocational qualifications at any level are useful.

Band 2: Although academic qualifications are not specified for this job, it is an advantage to have some S grades (1-3) in subjects that include English and maths, or similar.

Adult Qualifications

No formal academic qualifications are required. You need to show that you are capable of learning the theory and dealing with the practical demands of the job. Specific entry requirements for courses may be relaxed for mature applicants. You can improve your skills and qualifications by working through the Foundation Learning programme. This involves taking credit-based units and qualifications to help you progress.

Work Experience

Work experience helps you find out what you enjoy and do not enjoy about a type of work. Paid or voluntary work where you meet members of the public may be useful. Experience of working with cars and following manuals and instructions may help you stand out.

In some areas you can do a young apprenticeship (14-16) scheme in the motor industry. You do an extended work placement and a level 2 qualification whilst at school. For health and safety reasons there may be some jobs you cannot do until you are over 16.

Entry and Training

People can enter this type of work straight from school. Training is largely on the job with experienced workers. You may attend courses at a college or training centre. Many work towards qualifications such as S/NVQ levels 2-3 in automotive glazing or study for a technical certificate such as a Glass Qualifications Authority level 3 certificate in glass related operations (automotive glazing). Apprenticeships leading to level 2 and advanced apprenticeships leading to level 3 qualifications may be available in your area. Depending on their job role, some windscreen technicians may work towards other motor vehicle engineering qualification at levels 1-3. Mobile technicians need a full, clean driving licence.

Auto Windscreens is one of the largest NVQ training providers in this field. They offer comprehensive, ongoing training in the automotive glazing industry. The induction training lasts for four weeks and involves intensive on the job training. After this, technicians are assessed to ensure they meet the required standard. Once in the workplace, technicians undergo regular assessments. The Automotive Glazing Development Centre is now approved to offer the Automotive Technician Accreditation (ATA) scheme , overseen by the Institute of Motor Industries (IMI).

The IMI has developed Autocity, a useful and informative website on careers in the motor industry. There is a section on glazing technicians detailing training routes and industry links. Visit the website for more information. Similarly, Thatcham is a leading provider in skills training in the automative industry and offers a variety of apprenticeships and courses. There is specific training in windscreen glazing available. Check the website for details of course availability and dates. Glass Training Ltd. offers automotive glazing training courses at levels 2 and 3. Candidates should be working in the automative glazing sector as technicians, fitters or windscreen repairers. Optional units are studied in line with your work experience. Check the website for details.

A Diploma/Welsh Baccalaureate may be available in your area in engineering. This qualification is based around work and can include an automotive specialist learning component. See the diplomas website for further information.

Adults can enter this area of work and train on the job. The Glass Qualifications Authority level 3 certificate in glass related operations (automotive glazing) does not require any previous learning or experience.

Opportunities and Pay

There are over 35 million vehicles on the road. Windscreen checks are part of the MOT test and around 400 firms offer windscreen repair or replacement services. They employ about 1,650 fitters throughout the UK. There are jobs with windscreen repair firms, garages and vehicle manufacturers. Companies running buses, coaches, trains and planes also need glazing fitters. Some work as general mechanics as well.

You may progress from garage work to doing mobile work on your own. With experience you may supervise, train or manage others. Some move into customer service or vehicle maintenance and repair.

Trainees earn around £12k-£14k a year. Earnings for trained staff range from £14k-£20k for more experienced workers. Depending on the employer, those with a supervisory or training role can earn £22k-£35k a year. Managers can earn £25k-£45k a year.

Health

Good general fitness and normal colour vision are required. There may be an allergy risk from chemicals such as adhesives and resins.

Skills and Qualities

able to follow instructions, able to work well on your own, attention to detail, enjoy working outdoors, good communication skills, logical, manual dexterity, methodical, safety conscious, self-motivated

Relevant Subjects

Design and technology

Further Information

Apprenticeship Schemes (National Apprenticeship Service) - www.apprenticeships.org.uk

Auto Windscreens - www.autowindscreens.co.uk/about/training_school.aspx

Autocity (IMI) - http://autocity.org.uk

Automotive Technician Accreditation (ATA) (Institute of the Motor Industry) - www.automotivetechnician.org.uk

Careers in Glass (Proskills) - www.prospect4u.co.uk

Diplomas (Foundation, Higher and Advanced) - http://yp.direct.gov.uk/diplomas

Institute of the Motor Industry (IMI) - www.motor.org.uk

Proskills UK - sector skills council for process and manufacturing industries - www.proskills.co.uk

Thatcham - www.thatcham.org

Addresses

Glass Qualifications Authority (GQA)
Provincial House, Solly Street, Sheffield S1 4BA
Phone: +44 (0)114 272 0033
Web: www.glassqualificationsauthority.com

Glass Training Ltd
Suite 28, The Quadrant, 99 Parkway Avenue,
Parkway Business Park, Sheffield S9 4WG
Phone: 0844 809 4944
Web: www.glass-training.co.uk

Similar Jobs

Glassmaker: Operative, Glazier, Vehicle Breakdown Engineer, Vehicle Mechanic/Motor Vehicle Technician, Vehicle Tyre/Exhaust Fitter

Wine Producer

CRCI:Manufacturing and Production
CLCI:SAC Job Band: 4 to 5

Job Description

Wine producers manage and supervise the making of wine from cultivated red and white grape vines. In viticulture (growing of grapes) the producer organises the vineyard work, such as planting vines, pruning, spraying with fungicides and fertilising. Monitors growth of grapes, tests for readiness and organises the harvesting. In vinification (wine-making process in the winery) supervises the preparation of juice, fermentation and filtering processes. Directs bottling of wine and checks quality. Often has a range of other tasks, including sales and marketing.

Work Details

Wine producers usually work a basic 39 hr week but may be expected to work longer hours at times, as well as some weekends and evenings. The work is in the wine production areas, in an office and sometimes outside in the vineyard. You supervise and organise staff, liaise with a team and take responsibility for planning, quality control and efficient production. Travel, including overseas travel, may be necessary depending on the company.

Qualification

- **England, Wales and Northern Ireland**

Band 4: For relevant BTEC higher national award: 1-2 A levels and some GCSEs (A*-C) usually including maths, a science and English, or equivalent.

Band 5: For degree course: 2-3 A levels and some GCSEs (A*-C), usually including maths, a science and English. Exact requirements depend on the degree you take.

- **Scotland**

Band 4: For SQA higher national award: usually 2-3 H grades and some S grades (1-3), often including a science, maths and English, or similar.

Band 5: For degree course: 3-5 H grades and some S grades (1-3), usually including maths, a science and English, or similar. Exact requirements depend on the degree you take.

Degree Information

A degree in wine production or viticulture and marketing/business/French is an advantage, as are other related disciplines, such as horticulture, food science/technology, biochemistry or brewing. Business and administration subjects provide useful knowledge.

Adult Qualifications
Entry requirements may be relaxed for adults applying for higher education courses and Access courses give adults without qualifications a route on to degree courses.

Work Experience
Employers and universities may prefer candidates who have relevant work or voluntary experience. However, work experience with a wine producer can be difficult to gain. Experience in an agricultural or horticultural laboratory, or in food science, is particularly useful, but any horticultural/agricultural work is also relevant.

Entry and Training
Entry to the wine business is often through family connections. However, some enter as vineyard operatives or assistant winemakers and work their way up. Others do relevant higher education courses before entry. Plumpton College (University of Brighton) has a state-of-the-art commercial winery and offers a BSc in viticulture and oenology, as well as WSET qualifications and other part-time courses, such as the principles of vine growing, practical wine analysis and principles of wine making. Two-year foundation degrees at Plumpton in wine production, or wine business can lead on to a BSc. Contact Plumpton College for details. Relevant postgraduate courses are also available at several universities.

There is no formal pattern of training. Most training is on the job with an employer and can include the trade qualifications in knowledge of wines offered by the Wine and Spirit Education Trust (WSET).

Government training opportunities, such as apprenticeships, may be available in your area. You can also gain recognition of previous experience through Accreditation of Prior Learning (APL) or by working towards relevant S/NVQs. Contact your local careers office, Jobcentre Plus, Next Step service or Learning and Skills Council (LSC) Local Enterprise Company (LEC) for details of training schemes.

Opportunities and Pay
Currently, this is a very small though developing area of work in the UK, which is increasing in importance. There are currently around 300 places that produce wine. It must be remembered that due to the UK climate, vineyards are almost exclusively in the south of England and in Wales, but there are good opportunities for work abroad. Professional qualifications may enable you to move into the wine retail or hospitality industries.

Earnings depend on the size of operation, though most wine producers earn from around £16k-£35k. Successful international producers may earn up to £50k a year.

Health
This job requires an excellent sense of smell and taste. You must be fit and healthy and have no allergies.

Skills and Qualities
able to manage people, able to take responsibility, awareness of production process, business awareness, good communication skills, interest in wine and wine making, methodical, observant, patient, technical aptitude

Relevant Subjects
Biology, Business and accounting, Chemistry, Economics, English, Geography, Manufacturing, Mathematics, Science

Further Information
Improve Ltd - sector skills council for food and drink manufacturing and processing - www.improveltd.co.uk

Lantra - The Sector Skills Council for environmental & land-based sector (Lantra) - http:/www.lantra.co.uk

Training Schemes - www.direct.gov.uk/en/educationandlearning

Wine & Spirit - www.harpers.co.uk/

▶ Working in manufacturing (2010) (Babcock Lifeskills) - www.babcock-lifeskills.com/

Addresses
English Wine Producers
PO Box 5729, Market Harborough LE16 8WX
Web: www.englishwineproducers.co.uk

Plumpton College
Ditchling Road, Near Lewes, , East Sussex BN7 3AE
Phone: +44 (0)1273 890 454
Web: www.plumpton.ac.uk

Wine & Spirit Education Trust (WSET)
International Wine & Spirit Centre, 39-45 Bermondsey Street, London SE1 3XF
Phone: +44 (0)20 7089 3800
Web: www.wset.co.uk

Similar Jobs
Agricultural Research Scientist, Brewer: Technical, Off-Licence Manager, Sommelier

Wood Machinist
also known as: Timber Machinist

CRCI:Manufacturing and Production

CLCI:SAJ — Job Band: 1 to 2

Job Description
Wood machinists cut and shape wood for the furniture, timber and construction trades. They set up and use all types of machines that cut and shape the wood, including sawing and mortise machines, planers, moulding machines and routers. They study plans for the item to be made and then put the right jigs, templates and cutting tools into the machine. Machinists use the machine to cut the wood and then check that the shape is correct.

Items such as skirting boards, floorboards, banisters, window and door frames are all produced by machinists. May make the same product all day or reset machines to produce different items. They make sure that pieces produced are properly finished and of a good quality. Wood machinists clean the machines and sharpen the blades regularly. Being aware of health and safety regulations and following procedures is very important. Many of the machines are controlled by computer systems.

Work Details
Wood machinists usually work a 39 hr week, Monday to Friday, though some overtime work may be required at times to meet deadlines. The environment may be noisy, dusty, and can be dangerous, so strict safety regulations must be observed. You are physically active most of the day, standing for many hours and sometimes having to lift heavy wood. There is a risk of accidents from equipment and you may need to wear overalls, goggles, boots, a face mask and ear protectors.

Qualification

- **England, Wales and Northern Ireland**

Band 2: Although academic qualifications are not specified for this job, it is an advantage to have some GCSEs (A*-C) in subjects that include English and maths, a science or technology subject or equivalent.

- **Scotland**

Band 2: Although academic qualifications are not specified for this job, it is an advantage to have some S grades (1-3) in subjects that include English and maths, a science or technology subject or similar.

Adult Qualifications
A good standard of secondary education is usually required.

Work Experience
Relevant work or voluntary experience is always useful. It can improve your chances when applying for jobs or apprenticeships. Your personal or adult guidance adviser should be able to advise you about how to get some work experience with an employer.

Entry and Training
Most people enter this job via a training scheme and receive on-the-job training with a skilled worker/supervisor. Others may choose to do a course in wood machining, such as that offered by City & Guilds, before entering the work. Apprenticeships may be available. A Diploma/Welsh Baccalaureate in manufacturing and product design may be available in your area. This can prove a relevant introduction to this type of work.

Appropriate S/NVQs in wood machining are available at levels 2-3. The Institute of Wood Science offers some distance learning materials at foundation and certificate level which cover many aspects of the timber industry. All entrants to this work undergo safety training as the machines used can be dangerous.

Government training opportunities, such as an apprenticeship in wood machining, may be available in your area. You can also gain recognition of previous experience through Accreditation of Prior Learning (APL) or by working towards relevant S/NVQs. Contact your local careers office, Jobcentre Plus, Next Step service or Learning and Skills Council (LSC) Local Enterprise Company (LEC) for details of training schemes.

Opportunities and Pay
Around 30,000 people are involved in wood machining in the UK. You may work for large, medium or small companies in the manufacturing and retail sectors, including timber yards, joinery companies, construction companies and sawmills. Work is available throughout the UK. As there is an increase in the use of wood products, particularly in the construction industry, there is a good demand for wood machinists. Promotion to supervisory/management level is possible for those with qualifications and experience.

Pay varies depending on area and employer but a trainee can expect to earn around £12k-£15k a year and, with experience, around £17k-£21k. Some machinists can earn up to £26k. Overtime and bonus payments are possible.

Health
This job may require normal colour vision. There is an allergy risk from wood dust which may affect your chest.

Skills and Qualities
able to operate equipment, able to work quickly, accurate, careful, good concentration level, good co-ordination, good stamina and physically fit, manual dexterity, numeracy skills, safety conscious

Relevant Subjects
Design and technology

Further Information
Apprenticeship Schemes (National Apprenticeship Service) - www.apprenticeships.org.uk

Careers in Wood (Proskills) - www.prospect4u.co.uk

Diplomas (Foundation, Higher and Advanced) - http://yp.direct.gov.uk/diplomas

Proskills UK - sector skills council for process and manufacturing industries - www.proskills.co.uk

The Wood Technology Society - www.iom3.org/content/wood-technology

Training Schemes - www.direct.gov.uk/en/educationandlearning

Welsh Baccalaureate - www.wbq.org.uk

►Working in manufacturing (2010) (Babcock Lifeskills) - www.babcock-lifeskills.com/

Addresses
Timber Trade Federation
The Building Centre 26 Store Street, London WC1E 7BT
Phone: +44 (0)20 3205 0067
Web: www.ttf.co.uk

Similar Jobs
Carpenter/Joiner, Picture Framer, Sawmilling Operative, Timber Frame Erector

Writer
also known as: Author, Novelist

CRCI:Media, Print and Publishing
CLCI:FAC Job Band: 4 to 5

Job Description
Writers/authors produce creative fiction (novels) or non-fiction books, some of which may be commissioned by a publisher/editor. Many specialise in children's or adult's books, whether fiction or non-fiction. Topics include historical novels, crime, travel writing, romance and science fiction. Usually they research a topic first and then type, dictate or write the text by hand. Then submit the finished work to editors, or a literary agent and may be asked to make changes and re-write their work. Can be involved in proofreading, and also a publicity campaign if the work is accepted.

Work Details
Many authors have another job or write on a part-time basis, usually indoors and at home, which enables them to choose their own working hours. Sometimes the hours are long when deadlines approach. For much of the time you have contact with few people, so this job requires strong motivation and self-discipline. You must be able to keep your audience in mind and cope with having your work criticised or rejected. This work demands research and your writing must reflect accuracy in historical settings, geographical locations, quotations and references.

Qualification
There are no formal qualifications to be a writer/author. There are a wide variety of courses for budding writers, from basic short courses at all levels of writing skill, including residential courses, to a degree/postgraduate degree in creative writing. Writing skills, talent and luck are often more important than academic ability.

• England, Wales and Northern Ireland
Band 4: For HND, Diploma of Higher Education or foundation degree: 1-2 A levels and some GCSEs (A*-C) usually including English and maths, or equivalent.

Band 5: For degree courses: 2-3 A levels and some GCSEs (A*-C) usually including English, or equivalent qualifications. Exact requirements depend on the degree you take.

• Scotland
Band 4: For entry to SQA higher national and professional development awards, usually 2-3 H grades and some S grades (1-3), including English and maths, or similar qualifications.

Band 5: For degree courses: 3-5 H grades and some S grades (1-3), usually including English, or similar. Exact requirements depend on the degree you take.

Degree Information
Any degree is acceptable for entry to this job. A degree in creative writing is available, though subjects such as English language/literature, journalism, communication or media studies give useful background knowledge. Relevant postgraduate degrees, including creative writing, are also available.

Adult Qualifications
Entry requirements may be relaxed for adults applying for higher education courses. Access or foundation courses give adults without qualifications a route on to degree courses.

Work Experience
Relevant work or voluntary experience is extremely useful and can include any work that uses research and word-processing skills, or work for a local newspaper/publication, student journalism, and drama/theatre work. You can join a local writers' group or become a member of a book club to gain an insight into diverse authors. A work experience scheme is offered to aspiring writers by organisations such as the BBC, who offer an unpaid placement scheme working in radio drama. This can last from a few days up to four weeks.

Entry and Training
There is not a clearly defined formal training route to becoming a writer. Some may choose to train and qualify as a journalist, leading to a job writing articles for magazines, periodicals and journals. They can then diversify. There are few specific courses and writers' workshops. Taking part in full or part-time script or creative writing courses at a local college can be helpful. It may be useful to attend a course like this to gain skills and feedback on your style. There are also courses at degree/postgraduate level in creative writing.

There are distance learning courses available, such as those offered by the Open College of the Arts. Commercial companies, such as the Arvon Foundation, offer fee-paying courses, some residential, and advice for intending writers, though you should choose courses carefully. The Writers' & Artists' Yearbook gives useful guidance and advice, and is usually available in public and reference libraries. The Writernet website is also a useful source of information.

A Diploma/Welsh Baccalaureate may be available in your area in creative and media. This can be a useful introduction to this type of career as you gain practical experience while studying. See the diplomas website or Skillset for further information.

Mature entry is an advantage as many writers of fiction draw on their experiences, as well as imagination, research skill and creative ability. Writers of non-fiction usually have a relevant work background, as well as research skills acquired through their previous work or study. Experience in word-processing or journalism may be an advantage.

Opportunities and Pay
This job is highly competitive and very few people are successful enough to earn a living from their writing. For many this is a part-time occupation in addition to a full-time job. It is particularly difficult to become established in the area of creative writing. Literary prizes can help to gain recognition.

The Society of Authors helps aspiring writers by holding meetings, seminars and competitions. The society also publishes The Author, a quarterly journal, with useful information. Any writer who has been offered a contract is eligible for membership.

Most writers/authors are self-employed freelancers who agree a fee for each piece of work. The Writers' Guild of Great Britain recommends minimum rates of pay. Salary depends on success and the volume of work produced. Many writers earn less than £5k a year, but an established author may earn up to £35k a year. The most successful writers earn up to £120k, and celebrity authors can earn more than this. You should be prepared to supplement your income with a second job until you become established as a writer.

Skills and Qualities
able to withstand criticism, able to work to deadlines, able to work well on your own, business awareness, creative and imaginative flair, enthusiastic, good concentration level, good written English, IT skills, perseverance, research skills, self-disciplined

Relevant Subjects
English, Media and communication studies, Performing arts

Further Information
AGCSI/Gradireland: Sector Career Guide: Journalism & Media (AGCSI - Gradireland) - www.gradireland.com

Arts Council - www.artscouncil.org.uk

BBC Writers Room - www.bbc.co.uk/writersroom

Diplomas (Foundation, Higher and Advanced) - http://yp.direct.gov.uk/diplomas

Literature Training - www.literaturetraining.com

National Council for the Training of Journalists (NCTJ) - www.nctj.com

Skillset - sector skills council for the creative media, fashion and textiles industries - www.skillset.org

Society of Women Writers and Journalists (SWWJ) - www.swwj.co.uk

The Author (quarterly) (Society of Authors) - www.societyofauthors.org

The New Writer Magazine (6 x year) (New Writer) - www.thenewwriter.com/

The Writer's Handbook 2010 (Macmillan) - www.thewritershandbook.com/

▶ Working in creative & media (2007) (Babcock Lifeskills) - www.babcock-lifeskills.com/

▶ Working in English (2007) (Babcock Lifeskills) - www.babcock-lifeskills.com/

Writers' & Artists' Yearbook (A&C Black) (A&C Black) - www.writersandartists.co.uk

Writersnet - www.writers.net

Addresses
Arvon Foundation for Writing
Free Word , 60 Farringdon Road, London EC1R 3GA
Phone: +44 (0) 020 7354 2554
Web: www.arvonfoundation.org

BBC Recruitment Services
Recruitment BBC HR Direct, PO Box 1133, Belfast BT1 9GP
Web: www.bbc.co.uk/jobs

Irish Writers Centre
19 Parnell Square, Dublin 1
Phone: +353 (0)1 872 1302
Web: www.writerscentre.ie

Open College of the Arts
Michael Young Arts Centre, Redbrook Business Park, Wilthorpe Road, Barnsley S75 1JN
Phone: 0800 731 2116 (UK only)
Web: www.oca-uk.com

Society of Authors
84 Drayton Gardens, London SW10 9SB
Phone: +44 (0)20 7373 6642
Web: www.societyofauthors.org

Writers' Guild of Great Britain
40 Rosebery Avenue, London EC1R 4RX
Phone: +44 (0) 20 7833 0777
Web: www.writersguild.org.uk

Similar Jobs
Broadcast Journalist, Editorial Assistant: Publishing, Journalist, Journalist: Magazine, Magazine Features Editor, Proofreader, Screenwriter, Writer: Technical

Writer: Technical

also known as: Technical Author, Technical Communicator

CRCI:Media, Print and Publishing

CLCI:FAC Job Band: 4 to 5

Job Description

Technical authors write accurate and easy to understand technical descriptions and instructions for manuals, documents, reports and leaflets, for a host of everyday products. These include consumer products, computers, cars, or business procedures. They gather the relevant information from designers, manufacturers and experts using the Internet, databases, frequent meetings and interviews, and library research. Then write in a suitable form for publication. This may be on paper, CD-ROM, or online for a website. Must ensure that it is clear and easy for readers to follow.

Technical authors work with illustrators, other writers and printers. May produce indexes for their work and also copy edit the work of other writers. Many work in engineering and computing; a few work in agriculture, medicine and science. They need to keep up to date with developments in the industry in which they work.

Work Details

You usually work a 35-40 hr week, Monday to Friday, though may work longer hours, including weekends, when there are deadlines to meet. You may work on more than one project at a time. Work in offices, workshops, industrial premises, or from home. You have to be self-motivated, methodical and able to work under pressure to meet deadlines. You spend a lot of your time sitting, writing or working at a word processor, and the rest of the time liaising with people who are specialists in the field of publishing and editing. The need for accuracy is paramount. You may have to travel to meetings, sometimes spending time away from home.

Qualification

Although it is possible to take courses to train in technical authorship, the majority of entrants hold an appropriate qualification in engineering, technology or science, at technician or professional level.

• England, Wales and Northern Ireland

Band 4: For HND, Diploma of Higher Education or foundation degree: 1-2 A levels, usually including maths, English and a science subject, and some GCSEs (A*-C) usually including English and maths, or equivalent.

Band 5: For degree courses: 2-3 A levels, sometimes including maths, and some GCSEs (A*-C) usually including English and science subjects, or equivalent qualifications. Exact requirements depend on the degree you take.

• Scotland

Band 4: For entry to SQA higher national and professional development awards, usually 2-3 H grades, usually including maths, English and a science subject, and some S grades (1-3), including English and maths, or similar qualifications.

Band 5: For degree courses: 3-5 H grades sometimes including maths, and some S grades (1-3), usually including English, or similar. Exact requirements depend on the degree you take.

Degree Information

The type of degree required depends on the area in which you intend to work. Useful subjects include engineering, computer science, technical computing, information systems/technology, artificial intelligence, physical sciences, biological sciences, journalism, and technology subjects. Courses in communication studies and English can also be useful. There are some postgraduate courses in technical communication.

Adult Qualifications

Entry requirements may be relaxed for adults applying for higher education courses. Access or foundation courses give adults without qualifications a route on to degree courses.

Work Experience

Employers or colleges/universities may prefer candidates with relevant work or voluntary experience. It is useful to have practical experience in the technical or scientific area in which you hope to work. Experience that develops your writing and research skills is also useful, such as working for school or student newspapers.

Entry and Training

Most entrants are already experienced and qualified in a particular field of work. Others have a specific qualification in technical communication, such as a postgraduate award. You can also train on the job with part-time study, and either day release or distance-learning courses. It is useful to have some knowledge of foreign languages. Distance-learning courses are offered by the College of Technical Authorship and the Institute of Scientific and Technical Communicators (ISTC). It is an advantage to have knowledge and experience of HTML and of IT packages such as Corel Draw, Quark Express and Acrobat.

Foundation degrees in relevant subjects are also available in some areas. Full details of all relevant courses can be obtained from the ISTC.

A Diploma/Welsh Baccalaureate may be available in your area in creative and media. This can be a useful introduction to this type of career as you gain practical experience while studying. See the diplomas website or Skillset for further information.

Mature entry is sometimes possible without any formal qualifications if you are experienced in a relevant field, such as engineering, science, or the use of computers. This is often a second career. There are technical authorship courses which can be studied through part-time day, evening or distance learning courses. Some companies, such as Eston Training, run courses specifically aimed at those looking for a second career.

Opportunities and Pay

Between 5,000 and 10,000 people work as technical writers in the UK and currently, there is a shortage of experienced and appropriately qualified personnel. Work tends to be focused in areas where high-technology companies are located such as Bristol, south-west England and the Thames Valley. Manufacturing, engineering, scientific and computer companies along with technical publishing companies, research organisations and some government departments employ technical writers.

With experience, many become self-employed and work on a freelance basis. It is possible to find part-time work and there are opportunities to work abroad. Some move into science journalism or publishing. The Association of British Science Writers has a job and awards section on their website for those seeking work or wanting to enter writing competitions.

Pay varies depending on area and employer, but salaries start around £18k-£28k, rising to £30k-£37k a year with experience. Very experienced writers may earn as much as £50k or more in a year.

Skills and Qualities

able to explain clearly, accurate, analytical skills, attention to detail, good concentration level, good organisational skills, good written English, information handling skills, IT skills, methodical, research skills, technical aptitude

Relevant Subjects

Chemistry, Design and technology, Engineering, English, ICT/Computer studies, Mathematics, Physics, Science

Further Information

Communicator (ISTC, quarterly) (Institute of Scientific & Technical Communicators (ISTC)) - www.istc.org.uk/Publications/communicator.htm

Diplomas (Foundation, Higher and Advanced) - http://yp.direct.gov.uk/diplomas

e-skills UK - sector skills council for business and information technology - www.e-skills.com

Eston Training - www.estontrg.com

European Medical Writers' Association - www.emwa.org

SEMTA - sector skills council for science, engineering and manufacturing technologies - www.semta.org.uk

Skillset - sector skills council for the creative media, fashion and textiles industries - www.skillset.org

▶Working in creative & media (2007) (Babcock Lifeskills) - www.babcock-lifeskills.com/

▶Working in English (2007) (Babcock Lifeskills) - www.babcock-lifeskills.com/

Addresses

Association of British Science Writers (ABSW)
Wellcome Wolfson Building 165 Queen's Gate, London SW7 5HD
Phone: +44 (0)870 770 3361
Web: www.absw.org.uk

College of Technical Authorship
PO Box 7 Cheadle, Stockport, Cheshire SK8 3BY
Phone: +44 (0)161 437 4235
Web: www.coltecha.u-net.com/

Institute of Scientific and Technical Communicators (ISTC)
Airport House, Purley Way, Croydon, Surrey CR0 0XZ
Phone: +44 (0)20 8253 4506
Web: www.istc.org.uk

Similar Jobs

Advertising Copywriter, Information Scientist, Journalist: Magazine, Journalist: Scientific, Patent Attorney, Translator, Website Author/Editor, Writer

Zoo Keeper

also known as: Keeper: Zoo, Safari Park Keeper, Wild Animal Keeper

CRCI:Environment, Animals and Plants
CLCI:WAM Job Band: 3 to 4

Job Description

Zookeepers are responsible for the care, welfare, conservation and management of animals, including wild or exotic species, in a zoo or perhaps a wildlife, birdlife, butterfly centre or a safari park. A modern zoo's work is that of conservation and education, and it may operate a captive breeding programme for animals considered to be in danger of extinction. Keepers provide for the animal's needs, both physical and mental. They prepare food for the animals and feed them. Also look out for subtle changes in an animal's physical or psychological condition and react as needed. They take care of any sick animals and assist a vet when animals are checked or require medical treatment. Also clean out the cages and provide fresh bedding and water, ensuring a hygienic environment.

Zookeepers make sure that the animals cannot escape and regularly checs for signs of damage to their enclosures. They may do repairs to buildings, barriers or fences. Also keep records of diet, health and animal behaviour. May take visitors round the zoo, answering questions and telling people about the animals or may give talks and lectures. Must ensure visitors do not feed the animals or climb any barriers or fences. Many keepers become highly specialised and concentrate on a specific group of animals.

Work Details

Usually work a basic 40 hr week, and are expected to work early mornings, weekends and possibly evenings. There is usually a shift system worked over seven days, and you may be expected to work on public holidays. Keepers are responsible for animal welfare and safety, as well as their own safety and that of the visiting public. The job can be physically demanding as it requires you to be active most of the time. You must also be capable of lifting heavy loads.

Work environment can be dirty and smelly, and possibly cold, wet and noisy. A lot of the time may be spent outside in all weather conditions. There may be a risk of attack from animals. You need to wear overalls or protective clothing. A uniform is usually provided.

Qualification

• England, Wales and Northern Ireland

Band 3: For direct entry: usually at least 5 GCSEs (A*-C) including English and biology, or equivalent.

Band 4: For HND, Diploma of Higher Education or foundation degree: 1-2 A levels and some GCSEs (A*-C) usually including English and maths, or equivalent.

• Scotland

Band 3: For direct entry: usually at least five S grades (1-3) including English and biology, or similar.

Band 4: For entry to SQA higher national and professional development awards, usually 2-3 H grades and some S grades (1-3), including English and maths, or similar qualifications.

Adult Qualifications

Mature entrants may be able to gain entry without any set minimum qualifications but need experience of working with animals.

Work Experience

Relevant work or voluntary experience is always useful and can improve your employment prospects when applying for entry to jobs. Individual zoos, wildlife parks etc, run volunteer schemes though experience of work with farm animals or at a stables is also useful. On the website of the British and Irish Association of Zoos and Aquariums is information about opportunities for volunteering and work placements.

London Zoo and Whipsnade Wild Animal Park offer work experience placements to further education students engaged in biological or animal-related courses, and to school Yr 10 pupils (London residents only). There are also opportunities for volunteer work at both London and Whipsnade. Contact the Zoological Society of London (ZSL) for details.

Entry and Training

Entry to work in zoos is very competitive and most entrants need good GCSEs at least, with many entering with A levels or higher. Common sense and enthusiasm are two of the most important attributes a keeper can possess together with a knowledge of animals and an interest in conservation. On-the-job training is usual, alongside a more experienced keeper and often combined with part-time study for a City & Guilds/NPTC award in animal care management. Subjects covered in these courses include nutrition, enclosure design, health and safety, restraint and transport, conservation and disease.

A number of colleges offer courses in animal management/care up to HND level, and may offer the option to specialise in zoo animal or wildlife management. A foundation science degree in zoo resource management is offered by Sparsholt College that takes three years part time, though can be completed within two years.

For work in a safari park, a driving licence is essential. Training programmes, including apprenticeships leading to level 2 and advanced apprenticeships leading to level 3, may be available in your area.

Mature applicants may be preferred by some zoos, especially those with experience of working with animals. You may also benefit through government training opportunities that may be available in your area. You can gain recognition of previous experience through Accreditation of Prior Learning (APL) or by working towards relevant S/NVQs. The advanced diploma in animal management is designed specifically for mature entrants. See the website of the British and Irish Association of Zoos and Aquariums for more information.

Opportunities and Pay

There are 350 zoos and aquariums in the UK, employing around 3,000 full-time keepers. Jobs are only available in certain locations and there is stiff competition for places. Apart from zoos, aquariums, wildlife and safari parks, there are also jobs with some local authorities, charitable trusts, zoological societies or private companies who have special collections of animals, birds or fish. Promotion opportunities are limited beyond head keeper and it may be necessary to move to another employer.

Some keepers move into other related areas of work such as kennels, stables or with the RSPCA/Scottish SPCA. Zoos may offer a keeper exchange programme with countries that include the USA, Australia and New Zealand.

Pay varies on location and the individual zoo. Trainee keepers are likely to earn around £11k-£13k a year, rising to around £15.5k a year. Higher earners can expect around £18k-£24k a year. Low cost or free accommodation may sometimes be provided.

Health

To do this job you have to have good levels of stamina and general fitness.

Skills and Qualities

enthusiastic, good at handling animals, good communication skills, not squeamish, observant, patient, punctual, responsible attitude, safety conscious, strong

Relevant Subjects

Biology, Land and Environment, Leisure, travel and tourism, Science

Further Information

Apprenticeship Schemes (National Apprenticeship Service) - www.apprenticeships.org.uk

Association of British Wild Animal Keepers - www.abwak.co.uk

Careers with animals (British and Irish Association of Zoos and Aquariums) - www.biaza.org.uk/

Lantra - The Sector Skills Council for environmental & land-based sector (Lantra) http:/www.lantra.co.uk

Real Life Guide to Working with Animals & Wildlife (Trotman) - www.trotman.co.uk

Training Schemes - www.direct.gov.uk/en/educationandlearning

Working with animals (2009) (Babcock Lifeskills) - www.babcock-lifeskills.com/

Zoo keeping as a career (ABWAK) - www.abwak.co.uk/

Addresses

British and Irish Association of Zoos and Aquariums (BIAZA)
Regents Park, London NW1 4RY
Phone: +44 (0)20 7449 6351
Web: www.biaza.org.uk

Sparsholt College Hampshire
Westley Lane , Sparsholt, Winchester, Hampshire SO21 2NF
Phone: +44 (0)1962 776441
Web: www.sparsholt.ac.uk

Zoological Society of London (ZSL)
Outer Circle, Regent's Park, London NW1 4RY
Phone: +44 (0)20 7722 3333
Web: www.zsl.org

Similar Jobs

Animal Care Assistant, Farm Worker: Livestock, Gamekeeper, Horse Groom, RSPCA/Scottish SPCA Inspector, Veterinary Nurse

Zoological Scientist

also known as: Zoologist

CRCI:Science, Mathematics and Statistics
CLCI:QOD Job Band: 5

Job Description

Zoological scientists specialise in the scientific study of all aspects of animals and their life, including their physiology, anatomy, behaviour, ecology, classification and distribution. They are involved in the study of animals as diverse as mammals (including whales and dolphins), amphibians (frogs, toads and salamanders etc), reptiles (snakes, turtles and crocodiles etc) to all species of fish. Also study micro-organisms. Scientists conduct research both in the laboratory and in nature, analysing and interpreting data taken from samples. They investigate the origin, structure and behaviour of animals and their relationship with the environment.

Design experiments and use sophisticated equipment in their research. May be involved in medical research or conservation which sometimes includes wildlife or nature reserve management. Can also be involved in generating project bids for grants and funds. May attend conferences or research, write and present papers at conferences and meetings. May also supervise other professional staff.

Work Details

Much of the work is laboratory or office based and you normally work a standard week of around 39 hours, Monday to Friday, although you may be required to work early mornings, evenings or weekends. Research can involve spending time away from home, sometimes on fieldwork and occasionally overseas. You may need to work outdoors in all weather. This work can be physically active and there may be a risk of accidents. It involves a high degree of accuracy, working usually as part of a team with other professional scientists. You may need to wear protective clothing.

Qualification

- **England, Wales and Northern Ireland**

Band 5: For degree courses: 2-3 A levels preferably biology and chemistry, maths or physics and some GCSEs (A*-C) usually including English, maths and science, or equivalent. Exact requirements depend on the degree you take.

- **Scotland**

Band 5: For degree courses: 3-5 H grades including biology and chemistry, maths or physics and some S grades (1-3), usually including English, maths and science, or similar. Exact requirements depend on the degree you take.

Degree Information

Other life sciences can be acceptable at degree level, but specialist courses in zoology are preferred. A relevant first degree can be followed by a specialist higher degree. There are degrees in zoology or applied zoology, such as agricultural zoology or animal psychology, but there are also many other relevant degrees such as agricultural science, applied biology, animal biology, biochemistry, biology, ecology, genetics or microbiology.

Adult Qualifications

A formal higher education qualification such as a higher national award or a relevant degree, plus up-to-date scientific knowledge are essential. Course entry requirements may be relaxed for mature applicants. A foundation year prior to the start of a science degree may be available at some HE institutions for those applicants who do not have the traditional science qualifications or equivalent. Check with colleges and universities for details.

Work Experience

Entry to this career is highly competitive and it is essential for degree course entry that you have some relevant work or voluntary experience. Laboratory research in any biological/ecological area is relevant, as is working with a variety of animals. You can contact a veterinary practice, farm, kennels, or a wildlife sanctuary for possibilities of paid and voluntary employment.

London Zoo and Whipsnade Wild Animal Park offer work experience placements to further education students engaged in biological or animal-related courses, and to school Yr 10 pupils (priority to London residents). There are opportunities for volunteer work at both London and Whipsnade. Contact the Zoological Society of London (ZSL) for details.

Entry and Training

A range of courses are available and you should choose your course carefully. Most entrants are graduates and degree courses last 3-4 years and can be full time or sandwich. Training is through practical experience in the workplace. Membership of the Society of Biology and Zoological Society London (ZSL) can be attained by graduates with appropriate qualifications and relevant experience. The Field Studies Council (FSC) offers a range of training programmes in biological recording skills.

There are a number of foundation degrees in subjects that include zoological conservation management or animal behaviour/ science. Postgraduate study is an advantage and is usually essential for any research posts. Those having a relevant HND are usually appointed at technician level.

Mature candidates with appropriate qualifications and experience are usually preferred and entry qualifications to courses may be relaxed.

Opportunities and Pay

Competition for posts is fierce and many zoological scientists/ zoologists have a higher degree in a particular specialist area. Employers include research institutions, agriculture, government departments and agencies, museums, universities, environmental organisations and some with industrial concerns such as oil companies. Some find work in the conservation of endangered species, or with safari parks, wildlife trusts, zoological collections, nature reserves or zoos. Others move into writing or broadcasting. There are also teaching and research opportunities, which may involve fieldwork.

Pay varies depending on location and employer but generally start around £17k, rising to £25k-£35k a year for zoologists in research posts. Senior researchers may earn up to £50k a year.

Health

The work involves a risk of infection and you should not have any allergies to animals. You need good colour vision for some areas of work.

Skills and Qualities

able to report accurately, adaptable, analytical skills, aptitude for fieldwork, attention to detail, efficient record keeping, good communication skills, initiative, IT skills, problem-solving skills

Relevant Subjects

Biology, Chemistry, English, ICT/Computer studies, Land and Environment, Mathematics, Physics

Further Information

International Zoo Yearbook (annual) (Zoological Society of London) - www.zsl.org/info/publications/

Journal of Zoology (Zoological Society of London, monthly)) (Blackwell Publishing for ZSL) - http://www3.interscience.wiley.com/journal/118535410/home

Working with animals (2009) (Babcock Lifeskills) - www.babcock-lifeskills.com/

Addresses

British and Irish Association of Zoos and Aquariums (BIAZA)
Regents Park, London NW1 4RY
Phone: +44 (0)20 7449 6351
Web: www.biaza.org.uk

Field Studies Council (FSC)
Preston Montford Montford Bridge, Shrewsbury, Shropshire
SY4 1HW
Phone: 0845 345 4071 (UK only)
Web: www.field-studies-council.org

Society of Biology
9 Red Lion Court, London EC4A 3EF
Phone: +44 (0)20 7936 5900
Web: http://societyofbiology.org/home

Zoological Society of London (ZSL)
Outer Circle, Regent's Park, London NW1 4RY
Phone: +44 (0)20 7722 3333
Web: www.zsl.org

Similar Jobs

Agricultural Research Scientist, Biologist, Ecologist, Marine Biologist, Oceanographer, Teacher: Biological Sciences

Occupational Areas Index

This index lists jobs under their CRCI job families. Where there are many groups in a family, there are subdivisions into lower groups. We have used subgroups to help you identify similar jobs and we hope you find this index useful.

Occupational Areas Index

Occupational Areas Index

Title	Job Band	Page
Vehicle Mechanic/Motor Vehicle Technician	1 to 3	1116
Vehicle Tyre/Exhaust Fitter	1 to 2	1119
Windscreen Technician	1 to 2	1151

Environment, Animals and Plants

Agriculture and Fisheries

Title	Job Band	Page
Agricultural Consultant/Adviser	4 to 5	25
Agricultural Research Scientist	4 to 5	27
Bee Farmer	1	95
Farm Manager	3 to 5	395
Farm Worker: Crops	1 to 3	396
Farm Worker: Livestock	1 to 3	398
Farm Worker: Poultry	1 to 3	399
Fish Farm Manager	3 to 5	434
Fish Farm Worker	1 to 3	435
Fisherman/Fisherwoman	1 to 2	436
Shepherd	1 to 3	966
Water Keeper/Bailiff	1 to 3	1137

Landscape and Plants

Title	Job Band	Page
Arboriculturist	2 to 5	54
Countryside Ranger	2 to 5	242
Countryside/Conservation Officer/Manager	4 to 5	244
Forest District Manager	5	453
Forest Officer	3 to 5	455
Forest Worker	1 to 3	456
Garden Centre Assistant	1 to 2	469
Gardener	1 to 3	470
Greenkeeper: Golf	1 to 3	492
Groundsman/Groundswoman	1 to 3	493
Horticultural Manager	3 to 5	519
Horticultural Scientist	4 to 5	520
Horticultural Worker: Commercial	1 to 3	522
Landscape Architect	5	595
Landscape Gardener	2 to 5	596
Park Warden	1	757
Parks Manager	3 to 5	759
Parks Officer	1 to 3	761
Tree Surgeon	1 to 2	1108

Veterinary Services and Animal Care

Title	Job Band	Page
Animal Care Assistant	1 to 3	45
Animal Nutritionist	5	47
Animal Physiotherapist	5	48
Dog Groomer	1	286
Farrier	2 to 3	400
Gamekeeper	1 to 3	467
Guide Dog Trainer	2 to 4	494
Horse Groom	1 to 2	516
Horse Trainer	2 to 5	517
Pet Behaviour Counsellor	4 to 5	776
RSPCA Animal Collection Officer	1	932
RSPCA/Scottish SPCA Inspector	3	933
Stable Hand	1 to 2	996
Taxidermist	2 to 3	1031
Veterinary Animal Nursing Assistant	1 to 2	1121

Occupational Areas Index

Occupational Areas Index

Transport and Logistics